India

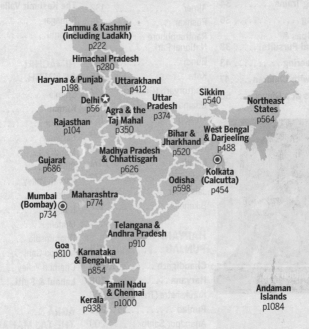

Jammu & Kashmir
(including Ladakh)
p222

Himachal Pradesh
p280

Haryana & Punjab
p198

Uttarakhand
p412

Delhi
p56

Agra & the
Taj Mahal
p350

Uttar
Pradesh
p374

Sikkim
p540

Northeast
States
p564

Rajasthan
p104

Bihar &
Jharkhand
p520

West Bengal
& Darjeeling
p488

Madhya Pradesh
& Chhattisgarh
p626

Kolkata
(Calcutta)
p454

Gujarat
p686

Odisha
p598

Mumbai
(Bombay)
p734

Maharashtra
p774

Telangana &
Andhra Pradesh
p910

Goa
p810

Karnataka
& Bengaluru
p854

Tamil Nadu
& Chennai
p1000

Andaman
Islands
p1084

Kerala
p938

THIS EDITION WRITTEN AND RESEARCHED BY

Sarina Singh, Abigail Blasi

Michael Benanav, Paul Clammer, Mark Elliott,

Paul Harding, Trent Holden, Anirban Mahapatra, Daniel McCrohan,

Isabella Noble, John Noble, Kevin Raub, Iain Stewart

KACHCHH P726

CITY PALACE, UDAIPUR P151

PRITI BHATT / GETTY IMAGES ©

RAJESH BHAND / GETTY IMAGES ©

Contents

Contents

ON THE ROAD

SADHU, VARANASI P390

Contents

Welcome to India

India pulsates with a spectacular mix of people, traditions and landscapes. Your journey through this mind-stirring country will blaze in your memory long after you've left its shores.

The Great Outdoors

From the soaring snow-dusted peaks of the northern mountains to the sultry sun-washed beaches of the southern coast, India's dramatic terrain is breathtaking. Along with abundant natural beauties, exquisitely carved temples rise majestically out of pancake-flat deserts and crumbling old fortresses peer over plunging ravines. Aficionados of the great outdoors can scout for big jungle cats on wildlife safaris, paddle in the shimmering waters of one of many beautiful beaches, take blood-pumping treks high in the Himalaya, or simply inhale pine-scented air on meditative forest walks.

Food, Glorious Food

Brace yourself – you're about to take one of the wildest culinary trips of your travelling life. Here you'll fry, simmer, sizzle, knead, roast and flip across a deliciously diverse repertoire of dishes. The hungry traveller can look forward to a tasty smorgasbord of regionally distinct creations, each with their own traditional preparation techniques and presentation styles – from the competing flavours of masterfully marinated meats and thalis to the simple splendour of vegetarian curries and deep-sea delights.

Expect the Unexpected

India tosses up the unexpected. This can be challenging, particularly for the first-time visitor: the poverty is confronting, Indian bureaucracy can be exasperating and the crush of humanity may turn the simplest task into a frazzling epic. Even veteran travellers find their nerves frayed at some point; yet this is all part of the India ride. With an ability to inspire, frustrate, thrill and confound all at once, adopting a 'go with the flow' attitude is wise if you wish to retain your sanity. Love it or loathe it – and most travellers see-saw between the two – to embrace India's unpredictability is to embrace her soul.

Simply Soul Stirring

Spirituality is the common characteristic painted across the vast and varied canvas that is contemporary India. The multitude of sacred sites and rituals are testament to the country's long, colourful, and sometimes tumultuous, religious history. And then there are the festivals! India hosts some of the world's most dazzling devotional celebrations – from formidable city parades celebrating auspicious events on the religious calendar to simple harvest fairs that pay homage to a locally worshipped deity.

Why I Love India
By Sarina Singh, Writer

The moment I start to think I'm right on the precipice of unravelling one of India's deep mysteries, she has an uncanny way of reminding me that it would take more than just a few lifetimes to do so. Indeed, demystifying India is a perpetual work in progress. And that is precisely what makes the country so deeply addictive for me. The constant exploration. The playful unpredictability. And knowing that, just when it's least expected, you can find yourself up close and personal with moments that have the power to alter the way you view the world and your place in it.

For more about our writers, see page 1248.

Above: Spectators at Dussehra festival (p28), Himachal Pradesh

India

External boundaries shown reflect the requirements of the Government of India.

⌖ N
0 0
250 miles
500 km

ELEVATION

6000m
5000m
4000m
3000m
2000m
1000m
0

Darjeeling
Quintessential hill station, famed for its tea (p500)

Delhi
Architecture, thrilling bazaars and cuisine (p56)

Agra
Taj Mahal – iconic marble masterpiece (p350)

Khajuraho
Sensuous sculptures wrap handsome temples (p638)

Varanasi
Historic holy town along the sacred Ganges (p390)

Himalayan Mountains
Dramatically majestic mountainscapes (p223)

Amritsar
Site of Sikhism's revered Golden Temple (p212)

Jaisalmer
Formidable fort; dreamy desert safaris (p182)

TAJIKISTAN
Dushanbe

AFGHANISTAN
Kabul

Islamabad

PAKISTAN

CHINA
TIBET
Lhasa
Gyantse

Thimphu Valley
BHUTAN
Thimphu

NEPAL
Kathmandu
Annapurna (8090m)
Mt Everest (8848m)

Arunachal Pradesh
Itanagar
Dibrugarh
Kaziranga National Park
Nagaland
Kohima
Guwahati
Shillong
Meghalaya
Manipur
Imphal
Aizawl? Agartala
BANGLADESH
West Bengal

Sikkim
Gangtok
Darjeeling
Siliguri
Jaldhapara Wildlife Sanctuary

Great Himalaya Range

K2 (Godwin Austin) (8611m)
Jammu & Kashmir
Kargil • Leh
Ladakh
Zanskar
Padum
Srinagar
Kishtwar
Jammu
Dalhousie Dharamsala
Pathankot
Attari Amritsar
Firozpur
Bathinda
Punjab
Chandigarh
Kufri
Manali
Himachal Pradesh
Shimla
Dehra Dun
Haridwar
Uttarakhand
Nanda Devi (7816m)
Nainital

Great Himalaya Range

Corbett Tiger Reserve

Haryana
Churu
Hansi
Delhi
Bareilly
Mathura
Agra
Gwalior
Jhansi
Uttar Pradesh
Lucknow
Kanpur
Ayodhya
Allahabad (Tirth Raj Prayag)
Gorakhpur
Varanasi
Bihar
Muzaffarpur
Patna
Gaya
Bodhgaya

Ganges
Yamuna

Keoladeo Ghana National Park
Jaipur
Ajmer
Rajasthan
Ranthambhore National Park
Bundi
Kota
Shivpuri
Khajuraho
Chittorgarh (Chittor)

Bikaner
Jodhpur
Great Thar Desert
Jaisalmer
Barmer
Mt Abu
Udaipur (Chittor)

Great Rann

MYANMAR (BURMA)

Mizoram

Nicobar
Islands

*Andaman
Sea*

Andaman
Islands

Port Blair ◉

Bay of Bengal

Sunderbans
Tiger Reserve

Kharagpur ✈ **(Calcutta)**

Digha

Balasore

Paradip

Jamshedpur ●

Simlipal
National
Park

Cuttack

Konark

Ajanta Caves
Ancient caves along a
horseshoe-shaped cliff (p788)

Hampi
Ruins peppered amid
enigmatic boulders (p896)

Puri

Berhampur

Bhubaneswar ◉

Odisha (Orissa)

Bheemunipatnam

Visakhapatnam

Chhattisgarh

Dindori

Bilaspur

Sambalpur

Raipur ◉

Rampur
Jharial

Kakinada

Machilipatnam

Jabalpur ●

*INDIAN
OCEAN*

Bhopal ◉

Mandu

Seoni

Kanha
National Park

Maharashtra

Nagpur ◉

Telangana

Warangal ●

Hyderabad ◉

Vijayawada ●

Ongole

Nellore

**SRI
LANKA**

Colombo ✪

*Gulf of
Mannar*

**Andhra
Pradesh**

Chittoor

Eastern Ghats

**Chennai
(Madras)** ◉

Mamallapuram

Puducherry
(Pondicherry)

Chidambaram

**Tamil
Nadu**

Trichy ● (Tiruchirappalli)

Madurai

Rameswaram

Kanyakumari

Ujjain

Dewas ●

Indore ●

Ahmedabad ◉

Vadodara
(Baroda) ●

Surat ●

Dhule ●

Jalgaon ●

Ajanta

Khandwa ●

Aurangabad ●

Upper
Godavari
Valley

Bijapur
(Vijapura)

Gadag ●

Hampi ●

Hospet
(Hosapete)

Sholapur ●

Pune ●

Kalyan ●

Nasik ●

Mahabaleshwar ●

Konkan Hills

**Panaji
(Panjim)** ◉

Goa

**Mumbai
(Bombay)** ◉ ✈

*Arabian
Sea*

Mumbai
India's cosmopolitan
capital of cool (p734)

Goan Beaches
Golden sands nuzzle
the Arabian Sea (p810)

Mangaluru
(Mangalore) ●

Thalasseri (Tellicherry)

Kozhikode (Calicut) ●

Lakshadweep
Islands

*Lakshadweep
Sea*

Hubli
(Hubballi) ●

Belgaum
(Belagavi) ●

Hassan ●

Karnataka

**Mysore
(Mysuru)** ●

Ooty
(Udhagamandalam) ●

Coimbatore ●

**Bengaluru
(Bangalore)** ◉ ✈

Nandi
Hills

Periyar
Wildlife
Sanctuary

Western Ghats

Kerala

Kochi (Cochin) ●

Kollam ●

Kovalam ●

Thiruvananthapuram (Trivandrum) ◉

Keralan Backwaters
Palm-fringed rivers,
lakes and lagoons (p938)

Dwarka ●

Porbandar ●

Junagadh ●

Sasan Gir
Wildlife
Sanctuary

Diu

Porbandar Coast

Daman

Dahanu

Little Rann
Wildlife
Sanctuary

Jamnagar ●

Rajkot ◉ ●

Bhavnagar ●

India's Top 17

GRANT FAINT / GETTY IMAGES ©

Taj Mahal

1 The poignant beauty of the Taj Mahal (p352) has long inspired writers and artists in and beyond India. Rabindranath Tagore described it as 'a teardrop on the cheek of eternity', while Rudyard Kipling referred to it as 'the embodiment of all things pure'. Built by Emperor Shah Jahan in adoration of his third wife, Mumtaz Mahal, this milky white marble mausoleum – inlaid with calligraphy, precious and semiprecious stones and intricate floral designs representing eternal paradise – is one of the world's most poetic parting tributes to love.

Enigmatic Hampi

2 The surreal boulderscape of Hampi (p896) was once the cosmopolitan Vijayanagar, capital of a powerful Hindu empire. Still magnificent in ruins, its temples and royal structures combine sublimely with the terrain: giant rocks balance on slender pedestals near an ancient elephant garage; temples tuck into crevices between boulders; and wicker coracles float by rice paddies and bathing buffalo near a gargantuan bathtub for a former queen. As the sunset casts a rosy glow over the dreamy landscape, you might just forget what planet you're on.

2

Himalayan Mountains & Monasteries

3 Up north, hill stations give way to snow-capped peaks. From Ladakh (p223) to Sikkim, the cultural influences came not from the coasts but via mountain passes. Tibetan Buddhism thrives, and monasteries emerge from the forest or steep cliffs as poetically as the sun rises over Khangchendzonga. Prayer flags flutter in the wind, the soothing sound of monks chanting reverberates in meditation halls, and locals abound with holy offerings, all in the shadow of the mighty Himalaya. Yumthang Valley (p553)

Caves of Ajanta

4 They may have been ascetics, but the 2nd-century-BC monks who created the Ajanta caves (p788) certainly had an eye for the dramatic. The 30 rock-cut forest grottoes punctuate the side of a cliff, and originally had individual staircases leading down to the river. The architecture and towering stupas made these caves inspiring places to meditate and live, but the real bling came centuries later, in the form of exquisite carvings and paintings depicting the Buddha's former lives. Renunciation of the worldly life was never so serenely sophisticated.

Tropical Kerala

5 It's a luscious experi-ence exploring the tropically radiant back-waters of Kerala (p964): 900km of interconnected rivers, lakes, canals and lagoons lined with the swaying palms of thick coconut groves. One of the most popular and scenic ways to peruse these parts is by cruising on a teak-and-palm-thatch houseboat. Drift along the waterways as the sun sinks behind the trees, snack on succulent Kera-lan seafood and later fall asleep under a twinkling night sky – and forget all about life on land for a while. Alappuzha (Alleppey; p958)

Architectural Mumbai

6 Mumbai (p734) has long embraced every-thing in her midst and inven-tively made them her own. The result is an architec-tural melange of buildings with a raft of design influ-ences. The art deco and modern towers lend the city its cool, but it's the eclectic Victorian-era structures – the neo-Gothic, Indo-Saracenic and other old flourishes – that have added to Mumbai's magic. All those spires, gables, arches and onion domes, set off by lofty palms and leafy banyans, are apt embellish-ments for this movie-star city. Chhatrapati Shivaji Terminus (Victoria Terminus; p739)

Wild Safaris

7 You have to be quite lucky to spot a tiger or leopard in India, but thou-sands do. Even if you don't see a big cat, it's a pleasure to simply wander through one of India's many forest reserves (p1169) on the back of an elephant, ob-serving spotted deer, pea-cocks and langur monkeys, while colourful birds and butterflies flit overhead. Or just forget jungle cats and elephants and get camel happy instead! Desert safaris around places such as Jaisalmer involve riding atop these lovably goofy beasts, stopping at night to camp among a rippled ocean of sand dunes. Tiger, Bandhavgarh National Park (p678)

/ GETTY IMAGES © BARTOSZ HADYNIAK

Breezy Hill Stations

8 The valleys, deserts and palm-lined beaches are all well and good, but it can get darn hot down there. India's erstwhile princes and British colonials long used cool mountain towns, such as Darjeeling (p500), as refuges from the heat, and the hill stations still serve up lush forests and crisp mountain air. So, curl up under a blanket with a steaming cup of local tea and watch birds swooping across misty hillsides, broody clouds drifting over bulbous tea trees and village kids running through mountain fog and meadow wildflowers. Darjeeling (p500)

Streets Alive

9 At first it can be overwhelming – dust in your eyes, incessant vehicle honking, the ever-jostling crowds – but you'll learn to adjust. And when that happens, you'll increasingly relish the jewels of Indian street life: scrumptious snacks sizzling in mobile carts, the fragrance of flowers being sold on footpaths, cars, rickshaws, motorbikes and bicycles dancing to a curious rhythm only they seem to hear, and, of course, the cows – those sweet, stubborn creatures that plod along, seemingly unperturbed, among the urban tumult. Old Delhi (p60)

Glorious Bazaars

10 Shopaholics: prepare to be dazzled! Those allergic to shopping, India will cure you! The bubbly bazaars have everything you want, guaranteed (though you may not have known you wanted it), usually with a side-serving of friendly haggling. The variety will astonish you: tremendous textiles from chiffon saris to cotton shirts, glittering gold and silver bling, mounds of colourful spices, beautifully carved woodwork, jangly glass bangles, belly-button bindis, hand-woven shawls, bargain leather-bound books and a treasure trove of cute little trinkets. Fabrics for sale at street bazaar in Rajasthan (p104)

Sacred Varanasi

11 Welcome to Varanasi (p390). This is arguably India's most revered sacred city, with pilgrims flocking here to worship, take a holy dip in the Ganges River, or cremate loved ones. Hindus believe the waters of the Ganges cleanse away sins, while dying here is deemed particularly propitious as it offers emancipation from the arduous life-and-death cycle. Varanasi will swiftly sweep you into its dizzying spiritual whirlwind – just take a deep breath and immerse yourself in pondering the meaning of life, death…and beyond.

Beaches of Goa

12 One of the most easygoing places in India to chill out is along Goa's sun-kissed tropical coast (p810). With palm groves on one side of the white sands and gently lapping waves on the other, the best of the beaches are, indeed, postcard-perfect. But it's not an undiscovered paradise: this cool coastal strip bustles with fellow travellers, vendors and beach-shack eateries. It's a slice of paradise that appeals to social creatures and fans of creature comforts who like their seafood fresh and their holidays easy. Palolem (p849)

PLAN YOUR TRIP INDIA'S TOP 17

Mystical Jaisalmer

13 Rising like a giant sandcastle from the vast desert of Rajasthan, the 'Land of Kings', Jaisalmer's 12th-century citadel (p182) is romantically picturesque. This mystical sandstone fort, with its crenellated ramparts and undulating towers, is a truly fantastical structure, elegantly blending in with the toffee-gold hues of its desert environs. Inside, a royal palace, atmospheric old *havelis* (traditional residences), delicately chiselled Jain temples and skinny lanes all conspire to create one of the country's best places to get lost.

Dilly-dallying in Delhi

14 India's capital (p56) has had several incarnations over the last few thousand years, which may explain why there's so much going on here. Ancient lures include captivating ruins on almost every corner, such as the crumbling splendour of Old Delhi – with the Jama Masjid, Red Fort and other architectural gems. Add to this the city's diverse dining choices, superb museums and marvellous shopping options, and it's easy to see why dilly-dallying in Delhi is so easy to do. Jama Masjid (p66)

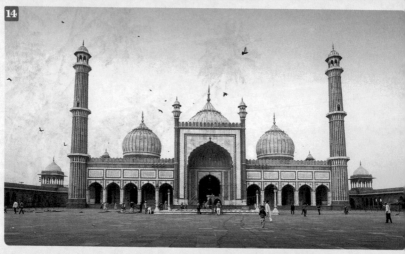

ABHINAV SAH / GETTY IMAGES ©

Sexy Khajuraho

15 Some say the sensuous carvings on Khajuraho's temples (p640) depict the Kamasutra, or Tantric practices for initiates; others, that they're educational models for children or allegories for the faithful. But pretty much everyone agrees that they're delightfully mischievous. Care to see a nine-person orgy? Couples imaginatively intertwined? Hot nymphs? Khajuraho is the place! Once the initial titillation wanes, you'll notice that the carving and architecture of these historic temples are breathtakingly exquisite and multifariously mind stirring.

Riding the Rails

16 India's quintessential journey is the long train ride (p34). Domestic flights are increasingly popular, but as the estimated 25 million daily train passengers can attest, you can't adequately soak up India's dramatically diverse landscape – from its parched sun-baked plains to its lush lime-green rice paddies – on a plane. Train travel also offers a splendid chance to leisurely chit-chat with Indian families and other fellow travellers, swapping stories the old-fashioned way – over a hot cup of chai, to the click-clacking soundtrack of the rattling rails. Mountain railway line to Ooty (Udhagamandalam; p1076)

Temple of Gold

17 The Sikhs' holiest of shrines, the Golden Temple (p213) in Amritsar, is divine in so many ways. Seeming to float atop a glistening pool named for the 'nectar of immortality', the temple is a stunning structure, made even more so by its intense goldness (the lotus-shaped dome is gilded in the real thing). Even when crowded with pilgrims it has a graceful tranquility, with the sounds of *kirtan* (Sikh devotional singing) and birds chirping outside, and the sacred waters gently lapping against the godly abode.

Need to Know

For more information, see Survival Guide (p1173)

Currency
Indian rupees (₹)

Languages
Hindi, English

Visas
Some nationalities can obtain a 30-day visa on arrival. For longer trips, most people obtain a six-month tourist visa, valid from the date of issue, not the date you arrive in India.

Money
ATMs in most large towns; carry cash or travellers cheques as back up. MasterCard and Visa are the most widely accepted credit cards.

Mobile Phones
Roaming connections are excellent in urban areas, poor in the countryside and the Himalaya. Local prepaid SIMs are widely available; they involve some straightforward paperwork and a wait of up to 24 hours for activation.

Time
India Standard Time (GMT/UTC plus 5½ hours)

When to Go

Leh
GO Jul–Sep

Delhi
GO Nov–Mar

Kolkata (Calcutta)
GO Nov–Mar

Mumbai (Bombay)
GO Nov–Feb

Bengaluru (Bangalore)
GO Nov–Mar

Alpine desert (including snow)
Desert, dry climate
Mild to hot summers, cold winters
Tropical climate, rain year-round
Tropical climate, wet & dry seasons
Warm to hot summers, mild winters

High Season (Dec–Mar)

➡ Pleasant weather with warm days and cool nights. Peak tourists. Peak prices.

➡ December and January bring chilly nights in the north.

➡ Temperatures climb steadily from February.

Shoulder Season (Jul–Nov)

➡ Passes to Ladakh and the high Himalaya open from July to September.

➡ Monsoon rain-showers persist through to September.

➡ The southeast coast and southern Kerala see heavy rain from October to early December.

Low Season (Apr–Jun)

➡ April is hot; May and June are scorching. Competitive hotel prices.

➡ From June, the monsoon sweeps from south to north, bringing draining humidity.

➡ Beat the heat (but not the crowds) in the cool hills.

Useful Websites

Lonely Planet (www.lonely-planet.com/india) Destination information, the Thorn Tree Travel Forum and more.

Incredible India (www.incredibleindia.org) Official India tourism site.

Templenet (www.templenet.com) Temple talk.

Rediff News (www.rediff.com/news) Portal for India-wide news.

World Newspapers (www.world-newspapers.com/india.html) Links to India's English-language publications.

Important Numbers

From outside India, dial your international access code, India's country code (②91) then the number (minus the initial '0').

Country code	②91
International access code	②00
Ambulance	②102
Fire	②101
Police	②100

Exchange Rates

Australia	A$1	₹50
Canada	C$1	₹52
Euro zone	€1	₹71
Japan	¥100	₹53
New Zealand	NZ$1	₹47
UK	UK£1	₹84
US	US$1	₹55

For current exchange rates see www.xe.com

Daily Costs

**Budget:
Less than ₹2000**

➡ Dorm bed: ₹100–200

➡ Double room in a budget hotel: ₹300–700

➡ All-you-can-eat thalis (plate meals): ₹120–300

➡ Bus & train tickets: ₹300–500

**Midrange:
₹2000–8000**

➡ Double hotel room: ₹1000–5000

➡ Meals in midrange restaurants: ₹400–1500

➡ Admission to historic sights and museums: ₹100–1000

➡ Local taxis/autorickshaws: ₹200–500

**Top End:
More than ₹8000**

➡ Deluxe hotel room: ₹5000–20,000

➡ Meals at superior restaurants: ₹1000–4000

➡ First-class train travel: ₹800–8000

➡ Renting a car & driver: ₹1200 upwards per day

Opening Hours

Opening hours are year-round for banks, offices and restaurants; many sights keep summer and winter opening hours.

Banks (nationalised) 10am–2pm/4pm Mon-Fri, to noon or 1pm Sat

Restaurants lunch noon–3pm, dinner 7pm–10pm or 11pm

Bars & Clubs noon–1am or later

Shops 10am–7pm or 8pm, some closed Sunday

Markets 10am–7pm in big cities, usually with one closed day; rural markets may be once weekly, from early morning to lunch

Arriving in India

Indira Gandhi International Airport (Delhi; p97) Prepaid taxis cost from ₹450 to the centre; express buses every 20 minutes (₹75); airport express metro trains (₹60/100 Sunday/Monday to Saturday) link up with the metro system. If you're transferring from terminal 1 to 3 allow at least three hours; the shuttle bus can take an hour.

Chhatrapati Shivaji International Airport (Mumbai; p771) Prepaid taxis to Colaba, Fort and Marine Dr cost ₹700/800 (non-AC/AC); ₹450 to ₹550 to Juhu or Bandra.

Chennai International Airport (pChennai) Suburban trains to central Chennai run every 10 to 20 minutes from 4am to midnight from Tirusulam station at the airport. Prepaid taxis cost ₹320 to ₹580.

Kempegowda International Airport (Bengaluru) (p868) Metered AC taxis to the centre cost ₹750 to ₹1000. Vayu Vajra's airport shuttle bus service runs to Kempegowda (Majestic) bus stand or MG Rd (₹210, hourly).

Getting Around

Transport in India is frequent and inexpensive, though not always fast. Consider domestic flights or sleeper trains as an alternative to long, uncomfortable bus rides.

Air Flights to major centres and state capitals; cheap flights with budget airlines.

Train Frequent services to most destinations; inexpensive tickets available even on sleeper trains.

Bus Buses go everywhere; some destinations are served 24 hours but longer routes may have just one or two buses a day.

For much more on **getting around**, see p1195

If You Like...

Forts & Palaces

India's architecture tells a tale of conquest, domination and inordinate riches.

Rajasthan Jaisalmer, Jodhpur and Amber are magnificent; Udaipur palace is surreally romantic. (p104)

Maharashtra The land of Shivaji has defensive masterpieces like Daulatabad (p784), and Janjira (p794), an island fortress.

Hyderabad The rugged Golconda Fort complements the many ethereal palaces of the City of Pearls. (p915)

Delhi This historically strategic city has several millennia worth of imperial forts. (p56)

Ladakh – Leh (p226) **& Stok** (p241) Palaces resemble mini versions of Tibet's Potala Palace.

Mysore Palace This majestic palace is the former residence of Mysore's maharajas. (p871)

Grand Temples & Monasteries

No one does temples like India – from psychedelic Technicolor Hindu towers to silently grand Buddhist cave temples and Amritsar's gold-plated fairy-tale Sikh shrine.

Tamil Nadu A temple wonderland, with towering, fantastical structures that climb to the sky in busy rainbows of sculpted deities. (p1000)

Golden Temple The queen of Sikh temples rises like a shining gem over a pool in Amritsar. (p213)

Rajasthan Jain temples at Jaisalmer, Ranakpur and Mt Abu are the stone-architecture equivalent of princesses draped in piles of jewellery. (p104)

Khajuraho Exquisite carvings of deities, spirits, musicians, regular people, mythological beasts – and lots of sex. (p638)

Tawang Gompa The world's second-largest Buddhist monastery, in Arunachal Pradesh, is set against snowy peaks. (p583)

Ajanta (p788) **& Ellora** (p785) Ancient, vast sculpted caves. Because monks like beautiful sculpture, too.

Delhi The almost-psychedelic structure of **Akshardham** (p78) versus the simplicity of the all-faith **Bahai House of Worship** (p77).

Ancient Ruins

You don't get to be a 5000-year-old civilisation without having lots of atmospheric ruins around. So many cultures and empires have left their marks here, making for easy time travel.

Hampi Rosy-hued temples and palaces of the capital of Vijayanagar are scattered among otherworldly looking boulders and hilltops. (p896)

Mandu Many of the tombs, palaces, monuments and mosques on Mandu's green plateau are among India's finest Afghan architecture. (p669)

Nalanda This 1600-year-old university once enrolled 10,000 monks and students. Its monasteries, temples and stupas are still elegant in ruins. (p535)

Delhi Conquered and built up repeatedly over the past 3000 years, Delhi resembles a subcontinental Rome, with ruins all over the place. (p56)

Fatehpur Sikri A ghostly abandoned Mughal city, close to Agra and the Taj Mahal. (p369)

Ellora (p785) **& Ajanta** (p788) Magnificent rock-cut Buddhist temple caves in Maharashtra.

City Sophistication

City people here had attained high planes of sophistication when culture was just a glimmer in the West's eye. India's cities have great arts scenes,

excellent restaurants and
heaps of style.

Mumbai (Bombay) Fashion, film
stars, incredible restaurants,
glamorous lounges and (along
with Delhi) the country's best art
galleries. (p734)

Delhi Urban sophisticate Delhi
has historic attractions to go with
its exceedingly good shopping,
museums, street food and fine
dining. (p56)

Kolkata (Calcutta) Long known
for its poetic and political tenden-
cies, Kolkata also has fabulous
colonial-era architecture and a
lively arts scene. (p454)

Bengaluru (Bangalore) This IT
hub has a boozy nightlife with
microbreweries, gastropubs and
rock bars full of locals looking to
party. (p856)

Chennai (Madras) Increasingly
sophisticated, with towering
temples, elegant bars, swish
hotels, fabulous shopping and
a booming fine-dining scene.
(p1003)

PLAN YOUR TRIP IF YOU LIKE...

Bazaars

Indian megamalls may be
popping up like monsoon
frogs, but the age-old bazaar – with its crowds and
spices, garbage and flowers,
altars and underwear – is
still where it's at.

Old Delhi The Mughal-era
bazaars sell pretty much
everything, while Chandni Chowk
has some of India's best street
food. (p94)

Goa Tourist flea markets are huge
on the north coast, while Panaji
(Panjim) and Margao bazaars
make for excellent wandering.
(p834)

Mumbai The megalopolis's old,
characterful markets are handily
themed: Mangaldas (fabric),
Zaveri (jewellery), Crawford

Top: Wild elephants, Kerala (p938)
Bottom: Vittala Temple (p897), Hampi

(produce) and Chor (random antique bits). (p769)

Hyderabad The colourful, swarming streets around the Charminar sell bangles, birds, vegetables, wedding saris, antiques and much more. (p925)

Mysuru (Mysore) Devaraja Market is about 125 years old and filled with about 125 million flowers, fruits and vegetables. (p872)

Beaches

India's coastlines are diverse and gorgeous, with lots of personality. Several Goan and Keralan beaches are downright paradisiacal, while elsewhere, the shoreline is more tinselled, with strolling and snack carts.

Varkala & Thottada In Kerala, Varkala (p950) is backed by dramatic cliffs and with a busy backpacker scene, while more deserted Thottada (p996), shaded by nodding palms, is a vision.

Goa Even when overrun with travellers, the beaches are still lovely. Mandrem and Palolem are two of the prettiest. (p810)

Havelock Island In the Andaman Islands, one of the world's most gorgeous beaches has clear, aquamarine water lapping against white powder. (p1093)

East Coast Gopalpur-on-Sea (p618), Puri (p610) and Visakhapatnam (p932) are more fun than precious: think esplanades, balloon-wallahs and extended families eating candy floss.

Gokarna Originally for Goa overflow, Gokarna's beaches are laid-back, beautiful and part of a sacred ancient village. (p892)

Hill Stations

India is blessed with a hot, tropical climate, and lots of hills where you can escape from it. Royalty and colonials of old laid the foundations for today's hill-station resort culture.

Tamil Nadu Kodaikanal (p1066) and Ooty (p1076) in the Western Ghats have lush, misty pine forests, tea plantations, gorgeous vistas and colonial-era bungalows.

Munnar Kerala's lofty, untouristy hill station is all rolling tea and spice plantations, unusual birds and dreamy mist. (p970)

Matheran This weekend retreat for Mumbaikars is not only scenic and car-free; it's also reached by narrow-gauge toy train. (p798)

Shimla With fascinating relics of the Raj, this is a great appetite-whetter for the magnificent Himalayan mountain tracts beyond. (p281)

Darjeeling Quintessential hot-season escape, surrounded by emerald-green tea plantations, with a backdrop of Himalayan splendour. (p500)

Boat Rides

India has such a diverse collection of waterways that the cruising possibilities are endless. From canoes to steamships to houseboats, there are lots of ways to experience India's aquatic side.

Kerala Languorous drifting on the backwaters around Alappuzha (Alleppey; p958), canoe tours from Kollam (Quilon; p955) and bamboo-raft tours in Periyar Wildlife Sanctuary (p966).

Goa Dolphin- and croc-spotting tours on the Mandovi River; cruise to a secluded beach by outrigger fishing boat. (p825)

Andaman Islands See mangroves, rainforest and reefs with 50 types of coral at Mahatma Gandhi Marine National Park. (p1092)

Uttar Pradesh Navigate UP's chaotic holiness with dawn tours of Varanasi's ghats (p391) and sacred river cruises in Chitrakut (p390), Mathura (p409) and Allahabad (p385).

Assam Four- to 10-night steamboat cruises are offered along the mighty Brahmaputra River as it meanders through the Northeast. (p571)

Odisha Spot rare Irrawaddy dolphin as you tour Chilika Lake, Asia's largest brackish lagoon. (p615)

Traveller Enclaves

Sometimes you just want to find travel partners, exchange stories, discuss strange bowel events. There are places for that.

Hampi The stunning beauty of Hampi's landscape and architecture makes everyone want to stay for a while. (p896)

Palolem & Arambol Goa is one big traveller enclave, but Palolem (p849) and cheaper Arambol (p840) are its current epicentres.

Yoga Centres Rishikesh (p414), Mysuru (p870), Pune (p801) and Goa (p810) all have major international yoga centres – and concomitant hang outs.

Sudder Street, Kolkata The accommodation on Kolkata's tourist lane is grungy but great for meeting fellow Mother Teresa volunteers. (p471)

Dharamsala Because who doesn't want to be near the Dalai Lama? (p318)

Pushkar Travellers, pilgrims, camels: everyone converges on this Rajasthan town for the Camel Fair, but it's a hang-out all year round. (p135)

Delhi Love it or hate it, almost every India traveller passes through Paharganj in Delhi at some point. (p81)

Arts & Crafts

Practically every town, village and neighbourhood here has its own tradition of devotional painting, silk weaving, camel-hide decorating, mirrored embroidering, or other art you won't find anywhere else.

Odisha Indians like bling – always have – and silver's an old favourite. Odisha's *tarakasi*, a kind of filigree work, is stunning. (p598)

Gujarat & Rajasthan India's textile traditions are legion. Villages in Gujarat and Rajasthan specialise in embroidery with tiny mirrors: such as jewellery for your clothes. (p686)

Bihar Folk paintings known as *Mithila* (or *Madhubani*) colourfully depict village scenes. The style is ancient but looks surprisingly contemporary. (p526)

Tamil Nadu The Tamil tradition of sculpting bronze figures of

Nataraja, the cosmic dancer, is about 1000 years old. (p1002)

Kashmir Renowned for its hand-woven carpets and jewel-bright papier mâché. (p222)

Mountains & Trekking

India has several beautiful mountain ranges that would be knock outs anywhere else. But here, there's only one range that matters: the Himalaya. The only question is how to approach it.

Ladakh Trek across 5000m passes between spiky crags and sleep in timeless villages whose barley fields create emerald-green oases in the arid moonscape. (p223)

Lahaul & Spiti Green Lahaul and drier, more rugged Spiti are separated from the rest of Himachal Pradesh by panoramic mountain passes. (p340)

Arunachal Pradesh This off-the-beaten-track 'land of dawn-lit mountains' is all forest, hills and peaks on the Tibetan border. (p577)

Darjeeling Take the Singalila Ridge Trek for incredible views of the mighty Himalaya. (p512)

Sikkim See Khangchendzonga, the world's third-highest mountain, in the early morning from Pelling or on treks to Goecha La and Dzongri. (p556)

Wildlife Safaris

You'll spot India's tigers and leopards if you're lucky, but its elephants, antelope, bison, one-horned rhino and deer are much more extroverted.

Madhya Pradesh & Chhattisgarh This is tiger country, and tiger-spotting safaris are offered in several national parks. (p626)

Assam Kaziranga National Park is the world's rhinoceros capital. Seeing them involves an hour's ride on a lumbering elephant. (p572)

Kerala Wayanad Wildlife Sanctuary is one of the few places where you have a good chance of spotting wild elephants. (p993)

Gujarat The only wild Asiatic lions, along with over 300 species of birds, live in the Sasan Gir Wildlife Sanctuary. (p715)

Karnataka Bandipur National Park is one of South India's best spots to see elephants, tigers and leopards. (p881)

Rajasthan Spot tigers and other wildlife amid the jungle and ruined temples of Ranthambhore. (p104)

Spiti The Kaza ecosphere in Kaza claims a 90% chance of snow leopard sightings if you spend a week or more in winter. (p347)

Maharashtra The Tadoba-Andhari Tiger Reserve is home to around 120 tigers. (p793)

Month by Month

Carnival, February or March

Holi, February or March

Ganesh Chaturthi, August or September

Navratri & Dussehra, September or October

Diwali, October or November

January

Postmonsoon cool lingers throughout the country, with downright cold in the mountains. Pleasant weather and several festivals make it a popular time to travel (book ahead!), while Delhi hosts big Republic Day celebrations.

Free India

Republic Day commemorates the founding of the Republic of India on 26

January 1950; the biggest celebrations are in Delhi, which holds a huge military parade along Rajpath, and the Beating of the Retreat ceremony three days later.

Kite Festival

Sankranti, the Hindu festival marking the sun's passage into Capricorn, is celebrated in many ways across India – from banana-giving to holy dips in the Ganges to cockfights. But it's the mass kite-flying in Gujarat, Andhra Pradesh, Uttar Pradesh and Maharashtra that steals the show.

Southern Harvest

The Tamil festival of Pongal, equivalent to Sankranti, marks the end of the harvest season. Families prepare pots of *pongal* (a mixture of rice, sugar, dhal and milk), symbolic of prosperity and abundance, then feed them to decorated and adorned cows.

Celebrating Saraswati

On Vasant Panchami, Hindus dress in yellow and place books, musical instruments and other educational objects in front of idols of Saraswati, the goddess of learning, to receive her blessing. The holiday may fall in February.

February

The weather is comfortable in most nonmountainous areas, with summer heat starting to percolate in the south (up to Maharashtra and West Bengal). It's still peak travel season; sunbathing and skiing are still on.

Tibetan New Year

Losar is celebrated by Tantric Buddhists all over India – particularly in Himachal Pradesh, Sikkim, Ladakh and Zanskar – for 15 days. Losar is usually in February or March, though dates can vary between regions.

Shivaratri

This day of Hindu fasting recalls the *tandava* (cosmic victory dance) of Lord Shiva. Temple processions are followed by the chanting of mantras and anointing of linga (phallic images of Shiva). Shivaratri can also fall in March.

🎭 Carnival in Goa

The four-day party kicking off Lent is particularly big in Goa. Sabado Gordo (Fat Saturday) starts it off with elaborate parades, and the revelry continues with street parties, concerts and general merrymaking. May also fall in March.

March

The last month of the travel season, March is full-on hot in most of the country, with rains starting in the Northeast. Wildlife is easier to spot as animals come out to find water.

🎭 Holi

One of North India's most ecstatic festivals; Hindus celebrate the beginning of spring according to the lunar calendar, in February or March, by throwing coloured water and *gulal* (powder) at anyone within range. Bonfires the night before symbolise the demise of demoness Holika. (Dates: 23 March 2016, 13 March 2017 and 2 March 2018.)

👁 Wildlife-Watching

When the weather warms up, water sources dry out and animals venture into the open to find refreshment: your chance to spot elephants, deer and, if you're lucky, tigers and leopards. Visit www.sanctuaryasia.com for detailed info.

🎭 Rama's Birthday

During Ramanavami, which lasts anywhere from one to nine days, Hindus celebrate Rama's birth with processions, music, fasting and feasting, enactments of scenes from the Ramayana and, at some temples, ceremonial weddings of Rama and Sita idols.

April

The heat has officially arrived in most places, which means you can get deals and avoid tourist crowds. The Northeast, meanwhile, is wet, but it's peak time for visiting Sikkim and upland West Bengal.

🎭 Mahavir's Birthday

In April or March, Mahavir Jayanti commemorates the birth of Jainism's 24th and most important *tirthankar* (teacher and enlightened being). Temples are decorated and visited, Mahavir statues are given ritual baths, processions are held and offerings are given to the poor.

🎭 Kumbh Mela

There are several versions of the huge Hindu pilgrimage, Kumbh Mela, held every few years, but all involve mass devotion – mass as in tens of millions of people. The next ritual group bathings are in Ujjain (April/May 2016) and Prayag (2019).

May

In most of the country it's hot. Really hot. Festivals slow down as humidity builds up in anticipation of the rain. Hill stations are hopping, though, and in the mountains it's pre-monsoon trekking season.

🎭 Buddha's Birthday

Commemorating the Buddha's birth, nirvana (enlightenment) and *parin-irvana* (total liberation from the cycle of existence, or passing away), Buddha Jayanti is quiet but moving: devotees dress simply, eat vegetarian food, listen to dharma talks and visit monasteries or temples. Sometimes falls in April. (Dates: 14 May 2016, 3 May 2017 and 22 May 2018.)

🏃 Northern Trekking

May and June, the months preceding the rains in the northern mountains, are good times for trekking, with sunshine and temperate weather. Consider Himachal Pradesh, Kashmir (but not Ladakh) and Uttarakhand.

June

June's not a popular travel month in India, unless you're trekking up north. The rainy season, or pre-monsoon extreme heat, has started just about everywhere else.

🎭 Ramadan (Ramazan)

Thirty days of dawn-to-dusk fasting mark the ninth month of the Islamic calendar. Muslims traditionally turn their attention to God, with a focus on prayer and purification. Ramadan begins around 7 June 2016, 27 May 2017 and 16 May 2018.

July

It's really raining almost everywhere, with many remote roads being washed out. Consider visiting Ladakh, where the weather's surprisingly fine, or do a rainy-season meditation retreat, an ancient Indian tradition.

★ Odisha's Festival of Chariots

During Rath Yatra (Car Festival), effigies of Lord Jagannath (Vishnu incarnated as lord of the world) and his siblings are carried through towns on massive chariots, most famously in Puri, Odisha (Orissa; p600). Millions come to see them. (Dates: 6 July 2016, 25 June 2017 and 14 July 2018.)

★ Brothers & Sisters

On Raksha Bandhan (Narial Purnima), girls fix amulets known as *rakhis* to the wrists of brothers and close male friends to protect them in the coming year. Brothers reciprocate with gifts and promises to take care of their sisters.

★ Eid al-Fitr

Muslims celebrate the end of Ramadan with three days of festivities. Prayers, shopping, gift-giving and, for women and girls, *mehndi* (henna designs) may all be part of the celebrations.

August

It's still high monsoon season, but it's prime time in Ladakh. Some travellers love tropical areas, like Kerala or Goa, this time of year: the jungles are lush, green and glistening in the rain.

★ Snake Festival

The Hindu festival Naag Panchami is dedicated to Ananta, the serpent upon whose coils Vishnu rested between universes. Women return to their family homes and fast, while serpents are venerated as totems against flooding and other evils. Falls in July or August (7 August 2016, 27 July 2017 and 15 August 2018).

★ Independence Day

This public holiday on 15 August marks the anniversary of India's independence from Britain in 1947. Celebrations include flag-hoisting ceremonies (the biggest one is in Delhi), parades and patriotic cultural programs.

★ Celebrating the Buddha's Teaching

Drupka Teshi commemorates Siddhartha Gautama's first teaching, in which he explained the Four Noble Truths to disciples in Sarnath. Celebrations are big in Sikkim. The festival may also fall in July.

★ Krishna's Birthday

Janmastami celebrations can last a week in Krishna's birthplace, Mathura; elsewhere the festivities range from fasting to

puja (prayers) and offering sweets, to drawing elaborate *rangoli* (rice-paste designs) outside the home. Janmastami is held August/September. (Dates: 25 August 2016, 15 August 2017 and 2 September 2018.) (p725)

★ Parsi New Year

Parsis celebrate Pateti, the Zoroastrian new year, especially in Mumbai (Bombay). Houses are cleaned and decorated with flowers and *rangoli,* the family dresses up and eats special fish dishes and sweets, and offerings are made at the Fire Temple.

★ Onam

In August or September, Onam is Kerala's biggest cultural celebration, when the entire state celebrates the golden age of mythical King Mahabali for 10 days.

◉ Nehru Trophy Boat Race

In Alappuzha (Alleppey); the most popular of Kerala's boat races. (p958)

September

The rain begins to ease up (with temperatures still relatively high), with places suh as Rajasthan all but finished with the monsoon. The second trekking season begins midmonth in the Himalaya and runs through October.

★ Ganesh Chaturthi

In August or September Hindus celebrate Ganesh Chaturthi, the birth of the elephant-headed god, with verve, particularly in Mumbai, Hyderabad and

Top: Street decorations for Southern Harvest (Pongal) festival (p24), Karnataka
Bottom: Holi festival (p25)

Chennai (Madras). Clay idols of Ganesh are paraded through the streets before being ceremonially immersed in rivers, tanks (reservoirs) or the sea. (Dates: 5–15 September 2016, 25 August–5 September 2017 and 13–23 September 2018.)

🎉 Eid al-Adha

Muslims commemorate Ibrahim's readiness to sacrifice his son to God by slaughtering a goat or sheep and sharing it with family, the community and the poor. (Dates: around 11 September 2016, 1 September 2017 and 20 August 2018.)

October

Some showers aside, this is when India starts to get its travel mojo on. October, aka shoulder season, brings festivals, mostly good weather with reasonably comfy temperatures, and lots of post-rain greenery and lushness.

🎉 Muharram

Shiite Muslims commemorate the martyrdom of the Prophet Mohammed's grandson Imam Hussain, an event known as Ashura, with fasting, beautiful processions and a month of grieving and remembrance. Sunni Muslims also mark this, but with fasting and celebrations marking when Moses (Moosa) fasted because Allah saved the Israelites from their enemy in Egypt. Approximate start dates: 1 October 2016, 20 September 2017 and 10 September 2018.

✳️ Gandhi's Birthday

The national holiday of Gandhi Jayanti is a solemn celebration of Mohandas Gandhi's birth, on 2 October, with prayer meetings at his cremation site in Delhi, Raj Ghat. (p67)

🏃 Water, Water Everywhere

Water bodies are full after the rains, making for spectacularly white-water falls. This is also the season for rafting in some areas; visit www.indiarafting.com.

✳️ Navratri

The Hindu 'Festival of Nine Nights' leading up to Dussehra celebrates the goddess Durga in all her incarnations. Festivities are particularly vibrant in West Bengal, Maharashtra and Gujarat; in Kolkata, Durga images are immersed in rivers and tanks. (p694)

✳️ Dussehra

Colourful Dussehra celebrates the victory of the Hindu god Rama over the demon-king Ravana and the triumph of good over evil. Dussehra is big in Kullu (p304), where over 200 village deities are carried into the town on palanquins and festivities go on for a week. (Dates: 11 October 2016 and 30 September 2017.) (p304)

✳️ Diwali

In the lunar month of Kartika, in October or November, Hindus celebrate Diwali (Festival of Lights) for five days, with gifts, fireworks, and burning butter and oil lamps (or hanging lanterns) to lead Lord Rama home from exile. One of India's prettiest and noisiest festivals. (Dates: 30 October 2016, 18 October 2017 and 7 November 2018.)

November

The climate is blissful in most places, but the southern monsoon hits Tamil Nadu and Kerala.

✳️ International Film Festival of India

Held in Panaji (Panjim) in Goa, India largest film festival draws Bollywood's finest for premieres, parties and screenings. (p815)

✳️ Guru Nanak's Birthday

Nanak Jayanti, birthday of Guru Nanak, founder of Sikhism, is celebrated with prayer, *kirtan* (devotional singing) and processions for three days, especially in Punjab and Haryana. The festival may also be held on 14 April, possibly Nanak's actual 1469 birth date.

👁 Pushkar Camel Fair

Held during Kartika (the eighth Lunar month, usually October or November), this fair attracts around 200,000 people, bringing some 50,000 camels, horses and cattle. It's a swirl of colour, magic and mayhem, thronged with musicians, mystics, tourists, camera crews, traders, devotees and animals. (p138)

December

December is peak tourist season for a reason: the weather's glorious (except for the chilly mountains), the humidity's low, the mood is festive and the beach is sublime.

👁 Weddings

Marriage season peaks in December, and you may see a *baraat* (bridegroom's procession), replete with white horse and fireworks, on your travels. Across the country, loud music and spectacular parties are the way they roll, with brides in *mehndi* and pure gold.

👁 Birding

Many of India's 1000-plus bird species have their winter migration from November to January or February, and excellent birdwatching spots are peppered across the country; www.birding. in is an excellent resource.

🏃 Camel Treks in Rajasthan

The cool winter (November to February) is the time to mount a camel and ride through Rajasthan's sands. See the Thar Desert from a new perspective: observe gazelles, cook dinner over an open fire and camp out in the dunes. (p188)

✳️ Christmas

Christian Goa comes alive at Christmas time, midnight masses are held on 24 December, and Christmas Day sees feasting and fireworks.

✳️ The Prophet Mohammed's Birthday

The Islamic festival of Eid-Milad-un-Nabi celebrates the birth of the Prophet Mohammed with prayers and processions, especially in Jammu and Kashmir. It falls around 24 December 2015, 12 December 2016 and 1 December 2017.

Itineraries

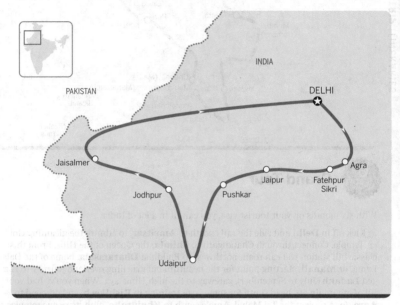

INDIA

PAKISTAN

DELHI

Jaisalmer

Agra

Jaipur

Fatehpur Sikri

Jodhpur

Pushkar

Udaipur

2 WEEKS Golden Triangle & Rajasthan

A tourist trail with genuine highlights to make up for the crowds, the Golden Triangle of Delhi, Agra and Jaipur combines some of India's top sights.

Kick off in **Delhi**, touring the must-sees – the Mughal-era Red Fort and Jama Masjid, and the magnificent Qutb Minar. Next, catch a train to **Agra** and gaze on the glory of the Taj Mahal, the world's most extravagant monument to love. Explore Agra Fort and devote a day to nearby **Fatehpur Sikri**, a mesmerising Mughal city. Continue on to **Jaipur**, and devote several days to the dusty bazaars and myriad monuments of the Pink City. Essential stops include the City Palace and Amber Fort.

Loop back to Delhi, or travel on to **Pushkar** for a few days of roaming around lakeside temples, then devote several days to graceful **Udaipur** and a lavish dinner at the hotel on the lake. Next visit magnificent hilltop Kumbhalgarh and the temple at Ranakpur, en route to **Jodhpur**. Soak up the colours of the Blue City from the battlements of magnificent Mehrangarh Fort. Spend the last few days in fortified **Jaisalmer** and indulge your *Arabian Nights* fantasies on a camel safari through the dunes. Finally, loop back to Delhi, with one last detour to the Qutb Minar, for a final dose of imperial splendour.

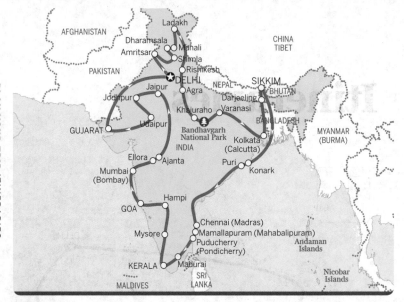

Grand Tour

With six months on your tourist visa, you can fit in a lot of India.

Kick off in **Delhi** and ride the rails north to **Amritsar**, to admire the gleaming Golden Temple. Connect through Chandigarh to **Shimla**, the Queen of the Hills. From this classic hill station you can roam northwest to Buddhist **Dharamsala**, home of the Dalai Lama, or **Manali**, starting point for the beautiful but gruelling overland journey to rugged **Ladakh** (July to September), gateway to the high Himalaya. When you've had your fill of mountain air, head south for some yoga training in **Rishikesh**, and descend to **Agra**, for a peek at the Taj Mahal. Amble south to **Khajuraho**, with its risqué temples, and scan the jungle for tigers in **Bandhavgarh National Park**. Continue to the holy city of **Varanasi** for a boat trip along the sacred Ganges.

Take time for detours as you wander east to **Kolkata** (Calcutta), bustling capital of West Bengal. Swing north as far as **Darjeeling** or **Sikkim** for sweeping Himalayan views, then drift down the coast to the temple towns of **Konark** and **Puri** in Odisha (Orissa). Consider a flight to transport you south to **Chennai** (Madras) for a dose of southern spice.

As you loop around the bottom of India, essential stops include **Mamallapuram** (Mahabalipuram), for temple carvings; **Puducherry** (Pondicherry), for colonial quaintness; and **Madurai**, for deity-encrusted temple towers. Allow a few days to kick back on **Kerala's beaches**, then swing inland to nostalgic **Mysore** to see how maharajas lived.

Continuing north, head to **Hampi**, where temples and ruined cities are strewn among the boulders, then get a second dose of beach life on the coast of **Goa**. Onward to **Mumbai** (Bombay), fast-paced capital of the west coast; take in a Bollywood movie, then admire the glory of the cave paintings and carvings at **Ajanta** and **Ellora**.

To finish, head to Rajasthan and complete the coloured-city triple – **Jaipur** (pink), **Jodhpur** (blue) and **Udaipur** (white). There might just be time to detour to the temples and nature reserves of **Gujarat**, before closing the circle with a last train ride to Delhi.

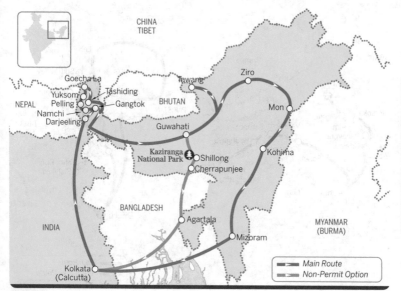

| | Main Route |
| | Non-Permit Option |

1 MONTH Sikkim & the Northeast States

Surprisingly few people explore mountainous Sikkim and the Northeast States. Kept from prying eyes by insurgencies and permit restrictions, India's last frontier is slowly opening up to the outside world. From Kolkata, you can swing north to Darjeeling, get a full dose of Himalayan vistas in Sikkim then enter the fascinating world of India's hill tribes. Advance planning is essential – permits are mandatory and there are security risks to consider.

Starting in **Kolkata**, make your first stop **Darjeeling** – here you can sample India's finest teas and pick up a permit for Sikkim, one of India's most serene quarters. **Gangtok**, the Sikkimese capital, is the starting point for jeep rides to a string of historic, dramatic Buddhist temples. Veer to **Namchi** to see the giant statues of Shiva and Padmasambhava, and to **Pelling** for inspiring views of the white-peaked Khangchendzonga and the beautiful Pemayangtse Gompa, ringed by gardens and monks' cottages. Take the week-long trek from **Yuksom** to **Goecha La**, a 4940m pass with incredible views, then exit Sikkim via **Tashiding**, with more wonderful views and another stunning gompa, before travelling to Siliguri for the journey east.

In **Guwahati**, the Assamese capital, arrange tours and permits for the Northeast States: the remote areas of Arunachal Pradesh, Nagaland, Mizoram and Manipur. If you can't get a permit, try this loop: from Guwahati, head to **Kaziranga National Park** to spot rare rhinos. Detour to sleepy **Shillong**, and the waterfalls and incredible living root bridges of **Cherrapunjee**. From **Agartala**, capital of Tripura, return to Kolkata by air or overland through Bangladesh.

With the right permits, head from Guwahati to Arunachal Pradesh to pay your respects at the Buddhist monastery at **Tawang**, or the tribal villages near **Ziro**, where the elders have dramatic facial tattoos and piercings. A Nagaland permit opens up tribal villages around **Mon**, countryside dotted by traditional longhouses and remote settlements, and the capital **Kohima**, with its WWII relics. Manipur permits are rarely granted, but there's a fair chance of encountering Mizo culture in **Mizoram**, before you fly back to Kolkata.

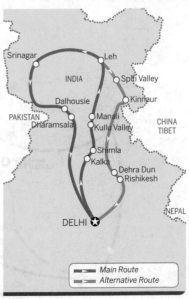

Main Route
Alternative Route

3 WEEKS Central Shrines

Visit some of India's most spiritual places on this temple-hopping trip around the central plains.

Start in the chaotic but cultured city of **Kolkata**, then swap the big-city bustle for the peace of **Bodhgaya**, where the Buddha attained enlightenment. Roll across the plains to **Sarnath**, where the Buddha first taught the dharma.

Hinduism replaces Buddhism as you approach the sacred city of **Varanasi**. Meditate on the banks of the River Ganges, then ramble to **Khajuraho**, where Hindu temples drip with erotic carvings. Head southwest to **Sanchi**, where Emperor Ashoka first embraced Buddhism, then zip through Bhopal to Jalgaon, jumping-off point for the carving-filled caves of **Ajanta**.

Next, detour into Rajasthan; stop off in whimsical **Udaipur**, with its lakes and palaces, then explore the extraordinary Jain temples of **Ranakpur** or **Mt Abu**. Continue to pilgrim-crammed **Pushkar**, then make a trip to nearby **Ajmer**, one of India's most holy Islamic sites. Take a final stop in atmospheric **Jaipur**, then end the trip in **Delhi**, with its magnificent Islamic ruins.

4 WEEKS Northern Mountains

This mountainous loop takes in some of India's most spectacular views.

Start by riding the rails from **Delhi** to **Kalka**, to board the narrow-gauge train to colonial-era **Shimla**. Spend a day or two rambling around the hills, then join the traveller pilgrimage north to the **Kullu Valley** for adventurous mountain activities.

From the hill resort of **Manali**, embark on the epic, two-day journey to **Leh** in Ladakh (July to September), to hike to dramatic Buddhist monasteries and trekking peaks. For a short loop, continue from Leh to Kargil and on to Kashmir (checking first that it's safe to travel). Stay on a **Srinagar** houseboat, then loop through Jammu to elegant **Dalhousie**, and soak up Buddhist culture in nearby **Dharamsala**, before returning to Delhi.

With more time to spare, head southeast from Leh into the dramatic **Spiti Valley**, where ancient monasteries blend into the arid landscape. Ride the rattletrap bus to rugged **Kinnaur**, with its plunging landscapes, and make stops in **Dehra Dun** and **Rishikesh** to soak up some Hindu culture, before finishing in Delhi.

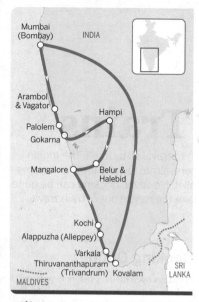

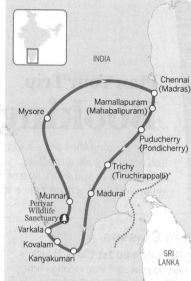

 Southern Coastal

 The Southern Tip

This trip gambols to some of India's finest beaches and charismatic coastal towns.

Start in **Mumbai** and sample *bhelpuri* (crisp noodle salad) on the sand at Girgaum Chowpatty beach. Cruise to the stunning rock-cut temples on Elephanta Island, then travel south by train to beach-blessed Goa.

Enjoy the best of the sand at **Arambol**, **Vagator** and **Palolem**, then continue along the coast to the sacred town of **Gokarna**. Now change the pace entirely; head inland to **Hampi**, with its serene Vijayanagar ruins, and witness the zenith of medieval stone-carving in the Hoysala temples of **Belur** and **Halebid**. Return by train to **Mangalore** to sample spectacular seafood, then chug south to melting-pot **Kochi** (Cochin), which draws influences from as far afield as China and the Middle East.

Cruise Kerala's backwaters from **Alappuzha** (Alleppey), before dipping your toes in the waters around beach resorts **Varkala** or **Kovalam**. Make your last stop **Thiruvananthapuram** (Trivandrum), home to often-overlooked museums, before closing the loop with a flight back to Mumbai.

Chennai is the capital of the south, and the easiest starting point for exploring India's steamy southern tip. Time your trip to avoid the monsoon – the sunniest skies are from October to February.

Kick off sampling incendiary thalis in **Chennai**, then surround yourself with intricate temple carvings in **Mamallapuram**, one-time home of the Pallava kings.

Next, head for the decadent grace of French-flavoured **Puducherry**, then leave the coast behind and head inland to the temple-towns of Tamil Nadu: essential stops include boulder-covered **Trichy** (Tiruchirappalli), and **Madurai**, with its soaring, deity-covered *gopurams* (temple towers). From here, it's easy to zip down to **Kanyakumari**, the southernmost point of India.

Kick back on the coast at **Kovalam** or **Varkala**, then head to **Periyar Wildlife Sanctuary**, home to tigers and elephants, or take a trip up to **Munnar**, Kerala's centre of tea plantations, to enjoy rambles in the hills. En route back to Chennai visit **Mysore**, with its maharaja's palace and giant stone Nandi (bull statue). Bingo – a neat circuit, stringing together the jewels of the south.

Plan Your Trip
Booking Trains

In India, riding the rails is a reason to travel all by itself. The Indian rail network goes almost everywhere, almost all the time, and trains have seats to suit every size of wallet. However, booking can be quite an undertaking – book online to take the hassle out of train travel.

Train Classes

Air-Conditioned 1st Class (1AC)
The most expensive class, with two- or four-berth compartments with locking doors and meals included.

Air-Conditioned 2-Tier (2AC)
Two-tier berths arranged in groups of four and two in an open-plan carriage. Bunks convert to seats by day and there are curtains, offering some privacy.

Air-Conditioned 3-Tier (3AC)
Three-tier berths arranged in groups of six in an open-plan carriage with no curtains; popular with Indian families.

AC Executive Chair
Comfortable, reclining chairs and plenty of space; usually on Shatabdi express trains.

AC Chair
Similar to the Executive Chair carriage but with less-fancy seating.

Sleeper Class
Open-plan carriages with three-tier bunks and no AC; the open windows afford great views.

Unreserved/reserved 2nd Class (II/SS or 2S)
Wooden or plastic seats and a lot of people – but cheap!

Booking Online

Bookings open 60 days before departure for long-distance trains, sometimes earlier for short-haul trips. Seats fill up quickly – reserve at least a week ahead where possible, though shorter journeys are usually easier to obtain.

Express and mail trains form the mainstay of Indian rail travel. Not all classes are available on every train service, but most long-distance services have general (2nd-class) compartments with unreserved seating and more comfortable reserved compartments, usually with the option of sleeper berths for overnight journeys. Sleeper trains offer the chance to travel huge distances for not much more cost than the price of a midrange hotel room.

Shatabdi express trains are same-day services with seating only; Rajdhani express trains are long-distance overnight services between Delhi and state capitals with a choice of 1AC, 2AC, 3AC and 2nd class. More expensive sleeper categories provide bedding. In all classes, a padlock and a length of chain are useful for securing your luggage to the baggage racks provided.

These websites are useful for online international bookings.

Cleartrip (www.cleartrip.com) A reliable private agency and the easiest way to book; accepts international MasterCard and Visa credit cards. Can only book direct journeys.

RAILWAY RAZZLE DAZZLE

You can live like a maharaja on one of India's luxury train tours, with accommodation on board, tours, admission fees and meals included in the ticket price. A new Mumbai–Goa train is also on the cards; check online to see if this is up and running.

Palace on Wheels (www.palaceonwheels.net) Eight- to 10-day luxury tours of Rajasthan, departing from Delhi. Trains run on fixed dates from September to April; the fare per person per night starts at US$615/451/411 (in a single/double/triple cabin). Try to book 10 months in advance.

Royal Rajasthan on Wheels (www.royalrajasthanonwheels.co.in) Runs lavish one-week trips from October to March, starting and finishing in Delhi. The fare per person per night starts from US$875/625 for single/twin occupancy in deluxe suites.

Deccan Odyssey (www.coxandkings.co.uk) Nine nights covering the main tourist spots of Maharashtra and Goa. Fares per person start at a decidedly upmarket UK£6090/3495 for single/double occupancy (includes flights). There are also several other shorter luxurious trips on offer.

Golden Chariot (www.coxandkings.co.uk) Tours the south in sumptuous style from October to March, starting in Bengaluru (Bangalore); 10-night trips visit Mysuru (Mysore), Hampi and Goa. Rates per person start at UK£4445 (includes flights).

Mahaparinirvan Express (Buddhist Circuit Special; www.railtourismindia.com) Running September to March to Buddhist sites over eight days, starting in Delhi, with overnight stays in hotels. Rates start from US$160/120/115 per person per night in 1st class/2AC/3AC. Additional charges apply for single occupancy of hotel rooms.The trip includes Nepal (the visa fee is not included in the price).

If booking from outside India before you have a local mobile number, a work-around is to enter a random number, and use email only to communicate.

IRCTC (www.irctc.co.in) Government site offering bookings for regular trains and luxury tourist trains; only American Express cards issued in UK and Australia for international ticketing, but accepts these erratically.

Make My Trip (www.makemytrip.com) Reputable private agency; accepts international cards. Again, you'll need an Indian mobile number. You'll then need to create an IRCTC User ID: choose a User ID (username), put in your name, birth date and address. For the 'Pincode' (postcode) '123456' will work. For the State choose 'Other'.

Yatra (www.yatra.com) Books flights and trains; accepts international cards.

Reservations

You must make a reservation for all chair-car, sleeper, 1AC, 2AC and 3AC carriages. No reservations are required for general (2nd-class) compartments. Book well ahead for overnight journeys or travel during holidays and festivals. Waiting until the day of travel to book is not recommended.

Train Passes

IndRail passes permit unlimited rail travel for a fixed period, ranging from one day to 90 days, but offers limited savings and you must still make reservations. Prices start at US$19/43/95 (sleeper/2AC, 3AC & chair car/1AC) for 24 hours.The easiest way to book these is through the IndRail pass agency in your home country – click on the Passenger Info/Tourist Information link on www.indian railways.gov.in/railwayboard for details.

Plan Your Trip
Trekking

India has world-class trekking opportunities, particularly in the Himalaya, where staggering snow-clad peaks, traditional tribal villages, sacred Hindu sites, ancient Buddhist monasteries and blazing fields of wildflowers are just some of the features that create extraordinary mountain experiences. Hit the trails for easy half-day jaunts or strenuous multiweek expeditions.

Best Treks

The Himalaya

Jammu & Kashmir The high, dry and rugged ranges rising in Ladakh boast unforgettable treks, including routes through the popular Markha Valley and wildly beautiful Zanskar region (p246).

Himachal Pradesh Alpine bliss is easily accessible, including on treks from McLeod Ganj to Bharmour (p328), between the Parvati and Pin Valleys (p304), and on the Buddhist-infused Homestay Trail in the Spiti region (p347).

Uttarakhand Immerse yourself in pristine scenery on the Kauri Pass, Milam Glacier and Har-ki-Dun treks (p440) or join pilgrims en route to sacred religious sites such as Kedarnath Temple (p435) or Hem Kund (p439).

Sikkim Gape at Khangchendzonga (8598m), the world's third-highest mountain, on the Goecha La trek (p561).

South India

Karnataka Explore the serene hills and forests of Kodagu (p883).

Kerala Check out tigers, elephants and boar in Periyar Wildlife Sanctuary (p966).

Tamil Nadu The hill station Ooty (Udhagamandalam; p1076) is popular for forest hikes, but may be closed to trekking due to tiger activity.

Trail Tips

With a commercial trekking industry that's far less developed than in neighbouring Nepal, many places still feel wild and relatively unspoilt. Still, on most routes, you can hire porters or pack animals to haul your gear. If you go with a trekking company, some gear may be supplied. Specify *everything* that's included beforehand, and get it in writing if possible.

Wherever you go, make sure you have any permits you may need.

Monitor your health – Acute Mountain Sickness (p1208) is a serious risk on trails over 3000m.

And beware of herding dogs!

Route Planning

Detailed maps of the Indian Himalaya are difficult to buy in-country. Some maps found online are good enough for planning, and even navigating if you're experienced at reading them. For Ladakh, pricey 1:300,000 scale maps can be bought in Leh; some maps from the 1:200,000 Leomann series are often available in Manali and McLeod Ganj.

On popular pilgrims' trails, it's virtually impossible to get lost, but less-travelled tracks can fork or vanish altogether, so hiring a local guide can be wise.

Lonely Planet's *Trekking in the Indian Himalaya* is a great resource for planning and executing treks.

For information on climbing Himalayan summits over 6000m, check the website of the **Indian Mountaineering Foundation** (www.indmount.org).

Packing

➡ Bring gear and clothing that are appropriate for the conditions you expect to encounter.

➡ On well-established trails, heavy hiking boots are overkill, but on remote mountain tracks they can be lifesavers.

➡ First-aid and water-purification supplies are often essential.

➡ Rain gear is a must, and warm layers are crucial for comfort at altitude.

➡ Remember sunscreen!

Trekking Ethics

➡ Follow low-impact trekking practices (you know the mantra – take only photographs, leave only footprints).

➡ Cook over stoves, since local people rely on limited fuel-wood sources.

➡ Respect local cultural sensibilities by dressing modestly; ask permission before snapping photos; remember that while locals' hospitality may be endless, their food supply might not be; and refrain from giving gifts to children.

When to Go

With India's diverse variety of terrain and altitudes, there's no single time throughout the country that's best for trekking; seasonal conditions vary greatly depending on what region you're in. Here's an overview of what you can expect, when:

May–June Before the monsoon hits, this is a good time for mountain trekking. Trails to holy Hindu sites can be packed with pilgrims.

> ### MOST ADVENTUROUS TREKS
>
> Only an intrepid few hike the tough terrain in the isolated, northeast mountain state of Arunachal Pradesh. One of the top spots to check out is Namdapha National Park (p581), which is mind-bogglingly rich in biodiversity.

Mid-July–mid-September This is monsoon season, so trekking in the wrong place can range from uncomfortable to deadly. Jungle trails can be forbiddingly muddy, while in many parts of the Himalaya cloudbursts cause massive landslides. Meanwhile, peaks are obscured by thick clouds, greatly diminishing the rewards trekkers seek for their efforts. The best places to trek during this time are Ladakh and Spiti, which generally stay pretty dry. The one place worth braving the rain is Uttarakhand's famous Valley of Flowers National Park (p439), which draws most of its visitors during the rainy season, when its dazzling botanical carpet spreads most vibrantly across the valley floor.

Mid-September–late October Once the monsoons clear out, searing blue skies usually bless the Himalaya. While nights at high altitude may dip below freezing, days are usually sunny and warm. Facilities and services (and some roads) in many mountain regions close for winter in October or November, so if you hope to trek then, check in advance to see what will be open.

December–March The most comfortable season to trek in South India. February is prime time to tackle the frozen Chadar Trek (p261) in the Zanskar region of Ladakh.

April Head for the hill stations (at middle altitudes), as it's ripping hot down low and usually still snow packed up high.

Plan Your Trip

Yoga, Spas & Spiritual Pursuits

Birthplace of at least three religions, India offers a profound spiritual journey for those so inclined. Even sceptical travellers can enjoy the benefits of trips to spas and yoga centres.

What to Choose

Ashrams
India has hundreds of ashrams – places of communal living established around the philosophies of a guru (a spiritual guide or teacher).

Ayurveda
Ayurveda is the ancient science of Indian herbal medicine and holistic healing, based on natural plant extracts, massage and therapies to treat body and mind.

Meditation
Many centres in Buddhist areas offer training in *vipassana* (mindfulness meditation) and Buddhist philosophy; many require a vow of silence and abstinence from tobacco, alcohol and sex.

Spa Treatments
India's spas offer an enticing mix of international therapies and local techniques based on ancient ayurvedic traditions.

Yoga
Yoga's roots lie firmly in India and you'll find hundreds of schools to suit all levels.

Ayurveda

Ayurveda – Indian herbal medicine – aims to restore balance in the body. For more, see the boxed text on p954.

Goa

Ayurvedic Massage Centre
(✆9420896843; 1/1½hr massage from ₹1000/1500; ☺9am-8pm) Two centres in Mandrem.

Gujarat

International Center for Ayurvedic Studies (p724; Jamnagar) Ayurveda, yoga and naturopathy.

Himachal Pradesh

Amchi (Tibetan traditional medicine) is closely linked to ayurveda. The Men-Tsee-Khang (Tibetan Medical & Astrological Institute; p321) is the primary authority on Tibetan medicine and has its HQ and two centres in McLeod Ganj, plus 46 other clinics across India.

Karnataka

Ayurvedagram (p861; Bengaluru) In a garden setting.

Soukya (p861; Bengaluru) Ayurveda and yoga.

Indus Valley Ayurvedic Centre (p876) (Mysore) Therapies from ancient scriptures.

Swaasthya (p885; Coorg) & Swaasthya (p876; Mysuru) Retreats and therapies.

SwaSwara (p894; Gokarna) Therapies and artistic pursuits.

Kerala

Dr Franklin's Panchakarma Institute (p950; Chowara) South of Kovalam.

Eden Garden (p951; Varkala) Treatments and packages.

Santhigiri Ayurveda Centre (p955; Kollam) Seven-to-21-day packages and day treatments. Branches at Kovalam (p946) and Periyar (p967).

Ayur Dar (p978; Kochi) Treatments of one to three weeks.

Madhya Pradesh

Orchha Resort (Map p634; ☑07680-252222; www.orchharesort.com; ☺8.30am-9pm) Ayurveda in Orchha.

Mumbai (Bombay)

Yoga Cara (p752) Ayurveda and massage.

Tamil Nadu

Sita (p1036; Puducherry) Ayurveda and yoga.

Uttar Pradesh

Swasthya Vardhak (p397; Varanasi) Ayurveda.

Yoga

You can practise yoga almost everywhere, from beach resorts to mountain retreats. In 2014, at India's initiative, the UN adopted a resolution declaring 21 June International Yoga Day.

Andaman Islands

Flying Elephant (p1095; Havelock Island) Yoga and meditation set in tropical surroundings.

Goa

Himalaya Yoga Valley (p839; Mandrem) Popular training school.

Swan Yoga Retreat (p835; Assagao) Retreat in a soothing jungle location.

Himalayan Iyengar Yoga Centre (p840) (Arambol) Courses.

Bamboo Yoga Retreat (p849; Patnem) Beachfront yoga.

Jammu & Kashmir

Mahabodhi Centre (p229; Leh) Yoga courses.

Karnataka

Mysuru (Mysore) was the birthplace of Ashtanga yoga, and there are centres all over the state (p877).

Kerala

Trivandrum, Varkala and Kochi (Cochin) are popular places for yoga. Sivananda Yoga Vedanta Dhanwantari Ashram (p946) near Trivandrum is renowned for longer courses.

Madhya Pradesh & Chhattisgarh

Amar Mahal (p637) (Orchha) Yoga training in luxurious surroundings.

Maharashtra

Kaivalyadhama Yoga Hospital (p799; Lonavla) Yogic healing.

Ramamani Iyengar Memorial Yoga Institute (p804; Pune) Advanced courses.

Mumbai

Yoga Institute (p753) Daily and longer-term programs.

Yoga House (p752) Hatha yoga in a lovely setting.

Yoga Cara (p752) More hatha yoga.

Tamil Nadu

International Centre for Yoga Education & Research (p1037; Puducherry) Has 10-day introductory courses as well as advanced training.

Krishnamacharya Yoga Mandiram (p1009; Chennai) Runs yoga courses, therapy and training.

Uttarkhand

Rishikesh has yoga centres and ashrams offering yoga for all levels (p415).

Meditation

Whether for an introduction or more advanced study, there are India-wide courses and retreats. McLeod Ganj is the main centre for the study of Tibetan Buddhism; public teachings are given by both the Dalai Lama (see p324) and the 17th Karmapa.

Bihar

Root Institute for Wisdom Culture (p531; Bodhgaya) Courses from two to 21 days.

International Meditation Centre (p531; Bodhgaya) informal 10-day courses.

Himachal Pradesh

Library of Tibetan Works & Archives (p326; McLeod Ganj) Serious Buddhist philosophy courses.

Himachal Vipassana Centre (p332; Dharamkot, near McLeod Ganj) Strict 10-day retreats.

Tushita Meditation Centre (p332; Dharamkot) Basic and advanced courses on Buddhist philosophy and meditation.

Jammu & Kashmir

Mahabodhi Centre (p229; Leh) Classes and three- or 10-day *vipassana* courses.

Maharashtra

Vipassana International Academy (p780; Igatpuri) Holds 10-day *vipassana* (mindfulness meditation) courses.

Mumbai

Global Pagoda (p750; Gorai Island) *Vipassana* courses from one to 10 days.

Telangana & Andhra Pradesh

Numerous Burmese-style *vipassana* courses, including the **Vipassana International Meditation Centre** (Dhamma Khetta; ☑24240290; www.khetta.dhamma.org; Nagarjuna Sagar Rd, Km12.6) near Hyderabad, **Dhamma Vijaya** (p931) near Eluru, and **Dhamma Nagajjuna** (p932; Nagarjuna Sagar).

Spa Treatments

From solo practitioners to opulent spas, there are choices nationwide. Be cautious of dodgy one-on-one massages that are offered by private (often unqualified) operators – seek recommendations and trust your instincts.

Delhi

Lodhi Spa (p79) A luxury-defining spa.

Goa

Nilaya Hermitage (☑0832-2269793; www.nilaya.com; Arpora; ✳@☎✉) Famous celebrity hangout.

Karnataka

Emerge Spa (p876) Pampering Asian-influenced treatments near Mysuru (Mysore).

Kerala

Neeleshwar Hermitage (p998) (near Bekal) Beachfront eco-resort.

Madhya Pradesh & Chhattisgarh

Jiva Spa (Map p630; Usha Kiran Palace; massage treatments from ₹1900; ☺8am-8pm) Massages, scrubs and wraps in beautiful surrounds in Gwalior.

Amar Mahal (p637) (Orchha) Lavish setting.

Mumbai

Antara Spa (p752) International treatments.

Palm Spa (p752) Renowned Colaba spa.

Uttar Pradesh

Aarna Spa (p397; Varanasi) Ayurveda, aromatherapy and pampering.

Top: Ayurvedic treatment (p954), Kerala

Bottom: Yoga practice

PANKAJ & INSY SHAH / GETTY IMAGES ©

Monks praying, Bodhgaya (p529)

Uttarakhand

Haveli Hari Ganga (p424; Haridwar) Over-looking the Ganges.

Ashrams

Many ashrams ('places of striving') are headed by charismatic gurus. Some tread a fine line between spiritual community and personality cult. Many gurus have amassed fortunes collected from devotees, and others have been accused of sexually exploiting their followers. Always check the reputation of any ashram you wish to join. Most ashrams offer philosophy, yoga or meditation courses, and visitors are usually required to adhere to strict rules. A donation is appropriate to cover your expenses.

Kerala

Matha Amrithanandamayi Mission (p957) (Amrithapuri) Famed for its female guru Amma, 'The Hugging Mother'.

Kolkata (Calcutta)

Belur Math (p464) Ramakrishna Mission head-quarters, founded by Swami Vivekananda.

Maharashtra

Brahmavidya Mandir Ashram (p793; Sevagram) Established by Gandhi's disciple Vinoba Bhave.

Sevagram Ashram (p792; Sevagram) Founded by Gandhi.

Osho International Meditation Resort (p803; Pune) Follows the sometimes controversial teachings of Osho.

Tamil Nadu

Sri Aurobindo Ashram (p1035; Puducherry) Founded by Sri Aurobindo.

Isha Yoga Center (p1073; Coimbatore) Offers intensive all-level yoga programs.

Sri Ramana Ashram (p1033; Tiruvannamalai) Founded by Sri Ramana Maharshi.

Plan Your Trip

Volunteering

For all India's beauty, rich culture and history, poverty and hardship are unavoidable facts of life. Many travellers feel motivated to help, and charities and aid organisations across the country welcome committed volunteers. Here's a guide to help you start making a difference.

Aid Programs in India

India faces considerable challenges and there are numerous opportunities for volunteers. It may be possible to find a placement after you arrive, but charities and nongovernment organisations (NGOs) generally prefer volunteers who have applied in advance and been approved for the kind of work involved. Reputable organisations may insist on a criminal background check for working with children. **Ethical Volunteering** (www.ethicalvolunteering.org) provides useful guidelines for choosing an ethical sending agency.

As well as international organisations, local charities and NGOs often have opportunities, though it can be harder to assess the work that these organisations are doing. For listings of local agencies, check www.ngosindia.com or contact the Delhi-based Concern India Foundation (p79).

The following programs are just some of many that may have opportunities for volunteers; contact them in advance to arrange a placement. Note that Lonely Planet does not endorse any organisations that we do not work with directly, so it is essential that you do your own thorough research before agreeing to volunteer with any organisation.

How to Volunteer

Choosing an Organisation

Consider how your skills will benefit the people you are trying to help, and choose an organisation that can specifically benefit from your abilities.

Time Required

Think realistically about how much time you can devote to a project. You're more likely to be of help if you commit for at least a month, ideally more.

Money

Giving your time for free is only part of the story; most organisations expect volunteers to cover their accommodation, food and transport.

Working 9 to 5

Make sure you understand what you are signing up for; many organisations expect volunteers to work full time, five days a week.

Transparency

Ensure that the organisation you choose is reputable and transparent about how it spends its money. Where possible, get feedback from former volunteers.

Caregiving

If you have medical experience, there are numerous opportunities to provide health care and support for the most vulnerable in Indian society.

Delhi

➡ **Missionaries of Charity** (☎011-33237839; www.motherteresa.org; 1 Magazine Rd) This Kolkata-based organisation also offers volunteer opportunities in Delhi.

Kolkata (Calcutta)

➡ **Missionaries of Charity** (p464) Mother's Teresa's charity (Mother Theresa's Motherhouse) places volunteers in hospitals and homes for impoverished children and adults.

➡ **Calcutta Rescue** (p470) Placements for medical and health professionals in Kolkata and other parts of West Bengal.

Community

Many community volunteer projects work to provide health care and education to villages.

Bihar & Jharkhand

➡ **Root Institute for Wisdom Culture** (p531; Bodhgaya) Occasional placements to train local health workers.

Delhi

➡ **Hope Project** (p80) A broad-based community project, welcoming short- or long-term volunteers who can offer childcare, medical, English Language Teaching, IT or other skills.

Karnataka

➡ **Kishkinda Trust** (p903; Hampi) Volunteers needed to assist with sustainable community development.

Madhya Pradesh & Chhattisgarh

➡ **Friends of Orchha** (p636; Orchha) Offers volunteer placements to help improve the livelihoods of rural villagers.

Mumbai (Bombay)

➡ **Slum Aid** (http://www.slumaid.org) Working in Mumbai slums to improve lives; placements from two weeks to six months.

West Bengal

➡ **Human Wave** (☎033-26854904; www.humanwaveindia.org; Mankundu) Short-term placements on community development and health schemes around West Bengal.

➡ **Makaibari Tea Estate** (p500; Kurseong) Volunteers assist with primary school teaching, health work and organic farming.

AGENCIES OVERSEAS

There are so many international volunteering agencies, it can be bewildering trying to assess which ones are reputable. Agencies offering the chance to do whatever you want, wherever you want, are almost always tailoring projects to the volunteer rather than finding the right volunteer for the work that needs to be done. Look for projects that will derive real benefits from your skills. To find sending agencies in your area, read Lonely Planet's *Volunteer: A Traveller's Guide,* or try one of the following:

Himalayan Education Lifeline Programme (HELP; www.help-education.org) British-based charity organising placements for volunteer teachers at schools in Sikkim.

Indicorps (www.indicorps.org) Matches volunteers to projects across India, particularly in social development.

Jamyang Foundation (www.jamyang.org) Arranges volunteer placements for experienced teachers in Zanskar and Himachal Pradesh.

Voluntary Service Overseas (VSO; www.vso.org.uk) British organisation offering long-term professional placements in India and worldwide.

Workaway (www.workaway.info) Connects people with hotels, guesthouses, organic farms, restaurants and more, where they will get free accommodation and food in return for working five days a week.

Teaching

Many Buddhist schools need teachers of English for long-term placements; enquire locally in Sikkim, Himachal Pradesh, West Bengal and Ladakh. Teaching experience is preferred.

Himachal Pradesh

➡ **Himalayan Buddhist Cultural School** (☎9418103512; palkithakur@yahoo.com; Manali) Placements of six months or more for experienced teachers at this boarding school for children from remote villages.

➡ **Jamyang Foundation** (www.jamyang.org; Kaza) Arranges placements teaching Buddhist women and girls in the Spiti Valley.

➡ **Learning & Ideas for Tibet** (p325; McLeod Ganj) Current needs are for teachers of English, French, German and computer skills, to work with Tibetan refugees.

➡ **Tibet Hope Center** (p325; McLeod Ganj) English teaching and conversation with the Tibetan community.

Jammu & Kashmir

➡ **Druk White Lotus School** (p243; Shey) Buddhist monastery school in Ladakh with long-term placements (May to September only) for English teachers.

➡ **We For Kargil** (www.weforkargil.in; Kargil) Places volunteers in rural villages around the region.

➡ **Phuktal Monastery** (http://phuktalmonastery.com/can-you-help; Zanskar) Accepts short-term EFL teaching volunteers.

➡ **Csoma's Room** (http://csomasroom.kibu.hu) This Hungarian outfit takes teachers (as well as restorers) in Zangla.

Rajasthan

➡ **Sambhali Trust** (p179) (Jodhpur) Volunteers needed to teach and help organise workshops for disadvantaged women.

West Bengal & Darjeeling

➡ **Hayden Hall** (p509; Darjeeling) Offers minimum two-month opportunities for volunteers with medical, teaching and business experience.

Working with Children

The following charities provide support for disadvantaged children.

Delhi

➡ **Salaam Baalak Trust** (p80) Volunteer English teachers, doctors, counsellors and computer experts provide education and support for street children.

➡ **Torch** (www.torchdelhi.org; 30D Nizamuddin Basti, Nizamuddin West) Works with homeless children, and looks for volunteers who can help with art activities, music and writing.

Goa

➡ **Mango Tree Goa** (p823; Mapusa) Opportunities for volunteer nurses and teaching assistants to help impoverished children.

➡ **El Shaddai** (p823; Assagao) Placements helping impoverished and homeless children; one-month minimum commitment.

Himachal Pradesh

➡ **Kullu Project** (☎9418102083; www.kulluproject.org; Kullu) Puts would-be long-term volunteers in contact with schools, orphanages and other organisations working with disadvantaged kids in the Kullu Valley.

➡ **Rogpa** (p325; McLeod Ganj) Volunteers provide childcare for Tibetan families.

Mumbai

➡ **Child Rights & You** (p752) Volunteers can assist with campaigns to raise funds for projects around India; four-week minimum commitment.

➡ **Vatsalya Foundation** (p752) Long- and short-term opportunities teaching and running sports activities for street children.

Tamil Nadu

➡ **RIDE** (p1029; Rural Institute for Development Education; Kanchipuram) Volunteer teachers and support staff help rural communities and children rescued from forced labour.

Uttar Pradesh

➡ **Learn for Life Society** (p397; Varanasi) Volunteer opportunities at a small school for disadvantaged children.

Environment & Conservation

The following charities focus on environmental education and sustainable development:

Andaman Islands

➡ **ANET** (Andaman & Nicobar Environmental Team; ☎03192-280081; www.anetindia. org; North Wandoor) Volunteers assist with environmental activities from field projects to general maintenance.

➡ **Reef Watch** (☎9930678367; www. reefwatchindia.org; Lacadives, Chiriya Tapu) Marine conservation NGO accepts volunteers for anything from beach clean ups and fish surveys to teaching; three-week minimum.

Himachal Pradesh

➡ **Ecosphere** (p347; Kaza) This multifaceted sustainable-development NGO has openings for short- and long-term volunteers including in cafe work, translating, agriculture and palliative care.

Jammu & Kashmir

➡ **International Society for Ecology & Culture** (www.isec.org.uk; Leh) One-month placements on rural farms to promote sustainable agriculture; relaunched in 2015.

Karnataka

➡ **Rainforest Retreat** (p885; Coorg) Organic farming, sustainable agriculture and waste management are catchphrases at this lush hideway amid spice plantations; check the website for volunteering options.

Tamil Nadu

➡ **Keystone Foundation** (p1075; Kotagiri) Offers occasional opportunities to help improve environmental conditions, working with indigenous communities.

Working with Animals

From stray dogs to rescued reptiles, opportunities for animal lovers are plentiful.

Andhra Pradesh

➡ **Blue Cross of Hyderabad** (☎23544355; www.bluecrosshyd.in; Rd No 35, Jubilee Hills) A shelter with over 1300 animals; volunteers help care for animals or work in the office.

Goa

➡ **Animal Rescue Centre** (p846; Chapolim) Animal welfare group that also has volunteer opportunities.

Mumbai

➡ **Welfare of Stray Dogs** (p753; Mumbai) Volunteers can work with the animals, manage stores or educate kids in school programs.

Rajasthan

➡ **Animal Aid Unlimited** (p154; Udaipur) Accepts volunteers to help injured, abandoned or stray animals.

Tamil Nadu

➡ **Madras Crocodile Bank** (p1022; Vadanemmeli) A reptile conservation centre with openings for volunteers (minimum two weeks).

Heritage & Restoration

Those with architectural and building skills should look at the following.

Jammu & Kashmir

➡ **Tibet Heritage Fund** (www. tibetheritagefund.org; Leh) Openings for highly skilled volunteers to help preserve traditional buildings.

➡ **Csoma's Room** (p45) Volunteers restore and preserve traditional architecture in Zanskar.

Rajasthan

➡ **Haveli Nadine Le Prince** (p171; Shekhawati) Has opportunities to assist the running of this historic *haveli* (traditional, ornately decorated residence).

Tamil Nadu

➡ **ArcHeS** (www.arche-s.com; Karaikkudi) Aims to preserve the architectural and cultural heritage of Chettinadu; openings for historians, geographers and architects.

Plan Your Trip
Travel with Children

Fascinating and thrilling; India can be every bit as exciting for children as it is for their wide-eyed parents. The scents, sights and sounds of India will inspire and challenge young enquiring minds, and with careful preparation and vigilance, a lifetime of vivid memories can be sown.

India for Kids

In many respects, travel with children in India can be a delight, and warm welcomes are frequent. Locals will thrill at taking a photograph or two beside your bouncing baby. But while all this is fabulous for outgoing children it may prove tiring or even disconcerting to younger kids and those with more retiring dispositions.

As a parent on the road in India, the key is to stay alert to your children's needs and to remain firm in fulfilling them, even if you feel you may offend a well-meaning local by doing so. The attention your children will inevitably receive is almost always good-natured; kids are the centre of life in many Indian households, and your own will be treated just the same. Hotels will almost always come up with an extra bed or two, and restaurants with a familiar meal.

Children's Highlights
Best Story-book Splendours

➡ **Jaisalmer** Revel in *Arabian Nights* grandeur in Jaisalmer's centuries-old fort (p183) on the edge of the Thar Desert.

Best Regions for Kids
Rajasthan

Vibrant festivals, medieval forts, fairy-tale palaces, camel rides across desert dunes and a well-oiled tourist infrastructure for hassle-free travel. For older kids there's the thrill of the incredible Flying Fox (zip wires) at Jodhpur.

Goa

Palm-fringed, white-sand beaches and inexpensive exotic food; an ideal choice for family holidays, whatever the budget.

Uttar Pradesh

The picture-perfect Taj Mahal and the nearby abandoned city of Fatehpur Sikri will set young imaginations ablaze.

Kerala

Canoe and houseboat adventures, surf beaches, Arabian Sea sunsets, snake boat races, wildlife-spotting and elephant festivals.

Himachal Pradesh

Pony and yak rides around colonial-era hill stations, rafting, horse riding, tandem paragliding (kids can do it), walks, canyoning and zorbing around Manali.

➡ **Delhi** See the famous Red Fort (p60) and imagine epic battles, or ride in a toy train at the National Rail Museum (p75).

➡ **Ranthambhore National Park** Step into a *Jungle Book* world, home to a monkey kingdom and hop aboard a jeep to scout for Shere Khan (p140).

➡ **Udaipur** Explore palaces, take a horse-riding excursion, and spoil your children rotten with a stay at the glorious Taj Lake Palace.

➡ **Orchha** Wander the crumbling palaces and battlements of little-known Orchha (p633).

Best Natural Encounters

➡ **Tiger parks, Madhya Pradesh** Delve deep into the jungle or roam the plains at the tiger parks of Kanha (p676), Pench (p680) or Bandhavgarh (p678). You might not see a tiger, but there's plenty of other wildlife worth spotting.

➡ **Elephants** At Elefantastic (Amber, near Jaipur) in Rajasthan, you can spend a brilliant day caring for elephants, washing them, feeding them etc. At parks in Kerala (Periyar; p966) and Goa (Colem p812 and Ponda p823) kids can ride, feed and bathe (and get sprayed by) elephants.

➡ **Dolphins, Goa** Splash out on a dolphin-spotting boat trip from almost any Goan beach to see them cavorting among the waves (p825).

➡ **Hill-station monkeys** Head up to Shimla (p286; Himachal Pradesh) or Matheran (p798; Maharashtra) for close encounters with cheeky monkeys.

Fun Forms of Transport

➡ **Autorickshaw, anywhere** Hurtle at top speed in these child-scale vehicles (p1199).

➡ **Bike, Delhi** Take a DelhiByCycle tour (p80) (for older children who are competent riders, or toddlers who can fit in a child seat).

➡ **Toy Train, Darjeeling** Ride the huffing, puffing steam toy train between Kurseong and Darjeeling, past colourful mountain villages and gushing waterfalls (p511).

➡ **Hand-pulled rickshaw, Matheran** A narrow-gauge diesel toy train takes visitors most of the way up to this cute, monkey-infested hill station, after which your children can choose to continue to the village on horseback or in a hand-pulled rickshaw (p798).

➡ **Houseboat, Alappuzha (Alleppey)** Hop on a houseboat to luxuriously cruise Kerala's beautiful backwaters (p958). If you happen to

hit town on the second Saturday in August, take the kids along to see the spectacular Nehru Trophy boat race.

Best Beaches

➡ **Palolem & Patnem, Goa** Hole up in a beachfront palm-thatched hut and watch your kids cavort at beautiful Palolem and neighbouring Patnem beaches, featuring the shallowest, safest waters in Goa (p849).

➡ **Mandrem, Goa** A broad, relaxed and child-friendly beach in North Goa, Mandrem (p839) also offers easy access to Arambol and Calangute, making it a great base.

➡ **Havelock Island** Splash about in the shallows at languid Havelock Island (p1093), part of the Andaman Island chain, where, for older children, there's spectacular diving on offer.

Planning

Before You Go

➡ Look at climate charts; choose your dates to avoid the extremes of temperature that may put younger children at risk.

➡ Visit your doctor to discuss vaccinations, health advisories and other heath-related issues involving your children well in advance of travel.

➡ For more tips on travel in India, and first-hand accounts of travels in the country, pick up Lonely Planet's *Travel with Children* or visit the Thorn Tree Forum at lonelyplanet.com.

What to Pack

You can get some of these items in many parts of India too, but often prices are at a premium and brands may not be those you recognise:

➡ For babies or toddlers: disposable or washable nappies, nappy rash cream (Calendula cream works well against heat rash too), extra bottles, a good stock of wet wipes, infant formula and canned, bottled or rehydratable food.

➡ A fold-up baby bed or the lightest possible travel cot you can find (companies such as KidCo make excellent pop-up tent-style beds), since hotel cots may prove precarious. Don't take a stroller/pushchair, as this will be impractical to use as pavements are often scarce. A much better option is a backpack, for smaller kids, so they're lifted up and out of the daunting throng, plus with a superb view.

➡ A few less-precious toys that won't be mourned if lost or damaged.

➡ A swimming jacket, life jacket or water wings for the sea or pool.

➡ Good sturdy footwear.

➡ Audiobooks are great for whiling away long journeys.

➡ Child-friendly insect repellent, mosquito nets, hats and sun lotion are a must.

Eating

➡ You may have to work hard to find something to satisfy sensitive childhood palates, but if you're travelling in the more family-friendly regions of India, such as Rajasthan, Himachal Pradesh, Goa, Kerala or the big cities, you'll find it easier to feed your brood. Here you will find familiar Western dishes in abundance.

➡ While on the road, easy portable snacks such as bananas, samosas, *puri* (puffy dough pockets) and packaged biscuits (Parle G brand are a perennial hit) are available.

➡ Adventurous eaters and vegetarian children will delight in paneer (unfermented cheese) dishes, simple dhals (mild lentil curries), creamy kormas, buttered naans (tandoori breads), *pilaus* (rice dishes) and Tibetan *momos* (steamed or fried dumplings).

➡ Few children, no matter how culinarily unadventurous, can resist the finger food fun of a vast South Indian dosa (paper-thin lentil-flour pancake) served up for breakfast.

Accommodation

➡ India offers such an array of accommodation options – from beach huts to heritage boutiques to five-star fantasies – that you're bound to be able to find something that will appeal to the whole family.

➡ The swish upmarket hotels are almost always child-friendly, but so are many upper midrange hotels, whose staff will usually rustle up an extra mattress or two; some places won't mind cramming several children into a regular-sized double room along with their parents.

➡ The very best five-stars come equipped with children's pools, games rooms and even

children's clubs, while an occasional night with a warm bubble bath, room service, macaroni cheese and the Disney channel will revive even the most disgruntled young traveller's spirits.

On the Road

➡ Travel in India, be it by taxi, local bus, train or air, can be arduous for the whole family. Concepts such as clean public toilets, changing rooms and safe playgrounds are rare in much of the country. Public transport is often extremely overcrowded so plan fun, easy days to follow longer bus or train rides.

➡ Pack plenty of diversions (iPads or laptops with a stock of movies downloaded make invaluable travel companions, as do audiobooks, plus the good old-fashioned story books, cheap toys and games available widely across India).

➡ If you are hiring a car and driver – a sensible and flexible option – and you require safety capsules, child restraints or booster seats, you will need to make this absolutely clear to the hiring company as early as possible. Don't expect to find these items readily available. And finally, don't be afraid to tell your driver to slow down and drive responsibly.

Health

➡ The availability of a decent standard of health care varies widely in India. Talk to your doctor at home about where you will be travelling to get advice on vaccinations and what to include in your first-aid kit.

➡ Access to health care is certainly better in traveller-frequented parts of the country where it's almost always easy to track down a doctor at short notice (most hotels will be able to recommend a reliable one).

➡ Prescriptions are quickly and cheaply filled over the counter at numerous pharmacies, often congregating near hospitals.

➡ Diarrhoea can be very serious in young children. Seek medical help if it is persistent or accompanied by fever; rehydration is essential. Heat rash, skin complaints such as impetigo, insect bites or stings can be treated with the help of a well-equipped first-aid kit.

Regions at a Glance

From high-tech cities to palm-fringed backwaters, from dizzying knife-edge mountain ranges to remote tribal villages, and from ancient temples to towering fortresses, India's regions are packed with an astounding mass of contrasts, colour and experiences.

Delhi

Ruins
Cuisine
Shopping

Not only does Delhi harbour the ruins of seven imperial cities, but also here you can feast on everything from creative cuisine to fresh-from-the-fire street food. It's shopping heaven too: all of India's riches sparkle in Delhi's bazaars and emporia.

p56

Rajasthan

Palaces & Forts
Wildlife
Arts & Crafts

Rajasthan's forts and palaces are a legacy of the region's maharajas, while their royal hunting reservations are now national parks, ripe for spotting tigers and other wildlife. You'll also find princely riches in Rajasthan's bazaars, from miniature paintings to traditional puppets.

p104

Haryana & Punjab

Architecture
Cuisine
Borders

Besides the stunning Golden Temple, the Punjab has palaces and follies, and the region is also home of butter chicken, basmati rice, and the tandoor (clay oven). The Attari–Wagah border crossing is worth a trip for its fabulous transborder pomp.

p198

Jammu & Kashmir (including Ladakh)

Landscapes
Trekking
Religion

From alpine Kashmir to the moonscapes of Ladakh and Zanskar, be humbled by the scale of nature and take hikes through Buddhist villages. Such beauty inspires spirituality; mantras fill Ladakh's gompas, pilgrims visit Amarnath's ice lingam and Sufi spirituality suffuses Srinagar.

p222

Himachal Pradesh

Adventure
Scenery
Cultures

High Himalayan passes and plunging valleys make for great trekking, climbing, mountain biking, paragliding and skiing. The scenery is consistently awe-inspiring, and the cultural variety huge, from colourful Hindu festivals to ancient Buddhist monasteries.

p280

Agra & the Taj Mahal

Architecture
Tombs
Forts

Agra's astounding Mughal architecture dates from the pinnacle of imperial virtuosity. The Taj Mahal is one of the wonders of the world, but don't miss out on other local masterpieces, such as Akbar's Mausoleum or the mighty Agra Fort.

p350

Uttar Pradesh

Architecture
Religion
Ghats

Uttar Pradesh contains ancient Islamic cities, two of Buddhism's most sacred pilgrimage centres, and two of the seven sacred cities of Hinduism. The river Ganges and its tributaries flow across UP, lined with holy ghats (ceremonial steps).

p374

Uttarakhand

Trekking
Yoga
Wildlife

Trekkers can take their pick from temples, sacred lakes, remote glaciers and rolling alpine meadows. Head to Rishikesh for a spiritual tune-up, and seek snow leopards, Asiatic black bears, brown bears and blue sheep in the national parks.

p412

Kolkata (Calcutta)

Culture
Architecture
Cuisine

Once the British Indian capital, Kolkata is full of colonial-era architecture, but the modern city mingles chaos and culture in an enticing and very Indian mix. Cuisine here is renowned across the subcontinent, with the focus on fresh fish and prawns.

p454

West Bengal & Darjeeling

Hill Stations
Hotels
Tigers

Darjeeling is the quintessential Indian hill station, offering spectacular Himalayan views. Stay in faded Raj-era cottages and elegant tea estates; and where better to spot an awesome Royal Bengal tiger?

p488

Bihar & Jharkhand

Religion
Ruins
Wildlife

Buddhist pilgrims flock to Bodhgaya, where Buddha attained enlightenment. The Unesco-listed ruins of the ancient Nalanda university are just one of many early Buddhist relics, and Jharkhand's serene Betla (Palamau) National Park is famous for its pachyderms.

p520

Sikkim

Views
Treks
Monasteries

This former Buddhist kingdom is dotted with Tibetan-style monasteries, and Sikkim's curtain wall of Himalayan peaks guarantees epic views. Khangchendzonga draws trekkers like bears to Himalayan honey.

p540

Northeast States

Tribes
Wildlife
Adventure

This is India's tribal heartland, and the one-horned Indian rhino is just one of the local roll-call of exotic animals. Get truly off the beaten track on this remote frontier.

p564

Odisha (Orissa)

Temples
Tribes
Wildlife

Odisha's dazzling temples tell a captivating tale of rulers who spared no expense in their veneration of the divine. The tribal markets of Onkadelli and Chatikona offer fascinating opportunities to mingle, and there are tiger reserves, mangrove forests and coastal wetlands.

p598

Madhya Pradesh & Chhattisgarh

Tigers
Temples
Tribes

A region of eclectic charms, with tiger parks, the raunchy relief work on the World Heritage–listed Khajuraho temples, and a wealth of tribal villages and markets.

p626

Gujarat

Wildlife
Crafts
Treks

Here you can see Asia's only wild lions and India's only wild asses, as well as Gujarati embroiderers, weavers, printers and dyers producing some of India's finest textiles. Or join Hindu and Jain pilgrims on treks up stunning, temple-topped peaks.

p686

Mumbai (Bombay)

Architecture
Divine Dinners
Nightlife

Thank the British – and Indian stonemasons – for Mumbai's glorious colonial-era architecture. Flavours from India and beyond mingle here too, from local snacks to global flavours. Keep an eye out for Bollywood stars in sleek bars and neon-filled nightclubs.

p734

Maharashtra

Caves
Beaches
Wine

Ajanta and Ellora hide exquisite cave paintings and rock sculptures, while the Konkan Coast has some of the most secluded beaches in India. Nasik is the *grand cru* of India's vineyards, from where exciting wines are starting to cause a real stir.

p774

Goa

Beaches
Cuisine
Architecture

Goa's beaches have undeniably been discovered, but with the surf breaking over your toes and palm fronds swaying overhead, it doesn't seem to matter. Add fresh-off-the-boat seafood, and beautiful colonial-era villas and basilicas, and you can see what all the fuss is about.

p810

Karnataka & Bengaluru

Temples
Wildlife Safaris
Cuisine

The temples of Karnataka overflow with carved embellishments, while the Nilgiri Biosphere Reserve is home to one of Asia's biggest populations of elephants, plus tigers and leopards. The table is laden too, with everything from Udupi vegetarian thalis to Mangalorean seafood.

p854

Telangana & Andhra Pradesh

City Buzz
Cuisine
Religions

Hyderabad's past splendours and contemporary style make it one of India's most engaging cities, while its famed biryani and spicy vegie dishes provide a rich cuisine. Ancient Buddhist remains are dotted throughout the region, and Tirumala is a major Hindu pilgrimage site.

p910

54

PLAN YOUR TRIP REGIONS AT A GLANCE

Kerala

Backwaters
Cuisine
Wildlife

The inlets and lakes of Kerala's backwaters spread far inland; boat trips here are one of India's most relaxing pleasures. On land is a fine assortment of wildlife-filled national parks, while the Keralan kitchen offers delicate dishes flavoured with coconut and spices.

p938

Tamil Nadu & Chennai

Temples
Colonial Echoes
City Life

Age-old tradition collides with cosmopolitan flair in Chennai, while Tamil Nadu's intricately carved, colour-bursting temples draw pilgrims from across India. Escape into the cool, Raj-era hill stations of the Western Ghats, or crash out in the peaceful, pretty French Quarter at Puducherry (Pondicherry).

p1000

Andaman Islands

Diving
Beaches
Tribes

India's prime diving destination has easy dips for first-timers and challenging drift dives for veterans. If you're searching for that picture-postcard beach or kilometres of deserted coastline, you'll find it here, and the Andamans are home to dozens of fascinating tribal groups.

p1084

On the Road

Delhi

📔 011 / POP 25 MILLION / ELEV 293M

Best Places to Eat

➜ Hotel Saravana Bhavan (p88)

➜ Bukhara (p90)

➜ Indian Accent (p91)

➜ Alkauser (p89)

➜ Sodabottleopenerwala (p89)

Best Places to Stay

➜ Lodhi (p84)

➜ Hotel Amax Inn (p81)

➜ Devna (p85)

➜ Bloom Rooms (p83)

Why Go?

Mystery, magic, mayhem. Welcome to Delhi, City of Djinns, and 25 million people. Like an eastern Rome, India's capital is littered with the relics of lost empires. A succession of armies stormed across the Indo-Gangetic plain and imprinted their identity onto the vanquished city, before vanishing into rubble and ruin. Modern Delhi is a chaotic tapestry of medieval fortifications, Mughal mausoleums, dusty bazaars, colonial-era town planning, and mega malls.

Travellers sometimes leave Delhi underwhelmed, after ticking off the sights and tussling with the touts. But give the city a chance and you might fall in love. It's often the lesser-known corners that are most rewarding, such as Lodi Gardens at dusk, the *qawwali* (Islamic devotional singing) at Nizamuddin or the great fort of Purana Qila. A recommended way to glimpse beneath the surface is to take one of the city's tours, from a former street child's view of Old Delhi to a cycle tour along the Yamuna.

When to Go
Delhi

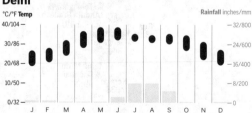

Oct–Mar Delhi at its best: warm with clear skies. Morning fog can play havoc with flight schedules.

May–Aug The months to avoid – hot, humid and uncomfortable.

Jun–Sep Monsoon season sees high temperatures and regular rain – a sticky combination.

History

Hindus claim Delhi as the site of ancient Indraprastha, home of the Pandavas in the Mahabharata, and excavations near the Purana Qila have revealed evidence of human habitation dating back 3000 years. The name Delhi is linked to the Maurya king Dhilu, who ruled the region in the 1st century BC, but for most of its existence, the city has been known by the names given to it by its conquerors.

The first city for which clear archaeological evidence remains was Lal Kot, or Qila Rai Pithora, founded by the Hindu king Prithvi Raj Chauhan in the 12th century. The city fell to Afghan invaders in 1191, and for the next 600 years, Delhi was ruled by a succession of Muslim sultans and emperors. The first, Qutub-ud-din Aibak, razed the Hindu city and used its stones to construct Mehrauli and the towering Qutb Minar.

Qutub-ud-din Aibak's Mamluk (Slave) dynasty was quickly replaced by the Khilji dynasty, following a coup. The Khiljis constructed a new capital at Siri, northeast of Mehrauli, supplied with water from the royal tank at Hauz Khas. Following another coup, the Tughlaq sultans seized the reins, creating a new fortified capital at Tughlaqabad, and two more cities – Jahanpanah and Ferozabad – for good measure.

The Tughlaq dynasty fell after Tamerlane stormed through town in 1398, opening the door for the Sayyid and Lodi dynasties, the last of the Delhi sultanates, whose tombs are scattered around the Lodi Gardens. The scene was set for the arrival of the Mughals. Babur, the first Mughal emperor, seized Delhi in 1526, and a new capital rose at Shergarh (the present-day Purana Qila), presided over by his son, Humayun.

Frantic city building continued throughout the Mughal period. Shah Jahan gained the Peacock Throne in 1627 and raised a new city, Shahjahanabad, centred on the Red Fort. The Mughal city fell in 1739, to the Persian Nadir Shah, and the dynasty went into steep decline. The last Mughal emperor, Bahadur Shah Zafar, was exiled to Burma (Myanmar) by the British for his role in the 1857 First War of Independence (Indian Uprising); there were some new rulers in town.

When the British shifted their capital to Delhi from increasingly rebellious Calcutta in 1911, it was time for another bout of construction. The architect Edwin Lutyens drew up plans for a new city of wide boulevards and stately administrative buildings to accommodate the colonial government – New Delhi was born.

Delhi has faced numerous challenges since Independence, from the violence of Partition to the deepening gulf between rich and poor, but the city on the Yamuna continues to flourish, with its new satellite cities adding ever increasing skyscrapers to the city's outskirts.

DELHI HISTORY

DELHI'S TOP FESTIVALS

To confirm dates contact India Tourism Delhi (p97).

Republic Day (⊗26 Jan) A spectacular military parade in Rajpath.

Beating of the Retreat (⊗29 Jan) More military pageantry in Rajpath.

St.Art (⊗ Jan/Feb) Street-art festival.

Independence Day (⊗15 Aug) India celebrates Independence from Britain and the prime minister addresses the nation from the Red Fort.

Dussehra (Durga Puja; ⊗ Sep/Oct) Hindus celebrate the victory of good over evil with parades of colourful effigies.

Ananya Dance Festival (⊗Oct) Free classical Indian dance festival takes place at Purana Qila.

Qutb Festival (⊗Oct/Nov) Several days of Sufi singing and classical music and dance at the Qutb Minar complex.

Diwali (⊗Nov/Dec) Fireworks across the city for the festival of light.

Delhi International Arts Festival (DIAF; ⊗Dec) Three weeks of exhibitions, performing arts, films, literature and culinary events at venues Delhi-wide.

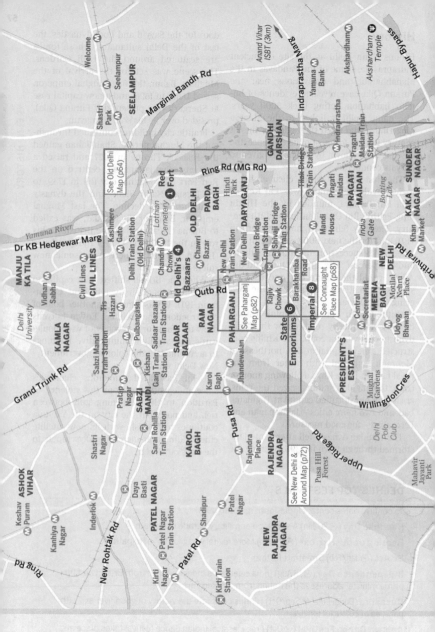

Delhi Highlights

1. Seeing how Mughals lived in the **Red Fort** (p60), the sandstone palace of the last emperors of Delhi

2. Wandering in peace around **Humayun's Tomb** (p69), inspiration for the Taj Mahal

3. Standing at the base of the magnificent **Qutb Minar** (p102), then plunge into the overgrown ruins of neighbouring **Mehrauli Archaeological Park** (p103)

4. Losing yourself in the mazelike **bazaars** (p94) of Old Delhi

5. Experiencing a living piece of Islamic history while hearing **qawwali** (Islamic devotional singing)

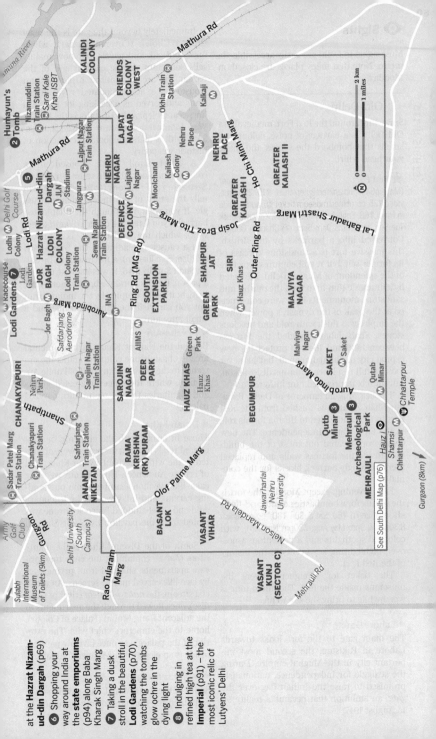

at the **Hazrat Nizam-ud-din Dargah** (p69)

6 Shopping your way around India at the **state emporiums** (p94) along Baba Kharak Singh Marg

7 Taking a dusk stroll in the beautiful **Lodi Gardens** (p70), watching the tombs glow ochre in the dying light

8 Indulging in refined high tea at the **Imperial** (p91) – the most iconic relic of Lutyens' Delhi

⊙ Sights

Most sights in Delhi are easily accessible via metro. Note that many places are closed on Monday.

◎ Old Delhi

Sprawling around the Red Fort, medieval-era Old Delhi is a barrage of noise, colour and smells that bombard the senses and make your head whirl.

★ Red Fort   FORT
(Map p64; Indian/foreigner/child ₹10/250/free, video ₹25, combined museum ticket ₹5, audio guide in Hindi ₹68, English or Korean ₹113; ⊙ dawn-dusk Tue-Sun, museums 9am-5pm; Ⓜ Chandni Chowk) Converted into a barracks by the British, this massive fort is a sandstone carcass of its former self, but it still conjures a picture of the splendour of Mughal Delhi. Protected by a dramatic 18m-high wall, the marble and sandstone monuments here were constructed at the peak of the dynasty's power, when the empire was flush with gold and precious stones. Shah Jahan founded the fortress between 1638 and 1648 to protect his new capital city of Shahjahanabad, but he never took up full residence, after his disloyal son, Aurangzeb, imprisoned him in Agra Fort.

The last Mughal emperor of Delhi, Bahadur Shah Zafar, was flushed from the Red Fort in 1857 and exiled to Burma for his role in the First War of Independence. The new conquerors cleared out most of the buildings inside the fortress walls and replaced them with ugly barrack blocks for the colonial army.

Every evening, except Monday, the fort is the setting for a bombastic **sound-and-light show** (Tue-Fri ₹60, Sat & Sun ₹80; ⊙ in English 8.30pm & 9pm May-Aug, 7.30pm Nov-Jan), with coloured spotlights and a portentous voice-over, highlighting key events in the history of the Red Fort.

The ticket for foreigners covers the museums inside the fort. The audio tour is worthwhile to bring the site to life.

➡ Lahore Gate

The main gate to the fort looks towards Lahore in Pakistan, the second most important city in the Mughal empire. During the struggle for Independence, nationalists promised to raise the Indian flag over the gate, an ambition that became a reality on 15 August 1947.

Immediately beyond the gate is the regal **Chatta Chowk** (Covered Bazaar), which once sold silk and jewels, but now mainly sells souvenirs. At the eastern end of the bazaar, the arched **Naubat Khana** (Drum House) once accommodated royal musicians and served as a parking lot for royal horses and elephants. Upstairs is the **Indian War Memorial Museum** (⊙ 8am-5pm Tue-Sun), with a fearsome-looking collection of historic weaponry.

A short stroll north, housed in a colonial-era block, the **Museum on India's Struggle for Freedom** (⊙ 9am-5pm Tue-Sun) tells the story of the Independence struggle. If you walk on through the dilapidated barracks, you'll reach a deserted *baoli* (stepwell), which the British used as a prison, and a causeway leading to the **Salimgarh** (⊙ 10am-5pm Tue-Sun), a fortress built by Salim Shah Suri in 1546. It was likewise used as a prison, first by Aurangzeb, and later by the British; it's still occupied by the Indian army, but you can visit the ruined mosque and a small museum.

➡ Diwan-i-Am

Beyond the Naubat Khana, a monumental arcade of sandstone columns marks the entrance to the Diwan-i-Am (Hall of Public Audience), where the emperor greeted guests and dignitaries from a pietra-dura covered balcony.

➡ Diwan-i-Khas

Those in favour with the emperor, or conquered rivals begging for peace, were admitted to the white marble Diwan-i-Khas (Hall of Private Audience). This delicate, wedding cake–like pavilion features some outstanding carving and inlay work. The legendary gold and jewel-studded Peacock Throne was looted from the pavilion by Nadir Shah in 1739.

South of the Diwan-i-Khas is the dainty **Khas Mahal**, containing the emperor's private apartments, shielded from prying eyes by lace-like carved marble screens. An artificial stream, the *nahr-i-bihisht* (river of paradise), once flowed through the apartments to the adjacent **Rang Mahal** (Palace of Colour), home to the emperor's chief wife. The exterior of the palace was once lavishly painted; inside is an elegant lotus-shaped fountain.

➡ Mumtaz Mahal

South of the Rang Mahal, this pavilion once contained the quarters for other women of the royal household. Today it houses the **Museum of Archaeology** (☺9am-5pm Tue-Sun), with royal vestments, miniature paintings, astrolabes, Mughal scrolls and a shirt inscribed with verses from the Quran to protect the emperor from assassins.

➡ Royal Baths & Moti Masjid

North of the Diwan-i-Khas are the royal baths, which once contained a sauna and hot baths for the royal family, and the Moti Masjid (Pearl Mosque), an elegant private place of worship for the emperor. The outer walls align with the fort walls, while the inner walls are slightly askew to correctly align with Mecca. Both are closed to visitors, but you can peer through the screen windows.

➡ Shahi Burj

North of the royal baths is the Shahi Burj, a three-storey octagonal tower, where Shah Jahan planned the running of his empire. In front of the tower is what remains of an elegant formal garden, centred on the Zafar Mahal, a sandstone pavilion surrounded by a deep, empty water tank.

Chandni Chowk   AREA

(Map p64; Ⓜ Chandni Chowk) Old Delhi's main thoroughfare is a chaotic shopping street, mobbed by hawkers, motorcycles, stray dogs and porters and with narrow lanes running off it offering the full medieval bazaar experience. In the time of Shah Jahan, a tree-lined canal ran down its centre, reflecting the moon, hence the name Chandni Chowk, or 'moonlight place'.

Digambara Jain Temple   JAIN TEMPLE

(Map p64; Chandni Chowk; ☺6am-noon & 6-9pm; Ⓜ Chandni Chowk) In the cluster of temples at the Red Fort end of Chandni Chowk, the scarlet Digambara Jain Temple houses a fascinating **bird hospital** (by donation; ☺10am-5pm) established to further the Jain principle of preserving all life, with a capacity of 10,000. Only vegetarian birds are admitted (up to 60 per day), though predators are treated as outpatients. Remove shoes and leather items before entering the temple.

Nearby, the 18th-century **Sisganj Gurdwara** marks the the martyrdom site of the ninth Sikh guru, Tegh Bahadur, executed by Aurangzeb in 1675 for resisting conversion to Islam.

Fatehpuri Masjid   MOSQUE

(Map p64; Chandni Chowk) The western end of Chandni Chowk is book-ended by the mid-17th-century Fatehpuri Masjid, built by one of Shah Jahan's wives; it was sold to a Hindu nobleman by the British for ₹19,000 and returned to Muslim worship in exchange for four villages in 1877.

Small green buses shuttle between Digambara Jain Temple and Fatehpuri Masjid (₹5).

(Continued on page 66)

DELHI'S MIGHTY MEN

Wander the districts north of Kashmere Gate in Old Delhi and you may notice a disproportionately high number of muscular men. No, it's not your imagination. This dusty quarter is the favoured stomping ground for Delhi's traditional mud wrestlers. *Kushti*, or *pehlwani*, is a full-contact martial art, fusing elements of yoga and philosophy with combat and intense physical training.

Young men enrol at *akharas* (training centres) in their early teens, and follow a strict regimen of daily exercise, climbing ropes, lifting weights and hauling logs to build up the necessary muscle bulk for this intensely physical sport. Even diet and lifestyle is strictly controlled; sex, tobacco and alcohol are forbidden, and wrestlers live together in rustic accommodation under the supervision of a coach who doubles as spiritual guide.

Bouts take place on freshly tilled earth, adding an extra element of grit to proceedings. As with other types of wrestling, the aim is to pin your opponent to the ground, but fights often continue until one wrestler submits or collapses from exhaustion. At regional championships, wrestlers compete for golden *gadas* (ceremonial clubs), a tribute to the favoured weapon of Hanuman, patron deity of wrestling.

Most *akharas* welcome spectators at the daily dawn and dusk training sessions, so long as this doesn't interfere with training. Seek permission first to avoid offending these muscle-bound gents – the blog www.kushtiwrestling.blogspot.com is a good introduction to the sport and the main *akharas*. Indomania Cultural Tours (p80) has Yamaya tours that also take in an *akhara*.

Red Fort

HIGHLIGHTS

The main entrance to the Red Fort is through **Lahore Gate** ❶ – the bastion in front of it was built by Aurangzeb for increased security. You can still see bullet marks from 1857 on the gate.

Walk through the Chatta Chowk (Covered Bazaar), which once sold silks and jewellery to the nobility; beyond it lies **Naubat Khana** ❷, a russet-red building, which houses Hathi Pol (Elephant Gate), so called because visitors used to dismount from their elephants or horses here as a sign of respect. From here it's straight on to the **Diwan-i-Am** ❸, the Hall of Public Audiences. Behind this are the private palaces, the **Khas Mahal** ❹ and the **Diwan-i-Khas** ❺. Entry to this Hall of Private Audiences, the fort's most expensive building, was only permitted to the officials of state. Nearby is the **Moti Masjid (Pearl Mosque)** ❻ and south is the **Mumtaz Mahal** ❼, housing the Museum of Archaeology, or you can head north, where the Red Fort gardens are dotted with palatial pavilions and old British barracks. Here you'll find the **baoli** ❽, a spookily deserted water tank. Another five minutes' walk – across a road, then a railway bridge – brings you to the island fortress of **Salimgarh** ❾.

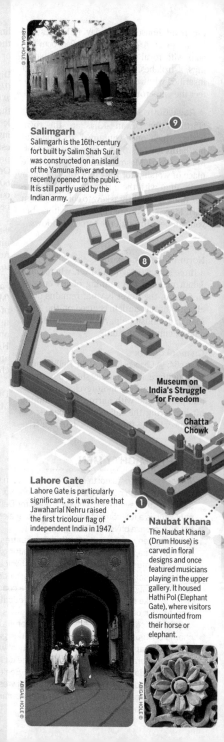

Salimgarh
Salimgarh is the 16th-century fort built by Salim Shah Sur. It was constructed on an island of the Yamuna River and only recently opened to the public. It is still partly used by the Indian army.

Museum on India's Struggle for Freedom

Chatta Chowk

Lahore Gate
Lahore Gate is particularly significant, as it was here that Jawaharlal Nehru raised the first tricolour flag of independent India in 1947.

Naubat Khana
The Naubat Khana (Drum House) is carved in floral designs and once featured musicians playing in the upper gallery. It housed Hathi Pol (Elephant Gate), where visitors dismounted from their horse or elephant.

Baoli

The Red Fort step well is seldom visited and is a hauntingly deserted place, even more so when you consider its chambers were used as cells by the British from August 1942.

Moti Masjid

The Moti Masjid (Pearl Mosque) was built by Aurangzeb in 1662 for his personal use. The domes were originally covered in copper, but the copper was removed and sold by the British.

Diwan-i-Khas

This was the most expensive building in the fort, consisting of white marble decorated with inlay work of cornelian and other stones. The screens overlooking what was once the river (now the ring road) were filled with coloured glass.

Baidon Pavilion

Zafar Mahal

Hammam

5

Rang Mahal

Mumtaz Mahal

6

7

4

3

2

PIT STOP

To refuel, head to Paratha Gali Wali, a foodstall-lined lane off Chandni Chowk noted for its many varieties of freshly made paratha (traditional flat bread).

Delhi Gate

← NORTH

Diwan-i-Am

These red sandstone columns were once covered in shell plaster, as polished and smooth as ivory, and in hot weather heavy red curtains were hung around the columns to block out the sun. It's believed the panels behind the marble throne were created by Florentine jeweller Austin de Bordeaux.

Khas Mahal

Most spectacular in the Emperor's private apartments is a beautiful marble screen at the northern end of the rooms; the 'Scales of Justice' are carved above it, suspended over a crescent, surrounded by stars and clouds.

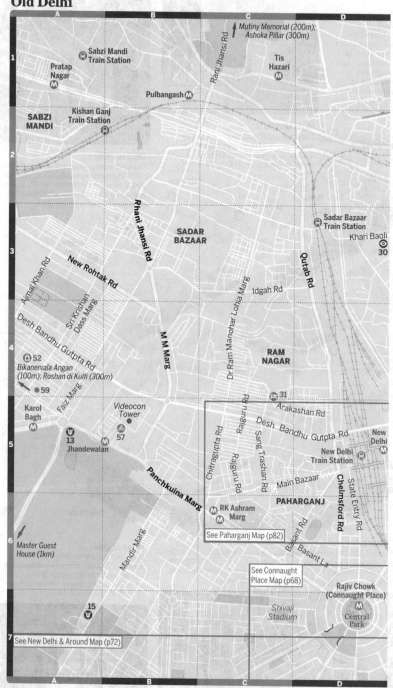

Mutiny Memorial (200m);
Ashoka Pillar (300m)

Sabzi Mandi
Train Station

Pratap
Nagar Ⓜ

Tis
Hazari Ⓜ

Pulbangash Ⓜ

Rani Jhansi Rd

Kishan Ganj
Train Station

**SABZI
MANDI**

Sadar Bazaar
Train Station

Khari Baoli
30

**SADAR
BAZAAR**

Rhani Jhansi Rd

Qutab Rd

New Rohtak Rd

Ajmal Khan Rd

Sri Krishan
Dass Marg

Idgah Rd

Dr Ram Manohar Lohia Marg

Desh Bandhu Gutpta Rd

M M Marg

**RAM
NAGAR**

Ⓐ 52
Bikanervala Angan
(100m); Roshan di Kulfi (300m)

● 59

Ⓐ 31

Arakashan Rd

Faiz Marg

Karol
Bagh Ⓜ

Videocon
Tower

Desh Bandhu Gutpta Rd

New
Delhi

⬆️ 13
Jhandewalan Ⓜ

● ⬆️
57

Chitragupta Rd

Rajguru Rd

Sang Trashan Rd

New Delhi
Train Station

New
Delhi Ⓜ

Rajguru Rd

Main Bazaar

State Entry Rd

Panchkuina Marg

Mandir Marg

Ⓜ RK Ashram
Ⓜ Marg

PAHARGANJ

Chelmsford Rd

Basant Rd

See Paharganj Map (p82)

Master Guest
House (1km)

Basant La

See Connaught
Place Map (p68)

Rajiv Chowk
(Connaught Place) Ⓜ

Shivaji
Stadium

Central
Park

⬆️ 15

See New Delhi & Around Map (p72)

DELHI

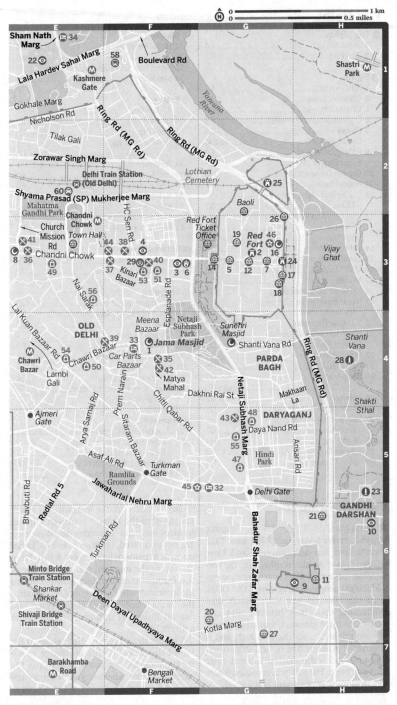

0 _____ 1 km
0 _____ 0.5 miles

Sham Nath Marg
🏛 34
22 ◉
Lala Hardev Sahai Marg
Kashmere Gate
58
Boulevard Rd
Gokhale Marg
Nicholson Rd
Tilak Gali
Ring Rd (MG Rd)
Ring Rd (MG Rd)
Yamuna River
Shastri Park Ⓜ
Zorawar Singh Marg
Delhi Train Station (Old Delhi)
Lothian Cemetery
60
Shyama Prasad (SP) Mukherjee Marg
Mahatma Gandhi Park
Chandni Chowk Ⓜ
Town Hall
Church Mission Rd
Baoli
🏛 25
Red Fort Ticket Office
26
19
Red Fort
46
🏛
HC Sen Rd
44 38 4
29 ◉ 40
37 53 51
Kinari Bazaar
Nai Sarak
56
41 ◉
36 ◉
8 ◉
49
Chandni Chowk
3 6
14
5 12 7
2 16
24
17
18
Vijay Ghat
OLD DELHI
Meena Bazaar
39
33
Chawri Bazaar Ⓜ
54
50
Lambi Gali
Car Parts Bazaar
Esplanade Rd
Jama Masjid
1
35
42
Matya Mahal
Netaji Subhash Park
Sunehri Masjid
Shanti Vana Rd
PARDA BAGH
Shanti Vana
28 ⓘ
Shakti Sthal
Ajmeri Gate
Arya Samaj Rd
Prem Narain
Sitaram Bazaar
Chitli Qabar Rd
Dakhni Rai St
Netaji Subhash Marg
Makhaan La
Ring Rd (MG Rd)
43
48
DARYAGANJ
Daya Nand Rd
55
47
Hindi Park
Ansari Rd
Asaf Ali Rd
Turkman Gate
Ramlila Grounds
Jawaharlal Nehru Marg
45 ⭐ 32
Delhi Gate
ⓘ 23
GANDHI DARSHAN
21 🏛
◉ 10
Bhavbuti Rd
Radial Rd 5
Turkman Rd
Minto Bridge Train Station
Shankar Market
Shivaji Bridge Train Station
Deen Dayal Upadhyaya Marg
Bahadur Shah Zafar Marg
◉ 9
11
Barakhamba Road Ⓜ
Bengali Market
20
Kotla Marg
27

DELHI SIGHTS

Old Delhi

(Continued from page 61)

★ **Jama Masjid**   MOSQUE
(Map p64; camera & video each ₹300, tower ₹100; ☉ non-Muslims 8am-dusk, minaret 9am-5.30pm; Ⓜ Chawri Bazaar) A calm respite from the surrounding mayhem, India's largest mosque can hold 25,000 people. Towering over Old Delhi, the 'Friday Mosque' was Shah Jahan's final architectural opus, built between 1644 and 1658. It has three gateways, four angle towers and two minarets standing 40m high, and is constructed of alternating vertical strips of red sandstone and white marble. You can enter from gate 1 or 3. The only prayer session where non-Muslims may be present is at 7.45am.

Buy a ticket at the entrance to climb 121 steps up the narrow southern minaret (notices say that unaccompanied women are not permitted, but they may be allowed up with a 'guide' who'll expect a tip). From the top of the minaret, you can see one of the features that architect Edwin Lutyens incorporated into his design of New Delhi – the Jama Masjid, Connaught Place and Sansad Bhavan (Parliament House) are in a direct line.

Visitors should remove their shoes at the top of the stairs. There's no charge to enter the mosque, but you'll have to pay the camera charge whether you want to use your camera or not. Once you buy a camera ticket, you should be allowed to go out and re-enter later that day if you choose.

Raj Ghat   MONUMENT

(Map p64; ☺6am-6pm) South of the Red Fort, situated on the banks of the Yamuna River, a simple black-marble platform marks the spot where Mahatma Gandhi was cremated following his assassination in 1948. It's a thought-provoking spot, inscribed with what are said to have been Gandhi's final words, *Hai Ram* (Oh, God). Across Kisan Ghat Rd is the Gandhi Darshan (☺10am-5pm Mon-Sat) **FREE**, a huge pavilion displaying photos relating to the Mahatma.

Shanti Vana   MONUMENT

(Forest of Peace; Map p64) Jawaharlal Nehru, the first Indian prime minister, was cremated just to the north of Raj Ghat, at Shanti Vana, in 1964. The cremation sites of Nehru's daughter, Indira Gandhi, and grandsons Sanjay and Rajiv are lined up along the riverbank in their own memorial parks.

National Gandhi Museum   MUSEUM

(Map p64; ✆23311793; Raj Ghat; ☺9.30am-5.30pm Tue-Sun) **FREE** A small but moving museum displaying historic photos and items such as Gandhi's spinning wheels and the dhoti (long loincloth) he was wearing at the time of his murder.

Feroz Shah Kotla   HISTORIC SITE

(Map p64; Bahadur Shah Zafar Marg; Indian/foreigner ₹5/100, video ₹25; ☺dawn-dusk; Ⓜ Pragati Maidan) Ferozabad, the fifth city of Delhi, was built by Feroz Shah in 1354 as a replacement for Tughlaqabad. Ringed by crumbling fortifications are a huge mosque, a *baoli* (step-well), and the pyramid-like Hawa Mahal, topped by a 13m-high sandstone Ashoka Pillar inscribed with Ashoka's edicts. There's an otherworldly atmosphere to the ruins, which are still a place of worship – on Thursday afternoon, crowds gather to light candles and incense and leave bowls of milk to appease Delhi's *djinns* (invisible spirits). Shoes should be removed when entering the mosque and Hawa Mahal.

Shankar's International
Dolls Museum   MUSEUM

(Map p64; ✆23316970; www.childrensbooktrust.com; Nehru House, Bahadur Shah Zafar Marg; adult/child ₹17/6; ☺10am-6pm Tue-Sun) From tacky Spanish bullfighting figurines to graceful Japanese geisha dolls, this cutesy but engaging museum has a collection of 6500 dolls from 85 countries, from Brazil to Japan.

National Bal Bhavan   MUSEUM

(Map p64; www.nationalbalbhavan.nic.in; Kotla Marg; adult/child ₹5/free; ☺9am-5.30pm Tue-Sat) Delhi's museum for children is a disorderly affair, with a toy train, animal enclosures, an exhibition on astrology and astronomy, and some delightful mini-dioramas showing key events in Indian history.

Nicholson Cemetery   CEMETERY

(Map p64; Lala Hardev Sahai Marg; ☺8am-6pm summer, 9am-5pm winter; Ⓜ Kashmere Gate) Close to Kashmere Gate, this forgotten cemetery is the last resting place for hundreds of Delhi's colonial-era residents, many of whom perished in childhood. One famous (ex-)resident is Brigadier General John Nicholson, who died from injuries sustained while storming Delhi during the 1857 First War of Independence (Indian Uprising). At the time he was hailed as the 'Hero of Delhi,' but author William Dalrymple has described him as an 'imperial psychopath'.

Take the metro to nearby Pulbangash station to see the British-erected Mutiny Memorial (Rani Jhansi Rd) and an Ashoka Pillar (Rani Jhansi Rd), transported here by Feroz Shah.

Coronation Durbar Site   MONUMENT

(Shanti Swaroop Tyagi Marg; Ⓜ Model Town) In a desolate field, around 10km north of Old Delhi, a lone obelisk marks the site where King George V was declared emperor of India in 1911, and where the great *durbars* (fairs) were held to honour India's British overlords in 1877 and 1903. Take an autorickshaw from Model Town metro station.

Lakshmi Narayan Temple   HINDU TEMPLE

(Birla Mandir; Map p64; Mandir Marg; ☺6am-9pm; Ⓜ Ramakrishna Ashram Marg) West of Connaught Place, the busy-looking, Orissan-style Lakshmi Narayan Temple was erected by the wealthy industrialist BD Birla. Gandhi inaugurated the complex in 1938 as a temple for all castes; a sign on the gate says, 'Everyone is Welcome'.

Connaught Place

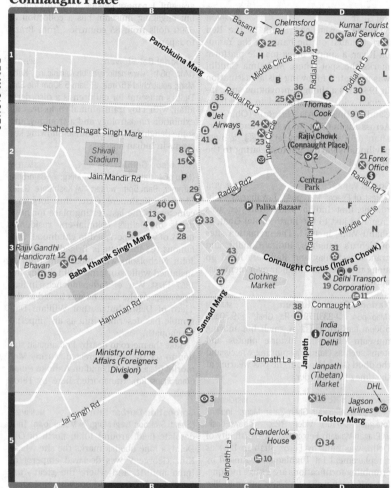

⊙ Connaught Place Area

Connaught Place AREA
(Map p68; Ⓜ Rajiv Chowk) New Delhi's colonial heart is Connaught Place, named after
George V's paternal uncle, and fashioned
after the colonnades of Cheltenham and
Bath to assuage British homesickness. Its
whitewashed, grey-tinged streets radiate out
from the central circle of Rajiv Chowk, lined
with shops and restaurants. The outer circle
(divided into blocks G to N) is technically

called Connaught Circus, and the inner circle (divided into blocks A to F) is Connaught
Place, but locals call the whole area 'CP'.

Almost every visitor to Delhi comes here,
which partly explains the rampant touts.

Jantar Mantar HISTORIC SITE
(Map p68; Sansad Marg; Indian/foreigner ₹5/100,
video ₹25; ⊙9am-dusk; Ⓜ Patel Chowk) The most
eccentric-seeming of Delhi's historic sites,
Jantar Mantar (derived from the Sanskrit
word for 'instrument') is an odd collection
of curving geometric buildings that are care-

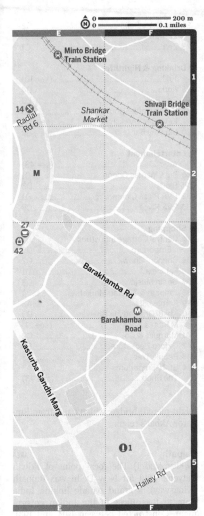

New Delhi & Around

★ Humayun's Tomb
HISTORIC BUILDING

(Map p72; Mathura Rd; Indian/foreigner ₹10/250, video ₹25; ☉dawn-dusk; Ⓜ JLN Stadium) The most perfectly proportioned and captivating of Delhi's mausoleums, Humayun's tomb seems to float above the gardens that surround it. Built in the mid-16th century by Haji Begum, the Persian-born senior wife of the Mughal emperor Humayun, the tomb brings together Persian and Mughal elements, creating a template that strongly influenced the Taj Mahal.

Following six years of restoration, completed in 2013, the tomb, other monuments and gardens are looking bright and beautiful. The arched facade is inlaid with bands of white marble and red sandstone, and the building follows strict rules of Islamic geometry, with an emphasis on the number eight. The surrounding gardens are alive with green parakeets and contain the tombs of the emperor's favourite barber and Haji Begum. This was where the last Mughal emperor, Bahadur Shah Zafar, took refuge before being captured and exiled by the British in 1857.

To the right as you enter the complex, Isa Khan's tomb is a fine example of Lodi-era architecture, constructed in the 16th century. Further south is the monumental Khan-i-Khanan's tomb (Indian/foreigner ₹5/100; ☉dawn-dusk), plundered in Mughal times to build Safdarjang's tomb.

A new visitor centre is due to be added to the site.

★ Hazrat Nizam-ud-din Dargah
SHRINE

(Map p72; off Lodi Rd; ☉24hr; Ⓜ JLN Stadium) Hidden away in a tangle of bazaars selling rose petals, *attars* (perfumes) and offerings, the marble shrine of the Muslim Sufi saint Nizam-ud-din Auliya offers a window through the centuries, full of music and crowded with devotees. The ascetic Nizam-ud-din died in 1325 at the ripe old age of 92, and his mausoleum became a point of pilgrimage for Muslims from across the empire. Later kings and nobles wanted to be buried as close to Nizam-ud-din as possible, hence the number of nearby Mughal tombs.

Other tombs in the compound include the graves of Jahanara (daughter of Shah Jahan) and the renowned Urdu poet Amir Khuysru. It's one of Delhi's most extraordinary pleasures to take a seat on the marble floor

fully calibrated to monitor the movement of the stars and planets. Maharaja Jai Singh II constructed the observatory in 1725.

Agrasen ki Baoli
MONUMENT

(Map p68; Hailey Lane; ☉dawn-dusk; Ⓜ Barakhamba Road) A remarkable thing to discover among the office towers southeast of Connaught Place, this atmospheric 14th-century step-well was once set in rural land, till the city grew up around it; 103 steps descend to the bottom, flanked by arched niches.

Connaught Place

and listen to Sufis singing rousing *qawwali* (Islamic devotional singing) at sunset. These are most spectacular on Thursday, but it's worth visiting on other evenings for a more intimate experience. Scattered around the surrounding alleyways are more tombs and a huge *baoli*. Entry is free, but visitors may be asked to make a donation.

A tour with the Hope Project (p80), which ends at the shrine, is recommended for some background.

Lodi Gardens   PARK
(Map p72; Lodi Rd; ⊙ 6am-8pm Oct-Mar, 5am-8pm Apr-Sep; Ⓜ Khan Market or Jor Bagh) This peaceful park is Delhi's favourite escape, popular with everyone from power-walking politicians to amorous teens. The gardens are dotted with the crumbling tombs of Sayyid and Lodi rulers, including the impressive 15th-century **Bara Gumbad tomb** (Map p72) and mosque, and the strikingly different tombs of **Mohammed Shah** and **Sikander Lodi**. There's a lake crossed by the Athpula

(eight-piered) bridge, which dates from Emperor Akbar's reign.

Rajpath   AREA
(Ⓜ Khan Market) The focal point of Edwin Lutyens' plan for New Delhi was Rajpath (Kingsway), a grand parade linking India Gate to the offices of the Indian government. Constructed between 1914 and 1931, these grand civic buildings, reminiscent of Imperial Rome, were intended to spell out in stone the might of the British empire – yet just 16 years later, the British were out on their ear and Indian politicians were pacing the corridors of power.

Shielded by a wrought-iron fence at the western end of Rajpath, the official residence of the president of India, Rashtrapati Bhavan (p71), is flanked by the mirror-image, dome-crowned **North Secretariat** (Map p72) and **South Secretariat** (Map p72), housing government ministries. The Indian parliament meets nearby at the **Sansad**

Bhavan (Parliament House; Map p72), a circular, colonnaded edifice at the end of Sansad Marg.

At Rajpath's eastern end, and constantly thronged by tourists, is **India Gate** (Map p72). This 42m-high stone memorial arch, designed by Lutyens, pays tribute to around 90,000 Indian army soldiers who died in WWI, the Northwest Frontier operations, and the 1919 Anglo-Afghan War.

Rashtrapati Bhavan   HISTORIC BUILDING
(President's House; Map p72; ☑23012960; www.presidentofindia.nic.in; 1hr tour ₹50; ⊙9am-4pm Fri-Sun; Ⓜ Central Secretariat) You have to book ahead online, but it's worth it to peek inside the grandiose President's House. Formerly home to the British Viceroy, it has 340 rooms, with 2.5km of corridors. However, visits are limited to the domed Durbar Hall, the presidential library and the gilded Ashoka Hall.

You'll have to leave cameras and phones at the entrance, but there's a chance to take pictures close up of the outside before/after your visit.

Rashtrapati Bhavan Museum   MUSEUM
(Map p72; ☑23013287; www.presidentofindia.nic.in; gate No 30, Mother Teresa Crescent Rd; tours ₹25; ⊙9am-4pm Fri-Sun; Ⓜ Central Secretariat) Housed in the palace's former stables (opposite Talkotara Stadium), this museum houses an array of the extravagant gifts received by the president, some of architect Lutyens' plans for the palace, and a few touch-screen exhibits about its history. Visits are by tour only and advance online bookings are required.

Mughal Gardens   GARDENS
(Map p72; ⊙Tue-Sun Feb-Mar; Ⓜ Central Secretariat) **FREE** Rashtrapati Bhavan's incredible, manicured gardens are open to the public for only two months a year, when they are in flower. If you're in town then, go see them. Lord Louis Mountbatten, India's last viceroy, was said to have employed 418 gardeners to care for the fabulous Mughal-style arrangements.

National Museum   MUSEUM
(Map p72; ☑23019272; www.nationalmuseumindia.gov.in; Janpath; Indian/foreigner ₹10/300, audio guide English, French or German ₹400, Hindi ₹150, camera Indian/foreigner ₹20/300; ⊙10am-5pm Tue-Sun; Ⓜ Central Secretariat) Offering a compelling if not always coherent snapshot of India's last 5000 years, this museum is

not overwhelmingly large, but full of splendours. Exhibits include rare relics from the Harappan Civilisation, Buddha's 4th to 5th century BC effects, antiquities from the Silk Route, exquisite miniature paintings (look out for the hand-painted playing cards), woodcarvings, textiles, statues, musical instruments, and an armoury with gruesomely practical weapons and a suit of armour for an elephant.

Allow at least two hours, preferably half a day. Bring identification to obtain an audio guide (worthwhile as labelling is minimal).

Next door is the **Archaeological Survey of India** (☑011-23010822; www.asi.nic.in; Janpath; ⊙9.30am-1pm & 2-6pm Mon-Fri), which stocks publications about India's main archaeological sites.

National Gallery of Modern Art   ART GALLERY
(Map p72; ☑23382835; www.ngmaindia.gov.in; Jaipur House, Dr Zakir Hussain Marg; Indian/foreigner ₹10/150; ⊙10am-5pm Tue-Sun; Ⓜ Khan Market) Delhi's flagship art gallery displays a remarkable collection of paintings, from colonial-era landscapes and 'Company Paintings', created by Indian artists to suit their new British rulers, to the primitive-inspired artworks of Nobel Prize–winner Rabindranath Tagore. Photography prohibited.

Gandhi Smriti   MUSEUM
(Map p72; ☑23012843; 5 Tees Jan Marg; ⊙10am-5pm Tue-Sun, closed 2nd Sat of month; Ⓜ Racecourse) **FREE** This poignant memorial is where Mahatma Gandhi was shot dead by a Hindu zealot on 30 January 1948, after campaigning against intercommunal violence. Concrete footsteps lead to the spot where Gandhi died, marked by a small pavilion. Video prohibited.

The adjacent house, where the Mahatma spent his last 144 days, contains rooms preserved as Gandhi left them, a detailed account of his last 24 hours, and vivid dioramas depicting scenes from Gandhi's life, set in boxes like 1950s TVs. Upstairs is the interpretative exhibition **Eternal Gandhi**.

In the room where Gandhi lodged, you can see his meagre possessions – not much more than a walking stick, spectacles, a spinning wheel and a pair of *chappals* (sandals).

Indira Gandhi Memorial Museum   MUSEUM
(Map p72; ☑23010094; 1 Safdarjang Rd; ⊙9.30am-4.45pm Tue-Sun; Ⓜ Racecourse) **FREE** The former residence of Indira Gandhi is now a museum dedicated to the former

New Delhi & Around

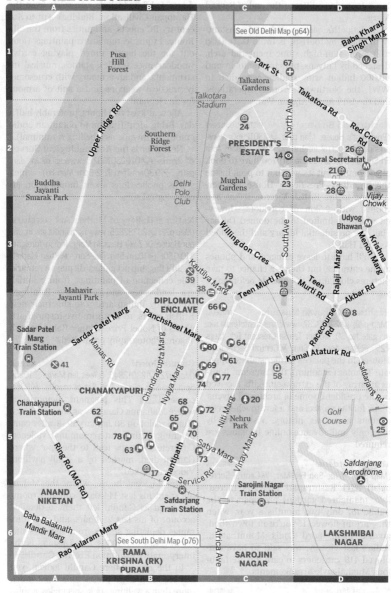

prime minister's life and family, India's Kennedys. It displays her personal effects, including the blood-stained sari she was wearing when she was assassinated in 1984. Many rooms are preserved in state, offering a window onto the elegant lives of Delhi's political elite. An exhibit at the rear charts the similarly truncated life of Indira's son, Rajiv, assassinated in 1991. In the garden, an enclosed crystal pathway marks Indira Gandhi's final footsteps.

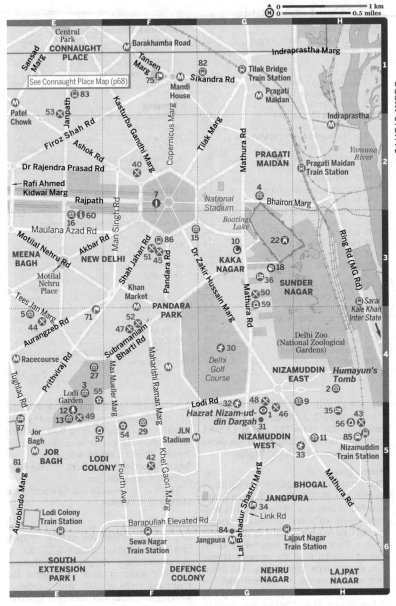

Nehru Memorial Museum   MUSEUM
(Map p72; ☎ 23016734; www.nehrumemorial.nic.in;
Teen Murti Rd; ⊙ 8am-5.15pm Tue-Sun; Ⓜ Udyog
Bhawan) FREE The stately Teen Murti Bhavan was the official residence of Jawaharlal
Nehru (India's first prime minister), and before that, the official residence of the British
commander-in-chief. As well as documents
and photos relating to Nehru's life and work,
there are several of his rooms preserved as if
he's just popped out.

New Delhi & Around

In the grounds is an old-fashioned **planetarium** (Map p72; ☑ 23014504; www.nehruplanetarium.org; 45min show ₹50; ⊗ Hindi 1.30pm & 4pm, English 11.30am & 3pm), which has shows about the stars in Hindi and English.

Purana Qila FORT
(Old Fort; Map p72; ☑ 24353178; Mathura Rd; Indian/foreigner ₹5/100, video ₹25, sound & light show ₹80; ⊗ dawn-dusk; Ⓜ Pragati Maidan) With its towering walls and dramatic gateways, Purana Qila was constructed by Afghan ruler Sher Shah (1538–45), who briefly seized control of Delhi from the emperor Humayun, and the monumental gatehouse opens onto a peaceful garden studded with ancient monuments. The graceful octagonal, red-sandstone **Sher Mandal** was used by Humayun as a library; it was a fall down its stairs that ended his reign, and life, in 1556. Beyond is the intricately patterned **Qila-i-Kuhran Mosque** (Mosque of Sher Shah). Across busy Mathura Road are more relics from the city of Shergarh, including the **Khairul Manazil mosque**, still used by local Muslims. A popular **boating lake** has been created from the former moat, with pedalos for hire. There's a **sound & light show** (⊗ in English 8.30pm Feb-Apr, Sep & Oct; 9pm May-Aug & 7.30pm Nov-Jan) at the fort.

The free **Ananya Dance Festival** takes place here in October.

Crafts Museum MUSEUM
(Map p72; ☑ 23371641; Bhairon Marg; ⊗ 10am-5pm Tue-Sun; Ⓜ Pragati Maidan) **FREE** Set up like a traditional village, this captivating, rambling museum aims to preserve the traditional crafts of India, from handloom weaving to Mithila wall painting. Highlights include an enormous carved temple rath (chariot), a mock-up of a Gujarati *haveli* (traditional, ornately decorated residence) and a shrine made from giant terracotta figures. In the rear courtyard, artisans sell their products. There's a good cafe.

National Rail Museum MUSEUM
(Map p72; ☎ 26881816; Service Rd, Chanakyapuri; adult/child ₹20/10, video ₹100; ⊙ 9.30am-5.30pm Tue-Sun) Trainspotters and kids will adore this recently renovated museum, with its collection of steam locos and carriages spread across 4.5 hectares. Among the venerable bogies are the former Viceregal Dining Car, the Maharaja of Mysore's rolling saloon, and the Fairy Queen locomotive, dating from 1855. The indoor gallery displays Indian Railways memorabilia, including the skull of an elephant that charged the *UP Mail* in 1894. A **miniature train** (adult/child ₹20/10) chuffs around the grounds.

National Zoological Gardens ZOO
(Map p72; ☎ 24359825; www.nzpnewdelhi.gov.in; Mathura Rd; Indian/foreigner ₹40/200, camera/video ₹50/200; ⊙ 9am-4.30pm Sat-Thu, to 4pm Oct-Mar; Ⓜ Pragati Maidan) Popular with families and couples, India's biggest zoo is set in 86 hectares. In fact, the grounds are so extensive you may have trouble finding the animals. Kept in reasonably considerate conditions are lions, tigers, elephants, hippos, rhinos, spectacular birds and monkeys who periodically take leave of their enclosures.

Safdarjang's Tomb TOMB
(Map p72; Aurobindo Marg; Indian/foreigner ₹5/100, video ₹25; ⊙ dawn-dusk; Ⓜ Jor Bagh) Built by the Nawab of Avadh for his father, Safdarjang, this grandiose mid-18th-century tomb was erected during the twilight of the Mughal empire. With not enough funds to pay for all-over marble, that which is on the dome was taken from the nearby mausoleum of Khan-i-Khana, and it was finished in red sandstone.

Tibet House MUSEUM
(Map p72; ☎ 24611515; 1 Lodi Rd; admission ₹10; ⊙ 9.30am-5.30pm Mon-Fri; Ⓜ JLN Stadium) Tibet House has a small museum displaying sacred manuscripts, votive carvings and historic *thangkas* (Tibetan cloth paintings), brought out of Tibet following the Chinese occupation. Photography prohibited.

South Delhi

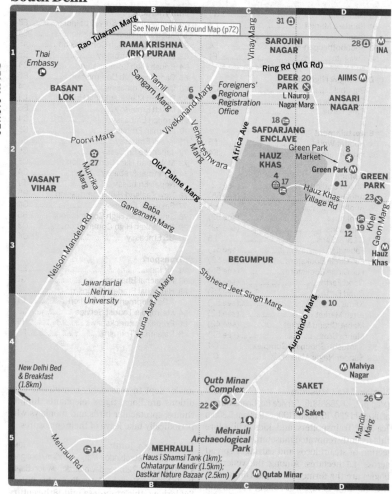

See New Delhi & Around Map (p72)

Nehru Park PARK
(Map p72; Vinay Marg; ⊙5am-8pm Apr-Sep, 6am-8pm Oct-Mar; Ⓜ Racecourse) On the edge of the Diplomatic Enclave, this green and pleasant park is a calm place to unwind away from the hubbub. In the centre is a statue of Lenin, revealing India's political sympathies during the Cold War.

Gurdwara Bangla Sahib SIKH TEMPLE
(Map p72; Ashoka Rd; ⊙4am-9pm; Ⓜ Patel Chowk) Topped by golden domes, this handsome white-marble gurdwara was constructed at the site where the eighth Sikh guru,

Harkrishan Dev, stayed before his death in 1664. Despite his tender years, the six-year-old guru tended to victims of Delhi's cholera and smallpox epidemic, and the waters of the gurdwara tank are said to have healing powers. Sikh pilgrims flock here at all hours, and devotional songs waft over the compound, adding to the contemplative mood.

◉ **South Delhi**

Hauz Khas AREA
(Map p76; Ⓜ Green Park) The lake at Hauz Khas, meaning 'royal tank,' was built by

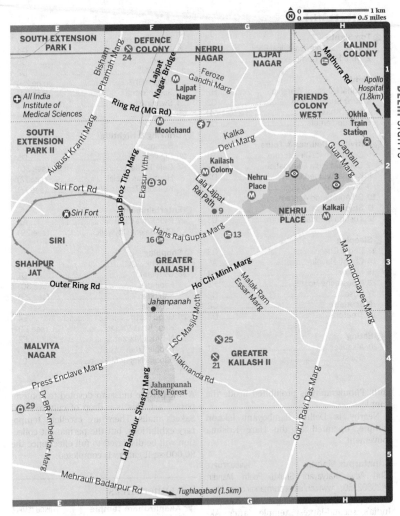

Sultan Ala-ud-din Khilji in the 13th century to provide water for Siri Fort. Thronged by birds and fringed by parkland, it is fronted by the ruins of Feroz Shah's 14th-century madrasa (religious school) and **tomb**, with a magnificent calligraphy-covered incised plaster ceiling.

To reach the lake shore, cut through the adjacent **Deer Park** (daylight hours), which has more ruined tombs, a well-stocked deer enclosure and a popular drumming circle. There are numerous Lodi-era tombs scattered along the access road to Hauz Khas Village, and in nearby Green Park.

Bahai House of Worship   BAHAI TEMPLE
(Lotus Temple; Map p76; ☐ 26444029; www.ba
haihouseofworship.in; Kalkaji; ☉ 9am-7pm Tue-Sun,
to 5.30pm winter; ☎; M Kalkaji Mandir) Designed
by Iranian-Canadian architect Fariburz Sah-
ba in 1986, Delhi's Bahai temple is a wonderful place to enjoy silence – a rare experience
in Delhi. Styled after a lotus flower, with 27
immaculate white-marble petals, the temple
was created to bring faiths together; visitors
are invited to pray or meditate silently according to their own beliefs. The attached
visitor centre tells the story of the Bahai

South Delhi

faith. Photography is prohibited inside the temple.

Nearby is Delhi's flamboyant **Iskcon temple**, operated by the Hare Krishna movement.

Chhatarpur Mandir HINDU TEMPLE
(Shri Adya Katyayani Shakti Peeth Mandir; ☎26802360; www.chhattarpurmandir.org; Main Chhatarpur Rd; ⊘4am-midnight; Ⓜ Chhatarpur) India's second-largest temple (after Akshardham), the Shri Adya Katyayani Shakti Peeth Mandir is dedicated to the goddess Katyayani (one of the nine forms of Parvati). There are dozens of shrines with towering South Indian *gopurams* (gateway towers), and an enormous statue of Hanuman stands guard over the compound. Weekdays tend to be fairly sedate, but the complex gets crowded at weekends and during the Navratri celebrations in September/October.

Kiran Nadar Museum of Art MUSEUM
(☎49160000; www.knma.in; 145 DLF, South Court Mall, Saket; ⊘10.30am-6.30pm Tue-Sun; Ⓜ Saket)

A fine private museum devoted to contemporary art, this is a drop of culture amid Saket's malls. There are excellent temporary exhibitions, but the permanent collection will be displayed to full effect once the 80,000-sq-ft gallery is completed.

○ **Other Areas**

★ **Akshardham Temple** HINDU TEMPLE
(☎22016688; www.akshardham.com; National Hwy 24, Noida turning; temple admission free, exhibitions ₹170, fountains ₹30; ⊘9.30am-6.30pm Tue-Sun; Ⓜ Akshardham) Rising dramatically over the eastern suburbs, the Hindu Swaminarayan group's controversially ostentatious Akshardham Temple draws elements from traditional Orissan, Gujarati, Mughal and Rajasthani architecture.

Surrounding this spiritual showpiece is a series of Disneyesque exhibitions, including a boat ride through 10,000 years of Indian history, animatronics telling stories from the life of Swaminarayan, and musical fountains.

The interior offers an almost psychedelic journey through Hindu mythology, with 20,000 carved deities, saints and mythical beings. Allow at least half a day to do the temple justice (weekdays are less crowded).

Sulabh International Museum of Toilets — MUSEUM

(☑ 25031518; www.sulabhtoiletmuseum.org; Sulabh Complex, Mahavir Enclave, Palam Dabri Rd; ☺ 10am-5pm summer, 10.30am-5pm winter) *FREE* Run by a pioneering charity that has done extraordinary work bringing sanitation to the poor of India, this quirky museum displays toilet-related paraphernalia dating from 2500 BC to modern times. It's around 20km west of Connaught Place. Take the metro to Janakpuri West, then take a rickshaw.

Activities

Lodhi Spa — SPA

(Map p72; ☑ 43633333; www.thelodhi.com; Lodhi Hotel, Lodi Rd, New Delhi; 1hr massage from ₹3800; Ⓜ JLN Stadium) The fragrant, rarified world of the Lodhi Spa is open to nonguests who book treatments, such as massages, facials, and traditional ayurvedic treatments.

Aura — SPA

(Map p72; ☑ 8800621206; www.aurathaispa.com; Middle Lane, Khan Market; 1hr oil massage ₹2400; ☺ 10am-9pm; Ⓜ Khan Market) Glitzy spa offering Thai-inspired massages and treatments. There are also branches at Karol Bagh, GK1, GK2 and Green Park.

Delhi Golf Club — GOLF

(Map p72; ☑ 24307100; www.delhigolfclub.org; Dr Zakir Hussain Marg; 18 holes weekdays/weekends ₹3050/4550; ☺ dawn-dusk; Ⓜ Khan Market) Founded in 1931, with beautiful, well-tended fairways, peacocks and Mughal pavilions. Weekends are busy.

Kerala Ayurveda — AYURVEDA

(Map p76; ☑ 41754888; www.keralaayurveda.biz; E-2 Green Park Extn; 1hr massage ₹1500; ☺ 8am-8pm; Ⓜ Green Park) Treatments from *sarvang ksheerdhara* (massage with butter milk) to *sirodhara* (warm oil poured on the forehead).

Park Hotel — SWIMMING

(Map p68; ☑ 23743737; 15 Sansad Marg; per person ₹850; ☺ 7am-7pm; Ⓜ Rajiv Chowk) The Park Hotel pool, handily convenient for Connaught Place, is surrounded by sunbeds and cabanas, and overlooked by the funky Aqua bar (p92).

Volunteering

There are plenty of ways to assist Delhi's less fortunate residents. The Salaam Balaak Trust (p80) in Paharganj, the Hope Project (p80) in Nizamuddin, and Torch (www.torchdelhi.org; 30D Nizamuddin Basti, Nizamuddin West) often have openings for volunteers. Mother Teresa's Missionaries of Charity run projects in Delhi that may accept volunteers – contact its Kolkata office (p459). Concern India Foundation (Map p76; ☑ 26210998; www.concernindiafoundation.org; A-52 Amar Colony, Lajpat Nagar IV) can also arrange placements for volunteers.

Courses

Hush Cooking — COOKING

(Vasant Vihar; 3hr lesson ₹3200) The lovely Prabeen Singh, a former development worker, offers 1½-hour cookery lessons in her home, in a suburb close to the airport. After the lesson, you eat your creations.

Nita Mehta — COOKING

(☑ 26141185; www.nitamehta.com; Block TU, Uttari Pitampura, North Delhi; 3hr lesson ₹2000) Cookery writer, teacher and TV chef Nita Mehta offers Indian cookery courses.

Central Hindi Directorate — LANGUAGE

(Map p76; ☑ 26178454; www.hindinideshalaya.nic.in; West Block VII, RK Puram, Vivekanand Marg; 60hr basic course ₹6000) Runs certificate and diploma courses in Hindi; the basic course lasts 60 hours with three classes a week.

Sivananda Yoga — YOGA

(Map p76; www.sivananda.org.in; A41 Kailash Colony; classes ₹400; Ⓜ Kailash Colony) Excellent yoga ashram, with beginners and advanced courses, plus drop-in classes.

OFF THE BEATEN TRACK

SHAHPUR JAT

A 1km rickshaw ride northeast from Hauz Khas metro, the urban village of Shahpur Jat was a focus of Delhi's 2014 street-art festival so has plentiful wall paintings; the enclave is also full of boutiques selling beautiful high-end, handmade dresses, jewellery, shoes and homewares. Little Black Book (www.littleblackbookdelhi.com) offers street-art walking tours.

DELHI ACTIVITIES

Sri Aurobindo Ashram
MEDITATION, YOGA
(Map p76; ☑ 26567863; www.sriaurobindoashram. net; Aurobindo Marg; Ⓜ Hauz Khas) Yoga and meditation for serious practitioners rather than hobbyists.

Studio Abhyas
MEDITATION, YOGA
(Map p76; ☑ 26962757; www.abhyastrust.org; F-27 Green Park; Ⓜ Green Park) Yoga and meditation classes and Vedic chanting in a comfortable suburban home. Prior experience preferred.

Tushita Meditation Centre
MEDITATION
(Map p76; ☑ 26513400; www.tushitadelhi.com; 9 Padmini Enclave; Ⓜ Hauz Khas) Tibetan/Buddhist meditation sessions – call or email for details. Donations are appropriate.

☞ Tours

Tours are an excellent way to explore Delhi. Admission fees and camera/video charges aren't included, and rates are per person. Book several days ahead.

★ DelhiByCycle
BICYCLE TOUR
(☑ 9811723720; www.delhibycycle.com; per person ₹1850; ⊙ 6.30-10am) Run by a Dutch journalist, these tours are a fantastic way to explore Delhi. Tours focus on specific neighbourhoods – Old Delhi, New Delhi, Nizamuddin, and the banks of the Yamuna – and start early to miss the worst of the traffic. The price includes chai and a Mughal breakfast. Child seats are available.

Salaam Baalak Trust
WALKING TOUR
(SBT; Map p82; ☑ 23584164; www.salaambaalak trust.com; Gali Chandiwali, Paharganj; suggested donation ₹200; Ⓜ Ramakrishna Ashram Marg) ∅ This charitable organisation offers two-hour 'street walks' guided by former street children, who will show you first-hand what life is like for Delhi's homeless youngsters. The fees help the Trust assist children on the streets.

Street Connections
WALKING TOUR
(www.walk.streetconnections.co.uk; 3hr walk ₹500) ∅ This fascinating walk through Old Delhi is guided by former street children who have been helped by the Salaam Baalak Trust. It explores the hidden corners of Old Delhi, starting at the Jama Masjid and concluding at one of the SBT shelters.

Hope Project
WALKING TOUR
(Map p72; ☑ 24353006; www.hopeprojectindia. org; 127 Hazrat Nizamuddin; 1½hr walk suggested donation ₹200; Ⓜ JLN Stadium) ∅ This charity runs fascinating walks around the Muslim *basti* (slum) of Nizamuddin. Take the walk in mid-afternoon to end at the *qawwali* at the Hazrat Nizam-ud-din Dargah, or at the more intimate session at the shrine of Hazrat Inayat Khan on Friday. Wear modest clothing.

Indomania Cultural Tours
TOUR
(☑ 8860223456; www.indomaniatours.com; half-day tours per person ₹2000) ∅ Excellent tours by the knowledgeable Priyush, exploring the parts of Delhi others don't reach. Visit a Rajasthani pottery village on Delhi's outskirts, cultural groups along the Yamuna River, or Delhi's Tibetan enclave, in tours that operate in association with local NGOs.

Delhi Tourism & Transport Development Corporation
BUS TOUR
(DTTDC; Map p68; www.delhitourism.nic.in; Baba Kharak Singh Marg; AC tours half-/full day ₹350/200; ⊙ 7am-9pm; Ⓜ Rajiv Chowk) Offers bus tours of New Delhi (9am to 1.30pm) and Old Delhi (2.15pm to 5.45pm) visiting all the big sights (avoid Monday, when most are shut). It also runs the air-conditioned Ho Ho (Hop-on, Hop-off) Dilli Dekho bus service, which circuits the major sights every 45 minutes or so from 8.30am to 6.30pm (Indian/foreigner ₹350/700, two-day ticket ₹600/1200) – buy tickets from the booth near the office.

Also runs rushed tours to Agra, Jaipur and Haridwar.

Intach
WALKING TOUR
(☑ 24641304; www.intachdelhichapter.org; tours ₹100) Intach runs walking tours with expert guides, exploring different areas, such as Chandhi Chowk, Nizamuddin, Hauz Khas and Mehrauli. Custom walks can also be arranged.

Delhi Transport Corporation Tours
BUS TOUR
(Map p68; ☑ 23752774; www.dtc.nic.in; Scindia House, Connaught Place; tour ₹200; ⊙ Tue-Sun; Ⓜ Rajiv Chowk) Inexpensive full-day air-con bus tours to the top sights from Connaught Place, leaving at 9.15am and returning at 5.45pm.

🛏 Sleeping

Delhi has plenty of choice, but it's wise to book ahead, as popular places can fill up in a flash. Reconfirm your booking 24 hours before you arrive. Most hotels offer pick-up from the airport with advance notice. Homestays are becoming an attractive alternative to hotels, and there's also an array of options on airbnb.com. For details of government-approved places contact India Tourism Delhi (p97), or check www.incredibleindianhomes.com and www.mahindra-homestays.com.

Hotels with a minimum tariff of ₹1000 charge luxury tax (10% at the time of research) and service tax (7.42% at the time of research), and some also add a service charge (up to 10%). Most hotels have a noon checkout and luggage storage is usually possible.

Old Delhi

Most hotels in the old town see few foreign visitors.

Hotel New City Palace   HOTEL $
(Map p64; ☎ 23279548; www.hotelnewcitypalace.in; 726 Jama Masjid; r ₹700; ❄; Ⓜ Chawri Bazaar) A palace it's not, but this mazelike hotel has an amazing location overlooking the Jama Masjid. Rooms are small, but some have windows and views; the bathrooms could do with a good scrub, but staff are friendly.

Hotel Broadway   HOTEL $$
(Map p64; ☎ 43663600; www.hotelbroadwaydelhi.com; 4/15 Asaf Ali Rd; s/d incl breakfast ₹2300/4000; ❄ @; Ⓜ New Delhi) A surprising find in the old city, Broadway was Delhi's first high-rise when it opened in 1956. Today it combines comfort with charm and eccentricity and has a great restaurant and bar. Some rooms have old-fashioned wood panelling, while others have been quirkily kitted out by French designer Catherine Lévy. Ask for one with views over Old Delhi.

Maidens Hotel   HOTEL $$$
(Map p64; ☎ 23975464; www.maidenshotel.com; 7 Sham Nath Marg; r from ₹12,000; ❄ @ 🛜 ❄; Ⓜ Civil Lines) Set in immaculate gardens, Oberoi-owned Maidens is a graceful wedding cake of a hotel, built in 1903. Lutyens stayed here while supervising the building of New Delhi, and the enormous high-ceilinged rooms have a colonial-era charm that is combined with contemporary comforts. There are two restaurants, a pool and a bar.

Paharganj & Around

With bumper-to-bumper budget hotels and a deserved reputation for hassle and dodgy characters, Paharganj isn't everyone's cup of chai. However, it's convenient for New Delhi train station, a great place to plug into the traveller grapevine, and the mayhem can grow on you. Note that if you're paying peanuts, you're in for a sun-starved, grimy cell. Splash a bit extra and you'll get more cleanliness and comfort. There are also better, more midrange rooms for not much more on nearby Arakashan Rd. Be warned that street noise can be diabolical – keep ear plugs handy.

Because of the pedestrian congestion, taxi-wallahs may be reluctant to take you right to the doorstep of your hotel, but if it's on the Main Bazaar or Arakashan Rd, they can make it. You can walk to everywhere from New Delhi train station or metro (for Arakashan Rd) or the Ramakrishna Ashram Marg metro stop. However tired you are when you get off the Airport metro or bus, don't believe rickshaw drivers or anyone who tells you differently. To avoid commission scams when you first arrive, ask rickshaws to drop you at Chhe Tooti Chowk and complete your journey on foot.

★**Hotel Amax Inn**   HOTEL $
(Map p64; ☎ 23543813; www.hotelamax.com; 8145/6 Arakashan Rd; s/d from ₹750/850; ❄ @ 🛜) Set back from chaotic Arakashan Rd, the Amax offers fairly standard, good-value budget rooms, with bullet-hard pillows, but the friendly staff run the place with the globetrotting traveller in mind. The rooftop terrace is a great spot to swap travel stories and there's wi-fi in reception.

Hotel Namaskar   HOTEL $
(Map p82; ☎ 23583456; www.namaskarhotel.com; 917 Chandiwalan, Main Bazaar; r ₹400-650, with AC

Paharganj

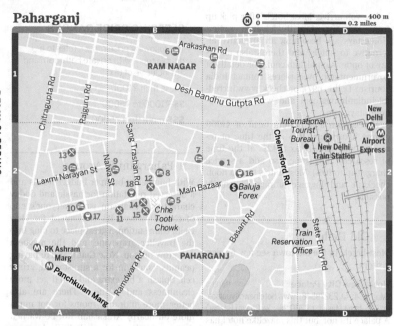

DELHI SLEEPING

Paharganj

🎯 Activities, Courses & Tours
1 Salaam Baalak Trust C2

🛏 Sleeping
2 Bloom Rooms..C1
3 Cottage Yes Please...............................A2
4 Hotel Ajanta..C1
5 Hotel All iz Well....................................B2
6 Hotel Grand Godwin..............................B1
7 Hotel Namaskar....................................B2
8 Hotel Rak International...........................B2
9 Jyoti Mahal Guesthouse B2
10 Metropolis Tourist Home.......................A2

🍴 Eating
11 Brown Bread Bakery..............................B2
Cafe Fresh .... (see 10)
Malhotra .... (see 10)
Metropolis Restaurant &
Bar .... (see 10)
12 Shimtur..B2
13 Sita Ram Dewan Chand.........................A2
14 Sonu Chat House B2
15 Tadka..B2

🍷 Drinking & Nightlife
16 Gem..C2
17 My Bar...A2
18 Sam's Bar..B2

₹650; ✹ 🛜) Up the alleyway opposite Dayal Boot House, this old favourite is run by two amiable brothers. It's not the Ritz (it's humid and noisy), but the simple rooms are usually freshly painted, the colour scheme will tickle you pink, and wi-fi works in the rooms.

Hotel Rak International HOTEL $
(Map p82; ☎ 23562478; www.hotelrakinternational. com; off Main Bazaar; s/d ₹550/650, with AC ₹800/900; ✹) Tucked off the Main Bazaar and overlooking a scruffy courtyard, the modest rooms at this popular hotel have

marble floors and bathrooms, chintzy built-in beds, including, unusually, twin rooms and...windows!

Cottage Yes Please HOTEL $
(Map p82; ☎ 23562300; www.cottageyesplease. com; 1843 Laxmi Narayan St; d from ₹950; ✹ @) One street north of Main Bazaar, this calm, comfortable place offers a selection of agreeable, if tired-looking, rooms. Rooms have TVs and fridges, and the decor runs to wood panelling and stained glass.

★ Bloom Rooms
HOTEL **$$**

(Map p82; ☑40174017; www.bloomrooms.com; 8591 Arakashan Road; s/d from ₹2200/2800; ☎) Sunny lemon-yellow and gleaming white, designer Bloom Rooms is sparklingly and clean, with soft pillows, white linen, great wi-fi and nice outdoor seating areas. This New Delhi branch is in a busy area but a haven inside. There's another balmy branch in Jangpura (Map p72; ☑41261400; 7 Link Rd) in South Delhi. Both have Amici restaurants (good pizza).

Hotel Grand Godwin
HOTEL **$$**

(Map p82; ☑23546891; www.godwinhotels.com; 8502/41 Arakashan Rd; d incl breakfast from ₹2500; ✳@☎) Located north of Main Bazaar, on the hotel strip of Arakashan Rd, the Grand Godwin is firmly midrange, and the glitzy feel of the lobby extends to the smart rooms. Run by the same owners, the nearby Godwin Deluxe offers similar facilities for similar prices.

Hotel All iz Well
HOTEL **$$**

(Map p82; ☑23580014; www.hotelallizwell.com; 4781 Main Bazaar; s/d ₹1300/1500; ✳☎) All iz Well offers clean, good-value, reasonably smart rooms, with room service, efficient wi-fi and reasonably helpful, unhassly staff. A calm and laid-back deal in Paharganj.

Jyoti Mahal Guesthouse
GUESTHOUSE **$$**

(Map p82; ☑23580523; www.jyotimahal.net; 2488-2490 Nalwa St; s/d ₹2200/2500; ✳@☎) Full of Rajasthani carvings and antiques, Jyoti is a cut above other places in Paharganj, with some genuine character: it feels like a traditional *haveli* home. Arranged around a central atrium, rooms have hand-made furniture, marble floors and some have four-poster beds.

Hotel Ajanta
HOTEL **$$**

(Map p82; ☑42350000; www.ajantahotel.com; 8647 Arakashan Rd; d/ste ₹2640/4650; ✳@☎) Some rooms are better than others at Ajanta; pay the higher rates and you'll be in for a more spacious room with a grand, polished-wood look. Some have private balconies. The downstairs Vagabond restaurant serves quality Mughlai food.

Metropolis Tourist Home
HOTEL **$$**

(Map p82; ☑23561794; www.metropolistourist-home.com; 16345 Main Bazaar; r from ₹2000; ✳@☎) A slightly haphazard but charac-terful lobby gives way to rooms with mood lighting, shiny bedspreads and slightly tired decor. The rooftop restaurant (mains ₹300 to ₹1000), hung with plants, is a tranquil retreat.

🛏 Connaught Place & Around

Sunny Guest House
GUESTHOUSE **$**

(Map p68; ☑23312909; sunnyguesthouse1234@hotmail.com; 152 Scindia House, Connaught Lane; r ₹800, without bathroom ₹400-600; Ⓜ Rajiv Chowk) Sunny Guest House is light on the pocket for the location, but this comes at a price – tiny, dingy rooms.

Prem Sagar Guest House
GUESTHOUSE **$$**

(Map p68; ☑23345263; www.premsagarguest-house.com; 1st fl, 11 P-Block, Connaught Place; s/d from ₹3520/4110; ✳@; Ⓜ Rajiv Chowk) A reliable, long-standing choice, with 12 snug rooms that aren't flash but are clean and relatively cheap for the location. There's a pot-plant-filled rear terrace, and internet in reception.

★ Imperial
HOTEL **$$$**

(Map p68; ☑23341234; www.theimperialindia.com; Janpath; r from ₹17,000; ✳@☎✳; Ⓜ Rajiv Chowk) The inimitable, Raj-era Imperial marries colonial classicism with gilded art deco. Rooms have high ceilings, flowing curtains, French linen and marble baths, and the hallways and atriums are lined with 18th- and 19th-century paintings and prints. The 1911 bar (p92) is highly recommended, and the Atrium cafe (p91) serves the perfect high tea.

Hotel Palace Heights
HOTEL **$$$**

(Map p68; ☑43582610; www.hotelpalaceheights.com; 26-28 D-Block; s/d ₹7150/8250; ✳@☎; Ⓜ Rajiv Chowk) This boutique hotel is cool enough to wear shades, offering Connaught Place's nicest rooms with gleaming white linen, black lampshades and caramel and amber tones. There's an excellent restaurant, Zäffrän (p89).

Hotel Alka
HOTEL **$$$**

(Map p68; ☑23344328; www.hotelalka.com; P-Block, Connaught Place; s/d from ₹3500/5500; ✳@☎; Ⓜ Rajiv Chowk) Hotel Alka has an old-fashioned charm, with lots of wooden furnishings. Rooms are small, but the pricier ones have some unique decor, including cheetah murals. There's a good pure veg (no onion or garlic) restaurant.

DELHI'S LITTLE LHASA

Home to Delhi's refugee Tibetan population, Majnu-ka-Tila takes a little effort to get to, but it's good for the little Lhasa vibe, and a good alternative traveller hub if the hustle of Paharganj is not your scene. This mellow enclave is packed with travel agents, restaurants and glittering trinket vendors and centres on a square with two colourful temples. You'll rub shoulders with maroon-clad Buddhist monks, local Tibetans and rather a lot of beggars; however, the streets have a peaceful, safe, small-town vibe.

Friendly **Wongdhen House** (☑23816689; 2wongdhenhouse@gmail.com; 15-A New Tibetan Colony; r ₹700-750, without bathroom ₹450; ✲) has simple, shabby, slightly overpriced rooms, and a good restaurant; next door **Lhasa House** (☑2393 9888, 2393 9777; lhasahouse@rediffmail.com; 16 New Aruna Nagar; r ₹350-550) is better value. **Ama** (H 40, New Aruna Nagar; snacks ₹20-95; ☉7am-9.30pm; ☎) is a splendid cafe hang-out, and there's the gorgeous, fantastic-value **Amala** (☉9am-8.30pm) boutique downstairs, selling everything from prayer flags to felt toys. Two good restaurants are **Tee Dee** (32 New Aruna Nagar; dishes ₹60-200; ☉8.30am-10.30pm) and **Dolma House** (Block 10, New Tibetan Colony; dishes ₹40-100; ☉8.30am-10.30pm).

To get here, take the metro to Vidhan Sabha, then one of the plentiful cycle-/autorickshaws (₹20/40) to the enclave on KB Hedgewar Marg.

🛏 West Delhi

Master Guest House　　　　GUESTHOUSE $$
(☑28741089;　　　www.master-guesthouse.com; R-500 New Rajendra Nagar; s/d incl breakfast from ₹3250/4250; ✲@☎; Ⓜ Rajendra Place) Around 5km west of Connaught Place, but a few minutes from Rajendra Place metro station, this smart and polished suburban home has three tastefully furnished rooms with spotless bathrooms. There's a leafy rooftop terrace.

Shanti Home　　　　　　　　HOTEL $$$
(☑41573366; www.shantihome.com; A-1/300 Janakpuri; s/d incl breakfast from ₹5500/6500; ✲@☎; Ⓜ Uttam Nagar East) Deep in West Delhi, around 17km from Connaught Place, this delightful small hotel is close to the metro and offers beautifully decorated rooms that get gradually swisher the more you spend. There are spacious lounge areas, an excellent rooftop restaurant, a gym and a reasonably priced steam and ayurvedic massage service (₹1500/1800 for a 60-/90-minute facial).

🛏 New Delhi

Youth Hostel　　　　　　　　　HOSTEL $
(Map p72; ☑26116285; www.yhaindia.org; 5 Nyaya Marg, Chanakyapuri; dm/d ₹300/900, with AC ₹600/1612; ✲@; Ⓜ Udyyog Bhawan) The dormitory here is a great deal if you're looking for somewhere quiet and cheap, but you'll get better rooms elsewhere at these prices.

The obligatory one-month temporary YHA membership costs ₹150.

★ Lodhi　　　　　　　　　　　　HOTEL $$$
(Map p72; ☑43633333; www.thelodhi.com; Lodi Rd; r from ₹27,000; ✲☎✈; Ⓜ JNL Stadium) Formerly the Aman, the Lodhi is one of Delhi's finest luxury hotels, with only 40 huge, lovely rooms and suites and acres of space. Each room has a balcony with private plunge pool, and those on the upper floors have great views, some over to Humayun's Tomb. Attention to detail is superb and the general managers greet everyone personally. There's also a top-notch spa.

Lutyens Bungalow　　　　GUESTHOUSE $$$
(Map p72; ☑24611341; www.lutyensbungalow. co.in; 39 Prithviraj Rd; s/d incl breakfast from ₹5500/7000; ✲@☎✈; Ⓜ Racecourse) This great rambling house is an atmospheric green oasis, ideal if you're travelling with kids and perfectly located for exploring New Delhi. The garden is great – lawns, flowers and fluttering parrots – but rooms are a little stuffy and overpriced, though looking much better since recent renovations.

🛏 South Delhi

Moustache Hostel　　　　　　HOSTEL $
(Map p76; www.facebook.com/moustachehostel; S25, GK1, M-Block Market Main Rd; dm ₹600, d ₹2500, incl breakfast; ✲☎; Ⓜ Kailash Colony) This cheerful hostel has appealing, nicely kept small dorms, a few doubles decorated with bright prints, and a funky, welcoming

vibe. It's a 15- to 20-minute walk from the metro. There's a book-lined common room and lots of local info. It's a great place to chat to other 20-something travellers.

Bed & Chai   HOSTEL $$
(Map p76; www.bedandchai.com; R55 Hans Raj Gupta Marg; dm ₹850, d with/without bathroom from ₹3000/2200) This French-owned guesthouse has simple, stylish rooms, decorated with flashes of colour and lamps made out of teapots. There's a sparkling clean dorm as well, a roof terrace and, of course, excellent chai. The owners also run Bed & Chai Masala, which has cheaper dorm beds.

Treetops   GUESTHOUSE $$
(Map p76; ☑9899555704; baig.murad@gmail. com; R-8b Hauz Khas Enclave; s/d incl breakfast ₹3500/4000; ❂@⑈; ⓂHauz Khas) Cookery writer Tannie and journalist Murad have a gracious home and to stay here feels rather like visiting distant, upper-crust relatives. Treetops offers two large rooms opening onto a leafy rooftop terrace overlooking the park. Evening meals are available.

★Devna   GUESTHOUSE $$$
(Map p72; ☑41507176; www.tensundernagar.com; 10 Sunder Nagar; s/d ₹5700/6000; ❂@⑈) Fronted by a pretty courtyard garden, and run with panache by the charming Atul and Devna, this is one of Delhi's prettiest guesthouses. The walls are lined with photos of maharajas and works of art (yes, those are original Jamini Roys) and the rooms are decked out with quirky antiques. The upstairs rooms front onto tiny terraces.

Manor   HOTEL $$$
(Map p76; ☑26925151; www.themanordelhi. com; 77 Friends Colony West; d incl breakfast from ₹12,000; ❂@) A more intimate alternative to Delhi's five-star chains, this 16-room boutique hotel oozes privacy and elegance. Set amid lush lawns off Mathura Rd, the Manor offers the kind of designer touches normally found in the homes of Bollywood stars. There's a colonial air to the opulent rooms and the restaurant, Indian Accent (p91), is one of Delhi's finest.

Bnineteen   GUESTHOUSE $$$
(Map p72; ☑41825500; www.bnineteen.com; B-19 Nizamuddin East; s/d incl breakfast from ₹7500/9000; ❂@; ⓂJNL Stadium) Located in posh and peaceful Nizamuddin East, with views over Humayun's tomb from the rooftop, this gorgeous place is owned by archi-

tects, and it shows. Rooms are modern and refined, and there is a state-of-the-art shared kitchen on each floor.

Scarlette   GUESTHOUSE $$$
(Map p76; ☑8826010278; www.scarlettenew delhi.com; B2/139 Safdarjung Enclave; d ₹8000; ❂⑈; ⓂGreen Park) In a serene residential area, close to the Deer Park and Hauz Khas, Scarlette is a lovely boutique *maison d'hotes* (guesthouse) with just four rooms and a large sitting room filled with books and interesting *objets*. It's French-owned and popular with French speakers. A set menu dinner (rather pricey at ₹900 to ₹1200) is served nightly.

Rose   HOTEL $$$
(Map p76; ☑65680444; www.therosenew delhi.com; T40 Hauz Khas Village; s ₹3750-8000, d ₹4250-8750; ❂⑈; ⓂGreen Park) This is a stylish guesthouse set in one of Delhi's most bohemian districts (packed with bars and boutiques, and good for live music), which sits alongside monument-scattered parkland. It's worthwhile paying for the more expensive rooms, as the cheaper ones have windows opening only onto the walkway.

Airport Area & Beyond

Delhi's brand-new Aerocity area is a bland but convenient conglomeration of hotels, only 4km from the airport. It's served by the Delhi Aerocity metro stop. Take your pick from brands such as JW Marriott, Red Fox and Lemon Tree; the cheapest option is the Ibis, which also offers a free 24-hour shuttle

---

OFF THE BEATEN TRACK

ESCAPE FROM DELHI

Tikli Bottom (www.tiklibottom.com; Manender Farm, Gairatpur Bas, Gurgaon; s/d full board ₹10,900/18,500) Less than 50km south of central Delhi, this peachy Lutyens-style bungalow surrounded by wooded hills is run by a British couple. The house and the owners seem to come from another era, one of toasted teacakes, lawns and chintz. There are four high-ceilinged guest rooms and spacious lounges, plus a beautiful pool overlooked by a pagoda and with hill views.

pick-up from either terminal. There are also a few choices in nearby Vasant Kunj.

There are also several options for sleeping at the airport, including Eaton Smart and SAMS sleeping pods; see www.newdelhiairport.in for details.

New Delhi Bed & Breakfast   HOMESTAY **$$**
(☑26894812; www.newdelhibedandbreakfast.com; C8/8225 Vasant Kunj; s/d ₹3000/3500; ✳@) A proper homestay: Renu Dayal is warm and welcoming and has two double rooms (one en suite) in her elegant house in a leafy enclave, only 10 minutes' drive from the airport.

Chhoti Haveli   HOMESTAY **$$**
(Map p76; ☑26124880; www.chhotihaveli.com; A1006, Pocket A, Vasant Kunj; s/d ₹3500/4000; ✳@⏚; Ⓜ Chhatarpur) Set in a block of low-rise apartments, in a quiet, leafy area near the airport, this well-kept place offers tastefully decorated rooms. Potted plants and scattered petals on the doorstep show a personal touch.

✖ Eating

Delhi is a foodie paradise, and locals graze throughout the day, from the city's famous *Dilli-ka-chaat* (street-food snacks and salads) to indulgent feasts at Delhi's fine-dining restaurants.

Midrange and upmarket restaurants charge a service tax of around 10%; drinks taxes can suck a further 20% (alcoholic) or 12.5% (nonalcoholic) from your money belt. Many restaurants also levy a 10% service charge, in lieu of a tip. Taxes haven't been included here unless indicated.

Reservations may be required for popular and high-end restaurants.

✖ Old Delhi

★ Karim's   MUGHLAI **$**
(Map p64; Gali Kababyan; mains ₹45-460; ◷9am-12.30am; Ⓜ Chawri Bazaar) Just off the lane leading south from the Jama Masjid, Karim's has been delighting carnivores since 1913. Expect meaty Mughlai treats such as mutton *burrah* (marinated chops), delicious mutton mughlai, and the breakfast mutton and bread combo *nahari* (₹125 half portion). There's a second branch in **Nizamuddin West** (Map p72; 168/2 Jha House Basti).

Gali Paratha Wali   STREET FOOD **$**
(Map p64; Gali Paratha Wali; parathas ₹15-35; ◷7am-11pm; Ⓜ Chandni Chowk) Head to this

food-stall-lined lane off Chandni Chowk for delectable *parathas* (traditional flatbread) fresh off the *tawa* (hotplate). Choose from a spectacular array of stuffings, from green chilli and paneer to lemon and banana.

★ Jalebiwala   SWEETS **$**
(Map p64; Dariba Corner, Chandni Chowk; jalebis per 100g ₹30; ◷8.30am-9.45pm; Ⓜ Chandni Chowk) Century-old Jalebiwala does Delhi's – if not India's – finest *jalebis* (deep-fried, syrupy fried dough), so pig out and worry about the calories tomorrow.

Natraj Dahi Balle Wala   STREET FOOD **$**
(Map p64; 1396 Chandni Chowk; plate ₹50; ◷10.30am-11pm; Ⓜ Chandni Chowk) This hole-in-the-wall with the big red sign and the big crowds is famous for its *dahi bhalle* (fried lentil balls served with yoghurt and garnished with chutney) and deliciously crispy *aloo tikki* (spiced potato patties).

Jain Coffee House   STREET FOOD **$**
(Map p64; Raghu Ganj, Chawri Bazaar; sandwiches ₹60; ◷9am-7.30pm; Ⓜ Chawri Bazaar) In a tiny lane, once Delhi's main granary, off Chawri Bazaar (Raghu Ganj is a tiny turning just before Nai Sarak), one grain trading family operates a sideline in delicious seasonal fruit sandwiches.

Kake di Hatti   INDIAN **$**
(Map p64; 654-655 Church Mission Rd; mains ₹40-130; ◷10am-11pm; Ⓜ Chawri Bazaar) This long-standing *dhaba* (snack bar) has been open since 1942 and is famous for its huge, delicious, stuffed (with peas and cheese, chili, cheese and onions, and many other combos) naans and *parathas,* which you can eat with various types of fragrant dhal. Look out for the hordes of people and the Hindi sign in red.

Haldiram's   FAST FOOD **$**
(Map p64; 1454/2 Chandni Chowk; mains ₹68-178; ◷10am-10.30pm; Ⓜ Chandni Chowk) This clean, bright cafeteria cum sweet shop is a popular stop for its top-notch dosas (large South Indian savoury crepe), *idli* (South Indian spongy, round, fermented rice cake) and thalis, and it also sells delectable *namkin* (savouries) and *mithai* (sweets) to eat on the hoof. There's a popular branch on **Connaught Place** (Map p68; 6 L-Block Connaught Place; ◷10am-10.30pm; Ⓜ Rajiv Chowk).

Bikanervala   FAST FOOD **$**
(Map p64; 382 Chandni Chowk; snacks ₹42-170; ◷8am-10.30pm; Ⓜ Chandni Chowk) This bright

little canteen offers tasty snacks such as *paratha* and *channa bhatura* (fried bread with chickpeas). There's a handy branch among the state emporiums on Baba Kharak Singh Marg (Map p68; ; M Rajiv Chowk).

Ghantewala   SWEETS $
(Map p64; 1862A Chandni Chowk; mithai per 100g from ₹25; ⊙8am-10pm; M Chandni Chowk) Delhi's most famous sweetery, 'the bell ringer' has been churning out *mithai* (Indian sweets) since 1790. Try some *sohan halwa* (ghee-dipped gram flour biscuits).

Moti Mahal   MUGHLAI $$
(Map p64; ☑23273661; 3704 Netaji Subhash Marg; mains ₹170-540; ⊙11am-midnight) The original, much-copied Moti Mahal has been open for six generations – the food is much more impressive than the faded surroundings. Delhiites rate the place for its superior butter chicken and dhal makhani. There's live *qawwali* (Islamic devotional singing) Wednesday to Monday (8pm to 11.30pm).

Al-Jawahar   MUGHLAI $$
(Map p64; Matya Mahal; mains ₹100-275; ⊙7am-midnight; M Chawri Bazaar) South of the Jama Masjid, Al-Jawahar serves up tasty Mughlai cuisine at laminate tables in an orderly dining room, and you can watch breads being freshly made at the front. Kebabs and mutton curries dominate the menu, but it also does good butter chicken and korma.

Chor Bizarre   KASHMIRI $$$
(Map p64; ☑23273821; Hotel Broadway, 4/15 Asaf Ali Rd; mains ₹305-675; ⊙7.30-10.30am, noon-3.30pm & 7.30-11.30pm; M New Delhi) A dimly lit cavern filled with bric-a-brac, including a vintage car, Chor Bizarre (meaning 'thieves market') offers delicious and authentic Kashmiri cuisine, including *wazwan* (preparations of mutton and chicken), the traditional Kashmiri feast. It offers an old-town walking tour combined with lunch for ₹2500.

✗ Paharganj & West Delhi

Paharganj's restaurants are a reflection of the globetrotting backpackers who eat here. As well as Indian staples, you'll find everything from banana pancakes to Israeli falafel...executed with varying degrees of success. There are more cheap eats in the bazaars at Karol Bagh.

★Sita Ram Dewan Chand   INDIAN $
(Map p82; 2243 Chuna Mandi; half/full plate ₹25/45; ⊙8am-6pm; M Ramakrishna Ashram Marg) A family-run hole-in-the-wall, serving inexpensive portions of just one dish – *chole bhature* (spicy chickpeas), accompanied by delicious, freshly made, puffy, fried bread. It's a traditional breakfast but you can feast on it any time of day.

Brown Bread Bakery   ORGANIC $
(Map p82; Ajay Guesthouse, 5084-A, Main Bazaar; snacks ₹65-150; ⊙7am-11pm; 🛜; M Ramakrishna Ashram Marg) With a rustic, wicker-heavy interior and a long menu of largely organic breads, cheeses, jams, soups, teas and more, the Brown Bread is a nice relaxing place to hang out among other travellers from all over the place. You can also buy ayurvedic products here.

Sonu Chat House   INDIAN $
(Map p82; 5045, 46 Main Bazaar; dishes ₹60-160; ⊙8am-1am; M Ramakrishna Ashram Marg) Perhaps Paharganj's most palatable *dhaba* (snack bar), this sunken small hive of activity is popular with foreign tourists and locals and serves up tasty thalis (from ₹70) and *masala dosa* (₹70).

Bikanervala Angan   FAST FOOD $
(82 Arya Samaj Rd, Karol Bagh; mains ₹80-170; ⊙8am-midnight; M Karol Bagh) From the Bikanervala stable, this small but buzzing Karol Bagh canteen is a useful pit stop for South Indian treats, fast food and snacks. Thalis start at ₹135.

Roshan di Kulfi   ICE CREAM $
(Ajmal Khan Rd, Karol Bagh; kulfi ₹70-80; ⊙8.30am-9.30pm; M Karol Bagh) A Karol Bagh institution for its scrumptious special *pista badam kulfi* (frozen milk dessert with pistachio, almond and cardamom). It's around 500m northeast of Karol Bagh metro.

★Shimtur   KOREAN $$
(Map p82; 3rd fl, Navrang Guest House, Tooti Galli; meals ₹240-500; ⊙10am-11pm; M Ramakrishna Ashram Marg) It's a mini-adventure to find this place, off the main drag and on top of the Navrang Guest House. Follow the stairs up several floors and you'll find a neat little bamboo-lined rooftop. The Korean food is fresh, authentic and delicious. Try the *bibimbap* (rice bowl with a mix of vegetables, egg and pickles; ₹240).

DELHI EATING

Tadka
INDIAN $$

(Map p82; 4986 Ramdwara Rd; mains ₹140-160; ☺9am-10.30pm; M Ramakrishna Ashram Marg) Named for everyone's favourite dhal, Tadka serves up tasty paneer dishes and other veg treats (thalis ₹170) under whirring fans, to an appreciative clientele of vegetarians and meat-avoiders.

Malhotra
MULTICUISINE $$

(Map p82; 1833 Laxmi Narayan St; mains ₹100-600; ☺7am-11pm; M Ramakrishna Ashram Marg) One street back from the Main Bazaar, Malhotra is smarter than most, with a good menu of set breakfasts, burgers, Indian and spirited attempts at continental dishes.

Cafe Fresh
CAFE $$

(Map p82; Laxmi Narayan St; dishes ₹100-200; ☺8am-11pm; 🛜) This vegetarian cafe has reasonably good food and is an appealingly calm place to retreat (down a few steps) from the busy streets. Free wi-fi.

Metropolis Restaurant & Bar
MULTICUISINE $$

(Map p82; Metropolis Tourist Home, Main Bazaar; mains ₹300-1000; ☺11am-11pm) On the rooftop at Metropolis Tourist Home, this energetic travellers' haunt is a cut above the competition, with prices to match, proffering cold beer and tasty tandoori chicken.

🍴 Connaught Place

★ Hotel Saravana Bhavan
SOUTH INDIAN $

(Map p68; 15 P-Block, Connaught Place; mains ₹65-165; ☺8am-11pm; M Rajiv Chowk) Delhi's best thali is served up in unassuming surroundings – a simple Tamil canteen on the edge of Connaught Place. There are queues every meal time to sample the splendid array of richly spiced veg curries, dips, breads and condiments that make it onto every thali plate. There's a second branch on Janpath (Map p68; 46 Janpath; M Rajiv Chowk).

Nizam's Kathi Kabab
FAST FOOD $

(Map p68; 5 H-Block, Connaught Place; kebabs ₹75-265; ☺11.30am-11pm; M Rajiv Chowk) This takeaway eatery creates masterful kebabs, biryani and kati rolls (kebabs wrapped in a hot paratha). It's always busy with meat-loving hordes, but there are also paneer, mushroom and egg options available so vegetarians don't have to miss out.

Coffee Home
INDIAN $

(Map p68; Baba Kharak Singh Marg; meals ₹35-70; ☺11am-8pm; M Rajiv Chowk) Popular with lo-cal workers, this has a lovely shady garden eating area, under the boughs of a peepal tree. It's always busy with locals feasting on South Indian snacks such as masala dosa (₹70), and is handily located next to the government emporiums.

Wenger's
BAKERY $

(Map p68; 16 A-Block, Connaught Place; snacks ₹30-90; ☺10.45am-7.45pm; M Rajiv Chowk) Legendary Wenger's has a wonderfully stuck-in-time feel having been baking since 1926. Come for cakes, sandwiches, biscuits and savoury patties. Around the corner you can eat in at Wenger's Deli (Map p68), which has the most delicious milkshakes, including mango (₹90).

Sagar Ratna
SOUTH INDIAN $$

(The Ashok, 50 B, Diplomatic Enclave; dishes ₹240-345; ☺8am-11pm; M Rajiv Chowk) Considered best of all the Sagar Ratna's around town, this venerable South Indian restaurant is always buzzing with families, couples and kitty parties, and does a great line in dosas, idlis, uttapams (savoury rice pancakes) and thalis. There are other branches in Connaught Place (Map p68; 15-K Block; dishes ₹100-250; ☺8am-11pm; M Rajiv Chowk) and Defence Colony Market (Map p76; Defence Colony Market; M Lajpat Nagar).

Kake-da-Hotel
MUGHLAI $$

(Map p68; ☎9136666820; 67 Municipal Market; mains ₹140-530; ☺noon-11.30pm; M Rajiv Chowk) This simple dhaba (snack bar) is a basic hole in the wall that's popular with local workers for its famous butter chicken (₹180) and other Mughlai Punjabi dishes.

★ Rajdhani
INDIAN $$$

(Map p68; ☎43501200; 1/90 P-Block, Connaught Place; thalis ₹395, dinner & weekends ₹445; ☺noon-4pm & 7-11pm; M Rajiv Chowk) This pristine, nicely decorated two-level place serves up excellent-value food-of-the-gods vegetarian thalis with a fantastic array of Gujarati and Rajasthani dishes. It's the same, sumptuous thali daily.

Véda
INDIAN $$$

(Map p68; ☎41513535; 27 H-Block, Connaught Place; mains ₹400-1300; ☺12.30-11.30pm; M Rajiv Chowk) Fashion designer Rohit Baal created Véda's sumptuous interior, making for Connaught Place's most dimly lit eatery, a dark boudoir with swirling neo-Murano chandeliers and shimmering mirror mosaics. The menu proffers tasty classic Mughlai dishes (butter chicken, dhal makhani and the like) and they mix a mean Martini.

Swagath   SOUTH INDIAN $$$
(Map p72; 23366761; Janpath Hotel, Janpath; mains ₹195-1395; noon-11.45pm; ; Patel Chowk) Serving supremely scrumptious Indian seafood (especially crab, prawns, lobster and fish), Swagath will take you on a culinary tour through the fishing villages of South India. There are several branches, including at **Defence Colony Market** (Map p76; noon-11.45pm; Lajpat Nagar) and **M Block Market** (Map p76; noon-11.45pm).

Zäffrän   MUGHLAI $$$
(Map p68; 43582610; Hotel Palace Heights, 26-28 D-Block; mains ₹435-800; noon-3.30pm & 7pm-midnight) An excellent restaurant serving Mughlai cuisine, with a lovely, calm bamboo-shuttered, glass-covered terrace and plenty of light.

United Coffee House   MULTICUISINE $$$
(Map p68; 23416075; 15 E-Block, Connaught Place; mains ₹345-1000; noon-midnight; Rajiv Chowk) Not a coffee shop, but an upscale, high-ceilinged, chandeliered restaurant, with an old-world dining room full of characters who look as elderly as the fixtures and fittings. The menu covers everything from butter chicken to English high tea. Serves alcohol (a pint of Kingfisher costs ₹225).

Zen   CHINESE $$$
(Map p68; 23357444; 25 B-Block, Connaught Place; mains ₹189-635; 11am-11pm; Rajiv Chowk) A high-ceilinged place with walls quilted like a Chanel handbag, Zen offers a more authentic take on Chinese cuisine than most Delhi eateries. Look out for dishes such as claypot tofu and spicy shredded lamb among the familiar standards.

✕ New Delhi & Around

To dine in style, head to Delhi's upmarket hotels or the posh enclaves around Khan Market, Lodi Rd and Mathura Rd. Shoppers at Khan Market, in particular, will be spoilt for choice.

Lodi Colony Kebab Stands   STREET FOOD $
(Map p72; Hazrat Nizam-ud-din Dargah; kebabs from ₹30; noon-11pm; JLN Stadium) The alley in front of Hazrat Nizam-ud-din Dargah becomes a hive of activity every evening as devotees leave the shrine in search of suste-

nance. Canteen-style kebab houses cook up lip-smacking beef, mutton and chicken kebabs at bargain prices, with biryani and roti as filling side orders.

Andhra Pradesh
Bhawan Canteen   SOUTH INDIAN $
(Map p72; 1 Ashoka Rd; breakfast ₹60, thalis ₹110; 7.30-10.30am, noon-3pm & 7.30-10pm; Patel Chowk) A hallowed bargain, the canteen at the Andhra Pradesh state house serves cheap and delicious unlimited South Indian thalis to a seemingly unlimited stream of patrons. Come on Sunday for the Hyderabadi biryani (₹180).

Nathu's   SOUTH INDIAN $
(Map p72; Sunder Nagar Market; dishes & snacks ₹60-100; 7am-11pm) A much-loved sweeterie serving up yummy *chaat* (Indian snacks), such as *golgappas* (crispy spheres with spicy filling, like eating a delicious water bomb), and filling 'mini meals.' Upstairs is Navanda's, with a broad menu of veg and nonveg Indian and Chinese treats.

Comesum   FAST FOOD $
(Map p72; Nizamuddin Train Station; dishes ₹180-300; 24hr) Fast food, from dosas to *kadhai* (metal pot) curries, served in double-quick time at all hours. There are branches at all the main train stations, but the biggest and best is at Nizamuddin.

★ Alkauser   STREET FOOD $$
(Map p72; www.alkausermughlaifood.com; Kautilya Marg; kebabs from ₹130, biryani from ₹250; 6-10.30pm) The family behind this hole-in-the-wall takeaway earned their stripes cooking kebabs for the Nawabs of Lucknow in the 1890s. The house speciality is the *kakori* kebab, a pâté-smooth combination of lamb and spices, but other treats include biryani (cooked *dum puhkt* style in a *handi* pot sealed with pastry) and perfectly prepared lamb *burra* (marinated chops) and *murg malai tikka* (chicken marinated with spices and paneer). There are several branches, including one in the **Safdarjand Enclave market** (Map p76; 6-10.30pm; AIIMS).

★ Sodabottleopenerwala   PARSI $$
(Map p72; Khan Market; dishes ₹125-500; 11am-11.15pm; Khan Market) Suggesting a typical Parsi surname (taken from a trade), this place emulates the Iranian cafes of Mumbai and the food is authentic Persian. The upstairs terrace has a good deal more charm. The menu includes Iranian cakes and

'Bombay specials' including delicious *kanda bhaji* (crispy onion fritters).

Kitchen Cafe
MULTICUISINE $$

(Map p72; ☑ 41757960; Khan Market; mains ₹400-600; ⊙11am-11pm; Ⓜ Khan Market) A buzzing small cafe offering an informal alternative to the glam eateries. The menu trots from Italy (pasta) to Thailand (pad thai) to England (fish and chips).

Khan Chacha
FAST FOOD $$

(Map p72; Khan Market; snacks ₹170-240; ⊙noon-11pm; Ⓜ Khan Market) A simple eatery serving lip-smacking roti-wrapped mutton, chicken and paneer kebabs to a youthful crowd who appreciate the moderate prices and no-fuss attitude.

Mamagoto
ASIAN FUSION $$

(Map p72; ☑ 45166060; Middle Lane, Khan Market; mains ₹300-500; ⊙12.30-11.30pm; Ⓜ Khan Market) The name means 'to play with food' in Japanese, and the kidult theme extends to the funky manga art on the walls. The eclectic menu spans Japan, China and Southeast Asia – including some authentically spicy hawker-style Thai food.

Amici
ITALIAN $$

(Map p72; ☑ 43587191; 47 Khan Market; pizzas ₹300-400; ⊙11am-11pm; Ⓜ Khan Market) Calm and unpretentious, Amici actually pays some attention to the way they make pizzas in Italy. The pulled pork sandwich is also recommended.

★ Bukhara
INDIAN $$$

(Map p72; ☑ 26112233; ITC Maurya, Sadar Patel Marg; mains ₹750-2400; ⊙12.30-2.45pm & 7-11.45pm) Widely considered Delhi's best restaurant, this glam hotel eatery serves Northwest Frontier–style cuisine at low tables, with delectable melt-in-the-mouth kebabs and its famous Bukhara dhal. Reservations are essential.

Dhaba
PUNJABI $$$

(Map p72; ☑ 39555000; The Claridges, 12 Aurangzeb Rd; dishes ₹425-1295; ⊙12.30-2.30pm & 7-11.30pm; Ⓜ Racecourse) Set in the ritzy Claridges hotel, Dhaba is a fun and tasty choice, offering a posh take on Punjabi highway cuisine, including delicious dhal, *b¶alti* (curry cooked in a small dish called a *kadhai*) and *kulfi* (frozen milk dessert with pistachio, almond and cardamom), in a room that looks like a Punjabi highway, with half a Tata truck on the wall and Bollywood hits on the stereo.

Lodi Garden Restaurant
MEDITERRANEAN $$$

(Map p72; ☑ 24652808; Lodi Rd; mains ₹400-1700; ⊙12.30pm-12.45am; Ⓜ Jor Bagh) Set in a funky garden with lanterns dangling from the trees and tables in curtained pavilions and wooden carts, this is the most romantic dinner spot in New Delhi. Although not quite as impressive as the surroundings, the menu traverses Europe and the Middle East, and there's a popular Sunday brunch.

Pandara Market
INDIAN $$$

(Map p72; Pandara Rd; mains ₹365-700; ⊙noon-1am; Ⓜ Khan Market) Less a market than a strip of upmarket restaurants, this is a good option for night owls – some eateries here are open to 1am or later. Prices, standards and atmosphere are very similar along the strip. For quality Mughlai and North Indian food, try **Gulati** (mains ₹150-500; ⊙noon-1am), **Havemore** (mains ₹160-390; ⊙noon-2am), nicely made-over **Pindi** (mains ₹150-500; ⊙noon-midnight), or the surpisingly glitzy **Chicken Inn** (mains ₹150-500; ⊙noon-1am). For Indian-style Chinese and Thai food, head to **Ichiban** (mains ₹150-500; ⊙noon-12.30am).

※ South Delhi

South Delhi's best eateries are tucked away in the southern suburbs of Hauz Khas, Greater Kailash II, Saket, Vasant Vihar and further afield.

★ Coast
SOUTH INDIAN $$

(Map p76; above Ogaan, Hauz Khas; set meals ₹340-440; ⊙noon-midnight; Ⓜ Green Park) A beautifully light, bright restaurant on several levels, with wonderful views over the parklands of Hauz Khas, Coast serves delicious, elegant cuisine, with light southern Indian dishes, such as *avial* (vegetable curry) with pumpkin *erisheri* (with black lentils) or European cuisine, such as salad with orange and walnuts.

Potbelly
BIHARI $$

(Map p76; 116C Shahpur Jat Village; mains ₹190-350; ⊙12.30-11pm; Ⓜ Hauz Khas) In the hip, boutique-filled urban village of Shahpur Jat: climb several flights of higgledy piggledy stairs to reach Potbelly, a rooftop cafe with good views and a lovely artsy mix of painted watering cans and cane furniture. The food is delicious – try the Bihari burger or *keema goli* (mutton meatballs).

Not Just Parathas INDIAN $$

(Map p76; 84 M-Block, Great Kailash II; dishes ₹90-625; ⊙noon-midnight) They don't just serve *parathas* (stuffed flatbread), they serve 120 types of *parathas!* Try them stuffed with kebabs, veg curries, shredded chicken and untold other fillings.

★ Indian Accent INDIAN $$$

(Map p76; ✆26925151; Manor, 77 Friends Colony; tasting menu veg/nonveg ₹2595/2695) Overlooking lush lawns at the Manor hotel (p85), this exclusive restaurant serves inspired modern Indian cuisine. Familiar and unfamiliar ingredients are thrown together in surprising and beautifully creative combinations. The tasting menu is recommended, though its portions are remarkably small. But the food is delicious: sample delights such as *cheeni ki roti* (a hard bread stuffed with jaggery), and bacon-stuffed *kulcha* (soft-leavened Indian-style bread).

Olive MEDITERRANEAN $$$

(Map p76; ✆29574443; One Style Mile, Mehrauli; dishes ₹450-1350; ⊙noon-midnight; Ⓜ Qutab Minar) Uberchic Olive with its uberchic clientele creates a little piece of the Mediterranean in the suburbs. The *haveli* setting, combined with beach-house colours, is unlike anywhere else in Delhi. Come for inventive Mediterranean dishes, such as scallops with mascarpone, quinoa, amaranth, pumpkin seeds and apricot-orange purée, and astoundingly good pizza.

Punjab Grill MUGHLAI $$$

(Map p76; ✆41572977; Select Citywalk, Saket; mains ₹420-1200; ⊙11am-11.30pm; Ⓜ Malviya Nagar) Don't be put off by the shopping-mall setting. This sleek eatery offers superior Mughlai food – kebabs, *kadhai* (metal pot) curries and unleavened breads – in classy surroundings. Take your pick from the gleaming dining room or the open-air terrace.

🍷 Drinking & Nightlife

Whether it's cappuccino and pastries for breakfast or beer and bites in the evening, Delhi has plenty of places to wet your whistle. For the latest places to go at night, check the hip and informative Little Black Book (www.littleblackbookdelhi.com) or Brown Paper Bag (http://bpbweekend.com/delhi). For gigs, check Wild City (www.thewildcity.com).

Cafes

Chain coffee shops abound – Café Coffee Day is the most prolific, but there are also numerous branches of Costa and Barista.

★ Imperial CAFE

Raise your pinkie finger! High tea at the Imperial (p83) is perhaps the most refined way to while away an afternoon in Delhi. Sip tea from bone-china cups and pluck dainty sandwiches and cakes from tiered stands, while discussing the latest goings-on in Shimla and Dalhousie. High tea is served in the Atrium from 3pm to 6pm daily (weekday/weekend ₹1100/1400 plus tax).

Café Turtle CAFE

(Map p72; Full Circle Bookstore, Khan Market; ⊙9.30am-9.30pm; Ⓜ Khan Market) Allied to the Full Circle Bookstore, this boho cafe ticks all the boxes when you're in the mood for coffee, cake and a calm reading space. There are branches in N-Block Market (Map p76; Greater Kailash Part I) and Nizamuddin East (Map p72).

Cha Bar CAFE

(Map p68; Oxford Bookstore, N81 Connaught Place; ⊙10am-9.30pm Mon-Sat, 11am-9.30pm Sun; Ⓜ Rajiv Chowk) Connaught Place's smart Oxford Bookstore contains the swish cafe Cha Bar, with more than 75 types of tea to choose from, as well as cakes and snacks, including a respectable fish and chips.

Kunzum Travel Cafe CAFE

(Map p76; www.kunzum.com; T49 Hauz Khas Village; ⊙11am-7.30pm Tue-Sun; 🎧; Ⓜ Green Park) ✐ Run by the team of travel writers behind the informative *Delhi 101* guidebook, Kunzum has a pay-what-you-like policy for the self-service French-press coffee and tea. There's free wi-fi and books and magazines to browse. They also run heritage walks.

Indian Coffee House CAFE

(Map p68; 2nd fl, Mohan Singh Place, Baba Kharak Singh Marg; ⊙9am-9pm; Ⓜ Rajiv Chowk) Stuck-in-time Indian Coffee House has lots of faded (to the point of dilapidation) charm. The roof terrace is a popular hang-out thanks to the staggeringly cheap menu of snacks (₹20 to ₹50) and it serves up South Indian coffee; there is a 'ladies and families' section.

Big Chill CAFE

(Map p72; Khan Market; ⊙noon-11.30pm; Ⓜ Khan Market) There are two branches of this film-poster-lined cafe at Khan Market, packed with chattering Delhi-ites. The menu is a directory of continental and Indian dishes. There's a branch at the **DLF Place mall** (Map p76; M Malviya Nagar) in Saket.

Keventer's Milkshakes   CAFE
(Map p68; 17 A-Block, Connaught Place; milkshakes ₹50-80; ◷9am-11pm; M Rajiv Chowk) If you want to find the best cheap treats, follow the teenagers. Keventer's has a cult following for its legendary milkshakes, slurped out of milk bottles on the pavement in front of the stand.

Bars
The nightlife scene in Delhi is fairly low-key, but a party mood prevails from Wednesday to Saturday, particularly in the bar-rammed enclave of Hauz Khas. There are also increasing numbers of bars in Paharganj.

A smart-casual dress code (no shorts, vests or flip-flops) applies at many places. Taxes can pack a nasty punch (alcoholic 20%, nonalcoholic 12.5%); they are not included here unless indicated. Most bars have two-for-one happy hours from around noon till 8pm.

★ Monkey Bar   BAR
(Map p68; P3 Connaught Circus; ◷noon-12.30pm; M Rajiv Chowk) With exposed brick walls and piping, Monkey Bar is CP's coolest choice, with a friendly, buzzy vibe, and a '90s neo-industrial look. It's the kind of place the cast of *Friends* might have hung out, if they lived in Delhi. Try the excellent buffalo burgers with Gruyère, Gouda, whisky glaze, Bloody Mary tomatoes and umami ketchup and sample out-there cocktails (goat cheese as an ingredient?).

Hauz Khas Social   BAR
(Map p76; 9A & 12 Hauz Khas Village; M Green Park) Enter down a muralled passageway and through an unsigned door, which opens onto several large rooms with plate-glass windows, overlooking Hauz Khas' lush park. There's space for the local hipster clientele to work or have laid-back meetings, lots of room for cocktails (served in measuring jugs) and snacks, and a busy smokers' terrace. There's also regular live music and DJs.

★ 1911   BAR
(Map p68; Imperial Hotel, Janpath; cocktails ₹750-1200, beer from ₹400; ◷noon-12.45am; M Rajiv Chowk) The elegant bar at the Imperial is the ultimate neocolonial extravagance. Sip perfectly prepared cocktails in front of murals of cavorting maharajas.

Barsoom   BAR
(Map p76; 3rd fl, 26 Hauz Khas Village; M Green Park) Barsoom was the dying Mars created by American pulp fiction author Edgar Rice Burroughs, and this bar has a cool, extra-terrestrial vibe, with mid-century-modern-style furniture upholstered in funky Aztec prints, and delectable snacks on the menu. It's a good place to catch live music, with eclectic sounds such as psychedelic sitar from Al Cometo.

Aqua   BAR
(Map p68; Park Hotel, 15 Sansad Marg; ◷11am-midnight; M Rajiv Chowk) If you feel the need for some five-star style after visiting Jantar Mantar or shopping in Connaught Place, Aqua is a good place to flop, forget the world outside, and sip cocktails by the pool.

My Bar   BAR
(Map p82; Main Bazaar, Paharganj; ◷10am-12.30pm; M Ramakrishna Ashram Marg) A dark and dingy bar, this is lively, loud and fun, with a cheery, mixed crowd of backpackers and locals, who'll even come here from outside Paharganj. There are several other branches, in CP and Hauz Khas, but this is the one to go for.

Sam's Bar   BAR
(Map p82; Main Bazaar, Paharganj; ◷noon-midnight; M Ramakrishna Ashram Marg) This sophisticated (for Paharganj) addition to the Vivek Hotel empire on the Main Bazaar is a good choice for a drink and a chat, with a mixed crowd of men and women, locals and foreigners. On the menu you'll find plentiful snacks and a choice of local (Kingfisher ₹100) or international beers or spirits. The best seats are by the plate-glass windows overlooking the street.

Gem   BAR
(Map p82; 1050 Main Bazaar, Paharganj; ◷9am-midnight; M Ramakrishna Ashram Marg) This dark, wood-panelled dive is a good, if seedy place to hang out with locals and other travellers; bottles of local beer cost from ₹100. The upstairs area has more atmosphere.

☆ Entertainment

To access Delhi's dynamic arts scene, check local listings. October and March is the 'season', with shows and concerts (often free) happening nightly.

Music & Cultural Performances

Blues   LIVE MUSIC
(Map p68; 18 N-Block, Connaught Place; ☺ noon-1am; Ⓜ Rajiv Chowk) A dark den with reasonably priced beers and random photos of rock stars on its brick walls. It's a lively, snob-free zone with a live band daily from 6.30pm.

Attic   CULTURAL PROGRAM
(Map p68; ☑ 23746050; www.theatticdelhi.org; 36 Regal Bldg, Sansad Marg; Ⓜ Rajiv Chowk) Small arts organisation set up to promote textiles and arts and crafts, with regular free or inexpensive exhibitions, music and dance lectures and workshops.

Habitat World   CULTURAL PROGRAM
(Map p72; ☑ 43663333; www.habitatworld.com; India Habitat Centre, Lodi Rd; Ⓜ Jor Bagh) Temporary art shows at the Visual Arts Gallery, and plays and arty performances in the public courtyards.

India International Centre CULTURAL PROGRAM
(Map p72; ☑ 24619431; www.iicdelhi.nic.in; 40 Max Mueller Marg; Ⓜ Khan Market) This cultural centre holds regular free exhibitions, talks and cultural performances.

Cinemas

Delite Cinema   CINEMA
(Map p64; ☑ 23272903; 4/1, Asaf Ali Rd; Ⓜ New Delhi) Founded in 1955, the Delite was renovated in 2006 but still has a resolutely old-school, grandiose feel. It's a great place to see a masala picture (full-throttle Bollywood, a mix of action, comedy, romance and drama), with famous extra-large samosas available in the interval.

Big Cinemas Odeon   CINEMA
(Map p68; www.bigcinemas.com/in; 23 D-Block, Connaught Place; Ⓜ Rajiv Chowk) A smart modern cinema screening Bollywood blockbusters and Hollywood hits.

PVR Plaza Cinema   CINEMA
(Map p68; www.pvrcinemas.com; H-Block, Connaught Place; Ⓜ Rajiv Chowk) Glossy chain cinema, screening the latest Bollywood releases as well as high-profile Hollywood imports. There are branches on **Baba Kharak Singh**

Marg (Map p68; Ⓜ Rajiv Chowk) and at **Basant Lok Community Centre** (Map p76; Vasant Vihar; ; Ⓜ Hauz Khas) and **Select Citywalk mall** (Map p76; www.pvrcinemas.com; ; Ⓜ Malviya Nagar) in Saket.

🛍 Shopping

Delhi is a fabulous place to shop, from its glittering, frenetic bazaars to its gleaming boutiques and amazing regional craft outlets. Away from government-run emporiums and other fixed-price shops, haggle like you mean it. Many taxi and autorickshaw drivers earn commissions (via your inflated purchase price) by taking travellers to dubious, overpriced places – don't fall for it.

🏛 Old Delhi

As well as the many shops and markets to explore, it's worth browsing the myriad **music shops** (Map p64; Netaji Subhash Marg; ☺ Mon-Sat) along Netaji Subhash Marg for sitars, tabla sets and other beautifully crafted Indian instruments.

Main Bazaar   HANDICRAFTS, CLOTHING
(Paharganj; ☺ 10am-9pm Tue-Sun; Ⓜ Ramakrishna Ashram Marg) The backpacker-oriented bazaar that runs through Paharganj is lined with shops and stalls selling everything from incense and hippy kaftans to religious stickers and cloth printing blocks. Haggle with purpose. The market is officially closed on Monday, but most stores stay open.

Aap Ki Pasand (San Cha)   DRINK
(Map p64; www.sanchatea.com; 15 Netaji Subhash Marg; ☺ 9.30am-7pm Mon-Sat) An elegant tea shop selling a full range of Indian teas, from Darjeeling and Assam to Nilgiri and Kangra. You can try before you buy, and teas come lovingly packaged in drawstring bags. There's another branch **Santushti Shopping Complex** (Chanakyapuri, Racecourse Rd; ☺ 10am-6.30pm Mon-Sat; Ⓜ Racecourse).

Karol Bagh Market   MARKET
(Map p64; ☺ around 10am-7pm Tue-Sun; Ⓜ Karol Bagh) This brash middle-class market shimmers with all things sparkly, from dressy *lehanga choli* (skirt-and-blouse sets) to princess-style shoes, spices, fruit and nuts packed in shiny paper, and chrome motorcycle parts.

OLD DELHI'S BAZAARS

Old Delhi's bazaars are a head-spinning assault on the senses: an aromatic barrage of incense, spices, rickshaw fumes, body odour and worse, with a constant soundtrack of shouts, barks, music and car horns. This is less retail therapy, more heightened reality. The best time to come is midmorning, when you actually move through the streets.

Whole districts here are devoted to individual items. **Chandni Chowk** (Map p68; Old Delhi; ⌚10am-7pm Mon-Sat; Ⓜ Chandni Chowk) is all clothing, electronics and break-as-soon-as-you-buy-them novelties. For silver jewellery, head for **Dariba Kalan** (Map p64), the alley near the Sisganj Gurdwara. Off this lane, the **Kinari Bazaar** (Map p64), literally 'trimmings market', is famous for *zardozi* (gold embroidery), temple trim and wedding turbans. Running south from the old Town Hall, **Nai Sarak** (Map p64) is lined with stalls selling saris, shawls, chiffon and *lehanga* (long skins with waist cords), while nearby **Ballimaran** (Map p64) has sequined slippers and fancy, curly-toed *jootis*.

Beside the Fatehpuri Masjid, on Khari Baoli, is the nose-numbing **Spice Market** (Gadodia Market; Map p64; Khari Baoli), ablaze with piles of scarlet-red chillies, ginger and turmeric roots, peppercorns, cumin, coriander seeds, cardamom, dried fruit and nuts. For gorgeous wrapping paper and wedding cards, head to **Chawri Bazaar** (Map p64), leading west from the Jama Masjid. For steel cooking pots and cheap-as-chapattis paper kites, continue northwest to **Lal Kuan Main Bazaar** (Map p64).

🔒 Connaught Place

⭐ **State Emporiums**   HANDICRAFTS, CLOTHING
(Map p68; Baba Kharak Singh Marg; ⌚11am-7pm Mon-Sat; Ⓜ Rajiv Chowk) Nestling side by side are the treasure-filled official emporiums of the different Indian states. Shopping here is like taking a tour around India – top stops include Kashmir, for papier mâché and carpets; Rajasthan, for miniature paintings and puppets; Uttar Pradesh, for marble inlaywork; Karnataka, for sandalwood sculptures; Tamil Nadu, for metal statues; and Odisha (Orissa), for stone carvings.

⭐ **Kamala**   HANDICRAFTS
(Map p68; Baba Kharak Singh Marg; ⌚10am-6.45pm Mon-Sat; Ⓜ Rajiv Chowk) Upscale crafts and curios, designed with real panache, from the Crafts Council of India.

Central Cottage Industries Emporium   HANDICRAFTS
(Map p68; ☎23326790; Janpath; ⌚10am-7pm; Ⓜ Rajiv Chowk) This government-run, fixed-price multilevel Aladdin's cave of India-wide handicrafts is a great place to browse. Prices are higher than in the state emporiums, but the selection of woodcarvings, jewellery, pottery, papier mâché, *jootis* (traditional slip-on shoes), brassware, textiles, beauty products and miniature paintings is superb.

Khadi Gramodyog Bhawan   CLOTHING
(Map p68; Baba Kharak Singh Marg; ⌚10am-7.45pm Mon-Sat; Ⓜ Rajiv Chowk) 🌿 Known for its excellent *khadi* (homespun cloth), including good-value shawls, plus handmade paper, incense, spices, henna and lovely natural soaps.

Oxford Bookstore   BOOKS
(Map p68; N81 Connaught Place; ⌚10am-9.30pm Mon-Sat, 11am-9.30pm Sun; Ⓜ Rajiv Chowk) The newly located CP Oxford Bookstore is a beautifully designed, swish bookshop where you could browse for hours, though staff are not as knowledgeable as at other Delhi bookshops. It also sells good gifts, such as handmade paper notebooks. The attached Cha Bar (p91) is a great meeting spot.

Janpath & Tibetan Markets   HANDICRAFTS
(Map p68; Janpath; ⌚10.30am-7.30pm Mon-Sat; Ⓜ Rajiv Chowk) These twin markets sell the usual trinkets: shimmering mirrorwork embroidery, colourful shawls, Tibetan bric-a-brac, brass oms and dangly earrings. There are some good finds if you rummage through the junk. Haggle hard.

The Shop   CLOTHING, HOMEWARES
(Map p68; 10 Regal Bldg, Sansad Marg; ⌚10am-7.30pm Mon-Sat; Ⓜ Rajiv Chowk) Lovely homewares and clothes (including children's clothes) from all over India in a chic boutique with fixed prices.

People Tree HANDICRAFTS, CLOTHING
(Map p68; Regal Bldg, Sansad Marg; ⏱10.30am-7pm Mon-Sat; Ⓜ Rajiv Chowk) 🖉 Teeny tiny fair-trade vedors People Tree sells cool T-shirts with funky Indian designs and urban attitude, as well as bags, jewellery and books. There's a branch in Hauz Khas village (Map p76; Ⓜ Hauz Khas).

Fabindia CLOTHING, HOMEWARES
(Map p68; www.fabindia.com; 28 B-Block, Connaught Place; ⏱11am-8pm; Ⓜ Rajiv Chowk) Reasonably priced ready-made clothes in funky Indian fabrics, from elegant kurtas and dupattas to Western-style shirts, plus stylish homewares. There are branches at Green Park (Map p76; Ⓜ Green Park), Khan Market (Map p72; Ⓜ Khan Market), N-Block Market (Map p76; Greater Kailash I; Ⓜ Kailash Colony) and Select Citywalk (Map p76, Saket; Ⓜ Malviya Nagar).

Godin Music MUSIC
(Map p68; Regal Bldg, Sansad Marg; ⏱11am-8pm; Ⓜ Rajiv Chowk) Fine musical instruments, from guitars to sitars, displayed in a modern showroom, though Godin has been going since 1940 and was once the tuner for Mountbatten's pianos.

M Ram & Sons CLOTHING
(Map p68; ☎23416558; 21 E-Block, Connaught Place; ⏱10.30am-8pm; Ⓜ Rajiv Chowk) A popular Delhi tailor, offering suits from ₹8000 (including material).

Marques & Co MUSIC
(Map p68; 14 G-Block, Connaught Place; ⏱noon-5pm Mon-Sat; Ⓜ Rajiv Chowk) This vintage music shop (since 1918) sells guitars, tabla sets, harmonicas and sheet music, in stuck-in-time glass cabinets.

New Delhi

⭐ **Khan Market** MARKET
(Map p72; ⏱around 10.30am-8pm Mon-Sat; Ⓜ Khan Market) 🖉 Favoured by expats and Delhi's elite, Khan Market's boutiques focus on fashion, books and homewares. For handmade paper, check out Anand Stationers, or try Mehra Bros for cool papier-mâché ornaments and Christmas decorations. Literature lovers should head to Full Circle Bookstore and Bahrisons (www.booksatbahri.com). For ethnic-inspired fashions and homeware, hit Fabindia, Anokhi and Good Earth, and for elegantly packaged ayurvedic remedies, browse Kama.

Good Earth HOMEWARES
(Map p72; www.goodearth.in; 9 ABC Khan Market; ⏱11.30am-8.30pm; Ⓜ Khan Market) Stuck for ideas for how to fill your designer apartment? Look no further than Good Earth, Delhi's most chichi homewares store. The see-and-be-seen Latitude 28° cafe is upstairs. There are branches at the Santushti Shopping Complex (Map p72; Ⓜ Racecourse) and Select Citywalk (Map p76; Saket; Ⓜ Malviya Nagar).

Full Circle Bookstore BOOKS
(Map p72; www.fullcirclebooks.in; 23 Khan Market; ⏱9.30am-9.30pm; Ⓜ Khan Market) Delhi's most welcoming bookstore, with racks of specialist books on the city, plus novels and kids' books. Relaxing Café Turtle is upstairs. There are branches at N-Block Market (p96; Ⓜ Kailash Colony) and Nizamuddin East (Map p72; Ⓜ JLN Stadium).

Meher Chand Market BOUTIQUES
(Map p72; Lodhi Colony; Ⓜ JLN Stadium) This enclave has recently emerged as a hot place to shop, with independent shops selling homewares and clothes; it's a particularly good place to pick up beautifully designed childrenswear. To eat, try chic Chez Nini (79-80, Meher Chand Market).

Anokhi CLOTHING
(Map p72; www.anokhi.com; 32 Khan Market; ⏱10am-8pm; Ⓜ Khan Market) Anokhi specialises in blockprint clothes and homewares, showcasing traditional designs that have a modern design sensibility. There are branches at the Santushti Shopping Complex (Map p72; ⏱10am-7pm Mon-Sat; Ⓜ Racecourse), N Block Market (Map p76; Greater Kailash I; ⏱10am-8pm; Ⓜ Kailash Colony) and a discount store in Nizamuddin East (Map p72; ⏱10am-8pm Mon-Sat; Ⓜ JLN Stadium).

DARYAGANJ SUNDAY BOOK MARKET

Daryaganj Kitab Bazaar (Book Market; Map p64; ⏱8am-6pm Sun) It's wonderful rummaging for gems here, from first editions to Mills and Boon, many at rock-bottom prices. It takes place for around 2km from Delhi Gate, northwards to the Red Fort, and a shorter distance west along Jawaharlal Nehru Marg.

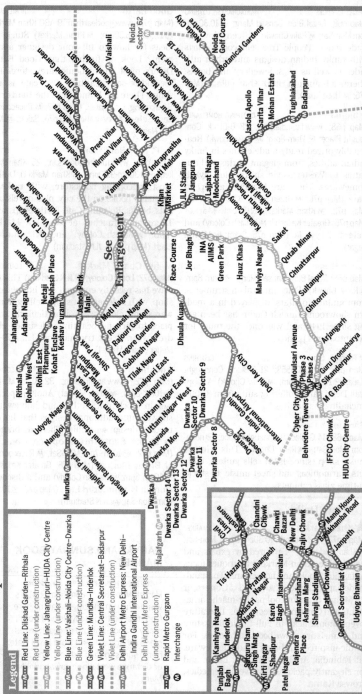

Delhi Metro Map

Legend

- Red Line: Dilshad Garden–Rithala
- Red Line (under construction)
- Yellow Line: Jahangirpuri–HUDA City Centre
- Yellow Line (under construction)
- Blue Line: Vaishali–Noida City Centre–Dwarka
- Blue Line (under construction)
- Green Line: Mundka–Inderlok
- Violet Line: Central Secretariat–Badarpur
- Violet Line (under construction)
- Delhi Airport Metro Express: New Delhi–Indira Gandhi International Airport
- Delhi Airport Metro Express (under construction)
- Rapid Metro Gurgaon
- Interchange

See Enlargement

Sunder Nagar Market HANDICRAFTS
(Map p72; Mathura Rd; ☺ around 10.30am-7.30pm Mon-Sat; Ⓜ Pragati Maidan) This genteel enclave specialises in Indian and Nepali handicrafts, replica 'antiques', and furniture, and has two outstanding tea shops, selling fine Indian teas.

**Santushti Shopping
Complex** HOMEWARES, CLOTHING
(Map p72; Kamal Ataturk Rd, Santushti Enclave; ☺ 10am-7pm Mon-Sat; Ⓜ Racecourse) Diplomats frequent this exclusive and serene complex facing the Ashok Hotel. Housed inside are stores such as Anokhi and Good Earth.

C Lal & Sons HANDICRAFTS
(Map p72; 9/172 Jor Bagh Market; ☺ 10.30am-7.30pm; Ⓜ Jor Bagh) After sightseeing at Safdarjang's tomb, drop into Mr Lal's 'curiosity shop' for cute Christmas-tree decorations, papier mâché and carvings.

🛍 South Delhi

Delhi's glitziest malls are lined up along Press Enclave Marg in Saket. Here you'll find the full air-con shopping experience, plus soft play for kids. **Select Citywalk** has a PVR cinema (p93), branches of Fabindia and Good Earth, and lots of big-name eateries. **DLF Place** has the Kiran Nadar Museum of Art (p78), plus more of the same, including a branch of Bahrisons bookstore, while nearby **MGF Metropolitan** has several showy bars.

★ Hauz Khas Village HANDICRAFTS, CLOTHING
(Map p76; ☺ 11am-7pm Mon-Sat; Ⓜ Green Park) The tight alleyways of this arty little enclave are crammed with boutiques selling designer Indian-clothing, handicrafts, handmade furniture and old Bollywood movie posters.

★ Dilli Haat HANDICRAFTS
(Map p76; Aurobindo Marg; admission ₹20; ☺ 10.30am-10pm; Ⓜ INA) Located opposite the colourful INA Market, this open-air food-and-crafts market is a cavalcade of colour, selling regional handicrafts. There are some gorgeous bits and pieces on offer; bargain hard. It's also a good place to sample cheap, delicious regional specialities, with lots of food stands.

Dastkar Nature Bazaar MARKET
(✆ 26808633; Andheria Modh; ☺ Tue-Sun; Ⓜ Chattarpur) Dastkar, a joint venture between an NGO and Delhi Tourism, holds

---

OFF THE BEATEN TRACK

JHANDEWALAN HANUMAN TEMPLE

Jhandewalan Hanuman Temple
(Map p64; Link Rd, Jhandewalan; ☺ dawn-dusk; Ⓜ Jhandewalan) While visiting the markets at Karol Bagh, it's worth making a detour to the surreal Jhandewalan Hanuman temple near Jhandewalan metro station. As well as a 34m-high Hanuman statue that soars above the train tracks, you can follow passageways through the mouths of demons to a series of atmospheric, deity-filled chambers.

monthly 12-day craft exhibitions. Each has a different theme and showcases cutting-edge regional culture, craft and food. There are also 15 permanent craft stalls.

N-Block Market MARKET
(Map p76; Greater Kailash I; ☺ 10.30am-8pm Wed-Mon) Swanky boutiques and posh eateries, including popular branches of Fabindia, Anokhi and Full Circle Bookstore, complete with a Café Turtle.

Sarojini Nagar Market CLOTHING
(Map p76; ☺ around 11am-8pm Tue-Sun; Ⓜ INA) Rummage here for cut-price Western-style clothes, with minor faults or blemishes, at bargain prices.

ℹ Information

DANGERS & ANNOYANCES

Shop & Hotel Touts Taxi-wallahs at the international airport and around tourist areas frequently act as touts for hotels, claiming that your chosen hotel is full, poor value, overbooked, dangerous, burned down or closed, or that there are riots in Delhi, as part of a ruse to steer you to a hotel where they will get a commission. Insist on being taken to where you want to go – making a show of writing down the registration plate number and phoning the autorickshaw/taxi helpline may help. Drivers and men who approach you at Connaught Place run a similar scam for private souvenir emporiums and tourist agents.

Travel Agent Touts Many travel agencies in Delhi claim to be tourist offices, even branding themselves with official tourist agency logos. There is only one tourist office – at 88 Janpath – and any other 'tourist office' is just a travel agency. Should you legitimately need the services of a travel agent, ask for a list of recommended agents from the bona-fide tourist office. Be wary of booking a multistop trip out of Delhi, particularly to Kashmir. Travellers are often hit for extra charges, or find out the class of travel and accommodation is less than they paid for.

Train Station Touts Touts (often dressed in official-looking uniform) at New Delhi train station endeavour to steer travellers away from the legitimate International Tourist Bureau (p100) and into private travel agencies where they earn a commission. An increasing problem is touts telling people that their tickets are invalid or that there's a problem with the trains, then helpfully assisting them in booking expensive alternative taxis or 3rd-class tickets passed off as something else. As a rule of thumb: don't believe anyone who approaches you trying to tell you anything at the train station

INTERNET ACCESS

Most hotels offer free wi-fi access these days. At cafes offering free access, you'll probably have to show ID.

MEDIA

To check out what's on, see **Little Black Book** (www.littleblackbookdelhi.com) or **Brown Paper Bag** (www.bpbweekend.com/delhi). For printed listings see the weekly calendar pamphlet *Delhi Diary* (₹30), which is available at local bookshops.

MEDICAL SERVICES

Pharmacies are found on most shopping streets and in most suburban markets.

All India Institute of Medical Sciences (IIMS; Map p76; ☑ 40401010; www.aiims.edu; Ansari Nagar; Ⓜ AIIMS)

Apollo Hospital (☑ 29871090; www.apollo-hospdelhi.com; Mathura Rd, Sarita Vihar)

Dr Ram Manohar Lohia Hospital (Map p72; ☑ 23365525; www.rmlh.nic.in; Baba Kharak Singh Marg; Ⓜ Patel Chowk)

East West Medical Centre (☑ 24690429; www.eastwestrescue.com; 37 Prithviraj Rd)

MONEY

Banks with ATMs are everywhere you look in Delhi. Foreign exchange offices are concentrated along the Main Bazaar in Paharganj and around Connaught Place. Travel agents and moneychangers offer international money transfers.

Baluja Forex (Map p82; 4596 Main Bazaar, Paharganj; ⊙ 9am-7.30pm; Ⓜ New Delhi)

Thomas Cook (Map p68; ☑ 66271900/23; C33, 335 Inner Circle, Connaught Circus; ⊙ 9.30am-6.30pm Mon-Sat; Ⓜ Rajiv Chowk)

POST & TELEPHONE

Delhi has tons of telephone kiosks where you can make cheap local, interstate and international calls. Look for the STD ISD PCO signs.

DHL (Map p68; ☑ 23737587; ground fl, Mercantile Bldg, Tolstoy Marg; ⊙ 8am-8pm Mon-Sat; Ⓜ Rajiv Chowk)

Post Office (Map p68; 6 A-Block, Connaught Place; ⊙ 8am-7pm Mon-Sat; Ⓜ Rajiv Chowk)

TOURIST INFORMATION

India Tourism Delhi (Government of India; Map p68; ☑ 23320008; www.incredibleindia. org; 88 Janpath; ⊙ 9am-6pm Mon-Fri, to 2pm Sat; Ⓜ Rajiv Chowk) This is the only official tourist information centre outside the airport. Ignore touts who (falsely) claim to be associated with this office. Anyone who 'helpfully' approaches you is certainly not going to take you to the real office. It's a useful source of advice on Delhi, getting out of Delhi, and visiting surrounding states. Has a free Delhi map and brochures, and publishes a list of recommended travel agencies and B&Bs. Come here to report tourism-related complaints.

ⓘ Getting There & Away

AIR

Indira Gandhi International Airport is about 14km southwest of the centre. International and domestic flights use the gleaming new Terminal 3. Ageing Terminal 1 is reserved for low-cost carriers. Free shuttle buses (present your boarding pass and onward ticket) run between the two terminals every 20 minutes, but can take an hour or more. Leave at least three hours between transfers to be safe.

The arrivals hall at Terminal 3 has 24-hour forex, ATMs, prepaid taxi and car-hire counters, tourist information, bookshops, cafes and a **Premium Lounge** (☑ 61233922; 3hr s/d ₹2350/3520) with short-stay rooms.

You'll need to show your boarding pass to enter the terminal. At check-in, be sure to collect tags for all your carry-on bags and ensure these are stamped as you go through security.

Delhi's airport can be prone to thick fog in December and January (often disrupting airline schedules) – it's wise to allow a day between connecting flights during this period.

Air India (Indian Airlines; Map p72; ☑ 24622220; www.airindia.in; Aurobindo Marg; ⊙ 8.30am-7pm; Ⓜ Jor Bagh)

Jagson Airlines (Map p68; ☑ 23721593; Vandana Bldg, 11 Tolstoy Marg; ⊙ 10am-6pm Mon-Sat; Ⓜ Rajiv Chowk)

Jet Airways (Map p68; ☑ 39893333; www. jetairways.com; 11/12 G-Block, Connaught Place; ⊙ 10am-9pm; Ⓜ Rajiv Chowk)

SpiceJet (☑ 1800 1803333; www.spicejet.com)

BUS

Most travellers enter and leave Delhi by train, but buses are a useful option to some destinations and if the trains are booked up.

Most state-run services leave from the **Kashmere Gate Inter State Bus Terminal** (ISBT; Map p64; ☎ 23860290) in Old Delhi, accessible by metro. The ISBT has undergone major renovations over the last few years, which makes travelling from here an altogether more pleasant experience, with sales and information offices for the bus companies as you enter the terminal building. The **Anand Vihar Inter State Bus Terminal** (ISBT) has some services to Nainital and Kumaun in Uttarakhand. Some cheaper buses to destinations in Uttar Pradesh, Madhya Pradesh and Rajasthan leave from the **Sarai Kale Khan ISBT** on the ring road near Nizamuddin train station.

Arrive at least 30 minutes ahead of your departure time. You can avoid the hassle by paying a little more for private deluxe buses that leave from locations in central Delhi – enquire at travel agencies or your hotel for details.You can also book tickets or check information on **Cleartrip** (www.cleartrip.com), **Make My Trip** (www.makemytrip.com) or **Goibibo** (www.goibibo.com).

There are buses to Agra, but considering the traffic at either end, you're better off taking the train. **Himachal Pradesh Tourism Development Corporation** (HPTDC; Map p72) runs a bus from Himachal Bhawan on Sikandra Rd (near Mandi House) to Dharamsala (deluxe non-AC, ₹700, 12 hours) at 5.30pm, Shimla (Volvo AC; ₹900, nine hours) at 8.30pm and Manali (Volvo AC, ₹1300, 10 hours) at 6.30pm. Tickets are sold at Himachal Bhawan and **Chanderlok House** (Map p68; 36 Janpath; Ⓜ Rajiv Chowk).

HRTC (Himachal Road Transport Corporation) also has buses starting from Himachal Bhawan: Shimla (Volvo, ₹847, five daily) and one to Manali at 7pm (Volvo;,₹1305). These stop at the ISBT Kashmiri Gate 30 to 90 minutes later, from where it's ₹20 less.

Rajasthan Tourism (Map p72; ☎ 23381884; www.rtdc.com; Bikaner House, Pandara Rd) runs deluxe buses from Bikaner House, near India Gate, to the following destinations. (Women receive a discount of 30%):

Ajmer Volvo, ₹1092, nine hours, three daily
Jaipur super deluxe/Volvo ₹590/815, six hours, every one to two hours
Jodhpur super deluxe/Volvo ₹815/1490, 11 hours, two daily
Udaipur Volvo, ₹1625, 15 hours, one daily

State bus companies operating out of Delhi include the following:
Delhi Transport Corporation (Map p68; ☎ 23370210; www.dtc.nic.in)
Haryana Roadways (☎ 23868271; www.hartrans.gov.in)
Himachal Road Transport Corporation (☎ 23868694; www.hrtc.gov.in)
Punjab Roadways (☎ 23867842; www.punbusonline.com)
Rajasthan State Road Transport Corporation (☎ 23864470; www.rsrtc.rajasthan.gov.in)
Uttar Pradesh State Road Transport Corporation (☎ 23235367; www.upsrtc.com)

TRAIN

There are three main stations in Delhi: (Old) Delhi train station (aka Delhi Junction) in Old Delhi; New Delhi train station near Paharganj; and Nizamuddin train station, south of Sunder

BUSES FROM DELHI (KASHMERE GATE)

DESTINATION	FARE (₹)	DURATION (HR)	FREQUENCY
Amritsar	420-905	10	hourly, 6am-9.30pm
Chandigarh	215-520	5	half-hourly, 6.30am-midnight
Dehra Dun	257-713	7	nine daily, 6am-midnight
Dharamsala	520-1150	12	6.30am, 5.30am & 11pm
Haridwar	213-542	6	hourly, 5am-11pm
Jaipur	196-655	6	hourly, 24hr
Manali	651-1285	15	6.40am, 7.45am, 11.30am, hourly 3.45-10pm
Rishikesh	770	10	9.30am, 9pm
Shimla	380-827	10	5am, 12.30pm, hourly 4.50-10.30pm

Nagar. Make sure you know which station your train is leaving from.

There are two options for foreign travellers: you can brave the queues at the main **reservation office** (Map p82; Chelmsford Rd; 8am-8pm, to 2pm Sun), or visit the helpful **International Tourist Bureau** (ITB; Map p82; 23405156; 1st fl, New Delhi Train Station; 8am-8pm Mon-Sat, to 2pm Sun).The entrance to the ITB is before you go onto platform 1, via a staircase just to the right of the entrance to the platform. Do not believe anyone who tells you it has shifted, closed or burnt down! Walk with confidence and ignore all 'helpful' or 'official' approaches. The ITB is a large room with about

MAJOR TRAINS FROM DELHI

DESTINATION	TRAIN NO & NAME	FARE (₹)	DURATION (HR)	FREQUENCY	DEPARTURES & TRAIN STATION
Agra	12280 Taj Exp	100/365 (A)	3	1 daily	7.05am NZM
	12002 Bhopal Shatabdi	505/1000 (B)	2	1 daily	6am NDLS
Amritsar	12029/12013 Swarna/Amritsar Shatabdi	865/1690 (B)	6	1-2 daily	7.20am/ 4.30pm NDLS
Bengaluru	12430 Bangalore Rajdhani	2895/4020/6675 (C)	34	4 weekly	8.50am NZM
Chennai	12434 Chennai Rajdhani	2795/3860/6355 (C)	28	2 weekly	5.55pm NZM
	12622 Tamil Nadu Exp	780/2020/2970 (D)	33	1 daily	10.30pm NDLS
Goa (Madgaon)	14854 Marudhar Exp	2605/3630/6075 (C)	26	3 weekly	10.55pm NZM
	12432 Trivandrum Rajdhani	170/535/735 (D)	27	1 daily	3pm NZM
Haridwar	12017 Dehradun Shatabdi	585/1175 (B)	4½	1 daily	6.45am NDLS
Jaipur	12958 ADI Swarna Jayanti Rajdani	795/1055/1695 (C)	4½	1 daily	7.55pm NDLS
	12916 Ashram Exp	235/590/820(D)	5	1 daily	3.20pm DLI
	12015 Ajmer Shatabdi	635/1280 (B)	4½	1 daily	6.05am NDLS
Kalka (for Shimla)	12011 Kalka Shatabdi	635/1280 (B)	4	2 daily	7.40am & 5.15pm NDLS
Khajuraho	12448 UP Sampark Kranti Exp	365/950/1340 (D)	10½	1 daily	8.10pm NZM
Lucknow	12004 Lucknow Swran Shatabdi	875/1830 (B)	6½	1 daily	6.15am NDLS
Mumbai	12952 Mumbai Rajdhani	2030/2810/4680 (C)	16	1 daily	4.45pm NDLS
	12954 August Kranti Rajdani	2030/2810/4680 (C)	17½	1 daily	4.50pm NZM
Udaipur	12963 Mewar Exp	415/1085/1545 (D)	12½	1 daily	6.55pm NDLS
Varanasi	12560 Shivganga Exp	415/1095/1555 (D)	12½	1 daily	6.55pm NDLS

Train stations: NDLS – New Delhi; DLI – Old Delhi; NZM – Hazrat Nizamuddin
Fares: (A) 2nd class/chair car; (B) chair car/1st-class AC; (C) 3AC/2AC/1AC; (D) sleeper/3AC/2AC

10 or more computer terminals – don't be fooled by other 'official' offices.

When making reservations here, you can pay in cash (rupees) only. Bring your passport.

When you arrive, take a ticket from the machine that gives you a place in the queue. Then complete a reservation form – ask at the information counter to check availability. You can then wait to complete and pay for your booking at the relevant counter. This is the best place to get last-minute bookings for quota seats to popular destinations, but come prepared to queue.

If you prefer to brave the standard reservation office, check the details for your journey (including the train number) in advance on the **Indian Railways** (www.indianrail.gov.in) website or **Erail** (www.erail.in), or in the publication *Trains at a Glance* (₹45), available at newsstands. You'll need to fill out a reservation form and queue – after 7pm is the quietest time to book.

ⓘ Getting Around

TO/FROM THE AIRPORT

International flights often arrive at ghastly hours, so it pays to book a hotel in advance and notify staff of your arrival time. Organised city transport runs to/from Terminal 3; a free shuttle bus runs every 20 minutes between Terminal 3 and Terminal 1.

Pre-arranged pick-ups Hotels offer pre-arranged airport pick-up, but you'll pay extra to cover the airport parking fee (up to ₹140) and ₹80 charge to enter the arrivals hall. To avoid the entry fee, drivers may wait outside Gates 4 to 6.

Metro The Airport Express line (www.delhimetrorail.com) runs every 10 to 15 minutes from 4.45am to 11.30pm, completing the journey from Terminal 3 to New Delhi train station in around 40 minutes (₹80 to ₹60); there are plans to reduce this journey time. It's usually empty because it's a separate line from the rest of the metro. You can buy a token for the other lines at the Airport station; check with customer services.

Bus Air-conditioned buses run from outside Terminal 3 to Kashmere Gate ISBT every 20 minutes, via the Red Fort, LNJP Hospital, New Delhi Station Gate 2, Connaught Place, Parliament St and Ashoka Rd (₹75).

Taxi In front of the arrivals buildings at Terminal 3 and Terminal 1 are **Delhi Traffic Police Prepaid Taxi Counters** (☏ 23010101; www.delhitrafficpolice.nic.in) offering fixed-price taxi services. You'll pay about ₹350 to New or Old Delhi, and ₹450 to the southern suburbs, plus a 25% surcharge between 11pm and 5am. Travellers have reported difficulty in persuading drivers to go to their intended destination. Insist that the driver takes you to your chosen destination and only surrender your voucher when you arrive.

You can also book a prepaid taxi at the Megacabs (p102) counter outside the arrivals building at both the international and domestic terminals. It costs ₹600 to ₹700 to the centre, but you get a cleaner car with air-con.

AUTORICKSHAW & TAXI

Local taxis (recognisable by their black and yellow livery) and autorickshaws have meters but these are effectively ornamental as most drivers refuse to use them. Delhi Traffic Police runs a network of prepaid autorickshaw booths, where you can pay a fixed fare, including 24-hour stands at the New Delhi, Old Delhi and Nizamuddin train stations; elsewhere, you'll need to negotiate a fare before you set off.

Fares are invariably elevated for foreigners so haggle hard, and if the fare sounds too outrageous, find another cab. For an autorickshaw ride from Connaught Place, fares should be around ₹40 to Paharganj, ₹60 to the Red Fort, ₹70 to Humayun's Tomb and ₹100 to Hauz Khas. However, it may be a struggle to get these prices. Visit www.taxiautofare.com for suggested fares for these and other journeys. To report overcharging, harassment or other problems take the license number and call the Auto Complaint Line on ☏ 42400400/25844444.

Taxis typically charge twice the autorickshaw fare. Note that fares vary as fuel prices go up and down. From 11pm to 5am there's a 25% surcharge for autorickshaws and taxis. The government has proposed to install microchips to track local taxis to make them safer.

CAR

Numerous operators will rent a car with driver, or you can negotiate directly with taxi drivers at taxi stands around the city. Note that some taxis can only operate inside the city limits, or in certain surrounding states. For a day of local sightseeing, there is normally an eight-hour, 80km limit – anything over this costs extra.

Kumar Tourist Taxi Service (Map p68; ☏ 23415930; www.kumarindiatours.com; 14/1 K-Block, Connaught Place; ⊙9am-9pm; Ⓜ Rajiv Chowk) Rates are among Delhi's lowest – a day of Delhi sightseeing costs from ₹1200 (the eight hours and 80km limit applies).

Metropole Tourist Service (Map p72; ☏ 24310313; www.metrovista.co.in; 224 Defence Colony Flyover Market; ⊙7am-7pm; Ⓜ Jangpura) Under the Defence Flyover Bridge (on the Jangpura side).

BICYCLE

DelhiByCycle (p80) offers cycle tours but bike hire has never taken off in traffic-snarled Delhi.

Jhandewalan Cycle Market (Map p64) To buy your own bike, head to the Jhandewalan Cycle Market, near Videocon Tower at Jhandewalan.

BUS

With the arrival of the metro, travellers rarely use Delhi's public buses, but the red air-con buses are comfortable and there are several useful routes, including the Airport Express bus (₹75) and bus GL-23, which connects the Kashmere Gate and Anand Vihar bus stations. Fares usually range from ₹15 to ₹25.

CYCLE-RICKSHAW

Cycle-rickshaws are useful for navigating Old Delhi and the suburbs, but are banned from many parts of New Delhi, including Connaught Place. Negotiate a fare before you set off – expect to pay around ₹5 to ₹10 per kilometre.

METRO

Delhi's magnificent **metro** (☑ 23417910; www. delhimetrorail.com) is fast and efficient, with signs and arrival/departure announcements in Hindi and English. Trains run from around 6am to 11pm and the first carriage in the direction of travel is reserved for women only. Note that trains can get insanely busy at peak commuting times (around 9am to 10am and 5pm to 6pm) – avoid travelling with luggage during rush hour if at all possible (however, the Airport Express is always empty, as it's not directly connected to the other lines).

Tokens (₹8 to ₹39) are sold at metro stations. There are also one-/three-day (₹150/300; ₹50 refundable when you return it) 'tourist cards' for unlimited short-distance travel, and a Smart Card (₹100; ₹50 refundable), which can be recharged for amounts from ₹200 to ₹1000 – making fares 10% cheaper than paying by token.

Because of security concerns, all bags are X-rayed and passengers must pass through an airport-style scanner.

MOTORCYCLE

Karol Bagh market is the place to go to buy or rent a motorcycle.

Lalli Motorbike Exports (Map p64; ☑ 28750869; www.lallisingh.com; 1740-A/55 Hari Singh Nalwa St, Abdul Aziz Rd; Ⓜ Karol Bagh) Run by the knowledgable Lalli Singh, this place sells and rents out Enfields and parts, and buyers get a crash course in running and maintaining these lovable but temperamental machines.

RADIOCAB

You'll need a local mobile number to order a radiocab, or ask a shop or hotel to assist. These air-conditioned cars are clean, efficient and use reliable meters, charging ₹20 at flagfall then ₹20 per kilometre.

Other telephone taxi services exist, such as car-sharing service Uber, which was banned in 2014 following an assault by one of its drivers but subsequently restarted.

Easycabs (☑ 43434343; www.easycabs.com)
Megacabs (☑ 41414141; www.megacabs.com) You can book a prepaid taxi at the Megacabs counter outside the arrivals building at both the international and domestic airport terminals. It costs ₹600 to ₹700 to the centre, but you get a cleaner car with air-con.
Quickcabs (☑ 45333333; www.quickcabs.in)

Greater Delhi

★**Qutb Minar Complex**   HISTORIC SITE
(Map p76; ☑ 26643856; Indian/foreigner ₹10/250, video ₹25, Decorative Light Show Indian/foreigner ₹20/250, audio guide ₹100; ☉ dawn-dusk; Ⓜ Qutab Minar) In a city awash with ancient ruins, the Qutb Minar complex is something special. The first monuments here were erected by the sultans of Mehrauli, and subsequent rulers expanded on their work, hiring the finest craftsmen and artisans to create an exclamation mark in stone to record the triumph of Muslim rule. The **Qutb Festival** of Indian classical music and dance takes place here every November/December. To reach the complex, take the metro to Qutab Minar station, then take an autorickshaw for the 1km to the ruins.

The complex is studded with ruined tombs and monuments. Ala-ud-din's sprawling madrasa (Islamic school) and tomb stand in ruins at the rear of the complex, while Altamish is entombed in a magnificent sandstone and marble mausoleum almost completely covered in Islamic calligraphy.

Bags should be left in the cloakroom. For the most atmosphere, try to visit in the morning before the crowds arrive.

➡ Qutb Minar
The Qutb Minar complex is dominated by the spectaclular Qutb Minar, a soaring Afghan-style victory tower and minaret, erected by sultan Qutb-ud-din in 1193 to proclaim his supremacy over the vanquished Hindu rulers of Qila Rai Pithora. Ringed by intricately carved standstone bands bearing verses from the Quran, the tower stands nearly 73m high and tapers from a 15m-diameter base to a mere 2.5m at the top. You can no longer climb the tower for safety reasons, but a webcam allows a view from the top (₹10).

The tower has five distinct storeys with projecting balconies, but Qutb-ud-din only completed the first level before being unfortunately impaled on his saddle while playing polo. His successors completed the job, and kept up the work of restoration and maintenance through the centuries.

➡ Quwwat-ul-Islam Masjid

(Might of Islam Mosque) At the foot of the Qutb Minar stands the first mosque to be built in India, intended to be a physical symbol of the triumph of Islam. An inscription over the east gate states that it was built with materials obtained from demolishing '27 idolatrous temples'. As well as intricate carvings that show a clear fusion of Islamic and pre-Islamic styles, the walls of the mosque are studded with sun disks, *shikharas* and other recognisable pieces of Hindu and Jain masonry, defaced as far as possible.

Altamish, Qutb-ud-din's son-in-law, expanded the original mosque with a cloistered court between 1210 and 1220, and Ala-ud-din added the exquisite marble and sandstone **Alai Darwaza gatehouse** in 1310. Nearby is the dainty tomb of the Turkic saint Imam Zamin, erected in the Lodi era.

➡ Iron Pillar

Standing in the courtyard of the Quwwat-ul-Islam mosque is a 7m-high iron pillar that is of such purity that it hasn't rusted in over 1600 years. This extraordinary pillar vastly predates the surrounding monuments. A six-line Sanskrit inscription indicates that it was initially erected outside a Vishnu temple, possibly in Bihar, in memory of Chandragupta II, who ruled from AD 375 to 413. What the inscription does not tell is how it was made – scientists have never discovered how the iron could be cast using the technology of the time.

➡ Alai Minar

When the Sultan Ala-ud-din made additions to the Qutb Minar complex in the 14th century, he also conceived an ambitious plan to erect a second tower of victory, exactly like the Qutb Minar – but twice as high. Construction got as far as the first level before the sultan died; none of his successors saw fit to bankroll this extravagant piece of showboating. The 27m-high plinth can be seen just north of the Qutb Minar.

★ Mehrauli Archaeological Park   PARK

(Map p76; ☉ dawn-dusk; Ⓜ Qutab Minar) Bordering the Qutb Minar complex, but overlooked by most of the tourist hordes, the Mehrauli Archaeological Park preserves some of the most atmospheric relics of the second city of Delhi.

Scattered around a forest park are the ruins of dozens of tombs, palace buildings and colonial-era follies. You can reach the park by turning right from the metro station onto Anuvrat Marg and walking around 500m; the entrance is via a small lane on your left, marked by a board showing the park regulations.

Entering the park from here, the first monuments you'll see are the time-ravaged tombs of Balban and Quli Khan, his son, which formerly incorporated a mosque. A short walk away is Mehrauli's most impressive structure, the Jamali Khamali mosque, attached to the tomb of the Sufi poet Jamali. Ask the caretaker to open the doors so you can see the intricate incised plaster ceiling decorated with Jamali's verses. To the west is the Rajon ki Baoli, a majestic 16th-century step-well with a monumental flight of steps. If you walk from here towards Mehrauli village, on the edge of the street is Adham Khan's mausoleum, which was once used as a British residence, than later as a police station and post office.

Southwest of the archaeological park is a complex of ruined tombs and summer palaces, constructed in the late Mughal period around the **Haus i Shamsi tank** (off Mehrauli-Gurgaon Rd). An empty space between two of the tombs was intended for the last king of Delhi, Bahadur Shah Zafar, who died in exile in Burma (Myanmar) in 1862.

Tughlaqabad   FORT

(Indian/foreigner ₹5/100, video ₹25; ☉ 8.30am-5.30pm; Ⓜ Tughlaqabad) This mammoth stronghold, the third city of Delhi, was built by sultan Ghiyus-ud-din Tughlaq in the 14th century. For its construction, the king poached workers from the Sufi saint Nizam-ud-din, who issued a curse that Tughlaqabad would be inhabited only by shepherds. This was indeed the case – today goats are as common as human visitors among the crumbling, vegetation-choked, but still magnificent ruins. To reach the fort, take an autorickshaw from the Tughlaqabad metro station (₹80).

The sultan's well-preserved sandstone mausoleum, which once stood in the middle of a lake, is separated from his fallen city by a busy highway.

Rajasthan

Best Forts & Palaces

➡ Jaisalmer (p183)

➡ Jodhpur (p173)

➡ Bundi (p142)

➡ Chittorgarh (p147)

➡ Udaipur (p151)

Best off the Beaten Track

➡ Keoladeo Ghana National Park (p126)

➡ Nawalgarh (p167)

➡ Osian (p181)

➡ Shekhawati (p167)

➡ Kumbhalgarh (p161)

Why Go?

It is said there is more history in Rajasthan than in the rest of India put together. Welcome to the Land of the Kings – a fabled realm of maharajas, majestic forts and lavish palaces. India is littered with splendid ruined bastions, but nowhere will you find fortresses quite as magnificent as those in Rajasthan, rising up imperiously from the desert landscape like fairy-tale mirages from a bygone era.

As enchanting as they are, though, there is more to this most royal of regions than its architectural wonders. This is also a land of sand dunes and jungle, of camel trains and wild tigers, of glittering jewels, vivid colours and vibrant culture. There are enough festivals here to fill a calendar (and an artist's palette), while the shopping and cuisine are nothing short of spectacular. In truth, Rajasthan just about has it all – it is the must-see state of this must-see country, brimming with startling, thought-provoking and, ultimately, unforgettable attractions.

When to Go
Jaipur

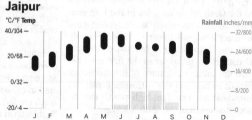

Oct Ranthambhore and Sariska National Parks reopen for tiger safaris.

Oct & Nov Don't miss the frenzy of Pushkar's famous Camel Festival.

Mar Jaipur's famous Elephant Festival precedes the typically boisterous Holi celebrations

History

Rajasthan is home to the Rajputs, warrior clans who claim to originate from the sun, moon and fire, and who have controlled this part of India for more than 1000 years. While they forged marriages of convenience and temporary alliances, pride and independence were always paramount; consequently,much of their energy was spent squabbling among themselves. The resultant weakness eventually led to the Rajputs becoming vassals of the Mughal empire.

Nevertheless, the Rajputs' bravery and sense of honour were unparalleled. Rajput warriors would fight against all odds and, when no hope was left, chivalry demanded *jauhar* (ritual mass suicide). The men donned saffron robes and rode out to face the enemy (and certain death), while the women and children perished in the flames of a funeral pyre. It's not surprising that Mughal emperors had such difficulty controlling this part of their empire.

With the Mughal empire declining, the Rajputs gradually clawed back independence – at least until the British arrived. As the British Raj inexorably expanded, most Rajput states allied with the British, which allowed them to continue as independent states, subject to certain political and economic constraints.

These alliances proved to be the beginning of the end for the Rajput rulers. Consumption took over from chivalry so that, by the early 20th century, many of the maharajas spent much of their time travelling the world with scores of retainers, playing polo and occupying entire floors of expensive hotels. While it suited the British to indulge them, the maharajas' profligacy was economically and socially detrimental. When India gained its independence, Rajasthan had one of the subcontinent's lowest rates of life expectancy and literacy.

At Independence, India's ruling Congress Party was forced to make a deal with the nominally independent Rajput states to secure their agreement to join the new India. The rulers were allowed to keep their titles and their property holdings, and they were paid an annual stipend commensurate with their status. It couldn't last forever, though, and in the early 1970s Indira Gandhi abolished the titles and the stipends, and severely sequestered rulers' property rights.

In their absence Rajasthan has made some headway, but the state remains poor. The strength of tradition means that women have a particularly tough time in rural areas. Literacy stood at 67% in 2011 (males 81%, females 53% – a massive rise from 18% in 1961 and 39% in 1991), the third-lowest in India, while the gender gap remains India's widest.

RAJASTHAN JAIPUR

EASTERN RAJASTHAN

Jaipur

📞 0141 / POP 3.07 MILLION / AREA 65 SQ KM

Jaipur, Rajasthan's capital, is an enthralling historical city and the gateway to India's most flamboyant state.

The city's colourful, chaotic streets ebb and flow with a heady brew of old and new. Careering buses dodge dawdling camels, leisurely cycle-rickshaws frustrate swarms of motorbikes, and everywhere buzzing autorickshaws watch for easy prey. In the midst of this mayhem, the splendours of Jaipur's majestic past are islands of relative calm, evoking a different pace and another world. At the city's heart, the City Palace continues to house the former royal family; the Jantar Mantar (the royal observatory) maintains a heavenly aspect; and the honeycomb Hawa Mahal gazes on the bazaar below. And just out of sight, in the arid hill country surrounding the city, is the fairy-tale grandeur of Amber Fort, Jaipur's star attraction.

History

Jaipur is named after its founder, the great warrior-astronomer Jai Singh II (1688–1744), who came to power at age 11 after the death of his father, Maharaja Bishan Singh. Jai Singh could trace his lineage back to the Rajput clan of Kachhwahas, who consolidated their power in the 12th century. Their capital was at Amber (pronounced 'am-er'), about 11km northeast of present-day Jaipur, where they built the impressive Amber Fort.

Rajasthan Highlights

① Explore the sandstone alleys of the magical fort at **Jaisalmer** (p182), then ride your camel into the desert dunes

② Make a lakeside pilgrimage to **Pushkar** (p135), Rajasthan's holiest town

③ Search for tigers in the forests and fortresses of **Ranthambhore National Park** (p140)

④ Take in the views of the Blue City from the imposing ramparts of **Mehrangarh** (p173), Jodhpur's mighty fortress

⑤ Look for royalty in the grand City Palace in **Udaipur** (p150), before enjoying a romantic sunset over gorgeous Lake Pichola

⑥ Shop till you drop in the bazaars of Jaipur, the **Pink City** (p109), and explore its marvellous Amber Fort

⑦ Get away from the tourist hustle in the ancient fort-town of **Bundi** (p142)

⑧ Uncover the architectural gems of **Shekhawati** (p167), with its many brightly-frescoed *havelis* (ornate traditional buildings)

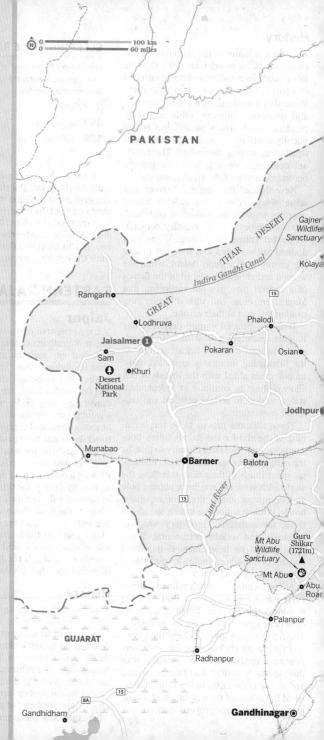

0   100 km
0   60 miles

PAKISTAN

THAR DESERT

GREAT

Indira Gandhi Canal

Gajner Wildlife Sanctuary

Kolaya

Ramgarh

Lodhruva

Phalodi

Jaisalmer ①

Pokaran

Osian

Sam

Khuri

Desert National Park

Jodhpur

Munabao

●**Barmer**

Balotra

Lauri River

Mt Abu Wildlife Sanctuary

Guru Shikar (1721m) ▲

Mt Abu

Abu Road

Palanpur

GUJARAT

Radhanpur

Gandhidham

Gandhinagar ◉

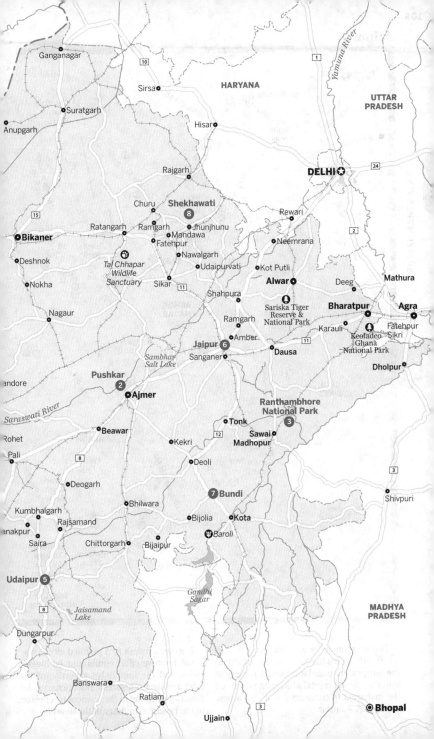

Jaipur

The kingdom grew wealthier and wealthier, and this, plus the need to accommodate the burgeoning population and a paucity of water at the old capital at Amber, prompted the maharaja to commence work on a new city in 1727 – Jaipur.

Northern India's first planned city, it was a collaborative effort combining Jai Singh's vision and the impressive expertise of his chief architect, Vidyadhar Bhattacharya. Jai Singh's grounding in the sciences is reflected in the precise symmetry of the new city.

Sights

Consider buying a **composite ticket** (Indian/foreigner ₹100/400), which allows you entry into Amber Fort, Central Museum, Jantar Mantar, Hawa Mahal and Nahargarh, and is valid for two days from the time of purchase. It's available for purchase at all of the sights listed.

Old City (Pink City)

The Old City (often referred to as the Pink City) is partially encircled by a crenellated wall punctuated at intervals by grand gateways. The major gates are Chandpol (*pol* means 'gate'), Ajmer Gate and Sanganeri Gate.

Avenues divide the Pink City into neat rectangles, each specialising in certain crafts, as ordained in the Shilpa Shastra (ancient Hindu texts). The main bazaars in the Old City include Johari Bazaar, Tripolia Bazaar, Bapu Bazaar and Chandpol Bazaar.

City Palace
PALACE
(Indian/foreigner incl camera ₹100/400, video camera ₹200, audio guide free, guide from ₹300, Royal Grandeur tour ₹2500; ⊙9.30am-5pm) A complex of courtyards, gardens and buildings, the impressive City Palace is right in the centre of the Old City. The outer wall was built by Jai Singh, but within it the palace has been enlarged and adapted over the centuries. There are palace buildings from different eras, some dating from the early 20th century. Despite the gradual development, the whole is a striking blend of Rajasthani and Mughal architecture.

The price of admission includes entry to Jaigarh, a long climb above Amber Fort. This is valid for two days.

➡ Mubarak Mahal

Entering through Virendra Pol, you'll see the Mubarak Mahal (Welcome Palace), built in the late 19th century for Maharaja Madho Singh II as a reception centre for visiting dignitaries. Its multi-arched and colonnaded construction was cooked up in an Islamic, Rajput and European stylistic stew by the architect Sir Swinton Jacob. It now forms part of the **Maharaja Sawai Mansingh II Museum** containing a collection of royal costumes and superb shawls, including Kashmiri *pashmina*. One remarkable exhibit is Sawai Madho Singh I's capacious clothing. It's said he was a cuddly 2m tall, 1.2m wide and 250kg.

In 1876 Maharaja Ram Singh had the entire Old City painted pink (traditionally the colour of hospitality) to welcome the Prince of Wales (later King Edward VII). Today all residents of the Old City are compelled by law to preserve the pink facade.

Jaipur

➡ Diwan-i-Khas (Sarvatobhadra)

Set between the Armoury and the Diwan-i-Am art gallery is an open courtyard known in Sanskrit as Sarvatobhadra. At its centre is a pink-and-white, marble-paved gallery that was used as the Diwan-i-Khas (Hall of Private Audience), where the maharajas would consult their ministers. Here you can see two enormous silver vessels, 1.6m tall and reputedly the largest silver objects in the world; Maharaja Madho Singh II, as a devout Hindu, used these vessels to take holy Ganges water to England for Edward VII's coronation in 1902.

➡ Diwan-i-Am

Within the lavish Diwan-i-Am (Hall of Public Audience) is this art gallery. Exhibits include a copy of the entire Bhagavad Gita (scripture) handwritten in tiny script, and miniature copies of other holy Hindu scriptures, which were small enough to be easily hidden in the event that zealot Mughal armies tried to destroy the sacred texts.

➡ The Armoury

The Anand Mahal Sileg Khana – the Maharani's Palace – houses the Armoury, which has one of the best collections of weapons in the country. Many of the ceremonial weapons are elegantly engraved and inlaid belying their grisly purpose.

➡ Pitam Niwas Chowk & Chandra Mahal

Located towards the palace's inner courtyard is Pitam Niwas Chowk. Here four glorious gates represent the seasons – the **Peacock Gate** depicts autumn, the **Lotus Gate**, signifying summer, the **Green Gate**, representing spring, and finally winter embodied by the **Rose Gate**.

Beyond this *chowk* (square) is the private Chandra Mahal, which is still the residence of the descendants of the royal family and where you can take a 45-minute **Royal Grandeur guided tour** of select areas.

Jantar Mantar HISTORIC SITE
(Indian/foreigner ₹40/200, guide ₹200, audio guide ₹150; ☉9am-4.30pm) Adjacent to the City Palace is Jantar Mantar, an observatory begun by Jai Singh in 1728 that resembles a collection of giant bizarre sculptures. Built for measuring the heavens, the name is derived from the Sanskrit *yanta mantr,*

meaning 'instrument of calculation,' and in 2010 it was added to India's list of Unesco World Heritage Sites. Paying for a local guide is highly recommended if you wish to learn how each fascinating instrument works.

Jai Singh liked astronomy even more than he liked war and town planning. Before constructing the observatory he sent scholars abroad to study foreign constructs. He built five observatories in total, and this is the largest and best preserved (it was restored in 1901). Others are in Delhi, Varanasi and Ujjain. No traces of the fifth, the Mathura observatory, remain.

Hawa Mahal HISTORIC BUILDING
(Johari Bazaar; Indian/foreigner incl camera ₹10/50, guide ₹200, audio guide Hindi/English ₹80/110; ☉9am-5pm) Jaipur's most distinctive landmark, the Hawa Mahal is an extraordinary, fairy-tale, pink sandstone, delicately honeycombed hive that rises a dizzying five storeys. It was constructed in 1799 by Maharaja Sawai Pratap Singh to enable ladies of the royal household to watch the life and processions of the city. The top offers stunning views over Jantar Mantar and the City Palace one way, and over Siredeori Bazaar the other.

There's a small **museum** (Saturday to Thursday), with miniature paintings and some rich relics, such as ceremonial armour, which help evoke the royal past.

RAJASTHAN JAIPUR

TOP STATE FESTIVALS

➡ **Desert Festival** (p182; Feb; Jaisalmer) A chance for moustache twirlers to compete in the Mr Desert contest.

➡ **Elephant Festival** (Mar; Jaipur) Parades, polo and human-versus-elephant tugs of war.

➡ **Gangaur** (Mar/Apr; statewide) A festival honouring Shiva and Parvati's love, celebrated with fervour in Jaipur.

➡ **Mewar Festival** (p155; Mar/Apr; Udaipur) Udaipur's version of Gangaur, with free cultural events and a colourful procession down to the lake.

➡ **Teej** (Aug; Jaipur and Bundi) Honours the arrival of the monsoon, and Shiva and Parvati's marriage.

➡ **Dussehra Mela** (p146; Oct; Kota) Commemorates Rama's victory over Ravana (the demon king of Lanka). It's a spectacular time to visit Kota – the huge fair features 22m-tall firecracker-stuffed effigies.

➡ **Marwar Festival** (p175; Oct; Jodhpur and Osian) Celebrates Rajasthani heroes through music and dance; one day is held in Jodhpur, the other in Osian.

➡ **Pushkar Camel Fair** (p138; Oct/Nov; Pushkar) The most famous festival in the statep; a massive congregation of camels, horses and cattle, pilgrims and tourists.

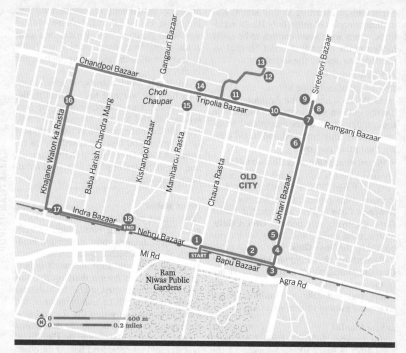

🏃 Walking Tour
Pink City

START NEW GATE
FINISH AJMER GATE
DISTANCE 4.5KM
DURATION THREE TO FIVE HOURS

Entering the old city from ❶ **New Gate**, turn into ❷ **Bapu Bazaar**, inside the city wall. Brightly coloured bolts of fabric, *jootis* (traditional shoes) and aromatic perfumes make the street a favourite destination for Jaipur's women. At the end of Bapu Bazaar you'll come to ❸ **Sanganeri Gate**. Turn left into ❹ **Johari Bazaar**, the jewellery market, where you will find jewellers, goldsmiths and artisans doing highly glazed *meenakari* (enamelling).

Continuing north you'll pass the famous ❺ **LMB Hotel**, and the ❻ **Jama Masjid**, with its tall minarets, and the bustling ❼ **Badi Chaupar**. Be very careful crossing the road here. To the north is ❽ **Siredeori Bazaar**, also known as Hawa Mahal Bazaar. The name is derived from the spectacular ❾ **Hawa Mahal** (p111), a short distance to the north. Turning left on ❿ **Tripolia Bazaar**,

you will see a lane leading to the entrance of Hawa Mahal. A few hundred metres west is the ⓫ **Tripolia Gate** (p151). This is the main entrance to the ⓬ **Jantar Mantar** and ⓭ **City Palace**, but only the maharaja's family may enter here. The public entrance is via the less ostentatious Atishpol (Stable Gate), a little further along.

After visiting the City Palace complex, head back to Tripolia Bazaar and resume your walk west past ⓮ **Iswari Minar Swarga Sal** (p114), which is well worth the climb for the view. Cross the bazaar at the minaret and head west. The next lane on the left is ⓯ **Maniharon ka Rasta**, the best place to buy colourful lac (resin) bangles.

Back on Tripolia Bazaar, continue west to cross Choti Chaupar to Chandpol Bazaar until you reach a traffic light. Turn left into ⓰ **Khajane Walon ka Rasta**, where you'll find marble and stoneware carvers at work. Continue south until you reach a broad road, ⓱ **Indra Bazaar**, just inside the city wall. Follow the road east towards ⓲ **Ajmer Gate**, which marks the end of this tour.

Claustrophobics should be aware that the narrow corridors can get extremely cramped and crowded inside the Hawa Mahal.

Entry is from the back of the complex. To get here, return to the intersection on your left as you face the Hawa Mahal, turn right and then take the first right again through an archway.

◉ New City

By the mid-19th century it became obvious that the well-planned city was bursting at the seams. During the reign of Maharaja Ram Singh (1835–80) the seams ruptured and the city burst out beyond its walls. Civic facilities, such as a postal system and piped water, were introduced. This period gave rise to a part of town very different from the bazaars of the Old City, with wide boulevards, landscaped grounds and grand European-influenced buildings.

Central Museum   MUSEUM

(Albert Hall; J Nehru Marg; Indian/foreigner ₹20/150, audio guide Hindi/English ₹90/124; ☺9.30am-5pm) This museum is housed in the spectacularly florid Albert Hall, south of the Old City. It was designed by Sir Swinton Jacob, and combines elements of English and North Indian architecture, as well as huge friezes celebrating the world's great cultures. It was known as the pride of the new Jaipur when it opened in 1887. The grand old building hosts an eclectic array of tribal dress, dioramas, sculptures, miniature paintings, carpets, musical instruments and even an Egyptian mummy.

SRC Museum of Indology   MUSEUM

(24 Gangwell Park, Prachyavidya Path; Indian/foreigner incl guide ₹40/100; ☺8am-6pm) This ramshackle, dusty treasure trove is an extraordinary private collection. It contains folk-art objects and other pieces – there's everything from a manuscript written by Aurangzeb and a 200-year-old mirrorwork swing from Bikaner to a glass bed. The museum is signposted off J Nehru Rd.

◉ City Edge

Nahargarh   FORT

(Tiger Fort; Indian/foreigner ₹10/30; ☺10am-5pm) Built in 1734 and extended in 1868, this sturdy fort overlooks the city from a sheer ridge to the north. The story goes that the fort was named after Nahar Singh, a dead prince whose restless spirit was disrupting construction. Whatever was built in the day

crumbled in the night. The prince agreed to leave on condition that the fort was named for him. The views are glorious here and it's a great sunset spot; there's a restaurant that's perfect for a beer.

Royal Gaitor   HISTORIC SITE

(Gatore ki Chhatryan; Indian/foreigner ₹20/30; ☺9am-5pm) The royal cenotaphs, just outside the city walls, beneath Nahargarh, are an appropriately restful place to visit and feel remarkably undiscovered. The stone monuments are beautifully and intricately carved. Maharajas Pratap Singh, Madho Singh II and Jai Singh II, among others, are honoured here. Jai Singh II has the most impressive marble cenotaph, with a dome supported by 20 carved pillars.

Jal Mahal   HISTORIC BUILDING

(Water Palace; ☺closed to public) Near the cenotaphs of the maharanis of Jaipur, and beautifully situated in the watery expanse of Man Sagar, is the beautiful Jal Mahal. It was built in 1799 by Madho Singh as a summer resort for the royal family, which they used to base duck-hunting parties. It's accessed via a causeway at the rear, and is currently undergoing restoration for tourism under the auspices of the **Jal Tarang** (www.jaltarang.in) project.

🏃 Activities

Several hotels will let you use their pool for a daily fee. Try the pools at the **Raj Mahal Palace** (Sadar Patel Marg; admission ₹270), the **Mansingh Hotel** (Sansar Chandra Marg; admission ₹225) and the **Narain Niwas Palace Hotel** (nonguests ₹200).

Yog Sadhna Ashram   YOGA

(☎9314011884; http://yogsadhnaindia.org; Bapu Nagar; ☺Wed-Mon) Classes take place among trees off University Rd (near Rajasthan University) and incorporate breathing exercises, yoga asanas (postures) and exercise. Most of the classes are in Hindi, but some English is spoken in the 7.30am to 9.30am class. You can visit for individual classes, or register for longer courses (free).

Kerala Ayurveda Kendra   AYURVEDA

(☎5106743; www.keralaayurvedakendra.com; F-34, Jamnalal Bajaj Marg, Azad Marg; ☺8am-noon & 4-8pm) Is Jaipur making your nerves jangle? Get help through ayurvedic massage and therapy. Treatments include *sirodhara* (₹1500), where medicated oil is steadily streamed over your forehead for 1½ hours to

RAJASTHAN JAIPUR

reduce stress, tone the brain and help with sleep disorders. Massages (male masseur for male clients and female for female clients) cost from ₹500 for 55 minutes. It offers free transport to/from your hotel.

🐾 Courses

Jaipur Cooking Classes COOKING
(☏ 9928097288; www.jaipurcookingclasses.com; 33 Gyan Vihar, Nirman Nagar, near Ajmer Rd; class ₹1800-3700) Popular cooking classes with chef Lokesh Mathur, who boasts over 25 years experience working in the restaurant and hotel business. Classes cover both classic dishes and Rajasthani menus and can be veg or nonveg. After a three-hour lesson, you sit down to a lunch or dinner of what you've prepared. Lokesh's kitchen is outside the western outskirts of Jaipur.

Sakshi BLOCK PRINTING
(☏ 2731862; www.handblockprintedproducts. com; Laxmi Colony, Sanganer Village; half-/full-day course per person ₹1500/2500) Basic block-printing or blue-pottery courses (eight hours per day) are available in Sanganer village, around 16km south of Jaipur. You can also do two- to three-month courses. Costs depend on the number of students; contact Sakshi for more details.

👉 Tours

RTDC SIGHTSEEING
(☏ 2200778; tours@rtdc.in; RTDC Tourist Office, Platform 1, Jaipur Train Station; half-/full-day tour ₹300/350; ⊗ 8am-6.30pm Mon-Sat) Full-day tours (9am to 6pm) take in all the major sights of Jaipur (including Amber Fort), with a lunch break at Nahargarh. The lunch break can be as late as 3pm, so have a big breakfast. Rushed half-day tours still

squeeze in Amber (8am to 1pm, 11.30am to 4.30pm, and 1.30pm to 6.30pm) – some travellers recommend these, as you avoid the long lunch break. The tour price doesn't include admission charges.

Departing at 6.30pm, the **Pink City by Night tour** (₹450) explores several well-known sights, and dinner at Nahargarh.

Tours depart from Jaipur train station; the company also picks up and takes bookings from the RTDC Hotel Teej, RTDC Hotel Gangaur and the tourist office at the main bus station.

Cyclin' Jaipur CYCLING
(☏ 28060965; www.cyclinjaipur.com; 4hr tour ₹1800; ⊗ tour 6.30am) Get up early to beat the traffic for a tour of the Pink City by bike, exploring the hidden lanes, temples, markets and food stalls of Jaipur. It's a unique and fun way to learn about the workings and culture of the city. Breakfast and refreshments during the tour are included, and helmets are provided on demand. Tours start at Karnot Mahal, on Ramganj Chaupar in the Old City.

🛏 Sleeping

Prepare yourself to be besieged by autorickshaw and taxi drivers when you arrive by train or bus. If you refuse to go to their choice of hotel, many will either snub you or double the fare. To avoid this annoyance, go straight to the prepaid autorickshaw and taxi stands at the bus and train stations. Even better, many hotels will pick you up if you ring ahead.

From May to September, most midrange and top-end hotels offer bargain rates, dropping prices by 25% to 50%.

DON'T MISS

HEAVEN-PIERCING MINARET

Piercing the skyline near the City Palace is the unusual **Iswari Minar Swarga Sal** (Heaven-Piercing Minaret; admission ₹20; ⊗ 9am-4.30pm), just west of Tripolia Gate. The minaret was erected by Jai Singh's son Iswari, who later ignominiously killed himself by snakebite (in the Chandra Mahal) rather than face the advancing Maratha army – 21 wives and concubines then did the necessary noble thing and committed *jauhar* (ritual mass suicide by immolation) on his funeral pyre. You can spiral to the top of the minaret for excellent views over the Old City. The entrance is around the back of the row of shops fronting Chandpol Bazaar – take the alley 50m west of the minaret along Chandpol Bazaar or go via the Atishpol entrance to the City Palace compound, 150m east of the minaret.

Around MI Road

★**Hotel Pearl Palace** HOTEL **$**
(☑2373700, 9414066311; www.hotelpearlpalace.
com; Hathroi Fort, Hari Kishan Somani Marg; dm
₹200, r ₹400-1400; ❋@☎) The delightful
Pearl Palace continues to raise the bar for
budget digs. There's quite a range of rooms
to choose from – small, large, shared bathroom, private bathroom, some with balconies, some with AC or fan cooling, and all
are spotless. Services include free pick-up,
moneychanging and travel arrangements,
and the hotel boasts the excellent Peacock
Rooftop Restaurant (p118). Advance booking is highly recommended.

Tony Guest House GUESTHOUSE **$**
(☑9928871717; www.facebook.com/tonyguest-
housejaipur; 11 Station Road; dm ₹150, s ₹250, d
₹500, without bathroom ₹250-420; ☻@☎) A
friendly choice on a busy road for backpackers on a tight budget, Tony's is well set
up for travellers with a rooftop garden, honest travel advice, internet and free-flowing
chai. Rooms are extremely basic, some with
plywood partition walls, and only one has
a private bathroom, although it's with a
cold-water shower. The common shower
is hot.

Jwala Niketan GUESTHOUSE **$**
(☑5108303; jwalaniketan@live.com; C6, Lal ji Ka
Bag, Motilal Atal Marg; s ₹200-500, d ₹400-580,
s/d with AC ₹1000/1200; ❋) This quiet yet
centrally located guesthouse has a range of
good-value, clean but very basic pastel-toned
rooms. The host family lives on the premises
and the atmosphere is decidedly noncommercial – almost monastic – though rooms
do have TVs. There is no restaurant, but
meals can be delivered to your room from
the nearby cheap and multicuisine Mohan
restaurant (p119) or you can sample the family's vegetarian fare.

★**Atithi Guest House** GUESTHOUSE **$$**
(☑2378679; www.atithijaipur.com; 1 Park House
Scheme Rd; s/d ₹1000/1400; ❋@☎) This
nicely presented modern guesthouse, well
situated between MI and Station Rds, of-
fers strikingly clean, simple rooms dotted
around a quiet courtyard. It's central but
peaceful, and the service is friendly and
helpful. Meals are available (the thali is par-
ticularly recommended) and you can have a
drink on the very pleasant rooftop terrace.

Hotel Arya Niwas HOTEL **$$**
(☑4073456; www.aryaniwas.com; Sansar Chandra
Marg; r from ₹1200, s/d with AC from ₹1500/1650;
❋@☎) Just off Sansar Chandra Marg, behind a high-rise tower, this very popular
travellers' haunt has a travel desk, bookshop
and yoga lessons. For a hotel of 92 rooms it
is very well run, though its size means it's
not as personal as smaller guesthouses. The
spotless rooms vary in layout and size so
check out a few.

For relaxing, there's an extensive terrace
facing a soothing expanse of lawn. The
self-service vegetarian restaurant doesn't
serve beer (so BYO).

Pearl Palace Heritage HOTEL **$$**
(☑9414066311, 2375242; www.pearlpalaceherit-
age.com; Lane 2, 54 Gopal Bari; s/d ₹2400/2800;
❋☎❋) The second hotel for the successful
Pearl Palace team is a midrange hotel with
several special characteristics and great at-
tention to detail. Stone carvings adorn the
halls and each room re-creates an individ-
ual cultural theme such as a village hut, a
sandstone fort, or a mirror-lined palace
boudoir. Modern luxuries and facilities have
been carefully integrated into the traditional
designs.

Karni Niwas GUESTHOUSE **$$**
(☑2365433; www.hotelkarniniwas.com; C5, Motilal
Atal Marg; r ₹1000, with AC ₹1500; ❋@☎) This
friendly hotel has clean, cool and comfortable rooms, often with balconies. There's
no restaurant, but there are relaxing plant-
decked terraces to enjoy room service on.
And being so central, restaurants aren't far
away. The owner shuns commissions for
rickshaw drivers; free pick-up from the train
or bus station is available.

All Seasons Homestay HOMESTAY **$$**
(☑9460387055; www.allseasonshomestayjaipur.
com; 63 Hathroi Fort; s ₹1300-1900, d ₹1400-2000;
❋☎) Ranjana and her husband Dinesh
run this welcoming homestay in their love-
ly bungalow on a quiet back street behind
deserted Hathroi Fort. There are only four
guest rooms, but each is lovingly cared for
and two have small kitchens. There's a pleas-
ant lawn and home-cooked meals. Advance
booking is recommended.

RTDC Hotel Swagatam HOTEL **$$**
(☑2200595; Station Rd; s/d incl breakfast
₹900/1300, with AC ₹1400/1700; ❋) One of
the closest digs to the train station (100m
down a quite inauspicious lane), this

government-run hotel has helpful, friendly management and a neatly clipped lawn. Rooms are well worn, but spacious, clean and acceptable.

Karan's Guest House
GUESTHOUSE $$

(☎9828284433; www.karans.info; D-76 Shiv Heera Path; s/d ₹1300/1500; ✹⊚) A sweet family-run guesthouse in a quiet residential part of town, but not too far from all the restaurants on MI Rd. Rooms are very spacious and homely and come with AC, TV and hot-water showers. There's a handy rickshaw stand at the end of the road.

Alsisar Haveli
HERITAGE HOTEL $$$

(☎2368290; www.alsisar.com; Sansar Chandra Marg; r from ₹7700; ✹⊚⊚⊚) A genuine heritage hotel that has emerged from a gracious 19th-century mansion. Alsisar Haveli is set in beautiful green gardens, and boasts a lovely swimming pool and grand dining room. Its bedrooms don't disappoint either, with elegant Rajput arches and antique furnishings. This is a winning choice, though a little impersonal, perhaps because it hosts many tour groups.

🛏 Bani Park

The Bani Park area is relatively peaceful (away from the main roads), about 2km west of the old city (northwest of MI Rd).

Hotel Anuraag Villa
HOTEL $$

(☎2201679; www.anuraagvilla.com; D249 Devi Marg; r ₹790-990, with AC ₹1650-2050; ✹⊚⊚) This quiet and comfortable option has no-fuss, spacious rooms and an extensive lawn where you can find some quiet respite from the hassles of sightseeing. It has a recommended restaurant with its kitchen on view, and efficient, helpful staff.

Tara Niwas
GUESTHOUSE $$

(☎2203762; www.aryaniwas.com; B-22-B Shiv Marg, Bani Park; s/d from ₹1150/1600, per month from ₹22,000/28,000; ✹⊚⊚) Run by the people behind Hotel Arya Niwas, Tara Niwas offers well-furnished apartments suitable for longer stays. Some rooms have attached kitchenettes, and there's also a cafe and dining room and a business centre.

Shahpura House
HERITAGE HOTEL $$

(☎2203069; www.shahpura.com; D257 Devi Marg; s/d from ₹4000/5000, ste from ₹5000; ✹⊚⊚⊚) Elaborately built and decorated in traditional style, this heritage hotel offers immaculate rooms, some with balconies, featuring murals, coloured-glass lamps, flat-screen TVs, and even ceilings covered in small mirrors (in the suites). This rambling palace boasts a durbar hall (royal reception hall) with huge chandelier and a cosy cocktail bar.

There's an inviting swimming pool and an elegant rooftop terrace that stages cultural shows.

Madhuban
HOTEL $$

(☎2200033; www.madhuban.net; D237 Behari Marg; r ₹2400/2900; ✹⊚⊚⊚) Madhuban has cute and cosy rooms with attractive wood furniture, and although they are small for the price, this is a comfortable stay. The pool is tiny (OK for a quick plunge), but the restaurant is good, and you can sometimes eat out on the lawn.

Jas Vilas
GUESTHOUSE $$$

(☎2204638; www.jasvilas.com; C9 Sawai Jai Singh Hwy; s/d ₹4440/5080; ✹⊚⊚⊚) This small but impressive hotel was built in 1950 and is still run by the same charming family. It offers 11 spacious rooms, most of which face the large sparkling pool set in a romantic courtyard. Three garden-facing rooms are wheelchair accessible. In addition to the relaxing courtyard and lawn, there is a cosy dining room and helpful management.

Hotel Meghniwas
GUESTHOUSE $$$

(☎4060100; www.meghniwas.com; C9 Sawai Jai Singh Hwy; s/d ₹4000/4500; ✹⊚⊚⊚) In a building erected by Brigadier Singh in 1950 and run by his gracious descendants, this very welcoming hotel has comfortable and spotless rooms, with traditional carved-wood furniture and leafy outlooks. The standard rooms are good, but the suite does not measure up to expectations. There's a first-rate restaurant and an inviting pool set in a pleasant lawn area.

🛏 Old City

Hotel Kailash
HOTEL $

(☎2577372; Johari Bazaar; r without/with bathroom ₹300/500) One of the few budget digs within the Old City, Kailash is right in the thick of it. But it's nothing fancy. Enter through a narrow stairway to the undersized rooms, which are basic and stuffy despite the central air-cooling. The cheapest rooms are windowless cells and the shared bathrooms can be challenging, while the bigger doubles with attached bath are adequate. Rooms at the back are quieter.

Hotel Sweet Dreams HOTEL $

(🖉 2314409; www.hotelsweetdreamjaipur.in; Nehru Bazaar; s/d ₹800/1000, with AC from ₹1400/1600; ❄️) A decent but basic budget choice in the Old City, if you ignore the rickety elevator that takes you upstairs. The rooms are pretty much identical (with balconies), with increasing amenities the higher up the price scale you go: adding air-cooling, hot water and finally AC. There's a bar and rooftop terrace restaurant.

LMB Hotel HOTEL $$

(🖉 2565844; www.hotellmb.com; Johari Bazaar; s/d from ₹2325/2525; ❄️) Situated above the renowned vegetarian restaurant (p119) of the same name, this hotel offers a prime vantage point from where you can check out the mayhem of the Old City bazaars. Rooms are generally large, bright and clean, though possibly overpriced. Check out a few (including the plumbing) before settling in.

🛏 Rambagh Environs

Hotel Diggi Palace HERITAGE HOTEL $$

(🖉 2373091; www.hoteldiggipalace.com; off Sawai Ram Singh Rd; s/d incl breakfast from ₹4000/5000; ❄️@) About 1km south of Ajmer Gate, this former splendid residence of the *thakur* (nobleman) of Diggi is surrounded by vast shaded lawns. The more expensive rooms at this former budget hotel are substantially better than the cheaper options. There's free pick-up from the bus and train stations.

Management prides itself on using organic produce from the hotel's own gardens and farms in the restaurant.

Nana-ki-Haveli HERITAGE HOTEL $$

(🖉 2615502; www.nanakihaveli.com; Fateh Tiba; r ₹1800-3000; ❄️@) Tucked away off Moti Dungri Marg is this tranquil place with attractive, comfortable rooms decorated with traditional flourishes (discreet wall paintings, wooden furniture). It's hosted by a lovely family and is a good choice for solo female travellers. It's fronted by a relaxing lawn and offers home-style cooking and discounted rooms in summer.

Rambagh Palace HERITAGE HOTEL $$$

(🖉 2211919; www.tajhotels.com; Bhawan Singh Marg; r from ₹38,500; ❄️@📶❄️) This splendid palace was once the Jaipur pad of Maharaja Man Singh II and, until recently, his glamorous wife Gayatri Devi. Veiled in 19 hectares of gardens, the hotel – now run by the luxury Taj Group brand – has fantastic views across the immaculate lawns. More expensive rooms are naturally the most sumptuous.

Nonguests can join in the magnificence by dining in the lavish restaurants or drinking tea on the gracious verandah. At least treat yourself to a drink at the spiffing Polo Bar (p119).

Narain Niwas Palace Hotel HERITAGE HOTEL $$$

(🖉 2561291; www.hotelnarainniwas.com; Narain Singh Rd; s/d incl breakfast from ₹5610/7670; ❄️@📶❄️) In Kanota Bagh, just south of the city, this genuine heritage hotel has wonderful ramshackle splendour. There's a lavish dining room with liveried staff, an old-fashioned verandah on which to drink tea, and antiques galore. The high-ceilinged rooms vary in atmosphere and the bathrooms also vary greatly – inspect before committing.

Out back you'll find a large secluded pool (nonguests ₹150), heavenly spa and sprawling gardens complete with peacocks.

✖️ Eating

✖️ Around MI Road

Old Takeaway The Kebab Shop KEBABS $

(151 MI Rd; kebabs ₹90-180; ⏱6-11pm) One of a few similarly named roadside kebab shops on this stretch of MI Road, this one (next to the mosque) is the original (so we're told) and the best (we agree). It knocks up outstanding tandoori kebabs, including *paneer sheesh,* mutton *sheesh* and tandoori chicken. Like the sign says: a house of delicious nonveg corner.

Indian Coffee House CAFE $

(MI Rd; coffee ₹11-15, snacks from ₹40; ⏱8am-9.30pm) Set back from the street, down an easily missed alley, this traditional coffee house (a venerable co-op owned institution) offers a very pleasant cup of filtered coffee in very relaxed surroundings. Aficionados of Indian Coffee Houses will not be disappointed by the fan-cooled ambience. Inexpensive samosas, *pakoras* (deep-fried battered vegetables) and dosas grace the snack menu.

Rawat Kachori SWEETS $

(Station Rd; kachori ₹20, lassi ₹25; ⏱6am-10pm) For great Indian sweets (₹10 each or ₹120 to ₹300 per kg) and famous *kachori* (potato masala in fried pastry case), head to this exceedingly popular place. A delicious milk crown (fluffy dough with cream) should fill you up for the afternoon.

Sankalp/Sam's Pizza
SOUTH INDIAN, PIZZA **$$**

(MI Rd; pizzas ₹130-385, mains from ₹170; ⊙11am-11pm) This clean and modern Western-style fast-food restaurant has a bit of a split personality. Waiters are dressed the part to serve up good vegetarian pizzas and offerings from the salad bar, but can also hand you a menu full of South Indian treats. Dosas or deep-pan pizzas? You decide, it's good both ways, and the service is quick.

Anokhi Café
ORGANIC **$$**

(2nd fl, KK Square, C-11, Prithviraj Marg; mains from ₹230; ⊙10am-7.30pm; 🖥🍴) A relaxing cafe with a quietly fashionable coffee-shop vibe about it, Anokhi is the perfect place if you're craving a crunchy, well-dressed salad, quiche, or thickly filled sandwich – or just a respite from the hustle with a latte or an iced tea. The delicious organic loaves are made to order and can be purchased separately.

Moti Mahal Delux
NORTH INDIAN **$$**

(☑4017733; MI Rd; mains ₹170-430; ⊙11am-11pm) The famous Delhi restaurant now has franchises all over India delivering its world-famous butter chicken to the masses. The tantalising menu features a vast range of veg and nonveg, including some succulent tandoori dishes. Snuggle into a booth and enjoy the ambience, spicy food and a delicious *pista kulfi* (pistachio-flavoured sweet similar to ice cream) for dessert. Beer and wine available.

Peacock Rooftop Restaurant
MULTICUISINE **$$**

(☑2373700; Hotel Pearl Palace, Hari Kishan Somani Marg; mains ₹80-260; ⊙7am-11pm) This multilevel rooftop restaurant at the Hotel Pearl Palace gets rave reviews for its excellent, inexpensive cuisine (Indian, Chinese and continental) and relaxed ambience. The mouth-watering food, attentive service, whimsical furnishings and romantic view towards Hathroi Fort make it a first-rate restaurant. There are great value thalis, and alcohol is served.

Surya Mahal
SOUTH INDIAN **$$**

(☑2362811; MI Rd; mains ₹90-170; ⊙8am-11pm) This popular option near Panch Batti specialises in South Indian vegetarian food; try the delicious *masala dosa* and the tasty *dhal makhani* (black lentils and red kidney beans). There are also Chinese and Italian dishes, and good ice creams, sundaes and cool drinks.

Handi Restaurant
NORTH INDIAN **$$**

(MI Rd; mains ₹140-300; ⊙noon-3.30pm & 6-11pm) Handi has been satisfying customers for years, with scrumptious tandoori and barbecued dishes and rich Mughlai curries. In the evenings it sets up a smoky kebab stall at the entrance to the restaurant. Good vegetarian items are also available. No beer.

It's opposite the main post office, tucked at the back of the Maya Mansions.

Natraj
VEGETARIAN **$$**

(☑2375804; MI Rd; mains ₹150-250; ⊙9am-11pm) Not far from Panch Batti is this classy vegetarian place, which has an extensive menu featuring North Indian, continental and Chinese cuisine. Diners are blown away by the potato-encased 'vegetable bomb' curry. There's a good selection of thalis and South Indian food – the *paper masala dosa* is delicious – as well as Indian sweets.

Four Seasons
VEGETARIAN **$$**

(☑2373700; D43A Subhas Marg; mains ₹100-210; ⊙noon-3.30pm & 6.30-11pm) Four Seasons is one of Jaipur's best vegetarian restaurants. It's a vastly popular place on two levels, with a glass wall to the kitchens. There's a great range of dishes on offer, including tasty Rajasthani specialities, dosas and a selection of pizzas. No alcohol.

Copper Chimney
INDIAN **$$**

(☑2372275; Maya Mansions, MI Rd; mains ₹150-400; ⊙noon-3.30pm & 6.30-11pm) Copper Chimney is casual, almost elegant and definitely welcoming, with the requisite waiter army and a fridge of cold beer. It offers excellent veg and nonveg Indian cuisine, including aromatic Rajasthani specials. Continental and Chinese food is also on offer, as is a small selection of Indian wine, but the curry-and-beer combos are hard to beat.

Niro's
INDIAN **$$$**

(☑2374493; MI Rd; mains ₹200-500; ⊙10am-11pm) Established in 1949, Niro's is a long-standing favourite on MI Rd that continues to shine. Escape the chaos of the street by ducking into its cool, clean, mirror-ceiling sanctum to savour veg and nonveg Indian cuisine. Classic Chinese and Continental food are available but the Indian menu is definitely the pick. Alcohol served.

Little Italy
ITALIAN **$$$**

(☑4022444; 3rd fl, KK Square, Prithviraj Marg; mains ₹300-500; ⊙noon-11pm) Easily the best Italian restaurant in town, Little Italy is part of a small national chain that offers excellent vegetarian pasta, risotto and wood-fired pizzas in cool, contemporary surroundings. The menu is extensive and includes some Mexican items and first-rate Italian desserts. There's a lounge bar attached so you can accompany your vegetarian dining with wine or beer.

Old City

Mohan
VEGETARIAN $
(144-5 Nehru Bazaar; mains ₹25-90; ⊘9am-10pm) Tiny Mohan is easy to miss: it's a few steps down from the footpath on the corner of the street. It's basic, cheap and a bit grubby, but the thalis, curries (half and full plate) and snacks are freshly cooked and very popular.

Ganesh Restaurant
VEGETARIAN $
(Nehru Bazaar; mains ₹60-120; ⊘ 9am-11.30pm) This pocket-sized outdoor restaurant is in a fantastic location on the top of the Old City wall near New Gate. The cook is in a pit on one side of the wall, so you can check out your pure vegetarian food being cooked. If you're looking for a local eatery with fresh tasty food such as paneer butter masala, you'll love it.

There's an easy-to-miss signpost, but no doubt a stallholder will show you the narrow stairway.

LMB
VEGETARIAN $$
(⌨2560845; Johari Bazaar; mains ₹180-340; ⊘8am-11pm; ✳) Laxmi Misthan Bhandar, LMB to you and me, is a *sattvik* (pure vegetarian) restaurant in the Old City that's been going strong since 1954. A welcoming AC refuge from frenzied Johari Bazaar, LMB is also an institution with its singular decor, attentive waiters and extensive sweet counter.

Popular with both local and international tourists, try the Rajasthan thali (₹450 and big enough to share) followed by the signature *kulfa* (a fusion of *kulfi* and *falooda* with dry fruits and saffron).

🍷 Drinking

Many bars around town tend to be oppressive, all-male affairs; most upper-end hotel bars are good for casual drinking.

★Lassiwala
CAFE
(MI Rd; small/jumbo lassi ₹18/36; ⊘ 7.30am till sold out) This famous, much-imitated institution is a simple place that whips up fabulous, creamy lassis in clay cups. Get here early to avoid disappointment! Will the real Lassiwala please stand up? It's the one that says 'Shop 312' and 'Since 1944', directly next to the alleyway. Imitators spread to the right as you face it.

Henry's the Pub
BAR
(Park Prime Hotel, C-59, Prithviraj Marg; ⊘noon-11.45pm) With coloured glass, dark wood and studded leather, this English pub wannabe has local Golden Peacock on tap and a small selection of international beer. You will also find Australian wine and a full array of Indian spirits. Food is also available.

Polo Bar
BAR
(Rambagh Palace Hotel, Bhawan Singh Marg; ⊘noon-midnight) A spiffing watering hole adorned with polo memorabilia and arched, scalloped windows framing the neatly clipped lawns. A bottle of beer costs from ₹300 according to the label, with cocktails around ₹450.

Café Coffee Day
CAFE
(Country Inn Hotel, MI Rd; coffee ₹60-90; ⊘10am-10pm) The franchise that successfully delivers espresso to coffee addicts, as well as the occasional iced concoction and muffin, has several branches in Jaipur. In addition to this one, sniff out the brews at Paris Point on Sawai Jai Singh Hwy (aka Collectorate Rd), and near the exit point at Amber Fort.

Brewberry's
CAFE
(G-2, Fortune Heights; coffee from ₹40; ⊘8am-midnight; 🛜) Modern wi-fi-enabled cafe with fresh coffee and a good mix of Indian and Western food and snacks. Has some patio seating. It's located opposite HDFC Bank.

100% Rock
BAR
(Hotel Shikha, Yudhishthir Marg, C-Scheme; beer from ₹160; ⊘10am-11.30pm) Attached to, but separate from, Hotel Shikha, this is the closest thing there is to a beer garden in Jaipur, with plenty of outdoor seating as well as AC-cooled side rooms and a clubby main room with a small dance floor. Two-for-one beer offers are common, making this popular with local youngsters.

⭐ Entertainment

Jaipur isn't a big late-night party town, although many of its hotels put on some sort of evening music, dance or puppet show. English-language films are occasionally screened at some cinemas in Jaipur – check the cinemas and local press for details.

Raj Mandir Cinema
CINEMA

(☑ 2379372; www.therajmandir.com; Baghwandas Marg; tickets ₹60-150; ⊘ reservations 10am-6pm, screenings 12.30pm, 3.30pm, 6.30pm & 9.30pm) Just off MI Rd, Raj Mandir is *the* place to go to see a Hindi film in India. This opulent cinema looks like a huge pink cream cake, with a meringue auditorium and a foyer somewhere between a temple and Disneyland. Bookings can be made one hour to seven days in advance at windows 9 and 10 – this is your best chance of securing a seat, but forget it in the early days of a new release.

Alternatively, sharpen your elbows and join the queue when the current booking office opens 45 minutes before curtain up. Avoid the cheapest tickets, which seat you very close to the screen.

Chokhi Dhani
THEME PARK

(☑ 2225001; Tonk Rd; adult/child ₹450/350, incl Rajasthani thali ₹650/400; ⊘ 6-11pm) Chokhi Dhani, meaning 'special village,' is a mock Rajasthani village 20km south of Jaipur, and is a fun place to take the kids. There are open-air restaurants, where you can enjoy a tasty Rajasthani thali, and there's a bevy of traditional entertainment – dancers, acrobats, snack stalls – as well as adventure park–like activities for kids to swing on, slide down and hide in. A return taxi from Jaipur, including waiting time, will cost about ₹700.

Polo Ground
SPORTS

(☑ ticket info 2385380; Ambedkar Circle, Bhawan Singh Marg) Maharaja Man Singh II indulged his passion for polo by building an enormous polo ground next to Rambagh Palace, which is still a polo-match hub today. A ticket to a match also gets you into the lounge, which is adorned with historic photos and memorabilia. The polo season extends over winter, with the most important matches played during January and March. Contact the Rajasthan Polo Club for info about tickets.

During Jaipur's Elephant Festival in March you can watch **elephant polo matches** at the Chaughan Stadium in the Old City. Contact the RTDC tourist office for details.

🔒 Shopping

Jaipur is a shopper's paradise. Commercial buyers come here from all over the world to stock up on the amazing range of jewellery, gems, artefacts and crafts that come from all over Rajasthan. You'll have to bargain hard – shops have seen too many cash-rich, time-poor tourists, particularly around major tourist centres, such as the City Palace and Hawa Mahal.

Most of the larger shops can pack and send your parcels home for you – although it may be slightly cheaper if you do it yourself.

The city is still loosely divided into traditional artisans' quarters. **Bapu Bazaar** is lined with saris and fabrics, and is a good place to buy trinkets. **Johari Bazaar** and **Siredeori Bazaar** are where many jewellery shops are concentrated, selling gold, silver and *meenakari* (highly glazed enamel), a Jaipur speciality. You may also find better deals for fabrics with the cotton merchants of Johari Bazaar.

Kishanpol Bazaar is famous for textiles, particularly *bandhani* (tie-dye). **Nehru Bazaar** also sells fabric, as well as jootis, trinkets and perfume. MI Rd is another good place to buy jootis. The best place for bangles is Maniharon ka Rasta, near the Shree Sanjay Sharma Museum.

Plenty of factories and showrooms are strung along the length of Amber Rd, between Zorawar Singh Gate and the Holiday Inn, to catch the tourist traffic. Here you'll find huge emporiums selling block prints, blue pottery, carpets and antiques; but these shops are used to busloads swinging in to blow their cash, so you'll need to wear your bargaining hat.

Rickshaw-wallahs, hotels and travel agents will be getting a hefty cut from any shop they steer you towards. Many unwary visitors get talked into buying things for resale at inflated prices, especially gems. Beware of these get-rich-quick scams.

Kripal Kumbh
HANDICRAFTS

(☑ 2201127; http://kripalkumbh.com; B18A Shiv Marg, Bani Park; ⊘ 9.30am-6pm Mon-Sat) This tiny showroom in a private home is a great place to buy Jaipur's famous blue pottery produced by the late Mr Kripal Singh, his family and his students. Most pieces cost between ₹250 and ₹500. Free **courses** (☑ 2201127; B18A Shiv Marg, Bani Park) are also available.

Khadi Ghar
CLOTHING, HANDICRAFTS

(MI Rd; ⊘ 10am-7.30pm Mon-Sat) The best of a handful of *khadi* (homespun cloth) shops in Jaipur, this branch sells good quality readymade clothing from the homespun *khadi* fabric, famously endorsed by Gandhi, as well

SHOPPING FOR GEMS

Jaipur is famous for precious and semiprecious stones. There are many shops offering bargain prices, but you do need to know your gems. The main gem-dealing area is around the Muslim area of Pahar Ganj, in the southeast of the old city. Here you can see stones being cut and polished in workshops tucked off narrow backstreets.

There is a **gem-testing laboratory** (☑ 0141-2568221; www.gtljaipur.info; Rajasthan Chamber Bhawan, MI Rd; ⊙ 10am-4pm Mon-Sat) in the Rajasthan Chamber Bhawan on MI Rd. Deposit your gems between 10am and 4pm, then return the following day between 4pm and 5pm to pick up an authenticity certificate. The service costs ₹1000 per stone, ₹1600 for same-day service, if deposited before 1pm.

A warning: one of the oldest scams in India is the gem scam, where tourists are fooled into thinking they can buy gems to sell at a profit elsewhere. Don't be taken in – the gems you buy will be worth only a fraction of what you pay. Often the scams involve showing you real stones and then packing up worthless glass beads to give you in their place. These scams can be elaborate productions and can begin when touts strike up conversations in excellent English while you're waiting for a bus or eating in a restaurant, until you develop a friendly relationship with them. It might be several hours (or even days if they know where you hang out and can arrange to see you again) before any mention is made of reselling items. Be wary, and never let greed cloud your judgment.

as a small selection of handicrafts. Prices are fixed and pressure to buy is minimal.

Rajasthali
HANDICRAFTS

(MI Rd; ⊙ 11am-7.30pm Mon-Sat) This state emporium, opposite Ajmer Gate, is packed with quality Rajasthani artefacts and crafts, including enamelwork, embroidery, pottery, woodwork, jewellery, puppets, block-printed sheets, miniatures, brassware, mirrorwork and more. The best reason to visit is to scout out prices before launching into the bazaar. Items can be cheaper at the markets, after haggling, and you'll find more choice.

★ Mojari
CLOTHING

(Shiv Heera Marg; ⊙ 10am-6.30pm Mon-Sat) Named after the traditional decorated shoes of Rajasthan, Mojari is a UN-supported project that helps rural leatherworkers, traditionally among the poorest members of society. A wide variety of footwear is available (₹500 to ₹750), including embroidered, appliquéd and open-toed shoes, mules and sandals. There's a particularly good choice for women, plus a small selection of handmade leather bags and purses.

Silver Shop
JEWELLERY

(Hotel Pearl Palace, Hari Kishan Somani Marg; ⊙ 6-10pm) A trusted jewellery shop backed by the hotel management that hosts the store. A money-back guarantee is offered on all items. Find it under the peacock canopy in the hotel's Peacock Rooftop Restaurant.

Anokhi
CLOTHING, TEXTILES

(www.anokhi.com; 2nd fl, KK Square, C-11, Prithviraj Marg; ⊙ 9.30am-8pm Mon-Sat, 11am-7pm Sun) Anokhi is a classy, upmarket boutique that's well worth visiting – there's a wonderful little cafe on the premises and an excellent bookshop in the same building. Anokhi sells stunning high-quality textiles, such as block-printed fabrics, tablecloths, bed covers, cosmetic bags and scarves, as well as a range of well-designed, beautifully made clothing that combines Indian and Western influences.

Fabindia
CLOTHING

(☑ 0141 5115991; www.fabindia.com; Sarojini Marg; ⊙ 11am-9pm) A great place to coordinate colours with reams of rich fabrics plus furniture and home accessories. You can also find certified-organic garments, beauty products and condiments. Located opposite Central Park, gate number 4.

ⓘ Information

INTERNET ACCESS

Internet cafes are thin on the ground, but almost all hotels and guesthouses provide wi-fi and/or internet access.

Dhoom Cyber Café (MI Rd; per hr ₹30; ⊙ 8.30am-8.30pm) Enter through an arch into a quiet courtyard just off the main drag.

Mewar Cyber Café (Station Rd; per hr ₹25; ⊙ 7am-11pm) Near the main bus station.

MEDIA

Jaipur Vision and *Jaipur City Guide* are two useful, inexpensive booklets available at bookshops and in some hotel lobbies (where they are free). They feature up-to-date listings, maps, local adverts and features.

MEDICAL SERVICES

Most hotels can arrange a doctor on site.

Santokba Durlabhji Memorial Hospital (SDMH; ☑2566251; www.sdmh.in; Bhawan Singh Marg) Private hospital, with 24-hour emergency department, helpful staff and clear bilingual signage. Consultancy fee ₹400.

Sawai Mansingh Hospital (SMS Hospital; ☑2518222, 2518597; Sawai Ram Singh Rd) State-run but part of Soni Hospitals group (www.sonihospitals.com). Before 3pm, outpatients go to the CT & MRI Centre. After 3pm, go to the adjacent Emergency Department.

MONEY

There are plenty of places to change money, including numerous hotels and masses of ATMs, most of which accept foreign cards.

Thomas Cook (☑2360940; Jaipur Towers, MI Rd; ☉9.30am-6pm)

POST

DHL Express (☑2361159; www.dhl.co.in; G8, Geeta Enclave, Vinobha Marg; ☉10am-8pm) Look for the sub-branch on MI Rd then walk down the lane beside it to find DHL Express. For parcels, the first kilo is expensive, but each 500g thereafter is cheap. All packaging is included in the price. Credit cards and cash are accepted.

Main Post Office (☑2368740; MI Rd; ☉8am-7.45pm Mon-Fri, 10am-5.45pm Sat) A cost-effective and efficient institution, though the back-and-forth can infuriate. Parcel-packing-wallahs in the foyer must first pack, stitch and wax seal your parcel for a fee (₹50 to ₹100 per small package) before sending.

TOURIST INFORMATION

The Tourism Assistance Force (police) are stationed at the railway and bus stations, the airport and at Jaipur's major tourist sights.

RTDC Tourist Office (www.rajasthantourism. gov.in) Main branch (☑5155137; www.rajasthan-tourism.gov.in; Room 21, former RTDC Tourist Hotel, MI Rd; ☉9.30am-6pm Mon-Fri); Airport (☑2722647; Airport); Amber Fort (☑2530264; Amber Fort); Jaipur train station (☑2200778; Jaipur Train Station, Platform 1; ☉24hr); main bus station (☑5064102; Main Bus Station, Platform 3; ☉10am-5pm Mon-Fri) Has maps and brochures on Jaipur and Rajasthan.

❶ Getting There & Away

AIR

It's possible to arrange flights to Europe, the USA and other places, such as Dubai, all via Delhi. It's best to compare ticket prices from travel agencies with what the airlines supply directly and through their websites – the latter is where you will usually find the best price.

Offices of domestic airlines:

Air India (☑2743500, airport 2721333; www.airindia.com; Tonk Rd, Nehru Place) Daily flights to Delhi and Mumbai.

MAIN BUSES FROM JAIPUR

DESTINATION	FARE (₹)	DURATION (HR)	FREQUENCY
Agra	196, AC 407	5½	11 daily
Ajmer	105, AC 269	2½	13 daily
Bharatpur	139	4½	5 daily
Bikaner	225	8	hourly
Bundi	161	5	5 daily
Chittorgarh	233, AC 584	7	6 daily
Delhi	210, AC 558-782	5½	at least hourly
Jaisalmer	471, AC 1239	15	3 daily
Jhunjhunu	135	5	half-hourly
Jodhpur	263, AC 669	7	every 2 hours
Kota	191	5	hourly
Mt Abu (Abu Road)	371	13	daily
Nawalgarh	105	4	hourly
Pushkar (direct)	116	3	daily (direct)
Sawai Madhopur	110	6	2 daily
Udaipur	315, AC 809	10	6 daily

MAJOR TRAINS FROM JAIPUR

DESTINATION	TRAIN NO & NAME	DEPARTURE TIME	ARRIVAL TIME	FARE (₹)
Agra (Cantonment)	19666 Udaipur-Kurj Exp	6.15am	11am	175/485 (A)
Ahmedabad	12958 Adi Sj Rajdhani	12.25am	9.40am	1190/1635 (B)
Ajmer	Ajmer-Agra Fort Intercity	9.40am	11.50am	90/305 (C)
Bikaner	12307 Howrah-Jodhpur Exp	12.45am	8.15am	265/680 (A)
Delhi (New Delhi)	12016 Ajmer Shatabdi	5.50pm	10.40pm	720/1365 (D)
Delhi (S Rohilla)	12985 Dee Double Decker	6am	10.30am	480/1175 (D)
Jaisalmer	14659 Delhi-Jaisalmer Exp	11.45pm	11.15am	340/910 (A)
Jodhpur	22478 Jaipur-Jodhpur SF Exp	6am	10.30am	495/600 (E)
Sawai Madhopur	12466 Intercity Exp	11.05am	1.15pm	170/305/535 (F)
Udaipur	12965 Jaipur–Udaipur Exp	11pm	6.45am	260/690 (A)

Fares: (A) sleeper/3AC, (B) 3AC/2AC, (C) 2nd-class seat/AC chair, (D) AC chair/1AC, (E) AC chair/3AC, (F) sleeper/AC chair/3AC

IndiGo (☎2743500, 5119993; www.goindigo.in; Airport) Flights to Delhi, Mumbai, Ahmedabad, Bengalaru and Hyderabad.

Jet Airways (☎5112225; www.jetairways.com; Room 112, Jaipur Tower, MI Rd; ◷9.30am-6pm Mon-Sat) Flights to Delhi, Mumbai and Bengalaru.

SpiceJet (☎9871803333; www.spicejet.com; Airport) Has one direct daily flight to Delhi.

BUS

Rajasthan State Road Transport Corporation (RSRTC aka Rajasthan Roadways) buses all leave from the **main bus station** (Station Rd), picking up passengers at Narain Singh Circle (you can also buy tickets here). There is a left-luggage office at the main bus station (₹10 per bag for 24 hours), as well as a prepaid autorickshaw stand.

Ordinary buses are known as 'express' buses, but there are also 'deluxe' buses (coaches really, but still called buses; usually with air-con but not always); these vary a lot but are generally much more expensive and comfortable than ordinary express buses. Deluxe buses leave from Platform 3, tucked away in the right-hand corner of the bus station. Unlike ordinary express buses seats on them can be booked in advance from the **reservation office** (☎5116032) here.

With the exception of those going to Delhi (half-hourly), deluxe buses are much less frequent than ordinary buses.

CAR

Most hotels and the RTDC tourist office can arrange car and driver hire. Depending on the vehicle, costs are ₹8 to ₹12 per kilometre, with a minimum rental rate equivalent to 250km per day. Expect to pay a ₹150 overnight charge, and note, you will have to pay for the driver to return to Jaipur even if you aren't.

MOTORCYCLE

You can hire, buy or fix a Royal Enfield Bullet (and lesser motorbikes) at **Rajasthan Auto Centre** (☎2568074, 9829188064; www.royalenfield-salim.com; Sanganeri Gate, Sanjay Bazaar; ◷10am-8pm, to 2pm Sun), the cleanest little motorcycle workshop in India. To hire a 350cc Bullet costs ₹500 per day within Jaipur.

TRAIN

For same-day travel, buy your ticket at the northern end of the train station on Platform 1, window 10 (closed 6am to 6.30am, 2pm to 2.30pm, and 10pm to 10.30pm). The railway inquiries number is ☎131.

Station facilities on Platform 1 include an RTDC tourist information bureau, Tourism Assistance Force (police), a cloakroom for left luggage (₹10 per bag per 24 hours), retiring rooms, restaurants and air-conditioned waiting rooms for those with 1st class and 2AC train tickets.

There's a prepaid autorickshaw stand and local taxis at the road entrance to the train station.

➡ Nine daily trains go to Delhi (sleeper ₹285; departs 1am, 2.50am, 4.40am, 5am, 6am, 2.35pm, 4.25pm, 5.50pm and 11.15pm), plus more on selected days. The 6am double-decker does the trip in 4½ hours, others take five to six.

➡ Two daily trains leave for Agra (sleeper ₹175; 4½ hours, 6.15am and 3.20pm).

➡ Three go to Bikaner (sleeper ₹265; 6½ to 7½ hours; 12.50am, 3.25am and 9.15pm).

➡ Seven go to Jodhpur (sleeper ₹240; five to six hours; 12.45am, 2.45am, 6am, 9.25am, 11.10am, 10.15pm and 11.45pm).

➡ Three go to Udaipur (2nd class ₹165; seven to eight hours; 6.45am, 2pm and 11pm).

➡ Six go to Ahmedabad (sleeper ₹370; 2.30am, 4.25am, 5.35am, 8.45am, 8.35pm and 12.25am). The 12.25am is the quickest (nine hours), while the others take 11 to 13 hours.

➡ For Pushkar, 11 daily trains make the trip to Ajmer (2nd class ₹90; two hours), plus many more on selected days so you rarely wait more than an hour.

➡ For Ranthambhore, six daily trains go to Sawai Madhopur (2nd class ₹90; two to three hours; 5.40am, 11.05am, 2pm, 4.50pm, 5.35pm and 11.55pm), plus plenty more on selected days.

➡ Two trains make the daily run to Jaisalmer (sleeper ₹360; 12 hours, 11.10am and 11.45pm).

❶ Getting Around

TO/FROM THE AIRPORT
There are no bus services from the airport, which is 12km southeast of the city. An autorickshaw costs at least ₹250; a taxi upwards of ₹450. There's a prepaid taxi booth inside the terminal.

AUTORICKSHAW
Autorickshaw drivers at the bus and train stations might just be the pushiest in Rajasthan. Use the fixed-rate prepaid autorickshaw stands instead. Keep hold of your docket to give to the driver at the end of the journey. In other cases be prepared to bargain hard – expect to pay at least ₹80 from either station to the Old City.

CYCLE-RICKSHAW
You can do your bit for the environment by flagging down a lean-limbed cycle-rickshaw rider. Though it can be uncomfortable watching someone pedalling hard to transport you, this *is* how they make a living. A short trip costs about ₹40.

TAXI
There are unmetered taxis available, which will require negotiating a fare, or you can try **Mericar** (☑ 4188888; www.mericar.in; flagfall incl 2km ₹50, afterwards per km ₹13, 25% night surcharge 10pm-5am). It's a 24-hour service and taxis can be hired for sightseeing for four-/six-/eight-hour blocks costing ₹600/1000/1500.

Around Jaipur

Amber

The formidable, magnificent, honey-hued fort of Amber (pronounced am-er), an ethereal example of Rajput architecture, rises from a rocky mountainside about 11km northeast of Jaipur, and is the city's must-see sight.

Amber, the former capital of Jaipur state, was built by the Kachhwaha Rajputs who hailed from Gwalior, in present day Madhya Pradesh, where they reigned for over 800 years. Construction of the fort, which was begun in 1592 by Maharaja Man Singh, the Rajput commander of Akbar's army, was financed with war booty. It was later extended and completed by the Jai Singhs before they moved to Jaipur on the plains below.

◉ Sights

Amber Fort   FORT
(Indian/foreigner ₹25/200, guide ₹200, audio guide Hindi/other ₹100/150; ⊘ 8am-6pm, last entry 5.30pm) This magnificent fort is largely made up of a royal palace, built from pale yellow and pink sandstone and white marble, and divided into four main sections, each with its own courtyard. You can trudge up to the fort from the road in about 10 minutes, but riding up on **elephant back** (one-way per 2 passengers ₹900; ⊘ 7.30am-noon & 3.30-5.30pm) is very popular. A return 4WD to the top and back costs ₹300 for five passengers, including one-hour waiting time.

Animal welfare groups have criticised the keeping of elephants at Amber, as recent government inspections have revealed inadequate housing conditions and abuse of the animals, so you may want to think twice before taking a ride.

Whether you walk or ride an elephant, you will enter Amber Fort through **Suraj Pol** (Sun Gate), which leads to the **Jaleb Chowk** (Main Courtyard), where returning armies would display their war booty to the populace – women could view this area from the veiled windows of the palace. The ticket office is directly across the courtyard from Suraj Pol. If you arrive by car you will enter through **Chand Pol** (Moon Gate) on the opposite side of Jaleb Chowk. Hiring a guide or grabbing an audio guide is highly recommended as there are very few signs and many blind alleys.

From Jaleb Chowk, an imposing stairway leads up to the main palace, but first it's worth taking the steps just to the right, which lead to the small **Siladevi Temple**, with its gorgeous silver doors featuring repoussé (raised relief) work.

Heading back to the main stairway will take you up to the second courtyard and the **Diwan-i-Am** (Hall of Public Audience), which has a double row of columns, each topped by a capital in the shape of an elephant, and latticed galleries above.

The maharaja's apartments are located around the third courtyard – you enter through the fabulous **Ganesh Pol**, decorated with beautiful frescoed arches. The **Jai Mandir** (Hall of Victory) is noted for its inlaid panels and multimirrored ceiling. Carved marble relief panels around the hall are fascinatingly delicate and quirky, depicting cartoonlike insects and sinuous flowers. Opposite the Jai Mandir is the **Sukh Niwas** (Hall of Pleasure), with an ivory-inlaid sandalwood door and a channel that once carried cooling water right through the room. From the Jai Mandir you can enjoy fine views from the palace ramparts over picturesque **Maota Lake** below.

The **zenana** (secluded women's quarters) surrounds the fourth courtyard. The rooms were designed so that the maharaja could embark on his nocturnal visits to his wives' and concubines' respective chambers without the others knowing, as the chambers are independent but open onto a common corridor.

Jaigarh   FORT

(Indian/foreigner ₹35/85, camera/video ₹50/200, car ₹50, Hindi/English guide ₹100/150; ⊙9am-5pm) A scrubby green hill rises above Amber and is topped by the imposing Jaigarh, built in 1726 by Jai Singh. The stern fort, punctuated by whimsical-hatted lookout towers, was never captured and has survived intact through the centuries. It's an uphill walk (about 1km) from Amber and offers great views from the Diwa Burj watchtower. The fort has reservoirs, residential areas, a puppet theatre and the world's largest wheeled cannon, Jaya Vana.

Anokhi Museum of Hand Printing   MUSEUM

(Anokhi Haveli, Kheri Gate; child/adult ₹15/30, camera/video ₹50/150; ⊙10.30am-4.30pm Tue-Sat, 11am-4.30pm Sun, closed 1 May-15 Jul) This interesting museum, in a restored *haveli*, documents the art of hand-block printing, from old traditions to contemporary design. You can watch masters carve unbelievably intricate wooden printing blocks and even have a go at printing your own scarf or T-shirt. There's a cafe and gift shop too. From the museum you can walk around the ancient town to the restored **Panna Meena Baori** (step-well) and **Jagat Siromani Temple** (known locally as the Meera Temple).

🛏 Sleeping

The decidedly untouristy village of Amber, with its colourful food market and scattering of temples and palace ruins, makes a low-key alternative to hectic Jaipur as a possible place to stay.

⭐**Mosaics Guesthouse**   GUESTHOUSE **$$**
(☑ 8875430000, 2530031; www.mosaicsguesthouse.com; Siyaram Ki Doongri, Amber; s/d incl breakfast ₹3200/3500; ❄ @ 🛜) Get away from it all at this gorgeous arty place (the French owner is a mosaic artist and will show off his workshop) with four lovely rooms and a rooftop terrace with beautiful fort views. Set-price Franco-Indian meals cost ₹500. It's about 1km past the fort near Kunda Village – head for Siyaram Ki Doongri, where you'll find signs.

ℹ Getting There & Away

There are frequent buses to Amber from near the Hawa Mahal in Jaipur (non-AC/AC ₹14/25, 15 minutes). They drop you opposite where you start your climb up to the entrance of Amber Fort.

The elephant rides and 4WDs start 100m further down the hill from the bus drop-off.

An autorickshaw/taxi will cost at least ₹400/700 for the return trip from Jaipur. RTDC city tours (p114) include Amber Fort.

Sanganer

The village of Sanganer is 12km south of Jaipur and has a **ruined palace**, a group of **Jain temples** with fine carvings (to which entry is restricted) and two ruined **tripolias** (triple gateways). The main reason to visit, however, is to see its handmade paper- and block-printing shops, workshops and factories (mostly found around the main drag, Stadium Rd), where you can see the products being made. You can also walk down towards the riverbank to see the enormous, brightly coloured fabrics drying in the sun as they hang on huge racks.

Salim's Paper (🖊2730222; www.handmade-paper.com; Gramodyog Rd, Sanganer; ⊙9am-5pm) is the largest handmade paper factory in India, and offers tours. The paper is made from fabric scraps, and often decorated with petals or leaves. The 200 or so employees produce 40,000 sheets a day, which are exported all over the world. There's also a beautiful range of paper products for sale in the showroom.

For block-printed fabrics and blue pottery, there are a number of shops, including **Sakshi** (🖊2731862; Laxmi Colony; ⊙shop 8.30am-8.30pm, factory 9am-6pm). You can see the block-printing workshop here, and even try your hand at block printing; it runs courses in block printing and blue pottery. There's a tremendous range of blue pottery and block-printed fabrics for sale.

ⓘ Getting There & Away

Local buses leave from the Ajmeri Gate in Jaipur for Sanganer every few minutes (₹12, one hour).

Bharatpur & Keoladeo Ghana National Park

🖊05644 / POP 205,200

Bharatpur is famous for its wonderful Unesco–listed Keoladeo Ghana National Park, a wetland and significant bird sanctuary. Apart from the park, Bharatpur has a few historical vestiges, though it wouldn't be worth making the journey for these alone. The town is dusty, noisy and not particularly visitor friendly. Bharatpur hosts the boisterous and colourful **Brij Festival** just prior to Holi celebrations.

The entrance to Keoladeo Ghana National Park lies 2km to the south of Bharatpur's centre.

◉ Sights

Lohagarh   FORT
The still-inhabited, 18th-century Lohagarh, Iron Fort, was so named because of its sturdy defences. Despite being somewhat forlorn and derelict it is still impressive, and sits at the centre of town, surrounded by a moat. There's a north entrance, at **Austdhatu (Eight-Metal) Gate** – apparently the spikes on the gate are made of eight different metals – and a southern entrance, at **Lohiya Gate**.

Maharaja Suraj Mahl, constructor of the fort and founder of Bharatpur, built two towers, the Jawahar Burj and the Fateh Burj, within the ramparts to commemorate his victories over the Mughals and the British. The fort also contains three much decayed palaces within its precincts.

One of the palaces, which is centred on a tranquil courtyard, houses a seemingly forgotten museum. Upstairs you will find a rather ragtag display of royal artefacts, including weaponry. More impressive is the Jain sculpture gallery, which includes some beautiful 7th- to 10th-century pieces. The most spectacular feature of the museum, however, is the palace's original hammam (bathhouse), which retains some fine carvings and frescoes.

◉ Keoladeo Ghana National Park

This tremendous bird sanctuary and **national park** (Indian/foreigner ₹55/400, video ₹400, guide ₹150, bike/mountain-bike rental ₹25/50, binoculars rental ₹100; ⊙6am-6pm Apr-Sep, 6.30am-5pm Oct-Mar) has long been recognised as one of the world's most important bird breeding and feeding grounds. In a good monsoon season, over one-third of the park can be submerged, hosting over 360 species within its 29 sq km. The marshland patchwork is a wintering area for aquatic birds, including visitors from Afghanistan, Turkmenistan, China and Siberia. The park is also home to deer, nilgai and boar, which can be readily spotted.

Keoladeo originated as a royal hunting reserve in the 1850s. It continued to supply the maharajas' tables with fresh game until as late as 1965. In 1982 Keoladeo was declared a national park and it was listed as a World Heritage Site in 1985.

Local campaigners have voiced concern in recent years at the increase in forest clearing to make way for small, tourism-related developments, such as the car park to your right as you enter the park. You'll notice that much of the park is no longer tree-shaded. They are also calling for a 2km 'no-construction zone' outside the park boundary. The current limit is 500m.

Visiting the Park

The best time to visit is from October to February, when you'll see many migratory birds.

Admission (₹400; sunrise to sunset) entitles you to one entrance per day. Guides cost ₹150 per hour. One narrow road (no motor-

Bharatpur

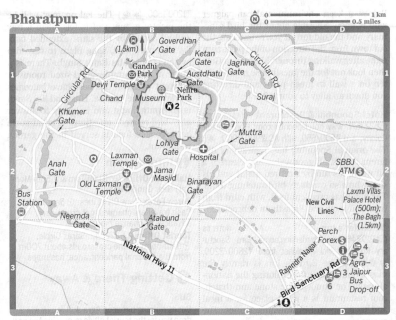

Bharatpur

◎ Sights
1 Keoladeo Ghana National Park Entrance C3
2 Lohagarh B1

⊟ Sleeping
3 Birder's Inn D3
4 Falcon Guest House D3
5 Hotel Spoonbill & Restaurant D3
6 Hotel Sunbird D3
7 Shagun Guest House..........................C2

ised vehicles are permitted past checkpoint 2) runs through the park, but a number of tracks and pathways fan out from it and thread their way between the shallow wetlands. Generally speaking, the further away from the main gate you go, the more interesting the scenery, and the more varied the wildlife becomes.

Only the government-authorised cycle-rickshaws (recognisable by the yellow license plate) are allowed beyond checkpoint 2. You don't pay an admission fee for the drivers, but they charge ₹70 per hour. Some are very knowledgeable. However, these cycle-rickshaws can only travel along the park's larger tracks.

An excellent way to see the park is by hiring a bicycle at the park entrance. Having a bike is a wonderfully quiet way to travel, and allows you to avoid bottlenecks and take in the serenity on your own. However, we recommend that lone female travellers who wish to cycle do so with a guide (who will cycle alongside you), as we've had more than one report of lone women being harassed by young men inside the park in recent years.

You get a small map with your entrance ticket, although the park isn't big so it's difficult to get lost.

🛏 Sleeping & Eating

There are tons of sleeping options near the Keoladeo Ghana National Park (suiting all budgets), either on the stretch of the highway beside Birder's Inn or on the dirt track that the Falcon Guest House is on.

Almost all guesthouses have restaurants and even those without a proper bar can sort you out with a cold beer if you ask.

Shagun Guest House GUESTHOUSE $
(📞 9828687488; rajeevshagun@hotmail.com; d ₹150, s/d without bathroom ₹150/90) This unusual tree-shaded courtyard guesthouse, in a quiet corner of the old town, is extremely basic, and has only four rooms, but it comes with bags of character. It's run by the affable

Rajeev, a keen environmental campaigner who is knowledgeable about the bird sanctuary and the old fort. If you're entering the old town from the direction of the park, turn right after walking through Mathurara Gate then look out for the guesthouse name written on a wall in green paint and directing you down an alley to your left.

Hotel Spoonbill & Restaurant GUESTHOUSE $
(☑ 223571; www.hotelspoonbill.com; Gori Shankur Colony; s/d ₹500/650, with AC ₹900/1000; ✳) The original Spoonbill has a variety of different rooms, all good value and clean, if a bit worn. It's run by a retired major and his son, who also conducts birdwatching tours. The hotel has excellent food, with curd from the family cow and Rajasthani delicacies..

★ Birder's Inn HOTEL $$
(☑ 227346; www.birdersinn.com; Bird Sanctuary Rd; s/d incl breakfast from ₹2800/3200; ✳ @ ☎ ✳) The Birder's Inn is rightly the most popular base for exploring the national park. The atmospheric stone and thatch-roof restaurant is a great place for a meal and to compare birdwatching stories. The rooms are airy, spacious, nicely decorated, and are set far back from the road in well-tended gardens. Guides from the hotel are available for Keoladeo.

Hotel Sunbird HOTEL $$
(☑ 225701; www.hotelsunbird.com; Bird Sanctuary Rd; s/d from ₹1800/2200; ✳) A well-run and popular place close to the Keoladeo park entrance. Rooms are clean and comfortable and there's an appealing garden bar and restaurant with a good range of tasty veg and nonveg dishes and cold beer. Packed lunches and guided tours for the park are available.

Falcon Guest House GUESTHOUSE $$
(☑ 223815; falconguesthouse@hotmail.com; Gori Shankur Colony; s/d from ₹600/800, with AC ₹1200-1500; ✳ @) The Falcon may well be the pick of a bunch of hotels all in a row and all owned by the same extended family. It's a well-kept, snug place to stay, run by the affable Mrs Rajni Singh. There is a range of comfortable, good-sized rooms at different prices – the best have balconies or views of the sunrise. Husband Tej Singh is an ornithologist and is happy to answer any bird-related questions. Flavoursome home-cooked food is served in the garden restaurant.

ⓘ Information

Main Post Office (☉10am-1pm & 2-5pm Mon-Sat) Near Gandhi Park.

Perch Forex (New Civil Lines; ☉5am-11pm) Cash travellers cheques, get credit-card advances or change money here.

Tourist Office (☑ 222542; Saras Circle; ☉9am-5pm) On the crossroads about 700m from the national park entrance; has maps.

ⓘ Getting There & Away

BUS
Buses running between Agra and Jaipur will drop you by the tourist office or outside the park entrance if you ask.

Buses from Bharatpur bus station include:

Agra (₹57, 1½ hours, every 30 minutes day and night)

Alwar (₹113, four hours, hourly until 8pm)

Deeg (₹28, one hour, hourly until 8pm)

Delhi (₹152 to ₹180, five hours, half-hourly from 6am to 7pm, then hourly until 11pm)

Fatehpur Sikri (₹25, 45 minutes, every 30 minutes day and night)

Jaipur (₹139, 4½ hours, every 30 minutes)

TRAIN
→ There are eight trains to Delhi (2nd class/sleeper ₹85/170, four hours) leaving throughout the day, plus three other services on selected days.

MAJOR TRAINS FROM BHARATPUR

DESTINATION	TRAIN NO & NAME	DEPARTURE TIME	ARRIVAL TIME	FARE (₹)
Agra (Cantonment)	19666 Udaipur-Kurj Exp	69.10am	11am	140/485 (A)
Delhi (Hazrat Nizamuddin)	12059 Kota-Jan Shatabdi	9.25am	12.30am	110/370 (B)
Jaipur	19665 Kurj-Udaipr Exp	6.57am	10.50am	140/485 (A)
Sawai Madhopur	12904 Golden Temple Mail	10.30am	12.55am	170/535 (A)

Fares: (A) sleeper/3AC, (B) 2nd-class/AC chair

➡ Five daily trains also make the two-hour trip to Agra (2nd class/sleeper ₹110/140; two hours; 4.45am, 6.50am, noon, 5.20pm and 8.15pm), plus once a day to Agra Cantonment (9.10am).

➡ Nine daily trains go to Jaipur (2nd class/sleeper ₹100/140; three to four hours) between 6am and 11pm.

➡ For Ranthambhore National Park, nine trains run daily to Sawai Madhopur (2nd class/sleeper ₹120/170; two to three hours) from 1am to 9pm. These trains all continue to Kota (four hours) from where you can catch buses to Bundi.

❶ Getting Around

An auto- or cycle-rickshaw from the bus station to the main hotel area should cost around ₹30 (add an extra ₹10 from the train station).

Alwar

♪ 0144 / POP 266,200

Alwar is perhaps the oldest of the Rajasthani kingdoms, forming part of the Matsya territories of Viratnagar in 1500 BC. It became known again in the 18th century under Pratap Singh, who pushed back the rulers of Jaipur to the south and the Jats of Bharatpur to the east, and who successfully resisted the Marathas. It was one of the first Rajput states to ally itself with the fledgling British empire, although British interference in Alwar's internal affairs meant that this partnership was not always amicable.

Alwar is the nearest town to Sariska Tiger Reserve (p130), and has a ruined fort and a rambling palace with an above-average museum hidden inside it. The town has relatively few tourists so there's a refreshing lack of hassle here.

◉ Sights

Bala Qila   FORT

This imposing fort stands 300m above Alwar, its fortifications hugging the steep hills that line the eastern edge of the city. Predating the time of Pratap Singh, it's one of the few forts in Rajasthan built before the rise of the Mughals, who used it as a base for attacking Ranthambhore. Mughal emperors Babur and Akbar have stayed overnight here, and Prince Salim (later Emperor Jehangir) was exiled in Salim Mahal for three years.

Now in ruins, the fort houses a radio transmitter station and parts can only be visited with permission from the superintendent of police. However, this is easy to get: just ask at the superintendent's office in the City Palace complex. You can walk the very steep couple of kilometres up to the fort entrance or take a 7km rickshaw ride.

City Palace   HISTORIC BUILDING

(Vinay Vilas Mahal) Below Bala Qila sprawls the colourful and convoluted City Palace complex, with massive gates and a tank reflecting a symmetrical series of ghats and pavilions. Today most of the complex is occupied by government offices, overflowing with piles of dusty papers and soiled by pigeons and splatters of *paan* (a mixture of betel nut and leaves for chewing).

Hidden within the City Palace is the excellent **Alwar Museum** (Indian/foreigner ₹5/50; ⊙10am-5pm Tue-Sun).

Alwar Museum's eclectic exhibits evoke the extravagance of the maharajas' lifestyle: stunning weapons, stuffed Scottish pheasants, royal ivory slippers, erotic miniatures, royal vestments, a solid silver table, and stone sculptures, such as an 11th-century sculpture of Vishnu. Somewhat difficult to find in the Kafkaesque tangle of government offices, the museum is on the top floor of the palace, up a ramp from the main courtyard. However, there are plenty of people around to point you in the right direction and from there you can follow the signs.

Cenotaph of Maharaja Bakhtawar Singh   HISTORIC BUILDING

This double-storey edifice, resting on a platform of sandstone, was built in 1815 by Maharaja Vinay Singh, in memory of his father. To gain access to the cenotaph, take the steps to the far left when facing the palace. The cenotaph is also known as the Chhatri of Moosi Rani, after one of the mistresses of Bakhtawar Singh who performed *sati* (self-immolation) on his funeral pyre – after this act she was promoted to wifely status.

🛏 Sleeping & Eating

As not many tourists stop here, Alwar's hotels are mostly aimed at budget business travellers and aren't particularly great value.

Alwar Hotel   GUESTHOUSE **$$**

(♪2700012; 25-26 Manu Rd; s/d incl breakfast ₹1900/2700; ❀@☎) Set back from the road in a neatly manicured garden, this well-run hotel has spacious, comfortable rooms. It's easily the best option in town, and staff can be helpful with general information and sightseeing advice. Tours to Sariska Tiger

Reserve can be arranged. The Alwar Hotel also boasts a great multicuisine restaurant, Angeethi.

Hotel Aravali HOTEL $$

(☎ 2332316; reservation.aravali@gmail.com; Nehru Rd; s/d ₹1800/2000, with AC from ₹2100/2400; ❀ ⊛ ⊛) One of the town's better choices, this hotel has large, well-furnished rooms and big bathrooms. It has a decent restaurant (mains ₹120 to ₹270) and bar. The pool is open in summer only, and breakfast is only included with the AC rooms. Turn left out of the train station and it's 300m down the road.

RTDC Hotel Meenal HOTEL $$

(☎ 2347352; Topsingh Circle; s/d ₹1400/1400; ❀) A respectable option with bland and tidy rooms typical of the chain. It's located about 1km south of town on the way to Sariska, so it's quiet and leafy, though a long way from the action.

Prem Pavitra Bhojnalaya INDIAN $

(near Hope Circle; mains ₹50-110; ⊙10.30am-4pm & 6.30-10pm; ❀) Alwar's renowned restaurant has been going since 1957. In the heart of the old town, it serves fresh, tasty pure veg food – try the delicious *aloo parathas* (bread stuffed with spicy potato) and *palak paneer* (unfermented cheese cubes in spinach purée). Servings are big; half-serves available.

You have to pay 10% extra to eat in the air-conditioned section – but it is worth it. Turn right out of the bus station, take the first left (towards Hope Circle) and it's on your left after 100m.

Angeethi MULTICUISINE $$

(Alwar Hotel, Manu Rd; mains ₹75-200; ⊙Tue-Sun; ❀) Alwar Hotel's restaurant serves first-rate Indian, Continental and Chinese food; the South Indian selection is particularly good. It's slightly gloomy in the restaurant but you can eat in the pleasant gardens.

ℹ Information

ICICI ATM Near the bus stand.

Merharwal's Internet Cyber Zoné (1 Company Bagh Rd; per hr ₹40; ⊙7am-10pm) Opposite Inderlok restaurant.

State Bank of Bikaner & Jaipur (Company Bagh Rd) Changes travellers cheques and major currencies and has an ATM. Near the bus stand.

Tourist Office (☎ 2347348; Nehru Rd; ⊙10am-5pm Mon-Sat) Helpful centre offering a map of Alwar and information on Sariska. Near the train station.

ℹ Getting There & Around

A cycle-rickshaw between the bus and train stations costs ₹30. Look out for the shared taxis that ply fixed routes around town (₹10). They come in the form of white minivans and have the word 'Vahini' printed on their side doors. One handy route goes past Hotel Aravali, the tourist office and the train station before continuing on to the bus station and terminating a short walk from Vinay Vilas Mahal (the palace complex).

A return taxi to Sariska Tiger Reserve will cost you around ₹1200.

BUS

Services from Alwar bus station:

Bharatpur (₹113, four hours, every hour from 5am to 8.30pm)

Deeg (₹60, 2½ hours, every hour from 5am to 8.30pm)

Delhi (₹129, four hours, every 20 minutes from 5am to 9pm)

Jaipur (₹120, four hours, half-hourly from 6am to 10.30pm)

Sariska (₹30, one hour, half-hourly from 6am to 10.30pm)

TRAIN

There are around a dozen daily trains to Delhi (3AC/sleeper ₹170/585, three to four hours), leaving throughout the day. Most services go to Old Delhi.

There are 16 daily trains to Jaipur (three to four hours). Prices are almost identical to those for Delhi.

Sariska Tiger Reserve

☎ 0144

Enclosed within the dramatic, shadowy folds of the Aravallis, the **Sariska Tiger Reserve** (Indian/foreigner ₹60/450, vehicle ₹250; ⊙ticket sales 7am-3.30pm Oct-Mar, 6.30am-4pm Apr-Sep, park closes at sunset) is a tangle of remnant semi-deciduous jungle and craggy canyons sheltering streams and lush greenery. It covers 866 sq km (including a core area of 498 sq km), and is home to peacocks, monkeys, majestic sambars, nilgai, chital, wild boars and jackals.

Although Project Tiger has been in charge of the sanctuary since 1979, there has been a dramatic failure in tiger protection. In 2004 there were an estimated 18 tigers in Sariska; however, this was called into question after an investigation by the WWF. That report prompted the federal government to investigate what has happened to the tigers of this reserve.

Sariska is in any case a fascinating sanctuary. Unlike most national parks, it opens year-round, although the best time to spot wildlife is from November to March, and you'll see most wildlife in the evening. During July and August your chances of spotting wildlife are minimal, as the animals move to higher ground, and the park is open primarily for temple pilgrimage rather than wildlife viewing.

Proposals to stop private-car access and to end the free access to pilgrims visiting the Hanuman temple often get press coverage, but to date there has been no further action taken.

◉ Sights

Besides wildlife, Sariska has some fantastic sights within the reserve and around its peripheries, which are well worth seeking out. If you take a longer tour, you can ask to visit one or more of these. A couple of them are also accessible by public bus.

Kankwari Fort   FORT
Deep inside the sanctuary, this imposing small jungle fort, 22km from Sariska, offers amazing views over the plains of the national park, dotted with red mud-brick villages. This is the inaccessible place that Aurangzeb chose to imprison his brother,

Dara Shikoh, Shah Jahan's chosen heir to the Mughal throne, for several years before he was beheaded.

A four- to five-hour **4WD safari** (one to five passengers plus guide) to Kankwari Fort from the Forest Reception Office near the reserve entrance costs ₹1600, plus guide fee (₹150).

Bhangarh   HISTORIC SITE
Around 55km from Sariska, beyond the inner park sanctuary and out in open countryside, is this deserted, well-preserved and notoriously haunted city. Founded in 1631 by Madho Singh, it had 10,000 dwellings, but was suddenly deserted about 300 years ago for reasons that remain mysterious. Bhangarh can be reached by a bus that runs twice daily through the sanctuary (₹35) to nearby Golaka village. Check what time the bus returns, otherwise you risk getting stranded.

☞ Tours

Private cars, including taxis, are limited to sealed roads. The best way to visit the park is by 4WD gypsy (open-topped, six-passenger 4WDs), which can explore off the main tracks. Gypsy safaris start at the park entrance and you'll be quoted ₹1050 for three

---

SARISKA'S TIGER TALE

Sariska Tiger Reserve took centre stage in one of India's most publicised wildlife dramas. In 2005 an Indian journalist broke the news that the tiger population here had been eliminated, a report that was later confirmed officially after an emergency census was carried out.

An inquiry into the crisis recommended fundamental management changes before tigers be reintroduced to the reserve. Extra funding was proposed to cover the relocation of villages within the park as well as increasing the protection force. But action on the recommendations has been slow and incomplete despite extensive media coverage and a high level of concern in India.

Nevertheless, a pair of tigers from Ranthambhore National Park were moved by helicopter to Sariska in 2008. By 2010, five tigers had been transferred. However, in November 2010 the male of the original pair was found dead, having been poisoned by local villagers, who are not supportive of the reintroduction. The underlying problem – the inevitable battle between India's poorest and ever-expanding village populace with the rare and phenomenally valuable wildlife on their doorstep. Plans to relocate and reimburse villagers inside the park have largely failed to come to fruition, and illegal marble mining and clashes between cattle farmers and park staff have remained a problem.

In early 2012 the first cubs were sighted. In recent years Sariska's tiger population was thought to be 13 – made up of seven females, two males and four cubs all born in the park.

Only time will tell if this reintroduction is successful – inbreeding in the small population is an understandably high concern. As things stand, Sariska remains a sad indictment of tiger conservation in India, from the top government officials down to the underpaid forest guards.

hours, or ₹3200 for a full day. Guides are available (₹150 for three hours).

Bookings can be made at the **Forest Reception Office** (⌨ 2841333; Jaipur Rd), directly opposite the Hotel Sariska Palace, which is where buses will drop you off.

🛏 Sleeping & Eating

RTDC Hotel Tiger Den   HOTEL $$
(⌨ 2841342; s/d incl breakfast ₹1900/2500, with AC ₹2400/3000; ❄) Hotel Tiger Den isn't a pretty place – it's an unattractive bloc backed by a rambling garden and the accommodation and meals are drab. On the plus side the rooms have balconies and occupy a pleasant setting close to the reserve entrance. Bring a mosquito net or repellent.

Alwar Bagh   HOTEL $$$
(⌨ 2945151412; www.alwarbagh.com; r from ₹4000; ❄≋) This is a very peaceful option located in the village of Dhawala, between Alwar (14km) and Sariska (19km). The bright heritage-style hotel boasts traditional styling, spotless rooms and romantic tents, an organic orchard, a garden restaurant and a gorgeous swimming pool. Pick-up and drop-off from Alwar can be arranged as well as safaris of Sariska.

Sariska Tiger Heaven   HOTEL $$$
(⌨ 9828225163; www.sariskatigerheaven.com; s/d with full board ₹6000/7500; ❄ 🏠 ≋) This isolated place about 3km west of the bus stop at Thanagazi village has free pick-up on offer. Rooms are set in stone-and-tile cottages and have big beds and windowed alcoves. It's a tranquil, if overpriced, place to stay. Staff can arrange 4WDs and guides to the reserve.

ⓘ Getting There & Away

Sariska is 35km from Alwar, a convenient town from which to approach the reserve. There are frequent (and crowded) buses from Alwar (₹30, one to 1½ hours, at least hourly) and on to Jaipur (₹85). Buses stop in front of the Forest Reception Office.

Ajmer

⌨ 0145 / POP 490,500

Ajmer is a bustling, chaotic city, 13km from the traveller haven of Pushkar. It surrounds the tranquil lake of Ana Sagar, and is itself ringed by the rugged Aravalli hills. Ajmer is Rajasthan's most important site in terms of Islamic history and heritage. It contains one of India's most important Muslim pilgrim-

age centres – the shrine of Khwaja Muin-ud-din Chishti, who founded India's most important Sufi order. As well as some superb examples of early Muslim architecture, Ajmer is also a significant centre for the Jain religion, possessing an amazing golden Jain temple. However, with Ajmer's combination of high-voltage crowds and traffic, most travellers choose to stay in laid-back Pushkar, and visit on a day trip.

⊙ Sights

Dargah of Khwaja
Muin-ud-din Chishti   ISLAMIC SHRINE
(www.dargahajmer.com; ⊙4am-9pm summer, 5am-9pm winter) This is the tomb of Sufi saint Khwaja Muin-ud-din Chishti, who came to Ajmer from Persia in 1192 and died here in 1236. The tomb gained its significance during the time of the Mughals – many emperors added to the buildings here. Construction of the shrine was completed by Humayun, and the gate was added by the Nizam of Hyderabad. Mughal emperor Akbar used to make the pilgrimage to the dargah from Agra every year.

You have to cover your head in certain parts of the shrine, so remember to take a scarf or cap – there are plenty for sale at the bazaar leading to the dargah, along with floral offerings and delicious toffees.

The main entrance is through **Nizam Gate** (1915). Inside, the green and white mosque, **Akbari Masjid**, was constructed in 1571 and is now an Arabic and Persian school for religious education. The next gate is called the **Nakkarkhana** because it has two large *nakkharas* (drums) fixed above it.

A third gate, **Buland Darwaza** (16th century), leads into the dargah courtyard. Flanking the entrance of the courtyard are the *degs* (large iron cauldrons), one donated by Akbar in 1567, the other by Jehangir in 1631, for offerings for the poor.

Inside this courtyard, the saint's domed tomb is surrounded by a silver platform. Pilgrims believe that the saint's spirit will intercede on their behalf in matters of illness, business or personal problems, so the notes and holy string attached to the railings around are thanks or requests.

Pilgrims and Sufis come from all over the world on the anniversary of the saint's death, the Urs, in the seventh month of the lunar calendar, Jyaistha. Crowds can be suffocating. Bags must be left in the cloakroom (₹10 each, with camera ₹20) outside the main entrance.

Ajmer

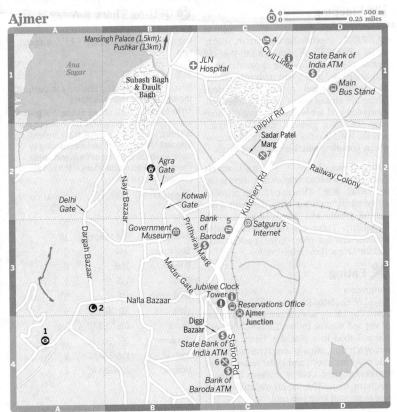

Adhai-din-ka-Jhonpra
HISTORIC SITE

(Two-and-a-Half-Day Building) Beyond the Dargah of Khwaja Muin-ud-din Chishti, on the town outskirts, are the extraordinary ruins of the Adhai-din-ka-Jhonpra mosque. According to legend, construction in 1153 took only two-and-a-half days. Others say it was named after a festival lasting two-and-a-half days. It was originally built as a Sanskrit college, but in 1198 Mohammed of Ghori seized Ajmer and converted the building into a mosque by adding a seven-arched wall covered with Islamic calligraphy in front of the pillared hall.

Nasiyan (Red) Temple
JAIN TEMPLE

(Prithviraj Marg; admission ₹10; ⊙8.30am-5.30pm) This marvellous Jain temple, built in 1865, is also known as the Golden Temple, due to its amazing display in the double-storey temple hall. The hall is filled with a huge golden diorama depicting the Jain concept of the ancient world, with 13 continents

and oceans, the intricate golden city of Ayodhya, flying peacock and elephant gondolas, and gilded elephants with many tusks. The hall is also decorated with gold, silver and precious stones. It's unlike any other temple in Rajasthan and is worth a visit.

Ajmer

◉ **Sights**

🛏 **Sleeping**

✕ **Eating**

🛏 Sleeping

Haveli Heritage Inn
HOTEL $$

(☑2621607; www.haveliheritageinn.com; Kutchery Rd; r ₹900-2875; 🖼) Set in a 140-year-old *haveli*, this is a welcoming city-centre oasis and arguably Ajmer's best midrange choice. The high-ceilinged rooms are spacious (some are almost suites), simply decorated, air-cooled and set well back from the busy road. There's a pleasant, grassy courtyard and the hotel is infused with a family atmosphere, complete with home-cooked meals.

Badnor House
GUESTHOUSE $$$

(☑2627579; www.badnorhouse.com; d incl breakfast ₹3000; 🖼🛜) This guesthouse provides an excellent opportunity to stay with a delightful family and receive down-to-earth hospitality. There are three heritage-style doubles and an older-style, spacious and comfortable self-contained suite.

🍴 Eating

Honeydew
MULTICUISINE $$

(☑2622498; Station Rd; mains ₹120-300; ⊙9am-11pm) The Honeydew offers a great selection of veg and nonveg Indian, Chinese and Continental food in a pleasant, clean, relaxed, but overly dim, atmosphere. It has long been one of Ajmer's best, and is the restaurant of choice for Mayo College students having a midterm treat. The ice cream, milkshakes and floats will keep you cool.

Mango Curry/Mango Masala
INDIAN, VEGETARIAN $$

(☑01452422100; Sadar Patel Marg; mains ₹100-280; ⊙9am-11pm) With dim, barlike lighting and nursery school decor, this is a popular Ajmer hang out. It's divided in two: Mango Curry is no alcohol and vegetarian, while Mango Masala has plenty of good nonveg options. Pizzas, Chinese, and North and South Indian are available throughout, plus cakes, ice cream and a bakery-deli.

🛈 Information

Bank of Baroda (Prithviraj Marg)
Bank of Baroda ATM (Station Rd)
JLN Hospital (☑2625500; Daulat Bagh)
Satguru's Internet (60-61 Kutchery Rd; per hr ₹20; ⊙9am-10pm)
State Bank of India ATM (Station Rd)
Tourist Office RTDC Hotel Khadim
(☑2627426; RTDC Hotel Khadim; ⊙9am-6pm Mon-Fri); Ajmer Junction Train Station (Ajmer Junction Train Station; ⊙9am-6pm)

🛈 Getting There & Away

For those passing through en route to Pushkar, haggle hard for a private taxi – ₹350 is a good rate.

BUS

Buses (₹14, 30 minutes) also leave throughout the day from the main bus stand.

The following table shows a sample of government-run buses leaving from the main bus stand in Ajmer. In addition to these, there are less-frequent 'deluxe' coach services running to major destinations such as Delhi and Jaipur. There is a 24-hour cloakroom at the bus stand (₹10 per bag per day).

DESTINATION	FARE (₹)	DURATION (HR)
Agra	297	10
Ahmedabad	455 Sleeper	13
Bharatpur	244	8
Bikaner	206	8
Bundi	135	5
Chittorgarh	146	5
Delhi	311/1051 AC	9
Jaipur	105/269 AC	2½
Jaisalmer	366/969 AC	10
Jodhpur	158/339 AC	6
Udaipur	229/554 AC	8

TRAIN

Ajmer is a busy train junction. To book tickets go to booth 5 at the train station's **reservations office** (⊙8am-8pm Mon-Sat, to 2pm Sun).

➤ Eleven trains run daily to Delhi (2nd class/sleeper ₹170/290, eight hours), mostly to Old Delhi or New Delhi stations, around the clock.

➤ At least two dozen trains leave throughout the day to Jaipur (2nd-class seat/sleeper/AC seat ₹90/170/305; less than three hours) – you won't have to wait for long.

➤ There are four daily trains to Udaipur (sleeper ₹205; five hours; 1.25am, 2.10am, 8.45am, 4.10pm).

➤ Only two direct trains go to Jodhpur (sleeper ₹175, five hours, 1.40pm and 2.25pm), while four go to Agra Fort (sleeper ₹265; 6½ hours; 2.10am, 6.30am, 12.50pm and 3pm).

➤ There are two daily trains to Mumbai (sleeper ₹460; 19 hours; 5.35pm and 11.15am).

➤ There are three reasonably timed daily trains to Chittorgarh (sleepers ₹140; 3½ hours; 1pm, 7.25pm and 9.05pm).

➤ For Mount Abu, there are 11 daily trains to Abu Road (sleeper ₹205; 11 hours).

MAJOR TRAINS FROM AJMER

DESTINATION	TRAIN NO & NAME	DEPARTURE TIME	ARRIVAL TIME	FARE (₹)
Agra (Fort)	12988 Ajmer-SDAH Exp	12.50pm	6.05pm	265/511 (A)
Delhi (New Delhi)	12016 Ajmer Shatabdi	3.45am	10.40am	865/1690 (B)
Jaipur	12991 Udaipur-Jaipur Exp	11.30am	1.30pm	90/305 (C)
Jodhpur	54802 Ajmer-Jodhpur Fast Passenger	2.25pm	7.55pm	120/485 (D)
Udaipur	09721 Jaipur-Udaipur SF SPL	8.45am	1.45pm	130/470/535 (D)

Fares: (A) sleeper/3AC, (B) AC chair/1AC, (C) 2nd-class seat/AC chair, (D) 2nd-class seat/AC chair/3AC

Pushkar

0145 / POP 14,800

Pushkar has a magnetism all of its own, and is quite unlike anywhere else in Rajasthan. It's a prominent Hindu pilgrimage town and devout Hindus should visit at least once in their lifetime. The town curls around a holy lake, said to have appeared when Brahma dropped a lotus flower. It also has one of the world's few Brahma temples. With 52 bathing ghats and 400 milky-blue temples, the town often hums with *pujas* (prayers) generating an episodic soundtrack of chanting, drums and gongs, and devotional songs.

The result is a muddle of religious and tourist scenes. The main street is one long bazaar, selling everything to tickle a traveller's fancy, from hippy-chic tie-dye to didgeridoos. Despite the commercialism and banana pancakes, the town remains enchantingly small and authentically mystic.

Pushkar is only 11km from Ajmer, separated by Nag Pahar, the Snake Mountain.

⊙ Sights

Shiva Temples   HINDU TEMPLE
About 8km southwest of the town (past the turn-off to Saraswati Temple) is a collection of Shiva temples near Ajaypal, which make a great trip by motorbike (or bike if you're fit and start early in the day), through barren hills and quiet villages. Be warned: the track is hilly and rocky.

Another Shiva temple is about 8km north of Pushkar, tucked down inside a cave, which would make for a good excursion.

Ghats
Fifty-two bathing ghats surround the lake, where pilgrims bathe in the sacred waters. If you wish to join them, do so with respect. Remember, this is a holy place: remove your shoes and don't smoke or take photographs.

Some ghats have particular importance: Vishnu appeared at Varah Ghat in the form of a boar, Brahma bathed at Brahma Ghat, and Gandhi's ashes were sprinkled at Gandhi Ghat, formerly Gau Ghat.

🏃 Activities

Shannu's Riding School   HORSE RIDING
(2772043; www.shannus.weebly.com; Panch Kund Marg; ride/lesson per hr ₹400) French-Canadian and long-time Pushkar resident Marc Dansereau can organise riding lessons and horse safaris on his graceful Marwari steeds. You can stay here too (p138). The ranch is on the southeastern fringes of Pushkar, off the Ajmer Road.

Government
Homeopathic Hospital   AYURVEDIC MASSAGE
(9413094664; Ajmer Rd; 1hr full-body massage ₹450, steam bath ₹50; 9am-1pm) For a totally noncommercial massage-treatment experience, try the ayurvedic department at the small and basic Government Homeopathic Hospital.

Roshi Hiralal Verma   REIKI, YOGA
(9829895906; Ambika Guesthouse, Laxmi Market) Offers reiki, yoga and shiatsu; costs depend on the duration and nature of your session.

Pushkar

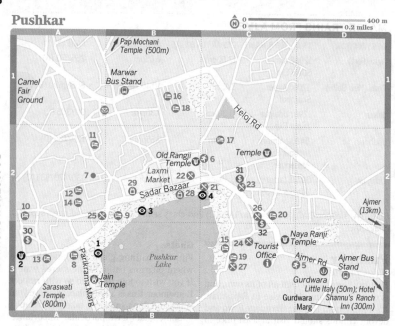

🐘 Courses

Saraswati Music School   MUSIC
(📱 Birju 9828297784, Hemant 9829333548; Mainon ka Chowk) Teaches classical *tabla* (drums), flute, singing and *kathak* (classical dance). For music, contact Birju, who's been playing for around 20 years, and charges from ₹350 for two hours. He often conducts evening performances (7pm to 8pm), and also sells instruments. For dance, contact Hemant.

Cooking Bahar   COOKING
(📱 2773124; www.cookingbahar.com; Mainon ka Chowk; 3hr class ₹1000) Part of the Saraswati Music School family, Deepa conducts cooking classes with three vegetarian courses.

🧭 Tours

Plenty of people in Pushkar offer short camel rides (around ₹200 per hour), which are a good way to explore the starkly beautiful landscape – a mixture of desert and rocky hills – around town. Sunset rides are the most popular. Ask for recommendations at your hotel. For longer camel treks, prices start at around ₹500 per person per day for a group of four. You can head out to Jodhpur (five to six days) or even Jaisalmer (10 to 12 days). Numerous operators line Ajmer Rd, but note, these places are less professional than the operators in Jaisalmer and Bikaner.

🛏 Sleeping

Owing to Pushkar's star status among backpackers, there are more budget than midrange options, though many have a selection of midrange-priced rooms. At the time of the camel fair, prices are up to threefold or more, and it's essential to book several weeks ahead.

⭐ **Shyam Krishna Guesthouse**   GUESTHOUSE **$**
(📱 2772461; skguesthouse@yahoo.com; Sadar Bazaar; s/d ₹500/600, without bathroom ₹300/500; 📶) Housed in a lovely old blue-washed building with lawns and gardens, this guesthouse has ashram austerity and genuinely friendly management. Some of the cheaper rooms are cell-like, though all share the simple, authentic ambience. The outdoor kitchen and garden seating are a good setting for a relaxing meal of hearty vegetarian fare, but watch out for passing troops of monkeys.

Bharatpur Palace   HOTEL **$**
(📱 2772320; bharatpurpalace_pushkar@yahoo.co.in; Sadar Bazaar; r ₹500-700, without bathroom ₹250-400; ❋) This rambling building occupies one of the best spots in Pushkar, on the upper levels adjacent to Gandhi Ghat. It features aesthetic blue-washed simplicity: bare-bones rooms with unsurpassed views of the holy lake. The rooftop terrace (with

Pushkar

restaurant) has sublime views, but respect for bathing pilgrims is paramount. Room 1 is the most romantic place to wake in: it's surrounded on three sides by the lake. Rooms 9, 12, 13 and 16 are also good.

Alka Guest House
GUESTHOUSE $

(☑ 9782642546, 2773082; Brahm Chowk, Badi Basti; s/d ₹300/400; ☎) Run by a welcoming but quiet family, Alka has rooms overlooking a large, tree-shaded courtyard. Each is small and basic but neat and tidy, and they come with unusual dressing areas that lend more space. Common bathrooms only, but showers are always hot.

Hotel Everest
HOTEL $

(☑ 2773417; www.pushkarhoteleverest.com; Sadar Bazaar; r ₹200-600, with AC ₹850; ❀ @ ☎) This welcoming budget hotel is nestled in the quiet laneways north of Sadar Bazaar and is convenient to the mela (fair) ground. It's run by a friendly father-and-son team who can't do too much for their appreciative guests. The rooms are variable in size, colourful and spotless and the beds are comfortable. The roof is a pleasant retreat for meals or just relaxing with a book.

Pushkar Inn's Hotel
HOTEL $

(☑ 2772010; hotelpushkarinns@yahoo.com; r ₹800, without bathroom ₹200, with AC ₹1500; ❀ ☎) A charming little hotel comprising a row of clean and bright rooms, backed

by a garden and orchard. The rooms catch the breeze from the lake and that is mostly a positive, though some wafts are less than holy. The best rooms have lake views.

Hotel Paramount Palace
HOTEL $

(☑ 0145-2772428; www.pushkarparamount.com; r ₹200-1000; ☎) Perched on the highest point in town overlooking an old temple, this welcoming hotel has excellent views of the town and lake (and lots of stairs). The rooms vary widely; the best (106, 108 and 109) have lovely balconies, stained-glass windows and are good value, but the smaller rooms can be dingy. There's a magical rooftop terrace.

Milkman Guesthouse
GUESTHOUSE $

(☑ 2773452; vinodmilkman@hotmail.com; off Heloj Rd; dm/r without bathroom ₹150/300, r ₹500-700; ❀ @ ☎) Milkman is a cosy guesthouse in a backstreet location with relaxing rooftop retreat featuring the Ooh-la-la Café and a lawn with high-altitude tortoises. The rooms are all brightly decorated with paintings. Some of the cheaper rooms are small and doorways are low, though the bright colours, cleanliness and friendly family atmosphere keep this place cheerful.

Hotel White House
GUESTHOUSE $

(☑ 2772147; www.pushkarwhitehouse.com; off Heloj Rd; r ₹250-850, with AC ₹1000-1300; ❀ @) This place is indeed white, with spotless rooms. Some are decidedly on the small side, but the nicest are generous and have balconies to boot. There is good traveller fare and green views from the plant-filled rooftop restaurant. It's efficiently run by a tenacious businesslike mother-and-son team. Yoga is offered.

Hotel Akash   HOTEL $

(☎ 2772498; filterboy21@yahoo.com; d ₹600, s/d without bathroom ₹300/500) A simple budget place with keen young management and a large tree sprouting up from the courtyard to shade the rooftop terrace. Rooms are basic fan-cooled affairs that open out to a balcony restaurant.

★ Inn Seventh Heaven   HERITAGE HOTEL $$

(☎ 5105455; www.inn-seventh-heaven.com; Chotti Basti; r ₹1100-3000; ❋ @ 🛜) You enter this lovingly converted *haveli* through heavy wooden doors and into an incense-perfumed courtyard, centred with a marble fountain and surrounded by tumbling vines. There are just a dozen individually decorated rooms situated on three levels, all with traditionally crafted furniture and comfortable beds. Rooms vary in size, from the downstairs budget rooms to the spacious Asana suite. On the roof you'll find the excellent Sixth Sense restaurant as well as sofas and swing chairs for relaxing with a book. Early booking (two-night minimum, no credit cards) is recommended.

Hotel Shannu's Ranch Inn   GUESTHOUSE $$

(☎ 2772043; www.shannus.weebly.com; Panch Kund Marg; s/d ₹1000/1500, ste ₹2000) Especially for horse lovers but not exclusively so, this relaxed, family-run hotel is just a short walk from the lake. There is a large garden compound featuring the family home, separate guest accommodation and, of course, the stables housing Marc's beloved Marwari horses (p135). There are usually a couple of friendly dogs wandering around. The large suites easily accommodate a family of five.

Hotel Navaratan Palace   HOTEL $$

(☎ 2772145; www.pushkarnavaratanpalace.co.in; r ₹750-950, with AC ₹1050; ❋ 🞐) Located close to the Brahma Temple, this hotel has a lovely enclosed garden with a fabulous pool (₹100 for nonguests), a children's playground and pet tortoises. The rooms are clean, small and crammed with carved wooden furniture.

Hotel Kishan Palace   HOTEL $$

(☎ 2773056; www.kishanpalacepushkar.com; Panch Kund Marg; s/d from ₹800/1200, ste ₹4500; ❋ @) A welcoming, brightly coloured hotel with abundant potted plants and a range of well-appointed rooms. The blue-domed

PUSHKAR CAMEL FAIR

Come the month of Kartika, the eighth lunar month of the Hindu calendar and one of the holiest, Thar camel drivers spruce up their ships of the desert and start the long walk to Pushkar in time for Kartik Purnima (Full Moon). Each year around 200,000 people converge here, bringing with them some 50,000 camels, horses and cattle. The place becomes an extraordinary swirl of colour, sound and movement, thronged with musicians, mystics, tourists, traders, animals, devotees and camera crews.

Trading begins a week before the official fair (a good time to arrive to see the serious business), but by the time the RTDC *mela* (fair) starts, business takes a back seat and the bizarre sidelines (snake charmers, children balancing on poles etc) jostle onto centre stage. Even the cultural program seems peculiar, with events such as a contest for the best moustache, and most beautifully decorated camel. Visitors are encouraged to take part: pick up a program from the RTDC office and see if you fancy taking part in the costumed wedding parade, or join a 'Visitors versus Locals' sports contest such as traditional Rajasthani wrestling.

It's hard to believe, but this seething mass is all just a sideshow. Kartik Purnima is when Hindu pilgrims come to bathe in Pushkar's sacred waters. The religious event builds in tandem with the camel fair in a wild, magical crescendo of incense, chanting and processions to dousing day, the last night of the fair, when thousands of devotees wash away their sins and set candles afloat on the holy lake.

Although fantastical, mystical and a one-off, it must be said that it's also crowded, touristy, noisy (light sleepers should bring earplugs) and occasionally tacky. Those affected by dust and/or animal hair should bring appropriate medication. However, it's a grand epic and is not to be missed if you're anywhere within camel-spitting distance.

It usually takes place in November but dates change according to the lunar calendar.

rooftop terrace is very communal, with guests mingling, munching and watching the satellite TV.

Hotel Pushkar Palace　　HERITAGE HOTEL **$$$**
(📞 2772001; www.hotelpushkarpalace.com; r incl breakfast ₹7000; ❄ @) Once belonging to the maharaja of Kishangarh, the top-end Hotel Pushkar Palace boasts a romantic lakeside setting. The rooms have carved wooden furniture and beds, and the suites look directly out onto the lake: no hotel in Pushkar has better views. A pleasant outdoor dining area overlooks the lake.

✖ Eating

Pushkar has plenty of atmospheric eateries with lake views and menus reflecting backpacker tastes and preferences. Strict vegetarianism, forbidding even eggs, is the order of the day.

Shri Vankatesh　　INDIAN **$**
(Chooti Basti; mains ₹40-90; ⏱ 9am-10pm) Head to this no-nonsense locals favourite and tuck into some dhal, paneer or kofta, before mopping up the sauce with some freshly baked chapatis and washing it all down with some good old-fashioned chai. The thalis (₹70 to ₹130) are excellent value too. There's some upstairs seating overlooking the street.

Falafel Wrap Stalls　　MIDDLE EASTERN **$**
(Sadar Bazaar; wraps ₹60-120; ⏱ 7.30am-10.30pm) Perfect for quelling a sudden attack of the munchies, and a big hit with Israeli travellers, these two adjacent roadside joints knock up a choice selection of filling falafel-and-hummus wraps.

Om Shiva Garden Restaurant　MULTICUISINE **$**
(📞 5105045; mains ₹70-170; ⏱ 7.30am-late) A traveller stalwart, Om Shiva continues to satisfy with its ₹80 buffet. Wood-fired pizzas and espresso coffee feature on the menu.

Sixth Sense　　MULTICUISINE **$$**
(Inn Seventh Heaven, Chotti Basti; mains ₹80-200; ⏱ 8.30am-4pm & 6-10pm; 🕾) This chilled rooftop restaurant is a great place to head to even if you didn't score a room in its popular hotel. The pizza and Indian seasonal vegetables and rice are all serviceable, as are the filter coffee and fresh juice. Its ambience is immediately relaxing and the pulley apparatus that delivers food from the ground-floor kitchen is very cunning.

Save room for the desserts, such as the excellent homemade tarts.

Naryan Café　　CAFE **$$**
(Mahadev Chowk, Sadar Bazaar; juices from ₹80, breakfast from ₹90) Busy any time of day, this is particular popular as a breakfast stop: watch the world go by with a fresh coffee or juice and an enormous bowl of homemade muesli, topped with a mountain of fruit.

Sunset Café　　MULTICUISINE **$$**
(mains ₹75-200; ⏱ 7.30am-midnight; 🕾) Right on the eastern ghats, this cafe has sublime lake views. It offers the usual traveller menu, including curries, pizza and pasta, plus there's a German bakery serving reasonable cakes. The lakeside setting is perfect at sunset and gathers a crowd.

Out of the Blue　　ITALIAN **$$**
(Sadar Bazaar; mains ₹100-200; ⏱ 8am-11pm; 🕾) Distinctly a deeper shade of blue in this sky-blue town, Out of the Blue is a reliable restaurant. The menu ranges from noodles and *momos* (Tibetan dumplings) to pizza, pasta (those *momos* occasionally masquerade as ravioli) and pancakes. A nice touch is the street-level espresso coffee bar and German bakery.

Honey & Spice　　MULTICUISINE **$$**
(Laxmi Market, off Sadar Bazaar; mains ₹90-340; ⏱ 7.30am-6.45pm) 🍃 Run by a friendly family, this tiny wholefood breakfast and lunch place has delicious South Indian coffee and homemade cakes. Even better are the salads and hearty vegetable stews served with brown rice – delicious, wholesome and a welcome change from frequently oil-rich Indian food.

🛍 Shopping

Pushkar's Sadar Bazaar is lined with enchanting little shops and is a good place to pick up gifts. Many of the vibrant textiles come from the Barmer district south of Jaisalmer. There's plenty of silver and beaded jewellery catering to foreign tastes, and some old tribal pieces, too. As Pushkar is touristy, you'll have to haggle.

Lala International　　CLOTHING
(Sadar Bazaar; ⏱ 9.30am-8pm) Brilliantly colourful women's clothing, with modern designs but Indian in theme. Dresses and skirts start from around ₹500. Prices are clearly labelled and fixed.

Khadi Gramodhyog　　CLOTHING
(Sadar Bazaar; ⏱ 10am-6pm Mon-Sat) Khadi Gramodhyog, almost hidden on the main

drag, is a fixed-price shop selling traditional hand-woven shirts, scarves and shawls.

ℹ Information

Foreign-card-friendly ATMs and unofficial moneychangers are dotted around Sadar Bazaar. Internet cafes are sprinkled around the lanes, and tend to charge ₹40 per hour, but most guesthouses and many restaurants and cafes have free wi-fi.

Post Office (off Heloj Rd; ◷ 9.30am-5pm) Near the Marwar bus stand.

State Bank of Bikaner & Jaipur (SBBJ; Sadar Bazaar; ◷ 10am-4pm Mon-Fri, to 12.30pm Sat) Changes travellers cheques and cash. The SBBJ ATM accepts international cards.

Thomas Cook (Sadar Bazaar; ◷ 9.30am-6.30pm Mon-Sat) Changes cash and travellers cheques and also provides train and flight ticketing.

Tourist Office (☑ 01452772040; Hotel Sarovar; ◷ 10am-5pm) Free maps and camel fair programs. Located in the grounds of RTDC Hotel Sarovar.

DANGERS & ANNOYANCES

Beware of anyone peddling flowers to offer as a *puja* (prayer): before you know it you'll be whisked to the ghats in a well-oiled hustle and asked for a personal donation of up to ₹1000. Some priests do genuinely live off the donations of others and this is a tradition that goes back centuries – but walk away if you feel bullied and always agree on a price before taking a red ribbon (a 'Pushkar passport') or flowers.

During the camel fair, Pushkar is besieged by pickpockets working the crowded bazaars. You can avoid the razor gang by not using thin-walled daypacks and by carrying your daypack in front of you. At any time of year, watch out for stray motorbikes in the bazaar.

ℹ Getting There & Away

Frequent buses to/from Ajmer (₹14, 30 minutes) stop on the road heading eastwards out of town; other buses leave from the Marwar bus stand to the north. A private taxi to Ajmer costs around ₹300 (note that it's almost always more expensive in the opposite direction). When entering Pushkar by car there is a toll of ₹20 per person.

Local travel agencies sell tickets for private buses – you should shop around. These buses generally leave from Ajmer, but the agencies should provide you with free connecting transport. Check whether your bus is direct as many services from Pushkar aren't. And note, even if they are direct buses they may well stop for some time in Ajmer, meaning it's often quicker to go to Ajmer first and then catch another bus from there.

ℹ Getting Around

There are no autorickshaws, but it's a breeze to get around on foot. If you want to explore the surrounding countryside, you could try hiring a scooter (₹250 per day) from one of the many places around town. For something more substantial, try **Shreeram Enfield Gairej** (Ajmer Rd; Enfield hire per day ₹500, deposit ₹50,000). They hire Enfield Bullets for ₹500 per day and sell them from ₹60,000.

Ranthambhore National Park

☑ 07462

This famous national park, open from 1 October to 30 June, is the best place to spot wild tigers in Rajasthan. Comprising 1334 sq km of wild jungle scrub hemmed in by rocky ridges, at its centre is the 10th-century Ranthambhore Fort. Scattered around the fort are ancient temples and mosques, hunting pavilions, crocodile-filled lakes and vine-covered *chhatris* (burial tombs). The park was a maharajas' hunting ground until 1970, a curious 15 years after it had become a sanctuary. Tiger numbers are reasonably healthy for a park of Ranthambhore's size (around 48 when surveyed in 2014), but the threat of poaching remains, requiring constant vigilance to protect the big cats.

Seeing a tiger is partly a matter of luck; leave time for two or three safaris to improve your chances. But remember there's plenty of other wildlife to see, including more than 300 species of birds.

It's 10km from Sawai Madhopur (the gateway town for Ranthambhore) to the first gate of the park, and another 3km to the main gate and Ranthambhore Fort. There's a bunch of cheap (and rather grotty) hotels near Sawai Madhopur train station, but the nicest accommodation is stretched out along Ranthambhore Rd, which eventually leads to the park. It's ₹50 to ₹100 for an auto from the train station to Ranthambhore Rd, depending on where you get off. Many hotels, though, will pick you up from the train station for free if you call ahead.

If you want to walk, turn left out of the train station and follow the road up to the overpass (200m). Turn left and cross the bridge over the railway line to reach a roundabout (200m), known as Hammir Circle. Turn right here to reach the Safari Booking Office (1.5km). But turn left to reach the better accommodation options.

🏃 Activities

Safaris take place in the early morning and late afternoon, starting between 6am and 7am, and between 2pm and 3pm, depending on the time of year. Each safari lasts for around three hours. The mornings can be exceptionally chilly in the open vehicles, so bring warm clothes.

The best option is to travel by gypsy (six-person open-topped 4WD; Indian/foreigner ₹528/927 per person). You have a chance of seeing a tiger from a canter (20-seat open-topped truck; Indian/foreigner ₹400/800), but other passengers can be rowdy. Be aware that the rules for booking safaris (and prices) are prone to change. At present, you have to book online through the park's official website (http://rajasthanwildlife.in), which we highly recommend you do, or go in person to the Safari Booking Office, which is inconveniently located 1.5km from Hammir Circle, in the opposite direction to the park from the accommodation on Ranthambhore Rd. You cannot book safaris in person in advance of the day you want to do the safari (you can only do that online). To be sure of getting a seat in a vehicle, start queuing at least an hour (if not two) before the safaris are due to begin – a very early start for morning safaris!

To visit the magical 10th-century Ranthambhore Fort (⊘6am-6pm) FREE on the cheap, join the locals who go there to visit the temple dedicated to Ganesh. Shared 4WDs (₹30 to ₹40 per person) leave from the train station for the park entrance – say 'national park' and they'll know what you want. From there, other shared 4WDs (₹20 per person) shuttle to and from the fort, which is inside the park.

🛏 Sleeping

Budget travellers may find the cheapest lodgings in Sawai Madhopur itself, but it isn't a particularly inspiring place to stay. All of the places on Ranthambhore Rd can help with safari bookings, though some are better at this than others. Some hotels may close when the park is closed.

Hotel Aditya Resort   HOTEL $
(☑9414728468; www.adityaresort.com; Ranthambhore Rd; r ₹400-700; ❋@🛜) This friendly place represents good value for money and is one of the better of the ultra-cheapies in town. There are just six simple, unadorned rooms (get one with an outside window;

only a couple have air-conditioning), and a basic rooftop restaurant. The keen young staff will help with safari bookings.

Hotel Tiger Safari Resort   HOTEL $$
(☑221137; www.tigersafariresort.com; Ranthambhore Rd; r ₹1600-2200; ❋@🛜🏊) A reasonable budget option, with spacious doubles and so-called cottages (larger rooms with bigger bathrooms) facing a garden and small pool. The management is adept at organising safaris, wake-up calls and early breakfasts before the morning safari, although like the other hotels they throw in a chunky commission. There's an expensive restaurant.

Hotel Ankur Resort   HOTEL $$
(☑220792; www.hotelankurresort.com; r incl breakfast ₹2000, cottages ₹2500; ❋@🏊) Ankur Resort is good at organising safaris, wake-up calls and early breakfasts for tiger spotters. Standard rooms are fairly unadorned but clean and comfortable with TVs. The cottages boast better beds, fridge and settee overlooking the surrounding gardens and pool.

Vatika Resort   HOTEL $$
(☑222457; www.ranthambhorevatikaresort.com; Ranthambhore Rd; r ₹1800, incl breakfast/all meals ₹2250/3000; ❋@🛜) A lovely little guesthouse with simple but immaculate rooms, each with terrace seating overlooking a beautifully tended, flower-filled garden. It's about 1km beyond the main strip of accommodation on Ranthambhore Rd (although still 5km before the park's main gate) so much quieter than elsewhere. It's 3km from Hammir Circle.

ℹ Information

There's an ATM just by Hammir Circle, as well as others by the train station.

Post Office (Sawai Madhoper) Located 400m northeast of the train station.

Ranthambore Adventure Tours (☑9414214460; ranthambhoretours@rediff.mail.com; Ranthambhore Rd) Safari agency that gets good reviews.

Safari Booking Office (www.rajasthanwildlife.com) Seats in gypsies and canters can be reserved on the website, though a single gypsy and five canters are also kept for direct booking at the Forest Office. Located 500m from the train station.

Tiger Track Internet (☑222790; Ranthambhore Rd; per hr ₹60; ⊘7am-10.30pm) Near Ankur Resort Hotel, 1.5km from Hammir Circle.

Tourist office (☎220808; Train Station; ⏰9.30am-6pm Mon-Fri) Has maps of Sawai Madhopur, and can offer suggestions on safaris.

❶ Getting There & Away

BUS

There are very few direct buses to anywhere of interest so it's always preferable to take the train. Three direct buses leave for Bundi (6am, 6.45am and 2pm; ₹93; five hours) from the Tonk bus stand (take the second left out of the train station and the bus stand is on your right after the petrol station).

TRAIN

➡ Trains run almost hourly to Kota (sleeper ₹100, less than two hours), from where you can catch buses to Bundi.

➡ There are six daily trains to Jaipur (2nd-class seats/sleeper ₹90/170; two hours; 2.05am, 5.55am, 9.40am, 10.40am, 2.35pm and 7.15pm), although plenty of others run on selected days so you rarely have to wait more than an hour.

➡ Ten trains run daily around the clock to Delhi (sleeper/3AC ₹250/635, 5½ to eight hours).

➡ A daily train goes to Agra (Agra Fort station; sleeper ₹200, six hours, 11.15pm).

➡ For Keoladeo Ghana National Park, nine daily trains go to Bharatpur (sleeper/3AC ₹170/535, 2½ hours).

UDAIPUR & SOUTHERN RAJASTHAN

Bundi

☑ 0747 / POP 88,900

A captivating town with narrow lanes of Brahmin-blue houses, lakes, hills, bazaars and a temple at every turn, Bundi is dominated by a fantastical palace of faded parchment cupolas and loggias rising from the hillside above the town. Though an increasingly popular traveller hang-out, Bundi attracts nothing like the tourist crowds of Jaipur or Udaipur, nor are its streets choked with noisy, polluting vehicles or dense throngs of people. Few places in Rajasthan retain so much of the magical atmosphere of centuries past.

Bundi came into its own in the 12th century when a group of Chauhan nobles from Ajmer were pushed south by Mohammed of Ghori. They wrested the Bundi area from the Mina and Bhil tribes, and made Bundi the capital of their kingdom, known as Hadoti.

Bundi was loyal to the Mughals from the late 16th century onwards, but it maintained its independent status until incorporated into the state of Rajasthan after 1947.

❂ Sights

Bundi has around 60 beautiful *baoris* (stepwells), some right in the town centre. The majesty of many of them is unfortunately diminished by their lack of water today – a result of declining groundwater levels – and by the rubbish that collects in them which noone bothers to clean up. The most impressive, **Raniji-ki-Baori** (Queen's Step-Well), is 46m deep and decorated with sinuous carvings, including the avatars of Lord Vishnu. The **Nagar Sagar Kund** is a pair of matching step-wells just outside the old city's Chogan Gate.

Bundi Palace   PALACE

(Garh Palace; Indian/foreigner ₹20/200, camera/video ₹50/100; ⏰8am-5pm) This extraordinary, partly decaying edifice – described by Rudyard Kipling as 'the work of goblins rather than of men' – almost seems to grow out of the rock of the hillside it stands on. Though large sections are still closed up and left to the bats, the rooms that are open hold a series of fabulous, fading turquoise-and-gold murals that are the palace's chief treasure. The palace was constructed during the reign of Rao Raja Ratan Ji Heruled (Ratan Singh; 1607–31) and added to by his successors.

If you are going up to Taragarh as well as the palace, get tickets for both at the palace entrance. Once inside the palace's **Hathi Pol** (Elephant Gate), climb the stairs to the Ratan Daulat or Diwan-e-Aam (Hall of Public Audience), with a white marble coronation throne. You then pass into the Chhatra Mahal, added by Rao Raja Chhatra Shabji in 1644, with some fine but rather weathered murals. Stairs lead up to the Phool Mahal (1607), whose murals include an immense royal procession, and then the Badal Mahal (Cloud Palace; also 1607), with Bundi's very best murals, including a wonderful Chinese-inspired ceiling, divided into petal shapes and decorated with peacocks and Krishnas.

Taragarh   FORT

(Star Fort; Indian/foreigner ₹20/200, camera/video ₹50/100; ⏰8am-5pm) This ramshackle, partly overgrown 14th-century fort, on the hilltop above Bundi Palace, is a wonderful place to ramble around – but take a stick to battle

Bundi

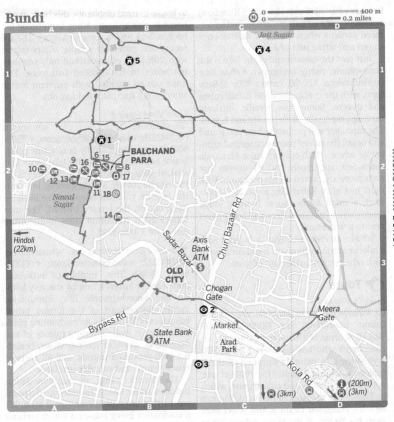

Bundi

◉ Sights
1 Bundi Palace	B2
2 Nagar Sagar Kund	C3
3 Raniji-ki-Baori	C4
4 Sukh Mahal	C1
5 Taragarh	B1

🛏 Sleeping
6 Bundi Vilas	A2
7 Haveli Braj Bhushanjee	A2
8 Haveli Elephant Stable	B2
9 Haveli Katkoun	A2
10 Hotel Bundi Haveli	A2
11 Kasera Heritage View	A2

12 Lake View Paying Guest House	A2
13 Nawal Sagar Palace	A2
14 RN Haveli	B2

✗ Eating
15 Out of the Blue	B2
16 Rainbow Cafe	A2

🛍 Shopping
17 Yug Art	B2

ℹ Information
Front Page Cyber Cafe	(see 8)
18 Roshan Tour & Travel	B2

the overgrown vegetation, help the knees on the steep climb and provide confidence when surrounded by testosterone-charged macaques. To reach it, just continue on the path up behind the Chitrasala.

Jait Sagar   LAKE
Round the far side of the Taragarh hill, about 2km north from the centre of town, this picturesque, 1.5km-long lake is flanked by hills and strewn with pretty lotus flowers during the monsoon and winter months. At

its near end, the Sukh Mahal (◷10am-5pm) is a small summer palace surrounded by terraced gardens where Rudyard Kipling once stayed and wrote part of *Kim*.

Just past the eastern end of the lake is the atmospheric, partly overgrown Kshar Bag (Indian/foreigner ₹20/50, camera ₹50; ◷9am-5pm), with the cenotaphs of 66 Bundi rulers and queens. Some have terrific, intricate carvings, especially of elephants and horses. The caretaker will probably show you round and detail the rulers' names, dates and number of wives – 17th-century ruler Maharaja Satru Sele apparently had 64 queens but even more are carved on his cenotaph. Fork right just after Kshar Bag to reach Shikar Burj, a small former royal hunting lodge (once there were tigers, deer and boars here) next to a water tank.

It's nice to visit Jait Sagar by bicycle; with a bike or autorickshaw you could combine it with other sights further out of town.

☞ Tours

Kukki's World TOUR
(☑9828404527; www.kukkisworld.com; 43 New Colony; half-/full-day tour ₹1000/1600) OP 'Kukki' Sharma is a passionate amateur archaeologist who has discovered around 70 prehistoric rock painting sites in a lifetime's exploring around Bundi. His trips get you out into the villages and countryside, which he knows like the back of his hand. You can visit his collection of finds and select sites from his laptop at his house (about 300m south of the tourist office) beforehand. Vehicle hire is not included in the tour price.

🛏 Sleeping

Most accommodation clusters in the Balchand Para area beneath the palace. Most places will pick you up from the train station or bus stand if you call ahead. Mosquitoes can be a nuisance in places near Nawal Sagar: keep repellent handy.

RN Haveli GUESTHOUSE $
(☑2443278, 9784486854; rnhavelibundi@yahoo.co.in; Rawle ka Chowk; s/d ₹500/700, without bathroom ₹250/350, with AC ₹800/1000; ☒) This old, slightly rundown house has reasonably well-decorated rooms and a cute garden where you can eat the delicious home cooking. A sound budget choice.

Haveli Elephant Stable GUESTHOUSE $
(☑9928154064; rajnandini1979@gmail.com; Surang Gate; dm ₹250, r ₹300-600) Once used

to house 15 royal elephants, this basic guesthouse is now a shanty home-from-home for backpackers with a sense of history. The six rooms are extremely simple affairs (some with 20ft-high ceilings!) and only one has hot water in its attached bathroom. The huge garden – dotted with elephant tether stones – is a fine place to hang out.

Lake View Paying Guest House GUESTHOUSE $
(☑2442326; lakeviewbundi@yahoo.com; r ₹300-600) Overseen by a kindly family, this guesthouse has some rooms with lake views and stained-glass windows. The side rooms by the restaurant are a little gloomy, but with the lake on your doorsteps you're likely to hang out on the terrace instead. The nice little garden restaurant does multicuisine dishes for ₹70 to ₹150.

★ Haveli Braj Bhushanjee HERITAGE HOTEL $$
(☑2442322; www.kiplingsbundi.com; r ₹1200-5000; ☒☎) This rambling, authentic, 200-year-old *haveli* is run by the very helpful and knowledgeable Braj Bhushanjee family, descendants of the former prime ministers of Bundi. It's an enchanting place with original stone interiors (plenty of low doorways), splendid rooftop views, beautiful, well-preserved murals, and all sorts of other historic and valuable artefacts.

The terrific range of accommodation includes some lovely, recently modernised rooms that are still in traditional style. It's a fascinating living museum where you can really get a feel for Bundi's heritage.

Haveli Katkoun GUESTHOUSE $$
(☑2444311; www.katkounhavelibundi.com; s from ₹700, d ₹1200-3200; ☒☎) Just outside the town's western gate, Katkoun is a completely revamped *haveli* with friendly management. It boasts large, spotless rooms offering superb views to either the lake or palace, and has a good rooftop restaurant (mains ₹65 to ₹200).

Kasera Heritage View GUESTHOUSE $$
(☑2444679; www.kaseraheritageview.com; s/d from ₹600/800; ☒@☎) A revamped *haveli*, Kasera has an incongruously modern lobby, but offers a range of slightly more authentic rooms. The welcome is friendly, it's all cheerfully decorated, the rooftop restaurant has great views, and discounts of 40% to 50% are frequently offered.

Bundi Vilas HERITAGE HOTEL $$
(☑5120694; www.bundivilas.com; r incl breakfast ₹4500-5500; ☒@) This 300-year-old *haveli*

up a side alley has been tastefully renovated with Jaisalmer sandstone, earth-toned walls and deft interior design. Sat in the lee of the palace walls, this guesthouse has commanding views of the town from the rooftop terrace (though furniture is kept inside due to the preponderance of visiting monkey).

Hotel Bundi Haveli   HOTEL **$$$**
(☑ 2447861; www.hotelbundihaveli.com; r ₹2500-4500; ❄ 🛜) The exquisitely renovated Bundi Haveli certainly leads the pack in terms of up-to-date style and sophistication. White walls, stone floors, colour highlights and framed artefacts are coupled with modern plumbing and electricity. Yes, it is very comfortable and relaxed and there's a lovely rooftop dining area boasting palace views and an extensive, mainly Indian menu (mains ₹90 to ₹250).

Nawal Sagar Palace   HERITAGE HOTEL **$$$**
(☑ 2447050; www.nawalsagarpalace.com; r ₹2000-3000; 🛜) This 300-year-old former royal residence, once home to the ladies of the court, has a beautiful location, with buildings overlooking a grassy lawn (with restaurant seating), which in turn overlooks the lake. Rooms are huge, with some interesting old furniture and artwork; some have balconies with lake views.

✖ Eating

Guesthouses and hotels provide the main eating options and many of them happily serve nonguests as well as guests. Bundi was once a dry town, so it's not a place for evening revelry; however, a cold beer can usually be arranged.

Out of the Blue   ITALIAN **$$**
(mains ₹130-220; ⊙ 8am-10.30pm; 🛜) Bundi's Out of the Blue was set up by the owners of its namesake in Pushkar (p139), but has since outgrown and outpaced the original. It serves up some of the best Italian pizza and pasta we've had in Rajasthan (the presence of pork products on the nonveg menu adds to the authenticity) as well as the best coffee in town (₹50 to ₹100).

Rainbow Cafe   MULTICUISINE **$$**
(mains ₹100-260; ⊙ 7am-11pm; 🛜) Bohemian ambience with chillout tunes, floor-cushion seating and two types of bhang lassi (a blend of lassi and bhang, a derivative of marijuana). Located on the rooftop of the town's western gate and caged off from marauding macaques with a bamboo trellis.

🛍 Shopping

Yug Art   ART
(http://yugartbundi.com; near Surang Gate; ⊙10am-7.30pm) Many art shops will offer you Rajasthani miniatures, but Yug Art is the first place that's offered to turn us into one. Provide a photo and you can be pictured on elephant back or in any number of classical scenes. Alternatively, Yug will record your India trip in a unique travel comic – you help with the script and he'll provide the artwork.

ℹ Information

There's an Axis Bank ATM on Sadar Bazaar and a State Bank ATM west of Azad Park.
Front Page Cyber Cafe (Balchand Para; per hr ₹40; ⊙ 8am-10pm)
Roshan Tour & Travel (⊙ 8am-10pm) Internet cafe that also exchanges currency and books train tickets. Located about 300m south of the palace.
Tourist Office (☑ 2443697; Kota Rd; ⊙ 9.30am-6pm Mon-Fri) Offers bus and train schedules, free maps and helpful advice.

ℹ Getting There & Away

BUS
For Ranthambhore, it's usually quicker to catch a bus to Kota, then hop on a train to Sawai Madhopur.

Direct services from Bundi bus stand:
Ajmer (₹135, four hours, hourly)
Jaipur (₹161, five hours, hourly)
Kota (₹30, 40 minutes, every 15 minutes)
Pushkar (₹146, 4½ hours, three daily)
Sawai Madhopur (₹104, four to five hours, three daily)
Udaipur (₹215, six hours, three daily)

TRAIN
There are no daily trains to Jaipur, Ajmer or Jodhpur. It's better to take a bus, or to catch a train from Kota or Chittorgarh.
➜ Two trains travel daily to Chittorgarh (sleeper ₹170). The 7.12am takes 3½ hours; the 9.16am takes 2½ hours.
➜ There are three daily trains to Sawai Madhopur (sleeper ₹100; 2½ to five hours; 5.35pm, 5.48pm and 10.35pm); the last train is the fastest.
➜ Two daily trains go to Delhi (Hazrat Nizamuddin). The 5.48pm (sleeper ₹260) takes nearly 12 hours; the 10.35pm (sleeper ₹315) takes just eight.
➜ There's one daily train to Agra (Agra Fort; sleeper ₹150, 12½ hours, 5.35pm).

» Only one train goes daily to Udaipur, the 12963 Mewar Express (sleeper ₹210, five hours, 2.08am).

ℹ Getting Around

An autorickshaw to the train station costs ₹50 to ₹70 by day and ₹100 to ₹120 by night.

Kota

📞 0744 / POP 703,150

An easy day trip from Bundi, Kota is a gritty industrial, commercial town on the Chamba, Rajasthan's only permanent river. You can take boat trips along the river for some good bird- and crocodile-watching, or explore the city's old palace. It's best experienced as a day trip from Bundi.

◉ Sights & Activities

A lovely hiatus from the city is a Chambal River **boat trip** (10min per person ₹60, 1hr ₹1000, max 6 people; ⊙ 10.30am-dusk). The river upstream of Kota is part of the Darrah National Park and once you escape the city it's beautiful, with lush vegetation and craggy cliffs on either side. It's an opportunity to spot a host of birds, as well as gharials (thin-snouted, fish-eating crocodiles) and muggers (keep-your-limbs-inside-the-boat crocodiles). Boats start from **Chambal Gardens** (Indian/foreigner ₹2/5), 1.5km south of the fort on the river's east bank.

City Palace & Fort   PALACE, FORT
(Indian/foreigner ₹30/200; ⊙ 10am-4.30pm Sat-Thu) The fort and the palace within it make up one of the largest such complexes in Rajasthan. This was the royal residence and centre of power, housing the Kota princedom's treasury, courts, arsenal, armed forces and state offices. Some of its buildings are now used as schools. The City Palace, entered through a gateway topped by rampant elephants, contains the offbeat **Rao Madho Singh Museum** (Indian/foreigner ₹10/100, camera ₹50; ⊙ 10am-4.30pm), where you'll find everything for a respectable Raj existence, from silver furniture to weaponry, as well as perhaps India's most depressingly moth-eaten stuffed trophy animals.

The oldest part of the palace dates from 1624. Downstairs is a durbar (royal audience) hall with beautiful mirrorwork, while the elegant, small-scale apartments upstairs contain exquisite, beautifully preserved paintings, particularly the hunting scenes for which Kota is renowned.

To get here, it's around ₹30 to ₹40 in an autorickshaw from the bus stand, and at least ₹60 from the train station.

✦ Festivals & Events

If you happen to hit Kota in October or November, check whether your visit coincides with the city's huge **Dussehra Mela**, during which massive effigies are built then spectacularly set aflame. Thousands of pilgrims descend on the city in the month of Kartika (October/November) for **Kashavrai Patan**. See the tourist office for festival programs.

ℹ Information

Tourist Office (📞 2327695; RTDC Hotel Chambal; ⊙ 9.30am-6pm Mon-Sat) Has free maps of Kota. Turn left out of the bus stand, right at the second roundabout and it's on your right.

ℹ Getting There & Away

BUS
Services from the main bus stand:
Ajmer (₹165, four to five hours, at least 10 daily)
Bundi (₹30, 40 minutes, every 15 minutes throughout the day)
Chittorgarh (₹135, four hours, half-hourly from 6am)
Jaipur (₹191, five hours, hourly from 5am)
Udaipur (₹241, six to seven hours, at least 10 daily)

TRAIN
Kota is on the main Mumbai–Delhi train route via Sawai Madhopur, so there are plenty of trains to choose from, though departure times aren't always convenient.

» For Ranthambhore, there are more than two dozen daily trains to Sawai Madhopur (2nd-class seat/sleeper ₹65/140; one to two hours), so you rarely have to wait more than an hour.

» Trains run almost hourly to Delhi (sleeper ₹270; five to eight hours), mostly to New Delhi or Hazrat Nizamuddin.

» Six trains run daily to Jaipur (sleeper ₹205; four hours; 2.55am, 7.40am, 8.55am, 12.35pm, 5.20pm and 11.50pm), but there are many others on selected days so you'll rarely have to wait long.

» Three daily trains go to Chittorgarh (sleeper ₹170; three to four hours; 1.25am, 6.10am and 8.45am).

» Five fast trains go daily to Mumbai (sleepers ₹465; 14 hours; 7.50am, 2.25pm, 5.30pm, 11.20pm and 11.45pm).

MAJOR TRAINS FROM KOTA

DESTINATION	TRAIN NO & NAME	FARE (₹)	DURATION (HR)	DEPARTURE
Agra	19037/39 Avadh Exp	174/445/601 (A)	7¼	2.50pm
Chittorgarh	59812 Haldighati Pass	170 (B)	4	6.10am
	29020 Dehradun Exp	170/395/650 (C)	3¼	8.45am
Delhi (Nizamuddin)	12903 Golden Temple Mail	270/576/770/1294 (E)	7¼	11.12am
	12964 Mewar Exp	270/576/770/1294 (E)	6½	11.55pm
Jaipur	12181 Dayodaya Exp	205/390/512 (A)	4	7.40am
	12955 Mumbai–Jaipur Exp	205/390/512/852 (E)	4	8.55am
Mumbai	12904 Golden Temple Mail	349/913/1237/2078 (E)	15	2.35pm
Sawai Madhopur	12059 Shatabdi	65/240 (D)	1¼	6am
	12903 Golden Temple Mail	150/280/338/551 (E)	1¼	11.12am
Udaipur	12963 Mewar Exp	179/433/573/955 (E)	6	1.25am

Fares: (A) sleeper/3AC/2AC, (B) sleeper, (C) sleeper/2AC/1AC, (D) 2nd class/AC chair, (E) sleeper/3AC/2AC/1AC

❶ Getting Around

Minibuses and shared autorickshaws link the train station and central bus stand (₹6 to ₹10 per person). A private autorickshaw costs around ₹40.

Chittorgarh (Chittor)

📞 01472 / POP 96,200

Chittorgarh, the fort (garh) at Chittor, is the largest fort complex in India, and a fascinating place to explore. It rises from the plains like a huge rock island, nearly 6km long and surrounded on all sides by 150m-plus cliffs.

Its history epitomises Rajput romanticism, chivalry and tragedy, and it holds a special place in the hearts of many Rajputs. Three times (in 1303, 1535 and 1568) Chittorgarh was under attack from a more powerful enemy; each time, its people chose death before dishonour, performing jauhar. The men donned saffron martyrs' robes and rode out from the fort to certain death, while the women and children immolated themselves on huge funeral pyres. After the last of the three sackings, Rana Udai Singh II fled to Udaipur, where he established a new capital for Mewar. In 1616, Jehangir returned Chittor to the Rajputs. There was no attempt at resettlement, though it was restored in 1905.

◉ Sights

Chittorgarh FORT
(Indian/foreigner ₹5/100, Sound & Light Show ₹75/200; ☉ dawn-dusk, Sound & Light Show dusk)
A zigzag ascent of more than 1km starts at **Padal Pol** and leads through six outer gateways to the main gate on the western side, the **Ram Pol** (the former back entrance). Inside Ram Pol is a still-occupied village that takes up a small northwestern part of the fort – turn right for the ticket office. The rest of the plateau is deserted except for the wonderful palaces, towers and temples that remain from its heyday, with the addition of a few more recent temples. A loop road runs around the plateau, which has a deer park at the southern end.

➔ **Meera & Kumbha Shyam Temples**
Both of these temples southeast of the **Rana Kumbha Palace** (Fort) were built by Rana Kumbha in the ornate Indo-Aryan style, with classic, tall sikharas (spires). The

Chittorgarh (Chittor)

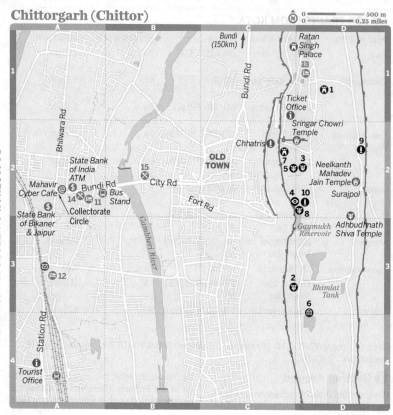

Chittorgarh (Chittor)

Meera Temple, the smaller of the two, is now associated with the mystic-poetess Meerabai, a 16th-century Mewar royal who was poisoned by her brother-in-law, but survived due to the blessings of Krishna. The **Kumbha Shyam Temple** is dedicated to Vishnu and its carved panels illustrate 15th-century Mewar life.

➜ Tower of Victory

The glorious **Tower of Victory** (Jaya Stambha; Fort), symbol of Chittorgarh, was erected by Rana Kumbha in the 1440s, probably to commemorate a victory over Mahmud Khilji of Malwa. Dedicated to Vishnu, it rises 37m in nine exquisitely carved storeys, and you can climb the 157 narrow stairs (the interior is also carved) to the 8th floor, from where there's a good view of the area.

Below the tower, to the southwest, is the Mahasati (Fort) area where there are many *sati* stones – this was the royal cremation ground and was also where 13,000 women committed *jauhar* in 1535. The Samidheshwar Temple (Fort), built in the 6th century and restored in 1427, is nearby. Notable among its intricate carving is a Trimurti (three-faced) figure of Shiva.

➧ Gaumukh Reservoir

Walk down beyond the Samidheshwar Temple and at the edge of the cliff is a deep tank, the Gaumukh Reservoir, where you can feed the fish. The reservoir takes its name from a spring that feeds the tank from a *gaumukh* (cow's mouth) carved into the cliffside.

➧ Padmini's Palace

Continuing south, you reach the Kalika Mata Temple, an 8th-century sun temple damaged during the first sacking of Chittorgarh and then converted to a temple for the goddess Kali in the 14th century. Padmini's Palace stands about 250m further south, beside a small lake with a central pavilion. The bronze gates to this pavilion were carried off by Akbar and can now be seen in Agra Fort.

➧ Surajpol & Tower of Fame

Surajpol, on the fort's east side, was the main gate and offers fantastic views across the empty plains. A little further north, the 24m-high Tower of Fame (Kirtti Stambha; Fort), dating from 1301, is smaller than the Tower of Victory. Built by a Jain merchant, the tower is dedicated to Adinath, the first Jain *tirthankar* (one of the 24 revered Jain teachers) and is decorated with naked figures of various other *tirthankars*, indicating that it is a monument of the Digambara (sky-clad) order. A narrow stairway leads up the seven storeys to the top. Next door is a 14th-century Jain temple.

🛏 Sleeping & Eating

Hotel Amber Plaza   HOTEL $
(☎248862; 32 Kidwai Nagar; r with/without AC ₹900/500; ❄) Down a quietish street near the bus stand, this hotel has quite comfy, medium-sized rooms with bright decorations and a restaurant.

Hotel Pratap Palace   HOTEL $$
(☎240099; www.hotelpratappalacechittaurgarh. com; off Maharana Pratap Setu Marg; s/d incl breakfast ₹3820/4400; ❄@⏚) This is Chittorgagh's best option, with a wide range of rooms, a convenient location and travel-savvy staff.

The more expensive rooms have window seats and leafy outlooks. There's a decent garden-side multicuisine restaurant too. It's near the main post office.

Padmini Haveli   HERITAGE HOTEL $$$
(☎94141410090, 241251; www.thepadminihaveli. com; Annapoorna Temple Rd, Shah Chowk, Village, Chittorgarh Fort; r incl breakfast ₹4000, ste ₹5000; ❄@⏚) A fantastically set 16th-century palace apparently plucked from the whimsy of Udaipur and dropped into a rural retreat 41km by road east of Chittorgarh. It's a great place to settle down with a good book, compose a fairy-tale fantasy or just laze around. Rooms are romantic and luxurious, and there's a pleasant garden courtyard and an airy restaurant serving Rajasthani food.

Reservations should be made through the website or Hotel Pratap Palace. The owners can arrange transfer from Chittor as well as horse and 4WD safaris, birdwatching, cooking classes, massage and yoga.

Saffire Garden Restaurant   MULTICUISINE $$
(City Rd; mains ₹100-150; ⏰8am-10pm; ❄) Sit at tables on the small, tree-shaded lawn or inside the air-conditioned room at the back, and tuck into a variety of standard, but tasty enough, Indian and Chinese dishes.

Chokhi Dhani Garden Family Restaurant   DHABA $
(Bundi Rd; mains ₹50-130; ⏰11am-10pm; ❄) This fan-cooled roadside *dhaba* (snack bar) with extra seating in the back does a good-value selection of vegetarian dishes, including filling thalis and a variety of South Indian dishes.

ℹ Information

You can access an ATM and change money at the SBBJ (SBBJ; Bhilwara Rd), and there's an ATM at SBI (Bundi Rd).

Mahavir Cyber Cafe (Collectorate Circle; ⏰8am-10pm)

Tourist Office (☎241089; Station Rd; per hr ₹40; ⏰10am-1.30pm & 2-5pm Mon-Sat) Friendly and helpful, with a town map and brochure to give out.

ℹ Getting There & Away

BUS

Services from Chittorgarh:

Ajmer (₹146, four hours, hourly until mid-afternoon)

Jaipur (₹233, seven hours, around every 90 minutes)

Kota (₹135, four hours, half-hourly)

RAJASTHAN CHITTORGARH (CHITTOR)

MAJOR TRAINS FROM CHITTORGARH

DESTINATION	TRAIN NO & NAME	DEPARTURE TIME	ARRIVAL TIME	FARE (₹)
Ajmer	12991 Udaipur-Jaipur Exp	8.20am	11.25pm	100/365/505 (A)
Bundi	29019 NMH-Kota Exp	3.45pm	5.45pm	140/690 (B)
Delhi (Nizamuddin)	12964 Mewar Exp	8.50pm	6.35am	370/970 (B)
Jaipur	12991 Udaipur-Jaipur Exp	8.20am	1.30pm	140/505/705 (A)
Sawai Madhopur	29019 NMH-Kota Exp	3.45pm	9.25pm	130/690 (B)
Udaipur	19329 Udaipur City Exp	4.50pm	7.10pm	140/485 (B)

Fares: (A) 2nd-class seat/AC chair/1st-class seat, (B) sleeper/2AC

Udaipur (₹86, 2½ hours, half-hourly)
There are no direct buses to Bundi.

TRAIN

➡ Three trains run daily to Bundi (sleeper ₹100; 2.10pm, 3.45pm and 8.50pm). The first one takes 3½ hours, the others just two hours.

➡ Five daily trains go to Udaipur (sleeper ₹140; two hours; 4.25am, 5.05am, 5.33am, 4.50pm and 9pm).

➡ Three trains make the trip to Jaipur daily (sleeper ₹210; 5½ hours; 8.20am, 12.35am and 2.45am).

➡ In addition to departures at 10.10am and 7.30pm, the trains to Jaipur also make the three-hour trip to Ajmer (sleeper ₹140).

➡ Two fast trains go to Delhi (10 hours, 7.30pm and 8.50pm), arriving at Delih Sarai Rohilla and Hazrat Nizamuddin respectively.

➡ For Ranthambhore, three trains travel daily to Sawai Madhopur (sleeper ₹130; 2.10pm, 3.45pm and 8.50pm). They take nine, six and four hours respectively.

ⓘ Getting Around

A full tour of the fort by autorickshaw should cost around ₹400 return. You can arrange this yourself in town. Hotel Pratap Palace (p149) gives 4WD tours of the fort for ₹600.

Udaipur

🎵 0294 / POP 389,400

Beside shimmering Lake Pichola, with the ochre and purple ridges of the wooded Aravalli Hills stretching away in every direction, Udaipur has a romantic setting unmatched in Rajasthan and arguably in all of India. Fantastical palaces, temples, *havelis* and countless narrow, crooked, colourful streets add the human counterpoint to the city's natural charms.

Udaipur's tag of 'the most romantic spot on the continent of India' was first applied in 1829 by Colonel James Tod, the East India Company's first Political Agent in the region. Today the romance is wearing ever so slightly thin as Udaipur strains to exploit it for tourist rupees. In the parts of the city nearest the lake, almost every building is a hotel, shop, restaurant, travel agent, or all four rolled into one. Ever-taller hotels compete for the best view, too many mediocre restaurants serve up near-identical menus, and noisy, dirty traffic clogs some of the streets that were made for people and donkeys.

Take a step back from the hustle, however, and Udaipur still has its magic, not just in its marvellous palaces and monuments, but in its matchless setting, the tranquillity of boat rides on the lake, the bustle of its ancient bazaars, its lively arts scene, the quaint old-world feel of its better hotels, its endless tempting shops and some lovely countryside to explore on wheels, feet or horseback.

Udaipur was founded in 1568 by Maharana Udai Singh II following the final sacking of Chittorgarh by the Mughal emperor Akbar. Though this new capital of Mewar had a much less vulnerable location than Chittorgarh, Mewar still had to contend with repeated invasions by the Mughals and, later, the Marathas, until British intervention in the early 19th century. This resulted in a treaty that protected Udaipur from invaders while allowing Mewar's rulers to remain effectively all-powerful in internal affairs. The ex-royal family remains influential and in recent decades has been the driving force behind the rise of Udaipur as a tourist destination.

◉ Sights

Lake Pichola
LAKE

Limpid and large, Lake Pichola reflects the cool grey-blue mountains on its rippling mirror-like surface. It was enlarged by Maharana Udai Singh II, following his foundation of the city, by flooding Picholi village, which gave the lake its name. The lake is now 4km long and 3km wide, but remains shallow and dries up completely during severe droughts. The City Palace complex, including the gardens at its southern end, extends nearly 1km along the lake's eastern shore.

Boat trips (adult/child 10am-2pm ₹400/200, 3-5pm ₹650/350; ⊙10am-5pm) leave roughly hourly from Rameshwar Ghat, within the City Palace complex (note, you have to pay ₹30 to enter). The trips make a stop at Jagmandir Island, where you can stay for as long as you like before taking any boat back. Take your own drinks and snacks, though, as those sold on the island are extortionately expensive. You can also take 30-minute boat rides (₹250 per person) from **Lal Ghat**, throughout the day without the need to enter the City Palace complex: it's worth checking in advance what time the popular sunset departure casts offs.

City Palace
PALACE

(www.eternalmewar.in; adult/child ₹30/15, free if visiting City Palace Museum; ⊙7am-11pm) Surmounted by balconies, towers and cupolas towering over the lake, the imposing City Palace is Rajasthan's largest palace, with a facade 244m long and 30.4m high. Construction was begun in 1599 by Maharana Udai Singh II, the city's founder, and it later became a conglomeration of structures (including 11 separate smaller palaces) built and extended by various maharanas, though it still manages to retain a surprising uniformity of design.

You can enter the complex through **Badi Pol** (Great Gate; 1615) at the northern end, or the **Sheetla Mata Gate** to the south. Tickets for the City Palace Museum are sold at both entrances. Note: you must pay the ₹30 City Palace entrance ticket in order to pass south through **Chandra Chowk Gate**, en route to the Crystal Gallery or Rameshwar Ghat for the Lake Pichola boat rides, even if you have a City Palace Museum ticket.

Inside Badi Pol, eight arches on the left commemorate the eight times maharanas were weighed here and their weight in gold or silver distributed to the lucky locals. You then pass through the three-arched **Tripolia Gate** (1711) into a large courtyard, **Manek Chowk**. Spot the large tiger-catching cage, which worked rather like an oversized mousetrap, and the smaller one for leopards.

City Palace Museum
MUSEUM

(adult/child ₹115/55, camera or video ₹225, ticket plus audio guide ₹225, human guide ₹200; ⊙9.30am-5.30pm, last entry 4.30pm) The main part of the palace is open as the City Palace Museum, with rooms extravagantly

DURBAR GLITZ

Many palaces in India have a durbar hall (royal reception hall). Usually the grandest room in the place, with a respectable number of chandeliers and gilt overlay, the durbar hall was dressed to impress – it was used by Indian rulers for official occasions, such as state banquets, and to hold meetings.

The restored Durbar Hall (p153) in the City Palace complex is one of India's most impressive, vast and lavish, with some of the country's biggest chandeliers. The walls display royal weapons and striking portraits of former maharanas of Mewar – a most distinguished-looking lot, who come from what is believed to be the oldest ruling dynasty in the world, spanning 76 generations.

The foundation stone of the hall was laid in 1909 by Lord Minto, the viceroy of India, during the reign of Maharana Fateh Singh, and it was originally named Minto Hall. The upper level of this high-ceilinged hall is surrounded by viewing galleries, where ladies of the palace could watch, in veiled seclusion, what was happening below. Nowadays, these are the Crystal Gallery (p152).

The Durbar Hall is included in visits to the Crystal Gallery and you will also see it if you go to the **Gallery Restaurant** (Durbar Hall; Durbar tea ₹325; ⊙9am-6pm). The hall still has the capacity to hold hundreds of people and can even be hired for conferences or social gatherings.

Udaipur

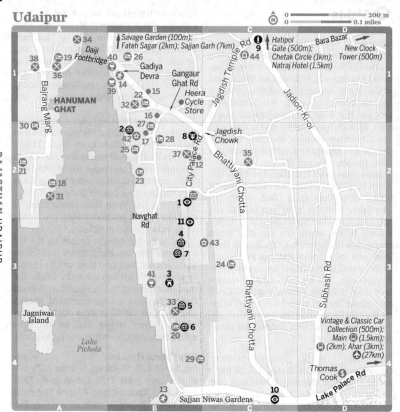

decorated with mirrors, tiles and paintings, and housing a large, varied collection of artefacts. It's entered from **Ganesh Chowk**, which you reach from Manek Chowk.

The City Palace Museum begins with the **Rai Angan** (Royal Courtyard), the very spot where Udai Singh met the sage who told him to build a city here. Rooms along one side contain historical paintings, including several of the Battle of Haldighati (1576), in which Mewar forces under Maharana Pratap, one of the great Rajput heroes, gallantly fought the army of Mughal emperor Akbar to a stalemate.

As you move through the palace, highlights include the **Baadi Mahal** (1699), where a pretty, central garden gives fine views over the city. **Kishan (Krishna) Vilas** has a remarkable collection of miniatures from the time of Maharana Bhim Singh (1778–1828). The story goes that Bhim Singh's daughter Krishna Kumari drank a fatal cup of poison here to solve the dilemma of rival princely suitors from Jaipur and Jodhpur, who were both threatening to invade Mewar if she didn't marry them. The **Surya Choupad** boasts a huge, ornamental sun (the symbol of the sun-descended Mewar dynasty) and opens into **Mor Chowk** (Peacock Courtyard) with its lovely mosaics of peacocks, the favourite Rajasthani bird.

The southern end of the museum comprises the **Zenana Mahal**, the royal ladies' quarters built in the 17th century. It now contains a long picture gallery with lots of royal hunting scenes (note the comic strip-like progression of the action in each painting). The Zenana Mahal's central courtyard, **Laxmi Chowk**, contains a beautiful white pavilion and a stable of howdahs, palanquins and other people carriers.

Crystal Gallery   GALLERY
(City Palace Complex; adult/child incl audio guide & drink ₹550/350, photography prohibited; ⊙9am-7pm) The Crystal Gallery houses rare crystal

Udaipur

RAJASTHAN UDAIPUR

that Maharana Sajjan Singh ordered from F&C Osler & Co in England in 1877. The maharana died before it arrived, and all the items stayed forgotten and packed up in boxes for 110 years. The extraordinary, extravagant collection includes crystal chairs, sofas, tables and even beds. The rather hefty admission fee also includes entry to the grand **Durbar Hall** (City Palace Complex). Tickets are available at the City Palace gates or the Crystal Gallery.

Government Museum MUSEUM
(◎10am-5pm Tue-Sun) FREE Entered from Ganesh Chowk, this has a splendid collection of jewel-like miniature paintings of the Mewar school and a turban that belonged to Shah Jahan, creator of the Taj Mahal. Stranger exhibits include a stuffed monkey holding a lamp. There are also regal maharana portraits in profile, documenting Mewar's rulers along with the changing fashions of the moustache.

Jagdish Temple HINDU TEMPLE
(◎5.30am-2pm & 4-10pm) Reached by a steep, elephant-flanked flight of steps, 150m north of the City Palace's Badi Pol entrance, this busy Indo-Aryan temple was built by Maharana Jagat Singh in 1651. The wonderfully carved main structure enshrines a black stone image of Vishnu as Jagannath, Lord of the Universe. There's also a brass image of the Garuda (Vishnu's man-bird vehicle) in a shrine facing the main structure.

Bagore-ki-Haveli HISTORIC BUILDING
(admission ₹30; ◎10am-5pm) This gracious 18th-century *haveli*, set on the water's edge in the Gangaur Ghat area, was built by a Mewar prime minister and has since been carefully restored. There are 138 rooms set around courtyards, some arranged to evoke the period during which the house was inhabited, while others house cultural displays, including – intriguingly enough – the world's biggest turban.

The *haveli* also houses a gallery featuring a fascinating collection of period photos of Udaipur and a surreal collection of famous monuments carved out of polystyrene.

Sajjan Garh   PALACE
(Monsoon Palace) Perched on top of a distant mountain like a fairy-tale castle, this melancholy, neglected late 19th-century palace was constructed by Maharana Sajjan Singh. Originally an astronomical centre, it became a monsoon palace and hunting lodge. Now government owned, it's in a sadly dilapidated state but visitors stream up here for the marvellous views, particularly at sunset. It's 5km west of the old city as the crow flies, about 9km by the winding road.

At the foot of the hill you enter the 5-sq-km **Sajjan Garh Wildlife Sanctuary** (Indian/foreigner ₹20/160, car ₹60, camera/video free/₹200). A good way to visit is with the daily sunset excursion in a minivan driven by an enterprising taxi driver who picks up tourists at the entrance to Bagore-ki-Haveli at Gangaur Ghat every day at 5pm. The round trip costs ₹200 per person, including waiting time (but not the sanctuary fees). His minivan has 'Monsoon Palace–Sajjangarh Fort' written across the front of it. Alternatively, autorickshaws charge ₹200 including waiting time for a round trip to the sanctuary gate, which they are not allowed to pass. Taxis ferry people the final 4km up to the palace for ₹100 per person.

Vintage & Classic Car Collection   MUSEUM
(Garden Hotel, Lake Palace Rd; adult/child ₹250/150, incl lunch or dinner ₹400/300; ☺9am-9pm) The maharanas' car collection makes a fascinating diversion, for what it tells about their elite lifestyle and for the vintage vehicles themselves. Housed within the former state garage are 22 splendid vehicles, including a seven-seat 1938 Cadillac, complete with purdah system, the beautiful 1934 Rolls-Royce Phantom used in the Bond film *Octopussy,* and the Cadillac convertible that whisked Queen Elizabeth II to the airport in

1961. The museum is a 10-minute walk east along Lake Palace Rd (bear to the right at the staggered junction).

If you enjoy a vegetarian thali, the combined museum-and-meal ticket is a very good option (lunch 11.30am to 3pm, dinner 7.30pm to 10pm).

🏃 Activities

Bike Tours

Art of Bicycle   CYCLING
(☎8105289167; www.artofbicycletrips.com; 27 Gadiya Devra, inside Chandpol; half-day per person ₹1950) This well-run outfit offers a great way to get out of the city. The Lakecity Loop is a 30km half-day tour that quickly leaves Udaipur behind to have you wheeling through villages, farmland and along the shores of Fateh Sagar and Badi Lakes. Other options include a vehicle-supported trip further afield to Kumbulhgarh and Ranakpur. Bikes are well-maintained and come with helmets.

Horse Riding

The wooded hills, villages and lakes around Udaipur are lovely riding country. You'll saddle up on Rajasthan's celebrated Marwari horses, known for their intelligence, stamina and cute inward-curving ears.

Pratap Country Inn   HORSE RIDING
(☎2583138; www.horseridingindia.in; Jaisamand Rd, Titaradi Village; 2hr rides ₹900, full day ₹2000) Run by the pioneer of horse safaris in Rajasthan, Maharaja Narendra Singh, this inn about 7km south of town organises day or part-day rides and long-distance safaris.

Krishna Ranch   HORSE RIDING
(☎9828059505; www.krishnaranch.com; full-day rides incl lunch ₹1200) Situated in beautiful countryside near Badi village, 7km northwest of Udaipur, and run by the owners of Kumbha Palace guesthouse (p157). Experienced owner-guide Dinesh Jain leads most trips himself, riding local Marwari horses through the surrounding hills. There are also attractive cottages (p154) at the ranch.

HELPING UDAIPUR'S STREET ANIMALS

The spacious **Animal Aid Unlimited** (☎9950531639, 9352511435; www.animalaidunlimited.com; Badi Village) refuge treats around 200 street animals a day (mainly dogs, donkeys and cows) and answers more than 3000 emergency rescue calls a year. The refuge welcomes volunteers and visitors: make contact in advance to fix a time between 9am and 5pm any day. It's in Badi village, 7km northwest of Udaipur. A round trip by autorickshaw, including waiting time, costs around ₹400.

Call Animal Aid Unlimited if you see an injured or ill street animal in Udaipur.

Massage

Ayurvedic Body Care   AYURVEDA, MASSAGE
(☑ 2413816; www.ayurvedicbodycare.com; 38 Lal Ghat; ⊙ 10am-8pm) A small and popular old city operation offering ayurvedic massage at reasonable prices, including a 15-minute head or back massage (₹250) and a 45-minute full-body massage (₹750). It also sells ayurvedic products such as oils, moisturisers, shampoos and soaps.

Walking

The horse-riding specialists at Krishna Ranch also offer guided hikes through the same beautiful countryside, passing through small tribal villages en route. Multiday hikes can be arranged too.

Millets of Mewar   WALKING
(☑ 8890419048; www.milletsofmewar.com; Hanuman Ghat; ₹1000 per person, min 2 people) Health-food specialists Millets of Mewar (p158) organises 2½-hour city tours on which you can meet local artisans who live and work in Udaipur. Tours should be booked a day in advance; they leave from the restaurant at 10am.

Courses

Cooking
Shashi Cooking Classes   COOKING
(☑ 9929303511; www.shashicookingclasses.blogspot.com; Sunrise Restaurant, 18 Gangaur Ghat Rd; 4hr class ₹1500, max 4 students) Readers rave about Shashi's high-spirited classes, teaching many fundamental Indian dishes.

Sushma's Cooking Classes   COOKING
(☑ 7665852163; www.cookingclassesinudaipur.com; Hotel Krishna Niwas, 35 Lal Ghat; 2hr class ₹1000) A highly recommended cooking class run by the enthusiastic Sushma. Classes offer up anything from traditional Rajasthani dishes and spice mixes, through bread-making to the all-important method of making the perfect cup of chai.

Music
Prem Musical Instruments   MUSIC
(☑ 2430599; 28 Gadiya Devra; lessons per hr ₹400; ⊙ 10.30am-6pm) Rajesh Prajapati (Bablu) is a local musician who gives sitar, tabla and flute lessons. He also sells and repairs instruments and can arrange performances.

Painting
Ashoka Arts   PAINTING
(Hotel Gangaur Palace, Gadiya Devra; lessons per hr ₹200) Learn the basics of classic miniature painting from a local master.

Yoga
Prakash Yoga   YOGA
(☑ 2524872; inside Chandpol; class by donation; ⊙ classes 8am & 7pm) A friendly hatha yoga centre with hour-long classes. The teacher has over 20 years' experience. It's tucked inside Chandpol, near the footbridge, but well-signed.

☞ Tours

Heritage Walks   WALKING
(☑ 9414164680; www.heritageroyalrajasthan.com; City Palace Rd; tours per person ₹200; ⊙ tours 8am & 5pm) If you want to really drill into Udaipur's history, architecture and religious sites, you could do a lot worse than joining one of the twice-daily expert-led tours from Heritage Walks, which will show you the Lal Ghat area that exists beyond the souvenir shops. Tours last two hours.

⚑ Festivals & Events

If you're in Udaipur in February or March, you can experience the festival of Holi Udaipur-style, when the town comes alive in a riot of colour. Holi is followed in March/April by the procession-heavy Mewar Festival – Udaipur's own version of the springtime Gangaur festival.

⌨ Sleeping

Accommodation clusters where most people want to stay – close to the lake, especially on its eastern side, in and near the narrow Lal Ghat. This area is a tangle of streets and lanes (some quiet, some busy and noisy), close to the City Palace and Jagdish Temple. It's Udaipur's tourist epicentre and the streets are strung not just with lodgings but also with tourist-oriented eateries and shops whose owners will be doing their best to tempt you in.

Directly across the water from Lal Ghat, Hanuman Ghat has a slightly more local vibe and often better views, though you're certainly not out of the tourist zone.

⌂ Lal Ghat Area
Many budget and midrange lodgings cluster here, with a particular concentration along the relatively peaceful Lal Ghat.

Nukkad Guest House   GUESTHOUSE $
(☑ 2411403; nukkad_raju@yahoo.com; 56 Ganesh Ghati; s/d without bathroom ₹100/200, r ₹300-500; @ 🛜) Nukkad has simple,

fan-cooled, very clean, good-value rooms, plus a sociable, breezy, upstairs restaurant with very good Indian and international dishes. You can join afternoon cooking classes and morning yoga sessions (by donation) without stepping outside the door – just don't stay out past curfew or get caught washing your clothes in your bathroom.

Lal Ghat Guest House   GUESTHOUSE $

(☑2525301; www.lalghat.com; 33 Lal Ghat; dm ₹150, r from ₹750, without bathroom ₹250; ❋@☎) This mellow guesthouse by the lake was one of the first to open in Udaipur, and it's still a sound choice, with an amazing variety of older and newer rooms. Accommodation ranges from a spruce, nonsmoking dorm (with curtained-off beds and lockers under the mattresses) to the best room, which sports a stone wall, big bed, big mirror and AC. Most rooms have lake views and those in the older part of the building generally have more character. There's a small kitchen for self-caterers.

Pratap Bhawan Paying Guest House   GUESTHOUSE $$

(☑2560566; 12 Lal Ghat; s ₹1000-1200, d ₹1450-1950; ❋☎) A curving marble staircase leads up from the wide lobby to large, sparkling-clean rooms with good, big bathrooms and, in many cases, cushioned window seats. A deservedly popular place, even if recent price hikes have spun the place slighlty out of the budget category. The rooftop terrace is nice for sitting out at night.

Poonam Haveli   HOTEL $$

(☑2410303; www.hotelpoonamhaveli.com; 39 Lal Ghat; r ₹1800-2500; ❋@☎) A fairly modern place decked out in traditional style, friendly Poonam has 16 spacious, spotlessly clean rooms with big beds and spare but tasteful decor, plus pleasant sitting areas. None of the rooms enjoy lake views, but the rooftop restaurant does, and boasts 'real Italian' pizzas among the usual Indian and traveller fare.

Jheel Palace Guest House   GUESTHOUSE $$

(☑2421352; www.jheelguesthouse.com; 56 Gangaur Ghat; r ₹1000-3000; ❋☎) Right on the lake edge (when the lake is full), Jheel Palace has three nice rooms with little balconies and four-poster beds, and three more ordinary ones. All are AC. Staff are accommodating and hands-off, and there's a good Brahmin pure-veg rooftop restaurant (no beer). Tight budgets will appreciate the basic ₹300 room.

Hotel Gangaur Palace   HERITAGE HOTEL $$

(☑2422303; www.ashokahaveli.com; Gadiya Devra; s ₹400-2000, d ₹500-2500; ❋@☎) This elaborate, faded *haveli* is set around a stone-pillared courtyard, with a wide assortment of rooms on several floors. It's gradually moving upmarket and rooms range from windowless with flaking paint to bright and recently decorated with lake views. Many have wall paintings and window seats.

The hotel also boasts an in-house palm reader, art shop, art school (p155), the good Cafe Namaste (p158) and a rooftop restaurant serving the same fare as the cafe as well as multicuisine dishes.

★ Jagat Niwas Palace Hotel   HERITAGE HOTEL $$$

(☑2420133; www.jagatniwaspalace.com; 23-25 Lal Ghat; r ₹3250-4250, without lake view ₹1850-2950; ❋@☎) This leading top-end hotel set in two converted lakeside *havelis* takes the location cake. The lake-view rooms are charming, with carved wooden furniture, cushioned window seats and pretty prints. Rooms without a lake view are almost as comfortable and attractive, and considerably cheaper.

The building is full of character with lots of attractive sitting areas, terraces and courtyards, and it makes the most of its position with a picture-perfect rooftop restaurant

🛏 Hanuman Ghat Area

Dream Heaven   GUESTHOUSE $

(☑2431038; www.dreamheaven.co.in; Hanuman Ghat; r ₹300-1000; ❋@☎) This popular place to come to a halt is in a higgledy-piggledy building with clean rooms with wall hangings and paintings. Bathrooms are smallish, though some rooms have a decent balcony and/or views. The food at the rooftop restaurant (dishes ₹40 to ₹110), which overlooks the lake and shows Udaipur at its best, is fresh and tasty – the perfect place to chill out on a pile of cushions.

Hibiscus Guest house   GUESTHOUSE $$

(☑9782222299; www.hibiscusudaipur.in; 190 Naga Nagri; r ₹1800-2200; ❋) A friendly, family-run house in a quiet setting back from Hanuman Ghat. The well-sized rooms have pretty Rajasthani decor, and the roof provides nice lake views. The flowers in the charming walled garden might equally have dubbed this place the Frangipani Guest House. Meals are available.

Amet Haveli
HERITAGE HOTEL $$$

(☏2431085; www.amethaveliudaipur.com; Hanuman Ghat; s/d ₹5400/6600; ❄@☎) A 350-year-old heritage building on the lake shore with delightful rooms featuring cushioned window seats and coloured glass with little shutters. They're set around a pretty little courtyard and pond. Splurge on one with a balcony or giant bathtub. One of Udaipur's most romantic restaurants, Ambrai (p158), is part of the hotel.

Udai Kothi
HOTEL $$$

(☏2432810; www.udaikothi.com; Hanuman Ghat; r ₹5500-7000; ❄@☎⊠) A bit like a five-storey wedding cake, Udai Kothi is a glittery, modern building with lots of traditional touches – cupolas, interesting art and fabrics, window seats in some rooms, marble bathrooms and carved-wood doors in others, and thoughtful touches such as bowls of floating flowers. Rooms are pretty, individually designed and well equipped.

The apex is the rooftop terrace, where you can dine well at the **restaurant** (Udai Kothi Hotel; mains ₹125-250) and swim in Udaipur's only rooftop pool (nonguests ₹300).

City Palace

Kumbha Palace
GUESTHOUSE $$

(☏9828059506, 2422702; www.hotelkumbhapalace.com; 104 Bhattiyani Chotta; r ₹550-600, with AC ₹1000; ❄@☎) This excellent place, run by a Dutch-Indian couple, is tucked up a quiet lane off busy Bhattiyani Chotta and backed by a lovely lush lawn. The 10 rooms are simple but comfortable (just one has AC), and the restaurant knows how to satisfy homesick travellers. The owners also run Krishna Ranch, where horse riding and cottage accommodation are available.

Shiv Niwas Palace Hotel
HERITAGE HOTEL $$$

(☏2528016; www.eternalmewar.in; City Palace Complex; r ₹15,000-42,000; ❄@☎⊠) This hotel, in the former palace guest quarters, has opulent common areas like its pool courtyard, bar and lawn garden. Some of the suites are truly palatial, filled with fountains and silver, but the standard rooms are poorer value. Go for a suite, or just for a drink (p159), meal (mains ₹500-1000; noon to 3pm and 7pm to 10.30pm), massage or swim in the gorgeous marble pool (nonguests ₹300).

Rates drop dramatically from April to September.

Fateh Prakash
Palace Hotel
HERITAGE HOTEL $$$

(☏2528016; www.hrhhotels.com; City Palace Complex; r ₹15,000, premier ste ₹31,500; ❄@☎) Built in the early 20th century for royal functions (the Durbar Hall is part of it), the Fateh Prakash has luxurious rooms and gorgeous suites, all comprehensively equipped and almost all looking straight out onto Lake Pichola. Views aside, the general ambience is a little less regal than at Shiv Niwas Palace Hotel – although the Sunset Terrace (p159) bar is a great place for an evening drink.

Other Areas

★ Krishna Ranch
COTTAGE $$

(☏9602192902, 3291478; www.krishnaranch.com; s/d incl meals ₹2000/2500) 🖉 This delightful countryside retreat has five cottages set around the grounds of a small farm. Each comes with attached bathroom (with solar heated shower), tasteful decor and farm views. All meals are included and are prepared using organic produce grown on the farm. The ranch is 7km from town, near Badi village, but there's free pick-up from Udaipur.

It's an ideal base for the hikes and horse treks that the management – a Dutch-Indian couple – organises from here, though you don't have to sign up for the treks to stay here.

Eating

Udaipur has scores of sun-kissed rooftop cafes, many with mesmerising lake views but often with uninspired multicuisine fare. Fortunately there's also a healthy number of places putting a bit more thought into their food.

Lal Ghat Area

Cafe Edelweiss
CAFE $

(73 Gangaur Ghat Rd; coffee from ₹50, sandwiches from ₹180; ⊙8.30am-8pm; ☎) The Savage Garden restaurant folks run this itsy piece of Europe that appeals to homesick and discerning travellers with superb baked goods and good coffee. Offerings included sticky cinnamon rolls, squidgy blueberry chocolate cake, spinach-and-mushroom quiche or apple strudel, good muesli or eggs for breakfast, and great sandwiches (the unexpected appearance of ham and bacon feels deliciously transgressive).

Lotus Cafe
MULTICUISINE $

(15 Bhattiyani Chotta; dishes ₹50-210; ⊙9am-10.30pm) This funky little restaurant serves up fabulous chicken dishes (predominantly Indian), plus salads, baked potatoes and plenty of vegetarian fare. It's ideal for meeting other travellers, with a mezzanine to loll about on, and cool background sounds.

Cafe Namaste
CAFE $

(Hotel Gangaur Palace; coffee ₹40-70, breakfasts ₹50-100; ⊙7am-10pm) A European-themed streetside cafe that delivers the goods with scrumptious muffins, apple pies, cinnamon rolls, brownies etc. And to wash it down there's coffee from a shiny silver espresso machine taking pride of place. The noisy street is a minus.

Jagat Niwas Palace Hotel
INDIAN $$

(⊡2420133; 23-25 Lal Ghat; mains ₹150-375; ⊙7am-10am, noon-3pm & 6-10pm) A wonderful, classy, rooftop restaurant with superb lake views, delicious Indian cuisine and good service. Choose from an extensive selection of rich curries (tempered for Western tastes) – mutton, chicken, fish and veg – as well as the tandoori classics. There's a cocktail menu and the beer is icy. Book ahead for dinner.

O'Zen Restaurant
MULTICUISINE $$

(City Palace Rd; coffee ₹50-70, mains ₹100-300; ⊙8.30am-11pm; 🛜) A swish location on City Palace Rd, this stylish 1st-floor restaurant-cafe does a range of Indian curries plus Italian pizza and pasta. It's bright and modern, does good coffee and beer (₹180), and has views of the street below.

★ Savage Garden
MEDITERRANEAN $$$

(⊡2425440; 22 inside Chandpol; mains ₹220-520; ⊙11am-11pm) Tucked away in the backstreets near Chandpol, Savage Garden does a winning line in soups, chicken and homemade pasta dishes. We loved the ravioli with lamb ragu, and the sweet-savoury stuffed chicken breast with nuts, cheese and carrot rice. The setting is a 250-year-old *haveli* with indigo walls and bowls of flowers, and tables in alcoves or a pleasant courtyard. The bar is slick, with red, white and sparkling Indian wines from Nasik, Maharashtra.

🍴 Hanuman Ghat Area

Millets of Mewar
INDIAN $

(www.milletsofmewar.com; Hanuman Ghat; mains ₹80-140; ⊙8.30am-10.30pm; 🛜) 🍃 This place does the healthiest food in town. Local millets are used where possible instead of less environmentally sound wheat and rice. There are vegan options, gluten-free dishes, fresh salads and juices and herbal teas. Also on the menu are multigrain sandwiches and millet pizzas, plus regular curries, Indian street-food snacks, pasta and even pancakes.

The sweet Indian coffee is delicious, and there's ice cream and chocolate pudding to go with the millet cookies on the dessert menu.

Jasmin
MULTICUISINE $

(mains ₹60-90; ⊙8.30am-11pm) Very tasty vegetarian dishes are cooked up in a lovely, quiet, open-air spot looking out on the quaint Daiji Footbridge. There are plenty of Indian options, and some original variations on the usual multicuisine theme including Korean and Israeli dishes. The ambience is super-relaxed and service friendly.

Queen Cafe
INDIAN $

(14 Bajrang Marg; mains ₹60-75; ⊙8am-10pm) This tiny restaurant-cum-family-front-room serves up good home-style Indian vegetarian dishes. Try the pumpkin curry with mint and coconut, and the Kashmir *pulao* (rice dish) with fruit, vegies and coconut. Host Meenu also offers cooking classes and slightly overpriced walking tours, but some diners may find that the hard sell she serves up with the food leaves a slightly bitter taste.

Ambrai
NORTH INDIAN $$$

(⊡2431085; www.amethaveliudaipur.com; Amet Haveli; mains ₹250-400; ⊙12.30-3pm & 7.30-10.30pm) The cuisine at this scenic restaurant – set at lake-shore level, looking across to Lal Ghat and the City Palace – does justice to its fabulous position. Highly atmospheric at night, Ambrai feels like a French park, with its wrought-iron furniture, dusty ground and large shady trees, and there's a terrific bar to complement the dining, which is strong on Rajashani dishes.

🍴 Other Areas

1559 AD
MULTICUISINE $$$

(⊡2433559; PP Singhal Marg; mains ₹200-650; ⊙11am-11pm) Waiters in embroidered-silk waistcoats serve up lovely Indian, Thai and Continental dishes in elegant surroundings at this secluded restaurant near the north-western side of Fateh Sagar. There are garden tables as well as several different rooms with just a few candlelit tables in each, and Indian classical music in the evenings. Includes a coffee shop with the best coffee we tasted in Udaipur.

🍷 Drinking

Most guesthouses have a roof terrace serving up cold Kingfishers with views over the lazy waters of Lake Pichola, but for a real treat try the top-end hotels. Note that you have to pay ₹25 to enter the City Palace complex (p151) if you're not staying in one of its hotels.

Paps Juice   JUICE BAR
(inside Chandpol; juices ₹40-100; ⊘9am-8pm)
This bright-red spot is tiny but very welcoming, and a great place to refuel during the day with a shot of Vitamin C from a wide range of delicious juice mixes. If you want something more substantial, the muesli mix is pretty good too.

Jheel's Ginger Coffee Bar   CAFE
(Jheel Palace Guest House, 56 Gangaur Ghat; coffee ₹50-100; ⊘8am-8pm; 🛜) This small but slick air-con-cooled cafe by the water's edge is on the ground floor of Jheel Palace Guest House. Large windows afford good lake views, and the coffee is excellent. Also does a range of cakes and snacks. Note, you can take your coffee up to the open-air rooftop restaurant if you like, but there's no alcohol served here.

Panera Bar   BAR
(Shiv Niwas Palace Hotel; beer from ₹475, shots from ₹250; ⊘11.30am-10pm) Sink into plush sofas surrounded by huge mirrors, royal portraits and beautiful paintwork, or sit out by the pool and be served like a maharaja.

Sunset Terrace   BAR
(Fateh Prakash Palace Hotel; ⊘7am-10.30pm) On a terrace overlooking Lake Pichola, this is perfect for a sunset gin and tonic. It's also a restaurant, with live music performed nightly.

☆ Entertainment

Dharohar   DANCE, PUPPETRY
(☑2523858; Bagore-ki-Haveli; Indian/foreigner ₹60/100, camera ₹100; ⊘7-8pm) The beautiful Bagore-ki-Haveli (p153) hosts the best (and most convenient) opportunity to see Rajasthani folk dancing, with nightly shows of colourful, energetic Marwari, Bhil and western Rajasthani dances, as well as traditional Rajasthani puppetry.

Mewar Sound & Light
Show   CULTURAL PROGRAM
(Manek Chowk, City Palace; adult/child ₹100/200; ⊘shows 7pm Sep-Feb, 7.30pm Mar-Apr, 8pm May-Aug) Fifteen centuries of intriguing Mewar

history are squeezed into one atmospheric hour of commentary and light switching – in English from September to April.

🛍 Shopping

Tourist-oriented shops, selling miniature paintings; wood carvings; silver and other jewellery; bangles; traditional shoes; spices; leather-bound, handmade-paper notebooks; ornate knives; camel-bone boxes; and a large variety of textiles, line the streets radiating from Jagdish Chowk. Udaipur is known for its local crafts, particularly its miniature paintings in the Rajput-Mughal style, as well as some interesting contemporary art.

The local market area extends east from the **old clock tower** at the north end of Jagdish Temple Rd, and buzzes loudest in the evening. It's fascinating as much for browsing and soaking up local atmosphere as for buying. Bara Bazar, immediately east of the old clock tower, sells silver and gold, while its narrow side street, Maldas St, specialises in saris and fabrics. A little further east, traditional shoes are sold on Mochiwada. Foodstuffs and spices are mainly found around the new clock tower at the east end of the bazaar area, and at Mandi Market, about 200m north of the tower.

Sadhna   CLOTHING
(☑2454655; www.sadhna.org; Jagdish Temple Rd; ⊘10am-7pm) 📍 This is the crafts outlet for Seva Mandir, a long-established NGO working with rural and tribal people. The small shop sells attractive fixed-price textiles; profits go to the artisans and towards community development work.

ℹ Information

EMERGENCY

Police (☑2414600, 100) There are police posts at Surajpol, Hatipol and Delhi Gate, three of the gates in the old-city wall.

INTERNET ACCESS

You can surf the internet at plenty of places, particularly around Lal Ghat, for ₹30 per hour. Many places double as travel agencies, bookshops, art shops etc.

MEDICAL SERVICES

GBH American Hospital (☑24hr enquiries 2426000, emergency 9352304050; www.gbhamericanhospital.com; Meera Girls College Rd, 101 Kothi Bagh, Bhatt Ji Ki Bari) Modern, reader-recommended private hospital with 24-hour emergency service, about 2km northeast of the old city.

MONEY

There are lots of ATMs, including Axis Bank and State Bank ATMs on City Palace Rd near Jagdish Temple; HDFC, ICICI and State Bank ATMs near the bus stand; and two ATMs outside the train station. Places to change currency and travellers cheques include **Thomas Cook** (Lake Palace Rd; ☺9.30am-6.30pm Mon-Sat).

POST

Main Post Office (Chetak Circle; ☺10am-1pm & 1.30-6pm Mon-Sat) North of the old city.

Post Office (City Palace Rd; ☺10am-4pm Mon-Sat) Tiny post office that sends parcels (including packaging them up) and there are virtually no queues. Beside the City Palace's Badi Pol ticket office.

TOURIST INFORMATION

Small tourist information counters operate erratically at the train station and airport.

Tourist Office (☎2411535; Fateh Memorial Bldg; ☺10am-5pm Mon-Sat) Not situated in the most convenient position, 1.5km east of the Jagdish Temple (though only about 500m from the bus stand), this place dishes out a limited amount of brochures and information.

ℹ Getting There & Away

AIR

→ **Air India** (☎2410999, airport office 2655453; www.airindia.com; 222/16 Mumal Towers, Saheli Rd) flies to Mumbai daily as well as to Delhi (via Jodhpur) daily.

→ **Jet Airways** (☎5134000; www.jetairways.com; Airport) flies direct to Delhi twice daily, and Mumbai daily.

→ SpiceJet (p123) has one direct daily flight to Delhi.

BUS

Private bus tickets can be bought at any one of the many travel agencies lining the road leading from Jagdish Temple to Daiji Footbridge.

The main bus stand is 1.5km east of the City Palace. Turn left at the end of Lake Palace Rd, take the first right then cross the main road at the end, just after passing through the crumbling old Surajpol Gate. It's around ₹40 in an autorickshaw.

If arriving by bus, turn left out of the bus stand, cross the main road, walk through Surajpol Gate then turn left at the end of the road before taking the first right into Lake Palace Rd.

TRAIN

The train station is about 2.5km southeast of the City Palace, and 1km directly south of the main bus stand. An autorickshaw between the train station and Jagdish Chowk should cost around ₹50. There's a prepaid autorickshaw stand at the station, though, so use that when you arrive.

There are no direct trains to Abu Road, Jodhpur or Jaisalmer.

→ For Pushkar, four daily trains make the journey to Ajmer (sleeper/2nd class ₹480/135, five hours; 6am, 2.15pm, 5.15pm and 10.20pm). The same departures also make the trip to Chittorgarh (2nd class ₹85, two hours).

→ Trains run daily to Jaipur (sleeper/2nd class ₹260/165, seven hours, 2.15pm and 10.20pm).

→ Two daily trains run to Delhi (sleeper ₹385, 12 hours, 5.15pm and 6.15pm).

→ Only one train runs daily to Bundi (sleeper ₹210, 4½ hours, 6.15pm).

→ Only one daily train runs to Agra (sleeper ₹360, 12½ hours; 10.20pm).

ℹ Getting Around

TO/FROM THE AIRPORT

The airport is 25km east of town. A prepaid taxi to the Lal Ghat area costs ₹400.

BICYCLE & MOTORCYCLE

A cheap and environmentally friendly way to buzz around is by bike; many guesthouses can arrange bicycles to rent, costing around ₹50 per day. Scooters and motorbikes, meanwhile, are great for exploring the surrounding countryside.

RSRTC BUSES FROM UDAIPUR

DESTINATION	FARE (₹)	DURATION (HR)	FREQUENCY
Ahmedabad	196	5	hourly from 5am
Ajmer	233	7	hourly from 6am
Bundi	160	6	4 daily (mornings)
Chittorgarh	86	2½	half-hourly from 6am
Delhi	521	15	4 daily
Jaipur	315	9	hourly
Jodhpur	206	6-8	hourly
Kota	230	7	hourly
Mt Abu (Abu Rd)	133	4	6 daily (mornings)

MAJOR TRAINS FROM UDAIPUR

DESTINATION	TRAIN NO & NAME	DEPARTURE TIME	ARRIVAL TIME	FARE (₹)
Agra (Cantonment)	19666 Udaipur-Kurj Exp	10.20pm	11am	360/970 (A)
Ajmer	Udaipur-Jaipur SF SPL 2.15pm	2.15pm	7.10pm	175/485 (B)
Bundi	12964 Mewar Exp	6.15pm	10.33pm	210/535 (A)
Chittogarh	12982 Chetak Exp	5.15am	7.10pm	170/535 (A)
Delhi (Nizamuddin)	12964 Mewar Exp	6.15pm	6.35am	385/1085 (A)
Jaipur	19666 Udaipur-Kurj Exp	10.20pm	5.45am	260/690 (A)

Fares: (A) sleeper/3AC, (B) 2nd-class seat/AC chair

Heera Cycle Store (☉7.30am-9pm), just off Gangaur Ghat Rd, hires out bicycles/mountain bikes/mopeds/scooters/motorbikes/Bullets for ₹50/100/200/350/350/450 per day (with a deposit of US$50/100/200/300/400/500); you must show your passport and driver's licence.

TAXI

Most hotels, guesthouses and travel agencies (many of which are on the road leading down to the lake from Jagdish Temple) can organise a car and driver to just about anywhere you want. As an example, a return day trip to Ranakpur and Kumbhalgarh will cost you around ₹1800 per vehicle.

Around Udaipur

Kumbhalgarh

☏ 02954

About 80km north of Udaipur, **Kumbhalgarh** (Indian/foreigner ₹5/100, Light & Sound Show ₹200; ☉9am-6pm, Light & Sound Show 6.30pm) is a fantastic, remote fort, fulfilling romantic expectations and vividly summoning up the chivalrous, warlike Rajput era. One of the many forts built by Rana Kumbha (r 1433–68), under whom Mewar reached its greatest extents, the isolated fort is perched 1100m above sea level, with endless views melting into the blue distance. The journey to the fort, along twisting roads through the Aravalli Hills, is a highlight in itself.

Kumbhalgarh was the most important Mewar fort after Chittorgarh, and the rulers, sensibly, used to retreat here in times of danger. Not surprisingly, Kumbhalgarh was only taken once in its entire history. Even then, it took the combined armies of Amber, Marwar and Mughal emperor Akbar to breach its strong defences, and they only managed to hang on to it for two days.

The fort's thick walls stretch about 36km; they're wide enough in some places for eight horses to ride abreast and it's possible to walk right around the circuit (allow two days). They enclose around 360 intact and ruined temples, some of which date back to the Mauryan period in the 2nd century BC, as well as palaces, gardens, step-wells and 700 cannon bunkers. If you are staying here and want to make an early start on your hike around the wall, you can get into the fort before 9am, although no one will be around to sell you a ticket.

There's a **Light & Sound Show** (₹200) at the fort every evening at 6.30pm. The large and rugged Kumbhalgarh Wildlife Sanctuary (p162) can be visited from Kumbhalgarh. Ask at the Aodhi hotel about organising 4WD, horse or walking trips in the sanctuary.

🛏 Sleeping & Eating

Kumbhal Castle   HOTEL **$$**

(☏242171; www.thekumbhalcastle.com; Fort Rd; r ₹2900-3500; ❄❄) The modern Kumbhal Castle, 2km from the fort, has plain but pleasant white rooms featuring curly iron beds, bright bedspreads and window seats, shared balconies and good views. The super deluxe rooms are considerably bigger and worth considering for the few hundred extra rupees. There's a good in-house restaurant (lunch/dinner ₹350/400).

Aodhi   HOTEL **$$$**

(☏8003722333, 242341; www.eternalmewar.in; Kumbhalgarh; r from ₹7500; ❄@🛜❄) Just under 2km from the fort is this luxurious and blissfully tranquil hotel with an inviting pool, rambling gardens and winter campfires. The spacious rooms, in stone

OFF THE BEATEN TRACK

KUMBHALGARH WILDLIFE SANCTUARY

Ranakpur is a great base for exploring the hilly, densely forested **Kumbhalgarh Wildlife Sanctuary** (Indian/foreigner ₹20/180, 4WD or car ₹150, camera/video free/₹400, guide per day ₹200; ☺ dawn-dusk), which extends over some 600 sq km to the northeast and southwest. It's known for its leopards and wolves, although the chances of spotting antelopes, gazelles, deer and possibly sloth bears are higher, especially from March to June. You will certainly see some of the sanctuary's 200-plus bird species.

There are several safari outfits on the road leading up to Kumbhalgarh Fort (don't believe posters suggesting tiger sightings), but some of the best safaris and treks are offered (to guests and nonguests) by Shivika Lake Hotel: options include three-hour 4WD safaris (₹850 per person), a three-hour forest and lake walk (₹350), a six-to-seven–hour round-trip walk leading to Parshuram Shiva Temple (₹650), and a one-way hike to Kumbhalgarh (about five hours; ₹850), with a two-person minimum and park fees included.

Note, there is a ticket office for the sanctuary right beside where the bus drops you off for the Jain temples, but the nearest of the sanctuary's four entrances is 2km beyond here, near Shivika Lake Hotel.

---

buildings, all boast their own palm-thatched terraces, balconies or pavilions, and assorted wildlife and botanical art and photos.

Nonguests can dine in the restaurant, where good standard Indian fare is the pick of the options on offer, or have a drink in the cosy Chowpal Bar. Room rates plummet from April to September.

❶ Getting There & Away

From Udaipur's main bus stand, catch an hourly Ranakpur-bound bus as far as Saira (₹57, 2¼ hours), a tiny crossroads town where you can change for a bus to Kumbhalgarh (₹30, one hour, hourly). That bus, which will be bound for Kelwara, will drop you at the start of the approach road to the fort, leaving you with a pleasant 1.5km walk to the entrance gate.

The last bus back to Saira swings by at 5.30pm (and is always absolutely jam-packed with villagers). The last bus from Saira back to Udaipur leaves at around 8pm.

To get to Ranakpur from Kumbhalgarh, head first to Saira then change for Ranakpur (₹14, 40 minutes, at least hourly).

A day-long round trip in a private car from Udaipur to Kumbhalgarh and Ranakpur will cost around ₹1800 per car.

Ranakpur

📞 02934

Ranakpur　　　　　　　　　　　JAIN TEMPLE
(camera/video ₹100/300; ☺ Jains 6am-7pm, non-Jains noon-5pm) At the foot of a steep wooded escarpment of the Aravalli Hills, Ranakpur is one of India's biggest and most important

Jain temple complexes. It's 75km northwest of Udaipur, and 12km west of Kumbhalgarh as the crow flies (but 50km by road, via Saira). **Chaumukha Mandir** (Four-Faced Temple), the main temple, is dedicated to Adinath, the first Jain *tirthankar* (depicted in the many Buddha-like images in the temple), and was built in the 15th century in milk-white marble.

An incredible feat of Jain devotion, the Chaumukha Mandir is a complicated series of 29 halls, 80 domes and 1444 individually engraved pillars. The interior is completely covered in knotted, lovingly wrought carving, and has a marvellously calming sense of space and harmony. Shoes, cigarettes, food and all leather articles must be left at the entrance; women who are menstruating are asked not to enter.

Also exquisitely carved and well worth inspecting are two other Jain temples, dedicated to **Neminath** (22nd *tirthankar*) and **Parasnath** (23rd *tirthankar*), both within the complex, and a nearby **Sun Temple**. About 1km from the main complex is the **Amba Mata Temple**.

Buses from Udaipur and Saira will drop you by the entrance to the temple complex, before continuing past Shivika Lake Hotel (2km), and then going on to Jodhpur.

🛏 Sleeping & Eating

Shivika Lake Hotel　　　　GUESTHOUSE **$$**
(📞 285078, 9799118573; r ₹600-1200, tent ₹1200; ❄ @ ☲) Two kilometres north of the temple, Shivika is a welcoming, rustic and

family-run hotel that provides free pick-ups and drop-offs at the bus stop near the temple. You can stay in small, cosy rooms amid leafy gardens, or safari-style tents. Two of the tents have prime positions beside beautiful Nalwania Lake, on the edge of the property.

Due to the presence of a few crocodiles, the lake isn't safe for swimming, but there's a swimming pool right beside it and some meals (mains ₹70 to ₹160, thali ₹170, buffet lunch ₹300) are served here too.

ⓘ Getting There & Away

There are direct buses to Ranakpur from the main bus stands in both Udaipur (₹68, three hours, hourly) and Jodhpur (₹139, four to five hours). You'll be dropped outside the temple complex unless you state otherwise. Return services start drying up at around 7pm.

A day-long round trip in a private car from Udaipur to Ranakpur and Kumbhalgarh costs around ₹1800.

Mt Abu

⌥ 02974 / POP 22,200 / ELEV 1200M

Rajasthan's only hill station sits among green forests on the state's highest mountain at the southwestern end of the Aravalli Range, close to the Gujarat border. Quite unlike anywhere else in Rajasthan, Mt Abu provides Rajasthanis, Gujaratis and a steady flow of foreign tourists with respite from the scorching temperatures and arid, beige terrain found elsewhere. It's a particular hit with honeymooners and middle-class families from Gujarat.

Mt Abu town sits towards the southwest end of the plateau-like upper part of the mountain, which stretches about 19km from end to end and 6km from east to west. The town is surrounded by the flora- and fauna-rich, 289-sq-km Mt Abu Wildlife Sanctuary, which extends over most of the mountain from an altitude of 300m upwards.

The mountain is of great spiritual importance for both Hindus and Jains and has over 80 temples and shrines, most notably the exquisite Jain temples at Delwara, built between 400 and 1000 years ago.

Try to avoid arriving in Diwali (October or November) or the following two weeks, when prices soar and the place is packed. Mt Abu also gets pretty busy from mid-May to mid-June, before the monsoon. This is when the Summer Festival hits town, with music, fireworks and boat races. In the cooler months, you'll find everyone wrapped up in shawls and hats; pack something woolly to avoid winter chills in poorly heated hotel rooms.

◉ Sights & Activities

Nakki Lake   LAKE
Scenic Nakki Lake, the town's focus, is one of Mt Abu's biggest attractions. It's so named because, according to legend, it was scooped out by a god using his *nakh* (nails). Some Hindus thus consider it a holy lake. Another version of its origins is that it was constructed by the British in the 19th century.

It's a pleasant 45-minute stroll around the perimeter – the lake is surrounded by hills, parks and strange rock formations. The best known, **Toad Rock**, looks like a toad about to hop into the lake.

Sunset Point   VIEWPOINT
Sunset Point is a popular place to watch the brilliant setting sun. Hordes stroll out here every evening to catch the end of the day, the food stalls and all the usual jolly hill-station entertainment. To get there, follow Sunset Point road west of the Polo Ground out of town.

Brahma Kumaris
Peace Hall & Museum   MUSEUM
The white-clad people you'll see around town are members of the **Brahma Kumaris World Spiritual University** (www.bkwsu.com), a worldwide organisation whose headquarters are here in Mt Abu. The university's **Universal Peace Hall** (Om Shanti Bhawan; ⊘8am-6pm), just north of Nakki Lake, where free 30-minute tours are available, includes an introduction to the Brahma Kumaris philosophy (be prepared for a bit of proselytising). The organisation also runs the **World Renewal Spiritual Museum** (⊘8am-8pm) **FREE** in the town centre.

⌂ Tours

The RSRTC runs full-day (₹100) and half-day (₹45) bus tours of Mt Abu's main sights, leaving from the bus stand at 9.30am and 1pm respectively. Both tours visit Achalgarh, Guru Shikhar and the Delwara Temples and end at Sunset Point. The full-day tour also includes Adhar Devi, the Brahma Kumaris Peace Hall and Honeymoon Point. Admission and camera fees and the ₹20 guide fee are extra. Make reservations at the main bus stand.

RAJASTHAN MT ABU

Mt Abu

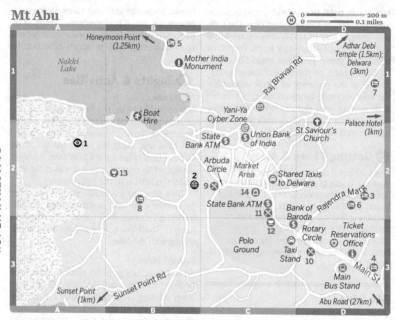

Mt Abu

◉ Sights
Brahma Kumaris Peace Hall &
Museum ....(see 2)
1 Toad Rock...A2
2 World Renewal Spiritual Museum B2

✪ Activities, Courses & Tours
Mt Abu Treks ....(see 5)
Shri Ganesh Hotel ....(see 8)

🛏 Sleeping
3 Connaught House D2
4 Hotel Hilltone.......................................D3
5 Hotel Lake Palace B1
6 Kishangarh House D2

7 Mushkil Aasan.......................................D1
8 Shri Ganesh Hotel B2

🍽 Eating
9 Arbuda C2
10 Kanak Dining Hall D3
Mulberry Restaurant.....................(see 4)
11 Sankalp C2

🍷 Drinking & Nightlife
12 Cafe Coffee Day C3
13 Polo Bar B2

🛍 Shopping
14 Chacha Museum C2

🛏 Sleeping

Room rates can double (or worse) during the peak seasons – mid-May to mid-June, Diwali and Christmas/New Year – but generous discounts are often available at other times in midrange and top-end places. Book way ahead at Diwali.

Shri Ganesh Hotel　　　　　　　HOTEL $
(📞237292; lalit_ganesh@yahoo.co.in; dm ₹250, s ₹500, d ₹600-1500; @🤝) A fairly central and popular budget spot, Shri Ganesh is well set up for travellers, with an inexpensive

cafe and plenty of helpful travel information. Rooms are well used but kept clean. Some have squat toilets and limited hours for hot water. Daily forest **walks** (📞237292; lalit_ganesh@yahoo.co.in; 1hr per person ₹500, 4hr ₹1000) and cooking lessons are on offer.

Mushkil Aasan　　　　　GUESTHOUSE $$
(📞235150, 9429409660; ccrrps@yahoo.com; s/d/q ₹1100/1200/1800; ✱🤝) A lovely guesthouse nestled in a tranquil vale in the north of town (near Global Hospital), with nine homely decorated rooms and a delightfully planted garden. Home-style Gujarati meals

are available, and check-out is a civilised 24 hours. Rooms next to reception can be noisy.

Hotel Lake Palace
HOTEL $$

(☑ 237154; http://savshantihotels.com; r incl breakfast ₹2500-2700; ❄ 🕸) Spacious and friendly, Lake Palace has an excellent location, with small lawns overlooking the lake. Rooms are simple, uncluttered, bright and clean. All have AC and some have semiprivate lakeview terrace areas. There are rooftop and garden multicuisine restaurants too, and even an aquarium next door.

Kishangarh House
HERITAGE HOTEL $$$

(☑ 238092; www.royalkishangarh.com; Rajendra Marg; cottages ₹3500, r ₹4500-6500; ❄🕸) The former summer residence of the maharaja of Kishangarh has been successfully converted into a heritage hotel. The deluxe rooms in the main building are big, with extravagantly high ceilings. The cottage rooms at the back are smaller but cosier. There's a delightful sun-filled drawing room and the lovely terraced gardens are devotedly tended.

Hotel Hilltone
HOTEL $$$

(☑ 238391; www.hotelhilltone.com; Main St; s/d from ₹4500/5500; 🅿🕸✉) A modern, well-run hotel in spacious grounds, the punningly named Hilltone takes a leaf out of the more famous hospitality brand with stylishly comfortable and modern rooms that punch above the price tag. The inhouse Mulberry Restaurant (p166) serves alcohol and nonveg Indian food – a rarity in Mt Abu.

Connaught House
HERITAGE HOTEL $$$

(☑ 235439; www.welcomheritagehotels.com; Rajendra Marg; r incl breakfast ₹7400; ❄@) Connaught House is a charming colonial-era bungalow that looks like an English cottage with lots of sepia photographs, dark wood, angled ceilings and a gorgeous shady garden. It's owned by Jodhpur's ruling family. The five rooms in the original 'cottage' have the most character – and big baths. The other five sit in a newer building with good views from their own verandahs.

🍴 Eating

Kanak Dining Hall
INDIAN $

(Lake Rd; Gujarati/Punjabi thali ₹60/130; ⏱8.30am-3.30pm & 7-11pm) The excellent all-you-can-eat thalis are contenders for Mt Abu's best meals. There's seating indoors

---

DON'T MISS

DELWARA TEMPLES

Delwara Temples (donations welcome; ⏱Jains 6am-6pm, non-Jains noon-6pm) These Jain temples are Mt Abu's most remarkable attraction and feature some of India's finest temple decoration. They predate the town of Mt Abu by many centuries and were built when this site was just a remote mountain vastness. It's said that the artisans were paid according to the amount of dust they collected, encouraging them to carve ever more intricately. Whatever their inducement, there are two temples here in which the marble work is dizzyingly intense.

The older of the two is the **Vimal Vasahi**, on which work began in 1031 and was financed by a Gujarati chief minister named Vimal. Dedicated to the first *tirthankar*, Adinath, it took 1500 masons and 1200 labourers 14 years to build, and allegedly cost ₹185.3 million. Outside the entrance is the **House of Elephants**, featuring a procession of stone elephants marching to the temple, some of which were damaged long ago by marauding Mughals. Inside, a forest of beautifully carved pillars surrounds the central shrine, which holds an image of Adinath himself.

The **Luna Vasahi Temple** is dedicated to Neminath, the 22nd *tirthankar*, and was built in 1230 by the brothers Tejpal and Vastupal for a mere ₹125.3 million. Like Vimal, the brothers were both Gujarati government ministers. The marble carving here took 2500 workers 15 years to create, and its most notable feature is its intricacy and delicacy, which is so fine that, in places, the marble becomes almost transparent. The many-layered lotus flower that dangles from the centre of the dome is a particularly astonishing piece of work.

As at other Jain temples, leather articles (including belts and shoes) cameras and phones must be left at the entrance, and menstruating women are asked not to enter.

Delwara is about 3km north of Mt Abu town centre: you can walk there in less than an hour, or hop aboard a shared taxi (₹10 per person) from up the street opposite Chacha Cafe. A taxi all to yourself should be ₹100, or ₹200 round-trip with one hour's waiting.

in the busy dining hall or outside under a canopy. It's near the bus stand for the lunch break during the all-day RSRTC tour.

Sankalp
SOUTH INDIAN $$

(Hotel Maharaja, Lake Rd; mains ₹90-220; ⊙9am-11pm) A branch of a quality Gujarat-based chain serving up excellent South Indian vegetarian fare. Unusual fillings like pineapple or spinach, cheese and garlic are available for its renowned dosas and *uttapams* (savoury South Indian rice pancake), which come with multiple sauces and condiments. Order *masala papad* (wafer with spicy topping) for a tasty starter.

Mulberry Restaurant
INDIAN $$

(Hilltone Hotel, Main St; mains ₹250-320) Mt Abu's Gujarati tourists make veg thalis the order of the day in the town, so if you're craving a bit of nonveg, the smart Mulberry Restaurant at the Hilltone Hotel is the place to go. There are plenty of meaty Indian options on the menu (although the biryanis are a bit bland) and alcohol is often served to wash it down.

Arbuda
INDIAN $$

(Arbuda Circle; mains ₹100-150; ⊙7am-10.30pm) This big restaurant is set on a sweeping open terrace filled with chrome chairs. It's very popular for its Gujarati, Punjabi and South Indian food, and does fine Continental breakfasts and fresh juices.

☕ Drinking

Most of the more upmarket hotels have bars; the prices are predictably high, but the heritage hotels can justify this with their quaint atmospheres.

Polo Bar
BAR

(☎02974-235176; www.royalfamilyjaipur.com; ⊙11.30-3.30pm & 7.30-11pm) The terrace at the Jaipur Hotel, formerly the maharaja of Jaipur's summer palace, is a dreamy place for an evening tipple, with divine views over the hills, lake and the town's twinkling lights. Meals are served (₹135 to ₹300).

Cafe Coffee Day
CAFE

(Rotary Circle; coffee from ₹60; ⊙9am-11pm) A branch of the popular caffeine-supply chain. The tea and cakes aren't bad either.

🛍 Shopping

The street leading down to Nakki Lake is lined with bright little shops mostly flogging all sorts of kitsch curios, and there's more of the same around the market area. **Chacha Museum** (⊙10am-8pm), a larger, fixed-price shop with some crafts and souvenirs, is worth a browse.

ℹ Information

There are State Bank ATMs on Raj Bhavan Rd, opposite Hotel Samrat International and outside the tourist office. There's a Bank of Baroda ATM on Lake Rd.

Main Post Office (Raj Bhavan Rd; ⊙9am-5pm Mon-Sat)

Union Bank of India (Main Market; ⊙10am-3pm Mon-Fri, to 12.30pm Sat) The only bank changing travellers cheques and currency.

Yani-Ya Cyber Zone (Raj Bhavan Rd; internet-per hr ₹40; ⊙9am-10pm)

ℹ Getting There & Away

Access to Mt Abu town is by a dramatic 28km-long road that winds its way up thickly forested hillsides from the town of Abu Road, where the nearest train station is. Some buses from other cities go all the way up to Mt Abu, others only go as far as Abu Road. Buses (₹30, one hour) run between Abu Road and Mt Abu town half-hourly from about 6am to 7pm. A taxi from Abu Road to Mt Abu is ₹300/400 by day/night.

MAJOR TRAINS FROM ABU ROAD

DESTINATION	TRAIN NO & NAME	DEPARTURE TIME	ARRIVAL TIME	FARE (₹)
Ahmedabad	19224 Jammu Tawi-Ahmedabad Exp	10.50am	3pm	140/485 (A)
Delhi (New Delhi)	12957 Swarna J Raj Exp	8.50pm	7.30am	1370/1875 (B)
Jaipur	19707 Aravali Exp	10.10am	6.55pm	260/690 (A)
Jodhpur	19223 Ahmedabad-Jammu Tawi Exp	3.25pm	7.40pm	185/485 (A)
Mumbai	19708 Aravali Exp	4.55pm	6.35am	355/960 (A)

Fares: (A) sleeper/3AC, (B) 3AC/2AC

TREKKING AROUND MT ABU

Getting off the tourist trail and out into the forests and hills of Mt Abu is a revelation. This is a world of isolated shrines and lakes, weird rock formations, fantastic panoramas, nomadic villagers, orchids, wild fruits, plants used in ayurvedic medicine, sloth bears (which are fairly common), wild boars, langurs, 150 bird species and even the occasional leopard.

Mahendra 'Charles' Dan of **Mt Abu Treks** (☑9414154854; www.mount-abu-treks.blog spot.com; Hotel Lake Palace; 3-4hr trek per person ₹500, full-day incl lunch ₹1000) arranges tailor-made treks ranging from gentle village visits to longer, wilder expeditions into Mt Abu Wildlife Sanctuary. He's passionate and knowledgeable about the local flora and fauna. Treks include a three- to four-hour trek, a full day including lunch, and an overnight village trek including all meals (₹2000). The sanctuary entrance fee (Indian/foreigner ₹20/160) is not included.

The Shri Ganesh Hotel (p164) also organises good one- or four-hour hikes (₹100/500) hikes starting at 7am or 4pm.

A warning from the locals: it's very unsafe to wander unguided in these hills. Travellers have been mauled by bears, or mugged (and worse) by other people.

BUS

Services from Mt Abu bus stand include:

Ahmedabad (₹138, seven hours, hourly from 6am to 9pm)

Jaipur (seat/sleeper ₹386/411, 11 hours, one daily)

Jodhpur (₹203, six hours, roughly hourly)

Udaipur (₹120, 4½ hours, four daily)

TRAIN

Abu Road station is on the line between Delhi and Mumbai via Ahmedabad. An autorickshaw from Abu Road train station to Abu Road bus stand costs ₹10. Mt Abu has a **railway reservation centre** (⊙8am-2pm Mon-Sat), above the tourist office, with quotas on most of the express trains.

Around Mt Abu

Guru Shikhar

At the northeast end of the Mt Abu plateau, 17km from the town, rises 1722m-high Guru Shikhar, Rajasthan's highest point. A winding road goes almost all the way to the summit where you'll find the **Atri Rishi Temple**, complete with a priest and fantastic, huge views. A popular spot, it's a highlight of the RSRTC tour (p163); if you decide to go it alone, a 4WD will cost ₹500 return.

NORTHERN RAJASTHAN (SHEKHAWATI)

Far less visited than other parts of Rajasthan, the Shekhawati region is most famous for its extraordinary painted *havelis* (traditional, ornately decorated residences that enclose one or more courtyards), highlight-ed with dazzling, often whimsical, murals. Part of the region's appeal and mystique is due to these works of art being found in tiny towns, connected to each other by single-track roads that run through lonely, arid countryside. Today it seems curious that such care, attention and money was lavished on these out-of-the-way houses, but from the 14th century onwards Shekhawati's towns were important trading posts on the caravan routes from Gujarati ports.

What makes the artwork on Shekhawati's *havelis* so fascinating is the manner in which their artists combined traditional subjects, such as mythology, religious scenes and images of the family, with contemporary concerns, including brand-new inventions and accounts of current events, many of which these isolated painters rendered straight from their imaginations.

Nawalgarh

☑01594 / POP 56,500

Nawalgarh is a small, nontouristy town almost at the very centre of the Shekhawati region, and makes a great base for exploring. It boasts several fine *havelis,* a colourful, mostly pedestrianised bazaar and some excellent accommodation options.

◉ Sights

Dr Ramnath A Podar Haveli Museum   MUSEUM
(www.podarhavelimuseum.org; admission ₹100, camera ₹30; ⊙8.30am-6.30pm) Built in 1902 on the eastern side of town, and known locally as 'Podar Haveli', this is one of the

region's few buildings to have been thoroughly restored. The paintings of this *haveli* are defined in strong colours, and are the most vivid murals in town, although purists point to the fact that they have been simply repainted rather than restored. On the ground floor are several galleries on Rajasthani culture, including costume, turbans, musical instruments and models of Rajasthan's forts.

Morarka Haveli Museum   MUSEUM
(admission ₹50; ☺ 8am-7pm) This museum has well-presented original paintings, preserved for decades behind doorways blocked with cement. The inner courtyard hosts some gorgeous Ramayana scenes; look out for the slightly incongruous image of Jesus on the top storey, beneath the eaves in the courtyard's southeast corner. Turn left out of Dr Ramnath A Podar Haveli Museum, then take the first right and it's on your right.

Bhagton ki Choti Haveli   HISTORIC BUILDING
(Bhagat Haveli; admission ₹50) On the western wall of Bhagton ki Choti Haveli is a locomotive and a steamship. Above them, elephant-bodied *gopis* (milkmaids) dance. Adjacent to this, women dance during the Holi festival. Inside you'll find other murals, including one strange picture (in a room on the western side) of a European man with a cane and pipe, and a dog on his shoulder.

To get here, turn left out of Morarka Haveli, take the first right, then left, then first right again and it's on your left.

🏃 Activities & Tours

Ramesh Jangid at **Apani Dhani** and his son Rajesh at **Ramesh Jangid's Tourist Pension** (🏠 224060; www.touristpension.com) are keen to promote sustainable rural tourism. They organise guided hiking trips (two to three days from ₹1900 per person), guided camel-cart rides (half-day ₹1500) to outlying villages, and guided tours by car (full day from ₹800 per person) to other towns in the region. They can also arrange lessons in Hindi, tabla drumming, cooking and local crafts such as *bandhani*.

   Roop Niwas Kothi (🏠 222008; www.royalridingholidays.com; 1hr/half-day/full day ₹1000/3000/6000) specialises in high-end horse excursions. Elaborate excursions are available, ranging from one night to a week, including accommodation in luxury tents.

🛏 Sleeping & Eating

DS Bungalow   GUESTHOUSE $
(🏠 9983168916; s ₹350-450, d ₹400-500) Run by a friendly, down-to-earth couple, this simple place with boxy air-cooled rooms is a little out of town on the way to Roop Niwas Kothi. It's backed by a garden with a pleasant outdoor mud-walled restaurant serving decent home cooking. The more energetic can arrange camel tours here.

★ **Apani Dhani**   GUESTHOUSE $$
(🏠 222239; www.apanidhani.com; r/cottages with AC ₹1800/2400, with fan ₹1600/2200; ❀🏠) 🌿 This award-winning ecotourism venture is a delightfully relaxing place. Rooms with comfortable beds are in cosy mud-hut, thatched-roof bungalows set around a bougainvillea-shaded courtyard. The adjoining organic farm supplies food and there are solar lights, water heaters and compost toilets. It's on the western side of the Jaipur road. Five per cent of the room tariff goes to community projects. Tours around the area, via bicycle, car, camel cart or foot, are available.

Shekhawati Guesthouse   GUESTHOUSE $$
(🏠 224658; www.shekhawatiguesthouse.com; r ₹600/800, cottage ₹1000-1400; ❀@🏠) This corner of rural loveliness is more like a homestay run by a very friendly couple. There are six rooms in the main building plus five lovely, mud-walled thatched cottages in the garden. The organic garden supplies most of the hotel's produce needs, which can be enjoyed in the lovely outdoor restaurant. It's 4km east of the bus stand (₹60 by taxi). Pick-up from the bus or train station can be arranged, as can cooking lessons.

**Ramesh Jangid's
Tourist Pension**   GUESTHOUSE $$
(🏠 224060; www.touristpension.com; s/d/tr from ₹800/1050/1350; @🏠) 🌿 Near the Maur Hospital, on the western edge of town, this pension is well known, so if you get lost, just ask a local to point you in the right direction. The guesthouse, run by genial Rajesh, Ramesh's son, offers homely, clean accommodation in spacious rooms with big beds. Some rooms have furniture carved by Rajesh's grandfather, and the more expensive rooms also have murals created by visiting artists. Pure veg meals, made with organic ingredients, are available, including a delectable vegetable thali for ₹180. The family also arranges all sorts of tours around Shekhawati.

Shekhawati

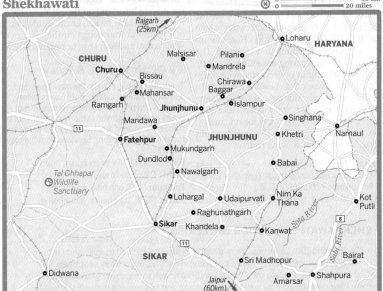

ⓘ Getting There & Away

The main bus stand is little more than a dusty car park accessed through a large, yellow double-arched gateway. Services run roughly every hour to Jaipur (₹105, 3½ hours), Jhunjhunu (₹30, one hour) and Mandawa (₹25, 45 minutes). Nawalgarh is on a narrow-gauge train line with slow daily trains running between Jhunjhunu to Jaipur (2nd-class seats only).

Jhunjhunu

📞 01592 / POP 100,500

Shekhawati's most important commercial centre has a different atmosphere to that of the smaller towns, with lots of traffic, concrete, and hustle and bustle befitting the district capital. It does, though, have some appealing *havelis* and a colourful bazaar.

⊙ Sights

Rani Sati Temple   HINDU TEMPLE
(Ram Niwas Bagh; ⊙ 4am-10pm) The enormous, multistorey Rani Sati Temple is notorious for commemorating an act of *sati* by a merchant's wife (after whom the temple is named) in 1595. It's fronted by two courtyards, around which 300 rooms offer shelter to pilgrims. The main hall, in the far courtyard, is made of marble with elaborate silver repoussé work before the inner sanctum. There's a tile-and-mirror mosaic on the ceiling and a relief frieze on one wall depicts the story of Rani Sati.

It's a 10-minute walk north of the private bus stand. Turn left out of the bus stand, take the first left, then keep asking for Rani Sati Mandir.

Modi Havelis   HISTORIC BUILDING
(Nehru Bazaar; admission ₹50) The Modi Havelis face each other and house some of Jhunjhunu's best murals and woodcarving. The *haveli* on the eastern side has a painting of a woman in a blue sari sitting before a gramophone; a frieze depicts a train, alongside which soldiers race on horses. The spaces between the brackets above show the Krishna legends. The *haveli* on the western side has some comical pictures, featuring some remarkable facial expressions and moustaches.

Around the archway, between the inner and outer courtyards, there are some glass-covered portrait miniatures, along with some fine mirror-and-glass tilework. In the second half of the antechamber, Krishna dances with the *gopis* while angels fly overhead. The inner courtyard shows the hierarchy of the universe, with deities in the upper frieze, humans in the middle band, and animal and floral motifs below.

🛏 Sleeping

Hotel Jamuna Resort HOTEL $$
(☑512696; www.hoteljamunaresort.com; near Nath Ka Tilla; r ₹1500-3500; ✳@🛜🏊) Hotel Jamuna Resort has everything that you need. The rooms in the older wing are either vibrantly painted with murals or decorated with traditional mirrorwork (but beware rooms with vanishingly tiny windows), while the rooms in the newer wing are modern and airy. There's an inviting pool (₹50 for nonguests) set in the serene garden and purpose-built kitchens set up for cooking courses.

Hotel Shiv Shekhawati HOTEL $$
(☑232651; www.shivshekhawati.com; Khemi Shakti Rd; s/d from ₹800/1000; ✳@) Shiv Shekhawati is the best budget option with plain but squeaky-clean rooms. It's 600m from the private bus stand on the eastern edge of town. The affable owner, Laxmi Kant Jangid, is a wealth of knowledge on the villages of Shekhawati and tours can be organised here.

ℹ Getting There & Away

There are two bus stands: the main bus stand and the private bus stand. Both have similar services and prices, but the government-run buses from the main bus stand run much more frequently. Shared autorickshaws run between the two (₹8 per person). Services from the main bus stand:

Bikaner (₹174, five to six hours, hourly)
Delhi (₹183, five to six hours, hourly)
Fatehpur (₹42, one hour, half-hourly)
Jaipur (₹135, four hours, half-hourly)

SHEKHAWATI'S OUTDOOR GALLERIES

In the 18th and 19th centuries, shrewd Marwari merchants lived frugally and far from home while earning money in India's new commercial centres. They sent the bulk of their vast fortunes back to their families in Shekhawati to construct grand *havelis* to show their neighbours how well they were doing and to compensate their families for their long absences. Merchants competed with one another to build ever more grand edifices – homes, temples, step-wells – which were richly decorated, both inside and out, with painted murals.

The artists responsible for these acres of decoration largely belonged to the caste of *kumhars* (potters) and were both the builders and painters of the *havelis*. Known as *chajeras* (masons), many were commissioned from beyond Shekhawati – particularly from Jaipur, where they had been employed decorating the new capital's palaces – and others flooded in from further afield to offer their skills. Soon, there was a cross-pollination of ideas and techniques, with local artists learning from the new arrivals.

The early paintings are strongly influenced by Mughal decoration, with floral arabesques and geometric designs. The Rajput royal courts were the next major influence; scenes from Hindu mythology are prevalent – Krishna is particularly popular.

With the arrival of Europeans, walls were embellished with paintings of the new technological marvels to which the Shekhawati merchants had been exposed to in centres such as Calcutta. Pictures of trains, planes, telephones, gramophones and bicycles featured, often painted directly from the artist's imagination. The British are invariably depicted as soldiers, with dogs or holding bottles of booze.

Haveli walls were frequently painted by the *chajeras* from the ground to the eaves. Often the paintings mix depictions of the gods and their lives with everyday scenes featuring modern inventions, such as trains and aeroplanes, even though these artists themselves had never seen them. Hence, Krishna and Radha are seen in flying motorcars and Europeans can be observed inflating hot-air balloons by blowing into them.

These days most of the *havelis* are still owned by descendants of the original families, but not inhabited by their owners, for whom small-town Rajasthan has lost its charm. Many are occupied by a single *chowkidar* (caretaker), while others may be home to a local family. Though they are pale reflections of the time when they accommodated the large households of the Marwari merchant families, they remain a fascinating testament to the changing times in which they were created. Only a few *havelis* have been restored; many more lie derelict, crumbling slowly away.

For a full rundown on the history, people, towns and buildings of the area, track down a copy of *The Painted Towns of Shekhawati*, by Ilay Cooper, an excellent book which can be picked up at bookshops in the region or Jaipur.

Mandawa (₹20, one hour, half-hourly)
Nawalgarh (₹35, one hour, half-hourly)

The train line to Jaipur via Nawalgarh is narrow gauge, and is not connected to the rest of the rail network. There are slow daily services, but generally it's quicker and more convenient to travel by bus.

Fatehpur

🎵 01571 / POP 78,400

Established in 1451 as a capital for nawabs (Muslim ruling princes), Fatehpur was their stronghold for centuries before it was taken over by the Shekhawati Rajputs in the 18th century. It's a busy little town, with plenty of *havelis*, many in a sad state of disrepair, but with a few notable exceptions.

👁 Sights

Apart from the magnificent Haveli Nadine Le Prince, other sights include the nearby **Jagannath Singhania Haveli**; the **Mahavir Prasad Goenka Haveli** (often locked, but with superb paintings); **Geori Shankar Haveli**, with mirrored mosaics on the antechamber ceiling; and **Harikrishnan Das Saraogi Haveli**, with a colourful facade and iron lacework.

Haveli Nadine Le Prince   HISTORIC BUILDING
(🎵233024; www.cultural-centre.com; admission incl guided tour ₹200; ⏰9am-6pm) This 1802 *haveli* has been stunningly restored by French artist Nadine Le Prince and is now one of the most exquisite in Shekhawati. Nadine is only here for part of the year, but enlists foreign volunteers to manage the building and conduct the detailed guided tours. There's a cafe of sorts secreted away in a garden courtyard, plus a small gallery. Some of the rooms have been converted into small but beautifully decorated guest rooms (p171).

The *haveli* is around 2km north of the two main bus stands, down a lane off the main road. Turn right out of the bus stands, and the turning will eventually be on your right, or hop into an autorickshaw.

🛏 Sleeping & Eating

Haveli Cultural Centre
Guest House & Art Café   BOUTIQUE HOTEL **$$**
(🎵233024; www.cultural-centre.com; Haveli Nadine Le Prince; r from ₹1300; ❄) The beautifully restored Haveli Nadine Le Prince has opened its artist residence rooms to travellers. Several traditional-style rooms over-

look the central courtyard. To just visit the Art Café you'll have to pay to get into the *haveli,* but this is a good option for a light lunch (meals ₹100 to ₹400). It's a cosy place with low tables, next to the garden, as well as Indian snacks.

ℹ Getting There & Around

From the private bus stand on the Churu–Sikar road, buses leave for Jhunjhunu (₹28, one hour), Mandawa (₹22, one hour), Churu (₹25, one hour) and Ramgarh (₹16, 45 minutes). From the RSRTC bus stand, which is further south down the same road, buses leave for Jaipur (₹88, 3½ hours, hourly), Delhi (₹184, seven hours, six daily) and Bikaner (₹125, 3½ hours, hourly).

Mandawa

🎵 01592 / POP 20,800

Of all the towns in the Shekhawati region, Mandawa is the one best set up for tourists, with plenty of places to stay and some decent restaurants. It's a little touristy (although this is a relative term compared with other parts of Rajasthan), but this small 18th-century settlement is still a pleasant base for your *haveli* explorations.

There is only one main drag, with narrow lanes fanning off it. The easy-to-find Hotel Mandawa Haveli is halfway along this street and makes a handy point of reference. Most buses drop passengers off on the main drag as well as by the bus stand.

👁 Sights

Binsidhar Newatia Haveli   HISTORIC BUILDING
This 1920s *haveli* on the northern side of the Fatehpur–Jhunjhunu road houses the State Bank of Bikaner & Jaipur. There are fantastically entertaining paintings on the external eastern wall, including a European woman in a chauffeur-driven car, the Wright brothers in flight watched by women in saris, a strongman hauling along a car, and a bird-man flying in a winged device.

Murmuria Haveli   HISTORIC BUILDING
The Murmuria Haveli dates back to the 1930s. From the sandy courtyard out front, you can get a good view of the southern external wall of the adjacent double *haveli:* it features a long frieze depicting a train and a railway crossing. Nehru is depicted on horseback holding the Indian flag. Above the arches on the southern side of the courtyard are two paintings of gondolas on the canals of Venice.

🛏 Sleeping & Eating

There are at least half a dozen *haveli* hotels here, either on or near the main drag. Rooms in them range from ₹1200 to ₹4000. Mandawa is small so wandering around town to find a room is relatively easy.

Hotel Shekhawati　　　　HOTEL $
(📞9314698079; www.hotelshekwati.com; r ₹400-1800; ❄@🖥) Near Mukundgarh Rd, the only real budget choice in town is run by a retired bank manager and his son (who's also a registered tourist guide). Bright, comically bawdy murals painted by artistic former guests give the rooms a splash of colour. Tasty meals are served on the peaceful rooftop, and competitively priced camel, horse and 4WD tours can also be arranged.

Hotel Mandawa Haveli　　HERITAGE HOTEL $$
(📞223088; www.hotelmandawa.com; s/d from ₹2200/3700; ❄) Close to Sonathia Gate, on the main road, this retreat is set in a glorious, restored 1890s *haveli* with rooms surrounding a painted courtyard. The cheapest rooms are small, so it's worth splashing out on a suite, filled with arches, window seats and countless small windows. There's a rooftop restaurant serving good food; it's especially romantic at dinner time, when the lights of the town twinkle below. A set dinner costs ₹450.

Hotel Castle Mandawa　　HERITAGE HOTEL $$$
(📞223124; www.castlemandawa.com; s/d from ₹4500/6000; ❄@🖥🏊) Mandawa's large upmarket hotel in the town's converted fort is a swish and generally comfortable choice. Some rooms are far better appointed than others (the best are the suites in the tower, with four-poster and swing beds), so check a few before you settle in. The gardens and grounds boast restaurants, a coffee shop and cocktail bar, pool and ayurvedic spa.

Monica Rooftop Restaurant　　INDIAN $$
(mains ₹100-300; ☺8am-9pm) This delightful rooftop restaurant, in between the fort gate and main bazaar, serves tasty meals. It's in a converted *haveli,* but sadly only the facade, rather than the restaurant itself, has frescoes.

Bungli Restaurant　　INDIAN $$
(Goenka Chowk; mains ₹130-300; ☺5am-10pm) A popular outdoor travellers' eatery near the Bikaner bus stand, Bungli serves piping-hot tandoori and cold beer from a down-at-heel setting. The food is cooked fresh by a chef who hails from Hotel Castle Mandawa. Early risers can have an Indian breakfast and yoga class for a total of ₹375.

ℹ Getting There & Away

The main bus stand, sometimes called Bikaner bus stand, has frequent services (roughly half-hourly). The main bus stand is at one end of the main drag, on your left as the road bears right. It's a few hundred metres walk left from Hotel Mandawa Haveli.

There is also a separate Nawalgarh bus stand, just off the main drag, with services to Nawalgarh only. Both bus stands are so small they are unrecognisable as bus stands unless a bus is waiting at them. Look for the chai stalls that cluster beside them and you should have the right spot.

Bikaner (₹154, four hours)
Fatehpur (₹22, 30 minutes)
Jhunjhunu (₹20, one hour)
Nawalgarh (₹25, 45 minutes)

WESTERN RAJASTHAN

Jodhpur

📞0291 / POP 1,033,900

Mighty Mehrangarh, the muscular fort that towers over the Blue City of Jodhpur, is a magnificent spectacle and an architectural masterpiece. Around Mehrangarh's base, the old city, a jumble of Brahmin-blue cubes, stretches out to the 10km-long, 16th-century city wall. Inside is a tangle of winding, glittering, medieval streets, which never seem to lead where you expect them to, scented by incense, roses and sewers, with shops and bazaars selling everything from trumpets and temple decorations to snuff and saris.

Traditionally, blue signified the home of a Brahmin, but non-Brahmins have got in on the act too. Glowing with a mysterious light, the blue tint is thought to repel insects.

Modern Jodhpur stretches well beyond the city walls, but it's the immediacy and buzz of the old Blue City and the larger-than-life fort that capture travellers' imaginations. This crowded, hectic zone is Jodhpur's main tourist area, and it often seems you can't speak to anyone without them trying to sell you something. Areas of the old city further west, such as Navchokiya, are just as atmospheric, with far less hustling.

History

Driven from their homeland of Kannauj, east of Agra, by Afghans serving Mohammed of Ghori, the Rathore Rajputs fled west around AD 1200 to the region around Pali, 70km southeast of Jodhpur. They prospered to such a degree that in 1381 they managed to oust the Pratiharas of Mandore, 9km north of present-day Jodhpur. In 1459 the Rathore leader Rao Jodha chose a nearby rocky ridge as the site for a new fortress of staggering proportions, Mehrangarh, around which grew Jodha's city: Jodhpur.

Jodhpur lay on the vital trade route between Delhi and Gujarat. The Rathore kingdom grew on the profits of sandalwood, opium, dates and copper, and controlled a large area that became cheerily known as Marwar (the Land of Death), due to its harsh topography and climate. It stretched as far west as what's now the India–Pakistan border area, and bordered with Mewar (Udaipur) in the south, Jaisalmer in the northwest, Bikaner in the north, and Jaipur and Ajmer in the east.

◉ Sights & Activities

★ **Mehrangarh** FORT
(www.mehrangarh.org; Indian/foreigner incl audio guide ₹/60/400, camera/video ₹100/250, human guide ₹225; ☉9am-5pm) Rising perpendicular and impregnable from a rocky hill that itself stands 120m above Jodhpur's skyline, Mehrangarh is one of the most magnificent forts in India. The battlements are 6m to 36m high, and as the building materials were chiselled from the rock on which the fort stands, the structure merges with its base. Still run by the Jodhpur royal family, Mehrangarh is packed with history and legend. Mehrangarh's main entrance is at the northeast gate, **Jai Pol**. You don't need a ticket to enter the fort, only the museum section.

It's about a 300m walk up from the old city to the entrance, or you can take a winding 5km autorickshaw ride (around ₹100). The superb audio guide (available in 11 languages) is included with the museum ticket, but bring ID or a credit card as deposit.

Jai Pol was built by Maharaja Man Singh in 1808 following his defeat of invading forces from Jaipur. Past the **museum ticket office** and a small cafe, the 16th-century **Dodh Kangra Pol** was an external gate before Jai Pol was built, and still bears the scars of 1808 cannonball hits. Through here, the main route heads up to the left through the 16th-century **Imritia Pol** and then **Loha Pol**, the fort's original entrance, with iron spikes to deter enemy elephants. Just inside

the gate are two sets of small hand prints, the *sati* (self-immolation) marks of royal widows who threw themselves on their maharajas' funeral pyres – the last to do so were Maharaja Man Singh's widows in 1843.

Past Loha Pol you'll find a restaurant and **Suraj Pol**, which gives access to the museum. Once you've visited the museum, continue on from here to the panoramic **ramparts**, which are lined with impressive antique artillery.

Also worth exploring is the right turn from Jai Pol, where a path winds down to the **Chokelao Bagh**, a restored and gorgeously planted 18th-century Rajput garden (you could lose an afternoon here lolling under shady trees reading a book), and the **Fateh Pol** (Victory Gate). You can exit here into the old city quarter of Navchokiya.

➡ **Museum**
This beautiful network of stone-latticed courtyards and halls, formerly the fort's palace, is a superb example of Rajput architecture, so finely carved that it often looks more like sandalwood than sandstone. The **galleries** around **Shringar Chowk** (Anointment Courtyard) display India's best collection of elephant howdahs and Jodhpur's royal palanquin collection.

One of the two galleries off **Daulat Khana Chowk** displays textiles, paintings, manuscripts, headgear and the curved sword of the Mughal emperor Akbar; the other gallery is the armoury. Upstairs is a fabulous **gallery of miniature paintings** from the sophisticated Marwar school and the beautiful 18th-century **Phul Mahal** (Flower Palace), with 19th-century wall paintings depicting the 36 moods of classical *ragas* as well as royal portraits; the artist took 10 years to create them using a curious concoction of gold leaf, glue and cow's urine.

Takhat Vilas was the bedchamber of Maharaja Takhat Singh (r 1843–73), who had just 30 maharanis and numerous concubines. Its beautiful ceiling is covered with Christmas baubles. You then enter the extensive *zenana,* whose lovely latticed windows (from which the women could watch the goings-on in the courtyards) are said to feature over 250 different designs. Here you'll find the **Cradle Gallery**, exhibiting the elaborate cradles of infant princes, and the 17th-century **Moti Mahal** (Pearl Palace), which was the palace's main durbar hall (royal reception hall) for official meetings and receptions, with gorgeously colourful stained glass.

Jodhpur

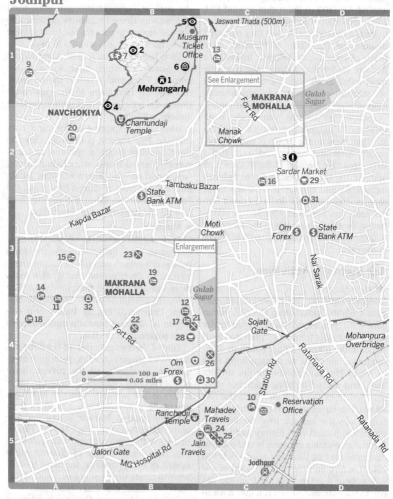

★ **Rao Jodha Desert Rock Park** PARK
(☑ 9571271000; www.raojodhapark.com; Mehrangarh; admission ₹50, guide ₹100; ⊘ 8am-6pm Oct-Mar, 7am-7pm Apr-Sep) This 72-hectare park – and model of intelligent ecotourism – sits in the lee of Mehrangarh. It has been lovingly restored and planted with native species to show the natural diversity of the region. The park is criss-crossed with walking trails that take you up to the city walls, around Devkund Lake, spotting local birds, butterflies and reptiles. For an extra insight into the area's native flora and fauna, take along one of the excellent local guides.

Walks here are the perfect restorative if the Indian hustle has left you in need of breathing space. Visit early in the morning or in the late afternoon for the most pleasant temperatures. The visitors centre is thoughtfully put together, and there's a small cafe too.

Jaswant Thada HISTORIC BUILDING
(Indian/foreigner ₹15/30, camera/video ₹25/50; ⊘ 9am-5pm) This milky-white marble memorial to Maharaja Jaswant Singh II, sitting above a small lake 1km northeast of Mehrangarh, is an array of whimsical domes. It's

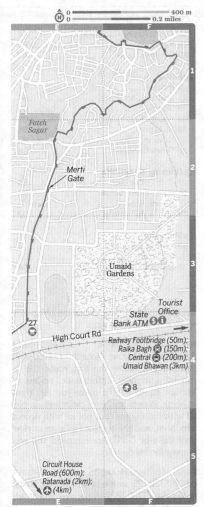

and southern ends. The narrow, winding lanes of the old city spread out in all directions from here. Westward, you plunge into the old city's commercial heart, with crowded alleys and bazaars selling vegetables, spices, sweets, silver and handicrafts.

Umaid Bhawan Palace
PALACE

(museum Indian/foreigner ₹25/60; ⊙ museum 9am-5pm) Take an autorickshaw to this hilltop palace, 3km southeast of the old city. The current royal incumbent, Gaj Singh II, still lives in part of the building. Built in 1929, the 365-room edifice was designed by the British architect Henry Lanchester for Maharaja Umaid Singh. It took more than 3000 workers 15 years to complete, at a cost of around ₹11 million. The building is mortarless, and incorporates 100 wagon-loads of Makrana marble and Burmese teak in the interior. Apparently its construction began as a royal job-creation program during a time of severe drought. Much of the building has been turned into a suitably grand hotel.

Casual visitors are not welcome at either the royal residence or the hotel, but you can visit the **museum**, housed in one side of the building. It includes photos showing the elegant art deco design of the palace interior, plus an eccentric collection of elaborate clocks. Don't miss the maharaja's highly polished classic cars, displayed in front of the museum, by the entrance gate.

Flying Fox
ADVENTURE

(www.flyingfox.asia; tour ₹1800; ⊙ 9am-5pm) This circuit of six zip-lines flies back and forth over walls, bastions and lakes on the northern side of Mehrangarh. A brief training session is given before you start and safety standards are good: awesome is the verdict of most who dare. Flying Fox has a desk near the main ticket office and its starting point is in the Chokelao Bagh. Tours last up to 1½ hours, depending on the group size. Book online for a discount on the walk-up price.

a welcome, peaceful spot after the hubbub of the city, and the views across to the fort and over the city are superb. Built in 1899, the cenotaph has some beautiful *jalis* (carved marble lattice screens) and is hung with portraits of Rathore rulers going back to the 13th century. Look out for the memorial to a peacock that flew into a funeral pyre.

Clock Tower
MONUMENT

The century-old clock tower is an old city landmark surrounded by the vibrant sounds, sights and smells of Sardar Market, which is marked by triple gateways at its northern

🎉 Festivals & Events

In September or October Jodhpur hosts the colourful **Marwar Festival**, which includes polo and a camel tattoo. It coincides with the excellent **Rajasthan International Folk Festival** (www.jodhpurriff.org), five days of music concerts by Indian and international artists held at Mehrangarh. This most spectacular of music venues also hosts April's **Jodhpur Flamenco and Gypsy Festival** (http://jfgfestival.com).

Jodhpur

🛏 Sleeping

The old city has something like 100 guesthouses, most of which scramble for your custom as soon as you get within breathing distance of Sardar Market.

If a rickshaw rider or friendly local is clamouring to take you to a guesthouse or hotel, it's probably because he is aiming to receive a commission from them. There's a growing anti-commission movement among hoteliers here, but many still pay touts, or your rickshaw/taxi driver an absurd 50% of what you pay for your room. Don't believe drivers or strangers on the street who tell you the place you want has closed, is full, is under repair, is far from the centre etc.

Many lodgings can organise a pick-up from the train station or bus stops, even at night, if you call ahead. Otherwise, for most places in the old city you can avoid nonsense by getting dropped at the clock tower and walking from there.

Old City (Sardar Market)

Mangal Haveli Guest House GUESTHOUSE $
(☑ 2611001; www.mangalhaveli.com; Killi Khana, Fort Rd; r ₹500-700; ☗) A good budget option between the fort and the clock tower. Rooms are simple but good value for the price; those facing inside are darker but quieter, compared to the airier rooms facing

the busy thoroughfare. It has the obligatory rooftop terrace restaurant.

Hill View Guest House GUESTHOUSE $
(☑ 2441763; Makrana Mohalla; r ₹250-600) Perched just below the fort walls, this is run by a friendly, enthusiastic, no-hassle, Muslim family, who'll make you feel right at home. Rooms are basic, clean and simple, all with bathrooms (but not all with decent windows), and the terrace has a great view over the city. Good, home-cooked veg and nonveg food is on offer.

Kesar Heritage Hotel GUESTHOUSE $
(☑ 09983216625; www.kesarheritage.com; Makrana Mohalla; r ₹700-1200) A popular recent addition to Jodhpur's budget accommodation scene, Kesar plays a good hand with large airy rooms (a few have balconies) and friendly, helpful management, plus a side-street location that puts noisily sputtering rickshaws out of earshot of light sleepers. The rooftop restaurant looks up to Mehrangarh.

Nirvana Hotel HOTEL $
(☑ 5106280; nirwanahome.jod@gmail.com; 1st fl, Tija Mata ka Mandir, Tambaku Bazar; r ₹800-1200; ❄☗) It's not often you get to lay your head down in a converted Hindu temple, but Nirvan Hotel gives you the chance. Rooms run off a lovely courtyard thick with pot plants, and although windows face inside,

your views are instead of original 150-year-old temple frescoes (fixtures and fittings are thankfully newer). Room 11 is the highlight – it's under an original temple dome, and looks straight over the rooftops to Mehrangarh.

Hare Krishna Guest House GUESTHOUSE $
(📞 2635307; www.harekrishnaguesthouse.net; Makrana Mohalla; r ₹600-1200; 🛜) An old house that has been extended upwards and squeezes in rooms and stairs wherever possible. The range of rooms is impressive, from the cavelike cheapie to the spacious fort-view rooms. Friendly staff, free wi-fi and, of course, a rooftop restaurant.

Pushp Paying Guest House GUESTHOUSE $
(📞 2648494; sonukash2003@yahoo.co.in; Pipli-ki-Gali, Naya Bass, Manak Chowk; r ₹500-800; ❄️ @ 🛜) This small family-home-cum-guesthouse has five clean, colourful rooms with windows. It's tucked down the narrowest of alleys, but you get an up-close view of Mehrangarh from the rooftop restaurant, where owner Nikhil rustles up great vegetarian fare (dishes ₹30 to ₹80).

Haveli Inn Pal HERITAGE HOTEL $$
(📞 2612519; www.haveliinnpal.com; Gulab Sagar; r incl breakfast ₹2050-2550; ❄️ @ 🛜) The smaller, 12-room sibling of Pal Haveli is accessed through the same grand entrance, but is located around to the right in one wing of the grand *haveli*. It's a simpler heritage experience, with comfortable rooms and lake or fort views from the more expensive ones. It also has its own good rooftop restaurant, a mere chapati toss from Indique at Pal Haveli. Free pick-ups from Jodhpur transport terminals are offered, and discounts are often available for single occupancy.

Raas BOUTIQUE HOTEL $$$
(📞 2636455; www.raasjodhpur.com; Tunvarji-ka-Jhalra; r incl breakfast ₹21,000-40,000; ❄️ @ 🛜 ▨) Developed from a 19th-century city mansion, Jodhpur's first contemporary-style boutique hotel is a splendid retreat of clean, uncluttered style, hidden behind a big castlelike gateway. The red-sandstone-and-terrazzo rooms come with plenty of luxury touches. Most have balconies with great Mehrangarh views – also to be enjoyed from the lovely pool in the neat garden-courtyard.

Pal Haveli HERITAGE HOTEL $$$
(📞 3293328; www.palhaveli.com; Gulab Sagar; r incl breakfast ₹5500-8500; ❄️ @ 🛜) This stunning *haveli*, the best and most attractive

in the old city, was built by the Thakur of Pal in 1847. There are 21 charming, spacious rooms, mostly large and elaborately decorated in traditional heritage style, surrounding a cool central courtyard. The family still live here and can show you their small museum. Three restaurants serve excellent food and the rooftop Indique (p178) boasts views.

Old City (Navchokiya)

Cosy Guest House GUESTHOUSE $
(📞 9829023390, 2612066; www.cosyguesthouse.com; Chuna Ki Choki, Navchokiya; r ₹400-1550, without bathroom ₹250; @ 🛜) A friendly place in an enchanting location, this 500-year-old glowing blue house has several levels of higgledy-piggledy rooftops and a mix of rooms, some monastic, others comfortable. Ask the rickshaw driver for Navchokiya Rd, from where the guesthouse is signposted, or call the genial owner, Mr Joshi.

★ **Singhvi's Haveli** GUESTHOUSE $$
(📞 2624293; www.singhvihaveli.com; Ramdev-ji-ka-Chowk, Navchokiya; r ₹900-2600; ❄️ @ 🛜) This red-sandstone, family-run, 500-odd-year-old *haveli* is an understated gem. Run by two friendly brothers, Singhvi's has 13 individual rooms, ranging from the simple to the magnificent Maharani Suite with 10 windows and a fort view. The relaxing vegetarian restaurant is decorated with sari curtains and floor cushions.

Train Station Area

Govind Hotel HOTEL $$
(📞 2622758; www.govindhotel.com; Station Rd; r ₹600-2000; ❄️ @ 🛜) Well set up for travellers, with helpful management, an internet cafe, and a location convenient to the Jodhpur train station. All rooms are clean and tiled, with fairly smart bathrooms. There's a rooftop restaurant and coffee shop (p178) with excellent espresso and cakes.

🍴 Eating

It's convenient to eat in your guesthouse or hotel restaurant (which is usually on the roof, with a fort view), but there are also a number of places well worth going out to.

Jharokha MULTICUISINE $
(Hotel Haveli; mains ₹70-170; ⊙until 11pm) The rooftop terraces of the Hotel Haveli host one of the best veg restaurants in Jodhpur. As

well as the excellent food and views there's nightly entertainment in the form of traditional music and dance. The dishes include Rajasthani specialities and traditional North Indian favourites, as well as pizza, pasta and pancakes for the homesick.

Jhankar Choti Haveli   MULTICUISINE **$**
(Makrana Mohalla; mains ₹90-150; ⊙8am-10pm; 🔊) Stone walls and big cane chairs in a leafy courtyard, prettily painted woodwork and whirring fans set the scene at this semi-open-air travellers' favourite. It serves up good Indian vegetarian dishes plus pizzas, burgers and baked cheese dishes.

Omelette Shops   STREET FOOD **$**
(omelettes from ₹25; ⊙10am-10pm) On your right and left as you leave Sadar Market through its northern gate, these two omelette stalls compete for the attentions of passing travellers by knocking up seemingly endless numbers and varieties of cheap, delicious omelettes. Both do a decent job, and are run by characters worth spending a few minutes with.

Three tasty, spicy boiled eggs cost ₹15, and a two-egg masala and cheese omelette with four pieces of bread is ₹30.

Nirvana   INDIAN **$$**
(1st fl, Tija Mata ka Mandir, Tambaku Bazar; mains ₹120-160, regular/special thali ₹160/250; ⊙10.30am-10pm) Sharing premises with a Rama temple, Nirvana has both an indoor cafe, covered in 150-year-old Ramayana wall paintings, and a rooftop eating area with panoramic views. The Indian vegetarian food is among the most delicious you'll find in Rajasthan. The special thali is enormous and easily enough for two. Continental and Indian breakfasts are served in the cafe.

Kalinga Restaurant   INDIAN **$$**
(off Station Rd; mains ₹130-300; ⊙8am-11pm; ❋) This restaurant near Jodhpur train station is smart and popular. It's in a dimly lit setting and has AC, a well-stocked bar, and tasty veg and nonveg North Indian tandooris and curries. Try the *lal maans,* a mouthwatering Rajasthani mutton curry.

On the Rocks   INDIAN **$$**
(📞5102701; Circuit House Rd; mains ₹115-325; ⊙12.30-3.30pm & 7.30-11pm) This leafy garden restaurant, 2km southeast of the old city, is very popular with locals and tour groups. It has tasty Indian cuisine, including lots of barbecue options and rich and creamy curries, plus a small playground and a cavelike bar (open 11am to 11pm) with a dance floor (for couples only).

Mid Town   INDIAN **$$**
(off Station Rd; mains ₹100-150; ⊙7am-10.30pm; ❋) This clean restaurant does great veg food, including some Rajasthani specialities, some particular to Jodhpur, such as *chakki-ka-sagh* (wheat dumpling cooked in rich gravy), *bajara-ki-roti pachkuta* (*bajara* wheat roti with local vegetables) and *kabuli* (vegetables with rice, milk, bread and fruit).

★**Indique**   INDIAN **$$$**
(📞3293328; Pal Haveli Hotel; mains ₹250-350; ⊙11am-11pm) This candle-lit rooftop restaurant at the Pal Haveli hotel is the perfect place for a romantic dinner, with superb views to the fort, clock tower and Umaid Bhawan. The food covers traditional tandoori, biryanis and North Indian curries, but the Rajasthani *laal maas* (mutton curry) is a delight. Ask the barman to knock you up a gin and tonic before dinner.

 Drinking

Try a glass of *makhania* lassi, a thick and filling saffron-flavoured version of that most refreshing of drinks.

Coffee drinkers will enjoy the precious beans and espresso machines at the deliciously air-conditioned **Cafe Sheesh Mahal** (Pal Haveli Hotel; coffee from ₹80; ⊙9am-9pm); the rooftop coffee shop at the **Govind Hotel** (Govind Hotel, Station Rd; ⊙10am-10pm); and, for those who need their dose of double-shot espresso, a branch of **Cafe Coffee Day** (Jaljog Circle, High Court Rd; ⊙10am-11pm).

For other forms of liquid refreshment, pull up a stool at the **Trophy Bar** (Umaid Bhawan Palace, Umaid Bhawan Rd; ⊙11am-3pm & 6-11pm).

Shri Mishrilal Hotel   CAFE
(Sardar Market; lassi ₹30; ⊙8.30am-10pm) Just inside the southern gate of Sardar Market, this place is nothing fancy but whips up the most superb creamy *makhania* lassis. These are the best in town, probably in all of Rajasthan, possibly in all of India.

 Shopping

Plenty of Rajasthani handicrafts are available, with shops selling textiles and other wares clustered around Sardar Market and along Nai Sarak (bargain hard).

Jodhpur is famous for antiques, with a concentration of showrooms along Palace

JODHPUR'S JODHPURS

A fashion staple for self-respecting horsey people all around the world, jodhpurs are riding breeches – usually of a pale cream colour – that are loose above the knee and tapered from knee to ankle. It's said that Sir Pratap Singh, a legendary Jodhpur states-man, soldier and horseman, originally designed the breeches for the Jodhpur Lancers. When he led the Jodhpur polo team on a tour to England in 1897, the design caught on in London and then spread around the world.

If you fancy taking home an authentic pair from the city they originated in, head to **Monarch Garments**, (☑ 9352353768; www.monarch-garments.com; A-13 Umaid Bhavan Palace Rd; ⊙10.30am-8.45pm) opposite the approach road leading up to Umaid Bhawan Palace, where you can buy ready-made jodhpurs or have a pair tailored for you within two days. Prices are polo-club–worthy, starting at around ₹7000.

Rd, 2km southeast of the centre. These ware-house-sized shops are fascinating to wander around, but they're well known to Western antiques dealers, so you'll be hard-pressed to find any bargains. Also remember that the trade in antique architectural fixtures may be contributing to the desecration of India's cultural heritage (beautiful old *havelis* are often ripped apart for their doors and win-dow frames), and restrictions apply to the export of items over 100 years old. However, most showrooms deal in antique reproduc-tions, and can make a piece of antique-style furniture and ship it home for you. The best bets for quality replica antiques are **Ajay Art Emporium** (Palace Rd; ⊙10am-7pm) or **Rani Handicrafts** (Palace Rd; ⊙10am-7pm). These shops also have more portable (often less expensive) items than furniture, such as tex-tiles, carvings and silverware.

MV Spices FOOD & DRINK
(www.mvspices.com; Nai Sarak; ⊙9am-9pm) The most famous spice shop in Jodhpur (and be-lieve us, there are lots of pretenders!), MV Spices has several small branches around town that are run by the seven daughters of the founder of the original stall. It will cost around ₹80 to ₹100 for 100g bags of spices, and the owners will email you recipes so you can use your spices correctly when you get home.

Sambhali Boutique CLOTHING, ACCESSORIES
(Makrana Mohalla; ⊙10am-8pm Mon-Sat, noon-8pm Sun) ✦ This small but interesting shop sells goods made by women who have learned craft skills with the **Sambhali Trust** (☑ 0291-2512385; www.sambhali-trust. org; c/o Durag Niwas Guest House, 1st Old Pub-lic Park, Raika Bagh, Jodhpur), which works to empower disadvantaged women and girls. Items include attractive *salwar* trousers,

cute stuffed silk or cloth elephants and horses, bracelets made from pottery beads, silk bags, and block-printed muslin curtains and scarves.

Krishna Book Depot BOOKS
(Sardar Market; ⊙10.30am-7.30pm) Upstairs is an Aladdin's Den of new and used books, piled high in no apparent order – great for browsing. Downstairs is handicrafts.

ℹ Information

There are foreign-card-friendly ATMs dotted around the city, though there are few in the old city, one exception being near Shahi Guest House. Internet cafes, found all around town, especially in the old city, charge around ₹40 per hour.

Main Post Office (Station Rd; ⊙9am-4pm Mon-Fri, to 3pm Sat, stamp sales only 10am-3pm Sun)

Om Forex (Sardar Market; internet per hr ₹30; ⊙9am-10pm) Also exchanges currency and travellers cheques.

Police (Sardar Market; ⊙24hr) Small police post inside the market's northern gate.

Tourist Office (☑ 2545083; High Court Rd; ⊙9am-6pm Mon-Fri) Offers a free map and willingly answers questions.

ℹ Getting There & Away

AIR

Jet Airways (☑ 5102222; www.jetairways.com; Residency Rd) and **Indian Airlines** (☑ 2510758; www.indian-airlines.nic.in; Circuit House Rd) fly daily to Delhi and Mumbai.

BUS
Government-Run Buses

Government-run buses leave from **Central Bus Stand** (Raika Bagh), directly opposite Raika Bagh train station. Walk east along High Court

MAJOR TRAINS FROM JODHPUR

DESTINATION	TRAIN NO & NAME	DEPARTURE TIME	ARRIVAL TIME	FARE (₹)
Ajmer	54801 Jodhpur-Ajmer Fast Passenger	7am	12.35pm	175/485
Bikaner	14708 Ranakpur Exp	10am	3.35pm	190/485
Delhi	12462 Mandor Exp	8pm	6.45am	370/485
Jaipur	14854 Marudhar Exp	9.45am	3.30pm	210/555
Jaisalmer	14810 Jodhpur-Jaisalmer Exp	11.45pm	5.25am	205/540
Mumbai	14707 Ranakpur Exp	2.45pm	9.40am	445/1195

Fares: sleeper/3AC

Rd, then turn right under the small tunnel. Services include:

Ajmer (₹158, five hours, hourly until 6.30pm)
Bikaner (₹191, 5½ hours, frequently from 5am to 6pm)
Jaipur (₹259, seven hours, frequently from 5am to midnight)
Jaisalmer (₹208, 5½ hours, six daily)
Mt Abu/Abu Road (₹203, 7½ hours, 14 daily until 9pm)
Osian (₹45, 1½ hours, half-hourly until 10pm)
Rohet (₹36, one hour, every 15 minutes)
Udaipur (₹210, seven hours, 10 daily until 6.30pm)

Private Buses

You can book private buses through your hotel, although it's cheaper to deal directly with the bus operators on the road in front of Jodhpur train station. **Jain Travels** (☏ 2633831; www.jaintravels.com; ⊙ 7am-11pm) and **Mahadev Travels** (☏ 2633927; MG Hospital Rd; ⊙ 7am-10pm) are both reliable. Buses leave from bus stands out of town, but the operator should provide you with free transport (usually a shared autorickshaw) from their ticket office. Example services are as follows:

Ajmer (₹220, six hours, at least six daily)
Bikaner (₹200, five hours, at least five daily)
Delhi (seat/sleeper ₹578/788, 12 hours, daily)
Jaipur (seat/sleeper ₹240/368, 7½ hours, five daily)
Jaisalmer (₹240, 5½ hours, hourly)
Mt Abu direct (seat/sleeper ₹250/430, 7½ hours, daily)
Mumbai (seat only ₹1600, 18 hours, at least four daily)

TAXI

You can organise taxis for intercity trips (or longer) through most accommodation places or deal directly with drivers. There's a taxi stand outside Jodhpur train station. A reasonable price is ₹7 to ₹8 per kilometre (for a non-AC car), with a minimum of 250km per day. The driver will charge at least ₹100 for overnight stops and will charge for his return journey.

TRAIN

The computerised **booking office** (Station Rd; ⊙ 8am-8pm Mon-Sat, to 1.45pm Sun) is 300m northeast of Jodhpur train station. Window 786 sells the tourist quota.
➡ Four daily trains make the trip to Jaisalmer (5½ hours; 5.30am, 7.35am, 5.45pm and 11.45pm).
➡ Four daily trains go to Bikaner (5½ hours; 10am, 10.45am, 1.50pm and 8.15pm). The 1.50pm takes more than seven hours.
➡ Eleven daily trains go to Jaipur (five to six hours), departing between 6.10am and midnight.
➡ Four daily trains go to Delhi (11 to 14 hours; 6.25am, 7pm, 8pm and 11pm); the early evening departures are fastest.
➡ Six go to Mumbai (16 to 19 hours; 5.35am, 2.45pm, 6.20pm, 6.45pm, 7.20pm and 11.55pm). Each of these goes via Abu Road, for Mt Abu (4½ hours).
➡ For Pushkar, there are two daily trains to Ajmer (5½ hours, 6.25am and 7am).

There are no direct trains to Udaipur; change at Marwar Junction.

🛈 Getting Around

Despite the absurd claims of some autorickshaw drivers, the fare between the clock tower area and the train stations or Central Bus Stand should be about ₹50. **Suncity Cab** (☏ 6888888) and **Rajasthan Cab** (☏ 6222222) have reliable fixed-price taxis that can be pre-booked.

The airport is 5km south of the city centre; a taxi/autorickshaw will cost about ₹300/150.

Around Jodhpur

The mainly arid countryside around Jodhpur is dotted with surprising lakes, isolated forts and palaces, and intriguing villages. It's home to a clutch of fine heritage hotels where you can enjoy the slower pace of rural life.

Southern Villages

A number of traditional villages are strung along and off the Pali road southeast of Jodhpur. Most hotels and guesthouses in Jodhpur offer tours to these villages, often called Bishnoi village safaris. The Bishnoi are a Hindu sect who follow the 500-year-old teachings of Guru Jambheshwar, who emphasised the importance of protecting the environment long before it was popular to do so. Many visitors are surprised by the density – and fearlessness – of wildlife such as blackbuck, bluebulls (nilgai), chinkara gazelles and desert fox around the Bishnoi villages. The Bishnoi hold all animal life sacred. The 1730 sacrifice of 363 villagers to protect khejri trees is commemorated in September at Khejadali village, where there is a memorial to the victims fronted by a small grove of khejri trees.

At **Guda Bishnoi**, the locals are traditionally engaged in animal husbandry. There's a small lake (full only after a good monsoon) where migratory birds such as demoiselle cranes, and mammals such as blackbucks and chinkaras, can be seen, particularly at dusk when they come to drink.

The village of **Salawas** is a centre for weaving beautiful *dhurries* (rugs), a craft also practised in many other villages. A co-operative of 42 families runs the **Roopraj Dhurry Udyog** (☏0291-2896658; rooprajdurry@sify.com), through which all profits go to the artisans. A 3ft by 5ft *dhurrie* costs a minimum of ₹2800, a price based on two weavers working several hours a day for a month at ₹50 per day each. Other families are involved in block-printing.

Bishnoi village tours from Jodhpur tend to last four hours and cost around ₹800 per person. Those run by Deepak Dhanraj of **Bishnoi Village Safari** (☏9829126398; www.bishnoivillagesafari.com) receive good feedback, but many other places offer them.

Rohet

Rohet Garh (☏02936-268231; www.rohetgarh.com; Rohet Village; s/d ₹8500/9500, ste ₹12,000; ✻@🛜≋), in Rohet village, 40km south of Jodhpur on the Pali road, is one of the area's most appealing heritage hotels. This 350-year-old, lovingly tended manor has masses of character and a tranquil atmosphere, which obviously helped Bruce Chatwin when he wrote *The Songlines* here, and William Dalrymple when he began *City of*

> ### ⓘ BORDER CROSSING – JODHPUR TO KARACHI, PAKISTAN
>
> The 14889 Thar Express (alias the Jodhpur–Munabao Link Express) leaves Bhagat Ki Kothi station, 4km south of the Jodhpur Train Station, at 1am on Saturdays for Karachi (Pakistan).
>
> You need to arrive at the station six hours before departure – the same amount of time it takes to reach the sole stop of Munabao on the border. There you undergo lengthy border procedures before continuing on to Karachi (assuming you have a Pakistan visa) in a Pakistani train, arriving about 2am on Sunday. Accommodation is sleeper only, with a total sleeper fare of around ₹450 from Jodhpur to Karachi.
>
> In the other direction the Pakistani train leaves Karachi at about 11pm on Friday, and Indian train 14890 leaves Munabao at 7pm on Saturday, reaching Jodhpur at 11.50pm.

Djinns in the same room, No 15. Rohet Garh has a gorgeous colonnaded pool, charming green gardens, great food (lunch/dinner ₹750/900) and lovely, individual rooms. It also possesses a stable of fine Marwari horses and organises rides ranging from two-hour evening trots (₹2000) to six-day countryside treks, sleeping in luxury tents. The quirky Om Bana Temple (p182) is a short bus ride from here.

A taxi from Jodhpur will cost around ₹800. There are also frequent buses; once here, turn right out of Rohet's tiny bus stand, take the first right and keep walking for about 1km.

Osian

The ancient Thar Desert town of Osian, 65km north of Jodhpur, was an important trading centre between the 8th and 12th centuries. Known as Upkeshpur, it was dominated by the Jains, whose wealth left a legacy of exquisitely sculpted, well-preserved temples.

The **Mahavira Temple** (Indian/foreigner free/₹10, camera/video ₹50/100; ☉6am-8.30pm) surrounds an image of the 24th *tirthankar*, formed from sand and milk. **Sachiya Mata Temple** (☉6am-7.15pm) is an impressive

THE MOTORBIKE TEMPLE

Om Bana Temple (Motorbike Temple) One of the strangest temples in all India stands 8km south of Rohet beside the Pali road, near Chotila village. The deity at Om Bana Temple is a garland-decked Enfield Bullet motorcycle, known as Bullet Baba. The story goes that local villager Om Bana died at this spot in the 1980s when his motorbike skidded into a tree. The bike was taken to the local police station, but then mysteriously twice made its own way back to the tree, and travellers along the road started seeing visions of Om Bana – inevitably leading to the machine's deification.

Any time of day or night people can be seen at the open-air shrine here, simultaneously praying for safe journeys and making offerings of liquor.

Buses from Jodhpur to Rohet should continue on to Om Bana, but check with the driver. Otherwise, you can hop on almost any passing bus from Rohet (₹10).

walled complex where both Hindus and Jains worship.

Prakash Bhanu Sharma, a personable Brahmin priest, has an echoing **guesthouse** (☑ 02922-274331, 9414440479; s/d without bathroom ₹250/300) geared towards pilgrims, opposite the Mahavira Temple. **Safari Camp Osian** (☑ 9928311435; www.safaricamposian.com; tent s/d incl dinner, breakfast & camel ride ₹7000/9000) is a fancier, tented camp option.

Gemar Singh (☑ 9460585154; www.hacra. org; per person per day approx ₹1400, minimum 2 people) arranges popular camel safaris, homestays, camping, desert walks and 4WD trips in the deserts around Osian and the Rajput and Bishnoi villages. The cost is around ₹1400 per person per day (minimum two people). Pick up from Osian bus station, or from Jodhpur, can be arranged.

There are frequent buses from Jodhpur to Osian (₹45, 90 minutes). Trains between Jodhpur and Jaisalmer also stop here. A return taxi from Jodhpur costs about ₹1200.

Jaisalmer

☑ 02992 / POP 89,000

The fort of Jaisalmer is a breathtaking sight: a massive sandcastle rising from the sandy plains like a mirage from a bygone era. No place better evokes exotic camel-train trade routes and desert mystery. Ninety-nine bastions encircle the fort's still-inhabited twisting lanes. Inside are shops swaddled in bright embroideries, a royal palace and numerous businesses looking for your tourist rupee.

Despite the commercialism it's hard not to be enchanted by this desert citadel. Beneath the ramparts, particularly to the north, the narrow streets of the old city conceal magnificent *havelis,* all carved from the same golden-honey sandstone as the fort – hence Jaisalmer's designation as the Golden City.

A city that has come back almost from the dead in the past half-century, Jaisalmer may be remote but it's certainly not forgotten – indeed it's one of Rajasthan's most popular tourist destinations, and few people come here without climbing onto a camel in the surrounding Thar Desert. Competition to get your bum into a camel saddle can be fierce, with some operators adopting unpleasant hard-sell tactics. Generally speaking, though, this is a much more laid-back, hassle-free place to stay than the likes of Jaipur or Jodhpur.

Jaisalmer celebrates its desert culture in January or February each year with the action-packed **Desert Festival** featuring camel races, camel polo, folk music, snake charmers, turban-tying contests and the famous Mr Desert competition. Many events take place at the Sam Sand Dunes.

History

Jaisalmer was founded way back in 1156 by a leader of the Bhati Rajput clan named Jaisal. The Bhatis, who trace their lineage back to Krishna, ruled right through to Independence in 1947.

The city's early centuries were tempestuous, partly because its rulers relied on looting for want of other income, but by the 16th century Jaisalmer was prospering from its strategic position on the camel-train routes between India and Central Asia. It eventually established cordial relations with the Mughal empire. In the mid-17th century Maharawal Sabal Singh expanded the Jaisalmer princedom to its greatest extents by annexing areas that now fall within the administrative districts of Bikaner and Jodhpur.

Under British rule the rise of sea trade (especially through Mumbai) and railways saw Jaisalmer's importance and population decline. Partition in 1947, with the cutting of trade routes to Pakistan, seemingly sealed the city's fate. But the 1965 and 1971 wars between India and Pakistan gave Jaisalmer new strategic importance, and since the 1960s the Indira Gandhi Canal to the north has brought revitalising water to the desert.

Today tourism and the area's many military installations are the pillars of the city's economy.

⊙ Sights

★ Jaisalmer Fort   FORT

Jaisalmer's unique fort is a living urban centre, with about 3000 people residing within its walls. It's honeycombed with narrow, winding lanes, lined with houses and temples – along with a large number of handicraft shops, guesthouses and restaurants. You enter the fort from the east, near Gopa Chowk, and pass through four massive gates on the zigzagging route to the upper part. The final gate opens onto the square that forms the fort's centre, **Dashera Chowk**.

Founded in 1156 by the Rajput ruler Jaisal and reinforced by subsequent rulers, Jaisalmer Fort was the focus of a number of battles between the Bhatis, the Mughals of Delhi and the Rathores of Jodhpur. In recent years, the fabric of the fort has faced increasing conservation problems due to unrestricted water use caused by high tourist numbers.

Fort Palace   PALACE

(Indian/foreigner incl compulsory audio guide ₹50/300, camera/video ₹100/200; ⊙8am-6pm Apr-Oct, 9am-6pm Nov-Mar) Towering over the fort's main square, and partly built on top of the Hawa Pol (the fourth fort gate), is the former rulers' elegant seven-storey palace.

Much of the palace is open to the public – floor upon floor of small rooms provide a fascinating sense of how such buildings were designed for spying on the outside world. The doorways connecting the rooms of the palace are quite low. This isn't a reflection on the stature of the Rajputs, but was a means of forcing people to adopt a humble, stooped position in case the room they were entering contained the maharawal.

The 1½-hour audio-guide tour, available in six languages, is worthwhile, but you must deposit ₹2000 or your passport, driver's licence or credit card.

Highlights of the tour include the mirrored and painted **Rang Mahal** (the bedroom of the 18th-century ruler Mulraj II), a gallery of finely wrought 15th-century sculptures donated to the rulers by the builders of the fort's temples, and the spectacular 360-degree views from the rooftop. One room contains an intriguing display of stamps from the former Rajput states. On the eastern wall of the palace is a sculpted pavilion-style balcony. Here drummers raised the alarm when the fort was under siege. You can also see numerous round rocks piled on top of the battlements, ready to be rolled onto advancing enemies.

The last part of the tour moves from the king's palace (Raja-ka-Mahal) into the queen's palace (Rani-ka-Mahal), which contains an interesting section on Jaisalmer's annual Gangaur processions in spring.

Jain Temples   JAIN TEMPLE

(Indian/foreigner ₹30/200, camera ₹50; ⊙Chandraprabhu 7am-1pm, other temples 11am-1pm) Within the fort walls is a mazelike, interconnecting treasure trove of seven beautiful yellow sandstone Jain temples, dating from the 15th and 16th centuries. Opening times have a habit of changing, so check with the caretakers. The intricate carving rivals that of the marble Jain temples in Ranakpur and Mt Abu, and has an extraordinary quality because of the soft, warm stone. Shoes and all leather items must be removed before entering the temples.

Chandraprabhu is the first temple you come to, and you'll find the ticket stand here. Dedicated to the eighth *tirthankar,* whose symbol is the moon, it was built in 1509 and features fine sculpture in the *mandapa,* whose intensely sculpted pillars form a series of *toranas*. To the right of Chandraprabhu is the tranquil **Rikhabdev temple**, with fine sculptures around the walls, protected by glass cabinets, and pillars beautifully sculpted with *apsaras* and gods.

Behind Chandraprabhu is Parasnath, which you enter through a beautifully carved *torana* culminating in an image of the Jain *tirthankar* at its apex. A door to the south leads to small **Shitalnath**, dedicated to the 10th *tirthankar,* whose image is composed of eight precious metals. A door in the northern wall leads to the enchanting, dim chamber of **Sambhavanth** – in the front courtyard, Jain priests grind sandalwood

Jaisalmer

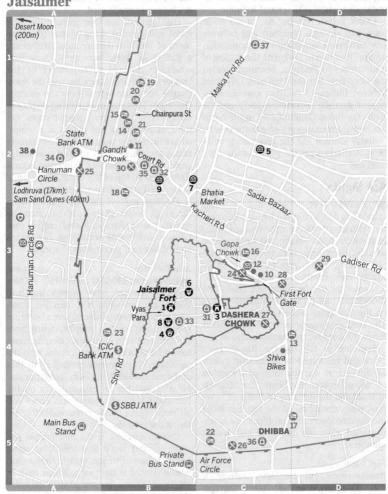

in mortars for devotional use. Steps lead down to the **Gyan Bhandar**, a fascinating, tiny, underground library founded in 1500, which houses priceless ancient illustrated manuscripts. The remaining two temples, **Shantinath** and **Kunthunath**, were built in 1536 and feature plenty of sensual carving. Note, the restrictive visiting times are for non-Jains. The temples are open all day for worshippers.

Laxminarayan Temple
HINDU TEMPLE

The Hindu Laxminarayan Temple, in the centre of the fort, is simpler than the Jain temples here and has a brightly decorated dome. Devotees offer grain, which is distributed before the temple. The inner sanctum has a repoussé silver architrave around its entrance, and a heavily garlanded image enshrined within. There's also a small 16th-century Hindu temple devoted to **Surya**, the sun god, inside the fort.

Havelis

Inside the fort but outside it, too (especially in the streets to the north), Jaisalmer is replete with the fairy-tale architecture of *havelis* – gorgeously carved stone doorways,

jali screens, balconies and turrets. There are some outstanding examples of incredibly fine sandstone *havelis* built by wealthy merchants and local notables in the 18th to 20th centuries.

Patwa-ki-Haveli   HISTORIC BUILDING

(Indian/foreigner ₹20/50; ⊙10am-5pm) The biggest fish in the *haveli* pond is Patwa-ki-Haveli, which towers over a narrow lane, its intricate stonework like honey-coloured lace. Divided into five sections, it was built between 1800 and 1860 by five Jain brothers who made their fortunes in brocade and jewellery. It's most impressive from the outside. The first of the five sections is open as the privately owned **Kothari's Patwa-ki-Haveli Museum** (Indian/foreigner ₹50/150, camera/video ₹50/70), which richly evokes 19th-century life.

Nathmal-ki-Haveli   HISTORIC BUILDING

(donation requested; ⊙8am-7pm) This late-19th-century *haveli*, once used as the prime minister's house, is still partly inhabited. It has an extraordinary exterior, dripping with carvings, and the 1st floor has some beautiful paintings using 1.5kg of gold leaf. The left and right wings were the work of two brothers, whose competitive spirits apparently produced this virtuoso work – the two sides are similar, but not identical. Sandstone elephants guard the entrance.

Museums

Desert Cultural Centre & Museum   MUSEUM

(Gadi Sagar Rd; Indian/foreigner ₹20/50, puppet show ₹30/50, camera/video ₹20/50, combined museum-show ticket ₹70; ⊙9am-8pm, puppet shows 6.30pm & 7.30pm) This interesting museum tells the history of Rajasthan's princely states and has exhibits on traditional Rajasthani culture. Features include Rajasthani music (with video), textiles, a *kaavad* mobile temple, and a *phad* scroll painting depicting the story of the Rajasthani folk hero Pabuji, used by travelling singers as they recite Pabuji's epic exploits. It also hosts nightly half-hour **puppet shows** with English commentary. The ticket includes admission to the Jaisalmer Folklore Museum.

Thar Heritage Museum   MUSEUM

(off Court Rd; admission ₹40, camera ₹20) This private museum has an intriguing assortment of Jaisalmer artefacts, from turbans, musical instruments, fossils and kitchen equipment to displays on birth, marriage, death and opium customs. It's brought alive by the guided tour you'll get from its founder, local historian and folklorist LN Khatri. We enjoyed the snakes and ladders game that acts as a teaching guide to Hinduism's spirutal journey. If the door is locked, you'll find Mr Khatri at his shop, Desert Handicrafts Emporium, nearby on Court Rd.

⌦ Tours

The tourist office runs sunset tours to the Sam Sand Dunes (₹200 per person, minimum four people). Add ₹100 if you'd like a short camel ride too.

Jaisalmer

🛏 Sleeping

While staying in the fort might appear to be Jaisalmer's most atmospheric choice, tourism has helped exert massive pressure on the fort's infrastructure. As a result, we don't recommend staying inside the fort. Fortunately, there's a wide choice of good places to stay outside the fort.

You'll get massive discounts between April and August, when Jaisalmer is hellishly hot. Some budget hotels are heavily into high-pressure selling of camel safaris and things can turn sour if you don't take up their offers: room rates that sound too good to be true almost always are.

Dylan Cafe & Guesthouse   GUESTHOUSE $

(✆ 9828561818; dylancafe.guesthouse@yahoo. in; Gandhi Chowk Rd; r ₹200-500, with AC ₹700; @ 🛜) Dirt cheap digs for young backpackers who like to chillout or party or both. Rooms are acceptable, but most of your time will be spent drinking with the young owners on the rooftop. Free wi-fi, fresh coffee and good company.

Hotel Swastika   HOTEL $

(✆ 252483; swastikahotel@yahoo.com; Chainpura St; dm ₹100, s/d/tr ₹200/300/400, r with AC ₹600; ❄) In this well-run place the only

thing you'll be hassled about is to relax. Rooms are plain, quiet, clean and very good for the price; some have little balconies. There are plenty of restaurants nearby.

Hotel Fort View   HOTEL $

(✆ 252214; Gopa Chowk; s/d from ₹300/400) A friendly stalwart of the budget scene located close to the fort gate. The cheapest rooms are small and in the back, but clean; those at the front squeak in fort views. There's a popular fort-facing multicuisine restaurant. Watch for the 9am checkout.

Hotel Renuka   HOTEL $

(✆ 252757; hotelrenuka@rediffmail.com; Chainpura St; r ₹250-650, with AC ₹800; ❄ @) Spread over three floors, Renuka has squeaky clean rooms – the best have balconies, bathrooms and AC. It's been warmly accommodating guests since 1988, so management knows its stuff. The roof terrace has great fort views and a good restaurant, and the hotel offers free pick-up from the bus and train stations.

Hotel Tokyo Palace   HOTEL $

(✆ 255483; www.tokyopalace.net; Dhibba Para; dm ₹200, s ₹400-1500, d ₹600-2000; ❄ @ 🛜 ▨) Well-run by honest, traveller-friendly management, this new place has clean midrange rooms as well as plenty of budget options, including separate basement dorms for men and women (bathrooms are the next level up). Wi-fi only extends to some rooms, and although it does have a pool, it's tiny.

Hotel Jaisal Palace
HOTEL $

(☑ 252717; www.hoteljaisalpalace.com; s ₹600-1050, d ₹750-1250; ❄) This is a well-run, good-value hotel, though the rooms tend to be on the small side and characterless. It's near Gandhi Chowk.

Arya Haveli
GUESTHOUSE $$

(☑ 9782585337; www.aryahaveli.com; Chainpura St; r ₹900-1800; ❄ 🖥) Helpful staff at this spruced-up guesthouse add to a stay at Arya Haveli. Rooms are well-appointed and looked after; the cheaper ones face an internal courtyard, the best have their own balcony. The top-floor Blues Cafe is a nice place to relax to some good music and tasty food.

Desert Moon
GUESTHOUSE $$

(☑ 250116, 9414149350; www.desertmoonguesthouse.com; Achalvansi Colony; s ₹600-1000, d ₹1000-1600; ❄ @ 🖥) On the northwestern edge of town, 1km from Gandhi Chowk, Desert Moon is in a remote-feeling location beneath the Vyas Chhatari sunset point. The guesthouse is run by a friendly Indian-Kiwi couple who offer free pick-up from the train and bus stations. The 11 rooms are cool, clean and comfortable, with polished stone floors, tasteful decorations and sparkling bathrooms. The rooftop vegetarian restaurant has fort and *chhatari* views.

Hotel Pleasant Haveli
HOTEL $$

(☑ 253253; www.pleasanthaveli.com; Chainpura St; r ₹2400, ste ₹2950; ❄ 🖥) This welcoming place has lots of lovely carved stone, a beautiful rooftop (with restaurant) and just a handful of spacious, attractive, colour-themed rooms, all with modern, well-equipped bathrooms and AC. Free pick-ups from transport terminals are available.

Hotel Gorakh Haveli
HOTEL $$

(☑ 9982657525; www.hotelgorakhhaveli.com; Dhibba; s/d ₹1000/1500, with AC ₹1500/2500; ❄) A pleasantly low-key spot south of the fort, Gorakh Haveli is a modern place built with traditional sandstone and some attractive carving. Rooms are comfy and spacious, staff are amiable, and there's a reasonable multicuisine rooftop restaurant (mains ₹60 to ₹120), with fort views, of course.

Shahi Palace
HOTEL $$

(☑ 255920; www.shahipalacehotel.com; off Shiv Rd; r ₹600-2500; ❄ @ 🖥) Shahi Palace is a deservedly popular option. It's a modern building in the traditional style with carved sandstone. It has attractive rooms with raw sandstone walls, colourful embroidery, and carved stone or wooden beds. The cheaper rooms are mostly in two annexes along the street, Star Haveli and Oasis Haveli. The rooftop restaurant (mains ₹80 to ₹200) is excellent. Indian veg and nonveg dishes are available plus some European fare, cold beer and a superb evening fort view.

Killa Bhawan Lodge
HOTEL $$$

(☑ 253833; www.killabhawan.com; r incl breakfast without/with AC ₹3000/3500; ❄ 🖥) Near Patwa-ki-Haveli, this small hotel is a delight. There are five big and beautifully decorated rooms, a pleasant rooftop restaurant that looks up to the fort, and free tea and coffee all day.

ℹ ARRIVAL IN JAISALMER

Touts work the buses heading to Jaisalmer from Jodhpur, hoping to steer travellers to guesthouses or hotels in Jaisalmer where they will get a commission. Some may even approach you before the bus leaves Jodhpur; others ride part or all of the way from Jodhpur, or board about an hour before Jaisalmer. On arrival in Jaisalmer, buses can be surrounded by touts baying for your attention. Don't believe anyone who offers to take you 'anywhere you like' for just a few rupees, and do take with a fistful of salt any claims that the hotel you want is 'full', 'closed' or 'no good any more.' Many hotels will offer pick-ups from the bus or train station.

Be very wary of offers of rooms for ₹100 or similar absurd rates. Places offering such prices are almost certainly in the camel-safari hard-sell game and their objective is to get you out of the room and onto a camel as fast as possible. If you don't take up their safari offers, the room price may suddenly increase or you might be told there isn't a room available any more.

Touts are less prevalent on the trains, but the same clamour for your custom ensues outside the station once you have arrived.

JAISALMER CAMEL SAFARIS

Trekking around by camel is the most evocative and fun way to sample Thar Desert life. However, don't expect dune seas – the Thar is mostly arid scrubland sprinkled with villages and wind turbines, with occasional dune areas popping out here and there. You will often come across fields of millet, and children herding flocks of sheep or goats whose neckbells tinkle in the desert silence – a welcome change after the sound of belching camels.

Most trips now include 4WD rides to get you to less frequented areas. The camel riding is then done in two-hour segments: one before lunch, one after. It's hardly camel *trekking*, but it is a lot of fun. A cheaper alternative to arranging things in Jaisalmer is to base yourself in the small village of Khuri, 48km southwest, where similar camel rides are available, but you're already in the desert when you start.

Before You Go

Competition between safari organisers is cut-throat and standards vary. Most hotels and guesthouses are very happy to organise a camel safari for you. While many provide a good service, some may cut corners and take you for the kind of ride you didn't have in mind. A few low-budget hotels in particular exert considerable pressure on guests to take 'their' safari. Others specifically claim 'no safari hassle'.

You can also organise a safari directly with one of the several reputable specialist agencies in Jaisalmer. Since these agencies depend exclusively on safari business it's particularly in their interest to satisfy their clients. It's a good idea to talk to other travellers and ask two or three operators what they're offering.

A one-night safari leaving Jaisalmer in the afternoon and returning the next morning, with a night on some dunes, is the minimum you'll need to get a feel for the experience: you'll probably get 1½ to two hours of riding each day. You can trek for several days or weeks if you wish. The longer you ride, the more you'll gain an understanding of the desert's villages, oases, wildlife and people.

The best-known dunes, at Sam (40km west of Jaisalmer), are always crowded in the evening and visiting them is more of a carnival than a back-to-nature experience. The dunes near Khuri are also quite busy at sunset, but quiet the rest of the time. Operators all sell trips now to 'nontouristy' and 'off the beaten track' areas. Ironically, this has made Khuri quieter again, although Sam still hums with day-tripper activity.

With 4WD transfers included, typical rates are between ₹1100 and ₹1700 per person for an overnight trip (leaving one morning, and returning the next). This should include meals, mineral water and blankets, and sometimes a thin mattress. Check that there will be one camel for each rider. You can pay for greater levels of comfort (eg tents, better food), but *always* get it all down in writing.

You should get a cheaper rate (₹900 to ₹1500 per person) if you leave Jaisalmer in the afternoon and return the following morning. A quick sunset ride in the dunes at Sam costs around ₹550 per person, including 4WD transfer. At the other end of the scale, you can ar-

1st Gate
HOTEL **$$$**

(☏ 9462554462; www.1stgate.in; First Fort Gate; r incl breakfast ₹8500; ❋@☜) Italian-designed and super slick, this is Jaisalmer's most sophisticated modern hotel and it is beautiful throughout with a desert-meets-contemporary boutique vibe. The location lends it one of the finest fort views in town, especially from its split-level open-air restaurant-cafe (p190) area. Rooms are immaculate and the food (Italian and Indian) and coffee are both top-notch.

Eating

As well as the many hotel-rooftop eateries, there's a good number of other places to enjoy a tasty meal, often with a view.

Free Tibet
TIBETAN **$**

(Fort; mains ₹120-250; ⊙6.30am-10pm) There's multi-multicuisine here, with everything from French baguettes to Mexican tacos, but the speciality is Tibetan, including good noodle soups and *momos* (dumplings). It's near the fort's southeast corner, with good views from the window tables.

range a 20-day trek to Bikaner. Expect to pay between ₹1000 and ₹2000 per person per day for long, multiday trips, depending on the level of support facilities (4WDs, camel carts, etc).

What to Take

A wide-brimmed hat, long trousers, long-sleeved shirt, insect repellent, toilet paper, torch, sunscreen, water bottle (with a strap) and some cash (to tip the camel men, if nothing else) are recommended. It can get cold at night, so if you have a sleeping bag, bring it, even if you're told that blankets will be supplied. Women should consider wearing a sports bra, as a trotting camel is a bumpy ride. During summer, rain is not unheard of, so come prepared.

Which Safari?

There are several options, and recommendations here shouldn't be a substitute for your own research. Whichever agency you go for, insist that all rubbish is carried back to Jaisalmer.

Sahara Travels (☑ 252609; www.saharatravelsjaisalmer.com; Gopa Chowk; ☺ 6am-8pm) Run by the son of the late LN Bissa (aka Mr Desert), this place is very professional and transparent. Trips are to 'nontouristy' areas only. Prices for an overnight trip (9am to 11am the next day): ₹1500 per person, all inclusive.

Trotters (☑ 9828929974; www.trotterscamelsafarijaisalmer.com; Gopa Chowk; ☺ 5.30am-7.30pm) This company is transparently run by Del Boy – who else? – with a clear price list showing everything on offer. Does trips to 'nontouristy' areas as well as cheaper jaunts to Sam or Khuri. Overnight trip (8am to 10am the next day): cost ₹1150 to ₹1300 per person, all inclusive.

Thar Desert Tours (☑ 255656; www.tharcamelsafarijaisalmer.com; Gandhi Chowk; ☺ 8.30am-7.30pm) This well-run operator charges ₹1100 per person per day, adjusting prices depending on trip times. They are slightly pricier than some of the other outfits, but we also receive good feedback about them. Customers pay 80% up front.

In the Desert

Camping out at night, huddling around a tiny fire beneath the stars and listening to the camel drivers' songs is magical.

There's always a long lunch stop during the hottest part of the day. At resting points the camels are unsaddled and hobbled; they'll often have a roll in the sand before limping away to graze on nearby shrubs, while the camel drivers brew chai or prepare food. The whole crew rests in the shade of thorn trees.

Take care of your possessions, particularly on the return journey. Any complaints you do have should be reported in Jaisalmer, either to the **Superintendent of Police** (☑ 252233), the tourist office (p191), or the intermittently staffed **Tourist Assistance Force** (Gadi Sagar Rd) posts inside the First Fort Gate and on the Gadi Sagar access road.

Camel drivers will expect a tip or gift at the end of the trip; don't neglect to give them one.

Chandan Shree Restaurant PUNJABI $
(near Hanuman Circle; mains ₹70-190; ☺ 7am-11pm) An always busy (and rightfully so) dining hall serving up a huge range of tasty, spicy South Indian, Gujarati, Rajasthani, Punjabi and Bengali dishes.

Bhang Shop CAFE $
(Gopa Chowk; lassi from ₹100) Jaisalmer's infamous lassi shop is a simple, pocket-sized place. The added ingredient is bhang: cannabis buds and leaves mixed into a paste with milk, ghee and spices. It also does a range of bhang-laced cookies. Bhang is legal here, but it doesn't agree with everyone so if you're not used to this sort of thing, go easy or avoid it altogether.

Desert Boy's Dhani INDIAN $$
(Dhibba; mains ₹100-135; ☺ 11am-4pm & 7-11pm) A walled-garden restaurant where tables are spread around a large, stone-paved courtyard with a big tree. There's also traditional cushion seating under cover. Rajasthani music and dance is performed from 8pm to 10pm nightly, and it's a very pleasant place to eat excellent, good-value Rajasthani and other Indian veg dishes.

A CASTLE BUILT ON SAND

A decade ago the whole structure of Jaisalmer Fort was in danger of being undermined by water leakage from its antique drainage system. The main problem was material progress in the form of piped water for the fort's inhabitants. Three of the ancient bastions had collapsed and parts of the fort palace were leaning at an alarming rate.

Since then, British-based **Jaisalmer in Jeopardy** (www.jaisalmer-in-jeopardy.org) and several Indian organisations, including the **Indian National Trust for Art & Cultural Heritage** (INTACH; www.intach.org), have raised funds and carried out much-needed conservation works to save the fort. Most important has been the renewal of the fort's drainage system and repaving of the streets, as well as repair works inside the fort palace.

Things have improved, although some conservationists still believe the fort's structure is in danger, and calls remain for the fort's inhabitants, and those who work in the fort, to be forced to leave. The fort's current population has been established since the 1960s; before then, the fort's inhabitants numbered in the few hundreds, made up mostly of royal family and their workers, plus monks and priests connected to the fort's temples. Visitors should be aware of the fort's fragile nature and conserve resources, especially water, as much as possible. Given that the most recent section of wall collapse took place in 2011, we recommend staying in accommodation outside the fort.

Natraj Restaurant
MULTICUISINE $$

(mains ₹70-270; ⊙10am-10pm) This is a brilliant place to eat, and the rooftop has a satisfying view of the upper part of the Salim Singh-ki-Haveli next door. The pure veg food is consistently excellent and the service is great. The delicious South India dosas (large savoury crepe) are fantastic value.

Monica Restaurant
MULTICUISINE $$

(Amar Sagar Pol; mains ₹100-280) The airy open-air dining room at Monica just about squeezes in a fort view, but if you end up at a non-view table, console yourself with the excellent veg and nonveg options. Meat from the tandoor is particularly well-flavoured and succulent, the thalis well-varied, and the salads fresh and clean.

1st Gate
ITALIAN $$$

(☑9462554462; First Fort Gate; mains ₹300-650; ⊙7am-11pm; 🕿) A small but good menu of authentic vegetarian Italian dishes as well as some delicious Indian food served on a split-level, open-air terrace with dramatic fort views. Also does good strong Italian coffee (₹100 to ₹150). A wood-fired oven was being built when we visited.

Saffron
MULTICUISINE $$$

(Hotel Nachana Haveli, Gandhi Chowk; mains ₹250-370) On the spacious roof terrace of Hotel Nachana Haveli, the veg and nonveg food here is excellent. The Indian food is hard to beat, though the Italian isn't too bad either. It's a particularly atmospheric place in the evening. Alcohol is served.

🔒 Shopping

Jaisalmer is famous for its stunning embroidery, bedspreads, mirror-word wall hangings, oil lamps, stonework and antiques. Watch out when purchasing silver items: the metal is sometimes adulterated with bronze.

There are several good *khadi* shops where you can find fixed-price tablecloths, rugs, clothes, cushion covers and shawls, with a variety of patterning techniques including tie-dye, block-printing and embroidery. Try **Zila Khadi Gramodan Parishad** (Malka Prol Rd; ⊙10am-6pm Mon-Sat), **Khadi Gramodyog Bhavan** (Dhibba; ⊙10am-6pm Mon-Sat) or **Gandhi Darshan Emporium** (near Hanuman Circle; ⊙11am-7pm Fri-Wed).

Jaisalmer Handloom
HANDICRAFTS

(www.jaisalmerhandloom.com; Court Rd; ⊙9am-10pm) This place has a big array of bedspreads, tapestries, clothing (ready-made and custom-made) and other textiles, made by its own workers and others. Staff don't hassle you with too much of a hard sell.

Desert Handicrafts Emporium
HANDICRAFTS

(Court Rd; ⊙9.30am-9.30pm) With some unusual jewellery, paintings and all sorts of textiles, this is one of the most original of numerous craft shops around town.

Dharan Book Store
BOOKS

(Vyas Para, Fort) Bookshops are 10 to the rupee in Jaisalmer, but this one wins us over with the cubbyhole cafe at the back, where you can browse through your latest purchase or get online while sipping a decent espresso. It's opposite Surya Temple.

Bellissima HANDICRAFTS
(Dashera Chowk, Fort; ⊙8am-9pm) This small shop near the fort's main square sells beautiful patchworks, embroidery, paintings, bags, rugs, cushion covers and all types of Rajasthani art. Proceeds assist underprivileged women from surrounding villages, including those who have divorced or been widowed.

❶ Information

INTERNET ACCESS
There are several internet cafes in the fort, but not so many outside it. Typical cost is ₹40 per hour.

MONEY
ATMs include State Bank and SBBJ near Hanuman Circle, SBBJ and ICIC Bank on Shiv Rd, and State Bank outside the train station. There are lots of licensed money changers in and around Gandhi Chowk.

POST
Main Post Office (Hanuman Circle Rd; ⊙10am-5pm Mon-Sat) West of the fort.
Post Office (Gopa Chowk; ⊙10am-5pm Mon-Fri, to 1pm Sat) Just outside the fort gate; sells stamps and you can send postcards.

TOURIST INFORMATION
Tourist Office (☑252406; Gadi Sagar Rd; ⊙9.30am-6pm) Friendly office with a free town map.

❶ Getting There & Away

BUS
RSRTC buses leave from the main bus stand. One daily air-conditioned coach goes to Delhi (₹2001, 15 to 17 hours, 5pm) via Jodhpur, Ajmer (₹366) and Jaipur (₹467), but it has reclining seats only. There are daily services to Jodhpur (₹208, 5½ hours) throughout the day

A number of private bus companies have ticket offices at **Hanuman Circle**. **Hanuman Travels** (☑9413362367) and **Swagat Travels**

(☑252557) are typical. The buses themselves leave from the private bus stand. Typical services include the following:
Ajmer (₹370, nine hours, two or three daily)
Bikaner (₹210, six hours, three to four daily)
Jaipur (seat/sleeper ₹220/500, 11 hours, two or three daily)
Jodhpur (₹400 to ₹500, five hours, half-hourly from 6am to 10pm)
Udaipur (sleeper ₹650, 12 hours, one or two daily)

TAXI
One-way taxis should cost about ₹1800 to Jodhpur, ₹4000 to Bikaner and ₹6500 to Udaipur. There's a stand on Hanuman Circle Rd.

TRAIN
The **station** (⊙ticket office 8am-8pm Mon-Sat, to 1.45pm Sun) is on the eastern edge of town, just off the Jodhpur road. There's a reserved ticket booth for foreigners.
➡ Three daily trains go to Jodhpur (2nd class ₹205; five to six hours; 1.20am, 6.15am and 5pm).
➡ One train a day runs to Bikaner (six hours, 11.20pm).
➡ One daily train goes to Delhi (18 hours, 5pm) via Jaipur (12 hours).

❶ Getting Around

AUTORICKSHAW
It costs around ₹40 from the train station to Gandhi Chowk.

CAR & MOTORCYCLE
It's possible to hire taxis or 4WDs from the stand on Hanuman Circle Rd. To Khuri, the Sam Sand Dunes or Lodhruva, expect to pay ₹800 to ₹1000 return, including a wait of about an hour.
Shiva Bikes (First Fort Gate; motorbike per day ₹500-2000; ⊙8am-9pm) is licensed to hire motorbikes (including Royal Enfield Bullets) and scooters for exploring town and nearby sights. Helmets and area maps are included.

MAJOR TRAINS FROM JAISALMER

DESTINATION	TRAIN NO & NAME	DEPARTURE TIME	ARRIVAL TIME	FARE (₹)
Bikaner	22479 Jaisalmer-Bikaner Exp	11.20pm	4.35am	135 (A)
Delhi	14660 Jaisalmer-Delhi Exp	5pm	11.10am	440/1185 (B)
Jaipur	14660 Jaisalmer-Delhi Exp	5pm	4.50am	340/910 (B
Jodhpur	14809 Jaisalmer-Jodhpur Exp	6.15am	12.15pm	205/540 (B)

Fares: (A) sleeper, (B) sleeper/3AC

Around Jaisalmer

Sam Sand Dunes

The silky **Sam Sand Dunes** (admission vehicle/camel ₹50/80), 41km west of Jaisalmer along a good sealed road (maintained by the Indian army), are one of the most popular excursions from the city. The band of dunes is about 2km long and is undeniably one of the most picturesque in the region. Some camel safaris camp here, but many more people just roll in for sunset, to be chased across the sands by dressed-up dancing children and tenacious camel owners offering short rides. Plenty more people stay overnight in one of the couple of dozen tent resorts near the dunes.

All in all the place acquires something of a carnival atmosphere from late afternoon till the next morning, making it somewhere to avoid if you're after a solitary desert sunset experience.

If you're organising your own camel ride on the spot, expect to pay ₹200 to ₹300 for a one-hour sunset ride, but beware the tricks pf some camel men such as demanding more money en route.

Khuri

☑ 03014

The village of Khuri, 48km southwest of Jaisalmer, has quite extensive dune areas attracting their share of sunset visitors, and a lot of mostly smallish 'resorts' offering the same sort of overnight packages as those at Sam. It also has a number of low-key guesthouses where you can stay in tranquility in a traditional-style hut with clay-and-dung walls and thatched roof, and venture out on interesting camel trips in the relatively remote and empty surrounding area. Khuri is within the **Desert National Park**, which stretches over 3162 sq km southwest of Jaisalmer to protect part of the Thar ecosystem, including wildlife such as the desert fox, desert cat, chinkara gazelle, nilgai or bluebull (a large antelope), and some unusual bird life including the endangered great Indian bustard.

Be aware that the commission system is entrenched in Khuri's larger accommodation options. If you just want a quick camel ride on the sand dunes, expect to pay around ₹150 per person.

🛏 Sleeping

★ Badal House   HOMESTAY $

(☑ 8107339097; r or hut per person incl full board ₹450) Here you can stay in a family compound in the centre of the village with a few spotlessly clean, mud-walled, thatch-roofed huts and equally spotless rooms (one with its own squat toilet), and enjoy good home cooking. Former camel driver Badal Singh is a charming, gentle man who charges ₹500 for a camel safari with a night on the dunes. He doesn't pay commission so don't let touts warn you away.

❶ Getting There & Away

You can catch local buses from Jaisalmer to Khuri (₹32, one hour) from a road just off Gadi Sagar Rd. Walking from Jaisalmer Fort towards the train station, take the second right after the tourist office, then wait by the tree on the left, with the small shrine beside it. Buses pass here at around 10am, 11.30am, 3.30pm and 4pm.

Return buses from Khuri to Jaisalmer leave at 8am, 9am, 10.30am, 11.30am and 2.30pm.

Bikaner

☑ 0151 / POP 647,800

Bikaner is a vibrant, dust-swirling desert town with a fabulous fort and an energising outpost feel. It's less dominated by tourism than many other Rajasthan cities, though it has plenty of hotels and a busy camel-safari scene, which attracts travellers looking to avoid the Jaisalmer hustle.

Around the full moon in January or very late December, Bikaner celebrates its three day **Camel Festival**, with one day of events at the Karni Singh Stadium and two days out at Ladera, 45km northeast of the city.

History

The city was founded in 1488 by Rao Bika, a son of Rao Jodha, Jodhpur's founder, though the two Rathore ruling houses later had a falling out over who had the right to keep the family heirlooms. Bikaner grew quickly as a staging post on the great caravan trade routes from the late 16th century onwards, and flourished under a friendly relationship with the Mughals, but declined as the Mughals did in the 18th century. By the 19th century the area was backward, but managed to turn its fortunes around by hiring out camels to the British during the First Anglo-Afghan War. In 1886 it was the first desert princely state to install electricity.

Sights

Junagarh
FORT

(Indian/foreigner ₹50/300, video ₹100, audio guide ₹50; ☉10am-5.30pm, last entry 4.30pm) This most impressive fort was constructed between 1589 and 1593 by Raja Rai Singh, ruler of Bikaner and a general in the army of the Mughal emperor Akbar. You enter through the **Karan Prole** gate on the east side and pass through three more gates before the ticket office for the palace museum. An informative audio guide (requiring an identity document as a deposit), is available in English, French, German and Hindi.

Old City
AREA

The old city still has a medieval feel despite the motorbikes and autorickshaws. This labyrinth of narrow, winding streets conceals a number of fine old *havelis,* and a couple of notable Jain temples just inside the southern wall, 1.5km southwest of Bikaner Junction train station. It makes for an interesting wander – we guarantee you'll get lost at least once. The old city is encircled by a 7km-long, 18th-century wall with five entrance gates,

the main entrance being the triple-arched Kothe Gate.

Bhandasar Temple
JAIN TEMPLE

(☉5am-1pm & 5.30-11.30pm) Of Bikaner's two Jain temples, Bhandasar is particularly beautiful, with yellow-stone carving and dizzyingly vibrant paintings. The interior of the temple is stunning. The pillars bear floral arabesques and depictions of the lives of the 24 *tirthankars*. It's said that 40,000kg of ghee was used instead of water in the mortar, which locals insist seeps through the floor on hot days. The priest may ask for a donation for entry, although a trust pays for the temple upkeep.

On the 1st floor of the three-storey temple are beautiful miniatures of the sentries of the gods. There are fine views over the city from the 3rd floor, with the desert stretching to the west. The temple is dedicated to the fifth *tirthankar*, Sumtinath, and was commissioned in 1468 by a wealthy Jain merchant, Bhandasa Oswal. It was completed after his death in 1514.

BIKANER SAFARIS

Bikaner offers an excellent alternative to the Jaisalmer camel safari scene. There are fewer people running safaris here, so the hassle factor is quite low. Camel trips tend to be in the areas east and south of the city and focus on the isolated desert villages of the Jat, Bishnoi, Meghwal and Rajput peoples. Interesting wildlife can be spotted here, such as bluebull antelopes (nilgai), chinkara gazelles, desert foxes, spiny-tailed lizards and plenty of birds including (from September to March) the demoiselle crane.

Three days and two nights is a common camel-safari duration, but half-day, one-day and short overnight trips are all also possible. If you're after a serious trip, Jaisalmer is a two-week trek away. The best months to head into the desert are October to February. Avoid mid-April to mid-July, when it's searingly hot.

Typical costs are ₹1400 to ₹2000 per person per day including overnight camping, with tents, mattresses, blankets, meals, mineral water, one camel per person, a camel cart to carry gear (and sometimes tired riders), and a guide, in addition to the camel men.

Many trips start at Raisar, about 8km east of Bikaner, or Deshnok, 30km south. Travelling to the starting point by bus rather than 4WD is one way of cutting costs.

The standout operator in terms of quality, reliability and transparency is Vijay Singh Rathore, aka **Camel Man** (☎2231244, 9829217331; www.camelman.com; Vijay Guest House, Jaipur Rd; half-/full-/multiday trip per person per day from ₹700/1000/1200, 1-day, 1-night per person ₹1600), who operates from Vijay Guest House. Also popular and long-established is **Vino Desert Safari** (☎2270445, 9414139245; www.vinodesertsafari.com; Vino Paying Guest House; 1-day, 1-night per person ₹1800, multiday trek per person ₹1500-2000) run by Vinod Bhojak, of Vino Paying Guest House. **Vinayak Desert Safari** (☎2202634, 9414430948; www.vinayakdesertsafari.com; Vinayak Guest House; half-day 4WD safari per person ₹500, full- or multiday 4WD safari per person ₹900-2000) runs appealing 4WD safaris with zoologist Jitu Solanki. This safari focuses on desert animals and birds including the enormous cinereous vulture, with its 3m wingspan, which visits the area in numbers from November to March.

Bikaner

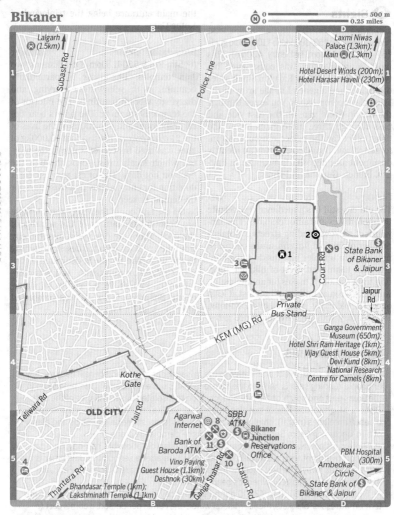

Lakshminath Temple
HINDU TEMPLE

(⊙ 5am-1pm & 7.30-11.30pm) The splendid Hindu Lakshminath Temple, behind Bhandasar Temple, was built during the reign of Rao Lunkaran between 1505 and 1526. Lakshminath was the patron god of the rulers of Bikaner, and during major religious festivals a royal procession headed by the maharaja pays homage here. The elaborate edifice was maintained with tributes received from five villages and several shops, which were granted to the temple by Maharaja Ganga Singh. Photography is prohibited here.

🛌 Sleeping

★ **Vijay Guest House**
GUESTHOUSE $

(☏ 2231244, 9829217331; www.camelman.com; Jaipur Rd; r ₹400-800, with AC ₹1200; ❄) About 4km east of the centre, this is a home away from home with spacious, light-filled rooms, a warm welcome and good home-cooked meals. Owner Vijay is a camel expert and a recommended safari operator (p193). As well as camel trips, it offers 4WD outings to sights around Bikaner, and tours to the owner's house in the untouristy village of Thelasar, Shekhawati.

Bikaner

Vino Paying Guest House GUESTHOUSE $
(☎ 2270445, 9414139245; www.vinodesertsafari.com; Ganga Shahar; s ₹200-250, d ₹350-400; @ ⛄) This guesthouse, in a family home 3km south of the main train station, is a cosy choice and the base of a good camel-safari operator (p193). It has six rooms in the house and six in cool adobe huts around the garden, where there's also a plunge pool. It's excellent value, and the family is helpful and welcoming. Home-cooked food is served and cooking classes are on offer. It's opposite Gopeshwar Temple; free pick-ups are offered.

Vinayak Guest House GUESTHOUSE $
(☎ 2202634, 9414430948; vinayakguesthouse@gmail.com; r ₹150-400, s without bathroom ₹100; ❄ @ ☎) This place offers six varied and clean rooms in a quiet family house with a little sandy garden (hot water only by bucket in some rooms). On offer are a free pick-up service, good home-cooked food, cooking lessons, bicycles (₹25 per day), and camel safaris and wildlife trips with Vinayak Desert Safari (p193). It's 500m north of Junagarh.

Hotel Harasar Haveli HOTEL $$
(☎ 2209891; www.harasar.com; r ₹2000-2500; ❄ ☎) At this modern hotel with the frontage of an old sandstone haveli, you'll find unexpectedly grand accommodation. The decor is extravagant: that's not fancy blue-and-gold wallpaper in your room, but exquisitely handpainted floral patterns. Old dark-wood furniture continues the classy character. Service is great, and the in-house restaurant on the terrace serves alcohol. Located opposite Karni Singh Stadium, nearly 1km north of Junargrah.

Hotel Jaswant Bhawan HOTEL $$
(☎ 2548848, 9001554746; www.hoteljaswantbhawan.com; Alakh Sagar Rd; s/d ₹800/1000; ❄ @) This is a quiet, welcoming place run by descendants of Bikaner prime ministers. It has a small garden and a comfy, old-fashioned sitting room with historic family photos. The air-conditioned rooms are spacious, plain and airy, though some of the paintwork

RAJASTHAN BIKANER

DON'T MISS

THE TEMPLE OF RATS

The extraordinary **Karni Mata Temple** (camera/video ₹20/50; ⊙4am-10pm) at Deshnok, 30km south of Bikaner, is one of India's weirder attractions. Its resident mass of holy rodents is not for the squeamish, but most visitors to Bikaner brave the potential for ankle-nipping and put a half-day trip here on their itinerary. Frequent buses leave from Bikaner's main bus stand. A return autorickshaw from Bikaner with a one-hour wait costs ₹400.

Karni Mata lived in the 14th century and performed many miracles during her lifetime. When her youngest son, Lakhan, drowned, she ordered Yama (the god of death) to bring him back to life. Yama said he was unable to do so, but that Karni Mata, as an incarnation of Durga, could restore Lakhan's life. This she did, decreeing that members of her family would no longer die but would be reincarnated as *kabas* (rats). Around 600 families in Deshnok claim to be descendants of Karni Mata and that they will be reincarnated as *kabas*.

The temple isn't swarming with rats, but there are a lot of them here, especially in nooks and crannies and in areas where priests and pilgrims leave food for them. And yes, you do have to take your shoes off to enter the temple: it's considered highly auspicious to have a *kaba* run across your feet – you may be graced in this manner whether you want it or not.

You can find food and drinks for yourself at the numerous snack stalls outside.

needs attention. Good meals are available. It's a two-minute walk from the main train station, via the station's 'foot over bridge'.

Hotel Kishan Palace
HOTEL $$

(☎2527762; www.kishanpalaceheritage.com; 8B Gajner Rd; r with fan ₹650, with AC ₹1500; ❀☎) An old Bikaner house, this hotel was once the home of a colonel of the Bikaner Camel Corps, and is now run by his grandson. Rooms are unfussy but generously sized, and the place is festooned with old photos and military memorabilia – check out grandfather's MBE, and watercolours by the Japanese prisoners of war he once guarded. Get a room at the back away from the main road.

Bhairon Vilas
HERITAGE HOTEL $$$

(☎2544751, 9928312283; http://hotelbhaironvilas.tripod.com; r from ₹2000; ❀@☎) This hotel on the western side of Junagarh is run by a former Bikaner prime minister's great-grandson. Rooms are mostly large and are eclectically decorated with antiques, gold-threaded curtains and old family photographs. There's a bar straight out of the Addams Family, a garden restaurant and a boutique specialising in original wedding saris.

Laxmi Niwas Palace
HERITAGE HOTEL $$$

(☎2202777; www.laxminiwaspalace.com; r ₹10,000-14,000, ste ₹18,000-25,000; ❀@☎) Located 2km north of the city centre, this pink-sandstone hotel is part of the royal palace, dating from 1902. It has opulent interiors with stone carvings, and is set in large lovely grounds. Rooms are large, elegant and evocative, while the bar and billiards room contain more trophy skins from tigers than are probably still alive in Rajasthan.

Bhanwar Niwas
HERITAGE HOTEL $$$

(☎2529323; www.bhanwarniwas.com; Rampuria St; r ₹4500; ❀@) This superb hotel has been developed out of the beautiful Rampuria Haveli – a gem in the old city, 300m southwest of the City Kotwali police station. It has 26 all-different, spacious and delightfully decorated rooms, featuring stencil-painted wallpaper, marble or mosaic floors and antique furnishings. Comfortable common rooms drip with antiques and are arranged around a large courtyard. The *haveli* was completed in 1927 for Seth Bhanwarlal Rampuria, heir to a textile and real-estate fortune. Inside the entrance gate is a stunning blue 1927 Buick.

✖ Eating

Bikaner is noted for its *bhujiya*, a special kind of *namkin* (spicy nibbles), sold in the shops along Station Rd among other places.

Heeralal's
MULTICUISINE $

(Station Rd; mains ₹50-150; ☉7.30am-10.30pm) This bright and hugely popular 1st-floor restaurant serves up pretty good veg and nonveg Indian dishes, plus a few Chinese and pizzas (but unfortunately no beer), amid large banks of plastic flowers. The ground-floor fast-food section is less appetising but it has a good sweets counter.

Laxmi Hotel
DHABA $

(Station Rd; mains ₹50-90, thali ₹60-100; ☉8am-10pm) A simple place, Laxmi is open to the street and dishes up tasty, fresh vegetarian thalis. You can see the roti being flipped.

★ Gallops
INDIAN $$

(Court Rd; mains ₹200-400; ☉10am-10pm) This fairly modern cafe and restaurant close to the Junagarh entrance is known as 'Glops' to rickshaw-wallahs. There are snacks such as pizzas, *pakoras* (deep-fried battered vegetables) and sandwiches, and a good range of Indian and Chinese veg and nonveg dishes. You can sit outside or curl up in an armchair in the air-conditioned interior with a cold beer or espresso coffee.

Evergreen
INDIAN $$

(☎2542061; Station Rd; mains from ₹110; ☉7am-10.30pm; ❀✎) Evergreen is a neat and clean restaurant whose delicious air conditioning hits you the moment you walk through the door. Despite the Egyptian heiroglyphic wallpaper, the cuisine leans strongly towards

MAJOR TRAINS FROM BIKANER JUNCTION

DESTINATION	TRAIN NO & NAME	DEPARTURE TIME	ARRIVAL TIME	FARE (₹)
Delhi (S Rohilla)	12456 Bikaner-Dee SF Exp	5pm	7.20am	382/1006
Jodhpur	14887 KLK-BME Exp	11am	4pm	190/278
Jaipur	SGNR Kota SF	11.05pm	5.30am	265/680

Fares: sleeper/3AC

South India, with a few classics like *paneer tikka* and *malai kofta*. Diners sometimes receive their dishes in sequence rather than all together, but the taste is worth the wait.

Palace Garden Restaurant INDIAN, CHINESE **$$$**
(Laxmi Niwas Palace; mains ₹250-800; ⏱7.30-10pm) This excellent garden restaurant at one of Bikaner's best hotels is a lovely place to eat – at least until the nights become too chilly. The fare spans South Indian, veg and nonveg North Indian, and Chinese, and if you're lucky there will be live music.

Shopping

Bikaner Miniature Arts ART
(Fort Rd) The Swami family has been painting miniatures in Bikaner for four generations, and now runs this art school-cum-gallery. The quality of work is astounding, and cheaper than you'll find in some of the bigger tourist centres. Art classes can be arranged.

Information

You'll find a **State Bank ATM** (Ambedkar Circle) outside the main train station, and Bank of Baroda ATMs opposite the station and next to the tourist office. There are several internet cafes on Ganga Shahar Rd.

Main Post Office (⏱9am-4pm Mon-Fri, to 2pm Sat) Near Bhairon Vilas hotel.

PBM Hospital (☎2525312; Hospital Rd) One of Rajasthan's best government hospitals, with 24-hour emergency service.

Tourist Office (☎2226701; ⏱9.30am-6pm Mon-Fri) This friendly office (near Pooran Singh Circle) can answer most tourism-related questions and provide transport schedules and maps.

Getting There & Away

BUS
There's a private bus stand outside the south wall of Junagarh with similar services (albeit slightly more expensive and less frequent) to the government-run services departing from the main bus stand, which is 2km directly north of the fort. An autorickshaw will cost around ₹20.

Services from the main bus stand include:

Ajmer (₹206, six hours, half-hourly until 6pm)
Delhi (₹352, 11 hours, at least four daily) Departs early morning.
Deshnok (₹26, one hour, half-hourly until 5.30pm)
Fatehpur (₹136, 3½ hours, half-hourly until 5.45pm)
Jaipur (₹255, seven hours, hourly until 5.45pm)
Jaisalmer (₹263, 7½ hours, 12pm)
Jhunjhunu (₹173, five hours, 7.30am, 8.30am, and 6.30pm)
Jodhpur (₹191, five hours, half-hourly until 4.30pm)
Pokaran (₹176, five hours, hourly until 2.15pm).

TRAIN
The main train station is Bikaner Junction, which has a **computerised reservations office** (⏱8am-10pm Mon-Sat, to 2pm Sun) in a separate building just east of the main station building. The foreigner's window is 2931. A couple of other useful services depart from Lalgarh station in the north of the city (₹50 in an autorickshaw).

➡ For Jaisalmer, an evening train with reserved ticketing runs only on Tuesday (sleeper/3AC ₹240/600, five hours, 6.30pm) from Bikaner Junction. On all other days there is the 22480 Bikaner-Jaisalmer Express (2nd class ₹135, five hours, 10.55pm), with unreservable seats. Turn up no less than 30 minutes before departure.

➡ Five daily trains go to Jodhpur (five hours; 12.45am, 6.30am, 9.30am, 11am and 4pm).

➡ Four daily trains go to Delhi (Delhi Sarai Rohilla; 9.15am, 5pm, 7.45pm and 10.20pm). The trip takes eight to 14 hours depending on the departure: the 9.15am and 10.20pm services are the fastest.

➡ Five daily trains go to Jaipur (6½ hours; 5.20am, 6am, 5.15pm 6.45pm and 11.05pm).

There are no direct trains to Ajmer for Pushkar.

Getting Around

An autorickshaw from the train station to Junagarh palace should cost ₹40, but you'll probably be asked for more.

Around Bikaner

National Research Centre on Camels

The **National Research Centre on Camels** (☎01512230183; www.nrccamel.res.in; Indian/foreigner ₹20/50, camera ₹30, rides ₹30; ⏱2-6pm) is 8km southeast of central Bikaner, beside the Jodhpur–Jaipur Bypass. While here you can visit baby camels, go for a short ride and look around the small museum. There are about 400 camels, of three different breeds. The British Army had a camel corps drawn from Bikaner during WWI. Guides are available for ₹50-plus. The on-site Camel Milk Parlour offers samples to try, as well as lassis. Camel grazing time is 3pm to 6pm and is the best time to come. The round trip, including a half-hour wait at the camel farm, is around ₹150/₹300 for an autorickshaw/taxi.

Haryana & Punjab

Best Forts & Temples

➜ Golden Temple (p213)

➜ Govindgarh (p211)

➜ Patiala Fort (p210)

➜ Kesgarh Sahib (p209)

➜ Mata Temple (p215)

Best Off the Beaten Track

➜ Bathinda (p211)

➜ Patiala (p210)

➜ Faridkot (p212)

➜ Kapurthala (p211)

➜ Morni Hills (p208)

Why Go?

The neighbouring states of Haryana and Punjab were carved from the Indian half of Punjab in the aftermath of Partition. Since then, Punjab has gone from strength to strength as the homeland of India's welcoming Sikh community, while Haryana has emerged as a dynamic hub for business and industry.

Studded with gleaming gurdwaras (Sikh temples) – including the unmissable Golden Temple in Amritsar – Punjab has become a popular stop on the traveller circuit. Haryana is more of a touristic mystery, best known for its modernist capital, Chandigarh. The hinterland around these two hubs is dotted with historic towns that tell a story of battling empires and playboy maharajas, and some of India's most alluring abandoned forts hide among their dusty bazaars.

Punjab and Haryana are united by their love of food. This is the region that gave the world tandoori chicken, tadka dhal (fried yellow lentils) and butter chicken; the prototype for chicken tikka masala. Enjoy the feast.

When to Go
Chandigarh

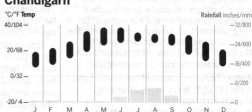

Mar Three days of Sikh celebrations for Holla Mohalla at Anandpur Sahib.

Apr Punjab's largest festival, Baisakhi, marks the Sikh New Year and the founding of the Khalsa.

Oct Diwali means lights, candles and fireworks; it's particularly magical at the Golden Temple.

Haryana & Punjab Highlights

❶ Feeling the energy of absolute belief at Amritsar's spectacular **Golden Temple** (p213), Sikhism's holiest site

❷ Climbing the towering walls of the little-known but magnificent 12th-century fort in **Bathinda** (p211)

❸ Getting off the beaten track by diving into the old town of **Patiala** (p210) before sizing up its impossibly charming 18th-century fort

❹ Watching the theatrical battle for supremacy between Indian and Pakistani border guards at Wagah's **border-closing ceremony** (p220)

❺ Tumbling into an alternative reality in Chandigarh's unique **Nek Chand Rock Garden** (p200)

❻ Visiting the **Khalsa Heritage Complex** (p209) at Anandpur Sahib, an enormous, lotus-flower-shaped museum of Sikh history, and one of India's most striking modern structures

CHANDIGARH

📞 0172 / POP 1.1 MILLION

Chandigarh is a place to see India as it would like to see itself – prosperous, comfortable and cosmopolitan. Officially a Union Territory controlled by the central government, Chandigarh is the joint capital of Punjab and Haryana. It is also the first planned city of independent India.

When the Swiss architect Le Corbusier was commissioned in 1950, he conceived a people-oriented city of sweeping boulevards, lakes and gardens and grand civic buildings, executed in his favourite material, reinforced concrete. So Chandigarh came into being; turn the clocks forward 60 years and the parks, monuments and civic squares are still here, albeit aged somewhat.

Each sector of the city is self-contained and pedestrian-friendly. Most visitors concentrate their attention on Sector 17 (for shops and restaurants) and Sector 22 (for hotels).

◎ Sights

A ₹10-ticket covers entrance to the Government Museum & Art Gallery, Chandigarh Architecture Museum and Natural History Museum.

★ **Nek Chand Rock Garden**   GARDENS
(www.nekchand.com; adult/child ₹20/5; ⊙9am-6pm Oct-Mar, to 7pm Apr-Sep) Nek Chand Rock Garden is unique: the surreal fantasy of a local transport official who, starting in 1957, spent almost 20 years personally creating more than 2000 sculptures using stones, debris and other discarded junk that was left over from the 50-odd villages that were destroyed in order to build the city of Chandigarh. Now, entering this fantastical, 10-hectare sculpture garden is like falling down a rabbit hole into the labyrinthine interior of one man's imagination.

Materials used in the construction of the garden range from concrete and steel drums to light switches, broken bathroom sinks and bicycle frames. Highlights include a legion of dancing girls made from broken glass bangles and a graceful arcade of towering arches with dangling rope swings. Ned Chand worked at night to begin with, to keep his eccentric masterpiece from the prying eyes of the city authorities, before eventually they realised the worth of his project and came on board, helping him to expand the site to its current proportions. Visit the website for more on the Nek Chand story, as well as for information on how you can volunteer and even help create new sculptures.

Electric carts (₹10 per person) shuttle tourists between here and Sukhna Lake.

★ **Capital Complex**   NOTABLE BUILDING
(⊙9am-5pm Mon-Fri) At the epicentre of Le Corbusier's planned city are the imposing concrete **High Court**, **Secretariat** and **Vidhan Sabha** (Legislative Assembly), which are shared by the states of Punjab and Haryana. All three are classic pieces of 1950s architecture from the proto-brutalist school, with bold geometric lines and vast sweeps of moulded concrete. To visit the complex, you must first register, with your passport, at the **High Court Tourist Office**. You will then be

---

TOP STATE FESTIVALS

Kila Raipur Sports Festival (Rural Olympics; ⊙Feb) Three days of bullock-cart races, kabaddi, strongman contests, folk dancing and more, in Kila Raipur, near Ludhiana.

Surajkund Crafts Mela (⊙1-15 Feb) Visiting artisans demonstrate and sell colourful handicrafts, with accompanying cultural performances in Surajkund.

Holla Mohalla (⊙Mar; p209) Sikhs celebrate the foundation of the Khalsa (Sikh brotherhood) with martial-arts and battle re-enactments in Anandpur Sahib.

Baisakhi (⊙13-14 Apr) State-wide, Sikhs head to gurdwaras (temples) to celebrate the Punjabi New Year.

Gita Jayanti (⊙Nov/Dec; p208) One week of cultural events in Kurukshetra for the anniversary of the Bhagavad Gita.

Pinjore Heritage Festival (⊙Dec) Three-day cultural festival with music and dance performances, handicrafts and food stalls at Pinjore Gardens, near Chandigarh.

Harballabh Sangeet Sammelan (www.harballabh.org; ⊙late Dec) The 130-year-old music festival in Jalandhar showcases Indian classical music over four days.

given a free accompanied tour, which lasts for around 1½ hours.

The tour includes a visit to Le Corbusier's unmistakable mid-century **Open Hand sculpture**, the city's official emblem, signifying that the people of Chandigarh are always 'open to give, open to receive'.

On the approach road to the High Court, the small **High Court Museum** (⊙10am-5pm Mon-Sat) `FREE` displays assorted judicial memorabilia including original Le Corbusier sketches, a signed copy of the Indian constitution, and the handcuffs worn by Nathuram Godse, Mahatma Gandhi's assassin. Like the sculpture, this can be visited unaccompanied.

Government Museum & Art Gallery · ART GALLERY
(Sector 10-C; admission ₹10, camera ₹5; ⊙10am-4.40pm Tue-Sun) You'll find a fine collection of artworks and treasures at this impressive state museum, including trippy paintings of the Himalaya by Russian artist Nicholas Roerich, elegant carvings from the Buddhist Ghandara civilisation, *phulkari* (embroidery work) and Sobha Singh's much-reproduced portrait of Guru Gobind Singh. At one end, through a separate entrance, is the **Child Art Gallery**, with colourful artworks from local schoolchildren.

Chandigarh Architecture Museum · MUSEUM
(City Museum; Jan Marg, Sector 10-C; admission ₹10, camera ₹5; ⊙10am-4.40pm Tue-Sun) Using photos, letters, models, newspaper reports and architectural drawings, this museum tells the story of Chandigarh's planning and development, including the abandoned first plan for Chandigarh by Albert Mayer and Matthew Nowicki.

Natural History Museum · MUSEUM
(Jan Marg, Sector 10-C; admission ₹10, camera ₹5; ⊙10am-4.40pm Tue-Sun) This museum features fossils, model dinosaurs, exquisite hand-embroidered pictures of birds, and a diorama with a caveman using an electric torch to illuminate his cave art!

Le Corbusier Centre · MUSEUM
(☑2777071; www.lecorbusiercentrechd.org; Madhya Marg, Sector 19-B; ⊙10am-6pm Tue-Sun) `FREE` One for fans of architecture and design, this fascinating museum displays documents, sketches and photos of Le Corbusier, along with fascinating letters revealing the politics behind the project, including one from Jawaharlal Nehru to the Chief Minis-

ter of Punjab which states, 'I do hope that you will not overrule Corbusier. His opinion is of value.'

National Gallery of Portraits · ART GALLERY
(Sector 17-B; ⊙10am-5pm Tue-Sun, free guided tours 11am & 3pm) `FREE` Located behind the State Library, with photos and paintings illustrating key players and events in the struggle for independence.

Sukhna Lake · LAKE
(⊙8am-10pm) Fulfilling the leisure objective of Le Corbusier's masterplan, this landmark artificial lake is a popular rest and recreation stop for Chandigarh families. It has ornamental gardens, a children's fairground, places to eat and drink, and **pedalos** (pedal boats; 2-/4-seaters per 30min ₹100/200; ⊙8.30am-5.30pm) for rent. Electric carts (₹10 per person) shuttle passengers between here and Nek Chand Rock Garden.

Rose Garden · GARDENS
(Sector 16; ⊙5am-9pm Apr-Sep, 6am-8pm Oct-Mar) In line with Le Corbusier's vision of a garden city, Chandigarh is dotted with pleasant public parks. Perhaps most pleasant is this garden, which contains over 1500 rose varieties.

Bougainvillea Garden · GARDENS
(Sector 3; ⊙8am-5pm) The Bougainvillea Garden has a thought-provoking memorial to Indian soldiers killed in cross-border conflicts since Independence.

🏃 Activities

Chandigarh Ayurved Centre · MASSAGE
(☑09876 466178; 1701, Sector 22-B; treatments from ₹450; ⊙8.30am-1.30pm & 4-8pm) Small, welcoming ayurvedic treatment centre that also does relaxation therapies for visitors. A 40-minute, full-body massage costs ₹800. The 20-minute *takra dhara,* where buttermilk is poured continuously over your forehead, costs ₹450.

Chandigarh

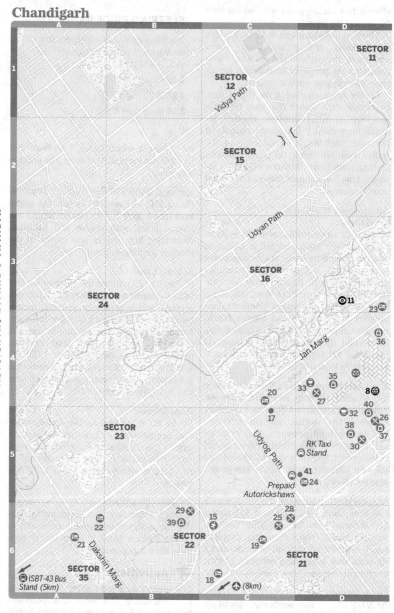

SECTOR 11

SECTOR 12

Vidya Path

SECTOR 15

Udyan Path

SECTOR 16

SECTOR 24

◎11

23

36

SECTOR 23

20

33 35

27

8

40

32

26

17

38

30

37

Jan Marg

Udyog Path

RK Taxi Stand

41

24

Prepaid Autorickshaws

29

39

15

SECTOR 22

28

25

22

21

19

SECTOR 21

Dakshin Marg

SECTOR 35

18

✈ (8km)

ISBT-43 Bus Stand (5km)

👉 Tours

Tourist Bus   BUS TOUR

(📞2703839, 4644484; 1 stop ₹10, half-/full-day tour ₹50/75; ⊙10am-1pm & 2.30-5.30pm) Chandigarh Tourism runs an open-top, double-decker tourist bus leaving from outside Hotel Shivalikview (Sector 17-E); buy a ticket when you get on. There are two half-day trips daily, visiting the Rose Garden, Government Museum & Art Gallery, Nek Chand Rock Garden and Sukhna Lake.

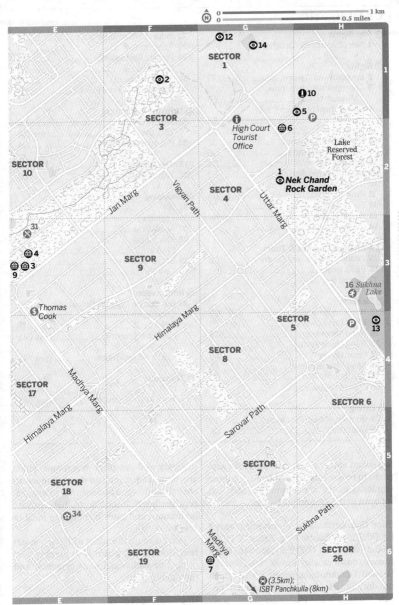

SECTOR 1

SECTOR 3

SECTOR 10

SECTOR 4

High Court Tourist Office

Lake Reserved Forest

1 Nek Chand Rock Garden

SECTOR 9

Thomas Cook

Himalaya Marg

SECTOR 8

SECTOR 5

16 Sukhna Lake

SECTOR 6

SECTOR 17

SECTOR 18

SECTOR 7

SECTOR 19

SECTOR 26

(3.5km); ISBT Panchkulla (8km)

Jan Marg

Vigyan Path

Uttar Marg

Madhya Marg

Himalaya Marg

Sarovar Path

Sukhna Path

Madhya Marg

Sleeping

Chandigarh hotels are pricier than elsewhere. Apart from the bus station's Transit Lodge, which readily accepts foreigners, there are two genuine budget options that are clean (for the price) and well run,

but they are sometimes reluctant to take foreign guests.

Kisan Bhavan REST HOUSE $
(☏5039153, 5002668; Dakshin Marg, Sector 35-A; r ₹550-850) Large, easy-to-spot Kisan Bhavan

Chandigarh

is a sound choice if you can get in. It's supposed to be a subsidised rest house for those employed in the agricultural industry, but it's open to the general public too.

Sood Dharamshala   PILGRIMS' REST HOUSE $
(☏2703711; off Dakshin Marg, Sector 22-D; dm ₹100, d ₹400-600, q ₹800-950) Opposite Kisan Bhavan, down an alley beside Hotel Samrat, is Sood Dharamshala, a rest house which has dormitories as well as a selection of private rooms. It's sometimes reluctant to accept foreign guests, but it won't hurt to try.

Transit Lodge   GUESTHOUSE $
(☏4644485; 1st fl, ISBT-17, Udyog Path; dm ₹230, tw ₹750, tw/tr with AC ₹980/1000) Located beside the train reservation office, on the 1st floor of the ISBT-17 bus station, this sur-

prisingly well-run place has rooms which are basic and a bit run-down, but clean enough and very spacious. All rooms, except the huge, 20-bed dorm, have private bathrooms, and rates include one meal (a vegetable thali).

Don't confuse this place with the bus station 'Guesthouse', which is in another part of the bus station and more expensive and thoroughly grotty.

Hotel Satyadeep   HOTEL $$
(☏2703103; hddeepsdeep@yahoo.com; SCO 1102-3, Sector 22-B; s/d from ₹1200/1400; ❄@) Run by courteous Sai Baba devotees, Satyadeep has wood-panelled corridors leading to simple, well-kept, bright and breezy rooms which open out onto shared balconies. It's upstairs from Sai Sweets.

Hotel Divyadeep   HOTEL **$$**

(☎2705191; hddeepsdeep@yahoo.com; SCO 1090-1, Sector 22-B; s/d from ₹1200/1400; ❄) In the same building as Satyadeep (but with a separate entrance), and run by the same group of Sai Baba devotees, Divyadeep also has smart yet austere rooms, though staff here tend to be more welcoming. It's above Bhoj Vegetarian Restaurant.

Hotel Aquamarine   HOTEL **$$$**

(☎5014000; www.hotelaquamarine.com; Himalaya Marg, Sector 22-C; s/d from ₹4460/5010, ste ₹10,600; ❄@☎) A proper boutique hotel, shielded from the road by a leafy terrace and full of luscious fabrics and framed artworks. There's a good restaurant and coffee shop, but no pool or gym.

Taj Chandigarh   HOTEL **$$$**

(☎6613000; www.tajhotels.com; Sector 17-A; r from ₹14,000; ❄@☎≋) Not as grand as some Taj Group properties, but still luxurious, with flawless service and rooms with floor-to-ceiling windows, minibars, flat-screen TVs, electronic safes and all the other mod-cons you'd expect at this price. There are several restaurants, the **Lava Bar** (⊙11am-11.30pm), a spa and a 24-hour business centre.

Hotel Shivalikview   HOTEL **$$$**

(☎4672222; www.citcochandigarh.com/shivalikview; Sector 17-E; s/d incl breakfast & dinner ₹3320/3790; ❄@☎≋) This hulk of a building is much more pleasant inside than it looks from the outside. Rooms are unexciting but large, clean and comfortable. The hotel has friendly staff, an outdoor pool, a gym, an Indian restaurant and a rooftop Chinese restaurant.

✗ Eating

Indian Coffee House   SOUTH INDIAN **$**

(SCO 12, Sector 17; mains ₹20-50; ⊙9am-10pm) Always busy with locals, this 40-year-old branch of the wonderful institution that is the Indian Coffee House is a great place for breakfast or lunch, with egg, toast and fabulously affordable filter coffee (₹20) sharing a menu of South Indian favourites such as *idli* (spongy, fermented rice cake), *vada* (doughnut-shaped, deep-fried lentil savoury) and dosa (large savoury crepe).

Punjabi Restaurant   PUNJABI **$**

(Shashtri Market Rd, SCF 15, Sector 22-D; mains ₹100-200; ⊙noon-5pm & 7-11pm) This small, friendly, no-frills restaurant whips up a choice of tasty Indian staples plus some Punjabi specialities. The *makki di roti sarson da saag* (a mustard-flavoured spinach dish served with corn chapati) and dhal makhani (black lentils and red kidney beans with cream and butter) is known as the Punjabi thali and is rich in flavour. The *dhal Punjabi* is for spice fiends, while the *karahi chicken,* with a thick sauce, is another delicious house special – the half portion is plenty for two to share.

Bhoj Vegetarian Restaurant   INDIAN **$**

(SCO 1090-1, Sector 22-B; thali ₹170-200; ⊙7.30am-10.30pm) This cosy haven run by Sai Baba devotees serves a house thali with artfully spiced curries that change throughout the day. Thalis come large or *choti* (small). It also has a selection of Indian desserts.

Shree Rathnam   SOUTH INDIAN **$**

(SCO 47, Sector 17-E; mains ₹100-200, thalis ₹225; ⊙9.30am-11pm) A swankier-than-average branch of this reliable all-veg chain, serving first-rate dosas and satiating thalis.

Stop 'N Stare Food Point   CAFE

(Sector 10; snacks ₹20-50; ⊙10am-6pm) Perfect for a pit stop after a tour of the museums, this simple cafe with shaded garden seating serves lassi, tea and instant coffee as well as Indian snacks such as patties, *paratha* (flaky flatbread) and *kulcha* (soft-leavened bread eaten with a chickpea masala). It's behind the Government Museum & Art Gallery.

Sai Sweets   SWEETS **$**

(SCO 1102-3, Sector 22-B; sweets per kg ₹300-400, snacks ₹20-60; ⊙7.30am-8.30pm) A clean and wholesome sweet shop below Hotel Satyadeep, serving tasty *mithai* (Indian sweets) and more substantial veg snacks, such as *tikki chaat* (potato cutlets), *golgappa* (also known as *panipuri* – round, hollow puri, fried crisp and filled with a mixture of chutney, chilli, potato, onion and chickpeas) and *pav bhaji* (tomato-based vegetable dish served with bread rolls).

★ Ghazal   MUGHLAI **$$**

(☎2704448; SCO 189-91, Sector 17-C; mains ₹200-400; ⊙11.30am-11.30pm) A Chandigarh stalwart and still going strong, Ghazal has a dignified air and a fine menu of Mughlai classics, including chicken and mutton, plus some Continental and Chinese dishes. The veg *jalfrezi* is a fiery sensation. At the back of the restaurant, a suited bartender guards a long line of imported single malts.

Pomodoro
ITALIAN $$$

([☎] 2707571; Piccadily Hotel, Sector 22-B; mains ₹300-500; ⊘11.30am-3.30pm & 7-11pm) This inviting restaurant located in the basement of the Piccadily Hotel serves hearty Italian food for grown-ups. Wine is available by the glass (from ₹300).

🍷 Drinking & Nightlife

Barista Crème
CAFE

(1st fl, SCO 63-4, Sector 17; coffee ₹90, snacks ₹90-200; ⊘9am-9pm) This Western-style chain coffee shop is a handy retreat from the orgy of consumerism in Sector 17. As well as good strong coffee, it does a few sandwiches and muffins.

Piccadily Blue Ice
BAR

([☎] 2703338; SCO 7, Sector 17-E; mains ₹300-500; ⊘11am-midnight) A slick, sleek, split-level resto-bar that appeals to smartly dressed drinkers. Beers from ₹200.

☆ Entertainment

Tagore Theatre
THEATRE

([☎] 2724278, 4347714; Sector 18-B) For a cultured night out, Tagore Theatre hosts music, dance and theatrical performances. See www.timescity.com for a schedule.

🛍 Shopping

The spacious, pedestrianised centre of Sector 17 is a cathedral to consumerism.

★1469
SOUVENIRS, CLOTHING

(www.1469workshop.com; SCO 81, Sector 17-D; ⊘10.30am-9pm) Named after the birth date of Guru Nanak (the founder of the Sikh faith), this funky independent clothing store sells fabulously colourful scarves, shawls and traditional Punjabi clothing, as well as modern T-shirts with a Punjabi twist. Also stocks some lovely jewellery, including the steel *kara* bracelets worn by Sikhs.

Fabindia
CLOTHING

(www.fabindia.com; SCO 50-1, Sector 17-A; ⊘10.30am-8.30pm) Gorgeous garments (Indian-meets-Western style) and homewares.

Khadi India
CLOTHING

(SCO 28, Sector 17-E; ⊘10am-7pm Mon-Sat) Good-value, homespun textiles and herbal beauty products, supporting small community producers. There's another **branch** (SCO 192-193, Sector 17; ⊘10am-7pm) a few minutes' walk east of here.

Tiny Shop
HANDICRAFTS

(Basement SCO 186-188, Sector 17-C; ⊘10.30am-8pm Mon-Sat) As cute as the name suggests, this basement shop, opened by Chandigarh local Mohina Sidhu in 1980, is secreted away underneath a row of shops and restaurants and sells artistic knick-knacks and household goods which make unusual souvenirs.

Phulkari
HANDICRAFTS

(SCO 27, Sector 17-E; ⊘10.30am-8pm Mon-Sat) Government of Punjab emporium with everything from inlaid wooden tables to *jootis* (traditional slip-on shoes).

Sector 22 Market
MARKET

(off Sector 22 Market Rd; ⊘10am-10pm) Bustling, sprawling street market selling household goods and clothing and sprinkled with pop-up street-food stalls.

ⓘ Information

INTERNET ACCESS

Each of the central sectors has at least one internet cafe.

E-Net (2nd fl, SCO-12, Sector 17-E; per hour ₹40; ⊘10.30am-8pm) Up the steps beside the Indian Coffee House. Photo ID required.

LEFT LUGGAGE

Bus Station Luggage Office (Sector 17; per day ₹9; ⊘24hr) For locked bags only.

MEDICAL SERVICES

Silver Oaks Hospital ([☎] 5097112; www.silveroakshospital.com; Phase 9, Sector 63, Mohali) Top-quality hospital, about 7km southwest of the centre. Well set up to treat foreign visitors.

MONEY

Most sectors have ATMs. Sector 17 has many.

Thomas Cook ([☎] 6610904; SCO 28-30, Sector 9-D; ⊘10am-6pm Mon-Fri, to 4pm Sat) Foreign exchange (cash and cheques) and international money transfers.

POST

Main Post Office ([☎] 2702170; Sector 17; ⊘9am-5pm Mon-Sat)

TOURIST INFORMATION

Chandigarh Tourism ([☎] 2703839; 1st fl, ISBT-17; ⊘9am-5pm) For hotel bookings.

Himachal Tourism ([☎] 2707267; 1st fl, ISBT-17; ⊘10am-5pm Mon-Sat, closed 2nd Sat of month) For hotel bookings.

Uttar Pradesh & Uttarakhand Tourism
(☑2707649; 2nd fl, ISBT-17; ⊙10am-5pm Mon-Sat, closed 2nd Sat of month)

ⓘ Getting Th ere & Away

AIR

Chandigarh airport is about 9km southeast of the centre. Air-con bus 201 runs from both main bus stands to the airport from 7.30am to 6pm (₹15), or take an autorickshaw for around ₹150 or a taxi for around ₹500.

The airport is being expanded to accommodate international flights. For now, there are daily flights to Delhi, Mumbai (Bombay), Bengaluru (Bangalore) and Srinagar. Many airlines have ticket offices at the airport:

Air India (☑1800 1801407; www.airindia.in)

GoAir (☑09223222111; www.goair.in)

IndiGo (☑09910383838; www.goindigo.in)

Jet Airways (☑5075674; www.jetairways.com)

SpiceJet (☑09871803333; www.spicejet.com)

BUS

Chandigarh has two main Inter State Bus Terminals (ISBT) – one in Sector 17 and one in Sector 43. Numerous red air-con buses run between the two terminals (₹20). ISBT Panchkulla is further from the centre and has buses to Morni. Local buses 2F and 30B link ISBT-17 and ISBT Panchkulla (₹30).

From ISBT-17, frequent buses run throughout the day to:

Delhi non-AC/AC ₹220/520

Delhi airport AC ₹600, six hours

Haridwar ₹210, five hours

Jaipur ordinary/Volvo ₹400/1200, 12 hours

Pipli (for Kurukshetra) ₹90, two hours

Rishikesh ₹240, eight hours, two direct buses (10.30am and 8pm)

From ISBT-43, non-AC buses run frequently to the following destinations (some destinations also have AC buses for roughly twice the price):

Amritsar ₹230, five hours

Anandpur Sahib ₹90, two hours

Dehra Dun ₹210, five hours

Dharamsala ₹295, eight hours

Jammu ₹320, eight hours

Kalka (for Shimla) 'toy train', ₹30, one hour

Manali ₹350, eleven hours

Pathankot ₹250, five hours

Patiala ₹65, two hours

Shimla ₹330, four hours

Sirhind ₹45, two hours

TRAIN

The train station is 7km southeast of the city centre, but there's a handy **reservation office** (☑2720242; ⊙8am-8pm Mon-Sat, to 2pm Sun) on the 1st floor of ISBT-17. There's no prepaid autorickshaw fee from the centre to the train station, but expect to pay around ₹100.

Several fast trains go to New Delhi daily: the quickest and slickest is the twice-daily Kalka Shatabdi (AC chair/1AC ₹595/1190, 3½ hours), which leaves at 6.53am and 6.23pm. To get to Delhi more cheaply, buy an unreserved 'general' ticket (₹110 to ₹145) when you turn up at the station and then just pile into the 2nd-class carriage of the next available train.

More than half a dozen trains go to Kalka (2nd-class seat/sleeper ₹45/140, 35 minutes), from where narrow-gauge trains rattle up through the hills to Shimla.

Two daily trains go to Amritsar (2nd class/AC chair ₹120/430, 4½ hours), at 7am and 5.10pm.

ⓘ Getting Around

Bicycles (₹100 per eight hours, ₹500 refundable deposit) are available at Sukhna Lake.

Expect to pay ₹30 for a short hop on a cycle-rickshaw. Hiring one for half a day (up to four hours), to take in sights such as Nek Chand Rock Garden and Sukhna Lake, will cost around ₹300.

Numerous local buses, including 203 and 22, link ISBT 17 with the train station (₹10).

There's a prepaid autorickshaw stand opposite ISBT 17, but it only does fares within the city centre, such as to ISBT-43 (₹54). For places further afield, such as the train station (about ₹80) or the airport (about ₹150), you'll have to negotiate with the driver.

RK Taxi Stand (☑09815832555) is behind ISBT-17 and charges ₹500 for the airport, ₹1600 return for Morni and ₹900/1200 for a half/full-day city tour.

AROUND CHANDIGARH

Yadavindra Gardens

These beautifully restored 17th-century Mughal-era walled **gardens** (Pinjore Gardens; ☑01733-230759; admission ₹20; ⊙7am-10pm), on the edge of the small town of Pinjore, are built on seven levels with water features and serene views of the Shivalik Hills.

Within the grounds there's a **restaurant** (mains ₹70-200; ⊙10am-7pm) in the Rang Mahal pavilion, which also has a bar. Visit

HARYANA & PUNJAB YADAVINDRA GARDENS

in December for regional delicacies and cultural performances as part of the Pinjore festival.

Should you fancy an overnight stay, there are pleasant rooms with Mughal-style flourishes and views of the gardens at the **Budgerigar Motel** (☑ 01733-231877; pinjore@hry.nic.in; d ₹2150-3000; ❀). The main entrance is just outside the walls, to the right as you face the entrance to the gardens, but it can also be accessed from inside the gardens, through the restaurant.

Nearby is the **Bhima Devi Museum** (☉ 10am-5pm; **FREE**), made up of a collection of small buildings in the grounds of the scattered ruins of the ornate, 10th-century Bhima Devi Temple, which was torn down when the gardens were originally constructed. To get here, turn left as you exit the gardens and walk past the new water park.

Frequent buses leave from Chandigarh's ISBT-43 to Pinjore (₹30, one hour). The gardens are on your left as you drive into the town. Less frequent services depart from ISBT-17.

Morni Hills

Perched at 1220m, Haryana's only hill station is set amid monkey-filled forests on a spur running west from the Shivalik Hills. Here you'll find a handful of rustic resorts, the village of Morni and, 7km downhill from the village, **Tikka Tal**, a pair of two pretty lakes with boats for rent (from ₹200).

With a pleasant location on the shore of the second lake, **Tikkar Taal Complex** (☑ 01733-250166; dm non-AC/AC ₹220/430, d ₹1610) has clean, comfortable dormitories and rooms with private bathrooms and views of the lake. There's a restaurant with terraced seating and gardens leading down to the lake. There's nothing much to do here, but it's a wonderfully peaceful place to stay if you want to escape the freneticism for a day or two.

There are daily buses to Morni (₹30, two hours) from Chandigarh's ISBT Panchkulla bus station. From Morni Village, there are three minibuses to Tikka Tal (₹10), at 6.30am, 7.30am and 3.30pm. They return from outside Tikkar Taal Complex at 7.30am, 8.30am and 4.15pm. The 4.15pm connects with the last bus back to Chandigarh, which leaves Morni Village at 5pm.

Private cars from Morni Village to Tikka Tal cost a whopping ₹700 return. Alternatively, it's a lovely two-hour, 7km downhill walk: walk back up the road towards Chandigarh, then turn left as the road bears sharp right (after less than 1km). Hitching is also possible.

HARYANA

Bordering India's burgeoning capital, Haryana was the setting for pivotal events in the conquest of northern India, but its sights see few foreign visitors.

Kurukshetra (Thanesar)

☑ 01744 / POP 964,200

According to Hindu legend, Kurukshetra (Thanesar in ancient times) was where Brahma created the universe, and where Krishna delivered his Bhagavad Gita sermon before the 18-day Mahabharata battle, an event commemorated by the **Gita Jayanti** (☉ Nov/Dec) festival. Accordingly, the town is mobbed by pilgrims and sadhus, who vastly outnumber the few foreign visitors.

For an English map of the area, turn right out of the main entrance to Bhramasarovar and you'll see one on the wall of a building on your right.

○ Sights

Bhramasarovar   HISTORIC SITE
The focus of attention at Kurukshetra is the sacred Bhramasarovar, India's largest ceremonial tank. According to Hindu holy texts, the ghat-flanked tank was created by Lord Brahma. Sadhus crowd the ghats and the ashrams beside the tank display dioramas of scenes from the Hindu epics and walkthrough models of sacred sites.

Kurukshetra Panorama & Science Centre   MUSEUM
(Pehowa Rd; admission ₹30, camera ₹20; ☉ 10am-5.30pm) The circular-shaped Kurukshetra Panorama & Science Centre contains a gory diorama of the Mahabharata battle; vultures pick at severed heads below a fiery, air-brushed sky. The less disturbing ground floor has interactive science exhibits for kids. It's a few hundred metres from Bhramasarovar; turn right out of the main entrance to Bhramasarovar then left at the roundabout.

Sri Krishna Museum
MUSEUM

(Pehowa Rd; admission ₹30; ⊘10am-5pm) Next to the Panorama & Science Centre is the Sri Krishna Museum, with an impressive collection of sculptures, carvings and paintings, and a low-tech multimedia exhibition with dioramas, giant statues, surreal sounds and a walk-through maze. There's a simple canteen (thali ₹70, chai ₹10) with terraced seating in the museum gardens.

Sheikh Chaheli's Tomb
TOMB

(Indian/foreigner ₹5/100; ⊘9am-5pm) About 2km northwest of the Panorama & Science Centre (turn right as you exit, then left to cross the railway line, then left again and follow the road round to the right) is the impressive mausoleum of the Sufi mystic Sheikh Chaheli, who provided spiritual guidance for the Mughal prince Dara Shikoh.

Behind the brick and sandstone tomb, and predating it by more than a thousand years, is a raised mound known as **Harsh Ka Tilla**, where you can view excavated 7th-century ruins from historical Thanesar. The ruins stretch for about 1km.

🛏 Sleeping

Hotel Welcome
HOTEL **$**

(☑9416408078; r ₹400-700) In a laneway opposite the main entrance to Bhramasarovar is the brightly painted Hotel Welcome, which has large but basic rooms and a small restaurant.

❶ Getting There & Around

Buses between Chandigarh (₹90, two hours) and Delhi (₹130, three hours) stop at Pipli on the national highway, about 5km outside Kurukshetra; shared autos (₹15) shuttle passengers between the bus stand and Bhramasarovar.

PUNJAB

Forged from the Indian half of Punjab province after Partition, Punjab is the homeland of India's Sikh population.

Anandpur Sahib

☑ 01887 / POP 17,000

The second most important pilgrimage site for Sikhs after the Golden Temple, Anandpur Sahib was founded in 1664 by the ninth Sikh guru, Tegh Bahadur, shortly before he

was beheaded by the Mughal emperor Aurangzeb. To resist the persecution of the Sikhs, his son, Guru Gobind Singh, founded the Khalsa (Sikh brotherhood) here in 1699, an event celebrated during the **Holla Mohalla** (⊘Mar) festival.

◉ Sights

Kesgarh Sahib
SIKH TEMPLE

The largest and most dramatic gurdwara is the Kesgarh Sahib, set back from the main highway on the edge of the old town. It marks the spot where the Khalsa was inaugurated, and enshrines an armoury of sacred Sikh weapons.

Anandpur Sahib Fort
FORT

Behind the Kesgarh Sahib, a broad paved path climbs the hillside to the small Anandpur Sahib fort, which affords glorious views over a sea of gurdwara domes.

Khalsa Heritage Complex
MUSEUM

(Virasat-e-Khalsa; ⊘8am-8pm Tue-Sun) **FREE** Over the other side of the fort is the striking five-petal form (inspired by the five warrior-saints in the Khalsa) of the Khalsa Heritage Complex, which opened in 2011. One of India's most impressive modern buildings, this fascinating museum complex uses elaborate murals and friezes to bring Sikh history to life.

🛏 Sleeping & Eating

The many gurdwaras in Anandpur Sahib provide accommodation and meals (donations are appropriate), though they are often full with pilgrims. Anandpur Sahib is strangely short on restaurants.

Hotel Paramount Residency
HOTEL **$**

(☑01887-233619; Academy Rd; r from ₹800) Above the road linking Kesgarh Sahib to the fort, Hotel Paramount Residency has austere, spartan rooms but a friendly welcome and a good location close to the Khalsa Heritage Complex.

Pal Restaurant
INDIAN **$**

(mains ₹50-100; ⊘7.30am-11.30pm) Pal Restaurant, above Pal Sweetshop, is close to the bus station and does good-value Indian cuisine, including thali. Turn left out of the bus stand, left again, and it's on your left.

ℹ️ Information

Mata Nanki Charitable Hospital (☏ 01887-233500) About 2km from the centre, Mata Nanki Charitable Hospital is a small but reputable general hospital run by a British-based charity.

ℹ️ Getting There & Away

The bus and train stations are 300m apart on the main road outside town. Buses leave frequently for Chandigarh (₹90, two hours), Amritsar (₹178, 4½ hours) and Patiala (₹120, three hours).

Three daily trains go to Chandigarh (2nd class/AC chair ₹95/310), at 5.46am, 7.43am and 3pm. The 5.46am takes 1¾ hours. The other two take three hours.

The overnight Himachal Express (sleeper/3AC/2AC ₹215/575/820, 7½ hours, 10.05pm) goes to New Delhi train station.

Patiala

☏ 0175 / POP 405,200

Punjab's best-kept secret, Patiala was once the capital of an independent Sikh state, ruled by an extravagant family of maharajas. As the Mughal empire declined, the rulers of Patiala curried favour with the British and filled their city with lavish palaces and follies. Family fortunes have declined and the grand monuments are crumbling, but the old city, ringed by 10 historic gates, is swooningly atmospheric. In January/February, the skies above Patiala burst into life for the **Basant** kite festival.

◉ Sights

Patiala's sights are dotted around the maze-like streets of the old town, south of the bus stand.

★ Qila Mubarak   FORT
The ancestral home of the maharajas of Patiala, this richly ornamented but fading 18th-century fort is an *Arabian Nights* fantasy of soaring buttresses and latticed balconies. You can't enter the interior of the fort, but you are allowed to walk between the hugely impressive inner and outer walls, surrounded by crumbling masonry and flocks of emerald-green parakeets.

Just inside the main entrance, to your right, the 1859 **Durbar Hall** (admission ₹10) has a wonderful collection of royal weaponry, outrageous chandeliers and other treas-ures rescued from the decaying palaces. It's open from 10.15am to 4.45pm, every day except Monday. The grounds of the fort itself are always open.

Other Sights
A self-guided walking tour will take you from the fort to various other historic sights. Turn right out of the fort, then right again, and follow the road south to the monumental gateway by the **Shahi Samadhan**, the three-storey tomb of Maharaja Aala Singh Samad (d 1822). You can climb to the top.

Continue along the same road and bear left by the Samania Gate to reach Mohindra College Rd and the twin towers of the **Mohindra College**, a former palace converted into a private school.

A short stroll further south, the **Netaji Subhas National Institute of Sports** (Old Moti Bagh; ◷ 9.30am-5pm Tue-Sun) ꜰʀᴇᴇ occupies a wing of the vast Moti Bagh palace, constructed by Maharaja Narendra Singh in 1847. The museum contains exhibits on Indian sporting heroes, including Punjabi sprinter Milkha Singh, 'the Flying Sikh'.

Bordering the palace compound is yet another palace, the totally over-the-top **Sheesh Mahal** (Sheesh Mahal Rd; admission ₹10; ◷ 10.30am-5pm Tue-Sun), graced by two wedding-cake towers and an ornamental suspension bridge. Inside the lavishly decorated interior is a gallery displaying royal treasures.

A short walk north of the bus stand, away from the old town, and over the flyover, the **Dukh Niwaran Gurdwara** is credited with healing powers thanks to a miraculous cure carried out by the ninth Sikh guru, Tegh Bahadur, in 1672.

🛏️ Sleeping & Eating

Hotel Chinar Regency   HOTEL $
(☏ 0175-2225592; outside Lahori Gate; r from ₹700; ❄) One of the few cheapies near the bus stand that accepts foreigners, Chinar has large rooms with quirky decor. It's in a lane behind the bus stand. To get to the old town from here, turn left out the door, left at the end of the road and Lahori Gate will be the road in front of you. The fourth turning on the right will eventually wind its way down to the fort, but you'll need to keep asking.

★ **Baradari Palace**   HERITAGE HOTEL $$$
(☑2304433; www.neemranahotels.com; Baradari Gardens; r incl breakfast from ₹4600; ❄️🛜) Built as a garden palace for Maharaja Rajinder Singh, this nostalgic heritage hotel is Punjab's most graceful place to stay. The artfully restored rooms have room to swing a Bengal tiger, and the terraces overlook elegant gardens. It's a 20-minute walk from the bus stand, or ₹20 to ₹30 in a cycle-rickshaw.

Chinese Hub   INDIAN, CHINESE $
(Lahori Gate; mains ₹50-200; ⏱11am-11pm) Cute, clean and friendly, this good-value restaurant knocks out delicious Indian staples as well as noodles, spring rolls and the like. It's on lively Lahori Gate, opposite the red-walled, 19th-century Patiala Methodist Church.

❶ Getting There & Away

Frequent buses run from Patiala to Chandigarh (₹65, two hours), Amritsar (₹230, five hours), Sirhind (₹30, one hour) and Anandpur Sahib (₹120, three hours)

Bathinda
☑0164 / POP 200,000

Bathinda is a quiet, friendly city, which sees few foreign tourists, but there are plenty of hotels and restaurants near the bus station, and the bazaars between the bus station and the city's fabulous fort are fun to wander through.

◎ Sights

Govindgarh   FORT
Of all the ruined forts in Punjab, Bathinda's Govindgarh is the mightiest and most impressive. It's also one of the oldest, dating way back to the 7th century, although rebuilt in its current red-brick form during the 12th century. It's an enormous structure, located smack bang in the middle of the city, and an unexpected highlight of a visit to this region. The fort's 36m-tall, 6m-thick walls tower over the old city bazaars and, best of all, it can be explored.

The fort contains two gurdwaras so, unlike other ancient forts in the region, it is

---

OFF THE BEATEN TRACK

KAPURTHALA

Once the capital of a wealthy independent state, Kapurthala is an unusual place to explore. The resident maharaja, Jagatjit Singh, was a travel junkie; he married Spanish flamenco dancer Anita Delgado and constructed numerous buildings inspired by his travels. The Jagatjit Palace (now the exclusive Sainik School) was modelled on Versailles, while the Moorish Mosque copies the Grand Mosque in Marrakesh (Morocco). Other sights of note include the British-style Jagatjit Club and Jubilee Hall, the Shalimar Gardens (containing the cenotaphs of the Kapurthala dynasty), and the handsome Indo-Saracenic court house.

Pick up a street map of Kapurthala in the tourist office in Amritsar. Otherwise, follow this leisurely one- to two-hour walking tour: Turn left out of the bus station, then take the first right after Hotel Royal. Turn left at the end to see **Jagatjit Club** (on your left) and **Jagatjit Palace** (at the end on your right). Just before Jagatjit Palace, turn right down a tree-shaded lane and bear right past a 150-year-old **royal guesthouse**, then left past the derelict **Gol Kothi** (a former residence of the maharaja) and continue straight on to the striking **Jubilee Hall**. Turn right here, then left at the end of the road (passing the beautiful whitewashed **state gurdwara** on your right en route), then take a diagonal left turn to reach the **Moorish Mosque**, a still-active mosque and one of the few historic buildings you can actually enter. Walk back the way you came; up the diagonal road, and right at the end, to pass the **court house** on your left. Turn left at the end, then first right to take you back to the town's main road. Turn left here for **Shalimar Gardens**, or right to get back to the bus stand.

Decent rooms and very tasty meals are available at **Hotel Royal** (☑01822-505110; Jallandhar Rd; r ₹850-1350; ❄️), 200m from the bus stand.

To get to Amritsar, you need to take a bus to Subhanpur (₹10, 30 minutes) then change for Amritsar (₹50, 1½ hours). There are four morning buses to Faridkot (₹100) at 6am, 7am, 8.40am and 10.20am.

open to the public; as well as visiting the gurdwaras themselves, you can wander the lawned gardens within the walls and even climb up on top in one spot for magnificent views of the city. Don't miss walking around the outside of the fort to the western face, where the immense walls are at their most impressive, towering above dhobi-wallahs (clothes washers) and cotton-loomers working on the dusty streets below.

Sleeping & Eating

Hotel Appreciate   HOTEL $
(☑ 0164 3201875; r from ₹500; ❋ ☎) Hotel Appreciate is the best value of a bunch of hotels behind the bus station; you can see its sign from the station.

Roadways Coffee   PUNJABI $
(mains ₹50-100; ☺ 8.30am-9pm) Roadways Coffee is an airy, fan-cooled restaurant with a charming art deco interior, 200m from the bus station (turn right as you exit the station). It does decent Punjabi food, but the coffee is instant only.

ⓘ Getting There & Around
To get to the fort, turn left out of the bus station, left at the roundabout, and keep walking straight (about 1km).

Five daily trains leave for New Delhi (2nd class/sleeper/AC chair ₹130/200/475, 5½ to seven hours) between 5am and 8am, plus another at 2.20pm. Five daytime trains go to Patiala (2nd class/AC chair ₹80/255, three hours), leaving at 6.30am, 7.30am, 2.10pm, 4.20pm and 5.25pm.

Frequent buses go to:
Amritsar ₹165, four hours
Chandigarh non-AC/AC ₹220/460, five hours
Faridkot ₹55, 1½ hours
Patiala ₹155, three hours

Faridkot

Faridkot was the capital of another vanished Sikh state. Today peacocks stalk the faded battlements of the once mighty **Qila Mubarak**, a fort protected by 15m-high walls, which was the ancestral home of the maharajas of Faridkot. Nearby the **Tilla Baba Farid Ji** is a recent rebuild of an age-old gurdwara, dedicated to the 13th-century Sufi poet Baba Sheikh Farid, whose poems were an inspiration for Guru Nanak,

founder of Sikhism. Also in town is the **Raj Mahal**, the current residence of the former royal family, who moved here from the fort in the 1880s, and the beautiful, 30m-tall, French-designed **Victoria Memorial Clock Tower** (c 1902), as well as the attractive, pastel-green **Memorial Library**.

The main sights can all be seen on an easy one-hour walking tour: To get the fort, turn left out of the bus station, then right at the roundabout, and keep walking, past the Memorial Library, and on through an old green archway. Turn left at the end, then bear right and the fort will be in front of you. You can't enter the fort, but you can complete a circuit around the outside of its formidable walls. To the left of the fort as you face it is a small bazaar, along which, on your left, you'll soon reach Tilla Baba Farid Ji, which you can enter, along with the visiting devotees. Returning from the fort, walk back through the green archway, then turn left to pass the Raj Mahal, which you can't enter, before reaching the splendid Victoria Memorial Clock Tower.

The only hotels in town are about a 750m-walk from the bus station. Turn left out of the bus station, left at the roundabout, then first right and you'll soon reach them all. Best value is **Sangam Hotel & Restaurant** (☑ 01639-252144; Kotkapura Rd; r from ₹700). A few doors further on, **Hotel Trump Plaza** (☑ 9216800789; Kotkapura Rd; r ₹1200-1500; ❋) has the best restaurant of the lot, and a bar.

Frequent buses run to Amritsar (₹110, three hours), Bathinda (₹55, 1½ hours), Chandigarh (₹200, four hours) and Patiala (₹160, two hours).

Amritsar
☑ 0183 / POP 1.13 MILLION
Founded in 1577 by the fourth Sikh guru, Ram Das, Amritsar is home to Sikhism's holiest shrine, the spectacular Golden Temple, one of India's most serene and humbling sights. The same cannot be said for the hyperactive streets surrounding the temple.

Amritsar is divided in two by a tangle of railway lines. The old city, containing the Golden Temple and other historic sights and bound by 12 medieval gates, is southeast of the railway lines. This is a fascinating area to explore, with a capillary network of narrow bazaars that seems to float between the centuries.

To the north of the railway lines, 'modern' Amritsar has grown up in haphazard fashion around a scattering of colonial-era boulevards. Gleaming malls and upmarket hotels stand testament to the prosperity of the city, but the hectic traffic makes this area hard to love at street level. Crossing between the old and new cities is best done by cycle-rickshaw, but once you're in the old city, walking is often the quickest way to get around.

Taxis taking you to the Golden Temple area will often drop you at Furwara Chowk from where you can walk the last few hundred metres.

◉ Sights & Activities

★ Golden Temple   SIKH TEMPLE
(ℐ information office 2553954; ◷ 24hr, information office 8am-7pm) The legendary Golden Temple is actually just a small part of this huge gurdwara complex, known to Sikhs as Harmandir Sahib (or Darbar Sahib).

Spiritually, the focus of attention is the tank that surrounds the gleaming central shrine – the **Amrit Sarovar** (Pool of Nectar), from which Amritsar takes its name, excavated by the fourth guru Ram Das in 1577. Ringed by a marble walkway, the tank is said to have healing powers, and pilgrims come from across the world to bathe in the sacred waters.

Floating at the end of a long causeway, the Golden Temple itself is a mesmerising blend of Hindu and Islamic architectural styles, with an elegant marble lower level adorned with flower and animal motifs in pietra dura work (as seen on the Taj Mahal). Above this rises a shimmering second level, encased in intricately engraved gold panels, and topped by a dome gilded with 750kg of gold. In the gleaming inner sanctum (photography prohibited), priests and musicians keep up a continuous chant from the Guru Granth Sahib (the Sikh holy book), adding to the already intense atmosphere. After paying their respects, pilgrims retreat to the intricately painted gallery on the second level to contemplate.

The Guru Granth Sahib is installed in the temple every morning and returned at night to the **Akal Takhat** (Timeless Throne), the temporal seat of the Khalsa brotherhood. The ceremony takes place at 5am and 9.40pm in winter, and 4am and 10.30pm in summer. Inside the Akal Takhat, you can view a collection of sacred Sikh weapons.

The building was heavily damaged when it was stormed by the Indian army during Operation Blue Star in 1984; it was repaired by the government but Sikhs refused to use the tainted building and rebuilt the tower from scratch.

More shrines and monuments are dotted around the edge of the compound. Inside the main entrance clock tower, the **Sikh Museum** (◷ 7am-7pm summer, 8am-6pm winter) **FREE** shows the persecution suffered by the Sikhs at the hands of Mughals, the British and Indira Gandhi. At the southeast end of the tank is the **Ramgarhia Bunga**, a protective fortress topped by two Islamic-style minarets; inside is a stone slab once used for Mughal coronations, seized from Delhi by Ranjit Singh in 1783.

➡ Baba Atal Tower
Just outside the compound is the octagonal Baba Atal Tower, constructed in 1784 to commemorate Atal Rai, the son of sixth Sikh guru Har Gobind, who according to legend revived a playmate from the dead, then gave his own life as penance for interfering in god's designs. The nine storeys each represent one year of Atal's short life.

➡ Guru-Ka-Langar
At the southeast end of the compound is the Guru-Ka-Langar, an enormous dining room where an estimated 60,000 to 80,000 pilgrims a day come to eat after praying at the Golden Temple. There's no charge to eat here, but a donation is appropriate and help with the staggering pile of washing up is always appreciated. Catering to everyone from paupers to millionaires, it's a

---

ⓘ GOLDEN TEMPLE ETIQUETTE

Before entering the compound, remove your shoes and socks – there are *chappal* (sandal) stands at the entrances – wash your feet in the shallow foot baths and cover your head; scarves can be borrowed (no charge) or hawkers sell souvenir scarves for ₹10. Tobacco and alcohol are strictly prohibited. If you want to sit beside the tank, sit cross-legged and do not dangle your feet in the water. Photography is permitted from the walkway surrounding the pool, but not inside the Golden Temple itself.

Amritsar

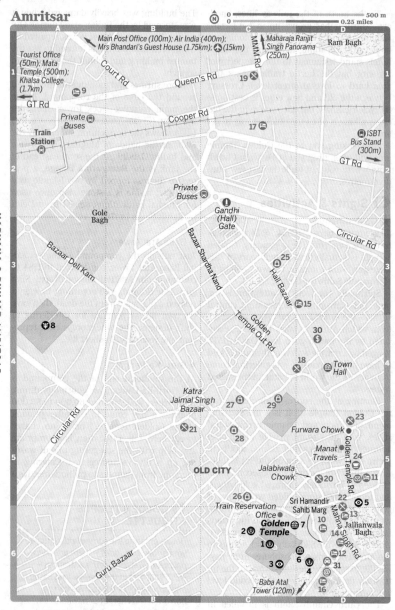

humbling demonstration of the Sikh principle of hospitality.

Jallianwala Bagh HISTORIC SITE
(Golden Temple Rd; ⊙6am-9pm summer, 7am-8pm winter) Reached through a gatehouse on the road to the Golden Temple, this poignant park commemorates more than 1500 Indians killed or wounded when a British officer ordered his soldiers to shoot on unarmed protesters in 1919. Some of the bullet holes are still visible in the walls, as is the well into

Amritsar

which hundreds desperately leapt to avoid the bullets. There's an eternal (24-hour) flame of remembrance, an exhibition telling the stories of victims, and a Martyrs' Gallery, with portraits of Independence heroes.

Sri Durgiana Temple   HINDU TEMPLE
(Gobindgarh Rd; ⊙ dawn-dusk) Dedicated to the goddess Durga, this 16th-century temple is a Hindu version of the Golden Temple. Surrounded by a holy water tank, it's often called the Silver Temple because of its exquisitely engraved silver doors. Soothing bhajans (devotional songs) are sung here just after the temple opens and just before it closes.

Mata Temple   HINDU TEMPLE
(Mata Lal Devi Ji; Rani-ka-Bagh, Model Town; ⊙ dawn-dusk) Credited with strong fertility-improving powers, this fascinating, labyrinthine Hindu temple commemorates the bespectacled 20th-century female saint Lal Devi. From the main hall, a narrow series of stairways and passages winds past mirrored mosaics, fairground-style carvings and untold deity statues to a semi-submerged mock-up of the Vasihno Devi cave temple.

Walking west along GT Rd, turn right after the train station, up Albert Rd, then take the first left and the temple will be to your left at the end of the lane.

Maharaja Ranjit Singh Panorama   MUSEUM
(Ram Bagh; admission ₹10; ⊙ 9am-5pm Tue-Sun) Located in the northwest corner of Ram Bagh, this museum is dedicated to Maharaja Ranjit Singh (1780–1839), the 'Lion of Punjab', who founded the Sikh empire, wresting large areas of northwest India from the Mughals. A vast diorama depicts the maharaja's greatest battles, complete with booming battle cries and other sound effects. Cameras and shoes are not permitted inside.

Khalsa College   HISTORIC BUILDING
(www.khalsacollegeamritsar.org; GT Rd; ⊙ dawn-dusk) This vast, sprawling castle of a college, on your right as you head west along GT Rd, was founded in 1890 to educate the cream of Punjabi society; it's a glorious example of the Indo-Saracenic style.

☞ Tours

The Grand Hotel (p216) runs day tours of the main sights (₹350 per hour) and evening tours (₹650 per person, starting at 3pm) to the Attari–Wagah border-closing ceremony, Mata Temple and Golden Temple.

THE JALLIANWALA BAGH MASSACRE

Following the introduction of the *Rowlatt Act* 1919, which gave British authorities the power to imprison Indians suspected of sedition without trial, Amritsar became a focal point for the Independence movement. After a series of *hartals* (general strikes) in which many protesters and three British bank managers were killed, Brigadier-General Reginald Dyer was called upon to return order to the city.

On 13 April 1919 (Baisakhi Day), over 5000 Indian protesters gathered in Jallianwala Bagh, an open courtyard surrounded by high walls. Under orders to make an example of the protesters, Dyer arrived with 150 troops and ordered his soldiers to open fire. When the barrage of bullets ceased, nearly 400 protesters were dead, according to the British authorities (although Indian National Congress placed the figure at more than 1000), and around 1500 were wounded, including many women and children.

Dyer's action was supported by the British establishment but described as 'monstrous' by Winston Churchill, and as 'a savage and inappropriate folly' by Sir Edwin Montagu, the Secretary of State for India, while the Nobel Prize-winning poet Rabindranath Tagore renounced his knighthood in protest of the massacre. The incident galvanised Indian nationalism – Gandhi responded with a program of civil disobedience, announcing that 'cooperation in any shape or form with this satanic government is sinful'.

Reginald Dyer died in retirement in England in 1927; Sir Michael O'Dwyer, governor of the Punjab at the time of the massacre, was assassinated by the Sikh revolutionary Udham Singh in London in 1940. Richard Attenborough's acclaimed film *Gandhi* (1982) dramatically re-enacts the events at Jallianwala Bagh.

The tourist office (p219) runs an interesting two-hour Heritage Walk (Indian/foreigner ₹25/75), covering the old-city bazaars. It starts from the Town Hall at 8am and 5pm daily (9am and 4pm December to February) and finishes outside the Golden Temple. Just turn up at the Town Hall 10 minutes before the start.

🛏 Sleeping

Sri Guru
Ram Das Niwas   PILGRIMS' REST HOUSE **$**
(dm free but donations appropriate, r ₹300, with AC ₹500; ❄@) Inexpensive rooms are available in the *niwas* (pilgrim hostels) at the southeast end of the Golden Temple compound. Foreigners are generally accommodated in the dorm at Sri Guru Ram Das Niwas, or at rooms in other buildings – check in at the Guru Arjan Dev Niwas to see what is available. Staying here is a fascinating experience but rooms and dorms are basic, with shared bathrooms, and there's a three-day maximum stay. Each person gets use of a locker in the dorms, but you need your own padlock.

Tourist Guesthouse   GUESTHOUSE **$**
(☎2553830; bubblesgoolry@yahoo.com; 1355 GT Rd; dm/s/d ₹180/250/450; @🛜) This good-value backpacker stalwart offers pocket-friendly prices and humble rooms with high ceilings and fans. There's a garden restaurant, rooftop seating and traveller-oriented vibe. On the downside, this is one of the few places in town that charges for wi-fi (₹100 per day) and the location, between a flyover and the railway line, is hardly the quietest.

Lucky Guest House   HOTEL **$**
(☎2542175; Mahna Singh Rd; r from ₹500; ❄) This solid, old-city budget option has basic rooms that are a bit pokey, but the location is good. Not all rooms have an outside window, so ask to see a few.

Hotel Grace   HOTEL **$**
(☎2559355; www.hotelgrace.net; No 35, Bharam Bhutta Bazaar; r with/without AC from ₹1000/800; ❄@🛜) This modest hotel opposite the Golden Temple has a real mix of rooms – the best are at the front, with plenty of natural light.

⭐ Grand Hotel   HOTEL **$$**
(☎2562424; www.hotelgrand.in; Queen's Rd; r from ₹1430; ❄@🛜) Across the road from the train station, but far from grungy, the Grand is an oasis of calm amid an otherwise chaotic location. Rooms are spacious – if not exactly grand – and surround a wonderfully charming courtyard garden. The restaurant,

with seating overlooking the garden, is also recommended.

Even if you don't stay here, drop into the genuinely inviting bar – the cheerfully named Bottoms Up. The owner also runs recommended tours (p215).

★**Mrs Bhandari's Guesthouse** GUESTHOUSE $$
(✆2228509; www.facebook.com/bhandariguest house; 10 Cantonment; camping per person ₹200, s/d from ₹1840/2300; ❋@🖰🛜) Founded by the much-missed Mrs Bhandari (1906-2007), this friendly guesthouse is set in spacious grounds in the Amritsar cantonment, about 2km from the centre. The large rooms have a hint of colonial-era bungalow about them, and the welcome is warm. The well-kept gardens are vast, and include swings, see-saws, plenty of seating and a small swimming pool, making this an excellent choice for families, while budget travellers can camp here if they bring their own camping equipment.

Pick-up is free from the train station and meals are available (breakfast/lunch/dinner ₹450/575/575). It's ₹50 to ₹60 in a cycle-rickshaw from the centre. Tell the rickshaw driver you want to take Gawal Mandi Chowk to Cantonment, and the guesthouse should be right opposite you.

MK Sood Guesthouse HOTEL $$
(✆5093376; Bharam Bhutta Bazaar; r ₹1000; ❋🛜) Small, quaint and clean, this place benefits from a quieter location than most old-city hotels. Rooms all have air-con but some are better than others so ask to see a few before deciding. Wi-fi in lobby only.

Hotel Indus HOTEL $$
(✆2535900; www.hotelindus.com; 211-13 Sri Hamandir Sahib Marg; r from ₹2140, with temple view ₹2880; ❋@🛜) The dramatic million-dollar view of the Golden Temple from the rooftop is reason enough to stay at this modern-style hotel. Rooms are compact but comfy. Book well ahead to secure one of the two rooms with temple vistas.

Hotel CJ International HOTEL $$
(✆2543478; www.hotelcj.in; Sri Hamandir Sahib Marg; r from ₹2250, with temple view ₹3700; ❋@🛜) The rooms are blandly comfortable and overpriced, but the draw is its proximity to the Golden Temple. Pre-book one of the five temple-facing rooms on level three.

Hotel Golden Tower HOTEL $$
(✆2534446; www.hotelgoldentower.com; off Golden Temple Rd, Furwara Chowk; r from ₹1550; ❋@🛜) More glam outside than in, this is a reasonable choice in a good location. Sparsely decorated but large, clean rooms come with TV and fridge. Wi-fi in the lobby.

Ramada Amritsar HOTEL $$$
(✆0183-5025555; www.ramadaamritsar.com; Hall Bazaar; s/d from ₹3000/4000; ❋@🛜🏊) New in 2013, this grand-looking hotel is the best top-end option in the old city. The lobby is somewhat chintzy, but rooms are smart and modern, and the service is excellent. Rates include breakfast, wi-fi, and use of the pool and gym.

✖ Eating

Amritsar is famous for its *dhabas* (snack bars) serving such Punjabi treats as *kulcha* (filled *parathas*) and 'Amritsari' fish (deep-fried fish with lemon, chilli, garlic and ginger). Hotels and restaurants in the Golden Temple area don't serve alcohol.

★**Kesar Da Dhaba** PUNJABI $
(Chowk Passian; mains ₹70-200; ⊙11am-6pm & 7-11pm) Hard to find (ask for directions in the old city), this takeaway and no-nonsense *dhaba* has delicious *paratha* thalis (₹200 to ₹250) and silver-leaf-topped *firni* (ground rice pudding; ₹20) served in small clay bowls, as well as arguably the best lassi (₹50) in town.

★**Bharawan da Dhaba** PUNJABI $
(Golden Temple Out Rd, Town Hall Chowk; mains ₹100-180; ⊙8am-midnight) This down-to-earth Amritsar institution has been serving up tasty *kulcha* and other Punjabi treats since 1912. Does handy half portions.

Neelam's PUNJABI $
(Golden Temple Rd, Jallianwala Bagh; mains ₹70-200; ⊙9am-11pm) Not far from the Golden Temple, this tiny two-tone eatery is a convenient spot to recharge your batteries. It does some multicuisine dishes, including a backpacker breakfast, but don't miss the great-value *kulcha* (₹50), served with a chickpea side dish and a spicy chutney.

Gurdas Ram SNACKS $
(Jalabiwala Chowk; jalebi per serving ₹10; ⊙9.30am-10.30pm) Get your fingers sticky

EXPLORING AMRITSAR'S BAZAARS

The Golden Temple sits on the edge of a mesmerising maze of market streets, where anything and everything can be found, from ceremonial swords to wedding gowns. Start your explorations at the main entrance to the Golden Temple. From here stroll northwest (so, to your left if you have your back to the Golden Temple) to the end of the temple compound and duck into the **Kathian Bazaar**, for blankets, stationery, tin pots and red-and-silver coloured wedding bangles. At the end, turn right onto Guru Bazaar Rd, past shops full of glittery ladies-wear, then take the first left into **Shashtri Bazaar**, where dupattas (long scarves for women) give way to fancy woollen shawls. At the end of the bazaar, turn right and continue past a string of food and fruit stalls to frenetic **Katra Jaimal Singh Bazaar**, crammed with tailors and fashion stores. At the T-junction, turn left into **Tahali Sahib Bazaar**, piled high with glittering satin dupattas, at the end of which Brothers' Dhaba (p218) and Bharawan da Dhaba (p217) offer well-earned sustenance.

at this 60-year-old *jalebi* (orange-coloured coils of deep-fried batter dunked in sugar syrup) joint, so famous they named the junction after it (Jalabiwala Chowk). The ₹10 single serving is perfect for a taster.

★ Brothers' Dhaba   PUNJABI $$

(Bade Bhai Ka; Town Hall Chowk; mains ₹100-200; ⊙7.30am-12.30pm) This fast and friendly upmarket *dhaba* serves some of Amritsar's tastiest *kulcha* (Punjabi-style *parathas* with herbs, potato and pomegranate seeds that burst in the mouth as tiny explosions of sweetness).

Shudh Veg Food Court   MULTICUISINE $$

(Golden Temple Rd, Furwara Chowk; mains ₹100-200; ⊙8am-11.30pm) Clean, modern food court where counters selling thali (₹115 to ₹210) and *kulcha* (from ₹50) stand beside others serving pasta, pizza and Chinese.

Crystal Restaurant   MUGHLAI $$$

(☑2225555; Crystal Chowk; mains ₹300-600; ⊙11am-11.30pm) Worth the splurge, this classy, ground-floor restaurant has a fin de siècle air, with mirror-lined walls and ornate stucco trim. The multicuisine menu is dominated by Mughlai favourites – the house speciality is delicious *mugh tawa frontier* (morsels of chicken in a dense onion gravy). It also has a decent wine list.

Upstairs is the Crystal Restaurant Plaza, run by a rival branch of the same family and serving the same menu in more modern surroundings. Outside is a no-nonsense takeaway joint where you can enjoy some of the same dishes while standing up at high, roadside tables.

🍷 Drinking & Nightlife

Bottoms Up Pub   BAR

(Grand Hotel, Queen's Rd; ⊙11am-11pm) The congenial bar serves icy cold, glycerine-free, draught Kingfisher beer (₹100) and good meals from the hotel kitchen.

Café Coffee Day   CAFE

(Golden Temple Rd; coffee from ₹100; ⊙9-11pm) Air-con-cooled old-city oasis with fresh coffee, a few cakes and street-view seating.

🔒 Shopping

Wandering around the winding alleys of the old-city bazaars is a head-spinning assault on the senses. Things to look out for include jootis (north Indian leather slippers), dupattas (women's scarves), woollen shawls and bangles (including the steel *kara* bangles worn by Sikhs).

Booklovers Retreat   BOOKS

(Hall Bazaar; ⊙9am-8pm Mon-Sat) Old-school bookshop full of interesting tomes.

ℹ Information

INTERNET ACCESS

Free wi-fi is widely available at Amritsar hotels.
Guru Arjun Dev Niwas Net Cafe (Guru Arjun Dev Niwas; per hour ₹25; ⊙6am-1am) Handy internet cafe in the Golden Temple complex.

MEDICAL SERVICES

Fortis Escorts Hospital (☑0183-3012222, 9915133330; www.fortishealthcare.com; Majitha Verka Bypass) International-standard hospital in the city suburbs, 7km northeast of the old city.

MONEY

Amritsar has an ever-mushrooming supply of ATMs, including one at the train station and at the airport, though there are no moneychangers at the airport. Manat Travels is a trustworthy moneychanger in the old city.

HDFC (ground fl, RS Towers, Hall Bazaar; ⊙9.30am-3.30pm Mon-Fri, to 12.30pm Sat) Foreign exchange and 24hr ATM.

ICICI Bank (ground fl, RS Towers, Hall Bazaar; ⊙9am-6pm Mon-Fri, to 2pm Sat) Foreign exchange and 24hr ATM.

POST

Main post office (☑2566032; Court Rd; ⊙9am-3pm Mon-Fri, to 2pm Sat) On the left, at the junction with Albert Rd.

Post office (Golden Temple Rd, Furwara Chowk; ⊙9am-5pm Mon-Fri, to 1pm Sat)

TOURIST INFORMATION

Tourist office (☑2402452; www.punjab-tourism.gov.in; Train Station exit, Queen's Rd; ⊙9am-5pm Tue-Sun) By the entrance to the train station, this tourist office has brochures and free maps covering Punjab, including detailed street maps of Amritsar, Patiala and Kapurthala.

Manat Travels (☑0183-5006006, 9815641310; www.mannattravels.com; 5 Dharam Singh Market, Furwara Chowk; ⊙Mon-Sat) Trustworthy travel agent who can book air and train tickets for ₹150 and ₹50 commission respectively. Also changes money.

⊙ Getting There & Away

AIR

About 11km northwest of the centre, Amritsar's Sri Guru Ram Dass Jee International Airport services domestic and international flights (to the Middle East and Central Asia mostly, but Air India also flies to London). Direct flights to Delhi cost around ₹3200 and to Mumbai around ₹7000.

Air India (☑2213392; www.airindia.in; 39A Court Rd; ⊙9.30am-1.15pm & 2-5pm Mon-Sat)

Jet Airways (☑3209847; www.jetairways.com; Airport)

SpiceJet (☑1800-1803333; www.spicejet.com)

BUS

Private bus companies operate from near Gandhi Gate, and from Cooper Rd, near the train station. Evening air-con buses run to Delhi (₹800, 10 hours), Chandigarh (₹600, four hours) and Jaipur (seat/sleeper ₹700/900, 16 hours), while non-AC ones run to Jammu (₹250, six hours).

The main **Inter State Bus Terminal** (ISBT; GT Rd) is about 2km north of the Golden Temple, near Mahan Singh Gate. There's at least one daily bus to Chamba (₹270, six hours), Dharamsala (₹225, seven hours) and Manali (₹550, 12 hours). Frequent buses serve:

Attari ₹30, one hour

Chandigarh non-AC/AC ₹230/460, five hours

Delhi non-AC/AC ₹420/850, 10 hours

Faridkot ₹110, three hours

Jammu ₹185, six hours

Pathankot ₹100, three hours

Patiala ₹230, five hours

BORDER CROSSING – ATTARI-WAGAH (PAKISTAN)

Because of the tense relations between India and Pakistan, few foreigners actually cross the border between Attari and Wagah. However, plenty of people come to watch the curious border-closing ceremony (p220) every evening.

The border is 30km west of Amritsar; buses run from Amritsar to Attari (₹30), from where it's a 2km walk to the customs post (or ₹10 in a shared auto). The border ceremony is held a few hundred metres beyond the customs post.

Border Hours

Officially, the border is open from 10am to 3.30pm daily, but confirm that the border is open at all before you leave Amritsar, and arrive at least an hour before the border closes.

Foreign Exchange

There are banks with moneychanging facilities and ATMs at both sides of the border, but it's wise to also change some money in Amritsar first.

Onward Transport

From Wagah (Pakistan) there are buses and taxis to Lahore, 30km away.

Visas

Visas are theoretically available at the Pakistan embassy in Delhi; however, it is almost always easier to obtain a Pakistan visa in your home country.

DON'T MISS

BATTLE OF POMP & CEREMONY

Every afternoon, just before sunset, members of the Indian and Pakistani military meet at the border post between Attari and Wagah to engage in a 30-minute display of military showmanship that verges on pure theatre. Officially, the purpose of the ceremony is to lower the national flag and formally close the border for the night, but what actually occurs is a bizarre mix of formal marching, flag-folding, chest beating, forceful stomping and almost comical high-stepping, as the two sides try to out-do each other in pomp and circumstance. The oiled moustaches and over-the-top dress uniforms (with fan-like flourishes atop each turban) only add to the theatrical mood.

While the participants treat the ceremony with absolute seriousness, the crowds who gather to watch from the grandstands on either side of the border come for the carnival mood. During the build-up to the ceremony, spontaneous anthem chanting, rapturous rounds of applause and Bollywood-style dancing in the street are de rigueur. Then a roar goes up from the crowd as the first soldier from each side marches furiously towards the border, to begin the first round of who-can-high-step-the-highest. It's all highly nationalistic, but considering the tense relations between the two countries, remarkably good-natured.

The ceremony starts at around 4.15pm in winter and about 5.15pm in summer. Not everyone gets in, though, so arrive at least one hour before the ceremony begins. It's a mad scrum at the main entrance gate (women must queue on the right; men on the left) as people are let through in sudden bursts, but once you're through, things calm down, and you are channelled into the appropriate stands (foreign tourists are allowed to sit in the second-best seats, just behind the VIPs) – bring your passport.

Taxis and private buses from Amritsar drop you off by the customs post, a few hundred metres before the entrance gate to the ceremony area. Cameras are permitted but bags, large and small, are banned; lockers (₹50) are available beside the entrance gate.

Most people arrange a taxi with their hotel in Amritsar (around ₹600), but you can also charter a taxi (₹1200), or take a shared taxi from the southeast gate of the Golden Temple (₹120 per person; just hang out around the prepaid taxi booth sometime before 3pm and drivers will find you). Buses to Attari (₹30, one hour) are the cheapest option but leave you with a ₹10 shared auto ride to the customs post – although some local buses (₹35) return to Amritsar afterwards, departing directly from the customs post.

It should be noted that the tragic suicide bombing in November 2014, which claimed the lives of 60 people just outside the entrance to the ceremony on the Pakistan side of the border, is thought to have nothing to do with relations between India and Pakistan. Instead, it is believed to be a response from militant groups to Pakistan's military operations in northwest Pakistan.

TRAIN

Apart from the train station, there's a less busy **train reservation office** (⊙ 8am-8pm, to 2pm Sun) at the Golden Temple.

The fastest train to Delhi is the Amritsar Shatabdi (AC chair/1AC ₹865/1690, six hours, two daily). Trains leave Amritsar at 5am and 4.50pm; from New Delhi train station, they leave at 7.20am and 4.30pm. There are around a dozen other daily trains to Delhi (sleeper/3AC/2AC ₹300/800/1200), taking eight to nine hours.

Two daily trains go to Chandigarh (2nd class/AC chair ₹120/430, four hours) at 5.15am and 5.30pm.

The daily 6.45pm Amritsar–Howrah Mail links Amritsar with Varanasi (sleeper/3AC/2AC ₹500/1340/1950, 22 hours) and Kolkata's Howrah train station (₹695/1850/2720, 37 hours).

Ten daily trains go to Pathankot (2nd class/AC chair ₹65/255, three hours), leaving between 4.40am and 8.30pm.

ⓘ Getting Around

Free yellow buses run between the train station and the Golden Temple from 4am to 9pm. Otherwise, from the train station to the Golden Temple, a rickshaw/autorickshaw will cost around ₹50/70 but you'll have to haggle like fury for a fair price. Taxis loiter around the station, or there's a **prepaid taxi booth** (☎ 9888561615) at the southeast entrance to the Golden Temple. To the airport, an autorickshaw costs around ₹250 and a taxi about double.

Pathankot

☎ 0186 / POP 148,500

The dusty frontier town of Pathankot is a transport hub for the neighbouring states of Himachal Pradesh and Jammu & Kashmir, but there's little to make you linger. There's a **Himachal Tourism** (☎0186-2220316; ☺10am-5pm Mon-Sat) booth at Pathankot Junction train station. The bus station has a simple restaurant and a **guesthouse** (☎9814131093; r ₹400) with very basic rooms and a common shower room. Just outside the bus station, **Hotel Comfort** (☎0186-2226403; Gurdaspur Rd; d with/without AC ₹1580/1200) has modern rooms and room-service meals.

ⓘ Getting There & Away

From Pathankot Junction station, on Gurdaspur Rd, there are 10 daily trains to Amritsar (2nd class/AC Chair ₹65/255, two to three hours) from 4.15am to 11.15pm; just buy a second-class 'general' ticket and hop on the next one.

Eight daily trains leave for New Delhi (sleeper/3AC/2AC ₹300/780/1100, eight hours) at 10.40am, 4.45pm and then frequently between 7pm and midnight.

For Dharamsala and McLeod Ganj, four daytime trains run along the narrow-gauge line to Kangra Mandir (seat ₹35, five hours), leaving at 6.45am, 10am, 1.20pm and 3.50pm.

From the bus station, also on Gurdaspur Rd, there are three or four direct buses for McLeod Ganj (₹150, 4½ hours) each morning; otherwise, go via Dharamsala. There are frequent bus services throughout the day to:

Amritsar ₹100, three hours

Chamba ₹170, 4½ hours

Chandigarh ₹260, six hours

Dalhousie ₹100, 3½ hours

Delhi ordinary/Volvo AC ₹465/1000, 11 hours

Dharamsala ₹135, four hours

Jammu ₹90, three hours

Manali ₹370, 11 hours

Jammu & Kashmir (including Ladakh)

Why Go?

J&K combines three incredibly different worlds into one state. Hindu Jammu, the state's major railhead, is a busy hub for domestic pilgrims. Muslim Kashmir is India's Switzerland, attracting hoards of local tourists seeking cool summer air, alpine scenery and Srinagar's romantic houseboat accommodation. For most foreigners, J&K's greatest attraction is the Himalayan land of Ladakh, whose disarmingly friendly, ethno-linguistically Tibetan people are predominantly Buddhist. Their timeless monasteries are set between arid canyons and soaring peaks with emerald-green villages nestled photogenically in highland deserts.

Although Kashmir has been relatively calm of late, be aware that it is politically volatile and arguments over its status caused three 20th-century wars. Ladakh is different, a meditatively calm world, where the main concern is giving yourself ample time for high-altitude acclimatisation. Note that Ladakh is inaccessible by road outside the summer season.

Best Buddhist Monasteries

➜ Yungdrung (Lamayuru) Gompa (p256)

➜ Thekchhok (Chemrey) Gompa (p245)

➜ Thiksey Gompa (p244)

➜ Phuktal Gompa (p262)

➜ Diskit Gompa (p248)

Best Mountain Scenery

➜ Pangong Tso (p251)

➜ Dal Lake (p265)

➜ Turtuk and the Shyok Valley (p250)

➜ Leh–Manali road (p244)

When to Go

Leh

Apr–Jun Kashmir is in full bloom but overloaded with domestic tourists. Prices peak.

Jul–Aug Perfect for Ladakh; rain drenches Jammu. Countless pilgrims flood to Amarnath.

Winter Ski season at Gulmarg. Ladakh has festivals but no road access for tourists.

LADAKH

Spectacularly jagged, arid mountains enfold this magical, Buddhist ex-kingdom. Picture-perfect gompas (Tibetan Buddhist monasteries) dramatically crown rocky outcrops amid whitewashed stupas and meditational *mani* walls topped with countless mantra-inscribed pebbles. Colourful fluttering prayer flags spread their spiritual messages metaphorically with the mountain breeze. Prayer wheels spun clockwise release more merit-making mantras. Gompa interiors are colourfully awash with murals and statuary of numerous bodhisattvas.

Ladakh's remarkably well-balanced traditional society has much to teach the West in terms of ecological awareness. While most Ladakhis are cash poor, traditional mudbrick homesteads are large, comfortable and self-sufficient in fuel and dairy products, organic vegetables and barley used to make *tsampa* (roast barley flour) and *chhang* (barley booze). Such self-sufficiency is an incredible achievement given the short growing season and very limited arable land in this upland desert, where precious water supplies must be laboriously channelled from glacier-melt mountain streams.

Ladakh is hemmed in by walls of dramatic mountains. This makes for unforgettable landscapes, but be aware that road access requires crossing tortuous high passes that close altogether from around October to May (or longer when snows are heavy).

History

Ladakh's (now-deposed) royal family traces its dynasty back 39 generations to AD 975. They took the name Namgyal (Victorious) in 1470 when their progenitor Lhachen Bhagan, ruling from Basgo, conquered a competing Ladakhi kingdom based at Leh/Shey. Although Ladakh had been culturally 'Tibetanised' in the 9th century, Buddhism originally arrived in an Indian form that's visible in ancient temple artisanship at Alchi. Over time, however, different Buddhist sects struggled for prominence, with the Tibetan Gelukpa order eventually becoming the majority philosophy after its introduction in the 14th century by Tibetan pilgrim Tsongkhapa (who left a curious relic at Spituk).

Ladakh's greatest king, Sengge Namgyal (r 1616–42) gained riches by plundering gold reserves from western Tibet and re-established a capital at Leh. Ladakh remained an independent kingdom until the 1840s when the region was annexed by the Jammu maharajas. The Namgyals eventually passed Leh Palace to the Indian Archaeological Survey and retired to their summer palace at Stok.

Ladakh is now a pair of subdistricts within J&K. That's a culturally odd situation for this 'little Tibet', which is one of the last relatively undisturbed Tantric Buddhist societies on Earth. When tourism was first permitted in 1974 commentators feared that the area would lose its identity, but the traditional lifestyle of the Ladakhis has proved unexpectedly robust to outside influences. Meanwhile locally relevant technologies, such as solar energy and Trombe thermal-storage walls, have helped to improve rural living standards.

Ladakh news and weather reports are available through www.reachladakh.com.

LADAKHI FESTIVALS

Buddhist temple festivals abound in Ladakh and Zanskar. Most follow a relatively similar formula with masked dances in a square or monastery precinct watched by a fair proportion of locals dressed in traditional *goncha*-robe costumes. Men might sport tall *gonda* hats with some women wearing *perak* 'crowns' encrusted with turquoise. The most genuine festivals are usually in December at Losar (Ladakhi New Year) and February/March during Dosmoche (Buddhist New Year) notably in Leh, Diskit and Likir where effigies representing the evil spirits of the old year are burnt or cast into the desert. Around the same time at Matho's monastery, oracles perform blindfolded acrobatics and ritual mutilations. Several other monastery festivals are now held in the summer, but tourists often form a large proportion of the crowd. For a detailed online festival calendar, see www.reachladakh.com/festival_dates.htm.

Leh's tourist-friendly **Ladakh Festival** (Leh), held in late September, is a fun celebration including several days of Buddhist dances, polo, music and archery.

Silk Route Festival (p251) is a new, vibrant celebration of Nubra Valley culture including archery contests, camel riding and dances.

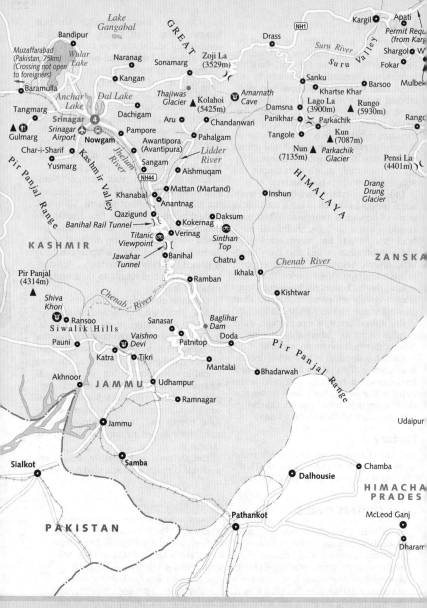

Jammu & Kashmir Highlights

1 Murmuring meditative mantras in the mural-decked gompas (Tibetan Buddhist monasteries) of the Indus Valley, such as at **Chemrey** (p245) or **Thiksey** (p244)

2 Escaping India's humid summer heat in entrancing **Leh** (p226), a traveller hub with dusty medieval backstreets, a Potala-style palace and a deep sense of ecological awareness

3 Experiencing the stark magnificence of Ladakh with a hassle-free homestay trek in the glorious traffic-free **Markha Valley** (p246)

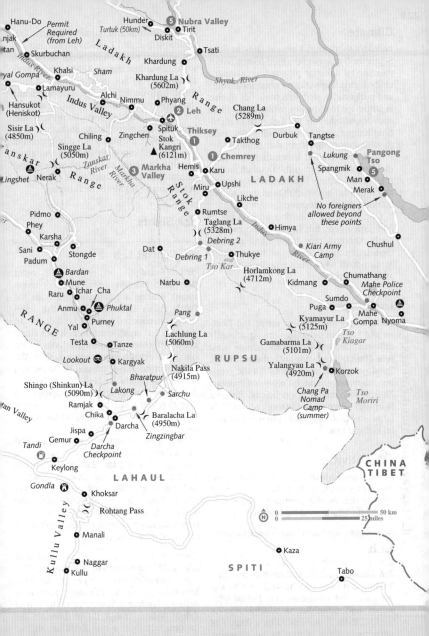

④ Enjoying an amusingly caricatured Raj-type experience relaxing on a deluxe Dal Lake houseboat in **Srinagar** (p264)

⑤ Gawping at the mountain-valley scenery backing surreally blue **Pangong Tso** (p251) or the splendid **Nubra Valley** (p248)

Climate

Ladakh's short tourist season (July to early September) typically sees mild-to-hot T-shirt weather by day, but pleasant, occasionally chilly nights. Early July is great for flowers and peaks still dusted with snow, but August is better for high passes, which can still be snowbound into July. On higher treks nighttime temperatures can dip below 0°C even in midsummer. By September snow is likely on higher ground although major passes usually stay open until October. Access roads close entirely in winter when temperatures can fall below –20°C and most tourist infrastructure shuts down.

Ladakh enjoys sunshine an average of 300 days a year, but storms can brew suddenly. Although rare, heavy rain can cause devastating mud slides, as happened in August 2010 when such cloudbursts killed around 200 people.

Language

Though they use the same script, the Tibetan and Ladakhi languages are significantly different. The wonderfully all-purpose word *jule* (pronounced '*joo*-lay') means 'hello', 'goodbye', 'please' and 'thanks'. To the greeting *khamzang,* simply reply *khamzang. Zhimpo-rak* means 'it's delicious'. Rebecca Norman's excellent *Getting Started in Ladakhi* (₹200) has more phrases and useful cultural tips.

Activities

In summer Ladakh is an adventure playground for outdoor types. Leh's vast range of agents can quickly arrange climbing, rafting, high-altitude trekking and jeep tours.

Leh

01982 / POP 30,870 / ELEV 3520M

Few places in India are at once so traveller-friendly and yet so enchanting and hassle-free as mountain-framed Leh. Dotted with stupas and crumbling mudbrick houses, the Old Town is dominated by a dagger of steep rocky ridge topped by an imposing Tibetan-style palace and fort. Beneath, the bustling bazaar area is draped in a thick veneer of tour agencies, souvenir shops and tandoori-pizza restaurants, but a web of lanes quickly fans out into a green suburban patchwork of irrigated barley fields. Here, gushing streams and narrow footpaths link traditionally styled Ladakhi homes and hotels with flat roofs, sturdy walls and ornate wooden window frames. Leh's a place that's all too easy to fall in love with, but take things easy on arrival. The altitude means that most visitors initially suffer mild headaches and breathlessness. To prevent this becoming full-blown acute mountain sickness (AMS), drink plenty of fluids (ginger tea is considered especially helpful) and avoid strenuous exertion at first. It's wise to wait several days before trekking or taking jeep excursions to Tso Moriri or Pangong.

⊙ Sights

⊙ Central Leh

★ **Leh Palace**   PALACE
(Map p232; Indian/foreigner ₹5/100; ⏱ sunrise-sunset) Bearing a passing similarity to the Potala Palace in Lhasa (Tibet), this nine-storey dun-coloured palace is Leh's dominant structure and architectural icon. It took shape under 17th-century king Sengge Namgyal but has been essentially unoccupied since the Ladakhi royals were stripped of power and shuffled off to Stok in 1846. Today the sturdy walls enclose some exhibition spaces and a small prayer room, but the most enjoyable part of a visit is venturing up to the uppermost rooftops for the view.

Interesting structures ranged around the palace's base include the prominent **Namgyal Stupa** (Map p232), the colourfully muralled **Chandazik Gompa** (Chenrezi Lhakhang; Map p232; admission ₹20; ⏱ hours vary) and the 1430 **Chamba Lhakhang** (Map p232) with medieval mural fragments between the inner and outer walls. Don't count on any of these being open.

Tsemo Fort   CASTLE, RUIN
(Map p232; admission ₹20; ⏱10am-7pm) Visible from virtually everywhere in Leh, 16th-century Tsemo (Victory) Fort is a defining landmark that crowns the top of Palace Ridge, though there's little to see inside apart from a tiny Buddhist shrine. Directly beneath, **Tsemo Gompa** (Map p232; admission ₹30; ⏱7.30am-6pm) consists of two little 15th-century temple buildings, one enshrining an 8m-tall gold-faced Maitreya, the other an atmospheric Gonkhang of protector deities.

Central Asian Museum   MUSEUM
(Map p232; www.tibetheritagefund.org/pages/pro-jects/ladakh/central-asian-museum.php; suggested donation ₹50; ⊙open on request) This tapered four-storey stone tower is new but has a design based on an historic Lhasa mansion with the added flourish of a fortress-style drawbridge. Exhibits are relatively limited but the top floor 'Faces of Ladakh' mini photo-essays are thought provoking.

The museum hides in a courtyard that also contains Leh's oldest mosque and a traditionally styled Ladakhi show-kitchen (nearing completion).

Leh Old Town   AREA
Behind Leh's fanciful **Jamia Masjid** (Map p232), a Sunni men's mosque, winding alleys and stairways burrow between and beneath a series of old mudbrick Ladakhi houses and eroded old chortens (stupas). The alleys themselves are a large part of the attraction, but some individual buildings have been particularly well restored, notably the 17th-century Munshi Mansion, once the residence of the Ladakhi royal secretary and now housing the **LAMO Arts Centre** (Ladakh Arts & Media Organisation; Map p232; ☑ 01982-251554; www.lamo.org.in).

⊙ Greater Leh

Sankar   AREA
For a charming wander, follow canal streams in the captivating yet relatively accessible area around little **Sankar Gompa** (Map p228; admission ₹30) and its one-room **geological museum** (LRMPS Museum; Map p228; www.ladakhrocksminerals.com; Sankar; Indian/foreigner ₹30/50; ⊙9am-1pm & 2-7pm). For memorable views, continue around 1km uphill to the laudable **Donkey Sanctuary** (☑ 9419658777; www.donkeysanctuary.in; Korean Temple Rd) or the nearby 11th-century **Tisuru Stupa** (Tisuru Rd), a bulky, partly restored mudbrick ruin that looks like a half-built *ziggurat* (stepped pyramid).

Shanti Stupa   BUDDHIST, VIEWPOINT
(Map p228; ⊙dawn-9pm) Dominating Leh from a high, rocky ridge, this gigantic white spired pudding of a stupa was built in 1991 by Japanese monks to promote world peace.

You can circumambulate to canned mantras and meditate in the Buddha Hall, but the greatest attraction is the stunning view over Leh. Ideally, make the breathless 15-minute climb when golden afternoon light still illuminates the city but the steps up from Changspa are already bathed in cooling shadow. There's a small simple cafe.

Gomang Stupa   BUDDHIST MONUMENT
(Map p228) This 9th-century stupa rises in concentric serrated layers flanked by numerous chortens. Recent restoration masks its aura of great antiquity, but its peaceful, shady setting remains a refreshingly spiritual escape from the tourist-centric developments of surrounding Changspa.

Nezer Latho   VIEWPOINT, SACRED SITE
(Map p228) This mysterious whitewashed cube is the shrine of Leh's guardian deity. While not much to see in itself, its rocky outcrop setting offers superb 360-degree views over the city through colourful strings of prayer flags.

⊙ Out of Town

3D Mandala   BUDDHIST SCULPTURE
(Nubra Highway, Km6) A truly vast Wheel-of-Life mandala, the size of a football pitch, is under construction at the northern edge of town.

Spituk Gompa   BUDDHIST MONASTERY
(admission ₹30) Founded in the late 14th century as See-Thub ('Exemplary') Monastery, impressive Spituk Gompa is incongruously perched overlooking Leh's airport runway around 5km from town. Multiple mudbrick buildings tumble merrily down a steep hillock towards Spituk village on the Indus riverbank. The courtyard below the gilt-roofed Skudung Lhakhang leads to a colourful *dukhang* (prayer hall) containing a yellow-hatted statue of Tsongkhapa (1357–1419), who spread Gelukpa Buddhism. A Buddha statue across the same room supposedly incorporates a very odd relic: Tsongkhapa's nose-bleed.

On the very top of the gompa hill is a three-tiered latho (spirit shrine) and the small Palden Lamo temple hiding veiled

Leh

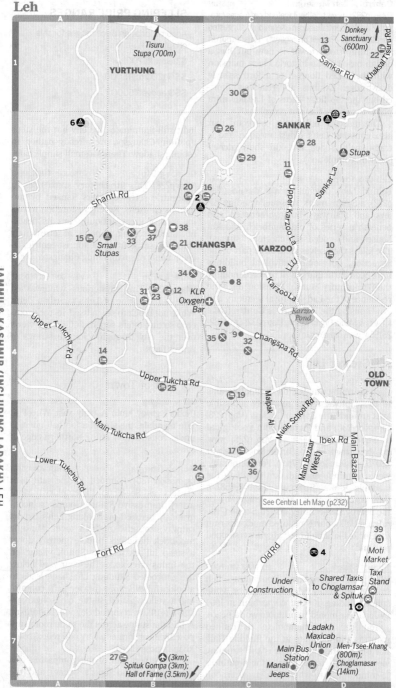

JAMMU & KASHMIR (INCLUDING LADAKH) LEH

YURTHUNG

Tisuru Stupa (700m)

Donkey Sanctuary (600m)

Khaksal Tsuru Rd

Sankar Rd

13

22

30

SANKAR

26

5 3

28

Stupa

29

11

Shanti Rd

20 16

2

38

CHANGSPA

KARZOO

Upper Karzoo La

Sankar La

10

15

Small Stupas

33

37

21

34 18

8

Karzoo La

Karzoo Pond

31 23 12

KLR Oxygen Bar

7

35 9 32

Changspa Rd

OLD TOWN

Upper Tukcha Rd

14

Upper Tukcha Rd

25

19

Malpak Al

Music School Rd

Main Bazaar (West)

Ibex Rd

Main Bazaar

17

24 36

See Central Leh Map (p232)

Main Tukcha Rd

Lower Tukcha Rd

Fort Rd

Old Rd

4

Under Construction

39

Moti Market

Shared Taxis to Choglamsar & Spituk

Taxi Stand

1

27

Spituk Gompa (3km); Hall of Fame (3.5km)

Ladakh Maxicab Union

Main Bus Station

Manali Jeeps

Men-Tsee-Khang (800m); Choglamsar (14km)

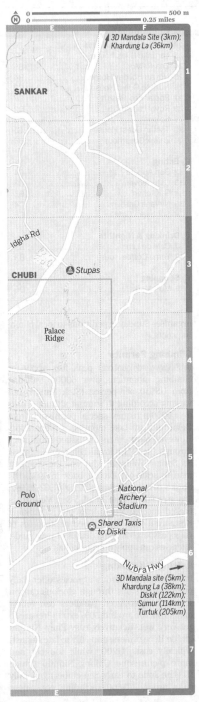

Hindu-style deities and festival masks in an intimate rear section.

Hall of Fame   MUSEUM
(Leh–Spituk Hwy Km428; Indian/foreigner/camera ₹25/50/50, adventure park adult/child ₹30/20; ☺9am-7pm Wed-Mon, to 5pm Nov-Mar) This well-presented museum mostly commemorates the army's role in Ladakh from helping with cloudburst relief in 2010 to the high-altitude battles fought with Pakistan during the 20th century and includes a 30-minute film introducing the 1999 'Kargil War'. Room 15 displays clothing worn by soldiers at -50°C.

An attached 'Adventure Park' combines assault course and archery range.

🏃 Activities

Cycling

For an exhilarating yet almost effortless excursion take a jeep ride up to Khardung La (the 'world's highest road-pass') and let gravity bring you back down. The potholes of the uppermost 14km (above South Pullu army camp) mean that initially you won't whizz down too fast, but the last 25km to Leh is well paved. Packages cost around ₹1300 per person and include bike hire, support vehicle and permits assuming at least four riders. Book one day ahead through **Summer Holidays** (Map p232; ☎9906985822; www.mtb ladakh.com; Zangsti Rd) or **Himalayan Bikers** (Map p228; ☎9469049270; www.himalayan -bikers.com; Changspa). Both also rent mountain bikes (per day ₹500 to ₹700).

Meditation & Yoga

Various yoga, reiki and meditation places pop up each summer. The following have been established for longer.

Mahabodhi Centre   YOGA, MEDITATION
(Map p228; ☎01982-251162, 9622995460; www. mahabodhi-ladakh.org; Changspa Rd; ☺Jun–mid-Sep) Daily, except Sundays, there are drop-in meditation sessions (by donation) at 7.30am and 6pm, pranayama-breathing exercises at 8.30am, and yoga classes (₹250) at 9am (intermediate), 2.30pm (beginners) and 4.30pm (all-level hatha). Three-day residential courses in *vipassana* meditation (₹4000) are held roughly weekly at their Choglamsar Centre (approximately 1km north of Km464.2), as are Sunday 'introduction-to-meditation' sessions (₹500 including Leh bus transfer).

Leh

Open Ladakh MEDITATION
(Map p232; ☏ 9622978828, 9906981026; www.openladakh.com; Hemis Complex, 23-24, Upper Tukcha Rd) Weekend *vipassana* residential retreats and lay-Buddhist teachings at the private little Dhamma House in Stok, along with occasional meditation-centred treks and activities.

Mountaineering

Ladakh has over 100 climbable peaks above 6000m, many rarely, if ever, scaled. A popular destination is 6121m Stok Kangri (Kanglha-jhal), the triangular snow-capped 'trekking peak' usually visible straight across the valley from Leh. Although accessible to those with minimal climbing experience, scaling its uppermost slopes requires ice axes, ropes, crampons, considerable fitness and an experienced guide. Pre-climb acclimatisation is essential as AMS can be a serious worry. Five-day agency packages from Stok or Zingchen, cost around ₹15,000 per person in a large group (permits and gear extra).

A good place to meet fellow climbers or to exercise your grips is the small bouldering-cafe GraviT (Map p232; www.facebook.com/GraviT.Leh; Raku Complex 2nd fl, Fort Rd; inside climbing wall per hr ₹80, excursions per day ₹1800; ⊙ 11am-10pm Mon-Sat, 6-10pm Sun), which also

organises Sunday expeditions to local climbing spots.

Climbing Permits

IMF (www.indmount.org) peak fees apply for climbing mountains over 6000m, starting from US$50 per person (Stok Kangri) but varying according to summit altitude. Peaks over 7000m require special permission from Delhi and can take months of preparation. However, most others are issued in minutes through the IMF's jovial Leh representative, Sri Sonam Wangyal, who was the youngest man to scale Mt Everest back in 1965. His house-office (IMF; Map p232; ☏ 01982-252992; Changspa Rd; ⊙ 10am-2pm & 5-8pm Mon-Sat) is tucked incongruously into the Mentokling Restaurant yard. You'll need photocopies of your passport/visa plus details of your guide. Agencies can apply on your behalf.

Rafting & Kayaking

In summer, numerous agencies offer daily rafting excursions through glorious canyon scenery. Experienced paddlers can follow in a kayak for around 50% extra. Prepare to get very wet. Relatively easy Phey–Nimmu (grade II, beginners, mid-July to late August) typically costs ₹1200; while tougher and more picturesque Chiling–Nimmu (grade III, late June to early September) generally costs around ₹1600 including equipment and lunch (bring extra drinking water). Reliable specialist companies include Rimo (Map p232; ☑01982-253348; www.rimoriver expeditions.com; Zangsti Rd), Wet'n'Wild (Map p232; ☑9419819721, 01982-255122; www.wetnwild explorations.com; Fort Rd, 1st fl) and Splash Adventures (Map p232; ☑9622965941; www. splashladakh.com; Zangsti Rd), while Luna Ladakh (Map p232; ☑9419977732; www.luna ladakh.com; Zangsti Rd) adds rafting as the finale to a package including mountain biking (Spituk–Zingchen) and trekking (Zingchen–Chiling with homestays) costing ₹16,000/20,000 for two people, on a three-/four-day package. Cheaper for groups.

Once or twice a year given enough interest, group expeditions descend the Zanskar River from Zangla to Nimmu (three days rafting, three days travel; see www.rimoriverexpeditions.com for more details).

Trekking & Jeep Safaris

Countless agencies offer trekking packages, jeep tours, rafting, biking and permit procurement. Few seem systematically bad but many are very inconsistent. A deciding factor is often simply which agent happens to have a group leaving on the day you need. We have found small operators Higher Himalayas (Map p232; ☑9419333393; www. higherhimalayas.com; Zangsti Rd), Snowfield (Map p232; ☑9469723819; Hemis Complex, Upper Tukcha Rd) and especially Shayok (Map p232; ☑9419342346, 9419888902; shayoktravels@redif-fmail.com; Changspa Rd) to be honest, competitive and helpful with trekking information and as jeep-tour fixers. Ask fellow travellers for recent recommendations.

Ladakhi Women's Travel Company TREKKING
(Map p232; ☑9469158137, 01982-257973; www. ladakhiwomenstravel.com; Hemis Complex, unit 22, Upper Tukcha Rd; ☺10am-6pm) Small highly reputable female-run operation specialising in Markha and Sham homestay trek packages. Male customers accepted if their group includes women.

Hidden North TREKKING
(Map p232; ☑9419218055, 01982-226007; www. hiddennorth.com; Music School Rd) Tashi has two decades of guiding experience and loads of interesting alternative trekking ideas to get you away from the typical routes. Some start from his own guesthouse in Phyang.

Wild East Adventure TREKKING
(Map p232; ☑01982-257939; www.wildeastad-venture.com; Hemis Complex, Upper Tukcha Rd) Long-established specialist for tailor-made treks using only their own guides. Helpful and obliging.

Yama Adventures TREKKING
(Map p228; ☑01982-250833, 9419178763; www. yamatreks.com; Changspa Rd) Namgial at Yama Adventures gets regular recommendations from Lonely Planet readers.

☞ Tours

Old City Heritage Walk WALKING TOUR
(Map p232; ☑9419952794; per person ₹450; ☺2.30pm Mon-Sat) Informative small-group walking tours peek into some 'secret' corners and get you inside a couple of usually closed ancient houses/temples. Start from Lala's Art Cafe (p238), where you should book ahead. Tours last around two hours.

🛏 Sleeping

Choice is phenomenal and almost nowhere is really dire, so don't panic if our suggestions are full. Room standards can vary significantly within each property so, when possible, look before you book. For ultra-budget places, try the back alleys of Upper

JAMMU & KASHMIR (INCLUDING LADAKH) LEH

LADAKH PERMITS

To visit Nubra Valley, Pangong Tso, Dha-Hanu, Tso Moriri and the Upper Indus (beyond Upshi) you'll need an inner line permit (valid seven days, nonextendable). Indian citizens can go direct to the DCO (Deputy Commissioner's Office; Map p232; Polo Ground; ☺10am-3pm Mon-Sat). Foreigners' permit applications must be made through travel agencies. Apply by 2pm the day before travel or on Saturday for Monday departures. Foreigners typically pay around ₹500. That's ₹20 per day of validity plus ₹70 Red Cross fee, agency fee and ₹300 environmental fee. You only need to pay the latter charge once and might have already done so on arrival in Ladakh (most commonly at Upshi), so make sure you keep the receipt voucher.

Technically at least two people must apply together, but agencies can usually fudge this for individual travellers. Making extra copies of your inner line permit is wise.

Central Leh

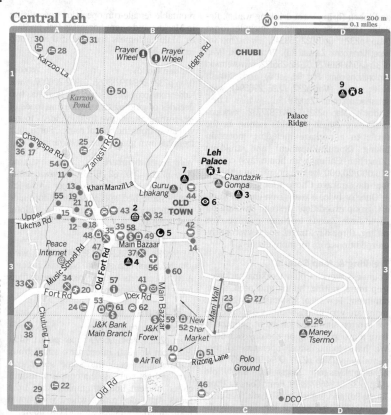

Changspa. For garden homestay-guesthouses around the ₹800 mark look in Upper Karzoo. For slightly plusher family guesthouses Upper Tukcha is a good bet. Staying out at Sankar or Yurthung can be idyllically peaceful but there'll be a fairly long, dark walk home from town (₹150 by taxi by day).

Many guesthouses will provide towels on request, but you'll usually have to buy your own toilet paper which should generally not be flushed: when there's a plastic bin, use that. In winter most accommodation closes; guesthouses that stay open often charge a ₹100 heating supplement and may only offer bucket water because pipes freeze.

Central Leh

Palace View Guest House
GUESTHOUSE $
(Map p232; ☎ 9622964542; palace.view@hotmail.com; d ₹600-1000) This fine-value family place keeps its promises with stupendous views across the old city from rooftop sitting areas and from some of the neat ensuite rooms, mostly rebuilt since 2011. Showers run very hot.

Zik-Zik
GUESTHOUSE $
(Map p232; ☎ 9622990273, 01982-255812; Upper Karzoo Lane; old/new d ₹600/1200; ☎) One of the most central guesthouses to have an extensive vegetable garden and orchard-shaded seating, Zik-Zik's rooms are mostly light and airy. Newer ones have slightly smarter bathrooms.

Travellers' House
GUESTHOUSE $
(Map p232; ☎ 01982-252048; thetravellershouse@gmail.com; Karzoo Lane; d ₹700-900) Striking a good quality-for-price balance, the eight well-kept, no-nonsense guest rooms come with geyser-equipped bathrooms and face the home of friendly, English-speaking family owners and Lukhee, their pet poodle.

Central Leh

JAMMU & KASHMIR (INCLUDING LADAKH) LEH

Saser GUESTHOUSE $
(Map p232; ☎01982-250162, 9596967447; nam_gyal@rediff.com; Karzoo Lane; lower/upper d ₹600/800) The lower rooms are bland, but upstairs rooms have log-beams, framed photos and a shared balcony, most facing the castle across the sweet little flower-edged lawn. There's roof-seating and a small library of English books in the breakfast room.

Namgyal Guest House GUESTHOUSE $
(Map p232; ☎9906973364; r without bathroom ₹300-500) This cube of traditional Ladakhi building offers simple, recently repainted rooms sharing three bathrooms with geyser and seatless toilets. New ensuite rooms due by 2015. The friendly lady owner speaks English. Wi-fi costs ₹100 per day.

Babu Guesthouse HOSTEL $
(Map p232; ☎01982-252419; s/d ₹300/400) Ever popular, based on price and location, Babu's basic but not unpleasant box rooms share outside squat and bucket shower-room.

The Auspicious Hotel
HOTEL $$

(Map p232; ☎9419177864, 01982-253687; www.
theaushotel.com; Chulung Lane; r ₹1800-
2200) This professionally managed and as-
siduously clean hotel is attractively fronted
with a wraparound Ladakhi-carved balcony.
Cheaper rooms have traditional varnished
log ceilings, while the huge new ones have
Leh's biggest super-king beds and schman-
zy bathrooms with square-headed rainfor-
est showers (though hot-water timings are
limited).

Kang-Lha-Chen
HOTEL $$

(Map p232; ☎01982-252144, 01982-202289; www.
hotelkanglhachen.com; Zangsti; s/d ₹3330/3390;
☺closed Oct-Apr; ☎) Central yet set around a
peaceful garden-courtyard, this long-standing favourite has older but well-maintained
rooms with excellent box-spring mattresses, wood-effect hard floors and simple but
clean bathrooms (hot water morning and
evening). Tasteful Tibetan touches add interest and there's a delightful sitting room
designed like an antique Ladakhi kitchen.

Almighty Guesthouse
GUESTHOUSE $$

(Map p232; ☎9419179501; Chulung Lane; ₹1000-
2000) This relatively luxurious new family
guesthouse has six capacious rooms with
standards better than most hotels. Bright,
airy room 5 has a balcony. There's free wi-fi
and glimpses of Stok Kangri from the roof-
top.

Cozy Corner
HOTEL $$

(Map p232; ☎01982-251587; hotelcozycorner@
gmail.com; Fort Rd; d ₹2500; ☎) Nine good-
sized, professionally appointed rooms are
accessed by art-adorned lime-green stairways from beside the well-known Summer
Harvest restaurant. Palace views from room

106 are impressive. There's no reception (ask
at Singge Tours office, upstairs).

Greater Leh

Chow Guest House
GUESTHOUSE $

(Map p228; ☎01982-252399; small/large d
₹600/800, without bathroom ₹400; ☎) This
excellent-value, family-run guesthouse has
sparkling clean, airy budget rooms with
good mattresses and log ceilings. Housed
in two new but unobtrusive buildings set in
a flower-filled walled garden, you'll find it
down a narrow path off Changspa Rd. Free
wi-fi.

Gyalson
GUESTHOUSE $

(Map p228; ☎9622951748; gyalsean@yahoo.
com; Changspa Rd; d with/without bathroom
₹600/1000) Spick-and-span rooms in a new
but traditionally styled family house with
a prime location just behind Wonderland
restaurant. Bathrooms have geysers and
there are two parasol-tables in the vegetable garden.

Haldupa Guest House
GUESTHOUSE $

(Map p228; ☎01982-251374; Upper Tukcha Rd; r
with/without TV ₹1200/900, r without bathroom
₹300-700) A handful of cheaper rooms are
inside the enchanting owners' wonderfully
authentic original house. The rest are new,
with decent bathrooms, hot showers and
poplar-willow ceilings in a separate, continuously cleaned block facing the peaceful
vegetable garden.

Nurboo Guest House
GUESTHOUSE $

(Map p228; ☎9419340947, 9906988963; Upper
Changspa; r without bathroom ₹400-500) Simple family place serenaded by the sound of
rushing water. Great mountain views from
the rooftop and from upper corner rooms.

LEH – WATER & ECO-AWARENESS

Water is precious – those streams you see cascading beside virtually every lane aren't
a sign of plenty but an elaborate network of irrigation channels that keep Leh from re-
verting to a dusty mountain desert. Anything you can do to save water is a positive step.
Bucket baths save a lot of water over showers, and some guesthouses offer traditional
water-free Ladakhi long-drop toilets that recycle human waste into compost. But don't
put anything nonbiodegradeable down the hole: whatever goes in will end up on the
farmer's field in a year or two.

To save Leh from vanishing under a sea of plastic bottles, refills of purified, pressure-
boiled water are provided by environmental organisations Dzomsa (p239) and LEDeG
(p238). Both provide recycling and disposal services. Dzomsa has an ecofriendly laundry
(₹95 per kg) and serves locally sourced *tsestalulu* (sea buckthorn) and apricot juices
that avoid packaging.

Norzin Holiday Home
GUESTHOUSE $

(Map p228; ☑ 01982-252022, 9419178751; Upper Tukcha Rd; r with/without bathroom ₹1000/800; ☎) Well-kept mod-trad family home with views from the roof terrace, an enclosed garden and, unusually, a grape-vine dominating the glassed-in verandah. Free drinking water refills; wi-fi costs ₹2 per minute.

Gangs-Shun
HOMESTAY $

(Map p228; ☑ 01982-252603, 9858060706; http://tiny.cc/GangsShun; Upper Tukcha Rd; d ₹1000; @) Seven very well-appointed guest rooms of significantly variable sizes in a plush, friendly family home. Room 1 is family-sized. Lovely lawn-seating and vegetable garden.

Lak Rook Guest House
GUESTHOUSE $

(Map p228; ☑ 01982-252987, 9419177870; Khaksal Tisuru Rd, Sankar; r without bathroom ₹300-600) ✏ This cult traveller favourite is a large, ramshackle Ladakhi farmhouse almost lost amid the flowers and fruit trees of its organic vegetable garden. Rooms are attractively designed but seriously let down by thin straw mattresses. The solar shower room is outside.

Goba
GUESTHOUSE $

(Map p228; ☑ 01982-253670; Goba Alley; r ₹1000, s/d without bathroom from ₹200/300; There's a great spirit to the traditional main house, topped with prayer room and lovely rooftop panoramas. A more neutral hotel-style block has functional ensuite rooms. The garden is a veritable field from which homegrown organic vegetables form the mainstay of family-cooked dinners (book ahead).

Tsetan Guest House
GUESTHOUSE $

(Map p228; ☑ 9622249125, 9469049131; tsetan_n@yahoo.com; Upper Changspa; d ₹800, r without bathroom ₹300-600) Eponymous owner Tsetan has a polite but unquenchable enthusiasm that transforms this simple, quiet back-lane guesthouse into a community brimming with traveller camaraderie.

Shared bathrooms have geysers.

Lardakh Guesthouse
GUESTHOUSE $

(Map p228; ☑ 01982-250780; off Changspa Rd; s/d without bathroom ₹250/300) The big, old house is an absolute Ladakhi classic with extensive garden, rooftop and rooms that, while simple, are as cheap as you'll find. Outdoor toilet and bucket-shower. Note that by day there's rarely anyone at home.

Zaltak Guesthouse
GUESTHOUSE $

(Map p228; Changspa; d ₹1000, r without bathroom ₹300-600) The old block is a standard Ladakhi house set in a pleasant garden. The brand new back building has excellent-value ensuite rooms with sitting areas, large beds and hotel-standard bathrooms.

All View
GUESTHOUSE $

(Map p228; ☑ 9419178854, 01982-252761; Chubi; s/d ₹350/500) This family guesthouse is arranged around a lawn and apple tree at the end of a quiet, dead-end footpath. It's such great value that many guests (predominantly Koreans) stay all season.

Gomang Guest House
GUESTHOUSE $

(Map p228; ☑ 01982-252657; Old Karzoo; small/large r without bathroom ₹400/600; ☎) Wobbly stairways in a genuine Ladakhi home link simple rooms sharing bathrooms with geysers and solar-heated water. Some rooms and two small communal sitting areas overlook peaceful Gomang Stupa through trees. Free wi-fi.

Chamtse Guesthouse
HOMESTAY $

(Map p228; ☑ 9419372430; Upper Karzoo Lane; r lower/upper ₹700/800) Perched above the barley-field garden of the similarly priced Skitsal Guesthouse, Chamtse feels like 'lived in' and the new carpets aren't properly fitted, but luminous rooms sparkle and the family is friendly.

Solpon
GUESTHOUSE $$

(Map p228; ☑ 01982-253067, 9906994466; www.ghoomleh.com; Upper Changspa; d ₹1000-1500, without bathroom ₹500) The simplest rooms have geyser-heated water in shared bathrooms while the plush new section is almost hotel standard, adorned with beautiful landscape photography.

★ Deskit Villa
BOUTIQUE HOTEL, GUESTHOUSE $$

(Map p228; ☑ 01982-253498, 9419178998; www.skywalkertravel.com; Sankar; r guesthouse/hotel ₹1500/3600; ✱) Hidden behind a family garden guesthouse that's delightful in itself, this 'secret' eight-room boutique hotel offers some of the best pampering in Leh with super-comfortable beds, a stupendous rooftop panorama and lots of air-conditioned (!!) public space in which to unwind. The dining room is designed like a traditional Ladakhi kitchen.

Royal Ladakh
HOTEL $$

(Map p228; ☑ 01982-251646, 01982-257576; www.hotelroyalladakh.com; Upper Karzoo Lane; s/d

₹3670/3800; 🛜) Numerous imitators are springing up along Sankar Lane and around Upper Karzoo, but Royal Ladakh remains one of the best choices in its price range if you want a more 'hotel-style' experience yet also feel away from it all. Rooms are spacious and well maintained and there's a majestic lawn panorama.

Grand Willow
HOTEL $$
(Map p228; ☎01982-251835, 9419178242; www. grandwillowladakh.com; Fort Rd; standard s/d ₹2540/3600, deluxe ₹3030/3680) Round a small floral yard right off Fort Rd, the 'standard' block is fronted with wooden-balconies, and rooms have colour-wash walls that might have been painted by Matisse. The more formal deluxe rooms occupy a new, three-storey block with pink marble floors and monogrammed bed-boards.

There's a walk-in discount of 30%.

Lha-Ri-Mo
HOTEL $$
(Map p228; ☎9419178233, 01982-252101; lha-rimo@yahoo.com; Fort Rd; s/d ₹2420/3350) Magenta window frames stacked upon whitewashed walls create a magical monastery-like impression enclosing a lawn garden. There's also an impressive neo-Tibetan lounge. Guest rooms don't have quite the same delight but they've been recently refitted with repainted walls, brass lamps and the odd wrought-iron mirror. Beds have somewhat spongy mattresses and service can be a little offhand.

Poplar Eco-Resort
RESORT $$
(Map p228; ☎01982-253518; www.eprleh.com; Shenam Rd; s/d ₹2250/3050) Lost in the birdsong of an overgrown orchard of apple, apricot and poplar trees is this series of well-spaced two-room bungalows each sharing a verandah with wicker chairs.

The setting is better than the slightly dated decor, but the attached bathrooms are clean and offer all-day hot water. Most food and juice served is sourced from the organic garden.

Hotel Gomang
BOUTIQUE HOTEL $$$
(Map p228; ☎01982-253536; hotelgomang @gmail.com; Upper Changspa; s/d/ste ₹6550/ 8360/9350) Leh abounds with new hotels, but Gomang stands out for the loving care of its management and the careful attention to detail. Boutiquey features include Gomang-branded toiletries, tab-folded loo rolls and fine bed sashes, but what really impresses are the swish yet homely public

spaces with heaped colourful cushions on black leather sofas.

Ladakh Residency
HOTEL $$$
(Map p228; ☎01982-254111, 9419233499; www.ladakhresidency.com; Changspa; s/d/ste ₹5124/6590/8785, walk-in ₹3500/4500/6000; 🛜) Decorated with *thangka* (Tibetan cloth paintings) and Roerich prints, this layered collage of wooden balconies and marble floors has proper king-size beds, bathrooms with toiletries and shower booths and Stok Kangri views from many rooms. It's professionally managed and one of very few wheelchair-friendly buildings in Ladakh. Pleasant raised lawn-garden.

🏠 Out of Town

For something special in the villages around Leh, there's a heritage hotel at Nimmu (p253), a delightful getaway guesthouse at Phyang (p253), a monastery hotel at Thiksey (p244), and five mural-adorned guest rooms within Stok's Royal Palace (p241).

🍴 Eating

From June to September, traveller cafes abound, Israeli and Chinese options supplementing curries, banana pancakes, tandoori pizzas and Tibetan favourites. Competition keeps standards generally high especially in the garden and rooftop restaurants of Changspa. Food around Main Bazaar tends to get more mixed reviews.

🍴 Central Leh

Bakery Shacks
BAKERY $
(Map p232; bread small/large ₹5/10; ⏰about 6-10am & 5-7pm) Fresh-baked *shirmal* (bread rounds) are sold hot from photogenically traditional wood-fired tandoori bakeries on the Old Town alley behind the Central Asian Museum.

Norlakh
TIBETAN $
(Map p232; Main Bazaar; mains ₹60-110, rice ₹40; ⏰about 10am-10.30pm) This loveable family restaurant is great for pure-veg Tibetan food such as cheese-and-spinach whole-wheat *momos* (Tibetan dumplings) or special *gyathuk* (a rich noodle soup). It's upstairs, hidden behind a willow tree almost opposite Ladakh Bookshop.

★ Chopsticks
ASIAN $$
(Map p232; ☎9622378764; Raku Complex, Fort Rd; mains ₹160-310, rice ₹60; ⏰noon-10.30pm)

This effortlessly stylish pan-Asian restaurant, with a solid reputation for quality wok dishes and Thai curries, now even offers trad-Ladakhi *skyu* (flat barley 'gnocci' in vegetable stew). The outdoor terrace is raised above the melee of Fort Rd.

Penguin Garden MULTICUISINE $$
(Map p232; Chulung Lane; mains ₹100-200, half/full tandoori chicken ₹250/490, rice/beer ₹60/150; ☺about 10am-11pm; ☎) Sit beneath the apricot trees and listen to the gushing stream at this slightly hidden but constantly popular garden restaurant. If the fresh-cooked tandoori chicken has run out (typical by early evening) there is still a world of cuisines to explore. Snappy, if casual, service.

Sunbeam Café MULTICUISINE $$
(Map p228; Fort Rd; mains ₹110-290, rice/beer ₹70/170; ☺about 10am-10.30pm; ☎) Convivial shaded rooftop with Chinese lamps and a well-cooked international menu.

Il Forno ITALIAN, INDIAN $$
(Map p232; Zangsti Rd; mains ₹170-290, rice/beer ₹80/150; ☺about 11am-11pm) Il Forno is a partly unshaded rooftop with views of both town and fortress. There's a fairly reliable supply of (sometimes cold) beer and the wood-oven pizzas (₹220 to ₹290) are thin-crust with ample cheese.

Gesmo MULTICUISINE $$
(Map p232; Fort Rd; mains ₹120-250; ☺about 9am-10.30pm) This age-old traveller haunt has been unchanged so long that its vinyl floors and chequerboard ceilings now seem almost like novel retro-design features. Good-value meals range from curries to moist lemon-iced sponge cake (₹50) to yak-cheese pizza.

🍴 Changspa

G-Kitchen MULTICUISINE $$
(Map p228; Changspa Rd; mains ₹90-300, rice ₹60; ☺about 11am-11pm; ☎) Changspa has several old-faithful rooftop restaurants but G-Kitchen is a notch above the competition thanks to its pleasantly appointed indoor section (for colder nights) and its imaginative gourmet specials. We tried seared lamb strips topped with Italian sauce and mozzarella served with balsamic-drizzled rocket. Delicious.

Nirvana Garden MULTICUISINE $$
(Map p228; Changspa Rd; mains ₹100-200, rice/beer ₹60/160; ☺about 10am-11pm) Leh's most New Age chill-out has open-air ground-

LADAKHI FOOD

Ladakh's Tibetan favourites include salt-tea, *momos* (dumplings wrapped ravioli-style in thin pasta) and *thukpa* (noodle soup), though a more genuinely Ladakhi dish is *skyu*, pieces of flat barley 'gnocci' in a vegetable stew. Hard-to-find *paba* is a pea-and-barley meal that you dunk in *tangtur* (boiled vegetables in curd). Ladakh's barley-beer, *chhang*, is available at rural homestays but not for general sale.

seating ringed by low adobe-style walls, an open fire pit and a little pool. Music ranges from informal acoustic jams through trippy-trance to nature-mantra mixes. Excellent curries.

Café Jeevan MULTICUISINE $$
(Booklovers Retreat; Map p228; Changspa Rd; mains ₹120-230, rice ₹80; ☺about 9.30am-10.30pm; ☎) Good for all-veg Italian food and individual-size pizzas, and especially for interesting, locally grown salads (like mint, cucumber and yak cheese). Do pay the ₹30 extra for a scrumptious side of hummus. Glass-walled kitchen, cosy yet gently suave interior and covered roof terrace for catching sunset rays.

★Bon Appetit MULTICUISINE $$$
(Map p228; ☎01982-251533; mains ₹220-460; ☺11am-late) Hidden down unlikely footpaths south of Changspa Rd, Leh's top restaurant is a stylish exercise in Ladakhi minimalist architecture. The menu is short but well chosen, offering artistically prepared fried aubergine-stacks, sublime cashew chicken and succulent tandoori grills.

Not to be confused with the Fort Road 'Bon Appetit' beside Dolphin Bakery.

🍷 Drinking

Bon Appetit is applying for a cocktail licence. Virtually no other restaurant has alcoholic drinks on the menu, but many rooftop and Changspa-garden places unofficially serve beer on request; Nirvana Garden, **La Piazzetta** (Map p232; mains ₹170-350, rice ₹90, pizzas ₹260-370; ☺about 11am-11.30pm; ☎) and Il Forno are good bets. For takeaway booze, the handy **Indus Wine Shop** (Map p232; Ibex Rd; beer/wine ₹85/850; ☺10am-1pm & 3-9.30pm) opens daily except on the 8th, 15th and last days of the Tibetan calendar.

Contenders for Leh's best baristas include small but tastefully stylish **CoffeeSutra** (Map p232; Main Bazaar, 1st fl; coffee ₹60-90; ☺10am-9pm), informal handicraft-shop **Open Hand** (Map p232; www.openhand.in; Chulung Lane; coffee ₹44-110, meals ₹160-250; ☺7.30am-9.30pm; ⊚), snazzy **Cafe de Leh** (Map p232; Changsna Rd; coffee ₹60-250, mains ₹150-300; ☺7am-10pm; ⊚), homely **Desert Rain** (Map p232; New Shar Market; tea/coffee from ₹20/40; ☺ 9.30am-noon & 2-8.30pm Mon-Sat) and unique Lala's. But for us, **Yama Coffee House** (Map p228; Changspa Rd; coffee ₹70-100; ☺7.30am-10pm; ⊚) has the caffeine edge. They do great fruit salads too.

For great masala chai, join the locals at basic **tea stalls** (Map p232; Chandu Market; masala chai ₹10; ☺6.30am-7.30pm) in dusty Chandu Market alley.

★**Lala's Art Cafe**   CAFE
(Leh Heritage House; Map p232; www.tibetheritagefund.org/pages/projects/ladakh/lala-s-cafe.php; Old Town; ☺9.30am-7pm Mon-Sat) Idea for old-town ambience, this tiny, mudbrick house was saved from demolition and brilliantly restored in 2006. It has trip-you-up stone steps and an open roof terrace serving French-press coffee (₹50) and original cakes-of-the-day. Check out art and photography exhibitions, plus the ancient carved steles downstairs.

★**Nati Cafe**   CAFE
(Map p232; Zangsti Parking; tea/coffee ₹10/35; ☺10am-7pm) Inexpensive beverages, cake-of-the-day and local snacks served in an authentically styled old-Ladakhi kitchen.

Old Town Cafe   CAFE
(Map p232; www.heritagehimalaya.org; drinks from ₹15; ☺ about 10am-6pm) Hidden in the shadows of Leh Palace, the historic Lonpo House has a 17th-century kitchen room that's a quiet getaway, ideal if you want to read and unwind. Currently only teas, coffee and juices are served, but on Friday night there's a Ladakhi supper club (sign up at Himalayan Shop on Main Bazaar near Chokhang Vihara gate, opposite SBI).

🛍 Shopping

Leh is a paradise for souvenir shopping. Dozens of colourful little shops, street vendors and **Tibetan Refugee Markets** (Map p232) sell wide selections of *thangkas,* Ladakhi hats, 'antiques' and heavy turquoise jewellery (from ₹80 per gram), as well as Kashmiri shawls and various Nepali, Tibetan and Chinese knick-knacks. Compare prices in fascinating, very local-focused **Moti Market** (Map p228), the little family shops of **Nowshera** (New Shar Market; Map p232) (New Shar) Market or the suavely up-market **Norbulingka Boutique** (Map p232; www.norbulingka.org; Rizong Complex).

Bookshops are well stocked with postcards, novels, spiritual works and books on Ladakh, Kashmir and Tibet. Old Fort Rd, Main Bazaar and Changspa Rd have several outdoors equipment stores. Some, including **Venture Ladakh** (Map p232; ☎9858323091; www.ventureladakh.com; Changspa Rd), rent climbing and trekking gear.

LEDeG   HANDICRAFTS
(Ladakh Ecological Development Group; Map p232; www.ledeg.org; Karzoo Pond; ☺9.30am-6pm Mon-Sat) Locally produced crafts and clothes.

Ladakh Bookshop   BOOKS
(Map p232; ☎9868111112; hanishbooks@yahoo.co.in; Main Bazaar; ☺9am-9pm) Hidden upstairs near the SBI ATM, this wonderfully well-stocked bookshop publishes locally relevant works and stocks Olizane's indispensible *Ladakh Trekking Maps* (₹1500 per sheet).

Book Worm   BOOKS
(Map p232; Old Fort Rd; ☺about 10am-9.30pm) Buys and sells secondhand books.

ℹ Information

INTERNET ACCESS

There are many internet cafes on Fort Rd, Changspa Rd and around Main Bazaar (₹60 per hour) with slow, unreliable connections; wi-fi is often worse. Don't plan on downloading or streaming.

Peace Internet (Map p232; Music School Rd) Comparatively good internet connection by Leh standards.

MEDICAL SERVICES

Het Ram Vinay Kumar Pharmacy (Map p232; ☎01982-252160; Main Bazaar; ☺10am-9pm) Dispenses Diamox (₹40 for 10) and numerous other essential medicines without prescription.

KLR Oxygen Bar (Map p228; KC Garden Restaurant; per minute ₹20; ☺11am-11pm) Breathe pure oxygen to relieve altitude sickness, or just for the buzz.

Men-Tsee-Khang (☎01982-253566; www.men-tsee-khang.org; consultation/museum

₹100/20; ☉9am-1pm & 2-5pm Mon-Fri, plus 1st & 3rd Sat) Amchi (Tibetan herbal medicine) centre, dispensary and one-room museum, 800m south of the bus station. Consultations with no appointment required, but for astrological readings (₹2000, 45 minutes) call two days ahead.

MONEY

There are numerous moneychangers on Changspa Rd and around Main Bazaar, plus at least five ATMs, notably **SBI** (Map p232; Main Bazaar).

J&K Forex (Map p232; 1st fl, Himalaya Complex, Main Bazaar; ☉10.30am-2pm & 2.30-4pm Mon-Fri, to 1pm Sat) Good exchange rates, better still for travellers cheques. Might move facilities to J&K Bank Main Branch (Map p232; Ibex Rd) during 2015.

POST

Tourist Post Office (Map p232; Main Bazaar; ☉10am-1pm & 2-5.30pm Mon-Fri, 10am-noon Sat)

TELEPHONE

Inexpensive sim cards are available from **Air-Cell** (Map p232; Main Bazaar) and **AirTel** (Map p232; Girls' School Lane; ☉10am-6pm) for use within 20km of Leh. Requires four photographs plus photocopies of passport and visa. Connection approval can take several days.

TOURIST INFORMATION

On noticeboards outside **Dzomsa** (Map p232; Zangsti; ☉8.30am-9.30pm), in agencies and pasted all over town are adverts for tours, treks and activities. Indiamike's online forum (www.indiamike.com/india/ladakh-and-zanskar-f31) is very active with Ladakh travellers.

LEDeG Film Screenings (Map p232; Karzoo Pond; by donation; ☉2pm Mon-Sat, Jul-early Sep) The excellent 1993 documentary *Ancient Futures: Learning from Ladakh* and other thought-provoking films are screened to give background to the ecological and economic position of Ladakh. A discussion follows.

Mini Tourist Information Office (Map p232; ☑01982-253462, 01982-252297; Ibex Rd; ☉10am-4pm Mon-Sat) Listings, basic maps and minimal English.

ⓘ Getting There & Away

AIR

Flights are dramatically scenic, but can be cancelled at short notice. Although flying into Leh means you're likely to suffer mild altitude problems on arrival, the Delhi–Manali–Leh drive is arguably worse, as you'll cross passes over 5000m. Flying to Leh is the only way to reach Ladakh once roads close in winter. **Jet**

Airways (Map p232; ☑01982-255444; Main Bazaar; ☉10am-1.30pm & 2-4pm), **GoAir** (Map p232; ☑01982-253940; Airport) and **Air India** (☑01982-252076; Airport; ☉6am-noon) fly to Delhi. Air India also serves Srinagar (Wednesday) and Jammu (Monday and Friday). Fly to Jammu for Dharamsala.

BUS

The **main bus station** (Map p228) is 700m south of the town centre via the Kigu-Tak stepped bazaar from **Friendship Gate** (Map p228).

MOTORCYCLE

Numerous companies along Music School Rd and Changspa Rd hire Enfield Bullet motorcycles (₹1000 to ₹1500 per day) and scooters (₹700). Double-check insurance, fittings and brakes. Carry spare fuel for longer trips: Ladakh's only petrol stations are at Leh, Choglamsar, Serthi near Karu (NH1 Km440.5), Diskit (opening unreliable), Spituk, Phyang junction, Khalsi (NH1 Km338.7), Wakha and Kargil (two).

SHARED JEEP

Services from the bus station (arranging one day ahead):

Kargil (₹900 to ₹1000 per seat, seven hours) Runs throughout the morning.

Srinagar (front/back seats ₹2500/2000, 15 hours) Departures around 4.30pm.

From the parking lot near the *zabakhana,* just southeast of the Polo Ground (without booking):

Diskit (₹400) and possibly Sumur (₹500) or other Nubra jeeps. Departures are before 8am.

From the southern end of Moti Market:

Choglamsar & Spituk (₹20) Shared taxis depart relatively frequently to Choglamsar, but only sporadically to Spituk.

REACHING LADAKH

Only two road routes, both beautiful but seasonal, link Ladakh to the rest of India. The route to Manali is spectacular but long and arduous; to Srinagar, crossing the perilous Zoji La scares the *momos* out of many first-time travellers. Both roads close altogether from October or November until May, leaving flying as the only option for reaching Leh. Allow at least a couple of spare days in case of delays.

On entering Ladakh, if you are asked to pay an 'environmental fee' (Indian/foreigner ₹200/300), keep the receipt and present it when applying for permits.

BUSES FROM LEH

DESTINATION	FARE (₹)	DURATION	DEPARTURES
Alchi	100	3hr	8am, 4pm (return 7.30am, 3pm)
Chemrey	45	1½hr	use Sakti buses
Chiling	85	2½hr	9am Wed & Sun (return 1pm)
Chiktan (A)	278	8hr	8am Tue, Thu, Sun (return Wed, Sat, Mon)
Choglamsar (G)	20	25min	as full
Chushul (B)	394 (406)		6.30am Wed direct (7am Sun via Merak)
Dha (A)	245	7hr	9am. On Friday diverts to Hanu.
Diskit/Hunder (B)	210	6hr	7am Sat, Wed (return Sun, Thu)
Fokha via Shargol & Mulbekh	364	8hr	7.30am Sat
Hemis Shukpachan (A)	101	4hr	2pm alternate days (return 8.30am)
Kargil	470 (B), 400 (C)	10h	2pm (B), 5am (C)
Keylong (F)	525	14hr	5am
Khalsi (A)	150	4hr	3pm (return 11.30am)
Lamayuru	195-300	5hr	use Chiktan, Fokha or Srinagar buses
Likir Gompa	80	2hr	4pm (return 7am)
Manali			see p244
Matho (B)	32	50min	5pm (return 9am)
Pangong Tso (B)	258	8hr	6.30am Sun
Phyang	35	45min	7.30am, 4pm
Sakti	50	1¾hr	10am, 2.30pm, 3pm (return 7.30am, 9am, 3pm)
Shang Sumdo		3hr	3pm Mon & Thu (return 8am same day)
Shey	20	25min	use Karu, Thiksey, Upshi or Sakti buses
Srinagar (B)	1058-1294	16-20hr	2pm
Stakna	35	40min	'Thiksey' buses terminate nearby
Stok (B)	26	30min	8am, 5pm (return 9am, 6pm), none Sun
Tangtse	186	4hr	6.30am Wed, Sat, Sun
Thiksey	30	40min	half-hourly 8am-6pm, last return 5pm
Tia & Timishgan (A)	143	4hr	1pm (return 8am)
Turtuk (B)	370	10hr	7am Sun
Wanla/Phanjila (A)	188	5hr	8.30am Thu, Sun (return Fri, Mon)

Companies: (A) LBOC Bus (252792), (B) J&KSRTC (252085), (C) Kargil Bus Operators Union, departs from the Polo Ground, buy ticket afternoon before from driver (F) HRTC (G) From 'Old' Bus Station.

All others are other local minibuses (253262), no pre-booking required. Unless noted, departures from main bus station. Some services depart earlier in winter. Durations are approximate.

TAXI & CHARTER JEEPS

Given irregular buses and many fellow travellers, chartering a vehicle makes eminent sense for visiting rural Ladakh. Fares are set by the drivers' unon and published in an annually updated booklet so there's no haggling, though sometimes booking via a small local agency can get you a minor discount (and a reliable driver). We quote the lowest standard rates, ie for taxi-vans or Sumo charter-jeeps. Prices are 5% to 10% higher for Scorpio/Innova jeeps. Rates include reasonable photo- and visit-stops but longer waits are officially chargeable (₹256/1033/2065 per hour/half-day/full day) and for extra overnight stops add ₹350. Requesting unplanned diversions from the agreed route once en route can cause unexpected difficulties.

TAXI & CHARTER-JEEPS FROM LEH

DESTINATION	ONE WAY (₹)	RETURN (₹)
Alchi	1830	2379
Basgo	1127	1464
Chiling	2432	3147
Hemis	2197	2853
Kargil	6479	9015
Keylong	15,135	19,676
Lamayuru	3549	4589
Likir	1549	2013
Magnetic Hill	888	1191
Manali (2 day)	17,712	23,028
Matho	912	1186
Nimmu	1014	1316
Phey	450	585
Phyang	700	913
Shang Sumdo	1617	2144
Shey	384	500
Spituk	280	370
Srinagar	12,839	19,608
Stakna	944	1227
Stok Palace	522	677
Sumur	4768	6197
Thiksey	603	789
Wanla	3525	4582
Zingchen	1407	1830

Note: assumes Sumo; upper class jeeps cost 5% to 10% more. Combining destinations reduces the total price, for example Leh–Shey–Thiksey–Hemis–Stok–Leh costs ₹2463.

TRAIN

There's no railway. Some agencies, plus a cash-only **train booking room** (⊘ 8am-6pm) at Trishul Army Camp near the airport, sell all India train tickets. Check the train number required before going.

ⓘ Getting Around

TO & FROM AIRPORT

The airport (Km430, Leh–Spituk Hwy) is 4km south of the centre. Taxi transfers cost ₹230/300 to central Leh/Changspa.

TAXI

Leh's little micro-van taxis charge from ₹100 per hop. Flagging down rides rarely works; go to a taxi stand to make arrangements.

Around Leh – South & East

📞 01982

Combine several of the following destinations to make a full-day taxi-trip, or visit one or two as part of a jeep excursion to Pangong, Tso Moriri or Nubra via Wari La.

Stok

Stately three-storey **Stok Palace** (admission ₹50; ⊘ 8am-1pm & 2-7pm May-Oct) is a smaller and more intimate version of Leh's. And, as the summer home to Ladakh's former royal family, it feels much more 'lived-in', though the overall scene is marred by a giant telecommunication tower. A handful of 'museum' rooms display family treasures, including the queen's ancient turquoise-and-gold *yub-jhur* (crown) and a sword that the king's oracle managed to bend into a knot, Uri Geller style. The palace's **cafe** (tea ₹20, sandwiches ₹80-100) is well appointed with open terrace seating and spendid views. But for a really unique experience, rent one of five 'secret' **guest rooms** (📞 01982-254976, 9797559799; nirlac@vsnl.net; r ₹15,000-30,000), lavished with brooding original murals (plus excellent new bathrooms). There's no reception so you'll need to make advance arrangements.

Across from the palace's base, 350-year-old **Stok Abagon** (📞 9906988325; suggested donation ₹20), is the decrepit former home of the royal physician. Calling its unlit old kitchen and storeroom a 'museum' is a serious overstatement, but the fun of a visit is simply getting in and meeting the wizened old lady key-keeper. Bring a torch.

Around Leh

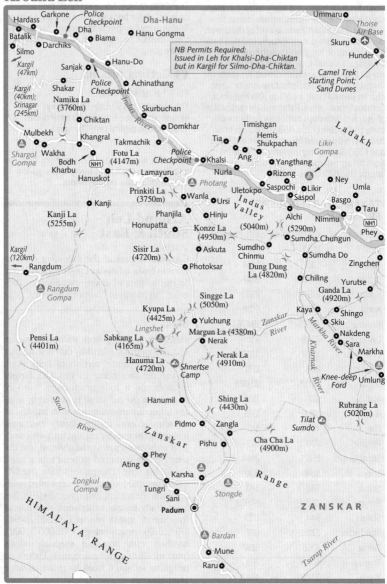

NB Permits Required:
Issued in Leh for Khalsi-Dha-Chiktan
but in Kargil for Silmo-Dha-Chiktan.

Stok's peaceful main lane winds up past whitewashed farmhouses, crumbling old stupas and a new seated Buddha statue. After 1.4km it bypasses the modest **Stok Gompa**, where royal oracles make predictions about the future during Stok's important

Guru Tse-Chu festival (☉Feb/Mar). Another kilometre south, buses from Leh terminate at a pair of simple food shacks known as the **trekking point**. Three homestays near here cater to late-arriving hikers. Ten minutes' walk upstream from here on the path

Matho

Matho Gompa (☎01982-246085; admission ₹50; ⊙9am-6pm) is a large Sakya-Buddhist monastery perched on a colourfully stratified ridge above Matho village. Incomparable views from here encompass a vast swathe of the mountain-backed Indus Valley, from emerald-green field patchworks to areas of sandy desert. The monastery itself is attractive, but most of the early-15th-century structure has been replaced and the top-floor museum is only one room. A *thanka* restoration workshop opens sporadically. During the monastery's famous **Matho Nagrang festival** (Matho; ⊙Feb-Mar), a pair of monk-oracles performs daring physical challenges while effectively blindfolded by mop-wigs, 'seeing' only through the fearsome 'eyes' painted on their chests. They also engage in ritual acts of self-mutilation and make predictions for the coming year.

Stakna

Small but visually impressive, **Stakna Gompa** (admission ₹30; ⊙8am-7pm) rises like an apparition out of the Indus Valley floor. Off the gompa's small central courtyard, four rooms have vivid new Tantric murals. Behind the main prayer hall, sub-shrines retain 400-year-old sandalwood statues, original frescoes and statuettes of the Bhutanese lamas who founded the monastery in 1618. From the Leh–Thiksey road (Km449), the complex is a 1.7km drive, half that on foot), crossing the Indus on a narrow suspension bridge decked with prayer flags.

Shey

Once one of Ladakh's royal capitals, Shey is an attractive, pond-dappled oasis from which rises a central dry rocky ridge, inscribed with roadside **Buddha carvings** (Km459). Along the rising ridge-top, a series of fortress ruins bracket the three-storey, 17th-century **Naropa Royal Palace**, whose wholesale reconstruction is nearing completion. The palace temple contains a highly revered 7.5m-tall gilded-copper Buddha, originally installed in 1645. The upper door opens to his inscrutably smirking face.

Experienced teachers are in demand for volunteer work at **Druk White Lotus School** (www.dwls.org).

towards Rumbak, the village's last riverside house is **Gyalpo Homestay** (☎9797456379; r per person incl full-board ₹800), simple but very authentic with wall murals and a full-blown Ladakhi kitchen.

LEH–MANALI

Utterly beautiful but exhaustingly spine-jangling, this is a ride you won't forget. The Up-shi–Keylong section crosses four passes over 4900m, and then there's the infamously unpredictable Rohtang La Pass before Manali. Although the road is 'normally' open from June to late September, unseasonable snow or major landslides can close it for days (or weeks). **BCM** (www.bcmtouring.com), **LAHDC** (http://leh.nic.in) and **High Road** (http://vistet.wordpress.com/) report the road's current status.

Transport Options

Bus & Minibus The cheapest option is taking the 5am HRTC bus to Keylong (₹525, 12 hours) then changing there. Buy tickets from the driver the afternoon before. To identify the bus, spot its HP42 number plate.

Marginally more comfortable **HPTDC** (Map p232; ☑ 9622374300; Fort Rd; ⊙ 10am-1.30pm & 2.30-7pm) buses (₹2500, two days) leave every second day at 5am from outside J&K Bank (Ibex Rd). Prebook upstairs opposite Iceland Travel. The fare includes overnight accommodation at Keylong in rather cold tents.

Nonstop 11-seater Tempo minibuses depart from Zangsti Parking at around 1am (15 to 21 hours). Tickets cost ₹2000 through agencies, ₹1800 direct from **Ladakh Maxicab Union** (Map p228; ☑ 01982-253192). Book two days ahead for a decent seat.

Rental Jeeps Officially, charter jeeps making one or more overnight stops want at least ₹17,700. Asking around the Manali drivers' area of the bus station, many vehicles demanded ₹20,000 but with persistance we found a ₹12,000 deal.

Driving There's no petrol station for 365km between Karu and Tandi (8km south of Keylong). Driving northbound, the Rohtang Pass requires permits. On Tuesdays the pass is closed northbound for all private vehicles, including taxis.

Route Highlights

The Manali road heads south at **Upshi** (Km425) via **Miru** (Km410), a pretty village with a shattered fortress and numerous stupas. Beyond is a beautiful, narrow valley edged with serrated vertical mineral strata in alternating layers of vivid red purple and ferrous green. A millennium ago, **Gya** (Km398) was the capital of King Gyapacho's upper Ladakhi

Thiksey

Glorious **Thiksey Gompa** (☑ 01982-267011; www.thiksey-monastery.org; admission ₹30, video ₹100; ⊙ 6am-1pm & 1.30-6pm, festival Oct/Nov) is one of Ladakh's biggest and most recognisable monasteries. Covering a large rocky outcrop with layered Tibetan-style buildings, it's a veritable monastic village incorporating shops, a school, a restaurant and a hotel. The main gompa starts with a prayer chamber containing a 14m-high Buddha whose expression is simultaneously peaceful, smirking and vaguely menacing. Smaller but much more obviously ancient is the Gonkhang and little rooftop library. A **museum** (Thiksey Gompa) hidden away beneath the monastery restaurant displays well-labelled Tantric artefacts including a wine-vessel made from a human skull. Notice the 10 weapons symbolically used to combat evil spirits.

Over 40 monks gather for morning chanted-prayers at 6am, lasting around two hours. It's a fascinating ceremony and visitors are welcome, but it's so popular that tourists often outnumber worshippers.

Pedestrian access is a steep climb from near Km455. By car it's a 1.5km loop starting from Km454.2 where monastery-run **Chamba Hotel** (☑ 9418178481, 01982-267385; www.thiksay.org; NH1 Km454.2, Thiksey; s/d ₹2750/3630, old d ₹700) has an appealing restaurant with Ladakhi-style decor that makes a popular breakfast stop for group tours. The majority of rooms are new and unexpectedly plush with geyser-heated water. For great monastery views request rooms 401 or 402. A few simple, older rooms have ensuite squat toilets.

Hemis

The 1672 **Hemis gompa** (www.drukpa-hemis.org; admission ₹100; ⊙ 8am-1pm & 2-6pm) is the

monarchy before he joined forces with Tibetan Prince Skiddeyimagon (who shifted the power centre to Shey). Today it's a small, picturesque village across the river from which a steep 15-minute hike leads up to the 1000-year-old castle ruin now partly occupied by a lovable little gompa. **Rumtse** (Km394), with its handful of homestays and camping spots, is the last green oasis and there are no further villages for 250km, just tiny seasonal camp-settlements. Numerous hairpins climb to **Taglang La** (Km364), which at 5328m is claimed to be the world's second-highest road pass (after Khardung La). Further south, the wide Moray Plains are edged with smooth peaks. At Km287, 10km beyond Pang, the road rises through a memorable, spiky-edged canyon before crossing **Lachlung La** (5060m) and **Nakila La** (4915m), descending the 21 switchbacks of the **Gata Loops** and trundling through two very photogenic valleys featuring Cappadocia-style erosion formations.

Southbound Advantages

If doing the trip southbound, you'll be better acclimatised for high-altitude sleeps (Pang or Sarchu); you could visit Tso Moriri en route; and, if there's a major landslide on the Rohtang Pass, you could 'escape' by walking two hours down to Marhi, a group of cafes jammed with day-trip tourist traffic from Manali.

Which Overnight Stop?

Overnighting in **Sarchu** handily breaks the Leh–Manali journey into two roughly equal sections, but the altitude (around 4000m) can cause problems. Note that there are essentially two Sarchus: cheap parachute tent-cafes at Km222, and upper-market tent camps on an attractive plateau at Km216-214. **Keylong**, **Jispa** (Km138-139) and **Gemur** (Km134) offer more comfortable accommodation at significantly lower altitudes, but Leh–Keylong is a very long day's ride.

To make Leh–Manali a three-day ride you might stop in Keylong and **Pang** (4634m), but Pang's parachute cafes are very basic and the unacclimatised might need Pang army camp's free oxygen if altitude sickness hits.

Other parachute cafes are available at **Debring** (Km343 & Km340), Km270, **Bharatpur** (Km197), **Zingzingbar** (Km174), Km159.5 and **Darcha Bridge** (Km143).

spiritual centre of Ladakh's Drukpa Buddhists. The vibrant, wealthy complex is hidden in a high sharp valley behind curtains of craggy red rocks that look especially dramatic when the mountains behind are misty with low cloud. The main monastery's rectilinear exterior lacks the vertically stacked perfection of Chemrey or Thiksey, but inside, the fine central courtyard is full of colourfully detailed timbers. The monastery's extensive **museum** mixes precious religious treasures with spurious tiger skins, swords, a bra-shaped wooden cup-case and a stuffed 'vulture pup'. The main prayer hall has wobbly four-storey pillars, a garish 8m-high statue of Padmasambhava with hypnotic boggle eyes and there is plenty more to explore amid the atmospheric upper, rear shrines. There are great views from the the lovely stream path beyond the school construction site.

The annual **Tse-Chu festival** (☉ Jul) sees three days of masked dances, and every 12th year (next in 2016) the festival culminates in the unfurling of Hemis' famous three-storey-high, pearl-encrusted *thangka*.

The nearest bus service is from Karu, 7km away by a road that partly follows two astonishingly long *mani* walls.

Chemrey & Takthog

Spectacularly viewed across barley fields and buckthorn bushes, Chemrey village is dominated by the beautifully proportioned **Thekchhok Gompa** (admission ₹50; ☉ museum 8.30am-1pm & 2-6pm, festival Nov) covering a steep hillock with a maze of pathways and Tibetan buildings. Above the appealingly wobbly 17th-century prayer hall, the Lama Lhakhang has murals blackened to semi-invisibility by butter-lamp smoke. On the penultimate floor the Guru Lhakhang has contrastingly vivid colours and a

TREKKING IN LADAKH & ZANSKAR

Bargain value, thrillingly scenic treks can take you into magical roadless villages, through craggy gorges and across stark breathless mountain passes flapping with prayer flags.

Seasons

Trekking season is almost exclusively July and August, but in the Markha and Sham areas routes can be feasible from May to early October. Late August is usually preferable for trails with significant river crossings due to lower water levels. In February you could attempt the challenging Chadar ice-trek.

Preparation

Most trekking routes start around 3500m, often climbing above 5000m, so proper acclimatisation is essential to avoid Acute Mountain Sickness (AMS). You could acclimatise with 'baby' treks or by adding extra (if less interesting) days to the core treks, for instance starting from Lamayuru, Spituk or Martselang rather than Hinju/Photoksar, Zingchen or Shang Sumdo.

➡ Consider pre-booking a jeep transfer back from your finishing point.

➡ Carry a walking stick and backed sandals for wading rivers.

➡ Water-filtering bottles are very helpful.

Horses Treks

At these altitudes, carrying heavy packs is much more exhausting than many anticipate. For wilder routes, engaging packhorses reduces the load and the accompanying horseman can often double as a guide. Agencies will very happily arrange all-inclusive packages with horses, guides, food and (often old) camping gear. If you're self-sufficient and patient it's often possible to find your own horseman from ₹400 to ₹700 per horse per day. Note that you'll generally need to engage a minimum of four horses, and pay for any extra days needed for them to return to their next starting point. During harvest season (August) availability drops and prices rise.

Homestay Treks

Almost all rural villages along well-trodden trekking routes offer very simple but wonderfully authentic homestays. In Zanskar/Markha Valley the cost is fixed at ₹500/800 per head including simple meals that are often taken in the traditional family kitchen where pots and pans are proudly displayed above the Aga-style winter stove. Mudbrick rooms generally have rugs, blankets and solar-battery electric lamps.

Smaller villages do occasionally run out of homestay beds, but even then you can usually find floor space in the kitchen or dining room. Bigger villages such as Rumbak, Hinju and

3m-high golden Padmasambhava statue encrusted with turquoise ornamentation.

The monastery access lane starts from near Km7.3 on the Karu–Pangong road. At Km10.4, a paved side-lane leads through Sakti, a spread-out village of gently terraced fields, waterlogged meadows and dry-stone walls. The lane skirts Sakti's shattered stone fortress ruins, and after nearly 5km, passes beside Takthog (Dakthok) Gompa (donation appropriate; ☉festival Jul), the region's only Nyingmapa monastery. The name Takthog ('stone roof') refers to a pair of small but highly revered and smoke-blackened cave-

shrines in which the great 8th-century sage Padmasambhava reputedly meditated.

Markha Valley & Rumbak

Ladakh's most celebrated trekking routes follow a comparatively straight-forward yet scenically glorious route through the Markha Valley then over the breathless but walk-up Kongmaru La (5260m). Starting from Chiling/Kaya, as far as Hankar you'll find villages in barley-field oases every two or three hours, contrasting very photogenically with the stark, dry, spikily up-

Skiu/Kaya can generally handle all comers, but they work on a rota system so sometimes you'll find one homestay jammed full while others remain entirely empty.

You might also find seasonal parachute cafes, so named because they are tents made from old army parachutes, these provide tea and simple snacks and sometimes offer very basic lodging.

Having an experienced local guide is not just useful for route finding but also for making social interactions more meaningful at homestays. With a couple of days' notice you can engage a guide through **Hemis National Park Guide Service** (Map p232; ☑ 9906975427; hemis_npark@yahoo.co.in; Hemis Complex, 1st fl, Unit 11, Leh; ☺10am-6pm). Pay ₹1200 per day including food, plus necessary travel expenses.

Which Trek?

Popular options:

DAYS	ROUTE	HOMESTAYS	HIGH PASSES	SEE
2	Zingchen–Rumbak–Stok	plenty	4900m	p246
2 (3)	Hinju–Sumdho Chinmu–(Sumdha Chungun)–Sumdha Do	limited	4950m	p256
2	Anmu–Phuktal–Anmu	yes	no	p262
3	Zingchen–Yurutse–Skiu–Chiling	yes	4920m	p246
4+	Chiling–Kaya–Markha–Hankar–Nimaling–Shang Sumdo	yes (or tent-camp)	5260m	p246
5 (8)	(Rumtse)–Tso Kar–Korzok	no	4 (7)	p252
5 (8)	(Padum)–Anmu–Phuktal–Ramjak (Darcha)	some days	5090m	p262
4 (9)	(Lamayuru)–Photoksar–Lingshet–Pidmo-(Padum)	most days	5050m	p256

For something relatively easy, Zingchen–Rumbak–Yurutse–Zingchen makes a great one- or two-day sampler from Leh.

Further Information

➤ Lonely Planet's *Trekking in the Indian Himalaya*

➤ Jean Louis Taillefer's *Ladakh Zanskar* (ladak.free.fr) is excellent if you read French

➤ Cicerone's *Trekking in Ladakh*

➤ www.myhimalayas.com/travelogues/ladakh.htm

turned strata all around them. Highlights include tiny **Tacha Gompa**, 25 minutes before Umlung (Umblung) and the shattered fortress ruin at Upper Hankar. Both are perched improbably atop razor-sharp ridges.

For now, there is no road in the valley, so absolutely zero traffic, but you'd better hurry. A new Zanskar River bridge 4km south of Chiling was completed in late 2014...so before long 'progress' will likely be bulldozed to the timeless Markha hamlets.

Doing the whole three-to-seven-day route is perfectly feasible without carrying sleeping bags, tents or significant

provisions. That's thanks to homestays (₹800 per person including dinner, breakfast and an egg-potato-chapati packed lunch) in virtually every settlement plus a ₹1000 tent-stay camp (similar deal) at **Nimaling**, the freezing-nights 'base camp' for the Kongmaru La. In season and good weather, finding the route is usually easy without a guide – just follow the donkey droppings. Unless water levels are very high, there are only two unbridged river crossings (four if starting from Zingchen), but those can be calf deep so carry a spare pair of backed sandals for wading. If there's even a hint of cloud on the high passes, crossing them without a guide is very unwise.

Assuming you drive to the trailhead from Leh, visiting fascinating Chiling en route, and have a car waiting for you at Shang Sumdo, reasonably fit hikers should budget on four days of roughly seven-hour walks, sleeping at Sara/Nakdeng, Hankar and Nimaling. For shorter sections take five or six days and stop at Skiu, Markha, Umlung/Hankar and Nimaling plus, perhaps, Chokdo to break up the long last-day descent. Incoming jeeps sometimes wait for passengers at Shang Sumdo but otherwise the only public transport is an 8am bus on Mondays and Thursdays (nearest alternative Karu).

As the first two days have only gentle inclines, the Markha Trek helps you acclimatise as you go. Still, don't start too soon after arrival in Ladakh! If you're well acclimatised, you could add two or three beautiful extra days by driving from Leh to Zingchen, sleeping at the single lonely (often packed) homestay at Yurutse (three to four hours' walk from Zingchen), then crossing the Ganda La (4920m) to Shingo (six to seven hours), from which Skiu is around another three hours.

Yurutse and the entire Markha Valley falls within the **Hemis National Park** (camping per person per day ₹20), for which the modest park fees are usually collected at Shang Sumdo or Stok trekking point. Also within the park is Rumbak, a magical village with an unusually close-packed concentration of traditional Ladakhi houses. You might stay in Rumbak before scaling 6121m Stok Kangri. Rumbak to Stok village is a long day's trek across a 4900m pass, but Rumbak–Zingchen is a contrastingly easy stroll taking less than three hours (two river fords en route).

Nubra Valley
☑ 01980

The deep cut Shyok and Nubra River Valleys (permit required) offer tremendous yet accessible scenery with green oasis villages surrounded by thrillingly stark scree slopes, boulder fields and harsh arid mountains. There are sand dunes, monasteries, a ruined palace and – at Turtuk – a whole different culture (Balti) to discover.

ⓘ Getting There & Around

By public transport start out with a shared jeep to Diskit then change. However, for photo stops and to add side excursions, it's well worth visiting from Leh by chartered jeep, at least one way. Leh–Diskit–Hunder one-way/two-day/three-day return costs from ₹4873/7279/9700 per vehicle. Leh–Turtuk one way/three-day/four-day return costs ₹7880/12,515/14,930. Add Tegar/Sumur for around ₹1500.

While most visitors go out and back via Khardung, a narrow road across the remote Wari La is now partly asphalted and allows a loop returning via pretty Tangyar to Takthog. Check conditions before departing: fords can prove tough to cross when water levels are high. A second possibility, the Khalsar–Durbuk route to Pangong Tso proved impassable due to an unbridged river when we attempted it.

Leh to Diskit

The Nubra road zigzags up stark bare-rock mountains for around 1½ hours to **Khardung La** (Km39), which at 5602m is claimed, albeit disputably, to be the world's highest motorable pass. Descending again, look for marmot and *dzo* (yak-cow mix-breeds) around the pretty pond known rather misleadingly as **Tsolding Buddha Park** (Km50.5). Permits and passports are checked at both South and North Pallu Army Camps (Km24 and Km53) and there are several basic shop-cafes and homestays in **Khardung** village (Km71), where the scenery starts to take on a certain Grand Canyon grandeur. There are splendid Shyok Valley views at Km86 with the green fields of **Tsati** village far below fading at their peripheries into the grey white river sands. There are more snack shacks at **Khalsar** (Km95).

Diskit

ELEV 3144M

Diskit is centred on a brash bazaar street that leads down from the area's only bus/taxi station, perpendicular to the Leh–Turtuk road. From the bottom of the bazaar, swing right past the Spangla Guesthouse to find an altogether softer Diskit along a lane that leads 1.5km to an area of stupas, a big *mani* wall, and a crumbling old Ladakhi mansion, rejoining the main road just beyond Sunrise Guest House. Above this latter junction, a 2km spaghetti of hairpins winds up to the 17th-century **Diskit Gompa** (Ganden Tashi Chosling Gompa; admission ₹30; ⊙ 7am-noon & 1-7pm), a brilliant jumble of Tibetan-style box buildings piled higgledy-piggledy up a steep rocky peak that ends in a toe-curlingly vertical chasm. At the back, right-hand corner of the monastery's *gonkhang* (guardian spirits' temple), a white six-armed deity statue clasps a withered forearm and human scalp, supposedly body-parts of a Mongol warrior who mysteriously dropped dead when attempting to seize the monastery. The gompa entry fee includes access to a gigantic (32m) full-colour Statue of Chamba (Maitreya-Buddha) on an intermediate hill, formally inaugurated by the Dalai Lama in July 2010.

🛏 Sleeping & Eating

Of six accommodation options in the bazaar area, **Sand Dune Hotel** (☑ 01980-220022, 9419568208; r ₹400-900) has the loveliest garden – including apricot trees and hop vines – but rooms are slightly fresher in the **Spangla Guesthouse** (☑ 01980-220058; r with cold/hot shower ₹700/1200, d/tr without bathroom ₹500/600). Near the base of the gompa access lane, facing the more conspicuous Olthang Hotel is the excellent-value stream-serenaded **Kharyok Guesthouse** (☑ 9469176131, 01980-220050; r with/without TV ₹900/700). Very nearby, the old faithful **Sunrise Guesthouse** (☑ 9469261853; r with/without bathroom ₹500/300; ☺ year-round) has Diskit's cheapest rooms – musty but OK – along with ensuite options sharing a rough balcony with good gompa views.

🛈 Getting There & Away

Shared jeeps to/from Leh's *zabakhana* (₹400, 4½ hours) leave when full. Departures fom Diskit bus station are mostly 6.45am to around 9am. Overloaded minibuses also depart early afternoon to virtually every main Nubra village (including Turtuk 2.30pm and Panamik 3pm) returning early morning. By charter jeep Turtuk costs ₹3159/4107 one-way/return if the Kafka-esque **Nubra Taxi Union** (☑ 9469727786, 220339) can be bothered to assign you a driver. A return taxi to Diskit Gompa/Tegar costs ₹300/1800.

Hunder (Hundur)

Lost in greenery and closely backed by soaring valley cliffs, Hunder village is a popular overnight stop 10km from Diskit. Hunder's big draw, especially for domestic visitors, is the chance to ride Bactrian camels (per 15min/hr ₹200/600) through a series of photogenic sand dunes. Host camels are re-

🛈 NUBRA NAMES

Note that on many maps, the names for several western Nubra settlements don't correspond at all with local reality.

ON MAPS	LOCAL USAGE
Thoise village	Terchey
Khar	Skuru
Yaglung	Changmar
Biadango	Bogdang

puted offspring of animals that plied the Ladakh–Xinjiang caravans up until the closure of the India–China border in the 1940s. Hunder's dunes aren't exactly Sahara-sized, but the landscape can prove disorientating so, if attempting to walk through them back to Diskit, bring plenty of water, stick relatively near to the road and beware following dead-end camel tracks into impenetrable thorn thickets.

The camel-mounting point is around 600m southeast of the army camp. That's nearly 3km from old Hunder where a precarious little ridgetop **fort ruin** rises high above the main road near the modest **gompa**.

With advance planning there are some interesting trekking routes, including a week-long hike to Phyang near Leh.

🛏 Sleeping & Eating

Hunder has nearly 20 garden guesthouses plus nearly a dozen 'luxury' camps charging around ₹4000 full-board in bedded tents.

Arrange meals with your accommodation or eat at the somewhat hidden **Himalayan Guest House** (mains ₹80-200, thali/rice ₹150/40), which also attempts pasta and sandwiches.

Goba Guest House　　　GUESTHOUSE $
(☑ 9469534590, 01980-200021; d with/without bathroom ₹700/800) Surveying a garden of dahlias and apple trees, four new rooms are relatively smart. Four more in the older house are dated, but rooms 8 (₹800) and 9 (₹700) have wraparound windows and share a coveted view terrace.

Nepali chefs prepare above-average food served up in a bland dining room. Obliging staff, soothing setting.

Mehreen Guesthouse　　　HOMESTAY $
(☑ 9469172690; beds ₹150) One of Hunder's last un-reconstructed genuine family homestays,

JAMMU & KASHMIR (INCLUDING LADAKH) NUBRA VALLEY

Mehreen is great value with a lovely host family and just two rooms (a double and a quad). Find it by following the *mani* wall behind Karma Inn.

Nubra Organic Retreat BEDDED TENTS $$
(☑ 9469176076, 01980-200118; www.nubraorganicretreat.com; s/d/tr ₹3000/3200/4000, with meals ₹3900/4600/6500) The prettiest of Hunder's dozen tent camps, the grounds here are a web of trickling streams and labelled vegetable plots with hammocks and wicker chairs dangling from contorted old apricot trees. Ensuite tents have hot showers and pebble toilet surrounds.

Karma Inn HOTEL $$
(☑ 9419612342, 01980-221042; www.hotelkarmainn.com; s/d/tr ₹2820/2916/3985; ⊘ Apr–mid-Oct; ☎) This is the closest Hunder comes to a 'real' hotel; the attraction here is more the balcony or bay-window views and pleasant lawn than the large, adequate if unadorned rooms. Basic toiletries provided. Lobby wi-fi works occasionally.

Turtuk

The turbulent Shyok valley between Hunder and Turtuk is 80km of scenic magnificence, marred only very occasionally by military installations. The grand raw-rock valley briefly narrows near tiny **Changmar**, the western limit of Ladakhi-Buddhist culture. Thereafter, the rare green splashes of village are culturally and linguistically Muslim-Balti. The main centres of both Turtuk and less visited **Bogdang** villages are raised patchworks of fields and houses on terrace ledges above the main road. Summer sees locals carting huge bundles of barley on their backs between the apricot trees. Upper Turtuk has unforgettable views towards serrated high peaks in Pakistan: the front line is only 7km away. Indeed Turtuk itself was in Pakistan until the 1971 war.

Although there are other shortcuts, on arrival by minibus you'd be advised to get off at the 'bus stop' and follow the side river for a five-minute walk upstream to a suspension bridge. **Turtuk Youl**, a section of town to the right past the **Apolee Guesthouse** (☑ 9469771666, 01980-248105; Turtuk Youl; s/d incl half board ₹500/600), has the oldest knot of houses, including a small palace *(khar)* building beside friendly **Balti Residency** (☑ 9797330141, 01980-248024; khaliq.khan777@gmail.com; Turtuk Youl; d/tr ₹400/550). How-

ever, the main area, **Turtuk Farol**, is back across the suspension bridge. Turtuk Farol has the better views and most of the best accommodation, including travellers' favourite **Kharmang Guest House** (☑ Salim 01980-248104; s/d full board ₹1500/2400, without bathroom ₹500/600), with convivial communal sitting area and a 360-degree panoramic rooftop view. It is building a few ensuite rooms too. Other good, simple options include **K2** (☑ 01980-248126; Turtuk Farol; r per person ₹200, breakfast/dinner ₹100/150) at the base of the central pond-pool, and fresh, clean **Issu Homestay** (☑ 01980-248039; Turtuk Farol; per person incl 2 meals ₹350) at Turtuk Farol's eastern edge. Tent-beds at **Kashmiri Homestay** (☑ Heydar 01980-248117; Turtuk Farol; house/tent dm incl half board ₹350/250) are Turtuk's cheapest option.

ℹ Getting There & Away

Shared jeeps (₹200, three hours) and overloaded minibuses (₹100, four hours) leave Turtuk at 6am for Diskit (returning 2.30pm) on a mostly well-paved lane. Bring spare permit photocopies.

Sumur, Tegar & Panamik

The Nubra River proper descends towards the Shyok from the heavily disputed **Siachen Glacier**, the world's highest battleground (between India and Pakistan). The upper secton follows what is reputedly one of Ladakh's most spectacular mountain valleys. However, foreigners can't visit this area as standard Nubra permits only allow travel as far as Hargam Bridge. That's just after diffuse Panamik (Km44) with its pitifully underwhelming hot spring.

Much more interesting is Tegar (Tiger) village, where the unguarded three-storey shell of **Zamskhang Palace** (Km25) sits above the eerie rubble of Nubra's former royal citadel (Km25). Hidden within Tegar village **Zimskang Museum** (donation ₹50; ⊘ 4-9pm by request) is an historic house, found by descending a path alongside chortens and a *mani* wall from the ancient little Manekhang Gompa/Angchunk Restaurant to the last unmarked wooden door on the left. Some 1.5km above the palace, where Tegar and Sumur back lanes merge, there are lovely panoramas from the parking area at colourful, extensively rebuilt **Samstemling Gompa** (donation appropriate; ⊘ 6am-6pm).

Sumur has some charming back lanes and, around 2km southwest, its very own **sand dunes** with **camel rides** (per 15min ₹150) undercut the Hunder competition. It's home to the Silk Route Festival (www.heritagehimalaya.org; Sumur; ⊙23rd-25th Jun), celebrating Nubra's archery, food and camel-culture.

🛏 Sleeping & Eating

Tegar has two midrange hotels, Panamik and Sumur have half a dozen guesthouses each. Sumur also has several tent camps and a trio of very basic cafes at the main junction.

K,Sar Guesthouse GUESTHOUSE $
(☑9469291358; Sumur Link Rd Km0.6, Sumur; d ₹500, d/q without bathroom ₹300/400) Four fair-priced rooms in a bungalow with traditional windows and a delightfully overgrown garden field from which to contemplate the snow-capped peaks.

AO Guesthouse GUESTHOUSE $
(☑9469731976; Sumur; r ₹500-700) On Sumur Link Rd, close to the main junction (Km99.7) this friendly place has a pleasant courtyard setting, views from the best upstairs rooms and a shared upper terrace. The helpful owner has a vehicle if you need transfers.

Kailash Mansarovar Hotel GUESTHOUSE $$
(☑9469220835, 01980-223522; Sumur Link Rd Km1.6, Sumur; s/d/tr ₹1800/2200/3000, walk-in r ₹800) In the heart of old Sumur, the Kailash is a brand-new low-rise with traditional windows, high willow-poplar ceilings and a spacious dining room all set on a three-level terraced garden. Excellent value at walk-in rates.

Yarab Tso HOTEL $$
(☑01980-223544, 9419977423; www.hotelyarabtso.com; Main Rd Km24.5, Tegar; s/d/ste ₹1600/1800/2600) From outside this is an impressive traditional-style Ladakhi building set in farm-sized grounds. Inside, the lurid pink-trim and somewhat institutional corridors are less appealing and room standards vary significantly.

Nubra Eco-Lodge BOUTIQUE GUESTHOUSE $$$
(☑9419215912; www.goodearth.me; Khalsar–Sumur Rd Km21; s/d ₹2200/3000, without bathroom ₹1500/2000, safari tent ₹5000-6000; ⊙Apr–mid-Oct) Behind Sumur's Sand Dune Park, around 2km west of town, this new eco-lodge uses a few designer-rustic touches to add considerable charm to their three-bedroom guesthouse. There's a traditional Ladakhi kitchen and four luxury tent-rooms really are luxurious.

❶ Getting There & Away

Buses to Diskit depart between 8am and 8.30am. A shared taxi direct to Leh leaves 7.30am most mornings.

Pangong Tso

Stretching around 150km (with the eastern third in China), this mesmerising lake plays artist with a surreal palette of vivid blues. These contrast magically with the colourful mineral swirls of the starkly arid, snow-brushed surrounding mountains. The scene is striking for the almost total lack of habitation along shores that can look almost Caribbean. Visitor activities don't stretch much beyond oggling the ever changing lake-scapes, but one 'sight' is a sand spit nicknamed 'Shooting Point' as it was used as a film set for the 2009 Bollywood hit *The Three Idiots*.

The jeep safari from Leh is a joy in itself – scenically magnificent and constantly varied with serrated peaks, trickling streams, horse meadows, reflective ponds, drifting sands and a 5369m pass. However, it's a tiring drive and doing the return in one day is masochism. Ideally stay at least one night in Spangmik or Man, then drive on unpaved lakeside trails to end-of-the-world Merak (10km beyond Man). It's a beautiful ride but get back early as the route can become impassable by mid-afternoon when water levels rise dramatically in the river-fords.

🛏 Sleeping & Eating

Note that the area has no phone or internet connection so where contacts are given they're for Leh agencies. Few guests stay more than one night so there's almost always a vacancy if you arrive by early afternoon, but don't leave it too late.

⌂ Lukung

Lukung isn't a village but a series of parachute cafes. Most are there to feed day trippers but some offer ₹200 bed spaces. There's also one very overpriced 'Inn' and two fair-value bedded tent camps. Around 2km further are a few more lunch shacks and Highland Camp (walk-in s/d from ₹800/1500), where ensuite tents with metal camp-beds look straight out across the lake (and road).

Spangmik

Pretty Spangmik is Pangong's most popular accommodation spot. A victim of its own success, there are now some 20 summer **tent camps** (d incl full board ₹3000-4000) marring the once-picturesque, dry-stone-walled meadows. Although it's crowded, the setting is still idyllic. Each of the dozen homesteads doubles as a basic homestay, charging around ₹200 per person for crammed bed spaces. Only two hotel-like options have full ensuite-bathrooms. **Ser Bhum Tso Resort** (☑9419176660; serbhumtso@gmail.com; d rack-rate/walk-in ₹5400/3500), with its good mattresses and picture windows, is right in central Spangmik. The somewhat more indulgent pine-fresh bungalows of **Changla Queen** (☑99419818253; bungalow incl half-board ₹3500) are well appointed, but suffer from an isolated, arid location 2km west, set way back from the Shooting Point.

Man

Man is quieter but more diffuse than Spangmik, and set slightly further back from the lake. There are two pleasant luxury tent camps (around ₹4000) and five basic homestays, of which our favourite is **Yokma** (bed/breakfast/dinner ₹250/100/150) with views from a parachute sitting area.

❶ Getting There & Away

Permits are required. One-/two-day jeep tours from Leh cost ₹6811/8108 to Spangmik, or ₹7867/9636 to Man and Merak. For a little more money add side trips to Chemrey and Takthog and request a stop around halfway at the colourful rock-cleft Tangtse Gompa, which is a 10-minute walk on a footpath that starts 200m beyond the booth outside Tangtse, where you'll stop anyway to pay the ₹10 Pangong 'ticket'. Consider making these stops on the way back towards Leh so that outbound you get a wider choice of accommodation.

Foreigners may not continue to Chushul nor to fabled Hanle.

Tso Moriri Loop

ELEV 4595M (LAKE)

The following two- or three-day jeep-loop from Leh can also be made as a scenic diversion en route to Manali, but for permit reasons it's only possible southbound. The highlights are two huge upland lakes, possible nomad-encounters and bird-watching

opportunities. You'll find far fewer visitors here than at Pangong, but the journey from Leh is considerably longer yet less scenically varied than the glorious Leh–Pangong trip.

On the first day out of Leh you'll pass a handful of attractive villages, including **Likche** (Km69) and **Himya** (Km80). Neither have any facilities and most jeep-tours whizz straight past, stopping instead to eat at one of the ramshackle eateries above Chumathang's unappetising, garbage-strewn hot-springs area. Far nicer **Chumathang village** is hidden from the road but worth the 2km detour to admire panoramic views from its gompa.

At Mahe Bridge, foreigners must show their permits. Indian nationals have to pay a nature reserve charge here (₹20 per day's intended stay) but for foreigners that's already included in their permits' environmental fee. Apart from **Sumdo** hamlet, with its basic roadside cafe-guesthouse, there's no further habitation till Tso Moriri. However, in late July you're likely to encounter Chang Pa nomads shearing sheep after smaller **Tso Kiagar**.

Tso Moriri is a giant high-altitude lake whose main attraction is the magical ever-changing series of reflections in its crystal-clear waters. The cloudscapes, snow-topped bald peaks and geological swirls are hypnotic. The scene is best before sunset from a viewpoint knoll around 2km south of tatty little **Korzok**, Tso Moriri's only settlement.

Korzok has half a dozen very simple mat-on-floor homestay-guesthouses, most named for local birds. Our current favourite is the super-friendly **Goose** (Korzok; r per person without/with food ₹200/350), which has the luxury of an indoor toilet.

Korzok also has two small hotels. Though still partly unfinished, the new **Hotel Lake View** (☑9419345362, 9469457025; tso-moririhotellakeview@gmail.com; Korzok; rack rate s/d ₹2720/3500, walk-in r with/with view ₹1500/2000; ⊗ May–mid-Oct) is marginally more comfortable. The other, with its dingy corridor but wide lake-view common verandah, is run by **Nomadic Life** (☑9419178984; www.nomadiclifecamp.com; Korzok; d ₹1500-2000, half board ₹2500-3000), which also has one of the settlement's four summer camps of bedded tents. Prices are highly dependent upon demand.

Tso Moriri is sometimes touted to ornithologists as a place for spotting super-rare black-necked cranes, though you're probably more likely to see those around the salt-whitened marshes that front **Tso Kar**. Three mating pairs have been spotted within binocular range of the **Tsokar Resort** (☑9622925002, 9906060654; tsokar resort@yahoo.com; s/d ₹2000/2600) where the newest six ensuite rooms face the birds' early-July breeding ground. Its little restaurant, along with the next-door **Lotus Camp** (☑9419819078; chotsering100@yahoo.com; Thukye; d half board ₹3000; ☉May-early Sep), represent virtually all the commercial activity in the tiny settlement of **Thukye**, which is less village than a small gompa and a labyrinth of stone-walled sheep-pens, used as a winter retreat for Chang Pa nomads.

From Thukye, 18km of bouncy, partly asphalted lane lead to South Debring parachute cafe on the Manali–Leh highway. Some groups trek between Korzok and Tso Kar in around five days by a somewhat different route. Before you join such an expedition be aware that you'll cross several very high passes, be subjected to very cold nights, even midsummer, and that there are essentially no villages en route to add interest or shelter to the trip.

❶ Getting There & Away

A two-day jeep charter looping Leh–Korzok–Thukye then returning to Leh across Taglang La costs ₹11,719/12,985 by Sumo/Innova. A three-day, one-way excursion doing the same but then continuing south to Keylong/Manali costs from ₹22,347/26,223. The only public bus runs to Korzok (₹310), leaving Leh at 6.30am on the 10th, 20th and 30th of each month, returning next morning, but there are no buses to Thukye.

Leh to Kargil

There are many fascinating sights close to the Leh–Srinagar road, but hopping by very limited public transport is slow going: other than Leh–Kargil and Leh–Srinagar through buses, the only options west from Khalsi are Leh–Dha buses (daily) and four other weekly services to Chiktan or Fokha. Lamayuru and Khalsi both have a couple of taxis but tracking them down is hit-and-miss. It makes great sense to get a group together in Leh and arrange a shared jeep with side trips at least as far as Mulbekh/Shargol, from where there are morning/afternoon buses to Kargil.

If you're driving, don't miss short diversions to Basgo and Alchi and consider canyonland side trips to Chiling (30km) and/or Wanla-Honupatta.

The widest selection of accommodation is in Likir, Alchi and Lamayuru, but you'll also find homestays in all trekking villages. For something special there are boutique hotels at Nimmu and Nurla. The bigger village of Khalsi has shops and the **Samyas Garden Restaurant** (Khalsi; mains ₹80-150, rice/thali/tea ₹60/100/15; ☉7.30am-10pm), an unexpectedly pleasant oasis handily placed right beside its bazaar and bus stand.

Phyang

Pretty Phyang village is an emerald expanse of layered, tree-hemmed barley fields, 40 minutes' drive from Leh in the next parallel valley west. Follow the idyllic lane north from Phyang's large, recently restored gompa to find **Hidden North Guest House** (☑01982-226007; www.hiddennorth.com; Phyang Tsakma; r ₹1000, without bathroom ₹600-800) where a young Ladakhi-Italian family have created a delightfully relaxing getaway. Panoramic views encompass a spiky mountain horizon, meals are available and guided treks get you into accessible yet little-known corners of Ladakh. From Leh the 9am 'teachers' bus' or 5pm J&K SRTC Pulungs-bound bus get you very close.

Nimmu & Chiling

If you just drive through on the main Leh highway, Nimmu seems a scrappy place. But away from the road it's very pretty. Take the lane signed Chamba Gompa for around 300m to find an (unmarked) former palace-mansion that belonged to cousins of the Ladakhi royals. Left decrepit for decades, it's now being converted into **Nimmu House** (☑8447757518; http://ladakh.nimmu-house.com; Nimmu; s/d incl full board ₹8880/9600), a super-stylish 12-room heritage boutique hotel and massage-spa incorporating many remnants of the atmospheric original interior. There are also five design-book safari-size tent-rooms set in the idyllic orchard garden.

A couple of kilometres south of Nimmu are the arrival points for rafting groups who come splashing down the beautiful River Zanskar through a feast of stark, colourful geology. The same photogenic canyons can be enjoyed by road too if you drive towards Chiling, some 30km south.

At first glance tiny Chiling seems little more than a teahouse (Km28.6). But hidden above, the village proper is a fascinating place, set on a fertile green plateau, more easily accessed from a low-profile path starting at Km27.9. Chiling village was founded by the families of Nepali copper craftsmen. They originally arrived in Ladakh to build Shey Palace's classic Buddha statue and never went home. The handicraft continues, with roughly turned-out heart-shaped spoons (around ₹250) made at photogenically antiquated little forges in a timeless area of old mudbrick buildings and giant trees. Several families here offer homestays.

If you're trekking into the Markha Valley, note that the bridge is 4km further south along a dusty sun-blasted road.

Basgo & Ney

Rising above Basgo village on a surreal collection of eroded earthen pinnacles are remnant stubs of once-great citadel walls, along with a largely derelict mud-walled palace, dating from when Basgo was a capital of lower Ladakh. It's worth coming just for the unusual views, but you can also visit two splendid one-room temples (admission per temple ₹30), each containing a two-storey seated Maitreya statue.

Driving 6km north into the verdant oasis village of Ney, you'll spy the gleaming golden form of a new giant Buddha Statue. It's claimed to be nearly 26m tall, though that includes the three-storey building that forms his 'stool'.

Sham (Likir, Yangthang, Hemis Shukpachan & Timishgan)

☏ 01982

The three-to-four day 'Sham baby trek' between Likir and Timishgan (Tingmosgan, Temisgam) is popularly used as a warm-up hike. With ample homestays along the way, you don't need to carry any camping equipment. Scenery is stark and arid with some grand Nevada-style crescendos but there's minimal shade, and much of the route follows a paved lane. The only roadless section is the short section from Hemis Shukpachan over two minor 3830m passes to Ang.

Starting-point Likir has seven guesthouses in the lower village plus the appealing Hotel Lhukhil (☏ 9419892278, 9419892237; www.hotellhukhil.com; dm/d ₹500/1500; ⊙ May-

Sep), styled like a Chinese temple and offering a range of yoga and meditation retreats and well-maintained ensuite rooms. There are three further atmospheric, inexpensive homestays 4km further north behind Likir's memorable mostly-15th-century gompa complex (⊙ 8am-1pm & 2-6pm), whose trademark is the large gilded 20th-century Maitreya-Buddha statue.

Plenty more homestays are available in the timeless intermediate villages of Yangthang and Hemis Shukpachan, beyond which Timishgan, a former co-capital of 14th-century lower Ladakh, has a dozen widely spread homestays supplemented by the comfortable, colourfully neo-traditional Namra Hotel (☏ 01982-229033, 9419178324; www.namrahotel.com; s/d/ste ₹2915/3465/4785, with half-board ₹4015/4565/5885) set in beautiful rustic gardens.

Timishgan, Likir Gompa and Hemis Shukpachan all have bus services from Leh.

Alchi

This rural village has become a regional tourism magnet thanks to the world famous Choskhor Temple Complex (foreigner/Indian ₹50/20; ⊙ 8am-1pm & 2-6pm), founded in the 11th century by 'Great Translator' Lotsava Ringchen Zangpo. The four main temple buildings are small and unobtrusive but they contain original interior murals that are considered the crowning glory of Ladakh's Indo-Tibetan art. Visits (no photography allowed) start with Sumrtsek Temple fronted by a wooden porch whose carving style is very much Indian rather than Tibetan. Inside, murals cover all three levels with hundreds of little Buddhas. Oversized wooden statues of Maitreya, Manjushri and Avalokitesvara burst their heads through into the inaccessible upper storey. Next along, Vairocana Temple is impressive for its mandalas – as antique murals in the rear chamber, as contemporary exercises in coloured sand at the front. In the Lotsa Temple, Lotsava Ringchen Zangpo himself appears as the slightly reptilian figure to the left behind the central Buddha cabinet. Beneath him, a row of comical-faced figures underline the importance of taking nothing too seriously. The attached Manjushri Temple enshrines a joyfully colourful four-sided statue of Manjushri (Buddha of Wisdom). The temple compex is reached by an obvious pedestrian lane lined by guesthouses, souvenir peddlers and the Golden Oriole (mains ₹90-200, pizza ₹200-400, rice ₹50; ⊘7am-8pm Jul-Sep), combining 'German' bakery, multi-cuisine restaurant and (rarely functioning) internet cafe.

There are a dozen accommodation options. Beside the temple complex, Heritage Home (☏9419811535, 01982-227125; www.hotelheritagealchi.com; s/d ₹1500/1750, half board ₹2150/2550) is a pleasant midrange choice though it's not as comfortable as the idyllic garden frontage might suggest. Hidden in the apricot orchard behind, the ultra-simple Dragung Homestay (☏9491838309; dm/s/d ₹200/350/700) is a bargain if you don't mind an outdoor walk to the bathroom.

Alchi Resort (☏9419218636; www.alchiresort.tripod.com; s/d ₹1600/2468, walk-in r from ₹1000) is a collection of comfortable white-washed duplex cottages ranged around apple trees and the gazebo of an enclosed garden area. Set amid flowers, 800m back towards Leh, friendly Choskor Guest House (☏9419826363; r ₹1800-2000, walk-in r ₹600-1000) comes complete with shrine room and sits beside the once-grand Lonpo House, formerly home to the Ladakhi King's local tax collector.

Central Alchi is 4km down a dead-end spur lane that leaves the Leh–Kargil road at Km370, immediately crossing a bridge over the Indus.

Uletokpo, Rizong & Nurla

An erosion-prone 6km side lane from Ule-tokpo village dead-ends at the photogenic 19th-century Rizong Gompa (admission by donation; ⊘7am-1pm & 1.30-6pm), stepped handsomely up an amphitheatre of rocky cliff. A steep, sometimes treacherous footpath continues from there up to Yangthang.

Uletokpo has two 'luxury camps'. Uley Adventure Resort (☏01982-252453; http://uleresort.com; huts/cottages/ste incl full board ₹5500/8500/11,000) is a major accommodation and activities centre for Indian family tourists, but seems overpriced and if you just want to sleep, the super-stylish, ha-cienda-style Apricot Tree (☏9419866688, 01982-229525; www.theapricottreehotel.com; NH1 Km350, Nurla; s/d ₹4950/5500, incl half-board ₹6435/7150) at Nurla is far better value despite offering one of the most luxurious hotel experiences along the whole Leh–Srinagar route.

Dha, Chiktan & Batalik

Driving up the Indus Valley northwest from Khalsi, the scenery becomes increasingly impressive with stark rocky valley-walls contrasting with apricot- and walnut-orchard villages. Picturesque Skurbuchan village is topped by a rickety gompa-fort overlooking the Indus canyon. Scattered ancient petroglyphs are inscribed on brown, time-polished roadside rocks, helpfully signposted at the Domkhar Rock Art Sanctuary but also unmarked along the roadside such as at Km54.8.

The villages of Hanu Gongma, Biama (Beema), Dha, Garkone, Hardass and beautiful Darchiks are culturally notable for their Brokpa people (aka Drokpa or Dard), a unique 'Red Aryan' community sometimes speculated to have been descended from Alexander the Great's invasion force. Though Buddhism (and in places Islam) has partially overlayed their traditional Bon-based religion, a few older Brokpa people still wear pearly button ear decorations, floral headwear and traditional hats, with older women tying their hair in long multistranded braids reminiscent of knotted dreadlocks. Biama is developing a Brokpa interpretation centre.

Across the Indus from Biama, a well-paved road back to the NH1 crosses the Indus at Sanjak and passes beside the shattered yet impressive ruins of Razi Khar, a dramatic 16th-century palace-fortress 2km south of Chiktan.

The alternative route to Kargil runs through Darchiks, swinging south just before Batalik then climbing through a seemingly impossible mountain gully then photogenic Silmo village, crossing a pass above Lalung mudbrick village then descending past the small Muslim fertility shrine of Astana. The road winds down passing within 2km of Apati, in which hides a 5m Buddha rock-face carving. It's at the back of the village, reached by a newly stone-paved footpath that burrows 'through' a couple of older houses.

🛏 Sleeping & Eating

Dha's old traveller hangout is the pretty but very basic Skyabapa Guesthouse (☏9469535269; Dha; d ₹500) with outside dining beneath a giant grape vine. The friendly English-speaking manager makes jams and wine, and international volunteers sometimes stay to help. There are also homestays in Biama, while the region's only ensuite

JAMMU & KASHMIR (INCLUDING LADAKH) LEH TO KARGIL

guest rooms are at a new hotel nearing completion in Darchiks. There is a selection of shops and very basic tea-stands in Sanjak.

❶ Getting There & Away

In principle, a good way to visit would be while driving the 'alternative' route between Khalsi and Kargil via Batalik. However, infuriating bureacracy means that foreigners require two permits. You must apply in Leh for the Khalsi–Dha section but in Kargil for Batalik–Darchiks–Garkone. Agencies can organise the combination but it is often just easier to do one side or the other then exit via the road through Sanjak.

Leh–Kargil charter taxis via Dha and Batalik/Chiktan cost ₹9428/7586. The daily bus from Leh to 'Dha' actually drops passengers at a dislocated gateway from which Dha is still a 20-minute walk away through the apricot trees. The bus starts daily at 9am except Fridays, when it heads to Hanu Gongma instead. From Sanjak and Darchiks, shared taxis to Kargil run sporadically. Linking any of the settlements you'll essentially have to walk if you don't have your own vehicle.

Yapola Valley

Running south from Lamayuru is a recently improved road that will eventually lead to Zanskar. It links several relatively unspoilt villages that were 'trek-only' until the early 21st century. The biggest, Wanla, is worth a brief diversion if you're driving slowly along the Leh–Kargil road, to see its tiny medieval gompa (www.achiassociation.org; admission ₹20; ☉ dawn-dusk) perched on a knife-edge ridge above town. Flanked by tower remnants of a now-destroyed 14th-century fortress, the monastery has a carved porch reminiscent of Alchi's and its spookily dark prayer-chamber contains three large statues backed by ancient smoke-blackened murals and naive statuettes. Monks in a hut-chamber nearby keep the key.

At minuscule Phanjila a spur road diverges to appealing Hinju where homestays can arrange horses for the two-/three-day trek to Sumdha Do/Chiling, crossing the 4950m Konze La (strenuous). South of Phanjila, a newly improved road is being widened to and through the spectacular Yapola Gorge with its soaring rocky sides, spikey mountain vistas and colourful geological pyrotechnics. Beyond is the traditional, closely clumped village of Honupatta. The scenery remains glorious as you traverse the 4720m

Sisir La and descend to Photoksar. It's likely that jeeps will soon be able to drive as far as Nerak, but reaching Zanskar is still a multi-day trek.

Lamayuru

📞 01982 / POP 700 / ELEV 3390M

Set among nation-backed badlands, low-paced Lamayuru is one of Ladakh's most memorable villages and an ideal place to break the Kargil–Leh journey. Picturesque homes huddle around a crumbling central hilltop that's pitted with caves and topped by the ultra-photogenic Yungdrung Gompa (Lamayuru Monastery; admission ₹100). Behind glass within the gompa's main prayer hall is a tiny cave in which 11th-century mystic Naropa (AD 1016–1100) meditated. Before that, legend claims, this whole area had been the bottom of a deep lake whose waters receded miraculously thanks to the powerful prayers of Buddhist saint Arahat Nimagung. Sculpted by time into curiously draped erosion patterns, the sands of that former lake bed now form 'moonland' landscapes at the roadside around 1km east of town.

New roads to Wanla, Hinju and Photoksar challenge Lamayuru's traditional role as a trekking trailhead, but if you're reliant on public transport, Lamayuru still makes a possible starting point for classic hiking routes to Chiling or Zanskar with packhorses sporadically available for hire.

🛏 Sleeping & Eating

Mains electricity (and thus wi-fi) is only available from 7.30pm to 11pm.

Lion's Den GUESTHOUSE $
(📞 01982-224542, 9419880499; liondenhouse@gmail.com; d ₹700, d/tr without bathroom ₹400/500; 🛜) At the very edge of town towards Leh, the super-clean Lion's Den is great value with some super views of the 'moonland' erosion zone. There's a comfy tent-roofed garden-cafe area out front.

Tharpaling Guest House GUESTHOUSE $
(📞 01982-224516, 9419343917; Km311; d with/without bathroom ₹500/300, half-board per person ₹400-500) Ever-smiling matriarch Tsiring Yandol gives this roadside place a jolly family feel, serving communal dinners in a dining room that's new but with traditional-style painted motifs. She also runs the popular little bus-stop cafe.

Singay Homestay
HOMESTAY **$**

([✔]01982-224509, 9419854809; d ₹600, without bathroom ₹300-500; [📶]) Genuine local family home with simple but clean rooms and gompa views from the rooftop. It is very central, tucked away behind Dragon Hotel.

Hotel Moonland
HOTEL **$$**

([✔]01982-224576; www.hotelmoonland.in; s/d ₹1200/1500, wi-fi ₹200, dinner/beer ₹330/200; [📶]) Set in a pretty garden at the first hairpin, 400m beyond the bus stop, Moonland's rooms offer little in terms of decor and show signs of wear, but all guest-rooms come with tiled hot-shower bathrooms and the agreeable restaurant has views back across barley fields towards the monastery complex.

ⓘ Getting There & Away

Buses stop only briefly in passing, and times can be plus or minus an hour:

Chiktan Departs around 2pm Tuesday, Thursday and Sunday.

Fokha via Shargol and Mulbekh Departs around 1.30pm Saturday.

Kargil Departs between 9am and 10am.

Leh Departs between 8.30am and 9.30am daily, plus around 11am four days a week.

Srinagar Early evening. Hopefully.

Lamayuru to Mulbekh

From Lamayuru, the NH1 road zigzags up towards Iguanodon-back spires that tower impressively over Fotu La (4147m). At Km281, a 12km spur road leads through memorable canyons to the very authentic village of Kanji (population 280). Little visited, except by occasional trekking groups, the village has a photogenic mini-citadel and three small gompas, including the minuscule one-room Chuchik-Zhal Temple (www.achiassociation.org; donation appropriate) containing three superb Alchi-style statues and two mandala murals. Konchok Trinley keeps the key.

All that most people usually see of Hansukot is the roadside tourist bungalow, but a rough side lane leads high up to the village passing the crumbling ruins of its shattered ancient fortress.

A comparatively wide, fertile valley extends as far as Khangral, where passports are checked beside the Chiktan–Sanjak–Dha turn-off. The NH1 then crosses the 3760m Namika La (Sky-Pillar Pass), named for the distinctive rocky outcrop that looks like an erupting tooth emerging through undulating elephant skin. A 15km descent brings you into the glorious Wakha Valley.

Wakha, Mulbekh & Shargol

The Wakha–Mulbekh Valley looks like a calm grass-green sea over which a vast tsunami of frothing red mountains is about to crash. It's breathtaking at sunset.

Mulbekh is best known for an 8m-high Maitreya-Buddha relief (NH1 Km243.3). That was carved over 1000 years ago into a fang of rock that's now right beside the road, its lower half shielded from view by the minuscule Chamba Gompa. Soaring above Mulbekh is the impregnable site of King Tashi Namgyal's 18th-century castle. Burnt during an 1835 raid, only two tower stubs remain but the site sports a small gompa and the valley views are symphonic. The 2.8km spaghetti of narrow access lane starts 100m west of Chamba Gompa opposite a red-roofed new refreshment-souvenir place.

The valley has plenty of old Ladakhi architecture including Rgyal Gompa, where tiny troglodyte hermit cells are built improbably into eroded pillars of composite rock, located 2km east of Wakha Police Station (NH1 Km245.8). Around 10km further west, Shargol has a tiny one-monk gompa built into a cliff-face, 2km off the NH1 (turn at Km235.5).

The area's best accommodation is Horizon Camp ([✔]9469405459; horizonladakh camp@gmail.com; NH1 Km245, Wakha; s/d ₹2400/2650, walk-in d ₹1500-2000), an unusually fair-value bedded tent camp in a beautiful roadside flower garden, 150m from Wakha's petrol station. Central Mulbekh has several inexpensive guesthouses, including the photogenically traditional Karzoo ([✔]9419827683, 01985-270027; NH1 Km242.2, Mulbekh; d/tr ₹400/550) and the friendly Othsnang ([✔]01985-270028, 9469280822; NH1 Km242.4, Mulbekh; r per person ₹150). On the NH1, just east of Wakha (Km246), are several cheap tea-house restaurants.

ⓘ Getting There & Away

Several overloaded Kargil-bound buses (from Chiktan, Shakar etc) pass through between 7am and 8.30am, returning from Kargil around 3pm. In the afternoon, a J&K SRTC bus leaves Shargol for Kargil at 3pm (returning 7am). Walking Mulbekh–Shargol makes an interesting 2½ hour trek following the south side of the river (one very small pass). Towards Lamayuru you're essentially limited to hitch-hiking or flagging down Leh-bound buses at around 6am.

KARGIL & ZANSKAR

Ladakh's less visited 'second half' comprises remote, sparsely populated Buddhist Zanskar and the slightly greener Suru Valley, where villagers predominantly follow Shia-Islam, as they do in the regional capital, Kargil (Km204). Scenery reaches some truly majestic mountain climaxes.

Kargil

☑ 01985 / POP 10,655 / ELEV 2704M

Love it or loathe it, you'll almost inevitably need to stop in proudly Muslim Kargil between Zanskar and Srinagar or Leh. If you're arriving from Srinagar, Ladakh's second city seems quaintly backward with workshops, old merchant stores and wild-eyed beggars cramming the packed, ramshackle central area. Coming from Leh, however, Kargil feels grimy and mildly hassled.

The landscape looks more attractive if you climb to the little **Central Asian Museum** (Munshi Aziz Bhat Museum; ☑ 9469730109; www. kargilmuseum.org; admission ₹50; ⊙ by arrangement), which celebrates Kargil's former glory as a trading post on major pre-1947 caravan routes. It's around 10 minutes' walk off the central street Main Bazaar (aka Imam Khomeini Chowk, or Khumani Chowk), which has two ATMs, a few internet cafes and several ho-hum restaurants. The **tourist office** (☑01985-232721; ⊙ 10.30am-5pm Mon-Sat) is upstairs in a vine-draped building between Main Bazaar and the well-marked Hotel Greenland, though 500m further north, tour agency **Sewak Travel** (We For Kargil; www.sewak. org.in) is a more useful contact. Their tours cover much of the district and they can arrange permits for the Batalik area via the DC Office in Baroo.

🛏 Sleeping & Eating

Cheap, central but miserable options around the bus station include the ramshackle old **Hotel Crown** (☑9419845108; muntazir98@yahoo.com; d with/without bathroom ₹500/400) and dreary, green-concrete box rooms at **Ever Green** (☑9419570515; tw ₹400) beside Hotel Greenland. Four marginally better cheapies stretch up Hospital Rd from the jeep stand, notably **Kacho Guesthouse** (☑9419889045; kachoalikhan@yahoo.com; Hospital Rd; d with/without TV ₹1000/700) with its cheery little patch of garden.

Tourist Facilitation Centre
HOTEL $

(TFC; ☑01985-232137, 9419219492; d/VIP ₹820/1500) Organisationally awkward as befits a government institution, TFC rooms are nonetheless great value. Doubles are hotel standard with fan, geyser and carved wooden bedsteads – many with river views. VIP rooms come with ludicrously oversized lounges with upward of 12 sofas in each. It's 2km south of the centre towards Baroo.

There's a terraced restaurant (mains ₹120 to ₹240, rice ₹45) at the riverside and a sweep of spiral staircase that seems designed for a musical performance.

Hotel Jan Palace
HOTEL $$

(☑01985-234135, 9419176277; www.janpalacekargil.com; Bus Station Approach; r ₹1500-2500, mains ₹165-430, rice ₹120) Elsewhere the Jan Palace might seem unremarkable, but in central Kargil its functional combination of cleanliness, big new ensuite rooms, rooftop views and friendly staff make it stand above the competition. Reliable food and beer available (₹320). As you leave the government bus station's main exit, it's in an alley to your right.

Hotel Greenland
HOTEL $$

(☑01985-232324, 9419979905; www.greenlandkargil.in; old/new r ₹2000/2800) Very central, this long-term traveller favourite remains helpful and acceptably clean, but you can do better for the money.

Zojila Residency
HOTEL $$

(☑01985-232281; www.zojilaresidency.com; Bemathang, Baroo; s/d/ste ₹2420/3260/5860; 🖤) A professional hotel-style lobby leads through to fresh new rooms with good bathrooms and a mild fashion consciousness, slightly undermined by the use of pale custard-yellow wall-paint. It's the best of the four upper midrange options that lie south of centre beyond Bardo Bridge, around half way to Baroo. Wi-fi costs ₹100 per day.

❶ Getting There & Away

The jeep stand (Hospital Rd) and main Leh/Srinagar bus station ('Public Park') are central, one block apart, linked via a narrow alley of butchers' and barbers' shops. Both are a short distance off Main Bazaar towards the river. A station for Omni minivans is 400m further west and the local bus station another 400m on, towards Bardo Bridge.

Leh Buses (private/government ₹400/470, 10 hours) depart at around 4.30am, driving via

Mulbekh (two hours) and Lamayuru (around five hours). You might still find a shared jeep (₹900 to ₹1000) as late as 7am. Charters cost ₹7100.

Mulbekh Minibuses (₹60) leave at 2pm and 3pm from the local bus station, returning next morning.

Srinagar Buses (₹550, 10 hours) depart at 10.30pm driving overnight to reach the hair-raising Zoji La Pass before the one-way system for large vehicles reverses. That doesn't apply to share taxis (₹900, seven hours), which can leave any time. Road conditions permitting, it's worth hiring your own taxi (₹6350) to experience the scenery, which is especially memorable between Drass and Kangan.

Suru Valley For Sanku and nearer villages, red-and-white minibuses depart sporadically from the local bus station. For Panikhar (₹87) the 7am bus loads up on Main Bazaar at the Hospital Rd corner. For the noon bus and for Parkachik (11.30am, alternate days) pre-purchase tickets from the green J&K SRTC stand hidden behind the back wall of the main bus station. Around midday you might find shared Omni micro-vans to Panikhar; chartering to Panikhar/Parkachik costs ₹2100/2800.

Zanskar Kargil–Padum buses are sporadic. Shared seven-seater jeeps (₹2000, 10 to 14 hours) park in the main bus station departing before dawn if at all. Chartering costs ₹13,400, with an extra ₹2275 to overnight en route at Rangdum or Parkachik (well worth considering) through the central **Jeep Drivers' Cooperative** (☑ 01985-232079). Non-Kargil or non-union drivers aren't allowed to take tourists to Zanskar and checkpoints en route might turn back unofficial rides.

ℹ Getting Around

By day, micro-vans (per seat ₹10) shuttle down the riverside to Baroo from the riverside corner of Hospital Rd.

Suru Valley

Potentially a bigger attraction than better-known Zanskar, to which it is the main access route, Suru Valley's green, semi-alpine Muslim villages are dotted among wide valleys with fabulous snow-topped mountainscapes. These are most apparent around Damsna and are spectacularly surveyed from Parkachik and from the steep but satisfying day trek to get there across the 3900m Lago La from Pursa on the Panikhar bypass road (four to six hours' hike). If driving from Sanku, consider a 5km detour east to the Khartse Khar Buddha off Barsoo Rd.

🛏 Sleeping & Eating

Options are sparse. Assuming you can find the *chowkidar* (caretaker) to open the doors, there are unpretentious but decently maintained J&K Tourist Bungalows (d/dm ₹500/200) at five Suru locations, the best choices being lonely Purtickchay (with distant but well-framed Nun–Kun views), Tangole (a possible mountaineering base) and especially Parkachik, with its stunning mountain views. Very basic guest meals are available at each.

Kamal Guesthouse (☑ Sajad Hussein 9469109034; sleeping/meal ₹200/100) at

---

TREKKING TO ZANSKAR

From Photoksar or Singge La base camp, the trek to Padum, Zanskar is most often undertaken in around a week as a group expedition with packhorses and full camping gear. If you're fit, well acclimatised and a little lucky it is just about possible to walk from Singge La to Padum sleeping entirely in homestays and tent-stays. To achieve this, hiking stages from Singge La base camp (tea tent in mid-season only) would be as follows:

Day 1 Seven hours' walk to Skyunpata campsite where there's a single 'dormitory tent'.

Day 2 Four hours to Lingshet – plenty of homestay options. If you have a tent you'd be advised to continue to Lamak base camp (no facilities) to reduce the next day's tough hike, but there are no non-camping options.

Day 3 Ten hours' hike from Lingshet including three hard, steep hours up the Hanuma La to Shnertse (two tea tents).

Days 4 & 5 Seven hours' hike including the Panfila Pass to Hanumil village (three homestays). Thence to Pidmo Bridge for a (pre-booked) car to Padum or walk on to Zangla.

Note that setting off on this trek without supplies and your own tent is risky, given very limited bed-space availability.

KARGIL DISTRICT – LADAKH'S BAMIYAN?

Hidden away across Kargil region are several ancient rock-cut Buddha statues. While nowhere near as huge as Afghanistan's now-destroyed Bamiyan site, the impressive 7th-century figure at Mulbekh is 8m tall and easy to visit en route to Leh. Around 2km off the Batalik–Kargil Rd, the smaller, more eroded Yurbaltak figure lies at the back of Apati village, a short but picturesque walk from the end of the access road following a stone-paved path through the village's most traditional knot of homes. Arguably the most impressive Buddha is 5km east of Sanku in the Suru Valley, close to the tiny school on the north side of the river facing the historic settlement of Khartse Khar. The spot is five minutes' walk off the Barsoo Rd.

Damsna has just two empty carpeted rooms for homestay guests to bed down on the floor. No English spoken. The main draw is a nearby picnic spot and the perfectly framed view of Nun and Kun – albeit only from the toilet.

Near the hospital in Panikhar, **Hotel Khayoul** (☑ 9469192810, 9419864611; saki_muna@yahoo.com; Prantee district, Panikhar; d/tr ₹400/500) is the four-room homestay of Hulam Ali, a friendly, English-speaking travel fixer with years of experience to help you make the most of any Suru exploration, including treks to Pahalgam. As business is thin, he spends much of his week working in Kargil (at the teashop beside Kacho Guesthouse), so it's worth making contact before turning up in Panikhar.

There are very simple tea-stall shops at Sanku and a summer parachute cafe in Parkachik, but you'd be well advised to bring your own food supplies if planning much Suru exploration.

ⓘ Getting There & Away

Government buses to Kargil leave Panikhar around 6.30am and 11am, and Parkachik on alternate days at 7am. Taxis aren't easily available, and, for Zanskar, onward transport is generally limited to highly uncertain hitch-hiking. Panikhar's Hotel Khayoul can organise vehicles given advanced notice.

Zanskar

Majestically rugged, the greatest attraction of this mountain-hemmed Ladakhi-Buddhist valley is simply getting there, preferably on a trek. While days can be scorching hot, come prepared for cold nights even in summer. Until the Wanla–Photoksar road is extended to Zangla, the only motorable road in is from Kargil into the glorious Suru Valley, then a rough track to isolated Buddhist Rangdum and across the 4401m Pensi La.

Rangdum

POP 280 / ELEV 3670M

Wind-scoured Rangdum makes a handy overnight break on the 12-hour Kargil–Padum jeep ride. The 20 or so low-rise buildings look as though they were dropped randomly onto the remarkably wild, big-sky valley, whose meandering streams are backed to the west by a breathtaking horizon of Patagonian-style jagged peaks. There are several tea-stalls, a homestay and a **J&K Tourism Bungalow** (d ₹500) with four ensuite rooms but not necessarily any water or electricity. Isolated **Rangdum Gompa** (admission ₹50), 5km further east, looks like a tiny floating island backed by a pastiche of oddly contorted strata. Above a stream at the foot of the gompa, summer-only **Nun-Kun Delux Camp** (☑ 982252153; lakpale@yahoo.co.in; Rangdum Gompa; s/d ₹1980/3036, full board ₹3980/4620) has clean but cramped, overpriced bedded tents sharing outside bathrooms.

Padum

☑ 01983 / POP 1500 / ELEV 3505M

Zanskar's dusty little capital has an impressive mountain backdrop but lacks much architectural character. Within a block of the central crossroads you'll find the bus/share-taxi stand, phone offices, shops, an unreliable internet cafe, the majority of Padum's dozen hotel-guesthouses and restaurants plus the helipad on which the carcass of an Indian Army chopper adds interesting foreground to landscape photos.

From the centre, the main road straggles 700m south past a sizeable 1991 mosque to the crumbling little 'old town' and a hillock of stupas and water-eroded boulders. Just before, if you fork left you'll find the road towards Anmu (trekking trailhead). Around 300m further another left turn doubles back past the police station and a few carved Buddha stones. There are more Buddha figures carved into rocks beneath (towards the river – follow the new pathway from the small cemetery).

Around 2km north of Padum is more traditional **Pibiting** village whose small gompa is dwarfed by a large hilltop stupa topped with a beacon lamp.

Activities

Zanskar's top activity is trekking. Although road-building is steadily proceeding, walking remains a popular way to reach the Yapola Valley (north) or Ramjak (south) for connections to Lamayuru/Keylong. Tents and provisions are needed for some sections and guides and horses can sometimes be organised on the spot. Ask around, at your guesthouse or at a couple of agencies along the road to the mosque.

Sleeping & Eating

Most hotels close from late October to June, except when booked for winter trekking groups.

Hotel Ibex GUESTHOUSE $
(245214, 9419803731; ibexpadumzanskar@gmail.com; walk-in/rack-rate d ₹800/1380) Rooms are slightly dark but the Ibex's large sheltered garden courtyard is a peaceful oasis, and the restaurant a great place to meet fellow travellers. Good hot showers.

Mont-Blanc Guest House HOMESTAY $
(9469239376; r with/without bathroom ₹500/450;) Friendly place with four traditionally furnished rooms just back from the main road at a large prayer wheel 200m before the mosque.

Gakyi Hotel HOTEL $
(9469096539; d from ₹800) Good-looking, well-furnished rooms seem oddly forgotten beneath the pleasant restaurant of the same

name. Some can smell a little musty but they are good value. A new section is under construction above, where rooms won't be so dark.

Zambala Hotel HOTEL $$
(9906990623, 9419242838; zambalahotel@yahoo.com; r ₹2100-2700, walk-in ₹800-1500) At discounted walk-in rates, the Zambala is one of Padum's best deals. OK, so there's no real reception, and cleaning could be more thorough but sheets are fresh, bathrooms large (bucket hot water) and the guest-only restaurant serves some of Padum's best food... albeit slowly.

Hotel Rigyal HOTEL $$
(9469224500; hotel_rigyal@yahoo.com; walk-in/rack-rate d ₹1000/3200) Set back peacefully away from the main market beyond the helipad, Rigyal's new if relatively unsophisticated rooms have very clean bathrooms and views of glacier-topped Ubarak Kangri (behind) or Pibiting (in front). There's a pure-veg restaurant for guests.

Getting There & Away

Until the Wanla–Padum–Darcha road is finished, transport options will remain very limited, and available in summer only. Every few days a Kargil-bound bus departs Padum at around 3.30am, often continuing to Leh. Afternoon buses run to Karsha and Zangla, returning the next morning.

By jeep, Padum to Kargil costs ₹13,400/2000 per vehicle/seat, but bargaining might be possible with returning Kargil drivers. Alternatively head to Parkachik by jeep (₹11,000), then continue by bus. Other one-way/return rates from Padum:

Karsha ₹1200/1500
Pidmo Bridge ₹3500/4500
Rangdum ₹10,500/12,700

JAMMU & KASHMIR (INCLUDING LADAKH) ZANSKAR

ZANSKAR IN WINTER

In winter, snow cuts Zanskar's tenuous road links altogether. Yet in late February, Zanskar's teachers and school kids returning from their winter break manage to walk in from Chiling following an ancient seasonal trade trail that essentially follows the frozen Zanskar River – often on the ice, crossing side streams on precarious snow bridges and camping in caves en route. This hazardous 'Chadar Trek' is likely to die out altogether once the Wanla–Zangla road is connected, but till then it attracts a handful of hardy winter hiking-groups every year. Never attempt this alone. While there are no high-altitude stages, you'll need serious winter kit and an experienced local guide who can 'read' the ice. Allow around six days each way.

North of Padum

SANI

At Sani, beside the Kargil road, Zanskar's oldest gompa (Turtot Gyal) is a small, two-storey prayer hall ringed by a tunnelled cloister and a whitewashed stone wall studded with stupas.

KARSHA

At the far side of a wide, sun-blasted plain around two hours' walk from Padum, Karsha Gompa is Zanskar's largest Buddhist monastery. Dating back to at least the 10th century, it's a jumble of whitewashed blocks rising almost vertically up a red rock mountain cliff. Concrete steps lead to the monastery's upper cloister and prayer hall with its cracked old murals and wobbly wooden columns. It's a great vantage point from which to survey Karsha's old-fashioned homes, barley fields and threshing circles worked by *dzo*. Homestay-guesthouses available.

ZANGLA

For a fine half-day excursion from Padum, drive to Zangla admiring the curled, contorted geological strata that are especially striking above Rinam and Shilingskit villages. A trip highlight is Stongde Gompa crowning a bird's-eye perch some 300m above the valley, 12km from Padum. The entrance to Zangla is guarded by a small hilltop fortress-palace in which the Hungarian scholar Alexander (Sándor) Csoma de Kőrös took a room while compiling the first Western dictionary of the Tibetan language. At the far end of the village there's a small, friendly Buddhist nunnery.

South of Padum

The road south from Padum passes Bardan Gompa, spectacularly set on a rocky outcrop high above the river. Ichar (Khor) has a looming monastery of its own and, on slightly higher ground, a small reflective pond and a small knot of very evocative old-town. As of 2014 the road ends just beyond Anmu where a small Amchi-medicine dispensary doubles as a teahouse. From that building a path descends to a very wobbly pedestrian suspension bridge though this might soon be superseded by a road bridge under construction at nearby Tsetang for the new link lane to Surley.

PHUKTAL

Hanging on a cliff face, Phuktal Gompa (http://phuktalmonastery.com; ☉prayers at 4.30am, noon & 7pm in summer) appears to be tumbling out of the mouth of a gaping cave. The main hall contains fragments of some 700-year-old murals in the Alchi style, though the tiny upper prayer room feels far more ancient. A road is slowly being built, but for now access is only by a scenically impressive five-hour trek from the trailhead at Anmu. Allow around 2½ attractive-yet-unchallenging hours to reach the large village of Cha (with homestays), then around two hours more to climb gently up and over a shoulder of upland plateau and make the long, steady descent to the river eventually passing (but not crossing) a bridge. Just two minutes later a last short climb brings you to Phuktal's monastery guesthouse (r per person ₹200, dinner ₹100). The gompa, visible ahead, is 15 minutes stroll away. If the guesthouse's four basic (yet ensuite) rooms are full, the nearest alternative accommodation involves crossing the bridge and walking 1½ hours to the village of Purney. Each of the three farmsteads offers rooms and camping places and they run two basic shop-teahouses. Directly below lower Purney, where two rivers meet, cross another bridge. Turning left here would take you eventually to Darcha (requires pre-planning – four days, a guide and gear for the 5090m Shingo La). Or turn right to return to Anmu in around three hours via the pretty one-homestead village of Gyalbok (1¼ hours) and the suspension footbridge. Neither Anmu–Phuktal route currently needs a guide if you have hiking experience, but beware that path details may change rapidly due to ongoing road-crew blasting.

THE KASHMIR VALLEY

Rimmed by layers of alpine peaks, the 140km-long Kashmir Valley opens up as a giant, flat upland bowl of lakes and orchards. Tin-roofed villages guard terraced paddy fields delineated by apple groves and pin-straight poplars. Proudly independent-minded Kashmiris mostly follow a Sufi-based Islamic faith, worshipping in distinctive box-shaped mosques with central spires. Some Kashmiris have startlingly green eyes and in winter, Kashmiri men traditionally keep warm by clutching a *kangri* (wicker fire-pot holder) beneath their flowing grey-brown *pheran* (woollen capes).

SAFETY IN KASHMIR

Kashmir's difficult 20th-century history and the delicate relationship between nationalist Muslims and Jammu Hindus creates a cauldron of intercommunal tensions contained or exacerbated (according to one's viewpoint) by a very visible Indian army presence. When things are calm, Kashmir is probably safer than most places in India. But cycles of unrest, stone-throwing and curfews can erupt remarkably rapidly. At such times the Old City is worth avoiding but Dal Lake generally remains trouble-free even during fairly significant disturbances: foreign tourists have never been targets. Use common sense, avoid public demonstrations and military installations and consult a wide range of resources to get a feel for the situation before arriving. Useful starting points include the forum of **India Mike** (www.indiamike.com/india/jammu-and-kashmir-f30) and local news feeds including **Kashmir Times** (www.kashmirtimes.com), **Greater Kashmir** (www.greaterkashmir.com), **Kashmir Monitor** (www.kashmirmonitor.in) and **Daily Excelsior** (www.dailyexcelsior.com). Travellers should avoid the India–Pakistan Line of Control in Kashmir as it is an active combat zone and there is no entry into the Pakistan-administered area from India

History

Geologists and Hindu mystics agree that the Kashmir Valley was once a vast lake. Where they disagree is whether it was drained by a post–ice age earthquake or by Lord Vishnu and friends as a ploy to kill a water demon.

In the 3rd century BC the Hindu kingdom of Kashmir became a major centre of Buddhist learning under Emperor Ashoka. In the 13th and 14th centuries, Islam arrived through the inspiration of peaceable Sufi mystics. Later some Muslim rulers, such as Sultan Sikandar 'Butshikan' (r 1389–1413), set about the destruction of Hindu temples and Buddhist monasteries. However, others such as the great Zain-ul-Abidin (r 1423–74) encouraged such religious and cultural tolerance that medieval visitors reported finding it hard to tell Hindus and Muslims apart. Mughal emperors, including Akbar (1556–1605), whose troops took Kashmir in 1586, saw Kashmir as their Xanadu and developed a series of extravagant gardens around Srinagar.

When the British arrived in India, Jammu and Kashmir were a loose affiliation of independent kingdoms, nominally controlled by the Sikh rulers of Jammu. In 1846, after the British had defeated the Sikhs, they handed Kashmir to Maharaja Gulab Singh in return for a yearly tribute of six shawls, 12 goats and a horse. Singh's autocratic Hindu-Dogra dynasty ruled until Independence, showing an infamous disregard for the welfare of the Muslim majority.

Partition & Conflict

As Partition approached in 1947, Maharaja Hari Singh favoured Kashmiri independence rather than joining either India or Pakistan, but he failed to make a definitive decision. Finally, to force the issue, Pashtun tribesmen, backed by the new government in Pakistan, attempted to grab the state by force, setting off the first India–Pakistan war. The invaders were pushed out of the Kashmir Valley but Pakistan retained control of Baltistan, Muzaffarabad and the valley's main access routes. Kashmir has remained divided ever since along a tenuous UN-demarcated border, known as the Line of Control. A proposed referendum to let Kashmir's people decide (for Pakistan or India) never materialised and Pakistan invaded again in 1965, triggering another protracted conflict.

In the 1970s, a generation of visitors rediscovered Indian Kashmir as an idyllic summer getaway. But armed rebellion became intense during the later 1980s and Kashmir was placed under direct rule from Delhi in 1990. For several bloody years massacres and bomb attacks were countered by brutal counter-insurgency tactics from the Indian armed forces. Significant human-rights abuses were reported on both sides.

After the brief India–Pakistan 'Kargil War' of 1999, a ceasefire and increasing autonomy for Kashmir was matched by a significant reduction in tensions. Coordinating relief after a tragic 2005 earthquake also helped bring the Indian and Pakistani governments a little closer. Militant attacks dwindled and domestic tourism blossomed anew despite disturbances in 2008 (over an arcane land dispute at Amarnath) and 2010 (after the shooting of juvenile stone-throwers). In 2014, a uniquely wet summer caused unprecedented flooding in Srinagar.

Srinagar

📞 0194 / POP 1,192,000 / ELEV 1730M

Indulgent houseboats, historic gardens, distinctive Kashmiri wooden mosques and a mild summer climate combine to make Srinagar one of India's top domestic tourist attractions. Except, that is, when intercommunal tensions paralyse the city with strikes and shut-downs. Srinagar's three main areas converge around Dalgate, where the southwestern nose of Dal Lake passes through a lock gate. Northwest lies the fascinatingly chaotic Old City. The busy commercial centre is southwest around

Lal Chowk. The city's greatest drawcard is mesmerisingly placid Dal Lake, which stretches a southwestern channel-spur towards the city centre, paralleled by the hotel-lined Boulevard. A bright array of houseboats here form a particularly colourful scene. The famous Mughal gardens are strung out over several kilometres around the lake.

In 2014, the city was hit by devastating floods as the Jhelum River surged over its banks; repairs are ongoing but more floods were reported in 2015 so check the latest situation before you visit.

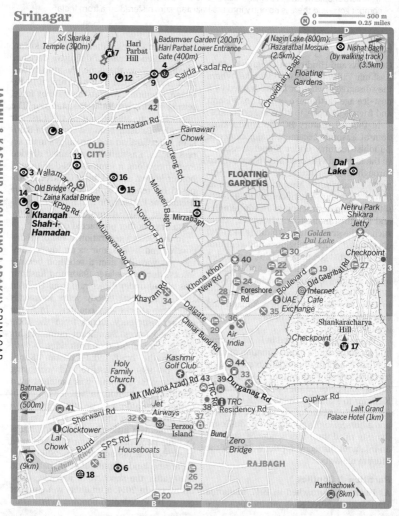

Srinagar

◎ Sights

◉ Dal Lake & Around

Whether you sleep on one of its wonderful time-warp houseboats or just stroll along the Boulevard savouring the sunset, beautifully serene **Dal Lake** is likely to be your main memory of Srinagar. Mirror-flat waters beautifully reflect the misty peaks of the Pir Panjal mountains while gaily painted *shikaras* (colourful gondolas) glide by. These are gondola-like boats, hand-powered with heart-shaped paddles used to transport goods to market, children to school, and visitors on explorative tours of the lake's floating communities. Canal-like passages link all the way to Nagin Lake. The gardens supplying the lake's **floating vegetable market** (◷5-6.30am) were affected by flooding in 2014; if the market resumes, expect approaches from *shikara* operators offering dawn tours. Alternatively, just watch veg-boats unloading by day at **Mirzabagh**.

For a visual portrait of Dal Lake life, watch the prize-winning 2012 movie *Valley of Saints*.

Floating Gardens & Lake Villages GARDENS, VILLAGES

Much of Dal Lake is thick with foliage, lotus patches and large areas of cultivated vegetable gardens linked by channels and served by villages of stilted walkways. Assuming that 2014 flood damage is repaired, a great way to see these areas is by walking along Chowdary Bagh. Eventually you'll reach a footbridge and causeway leading to the pumping station near Nishat Bagh Mughal Garden, though the last 3km (after Nandpora) can be muddy and is uncomfortably rough for bicycles.

Shankaracharya Hill VIEWPOINT, SACRED SITE

(◷7am-5.30pm) Thickly forested Shankaracharya Hill is topped by a small Shiva temple, **Shankaracharya Mandir**, built from hefty blocks of visibly ancient grey stone. Previously known as Takht-i-Sulaiman (Throne of Solomon), it's now named for a sage who reached enlightenment here in AD 750, but signs date the octagonal structure as 5th century and the site is even older.

Some claim, controversially, that a previous temple here was once renovated by Jesus and St Thomas. Access is by a winding 5.5km road from Nehru Park (₹300 return by autorickshaw). From road's end the temple is five minutes up a stairway from a police checkpoint where you must leave phones and cameras before reaching the panoramic views of Srinagar and Dal Lake.

Mughal Gardens   GARDENS
Srinagar's famous gardens date back to the Mughal era. Most have a fundamentally similar design with terraced lawns, fountain pools and carefully manicured flowerbeds interspersed with mighty *chinar* trees, pavilions and mock fortress facades. The most famous garden is **Shalimar Bagh** (adult/child ₹10/5; ⊙10am-7pm), 10km beyond Nehru Park, built for Nur Jahan by her husband Jehangir. However, **Nishat Bagh** (adult/child ₹10/5; ⊙9am-dusk) is more immediately impressive, with steeper terracing and a lake-facing panorama (7.5km from Nehru Park).

Pari Mahal (adult/child ₹10/5; ⊙9am-7.30pm) is set amid palace ruins high above the lakeshore (about 9km from Nehru Park). The ensemble looks most intriguing viewed from afar when floodlit at night. By day, the long, steep autorickshaw ride is worthwhile more for the lake views than for the gardens themselves. Bring ID for police checks. En route you'll pass the petite **Cheshmashahi Garden** (adult/child ₹10/5; ⊙8.30am-7.30pm) and the extensive, less formal **Botanical Garden** (adult/child ₹10/5; ⊙8.30am-dusk), behind which, from March to April, a 12-hectare **Tulip Garden** (⊙Mar-Apr) blooms colourfully.

Hazratbal Mosque   MOSQUE
(⊙5am-9.30pm) Backing onto Dal Lake several kilometres north of the Old City, this large, white-domed 20th-century mosque enshrines Kashmir's holiest Islamic relic, the Moi-e-Muqqadas, supposedly a beard hair of the Prophet Mohammed. The hair's brief disappearance in December 1963 nearly sparked a civil war. Visitors are admitted outside of prayer times.

⊙ Old City

When visiting mosques, follow normal Islamic formalities (dress modestly, remove shoes) and ask permission before entering or taking interior photos. Women will usually be expected to cover their hair and use a separate entrance.

★**Khanqah Shah-i-Hamadan**   MOSQUE
(Khanqah-e-Muala; Khawaja Bazaar area; ⊙5.30am-9.30pm; 🚌13) This distinctively spired 1730s Muslim meeting hall is one of Srinagar's most beautiful. It was constructed without using any nails and both frontage and interiors are covered in papier-mâché reliefs and elaborately coloured *khatamband* (faceted wood panelling). Non-Muslim visitors can peek through the door but may not enter.

The building stands on the site of one of Kashmir's first mosques, founded by Persian saint Mir Sayed Ali Hamadani, who arrived in 1372, one of 700 refugees fleeing Timur's conquest of Iran. He is said to have converted 37,000 people to Sufi-based Islam, and it's likely that his retinue introduced Kashmiris to the Persian art of fine carpet-making.

Pather Masjid   MOSQUE
Unlike most typical Kashmiri spired mosques, Pather Masjid is a heavy Mughal structure built by Nur Jahan in 1623. The road-facing side is partly hidden by shop-units, but behind, a triple-rank of nine arches opens onto a walled, four-tree *chinar* garden.

It's worth following the lane directly south, walking beneath the razor-wired guard post to the riverside for views across to Khanqah Shah-i-Hamadan.

Badshah Tomb   ARCHITECTURE
(⊙9am-6pm; 🚌25) Looking more Bulgarian than Kashmiri, the multi-domed 15th-century brick tomb of King Zeinalabdin's mum was built on the plinth of a much older former Buddhist temple. It's within an ancient graveyard hidden in Gadu Bazaar's maze of copperware, spice and cloth vendors' shops. A number of graves were washed away during the 2014 floods but work is underway to restore the compound. To view the interior, you will need to find the caretaker; ask at the shops in front of the cemetery.

The tomb's domes form part of the classic view of Old Town Srinagar as viewed looking north from the new Zaina Kadal (bridge), with the city's oldest wooden bridge as foreground.

Jama Masjid MOSQUE

(Nowhatta; ☺8am-9pm) Looking like the movie set for an imagined Central Asian castle, this mighty 1672 mosque forms a quadrangle around a large fountain garden courtyard with monumental spired gatehouses marking each of the four cardinal directions. There's room for thousands of devotees between 378 roof-support columns, each fashioned from the trunk of a single deodar tree.

Naqshband Sahib SACRED SITE

(Khanyar Chowk area; ☺6.30am-8.30pm) This beautifully proportioned but uncoloured 17th-century shrine was built in Himachal Pradesh style with alternating layers of wood and brick to dissipate the force of earthquakes.

Rozabal SACRED SITE

(Ziyarat Hazrati Youza Asouph) At the north end of the triangular patch of grass in front of the Sufi shrine of Pir Dastgir Sahib (☺5.30am-7.30pm) is a small, green shrine known as Rozabal. A highly controversial theory claims that the shrine's crypt holds the grave of Jesus Christ. Tourists are actively discouraged from approaching, but the mere existence of this little place poses some intriguing questions.

◉ Hari Parbat Hill

North of centre but visible from virtually anywhere in Srinagar, this prominent hilltop was once an island in a giant lake where, Hindus believe, Vishnu and Sharika (Durga) defeated Jalodbhava, Kashmir's mythical demon. The imposing Hari Parbat Fort (Koh-e-Maran Fort; permission note ₹100; ☺10am-3pm Sat-Thur) that now crowns the hill, mostly dates from 1808, built by Pathan governor Atta Mohammad Khan, though remnants of 6th-century fortifications have been found. The fort remains a minor military base but reopened to tourists in July 2014. Before going you'll need a stamped permissory note from the TRC (passport copy and ₹100 required for application). Entrance is from the northeast side, via a traffic-free lane starting north of Badamvaer (Badanwari; adult/child ₹10/5; ☺8am-8.30pm), orchard gardens whose most interesting feature is the antique well-house. The fort access lane starts with a checkpoint, then a sweaty 10-minute walk using fairly obvious short cuts brings you to a second sign-in, 15 minutes' walk to the fort's uppermost tower.

More easily accessible on the hill's southern mid-slopes, but also offering fine views, are the extensive ruins of the 1649 Akhund Mulla Shah Mosque along with the large, very active Makhdoom Sahib Shrine. Both can be reached by a three-minute cablecar ride (single/return ₹50/100; ☺10am-5pm) – though this operates erratically – or by climbing one of three beggar-lined step routes. The most easterly starts near Kathi Darwaza, an historical gateway through a remnant section of Srinagar's Old City walls, originally built by Akbar in the 1590s. Multiple Mughal-style domes on the large, white Chetipacha Gurdwara (Chattipatshahi Gurdwara), add to the scene.

Beside the lower cable car station, the brand new, museum-like Naagar-Nagar Interpretation Centre (tips requested; ☺10am-5pm) gives some interesting historical context

JAMMU & KASHMIR (INCLUDING LADAKH) SRINAGAR

JESUS IN KASHMIR?

To many, the theory sounds crackpot or even blasphemous, but several authors have claimed that Jesus spent his 'lost years' (between his youth and the start of his ministry aged 30) in India where Buddhism moulded his ideas. This theory gained a lot of publicity in the 1890s when Russian traveller/spy Nicolas Notovitch 'discovered' supposedly corroborating documents at Hemis Gompa (Ladakh), described in his book *Unknown Life of Jesus Christ*. These Hemis documents have since gone missing.

The Koran (surah 4, verses 156–157) states that Jesus' death on the cross was a 'grievous calumny' and that 'they slew him not'. Khwaja Nazir Ahmad's *Jesus in Heaven & Earth* further postulates that Jesus (as Isa, Yuz Asaf or Youza Asouph) retired to Kashmir post-crucifixion and was buried in Srinagar. Holger Kersten's *Jesus Lived in India*, widely sold in Indian traveller bookshops, argues the case carefully and even gives a floor plan of Rozabal (p267). The roughly four-million-strong Ahmadiyya sect (who consider themselves Muslim but are not recognised by other branches of the faith) also subscribe to the idea of Jesus dying in Kashmir. See www.alislam.org/topics/jesus.

HOUSEBOATS

Srinagar's signature houseboats first appeared in colonial times because the British were prohibited from owning land. The best deluxe boats are palatial, with chandeliers, carved walnut panels, ceilings of *khatamband* (faceted wood panelling) and chintzy sitting rooms redolent of the 1930s Raj era. Category A boats are comfy but less grand. Lower categories (C, D) might lack interior sitting areas.

Be aware that the Srinagar houseboat experience is like staying in a small, romantic guesthouse complete with cook and waiter. Unlike in Kerala, these boats never move, and most are moored in sizeable groups. A colourful attraction is watching comings and goings, but don't expect quiet seclusion.

Better houseboats typically have three or four ensuite double bedrooms. When things are busy, the best rooms (usually at the back of deluxe boats) may be booked out well in advance. But off season, or when the political climate drives tourists away, you're likely to get the whole boat to yourself, chef and all.

Choosing from 1400 boats is challenging. Some owners are super-friendly families, others are crooks – ask fellow travellers for recent first-hand recommendations. Outside peak season (April to June), it's best to check out a selection and pick one that suits rather than prebooking.

Houseboat Tips

For most visitors, staying on a houseboat is a relaxing Srinagar highlight. But a few have reported feeling cheated, being held virtual hostage or suffering inappropriate advances from houseboat staff. Some tips:

➡ Beware of houseboat packages and never book in Delhi.

➡ Check out houseboats in person or via trusted websites before agreeing to anything.

➡ Get a clear, possibly written, agreement stating what the fees cover (tea, drinking water, *shikara* transfer, canoe usage, second helpings at dinner?).

➡ Check whether the boat really is the category that the owner claims (certificates should be posted) or risk paying deluxe prices for a B-grade boat!

➡ Don't be pressured into giving 'charity' donations or signing up for overpriced treks.

➡ Don't leave valuables unattended: boat-borne thieves can be fast.

➡ Don't leave your passport with the boat owner.

➡ Tell a friend or trusted hotelier where you're staying.

➡ Trust your instincts.

Choosing the Area

Major choices:

➡ **Dal First Row** Facing the Boulevard, easy to-and-fro by *shikara* but busy and noisy in season.

to the sites mentioned above and plays two 15-minute films. Entrance is currently free, but opening hours can be erratic.

On the western flank of Hari Parbat is **Sri Sharika** (Chakreshwar; www.hariparbat.org), the 'abode' of the city's 18-armed guardian goddess, represented here by a vermilion-orange painted Shila rock beneath a rather gaudy temple-pavilion.

Central Srinagar

Sri Pratap Singh Museum   MUSEUM
(☏0194-2312859; http://spsmuseum.org; SPS Rd; Indian/foreigner ₹10/50; ⊙10.30am-4pm Tue-Sun) It's worth visiting this richly endowed historical museum for Mughal papier-mâché work, 4th-century tiles, 8th-century gods, stuffed birds, mammoth bones, weaponry and traditional Kashmiri

→ **Dal Second Row** (Golden Dal Lake) Though only slightly further back, boats here are invisible from the Boulevard and generally better placed for sunset views. Plenty of colourful bustle, and it costs less than ₹100 to reach by *shikara* from ghats 9 or 12. Our favourite is **Young Beauty Star** (☑ 9419060790; www.dallakehouseboat.ragu.com; Dal Lake 2nd Row; d incl half-board ₹2800; ☐ Ghat 9) with a junction location that's particularly ideal for watching life go by.

→ **Dal Lake Garden-Village** Many more boats lie in village-like clusters further back: peaceful except during prayers but somewhat trickier to 'escape' from should you go stir crazy. Low-key **Moon of Kashmir** (☑ 9906686454; www.moonofkashmir.com; Dal Lake; B-/A-cat d incl half-board ₹2000/3500; ☐ Ghat 7) is very welcoming and has been recommended for fair-value trekking.

→ **Foreshore Rd** Easy access. Boats often basic but very inexpensive, perhaps under ₹1000.

→ **Hazaratbal Butts Clermont** (☑ 9419056761, 0194-2415325; www.buttsclermonthouseboat.com; Naseem Bagh; d from ₹6000) Lonely houseboats are moored beside their own private Mughal Garden. This is where Ravi Shankar taught George Harrison sitar and many ambassadors and statesmen have stayed, yet the pricey boats aren't particularly luxurious and thick, smelly water-weeds breed lots of midges.

→ **Nagin** (Negin, Nageen) Quieter than Dal Lake but a long schlep from the city centre.

→ **Nagin East Bank** Boats are easily accessible by road and have views of Hari Parbat. Houseboat group **Majestic & Ritz** (☑ 9999990232, 9906874747; www.majesticgroupofhouseboats.com; Nagin Lake, east bank, directly south of Nagin Club; s/d from ₹3100/3500) are friendly and reliable, **Butterfly** (☑ 0194-2429889, 0194-2420212; Nagin Lake, east bank; r ₹3000-5000) is funky if ever-busy. Drop in bargains are possible at several boat-groups.

→ **Nagin West Bank** Boats have glorious sunset views with wooded mountain scarps reflected in the lake. They are usually approached by *shikara* from the east bank but most also have laneway access into a wealthy, if visibly religious, residential area. Getting into town is a pain so if you pick this area plan to spend your days relaxing aboard. **New Jacquline** (☑ 0194-2421425, 9419001785; www.newjacqulinehouseboats.com; Nagin Lake west shore; d ₹3400-8000) is a particularly comfortable choice here.

→ **Jhelum River** Easy access, little charm.

In almost any location, visits from *shikara*-borne souvenir sellers are an unavoidable irritation.

Prices
Officially, prices are 'set' by the **Houseboat Owners Association** (☑ 0194-2450326; www.houseboatowners.org; TRC Rd; ⊙ 10am-5pm Mon-Sat) ranging from ₹600/900 (category D) to ₹3150/4800 (deluxe) for a double room including half-board. In reality, however, that's merely a guide. Some places openly ask for more, others will ask only a fraction of that when occupancy is low.

costumes. The collection is housed in the touchingly unkempt 1872 Lalmandi Palace of Maharajah Pratap Singh, but the museum was damaged badly by flooding in 2014 and some exhibits may move once restoration is complete.

Government Silk Weaving Factory   SILK WORKSHOP
(SPS Rd; ⊙ 10am-4pm Mon-Sat) FREE Although damaged by the 2014 floods, this histor-ic factory still churns out bolts of silk on old-fashioned weaving machines, much as it has done since 1938. Ask permission at the 'time gate' or, at the government emporium in front.

🏃 Activities

The alpine lakes, meadows and uplands of Kashmir offer some stunning hiking opportunities, but unlike in Ladakh, it can be hard to find fellow walkers to join a group. Virtually every houseboat owner will have a 'brother' who can take you, and there are ever more online sites offering trek packages, but you may be able to get a better deal simply by heading to Naranag and organising things for yourself. If you are planning to do that, you might be advised to rent camping equipment from the Mountaineering Information Office, beside Srinagar TRC (p271), as supplies in Naranag are in short supply.

🛌 Sleeping

Staying on a houseboat is one of the city's main attractions, but when first arriving you might prefer to sleep at least the first night or two in a hotel while carefully selecting a suitable boat. Budget options are relatively limited (try Dalgate or Old Gagribal Rd). There are midrange hotels in profusion, but many are unkempt and rely primarily on noisy, self-catering groups of domestic tourists, especially from April to June and in October. Note that many hotels were affected by the 2014 floods – ask to see a few rooms before making a decision.

John Friends House Guesthouse   HOSTEL $
(☑0194-2458342; dm ₹200, d from ₹300) Hidden within a maze of stilt walkways, this basic guesthouse was a backpacker favourite, but it was flooded out in 2014 and repairs are ongoing. Assuming it reopens as planned, expect simple, mosquito-nibbled rooms and a friendly welcome.

Noor Guest House   GUESTHOUSE $
(☑0194-2450872, 9491034268; yulabshakeel@yahoo.in; off Dalgate; d ₹400-600, without bathroom ₹300-500) In a creaky but characterful old house; some rooms have thin hardboard divider walls, but the family owners are kind and there's a laundry and bicycle rental available. Rooms on the lower floor were flood damaged so check the room before you commit. Wi-fi ₹100.

★Hotel Swiss   GUESTHOUSE $$
(☑0194-2500115; www.swisshotelkashmir.com; 172 Old Gagribal Rd; foreigners d ₹800-1700, Indians ₹1500-5000; @) One of India's friendliest family guesthouses, the Swiss isn't showy but offers high-quality hotel rooms with fresh, varnished pine walls at walk-in prices that are significantly discounted for

foreigners. It's handy for the lake yet set back far enough to avoid traffic noise.

There's free wi-fi in the communal sitting room where travellers swap notes. Get lots of informed opinion from the tirelessly helpful manager.

★Green Acre   HOTEL $$
(☑0194-2313848; www.wazirhotels.com; Rajbagh; r ₹3500-8000, ste ₹9500-35,000; ❄🍵) Set deep within the lawns of a glorious rose garden, Green Acre's centrepiece is a 1942 classic-Raj mansion with a perfect reading perch on the 1st-floor common balcony. The property was inundated during the 2014 floods, but the rooms have been carefully restored. Heritage rooms have *khatamband* ceilings and elements of period furniture.

Even in the rear concrete block, rooms are large with family artworks, crewel embroideries and excellent bathrooms. Suites have garden views and air-con.

Chocolate Box   BOUTIQUE HOTEL $$
(☑9796577334; tcb.rooms@gmail.com; Boulevard; d ₹3500-4500) Pseudo-Burberry blankets, towels in wicker baskets and well-chosen elements of designer style make this 10-room newcomer the most up-to-date option on the Boulevard. Rooms 107 and 108 have private lake-facing balconies.

Hotel Ibni-Kabeer   HOTEL $$
(☑0194-2313193; www.hotelibnikabeer.com; Rajbagh; d ₹3800; 🍵) Fair value at discount rates, this unfussy midrange choice has 22 large rooms, repainted with ceiling mouldings and framed crewel-work on lilac walls.

Comrade Inn   HOTEL $$$
(☑0194-2459001; www.comradeinn.com; Rajbagh; d discount/rack rate ₹5000/8000; ❄🍵) Well-trained staff lead you through corridors tastefully decked in modern art to fully equipped new rooms with excellent box-spring beds, crisp cotton sheets, rainforest showers, fridge, kettle and stylish lighting. Back-up power supply keeps the lift and AC-heater units working. Flood repairs were completed in 2015 and a roof terrace and coffee shop are under construction.

Lalit Grand Palace Hotel   HERITAGE HOTEL $$$
(☑0194-2501001; www.thelalit.com; r ₹18,350-22,500, ste ₹22,500-183,000; 🍵❄) Vast period suites in the Maharaja's 1910 palace and a long new wing of (slightly) cheaper business-standard rooms are all beautifully

set above hectares of manicured lawns. Internet discounts are possible.

Eating

Inexpensive *dhaba* (snack bars) are dotted along the Boulevard.

New Krishna Vaishno Bhojnalay
VEGETARIAN $

(Durganag Rd; mains ₹50-90, small/large rice ₹25/50; ⊘8am-4pm & 7-10.30pm) Crowds clammer for the tasty, inexpensive pre-cooked vegetarian meals, dosas and South Indian breakfasts at Srinagar's small, 'original' *dhaba*. Pre-pay at counter.

Shahi Darbar
BARBECUE $

(Khayam Chowk; half/whole chicken ₹180/340, shish/kashmiri kebab ₹150/130; ⊘9am-10pm) One of at least four barbecue takeaways for inexpensive tikka and tandoori snacks around the Khayam Chowk street corner, two blocks northwest of Dalgate.

Mughal Darbar
KASHMIRI, INDIAN $$

(☑0194-2476998; 1st fl, Residency Rd; mains ₹105-340, 1-/4-person wazwan ₹640/2875; ⊘10.30am-10.30pm) This upstairs restaurant is a great place to try a full spread of Kashmir's mutton-based cuisine, though good Indian vegie dishes are also served. A special sit-on-carpet room with copper-work serving dishes is available if booking ahead for a full *wazwan* (Kashmiri feast). The main dining-room features an excellent 'Where is heaven?' oriental mural.

Shamiana
KASHMIRI $$

(Boulevard; meals ₹500-750; ⊘11.30am-10pm) Next to the Heemal Hotel Complex, Shamiana is a popular stop for authentic Kashmiri food. You can hop off the first row houseboats or a *shikara* on the edge of the Dal lake and walk across the street for local delicacies like mutton *seekh* kebabs, *wazwan* and *pulao*.

14th Avenue Cafe & Grill
INTERNATIONAL $$

(SPS Rd; snacks ₹125-200, mains ₹200-415, coffee/cake from ₹60/90; ⊘10.30am-9.30pm) This fashion-conscious, five-table coffee-cube overlooking the Jhelum River serves hummus, nachos, falafel-wraps, piri-piri chicken and thin-crust pizzas, but you might just drop in for coffee and cakes.

Stream
MULTICUISINE $$

(Boulevard; mains ₹170-320, rice ₹80; ⊘11am-10pm) This reliable, semi-smart eatery is set back from the Boulevard with a particular-

ly decent range of pan-Indian options, plus pizza, coffee and ice cream. Comfortably air-conditioned and with water-cascade down the front windows.

Drinking

Srinagar's Muslim mores mean that alcohol isn't served in restaurants, the few **wine shops** (Heemal Hotel Shopping Complex, Boulevard; ⊘10am-8pm Sat-Thu, closed during Ramadan) are not obvious to find and the tiny handful of bars are mostly in upmarket hotels.

Dar Bar
BAR

(cocktails/beer ₹715/490; ⊘11am-11pm) Even if you can't afford to stay at the Lalit Grand Palace Hotel, consider sipping a drink at its little bar or, better still, on the hotel's glorious lawns with indulgent views towards Dal Lake. Add 30% tax to menu prices.

Shopping

The Boulevard has several emporia flogging Kashmiri souvenirs, including elegantly painted papier-mâché boxes and carved walnut woodwork, plus cashmere and pashmina shawls, originally popularised in Europe by Napoleon's wife Josephine. Chain-stitched *gabbas* (Kashmiri rugs with appliqué), crewel embroidery work or floral *namdas* (felted wool carpets) also make good souvenirs. Saffron, cricket bats and dried fruits are widely sold around Lal Chowk.

Kashmir Government Arts Emporium
HANDICRAFTS

(☑0194-2452783; Bund; ⊘10am-8pm Mon-Sat) A veritable museum of Kashmiri crafts at

---

KASHMIRI FOOD

Kashmir has a distinct cuisine all of its own. A full traditional *wazwan* (feast) can have dozens of courses, notably *goshtaba* (pounded mutton balls in saffron-yoghurt curry), *tabak maaz* (fried lamb's ribs) and *rogan josh* (rich, vividly red-coloured mutton curry). Kashmiri chefs also serve deliciously aromatic cheese-based curries and seasonal *nadir* (lotus stems), typically served in *yakhni* (a curd-based sauce made mildly minty with fennel). Kashmiri *kahwa* is a luxurious golden tea, flavoured with saffron, cinnamon and crushed almonds.

marked, fixed prices in the century-old half-timbered former British Residency Building (gutted by fire 1998, restored 2004, damaged again in the 2014 floods). There's a splendid park opposite.

ℹ Information

ATMs are widespread, especially on Residency Rd. Beware of freelance moneychangers offering improbably good rates – you're likely to get forged banknotes.

Abdul Zandari (☑0194-2451370, 9469111596; www.riversongskashmir.webs. com) Fluent, knowledgeable if a little full-on, Abdul is an enthusiastic city guide who is likely to find you as you wander around Srinagar. Recommended by several readers. Pay him 'what you feel'.

Internet Cafe (Old Gagribal Rd; per hr ₹30; ⊙9am-11pm)

TRC (Tourism Reception Centre; ☑0194-2456291, toll-free 1800-1031060; www. jktourism.org; ⊙24hr) With perseverance you might actually find answers to your questions. Apply here for Hari Parbat permits. Next door the mountaineering centre rents camping and hiking equipment.

UAE Exchange (Boulevard; ⊙9.30am-1.30pm & 2-6pm Mon-Fri, to 4pm Sat) Hidden down the driveway directly east of Hotel Sunshine, this moneychanger offers good cash rates and exchanges travellers cheques with commission.

ℹ Getting There & Away

AIR

Arrival Foreigners must fill a J&K arrival form, which demands you give the name of your hotel. If you don't know, write TRC (Tourist Reception Centre).

Departure Srinagar's airport is 1.2km behind a security barrier where there can be long queues for baggage and body screening. You'll need to show an air ticket (or e-ticket confirmation print-out) to get through so don't come to the airport hoping to buy a ticket on departure. Allow at least two hours' leeway.

Airlines

Air India (☑0194-2450247; www.airindia.in; Boulevard) Delhi, Jammu; Leh on Wednesdays.

GoAir (www.goair.in) Delhi, Jammu.

IndiGo (www.goindigo.in) Delhi, Jammu, Mumbai.

Jet Airways (☑0194-2480801; Residency Rd) Delhi, Jammu.

SpiceJet (www.spicejet.com) Delhi, Jammu, Amritsar, Chandigah.

BUS & SHARED JEEP

Anantnag Shared sumo (₹80, 90 minutes) from **Tourist Taxi Stand 7** (Dalgate). Change in Anantnag for Pahalgam and Vailoo. For Kishtwar you'll have to stay overnight in Vailoo or nearby Kokernag as Kishtwar shared jeeps (₹300/3500 per person/vehicle, six hours) all depart from Vailoo between 6am and 10am.

Jammu Private buses (mostly overnight) start from Panthachowk bus station, 8km south of centre. There are also rickety J&KSRTC buses (class B/A/18-seater bus ₹300/420/510, 10 to 13 hours) at 6.30am, 7.30am and (some evenings) 7.30pm from the far more convenient **J&KSRTC bus station** (☑0194-2455107). Or take a shared jeep (₹700/4950 per person/vehicle) from across the road with departures all morning but easiest from 6.30am to 9am. The well-paved Srinagar–Jammu road has many scenic points and snow is cleared year-round, but jams are common following landslides and hartals (strikes). Be prepared to fly at such times.

Kargil Shared jeeps (₹900/6400 per person/car) depart before 9am from **Tourist Taxi Stand 1** (Residency Rd) and from Kaksarai near SMHS hospital in Karan Nagar (western Srinagar) from which there are also two private buses around 5am (₹400).

Leh J&KSRTC has a 7am bus (class B/A ₹1060/1600, two days, book one day ahead) that stops the night en route in Kargil. From Tourist Taxi Stand 1 shared jeeps (₹2100 per person, 14 hours) mostly leave before 7am. Book at least a day ahead to score good seats.

Delhi J&KSRTC 7.30am (seat/sleeper ₹1490/1670, around 24 hours).

J&KSRTC also advertises excursion buses to Sonamarg (one-way/return ₹180/289), Gulmarg (₹179/271) and Pahalgam (₹180/289) and other tourist destinations, all departing between 7.30am and 9am, but lack of customers means that few actually run outside the peak May to June period. Before paying the ticket, ask fellow passengers whether they might prefer to share a sumo from the taxi stand opposite.

The giant Batmalu bus station, west of centre, has services thrice daily to Sonamarg and frequent sumos to Tangmarg for Gulmarg.

JEEP HIRE

Dozens of stands offer jeep rental. Return prices include Pahalgam (₹2950), Sonamarg (₹2850) and Gulmarg (₹2050). Your hotel might offer better deals.

TRAIN

The nearest train station is at Nowgam, and around 10km south of the Old City. Trains currently run Banihal–Qazigund–Anantnag–Nowgam–Baramulla but by 2018 the whole Jammu–Katra–Nowgam–Baramulla line should be complete. Well maybe.

ℹ Getting Around

Autorickshaws cost ₹50 for short hops, and around ₹200 per hour for tours.

Shikaras are colourful gondolas propelled by a heart-shaped paddles. Officially they charge ₹50 for the shortest houseboat-to-shore hops or ₹500 per hour. In reality some *shikara*-wallahs accept as little as ₹200 per hour (notably from Khona Khon New Rd) but expect some sales pressure.

Overcrowded minibuses ply the main routes including Lal Chowk–Hazratbal and Lal Chowk–Shalimar Bagh via Dal Lake's south bank.

If you can handle the manic traffic, a bicycle offers a liberating way to go sightseeing in the sprawling but relatively flat old city and lakeshore areas. Bike-rental opportunites are limited but a few are available (usually for guests only) from Hotel Swiss, Comrade Inn and Noor Guest House (₹250 per day).

AIRPORT TRANSPORT

A J&KSRTC bus (₹70) supposedly meets most flights then runs to Lal Chowk, with tickets sold in the terminal. Last service before 4pm. Pre-paid taxis are listed as costing ₹445/525 to central Srinagar/Nehru Park but 'with extras' you'll actually pay ₹600. From the outside taxi counter, locals share rides paying ₹100 per seat to Lal Chowk in central Srinagar, but drivers seem extremely reluctant to take foreigners.

Around Srinagar

Sonamarg, set amid spectacular mountains, can be visited between Leh and Srinagar and in mid-summer is linked to tiny but historic Naranag by a multiday trek through some spectacular lake-dappled alpine highlands. Gulmarg is great for extreme skiing in winter but in summer its cable car is often over-loaded by queues of Indian tourists waiting for hours on end. Overcrowding is also a curse in once-lovely Pahalgam but canny foreigners zip on from there up to tiny Aru with its tremendous alpine backdrop and instant hiking appeal. While it's not a destination in itself, Anantnag (aka Islamabad), along with twin-town Khanabal, 4km away on the main Jammu–Srinagar highway, makes a useful transit point if diverting to Pahalgam or to Kishtwar via the lovely Kokernag Botanical Gardens and the countless hairpins of Sinthan Top. If you're driving Srinagar–Anantnag, you'll pass saffron-producers at Pampore, cricket-bat makers at Sangam and two ancient temple ruins at the roadside in Awantipora. If those appeal, then consider an 8km diversion from Khanabal to Mattan, 2.5km above which ruins of an 8th-century sun temple (☉dawn-dusk) **FREE** are set in splendidly tended grounds (follow signs to Kehrbal).

Naranag & Lake Gangabal

Home to seminomadic Gujar people, and a pair of remarkable (unfenced) 8th-century Shiva temple ruins (Naranag), little Naranag sits in a deep-cut river valley thick with mature conifer forests. It is mostly used by visitors as a trailhead for multiday treks in Kashmir's 'Great Lakes' uplands.

A major highlight is beautiful Lake Gangabal, which could be accessed in around seven strenuous hours' hike from Naranag village steeply following the last cascading side stream before the temple ruins. You'll gain around 1200m elevation so take things slowly! It's possible to continue in around five days to Sonamarg (or vice versa) but certain passes can be impassably snowy till late July and permits are required on certain routes (apply through Srinagar TRC or Manigal camp near Kangan). Prospective guides will likely find you on arrival in Naranag and will happily arrange pack-horses, but standards of English aren't great and pricing can be very sketchy. Most local guides have tents and sleeping bags but bringing your own would be very wise (rentable from Srinagar TRC). The advertised J&KSRTC tourist bus Srinagar–Naranag is essentially fictional due to lack of customers.

Naranag has at least eight scruffy homestay-guesthouses, most in a deplorable state of disarray. Upstairs rooms at Khan Guesthouse (☎9697559256; d without bathroom ₹500) are cleaner than most. Ashraf Jagil's Homestay (r ₹500), directly above the temple ruins, has ultra-basic floor-space accommodation sleeping up to eight people per bare room for ₹500 total (bring a sleeping bag). Scarlet-and-mustard New Pine Palace (☎7296309503, 9797121636; d ₹700-1000) has an attractive restaurant section but ensuite rooms are unkempt. At the start of town, four-room Gulshan Lodge (☎9858375734; r ₹500-1000) has balconies on two of its functional ensuite rooms.

A charter jeep from Srinagar costs ₹2400. The one daily bus service leaves at 8am for Kangan (₹20, 80 minutes) returning at 3pm. Kangan–Srinagar shared sumos (₹70, one hour) run to Lal Chowk, plus there are buses to Batmalu bus station.

Sonamarg

☑ 0194 / POP 800 (SUMMER ONLY) / ELEV 2800M

Surrounded by soaring sharpened peaks and *Sound of Music* scenery, Sonamarg (Km85) is a strip-town marring an otherwise gorgeous alpine valley. Sitting astride the Kargil–Srinagar road, it makes a possible trekking base or a meal-stop before/after crossing the nerve-jangling 3529m Zoji La (☺ often closed for maintenance 11am-3pm Mon-Sat) pass. It's also a staging point for *yatra*-hike pilgrims en route to Amarnath's holy ice lingam via Baltal Camp, a summer-only mayhem of tents around 15km east.

An easy way to savour the spectacular scenery is by walking up the parallel valley to the fingertips of Thajiwas Glacier. Walking takes around an hour starting along the track between the Hotel Glacier Heights and the Army camp through a zone of newly developing buiildings then curling left around the forest ridge. A more obvious (and far busier) route starts from around Km83, where you could alternatively engage small horses (₹500, only slightly faster) or take a taxi roughly half-way (₹800 return, private cars not permitted).

🛏 Sleeping & Eating

In central Sonamarg, facing the sumo stand and tourist office, is a scrappy strip of mostly jerry-built box restaurants and souvenir shops above which small, poorly maintained guest rooms typically cost ₹2000 to ₹4000 in high season (May to June) but only ₹1000 or so by September. Hotel Sonamarg (☑ 9419448827; r ₹1200-2500) is currently the best of this dreary lot.

Stretching west to Km83, a building frenzy is filling once-pristine upland sheep-meadows with cheek-by-jowl new hotels. We counted 17 construction sites. At the far end of this strip, longer-established Hotel Snowland (☑ 0194-2417262; Srinagar-Kargil Rd Km83; rack-rate r ₹6000-12,000, off-peak from ₹4000; ☺ May-Oct; 🛜) has grown into a veritable estate of nine comfortable sub-hotels.

Around 20 minutes' walk from Km83 towards Thajiwas Glacier, an aging green wooden building is home to Sonamarg's cheapest and most peaceful option, the misnamed J&K Tourist Dormitories (☑ Mr Hidayat 9469413011; dm/cottages ₹200/7000), with its basic old twin rooms around a central courtyard that you can pre-book at the J&KTRC office in central Sonamarg.

Sitting alone between the river and main road, 2km east of Sonamarg, the half-timbered International Youth Hostel (☑ 9419707307; iyhssonmarg@gmail.com; Srinagar-Kargil Rd Km86.3; dm/q ₹550/2400) has giant, super-airy dorms are often mostly empty even in season. Facilities include snooker, table-tennis and a well-equipped weight-training gym. There's a campsite 600m further upstream and beyond near Km87 you'll find a boating pond with zorbing cylinders and a rafting point.

There are a dozen more hotels in Gagangir (Km74), which has a cramped feel but a spectacular setting.

ℹ Getting There & Away

Srinagar Buses (₹120, over five hours) depart 7am, 9am, 11am, 2pm and 4pm. Locals prefer a shared sumo to Kangan (₹80, 90 minutes) and another from there to Srinagar (₹70, one hour).

Kargil Chartered jeeps want ₹5000. Kargil-/Leh-bound buses pass through at around 8am/10.30am respectively, but are often full on arrival. So too are most shared jeeps ex-Srinagar but it's worth looking for 07 number plates stopped at the restaurant strip or bus stand. If you find a seat the charge should be ₹600 per person to Kargil. An alternative is to have a friendly hotelier phone-reserve a seat in a jeep ex-Srinagar. Give him the fare (₹1000 per seat) as a deposit as reassurance that you won't make alternative arrangements.

Gulmarg

For Indian tourists, Gulmarg's double-shot Gondola (www.gulmarggondola.com; cable car 1/2 stages in summer ₹600/1400, 1-day ski pass 1/2 stages for foreigners ₹1000/1600, locals ₹600/1000; ☺ 9am-3pm, last return around 5pm) is a great summer attraction. Foreigners who have seen mountaintops and snow before might think otherwise due to gruelling queues at the cable car and the somewhat half-hearted nature of local donkey treks once you reach the top. Mid-December to mid-March everything changes. In winter Gulmarg comes into its own as a ski centre, famed for its perfect high-altitude powder. Although a chairlift partially paralleling the gondola's second stage does offer easier alternatives, this is really a venue for extreme skiers. The basin enfolding the gondola is patrolled and blasted for avalanche prevention, but the vast majority of other couloirs and forest tracks are unsecured so it's essential to be snow-savvy and to check conditions carefully. Gulmarg Avalanche (http://gulmargavalanche.org) gives detailed updates throughout the season. **GM Ahanger** (☑9596295371, 9697767268; ahangergrm@gmail.com) has been recommended as a ski-guide and several outlets rent decent gear. Swiss **FSH** (Free Ski Himalaya; www.freeskihimalaya.com) and Australia-based **Bills Trips** (www.billstrips.com) offer complete ski packages.

Gulmarg is only 1½ hour's drive from Srinagar, but stay overnight to get a head start on the pistes. Modest but switched-on **Raja's Hut** (☑9797297908; dadakhan53@yahoo.com; d/half-board ₹2500/2800) is run by a genial snowboarder and is favoured by many budget-minded international adventure folk. Other decent choices include the cheery if slightly worn, pine-decor **Heevan Retreat** (☑01954-254455; www.ahadhotelsandresorts.com; s/d/ste ₹7500/8500/11,000, breakfast/dinner buffet ₹500/850; 🛜), plain family-style **Shaw Inn** (☑01954-254532, 9596972200; www.shawinn.in; s/d ₹7000/7500) or the dauntingly suave palace-hotel **Khyber Himalayan** (☑01954-254666; http://khyberhotels.com; d ₹12,500-23,000, cottages ₹50,000-75,000; 🛜).

ⓘ Getting There & Away

A day-return jeep hire from Srinagar costs ₹2085 per vehicle. Alternatively, from Srinagar's Batmalu bus station take shared jeeps to Tangmarg (₹70) then change for the last 13km of hairpins to Gulmarg (₹30).

In summer a barrier is closed beside the jeep-stand forcing you to walk the last 15 minutes to the gondola, or to fall prey to cheeky horsemen who exaggeratedly claim it's 3km and want ₹150 for the trot.

Pahalgam & Aru

☑01936 / POP 6000 / ELEV 2400-2750M

Surrounded by alpine peaks, the Lidder and Seshnag rivers tumble down picturesque, deep-cut mountain valleys covered with giant conifers. The surrounding mountains contain many beauty spots and over 20 lakes to which countless guides and horsemen are more than keen to take you for a ride.

Not quite spoiling the great natural beauty is Pahalgam, a major resort town and staging point for the Amarnath pilgrimage. Sprawling 4km around the river junction, it offers golf, rafting and over 230 hotels ranging from vaguely Scandinavian-styled **Himalaya House** (☑01936-243072; www.himalayahouse.in; standard/deluxe ₹3000/4900; 🛜) and fashion-conscious **Pine Spring** (☑01936-243386; www.hotelpinespring.com; Lari-pora Rd; s/d/ste ₹7000/9000/11,000) to old-fashioned chocolate-box cottage-style **Alpine Inn** (☑9906756030, 01936-243065; www.alpineinnpahalgam.com; Heevan Link Rd; d ₹3200-4500) and the basic but peacefully secluded **Ramba Palace** (Bentes Lodge; ☑01936-243296, 9419745142, 9419727379; rambapalace@yahoo.com; Mamal; d ₹500-1000, without bathroom ₹400-600), an aging budget place with breathtaking views (ask at the co-owned Palestine Hotel facing the main sumo station and you'll probably be given a free transfer as it's somewhat hard to find).

Almost any hotel is likely to urge you to try a donkey hike or full-blown trek. The best hiking often starts 12km away in **Aru**, a tiny village set beautifully amid the foothill peaks. In the last couple of years, foreign budget travellers have started blowing straight through over-crowded Pahalgam to stay in one of Aru's half-dozen basic accommodation options including welcoming **Friends Guesthouse** (☑01936-210928; www.friendsguesthousepahalgam.com; Aru; d ₹300-500) and **Rohella Guesthouse** (☑01936-211339, 9622761355; www.rohella.brinkster.net; Aru; s/d ₹500/600; ☺Apr-Oct), a firm favourite with the dreadlock crowd. **Milky Way Hotel** (☑01936-210899, 9419435832; www.milkywaykashmir.com; Aru; r ₹2500-3200, without bathroom ₹800) is a slight cut above with ensuite bathrooms and an OK restaurant. Though Aru hibernates from November to March, in summer it's an easy place to find guides and horses or to simply wander off by yourself into magical upland landscapes.

ⓘ Getting There & Away

Sometimes-cancelled J&KSRTC buses run to Srinagar (₹180 to ₹260, 4.30pm) and Jammu (₹270, 7.30am). A better idea is heading first to Anantnag by shared jeep (₹80, one hour) or by rare local buses (₹42, 1½ hours). The only vehicles permitted to go to Aru (from ₹600) and Chandawari (₹700, 19km) start from the **Tourist Taxi Stand** (☑01936-243126; www.taxistand-pahalgam.com), 10 minutes' walk up the main road from the sumo station.

SOUTHERN JAMMU & KASHMIR

The state's predominantly Hindu southern region swelters at the edge of the plains. Floods of *yatri* (pilgrims) arrive en route to Katra (April to June and October to December) and Amarnath (July), but foreign visitors are rare.

Jammu

🔲 0191 / POP 504,000 / ELEV 327M

Jammu is the state's winter capital and pre-Independence was once the seat of J&K's Dogra dynasty. Religiously Hindu, Jammu dubs itself as the 'city of temples'. Few of these temples are historically compulsive, and for foreign tourists there's little pressing need to hang around longer than necessary to make transport connections to Amritsar, Srinagar or Dharamsala.

But if you've time to kill, consider one of the set three- to four-hour sightseeing circuits offered by certain autorickshaw drivers (₹350 to ₹500). These usually include the tall towered **Ranbireshwar Mandir** (Shalimar Road), the glitteringly colourful Krishna and Shiva caves of **Gupawala Mandir** (Pinkho Rd), the large but squat 19th-century **Bahu Fort** and the Disney-esque concrete gods of riverside **Har-ki-Paori Mandir**.

Mubarak Mandi · PALACE RUINS

Started in 1710 by the Dev dynasty and vastly expanded under the 19th-century Dogras, this extensive complex of palace buildings is fascinating for both its scale and its startling state of semi-collapse. The only part that's currently accessible contains the **Dogra Art Gallery** (foreigner/Indian ₹50/10; ⊙10am-5pm Tue-Sun), a museum featuring bronzes, armaments, instruments, 9th-century carvings and Kushan coins.

Renovation of the raja's impressive former 'foreign office' and Army Headquarters is nearing completion and that of the decrepit Royal Courts is due next, but restoring the gigantic shattered Gol Ghar section, hidden at the rear, could take decades.

Amar Mahal · PALACE

(www.karansingh.com/amml; standard/special entry ₹20/100; ⊙9am-1pm & 2-6pm Tue-Sun, to 5pm Apr-Sep) In the 20th century the Marharajas moved from Mubarak Mahal, further up the

Jammu

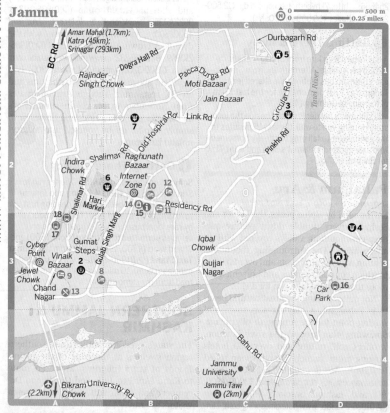

ridge to this very European brick mansion complete with token castle-style tower. An interesting museum-like interior introduces the characters who once lived here and with the 'special' ticket you'll be escorted upstairs to peruse the Maharani's chambers with Queen Victoria portrait and bathroom complete with perfume collection. Before leaving, peep through the front curved verandah window to see the raja's canopied throne made from 101kg of gold.

Then, perhaps, retire for a cocktail at the refreshingly air-conditioned Polo Lounge bar of the Hari Niwas Palace Hotel that shares the same manicured cliff-top lawns.

Raghunath Mandir   HINDU TEMPLE
(Raghunath Bazaar; admission by donation; ⊙6am-9.30pm) The large, 19th-century Raghunath Mandir marks the heart of older Jammu and features several pavilions containing thousands of what look like grey pebbles set in concrete. In fact, these are saligrams (ammonite fossils) symbolically representing the myriad deities of the Hindu pantheon.

Requests for donations are almost as plentiful. You'll be asked to deposit bags, cameras, phones and even pens before entering.

Chand Kaur Gurdwara   SIKH TEMPLE
Still unfinished, this vast complex dominates the lower city centre area with distinctive domes reminscent of the Royal Pavilion in Brighton, England.

🛏 Sleeping

Basic budget options are plentiful, especially around Vinaik Bazaar (a block southeast of the bus station), but very few can be recommended. Near the Jammu Tawi station, pilgrim lodges like Vishnavi Dahm might have dorm-space free outside *yatra* season. For midrange bargains look in lanes off Residency Road for the most recently built mini-hotels. Currently these include Upkar Plaza Lodge (☑ 0191-2543321, 9419197065; upkarplaza@gmail.com; 5 Panj Bakhtar Rd; r ₹1300-1750; ✳🛜) and Hotel Natraj (☑ 0191-2547450, Anil 9419165708; www.natrajhoteljammu.com; Residency Road; d ₹1500-2000; ✳🛜). If booking online, beware that many 'Jammu' hotels listed are actually 45km away in Katra.

Green View Hotel   GUESTHOUSE $
(☑ 0191-2573906, 9419198639; 69 Chand Nagar; s/d/tr/q ₹200/600/800/1000, with AC ₹1000/1200/1600/1800; ✳) Hidden down an unprepossessing lane off Vinaik Bazaar, this backpacker fall-back has freshly tiled ensuite rooms that are considerably better than you'd guess from their padlocked grey doors. The mini box singles share OK bathrooms and are about the cheapest foreigner-permitted rooms in Jammu. Wi-fi in the lobby-yard.

Park Inn   HOTEL $$
(☑ 0191-2560430; Residency Rd; s/d/tr ₹1760/1980/2750, walk-in rates from ₹1230; ✳🛜) A bargain at their discount rates, this super-central pad has reliable wi-fi, good aircon and friendly management. The 11 rooms are newly redecorated with ceiling mouldings and strong colours, but bathrooms are older with rattling fans and the odd cracked loo seat. Soap and toilet paper provided. Enjoy the welcome pot of tea.

Jammu

⦿ Sights
1 Bahu Fort D3
2 Chand Kaur Gurdwara A3
  Dogra Art Gallery ....(see 5)
3 Gupawala Mandir C1
4 Har-ki-Paori Mandir D3
5 Mubarak Mandi C1
6 Raghunath Mandir B2
7 Ranbireshwar Mandir B2

🛏 Sleeping
8 Fortune Riviera..A3
9 Green View Hotel A3
10 Hotel Natraj B2
11 Park Inn B2
12 Upkar Plaza Lodge.................................B2

✖ Eating
13 City Square Mall A3
  Falak..(see 11)

🛍 Shopping
  J&K Government Arts
    Emporium...................................(see 14)
14 Jay Kay Bookhouse................................B2

ℹ Information
15 J&K Tourism B2

ℹ Transport
  Air India..(see 15)
16 Matador 108 Terminus D3
17 Private Buses & Shared Jeeps A3
18 Public Bus Station A3

Fortune Riviera
HOTEL $$$

(☏0191-2561415; www.fortunehotels.in; Gulab Singh Marg; s/d from ₹5280/5720; ❄🛜) Central Jammu's most stylish and attentively businesslike hotel includes a glass elevator in the four-storey atrium, three restaurants, a coffee shop and a gym, all for just 29 soothingly cream-beige rooms with artistically conceived bedposts.

Wi-fi is free for one hour then ₹200 per day.

🍴 Eating & Drinking

Between Jewel Chowk and Vinaik Bazaar are several inexpensive *dhabas*, a fast-food place, wine shops and two bars. City Square Mall has Domino's Pizza, Barista Coffee and three other air-conditioned restaurants. Residency Rd has a wide range of options from cheap barbecues (near Raghunath Mandir) to vegetarian restaurants, fast food and a Café Coffee Day opposite KC Plaza.

Falak
INDIAN $$$

(☏0191-2520770; www.kcresidency.com; 7th fl, KC Residency Hotel, Residency Rd; mains veg/nonveg/fish from ₹345/425/525, rice ₹195; ⊙12.30-11pm) This revolving restaurant serves superb pan-Indian cuisine and offers 360-degree views of the crowded Jammu townscape. Although views are best before sunset, the floor only starts spinning around 7pm.

🛍 Shopping

Just near the J&K Tourism office is a well-presented government arts emporium (Residency Rd; ⊙10am-8.30pm Mon-Sat) and English-language bookshop Jay Kay Bookhouse (Residency Rd; ⊙10am-8pm Mon-Sat).

ℹ Information

Internet Zone (Shiva Lodge 1st fl, Residency Rd; per 30min ₹20; ⊙10am-7pm Mon-Sat) Bearable connection on old computers, but the owner is friendly.

Cyber Point (Jewel Chowk; per hour ₹20; ⊙9am-10pm) Tiny but cheap central internet access.

J&K Tourism (☏0191-2548172; www.jktdc. org; Residency Rd; ⊙8am-8pm Mon-Sat) The J&K Tourism complex includes a refreshingly air-conditioned reception centre, tourist jeepstand and a musty, institutional hotel hiding an attractive under-lit Kashmiri restaurant and typical old-Indian bar.

ℹ Getting There & Away

AIR

Air India (☏0191-2456086; www.airindia. com; J&K Tourism complex; ⊙10am-1pm & 2-4.45pm Mon-Sat) Delhi, Srinagar, Leh (Monday & Friday).

GoAir (www.goair.in) Delhi, Srinagar, Mumbai.

IndiGo (www.goindigo.in) Delhi, Srinagar.

Jet Airways (www.jetairways.com) Delhi.

SpiceJet (www.spicejet.com) Delhi, Srinagar.

BUS & JEEP

Private buses and shared jeeps depart from a chaotic strip in the shadow of the BC Rd (NH44 Hwy) overpass. Public buses use the big, rotting concrete bus station complex immediately east. Destinations:

Amritsar Up to 30 buses daily (₹175, six hours) via Pathankot in Punjab (₹90, 2½ hours).

Chandigarh Various private buses (seat/sleeper ₹450/600, eight hours) mostly at 9pm and 10pm.

AMARNATH

Amarnath's unique attraction is a natural stone lingam that becomes opalescent when encrusted with ice and is believed to wax and wane with the phases of the moon. Seen as symbolising Lord Shiva, it's hidden in an isolated mountain cave at 3888m, 14km from the nearest road. Joining the summer-only *yatra* (Hindu pilgrimage) is an unforgettable experience and the two possible routes are both very beautiful, but it's certainly not a meditative country hike. After all there are around 20,000 fellow pilgrims on the trail every day. Both blizzards and Kashmiri militants have killed pilgrims in the past so prospective *yatri* (pilgrim-hikers) need to be suitably equipped and must apply for a special permit that requires five photos, a medical check (at Srinagar public hospital), approved insurance, passport copy and ₹150, which should all be presented at the TRC Office in Nowgam, 12km outside Srinagar. See www.shriamarnathjishrine.com for more detail.

From the vast Baltal Camp 15km east of Sonamarg, Amarnath is just 14km away. Wealthier pilgrims complete that journey by pony, helicopter or *dandy* (palanquin). The longer approach starts with a 16km taxi ride from Pahalgam to Chandanwari (₹700) then a 36km, three-day hike. Either way, camps en route provide all essentials so essentially you don't need to carry much more than spare warm clothes.

Delhi Public buses 13 times daily (₹550, 13 hours) plus many private services leaving between 5pm and 10.30pm (luxury seat/sleeper/recliner ₹850/1200/1500).

Dharamsala Direct bus at 8.30am (₹260, six hours) or take an Amritsar service and change at Pathankot.

Katra Buses, minibuses and taxis depart very regularly from both bus and train stations.

Kishtwar Nine buses (₹260, seven hours) depart between 2am and 9.10am.

Manali Private bus at 8.30pm (₹750, 11 hours) from Krishna & Ashish Travel (bus station unit 13A).

Srinagar Ever-changing situation. Target journey time is 12 hours but traffic jams can extend that considerably. J&KSRTC buses should leave at 5am, 6.30am and 7am; there's a KMD basic bus at 8pm (₹400); and several private agencies have 10pm overnight departures including Sahiba and Luxmi (seat/sleeper ₹500/700). Chartered Indica/Qualis vehicles holding three/six passengers charge ₹5500/6500 one way. Drivers offering shared rides (from ₹600 to ₹800 depending on occupancy) gather along the bus station ramp and near Jewel Chowk, but while quicker than buses, departure times are highly uncertain.

TRAIN

Jammu Tawi, Jammu's main train station, is well south of the river, 5km from the bus station.

Amritsar Tata Mouri Express (18110) leaves at 2.25pm (sleeper/3AC/2AC ₹184/485/690, five hours). Returning from Amritsar it departs at 8.20am.

Delhi Uttar Sampark Kranti Express (12446) departs at 9.05pm arriving 6.50am (sleeper/3AC/2AC ₹355/920/1300). Slower but somewhat cheaper, the Jhelum Express (11078, departing 9.45pm) gives two hours more sleep and continues to Agra (sleeper/3AC/2AC ₹395/1060/1535) arriving 1.50pm.

The new northbound railway now extends to Katra and should reach Srinagar around 2018, crossing the Chenab River on the world's tallest rail bridge.

❶ Getting Around

To the airport from Jewel Chowk, autorickshaws/taxis cost around ₹175/300, or use 'Satwari'-bound minibuses. From the airport, turn left on exiting the grounds to find local taxis waiting at Durga Filling Station.

Around town, overloaded minibuses and curiously stretched 'Matadors' charge ₹10 per hop: route 117 links bus and train stations, 108 goes to the fort.

Around Jammu

Accessed by foot, palanquin or helicopter from nearby **Katra**, the latter-day **Vaishno Devi Shrine** (www.maavaishnodevi.org) is one of India's busiest pilgrim sites. It attracts millions of domestic visitors but its appeal is hard to understand for most non-Hindus.

Southwest of Udhampur, the restored historic palace **Ramnagar** is attractive but hardly justifies the long journey. Be aware that Ramnagar's train station is around 30km from Ramnagar itself.

Between Udhampur and Srinagar, the road winds up a vertical kilometre into mature coniferous woodlands where, between Kud and **Patnitop**, there lies a sprinkling of resort hotels.

JAMMU & KASHMIR (INCLUDING LADAKH) AROUND JAMMU

Himachal Pradesh

Why Go?

With spectacular snowy peaks and plunging river valleys, Himachal is India's outdoor adventure playground. From trekking and climbing to rafting, paragliding and skiing, if it can be done in the mountains, it can be done here. A convoluted topography of interlocking mountain chains also makes Himachal a spectacular place simply to explore, by bus, car, motorbike or jeep safari. Every pass crossing into a new valley brings you into a different world, with its own customs, gods and even language. Villages perched on staggering slopes enchant with fairy-tale architecture and their people's easygoing warmth. Hill stations appeal with holiday atmosphere and colonial echoes, while backpacker magnets lure with their blissed-out vibe and mountain beauty. Such is the variety of the Himachali jigsaw that in McLeod Ganj, the Dalai Lama's home-away-from-home, and in Lahaul and Spiti, with their centuries-old Buddhist cultures, you might even think you've stumbled into Tibet.

Best Places to Stay

➡ Chonor House (p327)

➡ Orchard Hut (p338)

➡ Alliance Guesthouse (p307)

➡ Johnson Hotel (p309)

Best Off the Beaten Track

➡ Chitkul (p294)

➡ Khir Ganga (p302)

➡ Mudh (p347)

➡ Chandratal (p344)

➡ Nako (p296)

When to Go
Manali

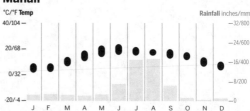

May–Jun & mid-Sep–Oct Outside the monsoon season; perfect for trekking and other activities.

Mid-Jul–mid-Sep In the monsoon season visit Lahaul and Spiti, which stay dry.

Nov–Apr Great for skiers, but snow blocks the high passes to Lahaul and Spiti.

History

Ancient trade routes dominate the history of Himachal Pradesh. Large parts of northern Himachal came under Tibetan control in the 10th century, and Buddhist culture still dominates the mountain deserts of Lahaul and Spiti. The more accessible areas in the south and west were ruled by a host of rajas, ranas and *thakurs* (noblemen), creating a patchwork of tiny states, with Kangra, Kullu and Chamba the most important. Sikh rajas conquered large areas in the early 19th century, but lost them with the Anglo-Sikh Wars of the 1840s, which brought most of Himachal under British control.

The British started creating little bits of England in the hills of Shimla, Dalhousie and Dharamsala. In 1864 Shimla became the British Raj's summer capital, and narrow-gauge railways were later pushed through to Shimla and the Kangra Valley. The areas under direct British rule were administered as part of the Punjab, while Chamba and the southern princedoms remained nominally independent, known as the Punjab hill states. Himachal Pradesh was formed from these princely states after Independence, liberating many villages from the feudal system. In 1966 the districts administered from Punjab – principally Kangra, Kullu, Lahaul and Spiti – were added, and full statehood was achieved in 1971. Initially neglected by central government, Himachal has been reinvented as the powerhouse of India, with huge hydroelectric plants providing power for half the country.

SOUTHERN HIMACHAL PRADESH

As soon as you cross the state line from Haryana the landscape starts to crinkle and fold in steep, forest-covered ridges – the foothills that herald the grand Himalayan ranges further north. The main travel destination in the south is Shimla, the former summer capital of British-ruled India. The official district website is http://hpshimla.gov.in.

Shimla

0177 / POP 170,000 / ELEV 2205M

Strung out along a 12km ridge, with steep forested hillsides falling away in all directions, the Himachal capital is a good appetite-whetter for the awe-inspiring mountain tracts of the state's interior. Shimla is one of India's most popular hill resorts, buzzing with a happy flow of Indian vacationers and full of echoes of its past role as the summer capital of British India. The long, winding main street, the Mall, runs east and west just below the spine of the

HIMACHAL PRADESH SHIMLA

TOP STATE FESTIVALS

Losar (Tibetan New Year; late Jan, Feb or early March) Tibetans across Himachal, including in McLeod Ganj and Spiti, celebrate their New Year with processions, music, dancing and *chaams* (ritual masked dances by monks).

Minjar Festival (Jul/Aug) A week of processions, music, dance and markets at Chamba.

Manimahesh Yatra (Aug/Sep) Shaivites trek for three days to bathe in Manimahesh Lake near Bharmour, one of Shiva's mythical abodes.

Phulech Festival (Sep/Oct) Villagers in Kalpa and throughout Kinnaur fill temple courtyards with flowers; oracles perform sacrifices and make predictions for the coming year.

Dussehra (Oct) Intense and spectacular week-long celebration of the defeat of the demon Ravana, at Kullu.

International Himalayan Festival (10-11 Dec) Celebrating the Dalai Lama's Nobel Peace Prize, this McLeod Ganj festival features cultural performances by groups from all around the Himalaya.

Himachal Pradesh Highlights

1 Travel the hair-raisingly spectacular passes, gorges and clifftop roads of the **Spiti–Kinnaur loop** (p344).

2 Trek the **Hamta Pass** (p317), **Pin-Parvati Pass** (p304), **Indrahar La** (p328) or a dozen other spectacular mountain crossings.

3 Immerse yourself in Tibetan culture or yoga, volunteer with refugees or just chill out in the mountains at **McLeod Ganj** (p320).

4 Ski, trek, climb, paraglide or raft from the backpacker playground of **Manali** (p308).

5 Turn back the centuries at the Buddhist monasteries of **Dhankar** (p348) and **Tabo** (p348) in remote Spiti.

6 Ride the toy train up to **Shimla** (p281), one of India's favourite hill stations.

7 Bliss out in the **Parvati Valley** (p299) and the strange mountain village of **Malana** (p301).

8 Visit **Kalpa** (p295) or **Chitkul** (p294), intriguing Kinnaur villages with awesome Himalayan views.

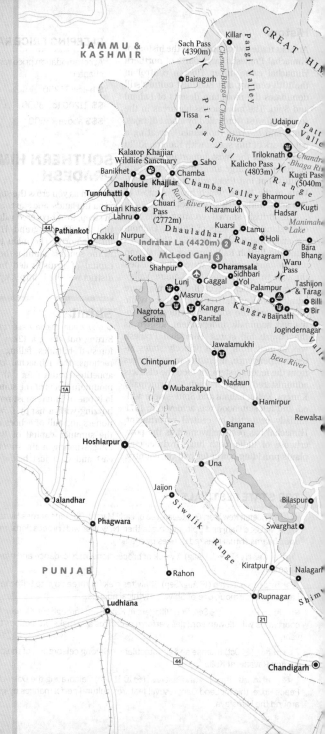

Shimla

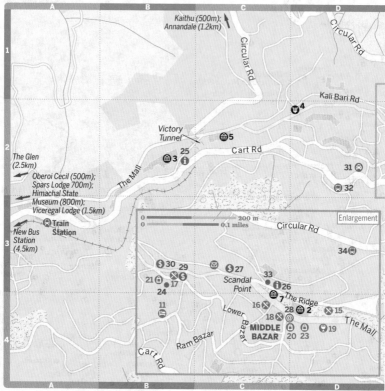

hill. South of it, the maze-like alleys of the bustling bazaar cascade steeply down to traffic-busy Cart Rd, which has the train station, Old Bus Station and taxi stands. Traffic is banned from the central part of town, so walking anywhere is pleasant – even when huffing and puffing uphill. A passenger lift provides a quick route between the eastern Mall and Cart Rd. Porters will carry your luggage uphill (about ₹100 from Cart Rd to the Mall) but many double as hotel touts.

> ### ⓘ USEFUL HIMACHAL WEBSITES
>
> **Himachal Pradesh Tourism Development Corporation** (www.hptdc.gov.in)
>
> **Himachal Tourism** (www.himachaltourism.gov.in)

The official centre of town is the junction called Scandal Point. From here, the flat open area known as the Ridge stretches east to Christ Church. A jagged line of distant snowy peaks is clearly visible for about half the year. From mid-July to mid-September Shimla is frequently wreathed in cloud, and in winter it often gets a carpeting of snow.

History

Until the British arrived, there was nothing at Shimla but a sleepy forest glade known as Shyamala (a local name for Kali – the Hindu destroyer-of-evil goddess). Then a Scottish civil servant named Charles Kennedy built a summer home here in 1822 and nothing was ever the same again. In 1864 Simla (its colonial-era name) became the official summer capital of the Raj, and from then until 1939 the entire government of India fled here for half of every year from the sweltering heat of the plains, bringing with them

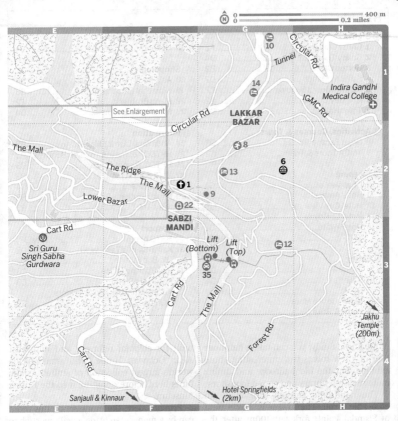

hundreds of muleloads of files, forms and other paraphernalia of government.

When the Kalka–Shimla railway was opened in 1906, Shimla's status as India's premier hill station was assured. The town became a centre not only of government but also of social frolics for the elite of the Raj. Maharajas as well as colonial grandees built mansions here, and the season was filled with grand balls at the Viceroy's lodge, picnics in the woods, amateur dramatics at the Gaiety Theatre and much flirtation and frivolity. Rudyard Kipling, who spent many years here, used Shimla as the setting for parts of *Kim* and his short-story collection *Plain Tales from the Hills*.

⊙ Sights & Activities

Gaiety Theatre   HISTORIC BUILDING
(📞 2650173; www.gaiety.in; the Mall; Indian/foreigner ₹10/25, camera ₹15/25; ⊙ tours every 45min 11am-12.30pm & 1.45-6.15pm Tue-Sun) This lovely Victorian theatre, opened in 1877 and now splendidly restored, has long been a focus of Shimla social life. Rudyard Kipling, Shashi Kapoor and various viceroys are among those who have trodden its Burmese teak boards. Today it hosts visiting theatre companies as well as 15 local dramatic societies. Mr R Gautam gives excellent guided tours, explaining its history as you appreciate the view from the viceroy's private box.

★ Viceregal Lodge   HISTORIC BUILDING
(tour Indian/foreigner ₹30/65, grounds only ₹10; ⊙ 10am-1pm & 2-5pm Tue-Sun, tours about every 45min) The official summer residence of the British viceroys was completed in 1888 and the Indian subcontinent was ruled from here for half of every year from then till WWII. Henry Irwin's grey-sandstone creation resembles a cross between Harry Potter's Hogwarts and a Scottish baronial castle. Today it houses the Indian Institute

Shimla

of Advanced Study: you can take a half-hour tour of a few rooms with interesting photo exhibits, but the old ballroom and dining hall are now a library and closed to visitors.

The handsome gardens still make an enjoyable stroll. The Lodge is 3.5km west of Scandal Point: fork left 100m after the Oberoi Cecil hotel, go 700m to the lodge gate, then 400m more to the lodge itself. Opposite the lodge gate is the glum **Himalayan Bird Park** (admission ₹15; ◷10am-5pm Wed-Mon), where you can see the iridescent monal pheasant, Himachal's state bird.

Jakhu Temple   HINDU TEMPLE

Shimla's most famous temple, a steep 30-minute hike up from the east end of the Ridge, is dedicated to the monkey god Hanuman, so it's quite appropriate that hundreds of rhesus macaques loiter around, harassing devotees for *prasad* (temple-blessed food offerings). Nearby a 33m-high pink statue of Hanuman looms above the treetops and is visible from most of Shimla.

The hilltop is awash in devotional music and the temple houses a small shrine surrounded by funky relief murals of Hanuman performing feats from the Ramayana.

On the way up to the temple, have a peep through the gates of **Rothney Castle**,

built for colonial reformer and naturalist Allan Octavian Hume, who amassed the world's largest collection of stuffed Asiatic birds here before donating it to the British Museum.

Primate alert: the monkeys on this route can be a menace, so bring a walking stick to discourage them.

Himachal State Museum   MUSEUM

(Indian/foreigner ₹20/50, camera ₹50/100; ◷10am-5pm Tue-Sun) About 2.5km west of Scandal Point, up near the telecommunications mast, the state museum occupies an 1860s mansion and houses an impressive collection of Himachali, Rajasthani and Punjabi miniatures, as well as colourful traditional costumes and jewellery, delicate stone and wood carvings, and interesting photos of Himachal temples.

Christ Church   CHURCH

(✆2652953; the Ridge; ◷10.30am-1pm & 2.15-5.30pm, services in English 9am Sun) This very English church, opened in 1846, dominates the Ridge and is the oldest surviving church in northern India. Its creamy-lemon paint job is uninspiring but it contains some moving Raj-era memorials and typical Victorian stained glass.

Kali Bari Mandir HINDU TEMPLE

The Bengali-hut-style Kali Bari Mandir, on the hillside above the Mall, 500m west of Scandal Point, enshrines an image of Kali as Shyamala. There are good views over Shimla.

Walking WALKING

Apart from the 'Heritage Walk' from Scandal Point to the Viceregal Lodge and walks to and around Jakhu Temple, there are several routes around Shimla's periphery using minor roads and forest paths. The Scandal Point tourist office (p289) can help with routes and the current condition of tracks.

A down-and-up circuit of around 9km leads down through the suburb/village of Kaithu to the green meadow of Annandale, once the site of colonial polo games and now home to a golf course and the Himachal chief minister's helipad. It then goes up a road through lovely cedar woods and down trails to The Glen, a forested valley that was once a playground of British colonialists, then back up to the Mall, about 2km west of Scandal Point.

The road northwest from the Viceregal Lodge gate leads 2km to Summer Hill village (on the Shimla–Kalka railway and site of Himachal Pradesh University). The road southwest from the lodge gate leads in about 2km, via Boileauganj village, to the interesting Kamna Devi Temple at Prospect Hill, with good views.

Shimla Walks WALKING

(☑9817141099, 2841858; www.shimlawalks.com) A professional operation run by local writer Sumit Vashisht, Shimla Walks offers excellent guided walks on and off the beaten track. Day or half-day trips (₹2000 to ₹3500 for up to four people) provide rare insights along the popular route to the Viceregal Lodge, or take you to writers' and artists' houses or Shimla's hidden Raj-era cemeteries. Also on offer are trips up the area's highest peak, Shali Tibba (2872m), hiking trips among remote mountain villages in the Inner Seraj region, and tours combining walking with stays in the homes of former local royal families.

Great Escape Routes OUTDOOR ADVENTURE

(☑9418012500, 6533037; www.greatescaperoutes. com; 6 Andi Bhavan; ⊙10am-9pm; ☎) Specialises in trekking and adventure tours around the state, including some local hikes overnighting in homestays, and can put you in touch with local mountain-bike guides. Ask for Nitin or Raman.

YMCA Tours & Treks OUTDOOR ADVENTURE

(Captivate Adventure Travels; ☑9857102657; www. himalayansites.com; YMCA, The Ridge; ⊙9am-6pm) The affable Anil Kumar runs day trips around Shimla and arranges reasonably priced treks, jeep safaris and mountain biking throughout Himachal and beyond. He can help travellers get together to cut costs.

🛏 Sleeping

You're paying for the location when staying in Shimla and hotels don't generally offer great value by Himachal standards, especially during the peak seasons (late April to June, Christmas/New Year and major holidays). But outside peak seasons, discounts of up to 40% are available at many places.

YMCA HOSTEL $

(☑2650021; ymcashimla@yahoo.co.in; the Ridge; s/d without bathroom incl breakfast ₹600/800) Up steps beside the Ritz Cineplex, the bright-red YMCA takes all comers, regardless of age, gender or religion. Rooms are neat and pleasant, the shared bathrooms are immaculate, and there's a nice sunset terrace. The atmosphere can be dreary in slow periods, but it's a reliable, clean, budget choice.

THE MALL

Traffic-free for a good part of its winding 7km length, the Mall is the heartbeat of Shimla life, strung with hotels, shops, and colonial-era buildings; both decaying and refurbished, and busy with people everywhere. It runs up from Chotta Shimla, southeast of the centre, to Scandal Point, then west along to the Viceregal Lodge. The Town Hall, beside Scandal Point, dates from 1910 and is oddly reminiscent of the mansion in Hammer Horror films.

West of Scandal Point, just above the Mall, a pretty quasi-Tudor folly houses the post office (1883). A further 700m west the turreted Railway Board Building (1897), built with fire-resistant cast iron and steel, now houses government and police offices. Just past here is the grand neo-Gothic Gorton Castle (1904), formerly the colonial government secretariat and now Himachal's State Accountant-General's Office.

Hotel City View
HOTEL **$**

(☑ 2811666; jagdishthakur80@gmail.com; US Club Rd; r ₹700-1500) This friendly place has a variety of reasonably well-kept rooms, the best of which are at the front and have bright views. The top floor has a small shared terrace and there are discounts for singles, making this solid value for Shimla.

★ Spars Lodge
GUESTHOUSE **$$**

(☑ 2657908; www.sparslodge.com; Museum Rd; s/d ₹990/1410, ste ₹2000-2590; ☎) Though it's 2km west of Scandal Point, on the road up to the State Museum, Spars is worth the trip for its inviting, homey feel, welcoming owners, bright, clean, airy rooms, and lovely sunny dining-cum-sitting area upstairs. The restaurant (mains ₹175 to ₹400) serves great food, including local trout and all-day English breakfasts, and has wi-fi. Room rates are fixed throughout the year.

Hotel Le Royale
HOTEL **$$**

(☑ 2651002; hotel-le-royale-shimla.hotelsgds.com; Jakhu Rd; r ₹2590-4520; ☎) The front rooms at this hotel on the road to Jakhu Temple, a steep 500m up from the Ridge, are large, bright and comfy and enjoy great views. The cheaper 'deluxe' quarters face to the rear and are smaller but still adequately comfortable. It's friendly, efficiently run and the in-house Green Leaf restaurant is handy. Wi-fi reaches the lobby, the two rooms beside it, and the restaurant.

Hotel White
HOTEL **$$**

(☑ 2656136; www.hotelwhitesimla.com; Lakkar Bazar; d ₹1760-2350) Northeast of the Ridge, through a bustling bazaar, the White is well run and rates are fixed all year. Rooms are clean and well kept and the better ones have terraces or balconies. The huge suites are perfect for families, and there are discounts for singles. Light sleepers might be disturbed by traffic noise from Circular Rd.

Hotel Amber
HOTEL **$$**

(☑ 2654994; hotelambershimla@gmail.com; Ram Bazar; s ₹780-1350, d ₹980-1680) In the thick of the bazaar, Amber provides cosy, carpeted (if smallish) rooms, with good, clean bathrooms, at moderate prices. It overlooks the Ram Mandir, a couple of minutes' walk up from the Old Bus Station, and has a decent, inexpensive little restaurant.

★ Oberoi Cecil
HOTEL **$$$**

(☑ 2804848; www.oberoicecil.com; the Mall, Chaura Maidan; s/d/ste incl breakfast from ₹16,440/17,620/31,710; ✻@☎✉) This grand high-rise, 2km west of Scandal Point, is Shimla's glitziest hotel. Discreet colonial-era charm outside gives way to modern, wood-clad luxury within. Rooms are luxurious, with tastefully trad furnishings, and the hotel has a lovely indoor pool and fine restaurant. Discounts are available for bookings 21 days or more in advance.

The Cecil is where Mohan Singh Oberoi got his first hotel job, as a clerk, in 1922. He went on to found the luxury hotel chain that bears his name, buying the Cecil along the way in 1944. It was radically modernised in the 1990s.

Hotel Springfields
HERITAGE HOTEL **$$$**

(☑ 2621297; www.hotelspringfields.com; opposite Tibetan School, Chotta Shimla; r/ste ₹4670/7640; ☎) The erstwhile summer retreat of the Raja of Sheikhupura, now run by his charming descendants, Springfields features neatly trimmed lawns and bright, spacious rooms with appealing heritage-style furnishings, parquet floors, tea- and coffee makers and large, marble-floored bathrooms. Best of all is the huge family suite with balcony, upstairs. It's a 30-minute walk or ₹200 taxi ride from Shimla centre.

Chapslee
HERITAGE HOTEL **$$$**

(☑ 2658663; www.chapslee.com; r half-board ₹17,500-26,775; ☎) For the full Raj treatment, you can't beat the outrageously ostentatious former home of Raja Charanjit Singh of Kapurthala. This exclusive hilltop retreat is crammed with chandeliers, tapestries, Persian carpets, Mughal ceramics and baroque furniture. There are just five sumptuous bedrooms, all with completely original fittings, plus a library, card room, sun lounge, tennis court and, of course, a croquet lawn.

Chapslee is perched atop Elysium Hill, on the northern outskirts of Shimla, within walking distance of the Ridge and Mall.

Marina
HOTEL **$$$**

(☑ 6629999; www.marinashimla.com; the Mall; r ₹9280-11,630; ✻☎) An adventurous departure from Shimla's touristic obsession with the past, the Marina provides immaculate contemporary-style rooms in blue and purple tones with flock wallpaper and black leather sofas. Service is polished and all rooms have balconies, views and tea- and coffee-makers. The hotel is also equipped with a good multicuisine restaurant, a spa, gym, and DJ music in the lounge-bar till 10.30pm.

✖ Eating & Drinking

As well as the formal restaurants, there are dozens of Indian snack places in the bazaar area serving samosas, potato cakes, *channa bhatura* (spiced chickpeas with a puffed, light, deep-fried bread) and other titbits.

Indian Coffee House   CAFE $
(the Mall; dishes ₹20-60; ⊗8am-9pm) This Shimla institution is like an old boys' club with its ageing leather seats, uniformed waiters and blackboard menu. Packed with chattering locals for much of the day, it's the most atmospheric place in town for breakfast, cheap dosas and coffee (don't even ask for tea!).

Wake & Bake   MULTICUISINE $$
(34/1 the Mall; dishes ₹100-300; ⊗9.30am-10.30pm; 🐕) This upstairs cafe is about the hippest eatery in Shimla (which isn't saying too much), serving up organic South Indian coffee, pizza by the slice, hummus, toasties and excellent crêpes. Wi-fi is ₹60 per hour.

Ashiana   INDIAN $$
(the Ridge; mains ₹100-250; ⊗9am-11pm) In a fanciful circular building, Ashiana is an almost-elegant restaurant and good people-watching spot, with a delightful sunny terrace. As well as tasty Indian dishes there are Chinese and a few Thai favourites. In Ashiana's basement, Goofa (the Ridge; dishes Rs80-230; ⊗9am-9.30pm) serves most of the same dishes for about ₹20 less.

Baljee's   INDIAN $$
(26 the Mall; mains ₹130-240; ⊗9am-10.30pm) Clean, cosy and air-conditioned, with bow-tied waiters, Baljee's gets packed with Indian families, many of whom come for the snacks and South Indian specialities. Breakfasts of omelettes, toast and dosas are good, too.

Cecil Restaurant   MULTICUISINE $$$
(☑2804848; Oberoi Cecil, the Mall, Chaura Maidan; mains ₹940-1600; ⊗dinner 7.30-10.30pm) For a formal night out, look no further than the colonial-era elegance of the Cecil Restaurant at the Oberoi. The menu is strong on Indian and Thai curries and there are Continental options as well. Book ahead.

Himani's   BAR
(the Mall; beer from ₹110; ⊗6am-10pm) The neon and marble decor is straight out of the 1980s, but Himani's is a decent place for a casual drink or meals like chicken tikka (mains ₹125 to ₹215) . The inside can be smoky and male-dominated, but the top-floor terrace overlooking the Mall is perfect on a sunny afternoon.

🛍 Shopping

Local holidaymakers head to the fashionable shops along the Mall for Himachali and Kashmiri shawls and other apparel. For a slice of more traditional Indian commerce, wander the labyrinthine bazaar area sprawling below the Mall. You can buy anything here from peacock feathers and henna kits to bangles and bicycles. It's fascinating to explore the different zones devoted to fruit and veg (Sabzi Mandi), spices, fabrics and more.

Himachal Emporium   HANDICRAFTS
(☑2011234; www.himcrafts.com; the Mall; ⊗10am-1pm & 2.30-7.30pm Mon-Sat) Kullu and Kinnauri shawls, thick Lahauli wool socks and other appealing Himachal crafts are sold at reasonable prices at this state-government crafts enterprise.

Asia Book House   BOOKS
(the Mall; ⊗10am-8.30pm Mon-Sat, 10am-1pm Sun) Novels, guides and other books on India.

Minerva Book House   BOOKS
(☑2803078; the Mall; ⊗10.30am-1.30pm & 2.30-8pm Mon-Sat, noon-8pm Sun) Good for novels and books on Himachal Pradesh.

Maria Brothers   BOOKS
(78 the Mall; ⊗10.30am-1pm & 3.30-7.30pm Mon-Sat) One of India's great antiquarian booksellers: the dusty shelves are packed with Himalayan travelogues, maps and engravings, at prices aimed firmly at collectors.

ℹ Information

Numerous ATMs are dotted around Scandal Point and the Mall. Laws exist banning plastic bags, littering, spitting and spitting in public places; police can hit offenders with a ₹200 fine.

HPTDC Tourist Office (Himachal Pradesh Tourist Development Corporation, Himachal Tourism; ☑2652561; www.hptdc.gov.in; Scandal Point; ⊗9am-8pm, to 7pm mid-Jul–mid-Sep & Dec-Mar) Very helpful for local information and advice; also books HPTDC buses, hotels and tours.

Indira Gandhi Medical College (☑2803073; IGMC Rd) Large public hospital with 24-hour outpatient department.

Photo Palace (the Mall; internet per hour ₹40; ⊗10am-8pm) Decent internet facilities in the town centre.

Post Office (Scandal Point; ⊗9.30am-5.30pm) There are several suboffices along the Mall.

Punjab National Bank (the Mall; ⊙10am-2pm & 3-4pm Mon-Fri, 10am-1pm Sat) Changes cash for major currencies, and American Express travellers cheques.

ⓘ Getting There & Away

AIR

At the time of research there were no flights to Jubbarhatti airport, 23km west of Shimla. Seasonal services from Delhi may resume at some point. The nearest other airport is at Chandigarh, a four-hour drive from Shimla.

BUS

The Himachal Road Transport Corporation (HRTC) runs five comfortable Volvo AC buses to Delhi (₹842, 10 hours) each day, as well as 12 cheaper deluxe and ordinary services (₹384 to ₹592). Other HRTC AC buses head to Manali (₹550, nine hours) at 9.30am and Dharamsala (₹926, nine hours) at 5.30pm. All HRTC buses leave from the **New Bus Station**, a 5km trip west from the town centre: make reservations at the **HRTC booth** (⊙11am-2pm & 3-6.30pm) at Scandal Point.

The HPTDC runs a Volvo AC bus to Delhi (₹900, 10 hours) at 8.30pm, and a non-AC deluxe bus to Manali (₹550, nine hours) at 8.30am, both starting from near the tourist information booth on Cart Rd west of Victory Tunnel: get tickets at the HPTDC Tourist Office (p289).

TAXI

The **Kalka-Shimla Taxi Union** (☏2658225) has its stand near the Old Bus Station, while **Vishal Himachal Taxi Operators Union** (☏2805164) operates from the bottom of the passenger lift. Most hotels and travel agencies can organise car transfers to other towns, or a car and driver for an extended tour. A cab for up to four people

to Manali costs around ₹5000, to Chandigarh ₹2500 and to Delhi around ₹6000. You pay around ₹500 more for AC. Vishal charges ₹1550 for day trips up to 80km, plus ₹12 for each extra kilometre.

TRAIN

One of the little joys of Shimla is getting to or from it by the narrow-gauge toy train from Kalka, just north of Chandigarh, along the Kalka–Shimla Railway, which has been operating since 1906 and is one of the World Heritage–listed Mountain Railways of India. Although the steam trains are long gone, it's a scenic five-to-six-hour trip, with 102 tunnels and 988 bridges on its winding 96km route. Shimla station is 1.5km west of Scandal Point on Cart Rd – a 20-to-30-minute uphill walk to town.

Trains leave Kalka for Shimla at 4am, 5.10am, 5.30am, 6am and 12.10pm, and start the return trip at 10.35am, 2.25pm, 4.25pm, 5.40pm and 6.15pm. The most comfortable option is the Shivalik Express (train 52451 from Kalka at 5.30am, train 52452 from Shimla at 5.40pm) with AC chair cars only, costing ₹415/500 uphill/downhill including food. All other trains have 2nd-class coaches (₹25 unreserved, ₹40 to ₹65 reserved) and fairly spartan 1st-class coaches (₹255 to ₹315).

The Himalayan Queen service runs from/to Delhi Sarai Rohilla, with comfortable connection times at Kalka and fares of ₹435/120 (chair car/2nd class) for the Delhi–Kalka (or vice-versa) leg.

A quicker alternative (4¼ hours) for the Delhi–Kalka (or vice-versa) leg is the Kalka Shatabdi: train 12011 departs New Delhi station for Kalka (chair car ₹635) at 7.40am and train 12012 leaves Kalka for New Delhi (₹720) at 5.45pm.

There's a **rail booking office** (⊙9am-1pm & 2-4pm Mon-Sat) on the Ridge.

BUSES FROM SHIMLA NEW BUS STATION

DESTINATION	FARE (₹)	DURATION (HR)	FREQUENCY
Chandigarh	163-330	4	every 15min
Dehra Dun	310-480	9	3 daily
Delhi	384-842	10	17 daily
Dharamsala	358-926	10	7 daily
Kalpa	370	11	6.15am
Kullu	325-460	8-9	5 daily
Manali	357-550	9-10	4 daily
Mandi	215-300	6	11 daily
Rekong Peo	375-460	10	8 buses, 4am to 10.50am
Sangla	350	10	6.30am
Sarahan	260	7	9.20am & 9.30am

TIMINGS FOR HIMALAYAN QUEEN EXPRESS

DEPART	ARRIVE/DEPART KALKA	ARRIVE	TRAIN NOS
Delhi Sarai Rohilla 5.35am	11.10am/12.10pm	Shimla 5.20pm	14095 & 52455
Shimla 10.35am	4.10pm/4.50pm	Delhi Sarai Rohilla 10.40pm	52456 & 14096

❶ Getting Around

The only way to get around central Shimla is on foot. Taxis are banned from the Ridge and much of the Mall. Fortunately a two-part **lift** (per person ₹10; ⊙ 8am-10pm, to 9pm Dec-Mar & mid-Jul–mid-Sep) connects Cart Rd with the Mall about 600m east of Scandal Point. Taxis from the train station/New Bus Station to the bottom of the lift cost ₹150/250. Green local buses (₹7) run every few minutes between the New Bus Station and the Old Bus Station on Cart Rd.

Around Shimla

Several villages and small towns outside Shimla attract crowds of day-trippers: the HPTDC Tourist Office (p289) organises bus tours (₹270 to ₹310) to places including Naldehra, Narkanda and Chail, if you have time on your hands. **Naldehra**, 25km northeast of Shimla, is famous chiefly for **Naldehra Golf Club** (☑ 0177-2747656; http://naldehragolfclub. in; green fees Indian/foreigner ₹393/562, club hire ₹281; ⊙ 7am-7pm Apr-Sep, 8am-5pm Oct-Mar), established in 1905 by British viceroy Lord Curzon. Set among tall cedars, it's a challenging course with the added quirk that many holes share the same fairway, simply criss-crossing it at different angles. Hire a caddy (₹150 per nine holes) or you won't know where you're going. You can have a drink or snack in the clubhouse whether you're playing or not.

Kalka-Shimla Taxi Union (p290) charges ₹1400 for a tour to Naldehra and nearby Mashobra. Five daily buses to Naldehra (₹33, one hour, 6.30am to 12.45pm) leave from Shimla's small **Rivoli bus stand** (Circular Rd).

Châlets Naldehra   RESORT **$$$**
(☑ 0177-2747715; www.chaletsnaldehra.com; apt/cottage for 2 ₹9670/12,890, chalet for 4 ₹18,270; ⍰⍰) Half a kilometre from Naldehra golf club, Châlets offers a selection of spacious, bright, attractive accommodation in pine buildings on beautifully landscaped terraces. There's an inviting two-part heated indoor pool, plus an elevated **revolving restaurant** (mains ₹500-650; ⊙ 12.30-10.30pm) as well as the main **multicuisine restaurant** (mains ₹450-530).

Wildflower Hall   HERITAGE HOTEL **$$$**
(☑ 0177-2648585, restaurant 9816802124; www. oberoihotels.com; s/d from ₹28,770/30,530; ✳⍰⍰) The most regal lodgings in Himachal Pradesh, Wildflower Hall looms above the hamlet of Chharabra, 14km east of Shimla, exuding wealth from its teak-panelled lobby to its chandelier-lit indoor pool and its opulent colonial-style rooms with marble bathrooms. The **restaurant** (mains ₹1100-2650; ⊙ 12-30-3pm & 7-10.30pm), with a lovely panoramic terrace, serves a daily-changing menu of Indian, Continental and Asian fare and is open to non-guests by reservation.

KINNAUR

The district of Kinnaur, stretching up to the Tibetan border in southeastern Himachal, is blessed with magnificent mountain and valley scenery and a cultural and ethnic mix that changes gradually from Aryan Hindu to Tibetan Buddhist as you progress eastward. Hwy 05 (formerly Hwy 22 and still so marked in places) threads a spectacular route up the Sutlej valley, following, for long sections, the course of the historic Hindustan–Tibet Road, a track constructed by the British in the 19th century in the hope of providing access to Tibet.

This is a land of mountain villages with slate-roofed temples, vast apple orchards, plunging gorges between towering snow-capped peaks, and hair-raising roads. Beyond it lies Spiti, the two combining into a loop from Shimla to Manali or Keylong in an unending sequence of breathtaking scenery. Check road conditions beforehand, as monsoon landslides, floods in the Sutlej valley or heavy winter snows can block the roads for days or even weeks. To travel between Rekong Peo in Kinnaur and Sumdo in Spiti, foreigners need an inner line permit, easily obtained in Rekong Peo.

The Kinnauris are proud but friendly people who mainly survive from farming and apple growing. You can recognise them all over India by their green felt *basheri* hats. To truly appreciate their land, you need to leave the main road, much of which is scarred by the multiple dam projects that

PABBAR VALLEY

This mellow, little-visited valley runs northeast from tiny **Hatkoti**, set in rolling fields about 105km east of Shimla. Hatkoti's 8th-century Kinnauri-style **Hatkeshwari Mata Temple**, dedicated to Durga as Mahishasurmardini (slayer of the buffalo demon Mahishasur), and the neighbouring Shiva temple, are well worth a trip, especially when Shaivite pilgrims convene during the Chaitra Navratra and Asvin Navratra festivals in April and October. Pilgrims' quarters are available at the temple or you can stay in large rooms at the HPTDC's **Hotel Chanshal** (☑01781-240661; www.hptdc.gov.in; s ₹1060-1410, d ₹1410-1880; ❀), 14km up the valley in Rohru. Beyond Rohru, the scenic valley runs up between 4000m-plus peaks to meet the range forming the west side of Kinnaur's Sangla Valley; there is some excellent hiking. En route from Shimla, 12km before Hatkoti, **Jubbal** is home to a fanciful 1930 palace built in a mix of Chinese, Indian and European styles for the Rana of Jubbal.

are turning the powerful Sutlej into a massive generator.

Lower Kinnaur gets monsoon rains in July and August, but east of Rekong Peo the landscape quickly becomes much more arid as you enter the rain shadow of the Great Himalaya Range. During the peak tourist seasons here – May, June and October – it's worth booking ahead for rooms in popular spots like Sarahan, the Sangla Valley and Kalpa.

A good source of information on Kinnaur, is the local government website www.hpkinnaur.gov.in.

Rampur

☑ 01782 / POP 5700 / ELEV 1005M

The gateway to Kinnaur, this bustling bazaar town was the winter capital of the Bushahr rajas who ruled Kinnaur. Today, Rampur is mainly a place to change buses, but if you have time check out the delightful, terraced and turreted **Padam Palace**, built for the Maharaja of Bushahr in the early 20th century; only the garden is open to visitors. It's just beside the Old Bus Stand in the centre. The **Lavi Fair**, a huge commercial and cultural get-together in the second week of November, attracts traders and pilgrims from all over northwest India.

If you need to stay, **Hotel Satluj View** (☑233924; r ₹550-2350; ❀ 🛜), just past the temple opposite the Old Bus Stand and down some steps, has rooms ranging from dingy but clean to large and air-conditioned, with big windows and balconies overlooking the rushing Sutlej River. Its **restaurant** (mains ₹125-295; ⏱7am-10.30pm) is the best place to eat in the town centre.

Rampur's bus station is 2km east of the centre but many people jump on through buses at the chaotic Old Bus Stand in the centre. From the bus station there are services to Rekong Peo (₹165, five hours) at least hourly till 4.30pm, to Shimla (₹200, five hours) every half-hour till 9.30pm, to Sarahan (₹65, two hours) about every 20 minutes till 6.15pm, and to Sangla (₹170, five hours) at 4.30am and 12.30pm.

Sarahan

☑ 01782 / POP 1700 / ELEV 1920M

The former summer capital of the Bushahr kingdom, Sarahan is dominated by the fabulous **Bhimakali Temple** (⏱7.30am-7pm), built in the traditional Kinnauri manner from layers of stone and timber to absorb the force of earthquakes. There are two towers here, one recently rebuilt after the 12th-century original collapsed, and one from the 1920s (on the left) containing a highly revered shrine to Bhimakali (the local version of Kali) beneath a beautiful silver-filigree canopy on its top floor. The curved, peaked roofs suggest the Tibetan influence on Kinnauri architecture, which becomes more marked as you move up the valley.

For entry to the innermost courtyard with the towers, male visitors must wear a cap (available on the spot) and cameras and leather items must be left in lockers. To the right of the two towers is the squat **Lankra Vir Temple**, where human sacrifices were carried out right up to the 18th century.

🛏 Sleeping & Eating

Most lodgings will provide meals, or you can choose from a handful of *dhabas* (small eateries serving snacks and simple local meals) in the bazaar area below the temple.

Temple Guesthouse GUESTHOUSE $
(☑ 274248; dm ₹70, r ₹350-550) Rooms here, within the ancient temple precinct itself, are plain and simple but, unlike most temple accommodation, far from gloomy. The upper-storey rooms in particular are bright, spacious and airy, with hot water.

Hotel Sagarika HOTEL $$
(☑ 9805694216; www.deblokgroupofhotels.in; r ₹1200-1800) Rooms here are clean, carpeted and well maintained, and the welcome is friendly. It has great views of the temple from the upper front rooms, and vistas of snow-capped mountains from the back. Discounts of up to 50% are available outside peak seasons.

Hotel Srikhand MULTICUISINE $$
(☑ 274234; www.hptdc.gov.in; mains ₹110-290; ⊙ 7.30am-9.30pm) The classiest place for a civilised dinner, or to savour a beer (they serve full-bodied Zingaro) while enjoying panoramic views over the valley. **Rooms** (s ₹1410-2380, d ₹1880-3170) are carpeted and have mountain views, and in most cases balconies, but are nothing fancy.

ℹ️ Information

There's a **State Bank ATM** (Main Bazar) opposite the Civil Hospital.

ℹ️ Getting There & Away

There are three daily buses to Shimla (₹260, seven hours) but you can also get one of the frequent services to Rampur (₹65, two hours) and change there. To head on eastward into Kinnaur, take any bus as far as Jeori (₹30, 45 minutes), on the highway below Sarahan, and catch an eastbound bus there. The last bus from Jeori up to Sarahan leaves around 7pm. Taxis are about ₹350.

Sangla Valley

☑ 01786
The Sangla (aka Baspa) Valley is a deeply carved cleft between burly mountain slopes, where evergreen forests rise to alpine meadows crowned by snowy summits. Villages here feature houses and temples built in traditional Kinnauri timber-and-stone-style. The hair-raising road to the valley leaves Hwy 05 at Karcham, passing the gushing outflow pipes from a big hydroelectric plant.

Sangla

POP 2250 / ELEV 2680M
The largest settlement in the valley, Sangla is a place where you might find yourself staying overnight if you can't find onward transport. It has a couple of cybercafes and a State Bank ATM on the main street. Clinging to a rocky spur 2km north (about 30 minutes' walk), **Kamru** village was the original capital of the Bushahr kingdom and its impressive tower-style **Kamru Fort** contains an important shrine to the goddess Kamakhya Devi (shoes and leather items must be removed, heads covered and a waist sash worn).

One of the most appealing places to stay is **Sangla Resort Guesthouse** (☑ 242401; dm ₹330, d ₹900-1000; ⊙ closed Dec-Mar), 200m down the road from the bridge below the bus stand, then 150m up a track to the right. The nine double rooms and one four-bed dorm are spotless, and there are nice views over the surrounding orchards. Breakfast is available and there are discounts outside May, June and October. Sangla centre has several near-identical 'Tibetan restaurants' centred on the **Tibetan Cafetaria** (dishes ₹50-60; ⊙ 8am-8pm).

ℹ️ Getting There & Away

Buses run to Rampur (₹170, five hours) at 6.30am, 11.30am, 12.30pm and 5.30pm, to Rekong Peo (₹65, 2½ hours) at 7am, 8am, 9am and 2.45pm, and up the valley to Chitkul (₹35, one hour) at 8am, 11.30am, 4.30pm and 5.30pm. There's a 7am bus to Shimla (₹350, 11 hours). Taxis ask ₹1500 to Chitkul and ₹800 to Karcham.

Sangla to Chitkul

The valley's best accommodation is upstream from Sangla. There are some lovely day and half-day walks from these places – in the valley or up to glaciers or mountain meadows – and you can day-trip up to Chitkul.

Rupin River View Hotel HOTEL $$
(☑ 9816686789; www.hotelinsangla.com; r ₹1000-2400; ⊙ closed Dec-Feb) Lovely river and mountain views from clean, medium-sized rooms with balconies, plus a bright Indian restaurant, are the successful recipe at this friendly, good-value hotel in Rakchham village, 13km up the valley from Sangla.

Banjara Camps TENT RESORT $$$
(☑ 9816881936; www.banjaracamps.com; full-board s ₹6300-12,075, d ₹7350-13,125; ⊙ closed Nov–mid-Mar) Banjara's comfortable, large tents, with beds, furniture and proper bathrooms, are spaced around a flower-strewn apple orchard on a beautiful river bend 6km up the valley from Sangla. There are also two riverbank cottages and 14 rooms in a handsome stone building called the Retreat. It's excellent accommodation, with good food, in a near-idyllic setting.

Pretty Batseri village, across the river, has won awards for cleanliness. Its Badrinarayan Temple burnt down in 1998, but has been rebuilt in full traditional style, even down to the band of erotic carvings on its outside wall.

Chitkul
POP 600 / ELEV 3450M
Chitkul, 25km from Sangla, is easily the most scenic settlement in the valley and sees a steady flow of international and domestic tourists.

◉ Sights & Activities
A good number of traditional Kinnauri-style wooden houses topped with slate roofs survive despite the encroachment of concrete and tin. The Mohatmin Mandir temple in the middle of the village, dedicated to the local god Mathi, has some excellent carving in wood and stone.

Walks & Treks
A short walk up the hillside above the village opens up some great views, and even better is the 3km track up the beautiful valley to the Indo-Tibet Border Post at Nagasti. Civilians are not allowed past the border post even though Tibet is still about 40km away. For longer day walks you can head up the Baspa's side valleys. Chitkul is also where the three-day trekking trail circumambulating Kinner Kailash descends into the Sangla Valley, and trekking routes to Uttarakhand's Garhwal region head over passes on the south side of the valley (it's eight to 10 days to Harsil near Gangotri).

🛏 Sleeping & Eating
The best of the guesthouses is Kinner Heights (☑ 9805628801; r ₹550-850; ⊙ closed Jan-Mar), with good clean rooms. Owner Baabe makes good meals and can give tips on walks and arrange guides and porters

for treks. Other decent options, also at the bottom of the village, include the simple Thakur Guest House (☑ 8988209604; r ₹300-600), and the more upmarket Shahensha Resort (☑ 9805649505; www.geetanjaligroupofhotels.com; r ₹1100-2200; ⊙ closed Nov-Mar), with multicuisine food (mains ₹80 to ₹200).

ⓘ Getting There & Away
Buses leave Chitkul for Rekong Peo (₹104, four hours) at 6am and 1.30pm, and for Shimla (₹375, 12 hours) at 3.30pm, all going through Sangla.

Rekong Peo
☑ 01786 / POP 2400 / ELEV 2290M
Rekong Peo is the main administrative and commercial centre for Kinnaur and a transport hub; the main reason for travellers to visit is as a stepping stone to the pretty village of Kalpa, or to obtain an inner line permit for onward travel to upper Kinnaur and Spiti. Known locally as 'Peo', the town spreads along a looping road about 10km above Hwy 05. Most hotels, and an SBI ATM, are in the main bazaar below the bus stand.

🛏 Sleeping & Eating
Ridang Hotel HOTEL $
(☑ 8627968336; d ₹400-1000) The best of a grotty bunch of hotels lining the main bazaar, Ridang has a range of acceptable rooms and a reasonable ground-floor restaurant.

Little Chef's Restaurant MULTICUISINE $$
(Main Bazaar; mains ₹100-200; ⊙ 8am-10pm) The sunny rooftop here is the nicest place to eat, with a good range of breakfasts, thalis, snacks and Indian dishes, including Kinnauri-style *rajma* (spiced kidney beans).

ⓘ Information
The government Tourist Information Centre (☑ 222897; ⊙ 10am-1.30pm & 2-5pm Mon-Sat, closed 2nd Sat of month) below the bazaar has a rail reservation office. Several agencies in the same building are good for arranging inner line permits. Monk Travels (☑ 9805530056; www.themonktravels.com; internet per hr ₹60) will obtain your permit for ₹350 within about an hour if you bring your passport between 10am and 3pm (best in the morning), except on Sundays and the second Saturday of each month, when the permit-issuing office is closed. The agency helps solo travellers hook up with others for paperwork purposes only, since the powers-

that-be prefer groups of two or more. All travellers need to come in person to be photographed. The permits are valid for 14 days.

ⓘ Getting There & Away

The bus stand is 2km uphill from the main bazaar by road, or 500m by the steps starting next to the police compound at the top of ITBP Rd.

Buses run roughly hourly until 6.30pm for Shimla (₹375, 10 hours), with deluxe services (₹460) at 5.30am and 1.30pm. For Sarahan, change at Jeori (₹140, four hours). Buses to Sangla (₹65, 2½ hours) and Chitkul (₹104, four hours) leave at 9.30am and noon, and there's a 4pm bus just to Sangla.

For Spiti, there's a 7am bus to Kaza (₹335, 11 hours) via Nako (₹165, five hours) and Tabo (₹263, eight hours). A second bus heads to Nako at 11.30am.

Taxis charge ₹3500 to Chitkul, ₹5500 or ₹6000 to Shimla, and ₹7000 to Kaza.

Kalpa

ⓙ 01786 / POP 1250 / ELEV 2960M

Reached by a winding 7km road up through pine woods and apple orchards from Rekong Peo, Kalpa is a little gem of a village. Majestic views of the Kinner Kailash massif grab your eyeballs and don't let go. There are several guesthouses in Chini, the main part of the village, plus a number of modern hotels on Roghi Rd, a 500m walk or longer drive above the centre. For an ambitious full-day hike, ask locals about the trail up to the meadows and ponds of Chakkha, starting from Hotel Kinner Kailash on Roghi Rd.

Kalpa's central temple group encompasses the colourful Buddhist Hu-Bu-Lan-Khar Gompa (Samdub Choeling), the ornately carved Hindu Narayan-Nagini temple complex just below it, and a recently rebuilt, tower-style Durga temple just above it. In September/October, villagers pile wildflowers in the stone courtyard in the centre of the village during the Phulech (Flaich) Festival.

🛏 Sleeping & Eating

Hotel Blue Lotus   HOTEL $
(ⓙ226001; r ₹600-1000) Only 100m from the bus stand, this friendly, concrete place is hard to beat for sheer convenience. Rooms are a touch shabby but not bad value, and the wide, sunny terraces face directly across to the mountains – ideal for meals with a view (mains ₹80 to ₹200).

Hotel Rollingrang   HOTEL $$
(ⓙ9816686789; www.hotelinkalpa.com; Roghi Rd; r ₹1320-1650; ⊙closed Dec-Feb) Up in a peaceful spot next to the HPTDC's Hotel Kinner Kailash, rooms here are spacious and sparkling clean, with geyser-heated showers, and the best have balconies with perfect mountain views. Rates drop 20% outside peak seasons.

Grand Shangri-La   HOTEL $$$
(ⓙ9805695423, 226134; www.thegrandshangri-la.com; Roghi Rd; r ₹3300-4950; ☎) The very comfortable rooms here are beautifully pine-panelled and decked with Tibetan-design fabrics, and the best enjoy stupendous views from picture windows. Beds are soft, the bathrooms have great hot showers and the food – Indian, Tibetan and Chinese (mains ₹120 to ₹270) – is excellent. There's also a good library with books on India and Tibet and, a rarity hereabouts, wi-fi (free).

ⓘ Getting There & Away

Buses run at least hourly from about 6.30am to 6pm between the roundabout in Rekong Peo's main bazaar and Kalpa (₹12, 30 minutes), or you can take a taxi (₹300/500 to lower/upper Kalpa). For walkers, a well-worn stepped path short-cuts the winding road.

Buses depart for Shimla (₹385, 11 hours) at 6.30am and 2.30pm, and for Sangla (₹75, three hours) and Chitkul (₹115, 4½ hours) at around 8.30am. More buses run from Rekong Peo.

Rekong Peo to Sumdo

The road into Spiti is a continuous procession of awe-inspiring vistas, with the road often clinging precariously to cliffsides and the river flashing hundreds of metres below. Foreigners must show their inner line permits at the Akpa checkpoint, 17km past the Rekong Peo turn-off. About 7km beyond, look for the fort-like temples across the river at Moorang. The Moorang road continues to Lambar, the start of the *parikrama* (ritual circumnavigation) trek around 6050m Kinner Kailash via the Charawng La. High above the road near Spillow, Khanum is well worth a detour for its several important Buddhist monasteries and temples, including the Kangyur Gompa, founded by Ringchen Zangpo, the 'Great Translator', in the 10th or 11th century.

Near Khab, Hwy 05 heads up to the Chinese border at the Shipki La (off-limits to foreigners). The road continues to the confluence of the Sutlej and Spiti Rivers, 2km on, then threads the Spiti gorge upstream.

ℹ️ INNER LINE PERMITS IN SHIMLA

The permits required for foreigners to travel between Rekong Peo in Kinnaur and Sumdo in Spiti are easily obtained in an hour or two, any day except Sunday or the second Saturday of the month, in Rekong Peo itself or in Kaza (Spiti). You can also try getting the permit at the office of Shimla's **Additional District Magistrate** (☑ 2657005; Room 207/208, Collectorate Building; ⏱ 10am-1.30pm & 2-4pm Mon-Sat, closed 2nd Sat each month). Take copies of your passport identity and visa pages. You may be told that only a minimum of four people together may apply, but if you get the go-ahead, you'll be sent to the Sugam Centre in the Collectorate to fill out a form and have your photo taken; you then return to the ADM office, where permits (₹300) are usually issued within 30 minutes.

Nako

POP 570 / ELEV 3660M

High above the Hangrang Valley, this quaint medieval village of stone and mud-brick houses is a great place to break the journey for a day or two. Nako is centred on a small sacred lake, behind which rise towering rock-strewn mountains dotted by stupas. A remote hiking trail leads up over a pass to Tashigang village and monastery (about four hours), from where hardcore hikers can continue about two hours to caves and a shrine at Tsomang; take a guide at the Youth Club Office in Nako centre. On the western edge of Nako you'll find the four 11th-century chapels of Nako Gompa, containing some fine murals and sculptures in similar styles to those of Spiti's famous Tabo Gompa.

Nako has several simple homestays and guesthouses such as Amar Home Stay (☑ 9418629453; s/d ₹400/500), signposted down steps 20m from the bus stop, where clean rooms with hot-water bathrooms open onto a pretty flower and vegetable garden. Better, but sometimes full with groups, are the bright Lake View Hotel (☑ 9418759493; ranjeetnako@gmail.com; r ₹700-1500; ⏱ late Apr-late Oct) overlooking the lake, with a pretty garden and meals available, and Knaygoh Kinner Camps (☑ 9418440767; www.knaygohkinnercamps.com; s/d incl breakfast ₹3150/3900, mains ₹130-230; ⏱ late Apr-late Oct), a short walk above the lake, with cosy en-suite tents and a dining room serving good Indian and Chinese food.

Buses start from Nako at 7am to Tabo (₹100, three hours) and Kaza (₹170, 5½ hours), and at 7.30am to Rekong Peo (₹165, five hours); the Rekong Peo–Kaza and Kaza–Rekong Peo buses stop here at about noon.

North of Nako the road descends to the Spiti River at Chango. Sumdo, 14km further on, marks the border between Kinnaur and Spiti: foreigners must show their inner line permits here.

CENTRAL HIMACHAL PRADESH

Central Himachal is essentially the Kullu and Parvati Valleys – famous for the production of woollen shawls and charas (hashish), and for their wonderful mountain and valley scenery. The area attracts all types of Indian and foreign travellers – hippies, honeymooners, trekkers and adrenaline junkies. At the heart of the scene is Manali, one of northern India's main travel centres, a base for all types of energetic activity from skiing to rafting to paragliding, and also a stepping stone to Lahaul, Spiti and Ladakh via the Rohtang La (3978m). In the hundreds of mountain villages life still goes on in a pretty traditional way, and the chance to get away from the towns and main roads amid the spectacular landscape shouldn't be missed.

For more information on Kullu district, see www.kullu.net, http://hpkullu.gov.in and www.kullutourism.com.

Mandi

☑ 01905 / POP 26,500 / ELEV 800M

The rambunctious bazaar town of Mandi (its name means 'market'), at the junction of main roads from Kullu, Shimla and Dharamsala, is no tourist town, and it has a sticky air reminiscent of the plains. But it's dotted with (according to official figures) 81 temples, many of them ancient Shaivite shrines, and it's fun tracking these down in the bazaars and along the banks of the Beas River.

Mandi is centred on a sunken-garden-cum-shopping-complex called Indira Market, with steps on the north side up to the Raj Mahal Palace. The bus stand is 500m east across the Suketi Khad stream, a ₹30 autorickshaw ride.

◉ Sights

As well as the following, you'll find many more ancient temples just by wandering the streets.

Bhoothnath Mandir HINDU TEMPLE

At the entrance to Bhoothnath Bazar, 100m northwest of Indira Market, this 16th-century temple recently had its garish paintwork removed, showing off its fine stone carving to much better effect. It's the focal point for the animated Shivaratri Festival honouring Lord Shiva in February/March.

River Temples

If you follow Bhoothnath Bazar to the Beas River you'll find the very colourful **Ekardash Rudra Mandir**, the British-built Victoria Bridge, some cremation ghats and several carved stone *sikhara* (corn-cob- or beehive-shaped) temples. Most impressive of these are the intricately sculpted, centuries-old **Panchvaktra Mandir** and **Triloknath Mandir**, facing each other across the Beas, 150m east of the ghats.

🛏 Sleeping & Eating

Evening Plaza Hotel HOTEL **$**

(☎225123; r ₹440-660, with AC ₹1100-1320; ❋) Right on the main square, this place is reliable value offering acceptable rooms with TVs. Front-facing rooms are best, but noisiest. If it's full, try the similar **Hotel Shiva** (☎224211; r ₹550-880) a few doors along.

★**Raj Mahal Palace Hotel** HERITAGE HOTEL **$$**

(☎222401; www.rajmahalpalace.com; r ₹1590-4230; ❋🖥) Mandi's most romantic hotel occupies part of the palace of its ex-royal family. 'Standard' rooms are nothing fancy, but the large deluxes and super-deluxes have that aristocratic touch – some with the air of a colonial hunting lodge, others with a modern chalet design. Book in advance as they can fill up with groups.

The **Copacabana Bar & Restaurant** (mains ₹120-280; ⊙7am-10pm) here, with tables on a large, tree-shaded lawn, is part of the appeal – peaceful for breakfast, animated for dinner.

❶ Information

There are international ATMs at the State Bank of Patiala and HDFC around the market square.

Kapoor Cyber Cafe (internet per hour ₹30; ⊙10am-8.30pm Mon-Sat) is on the ground floor of the Indira Market.

❶ Getting There & Away

For Dharamsala, if there are no immediate buses, head to Palampur and change there. Taxis outside the bus station and on the north side of the Indira Market charge ₹2500 to Manali and ₹3500 to McLeod Ganj.

Rewalsar Lake

☑ 01905 / ELEV 1350M

Hidden in the hills 24km southwest of Mandi, the sacred lake of Rewalsar is revered by Buddhists, Hindus and Sikhs. Tibetan Buddhists know it as Tso-Pema (Lotus Lake) and believe it was created when the king of Mandi tried to burn alive the revered Buddhist sage Padmasambhava (Guru Rinpoche), to prevent his daughter Mandarava running off with the long-haired Tantric master. Today the lake's 800m perimeter is surrounded by a collection of mostly modern temples, monasteries and monuments, in which all three faiths are represented. Despite the untidy architectural hodgepodge, the lake retains a spiritual atmosphere.

The ochre-red Tibetan-style **Drikung Kagyu Gompa** (www.dk-petsek.org), with its academy of Buddhist studies, stands immediately inside the entrance arch to the lake. Its temple features a large, central Sakyamuni statue, with Padmasambhava to the left. Moving clockwise around the lake, you pass a lakeshore shrine to Padmasambhava and then the **Tso-Pema Ogyen Heruka Nyingmapa Gompa**, with artful murals and

HIMACHAL PRADESH REWALSAR LAKE

BUSES FROM MANDI

DESTINATION	FARE (₹)	DURATION (HR)	FREQUENCY
Delhi	492-960	13	18 daily
Dharamsala	200	6	12 daily
Kullu	103	2½	half-hourly
Manali	163	4	half-hourly
Shimla	215	6	15 daily

atmospheric afternoon and morning *pujas* (prayer sessions). A few minutes' detour uphill from the lake, passing the **Zigar Drukpa Kagyu Institute**, with outsized statues of Tantric protectors in its temple, takes you to a dramatic 12m-high **statue of Padmasambhava**, with grand views over the lake.

Continuing clockwise around the lake you pass a group of smallish **Hindu temples** before arriving at lakeshore ghats, where hundreds of fish practically jump out of the water to get at the puffed rice thrown by pilgrims. On the far side of the lake is the gold-domed **Guru Gobind Singh Gurdwara**, a Sikh temple built in the 1930s. Rewalsar is of special significance to Sikhs as the place where, in 1701, Guru Gobind Singh, the 10th Sikh guru, issued an (unsuccessful) call to the Hindu rajas of the Punjab hills for joint resistance to the Mughals.

The other main pilgrim site is the **Padmasambhava Cave**, high above the lake on the ridge, where Padmasambhava allegedly meditated. Take a taxi (one-way/return ₹500/600) or jump on one of the five daily buses to Naina Devi Temple (₹30) and get off 1km before the temple.

🛏 Sleeping & Eating

Hotel Lotus Lake
HOTEL $
(📞 240239; hlotuslake@yahoo.com; r ₹450-700) The best rooms at this Buddhist-run place near the lakeshore Padmasambhava shrine are bright, with lake views. The cheapest are shabbier and viewless. All are adequately clean, with hot-water bathrooms.

Drikung Kagyu Gompa Guesthouse
MONASTERY GUESTHOUSE $
(📞 9816735264; www.dk-petsek.org; r with/without bathroom ₹300/150) Of several monastery guesthouses this is probably the best, offering a shared terrace with peaceful lake views.

Kora Community Cafe
MULTICUISINE $
(veg dishes ₹60-90; ⏱ 6am-9pm) Near Hotel Lotus Lake, the Kora is good for coffee, breakfasts and veg thali.

OFF THE BEATEN TRACK

TIRTHAN VALLEY

East of Mandi the main Hwy 3 (formerly Hwy 21) threads a dramatic gorge along the Beas River before turning north towards Kullu at Larji. A side-road southeast from here leads up the Tirthan (or Banjar) Valley into the remote, beautiful **Inner Seraj** region, ripe for walks in the hills and valleys between isolated traditional villages. There is a scattering of budget and midrange accommodation in and around such villages as Banjar, Sairopa, Gushaini, Jibhi and Shoja. You can hike a steep 6km up from Banjar to **Chehni** village to see one of the tallest temple-towers in Himachal – six, seven or 11 storeys high (depending how you count them). **Gushaini** is one access point to the **Great Himalayan National Park** (www.greathimalayannationalpark.com; per day Indian/foreigner ₹50/200), which gained World Heritage status in 2014. The pristine 754-sq-km national park stretches east up to the 6000m-plus peaks of the Great Himalaya Range, with a variety of wildlife including snow leopards, brown and black bears and over 250 bird species such as the rare western tragopan. Lush forests lower down give way to alpine meadows and high-altitude glaciers. There are plenty of hiking and trekking opportunities here, from easy day walks in the buffer zone (called the Ecozone) to demanding treks in the spectacular upper reaches. The park has an information centre at Larji and a visitors centre at Sai Ropa on the Banjar–Gushaini road. For guided tours and treks and other activities contact **Sunshine Himalayan Adventures** (📞 9418102083; http://ankitsood. wix.com/sunshinehimalayanadventures; Akhara Bazar, Kullu) 🖉, which works closely with the NGO representing local residents. For groups of four or more Sunshine typically charges US$50 per person per day for treks and US$65 for birdwatching tours, including food, permits, local transport, camping equipment and staff. It also offers wildlife tours and mountaineering expeditions.

South from Shoja the road climbs to the panoramic 3223m **Jalori Pass** (normally closed for two or three winter months), from where you can walk 6km east (mostly level) to the sacred **Saryolsar Lake**, or 3km west (uphill) to the faint ruins of **Raghupur Fort**.

MANDI TO BAJAURA

Hidden away in the high pastures between Mandi and Bajaura, a 23km zig-zag drive up from the back road between the two towns, is scenic **Prashar Lake** (2730m), home to the striking, pagoda-style **Prashara Temple**, built in the 14th century in honour of the sage Prashar Rishi. The lake is also home to a curious floating island, which moves around of its own accord. A bus to Prashar (₹70, three hours) leaves Mandi bus station at 7.30am. A return taxi from Mandi costs around ₹2000.

At Bajaura, 5km south of Bhuntar on Hwy 3, the 9th-century **Bisheshwar Mahadev Temple** is well worth a stop. A rare and outstandingly handsome Kullu Valley example of the classic stone *sikhara* temples of the North Indian plains, it's dedicated to Shiva as Lord of the Universe. The temple is covered all over with ornate carving, and niches on the outside contain superb reliefs of Vishnu (west side), Ganesh (south) and Durga (north).

🛈 Getting There & Away

Buses from Mandi to Rewalsar (₹35, 1¼ hours) leave frequently until late afternoon from the street between Indira Market and the Suketi Khad bridge. The last one back leaves about 6pm. A taxi is ₹700.

Bhuntar

📞 01902

This market town is the location of the Kullu Manali airport, and the main junction for transport to the beautiful Parvati Valley. There's an SBI ATM on the main street about 100m north of Hotel Malabar.

🛏 Sleeping & Eating

The best hotel in town is **Hotel Malabar** (📞 266199; www.hotelmalabarkullu.com; r ₹1880-2350; ❄), 500m north of the airport, with a good Indian restaurant (mains ₹120 to ₹300). There's a collection of acceptable cheaper places about 700m further up the main street, centred on **Hotel Amit** (📞 265123; www.hotelamitkullu.com; r ₹660-2400; ❄), with its decent restaurant.

🛈 Getting There & Away

The airport is at the south end of town, 600m from the bus stand. Air India flies to/from Delhi five times weekly, though flights are sometimes cancelled in bad weather.

Frequent buses head to Manali (₹70, 2½ hours, last bus 10pm), Kullu (₹20, 30 minutes) and Mandi (₹90, two hours). For the Parvati Valley, there are buses every half-hour until 6pm to Manikaran (₹50, 1½ hours) via Jari (₹30, one hour) and Kasol (₹40, 1¼ hours). Buses to Dharamsala, Shimla and Delhi pass through 2½ hours after leaving Manali. The taxi stand is opposite the bus stand: fares are ₹950 to Kasol and ₹1350 to Manali.

Parvati Valley

📞 01902

The Parvati River enters the Beas just above Bhuntar and its ethereally beautiful valley stretches back up to the hot springs at Manikaran and beyond. The valley has a well-deserved reputation for its wild and cultivated crops of charas, and a couple of villages along the river have been transformed into hippie/backpacker hang-outs, offering cheap accommodation, international food and nonstop music to crowds of dreadlocked and pierced travellers. Like Manali, the Parvati is an established stop on the 'hummus trail' followed by post-military-service Israeli travellers. Police sometimes set up checkpoints along the roads to search for charas.

There are some excellent treks in the area, including over the Chandrakani Pass to/from Naggar, or the Pin-Parvati Pass to/from Spiti. For safety reasons, solo trekking is not recommended.

Jari

Jari is a ramshackle roadside bazaar village 20km up the Parvati Valley from its mouth. Travellers head for the peaceful hillside hamlet of Mateura Jari, a 700m uphill hike from Jari bus stop (follow the 'Village Guest House' signs).

For guide services to Malana or trekking anywhere in the Parvati Valley, contact **Negi's Himalayan Adventure** (📞 9805105800, 9816081894; www.negis-himalayan-adventure.com; Hotel Negi's Nest, Chowki) at **Hotel Negi's Nest** (📞 9816081894; r ₹1500-3000; 🛜), across

Kullu & Parvati Valleys

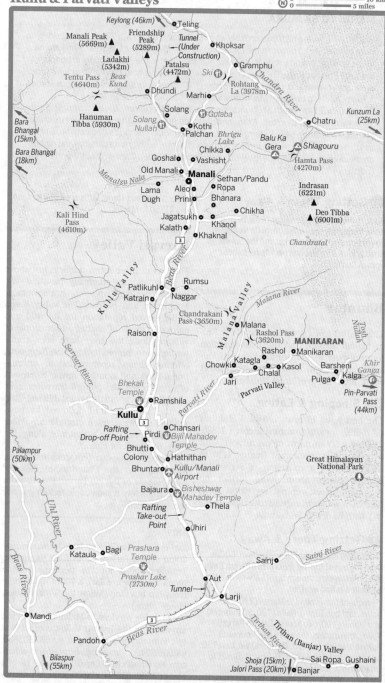

the river from Jari (a ₹150 taxi ride). Owner Chhape Negi is head of the area's mountain rescue team, so he's as reliable as it gets. A guide for a day costs ₹1500 to ₹2000, and trekking is around ₹2750 per person per day, plus transport. The rooms here are good, comfortable and pine-panelled with clean bathrooms, and there's a restaurant and kitchen for guests' use.

🛏 Sleeping & Eating

In addition to the places listed here you'll find more homestays and guesthouses tucked away along the pathways and in Punthal, 1km further.

Village Guest House   GUESTHOUSE $
(✆9805190051; r with/without bath ₹500/300; @) This large, welcoming property is the first place you come to in Mateura Jari and has the most comfortable rooms, especially those with attached bathroom ranged along the pretty garden. The family here are charming and they serve up good Indian and traveller food too (mains ₹70 to ₹170).

Rooftop Family House   GUESTHOUSE $
(✆9816474771; r ₹150) Near the ornate temples in the village centre, this has a pleasant, village vibe.

Chandra Place   GUESTHOUSE $
(✆8894280028; r ₹100-350) This laid-back spot has an awesome covered terrace with blissful views, and its own cafe.

Malana

Remote Malana, high on a hillside 20km up a side valley north of Jari, is one of the strangest villages in India. Its people – descended, according to legend, from deserters from Alexander the Great's army – speak their own unique language, operate what's called the world's oldest democracy, and consider outsiders unclean. Malana's famous charas, known as 'cream', is the backbone of its economy, and is what many visitors mainly come for. A rough road now reaches within striking distance of Malana, but for centuries it was one of the most isolated spots in the region. Be ready for random police checkpoints on the road, and bring your passport because security at the hydroelectric station en route may want to see it.

Once in the village, you must obey a litany of esoteric rules or face fines of ₹2500. Don't step off the main path, don't touch the temples or photograph them without permission, don't stray onto any sacred spots (even though there's nothing obvious to identify them), and don't touch any villagers or their belongings. To get the most out of the cultural experience and avoid breaking any rules, it's worthwhile visiting with a knowledgable guide.

Over half of Malana's traditional wood and stone houses were burned in a fire in 2008 and some have been replaced by cinderblock boxes, but the temples were rebuilt in traditional wood and stone, with intricately carved balconies. They are dedicated to the local deity Jamdagni (Jamlu) Rishi, and attract pilgrims from around the region, especially during Malana's main festival around 20 August. One of the two main temples stands on the village's central open space, facing a stone platform and stepped seating for village assemblies (Malana's 'parliament').

Malana has a half-dozen guesthouses, mostly at the top of the village and run by outsiders, with rooms for ₹200 to ₹300. Friendly **Chand View Guest House** (✆9805261446; r ₹250-500) has some attached bathrooms and decent Indian and traveller food (mains ₹100 to ₹180).

The easy way to reach Malana is by taxi from Jari to Nerang (₹800 one-way, ₹1300 return with a three-hour wait), a collection

ℹ WARNING – DEADLY VACATIONS

Since the mid-1990s more than two dozen foreign tourists have disappeared from the Kullu and Parvati Valleys. While some got too deep into the local drug trade and crossed the wrong people, others became lost or fatally injured while trekking alone through the confusing and rugged mountain terrain.

If you plan to head into the hills, we recommend going with a guide who can steer you away from natural – and human – hazards. It's a good idea to let your guesthouse know where you are going and when you plan to return. Avoid walking alone, and be cautious about befriending sadhus (holy people) or others wandering in the woods. So go, hike, and enjoy this incredible area – just be smart about it, for your family's sake!

of shacks from which it's a 30-to-45-minute walk up to the village. There are good walks in the area, and Parvati Valley taxi unions promote 'Magic Valley' day trips on which they'll take you to Nerang (for Malana) and then another 2km up to the road's end, where you continue a kilometre or two on foot. The Chandrakani Pass, a steep two-hour hike up from Malana, leads to Naggar in two or three days, and adventurers can head southeast over the Rashol Pass to Kasol (17km), staying in a homestay in Rashol en route.

Kasol

Stretched along the lovely Parvati River and with mountain views to the northeast, Kasol is the main traveller hang-out in the valley. It's a small village, but almost overrun with reggae bars, bakeries and cheap guesthouses catering to a largely hippie/Israeli crowd. It's also a summertime venue for trance parties transplanted from Goa, and at any time an easy base for exploring the forested valley or just chilling out. The village is divided into Old Kasol on the Bhuntar side of its bridge, and New Kasol on the Manikaran side.

For an easy 3.5km stroll, cross the footbridge over the Parvati River and walk downstream to Chalal and Katagla villages. Several rustic guesthouses and cafes along here, mostly foreign-run, are perfect for those who want to really 'turn on, tune in and drop out'. Recross the river at Katagla

to catch a passing bus back to Kasol (₹8). More remote paths continue from Katagla to Chowki.

Sleeping

There's plenty of budget accommodation. Some guesthouses close down for winter from November to March.

Taji Place GUESTHOUSE $
(☑9816461684; d with/without bathroom ₹700/350, cottage ₹1500; ☎) A big green-and-yellow house on a sweet and spacious riverside property, Taji has a range of tidy rooms and a couple of well-equipped cottages, plus a private hot spring (₹2 per minute). It's down an unsigned lane 80m past Evergreen restaurant in New Kasol.

Panchali Holiday Home HOTEL $
(☑273195; www.panchaliholidayhome.com; r ₹500-1500; ☎) Just west of the bridge, this friendly hotel doesn't have a ton of character but the rooms are clean and comfortable, and the front rooms have nice balconies. Rates double in June and July.

Alpine Guest House HOTEL $$
(☑9882892924; alpinehimachal@gmail.com; r ₹800-2000) Rooms at this helpful place among pines in Old Kasol are spacious and pretty well kept, but the great plus is the expansive terrace and open-air restaurant right on the bank of the rushing, tumbling, beautiful river.

HIMACHAL PRADESH PARVATI VALLEY

WORTH A TRIP

KHIR GANGA

This sloping alpine meadow is a beautiful three-to-four-hour walk up the Parvati Valley from Barsheni, which is 13km up from Manikaran. The meadow is home to delectable hot springs and a rundown collection of shack guesthouses (rooms ₹200 to ₹400) and cafe-restaurants, open from about April to October – it's a popular spot to drop out for a few days. A day trip to Khir Ganga and back is also well worthwhile. The walk from Barsheni, in which you ascend about 800m, is also the first stage of the Pin-Parvati trek. Paths run along both sides of the valley, through Nakthan village on the north side, and Kalga village on the south side, meeting just below Flower Cafe, about 45 minutes before Khir Ganga. The Nakthan route is prettier, sunnier and more frequented.

The **hot springs** (☉dawn-dusk) FREE, at the top of the meadow, are the perfect temperature – hot but not too hot – and feature a large men's pool with fantastic views and a smaller, enclosed women's pool from which you can at least see the sky. The pools are part of a temple, so decorum is required – no mixed bathing, nudity or smoking!

Buses to Barsheni (₹25, one hour) leave roughly hourly from about 7.30am to 5.30pm, from the road above Manikaran bus station. Some of them come from Bhuntar and pass through Jari and Kasol en route. The last bus back down leaves Barsheni at 5pm. Taxis from Manikaran cost ₹500.

Hotel Devlok International HOTEL $$
(☎273720; www.devlokinternational.com; r ₹1000-2500; ☎) Devlok's rooms are a cut above most other places with their comfy beds, pine panelling and hot-spring water piped into the showers. It's along the southern side-street just east of the bridge.

✗ Eating

★**Evergreen** MULTICUISINE $$
(mains ₹100-240; ⊙9am-11pm) Our favourite for its excellent chicken *sipoodim* (barbecue) served with chips and hummus, plus sizzlers, pizza, lasagne, homemade tofu dishes and good Israeli specials. You can eat at tables or settle back in the indoor or outdoor cushioned lounge areas. It's on the main road in New Kasol, 150m from the bridge.

**Moon Dance Café &
German Bakery** MULTICUISINE $$
(mains ₹100-300; ⊙9am-10pm) Moon Dance, just west of the bridge, stands tall among the many traveller restaurants serving similar 'three Is' menus (Italian-Israeli-Indian) for its great baked goods, strong coffee and excellent-value breakfasts served in the sunny courtyard.

❶ Information

Kasol has plenty of internet cafes, charging ₹40 per hour. The Central Bank of India ATM, in a side-street just east of the bridge, accepts international cards.

❶ Getting There & Away

Buses between Bhuntar and Manikaran pass through Kasol. Taxi fares from the stand near the bridge include ₹150 to Manikaran, ₹700 to Barsheni, ₹900 to Bhuntar and ₹1950 to Manali.

Manikaran

POP 6100 / ELEV 1737M
With steam continually issuing from the river bank beneath its large temple, the busy little pilgrim town of Manikaran, 4km east of Kasol, is famous for its hot springs and is sacred for both Sikhs and Hindus. According to legend, a giant snake stole the goddess Parvati's earrings while she was bathing (during an 11,000-year meditation session with Shiva), then snorted them out from underground, along with various other jewels, which released the hot springs. The water emerging from the ground is hot enough to boil rice and has to be cooled with riv-

---

CHARAS

Over the years, many tourists have been lured to the Parvati Valley and the Manali area by the famous local charas (hashish), which is seriously potent stuff. Though it's smoked fairly openly in the Parvati Valley, Old Manali and Vashisht, it's still illegal and local police do arrest people for possession (or hit them for hefty bribes).

---

er water for bathing. Locals say it can cure everything from rheumatism to bronchitis.

❍ Sights & Activities

The multistorey **Sri Guru Nanak Ji Gurdwara**, on the north bank of the river, was built in 1940. The main prayer hall, with its carpets and glittering glass columns, is on the top floor (shoes off, head-coverings on, for men and women). One level down is the eating hall where free rice, dahl, curry, chapatis and tea are served round the clock to all comers (and these meals are as good as any in town). Below that are men's and women's indoor bathing pools and, to one side, a sauna-like 'hot cave'. Across the footbridge are a more inviting open-air men's pool and another enclosed women's pool. Bring a swimming costume, towel and flip-flops if you want to bathe.

Next to the gurdwara is a **Shiva temple** where the rice for the gurdwara cooks in big pots in pools of boiling hot-spring water. A happy, quite light-hearted atmosphere prevails in both temples.

Along the main street of the traffic-free north side of town you'll find the ornate wooden **Naina Bhagwati Temple**, dedicated to the goddess, born from Shiva's third eye, who located Parvati's missing earrings.

🛏 Sleeping & Eating

Manikaran is an easy half-day trip from Kasol, but there are several guesthouses if you want to stay, mostly in the traffic-free main village on the north side of the river. Note that alcohol is banned this side of the river.

Fateh Paying Guesthouse GUESTHOUSE $
(☎9816894968; r ₹300; @) Signposted up an alley in the old part of town, this big blue house has just five simple but pleasant rooms, with welcoming owners, a sunny

rooftop terrace and a tiny hot-spring pool. Unlike most places here, Fateh keeps the same rates all year. Local meals are available.

Sharma Guest House   GUESTHOUSE $
(☏ 9418422343; r ₹200-400) In the kitschy bazaar area near the gurdwara, Sharma has adequate rooms in its main building, but the top-floor rooms in its new building nearby are the best budget lodgings in town – comfy and clean, with good mattresses and views across the valley from the shared balcony. Rates can triple or more in the June–July peak season.

🛈 Getting There & Away

Buses run at least hourly until 6.30pm from Manikaran to Bhuntar (₹50, 1½ hours), via Kasol (₹5, 10 minutes). There are also several daily to Kullu (₹70, 2½ hours) and Manali – or you can change in Bhuntar. Taxis from Manikaran bus station charge ₹500 to Barsheni, ₹1000 to Bhuntar and ₹2200 to Manali.

Kullu

☏ 01902 / POP 18,500 / ELEV 1220M

The bustling administrative capital of the Kullu Valley makes a gritty change from the hippie holiday resorts elsewhere in the valley, and in October it stages the area's most colourful and fascinating festival, the Kullu Dussehra.

The Beas River runs down the east side of Kullu, and its tributary the Sarvari River runs across the middle of town, dividing Kullu into southern and northern halves. The southern part has the taxi stand, tourist office, Dussehra grounds (two large, adjoining, open spaces) and most restaurants and hotels. The bus station and Raghunath Temple are north of the Sarvari. A footbridge near the bus station crosses to a bazaar street which brings you out near the Hotel Shobla International.

PIN-PARVATI TREK

Only accessible from late June to late September/early October (with September the best month), this strenuous but rewarding six-to-nine-day wilderness trek crosses the snow-bound Pin-Parvati Pass (5319m) from the Parvati Valley to the Pin Valley in Spiti. There is accommodation at Khir Ganga and Mudh, but none in between, so you'll have to be self-sufficient or go with a trekking agency. Organised treks are relatively pricey because your crew (often Nepali) needs to be transported back to their starting point. Sometimes two sets of porters are required, handing over loads near the pass.

From Barsheni, the route ascends through forest and pasture, past Khir Ganga hot springs to Thakur Khan. Two more days through an arid alpine zone takes you to High Cam (also called Plateau Camp). A challenging tramp over snow and scree will take you up to the pass, then down into the Pin Valley. A day or two for acclimatisation and/or rest on the way up will probably be beneficial, and the final stage could easily be broken into two days of hiking through the Pin Valley National Park to Mudh.

The trek can also be done in the east-to-west direction.

STAGE	ROUTE	DURATION (HR)	DISTANCE (KM)
1	Barsheni to Khir Ganga	3-4	12
2	Khir Ganga to Thakur Khan	6	15
3	Thakur Khan to Mantalai Lake	7	16
4	Mantalai Lake to High Camp	4	12
5	High Camp to Pin Valley Camp via Pin-Parvati Pass	5-6	12
6	Pin Valley Camp to Mudh	8	20

SHOPPING FOR SHAWLS

The Kullu Valley is famous for its traditional wool shawls – lightweight but wonderfully warm and attractively patterned – and the highway between Bhuntar and Manali is lined with scores of shops and showrooms. Kullu shawls are woven on wooden hand-looms using wool from sheep or hair from pashmina goats or angora rabbits. This industry provides an income for thousands of local women, many of whom have organised themselves into shawl-weaving cooperatives.

For high quality without the hard sell, head to the nearest branch of **Bhuttico** (www.bhutticoshawls.com), the Bhutti Weavers' Cooperative, which was established in 1944 and has showrooms in every town in the valley and several beyond, plus a **factory showroom** (☉9am-7pm) at Bhutti Colony, 8km south of Kullu. Bhuttico charges fixed prices, so it's a good place to gauge price and quality. Expect to pay upwards of ₹700 for a lambswool shawl, ₹1200 to ₹1600 for an angora-lambswool blend, ₹3500 for pashmina-lambswool and ₹6000 for pure pashmina. Bhuttico also makes scarves, topis, jackets, bags, gloves, *pullas* (slippers made from cannabis stalks) and *pattus*, the wonderfully patterned wraparound wool garments that are Kullu women's traditional clothing.

◉ Sights & Activities

Raghunath Temple
HINDU TEMPLE
(☉6.30am-9pm mid-Apr–mid-Sep, 7.30am-7.30pm mid-Sep–mid-Apr) Kullu's pre-eminent temple enshrines the Kullu Valley's most important idol, a tiny bronze image of Raghunath Ji (Rama) that lords it over the Dussehra celebrations. The 17th-century temple is on the hill above the bus station and near the Raja Rupi, the former Kullu rajas' palace; it's not particularly spectacular, and the main shrine is closed from 11.30am to 5.30pm (12.30pm to 4pm from mid-September to mid-April), but you will probably still be able to peer in through its barred window.

Bijli Mahadev Temple
HINDU TEMPLE
There are several important temples in Kullu's surrounding hills. Reached by a 3km hike up from Chansari, a 22km drive southeast from Kullu, the hilltop Bijli Mahadev is surmounted by a 20m wooden pole that attracts occasional divine blessings in the form of lightning. The surge of power shatters the stone Shiva lingam inside the temple, which is then glued back together with butter. There are spectacular panoramas over both the Kullu and Parvati Valleys from here.

Bijli Mahadev attracts crowds of pilgrims during the Shaivite Sawan Kamaina festival from mid-July to mid-August. A return taxi from Kullu costs ₹1100, or look for a shared taxi at Ramshila, 2km northeast on the main road, where the road to Bijli Mahadev starts.

☞ Tours

Sitated by the Dussehra grounds in the southern part of town, the **Kullu Taxi Operators' Union** (☎222332; www.kullutaxiunion.com) offers sightseeing day tours to four local temples (not including Bijli Mahadev) for ₹1100, or to Prashar Lake for ₹2400.

🛏 Sleeping & Eating

Hotel Vikrant
HOTEL $
(☎9816438299; vikramrashpa@gmail.com; d ₹450-1000) Up a tiny path behind the HPTDC office, Vikrant is a backpacker-friendly place with a welcoming vibe. Wood panelling and shared balconies give the rooms a simple charm: those upstairs are bigger and brighter, but all have fans and hot showers.

Hotel Aaditya
HOTEL $
(☎9418001244; http://hotelaadityakullu.com; d ₹660-2640; 🖥) Just across the footbridge from the bus station, Aaditya tries harder than most in this price range, with friendly service, comfy beds, and a range of rooms, many with balconies overlooking the Sarvari River. Rates drop 20% or 30% from mid-July to mid-April, except for Dussehra when they double.

Hotel Shobla International
HOTEL $$
(☎222800; www.shoblainternational.com; r ₹1780-2370; ❄🖥) The best of Kullu's business hotels, this modern place near the Dussehra grounds has clean rooms, a good restaurant (mains ₹160 to ₹300) and a bar. The cheapest ('standard') rooms are good value since they come with balconies and a view. Expect

discounts of 20% from about July to April (except during Dussehra).

Hot Spice MULTICUISINE $$
(mains ₹100-200; ⊗9am-10pm) For good-value thalis and breakfasts, head for this pleasant open-air cafe up the lane behind the tourist office.

ⓘ Information

The **HPTDC tourist office** (☏222349; ⊗10am-5pm), near the Dussehra grounds, is helpful with local information and can book seats on the comfortable HPTDC buses from Manali to Delhi and Shimla. The SBI has ATMs nearby.

ⓘ Getting There & Away

BUS

A mixture HRTC and private buses runs about every 15 minutes to Bhuntar (₹20, 30 minutes), Manali (₹50, 90 minutes) and Mandi (₹90, two hours). There are several buses to Manikaran (₹70, 2½ hours) via Jari and Kasol, or you can go to Bhuntar and change. Buses from Manali to destinations beyond the Kullu Valley stop in Kullu about 1½ hours after departure.

TAXI

Sample one-way fares include ₹700 to Naggar, ₹900 to Kasol and ₹1050 to Manali.

Naggar

☏01902 / POP 550 / ELEV 1760M

High on the east side of the Kullu Valley, sleepy Naggar was once capital of the Kullu kingdom and is perhaps the most charming village in the valley today. Russian painter and explorer Nicholas Roerich (Nikolai Rerikh) liked it so much he settled here in the early 20th century. It's an easy day trip from Manali, but with interesting sights and some good guesthouses and restaurants, it's a fine place for a few days' relaxing stay.

⊙ Sights

Naggar Castle FORT
(admission ₹30; ⊗9am-6pm) Built by the rajas of Kullu around 1500, this fort-cum-mansion is a fine example of the earthquake-resistant alternating-stone-and-timber style of Himachali architecture. Sold to the British assistant commissioner in 1846, it later became a courthouse and then, in 1976, a hotel. The **Jagti Patt Temple**, inside, houses a 2.4m-long sacred stone slab said to have been carried here by a swarm of deities in the form of honey bees.

KULLU DUSSEHRA

Raghunath Ji, the most important god in Kullu town and valley, is a version of Rama, the hero god of the Ramayana, so you might expect **Kullu Dussehra**, the October festival that celebrates Rama's victory over the demon-king Ravana, to be something special here. Unlike the one-day celebrations elsewhere, Kullu Dussehra goes on for a week. The opening day is the most exciting, with 200 or more village deities (*devtas*), including Hadimba from Manali, arriving in Kullu on palanquins, having been carried here on foot (for several days from the remotest villages). They pay homage at Raghunath Ji's temple in the early afternoon, before moving down to the Dussehra grounds in a wonderful cavalcade, with drums beating and giant trumpets blaring, decked in gorgeous garlands and draperies studded with silver masks. Here the tiny Raghunath Ji idol is placed in a large wooden chariot and pulled to its allotted place by teams of rope-hauling devotees amid excited crowds.The village *devtas* 'dance' – tilting from side to side and charging backwards and forwards – before settling down in their own allotted positions around the grounds, where they and their attendants camp for the week of the festival.

The rest of the week is focused mainly on a huge retail fair spread over the Dussehra grounds, outbreaks of music and dancing around the *devta* tents, plus evening dance, music and other performances in the adjacent auditorium. On the seventh day everyone goes home. The end of the festivities no longer sees the traditional sacrifice of a buffalo, goat, cock, fish and freshwater crab on the banks of the Beas, as animal sacrifices at religious festivals were banned in Himachal Pradesh in 2014.

Accommodation in Kullu is scarce and expensive during Dussehra, but it's an easy day trip from Manali or even Kasol.

★ **International Roerich Memorial Trust** MUSEUM
(☎248290; www.roerichtrust.org; admission/camera/video ₹50/30/60; ☺10am-1pm & 1.30-6pm Tue-Sun, to 5pm Nov-Mar) This fascinating memorial and museum complex 1km above the castle focuses on the former home of Russian painter, writer and Inner Asian explorer Nicholas Roerich and his wife Elena. They settled here in 1928 and stayed until his death in 1947. The couple's semimystical aesthetico-orientalist philosophising had an international following in their lifetimes but it is Nicholas' art that has had the more enduring appeal.

The house's lower floor displays some of his landscape paintings (many depicting Himalayan mountains), while the upper floor preserves some of the private rooms. Also on the property are Nicholas' samadhi (tomb) and an exhibit on the Roerichs' artist son Svyatoslav and his wife, the Indian film star Devika Rani.

Down the road there's a good little book and souvenir shop, while a five-minute uphill walk takes you to the **Urusvati Himalayan Research Institute**, with further exhibits on the work of the Roerichs and their associates.

Temples

Naggar is home to several intriguing and beautiful small temples. Down the street beside the castle, the 11th-century *sikhara*-style **Vishnu Mandir** is covered in ornate carvings. Turn left just past this, then left at the next fork, to the lovely little **Gauri Shankar Temple**, of similar style and date. It's dedicated to Shiva and the exterior wall recesses contain carvings of dancers, musicians and birds.

About 400m up the road from the castle, the pagoda-style **Tripura Sundari Temple** is sacred to the local earth-mother goddess. The existing building is only about 35 years old, but the site has probably been sacred since pre-Hindu times. The track leading uphill off the road here leads 1km to a junction where a right turn takes you 150m to the **Murlidhar Krishna Temple**, dating from about the 11th century, on the site of the ancient town of Thawa, which pre-dated Naggar by around 1000 years.

🏃 **Activities**

Naggar is the starting point for the excellent three-day trek to Malana village via the 3650m Chandrakani Pass, accessible between May and October (though rainy July is better avoided). **Himalayan Mountain Treks** (☎9418149827; www.poonammountain.in; Poonam Mountain Lodge), down the small street beside Naggar Castle, and **Ragini Treks & Tours** (☎9817076890; raginitours@hotmail.com; Hotel Ragini), just above the castle, are experienced operators who can organise this and other regional treks, and guided day walks.

It's feasible to reach Malana in two days and, depending on the season, there are teashops en route where you can sleep if you have a sleeping bag, but a slower pace gives more time to enjoy the mountains. Once over the pass, detours to Nagruni village (one extra day) or the Malana glacier (three or four extra days) are worthwhile. Himalayan Mountain Treks charges US$50 to US$60 per person per day for guided and equipped treks with porters.

For a straightforward half-day walk you could do just the first few kilometres of the trek, as far up as traditional **Rumsu** village, with its impressive wooden temple.

🛏 **Sleeping & Eating**

★ **Alliance Guesthouse** GUESTHOUSE $
(☎9817097033, 248263; www.alliancenaggar.com; s ₹300-1000, d ₹400-1200, tr/q ₹1300/1500; @ 🛜) On the road up to the Roerich Museum, this friendly French- and Indian-run place has a range of spotless rooms, from shared-bathroom cheapies to duplexes perfect for families. A lot of thought has gone into guests' comfort, with touches including kettles, tea, coffee and even cotton buds in the rooms, plus a library, laundry service and sitting areas; everything you could want.

The **restaurant** (mains ₹60-350; ☺7am-8pm) offers excellent Indian dishes and some with a French touch, including local trout and 40 varieties of salad.

Chander Lok Guesthouse GUESTHOUSE $
(☎9459341714; d ₹300-500) The eight rooms in this family-run place are clean and pleasant but the best thing is the garden, which leads down to charming 1500-year-old stone shrines to Shiva and Ganesh. It's a 400m walk below the castle in Chanalti village.

The Castle HERITAGE HOTEL $$
(☎248316; www.hptdc.gov.in; incl breakfast s ₹1680-3440, d ₹2230-4580) The HPTDC hotel occupying the castle has historical atmosphere but decor and furnishings are mostly

spartan. Prices depend mainly on room size and views (which are superb from some rooms). There's an affordable **restaurant** (mains ₹160-450; ☺8am-10pm) with a terrace overlooking the valley.

Hotel Ragini   HOTEL **$$**
(☎248185; www.naggarragini.com; r ₹1000-1500; @☎) Ragini is a clean, modern hotel just up from the castle, with bright, balconied rooms and a neat garden. The **Ragini Bakery** (snacks & light meals ₹20-200; ☺7.30am-10pm) overlooking the street does good coffee, lassi, baked goods and other snacks.

❶ Getting There & Away

Buses run about half-hourly between Manali and Naggar between 8am and 6pm (₹30, one hour) and there are several buses to and from Kullu (₹30, one hour). In either case, if there's no bus to Naggar itself, you can always get one to Patlikuhl, on the Kullu–Manali main road, and then a shared taxi (₹20) or autorickshaw (₹70) from there. A taxi from Manali to Naggar costs ₹800. Autorickshaws up to the castle from the bus stop are ₹50.

Manali

☎01902 / POP 8100 / ELEV 2050M
Surrounded by high peaks in the beautiful green valley of the Beas River, with mountain adventures beckoning from all directions, Manali is a year-round magnet. Backpackers come to hang out in the hippie villages around the main town; adventurers come for trekking, climbing, mountain biking, canyoning, paragliding, rafting and skiing; and Indian families and honeymooners come for the cool mountain air and a taste of snow on a day trip to the Rohtang La. Manali is also the main jumping-off point (from June to October) for Ladakh and Spiti. It makes sense to unwind and feed up here for a few days while organising your trip into the mountains.

So popular has Manali become among Indian tourists that this once bucolic retreat now has an estimated 800 to 1000 hotels and guesthouses in the town and outskirts, and from mid-April to mid-July, mid-September to mid-October, and over Christmas–New Year it gets pretty well overrun, with dire traffic jams along its narrow lanes and the main roads approaching town. Most travellers stay in the villages of Vashisht or Old Manali, which have a laid-back vibe and

plenty of services, but partially close for winter from about November to April.

◉ Sights & Activities

★**Hadimba Temple**   HINDU TEMPLE
(Map p310) This much-revered wood-and-stone mandir, constructed in 1553, stands in a clearing in the cedar forest about 2km west of central Manali. Pilgrims come from across India to honour Hadimba, the demon wife of the Pandava Bhima from the Mahabharata. The temple's wooden doorway, under a three-tier pagoda-style roof, is richly carved with figures of gods, animals and dancers; antlers and ibex horns adorn the outside walls.

Inside is a large sacrificial stone where grisly animal slaughterings have traditionally taken place during the three-day Dhungri Mela in May. Gatothkach, the warrior son of Hadimba and Bhima, is worshipped in the form of a **sacred tree** (Map p310) near the temple.

Old Manali   AREA
About 2km northwest of the Mall on the far side of the Manalsu Nala stream, Old Manali still has some of the feel of an Indian mountain village once you get past the core backpacker zone. There are some remarkable old houses of wood and stone, and the towered **Manu Maharishi Temple** (Map p310) is built on the site where, legend says, the ark of the Noah-like Manu, the creator of civilisation, landed after the great flood.

Nature Park   PARK
(Map p310; admission ₹5; ☺9am-7pm, to 5pm approx Nov-Mar) This woodland of magnificent towering deodars (cedars) is easily the nicest route between the centre and Old Manali, though it is not recommended for a woman walking alone. South of the centre is the similar **Van Vihar Park** (admission ₹10; ☺9am-7pm, to 5pm approx Nov-Mar).

Buddhist Monasteries
There's a small Tibetan community south of the town centre. The much-visited **Himalayan Nyinmapa Buddhist Temple** (☺6am-6pm) contains a two-storey statue of Sakyamuni, the historical Buddha. Just west is the more traditional **Von Ngari Monastery** (☺6am-7pm), with an atmospheric juniper-scented prayer room crammed with statues of bodhisattvas (enlightened beings) and revered lamas.

☞ Tours

In high season, the HPTDC (p315) offers bus day tours to the Rohtang La (₹310), Manikaran and the Parvati Valley (₹350) and Naggar, Jagatsukh and Solang Nullah (₹260), if there are enough takers. Private travel agencies offer similar tours.

The Him-Aanchal Taxi Operators Union (p316) has fixed-price tours, including to Rohtang La (₹1800), Solang Nullah (₹900) and Naggar (₹1100).

The following places can all arrange treks, tours and adventure activities:

Antrek Tours & Travels   OUTDOOR ADVENTURE
(☑ 9816022292; www.antrek.co.in; 1 Ram Bagh, the Mall) Good for trekking and skiing, and transport to Ladakh.

Himalayan Adventurers   OUTDOOR ADVENTURE
(☑ 252750; www.himalayanadventurers.com; 44 the Mall) Trekking specialist; also good for mountain biking, jeep safaris and motorcycle tours.

Himalayan Caravan   OUTDOOR ADVENTURE
(Map p310; ☑ 251579; www.himalayancaravan. com; Old Manali) Trekking, rock-climbing, mountaineering, skiing.

Himalayan Extreme Centre   OUTDOOR ADVENTURE
(Map p310; ☑ 9816174164; www.himalayan-extreme-centre.com) This long-running, professional outfit can arrange almost any activity you fancy. In Old Manali; it also has a branch in Vashisht (Map p310).

Himalayan Trails   OUTDOOR ADVENTURE
(Map p310; ☑ 250258; www.himalayantrails.in; Dragon Market, Old Manali) Energetic young company doing trekking, mountain biking, mountaineering and more; runs open-group treks that individuals can join.

🛏 Sleeping

Many midrange and top-end hotels slash prices dramatically outside the peak seasons. The best budget places, by far, are a short distance north of Manali town in the villages of Old Manali and Vashisht, where prices are often negotiable. The best upmarket hotels are found along Circuit House and Club House Rds, heading towards Old Manali.

🏠 Manali

★**Sunshine Guest House**   HERITAGE GUESTHOUSE $$
(Map p310; ☑ 252320; www.sunshineguesthouse. co.in; Club House Rd; d/tr/q ₹3000/4500/5500; ☎) Full of colonial character, the Sunshine has large triples and quads in its original 1920s building, where rooms have beautiful polished walnut and pine floors and old-fashioned bathrooms (pending renovation). There are also four modern doubles in a new building next door. All rooms have tea- and coffee-makers and 24-hour solar hot water, and meals can be enjoyed on the wide verandahs or in the lovely flowery garden with views down the valley.

Pushpak Hotel   HOTEL $$
(☑ 253656; r ₹2000-3000) Along an alley opposite the bus station (and accessed through a restaurant), this is the best budget place on the Mall outside the high season, when rates can drop by 75%. Rooms overlooking the Mall have balconies and great light, but are noisier than those towards the back.

The streets behind have dozens of further options in similar price ranges.

★**Johnson Hotel**   HOTEL $$$
(☑ 253764; johnsonhotel.in; Circuit House Rd; r/apt ₹3760/8220; ✳☎) One of a few places belonging to descendants of a prominent Raj-era landowner, the Johnson is a classy wood-and-stone hotel with 12 snug rooms, four two-bedroom apartments in the original century-old lodge, and lovely gardens, as well as an excellent restaurant (p313). It's well run and everything's in immaculate shape, making it well worth the price.

It's also very popular, so book well ahead.

★**Banon Resorts**   HOTEL $$$
(Map p310; ☑ 253026; www.banonresortmanali. com; Club House Rd; r incl breakfast ₹7050, ste ₹8220-10,570, cottages ₹21,140; ✳☎) This quiet, luxury hotel is a little slicker than its competition. Centrally heated rooms in the main building are spacious and uncluttered, with huge bathrooms, while the two-bedroom cottages are the last word in luxurious peace and privacy. The balconies and restaurant terrace overlooking the large, lovely garden provide the charm.

Johnson Lodge   HOTEL $$$
(☑ 251523; www.johnsonslodge.com; Circuit House Rd; d ₹4700, 4-person cottage ₹8810; ✳☎) Built in stone and timber in the

Manali & Vashisht

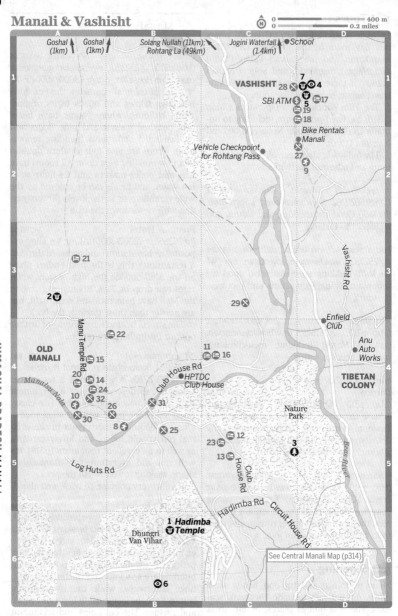

See Central Manali Map (p314)

traditional Himachal manner, but more contemporary inside, four-storey Johnson Lodge offers bright pastel-hued rooms that are starting to show a little wear, as well as luxurious two-bedroom cottages. The modern bar and multicuisine restaurant (mains ₹210 to ₹470) host live music or DJs a few times a week.

Baikunth Magnolia   HERITAGE HOTEL $$$
(Map p310; ☑ 9459494151; www.baikunth.com; Club House Rd; r ₹6110; ☎) A classy old heritage

Manali & Vashisht

property, with big lawns and comfortable, old-fashioned-style furnishings. Rooms have tea- and coffee-makers and good, contemporary bathrooms, and most of them have private balconies too. Low-season discounts run up to 50%.

Old Manali

Old Manali has many, mostly budget, guesthouses along its one street, Manu Temple Rd, or on various lanes and pathways off it. Some of them close from about December to April.

Apple View Guest House GUESTHOUSE $
(Map p310; ☑253899; www.appleviewmanali.com; r with/without bathroom ₹500/300; ☺closed approx Dec-Apr; ☜) Up steps opposite the HPTDC Club House, this homey family-run guesthouse has 12 plain, well-kept rooms and a nice little front patio, and offers a simple but good menu of Indian and continental food (mains ₹60 to ₹70). If it's full, try the also-good **Eagle Guest House** (Map p310; ☑250081; liatasher@hotmail.com; r ₹400-600; ☺closed approx Dec-May; ☜) 50m along the path.

Tourist Nest Guest House GUESTHOUSE $
(Map p310; ☑252383; touristnest@gmail.com; r ₹900-1100; ☜) In the heart of Old Manali,

Tourist Nest has bright, clean, tiled, well-kept rooms with private balconies. Negotiable rates can lead to some of the best value around.

Mountain Dew Guesthouse GUESTHOUSE $
(Map p310; ☑9816446366; d ₹500-800; ☜) This yellow three-storey place offers good-sized, decently maintained rooms with nice east-facing shared terraces. It's one of the best-value places in Old Manali.

Shiva Blues Café GUESTHOUSE $
(Map p310; ☑8628001973; www.facebook.com/theshivablues; r ₹800) Shiva Blues is popular with an arty, young, mainly Indian crowd, and can develop a party atmosphere. It has a nice little garden and decent, bright ensuite rooms, and serves Italian and Indian food.

Rocky's Guest Home GUESTHOUSE $
(Map p310; ☑254135; rajyadav788.rk@gmail.com; r ₹350; ☜) If you'd like to be in Old Manali but clear of the thickest crowds – and enjoy the best views – friendly Rocky's provides clean, carpeted rooms with hardish beds, and panoramic terraces, at the very top of the village.

Drifters' Inn HOTEL $$
(Map p310; ☑9805033127; www.driftersinn.in; r ₹800-1300, f ₹1600; ☜) The hipness of the ground-floor restaurant (p314) doesn't quite

OUTDOOR ACTIVITIES AROUND MANALI

Manali is the adventure sports capital of Himachal Pradesh, and all sorts of activities can be organised through operators here.

Canyoning

You can do this in several places around Manali with agencies including Himalayan Extreme Centre (p309), which charges ₹2500 to ₹2800 per person for day outings.

Mountain Biking

Agencies offer bike hire for ₹350 to ₹850 per day (and can give current info on routes) or will take you on guided tours – ranging from the exciting 51km descent from the Rohtang La (best in late September and October after the monsoon and summer traffic have died down) to two-week trips to Ladakh or Kinnaur and Spiti costing around ₹3000 per person per day with vehicle support.

Mountaineering

Agencies such as Himalayan Caravan (p309), Himalayan Trails (p309) and Himalayan Adventurers (p309) can arrange expeditions of 10 to 14 days to peaks around the head of the Solang valley, including Friendship Peak (5289m) and Ladakhi (5342m), which are suitable for those with limited experience (training is available), and the more difficult Hanuman Tibba (5930m) and Manali Peak (5669m). Typical prices are around ₹5000 per person per day including instructor/guides, equipment, transport, food and camping.

Paragliding

Paragliding is popular at Solang Nullah and at Gulaba and Marhi (below the Rohtang La) from April to October (except during the monsoon). Tandem flights at Solang Nullah cost ₹1000 (a two-minute flight) or ₹3000 (10 minutes). Adventure-tour operators can organise 20-or-30-minute tandem flights for ₹3500 to ₹4000 – and also solo-flight training courses, as can Hotel Iceland (p318).

Rafting

There is 14km of Grade II and III white water between Pirdi, on the Beas River 3km south of Kullu, and the take-out point at Jhiri; trips with adventure agencies from Manali cost around

extend into the rooms, but it's a spotless place with outdoor terraces on every floor. Wi-fi reaches all rooms, and they get their apostrophes right.

Dragon Guest House   HOTEL **$$**
(Map p310; ☑252290; www.dragontreks.com; r ₹600-1500, ste ₹4000; 🛜) Dragon has good, comfortable rooms opening out onto long verandahs on four floors – the higher the better, and the best are in the Swiss-chalet-style top floors. There's a little orchard out front, plus a restaurant and a reliable travel agency for treks and tours.

✖ Eating

Manali has some fine Indian and international restaurants, and there are lots of inexpensive travellers' cafes in Old Manali. Many restaurants serve trout from local farms.

⚲ Manali

★ Mayur   MULTICUISINE **$$**
(Mission Rd; mains ₹100-300; ⊘9am-10pm) Locals and visitors alike rate Mayur highly for its well-prepared North and South Indian specialities. The decor downstairs is solidly old-school and classy, with uniformed waiters, while the upstairs is bright and more contemporary. The Indian dishes are excellent and there are some refreshingly unusual continental options including ratatouille, fish in coconut milk, and lamb goulash.

Chopsticks   ASIAN **$$**
(the Mall; mains ₹110-400; ⊘9.30am-10pm; 🛜) The most popular traveller choice in Manali town centre, this tightly packed Tibetan-Chinese-Japanese place has Tibetan lutes on the walls and serves up good *momos* (dumplings) and *gyoza* (their Japanese

₹1000 per person, plus transport. May, June, late September and October are the best times (it's banned from mid-July to mid-September because of the monsoon).

Rock-Climbing

Cliffs at Solang, Aleo and Vashisht have a good range of bolted and traditional routes ranging from French 5a to 7b (British 4a to 6b). A day's climbing for beginners or experienced climbers costs ₹1500 to ₹2000 with Manali agencies, including transport. Longer courses are also offered. Solang and the Chatru area in Lahaul are tops for bouldering.

Skiing & Snowboarding

From around mid-January to mid-March, Solang Nullah transforms into Himachal's main ski and snowboarding resort. Equipment can be hired from Manali agencies or Solang Nullah hotels for ₹1000 per day. The piste offers limited options for experienced skiers, but there is off-piste powder and backcountry skiing from the top of the cable car. In April and May Gulaba becomes the off-piste centre with snowshoe-trekking up nearby peaks. Agencies such Himalayan Adventurers (p309) and Himalayan Extreme Centre (p309) offer one-to-two-week ski touring packages. Heli-skiing packages to high-altitude powder can be arranged through **Himalayan Heli Adventures** (☑ 251593; www.himachal.com).

Walking & Trekking

Manali is a popular starting point for organised mountain treks. Most agencies offer multi-day treks for between ₹2000 and ₹3000 per person per day including guides, transport, porters or pack animals, food and camping equipment. June, September and October are overall the best months. Popular options include Beas Kund (three days), the 4250m-high Bhrigu Lake (three days), the Hamta Pass to Lahaul (four days), the Chandrakani Pass from Naggar to Malana (three days) and, more demanding, the Pin-Parvati Trek (six to nine days) or routes west to the isolated village of Bara Bhangal and on to the Chamba or Kangra valleys (11 days or more).

Plenty of shorter walks are possible from Manali. The usual rules on safe trekking apply – tell someone where you are going and never walk alone. Guides for day hikes typically cost ₹1500. One recommended day-hike is up to Lama Dugh meadow west of town (about four hours up, three hours down). A good short walk goes from Vashisht to Jogini waterfall (p317) and back.

equivalent), *thenthuk* (a Tibetan soup with short, flat noodles) and Sichuan chicken and lamb. Cold beers and fruit wines too.

Khyber MULTICUISINE **$$**
(the Mall; mains ₹160-420; ☺8am-11pm) Upstairs by the roundabout at the top of the Mall, Khyber is central Manali's best place for a cold beer, fruit wine or even a *mojito*. The food is also good – the speciality is meat-heavy Punjabi and Afghani cuisine but there's also Chinese, Continental, and tandoori trout.

Drinks are reasonably priced, and the window booths are a good place to watch the Mall.

Johnson's Cafe CONTINENTAL **$$$**
(Circuit House Rd; mains ₹300-530; ☺8am-10.30pm; ☏) The restaurant at Johnson Hotel is tops for European food, with specialities

such as lamb and mint gravy, wood-oven-baked trout with almond sauce, and apple crumble with custard. The restaurant-bar is cosy but the garden terrace is the place to be, especially during happy hours.

🍴 Old Manali

Numerous half-open-air restaurants serve all the usual backpacker-town suspects – *momos,* omelettes, banana pancakes, apple pie and the three I's (Italian/Israeli/Indian dishes). Nearly all these places close by November. The best include friendly and efficient **Shiva Garden Cafe** (Map p310; mains ₹90-280; ☺7.30am-10.30pm; ☏) and **River Music** (Map p310; mains ₹130-300; ☺8am-10pm), which is especially good for breakfasts and baked goods.

Central Manali

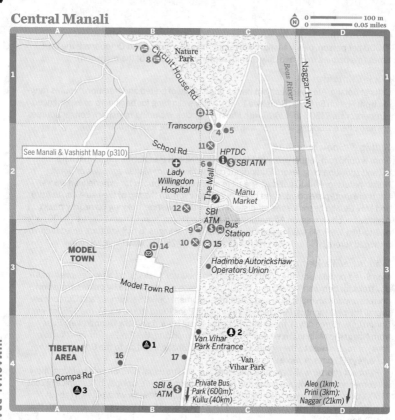

See Manali & Vashisht Map (p310)

Map labels: Nature Park, Circuit House Rd, Bus River, Naggar Hwy, Transcorp, HPTDC, SBI ATM, School Rd, The Mall, Lady Willingdon Hospital, Manu Market, SBI ATM, Bus Station, MODEL TOWN, Hadimba Autorickshaw Operators Union, Model Town Rd, TIBETAN AREA, Van Vihar Park Entrance, Van Vihar Park, Gompa Rd, SBI & ATM, Private Bus Park (600m); Kullu (40km), Aleo (1km); Prini (3km); Naggar (21km)

0   100 m
0   0.05 miles

Dylan's Toasted & Roasted CAFE $
(Map p310; www.dylanscoffee.com; coffees & breakfasts ₹50-150; ⊙9am-11pm Mon-Sat; 🐾) This ever popular hole-in-the-wall cafe serves the best coffee in town, plus cinnamon tea, hearty breakfasts and wicked desserts including 'Hello to the Queen' – ice cream, melted chocolate and fried banana chunks on a bed of broken biscuits.

Drifters' Inn MULTICUISINE $$
(Map p310; mains ₹180-410; ⊙9.30am-4pm & 6-11pm; 🐾) A loungey restaurant-cafe that's good for hearty breakfasts, strong coffee, international dishes from eggs Florentine to Thai curries, and imaginative beverages such as sea-buckthorn fizz.

★La Plage FRENCH $$$
(Map p310; 📱9805340977; www.facebook.com/la.plage.manali; mains ₹300-500; ⊙noon-11pm mid-May–Aug, closed Mon Jul-Aug) Dinner at this outpost of one of Goa's chic-est eateries is

like being invited to the hip Paris apartment of your much, much cooler friend. Classic French standards such as liver pâté are joined by specialities like overnight-cooked lamb, smoked trout, pumpkin ravioli and a chocolate thali dessert.

It's 1km from the Old Manali bridge in an apple orchard, but you can call ahead for free transport from and back to the bridge. It's worth the trip!

★Lazy Dog Lounge MULTICUISINE $$$
(Map p310; mains ₹220-670; ⊙11am-10.30pm; 🐾) This slick restaurant-bar features big plates of fresh, flavourful international food – from pumpkin-and-coconut soup to oven-baked trout and Thai rice bowls – that's steps above typical backpacker fare. Sit on chairs, benches or cushions in a space that's classy yet earthy, or relax in the riverside garden. The beer, wine and cocktail lists are as good as you'll get in the mountains.

Central Manali

Casa Bella Vista ITALIAN $$$
(Map p310; Log Huts Rd; mains ₹300-520; ⊙noon-11pm May-Sep) Not the cheapest, but the best pizzas in the Old Manali area – thin crust, log-oven pies with tasty topping combinations – and the salads and pasta are pretty good too. It's all vegetarian, in a bright, indoor-outdoor setting.

🍷 Drinking & Nightlife

Restaurants double as bars to provide Manali's nightlife, and most serve alcohol. Himachal's bounteous orchards produce huge quantities of apples, pears, plums and apricots, some of which are made into cider, perry (pear cider) or a wide range of strong fruit wines. In Manali town, the best places for a beer or fruit wine are Khyber (p313) and Chopsticks (p312). The upmarket Johnson's Cafe (p313), Johnson Lodge (p309) and Banon Resorts (p309) also have good bars.

In Old Manali, **The Hangout** (Map p310; ⊙noon-midnight, from 5pm Fri) is popular for its outdoor firepits, frequent live music including jam sessions, and decent food.

🛍 Shopping

Manali is crammed with shops selling souvenirs from Himachal, Tibet and Ladakh, including turquoise jewellery and lots of brass Buddhas. The local speciality is Kullu shawls (p305), for which a good place to start is **Bhuttico** (☑252196; the Mall; ⊙9am-7pm Mon-Sat), which charges fair, fixed prices and has several shops around town.

Bookworm BOOKS
(☑252920; Shop No 5, near Post Office; ⊙11am-7pm Mon-Sat) Excellent selection of books,

including many about the Himalaya, and maps including Leomann trekking maps.

ⓘ Information

Banks in Manali don't offer foreign exchange but there are private moneychangers, and SBI has three central ATMs – the one at the bank branch south of the pedestrian mall has shorter queues. It's easy to buy SIM cards for foreign phones at phone shops on and around the Mall. **Shashni Communications** (the Mall; ⊙9am-7pm), for example, only needs to see your passport.
HPTDC (☑252116; the Mall; ⊙8am-8pm, 9am-7pm approx Nov-Mar) Can book HPTDC buses and hotels.
Lady Willingdon Hospital (☑252379; www.manalihospital.com; School Rd) Church-run hospital with 24-hour emergency service.
Post Office (Model Town; ⊙9.30am-5.30pm Mon-Sat) Come before 2pm if posting parcels.
Transcorp (the Mall; ⊙9.30am-6.30pm Mon-Sat) Changes cash and travellers cheques.

ⓘ Getting There & Away

There's a **Railway Reservation Office** (the Mall; ⊙8am-1.30pm Mon-Fri, 8am-12.30pm Sat) at the top of the Mall.

AIR
Manali's closest airport is 50km south at Bhuntar.

BUS
Government-run HRTC buses go from the **bus station**. HPTDC buses also go from the bus station but tickets are sold at their office. Private buses start from a large bus park 1.2km south of the bus station; tickets are sold at travel agencies along the Mall.
Delhi The most comfortable options are the HPTDC's AC Volvo coaches at 5.30pm and 6.30pm (₹1300, 15 hours). Private travel

HIMACHAL PRADESH MANALI

agencies run similar overnight services for
₹800 to ₹1600, depending on season. HRTC
also has AC Volvos (₹1285/798 to Delhi/
Chandigarh) at 4pm, 5pm and 6.30pm, plus
an AC deluxe (₹1005/640) at 5.50pm, and 12
ordinary services daily (₹655/442).

Kullu & Parvati Valleys Buses go to Kullu
(₹50, 1½ hours) every few minutes, many
continuing to Bhuntar (₹70, 2½ hours) and
Mandi (₹163, four hours). Buses to Naggar
(₹30, one hour) go about half-hourly from
about 7am to 6pm. For the Parvati Valley,
change at Bhuntar.

Lahaul & Spiti The Rohtang La, between
Manali and Lahaul, is normally open from
mid-May to early November, and the Kunzum
La, between Lahaul and Spiti, from mid-June to
mid-October (exact dates depend on snow conditions). A new tunnel bypassing the Rohtang
La is due to open in 2017, opening up Lahaul
to year-round visits. In season, HRTC runs up
to seven daily buses to Keylong, Lahaul (₹170,
seven hours), and one at 5.30am to Kaza, Spiti
(₹300, 11 hours).

Leh The bone-shaking, exhausting and spectacular road to Leh is normally open from
early June to some time in October (exact
dates depend on road conditions). From July
to mid-September, an HPTDC bus (₹2500,
33 hours) departs at 9am every second day,
with an overnight stop at Keylong, where tent
accommodation, dinner and breakfast are
included in the fare. Throughout the season
the Him-aanchal Taxi Operators Union runs
minibuses to Leh departing at 2.30am without
an overnight halt (₹1000 to ₹1500, about 18
hours), or departing at 6am with an overnight
halt (₹1500 to ₹2200, or ₹2200 to ₹3200
with accommodation, dinner and breakfast
included); book a day in advance. Travel agencies run similar minibuses in July and August.
On all journeys to Leh, bring snacks and warm
clothing and be alert to the symptoms of Acute
Mountain Sickness (AMS).

Other Destinations For Shimla, the HPTDC
runs a daily bus at 8am (₹550, nine hours)
and there are also six HRTC buses (ordinary/
AC ₹390/550). For Dharamsala, HRTC buses
(₹355, 10 hours) go at 8am and 6.30pm, and
there's usually a private bus (₹550) at 7.30pm.

MOTORCYCLE

Many people tackle the mountain passes to
Ladakh or Spiti on bought or rented bikes. You
can book into a group tour with accommodation,
food and backup vehicles included at around
₹5000 per day, or just rent a bike and head off
on your own.

For rentals, expect to pay ₹1200/1500 per
day for a 350/500cc Enfield, down to ₹800
for a 150cc Pulsar. Make sure the deal includes

spares, tools and at least third-party insurance.
Reliable rental places include the following:

Anu Auto Works (Royal Moto Touring; Map
p310; ☑9816163378; www.royalmototouring.
com; Vashisht Rd) Offers Enfield motorbike
tours, and rents Enfields too.

Bike Rentals Manali (Map p310;
☑9459673440; www.bikerentalsmanali.com;
Vashisht) Enfield rentals and tours.

Enfield Club (Map p310; ☑9805206004;
chootutheenfieldclub@gmail.com; Vashisht
Rd) Enfield rentals, repairs and tours; also sells
secondhand machines.

Himalayan Inder Motors (☑9816113973;
Gompa Rd) Rents Enfields and other makes.

TAXI

The **Him-aanchal Taxi Operators Union**
(☑252120; the Mall) charges around ₹17,000
for a comfortable Sumo, Innova or Tavera jeep,
carrying six people in comfort or up to 10 in less
comfort, to Leh in high season (July and August).
Early or late in the season you might get one for
as little as ₹10,000. Private travel agencies generally charge a bit more. Antrek Tours & Travels
(p309) offers seats in similar vehicles for ₹2400
to ₹4000, including a night at their comfortable
Sarchu tent camp.

For Kaza, a Sumo/Innova/Tavera is ₹8000 to
₹8500 with Him-aanchal. For 6am share jeeps to
Kaza (₹800 per seat), enquire the day before at
Hotel Kiran (☑253066) in the south of Manali,
where drivers from Spiti hang out.

Other one-way taxi fares:

DESTINATION	FARE (₹)
Bhuntar airport	1500
Dharamsala	5000
Keylong	5000
Kullu	1000
Manikaran	1800
Naggar	800
Solang Nullah	800

ⓘ Getting Around

Hadimba Autorickshaw Operators Union
(☑253366; the Mall) has an office at the south
end of the Mall with a large sign listing fares
to various destinations, but drivers here often
refuse to go for the posted prices. Drivers
waiting at the top of the Mall tend to be a little
more logical and with luck will go to Old Manali
bridge for ₹50, Hadimba Temple for ₹60 or
Vashisht for ₹70. But they'll get more out of
you if they can, especially after dark (if you can
get one at all).

Around Manali

Vashisht

☎ 01902 / POP 1600

About 2km north of Manali on the slopes above the Beas River, Vashisht village is a slightly quieter and more compact version of Old Manali and a popular travellers' hangout. Indian tourists mostly come to bathe in the hot springs and tour the temples, while foreign travellers largely come for the cheap accommodation, chilled atmosphere and charas. Many guesthouses and restaurants close down from about November to April.

◉ Sights & Activities

Vashisht Mandir   HINDU TEMPLE

(Map p310; ☺5am-9pm) Vashisht's sulphur-laden hot springs are channelled into small **public baths** (Map p310; ☺5am-9pm) FREE, with separate areas for men and women, inside the ancient stone Vashisht Mandir, which is dedicated to the sage Vashisht. There's another open-air **public pool** (Map p310) just uphill, past a set of hot-water spouts where locals wash clothes and dishes. Nearby are similar temples to **Shiva** (Map p310) and **Rama** (Map p310).

Jogini Waterfall   WALKING

For a pretty walk of about an hour each way, head to the school built over a stream at the north end of Vashisht, and take the path up to the right along its far wall. This leads through woods and across a second stream to a small temple beside a third stream.

From here it's 30 minutes uphill to the pretty and quite powerful waterfall.

🛏 Sleeping

Many small, inexpensive guesthouses and homestays are tucked away along the village lanes and up paths towards the hills.

Hotel Dharma   HOTEL $

(Map p310; ☎252354; www.hoteldharmamanali. com; r ₹400-1200; ☺closed Jan & Feb; @) A short, steep walk above the Rama Temple is rewarded with some of the best views from any hotel on either side of the Beas River. The older wing, with a big terrace out front, has basic but clean rooms that get more expensive as you get higher, while the pricier new section has nicer, carpeted rooms with balconies. All have hot showers.

The top-floor duplexes fit four people for ₹1500.

Hotel Surabhi   HOTEL $

(Map p310; ☎9816042796; www.surabhihotel. com; s ₹880-1320, d ₹990-1430; ☎) One of several big, modernish places on the main street, Surabhi's slightly faded but spacious and clean rooms have balconies with great views, and there's free wi-fi in the rooftop cafe. This is one place where you don't really need to spring for the more expensive rooms. It's open year-round, with discounts possible in slow periods.

Hotel Valley of Gods   HOTEL $$

(Map p310; ☎01902-251111; www.hotelvalleyof-gods.com; r ₹2940-4110; @☎) This impressive stone-and-wood building, owned and run by a local family, has bright, spacious,

HIMACHAL PRADESH AROUND MANALI

HAMTA PASS TREK

Easily accessible from Manali, this camping trek crosses from the Kullu Valley to Lahaul's Chandra Valley via the 4270m Hamta Pass. Most people now drive up the Hamta valley from Prini village to the recently constructed dam just below Jabri Nullah. Two easy days to start off, with a combined ascent of around 500m, are good for acclimatisation. The climb to the pass from the campsite at Balu Ka Gera (3540m) is steep and tiring, but there are sublime snow-peak views from the top. Best times for this trek are the second half of September and October, after the monsoon. Chatru is on the road between Gramphu (on the north side of the Rohtang La) and Spiti.

STAGE	ROUTE	DURATION (HR)	DISTANCE (KM)
1	Dam to Chikka	3	5
2	Chikka to Balu Ka Gera	4	9
3	Balu Ka Gera to Shia-gouru via Hamta Pass	8	15
4	Shiagouru to Chatru	4	10

pine-floored rooms with good, big bathrooms and fine balconies overlooking the valley. The rooftop restaurant, internet cafe, in-room wi-fi and on-site trekking-and-travel agency provide a pretty good package of services. Off-season discounts can slash rates by more than half.

✗ Eating

Vashisht's main street has plenty of semi-open-air cafes serving similar menus of Indian, Italian, Tibetan, Chinese and Israeli dishes at reasonable prices, with free erratic wi-fi.

German Bakery   BAKERY $
(Map p310; baked goods ₹20-70; ⊙8am-10.30pm; ☎) Come here for all your carrot cake, apple pie and cinnamon roll requirements. The couple of tables and benches out front are an evening gathering spot for the local semi-resident backpacker crowd.

World Peace Cafe   MULTICUISINE $$
(Map p310; mains ₹100-280; ⊙8am-10pm; ☎) On Hotel Surabhi's rooftop, this popular choice has great valley views from its expansive patio, plus an inside room with low tables and floor cushions. The kitchen does a decent job on a wide-ranging international menu, and they sometimes hold music jams in summer.

Freedom Cafe   MULTICUISINE $$
(Map p310; mains ₹100-200; ⊙7.30am-11pm; ☎) Freedom, a little away from the main pack and standing on stilts to bring it up to road level, has the best views of all the traveller cafes, plus decently prepared fare and friendly service. Good for an early breakfast, too.

❶ Getting There & Away

The regular autorickshaw fare to or from Manali is ₹70; don't rely on being able to get one in either direction after 7pm. On foot it's about 30 minutes; a footpath down beside Bike Rentals Manali comes out on the main road about 250m north of the Vashisht turn-off.

Solang Nullah
☎01902
From January to March, skiers and snowboarders can enjoy 1.5km of alpine-style runs here, 13km north of Manali, taking the recently installed **cable car** (Ropeway, Gondola; ₹500 one-way or return; ⊙10am-6.30pm) up to 3200m (the cable car operates in all seasons).

Solang is also a year-round 'beauty spot', with paragliding, zorbing, quad bikes and a general carnival-like atmosphere in summer. The surrounding hills are good for walking – Patalsu peak (4472m) to the north is an excellent if quite strenuous one- or two-day hike.

If you want to stay, go for **Hotel Iceland** (☎256008; www.icelandsolang.com; r ₹2120-4110), a genuine ski lodge with great rooms, equipment rental and a restaurant, and off-season discounts of 20% to 40%.

Buses to Solang Nullah (₹20, one hour) leave Manali's bus station at 8am, 9.30am, 2pm and 4pm, heading back immediately on arrival. Snow may make the road impassable in January and February, which usually means taking a jeep or walking the 3km up from Palchan village on the highway.

WESTERN HIMACHAL PRADESH

Western Himachal Pradesh is most famous as the home of the Tibetan government-in-exile and residence of the Dalai Lama, near Dharamsala, but consider travelling further afield to the fascinating Chamba Valley. Information can be found online for the **Kangra Valley** (www.hpkangra.gov.in) and **Chamba Valley** (www.hpchamba.gov.in).

Dharamsala
☎01892 / POP 30,800 / ELEV 1219M
Dharamsala is known as the home of the Dalai Lama, but the untidy market town where the buses pull in is actually Lower Dharamsala. The Tibetan government-in-exile is based just uphill in Gangchen Kyishong, and travellers make a beeline further uphill to the busy little traveller town of McLeod Ganj, also known as Upper Dharamsala.

The **Museum of Kangra Art** (Indian/foreigner ₹50/100; ⊙10am-1.30pm & 2-5pm Tue-Sun), just off the main street, displays some fine miniature paintings from the Kangra school, and Chamba *rumal* embroideries, along with traditional costumes and photos from the devastating 1905 Kangra earthquake.

🛏 Sleeping & Eating

The well-kept HPTDC hotel **Kashmir House** (☎222977; www.hptdc.gov.in; s ₹1330-2120, d ₹1770-2820), a short hike up the hill

Dharamsala

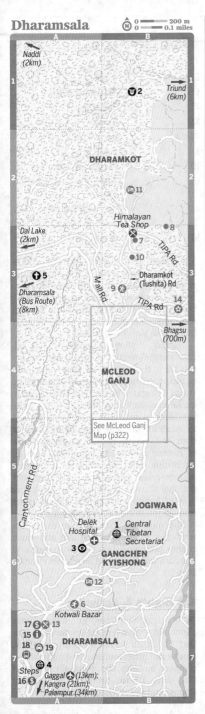

◉ Sights
1 Cultural Museum B6
2 Gallu Devi Temple B1
   Library of Tibetan Works &
   Archives ....(see 1)
3 Men-Tsee-Khang A6
   Men-Tsee-Khang Museum ....(see 3)
4 Museum of Kangra Art A7
   Nechung Gompa ....(see 1)
5 St John in the Wilderness A3

⊕ Activities, Courses & Tours
6 ANEC A6
7 Himachal Vipassana Centre B3
8 Himalayan Iyengar Yoga Centre B3
   Library of Tibetan Works &
   Archives ....(see 1)
   Library of Tibetan Works &
   Archives ....(see 1)
9 Regional Mountaineering Centre B3
10 Tushita Meditation Centre..................B3

🛏 Sleeping
11 Cool Talk Corner B2
12 Kashmir House....................................A6

🍴 Eating
13 Midtown Restaurant A7
   Nechung Cafe................................(see 1)

✪ Entertainment
14 Tibetan Institute of Performing
   Arts B3

ℹ Information
15 HPTDC..A7
16 SBI..A7
17 SBI ATM..A7

ℹ Transport
18 Dharamsala Bus Station.....................A7
19 Dharamsala Taxi Union.......................A7
   Railway Reservation Centre ....(see 15)

towards Gangchen Kyishong, once belonged to the Maharaja of Jammu and Kashmir and still packs a measure of Raj-era character. The best restaurant is **Midtown Restaurant** (mains ₹130-250; ⊙10am-10.30pm), good for kebabs, creamy curries or chicken tikka, with quite professional service.

ℹ Information
The **HPTDC** (☎224212; Hotel Dhauladhar; ⊙10am-6pm) has tourist information and there's a **Railway Reservation Centre** (☎226711; Hotel Dhauladhar; ⊙8am-2pm) in the same building.

BUSES FROM DHARAMSALA

DESTINATION	FARE (₹)	DURATION (HR)	FREQUENCY
Amritsar	230	7	5am
Chamba	260	8	3 daily
Dalhousie	250	6	7.30am & 12.30pm
Dehra Dun	515-535	13	3pm & 9pm
Delhi	510-1120	12	9 daily
Gaggal	15	40min	every 15min
Kangra	25	1	every 15min
Manali	355	10	7am, 6pm, 8.30pm
Mandi	200	6	4 HRTC daily; also private buses
Palampur	50	2	half-hourly until 6pm
Pathankot	130	3½	hourly 5am-5pm
Shimla	350-930	10	8 daily

ⓘ Getting There & Away

Dharamsala airport is at Gaggal, 13km south-west. Air India and SpiceJet both fly daily to/from Delhi, though flights are sometimes cancelled in bad weather.

Buses run from Dharamsala bus station to McLeod Ganj (₹14, 35 minutes) about every half-hour from 8am to 7pm. Services to Delhi include Volvo AC buses (₹1120) at 6.30pm and 8pm, and an AC deluxe bus (₹840) at 8.30pm.

Dharamsala Taxi Union (☑ 222105) is up a steep flight of steps from the bus stand. Cabs to McLeod Ganj cost ₹200. Irregular minibuses to McLeod Ganj (₹14, 35 minutes) wait nearby on the main street.

McLeod Ganj

☑ 01892 / ELEV 1770M

When travellers talk of heading up to Dharamsala (to see the Dalai Lama...), this is where they mean. Around 4km north of Dharamsala town – or 10km via the looping bus route – McLeod Ganj is the residence of His Holiness the 14th Dalai Lama and the site of the Tibetan exile community's main temple. The Tibetan government-in-exile is based just downhill at Gangchen Kyishong, and McLeod is home to a large Tibetan population, including many monks and nuns. It's also, along with Manali, one of the two big traveller hang-outs in Himachal Pradesh, where thousands of people come each year to volunteer with the Tibetan community, take courses in Buddhism, meditation or yoga, trek in the lofty and beautiful Dhauladhar mountains, or just hang out and enjoy the low-budget spiritual/alternative vibe. McLeod has many budget hotels and guesthouses, cafes and restaurants offering Indo-Italo-Israeli-Tibetan food (with free, erratic wi-fi), travel agencies and shops selling Tibetan souvenirs, all crammed into just a couple of blocks, like a mini-Kathmandu.

Named after Donald McLeod, Lieutenant-Governor of Punjab, McLeod began life in the 1850s as a civilian settlement outside the British garrison of Dharamsala. It was devastated by the 1905 Kangra earthquake and sank into obscurity after Independence – until the Dalai Lama arrived to establish his base here in 1960. Since then, McLeod has become a vibrant centre of Tibetan culture and Buddhism. With an interesting mix of travellers, volunteers, maroon-robed monks and nuns, the international dharma crowd and an increasing flow of Indian tourists, you are never far from an interesting conversation here.

The monsoon (late June to early September) is particularly wet here, and warm clothes are useful between November and March. Many shops and businesses close on Monday.

◉ Sights & Activities

★ **Tsuglagkhang Complex**   BUDDHIST TEMPLE
(Temple Rd; ⊙ 5am-8pm Apr-Oct, 6am-6pm Nov-Mar) The main focus of visiting pilgrims, monks and many tourists, the Tsuglagkhang complex includes the Tsuglagkhang itself (the main Tibetan temple), the Namgyal Gompa and the excellent Tibet Museum.

Tsuglagkhang   BUDDHIST TEMPLE

The revered Tsuglagkhang is the exiles' concrete equivalent of the Jokhang temple in Lhasa and was built in 1969. The central image is a gilded statue of the Sakyamuni Buddha (the name refers to the Buddha's birthplace Sakya). To its left are statues of Avalokitesvara (Chenrezig in Tibetan; the bodhisattva of compassion and Tibet's patron deity), and Padmasambhava, the Indian sage believed to have spread Buddhism in Tibet in the 8th century.

The silver Avalokitesvara is a replica of the 7th-century Avalokitesvara image in the Jokhang temple that was destroyed in 1966 during the Cultural Revolution. It contains relics rescued from the destruction and smuggled out of Tibet. The central Sakyamuni is flanked by collections of sacred texts, and on the right-hand wall are paintings of the three early kings credited with bringing Buddhism to Tibet.

Cameras and phones must be left at a counter before the temple entrance.

➤ Kalachakra Temple

Before visiting the Tsuglagkhang itself, pilgrims first visit the Kalachakra Temple on its west side, which contains mesmerising murals of the Kalachakra (Wheel of Time) mandala, specifically linked to Avalokitesvara, of whom the Dalai Lama is a manifestation. Coloured sand mandalas are created here annually on the fifteenth day of the third Tibetan month.

➤ Namgyal Gompa

Namgyal Gompa is the monastery in the Tsuglagkhang Complex. You can watch the monks in lively debate in the courtyard from 2pm to 3pm daily except Sunday, sealing points of argument with a foot stamp and theatrical clap of the hands. The Dalai Lama's residence, not open to the public, is on the south side of the courtyard.

➤ Tibet Museum

(www.tibetmuseum.org; ☺9am-1pm & 2-6pm Sun & Tue-Fri & 1st Sat of month, to 5pm Oct-Mar) **FREE** The museum tells the story of Tibetan history, the Chinese occupation and the subsequent Tibetan resistance and exodus, through photographs, video and clear English-language display panels. A visit here is a must. Documentaries (₹10) are screened at 11am and 3pm.

➤ Kora Circuit

Most Tibetan pilgrims make a clockwise *kora* (ritual circuit) around the outside of the Tsuglagkhang Complex. Take the downhill road to the left at the complex's entrance then follow the prayer-flag-draped path off to the right after 150m. About half way round the 1.5km circuit you pass a collection of chortens, prayer wheels and photos of more than 100 Tibetans who have self-immolated since 2009.

Central Tibetan Secretariat   MUSEUM

Inside the government-in-exile compound, nearly 2km downhill from the Tsuglakhang Complex, the **Library of Tibetan Works & Archives** (☎9218422467; www.ltwa.net; Gangchen Kyishong; ☺9am-1pm & 2-5pm Mon-Sat, closed 2nd & 4th Sat of month) began life as a collection of sacred manuscripts saved from the Cultural Revolution. Today it has over 100,000 manuscripts, books and documents in Tibetan, and over 13,000 volumes on Tibet, Buddhism and the Himalaya region in English and other languages.

There's a fascinating **cultural museum** (admission ₹20) upstairs, with statues, old Tibetan artefacts and books, and some astonishing three-dimensional mandalas in wood and sand.

Regular library visitors can become temporary members (for ₹100 per month for reading; ₹300 per month plus ₹1000 deposit for borrowing; passport photocopy needed for ID) to access the foreign-language collection.

Also worth a visit is the colourful **Nechung Gompa** below the library building, home to the Tibetan state oracle. Nearby, Nechung Cafe (p328) is an excellent spot for lunch.

Taxis from the Secretariat entrance charge ₹100 to McLeod or Dharamsala.

Men-Tsee-Khang   TIBETAN MEDICINE

(Tibetan Medical & Astrological Institute; ☎223113; www.men-tsee-khang.org; Gangchen Kyishong; ☺9am-1pm & 2-5pm Mon-Sat, closed 2nd & 4th Sat of the month) Established to preserve the traditional arts of Tibetan medicine and astrology, Men-Tsee-Khang is a college, clinic, museum, research centre and an astrological institute rolled into one. The astrological folk can do you a 45-minute oral consultation (₹2000; arrange at least two hours ahead), or a detailed life-horoscope based on your birth time and place, which you'll receive by email and hard copy seven or eight months later (₹5015).

The **Men-Tsee-Khang Museum** (admission ₹10) has interesting displays on Tibetan

McLeod Ganj

N

0 — 100 m
0 — 0.05 miles

A   B   C   D

↑ Dharamsala
(Bus Route)
(9km)

↑ Dharamkot
(800m)

↑ Dharamkot
(1.5km)

→ Bhagsu
(1km)

🕀 14

Taxi
Stand

29

46

🕀 18

Bhagsu Rd

TIPA Rd

Autorickshaw
Stand

🕀 48

📷 22
12

Mall Rd

Dharamkot (Tushita) Rd

43 📷 ◎ 3

20

Main
Square

49

38

34

37

25

2

📷 19

Nowrojee Rd

24

32

📷 23

SBI

45

30

Temple Rd

📷 27

Thomas
Cook

41

31

🕀 44

📷 42

Dolma
Chowk

40

✉ 36

📧 26

🕀 47

Jogiwara Rd

39 🕀🕀 16

🕀 28

Temple Rd

🍴 35

10

🕀

33 15 🕀 13

21

🕀 8

Hotel Bhagsu Rd

HDFC
ATM

💲 9

📷 17

Temple Rd

Tsuglagkhang
Complex

⛰ 1

⛰ 6

⛰ ⛰ 7
4

⛰ 5

🕀 11

→ Gangchen Kyishong (1km);
Dharamsala (4km)

HIMACHAL PRADESH MCLEOD GANJ

McLeod Ganj

medicine, told via illustrative *thangkas* (cloth paintings) as well as samples of medicines and the plants and minerals they're made from. Learn useful facts: cinnamon wards against flatulence and coriander combats anorexia, for example. Men-Tsee-Khang also runs occasional short courses in the basics of Tibetan medicine.

Gu-Chu-Sum Movement Gallery GALLERY
(☑220680; www.gu-chu-sum.org; Jogiwara Rd; ⊙9am-1pm & 2-5pm Mon-Sat, closed 2nd & 4th Sat) FREE Run by a charity that assists current and former Tibetan political prisoners, this gallery houses harrowing photos chronicling oppression in Chinese-occupied Tibet and the brutally suppressed demonstrations of 1987, 1988 and 2008. It's open on request;

ask at the Gu-Chu-Sum office next to Lung Ta Restaurant.

Chorten BUDDHIST TEMPLE
The colourful, recently-built temple between Temple and Jogiwara Rds is generally known as the 'Chorten' (Tibetan for 'Stupa'), since it indeed encases an old chorten. You can climb steps inside to inspect the chorten's upper levels.

Clean Upper Dharamsala Programme EXHIBITION
(www.cudp.in; Bhagsu Rd; ⊙9am-5pm Mon-Fri & 1st Sat of month) 🖉 This centre has exhibits on its admirable work keeping McLeod clean, and offers interesting free tours at 3pm on Wednesdays.

MEETING THE DALAI LAMA

Meeting the Dalai Lama is a lifelong dream for many travellers and certainly for Buddhists, but private audiences are rarely granted. Put simply, the Dalai Lama is too busy with spiritual duties to meet everyone who comes to Dharamsala. Tibetan refugees are automatically guaranteed an audience, but travellers must make do with the occasional public teachings held at the Tsuglagkhang, normally in September or October and after Losar (Tibetan New Year) in February or March, and on other occasions depending on his schedule. For schedules and just about everything you need to know about His Holiness, check out www.dalailama.com. To attend a teaching, you must register with your passport and two photos at the **Branch Security Office** (☎221560; Bhagsu Rd, McLeod Ganj; ☉9am-1pm & 2-5pm Mon-Fri & 1st Sat each month). It's advisable to do this three or four days before the teaching for the best chance of getting in. To get the most out of the teachings bring a cushion and rent a radio and headset for simultaneous translation.

St John in the Wilderness   CHURCH
Just 1.5km west of McLeod on the road to Forsyth Ganj, this brooding Gothic church (dating from 1852) is one of the few remaining traces of McLeod's days as a British hill station. It's open on Sunday mornings for a weekly 10am service. The cemetery contains the graves of many victims of the 1905 earthquake, as well as the rocket-like tomb of the Earl of Elgin, the second Viceroy of India.

Yoga, Ayurveda & Massage
McLeod Ganj has dozens of practitioners of holistic and alternative therapies, some reputable and some making a fast buck at the expense of gullible travellers. Adverts for courses and sessions are posted all over McLeod Ganj and in *Contact* magazine, but talking to other travellers is a better way to find good practitioners. Lha (offers reliable Swedish massages with Tibetan herbal oils for ₹1000. The Men-Tsee-Khang Therapy Centre (p326) is good for Tibetan massages.

Several of the most reputable and longest-established yoga and meditation centres are in Dharamkot and Bhagsu (p332), just outside McLeod.

Holistic Centre of Ayurveda   MASSAGE
(☎9418493871; Ladies Venture Hotel, Jogiwara Rd; 30/60min ₹400/700; ☉10.30am-6pm) Resident masseur Shami is very popular, so book a day or two ahead.

Universal Yoga Centre   YOGA
(☎9882222323; www.vijaypoweryoga.com; Youngling School, Jogiwara Rd; 1½hr class ₹200-300; ☉Apr-Nov) Gets good reports for daily drop-in classes in a variety of techniques; also does teacher-training courses.

Om Yoga Centre   YOGA, MEDITATION
(☎9805693514; www.omyogaindia.com; Ketan Lodge, Jogiwara Rd) This centre, run by a husband-and-wife team, holds daily drop-in classes in yoga (₹200), meditation (₹150) and Indian classical dance (₹500).

Walks
Short walks around McLeod include the 1.5km strolls east to Bhagsu or west to St John in the Wilderness, and the uphill walk to Dharamkot (2km by TIPA Rd, 1km by the steeper Dharamkot Rd). All these follow roads but pass through lovely pine and cedar forests. Some good off-road walks start from Bhagsu and Dharamkot (p331).

Trekking
It's possible to trek to the Chamba or Kullu Valleys and even Lahaul, and several agencies in town can make the necessary arrangements for camping, guides and porters or pack animals. Apart from the demanding Indrahar La trek to the Chamba Valley, the most popular option is the easy four-to-six-day loop to Kareri Lake. All-inclusive treks cost between ₹1500 and ₹2500 per person per day.

High Point Adventure   TREKKING
(☎9816120145; www.trek.123himachal.com; Kareri Lodge, Hotel Bhagsu Rd) An experienced, knowledgable team offering some of the best prices in town. They also have an office (Temple Rd; ☉9am-6pm) on Temple Rd.

Regional Mountaineering Centre   TREKKING
(☎9418020822; Dharamkot (Tushita) Rd; ☉10am-5pm Mon-Sat) This government-run organisation can arrange treks, hikes, rock-climbing and rappelling.

Volunteering

McLeod Ganj has more volunteering opportunities than almost anywhere else in India. Some English conversation classes welcome drop-in participants. For other opportunities it's ideal to make contact a couple of weeks in advance; always check out volunteer organisations carefully before agreeing to participate. Volunteers generally arrange their own accommodation and meals, though Lha offers homestays with Tibetan families (US$20 per day including breakfast and dinner, minimum one week).

Many organisations seeking volunteers advertise in the free magazine *Contact* (www.contactmagazine.net); the magazine itself looks for volunteers to help with writing and proofreading. For more on volunteering, see p46.

Lha (☑220992; www.lhasocialwork.org; Temple Rd; ☺office 9am-1pm & 2-5pm Mon-Sat, closed 2nd & 4th Sat each month) is a good place to start. This NGO arranges placements at a host of community projects, including for teachers of English and other languages, fundraisers, cooks and healthcare or IT professionals. Minimum periods range from one week to two months. Come to the office by 4pm Monday to Friday to join an English conversation class with local refugees.

Tibet Hope Center (☑9882162770; www. facebook.com/tibethopecenter; Jogiwara Rd) is a well-organised NGO aiding Tibetan refugees; it needs English teachers for a month or more and volunteers for English conversation classes (11am Monday to Friday). It welcomes ideas for new projects.

Rogpa (☑9857973026; www.tibetrogpa. org; Mithanala Rd, off Bhagsu Rd; ☺9am-5pm Mon-Sat) places volunteers with childcare experience to help at its baby care centre, freeing up refugee parents to earn an income. At least three weeks' commitment is requested, for half-days or full days.

Learning & Ideas for Tibet (LIT; ☑9418794218; http://lit-dharamsala.org; Jogiwara Rd; ☺9am-5pm Mon-Fri) has positions teaching English, French or German, and in computing for beginners. Volunteers can drop in for the 2pm English conversation classes.

Tibet World (☑9816999928; http://tibetworld. org; Jogiwara Rd; ☺office 9am-5pm Mon-Fri), with over 300 refugee students, needs volunteers for teaching English, German, French and Mandarin for two weeks minimum, and for its 4pm conversation classes. They're open to ideas for workshops or classes in fields such as music, web design or film-making.

Active Nonviolence Education Center (ANEC; www.facebook.com/anec2007; Jogiwara Rd) promotes and provides training in nonviolent conflict resolution. It seeks volunteers with good English for editing, research, fundraising, website design and outreach activities. Some work is at their **main office** (☑228181, 9805147048; tcsamkhar@gmail.com; 1st fl, House No 262,

---

TIBETAN EXILES

In October 1950, about a year after Mao Zedong declared the founding of the People's Republic of China, Chinese troops invaded Tibet. At the time, Tibet was a de facto independent state led by the Dalai Lama, with a hazy, complicated relationship with China. A year later, in October 1951, Lhasa, the Tibetan capital, fell. After resistance simmered for years in the countryside, protests against the Chinese occupation broke out in Lhasa in 1959. As the Chinese army moved against the uprising, it fired upon the Norbulingka, the Dalai Lama's summer palace. Believing his life or his freedom was at risk, the Dalai Lama secretly fled across the Himalayas to India, where he received asylum.

China says its army was sent to Tibet as liberators, to free Tibetans from feudal serfdom and improve life on the vast high plateau. It hasn't worked out that way. While the sometimes-quoted figure of 1.2 million Tibetans killed since 1950 is seriously disputed, no independent observers question the suffering and human-rights abuses, as well as huge losses to Tibet's cultural legacy, that have occurred under Chinese occupation. Many Tibetans still risk the dangerous crossing into India. Today there are an estimated 130,000 Tibetans in India, including those born here. Many new arrivals come first to the Dharamsala area, where they find support from their community (over 10,000 strong), their government-in-exile and a legion of NGOs. There are also large Tibetan communities in Karnataka state, where several settlements have been set up since the 1960s.

Khajanchi Mohalla, Khanyara Rd; ⏰10.30am-1pm & 2-4.30pm Mon-Fri) in Lower Dharamsala, but they'll pay bus fares from McLeod.

Gu-Chu-Sum (p323) places volunteers for English conversation with Tibetan former political prisoners and activists and their families, from 5pm to 6pm daily except Sunday.

Courses

The most reputable schools of yoga and meditation are mainly found in Dharamkot and Bhagsu (p332). The **Library of Tibetan Works & Archives** (☎9218422467; www.ltwa. net; Central Tibetan Secretariat; per month ₹300, registration ₹50; ⏰classes 9am & 11am Mon-Sat) conducts serious Buddhist philosophy courses in English (one hour daily) at the Gangchen Kyishong complex.

Cooking

There are several places where you can learn to cook your own *momos* and *thukpa*, and get to eat your work afterwards. Book the following classes at least a couple of hours ahead.

Lhamo's Kitchen COOKING COURSE (☎9816468719; lhamokitchen@gmail.com; Bhagsu Rd; 2hr class ₹300; ⏰10am-noon, 5-7pm Mon-Sat) Runs recommended courses in vegetarian Tibetan cooking. Each day focuses on *momos*, soups or breads, with two or three types of each.

Sangye's Kitchen COOKING COURSE (☎9816164540; Jogiwara Rd; classes ₹250; ⏰10am-noon, 4-6pm Thu-Tue) Tibetan treats, focusing on *momos* (including chocolate

momos!) every Sunday and Thursday, and noodles on Tuesday and Saturday.

Language

The **Library of Tibetan Works & Archives** (☎9218422467; www.ltwa.net; Central Tibetan Secretariat; per month ₹500, registration ₹50) runs three-month Tibetan-language courses (five hours a week) for beginner, intermediate and experienced students, starting around 20 March, 20 June and 20 September. Tibet Hope Center (p325) has one-hour basic Tibetan speaking classes at 3pm Monday to Friday. Om Yoga Centre (p324) offers daily two-hour Hindi classes (₹300).

There are several independent Tibetan teachers – ask around and check *Contact* magazine.

Festivals & Events

In late January, February or early March McLeod celebrates **Losar** (Tibetan New Year) with processions and masked dances at local monasteries. The Dalai Lama often gives public teachings at this time.

In December, the **International Himalayan Festival** commemorates the Dalai Lama's Nobel Peace Prize, featuring cultural troupes from all around the Himalaya.

Several film festivals liven up McLeod in different seasons. The **Dharamsala Film Festival** (www.dharamsalafilm.festival. com; ⏰May or Jun), **Free Spirit Film Festival** (www.freespiritfilmfestival.com; ⏰late Oct) and **Dharamsala International Film Festival** (www.diff.co.in; ⏰late Oct/early Nov) screen eclectic selections of independent features, documentaries and shorts. The **Tibet Film Festival** (www.tibetfilmfestival.org;

TIBETAN MEDICINE

Traditional Tibetan medicine is a centuries-old holistic healing practice and a popular treatment for all kinds of minor and persistent ailments. Its methods include massages, compresses, bath and steam therapies, pills made from plants and minerals, and diet and lifestyle advice. There are several clinics around town, including the **Men-Tsee-Khang Therapy Centre** (☎221484; www.men-tsee-khang.org; TIPA Rd; ⏰9am-1pm & 2-5pm Mon-Sat, closed 2nd & 4th Sat each month), run by the Tibetan Medical & Astrological Institute.

The most popular *amchi* (Tibetan doctor) in town is the former physician to the Dalai Lama, **Dr Yeshi Dhonden** (☎221461; Ashoka Niwas; ⏰9am-1pm Sun-Fri), whose tiny clinic is squirrelled away in a passage off Jogiwara Rd. To get a consultation you have to queue up early at the nearby Ashoka Guest House, where the first 45 people in line at 10am receive a token for an appointment three days later. For your appointment, bring a sample of urine, which, along with a quick examination, is all the doctor needs to prescribe the appropriate herbal pills. Many locals and expats swear by his treatments.

⊙late Oct) spotlights Tibetan and Nepalese documentaries.

🛏 Sleeping

Popular places fill up quickly; advance bookings are advised, especially from April to June and in October.

Kareri Lodge   HOTEL $
(🖉221132; karerilodge@gmail.com; Hotel Bhagsu Rd; r ₹660-990, ste ₹1540; 🛜) Kareri, squeezed in among a string of more upmarket hotels, has five spotless and comfy rooms with soft beds, some enjoying prime views from huge windows. There's a good vibe here, helped by the friendly manager who offers a reliable trekking service.

Kunga Guesthouse   GUESTHOUSE $
(🖉221180; www.kungaguesthouse.com; Bhagsu Rd; r ₹350-1500; 🛜) 🍴 Above (and below) Nick's Italian Kitchen (p328; which is its greatest asset), Kunga offers a huge range of dull but clean rooms in several buildings, and has a helpful travel-booking service. The cheapest rooms share bathrooms.

Om Hotel   HOTEL $
(🖉9816329985; Nowrojee Rd; r ₹500-550, without bathroom ₹300-350; 🛜) Friendly, family-run Om, just down a lane from the main square, has simple but pleasing rooms with good views. The popular **Namgyal Cafe** (Om Hotel, Nowrojee Rd; mains ₹80-300; ⊙7.30am-9pm) 🍴 serves well-laden but chewy pizzas, plus decently prepared tofu and potato dishes, soups and more, and its terrace catches the sunset over the valley.

Tibet World   HOSTEL $
(🖉9816999928; http://tibetworld.org; Jogiwara Rd; r ₹400-700) Tibet World is an energetic NGO that also has 13 plain, clean accommodation rooms with attached bathroom in its large building, available to its volunteers and others. Best are the top-floor pair with a large panoramic terrace outside. A Tibetan cafe should be open by the time you get there.

Hotel Tibet   HOTEL $
(🖉221587; www.hoteltibetdhasa.com; Bhagsu Rd; r ₹880-1770) Bang in the centre of town, this place has a faintly upmarket feel, but very reasonable prices. Rooms have parquet floors and there's a cosy multicuisine restaurant. Profits go to Tibetan settlements in India.

Loseling Guest House   GUESTHOUSE $
(🖉9218923305; d ₹300-400; 🛜) Just off Jogiwara Rd, Loseling is run by a Tibetan monastery in Karnataka. It's a good cheapie and all rooms have a hot shower; the three rooftop rooms are easily the best.

Tibetan Ashoka Guest House   GUESTHOUSE $
(🖉221763; r with/without bathroom ₹770/220) This 40-room guesthouse, down an alley off Jogiwara Rd, looks out on the valley and catches plenty of sunlight on its ample upper terrace. It's extremely bare and functional, but very clean, and fills up in season. The shared bathrooms have cold water only. Advance reservations aren't accepted.

Hotel Dream Land   HOTEL $
(🖉9816672708; r ₹500-2000; 🛜) Down a tiny alley off Jogiwara Rd, Dream Land is surprisingly large, with surprisingly good valley views. The clean, sizeable rooms have comfy beds and tile floors, and the lower-priced ones are pretty decent value.

Green Hotel   HOTEL $$
(🖉221200; www.greenhotel.in; Bhagsu Rd; r ₹800-2800; ❀🛜) A favourite with midrange travellers and small groups, the Green has a diverse range of sunny, super-clean rooms in three buildings, most with balconies and valley and mountain views. It's well run and has an excellent cafe.

★ Chonor House   BOUTIQUE HOTEL $$$
(🖉221006; www.norbulingkahotels.com; r ₹5290-7750; ❀@🛜) Up a lane near the Tsuglagkhang, Chonor House is a real gem. It's run by the Norbulingka Institute, and is decked out with wonderful handmade Norbulingka furnishings and fabrics. Each of the 13 bright and sunny rooms has a Tibetan theme that runs from the carpets to the bedspreads to the murals. Even the cheapest rooms are spacious.

There's also a lovely garden, with a reasonably priced terrace restaurant.

★ Serkong House   HOTEL $$$
(🖉9857957131; www.norbulingkahotels.com; Nowrojee Rd; s ₹2350-3530, d ₹2940-4110, ste s/d ₹4700/5290; 🛜) Belonging to the Norbulingka Institute, the recently opened Serkong is tasteful, comfortable and well run. Spacious rooms boast Tibetan rugs, Norbulingka-made tables and tea- and coffee-makers, and the more expensive ones have fine views. Staff are polite and efficient, and there's an excellent Tibetan-Indian restaurant (mains ₹130 to ₹250).

✕ Eating & Drinking

McLeod Ganj is crammed with traveller restaurants serving near-identical menus – omelettes, pancakes, Indian, Tibetan and Chinese staples, pizzas, pasta and assorted other European food. Happily, many of them do a pretty good job. McLeod also has some of North India's best cafes, with good coffee and English-style tea. For a quick snack, local women sell veg *momos* on the upper part of Jogiwara Rd and at the entrance to the Tsuglagkhang. Takeaway beer and spirits are available from several small 'wine shops'.

Snow Lion Restaurant   MULTICUISINE $
(Jogiwara Rd; mains ₹70-130, breakfasts ₹145-175; ☺7am-9pm; 🛜) Especially popular for its good-value set breakfasts and decent coffee, the Snow Lion does good *momos* and *thukpa* too, and has shelves full of books.

Café Budan   CAFE $
(Jogiwara Rd; items ₹60-120; ☺7.30am-7.30pm) A cool and cosy wicker-chaired hang-out that serves up tasty all-day breakfast dishes like spinach-and-cheese omelettes or French toast, plus cakes, tarts, coffees and teas.

Peace Cafe   TIBETAN $
(Jogiwara Rd; mains ₹70-100; ☺7am-8pm) This cosy little cafe is popular with Tibetans, including monks and nuns, as well as travellers, for dining on tasty *momos, thukpa* and *thenthuk* (veggies, cheese, egg and tofu).

Nechung Cafe   MULTICUISINE $
(mains ₹75-125; ☺ 7.30am-8.30pm Mon-Sat) Nechung Cafe, in the Central Tibetan Secretariat area, is an excellent spot for lunch, with tasty Tibetan, Thai and other dishes.

★ Indique   MULTICUISINE $$
(Temple Rd; mains ₹190-290; ☺8am-11pm) With a romantic open rooftop and plenty more tables and a loungy bar indoors, Indique is McLeod's most stylish eating venue and has live music some nights. Breakfasts and tortilla wraps are good, but the Indian lunch and dinner dishes are probably the best in town, with the chicken mint tikka a standout.

Nick's Italian Kitchen   ITALIAN $$
(Bhagsu Rd; mains ₹75-175; ☺7.30am-9pm; 🛜) Unpretentious, well-run Nick's has been serving up tasty vegetarian pizzas, lasagne and gnocchi for years. Follow up a ground coffee with a heavenly slice of lemon cheesecake – apparently Richard Gere's favourite when he stayed here. Eat inside or out on the large terrace.

MCLEOD GANJ TO BHARMOUR TREK

This popular five-day route crosses the Indrahar La (4420m) to the Chamba Valley, and can be done in either direction. The pass is normally open from June to early November, but the best months are September and October.

The first day climbs three or four hours to Triund, where there are a couple of simple rest houses and camping spots. The next stage climbs to the alpine meadow of Laka Got (3350m) and then the rocky shelter known as Lahesh Cave (3600m). With an early start the next day, you can cross the Indrahar La – and be rewarded for the tough climb with astounding views – before descending steeply to the meadow campground at Chata Parao.

The track on down to Kuarsi, crossing summer meadows, can be tricky to find in places. On the final day you reach an unpaved road 3km before Lamu. It's 5km down from Lamu to Holi-Chamba road, plied by several buses a day. To continue to Bharmour, take a bus down to Kharamukh and change there.

STAGE	ROUTE	DURATION (HR)	DISTANCE (KM)
1	McLeod Ganj to Triund	3-4	9
2	Triund to Lahesh Cave	3-4	8
3	Lahesh Cave to Chata Parao over Indrahar La	6	10
4	Chata Parao to Kuarsi	5-6	15
5	Kuarsi to Lamu	4	10

Green Hotel Restaurant   MULTICUISINE $$
(Bhagsu Rd; mains ₹100-180; ☺6.30am-9pm;
🖉) This traveller-oriented hotel restaurant,
with a sunny terrace and comfy couches in-
side, serves very good vegetarian food and
the earliest breakfasts in town.

Common Ground Cafe   ASIAN $$
(www.facebook.com/commongroundcafe09; Dhar-
amkot Rd; mains ₹70-190; ☺11am-9pm; 🖉)
The menu is a sizzling variety of Chinese and
Tibetan speciality dishes, from Taiwan-style
tofu to *sha tag* (a rich meat-and-veg stir fry),
available without MSG if you like, plus all-
day Western-type breakfasts. The coffee's
good, too. The atmosphere is pleasingly laid-
back but sociable, with communal tables,
floor cushions and a small library.

Moonpeak   MULTICUISINE $$
(www.moonpeak.org; Temple Rd; mains ₹120-250;
☺7.30am-8.30pm; 🖉) A little chunk of Se-
attle, transported to India. Come for excel-
lent coffee, cakes, imaginative brown-bread
open sandwiches (like poached chicken
with mango, lime and coriander sauce), plus
plenty of well-prepared main dishes – and
the Himachali thali (₹200), a sampler of re-
gional dishes.

Tibet Kitchen   TIBETAN $$
(Jogiwara Rd; mains ₹110-200; ☺noon-9.30pm)
It's worth queuing here to try the spicy
Bhutanese food including *kewa datse* (potatoes, beans and chilli in cheese sauce) and
unusual Tibetan dishes like *shapta* (roasted
lamb slices with capsicum and onion). The
momos are good too, and there are also
plenty of Indian, Thai and Chinese flavours.
Its three floors of tables are often full with
travellers, monks and locals.

McLlo Restaurant   MULTICUISINE $$
(Main Square; mains ₹190-370; ☺9.30am-11pm)
Crowded nightly and justifiably popu-
lar, this large, three-floor place serves a
mind-boggling menu of Indian, Chinese
and international fare, including pizzas and
pasta. The semi-open-air top floor is one of
McLeod's best places to enjoy a cold beer
(₹180).

Jimmy's Italian Kitchen   ITALIAN $$
(Jogiwara Rd; mains ₹150-250; ☺8am-10pm; 🖉)
Jimmy's is a dependable Italian place with
pleasant seating and a sunny rooftop. The
baked potatoes, Greek salads and dishes like
chicken Florentine are a nice change, and
the pasta includes ravioli and lasagne.

Lung Ta   JAPANESE $$
(Jogiwara Rd; set meals ₹170; ☺noon-8.30pm Mon-
Sat) The daily set menus are the best choice
at this vegetarian Japanese restaurant, es-
pecially on Tuesdays and Fridays when they
include sushi rolls and miso soup. The food
and ambience are authentic enough to at-
tract Japanese travellers looking for a taste
of home. Profits go to the NGO Gu-Chu-Sum.

Four Seasons Cafe   MULTICUISINE $$
(Jogiwara Rd; mains ₹70-300; ☺8.30am-9pm)
This bustling little place serves up excellent
pasta and Tibetan dishes at very fair prices.
There are only seven tables so be prepared
to share.

☆ Entertainment

Irregular live music nights or jam sessions at
cafes and restaurants are advertised around
town. Free documentary films are shown at
6.30pm Wednesdays at Tibet Hope Center
(p325), and at 6.30pm or 7pm Monday, Tuesday and Thursday at Learning & Ideas for
Tibet (p325). Tibet World (p325) puts on a
Tibetan folk show of songs, dances and stories at 6.30pm on Thursdays (₹150).

**Tibetan Institute of
Performing Arts**   THEATRE
(TIPA; 📞221478; tibetanarts2012@gmail.com; TIPA
Rd) Stages occasional Tibetan cultural per-
formances including colourful lhamo (folk
opera).

**Tibetan Song &
Dance Show**   CULTURAL PROGRAM
(www.facebook.com/lion.man.show;   Youngling
School, Jogiwara Rd; admission ₹200) A mix of
music, song, dance and circus theatrics,
Tsering Dorjee's one-man show is both entertaining and moving. Well worth an hour
of your time if he's performing when you're
in town. He publicises his show through
posters and normally does shows at 6pm
Wednesday, Saturday and Sunday.

🛍 Shopping

Dozens of shops and stalls sell Tibetan artefacts, including *thangkas*, bronze statues,
metal prayer wheels and 'singing' bowls.
Some are Tibetan-run, but many are run by
Kashmiri traders who apply a degree of sales
pressure. Several local cooperatives offer the
same goods without the hassle. And – book
lovers rejoice! – McLeod undoubtedly has
the highest bookshop-to-population ratio in
India.

HIMACHAL PRADESH MCLEOD GANJ

Tibetan Handicraft Center   HANDICRAFTS
(☏ 221415; www.tibetan-handicrafts.com; Jogiwara Rd; ⏰ 9am-5pm Mon-Sat) ✎ This cooperative employs refugees in the weaving of Tibetan carpets. You'll pay around ₹11,500 for a 0.9m-by-1.8m traditional wool carpet, and they'll ship it if you like (around ₹3500 to Europe). Visitors are welcome to watch the weavers in action. There's also a shop with a wide variety of attractive other goods.

The tailoring section across the street can make a Tibetan dress in four or five days for around ₹800 (cotton) or ₹2500 (silk).

Bookworm   BOOKS
(☏ 221465; Hotel Bhagsu Rd; ⏰ 9.30am-6pm Tue-Sun) The best all-round bookshop.

Green Shop   ORGANIC PRODUCTS
(Bhagsu Rd; ⏰ 9am-6pm Tue-Sun) ✎ Sells handmade recycled paper products, plus other Tibetan-made products including organic peanut butter and tahini.

Lha Tibet Fair Trade   HANDICRAFTS
(www.tibetfairtrade.com; Temple Rd; ⏰ 9am-1pm & 2-5pm Mon-Sat, closed 2nd & 4th Sat) Sells attractive crafts made by Tibetans in India.

ⓘ Information

MEDIA
Contact (www.contactmagazine.net) is an informative, free local magazine with useful information about courses and volunteer work. Available at several cafes, restaurants and hotels in McLeod Ganj.

MEDICAL SERVICES
Traditional Tibetan medicine (p326) is a popular form of treatment in McLeod Ganj.

Delek Hospital (☏ 222053; www.delekhospital.org; Gangchen Kyishong; consultations before/after noon ₹10/50; ⏰ outpatient clinic 9am-1pm & 2-5pm Mon-Fri, 9am-1pm Sat) A small, Tibetan-run hospital practising allopathic medicine.

MONEY
Several places around town offer Western Union money transfers.

HDFC ATM (Temple Rd)

SBI (Temple Rd; ⏰ 10am-4pm Mon-Fri, to 1pm Sat) Has a busy ATM.

Thomas Cook (Temple Rd; ⏰ 9.30am-6pm Mon-Sat) Changes cash/travellers cheques for ₹25/50 commission plus 0.12% tax (minimum ₹30), and gives advances on credit cards for a 5% charge.

POST
Post Office (Jogiwara Rd; ⏰ 9.30am-5pm Mon-Sat) Parcel post is until 1pm Monday to Friday.

TOURIST INFORMATION
HPTDC Tourist Information Centre (☏ 221091; Hotel Bhagsu Rd; ⏰ 10am-5pm) Offers basic local information and makes bookings for the HPTDC bus to Delhi.

TRAVEL AGENCIES
Numerous agencies can book bus tickets and arrange tours and treks.

Himachal Travels (☏ 221428; himachaltravels@sancharnet.in; Jogiwara Rd)

Himalaya Tours & Travels (☏ 220714; www.himalayatravels.net; Bhagsu Rd)

ⓘ Getting There & Around

Many travel agencies in McLeod will book train tickets for a commission of ₹100.

AIR
Dharamsala airport (p320) has flights to/from Delhi.

AUTORICKSHAW
The autorickshaw stand is just north of the main square. Fares are ₹50 to Bhagsu and ₹70 to Dharamkot.

BUS
Buses start from and arrive at the New Bus Stand, 150m north of the main square. Buses and minibuses to Dharamsala (both ₹14, 35

HRTC BUSES FROM MCLEOD GANJ

DESTINATION	FARE (₹)	DURATION (HR)	FREQUENCY
Dehra Dun	530	12	8pm
Delhi	510-1150	12-13	4am, 6pm & 7.30pm (ordinary); 5pm (semi-deluxe); 6.30pm & 7.45pm (deluxe); 5.30pm & 7pm (Volvo AC)
Manali	330	11	4.30pm
Pathankot	150	4	5 buses daily (10am to 4pm)

minutes) run about every half-hour from 8am to 8pm; the minibuses wait at the bus stand exit.

Some long-distance buses start from McLeod but there are more frequent departures from Dharamsala bus station. You can book government (HRTC) buses from both places at McLeod's **HRTC ticket office** (Main Square; ⊗ 9am-4pm). In addition, the HPTDC runs a non-AC deluxe bus to Delhi (₹700, 13 hours) at 6pm every one or two days, and travel agencies sell seats on deluxe private buses to Delhi (Volvo AC ₹1100, 12 hours, departs 6pm), Manali (₹400, 11 hours, departs 6am) and elsewhere.

TAXI

McLeod's **taxi stand** (🗗 221034; Mall Rd) is just north of the main square. A taxi for the day, travelling less than 80km, should cost ₹1600. One-way fares include ₹100 to Gangchen Kyishong, Dharamkot or Bhagsu, ₹200 to Dharamsala bus station, ₹700 to Dharamsala airport, ₹3500 to Chamba and ₹4000 to Manali.

Around McLeod Ganj

Bhagsu & Dharamkot

🗗 01892

Through pine trees north and east of McLeod lie the neighbouring villages of Bhagsu (officially Bhagsunag) and Dharamkot, more rural and laid-back than McLeod itself, and the abode of choice for many budget travellers and long-stayers – places where you can lounge in cafes, take drumming lessons and yoga classes, and forget there's any trouble in the world. Some of the area's best and most serious yoga and meditation schools are here too.

Dharamkot retains a quiet village vibe, with the scattered houses of upper Dharamkot stretching almost to the little Gallu Devi Temple on the ridge above. Lower Bhagsu, in contrast, is busy with concrete hotels, shops and discos aimed squarely at domestic visitors. Its small, 16th-century Shiva temple has a cold, clean, spring-fed swimming pool in front of it, and from there it's a 1km walk to Bhagsu waterfall, most impressive during the monsoon. Two minutes up from the main road in Bhagsu you're back in Backpackerland: upper Bhagsu is very similar to upper Dharamkot, with which it effectively merges. En route, drop into the awesomely kitsch Vashnu Mata Temple, 200m up from the main road, where you access the inner grotto through a concrete lion's mouth and emerge via the jaws of a crocodile.

LET'S DRINK TO A PLASTIC-FREE PLANET

Plastic bags are banned in Himachal Pradesh, but bottles are not. Do your bit for the environment by refilling your drinking water bottle for ₹10 a litre at one of a dozen filtered-water stations around McLeod Ganj, including at Lha, the Green Shop, Green Hotel Restaurant, Common Ground Cafe and Nick's and Jimmy's Italian Kitchens. A map of all the locations is available at http://cudp.in.

🏃 Activities

There are many good walks in the hills around Dharamkot and Bhagsu.

To reach the little Gallu Devi Temple, you can either walk straight up the path from the top of Dharamkot, or take the track along the left side of the water tank opposite Dharamkot's Himalayan Tea Shop, then turn up a path to the right after 50m. A lovely stone path winds 1km up through the forest to emerge on a jeep track. Head 500m to the right to Gallu Devi, with a couple of cafes and guesthouses nearby and panoramas both north and south.

From Gallu Devi one track leads gently west downhill to Naddi village (2.5km) and the underwhelming Dal Lake (3km); another heads about 2km north down to a waterfall; and the main track climbs east through rhododendron woods up to the panoramic mountain meadow of Triund (2900m), a walk of about 6km that gains 800m altitude in a strenuous 2½ to three hours. Triund has a couple of simple rest houses and shops, which rent out sleeping bags and places to sleep or camp, and can provide basic meals. An overnight stop gives you the best chance of clear weather, and time to hike one hour up to the teashop and viewpoint at Laka Got (3350m), sometimes called 'Snowline', before heading back down. If you're starting from McLeod Ganj, you have the option of taking an autorickshaw to the Himalayan Tea Shop (₹70), or even a taxi by a rough road to Gallu Devi (₹400).

If you do go down to Dal Lake, it's just a short hop onward to the Tibetan Children's Village (🗗 221348; www.tcv.org.in; ⊗ office 9am-12.30pm & 1.30-5pm Mon-Fri), which provides free education for nearly 2000 refugee children and lodging for most of them. Visitors are welcome. You can also get there by autorickshaw (₹100) or taxi direct from McLeod Ganj.

Courses

Dharamkot and Bhagsu have many of the area's best options for learning yoga, meditation, Buddhist philosophy and ayurveda. Some places have strict rules on silence, alcohol and smoking.

Himalayan Iyengar Yoga Centre YOGA
(www.hiyogacentre.com; TIPA Rd, Dharamkot; 5-day course ₹4000, advance booking fee ₹1000; ⊙ Mar-Oct) Five-day courses start every Thursday. Intensive and teacher-training courses are held at their ashram west of McLeod.

Tushita Meditation Centre MEDITATION, PHILOSOPHY
(http://tushita.info; Dharamkot; 10-day course incl accommodation & meals from ₹5000; ⊙ Feb-Nov) Tushita offers 10-day residential retreats in Tibetan Buddhist philosophy and drop-in meditation at 9.30am daily except Sunday.

Himachal Vipassana Centre MEDITATION
(☑ 9218414051; www.sikhara.dhamma.org; Dharamkot; ⊙ Apr-Nov) This centre runs strict 10-day silent *vipassana* (mindfulness meditation) courses starting on the 1st and 15th of the month. Payment is by donation.

Ayuskama Ayurvedic Clinic AYURVEDA
(☑ 9736211210; www.ayuskama.com; Hotel Anand Palace Bldg, Bhagsu; ⊙ 9am-6pm) Dr Arun Sharma's ayurvedic treatments and courses get rave reviews. Courses range from a week on massage or nutrition (₹6500 to ₹7500) to three-month diploma courses (₹65,000) and two-year practitioner courses.

🛏 Sleeping & Eating

Both villages have plenty of inexpensive guesthouses (many unsigned) and backpacker restaurants serving Indo-Italo-Israeli-Tibetan food. Long-stayers can get rooms in small family-run guesthouses for around ₹6000 a month, often with kitchen use included.

Cool Talk Corner GUESTHOUSE $
(☑ 9418712171; Dharamkot; r ₹350-500) A friendly and relaxed little guesthouse up a lane above Dharamkot's main street. The two bright top-floor rooms with their own sunny balconies are the real deal. There's good food too (restaurant 9am to 9pm; mains ₹80 to ₹200), including a ₹90 veg thali.

DK House GUESTHOUSE $
(☑ 9418797494; Upper Bhagsu; d ₹250-400; 🛜) A relatively large place in upper Bhagsu, with

clean ensuite rooms, panoramic balconies and the good, cosy Evergreen Cafe (mains ₹90 to ₹190). Turn right up steps, 100m up from Vashnu Mata Temple, and head uphill for 300m.

Sky Pie Guesthouse GUESTHOUSE $$
(☑ 9418605966;www.skypieguesthouse.in;Bhagsu; d ₹400-1800; @🛜) Across the street from Vashnu Mata Temple, Sky Pie has decent budget rooms, with hot showers and wifi, and sparkling, comfy abodes in its new building at the side. It also has a yoga hall and a good little multicuisine restaurant.

Norbulingka Institute

The wonderful **Norbulingka Institute** (☑ 9418436410; www.norbulingka.org; local & Tibetan ₹20, tourist ₹50; ⊙ 9am-5.30pm), 6km southeast of Dharamsala, was established in 1988 to teach and preserve traditional Tibetan art forms. You can watch artisans at work on woodcarving, metal-statue-making, *thangka* painting and embroidery on free tours. The **shop** (www.norbulingkashop.com) sells the centre's expensive but beautiful craftworks, including jewellery, painted boxes and embroidered clothes and cushions, and sales benefit refugee artists. Also set among the institute's delightful Japanese-influenced gardens are the **Deden Tsuglakhang temple**, with a 4m-high gilded Sakyamuni statue, and the **Losel Doll Museum** (local & Tibetan/tourist ₹5/20), which uses charming puppet dioramas to illustrate aspects of traditional Tibetan culture. A short walk outside the complex is the **Dolmaling** Buddhist nunnery, also open to visitors. On Sundays and the second Saturday of each month, the workshops and shop are closed but the rest of the complex is open.

Peaceful and stylish **Norling House** (☑ 9816646423; www.norbulingkahotels.com; r ₹3640, ste ₹5360; ❄🛜) offers comfortable rooms decked out with Buddhist murals and Norbulingka handicrafts, arranged around a sunny atrium. Vegetarian meals and snacks are available at the **Hummingbird Cafe** (mains ₹150-200; ⊙ 7am-9pm; 🛜).

To get here, catch a Palampur-bound bus from Dharamsala and get off at Sacred Heart School, Sidhpur (₹7, 15 minutes), from where it's a 1km gentle uphill walk (or ₹80 taxi ride). A taxi from McLeod Ganj costs ₹400/600 one-way/return.

Sidhbari

The **Gyuto Tantric Gompa** (☎01892-235307; www.kagyuoffice.org; ⊙9am-6pm) at Sidhbari, just north of the Palampur road 7km from Dharamsala, is the adopted home of Ogyen Trinley Dorje, who is widely accepted as the 17th Karmapa (leader of the Karma Kagyu school of Tibetan Buddhism), who fled from Tibet in 2000. Although the Karmapa's official seat is Rumtek Monastery in Sikkim (p549), he does not reside there owing to a rival claim to the Karmapa title.

When in residence, Ogyen Trinley Dorje gives half-hour public audiences on Wednesday and Saturday at 2.30pm; foreign visitors are welcome but security is tight: bring your passport and be ready to leave bags, phones and cameras outside the auditorium. Gyuto monks are famous for their deep-throated chanting and have performed at Glastonbury Festival, the Sydney Opera House and elsewhere.

Frequent Dharamsala–Palampur buses pass through Sidhbari (₹8, 20 minutes), or you can take a taxi from McLeod Ganj for ₹650 return.

Southwest of Dharamsala

Kangra

☎01892 / POP 9500 / ELEV 734M

Once capital of the princely state of Kangra, this bustling town 18km from Dharamsala is a good day trip from McLeod Ganj. Hindus visit to pay homage at the **Brajeshwari Devi Temple**, one of the 51 *Shakti peeths,* temples on the sites where body parts from Shiva's first wife, Sati, fell after the goddess was consumed by flames (this temple marks the final resting place of her left breast). It's reached through an atmospheric bazaar winding 10 minutes up from the main road, 1km south of the bus stand.

At the south end of town, around a ₹100 autorickshaw ride from the bus stand, the impregnable-looking **Kangra Fort** (www.royalkangra.com; Indian/foreigner ₹5/100, audio guide ₹150; ⊙dawn-dusk) soars on a high outcrop between the Manjhi and Banganga Rivers. At least 1000 years old, the fort was occupied by Hindu rajas, Mughal and Sikh conquerors and even the British (from 1846), before it was finally toppled by the 1905 Kangra earthquake. Head up to the palace

---

KANGRA VALLEY TOY TRAIN

Lumbering narrow-gauge trains run east from Pathankot, providing a scenic if slow route to Kangra (2½ hours), Palampur (four hours), Baijnath (seven hours) and Jogindernagar (nine hours). There are six trains a day – two as far as Jogindernagar and four as far as Baijnath. Ordinary trains cost ₹35 or less to any destination, but carriages are generally packed and seats cannot be booked in advance. Board early to grab a window seat and enjoy the views.

---

area at the top for views north to the mountains and south to the plains.

About 200m up the road from the fort is the **Maharaja Sansar Chand Museum** (☎265866; Indian/foreigner ₹30/100, audio guide ₹150; ⊙9am-5pm), whose peacock-feather fans, pashmina fly whisks and pretty Kangra School miniatures give a fine insight into the lifestyle of the erstwhile Kangra royal family, the Katochs – a dynasty so ancient that early members supposedly fought against the Pandavas of the Mahabharata.

Kangra hotels are dreary. Best is **Hotel Grand Raj** (☎260901; www.hotelthegrandraj. com; Dharamshala Rd; r ₹1870-5390; ❄), opposite the bus station, with a good restaurant, though the cheapest rooms are small and can be stuffy and noisy. **Hotel Abhi Residency** (☎261208; Hoshiarpur Rd; r ₹1200-2800; ❄), 600m south along the main road from the temple bazaar street, has sizeable, acceptably comfortable rooms with grubby walls.

❶ Getting There & Away

Buses run about every 30 minutes to Dharamsala (₹25, one hour), Palampur (₹50, 1½ hours) and Pathankot (₹125, three hours). Six trains a day in each direction pull into Kangra Mandir station, 2km east of the Brajeshwari Temple.

A return taxi from McLeod Ganj to Kangra Fort costs ₹1400, including waiting time.

Masrur

Winding roads through pleasant green hills lead 31km southwest from Gaggal to the impressive 10th-century **temples** (Indian/foreigner ₹5/100; ⊙dawn-dusk) at Masrur. Though badly damaged by the 1905 earthquake, the elaborately carved sandstone *sikharas* – very rare examples of rock-cut temples in northern India – bear more than a passing resemblance to the Hindu temples at Angkor Wat in Cambodia or to Ellora in Maharashtra. The tank in front provides photogenic reflections.

The easiest way to get here is a taxi day-trip (₹1600 return from McLeod Ganj, or ₹2000 combined with Kangra). Alternatively you can reach Lunj (₹65, 1½ hours) from Dharamsala by bus, then take a Nagrota Surian–bound bus 4km southwest to the junction at Pir Bindli, then either walk the last 2.5km or wait for one of the hourly buses to the temples.

Dharamsala to Mandi

The scenery along the Kangra Valley is dramatic, with the Dhauladhar Range rising to the north, and the wide valley sweeping away southward towards the plains. There are a few interesting places to stop, and a couple of good top-end hotels where car travellers might break a journey.

Palampur

☑ 01894

About 35km southeast of Dharamsala, Palampur is a bustling little market town surrounded by tea plantations and rice fields. You can take a free 20-minute tour to observe the tea-making process at the **Palampur Tea Cooperative Factory** (☑239034; ◷10am-5pm), 1.5km south of the bus station on the Kangra road. **Norwood Green** (☑9736031300; www.norwoodgreen.in; Bundla Tea Estate, Lohna village; half-board r ₹8000-9000; ✿), in the north of town, comprises four bright, contemporary and tasteful cottages, each with four comfy, sparkling clean rooms, and a nice sitting/dining area opening out onto a garden terrace – but in busy seasons they'll only take bookings for two rooms or more. From Palampur's bus station, 1km south of the centre, buses leave all day for Dharamsala (₹50, two hours) and Mandi (₹150, 3½ hours). Palampur is also a stop on the Pathankot–Jogindernagar railway.

Taragarh & Tashijong

About 12km past Palampur towards Mandi is **Taragarh Palace** (☑01894-242034, in Delhi 011-24692317; www.taragarh.com; r ₹5880-8220; ✳ ✿), the summer palace of the last maha-

raja of Jammu and Kashmir. It's now a luxury hotel on an estate full of camphor trees and equipped with tennis court, an open-air pool, spa and even a small polo ground. The Heritage Wing is the more atmospheric, but rooms in the modern Palace Wing are more comfortable and also stylish.

A side-road 1km past Taragarh leads 1km north to the impressive **Tashijong Gompa**, founded by lamas from Tibet's important Khampagar Monastery. Visitors can see several mural-filled prayer halls and a carpet-making, *thangka*-painting and wood-carving cooperative.

Baijnath

High above the Binwa River at Baijnath, 51km southeast of Dharamsala, the exquisitely carved 13th-century **Vaidyanath Temple** is sacred to Shiva in his incarnation as Vaidyanath, Lord of the Physicians. Thousands of pilgrims make their way here for the **Shivaratri Festival** (◷late Feb-early Mar). Plenty of buses between Mandi and Palampur or Dharamsala stop at Baijnath bus station, almost opposite the temple. Baijnath Paprola station on the Pathankot–Jogindernagar railway is 2km west.

Bir & Billing

From Ahju, 8km southeast of Baijnath, a road winds 3km uphill to the village of Bir (1500m). Bir has three peaceful **gompas** that welcome passing visitors, and a handful of guesthouses catering mainly to people who come for the **paragliding** and **hang-gliding** from Billing (2600m), an internationally renowned take-off point 14km up a winding road from Bir. Experienced paragliders may fly as far as Dharamsala or Manali from Billing, and international competitions take place here every autumn. In 2015 Billing is hosting its first Paragliding World Cup (24 to 31 October).

Several agencies in Bir offer tandem flights of around 30 minutes for ₹2500 to ₹3000, including transport up to Billing. McLeod Ganj travel agencies will also bring you here for flying. October and November have the best conditions. The monsoon prevents flying from mid-July to mid-September.

Most buses between Palampur and Mandi will drop you in Ahju. Alternatively, head to Jogindernagar, 12km further east, and get a taxi there.

Chamba Valley

The scenic Chamba Valley is a splendidly isolated valley system, cut off from the Kangra Valley by the Dhauladhar Range and from Lahaul and Kashmir by the Pir Panjal. This area was ruled for centuries as the princely state of Chamba, one of the most ancient states in North India. It's great for temple buffs and trekkers, but well off most tourists' radars.

Dalhousie

☑ 01899 / POP 10,500 / ELEV 2036M

With its plunging pine-clad valleys and distant mountain views, Dalhousie is another of those cool hill retreats left behind by the British. Founded in the 1850s by the viceroy whose name it bears, its heyday came in the 1920s, '30s and '40s when Lahore society flocked here for its hols. Come Partition, Lahore found itself in Pakistan and Dalhousie has never been quite the same again. Still, it carries on as a relatively staid escape for honeymooners and families from the plains.

There's not a lot to see or do except stroll the tree-shaded lanes. Unusually for a hill station there are few truly steep roads. The market areas at Subhash Chowk and Gandhi Chowk are linked by lanes – Thandi Sarak (Cold Rd), and Garam Sarak (Hot Rd). The latter lane receives more sunshine. There's a nice 2.5km road walk northeast from Gandhi Chowk to Jandrighat, a summer home of the former Chamba rulers (not open to visitors). You can also visit the British-era churches of St John (1863) and St Francis (1894), set among the pines at opposite ends of the ridge.

🛏 Sleeping

Dalhousie has more than 100 hotels spread across various ridges and lanes, but outside the May–June high season many of them wear a sadly unloved look.

Dalhousie

◉ Sights
1 St Francis Church A2
2 St John Church D2

🛏 Sleeping
3 Grand View Hotel A1
4 Hotel Crags B2
5 Silverton Estate Guest House B1

🍽 Eating
6 Hotel Mount View A1
7 Kwality Restaurant D2

ℹ Information
8 Manimahesh Internet Cafe.................D2

Dalhousie

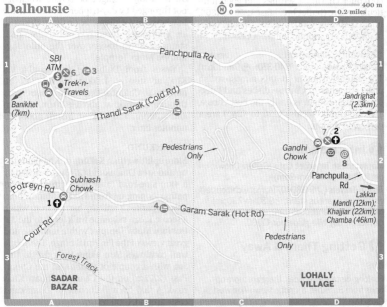

Hotel Crags
GUESTHOUSE $

(☏242124; hotelcrags@hotmail.com; Garam Sarak; r ₹600-900, cottage ₹1200) It's shabby, but the beds and bathrooms are clean. The rickety old house has huge rooms and a large terrace offering spectacular valley views; the best option is the self-contained cottage above.

Silverton Estate
Guest House
HERITAGE GUESTHOUSE $$$

(☏9418010674; www.heritagehotels.com/silverton; Above Circuit House, Moti Tibba; r ₹3300-5500; ☺Apr-Nov; ☏) Silverton is secluded among trees above Thandi Sarak and is the choice pick for colonial character and an old-fashioned kind of comfort. If it feels like staying in a cosy and beloved family home, it is - the welcoming owners also live here. Have a bash at croquet in the large gardens.

Grand View Hotel
HERITAGE HOTEL $$$

(☏240760; www.grandviewdalhousie.in; r incl breakfast ₹3640-4940, ste from ₹5880; ☏) The Grand has some rooms in its modern deluxe block and others with more colonial-era character, including some with four-poster beds. The 1920s building is fronted by a lovely terrace gazing across to the Pir Panjal peaks.

Eating

The restaurants at the Grand View Hotel and neighbouring Hotel Mount View (☏242120; www.hotelmountview.net; Club Rd; meals ₹500-600) offer charming settings and good multicuisine fare (buffet breakfast ₹250 to ₹300, lunch or dinner ₹500 to ₹600). Cheap Punjabi *dhabas* are around Subhash Chowk.

★ Kwality Restaurant
INDIAN $$

(Gandhi Chowk; mains ₹140-320; ☺9am-10pm) The extensive menu at this almost-stylish place stretches to Chinese dishes and burgers, though Indian is easily the best choice, and the combo meals (₹220 to ₹250) are a very good option.

ℹ Information

Manimahesh Internet Cafe (Gandhi Chowk; per hr ₹40; ☺8.30am-9pm)

Trek-n-Travels (☏9418040714; manu.dalhousie@gmail.com; near bus stand; ☺9.30am-7.30pm) Near the bus stand; does transport bookings and can supply day-hike guides for ₹1000.

ℹ Getting There & Away

BUS

For long-distance services, there are more options from Banikhet, a junction town 7km west (bus/taxi ₹8/220), though you aren't guaranteed a seat there. Four buses run from Dalhousie's bus stand to Chamba (₹80, 2½ hours) between 9am and 10.30am, two going via Khajjiar (₹40, one hour). Buses head to Dharamsala (₹250, six hours) at 7.15am, 11am and 1.45pm, and to Pathankot (₹100, three hours) eight times daily.

TAXI

There are taxi stands at the bus stand, Subhash Chowk and Gandhi Chowk. From the bus stand, you'll pay ₹100 to Subhash Chowk and ₹150 to Gandhi Chowk. Out-of-town fares may differ from one stand to another and the bus station stand was quoting the lowest rates at research time, including ₹520/720 (one-way/return) to Lakkar Mandi, ₹1130 to Chamba, ₹2500 to Dharamsala and ₹1550 for a day trip to Kalatop, Dhainkund and Khajjiar (₹2050 with a drop at Chamba).

Around Dalhousie

KALATOP KHAJJIAR WILDLIFE SANCTUARY

This sanctuary covers 31 sq km of forested hills east of Dalhousie. From the impoverished settlement of Lakkar Mandi, 12km from Dalhousie, a flat 3km unpaved road leads to the forest rest house (built in 1925) and tea shops at Kalatop, making for a nice forest walk. You have a chance of spotting langurs and musk deer. There's a ₹200 charge for vehicles to drive this track.

About 10km further down the road towards Chamba, the large, pine-ringed meadow at Khajjiar might be serene when it's not thronged by day-trippers and horse-ride hawkers. Half a kilometre on down the road, an enormous, recently erected 25m-high statue of Shiva towers over the little Jagdamba Mata Temple.

Buses from Dalhousie to Chamba via Khajjiar stop at Lakkar Mandi (₹15, 30 minutes). Chamba–Dalhousie buses pass through Khajjiar at about 8.30am, 2.30pm and 3.30pm, and Lakkar Mandi about 20 minutes later.

DHAINKUND

More uplifting than Kalatop or Khajjiar is the upland area Dhainkund (2745m), reached by a 4km side-road (and more direct shortcut paths) looping up from Lakkar Mandi. Taxis have to park at a military barrier, from which a scenic 1.5km ridgeline walk leads to the Jai Pohlani Mata Temple, with a teahouse and great views of the Pir Pinjal range. The scenic trail continues 5km along the ridge to tiny Jot, with a couple of *dhabas*, at the Chuari Pass (2772m) on the Chamba–Chuari Khas road. A taxi from Dalhousie to Dhainkund costs around ₹800 return.

Chamba

📞 01899 / POP 20,000 / ELEV 996M

Ensconced in the valley of the fast-flowing Ravi River, the capital of Chamba district is a beguiling old town with some beautiful temples, a good museum and bustling markets. Chamba was founded in AD 920 when Raja Sahil Varman moved his capital here from Bharmour, and it remained capital of the Chamba kingdom until merged with India in 1947, though under British control from 1846.

Chamba's de facto centre is the fine, open grassy field known as the Chowgan, a focus for festivals, cricket games, picnics and general hanging out. Every year since 935, Chamba has celebrated the harvest with the **Minjar Festival** in honour of Raghuvira (an incarnation of Rama) – nowadays a week of processions, folk dance and music, and a vast flea market on the Chowgan.

👁 Sights

⭐ Lakshmi Narayan Temple Complex
HINDU TEMPLE

(☉dusk-dawn) Standing on a rise at the top of the Dogra Bazar, this superb line of six beautiful stone *sikharas*, covered in carvings, dates from the 10th to the 19th centuries. The largest (and oldest), is dedicated to Lakshmi Narayan (Vishnu). The others, in north-to-south order, are sacred to Radha Krishna, Chandergupta, Shiva, Trimukeshwara and Lakshmi Damodar. All are topped by protective wooden canopy roofs.

Just outside the complex entrance is a distinctive Nepali-style pillar topped by a statue of Vishnu's Garuda.

Bhuri Singh Museum
MUSEUM

(📞 222590; Museum Rd; Indian/foreigner ₹20/100, camera ₹50/100; ☉10am-5pm Tue-Sun) This well-displayed museum includes a wonderful collection of Pahari (Hill Country) miniature paintings from the Chamba, Basholi, Kangra and Guler schools, plus intriguing copper-plate inscriptions (formerly a way of preserving important documents) and ornately carved centuries-old fountain slabs – a unique Chamba Valley tradition. There's comprehensive labelling in English and it's one of Himachal's best museums.

Akhand Chandi Palace
HISTORIC BUILDING

Lording it over the town is the unmissable stately white Akhand Chandi Palace, the former home of the Chamba raja, built in the mid-18th century. It now houses a postgraduate college; you can peep inside from the north-side entrance during school hours.

Rang Mahal
HISTORIC BUILDING

(Old Palace) Up on the hillside above the Chowgan, the fortresslike, rusty-coloured Rang Mahal, built in the 18th century and formerly the royal granary and treasury, now houses the State Handicraft & Handloom Centre, making local crafts, and the fairly modest **Himachal Emporium** (📞222333; ☉10am-5pm Mon-Sat), which sells them.

Other Temples

It's fascinating to seek out some of Chamba's beautiful smaller temples, many of them built during the town's earliest centuries.

A steep 378 steps up from near the bus stand (or take a taxi), the **Chamunda Devi Temple**, dating from 1762, affords wonderful views over the town and valley. It's dedicated to a wrathful aspect of the mother goddess Devi and its front *mandapa* (pavilion) features a forest of bells and rich ceiling carving. About 500m north along the road is the small, modern **Sui Mata Shrine**, with colourful paintings telling the tale of the Chamba queen Sui, who gave her life to appease a water spirit that was causing a terrible drought. The queen-goddess is highly venerated by local women, and the four-day Sui Mata Mela is celebrated on the Chowgan in her honour each March or April.

About 600m further along the same road, a small red-and-white roadside arch leads to the exquisite 12th-century *sikhara*-style **Bajreshwari Devi Temple**, dedicated to Bajreshwari, an incarnation of Durga. The very rich carving includes, on the rear wall, an image of Durga slaying the (minuscule-looking) giant Mahisasur and trampling on his buffalo.

By the Chowgan is the 11th-century **Harirai Mandir**, sacred to Vishnu. Three further finely-carved *sikhara* temples are dotted around the narrow lanes above the Chowgan. The 10th-century **Champavati Temple** was built by Raja Sahil Varman in honour of his daughter Champavati, who is worshipped locally as an incarnation of Durga; the 16th-century **Bansi Gopal Temple** is dedicated to Krishna; and the 17th-century **Sitaram Temple** is dedicated to Rama.

🏃 Activities

Mani Mahesh Travels
TREKKING

(📞 9816620401; www.himalayanlap.com; outside Lakshmi Narayan Temple Complex; ☉9am-9pm

Chamba

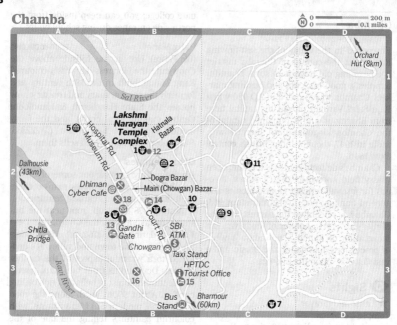

Mon-Sat) Professional and experienced Mani Mahesh can arrange treks with guides and porters in and across the surrounding Pir Panjal and Dhauladhar ranges, as well as informative tours of Chamba's temples (from ₹550). Treks cost ₹2000 to ₹2800 per person per day within the Chamba Valley, or ₹3500 to ₹4500 across the Pir Panjal or Dhauladhar passes, plus any transport costs.

Ask about stays in their isolated Ridgemoor Cottage, three or four hours' walk (with an elevation gain of 1000m) above the Orchard Hut; it's also run by this same family firm. Mani Mahesh also organises far-ranging jeep safaris and motorbike tours.

🛏 Sleeping

Chamba House
GUESTHOUSE $

(☎ 222564; Gopal Nivas; d ₹550-880, ste ₹1100) This creaky building, with fine views over the Ravi River from its balcony, is Chamba's best budget bolthole. The six rooms are small and have hard beds, but are quaint and clean, with wood floors, giving it a homey cottage feel.

⭐ Orchard Hut
GUESTHOUSE $$

(☎ 9816620401; www.himalayanlap.com; r ₹400-2350; ☎) 🌿 About 10km northeast of Chamba in the lovely Saal valley, this welcoming

country guesthouse and organic farm is a wonderfully peaceful place to unwind amid the plum and apricot orchards. There's a range of super-clean, thoughtfully designed rooms for all budgets, the home-cooked meals (₹550 half-board per person) are superb, and staff can lead you on walks.

Sister company Mani Mahesh Travels in Chamba will arrange transfers, either by taxi (₹350) or public bus (₹20), to Chaminu village, from where it's a 20-minute uphill walk to the house. You'll thank yourself if you schedule an extra day or two here.

Hotel City Heart
HOTEL $$

(☎ 222032; www.hotelcityheartchamba.com; r ₹1620-2920, ste ₹3270-4790; ☀☎) The cheapest ('business class') rooms are dingy holes, but the others (from ₹2090) are spacious, clean and recently decorated. The suites have expansive Chowgan views. Discounts of up to 30% are often available.

Hotel Iravati
HOTEL $$

(☎ 222671; www.hptdc.gov.in; Court Rd; s ₹1320-2120, d ₹1770-2820) Though it has that outdated, ascetic feel of most HPTDC hotels, the Iravati provides sizeable rooms in decent condition, nearly all with Chowgan-view balconies. Its Chowgan Restaurant is one of the town's best.

Chamba

⊙ Top Sights
1 Lakshmi Narayan Temple
  Complex B2

⊙ Sights
2 Akhand Chandi Palace B2
3 Bajreshwari Devi Temple D1
4 Bansi Gopal Temple B2
5 Bhuri Singh Museum A2
6 Champavati Temple B2
7 Chamunda Devi Temple C3
8 Harirai Mandir B2
9 Rang Mahal C2
10 Sitaram Temple B2
11 Sui Mata Shrine.................................... C2

⊕ Activities, Courses & Tours
12 Mani Mahesh Travels B2

⊜ Sleeping
13 Chamba House B3
14 Hotel City Heart B2
15 Hotel Iravati B3

⊗ Eating
16 Cafe Ravi View B3
  Chowgan Restaurant .... (see 15)
17 Desa Chicken Corner B2
18 Jagan Restaurant B2

⊙ Shopping
  Himachal Emporium .... (see 9)

✕ Eating

Chamba cuisine is known for its *chukh* – a chilli sauce with capsicum, lemon juice and mustard oil, served as a condiment almost everywhere.

Chowgan Restaurant　　　　INDIAN $$
(mains ₹100-250; ◷7.30am-9.30pm) Hotel Iravati's restaurant is one of Chamba's better eateries; it offers a few interesting Chamba specialities, including *chasnidar* (sweet-and-sour dried fruit).

Cafe Ravi View　　　　INDIAN $$
(Chowgan; mains ₹90-190; ◷9am-9pm) This HPTDC-run snack house is worth a visit for its icy-cold beers (₹130) and excellent river views as well as for its Indian and Chinese veg food – including dosas and bargain veg thalis (₹100). It has a sunny terrace as well as indoor air-con.

Desa Chicken Corner　　　STREET FOOD $$
(Museum Rd; mains ₹100-130; ◷10am-9.30pm) Tasty chicken tandoori or chicken curry, cooked in front of your nose, go down very well with chapatis and chutney at this friendly street-food stand on the back side of the Museum Rd shops.

Jagan Restaurant　　　　INDIAN $$
(Museum Rd; mains ₹90-200; ◷11.30am-10.30pm) It's nothing flash but the uniformed waiters at this upstairs restaurant serve up the tasty *chamba madhra* (kidney beans with curd and ghee) for ₹110, plus a good selection of veg curries and chicken dishes.

ⓘ Information

There's an international ATM (but no currency exchange) at SBI, near the courthouse.

Dhiman Cyber Cafe (Museum Rd; internet per hr ₹30; ◷9.30am-8.30pm Mon-Sat)
HPTDC Tourist Office (☏224002; Court Rd; ◷10am-5pm Mon-Sat) In the courtyard of Hotel Iravati.

ⓘ Getting There & Away

A mix of government-run HRTC and private buses runs to most destinations from the bus stand. For the spectacular trip to Bharmour (₹90, 3½ hours) buses leave about hourly till about 5pm; sit on the left for the best views and be prepared for delays during monsoon landslides. Eight buses daily head to Dalhousie (₹80, 2½ hours), with three going via Khajjiar (₹40, 1½ hours). At least 12 buses run to Pathankot (₹160, six to seven hours). For Dharamsala (₹200, eight hours) there are three government buses; alternatively catch a government or private bus to Gaggal (₹180, seven hours) where buses leave every few minutes to Dharamsala (₹15, 40 minutes). For the best scenery, try to get one going via Jot, over the 2772m Chuari Pass.

Taxis at the Court Rd stand charge around ₹1800 to Bharmour or Dalhousie and ₹3500 to Dharamsala. You can negotiate.

Bharmour

☏01895 / POP 2000 / ELEV 2195M
Hovering on the edge of the seemingly bottomless Budil Valley, Bharmour is reached by a mountain road as scenic as it is perilous, winding 60km east of Chamba (it gets really interesting once you leave the Ravi Valley at Kharamukh). This ancient settlement was the area capital until replaced by Chamba in AD 920, and there are some beautiful old temples, though the main reason to come here is for treks to the surrounding valleys and passes. The villages around Bharmour

HIMACHAL PRADESH CHAMBA VALLEY

are home to communities of seminomadic Gaddis, pastoralists who move their flocks to alpine pastures during the summer, and return here in winter.

⦿ Sights & Activities

Chaurasi Temples
HINDU TEMPLE

The Chaurasi temples, 500m up the street from the bus stand, occupy a wide flagstone courtyard that doubles as an outdoor classroom and cricket ground. There are three main Shaivite temples, plus a couple of dozen smaller temples and shrines. The central Manimahesh Temple is a classic stone *sikhara,* built in the 7th century AD. The squat Lakshna Devi Temple is of a similar date and features a weathered but wildly carved wooden doorway.

For the best valley views, hike 3km up from the Chaurasi entrance to the Brahmani Mata Temple above town. The route passes through the upper village, still full of traditional slate-roofed, wooden houses.

Trekking

The trekking season lasts from May to late October, though July and August see some monsoon rain. The many possible treks include: from Kugti to Jhalma in Lahaul over the 5040m Kugti Pass (five days); from Lamu in the Ravi Valley to McLeod Ganj over the 4420m Indrahar La (five days); and demanding longer treks via the isolated village of Bara Bhangal to Manali or Bir.

A popular shorter trek is to the sacred lake at Manimahesh, a three-day, 35km return hike starting at Hadsar, 13km east of Bharmour. It can be done without a tent thanks to the many *dhabas* en route. In August/September, thousands of pilgrims take a freezing dip in Manimahesh Lake as part of the Manimahesh Yatra in honour of Lord Shiva (leaving a sad trail of litter behind them).

Anna Adventures & Tours
TREKKING

(☑ 8894687758, 9817710758; www.bharmourtreks. com; Main Bazar) Treks from Bharmour can be arranged through Anna Adventures & Tours, on the street up to the Chaurasi temples; contact Gopal Chauhan.

⛏ Sleeping & Eating

Hotel Bharmour View
HOTEL $$

(☑ 225090; bharmourview.com; r ₹800-1600; 🖥) About 100m ahead from the bus stand, this is the most appealing of Bharmour's mediocre accommodation. Staff are friendly and

the rooms are clean and sizeable, and even boast wi-fi. A few have views.

Chaurasi Hotel & Restaurant
HOTEL $$

(☑ 9418025004; Main Bazar; r ₹500-2000) You can't miss this red multistorey building up the street towards the Chaurasi temples. Rooms are generous-sized and many have soaring views, but TLC is lacking. The ground-floor restaurant (mains ₹80 to ₹180) is Bharmour's best, which isn't saying much.

ℹ Information

There's an SBI ATM (Temple Rd) on the street below the Chaurasi temples.

ℹ Getting There & Away

Buses leave about hourly from 6am to 5pm for the rugged trip to Chamba (₹90, 3½ hours). Taxis charge between ₹1200 and ₹1800.

A bus to Dharamsala (₹300, 12 hours) departs at 5.30pm. At least five daily buses head to Hadsar (₹35, one hour); the 10.30am and 2pm departures continue to Dhanoul, halfway from Hadsar to Kugti. For buses up the Ravi Valley as far as Holi, take a Chamba-bound bus to Kharamukh and change there.

LAHAUL & SPITI

The vast, desolate northern and eastern tracts of Himachal Pradesh are among the most spectacular and sparsely populated regions on earth. Crossing the Rohtang La from Manali, you arrive first in Lahaul's relatively green Chandra Valley, but if you then travel east into Spiti you pass into the rain shadow of the Great Himalaya Range. Spiti is 7000 sq km of snow-topped mountains and high-altitude desert, punctuated by tiny patches of greenery and villages of whitewashed houses clinging to the sides of rivers and melt-water streams. As in Zanskar and Ladakh, Buddhism is the dominant religion.

From Manali, a seasonal highway runs north to Keylong, the capital of Lahaul, over the Rohtang La (3978m), which is normally open from about mid-May to early November. From Keylong the road to Ladakh continues over the mighty Baralacha La (4950m) and Taglang La (5328m) and is normally open from about early June to some time in October, though government buses stop running in mid-September (private buses, minibuses and jeeps continue longer). From Lahaul other roads branch west to the Pattan Valley and east to Spiti over the Kunzum La (4551m), which is open from about mid-June to mid-October. When the passes are closed, Lahaul is virtually cut off from the outside world, and Spiti is connected only by the rugged road from the south through Kinnaur. Check the status of the passes before visiting late in the season – once the snows arrive, you might be stuck for the winter! The website www.bcmtouring.com has updates.

A new tunnel being constructed between the Solang Valley, just north of Manali, and Teling in Lahaul, will bypass the Rohtang La and open Lahaul to year-round traffic. The hoped-for completion date is 2017.

For more information on Lahaul and Spiti, visit the local government website at www. hplahaulspiti.gov.in.

History

Buddhism is believed to have arrived in Spiti and Lahaul during the 8th century AD with the legendary Indian sorcerer, sage and missionary Padmasambhava (Guru Rinpoche in Tibetan) who spread Buddhism in Tibet. In the 10th century, upper Lahaul, Spiti, Zanskar and Ladakh were incorporated into the vast Guge kingdom of western Tibet, with Lahaul and Spiti eventually being ruled from Ladakh. The Great Translator, Ringchen Zangpo, founded a series of centres of Buddhist learning in Spiti, including Tabo, one of the most remarkable Buddhist monasteries in the Indian Himalaya.

The Kullu rajas took control of Lahaul in the 16th century and established a loose hold over Spiti in the 17th. The region came under British control following the 1846 Anglo-Sikh War, yet it maintained strong links with Tibet right up until the Chinese invasion there in 1950.

Recent decades have seen a resurgence in the region's cultural and religious life, aided by the work of the Tibetan government-in-exile in Dharamsala. Many gompas in Lahaul and Spiti have been restored, and money from tourism and hydroelectricity is improving conditions for the farming communities who get snowed in here each winter.

Climate

Rainfall is minimal, especially in Spiti, and the high altitude ensures low temperatures.

Winter temperatures can plummet below -30°C, but on the plus side, summer daytime temperatures often rise into the 20s, and when monsoons are soaking the rest of the state (mid-July to mid-September), it's usually dry and sunny here. Whenever you travel, bring some clothing for cold weather.

Lahaul

Lahaul is greener and a touch more developed than Ladakh or Spiti, but many travellers whistle straight through on the road between Manali and Leh, missing most of what Lahaul has to offer. The capital, Keylong, is an easy stop and you can detour to mountain villages and medieval monasteries that remain blissfully untouched by mass tourism.

Manali to Keylong

From Manali the road strikes north along the Beas River and climbs slowly through pine forests and endless switchbacks to the bare rocky slopes below the spectacular Rohtang La. The name literally translates as 'pile of dead bodies' – hundreds of travellers have frozen to death here over the centuries. In the height of summer, the pass is chock-a-block with Indian tourists riding horses and enjoying the novelty of a snowball fight. Look out for the small, dome-shaped temple that marks the source of the Beas River.

Once over the pass, the road deteriorates rapidly as it plunges down into Lahaul's awe-inspiring Chandra Valley, a rugged landscape of soaring crags, alpine meadows and mesmerising waterfalls plunging from glacial heights. After a zigzagging 14km, Gramphu (three or four stone buildings and a tiny *dhaba*) marks the turn-off to Spiti. Khoksar, in the valley bottom 5km past Gramphu, has more *dhabas*. The road passes along the sheer-sided valley, hemmed in by skyscraping rocky peaks. The planned tunnel bypassing the Rohtang La will join this road about 5km west of Khoksar.

About 18km before Keylong, Gondhla is famous for its seven-storey tower fort, built from alternating layers of stone and timber. The fort is no longer occupied, but it's still an impressive sight. Try to visit during the lively Gondla Fair in July. A strenuous but marvellous day hike leads from Keylong to Gondla over the 4405m Rangcha La; a guide

ROHTANG RULES

Northbound vehicles, including motorbikes, require a permit to go beyond Gulaba on the way up to the Rohtang La. Drivers can obtain the permit (₹50) at either of two check-points – one just north of Manali (Map p310) on the Rohtang road and the other at Gulaba itself – on production of their driver's licence, the vehicle registration document and the vehicle's pollution control certificate. Some Manali travel agencies, including Himalayan Extreme Centre (p309), will obtain the permit for you in advance for a small fee. The pass is closed on Tuesdays to all private northbound traffic, including taxis, to facilitate maintenance work. Southbound vehicles are exempt from both of these rules.

is not essential, but Brokpa Adventure Tours (p342) can supply one for ₹1000.

At Tandi, 7km before Keylong, the Chandra River is joined by the Bhaga River (together they become the Chandra-Bhaga). Tandi's petrol station is the last for 365km on the Ladakh road. You can walk 15 minutes up to **Tupchiling Gompa** and ask there for the keys to **Guru Ghantal Gompa**, a further hour's walk, which is the oldest monastery in Lahaul, allegedly founded by Padmasambhava. Although crumbling, the gompa contains ancient murals and unusual wooden statues of bodhisattvas.

Keylong

[☑]01900 / POP 1150 / ELEV 3350M

Keylong stretches along the north side of the green Bhaga Valley just below the Manali–Leh road, and it's an overnight stop for many buses plying that route. Many travellers only see Keylong briefly and in the dark, but a longer stay reveals grand mountain views, and some scenic walks.

The main street, optimistically named the Mall, winds for 1km below and roughly parallel to the highway, with the bus station (New Bus Stand) just above its east end. For tips on day hikes or to arrange longer treks to Zanskar, talk to Amar at **Brokpa Adventure Tours** ([☑]9418165176; www.brokpatreks.com; Hotel Dupchen Bldg, the Mall; internet or wi-fi per hr ₹60; ⊙9am-8pm May, Jun & Sep, 7am-10pm Jul & Aug; [☎]), which also has internet.

At the west end of the Mall is the sort-of-interesting **Lahaul & Spiti Tribal Museum** (⊙10am-1.30pm & 2-5pm Tue-Sun) **FREE**, with examples of a *thod-pa* (part of a skull formerly used by *amchis* or lamas to store healing or sacred liquids), old dance masks, historical photos and prints, and contemporary shots of local monasteries.

🛏 Sleeping & Eating

Hotel Nordaling   HOTEL $

([☑]222294; www.nordalingkeylong.in; r ₹800-1000, ste ₹1500; ⊙approx mid-May–Oct) Just 100m above the bus station is this pleasant place with large, spotless rooms, and a relaxing restaurant (mains ₹80 to ₹150) in the apple orchard outside. It's an excellent choice and rates can drop to ₹500 when quiet.

Hotel New Gyespa   HOTEL $

([☑]9418136055; www.gyespahotels.webs.com; r ₹700-1500) Only 20m up from the bus station, most of the clean, carpeted rooms here have views across the valley. The hotel also possesses an attractive pine-panelled restaurant (mains ₹100 to ₹300). Slightly cheaper rooms are available at the affiliated **Hotel Gyespa** (the Mall; r ₹800-1200), and both places offer discounts early and late in the season.

Hotel Tashi Deleg   HOTEL $$

([☑]222450; hoteltashideleg@yahoo.in; the Mall; r ₹1380-2800; ⊙approx May-Oct) This big white hotel, towards the western end of the Mall, is Keylong's nicest. Rooms in the new wing are large, with soft chairs, pretty bedding and good showers. The old wing is also fine, and mostly cheaper. The restaurant is Keylong's best, serving Indian, Chinese and continental food (mains ₹90 to ₹175), plus cold beers.

ℹ Information

There's an SBI ATM at the east end of the Mall.

ℹ Getting There & Away

From mid-June to mid-September, an HRTC bus departs for Leh (₹600, about 14 hours) at 4.30am – book tickets at the bus station the day before. Private minibuses and shared jeeps run until October, depending on snow conditions: one place you can book seats is Brokpa Adventure Tours. Seats can cost as much as ₹2000 in the peak season (June to August), and as little as ₹800 at the end of the season.

The HRTC also runs seven daily buses to Manali (₹170, seven hours) from mid-May to mid-November, seven to Udaipur (₹80, three hours) in the Pattan Valley from April/May to November, and three to Chika (₹50, two hours) in the Darcha Valley, jumping-off point for the Shingo La trek into Zanskar, from May to mid-November – road conditions permitting in all cases. For Kaza, take an early Manali bus and change at Gramphu (₹70, 2½ hours); the bus from Manali to Kaza pulls in around 8am.

Around Keylong

Shashur Gompa   BUDDHIST MONASTERY

About 3km (one hour of uphill walking) above Keylong, Shashur Gompa was founded in the 17th century by the Zanskari lama Deva Gyatsho. The original gompa, featuring 5m-high *thangkas*, is now enshrined inside a modern concrete one, with fine views over the valley. During the Tsheshu Festival in June or July, monks here perform frenetic ritual masked dances known as *chaams*.

The path to the gompa cuts uphill almost opposite the Yarkid Guesthouse on the main highway – follow it upwards until you see the white chortens visible on the ridge.

Kardang Gompa   BUDDHIST MONASTERY

Propped on concrete stilts facing Keylong across the valley, Kardang Gompa has ex-

isted for 900 years, but the current building dates from 1912. Maintained by an order of Drukpa Kagyu (Red Hat) monks and nuns, the monastery enshrines a mighty prayer wheel said to contain a million strips of paper bearing the mantra *Om mani padme hum* ('hail to the jewel in the lotus'). There are excellent frescoes, but you may have to track down a monk or nun to open it.

To get here, head for the hospital at the bottom of the west end of Keylong and take a path down to the left 30m before the hospital. This crosses the Bhaga on a footbridge, then climbs 1km to a road where you turn right into Kardang village. Ask directions to the gompa, 800m further uphill. For a different route back, return to Kardang village then head to the right along the road for 3km to Lapchang village, where a path descends 1km to another footbridge over the Bhaga, then climbs 1.25km to the main road. Keylong is 1.5km to the left (west).

JISPA

About 22km northeast of Keylong, pretty Jispa village is a popular overnight stop for mountain bikers and motorcyclists; 4km back towards Keylong is the 16th-century **Gemur Gompa**. For accommodation, there's the inviting **Hotel Ibex Jispa** (☑ 01900-233203; www.hotelibexjispa.com; d ₹2120) on the main road. There are several overnight halts further up the road towards Leh (p244).

OFF THE BEATEN TRACK

PATTAN VALLEY

At Tandi, 8km southwest of Keylong, a road branches northwest along the beautiful, green Pattan Valley, Lahaul's lowest-lying, most fertile area, carved by the Chandra-Bhaga River. Snowy peaks rise above its many side valleys, and passes over the Pir Panjal range to the south lead across to the Chamba Valley.

Around 36km from Tandi, a side road leads 5km to the hilltop village of **Triloknath**, whose squat stone temple is a remarkable example of Hindu-Buddhist syncretism: the white-marble main idol is revered by Buddhists as Avalokitesvara, the bodhisattva of compassion, while Hindus worship it as Shiva. It's a major pilgrimage site for both religions, especially during the **Pauri Festival** (⊙ 3rd week of Aug).

Pattan's largest settlement is the little town of **Udaipur**, 46km from Tandi, with a few basic lodgings including **Youngpha Guesthouse** (r without bath ₹300-400), with four clean, carpeted rooms. Udaipur's **Markula Devi Temple** looks plain on the outside, but the inside is covered with fabulous, detailed wood carvings from the 11th to 16th \centuries, including scenes from the Mahabharata and Ramayana around the top of the walls.

From Udaipur the road continues down the valley to Killar, beyond which unpaved roads head over the Sach Pass (open roughly mid-June to mid-October) to Chamba and on down to Kishtwar in Jammu and Kashmir.

Spiti

Separated from fertile Lahaul by the soaring 4551m Kunzum La, Spiti is another chunk of Tibet marooned in India. The scattered villages in this serrated moonscape arrive like mirages, clusters of whitewashed mud-brick homes huddled amid green barley fields below monasteries perched on crags a thousand feet above. The turquoise-grey ribbon of the Spiti River is your near-constant companion, running along a fairly broad valley before turning south at Sumdo into the precipitous gorges of the Hangrang Valley.

In many ways Spiti is even more rugged and remote than Ladakh, but buses do run over the Kunzum La from Manali from mid-June to mid-October, and the road from Kinnaur is open all year (except for temporary closures for winter snowfall and monsoon landslides and floods). The Spiti–Kinnaur loop is one of Asia's great road trips, and a steady stream of motorcyclists, mountain bikers and drivers of all kinds of four-wheelers pit themselves against some of the most challenging roads in India.

In either direction, an inner line permit (p346) is required for the stretch between Sumdo, east of Tabo, and the Akpa checkpoint east of Rekong Peo.

Gramphu to Kaza

From Gramphu, the road to Spiti runs up the dramatic, glacier-carved Chandra Valley. The tiny settlements of Chatru and Batal have popular *dhabas*. One kilometre past Batal, a rough track runs north to lovely Chandratal (Moon Lake), a tranquil glacial lake among snow peaks at 4270m. The track ends after 12km and a footpath runs the final 1km to the lake. From June to mid-October you can stay in tent camps 3km before the end of the track, among them Jamaica's Camp (☑9418200183; http://travelspiti.com; tents per person incl meals ₹1000), offering cosy two-person tents and a friendly welcome. From Chandratal, trekkers can reach the Baralacha La on the Manali–Leh road in three strenuous but heavenly days. Batal is also the starting point for treks to Bara Shigri (Big Glacier), one of the longest glaciers in the Himalaya, but the route is treacherous and it's essential to travel with an experienced guide.

The main road switchbacks precipitously up to the Kunzum La, where vehicles perform a respectful circuit of the stupas strewn with fluttering prayer flags before continuing down into Spiti. An alternative 10.5km footpath to Chandratal starts at the pass.

The first Spitian village of any size is Losar, a cluster of concrete and mud-brick houses, where there's a passport check and a handful of guesthouses and *dhabas*. Friendly Samsong Guesthouse (r with/without bathroom ₹700/500) has simple but clean rooms and hot meals (rates can drop to between ₹200 and ₹300 outside peak season).

The final stretch to Kaza follows the Spiti River, passing the large Yangchen Choling nunnery at Pangmo, and the Sherab Choling monastery school at Morang. Volunteer teaching placements at these schools can be organised through the US-based Jamyang Foundation (www.jamyang.org).

Kaza

☑ 01906 / POP 1700 / ELEV 3640M

The capital of Spiti, Kaza sits on the eroded flood plain of the Spiti River and is the biggest settlement you'll encounter in this empty corner of the planet. It feels a bit like a small frontier town with an easygoing pace. Jagged mountains rise on either side, while the river coils across the valley floor like twisted locks of Medusa's hair. The colourful Sakya Gompa stands just above the main road in New Kaza, while the ramshackle bazaar and whitewashed buildings of Old Kaza spread out on the north side of the stream. The bus and taxi stands are at the bottom of the bazaar in Old Kaza.

Most people stay at least one night to arrange the inner line permit for travel beyond Tabo. Kaza is also the starting point for trips to Ki Gompa and the villages of Kibber, Langza, Hikkim and Komic, high on the east side of the valley. Spiti Holiday Adventure (☑9418439247, 222711; www.spitiholidayadventure.com; Main Bazar; ⊙8.30am-8pm or later, Mar-Nov) organises all-inclusive treks in the region, plus jeep safaris and cultural tours, and is a good place for travel information.

In the third week of August, villagers from across Spiti descend on Kaza for the Ladarcha Fair. All sorts of goods are bought and sold, and traders wear their finest clothes.

🛏 Sleeping & Eating

There are plenty of places to stay in both halves of town. Most close for several months in winter.

Hotel Deyzor   HOTEL $
(☑9418402660; http://himalayanshepherd.co; New Kaza; s ₹600-1000, d ₹700-1400; ⊙late Apr-early

Nov; 📶) Bright, large, well-kept rooms with comfy beds, one of the better restaurants in town (mains ₹70 to ₹260), and helpful management who are real Spiti enthusiasts all keep a constant stream of travellers happy here. They can arranges treks, motorbike trips, wildlife-spotting or fossil-hunting trips, volunteer teaching placements and more. Wi-fi (₹80 per hour) is available for a few hours daily in the restaurant.

Mahabaudha Homestay
GUESTHOUSE $

(📞9418686272; drnorgyal@yahoo.com; Old Kaza; d without bathroom ₹400; ⊙Jun-Oct) Trained *amchi* (Tibetan doctor) Norbu Gyaltsen runs this homestay-style guesthouse beside his clinic just below the main road. The six rooms are well maintained and there are three shared hot-water bathrooms. Spitian meals can be booked in advance.

Zangchuk Guest House
HOTEL $

(📞9418439212; Old Kaza; r ₹500-800, without bathroom ₹300; ⊙Mar-Dec) This popular backpacker place near the upper footbridge over Kaza Nullah has 12 clean, bright ensuite rooms, some with balconies, in a new building, plus a few older rooms at the side.

Kunzaum Guest House
GUESTHOUSE $

(📞9459241933; New Kaza; r with/without bathroom ₹600/300; ⊙Apr-Oct) A clean, simple, friendly guesthouse; the best rooms are the three upstairs facing Kaza Nullah. It's just above the lower footbridge.

Sakya Abode
HOTEL $$

(📞9418208987; www.sakyaabode.com; New Kaza; s/d ₹1100/1320; ⊙Apr-Oct; 📶) On the main road near the Sakya Gompa, this is one of Kaza's longest-running and all-round best-value hotels. Bright, comfy rooms open onto shared terraces overlooking a grassy-lawned courtyard, and the Indian-Tibetan-Italian restaurant (mains ₹90 to ₹200; 7am to 9pm April to October) is excellent – try the addictively delicious 'copper Eliza' (a pancake with dried fruit, banana, honey and chocolate sauce).

Sol Cafe
CAFE $

(Main Bazar; hot drinks & snacks ₹15-50; ⊙10am-6pm) 🍴 Ecosphere operates this cool cafe, offering coffee, teas, and snacks that showcase local ingredients such as sea-buckthorn, a berry with an amazing list of health-giving properties. There are sometimes movie or open-mic nights, and you can fill water bottles with filtered water here.

Makang Restaurant
MULTICUISINE $$

(Main Bazar; mains ₹100-270; ⊙8am-10pm Apr-Oct) With balcony tables as well as an indoor dining room and bar, Makang is the choice spot for meals and drinks in the old town. They serve full-bodied Zingaro beer.

ℹ Information

There's an **internet cafe** (per hr ₹80; ⊙8am-8pm) opposite Shambhala Homestay in the bazaar, and an SBI ATM nearby.

ℹ Getting There & Away

The bus to Manali (₹300, 11 hours) leaves at 4.30am, mid-June to mid-October; buy tickets when it arrives about 4.30pm the day before. For Keylong, change at Gramphu (₹200, nine hours). A bus leaves for Rekong Peo (₹335, 11 hours) at 7.30am, via Tabo (₹71, 2½ hours) and Nako (₹170, 5½ hours). There's a second Tabo bus at 3pm.

Shramjeevi Taxi Operators Union (📞988054698), opposite the bus station, has fixed rates everywhere including to Dhankar (₹1450, 1½ hours), Tabo (₹1800, 1½ hours), Keylong (₹8000, eight hours) and Manali (₹8600, eight hours). For return trips with a one-hour wait, add 20%; for each extra hour, add ₹100 more. They also run a shared jeep to Manali (₹800) at 6am most days in season. For shared taxis to Spiti villages, try around lunchtime when villagers are returning home from town.

Around Kaza

The small, high-altitude villages on the east side of the Spiti valley (all well above 4000m) have a pristine, desolate beauty all their own – clusters of whitewashed, flat-roofed houses against a stark mountain backdrop with minimal vegetation except their carefully tended fields of barley and other crops. This is the abode of the Himalayan wolf, snow leopard, blue sheep, golden eagle and griffon vulture. Some of the villages have seasonal guesthouses or homestays and interesting old temples. They make good day trips from Kaza, and equally good places to stay over, take walks or trek between, and get a sense of the lifestyle of their amazingly resilient people.

KI

About 12km northwest of Kaza, on the road to Kibber, tiny Ki is dominated by the whitewashed buildings of Ki Gompa (⊙6am-7pm). Set picturesquely atop a conical hillock, this is the largest gompa in Spiti, with around 300 senior and student

ℹ INNER LINE PERMITS IN KAZA

To travel between Sumdo in eastern Spiti and Rekong Peo in Kinnaur, foreign travellers need an inner line permit. These are issued for free in around 20 minutes at the **Assistant Deputy Commissioner's Office** (☑222202; ◷10am-1.30pm & 2-5pm Mon-Sat, closed 2nd Sat each month) in New Kaza – the large green-roofed building diagonally opposite the Community Health Centre (hospital). Bring two passport photos and a photocopy of your passport's identity and visa pages, plus an application form (available at Ashoka stationers across the road). Solo travellers have no problems getting permits here.

monks. An atmospheric *puja* is held in the new prayer hall every morning around 8am. On request, the monks will open up the medieval prayer rooms, including the Zimshung Lhakhang, which houses a bed slept in by the Dalai Lama in 1960 and 2000. Dance masks are brought out for the annual **Ki Chaam Festival** (Tsheshu Festival; ◷Jun/Jul) and for **Losar**.

KIBBER

About 8km beyond Ki, this relatively large village (4200m) is the trailhead for the demanding nine-to-11-day trek over the 5578m Parang La to Tso Moriri lake in Ladakh (mid-July to mid-September), and also a good base for day hikes. You can walk to the even higher hamlets of **Gete** (about two hours, with small lakes nearby) or **Tashigang** (about three hours) or up to panoramic **Lama Tsong Tsong peak** (4750m high; six to seven hours round-trip). Chhetan Lama of **Norling Adventure Tours** (☑8988356455; lamachhetankibber@gmail.com) charges around ₹3500 per person per day for fully equipped treks, or ₹1000 to ₹1500 to guide day hikes. Kibber has one new and two old temples: the 14th-century one in the main village contains three prayer rooms with ancient wall paintings and sculptures.

Several guesthouses offer rooms and meals. Most close from some time in October to March or April. Easily the best rooms are at solar-powered **Norling Home Stay** (☑9418556107; r with/without bathroom ₹500/400) 🏊, a traditional whitewashed

home overlooking most of the village, which also dishes up excellent organic food. One daily bus to Kibber (₹32, 50 minutes) via Ki (₹23, 30 minutes) leaves Kaza at 5pm, starting back from Kibber at 8.30am. Taxis are ₹900 one-way.

LANGZA

Langza, a switchback 16km drive north of Kaza, sits at 4325m below the pointed 6300m peak of Chau Chau. A large modern **Buddha statue** stares across the valley from the top of the village; the temple behind it is around 500 years old. About a half-hour walk away is an area rich in **ammonite fossils** around 100 million years old. Village men participate in a drunken **horse race** to Komic and back on a variable date in the first half of August, imbibing homebrews before, during and after the race.

A bus leaving Kaza at 2pm on Tuesday and Saturday runs to Langza (₹23, one hour) and on to Komic (₹39, 1½ hours), starting back from Komic about 4pm. Taxis from Kaza cost ₹750 to Langza.

Norkhyil Home Stay   HOMESTAY $
(☑9418591066; anjaanchhering@gmail.com; r per person incl 3 meals ₹500; ◷May-Oct) 🏊 This excellent homestay has three rooms with comfy beds, carpets, mud floors, filtered drinking water and solar hot water. Anjaan, the owner, is an experienced, English-speaking guide who can show you local points of interest and take you to look for wildlife.

HIKKIM

About 6km south of Langza on a route to Komic, little Hikkim is home to the **world's highest post office** (◷9-10am & 5-6pm Mon-Sat), 4440m above sea level. It's actually a house, and all customers are offered a cup of tea. If the owners are around outside official opening hours, they'll probably still sell you some stamps. It's possible to hike direct from Kaza to Hikkim up the Kaza Nullah in three to four hours – steeper and harder, but shorter, than the 15km road route.

KOMIC

At 4513m, Komic is claimed to be the highest motorable village in Asia. It comprises about 10 houses and, above them, the important **Tangyud Gompa**, probably founded in the 14th century and with around 50 monks today. *Pujas* are offered at 8am to Mahakala, a wrathful emanation of Avalokitesvara. Above the fortlike main building, a smaller, older building has a stuffed snow leopard hanging inside the entrance: women are not permitted in its inner prayer rooms. Komic has at least one homestay – ask locally or at Ecosphere.

Taxis from Kaza cost ₹1400 via Langza, or ₹1050 by a shorter but rougher road avoiding Langza. From Komic it's about a 16km walk south to Demul, the next village on the 'Homestay Trail'.

Pin Valley

Southeast of Kaza, the snaking Spiti River is joined by the Pin River, flowing out of a wind-scoured but beautiful valley from the heights of the Great Himalaya Range. The road into the Pin Valley branches off the Tabo road 15km from Kaza. Mud slides at **Kirgarang Nullah**, 8km along, can block the road, sometimes for weeks, from some time in June, so take soundings before heading into the valley in early summer. **Gulling** village has a couple of simple guesthouses. At **Kungri**, 3km above Gulling, the 680-year-old **Ugyen Sangnak Choling Gompa** has a huge new monastery building and three much more interesting medieval shrines, featuring blackened murals, festival masks and carved wooden snow lions. Women are not allowed inside two of them. **Tringon**

Guest House (r without bathroom ₹450) at the monastery has tolerably clean rooms and a small food shop, but for meals you'll have to go down to Gulling.

The pretty, traditional village of **Sagnam** marks the turn-off to **Mudh** (3770m), the trailhead for the spectacular but logistically complicated six-to-nine-day trek to the Parvati Valley over the 5319m Pin-Parvati Pass (p304), and also for the easier four-day trek over the 4850m Bhaba Pass (Tari Khango) to Kaphnu in Kinnaur. Mudh is a beautiful spot to stay for a couple of days, even if you're not trekking. The excellent **Tara Homestay** (☑8988062293; www.spititaraadventure.com; s/d ₹500/600, r without bathroom ₹400, mains ₹80-130; ⊙May-Oct or Nov; @) is the pick of several guesthouses, and its owner Sonam Gialson can arrange full treks with porters.

A short distance from Mudh on either trek, you enter the 675-sq-km Pin Valley National Park, reputed as the 'land of ibex and snow leopards'. You may well see ibex (and blue sheep), but you'll be extremely lucky to spot a snow leopard.

Buses to Mudh (₹80, two hours) leave Kaza daily at 4pm, starting back at 6am. Some days there's a shared jeep (₹100 per person) from Mudh at about 6am, returning around 3pm. Kaza taxis charge ₹1800.

HIMACHAL PRADESH SPITI

SUSTAINABLE SPITI

While tourism brings money and development to remote areas like Spiti, it can also do unintentional damage to fragile cultures and ecosystems, and local communities may receive few of its benefits. Recognising this, a number of villages have partnered with **Ecosphere** (☑9418860099; www.spitiecosphere.com; Main Bazar, Kaza; ⊙office & shop 9am-7pm Mon-Sat May–mid-Oct, 10am-5pm Mon-Sat Apr & mid-Oct–mid-Dec) 🌿, a Spiti conservation and development NGO, to create a successful home-grown sustainable tourism program.

Homestays (₹600 per night, including meals) have been set up in six villages, five of which (Langza, Komic, Demul, Lhalung and Dhankar) can be linked into a 'Homestay Trail' trekking route. Visitors get a taste of authentic Spitian life, sleeping in traditional whitewashed houses and eating home-cooked food in the family kitchen. From the villages, wildlife-watching hikes offer a chance of spotting ibex, blue sheep (bharal) and possibly the *shanku* (Himalayan wolf), the world's oldest wolf species. Trained guides (per day ₹1000 to ₹1800), which are recommended but not required, explain about the culture and the land. Part of the homestay fee helps support the host family, and part goes into a village fund for activities to benefit the community as a whole, such as restoring the local Buddhist monastery, which is the heart of their cultural life.

Ecosphere also offers travellers numerous other activities including mountain-bike tours, culture or wildlife tours, and a 'day with the nuns' in Spiti's Buddhist convents. If you can get here in deep winter (February is best) and stay in high-altitude villages above Kaza for seven to 10 days, Ecosphere even offers a 90% chance of seeing snow leopards (₹2500 to ₹4000 per person per day for these trips).

Travellers can contribute to Ecosphere's work by volunteering on a range of projects from working in the Sol Cafe to building year-round greenhouses or working with shepherds, potters or herbal doctors.

Dhankar

High above the confluence of the Spiti and Pin Rivers, a steep 8km walk or drive up from Sichling on the Kaza–Tabo road, Dhankar village is the former capital of the Nono kings who ruled Spiti. The spectacular 1200-year-old Dhankar Gompa (admission ₹25; ⊙8am-7pm) perches precariously between eroded pinnacles on the edge of a cliff. Its top-floor courtyard has a stuffed blue sheep hanging above the stairwell, a room where the Dalai Lama slept, a meditation cave, and a shrine containing ceremonial masks. Another prayer hall stands on the hilltop above, accessed by separate concrete steps. The views from these buildings are phenomenal. Dhankar's lamas no longer inhabit the old gompa, having moved to the large, sparkling New Monastery, 800m away, in 2009. In November they celebrate the Guktor Festival (⊙Nov) with energetic masked dances.

On the hilltop above the gompa are the ruins of the mud-brick fort that sheltered the valley's population during times of war and gave the village its name (*khar* means 'citadel' and *dhak* means 'cliff'). An hour's walk up from the village, the small lake Dhankar Tso offers views over the valley and southeast to the twin peaks of Manirang (6593m).

Dhankar Monastery Guesthouse (☐9418817761; dm ₹150, r ₹350-800; ⊙Apr–mid-Oct), beside the New Monastery, has a relaxed traveller vibe, a wide choice of good food (mains ₹80 to ₹280) and rooms with picture-postcard views. There are also several homestays, charging ₹500 per person, including two or three meals. Manirang Home Stay (☐8988053409; r per person incl breakfast ₹400, inc 3 meals ₹500), below the road between the old and new monasteries, offers three pleasant rooms, a nice roof terrace and more views, and owner Anil Kumar can organise guides, treks and transport.

Buses between Kaza and Tabo pass through Sichling (₹38, one hour from Kaza); a taxi from Kaza is ₹1450/1740 one-way/return. You might find a taxi from Sichling to Dhankar for around ₹400.

Lhalung

Hidden up the Lingti Valley, 12km northeast of Dhankar along a fairly level dirt road, the charming traditional village of Lhalung is worth a detour for its fantastic medieval monastery (admission ₹50). The atmospheric main chapel contains superb old murals and an incredibly ornate carved wooden back frieze. The separate Langkharpo chapel holds a unique four-sided statue of the white deity atop a plinth of snow lions. Don't miss the skin prayer wheel in a side chapel. The village has several homestays charging around ₹500 per person, including meals, which you can arrange privately or through Ecosphere (p347).

Tabo

🎵 01906 / POP 600

Little Tabo, in a dramatic valley setting hemmed in by scree slopes, 48km southeast of Kaza, is the only other town in Spiti. The dull mud-brick walls of Tabo Gompa hide some of the finest of all Indo-Tibetan art, and Tabo makes a fine place to kick back for a couple of days.

⊙ Sights & Activities

★Tabo Gompa   BUDDHIST MONASTERY
(www.tabomonastery.com; donations accepted; ⊙6am-10pm, shrines 9am-5pm) The gompa was founded in AD 996 by Ringchen Zangpo, the Great Translator, as Tibet's Guge kingdom expanded into these outlying territories, and is reckoned to be the oldest continuously functioning Buddhist monastery in India. Bring a torch as lighting inside its shrines is dim at best. Five of the nine shrines date from the 10th and 11th centuries, when they were painted by some of the best Buddhist muralists of their era, blending Tibetan, Indian and Kashmiri styles.

The other shrines mostly date from the 15th to 17th centuries.

The main assembly hall, the Tsuglkang, is straight ahead from the temple entrance. Inside, near-life-size clay sculptures of 32 bodhisattvas line the walls around a statue of a four-bodied Vairochana Buddha turning the wheel of law – a 3D representation of the Vajradhatu mandala, which has the Vairochana at its centre. Murals below the bodhisattvas depict 10th-century life.

You'll probably have to ask a lama to open up other temples in the compound. The other highlight early temples are the Ser-Khang (Golden Temple), second to the left from the Tsuglkang, with outstanding murals of the green Tara and the goddess Usnishavijaya; the Kyil-Khang (Mystic Mandala Temple), behind the Ser-Khang, with a huge Vairochana mural surrounded by eight bodhisattvas; and the Byams-Pa Chen-po

Lha-Khang, immediately right of the Tsuglkang, with a 3m-high statue of the Bodhisattva Maitreya (future Buddha).

The modern gompa outside the ancient compound has a sparkling gilded chorten and holds a well-attended *puja* at 6.30am.

Caves
CAVE

A number of caves on the hillside above the main road were part of the monastery complex: you can reach them by steps opposite the Vijay Kumar shop.

🛏 Sleeping & Eating

⭐ **Tashi Khangsar Hotel**
HOTEL $

(☎9418817761; vaneetrana23@gmail.com; s/d ₹400/600, tent ₹200; ☺Apr-Oct) The four bright, inviting rooms here are set beside a lawn where table and chairs sit beneath a large parachute canopy. Tashi Khangsar has a good **restaurant** (mains ₹80-280; ☺7am-10pm) serving international fare, a grassy area for camping, and a relaxed, friendly vibe, adding up to excellent value. From the new monastery gate, head towards the river and turn right at the helipad.

Tiger Den
GUESTHOUSE $

(☎9459349711; naveen.chauhan82@gmail.com; r ₹700-800; ☺late Mar-late Oct) Clean, pink, medium-sized rooms with hot showers, almost next to the new monastery's entrance, and an attractive restaurant (mains ₹80 to ₹280; open 7.30am to 9pm) with floor cushions at low tables, offering Indian, Tibetan and traveller food.

Kesang Homestay Guest House
GUESTHOUSE $

(☎9418504451, 223451; sherabtabo@gmail.com; s/d ₹600/800, without bathroom ₹300/400; ☺mid-Apr-late Oct; @☎) Opposite the hospital 100m from the new monastery gates, Kesang is run by a super-friendly family and has clean, spacious rooms, plus wi-fi (₹80 per hour). Simple local meals are available. Rates drop by about one-third in April, May, September and October.

Sonam Homestay
GUESTHOUSE $

(☎9418503966; sonam@yahoo.co.in; r ₹600-800, r without bathroom ₹400) 🍃 Rooms here are some of the best value in Tabo, and the hot water is solar-heated.

Millennium Monastic Guesthouse
GUESTHOUSE $

(☎223315; dm ₹100, r with/without bathroom from ₹300/200, ste ₹700-1000) This ageing place has average rooms, but it does have piped hot water and is great for tight budgets. Guests are asked to refrain from smoking, drinking alcohol and other activities that might offend monastic sensibilities.

Dewachen Retreat
HOTEL $$

(☎9459566689; www.dewachenretreats.com; s/d ₹2000/2800; ☺approx mid-Apr–mid-Nov) The impressiveness of the carved wooden doorway doesn't quite extend inside, but the pine-panelled rooms, with good tiled bathrooms and temple and mountain views, are Tabo's nearest thing to luxury. It's on the main road at the back of town, and is sometimes full with groups. The good restaurant is open to all.

Cafe Kunzum Top
TIBETAN $

(mains ₹70-100; ☺7am-9.30pm) Kunzum Top serves tasty Tibetan and Spiti dishes in its sunny garden and cosy interior, and has decent coffee. Sonam Homestay is attached.

ℹ Information

Tabo has an SBI ATM, and internet is available at **Tabo Cyber Cafe** (Kesang Homestay Guest House; per hour ₹80; ☺ 9am-8pm Apr, May, Sep & Oct, 7am-9pm Jun-Aug).

ℹ Getting There & Away

Buses to Kaza (₹71, 2½ hours) pass through Tabo around 9am and 3pm, give or take an hour. There's a daily bus to Rekong Peo (₹270, nine hours) at 9am, via Nako (₹100, three hours), but this originates in Kaza so it can be packed, especially in May and October when seasonal workers are on the move. Taxis charge around ₹1600 to Kaza, ₹1300 to Dhankar, ₹1700 to Nako and ₹6000 to Rekong Peo.

Tabo to Sumdo

East of Tabo the highway continues to **Sumdo**, 27km east, where it turns south and enters Kinnaur. Foreigners must show their inner line permits at Sumdo. The southward stretch from here to Rekong Peo is one of India's most dramatic mountain roads.

If you've got your own transport, 3km before Sumdo look for the turn-off to **Giu**, 8km up a side valley, where you can see the mummified remains of a Buddhist monk who died over 500 years ago. The remains still have hair and fingernails and, according to local lore, spurted blood when unearthed by the shovels of a construction crew in 2004.

HIMACHAL PRADESH SPITI

Agra & the Taj Mahal

Best Places to Eat

➜ Pinch of Spice (p364)

➜ Time2Eat –
Mama Chicken (p365)

➜ Esphahan (p364)

➜ Lakshmi Vilas (p365)

➜ Dasaprakash (p365)

Best Places to Stay

➜ Bansi Homestay (p361)

➜ N Homestay (p361)

➜ Tourists Rest House (p363)

➜ Oberoi Amarvilas (p361)

➜ Saniya Palace Hotel (p359)

Why Go?

Agra's Taj Mahal rises from the dust-beaten earth of Uttar Pradesh as it does in dreams, but even the wildest imaginations leave travellers underprepared for that breath-stealing moment its gates are traversed and this magnificent world wonder comes into focus. Skipping it would be a bit like drinking chai without spoonfuls of sugar: absurd. Simply put, it's the most beautiful building in the world and it's almost impossible to see it without feeling awestruck.

But Agra, with its long and rich history, boasts plenty more besides. For 130 years this was the centre of India's great Mughal empire, and its legacy lives on in beautiful artwork, mouth-watering cuisine and magnificent architecture. The Taj is one of three places here that have been awarded Unesco World Heritage status, with the immense Agra Fort and the eerie ruined city of Fatehpur Sikri making up a superb trio of top-draw sights.

When to Go
Agra

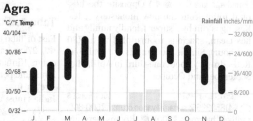

Sep–Oct The best time to visit. Most of the monsoon rains are over and summer temperatures have cooled.

Nov–Feb Daytime temperatures are comfortable but big sights are overcrowded. Evenings are nippy.

Mar–Apr Evening chill is gone but raging-hot mid-summer temperatures have yet to materialise.

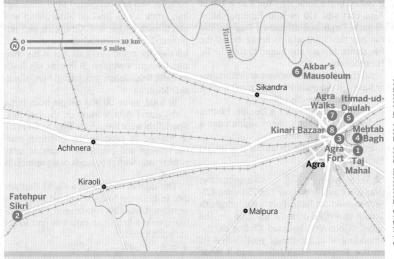

Agra & the Taj Mahal Highlights

1 Rising before dawn to take in the **Taj Mahal** (p352) minus the crowds, returning later for the cinematic sunset view

2 Exploring the fascinating abandoned city of **Fatehpur Sikri** (p369)

3 Gawking at the immensity of the red-sandstone walls that surround **Agra Fort** (p353)

4 Hiring a rickshaw for the day, taking in a tour of Agra's Mughal gardens, ending at sunset with **Mehtab Bagh** (p358)

5 Crossing the Yamuna River to **Itimad-ud-Daulah** (p355), an exquisite marble tomb nicknamed the Baby Taj

6 Hitting the suburbs for **Akbar's Mausoleum** (p355),

the beautiful resting place of the Mughals' greatest emperor

7 Strolling deeper into ancient Agra on a captivating jaunt with **Agra Walks** (p358)

8 Battling the throngs at hectic **Kinari Bazaar** (p366), one of India's most mesmerising markets

History

In 1501 Sultan Sikandar Lodi established his capital here, but the city fell into Mughal hands in 1526, when Emperor Babur defeated the last Lodi sultan at Panipat. Agra reached the peak of its magnificence between the mid-16th and mid-17th centuries during the reigns of Akbar, Jehangir and Shah Jahan. During this period the fort, the Taj Mahal and other major mausoleums were built. In 1638 Shah Jahan built a new city in Delhi, and his son Aurangzeb moved the capital there 10 years later.

In 1761 Agra fell to the Jats, a warrior class who looted its monuments, including the Taj Mahal. The Marathas took over in 1770, but were replaced by the British in 1803. Following the First War of Independence of 1857, the British shifted the administration of the province to Allahabad. Deprived of its administrative role, Agra developed as a centre for heavy industry, quickly becoming famous for its chemicals industry and air pollution, before the Taj and tourism became a major source of income.

Agra

📞 0562 / POP 1.7 MILLION

👁 Sights

The entrance fee for Agra's five main sights – the Taj, Agra Fort, Fatehpur Sikri, Akbar's Mausoleum and Itimad-ud-Daulah – is made up of charges from two different bodies, the Archaeological Survey of India (ASI) and the Agra Development Association (ADA). Of the ₹750 ticket for the Taj Mahal, ₹500 is a special ADA ticket, which gives you small savings on the other four sights if visited in the same day. You'll save ₹50 at Agra Fort and ₹10 each at Fatehpur Sikri, Akbar's Tomb and Itimad-ud-Daulah. You can buy this ₹500 ADA ticket at any of the five sights. Just say you intend to visit the Taj later that day.

All the other sights in Agra are either free or have ASI tickets only, which aren't included in the ADA one-day offer.

Admission to all sights is free for children under 15. On Fridays, many sights offer a tax-free discount of ₹10.

See also the illustrated highlight of the Taj Mahal (p356).

★ **Taj Mahal**   HISTORIC BUILDING
(Map p360; Indian/foreigner ₹20/750, video ₹25; ⊙dawn-dusk Sat-Thu) Poet Rabindranath Tagore described it as 'a teardrop on the cheek of eternity', Rudyard Kipling as 'the embodiment of all things pure', while its creator, Emperor Shah Jahan, said it made 'the sun and the moon shed tears from their eyes'. Every year, tourists numbering more than twice the population of Agra pass through its gates to catch a once-in-a-lifetime glimpse of what is widely considered the most beautiful building in the world. Few leave disappointed.

The Taj was built by Shah Jahan as a memorial for his third wife, Mumtaz Mahal, who died giving birth to their 14th child in 1631. The death of Mumtaz left the emperor so heartbroken that his hair is said to have turned grey virtually overnight. Construction of the Taj began the following year and, although the main building is thought to have been built in eight years, the whole

---

ⓘ BEST TIMES TO SEE THE TAJ

The Taj is arguably at its most atmospheric at **sunrise**. This is certainly the most comfortable time to visit, with far fewer crowds. **Sunset** is another magical viewing time. You can also view the Taj for five nights around **full moon**. Entry numbers are limited, though, and tickets must be bought a day in advance from the **Archaeological Survey of India office** (Map p358; ☑2227261; www.asi.nic.in; 22 The Mall; Indian/foreigner ₹510/750; ⊙9.30am-6pm Mon-Fri). See its website for details. Note, this office is known as the Taj Mahal Office by some rickshaw riders.

---

complex was not completed until 1653. Not long after it was finished Shah Jahan was overthrown by his son Aurangzeb and imprisoned in Agra Fort where, for the rest of his days, he could only gaze out at his creation through a window. Following his death in 1666, Shah Jahan was buried here alongside Mumtaz.

In total, some 20,000 people from India and Central Asia worked on the building. Specialists were brought in from as far away as Europe to produce the exquisite marble screens and pietra dura (marble inlay work) made with thousands of semiprecious stones.

The Taj was designated a World Heritage Site in 1983 and looks as immaculate today as when it was first constructed – though it underwent a huge restoration project in the early 20th century.

➡ Entry & Information
Note: the Taj is closed every Friday to anyone not attending prayers at the mosque.

The Taj can be accessed through the west, south and east gates. Tour groups tend to enter through the east and west gates. Independent travellers tend to use the south gate, which is nearest to Taj Ganj, the main area for budget accommodation, and generally has shorter queues than the west gate. The east gate has the shortest queues of the lot, but this is because the ticket office is inconveniently located a 1km walk away at Shilpgram, a dire government-run tourist centre. There are separate queues for men and women at all three gates.

Cameras and videos are permitted but you cannot take photographs inside the mausoleum itself, and the areas in which you can take videos are quite limited.

Do not forget to retrieve your free 500mL-bottle of water and shoe covers (included in Taj ticket price). If you keep your ticket you get small entry-fee reductions when visiting Agra Fort, Fatehpur Sikri, Akbar's Mausoleum or the Itimad-ud-Daulah on the same day. You can also store your luggage for free beside the ticket offices and pick up an audio guide (₹118).

From the south gate, entry to the inner compound is through a very impressive, 30m red-sandstone **gateway** on the south side of the forecourt, which is inscribed with verses from the Quran.

➡ Inside the Grounds
Once inside, the **ornamental gardens** are set out along classical Mughal *charbagh*

(formal Persian garden) lines – a square quartered by watercourses, with an ornamental marble plinth at its centre. When the fountains are not flowing, the Taj is beautifully reflected in the water.

The Taj Mahal itself stands on a raised marble platform at the northern end of the ornamental gardens, with its back to the Yamuna River. Its raised position means that the backdrop is only sky – a masterstroke of design. Purely decorative 40m-high white **minarets** grace each corner of the platform. After more than three centuries they are not quite perpendicular, but they may have been designed to lean slightly outwards so that in the event of an earthquake they would fall away from the precious Taj. The red-sandstone **mosque** to the west is an important gathering place for Agra's Muslims. The identical building to the east, the **jawab**, was built for symmetry.

The central Taj structure is made of semitranslucent white marble, carved with flowers and inlaid with thousands of semiprecious stones in beautiful patterns. A perfect exercise in symmetry, the four identical faces of the Taj feature impressive vaulted arches embellished with pietra dura scrollwork and quotations from the Quran in a style of calligraphy using inlaid jasper. The whole structure is topped off by four small domes surrounding the famous bulbous central dome.

Directly below the main dome is the **Cenotaph of Mumtaz Mahal**, an elaborate false tomb surrounded by an exquisite perforated marble screen inlaid with dozens of different types of semiprecious stones. Beside it, offsetting the symmetry of the Taj, is the **Cenotaph of Shah Jahan**, who was interred here with little ceremony by his usurping son Aurangzeb in 1666. Light is admitted into the central chamber by finely cut marble screens. The real tombs of Mumtaz Mahal and Shah Jahan are in a locked basement room below the main chamber and cannot be viewed.

★**Agra Fort**   FORT
(Map p358; Indian/foreigner ₹20/300, video ₹25; ☉dawn-dusk) With the Taj Mahal overshadowing it, one can easily forget that Agra has one of the finest Mughal forts in India. Construction of the massive red-sandstone fort, on the bank of the Yamuna River, was begun by Emperor Akbar in 1565.

TAJ MUSEUM

Within the Taj complex, on the western side of the gardens, is the small but excellent **Taj Museum** (Map p360; ☉9am-5pm, closed Fri) FREE, housing a number of original Mughal miniature paintings, including a pair of 17th-century ivory portraits of Emperor Shah Jahan and his beloved wife Mumtaz Mahal. It also has some very well preserved gold and silver coins dating from the same period, plus architectural drawings of the Taj and some nifty celadon plates, said to split into pieces or change colour if the food served on them contains poison.

Further additions were made, particularly by his grandson Shah Jahan, using his favourite building material – white marble. The fort was built primarily as a military structure, but Shah Jahan transformed it into a palace, and later it became his gilded prison for eight years after his son Aurangzeb seized power in 1658.

The ear-shaped fort's colossal double walls rise over 20m in height and measure 2.5km in circumference. The Yamuna River originally flowed along the straight eastern edge of the fort, and the emperors had their own bathing ghats here. It contains a maze of buildings, forming a city within a city, including vast underground sections, though many of the structures were destroyed over the years by Nadir Shah, the Marathas, the Jats and finally the British, who used the fort as a garrison. Even today, much of the fort is used by the military and so is off-limits to the general public.

The **Amar Singh Gate** to the south is the sole entry point to the fort these days and where you buy your entrance ticket. Its dogleg design was meant to confuse attackers who made it past the first line of defence – the crocodile-infested moat.

A path leads straight from here up to the large **Moti Masjid** (Pearl Mosque), which is always closed. To your right, just before you reach Moti Masjid, is the large open **Diwan-i-Am** (Hall of Public Audiences), which was used by Shah Jahan for domestic government business, and features a throne room where the emperor listened to petitioners. In front of it is the small and rather incongruous **grave of John Colvin**,

TOP TAJ VIEWS

Inside the Taj Grounds

You may have to pay ₹750 for the privilege, but it's only when you're inside the grounds themselves that you can really get up close and personal with the world's most beautiful building. Don't miss inspecting the marble inlay work (pietra dura) inside the *pishtaqs* (large arched recesses) on the four outer walls. And don't forget to bring a small torch with you so that you can shine it on similar pietra dura work inside the dark central chamber of the mausoleum. Note the translucency of both the white marble and the semiprecious stones inlaid into it.

From Mehtab Bagh

Tourists are no longer allowed to wander freely along the riverbank on the opposite side of the Yamuna River, but you can still enjoy a view of the back of the Taj from the 16th-century Mughal park Mehtab Bagh (p358), with the river flowing between you and the mausoleum. A path leading down to the river beside the park offers the same view for free, albeit from a more restricted angle.

Looking Up from the South Bank of the River

This is a great place to be for sunset. Take the path that hugs the outside of the Taj's eastern wall and walk all the way down to the small temple beside the river. You should be able to find boat hands down here willing to row you out onto the water for an even more romantic view. Expect to pay around ₹100 per boat. For safety reasons, it's best not to wander down here on your own for sunset.

From a Rooftop Cafe in Taj Ganj

Perfect for sunrise shots, there are some wonderful photos to be had from the numerous rooftop cafes in Taj Ganj. We think the cafe on Saniya Palace Hotel (p359) is the pick of the bunch, with its plant-filled design and great position, but many of them are good. And all offer the bonus of being able to view the Taj with the added comfort of an early-morning cup of coffee.

From Agra Fort

With a decent zoom lens you can capture some fabulous images of the Taj from Agra Fort, especially if you're willing to get up at the crack of dawn to see the sun rising up from behind it. The best places to shoot it from are probably Musamman Burj and Khas Mahal, the octagonal tower and palace where Shah Jahan was imprisoned for eight years until his death.

a lieutenant-governor of the northwest provinces who died of an illness in the fort during the 1857 First War of Independence (Indian Uprising).

A tiny staircase just to the left of the Diwan-i-Am throne leads up to a large courtyard. To your left, is the tiny but exquisite Nagina Masjid (Gem Mosque), built in 1635 by Shah Jahan for the ladies of the court. Down below was the Ladies' bazaar, where the court ladies bought goods.

On the far side of the large courtyard, along the eastern wall of the fort, is Diwan-i-Khas (Hall of Private Audiences), which was reserved for important dignitaries or foreign representatives. The hall once housed Shah Jahan's legendary Peacock Throne, which was inset with precious stones including

the famous Koh-i-noor diamond. The throne was taken to Delhi by Aurangzeb, then to Iran in 1739 by Nadir Shah and dismantled after his assassination in 1747. Overlooking the river and the distant Taj Mahal is Takhti-i-Jehangir, a huge slab of black rock with an inscription around the edge. The throne that stood here was made for Jehangir when he was Prince Salim.

Off to your right from here (as you face the river) is Shish Mahal (Mirror Palace), with walls inlaid with tiny mirrors. At the time of research it had been closed for some time due to restoration, although you could peek through cracks in the doors at the sparkling mirrors inside.

Further along the eastern edge of the fort you'll find Musamman Burj and Khas

Mahal, the wonderful white-marble octagonal tower and palace where Shah Jahan was imprisoned for eight years until his death in 1666, and from where he could gaze out at the Taj Mahal, the tomb of his wife. When he died, Shah Jahan's body was taken from here by boat to the Taj. The now closed Mina Masjid, set back slightly from the eastern edge, was his private mosque.

The large courtyard here is Anguri Bagh, a garden that has been brought back to life in recent years. In the courtyard is an innocuous-looking entrance – now locked – that leads down a flight of stairs into a two-storey labyrinth of underground rooms and passageways where Akbar used to keep his 500-strong harem.

Continuing south, the huge red-sandstone Jehangir's Palace was probably built by Akbar for his son Jehangir. It blends Indian and Central Asian architectural styles, a reminder of the Mughals' Afghani cultural roots. In front of the palace is Hauz-i-Jehangir, a huge bowl carved out of a single block of stone, which was used for bathing. Walking past this brings you back to the main path to Amar Singh Gate.

You can walk here from Taj Ganj, or it's ₹40 in a cycle-rickshaw.

Akbar's Mausoleum
HISTORIC BUILDING

(Indian/foreigner ₹10/110, video ₹25; ⊙ dawn-dusk) This outstanding sandstone and marble tomb commemorates the greatest of the Mughal emperors. The huge courtyard is entered through a stunning gateway. It has three-storey minarets at each corner and is built of red sandstone strikingly inlaid with white-marble geometric patterns.

The mausoleum is at Sikandra, 10km northwest of Agra Fort. Catch a bus (₹22, 45 minutes) headed to Mathura from Bijli Ghar bus stand; they go past the mausoleum.

Itimad-ud-Daulah
HISTORIC BUILDING

(Indian/foreigner ₹10/110, video ₹25; ⊙ dawn-dusk) Nicknamed the Baby Taj, the exquisite tomb of Mizra Ghiyas Beg should not be missed. This Persian nobleman was Mumtaz Mahal's grandfather and Emperor Jehangir's *wazir* (chief minister). His daughter Nur Jahan, who married Jehangir, built the tomb between 1622 and 1628 in a style similar to the tomb she built for Jehangir near Lahore in Pakistan.

It doesn't have the same awesome beauty as the Taj, but it's arguably more delicate in appearance thanks to its particularly finely carved *jali* (marble lattice screens). This was the first Mughal structure built completely from marble, the first to make extensive use of pietra dura and the first tomb to be built on the banks of the Yamuna, which until then had been a sequence of beautiful pleasure gardens.

You can combine a trip here with Chini-ka-Rauza, Mehtab Bagh and Ram Bagh, all on the east bank. A cycle-rickshaw covering all four should cost about ₹300 return from the Taj, including waiting time. An autorickshaw should be ₹450.

Chini-ka-Rauza
HISTORIC BUILDING

(⊙ dawn-dusk) FREE This Persian-style riverside tomb of Afzal Khan, a poet who served as Shah Jahan's chief minister, was built between 1628 and 1639. Rarely visited, it is hidden away down a shady avenue of trees on the east bank of the Yamuna.

(Continued on page 358)

TOP AGRA FESTIVALS

Taj Mahotsav (www.tajmahotsav.org; ⊙ Feb) This 10-day carnival of culture, cuisine and crafts is Agra's biggest and best party. Held at Shilpgram, the festival features over 400 artisan craft-makers from all over India, as well as a pot-pourri of folk and classical music, dances from various regions and enough regional food to induce a curry coma.

Kailash Fair (⊙ Aug/Sep) Held at the Kailash temple, 12km from Agra, this cultural and religious fair honours Lord Shiva, who legendarily appeared here in the form of a stone lingam. It attracts devotees from all over North India.

Ram Barat (⊙ Sep) Celebrated before the Hindu festival of Dussehra, Ram Barat is a dramatic recreation of the royal wedding procession of Shri Rama. Expect three days of colourful lights and pounding Hindu rhythms, highlighted by the 12-hour parade itself, featuring caparisoned elephants, horses, more than 125 mobile floats depicting mythological events and 30 marching bands.

Taj Mahal

TIMELINE

1631 Emperor Shah Jahan's beloved third wife, Mumtaz Mahal, dies in Buhanpur while giving birth to their 14th child. Her body is initially interred in Buhanpur itself, where Shah Jahan is fighting a military campaign, but is later moved, in a golden casket, to a small building on the banks of the Yamuna River in Agra.

1632 Construction of a permanent mausoleum for Mumtaz Mahal begins.

1633 Mumtaz Mahal is interred in her final resting place, an underground tomb beneath a marble plinth, on top of which the Taj Mahal will be built.

1640 The white-marble mausoleum is completed.

1653 The rest of the Taj Mahal complex is completed.

1658 Emperor Shah Jahan is overthrown by his son Aurangzeb and imprisoned in Agra Fort.

1666 Shah Jahan dies. His body is transported along the Yamuna River and buried underneath the Taj, alongside the tomb of his wife.

1908 Repeatedly damaged and looted after the fall of the Mughal empire, the Taj receives some long-overdue attention as part of a major restoration project ordered by British viceroy Lord Curzon.

1983 The Taj is awarded Unesco World Heritage Site status.

2002 Having been discoloured by pollution in more recent years, the Taj is spruced up with an ancient recipe known as multani mitti – a blend of soil, cereal, milk and lime once used by Indian women to beautify their skin.

Today More than three million tourists visit the Taj Mahal each year. That's more than twice the current population of Agra.

DANIEL MCCROHAN ©

GO BAREFOOT

Help the environment by entering the mausoleum barefoot instead of using the free disposable shoe covers.

Pishtaqs
These huge arched recesses are set into each side of the Taj. They provide depth to the building while their central, latticed marble screens allow patterned light to illuminate the inside of the mausoleum.

Minaret

Plinth

Entranc

Marble Relief Work
Flowering plants, thought to be representations of paradise, are a common theme among the beautifully decorative panels carved onto the white marble.

DANIEL MCCROHAN ©

BE ENLIGHTENED

Bring a small torch into the mausoleum to fully appreciate the translucency of the white marble and semiprecious stones.

Filigree Screen
This stunning screen was carved out of a single piece of marble. It surrounds both cenotaphs, allowing patterned light to fall onto them through its intricately carved *jali* (latticework).

Central Dome
The Taj's famous central dome, topped by a brass finial, represents the vault of heaven, a stark contrast to the material world, which is represented by the square shape of the main structure.

Yamuna River

NORTH →

Pietra Dura
It's believed that 35 different precious and semi-precious stones were used to create the exquisite pietra dura (marble inlay work) found on the inside and outside of the mausoleum walls. Again, floral designs are common.

Calligraphy
The strips of calligraphy surrounding each of the four pishtaqs get larger as they get higher, giving the impression of uniform size when viewed from the ground. There's also calligraphy inside the mausoleum, including on Mumtaz Mahal's cenotaph.

Cenotaphs
The cenotaphs of Mumtaz Mahal and Shah Jahan, decorated with pietra dura inlay work, are actually fake tombs. The real ones are located in an underground vault closed to the public.

Agra

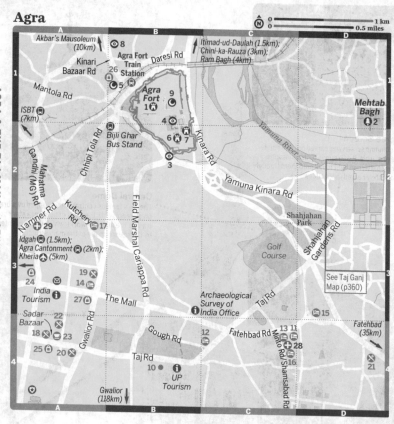

(Continued from page 355)

★ **Mehtab Bagh**   PARK
(Map p358; Indian/foreigner ₹5/100, video ₹25; ⊙ dawn-dusk) This park, originally built by Emperor Babur as the last in a series of 11 parks on the Yamuna's east bank, long before the Taj was conceived, fell into disrepair until it was little more than a huge mound of sand. To protect the Taj from the erosive effects of the sand blown across the river, the park was reconstructed and is now one the best places from which to view the great mausoleum.

The gardens in the Taj are perfectly aligned with the ones here, and the view of the Taj from the fountain directly in front of the entrance gate is a special one.

Jama Masjid   MOSQUE
(Map p358; Jama Masjid Rd) This fine mosque, built in the Kinari Bazaar by Shah Jahan's daughter in 1648, and once connected to Agra Fort, features striking marble patterning on its domes.

🏃 Activities

Hotels allowing nonguests to use their pools include Yamuna View (p363; ₹500), Howard Plaza (p362; ₹562), Amar (p362; ₹500) and Clarks Shiraz (p363; ₹1000).

☞ Tours

Agra Walks   WALKING TOUR
(☏ 9027711144; www.agrawalks.com; tours ₹1500) Many folks spend but a day in Agra, taking in the Taj and Agra Fort and sailing off into the sunset. If you're interested in digging a little deeper, this excellent walking/cycle-rickshaw combo tour will show you sides of the city most tourists don't see.

The guides are darling and Old Agra highlights include going deeper into Kinari Bazaar and a few off-the-beaten-path temples

Agra

such as Mankameshwar Mandir and Radha Krishna Mandir. A delectable food tour also debuted in 2014.

Amin Tours CULTURAL TOURS
(☎9837411144; www.daytourtajmahal.com) If you can't be bothered handling the logistics, look no further than this recommended agency for all-inclusive private Agra day trips from Delhi by car (₹6000) or train (₹6500). One caveat: if they try to take you shopping and you're not interested, politely decline.

UP Tourism COACH TOURS
(Map p358; ☎2421204; www.up-tourism.com; incl entry fees Indian/foreigner ₹500/2000; ⊙6.30am-9.30pm) UP Tourism runs coach tours that leave Agra Cantonment train station at 10.30am Saturday to Thursday, after picking up passengers arriving from Delhi on the Taj Express. The tour includes the Taj Mahal, Agra Fort and Fatehpur Sikri, with a 1¼-hour stop in each place.

Tours return to the station so that day trippers can catch the Taj Express back to Delhi at 6.55pm. Contact either of the UP Tourism offices to book a seat, or just turn up at the train station tourist office at 9.45am to sign up for that day. Tours only depart with 10 people or more.

🛏 Sleeping

The main place for budget accommodation is the bustling area of Taj Ganj, immediately south of the Taj, while there's a high concentration of midrange hotels further south, along Fatehabad Rd. Sadar Bazaar, an area boasting good-quality restaurants, offers another option. Be forewarned: free wi-fi hasn't really caught on in Agra's nicer hotels; expect to pay upwards of ₹500 for 12 hours.

🛏 Taj Ganj Area

Saniya Palace Hotel HOTEL $
(Map p360; ☎0562-3270199; www.saniyapalace.com; Chowk Kagziyan, Taj South Gate; d ₹400-600, without bathroom ₹200, with AC ₹800-1000; ❄@🛜) Set back from the main strip down an undesirable alleyway, this isn't the sleekest Taj Ganj option, but it tries to imbue character (marble floors and Mughal-style framed carpet wall hangings). The rooms (apart from the bathroomless cheapies) are clean and big enough, although the bathrooms in the non-AC rooms are minuscule.

The real coup is the very pleasant, plant-filled (and recently expanded) rooftop, which trumps its rivals for optimum Taj views.

Taj Ganj

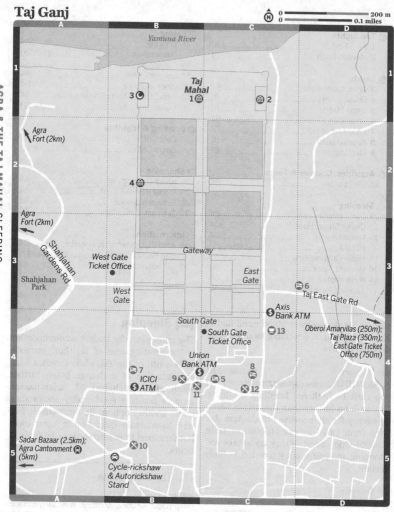

Hotel Kamal HOTEL $

(Map p360; ☎0562-2330126; hotelkamal@hotmail.com; Taj South Gate; d ₹600-900, with AC ₹1800; ❅@☎) The smartest hotel in Taj Ganj proper, Kamal has clean, comfortable rooms with nice touches such as framed photos of the Taj on the walls and rugs on the tiled floors (five in the newer annex are a definitive step-up with welcoming woodwork, extra space and stone-walled showers).

There's a cosy, bamboo-enclosed ground-floor restaurant and an underused rooftop restaurant with a somewhat obscured Taj view.

Hotel Sidhartha HOTEL $

(Map p360; ☎0562-2230901; www.hotelsidhartha.com; Taj West Gate; s/d/tr ₹700/850/960, with AC s ₹900, d ₹1300-1500; ❅@☎) Of the 21 rooms in this West Gate staple, those on the ground floor are stylish for the price, with marble walls, cable TV and clean bathrooms with hot water (room 111A is the standard to which all future ground-floor rooms will eventually be renovated). Upper-floor rooms are smaller and not as exciting.

Either way, all 21 surround or overlook a small, leafy courtyard overrun by a shade-providing tameshwari plant.

Taj Ganj

◉ Top Sights
1 Taj Mahal B1

◎ Sights
2 Jawab C1
3 Mosque B1
4 Taj Museum B2

🛏 Sleeping
5 Hotel Kamal C4
6 Hotel Sheela D3
7 Hotel Sidhartha B4
8 Saniya Palace Hotel C4

✴ Eating
9 Joney's Place B4
Saniya Palace Hotel .... (see 8)
10 Shankar Ji Restaurant B5
11 Shankara Vegis B4
12 Yash Cafe C4

☕ Drinking & Nightlife
13 Café Coffee Day C4

Hotel Sheela   HOTEL $

(Map p360; ☑ 0562-2333074; www.hotelsheelaagra.com; Taj East Gate Rd; s/d with fan ₹500/600, with AC ₹800/900; ☀ 🛜) It draws its fair share of complaints from travellers (cold in winter, indifferent management, questionable hygiene), but if you're not fussed about looking at the Taj Mahal 24 hours a day, and don't mind doing a little legwork for an autorickshaw, Sheela teeters on being an acceptable budget option.

Rooms are no-frills but are set around a landscaped garden. There are singing birds, plenty of shade and a restaurant area (better for atmosphere than food). Book ahead.

Taj Plaza   HOTEL $$

(☑ 0562-2232515; www.hoteltajplaza.com; Shilpgram VIP Rd; d ₹1500, with AC ₹2500, Taj-facing ₹3200; ☀ @ 🛜) Depending on demand, this well-positioned hotel fluctuates between budget and midrange. You won't be disappointed if you stay here. It has professional reception and clean rooms with TV, six of which eye the Taj, and there's a pleasant rooftop with decent Taj and sunset views.

It's a whole lot closer to the Taj than most hotels in the same price range.

The Retreat   BOUTIQUE HOTEL $$$

(☑ 0562-3022222; www.theretreat.co.in; Shilpgram Rd; s/d incl breakfast from ₹5000/6000; ☀ @ 🛜) Everything in this sleek 52-room hotel is done up boutique-style with Indian sensibilities (lots of soothing mauve and turquoise throughout)

and modern fixtures abound. There's a small pool and multicuisine restaurant offering countrywide specialities such as Goan fish curries and Lahori kebabs. Free wi-fi.

★ Oberoi Amarvilas   HOTEL $$$

(☑ 0562-2231515; www.oberoihotels.com; Taj East Gate Rd; d with/without balcony ₹62,960/53,960; ☀ @ 🛜 ☀) Following Oberoi's iron-clad MO of Maharaja-level service, exquisite dining and properties that pack some serious wow, Agra's best hotel by far oozes style and luxury. Elegant interior design is suffused with Mughal themes, a composition carried over into the exterior fountain courtyard and swimming pool, both of which are set in a delightful water garden.

All rooms (and even some bathtubs) have wonderful Taj views.

🛏 Fatahabad Road Area

★ Bansi Homestay   HOMESTAY $$

(Map p358; ☑ 0562-2333033; www.bansi-homestayagra.com; 18 Handicraft Nagar, Fatehabad Rd; r incl breakfast ₹3500; ☀ 🛜) 🅿 A retired director of Uttar Pradesh Tourism is your host at this wonderful upscale homestay tucked away in a quiet residential neighbourhood near Fatehabad Rd. The five large rooms boast huge bathrooms with pressurised solar-powered rain-style showers and flank pleasant common areas with bespoke furniture and Krishna paintings.

The immensely pleasurable 2nd-floor garden is a fabulous retreat to watch the world go by; and the food – notably the homemade pickles and *aloo paratha* (potato-stuffed flatbread) – excels along with the hospitality in general.

★ N Homestay   HOMESTAY $$

(Map p358; ☑ 9690107860; www.nhomestay.com; 15 Ajanta Colony, Vibhav Nagar; s/d incl breakfast ₹1600/1800; ☀ @ 🛜) Matriarch Naghma and her helpful sons are a riot at this wonderful homestay. Their beautiful home, tucked away in a residential

---

SLEEPING PRICE RANGES

Accommodation price ranges for this chapter are:

$ below ₹1500

$$ ₹1500 to ₹4000

$$$ above ₹4000

neighbourhood 15 minutes' walk from the Taj's western gate, is nothing short of a fabulous place to stay.

The three-storey house features marble floors throughout, and some of the six large and authentically appointed rooms have pleasant balconies (first-come, first-served). Naghma will even cook you dinner (₹350 to ₹400) – and what a cook she is! You'll rarely break through the cultural surface with such ease.

Dasaprakash HOTEL $$

(Map p358; ☑0562-4016123; www.dasaprakash-group.com; 18/163A/6 Shamshabad Rd; s/d incl breakfast ₹3220/3760; ❄️🛜) This friendly and clean retreat offers 28 modern and functional rooms with small desks, flat-screen TVs and nice bathrooms, all of which haven't been around long enough to show signs of deterioration. It all works well as a good-value escape from the diesel and dust, and is located far enough from Fatehabad Rd to offer relative R&R. Free wi-fi.

Howard Plaza HOTEL $$$

(Map p358; ☑0562-4048600; www.howardplazaagra.com; Fatehabad Rd; s/d incl breakfast from ₹7890/8990; ❄️@🛜🏊) Standard rooms in this very welcoming hotel are decked out in elegant dark-wood furniture and stylish decorative tiling. New deluxe rooms boast soothing aqua colour schemes – the results of recent renovations that squared away a new sleek marble lobby and coffee shop/ restaurant.

The pool is starting to show its age, but there's a small but well-equipped gym and a very pleasant spa offering a whole range of ayurvedic treatments (massages from ₹1799). The breezy open-air rooftop restaurant doubles as one of the few atmospheric bars in town at night (cocktails ₹325) – distant Taj views are on offer from the 4th-floor terrace. Wi-fi is enabled throughout.

Hotel Amar HOTEL $$$

(Map p358; ☑0562-2331884; www.hotelamar.com; Fatehabad Rd; s/d incl breakfast from ₹3820/4270; ❄️@🛜🏊) A little worn, the 66 wi-fi-enabled rooms at the friendly Amar come with big TVs and clean bathrooms. The marble-inlay entrance halls and funky mirrored-ceiling hallways drive home a palpable sense of place. There's a great pool area, complete

TAJ MAHAL MYTHS

The Taj is a Hindu Temple

The well-publicised theory that the Taj was in fact a Shiva temple built in the 12th century and only later converted into Mumtaz Mahal's famous mausoleum was developed by Purushottam Nagesh Oak. The Mughals had form in this regard, at Somnath and the Qutb Minar in Delhi among other places, but in 2000 India's Supreme Court dismissed his petition to have the sealed basement rooms of the Taj opened to prove his theory. Oak also claims that the Kaaba, Stonehenge and the Papacy all have Hindu origins.

The Black Taj Mahal

The story goes that Shah Jahan planned to build a negative image of the Taj Mahal in black marble on the opposite side of the river as his own mausoleum, and that work began before he was imprisoned by his son Aurangzeb in Agra Fort. Extensive excavations at Mehtab Bagh have found no trace of any such construction.

Craftsmen Mutilations

Legend has it that on completion of the Taj, Shah Jahan ordered that the hands of the project's craftsmen be chopped off, to prevent them from ever building anything as beautiful again. Some even say he went so far as to have their eyes gouged out. Thankfully, no historical evidence supports either story.

Sinking Taj

Some experts believe there is evidence to show that the Taj is slowly tilting towards and sinking into the riverbed due to the changing nature of the soil beside an increasingly dry Yamuna River. The Archaeological Survey of India has dismissed any marginal change in the elevation of the building as statistically insignificant, adding that it has not detected any structural damage at its base in the seven decades since its first scientific study of the Taj was carried out, in 1941.

THE SPA MAHAL

If India's most glorious monument looks particularly glowing on your visit, it could come down to a day at the spa. After years of research, Indian and American scientists have identified the culprit that has caused an ongoing discolouration of the mausoleum – marble-white by birth, but now brownish-yellow due to ageing – and it's the same pollutants responsible for global warming. Dubbed the Atmospheric Brown Cloud, black carbon, light-absorbing brown carbon and dust (the latter no surprise to anyone who has visited Agra) have slowly tarnished the surface of the Taj with years of open-stove cooking with wood and dung, vehicle exhaust, brick-making and trash burning in the vicinity.

In addition to an ongoing project to alleviate the larger issue, the Taj has received a mud-pack facial cleanse for the fourth time in its history. Based on a traditional recipe used by Indian women to restore their own facial radiance, a lime-rich clay mixture is added to pollution-affected areas of the monument overnight and is scrubbed off with nylon brushes the next day. And a massive clean-up to prepare for US president Barack Obama's scheduled visit in 2015 (he skipped the visit due to the death of Saudi Arabian King Abdullah), resulted in two tonnes of trash being removed from the Yamuna River. Voila! The Taj looks brand new.

with a lush green lawn and a 3.5m-tall water slide.

Sadar Bazaar Area

Tourists Rest House　　　HOTEL **$**
(Map p358; ☎0562-2463961; www.dontworrychickencurry.com; 4/62 Kutchery Rd; s/d ₹350/450, with AC from ₹850/1000; ❄@☎) If you aren't set on sleeping under the nose of the Taj, this centrally located travellers' hub offers better value than most Agra spots and has been under the watchful eye of the same family since 1965 (though you can't tell it is pushing 50 years).

If you can forgo aircon, the newly renovated cheapies are great value – and things only get better from there. All rooms come with free wi-fi, TV, hot water and large windows, and are set around a peaceful plant-filled, palm-shaded courtyard (a real highlight) and a North Indian pure veg restaurant. The bend-over-backwards owners speak English and French. They couldn't be more helpful, right down to occasionally carting you off somewhere in their hotel rickshaw. Phone ahead for a free station pick-up; otherwise, it's ₹40 in a cycle-rickshaw from the train station. Damn fine masala chai, too.

Clarks Shiraz Hotel　　　HOTEL **$$$**
(Map p358; ☎0562-2226121; www.hotelclarksshiraz.com; 54 Taj Rd; s/d incl breakfast from ₹8430/8990; ❄@☎≋) Agra's original five-star hotel, opened in 1961, has done well to keep up with the hotel Jones's. The standard

doubles are nothing special for this price range, but marble-floored deluxe versions are a pleasant step up and all bathrooms are retiled and spotless.

There are three very good restaurants, two bars (three in season), a gym, a shaded garden and pool area (one of Agra's best) and ayurvedic massages. Some rooms have distant Taj views.

Hotel Yamuna View　　　HOTEL **$$$**
(Map p358; ☎0562-3293777; www.hotelyamunaviewagra.com; 6B The Mall; s/d from ₹6183/6745; ❄@☎≋) A veteran Marriott manager runs a tight ship in this good-value spot in a quiet part of Sadar Bazaar, where spacious rooms with gleaming bathrooms and marble art tables are worth shelling out a few extra rupees for. There's hardly a need to upgrade to deluxe – they're not noticeably better than standard rooms.

There's a great garden pool, a sleek cocktail bar, a plush Chinese restaurant (with a real Chinese chef – good for an Indian food sabbatical) and free wi-fi (lobby only).

Eating

Dalmoth is Agra's famous version of *namkin* (spicy nibbles). *Peitha* is a square sweet made from pumpkin and glucose that is flavoured with rosewater, coconut or saffron. You can buy it in shops all over Agra. From October to March look out for *gajak,* a slightly spicy sesame-seed biscuit strip.

Taj Ganj Area

This lively area directly south of the Taj has plenty of budget rooftop restaurants, where menus appear to be carbon copies of one another. None are licensed but most will find you a beer if you are discreet.

Shankar Ji Restaurant
DHABA $

(Map p360; mains ₹35-100; ⊙7am-10pm) Shankar Ji is a *dhaba* (snack bar) perfect for when you're bored of the multicuisine foreigner-friendly tourist restaurants, and want something more down to earth and authentic. As basic as any *dhaba*, but it's all smiles (the cook is a real character), has an English menu and dishes out the *dhaba* experience without taking a toll on your gut.

It's near the autorickshaw stand.

Shankara Vegis
INDIAN $

(Map p360; Chowk Kaghzi; meals ₹60-120; ⊙8am-10.30pm; ☎) Most restaurants in Taj Ganj ooze a distinctly average air of mediocrity. Shankara Vegis is different. This cosy old-timer, with its red tablecloths and straw-lined walls, stands out not only for its decor, but for great vegetarian thalis (₹110 to ₹150) and, most pleasantly, the genuinely friendly, nonpushy ethos of its hands-on owners.

Joney's Place
MULTICUISINE $

(Map p360; Kutta Park, Taj Ganj; mains ₹30-110; ⊙5am-10.30pm) This pocket-sized institution whipped up its first creamy lassi in 1978 and continues to please despite cooking its meals in what must be Agra's smallest kitchen. The cheese and tomato 'jayfelles' (toasted sandwich), the banana lassi and the *malai* kofta all come recommended, but it's more about crack-of-dawn sustenance than culinary dazzle.

Yash Cafe
MULTICUISINE $

(Map p360; 3/137 Chowk Kagziyan; mains ₹60-300; ⊙7am-11pm; ☎) This chilled-out 1st-floor cafe has wicker chairs, sports channels on TV, DVDs shown in the evening and a good range of meals, from good-value set breakfasts to thali (₹90), pizza (₹90 to ₹300) and Indian-style French toast (with coconut; we think they made that up). It also offers a shower and storage space (₹50 for both) to day visitors.

Saniya Palace Hotel
MULTICUISINE $$

(Map p360; mains ₹50-200; ⊙6am-11pm; ☎) With cute tablecloths, dozens of potted plants and a bamboo pergola for shade, this is the most pleasant rooftop restaurant in Taj Ganj. It also has the best rooftop view of the Taj bar none. The kitchen isn't the cleanest in town, but its usual mix of Western dishes and foreigner-friendly Indian dishes usually go down without complaints.

★ Esphahan
NORTH INDIAN $$$

(☎2231515; Oberoi Amarvilas Hotel; Taj East Gate Rd; mains ₹1125-2250; ⊙dinner 6.30pm & 9pm) There are only two sittings each evening at Agra's finest **restaurant** (⊙6.30pm and 9.30pm) so booking a table is essential. The exquisite menu is chock-full of unique delicacies and rarely seen regional heritage dishes. Anything that comes out of the succulent North Indian tandoor is a showstopper (especially the *bharwan aloo*, a potato kebab stuffed with nuts, spices, mint and coriander). Melt-in-your-mouth dishes such as *aloobukhara maaz* (a Mughlai lamb kebab stuffed with prunes) and *safri gosht* (braised lamb with pickled onions, dried tomatoes and spiced pickle) redefine lamb as most know it. It's all set to a romantic background soundtrack of a live santoor player.

Fatehabad Road

Dasaprakash
INDIAN $$

(Map p358; www.dasaprakashgroup.com; 18/163A /6 Shamshabad Rd; thali ₹190-270, mains ₹170-350; ⊙7am-11pm) The Vibhav Nagar branch of this perennial South Indian upper-scale staple ups the ante with a North Indian tandoor. You get the pure veg love of other Dasaprakash branches plus North Indian options such as veg tandoori kebabs, available from noon (that tandoor needs a few hours to heat up). It's inside the hotel of the same name.

Vedic
NORTH INDIAN $$

(Map p358; www.vedicrestaurant.com; 1 Gwalior Rd; meals ₹150-275; ⊙10am-11pm) Modern decor meets traditional ambience at this North Indian veg hot-spot, with paneer (unfermented cheese) dishes featuring highly. The paneer tikka masala and Navaratan korma are particularly good. There's also a range of delicious vegetarian kebabs.

★ Pinch of Spice
NORTH INDIAN $$$

(Map p358; www.pinchofspice.in; Opp ITC Mughal Hotel, Fatehabad Rd; mains ₹280-410; ⊙noon-11.30pm) This modern North Indian superstar at the beginning of Fatehabad Rd is the best spot outside five-star hotels to indulge yourself in rich curries and succulent tandoori kebabs. The *murg boti masala* (chicken tikka swimming in a rich and spicy country gravy) and the *paneer lababdar* (fresh cheese cubes in a spicy red gravy with sauteed onions) are outstanding.

Sadar Bazaar Area

This area offers better-quality restaurants and makes a nice change from the please-all, multicuisine offerings in Taj Ganj.

★Time2Eat – Mama Chicken   DHABA $
(Map p358; ☏8899199999; Stall No 2, Sadar Bazaar; items ₹30-200; ☉2-10pm) This superstar *dhaba* is a must: duelling veg and nonveg glorified street stalls employing 24 cooks during the rush, each of whom is manning outdoor tandoors or other traditional cookware. They whip up outrageously good *kati* rolls (flatbread wrap; try chicken tikka or paneer tikka), whole chickens numerous ways, curries and chow meins for a standing-room-only crowd hell bent on sustenance. Bright lights, obnoxious signage and funky Indian tunes round out the festive atmosphere – a sure-fire Agra must.

Lakshmi Vilas   SOUTH INDIAN $
(Map p358; 50A Taj Rd; meals ₹50-110; ☉8.30am-10.30pm) This no-nonsense, plainly decorated, nonsmoking restaurant is *the* place in Agra to come for affordable South Indian fare. The thali (₹135), served noon to 3.30pm and 7pm to 10.30pm, is good though it comes across as relatively expensive.

Brijwasi   SWEETS $
(Map p358; www.brijwasisweethouse.com; Sadar Bazaar; sweets from ₹320 per kg, meals ₹80-150; ☉7am-11pm) Sugar-coma-inducing selection of traditional Indian sweets, nuts and biscuits on the ground floor, with a decent-value Indian restaurant upstairs. It's most famous for its *peda* milk sweets.

★Dasaprakash   SOUTH INDIAN $$
(Map p358; www.dasaprakashgroup.com; Meher Theater Complex, Gwailor Rd; meals ₹100-300; ☉noon-10.45pm) Fabulously tasty and religiously clean, Dasaprakash whips up consistently great South Indian vegetarian food, including spectacular thalis (₹190 to ₹270), dosas (large savoury crepes) and a few token Continental dishes. The ice-cream desserts (₹80 to ₹210) are another speciality.

Comfortable booth seating and wood-lattice screens make for intimate dining.

♟ Drinking & Nightlife

A night out in Agra tends to revolve around sitting at a rooftop restaurant with a couple of bottles of beer. None of the restaurants in Taj Ganj are licensed, but they can find alcohol for you if you ask nicely, and don't mind if you bring your own drinks, as long as you're discreet. You can catch live Indian classical music and *ghazals* (Urdu love songs) at restaurants in several of Agra's top-end hotels, most of which also have bars, albeit of the rather soulless variety.

Café Coffee Day   CAFE
(Map p360; www.cafecoffeeday.com; 21/101 Taj East Gate; coffee ₹65-140; ☉6.30am-8pm) This AC-cooled branch of the popular cafe chain is the closest place to the Taj selling proper coffee. There's another branch at **Sadar Bazaar** (Map p358; coffee ₹65-140; ☉9am-11pm).

Costa Coffee   CAFE
(Map p358; www.costacoffee.com; 8 Handicraft Nagar, Fatehabad Rd; coffee ₹90-240; ☉8am-11pm; ☎) Agra's only outlet of this UK coffee chain offers a cool and clean caffeine fix off Fatehabad Rd – and wi-fi.

Amarvilas Bar   BAR
(Oberoi Amar Vilas Hotel; Taj East Gate Rd; ☉noon-midnight) For a beer (₹375) or cocktail (₹575) in sheer opulence, look no further than the bar at Agra's best hotel. A terrace opens out to views of the Taj. Nonguests can wander onto the terrace, but staff can be funny about it.

⌂ Shopping

Agra is well known for its marble items inlaid with coloured stones, similar to the pietra dura work on the Taj. Sadar Bazaar, the old town and the area around the Taj are full of emporiums. Taj Mahal models are all made of alabaster rather than marble. Very cheap ones are made of soapstone, which scratches easily.

Other popular buys include rugs, leather and gemstones, though the latter are imported from Rajasthan and are cheaper in Jaipur.

Be sure to wander the narrow streets behind the Jama Masjid where the crazy maze of overcrowded lanes bursting with colourful

ℹ STAYING AHEAD OF THE SCAMS

As well as the usual commission rackets and ever-present gem-import scam, some specific methods to relieve Agra tourists of their hard-earned cash include the following.

Rickshaws

When taking an auto- or cycle-rickshaw to the Taj, make sure you are clear which gate you want to go to when negotiating the price. Otherwise, almost without fail, riders will take you to the roundabout at the south end of Shahjahan Gardens Rd – where expensive tongas (horse-drawn carriages) or camels wait to take tour groups to the west gate – and claim that's where they thought you meant. Only nonpolluting autos can go within a 500m radius of the Taj because of pollution rules, but they can get a lot closer than this.

Fake Marble

Lots of 'marble' souvenirs are actually alabaster, or even just soapstone. So you may be paying marble prices for lower quality stones. The mini Taj Mahals are always alabaster because they are too intricate to carve quickly in marble.

markets is known collectively as **Kinari Bazaar** (Map p358; ⏰11am-9pm, closed Tue).

Subhash Emporium   HANDICRAFTS
(Map p358; www.subhashemporium.com; 18/1 Gwalior Rd; ⏰9am-7pm) This expensive but honest marble-carving shop has been knocking up quality pieces for more than 35 years. Its prices are fairer than others in town, considering their experience.

Subhash Bazaar   MARKET
(Map p358; ⏰8am-8pm summer, 9am-8pm winter) Skirts the northern edge of Agra's Jama Masjid and is particularly good for silks and saris.

Khadi Gramodyog   CLOTHING
(Map p358; MG Rd; ⏰11am-7pm, closed Tue) Stocks simple, good-quality men's Indian clothing made from the homespun *khadi* fabric famously recommended by Mahatma Gandhi. No English sign: on Mahatma Gandhi (MG) Rd, look for the *khadi* logo of hands clasped around a mud hut.

Modern Book Depot   BOOKS
(Map p358; Sadar Bazaar; ⏰10.30am-9.30pm, closed Tue) Great selection of novels, plus Lonely Planet guides, at this friendly 60-year-old establishment.

ℹ Information

Agra is more wired than most places, even in restaurants. Taj Ganj is riddled with internet cafes, most charging from ₹40 per hour.

EMERGENCY

Tourist Police (☎0562-2421204; Agra Cantonment Train Station; ⏰6.30am-9.30pm) The guys in sky-blue uniforms are based on Fate-

habad Rd, but have an office here in the Tourist Facilitation Centre. Officers also hang around the East Gate ticket office and the UP Tourism office on Taj Rd, as well as at major sites.

MEDICAL SERVICES

Amit Jaggi Memorial Hospital (Map p358; ☎9690107860; www.ajmh.in; Vibhav Nagar, off Minto Rd) If you're sick, Dr Jaggi, who runs this private clinic, is the man to see. He accepts most health-insurance plans from abroad; otherwise a visit runs ₹1000 (day) or ₹2000 (night). He'll even do house calls.

SR Hospital (Map p358; ☎0562-4025200; Laurie's Complex, Namner Rd) Agra's best private hospital.

MONEY

ATMs are everywhere. There are four close to the Taj, one near each gate (though the East Gate Axis Bank ATM is often on the fritz) and another next to the East Gate ticket office complex. If you need to change money and are worried about being swindled in Taj Ganj, there is a government-sanctioned money-changer at the East Gate ticket office complex as well.

POST

India Post (Map p358; www.indiapost.gov.in; The Mall; ⏰10am-5pm Mon-Fri, to 4pm Sat) Agra's historic GPO (General Post Office) dates to 1913 and includes a handy 'facilitation office' for foreigners.

TOURIST INFORMATION

India Tourism (Map p358; ☎0562-2226378; www.incredibleindia.org; 191 The Mall; ⏰9am-5.30pm Mon-Fri, to 2pm Sat) Very helpful branch; has brochures on local and India-wide attractions and can arrange guides (half-/full day ₹1035/1311).

Tourist Facilitation Centre (Taj East Gate; ⊗9.30am-5pm, closed Fri) This helpful tourist office is part of the East Gate ticket office complex at Shilpgram.

UP Tourism (www.up-tourism.com; ⊗6.30am-9.30pm) The friendly train-station branch inside the Tourist Facilitation Centre offers helpful advice most hours of important train arrivals. This branch, which doubles as the Tourism Police, and the one on Taj Rd (Map p358; ☑0562-2226431; 64 Taj Rd; ⊗10am-5pm Mon-Sat) can arrange guides (half-/full day ₹1035/1310).

TRAVEL AGENCIES

Bag Packer Travel (Map p358; ☑9997113228; www.bagpackertravels.com; 4/62 Kutchery Rd; ⊗9am-9pm) An honest agency for all your travel and transport needs, run by the friendly Anil at Tourists Rest House (p363). English and French spoken.

ⓘ Getting There & Away

AIR

Commercial flights to Agra's Kheria Airport began again in late 2012 after a long absence. **Air India** (www.airindia.com) now flies to Varanasi (2.05pm, from ₹4000) via Khajuraho (from ₹3000) Monday, Wednesday and Saturday, and to Mumbai (12.30pm, from ₹1500) via Gwailor (from ₹3200) on Monday and Wednesday. At time of research there was no return flight via Khajuraho.

To access the airport, part of Indian Air Force territory, your name must be on the list of those with booked flights that day. Tickets must be purchased online or by phone.

BUS

The opening of the tolled 165km Yamuna Expressway in 2012 cut drive time from Agra to Noida, a southeastern suburb of Delhi, by 30%. Some luxury coaches now use this route and reach central Delhi faster.

Some services from **Idgah Bus Stand** (☑0562-2420324; off National Hwy 2, near Sikandra):

Bharatpur ₹62, 1½ hours, every 30 minutes, 6am to 6.30pm

Delhi non-AC (₹171, 4½ hours, every 30 minutes, 5am to 11.30pm

Fatehpur Sikri ₹40, one hour, every 30 minutes, 6am to 6.30pm

Gwalior ₹115, three hours, hourly, 5.30am to 6.30pm

Jaipur ₹228, six hours, hourly, 6am to 6.30pm

Jhansi ₹200, six hours, noon, 2.15pm, 8.30pm

A block east of Idgah near Hotel Sakura, the **Rajashstan State Road Transport Corp** (RTDC; ☑0562-2420228; www.rsrtc.rajasthan.gov.in) runs more comfortable coaches to Jaipur throughout the day. Services include non-AC (₹256, 5½ hours, 7.30am, 10am, 1pm and 11.59pm), AC (₹440, five hours, 6.30am and 8.30am) and luxury Volvo (₹530, 4½ hours, 11.30am and 2.30pm).

From **ISBT Bus Stand** (☑0562-2603536), luxury Volvo coaches leave for Delhi (₹557, four hours, 7am, 9.30am, 1pm, 2.30pm, 6.30pm and 7.30pm) and Lucknow (₹906, 7½ hours, 10am and 10pm); as well as standard non-AC services to Allahabad (₹450, nine hours, 4pm) which continue on to Varanasi (₹550, 13 hours, 4pm) and Gorakhpur (₹625, 16 hours, 11.30am, 1.30pm, 2.30pm, 5pm and 10pm). Dehra Dun buses also depart from here (Volvo/AC/non-AC ₹1130/750/375, 2.30pm, 3.30pm, 4.30pm, 5.30pm, 6pm, 8pm, 8.30pm and 9.30pm). If you're shut out of the train to Rishikesh, you'll need to catch the bus to Haridwar (AC/non-AC ₹950/350, 10 hours, 6.30pm, 7.30pm, 8.30pm and 10pm) and switch there.

Bijli Ghar Bus Stand (Map p358; ☑0562-2464557) serves Mathura (₹64, 90 minutes, every 30 minutes, 5am to 11.30pm), Tundla (₹35, one hour, every 30 minutes, 7am to 8pm), from where you can catch the 12382 Poorva Express at 8.15pm to Varanasi if the trains from Agra are sold out.

DELHI–AGRA TRAINS FOR DAY TRIPPERS

ROUTE	TRAIN NO & NAME	FARE (₹)	DURATION (HR)	DEPARTURES
New Delhi–Agra	12002 Shatabdi Exp	505/1000 (A)	2	6am
Agra–New Delhi	12001 Shatabdi Exp	545/1040 (A)	2	9.15pm
Hazrat Nizamuddin–Agra	12280 Taj Exp	100/385 (B)	3	7.05am
Agra–Hazrat Nizamuddin	12279 Taj Exp	100/365 (B)	3	6.55pm

Fares: (A) AC chair/1AC, (B) 2nd-class/AC chair

MORE HANDY TRAINS FROM AGRA

DESTINATION	TRAIN NO & NAME	FARE (₹)	DURATION (HR)	DEPARTURES
Gorakhpur*	19037/19038 Avadh Exp	335/905/1295 (A)	15½	9.50pm
Jaipur*	12036 Shatabdi Exp	650/1215 (C)	3½	5.40pm (except Thu)
Khajuraho	12448 UP SMPRK KRNTI	280/715/1000 (A)	8	11.20pm (except Wed)
Kolkata (Howrah)	13008 UA Toofan Exp	555/1490 (B)	31	12.30pm
Lucknow	12180/12179 LJN Intercity	145/510 (D)	6	5.50am
Mumbai (CST)	12138/12137 Punjab Mail	580/1515/2195 (A)	23	8.55am
Varanasi*	14854 Marudhar Exp	350/940/1350 (A)	14	8.30pm (Mon, Thu, Sat)

Fares: (A) sleeper/3AC/2AC, (B) sleeper/3AC only; (C) AC chair/1AC only; (D) 2nd-class/AC chair; *leaves from Agra Fort station

Shared autos (₹10) run between Idgah and Bijli Ghar bus stands. To get to the ISBT, take the aircon public bus from Agra Cantt train station to Dayalbagh (₹22) but get off at Baghwan Talkies (₹16), from where shared autos (₹8) can take you to the ISBT; or catch an autorickshaw from Taj Ganz (₹150).

TRAIN

Most trains leave from Agra Cantonment (Cantt) train station, although some go from Agra Fort station. A few trains, such as Kota PNBE Express, run as slightly different numbers on different days than those listed, but timings remain the same. If you are heading to Jaipur on Thursday, the best option is the 12403/12404 ALD JP Express, departing Agra at 7.15am.

Express trains are well set up for day trippers to/from Delhi but trains run to Delhi all day. If you can't reserve a seat, just buy a 'general ticket' for the next train (about ₹90), find a seat in sleeper class then upgrade when the ticket collector comes along. Most of the time, he won't even make you pay any more. A new semi-express train between Delhi and Agra, the Gatimaan Express, should be up and running by the time you read this. It travels 160km per hour (India's fastest) and a full 30km per hour faster than the Shatabdi Express.

For Orchha, catch one of the many daily trains to Jhansi (sleeper from ₹110, three hours), then take a shared auto to the bus stand (₹10) from where shared autos run all day to Orchha (₹20). An autorickshaw costs ₹200 for same route.

ℹ Getting Around

AUTORICKSHAW

Agra's green-and-yellow autorickshaws run on CNG (compressed natural gas) and are less environmentally destructive. Just outside Agra Cantt station is the prepaid autorickshaw booth, which gives you a good guide for haggling elsewhere. Usually, trips under three kilometres should not cost more than ₹50. Note, autos aren't allowed to go to Fatehpur Sikri.

Sample prices from Agra Cantt station: Fatehabad Rd ₹150; ISBT bus stand ₹200; Sadar Bazaar ₹70; Sikandra ₹200; Taj Mahal ₹100 (Taj West Gate) and ₹130 (Taj South Gate), Shilpgram (Taj East Gate) ₹150; half-day (four-hour) tour ₹400; full-day (eight-hour) tour ₹600. If you just want to shoot to the Taj and back with waiting time, they will charge ₹250. Prices listed here do not include the ₹5 booking fee, which is extra.

CYCLE-RICKSHAW

Prices from the Taj Mahal's South Gate include: Agra Cantt train station ₹80; Agra Fort ₹40; Bijli Ghar bus stand ₹50; Fatehabad Rd ₹30; Kinari Bazaar ₹100; Sadar Bazaar ₹50; half-day tour ₹400. Tack on another ₹10 to ₹20 if two people are riding.

TAXI

Outside Agra Cantt the prepaid taxi booth gives a good idea of what taxis should cost. Non-AC prices include: Delhi ₹3500; Fatehabad Rd ₹200; Sadar Bazaar ₹100; Taj Mahal ₹200; half-day (four-hour) tour ₹750; full-day (eight-hour) tour ₹1000. Prices do not include the ₹10 booking fee and tolls or parking charges (if applicable).

Around Agra

Fatehpur Sikri

♫ 05613 / POP 29,000

This magnificent fortified ancient city, 40km west of Agra, was the short-lived capital of the Mughal empire between 1571 and 1585, during the reign of Emperor Akbar. Akbar visited the village of Sikri to consult the Sufi saint Shaikh Salim Chishti, who predicted the birth of an heir to the Mughal throne. When the prophecy came true, Akbar built his new capital here, including a stunning mosque – still in use today – and three palaces for each of his favourite wives, one a Hindu, one a Muslim and one a Christian (though Hindu villagers in Sikri dispute these claims). The city was an Indo-Islamic masterpiece, but erected in an area that supposedly suffered from water shortages and so was abandoned shortly after Akbar's death.

It's easy to visit this World Heritage Site as a day trip from Agra, but there are some decent places to stay, and the colourful bazaar in the village of Fatehpur, just below the ruins, as well as the small village of Sikri, a few kilometres north, are worth exploring. The red-sandstone palace walls are at their most atmospheric and photogenic at sunset.

The bus stand is at the eastern end of the bazaar. Walking another 1km northeast will bring you to Agra Gate and the junction with the main Agra–Jaipur road, from where you can catch buses.

◉ Sights

The palace buildings lie beside the Jama Masjid. Both sit on top of a ridge that runs between the small villages of Fatehpur and Sikri. For more detail, see the illustrated highlight (p370).

Jama Masjid   MOSQUE

This beautiful, immense mosque was completed in 1571 and contains elements of Persian and Indian design. The main entrance, at the top of a flight of stone steps, is through the spectacular 54m-high Buland Darwaza (Victory Gate), built to commemorate Akbar's military victory in Gujarat.

Inside the courtyard of the mosque is the stunning white-marble tomb of Sufi saint Shaikh Salim Chishti, which was completed in 1581 and is entered through an original door made of ebony. Inside it are brightly coloured flower murals, while the sandalwood canopy is decorated with mother-of-pearl shell. Just as Akbar came to the saint four centuries ago hoping for a son, childless women visit his tomb today and tie a thread to the *jali* (carved lattice screens), which are among the finest in India. To the right of the tomb lie the gravestones of family members of Shaikh Salim Chishti and nearby is the entrance to an underground tunnel (barred by a locked gate) that reputedly goes all the way to Agra Fort. Behind the entrance to the tunnel, on the far wall, are three holes, part of the ancient ventilation system. You can still feel the rush of cool air forcing its way through them. Just east of Shaikh Salim Chishti's tomb is the red-sandstone tomb of Islam Khan, the final resting place of Shaikh Salim Chishti's grandson and one-time governor of Bengal.

On the east wall of the courtyard is a smaller entrance to the mosque – the Shahi Darwaza (King's Gate), which leads to the palace complex.

Palaces & Pavilions   PALACES

(Indian/foreigner ₹20/260, video ₹25; ◷ dawn-dusk) The main sight at Fatehpur Sikri is the stunning imperial complex of pavilions and palaces spread among a large abandoned 'city' peppered with Mughal masterpieces: courtyards, intricate carvings, servants quarters, vast gateways and ornamental pools.

A large courtyard dominates the northeast entrance at Diwan-i-Am (Hall of Public Audiences). Now a pristinely manicured garden, this is where Akbar presided over the courts from the middle seat of the five equal seatings along the western wall, flanked by his advisors. It was built to utilise an echo sound system, so Akbar could hear anything at any time from anywhere in the open space. Justice was dealt with swiftly if legends are to be believed, with public executions said to have been carried out here by elephants trampling to death convicted criminals.

The Diwan-i-Khas (Hall of Private Audiences), found at the northern end of the Pachisi Courtyard, looks nothing special from the outside, but the interior is dominated by a magnificently carved stone central column. This pillar flares to create a flat-topped plinth linked to the four corners of the room by narrow stone bridges. From this plinth Akbar is believed to have debated with scholars and ministers who stood at the ends of the four bridges.

(Continued on page 372)

Fatehpur Sikri

A WALKING TOUR OF FATEHPUR SIKRI

You can enter this fortified ancient city from two entrances, but the northeast entrance at Diwan-i-Am (Hall of Public Audiences) offers the most logical approach to this remarkable Unesco World Heritage site. This large courtyard (now a garden) is where Emperor Akbar presided over the trials of accused criminals. Once through the ticket gate, you are in the northern end of the **Pachisi Courtyard 1**. The first building you see is **Diwan-i-Khas 2** (Hall of Private Audiences), the interior of which is dominated by a magnificently carved central stone column. Pitch south and enter **Rumi Sultana 3**, a small but elegant palace built for Akbar's Turkish Muslim wife. It's hard to miss the **Ornamental Pool 4** nearby – its southwest corner provides Fatehpur Sikri's most photogenic angle, perfectly framing its most striking building, the five-storey Panch Mahal, one of the gateways to the Imperial Harem Complex, where the **Lower Haramsara 5** once housed more than 200 female servants. Wander around the Palace of Jodh Bai and take notice of the towering ode to an elephant, the 21m-high **Hiran Minar 6**, in the distance to the northwest. Leave the palaces and pavilions area via Shahi Darwaza (King's Gate), which spills into India's second-largest mosque courtyard at **Jama Masjid 7**. Inside this immense and gorgeous mosque is the sacred **Tomb of Shaikh Salim Chishti 8**. Exit through the spectacular **Buland Darwaza 9** (Victory Gate), one of the world's most magnificent gateways.

Buland Darwaza

Most tours end with an exit through Jama Masjid's Victory Gate. Walk out and take a look behind you: Behold! The magnificent 15-storey sandstone gate, 54m high, is a menacing monolith to Akbar's reign.

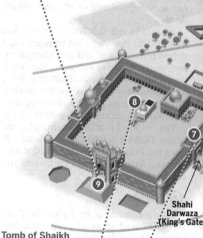

Shahi Darwaza (King's Gate)

Tomb of Shaikh Salim Chishti

Each knot in the strings tied to the 56 carved white marble designs of the interior walls of Shaikh Salim Chishti's tomb represents one wish of a maximum three.

Jama Masjid

The elaborate marble inlay work at the Badshahi Gate and throughout the Jama Masjid complex is said to have inspired similar work 82 years later at the Taj Mahal in Agra.

Hiran Minar
This bizarre, seldom-visited tower off the north-west corner of Fatehpur Sikri is decorated with hundreds of stone representations of elephant tusks. It is said to be the place where Minar, Akbar's favourite execution elephant, died.

Pachisi Courtyard
Under your feet just past Rumi Sultana is the Pachisi Courtyard where Akbar is said to have played the game *pachisi* (an ancient version of ludo) using slave girls in colourful dress as pieces.

Diwan-i-Khas
Emperor Akbar modified the central stone column inside Diwan-i-Khas to call attention to a new religion he called Din-i-Ilahi (God is One). The intricately carved column features a fusion of Hindu, Muslim, Christian and Buddhist imagery.

Panch Mahal

Diwan-i-Am (Hall of Public Audiences)

Lower Haramsara
Akbar reportedly kept more than 5000 concubines, but the 200 or so female servants housed in the Lower Haramsara were strictly business. Knots were tied to these sandstone rings to support partitions between their individual quarters.

Ornamental Pool
Tansen, said to be the most gifted Indian vocalist of all time and one of Akbar's treasured nine *Navaratnas* (Gems), would be showered with coins during performances from the central platform of the Ornamental Pool.

Rumi Sultana
Don't miss the headless creatures carved into Rumi Sultana's palace interiors: a lion, deer, an eagle and a few peacocks were beheaded by jewel thieves who swiped the precious jewels that originally formed their heads.

(Continued from page 369)

Next to Diwan-i-Khas is the **Treasury**, which houses secret stone safes in some corners (one has been left with its stone lid open for visitors to see). Sea monsters carved on the ceiling struts were there to protect the fabulous wealth once stored here. The so-called **Astrologer's Kiosk** in front has roof supports carved in a serpentine Jain style.

Just south of the Astrologer's Kiosk is **Pachisi Courtyard**, named after the ancient game known in India today as ludo. The large, plus-shaped game board is visible surrounding the block in the middle of the courtyard. In the southeast corner is the most intricately carved structure in the whole complex, the tiny but elegant **Rumi Sultana**, which was said to be the palace built for Akbar's Turkish Muslim wife. Other theories say it was used by Akbar himself as a palace powder room or R&R room during court sessions. On one corner of the **Ladies Garden** just west of Pachisi is the impressive **Panch Mahal**, a pavilion whose five storeys decrease in size until the top consists of only a tiny kiosk. The lower floor has 84 different columns; in total there are 176 columns.

Continuing anticlockwise will bring you to the **Ornamental Pool**. Here, singers and musicians would perform on the platform above the water while Akbar watched from the pavilion in his private quarters, known as **Daulat Khana** (Abode of Fortune). Behind the pavilion is the **Khwabgah** (Dream House), a sleeping area with a huge stone bunk bed. Nowadays the only ones sleeping here are bats, hanging from the ceiling. The small room in the far corner is full of them.

Heading west from the Ornamental Pool beholds the **Palace of Jodh Bai**, and the one-time home of Akbar's Hindu wife, said to be his favourite. Set around an enormous courtyard, it blends traditional Indian columns, Islamic cupolas and turquoise-blue Persian roof tiles. Just outside, to the left of Jodh Bai's former kitchen, is the **Palace of the Christian Wife**. This was used by Akbar's Goan wife Mariam, who gave birth to Jehangir here in 1569. Some believe Akbar never had a Christian wife and that Mariam was short for Mariam-Ut-Zamani, a title he gave to Jodh Bai meaning 'Beautiful like a Rose', or 'Most Beautiful Woman on Earth'. Like many of the buildings in the palace complex, it contains elements of different religions, as befitted Akbar's tolerant religious beliefs. The domed ceiling is Islamic in style, while remnants of a wall painting of the Hindu god Shiva can also be found.

Walking past the Palace of the Christian Wife once more will take you west to **Birbal Bhavan**, ornately carved inside and out, and thought to have been the living quarters of one of Akbar's most senior ministers. The **Lower Haramsara**, just to the south, housed Akbar's large inventory of live-in female servants.

Plenty of ruins are scattered behind the whole complex, including the **Caravanserai**, a vast courtyard surrounded by rooms where visiting merchants stayed. Badly defaced carvings of elephants still guard **Hathi Pol** (Elephant Gate), while the remains of the small **Stonecutters' Mosque** and a **hammam** (bath) are also a short stroll away. Other unnamed ruins can be explored north of what is known as the **Mint** but is thought to have in fact been stables, including some in the interesting village of Sikri to the north.

Archaeological Museum MUSEUM
(⊙9am-5pm, closed Fri) **FREE** Inaugurated in 2014 inside Akbar's former Treasury house, this museum about 100m from Diwan-i-Am showcases pre-Mughal artefacts excavated over many years at Fatehpur Sikri. Well-presented highlights include a few remarkably preserved sandstone Jain *tirthankars* (the 24 holy Jain supreme beings) dating between 982 and 1034.

☞ Tours

Official Archaeological Society of India guides can be hired from the ticket office for ₹250 (English), but they aren't always the most knowledgeable (some are guides thanks to birthright rather than qualifications). Official UP Tourism guides have gone through more rigorous training and can be hired for ₹750. Our favourite is **Pankaj Bhatnagar** (✆8126995552; www.tajinvitation.com).

🛏 Sleeping & Eating

Fatehpur Sikri's culinary speciality is *khataie,* the biscuits you can see piled high in the bazaar.

Hotel Goverdhan HOTEL **$**
(✆05613-282643; www.hotelfatehpursikriviews.com; Agra Rd; s/d/tr ₹500/800/900, with AC ₹1000/1250/1400; ❀@🗑) There are a variety

of rooms at this old-time favourite (check them out before you book), all of which surround a very well-kept garden. There's a communal balcony and terrace seating, free wi-fi, new beds in every room, air-coolers in the non-AC rooms and CCTV. The restaurant does decent work as well (meals ₹50 to ₹180).

Hotel Ajay Palace GUESTHOUSE $
(☎9548801213; Agra Rd; s/d ₹200/300, d with air-cooler ₹400) This friendly family guesthouse isn't pretty but offers a few very simple and cheap double rooms with marble floors and sit-down flush toilets. It's also a very popular lunch stop (mains ₹50 to ₹140). Sit on the rooftop at the large, elongated marble table and enjoy a view of the village streets with the Jama Masjid towering above.

Note it is not 'Ajay Restaurant By Near Palace' at the bus stand – it's 50m further along the road.

❶ Information

DANGERS & ANNOYANCES
Take no notice of anyone who gets on the Fatehpur Sikri–Agra bus before the final stop at Idgah Bus Stand, telling you that you have arrived at the city centre or the Taj Mahal. You haven't. You're still a long autorickshaw ride away, and the man trying to tease you off the bus is, surprise surprise, an autorickshaw driver.

❶ Getting There & Around

Tours and taxis all arrive at the Gulistan Tourist Complex parking lot, from which shuttle buses (₹10) depart for Fatehpur Sikri's Diwan-i-Am entrance (right side of the street) and Jodh Bai entrance (left side of the street). Note that if you have hired an unauthorised guide, you will not be allowed to enter at Diwan-i-Am.

Buses run to Agra's Idgah Bus Stand every half-hour (₹40) from 5.30am to 6.30pm. If you miss those, walk out through Agra Gate and another 350m to Bypass Crossing Stop on the main road and wave down a Jaipur–Agra bus. They run every 30 minutes or so, day and night.

For Bharatpur (₹25, 40 minutes) or Jaipur (₹190, 4½ hours), wave down a westbound bus from Bypass Crossing Stop.

Regular trains for Agra Fort Station leave Fatehpur Sikri at 4.49am (59811 Haldighati Pass) and 8.16pm (19037 Avadh Express), but there are simpler passenger trains at 10.17am and 3.55pm as well as four other trains that fly through at various times. Just buy a 'general' ticket at the station and pile in (₹20, one to two hours).

Uttar Pradesh

Best Places to Eat

➡ Oudhyana (p382)

➡ El Chico (p389)

➡ Sakhawat (p381)

➡ Moti Mahal Restaurant (p381)

➡ Eat On (p388)

Best Places to Stay

➡ Kanchan Villa (p388)

➡ Hotel Ganges View (p399)

➡ Ganpati Guesthouse (p398)

➡ Homestay (p398)

➡ Stops Hostel (p399)

Why Go?

The enormous state of Uttar Pradesh is one of India's mystical cradles and, as a result, is justifiably one of India's roads most taken. Its unmistakable spirituality and religious fervour leaves long-lasting impressions: being wow-ed along atmospheric riverside ghats such as Manikarnika and Dashashwamedh in India's holiest city, Varanasi; the contemplative aura that emanates from ancient Buddhist stupas in Kushinagar and Sarnath; the serenity of waking up before dawn to watch locals perform *puja* (offerings or prayers) in sacred Chitrakut; or the intense power of piety in Allahabad, where throngs of feverish devotees bow to the chaotic confluence of two of India's holiest rivers, the Ganges and Yamuna.

Along the way, a groundswell of Mughal and Nawab architectural and gastronomic highpoints – notably in Lucknow, Allahabad and of course Agra – ensure all-sensory satisfaction in India's imperial heartland.

When to Go
Varanasi

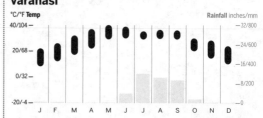

Sep & Oct Monsoon rains are mostly over and temperatures have cooled...just enough.

Nov–Feb Comfortable winter days and nippy nights means it's cool but overcrowded.

Mar & Apr With evening chills subsided and raging midsummer heat still at bay, some say it's perfect.

History

Over 2000 years ago this region was part of Ashoka's great Buddhist empire, remnants of which can be found in the ruins at the pilgrimage centre of Sarnath near Varanasi. Muslim raids from the northwest began in the 11th century, and by the 16th century the region was part of the Mughal empire, with its capital in Agra, then Delhi and, for a brief time, Fatehpur Sikri.

Following the decline of the Mughal empire, Persians stepped in briefly before the Nawabs of Avadh rose to prominence in the central part of the region, notably around the current capital of Lucknow. The Nawabs were responsible for turning Lucknow into a flourishing centre for the arts, culture and culinary delights, which continues to this day. But their empire came to a dramatic end when the British East India Company deposed the last nawab, triggering the First War of Independence (Indian Uprising) of 1857. During the 147-day Siege of Lucknow, British Chief Commissioner Sir Henry Lawrence was killed defending the British Residency, which remains in remarkable preservation in Lucknow.

Agra was later merged with Avadh and the state became known as United Province. It was renamed Uttar Pradesh after Independence and has since been the most dominant state in Indian politics, producing half of the country's prime ministers, most of them from Allahabad. The local population doesn't seem to have benefited much from this, though, as poor governance, a high birth rate, a low literacy rate and an erratic electricity supply have held back economic progress in UP in the past 60 years.

In 2000, the mountainous northwestern part of the state was carved off to create the new state of Uttaranchal.

LUCKNOW

📞 0522 / POP 2.9 MILLION

Liberally sprinkled with British Raj-era buildings – including the famous Residency – and boasting two superb mausoleums, the capital of Uttar Pradesh plays a somewhat unwarranted third fiddle to Agra and Varanasi, but caters well to history buffs, without attracting the hordes of tourists that sometimes make sightseeing tiresome. By contrast, Lucknow's modern side boasts a unique Iron Curtain-esque feel, with grandiose monuments and overstated parks and

SLEEPING PRICE RANGES

Accommodation price ranges for this chapter are:

$ below ₹1500

$$ ₹1500 to ₹4000

$$$ above ₹4000

gardens, many boasting marble sidewalks and pink sandstone a plenty (we imagine they were going for a Washington, DC aesthetic but ended up more Pyongyang). It's nothing if not interesting.

The city rose to prominence as the home of the Nawabs of Avadh (Oudh) who were great patrons of the culinary and other arts, particularly dance and music. Lucknow's reputation as a city of culture, gracious living and rich cuisine has continued to this day (it conveniently rhymes in Hindi: 'Nawab, Aadaab [Respect], Kebab and Shabab [Beauty]').

⊙ Sights

★ **Residency** HISTORIC SITE

(Indian/foreigner ₹5/100, video ₹25; ☺ dawn-dusk) The large collection of gardens and ruins that makes up the Residency offers a fascinating historical glimpse of the beginning of the end for the British Raj. Built in 1800, the Residency became the stage for the most dramatic events of the 1857 First War of Independence (Indian Uprising), the Siege of Lucknow, a 147-day siege that claimed the lives of thousands.

The compound has been left as it was at the time of the final relief and the walls are pockmarked from bullets and cannon balls.

The focus is the well-designed museum (open 8am to 4.30pm) in the main Residency building, which includes a scale model of the original buildings. Downstairs are the huge basement rooms where many of the British women and children lived throughout the siege.

The cemetery around the ruined St Mary's church is where 2000 of the defenders were buried, including their leader, Sir Henry Lawrence, 'who tried to do his duty' according to the famous inscription on his weathered gravestone.

★ **Bara Imambara** ISLAMIC TOMB

(Hussainabad Trust Rd; Indian/foreigner ₹50/500; ☺ 6am-6.30pm) This colossal *imambara*

Uttar Pradesh Highlights

1 Ogling a dramatic hubbub of holiness on a pre-dawn boat ride along the River Ganges followed by a fascinating backstreets walking tour in **Varanasi** (p396)

2 Walking off an Avadh culinary binge by exploring dramatic ornamented Mughal architecture on a Heritage Walking Tour in **Lucknow** (p379)

3 Getting stupa-fied outside the urban chaos in the tranquil pilgrimage centres of **Kushinagar** (p406) and **Sarnath** (p403)

4 Imagining 100 million Kumbh Mela devotees on your tail as you're rowed out to the confluence of two holy rivers in **Allahabad** (p385)

5 Experiencing a more relaxed spirituality without the hassle at the chilled-out riverside ghats of **Chitrakut**

6 Making a pilgrimage to spiritual **Vrindavan** (p410), the international home of the Hare Krishnas

7 Getting off the beaten path on a visit to Lord Rama's highly-contentious birthplace in **Ayodhya** (p384)

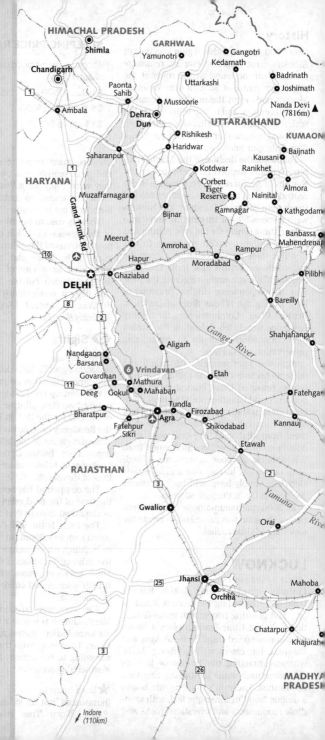

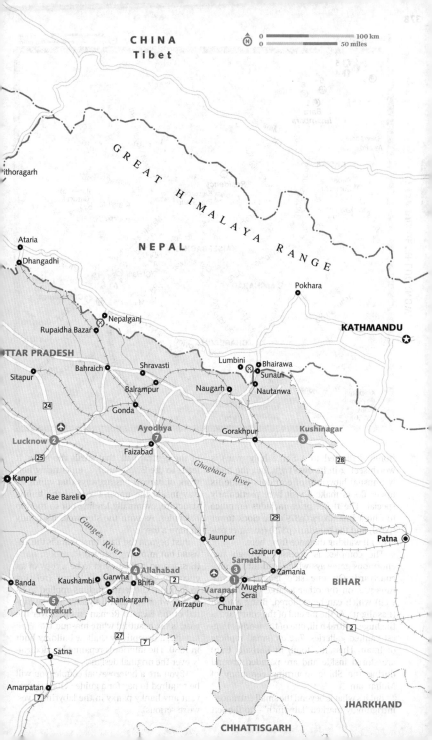

CHINA
Tibet

0 _____ 100 km
0 _____ 50 miles

GREAT HIMALAYA RANGE

ithoragarh

NEPAL

Ataria
Dhangadhi

Pokhara

KATHMANDU

Rupaidha Bazar
Nepalganj

UTTAR PRADESH

Sitapur

Bahraich
Shravasti
Lumbini
Bhairawa
Sunauli

Balrampur
Naugarh
Nautanwa

Gonda
Ayodhya
Gorakhpur
Kushinagar

24

Lucknow 2
Faizabad
7
3

28

25

Kanpur

Rae Bareli

Ghaghara River

29

Ganges River

Jaunpur
Gazipur

Patna

Sarnath
Zamania

Banda
Kaushambi
Garwha
4 Allahabad
3
BIHAR

Bhita
1

Shankargarh
2
Varanasi
Mughal
Serai

5
Mirzapur
Chunar

Chitrakut

27
7

Satna

Amarpatan
2

7

JHARKHAND

CHHATTISGARH

Lucknow

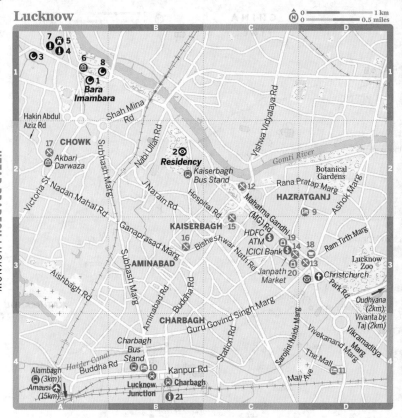

(tomb dedicated to a Shiite holy man) is worth seeing in its own right, but the highly unusual labyrinth of corridors inside its upper floors make a visit here particularly special. The ticket price includes entrance to Chota Imambara (p379), the clock tower (p379) and the baradari (p379) (summer palace), all walking distance from here.

The complex is accessed through two enormous gateways which lead into a huge courtyard. On one side is an attractive mosque, on the other a large baori (stepwell) which can be explored. Bring a torch (flashlight). At the far end of the courtyard is the huge central hall, one of the world's largest vaulted galleries. *Tazias* (small replicas of Imam Hussain's tomb in Karbala, Iraq) are stored inside and are paraded around during the Shiite mourning ceremony of Muharram.

But it's what is beyond the small entrance – intriguingly marked 'labyrinth' – to the left of the central hall, that steals the show. It leads to the Bhulbhulaiya, an enticing network of narrow passageways that winds its way inside the upper floors of the tomb's structure, eventually leading out to rooftop balconies. As with the step-well, it's handy to have a torch.

Just beyond the Bara Imambara is the unusual but imposing gateway Rumi Darwaza (Hussainabad Trust Rd), said to be a copy of an entrance gate in Istanbul. 'Rumi' (relating to Rome) is the term Muslims applied to Istanbul when it was still Byzantium, the capital of the Eastern Roman empire. Over the road is the beautiful white mosque Tila Wali Masjid, a deceptively shallow building built in 1680. The interior is repainted periodically over the original designs.

If you are a heterosexual couple, you will be required to pay for a guide (₹100) to prevent any hanky panky in the labyrinth (yes, we're serious).

Lucknow

Top Sights

1	Bara Imambara	A1
2	Residency	B2

Sights

3	Chota Imambara	A1
4	Clock Tower	A1
5	Hussainabad Picture Gallery	A1
6	Rumi Darwaza	A1
7	Satkhanda	A1
8	Tila Wali Masjid	A1

Activities, Courses & Tours

	UP Tourism Heritage Walking Tour	(see 9)

Sleeping

9	Hotel Gomti	D2
10	Hotel Mayur	B4
11	Lucknow Homestay	D4

Eating

12	Falaknuma	C2
13	Moti Mahal Restaurant	D3
14	Royal Cafe	C3
15	Sakhawat	C3
16	Tunday Kababi	B3
17	Tunday Kebabi	A2

Drinking & Nightlife

18	Cafe Coffee Day	D3
	EOS	(see 13)
	Strokes Sports Bar	(see 14)
	Tashna Bar	(see 9)

Shopping

19	Ram Advani Bookshop	C3
20	Sugandhco	C3

Information

21	Foreign Tourist Help	B4
	UP Tourism	(see 9)
	UP Tourism Kiosk	(see 18)

Chota Imambara ISLAMIC TOMB
(Hussainabad Imambara; Hussainabad Trust Rd; Indian/foreigner ₹20/200, admission free with Bara Imambara ticket; ⏰6.30am-8pm) This elaborate tomb was constructed by Mohammed Ali Shah (who is buried here, alongside his mother) in 1832. Adorned with calligraphy, it has a serene and intimate atmosphere. Mohammed's silver throne and red crown can be seen here, as well as countless chandeliers and some brightly decorated *tazias*.

In the garden is a water tank and two replicas of the Taj Mahal that are the tombs of Mohammed Ali Shah's daughter and her husband. A traditional **hammam** is off to one side.

Outside the complex, the decaying watchtower on the other side of the road is known as **Satkhanda** (Seven Storey Tower; Hussainabad Trust Rd). It has only four storeys because construction was abandoned in 1840 when Mohammed Ali Shah died.

The 67m red-brick **clock tower** (admission free with Bara Imambara ticket; ⏰dawn-dusk), the tallest in India, was built in the 1880s. Nearby is the **Hussainabad Picture Gallery** (Baradari; summer palace Indian/foreigner ₹20/200, admission free with Bara Imambara ticket; ⏰7am-6.30pm), a striking red-brick *baradari* (pavilion) built in 1842 that was once a royal summer house. It overlooks an artificial lake and houses portraits of the nawabs.

Tours

★ UP Tourism Heritage Walking Tour WALKING
(☎9415013047; Hotel Gomti, 6 Sapru Marg; 3hr tour ₹150; ⏰tours 7am Aug-Sep, 8am Oct-Mar) This fabulous two-hour Heritage Walking Tour run by UP Tourism could well turn out to be the best ₹150 you ever spend. Meet your English-speaking guide outside Tila Wali Masjid then follow them first around the mosque, then the Bara Imambara, before delving in to the architectural delights of the crazy maze of alleyways in the incredibly fascinating Chowk district.

You'll sample interesting nibbles such as refreshing *thandai* (made from milk, cardamom, almonds, fennel, saffron etc and – in this case – with or without marijuana!) and getting an insider glimpse into various traditions, from indigo block printing to traditional *unani* medicine or *vark* making (edible silver foil). This is an eye-popping way to get your bearings among Lucknow's oldest neighbourhoods. Note: tours are best booked directly or most easily via Naheed at Lucknow Homestay.

Sleeping

Lucknow Homestay HOMESTAY $
(☎9838003590; www.lucknowhomestay.wordpress.com; 110D Mall Ave; s/d ₹600/700, without bathroom ₹500/600, with AC ₹1000/1100, incl breakfast; ❄📶) Lucknow's most welcoming

TOP STATE FESTIVALS

Magh Mela (p387; ⊙ Jan/Feb, Allahabad) A huge annual religious fair that transforms into the world's largest human gathering, the Purna Kumbh Mela, every 12th year (next in 2025).

Holi (Feb/Mar; Mathura and Vrindavan) This national festival is celebrated with particular fervour around Mathura and Vrindavan, spiritual home of Krishna.

Purnima (Sarnath; ⊙ Apr/May) Also known as Vesak, Buddha Jayanti or, informally, Buddha's birthday, Purnima actually celebrates the birth, enlightenment and death of Buddha. Sarnath, just outside Varanasi, takes on a particularly festive air on this day, when Buddhists from many countries take part in a procession and a fair is held.

Janmastami (p410; ⊙ Aug/Sep, Mathura) You can barely move here during Krishna's birthday, when temples are swathed in decorations and musical dramas about Krishna are performed.

Ram Lila (p391; ⊙ Sep/Oct, Varanasi) Every year since the early 1800s the Ram Lila, a lengthy version of the Rama-yana, has been performed beside Ramnagar Fort in Varanasi. The epic saga of Rama's marriage to Sita and his battle against the demon king Ravana is performed mainly by Brahmin youths aided by masks, music, dancing and giant papier-mâché figures.

budget option is in the leafy neighbourhood home of Naheed and her family, who keep their distance but offer six rustic rooms – four with private bathrooms. The house number isn't marked, but a sign reading 'Munni's Dream' is above the front door.

Rickshaw drivers know Mall Ave, which is actually a neighbourhood (not merely an avenue), but you'll need to orient yourself upon arrival if you want to find your way back home, as the address is amid the maze if you enter the neighbourhood from anywhere other than the Mahatma Gandhi (MG) Rd side. Better yet, get to know Naheed's favourite rickshaw driver, the honest, reliable and English-speaking Guatam, and keep him close. Best part? He doesn't touch his horn. Book ahead – it's popular for long-stays (₹10,000 per month all in).

Hotel Mayur HOTEL $
(☎ 0522-4048129; 215/478 Charbagh; s/d ₹700/800, without bathroom ₹400/500, with AC ₹900/980; ﹢) Good-value rooms in this well-run establishment with limited English are basic but come with cable TV and some have huge bathrooms. Definitely one of the better cheapies near the train station. It's hard to spot – look up for a small sign on Subhash Marg, just around the corner from Kanpor Rd/Charbagh bus stand.

Hotel Gomti HOTEL $$
(☎ 0522-2611463; hotelgomti@up-tourism.com; 6 Sapru Marg; s/d ₹900/1125, with AC from

₹2480/2590, incl breakfast & bed tea; ﹢) A better government-run hotel than most, though bottom of the barrel rooms with air coolers are a bit musty. From there, the two categories of air-con rooms won't knock you out, but all come reasonably well equipped, with TV, desks, tables and chairs.

A restaurant; **Tashna Bar** (Hotel Gomti 6 Sapru Marg; ⊙ noon-11pm), a bar with garden; and a UP Tourism office are all here, too.

Vivanta by Taj HOTEL $$$
(☎ 0522-6771000; www.vivantabytaj.com; Vipan Khand, Gomti Nagar; s/d from ₹13,490/15,177; ﹢@☎﹢) Lucknow's top hotel resides in an enormous stately building built as a domed homage to Taj's famous Taj Mahal Hotel in Mumbai and instills of sense of head-of-state in those alighting here. Rooms are modest but well-honed at the 110-room property, with newer rooms offering whimsical refinement without stuffiness, with fun cubicle showers and hardwood headboards.

The excellent Nawab restaurant, Oudhyana (p382), is special.

✖ Eating

Lucknow is the undisputed king of UP cuisine. The refined palates of the Nawabs left the city with a reputation for rich, meaty and impossibly tasty Mughlai cuisine, and the city's dinner tables are heavily influenced by the Arab world. Lucknow's excellent Mughlai kitchens are famous for a wide range of mouth-watering kebabs and their biryani dishes as well. It's also known for *dum pukht* – the 'art' of steam-pressure cooking, in which meat and vegetables are cooked in a sealed clay pot. In winter, look out for *namash* (a surprisingly light and tasty concoction made from milk, cream and morning dew).

⭐ **Tunday Kababi**　　　　　NORTH INDIAN $
(Naaz Cinema Rd, just off Aminabad Rd; dishes ₹90-110; ⏱11am-11.30am) This is the cleaner, more hospitable outlet of Lucknow's renowned, 100-year-old impossible-to-find kebab shop in Chowk (near Akbari Gate, Chowk; kebabs ₹2; ⏱10am-11pm), where buffalo beef kebabs go for ₹2. Here the prices are higher, but the boys put on a quite a show streetside for to-go orders, while the proper restaurant behind dishes up scrumptious plates of mutton biryani, kebabs and tandoori chicken for throngs of carnivores.

The minced mutton kebab (₹90 for four, eat them with *paratha*) here is impossibly delicious and a spicy punch in the gut. Rickshaw riders know how to find this place. It's tucked away down a narrow street in the bustling Aminabad district. You'll find other Tunday kebab restaurants around the city, most of which are copies.

Sakhawat　　　　　　　NORTH INDIAN $
(www.sakhawatrestaurant.com; 2 Kaiserbagh Ave, behind Awadh Gymkhana Club; kebabs ₹100-120; ⏱4.30m-10.30pm, closed Tue) This highly recommended hole-in-the-wall doesn't look like much, but the daily-changing kebabs (*galawat* et all) at this locals' haunt are the best

we had – the smoky, perfectly crispy char makes the difference – and, despite appearances, it has won international accolades and doubles as an Awadh cooking institute. Also serves biryanis and several curries.

The present owner's great-grandfather was a brigadier in the British Army and a Nawab chef.

⭐ **Moti Mahal Restaurant**　　　　INDIAN $$
(75 MG Rd; mains ₹115-200; ⏱11am-11pm) If Mughlai meat country has got you down, seek refuge in this popular veg hideaway on MG Rd. It's perfect for a late breakfast (best *poori sabji* – deep fried bread rounds served with potato curry – we had in UP) or lunch. Come evening, head upstairs for more-refined dining in the good-quality, low-lit air-con restaurant.

You could do worse here than try the Lucknow *dum aloo* (potatoes stuffed with nuts and paneer in a tomato-based sauce) and the *kadhai paneer* (paneer in a gravy made of capsicum, tomato, onion and traditional Indian spices) makes a stunning case for vegetarianism. It's all excellent.

Royal Cafe　　　　　　　MULTICUISINE $$
(51 MG Rd; chaat ₹20-90, mains ₹160-330; ⏱noon-11pm) Even if you don't step inside this excellent restaurant, don't miss its exceedingly popular *chaat* (spicy snack) stand at the front where mixed *chaats* are served in an *aloo* (potato) basket or in mini *puris*.

Inside, you'll find it does a mouth-watering job of Mughlai cuisine and everything else, including Chinese, Continental, pizza and

UTTAR PRADESH LUCKNOW

LUCKNOW'S KEBABS DECONSTRUCTED

Kakori Kebab

Originates from Kakori, a small town outside Lucknow. Legend has it that the old and toothless Nawab of Kakori asked his royal *bawarchi* (chef) to make kebabs that would simply melt in the mouth. So these kebabs are made adding papaya as a tenderiser to raw mincemeat and a mix of spices. They are then applied to skewers and barbecued over charcoals.

Galawat Kebab

This is the mouth-watering creation that is served up in Lucknow's most famous kebab restaurant, Tunday Kababi (p381). There it is simply referred to as a mutton kebab, and in other restaurants it is often called Tunday. Galawat is the name of the tenderiser that's used for these kebabs. Essentially, they are the same as Kakori kebabs except that rather than being barbecued they are made into patties and shallow fried in oil or ghee.

Shami Kebab

Raw mincemeat is boiled with spices and black gram lentil. It is then ground on stone before being mixed with finely chopped onions, coriander leaves and green chillies, and shaped into patties and then shallow fried.

shakes and sundaes, which are whipped out along with classy service to a wildly mixed crowd that runs the gamut: Sikhs and Muslims over there, Hindus and hipsters over here. Our boneless *murg mirch masala* (chicken cooked with chilli peppers and ground spices with onion and tomatoes) was perfect.

★**Oudhyana**   MUGHLAI, NORTH INDIAN $$$
(www.vivantabytaj.com; Vivanta by Taj Hotel, Vipin Khand, Gomti Nagar; mains ₹575-995) If you want to savor the flavours of the Nawabs performing at their culinary best, look no further than Oudhyana, where Chef Nagendra Singh gives Lucknow's famous Awadh cuisine its royal due at this signature restaurant inside the city's top hotel.

The flavours of everything Singh does, from the famous *galawat* and *kakori* kebabs to an entire menu of long-lost heritage dishes, unravel like an intricate gastronomic spy novel in your mouth. The intimate room is impossibly striking as well, dressed up in soothing baby blues with chandelier accoutrements. A special night out.

Falaknuma   MUGHLAI, NORTH INDIAN $$$
(Hotel Clarks Avadh, 8 MG Rd; mains ₹330-520; ☺1-3.30pm & 8-11.30pm) The stylish rooftop dining room at Clarks Avadh Hotel has fabulous bird's-eye views and serves up sumptuous Nawab cuisine, including the famous kebabs and an outstanding list of rich, vibrant curries. There's a small bar to enjoy brews and views as well.

🍷 Drinking & Nightlife

Cafe Coffee Day   CAFE
(www.cafecoffeeday.com; 31/82 MG Rd; coffee ₹64-140; ☺8am-11pm) Our favourite Indian coffee chain – known as CCD by locals – sits in prime position at the beginning of MG Rd's upscale shopping district.

Strokes Sports Bar   BAR
(Capoor's Hotel, MG Rd; ☺11am-11pm, to midnight Sat) With metallic decor, zebra-print chairs, ultraviolet lights and a backlit bar, this must be one of the strangest places in India to come to watch the latest cricket match on TV. Set it all to an international, pop-heavy soundtrack and the results are surreal. Even the middle-modern Indian ladies can be found here, albeit in smaller numbers.

Good times – though under renovation and battling rumoured licensing problems when we came through. Check ahead.

EOS   BAR
(72 MG Rd; ☺noon-11:45pm Mon-Fri, to 1am Sat) This chic bar on the rooftop of the Best Western Levana is Lucknow's attempt at a genuinely trendy bar. It draws the young and restless, especially for Saturday night DJ sets. Otherwise, the breezy, plant- and bamboo-filled spot is pleasant enough for a cocktail (₹350 to ₹450), either in the open air or within the smart air-con lounge.

🛍 Shopping

Lucknow is famous for *chikan,* an embroidered cloth worn by men and women. It is sold in a number of shops in the bazaars near Tunday Kebab, in the maze of streets in Chowk and in the small, traffic-free Janpath Market, just south of MG Rd in Hazratganj.

Sugandhco   PERFUME
(www.sugandhco.com; D-4 Janpath Market; ☺noon-7.30pm Mon-Sat) A family business since 1850, the sweet-scented Sugandhco sells *attar* (pure essence oil extracted from flowers by a traditional method) in the form of women's perfume, men's cologne, household fragrances and incense sticks. Sweet-smelling stuff.

Ram Advani Bookshop   BOOKS
(Mayfair Bldg, MG Rd; ☺10am-7.30pm Mon-Sat) This Lucknow institution is worth visiting just to meet the fantastically friendly and exceedingly knowledgeable owner, Mr Advani (in his 90s!). Be aware, though, that he takes his siestas very seriously and is rarely seen between noon and 4pm. There's a strong collection of books on Lucknow history here as well as some popular India-based contemporary literature.

ℹ Information

Foreign-friendly ATMs are dotted around Hazratganj. There's also one at the train station and the airport.

ICICI Bank (Shalimar Tower, 31/54 MG Rd, Hazratganj; ☺8am-8pm Mon-Fri, 9am-2pm Sat) Changes travellers cheques (Monday to Friday only, 10am to 5pm) and cash, and has an ATM.

Main Post Office (www.indiapost.gov.in; MG Rd; ☺10am-4pm Mon-Sat) Grand Raj-era architecture.

Sahara Hospital (📞0522-6780001; www.saharahospitals.com; Gomti Nagar) The best private hospital in Lucknow.

UP Tourism (📞0522-2615005; www.up-tourism.com; 6 Sapru Marg; ☺9am-7pm Mon-Sat)

Not a particularly helpful or well-informed government tourist office, but it happens to run Lucknow's excellent Heritage Walking Tour (though they couldn't tell us one single detail about it!). It operates a smaller kiosk (MG Rd; ⊘8am-9pm Mon-Sat) on MG Rd's main drag as well as a Tourist Helpline (☏0522-3303030).

❶ Getting There & Away

AIR

The modern Chaudhary Charan Singh International Airport is 15km southwest of Lucknow. **Jet Airways** (www.jetairways.com; Chaudhary Charan Sungh Airport) is one of a number of airlines that has offices at the airport. Direct daily flights serve Lucknow from Abu Dhabi (United Arab Emirates; from ₹10,725), Bengaluru (Bangalore; from ₹6000), Delhi (from ₹2250), Mumbai (Bombay; from ₹3600), Patna (from ₹2500) and Riyadh (Saudi Arabia; from ₹17,096).

BUS

Long-distance buses leave from **Alambagh Bus Station** (☏0522-2454444), 4km southwest of the town centre. Services include:

Agra Non-AC (₹350, seven hours, 8.30am, 10.30am, 5.30pm and 10.30pm), Volvo AC (₹906, six hours, 10am and 10pm)

Allahabad Non-AC (₹148, five hours, every 30 minutes), Volvo AC (₹479, 4½ hours, 6am, 7am, 8am, 11am, 11.30am, noon, 1pm, 2pm, 4.45pm, 6pm and 9pm)

Ayodhya Non-AC (₹176, six hours, every 30 minutes)

Faizabad Non-AC (₹145, three to four hours, every 30 minutes), Volvo AC (₹336, three hours, 10am and 10pm)

Gorakhpur Non-AC (₹283, 7½ hours, every 30 minutes), Volvo AC (₹718, six hours, 10am, 10pm and 11pm)

Jhansi Non-AC (₹320, eight hours, 7am, 9.30am, 6pm, 7pm, 8pm and 8.30pm)

Varanasi Non-AC (₹270, eight hours, every 30 minutes), Volvo AC (₹720, six hours, 3pm and 10pm)

Regular local buses (₹10) run to Alambagh bus station from the road in front of **Charbagh Bus Stand** (Kanpor Rd, at Subhash Marg), near the train station.

Kaiserbagh Bus Stand (☏0522-2622503; J Narain Rd)also has services to Faizabad (₹121, four hours) and Gorakhpur (₹260, eight hours, every 30 minutes, 6am to 10pm); as well as buses to Rupaidha (₹170, seven hours, 9.30am, 11am, 7.30pm, 8.30pm, 9.30pm and 11pm), where there is a rarely used Nepal border crossing.

TRAIN

The two main stations, Charbagh and Lucknow Junction, are side by side about 4.5km or so south of the main sites. Services for most major destinations leave from Charbagh, including several daily to Agra, Varanasi, Faizabad, Gorakhpur and New Delhi. Lucknow Junction handles the one daily train to Mumbai. **Foreign Tourist Help** (Rail Rservation & Booking Center, Charbagh Station; ⊘8am-1.50pm & 2-8pm) is at window 601 inside the Rail Reservation and Booking Center complex 150m to your right as you exit Charbagh.

❶ Getting Around

TO/FROM THE AIRPORT

An autorickshaw to the airport in Amausi from the prepaid taxi stand outside the train station costs ₹125 (plus ₹20 airport entry) and takes about 30 minutes.

LOCAL TRANSPORT

A short cycle-rickshaw ride is ₹20 to ₹30. From the prepaid autorickshaw stand outside the train station (no English sign – look for the small blue

UTTAR PRADESH LUCKNOW

HANDY TRAINS FROM LUCKNOW (LKO/LJN)

DESTINATION	TRAIN NO & NAME	FARE (₹)	DURATION (HR)	DEPARTURES
Agra	13239 PNBE Kota Exp	215/575/820 (A)	6	11.55pm
Allahabad	14210 Intercity Exp	335 (B)	4	7.30am
Faizabad	13010 Doon Exp	140/485/690 (A)	2½	8.45am
Gorakhpur	13020 Bagh Exp	190/485/690 (A)	6	6.20am
Jhansi	11016 Kushinagar Exp	195/485/690 (A)	6½	12.40am
Kolkata (Howrah)	13006 ASR-HWH Mail	480/1290/1875 (A)	20½	10.50am
Mumbai (CST)**	12533 Pushpak Exp	626/1627/2337 (A)	24	7.45am
New Delhi	12553 Vaishali Exp	335/860/1210 (A)	8	10.25pm
Varanasi	14236 BE-BSB Exp	210/565 (C)	7½	11.25pm

Fares: are (A) sleeper/3AC/2AC, (B) AC chair class only, (C) sleeper/3AC, **leaves from Lucknow Junction

booth just off to your left as you exit), a trip to the Residency costs about ₹95, as does Bara Imambara; Hazratganj is ₹65 and Mall Ave ₹75. A half-day (four-hour) autorickshaw tour covering all the main sights costs ₹305. Prices do not include a ₹5 booking fee.

AYODHYA & AROUND

♪ 05278 / POP 58,000

With monkeys galore, the usual smattering of cows and even the odd working elephant, the relatively traffic-free streets of Ayodhya would be an intriguing place to spend some time even if it wasn't for the religious significance of the place. This is not only the birthplace of Rama, and as such one of Hinduism's seven holy cities, nor just the birthplace of four of Jainism's 24 *tirthankars* (religious teachers), this is also the site of one of modern India's most controversial religious disputes.

Ayodhya became tragically synonymous with Hindu extremism in 1992, when rioting Hindus tore down the Babri Masjid, a mosque built by the Mughals in the 15th century, which Hindus claimed stood on the site of an earlier Rama temple, marking Lord Rama's birthplace. Hindus built Ram Janam Bhumi in its place. Tit-for-tat reprisals soon followed, including reactionary riots across the country that led to more than 2000 deaths, and the problem eventually reached the High Court. Archaeological investigations were carried out at the site and, in September 2010, the Allahabad High Court ruled that the site should be split equally between three religious groups; two Hindu, one Muslim. The Muslim group,

Sunni Waqf Board, appealed parts of the ruling but the Supreme Court of India ruled in favour of the Allahabad ruling in 2011. Since the verdict, things have remained relatively calm. Meanwhile, security around the Ram Janam Bhumi remains incredibly tight.

The slightly larger town of Faizabad, 7km away, is the jumping-off point for Ayodhya and where you'll find more accommodation. From the Faizabad bus stand, turn left onto the main road where you'll find shared rickshaws (₹10 to ₹20, 20 minutes) to Ayodhya, where you can make a walking tour of the temples.

◉ Sights

Hanumangarhi HINDU TEMPLE
(⊙ dawn-dusk) This is one of the town's most popular temples, and is the closest of the major temples here to the main road. Walk up the 76 steps to the ornate carved gateway and the fortresslike outer walls, and join the throng inside offering *prasad* (temple-blessed food).

Dashrath Bhavan HINDU TEMPLE
(⊙ dawn-dusk) A further 200m up the side road from Hanumangarhi, this temple is approached through a colourful entranceway. The atmosphere inside is peaceful, with musicians playing and orange-clad sadhus reading scriptures.

Kanak Bhavan HINDU TEMPLE
(Palace of Gold; ⊙ 8.30-noon & 4.30-8pm) A few minutes' walk straight on from Dashrath Bhavan is this impressive, ancient but often rebuilt palace-cum-temple.

---

❶ JHANSI: TRANSIT HUB

This nondescript town near the Madhya Pradesh border is famous for its link to the Rani of Jhansi, a key player in the 1857 First War of Independence (Indian Uprising), and it is commonly used as a gateway to Orchha, Khajuraho and Gwalior.

Buses leave from the bus stand for Chhatarpur (₹130, three hours, hourly, 5am to 10pm), where you can switch for Khajuraho (₹50, 1½ hours); to Chitrakut (₹250, six hours, 8.30am); and Gwalior (₹100, three hours, hourly). Tempos (₹20) go between Jhansi bus stand and Orchha all day. Private autorickshaws charge ₹200. Coming from Khajuraho/Chhatarpur, you can ask the bus driver to drop you off at the Orchha turn-off on the National Hwy, where you should be able to wave down a vehicle to take you to Orchha.

Handy trains include 12137 Punjab Mail to Gwalior (sleeper/3AC/2AC ₹170/535/735, 1½ hours, 2.30pm) and Agra (₹195/535/735, 3½ hours, 2.30pm); 12138 Punjab Mail to Mumbai ₹530/1385/1995, 19 hours, 12.35pm); 12615 Grand Trunk Exp to Delhi (sleeper/3AC/2AC ₹275/705/985, 6½ hours, 11.42pm); 11107 Bundelkhand Exp to Varanasi (sleeper/3AC/2AC ₹305/825/1180, 12½ hours, 10.30pm) and 19666 Udz Kurj Express to Khajuraho (sleeper/3AC/2AC ₹160/485/690, five hours, 2.35pm).

Ram Janam Bhumi   HINDU TEMPLE
(☉ 7-11am & 3-6pm) If you turn left at Dashrath Bhavan, when coming from Hanumanghari, you soon reach the highly contentious temple that marks the birthplace of Rama. Security here is staggering (think crossing from West Bank into Israel). You must first show your passport, then leave all belongings apart from your passport and money (even your belt) in nearby lockers.

You are then searched several times before being accompanied through a caged corridor that leads to a spot 20m away from a makeshift tent of a shrine, which marks Rama's birthplace.

Ramkatha Museum   MUSEUM
(☎ 9415328511; ☉ 10.30am-5pm Tue-Sun, performances 6-9pm) FREE A 10-minute walk on the other side of the main road from the temples in this area brings you to Ramkatha Museum, a large, unsigned in English yellow-and-red building with paintings and ancient sculptures. Every evening except Monday, the museum hosts free performances of the Ram Lila (a dramatic re-enactment of the battle between Lord Ram and Ravan, as described in the Hindu epic, the Ramayana).

Walk about 500m or so along the main road deeper into Ayodhya, turn right at the police station across from Akash Cycle Company, and it's another 500m or so on your right.

🍽 Sleeping & Eating

Hotel Shane Avadh   HOTEL $
(☎ 05278-222075; www.hotelshaveavadh.com; Civil Lines, Faizabad; s/d from ₹400/500, with AC from ₹1236/1574; ﹡) There's a huge range of rooms at this well-run establishment in Faizabad (though only a few recently renovated ones are as smart as their website would have you believe). Even the cheapest ones are neat and spacious, though, if a little basic. Beds are rock hard (if you're into that). There's also a decent restaurant (mains ₹90 to ₹325). Book ahead.

★ Awantika   MULTICUISINE $
(Civil Lines, Faizabad; mains ₹95-210; ☉ 11am-10.30pm) Clean and hip, this out-of-place restaurant does a seriously good all-veg menu that runs the gamut from Chinese to Italian to Indian. The special thali (₹180) is a real treat and it's all set to trendy tunes in a funky lounge atmosphere. It's across the street from Bharat Petroleum.

ℹ Information
There's an HDFC Bank ATM next to Bharat Petroleum, between Hotel Shan-e-Avadh and the bus stand.

Cyber Zone (Civil Lines, Faizabad; per hour ₹20; ☉ 10am-8.30pm) A rudimentary internet cafe at the first intersection 50m on the right after Hotel Shan-e-Avadh on the road heading towards Ayodhya.

ℹ Getting There & Away
From Faizabad bus stand, buses run to Lucknow (₹135, three hours), Gorakhpur (₹144, 3½ hours, every 30 minutes, 5am and 8pm). Buses to Allahabad (₹147, five hours) depart on the same schedule between 7am and 10pm.

Daily trains include Lucknow (13307 Gangasutlej Express, sleeper/3AC/2AC ₹140/485/690, four hours, 11.08am), Varanasi (13010 Doon Express, sleeper/3AC/2AC ₹140/485/690, five hours, 11.10am) and Delhi (14205 Faizabad-Delhi Express, sleeper/3AC/2AC ₹340/910/1310, 12 hours, 9.45pm).

A cycle-rickshaw from the bus stand to the train station is ₹30.

ALLAHABAD
☎ 0532 / POP 1.2 MILLION
For all its importance in Hindu mythology, Indian history and modern politics, Allahabad is a surprisingly relaxed city that offers plenty in terms of sights, but little in the way of in-yer-face hassle.

Brahma, the Hindu god of creation, is believed to have landed on earth in Allahabad, or Prayag as it was originally known, and to have called it the king of all pilgrimage centres. Indeed, Sangam, a river confluence on the outskirts of the city, is the most celebrated of India's four Kumbh Mela locations. The vast riverbanks here attract tens of millions of pilgrims every six years for either the Kumbh Mela or the Ardh (Half) Mela, but every year there is a smaller Magh Mela.

Of more immediate interest to casual visitors are Allahabad's grand Raj-era buildings, its Mughal fort and tombs, and the historic legacy of the Nehru family.

◉ Sights & Activities

★ Sangam   SACRED SITE
This is the particularly auspicious point where two of India's holiest rivers, the Ganges and the Yamuna, meet one of Hinduism's mythical rivers, the Saraswati. All year

UTTAR PRADESH ALLAHABAD

Allahabad

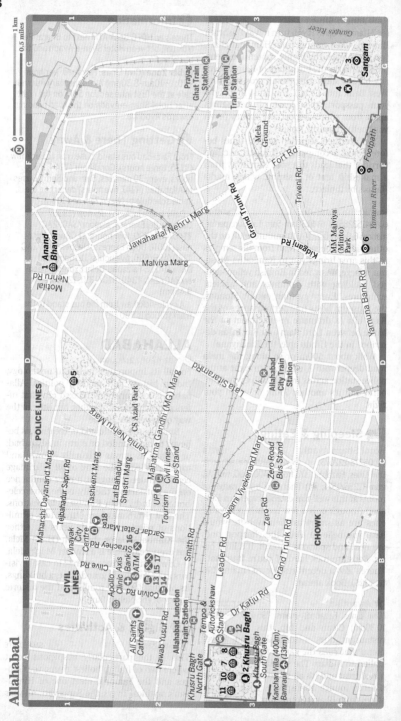

1 km
0.5 miles

CIVIL LINES

POLICE LINES

CHOWK

Sangam
Ganges River
Yamuna River

1 Anand Bhavan
2 Khusru Bagh
3
4
5
6
9

Motilal Nehru Rd
Jawaharlal Nehru Marg
Malviya Marg
Grand Trunk Rd
Fort Rd
Triveni Rd
Kidganj Rd
MM Malviya (Minto) Park
Yamuna Bank Rd
Mela Ground
Footpath

Prayag Ghat Train Station
Daraganj Train Station
Allahabad City Train Station

Lala Stara Rd

CS Azad Park
Kamla Nehru Marg
Mahatma Gandhi (MG) Marg
Tourism
UP
Civil Lines Bus Stand
Lal Bahadur Shastri Marg
Tashkent Marg
Tejbahadur Sapru Rd
Maharshi Dayanand Marg
Sardar Patel Marg
Vinayak City Centre
Strachey Rd
Axis Bank
ATM
13
15 17
14
16

Smith Rd
Leader Rd
Swami Vivekanand Marg
Zero Road Bus Stand
Zero Rd
Grand Trunk Rd

Clive Rd
Colvin Rd
Apollo Clinic
All Saints Cathedral
Nawab Yusuf Rd
Allahabad Junction Train Station
Tempo & Autorickshaw Stand
Dr Katju Rd
12
Khusru Bagh North Gate
Khusru Bagh South Gate
Kanchan Villa (400m);
Bamrauli (13km)
11 10 7 8

Allahabad

UTTAR PRADESH ALLAHABAD

round, pilgrims row boats out to this holy spot, but their numbers increase dramatically during the annual **Magh Mela** (Allahabad; ⊙ Jan/Feb), a six-week festival held between January and March, which culminates in six communal 'holy dips'.

Every 12 years the massive **Kumbh Mela** takes place here, attracting millions of people, while the **Ardh Mela** (Half Mela) is held here every six years.

In the early 1950s, 350 pilgrims were killed in a stampede to the soul-cleansing water (an incident re-created vividly in Vikram Seth's immense novel *A Suitable Boy*). The last Ardh Mela, in 2007, attracted more than 70 million people – considered to be the largest-ever human gathering until the 2013 Kumbh Mela, which attracted a guestimated 32 million on Mauni Amavasya, the main bathing day, and 100 million across the 55-day festival; expect equally astonishing numbers at the next Allahabad Kumbh Mela in 2025. Old boat hands will row you out to the sacred confluence for ₹50 per person (hard-bargaining Indian) or ₹100 (hard-bargaining foreigner), or ₹600 to ₹800 per boat.

Around the corner from Sangam (skirt the riverbank around the front of Akbar's Fort) are the **Saraswati** and **Nehru Ghats**, home to a nightly *aarti* (an auspicious lighting of lamps/candles).

★ Khusru Bagh   PARK
(Mughal tombs admission free; ⊙ Mughal tombs dawn-dusk) This intriguing park, surrounded by huge walls, contains four highly impressive **Mughal tombs**. One is that of **Prince Khusru**, the eldest son of Emperor Jehangir, who tried to assassinate his father but was blinded and imprisoned, finally dying in 1622. If Khusru's coup had succeeded, his brother, Shah Jahan, would not have become emperor and the Taj Mahal would not exist.

A second tomb belongs to **Shah Begum**, Khusru's mother (Jehangir's first wife), who committed suicide in 1603 with an opium overdose because of the ongoing feud between her son and his father. Between these two, a third, particularly attractive tomb was constructed by **Nesa Begum**, Khusru's sister, although was never actually used as a tomb. A smaller structure, called **Tamolon's Tomb**, stands to the west of the others, but its origin is unknown.

★ Anand Bhavan   MUSEUM
(Indian/foreigner ₹10/100; ⊙ 9.30am-1pm & 1.30-5pm Tue-Sun) This picturesque two-storey building is a shrine to the Nehru family, which has produced five generations of leading politicians from Motilal Nehru to the latest political figure, Rahul Gandhi. This stately home is where Mahatma Gandhi, Jawaharlal Nehru and others successfully planned the overthrow of the British Raj. It is full of books, personal effects and photos from those stirring times. Indira Gandhi was married here in 1942. The run-down Swaraj Bhavan next door is where former Prime Minister Indira Gandhi was born.

Akbar's Fort & Patalpuri Temple   FORT
(Patalpuri temple admission by donation; ⊙ Patalpuri temple 6am-5.30pm) Built by the Mughal Emperor Akbar, this 16th-century fort on the northern bank of the Yamuna has massive walls with three gateways flanked by towers. Most of it is occupied by the Indian army and cannot be visited, but a small door in the eastern wall by Sangam leads to one part you can enter, the underground Patalpuri Temple.

DIP DATES

The following are the auspicious bathing dates for upcoming mela to be held at Sangam in Allahabad.

BATHING DAY	2016	2017	2018	2019
Makar Sankranti	4 Jan	14 Jan	14 Jan	14 Jan
Mauni Amavasya	8 Feb	27 Jan	16 Jan	4 Feb
Vasant Panchami	12 Feb	1 Feb	22 Jan	10 Feb
Magh Purnima	22 Feb	10 Feb	31 Jan	19 Feb
Mahashivatri	8 Mar	25 Feb	14 Feb	5 Mar

This unique temple is crowded with all sorts of idols – pick up some coins from the change dealers outside so you can leave small offerings as you go. You may be pressured into giving ₹10 to ₹100 at some shrines. A few coins are perfectly acceptable.

Outside the temple – though its roots can be seen beneath ground – is the **Undying Banyan Tree** from which pilgrims used to leap to their deaths, believing it would liberate them from the cycle of rebirth.

Allahabad Museum MUSEUM
(Kamla Nehru Marg; Indian/foreigner ₹15/100; ⊙10am-5pm Tue-Sun, closed every 2nd Sun) This extensive museum in the grounds of a pleasant park has archaeological and Nehru family items, modern paintings, miniatures and ancient sculptures.

🛏 Sleeping

Hotel Prayag HOTEL $
(☎0532-2656416; www.prayaggroupofhotels.com; 73 Noorullah Rd; s/d/tr from ₹400/650/900, s/d without bathroom ₹275/375, s/d with AC ₹1137/1350; ❋@🛜) A stone's throw south of the train station, this sprawling, well-run place is helpful and boasts an internet cafe (per hour ₹30, wi-fi free), a State Bank of India ATM and a funky restaurant. There's a wide variety of old-fashioned, basic rooms in various states of dilapidation, but staff are friendly and will even help negotiate autorickshaws.

Royal Hotel HOTEL $
(☎0532-2427201; royalhotel.666@rediffmail.com; Nawab Yusef Rd; s/d from ₹300/450; @) This decrepit old building near the train station used to be royal stables but was converted into a hotel by the king of Kalakankar, a former princely state, after he was refused entry into a British-run hotel nearby. It's dire and run down, but offers dirt cheap antiquated

character and is foreign-traveller ready. The rooms (with 6m-high ceilings) and their bathrooms are absolutely enormous.

⭐**Kanchan Villa** HOMESTAY $$
(☎9838631111; www.allahabadbnb.com; 64 Lukerganj; s/d from ₹2850/3550, apt ₹5300, all incl breakfast; ❋@🛜) Ivan, a guitar-wielding Indian rum enthusiast, and his wife, Purnima, are your South Indian/Bengali hosts at this fabulous homestay offering a window into a rarely seen side of Christian Indian culture. In a historic home nearing its centennial milestone, six rooms are decked out with period furnishings (our fave: Bengali); breakfast can be taken on the lush, 2nd-floor patio. The lovely staff will cook for you as well, serving up fresh kebabs from the outdoor tandoor, for example, and you'll feel right at home in the living room/bar. Pickup and drops-offs included; otherwise it's a short ₹20 cycle-rickshaw ride from the train station.

Hotel U.R. HOTEL $$
(☎0532-2427334; mj1874@gmail.com; 7/3, A/1 MG Marg; r ₹1569-2243; ❋🛜) This professionally-run 20-room midranger is in a good location along MG Marg and offers a slight step-up from similarly-priced competition. A glass elevator leads to somewhat cramped (due to big beds) but clean rooms, the cheapest of which have renovated bathrooms, and small desks and seating areas. Staff is palpably better trained than elsewhere in this price range.

🍴 Eating

⭐**Eat On** MUGHLAI $
(MG Marg; mains ₹40-200; ⊙11.30am-10pm Wed-Mon) This standing-room only food shack does four things – and does them astonishingly cheap and well. Mouth-watering *shami* kebabs (minced mutton with black

gram lentil and spices), perfectly spiced chicken biryani, roasted chicken (evenings only) and a lovely thin *paratha* to accompany it all. Prepare to wait – this is one of Allahabad's best.

Indian Coffee House   CAFE $
(15 MG Marg; coffee from ₹17.50, mains ₹25-55; ⊙8am-9pm) Rickshaw drivers call this large, airy 50-year-old coffee hall simply 'Coffee House' (like the French call them fries). It's a classic South Indian choice for a budget breakfast (including Continental choices like eggs, omelettes and toast) and good filtered coffee.

The annex closest to the road is often closed, but the main building set back from the street should be open.

Kamdhenu Sweets   SWEETS $
(37, Palace Cinema Compound, MG Marg; snacks ₹20-80; ⊙8am-10pm) Very popular snack shop selling absolutely delicious homebaked sweets, as well as cakes, samosas, sandwiches and ice cream.

★ **El Chico**   MULTICUISINE $$
(26/28 MG Marg; mains ₹185-430; ⊙9am-10.30pm) This refined restaurant serves up absolutely wonderful Indian (the chicken chilli garlic kebab is every bit as delicious as it sounds), tasty-looking Chinese, popular sizzlers and Continental cuisine, along with coffee in pewter carafes.

El Chico Cafe   FUSION/BAKERY $$
(24/28 MG Marg; mains ₹150-450; ⊙10am-11pm) Cure your homesick hungries in a heartbeat among a forward-thinking Indian crowd. Big breakfasts all day (cinnamon pancakes, waffles, espresso); and sandwiches, wood-fired pizzas and more sophisticated fusion fare throughout the day. Try the sizzlin' brownie! It's next door to El Chico.

🍷 Drinking & Nightlife

Patiyala Peg Bar   BAR
(Grand Continental Hotel, Sardar Patel Marg; ⊙7-11pm) The most interesting bar for tourists has live *ghazal* (Urdu songs) music nightly from 7.30pm to 10.30pm. Mostly beers (from ₹300) and whisky.

ℹ Information

ATMs dot the Civil Lines area.

Apollo Clinic (www.apolloclinic.com; 28B MG Marg; ⊙24hr) A modern private medical facility/24-hour pharmacy.

Post Office (www.indiapost.gov.in; Sarojini Naidu Marg; ⊙10am-1.30pm & 2-5pm Mon-Fri, 10am-4pm Sat) Postal services.

UP Tourism (☑0532-2408873; www.up-tourism.com; 35 MG Marg; ⊙10am-5pm Mon-Sat, closed 2nd Sat) At the Rahi Ilawart Tourist Bungalow. Very helpful.

ℹ Getting There & Away

AIR

Allahabad Airport is 15km west of Allahabad. **Air India** (☑0532-258360; www.airindia.com) has one daily flight to Delhi (4pm; from ₹2500) and a Mumbai flight on Tuesday, Thursday, Friday and Saturday (1pm; from ₹6000). An autorickshaw to the airport costs ₹400 and taxis ₹600.

BUS

From the **Civil Lines Bus Stand** (MG Marg) regular non-AC buses run to Varanasi (₹115, three hours, every 10 minutes, 4am to 10pm), Faizabad (₹150, five hours, every 30 minutes, 5am to 11pm), Gorakhpur (₹243, 10 hours, every

HANDY TRAINS FROM ALLAHABAD (ALD)

DESTINATION	TRAIN NO & NAME	FARE (₹)	DURATION (HR)	DEPARTURES
Agra	12403 ALD JP EXP	316/802/1107 (A)	7½	11.30pm
Kolkata (Howrah)	12312 Kalka Mail	435/1145/1630 (A)	14	5.20pm
Lucknow	14209 ALD-LKO Intercity	335 (B)	4½	3.20pm
New Delhi	12559 Shiv Ganga Exp	375/980/1385 (A)	9	10.30pm
Satna	12428 ANVT REWA EXP	170/535/735 (A)	3	6.55am
Varanasi	15017 Gorakhpur Exp	140/485/690 (A)	4	8.35am

Fares: (A) sleeper/3AC/2AC, (B) AC chair only

CHITRAKUT: VARANASI IN MINIATURE

Known as a mini Varanasi because of its many temples and ghats, this small, peaceful town on the banks of the River Mandakini is the stuff of Hindu legends. It is here that Hinduism's principal trinity – Brahma, Vishnu and Shiva – took on their incarnations. It is also the place where Lord Rama is believed to have spent 11½ years of his 14-year exile after being banished from his birthplace in Ayodhya at the behest of a jealous stepmother.

Today Chitrakut attracts throngs of pilgrims, giving the area a strong religious quality, particularly by **Ram Ghat**, the town's centre of activity, and at the holy hill of **Kamadgiri**, 2km away.

Dozens, sometimes hundreds, of devotees descend onto Ram Ghat to take holy dips at dawn before returning at the end of the day for the evening *aarti* (an auspicious lighting of lamps/candles). Colourful **rowboats** (with rabbits!) wait here to take you across to the opposite bank, which is actually in Madhya Pradesh, or to scenic spots along the river. The 2km-trip to the **Glass Temple**, a building covered in religious mosaics made with thousands of pieces of coloured glass, is popular. During the day, many people make their way to Kamadgiri, a hill revered as the holy embodiment of Lord Rama. A 5km-circuit (90 minutes) around the base of the hill takes you past prostrating pilgrims, innumerable monkeys and temples galore.

30 minutes, 4am to midnight) and Lucknow (₹176, five hours, hourly, noon to 8pm). There are two more comfortable AC buses running to Lucknow (₹459, five hours, 6am to 8pm) daily. To get to Delhi or Agra, change in Lucknow, or take a train.

There are two direct buses to Chitrakut (₹110, three hours, 12.30 and 1.30pm) from **Zero Road Bus Stand** (Zero Rd). Otherwise, head instead to Karwi (₹110, three hours, every 30 minutes, 7am to 8.30) where you can do the final 10km by shared autorickshaw (₹10).

TRAIN

Allahabad Junction is the main station. A few daily trains run to Lucknow, Varanasi, Delhi, Agra and Kolkata. Frequent trains also run to Satna, from where you can catch buses to Khajuraho.

ⓘ Getting Around

Cycle-rickshaws (₹10 for a short trip of 1km to 2km but be prepared to go to war for it) are plentiful. The train station is your best bet for autorickshaws. Consider hiring one for half a day (₹500, four hours) to take in more of the sights. *Vikrams* (large shared autos) hang about on the south side of the train station. Destinations include Zero Road Bus Stand (₹10), Civil Lines Bus Stand (₹10) and Sangam (₹15).

VARANASI

🎵 0542 / POP 1.4 MILLION

Brace yourself. You're about to enter one of the most blindingly colourful, unrelentingly chaotic and unapologetically indiscreet places on earth. Varanasi takes no prisoners. But if you're ready for it, this may just turn out to be your favourite stop of all.

Also known at various times in history as Kashi (City of Life) and Benares, this is one of the world's oldest continually inhabited cities and is regarded as one of Hinduism's seven holy cities. Pilgrims come to the ghats lining the River Ganges here to wash away a lifetime of sins in the sacred waters or to cremate their loved ones. It's a particularly auspicious place to die, since expiring here offers moksha (liberation from the cycle of birth and death), making Varanasi the beating heart of the Hindu universe. Most visitors agree it's a magical place, but it's not for the faint-hearted. Here the most intimate rituals of life and death take place in public, and the sights, sounds and smells in and around the ghats – not to mention the almost constant attention from touts – can be overwhelming. Persevere. Varanasi is unique, and a walk along the ghats or a boat ride on the river will live long in the memory.

The old city of Varanasi is situated along the western bank of the Ganges and extends back from the riverbank ghats in a labyrinth of alleys called *galis* that are too narrow for traffic. They can be disorienting, but the popular hotels and restaurants are usually signposted and, however lost you become, you will eventually end up at a ghat and get your bearings. You can walk all the way along the ghats, apart from during and immediately after the monsoon, when the river level is too high.

India's current prime minister, Narendra Modi, is a Varanasi Member of Parliament, so it has been getting some extra attention of late, with new projects, roadworks and a general (much needed) sprucing up.

History

Thought to date back to around 1200 BC, Varanasi really rose to prominence in the 8th century AD, when Shankaracharya, a reformer of Hinduism, established Shiva worship as the principal sect. The Afghans destroyed Varanasi around AD 1300, after laying waste to nearby Sarnath, but the fanatical Mughal emperor Aurangzeb was the most destructive, looting and destroying almost all of the temples. The old city of Varanasi may look antique, but few buildings are more than a couple of hundred years old.

◉ Sights

★ **Vishwanath Temple**   HINDU TEMPLE
(Golden Temple; Map p394; ◷ 3am-11am, 12.30-8pm & 9-11pm) There are temples at almost every turn in Varanasi, but this is the most famous of the lot. It is dedicated to Vishveswara – Shiva as lord of the universe. The current temple was built in 1776 by Ahalya Bai of Indore; the 800kg of gold plating on the tower and dome was supplied by Maharaja Ranjit Singh of Lahore 50 years later.

The area is full of soldiers because of security issues and communal tensions. Bags, cameras, mobile phones, pens or any other electronic device must be deposited in lockers (₹20) before you enter the alleyway it's in. Accounts vary as to whether or not foreigners can go in the temple itself. Officially, non-Hindus, which counts most foreigners, cannot enter the temple, but many expats living in Varanasi as well as travelers have reported they were allowed in. We get the impression it's up to the whim of the security guards that day. For what's it's worth, they would not let us in until we returned with a local handler to sort things out. Declaring an interested or curiosity in Hindu beliefs may help you gain access (and it helps if you have an offering in hand, which can be purchased inside or outside the temple). Either way, bring your original passport (not a copy) if you want to enter. Once inside, it's quite a show, with people pushing, tripping over and sometimes violently asserting themselves for a chance to give an offering and touch the lingam, which resolves one of all sins. Hindus routinely wait in lines for 48 hours to enter on particularly holy days.

On the northern side of Vishwanath Temple is the **Gyan Kupor Well** (Well of Knowl-edge; Map p394). The faithful believe drinking its water leads to a higher spiritual plane, though they are prevented from doing so by a strong security screen. Non-Hindus are also not allowed to enter here, and here the rule is enforced more strictly.

Benares Hindu University   HISTORIC SITE
(BHU; Map p392; www.bhu.ac.in) Long regarded as a centre of learning, Varanasi's tradition of top-quality education continues today at Benares Hindu University, established in 1916. The wide tree-lined streets and parkland of the 5-sq-km campus offer a peaceful atmosphere a world away from the city outside. On campus is **Bharat Kala Bhavan** (Map p392; Indian/foreigner ₹10/150; ◷ 10am-5.30pm Mon-Fri), a roomy museum with a wonderful collection of miniature paintings, as well as 12th-century palm-leaf manuscripts, sculptures and local history displays.

Ramnagar Fort & Museum   MUSEUM
(Map p392; museum Indian/foreigner ₹20/150; ◷ 10-5.30pm) This crumbling 17th-century fort and palace, on the eastern bank of the Ganges, isn't worth coming out to if you only have a few days in Varanasi, but it is a beautiful place to watch the sun set over the river. It also houses an eccentric **museum**. There are vintage American cars, jewel-encrusted sedan chairs, a superb weaponry section and an extremely unusual astrological clock.

The current maharaja, Anant Narayan Singh – still known in these parts as the Maharaja of Benares despite such royal titles being officially abolished in 1971 – continues his family tradition of attending the annual month-long **Ram Lila drama festival** (Varanasi; ◷ Sep/Oct) held in the streets behind the fort.

Boats operate a shuttle service across the river (₹20 return, 10 minutes) between 5am and 8pm, but from October to mid-June, you can also cross on a somewhat steady pontoon bridge or take the long way round on a rickshaw (₹200). A new bridge, under construction now for years, means most folks will just drive across – if it's ever finished. A boat all the way back to Dashashwamedh Ghat is ₹200.

Ghats

Spiritually enlightening and fantastically photogenic, Varanasi is at its brilliant best by the ghats, the long stretch of steps leading down to the water on the western bank

UTTAR PRADESH VARANASI

Varanasi

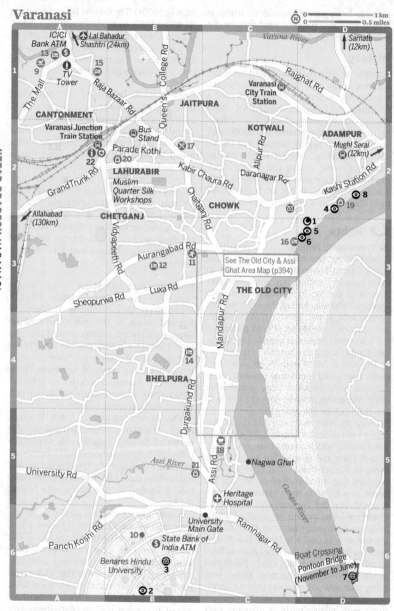

See The Old City & Assi Ghat Area Map (p394)

of the Ganges. Most are used for bathing but there are also several 'burning ghats' where bodies are cremated in public. The main one is Manikarnika: you'll often see funeral processions threading their way through the backstreets to this ghat.

The best time to visit the ghats is at dawn when the river is bathed in a mellow light as pilgrims come to perform puja to the rising sun, and at sunset when the main *ganga aarti* (river worship ceremony) takes place at Dashashwamedh Ghat.

Varanasi

About 80 ghats border the river, but the main group extends from Assi Ghat, near the university, northwards to Raj Ghat, near the road and rail bridge.

A boat trip along the river provides the perfect introduction, although for most of the year the water level is low enough for you to walk freely along the whole length of the ghats. It's a world-class 'people-watching' stroll as you mingle with the fascinating mixture of people who come to the Ganges not only for a ritual bath but also to wash clothes, do yoga, offer blessings, sell flowers, get a massage, play cricket, wash their buffaloes, improve their karma by giving to beggars or simply hang around.

Southern Stretch

★ **Assi Ghat** SACRED SITE
(Map p394) Assi Ghat, the furthest south of the main ghats and one of the biggest, is particularly important as the River Assi meets the Ganges near here and pilgrims come to worship a Shiva lingam (phallic image of Shiva) beneath a peepul tree. Evenings are particularly lively, as the ghat's vast concreted area fills up with hawkers and entertainers. It's a popular starting point for boat trips and there are some excellent hotels.

Tulsi Ghat SACRED SITE
(Map p394) Named after a 16th-century Hindu poet, Tulsi Ghat has fallen down towards the river but in the month of Kartika (October/November) a festival devoted to Krishna is celebrated here.

Bachraj Ghat SACRED SITE
(Map p394) This small ghat is marked by three Jain temples.

Shivala Ghat SACRED SITE
(Map p394) A Shiva temple and a 19th-century mansion built by Nepali royalty sit back from Shivalaya Ghat.

Dandi Ghat SACRED SITE
(Map p394) The Dandi Ghat is used by austere ascetics known as Dandi Panths

Hanuman Ghat SACRED SITE
(Map p394) Popular with Rama devotees (Hanuman was Rama's monkey servant).

Harishchandra Ghat SACRED SITE
(Map p394) Harishchandra Ghat is a cremation ghat – smaller and secondary in importance to Manikarnika, but one of the oldest ghats in Varanasi.

Kedar Ghat SACRED SITE
(Map p394) Above Harishchandra Ghat, with a shrine popular with Bengalis and South Indians.

Old City Stretch

★ **Dashashwamedh Ghat** SACRED SITE
(Map p394) Varanasi's liveliest and most colourful ghat is Dashashwamedh Ghat, easily reached at the end of the main road from Godaulia Crossing. The name indicates that Brahma sacrificed (medh) 10 (das) horses (aswa) here. In spite of the oppressive boat owners, flower sellers and touts trying

The Old City & Assi Ghat Area

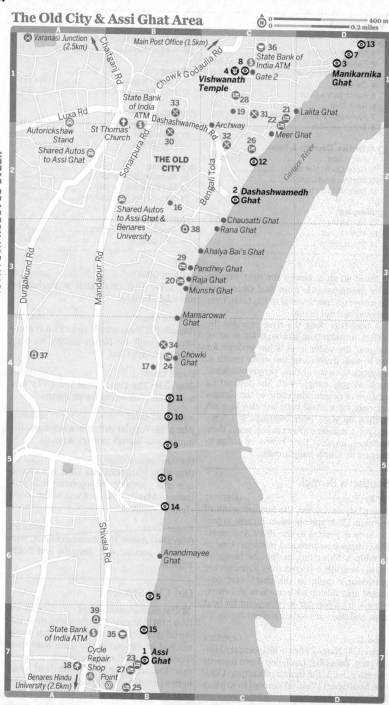

N
0   400 m
0   0.2 miles

Varanasi Junction (2.5km)

Chatganj Rd

Main Post Office (1.5km)

Chowk Godaulia Rd

36

State Bank of India ATM

8
Gate 2

13

7

3

Manikarnika Ghat

4

Vishwanath Temple

28

Luxa Rd

State Bank of India ATM

33

Dashashwamedh Rd

19

31

Archway

21

Lalita Ghat

22

Autorickshaw Stand

St Thomas' Church

30

32

Meer Ghat

26

Shared Autos to Assi Ghat

Sonarpura Rd

THE OLD CITY

12

Bengali Tola

Ganges River

2 Dashashwamedh Ghat

Shared Autos to Assi Ghat & Benares University

16

38

Chausatti Ghat

Rana Ghat

Ahalya Bai's Ghat

29

Pandhey Ghat

20

Raja Ghat

Munshi Ghat

Durgakund Rd

Mandapur Rd

Mansarowar Ghat

37

34

Chowki Ghat

17

24

11

10

9

6

14

Shivala Rd

Anandmayee Ghat

5

39

State Bank of India ATM

35

15

Cycle Repair Shop

23

1 Assi Ghat

18

27

25

Benares Hindu University (2.6km)

The Old City & Assi Ghat Area

UTTAR PRADESH VARANASI

to drag you off to a silk shop, it's a wonderful place to linger and people-watch while soaking up the atmosphere. Every evening at 7pm an elaborate *ganga aarti* ceremony with *puja*, fire and dance is staged here.

Man Mandir Ghat   SACRED SITE
(Map p394) Just north of Dashashwamedh Ghat, Man Mandir Ghat was built in 1600 by Raja Man Singh, but was poorly restored in the 19th century. The northern corner of the ghat has a fine stone balcony.

★ **Manikarnika Ghat**   SACRED SITE
(Map p394) Manikarnika Ghat, the main burning ghat, is the most auspicious place for a Hindu to be cremated. Dead bodies are handled by outcasts known as *doms*, and are carried through the alleyways of the old city to the holy Ganges on a bamboo stretcher swathed in cloth. The corpse is doused with water from the Ganges prior to cremation.

Huge piles of firewood are stacked along the top of the ghat; every log is carefully weighed on giant scales so that the price of cremation can be calculated. Each type of wood has its own price, sandalwood being the most expensive. There is an art to using just enough wood to completely incinerate

a corpse. You can watch cremations but always show reverence by behaving respectfully. Photography is strictly prohibited. You're almost guaranteed to be led by a priest, or more likely a guide, to the upper floor of a nearby building from where you can watch cremations taking place, and then asked for a donation (in dollars) towards the cost of wood. If you don't want to make a donation, don't follow them.

Above the steps here is a tank known as the **Manikarnika Well**. Parvati is said to have dropped her earring here and Shiva dug the tank to recover it, filling the depression with his sweat. The **Charanpaduka**, a slab of stone between the well and the ghat, bears footprints made by Vishnu. Privileged VIPs are cremated at the Charanpaduka, which also has a temple dedicated to Ganesh.

Dattatreya Ghat   SACRED SITE
(Map p394) Dattatreya takes its name from a Brahmin saint, whose footprint is preserved in a small temple nearby.

Scindhia Ghat   SACRED SITE
(Map p394) Scindhia Ghat was originally built in 1830, but was so huge and magnificent that it collapsed into the river and had to be rebuilt.

Northern Stretch

Ram Ghat
SACRED SITE

(Map p392) North from Scindhia Ghat, Ram Ghat was built by a maharaja of Jaipur.

Panchganga Ghat
SACRED SITE

(Map p392) This marks where five holy rivers are supposed to meet.

Alamgir Mosque
MOSQUE

(Map p392) Dominating Panchganga Ghat, this small mosque was built by Aurangzeb on the site of a large Vishnu temple.

Gai Ghat
SACRED SITE

(Map p392) A painted stone Nandi statue and lingam mark this ghat north of the mosque.

Trilochan Ghat
SACRED SITE

(Map p392) At Trilochan, two turrets emerge from the river, and the water between them is especially holy.

Activities

It's worth an early rise two of your mornings in Varanasi, one to take in the action on a river boat trip and another to experience the hubbub of activity on the ghats themselves. Nonguests can use the outdoor swimming pools (₹300) at Hotel Surya and Hotel Clarks Varanasi (Map p392; The Mall; nonguests ₹500; ☎).

★ River Trips
BOATING

A dawn rowing boat ride along the Ganges is a quintessential Varanasi experience. The early-morning light is particularly inspiring, and all the colour and clamour of pilgrims bathing and performing *puja* unfolds before you. An hour-long trip south from Dashashwamedh Ghat to Harishchandra Ghat and back is popular, but be prepared to see a burning corpse at Harishchandra.

Early evening is also a good time to be on the river, when you can light a lotus flower candle (₹10) and set it adrift on the water before watching the nightly *ganga aarti* ceremony (7pm) at Dashashwamedh Ghat directly from the boat.

The official government price of boats is ₹250 per hour for two to four people, but it is not enforced. Count yourself lucky if you manage ₹300 per person per hour and be prepared for some hard bargaining. And be warned: it's best to arrange a boat the day before. If you show up as the sun is about to rise, you'll find yourself in a Varanasi Standoff: a battle of wills between yourself, a boatsman and the unforgiving rising sun – to the tune of ₹1000 per person.

THE VARANASI SHAKEDOWN

If you thought the touts and rickshaw-wallahs were annoying in Agra, wait till you get to Varanasi. The attention here, particularly around the ghats and the Old City, is incredible: you will have to put up with persistent offers from touts and drivers of 'cheapest and best' boat trips, guides, tour operators, travel agents, silk shops and money changers (to name a few). Take it in good humour but politely refuse.

Words to live by in Varanasi:

➡ Don't take photos at the 'burning' ghats and resist offers to 'follow me for a better view', where you'll be pressured for money and may be placed in an uncomfortable situation.

➡ Do not go to any shop with a guide or autorickshaw driver. Be firm and don't do it. *Ever.* You will pay 40% to 60% more for your item due to insane commissions and you will be passively encouraging this practice. Do yourself a favour and walk there; or have your ride drop you a block away.

➡ Imposter stores are rampant in Varanasi, usually spelled one letter off or sometimes exactly the same. The shops we have recommended are the real deal. Ask for a visiting card (ie business card) – if the info doesn't match, you have been had.

➡ When negotiating with boatmen, confirm the price *and* currency before setting out. They just love to say '100!' and then at the end claim they meant dollars or euros.

➡ Do not book unofficial guides, which most guesthouses hire. If you want a guide, go through UP Tourism (p402) to avoid most of the hassles above. If not, have fun shopping!

➡ Be wary of bhang lassis – these are made with hash (degraded cannabis) and can be very strong (robberies of intoxicated people have been reported).

Many guesthouses offer boat trips, although they're more expensive than dealing with the boatmen directly. Brown Bread Bakery (p400) can arrange a hassle-free ride in their own boats for less than riverside (₹150 per hour for one person, ₹50 per hour per additional person) with some à la carte coffee and cakes to boot.

Aarna Spa   MASSAGE
(Map p392; ☑0542-2508465; www.hotelsuryavns. com; Hotel Surya, S-20/51A-5 The Mall Rd; massage from ₹1400; ⏰8am-8pm) Hotel Surya's spa is a nice choice for soothing Ayurvedic massages.

Swasthya Vardhak   AYURVEDA
(Map p394; ☑0543-2312504; www.swasthyavard-hak.com; Assi Crossing; ⏰8am-8pm) Varanasi is full of Ayurvedic imposters. Serious seekers should come here, the city's real deal Ayurvedic pharmacy. Consultations with a doctor are free; prescriptions from the 500 stocked medicines run from ₹20 to ₹2000. Additionally, it works with a government initiative that encourages struggling local farmers to turn over a new leaf planting Ayurvedic herbs.

Volunteering

Learn for Life Society   VOLUNTEERING
(Map p392; ☑2390040; www.learn-for-life.net; D55/147 Aurangabad) This small charity, run by two foreigners and contacted through Brown Bread Bakery (p400), has established a small school for disadvantaged children and a women's empowerment group, offering fairly paid work to local women, some of whom are mothers of the school's students.

The women make produce such as jams and muesli, which are available at the bakery. Pop into Brown Bread's Infocentre nightly at 7pm when representatives meet interested travellers. No cash donations.

Courses

Yoga Training Centre   YOGA
(Map p394; ☑9919857895; www.yogatrainingcen-tre.com; 5/15 Sakarkand Gali; 2hr class ₹300, reiki from ₹800; ⏰8am, 10am & 4pm) Former Army clerk and yoga master Sunil Kumar and partners run set classes three times a day on the 2nd and 3rd floors of this small backstreet building near Meer Ghat (but you can drop-in anytime for a session). He teaches an integrated blend of hatha, shivananda, satyananda, pranayama and Iyengar, and serious students can continue on certificate and diploma courses in both yoga and reiki.

Pragati Hindi   LANGUAGE
(Map p394; ☑9335376488; www.pragatihindi.com; B-7/176 Harar Bagh) Readers recommend the flexibility of the one-to-one classes taught here by the amiable Rajeswar Mukherjee (Raju). Private classes start from ₹300 per hour. Call ahead, or just drop in, to meet Raju and arrange a schedule. Walk up the stairs opposite Chowki Ghat and take the first left, following the "Hindi" signs.

International Music
Centre Ashram   INDIAN MUSIC
(Map p394; ☑0542-2452302; keshavaraonayak@ hotmail.com; D33/81 Khalishpura; per hour ₹300-400) This family-run centre is hidden in the tangle of backstreets off Bengali Tola. It offers sitar, tabla, flute and classical-dance tuition, and performances are held every Saturday and Wednesday evening at 8pm (₹150). There's a small, easy-to-miss sign on Bengali Tola directing you here.

If you can't find it, there are loads of **musical instrument shops** (Map p394) on Bengali Tola, many of which offer tuition.

International Centre   VARIOUS
(Map p392; ☑0542-2368130; www.bhu.ac.in; C/3/3 Tagore House; ⏰10am-5pm Mon-Sat) If you're interested in studying at Benares Hindu University, contact this centre. Courses on offer include Hindi, Sanskrit, and yoga, among others.

Tours

If time is short, UP Tourism (p402) can arrange guided tours by taxi of the major sites, including a 5.30am boat ride and an afternoon trip to Sarnath.

★ Varanasi Walks   WALKING
(☑8795576225; www.varanasiwalks.com; tours ₹1600-2000) The cultural walks on offer from this foreigner-run agency specialising in themed walks explore beyond the most popular ghats and temples. Walks are usually available on a reservation basis and can be booked online. Five of the eight guides were born and raised in Varanasi. It's a truly fascinating way to explore beyond the Old City.

Sleeping

The majority of Varanasi's budget hotels – and some midrange gems – are concentrated in the tangle of narrow streets back from the ghats along the River Ganges. There's a concentration around Assi Ghat, while others are in the crazy, bustling northern stretch of alleys between Scindhia and Meer Ghat, part of an area we refer to as the Old City, though at time of writing, city officials had marked numerous unlicensed ghat-side options, including some of our favourites, for demolition (whether it's carried out is another matter but 73 structures had been knocked down at time of writing). Check ahead for the current situation.

For those that prefer five-star luxury or aren't fussed about sleeping next to the river, there are some great choices in the neighbourhoods west of the river, such as Bhelpura, Aurangabad Rd and Cantonment.

Varanasi has an active paying-guesthouse scheme with more than 150 family homes available for accommodation from ₹150 to ₹900 a night (most are under ₹400). UP Tourism has a full list.

Old City Area

★ Ganpati Guesthouse
GUESTHOUSE $

(Map p394; ☎0542-2390057; www.ganpatiguesthouse.com; 3/24 Meer Ghat; r/tr with AC ₹1350/1686, with view ₹3935-5510; ❄@🛜) This old red-brick favourite has a pleasant, shaded courtyard as well as plenty of balcony space dotted around offering fine river views. Newly madeover rooms, even in the cheapest category, are clean, brightly painted from the ceilings down and feature tasteful framed wall hangings and modern bathrooms.

Six new rooms replacing space once occupied by reception are exquisite with silent split air-con – topped by Nos 12 and 13, the best of the bunch. Another seven new rooms are in an annexed building down the alley – best avoided as you're detached from the ambiance. Be *very* wary of the aggressive monkeys – one ran off with a chunk of someone's skin in its mouth during our visit!

Hotel Alka
GUESTHOUSE $

(Map p394; ☎0542-2401681; www.hotelalkavns.com; 3/23 Meer Ghat; r ₹650-1349, with AC ₹1574-5733, s/d without bathroom ₹600/700; ❄@🛜) This excellent ghat-side option could use an attentive eye on its exteriors, but the pretty much spotless rooms, either opening onto, or overlooking, a large, plant-filled courtyard or the Ganges, draw the lion's share of care here. In the far corner, a terrace juts out over Meer Ghat for one of the best views in all of Varanasi, a view shared from the balconies of eight of the pricier rooms.

Teerth Guesthouse
GUESTHOUSE $

(Map p394; ☎0542-2400741; www.teerthguesthouse.com; 8/9 Kalika Gali; r ₹800, without bathroom ₹350, with AC ₹950; ❄🛜) This inner core guesthouse is a pleasant diversion from the undesirable maze of alleyways that lead to it. For the price, it's considerably clean and the 27 rooms, on the smaller size, are quiet and confined from surrounding chaos. The marble-laced lobby hogs a load of sunlight through the open atrium and there's Old City views from the underused rooftop.

Vishnu Rest House
GUESTHOUSE $

(Map p394; ☎0542-2450206; D24/17 Pandhey Ghat; dm ₹90-100, s/d from ₹250/40, r with view ₹1200; @🛜) Accessed through a small courtyard with family homes coming off it, or directly from Pandhey Ghat itself, this simple Vishnu-blue guesthouse offers poky rooms that aren't the cleanest, but the atmosphere is friendly and the stone terrace overlooking the ghat is a winner. Free wi-fi and 24-hour hot water in winter.

Eden Halt
GUESTHOUSE $

(Map p394; ☎0542-2454612; dtripathi23@yahoo.co.in; D25/21-22 Ganga Mahal, Raja Ghat; s/d from ₹250/400; @🛜) We are not as bowled over by this dead-simple, pocket-sized guesthouse as many travellers, but the four rooms (two have private bathrooms, two have river views) here are spacious, some with interesting alcoves and built-in shelving. A roof terrace overlooks peaceful Raja Ghat, but be prepared to fight monkeys for space on it.

★ Homestay
HOMESTAY $$

(Map p392; ☎9415449348; www.homestayvaranasi.in; 61/16 Sidhgiri Bagh; s ₹2300-2800, d ₹2500-3000; ❄@🛜) This homestay in a 1936 colonial-era home in a residential neighbourhood 1.5km from the Old City back alleys is a true catch. Good-hearted host Harish, a 30-year veteran of the textile industry (well-regarded, fixed-price shop on premises) has six exquisitely maintained deluxe and enormous super deluxe rooms that are shielded from light, noise and mosquitoes. You'll truly appreciate the rest. His wife, Malika, whips up exquisite home-cooked meals and has been known to give impromptu cooking classes.

Kedareswar
HOTEL $$

(Map p394; ☎0542-2455568; www.kedareswarguesthouse.com; B14/1 Chowki Ghat; r ₹1400, with AC ₹2800, all incl breakfast; ❄@🛜) Housed in a brightly painted, aquamarine green building, this friendly six-room place has cramped but immaculate rooms with sparkling bathrooms. Breakfast is served on the rooftop when it's not too hot or rainy. There's only two cheaper non-AC rooms, so it might be worth phoning ahead. Chowki Ghat is right beside Kedar Ghat.

Rashmi Guest House HOTEL $$$

(Map p394; ☑ 0542-2402778; www.rashmiguesthouse.com; 16/28A Man Mandir Ghat; r incl breakfast ₹2810-6700; ✳@🖥) Fragrant white-tiled corridors and marble staircases lead to a variety of cramped but smart rooms boasting high marks for cleanliness and modernity (many have views of Man Mandir Ghat). Dolphin (p400), the hotel's rooftop restaurant, is a fine place for a beer-chased evening meal (emphasis on Kingfisher, not culinary catharsis) and one of the Old City's few nonveg options.

Assi Ghat Area

★ Stops Hostel HOSTEL $

(Map p392; ☑ 9506118025; www.stopshostels.com; B20/47A2, Vijaya Nagaram Colony; tent Nov-Feb ₹250, dm from ₹350, d with AC ₹950, incl breakfast; ✳@🖥) A true hostel has landed in Varanasi in a four-story residential mansion 2km or so from Assi Ghat. Dorms in six-, eight- and 12-bed variations are livened up by colourful lockers, and there's ample hang spaces on various floors that cultivate the right vibe – a previously scarce atmosphere in much of India. The few privates are basic; the real coup here are the dorms, common areas and the rooftop showers, each uniquely painted by various artistic volunteers. The hostel plans all sorts of activities (from cooking classes to city tours), many of which are free save gratuities. It's a solid choice for the socially inclined – required training for staff includes legging it around India for a few weeks to gain traveller perspective.

Sahi River View Guesthouse GUESTHOUSE $

(Map p394; ☑ 0542-2366730; www.sahiriverview.co.in; B1/158 Assi Ghat; s/d ₹400/650, r with AC from ₹1250, all incl breakfast; ✳@🖥) There's a huge variety of rooms at this friendly place, which is better than it looks from the entrance down a side alley. Most rooms are good quality and clean, and some have interesting private balconies. Each floor has a pleasant communal seating area with river view, creating a great feeling of space throughout.

★ Hotel Ganges View HOTEL $$$

(Map p394; ☑ 0542-2313218; www.hotelgangesview.com; Assi Ghat; r with AC ₹4500-6500; ✳@🖥) Simply gorgeous, this beautifully restored and maintained colonial-style house overlooking Assi Ghat is crammed with books, artwork and antiques. Rooms are spacious and immaculate and there are some charming communal areas in which to sit and relax, including a lovely 1st-floor garden terrace. Book ahead.

Palace on Ganges HOTEL $$$

(Map p394; ☑ 0542-2315050; www.palaceonganges.com; B1/158 Assi Ghat; r ₹8993; ✳@🖥) Each of the 24 rooms (the four river views are first-come, first-served) in this immaculate heritage accommodation is individually themed on a regional Indian style, using antique furnishings and colourful design themes. The colonial, Rajasthan and Jodhpur rooms are the best, though the lingering waff of insecticide indicates you might encounter some unwanted roommates.

WelcomHeritage Jukaso Ganges HERITAGE HOTEL $$$

(Map p392; www.welcomheritagehotels.in; CK/14, Patni Tola Chowk; s/d incl breakfast ₹11,242/13,490; ✳@🖥) This exclusive 15 room retreat is the Old City's first truly luxury option, a 700-year-old renovated *haveli* (traditional, ornately decorated residence) sitting dominion over Guleria Ghat with choice river views. Rooms of various sizes are spread among among several floors (only a few on each), so it never feels crowded.

But the common spaces – various courtyards and patios that wrangle in those postcard river views – are the real coup, highlighted by a breezy ghatside cafe and a 2nd floor Vishnu temple.

Cantonment Area

Hotel Surya HOTEL $$

(Map p392; ☑ 0542-2508465; www.hotelsuryavns.com; S-20/51A-5 The Mall Rd; s/d incl breakfast from ₹2473/3035; ✳@🖥➤) Varanasi's cheapest hotel with a swimming pool, Surya has standard three-star Indian rooms, but a modern makeover in the superior and premium rooms means stylish new furnishings, upholsteries and the like.

Value here is palpable, as all is built around a huge lawn area that includes a colourful lounge-style bar and cafe flanked by a gorgeous, nearly 200-year-old heritage building (the former stomping grounds of a Nepali king), where the excellent-value Canton Royale (p401) is housed. There's also the good (but smoky) Sol Bar and the recommended Aarna Spa (p397).

Taj Gateway Hotel Ganges   HOTEL $$$

(Map p392; ☑0542-6660001; www.thegatewayhotels.com; Raja Bazaar Rd; r from ₹14,062; ❋@☎☞≋) Varanasi's best hotel is on nearly 2 hectares of beautiful gardens with fruit trees, a tennis court, a pool, an outdoor yoga centre and the old maharaja's guesthouse. All the rooms were madeover between 2010 and 2013. There's little size difference between standard and deluxe categories, but the latter are far classier with refined art on the walls and more soothing colour schemes (a rich turquoise, for example). Service is expectedly top class and there are two fine restaurants, two bars and two spa treatment rooms (massages from ₹3000).

✗ Eating

Look out for locally grown *langda aam* (mangoes) in summer or *sitafal* (custard apples) in autumn. *Singharas* are water chestnuts that are sold raw (green) or cooked (black) – be wary of the risk of intestinal parasites with the latter. Many places in the Old City shut during summer months due to unbearable humidity and water levels that often flood the ghats and around.

✗ Old City Area

Keshari Restaurant   INDIAN $

(Map p394; 14/8 Godaulia; mains ₹35-170; ☉9.30am-11pm) Known as much for excellent cuisine as surly service, this atmospheric spot (carved wood panelling dons the walls and ceilings) has been famously at it for nearly a half-century. Indians pack in here for high-quality veg from all over India – a dizzying array of dishes are on offer (over 40 paneer curries alone).

Those who like to dance with the devil should spring for the paneer Kadahi (spicy tomato-based gravy), sure to make your nose run. Do not confuse it with the less-desirable Keshari Ruchiker Byanjan around the corner on Dashashwamedh Rd.

Ayyar's Cafe   SOUTH INDIAN $

(Map p394; Dashashwamedh Rd; mains ₹2-100; ☉9.30am-7pm) Excellent, no-nonsense choice off the tourist beaten path for South Indian masala *dosa* (₹40), and its spicier cousin, the Mysore *dosa* (₹90); and one of the few cheapies to serve filtered coffee. It's tucked away at the end of a very short alley signed 'New Keshari Readymade'.

Dosa Cafe   SOUTH INDIAN $

(Map p394; 15/49 Man Mandir; dosas ₹20-150; ☉9am-9pm) This easy-to-miss three-table cafe woos travelers with Chef Ranjana's out-of-the-box South Indian preparations (chocolate *idli*, *dosa* with ratatouille, spinach or fruit) and won us over with their choice of oil: pick from refined soybean oil (no), butter (maybe), ghee (maybe) or olive oil (yes!). Creative, progressive and tasty.

★ Brown Bread Bakery   MULTICUISINE $$

(Map p394; ☑9838888823; www.brownbreadbakery.com; 5/127 Tripura Bhairavi; mains ₹110-445; ☉7am-10pm; ☎) ✐ This restaurant and organic shop's fabulous menu includes more than 40 varieties of European-quality cheese and more than 30 types of bread, cookies and cakes. The ambience – with seating on cushions around low tables on the nonsmoking bottom floor, expansive views from the rooftop patio and live classical-music performances in the evenings – is spot on.

Pop in for the European breakfast buffet (7am to noon; ₹400), a hearty burger or just for a chai and respite from the heat and hassle. Part of the profits go to the charity Learn for Life (p397). Warning: not to be confused with the location across the street, abandoned by Micha, the 5th-generation German baker. If there are not four floors and a rooftop and the phone number doesn't match, you're in the wrong place.

Dolphin Restaurant   INDIAN $$

(Rashmi Guest House; Map p394; 16/28A Man Mandir Ghat; mains ₹110-325; ☉7am-10pm) The atmosphere trumps the food at Dolphin – the rooftop restaurant at Rashmi Guest House (p399) – which is perched high above Man Mandir Ghat, but it's still a fine place for an evening meal. The breezy balcony is the most refined table in the Old City and one of the few that serves nonveg as well.

Lotus Lounge   MULTICUISINE $$

(Map p394; D14/27 Mansarowar Ghat; mains ₹50-260; ☉8.30am-10pm; ☎) The food doesn't move mountains, but Lotus is a supremely great place to chill while walking the ghats. Its terrace, full of lounge cushions and tatami mats, juts right over Mansarowar Ghat. Free wi-fi.

Assi Ghat Area

Aum Cafe
CAFE **$**

(Map p394; www.touchoflight.us; B1/201 Assi Ghat; mains ₹60-180; ⊗7am-3.30pm Tue-Sun; 🕾) ✦
Run by a hippie dippie American woman who has been coming to India for more than 20 years, this colourful cafe has breakfast all day (good lemon pancakes!), astounding lemon and organic green tea lassis and a handful of light sandwiches and mains that offer a curry respite.

★Open Hand
CAFE **$$**

(Map p392; www.openhand.in; 1/128-3 Dumraub Bagh; breakfasts ₹105-210; ⊗8am-8pm Mon-Sat; 🕾) ✦ This shoes-off cafe-cum–gift shop serves the best espresso and French Press we had in India, as well as a range of excellent muffins, pancakes, muesli and juices that will delight you to no end. Take breakfast on the narrow balcony or lounge around the former home all day on the free wi-fi. There's also a large selection of gorgeous handicrafts (jewellery, toys, clothing) made in the local community. Couldn't be more pleasant.

Cantonment Area

Canton Royale
INDIAN **$$**

(Map p392; www.hotelsuryavns.com; S-20/51A-5 The Mall Rd; mains ₹190-380; ⊗11am-11pm) Housed in a nearly 200-year-old heritage building, Hotel Surya's excellent main restaurant has a colonial elegance, and on warm evenings you can eat out on the large lawn. Value for money, it's one of the best of Varanasi's top-end choices, offering a global hodgepodge that extends from Mexican and Thai to Chinese and Continental.

But really, it's the Indian that's excellent, including a wonderful thali (₹300 to ₹350).

Eden Restaurant
INDIAN **$$**

(Map p392; www.hotelpradeep.com; Jagatganj, Hotel Pradeep; mains ₹175-325; ⊗6am-11pm) Hotel Pradeep's rooftop dining space, complete with garden, manicured lawns and wrought-iron furniture, is a very pleasant place for a candle-lit evening meal. The good-quality Indian menu comes from the lobby-level Poonam restaurant.

🍷 Drinking & Nightlife

Wine and beer shops are dotted discreetly around the city, usually away from the river. Note that it is frowned upon to drink alcohol on or near the holy Ganges, and liquor laws regarding proximity of temples insure nobody is licensed, but rooftops here can usually discreetly fashion up a beer. For bars, head to midrange and top-end hotels away from the ghats.

There's nightly live **Indian classical music** at Brown Bread Bakery (p400).

The International Music Centre Ashram (p397) has small **performances** (₹150) on Wednesday and Saturday evenings.

Prinsep Bar
BAR

(Map p392; www.tajhotels.com; Gateway Hotel Ganges, Raja Bazaar Rd; ⊗noon-11pm Mon-Sat, to midnight Sun) For a quiet drink with a dash of history, try this tiny bar named after James Prinsep who drew wonderful illustrations of Varanasi's ghats and temples.

Mangi Ferra
CAFE

(Map p392; www.hotelsuryavns.com; S-20/51A-5 The Mall Rd; ⊗11am-11pm) This colourful, laidback lounge in the garden at Hotel Surya (p399) is a relaxing place where you can sip on espresso (₹50) or cocktail (₹150 to ₹480).

UTTAR PRADESH VARANASI

NO 1 LASSI IN ALL VARANASI

Your long, thirsty search for the best lassi in India is over. Look no further than **Blue Lassi** (Map p394; lassis ₹25-85; ⊗9am-10.30pm; 🕾), a tiny, hole-in-the-wall yoghurt shop that has been churning out the freshest, creamiest, fruit-filled lassis since 1925. The grandson of the original owner still works here, sitting by his lassi-mixing cauldron in front of a small room with wooden benches for customers and walls plastered with messages from happy drinkers. There are over 80 delicious flavour combos, divided by section – plain, banana, apple, pomegranate, mango, papaya, strawberry, blueberry, coconut and saffron – we think banana and apple, the latter flecked with fresh apple shreds, just about top the long list (what the hell, make it banana-apple!). The whole scene here is surreal: the lassi takes ages to arrive while club-like tunes burrow into the eardrums of a UN-rivaling group of thirsty nationalities; when it does, it's handed off to you with the care of a priceless work of art as the deceased are carried by the front of the shop on the way to Burning Ghat (Manikarnika). *Namaste!*

🛍 Shopping

Varanasi is justifiably famous for silk brocades and beautiful Benares saris, but don't believe much of what the silk salesmen tell you about the relative quality of products, even in government emporiums. Instead, shop around and judge for yourself.

Varanasi is also a good place to shop for sitars (ranging from ₹6000 to ₹60,000) and tablas (from ₹5000 to ₹15,000). The cost depends primarily on the type of wood used. Mango is cheapest (and cracks or warps correspondingly), while black shisham or mahogany are of the highest quality. Serious buyers should be sure to double-check their chosen wood isn't banned for export.

★ Baba Blacksheep   SILK

(Map p394; www.babablacksheep.co; B12/120A9, Bhelpura; ⊙9am-8pm) If the deluge of traveller enthusiasm is anything to go by, this is the most trustworthy, non-pushy shop in India. Indeed it is one of the best places you'll find for silks (scarves/saris from ₹400/3500) and *pashminas* (shawls from ₹1500).

Prices are fixed (though unmarked) and the friendly owner refuses to play the commission game, so autorickshaws and taxis don't like to come here (ignore anyone who says you cannot drive here). It's located at Bhelpura crossing under the mosque. It's not the cheapest (Indians find better deals elsewhere), but it's a pleasant experience.

Mehrotra Silk Factory   SILK

(Map p392; www.mehrotrasilk.in; 21/72 Englishia Line; ⊙10am-8pm) Tucked away down a tiny alleyway near the main train station, this pocket-sized, fixed-priced shop is a fun place to buy silk scarves (from ₹400), saris (from ₹3000) and bedspread sets (from ₹9000). The Lal Ghat location (Map p392; www.mehrotrasilk.in; 4/8A Lal Ghat; ⊙10am-8pm) is more convenient for Old City shoppers.

Organic by Brown Bread Bakery   COSMETICS

(Map p394; www.brownbreadbakery.com; 2/225 Shivali; ⊙7am-8pm; ☎) 🍃 This small shop sells natural and natural cosmetics from the government-sponsored Khadi program and select foodstuffs to go, as well as baked goods, fresh juices and coffee from Brown Bread Bakery's lengthier Old City menu.

Shri Gandhi Ashram Khadi   CLOTHING

(Map p392; Sankat Mochan Rd; ⊙10am-7.30pm) Stocks shirts, kurta pyjamas, saris and head scarves, all made from the famous home-spun *khadi* fabric.

ℹ Information

Varanasi is pretty wired – even Blue Lassi (p401) has wi-fi! Some charge. Many don't. Internet cafes are everywhere, charging around ₹20 per hour. There are several ATMs scattered around town, including State Bank of India in the lobby as you exit the train station.

Heritage Hospital (Map p392; ☑ 0562-2369996; www.heritagehospitals.in; Lanka) English-speaking staff; 24-hour pharmacy.

Main Post Office (GPO; Map p392; www.indiapost.gov.in; Visheshwarganj; ⊙10am-6pm Mon-Sat) Best PO for sending parcels abroad.

Point (Map p394; B1/156 Assi Ghat Rd; per hour ₹30; ⊙7am-10pm) Friendly internet.

Tourist Police (Map p392; UP Tourism office, Varanasi Junction train station; ⊙5am-9pm) Tourist police wear sky-blue uniforms.

UP Tourism (Map p392; ☑ 0543-2506670; www.up-tourism.com; Varanasi Junction Train Station; ⊙9am-7pm) The patient Mr Umashankar at the office inside the train station has been dishing out reasonably impartial information to arriving travellers for years; he's a mine of knowledge, so this is a requisite first stop if you arrive here by train. Get the head's up on autorickshaw prices, the best trains for your travels, details on Varanasi's paying-guesthouse scheme or arrange a guided tour.

ℹ Getting There & Away

AIR

Lal Bahadur Shashtri Airport, 24km north of town, is served by **Jet Airways** (www.jetairways.com; Lal Bahadur Shastri Airport), with direct flights to Delhi (from ₹4732, daily), Kolkata (from ₹4266, daily) and Khajuraho (from ₹4266, daily); and **Air India** (www.airindia.com; Airlines Bhavan 52, Yadunath Marg) to Delhi (from ₹4585, daily), Mumbai (from ₹4424, daily), Agra (from ₹2528, Monday, Wednesday and Saturday), Khajuraho (from ₹2528, Monday, Thursday and Saturday) and Kathmandu (from ₹10,947, Tuesday, Thursday, Friday and Sunday). Thai Airways flies to Bangkok (from ₹13,033, daily except Wednesday and Friday).

Other airlines are based at the airport include IndiGo and SpiceJet.

BUS

The main **bus stand** (Map p392) is opposite Varanasi Junction train station. Lucknow Volvo AC buses can be reserved in advance at a dedicated ticket window at the station.

Allahabad ₹116, three hours, every 30 minutes, 4am-10pm

Faizabad ₹191, seven hours, daily at 7am, 11.30am, noon and 2pm

Gorakhpur ₹185, seven hours, every 30 minutes, 4am-10pm

HANDY TRAINS FROM VARANASI (BSB)

DESTINATION	TRAIN NO & NAME	FARE (₹)	DURATION (HR)	DEPARTURES
Agra	13237/13239 PNBE Kota Exp	355/950/1365 (A)	13	4.40pm
Allahabad	15159 Sarnath Exp	140/485/690 (A)	3	12.25pm
Gorakhpur	15003 Chaurichaura Exp	170/485/690 (A)	6½	12.40am
Jabalpur	11062/11066 MFP/DBG-LTT Exp	285/755/1185 (A)	10½	11.20pm
Khajuraho	21108 BSB-Kurj Link E	265/715 (B)	12	5.45pm*
Kolkata (Howrah)	12334 Vibhuti Exp	415/1095/1555 (A)	14	6.08pm
Lucknow	14235 BSB-BE Exp	210/565 (B)	7¼	11.40pm
New Delhi	12561 Swatantra S Exp	415/1095/1555 (A)	12½	12.40am

Fares: (A) sleeper/3AC/2AC, *Mon, Wed, Sat only; (B) sleeper/3AC

Lucknow Non-AC ₹265, 7½ hours, every 30 minutes, 4am-11pm; Volvo AC ₹720, 7½ hours, 8am and 10.30pm

TRAIN

Luggage theft has been reported on trains to and from Varanasi so you should take extra care. Reports of drugged food and drink aren't uncommon, so it's probably still best to politely decline any offers from strangers.

Varanasi Junction, also known as Varanasi Cantonment (Cantt), is the main station.

There are several daily trains to Allahabad, Gorakhpur and Lucknow. A few daily trains leave for New Delhi and Kolkata, but only two daily trains go to Agra. The direct train to Khajuraho only runs on Monday, Wednesday and Saturday. On other days, go via Satna, a much larger rail transit hub from where you can catch buses to Khajuraho (₹120, 4 hours, 6.30am and 2.20pm).

Foreign Tourist Centre (Map p392; ☺8am-1.50pm & 2-8pm Mon-Sat, 8am-2pm Sun) Foreign tourist quota tickets must be purchased at the Foreign Tourist Centre, a ticket counter just past the UP Tourism office, on your right as you exit the Varanasi Junction train station.

❶ Getting Around

TO/FROM THE AIRPORT

An autorickshaw to the airport in Babatpur, 22km northwest of the city, costs ₹350. A taxi is about ₹840.

BICYCLE

You can hire bikes (per day ₹20) from a small **cycle repair shop** (Map p394; ☎7860154166; 1/105 Assi-Dham; ☺8am-7pm) near Assi Ghat.

CYCLE-RICKSHAW

A small ride – up to 2km – costs ₹50. Rough prices from Godaulia Crossing include: Assi Ghat ₹50, Benares Hindu University ₹60 and Varanasi Junction train station ₹60.

TAXI & AUTORICKSHAW

Prepaid booths for autorickshaws and taxis are directly outside Varanasi Junction train station and give you a good benchmark for prices around town, though it doesn't work as well as some other cities as there are usually no officials policing it.

First pay an administration charge (₹5 for autorickshaws, ₹10 for taxis) at the booth then take a ticket which you give to your driver, along with the fare, once you've reached your destination. Note that taxis and autorickshaws cannot access the Dashashwamedh Ghat area between the hours of 9am and 9pm due to high pedestrian traffic. You'll be dropped at Godaulia Crossing and will need to walk the remaining 400m or so to the entrance of the Old City; or 700m or so all the way to Dashashwamedh Ghat. During banned hours, autorickshaws line-up near Godaulia Crossing at a stand on Luxa Rd.

Sample fares:

Airport auto/taxi ₹225/650
Assi Ghat auto/taxi ₹90/300
Godaulia Crossing auto/taxi ₹95/250
Sarnath auto/taxi ₹120/400
Half-day tour (four hours) taxi ₹500
Full-day tour (eight hours) taxi ₹900

Autorickshaws do not have a half/full day tour scheme. Shared autos to Assi Ghat (₹15) and Benares University (₹15) leave from Mandapur Rd and Durgakund Rd, respectively.

SARNATH

☎0542

Buddha came to Sarnath to preach his message of the middle way to nirvana after he achieved enlightenment at Bodhgaya and gave his famous first sermon here. In the 3rd century BC, emperor Ashoka had magnificent stupas and monasteries erected

Sarnath

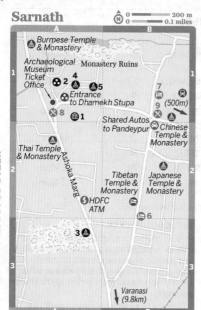

N
0 ———————— 200 m
0 ———————— 0.1 miles

Sarnath

⊙ Sights

🛏 Sleeping

✗ Eating

here as well as an engraved pillar. When Chinese traveller Xuan Zang dropped by in AD 640, Sarnath boasted a 100m-high stupa and 1500 monks living in large monasteries. However, soon after, Buddhism went into decline and, when Muslim invaders sacked the city in the late 12th century, Sarnath disappeared altogether. It was 'rediscovered' by British archaeologists in 1835.

Today it's one of the four key sites on the Buddhist circuit (along with Bodhgaya, Kushinagar and Lumbini in Nepal) and attracts followers from around the world, especially on Purnima (Buddha's birthday), when Buddha's life, death and enlightenment are celebrated, usually in April or May.

⊙ Sights

Purnima, Buddha's birthday, is celebrated with particular zeal in Sarnath, with a large fair and procession of Buddha relics.

Dhamekh Stupa & Monastery Ruins
BUDDHIST SACRED SITE

(Indian/foreigner ₹5/100, video ₹25; ⊙ dawn–dusk) Set in a peaceful park of monastery ruins is the impressive 34m Dhamekh Stupa, which marks the spot where the Buddha preached his first sermon. The floral and geometric carvings are 5th century AD, but some of the brickwork dates back as far as 200 BC.

Nearby is the 3rd-century BC Ashoka Pillar, with an edict engraved on it. It once stood 15m tall and had the famous four-lion capital (now in the museum), but all that remains now are five fragments of its base.

Chaukhandi Stupa
BUDDHIST SACRED SITE

(⊙ dawn–dusk) This large ruined stupa dates back to the 5th century AD, and marks the spot where Buddha met his first disciples. The incongruous tower on top of the stupa is Mughal and was constructed in the 16th century for the visit of Emperor Humayun.

Mulgandha Kuti Vihar
BUDDHIST TEMPLE

(camera/video ₹20/100; ⊙ 4-11.30am & 1.30-8pm) This modern temple was completed in 1931 by the Mahabodhi Society. Buddha's first sermon is chanted daily, starting between 6pm and 7pm depending on the season. A bodhi tree growing outside was transplanted in 1931 from the tree in Anuradhapura, Sri Lanka, which in turn is said to be the offspring of the original tree in Bodhgaya.

Archaeological Museum
MUSEUM

(admission ₹5; ⊙ 9am-5pm) This modernised, 100-year-old sandstone museum houses wonderfully displayed ancient treasures such as the very well preserved 3rd-century BC lion capital from the Ashoka Pillar, which has been adopted as India's national emblem, and a huge 2000-year-old stone umbrella, ornately carved with Buddhist symbols.

🛏 Sleeping & Eating

Jain Paying Guest House
GUESTHOUSE $

(☎ 0543-2595621; www.visitsarnath.com; d ₹500, without bathroom ₹450; 🛜) This simple, good-value guesthouse is run by a friendly doctor of geography, whose wife whips up home-cooked pure veg thalis (₹150). The five rooms are rustic but spacious (with mosquito window screen). Prices drop to ₹300 between April and September.

Agrawal Paying Guest House GUESTHOUSE $$
(☑0542-2595316; agrawalpg@gmail.com; Sn 14/94, Agrawal Kunj; r ₹700-800, with AC ₹1400; ❄🖧) Peaceful place with a refined owner and spotless marble-floored rooms overlooking a large garden.

Vaishali Restaurant INDIAN, CHINESE $
(mains ₹40-230; ◷8am-9pm) Large and modern 1st-floor restaurant serving mostly Indian dishes, but some Chinese. Best in town.

Green Hut INDIAN, CHINESE $
(meals ₹40-190; ◷8.30am-8.30pm) A breezy open-sided cafe-restaurant offering snacks, thalis (₹90 to ₹140) and Chinese dishes.

ℹ Information

Power cuts mean internet cafes are unreliable, but there are a few in town.

ℹ Getting There & Away

Local buses to Sarnath (₹15, 40 minutes) pass in front of Varanasi Junction train station, but you may wait a long time for one. A prepaid autorickshaw costs ₹120 from Varanasi Junction train station (use that as your bargaining base if you catch one from the Old City). On the way back, you can snag a lift in a shared auto or *vikram* (₹15) to Pandeypur, where you'll need to switch to another shared auto to Benia Bagh (₹15), which is just a ₹20 cycle rickshaw ride from Godaulia. Some trains running between Varanasi and Gorakhpur also stop here. Trains for Sarnath leave Varanasi Junction at 7am, 11.30am and 1.20pm. Returning to Varanasi, trains leave Sarnath at 9am, 7.30pm and 9.50pm.

GORAKHPUR

☑0551 / POP 623,000

There's little to see in Gorakhpur itself, but this well-connected transport hub is a short hop from the pilgrimage centre of Kushinagar – the place where Buddha died – making it a possible stopover on the road between Varanasi and Nepal.

🛏 Sleeping & Eating

There are loads of standard-issue hotels across from the railway station.

Hotel Adarsh Palace HOTEL $
(☑0551-2201912; hotel.adarshpalace@rediffmail.com; Railway Station Rd; dm ₹250, r from ₹550,

ℹ GETTING TO NEPAL

From Varanasi's bus stand there are regular services to Sunauli (₹293, 10 hours, every 30 minutes, 4am to 11pm).

By train, go to Gorakhpur then transfer to a Sunauli bus.

Air India has four weekly flights to Kathmandu (from ₹10,947). Nepali visas are available on arrival.

with air-cooler ₹750, with AC from ₹950; ❄) One of the better budget hotels opposite the train station, 200m to the left as you exit. It's friendly and basic but with something for everyone: a 10-bed dorm with lockers above each bed, cheap singles with TV and bathroom, and there are some decent-quality aircon rooms. Checkout is 24 hours.

Chowdhry Sweet House MULTICUISINE, DESSERTS $
(Cinema Rd; mains ₹50-200; ◷7am-11pm) This bi-level madhouse is packed with locals taking in an extensive array of delicious Indian and Chinese veg dishes in a diner atmosphere, including ginormous *dosas* and excellent thalis (₹150 to ₹210). It specialises in sundaes, too, and there is a tasty boatload from which to choose. It's a ₹30 cycle-rickshaw ride from the railway station.

Mirch Masala DHABA $
(mains ₹30-200; ◷8am-1am) One of the better, cleaner *dhabas* opposite the railway station. It does good thalis (₹45 to ₹130), can pack food to go and is open late. The friendly owner tends to dote on foreigners.

ℹ Information

There are State Bank of India ATMs in the train station parking lot and across from Adarsh Palace.

For the main bus stand, come out of the train station and keep walking straight for about 400m. For Varanasi buses you need the Katchari bus stand, about 3km further south.

Varden Cyber Hut (per hour ₹20; ◷9am-11pm) Internet cafe opposite the train station, below Hotel Varden.

ℹ Getting There & Away

Frequent bus services run from the main bus stand to Faizabad (₹145, 3½ hours, every 30 minutes), Kushinagar (₹53, two hours, every 30 minutes) and Sunauli (₹90, three hours, hourly), along with Volvo AC buses to Lucknow (₹718, six hours, 9am, 11am and 10pm). Faster collective cars and jeeps leave for Sunauli when full between 5am and 6pm, directly across from the train station (per person ₹150 to ₹300, two hours).

Buses to Varanasi (₹185, seven hours, express at 7.30am then hourly 10am to 10pm) leave from the Katchari bus stand, as do buses to Allahabad (₹243, 10 hours, express at 7am, then hourly 10am to 10pm).

There are four daily trains (five on Tuesday and Thursday, and six on Saturday) from big and bustling Gorakhpur Junction to Varanasi (sleeper/3AC/2AC ₹170/485/610, 5½ hours), including one slower, cheaper night train (55149 Gkp Muv Pass, seven hours, 11.10pm). A number of daily trains also leave for Lucknow (sleeper/3AC/2AC ₹220/535/735, five hours) and Delhi (₹430/1125/1605, 14 to 17 hours) and one for Agra Fort (19038 Avadh Express, ₹335/905/1295, 1.20pm, 14½ hours).

The train ticket reservation office is 500m from the train station; to the right of the station as you exit.

JetKonnect (www.jetkonnect.com) operates one daily flight from Delhi Monday to Saturday, but it is comparatively expensive.

KUSHINAGAR

☑ 05564 / POP 18,000

One of the four main pilgrimage sites marking Buddha's life – the others being Lumbini (Nepal), Bodhgaya and Sarnath – Kushinagar is where Buddha died. There are several peaceful, modern temples where you can stay, chat with monks or simply contemplate your place in the world, and there are three main historical sights, including the simple but wonderfully serene stupa where Buddha is said to have been cremated.

◉ Sights

In addition to the main principle ruins, Kusinagar's one road is lined with elaborate temples run by various Buddhist nations, many of which offer accommodations, sometimes to the public at large, sometimes only to pilgrims of their respective nations.

★**Mahaparinirvana Temple**   BUDDHIST TEMPLE
(Buddha Marg; ⊙ 6am-6pm) `FREE` The highlight of this modest temple, rebuilt in 1927 and set among extensive lawns and ancient excavated ruins with a circumambulatory path, is its serene 5th-century reclining Buddha, unearthed in 1876. Six metres long, it depicts Buddha on his ancient death-bed

and is one of the world's most moving Buddhist icons. Behind the temple is an ancient 19m-tall **stupa**, and in the surrounding park is a large **bell** erected by the Dalai Lama.

★**Ramabhar Stupa**   BUDDHIST SACRED SITE
Architecturally, this half-ruined, 15m-high stupa is little more than a large, dome-shaped clump of red bricks, but there is an unmistakable aura about this place which is hard to ignore. This is where Buddha's body is said to have been cremated and monks and pilgrims can often be seen meditating by the path that leads around the stupa.

★**Wat Thai Complex**   BUDDHIST TEMPLE
(☑ 9005007063; www.watthaikusinara-th.org; Buddha Marg; ⊙ 8am-9pm) Features an elaborate temple, beautifully maintained gardens with bonsai-style trees, a monastery and a temple containing a gilded Buddha. There's also a Sunday school and health clinic (across the street), each of which welcomes visitors. Unfortunately for the rest of us, rooms are reserved for Thai citizens only.

Buddha Museum   MUSEUM
(Buddha Marg; Indian/foreigner ₹3/10, photography ₹20; ⊙ 10.30am-4.30pm Tue-Sun) Exhibits Buddhist relics, sculptures and terracottas unearthed from the Kushinagar region, as well as some Tibetan *thangkas* (rectangular cloth paintings) and Mughal miniature paintings.

Mathakuar Temple   BUDDHIST TEMPLE
(Buddha Marg; ⊙ dawn-dusk) This small shrine, set among monastery ruins, marks the spot where Buddha is said to have made his final sermon and now houses a 3m-tall bluestone Buddha statue, thought to date from the 10th century AD.

🛏 Sleeping & Eating

Some of the temples, which have basic accommodation for pilgrims, also welcome tourists. Wat Thai is the most serene and beautiful, but only excepts Thai citizens.

Tibetan Temple   PILGRIMS' REST HOUSE $
(☑ 8795569357; Buddha Marg; d/tr ₹600/800) By far the nicest of the pilgrim accommodation offerings make this a great temple choice – some rooms are nicer than neighbouring hotels. There is also a dormitory offering beds by donation. Tibetan monks from Dharamsala do a one- to two-year managerial stint here and usually speak decent English.

Kushinagar

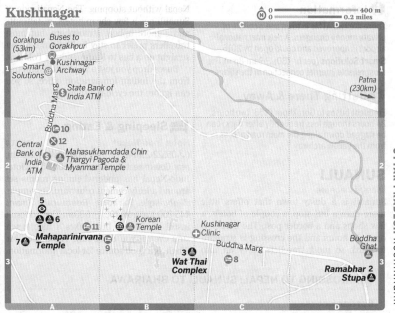

Kushinagar

◎ Top Sights
1 Mahaparinirvana Temple A3
2 Ramabhar Stupa D3
3 Wat Thai Complex B3

◎ Sights
4 Buddha Museum B3
5 Dalai Lama Bell A2
6 Maharparinirvana Stupa A3
7 Mathakuar Temple A3

🛏 Sleeping
8 Imperial Hotel C3
9 Japan-Sri Lanka Buddhist Centre B3
10 Linh Son Vietnam Chinese Temple A2
11 Tibetan Temple A3

🍴 Eating
12 Yama Cafe A2

Linh Son Vietnam Chinese Temple PILGRIMS' REST HOUSE $
(☑9936837270; www.linhsonnepalindiatemple.org; Buddha Marg; s/d/tr ₹400/550/800; ☎) Simple, clean triples with private bathroom, hot water and a rare wi-fi signal.

Japan-Sri Lanka Buddhist Centre PILGRIMS' REST HOUSE $
(☑9415312564; assajikushinagar@hotmail.com; Buddha Marg; tr/q ₹500/600) Set up for large groups (so call ahead). Decent-quality, clean rooms which technically are donation-only.

Imperial Hotel HOTEL $$$
(☑05564-273096; www.imperialhotel.com; Buddha Marg; s/d ₹6183/6745; ❉☎) This 44-room hotel is the flashpacker pilgrim's choice. With its breezy lobby, gleaming floors and modern rooms with flat-screen TVs, tubs and minibars, it's the nicest in the village.

★Yama Cafe MULTICUISINE $
(☑9956112749; Buddha Marg; mains ₹50-130; ⊙8am-8pm) Run by the welcoming Mr and Mrs Roy, this Kushinagar institution has a traveller-friendly menu which includes toast, omelettes, fried rice and *thukpa* (Tibetan noodle soup) and is the best place to come for information about the area. Ask about the so-called Holy Hike, a 13km-walk in the surrounding farmland, or give him a ring about other local information as well.

ℹ Information

There are two ATMs in town and a couple of private money changers. A new international airport is approved and *could* open by 2016.
Smart Solutions (per hr ₹30; ☺9am-8pm) The most reliable internet connection in the village.

ℹ Getting There & Away

Frequent buses to Gorakhpur (₹53, two hours, 24 hours though less frequently after dark) can be flagged down along the main road across from the yellow archway.

SUNAULI

🗹 05522 / POP 696

Sunauli is a dusty town that offers little more than a bus stop, a couple of hotels, a few shops and a border post. The border is open 24 hours and the crossing is straightforward, so most travellers carry on into Nepal without stopping. The Nepali side of Sunauli has a few cheap hotels, restaurants and a more upbeat atmosphere, but most travellers prefer to stay in Bhairawa, or get straight on a bus to Kathmandu or Pokhara.

Buses drop you just a few hundred metres from the Indian immigration office, so you can ignore the cycle-rickshaws.

🛏 Sleeping & Eating

Hotel Indo-Nepal HOTEL $
(🗹 05522-238142; ht.indonepal@gmail.com; near Government Bus Stand; r ₹500-850) Hotel Indo-Nepal has underwhelming rooms set around a leafy cement courtyard. Its simple, *dhaba*-style **Paradise Restaurant** (mains ₹45-200, thali from ₹90; ☺ 6.30am-10pm) doesn't instill confidence but makes a nice lunch stop even if you don't stay. The owner, Mr Singh, is a good source for local information.

ℹ CROSSING TO NEPAL: SUNAULI TO BHAIRAWA

Border Hours

The border is open 24 hours but closes to vehicles from 10pm to 6am, and if you arrive in the middle of the night you may have to wake someone to get stamped out of India. For further information, head to shop.lonelyplanet.com to purchase a downloadable PDF of the Kathmandu chapter from Lonely Planet's *Nepal* guide.

Foreign Exchange

There's no official moneychanger in Sunauli, but you can change Indian to Nepali (only) at Hotel Indo-Nepal. On the Nepal side, there are three ATMs in Belahiya: State Bank of India adjacent to Hotel Akash; Nabil Bank and Siddhartha Bank at the Mamta Hotel. Small denominations of Indian currency are accepted for bus fares on the Nepal side.

Onward Transport

The most comfortable option to Kathmandu is the **Golden Travels** (🗹 071-520194) AC bus (US$15, six to seven hours); it leaves from 100m beyond Nepali Immigration at 7am. AC Micros (mini-vans) depart from the same spot every 30 minutes from 6am to 10am (NRs 800, six hours).

Local buses (NRs20) and autorickshaws (NRs100) can take you from the border to Bhairawa, 4km away, where you can also catch non-AC buses to Kathmandu (NRs550, eight hours) via Narayangarh (NRs 350, three hours); and Pokhara (NRs 550, nine hours) via Tansen (NRs 250, five hours) along the Siddhartha Hwy or via the Mugling Hwy (NRs 650, eight hours). Local buses for Lumbini (NRs 80, one hour) leave from the junction of the Siddhartha Hwy and the road to Lumbini, about 1km north of Bank Rd.

Buddha Air (www.buddahair.com) and **Yeti Airlines** (www.yetiairlines.com) offer flights to Kathmandu from Bhairawa (from US$135).

Visas

Multiple-entry visas (15-/30-/90-days US$25/40/100 – cash, not rupees) are available at the Nepal immigration post. You can now save time by applying online at http://online.nepalimmigration.gov.np/tourist-visa. Your receipt, which you must produce at the border within 15 days of your application, outlines the border procedures. Always check with **Nepal Department of Immigration** (🗹 0977 1 4429659; www.nepalimmigration.gov.np; Kalikasthan, Kathmandu) for the latest information.

ℹ️ Information

Nepal Tourism Board Information Centre
(www.welcomenepal.com; ⏰10am-5pm Sun-Fri)
If you're leaving India, the very helpful tourist info centre is on your right in no-man's land.

ℹ️ Getting There & Around

Regular buses run from Sunauli to Gorakhpur (₹94, three hours, every 15 minutes, 4am to 7pm) from where you can catch trains to Varanasi. A few morning (4.30am, 5.30am, 6.30am and 7.30am) and afternoon (4.30pm, 5.30pm and 6.30pm) buses run direct to Varanasi (₹271, 11 hours), but it's a long, bumpy ride. Faster collective cars and jeeps to Gorakhpur hang out alongside the road after Indian immigration and leave when full (₹150 to ₹300, two hours).

WESTERN UTTAR PRADESH

On the road from Delhi to Agra in the west of the state is a pair of sacred towns that played a pivotal role in India's religious history.

Mathura

📞 0565 / POP 395,000

Famed for being the birthplace of the much-loved Hindu god Krishna, Mathura is one of Hinduism's seven sacred cities and attracts floods of pilgrims, particularly during Janmastami (Krishna's birthday) in August/September; and Holi in February/March. The town is dotted with temples from various ages and the stretch of the sacred Yamuna River which flows past here is lined with 25 ghats, best seen at dawn, when many people take their holy dip, and just after sunset, when hundreds of candles are sent floating out on the river during the *aarti* ceremony.

Mathura was once a Buddhist centre with 20 monasteries that housed 3000 monks but, after the rise of Hinduism, and later sackings by Afghan and Mughal rulers, today all that's left of the oldest sights are the beautiful sculptures recovered from ruins, now on display in the Archaeological Museum.

◎ Sights

★ **Kesava Deo Temple**　　　HINDU TEMPLE
(Shri Kirshna Janmbhoomi; ⏰5am-9.30pm summer, 5.30am-8.30pm winter) Among the foundations of the mural-filled Kesava Deo temple complex is a small, bare room with a slab of rock on which Krishna is said to have

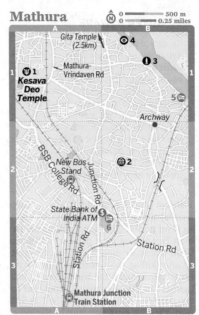

Mathura

◎ Top Sights
　1 Kesava Deo Temple..............................A1

◎ Sights
　2 Archaeological Museum.....................B2
　　Katra Masjid....................................(see 1)
　3 Sati Burj..B1
　4 Vishram Ghat & Around......................B1

🛏 Sleeping
　5 Agra Hotel..B1
　6 Hotel Brijwasi Royal............................B3

been born, some 3500 years ago. Near by is **Katra Masjid**, a mosque built by Aurangzeb in 1661 on the site of a temple he ordered to be destroyed.

The mosque is now guarded round the clock by soldiers to prevent a repeat of the tragic events at Ayodhya (p384) in 1992. Cameras and mobiles must be checked here.

Archaeological Museum　　　MUSEUM
(Museum Rd; Indian/foreigner ₹5/25, camera ₹20; ⏰10.30am-4.30pm Tue-Sun) This large museum houses superb collections of religious sculptures by the Mathura school, which flourished from the 3rd century BC to the 12th century AD.

> **ⓘ BUYER BEWARE**
>
> Be wary of buying 'through' tickets from Kathmandu or Pokhara to Varanasi. Some travellers report being intimidated into buying another ticket once over the border. Travelling in either direction, it's better to take a local bus to the border, walk across and take another onward bus (pay the conductor on board). Travellers have also complained about being pressured into paying extra luggage charges for buses out of Sunauli. You shouldn't have to, so politely decline.

Vishram Ghat & Around   AREA

A string of ghats and temples lines the Yamuna River north of the main road bridge. The most central and most popular is Vishram Ghat, where Krishna is said to have rested after killing the tyrannical King Kansa. Boats gather along the banks here to take tourists along the Yamuna (₹150 per hour for two people). Beside the ghat is the 17m **Sati Burj**, a four-storey tower built by the son of Behari Mal of Jaipur in 1570 to commemorate his mother's *sati* (self-immolation on her husband's funeral pyre).

Gita Temple   HINDU TEMPLE

(☉ dawn–dusk) This serene marble temple, on the road to Vrindavan, has the entire Bhagavad Gita (Hindu Song of the Divine One) written on a red pillar in the garden.

🎉 Festivals & Events

Mathura's most important festival, **Janmastami** (August/September), celebrates the birth of Lord Krishna and attracts huge crowds of devotees from all over the world for re-enactments of Kirshna's life, musical programs and fervent offerings and *puja* throughout Mathura and Vrindaven.

India's colourful national **Holi** festival (February/March) is a 16-day affair around Mathura and Vrindavan, where it takes on particular importance due to being the birthplace of Lord Krishna.

🛏 Sleeping & Eating

Agra Hotel   GUESTHOUSE $

(☎ 0565-2413318; Bengali Ghat; s ₹350-400, without bathroom ₹200-250, d ₹550-950, tr ₹650-950; ❄) This area, with narrow lanes winding their way down to the ghats and temples that line the Yamuna River, is the most interesting but least comfortable place to stay. Rooms here are basic (higher priced rooms have air-con and 24-hour geysers; otherwise hot water only flows from 6am to noon) but have character and some overlook the river. Staff members are very welcoming. Room 204 wins best in show.

Hotel Brijwasi Royal   HOTEL $$

(☎ 0565-2401224; www.brijwasiroyal.com; SBI Crossing, Station Rd; s/d incl breakfast from ₹2417/2886; ❄ 🖥) A clean and contemporary hotel with 40 business-like rooms that come with either marble floors or carpets, and bathtubs, some overlooking a buffalo pond behind. The **restaurant** (meals ₹130-205) does good quality Indian veg dishes and is deservedly popular. There's also a smoky, male-dominated **bar** (beer from ₹180). Wi-fi is temperamental but free.

ⓘ Information

There is a **State Bank of India** (Station Rd) ATM at SBI Crossing, next door to Brijwasi Royal and not far from the New Bus Stand. There is a second one at Sri Krishna Janmbhoomi.

ⓘ Getting There & Around

BUS

The so-called **New Bus Stand** (Vrindavan Rd) has regular buses to Delhi (₹133, four hours, every 30 minutes, 5am to 10pm) and Agra (₹64, 90 minutes, every 15 minutes, 4am to 9pm). Shared autos and tempos plying Station and Mathura–Vrindaven Roads charge ₹15 for the 13km Mathura–Vrindavan run.

TRAIN

Regular trains go to Delhi (sleeper/AC chair ₹191/206, two to three hours), Agra (sleeper/AC chair ₹161/305, one hour), and Bharatpur (sleeper/AC chair ₹161/257, 45 minutes). The Bharatpur trains continue to Sawai Madhopur (for Ranthambore National Park, two hours) and Kota (5½ hours).

Vrindavan

☎ 0565 / POP 65,000

The village of Vrindavan is where the young Krishna is said to have grown up. Pilgrims flock here from all over India and, in the case of the Hare Krishna community, from all over the world. Dozens of temples, old and modern, dot the area. They come in all shapes and sizes and many have their own unique peculiarities, making a visit here more than just your average temple hop.

☉ Sights

In addition to what's listed below, the **Rangaji Temple**, dating from 1851, **Radha Ballabh Temple**, built in 1626, **Madan Mohan Temple** and **Nidhivan Temple**, are also worth a visit.

★ Krishna Balaram Temple Complex   HINDU TEMPLE

The **International Society for Krishna Consciousness** (Iskcon; ☎0565-2540343; www.iskcon.org), also known as the Hare Krishnas, is based at the Krishna Balaram temple complex (Ishkon Temple), accessed through a beautiful white-marble gate, which houses the tomb of Swami Prabhupada (1896–1977), the founder of the Hare Krishna organisation. Several hundred foreigners attend courses and seminars here annually. The temple is closed to the public at various times of the day, most significantly from 12:45pm to 4pm (4.30pm in summer).

Govind Dev Temple   HINDU TEMPLE

This cavernous, red sandstone temple, built in 1590 by Raja Man Singh of Amber, has cute bells carved on its pillars. Resident monkeys here are as cheeky as any in India.

Pagal Baba Temple   HINDU TEMPLE

(admission ₹5) This 10-storey temple, a fairy-tale-castle lookalike, has an amusing succession of animated puppets and dioramas behind glass cases on the ground floor, which depict scenes from the lives of Rama and Krishna.

🛏 Sleeping & Eating

It's possible to stay at the **guesthouse** (☎0565-2540022; www.iskconvrindavan.com; d ₹700, d/tr with AC ₹950/1600; ❄) at the back of the Hare Krishna temple complex (though devotees are prioritised). Here you'll also find the clean, cool and healthy **Sri Govinda Restaurant** (mains ₹90-220; ⊙8am-2.30pm & 6-9.30pm), which does Indian veg dishes, pasta, cakes, shakes, salads and soups. There's a small bakery beside it.

ℹ Information

The closest ATM is **Andhra Bank**, 250m down from the main entrance of the temple complex, near the Bhaktivedanta Swami gate.

Krishna Balaram Welcome Office
(☎9557849475; ⊙10am-1pm & 5-8pm) Has lists of places to stay in Vrindavan and can help with booking Gita (studies in the Bhagavad Gita, an ancient Hindu scripture) classes as

Vrindavan

well as all travel agency services. There are internet services (per hour ₹30; ⊙10am-1pm & 5-8.30pm; 🖥) attached.

ℹ Getting There & Around

Most temples are open from dawn to dusk and admission is free, but they are well spread out so a cycle-rickshaw tour is a good way to see them. Expect to pay ₹200 to ₹250 for a half-day tour (₹350 to ₹400 in an autorickshaw).

Tempos, shared autos and buses all charge ₹15 from Vrindavan to Mathura.

Uttarakhand

Why Go?

Soaring Himalayan peaks and steamy lowland jungles. Revered temples and renowned ashrams. Peaceful hill stations and busy cities. Uttarakhand is an enticingly diverse state, with some of India's best trekking, yoga schools, holiday towns and wildlife-watching all tucked into one little corner of the country.

Hindus think of Uttarakhand as *Dev Bhoomi* – the Land of Gods – and the dramatic terrain is covered with holy mountains, lakes and rivers. Twisting roads and high-altitude hiking trails lead to spectacular pilgrimage sites where tales from the Hindu epics are set. And something of these ancient stories seems to have been absorbed by the land, which exudes a subtle sense of actually being sacred – even to ultra-orthodox agnostics.

Many travellers flock here for this vibe, finding it a powerful place to pursue a spiritual practice. Others come here to spot tigers.

Best Cultural Experiences

➡ Kedarnath (p435)

➡ Hem Kund (p439)

➡ Haridwar (p422)

➡ Nanda Devi Fair (p449)

Best Off the Beaten Path

➡ Munsyari (p451)

➡ Tungnath & Chandrisilla (p439)

➡ Binsar Wildlife Sanctuary (p450)

➡ Har-Ki-Dun (p440)

When to Go
Rishikesh

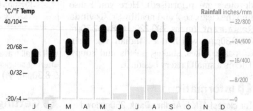

Apr–mid-Jun
The best season for tiger spotting at Corbett Tiger Reserve.

Jul–mid-Sep
Monsoons may make travel difficult; Valley of Flowers blooms July and August.

Mid-Sep–Oct
The perfect time to trek through the Himalayas.

Uttarakhand Highlights

1 Visiting **Gangotri Temple** (p434) and trekking beyond it to **Gaumukh** (p434), source of the holy Ganges

2 Floating a candle down the Ganges at the gorgeous nightly ceremony at Haridwar's **Har-ki-Pairi Ghat** (p422)

3 Scouting for rare Bengal tigers and riding an elephant in **Corbett Tiger Reserve** (p441)

4 Getting your asanas and chakras sorted at **Rishikesh** (p414), the yoga and ashram capital of the universe

5 Cooling off in a scenic Raj-era hill station in **Mussoorie** (p430) or **Nainital** (p444)

6 Trekking to sublime **Valley of Flowers National Park** (p439) and nearby **Hem Kund** for an unforgettable scenic and sacred combo

7 Immersing yourself in a mind-blowing Himalayan landscape while trekking the **Kuari Pass** (p440)

History

Uttarakhand consists of two culturally distinct districts: Garhwal (in the west) and Kumaon (to the east). Over the centuries various dynasties have dominated the region, including the Guptas, Kuturyi and Chand rajas. In the 18th century the Nepalese Gurkhas attacked first the kingdom of Kumaon, then Garhwal, prompting the British to step in and take most of the region as part of the Sugauli Treaty in 1816.

After Independence, the region was merged with Uttar Pradesh, but a vocal separatist movement followed, and the present-day state of Uttaranchal was formed in 2000. In 2007 it was officially renamed Uttarakhand, a traditional name meaning 'northern country'.

Climate

Temperatures are determined by altitude in this state of elevation extremes. Trekking the Himalayas is possible from May to October, but can be dangerous between July and mid-September, during the monsoon, when violent cloudbursts cause landslides. Hill stations offer a welcome escape from summertime heat, while low-lying Rishikesh is most comfortable from October to March.

ⓘ Information

Most towns in the region have an Uttarakhand Tourism office; however the main responsibility for the region's tourism rests with the **Garhwal Mandal Vikas Nigam** (GMVN; www.gmvnl.com), in the Garhwal district and **Kumaon Mandal Vikas Nigam** (KMVN; www.kmvn.org), in the Kumaon district.

ⓘ Getting Around

Tough old government buses are the main means of travelling around Uttarakhand. In addition, crowded shared jeeps criss-cross the state, linking remote towns and villages to important road junctions. Pay 10 times the share-taxi rate to hire the whole vehicle and travel in

comfort. Roads that snake through the hills can be nerve-racking and stomach-churning, and are sometimes blocked by monsoon-season landslides.

RISHIKESH

☎ 0135 / POP 102,160 / ELEV 356M

Ever since the Beatles rocked up at the ashram of the Maharishi Mahesh Yogi in the late 1960s, Rishikesh has been a magnet for spiritual seekers. Today it styles itself as the 'Yoga Capital of the World', with masses of ashrams and all kinds of yoga and meditation classes. Most of this action is north of the main town, where the exquisite setting on the fast-flowing Ganges, surrounded by forested hills, is conducive to meditation and mind expansion. In the evening, an almost supernatural breeze blows down the valley, setting temple bells ringing as sadhus (spiritual men), pilgrims and tourists prepare for the nightly *ganga aarti* (a fire offering or ritual performed on the Ganges). You can learn to play the sitar or tabla; try Hasya yoga (laughter therapy), practise humming or gong meditation, or even take a punt on crystal healing.

But Rishikesh is not all spirituality and contorted limbs; it's now a popular whitewater rafting centre, backpacker hang-out, and gateway to treks in the Himalaya.

Rishikesh is divided into two main areas: the crowded, unattractive downtown area (Rishikesh town), where you'll find the bus and train stations as well as the Triveni Ghat (a popular and auspicious bathing ghat and place of prayer on the Ganges); and the riverside communities 2km upstream around Ram Jhula and Lakshman Jhula, where most of the accommodation, ashrams, restaurants and travellers are ensconced. The two *jhula* (suspension bridges) that cross the river are pedestrian-only – though scooters and motorcycles freely use them. Swarg Ashram, located on the eastern bank, is the traffic-free 'spiritual centre' of Rishikesh, while High Bank, west of Lakshman Jhula, is a small enclave popular with backpackers.

⊙ Sights

Lakshman Jhula & Around

The defining image of Rishikesh is the view across the Lakshman Jhula hanging bridge to the huge, 13-storey wedding-cake temple of **Swarg Niwas & Shri Trayanbakshwar**. Built by the organisation of the guru Kai-

TOP STATE FESTIVALS

Magh Mela (Haridwar; ⊙ Jan & Feb) Hundreds of thousands of pilgrims come to bathe in the soul-cleansing Ganges during this huge annual religious fair. The Ardh Kumbh Mela is held every six years; and millions of pilgrims attend the mega Kumbh Mela every 12 years.

International Yoga Festival (p418; hMar) Rishikesh hosts the International Yoga Festival, attracting swamis and yoga masters from around the world for discourses and lectures. Most of the action is centred on the Parmarth Niketan Ashram (p417) in Swarg Ashram. Check the festival website for dates.

Shivaratri (Tapkeshwar Temple; ⊙ usually Mar) A festival celebrated in style with carnival rides and stalls at a picturesque riverside cave temple on the outskirts of Dehra Dun.

Nanda Devi Fair (p449; ⊙ Sep) During this five-day fair, devotees parade the image of the goddess in towns around Kumaon. There's also dancing and cultural shows.

lashanand, it resembles a fairyland castle and has dozens of shrines to Hindu deities on each level, interspersed with jewellery and textile shops. Sunset is an especially good time to photograph the temple from the bridge itself, and you'll hear the bell-clanging and chanting of devotees in the morning and evening. Shops selling devotional CDs add to the cacophony of noise on this side of the river. Markets, restaurants, ashrams and guesthouses sprawl on both sides of the river; in recent years the area has grown into the busiest and liveliest part of upper Rishikesh.

Swarg Ashram

A pleasant 2km walk south of Lakshman Jhula, along the path skirting the east bank of the Ganges, leads to the spiritual community of Swarg Ashram, made up of temples, ashrams, a crowded bazaar, sadhus and the bathing ghats (steps or landing on a river) where religious ceremonies are performed at sunrise and sunset. The colourful, though rather touristy, *ganga aarti* is held at the riverside temple of the Parmarth Niketan Ashram (p417) every evening around sunset, with singing, chanting, musicians and the lighting of candles.

Other Sights

Maharishi Mahesh Yogi Ashram　　　　HISTORIC BUILDING
(entry ₹100; ⊙ 8am-6pm) Just south of Swarg Ashram, slowly being consumed by the forest undergrowth, is what's left of the original Maharishi Mahesh Yogi Ashram. It was abandoned in 1997 and is now back under the control of the forest department. However, the shells of many buildings, medita-

tion cells and lecture halls can still be seen, including Maharishi's own house and the guesthouse where the Beatles stayed and apparently wrote much of the *White Album*.

The once-striking art installation called *The Beatles Cathedral Gallery* has become a graffiti free-for-all, but it's still worth a look.

🏃 Activities

Yoga & Meditation

Yoga and meditation are ubiquitous in India's yoga capital. Teaching and yoga styles vary tremendously, so check out a few classes and ask others about their experiences before committing yourself to a course. Many places also offer ayurvedic massage, and some residential ashrams have strict rules forbidding students from consuming drugs, alcohol, tobacco and meat during their stay.

Sri Sant Seva Ashram　　　　YOGA
(☑ 0135-2430465; santsewa@hotmail.com; Lakshman Jhula; d ₹200-500, with AC ₹1000; 🛜) The yoga classes are mixed styles and open to all. Beginner (₹100), and intermediate and advanced (₹200) sessions run daily. There are also courses in reiki, ayurvedic massage and cooking. Overlooking the Ganges in Lakshman Jhula, the large rooms here are popular, so book ahead. The more expensive rooms have balconies with superb river views.

Omkarananda Ganga Sadan　　　　YOGA
(☑ 0135-2430763; www.iyengaryoga.in; Lakshman Jhula Rd; r with/without AC ₹1500/350, minimum 3-day stay) On the river at Ram Jhula, this ashram has comfortable rooms and

Rishikesh

UTTARAKHAND RISHIKESH

1 km
0.5 miles

Neer Garh Waterfall (3km); Neelkantha Mahadev Temple by road (20km)

Swarg Niwas & Shri Trayanbakshwar Temple 1

Lakshman Jhula

See Enlargement

Enlargement

100 m
0.05 miles

Ganges River

21
10 17
25
24
22
16

Axis Bank ATM

20
15
13
12
4
3
27
14
8

HIGH BANK

19
11

Lakshman Jhula Rd

Ganges River

28
Ram Jhula

State Bank of India ATM
16
9

SWARG ASHRAM

Ferry
23
6
Axis Bank ATM
26
7
18
Blue Hills Travels

2

Neelkantha Mahadeva Temple on foot (7km)

Kailash Gate

Lakshman Jhula Rd
5

RISHILOK

MUNI-KI-RETI

Uttarakhand Tourism Office
29

Chandrabhaga River

Dehra Dun Rd

Bank of Baroda ATM

Railway Rd

Handwar Rd

HDFC ATM

Dhalwala Bypass Rd

Train Station

30

Haridwar (19km)

Haridwar (19km)

Rishikesh

specialises in highly recommended Iyengar yoga classes at the Patanjala Yoga Kendra centre. There are intensive seven- to 10-day courses (₹1200) on offer from October to May, advance reservations recommended. In the gaps between the intensives, day classes are offered (6pm to 7.30pm, Monday to Saturday, ₹250). The ashram has its own ghat and evening *ganga aarti*.

Parmarth Niketan Ashram YOGA
(☑ 0135-2434301; www.parmarth.com; Swarg Ashram; s/d ₹400/500) Dominating the centre of Swarg Ashram and drawing visitors to its evening *ganga aarti* on the riverbank, Parmarth has a wonderfully ornate and serene garden courtyard. The price includes a room with a private bathroom and basic hatha yoga sessions.

Anand Prakash Yoga Ashram YOGA
(☑ 0135-2442344; www.anandprakashashram. com; Badrinath Rd, Tapovan; private/share r incl full board ₹1100/800) About 1km north of Lakshman Jhula, you can stay here as long or short as you like, taking part in morning and afternoon Akhanda yoga classes (included in the price). Food is excellent and rooms are simple but comfortable and clean. Silence is

the rule from 9pm to 9am. If you're not staying, drop in for classes for ₹150 to ₹200.

Rishikesh Yog Peeth YOGA
(☑ 0135-2440193; www.rishikeshyogpeeth.com; Swarg Ashram; 40-day course US$1400) With its excellent reputation, this popular yoga-teacher-training school has become something of a local industry.

Rafting, Kayaking & Trekking
More than 100 operators offer full- and half-day rafting trips, launching upstream and paddling down to Rishikesh. Some also offer multiday rafting trips, with camping along the river. The official rafting season runs from 15 September to 30 June. A half-day trip starts at about ₹1000 per person, while a full day costs from ₹1800. Most companies also offer all-inclusive Himalayan treks to places such as Kuari Pass, Har-ki Dun and Gangotri/Tapovan from around ₹3500 per day.

Red Chilli Adventure TREKKING, RAFTING
(☑ 0135-2434021; www.redchilliadventure.com; Lakshman Jhula Rd; ⊙9am-8pm) Reliable outfit offering Himalayan trekking and rafting trips throughout Uttarakhand and to Himachal Pradesh and Ladakh.

De-N-Ascent Expeditions KAYAKING, TREKKING
(☏0135-2442354; www.kayakhimalaya.com; Lakshman Jhula, Tapovan Sarai) Specialist in kayaking lessons and expeditions. Learn to paddle and eskimo roll with an experienced instructor, or go on multiday kayaking or rafting adventures. Also organises trekking trips.

GMVN Trekking & Mountaineering Division TREKKING
(☏0135-2430799; www.gmvnl.com; Lakshman Jhula Rd, Muni-ki-Reti; ☉10am-5pm) Can arrange high-altitude treks in the Garhwal Himalaya, and hires out trekking equipment, guides and porters.

Walks & Beaches

An easy, 15-minute walk to two small **waterfalls** starts 3km north of Lakshman Jhula bridge on the south side of the river. The start is marked by drink stalls and a roadside shrine, and the path is easy to find. 4WD taxis cost ₹100 from Lakshman Jhula.

On the other side of the river, it's about 2km north to the signposted walk to lovely **Neer Garh Waterfall** (admission ₹30), from where it's a 20-minute uphill walk.

For a longer hike, follow the dedicated pilgrims who take water from the Ganges to offer at **Neelkantha Mahadev Temple**, a 7km, approximately three-hour walk along a forest path from Swarg Ashram. You can also reach the temple by road (20km) from Lakshman Jhula.

✦✦ Festivals & Events

International Yoga Festival YOGA
(www.internationalyogafestival.com; ☉Mar) In the first week of March, swamis and yoga masters from around the world flock to Rishikesh for lectures and training. Most of the action is centred on the Parmarth Niketan Ashram (p417) in Swarg Ashram. Check the festival website for dates.

🛏 Sleeping

Most of the accommodation is spread on both sides of the river around Lakshman Jhula; there are a handful of hotels among the ashrams at Swarg Ashram and directly across the river around Ram Jhula, and some good budget places at High Bank.

Midrange and top-end hotels are in relatively short supply in budget-minded Rishikesh.

🛏 High Bank

This small, leafy travellers' enclave is a 20-minute walk up the hill from Lakshman Jhula and has some of the best backpacker accommodation in Rishikesh.

Bhandari Swiss Cottage HOTEL $
(☏0135-2432939; www.bhandariswisscottagerishi kesh.com; r from ₹200, with AC from ₹1000; ✳@☎) The first place you come to, this is a well-run backpacker favourite with rooms in several budgets – the higher up you stay, the higher the price. Rooms with big balconies have expansive views of the river backed by green mountains. It has an excellent little restaurant, internet cafe and yoga classes.

New Bhandari Swiss Cottage HOTEL $
(☏0135-2435322; www.newbhandariswisscottage. com; r ₹400-800, with AC ₹1000-1500; ✳@☎) One of the last places on the High Bank lane, this is a large, popular place with rooms ranging from clean and simple to simply impressive. There's a massage centre, a good restaurant and a helpful travel desk in its internet cafe.

THE MAHARISHI & THE BEATLES

In February 1968, Rishikesh hit world headlines when the Beatles and their partners stayed at Maharishi Mahesh Yogi's ashram in Swarg Ashram, following an earlier visit by George Harrison. Ringo Starr and his wife didn't like the vegetarian food, missed their children and left after a couple of weeks, but the others stayed for a month or two. They relaxed and wrote tons of songs, many of which ended up on their double album *White Album*. But rumours of the Maharishi's demands for money and his behaviour towards some female disciples eventually disillusioned all of them. 'You made a fool of everyone', John Lennon sang about the Maharishi. In later years, Harrison and Paul McCartney said, on record, that the rumours were unfounded. The original ashram is now abandoned, but nearly 40 years on, idealistic foreigners still swarm into Rishikesh seeking spiritual enlightenment from teachers and healers in their tranquil ashrams scattered along the Ganges River.

Lakshman Jhula

There are several good budget options on both sides of the river here, which is the liveliest part of Rishikesh. Some of the best-value places are at the paying guesthouses along the lane that leads to Divine Ganga Cottage.

Hotel Ishan   HOTEL $
(☑0135-2431534; r ₹400-1200; ✳@🔊) This long-running riverfront place near Lakshman Jhula has a wide range of rooms at a wide range of prices. Here, you get what you pay for: the best are large and clean with terraces overlooking the river, the cheapest are unpleasantly musty. The top-floor room with TV and balcony has great views.

Hotel Surya   HOTEL $
(☑0135-2440211; www.hotelsuryalaxmanjhula.com; r ₹400-950; ✳@🔊) Above Café Coffee Day, the Surya is in a good location by the bridge. The midrange rooms are the best value, as they're quieter and in better condition than the pricey front-balcony rooms.

Divine Ganga Cottage   HOTEL $$
(☑0135-2442175; www.divinegangacottage.com; r ₹1500, with AC ₹2500; ✳@🔊) This is tucked away from the hubbub, and surrounded by small rice paddies and local homes with gardens. The huge upstairs terrace has supreme river views. Downstairs rooms are small and overpriced but the larger, stylish upstairs air-con rooms are some of the best in town, with writing tables and modern bathrooms. There's an ayurvedic spa and yoga instruction on some days.

Dewa Retreat   HOTEL $$$
(☑0135-2442382; www.dewaretreat.com; r from ₹4825; ✳🔊🏊) Lakshman Jhula's newest top-end hotel features immaculate rooms that blend simplicity with luxury. The best rooms have balconies with Ganges valley views, and the outdoor swimming pool takes the edge off of a sultry day.

Divine Resort   HOTEL $$$
(☑0135-2442128; www.divineresort.com; r ₹3750-7500; ✳🔊) Some rooms in this top-end hotel have stunning river views – but none as impressive as the view from the glass elevator, which could be a tourist attraction all its own. There's a glassed-in restaurant facing the Ganges River and an excellent pastry shop-cafe in front.

Swarg Ashram

If you're serious about yoga and introspection, stay at one of Swarg's numerous ashrams. Otherwise, there's a knot of hotels a block back from the river towards the southern end of Swarg.

★**Vashishth Guest House**   BOUTIQUE HOTEL $
(☑0135-2440029; www.vashishthgroup.com; r from ₹550, with kitchen from ₹1000; ✳🔊) This sweet little boutique hotel has colourfully painted walls, comfortable mattresses and a small lending library. A couple of the rooms boast good-sized kitchens with cooking utensils, table and chairs. For what you get, this is one of the best deals in Rishikesh.

Hotel Narayana Kunj   HOTEL $
(☑0135-2440822; www.narayanakunj.com; Swarg Ashram; r from ₹600) Tucked down a quiet lane, you'll find rooms with balconies overlooking a grassy courtyard, along with a spa offering massage and ayurvedic treatments.

✗ Eating

Virtually every restaurant in Rishikesh serves only vegetarian food, but there are lots of travellers' restaurants whipping up various interpretations of Continental and Israeli food, as well as Indian and Chinese.

Lakshman Jhula

★**Devraj Coffee Corner**   CAFE $
(snacks & mains ₹40-190; ⏰8am-9pm) Perched above the bridge and looking across the river to Shri Trayanbakshwar temple, this German bakery is a sublime spot for a break at any time of the day. The coffee is the best in town and the menu ranges from specialities such as brown bread with yak cheese to soups and sizzlers, along with croissants, apple strudel and more.

There's a good new and used bookshop next door.

Prem's Namaste Cafe   MULTICUISINE $
(mains ₹55-150; ⏰8am-11pm; 🔊) With a menu and atmosphere similar to most of the other restaurants on this strip, what sets Prem's apart are the superfriendly staff and the frequent jam sessions in the cushioned top-floor eating lounge.

Pyramid Cafe   MULTICUISINE $
(mains ₹60-95; ⏰8.30am-10pm; 🔊) Sit on cushions inside pyramid-shaped tents and

UTTARAKHAND RISHIKESH

choose from a menu of home-cooked Indian food, plus a few Tibetan and Western dishes including pancakes. The family that runs it is superfriendly and they also rent out a couple of peaceful, well-kept pyramid tents with double bed and attached bath (₹250 and ₹500).

★ **Little Buddha Cafe** MULTICUISINE $$
(mains ₹100-200; ⊗8am-11pm; 🛜) This funky treehouse-style restaurant has an ultraloungey top floor, tables overlooking the Ganges River and really good international food. Pizzas are big and the mixed vegetable platter is a serious feast. It's one of the busiest places in Lakshman Jhula, for good reason.

Ganga Beach Restaurant MULTICUISINE $$
(mains ₹100-160; ⊗7.30am-10.30pm; 🛜) Great riverside location with a spacious terrace and big menu including crepes and ice-cold lassis.

✕ Swarg Ashram & Ram Jhula

Madras Cafe INDIAN $
(Ram Jhula; mains ₹100-150; ⊗7.30am-9.30pm; 🛜) This local institution recently underwent a modern facelift but still dishes up tasty South and North Indian vegetarian food, thalis, a mean mushroom curry, wholewheat pancakes and the intriguing Himalayan 'health pilau', as well as superthick lassis.

Tip Top Restaurant MULTICUISINE $
(Swarg Ashram; mains ₹70-160; ⊗9am-9.30pm) The friendly little joint is perched up high, catching river views and breezes. Customise your own sandwich, or dig into Indian, Italian or Israeli dishes.

✕ High Bank

Backpackers gather at the popular restaurants on High Bank. This is the only area in town where you'll find meat on the menu.

Bistro Nirvana INTERNATIONAL $$
(mains ₹80-250; ⊗8am-10.30pm) This new joint hits the right groove, with a shaded patio and elevated tables with cushioned bench seating. The theme is bamboo, the multiregional food is tasty.

Oasis Restaurant MULTICUISINE $$
(mains ₹90-170; ⊗8am-10pm) At New Bhandari Swiss Cottage, this place has some character, with candlelit tables in the garden and hanging lanterns inside. The menu covers oodles of world cuisines, from Mexican

and Thai to Israeli and Tibetan, and features a number of chicken dishes. Great desserts include apple crumble.

🛍 Shopping

Swarg Ashram is the place to go for bookshops, ayurvedic herbal medicines, clothing, handicrafts and tourist trinkets such as jewellery and Tibetan singing bowls, though there are also plenty of stalls around Lakshman Jhula. Many stalls sell *rudraksh mala,* the strings of beads used in *puja* (literally 'respect'; offering or prayers). They are made from the nuts of the rudraksh tree, which originally grew where Shiva shed a single tear following a particularly long and satisfying period of meditation. Beads with *mukhi* (different faces) confer various blessings on the wearer.

If you need outdoor gear, your best bet is **Adventure Axis** (Badrinath Rd, Lakshman Jhula; ⊗10am-8pm), which stocks everything from sleeping bags and carabiners to drysuits and trekking boots.

ℹ Information

DANGERS & ANNOYANCES
Be cautious of befriending sadhus – while some are on genuine spiritual journeys, the orange robes have been used as a disguise by fugitives from the law since medieval times, and people have been robbed and worse.

The current in some parts of the Ganges is very strong and people occasionally drown here. Don't swim beyond your depth.

INTERNET ACCESS
Internet access is available all over town, usually for ₹20 or ₹30 per hour.
Blue Hills Travels (Swarg Ashram; per hour ₹30; ⊗8am-10pm) Skype is available.
Lucky Internet (Lakshman Jhula; per hour ₹30; ⊗8.30am-9.30pm; 🛜) Wi-fi access.

MEDICAL SERVICES
Himalayan Institute Hospital (📞0135-2471200, Emergency 0135-2471225; ⊗24hr) The nearest large hospital, 17km along the road to Dehra Dun and 1km beyond Jolly Grant airport.
Shivananda Ashram (📞0135-2430040; www.sivanandaonline.org; Lakshman Jhula Rd) Provides free medical services and has a pharmacy.

MONEY
Several travel agents around Lakshman Jhula and Swarg Ashram will exchange travellers cheques and cash.

POST

Main Post Office (Ghat Rd; ◷10am-4pm Mon-Fri, to 1pm Sat) Near Triveni Ghat.

Post Office (Swarg Ashram; ◷10am-4pm Mon-Fri, to 1pm Sat)

TOURIST INFORMATION

Uttarakhand Tourism Office (☎0135-2430209; main bus stand; ◷10am-5pm Mon-Sat) A building behind the bus stand, with eager staff.

❶ Getting There & Away

BUS

There are regular buses to Haridwar and Dehra Dun; for Mussoorie change at Dehra Dun. Buses run north to pilgrimage centres during the *yatra* (pilgrimage) season (April to November), and to Joshimath and Uttarkashi year-round. Buses to Gangotri were infrequent at the time of research.

Private AC and Volvo buses run to Delhi (₹600 to ₹830, seven hours) several times a day. There's also one direct overnight bus daily from Rishikesh to Dharamsala (₹950) at 4pm.

Private night buses to Jaipur (seat/sleeper/AC sleeper ₹500/600/1100, 13 hours) and Pushkar (₹500/600, 16 hours) can be booked at travel agents in Lakshman Jhula, Swarg Ashram and High Bank, but they leave from Haridwar. You can also book a bus to Agra (₹840, 12 hours) that departs from Dehradun.

SHARE JEEPS & TAXI

Share jeeps leave, when overfull, from the corner of Dehra Dun Rd and Dhalwala Bypass Rd, to Uttarkashi (₹300, five hours) and Joshimath (₹400, eight hours), mostly early in the morning, starting from 4am.

Private taxis can be hired from Lakshman Jhula, Ram Jhula, and in between the main and *yatra* (pilgrimage) bus stands. Rates to destinations include: Haridwar (₹810, one hour), Dehra Dun

(₹1220, 1½ hours), Jolly Grant Airport (₹710, one hour), Uttarkashi (for Gangotri; ₹3570, seven hours), Joshimath (₹5610, nine hours) and Almora (₹7200, 10 hours). For long-distance trips you may find a cheaper rate by asking around at travel agents and guesthouses. *Vikrams* (large autorickshaws) charge ₹400 to make the trip to Haridwar.

TRAIN

Very few trains run from Rishikesh itself, so your best bet is to take a bus or taxi to the railway station in Haridwar and hop on board there. Bookings, even for trains from Haridwar, can be made at the railway station in Rishikesh, or at travel agents around Lakshman Jhula and Swarg Ashram (for a fee).

❶ Getting Around

Shared *vikrams* run from the downtown Ghat Rd junction up past Ram Jhula (₹10 per person) and the High Bank turn-off to Lakshman Jhula. To hire the entire *vikram* from downtown to Lakshman Jhula should cost ₹80 to 'upside' – the top of the hill on which the Lakshman Jhula area sits – and ₹100 to 'downside' – closer to the bridge. From Ram Jhula to High Bank or Lakshman Jhula is ₹40.

To get to the eastern bank of the Ganges you either need to walk across one of the suspension bridges or take the **ferry** (one way/return ₹10/15; ◷7.30am-6.15pm) from Ram Jhula.

On the eastern bank of the Ganges, taxis and share jeeps wait to take passengers to waterfalls and Neelkantha temple (shared/private ₹120/1000), but it's a 16km trip by road to get from one side of the river to the other. Lakshman Jhula to Swarg Ashram costs ₹10 in a shared jeep, or ₹80 if you don't wish to share.

Bicycles (per day ₹100), scooters (per day ₹300) and motorcycles (per day ₹400 to ₹700) can be hired around the Lakshman Jhula area. There are no actual shops – rent from guys on the street or ask at guesthouses.

BUSES FROM RISHIKESH

The following buses depart from the main bus stand (A) or the GMOU (yatra) bus stand (B). The latter leave when full.

DESTINATION	FARE (₹)	DURATION (HOUR)	FREQUENCY
Badrinath	420	12	5am
Dehra Dun (A)	51	1½	half-hourly
Delhi (A)	240/470 ordinary/AC	7	half-hourly
Gangotri (B)	300	12	5.30am, 6.15am
Haridwar (A)	35	1	half-hourly
Joshimath (B)	340	6	6am
Kedarnath (B)	350	12	5am
Uttarkashi (A)	240	7	3.30am, 12pm
Yamnotri (B)	340	12	5am

HARIDWAR

☑ 01334 / POP 225,235 / ELEV 249M

Propitiously located at the point where the Ganges emerges from the Himalaya, Haridwar (also called Hardwar) is Uttarakhand's holiest Hindu city, and pilgrims arrive here in droves to bathe in the fast-flowing Ganges. The sheer number of people gathering around Har-ki-Pairi Ghat give Haridwar a chaotic but reverent feel. Within the religious hierarchy of India, Haridwar is much more significant than Rishikesh, an hour further north, and every evening the river comes alive with flickering flames as floating offerings are released onto the Ganges. It's especially busy during the *yatra* season from May to October, and is the site of the annual Magh Mela religious festival.

Haridwar's main street is Railway Rd, becoming Upper Rd, which runs parallel to the Ganges canal (the river proper runs further to the east). Generally only cycle-rickshaws are allowed between Laltarao Bridge and Bhimgoda Jhula (Bhimgoda Bridge), so vehicles travel around the opposite bank of the river. The alleyways of Bara Bazaar run south of Har-ki-Pairi Ghat.

⊙ Sights & Activities

★ Har-ki-Pairi Ghat   GHAT

Har-ki-Pairi (The Footstep of God) is where Vishnu is said to have dropped some divine nectar and left behind a footprint. Every evening hundreds of worshippers gather for the *ganga aarti*. Officials in blue uniforms collect donations and, as the sun sets, bells ring out a rhythm, torches are lit, and leaf baskets with flower petals inside and a candle on top (₹10) are lit and placed on the river to drift away downstream.

Tourists can mingle with the crowd to experience the rituals of an ancient religion that still retains its power in the modern age. Someone may claim to be a priest and help you with your *puja* before asking for ₹200 or more. If you want to make a donation, it's best to give to a uniformed collector.

The best times to visit the ghat are early morning or just before dusk.

Mansa Devi & Chandi Devi Temples   HINDU TEMPLE

Take the **cable car** (return ₹58; ⊙ 7am-7pm Apr-Oct, 8am-6.30pm Nov-Mar) to the crowded hilltop temple of **Mansa Devi**, a wish-fulfilling

goddess. The path to the cable car is lined with stalls selling packages of *prasad* (a food offering used in religious ceremonies) to bring to the goddess on the hill. You can walk up (1.5km) but beware of *prasad*-stealing monkeys.

Many visitors and pilgrims combine this with another **cable car** (return ₹102; ⊙ 8am-6pm) up Neel Hill, 4km southeast of Haridwar, to **Chandi Devi Temple**. The temple was built by Raja Suchet Singh of Kashmir in 1929.

Pay ₹210 at Mansa Devi and you can ride both cable cars and take an AC coach between the two temples. Photography is forbidden inside the shrines.

⌖ Tours

Mohan's Adventure Tours   ADVENTURE TOUR

(☑ 9412022966, 9837100215; www.mohansadventure.in; Railway Rd; ⊙ 8am-10.30pm) Sanjeev Mehta of Mohan's Adventure Tours can organise any kind of tour, including trekking, fishing, birdwatching, cycling, motorcycling and rafting. An accomplished wildlife photographer, he specialises in five-hour safaris (₹2350 per person with two or more, singles pay ₹2950) within Rajaji National Park. Sanjeev also runs overnight trips to Corbett Tiger Reserve (from ₹9950). Tours operate year-round.

⌂ Sleeping

Haridwar has loads of hotels catering to Hindu pilgrims. The busiest time of year is the *yatra* season from April to November – outside this you should have no problem finding a room at discounts of 20% to 50%.

Jassa Ram Rd and the other alleys running off Railway Rd have plenty of budget hotels, and although some of the fancy foyers and neon signs may raise your hopes, none are great. Rishikesh has far superior budget accommodation.

Down by the ghats are a number of high-rise hotels that have good views but worse-than-average rooms.

Hotel Arjun   HOTEL $

(☑ 01334-220409; www.hotelarjun.com; Jassa Ram Rd; r with/without AC from ₹700/500; ❋ ☞) Currently the best of the budget choices, the Arjun beats its neighbours for cleanliness and comfort. Some rooms have balconies. Most have their quirks, though – one a broken TV, another a dead overhead light – so

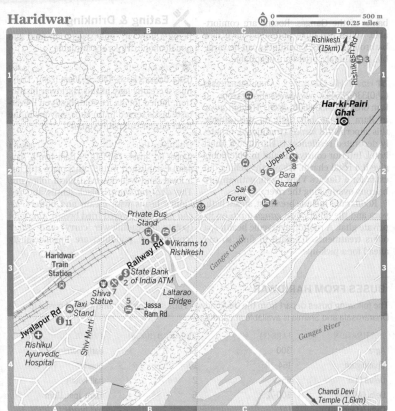

0 — 500 m
0 — 0.25 miles

UTTARAKHAND HARIDWAR

Haridwar

◎ Top Sights
1 Har-ki-Pairi Ghat D1

◆ Activities, Courses & Tours
2 Mohan's Adventure Tours B3

⊜ Sleeping
3 Bhaj-Govindam D1
4 Haveli Hari Ganga C2
5 Hotel Arjun B3
6 Hotel La Casa B3

⊗ Eating
7 Big Ben Restaurant B3
Haveli Hari Ganga Restaurant ....(see 4)
8 Hoshiyar Puri D2

⊖ Drinking & Nightlife
9 Prakash Lok C2

ⓘ Information
10 GMVN Tourist Office B3
11 Uttarakhand Tourism Office A4

take a look at a few if you can. It's walking distance from the train and bus stations.

Hotel La Casa　　　　　　　HOTEL $$
(☏ 01334-221197; www.lacasahotels.in; Bilkeshwar Rd, opposite Gurdwara; r from ₹2000; ❋ ☎) One of Haridwar's few solid midrange choices, La Casa boasts some of the least scuffed rooms in town. It strives for character, with splashes of colour, tasteful furnishings

and modern bathrooms. In all, good value (though not quite as nice as it looks on the hotel website).

Bhaj-Govindam　　　　　　　HOTEL $$
(☏ 01334-261682; www.bhajgovindam.com; Upper Rd; r from ₹1200; ❋) About 100m north of Bhimgoda Jhula, Bhaj-Govindam is the most peaceful hotel in town, set around a grassy garden, with river frontage on the

banks of the Ganges. Rooms are comfortable, suites are huge and some have new bathroom fixtures. Cleanliness can be variable. Fortunately, prices are negotiable.

★ **Haveli Hari Ganga**   HERITAGE HOTEL $$$
(☎ 01334-226443; www.havelihariganga.com; 21 Ram Ghat; r ₹6450-8600; ❋ ☎) Hidden away in Bara Bazaar, but right on the Ganges, this superb 1918 *haveli* (traditional, ornately decorated residence) is Haridwar's finest hotel. Interior courtyards and marble floors give it a regal charm. It's worth shelling out extra for a Ganges View room, with an airy balcony overlooking the river.

Room rates include breakfast, steam bath, yoga and the hotel's own *ganga aarti* on its private ghat. A rooftop ayurvedic health spa offers treatments. It's hard to find, so call ahead for a pick-up.

✖ Eating & Drinking

Being a holy city, only vegetarian food and nonalcoholic drinks are available.

★ **Prakash Lok**   LASSI
(Bara Bazaar; lassis ₹40; ⊙10am-12am) Don't miss a creamy lassi at this Haridwar institution, famed for its ice-cold, best-you'll-ever-taste lassis served in tin cups. Anyone in the Bara Bazaar can point you to it.

Hoshiyar Puri   INDIAN $
(Upper Rd; mains ₹65-150; ⊙11am-4pm & 7pm-4am) Established in 1937, this place still has a loyal (and well-deserved) local following. The *dhal makhani* (black lentils and red kidney beans with cream and butter), *lacha paratha* (layered fried bread), *aloo gobi* (potato-and-cauliflower curry) and *kheer* (creamy rice pudding) are lip-smackingly good.

BUSES FROM HARIDWAR

The following buses depart from the UK Roadways bus stand. Information about buses to Dharamsala and Shimla is available at counter six.

DESTINATION	FARE (₹)	DURATION (HOUR)	FREQUENCY
Agra	300	12	early morning
Chandigarh	164	10	hourly
Dehra Dun	55	2	half-hourly
Delhi (AC Volvo)	600-725	6	11am, 1pm, 11pm
Delhi (standard)	147	6	half-hourly
Dharamsala	400	15	2.30pm, 4.30pm
Haldwani (for Nainital & Almora)	263	7	hourly
Jaipur	345	12	early morning
Ranikhet	240	10	6am, 4.30pm
Rishikesh	30	1	half-hourly
Shimla	255	14	1.30am, 12.30pm, 5.30pm
Uttarkashi	257	10	5.30am, 7.3-0am, 9.30am

In the *yatra* (pilgrimage) season from May to October, the following buses run from the GMOU bus stand. During monsoon season (July to mid-September), service is occasionally suspended. For current info, call ☎ 9897924247. For Yamunotri, go to Dehra Dun, then take a bus to Barkot.

DESTINATION	FARE (₹)	DURATION (HOUR)	FREQUENCY
Badrinath (via Joshimath)	450	15	5.15am, 7.30am
Gangotri	400	10	5am
Joshimath	390	10	7.30am
Kedarnath	330	10	5am
Uttarkashi	280	8	7am, 10am

TRAINS FROM HARIDWAR

DESTINATION	TRAIN NAME & NUMBER	FARE (₹)	DURATION (HOUR)	DEPARTURE/ ARRIVAL
Amritsar	12053 Jan Shatabdi	2nd class/chair car 185/610	7½	2.35pm/10pm (Fri-Wed)
Amritsar	14631 Dehra Dun–Amritsar Express	sleeper/3AC/1st class 270/725/850	9¾	9.50pm/7.30am
Delhi (New Delhi Station)	12056 Jan Shatabdi Express	2nd class/chair car 140/465	4½	6.23am/11.10am
Delhi (New Delhi Station)	12018 Shatabdi Express	chair car/executive 670/1260	4½	6.15pm/10.45pm
Delhi (Old Delhi Station)	14042 Mussoorie Express	sleeper/3AC/2AC 190/485/690	8½	11.10pm/7.40am
Haldwani (for Nanital & Almora)	14120 Dehra Dun–Kathgodam Express	sleeper/2AC/1AC 190/690/1150	6½	12.25am/6.48am
Kolkata/Howrah	13010 Doon Express	sleeper/3AC/2AC 595/1585/2325	32	10.30pm/6.55am (2 nights later)
Lucknow	13010 Doon Express	sleeper/3AC/2AC 285/755/1085	10¼	10.30pm/8.45am
Varanasi	13010 Doon Express	sleeper/3AC/2AC 405/1095/1580	17¾	10.30pm/4.10pm

Big Ben Restaurant   MULTICUISINE $$
(Railway Rd, Hotel Ganga Azure; mains ₹85-200; ☺8am-10.30pm) Watch the passing parade through the big windows and enjoy some of Haridwar's best food in this restaurant of mirrors, soft music and polite staff. It's a solid choice for breakfast, with good coffee. There's wi-fi in the adjoining lobby.

Haveli Hari Ganga Restaurant   INDIAN $$$
(☎01334-226443; www.havelihariganga.com; 21 Ram Ghat; lunch thali ₹350, dinner buffet ₹450; ☺1-3pm & 7.30-10pm) The restaurant at this lovely heritage hotel is the classiest in Haridwar. Come for thali lunch or buffet dinner.

ⓘ Information

There are a number of internet places on Railway Rd near the train station and down the side lanes, but most have only one or two terminals.

GMVN Tourist Office (Garhwal Mandal Vikas Nigam; ☎01334-224240; Railway Rd; ☺10am-5pm Mon-Sat)

Main Post Office (Upper Rd; ☺10am-6pm Mon-Sat)

Rishikul Ayurvedic Hospital (☎01334-221003; Railway Rd) A long-established medical college and hospital with a good reputation.

Sai Forex (Upper Rd; ☺10am-2pm & 4-9pm) Changes cash and travellers cheques for a commission of 1%. Also has internet for ₹40 per hour.

Uttarakhand Tourism Office (☎01334-265304; Railway Rd, Rahi Motel; ☺10am-5pm Mon-Sat)

ⓘ Getting There & Away

Haridwar is well connected by bus and train, but book ahead for trains during the pilgrimage season (May to October).

BUS

Private deluxe buses buses run to Delhi (₹400), Agra (seat/sleeper ₹450/550), Jaipur (₹450/550) and Pushkar (₹550/650). Some leave from a **bus stand** around the corner from the GMVN tourist office by the gurdwara (Sikh temple). It's best to ask the travel agent who makes your booking where to find your bus.

TAXI

The main **taxi stand** (Railway Rd) is outside the train station. Destinations include Chilla (for Rajaji National Park, ₹570), Rishikesh (₹820, one hour) and Dehra Dun (₹1320), but it's usually possible to arrange a taxi for less than these official rates. You can hire private jeep Sumos to go to one or all of the pilgrimage sites on the Char Dham between April and October. One-way rates to single temples range from ₹6550 to ₹7550; a nine-day tour of all four is ₹22,600. Taxis to Jolly Grant Airport cost ₹1120.

❶ Getting Around

Cycle-rickshaws cost ₹10 for a short distance and ₹30 for longer hauls, such as from the Haridwar train station to Har-ki-Pairi. Shared *vikrams* run up and down Railway Rd (₹10) and all the way to Rishikesh (₹40, one hour) from Upper Rd at Laltarao Bridge, but for that trip buses are more comfortable. Hiring a taxi for three hours to tour the local temples and ashrams costs around ₹800; an autorickshaw costs ₹350.

RAJAJI NATIONAL PARK

ELEV 300-1000M

Unspoilt **Rajaji National Park** (www.rajajinationalpark.in; Indian/foreigner per day ₹150/600, vehicle fee ₹250/500; ◷ 15 Nov–15 Jun), covering 820 sq km in the forested foothills near Haridwar, is best known for its wild elephants, numbering around 600 at last count.

As well as elephants, the park contains some 250 leopards and 11 tigers, and at the time of writing, Rajaji was under consideration for being declared an official tiger reserve. These big cats, which are not easily seen, have thousands of chital (spotted deer) and hundreds of sambars (India's largest species of deer) to feed on. The park is also home to a handful of rarely seen sloth bears and some 300 species of birds.

Rajaji's forests include the traditional winter territory of more than 1000 families of nomadic Van Gujjar buffalo herders – most of whom have been evicted from the park against their will. For more on this and other issues affecting the unique Van Gujjar tribe, visit www.sophiaindia.org.

The village of Chilla, 13km northeast of Haridwar, is the base for visiting the park. At the Forest Ranger's office, close to the tourist guesthouse at Chilla, you can pick up a brochure, pay entry fees and organise a jeep. These take up to eight people and cost ₹1100 for the standard safari (plus a ₹500 entry fee for the vehicle). Elephant rides are no longer offered at Rajaji.

Before visiting, contact the GMVN tourist office (p425) in Haridwar and Mohan's Adventure Tours (p422), which offers abridged safaris even when the park is officially closed. These five-hour trips (₹2350 per person) include a short safari, during which you'll hopefully see a parade of wild elephants, and maybe visit a Van Gujjar forest camp.

⏳ Sleeping & Eating

Chilla Guesthouse (☑ 0138-266678; www.gmvnl.com; r from ₹2090; ❄) is the GMVN rest house and the most comfortable place to stay in Chilla. The guesthouse has a good restaurant and a pleasant garden.

You can stay inside the park at one of the rest houses run by the Forest Department. For information and reservations, contact the director at the **Rajaji National Park Office** (☑ 0135-2621669; Dehra Dun). Mohan's Adventure Tours can also make bookings.

Also within the park, the **Camp King Elephant** (☑ 9871604712; cottage incl full board, Indian/foreigner from ₹8500/US$240) resort has solar electricity, private bathrooms, full meal service and optional jeep tours.

❶ Getting There & Away

Buses to Chilla (₹30, one hour) leave the GMOU bus stand in Haridwar every hour from 7am to 2pm. The last return trip leaves Chilla at 5.30pm. Taxis charge ₹650 one way for the 13km journey.

DEHRA DUN

☑ 0135 / POP 578,420 / ELEV 640M

Perhaps best known for the institutions the British left behind – the huge Forest Research Institute Museum, the Indian Military Academy, the Wildlife Institute of India and the Survey of India – the capital of Uttarakhand is a hectic, congested city sprawling in the Doon Valley between the Himalayan foothills and the Siwalik Range. Most travellers merely pass through on their way to nearby Rishikesh, Haridwar, Mussoorie or Himachal Pradesh, but if you have time, there's enough to do here to make Dehra Dun worth a stop.

◉ Sights & Activities

Mindrolling Monastery　　　MONASTERY
(☑ 0135-2640556; www.mindrolling.org) The region around Dehra Dun is home to a thriving Tibetan Buddhist community, mainly focused on this monastery, about 10km south of the centre in Clement Town. Everything here is on a grand scale: at over 60m tall its **Great Stupa** (◷ 5am-9pm) FREE is believed to be the world's tallest stupa and contains a series of shrine rooms displaying relics, murals and Tibetan art. Presiding over the monastery is the impressive 35m-high gold **Sakyamuni Buddha Statue**, dedicated to the Dalai Lama.

Dehra Dun

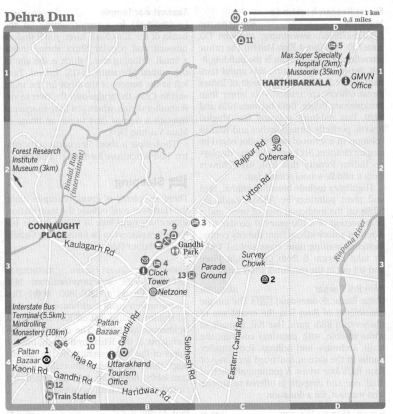

Dehra Dun

⦿ Sights
1 Ram Rai Darbar A4
2 Survey of India Museum C3

🛏 Sleeping
3 Hotel President C3
4 Moti Mahal Hotel B3
5 Samar Niwas Guest House D1

🍴 Eating
6 Chetan Puriwallah A4
7 Kumar Vegetarian & South Indian
    Restaurant B3
Moti Mahal .... (see 4)

🍷 Drinking & Nightlife
8 Barista B3
Polo Bar .... (see 3)

🛍 Shopping
English Book Depot .... (see 8)
9 Natraj Booksellers B3
10 Paltan Bazaar A4
11 Survey of India Map Counter C1

ℹ️ Transport
12 Mussoorie Bus Stand A4
13 Parade Ground Bus Stand B3
Taxi Stand .... (see 12)

The streets around the monastery are lined with Tibetan cafes. Unfortunately, due to new government regulations, foreigners are no longer allowed to stay overnight in Clement Town – but the manager of the Devaloka House hotel on the mon-astery grounds is willing to bend the rules. Simple rooms cost ₹350; the bed sheets have seen better days. Take *vikram 5* from the city centre (₹10). An autorickshaw costs about ₹150.

Forest Research Institute Museum
NOTABLE BUILDING

(☎0135-2759382; www.icfre.org; admission ₹10, guide ₹50; ☉9.30am-4.30pm Mon-Fri) The prime attraction of this museum is the building itself. Set in a 5-sq-km park, this grand remnant of the Raj era – where most of India's forest officers are trained – is larger than Buckingham Palace. Built between 1924 and 1929, this red-brick colossus has Mughal towers, perfectly formed arches and Roman columns in a series of quadrangles edged by elegant cloisters. Six huge halls have displays on Indian forestry that look like leftovers from a middle-school science fair.

Highlights include beautiful animal, bird and plant paintings by Afshan Zaidi, exhibits on the medicinal uses of trees, and a cross-section of a 700-year-old deodar tree. A return autorickshaw from the city centre, including waiting time, costs around ₹300. Or take *vikram* 6 from Connaught Place and get out at the institute's entry gate.

Ram Rai Darbar
MAUSOLEUM

(Paltan Bazaar; ☉dawn-dusk) FREE The unique mausoleum of Ram Rai, the errant son of the seventh Sikh guru, Har Rai, is made of white marble, with paintings covering the walls, archways, and ceilings. Four smaller tombs in the garden courtyard are those of Ram Rai's four wives. A communal lunch of dhal, rice and chapatis is offered to anyone who wants it, for a donation.

Survey of India Museum
MUSEUM

(Survey Chowk; ☉10.30am-5pm Mon-Fri) FREE Instruments used to accomplish the monumental task of mapping India in the 19th century are displayed here, including some designed especially for the mission by its leader, George Everest. See beautiful brass transits and scopes, plus a bar partly of iron, partly of brass, which allowed surveyors to compensate for inaccuracies in measurements caused by the expansion and contraction of their instruments in heat and cold. The museum is not officially opened to the public – you'll need permission to visit.

To get permission, go to the Surveyor General's office at the Survey of India Compound in Harthibarkala. There, you'll have to write a brief letter explaining why you want to view the collection. Permits are given only to those with an academic or professional interest in the subject – like a geography student or a historian – but proof of your vocation or college major isn't demanded.

Tapkeshwar Temple
HINDU TEMPLE

(☉dawn-dusk) In a scenic setting on the banks of the Tons Nadi River, you'll find an unusual and popular Shiva shrine inside a small, dripping cave, which is the site of the annual Shivaratri (p415) festival. Turn left at the bottom of the steps for the main shrine. Cross the bridge over the river to visit another shrine, where you have to squeeze through a narrow cave to see an image of Mata Vaishno Devi.

The temple is about 5km north of the centre. Take a rickshaw for ₹300 (round trip).

🛏 Sleeping

There are plenty of grungy cheapies along the Haridwar road outside the train station, some charging as little as ₹350 a double, but the better places can be found along Gandhi Rd and Rajpur Rd.

Samar Niwas Guest House
GUESTHOUSE $$

(☎0135-2740299; www.samarniwas.com; M-16 Chanderlok Colony; d ₹1200-1800; ❄@) This charming four-room guesthouse, in a peaceful residential area just off Rajpur Rd, is as welcoming as it gets. The owners are descendants of the Tehri royal family, but the rulers of the house seem to be the friendly pugs that roam the comfortable lounge-cum-lobby. Rooms are well appointed, but cleanliness is less than meticulous.

Moti Mahal Hotel
HOTEL $$

(☎0135-2651277; www.motimahal.net; 7 Rajpur Rd; s/d from ₹995/1495, with AC from ₹1595/1895; ❄🛜) Centrally located, Moti Mahal offers spotless rooms, most with air-con, and upholstered furnishings add a touch of class. Those facing Rajpur Road suffer from a bit of street noise, but not badly. Wi-fi is only in the lobby and the excellent restaurant (p429).

Hotel President
HOTEL $$$

(☎0135-2657082; www.hotelpresidentdehradun. com; Rajpur Rd, 6 Astley Hall; s from ₹3600, d from ₹3975; ❄) This Dehra Dun institution is one of the classiest hotels in town, despite being sandwiched within the complex of shops, restaurants and fast-food spots called Astley Hall. Rooms are thoroughly modern and even the least expensive have fridges, safes and complimentary slippers. There's a good restaurant, a coffee shop and the Polo Bar.

✖ Eating & Drinking

Dehra Dun has an eclectic range of restaurants, but by far the best hunting ground is along Rajpur Rd, northeast of the clock tower. The Astley Hall precinct is popular for fast food and has a couple of upmarket bars.

★ Chetan Puriwallah INDIAN $
(near Hanuman Chowk, Paltan Bazaar; ₹15 per puri; ⊙9am-4pm) If you're looking for that authentic (and delicious) local dining experience, you've found it. Unlimited thalis are served on plates made of leaves in this no-frills joint, and you just pay for the *puri* (deep-fried dough). The sweet *gulab jamun* (deep-fried dough in rose-flavoured syrup) is said to be some of the best in town.

Kumar Vegetarian & South Indian Restaurant INDIAN $$
(15B Rajpur Rd; mains ₹150-220; ⊙11am-4pm, 7-10.30pm) This popular, sparkling clean restaurant serves what surely comes close to the Platonic Form of a *masala dosa* (curried vegetables inside a crisp pancake), which is the main reason locals flock here. Other Indian dishes are also cooked to near perfection and even the Chinese food is quite good. The waitstaff are very attentive.

Moti Mahal SOUTH INDIAN $$
(7 Rajpur Rd; mains ₹160-425; ⊙9am-10.45pm; ⊚) Locals consistently rate Moti Mahal as one of the best midrange diners along Rajpur Rd. An interesting range of vegetarian and nonvegetarian includes Goan fish curry and Afghani *murg* (chicken), along with traditional South Indian fare and Chinese food.

Polo Bar BAR
(Rajpur Rd, 6 Astley Hall; ⊙11am-3pm & 7-11pm) One of the more salubrious of Dehra Dun's many hotel bars, this one is at Hotel President and is newly renovated.

Barista CAFE
(15A Rajpur Rd; drinks & snacks ₹70-190; ⊙9am-11pm) A popular modern cafe with an excellent bookshop in back.

🔒 Shopping

Among the best bookshops in town are **Natraj Booksellers** (17 Rajpur Rd; ⊙10am-8pm Mon-Sat), which gives plenty of shelf to local author Ruskin Bond, and **English Book Depot** (☑0135-2655192; www.englishbookdepot.com; 15 Rajpur Rd; ⊙10am-1.30pm & 2.30-8pm), attached to the Barista coffee shop.

★ Paltan Bazaar MARKET
The congested but relatively traffic-free area through Paltan Bazaar, running south from the clock tower, is a popular spot for an evening stroll. Here you can pick up everything from cheap clothing and souvenirs to camping and trekking gear.

Survey of India Map Counter MAPS
(off New Cantonment Rd; maps ₹20-70; ⊙9am-5.30pm Mon-Fri) The Survey of India Map Counter in Harthibarkala is mostly good at telling you which topographical maps you're not allowed to buy. However, you *can* pick up trekking maps that aren't bad for getting from village to village, but are worthless for backcountry navigation.

ℹ Information

The banks located on Rajpur Rd exchange travellers cheques and currency, and there are numerous ATMs that accept foreign credit cards.

3G Cybercafe (Meedo Arcade, Rajpur Rd; ₹20/hr; ⊙8am-10pm) Has air conditioning.

Ambulance (☑0135-6673666) Affiliated with Max Super Specialty Hospital

GMVN Office (74/1 Rajpur Rd; ⊙10am-5pm Mon-Sat) For some of the most helpful information on trekking in Garwhal, whether booking a GMVN trip or going independently, talk to Satish Khanduri on the ground floor of the tourism office (☑9568006696).

Main Post Office (Rajpur Rd; ⊙10am-5pm Mon-Sat)

Max Super Specialty Hospital (☑0135-6673000; Mussoorie Diversion Rd) North of centre.

Netzone (per hour ₹25; ⊙10am-8pm) One block southeast of the clock tower; also changes cash and travellers cheques.

Police (☑0135-2653333; Gandhi Rd)

Uttarakhand Tourism Office (☑0135-2653217; 45 Gandhi Rd; ⊙10am-5pm Mon-Sat, closed 2nd Sat of month) Located at the Hotel Drona – call for info about the airport shuttle. For any other info, the Tourism Office is barely more helpful than the attached office of KMVN, which should offer information about Kumaon, but is utterly useless.

ℹ Getting There & Away

AIR
A few airlines (Jet Airways, SpiceJet and Air India) fly daily between Delhi and Dehra Dun's Jolly Grant Airport – about 20km east of the city on the Haridwar road – with fares starting at around ₹3200 each way. A taxi to/from the airport costs ₹600, or take the AC coach for ₹100 (call the Uttarakhand Tourism office (p429) for times).

BUSES FROM DEHRA DUN

The following buses depart from the Interstate Bus Terminal (ISBT).

DESTINATION	FARE (₹)	DURATION (HOUR)	FREQUENCY
Chandigarh	230	6	hourly btwn 4am & 10pm
Delhi (AC-Volvo)	240/470 ordinary/AC	7	11 daily
Delhi (standard/deluxe)	257/400	7	hourly btwn 4am & 10pm
Dharamsala	750	14	5pm
Haridwar	60	2	half-hourly
Haldwani (for Nainital & Almora)	300	10	hourly
Manali	500	14	6.45am, 3pm, 10.15pm
Ramnagar	289	7	7 daily
Rishikesh	47	1½	half-hourly
Shimla	440	10	5 daily

BUS

Nearly all long-distance buses arrive and depart from the huge Interstate Bus Terminal (ISBT), 5km south of the city centre. To get there take a local bus (₹5), vikram 5 (₹10) or an autorickshaw (₹100). A few buses to Mussoorie leave from here but most depart from the Mussoorie bus stand (₹56, 1½ hours, half-hourly between 6am and 8pm) next to the train station. Some head to Mussoorie's Picture Palace bus stand while others go to the Library bus stand across town. There are also buses from the Mussoorie bus stand to Barkot – for Yamnotri – (₹218, five hours, 5.30am, 7.30am and 12pm); Purola – for Har-Ki-Dun – (₹227, seven hours, 6.30am and 1.30pm); Uttarkashi (₹250, seven hours, 5.30am) and Joshimath (₹480, 12 hours, 5.30am).

Private buses to Joshimath (₹370, 12 hours, 7am) and Uttarkashi (via Mussoorie ₹200, seven hours, 7am and 1.30pm; or via Chamba ₹280, eight hours, 8am and 12.30pm) leave from the Parade Ground bus stand.

TAXI

A taxi to Mussoorie costs ₹710, while a share taxi should cost ₹140 per person; both can be found in front of the train station. Taxis charge ₹1200 to Haridwar or Lakshman Jhula in Rishikesh.

TRAIN

Dehra Dun is well connected by train to Delhi, and there are a handful of services to Lucknow, Varanasi, Chennai (Madras) and Kolkata (Calcutta). Of the multiple daily trains from Dehra Dun to Delhi, the best are the expresses: Shatabdi (chair/executive ₹730/1390, six hours, train 12018, 5pm); Janshatabdi (2nd class/chair ₹160/515, six hours, train 12056, 5.10am) and Nanda Devi Express (3AC/2AC/1st Class ₹590/280/1365, six hours, train 12206, 11.30pm).

The overnight Dehradun–Amritsar Express (sleeper/3A/1st Class ₹270/725/850, 12 hours) to Amritsar departs nightly at 7.40pm.

❶ Getting Around

Hundreds of eight-seater vikrams (₹5 to ₹10 per trip) race along five fixed routes (look at the front for the number). Most useful is vikram 5, which runs between the ISBT stand, the train station and Rajpur Rd, and as far south as the Tibetan colony at Clement Town. Vikram 1 runs up and down Rajpur Rd above Gandhi Park, and also to Harthibarkala (check with the driver to see which route he's on). Autorickshaws cost ₹30 for a short distance, ₹120 from ISBT to the city centre or ₹160 per hour for touring around the city.

MUSSOORIE

📞 0135 / POP 29,500 / ELEV 2000M

Perched on a ridge 2km high, the 'Queen of Hill Stations' vies with Nainital as Uttarakhand's favourite holiday destination. When the mist clears, views of the green Doon Valley and the distant white-capped Himalayan peaks are superb, and in the hot months the cooler temperatures and fresh mountain air make a welcome break from the plains below.

Established by the British in 1823, Mussoorie became hugely popular with the Raj set. The ghosts of that era linger on in the architecture of the churches, libraries, hotels and summer palaces. The town is swamped with visitors between May and July, when it can seem like a tacky holiday camp for families and honeymooners, but at other times many of the 300 hotels have vacancies and their prices drop dramatically. During monsoon, the town is often shrouded in clouds.

Central Mussoorie consists of two developed areas: Gandhi Chowk (also called Library Bazaar) at the western end, and the livelier Kulri Bazaar and Picture Palace at the eastern end, linked by the 2km Mall, which is still dominated by pedestrians but has sadly seen a notable increase in vehicle traffic and noise. Beyond Kulri Bazaar a narrow road leads 1.5km to Landour Bazaar.

Sights

Gun Hill VIEWPOINT

From midway along the Mall, a **cable car** (return ₹75; ⊙ 8am-10pm May-Jul & Oct, 10am-7pm Aug-Sep & late Nov-Apr) runs up to Gun Hill (2530m), which, on a clear day, has views of several big peaks. A steep path also winds up to the viewpoint. The most popular time to go up is an hour or so before sunset. There's a minicarnival atmosphere in high season, with kids' rides, food stalls, magic shops and honeymooners having their photos taken in Garhwali costumes.

Activities

Walks

When the clouds don't get in the way, the walks around Mussoorie offer great views. **Camel's Back Rd** is a popular 3km promenade from Kulri Bazaar to Gandhi Chowk, and passes a rock formation that looks like a camel. There are a couple of good mountain viewpoints along the way, and you can ride a rickshaw (one way/return ₹150/300) along the trail if you start from the Gandhi Chowk end. An enjoyable, longer walk (5km one way) starts at the **Picture Palace Cinema**, goes past **Union Church** and the clock tower to Landour and the Sisters' Bazaar area.

West of Gandhi Chowk, a more demanding walk is to the **Jwalaji Temple** on Benog Hill (about 20km return) via Cloud's End Hotel. The route passes through thick forest and offers some fine views. Taking a taxi to Cloud's End (₹550) cuts the walk by more than half. A slightly shorter walk is to the abandoned **Everest House** (16km return), former residence of Sir George Everest, first surveyor-general of India and namesake of

the world's highest mountain. You can also take a cycle rickshaw (₹130) to Park Toll, cutting 5km off the distance.

Courses

Landour Language School LANGUAGE

(☑ 0135-2631487; www.landourlanguageschool. com; Landour; per hour group/private ₹285/460; ⊙ Feb-Dec) One of India's leading schools for teaching conversational Hindi at beginner, intermediate and advanced levels. There's an enrolment fee of ₹500, and course books are an extra ₹2000.

Tours

A full day of sightseeing around Mussoorie by taxi costs around ₹3000, including visits to the popular and overdeveloped Kempty Falls, 15km west, and to Dhanolti, a serene spot 25km east, set in deodar forests with Himalayan views.

The GMVN Booth (p433) can organise a number of local bus tours, including to Kempty Falls (three-hour tour ₹125), as well as further reaching full-day tours (from ₹250). Tours can also be booked at the Uttarakhand Tourism Office (p433) on the Lower Mall.

Sleeping

Peak season is summer (May to July) when hotel prices shoot to ridiculous heights. There's a midseason during the honeymoon period around October and November, and over Christmas and New Year, and these are the prices we list unless specified. At other times you should be able to get a bargain.

Budget places are scarce – you'll find some dives near Picture Palace. But many hotels offer budget rates out of season.

Hotel Broadway HOTEL $

(☑ 0135-2632243; Camel's Back Rd, Kulri Bazaar; d ₹650-1500) The best of the budget places by a country mile, this historic 1880s wooden hotel with colourful flowerboxes in the windows oozes character. It's in a quiet location but close to the Mall. Cheaper downstairs rooms could use a refresh, but upstairs rooms are nice; the best has sunlit bay windows.

★**Kasmanda**

Palace Hotel HERITAGE HOTEL $$$

(☑ 0135-2632424; www.kasmandapalace.com; s/d from ₹5850/7020) Located off the Mall, this is Mussoorie's most romantic hotel.

Mussoorie

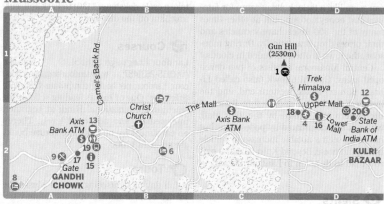

Mussoorie

The white Romanesque castle was built in 1836 for a British officer and was bought by the Maharaja of Kasmanda in 1915. The red-carpeted hall has a superb staircase flanked by moth-eaten hunting trophies. All the rooms have charm but the wood-panelled and antique-filled Maharaja Room is the royal best.

There's also a separate cottage with six renovated contemporary-style rooms. An excellent restaurant and pretty garden area – open to nonguests – complete the picture.

Hotel Padmini Nivas   HERITAGE HOTEL **$$$**
(☎ 0135-2631093; www.hotel-padmininivas.com; The Mall; d ₹3000-3750, ste ₹4500-5250; @) Built in 1840 by a British colonel, this heritage hotel has real old-fashioned charm.

Large rooms with quaint sun rooms are beautifully furnished; those in the main house are significantly nicer than those in the side building. The dining room, with its antique furniture, is an outstanding feature. The whole place is set on 2 hectares of landscaped gardens.

The Savoy   HERITAGE HOTEL **$$$**
(☎ 0135-2637000; www.fortunehotels/savoy. in; behind Gandhi Chowk; r from ₹11,700) This famous Mussoorie hotel, built in 1902, has recently reopened after undergoing a seven-year renovation. Inside and out, the public spaces are magnificent, imparting a regal aesthetic with none of the run-down air that often infuses historic properties. Bedrooms, however, feel strangely generic and, at the

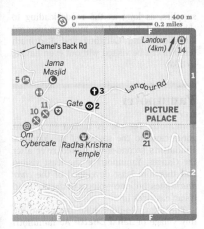

scores highly on everything – decor, service and food. The menu emphasises Continental dishes, with long lists of platters and sizzlers, plus big toasted sandwiches. For breakfast you can even have waffles. Upstairs features a tea room–cum–hookah lounge, and the attached hotel (rooms from ₹4500) has excellent rooms with valley views.

Shopping

Mussoorie has a wonderful collection of magic shops, where you can buy cheap but baffling magic tricks and wacky toys – great gifts for kids. The most interesting store is the antiques and miscellany shop run by **Vinod Kumar** (Clock Tower, Landour Bazaar; ⊙10am-7pm), near the clock tower at the bottom of Landour Bazaar – a 10- to 15-minute walk from Picture Palace.

Information

GMVN Booth (☑0135-2631281; library bus stand; ⊙9am-6pm) Can book local tours, treks and far-flung rest houses.

Main Post Office (☑0135-2632206; Upper Mall, Kulri Bazaar; ⊙9am-5pm Mon-Sat)

Om Cybercafe (off The Mall, Kulri Bazaar; per hour ₹60; ⊙10am-9pm) Behind Lovely Omelette Centre (p433).

Trek Himalaya (☑0135-2630491; Upper Mall; ⊙11am-9pm) Exchanges major currencies at a fair rate.

Uttarakhand Tourism Office (☑0135-2632863; Lower Mall; ⊙10am-5pm Mon-Sat) Near the cable-car station.

Getting There & Away

BUS

Frequent buses head to Mussoorie (₹56, 1½ hours) from Dehra Dun's Mussoorie bus stand. Some go to the **Picture Palace bus stand** (☑0135-2632259) while others go to the **Library bus stand** (☑0135-2632258) at the other end of town – if you know where you're staying, it helps to be on the right bus. There's no direct transport from Mussoorie to Rishikesh or Haridwar – change at Dehra Dun.

To reach the mountain villages of western Garhwal, grab one of the buses passing through Gandhi Chowk. For Yamunotri, hop on a bus to Barkot (₹140, 3½ hours, departs around 6.30am, 8.30am and 1pm), then transfer to another to Janki Chatti (₹60, three hours). A couple of buses go to Purola (₹200, five hours, departs around 7.30am and 2.30pm). For Uttarkashi, leave from the Tehri bus stand at Landour and change at Chamba, or go to Barkot and transfer there.

time of research, the reputation of the service wasn't stellar.

Eating & Drinking

Most of Mussoorie's best eating places are at the Kulri Bazaar and Picture Palace end of town. True to the holiday feel there are lots of fast-food places, and most hotels have their own restaurants. There is a **Café Coffee Day** (Kulri Bazaar; ⊙9am-11pm) in Kulri Bazaar and another **branch** (near Gandhi Chowk; ⊙9am-11pm) near Gandhi Chowk.

★**Lovely Omelette Centre**   FAST FOOD **$**
(The Mall, Kulri Bazaar; mains ₹40-90; ⊙9am-9.30pm Wed-Mon) Mussorie's most famous eatery is also its smallest – a cubbyhole along the Mall that serves what many say are the best omelettes in India. The speciality is the cheese omelette, with chillies, onions and spices, served over toast, but the maestro at the frying pan will whip up a chocolate omelette on request. Opening hours can be unpredictable.

Neelam   PUNJABI **$$**
(Kulri Bazaar; ₹130-280; ⊙9am-11pm) Around in one form or another since 1949, Neelam specialises in paneer dishes, and boasts a long list of chicken and lamb. In high season it breaks out the *tawa* – a heated metal plate, which slow-cooks meat to perfection. The affable manager, Sam, is exceptionally welcoming.

Imperial Square   CONTINENTAL **$$$**
(☑0135-2632632; Gandhi Chowk; mains ₹225-600; ⊙7am-11pm; 🛜) With huge windows overlooking Gandhi Chowk, Imperial Square

TAXI

From taxi stands at both bus stands you can hire taxis to Dehra Dun (₹710) and Rishikesh (₹2200), or Uttarkashi (₹4500). A shared taxi to Dehra Dun should cost ₹140 per person.

TRAIN

The **Northern Railway booking agency** (☑ 0135-2632846; Lower Mall, Kulri Bazaar; ⏱ 8am-2pm Mon-Sat) books tickets for trains from Dehra Dun and Haridwar.

❶ Getting Around

Central Mussoorie is very walkable – for a hill station, the Mall and Camel's Back Rd are surprisingly flat. Cycle-rickshaws along the Mall cost ₹30, but can only go between Gandhi Chowk and the cable-car station.

THE CHAR DHAM

High in the Garhwali Himalayas sit some of the holiest sites in the Hindu religion – Yamunotri, Gangotri, Kedarnath, and Badrinath – where temples mark the spiritual sources of four sacred rivers: the Yamuna, the Ganges, the Mandakini and the Alaknanda. Together, they make up one of the most important *yatra* circuits in all of India, known as the *char dham* (four seats). Every year between April and November, hundreds of thousands of worshippers brave hair-raising mountain roads and high-altitude trails to reach them. Or they did, anyway…

In June 2013, a torrential cloudburst produced an epic flood that swept away entire villages – and thousands of local people and pilgrims. The official death toll was around 6000, but locals insist the real number was closer to 50,000. Since then, many would-be pilgrims have stayed home, afraid that tragedy might repeat itself. The people and goverment of Uttarakhand are desperately hoping to rebuild confidence in the area's safety, to revive the region's main economic engine. We expect the *yatra's* popularity will begin to rebound after a few seasons without a major catastrophe.

Even now, travelling to one or more of these temples is a great way to get a feel for the religious pulse of the subcontinent, amid incredible alpine scenery. Numerous buses, share jeeps, porters, ponies and palanquins are on hand for transport, and there's a well-established network of guesthouses, ashrams and government rest houses. As a result, getting to these temples is easy enough without hiring guides or carrying supplies, as long as the roads leading to them aren't blocked by monsoon-inspired landslides. And Gangotri and Badrinath temples can be visited without even having to hike.

Yamunotri

ELEV 3185M

Yamunotri Temple is tucked in a tight gorge close to the source of the Yamuna, Hinduism's second-most sacred river after the Ganges. Yamunotri is the least visited and therefore least developed of the *char dham* sites, but once you get to the trailhead it's an easy trek in.

The 5km, 1½-hour hike begins at the tiny village of **Janki Chatti**. At Yamunotri Temple there are several **hot-spring pools** where you can take a dip, and others where pilgrims cook potatoes and rice as *prasad*. You'll find plenty of priests to help you make *puja* for a price. One kilometre beyond the temple, the Yamuna River spills from a frozen lake of ice and glaciers on the **Kalinda Parvat** mountain at an altitude of 4421m, but this is a very tough climb that requires mountaineering skills.

Across the river from Janki Chatti is the friendly village of **Kharsali**, which is worth a stroll if you have the time.

Accommodation is available at basic guesthouses or the GMVN tourist lodges in Janki Chatti and Hanuman Chatti.

During peak *yatra* season (May to June), buses run from Dehra Dun, Mussoorie and Rishikesh to Janki Chatti, but the most frequent transport services originate in Barkot. Buses (three hours, ₹60) depart Barkot for Janki Chatti at 9am, 1pm and 3pm; they make return runs to Barkot at 6am, 8.30am and 2pm. You can find sporadic share jeeps making the same runs (₹80, 2½ hours). A private taxi costs about ₹2000 each way.

Gangotri & Gaumukh Glacier Trek

☑ 01377 / ELEV 3042M

In a remote setting at an altitude of 3042m, **Gangotri Temple** is one of the holiest places in India. Near the source of the Ganges (known as the Bhagirathi until it reaches Devprayag), the shrine is dedicated to the origin of Hinduism's most sacred river. Nearby is the rock on which Shiva is said to have cushioned the impact of the water in his matted locks as it poured from the heavens, saving the earth from the destructive force of this great gift.

Erected by Gorkha commander Amar Singh Thapa in the 18th century, the temple – for a site of such significance – is surprisingly underwhelming. Unless you're a devout Hindu, to get a real sense of awe you'll probably have to trek from Gangotri to the true source of the river, at Gaumukh, 18km upstream. There, the water flows out of Gangotri Glacier beneath the soaring west face of Bhagirathi Parvat (6856m), with the peak of Shivling (the 6543m 'Indian Matterhorn') towering to the south.

Don't be daunted by the trek – the trail rises gradually and is completely solid. 14km (four to six hours) up the trail, at Bhojbasa (3790m), there's a GMVN Tourist Bungalow (☎01377-222221; Bhojbasa; dm ₹350) and other basic lodging; Gaumukh is 4km (1½ hours) past that. On clear days, the best time to visit the source is early to midafternoon, when it's out of the shadows. Porters (₹500 each way) and horses (one way/return ₹850/1250) can be hired in Gangotri. More ambitious hikers with camping gear often continue to the gorgeous meadow at Tapovan, 6km beyond Gaumukh.

Before trekking to Gaumukh, you must first get a permit, since access is limited to 150 people per day. This can be obtained from the District Forest Office (☎01377-225693; ☉10am-5pm Mon-Sat, closed 2nd Sat of month), 3km north of the Uttarkashi bus stand, or from the satellite office above the bus stand at Gangotri, which is open every day from 8am to 10am and 5pm to 7pm. At both places, you'll need to bring a copy of your passport ID page and visa. The permit is valid for two days and costs ₹150/600 per Indian/foreigner (then ₹50/250 for each extra day). Gangotri village has plenty of guesthouses, ashrams and dharamsalas (pilgrims' rest home)charging ₹300 or less per room. When hungry, follow the Indian families to the Hotel Gangaputra Restaurant (mains ₹60-150; ☉7am-11pm), which is busy for a good reason.

At the time of research, buses to and from Gangotri were sporadic and unpredictable. Service may become more regular once road improvements are complete. For now, the best way to get back and forth is by shared jeep (₹200) or private taxi (one way/return ₹3000/4000). To Rishikesh, shared jeeps/private taxis cost ₹400/5000.

Kedarnath

☑01364 / ELEV 3584M

In the epic Mahabharata, after the Pandavas defeated the Dhartarashtras, they sought forgiveness for killing their own family members, as their enemies also happened to be their cousins. Shiva refused, but the Pandavas were relentless in their quest for absolution, so Shiva, in the form of a bull, dove into the ground to elude them. He left his hump behind at Kedarnath, below the source of the sacred Mandakini River, where a magnificent stone temple – built in the 8th century by Guru Shankara – marks the spot. (Other portions of Shiva's bull-form body are worshipped at the other four Panch Kedar shrines, which take some effort to reach but can be visited: the arms at Tungnath, the face at Rudranath, the navel at Madmaheshwar and the hair at Kalpeshwar.)

Tucked at the base of 6970m peaks, 22km from the nearest road, Kedarnath is in the most dramatic location of any of the char dham temples. The puja offered inside, especially around the stone 'hump', is fervent and can be quite intense. The site is so auspicious that pilgrims used to throw themselves from one of the cliffs behind the temple in the hope of instantly attaining moksha (liberation).

Kedarnath was at the epicentre of the devastating flood of 2013. Thousands of people – pilgrims and locals, porters and horse guides, among others – perished here. Much of the village around the temple was destroyed by the raging waters and the huge rocks that washed down from the surrounding slopes. Today, nearly as much reverence is paid to a massive boulder that sits behind the temple – which, incredibly, shielded it from the worst of the onslaught and saved it from collapse – as to the temple itself.

The disaster has significantly altered the experience of visiting Kedarnath, as long swaths of the original trail slid off the mountainside, the base village of Gaurikund was ravaged and the road to it was heavily damaged. At the time of research, the pilgrims' route begins at Sonprayag, from where it is a 22km uphill hike to the temple; six to eight hours by foot or five hours if you hire a pony (₹1800). In Sonprayag, before heading up the trail, you must get a free 'biometric' ID card, then go next door to get your blood pressure tested (we're not sure why...). You then must go a couple doors down to register with the police.

The new route first follows the old road to Gaurikund. Beyond that, the government has set up canteens about every 5km along the trail, where free food and chai are served. If you stay overnight at Kedarnath, the best – and virtually only – place is the GMVN camp, set up about a kilometre before the temple; food and lodging (in a group tent with thin foam pads covering the floor) are free, and GMVN has sleeping bags so there's no imperative to carry your own (though we have no idea how often theirs are cleaned...). If you want to take photos of the sadhus at the temple, bring a pocketful of ₹10 notes.

Reaching Kedarnath by helicopter (₹7200) is becoming an increasingly popular option for Indians, though it doesn't offer the same experience as trekking. Passengers are only able to stay at Kedarnath for about an hour. Advance reservations are recommended. Contact Himalayan Heli Services (☑ 7895479452; www.himalayanheli.com; Guptkashi-Sonprayag Rd), or go to their office at the heli pad in Sersi, 20km from Guptkashi.

In Sonprayag, basic accommodation is available for ₹200 to ₹400. A handful of better places can be found about 2km before the trailhead, at Sitapur. If you prefer to stay at Guptkashi, the main transit hub, the New Viswanath (☑ 9720895992; Guptkashi Bus Stand; r from ₹500), at the bus stand, is a good choice; rooms on the 'back side' are quiet and share a terrace with valley views.

To get to Sonprayag, take a shared/private jeep (₹80/1000) from Guptkashi, or a GMOU bus from Rishikesh or Haridwar. From Sonprayag, morning buses run to Rishikesh (₹340, seven hours), Haridwar (₹340, eight hours), Dehradun (₹340, nine hours) and Badrinath (₹340) or take a share/private jeep back to Guptkashi and travel onwards from there.

Badrinath & Mana Village

☑ 01381 / ELEV 3133M

Basking in a superb setting in the shadow of snow-topped Nilkantha, Badrinath Temple appears almost lost in the tatty village that surrounds it. Sacred to Lord Vishnu, this vividly painted temple is the most easily accessible and popular of the *char dham* temples. It was founded by Guru Shankara in the 8th century, but the current structure is much more recent. Below the temple are hot springs that reach a scalding 40°C and serve as a laundry for locals.

A scenic 3km walk beyond Badrinath along the Alaknanda River (cross over to the temple side to pick up the path), past fields divided by dry-stone walls, leads to tiny but charismatic Mana Village (you can also take a taxi there for ₹200). The village is crammed with narrow stone laneways and traditional houses of varying designs – some have slate walls and roofs while others are wooden with cute balconies. You can wander around and watch the village ladies knitting colourful jerseys or hauling loads of fodder while the men tend goats or play cards or carom billiards. Carpets, blankets, jerseys, hats and gloves are all on sale.

Just outside the village in a small cave is the tiny, 5000-year-old Vyas Temple. Nearby is Bhima's Rock, a natural rock arch over a river that is said to have been made by Bhima, strongest of the Pandava brothers, whose tale is told in the Mahabharata. The 5km hike along the Alaknanda to the 145m Vasudhara Waterfall has a great reward-to-effort ratio, with views up the valley of the Badrinath massif jutting skywards like a giant fang. The villagers migrate to somewhere warmer – usually Joshimath – between November and April.

Badrinath can easily be visited in a day from Joshimath if you get an early start, but it's worth staying if you also want to see Mana Village and do any hiking. There is a slew of mediocre budget guesthouses lining the main road into town, charging ₹400 to ₹600 per room; they can be loud with pilgrims. Offering among the best value in town are Himgiri Guest House (☑ 7579257765; Badrinath Village; r ₹500), Narayan Palace Hotel (☑ 9426358998; www.narayanpalace.com; Badrinath Village; r ₹3600-4500), and Hotel Snow Crest (☑ 9412082465; www.snowcrest.co.in; Badrinath Village; r ₹4850-6450) – which is Badrinath's most expensive, but has heaters in the rooms. Even in summer, it can be quite cold here.

From the large bus station at the entrance to Badrinath, GMOU buses run to Haridwar (₹350) via Rishikesh (₹320) at 5.30am and Gaurikund (for Kedarnath, ₹255) at 7am, but check scheduled departure times or you may end up stranded. Private buses to Joshimath and beyond leave sporadically throughout the morning. For Joshimath or Govindghat (for Valley of Flowers) try to take a shared jeep around 7am.

UTTARKASHI

🎵 01374 / POP 17,120 / ELEV 1158M

Uttarkashi, 155km from Rishikesh and the largest town in northern Garhwal, is a major stop on the road to Gangotri Temple and the Gaumukh Glacier trek. The main bazaar is worth a wander and has all the supplies you might need. A number of outfitters can arrange treks in the region, including to Tapovan (beyond Gangotri/Gaumukh).

There's a State Bank of India ATM in the market.

The town is probably best known for the **Nehru Institute of Mountaineering** (☎ 01374-222123; www.nimindia.net; ⏱10am-5pm), which trains many of the guides running trekking and mountaineering outfits in India. The centre is across the river from the main market and has a museum and outdoor climbing wall. Basic and advanced mountaineering and adventure courses are open to all – check the website for details and admission information.

Uttarkashi also hosts the annual **Makar Sankranti** (⏱ Jan) festival in January.

🛏 Sleeping & Eating

There are plenty of hotels and *dhabas* (snack bars) around the bus stand and in the nearby market.

Monal Guest House   HOTEL $
(☎ 01374-222270; www.monaluttarkashi.com; Kot Bungalow Rd; r ₹600-1800; @) This hillside hotel feels like a large comfortable house with clean, airy rooms, a big-windowed restaurant and peaceful garden setting. Wing A has a more homely feel than Wing B. It's off the Gangotri road 3km north of town, about 100m from the office that issues permits to Gamukh.

Hotel Govind Palace   HOTEL $
(☎ 01374-223815, 9411522058; near bus stand; r from ₹400) One of the best value choices if you have to catch an early morning bus. It has good beds, hot showers and TVs, and the manager GS Bhandari is superhelpful. It also has one of the better restaurants in town.

ℹ Getting There & Away

At the time of research, regular bus services to Gangotri had ceased, but may begin again after road improvements are made. To get there, take a shared/private taxi (₹200/3000, five hours). Buses head to Rishikesh (₹230, seven hours)

every half-hour between 6.30am and 2pm. Five daily buses go to Haridwar (₹260, eight hours) and three go to Dehradun (₹260, nine hours). Buses to Srinagar (₹190, eight hours) leave at 5.30am and 8am, and those to Barkot (₹110, five hours) leave regularly until 3pm. In summer, two morning buses run directly to Janki Chatti (₹170, nine hours) for Yamunotri temple. Seats may sell out on some routes, so it's a good idea to buy tickets a day in advance.

JOSHIMATH

🎵 01389 / POP 13,860 / ELEV 1875M

As the gateway to Badrinath Temple and Hem Kund, Joshimath sees a steady stream of Hindu and Sikh pilgrims from May to October. And as the base for the Valley of Flowers and Kuari Pass treks, and Auli ski resort, it attracts adventure travellers year-round.

Reached from Rishikesh by a serpentine mountain road, Joshimath is a ramshackle two-street town with erratic power supply and limited places to eat. Although the mountain views are lost from the town itself, it's only a short **cable car** (return ₹500; ⏱ every 20min 8am-6.50pm) ride from here to Auli, which has magnificent vistas of Nanda Devi.

🏃 Activities

To trek the Kuari Pass and other routes in Nanda Devi Sanctuary, you need a permit and a registered guide. There are three excellent operators in town who can organise everything.

Himalayan Snow Runner   OUTDOOR ADVENTURE
(☎ 9756813236, 9412082247; www.himalayansnowrunner.com) Highly recommended outfit for trekking (from around ₹3000 per person per day), skiing and adventure activities, with camping gear provided. The owner, Ajay, also takes cultural tours to Bhotia and Garhwali villages, and runs a guesthouse in his home in Mawari village, 5km from Joshimath (rooms ₹1250 to ₹3850).

Adventure Trekking   OUTDOOR ADVENTURE
(☎ 9837937948; www.thehimalayanadventures.com; Main Bazaar) Treks of anything from two to 10 days can be arranged here for around US$50 per person per day (with more than one person), as well as white-water rafting, skiing and peak ascents. The owner, Santosh, is helpful and runs a guesthouse on the way up to Auli (rooms ₹1000 to ₹2000).

ⓘ GRAB A WINDOW!

If travelling through the hills or mountains, get to buses early to claim a window seat. The landscape, much of which you'll never stop to explore, is gorgeous.

Eskimo Adventures   OUTDOOR ADVENTURE
(☑ 9756835647; www.eskimoadventure.com) Offers treks and rock-climbing expeditions from about ₹3000 per day, equipment rental (for trekking and skiing), and white-water rafting trips on the Ganges.

🛏 Sleeping & Eating

There are lots of cheap lodgings and a few pricier hotels scattered around town. Joshimath's trekking outfits also operate upmarket homestay-style guesthouses that are worth considering. Several *dhabas* in the main bazaar serve similar vegetarian thalis and dosas from ₹30 to ₹100.

Hotel New Kamal   HOTEL $
(☑ 01389-221891; Main Market; r ₹400) Small and clean with bucket hot water and TVs; one of the better cheapies in the town centre.

Hotel Kamet   HOTEL $
(☑ 01389-222155; Main Market; r ₹500, annex ₹800-1600) Aim for the annex in the back, with newer rooms that are worth a few more rupees – but look at a few if you can, as each has unique flaws.

Malari Inn   HOTEL $$
(☑ 01389-222257; www.hotel-malari-inn.weebly. com; Main Market; r ₹1800-3500) This is the best place in Joshimath. Standard rooms are basic but spacious and clean; you pay more for more amenities, a fatter mattress and a balcony with valley views. All rooms have geysers. Discounts are offered outside peak season (May through to September).

Auli D's Food Plaza   MULTICUISINE $$
(Main Market; mains ₹70-450; ⊙ 7am-10pm) Featuring a full menu of Indian, Chinese and Continental food, including veg and nonveg choices, this 1st-floor restaurant has plastic tablecloths and covered seats, and feels like a banquet hall.

ⓘ Information

There's a **GMVN Tourist Office** (☑ 01389-222181; ⊙ 10am-5pm Mon-Sat) located just north of the town (follow the Tourist Rest House sign off Upper Bazaar Rd), and there's a State Bank of India ATM. Tour companies have internet services.

ⓘ Getting There & Away

Although the main road up to Joshimath is maintained by the Indian army, and a hydroelectric plant on the way to Badrinath has improved that road, the area around Joshimath is inevitably prone to landslides, particularly in the rainy season from mid-June to mid-September.

The best way to get to Badrinath/Govindghat (for Valley of Flowers and Hem Kund) is by shared jeep (₹100/50), leaving from the Badrinath taxi stand at the far end of Upper Bazaar Rd. Hiring the whole jeep costs ₹1400. A few buses (₹65) leave throughout the day from the same place.

Buses run from Joshimath to Rishikesh (₹360, 10 hours) and Haridwar (₹395, 11½ hours), at 4am, 4.30am, 6am and 7am, departing from the tiny **GMOU booth** (Upper Bazaar Rd; ⊙ 4am-8pm), where you can also book tickets. From the main jeep stand, private buses leave occasionally for Chamoli (₹75, two hours) and Karanprayag (₹130, four hours), with some continuing to Rishikesh.

To get to the eastern Kumaon region, take any bus or shared taxi to Chamoli then transfer onward to Karanprayag, from where a series of local buses and share jeeps can take you along the beautiful road towards Kausani, Bageshwar and Almora. You may have to change several times along the way. Transport winds down in late afternoon, so get an early start.

AROUND JOSHIMATH

Auli
☑ 01389 / ELEV 3048M

Rising above Joshimath, 14km by road – and only 4km by the gondola-style cable car – Auli is India's premier ski resort. But you don't have to visit in winter to enjoy the awesome views of Nanda Devi (India's second-highest peak) from the top of the cable-car station.

As a ski resort, Auli is hardly spectacular, with gentle 5km-long slopes, one 500m rope tow (₹100 per trip) that runs beside the main slope, and an 800m chairlift (₹200) that connects the upper and lower slopes. The snow is consistently good, though, and the setting is superb. The season runs from January to March, and equipment hire and instruction can be arranged here or in Joshimath.

The state-of-the-art cable car (p437), India's longest, links Joshimath to the upper slopes above Auli. There's a cafe, of sorts, at the top, serving hot chai and tomato soup.

The **Clifftop Club** (☑ 7417936606; www.clifftopclubauli.com; Auli; studio ₹11,600, ste ₹16,250) wouldn't look out of place in the Swiss Alps, with its solid timber interior finish, cosy atmosphere and spacious rooms, some with views of Nanda Devi. Meals and all-inclusive ski packages, including equipment, are available.

If on a tighter budget, stay at the surprisingly good **GMVN Tourist Rest House** (☑ 01389-223208; www.gmvnl.com; dm ₹280, r ₹1650-4400, incl breakfast) at the start of the chairlift. There's also the unique **Devi Darshan** (☑ 9719316777; www.mountainshepherds.com; r from ₹3650 incl meals), which has a restaurant and common room with full-on Nanda Devi views, though bedrooms are dark.

VALLEY OF FLOWERS & HEM KUND

British mountaineer Frank Smythe stumbled upon the Valley of Flowers in 1931. 'In all my mountain wandering,' he wrote, 'I have not seen a more beautiful valley where the human spirit may find repose'. The *bugyals* (high-altitude meadows) of tall wildflowers are a glorious sight on a sunny day, rippling in the breeze, and framed by mighty 6000m mountains that have glaciers and snow decorating their peaks all year.

The 300 species of flowers make this World Heritage Site a unique and valuable pharmaceutical resource. Unfortunately, most flowers bloom during the monsoon season in July and August, when the rains make access difficult and hazardous. There's a widespread misconception that the valley isn't worth visiting outside peak flower season, but even without its technicolour carpet it's still ridiculously beautiful. And it's more likely to be sunny.

To reach the 87-sq-km **Valley of Flowers National Park** (Indian/foreigner up to 3 days ₹40/600, subsequent days ₹20/175; ⊙ 7am-5pm Jun-Oct, last entry 2pm) first requires a full-day hike from Govindghat to the village of Ghangaria (also called Govinddham), less than 1km from the park. The fabled valley begins 2km uphill from the ticket office and continues for another 5km. Tracks are easy to follow.

A tougher hike from Ghangaria involves joining the hundreds of Sikh pilgrims toiling up to the 4300m Hem Kund, the sacred lake surrounded by seven peaks where Sikh guru Gobind Singh is believed to have meditated in a previous life. Ponies (₹400) are available if you prefer to ride up the 6km zigzag trail.

The trek to Ghangaria is a scenic but strenuous 14km uphill from Govindghat, which takes five to seven hours. You can

---

OFF THE BEATEN TRACK

TUNGNATH & CHANDRISILLA

One of the best day hikes in Uttarakhand, the trail to **Tungnath Mandir** (3680m) and **Chandrisilla Peak** (4000m) features a sacred Panch Kedar temple and a stunning Himalayan panorama.

The trail starts at Chopta, a small village with no electricity, which is found on the winding road between Chamoli (south of Joshimath) and Kund (south of Gaurikund). A well-paved path switchbacks 3.5km uphill, gaining 750m in elevation, to Tungnath, the highest Shiva temple in the world. A dirt trail continues 1.5km further to the top of Chandrisilla. From the summit, the Garhwali and Kumaoni Himalayas stretch out before you, with awesome vistas of major mountains including Nanda Devi, Trishul and the Kedarnath group. Start early before the clouds move in, or head up in the afternoon, stay at one of the spartan guesthouses around Tungnath and hit Chandrisilla for sunrise. There's basic accommodation in Chopta: **Hotel Neelkanth** (☑ 7500139051, 7351442200; r from ₹400) has the best rooms, but **Hotel Rajkamal** (r ₹200) is the friendliest.

The drive from Chamoli to Chopta is a worthwhile diversion in itself, as it traverses steeply terraced hillsides dotted with rural villages before entering a lushly forested musk-deer sanctuary pierced by dramatic cliffs.

TREKKING THE HIMALAYA

There are many sublime trekking routes in Uttarakhand. Here are details on a few, listed from west to east. For more information or more options, pick up Lonely Planet's *Trekking in the Indian Himalaya* or contact GMVN in Dehradun or local trekking outfitters.

Har-ki-Dun Valley Trek

The wonderfully remote Har-ki-Dun Valley (3510m), within **Govind Wildlife Sanctuary & National Park** (Indian/foreigner up to 3 days ₹150/600, subsequent days ₹50/250), is a botanical paradise criss-crossed by glacial streams, surrounded by pristine forests and snowy peaks. You might be lucky enough to glimpse the elusive snow leopard above 3500m.

The three-day, 38km trail to Har-Ki-Dun begins at Sankri (also called Saur), where the best place to stay is the new **Wild Orchid Inn** (☑9411500044; www.wildorchidin@gmail.com; Sankri; s/d ₹600/800). There are very basic GMVN Tourist Bungalows at Sankri and along the way in the villages of Taluka and Osla, but at the valley itself you have to stay in the Forest Department rest house or bring a tent. You can cut a day off the hike by taking a share jeep to Taluka and starting from there. A side trip to Jamdar Glacier takes another day. The trek can be busy during June and October.

A couple of reputable guides work out of Sankri – Chain Singh and Bhagat Singh – who run the **Har Ki Dun Protection & Mountaineering Association** (☑9458909022, 9410134589; www.harkidun.org). In addition to outfitting trips to Har-ki-dun, they can take you to the unique villages of the Rupin and Supin Valleys. They also lead treks from Sankri to the Baspa Valley in Himachal Pradesh and along other beautiful routes. Make arrangements in advance by email if possible – these guys are busy!

To get to Sankri, take a direct bus from Gandhi Chowk in Mussoorie or from Dehra Dun's Mussoorie Bus Stand – or hop onto a series of buses and shared or private jeeps until you get there.

Kuari Pass Trek

Also known as the Curzon Trail (though Lord Curzon's party abandoned its attempt on the pass following an attack of wild bees), the trek over the Kuari Pass (3640m) was popular in the Raj era. It's still one of Uttarakhand's finest and most accessible treks, affording breathtaking views of the snow-clad peaks around Nanda Devi – India's highest mountain – while passing through the outer sanctuary of Nanda Devi Sanctuary. The trailhead is at Auli and the 75km trek to Ghat past lakes, waterfalls, forests, meadows and small villages takes five days, though it's possible to do a shorter version that finishes in Tapovan in three days. A tent, guide, permit and your own food supplies are necessary, all of which can be organised easily in **Joshimath**.

quicken the trip and help the local economy by hiring a pony (₹610) through the Eco Development Committee office at the bridge over the Alaknanda River. The return trip takes four to five hours. You don't need to carry food because there are *dhabas* and drink stalls along the way serving the army of pilgrims heading to Hem Kund. Top tip: if you have the time, sleep at Badrinath the night before you trek to Ghangaria to acclimatise your body to the altitude; it'll make the hike easier.

Overnight stays are not permitted in the Valley of Flowers or at Hem Kund so you must stay in Ghangaria, a one-street village in a wonderful deodar forest with a busy market, a handful of budget hotels and mediocre restaurants, hundreds of ponies, a pharmacy and a doctor. Water and electricity supplies are erratic. It can get *cold*, so bring warm layers. The village shuts down outside the pilgrimage season, which lasts from 1 June to 1 October (or thereabouts).

Hotel Pritam (Ghangaria; s/d ₹300/400) is one of the better budget places to stay. **Hotel Priya** (Ghangaria; r from ₹250) is good, too. No hotels have heat, but they do have heaps of blankets.

Despite the distances and grades of the trails, treks to Ghangaria, the Valley of Flowers and Hem Kund are often undertaken by small children and people with weak legs or lungs – they ride up in a wicker chair hauled on the back of a *kandi* (porter; from ₹500)

Pindari Glacier Trek

This six-day, 94km trek passes through truly virgin country that's inhabited by only a few shepherds. It offers wonderful views of Nanda Kot (6860m) and Nanda Khat (6611m) on the southern rim of Nanda Devi Sanctuary. The 3km-long, 365m-wide Pindari Glacier is at 3353m, so take it easy to avoid altitude sickness. Permits aren't needed but bring your passport.

The trek begins and finishes at Loharket (1700m), a village 36km north of Bageshwar. Guides and porters can be organised easily there, or in the preceding village of Song (1400m), or you can organise package treks through companies in Almora. KMVN operates all-inclusive eight-day treks out of Loharket for ₹5100 per person, staying at government rest houses. KMVN dorms (mattresses on the floor for ₹200), basic guesthouses or *dhaba* huts (₹100 to ₹300) are dotted along the route, and food is available. KMVN tours are best arranged through KVMN Parvat Tours (p445) in Nainital.

Buses (₹50, two hours) or share jeeps (₹60, 1½ hours) run between Song and Bageshwar. Private taxis between Bageshwar and Song/Loharket cost ₹1500/2000.

Milam Glacier Trek

This challenging eight-day, 118km trek to the massive Milam Glacier (3450m) is reached along an ancient trade route to Tibet that was closed in 1962 following the war between India and China. It passes through magnificent rugged country to the east of Nanda Devi (7816m) and along the sometimes spectacular gorges of the river, Gori Ganga. You can also take a popular but tough side trip to Nanda Devi East base camp, adding another 32km or three days.

Free permits (passport required) are available from the District Magistrate in Munsyari. You will also need a tent and your own food supplies, as villages on the route may be deserted. KMVN organises all-inclusive eight-day treks (from ₹6325). These are best arranged at KMVN Parvat Tours (p445) in Nainital but the KMVN Rest House (☎05961-222339; Munsyari) in Munsyari should be able to set you up too.

The base for this excursion is the spectacularly located village of Munsyari, where a guide, cook and porters can be hired and package treks can be arranged through Nanda Devi Tour N Trek (☎05961-222324; trek_beeru@rediffmail.com) or Johar Tour & Treks (☎05961-222752).

Less travelled but equally (or more) stunning treks include the Begini/Dunagiri route north of Joshimath and the Panchachuli East/Chota Kailash route, north of Dharchula.

or reclining in a *dandi* (litter; from ₹5500), carried on the shoulders of four men like the royalty of old. It's also possible to fly by Deccan Air (☎9412051036; www.deccanair.com) helicopter from Govindghat to Gangharia (one way/return ₹3500/7000); the booking office is at the top of the road leading down to the village.

At Govindghat, there are lots of lodging options for around ₹200, as well as the huge gurdwara (payment by donation), where VIP rooms are basic. The Hotel Bhagat (☎9412936360; www.hotelbhagat.com; Badrinath Rd; r ₹1625-3000), up on the main road between Joshimath and Badrinath, has very clean rooms with river views, geysers and meals.

All buses and share jeeps between Joshimath and Badrinath stop in Govindghat, so you can easily find transport travelling in either direction, though this trickles off later in the day and stops dead at night.

CORBETT TIGER RESERVE

☎05947 / ELEV 400-1210M

The famous Corbett Tiger Reserve was established in 1936 as India's first national park, and now includes surrounding forest lands. It's named for legendary British hunter Jim Corbett (1875–1955), who put Kumaon on the map with his book *The Man-Eaters of Kumaon*. Greatly revered by local people for killing tigers that preyed on people, Corbett eventually shot more wildlife with his camera than with his gun and became a prominent voice for conservation.

Tiger sightings take some luck, as the 220 or so tigers in the reserve are neither baited nor tracked. Your best chance of spotting one is late in the season (April to mid-June), when the forest cover is low and animals come out in search of water.

Notwithstanding tiger sightings, few serious wildlife enthusiasts will leave disappointed, as the 1318-sq-km park has a variety of wildlife and birdlife in grassland, sal forest and river habitats, and a beautiful location in the foothills of the Himalaya on the river, Ramganga. Commonly seen wildlife include wild elephants (200 to 300 live in the reserve), sloth bears, langur monkeys, rhesus macaques, peacocks, romps of otters and several types of deer including chital (spotted deer), sambars, hog deer and barking deer. You might also see leopards, mugger crocodiles, gharials, monitor lizards, wild boars and jackals. The Ramganga Reservoir attracts large numbers of migrating birds, especially from mid-December to the end of March, and more than 600 species have been spotted here.

Of Corbett's six zones – Bijrani, Dhikala, Dhela, Durga Devi, Jhirna and Sonanadi – Dhikala is the highlight of the park, 49km northwest of Ramnagar and deep inside the reserve. This is the designated core area, where the highest concentration of the animals you probably hope to see are found. It's open from 15 November to 15 June and only to overnight guests, or as part of a one-day tour available through the park's **reception centre** (05947-251489; Ranikhet Rd; 6am-4pm), opposite Ramnagar's bus stand.

Jhirna and Dhela, in the southern part of the reserve, are the only zones that remains open all year, but your chances of seeing serious megafauna in those areas are iffy – at least for now. Dhela, which opened to the public in December 2014, may eventually include a large fenced section meant to house rescued tigers, which should be fairly easy to spot. There are also plans to create two nature trails in Dhela; we're told that these will mainly be for birdwatching, and that the trails will be protected by fences, so you don't have to worry about becoming tiger prey. At the time of writing, Dhela safaris could only be booked in Ramnagar, not online, but this may change in the future. Note that in some years, depending on conditions, the other four zones may open in October, but the only way to find out is to contact the reception centre.

Be sure to bring binoculars (you can hire them at park gates) and plenty of mosquito repellent and bottled water. If you're inter-

---

ⓘ PERMITS

Corbett Tiger Reserve controls tourist impact by limiting the number of vehicles into each zone each day. It's highly recommended that you make advance reservations. You can book via the park's website (www.corbettonline.uk.gov.in) or by signing up for a trip with a safari outfit. If you book online (fee ₹50), give your reservation confirmation to your driver, whether you hire one from the reservation centre or use a tour operator. Day trips can be booked three months in advance; if you can't plan ahead, go to the reception centre and try to pick up a leftover vehicle permit. If they are all gone, you still might be able to visit the park; safari operators will ask each other if anyone is running a jeep with open seats that you can fill. Overnight trips to Dhikala are best booked by calling the reception centre or a safari company.

For a day trip, the vehicle fee (not including passengers) costs ₹200/500 for Indians/foreigners; for an overnight jaunt, it's ₹500/1500. Then there's the visitor entry fee, which is about the craziest system we've seen in a while. Officially, the single-day fee (valid for four hours, available for every zone except Dikhala) is ₹100/450 per Indian/foreigner; three-day permits cost ₹200/900. But the park makes you pay visitor fees for every seat in the jeep, *even if they are empty*. Kindly, they imagine that unoccupied seats are filled by Indians, so two passengers in a jeep will pay their own entry fees, plus ₹100 for the driver's entry, plus an extra ₹400 for their invisible Indian companions!

How much does this all cost? Add up your jeep-hire fee, vehicle entry fee, visitor entry fees, driver's entry fee and empty seat fees, and that's your total. Arranging everything yourself is marginally cheaper than taking a safari or hotel tour, but they provide expert guides fluent in English, which can be well worth the few extra rupees.

ested in the life of Jim Corbett, his former house at Kaladhungi, 26km southeast of Ramnagar, is now a **museum** (Kaladhungi; admission ₹50; ⊙ 8am-5pm).

☞ Tours

The reception centre in Ramnagar runs daily **bus tours** (☑ 05947-251489; Ranikhet Rd; Indian/foreigner ₹1125/2250) to Dhikala – called Canter Safaris – at 6am and noon.

Jeeps can be hired at the reception centre in Ramnagar, or through your accommodation or a tour agency. Jeep owners have formed a union, so in theory rates are fixed (on a per-jeep basis, carrying up to six people). Half-day safaris (leaving in the morning and afternoon) should cost ₹1500 to Bijrani, ₹1800 to Jhirna, ₹1800 to Dhela, ₹2200 to Durga Devi, and ₹2200 to Sonanadi – not including the entry fees for you and your guide. Full-day safaris cost double. Overnight excursions to Dhikala cost ₹5200. Check current prices at the reception centre and at your hotel before hiring a jeep. Safaris offered by Karan Singh, who runs Karan's Corbett Motel (p443), are highly recommended.

Two-hour **elephant rides** (Indian/foreigner ₹300/1000) are available only at Dhikala and Bijrani, at 6am and 4pm on a first-come, first-served basis.

🛏 Sleeping & Eating

For serious wildlife viewing, Dhikala – deep inside the reserve – is the prime place to stay, though prices for foreigners are exorbitant. Book through the park's website (www. corbettonline.uk.gov.in) at least one month in advance. The town of Ramnagar has budget accommodation, while upmarket resorts are strung out along the road skirting the eastern side of the park between Dhikuli and Dhangarhi Gate.

🛏 Dhikala

Easily the cheapest beds in the park are at **Log Huts** (☑ 9212777223, 05947-251489; dm Indian/foreigner ₹200/400), resembling 3AC train sleepers, with 24 basic beds (no bedding supplied). **Tourist Hutments** (☑ 9212777223, 05947-251489; Indian/foreigner ₹1250/2500) offer the best value accommodation in Dhikala and sleep up to six people. Book via www.dhikalaforestlodge.in or

www.corbettonline.uk.gov.in. Dhikala has a couple of restaurants serving vegetarian food. No alcohol is allowed in the park.

Accommodation at the **New Forest Rest House** (☑ 9212777223, 05947-251489; r Indian/foreigner ₹1250/2500), **Annexe** (☑ 05947-251489, 9212777223; r Indian/foreigner ₹1000/2000), three cabins (Indian/foreigner ₹1250/2500) and the VIP **Old Forest Rest House** (r Indian/foreigner ₹1500/3000 or ₹2500/5000) can all be booked at the reception centre in Ramnagar.

🛏 Elsewhere in the Reserve

Most rest houses outside of Dhikala offer kitchen facilities but not restaurants, so check with your guide to see if you should bring your own food.

Bijrani Rest House   HOTEL **$$**
(☑ 05947-251489; s/d Indian ₹500/1250, foreigner ₹1000/2500) The first place in from Amdanda Gate; meals and elephant rides are available.

Khinnanauli Rest House   HOTEL **$$$**
(☑ 05947-251489; r Indian/foreigner ₹5000/ 12,000) VIP lodging near Dhikala, deep in the reserve.

Sarapduli Rest House   HOTEL **$$$**
(☑ 05947-251489; r Indian/foreigner ₹2000/4000) In a good location in the reserve's core area.

Gairal Rest House   HOTEL **$$$**
(☑ 05947-251489; r Indian/foreigner from ₹1250/2500) On the Ramnagar River, accessed from Dhangarhi Gate; meals are available.

🛏 Ramnagar

A busy, unappealing town, Ramnagar has plenty of facilities, including internet cafes (₹30 per hour), ATMs (State Bank of India ATM at the train station and a Bank of Baroda ATM on Ranikhet Rd) and transport connections – mostly along Ranikhet Rd.

★ **Karan's Corbett Motel**   HOTEL **$**
(☑ 9837468933; www.karanscorbettmotel.com; Manglar Rd; r ₹600-800; ❄) This longtime favourite has changed its name and moved to a new location. It's still surrounded by gardens and mango trees and still has the same terrific owner, Karan Singh – but the rooms and the restaurant are all brand new.

Hands-down, the best place to stay in Ramnagar. Karan runs highly recommended jeep safaris in Corbett.

Hotel Corbett Kingdom
HOTEL $$

(☏7500668883; www.corbettkingdom.com; Bhaghat Singh St; r from ₹1500; ❉🛜) This straightforward hotel is a comfortable, well-kept option right in Ramnagar. Marble floors add a touch of class.

Delhi Darbar Restaurant
INDIAN $

(Ranikhet Rd; mains ₹60-160; ⏱9am-11pm) The cleanest and quietest place to eat near the bus stand, with a typical Indian menu, plus pizza.

🛏 North of Ramnagar

A growing number of upmarket African-style safari resorts are strung along the Ramnagar–Ranikhet road that runs along the reserve's eastern boundary. Most are around a settlement called Dhikuli – not to be confused with Dhikala. When most of the reserve is closed (15 June to 15 November), discounts of up to 50% are offered. Most rates are for a room only, but most have packages that include meals and safaris. All places have resident naturalists, recreational facilities, restaurants and bars.

Infinity Resorts
HOTEL $$$

(☏05947-251279; www.infinityresorts.com; Dhikuli; s/d incl breakfast from US$118/135; ❉🛜🏊) The most impressive of the Corbett Park resorts, Infinity has luxurious rooms, a roundhouse with restaurant and bar, and a swimming pool in a lovely garden backing onto the Kosi River (where you can see hordes of golden mahseer fish). The rooms in the 'old block' are better located and have more character than those in the 'new block'. Big discounts are offered if booking online.

Corbett Hideaway
HOTEL $$$

(☏05947-284132; www.corbetthideaway.com; Dhikuli; cottages ₹15,000-20,000; ❉🛜🏊) The already-upscale resort was purchased by the Taj Group and is getting a makeover. We're told they're incorporating many of the green technologies that they've used around other national parks. Rooms are luxury cottages, spread among a lush garden. There's a poolside bar and a relaxing riverside terrace. Prices will probably rise before you read this.

Tiger Camp
RESORT $$$

(☏9411321606; www.habitathotels.com/tiger-camp; Dhikuli; cottages from ₹5275; ❉🛜) This intimate, excellent-value resort is nestled in a shady jungle-style garden by the Kosi River, 8km from Ramnagar. Cosy cottages and bungalows have modern facilities, and nature walks and village tours are offered.

ℹ Getting There & Away

Buses run almost hourly from Ramnagar to Delhi (₹241, seven hours), Haridwar (₹190, six hours) and Dehra Dun (₹254, seven hours). For Nainital (₹80, 3½ hours) there are three direct morning buses, or take one to Haldwani and change there. Frequent buses run to Haldwani (₹61, two hours).

Ramnagar train station is 1.5km south of the main reception centre. The nightly Ranikhet Express Slip 15013-Slip (sleeper/3AC/2AC ₹175/485/690) leaves Old Delhi at 10.30pm, arriving in Ramnagar at 4.55am. The return trip on train 25014 leaves Ramnagar at 10pm, arriving in Old Delhi at 3.55am. A daytime run from Old Delhi on train 15035-Slip (2nd class/chair ₹100/370) departs at 4pm, reaching Ramnagar at 8.40pm; the return on train 25036 departs Ramnagar at 9.50am, hitting Delhi at 3.20pm.

NAINITAL

☏05942 / POP 40,000 / ELEV 2084M

Crowded around a deep, green volcanic lake, Nainital is Kumaon's largest town and favourite hill resort. It occupies a steep forested valley around the namesake lake Naini and was founded by homesick Brits reminded of the Cumbrian Lake District.

Plenty of hotels are set in the forested hills around the lake. There's a busy bazaar and a spider's web of walking tracks covers the forested hillsides to viewpoints overlooking the distant Himalayan peaks. For travellers, it's an easy place to kick back and relax, eat well, and go horse riding or paddling on the lake. In peak seasons – roughly May to mid-July and October – Nainital is packed to the gills with holidaying families and honeymooners, and hotel prices skyrocket.

Tallital (Lake's Foot) is at the southeastern end of the lake where you'll find the bus stand and the main road heading east towards Bhowali. The 1.5km promenade known as the Mall leads to Mallital (Lake's Head) at the northwestern end of the lake. Most hotels, guest houses and restaurants are strung out along the Mall between Mallital and Tallital. You'll most find shops, including pharmacies, in Bara Bazaar.

◉ Sights & Activities

★ Naini Lake   LAKE

This pretty lake is Nainital's centrepiece and is said to be one of the emerald green eyes of Shiva's wife, Sati (*naina* is Sanskrit for eye) that fell to earth after her act of self-immolation. Boatmen will row you around the lake for ₹210 in the brightly painted gondola-like boats, or the **Nainital Boat Club** (☑05942-235318; www.boathouse-club.in; Mallital; ⊙10am-4pm) will sail you round for ₹350. Pedal boats can also be hired for ₹150 per hour.

Naina Devi Temple is on the precise spot where the eye is believed to have fallen. Nearby is the **Jama Masjid** and a **gurdwara**. You can walk around the lake in about an hour – the southern side is more peaceful and has good views of the town.

Snow View   VIEWPOINT

A **cable car** (adult/child return ₹150/100; ⊙8am-8pm May & Jun, 10.30am-4.30pm Jul-Apr) runs up to the popular Snow View at 2270m, which (on clear days) has panoramic Himalayan views, including of Nanda Devi. The ticket office is at the bottom. At the top you'll find the usual food, souvenir and carnival stalls, as well as **Mountain Magic** (rides ₹30-100), an amusement park with kids' entertainment including bumper cars, trampolines and a flying fox.

A highlight of the trip to Snow View is hiking to viewpoints such as Cheena/Naina Peak, 4km away. Local guides may offer to lead you there.

If you want to get up to Snow View for sunrise, taxis charge ₹200.

Tiffin Top & Land's End   HORSE RIDING, WALKING

A 4km walk west of the lake brings you to Tiffin Top (2292m), also called Dorothy's Seat. From there, it's a lovely 30-minute walk to Land's End (2118m) through a forest of oak, deodar and pine. Mangy horses gather 3km west of town on the road to Ramnagar to take you on rides to these spots.

A two-hour ride costs about ₹900, but you can take shorter rides (eg Tiffin Top for ₹500); you can always negotiate. Touts for these rides will no doubt accost you in Mallital near the ropeway.

★ Tranquility Treks   TREKKING

(☑9411196837; www.tranquilitytreks.in) Experienced guide Sunil Kumar leads hikes and focuses on bird- and wildlife-watching. He can take you on day walks (₹1500), overnight hikes where you stay in local villages (₹2000) and two-week all-inclusive nature trips (from ₹75,000).

Nainital Mountaineering Club   MOUNTAINEERING

(☑9412905949; www.ntmcindia.org; Mallital; per day ₹600) Offers rock-climbing courses at the rock-climbing area, a 15m-high rocky outcrop to the west of the town.

Snout Adventures   OUTDOOR ADVENTURES

(☑9411374560; www.snoutadventure.com; Ashok Cinema Bldg, Mallital) A recommended outfit offering treks in the Kumaon and Garhwal mountains (from ₹2200 per day, all inclusive). It also conducts rock-climbing courses (₹500 per day) and organises adventure camps.

KMVN Parvat Tours   TREKKING

(☑05942-231436; www.kmvn.org; Tallital; ⊙8am-7pm) A helpful office for information and booking KMVN's rest houses and trekking packages.

☞ Tours

Travel agencies along the Mall such as **Hina Tours & Travel** (☑05942-235860; www.hina-tour.com) and **Anamika Travels** (☑05942-235186; www.anamikatravelsnainital.com) offer bus tours of the local lakes and trips to Corbett National Park. KMVN offers the full-day Jim Corbett Legacy Trail tour (₹950), visiting sites important in the life of the legendary hunter/author/conservationist.

🛏 Sleeping

Nainital is packed with hotels but they fill up fast in peak seasons, making it hard to find a bargain at those times. Virtually all hotels offer around 50% discounts in the low season. The main peak season is generally 1 May to 30 June, and some hotels have a semipeak in October, at Diwali (October/November) and at Christmas.

Hotel City Heart   HOTEL $$

(☑05942-235228; www.cityhearthotelnainital.com; Mallital; d ₹3200-5500) Located off the Mall, the rooftop terrace restaurant has fine lake views. Rooms range from small but cute to fabulous deluxe rooms with a view.

Nainital

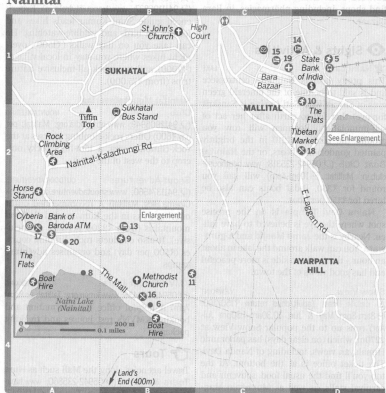

This place discounts more than most and is one of Nainital's best off-season bargains, with rooms from ₹800. The effusive owner will gladly play the CD of his band covering tunes by Pink Floyd and Dire Straits.

Traveller's Paradise
HOTEL $$
(☎ 9411107877; www.travellersinparadise.com; Mallital; r ₹2700-4500; ☜) A bit north of the Mall, this exceptionally friendly hotel has been recently renovated. Rooms feature flat-screen TVs, couches, faux-wood panelling, wi-fi and quality beds. It's run by the amiable Anu Consul, who spent 10 years living in Mexico, and his wonderful father. Off-season prices start at ₹1500.

Evelyn Hotel
HOTEL $$
(☎ 05942-235457; www.hotelevelynnainital.com; the Mall, Tallital; d ₹2000-3500, ste ₹5500-6000) This large Victorian-looking hotel overlooking the lake is quintessential Nainital – charming and slightly eccentric. It's big,

with stairways and terraces cascading down the hillside. It's a bit old-fashioned, but the well-tended rooms with retro furniture have a nice, cosy feel.

Palace Belvedere
HERITAGE HOTEL $$$
(☎ 05942-237434; www.palacebelvedere.com; Mallital; s/d/ste from ₹6500/7500/10,000; ☜) Built in 1897, this was the summer palace of the rajas of Awagarh. Animal skins and old prints adorn the walls and lend a faded Raj-era charm. Rooms are spacious, high-ceilinged, and have an aged, if worn, soul. Upstairs gets much more light. Downstairs has an elegant dining room, lounge and verandah. It can be cold in winter. Discounts are offered during off-season.

✕ Eating & Drinking

Nainital has a host of restaurants, mostly along the Mall on the north side of the lake. For cheap eats, head to the food stalls

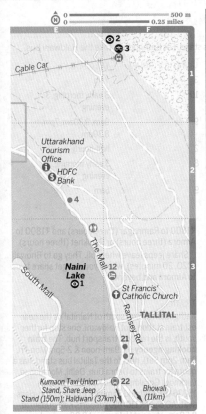

Nainital

◉ Top Sights
1 Naini Lake E3

◉ Sights
2 Mountain Magic F1
3 Snow View F1

⊕ Activities, Courses & Tours
4 Anamika Travels E2
5 Cable Car D1
6 Hina Tours & Travel B4
7 KMVN Parvat Tours F4
8 Nainital Boat Club A3
9 Nainital Mountaineering Club B3
10 Snout Adventures D1
11 Tiffin Top & Land's End B3

⊜ Sleeping
12 Evelyn Hotel F3
13 Hotel City Heart B3
14 Palace Belvedere D1
15 Traveller's Paradise C1

⊗ Eating
16 Embassy B3
17 Sakley's Restaurant A3
18 Sonam Chowmein Corner D2

⊕ Drinking & Nightlife
Nainital Boat Club .... (see 8)

ⓘ Information
19 BD Pandey Government
Hospital C1

ⓘ Transport
20 Cycle-Rickshaw Ticket Booth A3
21 Cycle-Rickshaw Ticket Booth F4
22 Tallital Bus Stand F4
Train Booking Agency .... (see 22)

---

around the Tibetan Market or to the *dhabas* in Bara Bazaar.

Sonam Chowmein Corner   FAST FOOD **$**

(The Flats, Mallital; mains ₹30-60; ⊙ 11am-7.30pm) In the covered alley of the Tibetan Market, this authentic Tibetan *dhaba* whips up fabulous chow mein and *momos* (dumplings) for the best cheap eats in town.

Embassy   INDIAN **$$**

(The Mall, Mallital; meals ₹100-350; ⊙ 9.30am-10.30pm) With a wood-lined chalet interior and snappily dressed staff, Embassy has been serving up five pages of menu items for more than 40 years. For drinks try 'dancing coffee' or a rosewater lassi. There's a good terrace for people-watching.

Sakley's Restaurant   MULTICUISINE **$$**

(Mallital; mains ₹150-650; ⊙ 9am-10pm) A spotless restaurant found off the Mall, serving up a range of unusual global items such as Thai curries, honey chicken, roast lamb, pepper steaks, and plenty of Chinese dishes, pizzas and sizzlers. The cakes and pastries are great; even if you don't dine here, swing by and pick up some dessert to take back to your room.

Nainital Boat Club   BAR

(The Mall, Mallital; temporary membership men/women/couples ₹850/425/850; ⊙ 10am-10pm) This club is a classic remnant of the Raj-era. Temporary membership is ridiculously steep, but the atmospheric bar – with timber beams, buttoned-up barmen with handlebar moustaches, and an outdoor deck overlooking the lake, is perfect for an afternoon drink. The dress code specifies no shorts or slippers, and signs warn that 'decorum should be maintained'.

BUSES FROM NAINITAL

The following buses leave from the Tallital bus stand. For Kathgodam, take the Haldwani bus.

DESTINATION	FARE (₹)	DURATION (HOUR)	FREQUENCY
Almora	110	3	7am
Dehra Dun	375-625	10	3 early morning, 3 evening
Delhi	325-465	9	9am, 9.30am, 7pm, 8.30pm
Haldwani	60	2	half-hourly
Haridwar	330-575	8	3 early morning, 3 evening
Rishikesh	310	9	5am

ℹ Information

BD Pandey Government Hospital (☎ 05942-235012; Mallital) Located off the Mall.

Cyberia (Mallital; per hour ₹30; ⊙10am-7.30pm) Nainital's best internet cafe offers printing and wi-fi access. Found off the Mall.

HDFC Bank (The Mall; ⊙10am-4pm Mon-Fri, to 1pm Sat) 24-hour ATM.

Main Post Office (Mallital; ⊙10am-5pm Mon-Sat)

State Bank of India (The Mall, Mallital; ⊙10am-4pm Mon-Fri, to 1pm Sat) Exchanges foreign currencies and travellers cheques.

Uttarakhand Tourism Office (☎ 05942-235337; The Mall; ⊙10am-5pm Mon-Sat) Doesn't always follow official hours.

ℹ Getting There & Away

BUS

Most buses leave from the **Tallital bus stand**.

Although there are direct buses from Nainital, many more services leave from the transport hubs of Haldwani and Bhowali. From Haldwani, regular buses head to Ramnagar, Delhi, Haridwar and the Nepal border at Banbassa. Haldwani is also a major train terminus. For points north, take a bus or share jeep from Nainital to Bhowali (₹20, 20 minutes) and catch one of the regular onward buses to Almora, Kausani and Ranikhet.

Seven private buses direct to Ramnagar (₹80, 3½ hours) leave from the **Sukhatal bus stand**, northwest of Mallital, between 8am and 3.30pm.

Travel agencies sell tickets for private overnight deluxe coaches (with reclining seats) to Delhi (₹350 to ₹800, nine hours), which leave from Tallital around 11am and 10pm.

TAXI & SHARE JEEP

From the Kumaon Taxi Union stand in Tallital, taxis cost ₹400 to Bhowali, ₹100/500 (shared/private) to Kathgodam or Haldwani (1½ hours), ₹1800 to Ramnagar (three hours) and ₹1800 to Almora (three hours) or Ranikhet (three hours).

Share jeeps leave when full. They go to Bhowali (₹20, 20 minutes), where you can get share taxis to Almora and beyond.

TRAIN

Kathgodam (35km south of Nainital) is the nearest train station, but Haldwani, one stop further south, is the regional transport hub. The **train booking agency** (⊙ 9am-noon & 2-5pm Mon-Fri, 9am-2pm Sat), next to the Tallital bus stand, has a quota for trains to Dehra Dun, Delhi, Moradabad, Lucknow, Gorakhpur and Kolkata. The daily 15036 Uttarakhand Sampark Express (2nd-class seat/AC chair ₹110/410) departs Kathgodam at 8.50am, stops at Haldwani at 9.08am, and arrives Old Delhi station at 3.20pm. In the other direction, train 15035 departs Delhi at 4pm, arriving Haldwani 8.10pm and Kathgodam at 8.40pm.

ℹ Getting Around

Cycle-rickshaws charge a fixed ₹10 along the Mall, but can only pick up and drop off at the ticket booths at either end. Taxi rides within town cost ₹50 to ₹250.

ALMORA

☎ 05962 / POP 33,000 / ELEV 1650M

Clinging to a steep-sided valley, Almora is the regional capital of Kumaon, first established as a summer capital by the Chand rajas of Kumaon in 1560. These days you'll find some colonial-era buildings, reliable trekking outfits and a couple of community-based weaving enterprises. Don't be put off by the ugly, shambolic main street when you're first deposited at the bus stand – head one block south to the pedestrian-only cobbled Lalal Bazaar, lined with intricately carved and painted traditional wooden shop facades. It's a fascinating place to stroll, people-watch and shop.

👁 Sights & Activities

Nanda Devi Temple   HINDU TEMPLE
(Lalal Bazaar) The stone Nanda Devi Temple dates back to the Chand raja era, and is covered in folk-art carvings, some erotic. Every September, the temple hosts the five-day **Nanda Devi Fair** (Almora; ⊙ Sep).

Panchachuli Weavers Factory   HANDICRAFTS
(☑ 05962-232310; www.panchachuli.com; off Bageshwar Rd; ⊙ 10am-5pm Mon-Sat) FREE The Panchachuli Weavers Factory employs some 700 women to weave, market and sell woollen shawls. The shop here has a wider range of products than at the small shop in the Mall. Taxis charge ₹150 return to the factory, or you can walk the 3km – follow the continuation of Mall Rd to the northeast and ask for directions.

High Adventure   TREKKING
(☑ 9412044610; www.trekkinghimalayas.in; The Mall) Organises treks around Uttarakhand, and mountain-bike trips near Almora and Nainital. Prices vary depending on route and group size, so call for details.

🛏 Sleeping

Unlike most hill stations, prices here are not seasonal.

Savoy Hotel   HOTEL $
(☑ 05962-262601; www.ashoknainital.com; The Mall; r ₹800-1700) At the southern end of the Mall, just past the tourist office, the Savoy is in a quiet location. Cheaper downstairs rooms are simple, musty affairs, but the pricier upstairs rooms strive for comfort and style; best of all, they have tables and chairs on a shared terrace that overlooks the valley below Almora.

Bansal Hotel   HOTEL $
(☑ 05962-230864; Lalal Bazaar; d ₹300-400) Above Bansal Cafe in the bustling bazaar, but easily reached from the Mall, this is a fine budget choice with small, tidy rooms (some with TV) and a rooftop terrace.

Hotel Shikhar   HOTEL $$
(☑ 05962-230253; www.hotelshikhar.com; The Mall; r ₹600-1800, ste ₹2500-3500; ❄) Dominating the centre of town and built to take

in the views, this large, boxlike hotel offers a maze of rooms covering all budgets. In the original building, higher-end rooms aren't much better than cheaper ones; all are a bit worn, but not too awful. The top-tier rooms in the new building are among Almora's nicest.

🍴 Eating

Almora's speciality sweet is *ball mithai* (fudge coated in sugar balls), available for ₹10 in sweet shops all along the Mall and bazaar.

Glory Restaurant   INDIAN $
(LR Sah Rd; mains ₹65-190; ⊙ 8.30am-9.30pm) This long-running family eatery features popular South and North Indian veg and nonveg dishes, including biryanis and lemon chicken. Pizzas are extra cheesy.

Saraswati Sweet & Restaurant   TIBETAN $
(Pithoragarh Rd; dishes ₹30-60; ⊙ 7am-8pm) This busy place with upstairs tables quickly dishes up veg and nonveg *momos* and other Tibetan food, along with Chinese. The *thukpa* (Tibetan noodle soup) is spicy enough to clear your sinuses. It also has mutton burgers and a full list of cold drinks.

ℹ Information

Internet access is available at several places in Lalal Bazaar and the Mall, usually from ₹25 per hour.

HDFC (The Mall; ⊙ 9.30am-3.30pm Mon-Fri, to 12.30pm Sat)

Sify iWay (The Mall; per hour ₹25; ⊙ 9am-8pm) One of several places with internet.

State Bank of India (The Mall; ⊙ 10am-4pm Mon-Fri, to 1pm Sat)

Uttarakhand Tourism Office (☑ 05962-230180; Upper Mall; ⊙ 10am-5pm Mon-Sat)

ℹ Getting There & Away

The vomit-splattered sides of the buses and jeeps pulling into Almora tell you all you need to know about what the roads are like around here.

KMOU buses operate from the Mall – starting early morning until 2.30pm or 3pm – to Ranikhet (₹65, two hours), Kausani (₹85, 2½ hours), Bageshwar (₹120, two hours) and Haldwani (₹125, three hours) via Bhowali (₹80, two hours) near Nainital. Buses to those places – except Ranikhet – also leave from the adjacent Roadways stand, where you'll find buses to Delhi (₹440, 12 hours) at 7am, 4pm, 5pm and 6pm. For

Pithoragarh, head to the Dharanaula bus stand east of the bazaar on Bypass Rd, where several buses (₹165, five hours) depart between about 8.30am and 11am. For Banbassa on the Nepal border, take a bus to Haldwani and change there.

You can get a taxi or jeep to Ranikhet (shared/private ₹100/1000, two hours), Kausani (₹120/1200, 2½ hours), Bageshwar (₹250/1500, two hours), Bhowali (₹200/1000, three hours), Kasar Devi (₹35/250), Pithoragarh (₹350/2500, five hours) and Munsyari (private only ₹5000, 10 hours). All leave from the Mall, except the shared taxis to Pithoragarh, which leave from Dharanaula bus stand.

The nearest railway stations are at Kathgodam and Haldwani. There's a **Railway Reservation Centre** (☑ 05962-230250; KMVN Holiday Home, The Mall; ☺ 9am-noon & 2-5pm Mon-Sat) at the southern end of town.

AROUND ALMORA

Kasar Devi

This peaceful spot about 8km north of Almora has been luring alternative types for close to 100 years – as a result, it's also known as Crank's Ridge. The list of luminaries who've visited, some for extended stays, includes Bob Dylan, Cat Stevens, Timothy Leary, Allen Ginsburg and Swami Vivekananda, who meditated at the hilltop **Kasar Devi Temple**. Today, the village is a low-key backpacker destination, with a mellow vibe and clear-day Himalayan views. There's not a lot to do here, but it's a great place to chill. And Mohan's Binsar Retreat (p450) can arrange multiday fishing, rafting, or trekking trips. Get there from Almora by share jeep (₹20) or private taxi (₹250).

🛏 Sleeping & Eating

There are some great budget to midrange guesthouses here, along with a few restaurants and shops.

Freedom Guest House   GUESTHOUSE $
(☑ 7830355686; Binsar Rd; r ₹800-1200) Big, immaculately clean rooms open onto shared terraces with west-facing valley views, catching the afternoon and sunset light. New rooms on the upper floors have a bit more luxury. If you ask nicely and pay for gas, Gita, the owner, may set you up with your own little kitchen.

Manu Guest House   GUESTHOUSE $
(☑ 9410920696; below Binsar Rd; r ₹400-600) Set amid an orchard with a couple of cows, this place feels like a rural homestay. The largest stone or brick cottages include kitchenettes, making it a great choice for long stays.

Kripal House   HOTEL $
(☑ 9690452939; off Binsar Rd; r from ₹600, without bathroom from ₹300) This basic guesthouse, down a dirt lane off the main road, boasts mindblowing views of the Himalayas from its unfurnished rooftop terrace.

★ **Mohan's Binsar Retreat**   GUESTHOUSE $$$
(☑ 9412162816; www.mohansbinsarretreat.com; Binsar Rd; r incl breakfast from ₹4400; @ 🛜) Arguably the nicest place in Kasar Devi, Mohan's has huge, beautiful rooms with luxurious beds and wooden ceilings and floors. The real draw is the indoor-outdoor terrace restaurant, with great views of the valley below and a shot of distant Himalayan peaks. There's an internet cafe and a library.

Rainbow Restaurant   INTERNATIONAL $$
(☑ 9720320664; www.kasarrainbowresort.com; Binsar Rd; ₹100-200; ☺ 9am-9.30pm) Currently Kasar Devi's main backpacker hang-out, sit at tables or cushions on the floor while ordering Indian, Asian, Western or Middle Eastern food. Everything we tried was delicious – especially dessert! The owners also run a top-notch guesthouse with rooms from ₹2100 to ₹5000.

Binsar Wildlife Sanctuary

Beyond Kasar Devi, picturesque Binsar, 26km from Almora, was once the hilltop summer capital of the Chand rajas. Now it's a sanctuary protecting 45 sq km. You may spot a leopard or some barking deer, but many people come here for the 200-plus species of birds. On clear days, the Himalayan panorama is breathtaking – from the tower at 'Zero Point,' Binsar's summit (2420m), you can see Kedarnath, Nanda Devi, Panchachuli and more. Hiking trails wend throughout the lush forest; their main nexus is the KMVN Rest House. There is one good map of Binsar put out by the Forest Department, with trails and topo lines, but this is very hard to find; it's not offered at the entry gate.

It's possible to trek between the villages that are in the sanctuary, sleeping in rural homestays (which vary in quality and price). For details, call guides Pooja at

☑9759749283 or Nandan at ☑9411516469 (be sure to compare details and prices).

The fee to enter the sanctuary is ₹150/600 per Indian/foreigner, plus a ₹250 to ₹500 vehicle fee depending on what you're driving. Guides, who can be hired at the sanctuary gate or the Rest House, charge ₹250 for a 1½-hour hike. A return taxi from Almora costs about ₹1100.

Jageshwar

An impressive and active temple complex is set along a creek in a forest of deodars at the village of Jageshwar, 38km northeast of Almora. The 124 temples and shrines date to the 7th century AD and vary from linga shrines to large *sikhara* (Hindu temples) dedicated to different gods and goddesses. Down the street is the Jageshwar Archaeological Museum (www.asi.nic.in; Jageshwar; ◷10am-5pm Sat-Thu) FREE, which houses a small collection of exquisite religious carvings taken from the temples for preservation. It is well worth a look; among the highlights are the 'Dancing Ganesha' and the highly detailed version of 'Uma/Maheshwar Sitting on Nandi' with the intense snake action.

A 3km trail that starts below the centre of the village leads to the top of the ridge behind it. The ridge has dizzying views of the sculpted valley on the other side and the big peaks in the distance.

There are a number of *dhabas* in Jageshwar, plus a handful of hotels. The best of the bunch is Tara Guest House (☑9411544736; www.jageshwar.co.uk; Jageshwar; r from ₹200; ☎), surrounded by gardens, with views of the forest and the temple. It has basic but decent rooms. The easiest way to get from Almora to Jageshwar is by taxi (₹1200 return) or shared taxi (₹75). There's one direct bus daily around noon. It returns to Almora at 8am the following day. You can also take any bus going through Artola, get off there, and either walk 4km to Jageshwar or take a taxi for ₹80.

KAUSANI

☑05962 / POP 4100 / ELEV 1890M

Perched high on a forest-covered ridge, this tiny village has lovely panoramic views of distant snowcapped peaks, fresh air and a relaxed atmosphere. Mahatma Gandhi found Kausani an inspirational place to write his Bhagavad Gita treatise *Anasakti Yoga* in 1929, and there is still an ashram devoted to him here. Baijnath village, 19km north, has an intriguing complex of 12th-century *sikhara*-style temples in a lovely location shaded by trees, with other shrines in the nearby old village.

OFF THE BEATEN TRACK

MUNSYARI

Perched on a mountainside surrounded by plunging terraced fields, where the 6000m Panchachuli peaks scrape the sky across the Johar Valley, Munsyari (2290m) is one of the most scenic villages in Uttarakhand. Visited mostly by trekkers heading to the Milam Glacier, the surrounding landscape makes this a worthwhile destination even if you don't plan on lacing up your boots and hitting the trail.

There are some nice day hikes in the area. Two kilometres downhill from the bazaar, the small Tribal Heritage Museum (☑9411337094; admission ₹10), run by the charming scholar SS Pangtey, has artefacts from the days when Munsyari was an important nexus of trade with Tibet. This is also a unique place to experience the Nanda Devi Festival in September.

The Hotel Pandey Lodge (☑9411130316; www.munsyarihotel.com; near the bus stand; r ₹200-1850), by the bus stand, has a wide range of good-value rooms, some with amazing views, and an extremely helpful owner. Munsyari's dining situation is sparse. If you want to eat until you're stuffed (plates refilled free), try the hole-in-the-wall *dhaba* (₹40) just to the left of the big 'Nanda Devi Trek n Tour' sign, at the main chowk.

Buses run to and from Bageshwar (₹150, six hours) and Almora (₹200, 11 hours). Share jeeps run to Pithoragarh (₹180, eight hours) and Thal (₹120, three hours), where you can change for onward transport. If travelling to Munsyari via Thal, get a right-side window seat for the best views along the road. If you came from Thal and are heading to Pithoragarh, consider taking the longer route via Jauljibi for a change of scenery, including some amazing vistas of the Kumaon and Nepali Himalayas.

⊙ Sights & Activities

Kausani Tea Estate
TEA ESTATE

(☏ 05962-258330; ⊙ 9am-6pm mid-Mar–mid-Nov) FREE At Kausani Tea Estate – a tea plantation that involves private enterprise, the government and local farmers – you can look around and sample and buy products that are exported around the world. It's 3.5km north of the village on the road to Baijnath, an easy and scenic walk.

Anasakti Ashram
HISTORIC SITE

(☏ 05962-258028; Anasakti Ashram Rd) About 1km uphill from the bus stand, Anasakti Ashram is where Mahatma Gandhi spent two weeks pondering and writing *Anasakti Yoga*. It has a small museum (Anasakti Ashram Rd; ⊙ 6am-noon & 4-7pm) FREE that tells the story of Gandhi's life through photographs and words. Visit at 6pm to attend nightly prayers in his memory.

⌁ Sleeping & Eating

Outside the two short peak seasons (May to June and October to November), accommodation is often discounted by 50%.

There are lots of cheap *dhabas* around the main bazaar and the road leading uphill from the bus stand.

Hotel Uttarakhand
HOTEL $$

(☏ 05962-258012; www.uttarakhandkausani.com; north of bus stand; d ₹1050-2550; @) Near the bus stand, but in a quiet location with a panoramic view of the Himalaya from your verandah, this is Kausani's best-value accommodation. The cheaper rooms are small, with bucket hot water, but upper-floor rooms are spacious and have hot showers and TVs. The manager is helpful and friendly.

Krishna Mountview
HOTEL $$$

(☏ 05962-258008; www.krishnamountview.com; Anasakti Ashram Rd; d ₹3400-5900, ste ₹8000-9650; ☏) Just past Anasakti Ashram, this is one of Kausani's smartest hotels, with clipped formal gardens (perfect for mountain views). Try to get a spacious upstairs room; they have balconies, bay windows and rocking chairs.

BORDER CROSSING – INTO NEPAL FROM BANBASSA

Banbassa is the closest Indian village to the Nepal border post of Mahendranagar, 5km away. Check the current situation in western Nepal before crossing here, as roads during monsoon or immediate postmonsoon season may be impassable due to landslides and washed-out bridges. Buses run between Banbassa and Delhi, Haldwani, Haridwar and Pithoragarh.

Border Hours

The border is open 24 hours, but before 6am and after 6pm you're unlikely to find anyone to stamp you in and out of the respective countries. While officially open to vehicles only from 6am to 8am, 10am to noon, 2pm to 4pm and 6pm to 7pm, rickshaws and motorcycles are usually allowed to make the 1km trip across the bridge between the border posts at any time. Otherwise, you have to walk it.

Foreign Exchange

Hotels in Banbassa exchange Indian and Nepali rupees, as will a small office near the Nepal border post. Nabil Bank in Mahendranagar has an ATM and foreign currency exchange.

Onward Transport

From the border, take an autorickshaw (₹100) or shared taxi to Mahendranagar. The bus station is about 1km from the centre on the Mahendra Hwy, from where eight daily buses depart for Kathmandu between 5.30am and 4.30pm. There's also a single Pokhara service at 2.20pm (16 hours).

Visas

Single-entry visas valid for 15/30/90 days cost US$25/40/100 and are available at the Nepali side of the border between 9am and 5pm.

Garden Restaurant MULTICUISINE **$$**
(north of bus stand, Hotel Uttarakhand; mains ₹70-250; ⊙ 7am-10pm) In front of Hotel Uttarkhand and enjoying fine Himalayan views, this bamboo and thatch-roofed restaurant is Kausani's coolest. The food comprises first-class dishes from Swiss rösti to chicken tikka and imported pasta, as well as some Kumaon specialities, using fresh ingredients.

ⓘ Information

Kausani has a State Bank of India ATM in the main bazaar, but no foreign currency exchange.
Sanchar Dhaba Cyber Cafe (Anasakti Ashram Rd; per hour ₹40; ⊙ 6am-8.30pm) At Hill Queen Restaurant.

ⓘ Getting There & Away

Buses and share jeeps stop in the village centre. Several buses run to Almora (₹120, 2½ hours), but in the afternoon they generally stop at Karbala on the bypass road, from where you need to take a share jeep (₹10). Heading north, buses run every hour or so to Bageshwar via Baijnath (₹55, 1½ hours). Share jeeps (₹25, 30 minutes) run to Garur, 16km north of Kausani, which is a much more active transport hub, and where you can find share jeeps to Gwaldam for onward buses and jeeps to Garhwal (via Karanprayag). A taxi to Almora costs around ₹1200; to Nainital or Karanprayag it costs ₹3000.

BAGESHWAR

☑ 05963 / POP 8000 / ELEV 975M
Hindu pilgrims visit Bageshwar, at the confluence of the Gomti and Sarju Rivers, for its ancient stone **Bagnath Temple**. For travellers, it's more important as a transit town to or from the Milam or Pindari Glacier trailheads. There are a couple of internet cafes around, and there's a State Bank of India ATM in the main bazaar.

The OK **Hotel Annapurna** (☑ 05963-220109; r ₹200-400, s/d without bathroom ₹70/150) is conveniently located next to the bus stand, but for something much better, head for **Hotel Narendra Palace** (☑ 9319083181; www.hotelnarendrapalace.in; Pindari Rd; ₹350-1500; ✳), about 1km from the bus stand on Pindari Rd.

Several daily buses go to Almora (₹115, three hours), and Ranikhet (₹115, three hours) via Kausani (₹45, 1½ hours). Fre-

quent buses run to Bhowali (₹175, six hours) and Haldwani (₹225, 7½ hours). For connections to Garhwal, take a bus to Gwaldam (₹60, two hours) and change there. There are several morning buses to Pithoragarh (₹160, seven hours) and one at 9am to Munsyari (₹150, six hours). There's a jeep stand near the bus stand, along with a few other spots around town. Share jeeps go to Garur (₹35, 45 minutes), Kausani (₹55, 1½ hours) and Gwaldam (₹85, two hours). A shared/private jeep costs ₹90/1500 to Song (two hours), ₹110/2000 to Loharket (2½ hours), ₹400/5000 to Munsyari (five hours), ₹350/4000 to Pithoragarh (six hours) and ₹150/1500 to Almora (two hours).

PITHORAGARH

☑ 05964 / POP 42,000 / ELEV 1514M
Spread across the hillsides above a scenic valley that's been dubbed 'Little Kashmir', Pithoragarh is the main town of a little-visited region that borders Tibet and Nepal. Its sights include several Chand-era temples and an old fort, but the real reason to come here is to get off the tourist trail. The busy main bazaar is good for a stroll, and townspeople are exceptionally friendly. Picturesque hikes in the area include the rewarding climb up to **Chandak** (7km) for views of the **Panchachuli (Five Chimneys)** massif.

The **tourist office** (☑ 05964-225527), 50m uphill from the jeep stand, can help with trekking guides and information; a State Bank of India ATM and a few internet cafes (₹30 per hour) are in the bazaar. Cheap hotels can be found around the bus stand (rooms from ₹300), but for something much better head 200m uphill to **Hotel Yash Yatharth** (☑ 05964-225005; www.punethahotels.com; Naya Bazaar; dm ₹200, r ₹1000-3400); rates can be halved if business is slow. For a good meal at a good price, locals swear by **Jyonar Restaurant** (Gandhi Chowk; mains ₹80-250; ⊙ 8am-10pm) in the bazaar.

Several buses leave in the morning for Almora (₹160, five hours). Frequent buses go to Delhi; there are hourly services from 5am to 2pm to Banbassa (₹255, six hours), the border crossing into Nepal; and buses to Haldwani (10 hours) depart at 5am, 6.30am and 9.30am. To get to Munsyari, take a share jeep (₹250, seven hours).

Kolkata (Calcutta)

033 / POP 14.1 MILLION

Includes ➔

Best Places to Eat

➔ Bhojohori Manna (p481)

➔ 1658 (p478)

➔ Oh! Calcutta (p480)

➔ Fire and Ice (p480)

Best Places to Stay

➔ Oberoi Grand (p473)

➔ Corner Courtyard (p476)

➔ Astor (p474)

➔ Central B&B (p474)

Why Go?

India's second-biggest city is a festival of human existence, simultaneously noble and squalid, cultured and desperate. By its old spelling, Calcutta conjures up images of human suffering to most Westerners. But locally, Kolkata is regarded as India's intellectual and cultural capital. While poverty is certainly in your face, the dapper Bengali gentry continue to frequent old gentlemen's clubs, back horses at the Calcutta Racetrack and tee off at some of India's finest golf courses.

As the former capital of British India, Kolkata retains a feast of colonial-era architecture contrasting starkly with urban slums and new-town suburbs with their air-con shopping malls. Kolkata is the ideal place to experience the mild, fruity tang of Bengali cuisine. Friendlier than India's other metropolises, this is a city you 'feel' more than simply visit. Walk the chaotic back alleys, ride the Hooghly ferries and, if you've got more time, take an excursion to the Sundarbans.

When to Go
Kolkata (Calcutta)

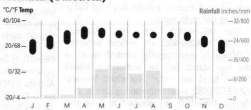

Sep & Oct The city dresses up magnificently for the colourful mayhem of Durga Puja.

Nov–Jan Cool and dry; there's a big film-fest in November and a music festival in January.

May–Sep Best avoided unless you're prepared for a very serious drenching.

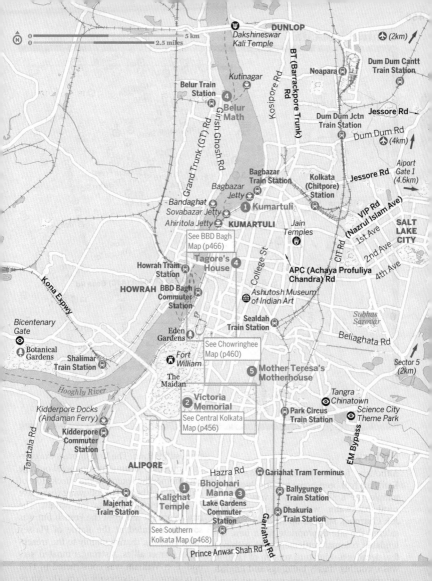

DUNLOP

Dakshineswar Kali Temple

⛩ (2km)

Kutinagar

BT (Barrackpore Trunk) Rd

Noapara

Dum Dum Cantt Train Station

Belur Train Station

4 **Belur Math**

Kosipore Rd

Dum Dum Jctn Train Station

Jessore Rd

Dum Dum Rd ⛩ (4km)

Grand Trunk (GT) Rd

Girish Ghosh Rd

Bagbazar Train Station

Kolkata (Chitpore) Station

Jessore Rd

Aiport Gate 1 (4.6km)

Bagbazar Jetty

- Bandaghat

Sovabazar Jetty

Ahiritola Jetty

1 Kumartuli

KUMARTULI

CIT Rd

VIP Rd (Nazrul Islam Ave)

1st Ave

2nd Ave

4th Ave

SALT LAKE CITY

Jain Temples

See BBD Bagh Map (p466)

Tagore's House **4**

College St

APC (Achaya Profuliya Chandra) Rd

Howrah Train Station

HOWRAH

BBD Bagh Commuter Station

Ashutosh Museum of Indian Art

Subhas Sarovar

Sealdah Train Station

Beliaghata Rd

Sector 5 (2km)

Kona Expwy

Bicentenary Gate

Botanical Gardens

Shalimar Train Station

Eden Gardens

Fort William

The Maidan

Hooghly River

See Chowringhee Map (p460)

5 Mother Teresa's Motherhouse

Tangra Chinatown

Science City Theme Park

EM Bypass

Kidderpore Docks (Andaman Ferry)

Kidderpore Commuter Station

Taratala Rd

Victoria Memorial **2**

See Central Kolkata Map (p456)

Park Circus Train Station

ALIPORE

Hazra Rd

Bhojohari Manna **3**

Gariahat Tram Terminus

Majerhat Train Station

1 Kalighat Temple

Lake Gardens Commuter Station

Gariahat Rd

Ballygunge Train Station

Dhakuria Train Station

See Southern Kolkata Map (p468)

Prince Anwar Shah Rd

N

0 ———— 5 km
0 ———— 2.5 miles

Kolkata Highlights

1 Watch goddesses coming to life in the curious lanes of **Kumartuli** (p464) or on Kalighat Rd, near the famous **Kalighat Temple** (p465)

2 Ponder the contradictions of the magnificent **Victoria Memorial** (p457)

3 Sample lip-smackingly authentic Bengali cuisine at **Bhojohari Manna** (p481)

4 Discover the enlightened universalist idealism of Ramakrishna in **Belur Math** (p464) and Rabindranath Tagore at **Tagore's House** (p463)

5 Volunteer to help the destitute with the organisation founded by **Mother Teresa** (p459)

Central Kolkata

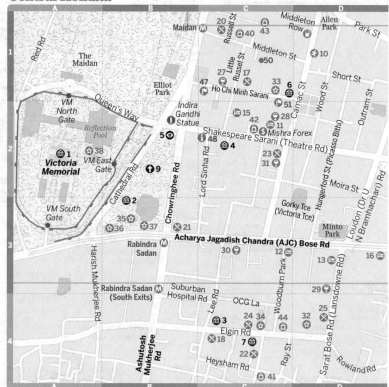

History

Although for centuries Kalikata (now Kalighat) had been home to a much-revered temple, the Kolkata area was very much a rural backwater when British merchant Job Charnock showed up in 1686. He considered the site appropriate for a new, defendable colonial settlement and within a few decades a miniature version of London was sprouting stately buildings and English churches amid wide boulevards and grand formal gardens. But the grand illusion vanished abruptly at Calcutta's frayed edges where Indians servicing the Raj mostly lived in cramped, overcrowded slums.

The most notable hiccup in the city's meteoric rise came in 1756, when Siraj-uddaula, the nawab of nearby Murshidabad, recaptured the city. Dozens of members of the colonial aristocracy were imprisoned in a cramped room beneath Fort William. By morning, around 40 of them were dead

from suffocation. The British press exaggerated numbers, drumming up moral outrage back home: the legend of the 'Black Hole of Calcutta' was born. The following year, Clive of India retook Calcutta for Britain. The nawab sought aid from the French but was soundly defeated at the Battle of Plassey (now Palashi), thanks mainly to the treachery of former allies. A stronger moated 'second' Fort William was constructed in 1758 in octagonal, Vaubanesque form. The whole village of Gobindapur was flattened to give the new fort's cannons a clear line of fire. Though sad for then-residents, this created the Maidan (moi-dan), a 3km-long park that is today as fundamental to Kolkata as Central Park is to New York City.

Calcutta became British India's official capital, though well into the late 18th century one could still hunt tigers in the bamboo forests around where Sudder St lies today.

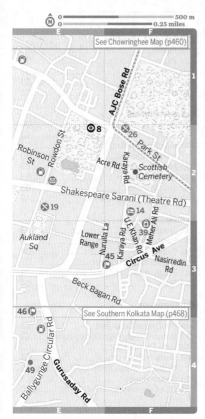

The late-19th-century Bengali Renaissance movement saw a great cultural reawakening among middle-class Calcuttans. This was further galvanised by the massively unpopular 1905 division of Bengal, sowing the seeds of the Indian Independence movement. Bengal was reunited in 1911, but the British promptly transferred their colonial capital to less troublesome Delhi.

Initially, loss of political power had little effect on Calcutta's economic status. However, the impact of 1947's partition was devastating. While West Pakistan and Punjab saw a fairly equal (if bloody) exchange of populations, migration in Bengal was almost entirely one way. Around four million Hindu refugees from East Bengal arrived, choking Calcutta's already overpopulated *bastis* (slums). For a period, people really were dying of hunger in the streets, creating Calcutta's abiding image of abject poverty. No sooner had these refugees been absorbed than a second wave arrived during the 1971 India–Pakistan War.

After India's partition, the port of Calcutta was hit very hard by the loss of its main natural hinterland, now behind the closed Pakistan (later Bangladesh) border. Labour unrest spiralled out of control while the city's dominant party (Communist Party of India) spent most of its efforts attacking the feudal system of land ownership. Well-intentioned attempts to set strict rent controls backfired: where tenants pay only a few rupees in monthly rent, landlords have no interest in maintaining or upgrading properties, so many fine old buildings spent years crumbling.

In 2001, Calcutta officially adopted the more phonetic spelling, Kolkata. Around the same time the city administration implemented a new, relatively business-friendly attitude that has encouraged a noticeable economic resurgence. The most visible results are numerous suburban shopping malls and apartment towers plus the rapid emergence of Salt Lake City's Sector 5 as Kolkata's alternative corporate and entertainment centre, albeit well off most tourists' radar.

◉ Sights

◉ Chowringhee

★**Victoria Memorial**   HISTORIC BUILDING
(VM; Map p456; ☎033-22235142; www.victoriamemorial-cal.org; Indian/foreigner incl park ₹10/150; ☉10am-5pm Tue-Sun, last tickets 4.30pm) The incredible Victoria Memorial is a vast, beautifully proportioned festival of white marble: think US Capitol meets Taj Mahal. Had it been built for a beautiful Indian princess rather than a dead colonial queen, this would surely be considered one of India's greatest buildings. It was designed to commemorate Queen Victoria's 1901 diamond jubilee, but construction wasn't completed until nearly 20 years after her death.

Inside, highlights are the soaring central chamber and the Calcutta Gallery, an excellent, even-handed exhibition tracing the city's colonial-era history. But even if you don't want to go in, the building is still worth admiring from afar: there's a magnificently photogenic view across reflecting ponds from the northeast. Or you can get closer by paying your way into the large, well-tended park. Entrance is from the north or south

Central Kolkata

◎ Top Sights
1 Victoria Memorial A2

◎ Sights
2 Academy of Fine Arts B3
3 Ahuja Museum for Arts C4
4 Aurobindo Bhawan C2
5 Birla Planetarium B2
6 Harrington Street Arts Centre C1
7 Netaji Bhawan C4
8 South Park Street Cemetery E2
9 St Paul's Cathedral B2

◎ Activities, Courses & Tours
10 Mystic Yoga Studio D1

⬒ Sleeping
11 Astor C2
12 Casa Fortuna C3
13 Central B&B D3
14 Diamond Suites F2
15 Kenilworth C2
16 Park Prime D3

⊗ Eating
17 Amigos C1
18 Bikers' Cafe C4
19 Chocolate Room E2
   Drive Inn .... (see 40)
20 Fire and Ice C1
21 Haldiram B3
22 Kewpies C4
23 Little Italy C2
24 Oh! Calcutta C4
25 Picadilly Square D4
26 Shiraz F2

◎ Drinking & Nightlife
27 Fusion C1
28 Plush C2
29 Soho D3
30 Underground C3
31 Urban Desi C2

◎ Entertainment
32 Akhra D4
33 ICCR C1
34 Inox (Forum Mall) C4
   Nandan Cinema .... (see 35)
35 Nandan Complex B3
36 Rabindra Sadan B3
37 Sisir Mancha B3
38 VM Sound & Light Show A2

◎ Shopping
39 Ankur Kala F3
40 Earthcare Bookstore C1
41 FabIndia C4
42 Nagaland Emporium C2
43 Pragjyotika C1
44 Story C4

ⓘ Information
45 Bangladeshi Consulate F3
46 Bhutanese Consulate E3
47 British Deputy High Commission C1
48 India Tourism C2
49 Manipur State Office E4
   Nagaland State Office .... (see 42)
50 Sikkim House C1
51 USA Consulate C2

gates (with ticket booths at both). The east gate is exit-only by day, but on dry season evenings, enter here for the 45-minute English-language **sound & light show** (Map p456; Indian/foreigner ₹10/20; ⊙7.15pm Tue-Sun mid-Oct–Feb, 7.45pm Tue-Sun Mar-Jun). Tickets available from 5pm. Show seating is outside and uncovered. No shows in summer.

St Paul's Cathedral   CHURCH
(Map p456; Cathedral Rd; ⊙9am-noon & 3-6pm)
With its central crenellated tower, St Paul's would look quite at home in Cambridgeshire. Built between 1839 and 1847, it has a remarkably wide nave and features a stained-glass west window by pre-Raphaelite maestro, Sir Edward Burne-Jones.

Indian Museum   MUSEUM
(Map p460; ☎033-22861702; www.indianmuseum kolkata.org; 27 Chowringhee Rd; Indian/foreigner ₹10/150, camera ₹50; ⊙10am-4.30pm Tue-Sun,

last entry 4pm) India's biggest and oldest major museum celebrated its bicentenary in February 2014. It's mostly a lovably old-fashioned place that fills a large colonnaded palace ranged around a central lawn. Extensive exhibits include fabulous sculptures dating back two millennia, notably the lavishly carved 2nd-century-BC Barhut Gateway. But there's so much more. Gag at the pickled human embryos beneath a dangling whale skeleton. Seek out an ancient Egyptian mummy. Peruse 37 types of opium in the library-like commercial-botany gallery. Notice over 7kg of rings and bangles found in the tummy of a gigantic man-eating crocodile. Woman-eating too, one supposes.

No bags are allowed inside: handbags can be stored at the entrance but don't arrive with a big backpack.

New Market
MARKET

(Hogg Bazaar; Lindsay St) Marked by a distinctive red-brick clocktower, this enormous warren of market halls dates originally from 1874 but was substantially rebuilt after a 1980s fire. By day, handicraft touts can be a minor annoyance. It's more interesting just after dawn when there's a harrowing fascination in watching the arrival of animals at the Hogg Meat Market, with its grizzly chopping blocks, gruesomely blood-splattered floors and grimly pillared high ceilings. Another curiosity to seek out is **Nahoum Bakery** (Stall F-20, New Market; ⊙9.30am-8pm Mon-Sat, 9.30am-1pm Sun), little changed since 1902 when the Jewish owners arrived from Bagdhad. The little teak cash-desk is 80 years old.

St Thomas Church
CHURCH

(7 Middleton Row) Opened in 1842, this Catholic church has a Doric columned portico topped by a short octagonal spire. It was here that the body of Mother Teresa lay 'in state' after her death in 1997.

Academy of Fine Arts
ART GALLERY

(2 Cathedral Rd; ⊙3-8pm) FREE Several bright, ground-floor gallery rooms in this 1933 building feature changing exhibitions by local living artists.

Ahuja Museum for Arts
ART GALLERY

(www.sdahujaart.com/; Elgin Rd; ⊙noon-6pm) FREE Changing exhibitions feature mostly excellent 21st-century works by Bengali artists. Free, even the coffee (when we visited)!

Harrington Street Arts Centre
ART GALLERY

(Map p456; www.hstreetartscentre.com; 2nd fl, 8 Ho Chi Minh Sarani; ⊙2-8pm Mon-Sat) Imaginative exhibitions, normally photographic, are spread through four spacious rooms of a classic Kolkata colonial building.

Birla Planetarium
PLANETARIUM

(Map p456; Chowringhee Rd; admission ₹30; ⊙in English 1.30pm & 6.30pm) Loosely styled on Sarnath's classic Buddhist stupa, this 1962 dome presents slow-moving, half-hour star shows.

Aurobindo Bhawan
HISTORIC BUILDING

(Map p456; 8 Shakespeare Sarani; ⊙8am-8pm) Revolutionary turned guru Sri Aurobindo was born in Calcutta in 1872. His childhood mansion-home has been preserved and its garden creates a small oasis of peace in the city centre.

Mother Teresa's Motherhouse
HISTORIC BUILDING

(Map p460; ☎033-22497115, 033-22172277; www.motherteresa.org; 54A AJC Bose Rd; ⊙8am-noon & 3-6pm Fri-Wed) A regular flow of mostly Christian pilgrims visit the Missionaries of Charity's 'Motherhouse' to pay homage at Mother Teresa's large, sober tomb. A small adjacent museum room displays Teresa's worn sandals and battered enamel dinner bowl. Located upstairs is the room where she worked and slept from 1953 to 1997, preserved in all its simplicity.

From Sudder St, walk around 15 minutes along Alimuddin St, then two minutes'

KOLKATA (CALCUTTA) SIGHTS

KOLKATA IN...

Three Days

On the first day, admire the Victoria Memorial (p457) and surrounding attractions, then visit India Tourism to grab a Marble Palace permit (to be used two days hence), before dining and dancing on Park St. On day two wander through the colonial-era wonderland of **BBD Bagh** (Map p466; Dalhousie Sq), experience the fascinating/disturbing alley-life of **Old Chinatown** and **Barabazar**, and observe Howrah Bridge (p463) from colourful Mullik Ghat flower market (p463). Day three visit Marble Palace (p463) and surrounding attractions, continuing to Kumartuli (p464) directly or by a vastly longer loop via Dakshineswar (p465) and Belur Math (p464).

One Week

In addition to the three-day itinerary, experience the contrasts of **Southern Kolkata**, its art galleries, golf clubs, dawn laughing clubs, the great Bengali food and the goat sacrifices at Kalighat (p465). Ponder the moral dilemmas of taking/not taking a hand-drawn rickshaw. Then take a multiday tour to the **Sundarbans** in West Bengal or consider volunteering for a few days having visited Mother Teresa's Motherhouse (p459).

Chowringhee

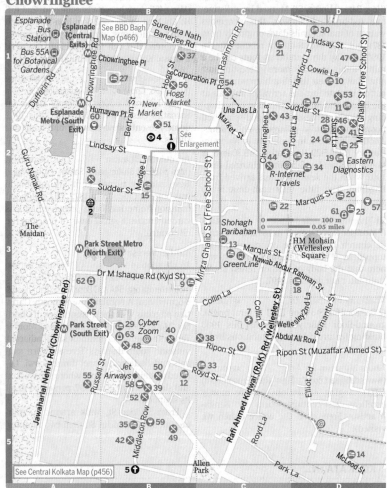

See BBD Bagh Map (p466)

See Central Kolkata Map (p456)

KOLKATA (CALCUTTA) SIGHTS

south. It's in the second alley to the right (after Hotel Heaven).

South Park Street Cemetery CEMETERY
(Map p456; donation ₹20, guide booklet ₹100;
⊙8am-4.45pm) Active 1757 to 1840, this historic cemetery remains a wonderful oasis of calm featuring mossy Raj-era graves from rotundas to soaring pyramids, all jostling for space in a lightly manicured jungle.

Netaji Bhawan MUSEUM
(Map p456; ☎033-24756139; www.netaji.org; 38/2 Elgin Rd; adult/child ₹5/2; ⊙11am-4pm Tue-Sun)

Celebrating the life and vision of controversial independence radical Subhas Chandra Bose, this house museum was Bose's brother's residence from which Subhas made his famous 'Great Escape' from British-imposed house arrest in January 1941. Some rooms retain a 1940s feel and the original getaway car is parked in the drive.

◉ BBD Bagh

One of Raj-era Calcutta's foremost squares, BBD Bagh is centred on a palm-lined central reservoir-lake ('tank') that once supplied the young city's water. Although concrete

Life Building (Map p466; 32 BBD Bagh) sports cherubic details that are coming back to life with a new restoration project. Although half collapsed, the ruins of the once-grand Currency Building (Map p466; BBD Bagh East; ⏰10am-5pm Mon-Fri) have been stabilised, making an interesting venue for an exhibition-bookshop of the Archaeological Survey of India. Standing proud to the north is St Andrews Church (Map p466; 14-15 BBD Bagh) with a fine Wren-style spire.

St John's Church   CHURCH
(Map p466; ☎033-22436098; KS Roy Rd; admission on foot/with car ₹10/25; ⏰8am-5pm) This stone-spired 1787 church is ringed by columns and contains a small, portrait-draped room once used as an office by Warren Hastings, India's first British governor-general (on the right as you enter). The tree-shaded grounds have several interesting monuments including the mausoleum of Job Charnock (Map p466) celebrating Kolkata's disputed 'founder'. The 1902 Black Hole Memorial (Map p466) was moved here in 1940.

High Court   HISTORIC BUILDING
(Map p466; http://calcuttahighcourt.nic.in; Esplanade Row West; ⏰10am-5pm Mon-Fri) One of Kolkata's greatest architectural triumphs, the High Court building was built between 1864 and 1872, loosely modelled on the medieval Cloth Hall in Ypres (Flanders). The grand Gothic exterior is best viewed from the south. Sometimes foreigners can simply wander in but more likely you'll be asked to go around to the eastern entrance security desk and apply for an entry pass (free).

Once inside it's fun to simply explore the endless arches following brigades of lawyers shuffling around in twin-tailed white collar-pieces and tuxedos overlayed with flapping university-style gowns. Sadly photography isn't allowed.

Banking Museum   MUSEUM
(Map p466; ☎033-22318164; 11th fl, SBI Bldg, Strand Rd; ⏰2.30-5pm Tue-Fri, or by request) **FREE** This professionally presented little museum brings alive the history of Indian banking using paintings, models, seals, weapons and archive materials. A star exhibit is the 'forgotten' chest in which some of Mahatma Gandhi's ashes were left for 46 years in the State Bank vault in Cuttack.

intrusions detract from the overall spectacle, many a splendid colonial-era edifice remains. Foremost is the 1780 Writers' Building (Map p466), whose glorious south facade looks something like a French provincial city hall. It was originally built for clerks ('writers') of the East India Company. Behind, past the joyously re-painted Eastern Railway Building (Map p466; NS Rd), the former Chartered Bank Building (Map p466; India Exchange Pl) has a vaguely Moorish feel and shrubs sprouting from the untended upper turrets. The 1860s GPO (Map p466) has a soaring rotunda and the Standard

Chowringhee

◎ Sights
1	Clocktower	B2
2	Indian Museum	A3
3	Mother Teresa's Motherhouse	F4
4	New Market	B2
5	St Thomas Church	B5

◈ Activities, Courses & Tours
6	Backpackers	C2
7	Calcutta Rescue	C4
8	Sishu Bhavan briefings	F3

◉ Sleeping
9	Aafreen Tower	B3
10	Afridi International	D1
11	Astoria Hotel	D2
12	Corporate	B4
13	DK International	C3
14	Enclave Guest House	D5
15	Fairlawn Hotel	B2
16	Georgian Inn	E2
17	Golden Apple Hotel	D1
18	Hotel Aafreen	D3
19	Hotel Galaxy	D2
20	Hotel Kempton	D2
21	Hotel Lindsay	C1
22	Hotel Pioneer International	C3
23	Hotel VIP Intercontinental	D3
24	Maria	D2
25	Modern Lodge	D2
26	Monovilla Inn	F3
27	Oberoi Grand	B1
28	Paragon Hotel	D2
29	Park Hotel	B4
30	Sapphire Suites	D1
31	Shams Hotel	D2
32	Shaw Guest House	F3
33	Sunflower Guest House	C4
34	Timestar Hotel	D2
35	YWCA	B5

◎ Eating
36	1658	A2
37	Aminia	B1
38	Arsalan	C4
39	Au Bon Pain	B4
40	Baba Rolls	B4
41	Bhoj Company	D2
42	Bistro by the Park	B5
	Blue & Beyond	(see 21)
43	Blue Sky Cafe	C2
44	Delish	C2
45	Hot Kati Rolls	A4
46	JoJo's Cafe	D2
47	Kathleen Confectioners	D1
48	Kusum Rolls	B4
49	Marco Polo	B5
50	Mocambo	B4
51	Nahoum Bakery	B2
52	Peter Cat	B5
53	Raj's Spanish Cafe	D1
54	Sidheshwari Ashram	C1
55	Teej	A4
56	UP Bihar	B1

◎ Drinking & Nightlife
57	Arabian Delight	D3
	Fairlawn Hotel Beer-Garden	(see 15)
58	Flury's	B4
59	Myx	B5
60	New Cathay	A2
	OlyPub	(see 48)
	Tantra	(see 29)

◎ Shopping
61	Ashalayam	D3
62	Doel's Choice	A3
63	Oxford Bookstore	B4

Museum entrance is free. Sign in with bank security at the entrance towards the northerly end of the big SBI tower building.

◎ Barabazar & Howrah

The following walk links several minor religious sights but much of the fun comes from exploring the vibrantly chaotic alleys en route that teem with traders, rickshaw couriers and baggage wallahs hauling impossibly huge packages balanced on their heads. Hidden away amid the paper-merchants of Old China Bazaar St, the Armenian Church of Nazareth (Map p466; Armenian St; ☺9am-4pm Mon-Sat) was founded in 1707 and is claimed to be Kolkata's oldest place of Christian worship. The larger 1797 Portuguese-Catholic

Holy Rosary Cathedral (Map p466; Brabourne Rd; ☺6am-11am & 5-6pm) has eye-catching crown-topped side towers and an interior whose font is festively kitsch.

Kolkata's Jewish community once numbered around 30,000 but these days barely 40 ageing co-religionists turn up at Maghen David Synagogue (Map p466; Canning St). Around the corner, the Neveh Shalome Synagogue (Map p466; Brabourne Rd) is almost invisible behind shop stalls. Once you've fought your way across Brabourne St, descend Pollock St between very colourful stalls selling balloons, tinsel and plastic plants to the decrepit Pollock St Post Office (Map p466), once a grand Jewish school building. Opposite, BethEl Synagogue (Map p466; Pollock St) has a facade that looks passingly similar to a 1930s cinema. The synagogue has a fine colonnaded interior but to get into this or the other synagogues you'll generally need to have contacted the Community Affairs office at 63 Park St, ☑ 9831054669, in advance.

Parallel to Pollock St, wider Ezra St has a brilliant old perfumerie (Map p466; 55 Ezra St), just before the Shree Cutchi Jain Temple (Map p466; Ezra St). From there follow Parsee Church St east to reach Old Chinatown or swing back up ever-fascinating Rabindra Sarani to find the shop-clad 1926 Nakhoda Mosque (Map p466; 1 Zakaria St) that was loosely modelled on Akbar's Mausoleum at Sikandra.

Howrah Bridge LANDMARK
(Rabindra Setu; Map p466) Howrah Bridge is a 705m-long abstraction of steel cantilevers, sweat and traffic fumes. Built during WWII, it's one of the world's busiest bridges and a Kolkatan architectural icon. Photography of the bridge is technically prohibited but you might sneak a discreet shot from one of the various ferries that ply the Hooghly River to the vast 1906 Howrah train station.

Mullik Ghat Flower Market FLOWER MARKET
(Map p466) Near the southeast end of Howrah Bridge, the flower market is fascinating and colourful virtually 24 hours a day. Many workers live in makeshift shacks, bathing in the river behind from a ghat with sunset views of Howrah Bridge. At around 7am local wrestlers practise their art on a small caged area of sand set back from the river.

◉ Old Chinatown

For nearly two centuries the area around Phears Lane was Kolkata's Chinatown. A fit of anti-Chinese fervour during the 1962 war drove many ethnic Chinese away and these days 'old' Chinatown is predominantly Muslim. However, just after dawn, there's a lively market scene on Tiretta's Bazaar. It's all closed by 10am, as is the archetypal old shop, Hap Hing (Map p466; 10 Sun Yat Sen St; ◎ 6am-10am) whose owner Stella Chen can tell you lots more about the Chinese community.

Other historic shops nearby, albeit non-Chinese, include musical instrument makers Mondal (p483) and the fascinating 1948 gun shop ML Bhunja (Map p466; ☑ 033-

22374144; 301 Bipin Behari Ganguli St; ◎ 12.30-6.30pm Mon-Fri), with its misty old cases of rifles, sabres, a flintlock and many an old bayonet laced with snake venom.

Around the once-grand 1924 Toong On Temple (Map p466; Blackburn Lane) destitute scavengers sift through rubbish heaps, sleeping in tent-and-box shacks on neighbouring pavements. Very humbling.

◉ Rabindra Sarani & Around

This ever fascinating street of close-packed shops and workshops is threaded through by tram 8 (Esplanade-Galiff St, every 20 minutes) which terminates at the site of Kolkata's curious Sunday morning pet and bird market. There are more interesting sights around the Kolkata University on College St, east of Rabindra Sarani.

★**Tagore's House** MUSEUM
(Jorasankho Thaurbari; ☑ 033-22695242; www.rbu.ac.in/museum; 246D Rabindra Sarani; Indian/foreigner adult ₹10/50, student ₹5/25; ◎ 10.30am-5pm Tue-Sun, last entry 4.30pm) The comfortable 1784 family mansion of Rabindranath Tagore has become a shrine-like museum to India's greatest modern poet. Even if his personal effects don't inspire you, some of the well-chosen quotations might spark an interest in Tagore's deeply universalist philosophy. There's also a decent gallery of paintings by his family and contemporaries, and an exhibition on his links with Japan. The 1930 photo of Tagore taken with Einstein could win a 'World's Wildest Hair' competition. You'd need an hour to see everything, but for many casual visitors a brief glimpse is enough.

★**Marble Palace** MUSEUM
(☑ 033-22393310; 46 Muktaram Babu St; ◎ 10am-3pm, closed Mon & Thu) This resplendent 1835 rajah's mansion is overstuffed with dusty statues of thinkers and dancing girls, much Victoriana, ample Belgian glassware and fine if bedraggled paintings, including supposedly original works by Murillo, Joshua Reynolds and Rubens.

Napoleons beat Wellingtons three to one in the music room, which is lavishly floored with marble inlay. The ballroom retains its vast array of candle chandeliers with globes of silvered glass to spread illumination: original 19th-century disco balls!

Admission is free, but before arriving you need to get a permission note from

West Bengal Tourism (p484) or India Tourism (p484). To find Marble Palace from MG Rd metro, walk north and turn left at the first traffic light (171 Chittaranjan Ave). Coming from the east, it's on the lane that leaves Rabindra Sarani between Nos 198 and 200.

Ashutosh Museum of Indian Art   MUSEUM
(☑ 033-22410071; www.caluniv.ac.in/museum/ museum.html; Centenary Bldg, 87/1 College St; admission ₹10; ⊙ 11am-4pm Mon-Fri) Priceless antique Indian sculptures, brasswork and Bengali terracotta are displayed with very little fanfare in this dry, but brilliantly endowed museum tucked behind Kolkata University's Central Library. Entrance is off College St down the first lane to the left as you walk north from Coolootola Rd.

Indian Coffee House   HISTORIC SITE
(1st fl, 15 Bankim Chatterjee St; coffee ₹12; ⊙ 9am-9pm Mon-Sat, to 12.30pm & 5-9pm Sun) If you're walking down College St to the Ashutosh Museum from intriguing MG Rd, after one block turn left, take the fourth doorway on the left and climb the stairs to this mythic cafe. The cheap, dishwater coffee can hardly be recommended, but it's perversely fascinating to look inside this unpretentious high-ceilinged place that was once a meeting place of freedom fighters, bohemians and revolutionaries.

◉ Northern Kolkata

This area's long distances and tedious traffic are somewhat mitigated if you take the boat downstream from Dakshineswar to Belur Math.

★ Kumartuli Idol-makers   AREA
Countless effigies of deities are immersed in the holy Hooghly during Kolkata's colourful *pujas* (offering or prayers). Most have been created in specialist *kumar* (sculptor) workshops in this enthralling district, notably along Banamali Sakar St, the lane running west from 499 Rabindra Sarani. Craftsmen are busiest from August to October, creating straw frames, adding clay coatings and painting the divine features for the Durga and Kali festivals. In November, old figures wash up on river banks and are refurbished.

Sheetalnathji Mandir   JAIN TEMPLE
(www.jaindharmonline.com/pilgri/shitala.htm; Badridas Temple St; ⊙ 6am-noon & 3-7pm) The best known of a closely grouped trio of Jain temples, this 1867 complex is a dazzling if unrefined pastiche of colourful mosaics, spires, columns and slivered figurines. The effect is Gaudi-esque. It's 1.6km from Shyambazar metro. The temple relies on donations.

★ Belur Math   SACRED SITE
(☑ 033-26545892; www.sriramakrishna.org/belur. htm; Grand Trunk Rd; ⊙ 6.30am-noon & 3.30-

---

MOTHER TERESA

For many people, Mother Teresa (1910–97) was the living image of human sacrifice. Born Agnes Gonxha Bojaxhiu to Albanian parents in then-Ottoman Üsküp (now Skopje in Macedonia), she joined the Irish Order of Loreto nuns and worked for over a decade teaching in Calcutta's St Mary's High School. Horrified by the city's spiralling poverty, she established a new order, the **Missionaries of Charity** (www.motherteresa.org) and founded refuges for the destitute and dying. The first of these, Nirmal Hriday (p465), opened in 1952. Although the order swiftly expanded into an international charity, Mother Teresa herself continued to live in absolute simplicity. She was awarded the Nobel Peace Prize in 1979 and beatified by the Vatican in October 2003, the first official step towards being made a saint.

But this 'Saint of the Gutters' is not universally beloved. For some Kolkatans it's slightly galling to find their cultured, predominantly Hindu city popularly linked in the world's mind with a Catholic heroine whose work underlined the city's least appealing facet. Germaine Greer has accused Mother Teresa of religious imperialism, while Christopher Hitchens' book, *The Missionary Position*, decried the donations from dictators and corrupt tycoons. Many have questioned the Missionaries of Charity's minimal medical background and Teresa's staunchly Catholic position against contraception. However, the organisation was never primarily focused on saving lives, simply offering a little love and dignity to the dying. Before Mother Teresa, even that was an unknown luxury for the truly destitute.

8.30pm) Set very attractively amid palms and manicured lawns, this large religious centre is the headquarters of the Ramakrishna Mission, inspired by 19th-century Indian sage Ramakrishna Paramahamsa, who preached the unity of all religions. Its centrepiece is the 1938 **Ramakrishna Mandir** (⊘closes 8pm) which somehow manages to look like a cathedral, Indian palace and Istanbul's Aya Sofya all at the same time. Several smaller shrines near the Hooghly riverbank include the **Sri Sarada Devi Temple** (⊘6.30-11.30am & 3.30-5.15pm), entombing the guru's wife.

Accessed from the car park, a beautifully presented **museum** (⊘8.30-11.30am & 3.30-5.30pm Tue-Sun) charts Ramakrishna's life and the travels of his great disciple Swami Vivekananda.

From the main road outside, six daily suburban trains run Belur Math–Howrah (25 minutes) most usefully at 10.45am and 4.45pm. Picking up next door to Belur Math train station, minibus 11 and buses 54/56 run to Esplanade/Howrah in miserable stop-start traffic. Southbound they pass almost beside Bandaghat from which you might prefer to take the thrice hourly ferry across to Ahiritola, then switch to the Bagbazar boat for Kumartuli. From **Belur Jetty**, ferries (hourly) and open boats (when full) operate to Dakshineswar. Southbound ferries to Howrah via Bagbazar depart at 6.30pm and 8pm (plus 9.15am/1.30pm weekdays/Sunday).

Dakshineswar   HINDU TEMPLE
(www.dakshineswarkalitemple.org;   ⊘6am-12.30pm & 3.30-8.30pm) The heart of this vibrant riverside complex is a cream-and-red 1847 Kali Temple shaped like an Indian Sacré-Coeur. The site is where Ramakrishna started his remarkable spiritual journey, and his small room in the outer northwest corner of the temple precinct is now a place of special meditative reverence. No photos, deposit shoes outside complex.

Several daily suburban trains from Sealdah run to Dakshineswar station (₹5, 20 minutes), 400m south of the temple. A metro extension is due to reach the same point by 2017, but for now you can either take painfully slow DN9/1 from Dum Dum metro. Or from the southwest side of Noapara metro, take an auto to Dunlop (₹10, a convoluted 15 minutes) then cross under the curling overpass and take bus 79 for five minutes. Hourly ferries from almost under the old Dakshineswar Bridge run to Belur Math (₹10). From around 200m further north, uncovered small boats do the same route much more frequently, but you'll have to sit cross legged in the sun (or rain), squashed with two dozen others for nearly half an hour. Bring a hat or umbrella.

◎ Kalighat

Surrounding Kalighat temple is a fascinating maze of alleys jammed with market stalls selling votive flowers, brassware and religious artefacts.

★**Kalighat Temple**   HINDU TEMPLE
(Map p468; ⊘5am-10pm, central shrine closed 2-4pm) This ancient Kali temple is Kolkata's holiest spot for Hindus and possibly the source of the city's name. Today's version is a 1809 rebuild with floral- and peacock-motif tiles that look more Victorian than Indian. More interesting than the architecture are the jostling pilgrim queues that snake into the main hall to fling hibiscus flowers at a crowned, three-eyed Kali image. There's no need to join them to feel the atmosphere.

Behind the bell pavilion but still within the mandir complex, goats are ritually beheaded (generally mornings) to honour the ever-demanding goddess. To the direct east is a pea-green 'holy pond' and by the sanctuary's north perimeter, a 'tree of fertility'.

Unless using their services to queue-jump into the central shrine hall, a token donation of ₹20 is sufficient for any impromptu temple guide. Donating ₹21 is even better – giving a sum ending in one is considered lucky and implies that you are familiar with local customs.

Nirmal Hriday   ARCHITECTURE
(Map p468; 251 Kalighat Rd; ⊘closed to visitors) Mother Teresa's world famous, if surprisingly small, home for the dying, was originally a Kalighat pilgrim hostel. Its roof-corners are pimpled with neo-Mughal mini-domes.

Kalighat Idol-makers   WORKSHOPS
(Map p468; Kalighat Rd) Though less famous than Kumartuli, there's a fascinating group of idol-makers' workshops where Kalighat Rd curves north from Hazra Rd.

Shanagar Burning Ghat   MONUMENT
(Map p468; Tolisnala Stream) Overlooking the putrid Tolisnala Stream, Shanagar Burning

BBD Bagh

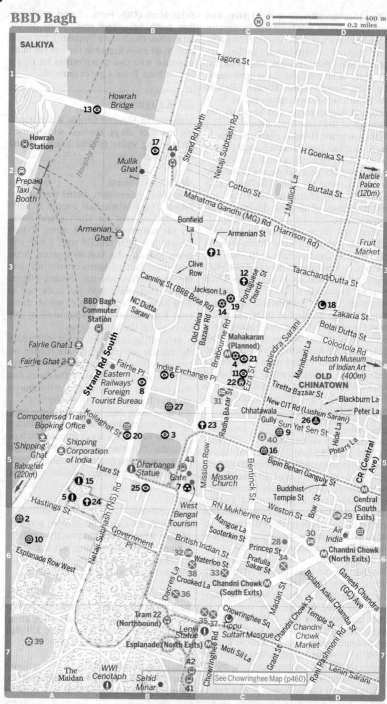

SALKIYA

0 — 400 m
0 — 0.2 miles

Tagore St

Howrah Bridge
13

Howrah Station

Strand Rd North

Netaji Subhash Rd

H Goenka St

Marble Palace (120m)

Prepaid Taxi Booth

Hooghly River

Mullik Ghat
17
44

Cotton St

J Mullick La

Burtala St

Mahatma Gandhi (MG) Rd (Harrison Rd)

Armenian Ghat

Bonfield La

Armenian St
1

Fruit Market

Clive Row

Canning St (BRB Bose Rd)

Jackson La

Portuguese Church
12

Tarachand Dutta St

NC Dutta Sarani

14 **19**

Old China Bazaar Rd

Zakaria St
18

BBD Bagh Commuter Station

Brabourne Rd

Mahakaran (Planned)
4 **21**

Rabindra Sarani

Bolai Dutta St

Cooltola Rd

Marinbari La

Ashutosh Museum of Indian Art (400m)

Fairlie Ghat 1

Fairlie Ghat 2

Strand Rd South

Fairlie Pl
Eastern Railways' Foreign Tourist Bureau
8

India Exchange Pl
6

Ezra St
11
22

Tiretta Bazaar St

OLD CHINATOWN

Blackburn La

Peter La

Computerised Train Booking Office

Koilaghat St

27

Radha Bazar St

31

New CIT Rd (Lushun Sarani)

Chhatawala Gully

26
Sun Yat Sen St
9

Hide La

Phears La

CR (Central Ave)

'Shipping' Ghat

Shipping Corporation of India

20

3

23

40

16

Bipin Behari Ganguly St

Babughat (220m)

Hare St

Dharbanga Statue

43
Gate
7

Mission Row

Mission Church

Bentinck St

Buddhist Temple St

Bow St

Central (South Exits)

25

West Bengal Tourism

RN Mukherjee Rd

Weston St

29

Air India

Hastings St

15

5
24

Government Pl

Mangoe La
Sooterkin St

Princep St

28

30
34

Chandni Chowk (North Exits)

2

10

British Indian St

32

Waterloo St
38

Prafulla Sakar St

Madan St

Ganesh Chandra (GC) Ave

Esplanade Row West

Dacres La

33

Chandni Chowk (South Exits)

Biplabi Anukul Chamba St

Crooked La

36

Chandni Chowk Temple St

Chandni Chowk Market

Tram 22 (Northbound)

35 37

Lenin Statue
1

Tippu Sultan Mosque

Chowringhee Sq

Chowringhee Rd

Grant St

Rani Rashmoni Sarani

Esplanade (North Exits)

Moti Sil La

39

The Maidan

WWI Cenotaph

Sahid Minar

42

41

Lenin Sarani

See Chowringhee Map (p460)

BBD Bagh

Ghat hosts an impressive gaggle of monuments to the celebrities who have been cremated here.

◉ Ballygunge, Gariahat & Lansdowne

East of Kalighat, these areas are a fascinating mixture of new, old and slowly gentrifying, with a scattering of restaurants, shopping areas and galleries.

Birla Mandir HINDU TEMPLE
(Map p468; Gariahat Rd; ⊙6-11am & 4.30-9pm) The 20th-century Birla Mandir is a large Lakshmi Narayan temple complex in cream-coloured sandstone whose three corn-cob shaped towers are more impressive for their size than their carvings.

CIMA ART GALLERY
(Map p468; ☎033-24858509; www.cimaartindia. com; Sunny Towers, 2nd fl, 43 Ashutosh Chowdhury Rd; ⊙11am-7pm Tue-Sat, 3-7pm Mon) CIMA is a cutting-edge contemporary Bengali art gallery with an eclectic giftshop.

Experimenter ART GALLERY
(Map p468; www.experimenter.in; 2/1 Hindustan Rd; ⊙11am-7pm Mon-Sat) Experimenter is a relatively small contemporary art gallery but its exhibitions are about as cutting edge as anything you'll find in Kolkata. It's tucked behind Kanishka's on Hindustan Rd just off Gariahat Rd.

Birla Academy of Art & Culture GALLERY
(Map p468; ☎033-24666802; www.birlaart. com; 109 Southern Ave; exhibition/museum free/₹5; ⊙3-8pm Tue-Sun) This multi-storey gallery displays frequently changing exhibitions both from contemporary artists and from its vast collection encompassing all Indian styles back to some classic medieval work.

Rabindra Sarovar PARK
(Map p468) The lake here prettily reflects hazy sunrises, while middle-class Kolkatans jog, row and meditate around the parklands.

Southern Kolkata

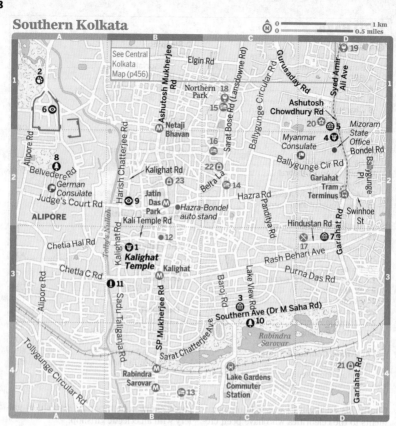

Some form circles to do group-yoga routines culminating in ho-ho ha-ha-ha laugh-ins, engagingly described by Tony Hawks as Laughing Clubs in *The Weekenders: Adventures in Calcutta*. Even if forced, a good giggle can be refreshingly therapeutic.

◉ Alipore & Around

Wealthy Alipore extends west from Tolly's Nullah stream. This affluent area was once the home of the British viceroy, and several colonial relics remain amidst the high-rise condos.

Alipore Zoo
ZOO
(Map p468; www.kolkatazoo.in; Alipore Rd; admission ₹20; ⊙9am-5pm Fri-Wed) Kolkata's 16-hectare zoo first opened in 1875. The spacious lawns and lakeside promenades are very popular with weekend picnickers

(hence all the rubbish). Bus 230 from Rabindra Sadan passes outside.

Grass is so high in the moated Bengal Tiger enclosure that it's hard to spot the animals but it's better than several more confining cages and the aviaries whose thick rusty-black wire-mesh rather obscures viewing.

Curzon Mansion
ARCHITECTURE
(Map p468; south of the Zoo) Directly south of the zoo's entrance, the access road to the National Library loops around the very regal Curzon Mansion, once the colonial Viceroy's residence. It's not (yet) a museum.

Horticultural Gardens
PARK
(Map p468; Belvedere Rd; admission ₹10; ⊙6-10am & 2-7pm) The lawn, tropical trees and flowering shrubs of the delightful Horticultural Gardens offer some respite from the traffic rumble.

Southern Kolkata

Botanical Gardens PARK
(☏033-26685357; Indian/foreigner ₹10/100; ⊙5.30am-5pm Tue-Sun; 🚌6, 55, 55A) If it weren't such an awkward trek by public transport, Kolkata's lovely 109-hectare Botanical Gardens would make a great place to escape from the city's sounds and smells. Founded in 1786, the gardens played an important role in cultivating tea long before the drink became a household commodity. Today there's a cactus house, palm collection, river-overlook and a boating-lake with splendid Giant Amazon Lily pads.

The most touted attraction is the 250-year-old 'world's largest banyan tree'. That's a little misleading: the central trunk rotted away in the 1920s, leaving an array of cross-branches and linked aerial roots so it looks more like a copse than a single tree. The banyan is five minutes' walk from the park's Bicentenary Gate on bus route 55A, or 25 minutes' walk from the gardens' main gate where bus 55 and minibus 6 terminate after a painfully slow drive from Esplanade via Howrah. Taxis from Shakespeare Sarani charge around ₹180 via the elegant Vidyasagar Setu (aka the Hooghly Suspension Bridge).

🏃 Activities

Cooking
Kali Travel Home (☏033-25550581; www.traveleastindia.com; courses ₹600-800; ⊙closed summer) arranges personal three-hour Bengali cooking courses led by local women in their homes. Costs include food. Several days' advance notice required.

Golf
The 1829 **Royal Calcutta Golf Club** (☏033-24731288, 033-24731352; www.rcgc.in; 18 Golf Club Rd; non-member green-fees ₹7303, 9-/18-hole caddy fee ₹225/449) is reputedly the world's oldest outside Britain.

Yoga & Meditation
Type 'Kolkata' into the website of **Art of Living** (www.artofliving.org/in-en/search/course) to find courses at various venues.

Mystic Yoga Studio YOGA
(Map p456; www.mysticyogastudio.in; 2nd fl, 20A Camac St; drop-in sessions ₹600; ⊙7am-noon & 4-8pm Mon-Sat) Mirror walled commercial studio offering one-hour guided yoga sessions (mostly basic). Attached juice bar and organic cafe playing recorded mantras. Hours can vary.

KOLKATA (CALCUTTA) ACTIVITIES

TOP FESTIVALS

Dover Lane Music Conference (www.doverlanemusicconference.org; Nazrul Mancha, Rabindra Sarovar; ☺late Jan) Indian classical music and dance at Rabindra Sarovar.

Kolkata Book Fair (www.kolkatabookfair.net; Milan Mela, EM Bypass; ☺late Jan/early Feb) Asia's biggest book fair.

Saraswati Puja (☺early Feb) Prayers for educational success, all dress in yellow.

Rath Yatra (☺Jun/Jul) Major Krishna chariot festival similar to the Puri equivalent.

Durga Puja (p472; www.durga-puja.org; ☺late-Sep or early-Oct) Kolkata's biggest festival.

Kolkata Film Festiva (www.kff.in; ☺mid-Nov)l Weeklong festival of Bengali and international movies.

There are also a wide range of village craft festivals in the area outside the city. **TourEast** (www.banglanatak.com) helps raise awareness and encourage visitors.

Sahaja Yoga Meditation   MEDITATION
(Map p466; ☑033-22254575; www.sahajay-oga.org; 2nd fl Shah House, Radha Bazar Rd; ☺6.30pm Tue, 5.30pm Sat, 10.45am Sun) **FREE** Kundalini awakening meditation sessions organised by devotees of Shri Mataji Nirmala Devi.

Volunteering

Several organisations welcome foreign volunteers. A good place to meet other volunteers informally is at Raj's Spanish Cafe (p478).

Mother Teresa's Missionaries of Charity (p464) welcome all comers. There's no minimum service period and no specific skills are required other than a warm heart and patience to empathise with those whose language you might not understand. Start by attending a briefing at **Sishu Bhavan** (Map p460; 78 AJC Bose Rd; ☺3pm Mon, Wed & Fri), two blocks north of the Motherhouse (p459).

US-based humanist **Responsible Charity** (www.responsiblecharity.org) looks for qualified medics or those with educational experience to volunteer for a month or more in the Jadavpur slums. Or simply donate old (decent) clothes to its collection bank at JoJo's Cafe (p477).

Calcutta Rescue (Map p460; ☑22491520, 40648277; www.calcuttarescue.org; 4th fl, 85 Collin St) provides medical care and health education for the disadvantaged of Kolkata and other parts of West Bengal. Volunteer postings are usually for six- to 12-months and limited to experienced professionals.

☞ Tours

Walking Tours

Small group, accompanied city-walks typically cost between ₹800 and ₹2000 per person depending on group size.

Kali Travel Home   WALKING
(☑033-25550581, 9432145532, 9748588366; www.traveleastindia.com) The 'original' Kolkata walking outfit offers tailored walks by day or night and a 3pm gallery exploration.

Calcutta Walks   WALKING
(Map p466; ☑98306 04197, 033-4005 2573, 9830184030; www.calcuttawalks.com; 9A Khairu Place) Well organised with a wide range of walking, cycling and motorbike tours, plus homestays with local characters. It produces what is arguably the best printed map of Kolkata.

Footsteps   WALKING, PHOTOGRAPHY
(☑9830008033, 9830052688; www.braindrop sindia.com/footsteps) Akash's early morning two to three hour photo-walks generally start at 7am.

Calcutta Photo Tours   WALKING, PHOTOGRAPHY
(☑9831163482; www.calcuttaphototours.com) Photography walks.

Tour/Hosting

Bomti   GUIDE
(Surajit Iyengar; ☑9831314990; bomtiyengar@ yahoo.com; per group per day ₹5000-8000, plus meals per person ₹1500-2500) Tailor-made personalised tours for up to four people typically end up with a traditional Bengali meal in Bomti's remarkable art-filled apart-

ment, which once featured in Elle Decor (www.elledecor.com/design-decorate/artful-patina).

Motorbike/Car Tours

Best known for their Sundarban mangrove trips (p491), the spirited 'brothers' at **Back-packers** (Map p460; ☑9836177140; www.tourdesundarbans.com; Tottee Lane) also offer innovative six-hour city tours on the back of a motorbike (₹2200). Tours pass several well-known sites and add curiosities such as Kolkata's giant trash-mountain, Tangra Chinatown, a burning ghat, a Shiva temple (join the prayers) and a brief drive through the red-light district. A similar, if adapted, tour by car costs ₹4000/4500 without/with AC for up to three people. Longer car tours to Belur Math, Dakshineswar and the Hooghly river-town sites as far as Bansberia's Kremlin-styled palace temple costs ₹5000 per car. Ask about early morning bazaar tours.

Bus Tours

Full-day sightseeing **bus tours** (tour ₹450; ⊗8.30am Tue-Sun) operated by West Bengal Tourism (p484) seem a relative bargain, but feel very rushed apart from the lengthy lunch stop. Cancelled if less than eight customers sign up.

🛏 Sleeping

Decent accommodation is expensive in Kolkata and budget places are often dismal. Even in many midrange hotels, peeling paint, loose wires, battered furniture and damp patches come as standard. Many cheaper hotels lock their gates by midnight, so if you're planning a night on the tiles, check if there's a late-entry procedure.

Top-end hotels can be very significantly discounted on websites such as www.yatra.com and www.booking.com, but midrange hotels are usually better value as walk-ins, while budget places rarely take bookings at all. The Salt Lake area has many business hotels but painfully slow transportation to most points of touristic interest means that travellers might regret staying there, at least until the metro Line 2 extension arrives.

Accommodation fills to bursting before and during Durga Puja (p472). Occupancy drops noticeably afterwards (late October), but picks up again from mid-November to February.

🛏 Around Sudder Street

The nearest Kolkata gets to a traveller ghetto is the area around helpfully located Sudder St. There's a range of backpacker-oriented services, and a big advantage of arriving here is that virtually every second building is a guesthouse or hotel, ranging from Kolkata's top five-star heritage palace to ultra-budget dives that represent a whole new league of nastiness. When we list Sudder St area accommodation under ₹800, we're usually identifying the least objectionable options rather than making a recommendation. For under ₹500 expect coffin-sized rooms where the main decor is the graffiti of previous inmates; long-standing ultra-cheapies in this gloomy bracket include **Maria** (Map p460; ☑033-22520860; 5/1 Sudder St; s/d ₹400/500, without bathroom ₹250/300) and **Paragon** (Map p460; ☑033-22522445; 2 Stuart Lane; without bathroom s/d ₹300/450; ⊗check-out 11am). **Pioneer** (Map p460; ☑033-22520557; 1st fl, 1 Marquis St; d without/with bathroom & AC ₹750/1100; ❄) is slightly more survivable despite its crumbling facade, while **Shams** (Map p460; ☑9331007721, 033-30222722; 3 Tottie Lane; r ₹500, with AC ₹1200; ❄☎) has ceilings so low that only the shortest guests can stand upright in the cheapest rooms.

Afridi International   HOTEL $
(Map p460; ☑033-66077525; afridiinthotel@goldenapplehotel.in; 3 Cowie Lane; r ₹995) Possibly the most professionally managed budget hotel in Sudder St, the furniture and fittings here are top knotch and the entrance is floored in crystaline Italian marble. Some rooms are small and suffer a little from damp but maintenance is regular and the 35-room 'old building' should be totally renovated by the time you read this.

SLEEPING PRICE RANGES

Accommodation price ranges for this chapter are:

$ below ₹2000

$$ ₹2000 to ₹10,000

$$$ above ₹10,000

Prices quoted are for double rooms including tax (5% on rooms over ₹1000, 17.42% on those over ₹3000). When bargaining, double-check whether the quote is 'plus plus'.

DURGA PUJA

Much as Carnival transforms Rio or New Orleans, Durga Puja brings Kolkata to a fever pitch of colourfully chaotic mayhem as the city's biggest festival celebrates the maternal essence of the divine. For five days in the Bengali month of Aswin, people venerate gaudily painted idols of the 10-armed goddess Durga and her entourage displayed in *pandals* (temporary shrines) that dominate yards and block roads. *Pandals* grow ever more ornate and complex each year, some carrying topical or political messages. West Bengal Tourism (p484) tours try to take tourists around a selection of the best *pandals*, but getting anywhere within the city can take hours given the general festive pandemonium. At the festival's climax, myriad Durga idols are thrown into the sacred Hooghly River amid singing, water throwing, fireworks and indescribable traffic congestion. If you just want *pandal* photos and not the festival aspect, consider visiting just after Durga Puja when the idols have gone but *pandals* have yet to be deconstructed. Or come back for **Kali Puja** three weeks later when the city does the whole thing all over again, this time with statues of blue-faced, red-tongued Kali.

Hotel Aafreen
HOTEL **$**

(Map p460; ☑ 033-32261780, 033-22654146; www.goldenapplehotel.in/aafreen.aspx; Nawab Abdur Rahman St; d ₹700, with AC ₹995, ste ₹2024; ❄) Offering midrange quality at budget prices, the Aafreen has patterned pink-marble floors and ample-sized rooms which are regularly repainted. Temperamental lift.

Hotel Galaxy
BACKPACKER GUESTHOUSE **$**

(Map p460; ☑033-22524565; hotelgalaxy.kol@gmail.com; 3 Stuart Lane; d/tr ₹850/1100, r without bathroom ₹500; ❄🛜) This quiet, ever-popular guesthouse looks dowdy from outside but several rooms have been unexpectedly well upgraded. Several others are large and good value despite being older with some peeling paint. Reliable hot water in ensuite bathrooms and free wi-fi; add ₹150 for air-conditioning. There's a very small front porch/sitting area, with mini library.

Aafreen Tower
HOTEL **$**

(Map p460; ☑ 033-22293280; www.aafreentower.co.in; 9A Kyd St; d ₹1000, with AC ₹1500; ❄🛜) The glass elevator plays music as it rises to mustard yellow corridors where good-sized rooms have a Disneyesque caricature of old-world style. There are obvious signs of wear but it's relatively good value in this price range. Wi-fi only in the small lobby.

Modern Lodge
GUESTHOUSE **$**

(Map p460; ☑ 033-22524960; Stuart Lane; r from ₹350) High-ceilinged main-house rooms are ropey and rooftop ones are like caged cells, but a vague feeling of byegone history haunts the dustily atmospheric 1st-floor sitting room, and there's a peaceful if ragged roof terrace.

Timestar Hotel
HOTEL **$**

(Map p460; ☑033-30222959, 033-22523817; timestarhotel@yahoo.co.in; 2 Tottie Lane; s/d from ₹475/700, r with AC ₹1000) This chunky-walled colonial-era mansion house has some tatty walls but newly tiled floors and high enough ceilings in the upstairs rooms that they don't overheat too badly.

Golden Apple Hotel
GUESTHOUSE **$$**

(Map p460; ☑ 66077500; www.goldenapplehotel.in; 9 Sudder St; cubicle ₹500, r ₹1800-2500) The Golden Apple has accommodation that's mostly fresh and stylishly appointed for the price. Even the cramped cheapest rooms somehow jam in a small desk. A handy backpacker feature is the set of 15 top-floor budget 'cubicles': like a dorm deluxe, each is a lockable bedspace partitioned off by smoked-glass walls and with a storage area beneath the mattress.

Hotel Kempton
HOTEL **$$**

(Map p460; ☑ 033-40177888; www.hotelkempton.in; 3 Marquis St; s/d from ₹3757/4461; ❄🛜) The Kempton welcomes guests with a light-suffused feast of white marble and artificial orchids. Landings have attractive watercolours and rooms are sturdily-built with Springwel mattresses and walk-in showers. Prices include a buffet breakfast.

Fairlawn Hotel
HOTEL **$$**

(Map p460; ☑033-22521510; www.fairlawnhotel.com; 13A Sudder St; s/d incl breakfast & afternoon tea ₹3550/4545; ❄🛜) Taking guests since 1936, the Fairlawn is a characterful 1783

Raj-era home fronted by tropical greenery. The stairs and sitting room are smothered with photos, family mementos and articles celebrating the hotel's long-term owner who passed away aged 94 in September 2014. Rooms are mostly spacious but less polished than you might anticipate. Indeed some are downright plain with little charm and old bathtubs over-painted rather than re-enamelled.

Astoria Hotel
HOTEL $$
(Map p460; www.astoria.in; 6/2 Sudder St; new block s/d ₹2500/3400, old block d ₹2000; ❋ 🛜) In an alley off Sudder St, the pleasant new block is dotted with square-framed artworks and has a boutiquey modern feel with lots of little extras (kettle, safe, fridge etc), though some walls suffer from damp-stains.

Beware that there's also a contrastingly unappealing old block. Rooms there, while large and partially refurbished, are approached via very dowdy stairs and unlike new-block rooms, walls are stark, wi-fi doesn't work and air-con is older.

DK International
HOTEL $$
(Map p460; ☎033-40019283, 033-22522540; www.dkinthotel.com; 11/1A Marquis St; r from ₹2473; ❋) This relatively new five-storey glass tower has a certain neo-art-deco feel in its corridors, soap-stone 'jade' ornamentation and rooms with golden curtains.

Hotel VIP Intercontinental
HOTEL $$
(Map p460; ☎033-22520150; vipintercontinental@rediffmail.com; 44 Mirza Ghalib St; s/d from ₹1520/2130; ❋🛜) Behind the very narrow, one-desk reception hall, the cramped but friendly VIP InterContinental has good air-conditioned little rooms in varying styles, all with stone floors, and hot water in presentable little bathrooms.

Hotel Lindsay
HOTEL $$
(Map p460; ☎033-30218866; www.hotellindsay.com; 8 Lindsay St; s/d ₹5870/7045) A thorough redecoration gives an attractive old-Kolkata 'heritage' ambience to the Lindsay's guestrooms and corridors, belying the 1970s architecture of the tower in which they lie. Rooms numbered xx01 overlook New Market. When the hotel is full, the elevator struggles to cope with demand. Walk-in rates from ₹4100.

Sapphire Suites
HOTEL $$
(Map p460; ☎033-22523052; www.sapphiresuites.in; 15 Lindsay St; s/d from ₹5870/6460, ste ₹8220-10,570) Overlooking New Market, this new hotel gives itself a smart feel with sparkling white walls set off by deep brown floors and B&W prints. However much feels cramped, the 'gymnasium' is a two-machine fitness cubicle and the 'steam room' little more than a high-tech shower. Walk-in rates from ₹4700.

★ Oberoi Grand
HERITAGE HOTEL $$$
(Map p460; ☎033-22492323; www.oberoihotels.com; 15 Chowringhee Rd; s/d/ste from ₹23,484/25,245/46,968; ❋@🛜🛍) Saluting guards usher you out of the chaos of Chowringhee Rd into a regal oasis of genteel calm that deserves every point on its five stars. Immaculate accommodation exudes timeless class, the swimming pool is ringed with 5-storey palms, and proactive staff anticipate your every need. Remarkably comfortable beds come with a five-choice pillow menu. Online bargains from ₹8454 can be picked up.

🛏 Around Park Street

Sunflower Guest House
GUESTHOUSE $
(Map p460; ☎033-22299401; www.sunflowerguesthouse.com; 5th fl, 7 Royd St; d ₹1000-1290, with AC ₹1380-1913; ❋@🛜) The Sunflower is slowly taking over and restoring a grand 1865 residential six-storey building with layered atrium and 1940s lift. Take it to the top then climb stairs one floor higher to check-in. Rooms can be slightly spartan but they're assiduously cleaned, with high ceilings.

Pleasant communal spaces are available on the first and third floors (the latter with wi-fi, which is not available in-room). The most delightful feature is sitting in the rooftop garden at dusk as the fairy lights start to twinkle.

YWCA
HOSTEL $
(Map p460; ☎033-22292494; www.ywcacalcutta.org; 1 Middleton Row; s/d ₹670/1000, without bathroom ₹410/770, with AC ₹1000/1350; ❋) No, you don't have to be female to get a room in this well kept, imposing but basic 1925 building. Old high-ceilinged rooms have slatted green doors opening onto a wide arched corridor whose other open side faces a central tennis court. Large, sparse sitting rooms have a sense of times gone by, without the slightest hint of luxury. Rates are a remarkable bargain for such

a perfect location and a very basic breakfast is included.

Corporate
HOTEL $$

(Map p460; ☑ 033-22267551; www.thecorporate-kolkata.com; 4 Royd St; s/d/ste ₹5284/5871/7632; ❋ 🛜) In the suave little designer lobby, the receptionist seems to float in luminous marble. Compact well-maintained rooms in beige and brown tones, have comfy thick mattresses with satin sashes and pale polished stone bathrooms.

Mini-kettle, safe and hair-dryer are provided. Suites have small balconies and there's a four-table 'garden' behind the kitchen windows. When all 24 rooms are full, the lift and staff can get overstretched.

Casa Fortuna
HOTEL $$

(Map p456; ☑ 033-40218000; www.casafortuna-hotel.com; 234/1 AJC Bose Rd; s/d ₹5871/7045; ❋ 🌐 🛜) Five-storey city-centre modern cube where 26 attractively fresh rooms have burlap style wallpaper and oversized windows, albeit some facing the expressway outside. Pleasant first floor bar-restaurant, obliging staff.

Park Hotel
HOTEL $$$

(Map p460; ☑ 033-22499000; www.thepark-hotels.com; 17 Park St; s/d from ₹9400/10,570; ❋ 🌐 🛜 🏊) The Park is a top central choice for hip, upmarket accommodation, though reverberating music might disturb light sleepers on the lower floors. Hidden on the rear 1st floor is a trio of well reputed restaurants and a passage past waterfall foliage to Aqua, one of India's coolest poolside bars.

Bizarrely the hotel's under-sized reception area is accessed from Park St through The Street, a cafe-deli.

🛏 Southern Chowringhee

Central B&B
B&B $$

(Map p456; ☑ 9836465400; www.kolkatabnb.com; Flat 28, 7th fl, Lansdowne Court, 5B Sarat Bose Rd; s/d/tr ₹2599/2799/3699; 🛜) Probably the best Kolkata apartment-guesthouse to have made its name through AirBnB, Central lives up to all its promises. Rooms are huge and comfortable with large shared lounge and communal kitchen. There's fast wi-fi, a basic breakfast, a basket of snacks and an ever obliging (if usually invisible) host.

Pre-paying a deposit (paypal/credit-card) is required. No drop in guests.

Diamond Suites
GUESTHOUSE $$

(Map p456; ☑ 033-64582564; 17A Karaya Rd; s/d ₹1500/1800; ❋ 🛜) This friendly 12-room family hotel has clean, compact rooms, some oddly shaped, others with hotplates and tiny kitchen sink units. There's a rooftop view of sorts.

Astor
HOTEL $$

(Map p456; ☑ 033-22829950; www.astorkolkata.com; 15 Shakespeare Sarani; s/d/ste ₹5871/6458/8220) Artful evening floodlighting brings out the best of the Astor's solid 1905 architecture, while inside, walls are lavished with B&W photos of old Kolkata. A creative palate of chocolate, beige and iridescent butterfly blue brings to life beautifully furnished rooms, fully refurbished in 2012. Some suites include a four-poster bed. Sizes and shapes vary. There's no lift.

Park Prime
HOTEL $$$

(Map p456; ☑ 033-30963096; www.chocolate-hotels.in; 226 AJC Bose Rd; s/d ₹11,742/12,330; ❋ 🌐 🛜 🏊) Sleep in an artistic statement whose exterior looks like a seven-storey computer punch-card and whose rooms have optical-illusion decor. Bedboards carry up across the ceiling and sweep down the wall to emerge as a dagger of desk. It's all done without compromising comfort, the foyer is spaciously inviting and the rooftop swimming pool nestles beside hip Henry's Lounge Bar. Walk-in rates drop to single/double ₹7045/7632.

Kenilworth
HOTEL $$$

(Map p456; ☑ 033-22823939; www.kenilworth-hotels.com/kolkata; 1 Little Russell St; s/d ₹12,330/13,500; ❋ 🛜) The deep lobby of marble, dark wood and chandeliers contrasts successfully with a more contemporary cafe that spills out onto an attractive quadrangle of lawn. Pleasingly bright, fully equipped rooms have some of Kolkata's most comfortable beds.

Gym but no pool. Online rates drop to as little as single/double ₹7000/7500.

🛏 Motherhouse Area

The following options are handier than Sudder St for Mother Teresa volunteers, but they're rather scattered without backpacker facilities or any sense of 'traveller community'.

Georgian Inn
BACKPACKER GUESTHOUSE **$**

(Map p460; ☑ 9830156625, 9830068355; www.georgianin.com; 1A Doctor Lane; s/d ₹750/1000, with AC ₹1200/1350) Very functional but friendly and cheap, a bonus is the fascinating melee of Talitala Market that surrounds the property. Street-scapes of Doctor Lane to the direct east have architectural hints of old Penang.

Shaw Guest House
GUESTHOUSE **$**

(Map p460; ☑ 033-22650841, 033-65650096; shawguesthouse@rediffmail.com; 1C Abdul Halim Lane; dm/d/tr ₹600/1200/1500) Very handy for Mother Teresa volunteers, this pleasant, clean if plainly furnished colonial-era house run by Christian owners retains original wrought iron beams and bannisters.

Enclave Guest House
HOMESTAY **$$**

(Map p460; ☑ 9339750040; www.enclaveguesthouse.co; 2nd & 3rd fl, 34A McLeod St; s/d ₹1400/1500) If you value space, hygiene and value over style, this unsophisticated trio of completely unmarked apartments is worth considering. All three have three decent-sized double-bedded guestrooms and a shared sitting room. There's no guest kitchen and no reception so phone before arriving.

Monovilla Inn
GUESTHOUSE **$$**

(Map p460; ☑ 033-40076752; www.monovillainn.com; Doctor Lane; s/d ₹1200/1500, with AC ₹1500/1800) Fresh 21st-century rooms back a 1940s three-storey building with just two guest-rooms per floor (two more under construction on the roof). Upstairs is better for light. Minimal communal space.

🖺 BBD Bagh

While accommodation choices are limited, this area has plenty to see and Chandni Chowk metro is handily close.

Broadway Hotel
HOTEL **$**

(Map p466; ☑ 033-22363930; www.broadwayhotel.in; 27A Ganesh Chandra Ave; s/d/tr/ste ₹825/925/1585/1940, s/d without bathroom ₹765/850) The Broadway is a simple colonial era hotel that's kept all its character without going even slightly upmarket. An antiquated lift accesses plain but well maintained rooms with high ceilings and re-upholstered 1950s-style furniture. Good value, free newspaper under the door, but hot water's by bucket in the cheaper rooms.

Bengal Buddhist Association
GUESTHOUSE **$**

(Bauddha Dharmankur Sabha; Map p466; ☑ 033-22117138; bds1892@yahoo.com; Buddhist Temple St; d/tr without bathroom ₹300/400) Primarily intended for Buddhist students, these simple rooms are unadorned except for the window bars shaped into lama form. Most share basic common bathrooms (with geysers), though a couple are ensuite with aircon (₹750). There's no way in once gates are locked (10pm to 6am), so forget nightlife.

Hotel Neeranand
GUESTHOUSE **$$**

(Map p466; ☑ 9903957848, 033-22254660; www.hotelneeranand.com; 5th fl, Shah House, Radha Bazar St; s/d ₹2250/2800, deluxe ₹2800/3372; ❄🛜) Rooms are 1980s style and some fittings a tad aged, but floors are very clean and you get air-con, wi-fi and a fascinating location handy for BBD Bagh, Barabazar and Old China Town. Rooms are on four floors; reception on the 5th.

Lalit Great Eastern
HOTEL **$$$**

(Map p466; ☑ 033-44447777; www.thelalit.com/the-lalit-great-eastern-kolkata; Old Court House St; r from ₹11,000; ❄) The 1840 Great Eastern Hotel was once one of India's finest hotels. It lay derelict for years and the original west-facing facade remains a work in progress. Behind that, however, is an entirely new, sleek business hotel. Rooms are spacious and modernist with very comfortable super-king beds and stylish black-pebble surround showers (albeit leaky). Enter via Waterloo St.

Rooms are even bigger in the Legacy Block, whose atrium features what appear to be Childcatcher cages dangling from old steel beams above two Tiffany-roofed pergolas. Service is fawning if sometimes flawed. The little-used swimming pool is hemmed in without poolside bar. Online rates can go as low as ₹6600.

🖺 Howrah

Howrah Hotel
HOSTEL **$**

(☑ 033-26413878; www.thehowrahhotel.com; 1 Mukhram Kanoria Rd; s/d/q from ₹300/500/1260, d with AC ₹1890, s without bathroom ₹225; ⊘ reception 24hrs) This characterful 1890 mansion has seen far better days but retains elements of original tile-work and Italian chequer-board marble flooring. The inner courtyard is an unexpected oasis of birdsong and the brilliantly antiquated reception has featured in several movies. The best value rooms are the ₹900 upstairs doubles and

KOLKATA (CALCUTTA) SLEEPING

the tiny, ultra-cheap ₹225 box singles. Many ₹550 rooms are claustrophobic.

From Howrah train station's northern (commuter-area) underpass, emerge at exit 1, cross the bus station and walk one block west, turning right after Hotel Bhimsain.

Southern Kolkata

Kolkata Backpakers
HOMESTAY HOSTEL $
(Map p468; ☑ 9836059791; http://kolkataback-packershomestay.weebly.com; 108/1D Bakul Bagan; dm ₹450; 🛜) Tiny, cramped but characterful travellers' homestay in an interesting part of Southern Kolkata near the Lansdowne Vegetable Market (Map p468). Access by the footpath opposite 28 Mahendra Rd.

★Corner Courtyard
BOUTIQUE HOTEL $$
(Map p468; ☑ 033-40610145; www.thecornercourt-yard.com; 92B Sarat Bose Rd; r ₹4000) Eight perfectly pitched rooms are named for colours but also take subthemes, Bengali movies in 'Charcoal', Kumartuli goddesses in 'Vermilion'. They're on two storeys above a superb little restaurant in a recently restored 1904 town house that includes a charming little roof garden drooping with bougainvillea.

Hotel Aston
HOTEL $$
(Map p468; ☑ 033-24863145; hotelaston@gmail.com; 3 Aston Rd; s/d ₹1854/1970; 🌣@🛜) Compact but gently attractive air-con rooms come in various sizes and shapes. A few need minor repairs, but standards are fair for the relatively reasonable price point.

Bodhi Tree
BOUTIQUE GUESTHOUSE $$
(Map p468; ☑ 033-24243871, 033-24246534; www.bodhitreekolkata.com; 48/44 Swiss Park; s/ste ₹2500/9000, d ₹3500-4500, incl breakfast; 🌣🛜) A handful of very characterful, stone-walled Buddha-themed guestrooms are attached to this intriguing little 'monastery of art' gallery cafe. Access is from behind Rabrindra Sarovar metro's southeast exit, walking east for around 10 suburban minutes.

Airport Area

Airport area hotels fall into two main clumps. Cheaper options are on or near Jessore Rd which approximately parallels the runway to the west. Bigger, flashier but rarely luxurious hotels are spread out along VIP Rd between 1.5km and 3km south of the terminal and can be accessed for ₹6 by 'Baguiati' autos from Airport Gate 1.

Hotel Sai Baba
HOTEL $
(☑ 9883031486; 10/1 Jessore Rd; r ₹800, with AC ₹1500; 🌣) This funky, colourful little 10-room guesthouse has naive murals in the foyer and hearts, butterflies and stencil designs in the comparatively cute rooms, which are far less miserable than most of the other airport-area cheapies. Around half way between Airport Gates 1 and 2, it's down a short side lane accessed via the gateway arch of the Jessore Rd gurdwara.

Hotels Tirupati & Balaji
HOTEL $$
(☑ 033-25120065; www.hotelbalajiinternational.in; 32 Jessore Rd; r Tirupati/Balaji from ₹2000/2350) Set back off Jessore Rd between Airport Gates 1 and 2, this new block has heavy timber doors, plants on the stairs and decent bathrooms, though the mattresses are thin and there's a Donald Duck painted incongrurusly on some mirrors. Along with the slightly cheaper co-owned Balaji next door, prices include a ride to the airport.

Tirupati is the god who stands in the foyer with his eyes masked.

Atithi Inn
HOTEL $$
(www.atithiinn.com; VIP Rd, Raghunathathpur; s/d ₹1800/2500; 🌣) Strengths of this family-oriented place are the hallway seating areas and the striking use of wooden door surrounds to create M-shape designs. Rooms don't quite live up to the promise, with rather basic bathrooms and there's no wi-fi. Noisy during weddings.

Celesta
BOUTIQUE HOTEL $$
(☑ 033-71000131; www.celesta.in; VIP Rd, Ragunathpur; s/d ₹5500/6000) Celesta is the suavest of over a dozen hotels in the Raghunathpur area, with big plate-glass lobby walls and an upper exterior looking like a Mondrian painting. Luxurious beds are piled with pillows in retro-art-deco rooms with rainforest showers.

It's beside the well-signed KFC on the east side of VIP Rd, 3km south of the airport.

Eating

Don't miss sampling Bengali cuisine, a wonderful discovery once you've mastered a whole new culinary vocabulary. Cheaper Bengali places often serve tapas-sized portions, so order two or three dishes per person along with either rice or *luchi* (Bengali flatbread), plus some sweet *khejur* (chutney).

A Kolkata delight is making streetside tea stops for ₹5 mini-cuppas served in disposable *bhaar* (environmentally friendly earthenware cups).

Plentiful branches of Starbuck-style chains Barista, Aqua Java and Café Coffee Day make air-conditioned oases in which to sip a decent macchiato. And some offer wi-fi.

Most restaurants add 19.4% tax to food bills (included in prices quoted here). Posher places add service fees too. Tips are welcome at cheaper places and expected at most expensive restaurants. **Times Food Guide** (www.timescity.com/kolkata; book ₹199) and **Zomato** (www.zomato.com/kolkata) offer hundreds of restaurant reviews.

✖ Around Sudder Street

A few relatively basic traveller cafes around Sudder St serve backpacker favourites including banana pancakes, muesli and toasted sandwiches complemented by fresh fruit juices and a range of good-value Indian dishes. Eateries across Mirza Ghalib St cater predominantly to Bangladeshi tastes. Cheap places for Indian-regional food lie around New Market (notably Hogg St), with grungy classics like the 1937 **UP Bihar** (Map p460; H12 Hogg St; mains ₹40-120, kati rolls ₹20-80, dhal/rice ₹5/6; ⊙6.30am-11pm) beef-curry specialist or the cacophonous 1940s-retro **Aminia** (Map p460; Hogg St; mains ₹75-155; ⊙10.30am-10.30pm). Many more food stalls line Madge Lane, Bertram St, and Humayan Pl. At food stalls near the Indian Museum you can fill up for ₹16 on dhal and chapati, freshly baked in oil-barrel tandoors.

Bhoj Company   BENGALI $
(Map p460; Sudder St; veg dishes ₹40-90, fish mains ₹100-330, small/large rice ₹20/30; ⊙8.30am-11.30pm) Excellent, inexpensive Bengali food served in a bijou little restaurant, where colourful naive art sets off white walls inset with little terracotta-statuette niches. If you're not familiar with Bengali menu names, a deliciously safe bet is *ruhi kalia* (ginger-based curry) with *doi begun* (eggplant in curd; ₹190 with rice). Or giant prawn *malaikari* (coconut milk; ₹220 with rice plus *jhuri alu bhaja* – crispy potato whisps to add crunch).

JoJo's Cafe   CAFE $
(Map p460; Facebook jojoskolkata; Stuart Lane; snacks ₹50-70, mains ₹80-120, rice ₹20; ⊙8am-11pm; 🛜) Pleasant, well-run backpacker cafe

BENGALI FOOD

Fruity and mildly spiced, Bengali food favours the sweet, rich notes of *jaggery* (palm-sugar), *daab* (young coconut), *malaikari* (coconut milk) and *posto* (poppy seed). Typical Bengali curry types include the light, coriander-scented *jhol,* drier spicier *jhal* and richer, ginger-based *kalia.* Strong mustard notes feature in *shorshe* curries and *paturi* dishes that come steamed in a banana leaf. *Gobindobhog bhaat* (steamed rice) or *luchi* (small puris) are the usual accompaniment. More characteristic than meat or *murgir* (chicken) are *chingri* (river prawns) and excellent fish, particularly *rohu* (white rui), fatty chital and cod-like *bhekti.* If you can handle the bones, *ilish* (hilsa) is considered the tastiest fish, *kachki* are very small and *lau ghonto* – an acquired taste – is fish head pounded with pumpkin. Excellent vegetarian choices include *mochar ghonto* (mashed banana-flower, sometimes with potato and coconut), *doi begun* (eggplant in curd) and *shukto,* a favourite lunchtime starter combining at least five different vegetables in a milk-based sauce.

For a colourful and very affectionate portrait of Kolkata's ever-vibrant street food scene, see www.streetfoodkolkata.com, which includes recipes, films and sells a brilliantly evocative book.

Bengal's trademark fast food is the *kati roll:* a *paratha* roti, fried with a coating of egg then filled with sliced onions, chilli and your choice of stuffing (curried chicken, grilled meat or paneer). Generally eaten as a takeaway from hole-in-the-wall serveries. Famed are **Kusum** (Map p460; 21 Park St; rolls from Rs25; ⊙noon-11.30pm) and **Hot Kati Rolls** (Map p460; 1/1 Park St; rolls from ₹23; ⊙11am-10.30pm), though some travellers prefer the substantially cheaper versions from **Baba** (Map p460; Mirza Ghalib St; rolls/chow mein from ₹17/23; ⊙noon-11pm).

Bengali desserts and sweets are legendary. Most characteristic are *mishti dhoi* (curd deliciously sweetened with *jaggery*), *rasgulla* (syrupy sponge balls) and *cham-cham* (double-textured curd-based fingers).

KOLKATA (CALCUTTA) EATING

with some original fresh fruit-veg juices and smoothies with evocative names ('Liquid Breakfast', 'Kung Flu Fighter' etc). Free wi-fi.

Raj's Spanish Cafe
CAFE $

(Map p460; off Sudder St; mains ₹80-150; ☺8.30am-10pm; ☎) Popular as a hang-out for medium-term charity volunteers, this unpretentious place serves good coffee (₹40 to ₹70), lassis, pancakes and a range of Italian, Mexican and Spanish dishes.

Vermillion walls are unadorned except for a traveller noticeboard. There's a small outdoor area with some cursory foliage. It's hidden behind Roop Shringar fabric shop.

Sidheshwari Ashram
BENGALI $

(Map p460; 19 Rani Rashmoni Rd; mains ₹16-65, fish mains ₹100-140, rice ₹6-18; ☺9.30am-4pm & 7-11pm) For a really local experience, venture into this archetypal old-fashioned eating house serving excellent Bengali food eaten with the (right) hand at old stone-topped tables. Women are rare, some waiters shoeless and the blackboard menu offers no explanations, so ideally bring a local friend. No AC. The entrance is easily missed between shops, then up an unlikely stairway.

Kathleen Confectioners
BAKERY $

(Map p460; 12 Mirza Ghalib St; snacks ₹20-50; ☺10am-9pm) Stand-n-snack chain bakery best known for its flakey pastry savouries like the ₹25 paneer patties. Walls ice creams (Cornetto ₹35) available.

Delish
MULTICUISINE $$

(Map p460; www.delishrestaurant.in; 9 Chowringhee Lane; mains ₹100-180) Hanging lanterns echoed in the cartoon-style Calcutta-scene mural give this small place the visual edge over other Sudder St backpacker restaurants, but it really needs better air-con. Or at least to turn it on.

Blue & Beyond
MULTICUISINE $$

(Map p460; 9th fl, Lindsay Hotel, Lindsay St; mains ₹225-680, beer/cocktails from ₹203/286; ☺noon-10.45pm) The drawcard here is an open-air rooftop terrace with wide views over New Market plus a small glass-walled cocktail bar that falls somewhere between 70s-retro and space-station acid-trip. The globe-trotting menu swerves from *khawsuey* (Burmese-style curried noodles) to Roquefort-prawn sizzler, Greek chicken to Mexican 'veg-steak'.

Blue Sky Cafe
CAFE $$

(Map p460; Chowringhee Lane; mains ₹70-270, curries ₹70-150, rice ₹35; ☺8am-11pm) Wise-cracking staff serve up a vast selection of reliable traveller standbys including great old-style banana pancakes at long glass tables set close enough to make conversation between strangers a little more likely.

★1658
EUROPEAN, FUSION $$$

(Map p460; ☎033-40611658; 26 Chowringhee Rd; most mains ₹350-450, lobster ₹1500, beer/wine/cocktails from ₹175/320/700; ☺noon-3pm Wed-Mon & 7.30-11.30pm daily, kitchen closes 10.30pm; ☎) Although offering inventive gourmet-standard cuisine, prices are sensible and the atmosphere relaxed yet very special. The name references the start of Italy's Baroque period, but the decor prefers an early 20th-century sense of retro with low-wattage filament lamps and Charlie Chaplin era movies playing on designer-stark walls beside the six-stooled cocktail bar that takes centre stage.

PARK ST DINING CLASSICS

Several classic multicuisine restaurants huddle within a block of the attractive art-deco teashop-restaurant **Flurrys** (Map p460; Park St; mains ₹374-650, coffee/tea/cake from ₹130/142/72; ☺7.30am-9.45pm), harking back to the 1970s, when Park St was *the* place to be seen after hours in Kolkata. Contrasting conspicuously with 21st-century decor trends so beloved of most upmarket Kolkata restaurants, **Mocambo** (Map p460; Mirza Ghalib St; curry/rice from ₹195/186, other mains ₹290-430; ☺11.30am-11.15pm) and **Peter Cat** (Map p460; Middleton Row; mains ₹160-360, beer ₹183; ☺11am-11.15pm) seem almost self-conscious parodies of vintage British steak-house design. The latter serves beers in pewter tankards and dresses its waiters in Khan-Afghani costumes. The draw at all is both a reputation among middle-class Kolkatans for ever-reliable food, and snappy service that can prove quietly witty. None of these eateries take reservations. Indeed meeting fellow diners in the queue for a late dinner spot is an integral part of the experience.

Creative skewer snacks arrive in lab beakers, flavour packed 'skinny pizza' starters perch on long thin slabs of slate, and scrumptious herb-seared cottage cheese is served on lemon potatoes with a pepper coulis so good you'll want to lick the plate.

Around Park Street

On or near Park St (between Russel St and Middleton Row) you'll find dozens of good restaurants, including many age-old Kolkata family classics (p478) facing off with Pizza Hut, KFC and a beef-free McDonald's.

Au Bon Pain   BAKERY, SALADS $
(Map p460; Park St; snacks ₹65-350, coffee from ₹70; ☺7.30am-10.30pm; 🛜) This large, central bakery-cafe could have made more of its large, heritage building but there's lots of well-lit space to sit and read over egg and pesto croissants (₹70) and very acceptable espressos. The free wi-fi only works if you have a locally accessible phone number for registration.

Arsalan   MUGHLAI $$
(Map p460; www.arsalanrestaurant.in; 119A Ripon St; mains ₹110-260; ☺11.30am-11.30pm) Consistently popular with locals, this branch is high ceilinged and attractively modern without being fashion-conscious. The main attractions are melt-in-mouth chicken tikka and celebrated biryanis that you season from a palate of fresh lime, mixed pickles and green chilli.

Bistro by the Park   MULTICUISINE $$$
(Map p460; ☑033-22296494; www.bistrobythepark.com; 2A Middleton Row; mains ₹390-600, rice ₹117, beers/cocktails from ₹160/230; ☺noon-11pm; 🛜) This enticing cafe has multi-textured walls and lamps like airbourne Thai spirit lanterns, albeit in colours that are tastefully muted. Menus (on iPads) cover many international bases, with a reduced selection (pizza, pasta, bijou fish-n-chips) from 3.30pm to 6.30pm.

Teej   RAJASTHANI $$$
(Map p460; ☑033-22170730; www.teej.in; 1st fl, 2 Russell St; mains ₹230-350, rice ₹175, thalis ₹360, beer ₹180; ☺noon-3.30pm & 7-10.30pm) Superbly painted with Mughal-style murals, the interior feels like an ornate Rajasthani *haveli* (traditional residence) and the excellent, 100% vegetarian food is predominantly Rajasthani, too.

Reservations accepted on weekdays but at weekends it's first come, first served.

Marco Polo   MULTICUISINE $$$
(Map p460; ☑033-22273939; 24 Park St; mains ₹430-700, rice ₹320; ☺noon-11pm) Stylish deep brown panels incised with flower patterns are back-lit to create a moody yet contemporary atmosphere in this split-level restaurant which takes a world tour of cuisines.

Southern Chowringhee

Beware that the most upmarket places listed below typically add almost 30% tax/service to menu prices and their bottled water can cost over ₹100.

Drive Inn   VEGETARIAN MULTICUISINE $
(Mission Cafe; Map p456; ☑033-32000025; 10 Middleton St; mains ₹90-180; ☺noon-10.30pm) Good value vegetarian fare served in a modest little part-covered urban 'garden' area that twinkles with fairy lights at night.

Chocolate Room   BAKERY CAFE $
(Map p456; http://thechocolateroomindia.com; Rawdon St; cake slices from ₹60; ☺8am-10pm) Chocolate everything! Waffles, fondue, choco-pizza, vareties of hot chocolate and hot, moist cake slices that are rich yet light and eggless.

Haldiram   FAST FOOD $
(Map p456; 58 Chowringhee Rd; thalis from ₹100; ☺7.30am-10pm) Chain cafeteria with inexpensive pay-then-queue vegetarian thalis.

Picadilly Square   CAFE $$
(Map p456; 15B Sarat Bose Rd; coffee ₹60-120, snack mains ₹130-190, pasta ₹270; ☺11am-10.30pm Mon-Fri, 8am-11.30pm Sat & Sun) Cute six-table cafe with two Victorian-style lamp-posts, a serving counter fashioned like a street cart, and floors designed to feel like a Parisian sidewalk. Serves imaginative savoury crepes (try the Ratatouille Blintz), pitas, ice creams, waffles and good espressos to a seemingly endless Bruno Mars soundtrack.

Shiraz   MUGHLAI $$
(Map p456; 135 Park St; mains ₹165-300; ☺5am-11.30pm) Synonymous with Kolkata biryani, Shiraz also offers a range of curries including a superb ₹100 mutton *keema* (minced-meat curry) breakfast (until noon). The much smarter, more comfortable co-owned AC branch two doors away only opens from lunchtime.

★ Oh! Calcutta
BENGALI $$$

(Map p456; ☎033-22837161; 4th fl, Forum Mall, Elgin Rd; mains ₹390-1000, rice ₹196, cocktails from ₹350; ⏱12.30-3.15pm & 7.30-10.45pm) Although it's situated within a shopping mall, shutter-edged mirror 'windows', bookshelves, large paintings and B&W photography create a casually upmarket feel for enjoying what remains some of the city's best Bengali-fusion food. Mild, subtle and creamy *Daab Chingri* (₹780) is served in a green coconut, the subtleties brought out particularly well by a side dish of fragrant lime salad (₹86).

★ Fire and Ice
ITALIAN $$$

(Map p456; ☎033-22884073; www.fireandice pizzeria.com; Kanak Bldg, Middleton St; mains ₹530-730, water/beer/cocktails from ₹130/210/480; ⏱11.30am-11.30pm) Founded and directed by an Italian from Naples, Fire and Ice's waiters sport black shirts, red aprons and bandanas, and bring forth real Italian-style pastas and Kolkata's best thin-crust pizzas. Old film posters give character to the spacious dining room set behind foliage in a huge heritage building. Few other Kolkata restaurants keep serving as late.

Kewpies
BENGALI $$

(Map p456; ☎033-24861600; 2 Elgin Lane; thalis ₹450-1050, minimum spend ₹580 per person; ⏱12.30-3pm & 7.30-10.30pm Tue-Sun) Kewpies is a Kolkata institution and dining here feels like a dinner party in a gently old-fashioned home. However, you might find the Bengali cuisine at some cheaper competitors to be every bit as good.

Bikers' Cafe
MULTICUISINE $$$

(Map p456; www.bikerscafe.co.in; 1st fl, 31 Elgin Rd; mains ₹466-880; ⏱7.30am-11pm) A gold-plated Enfield low-rider motorbike in the window, helmet lampshades and a Clapton and Led Zep sound track set the tone in this youthful cafe-diner. Mains include tajines, salmon teriyaki and Spanish prawns, while a great snack is the toasted veg-patty with cottage cheese mash and Thai curry sauce.

Alcohol license awaiting approval.

Amigos
MEXICAN $$$

(Map p456; ☎033-40602507; www.facebook. com/Amigos.calcutta; 11/1A Ho Chi Minh Sarani; mains ₹350-700; ⏱12.30-3.30pm & 7.30-10.30pm) The excellent Tex-Mex spread is sometimes missing the guacamole (avocados are apparently awkward imports) but makes amends with exquisite mango salsa. The atmosphere has a warm buzz, partly stone-clad walls are picked out with a band of colourful patterned tiles, softly illuminated by swallows-nest lamps and tickled with low-volume salsa music.

There's no alcohol but the bill arrives in a sombrero.

Little Italy
ITALIAN $$$

(Map p456; ☎033-22825152; 8th fl, Fort Knox Bldg, 6 Camac St; mains ₹470-720; ⏱noon-2.45pm & 7-10.45pm) While the pastas and pizzas at elsewhere might have more pizazz, those wanting a pure veg kitchen and an artily upmarket environment might prefer Little Italy. What appear to be rhino horns protrude from the walls, there are seven waving ceramic monoliths, a wall-of-water fountain and some city views. Lounge bar attached.

✖ BBD Bagh

For great variety of ₹20 street meals, **Dacres Lane** (James Hickey Sarani; Map p466; mains from ₹16; ⏱8am-9pm) is a classic address with stalls serving as late as 9pm interspersed by dodgy air-con 'bar-restaurants' whose fairy lights add a festive atmosphere to the grunge. Daytme (except Sundays) there's another good street-food area on Koilaghat St where some stalls have makeshift seating.

Anand
SOUTH INDIAN $

(Map p466; ☎033-22128344; 19 CR Ave; dosas ₹67-133, fresh juice ₹70; ⏱9am-9.30pm, closed Wed) Prize-winning pure-veg dosas served in a well-kept if stylistically dated family restaurant with octagonal mirror-panels and timber strips on the somewhat low upper ceiling. Good air-conditioning.

KC Das
BENGALI SWEETS $

(Map p466; Lenin Sarani; mishti doi ₹18; ⏱7.30am-9.30pm) This bustling Bengali sweet shop claims to have invented *rasgulla* (rosewater-scented cheese balls) in 1868. Try the *mishti doi* (a sweet-yoghurt desert). Seating available.

Bakery
BAKERY $

(Waterloo St; pastries/croissants/cakes from ₹40/58/58; ⏱7.30am-10.30pm) A bakery opened on this site in 1830, and the comfortably climate-controlled 21st-century incarnation has used original archaic oven shells to create bizarre room dividers. Pastries are good value but tea or coffee costs more than beer (tea/beer ₹285/250).

Amber/Essence
INDIAN $$

(Map p466; ☎033-22486520; 2nd fl, 11 Waterloo St; mains ₹200-450, rice ₹220, beer ₹220; ☺noon-11pm) This two-hall middle-class restaurant serves reliable Indian food though the signature brain curry isn't to everyone's taste. Amber (1st floor) is more family oriented, Essence (2nd floor) lower lit and predominantly businessman types. Menus are essentially the same.

Bhojohori Manna (takeaway)
BENGALI $$

(Map p466; www.bhojohorimanna.com; Lenin Sarani; dishes ₹50-270; ☺noon-10pm) The same sublime Bengali food that you'd expect from Bhojohori Manna is available as takeaway here; avoid the claustrophobic dining room.

Manthan/Songhai
CHINESE $$

(Map p466; ☎033-22105065; 3 Waterloo St; mains/beer from ₹140/160; ☺11am-11pm) This trio of restaurants in a single location has three different decors, two different names and a single kitchen turning out good if not really gourmet Chinese food. The cheapest option, upstairs at Manthan, could use a few artworks to give more character to the blank, chandelier-lit white walls. Manthan's downstairs rooms are comfortable upper middle-class, while Songhai goes for a dark, modern oriental feel.

✕ Southern Kolkata

★ Bhojohori Manna 6
BENGALI $$

(Map p468; ☎033-24663941; www.bhojohorimanna.com; 18/1 Hindustan Rd; dishes ₹50-270, small/large thali ₹220/265, rice ₹55; ☺12.30-10.30pm) Each Bhojohori Manna branch feels very different, but all feature top-quality Bengali food at sensible prices. Branch 6 on Hindustan Rd is comparatively spacious, decorated with tribal implements and offers live traditional music some Saturdays. The menu allows you to pair a wide selection of fish types with the sauce of your choice. Some dishes are rather small so order a spread, not missing the *echorer dalna* (green jackfruit curry).

Corner Courtyard
FUSION $$$

(Map p468; ☎9903990567; www.facebook.com/TheCornerCourtyard; 92B Sarat Bose Rd; mains ₹400-700, lobster ₹1950; ☺noon-11pm, reduced menu 3-7pm) This reincarnated 1904 mansion has had its walls artistically splattered with doorknobs, locks and old books. The wide ranging menu flits from Thai risotto to Brazilian salmon to Finnish fondue, with many a daring flavour combination.

Drinking & Nightlife

Cheaper bars are mostly dingy and overwhelmingly male-dominated with a penchant for over-loud music, often sung by scantily clad females.

Most better bars and clubs are in hotels. Clubs open till 2am or later on party nights (Wednesday, Friday and Saturday) but other evenings they're typically half empty and closed by midnight. Note the difference between entry charge and cover charge: the latter can be recouped in drinks or food to the same value. Either is charged per couple. Women can often enter free but single men (known as 'stags') are generally excluded altogether and certainly aren't expected to dance without a female partner, heaven forbid.

🍷 Central Kolkata & Chowringhee

Park St has several bars ranging from mysteriously popular long-term student steak-and-beer favourite **Oly Pub** (Map p460; 21 Park St; beer/steak ₹182/220; ☺11am-11pm) to upper-market alternatives in and around Park Hotel.

Fairlawn Hotel Beer-Garden
BAR

(Map p460; 13A Sudder St; beers ₹185; ☺10am-10pm) The small tropical garden of the historic Fairlawn Hotel is the most appealing place on Sudder St to down a cold brew.

Arabian Delight
SHISHA BAR

(Map p460; 21A Mirza Galib St; shisha ₹220-250, soft drinks ₹50-100; ☺11am-10pm) Pleasantly low lit, one-room hubble-bubble bar.

Myx
NIGHTCLUB

(Map p460; Facebook The Myx Kolkata; Middleton Row; cover ₹2000; ☺9pm-midnight daily, to 2.30am Wed, Fri & Sat) Central Kolkata's best looking nightclub has a second bar upstairs and a shisha terrace on the rooftop. It's atop a tower above three upmarket restaurants, hidden behind KFC.

Tantra
NIGHTCLUB

(Map p460; Park Hotel, 17 Park St; entry ₹500-1000; ☺7pm-midnight Tue, Thu & Sun, 7pm-3am Wed, Fri & Sat) Kolkata's best-established nightclub features contemporary sounds throbbing through the single small dance floor and not-so-chilled chill-out zone around a central-island bar with an overhead observation bridge. On Wednesdays women drink for free until 11.30pm.

The entrance is guarded not only by bouncers but by mannequin-style boxed statues. The one to your left is not a green bearded drag queen but a god of love.

New Cathay
BAR

(Map p460; 17 Chowringhee Rd; shots/beer from ₹55/135; ⊙11am-11.30pm) Classic old-style bar with double-height ceilings and long whirring fans.

Irish House
PUB

(Map p468; www.facebook.com/IrishHouseKolkata; Quest Mall, Syed Amir Ali Ave; ⊙noon-11.30pm) While not really Irish at all, this is the nearest Kolkata gets to a fully fledged non-hotel pub/sports bar. Lots of weekend ambience and a showman at the bar.

Plush
LOUNGE BAR

(Map p456; Astor Hotel, 15 Shakespeare Sarani; ⊙3pm-close) This stylish yet unthreateningly casual, low-lit bar is most appealing on Thursday evenings when young local musicians perform at the open mic (7pm to 11.30pm). Wednesdays there's a ₹1200 all-you-can-drink deal till 2am. Friday/Saturdays there's a cover charge (₹1500/2000 per couple). No 'stags'.

Urban Desi
SHISHA BAR

(Map p456; 9th fl, 6 Camac St; shisha ₹450-850, beer/wine/cocktails from ₹200/400/550; ⊙12.30pm-11.30pm) Pumping music energises this highly-rated shisha (waterpipe) lounge-bar. Moroccan lamps spangle the lighting and big windows offer extensive (if none too beautiful) views. Small open-terrace, table football available.

Soho
NIGHTCLUB

(Map p456; ☑030-40036605; Ideal Plaza, 11/1 Sarat Bose Rd; beer ₹500; ⊙6pm-close Mon-Sat) Upper-market party address with thunderous music and a sweep of bar behind reverse conical columns. Weekend cover charges apply.

Fusion
PUB

(Map p456; www.goldenparkk.com; Hotel Golden Park, 13 Ho Chi Minh Sarani; ⊙8pm-midnight) Unusually large hotel basement bar with dancefloor and DJ. No stags.

Underground
BAR, NIGHTCLUB

(Map p456; HHI Hotel, AJC Bose Rd) Small dance floor in a pub-bar with Hard Rock Café–style design feel.

🍴 BBD Bagh

If you want ear-shattering 'live' (ie karaoke quality) music, there are several choices along eastern Waterloo St and Dacres Lane.

Broadway Bar
BAR

(Map p466; Broadway Hotel, 27A Ganesh Chandra Ave; small/standard beer ₹75/135, shots ₹41-120; ⊙11am-10.30pm) Back-street Paris? Chicago 1930s? Prague 1980s? This cavernous, unpretentious old-men's pub defies easy parallels but has a compulsive left-bank fascination with cheap booze, 20 ceiling fans, bare walls, marble floors and, thankfully, no music.

🍴 Southern Kolkata

Basement
NIGHTCLUB

(Map p468; Samilton Hotel, Sarat Bose Rd; ⊙live music Thu 7pm) Relaxed and inexpensive club with live music Thursday evenings.

☆ Entertainment

Cultural Programs

Nandan Complex
CULTURAL CENTRE

(Map p456; ☑033-22235317; 1/1A AJC Bose Rd) Comprises theatre halls Rabindra Sadan (Map p456; ☑033-22239936) and Sisir Mancha (Map p456; ☑033-22235317), plus the arthouse Nandan Cinema (Map p456; ☑033-22231210).

ICCR
CULTURAL CENTRE

(Rabindranath Tagore Centre; Map p456; ☑033-22822895; www.tagorecentreiccr.org; 9A Ho Chi Minh Sarani) Large, multilevel cultural centre sporadically hosting exhibitions, dance shows and recitals. Often free.

Calcutta School of Music
MUSIC

(Map p468; www.calmusic.org; 6B Sunny Park) Musical events in a variety of styles, anything from classical to traditional Indian music. See website for events.

Akhra
CULTURAL EVENINGS

(Map p456; ☑033-24178561; www.banglanatak.com; 4 Elgin Rd) Showcasing an ever-changing melange of art, theatre and folk or fusion music, both rural and urban, a few evenings per month (October to January and March to June).

Cinema

Inox (www.inoxmovies.com) has modern multiplex cinemas in several shopping centres, including the **Forum** (Map p456) and **Quest Malls** (Map p468).

Spectator Sports

Even if you don't know Ganguly from a googly, the electric atmosphere of a **Knight Riders** (www.kkr.in) cricket match at **Ranji Stadium** (Eden Gardens; Map p466; Eden Gardens) is an unforgettable experience.

If it's football (soccer) you're into, **Atlético de Kolkata** (www.facebook.com/atleticodekolkata; tickets from ₹125) plays Indian Superleague matches at **Salt Lake Stadium**. Buy tickets through www.ticketgenie.in or from a kiosk outside Flury's cafe on Park St.

Maidan racecourse (033-22291104; www.rctconline.com; Acharya Jagdish Rd; admission from ₹15; 36) hosts some of India's best horse racing. Viewed from the 19th-century grandstands, the Victoria Memorial provides a beautiful backdrop. Over 40 annual meets.

🛍 Shopping

Several small traveller-oriented bookstalls huddle around the junction of Sudder St and Mirza Ghalib St. Small, family publisher **Earthcare Bookstore** (Map p456; 033-22296551; www.earthcarebooks.com; 10 Middleton St; 11am-7pm Mon-Sat) has an eclectic stock, **Seagull** (Map p468; www.seagullindia.com; 31A SP Mukherjee Rd; 10.30am-7.30pm; Jatin Das) has arts, humanities and politics specialities. Big air-conditioned cafe-bookstores **Oxford** (Map p460; 033-22297662; www.oxfordbookstore.com; 17 Park St; 10am-10pm) and **Story** (Map p456; 9830470000; storyostory.com; 8 Elgin Rd; 10.30am-8.30pm) have very extensive selections, including travel guides and plenty of Kolkata-relevant texts.

State-government emporia sells quality souvenirs at decent fixed prices, while several charity cooperatives allow you to feel good about your purchases.

Shops and workshops along Rabindra Sarani sell a great range of musical instruments. For tablas (drums; from ₹1200), rayas (from ₹500) and other percussion, try numbers 248 and 268B near Tagore's House (p463). For sitars (from ₹4000) or violins (from ₹2000) visit **Mondal & Sons** (Map p466; 033-22349658; 8 Rabindra Sarani; 10am-6pm Mon-Fri, to 2.30pm Sat) who

have counted Yehudi Menuhin among their satisfied customers.

Dakshinapan Shopping Centre SHOPPING CENTRE
(Map p468; Gariahat Rd; 10.30am-7.30pm Mon-Sat) It's worth facing the soul-crushing 1970s architecture for Dakshinapan's wide range of government emporia. There's plenty of tack but many shops offer excellent-value souvenirs, crafts and fabrics. Several shops close by 7pm.

Try **Tribes India** (Map p468; Dakshinapan, F48) for brass figures and greetings cards, **Aranya** (Map p468; 9831039822; www.aranyakolkata.com; Dakshinapan, F56; 10am-7.30pm) for charming gifts made from recycled materials, **Purbasha Tripura** (Map p468; Dakshinapan F4) for bargain caneware and **Kashmir Emporium** (Map p468; Dakshinapan F38) for colourful papier mâché work (boxes from ₹90).

Pragjyotika HANDICRAFTS
(Map p456; Assam House, 8 Russell St; 10.30am-6pm Mon-Fri, 11am-1pm Sat) This Assam State emporium is a great place to look for fixed-price cane vases, jute handbags, pearls, fabrics and Assam tea.

Nagaland Emporium SOUVENIRS
(Map p456; 11 Shakespeare Sarani; 10am-5.30pm Mon-Fri, to 2pm Sat) Naga crafts including shawls and 'face' necklaces for wannabe head-hunters are available from this state-government store.

Doel's Choice HANDICRAFTS
(Map p460; 1 Kyd St; 11am-7pm Mon-Sat) Hand-carved wooden products.

FabIndia FABRICS, HANDICRAFTS
(Map p456; www.fabindia.com; 11A Allenby Rd; 11am-8.30pm) Western-style boutique with clearly labeled/priced Indian textiles and some handicrafts.

Ankur Kala SOUVENIRS
(Map p456; 033-22878476; www.ankurkala.org; 3 Meher Ali Rd; 10am-1pm & 2-5pm Mon-Sat) This cooperative training centre empowers women from the slums. The small shop sells batik, embroidered goods, greeting cards and leather goods. It's hidden beneath a domestic residence in a non-commercial road. Entrance from the side.

Ashalayam HANDICRAFTS
(Map p460; www.ashalayamfrance.org; 1st fl, 44 Mirza Ghalib St; 10.30am-6pm Mon-Fri, to 4pm

KOLKATA (CALCUTTA) SHOPPING

Sat) Buying cards, handmade paper and fabrics here funds the (ex)street kids who made them. The shop doubles as a simple cafe serving instant coffee (₹20).

ℹ Information

DANGERS & ANNOYANCES

Kolkata feels remarkably unthreatening. Predictable beggar-hassle is a minor irritant around Sudder St. *Bandhs* (strikes) occasionally stop all land transport (including taxis to the airport). Monsoon-season flooding can be severe.

INTERNET ACCESS

Inexpensive widespread 3G means that internet cafes are becoming rarer. A central survivor is **Cyber Zoom** (Map p460; 27B Park St; per hr ₹15; ◐10am-9.30pm) which also does passport photos. Around Sudder St, some back alley cubby-hole places charge ₹20, but its worth paying a little more for fast connection and more comfortable seating at travel agency web-cafe **R-Internet Travels** (Map p460; ☑ 9830135365; rinternettravels.weebly.com; Tottee Lane; per ½/full hour ₹20/30; ◐9am-10pm).

MEDICAL SERVICES

Medical contacts are widely listed on www. calcuttaweb.com/directory/doctors-in-kolkata. **Apollo Gleneagles** (☑ 033-23203040, emergency 033-60601066; www.apollogleneagles. in) Hospital group with 24-hour ambulance service.

Eastern Diagnostics (Map p460; ☑ 033-22178080; www.easterndiagnostics.com; 13C Mirza Ghalib St; ◐9am-2pm Mon-Sat, longer some days) Polyclinic for doctors' consultations; handy for Sudder St.

MONEY

Many private moneychangers around Sudder St offer commission-free exchange rates significantly better than banks. Some will exchange travellers cheques. Shop around and double-check the maths. In the city centre, **Mishra Forex** (Map p456; 11 Shakespeare Sarani; ◐10am-8.30pm Mon-Sat, to 6pm Sun) gives reasonable rates and opens daily.

Airport moneychangers give predictably poor rates and charge up to 5% tax/commission. There's an ATM in arrivals (booth 22) between exit doors 3B and 4.

POST

General Post Office (Map p466; ◐7.30am-8.30pm Mon-Sat, 10am-4pm Sun, parcel service 10am-2.30pm, philatelic office 10am-6pm Mon-Fri) While the iconic old GPO building still sells basic stamps, the new postal centre is 100m further along Koilaghat St. Coin dealers, envelope sellers and parcel-wallahs wait outside. The philatelic bureau sells commemmorative issues, or can turn your own photos into a sheet of ₹5 stamps (₹300).

TELEPHONE

Sudder St agency-shops sell SIM cards (₹200) given ID copy, a passport photo and details of your address/hotel.

TOURIST INFORMATION

India Tourism (Map p456; ☑ 033-22825813; www.incredibleindia.org; 4 Shakespeare Sarani; ◐9am-6pm Mon-Fri, to 1pm Sat) Free maps of greater Kolkata.

West Bengal Tourism (Map p466; ☑ 033-22488271; www.wbtdc.gov.in; 3/2 BBD Bagh; ◐10.30am-1.30pm & 2-5.30pm Mon-Fri, to 1pm Sat) Useful websites. The office primarily sells its own tours (last sales 4.30pm) but have good free city maps and an interesting line in philosophical conversation.

USEFUL WEBSITES

Bengali Recipes (www.sutapa.com)
West Bengal Tourism (www.wbtourism.gov.in)
News & Listings (www.calcuttaweb.com)
Curiosities (www.rangandatta.wordpress. com/blog-index/calcutta-kolkata)

ℹ Getting There & Away

The tourist quota on train tickets can be a saviour around Durga Puja (September/October) when local travel is at a peak.

AIR

Rebuilt in 2013, **Netaji Subhash Bose International Airport** (NSBIA; ☑ 033-25118787; www. aai.aero/kolkata/index.jsp) has an impressive departures area but screening bottlenecks persist, so arrive in ample time.

Kolkata has a vast selection of domestic connections. It's a useful hub for regional flights including to Bhutan (Druk Air and Bhutan Airlines), Bangladesh (Regent, United Airways Bangladesh, Biman and Jet Airways), Myanmar (Air India) and Nepal (Air India). East Asian destinations include Bangkok (Air Asia, Bhutan Airlines, Thai, IndiGo and Jet Airways), Hong Kong (Dragonair), Kuala Lumpur (Air Asia), Singapore (Singapore Airlines and Druk Air) and various Chinese destinations via Kunming on China Eastern. Many long-haul connections to Europe go via the Gulf (Emirates, Etihad and Qatar Airways).

Air India (Map p466; ☑ 033-22114433; 39 Chittaranjan Ave; ◐10am-6pm Mon-Sat)

Jet Airways (Map p460; ☑ 033-39893333; www.jetairways.com; Park St; ◐9am-7pm Mon-Sat)

BOAT

A few ferries each month ferries to Port Blair (Andaman Islands) depart from **Kidderpore Docks** (www.kolkataporttrust.gov.in; Karl Marx Sarani), entered from Gate 3 opposite Kidderpore commuter train station. Tickets (bunk/cabin/deluxe ₹2268/5817/8841) go on sale around 10 days before at the Passage Department on the first floor of the **Shipping Corporation of India** (Map p466; ☎ 033-22482354; calcps. dept@sci.co.in; Hare St; ☺10am-1pm & 2-4pm Mon-Fri).

BUS

International

Bangladesh Buses advertised to Bangladesh actually run to Benapol (border), where you walk across and take a separate vehicle on to Dhaka. **Shohagh Paribahan** (Map p460; ☎ 033-22520757; shohagh12@sify.com; 21A Marquis St; ☺5am-10.30pm) have five morning 'Dhaka' services (13 hours, fan/AC ₹830/1430). **GreenLine** (Map p460; ☎ 033-22520571; 12B Marquis St; ☺4am-10.30pm) has three AC buses to Benapol (₹380), all leaving by 7am. Connecting tickets to Dhaka cost 1200TK (just under ₹1000).

Bhutan The 'Gross National Happiness Express' postbus to Phuentsholing (₹505, 18 hours) leaves at 7pm daily, except Sunday, from the walled northeast yard of Esplanade bus station where there are two special **ticket booths** (Map p466; ☎ 033-22627735, 033-22487737; ☺9.30am-1pm & 2-6pm Mon-Sat). It's faster and more comfortable to take the Kanchankanya Express train (13149) from Sealdah station to Hasimara (depart 8.30pm, arrive 10.18am, sleeper/3AC/2AC ₹370/1000/1440) then travel the last 18km by bus or taxi to Phuentsholing, where Indian citizens can get Bhutanese permits in a couple of hours.

MAJOR TRAINS FROM KOLKATA

USEFUL FOR	TRAIN	DURATION (HR)	DEPARTURES	FARES (₹; SLEEPER/ 3AC/2AC UNLESS OTHERWISE STATED)
Bhubaneswar	12839 Chennai Mail	6½	11.45pm (HWH)	290/735/1035
Chennai	12841 Coromandal	26½	2.50pm (HWH)	665/1730/2520
	12839 Chennai Mail	28	11.45pm (HWH)	665/1730/2520
Delhi	12303/12381 Poorva	23½	8.05am/8.15am (HWH)	630/1650/2395
	12313 SDAH Rajdhani	19½	4.50pm (SDAH)	3AC/1AC 2080/4830
Gorakhpur	15047/15049/15051 Puranchal/KKK-GKP	17¼-19	2.30pm (KOAA)	420/1130/1630
Guwahati	12345 Saraighat	17¾	3.50pm (HWH)	500/1305/1870
	15657 Kanchanjunga	21¾	6.35am (SDAH)	455/1225/1775
Hooghly	Bandel Local	51 mins	several hourly (HWH)	Unreserved ₹10
Lucknow	13151 Jammu Tawi	22¾	11.45am (KOAA)	470/1260/1825
	12327/12369Upasana/Kumbha	18¼	1pm (HWH)	510/1340/1960
Mumbai CST	12810 Mumbai Mail	33	8.15pm (HWH)	740/1930/2820
New Jalpaiguri	12343 Darjeeling Mail	10	10.05pm (SDAH)	350/910/1285
	12377 Padatik	10¼	10.55pm (SDAH)	350/910/1285
Patna	13131 ANVT mail	12½	7.50pm (KOAA)	315/845/-
	12351 Danapur	9½	8.35pm (HWH)	340/880/1240
Puri	18409 Sri Jagannath	9¾	7pm (HWH)	300/805/1150
	12837 Howrah-Puri	8¾	10.35pm (HWH)	330/850/1200
Varanasi Jn	13005 Amritsar Mail	14	7.10pm (HWH)	385/1045/1510

HWH=ex-Howrah, SDAH=ex-Sealdah, KOAA=ex-Chitpur

KOLKATA (CALCUTTA) GETTING THERE & AWAY

Domestic

For Darjeeling or Sikkim, start by taking a bus to Siliguri (12 to 14 hours). All drive overnight departing **Esplanade bus station** (Map p460) between 5pm and 8pm (seat/sleeper from ₹400/500, with AC₹1000/1200). An NBSTC bus for Cooch Behar leaves at 8pm (₹489, 18 hours)

Buses to Bihar and Odisha line up along the roadside directly south of Babaghat/Eden Gardens commuter train station. Most run overnight, departing between 5pm and 8.30pm. Arrive very early if you have baggage. Destinations include:

Bhubaneswar (fan/AC ₹350/400, 9½ hours)

Gaya (seat/sleeper ₹260/640, 13 hours) Leaves at 7pm with Maharani Express.

Puri (seat/sleeper ₹400/450, 12 hours) On Dolphin (www.odishabusservice.com).

Ranchi (seat/sleeper from ₹220/270, 10 hours)

STREET NAMES

Since independence, street names with Raj-era connotations have been officially changed, but while street signs and business cards use the new variant, citizens and taxis often still refer to the British-era names. This chapter uses what we found, quite unscientifically, to be the most commonly employed variant, *italicised* in the list below:

OLD NAME	NEW NAME
Allenby Rd	Dr Sisir Kumar Bose Sarani
Ballygunge Rd	Ashutosh Chowdhury Ave (AC Rd)
Brabourne Rd	Biplabi Trailokya Maharaja Rd
Camac St	Abinindranath Tagore St
Central Ave	*Chittaranjan (CR) Ave*
Chitpore Rd	*Rabindra Sarani*
Chowringhee Rd	Jawaharlal Nehru Rd
Dalhousie Sq	*BBD Bagh*
Free School St	*Mirza Ghalib St*
Harrington St	*Ho Chi Minh Sarani*
Harrison Rd	*Mahatma Gandhi (MG) Rd*
Hungerford St	Picasso Bithi
Kyd St	Dr M Ishaque Rd
Lansdowne Rd	*Sarat Bose Rd*
Loudon St	Dr UM Bramhchari St
Lower Circular Rd	*AJC Bose Rd*
Old Courthouse St	Hemant Basu Sarani
Park St	Mother Teresa Sarani
Rawdon St	Sarojini Naidu Sarani
Theatre Rd	*Shakespeare Sarani*
Victoria Terrace	*Gorky Terrace*
Waterloo St	Nawab Siraj-ud-Daula Sarani
Wellesley St	*RAK (Rafi Ahmed Kidwai) Rd*
Wood St	Dr Martin Luther King Sarani

TRAIN

Stations

Long-distance trains depart from three major stations. Gigantic Howrah (Haora; HWH) is across the river, often best reached by ferry; Sealdah (SDAH) is at the eastern end of MG Road; and 'Kolkata' (Chitpore; KOAA) Station is around 5km further north (nearest metro Belgachia).

Tickets

To buy international tickets or long-distance-train tickets with 'tourist quota', foreigners should use the **Eastern Railways' Foreign Tourist Bureau** (Map p466; ☏033-22224206; 6 Fairlie Pl; ⏰10am-5pm Mon-Sat, to 2pm Sun). Bring a book to read as waits can be very long but there are seats. On arrival, take and fill in a booking form (forms are numbered and double as queuing chits). Lines form well before opening. It's sometimes quicker to use the nearby standard **computerised booking office** (Map p466; Koilaghat St; ⏰8am-8pm Mon-Sat, to 2pm Sun) but that has no tourist quota.

For Dhaka, Bangladesh, the Maitree Express (2nd class/AC chair/1AC ₹485/755/1250, 12½ hours) departs Kolkata (Chitpore) Station at 7.10am Saturday and Tuesday, returning from Dhaka Cantt at 7am Wednesday and Sunday. If you need a Bangladeshi visa, it should have Darsana marked as the entry point. Buy tickets up to 10 days ahead.

For a certain commission, Sudder St travel agencies can save you the trek to the ticket office and can sometimes manage to find tickets on 'full' trains.

ⓘ Getting Around

Tickets for buses, trams and the metro on most city transport routes cost from ₹4 to ₹15. Men shouldn't sit in assigned 'Ladies' seats'.

Beware: around 1pm much of the city's one-way road system reverses direction, so bus routes invert and taxis can prove reluctant to make journeys around this time.

TO/FROM THE AIRPORT

NSBIA Airport (p484) is around 16km northeast of central Kolkata. A feeder loop road accesses the new combined terminal from the south (VIP Rd) via Airport Gate 1. Busy Jessore Rd approximately parallels the runway to a second, smaller access through Airport Gate 2, around 400m west of the largely disused old terminals.

AC Bus

Airport buses start from a stand that's a minute's walk north from arrivals door 1A (between the new and old terminals). Pay on board. **Bus VS1** (Map p466; one-way ₹50; ⊙8am-7.30pm) runs every half hour to Esplanade, returning from a walled government-bus compound in Esplanade Bus Station (around one hour). Bus VS2 runs to Howrah.

City Bus

Cheap but very slow minibus 151 to BBD Bagh (₹10) and relatively infrequent bus 46 to Esplanade via VIP Rd start from the VIP Rd/Jessore Rd junction near Airport Gate 1. Bus 30B from Jessore Rd runs to Babughat.

Metro

The airport metro-spur line from Noapara should be operational by 2017. For now the closest station is Dum Dum, 5km southwest by buses 30B and DN9/1 from Airport Gate 2/Jessore Rd.

Taxi

Fixed-price taxis cost ₹345/455 to Sudder St/Howrah taking around 50 minutes/one hour when traffic is kind. Pre-pay at booth 12 in the new arrivals area between exits 3B and 4.

AUTORICKSHAW

Tuk-tuk-style autorickshaws ('autos') operate as fixed-route hop-on share-taxis with three passengers in the back and one beside the driver. Fares are typically ₹6 to ₹10, depending on distance.

Key routes include the following:

Dharamtala–Loha Pool Starts from Park Circus using Park St (or after 1pm looping via Nasreddin and Karaya roads), goes up AJC Bose Rd, (near Mother Teresa's Motherhouse), along Elliot/Royd then up Mirza Ghalib/RAK Rd (mornings/afternoons) near Sudder St. Loops reverse after 1pm.

Hazra–Bondel (Map p468) Along Hazra Rd, starting a block east of Jatin Das Park Metro.

Hazra–Khiddapur West from Jatin Das Park Metro, past the Kalighat idolmakers and on through Alipore.

BUS & TRAM

Buses and minibuses are more frequent but photogenic battered old trams follow somewhat more predictable routes and are immune to one-way traffic.

FERRY

Crossing the Hoogly is generally faster and more agreeable by boat than by using the clogged road bridges. **Ferries** (tickets ₹5-10; ⊙8am-8pm) depart every 15 to 20 minutes from Howrah to jetties in central Kolkata; other useful routes are Howrah–Ahritola–Sovabazar–Bagbazar (for Kumartuli), Ahritola–Bandaghat and Belur–Dakshineswar.

METRO

Kolkata's busy **metro** (www.mtp.indianrailways.gov.in; ⊙7am-9.45pm Mon-Sat, 2-9.45pm Sun) has trains every five to 15 minutes. For Sudder St, use Esplanade or Park St.

Only one line is operational so far but several extensions are planned. Line 2 (http://kmrc.in) linking Howrah, Sealdah and Salt Lake is due by late 2015.

Theoretically you may not carry bags over 10kg.

RICKSHAW

Human-powered 'tana rickshaws' work within limited areas, notably around New Market. Although rickshaw pullers sometimes charge foreigners disproportionate fares, many are virtually destitute, sleeping on the pavements beneath their rented chariots at night, so tips are heartily appreciated.

SUBURBAN TRAINS

Sealdah–Dum Dum–Dakshineswar trains run roughly hourly. The Kidderpore–BBD Bagh–Bagbazar–Chitpore–Dum Dum route is rush hour only. Biman Bandar is the airport station but only a couple of daily services stop there.

TAXI

Kolkata's yellow Ambassador cabs charge ₹25 for up to 1.9km. Most have 'new' digital meters that simply show the fare due. However, a few have old mechanical meters for which there's a conversion chart: expect to pay around 240% of that reading. Taxis are generally easy to flag down except during the 5pm to 6pm rush hour and after 10pm when some cabs refuse to use the meter. After 9pm, drivers might reasonably ask double fare if they can't expect to find a return ride.

There are prepaid taxi booths at Howrah Station, Sealdah Station and at the airport.

West Bengal & Darjeeling

Best Places to Stay

➡ Elgin (p507)
➡ Holumba Haven (p517)
➡ Vedic Village (p493)

Best Places for a Cuppa

➡ Windamere Hotel (p507)
➡ Glenary's (p509)
➡ Cochrane Place (p500)

Why Go?

A sliver of fertile land running from the tea-draped Himalayan foothills to the sultry mangroves of the Bay of Bengal, West Bengal offers a remarkable range of destinations and experiences to find within a single state. In the tropical southern areas, the sea-washed hamlet of Mandarmani vies for attention with Bishnupur's ornate terracotta-tiled Hindu temples and palaces. The striped Bengal tiger stealthily swims through muddy rivulets in the Sunderbans, while a bunch of European-style ghost towns line the banks of the Hooghly (Ganges) further upstream as reminders of the state's maritime heyday. In the cool northern hills, the toy train chugs its way up to the charming British-era hill station of Darjeeling, revered for its ringside views of massive Khangchendzonga. There's also a vibrant art scene, delectable cuisine and a genuinely hospitable population where friends are easy to make and hard to lose.

When to Go

Darjeeling

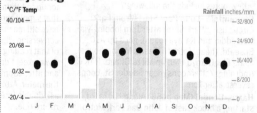

Oct–Dec & Mar–May Best for hill views, trekking and spring blooms up north.

Oct–Mar Best time for avoiding the heat on the lower southern plains.

Jan Ideal for navigating the dense mangrove forests of the Sunderbans Tiger Reserve.

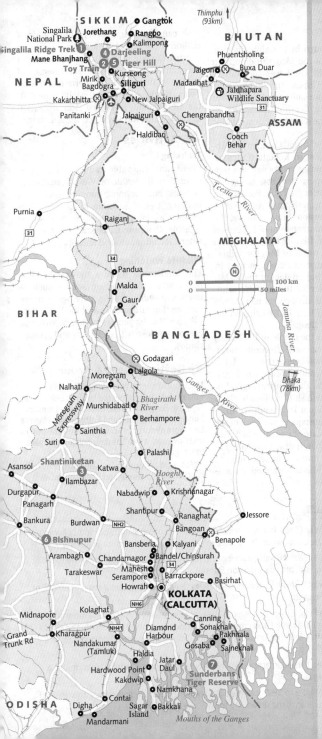

West Bengal Highlights

1 Enjoying 360-degree mountain views over breakfast at hilltop lodges on the **Singalila Ridge Trek** (p513)

2 Riding the steam-driven **toy train** (p511) as it puffs and pants its way between the tea towns of Kurseong and Darjeeling

3 Exploring rural wonders and getting arty on a visit to the university town of **Shantiniketan** (p493)

4 Visiting a tea estate, sipping a delicate local brew and enjoying fantastic mountain views from the historic hill station of **Darjeeling** (p500)

5 Watching dawn break over Khangchendzonga, the world's third-highest peak, from **Tiger Hill** (p501)

6 Admiring intricate scenes from the Hindu epics carved on the medieval terracotta temples of **Bishnupur** (p493)

7 Cruising the river channels of the **Sunderbans** (p491) through the world's most extensive mangrove forest, to spot darting kingfishers, spotted deer and the elusive Royal Bengal tiger

History

Referred to as Bongo in the Mahabharata, Bengal was part of the Mauryan empire in the 3rd century BC, and was successively controlled by the Guptas, the Buddhist Palas and the Muslim sultans of Delhi over time. Following the death of Aurangzeb in 1707, Bengal became an independent Islamic state.

The British East India Company established a trading post in Kolkata (Calcutta) in 1698, which quickly prospered and outshone other European outposts along the Hooghly River belonging to Portuguese, Dutch and Danish merchants. Annoyed by rapid British expansion, Siraj-ud-daula, the nawab of Bengal, marched out of his capital at Murshidabad and easily took Kolkata in 1756. Robert Clive defeated him the following year at the Battle of Plassey, helped by the treachery of Siraj-ud-daula's uncle, Mir Jafar, a commander in the nawab's army. Jafar succeeded his nephew as nawab, but after the Battle of Buxar in 1764 the British took full control of Bengal.

West Bengal was the cradle of the Indian Renaissance and national freedom movement, and has long been considered the country's cultural and intellectual heartland – Calcutta was the political capital of India until the British shifted office to Delhi in 1931. In 1947, Indian Independence from Britain – and the subsequent partition of the country – saw the state of Bengal (which had already been split for administrative purposes in 1905) divided into Hindu-predominant West Bengal and Muslim-oriented Bangladesh, causing the upheaval and migration of millions of Bengalis.

Since the late 1980s, Darjeeling's demand for political autonomy has seen phases of unrest in the state's northern mountains, eventually leading to the establishment of the Gorkhaland Territorial Administration in 2012, which has stabilised the situation.

🏃 Activities

Trekking

There are enjoyable walks along pine-scented trails in all of West Bengal's hill stations, but the most popular place for a multiday trek is Singalila Ridge, near Darjeeling, where teahouse-style trekking is possible. Camping treks are available elsewhere, including around Kalimpong.

Wildlife Watching

The Sunderbans remains the state's prime forest area for spying on species such as crocs, Gangetic dolphins, deer, water monitors, myriad bird species and the Royal Bengal tiger. In the jungles of Jaldhapara, you can get up close with elephants and grumpy rhinos.

ℹ️ Getting There & Around

Most tourists enter West Bengal through Kolkata, which is connected by air to Delhi, Mumbai, Bangkok, Dubai, Doha, Kuala Lumpur, Singapore, Hong Kong and Kathmandu. Siliguri's Bagdogra airport has services to Kolkata, Delhi and Guwahati, as well as daily helicopter flights to Gangtok.

Most land arrivals are by train: main lines run south to Bhubaneswar and Chennai, and west

TOP FESTIVALS

Ganga Sagar Mela (Sagar Island; ⊙ mid-Jan) Hundreds of thousands of Hindu pilgrims converge where the Ganges meets the sea, to bathe en masse in a riotous festival.

Bengali New Year (Naba Barsha; Statewide; ⊙ mid-Apr) A holiday celebrating the first day of the Bengali calendar, also called *Nabo Barsho*.

Rath Yatra (Chariot Festival; Statewide; ⊙ Jul/Aug) Celebrated by pulling the juggernaut of Lord Jagannath's chariot.

Dussehra (Durga Puja; ⊙ Sep/Oct) Across the state, especially in Kolkata, temporary *pandals* (pavilions) are raised and intense celebrations take place to worship the Hindu goddess Durga. After four colourful days, beautiful clay idols of the 10-armed deity are immersed in the rivers.

Jagaddhatri Puja (Chandarnagar; ⊙ Nov) Honours the Hindu goddess Jagaddhatri, an incarnation of Durga.

Poush Mela (p494; 23 to 26 December, Shantiniketan) Folk music, dance, theatre and Baul songs radiate across the university town.

to Gaya, Varanasi and Delhi. Other lines connect Assam in Northeast India and Jharkhand in the west. Numerous long-distance buses also connect surrounding states.

Overcrowded 'share jeeps' with cramped back seats ply the winding roads of the West Bengal hills.

SOUTH OF KOLKATA

Sunderbans Tiger Reserve

Home to one of the largest concentrations of Royal Bengal tigers on the planet, the 2585-sq-km **Sunderbans Tiger Reserve** (admission/video ₹50/200; ⊙ dawn-dusk) is a network of channels and semisubmerged mangroves that forms the world's largest river delta. The ecosystem here is contiguous with the Sunderbans delta in Bangladesh, which lies eastward across the international border along the same shoreline. Tigers (officially estimated to number close to 300) lurk in the impenetrable depths of the mangrove forests, and also swim the delta's innumerable channels. Although they do sometimes kill villagers and their livestock, tigers are typically shy and sightings are rare. Nevertheless, cruising the broad waterways through the world's biggest mangrove sanctuary (now a Unesco World Heritage Site) and watching wildlife, whether it be a spotted deer, 2m-long water monitor or luminescent kingfisher, is a world away from Kolkata's chaos.

The best time to visit the reserve is between November and March – entry is restricted through the late summer and monsoon months. Organised tours are the best way to navigate this tricky and harsh landscape, not least because all your permits, paperwork, guiding duties and logistical problems are taken care of. In fact, travelling alone is not recommended.

At Sajnekhali, the official gateway into the reserve, you'll find the **Mangrove Interpretation Centre** (Sajnekhali; ⊙ 8.30am-5pm) [FREE] with a small turtle and crocodile hatchery, a collection of pickled wildlife and a blackboard with the date of the last tiger-spotting chalked up. Motorboats (₹600) and guides (₹600) are available for hire near the site.

Tours

Tour prices vary widely. They typically include return transport from Kolkata, accommodation, food, park entry fees, as well as guide- and boat-hire charges. Do check what is and isn't included.

Backpackers WILDLIFE-WATCHING
(☎ 9836177140; www.tourdesundarbans.com; 11 Tottee Lane, Kolkata; 1/2 nights per person all-inclusive ₹4000/4500; ⊙ 10am-7pm) Reliable yet laid-back, fun yet spiritual, this very knowledgeable 'three brothers' outfit conducts highly recommended tours of the jungle, including birdwatching and local music. Accommodation is either in a cruise boat converted from a fishing trawler, or a traditional village-style guesthouse, with folk music in the evenings. Rates depend on group size and number of days.

West Bengal Tourism CRUISE
(☎ 033-22436440, 033-22488271; www.wbtdc.gov. in; per person per day all-inclusive from ₹3400) Organises weekly boat cruises from September to April, including food and on-board accommodation in dedicated vessels. The trips last one night and two half days; consider throwing in an extra day (₹4400 per head).

Sunderban Tiger Camp WILDLIFE-WATCHING
(☎ 033-32935749; www.waxpolhotels.com; 71 Ganesh Chandra Ave, Kolkata; 1/2 nights per person all-inclusive from ₹4290/7290) This well-managed outfit provides expert guides and quality accommodation (on dry land) in tents, huts and lovely red-brick cottages with forest-themed wall murals. The tents are cheapest, but come with a sense of adventure.

Help Tourism WILDLIFE-WATCHING
(Map p468; ☎ 033-24550917; www.helptourism. com; 67A Kali Temple Rd, Kalighat, Kolkata; 2 nights per person all-inclusive ₹16,400) Actively associated with local communities, this tour operator takes you up close to rural life in the

delta, and provides wonderful access into the forest. Accommodation is in a luxury eco-themed camp. Prices drop dramatically as group size increases; enquire with them directly.

Mandarmani
☑ 03220

About 180km south of Kolkata, the sleepy fishing village of Mandarmani sports a heavenly beach stretching nearly 15km. It remains one of the more unpolluted beaches in the country, and supports countless colonies of sand bubbler crabs. The beaches see some additional action at dawn, when fishing boats drop anchor and disgorge their catches of marine goodies.

Adventure Zone (☑ 9830033896; www.aboutadventure.org; Mandarmani) conducts parasailing (₹600) on the beaches, and offers an adventure-sports package (₹1200) that includes kayaking, zip-lining, rock climbing and rappelling.

Sana Beach (☑ 9330633111; www.mandarmanihotels.com; d incl breakfast from ₹2850; ❄ ☒), at the far end of the beach, is by far the best among all the resorts lining Mandarmani's sands. It has a mix of comfy rooms done up in cheerful hues, ethno-chic cottages and tents, a lovely swimming pool and a good bar-cum-restaurant.

SAGAR FESTIVAL

According to Hindu legend, Sagar Island – at the confluence of the Ganges – was where King Sagar's 60,000 sons were brought back to life by the flowing river after they had been reduced to ashes by a sage named Kapil Muni. Each year in January, the **Ganga Sagar Mela** is held here, near the Kapil Muni Temple, honouring the legend. The best way to see the festival is the two-day, one-night boat tour operated from Kolkata by **West Bengal Tourism** (www.wbtdc.gov.in), with accommodation on board (per person all-inclusive from ₹8000). The island hibernates for the rest of the year.

Buses (₹60, two hours) run frequently from Kolkata's Esplanade bus stand to Namkhana pier, from where ferries ply to the island. Buses and share taxis shuttle within the island between points of tourist interest.

To get there, take the 6.40am 12857 Tamralipta Express (2nd class/chair ₹100/365, 3½ hours) from Kolkata's Howrah Station to Digha. A one-way taxi ride from there costs about ₹500.

NORTH OF KOLKATA

Up the Hooghly

Serampore, on the Hooghly River, about 25km north of Kolkata, was a Danish trading centre until Denmark's holdings in India were transferred to the British East India Company in 1845. **Serampore College** was founded in 1818 by the first Baptist missionary to India, William Carey, and houses a library that was once one of the largest in the country.

Further upstream is the former French outpost of **Chandarnagar**. Here you can visit the **Eglise du Sacre Coeur** (Sacred Heart Church) and the nearby 18th-century mansion now housing the **Cultural Institut de Chandarnagar** (⊘ 11am-5.30pm, closed Thu & Sat) **FREE**, with collections documenting this colonial-era outpost. In November, there are gorgeous public lighting displays for **Jagaddhatri Puja**, a festival devoted to the worship of an incarnation of the Hindu mother goddess. Enthusiastic locals throng festive arenas to pay their respects to gigantic clay idols of the four-armed deity, housed in temporary pavilions called *pandals*.

In 1571 the Portuguese set up a factory in **Bandel**, 41km north of Kolkata and close to Saptagram, which was an important Portuguese trading port long before Kolkata rose to prominence. Here, you can climb the lofty clock tower of the romantically crumbling **Imambara** (admission ₹5; ⊘ 8am-6pm Apr-Jul, to 5.30pm Aug-Nov, to 5pm Dec-Mar), which has breathtaking views of the river. The building was constructed in 1861 as a centre for learning and worship. Only 1km south of Bandel, Chinsurah was ceded by the Dutch to the British in exchange for Sumatra in 1825. There are dilapidated ruins of a fort and a cemetery, about 1km to the west.

About 6km north of Hooghly, **Bansberia** has two interesting temples. The 13 *sikharas* (spires) of the **Hanseswari Temple** look like something you'd expect to see in St Petersburg, while the ornate terracotta tiles cov-

SPA TREATS

Looking to experience the best of rural Bengal while treating yourself to a spot of wellness and luxury? Head to one of these two recommended spa resorts, set amid scenic landscapes, and indulge in some of the best comforts and therapies, while soaking up the bucolic charms of the region.

Hemmed by blooming vegetable gardens and centred on a tree-lined lake only an hour's drive north of Kolkata is **Vedic Village** (☑9830025900; www.thevedicvillage.com; Shikharpur village; r from ₹8500; ❄@☲), a luxury resort known as much for its fine hospitality as its showcase facility – a speciality spa-cum-naturopathy clinic that's touted to be the first (and best) medical spa in the country. Long-stay treatment packages, built around several sessions of consultation with in-house doctors, can be customised upon prior notice. Casual holidaymakers can simply kick back in one of the luxury villas, de-stress to the chirping of myriad bird species, tuck into mouth-watering cuisine, or float in the ultramarine waters of the swimming pool.

En route to Diamond Harbour, about two hours south of Kolkata, stands **Ganga Kutir** (☑033-40404040; www.gangakutir.com; Sarisa village, Raichak; r incl breakfast from ₹15,299; ❄@☲), another popular destination for those wanting some solitude. Located on the banks of the Hooghly, this swish resort offers a range of wellness packages which – paired with yoga and meditation – are a great nourisher for tired sinews. Accommodation is in chic suites appointed with snazzy mural-covered walls and great river views.

ering the **Vasudev Temple** resemble those seen in Bishnupur.

To visit these settlements on a day tour from Kolkata, take any Bandel-bound local train (₹14, one hour, hourly) from Howrah Station, or hire a taxi for the day (₹2600). There aren't too many restaurants in the area, so carry a packed lunch.

Bishnupur

☑03244 / POP 61,900

Known for its beautiful terracotta temples, Bishnupur flourished as the capital of the Malla kings from the 16th to the early 19th centuries. The architecture of these intriguing **temples** (Indian/foreigner ₹10/250; ☉dawn-dusk) is a bold mix of Bengali, Islamic and Oriya (Odishan) styles. Intricately detailed facades of numerous temples play out scenes of the Hindu epics, the Ramayana and Mahabharata. The most striking structures include the **Jor Bangla**, **Madan Mohan Temple**, the multiarched **Ras Mancha** and the elaborate **Shyam Rai Temple**. You need to pay for your ticket at Ras Mancha and show it at the other temples. Cycle-rickshaw-wallahs offer tours (the best way to negotiate the labyrinth of lanes) for ₹300.

There's a small **museum** (admission ₹10; ☉11am-7pm Tue-Sun) that's worth a look for its painted manuscript covers, stone friezes, musical instruments and folk-art gallery.

Bishnupur is in Bankura district, famous for its Baluchari silk saris and its pottery, particularly the stylised terracotta Bankura horse. Reproductions of detailed terracotta tiles from the temples are sold everywhere.

Bishnupur Tourist Lodge (☑03244-252013; www.wbtourism.gov.in; College Rd; d from ₹800; ❄), flaunting a red-and-white exterior, is perhaps the best place to sleep in town, with clean pastel-shaded rooms and a good bar-cum-restaurant. It's close to the museum and a ₹50 rickshaw ride from the train station. It's often full, so book ahead.

Regular buses run from Bishnupur to Kolkata (₹140, five hours). For Shantiniketan (₹100, four hours) you have to change in Durgapur. Two fast trains run daily to Howrah station (2nd class/chair ₹140/505, four hours): the 6.25am 12883 Rupashi Bangla Express and the 4.50pm 12827 Howrah Purulia Express.

Shantiniketan

☑03463

In addition to epitomising its Bengali name – meaning 'abode of peace' – Shantiniketan is a veritable nerve centre of Bengal's art and culture. Nobel laureate, poet and artist Rabindranath Tagore (1861–1941) founded a school here amid pastoral settings in 1901. It later developed into the **Visva Bharati University**, with an emphasis on the study

PALACES GALORE

Thrown around the vicinity of Kolkata's city limits are a handful of rajbaris or palaces belonging to families of erstwhile zamindars (landowners). While most of them stand delapidated and forlorn, a few have recently made a promising turnaround and joined the top-end tourism bandwagon. Among the few palaces offering a luxury experience woven around the bygone regal life is the palace of **Itachuna** (☑ 9830142389; www.itachunarajbari.com; Halusai village; d from ₹2700; ❄), 110km from Kolkata. It packs a punch with its renovated stately interiors, fine Bengali food and an overall bucolic ambience. The palace of **Bawali** (☑ 9830383008; www.therajbari.com; Bawali village; d incl breakfast from ₹13,500; ❄), a one-hour drive south of Kolkata, also makes for a lovely getaway, with a striking doric-pillared facade, carefully preserved distressed decor and excellent overall hospitality.

of liberal arts as well as humanity's relationship with nature. A relaxed place, it attracts students from all over India and overseas.

Spread throughout the leafy university grounds are eclectic **statues**, the celebrated **Shantiniketan murals** and the Belgian glass-panelled **university prayer hall**. The **Museum & Art Gallery** (adult/student ₹10/5; ☉10.30am-1pm & 2-4.30pm Thu-Mon, to 1pm Tue) within the **Uttarayan complex** (Tagore's former home) are worth a peek if you are a Tagore aficionado. Reproductions of his sketches and paintings are sold here.

Subarnarekha bookshop near the post office has plenty of Tagore's titles (₹100 to ₹250) in English. Around Shantiniketan, several practitioners of classical dance, music, pottery and painting offer casual short-term courses to visiting students. Ask the helpful staff at Subarnarekha.

🎎 Festivals & Events

Poush Mela   CULTURAL
(Shantiniketan; ☉23-26 Dec) The highpoint of Shantiniketan's festive calendar, this four-day winter gala brings together artists, musicians, artisans and poets from places as diverse as nearby villages to far-flung continents. There's food, fun, frolic, song, dance and poetry round the clock, with sessions of vigorous souvenir shopping in between.

🛏 Sleeping & Eating

Park Guest House   GUESTHOUSE $$
(☑ 9434012420; www.parkguesthouse.in; Deer Park; d incl breakfast ₹1450; ❄ 🛜) Bordering a quaint tribal village, this peaceful and pretty place is clearly the best deal in town. The rooms are beautifully embellished with tribal decor, and the elaborate thali meals

(prepared upon advance notice) are simply awesome. There's a lovely lawn where you can nurse a quiet beer in the evening.

Shantiniketan Tourist Lodge   HOTEL $$
(☑ 03463-252699; www.wbtourism.gov.in; Bhubandanga; d from ₹950; ❄) Industrial but friendly, this large-scale government operation is worth considering if you go for one of its deluxe air-conditioned rooms (₹2650; located in cottages standing around a pretty lawn. There's a decent **restaurant** (mains ₹120) which works up delicious local Bengali fare.

Ghare Baire   BENGALI $$
(Geetanjali Cinema complex; meals ₹150; ☉11am-9.30pm) A restaurant specialising in traditional Bengali fare, this cafeteria-style eatery churns out sumptuous and utterly delectable platters for lunch and dinner. There are a few generic snacks and Chinese preparations on offer as well. There's a souvenir store on site, selling exquisite pottery that you might want to browse in between morsels.

ℹ Information

Post office (Santiniketan Rd; ☉10am-4pm Mon-Sat) On the main road, opposite the turn-off to the university entrance.
State Bank of India (Santiniketan Rd; ☉10am-2pm Mon-Fri, to noon Sat) Has an ATM and changes foreign currency.

ℹ Getting There & Away

Several trains ply the route between Bolpur station, 2km south of the university, and Kolkata daily. The best is 12337 Shantiniketan Express (2nd class/chair ₹95/305, 2½ hours) departing at 10.10am from Howrah station. For New Jalpaiguri, take the 9.20am 15657 Kanchenjunga Express (sleeper/3AC ₹250/665, nine hours).

Bolpur's Jambuni bus stand has connections to Berhampore/Murshidabad (₹110, four hours) and Bishnupur (₹100, four hours). Change in Suri and Durgapur respectively.

Train booking office (Santiniketan Rd; ⊙ 8am-noon & 12.30-2pm Thu-Tue) Near the post office, with information on trains to and from Kolkata or Darjeeling, and reservations.

Nabadwip & Mayapur

☑ 03472 / POP 125,300

Nabadwip, 114km north of Kolkata, is an important Krishna pilgrimage centre, attracting throngs of devotees, and is also an ancient centre of Sanskrit culture. The last Hindu king of Bengal, Lakshman Sen, moved his capital here from Gaur.

Across the river from Nabadwip, Mayapur is the headquarters of the Iskcon (Hare Krishna) movement. There's a large, colourful temple and the basic but clean **Iskcon Guest House** (☑ 03472-245620; mghb@pam ho.net; Main Complex; d/tr/q from ₹500/600/800; ✳). Iskcon runs a package tour in a private bus from Kolkata, leaving early on Friday, Saturday and Sunday mornings, returning the subsequent evening. For details or to make a booking call **Iskcon Kolkata** (☑ 9830955124).

Murshidabad & Berhampore

☑ 03482 / POP 170,300

In Murshidabad, rural Bengali life and 18th-century architecture meld on the verdant shores of the Bhagirathi River. When Siraj-ud-daula was nawab of Bengal, Murshidabad was his capital, and he was assassinated here after the defeat at Plassey (now Palashi).

The main draw here is the palace of **Hazarduari** (Indian/foreigner ₹10/250; ⊙ 10am-4.30pm Sat-Thu), a palace famous for its 1000 doors (real and false), built here for the nawabs in 1837. It houses an astonishing collection of antiquities from the 18th and 19th centuries. Other beautiful structures in the complex include the **Nizamat Imambara**, the clock tower, the **Wasef Manzil**, a former regal residence, and the elegant **Madina Mosque**.

Murshid Quli Khan, who moved the capital here in 1700, is buried beneath the stairs at the impressive ruins of the **Katra Mosque**. Siraj-ud-daula was assassinated

at the **Nimak Haram Deori** (Traitor's Gate). Within the **Kathgola Gardens** (admission ₹10; ⊙ 6.30am-5.30pm) is an interesting family mansion of a Jain trading family, dating back to 1873.

Berhampore is 15km south of Murshidabad and acts as its bus and railway hub.

🛏 Sleeping & Eating

Hotel Sagnik HOTEL $
(☑ 09434021911; Omrahaganj; d from ₹850; ✳) Conveniently located between Murshidabad and Berhampore, this friendly place has good-value rooms and a decent restaurant, but scores mostly on service, which is prompt and personalised. It's a 10-minute cycle-rickshaw ride from Murshidabad train station.

Hotel Samrat HOTEL $
(☑ 03482-251147; NH34 Panchanantala; d from ₹850; ✳) This is one of Berhampore's longest-running operations. It offers spacious and clean rooms opening along corridors painted in orange and cream. The **Mahal restaurant** (mains ₹80 -150) downstairs is a good place for meals. It's located on the main highway, though, so expect some vehicle noise at night.

ℹ Getting There & Around

The 13103 Bhagirathi Express (2nd class/chair ₹68/241, four hours) departs Kolkata's Sealdah station at 6.20pm. Regular buses leave for Kolkata (₹130, six hours) and Malda (₹90, four hours). To Shantiniketan/Bolpur (₹95, four hours) there are occasional direct buses but you may need to change in Suri.

Shared autorickshaws (₹30) whiz between Murshidabad and Berhampore. Cycle-rickshaws/taxis offer guided half-day tours to see the spread-out sites for ₹300/800.

WEST BENGAL HILLS

Siliguri & New Jalpaiguri

☑ 0353 / POP 701,000 / ELEV 120M

The crowded and noisy transport hub encompassing the twin towns of Siliguri and New Jalpaiguri (NJP) is the jumping-off point for Darjeeling, Kalimpong, Sikkim, the Northeast States, eastern Nepal and Bhutan. Despite this being one of the largest cities in the state, there's little to see or do here, apart from staying the night in transit.

GAUR & PANDUA

Rising from the flooded paddy fields of Gaur (355km from Kolkata) are mosques and other crumbling ruins of the 13th- to 16th-century capital of the Muslim nawabs of Bengal. Little remains from the 7th- to 12th-century pre-Muslim period, when Gaur was the capital of the successive Buddhist Pala and Hindu Sena dynasties.

Hiding behind lush mango orchards, the most graceful monuments in this area are the impressive **Baradwari Mosque** (1526) – the arcaded aisle of its corridor still intact – and the fortresslike gateway of **Dakhil Darwaza** (1425). The **Qadam Rasul Mosque** enshrines the flat footprint of the Prophet Mohammed. Remnants of colourful enamel cling to the **Chamkan Mosque** and the **Gumti Gate** nearby.

In Pandua (about 25km from Gaur) are the vast ruins of the 14th-century **Adina Masjid**, once India's largest mosque. About 2km away is the **Eklakhi Mausoleum**, so called because it cost one lakh (₹100,000) to build back in 1431.

To visit these forgotten relics, board the 3.25pm 13011 Howrah–Malda Intercity Express (2nd class/chair ₹130/465, 7½ hours) from Kolkata. Accommodation is available in Malda (15km from Gaur and 30km from Pandua) at **Hotel Kalinga** (☑03512-283567; hotelkalinga@gmail.com; NH34, Ram Krishna Pally; d ₹1000; ﹡), which has basic rooms, friendly service and palatable in-house food. For touring the monuments, it's best to hire a taxi from Malda for the day (₹2200).

Most of Siliguri's hotels, restaurants and services are spread along Tenzing Norgay Rd, better known as Hill Cart Rd. NJP Station Rd leads southward 6km to NJP station. Branching northeastward off Hill Cart Rd are Siliguri's other main streets, Sevoke and Bidhan roads.

If you have time in the evening, you might want to visit the colourful Salugara gompa, about 5km out of town, adorned with an imposing chortenlike spire. Alternatively, shop for Chinese knock-offs in the bustling Hong Kong Market off Sevoke Rd in the heart of town.

🛏 Sleeping

Evergreen Inn
HOTEL **$**

(☑0353-2510426; innevergreen@yahoo.in; Pradhan Nagar, Ashana Purna Sarani; d from ₹990; ﹡) Located just 100m from the bus terminal, this hotel down a side street is surprisingly peaceful. Each room is different, but they all are clean and fresh with flat-screen TVs and stylish bathrooms. The staff are friendly, though English isn't their forte. You'll find it down a lane on the opposite side of the bus terminal.

Hotel Conclave
HOTEL **$**

(☑0353-2516155; www.hotelconclave.in; Hill Cart Rd; s/d from ₹770/880; ﹡) Located conveniently close to the bus stand, it has quality beds and prim cedar-themed decor. The glass elevator adds a touch of class. The

cheaper rooms are quieter, while the pricier ones come with complimentary breakfast.

Hotel Himalayan Regency
HOTEL **$**

(☑0353-6502955; Hill Cart Rd, Pradhan Nagar; d from ₹800; ﹡) Don't judge this place by its vivacious sense of aesthetics. The rooms are clean and comfortable, and the bathrooms are a definite winner for this price range. You'll find it on a narrow lane near Pradhan Nagar police station.

Hotel Rajdarbar
HOTEL **$$**

(☑0353-2511189; www.hotelrajdarbarsiliguri.com; Hill Cart Rd; s/d incl breakfast ₹1900/2100; ﹡🛜) A fresher and better-run option than its popular neighbour, the Hotel Conclave, this place has tidy and well-maintained rooms, a good restaurant and lobby wi-fi. It offers excellent value for money overall, and the free breakfast is quite sumptuous.

Hotel Sinclairs
HOTEL **$$$**

(☑0353-2512675; www.sinclairshotels.com; off NH31; s/d incl breakfast from ₹5300/5600; ﹡🛜🏊) This comfortable three-star hotel, 1km north of the bus terminal, offers an escape from the noise of Hill Cart Rd. It's one of Siliguri's longest-standing luxury addresses, and offers comfortable and spacious carpeted rooms with good bathrooms and dedicated room service. There's an excellent patio restaurant-bar and a cool clean pool.

✖ Eating

★ **Khana Khazana** MULTICUISINE $$
(Hill Cart Rd; mains ₹120-180; ⊗noon-10pm) On a side alley off the busy main highway, the secluded outdoor garden here offers merciful relief from the chaos outside. The extensive menu ranges from Chinese and South Indian specials to Mumbai street snacks. There are plenty of hearty vegetarian options.

Amber INDIAN $$
(Hill Cart Rd; mains ₹120-250; ⊗noon-10pm) This trusted eating address attached to Hotel Saluja Residency serves mouth-watering dishes including fluffy naans, lip-smacking curries, tender meat dishes and subtly flavoured biryanis that go down extremely well with the city's food lovers. Evenings are an especially buzzy time to be here.

Sartaj INDIAN $$
(Hill Cart Rd; mains ₹120-220; ⊗noon-10pm) In a cluster of similar bar-cum-restaurant operations, this sophisticated eatery boasts a huge range of first-rate North Indian tandooris and curries, some decent Continental options and top-notch service, including a fantastic uniformed doorman. It's also a good place for a cold beer.

ℹ Information

Krishna Travels (Hill Cart Rd; per hour ₹40; ⊗9am-8pm) Internet access down a side street across from Hotel Conclave.

MEDICAL SERVICES

Sadar Hospital (☏0353-2436526; Hospital Rd) Siliguri's main state-run hospital with emergency and outpatient services.

MONEY

Bagdogra Airport has a money changer with decent rates.

Delhi Hotel (Hill Cart Rd; ⊗8am-8pm) Currency and travellers cheques exchanged, opposite the bus station. A ₹50 tax is levied per transaction.

TOURIST INFORMATION

Sikkim Tourist Office (☏0353-2512646; Hill Cart Rd, SNT Terminal; ⊗10am-4pm Mon-Sat) Issues permits for Sikkim on the spot. Bring copies of your passport, visa and one passport-sized photo.

West Bengal Tourist Office (☏bookings 0353-2517561, information 0353-2511974; www.wbtdc.gov.in; Hill Cart Rd; ⊗10.30am-5.30pm Mon-Fri, to 1.30pm Sat) Can book accommodation and tours for Jaldhapara Wildlife Sanctuary, including forestry lodges.

TRAVEL AGENCIES

Private transport booking agencies line Hill Cart Rd.

Help Tourism (☏0353-2535896; www.help tourism.com; 143 Hill Cart Rd) A recommended agency with a strong environmental and community-development focus, including voluntourism. It has links to dozens of homestays and lodges around the hills, including a historic tea estate at Damdin and the stylish Neora Valley Jungle Camp outside Lava.

ℹ Getting There & Away

AIR

Bagdogra Airport is 12km west of Siliguri. There are daily flights to Delhi, Kolkata and Guwahati. Fares vary widely; online deals are often the best.

Five-seater helicopters (₹3500, 30 minutes, 10kg luggage limit) travel daily from Bagdogra to Gangtok at 2.30pm in good weather. You need to book in advance through Sikkim Tourism Development Corporation (p546) in Gangtok; there's also a booking counter at the airport for spot bookings.

BUS

Most North Bengal State Transport Corporation (NBSTC) buses leave from **Tenzing Norgay Central Bus Terminal** (Hill Cart Rd), as do many private buses plying the same routes. Private long-distance bus companies line the entrance.

NBSTC buses include frequent buses to Malda (₹150, 6½ hours), plus six daily services to Kolkata (₹390 to ₹430, AC ₹770). Assam State Transportation Corporation runs a daily 4pm bus to Guwahati (₹490, 15 hours).

For a 6pm Patna departure (₹260, 12 hours) try **Gupta Travels** (☏0353-2513451; Hill Cart Rd), just outside the bus station. Deluxe Volvo buses for Kolkata (₹1320, 11 hours) leave around 7pm from this and many other agencies.

Sikkim Nationalised Transport (SNT) buses to Gangtok (₹160, 4½ hours) leave at 7.30am, 11.30am, 12.30pm and 1.30pm from the **SNT terminal** (Hill Cart Rd), 250m southeast of the bus terminal. Arrange your permit in advance at the Sikkim Tourist Office next door.

JEEP

An efficient and relatively comfortable way of getting around the hills is by share jeep. There are a number of jeep stands lining Hill Cart Rd: for Darjeeling (₹150, three hours) and Kurseong (₹80, 1½ hours) look around opposite the bus

WEST BENGAL & DARJEELING SILIGURI & NEW JALPAIGURI

> ### ⓘ TOY TRAIN WOES
>
> The toy train continues to remain suspended from Siliguri, due to damaged tracks near Tindharia. For the next few years, the only option will be to drive to Kurseong and then catch the toy train on to Darjeeling.

terminal or outside the Conclave Hotel until late afternoon; for Kalimpong (₹120, 2½ hours) head to the Panitanki Mall stand on Sevoke Rd (take an autoricksaw for ₹20); and for Gangtok (₹200, four hours) jeeps leave from next to the SNT terminal until around 4pm. Share and charter jeeps for all these destinations also leave from NJP train station. Mirik-bound jeeps (₹100, 2½ hours) leave most frequently from Siliguri train station, 200m southwest from the central bus terminal.

Chartering a jeep privately costs roughly 15 times that of a shared ticket. An option for XL-sized travellers is to pay for and occupy the front two or three seats next to the driver.

A prepaid taxi stand at Bagdogra Airport offers fixed fares to Darjeeling (₹2200), Gangtok (₹2400), Kakarbhitta (₹600) and even Bhadrapur in Nepal (₹1200), allowing you to bypass Siliguri completely. It's not difficult to hook up with other airline passengers to share the cost.

TRAIN

Buy tickets at Siliguri Junction station or at the **train booking office** (☑ 0353-2537333; cnr Hospital & Bidhan Rds; ☺ 8-11am, 11.30am-2pm & 2.15-8pm Mon-Sat, to 2pm Sun), 1.5km southeast of the Hotel Conclave.

The 8pm 12344 Darjeeling Mail is the fastest of the many daily services to Kolkata (sleeper/3AC ₹350/910, 10 hours), via Malda. For Delhi, the 1.15pm 12435 Rajdhani Express is your best and quickest bet (3AC/2AC ₹2155/2960, 21 hours). Alternatively, board the 5.15pm 12505 North East Express (sleeper/3AC ₹610/1600, 26 hours), via Patna (sleeper/3AC ₹305/780, 10 hours). For Guwahati, board the 8.35am 12506 North East Express going in the other direction (sleeper/3AC ₹275/705, eight hours).

ⓘ Getting Around

From the bus terminal to NJP train station a taxi/autorickshaw costs ₹200/100. Taxis/autorickshaws between Bagdogra Airport and Siliguri cost ₹400/250.

Jaldhapara Wildlife Sanctuary

☑ 03563 / ELEV 60M

The little-visited **Jaldhapara Wildlife Sanctuary** (☑ 03563-262239; www.jaldapara.in; Indian/foreigner ₹50/200, camera/video ₹50/500; ☺ mid-Sep–mid-Jun) protects 114 sq km of lush forests and grasslands along the Torsa River and is a refuge for 150 Indian one-horned rhinoceros (*Rhinoceros unicornis*).

The best time to visit is mid-November to April, with March and April being the best months for wildlife spotting. Your best chance of spotting a rhino is on an **elephant ride** (☑ 03563-262230; Indian/foreigner per hour ₹200/600; ☺ 5-8am), though these lumbering safaris are often booked out by the tourist lodges. Even if you are staying at Jaldhapara Tourist Lodge for a night you are not guaranteed a ride, as full occupancy is double that of their daily elephant quota. Weekdays offer the best chance, since local tourist footfall is almost nil.

Jeep safaris (☑ 03563-262230; 4/8 passengers ₹2000/2400) operate in the early morning and afternoon and stop at viewing platforms, but these can be hard to arrange unless you are on a tour.

The West Bengal tourist offices in Kolkata and Siliguri organise weekend **tours** (☑ 033-22488271; www.wbtdc.gov.in; Indian/foreigner ₹4300/5225; ☺ departs 10am Sat, returns 5pm Sun) from Siliguri to Jaldhapara, which include an elephant ride, transport, accommodation at the Hollong Tourist Lodge and all meals.

Mithun of Wild Planet Travel Desk (☑ 9735028733; easthimalayan3@yahoo.com) and Hotel Relax can often book accommodation and elephant rides when no one else can and is probably your best option for a DIY trip. Budget travellers should bear in mind that an hour-long elephant ride will cost at least US$50 per person, after all costs are added in.

Bring mosquito repellent.

🛏 Sleeping & Eating

The two lodges should be booked well in advance through the West Bengal Tourist Office in Siliguri (p497), Darjeeling (☑ 0354-2254102; www.wbtdc.gov.in; Chowrasta; ☺ 10am-5pm Mon-Fri) or Kolkata (p484), or online at www.westbengaltourism.gov.in.

Hotel Relax   HOTEL $

(☑ 9641796512; Madarihat; d ₹600) The Relax is the best private budget option, opposite the Jaldhapara Tourist Lodge, with simple yet well-kept doubles that lack air-conditioning but come with hot-water bathrooms. Tasty and wholesome meals are available in-house (veg/fish/chicken ₹50/90/130).

Hollong Tourist Lodge   LODGE $$

(☑ 03563-262228; d ₹2200) This charming, green-coloured wooden lodge right in the heart of the park is easily the best place to stay, though booking one of the six rooms can be a real challenge. You can spot animals right from the verandah and you are guaranteed a morning elephant ride. Book up to three months in advance.

The lodge doesn't take direct bookings, bookings are made via West Bengal Tourist Office (p484).

Jaldhapara Tourist Lodge   HOTEL $$

(☑ 9733008795; Madarihat; d from ₹1800; ✲) This functional but spiffy WBTDC (West Bengal Tourism Development Corporation) hotel is just outside the park in Madarihat town. It has rooms in wooden and concrete blocks or in new cottages. Weekends can be a bad time to check in, as the place is swamped with noisy local families and youth groups.

The lodge doesn't take direct bookings, bookings are made via West Bengal Tourist Office (p484).

ℹ Getting There & Away

Jaldhapara is 124km east of Siliguri. Local buses run frequently from Siliguri to Madarihat (₹80, four hours) between 11.40am and 4.30pm. There are also slow but scenic mail trains (unreserved seat ₹40 to ₹65, three to four hours), leaving Siliguri Junction at 8.20am, 5.10pm and 6pm, returning from Madarihat at 6.05am, 7.50am and 1.30pm.

From Madarihat, it's a 7km trip to the park headquarters. A return taxi costs ₹600, including waiting time, plus you'll also have to pay the ₹200 vehicle entry fee.

Kurseong

☑ 0354 / POP 40,100 / ELEV 1460M

Kurseong, 32km south of Darjeeling, is a tiny and bustling hill town best known for its formidable league of tea estates and a rush of Raj-era boarding schools that dot its extents. Its name derives from the Lepcha

BORDER CROSSING – BANGLADESH, BHUTAN & NEPAL

To/From Bangladesh

A number of private agencies in Siliguri, including **Shyamoli** (☑ 9932628243; Hill Cart Rd, 1km northwest of the central bus station, Hotel Central Plaza complex, Mallagauri More), run daily AC buses direct to Dhaka (₹1200, 18 hours), departing at 1.30pm. You'll need to complete border formalities at Chengrabandha. Book a day or two in advance.

Buses also run every 45 minutes from the Tenzing Norgay Central Bus Terminal to Chengrabandha (₹80, 2½ hours) between 7am and 6pm. The border post is open from 8am to 6pm daily. From near the border post you can catch buses on to Rangpur, Bogra and Dhaka. Visas for Bangladesh can be obtained in Kolkata and New Delhi.

To/From Bhutan

Bhutan Transport Services runs two daily buses from Sevoke Rd, Siliguri to Phuentsholing (₹90, departs 7.15am and noon), and there are many more local buses to Jaigon on the Indian side of the border, where you clear Indian immigration. Non-Indian nationals need visa clearance from a Bhutanese tour operator to enter Bhutan.

To/From Nepal

For Nepal, local buses pass the Tenzing Norgay Central Bus Terminal on Hill Cart Rd in Siliguri every 30 minutes for the border town of Panitanki (₹30, one hour). Nearby shared jeeps to Kakarbhitta (₹80 to ₹100) are faster but only leave when full. The Indian border post in Panitanki is officially open 24 hours but the Nepali post in Kakarbhitta is open from 7am to 7pm. Onward from Kakarbhitta there are numerous buses to Kathmandu (17 hours) and other destinations. Bhadrapur Airport, 23km southwest of Kakarbhitta, has regular flights to Kathmandu on **Buddha Air** (www.buddhaair.com). Visas for Nepal can be obtained at the border (bring two passport photos).

word *khorsang*, a reference to the small white orchid prolific in this area. Flanked by hilly slopes draped with manicured tea estates, it is also currently the southern terminus for the charming toy trains of the Darjeeling Himalayan Railway.

Hill Cart Rd (Tenzing Norgay Rd) – the noisy, traffic-choked main thoroughfare from Siliguri to Darjeeling – and its remarkably close shadow, the railway line, wind through town.

There are numerous good walks in the area. Eagle's Crag (2km return) affords splendid views down the Teesta Valley and the steamy plains to the south. St Mary's Hill (4km) takes you past atmospheric grottos and churches into charming pine forests that lead all the way up to a spectacular mountain ridge.

◉ Sights & Activities

Makaibari
TEA ESTATE
(📞9733004577; www.makaibari.com; Pankhabari Rd; ⏲Tue-Sat) **FREE** If you like tea you should visit this organic and biodynamic tea estate; the factory is open to visitors. In-between the huge sorting and drying machines, and the fields of green bushes you may run into the owner, tea guru and local character Rajah Banerjee. Mornings are the best time to see the production process. Visits are free, or you can opt for a program of tea plucking, tasting and lunch in a local homestay for ₹300.

The estate is 3km below Kurseong along Pankhabari Rd, and 1km below Cochrane Pl. A taxi here costs ₹200, or it's a pleasant downhill walk (it's much steeper coming back so take a ₹20 shared taxi from Cochrane Pl). En route, the lush, overgrown old graveyard at St Andrew's has poignant reminders of the tea-planter era.

Makaibari runs a pioneering homestay and volunteer program from a separate office 50m below the main entrance. Volunteers can find placements in teaching, health and community projects.

🛏 Sleeping & Eating

Makaibari Homestays
HOMESTAY $$
(📞033-22878560; Makaibari Tea Estate; per person incl full board US$25) This pioneering program aims to harness tourism to empower local women tea pickers. There are 21 family houses currently involved in the project, and more are planned in a new environmentally

sustainable village below. Houses are simple but comfortable and families speak basic English. Activities on offer include tea picking and birdwatching trips.

Kurseong Tourist Lodge
HOTEL $$
(📞0354-2345608; Hill Cart Rd; d from ₹1700) This old-fashioned, government-run lodge has inviting wood-lined rooms with valley views. The toy train whistles past the popular cafe, where you can snack on *momos* (Tibetan dumplings). The **restaurant** (mains ₹80 to ₹140), on the other hand, serves up good Indian treats for lunch and dinner. It's a 10-minute walk out of town along the main road towards Darjeeling.

★ Cochrane Place
BOUTIQUE HOTEL $$$
(📞9932035660, 0354-2330703; www.imperial chai.com; 132 Pankhabari Rd; s/d incl breakfast from ₹2700/3400; @) With 360-degree plantation views and the twinkling lights of Siliguri below, this charming getaway offers oodles of quaintness in the form of period furniture and antique artefacts in its bright and airy pastel-shaded rooms. There's a delicious mix of Anglo-Indian, Continental and Indian food on offer, and a fine selection of Darjeeling teas at Chai Country, the in-house cafe.

The hotel is wheelchair-friendly and can provide Bagdogra Airport and NJP train station pick-ups. It's worth taking an extra day to enjoy an excellent guided village and tea-estate walk, topped off by a local-style stick massage (working on pressure points with a set of sticks) or an expert tea-tasting session.

❶ Getting There & Away

Numerous share jeeps run to Darjeeling (₹60, 1½ hours) and Siliguri (₹60, 1½ hours), with 8am departures for Kalimpong (₹130, 3½ to four hours) and Mirik (₹70, 2½ hours).

The Darjeeling Himalayan Railway's toy train to Darjeeling (1st/2nd class ₹160/27, three hours) leaves at 7am and 3pm and takes twice as long as a shared jeep.

Darjeeling

📞0354 / POP 120,400 / ELEV 2135M

Spread in ribbons over a steep mountain ridge, surrounded by emerald-green tea plantations and towered over by the majestic Khangchendzonga (8598m), Darjeeling is the definitive Indian hill station. Dating back to the Raj era, it's arguably West Bengal's premier attraction, and promises some interesting exploration for the curious traveller. When you aren't gazing open-mouthed at Khangchendzonga, you can explore colonial-era architecture, visit Buddhist monasteries, and spot snow leopards and red pandas at the nearby zoo. On the steep and bustling streets winding through town, you can lose yourself amid an array of Himalayan faces from Sikkim, Bhutan, Nepal and Tibet. And finally, when energies start to flag, a good, steaming Darjeeling brew is never far away.

Most tourists visit Darjeeling in autumn (October and November) and spring (mid-March to mid-May) when skies are dry, panoramas are clear and temperatures are pleasant. Winters can be cold here, so bring an extra jumper if visiting from December to February. The rainy months (June to September) can be extremely wet and are best avoided.

Darjeeling sprawls over a west-facing slope in a confusing web of interconnecting roads and steep flights of steps. Expect an uphill hike to your hotel if arriving at the train station or jeep stand. The two main squares – Chowrasta, near the top of town, and Clubside junction – are linked by pedestrianised Nehru Rd (aka the Mall), which doubles as the main shopping street. Hill Cart Rd (aka Tenzing Norgay Rd) runs the length of the bustling lower bazaar and is Darjeeling's major vehicle thoroughfare.

History

Darjeeling originally belonged to the Buddhist chogyals (kings) of Sikkim until 1780, when it was annexed by invading Gurkhas from Nepal. The East India Company gained control of the region in 1816, but soon returned most of the lands to Sikkim in exchange for British control over any future border disputes.

During one such dispute in 1828, two British officers stumbled across the Dorje Ling monastery, on a tranquil forested ridge, and passed word to Kolkata (Calcutta) that it would be a perfect site for a sanatorium (they were sure to have also mentioned its strategic military importance in the region). The chogyal of Sikkim (still grateful for the return of his kingdom) agreed to lease the uninhabited land to the East India Company for the annual fee of £3000. In 1835, the hill station of Darjeeling was born and the first tea bushes were planted. By 1857, the population of Darjeeling had reached 10,000,

mainly because of a massive influx of Gurkha tea labourers from Nepal.

Since Independence, the Gurkhas have become the main political force in Darjeeling. Friction with the state government led to calls for a separate state of Gorkhaland in the 1980s. In 1986, violence and riots orchestrated by the Gorkha National Liberation Front (GNLF) brought Darjeeling to a standstill. As a result, the Darjeeling Gorkha Hill Council (DGHC) was given a large measure of autonomy from the state government. Calls for full secession have resurfaced in recent years, leading to the replacement in 2012 of the DGHC by the Gorkhaland Territorial Administration (GTA). The political situation is now calm.

◉ Sights

Tiger Hill   VIEWPOINT
To watch the dawn light break over a spectacular 250km stretch of Himalayan horizon, including Everest (8848m), Lhotse (8501m) and Makalu (8475m) to the far west, rise early and jeep out to Tiger Hill (2590m), 11km south of Darjeeling, above Ghum. The skyline is dominated by Khangchendzonga (great five-peaked snow fortress), India's highest peak and the world's third-highest. On either side of the main massif are Kabru (7338m), Jannu (7710m) and Pandim (6691m), all serious peaks in their own right.

This daily morning spectacle (views are best in autumn and spring) is a major tourist attraction, and you'll find hundreds of jeeps leaving Darjeeling for Tiger Hill every morning at 4am – traffic snarls en route are quite common. At the summit you can either pay ₹10 to stand in the pavilion grounds or warm up in one of the heated lounges in the pavilion (₹20 to ₹40). It can be a real bunfight here, so we suggest you simply find yourself a ringside spot in the open courtyard in front of the pavilion, from where the views are equally grand.

Organised sunrise trips (usually with a detour to Batasia Loop on the way back) can be booked through a travel agency or directly with jeep drivers at the Clubside taxi stand. Return trips cost ₹1200 per vehicle.

Observatory Hill   SACRED SITE
Sacred to both Buddhists and Hindus, this hill was the site of the original Dorje Ling monastery that gave the town its name. Today, devotees come to a temple in a small cave to honour Mahakala, a Buddhist protector deity also worshipped in Hinduism as

WEST BENGAL & DARJEELING DARJEELING

Darjeeling

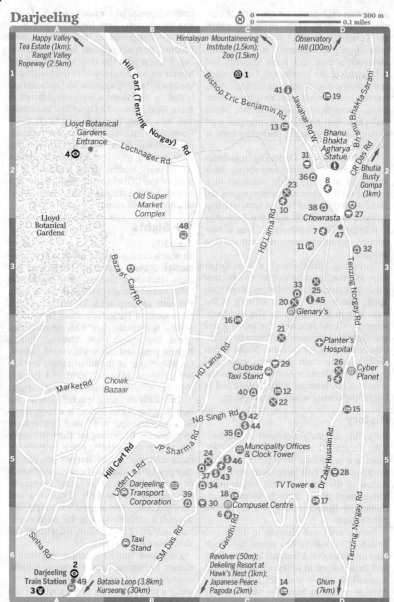

Happy Valley
Tea Estate (1km);
Rangit Valley
Ropeway (2.5km)

Himalayan Mountaineering
Institute (1.5km);
Zoo (1.5km)

Observatory
Hill (100m)

Hill Cart (Tenzing Norgay) Rd

Bishop Eric Benjamin Rd

Lloyd Botanical
Gardens
Entrance

Lochnager Rd

Bhanu Bhakta Sarani

Jawahar Rd W

CR Das Rd

Bhanu
Bhakta
Agharya
Statue

Bhutia
Busty
Gompa
(1km)

Lloyd
Botanical
Gardens

Old Super
Market
Complex

HD Lama Rd

Chowrasta

Bazaar Cart Rd

Tenzing Norgay Rd

Chowk
Bazaar

HD Lama Rd

Planter's
Hospital

Clubside
Taxi Stand

Cyber
Planet

Market Rd

NB Singh Rd

JP Sharma Rd

Muncipality Offices
& Clock Tower

Hill Cart Rd

Laden La Rd

Darjeeling
Transport
Corporation

TV Tower

Dr Zakir Hussain Rd

Compuset Centre

Sinha Rd

Taxi
Stand

SM Das Rd

Gandhi Rd

Revolver (50m);
Dekeling Resort at
Hawk's Nest (1km);
Japanese Peace
Pagoda (2km)

Ghum
(7km)

Darjeeling
Train Station

Batasia Loop (3.8km);
Kurseong (30km)

a wrathful avatar of Shiva the destroyer. The
summit is marked by several shrines, a flurry of colourful prayer flags and the ringing
notes from numerous devotional bells.

A path leading up to the hill through
giant Japanese cedars starts about 300m

along Bhanu Bhakta Sarani from Chowrasta; watch out for marauding monkeys. Dis-
appointingly, there are no mountain views,
but the still, pine-scented ambience is worth
taking in.

Darjeeling

Bhutia Busty Gompa MONASTERY
This temple originally stood on Observatory
Hill, but was rebuilt in its present location
by the chogyals of Sikkim in the 19th centu-
ry. It houses fine murals depicting the life of
Buddha, with Khangchendzonga providing
a spectacular backdrop. To get here, follow
CR Das Rd downhill for five minutes from
Chowrasta Sq, past a trinity of Buddhist
rock carvings.

Japanese Peace Pagoda BUDDHIST TEMPLE
(⊙puja 4.30-6am & 4.30-6.30pm) Perched on
a hillside at the end of AJC Bose Rd, this
gleaming white pagoda is one of more than
70 pagodas built around the world by the
Japanese Buddhist Nipponzan Myohoji
organisation. During the drumming *puja*
(prayer) sessions, visitors are offered a hand

drum and encouraged to join in the rituals. Getting here involves a pleasant, gentle 30-minute walk from Clubside junction
along Gandhi and AJC Bose Rds, past the
curiously named Institute of Astroparticle
Physics and Space Science.

**Padmaja Naidu Himalayan
Zoological Park** ZOO
(☑0354-2254250; www.pnhzp.gov.in; admission
incl Himalayan Mountaineering Institute Indian/
foreigner ₹40/100, camera/video ₹10/25;
⊙8.30am-4.30pm Fri-Wed, ticket counter closes
4pm) This zoo, one of India's best, was established in 1958 to study, conserve and preserve Himalayan fauna. Housed within its
rocky and forested environment are species
such as Himalayan bears, clouded leopards,
red pandas and Tibetan wolves. The zoo,

and its attached snow leopard–breeding centre (closed to the public), are home to the world's largest single captive population of snow leopards. The zoo is a pleasant 20-minute downhill walk from Chowrasta along Jawahar Rd West.

Alternatively, take a share jeep (₹20, about 10 minutes) from Chowk Bazaar bus/jeep station, or hire a taxi (₹250).

Himalayan Mountaineering Institute MUSEUM
(HMI; ☏0354-2254087; www.hmi-darjeeling.com; admission incl zoo Indian/foreigner ₹40/100, museum Indian/foreigner ₹20/50; ⊗8.30am-4.30pm Fri-Wed) Tucked away within the grounds of the zoo, this prestigious mountaineering institute was founded in 1954 and has provided training for some of India's leading mountaineers. Within the complex is the fascinating **Mountaineering Museum**. It houses sundry details and memorabilia from the 1922 and 1924 Everest expeditions, which set off from Darjeeling, as well as more recent summit attempts. While browsing the displays, look for the Carl Zeiss telescope presented by Adolf Hitler to the head of the Nepali Army.

Just beside the museum, near the spot where Tenzing Norgay was cremated, stands the **Tenzing Statue**. The intrepid Everest summiteer lived in Darjeeling for most of his life and was the director of the institute for many years.

The HMI runs 28-day basic and advanced **mountaineering courses** (HMI; ☏0354-2254087; www.hmi-darjeeling.com; Indian/foreigner ₹4000/US$650) from March to May and September to December. These courses are oriented to teach candidates a broad range of skills required for high-altitude climbing. Foreigners should apply at least three months in advance. There are also a number of 15-day adventure courses for those aged between 14 and 40. These courses combine a range of adventure activities such as trekking, camping, rock climbing and water sports.

Rangit Valley Ropeway CABLE CAR
(return-ticket adult/child ₹150/75; ⊗10am-2pm, closed 19th of every month) This scenic ropeway reopened in 2012, after a fatal accident halted operations in 2003. The 40-minute ride takes you from North Point down to the Takvar Valley tea estate, gliding over manicured tea bushes that look like giant broccoli growing on mountain slopes. Get here early if you want to explore the village and tea plantation.

Tibetan Refugee Self-Help Centre CRAFT WORKSHOP
(Lebong Cart Rd; ⊗9am-4.30pm Mon-Sat) Established in 1959, this refugee centre comprises a home for the aged, a school, an orphanage, a clinic, a gompa (Tibetan Buddhist monastery) and craft workshops that produce carpets, woodcarvings, leather work and woollen items. There's also an interesting, politically charged **photographic exhibition** portraying the early years of the Tibetan refugees in Darjeeling. Visitors are welcome to wander through the workshops. The handicrafts are for sale in the **showroom** and proceeds go straight back into the Tibetan community.

The quickest way to reach the centre is to walk steeply downhill from the north side of Bhanu Bhakta Sarani; take the alley down beside Hotel Dolphin. To return to Chowrasta Sq, take a side path 10 minutes to the Bhutia Busty Gompa and climb back uphill from there. A chartered taxi via North Point costs around ₹400/600 one way/return.

Happy Valley Tea Estate TEA ESTATE
(Pamphawati Gurungni Rd; ⊗8am-4pm Tue-Sun) FREE This 1854 tea estate below Hill Cart Rd is worth visiting, especially when the plucking and processing are in progress (March to November). An employee will guide you through the aromatic factory and its withering, rolling, fermenting and drying processes, explaining how green, black and white teas all come from the same leaf. Take the marked turn-off about 1km northwest of town on Hill Cart Rd.

Lloyd Botanical Gardens GARDENS
(☏0354-2252358; ⊗8am-4.30pm) FREE These pleasant gardens contain an impressive collection of Himalayan plants, most famously orchids and rhododendrons. Follow the signs along Lochnager Rd from the Chowk Bazaar bus and jeep station, until the hum of cicadas replaces the honking of jeeps at the main entrance. A map is posted at the office at the top of the park.

Batasia Loop MONUMENT
(admission ₹10) If you're travelling on the toy train, or walking back from Tiger Hill, look out for this famous railway loop that goes around the open-air **Gorkha War Memorial**, erected in honour of the brave soldiers from the region who laid down their lives in WWI

ℹ **SEEING THE SIGHTS IN DARJEELING**

Darjeeling's sights are quite spread out and road transport is a bit of a hassle. You'll make things easier by visiting certain sights together as clusters.

One excellent idea is to jump out of bed at 4am and take a jeep up to **Tiger Hill** in time for the spectacular sunrise over **Khangchendzonga**. After a regulation photo op with the mountain in the backdrop, continue down to Ghum and spend the morning/day visiting **Batasia Loop** and the monasteries there. Next drive, walk or take a **toy train** (p511) back to Darjeeling along the quiet Tenzing Norgay Rd, via the monastery of **Alu Bari** (1½ hours). Despite the lack of mountain views, this also makes a nice cycling route.

If you can't face a dawn trip to Tiger Hill, an early-morning stroll around **Bhanu Bhakta Sarani**, which runs from Chowrasta around the north side of Observatory Hill, offers several stunning viewpoints. Combine the stroll with a visit down to **Bhutia Busty Monastery** or up to **Observatory Hill**.

A good half-day itinerary is to walk out to the **zoo** and **Himalayan Mountaineering Institute**, then continue around the hill on the road above busy Hill Cart Rd to the **Rangit Valley Ropeway**. From here take a shared minivan from North Point back to Darjeeling, getting off at **Happy Valley Tea Estate**. Then walk the short-cut footpath to Chowk Bazaar jeep stand via **Lloyd's Botanical Garden**. Alternatively, walk 30 minutes from the ropeway along Lebong Cart Rd to the **Tibetan Refugee Self-Help Centre** and hike back steeply uphill to Chowrasta via Bhutia Busty Monastery.

---

and WWII. Some tours stop here after the sunrise trip to Tiger Hill. The views are almost as good and the atmosphere much more serene.

Ghum
MONASTERIES

The junction of Ghum, 7km southwest from Darjeeling, is home to a number of colourful Buddhist monasteries. **Yiga Choling Gompa**, the region's most famous monastery, has wonderful old murals and is home to some 30 monks of the Gelugpa school. Built in 1850, it enshrines a 5m-high statue of Jampa (Maitreya or 'Future Buddha') and 300 beautifully bound Tibetan texts. It's just west of Ghum, about a 10-minute walk off Hill Cart Rd.

Other gompas of interest nearby include the fortress-style **Guru Sakya Gompa**, which conducts prayer sessions between 5.30am and 7.30am (useful if returning from a dawn visit to Tiger Hill). The active **Samten Choling Gompa**, just downhill, has the largest Buddha statue in West Bengal, a memorial chorten dedicated to German mystic Lama Govinda and a small cafe selling piping hot veg *momos* (₹20). All three gompas are within 10 minutes' walk of each other on Hill Cart Rd.

About halfway between Ghum and Darjeeling is the huge **Druk Sangak Choling Gompa**, also known as Dali Gompa, inaugurated by the Dalai Lama in 1993. Known for its vibrant frescoes, it is home to 300 Himalayan monks who study philosophy, literature, astronomy, meditation, dance and music. Come for prayers between 4pm and 6pm.

You can get to Ghum from Darjeeling by toy train (₹30), shared taxi (₹30) or chartered taxi (₹300 one way).

Bengal Natural History Museum
MUSEUM

(Bishop Eric Benjamin Rd; adult ₹10; ⊙9am-4.30pm) Established in 1903, this minor sight houses a moth-eaten collection of Himalayan and Bengali species, hidden away in a compound just off Bishop Eric Benjamin Rd. The giant leeches and horrific baby animals pickled in jars are guaranteed to provoke a shudder.

Dhirdham Mandir
HINDU TEMPLE

Darjeeling's most conspicuous Hindu temple is a replica of the famous Pashupatinath Temple in Kathmandu. It's easy to find – just below the Darjeeling train station. There's a good view over Darjeeling from its grounds.

Activities

Pony Rides
HORSE RIDING

From Chowrasta, children can take a ride around Observatory Hill for ₹200, or through tea estates to visit a monastery for ₹500 per hour. A horseman accompanies the horse at all times, and the activity is fairly safe. No riding helmets are provided though.

Courses

Manjushree Centre of Tibetan Culture LANGUAGE

(☑0354-2252977; www.manjushree-culture.org; 12 Gandhi Rd; 3-/6-/9-month courses US$230/340/450, plus registration US$30; ⊙mid-Mar–mid-Dec) Beginner and advanced lessons in written and spoken Tibetan are offered at this Tibetan cultural centre, with beginner courses starting every two months. Students can lodge with local Tibetan families.

☞ Tours

The GTA Tourist Reception Centre (p510), taxi stands and travel agencies offer a variety of tours around Darjeeling, usually including the zoo, Himalayan Mountaineering Institute, Tibetan Refugee Self-Help Centre and several scenic viewpoints. Taxis can be hired for custom tours for ₹1000 per half-day.

🛏 Sleeping

Darjeeling has a large selection of hotels. The main backpacker enclave is Dr Zakir Hussain Rd, which follows the highest ridge in Darjeeling, so be prepared for a hike to the best budget places.

Prices given are for the high season (October to early December and mid-March to mid-May), when it's wise to book ahead. In the low season prices can drop by 50%. A recently introduced rule requires foreigners to sometimes present a passport photo when checking in to a hotel, so carry some with you until this rule is withdrawn.

Hotel Tranquillity HOTEL $

(☑0354-2257678; hoteltranquillity@yahoo.co.in; Dr Zakir Hussain Rd; d/tr ₹700/800; ☎) This good-value place is sparkling clean, with 24-hour hot water, nice lobby seating and small but neat baby-blue rooms. The helpful owner is a local schoolteacher, and can provide all kinds of info about the area. Wi-fi costs ₹100 per day.

Hotel New Galaxy HOTEL $

(☑7583995457; Dr Zakir Hussain Rd; d from ₹800) This is a simple budget option, with wood-panelled walls, smallish rooms and hot-water buckets in the cheaper rooms. Try for room 104 – it has the best views across to the mountains. The property could do with a facelift, though, considering its innards currently feel a bit musty.

★ Dekeling Hotel GUESTHOUSE $$

(☑0354-2254159; www.dekeling.com; Gandhi Rd; d from ₹1650; @☎) Spotless Dekeling is full of charming touches such as coloured diamond-pane windows, a traditional *bukhari* (enclosed cylindrical wood-fired oven) in the cosy and sociable lounge-library, wood panelling and sloping-attic ceilings, plus superb views. Tibetan owners Sangay and Norbu play perfect hosts, and the whole place is a combination of clean and homey, right down to the adorable dog, Drolma.

★ Revolver BOUTIQUE HOTEL $$

(☑0354-2253711; www.revolver.in; 110 Gandhi Rd; d ₹1400; ☎) This Beatles-themed hotel is a must for fans. The five small but stylish rooms are each named after one of the Fab Four (plus Brian Epstein), so you can choose your favourite Moptop (John fills up first; Ringo brings up the rear). The hotel is chock-a-block with Beatles memorabilia, including Beatles movies on the in-house TV channel.

The downstairs restaurant serves good fresh-ground coffee (₹120) and interesting Naga set meals (₹180). It's certainly well thought-out, but there's a certain coldness to the hospitality that's dispensed by the proprietors. The entrance is easily missed behind the Union Church.

Hotel Aliment HOTEL $$

(☑0354-2255068; alimentweb98@gmail.com; 40 Dr Zakir Hussain Rd; s/d from ₹800/1600; @) A budget travellers' favourite, with a good top-floor restaurant (and cold beer), lending library, helpful owners and wood-lined rooms. The upstairs rooms (₹1800) have a TV and valley views. All the double rooms have geysers, but they only operate between 6pm and 8pm. The overall hostel-like ambience is a throwback to the classic backpacker era.

Hotel Seven Seventeen HOTEL $$

(☑0354-2255099; www.hotel717.com; 26 HD Lama Rd; s/d from ₹2200/2500; ☎) This friendly Tibetan-themed place on the edge of the bazaar has pleasant wood-skirted rooms with clean toilets. Some of the rooms have great views overlooking the valley. There's a good restaurant specialising in Tibetan, Chinese and Indian staples. The reception is a flight of steps below road level.

Bellevue Hotel HOTEL $$

(☑0354-2254075; www.bellevuehotel-darjeeling.com; d from ₹2000; @) This spacious gompa-style Tibetan complex has a variety of renovated wood-panelled rooms, most of which come with grass-mat floors and a *bukhari*. The affable staff, communal breakfast and lounge area, and location (not to mention the outlook over Chowrasta towards Khangchendzonga) all make this a popular choice. Don't confuse it with the Olde (Main) Bellevue Hotel up the road.

Tibet Home GUESTHOUSE **$$**
(☑0354-2252977; 12 Gandhi Rd; r ₹1900) Clean, bright and modern rooms make this a solid, central option, with profits going to the attached Manjushree Centre of Tibetan Culture. There are great views from the rooftop. It is often booked out by visiting Buddhist delegates and monks, so ask in advance.

★**Windamere Hotel** HERITAGE HOTEL **$$$**
(☑0354-2254041; www.windamerehotel.com; Jawahar Rd West; s/d incl full board from ₹10,500/13,500; @) This quaint, rambling relic of the Raj on Observatory Hill offers one of Darjeeling's most atmospheric digs. The charming colonial-era Ada Villa was once a boarding house for British tea planters, and the well-tended grounds are spacious with lots of pleasant seating areas. The comfort-able rooms, fireplaces and hot-water bottles offer just the right measures of comfort and mothballed charm.

It's a particularly great place to spend Christmas. At any time of the year, feel free to drop by for evening high tea (per person ₹450) and to sample the vintage charm of the place. Keep your eyes peeled for the Jan Morris poem in the tea room.

Elgin HERITAGE HOTEL **$$$**
(☑0354-2257226; www.elginhotels.com; HD Lama Rd; s/d incl half board ₹8800/9200; @⊚) Grand yet friendly and full of classy ambience, the Elgin is a modern and formal hotel. The restaurant is elegant, as is the great bar and small library. The cute garden terrace is the perfect place to nurse a beer (₹200) or high tea (₹400, 4pm to 6pm). The 'attic room' underneath the dripping eaves is charming.

Dekeling Resort at Hawk's Nest HERITAGE HOTEL **$$$**
(☑0354-2253298; www.dekeling.com; 2 AJC Bose Rd; d from ₹3800; ⊚) Run by the good people at Dekeling Hotel, this is a quiet, exclusive place, 1km outside of Darjeeling en route to the Japanese Pagoda. The four 130-year-old, colonial-style, two-room suites have antique

TEA TOURISM

Darjeeling's most famous export is its aromatic muscatel tea, known for its amber colour, tannic astringence and a musky and spicy flavour. These days, however, sundry other teas including green, oolong and premium white varieties are produced alongside the traditional black tea. Most of the produce is now organic, and the best grades fetch several hundred dollars per kilo at auctions.

While in Darjeeling, a pot of this fine brew is best enjoyed at Sunset Lounge (p509) and House of Tea (p509). The true-blue afternoon-tea experience at **Windamere Hotel** (₹450; ⊙4-6pm) is a joy for aficionados of all things colonial era, with shortcake, scones, cheese and pickle sandwiches, and brews from the reputed Castleton Tea Estate.

For a more absorbing and enlightening experience, we recommend a day visit to one of the tea estates that currently welcomes visitors. The easiest places to learn about tea production are Makaibari Estate (p500) in Kurseong and Happy Valley (p504) outside Darjeeling. Spring, monsoon and autumn are the busiest times, when the three respective 'flushes' are harvested. There's no plucking on Sunday, which means most of the machinery isn't working on Monday.

If you wish to spend a night amid the plantations, try a tea pickers' family at a **homestay** (☑033-22878560; Makaibari Tea Estate; per person incl full board US$25) at Makaibari Estate, where you'll get to join your hosts for a morning's work in the tea bushes. Pick your own leaves, watch them being processed and then return home with a batch of your very own hand-plucked Darjeeling tea. If you're in the mood for splurging, accommodation doesn't get any more exclusive than top-end **Glenburn** (☑9830070213; www.glenburnteaestate.com; Darjeeling; s/d incl full board ₹19,900/31,500), between Darjeeling and Kalimpong, a working tea estate/resort that boasts five members of staff for every guest. A stay at Glenburn is rumoured to have given director Wes Anderson inspiration for his film *The Darjeeling Limited*.

touches and fireplaces, and there's a nice sunny terrace. Five new mountain-facing superdeluxe rooms were recently added. It's a great escape from Darjeeling's increasingly noisy centre.

Mayfair Darjeeling HOTEL $$$
(☎0354-2256376; www.mayfairhotels.com; Jawahar Rd West; d incl half board from ₹12,100; 🛜) Originally a maharaja's summer palace but renovated within an inch of its life, this plush choice sits among manicured gardens and a bizarre collection of kitschy sculptures. The outside and common areas don't have quite the charm of the Elgin, but the plush rooms are well decorated and many have balconies.

Soft carpets and coal fires add to the warm welcome, the bar has fine sunset views and the cosy library has a choice of DVDs for a rainy day. The children's playroom makes it good for families.

🍴 Eating

Most restaurants close by 8pm or 9pm. Tax will add on 13.5% to most bills.

Sonam's Kitchen CONTINENTAL $
(142 Dr Zakir Hussain Rd; mains ₹80-120; ⊙8am-2.30pm & 5.30-8pm Mon-Sat, 8am-2pm Sun) Sonam's serves up real brewed coffee, authentic French toasts, fluffy pancakes, fresh soups (nettle in season) and yummy pasta, all within its tiny ration-store-like interior that seats barely a dozen people. The deliciously chunky wholemeal sandwiches can be packed to go for picnics.

Kunga TIBETAN $
(51 Gandhi Rd; mains ₹100-140) Kunga is a cosy wood-panelled place run by a friendly Tibetan family, which goes strong on noodles and *momos,* with excellent juice, fruit muesli curd and *shabhaley* (Tibetan pies). The clientele includes locals, which is a mark of its culinary authenticity. You'll find it next to Hotel Dekeling.

Dekeva's TIBETAN $
(51 Gandhi Rd; mains ₹80-120; ⊙11am-9pm) Next door to Kunga, this small place offers good servings of Tibetan butter tea, *tsampa* (roast barley flour), good Chinese dishes and a range of noodles for connoisseurs who can tell their *thanthuk* (Tibetan noodles) from their *sogthug* (also Tibetan noodles).

Hasty Tasty INDIAN $
(Nehru Rd; mains ₹60-140) There's nothing fancy at this vegetarian self-service canteen, but the open kitchen churns out great paneer *masala dosas* (curried vegetables inside a crisp pancake) and several types of veg set-meal options. It's a hit with domestic tourists, so expect some rush during mealtimes.

★**Glenary's** MULTICUISINE $$
(Nehru Rd; mains ₹150-250; ⊙noon-9pm; 🛜) This elegant restaurant sits atop the famous bakery and cafe of the same name. It receives rave reviews and it caters to diners round the clock. Of note are the yummy Continental sizzlers, Chinese dishes, tandoori specials and veg gratin. The wooden floors and linen tablecloths add to the classy atmosphere. Oh, and there's booze to go with it all. Also has **wi-fi** (per hour ₹30; ⊙10am-8pm).

Foodsteps MULTICUISINE $$
(19 Nehru Rd; mains ₹160-240; ⊙8.30am-9.30pm) There's a refreshing focus on healthy options at this upstairs place, with gluten-free baked goods and brown breads on the menu. The best options are the all-day breakfasts, particularly the waffles and pancakes, but there are also good grilled sandwiches and dinner thalis. Cookies and muffins are served with a Darjeeling brew as afternoon set teas.

Shangri-La CHINESE $$
(Nehru Rd; mains ₹120-180; ⊙noon-8pm) This classy and modern bar-restaurant near the top of the Mall specialises in local Chinese offerings, but the menu is fringed with a few Indian and Continental entries. The surrounds are stylish, with sleek wooden floors, clean tablecloths and roaring fires in winter. There are also a couple of stylish **hotel rooms** (d ₹3500) upstairs.

Lunar Restaurant INDIAN $$
(51 Gandhi Rd; mains ₹120-160; ⊙11am-9pm) This bright and clean space just below Hotel Dekeling is perhaps the best vegetarian Indian restaurant in town, with good service and great views from the large windows. The *masala dosas* come with yummy dried fruit and nuts. Access to this 1st-floor joint is via the same staircase as Hotel Dekeling.

Mamta Pizza Place ITALIAN $$
(HD Lama Rd; pizza ₹150-220; ⊙9am-8pm) An unlikely address (or name) for a pizzeria, this cramped but sociable one-table place tosses up excellent European-accented pizza, pasta, panini and salads. Come at break-

fast for such rarities as bacon, beef merguez sausage and Nepali cheese. Expect to wait about 20 minutes for a pizza.

Park Restaurant INDIAN, THAI **$$**
(📞0354-2255270; 41 Laden La Rd; mains ₹120-180; ⊙noon-9pm) The intimate Park is deservedly very popular for its tasty North Indian dhal preparations and curries (great chicken tikka masala) and surprisingly authentic Thai dishes, including the tasty *tom kha gai* (coconut chicken soup) and spicy green papaya salad. Grab a table early or make a reservation during lunch and dinner hours.

🍷 Drinking & Nightlife

Glenary's TEAHOUSE
(Nehru Rd; small pot ₹65, pastries ₹20-50; ⊙8am-8pm; 📶) This teahouse and bakery has massive windows and good views. Order your tea, select a cake, grab your book and sink into a cosy wicker. It's a good place to grab breakfast.

Café Coffee Day CAFE
(Chowrasta Sq; coffee from ₹60; ⊙10am-9pm) This reliable chain has locations at the Rink Mall and Chowrasta, the latter recommended for its fine sunny terrace that promises gorgeous mountain views.

House of Tea TEAHOUSE
(Nehru Rd; tea ₹50-80; ⊙10am-7pm) Sit and sip a range of brewed teas from several local Goodricke estates before purchasing a package of your favourite leaves.

Sunset Lounge TEAHOUSE
(Chowrasta Sq; cup of tea ₹50-150; ⊙9am-8pm; 📶) This tearoom run by Nathmull's Tea offers aficionados a range of white, green and black teas by the cup, with baked treats, fine valley views and free wi-fi.

Bars
The top-end hotels all have classy bars; the Windamere (p507) is the most atmospheric place to kick back with an early-evening G&T (₹300).

Joey's Pub PUB
(SM Das Rd; beer ₹150; ⊙6-10pm) If your preferred beverage comes in a pint not a pot, this long-standing British-style pub near the post office is a great place to strike conversations with other travellers. It has sports on TV, cold beer and hot toddies in the winter.

Gatty's Cafe BAR
(Dr Zakir Hussain Rd; ⊙11am-11pm; 📶) The backpacker-friendly Gatty's is the only place in town that has a pulse after 9pm, with live music on the weekend and open mic and movie nights during the week. The food includes housemade ravioli and decent breakfasts (mains ₹150 to ₹200), with Lavazza coffee and free wi-fi on the side.

🛍 Shopping

Nathmull's Tea Room TEA
(www.nathmulltea.com; Laden La Rd; ⊙10am-8pm Mon-Sat, daily Mar-May & Oct-Nov) Darjeeling produces some of the world's finest teas and Nathmull's is the best place to pick up some, with more than 50 varieties. Expect to pay ₹100 to ₹400 per 100g for a decent tea, and up to ₹2000 per 100g for the finest flushes. You can ask for a free tasting, and buy attractive teapots, strainers and cosies as souvenirs.

Tibetan Refugee Self-Help Centre CARPETS
(📞0354-2252552; www.tibetandarj.yolasite.com; carpet incl shipping from US$220) ✎ This centre makes gorgeous Tibetan carpets to order, if you don't mind waiting six months for one to be made. Choose from the catalogue and they'll ship the finished carpet to your home address. Good quality *thangkas* (Tibetan cloth paintings) are also available, but production was on hold in late 2014 due to the health of the only artist.

Hayden Hall HANDICRAFTS
(www.haydenhall.org; Laden La Rd; ⊙10am-6pm) ✎ Sells Tibetan-style yak wool carpets as part of its charitable work (₹6000 for a 1m by 1.8m carpet) and offers shipping. There are also good knitwear items (jumpers, caps, gloves, shrugs etc) and bags made by local women.

Bhutan Tibet Arts HANDICRAFTS
(Chowrasta Sq; ⊙11am-7pm) Has an impressive *thangka* collection, sourced from Bhutan and Nepal. Expect to pay around US$100 for a decent *thangka*, and up to US$600 for a rare vintage piece.

Dorjee Himalayan Artefacts HANDICRAFTS
(Laden La Rd; ⊙11am-7pm Mon-Sat) This tiny Aladdin's cave is crammed full of Himalayan knick-knacks, from Tibetan *gau* (amulets) to cast Buddhas and silver prayer wheels. A good collection of masks and *thangkas* are also on offer.

WEST BENGAL & DARJEELING DARJEELING

ⓘ BORDER CROSSING – NEPAL FROM DARJEELING

Foreigners can only cross the border into Nepal at Kakarbhitta/Panitanki (not at Pasupati, en route to Mirik).

Samsara Tours, Travels & Treks (can book day and night buses from Kakarbhitta to Kathmandu (₹1000 to ₹1200, departure 4am and 4pm), leaving you to hire a jeep to Kakarbhitta or catch a shared jeep to Siliguri and then Karkabhittha. Samsara can also book Nepali domestic flights from Bhadrapur to Kathmandu (US$130), which will save you the overnight bus trip.

Any tickets you see advertised from Darjeeling to Kathmandu are not direct buses and involve transfers in Siliguri and at the border – leaving plenty of room for problems – it's just as easy to do it yourself.

Life & Leaf Fair Trade Shop HANDICRAFTS (www.lifeandleaf.org; Chowrasta Sq; ⊙10am-7pm Mon-Sat) Supports local artisans and environmental projects through the sale of organic honey and tea sourced from local small farmers, plus jute bags and Assamese silk shrugs and scarves.

Oxford Book & Stationery Company BOOKS (Chowrasta Sq; ⊙10am-7.30pm Mon-Sat, daily Mar-May & Oct-Nov) The best bookshop in Darjeeling, selling a good selection of novels and Himalayan titles.

Das Studios PHOTOGRAPHY (Nehru Rd; ⊙10am-7pm Mon-Sat) Digital photo accessories, printing and instant passport photos (six for ₹50). The reprinted 19th-century photographs depicting local anthropological and natural history make for great souvenirs (₹400 to ₹800); ask to look at the catalogue.

The Rope OUTDOOR GEAR (NB Singh Rd; ⊙10am-7pm Mon-Sat) This shop stocks quality imported gear alongside decent Chinese knock-offs, including backpacks, stoves and trek boots. The fakes come at nearly half price; you get what you pay for.

ⓘ Information

EMERGENCY
Police Assistance Booth (Chowrasta Sq) A friendly neighbourhood cop is stationed here for quick assistance.
Sadar Police Station (☑0354-2254422; Market Rd) Prompt, friendly and helpful.

INTERNET ACCESS
There are dozens of internet cafes around town.
Compuset Centre (Gandhi Rd; per hour ₹30; ⊙8am-8pm; 🖥) Does printing and will burn photos to a CD/DVD, but doesn't offer Skype.
Cyber Planet (Dr Zakir Hussain Rd; per hour ₹30; ⊙8am-10pm) Opposite Sonam's Kitchen.

MEDICAL SERVICES
Planter's Hospital (D&DMA Nursing Home; ☑0354-2254327; Nehru Rd) The best private hospital in town.

MONEY
ICICI Bank ATM (Laden La Rd) Accepts most international bank and credit cards.
Poddar's (☑0354-2252841; Laden La Rd; ⊙9.30am-8pm) Better rates, longer hours and shorter queues than the State Bank next door. Changes most currencies and travellers cheques at no commission. It accepts credit cards and is a Western Union agent. It's inside a clothing store.
Ridhi Siddhi (Laden La Rd; ⊙9.30am-8.30pm) Changes cash at good rates with no commission.
State Bank of India (Laden La Rd; ⊙10am-2pm Mon-Fri, to noon Sat) Changes major foreign currencies plus US-dollar Amex travellers cheques, with a commission of ₹100 per transaction. It has an adjacent ATM, another in Chowrasta.

POST
Main post office (Laden La Rd; ⊙10am-4pm Mon-Fri, to 2pm Sat) For snail mail and parcel dispatches (bring your passport as identification for the latter).

TOURIST INFORMATION
GTA Tourist Reception Centre (☑0354-2255351; Silver Fir Bldg, Jawahar Rd West; ⊙10am-5pm Mon-Sat, 9am-1pm every 2nd & 4th Sat, 9am-1pm Sun Mar-May & Oct-Nov) The staff are friendly, well organised and the best source of information on Darjeeling.
Sikkim Tourist Office Darjeeling (☑9832438118; Nehru Rd; ⊙10am-4pm Mon-Sat) For an on-the-spot permit to visit Sikkim, bring a photocopy of your passport and Indian visa, plus one photo. It's opposite Glenary's in the Olde (Main) Bellevue Hotel annexe.

TRAVEL AGENCIES

Most travel agencies in town can arrange local tours.

Adventures Unlimited (9933070013; www.adventuresunlimited.in; Dr Zakir Hussain Rd; ⊙10am-8pm Mon-Sat) Offers treks (US$50 to US$60 per person per day), kayaking, motor paragliding, Enfield motorbike hire and mountain-bike trips.

Himalayan Travels (☑ 0354-2252254; 18 Gandhi Rd, Darjeeling) Experienced company arranging treks (US$60 to US$70 per person per day) and mountaineering expeditions in Darjeeling and Sikkim.

Off Road Adventure (☑ 9832054944; off_road@rediffmail.com; Chowrasta Sq; ⊙10am-7pm) This adventure outfit under the GTA Tourist Reception Centre can book itineraries woven around trekking, paragliding, birding, camping and rural tours.

Samsara Tours, Travels & Treks (☑ 0354-2252874; www.samsaratourstravelsandtreks.com; Laden La Rd) This agency can book 'luxury' air-con buses from Siliguri to Kolkata (₹1000 to ₹1500, 12 hours) and ordinary night buses to Guwahati (₹600, 10 hours, 6pm) and Patna (₹450, 10 hours, 6pm). Note that these tickets don't include transfers to Siliguri.

Somewhere Over the Rainbow Treks & Tours (☑ 9832025739; kanadhi@yahoo.com; HD Lama Rd; ⊙8am-6pm, later in Mar-May & Oct-Nov) Organises off-the-beaten-track walks around Darjeeling, as well as rafting, rock climbing, cycling and trekking in Sikkim (including interesting routes from Uttarey). Treks start from US$60 per person per day, depending on group size.

❶ Getting There & Away

AIR

The nearest airport is 90km away at Bagdogra, about 12km from Siliguri. Allow four hours for the drive, to be safe.

Air India (☑ 0354-2254230; www.airindia.com; Chowrasta Sq; ⊙9.30am-1pm & 1.45-5.30pm Mon-Fri) Has flights to Kolkata and Delhi.

Pineridge Travels (☑ 0354-2253912; pineridge@mail.com; Nehru Rd; ⊙10am-5pm Mon-Sat) For domestic and international flight tickets.

BUS

Samsara Tours, Travels & Treks can book 'luxury' air-con buses from Siliguri to Kolkata (₹1000 to ₹1500, 12 hours) and ordinary night buses to

---

THE TOY TRAIN

The **Darjeeling Himalayan Railway**, known affectionately as the toy train, is one of the few hill railways still operating in India. The panting train made its first journey along its precipice-topping, 60cm-wide tracks in September 1881. These days, it passes within feet of local storefronts as it weaves in and out of the main road, bringing traffic to a standstill and tooting its whistle incessantly for almost the entire trip. The train has been a Unesco World Heritage Site since 1999.

Services on the line have been in flux since 2009, when landslides destroyed a section of the track near Tindharia village. Services to and from NJP station are not expected to resume at least until 2016, which leaves only two daily diesel services to/from Kurseong via Ghum:

TRAIN NO	DARJEELING	GHUM	KURSEONG
52544	10.15am	10.45am	1.10pm
52588	4.10pm	4.40pm	6.50pm

TRAIN NO	KURSEONG	GHUM	DARJEELING
52587	7am	9.10am	9.40am
52545	3pm	5.20pm	5.50pm

During high season (March to May and October to November) there are also joy rides (₹400) that leave Darjeeling at 8am, 10.40am, 1.20pm and 4.05pm for a two-hour steam-powered return trip. The service pauses for 10 minutes at the scenic Batasia Loop and then stops for 20 minutes in Ghum, India's highest railway station, to visit the small **railway museum** (admission ₹20; ⊙10am-1pm & 2-4pm). Enthusiasts can see the locomotives up close in the shed across the road from Darjeeling station.

Book at least a day or two ahead at the train station (p512) or online.

Guwahati (₹600, 10 hours) and Patna (₹550, 10 hours). These tickets don't include transfers to Siliguri.

JEEP & TAXI

Numerous share jeeps leave the crowded **Chowk Bazaar Bus & Jeep Station** (Old Super Market Complex) for Siliguri (₹150, three hours) and Kurseong (₹80, 1½ hours). Jeeps for Mirik (₹90, 2½ hours) leave from the northern end about every 1½ hours. A ticket office inside the ground floor of the Old Super Market Complex sells advance tickets for the frequent jeeps to Kalimpong (₹100, 2½ hours), while two roadside stands sell advance tickets for Gangtok (₹200, four hours). All jeeps depart between 7am and 3.30pm.

At the northern end of the station, three to four jeeps a day leave before noon for Jorethang (₹140, two hours) in Sikkim. You must already have a permit to enter Sikkim via this route.

To New Jalpaiguri or Bagdogra, get a connection in Siliguri, or charter a jeep or taxi from Darjeeling.

Darjeeling Transport Corporation (Laden La Rd) offers chartered jeeps to Gangtok (₹2200), Kalimpong (₹2200), Kurseong (₹1400), Kakarbhitta (₹2800) and Siliguri/Bagdogra Airport (₹2200/2400).

TRAIN

The nearest major train station is at New Jalpaiguri (NJP), near Siliguri. Tickets can be bought for major services out of NJP at the **Darjeeling Train Station** (☎ 0354-2252555; www.irctc.co.in; Hill Cart Rd; ☺ 8am-5pm Mon-Sat, to 2pm Sun). Fares from Darjeeling include Ghum (1st/2nd class ₹140/20, 30 minutes) and Kurseong (1st/2nd class ₹30/210, three hours).

🛈 Getting Around

There are several taxi stands around town, but rates are absurdly high for short hops. Darjeeling's streets can be steep and hard to navigate. You can hire a porter to carry your bags up to Chowrasta Sq from Chowk Bazaar for around ₹100.

Share minivans to anywhere north of the town centre (eg to North Point) leave from the northern end of the Chowk Bazaar Bus & Jeep Station. For Ghum, get a share jeep (₹20) from along Hill Cart Rd.

Singalila Ridge Trek

The most popular multiday walk from Darjeeling is the five-day Singalila Ridge Trek from Mane Bhanjhang to Phalut, through the scenic Singalila National Park (Indian/foreigner ₹100/200, camera/video ₹100/500). The highlights are the great views of the Himalayan chain stretching from Nepal to Sikkim and Bhutan. Sandakphu in particular offers a superb panorama that includes

Around Darjeeling

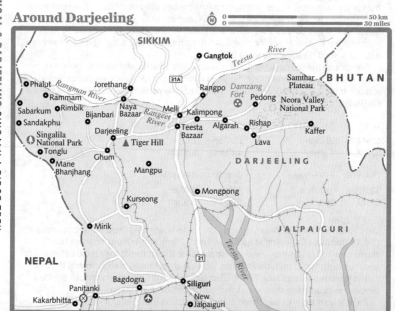

SINGALILA RIDGE TREK

DAY	ROUTE	DISTANCE
1	Mane Bhanjhang (2130m) to Tonglu (3070m)/Tumling (2980m) via Meghma Gompa	14km
2	Tonglu to Sandakphu (3636m) via Kalipokhari & Garibas	17km
3	Sandakphu to Phalut (3600m) via Sabarkum	17km
4	Phalut to Rammam (2530m) via Gorkhey	16km
5	Rammam to Rimbik (2290m) via Sri Khola	19km

Lhotse, Everest and Khangchendzonga peaks. October and November's clear skies and warm daytime temperatures make it an ideal time to trek, as do the long days and incredible rhododendron blooms of late April and May.

Local guides (₹800 per day) are mandatory within the park and must be arranged at the office of the **Highlander Trekking Guides Association** (☏9734056944; www.highlanderguidesandporters.com; Mane Bhanjang) at Mane Bhanjhang, along with porters (₹400) if required.

Mane Bhanjhang is 26km from Darjeeling and is served by frequent shared jeeps (₹90, 1½ hours) as well as a 7am bus from Darjeeling's Chowk Bazaar bus & jeep station. A chartered jeep costs ₹1200. From Rimbik, there are shared jeeps back to Darjeeling (₹120, five hours) at 7am and noon, and a bus at 6.30am (₹90). Book seats in advance.

If you have to overnight in Rimbik the best lodges are **Hotel Sherpa** (d ₹900), with pleasant lawns and Alpine-style huts, and **Green Hill** (dm ₹200, r ₹500), with quieter wooden rooms out back.

The usual trekking itinerary is 83km over five days. A shorter four-day option is possible by descending from Sandakphu to Sri Khola on day three. A rough jeep road follows the trek from Mane Bhanjhang to Phalut but traffic is very light and the walking trail partly avoids the road.

Private lodges, some with attached bathrooms, are available along the route for around ₹200 for a dorm bed or ₹400 to ₹700 per room. All offer food, normally a filling combo of rice, dhal and vegetables (₹200). Rooms have clean bedding and blankets so sleeping bags are not strictly necessary, though they are nice to have. At a minimum, bring a sleeping bag liner and warm clothes for dawn peak viewing. Bottled and boiled water is available along the route. Trekkers' huts can be booked at the GTA Tourist Reception Centre but even

staff here will tell you that you are better off at one of the private lodges. The main lodges for each overnight stop are listed below in ascending order of price and quality:

Day 1: Trekkers' Hut, Mountain Lodge, Siddharta Lodge and Shikhar Lodge in Tumling; Trekkers' Hut in Tonglu

Day 2: Chewang Lodge in Kalipokhari

Day 3: Trekkers' Hut, Namobuddha, Sunrise and Sherpa Chalet Lodge in Sandakphu

Day 4: Trekkers' Hut and Forest Rest House in Phalut

Day 5: Trekkers' Hut, Namobuddha Lodge and Sherpa Lodge in Rammam

All-inclusive guided treks on this route are offered by Darjeeling agencies for about ₹3000 per person per day, though it's easy enough to arrange a DIY trek for less. Lodges can get booked out in the busy month of October, so consider a November itinerary if you're planning the trek in autumn.

Remember to bring your passport, as you'll have to register at half a dozen army checkpoints. The ridge forms the India-Nepal border and the trail actually enters Nepal in several places.

For a relaxing end to a trek, consider a stay at **Karmi Farm** (www.karmifarm.com; per person incl full board ₹2000), a two-hour drive from Rimbik near Bijanbari. It's managed by Andrew Pulger-Frame, whose Sikkimese grandparents once ran an estate from the main house here. The simple but comfortable rooms are attractively decorated with colourful local fabrics, and bathrooms have 24-hour hot water. A small clinic for villagers is run from the farm, providing a volunteer opportunity for medical students and doctors. Singalila treks and other activities can be organised, but it is just as easy to sit here for a week with a book

WEST BENGAL & DARJEELING SINGALILA RIDGE TREK

and a pot of tea, overlooking the bird- and flower-filled gardens in the foreground and towering peaks in the distance. The adventurous could walk here in a day from Darjeeling, via North Point, Singtom Tea Estate and Pul Bazaar.

Kalimpong

☏ 03552 / POP 43,000 / ELEV 1250M

This bustling bazaar town sprawls along a saddle-shaped mountain ridge overlooking the roaring Teesta River and lorded over by

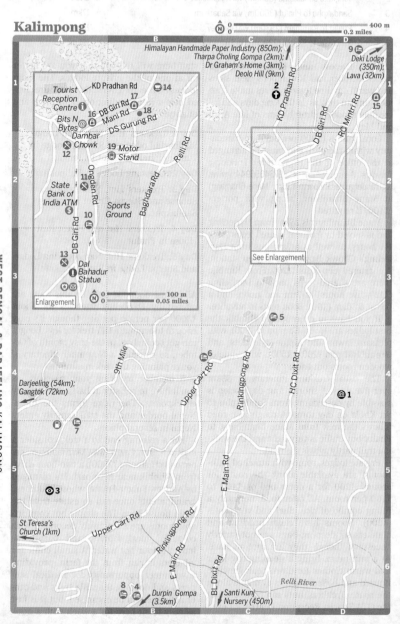

Kalimpong

Himalayan Handmade Paper Industry (850m);
Tharpa Choling Gompa (2km);
Dr Graham's Home (3km);
Deolo Hill (9km)

Deki Lodge (350m);
Lava (32km)

KD Pradhan Rd

Tourist Reception Centre

Bits N Bytes

DB Giri Rd

Mani Rd

DS Gurung Rd

Dambar Chowk

Motor Stand

Relli Rd

Baghdara Rd

State Bank of India ATM

Ongden Rd

Sports Ground

DB Giri Rd

Dal Bahadur Statue

Enlargement

See Enlargement

Darjeeling (54km);
Gangtok (72km)

9th Mile

Upper Cart Rd

Rinkingpong Rd

HC Dixit Rd

St Teresa's Church (1km)

Upper Cart Rd

Rinkingpong Rd

E Main Rd

E Main Rd

BL Dixit Rd

Durpin Gompa (3.5km)

Santi Kunj Nursery (450m)

Relli River

WEST BENGAL & DARJEELING KALIMPONG

the summit of Khangchendzonga. It's not a must-see, but it does boast Himalayan views, Buddhist monasteries, colonial architecture and a fascinating nursery industry, all linked by some fine hikes.

Kalimpong's early development as a major Himalayan trading centre focused on the tea trade with Tibet, across the Jelep La. Like Darjeeling, Kalimpong once belonged to the chogyals of Sikkim, but it fell into the hands of the Bhutanese in the 18th century and later passed to the British, before becoming part of India at Independence. Scottish missionaries, particularly the Jesuits, made great efforts to win over the local Buddhists in the late 19th century and the town remains an important educational centre for the entire eastern Himalaya.

Kalimpong is centred on its chaotic central market and Motor Stand. Most sights and quality accommodation are a kilometre or two from town, along DB Giri and Rinkingpong Rds.

⊙ Sights

Durpin Gompa   MONASTERY
FREE Kalimpong's largest monastery, formally known as Zangtok Pelri Phodang, sits atop panoramic Durpin Hill (1372m) and was consecrated by the Dalai Lama in 1976. There are impressive religious murals in the main prayer room downstairs (photography is permitted), interesting 3D mandalas (visual meditational aids) on the 2nd floor, and stunning Khangchendzonga views from the terrace. Prayers are held at 4pm.

The monastery is located about 5km south of the town centre, and is most easily

reached by taxi (₹250 one way). It's a pleasant downhill walk back to town, passing the army golf course. Stop for a drink at charming Morgan House, now a WBTDC hotel. A viewpoint about 300m below the gompa looks north towards the Jelep La and south over the Relli and Teesta rivers.

Tharpa Choling Gompa   MONASTERY
(off KD Pradhan Rd) **FREE** Built in 1922, this ambient Gelugpa-school Tibetan monastery contains statues of the past, present and future Buddhas. A Garuda protects each Buddha from above, his mouth devouring hatred and anger (in the form of a snake). It's a 30-minute walk (uphill) from town, 50m past Tripai Rd.

Dr Graham's Home   HISTORIC BUILDING
(⊙ museum 9am-noon & 1.15-3.30pm Mon-Fri) **FREE** This orphanage and school was built in 1900 by Dr JA Graham, a Scottish missionary, to educate children of tea-estate workers, and now has 1300-odd students. There's a **museum** that commemorates Graham and his wife, Katherine. The 1925 chapel above the school seems lifted straight out of a Scottish parish, with its grey slate, spire and fine stained-glass windows.

The gate is 4km up the steep KD Pradhan Rd. Many people charter a taxi to get here (₹200) and then do the downhill walk back to town via Tharpa Choling Gompa and the Himalayan Handmade Paper Industry workshop.

Deolo Hill   VIEWPOINT
(9km from Kalimpong; admission ₹50, tourist lodge breakfast ₹100-150; ⊙ tourist lodge from 8am)

Kalimpong

On a clear day the sunrise views of Khangchendzonga from this hilltop park are simply superb. After savouring the views you can have breakfast at the attached **Tourist Lodge** and then walk down to Kalimpong via Dr Graham's Home. A taxi here costs around ₹300. Casual horse rides (₹200) are sometimes offered by local horse owners on the greens.

Himalayan Handmade
Paper Industry
HANDICRAFTS WORKSHOP

(☑ 03552-255418; KD Pradhan Rd; ⏱ 9am-noon & 1-4pm Mon-Sat) FREE Visitors are welcome to drop into this small workshop to see traditional papermaking processes, from boiling and pulping of the local *argayli* (daphne) bush to sifting, pressing and drying. The resulting insect-resistant paper is used to block-print monastic scriptures. Morning is the best time to see production. It's a 10-minute walk from town, on the right side of the road.

MacFarlane Church
CHURCH

FREE One of Kalimpong's most imposing churches, this 1870 church was severely damaged by a 2011 earthquake, when one of its steeples came crashing to the ground. After much renovation work, the church is now open to visitors and believers alike, and its wood-buttressed Gothic interiors are a wonderful place to spend a few moments in quiet contemplation.

Nurseries
NURSERIES

Kalimpong is a major flower exporter and produces about 80% of India's gladioli and sundry orchid varieties. Visit **Nurseryman's Haven** (☑ 03552-256936; 9th Mile) at Holumba Haven to see some 200-odd species of orchids; **Santi Kunj** (BL Dixit Rd; ⏱ 8.30am-noon & 1.30-4pm Sun-Fri) to see anthuriums and the bird of paradise; and **Pineview Nursery** (☑ 03552-255843; Atisha Rd; admission ₹10; ⏱ 9am-5pm Mon-Sat) to gaze at its eminently photographable cactus collection.

Lepcha Heritage Museum
MUSEUM

(☑ 9933780295; ⏱ 10.30am-4.30pm Mon-Fri) FREE This offbeat collection of Lepcha treasures could be likened to rummaging through the attic of your grandfather's house (if he were a Lepcha elder). A guide explains Lepcha creation myths, while pointing out religious texts, sacred porcupine quill hats and old pangolin skins. It's a 10-minute walk downhill below the Sports Ground. Times vary so call ahead.

St Teresa's Church
CHURCH

A fascinating missionary church built in 1929 by Swiss Jesuits, St Teresa was constructed to incorporate designs from a Bhutanese gompa. The wooden apostles resemble Buddhist monks, and carvings on the doors resemble the *tashi tagye,* eight auspicious symbols of Himalayan Buddhism. The church is off 9th Mile, about 2km from town. If it's locked, ask the next-door neighbours.

Activities

Gurudongma Tours & Travels
TOURS

(☑ 03552-255204; www.gurudongma.com; Rinkingpong Rd, Hilltop) This local operator organises interesting trekking, mountain-biking and birdwatching tours, based around its luxury farmhouse on the Samthar Plateau. Pricey **homestays** (s/d including full board US$45/65) are also available.

Himalayan Eagle
PARAGLIDING

(☑ 9635156911; www.himalayaneagle.com) Kalimpong-based Swedish pilot Roger Lenngren offers paragliding flights from Deolo Hill. Tandem flights cost ₹3000/4500 for a 15-/30-minute flight, and transport to and from town is included in the price. Weather conditions have to be perfect for flights though.

🛌 Sleeping

Manokamana Lodge
GUESTHOUSE $

(☑ 03552-257047; manokamanalodge@gmail.com; DB Giri Rd; s/d ₹550/800; @) This family-run place exudes the air of a classic backpackers' dive. Its central location, combined with an **internet cafe** (per hour ₹30) and an excellent-value restaurant add to its appeal, even though accommodation is fairly basic, characterised by linoleum-floored rooms and bucket hot water in clean toilets. Ask for one of the quieter rear rooms.

Sherpa Lodge
HOTEL $

(☑ 8972029913; Ongden Rd; s/d ₹300/700) This simple but decent cheapie is slap bang in the centre of town, offering bright, clean rooms and buckets of hot water for the attached bathrooms. Service can be a little slack at times, however, and there's a fair bit of traffic noise coming from the busy road below.

Deki Lodge
GUESTHOUSE $

(☑ 03552-255095; dekilodge@hotmail.com; Tripai Rd; s/d from ₹350/950) This superfriendly

KALIMPONG WALKS

There's plenty of scope for some great walking around Kalimpong, so allow an extra day or two to stretch the legs. Helpdesk (p519) at Sherpa Lodge and Holumba Haven Hotel offer information on all these walks and can arrange guides and transport if needed.

In Kalimpong itself, Helpdesk can arrange a guided crafts walk, taking in a traditional incense workshop, working silversmiths, noodle makers and a *thangka* (Tibetan cloth painting) studio, all hidden in the backstreet bazaars.

One good half-day walk close to town leads from near Holumba Haven to the villages of **Challisey** and **Chibo Busty** to a grand viewpoint over the Teesta River. En route, you can drop by the **LK Pradhan Cactus Nursery** and a small **curd production centre** at Tharker Farm, with the option of descending to see two fascinating traditional **Lepcha houses** at Ngassey village.

Heading further afield, one potential DIY hike starts at a wide track 2km past Algarah on the road to Pelling. The track climbs gently along a forested ridge to the faint 17th-century ruins of **Damsang Dzong**, site of the last stand of the Lepcha kings against the Bhutanese. Continue along the ridge and then descend to views of Khangchendzonga at Tinchuli Hill, before following the dirt road back to the main Algarah–Pedong road. From here you can walk back 4km to Algarah to catch a shared jeep to Kalimpong, or continue 3km to Pedong via the **Shangchen Dorje Gompa** in Sakyong Busty. You can get a shared jeep from Kalimpong to Pedong (₹50) or Algarah (₹30). If you want to stay overnight, try the **Silk Route Retreat** (☑ 9932828753; www.thesilkrouteretreat.com; 21st Mile, Pedong; r/cottage ₹900/1700) in Pedong.

For the ultimate dawn and dusk views of Khangchendzonga, head to the **Tiffin Dara viewpoint**, just above the village of Rishap, about 30km from Kalimpong. A rough road climbs from the main Kalimpong–Lava road for 3km to a signed footpath 1km before Rishap. The path detours left after 20 minutes to the viewpoint and then continues through forest for 45 minutes to rejoin the main Lava–Kalimpong road. Just before this junction, by some prayer flags, a shortcut footpath drops down to Lava village via the Forest Lodge. For transport take the 7am shared jeep to Lava or the slower 8am bus. A chartered one-way jeep costs ₹1600 to Rishap or ₹2000 for a day's return hire, taking in Lava.

Lava (2353m) is a worthy destination in itself, especially if you time your walk with the bustling Tuesday market, or the 10am debating or 3.30pm prayers at the modern **Kagyupa Thekchenling Gompa**. Adjoining Lava is **Neora Valley National Park** (Indian/foreigner ₹100/200, vehicle entry ₹100, guide ₹600; ⊙ 15 Sep-15 Jun), whose lush forests are home to red pandas, clouded leopards and myriad bird species. Travel agents can arrange a four-day camping trek to Roche La (3155m), at the high junction of West Bengal, Sikkim and Bhutan. The cottages of the **Lava Forest Lodge** (☑ 033-23350064; www.wbfdc.com; Lava; d from ₹800) just above town offer the nicest accommodation but can be hard to book; try through **WBTDC** (☑ 03552-255654; www.wbtdc.gov.in) in Siliguri or Holumba Haven in Kalimpong. The private **Hotel Orchid** (☑ 03552-282213; Lava; d from ₹1100) is another decent choice. Avoid October, when Bengali tourists flood the town. Shared jeeps (₹100) run back to Kalimpong when full, until around 3.30pm.

Tibetan place is set around a peaceful flower-hemmed family mansion, and boasts some superb Tibetan eats in its airy terrace cafe. The rooms are plain and a tad overpriced for what's on offer, but the pricier upper-floor rooms have some quaintness and ambience to them. It's a 10-minute walk out of the town centre.

★ **Holumba Haven**   BOUTIQUE HOTEL **$$**
(☑ 03552-256936; www.holumba.com; 9th Mile; s/d from ₹1500/1700; 🛜) A curious yet utterly charming property combining a nursery and a family-run guesthouse, Holumba is located amid sylvan settings about 1km below town. The spotless, comfy rooms are arranged in cosy cottages spread around the lush gardens, and good homestyle meals (₹350,

preorders only) are available in the sociable dining room.

Kalimpong Park Hotel
HERITAGE HOTEL $$

(☑ 03552-255304; www.kalimpongparkhotel.com; Rinkingpong Rd; d from ₹2600; @ 🖎) This former summer home of the maharajas of Dinajpur is perched on a mountain shelf overlooking the Relli valley, and packs in oodles of Raj-era charm. Wicker chairs and scarlet blossoms line the verandah and there's a charming lounge bar, along with a restaurant offering British boarding-school staples such as jelly custard. Rooms in the main building have more ambience than their annex counterparts.

Cloud 9
HOTEL $$

(☑ 9832039634; cloudnine.kpg@gmail.com; Rinkingpong Rd; s/d ₹1500/2200) The five wood-panelled rooms on the 1st floor of this cheerful property are irreverently homey, and the restaurant below serves interesting Bhutanese and Sikkimese dishes and chilled beer. Binod the owner is a Beatles junkie and loves to bond over music late evenings – he might even buy you a beer if you're good with the guitar or vox!

Himalayan Hotel
HERITAGE HOTEL $$$

(☑ 03552-255248; www.himalayanhotel.com; Upper Cart Rd; s/d ₹2400/3600; 🖎) Opened by David MacDonald, an interpreter from Francis Younghusband's 1904 Lhasa mission, this fascinating property has vintage rooms with fireplaces and sloping Himalayan-oak ceilings. There's also a clutch of suites that mesh old-world charm with modern comfort and private balconies. You're in fine company here; the former guest list includes Himalayan legends such as Alexandra David-Neel, Heinrich Harrer and Charles Bell.

Elgin Silver Oaks
HERITAGE HOTEL $$$

(☑ 03552-255296; www.elginhotels.com; Rinkingpong Rd; s/d incl full board ₹7700/8200; @ 🖎)

This centrally located Raj-era homestead-turned-heritage hotel is clearly Kalimpong's most luxurious option. The rooms are plushly furnished and offer grand views down the valley towards the Relli River (ask for a garden-view room). The tariff includes all meals in the classy restaurant and the sociable bar packs bags of atmosphere.

🍴 Eating & Drinking

Gompu's Bar & Restaurant
TIBETAN $$

(Gompu's Hotel, off DB Giri Rd; mains ₹80-140, beer ₹150; ⊙7am-9pm) Gompu's starts its day with its signature oversized pork *momos* (₹110), which have been drawing locals and travellers alike for as long as anyone can remember. It's also a good place for a cold beer chased by a plate of garlic chilli potatoes or roast pork glazed in soy sauce.

Lee's
CHINESE $$

(☑ 9593305812; DB Giri Rd; mains ₹80-140; ⊙11am-7.30pm Mon-Sat) In true Chinese fashion, Mr Lee and his daughter serve up fantastic and unique Yunnan-style dishes at this eatery with a red interior. Stand-out dishes include the *mun* wontons (dumplings fried in egg), red pork, homemade rice noodles, a delectable golden chicken in garlic gravy and a refreshing pot of good-quality green tea. It's just above One Cup cafe.

3C's
BAKERY $

(DB Giri Rd; cakes & snacks ₹20-40; ⊙8.30am-7.30pm) If you need a quick break, this popular bakery and fast-food restaurant offers a variety of pastries and cakes, both sweet and savoury. There's mediocre coffee on tap, and seating to the rear overlooking the sports ground.

King Thaiw
CHINESE $$

(3rd fl supermarket; DB Giri Rd, mains ₹80-140; ⊙11am-9.30pm) A multicultural hang-out with a Thai name, Chinese food and Bob Marley posters on the walls, this place draws in monks, businessmen and Tibetan cool kids. The generously portioned food is mainly Chinese with some Thai and Indian accents, and there's a bar with comfy chairs and loud music in the evenings.

One Cup
CAFE

(DB Giri Rd; coffee ₹60; ⊙11am-6.30pm Mon-Sun) Kalimpong's first coffee house serves a decent espresso hit, alongside some quality cakes and ice-cream specials. It's frequented by young people, and gets noisy in the evenings.

Shopping

Lark's Provisions
FOOD & DRINK

(DB Giri Rd; ⊙10am-6pm) This is the best place to pick up local cheese (₹350 per kilogram), produced in Kalimpong since the Jesuits established a dairy here in the 19th century. It also sells locally made stickjaws and milky lollipops (₹40) and yummy homemade pickles.

Haat Bazaar
MARKET

(btwn Relli & RC Mintri Rds) On Wednesdays and Saturdays, this normally quiet bazaar roars to life with a plethora of merchandise ranging from food and textiles to objects of daily life and sundry other knick knacks.

Kashi Nath & Sons
BOOKS

(DB Giri Rd; ⊙10am-6.30pm Mon-Sat) This, and the shop next door, has a decent collection of books on Buddhism, Nepal and Tibet, plus some Indian and international bestselling novels and nonfiction titles.

ℹ Information

Bits N Bytes (DB Giri Rd; per hour ₹30; ⊙8.30am-7pm; 🛜) Reliable and fast internet connections.

Helpdesk (📞8972029913; helpdesk_kpg@hotmail.com; Sherpa Lodge; ⊙9am-5pm) This private information centre on the ground floor of the Sherpa Lodge offers guides, a useful map and information on trips around Kalimpong.

Post office (Rinkingpong Rd; ⊙9am-5pm Mon-Fri, to 4pm Sat) For snail-mail services. Show your passport if you're sending a parcel home.

State Bank of India ATM (DB Giri Rd) One of several ATMs located together on DB Giri Rd.

Tourist Reception Centre (DGHC; 📞03552-257992; DB Giri Rd; ⊙10am-4.30pm Mon-Sat, closed 2nd & 4th Sat) Sleepy staff can organise local tours and accommodation.

ℹ Getting There & Away

All the bus and jeep options and their offices are found next to each other at the chaotic Motor Stand.

BUS & JEEP

Bengal government NBSTC buses run hourly to Siliguri (₹80, 2½ hours). A single **Sikkim Nationalised Transport** (SNT; Ongden Rd) bus to Gangtok (₹90, three hours) leaves at 1pm from across the road.

Himalayan Travellers (📞9434166498; Motor Stand) This helpful transport company runs share jeeps to Gangtok (₹120, three hours, four daily) and Lava (₹80, 1½ hours, five per day) and a bus to Kaffer (₹60, 2½ hours, 8am).

Kalimpong Mainline Taxi Driver's Welfare Association (KMTDWA; Motor Stand) Frequent share jeeps to Siliguri (₹100, 2½ hours) and Gangtok (₹120, 2½ hours) and one daily to Jorethang (₹80, two hours, 7.15am).

Kalimpong Motor Transport (Motor Stand) Frequent share jeeps (₹100, 2½ hours) to Darjeeling until midafternoon, plus charters (₹1400).

KS & AH Taxi Driver's Welfare Association (Motor Stand) Share jeeps to Gangtok (₹120, hourly), Ravangla (₹130, 3½ hours, 2pm) and Namchi (₹100, four daily) in Sikkim.

TRAIN

Kalimpong Railway Out Agency (Mani Rd; ⊙10am-6pm Mon-Sat, to 1pm Sun) Sells train tickets out of New Jalpaiguri (NJP) train station and runs a daily shared jeep to NJP station at 1pm (₹120).

ℹ Getting Around

Taxis (mostly unmarked minivans) can be chartered for local trips from along DB Giri Rd. A half-day rental to see most of the sights should cost ₹800.

Bihar & Jharkhand

Why Go?

Glistening paddy-fields to the north and wild forested hills to the south provide a striking backdrop for a visit to this remote rural region. This is also one of the country's religious melting pots, and getting caught up in the spiritual atmosphere is the real draw for travellers.

Bihar is the birthplace of Buddhism and plays host to thousands of pilgrims from around the world who throng its many places of religious significance; the most extraordinary of which is traveller-friendly Bodhgaya, where Buddha achieved enlightenment. In tribal Jharkhand, holy Parasnath Hill is a revered Jain pilgrimage site, and joining devotees on the hike to the top is a surreal highlight for those who like to get off the beaten track.

Truth be told, the whole of this region is off the beaten track. Outside Bodhgaya, foreign tourists are almost nonexistent, so if you're looking to sidestep mainstream travel, this unfashionable pocket could be an unexpected highlight.

Best for Spiritual Atmosphere

➜ Bodhgaya (p529)

➜ Parasnath Hill (p537)

➜ Rajgir (p533)

Best Off the Beaten Track

➜ Parasnath Hill (p537)

➜ Betla (Palamau) National Park (p538)

➜ Vaishali (p526)

➜ Kesariya (p531)

➜ Motihari (p528)

When to Go

Patna

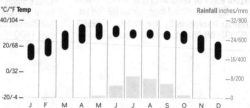

Jan & Feb Temperatures hover between a chilly-to-pleasant 12°C and 25°C.	**Jun–Sep** Monsoon season. Steer clear – Bihar is India's most flood-prone state.	**Oct & Nov** Comfortably cool again; the region's forests assume a moody autumn look.

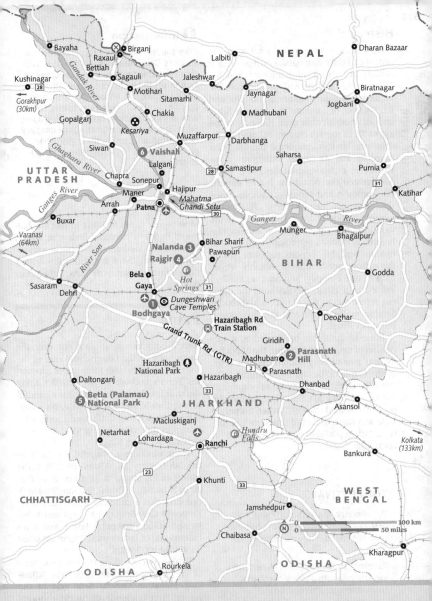

Bihar & Jharkhand Highlights

1 Witnessing Buddhists from around the world converging on the powerfully serene Mahabodhi Temple in the traveller haven of **Bodhgaya** (p529)

2 Getting up at 3am for the surreal Jain pilgrimage to the top of **Parasnath Hill** (p537)

3 Visiting the peaceful ruins of the once-huge ancient university at **Nalanda** (p535)

4 Hiring a tonga (horse-drawn carriage) for the day to explore the temples and stupas in laidback **Rajgir** (p533), before bathing with Hindu devotees at the revered hot springs

5 Prowling the forests of remote **Betla (Palamau) National Park** (p538) on the back of an elephant

6 Walking through northern Bihari villages to the Buddhist ruins at **Vaishali** (p526)

History

Bihar's ancient history kicks off with the arrival of Prince Siddhartha during the 6th century BC, who spent many years here before leaving, enlightened, as the Buddha. Mahavira, a contemporary of Buddha and the founder of Jainism, was born in Bihar and attained nirvana near Nalanda at the age of 72. In the 4th century BC, after Chandragupta Maurya conquered the Magadha kingdom and its capital Pataliputra (now Patna), he expanded into the Indus Valley and created the first great Indian empire. His grandson and successor, Ashoka, ruled the Mauryan empire from Pataliputra, which was one of the largest cities in the world at that time. Emperor Ashoka embraced Buddhism, erecting stupas, monuments and his famous Ashokan pillars throughout northern India, notably at Sarnath (Uttar Pradesh) and Sanchi (Madhya Pradesh). In Bihar, Ashoka built the original shrine on the site of today's Mahabodhi Temple in Bodhgaya and the lion-topped pillar at Vaishali.

Bihar continued to be coveted by a succession of major empires until the Magadha dynasty rose to glory again during the reign of the Guptas (7th and 8th centuries AD). With the decline of the Mughal empire in the 17th century AD, Bihar came under the control of Bengal until 1912, when a separate state was formed. Part of this state later became Orissa (Odisha) and, more recently, 2000, Jharkhand.

TOP FESTIVALS

Pataliputra Mahotsava (Patna; ⊘ Mar) A celebration of Patna's historic past with parades, sports, dancing and music.

Rajgir Mahotsava (p534) A performing-arts gala with dances, devotional songs and instrumental music.

Chhath Festival (p536) People perform spectacular rituals on the banks of rivers and water bodies to honour Surya, the Sun God.

Sonepur Mela (Sonepur; ⊘ Nov/Dec) With 700,000 attendees and countless thousands of animals taking part, this three-week festival is four times the size of Pushkar's Camel Fair.

ⓘ Information

Bihar and Jharkhand have a reputation for lawlessness. Conditions have improved in recent times, but bandit activity – such as holding up cars, buses and trains – is still a possibility, albeit a remote one. Although tourists are not specific targets, it's a good idea to keep up to date with the latest info; check the newspapers *Bihar Times* (www.bihartimes.in) or *Patna Daily* (www.patnadaily.com), or the English portal of *Ranchi Express* (www.ranchiexpress.com) before arrival.

BIHAR

Most people travel to Bihar to visit the hallowed Buddhist circuit of Bodhgaya, Rajgir, Nalanda and Vaishali, with Patna as a transport hub, but there are also a few quirky destinations to get your adventure juices flowing.

Patna

⌨ 0612 / POP 1.7 MILLION

Bihar's busy capital sprawls out over the south bank of the Ganges, just east of the river's confluence with three major tributaries. There's nothing for the traveller along the river itself, and Patna only has a handful of worthwhile sights. Otherwise, it's a chaotic, congested city that's used mostly as a transport hub, or as a base for day trips to sights in northern Bihar.

Patna was once a powerful city. Early in the 5th century BC, Ajatasatru shifted the capital of his Magadha kingdom from Rajgir to Pataliputra (Patna), fulfilling Buddha's prophecy that a great city would arise here. Emperors Chandragupta Maurya and Ashoka also called Pataliputra home, and it remained one of India's most important cities for almost 1000 years.

Patna stretches along the southern bank of the Ganges for about 15km. The 5.7km-long Mahatma Gandhi Setu, one of the longest river bridges in the world, connects Patna with northern Bihar.

⊙ Sights & Activities

★**Patna Museum**   MUSEUM
(Buddha Marg; Indian/foreigner ₹15/250; ⊙ 10.30am-4.30pm Tue-Sun) Housed in a majestic heritage building, this museum contains a splendid collection of Mauryan and Gupta stone sculptures, some beautiful bronze Buddhist

statuary, 2000-year-old terracotta figurines and a gallery of wonderful Rajasthani miniatures. Don't miss the fabulous collection of *thangkas* (Tibetan cloth paintings) brought to India by the scholar and traveller Rahul Sankrityayan in the early 20th century.

Upstairs in a locked gallery (an extra ₹500) you can glimpse a tiny casket believed to contain some of Buddha's ashes that were retrieved from Vaishali.

★**Golghar**   HISTORIC BUILDING
(Danapure Rd; admission ₹2; ⊘6am-6pm) For a dome with a view, climb this massive, bulbous granary, built by the British army in 1786. The reason behind its construction was to avoid a repeat of the 1770 famine – look for the old carved sign on one side, reading: 'For the perpetual prevention of famine in these provinces' – although fortunately it was never required.

Its dual spiralling staircases (142 steps each) were designed so that workers could climb up one side and down the other. The viewing gallery on top of the monument affords unparalleled vistas of the city and the Ganges.

Buddha Smriti Park   PARK
(Fraser Rd; admission ₹10; ⊘dawn-dusk Tue-Sun) This 9-hectare park, inaugurated by the Dalai Lama in 2010, is notable for its massive sandblasted charcoal stupa (admission ₹50), which houses a unique bulletproof chamber inside; and sapling plantings from both the Bodhi Tree in Bodhgaya and Anuradhapura in Sri Lanka. There is also a strikingly modern **Buddhist museum** (₹40), a **library** (₹50) and a **meditation centre** (free).

Khuda Bakhsh Oriental Library   MUSEUM
(Ashok Raj Path; ⊘9.30am-5pm Sat-Thu) FREE This tiny, but fascinating, library-cum-museum, founded in 1900, contains a renowned collection of Arabic and Persian manuscripts, Mughal and Rajput paintings, and even the Quran inscribed in a book just 25mm wide. A significant exhibit is Nadir Shah's sword – perhaps the very weapon he raised at Delhi's Sunehri Mosque in 1739 to order the massacre of the city's residents.

Gandhi Museum   MUSEUM
(Danapure Rd; ⊘10am-6pm Sun-Fri) FREE This museum contains a pictorial history of Mahatma Gandhi's life, plus some of his meagre belongings. On your way in, don't miss the glass-boxed statues of Gandhi and Nobel laureate Rabindranath Tagore in conversation.

🛏 Sleeping

Most budget hotels in Patna do not accept foreigners.

Hotel Clark Inn   HOTEL $
(☑9939726620; Jamal Rd; r from ₹660) The cheapest hotel we could find that welcomed foreigners, Clark Inn has simple but comfortable rooms with TVs, chairs and tables, and small balconies.

Hotel President   HOTEL $$
(☑0612-2209203;   www.hotelpresidentpatna. com; off Fraser Rd; s/d ₹1400/1700; ✳@) This smart, family-run hotel is in a relatively quiet location off Fraser Rd and close to Patna Museum. Rooms – all with AC – are spacious and clean, with TV, seating areas and hot water. Some have small balconies. No wi-fi, but there's an internet terminal in the lobby.

Hotel City Centre   HOTEL $$
(☑0612-2208687;   hotelcitycentrepatna@rediff mail.com; Station Rd; d incl breakfast with/without AC ₹2000/1100; ✳@) This modern glass tower to your right just as you exit the train station is perfect for a comfy transit overnighter. Rooms are good value for the price (non-AC rooms have squat toilets), and there's a restaurant within the premises.

Hotel Maurya Patna   HOTEL $$$
(☑0612-2203040; www.maurya.com; S Gandhi Maidan; s/d incl breakfast ₹12,000/14,000; ✳@🛜🏊) Fine appointments and luxurious surroundings distinguish Patna's top business hotel. The large gardens host a tempting pool, and there are a few nice restaurants and a bar. Rooms are tastefully furnished.

🍴 Eating & Drinking

Litti Chokha Stall   STREET FOOD $
(opp Gandhi Maidan; ₹10 per plate) One of numerous street-side stalls dotted around the city cooking up Patna's speciality snack;

Patna

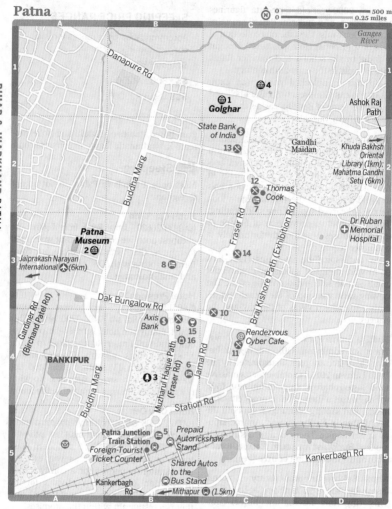

BIHAR & JHARKHAND PATNA

litti chokha (chickpea-powder dough balls served with a spicy side sauce of mashed tomatoes, aubergine and potatoes).

Baba Hotel
INDIAN $
(Dak Bungalow Rd; mains ₹50-100; ☉9am-10pm) Clean, good-value, pocket-sized restaurant serving veg and nonveg Indian and Chinese dishes, as well as ₹85 thalis.

Bollywood Treats
MULTICUISINE $
(Maurya Patna Hotel Arcade; mains ₹80-150; ☉noon-9pm) This spotless American-style diner dishes out South Indian snacks, Chinese stir-fries, decent pizza and tempting brownies to

Patna's blossoming middle class. There is a Baskin-Robbins ice-cream kiosk, and it also does fresh coffee (₹95). Opens at noon, but doesn't start serving food until 1pm.

Tandoor Hut
INDIAN $
(☏delivery 9304871717; Fraser Rd; mains ₹70-130; ☉noon-3pm & 7-11pm) Street-side stand serving delicious kebabs and other tandoor offerings. Take them back to your hotel, or stand at the tables provided on the pavement outside. The chicken tikka and *reshmi kebab* (tender chicken kebab cooked in the tandoor) are both superb.

Patna

★ **Bellpepper Restaurant**   INDIAN **$$**
(Hotel Windsor, Exhibition Rd; mains ₹100-250; ⊘11am-3pm & 7-11pm) Intimate and contemporary, this restaurant inside Hotel Windsor is hugely popular for its tandoori dishes. The *murg tikka lababdar* (boneless tandoori chicken basted with garlic, ginger, green chillies, and a pistachio- and cashew-nut paste) is melt-in-your-mouth sinful. The biryanis are good here too. No alcohol.

Anarkali   INDIAN **$$**
(Mamta Hotel; cnr Fraser & Dak Bungalow Rds; mains ₹90-180; ⊘noon-10pm) One of the friendliest restaurants in Patna, this oldie, housed inside Mamta Hotel, is a wonderful place to get sloshed in style (beers from ₹200). Serves excellent food too, although portions are on the small side.

Beer Shop   BAR
(Dak Bungalow Rd; beer from ₹95; ⊘10am-10pm) Off licence selling big bottles of Kingfisher light for ₹95.

 Shopping

Ajanta   HANDICRAFTS
(Fraser Rd; ⊘10am-9pm Mon-Sat) This unassuming little shop has a delightful selection of Mithila (Madhubani) paintings secreted away in drawers and cupboards. Most of the stock on display is bronzes, but if you ask, the owner will show you a colourful range of unmounted paintings starting from ₹350 (handmade paper) to ₹950 (silk).

ℹ **Information**

INTERNET ACCESS
Rendezvous Cyber Cafe (Hotel Windsor, Exhibition Rd; per hour ₹30; ⊘10am-8pm) Internet cafe attached to Hotel Windsor.

MEDICAL SERVICES
Dr Ruban Memorial Hospital (☏0612-2320446, 0612-2320404; Gandhi Maidan; ⊘24hr) Emergency room, clinic and pharmacy.

MONEY
Axis Bank (Fraser Rd; ⊘10am-4pm Mon-Sat) Exchanges currency and has ATMs.

State Bank of India (Gandhi Maidan; ⊘10am-2pm Mon-Fri, to noon Sat) Exchanges currency and travellers cheques. Has ATMs.

POST
Post office (Buddha Marg; ⊘10am-4pm Mon-Fri, to 2pm Sat) Ordinary and speed post facilities.

TRAVEL AGENCIES
Thomas Cook (☏0612-2221699; www.thomas cook.in; Hotel Maurya, Patna Arcade; ⊘10am-6pm Mon-Sat) Helpful for booking airline tickets and car rental. Also exchanges currency.

ℹ **Getting There & Away**

Patna's Jaiprakash Narayan International Airport is 8km from the city centre. Between them, **Air India** (☏2223199; www.airindia.in; Patna airport), **IndiGo** (☏1800 1803838; www.goindigo.in; Patna airport) and **JetKonnect** (☏2223045; www.jetkonnect.com; Patna airport) fly daily to Delhi, Mumbai, Chennai and Kolkata. The IndiGo flight to Mumbai goes via Lucknow.

MITHILA (MADHUBANI) PAINTINGS

Bihar's unique and most famous folk art is its Mithila (Madhubani) paintings, produced by women from the Maithili tribe. Traditionally, women from Madhubani and surrounding villages started to create line drawings on the walls of their homes from the first day of their marriage. Using pigments from spices, minerals, charcoal and vegetable matter, they painted local deities and scenes from mythology, often intermingled with special events and aspects of everyday life.

These paintings, in both black-and-white and strong primary colours, are now professionally produced on paper, canvas and silk, and marketed for sale. Original wall paintings can still be seen in homes around Madhubani, 160km northeast of Patna.

BUS

The main bus stand occupies a large, dusty space about 1.5km from the train station (₹5 shared autos run here from the back of the train station). It's a hugely hectic place, but if you walk into the chaos telling people where you want to go, you'll soon get shown to the right bus; buy tickets on board.

There are frequent services throughout the day, and some sleeper buses to Ranchi and Raxaul. Destinations include:

Gaya ₹100, three hours

Kesariya ₹100, three hours

Motihari ₹145, 4½ hours

Ranchi AC/non-AC ₹350/280, eight hours

Raxaul AC/non-AC ₹230/180, eight hours

Vaishali ₹60, two hours

CAR

Hiring a car and driver can be done through Thomas Cook (p525), starting from ₹10 per kilometre (minimum 200km) plus a driver allowance of ₹300 per overnight stay.

TRAIN

Patna Junction has a **foreign-tourist ticket counter** (window 3, Patna Junction; ⊙8am-8pm Mon-Sat, to 2pm Sun) at the 1st-floor reservation office, in the right-hand wing of the station.

Trains leave roughly hourly for Gaya (2nd class/AC chair ₹25/290, two to three hours) between 5am and 11.30pm. Just buy a 2nd-class

'general' ticket and hop on the next available service.

More than a dozen daily trains leave for New Delhi (sleeper/3AC/2AC ₹500/1260/1825, 12 to 18 hours); the quickest and most convenient time-wise, is the RJPB Rajdhani (3AC/2AC/1AC ₹1610/2235/3730) which leaves at 7.25pm and arrives in Delhi at 7.40am.

Ten daily trains go to Kolkata (sleeper/3AC/2AC ₹340/880/1240, eight to 14 hours). The best time-wise is probably the Vibhuti Express (10.35pm, nine hours).

At least 20 daily trains go to Varanasi (sleeper/3AC/2AC ₹160/485/690, four to six hours) between 5am and 11pm.

Three fast trains go to Ranchi (sleeper/3AC/2AC ₹310/835/1195, eight to 10 hours), leaving at 6am, 11.40am and 9.45pm.

ⓘ Getting Around

The airport is located 7km west of the city centre. Autorickshaws/taxis cost ₹150/350 from the prepaid stand by the train station.

Shared autos (often jam-packed) depart from the rear of the train station. They shuttle between the train station and Gandhi Maidan (₹5), and between the train station and the bus stand (also ₹5).

Vaishali

📞 06225

A quiet, yet significant Buddhist pilgrimage site, Vaishali, 55km northwest of Patna, makes a lovely rural escape from hectic Patna. The small museum is engaging, while the ruins of Kolhua are wonderfully serene. And simply walking around the surrounding villages and farmland is a treat in itself.

The bus will drop you at the so-called 'high school', from where it's a 1km walk along a straight lane to a large ancient coronation water tank. On the left side of the tank is the modern, whitewashed, Japanese-built **World Peace Pagoda** (Indian/foreigner ₹5/100; ⊙dawn-dusk). On the opposite side of the tank, and of more interest, is the **Buddha Relic Stupa** (⊙dawn-dusk) FREE and the **Archaeological Museum** (admission ₹10; ⊙9am-5pm Mon-Sat). The 5th-century stupa, once 12m tall, is now in ruins, but it was once one of the eight locations in which Buddha's ashes were buried, after he had been cremated at Kushinagar. The ashes now reside in Patna Museum. The small archaeological museum here contains 2000-year-old clay and terracotta figures,

1000-year-old Buddhist statuary, and an intriguing 1st- to 2nd-century AD toilet pan. It also has an interesting scale model of the nearby site of Kolhua.

Between the Buddha Stupa Relic and the Archaeological Museum, a single-lane countryside road winds its way through farming villages to the **Kolhua Complex** (Indian/foreigner ₹5/100; ⊙7am-5pm), 5km away. It's worth making time for this very pleasant walk, although shared autos also make the trip and it's relatively easy to hitch a ride on a motorbike. Set in a landscaped park, Kolhua comprises a large, hemispherical brick stupa guarded by a lion squatting atop a 2300-year-old Ashoka pillar. The pillar is plain and contains none of the Ashokan edicts usually carved onto these pillars. Nearby are the ruins of smaller stupas and monastic buildings. According to legend, Buddha was given a bowl of honey here by monkeys, who also dug out a rainwater tank for his water supply.

The best place to grab lunch in Vaishali is the **Buddha Fun & Food Village** (mains ₹65-200), located at one corner of the ceremonial tank. There's outdoor seating and a children's play area.

The last bus back to Patna swings by the main road at around 4pm.

Raxaul

📞 06255 / POP 41,600

Raxaul is a dusty, congested border town that provides passage into Nepal via a hassle-free border post. It's no place to linger, but if you must spend the night, **Hotel Kaveri** (📞06255-221148; Main Rd; with/without AC ₹1000/300; ✹), on the main road leading to the border (about 1km from the border), has decent AC rooms with modern bathrooms, and very basic non-AC rooms with tap-and-bucket showers, but shared toilets. Restaurants are scarce and none have English menus; the *dhaba* opposite Hotel Kaveri is probably your best bet.

The bus stand is 200m down a lane off the main road, about 2km from the border on the right. There are frequent buses, day and night, to Patna (AC/non-AC ₹230/180, seven to eight hours) via Motihari (₹60/50, 2½ hours). The road to Motihari is dreadfully bumpy so sit near the front of the bus if you can.

The train station is off the main road, 750m from the border, but isn't well

BORDER CROSSING – NEPAL FROM RAXAUL

Border Hours
The border at Raxaul is open from 6am to 10pm.

Foreign Exchange
No banks change money in Raxaul but there are many private money changers on both sides of the border. The **State Bank of India** (⊙10.30am-4.30pm Mon-Fri, to 1.30pm Sat), on the main road in Raxaul, has an ATM.

Onward Transport
On the Nepal side, the town of Birganj is about 3km from the border. You are free to walk across the border to Birganj, or shared autorickshaws and tongas (two-wheeled horse carriages) charge ₹20 per person from the border to Birganj. A cycle-rickshaw costs about ₹100.

From Birganj, there are frequent buses to Kathmandu (ordinary/deluxe/AC ₹550/600/800, six to seven hours, 5am to 8pm). However, the most comfortable and quickest option is to get a Tata Sumo '4WD' (₹550 to ₹800, four to five hours, every 20 minutes until 5pm). There are also morning buses to Pokhara (₹600, eight hours) via Narayangarh (₹250, four hours) at 5am, 6.30am and 7.30am.

Buddha Air has up to five daily flights between Simara (the airport for Birganj) and Kathmandu (US$100, 20 minutes). The airport is 22km from Birganj and a taxi costs around ₹1000.

Visas
Nepali 15-, 30- and 90-day visas (US$25/40/100 and one passport photo) are only available from 6am to 6pm on the Nepal side of the border.

GEORGE ORWELL MUSEUM

Not only will a trip to Motihari break the long bus ride between Patna and the Nepal border, it will also allow you to become one of the first-ever tourists to visit the world's first George Orwell Museum. The museum was still being built when we visited, on the site of the dilapidated family cottage in which Orwell was born. It was due to open in 2015 and will be the world's only museum dedicated to the celebrated British novelist.

Eric Arthur Blair (George Orwell was a pen name), was born here in 1903. His father, Richard W Blair, worked for the opium department, supervising poppy growers and collecting opium for export to China. The grounds of their family home, which will be landscaped into a small park, also contain the crumbling remains of one of his father's opium warehouses.

Motihari is part of a region from where, in 1917, Mahatma Gandhi launched the civil disobedience movement that ultimately resulted, 30 years later, in the departure of the British from India. Gandhi had been moved by the plight of cultivators in Bihar who were being forced to produce opium and indigo for the lucrative markets of China and Europe respectively. There is also a small Gandhi Museum in town.

The Orwell Museum is a 2.5km walk northwest of the bus stand (₹30 in a cycle-rickshaw; ask for Gyan Babu Chowk). Walk back up to the main road that your bus came in on, passing the cinema on your left. Walk over the crossroads (known as Chhatauni Chowk), and continue straight along Bagaha Dhala Rd, past the Gandhi statue and Hotel Puja and on to Gyan Babu Chowk. Here, just as the road starts bearing round to the left, take the straightest of the three right forks, and the museum will be on your left after 200m. If you reach the veterinary clinic you've walked 100m too far.

Hotel Puja (☎ 8521731700; Bagaha Dhala Rd; with/without AC ₹2000/700; ❄) has large colourful rooms. There are plenty of restaurants nearby. From Motihari, there are frequent buses to Patna (₹145, 4½ hours), Raxaul (₹50, 2½ hours) and Kesaria (₹40, two hours), from where you can catch passing buses to Vaishali.

---

connected. The Mithila Express runs daily to Kolkata (sleeper/3AC/2AC ₹365/990/1425, 18 hours, 10am). The Satyagrah Express runs daily to New Delhi (sleeper/3AC/2AC ₹455/1215/1765, 24 hours, 9.05am).

Gaya

☎ 0631 / POP 395,000

The hectic town of Gaya is a religious centre for Hindu pilgrims. They believe that the temple offerings here relieve the recently departed from the cycle of birth and rebirth. For foreign tourists, it merely serves as a transit point for Bodhgaya, 13km away.

🛏 Sleeping & Eating

Ajatsatru Hotel   HOTEL $

(☎ 0631-2222961; Station Rd; with/without AC ₹1400/840; ❄) If you get stuck for the night in Gaya, this hotel is the best-value of a cluster of hotels directly opposite the train station. It has clean rooms and a decent multicuisine restaurant. No internet.

ℹ Information

There's a **Bihar State Tourist Office** (☎ 2223635; ⊗ 10am-5pm Mon-Sat) and a State Bank of India ATM at the train station. The nearest internet cafes are along Swarajpuri Rd; turn right out of the train station, left at the end, then right again.

ℹ Getting There & Around

AUTORICKSHAWS

Shared autos leave when full from Gaya Railway Station for Bodhgaya (₹20 per person), Manpur bus stand (₹10) and Gandhi Maidan bus stand (₹5).

A private auto from Gaya to Bodhgaya should cost ₹120 to ₹150, although they usually ask for ₹200 or more.

BUS

Patna (₹100, three hours, hourly) Buses leave from the train station.

Rajgir (₹55, 2½ hours, hourly) Buses leave from Manpur bus stand, across the river.

Ranchi (₹180, seven hours, twice hourly) Buses leave from the Gandhi Maidan bus stand.

TRAIN

Trains leave roughly hourly for Patna (2nd class/AC chair ₹25/290, two to three hours) between 4am and 10pm. Buy a 2nd-class 'general' ticket and hop on.

Four daily trains go to New Delhi (sleeper/3AC/2AC ₹490/1280/1835, 11 to 15 hours) at 2.05pm, 2.20pm, 10.55pm and 11.11pm. The two evening trains are four hours quicker.

At least eight trains run daily to Kolkata (sleeper/3AC/2AC ₹300/760/1065, eight to 10 hours), the most convenient being the Doon Express (9½ hours, 9.27pm).

Almost a dozen daily trains go to Varanasi (sleeper/3AC/2AC ₹190/535/735, three to six hours). The quickest is the Purushottam Express (three hours, 2.05pm).

Bodhgaya

☏ 0631 / POP 30,900

The crucible of Buddhism, Bodhgaya was where Prince Siddhartha attained enlightenment beneath a bodhi tree and became Buddha 2600 years ago. In terms of blessedness, this tiny temple town is to Buddhists what Mecca is to Muslims. It attracts thousands of pilgrims from around the world every year, who come for prayer, study and meditation.

The most hallowed spot in town is a bodhi tree which flourishes inside the Mahabodhi Temple complex, amid a beautiful garden setting, its roots embedded in the same soil as its celebrated ancestor. Additionally, many monasteries and temples dot the bucolic landscape, built in their national style by foreign Buddhist communities. The ambience is a mix of monastic tranquillity and small-town commotion (a booming nonreligious tourism industry has brought along with it the usual invasion of tourist paraphernalia, souvenir stalls and English-speaking wannabe guides).

The best time to visit is November to March when Tibetan pilgrims come down from McLeod Ganj in Dharamsala. The high season is from December to January, which is also when the Dalai Lama often visits.

◎ Sights & Activities

★ **Mahabodhi Temple**   BUDDHIST TEMPLE
(camera ₹100; ◎4am-9pm) The magnificent Unesco World Heritage–listed Mahabodhi Temple, marking the hallowed ground where Buddha attained enlightenment and formulated his philosophy of life, forms the spiritual heart of Bodhgaya. Built in the 6th century AD atop the site of a temple erected by Emperor Ashoka almost 800 years earlier, it was razed by foreign invaders in the 11th century, and subsequently underwent several major restorations.

Topped by a 50m pyramidal spire, the inner sanctum of the ornate structure houses a 10th-century, 2m-high gilded image of a seated Buddha. Amazingly, four of the original sculpted stone railings surrounding the temple, dating from the Sunga period (184–72 BC), have survived amid the replicas. Others are now housed inside the archaeological museum.

Pilgrims and visitors from all walks of life and religions come to worship or just soak up the atmosphere of this sacred place. There's a well-manicured **Meditation Park** (Mahabodhi Temple; visitors/meditators ₹20/25; ◎visitors 10am-5pm, meditators 5-10am & 5-9pm) for those seeking extra solitude within the temple grounds. An enthralling way to start or finish the day is to stroll around the inside perimeter of the temple compound (in an auspicious clockwise pattern) and watch a sea of maroon and yellow dip and rise as monks perform endless prostrations on their prayer boards.

Monasteries & Temples   MONASTERIES, TEMPLES
One of Bodhgaya's great joys is its collection of monasteries and temples, each offering visitors a unique opportunity to peek into different Buddhist cultures and compare architectural styles. The **Indosan Nipponji Temple** (Japanese Temple; Buddha Rd; ◎5am-noon & 2-6pm) is an exercise in quiet Japanese understatement compared with the richly presented **Bhutanese Monastery** (Buddha Rd) nearby, which houses some wonderfully colourful and intricate frescoes. The most impressive of all the modern monasteries is the **Tergar Monastery** (Sujata Bypass Rd) of the Karmapa school of Tibetan Buddhism. It's a glory of Tibetan decorative arts that will leave you slack-jawed as you enter. A none-too-distant runner-up is the impressive **Thai Temple** (Bodhgaya Rd; ◎dawn-dusk), a brightly coloured *wat* with gold leaf shimmering from its arched rooftop and manicured gardens. Meditation sessions are held here mornings and evenings. The Tibetan **Karma Temple** (Temple St; ◎dawn-dusk) – note the double-dragon brass door knockers – and **Namgyal Monastery** (Tibetan Temple; Kalachakra Maidan Rd) each contain large prayer wheels. Monasteries are open dawn to dusk.

Bodhgaya

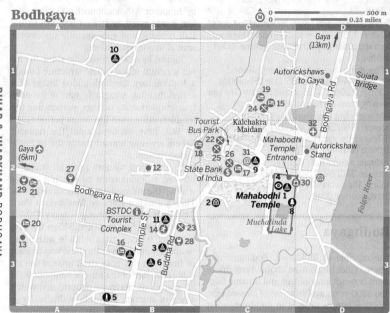

Bodhgaya

⊚ Top Sights
1 Mahabodhi Temple.................................C2

⊚ Sights
2 Archaeological Museum C2
3 Bhutanese Monastery..............................B3
4 Bodhi Tree...C2
5 Great Buddha Statue...............................B3
6 Indosan Nipponji Temple.......................B3
7 Karma Temple...B3
8 Meditation Park..C2
9 Namgyal Monastery.................................C2
10 Tergar Monastery.....................................B1
11 Thai Temple..B3

⊙ Activities, Courses & Tours
12 International Meditation Centre B2
13 Root Institute for Wisdom
    Culture..A3
14 Thai Massage B3

⊜ Sleeping
15 Gupta House...C1
16 Karma Temple...B3

17 Kirti Guest House.....................................C2
18 Mohammad House.....................................B2
19 Rahul Guest House...................................C1
20 Shantidevi Ashram's Guesthouse.........A3
21 Taj Darbar...A2

⊗ Eating
22 Be Happy Cafe..C2
23 Bodhgaya City Cafe Restaurant B3
24 Hari Om International Cafe C1
25 Mohammad Restaurant...........................C2
26 Ram Sewak Tea Corner...........................C2

⊙ Drinking & Nightlife
27 Bottle Shop...A2
28 Hotel Sujata..B3
29 Royal Residency.......................................A2

⊙ Shopping
30 Mahabodhi Bookshop..............................D2

⊙ Information
31 Namaste India Holiday Tours C2
32 Verma Health Care Centre.....................D2

Great Buddha Statue   MONUMENT
(off Temple St; ⊙7am-noon & 2-5pm) This
25m-high statue towers above a pleasant
garden at the end of Temple St. The impressive monument was unveiled by the Dalai
Lama in 1989 and is surrounded by 10 smaller sculptures of Buddha's disciples. The statue is partially hollow and is said to contain
some 20,000 bronze Buddhas.

WORTH A TRIP

KESARIYA

Rising high out of the earth from where the dying Buddha donated his begging bowl, the enormous **Kesariya Stupa** (⊘dawn-dusk) is an enthralling example of how nature can reclaim a deserted monument. Excavated from under a grassy and wooded veil is what is thought to be the world's tallest (38m) Buddhist stupa dating from the Pala period (200–750 AD). Above the 425m-circumference pedestal are five uniquely shaped terraces that form a gargantuan Buddhist tantric mandala. Each terrace has a number of niches containing disfigured Buddha statues, which were destroyed during attacks by foreign invaders in the middle ages. The rural setting is a joy, but there is nothing else to see here apart from the stupa.

Buses from Patna can drop you by the stupa, which is visible from the main road. The last bus back swings by at around 3.30pm. Buses from Motihari will drop you at the main crossroads in the village of Kesariya, where there are roadside *dhabas* (snack bars) you could have lunch in, leaving you with a 2km-walk (the signpost says 3km but it's not that far).

Archaeological Museum
MUSEUM

(off Bodhgaya Rd; admission ₹10; ⊘8am-5pm, closed Fri) This museum contains a number of stone Buddhist sculptures dating from the 8th to 12th centuries, but the highlight is the collection of original granite and sandstone railings and pillars rescued from the Mahabodhi Temple, some of which predate the temple by 700 years.

Thai Massage
MASSAGE

(Thai Temple; 1hr foot massage 300 Thai baht; 2hr body massage 500 Thai baht; ⊘8am-5pm) Authentic Thai massage in a massage clinic at the Thai Hospital, located within the grounds of the Thai Temple; take the entrance to the left of the main temple entrance. Rates are listed in Thai baht, which are roughly twice the value of Indian rupees, so expect to pay around ₹1000 for a full-body two-hour massage.

⚑ Courses

Root Institute for
Wisdom Culture
MEDITATION, YOGA

(☑0631-2200714; www.rootinstitute.com; ⊘office 8.30-11.30am & 1.30-4.30pm) Located in a tranquil, tree-shaded corner of town, this foreign-run institute holds various meditation courses (from two to 21 days) between October and March. Courses cost around ₹1000 per day, including meals and accommodation. The 6.45am meditation session is open to all; you can also catch drop-in yoga classes at 11.45am Tuesday to Saturday.

There's a charitable health program running six days a week; volunteering is welcome.

International Meditation Centre
MEDITATION

(☑0631-2200707; meditation by donation) The courses here are more informal than other meditation centres, and run sporadically throughout the year. Courses are often in blocks of 10 days, although you are free to join midway through a course.

⌨ Sleeping

You can stay at the very peaceful Root Institute for Wisdom Culture even if you're not attending any of its courses. Dorm beds cost ₹230, while double rooms go for ₹900, or ₹1500 with a private bathroom.

★Rahul Guest House
GUESTHOUSE $

(☑0631-2200709; rahul_bodhgaya@yahoo.co.in; near Kalchakra Maidan; s/d ₹500/600; ⊛) Clean, serene and unobtrusively welcoming, this family home makes for an excellent stay away from the din. The rooms upstairs, with whitewashed walls, nice breezes and simple furnishings, are better than those on the ground floor, but all are good value. No restaurant, but wi-fi throughout.

Mohammad House
GUESTHOUSE $

(☑9431085251, 9934022691; yasmd_2002@rediffmail.com; r ₹300-400) There's an authentic village atmosphere at this hard-to-find, no-frills guesthouse, which is hidden away from the more touristy parts of town. Ducks and chickens scuttle around the narrow lanes which link villagers' colourfully painted homes to the Kalchakra Maidan area.

The guesthouse has two buildings, almost side by side; the older one has very basic triple rooms with shared bathrooms for ₹300.

The newer one has simple, but clean twin rooms with attached bathrooms and powerful, hot-water showers for ₹400. Both have rooms on upper floors with lovely views of the surrounding paddy fields. To find the place, either take the lane beside Mohammad Restaurant (same owners), and walk through the village, turning left then right, or take the lane diagonally opposite the Thai Temple (signposted towards the International Meditation Centre) and keep walking straight.

Karma Temple   GUESTHOUSE $
(☎0631-2200795; Temple St; d ₹500) Simple but tidy twin rooms, with clean shared shower rooms, set around a courtyard at the back of the peaceful Karma Temple.

Gupta House   GUESTHOUSE $
(☎0631-2200933; jyoti_gupta2000in@yahoo.com; beside Kalchakra Maidan; d ₹500; ☎) Rooms are spartan, but comfortable enough at this homestay-style guesthouse, but its main selling point is the alfresco Hari Om International Cafe located out front.

★**Shantidevi Ashram's Guesthouse**   GUESTHOUSE $$
(☎9939248755; www.shantideviashramguesthouse.com; r ₹1000) This unassuming, but tastefully decorated boutiquelike guesthouse makes a pleasant retreat from the hustle and bustle of the main drags. Fancooled rooms come with quality wooden furniture, pieces of artwork and colourful rugs on concrete floors. Bathrooms are small, but super clean. There's no restaurant, but staff can usually whip up a simple breakfast for guests.

The five-bed group room costs ₹2500. All other rooms are ₹1000. Wi-fi is in the reception area only.

Kirti Guest House   HOTEL $$
(☎0631-2200744; kirtihouse744@yahoo.com; off Bodhgaya Rd; with/without AC ₹2000/1500; ✳@☎) Run by the Tibetan Monastery, this hotel offers a quiet atmosphere despite its central location. It's set back from the road slightly and has simple but neat and tidy rooms. air-con rooms are quieter and more spacious, but non-AC rooms open out onto a shared balcony overlooking the street below, so have more natural light. Wi-fi in lobby only.

Taj Darbar   HOTEL $$$
(☎0631-2200053, 7739320524; www.hoteltajdarbar.com; Bodhgaya Rd; s/d from ₹5000/5600; ✳☎) A good-value top-end choice, this smart hotel comes with polished marble hallways and spacious rooms with ivory-white bed sheets, small seating areas, working desks and sporadic bathtubs. Fish for discounts as you can sometimes get rooms for as little as ₹3500.

✖ Eating & Drinking

Royal Residency (Bodhgaya Rd; mains ₹150-250, beers ₹350) and **Hotel Sujata** (Buddha Rd; mains ₹150-300, beers ₹320), two of Bodhgaya's upmarket hotels, have the only restaurants in town which officially serve alcohol,

---

TREE OF WISDOM

Undoubtedly, the most sacred fig tree ever to grace the Earth was the **Bodhi Tree** at Bodhgaya, under which Prince Siddhartha, aka the Buddha, achieved enlightenment.

Known as Sri Maha Bodhi, the original tree was paid special attention by Ashoka, a mighty Indian emperor who ruled most of the subcontinent from 269 to 232 BC, a century or so after the date the Buddha is believed to have died. Ashoka's jealous wife, Tissarakkhā, felt the emperor should have been directing his devotion towards her, rather than towards a tree and, in a fit of rage, she caused the tree to perish by piercing it with poisonous thorns.

Thankfully, before its death, one of the tree's saplings was carried off to Anuradhapura in Sri Lanka by Sanghamitta (Ashoka's daughter), where it continues to flourish. A cutting was later carried back to Bodhgaya and planted where the original once stood. The red sandstone slab between the tree and the adjacent Mahabodhi Temple was placed by Ashoka to mark the spot of Buddha's enlightenment – it's referred to as the Vajrasan (Diamond Throne). Buddha was said to have stared unblinkingly at the tree in an awed gesture of gratitude and wonder after his enlightenment. Today, pilgrims and tourists alike flock here and attempt to do exactly the same thing, and the tree is considered the most important of Buddhism's four holiest sites.

although Mohammad's and Hari Om can usually rustle you up a beer if you ask discreetly. There's a **bottle shop** (beer from ₹100; ⊙10am-10pm) along Bodhgaya Rd, but it tends to only serve strong beer and whiskey, rather than the more drinkable light beers.

⭐**Mohammad Restaurant**   MULTICUISINE $
(mains ₹50-150; ⊙7am-9pm; 🛜) Tucked away behind the market stalls at the tourist bus park (take the lane beside Fujiya Green restaurant), Mohammed's whips up a fine array of food from across the Buddhist world – Tibetan, Chinese, Thai, Indian – as well as doing a strong line in Western favourites, including breakfasts. The fresh fruit juices are superb and there's outdoor seating.

This is also one of the few places in town that's willing to serve beer (₹150), albeit in an unofficial capacity.

Hari Om International Cafe   MULTICUISINE $
(Kalchakra Maidan; mains ₹70-100; ⊙8am-10pm) This informal, shantylike, alfresco restaurant in front of Gupta House guesthouse has a multicuisine menu, which includes local specialities such as *litti chokha*, *khichdi* (a blend of lightly spiced rice and lentils) and *rajma* (kidney bean curry).

Ram Sewak Tea Corner   SWEETS $
(dishes ₹30-60, thalis ₹75; ⊙7am-7pm) If you're seeking sustenance at rock-bottom prices, look no further than this *dhaba*-style eatery, little more than a glorified roadside stand, for excellent snacks (including samosa, dosa and *idli* – a South Indian spongy, round, fermented rice cake), sweets, lassis and basic thalis.

The outdoor seating is a great spot to lounge with a cup of masala chai and watch Bodhgaya go by.

Bodhgaya City Cafe Restaurant   INDIAN $
(Buddha Rd; mains ₹50-150; ⊙7am-10pm) Good-value local food with outdoor seating in a newly built restaurant-and-cafe complex set back from Buddha Rd.

⭐**Be Happy Cafe**   ITALIAN $$
(beside Kalchakra Maidan; mains ₹170-320; ⊙8am-8.30pm; 🛜) Quaint, cosy, European-style cafe serving fresh coffee (₹80), herbal teas and healthy Italian cuisine; salads, pastas and freshly baked pizza. Will refill water bottles with safe-to-drink filtered water (₹10). Free wi-fi.

🛍 Shopping

There are scores of souvenir stalls around, peddling the usual religious trinkets such as rosaries and prayer wheels, as well Tibetan-style jewellery.

Mahabodhi Bookshop   BOOKS
(Mahabodhi Temple; ⊙5am-9pm) Stocks a range of Buddhist literature within the temple complex.

ℹ Information

Main post office (cnr Bodhgaya & Godam Rds; ⊙10am-4pm Mon-Fri, to 2pm Sat)

Namaste India Holiday Tours (per hour ₹50; ⊙9am-9pm) Internet cafe diagonally opposite Kirti Guesthouse. Has wi-fi too.

State Bank of India (Bodhgaya Rd; ⊙10.30am-4.30pm Mon-Fri, to 1.30pm Sat) Best rates for cash and travellers cheques; has an ATM.

Verma Health Care Centre (📞0631-2201101, 9934290324; ⊙24hr) Emergency room and clinic. Staffed round the clock, but a doctor is only on location from 11.30am to 8pm.

ℹ Getting There & Away

Gaya airport is 8km west of Bodhgaya, on the back route to Gaya. **Air India** (📞2201155; www.airindia.com; Airport) flies daily to Delhi and Varanasi, and twice a week to Kolkata. During tDecember and January there are direct international flights from Bangkok (Thailand), Colombo (Sri Lanka), Thimphu (Bhutan) and Yangon (Myanmar).

Shared autorickshaws (₹20) leave from the T-junction of Bodhgaya Rd and Sujata Bridge for the 13km trip to Gaya. A private autorickshaw to Gaya costs ₹120 to ₹150.

Note, autos sometimes take the back route from Gaya to Bodhgaya, via Sikadia More, and then drop passengers on the approach to Mahabodhi Temple on Bodhgaya Rd.

Rajgir

📱06112 / POP 33,700

The fascinating surrounds of Rajgir are bounded by five semiarid rocky hills, each lined with ancient stone walls – vestiges of the ancient capital of Magadha. As both Buddha and Mahavira spent some serious time here, Rajgir is an important pilgrimage site for Buddhists and Jains. And a mention in the Mahabharata also means that Rajgir sees a large number of Hindu pilgrims, who come to bathe in the hot springs at the Lakshmi Narayan Temple.

Rajgir is littered with historic sites, so bank on spending a couple of days here, including a side trip to Nalanda. It's a lovely part of Bihar; cooler and greener than other places in the region, and relatively hassle-free.

The bus stand is in the centre of town, with the train station 1km away; turn left out of the bus stand and take the third left to reach the train station. Turn right out of the train station road to reach the bus stand and the town centre.

Rajgir Mahotsava (Rajgir; ⊙ Oct), in October, is the town's three-day cultural festival featuring classical Indian music, folk music and dance.

◉ Sights & Activities

The most pleasant way to see Rajgir's scattered sites is to rent a tonga. A four-hour tour including the hot springs at Lakshmi Narayan Temple, Vishwashanti Stupa, the museum at Veerayatan and any number of other sights you have time for is ₹600, although you can usually barter the price down to ₹500. For single-trip journeys to popular sights, shared tonga rides are also possible (expect to pay about ₹10 per person for a 2km ride).

★ Vishwashanti Stupa   BUDDHIST TEMPLE
(Shanti Stupa Rd; chairlift return ticket ₹60; ⊙ ropeway 8.15am-1pm & 2-5pm) Constructed in 1965, this blazing-white, 40m stupa stands atop the Ratnagiri Hill about 5km south of town. Recesses in the stupa feature golden statues of Buddha in four stages of his life – birth, enlightenment, preaching and death. A fun, but wobbly, single-person chairlift runs to the summit, which affords expansive views of hills and a few Jain shrines dotting the landscape.

Next to the stupa, a Japanese-built peace pagoda reverberates to the rhythmic sound of meditative drum beat. If you walk back down the hill, rather than taking the chairlift, you can detour to the ruined remains of a 1500-year-old stupa, thought to be where Buddha preached to his disciples.

Lakshmi Narayan Temple   HINDU TEMPLE
(free; ⊙ dawn-dusk) Hindu pilgrims are drawn to the noisy Lakshmi Narayan Temple, about 2km south of town (turn right out of the bus stand and keep walking), to enjoy the health benefits of the hot springs here. The murky grey Brahmakund, the hottest spring, is a scalding 45°C.

Temple priests will show you around, pour hot water on your head (in the manner of bathing a pilgrim) and ask for generous donations (don't feel pressured into giving anything if you don't want to; there's no obligation). It's a fascinating but confusing place with no English signs; tread carefully so you don't unintentionally offend.

Veerayatan   MUSEUM
(www.veerayatanbihar.org; Veerayatan Rd; admission ₹20; ⊙ 7am-6pm) About 1km from Lakshmi Narayan Temple (turn left out of the temple, then first left), this Jain museum tells the history of each of the 24 Jain *tirthankars* (teachers) through ornate dollhouselike 3D panel depictions made from wood and metal. The level of detail is astonishing.

Buddha Jal Vihar   SWIMMING
(admission/swimming ₹5/25; ⊙ men 5-10am & noon-9pm, women 10am-noon) Within the Lakshmi Narayan Temple complex (on your left as you approach the temple), the Jaipur-pink Buddha Jal Vihar is an inviting, crystal-clear swimming pool set in well-manicured gardens and perfect to beat the heat. There's another, similar pool by a restaurant, just before it, but it's not as popular (or attractive), and is sometimes closed.

⌂ Sleeping

Hotel Raj   HOTEL $
(☑ 9304376445; opposite the bus stand; r ₹400) One hundred metres down the road opposite the bus stand, this is the cleanest and most welcoming of the cheapies in the town centre. Simple but colourful fan-cooled rooms open onto an inner courtyard. Management speaks English, and everything is kept pretty much spotless. Squat toilets only.

Siddharth Hotel   HOTEL $$
(☑ 06612-255216, 9304013642; siddharthrajgir@gmail.com; s/d from ₹1450/1760; ❋ @ 🛜) Near Lakshmi Narayan Temple (turn left out of the temple, and it's on the right after 300m), Siddharth has fresh, clean rooms, a restaurant and wi-fi in the lobby. It's handy for the hot springs and the Buddha Jal Vihar swimming pool, but it's a 2km-hop into town.

Indo Hokke Hotel   BOUTIQUE HOTEL $$$
(☑ 06612-255245; indohokkehotel@gmail.com; Veerayatan Rd; s/d ₹6000/6500; ❋ @ 🛜 ⛨) Surrounded by lovely gardens, this modern, red-brick building features Japanese-style rooms furnished with tatami mats, teak furniture and Eastern decor. The restaurant

has an excellent Japanese menu, as well Indian. It's 500m beyond Veerayatan museum.

Eating

Hotel Anand PUNJABI $
(mains ₹40-100; ⊘8am-10pm) Small, fan-cooled, streetside restaurant serving good-value Punjabi and South Indian dishes, including thali (₹80 to ₹130). About 100m beyond Hotel Raj.

Green Restaurant INDIAN $
(mains ₹60-150, thali ₹250; ⊘7.30am-9.30pm) Diagonally opposite the Lakshmi Narayan Temple complex, this simple restaurant offers great Indian meals including an elaborate vegetarian thali. Has outdoor seating.

Lotus Restaurant INDIAN, JAPANESE $$$
(Veerayatan Rd; mains ₹150-500; ⊘11am-3pm & 7-10pm) If you fancy an upscale experience, look no further than this restaurant at the Indo Hokke Hotel. It has superb Indian food and a pricier Japanese menu featuring soba noodles, teriyaki and tempura, with authentic flavours and fresh ingredients (including pepper, pickles and tea).

ⓘ Information

There's a **tourist office** (⊘10am-5pm Mon-Sat) on the main road between the bus stand and the railway station, which has a free map of Rajgir and Nalanda. The main sights are signposted in English.

There are ATMs near the bus stand and one opposite the Lakshmi Narayan Temple complex.

ⓘ Getting There & Around

Frequent buses run to Gaya (₹50 to ₹55, 2½ hours) and Nalanda (₹10, 20 minutes) from the bus stand. Shared jeeps also shuttle between Rajgir and Nalanda (₹10).

Only one daytime train goes to Gaya (2nd class ₹25, three hours, 4.33pm except Sunday), while two fast trains run daily to Patna (2nd class/sleeper/AC chair ₹50/140/255, 2½ hours) at 8.10am and 2.40pm.

Nalanda

🎵 061194

Founded in the 5th century AD, Nalanda – 15km north of Rajgir – was one of the ancient world's great universities and an important Buddhist centre of academic excellence. When Chinese scholar and traveller Xuan Zang visited sometime between 685 and 762 AD, about 10,000 monks and students lived here, studying theology, astronomy, metaphysics, medicine and philosophy. It's said that Nalanda's three libraries were so extensive they burnt for six months when foreign invaders sacked the university in the 12th century.

Allow at least an hour or two for wandering the extensive **ruins** (Indian/foreigner ₹5/100, video camera ₹25; ⊘9am-5.30pm). They're peaceful and well maintained with a parklike atmosphere of clipped lawns, shrubs and roses. The red-brick ruins consist of nine monasteries and four main temples. Most impressive is the **Great Stupa**, with steps, terraces, a few intact votive stupas and monks' cells (sleeping quarters). Climbing the structures is not allowed.

Unofficial guides (₹100) will approach you, but each of the ruins have signboards beside them in English.

Across from the entrance to the ruins is the **archaeological museum** (admission ₹5; ⊘9am-5pm, closed Fri), a small but fascinating museum housing the Nalanda University seal and a host of beautiful stone sculptures and bronzes unearthed from Nalanda and Rajgir. Among the many Buddha figures and *kirtimukha* (gargoyles) is a bizarre multiple-spouted pot (probably once used to contain perfumed water).

About 1.5km further on from the museum and the ruins (take the first right) is the huge **Xuan Zang Memorial Hall** (Indian/foreigner ₹5/50; ⊘8am-5pm), built by the Chinese as a peace pagoda in honour of the famous Chinese traveller who walked to India from China before studying and teaching for some years at Nalanda, and

PILGRIMAGE ON RAILS

A unique way to explore the Buddhist circuit in North India is by hopping onto the **Mahaparinirvan Express** (www.railtourismindia.com/buddha), operated by Indian Railways on set dates between September and March. The eight-day package tour starts in Delhi, and guides you through Bodhgaya, Rajgir, Nalanda, Varanasi, Sarnath, Kushinagar, Lumbini (in Nepal) and Sravasti before returning to Delhi via Agra. Per person all-inclusive rates for the tour start from US$115 per day. Note that the tariff doesn't include your visa fees for Nepal.

BIHAR & JHARKHAND NALANDA

eventually returning home with Buddhist scriptures he would later translate into Chinese. His epic trip was immortalised in *Journey to the West*, one of China's classic pieces of literature. The story was then turned into the cult 1970s TV show, *Monkey*. Modern-day backpackers will appreciate the statue of Xuan Zang at the front of the memorial hall.

On the pathway leading to the archaeological museum, Cafeteria Nalanda (mains ₹100-250; ⊙6am-8pm) makes a pleasant spot for lunch. It does Indian and Chinese dishes and has tree-shaded outdoor seating.

Buses from Rajgir (₹10) drop you at Nalanda village. From there you can take a shared tonga (per person ₹5) for the final 2km to the ruins.

Kundalpur

About 1.5km beyond the Nalanda ruins (bear left, then right, then take the first right turn after Surya Kund pond), you'll find the striking Nandyavarta Mahal (⊙5am-9pm) at Kundalpur, believed by the Digambar Jain sect to be the birthplace of Lord Mahavira, the final *tirthankar* and founder of Jainism. The small temple complex houses three hot-white temples, the main featuring a to-scale postured idol of Mahavira. Inside the serene Trikal Chaubeesi Jinmandir within the same complex you'll find 72 *tirthankar* idols representing 24 each of the past age, the present age and the future age.

JHARKHAND

Hewn out of neighbouring Bihar in 2000 to meet the autonomy demands of the Adivasi (tribal) population, Jharkhand is a land of immense natural and anthropological wealth. However, despite boasting an incredible 40% of the country's mineral wealth (mostly coal, copper and iron ore), rich forests and cash rich industrial hubs, it is plagued by poverty, social injustice, corruption and sporadic outbursts of Maoist and Naxalite violence. For travellers, Jharkhand's prime attractions are the Jain pilgrimage centre at Parasnath Hill, its national parks and the chance to explore a relatively tourist-free and unspoilt part of India.

Ranchi

☏0651 / POP 863,500

Set on a plateau at 700m and marginally cooler than the plains, Jharkhand's capital, Ranchi, was the summer capital of Bihar under the British. Apart from the Jagannath Temple, there's little of interest here for travellers, but the city acts as a gateway to Betla (Palamau) National Park, and there are numerous waterfalls you can visit in the surrounding countryside.

◉ Sights

Jagannath Temple   HINDU TEMPLE
This 17th-century temple, about 12km southwest of town (₹250 return by autorickshaw), is a smaller version of the great Jagannath Mandir at Puri, and is open to non-Hindus. Every year during the Rath Yatra festival, in the same manner as in Puri in Odisha, Jagannath and his brother and sister gods are charioted to their holiday home, a smaller temple some 500m away.

☞ Tours

Suhana Tour & Travels   TOUR AGENCY
(☏9431171394;   suhana_jharkhandtour@yahoo.co.in; Station Rd; ⊙8am-8pm Mon-Sat, to 2pm Sun) Run by friendly Amardeep Sahay, this place organises day-long trips to local waterfalls (₹1250 per person; minimum two people), as well as a two-day trip to Betla (Palamau) National Park (₹4200 per person; minimum two people). The Betla trip includes transport, one night's accommodation, meals, one jeep safari and one elephant safari. Amardeep also helps with general transport and ticketing.

★★ Festivals & Events

Chhath Festival   HINDU FESTIVAL
(Bihar & Jharkhand; ⊙Oct/Nov) People line the banks of rivers and water bodies to honour Surya, the Sun God. For four days every November, it sees pious locals perform a series of rites that culminate in a social jamboree on the third day, marked by water rituals, traditional music and social mingling. At sunset on the sixth day after Diwali, married women, having fasted for 36 hours, immerse themselves in the water and offer fruits and flowers to the deity.

🛏 Sleeping

Station Rd, running between the train and bus stations, is lined with hotels and restaurants, but most budget hotels do not have permits for hosting foreigners. Turn left out of the train station to reach Chanakya BNR Hotel (100m), the Nook, and Suhana Tour & Travels (200m), Hotel AVN Plaza (300m) and the government bus stand (500m), just beyond the junction where shared autorickshaws pick up passengers.

Yatri Niwas GUESTHOUSE **$**
(☑ 06612-2462925; Train Station; dm ₹150-200, s ₹500-550, tw ₹700-750, with AC s/d ₹1000/1280) Surprisingly good for a train-station rest house, and the only budget hotel around here that will accept foreigners, Yatri Niwas has simple but comfortable rooms with TV

OFF THE BEATEN TRACK

HIKING THE HOLY HILL

For a fabulously off-beat experience with a spiritual leaning, consider joining the hundreds of Jain pilgrims who hike each morning to the top of holy **Parasnath Hill**.

Also known as Shikarji, Parasnath Hill is the highest mountain in Jharkhand, and a major Jain pilgrimage centre. It rises 1366m from the lush surrounding farmland in a secluded spot of eastern Jharkhand (although it's best reached from Gaya in Bihar) and its summit is studded with 31 temples of religious importance, including the striking **Parasnath Temple** which stands on the spot where 20 of the 24 Jain *tirthankars* (including Parasnath, at the age of 100) are believed to have reached salvation.

The approach to the hill is from the small, but auspicious temple town of Madhuban, 13km northeast of Parasnath train station, and located at the foot of the mountain. The daily pilgrimage begins from the town at 3am or 4am; it's a 9km hike to the top, followed by a 9km loop at the summit, visiting each of the temples. The entire 27km circuit – up, round and back down – takes about nine to 10 hours; three hours up, three or four hours circuiting the summit, and two hours back down. You could start later in the day and still get back before dark, but hiking while you're half asleep with hundreds of pilgrims as dawn breaks across the mountain is a big part of the experience here, and starting early means you avoid the worst of the midday heat. Water, chai and snacks are available along the way. During holidays and major festivals, you could end up walking with as many as 15,000 people.

You're likely to spend at least one night in Madhuban. There are three or four hotels in town (plus numerous *dharamsalas* – pilgrims' rest houses). The best value is the ageing **Yatri Nivas** (☑ 0658-232265; r ₹300-400) with simple, but huge rooms, some with mountain views. It's at the bottom end of the main road leading up to the mountain, just before you reach the museum; look for the easy-to-miss sign on the gate. Just before Yatri Nivas, turn left down a lane off the main road, and keep walking for 500m to reach **Shikarji Continental** (☑ 06558-232429; r ₹1400; ❋). This is the best quality hotel in town, with large, smart, air-con-cooled rooms; many have balconies with mountain views. It has a restaurant and a massage room (per hour ₹50); perfect after your hike. **Hotel Sapna & Veg Restaurant** (☑ 06558-232234; Main Rd; r from ₹600, mains ₹50-130; ⊙ 11am-10pm) is towards the top end of the main road and has a 1st-floor restaurant serving tasty South Indian and Punjabi dishes. While you're in Madhuban, it's worth popping into the small but well-kept **Jain Museum** (admission ₹5; ⊙ 8am-6.30pm Mar-Oct, 8.30am-6pm Nov-Feb), on your left at the bottom end of the main road.

There are frequent trains throughout the day running between Gaya and Parasnath (two hours). Just buy a 'general' 2nd-class ticket (₹65 to ₹80) and hop on the next train; you'll usually get a seat, and if not, it's only two hours. Shared vehicles (jeeps, autos and even the odd bus) wait for passengers to disembark at Parasnath station, then take them to Madhuban (per person ₹30).

From Parasnath there are also trains to Ranchi (2nd class/AC chair ₹110/370, four hours, 10.24am and 4.25pm) and Varanasi (2nd class/sleeper ₹130/255 six hours, 11.21am), and a handful of trains to Kolkata, the most convenient being the Doon Express (sleeper/3AC/2AC ₹210/555/790, seven hours, 11.55pm).

and clean bathrooms. Rooms facing the outside of the building cost ₹50 more than their station-facing counterparts, but are quieter and have more natural light.

Turn right out of the train station to find the entrance. It has 24-hour checkout.

Hotel AVN Plaza HOTEL $$

(☑ 06612-2462231; www.hotelavnplaza.com; off Station Rd; s/d from ₹800/1000; ❋ ☎) This neat, modern hotel has small but spotlessly clean rooms with TV, wi-fi and hot-water showers. There are only five standard rooms (₹1000 for a double), so call ahead to reserve one unless you want to pay for premium (₹1800 for a double). It's down a lane, off Station Rd, but signposted. It has 24-hour checkout.

★ Chanakya BNR Hotel HERITAGE HOTEL $$$

(☑ 06612-2461211; www.chanakyabnrranchi.com; Station Rd; s/d incl breakfast from ₹4500/5700; ❋ @ ☎ ☎) This charming hotel could be your sole reason for visiting Ranchi. A part-historic railway property located outside the train station, it's a superbly renovated terracotta-roofed Raj relic that oozes vintage and boutique appeal. The property's trees are home to parrots, and it has a small outdoor pool, two excellent restaurants and a bar.

While the deluxe rooms are luxurious enough, try and grab a 110-year-old heritage room (same price), with antique furniture, plush beds, high ceilings and glass-panelled views of manicured lawns outside. You can't prebook the heritage rooms; just ask for one when you arrive and keep your fingers crossed.

✗ Eating & Drinking

Hotel AVN Plaza and Chanakya BNR Hotel both have restaurants that are open to nonguests; Chanakya BNR's two restaurants are particularly good.

The Nook INDIAN $$

(Station Rd; mains ₹90-150; ☺ noon-3pm & 7-11pm) Arguably the best midrange hotel restaurant in the train-station area, this in-house dining facility at Hotel Kwality Inns is comfortable and the service attentive without being obsequious. The tandoori section is delightful and amazingly popular, and there's chilled beer and hard booze on offer too.

❶ Information

There are ATMs at the train station and on Station Rd, and **internet cafes** (Station Rd, Gurunanak Market; per hour ₹20; ☺ 8am-10pm) in the same building as Suhana Tour & Travels.

❶ Getting There & Away

AIR

Ranchi's Birsa Munda Airport is 6km from the city centre. **Air India** (☑ 2503255; www.airindia.com) and **GoAir** (☑ 1800 222111; www.goair.in) fly daily to Delhi and Mumbai. A taxi to the airport is around ₹250.

BUS

From the **Government bus stand** (Station Rd), there are frequent buses to Gaya throughout the day (₹160, six hours) and numerous evening services to Patna (₹220 to ₹250, nine hours), which leave from around 9pm onwards.

Private sleeper and AC buses to cities such as Patna (seat ₹650, nine hours), Kolkata (seat/sleeper ₹220/300, 10 hours, from 8pm onwards) and Bhubaneswar (sleeper ₹450, 13 hours, from 6pm onwards) leave from **Khartatoli bus stand**, 3km from Station Rd (cycle-rickshaw/shared auto ₹30/5).

For Betla National Park, buses to Daltonganj (₹160, 4½ hours) leave from **ITI bus stand**, about 8km from Station Rd (local bus/shared auto/private auto ₹15/30/200).

TRAIN

The handy 12366 PNBE Janshatabdi runs daily to Patna (2nd class/chair ₹185/625, eight hours, 2.25pm), via Parasnath (₹110/370, three hours) and **Gaya** (₹160/525, 5½ hours).

For **Kolkata**, the handiest of the two daily trains is the Howrah Express (sleeper/3AC/2AC ₹250/665/955, nine hours, 9.40am).

The once-daily Tapaswini Express goes to Bhubaneswar (sleeper/3AC/2AC ₹340/920/1325, 13 hours, 3.55pm).

Betla (Palamau) National Park

☑ 06562

Wild elephants freely roam the virgin forests of this lovely, rarely visited **national park** (☑ 06562-222650, 9939341211; ☺ 6-10am & 2-5pm), spread over the hilly landscape of picturesque Palamau district, 140km west of Ranchi. Tiger sightings are rare, but a trip to this primeval region of Jharkhand offers a glimpse into the rich tribal heritage of the state. The park covers around 1026 sq km, about 232 sq km of which was declared as

Betla National Park in 1989. Hiding behind stands of sal forest, rich evergreens, teak trees and bamboo thickets are some 17 tigers, 52 leopards, 216 elephants and four lonely nilgais (antelope) according to a 2007 census (newer figures are yet to be derived). You'll also see plenty of monkeys, spotted deer and possibly some gaur (Indian bison).

The park is open year-round, but the best time to visit is November to April. If you can stand the heat, May is prime time for tiger spotting as forest cover is reduced and animals venture out in search of waterholes.

Jeep safaris and elephant safaris can be arranged privately at the park gate.

Elephant safaris only last one hour but cost a flat-rate of ₹400 per elephant (up to four people), so are a bargain as well as being a lot of fun; the elephant takes you off-piste, into thick forest cover, although not as deep into the park as the jeeps do.

Jeep safaris can be taken either during the park's morning session (between 6am and 10am) or afternoon session (between 2pm and 5pm), but elephant safaris can only be taken in the morning, and should be prebooked the night before (although this isn't always necessary). If you take a morning safari, wrap up warm; it's freezing in the forest before the sun comes up properly. If you don't have any warm clothes, borrow a blanket from your guesthouse to wrap yourself in.

If you have time on your hands, consider an excursion to the ruined **Palamau Fort**, a 16th-century citadel of the local tribal Chero dynasty sited spectacularly within the forest. Alternatively, plan a picnic on the sandy banks of the scenic **Kechki River**. A jeep tour to the fort costs the same as a jeep safari. A jeep tour to Kechki River is the same, minus the ₹150 park entry fee.

🛏 Sleeping & Eating

The best accommodation is **Tourist Lodge** (✆ bookings 06562-222650; d from ₹1130; ❄), just inside the entrance gate. It's far from luxurious, but boasts large clean rooms with TV, spacious bathrooms and private balconies with views of the deer-filled meadow in front of the forest. The well-priced canteen does post safari breakfasts and arranges a hearty vegetarian thali (₹100) for lunch and dinner upon advance notice.

About 50 paces from the lodge, and also just inside the park entrance, is **Tree House**

ℹ JEEP SAFARI COSTS

Jeep safaris can be arranged privately at the Betla (Palamau) National Park gate. The breakdown of the costs for jeep safaris is as follows:

Park entry (per vehicle, per hour) ₹150

Compulsory guide (per vehicle, per hour) ₹100

Jeep hire (per vehicle, per hour) ₹450

Camera fee (per person, per safari) ₹100

So, for example; a two-hour jeep safari for two people, both with cameras, would cost a total of ₹1600. For a single person, it would cost ₹1500. Jeep safaris can last from one hour to up to three or four hours, depending on how long you wish to spend in the park.

(✆ bookings 06562-222650; r ₹590). It has two elevated sets of rooms built of teak, and contains two bedrooms (one double, one single), a bathroom and an observation deck with the same views as Tourist Lodge. It's more basic, but great value. Both can be booked through the park office.

If they are booked out, spend the night at the government-run **Van Vihar** (✆ 07352006141; d with/without AC ₹1030/600; ❄), 100m before the park entrnace. It's a hulking property that was undergoing wholesale renovations when we last visited, so should be spick and span by the time you arrive. It also has a restaurant.

ℹ Getting There & Away

The nearest town to the park entrance is Daltonganj, about 20km away, which has frequent bus services to Ranchi throughout the day (₹160, 4½ hours). From Daltonganj take a local bus (₹20, roughly hourly until around 4pm) or shared autorickshaw (₹30) to Betla. A private auto from Daltonganj will cost around ₹300. If you're able to explain where you're going to the bus conductor, you can save some time by getting off the Ranchi bus at the turn-off for Betla, about 10km before Daltonganj. From here you can wave down a passing bus (₹10) or shared auto (₹20), or hire a private auto (₹200) to the park.

If you don't fancy going it alone, Suhana Tour & Travels (p536), based in Ranchi, does two-day trips to Betla for ₹4200 per person (minimum two people).

Sikkim

Why Go?

Hailed as one of the world's last utopias by legendary Buddhist guru Padmasambhava, Sikkim is arguably among the loveliest destinations in India. And what variety in such a small state: plunging rhododendron-clad mountain valleys in the north; West Sikkim's atmospheric Buddhist monasteries; monumental religious statues in South Sikkim; and friendly and cheerful urban centres in the east. Then there are stunning views of Khangchendzonga, the world's third-highest mountain (8598m), visible from almost any viewpoint in the state. Little wonder that this tiny former Himalayan kingdom is such a haven for travellers.

A strong preserve of Tibetan Buddhism, Sikkim's public aesthetics are executed in shades of ritualistic vermilion, gold, blue and green, which make striking photo ops. Throw in yummy local food, exotic Himalayan wildlife, picture-postcard landscapes and some great hikes, and you have a superb mountain escape on the cards.

Best Places to Stay

➜ Elgin Mount Pandim (p558)

➜ Bamboo Retreat (p551)

➜ Biksthang (p561)

Best Monasteries

➜ Tashiding Gompa (p562)

➜ Pemayangtse Gompa (p558)

➜ Rumtek Gompa (p549)

When to Go
Gangtok

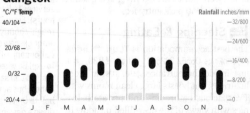

Oct–mid-Nov	Apr–May Spring	Mid-Jun–Sep
Clearest weather for views, but there are high-season crowds and prices.	blossoms and warmth make up for the cloudier skies.	Monsoon plays spoilsport, but there are great discounts on offer.

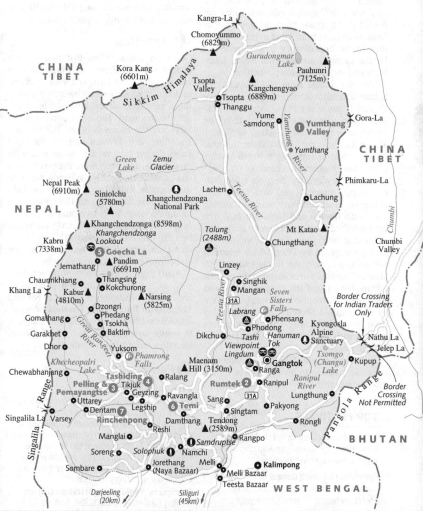

Sikkim Highlights

1 Enjoying a roller-coaster journey over mountain ridges and through abysslike valleys on a road trip to **Yumthang Valley** (p553)

2 Being enthralled by a colourful *chaam* (masked dance) ceremony at **Rumtek Gompa** (p549)

3 Waking up to dazzling Khangchendzonga views in **Pelling** (p556), and visiting **Pemayangtse Gompa** (p558)

4 Wandering among prayer flags and ancient chortens (stupas) within the magical **Tashiding Gompa** (p562)

5 Walking on high ground and getting close to sublime Himalayan peaks on the **Goecha La** (p561) trek

6 Sipping garden-fresh tea while taking in sweeping mountain vistas in **Temi** (p556)

7 Courting solitude and luxury at a stylish farmhouse in **Rinchenpong** (p561)

History

Sikkim was uninhabited until the 13th century, when the Lepchas migrated here from Assam or Myanmar (Burma), followed by Bhutias arriving from Tibet in the 15th century. In the 19th century, large numbers of Hindu migrants arrived from Nepal, forming a majority of Sikkim's population.

The Nyingmapa form of Vajrayana (Tibetan) Buddhism arrived with three refugee Tibetan lamas who met in modern-day Yuksom. Here in 1641 they crowned Phuntsog Namgyal as first chogyal (king) of Sikkim. The capital later moved to Rabdentse (near Pelling), then to Tumlong in North Sikkim, before finally settling in Gangtok.

In their heydays, the chogyals ruled eastern Nepal, upper Bengal and Darjeeling. However, much territory was lost during wars with Bhutan and Nepal. In 1835, the British bribed the chogyal to cede Darjeeling to the East India Company, a move that was strongly opposed by Tibet, which regarded Sikkim as a vassal state. In 1849, the British annexed the entire area between the present Sikkim border and the Ganges plains, and subsequently repulsed a counterinvasion by Tibet in 1886. Sikkim's last chogyal ruled from 1963 to 1975, after which the kingdom merged with the Indian dominion and was given statehood.

In the past decade, Sikkim has made considerable progress to become one of India's model states with high employment and low poverty. It is the first among Indian states to implement successful projects in organic farming, rural sanitation, public health and secondary education across its districts.

Activities

Going on a trek is the highpoint of any Sikkim sojourn. From day hikes between villages along centuries-old foot trails to multiday slogs across high mountain passes, there are plenty of trekking options available in the state. The most popular short hikes are the routes between Yuksom and Tashiding, and Yuksom and Khecheopalri Lake. Longer options that score well with experienced adventurers are the trek to Goecha La at the base of Khangchendzonga, and the Singalila Ridge trek that connects Yuksom to West Sikkim along the eponymous mountain ridge. Treks to remote areas such as Zemu Glacier and Green Lake are yet to be fully opened up, though it's possible to visit these areas if you have lots of money and permit-processing time to spare.

Apart from trekking, adventure activities such as mountain biking and paragliding are slowly becoming popular in Sikkim. The **Sikkim Paragliding Festival** (www.paraglidingassociationofindia.org), held in Gangtok in winter, sees plenty of participation from travellers and adventure junkies alike.

Permits

STANDARD PERMITS

Foreigners require an Inner Line Permit to enter Sikkim (Indians don't). These are free and getting one is a formality, although to apply you'll need photos and passport photocopies. Permits are most easily obtainable at the Melli police checkpost and Rangpo border post on arrival, but can also be obtained at Indian embassies abroad when getting your visa.

Foreigners' Regional Registration Offices (FRRO) (Delhi 011-26711384, Kolkata 033-22900549; www.immigrationindia.nic.in; 10am-5pm Mon-Fri) Sikkim permits.

Sikkim House (Delhi 011-26883026, Kolkata 033-22817905; www.sikkim.nic.in/sikkim house; 10.30am-4pm Mon-Fri, to 2pm Sat) Sikkim permits.

Sikkim Tourist Office (www.sikkimtourism. gov.in; 10am-5pm Mon-Sat) Darjeeling, Siliguri and Rangpo offices.

EXTENSIONS

Permits are generally valid for 30 days (sometimes 15 days from embassies abroad). These can be extended at government offices in

---

TOP FESTIVALS

Losar (Rumtek Gompa; Feb/Mar) Sikkim's biggest *chaam* (masked dance) rings in the Tibetan New Year.

Bumchu (Tashiding Gompa; Feb/Mar) Lamas open a *bum* (pot) containing *chu* (holy water) to foretell the year's fortunes.

Saga Dawa (all monastery towns; May/Jun) Religious ceremonies and parades commemorate Buddha's birth, enlightenment and death.

Pang Lhabsol (Ravangla; Aug) Prayers and religious dances are performed in honour of Sikkim's guardian deity Khangchendzonga.

Losoong (Old Rumtek; Dec/Jan) Sikkimese New Year, preceded by flamboyant *chaam* dances.

Gangtok and Tikjuk (6km below Pelling) for a further 30 days, giving a maximum of 60 days. Once you leave Sikkim, you must wait three months before applying for another permit.

PERMIT VALIDITY
The standard permit is valid for visits to the following areas:
- Gangtok, Rumtek and Lingdum
- All of South Sikkim
- North Sikkim as far as Singhik
- Most of West Sikkim where paved roads extend

SPECIAL PERMITS
High-altitude treks require **trekking permits**. These are valid for 15 days and can be easily organised by trekking agents.

For travel beyond Singhik up the Lachung and Lachen valleys in North Sikkim, foreigners need **restricted area permits**. These allow travel up to the Tsopta and Yumthang valleys. Indian citizens need a **police permit** to travel north of Singhik, but can venture further up the Thangu valley to Gurudongmar Lake, or to Yume Samdong (Zero Point) past Yumthang.

Foreigners also need a restricted area permit to visit Tsomgo (Changu) Lake. Only Indians are permitted to travel past Tsomgo Lake to the Tibetan border at Nathu La.

Trekking permits, as well as restricted area permits, are issued locally through approved tour agencies, and you must join a tour to get one. You'll need a minimum group of two, a passport photo, and copies of your existing permit, visa and passport details page. Permits take 24 hours to arrange.

EAST SIKKIM

Connected by a highway and speedy helicopter services with the rest of India, East Sikkim is focused around the urban hub of its capital Gangtok, and sees a higher tourist footfall than other parts of the state. The relaxed and casual grain of life, combined with a rush of cosmopolitan conveniences and points of touristy interest, makes this a nice place to kick back for a few days.

Gangtok

☑ 03592 / POP 98,600 / ELEV 1750M

Irreverent, cheerful and pleasantly boisterous, Sikkim's modern capital perches along a precipitous mountain ridge, descending down the hillside in steep tiers. A gradual-

ly growing sprawl of concrete, the town is blessed with a handful of sights, and doubles as a good base for excursions to places such as Rumtek and Tsomgo Lake. Travellers usually linger here for a few days, soaking up the local culture, stealing Khangchendzonga views from hotel terraces and arranging their travels (eg treks and tours) around the state.

The Rangpo–Mangan road (marked NH31A) forms the crooked north–south spine of Gangtok. Several restaurants, shops, banks, travel agents and tourist offices line the central pedestrianised Mahatma Gandhi (MG) Marg, a happy district patronised by shoppers, lovers, diners and fashionistas.

◉ Sights
★**Namgyal Institute of Tibetology** MUSEUM (www.tibetology.net; Deorali; admission ₹10; ◎10am-4pm) This fantastic museum housed in a traditional Tibetan-style mansion boasts a jaw-dropping collection of artefacts related to Vajrayana Buddhism and Tibetan culture. Established in 1958 to promote scholastic and cultural research, its ground-floor hall displays Buddhist manuscripts, icons, *thangkas* (Tibetan cloth paintings) and Tantric ritual objects, such as a *thöpa* (bowl made from a human skull) and *kangling* (human thighbone trumpet). The library on the 1st floor houses precious Buddhist tomes, some dating back several hundred years.

The revamped **souvenir store** within the building sells a collection of ritual objects, jewellery, mementos, books and documentaries on Sikkimese tradition and culture.

Five minutes up the same road is the **Do-Drul Chorten**, a large white stupa surrounded by monks' hostels and glass-walled galleries with countless flaming butter lamps burning within. Feel free to step in and light some as personal offerings (per lamp ₹7).

Gangtok

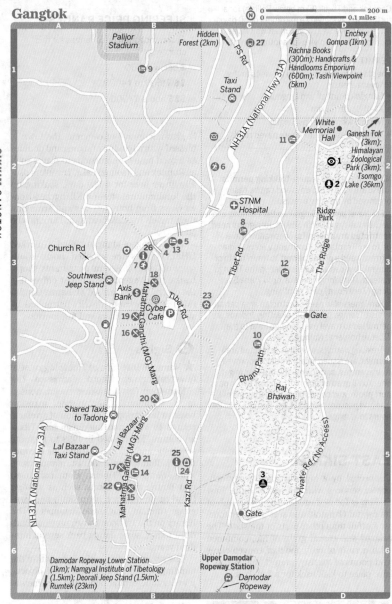

The institute sits in a shady grove and is close to the lower station of **Damodar Ropeway** (per person adult/child return ₹80/50, video ₹80; ⊙10am-4.30pm), a cable car running to the Secretariat ridge with great views of town.

Ridge PARK

With gorgeous views both to the east and west, the ridge – a shaded promenade cresting Gangtok's upper reaches – promises a pleasant stroll amid manicured parks and gardens. Located within one of the

Gangtok

green zones here is the **Flower Exhibition Centre** (admission ₹10; ☺9am-5pm), a modestly sized greenhouse full of exotic orchids, anthuriums and lilium. The impressive **Tsuglhakhang** temple to the south of the ridge is often open to the public early in the morning and during major festivals.

Nearby, the imposing Chogyal Palace (former royal residence) is closed to visitors, but it's a fine sight from a distance nonetheless.

Enchey Gompa   MONASTERY
(☺4am-4pm Mon-Sat, to 1pm Sun) FREE On the northern outskirts of Gangtok, approached through gently rustling conifers, stands this atmospheric and quaint monastery, with lovely murals and statues of Tantric deities. Some say the monastery's founder was known for his levitational skills. It's easily Gangtok's most attractive hermitage and comes alive for the colourful **Detor Chaam** masked dances in December/January.

To get here, hire a taxi from MG Marg (₹200) or simply walk for about 3km from MG Marg, first up to the ridge and then roughly in a northwestern direction (ask locals and they'll happily point you up the right path).

Himalayan Zoological Park   ZOO
(Indian/foreigner ₹25/50, vehicle ₹40, video ₹500; ☺9am-4pm Fri-Wed) One of the better main-tained zoos in the country, the Gangtok zoo occupies an entire hill opposite Ganesh Tok viewpoint. Red pandas, civet cats, Himalayan bears, clouded leopards and snow leopards roam around in extensive forested enclosures so large that you'll value a car to shuttle between them (although a walk through the dense greenery is recommended over motorised transport). There's a cafeteria within the zoo, with refreshments (snacks ₹30) and restroom facilities.

Ganesh Tok   VIEWPOINT
Festooned in colourful prayer flags and located opposite the zoo's main entrance is Ganesh Tok viewpoint, which offers superb city views, hot tea and Indian snacks (₹50). **Hanuman Tok**, another impressive viewpoint, sits on a hilltop around 4km beyond Ganesh Tok. The best Khangchendzonga views, however, are at **Tashi viewpoint**, 4km northwest of town, beside the road to Phodong.

🏃 Activities

Early-morning 'three-point' jeep tours show you Ganesh Tok, Hanuman Tok and Tashi viewpoints (₹800). Almost any travel agent, hotel or taxi driver offers variants, including a 'five-point' tour adding Enchey Gompa and Namgyal Institute (₹1000), or 'seven-point' tours taking on Old and New

Rumtek gompas (₹1600) or Rumtek plus Lingdum (₹1800). Prices are per vehicle for up to four passengers.

For high-altitude treks, visits to Tsomgo Lake or tours to North Sikkim you'll need a tour agency. Not all agents work with foreigners, so look for one that's registered with **Travel Agents Association of Sikkim** (TAAS; www.taas.org.in). All-inclusive trekking charges for foreigners range from US$60 to US$100 per person per day, depending on group size and services offered.

Altitude Tours & Travels   TREKKING
(☑ 9733380698; baichungb1@hotmail.com; MG Marg) A young and professional outfit offering standard trek and tour packages in Sikkim.

Blue Sky Treks & Travels   TREKKING
(☑ 9832370680; www.blueskysikkim.com; Tourism Bldg, MG Marg) For trekking and customised tours.

Potala Tours & Treks   TREKKING
(☑ 9434257036; www.potalatreks.in; PS Rd) A pricey but professional outfit with operations in Sikkim, Darjeeling and Bhutan, with an emphasis on local Tibetan culture.

Sikkim Tourism Development Corporation   OUTDOOR ADVENTURE
(STDC; ☑ 03592-203960; www.sikkimtourism. gov.in; MG Marg) Memorable eagle-eye views of Sikkim can be enjoyed from scenic **helicopter flights** operated by STDC. Choose between a buzz over Gangtok (₹9500, 15 minutes), a circuit of West Sikkim (₹66,000, 55 minutes), a circuit of North Sikkim (₹78,000, 65 minutes) and the Khangchendzonga ridge (₹90,000, 75 minutes). Prices are for five people (four for North Sikkim and Khangchendzonga). Book early.

STDC also has information on **paragliding** and **mountain biking**.

Yak & Yeti Travels & Expeditions   TREKKING
(☑ 9434117418; www.yaknyeti.com; Zero Point) Highly recommended for regional treks.

🛏 Sleeping

★ Hotel Pandim   HOTEL $
(☑ 9832080172; www.hotelpandim.com; Bhanu Path; d from ₹1500; 🔊) Richard Gere supposedly swung by this superb family-run budget address, located at a quiet roadside location along the ridge. Apart from his photo that hangs in the pretty terrace restaurant, the hotel offers great value, commendable ser-

vice, and the best beds and baths in town within a budget. The food menu is limited, but it's all fresh, homemade and delicious.

Top-floor deluxe rooms have the best mountain views, but the cheaper basement rooms are eminently liveable too. The reception is on the top floor, manned by Kesang, the friendly proprietor.

Modern Central Lodge   GUESTHOUSE $
(☑ 03592-204220; modernresidencysikkim@gmail. com; NH31A; d/tr ₹900/1000) First among equals in a group of budget hotels lining Gangtok's main drag, this place has the added advantage of an in-house travel agency that organises treks and tours. The spartan rooms sport hand-painted furniture, pastel walls and clean sheets. Combining a stay in the guesthouse with a tour often works in your favour money-wise.

Hotel Tashi Tagey   HOTEL $
(☑ 03592-231631; www.tashitagey.com; NH31A, Tadong; d from ₹1200; @) For quality Tibetan hospitality at unbelievable prices, it's worth seeking out this superfriendly place 3km below Gangtok. The spotless rooms here are adorned with cheerful upholstery, and the common areas sport floral arrangements and lots of quaint charm. The views from the rooftop garden are unbeatable and the Tibetan food is simply scrumptuous. A shared taxi from town costs ₹20.

★ Hidden Forest   HOMESTAY $$
(☑ 03592-205197; www.hiddenforestretreat.org; Middle Sichey Village; s/d from ₹2000/2500; @)
🌿 Some 2km from town, this family-run homestay – secluded amid fruit trees, orchids and flower nurseries – is a dream hideaway. The property overlooks a gorgeous valley vista and the pine-lined rooms boast understated luxury. The lip-smacking food (customised to your preferences) comes from a solar-powered kitchen, a resident cow provides dairy produce and all vegetable matter is composted.

The terrace is a great place for evening chhangs (barley beer), while the dining hall is accentuated by a splendid collection of botanical illustrations of rare Himalayan flora. A taxi from the centre of town costs ₹150.

Mintokling Guest House   GUESTHOUSE $$
(☑ 03592-208553; www.mintokling.com; Bhanu Path; s/d from ₹2050/2250; @ 🔊) Nestled amid exotic greenery and thrown around pretty lawns dotted with prayer flags, this lodge-like family home is an oasis of peace

and quiet. The plain but well-kept rooms sport pinewood wall panels and fresh upholstery made from traditional fabric. The local menu at the restaurant is a must-try; ask Pema at reception for recommendations.

Hotel Sonam Delek   HOTEL $$
(☑ 03592-202566; www.hotelsonamdelek.com; Tibet Rd; d incl breakfast from ₹1540; 🛜) Part art deco, part Tibetan, this long-standing favourite is great value for money. The cheaper rooms in the basement have common access to a superb rear terrace with sweeping views of Khangchendzonga across the valley. The pricier rooms (₹3440) above have private balcony views, king-size beds and prim furnishings. Service is prompt and efficient, and the food is yummy.

Oriental   BOUTIQUE HOTEL $$
(☑ 03592-221181; www.orientalsikkim.com; MG Marg; s/d incl breakfast ₹2850/3600; @) Stylish though understated, this appealing hotel behind a glass-and-teak facade sees a lot of guests who desire comfort and privacy without having to venture far from town. Rooms are smallish, but appointed with inviting beds (some with canopies), pinewood panelling and good views of Gangtok's central pedestrianised district below. It can be noisy during the day.

Hotel Nor-Khill   HERITAGE HOTEL $$$
(☑03592-205637; www.elginhotels.com; PS Rd; d incl half board ₹9200; 🛜) Checking into Nor-Khill is like time travelling back to the pre-Independence era, when this stately property served as the chogyal's royal guesthouse. Bearing testimony to its heyday are countless historical photos, period furniture and exquisite Tibetan carpets lending a vintage feel to the hallways and the lobby. The spaciously luxurious rooms are a worthy splurge, and attract diplomats and dignitaries.

For all its positives, however, the hotel overlooks a football stadium, which means things can get roaringly noisy with cheering and chanting during local league fixtures.

Chumbi Residency   BOUTIQUE HOTEL $$$
(☑ 03592-206618; www.thechumbiresidency.com; Tibet Rd; s/d incl breakfast from ₹4000/5000; 🛜) Despite being a tad overpriced, this spot of luxury lies only five minutes from the town centre and is extremely popular with top-end tour groups. A throwback to the 1980s in terms of appointment, its smallish rooms sport fresh white walls and tasteful furni-

ture. Ask for a room with a view. Tangerine, the bar-restaurant, is great for dinner.

🍴 Eating

★ Taste of Tibet   TIBETAN $
(MG Marg; mains ₹100-150; ⊙10am-9pm) This bustling upstairs place, incredibly popular with Gangtok's youth brigade, serves the best Tibetan morsels in Gangtok. On offer are generous servings of *momos* (dumplings), noodle soup, *shyabhale* (fried meat pasty), cold beef salad, fried pork and a selection of rice dishes – best paired with a bottle of local Dansberg beer. Finding a table during mealtimes can be difficult.

Parivar Restaurant   SOUTH INDIAN $
(MG Marg; dishes ₹80-120; ⊙8am-8pm) Eat here for good-value South Indian food, all of it purely vegetarian. Go for the various *masala dosas* (curried vegetables inside a crisp pancake) or *puri* (bread) with *choley paneer* (chickpeas with cottage cheese) for breakfast. For lunch and dinner, try the all-inclusive mini/full thali (₹120/180).

Bakers Cafe   BAKERY $
(MG Marg; pastries from ₹20, mains ₹80-150; ⊙9am-8pm) The hippest place to catch up with locals or fellow travellers on MG Marg, this cosy Western-style cafe has strong espresso (₹60), refreshing lemon iced tea, croissants, baguettes, panini, pizzas, hot dogs and pastries. Grab a window-side table overlooking the valley and pair your food with great mountain views.

FOODIE'S PARADISE

Sikkimese cuisine is a melange of robust Tibetan flavours and local tribal recipes, garnished with hints of Nepali and Bengali cooking. Traditional Sikkimese dishes include *sisnoo* (nettle soup), *ningro* (fried fiddlehead ferns), Tibetan-style *churpi* (dried yak cheese), *ema datshi* (cheese and chilli soup) and the Lepcha speciality *gundruk ko jhol* (fermented spinach soup). The must-try beverage here is tongba (or chhang), an alcoholic millet beer enjoyed across the eastern Himalaya. The brew is sipped through a bamboo straw, and the wooden container (the tongba) is topped up periodically with boiling water to let the brew gain strength.

★ 9'INE
SIKKIMESE $$

(MG Marg; set meals ₹250-320; ⊙11am-9pm) Offers friendly and laid-back dining directly above the pedestrianised stretch of MG Marg. This glass-fronted restaurant serves an awesome spread of local delicacies such as *sisnoo* (nettle soup), *gundruk ko jhol* (fermented spinach soup), fermented soyabean chutney and fiery pork or beef curry. There's a good selection of local whiskies, brandies and beer, to complement the platter of your choice.

Golden Dragon
MULTICUISINE $$

(MG Marg; mains ₹160-220; ⊙11am-9pm) Grab a cane table on the lovely sit-out overlooking MG Marg, and make short work of a wide range of tasty food that emerges from this restaurant's busy kitchen. Call in a serving of creamy chicken and mushroom sandwich followed by assorted *momos,* or simply go for the all-day breakfast platter (₹320).

Chopsticks
MULTICUISINE $$

(MG Marg; mains ₹180-220; ⊙11am-9pm) Craving a comfort meal of spare-pork ribs glazed in honey, or a giant serving of grilled sausages with barbecue sauce and mashed potato? Then walk into this fancy place and hog away to glory, all the while catching up on cricketing action and Bollywood shakes on the wall-mounted giant TV screen.

🍷 Drinking & Entertainment

Two of the nicest locations for a quiet drink are the large terrace of the **Tashi Delek Hotel** (MG Marg; beers ₹150) or the bar and garden of Hotel Nor-Khill (p547).

Pub 25
BAR

(MG Marg; beers ₹150; ⊙1-10.30pm) Smart decor, lounge-style sofas, moody lighting and cheeky posters on the walls lend themselves rather well to this tiny watering hole, patronised by locals and travellers alike. TV screens behind the bar relay sporting action, and there's pleasant music on the pipe.

Cafe Live & Loud
LIVE MUSIC

(www.thriceasmuch.com; Tibet Rd; beers from ₹160; ⊙1-11pm; 🛜) Gangtok's most happening venue for live music, this flashy lounge-bar hosts gigs by live-rock, blues and alternative bands every Thursday, Friday and Saturday evenings. There's a full bar and food menu, with some unusual Southeast Asian offerings (mains ₹150 to ₹200), and a pleasant cafe terrace if you wish to distance yourself from the soundblast within.

🛍 Shopping

Several souvenir shops on MG Marg and PS Rd sell Tibetan and Sikkimese handicrafts such as wooden tongba pots, prayer flags, Tibetan curios and Nepali-style *khukri* knives.

Owing to its tax-free status, Sikkim sells alcohol at rock-bottom prices. Apart from generic Indian and foreign labels being sold almost at half price, a few local brands are available in souvenir containers. Fireball brandy comes in a bowling-ball-style red sphere, while Old Gold whisky is bottled in a *khukri*-shaped glass dagger.

★ Golden Tips
FOOD & DRINK

(www.goldentipstea.com; Kazi Rd; tea per pack from ₹200; ⊙9am-9pm) This boutique tea store stocks a mind-blowing repertoire of premium Darjeeling teas (of the black, green, white and flavoured varieties), as well as selections of Sikkimese tea from Temi. The produce is sold in souvenir-sized packages (100g upwards), and the store reps are happy to brew you a cup of your chosen tea for sampling. There's another outlet run by the same proprietors on MG Marg.

Rachna Books
BOOKS

(www.rachnabooks.com; Development Area; ⊙10am-7pm) Gangtok's best-stocked and most convivial bookshop also has occasional film screenings and music events in its upstairs gallery. Its catalogue of titles on Sikkimese and Tibetan history, as well as Vajrayana Buddhism, is well worth browsing.

Handicrafts & Handloom Emporium
HANDICRAFTS

(Zero Point; ⊙10am-4pm, closed Sun Apr-Jun) This government initiative teaches traditional crafts to local students and markets their products – including toy red pandas, 1m by 2m handwoven carpets (₹6000), Tibetan furniture, handmade paper and traditional Sikkimese-style ensembles (₹2000 to ₹3000).

ℹ Information

Many ATMS and high-speed internet cafes (per hour ₹30) line MG Marg.

Axis Bank (MG Marg; ⊙10am-5pm Mon-Sat) Changes cash and travellers cheques and has an ATM. Note that exchange is virtually impossible elsewhere in Sikkim.

Cyber Cafe (MG Marg; per hour ₹30; ⊙9am-9pm) Internet access in a laneway.

Foreigners' Registration Office (Kazi Rd; ⊙10am-4pm Mon-Sat) In the lane beside Indian Overseas Bank; for permit extensions.

Main Post Office (PS Rd; ⊙10am-4pm Mon-Sat, to 2pm Sun for stamps) Normal, registered post and speed-post services.

Police Station (☑03592-202033; NH31A) Helpful, efficient and mostly English-speaking.

Sikkim Tourist Information Centre (☑toll free 03592-203960; www.sikkimtourism.gov.in; MG Marg; ⊙10am-7pm) Offers general and up-to-date advice. Open 10am to 4pm outside peak seasons (March to May and October to November).

STNM Hospital (☑03592-222059; NH31A) Emergency and outpatient facilities. Take a copy of your travel insurance for major treatments.

Getting There & Away

AIR
The nearest airport to Sikkim is Bagdogra, 124km from Gangtok, near Siliguri in West Bengal, which has flights to Kolkata, Delhi and Guwahati.

Helicopters operated by **Sikkim Helicopter Service** (☑03592-203960; www.mountainflightindia.com) shuttle daily from Gangtok to Bagdogra (₹3500, 40 minutes), departing at 11am and returning at 2.30pm. Services are cancelled in adverse weather. There's a strict maximum 10kg baggage allowance. Tickets are sold by Sikkim Tourism Development Corporation (p546).

Fixed-price taxis and sumos (jeeps) go directly to Bagdogra (₹3000, five hours).

Sikkim's first airport is planned at Pakyong, 35km from Gangtok, with a tentative completion date of 2016.

BUS
Buses run from the government **SNT bus station** (☑03592-202016; PS Rd) at 7am to Jorethang (₹100), Kalimpong (₹90) and Namchi (₹100), at 1.15pm to Pelling (₹160) and hourly to Siliguri (₹190, 6am to 1pm). Shared jeeps, however, are quicker and more frequent.

SHARED JEEPS
Some jeep departures are fixed, while others leave when all seats are filled. Departures usually start at 6.30am for the more distant destinations and continue until about 2pm.

From the well-organised **Private Jeep Stand** (NH31A), 1.5km below Gangtok, shared jeeps depart every 30 minutes or so to Darjeeling (₹160, five hours), Kalimpong (₹90, three hours) and Siliguri (₹180, five hours), some continuing to New Jalpaiguri train station.

ⓘ BORDER CROSSING – NEPAL & BHUTAN
There are daily jeeps from the Private Jeep Stand to Kakarbhitta (₹250, six hours, 6.30am) on the Nepalese border and Jaigaon (₹300, five hours, 7am) on the Bhutanese border.

West Sikkim vehicles depart from **Southwest Jeep Stand** (Church Rd) for Geyzing (₹190, 4½ hours, four daily), Ravangla (₹120, three hours, four daily), Namchi (₹130, three hours, every half-hour) and Jorethang (₹120, three hours, hourly). Jeeps for Yuksom, Tashiding and Pelling (₹200 to ₹220, five hours) usually depart around 7am. For independent (and comfortable) travel, it's best to charter a vehicle (per day ₹3500).

TRAIN
The nearest major train station is about 125km away at New Jalpaiguri (NJP). There's a computerised **railway booking counter** (⊙8am-2pm Mon-Sat, to 11am Sun & public holidays) at the SNT bus station.

Getting Around
There's a **taxi stand** in Lal Bazaar opposite the Denzong Cinema, and another in **PS Rd** just north of the post office. **Shared taxis** to Tadong (₹20, every 10 minutes) depart from just under the pedestrian bridge on NH31A.

Around Gangtok

Rumtek
Facing Gangtok distantly across a plunging green valley, Rumtek is a pretty village dominated by its extensive and eponymous gompa complex, considered to be one of Tibetan Buddhism's most venerable institutions and currently the home-in-exile of Buddhism's Kagyu (Black Hat) sect. Time permitting, you can make a quick sortie to Lingdum gompa as well, linked to Rumtek by beautiful country lanes that wind through mossy forests, bamboo groves and artistically terraced paddy fields.

⊙ Sights
★**Rumtek Gompa** MONASTERY
(☑03592-252329; www.rumtek.org; monastery admission ₹10; ⊙monastery 6am-6pm) Meant to replace the Tsurphu Monastery in Tibet, Rumtek's main monastery building was

THE KARMAPA CONTROVERSY

The 'Black Hat' sect takes its name from a priceless ruby-topped black headgear traditionally worn by the Karmapas (reincarnate spiritual leaders). Supposedly woven from the hair of *dakinis* (angels), the hat must be kept locked in a box to prevent it from flying back to the heavens.

Nobody, however, has actually seen the hat since 1993, when a bitter controversy spewed within the Kagyu sect over the legitimacy of two candidates, with both claiming their right to the throne following the death of the 16th Karmapa. The main candidate, Ogyen Trinley Dorje (www.kagyuoffice.org), fled Tibet in 2000 and remains based in Dharamsala: Indian authorities are believed to have prevented him from officially taking up his Rumtek seat for fear of upsetting Chinese government sensibilities. The rival candidate, Thaye Dorje (www.karmapa.org), lives in nearby Kalimpong in West Bengal. Supporters of the two are locked in a legal dispute over who can control Rumtek. To learn more about the controversy, read *The Dance of 17 Lives* by Mick Brown.

Only when the dispute is resolved and the 17th Karmapa is finally crowned would anyone dare to unlock the box and reveal the sacred black hat.

constructed between 1961 and 1966. Unusually for a monastery, the place is guarded by armed forces, following heated altercations and an invasion by partisan monks in the wake of the Karmapa controversy. To enter, foreigners must show their passport and Sikkim permit at the checkpost.

The rambling and walled gompa complex contains religious buildings, schools and a few small lodge-hotels, snack shops and souvenir stalls for travellers. There's a mural of the original Tsurphu Monastery – destroyed during the Chinese Cultural Revolution – beside the main entrance. In the main hall, a giant throne awaits the crowning of the Kagyu spiritual leader, the (disputed) 17th Karmapa, who currently resides in Dharamsala. An ornate scroll, hand-painted by the young leader, adorns the monastery in his absence.

Behind the monastery building, up a flight of stairs running past a snack shop (good tea, instant noodles and *momos*) stands the **Golden Stupa** (⊙6am-11.45am & noon-5pm) **FREE**. Stuffed with religious paraphernalia, the smallish room holds the ashes of the 16th Karmapa in an amber, coral and turquoise-studded reliquary to which pilgrims pay their deepest respects. The keys to the shrine are usually with obliging lamas enrolled at the Karma Shri Nalanda Institute of Buddhist Studies opposite. Leave a donation and you'll be blessed with a holy metal dorje (talisman symbolising lightning).

The knowledgeable, witty and dapper Monay Rai gives a wonderful tour of the monastery (₹250).

Old Rumtek Gompa MONASTERY
(⊙dawn-dusk) **FREE** About 1.5km beyond Rumtek Gompa, a long avenue of prayer flags and junipers leads photogenically down to the forlorn and atmospheric Old Rumtek Gompa, looking out to some fabulous views. The monastery is still in use, and the main prayer hall has been renovated. Two days before the Sikkimese New Year, the monastery comes to life with *chaam* dances.

Lingdum Gompa MONASTERY
(⊙dawn-dusk) **FREE** Completed as recently as 1998, peaceful Lingdum Gompa grows out of pine forests in impressive layers, with pleasant side gardens and a photogenic chorten. The extensively muralled main prayer hall enshrines huge statues of Sakyamuni Buddha, Guru Rinpoche and the 16th Karmapa.

★ Festivals & Events

Rumtek holds impressive masked *chaam* dances during the annual **Drupchen** (group meditation) in May/June, and two days before Losar (p542; Tibetan New Year). The much-fancied **Mahakala Dance** (Ralang) takes place in February, when giant figurines of the fierce protector deity come to life in the central courtyard.

🛏 Sleeping & Eating

Sangay Hotel GUESTHOUSE $
(☎03592-252238; Rumtek Gompa complex; s/d ₹600/800) This Tibetan establishment within the monastery complex is a good place to overnight if you want to explore the region at leisure. Rooms are simple and comfortable

with hot-water bathrooms. Some have balconies.

Rumtek Dzong HOTEL $$

(☎9475463126; www.hotelrumtekdzong.com; Rumtek Rd; d incl breakfast from ₹2500) Midway up the Rumtek road, overlooking the Shanti viewpoint, is this smart hotel commanding fabulous vistas of Gangtok across the valley. Rooms are prim and well appointed, and there's a cute lawn in front where you could laze away a sunny afternoon with a paperback in hand. Ask for a room with a view.

★ Bamboo Retreat RESORT $$$

(☎9434382036; www.bambooretreat.in; Sajong; per person incl breakfast from ₹3380; 🛜) This fabulous resort en route to Rumtek is lounged amid conifers and blooming gardens. It offers oodles of tranquillity along with a horde of optional activities such as mountain biking, guided hikes, Lepcha cultural programs, herbal baths and refreshing massages. The colourful rooms are ethnically appointed, and much of the yummy food comes from the property's organic gardens.

❶ Getting There & Away

Rumtek is 26km (1½ hours) from Gangtok by a winding but scenic road. Lingdum Gompa is a 2km walk from Rumtek along well-trodden mountain trails. Shared jeeps run from Gangtok to Rumtek (₹50) every hour or so, with the last jeep returning to Gangtok around 3pm. A reserved return taxi costs around ₹1000, or ₹1500 including Lingdum.

Towards Tibet

Tso+mgo (Changu) Lake

Pronounced Changu, this high-altitude lake (3780m) 38km from Gangtok is madly popular with Indian travellers, though foreigners require a permit to visit. It's not the prettiest mountain lake in the world, but if you're still keen on checking it out, sign up for a tour by 2pm and most Gangtok agents can get the permit for next-day departure (two photos required). A budget day tour will cost around ₹4000 per vehicle or ₹800 per person if you can get a group together.

At the lakeside, food stalls sell hot chai, chow mein and *momos,* while short yak rides (₹200) potter along the shore.

NATURE'S FURY

In September 2011 a 6.9-magnitude earthquake rocked North Sikkim, claiming more than 100 lives and leaving indelible marks of destruction on the landscape, architecture and the minds of citizens. Further damage was inflicted by another earthquake and a flash flood in September 2012. While the region has recovered considerably from the twin blows, future disasters are always a possibility. Check local conditions before you travel.

Nathu La

Indian citizens are permitted to continue 18km north along the rough road from Tsomgo Lake to the 4130m Nathu La (Listening Ears Pass), on the border with Tibet. It's currently sealed and no crossing over is allowed, although tourists can walk all the way to the barbed wires and pose with Indian and Chinese soldiers for photo ops.

A few kilometres southeast of Nathu La, **Jelep La** was the pass used by Francis Younghusband during the British invasion of Tibet (1903–04). Before being sealed along with Nathu La in 1962, Jelep La was the main regional trade route between Kalimpong and Lhasa. As of now, neither pass shows any sign of reopening.

NORTH SIKKIM

✔ 03592 / POP 43,700

Both breathtakingly beautiful and dauntingly dangerous, the pristine mountains of North Sikkim are blessed with nature's unspoilt bounties. Landscape lovers head to the idyllic valleys of Yumthang and Tsopta, but travelling here requires some stamina and a special permit, which is easy to obtain if you sign up for a tour. April, May, October and November are the best months to visit. Avoid the monsoon, when the rains are often accompanied by landslides and earthquakes.

Gangtok to Singhik

Shortly after exiting Gangtok begins a hair-raising journey along the frail and narrow NH31A. You'll pass through wooded

NORTH SIKKIM TOUR TIPS

➡ A group of four is ideal for sharing costs while not overfilling a jeep. Solo travellers must find at least one copassenger and qualify as a 'group' to apply for permits.

➡ Travelling as part of a tour organised by a registered travel agent is both mandatory and recommended. Agents in Gangtok can find you jeep-share partners quite easily, so ask around a few days before you plan to travel.

➡ Allow at least four days to comfortably visit both Yumthang/ Lachung and Lachen. Three days is enough to see just Yumthang. All-inclusive three-night, four-day tours start from around ₹9000 per person for groups of four.

➡ Break camp early in the morning and maximise your time on the road for photo ops and sightseeing.

➡ Bring a torch (flashlight) and warm clothes.

slopes high above the Teesta River, occasionally descending in long coils of hairpin bends to a bridge photogenically draped in prayer flags, only to switchback up again on the other side.

Kabi Lunchok, an atmospheric glade decorated with memorial stones 17km north of Gangtok, is the site of a 13th-century peace treaty between the chiefs of the Lepcha and Bhutia tribes. Consider breaking your journey here for a while. The small 290-year-old Nyingmapa-school **Phensang Gompa** is further north, 1km off the main road.

Just over 30km north of Gangtok, **Seven Sisters Waterfall**, a multistage cascade, cuts a chasm above a roadside cardamom grove and plummets into a rocky pool. Further down the road is **Phodong** (1815m), lined with a strip of roadside restaurants that serve quick-and-ready lunch. About 1km past Phodong, a 15-minute walk along a side road leads to **Phodong Gompa** (established in 1740). Belonging to the Kagyu sect, it houses extensive murals and a large statue of the ninth Karmapa.

With time to spare, drive or walk another 1.5km uphill to the much more atmospheric **Labrang Gompa** (established in 1884), home to 100 monks. The inner walls of the

eight-sided main building are lined with more than 1000 icons of Padmasambhava, while upstairs a fearsome statue of the guru sports a necklace of severed heads.

Between the two monasteries, just below the road, lie the 19th-century foundations of **Tumlong**, Sikkim's third capital. The enigmatic palace ruins are worth a quick scramble.

North Sikkim's district headquarters are located in **Mangan**, 28km from Phodong. **Singhik**, Mangan's twin village, is just a few bends down the road.

Beyond Singhik

With relevant permits and an organised tour you can continue north beyond Singhik. At Chungthang, the next settlement, the road branches up the Lachung Chu and Lachen Chu valleys. If you only have time to visit one valley, the Lachung Chu has more impressive scenery.

Accommodation is available in Lachung and Lachen. Unless you're specifically looking to stay in a plush hotel and pay over and above your package tariff, your tour operator will have preselected a budget hotel for you in both places.

Lachung

✆ 03592 / POP 2450 / ELEV 2910M

Soaring rock-pinnacled valley walls embroidered with long ribbons of waterfalls surround the scattered village of Lachung. To appreciate the full drama of its setting, take the metal cantilever bridge across the wild Yumthang River and then climb 1.5km for great views from the **Lachung (Sarchok) Gompa** (established 1880). Don't attempt this walk in bad weather though.

More than 50 hotels are dotted around Lachung. Most are simple family-run budget accommodations. Each is comparable to the other with basic rooms, bathroom and traditional Tibetan-style wood-fire kitchens, a cosy place to linger over a butter tea or chhang. Unless you specifically opt for top-end accommodation as part of the package, your tour operator will prechoose one of these hotels for the night and you'll have to accept this preference.

If you don't mind paying surplus cash to stay at a more luxurious place, the gompa-style hotel **Modern Residency** (✆ 03592-204220; www.modernresidency.com;

OFF THE BEATEN TRACK

THANGGU & TSOPTA

Beyond a sprawling army camp 32km north of Lachen, Thanggu (3850m) has an end-of-the-world feel. There are no phones (mobile or otherwise), the electricity is solar generated and the Chinese are only 15km away.

Thanggu Resort (Main Rd; snacks ₹100; ☺ May-Nov) is a simple wooden house incorporating a traditional-styled kitchen and tongba-drinking den (tongba ₹50) that offers the only toilet and breakfast stop (snacks ₹100) along the route.

From Thanggu, a boulder-strewn stream leads on 2km to the Tsopta Valley. Just above the tree line, the scenery takes on the added drama of a glacier-toothed mountain wall framing the western horizon. A two-hour hike leads up to a pair of meditation caves, one of which was used for two years by the famous French traveller and mystic Alexandra David-Neel.

Indian visitors can continue 30km north to spectacular **Gurudongmar Lake** (5150m), right on the border with Tibet, but the glacial lake is off-limits to foreigners.

Singring village; d incl full board ₹6800), 3km south of Lachung, has comfortable, well-decorated rooms done up in local motifs and appointed with snug beds, luxe creature comforts and fresh toilets. Pluses include a minimuseum, library and bar. You can book through Gangtok-based **Modern Treks & Tours** (☑ 03592-204220; www.modernresidency.com; MG Marg, Modern Central Lodge). Early birds stand to get good discounts.

The fancy resort **Mayfair Yarlam** (☑ 9434330033; www.yarlamresort.com; Main Rd; d incl full board from ₹8800; @), possibly the top place in Yumthang, is also a good place to stay, with smart cosy rooms and amenities such as round-the-clock hot water, flatscreen TVs and internet via satellite connections. However, it is preferred by top-end international tour operators for their groups and remains largely booked out during the high season.

Yumthang Valley

The main reason to come to Lachung is to continue 24km further north to admire the majestic Yumthang Valley, which starts some 10km past Lachung. This point is also the entry to the **Singba Rhododendron Sanctuary**, whose network of hiking trails offers a welcome chance to get out of the jeep. From March to early May a host of primulas, 24 species of rhododendrons and other alpine flora burst forth in riotous blossom, carpeting the valley floor.

At the Km24 point, a number of snack shacks and souvenir stalls operate in the high season. There's also a tiny **museum** (opening hours are irregular) with a display

of Tibetan and Sikkimese relics. From here, you can walk ahead and explore the pretty terrain, which slowly transforms into a montage of jagged peaks, lush pastures and bridges draped with colourful prayer flags. The glacial waters of the Yumthang River gurgle through the scene. Come early in the morning for the best photo-ops, before the clouds roll in.

Lachen

POP 2000 / ELEV 2700M

Despite a recent invasion of concrete, the traditional mountain village of Lachen retains its quaintness in the form of old wooden homes on sturdy stone bases, log sheds stacked with timber for winter fuel, and plenty of colour in the form of ornate Tibetan-style window frames and prayer flags. **Lachen (Nyudrup Choeling) Gompa** is a 15-minute walk above the town and is most likely to be open early morning or late afternoon for rituals.

While primarily serving as a night stop for exploring the higher valley of Tsopta, Lachen is also the trailhead for eight-day expeditionary treks to **Green Lake** (5050m) along the Zemu Glacier (thought to be filled with the yeti, or abominable snowman), towards Khangchendzonga's northeast face. Consider this trek with lots of money, time and patience to spare as permits are extremely difficult to obtain.

Of the few accommodation options available for tourists to choose from, most groups prefer the **Lachen View Point** (☑ 9434867312; d incl full board from ₹3000), which has good-value rooms and efficient service. Alternatively, try the luxurious and hospitable **Apple Orchard Resort** (☑ 9474837640; www.theappleorchardresort.com; d incl full board ₹9500), above the village next to the *ani gompa* (nunnery). It has cosy and inviting rooms (with graceful wooden flooring and panelling) located in smart buildings thrown around a leafy, tiered complex.

SOUTH SIKKIM

People visit the lofty hills of South Sikkim either to gaze at the sky-piercing statues of Namchi and Ravangla, or to find religion in the latter's atmospheric monasteries. This is also the state's only tea-growing region, and the gardens of Temi are a delightful stopover for anyone travelling the road between Gangtok and West Sikkim.

Namchi

☑ 03595 / POP 12,200 / ELEV 1525M

The hulking religious superstructures that dot the jagged horizon of Namchi are perhaps the only reason why travellers swing by this tiny settlement. There are several internet cafes in the central pedestrianised plaza, along with an Axis Bank ATM, two ancient bodhi and pipal trees and an aquarium with angel fish, parrot fish and piranhas.

⊙ Sights

Samdruptse MONUMENT
(Padmasambhava Statue; admission ₹30; ⊙ dawn-dusk) Painted in shimmering copper, pink and bronze, the 45m-high **statue of Guru Padmasambhava** lords over the forested Samdruptse ridge and is visible for miles around. Completed in 2004 on a foundation stone laid by the Dalai Lama, the statue of the hallowed Buddhist leader sits atop a giant lotus plinth and makes for a striking photo op. Within the complex, there's a permanent photo exhibition of archival images documenting Sikkim's cultural, natural and artistic history.

The site is 7km from Namchi, 2km off the Damthang/Ravangla road. Taxis from town charge around ₹700 return. Alternatively, pay ₹500 for a one-way trip and walk back to Namchi, following the road down to the atmospheric **Ngadak Gompa**. Pass the ruined **Ngadak Dzong**, which dates back to 1717 and still exudes a sense of antique Sikkim.

Char Dham MONUMENT
(Siddesvara Dham; ₹30 per vehicle; ⊙ 8am-noon & 1-7pm) Spread over the Solophuk hilltop 5km south of Namchi, the site of Char Dham is towered over by a massive 33m **Shiva statue**. The complex intends to bring together all revered Hindu pilgrimages from across India (albeit in the form of replicas), and is strewn with temples and pagodas built on an epic scale. A taxi here costs ₹700/500 for a return/one-way trip, and the **Yatri Nivas** guesthouse dishes out a superb thali (₹200) for lunch.

Apart from visiting these concrete behemoths (each of which enshrines sundry deities of the Hindu pantheon), there's a **4D simulator show** (₹50) that re-creates popular pilgrimages, plane flights and car races for kids.

🛏 Sleeping

Dungmali Heritage Resort GUESTHOUSE $
(☑ 9734126039; Solophuk Rd; d from ₹1000) Overlooking the Solophuk road about 4km from Namchi, this family-run guesthouse boasts solitude, silence and lots of ambient greenery. Accommodation is snug for the price, and the costlier rooms come with balconies and great valley views. The family grows organic vegetables, and runs a popular **cafe** (mains ₹100-150) 20m up the road.

Upon prior request, the proprietors can organise forest walks and birdwatching tours in the jungle adjacent to the property.

Seven Hills Resort RESORT $$
(☑ 8348171672; www.sevenhillsresort.com; Phalidara; d from ₹3850) Located on a remote ridge 7km northeast of Namchi, this ecothemed resort boasts a collection of rustic cottages sporting lots of canework and traditional tapestry, all thrown around manicured lawns and gardens dotted with passionfruit, bamboo and orchids. The mountain views from the balconies are commanding, and go well with a glass of house-made rhododendron brandy on a cold evening.

⊙ Getting There & Around

Share jeeps leave frequently when full to Ravangla (₹50, one hour), Gangtok (₹130, three hours) and Siliguri (₹150, three hours) from stands around the pedestrian mall. Services dry up shortly after noon.

Buses leave early in the morning from the SNT bus stand in the east of town, heading to Ravangla (₹40, one hour) and Gangtok (₹100, three hours).

Ravangla (Rabongla)

📞 03595 / POP 2280 / ELEV 2010M

Lined by conifer forests and spectacularly perched on a ridge overlooking a wide sweep of western Sikkim, Ravangla promises some of the best mountain views in the region. The gompas of Ralang, Tashiding, Pema-yangtse and Sangacheoling are all distantly visible against a horizon that's sawtoothed with high mountain peaks.

A cheerful and laid-back town, Ravangla is useful as a hub to visit surrounding sights. Joining the main highway is the Main Bazaar, a concentration of shops, cheap hotels, the jeep stand and the **Cyber Cafe** (Main Bazaar; per hour ₹30; ⏱ 9am-7pm).

◎ Sights

Mane Choekhorling Gompa   MONASTERY
(⏱ dawn-dusk) FREE This flamboyant stone-and-wood gompa stands at the top end of a long flight of steps leading up from the end of the Main Bazaar. The festival ground here hosts the annual Pang Lhabsol (p542) festival, held each August in honour of Kanchendzonga. *Chaam* dances take place on the 15th day of the seventh lunar month.

Tathagata Tsal   MONUMENT
(Buddha Park; admission ₹50; ⏱ 10am-4.30pm) On the edge of town is the sprawling Tathagata Tsal, a Buddhism-themed park dominated by a giant 41m-tall **Buddha statue**, which holds Buddhist relics from 13 countries. Within the superstructure is a gallery showcasing scenes from Buddha's life. Blessed by the Dalai Lama in 2010, the site boasts manicured lawns, fountains, ambient lighting, a meditation lounge and lots of photo ops.

🛏 Sleeping & Eating

Blue Spring Residency   HOTEL $$
(📞 9733121105; bluespring64@gmail.com; Main Bazaar; d from ₹1600) A better choice than most of Ravangla's boxy hotels, this spiffy place has 20 rooms on three floors, many of which have mountain views. Book early and you could get a discount on quoted tariffs.

Mt Narsing Resort   RESORT $$
(📞 8145294900; www.mtnarsingresorts.com; Kewzing Rd; d lower resort from ₹1450, upper annex from ₹2750) This charming property occupies a gladelike roadside plot 5km southwest of Ravangla. The lower bungalow is cheaper, but the ambience and views are far better at the upper annex, which boasts cottage-style rooms with wooden interiors. There's good food and fine views over the lawn towards the summits of Narsing and Pandim. A taxi to the lower/upper resort costs ₹150/300.

Kookay Restaurant   TIBETAN $
(Main Bazaar; mains ₹80-120; ⏱ 7am-8pm) A cheerful eatery perpetually packed with happy diners, this clean restaurant is easily the best in town. The menu includes a wide range of Tibetan delicacies, rice and curry sets, and Chinese staples. Slurp down a steaming bowl of noodle soup or beef *momos*, and leave a note of appreciation on the 'We Were Here' noticeboards lining the walls.

❶ Getting There & Away

Travel agents on the main highway book shared jeeps to Gangtok (₹120, 7am to noon) and Siliguri (₹190, 7am to 8am). For Yuksom, change at Geyzing (₹100, 9am). Jeeps to Namchi (₹50) and Legship (₹50) leave periodically from near Hotel 10Zing in the centre of town.

The SNT bus booking office is part of Hotel 10Zing. Morning buses run to Namchi (₹45, one hour, 9am) and Siliguri (₹190, five hours, 6.30am).

Around Ravangla

Beside the main Legship road, 5.5km from central Ravangla, the small but fascinating **Yungdrung Kundrakling** is the only Bon monastery in Sikkim. Animistic in nature, Bon preceded Buddhism in Tibet but has since been largely subsumed by it. The deities look slightly different and prayer wheels are turned anticlockwise. Flash photography is prohibited within. You can get here from Ravangla on a b Kewzing-bound shared jeep (₹20). Friendly monks will be happy to brief you on Bon while you're exploring the monastery.

Back in Ravangla, a steep four-hour hiking trail leads from above Tathagata Tsal to the top of **Maenam Hill** (3150m). En route, you'll pass the springtime rhododendrons and magnolia blooms of the **Maenam Wildlife Sanctuary**. From the summit, continue 2km to **Bhaledunga rock**, where you can enjoy sweeping views and a chance encounter with red pandas and monal pheasants (Sikkim's state bird). Hire a guide (₹600) at the forestry check post to avoid getting lost.

Ralang

At Ralang, 13km below Ravangla, the splendid 1995 **Palchen Choeling Monastic Institute** (New Ralang Gompa) is home to about 200 Kagyu-order monks. Arrive early morning or around 3pm to hear them chanting in mesmerising unison. There's a 9m-high golden statue of the historical Buddha in the main hall, and the gompa is famous for elaborate butter sculptures. Peek into the side room to see the amazing effigies used in November's impressive Mahakala dance held in the monastery's expansive courtyard.

About 1.5km downhill on the same road is the peaceful (and still active) **Old Ralang Gompa**, established in 1768 and definitely worth a hike from the new monastery. A chartered taxi to Ralang costs around ₹600 return from Ravangla with two hours' wait.

Temi

Located 16km south of Ravangla, the jade-green estate of Temi is as famous for its fine-quality tea and its gorgeous mountain scenery. The only tea garden in Sikkim, it drapes some 180 hectares of hill slopes that are fronted by a stupendous hill-lined horizon, towered over by the Khangchendzonga massif.

Accommodation is available at the stylish **Cherry Resort** (☑ 8016488737; www.cherryresort.com; Temi Tea Estate; s/d incl breakfast from ₹2900/3400), a government-run property slap-bang in the middle of the plantations overlooking the Teesta valley far below. The spacious rooms have fantastic patios and a terrace with magnificent views of summits and the plantations. The food is unimaginative but delicious, and there's great tea to go with your meals and snacks.

Shared jeeps from Ravangla (₹50, 30 minutes) bound for Siliguri via Damthang and Rangpo can drop you at the resort.

WEST SIKKIM

Towered over by the sublime Khangchendzonga, West Sikkim's breathtaking landscape is strung out along formidable mountain ridges draped in evergreen alpine forests. A handful of intriguing monasteries, villages and waterfalls add to its overall appeal, and make it an ideal spot for footloose hiking. The fabulous Goecha La trek, which takes hikers to the icy base of Khangchendzonga, begins in the village of Yuksom (which is also the trailhead for some pleasant day hikes). Comfort seekers, on the other hand, can simply settle for stupendous mountain views from Pelling.

Geyzing & Tikjuk

☑ 03595 / POP 1100

Located 6km from Pelling, Tikjuk is the District Administrative Centre for West Sikkim. Permits can be extended at the **Superintendent of Police office** (Side wing, 3rd fl; ☺ 10am-4pm Mon-Sat, closed 2nd Sat of month). Geyzing, its contiguous twin, is most useful as West Sikkim's transport hub. Frequent shared jeeps go to Jorethang (₹90, 1½ hours), Pelling (₹20, 20 minutes), Tashiding (₹70, 1½ hours) and Yuksom (₹100, 2½ hours). Several serve Gangtok (₹190, seven to nine hours, 7am to 12.30pm), Ravangla (₹70, one hour, 9am and 11.45am) and Siliguri (₹200, four hours, 7am and 12.30pm).

Pelling

☑ 03595 / POP 3500 / ELEV 2085M

Pelling's raison d'être is its stride-stopping, jaw-dropping view of Khangchendzonga at dawn (weather permitting, that is). It's otherwise a fairly nondescript town, with a 2km stretch of boxed-out tourist hotels that line its main thoroughfare, frequented by hordes of local tourists through the year.

Pelling is nominally divided into Upper, Middle and Lower areas. A focal point of Upper Pelling is a small roundabout where the main road from Geyzing turns 360 degrees in front of Hotel Garuda. At the same point, minor roads branch south to Dentam and southwest to the tourist office and the helipad, which has magnificent panoramic views at dawn.

☞ Tours

Popular day tours (offered by most hotels and travel agencies) include Yuksom via Khecheopalri Lake and three waterfalls (₹3000 per jeep) or Khecheopalri Lake, Pemayangtse Gompa and Rabdentse (₹2500 per jeep).

Hotel Garuda   SIGHTSEEING
(☑ 03595-258319; Upper Pelling; tours per day per jeep from ₹1500) Half-day tours to Khecheopalri Lake cost ₹1500. Adding Pemayangtse

and Rabdentse to the trip costs an extra ₹1000.

Simvo Tours & Travels　SIGHTSEEING

(☏9733076457; Upper Pelling; day tour per person/jeep ₹400/2500) This outfit offers guided and independent tours of local sights.

🛏 Sleeping

Most of Pelling's hotels are overpriced, drab and cater to midrange domestic tourists. Rates typically drop 30% (June to September) and are highly negotiable during low occupancy.

Hotel Garuda　HOTEL $

(☏9733076484; www.hotelgarudapelling.com; Main Rd, Upper Pelling; d from ₹850; @) This cheerful, old-school backpacker ghetto has clean, spacious rooms (all with hot showers and TV), a library with book-swap facilties, good Khangchendzonga views and a superb restaurant ideal for meeting other travellers. The pricier 'suites' upstairs have ethnic decor and Tibetan names such as Nima and Pema. The in-house travel agency organises customised sightseeing tours.

Hotel Rabdentse Residency　HOTEL $

(☏9681292163; www.saikripa.in; Main Rd, Lower Pelling; d from ₹1050) This clean and commercial place is largely patronised by domestic tourists, and stays mostly booked through the high season (March to May and October to November). Done up in smart colours and prim upholstery, the rooms are pleasant and well-appointed. It's on the lowermost fringes of Pelling, about 15 minutes on foot from the central part of town.

Hotel Phamrong　HOTEL $$

(☏9733085318; www.hotelphamrong.com; Main Rd, Upper Pelling; s/d incl breakfast from ₹2500/3100) This pretty hotel features stylish rooms with wicker and wood interiors that open out to a multilevel inner foyer adorned with Sikkimese artifacts and murals. Rooms become more gorgeous as you climb up the stairs, as do the mountain views. There's a decent in-house restaurant with a good vegetarian selection, and service is prompt and friendly.

Hotel Sonamchen　HOTEL $$

(☏03595-258346; www.hotelsonamchenpelling.com; Main Rd, Upper Pelling; d from ₹2800) A largish place patronised by domestic tourists, this hotel has good mountain views from

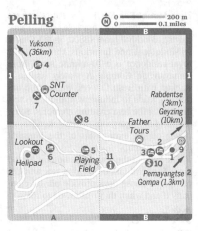

Pelling

🏃 Activities, Courses & Tours
Hotel Garuda ....(see 2)
1 Simvo Tours & Travels B2

🛏 Sleeping
2 Hotel Garuda B2
3 Hotel Phamrong B2
4 Hotel Rabdentse Residency A1
5 Hotel Sonamchen A2
6 Norbu Ghang Resort A2

🍴 Eating
7 Anjali Restaurant A1
8 Melting Point A1

ℹ Information
9 Paylink Cyber Zone...............................B2
10 SBI ATM B2
11 Tourist Office...B2

most rooms. Service and housekeeping are commendable, and the ornate lobby has an adjoining restaurant for snacks and meals. Rates are flexible and could dip to almost half the quoted rate if you bargain hard.

Norbu Ghang Resort　HERITAGE HOTEL $$$

(☏03595-258272; www.norbughanghotels.com; Main Rd, Upper Pelling; d incl breakfast ₹4700; 🐕) This charming property has pretty cottages dotting a lush hillside. Its rooms have been decorated with care and have traditional upholstery and polished wood flooring. The biggest draws are the giant glass-panelled windows with gorgeous Khangchendzonga views. The lawn has great vistas, perfect for an afternoon beer. The management is affable and service is excellent.

SIKKIM PELLING

Elgin Mount Pandim   HERITAGE HOTEL $$$

(☎03595-250756; www.elginhotels.com; Pemayangtse; d incl half board ₹8800; @🛜) Classy, self-indulgent and luxurious, this erstwhile royal residence is a 10-minute stroll from Pemayangtse Gompa. A stately lounge – stacked with fresh flowers, wicker and antiques – leads to indulgent, tranquil rooms, lined with the best creature comforts. Some rooms have gorgeous Khangchendzonga views; others have vistas of the Singalila Ridge to match.

The lawn at the rear of the hotel is a good place for breakfast or evening tea, and the pampered house dogs provide playful company if and when they're allowed to roam.

Eating

Pelling's best dining is in the hotels, and there are few standalone places.

Anjali Restaurant   MULTICUISINE $

(Middle Pelling; mains ₹80-120; ⊗8am-9pm) The seating is grubby, the service laid-back, but the food is finger-licking good. The quasi-Chinese dishes woo the palate with a plethora of spicy flavours that are best smothered by a chilled beer, while the Sikkimese specials (advance orders only) such as *sisnoo* and *ningro* go well with a glass of chhang.

Melting Point   MULTICUISINE $$

(Middle Pelling; mains ₹100-150; ⊗8am-9pm) Pelling's paltry equivalent to a fine-dining restaurant, this eatery has a cosy lounge and an adjoining alfresco terrace to the rear, with superb mountain views. The menu features wholesome Chinese, Indian and Western staples (the penne in mushroom sauce won't disappoint), and service is prompt. Early evenings are a quiet time to finish dinner, before the crowds file in.

ℹ Information

Paylink Cyber Zone (Main Rd; per hour ₹30; ⊗8am-7pm) Internet access on the main road.

SBI ATM (Main Rd) Opposite Hotel Garuda.

Tourist office (☎7797887401; Main Rd; ⊗10am-4pm Mon-Sat) The helpful tourist office can be found past the Middle Pelling roundabout, on the way to the helipad.

ℹ Getting There & Away

SNT buses run to Siliguri (₹190, five hours, 7am) via Jorethang (₹70, 2½ hours); book at the **SNT counter** (Hotel Pelling) in Lower Pelling from where the buses depart.

Father Tours (☎9733286872; Upper Pelling) runs shared jeeps at 7am for Gangtok (₹200, five hours) and Siliguri (₹200, 4½ hours).

Shared jeeps to Geyzing (₹20, 20 minutes) leave frequently from near the Hotel Garuda, passing close to Pemayangtse, Rabdentse and Tikjuk district administrative centre. For Khecheopalri Lake (₹70) or Yuksom (₹90), jeeps start from Geyzing, passing through Pelling between noon and 1pm.

Around Pelling

Pemayangtse Gompa

Literally translated as 'Perfect Sublime Lotus', the 1705 **Pemayangtse Gompa** (admission ₹20; ⊗7am-5pm) is one of Sikkim's oldest and most significant Nyingmapa gompas. Magnificently set on a hilltop (2100m) overlooking the Rabdentse ruins, the atmospheric compound is ringed by gardens and traditional cottages used by resident monks. The ground floor features a central Buddha, while on the 1st floor, fierce-looking statues depict all eight reincarnations of Padmasambhava. On the top floor is an astounding seven-tiered model representing Padmasambhava's heavenly abode of Zangtok Palri, handmade over five laborious years by a single dedicated lama.

During February and March, impressive *chaam* dances celebrating Losar (p542) culminate with the unfurling of a huge *gyoku*

OFF THE BEATEN TRACK

THE RHODODENDRON TRAIL

In the far southwest corner of Sikkim, close to the India–Nepal border, lies the **Varsey Rhododendron Sanctuary**, known to be the native habitat of more than 500 species of rhododendrons. Well off the tourist route, this exotic forest (at an altitude of about 3000m) can be accessed by a two-hour trek through enchanted pine forests from the village of Hilley, about 28km from Pelling. Hemmed by the Singalila Ridge, the forest bursts in a riot of colours in April and May. A few basic lodges provide overnight accommodation in the sanctuary – contact Sikkim Tourism Development Corporation (p546) for details.

(giant embroidered *thangka*) and the zapping of evil demons with a great fireball.

Pemayangtse is 1.5km from Upper Pelling, along the road to Geyzing, and is easily combined with a visit to Rabdentse. The signposted turn-off is near an obvious stupa.

If you are walking to or from Pemayangtse, pop into the self-service **Lotus Bakery** (Geyzing Rd; cakes ₹25-30; ☺8am-5pm), about 20 minutes from town, for a restorative slice of carrot or banana cake. All money raised goes to the nearby Denjog Pema Choling Academy, which works with underprivileged children.

Rabdentse

Rabdentse (☺dawn-dusk) **FREE** was the royal capital of Sikkim from 1670 to 1814. It is now in ruins and consists only of chunky wall-stubs with a few inset inscription stones. The selling point of the site, however, is the utterly fabulous viewpoint on which the ruins are located. The entrance is around 3km from Upper Pelling, along the road to Geyzing. The ruins are a 10-minute walk from the site's yellow gateway – beware of leeches in the undergrowth.

The Monastery Loop

The picturesque western frontiers of Sikkim can technically be enjoyed on a day-long or overnight jeep tour from Pelling. Time permitting, however, you can do an adventurous three-day trip from Pelling to Tashiding via Khecheopalri Lake, using a combination of jeeps and hiking. Alternatively, consider an outing to wonderful Yuksom via Khecheopalri Lake, and a subsequent multiday high-altitude trek that takes you up close and personal with Khangchendzonga.

Pelling to Yuksom

Apart from dipping your toes in the cascading waters of the **Rimbi**, **Khangchendzonga** and **Phamrong Falls**, the only major sight on this stretch is the hallowed **Khecheopalri Lake** (admission ₹10; ☺dawn-dusk). Located at 1950m, this placid natural reservoir – pronounced 'ketchup-perry' – is highly revered by both Sikkimese Buddhists and Lepcha animists who believe its shape to be akin to the footprint of the goddess Tara. Legend also has it that birds assiduously remove any leaves from its surface, keeping it clean through the year.

During the springtime festival **Khecheopalri Mela** (☺Mar/Apr), butter lamps are floated out across the lake. Prayer wheels line the lake's jetty, backed by fluttering prayer flags and Tibetan inscriptions, but the setting, ringed with forested hills, is serene rather than dramatic.

Day jeep tours typically drop you at a car park five minutes from the lake, allowing you 30 minutes of sightseeing time. The best way to appreciate the site, however, is to stay overnight and visit once the tourists have left.

Around the car park is a Buddhist nunnery, a couple of shops and the simple **Jigme Restaurant** (snacks ₹50). serving tea and chow mein From the car park, a path to the left leads uphill for 20 minutes to **Khecheopalri Gompa** and stupa, from where you can hike up to several viewpoints.

Just beside the gompa and overseen by a local lama is **Pala's Guest House** (☏9832471253; per person incl 3 meals ₹600), with more rooms available at the next-door annex. On the main approach to the car park, Teng Hang Limboo operates a basic homestay at the **Family Guest House** (☏9609874677; per person ₹400).

Shared jeeps to Pelling (₹60, two hours) leave the car park at 6am, or you could hitch a ride on a reserved tourist jeep returning to Pelling.

A hiking trail to Yuksom (9km, three to five hours) leaves the road just opposite Family Guest House, descending steeply to the main road (take the right branch after crossing the Runom Khola River) and emerging near Khangchendzonga Falls. After the road suspension bridge, follow the concrete steps uphill to meet the Yuksom road, about 2km below Yuksom village.

Yuksom

☏ 03595 / POP 1850 / ELEV 1780M

Loveable little Yuksom is historic, charming and unspoilt, although concretisation is fast taking over (the latest addition is an enclosed complex studded with gigantic prayer wheels along the settlement's main drag). Yuksom is the main trailhead for the treks towards Mt Khangchendzonga, and is a good place to kick back for a few quiet nights.

SIKKIM THE MONASTERY LOOP

◉ Sights

Norbugang Park
HISTORIC SITE

(⊙ dawn-dusk) **FREE** Yuksom means 'meeting place of the three lamas', referring to the trio of Tibetan holy men who crowned the first chogyal of Sikkim at this historic site in 1641. The charming complex contains a small temple, a huge prayer wheel, a chorten and the supposedly original **Coronation Throne** (Norbugang), from which it takes its current name.

Standing beneath a vast cryptomeria pine, the site looks something like an ancient Olympic podium hewn out of stone. Just in front is a spooky footprint fused into stone, believed to be that of one of the crowning lamas.

Dubdi Gompa
MONASTERY

(⊙ dawn-dusk) **FREE** High on the ridge above Yuksom, this atmospheric gompa (its name means 'hermit's cell') is set in beautifully tended gardens behind three coarsely hewn stupas. Established in 1701, it is said to be Sikkim's oldest monastery, though the current chapel looks much newer.

Start the steep 40-minute climb from upper Yuksom's primary health centre; the clear path rises through thickets of trumpet lilies and some lovely mature forest.

Kathok Wodsallin Gompa
MONASTERY

(⊙ dawn-dusk) **FREE** This newly contructed gompa opposite Hotel Tashi Gang has an impressively stern statue of Guru Padmasambhava surrounded by a collection of yogis, gurus and lamas in glass-fronted compartments. The coloured motifs on the walls provide a few striking photo ops.

🏃 Activities

Several trekking agencies in Yuksom can organise a **Khangchendzonga trek** given a couple of days. Prices start at around US$60 per person per day assuming a group of four.

Red Panda Tour & Travel
TREKKING

(📞 9733196470; sikkimtraveler@gmail.com; Main Rd; ⊙ 8am-6pm) Run by a former porter-turned-guide (nicknamed 'panda') with great expertise and experience. Also offers slow internet (per hour ₹50).

Alpine Exodus Tours & Travel
TREKKING

(📞 9735087508; nawang.bhutia@gmail.com; Main Rd; ⊙ 8am-8pm) The in-house adventure agency at Hotel Yangri Gang.

Mountain Tours & Treks
TREKKING

(📞 9641352656; www.sherpatreks.in; Main Rd; ⊙ 8am-6pm) A reputed outfit with a good repertoire of high-altitude gear, and patchy internet service (per hour ₹50).

🛏 Sleeping & Eating

Tourist traffic is heavy during peak trekking seasons (March to May and October to November), so book early.

Hotel Yangri Gang
HOTEL **$**

(📞 9434164408; Main Rd; s/d from ₹500/800; @) The better rooms at this functional hotel at the head of Yuksom's main street are on the upper floors. Beds are comfy, the wooden half-panelling is pleasant to the eye and there are hot showers through the day. Thanks to its in-house trekking agency, it's a good upper-budget option favoured by trekkers to start and end their treks.

WORTH A TRIP

YUKSOM TO TASHIDING HIKE

This wonderful one-day hike requires no permits and can be done quite easily if you start in Yuksom. Figure on six hours of walking (19km), plus another two hours visiting the monasteries. Porter-guides are available in Yuksom for around ₹600.

Start by ascending to **Dubdi Gompa**, from where a path dips into a side valley for 40 minutes to **Tsong**. The trail splits here; take the upper trail leading uphill past cardamom fields to lonely **Hongri Gompa**, a small, unusually unpainted ancient monastery on a beautiful ridge. Local folklore claims the gompa was moved here from a higher spot where monks were being ravaged by yeti.

A signpost points the way downhill for 20 minutes to **Nessa** hamlet, 10 minutes below which is the village of **Pokhari Dara** (four hours from Yuksom). Follow the road until a footpath branches towards **Sinon Gompa** (built 1716). From here the stepped path drops steeply behind the yellow monastic school, following village trails down to Tashiding.

THE FARMHOUSE CIRCUIT

A bucolic expanse of unspoilt sylvan beauty, the surrounds of Rinchenpong village in West Sikkim is home to a number of plush farmhouses that offer a luxurious stay amid pristine forests, orchards and farmlands, with copious mountain views all around. An hour's drive from Pelling, the area is slowly attracting leisure seekers who wish to give urban chaos the slip and enjoy nature's charms for a few days. **Biksthang** (☑9593779077; www.biksthang.com; Mangalbarey Village; s/d incl half board ₹4350/6150; 🐾), an utterly beautiful farmhouse built around a 19th-century family estate, boasts ultrasnug cottages with lavish interiors and superb home-cooked Sikkimese food. **Yangsum Heritage Farm** (☑9434179029; www.yangsumheritagefarm.com; Rinchenpong; d incl full board ₹5100), another popular hideaway, scores with its air of quaintness, expansive plantations and cottages that come with incremental degrees of comfort and luxury. Both farms can organise transport from Siliguri, Gangtok or Pelling upon advance request.

Hotel Demazong
HOTEL **$**

(☑9775473687; Main Rd; dm ₹150, d from ₹500) Used by domestic trekking groups, this place has simple but clean rooms behind its boxy facade. The more expensive rooms have balconies. Don't expect much in terms of service though, and if a quiet stay is what you're looking for, you may have to stop elsewhere.

Hotel Tashi Gang
HOTEL **$$**

(☑9733077249; hoteltashigang@gmail.com; Main Rd; s/d from ₹1500/2000) Done up in rich Sikkimese motifs and colourful *thangkas*, the rooms at this popular hotel offer unbelievable value for money and, as a result, are mostly booked out. There's good food at the in-house restaurant, and the rooms out front have balconies opening in the direction of Khangchendzonga. There's a patch of front lawn hemmed by flowering plants.

Yuksum Residency
HOTEL **$$**

(☑9933133330; www.yuksumresidency.com; Main Rd; s/d from ₹2700/3200; 🛜) Very plush, stylish and comfortable by Yuksom's standards, this upscale hotel has large rooms with giant windows overlooking soothing greenery. It has a pleasant terrace which doubles as a dining area in the evenings. All in all, the perfect place for returning trekkers in need of a hot shower and creature comforts. Service, however, can be somewhat impersonal.

Tibet Restaurant
TIBETAN **$**

(Main Rd; mains ₹80-120; ⊙6am-9pm) There's a great selection of Tibetan and Sikkimese fare at this busy and buzzy eatery on Yuksom's main drag. The signature dish, however, is the Bhutanese-style *ema datse*, featuring pork and vegetables stewed in a fiery chilli cheese sauce, best combined with steamed rice and chilled beer.

Gupta Restaurant
MULTICUISINE **$**

(Main Rd; mains ₹50-100; ⊙5am-9pm) This alfresco restaurant belts out curries, pizza, instant noodles, breakfast platters and dinner thalis for a steady stream of diners through the day. The sociable thatched cabana outside is good for a beer with fellow travellers.

❶ Getting There & Away

At around 6.30am, several shared jeeps leave for Jorethang (₹160, four hours) via Tashiding (₹60, 1½ hours), Geyzing via Pelling (₹90, 2½ hours) and Gangtok (₹250, six hours). Book the day before at the shop next to Gupta Restaurant or the hut opposite.

Dzongri & Goecha La – The Khangchendzonga Trek

For guided groups with permits, Yuksom is the starting point for Sikkim's classic seven- to 10-day trek to Goecha La, a 4940m pass with jaw-dropping views of Khangchendzonga.

Don't underestimate the rigours of the trek – it's considered one of the most challenging hikes in the Indian Himalaya. Don't climb too high too quickly: altitude sickness often strikes those who are fittest and fastest. Starting early makes sense, as rain is common in the afternoons, spoiling views and making trails annoyingly muddy. Check all your equipment before setting off – bring good-quality sleeping bags, torches (flashlights), some heavy woollens and rain gear. Also watch out for leeches in case you're trekking immediately after the monsoons; the local mosquito repellent Odomos does a good job at keeping the pesky creatures at bay.

Dzongri & Goecha La

March to May is an ideal time to trek. Monsoon clouds move in by the end of May, rendering the mountains unwalkable. The clearest skies are from October to December, but remember that snow starts to block the trails with the advent of winter.

The route initially follows the Rathong Valley through unspoilt forests before steeply ascending to **Baktim** (Bakhim; 2750m) and the rustic Tibetan village of **Tsokha** (3050m), established in 1969 by Tibetan refugees. Spending two nights here helps with acclimatisation.

The next stage climbs to pleasant meadows around **Dzongri** (4020m). Consider another acclimatisation day here, best spent by strolling up to **Dzongri La** (4550m, four-hour round trip) for fabulous views of Mt Pandim (6691m).

From Dzongri, the trail drops steeply to **Kokchurong** and follows the river to **Thangsing** (3930m). Next day takes you to camping at **Lamuni**, 15 minutes before **Samiti Lake** (4200m). From here, a dawn assault the following morning takes you to the head-spinning **Goecha La** (4940m) for those incredible views of Khangchendzonga. A further viewpoint, another hour's walk ahead, offers even closer views.

The return is essentially by the same route. An alternative is to cut south at Dzongri and follow the **Singalila Ridge** for a week to **Uttarey**, from where there are connections to Pelling and Jorethang.

There are government-run **trekkers' huts** at Baktim, Tsokha, Dzongri, Kokchurong and Thangsing, but most have neither furniture nor mattresses, and can be crowded during peak trekking seasons. It's far better to bring all camping equipment and food.

Tashiding

ELEV 1490M

Little Tashiding is a single, sloping market street forking north off the Yuksom–Legship road. A 2.5km uphill track from the main junction leads to a car park from where a footpath leads up between an avenue of prayer flags to the atmospheric Nyingmapa-school **Tashiding Gompa** (⊙dawn-dusk) **FREE**. It is about 30 minutes' away via a steep 1km walk.

KHANGCHENDZONGA TREK SCHEDULE

STAGE	ROUTE	DURATION
1	Yuksom to Tsokha, via Baktim	6-7hr
2	Optional acclimatisation day at Tsokha	1 day
3	Tsokha to Dzongri	4-5hr
4	Acclimatisation day at Dzongri, or continue to Kokchurong	1 day
5	Dzongri (or Kokchurong) to Lamuni, via Thangsing	6-7hr
6	Lamuni to Goecha La, then down to Thangsing	8-9hr
7	Thangsing to Tsokha	6-7hr
8	Tsokha to Yuksom	5-6hr

Founded in 1641 by one of the three Yuksom crowning lamas, the monastery's five colourful religious buildings are strung out between more functional monks' quarters. Beautifully proportioned, the four-storey **main prayer hall** has a delicate filigree topknot, with wonderful views across the semiwildflower garden towards Ravangla. The Dalai Lama chose this magical spot for a two-day meditation retreat in 2010. Notice the cracks left in the marble flooring by the 2011 earthquake.

Beyond the last monastic building, an unusual compound contains dozens of white chortens, including the **Thongwa Rangdol**, said to absolve the sins of anyone who gazes upon it. More visually exciting is the golden **Kench Chorgi Lorde** stupa. Propped up all around are engraved stones bearing the Buddhist mantra *om mani padme hum;* at the back of the compound is the engraver's lean-to.

In February the monastery celebrates the Bumchu (p542) festival, when lamas gingerly open a sacred pot containing holy water and make important predictions by studying the level of water within.

There are a few scruffy lodges within Tashiding. The best beds, however, are at the government-run **Yatri Niwas** (☑ 9832623654; Main Rd; d ₹2000). An excellent midrange place by the turn-off to the monastery, it offers spacious rooms, lovely gardens and a good restaurant.

Shared jeeps to Gangtok (₹190, four hours) and Geyzing (₹80, 1½ hours) leave from the main junction between 6.30am and 8am. For Siliguri, take a jeep to Jorethang (₹90, two hours) and change. A few jeeps to Yuksom (₹60, one hour) pass through during early afternoon.

Northeast States

Why Go?

Thrown across the farthest reaches of India, obscured from the greater world by ageless forests and formidable mountain ranges, the Northeast States are one of Asia's last great natural and anthropological sanctuaries. Sharing borders with Bhutan, Tibet, Myanmar (Burma) and Bangladesh, these remote frontiers are a region of rugged beauty, and a collision zone of tribal cultures, climates, landscapes and peoples. In this wonderland for adventurers, glacial Himalayan rivers spill onto Assam's vast floodplains, faith moves mountains on the perilous pilgrimage to Tawang, rhinos graze in Kaziranga's swampy grasslands and former head-hunters slowly embrace modernity in their ancestral longhouses in Nagaland.

Of course, it's not all smooth sailing, with a horde of obstacles to battle along the way (bad roads, poor infrastructure and rebel armies, to name a few). In other words, only those with a taste for raw adventure need apply.

Best Places to Stay

➜ Diphlu River Lodge (p573)
➜ Wild Mahseer (p572)
➜ Ri Kynjai (p595)
➜ Heritage (p585)
➜ Mancotta Heritage Chang Bungalow (p573)

Best Places to Eat

➜ Khorika (p569)
➜ Maihang (p569)
➜ Trattoria (p595)

When to Go
Assam (Guwahati)

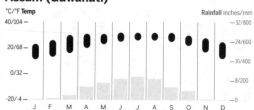

Mar The best season for rhino spotting in Kaziranga.

Oct A time for dazzling Himalayan vistas and trips to remote outposts.

Dec Fierce Naga warriors in ethnic regalia assemble for Kohima's Hornbill Festival.

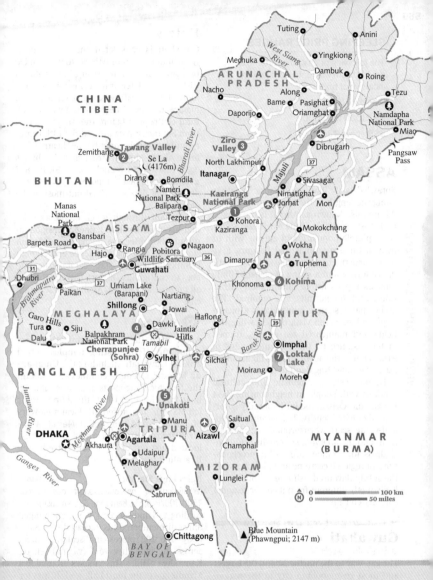

Northeast States Highlights

1 Riding atop an elephant in search of rhinos in **Kaziranga National Park** (p572)

2 Touching the clouds at the 4176m pass of Se La before descending to the valley of **Tawang** (p583), Arunachal Pradesh's Tibetan Buddhist hotspot

3 Visiting the scenic villages around **Ziro** (p579), where you can meet the intriguing Apatani tribe and learn about their unique way of life

4 Gazing down on the plains of Bangladesh from the lofty escarpment around **Cherrapunjee** (p597)

5 Staring in awe at the massive rock-cut sculptures of gods amid the wilderness at **Unakoti** (p595) in Tripura

6 Visiting a WWII cemetery and sampling Naga hospitality in and around **Kohima** (p585)

7 Exploring the unique ecosystem and islands of **Loktak Lake** (p589) in Manipur

SLEEPING PRICE RANGES

The following price ranges refer to a double room with bathroom and are inclusive of tax:

$ below ₹1000

$$ ₹1000 to ₹3000

$$$ above ₹3000

ASSAM

Sprawled lazily like a prehistoric leviathan along the length of the Brahmaputra valley, Assam (also known as Ahom) is the biggest and most accessible of the Northeast States. A hospitable population, a cuisine with its own distinctive aromas and flavours, a vibrant artistic heritage marked by exotic dance forms, and a string of elegant Hindu temples top its list of innumerable attractions, and no permits are required. The archetypal Assamese landscape is a picturesque golden-green vista of jigsaw-like rice fields and manicured tea estates, framed in the distance by the blue mountains of Arunachal in the north and the highlands of Meghalaya and Nagaland to the south.

Despite certain linguistic and cultural overlaps with people in neighbouring West Bengal and Orissa, Assam is proudly sovereign about its identity. The *gamosa* (a red-and-white scarf worn around the neck by men) and the *mekhola sador* (the traditional dress for women) are visible proclamations of regional costume and identity, while the subtly flavoured fish *tenga* (sour curry) is distinctly different from its other regional culinary cousins.

Guwahati

📞 0361 / POP 809,500

The gateway to the northeast and the largest and most cosmopolitan city in the region, Guwahati serves as the starting block for most Northeast itineraries. It's a somewhat featureless city – a prosaic heap of glass and concrete for the most part – but there are a scattering of interesting temples to explore. Walk its back alleys and old quarters, however, and you will be able to salvage a generous amount of local flavour that lingers amid its suburban sprawl of ponds, palm trees, small single-storey traditional houses and old colonial-era mansions.

History

Guwahati is considered the site of Pragjyotishpura, a semi-mythical town founded by Asura King Naraka (son of an avatar of Vishnu who later transformed into a demon), later killed by Krishna for a pair of magical earrings. The city was a vibrant cultural centre well before the Ahoms arrived from Southeast Asia around the 13th century, and it was subsequently the theatre of intense Ahom–Mughal strife, changing hands eight times in 50 years before 1681. In 1897 a huge earthquake – followed by a series of devastating floods – wiped out most of the old city.

Dormant through much of India's colonial history, Guwahati gained metropolitan prominence after the formation of Assam state in the post-Independence era. Though technically not the state capital (the title goes to contiguous Dispur), Guwahati is, for all purpose and intent, Assam's numero uno city.

⊙ Sights

Apart from the major sights, there are a handful of interesting temples dotted around Guwahati, including the **Umananda Mandir**, a temple complex that sits on the forested Peacock Island, accessible by boat from Kachari Ghat; the **Jain Mandir** (off MS Rd), patronised by local followers of Jainism; and the quaint **Nepali Mandir** (Rehabari Rd), consecrated to Krishna, located just out of the town centre by the Bharalu River.

Kamakhya Mandir   HINDU TEMPLE

(admission for no queue/short queue/queue ₹500/100/free; ⊙8am-1pm & 3pm-dusk) According to Hindu legend, when an enraged Shiva dismembered his deceased wife Sati's body into 108 pieces and scattered them across the land, her yoni (vagina) fell on Kamakhya Hill. This makes Kamakhya Mandir one of the most hallowed shrines for practitioners of *shakti* (tantric worship of female spiritual power). Goats are ritually beheaded here as offerings to the goddess in a gory pavilion and the hot, dark inner womb-like sanctum is painted red to signify sacrificial blood. It is here that the Ambubachi Mela takes place.

Kamakhya is 7km west of central Guwahati and 3km up a spiralling side road. Occasional buses from Guwahati's Kachari bus stand run all the way up (₹20, 30 minutes).

Guwahati

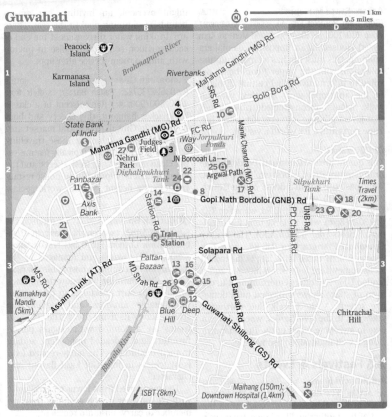

NORTHEAST STATES GUWAHATI

Guwahati

◉ Sights
1 Assam State Museum	B2
2 Courthouse	B2
3 Dighulipukhuri Park	B2
4 Guwahati Planetarium	B1
5 Jain Mandir	A3
6 Nepali Mandir	B3
7 Umananda Mandir	B1

◉ Activities, Courses & Tours
8 Jungle Travels India	C2
9 Network Travels	B3

◉ Sleeping
10 Baruah Bhavan	C1
11 Hotel Prag Continental	A2
12 Hotel Siroy Lily	B3
13 Kiranshree Portico	B3
14 Prashaanti Tourist Lodge	B2
15 Rains Inn	C3
16 Sundarban Guest House	B3

◉ Eating
17 Beatrix	C2
18 Khorika	D2
19 Maihang	D4
20 Paradise	D2
21 Tandoori	A3

◉ Drinking & Nightlife
22 Café Coffee Day	B2
23 Trafik	D2

◉ Shopping
24 Artfed	B2
25 Northeast Network	C2

◉ Information
Assam Tourism	(see 14)

◉ Transport
26 Airport Taxis	B3
27 Kachari Bus Stand	B2
Network Travels	(see 9)

Assam State Museum — MUSEUM

(Gopi Nath Bordoloi Rd; admission ₹5, camera/video ₹10/100; ⊙10am-5pm Wed-Mon, to 4pm winter) Housed in an imposing colonial-era building, this museum has a large sculpture collection, with the upper floors being devoted to informative tribal culture displays. In the anthropological galleries, you can walk through reconstructed tribal homes that give a glimpse into everyday rural life. Time permitting, it's worth a visit.

Old Guwahati — AREA

This quaint area of Guwahati, bordering the Brahmaputra River, is best explored on foot. Walk past the beehive dome of the **Courthouse** (MG Rd), which rises above attractive **Dighulipukhuri Park** (HB Rd; admission ₹10; ⊙9.30am-8pm), with its large tank full of colourful boats (per person ₹20). The nearby **Guwahati Planetarium** (MG Rd; shows ₹20; ⊙noon & 4pm, closed 1st & 15th of the month) looks somewhere between a mosque and a landed UFO and offers entertainment in the form of space shows projected on a dome-like screen. A short walk due northwest takes you to the **riverbanks**, where you can take in sweeping views of the Brahmaputra along a well-maintained promenade.

Festivals & Events

Ambubachi Mela — RELIGIOUS

(⊙Jun/Jul) The huge Ambubachi Mela takes place at Kamakhya Mandir, celebrating the end of the mother goddess' menstrual cycle with animal sacrifice.

Sleeping

Prashaanti Tourist Lodge — HOTEL $

(☑0361-2544475; Station Rd; s/d from ₹680/950; ✳) This central hotel is convenient for the train station. A fancy elevator takes you up to your room, which is clean and tidy and might overlook an inviting (but out-of-bounds!) swimming pool to the rear. There are drinking water dispensers at the end of each corridor, some train noise to put up with, and no room service after 9pm.

Sundarban Guest House — HOTEL $

(☑0361-2730722; Paltan Bazaar; s/dt/tr from ₹700/800/900; ✳) Reminiscent of a classic backpacker hangout, this cheery and busy hotel sits in Guwahati's central market area and offers great value for those travelling on a budget. Rooms are typically featureless but clean and tidy with fresh sheets, and the management is helpful. The in-house restaurant offers a decent range of working-class dishes.

★ Baruah Bhavan — GUESTHOUSE $$

(☑0361-2541182; www.baruahbhavan.com; Uzanbazar, Manik Chandra Rd; d incl breakfast from ₹2500; ✳@) Owned and managed by the affable and genuinely hospitable Baruah family, this charming bungalow dating back to the 1970s oozes nostalgia in the form of innumerable antiques and memorabilia strewn across its living areas. The six plush rooms are appointed with elegant period furniture and brocaded upholstery, adding to their quaintness. The home-cooked food is matchless in terms of local flavour and character.

The manicured front lawns go excellently with chilled beer in the evenings (just remember to carry mosquito repellent).

Rains Inn — HOTEL $$

(☑0361-2730023; www.rainsinn.com; Solapara Rd; d from ₹2450; ✳☎) This stylish hotel makes great use of ethno-chic decor (read cane furniture and reed blinds) in its well-appointed, airy and bright air-conditioned rooms. The loos are squeaky clean, some of the furniture is made from recycled wood, and water con-

TOP FESTIVALS

Losar (p583) Masked Tibetan Buddhist dances take place in Tawang.

Rongali Bihu (⊙mid-Apr) Assamese New Year festivities take place statewide.

Ambubachi Mela (p568) A melange of tantric fertility rituals takes place at Kamakhya Mandir in Guwahati.

Ziro Music Festival (p579) The region's very own Glastonbury in Ziro Valley.

Wangala (p596) Garo harvest festival with dance and drum rolls.

Ras Mahotsav (p575) Much song and dance in praise of Krishna on Majuli Island.

Hornbill Festival (p585) Naga tribes take to the stage in full warrior gear just outside Kohima in Nagaland.

servation is given top priority. Wi-fi, tea and coffee come complimentary. The smart restaurant downstairs has lip-smacking food.

Hotel Siroy Lily
HOTEL $$
(☑ 0361-2608492; www.hotelsiroygroup.com; Solapara Rd; s/d incl breakfast from ₹1380/1590; ✳) This trusted oldie is professionally run and offers superb value for money, and is thereby a favourite with midrange travellers transiting through Guwahati. Rooms are well serviced; those with AC offer a significantly better deal for a few hundred extra rupees. Book in advance, as it's packed most of the time.

Hotel Prag Continental
HOTEL $$
(☑ 0361-2540850; www.hotelpragcontinental.com; MN Rd; s/d incl breakfast from ₹2100/2600; ✳@☎) The well-furnished and excellently serviced rooms in this hotel are great value, more so since discounts can be easy to come by. It's on a quieter side street and has a good restaurant. The ice-cream parlour outside is a nice spot for an after-dinner dessert.

Kiranshree Portico
HOTEL $$$
(☑ 0361-2735300; www.kiranshreeportico.com; Guwahati Shillong Rd; s/d from ₹5300/6100; ✳☎) Currently favoured by business and top-end leisure travellers and located among upscale addresses in town, this luxurious, modern hotel in the heart of Guwahati boasts prim and elegant rooms with soft beds, ambient lighting, giant LCD TVs and well-stocked minibars. Guests have complimentary access to the fitness centre, while the coffee shop has a delectable range of bakes and brews.

✗ Eating

Beatrix
MULTICUISINE $
(MC Rd; dishes ₹80-120; ☺noon-10pm) Beatrix has come a long way, from hangout for college students to an understated dining with accented lighting and red table linen. The food is a predictable mix of Indian, Chinese and regional dishes, but it's all piping hot and eminently tasty.

Paradise
ASSAMESE $$
(GNB Rd; mains ₹100-200; ☺10.30am-10.30pm) The lunch thali at Paradise is considered by many to be the archetypal Assamese spread, bringing together a wide range of local culinary flavours on one platter. Try the subtly flavoured fish *tenga* and you're bound to become a fan for life.

Khorika
NORTHEAST INDIAN $$
(☑ 9706034838; GS Rd; mains ₹100-180; ☺noon-11pm) Named after the Assamese *khorika* (barbecued dishes), this restaurant serves a superb selection of regional dishes in upscale air-conditioned comfort. Try barbecued small fish or fried pigeon meat, or go for the delicious pork with sesame seeds.

★ Maihang
NORTHEAST INDIAN $$
(☑ 9854373978; GS Rd; mains ₹150-170; ☺noon-3pm & 7-10.30pm) A whiff of exotic aromas serenade your olfactories the moment you walk into this smart restaurant. A range of regional dishes are on offer here, ranging from pork with fermented bamboo shoots, wild herb or *akhoni* (fermented soybeans), fish *khorika,* chicken with sesame seeds, and duck in sesame gravy.

Tandoori
NORTH INDIAN $$
(☑ 0361-2516021; Dynasty Hotel, SS Rd; mains ₹200-300; ☺noon-3pm & 7-11pm) Inside the stately Dynasty Hotel on Sir Shahdullah (SS) Rd, this stylish restaurant has tasty North Indian dishes, served by waiters in Mughal uniforms with gentle Indian music playing in the background. It's a somewhat upscale affair, so dress for the occasion.

♟ Drinking & Nightlife

Café Coffee Day
CAFE
(Taybullah Rd; coffee ₹50-90; ☺10am-10pm) Guwahati's central coffee shop, pumping out contemporary music, attracts the city's students and nouveau riche youth with lattes and macchiatos. Some tasty snacks are on offer to go with your cuppa.

Trafik
BAR
(GNB Rd; beer ₹130; ☺11am-10pm; ☎) Dim and buzzy, this popular bar is a hit with the city's office workers and, true to its name, attracts heavy traffic after sundown. There's a vast TV screen for cricket matches and Bollywood music, and a tiny platform where live bands play local hits on the weekend.

⌂ Shopping

Artfed
SOUVENIRS
(☑ 0361-2548987; GNB Rd; ☺10am-8pm) Well stocked with bargain bamboo crafts, textiles, wickerwork, bell-metal and terracotta handicrafts, and many a carved rhino are on offer at this state-operated emporium. Several nearby shops specialise in Assam's famous golden-toned silks.

Northeast Network   CLOTHING
(☎ 0361-2603833; www.northeastnetwork.org; JN
Borooah Lane; ⏰ 11am-4pm Mon-Fri) This NGO
seeds self-help projects in rural villages to
empower rural women, and works as an
umbrella organisation for several hand-
loom-weaving cooperatives. Buying beautiful (and good-value) handloomed products
here supports this fine work.

ℹ Information

ATMs and banks abound. It's a good idea to
stock up on local currency here as ATMs in
smaller centres across the region can be unreliable.

Assam Tourism (☎ 0361-2544475; www.
assamtourism.gov.in; Prashaanti Tourist Lodge,
Station Rd; ⏰ 10am-5pm Mon-Sat) Informal
help desk in the Prashaanti Tourist Lodge and a
tour booth just outside.

Axis Bank (M Nehru Rd; ⏰ 10am-4pm Mon-
Sat) Has an ATM and handles foreign exchange.

Downtown Hospital (☎ 0361-2331003; Guwahati Shillong Rd, Dispur) Among the best hospitals in town for emergencies. Dispur, Assam's
state administrative district, is contiguous to
Guwahati along GS Rd in an eastward direction.

iWay (Lamb Rd; internet per hr ₹30; ⏰ 9am-
8pm)

Main Post Office (Ananda Ram Barua Rd;
⏰ 10am-4pm Mon-Sat) For sending snail mail
and parcels back home.

Police Station (☎ 0361-2540126; Hem Barua
Rd)

State Bank of India (SBI Bldg, MG Rd;
⏰ 10am-2pm Mon-Fri, to noon Sat) Has an ATM,
changes major currencies and cashes travellers
cheques.

ℹ Getting There & Away

AIR

Air India (☎ 0361-2266266; www.airindia.
in; Ganeshguri), IndiGo, GoAir, **Jet Airways**
(☎ 0361-2633252; www.jetairways.com;
Tayebullah Rd) and SpiceJet fly to Guwahati
from most major Indian cities (often with a stopover in Kolkata).

Arunachal Helicopter Service (☎ 0361-
2229501; www.pawanhans.co.in; Guwahati
Airport; ⏰ 9am-2pm) For those with permits,
Arunachal Helicopter Service has flights to
Itanagar (₹4000, 1½ hours, 1.30pm Monday
and Friday, 2pm Tuesday, Thursday and Saturday, and 2.30pm Sunday).

Meghalaya Helicopter Service
(☎ 9859021473; Guwahati Airport; ⏰ 8.30am-

2pm) Shuttles to Shillong (₹1500, 30 minutes,
9am and 12.30pm Monday to Saturday) and
Tura (₹1900, 45 minutes, 10.30am Monday,
Wednesday, Friday and Saturday). Note that
helicopters won't fly in bad weather.

BUS & SUMO

Long-distance buses leave from the **Interstate
Bus Terminal (ISBT)**, 8km from the town centre
along NH37. Private bus operators run shuttle
bus services from their offices to the ISBT. **Blue
Hill** (☎ 0361-2601490; HPB Rd; ⏰ 6am-8pm),
Deep (☎ 0361-2152937; HPB Rd; ⏰ 6am-9pm)
and **Network Travels** (☎ 0361-2522007; GS Rd;
⏰ 5am-9pm) have extensive networks. All companies hire out Sumos and other sturdy 4WD
vehicles for travel in the region, and charge the
same regulated fares of ₹4000 per day, including fuel and driver. If you're plan to mostly travel
within the region, rather than clocking road
miles, consider hiring a 'dry' vehicle for ₹1800
per day and buy your own fuel as you go.

Buses from Guwahati

DESTINATION	FARE (₹)	DURATION (HR)
Agartala (Tripura)	780	24-26
Aizawl (Mizoram)	760	28
Dibrugarh	510	10
Imphal (Manipur) via Mao	920	20
Jorhat	320	8
Kaziranga	260-350	6
Kohima (Nagaland)	410	13
Shillong (Meghalaya)	90-120	3½
Sivasagar	410	8
Tezpur	190	5

TRAIN

Four daily trains connect Guwahati to Delhi; the
12423 Dibrugarh Rajdhani Express (3AC/2AC
₹2635/3660, 27 hours, 5.55am) is the fastest
and most comfortable. The best daily train
to Kolkata (Howrah) is the 12346 Saraighat
Express (sleeper/3AC/2AC ₹500/1305/1870,
16½ hours, 12.35pm). If travelling to Darjeeling
and Sikkim, get off at New Jalpaiguri (sleep-
er/3AC/2AC ₹295/760/1065, 6½ hours).

Several trains also serve Dimapur (chair/
sleeper/3AC ₹90/180/485, four to six hours),
Jorhat (chair/sleeper/3AC ₹125/235/635,
eight to 11 hours) and Dibrugarh (3AC/2AC
₹165/315/850, 10 to 14 hours).

ℹ Getting Around

Getting into town from Guwahati's orderly Lok-priya Gopinath Bordoloi International Airport (23km) costs ₹500/150/100 for a taxi/shared taxi/airport bus. Shared taxis (per person/car ₹150/500) travel to the airport from outside the Hotel Mahalaxmi on Guwahati Shillong (GS) Rd. Autorickshaws charge ₹25 to ₹70 for short hops within the city. You could also dial in a time-efficient **Green Cab** (☑ 0361-7151515; www.7151515.com) and enjoy a comfortable ride at ₹15 per kilometre within town or to the airport.

Around Guwahati

Hajo

Some 30km northwest of Guwahati, the pleasant little town of Hajo attracts Hindu and Buddhist pilgrims to its five ancient temples topping assorted hillocks. **Haigriv Madhav Temple** is the main shrine, which is accessed by a long flight of steps through an ornate quasi-Mughal gateway. The images inside of Madhav, an avatar of Krishna, are believed to be 6000 years old. To get here, take local bus number 25 from the Adabari bus stand in Guwahati (₹60, one hour).

Pobitora Wildlife Sanctuary

Pobitora Wildlife Sanctuary   WILDLIFE RESERVE
(Indian/foreigner ₹50/500) Only 40km from northeast of Guwahati, this small wildlife sanctuary has a generous sprinkling of one-horned rhinoceros. Getting into the park involves a boat ride over the river boundary to the elephant-mounting station, from where you could embark on a one-hour trip atop an elephant, lumbering through boggy grasslands and stirring up petulant rhinos. The best way to get there is by taxi (return trip ₹1800).

Tezpur

☑ 03712 / POP 105.300

Little more than a utilitarian stopover for travellers journeying into Arunachal Pradesh or Upper Assam, Tezpur is a charming town with some beautifully kept parks, attractive lakes and enchanting views of the mighty Brahmaputra River as it laps the town's edge.

RIVER RIDES

To experience the innate beauty of Assam from a unique perspective (and all of it in style), consider signing up for a plush river cruise. Departing Guwahati on set dates between September and April, these multiday luxury rides take you upstream along the Brahmaputra River all the way to Dibrugarh, dropping anchor at essential hotspots such as Kaziranga National Park, Majuli Island and Sivasagar. Activities en route include wildlife tours, cultural excursions, or simply lazing on the sun-deck with a chiller in hand. Guwahati-based **Assam Bengal Navigation** (☑ 9207042330; www.assambengalnavigation.com; GNB Rd; per person per day all-inclusive from US$195) has all the information, and is recommended.

◉ Sights

Chitralekha Udyan   PARK
(Cole Park; Jenkins Rd; admission ₹20, camera/video ₹20/100; ⊙9am-7pm) Chitralekha Udyan has a U-shaped pond (paddle-boat hire per person ₹20) wrapped around pretty manicured lawns, dotted with fine ancient sculptures. From April to September, the park also contains bumper cars and water slides!

A block east, then south, stands **Ganesh-garh Temple**, which backs onto a ghat overlooking the surging river, a good place for Brahmaputra sunsets.

Agnigarh Hill   PARK
(Padma Park; admission ₹20, camera/video ₹20/100; ⊙8.30am-7.30pm) Nearly 1km east along the narrow, winding riverside lane is Agnigarh Hill, which might have been the fire fortress site of Banasura (the demon son of the monkey god Bali). The park has peaceful greens and great vistas of the Brahmaputra River that flows nearby.

🛏 Sleeping

Prashaanti Tourist Lodge   HOTEL $
(☑ 03712-221016; touristlodgetezpur@gmail.com; Jenkins Rd; d/tr ₹850/950) Facing Chitralekha Udyan south of the bus station, this government-run hotel has been spruced up to cater to international budget travellers. Manned by staff who are extremely efficient and obliging by governtment standards, the

place offers spacious, good-value rooms with clean attached bathrooms, fresh sheets and mosquito nets.

KF HOTEL $$
(☑ 03712-255203; Mission Charali; s/d from ₹2400/3000; ✳ ☎) With slick, contemporary rooms, good customer service and plenty of attention to detail, this hotel – located about 3km north of the town centre – has lots going for it. There's an in-house restaurant, a coffee shop and, most importantly, a well-stuffed department store downstairs where you can stock up on essential commodities before venturing into remote areas.

Hotel Centre Point HOTEL $$
(☑ 03712-232359; hotelcentrepoint.tez@gmail.com; Main Rd; d incl breakfast from ₹1650; ✳) Easily offering the best returns on investment, the smart, freshly painted rooms at this well-run, centrally located hotel feature flat-screen TVs, hot showers and polished wood floors, giving them a poor man's business hotel sort of feel. The in-house travel desk can organise local sightseeing trips as well as longer tours.

✖ Eating & Drinking

Spring Valley CAFETERIA $
(NC Rd; ⊙ 7.30am-9pm) This incredibly busy and popular cafeteria serves hot, tasty all-day snacks and mini meals (the puris are simply scrumptious) through the day. The bakery section has a decent range of puffs, pastries and bread, while the upstairs restaurant comes alive during lunch and dinner.

Oasis BAR
(Jonaki Cinema Rd; beers from ₹110; ⊙ 11am-10pm) Chilled bottles of Kingfisher are served with a wide array of kebabs at this popular and friendly bar a short walk from Hotel Centre Point. It's adjacent to Jonaki Cinema, alongside a row of shops specialising in garments and handloom products.

ℹ Information

Cinex Computers (Santa Plaza, SC Rd; internet per hr ₹30; ⊙10am-9pm)
HDFC Bank (Mission Chariali; ⊙10am-4pm Mon-Sat) Has an ATM.

ℹ Getting There & Away

Sumos booking counters are located on Jenkins Rd and run to Bomdila (₹350, eight hours) and Dirang (₹400, 10 hours) in Arunachal Pradesh and Tawang (₹700, 15 hours). Bargain for a private taxi on the same street for the Eco-Camp at Nameri National Park (₹2200) and Kaziranga National Park (₹2200). A little further on is the **bus station** (Jenkins Rd) with frequent services to Guwahati (₹160, five hours), Jorhat (₹160, four hours) and Kohora village (₹90, two hours) for Kaziranga.

Around Tezpur

Scenic **Nameri National Park** (Indian/foreigner admission ₹20/250, camera ₹50/500, video ₹500/1000; ⊙ Nov-Apr) specialises in low-key, walk-in birdwatching treks. Around 374 bird species have been recorded in the park, including such rarities as the greater spotted eagle and the white-winged duck. Mammals include wild elephants, a few rarely seen tigers and the critically endangered dwarf hog. Park fees include the compulsory armed guard. Access is from **Potasali**, 2km off the Tezpur–Bhalukpong road.

Eco-Camp (☑ 03714-292644; ecocampnameri@gmail.com; dm/d ₹250/1800) organises park visits, including two-hour birdwatching rafting trips (two people Indian/foreigner ₹1500/2000). Accommodation is in 'tents', but colourful fabrics, private bathrooms, sturdy beds and thatched-roof shelters make the experience relatively luxurious. The camp is set within lush gardens full of tweeting birds and butterflies drunk on tropical nectar.

Wild Mahseer (☑ 03714-234354; www.wild-mahseer.com; d incl meals from ₹8500; ✳), located amid rolling tea gardens about 5km from Balipara and 30km northeast of Tezpur, offers a luxurious stay in its four superbly renovated planter's bungalows set on a picturesque 22-acre campus canopied with evergreen trees. For a particularly memorable experience, consider spending a night in the Heritage Bungalow, a stately 100-year-old building that carefully preserves a slice of high life from its bygone era. To get to the estate, turn right from Balipara crossing and take the village road going left after the bridge over the Bhorelli River.

Kaziranga National Park
☑ 03776
The famed one-horned rhinoceros, one of India's best-known tourism mascots, calls the expansive grasslands of the **Kaziranga National Park** (Indian/foreigner admission ₹50/500, camera ₹50/500, video ₹500/1000;

⊘Nov-Apr, elephant rides 5.30-8.30am, 4WD access 7.30am-noon & 2.30pm-dusk) its home. The park's population of 1800-odd rhinos represents more than two-thirds of the world's total; in 1904 there were just 200.

The park consists of western, central and eastern ranges, the central range doubling as the venue for popular early-morning **elephant safaris**. Lasting an hour each, these rides offer unparalleled opportunities to get close to rhinos, which don't seem phased by the elephants, even when surrounded by several safari groups. Safaris can be arranged at the Kaziranga Tourist Complex or directly with your accommodation.

🛏️ Sleeping & Eating

In season, booking ahead and paying in advance is recommended. Most midrange and top-end hotels sell 'Jungle Plan' packages, which include full-board accommodation, park fees, a morning elephant safari and an afternoon 4WD safari.

🛏️ Tourist Complex

There are a number of budget and midrange options across the well-maintained Kaziranga Tourist Complex off the main road in Kohora village; all are within a short walk of the range office.

Aranya Tourist Lodge   HOTEL **$$**
(☑ 03776-262429; d from ₹1250; ❄) A somewhat characterless and boxy government operation masquerading as a forest getaway, this garden-fronted hotel features clean rooms, prompt service, decent food and a well-stocked bar. It's popular with large groups, so expect some noisy company.

Jupuri Ghar   RESORT **$$**
(☑ 9435196377, 0361-2605335; www.jupurigharkaziranga.com; d incl breakfast ₹3200; ❄) A holiday atmosphere adds to the appeal of this pretty property, comprising traditional-style cabins set around pleasant, mature gardens in a tranquil setting. It's well managed and has an open-air restaurant where you can compare your elephant safari notes with other guests over the complimentary breakfast.

🛏️ Beyond the Complex

Wild Grass Resort   RESORT **$$**
(☑ 03776-262085, 9954416945; wildgrasskaziranga@gmail.com; d incl breakfast ₹2450) This slightly ramshackle yet cheerful resort is so popular that it doesn't bother with a sign – it carefully labels all the trees instead! Colonial-era decor makes you feel the clock has slowed. Tasty Indian food is served in the dining room. The affable, bearded proprietor is a fount of local information. In season, bookings are absolutely essential. The resort is located about 10km to the east of Kohora.

Bonhabi Resort   RESORT **$$**
(☑ 03776-262675; www.bonhabiresort.com; d from ₹1610; ❄) A short way east of the tourist complex, this quiet, friendly place consists of an old villa with a colonial-era look and feel, plus a series of comfortable cottages set around gorgeous gardens. The food is well cooked but somewhat unimaginative. It's well signposted on the way to the eastern range.

⭐ **Diphlu River Lodge**   RESORT **$$$**
(☑ 0361-2667871, 9954205360; www.diphluriverlodge.com; jungle plan per person Indian/foreigner ₹8000/15,000; ❄📶) Easily the classiest (and

DON'T MISS

TEA GETAWAYS

No visit to Upper Assam is complete without a lavish night or two in a heritage tea-estate bungalow, of which there are many in the region. For a memorable experience, try the antique crammed **Banyan Grove** (☑ 033-22657389; www.heritagetourismindia.com; s/d incl full board ₹5600/6500; ❄❄) or the quaint colonial-era **Thengal Manor** (☑ 033-22657389; www.heritagetourismindia.com; Jalukanburi; s/d incl full board ₹4000/6500; ❄), both a short drive out of Jorhat. In Dibrugarh, the best place to enjoy a planter-style cuppa is the **Mancotta Heritage Chang Bungalow** (☑ 0373-2301120; purvi@sancharnet.in; Mancotta Rd, Dibrugarh; d incl meals from ₹8300; ❄📶), which also arranges tea tours and river cruises on request. Accommodation here is in a charming planter's bungalow fronted by grassy lawns. The patio, the 1st-floor balcony and the reading room make for exceptional places to while away leisure time, and the dining hall has an impressive collection of 19th-century sketches and prints with a predominantly equestrian theme.

SATRAS

A *satra* is a monastery for Vishnu worship, Assam's distinctive form of everyman Hinduism. Formulated by 15th-century Assamese philosopher Sankardev, the faith eschews the caste system and idol worship, focusing on Vishnu as God, especially in his Krishna incarnation. Much of the worship is based around dance and melodramatic play-acting of scenes from the holy Bhagavad Gita. The heart of any *satra* is its *namghar* (a large, simple, prayer hall), housing an eternal flame, the Gita and possibly a horde of instructive (but not divine) images. Traditionally, *satras* have also patronised the elegantly choreographed Satriya dance form and the folk-performing-arts tradition of Ankiya Bhawna, in which masked dancers play out tales from Hindu mythology. To purchase traditional dance masks (₹300 to ₹2000) as souvenirs, visit **Samaguri Satra**, a 15-minute drive from Garamur on Majuli Island.

priciest!) place to stay in the Kaziranga region, this fantastic resort combines fine luxuries with a rustic look and an ethno-chic theme. The bamboo cottages lining the Diphlu River boast soft beds, rain showers in stylish bathrooms, and pleasant sit-outs from where lucky guests might spot rhinos grazing the grasslands. Oh, and the food is delicious.

There's no marker: if you're travelling from Guwahati, look for the dirt track on the left after the Bagori police outpost, leading to a gate with a signage saying 'private property'. Boo Moni, the in-house forest guide, is a trove of local information.

Iora   RESORT $$$
(The Retreat; ☑ 9957193350; www.ioraholidays.com; s/d incl breakfast from ₹3850/4250; ❋ @ 🛜 ☒) Somewhat formal and oversized for a place like Kaziranga, this sprawling property has excellently maintained rooms (42 in all) featuring tasteful decor, modern amenities and efficient service. The swimming pool is a big draw for kids, while adults can spend a lazy afternoon indulging in a range of therapies at the in-house spa.

ℹ Information

The forest administration offices are clubbed together in the Kaziranga Tourist Complex (marked by an obvious Rhino Gate) about 800m south of Kohora village. Here you'll find the **range office** (☑ 03776-262428; ⊙ 24hr), **elephant-ride booking office** (rides incl park admission Indian/foreigner ₹550/1550; ⊙ 5-7pm, book the previous night) and **4WD rental stand** (per vehicle incl toll fee western/central/eastern ranges ₹1600/1500/2000). Pay your fees at the range office before entering the park, 2km north.

An armed guard accompanies all vehicles (and some elephants) entering the park. A ₹50 tip for mahouts, drivers and guards is customary.

ℹ Getting There & Away

Buses travel from Kohora village to Guwahati (₹350, five hours, hourly 7.30am to 4.30pm), Dibrugarh (₹320, four hours) and Tezpur (₹90, two hours).

Jorhat

☑ 0376 / POP 137,800

Apart from being the access point for Majuli Island, bustling Jorhat has little on offer for travellers. Gar Ali, the town's commercial street, meets the main AT Road (NH37) in front of a lively **central market**. AT Rd has an ATM and the **Netizen Cyberspace** (internet per hr ₹30; ⊙ 10am-8pm).

Conveniently tucked behind the Assam State Transport Corporation (ASTC) bus station, Solicitor Rd has a bunch of reasonable hotels. The best of the bunch is **Hotel Paradise** (☑ 0376-2321521; paradisejorhat@gmail.com; Solicitor Rd; s/d incl breakfast from ₹600/850; ❋ 🛜), with well-kept interiors, chequered blankets, friendly service, deep-fried snacks and free wi-fi. **Hotel Heritage** (☑ 0376-2301839; heritagejorhat2009@yahoo.in; Solicitor Rd; d from ₹1000; ❋) has well-maintained rooms, obliging staff and an old-fashioned character, while **New Park** (☑ 0376-2300721; hotelnewparkjorhat@gmail.com; Solicitor Rd; s/d from ₹950/1050; ❋) is a smart establishment with tidy, breezy rooms, hot showers and lots of daylight.

The **ASTC bus station** (AT Rd) has frequent services to Sivasagar (₹70, 1½ hours), Tezpur (₹170, four hours), and Guwahati

(₹380, eight hours, eight buses 6am to noon), passing Kaziranga en route.

The **Jorhat train station** is in the heart of town, about 500m to the south of AT Rd along Gar Ali. The 12068 Jan Shatabdi Express (AC Chair ₹580, 6¾ hours, 2.10pm Monday to Saturday) is the most convenient of the three trains to Guwahati.

The windswept sandbank of Nimatighat in Jorhat, pockmarked with chai shacks, is the departure point for overcrowded **ferries** to Majuli Island (adult/4WD ₹20/600, 1½ hours, 8.30am, 10.30am, 1.30pm and 3pm). It's a 12km ride from Jorhat by bus (₹30, 40 minutes).

Majuli Island

☑ 03775 / POP 168,000

Beached amid the mighty Brahmaputra River's ever-shifting puzzle of ochre sandbanks is Majuli, which at around 452 sq km is India's largest river island. For a place continually ravaged by the primal forces of nature (much of the island disappears under water every monsoon), Majuli flaunts unparalleled scenic beauty. The island is a relaxed, shimmering mat of glowing rice fields and water meadows bursting with hyacinth blossoms.

Aside from enjoying the laid-back vibe, highlights of a visit include birdwatching (the island is home to nearly 100 species of birds) and learning about neo-Vaishnavite philosophy at Majuli's 22 ancient *satras* (Hindu Vaishnavite monasteries and centres for art). But don't waste time getting Majuli Island surveys indicate that at current levels of erosion the island will cease to exist within the next two decades.

The two main villages are **Kamalabari**, 3km from the ferry port, and **Garamur**, 5km further north. The most interesting, accessible *satras* are the large, beautifully peaceful **Uttar Kamalabari** (1km north, then 600m east of Kamalabari) and **Auni Ati** (5km west of Kamalabari), where monks are keen to show you their little **museum** (Indian/foreigner ₹10/50, camera/video ₹50/200; ☉ 9.30-11am & 12-4pm) of Ahom royal artefacts. The best chances of observing chanting, dances or drama recitations are around dawn and dusk or during the big **Ras Mahotsav Festival** (☉ Nov), in celebration of the birth, life and feats of Krishna.

Majuli Tourism (☑ 9435657282; jyoti24365@gmail.com; full-day tour ₹500, bicycle hire per day ₹100), run by the friendly and knowledgeable Jyoti Narayan Sarma, conducts birdwatching tours and rents bicycles.

🛏 Sleeping & Eating

Some of the *satras* on Majuli Island have very basic guesthouses (per person ₹150). Remember to dress conservatively within the premises.

La Maison de Ananda GUESTHOUSE $
(☑ 9957186356; monjitrisong@yahoo.in; r ₹500-800) In Garamur, this thatched guesthouse on bamboo stilts has rooms decked out in locally made fabrics, giving it a hippie-chic atmosphere; there's also one new concrete block that sticks out like a sore thumb. It's run by a friendly tribal family, and the kitchen serves up a delicious range of local Mishing dishes.

Ygdrasill Bamboo Cottage GUESTHOUSE $
(☑ 8876707326; bedamajuli@gmail.com; d/q ₹500/1200) En route from Kamalabari to Garamur, this stilted guesthouse perches on a marshy, avian-spotted lake. Listen to the chorus of a thousand cicadas before lolling off to sleep in a comfy bamboo bed in one of the spartan, traditionally furnished cottages (bring that insect repellent along!). Dinner (₹200) can be organised upon prior request.

Mepo Okum GUESTHOUSE $$
(☑ 9435203165; d ₹1500) A pretty complex of eight cottages thrown around a grassy lawn hemmed by seasonal blossoms, this place is mostly booked out by top-end international tour groups, and is clearly the best of Majuli's overnight options. A very tasty and pricy local meal (₹500) can be arranged upon prior request.

❶ Getting There & Away

Ferries (adult/vehicle ₹20/600, 1½ hours) leave Nimatighat in Jorhat for Majuli Island at 8.30am, 10.30am, 1.30pm and 3pm; return trips are at 7.30am, 8.30am, 1.30pm and 3pm. Departures depend on tidal conditions and season.

❶ Getting Around

Jam-packed buses/vans (₹20/30) meet arriving ferries at the pier then drive to Garamur via Kamalabari. For long stays, consider arranging a bicycle (₹100) through Majuli Tourism (p575).

Sivasagar

📞 03772 / POP 53,800

Once the capital of the Ahom dynasty, sleepy Sivasagar (literally 'waters of Shiva') takes its name from the graceful central reservoir in the heart of town, commissioned by the Ahom Queen Ambika in 1734. Three typical Ahom **temple towers** rise proudly above the tank's partly wooded southern banks – to the west **Devidol**, to the east **Vishnudol** and in the centre, the 33m-high **Shivadol Mandir**.

Around 500m from Shivadol, a gaggle of hotels line AT Rd, the most appealing of which is the freshly renovated **Hotel Shiva Palace** (📞 03772-222629; hotelshiva-palace.1811@rediffmail.com; AT Rd; s/d from ₹900/1000; ❄️), incorporating a decent restaurant, the **Sky Chef Restaurant** (AT Rd; mains ₹160).

About 1.5km along Bhuban Gogoi (BG) Rd stands **Hotel Siddhartha** (📞 03772-222276; e7safari@rediffmail.com; BG Rd; d ₹1100; ❄️), a sparkly place with a range of good-value rooms.

The **ASTC bus station** (cnr AT & Temple Rds) has frequent services to Jorhat (₹70, one hour), Dibrugarh (₹90, two hours), Tezpur (₹250, five hours) and Guwahati (₹410, eight hours, frequent from 7am).

For local sightseeing to Talatalghar and Karenghar, use a tempo (per tour ₹200). You'll find them at an unmarked stop about 300m up BG Rd from AT Rd.

Around Sivasagar

Rang Ghar & Talatalghar

The famous Ahom ruins of Sivasagar are located about 4km down AT Rd from Sivasagar. First up along your way is the elegant **Rang Ghar** (Indian/foreigner ₹5/100; ☀️ dawn-dusk), a two-storey oval-shaped pavilion from where Ahom monarchs once watched buffalo and elephant fights in an arena that's now been converted into a manicured garden.

Past Rang Ghar along AT Rd, a left turning passes the barrack-shaped **Golaghar** (Ahom ammunition store). Beyond are the ruins of **Talatalghar** (Indian/foreigner ₹5/100; ☀️ dawn-dusk), an expansive, two-storey Ahom palace built by Ahom King Rajeswar Singha in the mid-18th century.

Karenghar

Karenghar   PALACE
(Indian/foreigner ₹5/100; ☀️ dawn-dusk) Dramatic if largely unadorned, this 1752 brick palace is the last remnant of the Ahom's pre-Sivasagar capital. The unique four-storey structure rises like a sharpened, stepped pyramid above an attractive forest-and-paddy setting. It's about 15km along the Sivasagar–Sonari highway down a village road: turn left just before Gargaon.

Dibrugarh

📞 0373 / POP 137,600

Cheerful and clement Dibrugarh, Assam's original tea city, usefully closes a loop between Kaziranga National Park and the Ziro–Along–Pasighat route in Arunachal Pradesh. It is also the terminus (or starting point) for the fascinating ferry ride along the Brahmaputra River to Pasighat.

Hotel Little Palace (📞 0373-2328700; www.hotellp.com; AT Rd; s/d from ₹800/950; ❄️📶), on the edge of town, is anything but little. Its 48 rooms are well appointed with clean linen, and the views of the Brahmaputra from the verandah at the end of the corridor comes free. **Hotel Rajawas** (📞 0373-2323307; www.hotelrajawas.com; AT Rd; s/d incl breakfast from ₹900/1100; ❄️@📶) has 30 delightful rooms with modern amenities, and boasts the highly recommended **Moti Mahal restaurant**, with superb North Indian food (mains ₹160).

State Bank of India (Thana Chariali; ☀️ 10am-2pm Mon-Fri, to noon Sat) cashes travellers cheques and foreign currency; there's also an SBI ATM in the main bus station complex. **Cyber@Generation Next** (HS Rd; internet per hr ₹30; ☀️ 10am-9pm) is one of several internet cafes.

From **Mohanbari airport**, 16km northeast of Dibrugarh and 4km off the Tinsukia road, Air India and Jet Airways fly to Guwahati, Kolkata and Delhi, while IndiGo flies to Guwahati.

From the **main bus station** (Mancotta Rd), both ASTC and private buses depart for Sivasagar (₹90, two hours, frequent 6am to 9am), Jorhat (₹170, three hours, frequent 6am to 9am), Tezpur (₹390, six hours, hourly 6am to 6pm) and Guwahati (₹490, 10 hours, hourly 6am to 8am and 8pm to 10pm). There's also an AC Volvo service to Guwahati (₹690, eight hours, 9.45pm).

From the train station in the town centre, the overnight 12423 Dibrugarh Rajdhani Express leaves for Guwahati (3AC/2AC ₹1150/1560, 10 hours) at 8.35pm.

Rough-and-ready ferries (per person ₹60, vehicle ₹1000; ☺ hourly 9am to 3pm) cruise daily to Bogibil Ghat on the Arunachal side of the Brahmaputra River, where they are met by a bus to Pasighat in Arunachal Pradesh. Cheekily challenging the basic laws of floatation, the rickety steamboats carry two 4WDs, a few dozen motorcycles and an army of humans. There's little shelter and the journey takes around 1½ hours, so bring shades, water and sunscreen. Exact departure times depend on the Brahmaputra's water level. During the dry season, ferries cruise further upstream to Majer Ghat or Oiram Ghat, which can take up to five hours. Many hotels in Dibrugarh sell 4WD-ferry-4WD combination tickets (per person ₹300) for travel to Pasighat.

ARUNACHAL PRADESH

The final frontier of Indian tourism, virginal Arunachal Pradesh shows up as a giant patch of unexplored green on the country's map. India's wildest and least explored state, Arunachal (literally the 'Land of Dawn-lit Mountains') rises abruptly from the Assam plains as a mass of densely forested, and impossibly steep, hills, which eventually top off as snow-capped peaks along the Tibetan border. Home to 26 indigenous tribes, Arunachal is perhaps the last sanctuary for India's natural and anthropological heritage. Much of the state still remains beyond tourism's reach, but new areas (comprising lush river gorges and craggy mountainscapes) are slowly being opened to visitors.

China has never formally recognised Indian sovereignty here, and it took the surprise Chinese invasion of 1962 for Delhi to really start funding significant infrastructure (the Chinese voluntarily withdrew). These days, border passes are heavily guarded by the Indian military but the atmosphere is generally calm. Compared to its neighbours, Arunachal has been relatively untouched by political violence, but Naga rebels continue to be active in the far northeast of the state, along the borders with Nagaland and Myanmar.

Itanagar

☎ 0360 / POP 35,000

Arunachal's capital takes its name from the mysterious Ita Fort, the brick ruins of which crown a hilltop above the rapidly booming town. A concrete-fest of sorts, this somewhat characterless urban hub merely serves as the state's power centre (your travel permits for Arunachal are issued here). There's a stack of ATMs and internet cafes along Mahatma Gandhi (MG) Marg.

The few sights in town include the decent but shoddily curated Jawaharlal Nehru State Museum (Indian/foreigner ₹10/75, camera/video ₹20/100; ☺ 9.30am-4pm Sun-Thu), and the brightly coloured gompa (Tibetan Buddhist monastery) of the Centre for Buddhist Culture set in the gardens nearby.

ARUNACHAL'S TRIBAL GROUPS

An astonishing patchwork quilt of ethnic populations, Arunachal is home to some 26 different tribal groups, including the Adi (Abor), Nishi, Tagin, Galo, Apatani and Monpa people. Many tribes are related to each other, while some consider themselves unique.

Modernity is slowly making inroads into the local society, but most tribes straddle the boundary between old and new – it's not uncommon to see a modern concrete building outfitted with a traditional open-hearth kitchen over stilted bamboo flooring.

The traditional animistic religion of Donyi-Polo (sun and moon worship) is still prevalent in the region, although Christian missionaries have had a significant impact on the religious beliefs and way of life in this area. For ceremonial occasions, village chiefs typically wear scarlet shawls and a bamboo wicker hat spiked with porcupine quills or hornbill beaks. Women favour hand-woven wraparounds like Southeast Asian sarongs, while some of the older men still wear their hair long, with a topknot above their foreheads. The artistic traditions of weaving and wickerwork are very much alive in these hills.

Architecture varies from tribe to tribe – traditional Adi villages are generally the most photogenic, with luxuriant palmyra-leaf thatching and wobbly bamboo suspension bridges strung across river gorges.

NORTHEAST PERMITS & TOURS

The Northeast States are a fascinating melting pot of tribal cultures, but currently foreigners can only access Arunachal Pradesh with a Protected Area Permit (PAP) from the Indian government, which is usually only granted if you are travelling in a group. Permits are only issued through registered travel agents, meaning that even if you plan to travel independently, you will have to approach a tour operator to process the PAP for you. In practice, almost everyone joins a tour because of the difficulties of dealing with local officials and avoiding political unrest and insurgent groups without a guide who speaks the local language.

The rules in other Northeastern states change regularly. Nagaland, Manipur and Mizoram enjoy 'permit free' status as of 2015, but the situation can easily change. Check ahead before you travel to any of the Northeast States.

Here is an overview of the regulations at the time of writing;

Minimum group size Permit applications need a two-person minimum group. It's possible for single travellers to get a permit, but only if you use a tour company, who will add staff to make up the numbers.

Permit requirements An application for a permit must be accompanied by a cover letter, photocopies of passport and valid visa, two passport-size photographs and a US$50 processing fee.

Validity Permits are valid for 30 days from a specified starting date. If you wish to overstay, you have to apply for a fresh permit. Permits only allow you to visit specified districts between specified dates; plan your itinerary carefully. Make multiple photocopies of your permit to hand in at each checkpoint, police station and hotel.

Where to apply Permits are issued at the state secretariat in Itanagar, which accepts applications only from reputed and registered travel agencies. Ergo, you must go through a tour operator even if you plan to travel independently in the region afterward. Some agents nowadays offer to secure permits for independent travellers for an additional fee.

Registration In every state, foreigners are technically required to register at the nearest police station upon their arrival in any state capital.

The good-value **Hotel Blue Pine** (📞 0360-2211118; Ganga Market; s/d from ₹1000/1200; ❄️) stands near the APST bus station, with simple but prim rooms, and positions itself 'between you and your sweet home'. Oversized **Hotel Arun Subansiri** (📞 0360-2212806; Zero Point Tinali; s/d ₹1300/1500; ❄️), en route to the Jawaharlal Nehru State Museum, has large rooms and an overall officious feel. For premium comforts, try **Hotel SC Continental** (📞 9436075875; infohotelsccontinental@gmail.com; Vivek Vihar; s/d from ₹2000/2400; ❄️ @), a 15-minute walk southwest of the bustling Ganga Market area.

The **APST bus station** (Ganga Market) has services to Guwahati (₹490, 11 hours, 6am), Bomdila (₹320, eight hours, 6am), Pashighat (₹270, 10 hours, 5.30am and 6am) and Shillong (₹390, 12 hours, 5pm).

Across the road, the **Royal Sumo Counter** has daily services to Ziro (₹320, five hours, 5.30am and 2.50pm), Along (₹620,

14 hours, 5.30am) and Pasighat (₹370, eight hours, 5.30am).

A new railway line now connects Naharlagun, about 12km east of Itanagar, to the rest of Northeast India, but regular services may only begin by late 2015.

Itanagar is also serviced by the **Naharlagun helipad**, which has daily flights (except Sunday) to Guwahati (₹4000). Ask your hotel reception or tour operator for tickets.

Central Arunachal Pradesh

For intrepid types, Central Arunachal Pradesh promises some great adventures, from tribal encounters in the picturesque Ziro Valley to rafting on the Siang River and thrilling treks to remote settlements, such as Mechuka.

Tour Companies

While joining a tour might seem restrictive, tour agents are highly experienced in dealing with permit red tape and negotiating with local officials, and will also help you bridge language barriers in a way that would be almost impossible if you were travelling independently. Indeed, it would be very difficult to have any meaningful encounters with tribal people without a local go-between to explain the proper etiquette. A tour agent will also help you steer clear of insurgent hotspots.

The following companies organise tours and permits throughout the Northeast:

Jungle Travels India (✆0361-2667871; www.jungletravelsindia.com; 3B Dirang Arcade, GNB Rd, Guwahati) An experienced agency covering the entire northeast with tailor-made tours and fixed-date departures for Nagaland and Arunachal Pradesh. It organises all the permits. Also runs Brahmaputra cruises for four to 10 nights at US$320 per person per night.

Aborcountry Travels & Expeditions (✆9436053870, 0360-2292969; www.aborcountrytravels.com; B Sector, Itanagar) Based in Itanagar, Aborcountry specialises in customised adventure tours and treks in remote areas, including Namdapha National Park.

Alder Tours & Travels (✆9402905046; www.aldertoursntravels.com; opp War Cemetery, Imphal Rd, Kohima; ⊙9am-5pm) Can provide matchless service (thanks to being located in Kohima) during the rushed Hornbill Festival.

Network Travels (✆0361-2605335; GS Rd, Guwahati; ⊙10am-7pm Mon-Sat) A reputed Guwahati agency with tailor-made, fixed-itinerary tours and a fantastic regional network.

Purvi Discovery (✆0373-2301120; www.purviweb.com; Medical College Rd, Jalan Nagar) This Dibrugarh-based agency offers culinary, wildlife and cultural tours in Upper Assam and also owns and operates the Mancotta Heritage Chang Bungalow (p573).

Times Travel (✆9864024838; timestravel24@gmail.com; GM Path, New Guwahati) A small but extremely efficient Guwahati-based agency for organising permits, which are delivered to your hotel's doorstep in Guwahati. Also organises no-frills budget tours for small groups.

Ziro Valley

✆03788

One of the prettiest landscapes in all of India, the fertile Ziro Valley nestles within Arunachal's formidable mountainscape like a mythical kingdom. A layered landscape of rice fields, rivers and picture-postcard villages of the Apatani tribe, it is an undisputed high point of any trip to Arunachal.

Scenery and village architecture apart, the main attraction here is meeting the friendly older Apatani folk who sport facial tattoos and nose plugs to rival any tattoo artist back home. The most authentic Apatani villages are **Hong** (the biggest and best known), **Hija** (more atmospheric), **Hari**, **Bamin** and **Duta**; none of which are more than 10km apart. It's vital to have a local guide to take you to any of these villages, otherwise you won't see much and might even be made to feel quite unwelcome.

For four days in September, Ziro is invaded by thousands of music lovers who come to attend the **Ziro Music Festival** (www.ziro-festival.com; ⊙Sep), which showcases the best of regional music as well as a great selection of bands from across India.

Sprawling **Hapoli** (New Ziro), about 7km south of Ziro, has basic urban infrastructure and road transport. Just below the Commissioner's Office, on a bend in MG Rd, is an **SBI ATM**.

Ngunu Ziro (✆9436224834; www.facebook.com/NgunuZiro; homestay per person Indian/foreigner ₹800/1000), a local self-help group that works towards sustainable community development in Apatani villages, provides superb access into the lives of local villagers. It runs a string of comfortable and thoroughly atmospheric homestays with friendly and hospitable hosts – an evening treat of local rice beer and smoked beef often comes free! Ngunu Ziro also provides guides (₹1000) and bicycles (₹500) for village tours.

MEET THE APATANI

Numbering around 25,000 and native to the Ziro Valley, the Apatani are one of Northeast India's most intriguing tribes. Believed to have migrated to the valley from the less hospitable northern highlands, the Apatanis are strongly rooted to their ancient culture. Most people are adherents of the animistic Donyi-Polo (sun-and-moon worship) religion, and continue to live in traditional houses fabricated out of bamboo and wood (the interiors are considerably modern though). Apatani villages are immensely photogenic, with T-shaped totem poles called *babos* towering over rows of huts that line every thoroughfare. Farmers by occupation, the Apatani practice a unique system of agriculture, where terraced rice fields are flooded with water to double as shallow fish farms. Apatanis also excel in arts such as weaving and wicker work.

Historically famous for their beauty, Apatani women were often kidnapped by warriors of the neighbouring Nishi tribes. As a 'defence', Apatani girls were deliberately defaced with facial tattoos and extraordinary nose plugs known as *dat*, fitted into holes cut in their upper nostrils. Peace with the Nishis in the 1960s meant an end to the brutal practice, and only a few surviving locals from the older generations can now be seen wearing *dat*. Photography is a sensitive issue, so always ask first.

For a memorable homestay experience (and a sampling of superb home cooked food), you could also consider a night or two at the lovely **Abasa Homestay** (☑ 9402709164; Siiro Village; per person incl half board ₹1000), run by the friendly and hospitable Kago Kampu and her husband, in Siiro village.

Hotel Blue Pine (☑ 03788-224812; Pai Gate; s/d from ₹1000/1200) offers the best-value lodging in Hapoli, with wood-panelled rooms with plenty of character. Out of town, the log-cabin style **Siiro Resort** (☑ 9856212352; siiroresort12@gmail.com; Siiro Village; d from ₹1600) has pastel-shaded rooms, lounge-sized bathrooms and prompt service.

Sumos depart from Hapoli, on MG Rd near the SBI ATM, for Itanagar (₹320, five hours, 5am and 11am), Lakhimpur (₹310, four hours, hourly 7am to 9am) and Daporijo (₹420, six hours, around 9.30am). A new airport, if completed by its 2016 deadline, should handle flights to Guwahati and Dibrugarh.

Ziro to Pasighat

Passing through a most pristine landscape marked by forested hills and tribal settlements, the highway linking Ziro to Pasighat via Along offers great photo-ops of dizzying suspension footbridges and thatched Adi villages. Tourism is low key in this rough and remote area and villagers are likely to be more welcoming if you visit with a local tour guide.

DAPORIJO

☑ 03792 / POP 15,700 / ELEV 700M

A necessary stopover midway along the long drive from Ziro to Pasighat, Daporijo is dirty, characterless and unsophisticated. However, its riverside location on the banks of the Subansiri River gives you the option of a few walks and hikes. Start early from Itanagar, and you'll be here by lunch. **Hotel Singhik** (☑ 03792-223103; singhikhotel@gmail.com; d from ₹1700; ✴ ☎), a new and surprisingly comfortable hotel with colourful interiors, an excellent restaurant and free wi-fi, is the best place to stop for the night. Otherwise, you could spend the night in the traditional thatched village of Ligu (coming from Ziro take the left turning just before the bridge at the entrance to Daporijo), where you'll find the basic but delightful **Ligu Tourist Resort** (☑ 03792-223114; r ₹1000). The proprietor's family cooks up fantastic meals.

Sumos leave New Market in the town centre at 6am for Itanagar (₹570, 12 hours) and Ziro (₹320, six hours).

ALONG

☑ 03783 / POP 17,000 / ELEV 300M

A nondescript highway town en route to Pasighat from Daporijo, Along is a dusty and scruffy settlement with little on offer for travellers. There's internet at **Eastern Infotech Cyber Cafe** (Nehru Chowk; per hr ₹50; ⊙ 8am-6pm Mon-Sat) opposite the APST bus station and an **SBI ATM** (Main Rd). Next to the Circuit House, also on Main Rd, is an informative little **district museum** (⊙ 10am-4pm Mon-Fri) FREE.

The saving grace of Along is the well-kept Hotel West (☑03783-222566; hotelwest@rediff mail.com; Medical Rd; d from ₹1200; ❀), which has spacious and comfortable rooms, good service and a central location. Hotel Toshi Palace (☑9436638196; Rime Market; d from ₹700; ❀), opposite the APST bus station, has clean rooms and a pleasant terrace restaurant where beers flow freely after sundown.

There are Sumos to Itanagar (₹610, 14 hours, 5.30am) and Pasighat (₹270, five hours, 5.30am and 11.30am).

Of the many Adi villages around Along, Kabu and Pobdi (2km and 7km north of town respectively) are best known and most easily accessible. It's easier to secure entry in the company of a local guide, and you can observe the Adis slowly warming to modernity (heralded by zippy cars and the ubiquitous satellite TV dish outside most huts) from a much closer range.

There are many more interesting and less-visited Adi villages along the onward journey to Pasighat. The top sight, however, is a wobbly, cable-trussed bamboo-decked suspension bridge running almost 200m across the Siang River.

Pasighat

☑0368 / POP 21,900

Laid out along forested plains by the banks of the Siang River, Pasighat feels more like Assam than Arunachal Pradesh. The town hosts the interesting Adi festival of Solung (⊙1-5 Sep), marked by rituals performed to seek agricultural prosperity and protection from evil spirits. Through the rest of the year, the most interesting sight around here is the sunrise over the Siang.

Most tourists passing through Pasighat sleep at Hotel Aane (☑0368-2222777; MG Rd; d from ₹1400; ❀), which has floral shades adorning its walls, clean sheets, and a good in-house restaurant. The friendly and centrally located Hotel Oman (☑0368-2900430; Main Market; d/tr ₹1050/1600) is a tad cheaper, but there's no hot water and you'll have to traipse to the market for meals.

For a more rewarding stay, head 25km south of Pasighat along NH52 to Oyan village, where you can spend a few days lounging amid lush tea gardens at the Siang Tea Garden Lodge (☑9436675824; Oyan Village; per person incl full board ₹2500; ☎), which has simple but comfy rooms with ethnic decor, garden-fresh tea and awesome food prepared by Babul. Contact Aborcountry Travels & Expeditions (p579) for bookings.

There's an internet cafe (MG Rd; per hr ₹60; ⊙7.30am-8pm) 50m from Hotel Aane and an ATM near the Sumo stand in the central market area.

Sumos run to Along (₹270, five hours, 6am and noon) and Itanagar (₹370, eight hours, 6am), as well as Tuting (₹980) when demand warrants it. Ferries (per person/ vehicle ₹60/1000) drift lazily down the Brahmaputra to Dibrugarh in Assam from Bogibil Ghat, and from Oiram Ghat and Majerbari Ghat during the dry season (Sumos take one hour from Pasighat, depart at 6am and cost ₹140). Ferry tickets are sold by agents at the Sumo stand in town.

NORTHEAST STATES CENTRAL ARUNACHAL PRADESH

OFF THE BEATEN TRACK

NAMDAPHA NATIONAL PARK

The staggering Namdapha National Park (☑03807-222249; www.changlang.nic.in/ namdapha.html; Indian/foreigner ₹10/50, camera ₹75-400, video ₹750), spread over 1985 sq km of dense forest in far eastern Arunachal Pradesh, is an ecological hotspot with a mind-boggling array of animal and plant species and habitats ranging from warm tropical plains to icy Himalayan highlands. Namdapha is famous for being the only park in India to have four big cat species (leopard, tiger, clouded leopard and snow leopard). It's also a birdwatcher's delight, with around 500 recorded species.

The park is a long haul from anywhere, and visiting can be a pain unless you're travelling with a tour operator. Aborcountry Travels & Expeditions (p579) has a good grasp of these jungles.

The gateway to Namdapha is Dibrugarh in Assam, from where you need to travel about 150km to get to the small town of Miao. From here it's a 26km drive to Deban, where the park headquarters is located. Simple accommodation is available in Miao at the Eco-Tourist Guest House (☑03807-222296; per person Indian/foreigner ₹400/600), or in Deban at the Forest Rest House (☑03807-222249; d Indian/foreigner ₹190/380).

Western Arunachal Pradesh

After two full days of hobbling along what could easily be called the worst road in the world, you will emerge into a humbling landscape of magnificent blue mountains guarding the ancient city of Tawang, the archetypal Shangri La. The most important sight in Western Arunachal Pradesh, Tawang is inhabited by the Monpa, a tribal people who are culturally closer to Tibet than to their neighbours in the lowlands of Arunachal. Ideally budget at least one week for a return trip from Guwahati (or Tezpur), breaking the journey each way with a full day in Dirang or Bomdila. Be prepared for intense cold and snow in winter, and vehicular breakdowns and roads being blocked by landslides at any time of the year.

Bomdila
☑ 03782 / ELEV 2680M

An alternative sleeping place to Dirang, 50km away, Bomdila is a tiny settlement incorporating a bunch of administrative offices, hotels, local markets and wayside eateries. The traditionally decorated **Doe-Gu-Khill Guest House** (☑ 9402292774; yipe_bg@yahoo.com; d from ₹800), located just below the large monastery, provides fabulous views of the town spread out below. **Hotel Tsepal Yangjom** (☑ 03782-223473; www.hoteltsepalyangjom.in; d from ₹2200), with wood-panelled rooms and a busy restaurant screening cricket matches on a cricket-field-sized TV, is the town's most popular inn.

Dirang
☑ 03780 / ELEV 1620M

Dirang is the gateway to the Tawang Valley, and serves as a useful overnight stop. Tiny **Old Dirang**, 5km south of New Dirang, is a picture-perfect Monpa stone village. The main road separates its rocky mini **citadel** from a huddle of picturesque streamside houses above which rises a steep ridge topped by a timeless **gompa** (Tibetan Buddhist monastery). Heading the other way, just north of New Dirang, the valley opens out and its floor becomes a patchwork of rice and crop fields through which gushes the icy blue Dirang River.

All of Dirang's commercial services are in **New Dirang**, with a strip of cheap eateries and Sumo counters around the central crossroads. **Hotel Pemaling** (☑ 03780-242615; www.hotelpemaling.com; d from ₹1500; ☎), located a kilometre south, is a nice family-run hotel with smart rooms, great service and a very pleasant garden where you can enjoy the views. The self-important **Awoo Resort** (☑ 03780-242036; www.awooresort.com; d from ₹1300), located a short hike away, has good-value rooms with cosy wood panelling, a decent restaurant and a park with swings and slides.

OFF THE BEATEN TRACK

TUTING & PEMAKO

In the far north of Arunachal lies the isolated region of Tuting, visited yearly by a handful of pilgrims and hardcore adventure seekers. Accessible from Pasighat by a long rough road, it sits near the Tibetan border, where the Tsang Po River, having left the Tibetan Plateau and burrowed through the Himalayas via a series of spectacular gorges, enters the Indian subcontinent and becomes the Siang (which in turn becomes the Brahmaputra in Assam). Steadily gaining a reputation as a thrilling white-water rafting destination, the perilous 180km route is littered with grade 4 to 5 rapids, strong eddies and inaccessible gorges. Needless to say, this is the stuff of pros.

Tuting also serves as the launchpad for the fabulous land of Pemako, known in Buddhist legend as a hidden earthly paradise and the earthly representation of Dorje Pagmo (a Tibetan goddess). This isolated mountain valley is populated by Memba Buddhists, who are almost completely isolated from the rest of the world. Pemako is accessible to those willing to endure days of incredibly tough hiking (and permit hassles) – in practice, most visitors are Buddhist pilgrims.

If you do manage to get here, consider kicking back for a few nights at **Yamne Abor** (☑ 9436053870; Damro Village; per person incl full board ₹2500), a lovely resort comprising a mix of luxury tents and eco-cottages in the remote Yamne valley amid pretty Adi villages, rice fields and verdant forests. Book through Aborcountry Travels & Expeditions (p579).

MECHUKA

For intrepid travellers, the drive from Along to Mechuka – a remote outpost very close to the Tibetan border – qualifies as one of the most enthralling road trips in Arunachal Pradesh. Recently opened for tourism by the government, Mechuka often goes by the moniker of 'forbidden valley' or the 'last Shangri La' – indeed, until recently, the only way to reach the village was on foot. Populated by the Buddhist Memba tribe, this tiny village sitting on the banks of the Siang River is notable for both the 400-year-old **Samten Yongcha Monastery** and the stunning landscapes surrounding the town, which culminate in a massive hulk of snow-draped mountains running along the border.

Sumos ply the 180km from Along (₹470, seven hours, 5.30am). Unless you are able to find accommodations with a local family, the only accommodation is the government **Circuit House**, which rents out rooms on an ad hoc basis (and tariff). Remember that bookings can be overriden by visiting government officials.

Dirang to Tawang Valley

Climbing from Dirang, Arunachal's worst road is a seemingly endless series of zigzags which cross several army camps and landslide zones to finally top off at **Se La**, an icy 4176m pass that breaches the mountains and provides access to Tawang. From here, the road plummets down the mountainside into the belly of Tawang Valley.

Tawang Valley

☑ 03794 / ELEV 3050M

A mighty gash in the earth fringed by hulking mountains, the Tawang Valley works a special magic on the minds of travellers. The valley is a gorgeous patchwork of mountain ridges, vast fields and clusters of Buddhist monasteries and Monpa villages. Autumn is a particularly beautiful season for travelling this route, when waterfalls are in spate and cosmos shrubs lining the tarmac come alive with a riotous blossom of red and pink.

Tawang town is a transport hub and service centre for the valley's villages, plus there are a number of small hotels, but the setting is more beautiful than the town itself. Nonetheless, murals of auspicious Buddhist emblems and colourful prayer wheels add interest to the central old market area. The prayer wheels are turned by a stream of Monpa pilgrims, many of whom sport traditional black yak-wool *gurdam* (skullcaps that look like giant Rastafarian spiders).

◉ Sights & Activities

Tawang Gompa   MONASTERY
(camera/video ₹20/100; ☺dawn-dusk) Tawang's biggest attraction is the mag-ical Tawang Gompa, backdropped by snow-speckled peaks. Founded in 1681, this medieval citadel is reputedly the world's second-largest Buddhist monastery complex after Lhasa's Potala Palace and famed in Buddhist circles for its library. Within its fortified walls, narrow alleys lead up to the majestic and magnificently decorated prayer hall containing an 8m-high statue of Buddha Shakyamuni. Across the central square is a small but interesting museum containing images, robes, telescopic trumpets and some personal items of the sixth Dalai Lama.

Come here at dawn (4am to 5am) to see monks performing their early-morning prayers. Spectacular masked chaam dances are held in the monastery courtyard during the Torgya, Losar and Buddha Mahotsava festivals.

Urgelling Gompa   MONASTERY
(☺dawn-dusk) Enchanting gompas and ani gompas (nunneries) offer great day hikes from Tawang, including the ancient if modest Urgelling Gompa, where the sixth Dalai Lama was born. By road, it's 6km from Tawang town but closer on foot downhill from Tawang Gompa. Note that the monastery is sometimes closed; ask around for the caretaker, who has the only set of keys.

✲ Festivals & Events

Losar   RELIGIOUS
(☺Jan/Feb) For a few days sometime between January and February, Tawang hosts the dazzling Tibetan New Year festival of Losar, marked by prayer sessions and colourful masked dances at the Tawang Gompa.

🛏 Sleeping

Hotel Nefa
HOTEL $

(☎03794-222419; Nehru Market; d from ₹700)
On the cheap end is Hotel Nefa, with tidy,
wood-panelled rooms and hot showers but
lackadaisical service.

Monyul Lodge
HOTEL $

(☎03794-222196; www.monyullodgetawang.in;
Old Market; d ₹1000) In the heart of the market area, Monyul Lodge has fresh linen and
plenty of air and sunlight.

Hotel Gakyi Khang Zhang
HOTEL $$

(☎03794-224647; www.gkztawang.com; d from
₹1300) A couple of kilometres out of town on
the road to Tawang Gompa, this hotel offers
by far the best rooms in town – colourful
sky-blue affairs with polished wood floors.
There's power back-up, and the distant
views of the monastery (from most rooms)
are a deal-maker.

✕ Eating & Drinking

Slaughtering of animals is banned in Ta-
wang, and all meat served in local restau-
rants comes by road from Tezpur; if you're
ordering nonveg, always enquire if the sup-
plies are fresh.

Dragon Restaurant
CHINESE $$

(Old Market; mains ₹80-160; ⊙8am-8pm) The
cosy Dragon Restaurant is Tawang's best eatery with freshly made local dishes such as
churpa (a delicious fermented cheese broth
with fungi and vegetables; ₹150), *momos*
(Tibetan dumplings), a fiery chilli chicken
and salted Tibetan yak-butter tea.

Snow Hill Restaurant
MULTICUISINE $

(Old Market; mains ₹70-120; ⊙8am-8pm) In the
heart of town, Snow Hill Restaurant has a
standard range of tasty Indian, Chinese and
Tibetan dishes.

Orange Restaurant & Lounge Bar
BAR

(Old Market; beers ₹100; ⊙10am-9pm) Located along the main drag, this convivial bar
comes alive in the evenings with chilled
beers, pleasant company, fairy lights on the
walls, loud music and TV.

🛈 Information

In the market area is **D-Zone** (internet per hr
₹50; ⊙9am-4pm), which has pool and video
games when it doesn't have internet. There's a

State Bank of India branch with an ATM just past
the market on the road to the monastery.

🛈 Getting There & Away

Sumos manned by kamikaze drivers ply daily
from Tawang to Tezpur (₹900, 14 hours,
5.30am), calling at Dirang (₹550, six hours),
Bomdila (₹650, eight hours) and Bhalukpong
(₹800, 11 hours). **Himalayan Holidays** (Main
Market), a reliable tour agency, sells sumo tickets and arranges local tours and hikes.

NAGALAND

The uncontested 'wild east' of India, Nagaland is probably one of the reasons you
came to the Northeast in the first place. A
place of primeval beauty, Nagaland's dazzling hills and valleys – right on the edge
of the India–Myanmar border – are an otherworldly place where, until very recently,
some 16-odd headhunting Naga tribes val-
iantly fought off any intruders. Of course,
Nagaland today is a shadow of its once savage self, and much of the south of the state
is fairly developed. In the north, however,
you still stand a good chance of meeting
tribesmen in exotic attire who continue to
live a lifestyle that is normally only seen
within the pages of a *National Geographic* magazine. Note that a number of insurgent groups are active in the state and you
should check the political situation before
you travel.

Dimapur

☎03862 / POP 98,100 / ELEV 260M

Unless you're transiting via its airport, 4km
from Dimapur, you would find little reason
to linger in this flat, uninspiring commercial
centre of Nagaland. If you have time to kill,
visit the mushroom-shaped stone megaliths
that are all that remains of **Rajbari**, the ancient capital of the kingdom of Kachari.

Of the central hotels, the new **Hotel Acacia** (☎8415935254; www.hotelacacia.in; d from
₹1200; ❉🛜) is the smartest option, with
mint-fresh rooms, speedy wi-fi, prompt service and good in-house food. You'll find it
opposite East Police Station.

Air India (☎03862-242441; www.airindia.in)
flies to Kolkata, Guwahati and Imphal. The
NST bus station (Kohima Rd) runs services
to Kohima (₹90, three hours, hourly) and
Imphal (₹230, seven hours, 6am).

Kohima

📞 0370 / POP 77,100 / ELEV 1450M

If not for its crazy traffic and rampant urbanisation, Nagaland's agreeable capital – scattered across a series of forested ridges and hilltops – could easily rub shoulders with the best hill stations of India. Avoid Kohima on Sunday if you can, as apart from hotels, everything is closed.

◉ Sights & Activities

★ War Cemetery   HISTORIC SITE
(⊙9am-5pm, to 4pm winter) This immaculate cemetery contains the graves of 1400 British, Commonwealth and Indian soldiers laid out across stepped and manicured lawns. It stands at the strategic junction of the Dimapur and Imphal roads, a site that saw intense fighting against the Japanese during one 64-day battle in WWII.

Central Market   MARKET
(Stadium Approach; ⊙6am-4pm) At this fascinating, tiny market, tribal people buy and sell local delicacies such as *borol* (wriggling hornet grubs), tadpoles and bullfrogs, exotic condiments such as fermented bamboo shoots and fermented soybeans, and a mind-boggling range of meats and vegetables.

State Museum   MUSEUM
(admission ₹5, camera/video ₹20/100; ⊙9.30am-3.30pm Mon-Sat) This superbly presented museum, 3km north of Kohima's centre, includes tribal artefacts, jewellery, tableaux with mannequins-in-action and a display of 'hunted' human skulls.

Explore Nagaland   CULTURAL TOUR
(📞9856343037; www.explorenagaland.com; per person per night incl full board ₹1000-1800) Cultural tours are slowly catching on in Nagaland, and it's now possible to visit remote villages, interact with villagers and stay with local families thanks to the co-opting of homestays in several villages such as Khonoma and Kisama. Contact Explore Nagaland for tailor-made excursions.

🛏 Sleeping & Eating

Accommodation becomes pricier and extremely scarce during the Hornbill Festival – book well in advance.

★ Heritage   GUESTHOUSE $$
(📞9436215259; www.theheritage.in; Raj Bhavan Rd; s/d ₹1200/1800; 🖵) This stately guest-house was once the official residence of Kohima's serving deputy commissioners, and overlooks the town from the summit of Officer's Hill. With nostalgia reigning supreme in each of its four charming and luxurious rooms, the place preserves a slice of the high administrative life from the bygone era. The host is a wonderful source of local information.

Razhu Pru   HERITAGE HOTEL $$
(📞0370-2290291; razhupru@yahoo.co.in; Mission Compound; d incl breakfast from ₹2000; ❄🖵) A family home thoughtfully converted into a heritage hotel, Razhu Pru packs in a diverse array of heirlooms and artefacts in its wood-panelled living areas. Elegant cane furniture and potted ferns add to its appeal. Rooms sport comfy beds, ethnic upholstery and fireplaces for cold winter nights.

Hotel Vivor   HOTEL $$$
(📞0370-2270317; NH 61; s/d incl breakfast from ₹3000/3500; ❄🖵) This upscale affair is located about 3km out of town. Rooms are lavishly fitted out with spongy beds, snow-white linen, ultra-clean loos and large

DON'T MISS

HORNBILL FESTIVAL

Hornbill Festival (www.hornbillfestival.com; ⊙1-10 Dec) Nagaland's biggest annual jamboree, the Hornbill Festival is celebrated at Kisama Heritage Village in December, with various Naga tribes converging for a 10-day cultural, dance and sporting bash, much of it in full warrior costume. Of all the festivals in the Northeast this is the most spectacular and photogenic. Capering in step with former headhunters are headbangers who play out acid riffs at the **rock and metal festival**, held simultaneously in Kohima. Kohima-based Alder Tours & Travels (p579) organises customised festival tours.

windows. Service is prompt, and there's a souvenir shop boasting a decent collection of handicrafts with reasonable price tags.

Ozone Cafe   CAFE $

(Imphal Rd, opp ICICI Bank; mains ₹70-100; ⊘noon-8pm; 🛜) Hip and happening, this centrally located cafe has a sprawling gymnasium-style dining area, where Kohima's young guns spend hours catching up over a variety of dishes including *momos*, pizza, noodles and ginger ale. There's free wi-fi.

Dream Café   CAFE $

(cnr Dimapur & Imphal Rds, opp War Cemetery; mains ₹80-120; ⊘10am-6pm Mon-Sat) The melting pot for most of Kohima's youth, this busy and cheerful place works up daily lunch specials such as fried noodles or pizzas as well as coffee and snacks. Great hill views from bay windows, displays by local artists and lots of friendly diners make this a good place to linger.

❶ Information

NIIT Internet Cafe (per hr ₹30; ⊘8am-7pm Mon-Sat) Located opposite the NST bus station.

SBI ATM (Police Bazar) One of several ATMs in town.

❶ Getting There & Away

The **NST bus station** (Main Rd) has services to Dimapur (₹90, three hours, hourly Monday to Saturday), Mokokchung (₹220, seven hours, 6.30am Monday to Saturday) and Imphal (₹190, six hours, 7.30am Monday to Saturday). The taxi stand opposite has shares taxis to Dimapur (₹200, 2½ hours). A car and driver for a day out to Kisama and Khonoma costs about ₹1500.

Around Kohima

Kisama

Kisama Heritage Village   AREA

Kisama Heritage Village has a representative selection of traditional Naga houses and *morungs* (bachelor dormitories) with full-size log drums. Nagaland's biggest annual festival, the Hornbill Festival (p585) is celebrated here. Within the premises is the **WWII Museum** (admission ₹10; ⊘10am-4pm), which has a collection of war memorabilia. Kisama is 10km from central Kohima along the Imphal road.

Kigwema

A 10-minute drive past Kisama along Imphal road brings you to Kigwema, an Angami village of historic importance where Japanese forces arrived and set up camp before the final showdown with Allied Forces in 1944. Several households here welcome tourists (preferably accompanied by local guides) and you can get a peek into the daily lives of resident tribespeople.

Khonoma

This historic Angami-Naga village was the site of two major British–Angami siege battles in 1847 and 1879. Built on an easily defended ridge, Khonoma looks beautifully traditional, with emerald paddy patchworks carpeting valley floors between towering ridges. There are a few simple homestay options in the village.

THE HISTORY OF HEADHUNTING

Long feared for their ferocity in war and their sense of independence, Naga tribes considered headhunting a sign of strength and machismo. Every intervillage war saw the victors lopping off the heads of the vanquished and instantly rising in social stature (as well as in the eyes of women). Among certain tribes such as the Konyaks of Mon, men who claimed heads were adorned with face tattoos and V-shaped marks on their torsos, in addition to being allowed to wear brass pendants called *yanra* denoting the number of heads the wearer had taken.

Headhunting was outlawed in 1953 (the last recorded occurrence was in 1963). Much of the credit for the change, however, goes to Christian missionaries in the region who preached non-violence and peaceful coexistence over decades. Almost 90% of the Nagas now consider themselves Christian, their unshakeable faith marked by behemoth-like churches that are a prominent landmark in any settlement. Now seen as immoral possessions, most hamlets have gotten rid of their grisly human trophies.

ℹ️ SAFE TRAVEL IN THE NORTHEAST STATES

In recent decades, many ethno-linguistic groups in the Northeast have jostled – often violently – to assert themselves in the face of illegal immigration from neighbouring countries, governmental apathy and a heavy-handed defence policy. Some want independence from India, others autonomy, but most are fighting what are effectively clan or turf wars. While peace mostly prevails, trouble in these regions can flare up suddenly and unpredictably. In 2010 bombings hit parts of Assam and the Garo Hills area of Meghalaya. Ethnic violence erupted in Assam, while a bomb blast and curfews shattered the veneer of peace in Manipur in late 2012. In December 2014, strikes by Bodo groups killed more than 70 people across Assam. To make things worse, Assam and Manipur are often paralysed by strikes and shutdowns. It pays to keep abreast of the latest headlines on TV and in local papers. If you're with a tour group, talk to the operators to make sure your guide is up to date with the latest situation.

Tuophema

Forty-five kilometres north of Kohima is the village of Tuophema, en route to Mon. The highlight here is the **Tuophema Tourist Village** (☏9436005002; d ₹1500), where you sleep in comfortable traditionally styled Naga thatched huts, and eat traditional food in a glass-paned cafeteria (meals ₹200). Notify them of your arrival in advance or it will probably be closed.

Kohima to Mon

The scenic but but insufferably bumpy road from Kohima to Mon passes through beautiful forested hills, at one point briefly entering Assam. A convenient stopover en route is **Mokokchung**, a laid-back town with a spectacular hillside setting. The spiffy **Hotel Metsuben** (☏0369-2229343; metsuben@yahoo.com; off Kohima Rd; d from ₹850; ✳@☎) is the best place to look for a bed, and a range of hearty and fiery Naga dishes.

Northern Nagaland

The most unspoiled part of the state, Northern Nagaland is a rugged and divinely beautiful country where antiquity still thrives in tribal villages composed of thatched longhouses, many of whose inhabitants continue to live a fairly traditional hunting and farming lifestyle. The most accessible villages are the Konyak settlements around Mon (where traditional houses abound). Some villages still have *morungs* and religious relics from pre-Christian times. Village elders may wear traditional costumes and Konyaks of all ages carry the fearsome-looking *dao* – a crude machete (originally used for headhunting) as a standard accessory.

Visiting a Naga village without a local guide is hopelessly unproductive. You'd also do well to have your own sturdy vehicle, as there's virtually no public transport and roads are atrocious.

Mon & Around

The haggard hill town of Mon merely serves as an access point for the many Konyak villages in the area. There's an **SBI ATM** in town which rarely works.

Of the numerous tribal villages in the area, the most popular is **Longwa**, about 35km from Mon, where the headman's longhouse spectacularly straddles the India–Myanmar border and contains a fascinating range of weapons, dinosaur-like totems and a WWII metal aircraft seat salvaged from debris scattered in nearby jungles. You can spend some time at a local house here and several tattooed former headhunters can be photographed for a fairly standard ₹100 fee. Tribal jewellery, carved masks and other collectibles (₹200 to ₹1000) can also be bought from many households. In the high season, the village charges a per person entry fee of ₹200.

Other villages that can be visited from Mon include **Old Mon** (5km), with countless animal skulls adorning the walls of the headman's house; **Singha Chingnyu** (20km), which has a huge longhouse decorated with animal skulls and three stuffed tigers; and **Shangnyu** (25km), with a friendly headman and a wooden shrine full of fertility references.

The only decent hotel in Mon itself is the scrappy but friendly **Helsa Cottage** (☏9862345965; d from ₹1000) run by the influential, affable Aunty. Running water and electricity are seldom your companions here, but the food is tasty. Aunty also co-manages the **Helsa Resort** (🖉9436000028; d from ₹1000), slightly out of town en route to Longwa, which has six traditional thatched Konyak huts with springy bamboo floors, sparse furnishings and hot water by the bucket. Meals can be arranged upon prior request.

Shared 4WD vehicles bounce painfully to Dimapur (₹380, 12 hours, 3pm) and Sonari in Assam (₹90, 6am and 9am), where you can change for Jorhat. No public transport leaves Mon on the weekend.

MANIPUR

A breeding ground for graceful classical dance traditions, intricate art forms, sumptuous cuisine and (supposedly) the sport of polo, Manipur sits pretty amid rolling hills along India's border with Myanmar. This 'Jewelled Land' is home to Thadou, Tangkhul, Paite, Kuki, Mao Naga and many other tribal peoples, but the predominant community is the Hindu Meitei tribe, who adhere to a neo-Vaishnavite order. Much of the state is carpeted with dense forests which provide cover for rare birds, drug traffickers and guerrilla armies, making it by far the Northeast's most dangerous state.

Foreign travellers are currently restricted to Imphal and its outskirts, an area which is deemed 'safe'. Most foreigners fly into Imphal; it is also possible to drive in from Kohima (Nagaland) or Silchar (Assam) if you have a guide. Travelling east of Kakching towards the Myanmar border is not permitted.

ℹ REGISTERING ON ARRIVAL IN MANIPUR

On arrival at Imphal airport, all foreigners must register with the police stationed next to the luggage collection point. You must then register again with the CID at the **main police station** (🖉0385-2220002; Thangal Bazaar) in Imphal town. In both cases it's a fairly painless affair (assuming your passport and visa are in order). If you're travelling by road, you must register at the security checkpoint on the state border.

Imphal

🖉0385 / POP 250,200

Set at the border of India and Southeast Asia, Imphal is a vibrant melting pot of cultures and customs, although heavy militarisation and random shutdowns and curfews means there little to do, especially after dark.

◉ Sights

Kangla PARK
(admission ₹10; ⊘9am-4pm Nov-Feb, to 5pm Mar-Oct) This expansive, low-walled fort was the on-again, off-again regal capital of Manipur until the Anglo-Manipuri War of 1891 saw the defeat of the Manipuri maharaja and a British takeover. Entrance is by way of an exceedingly tall gate on Kanglapat. The interesting older buildings are at the rear of the citadel, guarded by three restored large white *kangla sha* (dragons).

Manipur State Museum MUSEUM
(off Kangla Rd; admission ₹10; ⊘10am-4pm Tue-Sun) This government-run museum has a curious collection of tribal costumes, royal clothing, historical polo equipment and stuffed carnivores in action. Outside by the lawns, you'll find an ornate and spectacular 78ft royal boat. Fronting the museum is the **Polo Ground**, where polo is said to have been invented.

Khwairamband Bazaar MARKET
(Ima Market; ⊘7am-5pm) A spectacular photo-op for shutterbugs, this vast all-women's market is run by some 3000 *ima* (mothers). Divided by a road, one side sells vegetables, fruit, fish and groceries while the other deals in household items, fabrics and pottery.

Imphal War Cemetery CEMETERY, MEMORIAL
(Imphal Rd; ⊘8am-5pm) This peaceful, well-kept memorial contains the graves of more than 1600 British and Commonwealth soldiers killed in WWII battles that raged around Imphal in 1944. You'll find the cemetery across a shaded park at the end of a bylane off Imphal Rd.

🛏 Sleeping & Eating

Hotel Nirmala HOTEL $
(🖉0385-2459014; MG Ave; s/d incl breakfast from ₹850/1000; ✳) This no-frills establishment in the heart of Imphal's market area has a genuine sense of belonging, and the staff go about their chores with dedication. Rooms

are non-fussy and prim, and the air-con in-house Chamu Restaurant serves decent food.

★ **Classic Hotel**   HOTEL $$
(☎ 0385-2443967; www.theclassichotel.in; North AOC Rd; s/d incl breakfast from ₹1800/2100; ✳@🛜) Luxury couldn't come at a more affordable price. Featuring large, spotless rooms stuffed with requisite business-class comforts, this unexpectedly classy hotel is one of Northeast India's best-value hotels. The English-speaking staff love to please, and the restaurant serves the best dishes in town (place advance orders for regional delicacies). The clean and smartly plumbed bathrooms are a definite plus.

Hotel Imphal   HOTEL $$
(☎ 0385-2421373; www.hotelimphal.com; North AOC Rd; s/d incl breakfast from ₹1400/1800; ✳@🛜) This hulking former state-owned operation now sports a fresh look in the form of manicured lawns, pearl white exteriors, bright pine-skirted rooms with cane furniture, snug beds with fresh white linen and friendly, prompt service. Remember though that public receptions are all the rage here, and it could get a bit noisy during one of these galas.

ℹ Information

ATMs in Imphal see enormous queues and run out of cash quickly. It's better to bring enough money with you.
Internet Cafe (MG Ave; per hr ₹30; ⊙ 8am-7pm Mon-Sat) For speedy connections.
SBI ATM (MG Ave) About 100m from Hotel Nirmala.

ℹ Getting There & Away

The airport is 9km to the southwest of Imphal. From here, Air India, IndiGo and Jet Airways fly to Guwahati and Kolkata. Air India also flies to Aizawl and Dimapur.

Private buses head to Guwahati (₹740, 20 hours, hourly 6am to 10am) and Dimapur (₹430, 10 hours, 10am) via Kohima (₹370, five hours). If you're heading to Aizawl you must change in Dimapur first. All the bus company offices are found on North AOC Rd, on a turn midway between Classic Hotel and Hotel Imphal.

The international checkpost at Moreh (110km from Imphal) is technically open for passage between India and Myanmar (Burma), and full-fledged thoroughfare should be a reality by late 2015.

MIZORAM

Seated precariously along rows of north–south-running mountain ridges, pristine Mizoram is more of an experiential journey than a tourist destination. Ethnically, the majority of the local population shares similarities with communities in neighbouring Southeast Asian countries such as Myanmar (Burma), and the predominant religion is Christianity. Mizo culture is liberated from caste or gender distinctions: in Aizawl girls smoke openly, wear modern clothes and hang out in unchaperoned posses meeting up with their beaus at rock concerts.

Mizoram runs to its own rhythm. Most businesses open early and shut by 6pm; virtually everything closes tight on Sunday. Upon arrival, you must register at the **Office of the Superintendent of Police** (☎ 0389-2335339; CID Office, Bungkawn; ⊙ 10am-4pm Mon-Sat) in Aizawl. Domestic tourists require a temporary Inner Line Permit, issued for ₹170 on arrival at Aizawl airport.

★ Festivals & Events

Chapchar Kut   CULTURAL
(⊙ Mar) This statewide festival held in March celebrates the end of a long season of *jhum* (the traditional practice of clearing forest land for agriculture) through song and dance.

OFF THE BEATEN TRACK

LOKTAK LAKE

A most intriguing and picturesque ecosystem if there ever was one, the fascinating Loktak Lake is one of the few places a foreigner is allowed to visit outside Imphal. A shimmering blue lake broken up into small lakelets by (rapidly vanishing) clumps of thick matted weeds called *phumdis,* the lake is inhabited by local villagers who build thatched huts on these floating 'islands' and make their way about the lake in dugout canoes. More peculiar than floating villages are the large, perfectly circular fishing ponds created out of floating rings of weeds. The best view is atop **Sendra Island** (admission ₹15). You can embark on a boat ride (per person ₹20) in order to get a closer look at lake life. The lake is 45km by road from Imphal; a return taxi costs about ₹2200.

Pawl Kut
CULTURAL

(☉Nov/Dec) Held in December, this festival marks the end of the harvest season, and involves plenty of music, dance and alcohol statewide.

Aizawl

📞 0389 / POP 228,200

Clinging to a near-vertical ridge by its fingernails, Aizawl (pronounced 'eye-zole') is easily the most languid and unhurried among all Indian state capitals. There's very little to do here, apart from soaking up its relaxed grain and peaceful way of life. The area around Chanmari, the heart of Aizawl's residential and shopping district, is the most interesting, and most tourist establishments are located in and around it.

⊙ Sights

Mizoram State Museum
MUSEUM

(Macdonald Hill, Zarkawt; admission ₹10; ☉10am-5pm Mon-Fri) This museum has interesting exhibits on Mizo culture, but the display is a bit random and unkempt. It's up a steep lane from Sumkuma Point, past Aizawl's most distinctive **church**, whose modernist bell-tower spire is pierced by arched 'windows'.

Salvation Army Temple
CHURCH

(Zodin Sq) The Salvation Army Temple has bell chimes that are endearingly complex and can be heard throughout the city, es-

---

OFF THE BEATEN TRACK

RURAL MIZORAM

Mizoram's pretty, green hills get higher as you head east towards the Myanmar (Burma) border. **Champhai** is widely considered the most attractive district, where you'll find the **Murlen National Park**, known for its hoolock gibbons. The small town of **Saitual** is a good stopover on the road to Champhai. Very close to Champhai is pretty **Tamdil Lake**, ringed by lush mountains. Further afield is the stunning **Blue Mountain** (Phawngpui), Mizoram's highest peak at 2147m. It's considered by Mizos to be the abode of Gods, but its slopes are said to be haunted by ghosts.

---

pecially on a quiet Sunday morning. Its hulking white Gothic-inspired exteriors are worth a photo.

🛏 Sleeping & Eating

Hotel Clover
HOTEL $$

(📞0389-2305736; hotelclover@hotmail.com; Chanmari; s/d incl breakfast from ₹950/1500; @🛜) It may not be the plushest address in town, but it's definitely the friendliest. The well-kept rooms have colourful accent lighting and fancy bathroom fittings. The exteriors have recently got a touch of lime-coloured paint and look inviting. It's a flight of steps down from the road level.

Hotel Regency
HOTEL $$

(📞0389-2349334; www.regencyaizawl.com; Zarkawt Main St; s/d incl breakfast from ₹1750/2100; ❄🛜) Posh by Aizawl's standards, this stylish hotel has inviting rooms opening along marbled corridors, each with cosy beds, clean baths and LCD TVs. The staff are smart and cooperative, and there's a great in-house restaurant overlooking the main street that serves tasty Indian, Chinese and Continental fare.

Aizawl Masala
CHINESE $

(Zarkawt Main St; mains ₹80-120; ☉noon-8pm) One flight of stairs below road level, this trendy place serves a host of usual quasi-Chinese suspects (noodles, fried rice, meat in chilli/garlic/pepper sauce etc). There's good music to go with your food.

ℹ Information

Directorate of Tourism (📞0389-2333475; PA-AW Bldg, Bungkawn) Has some information and leaflets on local tourism. Located in Bungkawn, about 4km southwest of Chanmari.

ICICI Bank (Zarkawt; ☉10am-4pm Mon-Sat) Has an ATM.

Mizo Holidays (📞0389-2306314; Hauva Bldg, Chanmari; ☉10am-5pm Mon-Sat) Arranges a variety of state-wide tours including village visits. Also doubles as local representatives for Thomas Cook.

Sify E-port (Chanmari; per hour ₹30; ☉9am-5pm Mon-Sat) High-speed internet.

ℹ Getting There & Away

Lengpui airport is 35km west of Aizawl; a taxi/Sumo will charge ₹1300/100 to get here. **Air India** (📞0389-2322283; www.airindia.in) flies to Guwahati and Kolkata, while Jet Konnect goes to Kolkata.

Counters for long-distance Sumos are conveniently clustered around Zarkawt's Sumkuma Point. Services include:

Guwahati ₹1100, 20 hours, 6pm Monday to Saturday

Shillong ₹900, 16 hours, 6pm Monday to Saturday

Silchar ₹400, six hours, four daily

TRIPURA

Far from India's popular tourist circuits, Tripura is a culturally charming place which thrives on the hope that its handful of royal palaces and temples will draw the world's attention some day. For the moment, though, foreign travellers remain very rare, despite the fact that no permit is currently required. The state can be accessed by land from Meghalaya or Bangladesh; if you fly in, you must register with the police on arrival at the airport.

Agartala

☑ 0381 / POP 189,900

Tripura's only 'city', this low-key settlement with its semi-rural atmosphere feels like an India of yore. It's a congested but relaxed place, and in many ways feels more like a small town than a state capital. The pace of life is slow, and the people are friendly.

◎ Sights

Apart from the town's main sights, there are several royal mausoleums decaying quietly on the riverbank behind Battala market (walk west down HGB Rd, turn left at Ronaldsay Rd and right along the riverbank).

Ujjayanta Palace PALACE, MUSEUM
(admission ₹10; ⊙ 11am-5pm Tue-Sun) Agartala's centrepiece is this striking, dome-capped palace. Flanked by two large reflecting ponds, the whitewashed 1901 edifice was built by Tripura's 182nd maharaja. Within the superstructure is a museum (the only section open to public) with an imposing collection of regal and cultural memorabilia and artefacts.

Jagannath Mandir HINDU TEMPLE
(Sakuntala Rd; ⊙ 4am-2pm & 4-9pm) Of the four Hindu temples around the Ujjayanta Palace compound, the most fanciful is Jagannath Mandir. Its massive sculptured portico leads

Agartala

◎ **Sights**
1 Jagannath Mandir A2
2 Tripura Government Museum A3
3 Ujjayanta Palace B1

🛏 **Sleeping**
4 Hotel Rajdhani B1

🍴 **Eating**
5 Abhishek Restaurant A2
6 Restaurant Kurry Klub A3

ℹ **Information**
Axis Bank ATM .... (see 6)
7 SBI ATM A1

into a complex with wedding-cake architecture painted in ice-cream sundae colours.

Tripura Government Museum MUSEUM
(Post Office Circle, HGB Rd; admission ₹10; ⊙ 10am-1pm & 2-5pm Mon-Sat) This small state-operated museum has a variety of tribal displays plus some interesting musical instruments made from bamboo.

🛏 Sleeping & Eating

Ginger HOTEL $$
(☑ 0381-2411333; www.gingerhotels.com; Airport Rd; s/d from ₹2700/2900; ❄ @ 🛜) Part of the

Tata-owned Ginger chain of hotels, this well-run, low-cost business hotel has smart rooms done up in orange and blue pastel shades. There's wi-fi, real coffee, a small gym and an in-house SBI ATM. Coming from the airport, you'll find the hotel on your right about 2km short of town.

Geetanjali Guest House   HOTEL $$
(☑ 0381-2410009; Airport Rd; d ₹1830; ❄@) The only match for Ginger in terms of luxe quotient, this government-run guesthouse across the road has large, perfect rooms done up in floral upholstery and washed with disinfectants and sunlight. The in-house restaurant has some tasty but unimaginative fare.

Hotel Rajdhani   HOTEL $$
(☑ 0381-2323387; BK Rd; d from ₹1400; ❄) Located close to the Ujjayanta Palace compound, this trusted address has an assortment of clean and tidy rooms, some of which have direct views of the palace's ramparts. The staff are helpful but easy-going, and there's a good in-house eatery serving multicuisine fare.

Restaurant Kurry Klub   INDIAN, CHINESE $$
(Hotel Welcome Palace, HGB Rd; mains ₹100-140; ⊙10am-10pm) The in-house restaurant at Hotel Welcome Palace serves generous helpings of tasty Indian food, including some fantastic fish preparations. It's particularly busy during dinner.

Abhishek Restaurant   INDIAN $
(LN Bari Rd; mains ₹80-100; ⊙noon-10pm) Choose between a marine-themed AC dining room and an outdoor seating area with tables set amid bushes and sculptures, and then proceed to put away a hearty meal comprising some eminently enjoyable North Indian and local savouries. The lighting could be less tacky, though.

ⓘ Information

Axis Bank ATM (Hotel Welcome Palace, HGB Rd)

Netzone (6 Sakuntala Rd; internet per hr ₹30; ⊙10am-8pm) Best of several closely grouped internet cafes.

State Bank of India (☑ 0381-2311364; top fl, SBI Bldg, HGB Rd; ⊙10am-4pm Mon-Fri, to noon Sat) Changes cash and travellers cheques and has an ATM west of Mantri Bari Rd. There's also an ATM on Palace Compound West (Palace Compound West).

Tripura Tourism (☑ 0381-2225930; www.tripuratourism.nic.in; Swet Mahal, Ujjayanta Palace Complex; ⊙10am-5pm Mon-Sat) A helpful and enthusiastic lot.

ⓘ Getting There & Around

Agartala's airport is 12km north; a taxi costs ₹250. **Air India** (☑ 0381-2325470; VIP Rd), SpiceJet and Jet Konnect fly from here to Kolkata and Guwahati; IndiGo flies to Kolkata only .

Private bus operators are clustered on LN Bari Rd. From the **Interstate Bus Terminal**, 3km east of the centre (rickshaw ₹50), buses head to Guwahati (₹820, 24 hours, 6am and noon), Shillong (₹770, 20 hours, 6am and noon) and Silchar (₹230, 12 hours, 6am). Sumos use the **Motor Stand** (Motor Stand Rd) and **South Bus Station** (SBS; off Ronaldsay Rd).

Taxis can be hired on a day-long basis for sightseeing in and around Agartala, for about ₹7 per kilometre plus ₹600 per vehicle per day. Try **Hindustan Tours & Travels** (☑ 9206348911; Ginger Hotel, Airport Rd).

Around Agartala

Udaipur
☑ 03821

Udaipur was Tripura's historic capital and remains dotted with ancient temples and tanks. The main sight here is the **Tripura Sundari Mandir** (Matabari; ⊙4.30am-1.30pm & 3.30-9.30pm), a 1501 Kali temple where a steady stream of pilgrims make almost endless animal sacrifices that leave the grounds as bloody as the temple's vivid-red *sikhara* (spire). Even more people come here during the Diwali festival (October/November) to bathe in the fish-filled tank by the temple. The temple is 100m east of the NH44, 4km south of Udaipur, which has bus connections to Agartala (₹50, two hours) and Melaghar (₹30, 45 minutes). An autorickshaw from Udaipur costs ₹50.

Neermahal & Melaghar
☑ 0381

Tripura's most iconic building, the **Neermahal** (admission ₹5, camera/video ₹10/25; ⊙8.30am-4pm, to 4.30pm Apr-Sep), is a gorgeous red-and-white water palace, empty but shimmering on its own boggy island in the lake of Rudra Sagar. Like its counterpart in Rajasthan's Udaipur, this was a princely exercise in aesthetics; Tripuran king Bir Bikram Kishore Debbarman hired the finest craftsmen to construct his lavish summer palace in a blend of Hindu and Islamic architectural styles. The pavilion was christened by the Bengali Nobel laureate Rabindranath Tagore in 1930.

The delightful waterborne approach by speed boat (passenger/boat ₹20/400) or fancy rowboat (passenger/boat ₹20/100) is the most enjoyable part of visiting. Boats leave from a pier beside the remarkably decent **Sagarmahal Tourist Lodge** (☑ 9436185313; d from ₹900; ❄), where most rooms have lake-facing balconies, and there's a good restaurant presiding downstairs.

Melaghar has bus connections to Agartala (₹50, two hours) through the morning and afternoon.

MEGHALAYA

Separating the Assam valley from the plains of Bangladesh, hilly Meghalaya – the 'abode of clouds' – is a cool, pine-fresh mountain state set on dramatic horseshoes of rocky cliffs. Cherrapunjee and Mawsynram are statistically among the wettest places on earth; most of the rain falls between June and September, creating very impressive waterfalls and carving out some of Asia's longest caves.

The state's population predominantly comprises the Jaintia, Khasi and Garo tribes, who live in the eastern, central and western parts respectively. A good time to be in Meghalaya is during the Wangala festival in the Garo Hills in autumn. No permits were required for Meghalaya at time of writing.

Shillong

☑ 0364 / POP 267,600

Irreverent Shillong was the capital of British-created Assam until 1972. Since becoming the state capital of Meghalaya, it has rapidly developed into a typical modern Indian town, but still retains some its colonial-era charm in certain pockets. Overhauled cars are all the rage here – take a ride in one of Shillong's many taxis and you'll know.

⦿ Sights

★ **Don Bosco Museum of Indigenous Cultures** MUSEUM
(☑ 0364-2550260; www.dbcic.org; Mawlai; Indian/foreigner ₹60/150; ⦿ 9am-5.30pm Mon-Sat,

ⓘ BORDER CROSSING: AGARTALA TO BANGLADESH

From central Agartala, the border is just 3km along Akhaura Rd (₹60 by rickshaw). On the Bangladesh side the nearest town is Akhaura, 5km beyond the border, reached by 'baby taxi' (autorickshaw). From Akhaura trains head to Dhaka, Comilla and Sylhet. From Agartala, there's a 1.30pm bus connection to Dhaka (₹450, six hours). The border at Agartala is open from 8am to 6pm. There's no exchange booth, so ask local traders or border officials.

to 4.30pm Dec & Jan) This well-maintained museum is a fabulous repository of innumerable tribal artefacts interspersed with galleries on Christian missionary work. Compulsory tours depart on the half-hour and last over an hour. Sights in the seven-storey museum include tribal basketry, musical instruments, weapons, objects of daily life, costumes and jewellery, along with plenty of photographic documentation. A food gallery is to be added soon.

The museum is located about 3km north of Shillong off GS Rd. A return taxi costs about ₹400.

Ward's Lake LAKE
(admission ₹5, camera/video ₹10/20; ⦿ 8.30am-5.30pm Nov-Feb, to 7pm Mar-Oct) The central landscaping element of colonial-era Shillong, this attractive lake has a pretty ornamental bridge, flower beds, coy courting couples, boating facilities and gaggles of geese. Walk 15 minutes northeast of the lake to visit the rolling meadows of **Shillong Golf Course** (Golf Links), bordered by pine trees and fronted by a pretty clubhouse.

Historic Buildings

The city's half-timbered architecture has been rather swamped by lots of drab modern concrete, but areas such as Oakland and Lumsohphoh retain many older houses. More centrally located is the **Pinewood Hotel** (Rita Rd), a 1920s tea-growers retreat, which is particularly representative of colonial-era architecture and looks great at night. The 1902 **All Saints' Cathedral** (Kacheri Rd) would look perfect pictured on a biscuit tin. The **Anglican Church**, perched above Police Bazaar, is a graceful structure fronted by pretty lawns.

Shillong

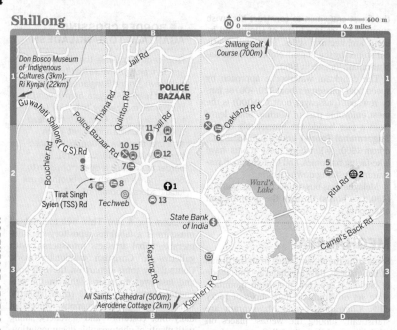

Shillong

◎ Sights
1 Anglican Church....................................B2
2 Pinewood Hotel.....................................D2

◉ Activities, Courses & Tours
3 Campfire Trails.....................................A2

⬭ Sleeping
4 Baba Tourist Lodge.............................A2
5 Blueberry Inn..D2
6 Earle Holiday Home............................C2
7 Hotel Centre Point...............................B2
8 Hotel Rainbow......................................B2

⊗ Eating
9 City Hut Dhaba.....................................C1
   La Galerie.......................................(see 7)
10 Trattoria..B2

ⓘ Information
11 Meghalaya Tourism...........................B2

ⓘ Transport
12 Deep..B2
13 Khasi Hills Tourist Taxi
   Cooperative.......................................B2
14 MTC Bus Station...............................B2
15 Network Travels.................................B2

🏃 Activities

Campfire Trails
OUTDOOR ADVENTURE
(☏ 9856001871; www.campfireshillong.com; DD
Laloo & Co, GS Rd; per person per night incl full
board ₹1700-2000) Campfire Trails specialises in authentic village tourism experiences
in rustic settings across Central Meghalaya.
Four previously unexplored villages are
run as self-sustaining units in cooperation
with local tribal stakeholders. Activities to
go with your village experience (complete
with delicious local food) include kayaking,
mountain biking, zip lining and trekking.

Pioneer Adventure
OUTDOOR ADVENTURE
(☏ 9049442647; www.pioneeradventuretours.com;
Jarman Villa, Hopkinson Rd) This out-there agency has broken new ground by introducing
diving in the hills! Open-water dive facilities
(per person ₹1500) are available at its camp
near Dawki, where the Umngot River offers
up to 10m visibility. PADI-recognised diving
courses are also available. Other activites
include snorkelling, rock climbing, rafting,
caving and camping. All-inclusive overnight
packages (per person ₹7000) allow you to
sample a bit of everything.

The agency is located in the Lower Lachumiere area of Shillong, about 3km southeast of Police Bazaar.

🛏 Sleeping

Taxes add a discouraging 27% to your bill (included in the prices listed here), but off-season discounts are available.

Baba Tourist Lodge   HOTEL $
(📞0364-2211285; GS Rd; d/tr from ₹1050/1350) Popular with backpackers and budget travellers, Baba hides many floors below the road level, and offers clean, spartan accommodation in rooms that open past a prim wood-panelled reception area lined with fish-filled aquariums. The pricier rooms have running hot water. There's basic in-house food.

Earle Holiday Home   HOTEL $
(📞0364-2228614; Oakland Rd; d from ₹750; ❄) This hotel has character but is amusingly disorganised. The cheaper rooms are original half-timbered affairs within a classic 1920 Shillong hill house adorned with sweet little turrets. Pricier rooms in the concrete annexe are less atmospheric but more comfortable.

Hotel Rainbow   HOTEL $$
(📞0364-2222534; www.hotelrainbowshillong.com; GS Rd; d from ₹1300) This lovely little place has a string of pleasantly styled rooms with wood panelling, moody lighting and tasteful ethnic decor. The best is room 103 which has a little balcony. Expect some street noise though, as it's on a main thoroughfare.

Aerodene Cottage   GUESTHOUSE $$$
(📞9774065366; www.aerodene.com; Lower Cleve Colony; d incl breakfast from ₹3200; 🛜) A charming garden-fronted Assam-style bungalow converted into a guesthouse, Aerodene has atmospheric rooms with soft beds, wood floors, period decor and lots of light and fresh air. The newer annexe block to the right has rooms that are less ambient but equally comfortable. The food is simply delicious; dinner costs an additional ₹250 per person.

Hotel Centre Point   HOTEL $$$
(📞0364-2220480; www.shillongcentrepoint.com; Police Bazaar Rd; s/d incl breakfast from ₹3700/4200; ❄🛜) Located bang on Police Bazaar, this is arguably the best business hotel in Shillong. Run by professional and helpful staff, it has smart rooms with wood flooring and large windows overlooking the town centre. All requisite creature comforts are at your disposal, and the Cloud 9 rooftop lounge bar is a good place for evening beers and (occasionally) live music.

Blueberry Inn   HOTEL $$$
(📞0364-2500655; www.blueberryinn.in; Rita Rd; d from ₹3800; ❄🛜) A spiffy address down a quiet lane past Pinewood Hotel, this place has excellent, bright rooms with fluffy beds, clean loos and a range of small comforts to match its premium price tag. The decor could come across as a bit over-the-top, though. The in-house kitchen serves good food.

★Ri Kynjai   RESORT $$$
(📞9862420300; www.rikynjai.com; Umiam Lake; d incl breakfast from ₹8700; ❄@) This divine resort on the banks of pristine Umiam Lake, 22km from Shillong, is a gem of a getaway. Spacious wood-pillared cottages with fabulous lake views lie scattered about its lush, green gardens and each is impeccably presented with elegant furnishings and lavish bathrooms. There's a spa done up in traditional decor, restaurant and bar with lake views.

🍴 Eating & Drinking

Trattoria   KHASI $
(Police Bazaar Rd; mains ₹100-120; ⏱11am-4pm) No visit to Shillong is complete without a midday meal at this busy proletarian eatery patronised by locals. Some of the best local Khasi dishes, including *ja doh* (rice stewed

---

OFF THE BEATEN TRACK

UNAKOTI

Located about 150km from Agartala, the archaeological site of Unakoti is one of Northeast India's best-kept travel secrets. Massive rock-cut sculptures of Hindu gods and goddesses (some dating back to the 7th century) adorn the faces of hillocks at the site, including a 10m-tall face of Shiva sculpted on a monolithic rock, and a trio of Ganeshas hewn in stone beneath a waterfall. To get here, it's best to hire a taxi from Agartala (₹2800) and organise a day trip. Bring your own food and water.

in pig blood) and curried pig innards, are (literally) hot favourites here. For an overall sampling, try the immensely popular lunch platter (₹120).

City Hut Dhaba MULTICUISINE $$
(Oakland Rd; mains ₹100-150; ☺10am-9pm) Tucked beside Earle Holiday Home and guarded by gnomes, City Hut serves a variety of Indian, Chinese, barbecue and ice creams in four different eating rooms, including a family-only room and an attractive, flower-decked straw pavilion. The quality of food is fairly commendable, and the place sees plenty of local diners.

La Galerie MULTICUISINE $$
(Hotel Centre Point, Police Bazaar Rd; mains ₹150-200; ☺10am-9pm) This suave glass-panelled restaurant compartmentalised into booths and adorned with photographs of local scenes serves excellent Indian, Continental and Chinese food. Cloud 9 is the top-floor bar-restaurant serving dainty Thai dishes, cold beers and cocktails.

Café Shillong CAFE
(☎2505759; Laitumkhrah; coffee ₹60, mains ₹120-200; ☺11am-9pm) This cool hangout in bustling Laitumkhrah (pronounced Lai-muk-rah) has the best coffee in town, yummy steaks, and rock, jazz and blues on tap. Its fashionable decor features a Les Paul guitar signed by performing musicians. Weekends are the busiest when there are live acts.

ℹ Information

There are many ATMs in Shillong.
Meghalaya Tourism (☎0364-2226220; www.megtourism.gov.in; Jail Rd) Lots of brochures and useful information.
State Bank of India (Kacheri Rd; ☺10am-4pm Mon-Fri, to noon Sat) Exchanges foreign currency and travellers cheques; has an ATM outside.
Techweb (basement, Zara's Arcade, Keating Rd; internet per hr ₹30; ☺9am-7pm)

ℹ Getting There & Away

The **MTC bus station** (Jail Rd) has a computerised train reservation counter (nearest train station is Guwahati). Private buses depart from Dhankheti Point; book tickets from counters around Police Bazaar, including **Deep** (Ward's Lake Rd) and **Network Travels** (☎0364-2210981; Shop 44, MUDA Complex, Police Bazaar Rd).

Departing from the MTC bus station, frequent buses and Sumos go to:
Aizawl ₹620, 15 hours
Cherrapunjee bus/Sumo ₹170/250, three hours
Dimapur ₹450, 12 hours

OFF THE BEATEN TRACK

GARO & JAINTIA HILLS

Far from well-trodden tracks, lush Garo Hills in the far west of Meghalaya is worth exploring if you have a few days (and a sense of adventure) to spare. Easier to reach from Guwahati than Shillong, its main urban hub is the tiny settlement of **Tura**, where the friendly **tourist office** (☎03651-242394; ☺10am-4pm Mon-Fri) can arrange local guides. Buses run here from Guwahati and accommodation is available at the **Rikman Continental** (☎03651-220744; www.hotelrikman.com; Circular Rd; s/d incl breakfast from ₹1200/1500; 🅿🛜), which has a mix of standard and semi-luxury rooms.

For most people, a visit to Garo Hills involves an encounter with the endangered Hoolock gibbon, a friendly primate that lives in the forests of the **Nokrek Biosphere Reserve**. The other highlight of the region is an excursion to **tribal villages** deep in the mountains, where you can see villagers practise the ancient slash-and-burn method of *jhum* cultivation. Intriguing *borangs* (traditional tree houses) dot the lush landscape around here. If you're with a reliable local guide, it's also possible to visit a traditional Garo village and sample their rice-beer-soaked hospitality. Remember to leave a tip in return. In autumn Garo Hills hosts the four-day **Wangala festival** (☺Oct/Nov), renowned for its impressive tribal dancing and traditional drum recitals.

The Jaintia Hills, meanwhile, is home to the village of **Nartiang**, where you can visit an intriguing complex of stone monoliths erected by different clans between the 16th and 19th centuries. It's unattended and overgrown – beware of snakes in the undergrowth. Nartiang is located 62km southeast of Shillong, and can be visited on a day trip by hiring a taxi (₹1600).

Guwahati ₹130/170, 3½ hours
Silchar ₹380, 10 hours
Siliguri ₹490, 12 hours
Tura bus/Sumo ₹350/450, 12 hours via Guwahati

Khasi Hills Tourist Taxi Cooperative (📞 0364-2223895; Kacheri Rd) charges ₹2200 to ₹2500 for a day trip to Cherrapunjee; for a ride to the Bangladesh border near Dawki it's ₹2000. For Guwahati airport, a full taxi costs ₹2200, or you can share with other passengers for ₹350.

ℹ BORDER CROSSING: DAWKI TO BANGLADESH
....
The border post is at Tamabil, 1.5km from Dawki market (a taxi costs ₹100). There are frequent Tamabil–Sylhet minibuses on the other side. The border is open from 9am to 6pm. There's no foreign-exchange booth here, but you might find helpful nonofficial personnel on the Bangladesh side.

Cherrapunjee (Sohra)

📞 03637 / POP 10,100

Laid out along razorlike ridges of a high mountain wall, Cherrapunjee sits on the edge of the Himalayas, overlooking the pancake-flat plains of Bangladesh. The village was once feted as the wettest place on earth because of the prodigious monsoon rainfall. The road from Shillong to this tiny village passes through pretty scenery that becomes dramatic at the **Dympep viewpoint**, where a photogenic V-shape valley slits deeply into the plateau.

The grassy moors surrounding Cherrapunjee justify Meghalaya's over-played 'Scotland of the East' tourist-office soubriquet, although they're dotted with monoliths and scarred by quarrying. The **Nohkalikai Falls** are particularly dramatic, especially in the monsoon when their capacity increases 20-fold. You can see them from the **viewpoint** (admission ₹10, camera/video ₹20/50; ⏰8am-5pm) located on a plateau at the end of a mountain ridge 4.4km from Sohra market. Local taxis (₹50) shuttle passengers to the viewpoint. Much more impressive, however, is the series of 'grand canyon' valleys around the region, which plunge into deep lush chasms of thick lush forest.

The most fascinating sight around Cherrapunjee are the incredible **root bridges** – living rubber fig-tree roots which ingenious Khasi villagers have, over decades, trained across streams to form natural pathways. Three of these root bridges (including an amazing 'double-decker') are near **Nongriat**. Access is via the pretty village of **Tyrna**, 2km from Mawshamok. The round trip into the canyon where these root bridges stand is an eight-hour slog from Tyrna, involving a 2000-step ascent and descent through very steep terrain.

Although straggling for several kilometres, Cherrapunjee (known locally as Sohra) has a compact centre. Huddling beside the marketplace is the Sumo stand, with connections to Shillong (₹250, three hours).

🛏 Sleeping & Eating

Cherrapunjee Holiday Resort   RESORT **$$**
(📞09436115925; www.cherrapunjee.com; Laitkynsew village; d from ₹2230; @) Run by a warm and affable Khasi lady and her South Indian husband, this delightful resort comprises an older building (with cheaper rooms thrown around a spacious refectory) and a new multistoreyed block (which has newer deluxe rooms). The home-cooked meals are simply fantastic. The resort provides guides for local hikes, and organises tented accommodation in the dry season.

A daily bus leaves nearby Laitkynsew village for Shillong (₹70, 6am). Going the other way it leaves Shillong at 1pm. Otherwise a taxi from Cherrapunjee costs ₹400.

NORTHEAST STATES CHERRAPUNJEE (SOHRA)

Odisha

Best off the Beaten Track

➔ Koraput (p619)

➔ Bhitarkanika Wildlife Sanctuary (p623)

➔ Pusphagiri Ruins (p623)

➔ Satkosia Gorge Sanctuary (p608)

Best Rural Retreats

➔ Gajlaxmi Palace (p606)

➔ Nature Camp Bhitarkanika (p624)

➔ Chandoori Sai (p621)

➔ Nature Camp Tikarpada (p608)

➔ Toshali Ratnagiri Resort (p623)

Why Go?

Odisha (Orissa) slipped off the tourist radar once Puri's hippy-hangout days began to fade, but it's beginning to re-establish itself as an off-the-beaten-track favourite for more adventurous types. Those who make the effort are rewarded with an intricate patchwork of history, culture and natural beauty, along with a sprinkling of sun and sand.

The forested hills of the southwest (and overly officious bureaucracy) keep Adivasi (tribal) groups hidden from mainstream tourism, but it is still possible to visit their fascinating weekly markets. Forests elsewhere – both inland and along the coast – are home to some of Odisha's intriguing nature reserves – 6m-long crocodiles, anyone?

Foodies will relish a whole new set of regional flavours cooked up in Odishan kitchens, while history buffs will be left salivating over long-lost Buddhist universities, ancient Jain rock carvings and centuries-old Hindu relics, including Konark's unparalleled Sun Temple.

When to Go
Bhubneswar

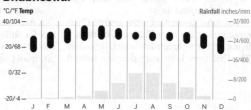

Nov–Mar Warm and dry, just like fresh laundry from the dhobi-wallah.

Jun & Jul It's baking, but Puri's Rath Yatra festival is Odisha's biggest celebration.

Dec Sun Temple is the magnificent backdrop for the seductive Konark Festival.

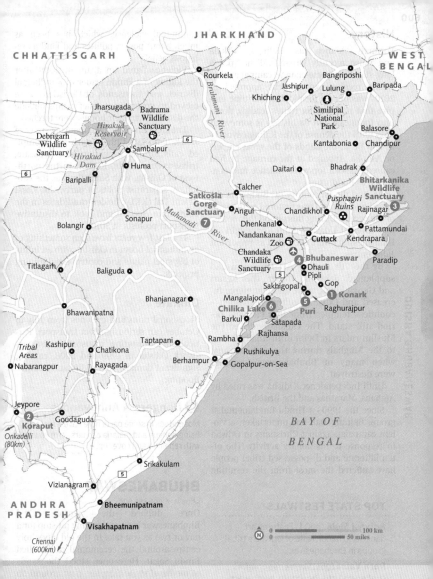

Odisha Highlights

1 Marvelling at the artistic magnificence of Konark's 800-year-old Unesco-protected **Sun Temple** (p615)

2 Venturing deep into the hills around **Koraput** (p619) to visit one of the region's fascinating tribal markets

3 Cruising past enormous estuarine crocodiles in the rarely visited mangrove swamps of **Bhitarkanika Wildlife Sanctuary** (p623)

4 Touring some of the 50-odd ancient temples that still remain in Odisha's full-of-surprises capital city, **Bhubaneswar** (p600)

5 Tapping into what's left of the traveller vibe in the one-time hippy hangout of **Puri** (p610)

6 Spotting rare Irrawaddy dolphins at **Chilika Lake** (p615)

7 Stepping out of your tent and gaze across the sands of the Mahanadi River in breathtaking **Satkosia Gorge Sanctuary** (p608)

History

Formerly known as Kalinga, Utkala and more recently Orissa, Odisha (per a long-standing name-change campaign that finally received government approval in 2010) was once a formidable maritime empire that had trading routes leading down into Indonesia, but its history is somewhat hazy until the demise of the Kalinga dynasty in 260 BC at the hands of the great emperor Ashoka. Appalled at the carnage he had caused, Ashoka forswore violence and converted to Buddhism.

Around the 1st century BC Buddhism declined and Jainism was restored as the faith of the people. During this period the monastery caves of Udayagiri and Khandagiri (in Bhubaneswar) were excavated as important Jain centres.

By the 7th century AD Hinduism had supplanted Jainism. Under the Kesari and Ganga kings, trade and commerce increased and Odishan culture flourished – countless temples from that classical period still stand. The Odishans defied the Muslim rulers in Delhi until finally falling to the Mughals during the 16th century, when many of Bhubaneswar's temples were destroyed.

Until Independence, Odisha was ruled by Afghans, Marathas and the British.

Since the 1990s a Hindu fundamentalist group, Bajrang Dal, has undertaken a violent campaign against Christians in Odisha in response to missionary activity. The often illiterate and dispossessed tribal people have suffered the most from the resulting communal violence, which has been as much about power, politics and land as religious belief.

Violence flared up again in 2008 after the killing of a Hindu leader in Kandhamal district, and thousands of Christians were moved to government relief camps outside the district after their homes were torched.

The creation of the neighbouring states of Jharkhand and Chhattisgarh has prompted calls for the formation of a separate, tribal-oriented state, Koshal, in the northwest of Odisha, with Sambalpur as the capital. A separatist political party, the Kosal Kranti Dal (KKD), fielded candidates in the 2009 state election and took to disruptive transport protests in 2010.

The last few years have seen something of an industrial boom in Odisha, with an influx of big steel plants and controversial mining projects.

Climate

Monsoonal rains and cyclones from July to October can seriously affect transport. Particularly devastating monsoonal disasters struck Odisha in 1999 and 2008, causing significant damage, loss of life and massive flooding.

🛈 Dangers & Annoyances

Mosquitoes in some parts here have a record of being dengue and malaria carriers. Arm yourself with repellent and cover up.

BHUBANESWAR

📞 0674 / POP 658,000

Once dubbed the 'Temple City', Bhubaneswar is an enthralling pit stop for a day or two as you take in the old city's holy centre around the ceremonial tank called Bindu Sagar. Here once stood thousands of medieval stone temples; now around 50 remain.

◉ Sights

The best way to tour the temples is on foot. That way you have the opportunity to stumble across and explore some of the numerous smaller temples that dot the way. You could also consider hiring a cycle-rickshaw for a half-day tour (around ₹300 for four hours).

TOP STATE FESTIVALS

Adivasi Mela (p604) Features art, dance and handicrafts of Odisha's tribal groups in Bhubaneswar.

Rath Yatra (p611) Immense chariots containing Lord Jagannath, brother Balbhadra and sister Subhadra are hauled from Jagannath Mandir (Puri's foremost Hindu temple) to Gundicha Mandir (a temple beside Puri's main bus stand).

Puri Beach Festival (p611) Song, dance, food and cultural activities on the beach in Puri.

Konark Festival (p614) Features traditional music and dance and a seductive temple ritual.

★ Lingaraj Mandir   HINDU TEMPLE

The 54m-high Lingaraj Mandir, dedicated to Tribhuvaneswar (Lord of Three Worlds), dates from 1090 to 1104 (though parts are over 1400 years old) and is surrounded by dozens of smaller temples and shrines. The granite block, representing Tribhuvaneswar, is bathed daily with water, milk and bhang (marijuana). The main gate, guarded by two moustachioed yellow lions, is a spectacle in itself as lines of pilgrims approach, *prasad* (temple-blessed food offering) in hand.

Because the temple is surrounded by a wall, and closed to non-Hindus, foreigners can see it only from a viewing platform (this can also include foreign Hindus). Face the main entrance, walk right, then follow the wall around to the left and find the viewing platform on your left, just before you reach Chitrakarini Temple. There have been reports of aggressive hassling for 'donations' at the viewing platform. The money will not go to the temple; stand your ground and do not pay.

Bus 333 goes here from Master Canteen bus stand.

Mukteswar Mandir   HINDU TEMPLE

The small but beautiful 10th-century Mukteswar Mandir is one of the most ornate temples in Bhubaneswar; you'll see representations of it on posters and brochures across Odisha. Intricate carvings show a mixture of Buddhist, Jain and Hindu styles – look for the Nagarani (Snake Queen), easily mistaken by Westerners for a mermaid, who you'll also see at the Raja Rani Mandir. The ceiling carvings and stone arch are particularly striking, as is the arched *torana* (architrave) at the front, clearly showing Buddhist influence.

Siddheswar Mandir, in the same compound, is a later but plainer temple with a fine red-painted Ganesh. Over the pathway is the whitewashed Kedargauri Mandir, one of the oldest temples in Bhubaneswar, although it has been substantially rebuilt.

Bus 225 goes past here en route to Dhauli.

Vaital Mandir   HINDU TEMPLE

This 8th-century temple, with a double-storey 'wagon roof' influenced by Buddhist cave architecture, was a centre of tantric worship, eroticism and bloody sacrifice. Look closely and you'll see some very early erotic carvings on the walls. Chamunda (a fearsome incarnation of Devi), representing old age and death, can be seen in the dingy interior, although her necklace of skulls and her bed of corpses are usually hidden beneath her temple robes.

Parsurameswar Mandir   HINDU TEMPLE

Just west of Lewis Rd lies a cluster of about 20 smaller but important temples. Best preserved is Parsurameswar Mandir, an ornate Shiva temple built around AD 650. It has lively bas-reliefs of elephant and horse processions, and Shiva images.

Raja Rani Mandir   HINDU TEMPLE

(Indian/foreigner ₹5/100, camera ₹25; ⊙dawn-dusk) Built around 1100, this temple surrounded by manicured gardens is famous for its ornate *deul* (temple sanctuary) and tower. Around the compass points are pairs of statues representing eight *dikpalas* (temple guardians). Between them, nymphs, embracing couples, elephants and lions peer from niches and decorate the pillars.

Brahmeswar Mandir   HINDU TEMPLE

Standing in well-kept gardens, flanked on its plinth by four smaller structures, this 9th-century temple is a smaller version of Lingaraj Mandir. It's notable for its finely detailed sculptures with erotic elements. Turn right at the 13th-century Bhaskareswa Temple.

★ Udayagiri & Khandagiri Caves   HISTORIC SITE

(admission both sites Indian/foreigner ₹5/100, video ₹25; ⊙dawn-dusk) Six kilometres west of the city centre are two hills riddled with rock-cut shelters. Many are ornately carved and thought to have been chiselled out for Jain ascetics in the 1st century BC.

Ascending the ramp at Udayagiri (Sunrise Hill), note Swargapuri (Cave 9) to the right with its devotional figures. Hathi Gumpha (Cave 14) at the top has a 117-line inscription relating the exploits of its builder, King Kharavela of Kalinga, who ruled from 168 BC to 153 BC.

SLEEPING PRICE RANGES

The following price ranges refer to a double room with bathroom and are inclusive of tax:

$ less than ₹1000

$$ ₹1000 to ₹3000

$$$ more than ₹3000

Bhubaneswar

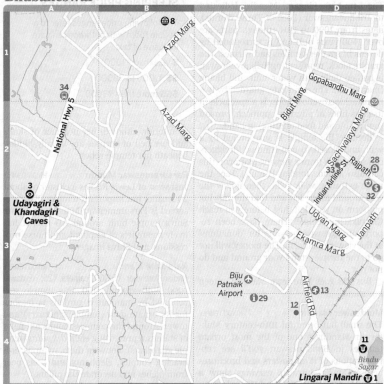

ODISHA BHUBANESWAR

Around to the left you'll see **Bagh Gumpha** (Tiger Cave; Cave 12), with its entrance carved as a tiger mouth. Nearby are **Pavana Gumpha** (Cave of Purification) and small **Sarpa Gumpha** (Serpent Cave), where the tiny door is surmounted by a three-headed cobra. On the summit are the remains of a defensive position. Around to the southeast is the single-storey elephant-guarded **Ganesh Gumpha** (Cave 10), almost directly above the two-storey **Rani ka Naur** (Queen's Palace Cave; Cave 1), carved with Jain symbols and battle scenes.

Continue back to the entrance via **Chota Hathi Gumpha** (Cave 3), with its carvings of elephants, and the double-storey **Jaya Vijaya Cave** (Cave 5), with a bodhi tree carved in the central area.

Across the road, Khandagiri offers fine views over Bhubaneswar from its summit. The steep path splits about one-third of the way up the hill. The right path goes to **Ananta Cave** (Cave 3), with its carved figures of athletes, women, elephants and geese carrying flowers. Further along is a series of **Jain temples**; at the top is another (18th-century) Jain temple.

Buses don't go to the caves, but some go close (Bus 801 to Baramunda bus stand, for example). A shared/private autorickshaw shouldn't cost much more than ₹20/200.

★ **State Museum** MUSEUM
(www.odishamuseum.nic.in; Lewis Rd; Indian/foreigner ₹5/50, camera ₹10/100; ⊙10am-4.30pm Tue-Sun) Odisha's best collection of rare palm-leaf manuscripts, as well as *patachitra* (Odishan cloth paintings), traditional and folk musical instruments, Bronze Age tools, an armoury, and an impressive collection of Buddhist, Jain and Brahmanical sculptures (look for the haunting 8th-century sculpture of Chamunda).

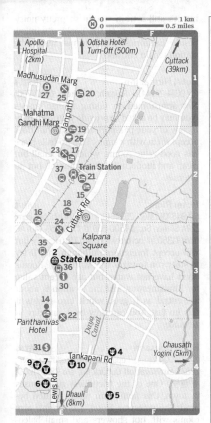

Bhubaneswar

◎ Top Sights
1 Lingaraj Mandir	D4
2 State Museum	E3
3 Udayagiri & Khandagiri Caves	A2

◎ Sights
4 Bhaskareswa Temple	F4
5 Brahmeswar Mandir	F4
6 Kedargauri Mandir	E4
7 Mukteswar Mandir	E4
8 Museum of Tribal Arts & Artefacts	B1
9 Parsurameswar Mandir	E4
10 Raja Rani Mandir	E4
Siddheswar Mandir	(see 7)
11 Vaital Mandir	D4

◎ Activities, Courses & Tours
12 Alternative Tours	D4
13 Kerala Panchakarma	D3
14 OTDC	E3

◎ Sleeping
15 Hotel Grand Central	E2
16 Hotel Nirmal Inn	E2
17 Hotel Richi	E2
18 Hotel Upasana	E2
19 Maurya Inn	E2
20 New Marrion	E1
21 Railway Retiring Rooms	E2

◎ Eating
22 Dalma	E3
23 Hare Krishna Restaurant	E2
24 Khana Khazana	E3
Maurya Gardens	(see 17)
25 Sri Ram Mandir Tiffin Centre	E1
Truptee	(see 24)

◎ Drinking & Nightlife
26 BNC	E2

◎ Shopping
27 Ekamra Haat	E1
28 Utkalika	D2

◎ Information
India Tourism	(see 30)
29 Odisha Tourism	C4
30 Odisha Tourism	E3
Odisha Tourism	(see 21)
31 SBI ATM	E4
32 State Bank of India	D2

◎ Transport
33 Air India	D2
34 Baramunda Bus Stand	A1
35 Buses to Cuttack	E3
36 Buses to Puri	E3
37 Master Canteen Bus Stand	E2

Museum of Tribal Arts & Artefacts MUSEUM
(⊙10am-5pm Tue-Sun) FREE For anyone considering a visit to the tribal areas, this museum is recommended. Dress, ornaments, weapons, household implements and musical instruments are displayed. The museum is located off National Hwy 5; bus 801 goes close to here – up Azad Marg, before turning left to Baramunda bus stand.

🏃 Activities

Kerala Panchakarma AYURVEDA, MASSAGE
(240/90 Airfield Rd; treatments from ₹500; ⊙6am-9pm) Small ayurvedic clinic offering stress-busting full-body massages.

☞ Tours

OTDC BUS TOUR
(☑0674-2431515; www.otdc.in; Lewis Rd; ⊙7am-8pm) OTDC, the transport arm of Odisha Tourism, runs various bus tours. The city

tour (₹300, 9am daily) covers the Nandankanan Zoo, Dhauli, the Lingaraj and Mukteswar temples, the State Museum, and Udayagiri and Khandagiri Caves. Another tour goes to Pipli, Konark and Puri (₹380, 9am daily), while a third takes in Chilika Lake (₹400, 7.30am daily). All tours leave from the OTDC office behind Panthanivas Hotel. You also need to prebook them from here, the day before you wish to take the tour. Tour prices do not include entry fees.

Alternative Tours   CULTURAL TOUR
(☑2590830; www.travelclubindia.com; Room 5, BDA Market Complex, off Airfield Rd; ⊙10.30am-4.30pm Mon-Sat) 🖉 A veteran for tribal tours in Odisha, Nagaland and Arunchal Pradesh. Prices start at around ₹9000 per person per day, all inclusive.

✨ Festivals & Events

Adivasi Mela   CULTURAL
(⊙26-31 Jan) Bhubaneswar goes tribal for the annual Adivasi Mela festival, celebrating the art, dance and handicrafts of Odisha's tribal groups.

🛏 Sleeping

Most hotels have 24-hour checkout. Many cheaper hotels don't accept foreigners.

Railway Retiring Rooms   RETIRING ROOM $
(Platform 1, Bhubaneswar Railway Station; dm ₹70-280, r ₹250-500, with AC ₹450-900; ❄) These large but simple rooms are the cheapest place foreigners can stay in Bhubaneswar. Rooms are in a quiet corner of the station,

but it's still a train station so pretty noisy. Secure your room at the booking window beside 'Enquiries', which is just inside the station's main entrance.

Hotel Nirmal Inn   HOTEL $
(☑0674-2534411; Rajpath; s/d from ₹600/700) Not accustomed to taking foreign guests (you may be asked to provide your own photocopy of your passport and visa), but does accept them with a smile. This no-frills place has good-value rooms, which are small but clean and modern. Has a restaurant, but no internet.

Hotel Richi   HOTEL $
(☑9437012316, 2534619; www.richihotels.com; 122A Station Sq; s ₹500-550, d ₹750-950, with AC from ₹1350, all incl breakfast; ❄) Unfriendly, but will accept foreigners (although they'll try to steer you towards the AC rooms). Rooms don't have hot water, but are decent value for Bhubaneswar, and the location is about as central as it gets, which also means it fills up fast. You can only book one day in advance.

Hotel Upasana   HOTEL $$
(☑2310044; upasana_bbsr@rediffmail.com; 2282 Laxmisagar, off Cuttack Rd; s/d ₹850/1000; ❄@🛜) One of the friendliest guesthouses in town, this family-run place, located behind Bhubaneswar Hotel, has bright, airy rooms with hot showers and small balconies. There are computer terminals in the lobby and wi-fi extends to some rooms. No restaurant.

ODISHA'S INDIGENOUS TRIBES

Sixty-two Adivasi (tribal) groups live in an area that encompasses Odisha, Chhattisgarh and Andhra Pradesh. In Odisha they account for one-quarter of the state's population and mostly inhabit the jungles and hilly regions of the centre and southwest. Their distinctive cultures are expressed in music, dance and arts.

Of the more populous tribes, the **Kondh** number about one million and are based around Koraput in the southwest, Rayagada and the Kandhamel district in the central west. The 500,000-plus **Santal** live around Baripada and Khiching in the far north. The 300,000 **Saura** live near Gunupur near the border with Andhra Pradesh. The **Bonda**, known as the 'Naked People' for wearing minimal clothing but incredibly colourful and intricate accessories, have a population of about 5000 and live in the hills near Koraput.

As of 2012, permission from the District Collector was required to visit specific areas designated as home to Particularly Vulnerable Tribal Groups (PVTGs) and bans on overnight lodging, private home visits, photographs and video had all been put in place. It is possible to visit tribal regions independently (see the Koraput section for details), but most travellers choose a customised tour, organised through private tour agencies in Bhubaneswar or Puri.

Maurya Inn   HOTEL **$$**

(☎9040402003, 0674 2535894; 59 Janpath; s/d ₹1200/1400, with AC ₹1300/1500; ❀) Simple, straightforward midrange hotel with clean spacious rooms, hot showers and cable TV. No internet or restaurant.

Hotel Grand Central   HOTEL **$$**

(☎0674-2313411; www.hotelgrandcentral.com; Old Station Bazaar; s/d incl breakfast from ₹2100/2300; ❀🛜) Whitewashed corridors and marble floors lead to smart, well-fitted rooms at this new business-class hotel, located just behind the train station. Rates include wi-fi. There's a restaurant, bar and car rental.

New Marrion   HOTEL **$$$**

(☎2380850; www.hotelnewmarrion.com; 6 Janpath; r from ₹3800; ❀@🛜🏊) Great value for a top-end hotel, Marrion has rooms with a contemporary, classy design – LCD TVs, dark-wood panelling and a small sofa space. Restaurants include South Indian, Italian-Mexican combo and Chinese, a great kebab house, a Café Coffee Day in the building out front and a contemporary Scottish bar. There's a Thai spa to round off the allure, and service is top-notch.

✗ Eating

★ Dalma   ODISHAN **$**

(Lewis Rd; mains ₹50-150, thali ₹110-200; ⏱noon-10.30pm) Down some steps from Lewis Rd, this small Bhubaneswar chain is widely regarded by locals as the best place in town to sample authentic Odia cuisine, including *aloo bharta* (a delicious mashed potato and aubergine combination), *dalma* (the restaurant's speciality dhal dish, cooked with coconut), *chhena poda* (Odisha's cottage-cheese dessert from heaven) and numerous Odishan thalis.

It's nothing flash – there's a canteen feel to the place, with dishes served on metal trays – but the food is nothing short of sensational, especially when you consider the prices. First-time visitors to the region will welcome the well-translated menu with clear, English descriptions of every dish.

Khana Khazana   INDIAN **$**

(Kalpana Sq; mains ₹40-140; ⏱5.30-10.30pm) This long-standing evening-only street stall – with plastic chairs and tables spread across the pavement – does a bang-up job with tandoori chicken, delicious chow mein and tasty biryanis. The *chicken dum bir-*

ODIA CUISINE

Mustard is the staple in Odishan kitchens, used ubiquitously in seed, paste and oil forms, giving many Odia dishes a distinct pungent flavour. A typical meal consists of *bhata* (rice) served alongside a variety of tasty side dishes such as *kaharu phula bhaja* (fried pumpkin flower); *dalma* (dhal cooked with pumpkin, potato, plantains and eggplant, then fried in a five-spice oil of fenugreek, cumin, black cumin, anise and mustard, topped with grated coconut); and *besara* (vegetables or river fish with mustard-paste gravy). *Saga bhaja* – leafy greens lightly fried with garlic paste and a five-seed mixture called *pancha phutan* (cumin, mustard, anis, black cumin and chilli) – is also a treat here. On the coast, fish and prawns are omnipresent: *sarison macha* is a superb favourite fish dish cooked in a mustard-based curry.

yani (₹90) is particularly popular with the locals, as are the great-value rolls (roti wraps that come with various fillings and are a speciality of Kolkata; ₹35 to ₹50).

Truptee   SOUTH INDIAN **$**

(Cuttack Rd; mains ₹50-130; ⏱7am-10.30pm) A great choice for South Indian breakfasts, this clean, family-friendly restaurant does a fine line in dosas (paper-thin lentil-flour pancake), *vada* (doughnut-shaped deep-fried lentil savoury) and *idli* (spongy, fermented rice cake) before bringing out the curries and tandoor flat breads later in the day. Also does thalis (₹80 to ₹120).

Sri Ram Mandir Tiffin Centre   ODISHAN **$**

(Janpath; dishes ₹5-20; ⏱6.30am-9pm) *Dahi vada* (*vada* in a slightly spicy yoghurt sauce) is the classic Odishan breakfast dish, and locals flock to this street-side stall beside Sri Ram Mandir Temple to have their fill of it, along with other tasty offerings such as samosas, *aloo chops* (deep-fried potato snack) and small portions of veg curry.

There's no seating; punters just stand on the pavement, breakfast tray in one hand, spoon in the other. There's also no menu, but the food is laid out on the counter, canteen style, so just point, pay and tuck in.

ODISHA BHUBANESWAR

SLEEP LIKE A KING

Located a mere 3km from the Dhenkanal train station (an easy train ride from Bhubaneswar), the wonderful **Gajlaxmi Palace** (☑ 9861011221; www.gajlaxmipalace. com; s/d incl meals & nature walk ₹3000/6000), tucked away amid stunning scenery in the untapped forests of the Dhenkanal district, dates back to 1935. The palace belonged to Rajkumar Shri Shesh Pratap Singh Deo, a member of the Dhenkanal royal family. Today, his grandson, JP Singh Deo, and Navneeta, his lovely wife, have opened up two rooms inside their tranquil slice of royal history to guests.

Sleeping here is like overnighting in a museum – the whole place is chock full of Singh Deo's antiques collected around the world and the whole place lives and breathes of decadent days gone by. The surrounding forest hides at least 22 wild elephants, a common sight on JP's morning and evening nature walks. Wild boar, jungle fowl and barking deer also roam freely outside the palace doors. JP grew up here and is ever too pleased to take you to rarely visited Sabara tribal villages or nearby Joranda Temples, or spin tales of elephant and tiger kills in crazier days over wonderful meals sourced from their own organic gardens. Paradise found.

★ **Odisha Hotel** ODISHAN $$
(☑ 9437419279; Market Bldg, Sahid Nagar; thali ₹140-340; ⏱ 12.30-4pm) This dead-simple lunchtime-only restaurant is one of the best spots to try authentic Odia cuisine, served in huge proportions thali-style in traditional bell-metal dishware. The menu board is entirely in Odia, so just order veg or nonveg (not always available) and sit back and await this Hindu last supper!

Make sure you ask for a small spread, and double check the price of it before you tuck in. Otherwise you'll be given the enormous ₹340 thali, which one person could never finish. To get here, walk or take a shared autorickshaw (₹5) along Janpath to Sahid Nagar (the name of the area the restaurant is in). Still on Janpath, turn right beside Panda Lifestyle shopping centre, which is just past the easier-to-spot Khimji wedding store. The restaurant is about 500m along this side road; go straight over the crossroads, then take the right fork and it's on your right.

★ **Hare Krishna Restaurant** INDIAN $$
(Lalchand Market Complex, Janpath; mains ₹100-220; ⏱ 11.30am-3.30pm & 7pm-10.45pm) The beautifully lacquered Gujarati *sankheda* furniture stands out at this stylish but unpretentious veg restaurant where you can enjoy delicious curries, biryanis and tandoor flat breads in a soothing atmosphere. Enter through Lalchand shopping complex.

Maurya Gardens INDIAN, CHINESE $$
(Station Sq; mains ₹100-250; ⏱ noon-11pm) This small, low-lit, AC-cooled restaurant is a welcome respite from the train station chaos outside. The curries (veg and nonveg) are nice and hot, but you can cool them down with a beer (from ₹165).

Drinking & Nightlife

Local bars and bottle shops are dotted around the city, often attached to a hotel or restaurant. There's a clutch of them by the train station and along Cuttack Rd.

BNC CAFE
(Brown n Cream; Janpath; ⏱ 8am-10.30pm) AC-cooled coffee shop with good-value fresh coffee (₹60), plus sandwiches, muffins and ice cream.

Shopping

Ekamra Haat MARKET
(www.ekamrahaat.in; Madhusudan Marg; ⏱ 10am-10pm) A wide-ranging exposition of Odishan handicrafts (and snack stalls) can be found at this permanent market, located within pleasant, well-tended gardens.

Utkalika HANDICRAFTS
(Odisha State Handloom Cooperative; Eastern Tower, Market Bldg; ⏱ 10am-8.30pm) Located in the busy all-day market streets known as Market Building, the state-government emporium features Odishan textiles, including appliqué and *ikat* (a technique involving

tie-dyeing the thread before it's woven), as well as some traditional palm-leaf paintings.

ⓘ Information

ATMs are plentiful along Janpath and Cuttack Rd. There's also a couple at the train station.

Apollo Hospital (☏ 0674-2301819, 0674-6660413; www.apollohospitals.com; Plot No 251, Old Sainik School Rd; ⊙24hr) A new modern private medical facility with 24-hour trauma centre and pharmacy; it's where you want to be if you're ill.

Cyber Cafe (Janpath; per hour ₹30; ⊙9am-10pm)

India Tourism (www.incredibleindia.org; Paryatan Bhavan, 2nd fl, Lewis Rd; ⊙9am-6pm Mon-Fri, to 1pm Sat) Dishes out national information. Located in the same building as Odisha Tourism.

Jayshree Internet (Cuttack Rd; per hour ₹10; ⊙8am-10pm)

Odisha Tourism (www.orissatourism.gov.in; Paryatan Bhavan, 2nd fl, Lewis Rd; ⊙10am-5pm Mon-Sat) Tourist information, maps and lists of recommended guides, but generally pretty useless. There are also branches at the airport (⊙by flight schedule) and train station (☏2431299; ⊙6am-10pm).

Police (Capitol Police Station, Rajpath)

Post Office (cnr Mahatma Gandhi & Sachivajaya Margs; ⊙9am-7pm Mon-Sat, 3-7pm Sun) Parcels 10am to 4pm; 3pm to 7pm on Sunday.

State Bank of India (Rajpath; ⊙10am-4pm Mon-Fri, to 1pm Sat) Exchanges cash (1st floor) and has ATMs.

ⓘ Getting There & Away

AIR

Bhubaneswar's modern Biju Patnaik Airport is just a couple of kilometres from the centre.

A number of airlines have ticket offices at the airport, including **IndiGo** (☏ 0674-2596174; www.goindigo.in), **GoAir** (www.goair.in) and **Air India** (www.airindia.com; Rajpath; ⊙10am-4.45pm Mon-Sat), which between them fly daily to Delhi, Kolkata, (Bengaluru) Bangalore and Mumbai.

BUS

For most destinations northeast of Bhubaneswar, it's quicker catching a bus to Cuttack's Badambari bus stand and then catching an onwards service from there. To get to Cuttack, either take a bus from Baramunda bus stand, or take Bus 324 from the Master Canteen bus stand, or jump on any bus heading east along Cuttack Rd.

To reach Baramunda bus stand, catch bus 801 from Master Canteen bus stand (₹10, 20 minutes).

Services from **Baramunda bus stand** (National Hwy 5) include:

Baripada ₹270, six hours, hourly 9am to 11pm

Berhampur ₹140, four hours, every two hours

Cuttack ₹20, one hour, frequent

Jeypore seat/sleeper ₹550/600, 13 hours, 6pm, 7pm, 8pm and 8.30pm

Kolkata non-AC seat/sleeper ₹300/700, AC seat/sleeper ₹400/900, 12 hours, frequent 6.30pm to 9.30pm

Konark ₹50, two hours, frequent

Puri ₹40, 1¼ hours, frequent

ODISHA BHUBANESWAR

TRAINS FROM BHUBANESWAR

DESTINATION	TRAIN NO & NAME	FARE (₹) SLEEPER/3AC/2AC	DURATION (HR)	DEPARTURE TIME
Chennai	12841 Coromandal Express	550/1435/2070	20	9.25pm
Kolkata (Howrah)	18410 Sri Jagannath Express	260/690/990	8	11.55pm
Koraput	18447 Hirakhand Express	360/970/1395	14	7.35pm
Mumbai	11020 Konark Express	700/1830/2745	37	3.25pm
New Delhi	12801 Purushotlam Express	695/1810/2645	30	11.15pm
Ranchi	18452 Tapaswini Express	340/920/1325	12	10pm
Rayagada	18447 Hirakhand Express	300/805/1150	9	7.35pm

Rayagada seat/sleeper ₹370/400, 12 hours, 6pm and 9pm

TRAIN

Foreigners queue at window 3 at the **computerised reservation office** (🕑 8am-10pm Mon-Sat, to 2pm Sun), in a separate building in front of the train station. Destinations include:

Berhampur 2nd-class unreserved seat ₹35 to ₹80, two to three hours, more than a dozen (7am to 9.25pm)

SATKOSIA GORGE SANCTUARY

This 525-sq-km forested **sanctuary** (📞 8763102681; www.satkosia.org; per day Indian/ foreigner ₹20/1000; 🕑 6am-6pm) is straddled by a breathtaking gorge, cut by the mighty Mahanadi River, and is one of the most beautiful natural spots in Odisha. The sanctuary as a whole is home to significant populations of gharial and mugger crocodiles, plus 38 species of mammal, including elephants, leopards, sambar deer, wild dogs, jackals, giant squirrels and around a dozen tigers. However, this is not a place to come for a wildlife safari; tourists are not allowed inside the park's core zone, where most of the wildlife is found, and 4WD safaris are not on offer. The main appeal of coming here is the opportunity to spend some time deep inside the protected forests of a stunning national park. The setting is gloriously peaceful and you can spot crocs in the crocodile sanctuary or on the riverbank if you take a boat trip from Tikarpada.

The main entry gate of the reserve is at Pampasar, 30km southwest of Angul. **Satkosia Wildlife Division** (📞 8763102681; Hakimpada, Angul) manages four or five sets of accommodation that are run by local communities. The nicest is the new **Nature Camp Chhotkei** (s/d incl meals, guide & nature hike ₹3000/3500) 🍃 , where you'll find five spacious eco-cottages. Meals are simple but tasty and served proudly and substantially by villagers. Simpler cottages and tents are available at **Nature Camp Purunakote** (tent/cottage per person ₹1000/1200). Meals here cost an extra ₹500 per person per day, although there are cheaper restaurants in the village. **Nature Camp Tikarpada** (tent incl meals & nature hike ₹1800-2200; 🕑 Dec-Mar) has the most spectacular setting, perched above the golden-sand beaches of the Mahanadi River with the gorge as a scenic backdrop. Tented accommodation here is basic – even the 'deluxe' tents have outhouse bathrooms, albeit private ones, and the standard tents have no showers. As at Chhotkei, rates include meals and a morning nature hike, which here includes a visit to the nearby crocodile sanctuary. Boat rides (₹1000) along the river are also available.

You'll need to stop by Satkosia Wildlife Division in Angul for permissions and reservations – a mere formality, but bring a copy of your passport and visa. The office is a 1km walk from the bus stand; turn left at the restaurant called Hotel Sagar, then left at the green cavalryman statue, keep walking to the end of the road, turn left and the office is on your right. From the train station it costs ₹100 in an autorickshaw. If you get stuck in Angul, **Hotel Santi** (📞 06764-230386; www.santihotels.com; Bus Stand, Angul; s/d ₹750/1000, with AC ₹1500/1800; ❄ 🖥), overlooking the bus stand, has comfortable rooms, a good restaurant and free wi-fi. It can also arrange a car and driver for you to visit Satkosia; expect to pay around ₹2000, leaving one day and returning the next.

Four buses go from Angul bus stand to Tikarpada (₹35, 2½ hours, 6am, 9.30am, 3.30pm and 5pm), via the park gate at Pampasar, where you're supposed to pay your park fees (travellers sometimes get away without paying this if travelling by bus), the turn-off for Chhotkei (5km from the main road) and Purunakote. Return buses leave Tikarpada at 6.30am, 10.30am and 1pm.

From Angul bus stand there are frequent buses to Bhubaneswar (₹100/140, four hours) and Cuttack (non-AC/AC ₹80/110, three hours) between 6am and 6pm.

The quickest way to get to Angul from Bhubaneswar is on either the 12893 Bhubaneswar–Balangir Express (2nd class/AC chair ₹70/222, 2¼ hours, 6.45am) or the 18106 Bhubaneswar–Rourkella Express (2nd class/AC chair ₹70/222, two hours and 10 minutes, 1.40pm). There are at least four other slightly slower daily trains. Returning, the Bhubaneswar–Balangir Express (now numbered 12894) leaves Angul for Bhubaneswar at 7.35pm.

Kolkata 2nd class/sleeper ₹140/290, seven to eight hours, seven daily (7.55am to 11.55pm)

Puri 2nd-class unreserved seat from ₹15, two hours, more than a dozen (7am to midnight)

❶ Getting Around

BUS

Bhubaneswar has a relatively foreigner-friendly numbered city-bus system that runs between 7am and 9pm from the bus stand known as Master Canteen, right by the train station. Double check your bus is going where you want it to, as some bus numbers run along more than one route.

Note that for Puri, it's cheaper to catch a private bus (₹40) from outside the State Museum.

City buses leaving from Master Canteen bus stand:

Airport Bus 207A, ₹10, 15 minutes

Baramunda bus stand Bus 801, ₹10, 20 minutes

Dhauli Bus 225, ₹10, 30 minutes

Lingaraj Temple Bus 333, ₹10, 20 minutes

Mayfair Hotel Bus 207N, ₹10, 20 minutes

Mukteswar Temple Bus 225, ₹10, 15 minutes

Pipli Bus 701, ₹50, 50 minutes

Puri Bus 701, ₹100, two hours

Udayagiri Caves Bus 801 or 405

CAR

OTDC (p603) offers car-and-driver services for tours around the area. For destinations within 200km, the charges are ₹110 per hour and ₹11 per kilometre for an AC Indigo, or ₹72 per hour and ₹7 per kilometre for a non-AC Ambassador. Book in person at least a day in advance.

TAXI/AUTORICKSHAW

An autorickshaw/taxi to the airport costs ₹50/250. There's a prepaid taxi stand at the airport. Autorickshaws are allowed to drop-off passengers at the airport, but they're not really supposed to pick-up from there, so you may have to walk to the main road to hail one.

AROUND BHUBANESWAR

Chausath Yogini

Rediscovered in the 1950s among rice fields 15km south of the city, this small but serene 9th-century open-roofed temple is dedicated to *yoginis* (female goddess attendants) and is one of only four of its kind in India. The temple – no larger than a village hut –

contains 64 (chausath) carved *yoginis*, each shown standing on top of her *vaharna* (vehicle; often in animal form). Few tourists make it out here, which adds to the tranquility of the location, beside a large pond and surrounded by farmland.

While you're here, don't miss visiting the fascinating **Soumya Handicraft** (Chausath Yogini, Hirapur; ☺8am-5pm), the small workshop-gallery of a local artist who paints, carves and sells his work from his home, close to the temple. On display are fabulously detailed *patachitra* (₹500 to ₹2000), quirky brightly painted whiskey and beer bottles (₹200 to ₹800) and some stunning palm-leaf scroll carvings (₹200 to ₹8000). Some pieces are distinctly tribal Odishan in design, others have Buddhist influences or a Hindu tantric flavour. His palm-leaf representations of the *yoginis* make wonderfully unique souvenirs.

No buses come out this way, so you'll have to take an autorickshaw. Expect to pay around ₹100 to ₹150 one-way from Tankapani Rd, and more like ₹200 from Cuttack Rd. Note that not everyone has heard of this place, so you may have to ask more than one driver before you get a response. The temple is pronounced *'chorsat jorgini'* in Odia.

Dhauli

In about 260 BC, 11 of of Ashoka's 14 famous edicts were carved onto a large rock at Dhauli, 8km south of Bhubaneswar. The rock, now a small tourist attraction called the **Ashokan Rock Edicts**, is protected by a grill-fronted facade. A large sign offers English translations of each edict. Above the edicts, on top of a mound, is a carved elephant, representing Buddha, seemingly emerging from a small rock.

Just beyond the rock edicts is the huge, white **Shanti Stupa** (Peace Pagoda), built by Japanese monks in 1972 on a hill to the right. Older Buddhist reliefs are set into the modern structure, and there are great views of the surrounding countryside from the top.

Bus 225 goes to Dhauli (₹10, 30 minutes) from Bhubaneswar's Master Canteen bus stand. From the turn-off, it's a pleasant, largely tree-shaded 3km walk to the rock edicts (on your left), and then a short, steep walk to the stupa (slightly further along on your right). Alternatively take a shared/private autorickshaw (₹5/50 one-way) from the turn-off. You can continue on to Puri from the turn-off, flagging down any bus passes.

Pipli

This colourful town, 16km southeast of Bhubaneswar, is notable for its brilliant appliqué craft, which incorporates small mirrors and is used for door and wall hangings and the more traditional canopies hung over Jagannath and family during festival time. Lampshades and parasols hanging outside the shops turn the main road into an avenue of rainbow colours. The work is still done by local families in workshops behind the shops; you may be able to go back and have a look. During Diwali, it's particularly vibrant. Pipli is easily accessible by any bus between Bhubaneswar and Puri or Konark.

SOUTHEASTERN ODISHA

Southeastern Odisha hugs the coast of the Bay of Bengal and is home to the state's most visited spots, including the backpacker outpost of Puri and the Unesco-protected Sun Temple at Konark.

Puri

☑ 06752 / POP 158,000

Hindu pilgrims, Indian holidaymakers and foreign travellers all make their way to Puri, setting up camp in different parts of town. For Hindus, Puri is one of the holiest pilgrimage places in India, with religious life revolving around the great Jagannath Mandir and its famous Rath Yatra (Car Festival). The town's other attraction is its long, sandy beach – better for strolling than swimming.

In the 1970s, travellers on the hippie trail through Southeast Asia were attracted here by the sea and bhang (marijuana), which is legal in Shiva's Puri. There's little trace of that scene today (though the bhang hasn't departed); travellers come just to hang out and recharge their backpacking spirit.

The action is along a few kilometres of coast. The backpacker part of town is

bunched up towards the eastern end of Chakra Tirtha (CT) Rd, while Bengali holidaymakers flock to busy New Marine Rd, where there is lots of hang-out action on the long esplanade.

❶ Dangers & Annoyances

Muggings and attacks on women have been reported along isolated stretches of beach, even during the day, so take care. Ocean currents can become treacherous in Puri, and drownings are not uncommon, so don't venture out beyond your depth. Ask one of the *nolias* (fishermen/lifeguards), with their white-painted, cone-shaped wicker hats, for the best spots and keep a look out for Sea Riders, a group of traditional fishermen turned lifeguards through an initiative of a local NGO.

◉ Sights

Jagannath Mandir   HINDU TEMPLE

This mighty temple belongs to Jagannath (Lord of the Universe), an incarnation of Vishnu. The jet-black deity with large, round, white eyes is hugely popular across Odisha; figures of Jagannath are tended and regularly dressed in new clothes at shrines across the state. Built in its present form in 1198, the temple (closed to non-Hindus) is surrounded by two walls, but you can spot its 58m-high *sikhara* (spire) topped by the flag and wheel of Vishnu.

Guarded by two stone lions and a pillar crowned by the Garuda that once stood at the Sun Temple at Konark, the eastern entrance (Lion Gate) is the passageway for the chariot procession of Rath Yatra.

Jagannath, brother Balbhadra and sister Subhadra reside supreme in the central *jagamohan* (assembly hall). Priests continually garland and dress the three throughout the day for different ceremonies. The temple employs about 6000 men to perform the complicated rituals involved in caring for the gods. An estimated 20,000 people – divided into 36 orders and 97 classes - are dependent on Jagannath for their livelihood.

Non-Hindus can spy from the roof of **Raghunandan Library** (cnr Temple & Swargadwar Rds; ◷ 9am-1.30pm & 4-6pm Mon-Sat) opposite; a 'donation', while not officially compulsory, is expected (₹10 is fine, though they will ask for more). The library is closed on Sunday, so touts who will help you to a nearby rooftop prey on tourists and demand ₹100 – easily negotiated down to ₹50. Enter around the back of the building to the right-hand side and follow the arrows and signs through a fascinating ruined monastery.

Model Beach
BEACH

(www.puribeach.net) Puri is no palm-fringed paradise – the beach is wide, shelves quickly with a nasty shore break and is shadeless – but the newly crowned Model Beach, part of a sustainable, community-run beach tourism initiative, offers a 700m stretch of sand that's easily Puri's finest and cleanest. Palm umbrellas provide shade and cabana boys/lifeguards, known as Sea Riders, hawk fixed-price beach chairs (₹20) and massages (₹50 to ₹200) and are responsible for keeping the beach clean.

Swargdwar
SACRED SITE

(off New Marine Rd; 24hr) These hallowed cremation grounds are the end stop of choice for Eastern India's Hindu population and beyond – some 40 bodies are cremated here daily. Anyone can watch or walk among the open-air ceremonies providing you behave in a respectful manner and avoid taking photos. It's an obviously solemn affair, but a fascinating glimpse into Puri's role as one of India's holiest cities.

Activities & Tours

Heritage Tours
CULTURAL TOUR

(9437023656, 223656; www.heritagetoursodisha.com; Mayfair Heritage Hotel, CT Rd; 8am-8pm) Bubu is a tribal and cultural tourism veteran whose tour company focuses on rural and special-interest ethnic tourism. In addition to multiday tribal tours and car hire, Heritage also offers cycle-rickshaw tours (two hours ₹300) around the backstreets of old Puri, and Odishan-cuisine cookery classes (half-day ₹500) at the excellent Wildgrass Restaurant (p613), also owned by Bubu.

Heritage is interesting for its 'Green Riders' program, in which 75 cycle-rickshaw riders are trained in fixed pricing, self-respect and why spiking prices for foreign tourists is uncool. That said, we found we still had to negotiate fares with them! Bubu's latest venture is the beautiful tribal-region countryside retreat, Desia (p621).

Grass Routes
CULTURAL TOUR

(9437029698; www.grassroutesjourneys.com; CT Rd) Australian-run tour agency offering all-inclusive tribal tours. Also manages the excellent countryside getaway, Chandoori Sai (p621).

Festivals & Events

Highlights of the festival-packed year include the celebrated festival of **Rath Yatra** (Car Festival; Jun/Jul) and the **Puri Beach Festival** (www.puribeachfestival.com; late Nov) featuring magnificent sand art, food stalls, traditional dance and other cultural programs.

Sleeping

Book well in advance for Rath Yatra, Durga Puja (Dussehra), Diwali or the end of December and New Year. Many hotels have early-morning checkout times.

Hotel Lotus
HOTEL $

(227033; www.hotellotuspuri.com; CT Rd; d/q from ₹550/1200, d with AC ₹1200;) Friendly and humbly run, Lotus is probably the most popular budget choice among foreign backpackers, offering a range of inexpensive rooms that are clean and comfortable. The non-AC rooms, with small balconies, are great value. Travellers fight over the one rooftop room (₹600).

Travellers Inn
GUESTHOUSE $

(06752 223592; CT Rd; r ₹250-350, without bathroom ₹200) Rooms are basic but swept clean at this simple CT Rd guesthouse with rock-bottom prices and a friendly welcome. The ones with attached bathrooms have more natural light as they open out onto a

ODISHA PURI

CHHENA PODA

Puri Cheesecake (Temple Rd, Dolamandap Sahi; per piece ₹16; 7am-11pm) The narrow lanes of Puri's holy quarter are full of makeshift sweet shops, perhaps none more famous than Puri Cheesecake. Bikram Sahoo and his six brothers have been churning out this unique Odishan delight, known as *chhena poda* (burnt cheese), for 45 years. It's cottage cheese, sugar and cardamom cooked in an iron pan over an open flame – a real treat. Though it's more like a flan than traditional cheesecake, it's off the mark by name only.

To find it, walk down Temple Rd from Jagganath Mandir, pass a small public square about 300m on the right, and it's another 100m on your right next door to Jagganath Pump House.

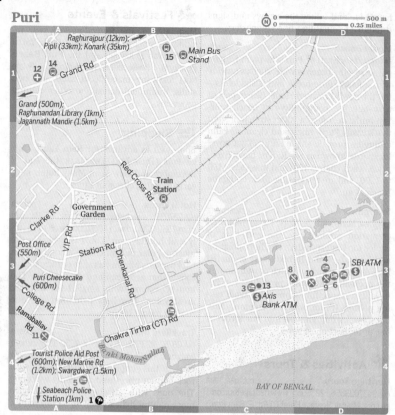

small tatty garden courtyard, which leads down to the beach.

★ Z Hotel
HERITAGE HOTEL $$

(☑ 222554; www.zhotelindia.com; CT Rd; dm women-only ₹100, r without/with bathroom from ₹700/2000; ✳ 🛜) This charming yet understated heritage hotel – the former maharaja's home – remains one of Puri's most atmospheric choices. Rooms are large and airy, and come with high ceilings, chunky wooden furniture and spotless bathrooms (including the shared one). Management is far from helpful, but once you're in you can safely ignore them. There's a restaurant, evening films shown in the TV room, and wi-fi in common areas.

★ Hotel Gandhara
HERITAGE HOTEL $$

(☑ 224117; www.hotelgandhara.com; CT Rd; heritage r ₹850-1250, new-block s/d incl breakfast ₹1500/1570, with AC ₹2290/2700; ✳ @ 🛜 🏊) Gandhara continues to steamroll the com-

petition in this price bracket for its friendliness, services and value. The 200-year-old pillared heritage building – the former holiday home of a rich Bengali family – has three wonderfully atmospheric fan-cooled rooms. More expensive modern AC rooms are in a new block at the back of the lawned garden, overlooking the delightful swimming pool.

The wi-fi is super quick (for India), you get newspapers slipped under your door and there are beers (₹100) waiting for you in a fridge.

★ Chanakya BNR Hotel
HERITAGE HOTEL $$$

(☑ 223006; www.therailhotel.com.com; CT Rd; r incl breakfast ₹4300; ✳ 🛜 🏊) Conjuring up images of the Raj, this splendid 150-year-old railway hotel is a magnificent place to stay. Rooms, entered through 2.7m-tall wooden doors, are enormous, while inside there's wood flooring, period furniture and old framed Indian Railways photographs. First-

Puri

floor rooms open out onto a large shared verandah with sea views from the rattan chairs.

There are beautiful bygone touches throughout, most notably the dark, 90-year-old lac mural art in the lobby stairwell and restaurant. There's a garden pool and wi-fi throughout.

Mayfair HOTEL $$$
(☑227800; www.mayfairhotels.com; off CT Rd; d incl breakfast & dinner from ₹11,000; ❄@🅿❄) The benchmark for Puri luxury, this modern hotel has two buildings side by side. The 12-year-old Mayfair Heritage has rooms (₹10,750) and cottages (₹12,900), all with sea views, dotted around freshly clipped gardens, while the brand new Mayfair Waves has luxury rooms (₹12,900) and suites (₹16,000) as well as a gym and spa.

Both buildings have garden pools and top-notch restaurants, and guests can use facilities at either.

✗ Eating & Drinking

A few restaurants (such as Peace and Jabari Garden) can 'find' a beer for you, but be discreet.

Peace Restaurant MULTICUISINE $
(CT Rd; mains ₹35-250; ⊙7am-4pm & 6-11pm) This Puri stalwart, with seating in a shaded front courtyard, is still the most pleasant budget option, doing nice work with Western breakfasts and pasta, but excelling at Indian food. Save room for the house dessert, a fried empanada-like banana or apple turnover laced with sugar, cinnamon and honey.

Jabari Garden Restaurant MULTICUISINE $
(CT Rd; mains ₹60-150; ⊙8.30am-3pm & 6-10.30pm) This place is popular with Puri long-termers and does decent Western comfort food as well as excellent local fare. The garden is a dazzle of fairy lights come evening.

★Wildgrass Restaurant ODISHAN $$
(☑9437023656; VIP Rd; mains ₹80-200, thali ₹100-220; ⊙11am-11pm) A delightful restaurant, Wildgrass has an AC-cooled main room, but it's more fun to sit outside at one of the thatched pavilions dotted around the lush garden. The menu is superb, with local and regional specialities categorised by their origins (Odishan, Chilikan and Puriwala).

Ask about its Odishan-cuisine cookery classes (₹500), which include a morning trip to the local food market to buy the ingredients with which you'll be cooking your lunch.

Honey Bee Bakery & Pizzeria CAFE $$
(CT Rd; pizza & mains ₹80-300; ⊙8.30am-2pm & 6-10pm) Pizzas and pancakes, espresso-machine coffee (₹70), toasted sandwiches and breakfast fry-ups (including bacon!) – all the comforts of home are here at this cute and clean cafe-restaurant with rooftop seating.

Grand NORTH INDIAN $$
(☑222829; Grand Centre, Grand Rd; mains ₹80-130; ⊙11.30am-3.30pm & 7.30-10.30pm) This large, pure-veg locals' favourite offers plenty of off-menu dishes, so even if you don't see the *bhindi chatpati* (okra), *gobi Hyderabadi* (cauliflower), or *kadhai* veg (creamy curried vegies) on the menu, ask for them anyway. Also has a healthy list of dosas (₹30 to ₹75).

A bonus to the fab food is the open-air terrace, from which there are striking views of Jagannath Mandir and the hubbub of Grand Rd below. From the temple, it's 100m down Grand Rd.

ODISHA PURI

ⓘ Information

The main hotel stretch of CT Rd has numerous moneychangers and internet cafes (₹30 to ₹40 per hour.)

Gandhara Travel Agents (www.gandharatravels.com; Hotel Gandhara, CT Rd; internet per hour ₹40; ⊙8am-7pm Mon-Sat, to 1pm Sun) Friendly travel agency, moneychanger and internet (with fast connection and cameras for Skype).

Post office (cnr Kutchery & Temple Rd; ⊙10am-6pm Mon-Sat)

Tourist Police Aid Post (CT Rd, Seabeach)

ⓘ Getting There & Away

BUS

The easiest way to Bhubaneswar is Bus 171 (₹100, two hours), which leaves from Medical Sq on Grand Rd every 30 to 45 minutes between 7.45am and 5.30pm and will drop you at the Master Canteen bus stand, next to Bhubaneswar's train station. But private buses, leaving from the same place, are cheaper (₹40, two hours).

Frequent buses to Konark (₹25, 45 minutes) leave from the Konark bus stand. The last bus back is at 6.30pm.

Next to the Konark bus stand is the sprawling **main bus stand** (☑ 224461), where frequent buses head to Bhubaneswar (₹40, two hours), Cuttack (₹50, 2½ hours) and Satapada (₹33, two to three hours), as well as AC (seat/sleeper ₹550/580, 13 hours, 6pm to 8pm) and non-AC (seat ₹350, 13 hours, from 3pm) buses to Kolkata.

For Pipli and Raghurajpur, take a Bhubaneswar bus.

TRAIN

At least a dozen daily trains go to Bhubaneswar (2nd-class unreserved seat ₹10 to ₹50, two hours, from 6am to 11.50pm). The daily 58417 Puri-GNPR Express goes to Brahmapur (2nd-class seat ₹40, 4½ hours) at 8am. The 12801 Purushottam Express heads to Delhi (sleeper/3AC/2AC ₹715/1860/2720, 31 hours) at 9.45pm, while the 18410 Sri Jagannath Express leaves for Kolkata (sleeper/3AC/2AC ₹300/805/1150, 10 hours) at 10.30pm.

ⓘ Getting Around

A few places along CT Rd rent bicycles (per day ₹50), mopeds (per day ₹250) and motorbikes (per day ₹350).

From CT Rd, cycle-rickshaws charge about ₹30 to the train station and ₹40 to ₹50 to the bus stands or Jagannath Mandir.

Raghurajpur

The fascinating artists' village of Raghurajpur, 14km north of Puri, is two streets and 120 thatched brick houses adorned with murals of geometric patterns and mythological scenes – a traditional art form that has almost died out in Odisha.

The village is most famous for its *patachitra* (Odishan cloth paintings). With eye-aching attention and a very fine brush, artists mark out animals, flowers, deities and demons, which are then illuminated with bright colours. It makes for very beautiful and unique souvenirs.

Take the Bhubaneswar bus from Puri and look for the 'Raghurajpur The Craft Village' signpost 11km north of Puri, then walk the last 1km. Don't get cornered by the few shops that have set up first but which are technically outside the village itself.

Konark

☑ 06758 / POP 15,000

The iconic Sun Temple at Konark – listed as a Unesco World Heritage Site – is one of India's signature buildings and Odisha's *raison d'être*. Most visitors are day-trippers from Bhubaneswar or Puri, which makes sense, as Konark isn't a particularly nice place to stay. However, you might want to consider staying a bit closer, at one of the excellent coastal retreats (p616) located just a few kilometres away, between here and Puri.

Originally nearer the coast (the sea has receded 3km), Konark was visible from far out at sea and known as the 'Black Pagoda' by sailors, in contrast to Puri's whitewashed Jagannath. The inland lighthouse near Chandrabhaga Beach is an odd testament to that fact.

⊙ Sights

Archaeological Museum MUSEUM
(admission ₹10; ⊙9am-5pm Sat-Thu) Contains many impressive sculptures and carvings found during excavations of the Sun Temple.

★ Festivals & Events

Konark Festival DANCE
(⊙1-5 Dec) Steeped in traditional music and dance, the Konark Festival takes place in the open-air auditorium with the gorgeous Sun Temple as a backdrop.

SUN TEMPLE

The massive **Sun Temple** (Indian/foreigner ₹10/250, video ₹25, guide per hr ₹150; ⊙dawn-8pm) was constructed in the mid-13th century, probably by Odishan king Narashimhadev I to celebrate his military victory over the Muslims, and was in use for maybe only three centuries. In the late 16th century the 40m-high *sikhara* (spire) partially collapsed: speculation about causes ranges from marauding Mughals removing the copper over the cupola to a ransacking Kalapahad displacing the Dadhinauti (arch stone), to simple wear and tear from recurring cyclones – the truth was apparently lost with Konark's receding shoreline.

The entire temple was conceived as the cosmic chariot of the sun god Surya. Seven mighty prancing horses (representing the days of the week) rear at the strain of moving this stone leviathan on 24 stone cartwheels (representing the hours of the day) that stand around the base. The temple was positioned so that dawn light would illuminate the *deul* (temple sanctuary) interior and the presiding deity, which may have been moved to Jagannath Mandir in Puri in the 17th century – the interior of the temple was filled in with stone in 1903 'in order to preserve this superb specimen of old Indian architecture'.

The *gajasimha* (main entrance) is guarded by two stone lions crushing elephants and leads to the intricately carved *nritya mandapa* (dancing hall). Steps, flanked by straining horses, rise to the still-standing *jagamohan* (assembly hall). Behind is the spireless *deul*, with its three impressive chlorite images of Surya aligned to catch the sun at dawn, noon and sunset.

The base and walls present a chronicle in stone of Kalinga life; you'll see women cooking and men hunting. Many are in the erotic style for which Konark is famous and include entwined couples as well as solitary exhibitionists.

Guides can be useful here as the temple's history is a complicated amalgam of fact and legend, and religious and secular imagery, and the guides' explanations can be thought provoking. But make sure you get a government-approved one; the tourist office at Yatrinivas hotel, beside the Archaeological Museum, can help.

🛏 Sleeping & Eating

Suntemple Hotel INDIAN $$
(☑236890; Bus Stand Rd; mains ₹60-200; ⊙8am-3.30pm & 6-10pm) A busy, friendly, AC restaurant with a big range of Indian veg and nonveg dishes, as well as traveller favourites such as chips and banana pancakes. Also has a few simple **rooms** (r ₹400-500, with AC ₹800) out back if you get stuck here. It's right by the bus drop-off, two minutes walk from Sun Temple.

ⓘ Information

There's an ATM and a couple of internet cafes in the dusty lane leading to Sun Temple. Restaurants and cheap hotels cluster the main road by the bus drop-off. The bus stand is set back from the main road, 200m further away from the temple.

ⓘ Getting There & Away

Bus 441 is the most comfortable to Puri (₹40, one hour), but cheaper, more frequent private buses (₹25) also ply the route. There are also frequent departures to Bhubaneswar (₹45, two hours).

Chilika Lake

Chilika Lake is Asia's largest brackish lagoon. Swelling from 600 sq km in April and May to 1100 sq km in the monsoon, the shallow lake is separated from the Bay of Bengal by a 60km-long sand bar called Rajhansa.

The lake is noted for the million-plus migratory birds – including grey-legged geese, herons, cranes and pink flamingos – that flock here in winter (from November to mid-January) from as far away as Siberia and Iran and concentrate in a 3-sq-km area within the bird sanctuary on Nalabana Island.

Other attractions are rare Irrawaddy dolphins near Satapada, the pristine beach along Rajhansa, and Kalijai Island temple where Hindu pilgrims flock for the Makar Mela festival in January.

Satapada

☑ 06752

Little more than a bus stand, a hotel, and a cluster of road-shack restaurants beside a jetty, the tiny village of Satapada, on a headland jutting southwestwards into Chilika Lake, is the starting point for dolphin-spotting boat trips; the boats usually cruise towards the new sea mouth for a paddle in the sea and some dolphin- and bird-spotting en route. Travellers have reported dolphins being (illegally) herded and otherwise harassed; make it clear you don't want this.

OTDC (☑ 262077; Yatrinivas Hotel; per person ₹180-250) runs a three-hour tour of the lake which leaves from between 9.30am and 10am each morning. Price per person depends on the group size.

Dolphin Motor Boat Association (☑ 7377653372; Satapada Jetty; 1½hr/3hr/4hr/8hr trips per boat ₹1900/2100/2400/3700), a cooperative of local boat owners, has set-price trips that include dolphin sightseeing, Nalabana Bird Sanctuary and Kalijai Island temple. Note, there are two rival associations running under the same name; they run similar tours, but we feel the one to the left of the jetty is more trustworthy, albeit slightly more expensive. Don't forget to take water on your boat trip.

The grandly named **Chilika Ecopark** (Satapada Jetty) is a small but pleasant palm-tree-shaded park by the jetty which has on display the 12m-long skeleton of a baleen whale that was washed up on the shore near here in 2007.

Considering the potential storybook lakeside setting, **Yatrinivas** (☑ 262077; d ₹550, with AC ₹1500; ❋) is surprisingly uninspired. Its three ageing non-AC rooms have seen better days, but are very spacious and, like the more modern AC rooms, have balconies with lake views. The **restaurant** (mains ₹50-150) is decent value.

The daily ferry crossings to Barkul stopped some time ago. However, there is one daily ferry to Balugaon (₹50, five hours), a few kilometres north of Barkul. It leaves Satapda at around 1.30pm. The return leaves Balugaon at 6.30am. An autorickshaw from Balugaon to Barkul is around ₹100.

If you want to charter your own boat from Satapada, expect to pay at least ₹3000 for a trip across the lake to Barkul.

More frequent ferries (pedestrians/bicycles/motorbikes/cars ₹4/5/15/300, 30 minutes) ply between Satapada and the

COASTAL RETREATS

For an idyllic getaway that's still within shouting distance of both Puri and Konark, consider one of these coastal retreats.

Nature Camp, Konark Retreat (☑ 9437029989; www.naturecampindia.com; s/d incl breakfast ₹2000/3000) Plopped down on the banks of the Ramchandi River, just across from a sandy Bay of Bengal beach, and only 10km south of Konark, this friendly, laid-back tented camp has a shanty feel to it with tented rooms dotted around a slightly unkempt forest clearing. The tents are fan-cooled only, and are comfortable rather than luxurious, but come with cute attached shower rooms with sit-down flush toilets.

The food comes in the form of two sumptuous Odia thalis (veg ₹250, nonveg ₹350), both cooked in a traditional charcoal-fired *chulha* (stove) and served on a banana leaf.

The camp is about 500m off the main Puri–Konark road; there's a big sign on the main road so you can take any bus (Puri ₹20, Konark ₹5) and jump off when you see it.

Lotus Resorts (☑ 06758-236161; www.lotusresorthotels.com; Puri-Konark Marine Dr; cottage incl breakfast from ₹3500; ❋) About 6km from Konark, on pretty Ramchandi Beach, this collection of rustic, weathered Canadian-pine cottages is a beautiful getaway across a calm and swimmable islet catering to a few local fisherman and not much else. Accommodation is stylish and amenities include a small ayurvedic spa (high-season only) and a nice sand-side restaurant (mains ₹120 to ₹350).

Each cottage has TV, AC and a modern bathroom, but there's no internet. To get here take any bus between Puri (₹20) and Konark (₹5) and look for the big sign on the main road.

Janhikuda jetty just to the west, where vehicles can then head west, and around to the north side of the lake. It's a wonderfully scenic route. Daily departures are at 7.30am, 10am, 1pm and 4pm, returning at 8am, 10.30am, 1.30pm and 4.30pm.

A bus to Berhampur (₹75, 3½ hours), near Gopalpur-on-Sea, travels on the 7.30am ferry before following the beautiful countryside road for two hours until it meets up with the main highway. Wait for the bus on the ferry, then jump on as it drives off. It will already be full of villagers by the time it reaches Satapada so don't expect a seat, but passengers get off along the way so you won't have to stand for long. The bus will drop you at the turn-off for Gopalpur-on-Sea, if you ask, from where you can wave down any passing bus (₹11, 20 minutes). The return bus leaves Berhampur at 12.40pm and crosses Chilika Lake on the 4.30pm ferry to Satapada.

Pretty much every hotel and travel agent in Puri does day trips to Chilika Lake, but it's easy to come here independently by bus (₹33, two to three hours). The last bus back to Puri leaves Satapada at around 6pm.

Barkul

☑ 06756

On the northern shore of Chilika, Barkul is just a scattering of houses, small guesthouses and food stalls on a lane which runs from the main highway down to the government-run hotel property Panthanivas Barkul. From here boats make trips to Nalabana Island (full of nesting birds in December and January) and Kalijai Island (which has a temple on it), though you could charter you own boat to anywhere; deal directly with the boat hands.

Panthanivas Barkul hotel runs two-hour round trips to Kalijia for ₹955 per boat (up to seven passengers), including some time on the island. The four-hour trip to Kalijia and Nalabana costs ₹2865 per boat, but tends only to be done in December and January when the birds are on Nalabana. You can also get out on the lake on a pedal boat (₹40 to ₹60).

Panthanivas Barkul (☑227488; pns. barkul@gmail.com; d ₹900, with AC ₹2250, AC cottage ₹2600, all incl breakfast; ❄@) has a great setting, and is one of the best government-run hotels in Odisha, with

comfortable rooms overlooking the lake. The AC rooms and cottages are newer and cleaner but all rooms are good here. The restaurant (mains ₹50-170) does decent Indian and Chinese food, including some seafood. And there's a bar (☺11am-10pm), which is dimly lit and has plastic chairs, but sells large bottles of Kingfisher Light (₹130) and is run by a friendly old guy.

There's a handful of cheaper guesthouses on the lane leading to Panthanivas Barkul.

Frequent buses dash along National Hwy 5 between Bhubaneswar (₹80, 1½ hours) and Berhampur (₹60, 1½ hours). You can get off anywhere en route.

Panthanivas Barkul is at least 2km walk from the main highway. If you don't have much luggage it's a lovely, signposted walk past village homes. Alternatively, hop in a passing autorickshaw (shared/private ₹10/50).

A ferry for Satapada (₹50, five hours) leaves from nearby Balugaon at 6.30am. It's about ₹100 to get to Balugaon in an autorickshaw.

Rambha

☑ 06810

The village of Rambha, on the northwestern shore of Chilika Lake, is the nearest place to stay for turtle-watching on Rushikulya beach.

Panthanivas Rambha (☑278346; rabi. dash09@gmail.com; dm ₹200, d ₹800, with AC ₹1560, AC cottage ₹3150, all incl breakfast; ❄) is a fine government-run property with good-value non-AC rooms with balconies and lake views. The AC rooms are more modern, but not worth the extra money. The huge eight-bed dorm is extremely spartan, but does have its own bathroom. The restaurant (mains ₹50-170) is decent, and there's also a bar here. Speedboat (per hour ₹2000) or motorboat (per hour ₹700) tours of the lake are available. If you want to charter your own boat across the lake, it costs around ₹2000 for Satapada.

The hotel is a 1km walk from the main highway (ignore the sign that says 5km), or hop in a passing autorickshaw (₹10).

From the highway you can easily wave down buses to Barkul (₹30, 30 minutes), Berhampur (₹30, one hour) and Bhubaneswar (₹110, two hours).

Gopalpur-on-Sea

📞 0680 / POP 6660

If you dig nosing about decaying seaside resorts, Gopalpur-on-Sea, a seaside town the British left to slide into history until Bengali holidaymakers rediscovered its attractions in the 1980s, could be just your thing. Prior to this, it had a noble history as a seaport with connections to Southeast Asia, the evidence of which is still scattered through the town in the form of romantically deteriorating old buildings.

It's no paradise, but the peaceful and relatively clean beach is great for a stroll or a paddle, and it's oddly charismatic in its own strange, antiquated way. And, unlike Puri, there's proper seaside accommodation right on the beach.

The main village is a couple of hundred metres back from the beach, along the road to Berhampur. Here you'll find the turn-off for Mayfair Palm Beach as well as a couple of internet cafes (per hour ₹20), a post office and a police station. For cash, there's an ATM on the seafront.

Sights

Lighthouse   LIGHTHOUSE
(Indian/foreigner/child ₹10/25/3, camera ₹20; ⏱ 3.30-5.30pm) Peering over the town is the lighthouse, with its immaculate gardens and petite staff cottages. It's a late-afternoon draw card and after puffing up the spiral staircase you're rewarded with expansive views and welcome cooling breezes.

🛏 Sleeping & Eating

Gopalpur-on-Sea can be booked out during holiday and festival times, and it gets quite busy at weekends generally.

In the main village, right at the end, there's a **Foreign Liquor Off Shop** (⏱ 10.30am-10.30pm), which sells big bottles of Kingfisher for ₹90.

ODISHA'S OLIVE RIDLEY MARINE TURTLES

One of the smallest sea turtles and a threatened species, the olive ridley marine turtle swims up from deeper waters beyond Sri Lanka to mate and lay eggs on Odisha's beaches. The main nesting sites are Gahirmatha (in Bhitarkanika Wildlife Sanctuary), Devi River mouth near Konark, and Rushikulya River mouth by Chilika Lake.

Turtle deaths due to fishing practices are unfortunately common. Although there are regulations, such as requiring the use of turtle exclusion devices (TEDs) on trawl nets and banning fishing from certain prohibited congregation and breeding areas, these laws are routinely flouted in Odisha.

Casuarina trees have been planted to help preserve Devi beach but they occupy areas of soft sand that are necessary for a turtle hatchery. Other potential threats include the upcoming Astaranga Seaport and Thermal Power Plant and the proposed Palur port, which is planned right next to the Rushikulya River mouth nesting site (which it would destroy if allowed to continue as planned).

In January and February the turtles congregate near nesting beaches and, if conditions are right, come ashore. If conditions aren't right, they reabsorb their eggs and leave without nesting.

Hatchlings emerge 50 to 55 days later and are guided to the sea by the luminescence of the ocean and stars. They can be easily distracted by bright lights; unfortunately National Highway (NH) 5 runs within 2km of Rushikulya beach. Members of local turtle clubs in Gokharkuda, Podampeta and Purunabandha village gather up disoriented turtles and take them to the sea. It's best to visit the nesting beach at dawn when lights are not necessary.

The best place to see nesting and hatching is on the northern side of Rushikulya River, near the villages of Purunabandha and Gokharkuda, 20km from the nearest accommodation in Rambha. During nesting and hatching, activity takes place throughout the night: don't use lights.

Ask staff at Panthanivas Rambha (p617) what conditions are like, or contact the **Wildlife Society of Odisha** (📞 6712311513; www.wildlifeorissa.org; Shantikunj, Link Rd, Cuttack). Rickshaws between Rambha and Rushikulya cost ₹400 return for a half day and ₹800 for the full day.

★ Hotel Seaside Breeze
HOTEL **$**

(☑ 2343075; s/d ₹600/750, with AC ₹1100/1350; ❀) Right on the beach, this friendly no-frills guesthouse has clean, brightly painted rooms with sea-facing terraces. Cute corner room No 15 has a private balcony with sweeping views of the beach – it's the smallest and cheapest (single/double ₹500/650), but we think the best. There's no restaurant, but the balconies have tables and chairs, and the great-value menu (mains ₹35 to ₹120) includes sea fish.

Hotel Sea Pearl
HOTEL **$$**

(☑ 2343557; www.hotelseapearlgopalpur.com; d ₹700-900, with AC ₹1400-1780; ❀ @) Right on the beach, Sea Pearl is a decent midrange option. Rooms are a little on the small side, but all have a sea view of some description (except the cheapest non-AC ones). Has a restaurant.

★ Mayfair Palm Beach
HOTEL **$$$**

(☑ 6660101; www.mayfairhotels.com; r incl breakfast & dinner from ₹11,000; ❀ @ 🌐 🏊) First opened as a luxury resort in 1914, this historic property was renovated by Mayfair in 2012 and transformed into one of this region's stand-out hotels. The grounds contain winding walkways, a beautiful pool and immaculate terraced gardens leading down to the beach. Rooms are tasteful, but understated – it's worth paying the extra ₹2000 for the deluxe-category rooms, which have fabulous beach-facing balconies.

There's also a large children's play area, a spa, an excellent **restaurant** (mains ₹350-900) and a huge indoor lounge with a striking teak-wood **bar** (beer from ₹200). The bar and restaurant are both open to nonguests.

Sea Shell Fast Food
INDIAN, CHINESE **$**

(mains ₹30-80; ⏰ 8am-10.30pm) Cheap-and-cheerful alfresco dining on the esplanade overlooking the beach.

❶ Getting There & Away

Comfortable, half-hourly buses shuttle between the beachfront and Berhampur (₹14, 30 minutes) between 7am and 7.45pm, from where you can catch onward transport by rail or bus.

From Berhampur's new bus stand there are frequent buses throughout the day to Bhubaneswar (₹140, three hours, frequent) via Rambha (₹30, one hour) and Barkul (₹60, 1½ hours). There are two buses to Rayagada (₹140, eight

hours, 9.45am and 1.45pm), and one daily bus to Satapada (₹75, three hours, 12.40pm) via the scenic route along southeast shore of Chilika Lake and then on the ferry.

SOUTHWESTERN ODISHA

As of 2012, prior permission from the District Collector was required for foreigners wishing to visit some specific parts of tribal regions. Some agencies were saying this rule may change, so check online travel forums before you fork out for an expensive tour; you may be able to do your trip independently. Assuming the rules don't change, the permissions process is taken care of either by a government-approved tour agency, a government-approved guide or a local tourism office, and usually takes two to three days to arrange (just give them a copy of your passport and visa, and wait), though it can take up to five days.

Photography and overnight stays in Adivasi households are strictly prohibited by law.

Koraput
☑ 06852 / POP 40,000

Up in the cool, forested hills, the small market town of Koraput is by far the nicest of the main towns in which to base yourself in this region. There's a friendly village feel to it, a weekly market for which you don't need special permission to visit, and the main temple here is fascinating, especially for non-Hindus who can't enter the Jagannath Mandir in Puri.

◉ Sights & Activities

Koraput's helpful **tourist office** (☑ 06852-250318; www.orissatourism.gov.in; Tourist Complex, near Station Circuit House; ⏰ 10am-5pm Mon-Sat) can put you in touch with government-approved guides for visits to the region's weekly markets (p620). The guides themselves will process the 'prior permission' that's required for foreigners to visit these markets. All you need to do is give them a copy of your passport and visa, and tell them where you wish to visit; it should only take one or two days to process, but can take up to five. Don't feel disheartened if you miss the market you wanted. There are weekly markets held at various villages in

ODISHA KORAPUT

Koraput district every day of the week; see the boxed text for details.

At the time of research foreigners had to be accompanied by a government-approved guide to visit any of the tribal areas where the markets are held, but ask for confirmation of this at the tourist office when you arrive in Koraput. It's possible to get to some of the markets by bus, but you will need to hire a car for the day to visit others.

Guides charge from between ₹1000 and ₹2000 per day. Expect to pay around ₹1500 per day on top of that for car hire. Guides are often reluctant to use public transport.

To get to the tourist office, continue walking past Raj Residency, round the corner and head up the hill (200m).

Jagannath Temple
HINDU TEMPLE

While you're hanging around in Koraput, waiting for permission to visit the markets, don't miss visiting Jagannath Temple, whose whitewashed *sikhara* (temple spire) overlooks the town. The courtyard around the *sikhara* contains numerous colourfully decorated statues of the wide-eyed Jagganath, the deity of Odisha, which you'll see painted on homes across the state. Below the *sikhara*, in a side hall, you'll walk past more than two dozen linga (phallic symbols of Shiva), before reaching some attractive displays of local *ossa* (traditional patterns made with white and coloured powders on doorsteps; also known as *rangoli*).

The temple is 200m behind the bus stand; at the bus stand, facing the police station, turn left up Post Office Rd then take the first left and look for the temple steps up to your right at the small staggered crossroads.

Sunday Market
MARKET

There's a market here every day, but it's Koraput's all-day Sunday Market that's the big one and worth exploring. Tribespeople and local traders alike buy and sell food produce and handmade goods in the lanes around the bus stand and behind the police station, and buying stuff from them is a rare opportunity for you to interact with tribespeople on your own.

🛏 Sleeping & Eating

The Jagganath Temple manages three great-value budget hotels just outside its grounds. Atithi Bhavan (📞 250610; atithibhaban@gmail.com; d ₹250, with AC ₹500; 🕸), just to the right of the steps that lead to the temple, is easily the best of them, with comfortable rooms and a pure veg restaurant (thalis ₹50). Atithi Nivas (📞 250610; atithibhaban@gmail.com; s ₹150), to the left of the temple steps, has singles only. Yatri Nivas (📞 9337622637; d ₹175), up towards the

---

LOCAL KNOWLEDGE

WEEKLY MARKETS

There are weekly *haats* (markets) held every day at different villages in Koraput district, sometimes two or three at different places on the same day. Tribespeople from surrounding villages will descend on the market of the day to trade handicrafts, clothes, jewellery and foodstuffs. They are fabulously colourful places to visit, and the best chance foreign tourists have of interracting with Odishan tribespeople.

Ondakelli Market – one of the most fascinating of all the *haats* – trades during the morning only. Other markets last all day. Kundli is the region's largest food market, while Koraput itself has a Sunday *haat* which, because of its location in the town centre, is open to foreigners even without special permission.

Selected *haats* include:

Monday Subai – small market, 34km from Koraput

Tuesday Ramgiri – 64km from Koraput

Wednesday Nandapur – 45km from Koraput

Thursday Onkadelli – numerous tribes represented, including Bonda, 65km from Jeypore

Friday Kundli – region's largest food marlet; numerous tribes represented

Saturday Laximpur – 56km from Koraput; accessible on any Rayagada-bound bus

Sunday Koraput – in the town centre; also one of the bigger markets

COUNTRYSIDE RETREATS IN THE TRIBAL SOUTHWEST

Strict regulations prohibit homestays in tribal regions these days, but for something approaching full immersion of Adivasi (tribal) culture, consider staying at one of these two fabulous countryside retreats, both of which are nestled in the village-dotted hills near Koraput.

Chandoori Sai (📞9439528602, 9443342241; www.chandoorisai.com; Goudaguda; s/d incl meals ₹3500/5000; @) On the scenic hill road and train line between Koraput and Rayagada, and just a couple of kilometres from the tiny town of Kakirigumma, Chandoori Sai is a beautiful, Australian-run rural retreat in a village called Goudaguda, and is one of Odisha's most stylish countryside getaways.

Run by Grass Routes (p611), a tour agency based in Puri, this unpretentious villagelike resort is a sustainable earthen-walled refuge with beautiful terracotta flooring and bamboo-sheeted ceilings. The food is fabulous, but the real coup is the guest interaction with tribal women, who act as cultural ambassadors on the property and guides through the village, and in doing so offer a brief assimilation into the vibrant Adivasi way of life.

To reach Chandoori Sai, take any bus between Koraput (40km) and Rayagada (70km) and get off at Kakirigumma; staff will then pick you up from there. Alternatively, catch the 18447 Hirakhand Express from Koraput to Bhubaneswar and get off at Kakirigumma Train Station. It leaves Koraput at 5.25pm, arriving in Kakirigumma an hour later. An unreserved 2nd-class seat costs ₹30; a sleeper is ₹140. From Bhubaneswar, the 18448 Hirakhand Express leaves at 7.35pm and arrives in Kakirigumma at 8.11am the next morning. Sleeper tickets cost ₹345.

Desia (📞9437023656; www.desiakoraput.com; Bantalabiri Village, Lamptaput; Apr-Sep s/d incl meals ₹2500/3500, Oct-Mar ₹3000/4700) A gorgeous rural retreat tucked away in the tribal hills of the Koraput region, this stylish villagelike resort is run by the excellent, Puri-based Heritage Tours (p611) and was just getting off the ground at the time of research. Activities on offer include hiking, cooking, craftwork and local market trips.

You can come here independently or with an all-inclusive 'tribal tour' package, starting at ₹19,000 for a four-day trip for two people. Desia is only 20km from Koraput, on the road to Rayagada. If you're not on a tour, it's best to call for a pick up from Koraput, although you could take any Rayagada-bound bus from Koraput to the village of Podagada, which is close by.

museum, has distinctly basic crash pads off a quiet courtyard compound.

Raj Residency　　　　HOTEL $$
(📞251591; www.hotelrajresidency.com; Post Office Rd; s/d ₹750/950, with AC from ₹1250/1500; ❋🛜) Raj Residency has the best digs in town, offering modern rooms with plasma TVs, friendly service and free wi-fi (lobby only). The Indian/Chinese *restaurant* (mains ₹60-170; ⏰7.30am-11am, noon-3pm & 7.30pm-10.30pm) is also the best place for food in Koraput. To get here, turn left up Post Office Rd, walk past the post office and keep going straight (400m).

ℹ Information

There are ATMs on the walk up to the tourist office, and a few internet cafes dotted around town. At the bus stand, there's a handy travel agency that can book train tickets for you (commission ₹30 to ₹50).

ℹ Getting There & Away

BUS

From the Koraput bus stand, there are half-hourly buses to Jeypore (₹15, 40 minutes) between 6am and 8.30pm. Seven buses make the scenic trip to Rayagada (₹90, four hours) between 6am and 7pm. And at least four evening buses leave for Bhubaneswar (₹520, 12 hours) between 5pm and 7pm.

To get a bus to Onkadelli Market, you'll have to first catch a bus to the scruffy town of Jeypore. From there, the 7.30am bus to Onkadelli (₹30, two to three hours) should get you there in time to catch the last couple of hours of the market. The Onkadelli buses leave from Jeypore's private bus stand, which is located in front of Jeypore's government bus stand. From Jeypore's government bus stand, there are frequent buses to Visakhapatnam (₹230, six hours, 5am to 11pm) in Andhra Pradesh.

TRAIN

The train station is 3km from the centre; it costs ₹10/50 in a shared/private autorickshaw to get here from the bus stand.

The 18448 Hirakhand Express plies daily between Bhubaneswar and Koraput. It leaves Koraput at 5.25pm, passes Rayagada at 10.05pm, and arrives in Bhubaneswar at 8.25am the next morning. Sleeper tickets cost ₹360.

There are three fabulously scenic, daily trains to Jagdalpur in Chhattisgarh, leaving at 9.50am, 1pm and 8.50pm. It takes around three hours. Sleeper tickets cost ₹100 to ₹140; unreserved, 2nd-class seats cost ₹40.

Rayagada

☎ 06856 / POP 58,000

The small town of Rayagada is the base for visiting the weekly Wednesday **Chatikona market** at Bissamcuttack (about 40km north). Here, highly ornamented Dongria Kondh and Desia Kondh villagers from the surrounding Niayamgiri Hills bring their produce and wares to sell. Alongside piles of chillies and dried fish are bronze animal sculptures made locally using the lost wax method. The market is considered tourist-friendly, but it's a bit of a process organising a permit; you'll need to track

---

SIMILIPAL NATIONAL PARK

The 2750-sq-km **Similipal National Park** (www.similipal.org; per day Indian/foreigner ₹40/1000, camera per 3 days ₹50/100; ☉ Oct–mid-Jun) has long been Odisha's prime wildlife sanctuary. However, due to several issues, including ongoing Maoist activity in the region, the park has been off-limits to foreign tourists in recent years. When it is open, there are waterfalls to see and wildlife safaris to take; wild elephants are relatively common, tigers less so.

Mayur Tours & Travels (☎ 9437218602, 253567; mayurtour@rediffmail.com; Lal Bazaar) is a recommended agency in the dusty town of Baripada, which acts as a transport hub for the park. Check the latest with them to see if you can visit.

---

down Rayagada's tourist officer, **Ramal Loechan Gamango** (☎ 9439838936), and provide a copy of your passport and visa. He will then facilitate your paperwork through the appropriate channels.

Rayagada's **daily market** is between the train station and the bus stand; turn right out of the bus stand, take the second right and it's on your left. Here you'll see colourfully dressed tribespeople weaving bamboo baskets alongside local traders selling fruit and veg, spices, dried fish and the like.

Tejasvi International (☎ 224925; www.hoteltejasvi.com; Collector Residence Rd; s/d incl breakfast from ₹1360/1600; ❋ 🛜) is a smart business hotel with good service, comfortable rooms and wi-fi throughout. Friendly **Hotel Rajbhavan** (☎ 223777; Main Rd; d/tr ₹600/900, with AC from ₹1160/1500; ❋) is cheaper, but also decent and has a good multicuisine **restaurant** (mains ₹50-170) open for lunch and dinner only. The latter is just across the main road from the train station – don't confuse it with nearby Hotel Raj, which isn't as good. Tejasvi is also walkable – take a right out of the station, then first left and keep walking to the end (500m).

There's an ATM just outside the train station.

The bus stand is a 1km walk from the train station; turn right out of the station, walk over the railway line and it's on your left.

From Rayagada bus stand, there are three early-morning local buses to Chatikona (₹30, two hours, 4.45am, 6.30am and 9.30am). Buses to Jeypore (₹100, five hours, 6.30am, 10.30am, noon, 2pm and 4pm) all go via Koraput (₹90, four hours); the route over the forested hills is fabulously scenic. There are frequent evening buses to Bhubaneswar (₹350, 12 hours) between 4pm and 7pm.

The 18447 Hirakhand Express departs Bhubaneswar daily at 7.35pm reaching Rayagada at 4.50am and Koraput at 9.50am. Sleeper tickets cost ₹300 and ₹360 respectively. The return leaves Rayagada at 10.30pm.

NORTHEASTERN ODISHA

Northeastern Odisha is best known for its nature sanctuaries, notably Bhitarkanika Wildlife Sanctuary and Similipal National Park (though foreigners were being denied entry to the latter at time of research) and the excellent Buddhist ruins at Ratnagiri, Udayagiri and Lalitgiri.

Pusphagiri Ruins

These fascinating Buddhist ruins are the remnants of one of India's earliest *mahaviharas* (Buddhist monasteries which were, effectively, the universities of their day). Pusphagiri Mahavihara had three campuses – Ratnagiri, Udayagiri and Lalitgiri – each built upon a small hilltop in the low-lying Langudi Hills. The Kelua River provided a scenic backdrop, and these days supports small farming communities and their mud-and-thatch villages which dot the rural landscape.

If you leave early, and restrict yourself to just one of the three sites, it's possible to visit the area in a day trip by bus from Bhubaneswar, but there are decent places to stay and doing so not only gives you the chance to explore each of the three sites properly, it also allows you the opportunity to soak up the peaceful charms of village life in the Odishan countryside.

Ratnagiri

Ratnagiri has the most interesting and extensive **ruins** (Indian/foreigner ₹5/100, video ₹25; ☺ dawn-dusk). Two large monasteries flourished here from the 6th to 12th centuries. Noteworthy are an exquisitely carved doorway and the remains of a 10m-high stupa. Stone remains are scattered across the hill here, some still half-buried in the grass, some even dotted around the village. The fine **museum** (admission ₹5; ☺ 9am-5pm Sat-Fri) contains beautiful sculptures from all the three sites.

Udayagiri

Another **monastery complex** is being excavated here in lush surrounds. There's a large pyramidal brick stupa with a seated Buddha and some beautiful doorjamb carvings. There's no entry fee, but unhelpful guides may attach themselves to you then ask for a donation (not compulsory). The ruins are a 1km to 2km walk from the main road.

Lalitgiri

Several **monastery ruins** (Indian/foreigner ₹5/100, video ₹25; ☺ dawn-dusk) are scattered up a hillside leading to a small museum and a hillock crowned with a shallow stupa. During excavations of the stupa in the 1970s, a casket containing gold and silver relics was found. Like Ratnagiri, Lalitgiri is also notable for its surrounding village atmosphere.

🍴 Sleeping & Eating

Toshali Ratnagiri Resort　　　　HOTEL $$$
(☑ 06725-281044, 9937023791; www.toshaliratnagiri.com; r incl breakfast ₹2500; ❋ @ ☎) The Toshali Ratnagiri Resort, opposite the Ratnagiri museum at the far end of Ratnagiri village, is surrounded by rice fields and a peaceful village pond. Tastefully decorated rooms flank an interior courtyard and there's a **restaurant** (mains ₹60-200) and a bar.

Toshali has three other similar hotels; two near the ruins of **Udayagiri** (☑ 9668013550; www.toshaliudayagiri.com; r ₹2500) and **Lalitgiri** (☑ 9937282626; www.toshalilalitgiri.com; r ₹3500) and another, called **Hotel Toshali Pusphagiri** (☑ 9937292311; www.toshalipushpagiri.com; Paradeep Rd; r ₹2500), on the main road 5km before Lalitgiri.

ℹ Getting There & Away

From Bhubaneswar, catch a bus to Cuttack (₹20, one hour, frequent) then change for a bus to Chandikhol (₹25, one hour, frequent) where, from the road leading off to the right, you can catch shared minivans to Ratnagiri (₹25, 45 minutes) via Udayagiri (₹20, 30 minutes), or to Lalitgiri (₹20, 30 minutes) via Hotel Toshali Pusphagiri. Minivans start drying up at around 3.30pm.

Udayagiri is 23km from Chandikhol. Ratnagiri is 9km past Udayagiri. Lalatgiri is 22km from Chandikhol, but down a different lane, 8km beyond the Ratnagiri/Udayagiri turn-off.

Bhitarkanika Wildlife Sanctuary

⭐ **Bhitarkanika Wildlife Sanctuary**　　　　NATURE RESERVE
(www.bhitarkanika.org; Indian/foreigner per day ₹20/1000, camera/video ₹50/1000; ☺ 1 Oct-30

WORTH A TRIP

ONKADELLI

This small village, 65km from Jeypore, has a most remarkable and vibrant Thursday market that throngs with Bonda, Gadaba, Mali and Didai villagers. In the morning it's all business on the vegetable side; in the afternoon, the alcohol market revs up, and entire families get sloshed. The best time to visit is between 10am and 1pm.

The market has been traditionally popular with tour groups; however, due to Maoist activity in the region, outcries of 'Human safari!' by some and an Odishan government that cannot (or will not) ensure security of tourists, visits to Onkadelli have declined in recent years and some conservative local tour operators have dropped it from their regularly scheduled tours. Check the latest with tour operators in Bhubaneswar or Puri, or on travel forums.

Onkadelli is best accessed by hire car, although the early morning bus from Jeypore is another option, and can only be visited with a professional guide, who will enrich your experience, keep the peace if things get ugly among the alcohol and the bows and arrows, and help enforce things such as the no-photography rules for tourists. It's feasible to come to Jeypore or Koraput independently and organise a guide (₹1000 to ₹1500). If you opt to go on your own, remember that photographs are strictly prohibited by law, and you'll need to stop by the tourist office (p619) in Koraput to handle the paperwork. Plan ahead – at least five days to be safe – and bring a copy of your passport and visa.

For those willing to put in the effort, Onkadelli is a sight for the senses and a true Odisha highlight.

Apr) Three rivers flow out to sea at Bhitarkanika forming a tidal maze of muddy creeks and mangroves. This is India's second largest mangrove region after the Sunderbans, and most of the 672-sq-km delta forms this wonderful sanctuary, a significant biodiversity hotspot. The only way to get around most of the sanctuary is by boat, and the main reason to come is to spot some of the hundreds of crocodiles that make these rivers their home.

There are three types: long-snouted gharials, short squat muggers, and the enormous estuarine crocodiles, or 'salties', which bask on mud flats before diving into the water for cover as your boat chugs past.

The best time to visit is from December to February, but you'll see crocs all year round, and may also see monitor lizards, spotted deer, wild boar and all sorts of birds, including eight species of brilliantly coloured kingfishers. Herons arrive in early June and nest until early December, when they move on to Chilika Lake, while raucous open-billed storks have set up a permanent rookery here.

It's also worth knowing that this area has the highest concentration of king cobras found anywhere in India, though hopefully you won't meet any of those.

The park entrance is at the beautiful, but very poor, mud-hut village of Dangmal (pronounced Dang-ger-mal).

🛏 Sleeping & Eating

There are only two accommodation options in Dangmal.

Forest Rest House GUESTHOUSE $
(d from ₹1900) The Forestry Department–run Forest Rest House is located just inside the sanctuary's main gate. Annoyingly, rooms have to be prebooked through the **Divisional Forest Officer** (📞9437037370, 06729-242460; Rajnagar) at Rajnagar village, about an hour's drive back up the road. Cheaper rooms are available for Indian tourists.

⭐**Nature Camp Bhitarkanika** CAMPGROUND $$$
(📞9437016054; www.bhitarkanikatour.com; s/d/tr/q incl meals ₹2000/4000/5000/6000) 🍃
A special experience awaits at this small, privately run tented camp at the heart of Dangmal village, built with the help of villagers, with a sustainable foot on the ground and just 200m before the sanctuary gate. The stylish Swiss Cottage tents are fully equipped with electricity, fans, sit-down flush toilets and pleasant terraces, and the wonderful rustic Odishan cuisine is almost worth the trip alone. Nature Camp happily welcomes walk-in guests, though you'd be wise to book, given the lack of other options.

You can organise boat trips here for only slightly more than if dealing directly at the park gate. A popular trip is the half-day morning tour (₹3500 per boat, up to 18 people), which includes a nature hike around the forests after the boat trip. Tours which include pick-up and drop-off in Bhubaneswar (two/three/four people ₹6700/4800/3900 per person, all inclusive) can also be arranged.

ⓘ Information

Permits (bring a copy of your passport), park entrance tickets and boat trips (₹2500 to ₹3000 per boat) can all be arranged in Dangmal at the park gate.

ⓘ Getting There & Away

Getting here is a bit of a mission, but the beautiful countryside scenery along the final, single-lane road leading to Dangmal makes it worthwhile.

Two or three direct buses to Dangmal leave from Cuttack between noon and 1pm. Other-wise, frequent buses go from Cuttack to Patta-mundai (₹60, three hours), from where you can catch onward buses to Dangmal (₹40, 2½ hours, last bus 5pm), passing Rajnagar en route.

There are three early-morning buses from Dangmal. The 5am and 7am both go as far as Kendrapara (a small town, just past Pattamun-dai), from where you can catch onward transport to Cuttack or Chandikhol (for the Pusphagiri Ruins). The 6am bus goes all the way to Cuttack. After that, you'll have to catch an autorickshaw from Dangmal to Rajnagar (around ₹500) from where the last bus to Cuttack leaves at 2pm.

The really adventurous might like to take the 4pm ferry (called a 'launch' in these parts) from Nalitapatia jetty (2km walk up the road from Dangmal) to Chandibali (₹16, 1½ hours), where you can find cheap guesthouses and onward buses in the morning to Bhadrak, which is on the main highway between Cuttack and Kolkata.

Madhya Pradesh & Chhattisgarh

Best Tiger Parks

➡ Kanha (p676)

➡ Bandhavgarh (p678)

➡ Pench (p680)

➡ Panna (p647)

➡ Satpura (p659)

Best Places to Stay

➡ Kipling Camp (p678)

➡ Friends of Orchha (p636)

➡ Laboo'z Cafe (p669)

➡ Manu Guest House (p667)

➡ Treehouse Hideaway (p679)

Why Go?

The spotlight doesn't hit Madhya Pradesh (MP) with quite the same brilliance as it does on its more celebrated neighbouring states, which is why it rewards travellers with unparalleled opportunities to detour from the tourist trail and delve into India's heartland.

Khajuraho's temples boast some of the finest stone carvings in India, but these exquisite erotic sculptures are a mere slice of architectural wonder in a region blessed with palaces, forts and stupas, the former most gloriously prominent in the postcard-perfect village of Orchha. Tigers are the other big attraction, and your chances of spotting a wild Royal Bengal in MP's national parks are as good as anywhere in India. Laid-back traveller havens like Maheshwar and Omkareshwar display the spiritual, scenic, and chilled-out flavours for which India is renowned, while the adventurous can foray into tribal Chhattisgarh, which split from Madhya Pradesh in 2000 and remains fascinatingly far removed from mainstream Indian culture.

When to Go
Bhopal

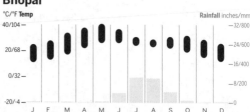

Nov–Feb The most pleasant time to visit central India, despite chilly mornings.

Apr–Jun Best chance of spotting tigers due to thin vegetation and fewer water sources.

Jul–Sep Monsoon time, but places such as Chhattisgarh are at their most beautiful.

Madhya Pradesh & Chhattisgarh Highlights

1 Tracking tigers at one of India's two best tiger parks: **Bandhavgarh National Park** (p678) or **Kanha National Park** (p676)

2 Blushing at the erotic carvings on the exquisite temples in **Khajuraho** (p638)

3 Sleeping in a mud hut homestay in **Orchha** (p636)

4 Dining like a prince at **Ahilya Fort** (p669) in Maheshwar

5 Cooling off under a waterfall in **Pachmarhi** (p657), Madhya Pradesh's only hill station

6 Cycling around India's finest Afghan ruins in **Mandu** (p669)

7 Marvelling at the Jain Rock Sculptures at the magnificent **Gwalior Fort** (p629)

8 Wandering the fascinating tribal markets of Baster near **Jagdalpur** (p683)

TOP STATE FESTIVALS

Festival of Dance (p645; ☉ Feb/Mar) Weeklong event with the cream of Indian classical dancers performing amid floodlit temples.

Shivaratri Mela (☉ Feb/Mar; Pachmarhi) Up to 100,000 Shaivite pilgrims, sadhus (spiritual men) and Adivasis (tribal people) attend celebrations at Mahadeo Cave. Participants bring symbolic tridents and hike up Chauragarh Hill to plant them by the Shiva shrine.

Magh Mela (p661; ☉ Apr/May) Huge annual religious fair held at Ujjain; pilgrim numbers are massive every 12th year for the Kumbh Mela (p661).

Ahilyabai Holkar Jayanti Mahotsav (p669) The Holkar queen's birthday is celebrated with processions through the town.

Navratri (p661; ☉ Sep/Oct) Celebrated with particular fervour in Ujjain, where lamps are lit at Harsiddhi Mandir.

Tansen Music Festival (p632; ☉ Nov/Dec) Gwalior music festival featuring classical musicians and singers from all over India.

Dussehra (p683; ☉ Oct) Dedicated to local goddess Danteshwari, this 75-day festival culminates in eight days of (immense) chariot racing in the streets of Jagdalpur.

History

Virtually all phases of Indian history made their mark on the region historically known as Malwa, starting with the rock paintings at Bhimbetka and Pachmarhi, which date back more than 10,000 years. They tell of a cultural succession through the late Stone Age to the start of recorded Indian history in the 3rd century BC, when the Buddhist emperor Ashoka controlled the Mauryan empire from Malwa and built Sanchi's Great Stupa.

The Mauryas were followed by the Sungas and the Guptas – Chandragupta II (r AD 382–401) ruled from Ujjain and had the caves cut at Udaigiri – before the Huns rampaged across the state. Around 1000 years ago the Parmaras reigned in southwest Madhya Pradesh – notably Raja Bhoj, who ruled for over half a century across this region and who founded the now-ruined town of Bhojpur, the magnificent fort of Mandu and, according to some scholars, the city of Bhopal.

The Chandelas ruled over much of central India from the 9th to the 13th centuries. It was their nimble-fingered sculptors who enlivened the facades of some 85 temples in Khajuraho with erotic scenes before the dynasty eventually moved its capital from Khajuraho to Mahoba. Between the 12th and 16th centuries, the region experienced continuing struggles between Hindu and Muslim rulers, and Mandu was the scene of some decisive clashes. The Mughals were eventually superseded by the Marathas after a 27-year war (1681–1707) – the longest in India's history. The Marathas went on to rule the region for more than a century before they fell to the British (1818), for whom the Scindia maharajas of Gwalior were powerful allies.

With the States Reorganisation Act of 1956, several former states were combined to form Madhya Pradesh. In 2000, Chhattisgarh became an independent state.

NORTHERN MADHYA PRADESH

Gwalior

📞 0751 / POP 1.05 MILLION

Famous for its medieval hilltop fort, and described by Mughal emperor Babur as 'the pearl amongst fortresses in India', Gwalior makes an interesting stop en route to some of the better-known destinations in this part of India. The city also houses the elaborate Jai Vilas Palace, the historic seat of the Scindias, one of the country's most revered families.

History

Gwalior's legendary beginning stems from the 8th century when a hermit known as Gwalipa is said to have cured the Rajput chieftain Suraj Sen of leprosy using water from Suraj Kund tank (which remains in

Gwalior Fort). Renaming the chieftain Suhan Pal, Gwalipa foretold that Suhan's descendants would remain in power as long as they retained the name Pal. Suhan's next 83 descendants did just that, but number 84 changed his name to Tej Karan and, naturally, lost his kingdom.

In 1398 the Tomar dynasty came to power. Gwalior Fort became the focus of continual clashes with neighbouring powers and reached its ascendancy under Raja Man Singh (r 1486–1516). Two centuries of Mughal rule followed, ending with the fort's capture by the Marathas in 1754.

Over the next 50 years the fort changed hands several times, including twice to the British, before finally passing to the Scindias.

During the First War of Independence (Indian Uprising) in 1857, Maharaja Jayajirao remained loyal to the British but his troops rebelled, and in mid-1858 the fort was the scene of some of the uprising's final events. Near here the British defeated rebel leader Tantia Topi and it was in the final assault on the fort that the rani (wife) of Jhansi was killed.

◉ Sights

★ Gwalior Fort   FORT
(☉ dawn-dusk) Perched majestically on top of a 3km-long plateau overlooking Gwalior, this 8th-century hilltop fort is an imposing, eye-catching sight, with the circular towers of the dominating Man Singh Palace ringed with turquoise tiles. Much of the fort is now occupied by the prestigious private Scindia School, established by Maharaja Madhavrao Scindia in 1897 for the education of Indian nobility.

There are two approaches to the fort, both of which are steep treks. Autorickshaws can drive you up to Urvai Gate, the western entrance, so it's tempting to go that way because vehicles cannot drive up from the eastern entrance. But the western entrance is an anticlimax compared with the formidable view of the fort from the eastern approach, which makes entering from the east well worth the climb. Don't, however, miss the rock sculptures, which are part of the way down the western side.

A sound-and-light show (Indian/foreigner ₹75/250; ☉ English 8.30pm Mar-Oct, 7.30pm Nov-Feb, Hindi 7.30pm Mar-Oct, 6.30pm Nov-Feb) is held nightly in the amphitheatre.

➜ Eastern Entrances
From the east a series of gates punctuates the worn steps of the path leading up to the fort. At the bottom, the first gate you pass through is Gwalior Gate (Alamgiri Gate), dating from 1660, and leads to the State Archeological Museum. The second, Bansur (Archer's Gate), has disappeared, so the next is Badalgarh, named after Badal Singh, Man Singh's uncle.

Further up is Ganesh Gate, built in the 15th century. Nearby is Kabutar Khana, a small pigeon house, and a small four-pillared Hindu temple to the hermit Gwalipa, after whom both fort and town are named.

You'll pass a 9th-century Vishnu shrine known as Chatarbhuj Mandir (Temple of the Four-Armed) before reaching the fifth gate, Hathiya Paur (Elephant Gate), now the entrance to the palace grounds (as the sixth gate, Hawa Gate, no longer exists).

➜ ★ Jain Rock Sculptures
While there are sculptures carved into the rock at a few points on the plateau, including on the way up from Gwalior Gate, the most impressive is the upper set on the western approach, between Urvai Gate and the inner fort walls. Mostly cut into the cliff face in the mid-15th century, they represent nude figures of *tirthankars* (the 24 great Jain teachers). They were defaced by Babur's Muslim army in 1527 but have been more recently repaired.

There are more than 30 images, including a splendid 17m-high standing sculpture of the first *tirthankar*, Adinath.

➜ ★ Man Singh Palace
(Indian/foreigner ₹5/100, video ₹25; ☉ dawn-dusk) This imperial-style palace is one of the more unusually decorated monuments you'll see in India: the outer walls include a frieze of yellow ducks! These – and mosaic tiling of elephants, tigers and crocodiles in blue, yellow and green – give it its alternative identity of Chit Mandir (Painted Palace).

SLEEPING PRICE RANGES

Price ranges in this chapter (double room with bathroom inclusive of tax) are as follows:

$ less than ₹1000

$$ ₹1000 to ₹5500

$$$ more than ₹5500

Gwalior

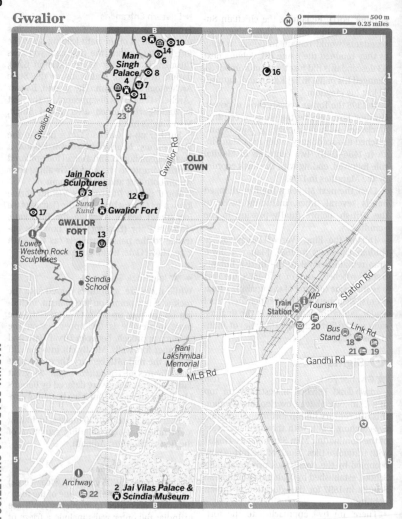

Built by Tomar ruler Man Singh between 1486 and 1516, this fine example of early Hindu architecture consists of two open courts surrounded by apartments on two levels. Below ground lie another two storeys constructed for hot weather, connected by 'speaking tubes' built into the walls, and used by the Mughals as prison cells.

The ticket counter is opposite the palace, while another ticket counter nearby sells tickets for the ruins of Shah Jahan Palace, Karan Palace and several other dilapidated palaces in the northwest of the fort. Also opposite the palace is the small **Archeo-**logical Survey of India museum (ASI; ₹5; ⊙9am-5pm Sat-Thu) that was a hospital under British rule.

★ **Jai Vilas Palace &**
Scindia Museum   PALACE
(Indian/foreigner ₹75/450, camera/video ₹70/50; ⊙10am-5.30pm Tue-Sun) The museum occupies some 35 rooms of the Scindias' opulent Jai Vilas Palace, built by Maharaja Jayajirao in 1874 using prisoners from the fort. The convicts were rewarded with the 12-year job of weaving the hall carpet, one of the largest in Asia.

Gwalior

Supposedly, eight elephants were suspended from the durbar (royal court) hall ceiling to check it could cope with two 12.5m-high, 3.5-tonne chandeliers, each with 250 light bulbs – said to be the largest pair in the world.

Bizarre items fill the rooms: cut-glass furniture, stuffed tigers and a ladies-only swimming pool with its own boat. The cavernous dining room displays the pièce de résistance, a model railway with a silver train that carried after-dinner brandy and cigars around the table.

Note: the gates to the north and south are locked so you have to enter the palace from the west.

State Archaeological Museum   MUSEUM
(Indian/foreigner ₹10/100, camera/video ₹50/200; ⊙10am-5pm) This museum is within Gujari Mahal, just through Gwalior Gate at the base of the fort. Built in the 15th century by Man Singh for his favourite rani, the palace is now rather deteriorated. There's a large collection of Hindu and Jain sculptures, including the famed Salabhanjika (an exceptionally carved female figure) plus copies of Bagh Caves frescoes.

Sasbahu Temples   HINDU TEMPLE
The Mayan-like Sasbahu (Mother-in-Law and Daughter-in-Law Temples), date from the 9th to 11th centuries. Mother-in-Law,

dedicated to Vishnu, has four gigantic pillars supporting its heavy roof, layered with carvings. The smaller Daughter-in-Law, dedicated to Shiva, is also stacked with sculptures.

Teli ka Mandir   HINDU TEMPLE
Used as a drinks factory and coffee shop by the British after the First War of Independence (Indian Uprising) of 1857, this 30m-high, 8th-century temple is the oldest monument in the compound.

The modern, gold-topped **gurdwara** (Sikh Temple) nearby is dedicated to Sikh hero Guru Har Gobind, who was imprisoned in Man Singh Palace from 1617 to 1619.

Tomb of Tansen   ISLAMIC TOMB
Tucked away in the winding lanes of the old town, and in the same compound as the resplendent tomb of Mohammed Gaus, is the smaller, simpler tomb of Tansen, a singer much admired by Akbar and held to be the father of Hindustani classical music. Chewing the leaves from the tamarind tree here supposedly enriches your voice.

ⓒ Tours

Gwalior Darshan   CITY TOUR
(☑0751-2340370; MP Tourism, Tansen Residency; adult/child ₹155/80) MP Tourism's little yellow bus, Gwalior Darshan, takes passengers on a full-day city tour, taking in all the main

MADHYA PRADESH & CHHATTISGARH GWALIOR

sights, including Gwalior Fort and Jai Vilas Palace. Enquire at the tourist office at Tansen Residency, where the tour begins. Minimum eight passengers.

 Festivals & Events

Tansen Music Festival   MUSIC
Four-day music festival in November or December attracting classical musicians and singers from all over India; free performances are usually staged at the tomb of Tansen, one of the most revered composer-musicians of Hindustani classical music.

🛏 Sleeping

Hotel DM   HOTEL $
(☏ 0751-2342083; Link Rd; s/d from ₹550/660, with AC from ₹1320; ❄) Rooms are a bit cramped so it feels slightly pricy – wi-fi would help ease that blow. However, they are slightly better than the other budget options around town, and the chirping birds at the end of the well-lit room corridor are nice. All have clean bathrooms and an old TV locked securely inside a cabinet (when was the last time you stole a hotel TV?).

SHIVPURI'S MARBLE CENOTAPHS

A possible day trip from Gwalior is to the old Scindia summer capital of Shivpuri. This rarely visited town is the site of the Scindia family's *chhatris* (cenotaphs), appropriately grand memorials to maharajas and maharanis gone by.

Two kilometres' walk from the bus stand (autorickshaw ₹30), and set in formal gardens, the **chhatris** (admission ₹40, camera/video ₹10/40; ⊙ 8am-noon & 3-8pm) are magnificent walk-in marble structures with Mughal-style pavilions and *sikharas* (Hindu temple spires) facing each other across a pool with a criss-cross of walkways. The *chhatri* to Madhorao Scindia, built between 1926 and 1932, is exquisitely inlaid with intricate pietra dura (marble inlay work).

Buses leave regularly from the Shivpuri bus stand for Gwalior (₹110, 2½ hours) and Jhansi (₹95, three hours), meaning you don't have to backtrack.

Hotel India   HOTEL $
(☏ 0751-2341983; Station Rd; s/d ₹660/940, with AC ₹1410/2000; ❄) Basic rooms and facilities are on offer at this 2nd-floor hotel across from the train station, where you'll have the added advantage of room service from Indian Coffee House, which owns and operates the hotel. Perch yourself on the 2nd-floor breezeway looking out on the street below and watch India run.

Tansen Residency   HOTEL $$
(☏ 0751-4056789; www.mptourism.com; 6A Gandhi Rd; s/d incl breakfast & bed tea from ₹3040/3510; ❄ 🖥 ❄) A distinctly average midrange run by MP Tourism, which means it's better than expected for a government hotel. Rooms are modern, all with updated bathrooms. There's a bar and restaurant and the location is central.

Hotel Gwalior Regency   BUSINESS HOTEL $$
(☏ 0751-2340670; www.hotelregencygroup.com; Link Rd; s/d incl breakfast from ₹3620/4780; ❄ @ 🖥) A paint-by-numbers Indian business hotel. Standard-issue rooms are perfectly decent, though the central air-con struggles to make much of an impact. You can pay an extra ₹700 to ₹1000 for 'grande deluxe' rooms with modern furnishings (wall-mounted wide-screen TV, glass-walled shower room, free wi-fi). There's a legitimate bar with DJs each night as well.

★ Usha Kiran Palace   HERITAGE HOTEL $$$
(☏ 0751-2444000; www.tajhotels.com; Jayendraganj; r from ₹14,680; ❄ @ 🖥) Live like royalty in this grand, nearly 130-year-old building that was built as a guesthouse for the Prince of Wales (later King George V). Every room has its own unique touches, but all feature understated heritage luxury – while the villas even come with their own private pool!

There's a gorgeous main pool with separate kids' pool, the soothing Jiva Spa (massage treatments from ₹1900), the excellent Silver Saloon restaurant and the spiffing Bada Bar (beer ₹415) with its century-old, four-ton, Italian-slate snooker table.

🍴 Eating & Drinking

Indian Coffee House   SOUTH INDIAN $
(Station Rd; mains ₹45-250; ⊙ 7.30am-10.30pm) Hugely popular branch that does all the breakfast favourites – real coffee, dosas, scrambled eggs – but also has a main-course menu, including excellent thalis (₹120 to ₹220), in a separate 1st-floor family section.

TRAINS FROM GWALIOR

DESTINATION	TRAIN NO & NAME	FARE (₹)	DURATION (HR)	DEPARTURE
Agra	12617 Mangala Ldweep	170/535/735 (A)	2	8.13am
Bhopal	12920 Malwa Express	265/680/950 (A)	7	12.35am
Delhi	12625 Kerala Express	240/600/835 (A)	5	8.25am
Indore	12920 Malwa Express	385/1000/1410 (A)	12	12.35am
Jhansi	12002 Delhi-Bhopal-Shatabdi	310/645 (B)	1	9.28am

Fares: (A) sleeper/3AC/2AC, (B) chair/1AC

★**Moti Mahal Delux**   NORTH INDIAN $$
(Link Rd; mains ₹170-440; ⊙noon-11pm) The flavours pop on anything coming out of the tandoor at this stylish nonveg Delhi transplant, as they have done for nearly 100 years. The founder *invented* tandoori chicken and they work magic with Northwest frontier cuisine, especially the chicken tikka biryani and chicken tikka masala. It's next to the bus stand.

Silver Saloon   INDIAN $$$
(Usha Kiran Palace, Jayendraganj; mains ₹350-1100; ⊙7am-11pm) Mouth-watering Indian and continental dishes, as well as some Thai, Nepali and Marathi specialities, are served in the AC restaurant or the palm-shaded verandah of this exquisite heritage hotel.

HQ   BAR
(Hotel Gwalior Regency, Link Rd; minimum spend ₹500; ⊙2pm-midnight) This small but trendy bar inside the Gwalior Regency does good cocktails (₹250 to ₹380) set to choice tunes. A DJ (well, a guy with iTunes) 'spins' nightly and there are theme nights throughout the week (Bollywood, Sufi, ladies night, etc). Nice bar service.

ⓘ Information

MP Tourism (☑0751-2340370; Tansen Residency, 6A Gandhi Rd; ⊙10am-5pm Mon-Sat) The main tourist office is located at Tansen Residency. There's also a branch at the train station (☑0751-4040777; Train Station; ⊙9am-5pm Mon-Sat) – it's hard to find, but it's tucked away next to the State Bank of India ATM near the exit.

Post Office (www.indiapost.gov.in; Station Rd; ⊙9.30am-6pm Mon-Fri, 10am-3.30pm Sat) A convenient branch near the train station. The GPO is at Jayaji Chowk.

ⓘ Getting There & Away

AIR
Air India (www.airindia.in) flies daily to Delhi (from ₹4440) and Mumbai (from ₹3970). Jet Airways also flies similar routes out of Bhopal.

BUS
Services from the **bus stand** (Link Rd) include:
Agra ₹110, 3½ hours, 8pm
Jaipur AC ₹460, 10 hours, 7.20pm
Jhansi ₹110, three hours; noon, 12.25pm, 1.25pm, 3pm, 5pm and 7pm
Shivpuri ₹110, 2½ hours, frequent 6am to 10pm

TRAIN
More than 20 daily trains go to Agra's Cantonment station and to Jhansi for Orchha or Khajuraho and Delhi, while more than 15 go to Bhopal.

ⓘ Getting Around

Cycle-rickshaws, autorickshaws and taxis are plentiful. An auto to the airport, 10km northeast of the centre, will cost at least ₹200.

Orchha
☑07680 / POP 10,200

This historic village, on the banks of the boulder-strewn Betwa River, showcases a supreme display of Mughal architecture, some of which is similar to that of nearby Khajuraho (albeit without such high-quality artistry), with much grander palaces and cenotaphs dotting the pastoral landscape as well. The atmosphere in Orchha, though, is far more laid-back and hassle-free, which makes for a relaxing stay. There are great homestay options as well

Orchha

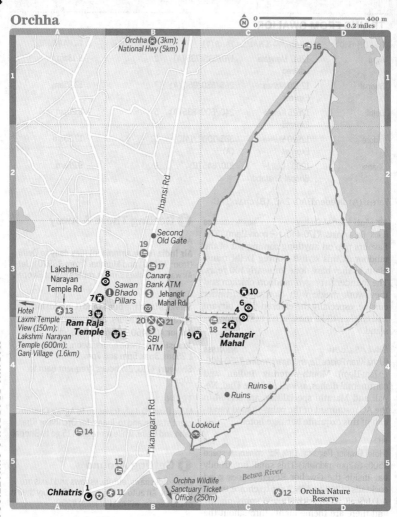

Orchha (3km);
National Hwy (5km)

Jhansi Rd

Second
Old Gate

19

17

Canara
Bank ATM

Jehangir
Mahal Rd

Lakshmi
Narayan
Temple Rd

8

Sawan
Bhado
Pillars

7

10

6

4

Hotel
Laxmi Temple
View (150m);
Lakshmi Narayan
Temple (600m);
Ganj Village (1.6km)

13

3

Ram Raja
Temple

20

21

18

2

Jehangir
Mahal

5

SBI
ATM

9

Tikamgarh Rd

Ruins

Ruins

Lookout

14

Betwa River

15

Chhatris

1

11

Orchha Wildlife
Sanctuary Ticket
Office (250m)

12

Orchha Nature
Reserve

MADHYA PRADESH & CHHATTISGARH ORCHHA

as opportunities to enjoy the surrounding countryside, with walking, cycling and rafting all on the agenda.

History

Orchha was the capital of the Bundela rajas from the 16th century to 1783, when they decamped to nearby Tikamgarh. Bir Singh Deo ruled from Orchha between 1605 and 1627, and built Jhansi Fort. A favourite of Mughal prince Salim, Bir Singh feuded with Salim's father, Emperor Akbar, who all but ruined his kingdom.

◉ Sights

The combined ticket (Indian/foreigner ₹10/250, camera/video ₹25/100) for Orchha's sites covers seven monuments – Jehangir Mahal, Raj Mahal, Raj Praveen Mahal, the camel stables, the *chhatris*, Chaturbhuj Temple and Lakshmi Narayan Temple – and is only for sale at the ticket office (⊙8am–5pm) at Raj Mahal. You can walk around the palace grounds for free.

Palaces

Crossing the granite bridge from the village centre over the often dry water channel

Orchha

◎ Top Sights
1	Chhatris	A5
2	Jehangir Mahal	C4
3	Ram Raja Temple	A3

◎ Sights
4	Camel Stables	C3
5	Chaturbhuj Temple	B4
6	Khana Hammam	C3
7	Palki Mahal	A3
8	Phool Bagh	B3
9	Raj Mahal	B4
10	Raj Praveen Mahal	C3

◎ Activities, Courses & Tours
	Kerala Ayurvedic Center	(see 14)
11	Orchha Resort	B5
12	Orchha Wildlife Sanctuary	C5
13	Raju Bikes	A3

◎ Sleeping
14	Amar Mahal	A5
15	Betwa Retreat	B5
16	Bundelkhand Riverside	D1
17	Fort View Guest House	B3
18	Hotel Sheesh Mahal	C4
19	Monarch Rama	B3

◎ Eating
20	Betwa Tarang	B4
	Jharokha Restaurant	(see 18)
21	RamRaja Restaurant	B4

◎ Drinking & Nightlife
	Bhola Restaurant	(see 20)

◎ Information
	MP Tourism	(see 18)
	MP Tourism	(see 15)
	Ticket Office	(see 9)

brings you to a fortified complex dominated by two wonderfully imposing 17th-century palaces – Jehangir Mahal and Raj Mahal. If you look closely at the top of some buildings, you can still see some of the few remaining turquoise-coloured tiles that once decorated the palaces here.

Jehangir Mahal (⊙dawn-dusk), an assault course of steep staircases and precipitous walkways, represents a zenith of medieval Islamic architecture. Behind the palace, sturdy **camel stables** (⊙dawn-dusk) overlook a green landscape dotted with monuments.

In the nearby **Raj Mahal** (⊙dawn-dusk), the caretaker will open the painted rooms where Rama, Krishna and Orchha royalty wrestle, hunt, fight and dance across the walls and ceilings. A **sound-and-light show** (Raj Mahal; Indian/foreigner ₹75/250; ⊙in English 7.30pm Mar-Oct, 6.30pm Nov-Feb, in Hindi 8.45pm Mar-Oct, 7.45pm Nov-Feb) that's more sound than light takes place here each evening. Those interested in Orchha's history will be the most enthusiastic about this tall tale that dramatically sets Raj Mahal alight under the stars. The story has it all – galloping horses, lion attacks, war, infidelity, attempted suicide and murder – but it still struggles to hold the attention of all but the most serious of historians.

Downhill from the palace compound are the smaller **Raj Praveen Mahal** (⊙9am-5pm), a pavilion and formal Mughal garden, and **Khana Hammam** (⊙dawn-dusk), with some fine vaulted ceilings.

On the other side of the village, **Palki Mahal** (⊙9am-6pm) was the palace of Dinman Hardol (the son of Bir Singh Deo), who committed suicide to 'prove his innocence' over an affair with his brother's wife. His memorial is in the adjacent **Phool Bagh** (⊙9am-6pm), a traditional *charbagh* (formal Persian garden, divided into quarters). Prince Hardol is venerated as a hero in Bundelkhand culture. Women sing songs about him, tie threads onto the *jali* (carved marble lattice screen) of his memorial and walk around it five times, clockwise, to make wishes they hope he'll grant.

Chhatris
Cenotaphs to Orchha's rulers, including **Bir Singh Deo** (⊙9am-5.30pm), the immense and serene *chhatris* rise beside the river about a kilometre south of the village. They're best seen at dusk, when the birds reel above the children splashing at the river ghats and cinematic sunsets drop across the Betwa River.

Temples
Orchha's impressive 16th-century temples still receive thousands of Hindu pilgrims.

★ Ram Raja Temple HINDU TEMPLE
(⊙9am-1pm & 7-11pm Oct-Mar, 8am-1pm & 8-11pm Apr-Sept) At the centre of a lively square is the pink- and gold-domed Ram Raja Temple, the only temple where Rama is worshiped as a king. Built as a palace for Madhukar Shah's wife, it became a temple when

MADHYA PRADESH & CHHATTISGARH ORCHHA

an image of Rama, temporarily installed by the rani, proved impossible to move. In addition to shoe removal, you must also remove any leather belts to enter, and photography is prohibited.

Chaturbhuj Temple
HINDU TEMPLE

(☉9am-5pm) Ram Raja is overlooked by the spectacular towers of Chaturbhuj Temple, an immensely solid building on a cruciform plan. Buy a cheap torch from the bazaar and climb the internal stairs to the roof where, from among the mossy spires and domes, you get the best view in town.

Lakshmi Narayan Temple
HINDU TEMPLE

(☉9am-5pm) Lakshmi Narayan Temple, on the road out to Ganj village, has fine rooftop views and well-preserved murals on the ceilings of its domed towers.

🏃 Activities

Several hotels open their pools to nonguests for a fee; otherwise, just cool off in the Betwa – it's one of India's cleanest rivers.

River-rafting trips (raft per 1½ hours ₹1200) start from the boat club, but tickets must be bought through MP Tourism at Hotel Sheesh Mahal or Betwa Retreat. Rafts take one to six people.

Orchha Wildlife Sanctuary
WALKING, CYCLING

(Indian/foreigner ₹15/150; ☉7am-6pm) A 44-sq-km island surrounded by the Betwa and Jamni Rivers. You need a ticket to enter the reserve (the ticket office is 250m on the right after the bridge), then you are free to explore. The nature trail is well marked and the roads are signposted, making this a nice place to cycle. Wildlife that you're likely to see on the trail includes monkeys, deer, monitor lizards and peacocks.

Kerala Ayurvedic Center
AYURVEDA

(☏9981894615; Amar Mahal Hotel; treatments ₹1500-2000; ☉8.30am-7.30pm) This small spa at Amar Mahal hotel offers a good range of ayurvedic therapies as well as pressure-point massages and herbal treatments.

Raju Bikes
BICYCLE RENTAL

(Lakshmi Narayan Temple Rd; per hr/day ₹10/50; ☉6am-10pm) Hires out rickety bicycles at unbeatable prices.

🛏 Sleeping

Hotel Laxmi Temple View
HOTEL $

(hotelorchhalaxmitempleview@gmail.com; Lakshmi Narayan Temple Rd; s/d ₹600/800, with AC ₹1200/1400; ❈☎) If you don't mind being a little on the outskirts of the action, this 10-room guesthouse on the road to Laxmi

VILLAGE IMMERSION HOMESTAYS IN GANJ

Thanks to **Friends of Orchha** (☏9993385405; www.orchha.org; s/d from ₹600/800, meals ₹50-220; ☎), a nonprofit organisation run by Dutchman Louk Vreeswijk and his Indian wife, Asha D'Souza, travellers have the opportunity to stay with local people in the village of Ganj.

This is a wonderful chance to experience Indian village life, so don't expect luxury, but the rooms – spread close by one another around the village – are better and more charming than a lot of budget hotels. The eight rooms offer insulated walls and tiled roofs and are equipped with fans and mosquito nets. Facilities vary but most have running water and sit-down flush toilets, and others have dry-composting squat toilets or a squat toilet linked to a bio-gas digester.

Friends of Orchha helped provide loans for some renovations, including installing ecofriendly dry toilets in the yards of each homestay house, but you will still be staying in mud huts and eating simple meals that your host family eats every day (veg and nonveg available). The interaction with villagers and immersion into village life is priceless (so stay off the wi-fi, which is ₹100 per day) and you can hop on one of their bikes (₹50 per day) when you need to explore Orchha.

Staying for a single night is discouraged for logistical reasons. If you really want to stay one night only, you can, but room rates will be slightly higher. In any case, the slow pace of life in Ganj is something that should be savoured.

Friends of Orchha also runs an after-school youth club for village children. Options to volunteer and donate are available. The Friends of Orchha office is in Ganj Village itself, on the left-hand side of the main road as you are coming from Orchha. It's about 1.5km from the main drag.

Narayan Temple offers the best budget rooms in town. It's fairly new, so everything is modern and shiny – spacious, freshly tiled bathrooms, flat-screen TVs – and small touches like painted crown moldings throughout give it a leg-up character-wise.

True to its name, the rooftop affords memorable views of the temple.

Monarch Rama   HOTEL $
(☑07680-252015; Jhansi Rd; s/d ₹400/500, with AC ₹900/1250; ❋@🖧) Rave traveller reviews about value here are not unfounded. The formula? It's not rocket science: the basic rooms on offer at this Main Rd cheapie are cleaner and more affordable than the competition and the staff are more friendly and accommodating, too. Even the soap provided is better quality than usual.

Fort View Guest House   HOTEL $
(☑07680-252701; fortvieworchha@rediffmail.com; Jhansi Rd; r ₹500, with AC incl breakfast ₹1500-2000; ❋🖧) This dilapidated budget hotel isn't wonderful, but it's worth considering if you can snag rooms 108, 111 or 112, which all have dramatic views to the river and Janhangir Mandir and Raja Mahal beyond. Otherwise, the juxtaposition is palpable: musty, well-worn rooms surround a cute courtyard. Also signposted as Fort View Hotel.

★Hotel Sheesh Mahal   HERITAGE HOTEL $$
(☑07680-252624; www.mptourism.com; Jehangir Mahal; s/d ₹1930/3100, ste ₹5390-5670, all incl breakfast; ❋🖧) Literally palatial and like sleeping with history, this hotel is located in a wing of Jehangir Mahal. As you'd expect, the surrounding architecture is stunning – arches, columns, lattice windows – but the rooms themselves are gorgeous too, and each is unique, some with regal touches such as throne-like toilets.

Bundelkhand Riverside   HOTEL $$
(☑07680-252612; www.bundelkhandriverside.com; s/d incl breakfast from ₹3900/4500, cottage s/d ₹2800/3500; ❋🖾) Owned by the grandson of Orchha's last king, Vir Singh, this hotel feels authentically heritage, although the main building is only 15 years old. Antique-style furniture abounds and some of the maharaja's personal art collection is displayed in the corridors. Exquisite rooms overlook either the river or the graceful gardens, which contain some 16th-century monuments as well as a small swimming pool (nonguests ₹250).

Cheaper cabins overlook the river but lack air-con. One of Orchha's best restaurants, Turquoise Diner, is here as well.

Betwa Retreat   HOTEL $$
(☑07680-252618; www.mptourism.com; tents/cottages ₹3040/3510, ste ₹5040; ❋🖧🖾) Set among shady gardens, this MP Tourism property, overlooking the river and views of the *chhatris,* makes an excellent family choice. The well-equipped Swiss-made safari-style tents, with iron bed-frames, TVs and minibars, are the way to go unless you can spring for the heritage suite, built within a 17th-century changing room surrounded by a large, beautifully manicured lawn.

There's a restaurant, a bar and an outdoor terrace, and it's only a five-minute walk from the main drag.

Amar Mahal   HOTEL $$$
(☑07680-252102; www.amarmahal.com; s/d from ₹4900/6100, ste ₹10,500; ❋@🖧🖾) Kick your feet up like a maharaja in rooms featuring lovely wood-carved four-poster beds set around a gorgeous courtyard with white pillar verandahs or the large pool. There's an ayurvedic massage and yoga centre beside the pool (which nonguests can use for ₹300). This is probably Orchha's most luxurious stay.

🍴 Eating & Drinking

Betwa Tarang   INDIAN $
(Jehangir Mahal Rd; mains ₹80-180; ⏰8am-10pm; 🖧) This place does the best pure-veg food out of any of Orchha's budget restaurants – the thalis (₹130 to ₹200) are particularly good. It also has the attraction of a rooftop terrace, where you can sit and enjoy stupendous views of Jahangir Mahal. Beers are off menu but available.

RamRaja Restaurant   INDIAN $
(Jahangir Mahal Rd; mains ₹60-320; ⏰7am-11.30pm; 🖧) No hygiene awards here, but this friendly, family-run streetside restaurant offers eggy breakfasts, tasty vegetarian fare and a decent espresso under the shade of a large tree. Can also scare up a beer.

Jharokha Restaurant   INDIAN $$
(Hotel Sheesh Mahal; mains ₹110-380; ⏰7am-10pm; 🖧) Good food, cold beer and friendly waiters belie the fact that this is in a government-run hotel. Indian, Chinese and continental dishes are on offer, but as usual the Indian (especially tandoori items) are

recommended, especially in this grand dining room where, when we visited, there was live Indian music courtesy of an Indian drag queen flanked by two musical minions (yes, we're serious!).

The restaurant gets bonus points for not being afraid to lay down the heat if you ask for Indian spicy.

Bhola Restaurant   INDIAN
(cnr Jehangir Mahal & Tikamgarh Rds; mains ₹50-100; ⊙7.30am-10pm) A great spot for people-watching and fresh juices.

ⓘ Information

MP Tourism (☑07860-252624; Betwa Retreat; ⊙7am-11pm) Books rafting trips on the river Betwa. Trips can also be booked at the MP Tourism office at Hotel Sheesh Mahal (☑07860-252624; Hotel Sheesh Mahal; ⊙7am-11pm).

Post Office (www.indiapost.gov.in; cnr Jhansi & Jehangir Mahal Rds; ⊙9am-5pm Mon-Sat)

ⓘ Getting There & Around

BUS

There are no buses between Orchha and Khajuraho. To get there you will first need to go to Jhansi; tempos (₹20) go between Orchha and the Jhansi bus stand all day or a private autorickshaw costs ₹200. From here, catch a bus to Chhatarpur (₹130, three hours, hourly 5am to 10pm), where you can switch for Khajuraho (₹50, 1½ hours). Alternatively, taxis to Khajuraho cost ₹2300. Coming from Khajuraho, you can ask the bus driver to drop you off at the Orchha turn-off on the National Hwy, where you should be able to wave down a vehicle to take you to Orchha.

TRAIN

You can take a slow passenger train (number 51821) to Khajuraho from Orchha's tiny train station, which is on the Jhansi Rd, about 3km from the village centre. The train leaves daily at 7.25am and takes five hours (if it's on time). It has 2nd-class seats only so you can't reserve tickets. Just turn up at the station and buy a 'general' ticket (₹40). The return train leaves Khajuraho at 12.30pm.

Khajuraho

☑07686 / POP 23,200

The erotic carvings that swathe Khajuraho's three groups of Unesco World Heritage Site–listed temples are among the finest temple art in the world. The Western Group of temples, in particular, contains some stunning sculptures. See our special colour illustration (p640) for more details.

Many travellers complain about the tiring persistence of touts here, and the village is fully on the tour bus map. Their complaints are well founded, but its not so bad that you should contemplate missing out on these beautiful temples.

History

Legend has it that Khajuraho was founded by Chardravarman, the son of the moon god Chandra, who descended and saw a beautiful maiden as she bathed in a stream. Historians tell us that most of the 85 original temples (of which 25 remain) were built from AD 950 to 1050 during the Chandela dynasty, and they remained active long after the Chandelas moved their capital to Mahoba.

Khajuraho's isolation may well have helped preserve it from the desecration Muslim invaders inflicted on 'idolatrous' temples elsewhere, but perhaps for the same reason the area was slowly abandoned and eventually fell into ruin, letting the jungle take over. The wider world remained largely ignorant until British officer TS Burt was apparently guided to the ruins by his palanquin bearers in 1838.

⊙ Sights

Temples

The temples are superb examples of Indo-Aryan architecture, but it's their liberally embellished carvings that have made Khajuraho famous. Around the outsides of the temples are bands of exceedingly artistic stonework showing a storyboard of life a millennium ago – gods, goddesses, warriors, musicians, and real and mythological animals.

Two elements appear repeatedly – women and sex. Sensuous, posturing *surasundaris* (heavenly nymphs), *apsaras* (dancing *surasundaris*) and *nayikas* (mortal *surasundaris*) have been carved with a half-twist and slight sideways lean that make the playful figures dance and swirl out from the temple. The *mithuna* (pairs, threesomes etc of men and women depicted in erotic poses) display the great skill of the sculptors and the dexterity of the Chandelas.

Western Group – Inside the Fenced Enclosure

Khajuraho's most striking, best-preserved temples are those within the fenced-off section of the Western Group (Indian/foreigner ₹10/250, video ₹25; ⊙dawn-dusk) and are the only temples you need to pay to see. An

Archaeological Survey of India (ASI) guidebook to Khajuraho (₹60) and a 1½-hour audio guide (₹100) are available at the ticket office. If you'd like a guide, official government prices are ₹900 for a half day and ₹1140 for a full day for up to five people plus a ₹360 to ₹480 language allowance.

A nightly **sound-and-light show** (Indian/foreigner ₹200/500, child ₹100/250; ☺ in English 6.30pm Oct-Mar, 7.30pm Apr-Sep, in Hindi 7.40pm Oct-Mar, 8.40pm Apr-Sep) sees technicolour floodlights sweep across the temples of the Western Group as Indian classical music soundtracks a potted history of Khajuraho, narrated by the 'master sculptor'. Photography is prohibited.

★Lakshmana Temple HINDU TEMPLE

The large Lakshmana Temple took 20 years to build and was completed in about AD 954 during the reign of Dhanga, according to an inscribed slab in the *mandapa* (pillared pavilion in front of a temple). It's arguably the best preserved of all the Khajuraho temples.

You'll see carvings of battalions of soldiers here – the Chandelas were generally at war when they weren't inventing new sexual positions. On the south side is a highly gymnastic orgy, including one gentleman proving that a horse can be a man's best friend, while a shocked figure peeks out from behind her hands. More sensuous figures intertwine between the elephants in the frieze ringing the basement, while some superb carvings can be found around the *garbhagriha* (inner sanctum). Lakshmana is dedicated to Vishnu, although it's similar in design to the Shiva temples Vishvanath and Kandariya-Mahadev.

Varaha, dedicated to Vishnu's boar incarnation, and the locked **Lakshmi** are two small shrines facing the large Lakshmana Temple. Inside Varaha is a wonderful, 1.5m-high sandstone boar, dating from AD 900 and meticulously carved with a pantheon of gods.

★Kandariya-Mahadev HINDU TEMPLE

The 30.5m-long Kandariya-Mahadev, built between 1025 and 1050, is the largest temple and represents the high point of Chandelan architecture. It also has the most representations of female beauty and sexual acrobatics. There are 872 statues, most nearly 1m high – taller than those at the other temples. One frequently photographed sculpture illustrates the feasibility of the handstand position.

The 31m-high *sikhara* here is, like linga, a phallic Shiva symbol, worshipped by Hindus

hoping to seek deliverance from the cycle of reincarnation. It's decorated with 84 subsidiary spires, which make up a mountain-like rooftop scene reminiscent of the Himalayan abode of the gods.

Mahadeva HINDU TEMPLE

Mahadeva, a small ruined temple on the same platform as Kandariya-Mahadev and Devi Jagadamba, is dedicated to Shiva, who is carved on the lintel of its doorway. It houses one of Khajuraho's finest sculptures – a *sardula* (mythical beast – part lion, part other animal – possibly human) caressing a 1m-high woman.

Devi Jagadamba HINDU TEMPLE

Devi Jagadamba was originally dedicated to Vishnu, but later to Parvati and then Kali. The carvings include *sardulas* accompanied by Vishnu, *surasundaris,* and *mithunas* frolicking in the third uppermost band. Its three-part design is simpler than Kandariya-Mahadev and Chitragupta. It has more in common with Chitragupta, but is less embellished with carvings so is thought to be a little older.

Chitragupta HINDU TEMPLE

North of Devi Jagadamba, Chitragupta (1000–25) is unique in Khajuraho – and rare among North Indian temples – in being dedicated to the sun god Surya. While its condition is not as good as the other temples, it has some fine carvings of *apsaras* and *surasundaris*, elephant fights and hunting scenes, *mithuna* and a procession of stone-carriers. In the inner sanctum, Surya drives his seven-horse chariot, while in the central niche on the south facade is an 11-headed statue of Vishnu, representing the god and 10 of his 22 incarnations.

Parvati Temple HINDU TEMPLE

Continuing around the enclosure from Chitragupta, the closed-up Parvati Temple is on your right, a small temple originally dedicated to Vishnu and now with an image of Gauri riding a *godha* (iguana).

Vishvanath Temple HINDU TEMPLE

Believed to have been built in 1002, the Vishvanath Temple is reached by steps on the northern and southern sides. Elephants flank the southern steps. Vishvanath anticipates Kandariya-Mahadev, with which it shares *saptamattrikas* (seven mothers) flanked by Ganesh and Virabhandra, and is

Khajuraho

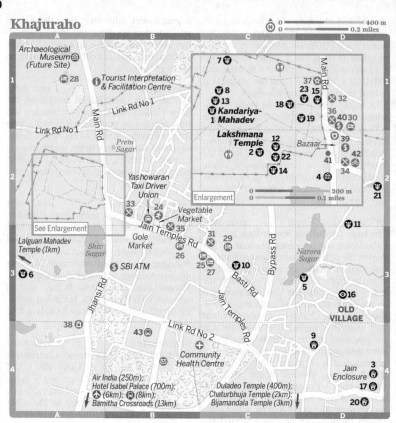

N
0 ————— 400 m
0 ————— 0.2 miles

Enlargement
0 ————— 200 m
0 ————— 0.1 miles

See Enlargement

MADHYA PRADESH & CHHATTISGARH KHAJURAHO

another superlative example of Chandelan architecture. Its sculptures include sensuous *surasundari* writing letters, cuddling babies and playing music while languishing more provocatively than at other temples.

At the other end of the platform, a 2.2m-long statue of Nandi, Shiva's bull vehicle, faces the temple. The basement of the 12-pillared shrine is decorated with an elephant frieze that recalls similar work on Lakshmana's facade.

Pratapeswar   HINDU TEMPLE
Near Vishvanath Temple, the white temple Pratapeswar is a much more recent bricksand-mortar structure built around 200 years ago.

Western Group –
Outside the Fenced Enclosure

Matangesvara   HINDU TEMPLE
Skirting the southern boundary of the fenced enclosure, Matangesvara is the only temple in the Western Group still in everyday use. It may be the plainest temple here (suggesting an early construction), but inside it sports a polished 2.5m-high lingam (phallic image of Shiva). From its platform you can peer into an open-air storage facility scattered with temple finds, but it's not open to the public.

Chausath Yogini   HINDU TEMPLE
The ruins of Chausath Yogini, beyond Shiv Sagar, date to the late 9th century and are probably the oldest at Khajuraho. Constructed entirely of granite, it's the only temple not aligned east to west. The temple's name means 64 – it once had 64 cells for the *yoginis* (female attendants) of Kali, while the 65th sheltered the goddess herself. It's reputedly India's oldest *yogini* temple.

Lalguan Mahadev Temple   HINDU TEMPLE
A further 600m west from Chausath Yogini, down a track and across a couple

Khajuraho

of fields (just ask the locals), is the sandstone-and-granite Lalguan Mahadev Temple (AD 900), a small ruined shrine to Shiva.

Eastern Group – Old Village Temples

The Eastern Group includes three Hindu temples scattered around the old village and four Jain temples further south, three of which are in a walled enclosure.

Hanuman Temple   HINDU TEMPLE

(Basti Rd) The Hanuman Temple contains a 2.5m-tall statue of the Hindu monkey god. It's little more than a bright orange shrine, but the interest is in the pedestal inscription dating to AD 922, the oldest dateable inscription in Khajuraho.

Brahma Temple   HINDU TEMPLE

The granite Brahma Temple, with its sandstone *sikhara* overlooking Narora Sagar, is one of the oldest in Khajuraho, dating from about AD 900. The four-faced lingam in the sanctum led to it being incorrectly named, but the image of Vishnu above the sanctum doorway reveals its original dedication to Vishnu.

Javari Temple   HINDU TEMPLE

Resembling Chaturbhuja Temple in the southern group, Javari Temple (1075–1100) stands just north of the old village. It's dedicated to Vishnu and is a good example of small-scale Khajuraho architecture for its crocodile-covered entrance and slender *sikhara*.

Vamana Temple   HINDU TEMPLE

Vamana Temple (1050–75), 200m further north of Javari Temple, is dedicated to the dwarf incarnation of Vishnu. It has quirky touches such as elephants protruding from the walls, but its *sikhara* is devoid of subsidiary spires and there are few erotic scenes. Its roofed *mahamandapa* (main hall) is an anomaly in Khajuraho but typical among medieval west Indian temples.

(Continued on page 644)

MADHYA PRADESH & CHHATTISGARH KHAJURAHO

Khajuraho Temples

WESTERN GROUP

The sheer volume of artwork at Khajuraho's best-preserved temples can be overwhelming. Initiate yourself with this introductory tour, which highlights some of those easy-to-miss details.

First, admire the **sandstone boar** ❶ in the Varaha shrine before heading towards **Lakshmana Temple** ❷ to study the south side of the temple's base, which has some of the raunchiest artwork in Khajuraho: first up, a nine-person orgy; further along, a guy getting very friendly with a horse. Up on the temple platform see a superb dancing Ganesh carved into a niche (south side), before walking to the west side for graceful surasundaris (nymphs): one removing a thorn from her foot; another draped in a wet sari; a third admiring herself in a mirror.

Next is Khajuraho's largest temple, **Kandariya-Mahadev** ❸. Carvings to look for here include the famous handstand position (south side), but the most impressive thing about this temple is the scale of it, particularly its soaring rooftops.

Mahadeva ❹ and **Devi Jagadamba** ❺ share the same stone plinth as Kandariya-Mahadev, as do four beautifully carved sardula (part-lion, part-human mythical beasts), each caressing a stone lion – one is at the entrance to Mahadeva; the other three stand alone on the plinth.

Walk north from here to **Chitragupta** ❻, with beautiful carvings hidden on the west side, as well as elephant friezes around the temple's base (north side). The interior here is particularly impressive.

Continue east to **Vishvanath Temple** ❼ for more fabulous carvings before admiring the impressive statue of Vishnu's bull in the **Nandi shrine** ❽ opposite.

DANIEL MCROHAN ©

Handstand Position
Perhaps Khajuraho's most famous carving, this flexible flirtation is above you as you stand on the south side of the awesome Kandariya-Mahadev.

Sikharas
Despite its many fine statues, perhaps the most impressive thing about Kandariya-Mahadev is its soaring sikharas (temple rooftops), said to represent the Himalayan abode of the gods.

NORTH →

Sardula Statue
There are four lion-stroking sardula (part-lion, part-human mythical beasts) on this huge stone plinth, but this one, guarding the entrance to Mahadeva, is our favourite.

Kama Sutra Carvings
Although commonly referred to as Kama Sutra carvings, Khajuraho's erotic artwork does not properly illustrate Vatsyayana's famous sutra. Debate continues as to its significance: to appease evil spirits or imply rulers here were virile, thus powerful? Interestingly, the erotic carvings are never located close to the temple deity.

DANIEL MCROHAN ©

LISTEN UP

The audio guide provides a detailed insight into the stories behind the temples and their carvings.

6 Chitragupta Temple

Toilets

7 Vishvanath Temple

Parvati Temple

JUST THE TICKET

For an extra-close look at Khajuraho artwork, use your ticket for same-day entrance to the small Archaeological Museum nearby.

8 Nandi Shrine

Lakshmana Temple **2**

Pratapeswar Temple

Lakshmi Shrine

Matangesvara Temple

1 Varaha Shrine

Entrance

Nandi Statue
This massive 2.2m-long statue of Nandi, the bull-vehicle of Shiva, is enshrined in a pavilion facing Vishvanath Temple.

Surasundaris
Beautifully graceful depictions of nymphs are found on a number of Khajuraho temples. And despite all the depictions of gymnastic orgies, the wonderfully seductive *surasundari* draped in a wet sari is arguably the most erotic of all.

Vishnu's Boar
This 9th-century statue of Varaha, the boar incarnation of Vishnu, is carved all over with figures of Bramanical gods and goddesses. Under Varaha's foot notice the serpent Seshanaga in a devotional posture, and the feet of a goddess, now missing.

(Continued from page 641)

Ghantai Temple
JAIN TEMPLE

Located between the old village and the Jain Enclosure, the small Ghantai Temple, also Jain, is named after the *ghanta* (chain and bell) decorations on its pillars. It was once similar to nearby Parsvanath, but only its pillared shell remains, and it's normally locked.

Eastern Group – Jain Enclosure

Parsvanath Temple
JAIN TEMPLE

While not competing in size and erotica with the western-enclosure temples, Parsvanath Temple, the largest of the Jain temples in the walled enclosure, is notable for the exceptional precision of its construction as well as for its sculptural beauty. Some of the best preserved of Khajuraho's most famous images can be seen here, including the woman removing a thorn from her foot and another applying eye make-up, both on the southern side.

Although the temple was originally dedicated to Adinath, a jet-black image of Parsvanath was substituted about a century ago. Both an inscription on the *mahamandapa* doorway and its similarities with the slightly simpler Lakshmana Temple date it to AD 950–70.

Adinath
JAIN TEMPLE

Adjacent to Parsvanath Temple, the smaller Adinath has been partially restored over the centuries. With fine carvings on its three bands of sculptures, it's similar to Khajuraho's Hindu temples, particularly Vamana. Only the striking black image in the inner sanctum triggers a Jain reminder.

Shanti Nath
JAIN TEMPLE

Shanti Nath, built about a century ago, houses components from older temples, including a 4.5m-high Adinath statue with a plastered-over inscription on the pedestal dating to about 1027.

Southern Group

Duladeo Temple
HINDU TEMPLE

A dirt track runs to the isolated Duladeo Temple, about 1km south of the Jain enclosure. This is the youngest temple, dating to 1100–1150. Its relatively wooden, repetitious sculptures, such as those of Shiva, suggest that Khajuraho's temple builders had passed their artistic peak by this point, although they had certainly lost none of their zeal for eroticism.

Chaturbhuja Temple
HINDU TEMPLE

Anticipating Duladeo and its flaws, the ruined Chaturbhuja Temple (c 1100) has a fine 2.7m-high, four-armed statue of Vishnu in the sanctum. It is Khajuraho's only developed temple without erotic sculptures.

Bijamandala Temple
HINDU TEMPLE

Just before Chaturbhuja there's a signed track leading to Bijamandala Temple. This is the excavated mound of an 11th-century temple, dedicated to Shiva (judging by the white marble lingam at the apex of the mound). Although there are some exquisitely carved figures, unfinished carvings were also excavated, suggesting that what would have been Khajuraho's largest temple was abandoned as resources flagged.

Other Sights

Raneh Falls
WATERFALL

The 30m-high Raneh Falls is a worthwhile nature excursion, 18km from Khajuraho, if it has just rained.

Archaeological Museum
MUSEUM

(Main Rd; admission free with same-day Western Group ticket; ☉9am-5pm Sat-Thu) **FREE** The Archaeological Museum, announced by a wonderful 11th-century statue of Ganesh dancing sensuously for an elephant-headed deity, has a small but well-presented collection of sculptures from around Khajuraho. There are plans to move this museum to a larger, seemingly ready-to-go site north of the Western Group, but they've been telling us that since 2006.

Old Village
AREA

If you can put up with the persistent requests from local children for pens and money, then a stroll or cycle around the dusty narrow streets of the old village can be very rewarding. Homes here are whitewashed or painted in colourful pastels and the lanes are dotted with small shrines, old wells and water pumps.

🏃 Activities

Many budget hotels offer cheap ayurvedic massage treatments of varying levels of authenticity. Top-end hotels offer more luxurious versions.

Ayur Arogyam
MASSAGE

(☎07686-272572; www.ayurarogyam.in; Jain Temples Rd; treatments ₹1170-2700) For the real deal, head to Ayur Arogyam, which, given that many ayurvedic treatments are more oil baptism than drool-inducing relaxation coma, is supremely soothing.

The lovely Keralan couple who run this small place from their home also have two simple double rooms to rent (₹200).

✷ Festivals & Events

Festival of Dance   DANCE
Come February/March, the Western Group of temples becomes the stage for the week-long Festival of Dance.

🛏 Sleeping

Hefty discounts (20% to 50%) are available out of season (April to September), although it's worth bargaining at any time of year. Hotel staff are more than happy to organise tours and travel.

Hotel Harmony   HOTEL $
(☑ 07686-274135; www.hotelharmonyonline. com; Jain Temples Rd; s/d ₹800/1000, with AC ₹1200/1500; ❈ 🛜) Cosy, well-equipped rooms off marble corridors are tastefully decorated and come with mostly effective mosquito screens and cable TV. Great food is available at the Zorba the Buddha restaurant and you can eat under the stars on the rooftop. Wi-fi is ₹50 per day.

Hotel Surya   HOTEL $
(☑ 07686-274144; www.hotelsuryakhajuraho.com; Jain Temples Rd; r ₹400-1000, with AC ₹800-1600; ❈ @ 🛜) There's quite a range of rooms in this sprawling, well-run hotel with whitewashed corridors, marble staircases and a lovely courtyard garden out the back. Some rooms have TV. Some have balconies. There's yoga, massage, cycling tours and cooking classes available. Wi-fi costs ₹50 per day.

Hotel Zen   HOTEL $
(☑ 07686-274228; www.hotlzenkhajuraho.co.in; Jain Temples Rd; d/tr ₹500/600, r with AC ₹1000-1300, all incl breakfast; ❈ @ 🛜) A popular backpacker hang-out. Upstairs rooms are brightest and overlook a series of courtyards with lotus ponds, winter bonfires, candles flickering at night and a decent restaurant. Rooms have cable TV.

Osaka Guesthouse   GUESTHOUSE $
(☑ 07686-272839; imrankhankhj@yahoo.co.in; off Basti Rd; r ₹500-600, with AC ₹1000-1200; ❈ 🛜) Spacious rooms here are pretty basic but have a homey feel to them. The owner and family are very welcoming, and there are some nice temple views from the rooftop.

It's set back off the main drag so is quieter than elsewhere.

Yogi Lodge   GUESTHOUSE $
(☑ 07686-274158; yogi_sharm@yahoo.com; off Main Rd; s ₹150, d ₹250-300, r with AC ₹600; ❈ @ 🛜) Rooms at this backpacker-favorite cheapie are simple, but the small courtyards, narrow corridors and the cute stone tables in the rooftop restaurant along with free wi-fi and yoga meditation give this place character and value. There's a lone AC room but it's not worth the extra cost.

★ Hotel Isabel Palace   HOTEL $$
(☑ 07686-274770; www.hotelisabelpalace.com; Temple Rd; r from ₹1500, with AC ₹2250-2800, all incl breakfast; ❈ 🛜) This newish hotel, tucked away off a quiet dirt road in a far more pastoral village than Khajuraho's main drag, is a star. Sparkling-clean rooms are spacious, varying according to view (garden or sunrise), all with sizeable bathrooms and comfortable furnishings (the ₹1500 non-ACs feel like stealing).

Surendra, the manager, is delightful and takes his family's hospitality business very seriously (as he does his great masala chai). You could eat off the floor in the stylish restaurant, which offers sunset views, as does the extraordinary rooftop terrace, the best by far in town and candlelit for romantic dinners for guests at night.

Lalit Temple View   HOTEL $$$
(☑ 07686-272111; www.thelalit.com; Main Rd; r from ₹8570, with temple view ₹14,080; ❈ @ 🛜 ☒) Sweeps aside all other five-star pretenders with supreme luxury, impeccable service and high prices. Rooms are immaculate with large-screen TVs, wood-carved furniture and tasteful artwork. If you're not fussed about temple views, it has a block of 'budget' rooms hidden away from the main grounds – all the same amenities for half the price.

🍴 Eating

The pleasant main drag is a compact dirt-track road lined with rooftop restaurants.

Madras Coffee House   SOUTH INDIAN $
(cnr Main & Jain Temples Rds; mains ₹50-200; ⏲8.30am-9.30pm) Three generations of great, honest South Indian fare – dosa, *idli* (spongy round fermented rice cakes), *uttapam* (thick savoury rice pancakes), thali – as well as coffee (Madras style with chicory) and chai, served in a narrow cafe. Ideal for

breakfast. The unique house speciality is the tasty egg, cheese and veg dosa (₹200).

Lassi Corner
INDIAN $

(Jain Temples Rd; meals ₹15-60, lassis ₹15-45; ☺9am-9.30pm) This tarpaulin-covered bamboo shack is a great place for a quick chai break, lazy lassi, breakfast and simple Indian fare.

★ Raja's Café
MULTICUISINE $$

(www.rajacafe.com; Main Rd; mains ₹140-380; ☺8am-10pm; 🛜) Raja's has been on top of its game for more than 35 years, with espresso coffee, English breakfasts, wood-fired pizzas, superb Indian, Italian and Chinese dishes, and an otherwise eclectic menu full of things you might miss, depending on your passport (rosti, fish and chips, lasagna).

The location, with a temple-view terrace, is great, as is the restaurant design, with a delightful courtyard shaded by a 170-year-old neem tree. But it's the food that steals the show. Wi-fi downstairs only.

Agrasen
MULTICUISINE $$

(Jain Temples Rd; thalis ₹130-380; ☺7am-10.30pm; 🛜) While perhaps not India's best – as declared in French – the thalis at this otherwise unthrilling restaurant are extremely good and do come with perhaps one of the best dhal fry in the country. The fact that it tends to fill nightly with locals, not tourists, speaks volumes. A 1st-floor terrace is lit up nicely after dark.

Mediterraneo
ITALIAN $$

(Jain Temples Rd; mains ₹200-440, pizza ₹350-460; ☺7.30am-10pm; 🛜) Far removed from its Italian roots, Mediterraneo manages acceptable Italian fare served on a lovely terrace overlooking the street. Dishes includes chicken, salads, organic wholewheat pasta and surprisingly good wood-fired pizzas. Beer and wine are also available.

Blue Sky Restaurant
MULTICUISINE $$

(Main Rd; mains ₹80-260, tree house per person ₹50; ☺7am-10.30pm) An ordinary restaurant with an extraordinary seating arrangement: a rickety wooden platform, three storeys up, leading out to the most unusual place to eat in Khajuraho – a one-table tree house with an unrivaled view of the western temples.

🛍 Shopping

Kandariya Art & Culture
HANDICRAFTS

(☑07686-274031; Jhansi Rd; ☺9am-9pm) Huge emporium where full-size replicas of some of Khajuraho's temple carvings can be bought – if you have a spare ₹10,000 to ₹1,000,000! Smaller, more affordable versions, along with textiles, wood carvings and marble inlay, can be found indoors.

Nightly one-hour folk-dancing performances (₹550) can be seen at the comfortable indoor theatre here, starting at 8pm and 9.45pm

ℹ Information

Khajuraho is very wired, even at budget hotels. Internet cafes around town tend to charge ₹40 per hour. There are several ATMs across from the lake on Jhansi Rd.

Community Health Centre (☑07686-272498; Link Rd No 2; ☺24hr) Helpful staff but with limited English. Hours for nonemergency consultations are 8am to 1pm and 5pm to 6pm.

Post Office (☺9am-5pm Mon-Sat)

State Bank of India (Main Rd; ☺10.30am-2.30pm & 3-4.30pm Mon-Sat) Changes cash and travellers cheques.

Tourist Interpretation & Facilitation Centre (☑07686-274051; khajuraho@mptourism.com; Main Rd; ☺10am-5pm Mon-Sat, closed 2nd & 3rd Sat of the month) Has leaflets on statewide tourist destinations. Also has a stand at the airport and train station.

Tourist Police (☑07686-272690; Main Rd; ☺24hr) Handy Tourist Police booth near the western temples.

ℹ Getting There & Away

AIR

Khajuraho has a new, wildly modern airport (for its surroundings) that's set to open by 2016.

Air India (www.airindia.in) Has cheaper 3.05pm flights to Delhi and Varanasi, but only on Monday, Wednesday and Saturday.

Jet Airways (www.jetairways.com) Has a daily 1.40pm flight to Delhi via Varanasi.

BUS

If the **bus reservation office** (☺8am & 4pm) is closed, the owner of the Madhur coffee stand, just opposite, is very helpful and trustworthy.

For Jhansi and Gwalior, you'll need to catch a bus to Chhatarpur (₹50, 1½ hours, hourly 7am to 5pm) and switch there. For Orchha, get a Jhansi bus in Chhatarpur, which can drop you at the junction to Orchha, from where you can wave down a shared autorickshaw (₹10) to go the rest of the way. Buses also run to Madla (for Panna National Park; ₹40, one hour, 7.30am, 8.45am, 10am, 12.30pm and 3pm).

There are two daily buses to Satna (₹150, four hours, 7.30am and 3pm), a much larger and more convenient rail hub. Coming the other way, buses depart for Khajuraho twice daily as well (₹120, four hours, 6.30am and 2.30pm).

Much more frequent buses can be caught at the Bamitha crossroads, 11km away on Hwy 75, where buses between Gwalior, Jhansi and Satna shuttle through all day. Catch a shared 4WD (₹20, 7am to 7pm) to Bamitha from the bus stand or as they drive down Jhansi Rd.

TAXI

Yashowaran Taxi Driver Union is opposite Gole Market, under a neem tree. Fares including all taxes and tolls: airport (₹300), train station (₹300), Raneh Falls (₹800), Panna National Park (in 4WD, ₹2000), Satna (₹2500), Orchha (₹3500), Chitrakut (₹3500), Bandhavgarh (₹4000), Varanasi (₹8000) and Agra (₹8000).

TRAIN

Four useful trains leave from Khajuraho train station:

Delhi (22447 Khajuraho–Nizamuddin Express) sleeper/3AC/2AC ₹365/935/1365, 11½ hours, 6.20pm daily, via Jhansi (sleeper/3AC/2AC ₹190/535/735, five hours) and Agra (sleeper/3AC/2AC ₹280/715/1000, 8½ hours)

Jhansi (19655 Kurj Udz Express) sleeper/3AC/2AC ₹160/485/690, 4½ hours, 9.10am daily, from where you can catch an autorickshaw to Orchha

Jhansi (51822, unreserved passenger train) ₹40, four hours, 12.30pm daily, stopping at the tiny Orchha train station

Varanasi (21107 Khajuraho–Varanasi Express) sleeper/3AC ₹265/715, 11 hours, 11.40pm Tuesday, Friday and Sunday

Train tickets can be bought from the **train reservation office** (07686-274416; 8am-noon & 1-4pm Mon-Sat, to 2pm Sun) at the bus stand. You must book tickets at least four hours before departure.

Coming to Khajuraho, the 21108 Varanasi–Khajuraho Express leaves Varanasi on Monday, Wednesday and Saturday at 5.45pm and arrives in Khajuraho at 5.15am. The 12448 U P Sampark Kranti leaves Delhi's Hazrat Nizamuddin station daily at 8.10pm and passes Agra (11.15pm) before reaching Mahoba (5.08am) where part of the train continues to Khajuraho (6.35am) as Slip Route 22448. If you book a seat through from Nizamuddin to Khajuraho, you'll automatically be seated in the right carriages.

From Jhansi, the 19666 Udz Kurj Exp departs at 2.35pm and arrives in Khajuraho at 7.30pm.

❶ Getting Around

Autorickshaws to the airport/train station charge ₹80/100, but if you don't have too much luggage, it's easy enough to wave down a bus or a shared 4WD (₹20) as they head along Jhansi Rd either into or out of town. b

Bicycle is a great way to get around. Mohammad at **Best Bicycles** (9893240074; Jain Temples Rd; per day ₹50-150; 8am-7pm) has been in the bike business since 1982. He rents bikes and mountain bikes in varying conditions.

Around Khajuraho

Panna National Park

Tigers are now making a comeback after being reintroduced to **Panna National Park** (07732-252135; www.pannatigerreserve.in; vehicle with up to 8 passengers Indian/foreigner ₹1250/2450, 6-person jeep hire ₹2000, guide ₹300; 16 Oct-31-Jun, closed Wed evenings) from Bandhavgarh, Pench and Kanha, and after some cubs have been born to these new settlers. At the time of research, there were an estimated 22 tigers in the park. This is also a good place to see crocodiles and, with the Ken River flowing through it, Panna is a peaceful, picturesque place to spend a day on your way to or from Khajuraho. In fact, it's easy enough to do an afternoon safari here as a day trip from Khajuraho, using public transport to get to and from Madla.

Even if you don't stay the night here, it's worth making **Jungle Camp** (07732-275275; jcmadla@mptourism.com; r incl breakfast ₹2924;) your base. It's on the edge of Madla village, 200m past the large Ken River bridge (if you're coming from Khajuraho), and right by Madla Gate, the main entrance to the park. There's a restaurant (mains ₹90 to ₹280), you can arrange jeep safaris and there's a nicely kept garden dotted with children's play areas in which the very comfortable air-conditioned tents for guests are located.

Regular buses run between Madla and Khajuraho (₹40, one hour) and between Madla and Satna (₹120, three hours), although for Satna you sometimes have to change at the nearby town of Panna.

CENTRAL MADHYA PRADESH

Bhopal

☑ 0755 / POP 1.80 MILLION

Split by a pair of lakes, Bhopal offers two starkly contrasting cityscapes. In the north is the Muslim-dominated old city, a fascinating area of mosques and crowded bazaars. Bhopal's population is 40% Muslim – one of India's highest concentration of Muslims – and the women in black *niqabs* (veils) are reminders of the female Islamic rulers who built up Bhopal in the 19th century. North of here is a reminder of a more recent, tragic history – the Union Carbide chemical plant, site of the world's worst industrial disaster.

South of the two lakes, Bhopal is more modern, with wide roads, shopping complexes and upmarket hotels and restaurants nestled comfortably in the Arera and Shamla Hills, which overlook the lakes and the old city beyond. The central district here is known as New Market.

The main train and bus stations are just off Hamidia Rd – the main budget hotel area – with the bustling *chowk* (marketplace) slightly further southeast. Hamidia Rd is accessed via the Platform 5 end of the train station. The Platform 1 end is where you'll find left luggage (you need your own padlock), MP Tourism, the post office and an ATM.

◎ Sights & Activities

It should come as no surprise that Bhopal is rife with impressive mosques, one of the main attractions of the city.

★ Tribal Museum   MUSEUM
(Shamla Hills; Indian/foreigner ₹10/100, camera ₹50; ☺ noon-8pm Tue-Sun) Step through the tribal looking glass at this extremely well-done museum dedicated to the seven tribes and subtribes of Madhya Pradesh. Opened in 2013, the artistic space was built by 1500 tribespeople over 2½ years using no materials from outside their villages. The stunning results are divided into five surreal galleries featuring hyper-examples of tribal life. There's also a very interesting museum shop.

Afterwards, compliment your visit by popping over to **Rashtriya Manav Sangrahalaya** (Museum of Man; www.igrms.com; Shamla Hills; Indian/foreigner ₹10/500, video ₹50;

☺ 10am-5pm Tue-Sun Nov-Feb, 11am-6pm Mar-Sep), a kind of tribal safari park spread out over an open-air hillside complex.

★ State Museum   MUSEUM
(Shamla Hills; Indian/foreigner ₹10/100, camera/video ₹50/200; ☺ 10.30am-5.30pm Tue-Sun) This first-class archaeological museum spread over 17 galleries includes some wonderful temple sculptures as well as 87 Jain bronzes unearthed by a surprised farmer in western Madhya Pradesh. Keep an eye out for the tiny, but remarkably animated, metal carpet seller in the Royal Art Gallery.

★ Taj-ul-Masjid   MOSQUE
(☺ closed to non-Muslims noon-3pm Fri) Bhopal's third female ruler, Shah Jahan Begum wanted to create the largest mosque in the world, so in 1877 she set about building Taj-ul-Masjid. It was still incomplete at her death in 1901, after funds had been diverted to other projects, and construction did not resume until 1971. Fortress-like terracotta walls surround three gleaming white onion domes and a pair of towering pink minarets with white domes. Try to make the dawn *azan* (Muslim call to prayer). From Hamidia Rd to Taj-ul-Masjid, an autorickshow costs ₹40.

Jama Masjid   MOSQUE
The gold spikes crowning the squat minarets of the Jama Masjid Mosque, built in 1837 by Qudsia Begum, glint serenely above the skull caps and veils swirling through the bazaar below.

Dhai Seedi Ki Masjid   MOSQUE
Bhopal's oldest and teeniest mosque inside the grounds of Hamidia Hospital.

MP Tourism Boat Club   BOATS
(☑ 0775-3295043; Lake Drive Rd; ☺ 10.30am-6.30pm) Offers motorboat rides (₹210, five minutes, minimum three people), pedal boats (₹60 per boat, 30 minutes), jet skiing (₹400 per person) and even parasailing (₹500). Children might enjoy feeding the gaggle of geese that make their home by the boat club. An autorickshaw here from New Market costs ₹80.

☞ Tours

Bhopal-On-Wheels   BUS TOUR
(☑ 0755-3295040; 3½hr tour ₹100; ☺ 11am-5pm Tue-Sun) A guided tour on a toy-train looka-like open bus, departing from Palash Residency and winding through the hills and the old city. Stops include Lakshmi Narayan

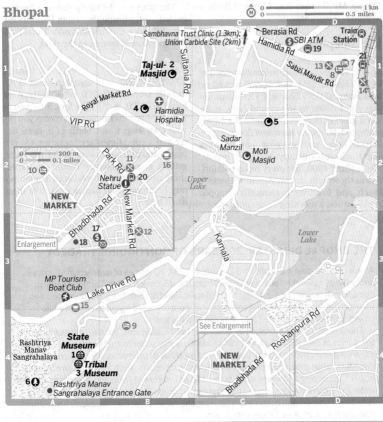

Bhopal

◉ Top Sights
1 State Museum	A4
2 Taj-ul-Masjid	B1
3 Tribal Museum	A4

◉ Sights
4 Dhai Seedi Ki Masjid	B1
5 Jama Masjid	C2
6 Rashtriya Manav Sangrahalaya	A4

◉ Activities, Courses & Tours
Bhopal-On-Wheels	(see 10)

◎ Sleeping
7 Hotel Ranjeet	D1
8 Hotel Sonali Regency	D1
9 Jehan Numa Palace Hotel	B4
10 Palash Residency	A2

⊗ Eating
11 Bapu Ki Kutia	B2
12 Indian Coffee House	B3
13 Manohar	D1
Under the Mango Tree	(see 9)
14 Zam Zam	D1

◎ Drinking & Nightlife
15 Café Coffee Day	A3
16 Café Coffee Day	B2

ⓘ Information
MP Tourism	(see 10)
17 State Bank of India	A3

ⓘ Transport
18 Air India	A3
19 Central Bus Stand	D1
Chartered Bus	(see 10)
20 Minibuses to Hamidia Rd	B2
21 Minibuses to New Market	D1

MADHYA PRADESH & CHHATTISGARH BHOPAL

Temple, MP Tourism Boat Club and Rashtriya Manav Sangrahalaya.

🛏 Sleeping

Hotel Sonali Regency
HOTEL $

(☎ 0755-2740880; www.hotelsonaliregency.com; Radha Talkies Rd; s/d from ₹650/750, with AC incl breakfast from ₹1350/1550; ❄ ☎) Excellent service, right down to the errand boys, make this a great option near Hamidia Rd. Newly renovated AC rooms have new floors, funky-shaped beds and working hot showers. Skip the lowest category; executive non-AC rooms (from ₹900) are every bit as comfortable as those with air-con. Amenities include towels and toiletries hygienically wrapped in plastic and a morning *Times of India*.

The manager definitely showers foreigners with extra hospitality. From Hamidia Rd, turn left down the lane alongside Hotel Ranjit and follow it around to the right.

Hotel Ranjeet
HOTEL $

(☎ 0755-2740500; www.ranjeethotels.com; 3 Hamidia Rd; s/d from ₹450/700, with AC incl breakfast from ₹750/1000; ❄ ☎) They look after you in Ranjeet. Even in the cheapest rooms you get your own soap, towel, bottle of mineral water and a complimentary breakfast. On our pass through, rooms were under the knife, getting a contemporary facelift, so expect shiny new floors and woodwork, contemporary bathrooms and higher rates than those listed here.

THE BHOPAL DISASTER: 30 YEARS OF CONTINUING TRAGEDY

At five minutes past midnight on 3 December 1984, 40 tonnes of deadly methyl isocyanate (MIC) gas leaked out over Bhopal from the US-owned Union Carbide chemical plant. Blown by the wind, a 40-foot wall of toxic cloud hugged the ground and coursed through the city. In the ensuing panic, people were trampled trying to escape while others were so disorientated that they ran into the gas.

There were 5295 initial fatalities according to official figures, but the continuing death toll stands at over 25,000. More than 450,000 people suffer from a catalogue of illnesses ranging from hypertension, diabetes and paralysis to premature menopause and skin disorders, while their children experience growth disorders, such as shrunken rib cages. In 2013, according to a water study by the Indian Institute of Toxicology Research, ground water in 22 communities around the abandoned Union Carbide factory was contaminated with cancer- and birth-defect-causing chemicals as well as chemicals known to damage the lungs, liver, kidneys and brain.

The leak at the plant was the result of a saga of untested technology, negligent maintenance and cost-cutting measures. Damages of US$3 billion were demanded, and in 1989 Union Carbide paid the Indian government US$470 million. Winning compensation for the victims, however, has been a tortuous process slowed by the Indian government's wrangling over who was a victim and Dow Chemical's acquisition of Union Carbide in 2001. Both buyer and seller deny ongoing liability.

A multimillion-dollar hospital was funded by the sale of confiscated shares of Union Carbide's Indian subsidiary, while charity **Sambhavna Trust Clinic** (☎ 0755-2730904; www.bhopal.org; Berasia Rd, Bafna Colony; ⊙ 8.30am-3pm), opened in 1996, treats more than 200 Union Carbide victims a day using yoga, ayurvedic treatments, conventional medicine and herbal remedies. Volunteers can work in a range of areas from water testing and medical research to gardening and internet communications; they are hugely appreciated and offered board and lodgings at the medical centre. Visitors are welcome and donations can be made.

Bafna Colony is off Berasia Rd. If walking from Hamidia Rd, turn right after about 500m and keep asking for Sambhavna.

To commemorate the 30th anniversary of the tragedy, the new and at times extremely sombre **Remember Bhopal Museum** (www.rememberbhopal.net; HIG 22, Housing Board Colony, Berasia Rd, near Triveni Heights; ⊙ 10am-5pm Tue-Sun) opened in 2014 in New Housing Board Colony near the the now-derelict Union Carbide factory site, preserving the belongings and pictures of victims as well as over 50 audio recording from survivors, doctors and forensic experts.

The restaurant here is good, there's a bar, and it's convenient to the bus and train stations.

Palash Residency
HOTEL **$$**

(☏0755-2553066; palash@mptourism.com; TT Nagar; s/d from ₹3860/4220; ✳@🛜🏊) This stately midrange MP Tourism hotel is walking distance from New Market. Breezy corridors lead to smart rooms with heavy wood furniture, wall-mounted flat-screen TVs, kettles and complimentary toiletries; bathrooms are less appealing. There's free wi-fi in the lobby, a spa, bar, three restaurants and a new pool. MP Tourism is based here.

★ Jehan Numa Palace Hotel
HERITAGE HOTEL **$$$**

(☏0755-2661100; www.hoteljehanumapalace.com; 157 Shamla Hill; patio s/d ₹5480/6700, s/d from ₹7920/9140, ste from ₹19,500, all incl breakfast; ✳@🛜🏊) This former 19th-century palace lost none of its colonial-era charm through its conversion into a top-class hotel. Arched walkways and immaculate lawns lead you to beautifully decorated rooms. The fact that you can sleep in a patio room – perfectly great – for under US$100 in a five-star hotel is ridiculous. Worth a splurge.

There's a palm-lined pool, an excellent health spa and three restaurants, two bars and a coffee shop.

✗ Eating & Drinking

★ Zam Zam
STREET FOOD **$**

(Hamidia Rd; mains ₹50-100; ⊘8am-midnight) A standing-room-only crowd swarms this fast-food hotspot day and night for some of Bhopal's best biryani, but it's the finger-lickin', outrageously good chicken tikka, grilled over hot coals before your eyes and dipped in house green-chilli yoghurt sauce, that's the true showstopper. It's so cheap, we ordered both!

★ Bapu Ki Kutia
INDIAN **$**

(Rashanpura Rd, TT Nagar; mains ₹50-160, thali ₹140-160; ⊘10am-11pm) Papa's Shack has been serving up delicious Indian veg dishes since 1964. Prepare to get cosy with the locals – it's so popular you'll often share a table. There's an English menu, but no English sign. Look for the picture of a beach hut and palm tree above the door.

Indian Coffee House
SOUTH INDIAN **$**

(New Market Rd, New Market; mains ₹50-260; ⊘7am-11pm) As always, Indian Coffee House is a top spot for breakfast, and this is one of the nicest outlets in India. Waiters in fantailed hats dish out filtered coffee plus South Indian favourites.

Manohar
INDIAN **$**

(6 Hamidia Rd; mains ₹30-150, thali ₹130-160; ⊘8am-11pm) This bright, clean, canteen-style restaurant does a brisk business in South Indian breakfasts, thalis, snacks, shakes and a load of presumably more-hygienic versions of many Indian street-food favourites. In truth, it's a bit of a madhouse and rightfully so. Has an impressive range of cakes, cookies and sweets at a side counter, one of the best in town.

★ Under the Mango Tree
INDIAN **$$$**

(Jehan Numa Palace Hotel, 157 Shamla Hill; mains ₹380-750; ⊘7.30-11pm) Jehan Numa Palace's best restaurant specialises in barbecue kebabs and tandoor. The *pankhi* chicken kebab (marinated chicken wings) is melt-off-the-bone astonishing, but drowning yourself in flavour with the sampler platter (from ₹830) is the way to go.

Good food, wine, draught beer (Woodpecker, a local swill) and cocktails all combine under a romantic white pavilion and the heavy boughs of a venerable centenarian mango tree.

Café Coffee Day
CAFE

(www.cafecoffeeday.com; Lake Drive Rd; coffee ₹60-110; ⊘10.30am-10.30pm) Quality fresh coffee. The lakeside location is vying for India's best espresso with a view. There's also a **New Market** (www.cafecoffeeday.com; 15/9B Rajbhavan Rd; coffee ₹60-110; ⊘10.30am-10.30pm) branch.

ⓘ Information

Post Office (TT Nagar, New Market; ⊘10am-8pm Mon-Sat, to 6pm Sun) Convenient postal services in New Market. Also a counter at the train station.

MP Tourism (☏0775-3295040; Palash Residency, TT Nagar; ⊘8am-10pm) Also has desks at the airport and train station.

State Bank of India (Rang Mahal Rd; ⊘10.30am-4.30pm Mon-Fri, to 1.30pm Sat) The International Division on the 1st floor changes travellers cheques and cash. Has an ATM, plus there are others at the train station and near the central bus stand.

TRAINS FROM BHOPAL

DESTINATION	TRAIN NO & NAME	FARE (₹)	DURATION (HR)	DEPARTURE
Agra	12627 Karnataka Express	330/850/1200	7	11.30pm
Delhi	12621 Tamil Nadu Express	400/1045/1485	10½	8.20pm
Gwalior	11077 Jhelum Express	235/635/905	6	9.10am
Indore	12920 Malwa Express	215/535/735	5	7.40am
Jabalpur	18233 Narmada Express	215/575/820	7	11.25pm
Mumbai (CST)	12138 Punjab Mail	445/1165/1665	14½	4.55pm
Raipur	18238 Chhattisgarh Express	365/980/1410	14½	6.45pm
Ujjain	12920 Malwa Express	170/535/745	3½	7.40am

Fares: sleeper/3AC/2AC

ⓘ Getting There & Away

AIR

Air India (🖰 0755-2770480; www.airindia.in; Bhadbhada Rd; ◷10am-5pm Mon-Sat) flies daily to Delhi and Mumbai.

BUS

There are two bus stands in Bhopal. Services from the ISBT bus stand in Habibganj, 5km east of New Market:

Jabalpur ₹300, 10 hours, four daily (5.30pm, 5.50pm, 7.30pm and 11.30pm)

Khajuraho ₹400, 10 hours, two daily (7.30pm and 8.40pm)

Pachmarhi ₹150, six hours, six daily (5.15am, 6.15am, 8.15am, 3pm, sleeper 1am and 2.30am)

Services from the **Central bus stand** (🖰 0755 4257602; Hamidia Rd) off Hamidia Rd:

Indore ₹200, five hours, frequent 6am to 10pm

Sanchi ₹40, 1½ hours, frequent 6am to 10pm

For a more comfortable ride to Indore, **Chartered Bus** (🖰 0755-4288888; www.charteredbus.in; Palish Residency) departs from Palish Residency Hotel every hour or so from 1.30am to 11.30pm (₹325, 3½ hours) and can be booked online or at its ticket counter at Palish.

TRAIN

There are nearly 20 daily trains to Gwalior, Agra and Delhi and at least five to Ujjain.

ⓘ Getting Around

Minibuses and buses (both ₹10) shuttle between New Market and Hamidia Rd all day and all evening. Catch ones to New Market at the eastern end of Hamidia Rd. Returning from New Market, they leave from the Nehru Statue. Autorickshaws cost about ₹60 for the same

journey. **My Cab** (🖰 0775-6666666; www.my-cabindia.com) has taxi services in Bhopal.

The airport is 16km northwest of central Bhopal. Expect to pay at least ₹250 for an autorickshaw and around ₹700 for a taxi.

Sanchi

 07482 / POP 7305

Rising from the plains, 46km northeast of Bhopal, is a rounded hill topped with some of India's oldest Buddhist structures.

In 262 BC, repentant of the horrors he had inflicted on Kalinga, in present-day Odisha, the Mauryan emperor Ashoka embraced Buddhism. As a penance he built the Great Stupa at Sanchi, near the birthplace of his wife. A domed edifice used to house religious relics, it was the first Buddhist monument in the region, although many other religious structures followed. Today, the remarkably preserved Great Stupa is the centerpiece of Sanchi's Buddhist Monuments, a Unesco World Heritage Site. As Hinduism gradually reabsorbed Buddhism, the site decayed and was forgotten, until being rediscovered in 1818 by a British army officer.

Although Sanchi can be visited as a day trip from Bhopal, this crossroads village is a relaxing spot to spend the night, and a number of side trips can be taken from here.

◉ Sights

Buddhist Monuments

The hilltop **Buddhist monuments** (Indian/foreigner ₹10/250, video ₹25; ◷dawn-dusk) are reached via a path and stone steps at the end of Monuments Rd (which is a continuation of the road that leaves the train station), where the **ticket office** (⊙dawn-dusk) is located. If you don't want to walk up the hill, autorickshaws will deposit you at the top for ₹30. If you are interested in a guide, official central government guides mill about and charge ₹1035/1310 for half-/full day.

If you're going up to the stupas for sunrise, buy a ticket the day before. Remember, it's auspicious to walk clockwise around Buddhist monuments.

Stupas

Beautifully proportioned, **Stupa 1** (Great Stupa) is the main structure on the hill, directly in front of you as you enter the complex from the north. Originally constructed by Ashoka, it was later enlarged and the original brick stupa enclosed within a stone one. Presently it stands 16m high and 37m in diameter. Encircling the stupa is a wall with four entrances through magnificently carved *toranas* (gateways) that are the finest Buddhist works of art in Sanchi, if not India.

Stupa 2 is halfway down the hill to the west (turn right at Stupa 1). If you come up from the village by the main route you can walk back down via Stupa 2, although be prepared for some fence-hopping at the bottom. Instead of gateways, 'medallions' decorate the surrounding wall – naive in design, but full of energy and imagination. Flowers, animals and people – some mythological – ring the stupa.

Stupa 3 is northeast of the Great Stupa (you pass it on your left as you approach the Great Stupa from the main entrance) and similar in design, though smaller, with a single, rather fine gateway. It once contained relics of two important disciples of Buddha:

Sari Puttha and Maha Moggallana. They were moved to London in 1853 but returned in 1953 and are now kept in the modern *vihara* (resting place).

Only the base is left of the 2nd-century-BC **Stupa 4**, which stands behind Stupa 3. Between Stupas 1 and 3 is the small **Stupa 5**, unusual in that it once contained a statue of Buddha, now displayed in the museum.

Toranas

The Great Stupa's four *toranas* (gateways) were erected around 35 BC, but had all fallen down by the time the site was rediscovered. They have since been repositioned. Scenes carved onto the pillars and their triple architraves are mainly tales from the Jatakas, episodes from Buddha's various lives.

At this stage in Buddhist art, Buddha himself was never represented directly – only his presence was alluded to through symbols. The lotus stands for his birth, the bodhi tree for his enlightenment, the wheel for his teachings, and the footprint and throne for his presence. The stupa itself also symbolises Buddha.

Northern Gateway   GATE

The Northern Gateway, topped by a broken wheel of law, is the best preserved of the *toranas*. Scenes include a monkey offering a bowl of honey to Buddha, who is represented by a bodhi tree.

Another panel depicts the Miracle of Sravasti – one of several miracles represented here – in which Buddha, again in the form of a bodhi tree, ascends a road into the air. Elephants support the architraves above the columns, while delicately carved

---

WORTH A TRIP

BEYOND BHOPAL

If you're interested in exploring further around Bhopal, check out the following attractions:

Islamnagar This now-ruined fortified city 11km north of Bhopal was the first capital of Bhopal state, founded as Jagdishpur by the Rajputs before Dost Mohammed Khan occupied and renamed it in the early 18th century. The still-standing walls enclose two villages as well as the remains of two palaces: Chaman Mahal and Rani Mahal.

Bhojpur Built by the founder of Bhopal, Raja Bhoj (1010–53), Bhojpur used to be home to a 400-sq-km manmade lake, which was destroyed in the 15th century by the dam-busting Mandu ruler Hoshang Shah. Thankfully, the magnificent Bhojeshwar Temple survived the attack.

Bhimbetka Secreted in a forest of teak and sal in craggy cliffs 46km south of Bhopal are more than 700 rock shelters. Around 500 of them contain some of the world's oldest prehistoric paintings.

Sanchi

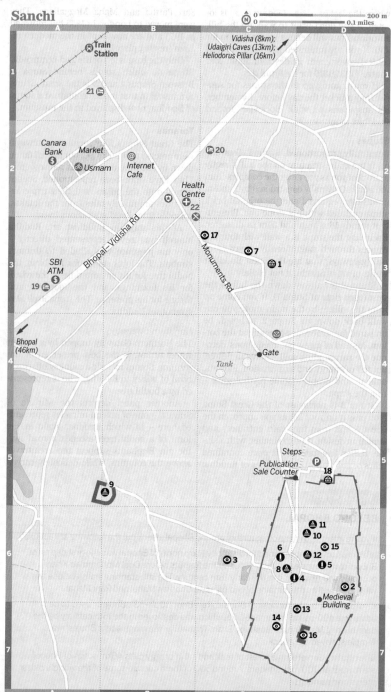

N

0 ————————————— 200 m
0 ————————————— 0.1 miles

Vidisha (8km);
Udaigiri Caves (13km);
Heliodorus Pillar (16km)

Train Station

21

Canara Bank

Market

Usmam

Internet Cafe

20

Health Centre

22

17

7

1

Bhopal–Vidisha Rd

Monuments Rd

SBI ATM

19

Gate

Tank

Bhopal (46km)

Steps

Publication Sale Counter

P

18

9

11

10

6

15

12

3

8

5

4

2

Medieval Building

14

13

16

Sanchi

◉ **Sights**
1	Archaeological Museum	C3
	Great Bowl	(see 3)
2	Monasteries 45 & 47	D6
3	Monastery 51	C6
4	Pillar 10	D6
5	Pillar 25	D6
6	Pillar 35	C6
7	Sir John Marshall Memorial	C3
8	Stupa 1	C6
9	Stupa 2	B5
10	Stupa 3	D6
11	Stupa 4	D6
12	Stupa 5	D6

13	Temple 17	D7
14	Temple 18	C7
15	Temple 31	D6
16	Temple 40	D7
17	Ticket Office	C3
18	Vihara	D5

🛌 **Sleeping**
19	Gateway Retreat	A3
20	Krishna Hotel	C2
21	New Jaiswal Lodge	A1

✴ **Eating**
22	Gateway Cafeteria	B2

yakshis (maidens) hang nonchalantly on each side.

Eastern Gateway
GATE

The breathtakingly carved figure of a *yakshi*, hanging from an architrave on the Eastern Gateway, is one of Sanchi's best-known images. One of the pillars, supported by elephants, features scenes from Buddha's entry to nirvana. Another shows Buddha's mother Maya's dream, which she had when he was conceived, of an elephant standing on the moon.

Across the front of the middle architrave is the Great Departure, when Buddha (a riderless horse) renounced the sensual life and set out to find enlightenment.

Southern Gateway
GATE

The back-to-back lions supporting the Southern Gateway, the oldest gateway, form the state emblem of India, which can be seen on every banknote. The gateway narrates Ashoka's life as a Buddhist, with scenes of Buddha's birth and another representation of the Great Departure.

Also featured is the Chhaddanta Jataka, a story in which Bodhisattva (Buddha before he had reached enlightenment) took on the form of an elephant king who had six tusks. The less favoured of the elephant king's two wives was so jealous of the other that she decided to starve herself to death, vowing to come back to life as the queen of Benares in order to have the power to avenge her husband's favouritism. Her wish came true, and as queen she ordered hunters to track down and kill the elephant king. A hunter found the great elephant but before he could kill it, the elephant handed over his tusks, an act so noble it led to the queen dying of remorse.

Western Gateway
GATE

Pot-bellied dwarves support the architraves of the Western Gateway, which has some of the site's most interesting scenes. The top architrave shows Buddha in seven different incarnations, manifested three times as a stupa and four times as a tree.

The rear of one pillar shows Buddha resisting the Temptation of Mara (the Buddhist personification of evil, often called the Buddhist devil), while demons flee and angels cheer.

Pillars

Of the scattered pillar remains, the most important is **Pillar 10**, erected by Ashoka but later broken. Two upper sections of this beautifully proportioned and executed shaft lie side by side behind Stupa 1; the capital (head of the pillar, usually sculpted) is in the museum. **Pillar 25**, east of Stupa 1, dating from the Sunga period (2nd century BC) and the 5th-century-AD **Pillar 35**, west of Stupa 1, are less impressive.

Temples

Temple 18, behind Stupa 1, is a *chaitya* (prayer room or assembly hall) remarkably similar in style to classical Greek columned buildings. It dates from around the 7th century AD, but traces of earlier wooden buildings have been discovered beneath it. To its left is the small, also Greek-like **Temple 17**. Beyond both of them, the large **Temple 40** dates back to the Ashokan period, in part.

The rectangular **Temple 31**, beside Stupa 5, was built in the 6th or 7th century, but reconstructed during the 10th or 11th century. It contains a well-executed image of Buddha.

MADHYA PRADESH & CHHATTISGARH SANCHI

Monasteries

The earliest monasteries were made of wood and are long gone. The usual plan was of a central courtyard surrounded by monastic cells. These days only the courtyards and stone foundations remain. Monasteries 45 and Monastery 47, standing on the eastern ridge to the left of Stupa 1, date from the transition from Buddhism to Hinduism, with strong Hindu elements in their design. The former has two sitting Buddhas. The one housed inside is exceptional. Behind Monastery 51, partway down the hill towards Stupa 2, is the Great Bowl, carved from a boulder, into which food and offerings were placed for distribution to the monks.

Other Sights

Vihara
MUSEUM

(⊙ 9am-5pm) The *vihara*, literally 'resting place', was built to house the returned relics from Stupa 3. They can be viewed on the last Sunday of the month. It's immediately on your left as you enter the complex.

Archaeological Museum
MUSEUM

(admission incl with Stupa ticket; ⊙ 9am-5pm Tue-Sun) This fine museum has a small collection of sculptures from the site. The centrepiece is the 3rd-century-BC lion capital from the Ashoka Pillar 10. Other highlights include a *yakshi* hanging from a mango tree, and beautifully serene Buddha figures in red sandstone. There are also some interesting photos showing the site, pre-restoration.

Next door is the preserved Gothic-style 'bungalow' of Sir John Marshall, former director of the Archaeological Survey of India. Marshall stayed here from 1912 to 1913 and was the instrumental figure in excavations.

🛏 Sleeping & Eating

New Jaiswal Lodge
GUESTHOUSE $

(☑ 9981941274; nic_cool111@yahoo.co.in; Monuments Rd; s/d/tr ₹450/550/650) This friendly place has basic but colourful rooms and small private bathrooms with sit-down flush toilets. Does basic meals and air-coolers can be provided.

Krishna Hotel
GUESTHOUSE $

(☑ 07482-266610; Bhopal-Vidisha Rd; s/d from ₹200/450; @) Simple rooftop rooms, some with sit-down flush toilets, are slightly more expensive than the darker, noisier rooms at the front. It's above Sai Chemist Shop. Pancakes and a few traveller favourites are available from the kitchen.

★ Gateway Retreat
HOTEL $$

(☑ 07482-266723; www.mptourism.com; Bhopal-Vidisha Rd; s/d ₹990/1170, with AC from ₹2140/2690, incl breakfast; ❋ 🛜 🛁) This family-friendly MP Tourism hotel is the most comfortable place to stay in Sanchi. AC bungalows are set among well-kept gardens, with a small children's play area and a rather big slide leading to a rather small kiddie pool. Note that non-AC rooms are not located here but rather nearby at Gateway Cafeteria.

The restaurant (mains ₹110 to ₹290) is Sanchi's best and there's a bar.

Gateway Cafeteria
INDIAN $

(Monuments Rd; mains ₹70-100; ⊙ 8am-10am, noon-3pm & 7-10.30pm) This simple MP Tourism place has a very basic Indian menu and coffee in addition to housing the non-AC rooms of Gateway Retreat.

ℹ Information

A couple of places in the market have **internet access** (per hr ₹30; ⊙ 8am-10.30pm).

ℹ Getting There & Around

BIKE

You can rent bicycles from **Usmam** (per hr/day ₹10/50) at the market.

BUS

Every half-hour buses connect Sanchi with Bhopal (₹45, 1½ hours, 6am to 10pm) and Vidisha (₹10, 20 minutes, 6am to 11pm). Catch them at the village crossroads.

TRAIN

Train is a decent option for getting to Sanchi from Bhopal. It takes less than an hour so there's no need to book a seat: just turn up with enough time to queue for a 'general' ticket (₹10 to ₹30) and then squeeze on. At least four daily trains leave from Bhopal (8am, 10am, 3.05pm, and 6.15pm) and four run in the other direction (8am, 10.30am, 4.30pm and 7.30pm) from Sanchi.

Around Sanchi

Vidisha

☑ 07592 / POP 155,959

This small but thriving market town, 8km northeast of Sanchi, was a commercial centre in the 5th and 6th centuries BC. These days it's an interesting place for a wander or a chai break en route to the Udaigiri Caves.

Many of the attractive whitewashed or painted buildings still have old wooden balconies that overlook the market streets where horse-drawn carts share space with scooters and rickshaws. There are also a number of brightly coloured temples dotted around the old town, which is located to the left of the main road from Sanchi.

Past the town, and over the railway line, is the dusty **District Museum** (Sagar-Vidisha Rd; Indian/foreigner ₹5/50, camera ₹50; ⊙10am-5pm Tue-Sun), which houses some beautiful sculptures recovered from local sites. The most impressive is a 3m-high, 2nd-century-BC stone statue of Kuber Yaksha (treasurer of the gods), on display as you enter.

It's a straightforward 30-minute cycle from Sanchi or else there are frequent buses (₹10, 20 minutes).

Udaigiri Caves

Cut into a sandstone hill, about 5km north-west of Vidisha, are some 20 Gupta **cave shrines** (⊙dawn-dusk), which date from the reign of Chandragupta II (AD 382–401). Most are Hindu but two, near the top of the hill, are Jain (Caves 1 and 20) – unfortunately both are closed due to unsafe roofs.

In Cave 4 is a lingam bearing Shiva's face complete with a third eye. Cave 5 contains the finest carving – a superb image of Vishnu in his boar incarnation topped with a frieze of gods, who also flank the entrance to Cave 6. Lotus-ceilinged Cave 7 was cut out for the personal use of Chandragupta II. On the top of the hill are ruins of a 6th-century Gupta temple dedicated to the sun god.

To get here by bike from Sanchi, head towards Vidisha, but turn left about 1km before the town, following a sign for Udaigiri. Follow the road to the Betwa River, cross the river then take the first left and keep going until you reach the caves. Alternatively, take a bus to Vidisha then a rickshaw (₹150 return). A return rickshaw from Sanchi is about ₹400.

If you want to cycle back via Vidisha, cross back over the river and keep going straight instead of bearing round to the right on the road you took from Sanchi.

Heliodorus Pillar

The Heliodorus Pillar (Khamb Baba), just beyond the Udaigiri Caves turn-off, was erected by a Greek ambassador, Heliodorus from Taxila (now in Pakistan), in about 140 BC, and dedicated to Vasudeva. The pillar is worshipped by local fishermen who chain themselves to the pillar on full-moon nights. It's said they then become possessed and are able to drive evil spirits from other locals. When someone has been exorcised, they drive a nail into the tamarind tree nearby, fixing to it a lime, a piece of coconut, a red thread and supposedly the spirit. The large tree is bristling with old nails.

The pillar is close to the Udaigiri Caves. Once you cross the Betwa River, carry straight on, rather than turning left for the caves, and you'll soon see a sign directing you up a small lane on your right, which leads to the pillar.

Pachmarhi

☎07578 / POP 13,700 / ELEV 1067M

Madhya Pradesh's only hill station is surrounded by waterfalls, cave temples and the forested ranges of the Satpura Tiger Reserve and offers a refreshing escape from steamy central India.

Even if you don't go on an organised trek or 4WD safari, you can easily spend a couple of days here cycling or hiking to the numerous sights before taking a dip in one of the natural pools that dot the area.

Explorer Captain J Forsyth 'discovered' Pachmarhi as late as 1857 and set up India's first Forestry Department at Bison Lodge in 1862. Soon after, the British army set up regional headquarters here, starting an association with the military that remains today.

◎ Sights

Many of the sights in Pachmarhi fall within Satpura National Park; to visit, you'll need a ticket from the office outside Bison Lodge. This allows entry to Bison Lodge, Bee Falls, Duchess Falls, Reechgarh, Astachal, Ramykund and Rajat Prapat (including Panchuli Kund and Apsara Vihar). Other sights in the area are free with the exception of the Satpuri Tiger Reserve.

Satpura National Park   NATURE RESERVE (www.satpura-national-park.com; Indian/foreigner per day ₹50/100, per 4WD ₹2400/4400; ⊙9am-7pm) Tickets for this national park, carved from a portion of the larger Satpuri Tiger Reserve, must be bought at the ticket office outside Bison Lodge. Forestry commission guides (trekking per day ₹700) can also be arranged at Bison Lodge ticket office;

Pachmarhi

Scale:
0 – 1 km
0 – 0.5 miles

Enlargement scale:
0 – 100 m
0 – 0.05 miles

Map labels

Rajat Prapat (300m) 1

Pahar (1127m)

3

7

SBI ATM

PACHMARHI TOWN

See Enlargement

Pandav Caves

Christchurch

MP Tourism

Axis Bank ATM

11

5

Handi Khoh (2km)

6
10
9
2

Train Reservation Office

Ben Falls

Pudmini Jheel

Reechgarh Viewpoint

Duchess Falls

Astachal Cave

Ramykund Pool

Enlargement

MP Tourism Kiosk

Bus Stand

PACHMARHI TOWN

Arvindar Marg

SBI ATM

Subhash Rd

Anurag Photo Stat

4

8

Patel Rd

Enlargement

Pachmarhi

⊙ Sights

⊕ Activities, Courses & Tours

⊜ Sleeping

⊗ Eating

some guides speak English. 4WD tours are available as well, though the area isn't world-class for wildlife – you'll need to make your way to Satpuri Tiger Reserve for that.

Satpura Tiger Reserve   NATURE RESERVE
(www.satpura-national-park.com; Indian/foreigner per 4WD ₹2400/4400; ⊙6am-7pm mid-Oct–Jun) This reserve, entered from Madhai 93km northwest of Pachmarhi by road, counts an estimated 40-odd tigers and unknown number of leopards; chances of sighting the latter, along with Indian gaurs, sloth bears, monkeys, deer and birds of all type, are decent. Safaris can be arranged through agencies, online (www.mponline.gov.in) or at the gate itself.

On top of your 4WD entrance fee, you will need to pay for one guide per vehicle (₹300). The 4WDs hold up to six people in addition to the guide and driver. Boat safaris can also be arranged for up to 10 people (₹4000 per boat, 45 minutes). Accommodation in the reserve is limited and expensive, but there's an affordable Forest Rest House bookable from Madhai Gate itself.

To reach Madhai, shared 4WDs leave when full between 6am and 8pm from the Pachmarhi bus stand (₹150 per person, three hours).

Chauragarh   VIEWPOINT
South of Jaistambha is the road that leads towards Chauragarh (1308m), Madhya Pradesh's third-highest peak. The Shiva shrine at the top attracts tens of thousands of pilgrims during Shivaratri Mela. On the way, stop at **Handi Khoh**, also known as Su-

icide Point, to gawk down the 100m canyon into the dense forest. You'll spy Chauragarh in the distance from here as well as Priyadarshini (Forsyth Point), further along the road.

About 3km beyond Priyadarshini the road ends at **Mahadeo Cave**, where a path 30m into the damp gloom reveals a lingam with attendant priest. This is the beginning of the 1365-step pilgrim trail to Chauragarh (five hours' return hike).

Jata Shankar   HINDU TEMPLE
This cave temple is in a beautiful gorge about 2.5km along a good track that's signed just north of the town limits. The small Shiva shrine is hidden under a huge overhanging rock.

Rajat Prapat   WATERFALL
(Big Fall) Steps up from the snack stall by Apsara Vihar lead to a point with magnificent views of the gorge and of Rajat Prapat, the tallest of Pachmarhi's waterfalls at 106m, and which tumbles down a gully over a sheer cliff.

Apsara Vihar   POND
(Fairy Pool) On the other side of Jaistambha, about 1km past Pandav Caves, is the trailhead for Apsara Vihar, a pool underneath a small waterfall, which is the best of Pachmarhi's natural pools for swimming.

Bison Lodge   MUSEUM
(⊙9am-5pm Thu-Tue, to 1pm Wed) Captain Forsyth named Bison Lodge after a herd of 'bison' (gaur) he spotted here. It's now an old-fashioned, dilapidated museum focusing on the history, flora and fauna of the Satpura region.

🏃 Activities

Pachmarhi sights can be reached by bicycle, although bikes have to be left at the trailheads from where the hiking begins. You can rent one from **Baba Cycles** (Subhash Rd; per hr/day ₹10/100; ⊙10.15am-7pm).

🛏 Sleeping & Eating

Places fill up and room rates rocket during high seasons (April to July and December to January). The same applies during national holidays and major festivals. A number of colonial-era buildings have been converted into delightful guesthouses and hotels – most of the latter are run by MP Tourism – which can be found in the Jaistambha area, 2km southwest of the small town.

MADHYA PRADESH & CHHATTISGARH PACHMARHI

Pachmarhi Town

Hotel Saket
HOTEL **$**

(📞07578-252165; www.pachmarhihotel.com; Patel Rd; r from ₹600, with AC from ₹1500; ❄) The wide range of updated rooms are better than the lobby suggests at this welcoming hotel, one of myriad paint-by-number options in town. The attached restaurant Raj Bhoj (mains ₹60 to ₹200) does good and cheap Gujarati, Bengali, Chinese and South Indian dishes.

Hotel Highlands
HOTEL **$$**

(📞07578-252099; www.mptourism.com; Pipariya Rd; r incl breakfast & bed tea ₹2140; ❄ 🗬) This family-friendly MP Tourism property on the approach road into Pachmarhi has great-value rooms with high ceilings, dressing rooms, modern bathrooms and verandahs, which are dotted around well-tended gardens. There's a children's play area and a bar-restaurant. Wi-fi is in the lobby only.

Jaistambha Area

Glen View
HERITAGE HOTEL **$$**

(📞07578-252533; www.mptourism.com; Rajbhaven Rd; s/d incl meals ₹4000/4600, heritage s/d ₹4700/5600; ❄ 🗬 ▦) Large, comfortable AC tents and cottages are dotted around the shaded, family-friendly gardens of a huge colonial-era cottage, which has also been converted to house the luxury 'heritage' rooms, all of which empty out onto a sweeping verandah. There's a restaurant and bar, and a pool and gym were under construction at the time of writing.

Evelyn's Own
GUESTHOUSE **$$**

(📞07578-252056; evelynsown@gmail.com; Sapture Retreat Rd; r ₹2000-4000; ❄ 🗬 ▦) This rustic colonial-era cottage, built by a British priest then converted into a charming guesthouse by the gruff-but-good-hearted Colonel Balwant Rao and his indomitable wife Pramila has the right ethos. The main cottage, full of family portraits and period furniture, and the lush grounds, holding loads of hideaway nooks for a peaceful read or afternoon drink, are antiquated delights.

Despite being comfortable, some of the guest rooms themselves, in buildings dotted around pleasant gardens, lead to bathrooms that are a little too crusty for the price. Wi-fi is fussy.

Rock-End Manor
HERITAGE HOTEL **$$$**

(📞07578-252079; www.mptourism.com; r incl meals ₹5600; ❄ 🗬) A gorgeous colonial-era building, whitewashed Rock-End is perched above the parched fairways of the army golf course. Six spacious rooms have wonderfully high ceilings, and furnishings are luxurious with quality upholstery, framed paintings and full-body massage showers. There are also great views to be had from seating areas around the covered walkway.

★Rasoi
DHABA **$**

(near Company Garden; mains ₹90-500; ☺8am-11pm) Not your average roadside *dhaba* (snack bar). A scrumptious, long-winded nonveg, South Indian and Chinese menu is served here by uniformed waiters in several open-air seating areas covered by corrugated roofs. Our waiter's recommendation, Tawa Veg (₹180), was downright delicious. The slap-slap-slap of the tandoor bread man provides the soundtrack to the excellent food here. Credit cards are even accepted!

Nandavan Restaurant
INDIAN **$**

(mains ₹50-300; ☺8am-11pm) An outdoor restaurant and a sort of reverse zoo, as monkeys sit outside watching humans eating in a cage. Good wide-reaching Indian menu.

ℹ Information

Anurag Photo Stat (Subhash Rd; internet per hr ₹30; ☺8am-10pm; 🗬) Has wi-fi as well.

MP Tourism (📞07578-252100; ☺10am-7pm) Regional Office near Jaistambha. Also has a kiosk by the bus stand (📞252100; ☺10am-5pm Mon-Fri).

ℹ Getting There & Away

From the bus stand in Pachmarhi town, six daily buses go to Bhopal (₹200, six hours). The two evening ones (6.30pm and 8pm) are sleepers (seat/bed ₹250/300). There are three buses to Nagpur (₹260, seven hours, 8am, 10am and 9pm) and two to Indore (seat/sleeper ₹460/500, 12 hours, 6.30am and 8am). The friendly guys at the bus-ticket counter are around from 7.30am to 9pm.

All Bhopal buses, plus hourly local ones, go via Pipariya (₹60, 1½ hours), from where you can catch trains to onward destinations such as Jabalpur and Varanasi without having to go all the way to Bhopal. Train tickets can be bought from the **train reservation office** (☺10am-2pm) inside the town post office.

If you're coming from Pipariya, shared 4WDs (₹60 to ₹150 per person depending on season and the number of people) to Pachmarhi leave far more frequently than buses.

ℹ️ Getting Around

Shared 4WDs cost ₹1000 to ₹2500 for a day depending on the season. Cycling or hiking will give you more freedom.

WESTERN MADHYA PRADESH

Ujjain

📞 0734 / POP 515,215

First impressions don't always impress. And that's the case with Ujjain. The area around the train and bus stations is chaotic and nothing special, but wander down towards the river ghats, via Ujjain's maze of alleyways, and you'll discover an older, more spiritual side to this city that has been attracting traders and pilgrims for hundreds of years. An undeniable energy pulses through the temples here – perhaps because this is one of Hinduism's seven sacred cities.

History

The Guptas, the Mandu sultans, Maharaja Jai Singh (of Jaipur fame), the Marathas and the Scindias have all had a controlling hand in Ujjain's long and chequered past, which stretches back to when the city, originally called Avantika, was an important trade stop. When the Scindias moved their capital to Gwalior in 1810, Ujjain's prominence declined rapidly.

👁 Sights

Mahakaleshwar Mandir   HINDU TEMPLE
While this is not the most stunning temple, tagging along behind a conga-line through the underground chambers can be magical. At nonfestival times, the marble walkways are a peaceful preamble to the subterranean chamber containing one of India's 12 sacred Shiva shrines known as *jyoti linga* – naturally occurring linga believed to derive currents of *shakti* (creative energies perceived as female deities) from within themselves rather than being ritually invested with *mantra-shakti* by priests.

The temple was destroyed by Altamish in 1235 and restored by the Scindias in the 19th century. You may be asked to give a donation, but it's not compulsory.

Vedh Shala   HISTORIC BUILDING
(Observatory; Jantar Mantar; admission ₹10; ⊙8am-5pm) Ujjain has been India's Greenwich since the 4th century BC, and this simple but interesting observatory was built by Maharaja Jai Singh in about 1730. He also built observatories in Jaipur, Delhi, Varanasi and Mathura, but Ujjain's is the only one still in use.

Gopal Mandir   HINDU TEMPLE
The Scindias built this marble-spired temple, a magnificent example of Maratha architecture, in the 19th century. Muslim pillagers originally stole the sanctum's silver-plated doors from Somnath Temple in Gujarat and installed them in Ghazni, Afghanistan. Mohammed Shah Abdati later took them to Lahore (in present-day Pakistan), before Mahadji Scindia brought them back here. The alleyways north, east and west of here are wonderful places to explore.

Harsiddhi Mandir   HINDU TEMPLE
Built during the Maratha period, this temple enshrines a famous image of goddess Annapurna. At the entrance, two tall blackened stone towers bristling with lamps are a special feature of Maratha art. They add to the spectacle of Navratri in September/October ,when filled with oil and ignited.

Ram Ghat   GHAT
The most central and popular of Ujjain's river ghats is best visited at dawn or dusk when the devout chime cymbals and light candles at the water's edge.

🎊 Festivals & Events

Magh Mela   RELIGIOUS
(⊙Apr/May) Huge annual religious fair held on the banks of the Shipra River at Ujjain; pilgrim numbers increase dramatically every 12th year for the massive Kumbh Mela.

Kumbh Mela   RELIGIOUS
(⊙Apr/May) Ujjain is also one of four sites in India that hosts the incredible Kumbh Mela, during which millions bathe in the Shipra River. It takes place here every 12 years, normally during April and May. The next one is in 2016 (22 April to 21 May).

Navratri   CULTURAL
(Festival of Nine Nights; ⊙Sep/Oct) The Festival of Nine Nights, leading up to Dussehra, is celebrated with particular fervour in Ujjain. Lamps on the large pillars in Harsiddhi Mandir are lit.

Ujjain

🛏 Sleeping & Eating

Ujjain suffers from a dearth of hotels.

Hotel Rama Krishna   HOTEL **$**
(☎ 0734-2553017; www.hotelramakrishna.co.in; Subhash Rd; s/d ₹500/650, with AC ₹900/1000; ❄) This cleaner-than-average Subhash Rd hotel has the best air-con rooms of those considered, with white-tiled floors, TVs, stylish trimmings and tight bathrooms. The non-ACs are well-worn versions of the same. Sit-down flush toilets throughout. New Sudama restaurant does inexpensive North Indian food (mains ₹60 to ₹100).

Hotel Pleasure Landmark   HOTEL **$**
(☎ 0734-2557867; www.hotelpleasurelandmark. com; 98 Mahakal Marg; r ₹900, with AC ₹1200; ❄) Basic rooms here cop a bit of noise and are a tad cluttered with chunky wooden furniture, but there's some historic character and it's a

great location from which to launch yourself into the old town. Squat toilets only.

Hotel Grand Tower   HOTEL **$$**
(☎ 0734-2553699; 1 Vikram Marg; s/d from ₹1420/1640; ❄) In a very busy part of town convenient to both the bus stand and train station, the all-AC GT has large, clean, well-kept rooms, plus efficient service and the very good Zharokha restaurant serving excellent Kashmiri, Punjabi and Chinese food (mains ₹90 to ₹140).

★ Shree Ganga   SWEETS, SOUTH INDIAN **$**
(50 Amarsingh Marg; sweets per kilo from ₹360, mains ₹40-120; ⊙ 7am-11pm) Since 1949 this epic sweet shop has been satiating Ujjaini sugar cravings. There's no English sign or menu, but the friendly owner can steer you in the right direction, albeit in a staunchly democratic way: What do you recommend? 'Everything.' What are you most famous for?

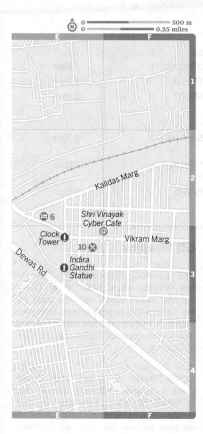

'Everything.' What do you sell the most? 'Everything.'

Upstairs, there's a great savoury menu that includes creative South Indian (green chutney masala dosa) and Chinese. It's just to the right of Baker's Lounge.

Shivam Restaurant INDIAN $
(Hotel Satyam; mains ₹60-160; ⊙8am-5pm & 7.30-10.30pm) This popular veg restaurant in the basement below Hotel Satyam has an extensive menu with detailed descriptions of every dish. Choose from tandoori kebabs, a selection of paneer dishes, koftas and a variety of stuffed vegetables. Skip the uneventful thali.

❶ Information

There are ATMs all over town, including two next to the Hotel Grand Tower.
Shri Vinayak Cyber Cafe (per hr ₹10; ⊙10am-10pm) Walk up Vikram Marg, turn left at the

roundabout and it's on your right on the ground floor.
MP Tourism (☑0734-2552263; www.mptourism.com; ⊙10am-6pm Mon-Sat) Located in the grounds of Mahakaleshwar Mandir.

❶ Getting There & Away

BUS
Services from the bus stand:
Bhopal ₹170, five hours, two daily (7.30am and 8.30am)
Dhar ₹90, three hours, four daily (5.45am, 8am, 9am and 3pm)
Indore ₹58, two hours, frequent 5am to 11pm
Mandu ₹140, 4½ hours, 2.30pm daily
Omkareshwar ₹140, four hours, four daily (6am, 8am, 10.30am and 4pm)

For Maheshwar (or Mandu at other times), change at Dhar.

TRAIN
There's one handy daily train to Gwalior and Agra; otherwise you're better off going via Bhopal which, like Indore, has many more options.

❶ Getting Around

Prepaid autorickshaws from the booth outside the train station charge ₹50 to Ram Ghat and ₹400 for a four-hour tour around Ujjain.

Indore

☑0731 / POP 1.96 MILLION
The Holkar dynasty left behind some fine buildings here, and you'll find some cool cafes thanks to the city's ever-burgeoning coffee culture, but Indore – Madhya Pradesh's business powerhouse – is primarily used by

TRAINS FROM UJJAIN

DESTINATION	TRAIN NO & NAME	FARE (₹)	DURATION (HR)	DEPARTURE
Agra	12919 Malwa Express	355/920/1300 (A)	11	2.10pm
Bhopal	12919 Malwa Express	170/535/735 (A)	3½	2.10pm
Delhi	12919 Malwa Express	460/1200/1715 (A)	15	2.10pm
Gwalior	12919 Malwa Express			
Indore	18234 Narmada Pas Express	100/485/690 (A)	2	8.30am
Jaipur	12465 Ranthambore Express	185/355/695/860 (B)	8½	7.45am
Mumbai (Central)	12962 Avantika Express	415/1085/1545 (A)	13	5.55pm

Fares: (A) sleeper/3AC/2AC, (B) 2nd class/sleeper/chair car/3AC

tourists as the gateway to Omkareshwar, Maheshwar or Mandu. That said, it's a fine spot to reload.

◉ Sights

Lal Bagh Palace   MUSEUM
(Indian/foreigner ₹5/100; ◷10am-5pm Tue-Sun) Built between 1886 and 1921, Lal Bagh Palace is the finest building left by the Holkar dynasty. Replicas of the Buckingham Palace gates creak at the entrance to the 28-hectare garden, where, close to the palace, there's a statue of Queen Victoria. The palace is dominated by European styles, with baroque and rococo dining rooms, an English library with leather armchairs, a Renaissance sitting room with ripped sofas and a Palladian queen's bedroom. An autorickshaw from the town centre costs about ₹50.

Central Museum   MUSEUM
(AB Rd; Indian/foreigner ₹10/100, camera/video ₹50/200; ◷10am-5pm Tue-Sun) Housed in a fine Holkar building, this museum has one of Madhya Pradesh's best collections of medieval and premedieval Hindu sculptures, along with tools, weaponry and copper-engraved land titles. Skirmishes took place here during the First War of Independence (Indian Uprising) – the well in the garden was poisoned during the struggle.

Gandhi Hall   HISTORIC BUILDING
(MG Rd) This gorgeous Gothic town hall, built in 1904 and originally called King Edward's Hall, stands incongruously on MG Rd like a ghost of the Raj.

🛏 Sleeping

Hotel Neelam   HOTEL $
(☏0731-2466001; 33/2 Patel Bridge Corner; s/d from ₹450/650, with AC ₹750/950; ❄) One of the few budget places near the train and bus stations that happily accepts foreigners. Neelam is well run and has simple but clean rooms with upgraded bathrooms off a central atrium.

Hotel Chanakya   HOTEL $
(☏0731-2704497; 57/58 RNT Marg, Chhawni Chowk; s/d from ₹800/900, with AC from ₹1270/1430; ❄) Rooms here aren't as flashy as the disco-lit Krishna waterfall in the entrance hallway but they are functional nonetheless. The cheapest have no windows and it's worth paying ₹100 more for the air-cooled 'semi-deluxe' rooms or AC rooms. Staff are friendly and it's right in the heart of an interesting section of the old town.

There's no English sign. Autorickshaws know it by the famous sweet shop below it, Mathurawala.

★ Hotel Shreemaya   BUSINESS HOTEL $$
(☏0731-2515555; www.shreemaya.com; 12 RNT Marg; s/d from ₹2880/3700; ❄@☎) Faults are hard to come by in this professionally run and extremely friendly business hotel with modern rooms in immaculate condition. Rooms feature flat-screen TVs, coffee-makers and balconies peppered with potted plants. Rates include breakfast and airport drop-off, while the multicuisine restaurant is one of the best in town (mains ₹155 to ₹350).

If you've been traveling on a hardcore budget, it's the perfect spot to recharge your

Indore

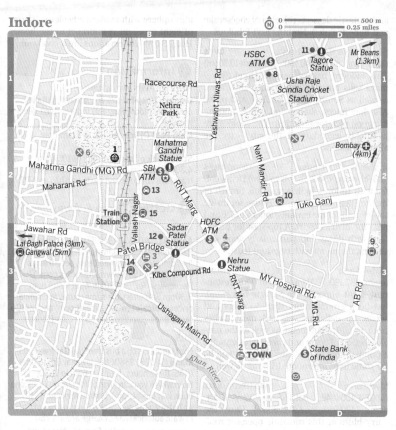

Indore

◎ Sights
1 Gandhi Hall B2

🛏 Sleeping
2 Hotel Chanakya C4
3 Hotel Neelam B3
4 Hotel Shreemaya C3

✕ Eating
5 Hotel Apna B3
6 Indian Coffee House A2
7 Mr Beans D2
Shreemaya Celebration .... (see 4)

① Transport
8 Air India C1
9 Chartered Bus D3
10 Hans Travels C2
11 Jet Airways D1
Metro Taxi .... (see 9)
12 Passenger Reservation
Center B3
13 Private Taxi Firms B2
14 Sarwate Bus Stand B3
15 Shared Minivans to
Gangwal Bus Stand B2

batteries without depleting your savings account.

✕ Eating & Drinking

★ Mr Beans
CAFE $

(www.mrbeans.in; 100 Saket Nagar; mains ₹100-400; ⊙12.30-11.30pm; 🕾) With sophisticated

French-style interiors throughout its seven rooms, this excellent cafe is one of India's nicest. Besides the Indorean in-crowd and excellent coffee (₹50 to ₹130) and tea, the menu specialises in homesick remedy overload: shepherd's pie, coq au vin, pastas, outstanding thin-crust pizzas (try the verde) and fantastic desserts (blueberry cheesecake and Banoffee pie!). Nothing isn't fabulous.

Shreemaya Celebration   CAFE $

(Tuko Ganj; mains ₹40-190; ⊙7.30am-10.30pm) This modern bakery next to Hotel Shreemaya sells pastries, sandwiches and cakes, as well as South Indian, Chinese and pizza. Also has juices, shakes and coffee, making it a good pick for breakfast. The cookies are justifiably legendary in the city – try the almond-cashew.

Indian Coffee House   SOUTH INDIAN $

(MG Rd; mains ₹50-200; ⊙8am-8pm) Drink coffee with Indore's judiciary at this branch of the excellent Indian Coffee House set inside the grounds of the commissioner's office and near the district court. A top spot for breakfast, with dosas and particularly good *idli* sharing the menu with eggs and toast.

Hotel Apna   INDIAN $

(mains ₹80-190; ⊙11am-11.30pm) This restaurant, right opposite the Sarvate bus stand, has been around more than 50 years and serves up delicious veg and meat dishes from an all-Indian menu, as well as the usual selection of beers and cheap whiskeys. It's a popular spot to stow away in dark booths for some hard afternoon drinking as well.

Mediterra   MEDITERRENEAN $$$

(☎0731-4004848; Hotel Sayaji, Vijay Nagar; mains ₹490-950; ⊙7.30-11.30pm) Cure the curry blues at this romantic open-air rooftop restaurant along Indore's main avenue of upscale shopping and hotels north of the centre. Mediterranean fare is on order, everything from honey roasted rack of lamb to great mezze and Moroccan stews.

Cool tunes, cocktails (₹330 to ₹400) and New World wines are the sidekicks to the excellent grub, all served up in a trendy lounge atmosphere with modern city views. It's one of eight excellent restaurants in the luxury Hotel Sayaji. Reservations are a good call.

❶ Information

There are ATMs all over town.

Bombay Hospital (www.bombayhospitalindore.com; Indore Ring Rd) Indore's best general hospital.

Main Post Office (AB Rd; ⊙10am-6pm Mon-Sat)

State Bank of India (AB Rd; ⊙10.30am-4.30pm Mon-Fri, to 1.30pm Sat) Changes travellers cheques and cash, and has an ATM.

❶ Getting There & Away

AIR

Air India (☎0731-2431595; www.airindia.in; Racecourse Rd; ⊙10am-1pm & 2-5pm Mon-Sat) flies daily to Mumbai and Delhi. **Jet Airways** (☎0731-2544590; www.jetairways.com; 17 Racecourse Rd; ⊙9.30am-6pm Mon-Fri, to 3.30pm Sat) offers the same routes and similar prices. **Spicejet** (www.spicejet.com) and **IndiGo** (www.book.goindigo.in) also fly out of Indore.

BUS

For Mandu, catch a bus from the **Gangwal bus stand** (☎0731 2380688; Jawahar Rd) to Dhar (₹65, three hours, frequent 6am to 11.30pm) from where you can change for Mandu (₹35, one hour, last bus at 7pm). Shared minivans (₹10) go between the centre and Gangwal bus stand. Private autorickshaws charge around ₹80.

Bus services from the **Sarwate bus stand** (☎2465688) include the following. For Maheshwar, change at Dhamnod.

Bhopal ₹186, five hours, frequent 5am to 10pm

Dhamnod ₹77, three hours, frequent 5am to 11pm

Gwalior ₹488, 12 hours, three daily (3.30am, 6am and 11am)

TRAINS FROM INDORE

DESTINATION	TRAIN NO & NAME	FARE (₹)	DURATION (HR)	DEPARTURE
Bhopal	12919 Malwa Express	215/535/735	5	12.25pm
Delhi	12919 Malwa Express	485/1265/1810	16½	12.25pm
Mumbai	12962 Avantika Express	440/1150/1640	15	4.25pm
Ujjain	12919 Malwa Express	170/535/745	2	12.25pm

Fares: sleeper/3AC/2AC

Khajuraho seat/sleeper ₹580/630, 12 hours, three daily (3.45pm, 4.45pm and 5.45pm)
Omkareshwar ₹77, three hours, hourly 6am to 12.30pm
Pachmarhi seat/sleeper ₹380/450, 12 hours, two daily (8pm and 9.30pm)
Ujjain ₹55, two hours, frequent 6am to 11pm

For Omkareshwar after 12.30pm, catch a bus to Motakka, 11km east of Omkareshwar, and change there.

Chartered Bus (☑ 0731-4288888; www. charteredbus.in; AB Rd) offers luxury AC Volvo coaches to Bhopal (₹325, four hours) almost hourly from 3.30am to 11.30pm. **Hans Travels** (☑ 0731-2510007; www.hanstravel.in; 15/3 South Tukoganj) offers similar comfort to Gwalior (non-AC sleeper ₹450, 12 hours, 7.15pm and 9pm), Agra (non-AC sleeper ₹500, 14 hours, 7.15pm) and Jaipur (non-AC sleeper ₹515, 14 hours, 7.30pm).

TAXI
Private taxis on the service road parallel to Valiash Nagar charge from ₹2500 return to Mandu or to Omkareshwar and Maheshwar. For a tad more, **Metro Taxi** (☑ 0731-4288888) has new cars and professional drivers.

TRAIN
There are five daily trains to Bhopal and nine to Ujjain. The **train reservation office** (⊙ 8am-10pm Mon-Sat, to 2pm Sun) is 200m east of the train station.

🛈 Getting Around
The airport is 9km from the city. Allow 45 minutes. Autorickshaws charge around ₹150, taxis ₹250 to ₹300.

Indore has implemented a glorious fixed-priced, hassle-free autorickshaw scheme called **Tele-Rickshaw** (☑ 9098098098; per km ₹12). Just call for a ride. The minimum fare is ₹40 and they even provide receipts.

Omkareshwar
☑ 07280 / POP 10,062
This Om-shaped island attracts pilgrims in large numbers and has become a popular chill-out destination for a certain kind of spiritual traveller. The controversial dam has changed the look of Omkareshwar considerably, but the island has retained its spiritual vibe and remains a pleasant and authentic – if overly commercialised – pilgrimage point.

Much activity takes place off the island, at the market square called Getti Chowk

(from where the old bridge crosses to the island), and on Mamaleshwar Rd, which links Getti Chowk to the bus stand. If you continue straight along Mamaleshwar Rd from the bus stand, without turning left to Getti Chowk, you'll find steps leading down to the ghats (where you can cross the river on boats for ₹5). Beyond is the new bridge and the dam.

The path leading from the old bridge to Shri Omkar Mandhata temple is the hub of the island.

⊙ Sights & Activities
Tourists can rub shoulders with sadhus in the island's narrow lanes, browse the colourful stalls selling chillums (pipes) and souvenir linga, or join pilgrims attending the thrice daily *puja* (prayer) at **Shri Omkar Mandhata**. This cave-like temple, which houses the only shapeless *jyothi lingam* (12 important shrines dedicated to Shiva), is one of many Hindu and Jain monuments on the island.

From the old bridge, instead of turning right to Shri Omkar Mandhata, head left and walk up the 287 steps to the 11th-century **Gaudi Somnath Temple**, from where you can descend the hill to the northern tip of the island, where sadhus bathe in the confluence of the holy Narmada and Keveri Rivers. You can climb the narrow, inner staircase of the temple or just sit and watch the langur monkeys play. Nearby is a 30m-tall Shiva statue.

The path passing in front of the Shiva statue near Gaudi Somnath Temple can be followed back to the ghats (45 minutes), up and down hills and past a number of temple ruins. Don't miss the beautifully sculpted **Siddhanatha Temple** (left at the T-junction in the pathway) with marvellous elephant carvings around its base.

🛏 Sleeping & Eating
★ **Manu Guest House** GUESTHOUSE $
(☑ 9826749004; omkar_bagh@yahoo.co.in; r with shared bathroom ₹350) A special experience awaits at this welcoming guesthouse, where Manu and family treat you like one of their own. Rooms are simple yet well looked after and bathrooms are shared only but kept clean. If you ask in advance, your hosts can whip up a delicious thali (₹100), served village-style on the open-air patio floor. The serene views are inspiring.

This is pretty much the only place to stay on the island itself that isn't a *dharamsala* (pilgrims' rest house). It's perched midway above the old bridge just to the left of the salmon-coloured temple. It's hard to find, though. Cross the bridge from Getti Chowk, come around and down the stairs and turn left. After 10m, turn left into a narrow alley with the painted blue wall saying, 'Kalyan Bhattacharya', and head around and up a very steep and trashy set of steps. Keep asking the way as you climb and be prepared for the odd territorial dog.

Ganesh Guest House GUESTHOUSE $
(☑07280-271370; sumitbhoi1137@gmail.com; r ₹250) Follow the signs as you zig-zag off the path leading down to the ghats from Mamaleshwar Rd to reach Ganesh, with its decidedly budget rooms with thin mattresses. Upstairs rooms are brighter and have air-coolers, while its shaded garden restaurant (mains ₹60 to ₹150), overlooking the ghats, has a multicuisine menu including Western breakfasts and a peaceful ambience.

Brahmin Bhojanalaya INDIAN $
(Mamaleshwar Rd; thali ₹50; ⊘9.30am-10pm) There are a number of no-nonsense, pureveg *dhabas* in Omkareshwar, both on the island and on the mainland, especially in Getti Chowk. None has an English sign, although this one does have a friendly English-speaking *chapati-wallah*. The thalis tend towards soupy (what do you expect for ₹50?). It's on your left as you walk up from the bus stand, 50m before the road bears left towards Getti Chowk.

ⓘ Information

Sarita Photo Studio (Mamaleshwar Rd; internet per hr ₹50; ⊘9am-9pm; 🛜) The very friendly and English-speaking Mamta has laptops and wi-fi at this magnet for tourist information. Also exchanges money and is a Western Union rep. It's on the right just as the main road bears left to Getti Chowk.

State Bank of India ATM (Mamaleshwar Rd) Near the bus stand.

ⓘ Getting There & Away

Services from the bus stand:

Dhamnod (for Mandu, via Oonera) ₹60, 3½ hours, half-hourly 6am to 3.30pm

Indore ₹80, two hours, half-hourly 6am to 7.30pm

Maheshwar ₹60, three hours, half-hourly 6am to 4.30pm

Ujjain ₹135, four hours, five daily (6am, 11.30am, 2.30pm, 3.30pm and 5.30pm)

Maheshwar

☑ 07283 / POP 23,600

The peaceful, riverside town of Maheshwar has long held spiritual significance – it's mentioned in the Mahabharata and Ramayana under its old name, Mahishmati, and still draws sadhus and *yatris* (pilgrims) to its ancient ghats and temples on the holy Narmada River. The town enjoyed a golden age in the late 18th century under Holkar queen Ahilyabai, who built the palace in the towering fort and many other monuments. Away from the ghats and historic buildings, Maheshwar's colourful streets display brightly painted wooden houses with overhanging balconies.

It's a mesmerising place that packs a lot of punch in a very small area around the ghats, palace and temples – a sort of refined, spitshined Varanasi in miniature.

◉ Sights & Activities

The town is dominated by a 16th-century fort. The huge, imposing ramparts were built by Emperor Akbar, while the Maheshwar Palace and several temples within its grounds were added during the reign of Holkar queen Ahilyabai (r 1767–95). The palace is part public courtyard, part posh hotel. Nearby is a Shiva temple with a golden lingam – the starting point for palanquin processions on Ahilyabai's birthday and Dussehra.

From the ramparts of the fort you can see boats (return trip per person/boat ₹50/500) and incense smoke drifting across the water to Baneshwar Temple, located on a tiny island in the middle of the river. Descending to the dhobi-wallahs (clothes washers) at the ghats, you pass two impressive stone temples. The one on the right, guarded by stone Holkar sentries and a frieze of elephants, houses more images of Ahilyabai and two candle towers, lit during festivals.

Between the palace and the two stone temples a small doorway announces the NGO Rehwa Society (☑07283-273203; www.rehwasociety.org; ⊘10am-6pm Wed-Mon, shop open daily), a craft cooperative where profits are ploughed back into the education, housing and welfare of the weavers. A local school, run by Rehwa, is behind the workshop. Maheshwar saris are famous for their unique weave and simple, geometric patterns.

You can watch the weavers at work and buy shawls (from ₹2100), saris (₹3000 to ₹11,000), scarves (₹800 to ₹2500) and fabrics made from silk, cotton and wool. Volunteers with some design background are always welcome, as are those interested in volunteering to teach at the school.

✪ Festivals & Events

Ahilyabai Holkar Jayanti Mahotsav   FESTIVAL
(⊙Apr/May) The birthday celebrations for the revered Holkar queen, Ahilyabai Holkar, one of India's greatest female rulers, are celebrated with particular fervor in Maheshwar, with percussion-soundtracked palanquin (enclosed seats carried on poles on four men's shoulders) processions throughout the town.

🛏 Sleeping & Eating

Hansa Heritage   HOTEL $
(⌨9827857097; Kila Rd; r ₹700, with AC ₹1050, ste ₹1450; ❇🛜) This place has been built with style and quality throughout. Smart, modern rooms have a rustic feel with mud-and-grass daubed interior walls, antique-looking wooden furniture and attractive coloured-glass window panes. Bathrooms are also very modern and spotlessly clean. Indian breakfasts and thali are available.

Akash Deep   GUESTHOUSE $
(⌨9827809455; Kila Rd; r ₹300-500, with AC ₹1200) Friendly Akash has clean, spacious rooms (from ₹500 up, anyway), some with TV and all with small balconies. Next door to Hansa Heritage.

★Laboo'z Café   GUESTHOUSE $$
(⌨7771004818; santosh.ahilyafort@gmail.com; s/d incl breakfast ₹900/1210, with AC from ₹1430/1650; ⊙cafe 6.30am-8pm; ❇🛜) Not only a delightful cafe in a glorious tree-shaded courtyard, but also a place with six wonderful rooms to stay in. Each room is different, being part of the fort gate and walls, but they are decorated with care and attention. The upper room features its own fort-wall verandah.

The cafe menu is snacks only (₹15 to ₹40), but staff whip up a delicious, unlimited thali (₹250), one of MP's best. It also organises river trips (₹150 to ₹200 per boat per hour). Another deal to consider: if you don't want to dish out to stay at Ahilya Fort itself, you can sleep at Laboo'z but take three meals at the fort for ₹7500 per person per night.

Ahilya Fort   HERITAGE HOTEL $$$
(⌨7771004811, reservations 9810306178; www.ahilyafort.com; r Indian/foreigner incl all meals from ₹11,750/18,050; ❇@🛜🏊) Demi Moore, Mick Jagger and Sting have all indulged in this heritage hotel owned by Prince Shivaji Rao Holka, a 14th-generation Indian-American direct descendent of Ahilyabai. Part of Maheshwar Palace, the best rooms are indeed palatial and some come with fabulous river views, while lush gardens house exotic fruit trees, organic vegetable patches and history at every turn. Rates include all meals as well as boat trips on the river. Booking ahead is essential. Nonguests who fancy a night to remember should not miss dining here. The sumptuous menu is set, as is the ₹1575 per person price (including alcohol), and all the food comes from the on-site, nearly 100% organic gardens. You'll need to book and pay in advance (subject to availability). Dinner begins at 7.30pm with candlelit cocktails courtesy of the Prince himself, who divides his time between here and Paris.

ℹ Information

There's a State Bank of India ATM on the main road 400m before the fort entrance gate.

ℹ Getting There & Away

There are buses to Omkareshwar (₹70, three hours, every 45 minutes, 9.15am to 7pm), Dhamnod (₹15, 30 minutes, frequent from 6am to 9.30pm) and Indore (₹90, two hours, hourly 6.15am to 5.15pm). For Mandu, first head to Dhamnod then take a Dhar-bound bus as far as a forked junction in the main road, known as Oonera (₹50, two hours). From there flag down a bus (₹15, 30 minutes) or hitch the final 14km to Mandu.

Mandu

⌨07292 / POP 10,300 / ELEV 634M
Perched on top of a pleasantly green, thinly forested 20-sq-km plateau, picturesque Mandu is home to some of India's finest examples of Afghan architecture as well as impressive baobab trees, originally from Africa. The area is littered palaces, tombs, monuments and mosques, many with Unesco World Heritage status. Some cling to the edge of ravines, others are beside lakes, while Rupmati's Pavilion, the most romantic of them all, sits majestically at the far end

Mandu

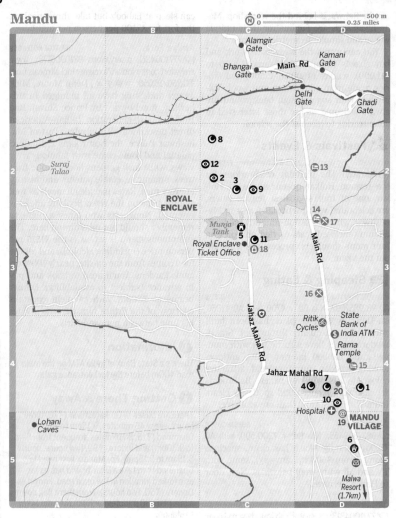

of the plateau, overlooking the vast plains below.

History

Raja Bhoj, of Bhopal fame, founded Mandu as a fortress retreat in the 10th century before it was conquered by the Muslim rulers of Delhi in 1304. When the Mughals captured Delhi in 1401, the Afghan Dilawar Khan, governor of Malwa, set up his own little kingdom and Mandu's golden age began.

Although Dilawar Khan established Mandu as an independent kingdom, it was his son, Hoshang Shah, who shifted the capi-

tal from Dhar to Mandu and raised it to its greatest splendour.

In 1526, Bahadur Shah of Gujarat conquered Mandu, only to be ousted in 1534 by the Mughal Humayun, who in turn lost the kingdom to Mallu Khan, an officer of the Khalji dynasty. Ten more years of feuds and invasions saw Baz Bahadur eventually emerge in the top spot, but in 1561 he fled Mandu to avoid facing Akbar's advancing troops.

After Akbar added Mandu to the Mughal empire, it kept a considerable degree of independence, until taken by the Marathas in

Mandu

◉ **Sights**
Archaeological Museum	(see 11)
1 Ashrafi Mahal	D4
2 Champa Baodi	C2
3 Hindola Mahal	C2
4 Hoshang's Tomb	D4
5 Jahaz Mahal	C3
6 Jain Temple	D5
7 Jama Masjid	D4
8 Mosque of Dilawar Khan	C2
9 Palace & Shop of Gada Shah	C2
10 Saturday Haat	D4
11 Taveli Mahal	C3
12 Turkish Bath	C2

🛏 **Sleeping**
13 Hotel Rupmati	D2
14 Malwa Retreat	D2
15 Rama Guesthouse	D4

🍴 **Eating**
16 Shivani Restaurant	D3
17 Yatrika	D3

🛍 **Shopping**
18 Publication Sale Counter	C3

ℹ **Information**
19 Harsh Communication/Malima Medical	D5
20 Village Group Ticket Office	D4

1732. The capital of Malwa was then shifted back to Dhar, and the slide in Mandu's fortunes that had begun with the absconding of Baz Bahadur became a plummet.

◉ Sights & Activities

There are three main groups of ruins: the Royal Enclave, the Village Group and the Rewa Kund Group. Each requires its own separate ticket. All other sights are free.

Royal Enclave

The **Royal Enclave ruins** (Indian/foreigner ₹5/100, video ₹25; ☉ dawn-dusk) are the only ones fenced off into one single complex. There's a **Publication Sale Counter** (☉ 9am-5pm) selling guidebooks and a shaded canteen selling tea, coffee and snacks just to the right of the main entrance.

Jahaz Mahal ISLAMIC PALACE
(Ship Palace) Dating from the 15th century, this is the most famous building in Mandu. Built on a narrow strip of land between Munja and Kapur tanks, with a small upper storey like a ship's bridge (use your imagination), it's far longer (120m) than it is wide (15m). Ghiyas-ud-din, who is said to have had a harem of 15,000 maidens, constructed its lookouts, scalloped arches, airy rooms and beautiful pleasure pools.

Taveli Mahal ISLAMIC HISTORIC SITE
These former stables now house a small **Archaeological Museum** (☉ 9am-5pm), which features a handful of artefacts found here, including 11th- and 12th-century sculptures and stone slabs with Quranic text dating back to the 15th century.

Hindola Mahal ISLAMIC HISTORIC SITE
(Swing Palace) Just north of Ghiyas' stately pleasure dome is Hindola Mahal, so-called because the slope of the walls is supposed to create the impression that they are swaying. While it doesn't give that impression, it's an eye-catching design nonetheless.

Palace & Shop of Gada Shah HISTORIC SITE
The house is within the enclave, but the shop is outside on the road to Delhi Gate. As the buildings' size and internal workmanship suggest, their owner was more than a shopkeeper. His name, which means 'beggar master', is thought to identify him as Rajput chief Medini Ray, a powerful minion of the sultans. The 'shop' was a warehouse for saffron and musk, imported and sold at a handsome profit when there were enough wealthy people to shop here.

Mosque of Dilawar Khan MOSQUE
Built by Dilawar Khan in 1405, this mosque is Mandu's earliest Islamic building. There are many Hindu elements to the architecture, notably the pillars and ceilings inside, which was typical for this era.

Champa Baodi HISTORIC SITE
So-called because its water supposedly smelled as sweet as the champak flower, Champa Baodi is a step-well surrounded by subterranean vaulted chambers, some of which you can explore.

Turkish Bath HAMMAM
Stars and octagons perforate the domed roofs of this tiny *hammam* (Turkish bath), which had hot and cold water and a hypocaust (underfloor heated) sauna.

MADHYA PRADESH & CHHATTISGARH MANDU

Village Group

The Village Group (Indian/foreigner ₹5/100, video ₹25; ☉dawn-dusk), located by the bus stand in the centre of the village, contains three monuments. The ticket office is at the entrance to Jama Masjid; one ticket covers all three sights.

Jama Masjid   MOSQUE

Entered by a flight of steps leading to a 17m-high domed porch, this disused redstone mosque dominates the village of Mandu. Hoshang Shah began its construction around 1406, basing it on the great Omayyad Mosque in Damascus in Syria, and Mohammed Khalji completed it in 1454. Despite its plain design, it's reckoned to be the finest and largest example of Afghan architecture in India.

Hoshang's Tomb   ISLAMIC TOMB

Reputed to be India's oldest marble building, this imposing tomb is crowned with a crescent thought to have been imported from Persia or Mesopotamia. Inside, light filters into the echoing dome through stone *jalis* (carved lattice screens), intended to cast an appropriately subdued light on the tombs. An inscription records Shah Jahan sending his architects – including Ustad Hamid, who worked on the Taj Mahal – here in 1659 to pay their respects to the tomb's builders.

Ashrafi Mahal   ISLAMIC HISTORIC SITE

Mohammed Shah originally built his tomb as a madrasa (Islamic college), before converting and extending it. The overambitious design later collapsed – notably the seven-storey circular tower of victory. The building is an empty shell, but intricate Islamic pillarwork can be seen at the top of its great stairway.

Rewa Kund Group

A pleasant 4km-cycle south of the village Mandu, past Sagar Talao, brings you to two more ruins (Indian/foreigner ₹5/100, video ₹25; ☉dawn-dusk). Tickets for both should be bought from outside Baz Bahadur's Palace.

Baz Bahadur's Palace   PALACE

Baz Bahadur was the last independent ruler of Mandu. His palace, constructed around 1509, is beside the Rewa Kund tank where a water lift at the northern end supplied water to the palace. A curious mix of Rajasthani and Mughal styles, it was actually built decades before Baz Bahadur came to power.

Rupmati's Pavilion   HINDU MONUMENT

Standing at the top of a cliff plunging 366m to the plains, Rupmati's Pavilion has a beauty unmatched by the other monuments – and some of the dinkiest stone staircases you'll ever climb. According to Malwa legends, the music-loving Baz Bahadur built it to persuade a beautiful Hindu singer, Rupmati, to move here from her home on the plains. From its terrace and domed pavilions, Rupmati could gaze down at the distant glint of the sacred Narmada River.

In fact, the pavilion was built in two or three phases and the style of its arches and pillars suggests it was completed 100 years before Rupmati's time. Nonetheless, the love story is a subject of Malwa folk songs – not least because of its tragic ending. Lured by tales of Rupmati's beauty, Akbar marched on the fort and Baz Bahadur fled, leaving his lover to poison herself.

This place is simply gorgeous at sunset.

Other Sights

Nil Kanth Palace   HINDU HISTORIC SITE

If you're looking for a great reason to cycle out into the countryside, consider visiting this unusual former palace turned temple. It stands at the head of a ravine, on the site of an earlier Shiva shrine – its name means God with Blue Throat – and is now once again used as a place of worship. A stream built by one of Akbar's governors trickles through a delightful spiral channel and is usually filled with sweet-scented water.

To get here, cycle south along Main Rd for less than 1km until you see a large white water tower. Turn right here and follow the road as it twists and turns past villages all the way to Nil Kanth (about 2km). You can continue from here, past more remote villages, for about another kilometre to reach the still-standing gateway of the now ruined Songarh Fort, from where there are more great views.

Jain Temple   JAIN TEMPLE

Entered by a kaleidoscopic potpourri of colour, this complex is a splash of kitsch among the Islamic monuments. The richly decorated temples feature marble, silver and gold *tirthankars* with jade eyes, and behind them is a theme parklike museum with a walk-on replica of Shatrunjaya, the hilltop temple complex at Palitana in Gujarat. In the colourful murals, bears devour sinners' arms, crocodiles chew their heads, and demons saw one evil character in half, lengthways.

Saturday Haat
MARKET

(☉10am-dusk) This colourful weekly *haat* (market), behind Jama Masjid, is similar to ones held all over the Bastar region, a tribal stronghold of Chhattisgarh. Adivasis (tribes-people) walk kilometres to come here to buy and sell goods ranging from mountains of red chillis to dried *mahua* (a flower used to make a potent liquor of the same name).

🛏 Sleeping & Eating

You get noticeably less for your money in Mandu and wi-fi is hard to come by. Be sure to stop by and have chai with the friendly Rami, whose tea stand is under the shady ficus tree between Jama Masjid and Ashrafi Mahal.

Rama Guesthouse
GUESTHOUSE $

(☑ 263251; r ₹300, without bathroom ₹200) Made up of a row of simple rooms off a courtyard that leads to the small Rama Temple, accommodation here is slightly more atmospheric than fellow budget choices. Some bathrooms have showers and sit-down flush toilets, but these are still very basic digs. Walk through an archway between two shops by the bus stand to get here.

Reception is beyond the rooms, inside the temple grounds, where you'll find a non-English speaking curmudgeon of a manager. *Namaste!*

Hotel Rupmati
HOTEL $$

(☑ 07292-263270; Main Rd; r from ₹1750, with AC ₹2100; ✲) Clean, colourful row of rooms with large bathrooms are perched on the edge of a cliff with great views of the valley below. Air-con itself (and a little less upkeep) is the only difference between the non-AC and AC rooms. There's a restaurant and delightful outdoor eating lawn with views.

Malwa Retreat
HOTEL $$

(☑ 07292-263221; www.mptourism.com; Main Rd; r/tents ₹2050/3650, with AC ₹3230; ✲) This is MP Tourism's cheaper option, with air-cooled and air-con rooms and nicely appointed tents with valley views. The newish spick-and-span Malwa Retreat Cafeteria is a step up for Mandu's dining scene and reception doubles as the Tourist Interpretation Centre, where you can arrange local guides (half-day ₹375). It's in a location handy to the village.

Malwa Resort
HOTEL $$

(☑ 07292-263235; www.mptourism.com; Main Rd; r with AC from ₹4070; ✲ 🔊 ✺) The best thing about this family-friendly MP Tourism property, 2km south of the village, is morning chai in the lakeside gazebo, watching local fishermen cast their nets over lake Sagar Talao. Otherwise, there are large gardens containing comfortable cottages, children's play areas, tree swings and a pool, restaurant and bar.

No compelling reason to consider upgrading categories here – you won't get anything noticeable over the standard rooms.

Shivani Restaurant
INDIAN $

(Main Rd; mains ₹60-180, thali ₹80-180; ☉9am-10pm) The subtle canteen-style interior of this no-nonsense diner with plastic tables and chairs is appreciatively understated compared with the gaudy exterior, but it's the good, honest and cheap food that overshadows both. The menu is extensive and includes solid thalis plus local specialities such as *Mandu kofta* (dumplings in a mild sauce).

South Indian breakfasts are also available, as are lassis and coffee. It also has open-air 'garden' seating across the street.

Yatrika
INDIAN $

(Main Rd; mains ₹90-280; ☉8-10am, noon-3pm & 7-10pm) This small cafe at Malwa Retreat dishes out veg and nonveg Indian meals in very flash (for Mandu) contemporary premises with an open kitchen. If you want a cold beer you'll need to head to the sister property, the Malwa Resort.

🛍 Shopping

Roopayan
HANDICRAFTS

(Main Rd; ☉9am-7pm) Next to Malwa Retreat, this small shop sells good-quality scarves, shawls, bed spreads, and clothing made from material that has been block-printed in the nearby village of Bagh.

ℹ Information

Harsh Communication/Malima Medical (Main Rd; per hr ₹40; ☉8am-9pm) This side-by-side family operation is the only internet game in town. Harsh has just one terminal while Malima, a pharmacy, can hook up your laptop.

Post Office (☑ 263222; www.indiapost.gov.in; Main Rd; ☉9am-5pm) Next to Jain Temple.

State Bank of India ATM The only ATM in the village.

ℹ️ Getting There & Away

There are four buses to Indore (₹100, 3½ hours, 8.30am, 9am, 2.30pm and 3.45pm), one to Ujjain (₹150, six hours, 6.30am) and regular services to Dhar (₹30, one hour, 6.30am to 7pm), where you can change for buses to Dhamnod (₹50, two hours), then, in turn, for Maheshwar (₹15, 30 minutes, last bus 6pm) or Omkareshwar (₹70, 3½ hours, last bus 6pm). If doing this, it's quicker to get off 14km before Dhar at a junction called Oonera (₹15, 30 minutes) from where you can flag down Dhamnod-bound buses (₹50, 1½ hours).

ℹ️ Getting Around

Cycling is the best way to get around, as the terrain is flat, the air clear and the countryside beautiful. We didn't see a single autorickshaw on our visit. **Ritik Cycles** (📞 9000157920; Main Rd; per day ₹100) rents bicycles right in the village.

EASTERN MADHYA PRADESH

Jabalpur

📞 0761 / POP 1.27 MILLION

Domestic tourists mostly come here to visit Marble Rocks, an attractive river gorge nearby, but for foreigners this industrial city of *chowks* and working men's taverns is used mainly as a launchpad for the famous tiger parks – Kanha, Bandhavgarh and Pench.

👁 Sights

Rani Durgavati Museum   MUSEUM
(Indian/foreigner ₹10/100, camera/video ₹50/200; ⊙10am-5pm Tue-Sun) Displays a collection of 10th-century sculptures from local sites, while upstairs are galleries for stone and copper inscriptions, ancient coins and a photograph exhibition of Bhedaghat's 64 Yogini Temple.

☞ Tours

Tiger Safari   4WD SAFARI
(📞 8120445454; www.thetigersafari.com)
If you can't be fussed with a DIY safari, this agency – inherently involved in tiger conservation – can customise safari tours throughout Eastern MP. Photography wildlife tours are a speciality, but it handles birding and cultural itineraries as well. Five per cent of the profits go towards three tiger-saving NGOs.

Expect to pay from ₹13,500 (budget) to ₹66,000 (top end) per day for custom safaris for two people all-inclusive, depending on a variety of factors (type of vehicle, accommodation, number of 4WD tours, number of days etc). Prices come down for groups of six or more people.

🛏 Sleeping & Eating

Lodge Shivalaya   HOTEL $
(📞 2625188; Napier Town; s/d from ₹460/560, r with AC incl breakfast from ₹1200; ❋) Rooms are basic, but are clean enough for one night

---

WORTH A TRIP

MARBLE ROCKS AT BHEDAGHAT

Known locally as Bhedaghat, the magnesium-limestone cliffs at this gorge on the holy Narmada River, 22km west of Jabalpur, change colours in different lights, from pink to black. They're particularly impressive by moonlight, and parts are floodlit at night.

More pleasant than awe-inspiring (during the day, anyway), the trip up the 2km-long gorge is made in a shared **motorboat** (per person 30/50min ₹50/70; ⊙7am-7pm, full moon 8pm-midnight, closed during monsoon 15 Jun-15 Oct) from the jetty at Panchvati Ghat (private boats run ₹750/1500 for the same timeframes). Sticking around? The **Dhuandhar (Smoke Cascade)** waterfall is a worthwhile 1.5km walk uphill from the ghat. Along the way is the much-revered **Chausath Yogini**, a circular 10th-century temple dedicated to the Hindu goddess Durga and accessed via a steep flight of steps on the right-hand side of the road. Once at the falls, you can take a short cable-car ride (₹75 return) to the other side of the gorge.

Local city buses 203/203A leave regularly for Bhedaghat (₹15, 45 minutes, 8am to 10pm) from Model Rd opposite Jabalpur bus stand. They drop you at a crossroads 100m from Panchvati Ghat (right side of fork). To return, wait at the crossroads for a passing bus or squeeze into Jabalpur-bound shared autorickshaws (₹20).

Jabalpur

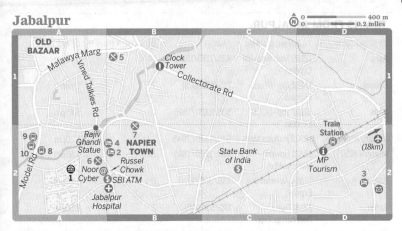

and come with TVs and small bathrooms. The cheapest 1st-floor rooms open onto a large shared balcony overlooking the bustling and noisy street below. Checkout is 24 hours.

Hotel Wardhman HOTEL $$
(☎0761-4006002; www.hotelwardhman.com; Russel Crossing; s/d incl breakfast from ₹1440/1680; ❄️🖥️) Down an alley off Russel Chowk, the Wardhman underwent a massive modernisation in 2013, catapulting itself into Russel Chowk's best deal. Rooms aren't massive, but everything is new and clean – save the odd musty bathroom – with all the modern fixings, most notably being the miraculous hot-water pressure and huge flat-screen TVs. Breakfast is great – ask Sussil for an *idli* demonstration! Free wi-fi throughout.

Kalchuri Residency HOTEL $$
(☎0761-2678491; www.mptourism.com; South Civil Lines; s/d incl breakfast from ₹3860/4200; ❄️🖥️🏊) One of the nicest MP Tourism properties in the state, this government hotel is located in the quieter Civil Lines area just south of the train station. It has large, modern deluxe AC rooms in soothing earth tones with TVs, kettles and spacious renovated bathrooms. Standard AC rooms are nearly as good.

There's a nice restaurant (mains ₹130 to ₹310) and a spacious pub (beer from ₹225).

Indian Coffee House SOUTH INDIAN $
(www.indiancoffeehousejabalpur.com; Hotel India; coffee from ₹10, mains from ₹60; ⊙7am-10pm) Classic for filtered coffee and South Indian breakfasts.

Jabalpur

◎ Sights
1 Rani Durgavati Museum A2

🛏 Sleeping
2 Hotel Wardhman................................B2
3 Kalchuri Residency D2
4 Lodge Shivalaya B2

🍴 Eating
5 Indian Coffee House B1
6 Saheb's Food Junction......................A2
7 Yellow Chili......................................B2

ⓘ Transport
8 Buses to Bhedaghat..........................A2
9 Old Bus Stand A2
10 Rohani Bus......................................A2

Saheb's Food Junction MUGHLAI $$
(Russel Chowk; meals ₹80-300; ⊙11am-11.30pm) Best nonveg in Russel Chowk isn't afraid to spice things up in their fiery gravies (mutton curry, *kadhai* chicken). Does Chinese as well.

★Yellow Chili NORTH INDIAN $$$
(www.theyellowchilli.com; Dixit Pride, Napier Town; mains ₹240-360; ⊙noon-midnight) This higher-end Indian chain, the domain of celeb chef Sanjeev Kapoor, might not be top choice in Delhi, but it's a gastro-godsend in Jabalpur. Creative takes on gourmet Indian fare rule here and everything is a flavour bomb. The *khurcha saag murh* (chicken tikka in spinach, fenugreek, coloured peppercorns and mustard seeds) was our favourite dish in all of MP.

TRAINS FROM JABALPUR

DESTINATION	TRAIN NO & NAME	FARE (₹)	DURATION (HR)	DEPARTURE
Agra	12189 Mahakaushal Express	425/1110/1580	14	6.10pm
Bhopal	11472 Jbp–Bhopal Express	215/575/820	7	11pm
Delhi	12192 Jbp–NDLS Express	505/1320/1895	18	5.45pm
Kolkata (Howrah)	12322 Kolkata Mail	540/1420/2045	22	1.20pm
Mumbai (CST)	12321 Howrah–Mumbai Mail	490/1290/1845	17½	5.55pm
Raipur	12854 Amarkantak Express	335/860/1210	9½	9.20pm
Satna	22131 Pune–Darbhanga Exp	170/535/745	3	8.50am
Umaria	18233 Narmada Express	100/485/690	4	6.35am
Varanasi	12165 Lokmanya Tilak Express	330/850/1200	10	8.50pm (Mon, Thu, Fri)

Fares: sleeper/3AC/2AC

❶ Information

Jabalpur Hospital (Napier Town; ⊙24hr) Jabalpur's top private hospital.

Noor Cyber (Russel Chowk; per hr ₹15; ⊙10am-10pm; ☎) Has wi-fi.

MP Tourism (☑0761-2677690; www.mptourism.com; ⊙8am-8pm Mon-Sat, 9am-5pm Sun) At the south entrance of the train station.

Post Office (www.indiapost.gov.in; Residency Rd; ⊙10am-4pm Mon-Fri, to 3pm Sat)

State Bank of India (South Civil Lines; ⊙10.30am-4.30pm Mon-Fri, to 1pm Sat) Changes American Express travellers cheques and cash, and has an ATM; there's also an ATM at the train station and others around the city.

❶ Getting There & Away

AIR

Air India (☑0761-2904090; 1455 Narmada Rd) flies to Delhi on Monday, Wednesday and Friday. **SpiceJet** (www.spicejet.com) flies to Delhi and Mumbai daily.

BUS

Services from the old bus stand include three daily buses to Kanha National Park (₹160, four hours, 7am, 11am and 12.30pm). Otherwise, catch a bus to Mandla (₹92, three hours, frequent 6am to 9pm) and switch.

For Pench Tiger Reserve, catch a bus to Khawasa (₹200, five hours, half-hourly 8.30am to 11.30pm), then take a shared 4WD (₹10) for the final 12km. For Bandhavgarh National Park, it's best to take a direct train to Umaria, but you can also take a bus to Katni (₹100, three hours, frequent 5am to 11pm), from where there are trains and buses to Umaria.

For more comfort on long-distance trips, **Rohani Bus** (☑8889186709; Model Rd) has daily services to Indore (seat/sleeper ₹500/600, 12 hours, 7pm) and Raipur (seat/sleeper ₹350/400, 10 hours, 7pm).

TRAIN

More than 10 daily trains leave for Satna, from where you can take a bus to Khajuraho. You may have to catch a bus from Satna to Panna and change again for Khajuraho. For Bandhavgarh National Park, take a train to Umaria.

❶ Getting Around

A cycle-rickshaw from the train station to Russel Chowk is ₹25. Autorickshaws are usually double the price.

Kanha National Park

☑07649

Madhya Pradesh is the king of the jungle when it comes to tiger parks, and Kanha (www.kanhanationalpark.com; Indian/foreigner ₹1250/2450, premium zones ₹1850/3650, 4WD from ₹1800, guide ₹300; ⊙mid-Oct–mid-Jun, closed Wed evening) is the most famous. The forests are vast, and while your chances of seeing a tiger are probably slightly slimmer than at nearby Bandhavgarh, at the time of research sightings were on the rise. Add to that the fact that you can really go deep into the forest, and you have a complete safari experience, rather than the rush-and-grab outings some complain of at Bandhavgarh.

The sal forests and vast meadows contain tigers (89 at last count) and leopards and support huge populations of deer and antelope, including the rare *barasingha* (deer). You'll see plenty of langur monkeys, the odd gaur (Indian bison), maybe even a family or two of wild boar and the odd lonesome jackal or two. The park is also home to more than 300 bird species.

Khatiya Gate in Khatiya village is easily the most popular; other gates into the park include Mukki, 45km southeast of Khatiya, and Sarahi, 60km northeast.

Bookings for **4WD safaris** are made online (www.mponline.gov.in) up to 120 days in advance, but foreign cards weren't being accepted at the time of writing. Save yourself immense hassle by allowing hotels/agencies to do this.

Ten percent of safari tickets (14 4WDs) are reserved for gate sales and are sold 30 minutes before opening – but this is a major hassle and lines form as early as midnight the evening prior. Vehicle fees may be higher if you need to drive further to enter from a more distant gate (depending on the zone you are visiting). New park formalities have also been implemented to fiscally discourage walk-ups: if you meet other folks with a reservation and extra space in their 4WD, you cannot just join in and share the costs. For anyone joining a booked reservation, you will pay an add-on fee, which is the park entrance fee per person (rather than per 4WD). So, two foreigners joining a booked group for the premium zone will pay ₹3650 each to join. Note, a 4WD containing Indian nationals and foreigners costs the foreign-tourist price.

There are two safari slots each day: morning (roughly 6am to 11am) and afternoon (roughly 3pm to 6pm). The morning safaris are longer and tend to produce more tiger sightings.

◎ Sights & Activities

MP Tourism Canter 4WD SAFARI
(Indian/foreigner ₹1200/3200) These two 12-seat canters operated by MP Tourism are a last-resort option for getting into the park.

They do not stray beyond the Kisli zone. Book through MP Tourism.

Nature Trails WALKING
(guide ₹400; ☺ 6-11am & 3-6pm) A well-marked 7km trail leads from just inside Khatiya Gate and skirts along the edge of the park before looping back to the village. Mostly you'll see a lot of monkeys and birds, but tigers do venture into this area on occasions and an accompanying guide is essential.

🛏 Sleeping & Eating

Most hotels have restaurants. There's a row of small *dhabas* just before Khatiya Gate serving cheap thalis (₹80) and chai. If you're on a morning safari, you can grab breakfast (₹20), tea and coffee when you stop at the interpretation centre inside the park.

🛏 Inside the Buffer Zone

Note, while lodgings in the buffer zone enjoy a wonderfully natural forest location, there are none of the facilities that are available in the village outside the park. You'll need to have a room booked here in advance in order to get past security at Khatiya Gate. If you're walking up, book at the MP Tourism Tourist Information Booth next to Khatiya Gate.

Tourist Hostel HOSTEL $$
(☑ 07649-277310; Kisli Village; American Plan dm ₹1300) This MP Tourism property, made up of a few huge, well-kept multibed dorms with clean shared bathrooms and lockers, is inside the buffer zone, right in Kisli village, which leads into the park's core zone. There are no facilities here apart from the dorms, the nearby canteen and the adjacent Baghira Log Huts (another MP Tourism property).

The attraction is that you're staying right in among the monkey-filled forest, and a stone's throw from meadows that attract deer and gaur throughout the day, though you are not allowed to wander far off.

Baghira Log Huts GUESTHOUSE $$
(☑ 07649-277227; www.mptourism.com; Kisli Village; American Plan s/d from ₹4800/6000; ❄) Apart from the nearby Tourist Hostel, this is the only place inside the buffer zone. Comfortable rather than luxurious log cabin-style rooms are set among the trees and overlook a beautiful meadow. There's a restaurant and bar. The single price is only available on a walk-up basis, not online.

MADHYA PRADESH & CHHATTISGARH KANHA NATIONAL PARK

In the Village by Khatiya Gate

Machan Complex   GUESTHOUSE **$**

(☑ 9993672827; dm ₹100, r ₹500-700) Like staying in a tiny village, Machan has bucket hot-water rooms in different buildings, all a bit shabby, set around a huge banyan tree. There's a new dorm building, basic mud-hut doubles, and larger rooms with sit-down flush toilets. The owner, Anil, is a naturalist and extremely welcoming. About 1km before Khatiya Gate, on the right.

Pugmark Resort   HOTEL **$$**

(☑ 07649-277291; www.pugmarkresort.com; r without/with AC incl breakfast ₹2300/2800, s/d American Plan with AC ₹4000/4500; ✳ 🛜) These spacious village-like cottages in Khatiya are just a step above basic but bright and airy and set around a pleasant, albeit slightly overgrown, garden. It's a well-oiled family-run operation, and Rahul, the owner/manager, is very knowledgeable and nails five-star service for three-star prices (in addition to being the resident painter).

From breakfast on down, the food is outstanding – they even use milk from their own two Holsteins. Wi-fi throughout.

Motel Chandan   HOTEL **$$**

(☑ 07649-277220, 9425855220; www.motelchandan.com; r ₹1000-1400, with AC ₹2100; ✳@🛜) Great-value modern rooms, some with teakwood accents, right in Khatiya village. The friendly owner is a smooth guy who organises safaris with four of his own 4WDs and two resident naturalists. American Plan (meals included) runs ₹500 extra per person.

★ Kipling Camp   HOTEL **$$$**

(☑ 011-65196377; www.kiplingcamp.com; Mocha Village; American Plan s/d ₹17,800/26,600; ✳🛜) 🍃 A wonderful, laid-back wildlife lodge hosted by one of India's most formidable tiger proponents, former Nat Geo photographer Belinda Wright. It's as informative as it is relaxing to stay in this jungle setting where wildlife discussions follow excellent communal meals (Indian for lunch, continental for dinner) and guests retire to rustic-chic lodges slightly scented with essence of English colonialism.

Nature abounds in the fenceless grounds where langur monkeys and chitals make regular appearances, only to be outshined by an occasional tiger and leopard flyby. You can also swim in the river with Tara, the camp's memorable 55-year-old elephant, a truly extraordinary experience.

ℹ Information

A Central Bank of India ATM next to Motel Chandan accepts foreign cards.

Tourist Information Booth (☑ 07469-277242; www.mptourism.com; Khatiya Gate; ⊙10am-8pm) In addition to tourist info and government hotel bookings, this MP tourism office books the 12-seat government canter for safaris.

ℹ Getting There & Away

The nearest train station, 56km north in Mandla, is only a narrow gauge station and therefore only reachable by a general seating train from Nainpur (Maharashtra).

There are six daily buses from Khatiya Gate to Mandla (₹60, 2½ hours, 2.15am, 6.30am, 8am, 9am, 12.45pm, 5.45pm). The 6.30am, 9am and 12.45pm continue to Jabalpur (₹160, 5½ hours). For Raipur, there's one daily bus from Mocha (₹210, four hours, 8.30am).

If you catch a bus only as far as Mocha, you can arrange a pick-up with your hotel or you'll have to hitchhike the remaining 5km to Khatiya.

Services from Mandla bus stand:

Jabalpur ₹90, 2½ hours, half-hourly 5am to 11pm

Kanha ₹60, two hours, 6.20am (to Mocha), 8.30am (to Mocha), 11.30am and 12.40pm

Nagpur (buses go via Khawasa for transfer to Pench National Park) ₹230, eight hours, eight daily (6am, 8.30am, 7.45am, 1pm, 9pm, 9.30pm, 10.30pm and 11pm)

Raipur ₹230, eight hours, five daily (5am, 7.30am, 11.40am, 7.45pm and 9.30pm)

Bandhavgarh National Park

☑ 07653

If your sole reason for visiting a national park in India is to see a tiger, look no further. Though it's not as easy as it used to be, a couple of days at **Bandhavgarh** (www.bandhavgarhnationalpark.com; Indian/foreigner per jeep ₹1250/2450, premium zones ₹2450/4850, jeep ₹2000, guide ₹300; ⊙16 Oct-30 Jun, closed Wed evenings) should net you a tiger sighting in this relatively small park, whose Tala Range boasts the highest density of Royal Bengal tigers in the world (68 as of 2013). Neck and neck with Rajasthan's Ranthambhore National Park for sightings, it is India's top tiger playground. There are also more than

40 rarely seen leopards and more commonly sighted animals such as deer, wild boar and langur.

The park is entered at the small, laid-back village of Tala, 32km from Umaria, the nearest train station. Like Kanha, Bandhavgarh has a lot of budget accommodation making this a good place for independent travellers to find others to share safari costs.

The park takes its name from an ancient fort perched on top of 800m-high cliffs. Its ramparts provide a home for vultures, blue rock thrushes and crag martins. You can visit on special 4WD trips during the day, but you'll have to pay all the usual park entry fees.

A **4WD safari** (www.mponline.gov.in) can be booked online up to 120 days in advance, but foreign credit cards weren't being accepted at the time of writing. Save yourself immense hassle by allowing hotels/agencies to do this. Ten percent of safari tickets (11 4WDs) are reserved for gate sales and are sold 30 minutes before opening. Lines form as early as midnight the evening prior and it's a free-for-all, with you against the locals when the gates open (read: you aren't likely to win). New park formalities have also been implemented to fiscally discourage walk-ups: if you meet other folks with a reservation and extra space in their jeep, you cannot just join them and share the costs. For anyone joining a booked reservation, you will pay an add-on fee, which is the park entrance fee per person (rather than per 4WD). So two foreigners joining a booked group for Tala Gate will pay ₹4850 each to join.

Note that Maghdi (7km from the village) and Khitauli Gates (6km from the village) have cheaper 4WD charges. With safari numbers drastically reduced in the 2012 review, booking early is essential. February to June are the best months for sightings.

◎ Sights & Activities

Interpretation Centre   MUSEUM
(⊙ 11am-1.30pm & 6-8pm, closed Wed evening)
`FREE` Interesting exhibits detailing the history and legends of Bandhavgarh, plus some superb tiger photos on the 1st floor. On your right just before the village.

MP Tourism Canter   4WD SAFARI
(☑ 07627-265366; www.mptourism.com; White Tiger Forest Lodge; Indian/foreigner ₹1200/2400) If all else fails, you can book one of MP Tourism's two 12-seat canters, which only

traverse the Magdhi and Khitauli zones of the park.

🛏 Sleeping & Eating

Kum Kum Home   HOTEL **$**
(☑ 9424330200; r ₹600-800) The lesser of the dismal budget evils in town. At least the bottom-barrel basic rooms have verandahs and access to garden swings!

★ **Nature Heritage Resort**   HOTEL **$$**
(☑ 07653-265351; www.natureheritageresort. com; s/d incl breakfast ₹4800/5800, American Plan ₹6500/7500; ❄ 🤍) A wonderful mid-range choice with a slick safari operation. The very comfortable adobe-toned cottages, strewn amid a wealth of bamboo-accented everything, approach boutique levels and service is on point. Rooms 109 and 110 catch the lobby-only wi-fi. The owner survived a tiger attack in 2003 – ask him about it!

★ **Tigergarh**   LODGE **$$**
(☑ 7489826868; www.tigergarh.com; s/d incl breakfast ₹4000/4500, American Plan ₹5000/5500; ❄ 🖥) ✈ This 11-room relative newcomer sits under the nose of the surrounding mountains and integrates with nearby villages without nonchalance. A sustainable mantra permeates throughout the peaceful place and the fashionable country-style cottages provide surprising comfort for the price, including four-poster beds and rain-style showers.

Treehouse Hideaway   LODGE **$$$**
(☑ 0124-4222657; www.treehousehideaway.com; s/d American Plan ₹15,000/17,000, Jungle Plan ₹28,000/30,000; ❄ 🤍) With undoubtedly the most special beds in Bandhavgarh, these five massive tree houses clock in at 625 sq m each and are dismantled and reassembled each season 5m off the ground in all their luxurious glory. Beautiful four-poster beds and spacious outdoor porches frame the

---

AMERICAN/JUNGLE PLAN

Many of the resorts at the tiger reserves have part- and all-inclusive packages rather than straight accommodation prices. The so-called American Plan includes accommodation and all meals, while the Jungle Plan includes accommodation and meals plus a morning and an afternoon 4WD safari.

jungly surrounds with poetic aplomb and privacy is tantamount.

Malaya Cafe
CAFE $$

(Tala Main Rd; snacks ₹10-120, breakfast ₹350; ◉9.30am-8pm) This welcoming cafe run by an extroverted Gujarati woman does fabulous three-course brunches (bookings essential) that are the perfect finish to a morning safari. Real filter coffee or lemongrass chai, fresh fruit, porridge and lentil pancakes typically find their way to your plate.

This is also an excellent souvenir shop – Neelam spends two to three months per year driving herself around India picking up wares – and the local Western Union rep.

Kolkata Restaurant
DHABA $$

(Tala Main Rd; mains ₹70-330, thali ₹140; ◉8am-9pm) Friendly chef-owner Amal Jana is a one-man show at this glorified *dhaba* in the middle of the village, where he whips up honest, down-home and extremely tasty thalis – he reckons it's due to the mustard oil – that can be kicked up a notch with a side of his spicy tomato chutney. Also omelettes, Chinese and limited Continental.

❶ Information

Most things in Tala are within one block of each other, including the post office, internet cafes (₹50 per hour), restaurants and a State Bank of India ATM.

❶ Getting There & Around

A cycle-rickshaw to Umaria's bus stand from the train station is ₹10 (10 minutes). There are frequent buses to Tala (₹35, 1½ hours, half-hourly 7am to 6pm). To reach Tala outside of those hours, you'll have to take an autorickshaw (₹500, one hour) or arrange a private taxi in advance (from ₹800).

The last bus from Tala Village back to Umaria bus stand is 7.30pm (₹40, 1½ hours).

TRAIN

Trains from Umaria include the 18477 Utkal Express to Delhi (Nizamuddin station; sleeper/3AC/2AC ₹425/1145/1655, 17 hours, 8.57pm) via Gwalior (₹320/860/1240, 11 hours), Agra (₹365/980/1410, 14 hours) and Mathura (₹380/1030/1480, 15 hours), and the 18234 Narmada Express, which goes to Jabalpur (₹100/485/690, 4½ hours, 4.17pm) before continuing to Bhopal (₹280/745/1070, 12 hours), Ujjain (₹360/970/1395, 16½ hours) and Indore (₹385/1045/1510, 18½ hours).

There are two daily trains to Varanasi: the 15160 Sarnath Express (₹275/735/1035, 12 hours, 4.19am) and the 15232 Gondia Bju Express (₹280/745/1070, 12½ hours, 7.15am), the latter being the best option to Satna (from where you can also catch buses to Khajuraho).

For Chhattisgarh, there are three daily trains to Raipur, the best being the 15159 Sarnath Express (₹230/610/870, eight hours, 10.16pm)

An alternative to Umaria is Katni, a busier railway junction from where there are direct trains to places like Jabalpur, Satna and Varanasi. You'll need to hop on a Manpur-bound bus in Tala village to Manpur Modh (₹10, 10 minutes, half-hourly 7am to 7.30pm), a crossroads 3km beyond Tala Village, where buses to Katni depart (₹100, four hours, hourly, 7am to 9am and noon to 4pm).

Pench Tiger Reserve
☑07695

The third of Madhya Pradesh's trio of well-known tiger parks, **Pench** (www.penchnationalpark.com; Indian/foreigner ₹1250/2450, jeep ₹200, guide ₹300; ◉16 Oct-30 Jun, closed Wed evenings) is made up mostly of teak-tree forest rather than sal and so it has a different flavour from nearby Kanha or Bandhavgarh. It also sees fewer tourists (and fewer tigers;only 33 as of the 2014 census); as you're driving around the park, you'll often feel like you have the whole forest to yourself. Turia Gate is the only one of the park's three gates that is regularly used.

Bookings for **4WD safaris** (www.mponline.gov.in) can be made online up to 120 days in advance, but foreign cards weren't being accepted at the time of writing. Allow hotels/agencies to do this and save yourself the hassle. Ten percent of safari tickets (five 4WDs) are reserved for gate sales and are sold 30 minutes before opening – expect lines to form as early as midnight the night before.

Note that if you meet other folks with a reservation and extra space in their 4WD, you cannot just join them and share the costs. For anyone joining a booked reservation, you will pay an add-on fee, which is the park entrance fee per person (rather than per 4WD). Two foreigners joining a booked group will pay ₹2450 each.

If you get shut out of a traditional 4WD safari, you can book a spot on the 12-seat **MP Tourism Canter** (☑07695-232830; www.mptourism.com; Kipling's Court; Indian/foreigner ₹1200/2400) at Kipling's Court as a last resort. There's a six-person mimimum.

JUNGLE CAT! (EAGLE). JUNGLE CAT! (EAGLE).

Once upon a time in Pench, another journalist and I spotted a jungle cat moments after entering the park. Notoriously shy, the cat waddled on down the road as we excitedly exclaimed, 'Jungle cat!' Our guide was nonplussed, however. '*Eagle*,' he said. 'No no,' we protested. 'Who cares about an eagle? Jungle cat!' '*Eagle*,' he insisted.

Then we got it. A crested hawk-eagle, a fierce bird of prey, was stalking the cat. A Discovery Channel–brutal moment was on the horizon. In a blink, the eagle went into a kamikaze dive, ambushing the cat mercilessly from above. As we pulled up alongside the kill, what we encountered still haunts me to this day. The eagle had a relentless grip on the cat's neck. Through binoculars, his menacing, otherworldly eyes – full of sheer, unadulterated yellow terror – stared right at us in a motionless trance.

The standoff – the eagle with the cat, us with the eagle – lasted 15 minutes. The eagle's stare never once strayed from us, as if sending a very serious warning through the most sinister set of eyes I had ever seen in my life. No horror movie could ever do the moment justice.

Kevin Raub

As at the other tiger parks, there are morning (sunrise to 10.30am) and afternoon (2.30pm to sunset) safaris.

🛏 Sleeping & Eating

Kipling's Court HOTEL **$$**
(☑ 07695-232830; www.mptourism.com; dm/r American Plan ₹1090/3990, r with AC from ₹5690; ❋ @) This government-run property wins in both the budget category (considering prices include all meals, the two well-kept six-bed dorms here are good value) and family category (it boasts the best playground in Turia and 30-odd rabbits!). The private cottages aren't bad either and are dotted around dutifully manicured gardens. There's also a bar. It's 2km past Turia, about 1km before the park gate.

Tathastu HOTEL **$$$**
(☑ 07695-232838; www.tathasturesorts.com; s/d villa ₹9000/12,000, tent ₹12,500/16,000, all American Plan; ❋ @ 🛜 ❄) 🦮 There's an uncomfortable haphazard kitsch to the interior design at this Pench newcomer, but that's immediately forgotten by the incredible value in the villas. Set in American Southwest desert style, each enormous three-bedroom villa comes with a living room, kitchen, dining room, dip pool and a dedicated cook, waiter and housekeeper. Yes, you read that right.

The Flintstones-y cave rooms, the 10m-high treehouses and well-appointed tents are great as well, but are all more expensive than the unbelievably priced villas.

Baghvan Taj LODGE **$$$**
(☑ 07695-232847; www.tajsafaris.com; American Plan s/d ₹29,250/39,000; ❋ @ 🛜 ❄) Taj Hotels has luxury properties at all of MP's major tiger parks, but this discerning choice is the most jungly and worth the splurge. Twelve massive bamboo and sal cottages are hidden away amid the forest and feature exquisite artwork and furniture (including gorgeous antique Rajasthani porch swings), indoor-outdoor showers and massive elevated *machans* (open-air patios).

The open-air common areas follow suit, only to be pleasantly offset by the occasional retro appliance, giving off a blast of whimsy to the place. Food is expectedly divine. A lush pool area and massage room (treatments from ₹2500) round out the luxury.

ⓘ Information

There's a Bank of Maharashtra ATM in Khawasa that accepts foreign cards. Internet can only be found at places of accommodation.

ⓘ Getting There & Away

Regular buses link Khawasa with Nagpur (₹90, two hours, half-hourly 8am to midnight) and Jabalpur (₹280, five hours, half-hourly 9am to 9pm). Shared 4WDs (₹20) run between Khawasa and Turia when full. The main gate to the park is about 3km beyond Turia. The nearest airport and major train station is in Nagpur.

You can go to Kanha National Park from Khawasa without going all the way to Jabalpur or Mandla. Flag down any north-bound bus to

Seoni (₹50, one hour, frequent from 7am) then take a Mandla-bound bus to Chiraidongri (₹95, 3½ hours, frequent 5am to 8.30pm) where there are four daily buses to Khatiya Gate (₹35, one hour, 11am, 4pm, 5pm, 6.45pm) and many more to Mocha.

CHHATTISGARH

Chhattisgarh is remote, its public transport system is poor and its tourist infrastructure outside the main cities is almost nonexistent, but for the intrepid traveller, time spent here may well prove to be the highlight of your trip to this part of India. The country's most densely forested state is blessed with natural beauty – waterfalls and unspoilt nature reserves abound. More interestingly, though, it's home to 42 different tribes whose pointillist paintings and spindly sculptures are as vivid as the colourful *haats* (markets) that take place across the region, particularly around Jagdalpur in Bastar.

Chhattisgarh is one of the eastern states associated with the Naxalite guerrillas (an ultra-leftist political movement that began in Naxal Village, West Bengal), but they rarely stray from their remote hideouts on Chhattisgarh's northern and southern borders.

Raipur

📞 0771 / POP 1.01 MILLION

Chhattisgarh's ugly capital is a centre for the state's steel industry and, apart from being a day trip away from Sirpur, has little in the way of tourist attractions. The Chhattisgarh

LOCAL KNOWLEDGE

ANT-EDOTE

Red ants are more than just a painful nuisance to the Bastar tribes. Known as *chapura*, they also play an important role in food and medicine. They are often eaten live, served on a leaf with white ant eggs. Alternatively, villagers grind them into a paste and mix them with chilli to make chutney. The bodies of *chapura* contain formic acid believed to have useful medicinal qualities. If suffering from a fever, locals will sometimes put their hand into an ants nest, allowing it to be bitten hundreds of times so that the acid is administered into their bloodstream. Patients presumably soon forget their fever.

Tourism Board head office here is worth visiting though.

🛏 Sleeping & Eating

Hotel Jyoti
HOTEL $

(📞 0771-2428777; hoteljyoti@gmail.com; Pandri; s/d from ₹650/850, with AC from ₹1200/1450; ❄🌐) A welcome retreat after a long bus journey. Basic rooms have flourishes of character and colour and the manager is helpful. Right opposite the Naya bus stand.

Hotel Radhika
HOTEL $

(📞 9575303807; Jaistambh Chowk; s/d from ₹630/950, with AC from ₹890/1120; ❄) A centrally located budget stop with rooms varying from in desperate need of renovation to decent AC midrangers. It's on a busy chowk (the acceptable air-cooler deluxe rooms are somewhat spoilt by noise) and there are ATMs opposite, a thali restaurant and a good bar. Book ahead – it's popular.

Girnar Restaurant
INDIAN $$

(Hotel Radhika, Jaistambh Chowk; mains ₹160-240, unlimited thali week/weekend ₹150/170; ⏰noon-4.30pm & 7.30-10.30pm) This well-groomed institution of a restaurant serves good-quality Indian food. It's right opposite Hotel Radhika reception. Upstairs, the separate thali restaurant is wonderful too.

ℹ Information

There are ATMs outside the bus and train stands, and a few opposite Hotel Radhika.

Chhattisgarh Tourism Board

(📞 18001026415; www.tourism.cg.gov.in; Train Station; ⏰7am-10pm) Gives statewide advice and can help organise tribal visits, transport, accommodation and guides. There's also a booth at the airport.

ℹ Getting There & Around

AIR

Air India (📞 0771-4060942; Pandri; ⏰10am-5.30pm Mon-Sat) Flies to Mumbai (from ₹3119, 1.20pm) via Visakhapatnam (from ₹2900) and to Delhi (from ₹3585, 9.20am). Turn left out of the bus stand and the office is 1km along on your left, just past the level crossing.

Jet Airways (📞 0771-2418612; www.jetairways. com; Airport) Flies to Mumbai (from ₹4000, 9.10am) and Delhi (from ₹4000, 7.55pm).

IndiGo (📞 0771-2418213; www.indigo.in; Airport) Flies to Delhi (from ₹7826, 9.30am and 6.55pm), Mumbai (from ₹3500, 8.35am) via Indore (from ₹2700), Kolkata (from ₹5061,

4.15pm), Banguluru (from ₹6000, 9.05am) via Hyderabad (from ₹3000) and Chennai (from ₹6000, 7.45pm) via Hyderabad.

BUS

The government bus ticket office is invariably unstaffed so it's far easier to use private bus companies, which all operate out of the bus stand area too. **Mahendra Travels** (www.mahendrabus.in) is a reliable private company with a ticket desk on the corner of the bus stand.

There are frequent departures to Jagdalpur (seat ₹300 to ₹375, AC Volvo ₹400, seven hours, 5.15am to midnight), Jabalpur (seat/sleeper ₹350/400, 11 hours, 6am to 9pm) and Nagpur (seat/sleeper ₹250/270, eight hours, 6am, 7am, 8.30pm, 10pm, 10.30pm).

AUTORICKSHAWS

From the prepaid booth outside the train station (the one with the hard-hat-shaped roof), autorickshaws run to the bus stand (₹50) and the airport (₹240 including parking fee). Shared autos (₹15) ply the same route as well as the main GE Rd between Jaistambh Chowk and the Chhattisgarh Tourism head office.

TRAIN

Useful trains include the 18237 Chhattisgarh Express to Delhi (Nizamuddin station; sleeper/3AC/2AC ₹565/1505/2200, 27½ hours, 4.20pm) via Nagpur (5½ hours), Bhopal (14½ hours), Jhansi (19½ hours), Gwalior (21½ hours) and Agra (24 hours), and the 12859 Gitanjali Express to Kolkata (Howrah station; ₹445/1160/1655, 13 hours, 11.35pm).

Jagdalpur

☎ 07782 / POP 125,345

The capital of the Bastar region is an ideal base for exploring tribal Chhattisgarh. The town itself hosts a *haat* every Sunday where you'll see Adivasis (tribal people) buying, selling and bartering alongside town traders, but it's in the surrounding villages where Adivasi life can be fully appreciated. Some villages are extremely remote, and only really accessible with a guide. Others, though, are just a bus ride away and, particularly on market days, can be explored independently.

Sanjay Market, which hosts the Sunday *haat,* is the heartbeat of Jagdalpur.

◉ Sights

★ Chitrakote Falls   WATERFALL
India's broadest waterfall (300m), two-thirds the size of Niagara, is at its roaring best just after the rains, but it's beautiful year-round, particularly at sunset. When the

THE VENERABLE LAXMAN TEMPLE

A possible day trip from Raipur, Sirpur is home to dozens of ruined Hindu temples and Buddhist monasteries, all dotted around the village and surrounding countryside. Many of the excavations are works in progress. All are free to see apart from the star of the show, the 7th-century **Laxman Temple** (Indian/foreigner ₹5/100; ⊙ dawn-dusk), one of the oldest brick temples in India.

Buses from Raipur bus stand drop you at Sirpur Modh (₹40, two hours), a junction 17km from Sirpur where you'll have to wait for a bus or shared 4WD (₹10, 25 minutes) to the village. For Laxman Temple, turn right past the snack stalls and keep walking for 1km. It's on the left, past the petrol pump.

water is low, it's possible to paddle in pools at the top of the drop. Take extreme care. In the river below the falls you can swim or get a local fisherman to row you up to the spray (₹55). Take the steps down from the garden of the government-only hotel.

The falls are 40km east of Jagdalpur. The last bus back to Jagdalpur is at 4pm.

Anthropological Museum   MUSEUM
(Chitrakote Rd; ⊙ 10.30am-5.30pm Mon-Fri) FREE This old-fashioned museum hoards a fascinating collection of artefacts collected from tribal villages in the 1970s and 1980s.

★☆ Festivals & Events

Dussehra   CULTURAL
(⊙ Oct) For eight particularly lively days in October, Jagdalpur's streets transform into race tracks as immense, homemade chariots are pitted against each other in an unusual climax to the 75-day festival of Dussehra.

🛏 Sleeping & Eating

Hotel Rainbow   HOTEL $
(☎ 07782-221684; hotelrainbow@rediffmail; r from ₹500/630, with AC from ₹1050; ❀ ⑦) Even the cheap, non-AC rooms are huge and well furnished at this well-worn, good-value hotel (wi-fi throughout, hygiene toilet nozzles!), while the in-house Indian restaurant (mains ₹90 to ₹275) is one of the best in town and there's a very blue bar to boot. Management

WORTH A TRIP

BASTAR HAATS & ADIVASI VILLAGES

There are eight tribes in Bastar spread over more than 3500 villages, ranging from the Ghadwa (specialists in bell metal) to the Doria, the only tribe to make their homes from the branches and leaves of trees (instead of mud thatch) in the remote forests of the far south of Chhattisgarh. One of the most fascinating ways to get a closer look are the colourful *haats* (markets). These markets are the lifeblood of tribal Chhattisgarh, and visiting them is an excellent way to get a taste of Bastar's vibrant Adivasi culture. Tribes walk up to 20km to trade everything from their distinctive, almost fluorescent, saris to live red ants (p682).

You'll find all kinds of fascination here, including bell-metal craftwork, a skill passed down through generations for some 300 years in some cases. The large piles of what look like squashed dates are in fact dried *mahuwa*, a type of flower, either eaten fresh, or dried then boiled to create steam, which is fermented to produce a potent liquor, the favourite tipple of many Bastar Adivasis.

You can get to many local Adivasi villages by bus – this is certainly an option on market days – but some are quite inaccessible, and if you want to actually meet tribespeople, rather than just look at them, a guide is essential as a translator if nothing else. They can also help you arrange homestays. A day with **Awesh Ali** (✆9425244925; aweshali@gmail.com; per day ₹1500) is a truly enlightening experience. He speaks nine languages (four of which are tribal) and comes highly recommended. Contact him directly, or go through the Chhattisgarh Tourism Board. A car and driver will cost from ₹1200 per day plus fuel.

Most *haats* run from around noon to 5pm. There are many markets – these are just some of the more popular ones. Ask at the Chhattisgarh Tourism Board in Raipur for details. Shared 4WDs normally hang around markets to take people back to Jagdalpur.

DAY	LOCATION	DISTANCE FROM JAGDALPUR	BUS FARE, DURATION	FEATURES
Mon	Tokapal	23km	₹25, 30min	Bell-metal craftwork from Ghadwa Adivasis
Wed	Darbha	40km	₹40, 1hr	Attended by Bhurwa Adivasis
Thu	Bastar	18km	₹30, 30min	Easy to reach from Jagdalpur
Fri	Nangur	35km	No direct bus	Attended by distant forest Adivasis
	Nagarnar	18km	No direct bus	Colourful Bhatra Adivasis
Sat	Kuknar	65km	₹60, 2hr	Bison-Horn Maria stronghold
Sun	Jagdalpur	-	-	City location, open late into the evening
	Chingitarai	52km	No direct bus	Open, meadow setting
	Pamela	12km	₹10, 20min	Animated crowds bet on cockfighting

can be extra helpful and there's 24-hour checkout. It's opposite Sanjay Market.

Hotel Chetak HOTEL $
(✆07782-223503; s/d ₹330/430, with AC ₹630/730; ❄) Chetak is handy to the bus stand, and though its dead-simple rooms are small, they're better than the price suggests. It has a dimly lit bar-restaurant where cold beer is available. Turn right out of the bus stand and walk 100m. No English is spoken.

🛍 Shopping

Shabari HANDICRAFTS
(Chandi Chowk; ⏱11am-8pm Mon-Sat) A fixed-price government emporium selling Adivasi handicrafts, from small, spindly iron figures to more expensive, heavy bell-metal statues. From the Sanjay Market end of Main Rd, take the third right and continue for 500m. Opposite the Bank of Baroda ATM.

ℹ Information

There's a Bank of Baroda ATM opposite Shabari emporium, and others around town.

Contact the Chhattisgarh Tourism Board (p682) in Raipur to arrange a guide to help with trips to tribal areas of the Bastar region, or arrange your own.

ℹ Getting There & Away

BUS

Buses to Chitrakote Falls (₹40, 1½ hours, hourly 7am to 4pm) leave from near Anumapa Talkies, a local cinema about 2km (cycle-rickshaw ₹20) from the bus stand. From Hotel Rainbow, turn left out of the hotel and take an immediate left on Palace Rd. Take your third right (Chitrakote Rd; 250m) and buses are 50m on your left not too far from Anupama Talkies, a well-known local cinema.

Mahendra Travels (www.mahendrabus. in) offers frequent private services to Raipur (seat/sleeper from ₹300/370, seven hours, half-hourly 4.45am to midnight).

TRAIN

The 18448 Jagdalpur–Bhubaneswar Express heads over the Eastern Ghats on India's highest broad-gauge line to Bhubaneswar (sleeper/3AC/2AC ₹395/1070/1545, 18 hours, 2.30pm) near the Odisha coast, via Koraput (₹140/485/690, three hours). In the opposite direction, the 18447 arrives in Jagdalpur at 1.30pm.

Gujarat

Includes →

Best Places to Eat

→ Vishalla (p696)

→ Shaam-e-Sarhad Village Resort (p731)

→ Gopi Dining Hall (p696)

→ Osho Restaurant (p732)

Best Tribal Fairs

→ Tarnetar Fair (p733)

→ Vautha Fair (p700)

→ Dangs Darbar (p704)

Why Go?

Barely glimpsed by many travellers scurrying between Mumbai (Bombay) and Rajasthan, Gujarat is an easy side-step off the well-beaten tourist trail. While the capital, Ahmedabad (Amdavad), retains some charm amid its chaos, the countryside holds most of this state's many treasures. Traditional artisans in tribal villages weave, embroider, dye and print some of India's finest textiles, and pristine parks harbour unique wildlife, including migratory birds, wild asses and the last remaining prides of Asiatic lions. For the spiritually inclined, sacred Jain and Hindu pilgrimage sites sit atop mountains that rise dramatically from vast flatlands. And colourful festivals burst with a cornucopia of culture.

Gujarat also claims a special relationship to the life and work of Mahatma Gandhi: he was born here, he ignited the satyagraha movement from here, he made his Salt March here – and his legacy remains a vibrant part of public discourse and private lives.

When to Go
Ahmedabad

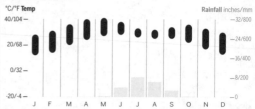

Sep & Oct Navratri festival brings music and dancing to every town and village.

Nov & Dec Mango milkshake time in Junagadh.

Nov–Mar Best for Gujarat's national parks and wildlife sanctuaries.

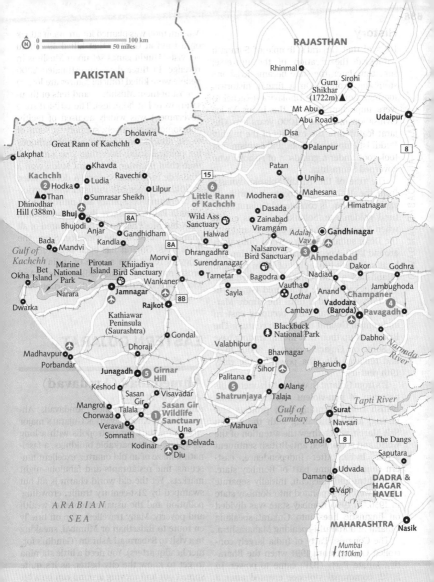

Gujarat Highlights

1 Taking a forest safari in search of Asia's only wild lions at **Sasan Gir Wildlife Sanctuary** (p714)

2 Exploring the villages of **Kachchh** (p726) to admire and acquire some of India's best textiles

3 Tackling a thali, exploring the old-city mosques and paying homage to Mahatma Gandhi in bustling **Ahmedabad** (p688)

4 Exploring an abandoned capital city and following pilgrims up a mountain at the World Heritage Sites of **Champaner** (p704) and **Pavagadh** (p704)

5 Undertaking a challenging dawn pilgrimage to the hilltop temples of **Shatrunjaya** (p707) near Palitana or **Girnar Hill** (p717) near Junagadh

6 Looking for Indian wild ass on the flat salt plains of the **Little Rann of Kachchh** (p733)

History

It's said that Gujarat's Temple of Somnath witnessed the creation of the universe; sometime later, the state became Krishna's stomping ground. On a firmer historical footing, Lothal and Dholavira (Kachchh) were important sites of the Indus Valley civilisation more than 4000 years ago. Gujarat featured in the exploits of the mighty Buddhist emperor Ashoka, and Jainism first took root under a grandson of Ashoka who governed Saurashtra.

The rule of the Hindu Solanki dynasty from the 10th to 13th centuries, with its capital at Patan, is considered Gujarat's cultural golden age. Solanki rule was ended when Ala-ud-din Khilji brought Gujarat into the Delhi sultanate after several campaigns around 1300. A century later the Muslim Gujarat sultanate broke free of Delhi rule and established a new capital at Ahmedabad. The Mughal empire conquered Gujarat in the 1570s and held it until the Hindu Marathas from central India occupied eastern and central Gujarat in the 18th century. The British set up their first Indian trading base at Surat on Gujarat's coast in about 1614, and replaced Maratha power in the early 19th century.

It's from Gujarat that Gandhi launched his program of non-violent resistance against British rule, beginning with protests and fasting, and culminating with the 390km Salt March, which drew the attention of the world and galvanised anti-British sentiment across India. After Independence, eastern Gujarat became part of Bombay state. Saurashtra and Kachchh, initially separate states, were incorporated into Bombay state in 1956. In 1960 Bombay state was divided on linguistic lines into Gujarati-speaking Gujarat and Marathi-speaking Maharashtra.

The Congress Party of India largely controlled Gujarat until 1991 when the Bharatiya Janata Party (BJP) came to power. In 2002, communal violence erupted after a Muslim mob was blamed for an arson attack on a train at Godhra that killed 59 Hindu activists. Hindu gangs set upon Muslims in revenge. In three days, an estimated 2000 people were killed (official figures are lower) – most of them Muslims – and tens of thousands were left homeless. The BJP-led state government was widely accused of tacitly, and sometimes actively, supporting some of worst attacks on Muslim neighbourhoods for political gain; later that year Gujarat's then chief minister, Nahendra Modi, won a landslide re-election victory. A decade later, in 2012, a former BJP minister was convicted of criminal conspiracy and murder in the Naroda Patiya massacre during the Godhra riots, but Modi has so far been cleared of all charges related to the violence. Since the 2002 riots, Gujarat has been peaceful, and enjoys a reputation as one of India's most prosperous and businesslike states. And Modi, of course, became India's prime minister in 2014.

EASTERN GUJARAT

Ahmedabad (Amdavad)

079 / POP 5.57 MILLION

Ahmedabad (also called Amdavad, Ahmadabad or Ahemdavad) is Gujarat's major city and a startling metropolis with a long history, many remarkable buildings, a fascinating maze of an old quarter, excellent museums, fine restaurants and fabulous night markets. Yet the old-world charm is all but swamped by 21st-century traffic, crowding, pollution and the usual extremes of wealth and poverty. Many travellers stop off briefly en route to Rajasthan or Mumbai, sneaking in a visit to Sabarmati Ashram (Gandhi's former headquarters). You need a little stamina to get to know the city better, as it's quite spread out and moving around can be a bit of a task.

The old city lies on the east side of the Sabarmati River and used to be surrounded by a 10km-long wall, of which little now remains except 15 formidable gates standing as forlorn islands amid swirling, cacophonous traffic. The new city on the west side of the river, nearly all built in the last 50 years, has wider streets, several major universities and many middle-class neighbourhoods.

History

Ahmedabad was founded in 1411 by Gujarati sultan Ahmed Shah at the spot where, legend tells, he saw a hare chasing a dog and was impressed by its bravery. The city quickly spread beyond its citadel on the east bank of the Sabarmati, and by the 17th century it was considered one of the finest cities in India, a prospering trade nexus adorned with an array of fine Islamic architecture. Its influence waned, but from the second half of the 19th century Ahmedabad rose again as a huge textile centre (the 'Manchester of the East'). By the late 20th century many of the mills had closed and the subsequent economic hardship may have been a contributing factor in the communal violence that split the city in 2002, when about 2000 people, mostly Muslims, were killed. Today Ahmedabad is booming again as a centre for IT, education and chemical production on top of its traditional textiles and commerce, and has been officially dubbed a 'megacity'.

⊙ Sights

The most interesting part of Ahmedabad is the old city, east of the Sabarmati River – particularly the areas of Lal Darwaja, Bhadra Fort and Teen Darwaja, and the market streets that radiate from them.

★**Sabarmati Ashram**   HISTORIC SITE
(www.gandhiashramsabarmati.org; Ashram Rd; ⊙8.30am-6.30pm) **FREE** In peaceful, shady grounds on the Sabarmati River's west bank, this ashram was Gandhi's headquarters from 1917 to 1930 during the long struggle for Indian independence. It's said he chose this site because it lay between a jail and a cemetery, and any *satyagrahi* (nonviolent resister) was bound to end up in one or the other. Gandhi's poignant, spartan living quarters are preserved, and there's a museum that presents a moving and informative record of his life and teachings.

It was from here, on 12 March 1930, that Gandhi and 78 companions set out on the famous Salt March to Dandi, on the Gulf of Cambay, in a symbolic protest, with Gandhi vowing not to return to the ashram until India had gained independence. The ashram was disbanded in 1933, later becoming a centre for Dalit welfare activities and cottage industries. After Gandhi's death some of his ashes were immersed in the river in front of the ashram.

Uttarayan (p692) Skies swarm with kites in Ahmedabad and other cities.

Modhera Dance Festival (p700) Indian classical dance jamboree in Modhera.

Bhavnath Mela (Bhavnath Fair; ⊙ Jan/Feb) Hindu festival at the foot of sacred Girnar Hill in Junagadh.

Mahakali Festival (⊙ Mar/Apr) Pilgrims pay tribute to Kali at Pavagadh hill.

Navratri (p694) Nine nights of dancing all around Gujarat.

Kartik Purnima (Somnath & Shatrunjaya; ⊙ Nov/Dec) A multifaceted holy day for Hindus, Jains and Sikhs (who celebrate it as Guru Nanak Jayanti). There's a large fair at Somnath (p714) and Jain pilgrims flock to Shatrunjaya hill (p707).

It's about 5km north of Lal Darwaja; bus 83 (₹11) runs here from Lal Darwaja bus stand. An autorickshaw from the city centre is about ₹40.

★**Calico Museum of Textiles**   MUSEUM
(☎22868172; www.calicomuseum.org; Sarabhai Foundation; ⊙tours 10.30am & 3pm Thu-Tue) **FREE** This museum contains one of the world's finest collections of antique and modern Indian textiles, all handmade and up to 500 years old. There are some astoundingly beautiful pieces, displaying incredible virtuosity and extravagance. You'll see Kashmiri shawls that took three years to make, and double-*ikat* cloths whose 100,000 threads were each individually dyed before weaving. Two tours are offered each day the museum is open; advance booking is required, either by phone or by email.

The main textile galleries can only be visited on the morning tour (maximum 20 people), which lasts two hours. The afternoon tour (maximum 10 people) is devoted to the Sarabhai Foundation's collection of religious art, which explores depictions of Indian deities, including textile galleries.

Kids under 10 are not welcome. Photography is not permitted and bags are not allowed inside. The museum is in the Shahibag area, 3.5km north of the old centre,

Ahmedabad (Amdavad)

Sabarmati Ashram (2km); 38
Gandhinagar (28km)

University Rd 27

Stadium Circle

Gandhi Bridge

Kasturba Gandhi Rd

Swastik Cross Rd

NAVRANGPURA 32

Ashram Rd

ICICI Bank 35

HDFC ATM (Sri RC Rd)

Sabarmati River

Khanpur Rd (Lady Vidyagauri Rd)

28

7
St Xaviers College Rd

Chimanlal Girdharlal (CG) Rd

HDFC Bank 30

31

18

Mithakali Six Rd

14

33

Gandhigram Train Station

Nehru Bridge

Enlargement

LAL DARWAJA

13

University Rd

Panchwati Circle

Law Garden

Gujarat College

Ellis Bridge

Ahmed Shah's Mosque

1
Swami Vivekananda Rd

Parimal Garden

Mangaldas Rd

29

24

Ashram Rd (Pritamraj Rd)

Sabarmati Riverfront

Lokayatan Folk Museum (250m)

Chimanlal Girdharlal (CG) Rd

34

37

40

5

Bhagtacharya Rd

Sardar Bridge

17

Jamalpur Rd

Jamalpur Gate

Vechaar Utensil Museum (4km);
Vishalla (4km); Sarkhej Roza (5km)

---

opposite the Shahibag Underbridge. An autorickshaw from Lal Darwaja should cost about ₹40.

Bhadra Fort FORT
(Lal Darwaja; ⊙ dawn-dusk) Built immediately after the founding of Ahmedabad in 1411, Bhadra Fort now houses government offices and a Kali temple. Its gate formed the eastern entrance of the Ahmedabad citadel, which stretched west to the river. From the roof you can see the formidable structure and views of surrounding streets. Between the fort and the **Teen Darwaja** (Triple Gateway; Lal Darwaja) to its east was the **Maidan Shahi** (Royal Square), where royal processions and polo games took place. Today it's a seething marketplace.

Lokayatan Folk Museum MUSEUM
(www.shreyasfoundation.in; Indian/foreigner ₹25/100; ⊙ 3-5.30pm Tue-Sat, 10.30am-1.30pm & 3-5.30pm Sun) This museum, 3km west of the

river in Bhudarpura, displays an impressive range of Gujarati folk arts, including wood carvings, metalwork and some wonderful embroidered textiles and amazing tie-dyed quilts. Included in the ticket is the **Kalpana Mangaldas Museum** (⊙ 3-5.30pm Tue-Sat, 10am-1.30pm & 3-5.30pm Sun), with festival masks from around India and, just to round things off, an elephant skeleton. It's all set in the peaceful, peacock-dotted grounds of the Shreyas Foundation. Photos are not allowed.

An autorickshaw from the centre costs around ₹40; say you want to go to Shreyas Foundation.

Lalbhai Dalpatbhai Museum MUSEUM
(LD Museum; www.ldmuseum.co.in; University Rd; ⊙ 10.30am-5.30pm Tue-Sun) FREE Part of the LD Institute of Indology, this museum houses a gorgeous collection of ancient and medieval Indian art treasures, including stone, marble, bronze and wood carvings and

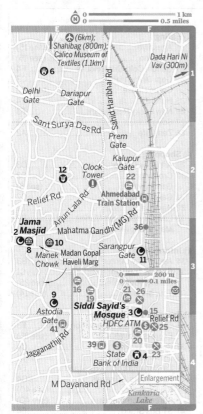

75,000 Jain manuscripts. A 6th-century-AD sandstone carving from Madhya Pradesh is the oldest-known carved image of the god Rama.

NC Mehta Gallery
MUSEUM

(University Rd; ⊙10.30am-5.30pm Tue-Sun) FREE
In the same building as the LD Museum, this gallery has an important collection of jewel-like illustrated manuscripts and miniature paintings. Best known is *Chaurapanchasika* (Fifty Love Lyrics of a Thief), written by Vilhana, an 11th-century Kashmiri poet sentenced to be hanged for loving the king's daughter. Before his execution he was granted one final wish: he chose to recite these 50 poems, which so impressed the king that he gave Vilhana his daughter in marriage.

Sarkhej Roza
HISTORIC BUILDING

(⊙9am-dusk) A mosque, tomb and palace complex dedicated to the memory of Ahmed Shah I's spiritual advisor, Ahmed Khattu Ganj Baksh. The elegant, dilapidated buildings cluster around a great (often dry) tank, constructed by Sultan Mahmud Begada in the mid-15th century. It's an atmospheric place once used as a retreat by Ahmedabad's rulers. The mausoleums of Mahmud Begada (by the entrance, with geometric *jalis* – carved lattice screens casting patterns of light on the floor – and Ganj Baksh (the largest in Gujarat) are both here.

It's located in the Sarkhej area, 8km southwest of the old centre; a return autorickshaw from the city centre will cost around ₹120. Sarkhej Roza could be combined with a visit to Vishalla restaurant (p696) and its Vechaar Utensil Museum (p692), about 1km back towards the city.

Hutheesingh Temple
JAIN TEMPLE

(Balvantrai Mehta Rd) Outside Delhi Gate, north of the old city, the Jain Hutheesingh Temple is constructed of delicately carved white marble. Built in 1848, it's dedicated to Dharamanath, the 15th Jain *tirthankar* (great teacher).

Swaminarayan Temple
HINDU TEMPLE

(Kalupur) The glorious, multicoloured, wood-carved Swaminarayan Temple, in the old city, was built in 1822 as the first temple of the Swaminarayan Hindu sect. Followers believe the sect's founder, Swaminarayan (1781–1830), was the supreme being. The daily Heritage Walk (p693) starts here at 8am and usually coincides with worship at the temple, with believers' passion on full display.

Sabarmati Riverfront
AREA

(www.sabarmatiriverfront.com) Replacing the slum camps that once lined the Sabarmati River, this new waterfront promenade will eventually stretch for 10km through the heart of Ahmedabad. It's a pleasant place to stroll, popular with families and young lovers, and boat rides (motor and pedal) are available. Still very much a work in progress, you can see the plans for the finished park on its website. The waterfront can currently be accessed from numerous points on the western bank of the river.

Kankaria Lake
LAKE

(admission ₹10, 10-min hot-air-balloon ride ₹100; ⊙8am-10pm, hot-air balloon 10am-10pm) Built in 1451 and recently dandified as a recreation space for the city, this large lake is a nice respite from the hectic streets. Attractions

Ahmedabad (Amdavad)

include a tethered hot-air balloon, mini-train and zoo. **One Tree Hill Garden** on the west side (entered from outside) contains some quite grand colonial Dutch tombs.

Vechaar Utensil Museum MUSEUM
(www.vishalla.com; By-Pass Rd; Indian/foreigner ₹10/20; ⊙2-4pm & 5-10.30pm Tue-Sun) At Vishalla restaurant (p696), opposite Vasna Tol Naka, this museum displays pots and utensils, with more than 4500 items from all over India, some 1000 years old.

City Museum MUSEUM
(Bhagtacharya Rd, Sanskar Kendra; ⊙10am-6pm Tue-Sun) FREE The City Museum covers Ahmedabad's history with simple but diverse displays, and explanatory material in English and Gujarati. It includes sections on the city's religious communities, Gandhi and the Independence struggle. The ground floor houses the disappointing Kite Museum, where flattened tissue-paper contraptions resemble trapped butterflies.

Dada Hari Ni Vav NOTABLE BUILDING
(⊙dawn-dusk) This step-well, built in 1499 by the supervisor of Sultan Mahmud Begada's harem, descends through five levels of carved stone columns to two small wells, now often dry. The depths are cool, even on the hottest day, and it's a somewhat eerie place. Behind the step-well, the 16th-century **Dai Halima Mosque** contains the mausoleum of a royal midwife named Halima, with nice *jalis*.

✦ Festivals & Events

Uttarayan KITE FESTIVAL
(Makar Sakranti; ⊙14-15 Jan) Every January, Ahmedabad hosts Uttarayan, a traditional kite festival that attracts international participants and is well worth the stiff neck.

Tours

★ **Nirav Panchal** TOUR
(📞 9825626387; nirupanchal@yahoo.co.in) One of Gujarat's most knowledgeable guides, the charming Nirav Panchal leads customised tours that fit your interests, from single-day experiences in Ahmedabad to multiday trips across all parts of the state. He speaks perfect English, and his French isn't bad either. Call or email him for details and prices, based on your wants.

Heritage Walk WALKING TOUR
(📞 9824032866; Swaminarayan Temple; Indian/foreigner ₹30/50; ⊘ daily 8am) Ahmedabad's Municipal Corporation runs a fascinating daily walking tour through the old city. It starts at 8am at the Swaminarayan Temple in Kalupur and finishes at the Jama Masjid around 10.30am. Meandering through the narrow, confusing streets and past dilapidated, carved wooden houses, it is an excellent way to get a feel for old Ahmedabad with its 600 *pols* – nook-like neighbourhoods with

GUJARAT AHMEDABAD (AMDAVAD)

MOSQUES & MAUSOLEUMS

Under the Gujarat sultanate in the 15th and 16th centuries, and especially under Ahmed Shah I (1411–42) and Mahmud Begada (1459–1511), Ahmedabad was endowed with a remarkable collection of stone mosques in a unique style incorporating elements of Hindu and Jain design. Note that women are not allowed into the actual prayer halls and at some mosques are restricted to the periphery.

Jama Masjid (Friday Mosque; MG Rd) Built by Ahmed Shah in 1423, the Jama Masjid ranks as one of India's most beautiful mosques, enhanced by an enormous, peaceful courtyard. Demolished Hindu and Jain temples provided the building materials, and the mosque displays some architectural fusion with these religions, notably in the lotuslike carving of some domes, which are supported by the prayer hall's 260 columns. There were once two 'shaking' minarets, but they lost half their height in the great earthquake of 1819; their lower portions still flank the prayer hall's central portico.

Mausoleum of Ahmed Shah (Badshah-na-Hazira; MG Rd) This atmospheric mausoleum, outside the Jama Masjid's east gate, may have been constructed by Ahmed Shah himself before his death in 1442. His cenotaph is the central one under the main dome. An 11pm drumming session in the mausoleum's eastern gateway used to signal the closing of the city gates and still happens nightly, carrying on a nearly 600-year-old tradition.

Rani-na-Hazira The tomb of Ahmed Shah's queen sits on a raised platform that's engulfed by market stalls. Though it's not in great shape, the *jali* (carved lattice screens) are worth a look.

Siddi Sayid's Mosque (Lal Darwaja) One of Ahmedabad's most stunning buildings, this mosque is famed for its exquisite *jali* windows, spiderweb fine, depicting the intricate intertwining branches of the 'tree of life'. Built in the year the Mughals conquered Gujarat (1573), by an Abyssinian in the Gujarati army, it was once part of the old citadel wall.

Ahmed Shah's Mosque (Swami Vivekananda Rd) Southwest of Bhadra Fort and dating from 1414, this is one of the city's earliest mosques, built for the sultan and nobles within Ahmedabad's original citadel. The prayer hall is a forest of beautifully carved stone pillars and *jali* screens, and its elaborately carved ceiling has a circular symmetry reminiscent of Hindu and Jain temples.

Rani Sipri's Mosque This small mosque near the ST bus stand is also known as the Masjid-e-Nagira (Jewel of a Mosque) because of its graceful construction, with delicately carved minarets and domed tomb with fine *jali* screens. It was commissioned in 1514 by Rani Sipri, the Hindu wife of Sultan Mahmud Begada; after her death, she was buried there.

Sidi Bashir Mosque Between Ahmedabad train station and Sarangpur Gate, the Sidi Bashir Mosque, built in 1452, is famed for its 21.3m-high shaking minarets (*jhulta minara*), built to shake to protect against earthquake damage. This certainly worked in 2001!

NAVRATRI & DUSSEHRA

Navratri (Festival of Nine Nights; ⊙ Sep/Oct) is celebrated India-wide, but Gujarat has made it its own. This nine-night festival celebrates the feminine divinity in the forms of the goddesses Durga, Lakshmi and Saraswati – particularly Durga's slaying of the demon Mahishasura. Celebrations centre on special shrines at junctions, marketplaces and, increasingly, large venues that can accommodate thousands.

People dress up in sparkling finery to whirl the night away in entrancing *garba* or *dandiya rasa* circle dances till the early hours. Celebrated in every town and village in Gujarat, Navratri is a festival where you may well find yourself joining in.

The night after Navratri is **Dussehra**, which celebrates the victory of Rama over Ravana, with more nocturnal dancing and fireworks, plus the burning of giant effigies of the defeated demon king.

common courtyards, wells and *chabutaras* (bird-feeding towers).

The tours are in English and there's a brief slide show beforehand. Wear slip-on footwear as you'll be visiting plenty of temples. Show up no later than 7.45am.

House of MG Walks   WALKING TOUR
(☑25506946; House of MG, Lal Darwaja; breakfast walk ₹350, night walk ₹250; ⊙breakfast walk 7.30-9.30am Oct-Mar, night walk 10-11pm year-round) The House of MG heritage hotel offers two excellent guided walking tours. The Breakfast Walk covers the old city's highlights and ends at the hotel, where breakfast is served. The hour-long Heritage Night Walk gives a glimpse of some of Ahmedabad's historic neighbourhoods at night, including the markets of Manek Chowk. The whole aesthetic is quite different from the daylight hours! Meet at the House of MG no later than 9.30pm.

Dehko Amdavad   BUS TOUR
(☑1800-2337951; www.gujarattourism.com; Law Garden; per person ₹400; ⊙noon-8pm Tue-Sun) The Municipal Corporation runs an eight-hour city tour by bus, with stops at major sights in and around Ahmedabad. It's a good way to see a lot in one fell swoop. Buses depart from Law Garden; be there no later than 11.45am.

🛏 Sleeping

Budget hotels are mostly clustered in the noisy, traffic-infested Lal Darwaja area, close to the old city, while the majority of midrange and top-end places are found on Khanpur Rd (paralleling the eastern bank of the Sabarmati) or west of the river, which is a more congenial environment but further from most of the interesting sights. Ahmedabad has most of the top-end hotels in Gujarat.

Hotel Volga   HOTEL $
(☑25509497; www.hotelvolga.in; off Relief Rd, Hanuman Lane, Lal Darwaja; s/d ₹1020/1750, s with AC ₹1300-1720, d with AC ₹1500-1950; ❋ 🗢) This surprisingly good option tucked down a narrow street behind the House of MG is worth searching out. Rooms are smart and respectably clean, with many recently upgraded and decorated with curved or padded headboards and accent lighting. The front desk is friendly and efficient, checkout is 24 hours, and you can order decent multicuisine food (mains ₹95 to ₹175) to your room.

Hotel Good Night   HOTEL $
(☑25507181; www.hotelgoodnight.co.in; Lal Darwaja; s ₹1030-1830, d ₹1200-2050; ❋ 🗢) This tidy hotel next door to the House of MG has a few categories of rooms, many of which have been newly renovated in sparkling whites. The top-grade 'executive' rooms are surprisingly arty; the ground-floor 'economy' ones can be a bit stuffy.

Hotel Cadilac   HOTEL $
(☑25507558; Advance Cinema Rd, Lal Darwaja; s ₹400-500, d ₹500-600) If you're counting every last rupee, you could do worse than this friendly option – an old-timer from 1934, which has kept its wooden balustrade. Mattresses are lumpy and smaller rooms are cell-like; larger rooms are OK, just grungy. Try to get a room on the balcony.

★ **Eldorado Hotel**   BOUTIQUE HOTEL $$
(☑26425517; www.eldorado-hotel.com; Mithakhali Six Rd; s ₹4180-6580, d ₹4780-7780; ❋ 🗢) Every inch of this new hotel breathes style – including the pattern-painted hallways. Rooms are coordinated concepts of tile, stone and wood, softened with cushioned seating and even beanbag chairs. The bathrooms may be the coolest in the whole city,

and the lobby-level restaurant is chic but not aloof. Steam rooms and saunas are in the basement. It's located opposite the Shree Krishna Centre.

Hotel Ambassador
HOTEL $$

(☑ 25502490; www.ambassadorahmedabad.com; Khanpur Rd; s/d from ₹2400/2900; ❄@🖃) With a bright white exterior and modern decor inside, the Ambassador greets you with a chilled lobby and friendly desk. It follows up with rooms that are quite stylish in browns and creams. With discounts often available, it's good value; ask to have breakfast included and it will be.

Hotel Royal Highness
HOTEL $$

(☑ 25507450; www.hotelroyalhighness.com; Lal Darwaja; s/d incl breakfast from ₹4200/4800; ❄@🖃) The lobby is a bit tacky, with wood panelling and glass chandeliers, but the rooms are tasteful, spacious and clean. Deluxe rooms feature zebra-print furnishings and sparkling bathrooms with big glassed-in showers. There is 24-hour room service, free airport shuttle service and helpful staff, all in a great location.

Ritz Inn
HOTEL $$

(☑ 22123842; www.hotelritzinn.com; Station Rd; s ₹3450-3700, d ₹4300-4550; ❄@🖃) Near the train station, this smart hotel has unusual class for the money. The art deco lobby, comfortable rooms with superb beds, and amiable service make it an outstanding option. Checkout is a civilised 24 hours, discounts are often available and it offers free airport and station transfers. The less expensive rooms are actually better (quieter) than the more expensive ones.

⭐ House of MG
HERITAGE HOTEL $$$

(☑ 25506946; www.houseofmg.com; Lal Darwaja; s/d from ₹7200/9000, ste from ₹15,000, all incl breakfast; ❄@🖃🏊) This 1920s building

opposite Siddi Sayid's Mosque was once the home of textile magnate Sheth Mangaldas Girdhardas – it was converted into a beautiful heritage hotel in the 1990s by his great-grandson. All the rooms are vast, verandah-edged and masterfully decorated, with homey yet luxurious ambience. It's an icon of the upper classes, and hugely popular. Service is first-rate, there are two excellent restaurants, and the indoor swimming pool and gym are divine. If you know your dates, book in advance online to receive a discount.

Diwan's Bungalow
HERITAGE HOTEL $$$

(☑ 25355428; www.neemranahotels.com; r ₹5400-7800; ❄🖃) Tucked away in a lively neighbourhood a 10-minute walk from Bhadra Fort, this restored 19th-century mansion has an air of casual elegance. The lobby and dining room are hung with period chandeliers and an interior terrace opens onto a garden courtyard. Every room is different, but each is large and tastefully appointed, blending modern amenities with historic touches.

Atrium
HOTEL $$$

(☑ 25505505; www.lemontreehotels.com; Khanpur Rd; s/d from ₹7800/9000, ste ₹24,000; ❄🖃🏊) Formerly Ahmedabad's Le Meridien, now owned by Lemon Tree, the Atrium is the most luxurious hotel around the old city. At the time of research, it was undergoing renovations to modernise an already plush property. The indoor swimming pool is a gem, and there's a spa and sauna too. Check the website for current prices and special offers.

🍴 Eating

Ahmedabad has the best range of restaurants in Gujarat and is a great place to sample Gujarati thalis.

GUJARATI CUISINE

Gujarat is strong on vegetarian cuisine, partly thanks to the Jain influence here, and the quintessential Gujarati meal is the all-veg thali. It's sweeter, lighter and less spicy and oily than Punjabi thali and locals – who are famously particular about food – have no doubt it's the best thali in the world. It begins with a large stainless-steel dish, onto which teams of waiters will serve most or all of the following: curries, chutneys, pickles, dhal, *kadhi* (a yoghurt and gram-flour preparation), raita, rotis, rice, *khichdi* (a blend of lightly spiced rice and lentils), *farsan* (savoury nibbles), salad and one or two sweet items – to be eaten concurrently with the rest. Buttermilk is the traditional accompanying drink. Normally the rice and/or *khichdi* don't come till you've finished with the rotis. In most thali restaurants the waiters will keep coming back until you can only say 'No more'.

ℹ ALCOHOL PERMITS

Gujarat is officially a dry state, but alcohol permits for foreign visitors are easy to get. They're free upon arrival at the airport, or can be picked up – usually for a small charge – at the 'wine shops' found in many large hotels. Just show your passport to receive a one-month permit. There are plans to issue permits over the internet in the near future. The permit allows you two units over the month, which equates to 20 bottles of standard beer or two 750mL bottles of liquor, which you must drink in private. Cheers!

The Law Garden Night Market and Manek Chowk are both good for street food after sunset. Halal grills are fired up nightly along Bhathiyar Gali, a small street parallel to MG Rd: you can get a good meaty feed for about ₹30 from the evening stalls.

★ **New Lucky Restaurant**   SOUTH INDIAN $
(Lal Darwaja; mains ₹50-120; ⊙8am-11pm) For the best breakfast for your buck in Ahmedabad, it's hard to beat the dosas (large South Indian savoury crepes) at New Lucky – though they're good at any time! There's booth-seating in a simple but clean dining hall, with friendly service and surprisingly drinkable black coffee.

Gandhi Cold-Drink House   ICE CREAM $
(near Teen Darwaja; ice cream ₹20-40; ⊙10am-11pm) Locals throng this shop between Bhadra Fort and Teen Darwaja for ice cream, lassis and, best of all, lassis with ice cream!

★ **Gopi Dining Hall**   GUJARATI $$
(off Pritamraj Rd; thali ₹160-250; ⊙10.30am-3.30pm & 6.30-10.30pm) Just off the western end of Ellis Bridge, this little restaurant is a much-loved thali institution, with a small garden and an air-con dining room. You can choose from 'fix', 'full' and 'with one sweet' options depending on how hungry you are.

Zen Cafe   CAFE $$
(www.zencafe.co.in; University Rd; drinks ₹60-120, snacks ₹100-160; ⊙4-8pm Tue-Sun) This peaceful spot in a tree-fringed garden is popular with students from Gujarat University and other colleges nearby. It's right next to the weird Amdavad ni Gufa (Amdavad Cave), an underground art gallery that looks like a heap of octopi with sawn-off tentacles.

Offerings include panini, chocolate walnut brownies, organic coffee and capriosch mocktails – perfect icy coolers of mint, lime and soda.

Green House   GUJARATI $$
(House of MG, Lal Darwaja; snacks ₹150-310, mains ₹220-600; ⊙7am-10.45pm) The casual front restaurant at the House of MG serves a selection of Gujarati veg dishes which are superb, as is the *chaat* (savoury snacks)and the house special *sharbat* (sherbet). The *malpuva* (a sweet, deep-fried pancake in saffron syrup, topped with rose petals) is divine. Don't forget the hand-churned ice cream!

Great anytime, there's nowhere in the city better for an afternoon break. Choose the fan-blasted outdoor courtyard or the air-con room with a 15% surcharge.

Hotel ZK   INDIAN, CHINESE $$
(Relief Rd, Lal Darwaja; mains ₹140-300; ⊙11am-11.30pm) This popular nonveg restaurant has air-con, tinted windows, low lighting and impeccable service. The boneless mutton *kadhai* is fantastic and (like a number of dishes here) comes served over a flame. The Afghani chicken curry is also recommended and locals love the chicken pesto Chinese. On weekends, there may be a wait.

Food Inn   INDIAN $$
(Lal Darwaja; mains ₹130-280; ⊙11.45am-4pm & 7-11pm) A clean, bright and bustling curry house in the Hotel Good Night building (opposite Siddi Sayid's Mosque) where carnivores can tuck into numerous chicken, mutton and fish dishes, including spicy Punjabi curries, lip-smackin' tandoori, biryani and sizzlers.

★ **Vishalla**   INDIAN $$$
(☑ 26602422; www.vishalla.com; Bye-Pass Rd; lunch/dinner ₹340/550; ⊙11am-3pm & 7.30-11pm) On the southwestern outskirts of town, just off the road to Sarkhej (opposite Vasna Tol Naka), Vishalla is a magical eating experience in an open-air setting that's something of a rural village fantasy. An endless thali of Gujarati dishes you won't find in other restaurants is served on plates of leaves, at low wood tables under open-air awnings. Dinner includes excellent performances of folk music, dance and puppet shows. The complex includes the fascinating Vechaar Utensil Museum (p692). An autorickshaw from the city centre costs about ₹100 return.

GUJARAT AHMEDABAD (AMDAVAD)

Souq MEDITERRANEAN $$$
(University Rd, below Vijay Char Rasta; mains ₹220-450; ⏱11am-3pm & 7-11.30pm) This cute bistro, decorated in blue and white with a vaguely Egyptian theme, serves up specialities inspired by Mediterranean cuisine. Though there are a few nonveg options – like lamb shawarma – most dishes are vegetarian, from a long list of creatively spiced kebabs to Moroccan tagines to creative hummus blends. And much more.

Agashiye GUJARATI $$$
(☏25506946; House of MG, Lal Darwaja; set meals regular/deluxe ₹770/1050; ⏱noon-3.30pm & 7-10.30pm) On the rooftop terrace of the city's finest hotel, Agashiye features a daily-changing, all-veg menu, begins with a welcoming drink and is a cultural journey around the traditional thali, with a multitude of diverse dishes delivered to your plate. It finishes with hand-churned ice cream. For dinner, it is advisable to book ahead.

🛍 Shopping

★ **Manek Chowk** HANDICRAFTS, FOOD
(Old City) This busy space and surrounding narrow streets are the commercial heart of the old city. Weave your way through the crowds to soak up the atmosphere and browse the vegetable and sweet stalls.

Gamthiwala TEXTILES
(Manek Chowk; ⏱11am-7pm Mon-Sat) Gamthiwala, by the entrance to the Mausoleum of Ahmed Shah in the old city, sells quality block-printed textiles.

**Law Garden
Night Market** HANDICRAFTS, CLOTHING
(Law Garden; ⏱dusk-11pm) An evening market packed with stalls selling glittering wares from Kachchh and Saurashtra. It's chock-a-block with fantastically decorated *cholis* (sari blouses) and *chaniyas* (long, wide traditional skirts), as well as embroidered wall hangings, costume jewellery and more.

Garvi Gurjari HANDICRAFTS, CLOTHING
(Ashram Rd; ⏱11am-7pm Mon-Sat) This state-government-run outlet has three floors of Gujarat crafts including silk and handloomed-cotton saris, painted metal jewellery boxes and clothing in folksy designs. There are some good finds if you rummage around.

Hansiba HANDICRAFTS
(8 Chandan Complex, CG Rd; ⏱11am-9pm Mon-Sat, 11.30am-7.30pm Sun) The retail outlet of the Self-Employed Women's Association (SEWA), Hansiba sells colourful woven and embroidered shawls, saris, other clothes and wall hangings.

Art Book Center BOOKS
(www.artbookcenter.net; off Mangaldas Rd; ⏱10am-6pm) This specialist treasure trove is upstairs in a brightly painted building near Ellis Bridge. Indian architecture, miniature painting and textile design are the main topics stocked.

Crossword BOOKS
(Shree Krishna Centre, Mithakali Six Rd; ⏱10.30am-9pm) This is a large, bustling book, music and DVD shop also boasting the Chocolate Room cafe (with chocolate drinks and coffee).

ℹ Information

The **Uexplore** (www.uexplore.in) website has some useful information, particularly for DIY walking tours. There are numerous ATMs in town.

Apollo City Center (☏66305800; www.apolloahd.com; 1 Tulsibaug Society) Small but recommended private hospital opposite Doctor House, near Parimal Garden.

Gujarat Tourism (☏26578044; www.gujarattourism.com; off Ashram Rd, HK House; ⏱10.30am-6pm Mon-Sat, closed 2nd & 4th Sat of the month) The very helpful HK House office has all sorts of information at its fingertips and you can also hire cars with drivers here. There is also an office at the Ahmedabad train station.

HDFC Bank (Relief Rd, Lal Darwaja)

ICICI Bank (Ashram Rd, 2/1 Popular House; ⏱9am-6pm Mon-Fri) Foreign currency and changing travellers cheques.

Main Post Office (Ramanlal Sheth Rd; ⏱10am-7.30pm Mon-Sat, to 1pm Sun)

Relief Cyber Café (Relief Rd; per hour ₹20; ⏱10am-midnight) Has air-con.

State Bank of India (Lal Darwaja; ⏱11am-4pm Mon-Fri, 11am-1pm Sat) Changes travellers cheques and currency.

Tourism Desk (☏32520878; Law Garden; ⏱10.30am-6pm Mon-Sat, closed 2nd & 4th Sat of the month) Ahmedabad Municipal Corporation's office has city maps and puts effort into answering questions.

ⓘ Getting There & Away

AIR

Ahmedabad's busy airport has direct flights to several Indian cities and international destinations, including Doha (Qatar), Dubai (UAE), Kuwait City (Kuwait), Muscat (Oman), Sharjah (UAE) and Singapore. Many agencies sell air tickets, including **Express Travels** (☑ 26588602; www.expresstravels.in; off Ashram Rd, Jivabhai Chambers).

IndiGo (☑ 9910383838; www.goindigo.in)

Jet Airways (☑ 022-39893333; www.jetairways.com; Ratnanabh Complex, Ashram Rd) Also its low-cost carrier, JetKonnect

SpiceJet (☑ 9871803333; www.spicejet.com)

BUS

Private buses coming from the north may drop you on Naroda Rd, about 7km northeast of the city centre – an autorickshaw will complete the journey for ₹50 to ₹60.

From the main ST bus stand, also known as Geeta Mandir or Astodia, frequent Gujarat State Road Transport Corporation (GSRTC, ST) buses go to Vadodara (₹82, two hours), Bhavnagar (₹100, five hours), Junagadh (₹160, eight hours), Jamnagar (₹163, seven hours), Rajkot (₹131, 4½ hours) and Bhuj (₹170, nine hours). Volvo AC buses go to Vadodara (₹170) throughout the day. Eleven daily buses go to Udaipur (₹200, 5½ hours), five head to Jodhpur (₹348), and three to Jaipur (₹480). A Volvo AC bus departs at 7pm for Udaipur (₹440), Jaipur (₹1115) and Delhi (₹1843, 20 hours).

For long distances, private buses are generally quicker; most offices are close to Paldi Char Rasta.

Gujarat Travels (☑ 26575951; www.gujarat-travels.co.in; Paldi Char Rasta) Has buses to Mt Abu (seat/sleeper ₹535/745, seven hours, 7am and 11pm).

Patel Tours & Travels (☑ 26576807; www.pateltoursandtravels.com; Paldi Char Rasta) Runs Volvo AC buses to Rajkot (₹450, four hours, 20 daily), Jamnagar (₹550, six hours, nine daily) and Mumbai (sleeper ₹1500, 11 hours), plus non-AC buses to Mumbai (seat/sleeper ₹900/1200, 6pm and 10pm) and six daily buses to Bhuj (non-AC seat/sleeper ₹350/450, AC seat/sleeper ₹480/580, AC Volvo ₹700, eight hours).

Raj Express (☑ 26579667; www.rajexpressbus.com; Paldi Char Rasta) Runs Volvo AC buses to Udaipur (seat/sleeper ₹600/1000, five hours, hourly 5pm to midnight) and AC buses to Jaipur (seat/sleeper ₹1200/1800).

Shree Swaminarayan (☑ 26576544; www.sstbus.in; 22 Anilkunj Complex) Heads to Diu in non-AC buses (seat/sleeper ₹400/500, 10 hours, 10pm).

TRAIN

There's a **computerised reservation office** (🕐 8am-8pm Mon-Sat, to 2pm Sun) just outside Ahmedabad train station. Window 6 handles the foreign-tourist quota. Computerised reservation is also available at the *relatively* quiet Gandhigram station, although there is no window dedicated to foreigners.

MAJOR TRAINS FROM AHMEDABAD

DESTINATION	TRAIN NO & NAME	FARE (₹)	DURATION (HR)	DEPARTURE
Bhavnagar	12971 Bandra-Bhavnagar Express	230/535/735 (A)	5½	5.45am
Bhuj	19115 Sayaji Nagari Express	225/600/855 (A)	7½	11.59pm
Delhi (DLI)	12915 Ashram Express	475/1240/1775/3015 (C)	15¾	6.30pm
Delhi (NDLS)	12957 Rajdhani	1595/2190/3635 (B)	14	5.40pm
Jamnagar	19005 Saurashtra Mail	215/575/820/1375 (C)	7	5.05am
Junagadh	19221 Somnath Express	220/590/840 (A)	6½	10pm
Mumbai	12010 Shatabdi	940/1825 (D)	7	2.30pm (Mon-Sat)
	12902 Gujarat Mail	315/825/1135/1915 (C)	8½	10pm
Udaipur	19944 Udaipur Express	200 (E)	10½	11pm
Vadodara	12010 Shatabdi	370/735 (D)	1¾	2.30pm (Mon-Sat)

Fares: (A) sleeper/3AC/2AC, (B) 3AC/2AC/1AC, (C) sleeper/3AC/2AC/1AC, (D) AC chair/exec, (E) sleeper

ⓘ Getting Around

The airport is 8km north of the centre; a prepaid taxi should cost around ₹550, depending on your destination. An autorickshaw costs about ₹170 to the old city.

Autorickshaw drivers are supposed to turn their meter to zero at the start of a trip then calculate the fare using a conversion chart at the end. Some meters have been rigged, but most work properly. If a driver refuses to use the meter, negotiate the fare in advance.

Around Ahmedabad

Adalaj Vav

Adalaj Vav   NOTABLE BUILDING
(⊙dawn-dusk) The Adalaj Vav, 19km north of Ahmedabad, is among the finest of the Gujarati step-wells. Built by Queen Rudabai in 1499, it has three entrances leading to a huge platform that rests on 16 pillars, with corners marked by shrines. The octagonal well is five storeys deep and is decorated with exquisite stone carvings; subjects range from eroticism to buttermilk.

From Ahmedabad, an autorickshaw costs ₹450 return, or take bus 85 from Lal Darwaja to Chandkheda, transfer to bus 501 towards Sarkej, and ask the driver to let you off at the Adalaj Vav turn-off, from where you can walk or take an auto about 1km.

Gandhinagar

With broad avenues and greenery, Gandhinagar forms a striking contrast to Ahmedabad. This is where state politicians live in large, fortified houses. Although Ahmedabad became Gujarat's capital when the old state of Bombay was split, this new capital was planned 28km north on the west bank of the Sabarmati River. Named Gandhinagar after Mahatma Gandhi, it's India's second planned city after Chandigarh. The secretariat was moved here in 1970.

Gandhinagar's only real tourist attraction is the spectacular **Akshardham** (www.akshardham.com; J Rd, Sector 20; ⊙9.30am-6.30pm Tue-Sun), belonging to the wealthy Hindu Swaminarayan group. Ornately carved and built by nearly 1000 artisans, the temple is constructed of 6000 tonnes of pink sandstone and surrounded by manicured gardens. Elaborate underground **exhibition areas** (admission ₹170; ⊙10am-5.30pm Tue-Sun) feature high- (and low-) tech multimedia dis-

ⓘ ADVANCE BUS RESERVATIONS

These days, it's becoming much more common for passengers using public intercity buses run by Gujarat State Road Transport Corporation (GSRTC, ST) to reserve seats in advance. Theoretically, you should be able to do this online by registering at www.gsrtc.in. None of our attempts to book tickets by computer were successful, but we had no problem connecting to their internet system via smartphone – using an Indian SIM card with a data plan. (The system is also very useful for checking most bus route timings.) Alternatively, if you don't have the technology, many bus stands have online reservation windows, where you can make advance bookings in person. Doing so is not absolutely necessary, but depending on the route, you just might get stuck standing for a few hours.

plays on the Swaminarayan movement and the Hindu epics. At sunset a 45-minute **Water Show** (adult/child ₹75/50; ⊙Tue-Sun) presents the story of the Upanishads through fountains, music, fire and lasers. It promises to reveal the secret of life after death. There's also a small amusement park for kids. Note that cameras, mobile phones and bags are not allowed into the compound.

Buses from Ahmedabad to Gandhinagar (₹20, 45 minutes, every 15 to 30 minutes) depart from the back northwest corner of Lal Darwaja, from the ST bus stand and from numerous stops along Ashram Rd. From the Gandhinagar bus stand to Akshardham, take an autorickshaw for ₹50.

Nalsarovar Bird Sanctuary

Nalsarovar Bird Sanctuary   WILDLIFE RESERVE
(Indian/foreigner ₹20/300, car ₹20, camera/video ₹100/2500; ⊙6am-6pm) This 121-sq-km sanctuary, 60km southwest of Ahmedabad, protects Nalsarovar Lake, a flood of island-dotted blue dissolving into the sky and iron-flat plains, and its surrounding wetlands. Between November and February, the sanctuary sees flocks of indigenous and migratory birds, with as many as 250 species passing through. Ducks, geese, eagles, spoonbills, cranes, pelicans and flamingos are best seen at daybreak and dusk.

The sanctuary is busiest at weekends and on holidays. To see the birds it's best to hire a boat (around ₹150, negotiable, per hour). Gujarat Tourism offers luxury tent (☑9427725090; s/d ₹1100/1650; ❄) accommodation 1.5km from the lake. A taxi from Ahmedabad costs around ₹4400 for a day trip, and gives you the option of combining Nalsarovar with Lothal (40km south).

Lothal

About 80km southwest of Ahmedabad, the city that stood at this archaeological site (☉ dawn-dusk) 4500 years ago was one of the most important of the Indus Valley civilisation, which extended into what is now Pakistan. Excavations have revealed the world's oldest known artificial dock, which was connected to an old course of the Sabarmati River. Artefacts suggest that trade may have been conducted with Mesopotamia, Egypt and Persia. The site museum displays intricate seals, weights and measures, games and jewellery, plus an artist's impression of how Lothal looked at its peak. Lacking dramatic buildings, the site is best appreciated by true archaeology buffs.

Palace Utelia (☑9825012611; www.thepalaceutelia.com; r from ₹6000; ❄), a heritage hotel 7km from the site, by the Bhugavo River, is an imposing palace – complete with aged retainers – that dwarfs the village it oversees. The shabby rooms are overpriced, but it's an unusual place with some charm if not comfort.

Lothal is a long day trip from Ahmedabad, and a taxi (around ₹4400 return) is the easiest bet. Trains from Ahmedabad's Gandhigram station depart at 7.15am and 9am run to Lothal-Bhurkhi station (2nd-class ₹45, two hours), 6km from the site, from where you can catch a bus. Take water and food.

Modhera

Built in 1026 and 1027 by King Bhimdev I, the Sun Temple (Indian/foreigner ₹5/100; ☉9am-5pm) in Modhera is one of the greatest monuments of the Solanki dynasty, whose rulers were believed to be descended from the sun. The exterior is intricately carved with demons and deities, and the main hall and shrine are reached through a pillared pavilion. Inside, 52 sculpted pillars depict scenes from the Ramayana and the Mahabharata, and a hall with 12 niches represents the different monthly manifestations of Surya (the sun god). Erotic sculpture panels complete the sensual decoration.

Like the better-known Sun Temple at Konark in Odisha (Orissa), which it predates by 200 years, the Modhera temple was designed so that the dawn sun shone on the image of Surya during the equinox. Surya Kund, an extraordinary rectangular step-well inside the complex, contains over 100 shrines, resembling a sunken art gallery.

Each year, around 20 January, the temple is the scene for a three-day classical dance festival featuring dancers from all over India.

Modhera is 100km northwest of Ahmedabad. You can take a bus (₹65, two hours, half-hourly) from Ahmedabad's ST bus stand to Mahesana (Mehsana), and then another bus 26km west to Modhera (₹30, one hour). There are also trains from Ahmedabad to Mahesana. A taxi from Ahmedabad is *much* easier, and will cost about ₹3500 round trip, including a visit to nearby Patan.

Patan

☑ 02766 / POP 125,502

About 130km northwest of Ahmedabad, Patan was Gujarat's capital for six centuries before Ahmedabad was founded in 1411. It was ruined by the armies of Ala-ud-Din Khilji around 1300, and today is a dusty, little town with narrow streets lined by elaborate wooden houses.

Patan is famed, far and wide, for its beautiful Patola silk textiles, produced by the torturously laborious double-*ikat* method.

WORTH A TRIP

VAUTHA FAIR

Vautha Fair (☉ Nov) Each year, Gujarat's largest livestock fair is held at Vautha, at the confluence of the Sabarmati and Vatrak Rivers, 50km south of Ahmedabad. Thousands of donkeys, camels and cows change hands here, and some 25,000 people – including many *maldhari* (herder) pastoralists – set up tents and stay for a few days of buying, selling, eating, dancing, and making sunset *puja* (prayers) in the river. Check with Gujarat Tourism for exact dates.

Both the warp (lengthways) and weft (transverse) threads are painstakingly tie-dyed to create the pattern before the weaving process begins. It takes about six months to make one sari, which might cost ₹100,000.

◉ Sights

Rani-ki-Vav   HISTORIC SITE
(Indian/foreigner ₹5/100; ⊙9am-5pm) The only real sign of Patan's former glory is this astoundingly beautiful step-well. Built in 1063 by Rani Udayamati to commemorate her husband, Bhimdev I, the step-well is the oldest and finest in Gujarat and is remarkably preserved. Steps lead down through multiple levels with lines of carved pillars and over 800 sculptures, mostly on Vishnu-avatar themes.

Patan Patola Heritage   HANDICRAFTS WORKSHOP
(✆232274; www.patanpatola.com; Patolawala St, Salvivado; ⊙10am-6pm) Run by the award-winning Salvi family, this is an excellent place to see Patola silk weaving in action.

Panchasara Parshvanath   JAIN TEMPLE
Among more than 100 Jain temples around Patan, this is the largest, with all the domes and sacred carvings your eyes can absorb.

🛏 Sleeping & Eating

There's really nowhere worth staying in town.

Food Zone   INDIAN $
(mains ₹80-120; ⊙11am-3pm & 7-11pm) This place near the railway tracks has modern booth seating, air-con and great set meals.

❶ Getting There & Away

Patan is 40km northwest of Mahesana. Buses leave Ahmedabad's ST bus stand about every hour (₹78, 3½ hours). There are also buses to/from Zainabad (₹65, 2½ hours, two daily), via Modhera. A day trip in a private taxi from Ahmedabad costs about ₹3500; combine with a visit to the Sun Temple in Modhera.

Vadodara (Baroda)

✆0265 / POP 1.66 MILLION

Vadodara (or Baroda as it's often known) lies 106km southeast of Ahmedabad, a little over an hour's drive along National Expressway 1. Vadodara has some interesting city sights, but the main reason for coming here is to visit the stunning Unesco World Heritage Site of Champaner and Pavagadh (p704) nearby. The city is way less hectic than Ahmedabad, and parts of the Sayajigunj area near the university have a college-town feel.

After the Marathas expelled the Mughals from Gujarat in the 18th century, their local lieutenants, the Gaekwad clan, made Vadodara their capital. Vadodara retained a high degree of autonomy even under the British, right up to Independence in 1947. Maharaja Sayajirao III (1875–1939) was a great moderniser and laid the foundations of Vadodara's modern reputation as Gujarat's cultural capital.

◉ Sights

★Laxmi Vilas Palace   PALACE
(Nehru Rd; admission ₹170; ⊙10am-5pm Tue-Sun) Still the residence of Vadodara's royal family, Laxmi Vilas was built in full-throttle 19th-century Indo-Saracenic flourish at a cost of ₹6 million. The most impressive Raj-era palace in Gujarat, its elaborate interiors boast well-maintained mosaics, chandeliers and artworks. It's set in expansive parklike grounds, which include a golf course. A one-hour audio guide is included with admission.

Sayaji Bagh   PARK
A welcome patch of shady green space in the heart of Vadodara, stroll the wide paved pathways for a bit of peace and relative quiet. If you have kids, hit the playgrounds!

Baroda Museum & Picture Gallery   MUSEUM
(Indian/foreigner ₹10/200; ⊙10.30am-5pm) Within Sayaji Bagh park, this museum houses a diverse collection, much of it gathered by Maharaja Sayajirao III, including statues and carvings from several Asian regions, an Egyptian room and some rather mangy zoology exhibits. The gallery has lovely Mughal miniatures and a motley crew of European masters.

Tambekar Wada   HISTORIC BUILDING
(Pratap Rd, Raopura; ⊙8am-6pm) This wooden multistoreyed townhouse is a typical Maratha mansion, once the residence of Bhau Tambekar, diwan of Baroda (1849–54). Inside are beautiful 19th-century murals featuring scenes from the Mahabharata, Krishna's life and the 19th-century Anglo-Maratha War. Many are worn and poorly lit by ambient light, but they're still impressive.

Vadodara (Baroda)

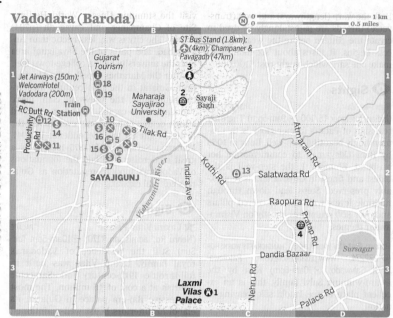

🛏 Sleeping

Most accommodation is in the conveniently central Sayajigunj area; there are a number of very cheap hotels (₹200 to ₹400) there, but they fill up early.

Hotel Valiant
HOTEL $
(☎2363480; www.hotelvaliant.com; 7th fl, BBC Tower, Sayajigunj; s/d ₹860/1070, with AC from ₹1180/1400; ❄🞡) The Valiant offers surprisingly fresh digs on the upper floors of a high-rise building. Take the lift up from the street entrance to find reception in a spacious lobby on the 7th floor. The clean if bland rooms are the best value in town.

Hotel Ambassador
HOTEL $$
(☎2362727; www.hotelambassadorindia.com; Sayajigunj; s/d from ₹1460/1780; ❄🞡) With stylish rooms and comfortable beds, the Ambassador offers very good value. The cheapest 'deluxe' rooms have a vaguely Japanese air, while the 'executive' quarters have a slick contemporary feel, all pinks, oranges, squares and rectangles. There's civilised 24-hour checkout and a very helpful front desk.

Oasis Hotel
HOTEL $$
(☎22225054; www.theoasishotel.net; Sayajigunj; s ₹3000-4300, d ₹3700-4880, ste ₹8950; ❄🞡🞡) For a touch of comfort, the Oasis delivers.

Rooms are modern and pleasingly designed, and there's a swimming pool on the roof! The more expensive Club rooms are not worth the extra rupees, but suites are fittingly luxurious, with sunken living rooms and personal putting greens.

WelcomHotel Vadodara
HOTEL $$$
(☎2330033; www.itchotels.in; RC Dutt Rd; r incl breakfast from ₹9550-13,150, ste ₹21,500; ❄@🞡🞡) A swish five-star complex with predictable, well-appointed rooms, an unusual outdoor pool, plenty of cool lounge areas, an expensive 24-hour multicuisine restaurant and a wine shop.

🍴 Eating

Dairy Den
ICE CREAM $
(scoops ₹70-130; ⊙10am-12.20am) Cool off with a few scoops, or a soft-serve, at Vadodara's best ice-cream parlour. Find it at Sardar Patel statue.

Kalyan
SOUTH INDIAN $
(Sayajigunj; dishes ₹60-200; ⊙7am-11pm) Kalyan is a breezy student hang-out serving healthy portions of South Indian food and less healthy attempts at Western fast food (though all dishes are vegetarian).

Vadodara (Baroda)

◎ **Top Sights**
1 Laxmi Vilas Palace...................................C3

◎ **Sights**
2 Baroda Museum & Picture Gallery........B1
3 Sayaji Bagh...B1
4 Tambekar Wada.....................................D3

🛏 **Sleeping**
5 Hotel Ambassador.................................B2
6 Hotel Valiant..B2
  Oasis Hotel.......................................(see 5)

🍴 **Eating**
7 Aamantran...A2
8 Dairy Den B2
9 Kalyan...B2

10 Kansaar...B2
11 That Place...A2

🛍 **Shopping**
12 Baroda Prints..A1
13 Baroda Prints & Workshop C2

ℹ **Information**
14 ATM...A2
15 Bank of Baroda ATM.............................A2
16 HDFC ATM...A2
17 ICICI Bank...B2
  Speedy Cyber Cafe ....(see 10)

ℹ **Transport**
18 ST Bus Stand A1
19 Sweta Travels A1

★ **Aamantran**   INDIAN $$
(Sampatrao Colony; mains ₹130-300, thalis ₹280;
🕐11am-3pm & 7-10.30pm) Hailed by many as
the best thali in Vadodara, it's an all-you-
can-eat taste of Gujarat. À la carte dishes
include a variety of veg tandoor selections,
along with North Indian and Jain speciali-
ties. Look for the sign in Gujarati.

Kansaar   GUJARATI $$
(101 Unique Trade Centre, Sayajigunj; thalis ₹170;
🕐11am-2.45pm & 7-10pm) A classy veg thali
joint on the 1st floor with impeccable service
and delicious food; the thali is bottomless
and you can eat inside or out on the terrace.

★ **That Place**   MULTICUISINE $$$
(☑2310222; Sampatrao Colony; breakfast ₹150-
280, lunch & dinner mains ₹250-430; 🕐11.30am-
10.30pm Mon-Fri, 9am-10.30pm Sat & Sun) At the
forefront of Vadodara's emerging dining
scene, That Place is a global tour for your
palate, with offerings from Persian lamb
to East African chicken poussin to creative
pastas, salads, burgers and more. Continen-
tal-style breakfasts are served on weekends.
Oh, and there's chocolate fondue...

🛍 **Shopping**

Baroda Prints   HANDICRAFTS
(3 Aires Complex, Productivity Rd; 🕐9am-9pm
Mon-Sat, 8am-6pm Sun) Hand-printed dress
materials in original, colourful and attrac-
tive designs. There's also a branch on **Salat-
wada Rd** (🕐10am-8pm Mon-Sat, 11am-5pm
Sun), where you can see printers at work
upstairs.

ℹ **Information**

There are ATMs at the train station, on RC Dutt
Rd, and in Sayajigunj.
Gujarat Tourism (www.gujarattourism.com;
🕐10am-6pm Mon-Sat, closed 2nd & 4th Sat of
the month) Located at the new ST bus stand.
Friendly, but don't expect much.
ICICI Bank (Sayajigunj; 🕐10am-4pm Mon-Fri,
to 1pm Sat) Has an ATM and changes travellers
cheques and cash.
Speedy Cyber Cafe (Sayajigunj; per hour ₹20;
🕐8.30am-11pm) Reliable internet cafe.

ℹ **Getting There & Away**

AIR
The airport is 4km northeast of the centre. **Jet
Airways** (☑022-39893333; www.jetairways.
com; 11 Panorama Bldg, RC Dutt RD) and **IndiGo**
(☑9910383838; www.goindogo.com) fly to
Mumbai and Delhi.

BUS
The new ST bus stand, integrated with a shop-
ping mall, is just north of the train station. Fre-
quent buses go to:
Ahmedabad ordinary/AC Volvo ₹82/170, two
hours, at least hourly
Bhavnagar express ₹137, five hours, about
hourly from 6am
Diu ₹225, 12 hours, 6am and 9pm
Mumbai ₹350, nine hours, 6pm, 6.40pm and
7.30pm
Udaipur ₹232, eight hours, 3am and 6am

Across from the train station, **Sweta Travels**
(☑2786917) sends AC Volvo buses to Mumbai
(seat/sleeper ₹1500/1800, eight hours, three
nightly). Many other companies have private
buses to other destinations in Gujarat and

Rajasthan from the plethora of offices at Pandya Bridge, 2km north of the train station.

TRAIN

About 30 trains a day run to Ahmedabad, including the 12009 Shatabdi (AC chair/exec ₹435/790, two hours, 11.20am Monday to Saturday). The 13 daily trains to Mumbai include the 12010 Shatabdi (AC chair/exec ₹815/1575, 5¼ hours, 4.17pm Monday to Saturday).

Around Vadodara

Champaner & Pavagadh

This spectacular Unesco World Heritage Site, 47km northeast of Vadodara, combines a sacred, 762m volcanic hill (Pavagadh) that rises dramatically from the plains and a ruined Gujarati capital with beautiful mosque architecture (Champaner). The whole area is referred to as Pavagadh.

◉ Sights

Pavagadh   HISTORIC SITE
This strategic hilltop may have been fortified as early as the 8th century. It became the capital of the Chauhan Rajputs around 1300, but in 1484 was taken by the Gujarat sultan Mahmud Begada, after a 20-month siege; the Rajputs committed *jauhar* (ritual mass suicide) in the face of defeat. Today, throngs of pilgrims ascend Pavagadh to worship at the important Kalikamata Temple, dedicated to the evil-destroying goddess Kali, who sits atop the summit.

Near the top of the hill you'll also find Pavagadh's oldest surviving monument, the 10th- to 11th-century Hindu Lakulisha Temple, and several Jain temples. The views are fantastic and so are, if you're lucky, the cooling breezes. During the nine days of Navratri (p694) and the Mahakali Festival (p689), the usual flow of pilgrims becomes a flood.

To ascend Pavagadh, you can either walk up the pilgrim trail, which will take two to three hours, or take a shuttle (₹20) from the Champaner Citadel south wall. The shuttle deposits you about halfway up the hill, where you can either join the walking path (here lined by souvenir and drink stalls), or hop on the **ropeway** (cable car; return ₹98; ⊙ 6am-6.45pm) which glides you up to within a 700m walk of the Kalikamata Temple.

Champaner   HISTORIC SITE
(Indian/foreigner ₹10/250; ⊙ 8am-6pm) Following his capture of Pavagadh, Sultan Mahmud Begada turned Champaner, at the base of the hill, into a splendid new capital. But its glory was brief: when it was captured by Mughal emperor Humayun in 1535, the Gujarati capital reverted to Ahmedabad, and Champaner fell into ruin. The heart of this historic site is the Citadel, whose most impressive features are its monumental mosques (no longer used for worship), with their beautiful blending of Islamic and Hindu decoration styles.

The huge **Jami Masjid**, just outside the Citadel's east gate, boasts a wonderful carved entrance porch that leads into a lovely courtyard surrounded by a pillared corridor. The prayer hall has two tall central minarets, further superb stone carving, multiple domes, and seven mihrabs (prayer niches) along the back wall.

Other beautiful mosques include the **Saher ki Masjid**, behind the ticket office inside the Citadel, which was probably the private

OFF THE BEATEN TRACK

SOUTH OF VADODARA

Gujarat stretches some 240km south from Vadodara to the border of Maharashtra, 150km short of Mumbai. **Surat**, 140km south of Vadodara, is where the British established their first Indian settlement in 1614. It's now Gujarat's hectic second-biggest city (population five million), and a busy commercial centre for textiles and diamonds. Around 40km south of Surat is **Dandi**, the destination of Gandhi's epic Salt March in 1930, with several Gandhi monuments by its strikingly empty beach. Just before the Maharashtra border is the ex-Portuguese enclave of **Daman**, an alcohol-infused resort town on a grey sea. Though it still retains a little of the piquancy of old Portugal, Daman is far less attractive than its counterpart, Diu in Saurashtra. In the southeast, the hilly Dangs district is the northern extremity of the Western Ghats, with a large tribal population and little tourist infrastructure. The main town is the minor hill resort of Saputara. The **Dangs Darbar** (⊙ Feb/Mar), in the week before Holi, is a spectacular, largely tourist-free tribal festival.

royal mosque, and the **Kevda Masjid**, 300m north of the Citadel and about 600m west of the Jami Masjid. Here you can climb narrow stairs to the roof, and higher up the minarets, to spot other mosques – **Nagina Masjid**, 500m north, with no minarets but exquisite geometric carving, and **Lila Gumbaj ki Masjid**, 800m east, with a fluted central dome. The twin minarets resembling factory chimneys, about 1km west, adorn the **Brick Minar ki Masjid**, a rare brick tomb.

ℹ Getting There & Away

Buses to Pavagadh run about every half-hour from Vadodara (₹41, 1½ hours); a return taxi costs around ₹1000. Some buses from Pavagadh travel via Vadodara to Ahmedabad (₹80, four hours).

SAURASHTRA

Before Independence, Saurashtra, also known as the Kathiawar Peninsula, was a jumble of over 200 princely states. Today it has a number of hectic industrial cities, but most of them retain a core of narrow old streets crowded with small-scale commerce. Outside the cities it's still villages, fields, forests and a timeless, almost feudal feel, with farmers and *maldhari* (herders) dressed head to toe in white, and rural women as colourful as their neighbours in Rajasthan.

Saurashtra is mainly flat and its rare hills are often sacred, including the spectacular, temple-topped Shatrunjaya and Girnar. The peninsula is liberally endowed with wildlife sanctuaries, notably Sasan Gir, where Asia's last wild lions roam. On the south coast lies the very quaint, laid-back ex-Portuguese island enclave of Diu. Saurashtra is also where Mahatma Gandhi was born and raised: you can visit several sites associated with his life.

Saurashtra has a reputation for being fond of its sleep, and siesta takes place from *at least* 1pm to 3pm.

Bhavnagar

☏ 0278 / POP 593,768

Bhavnagar is a hectic, sprawling industrial centre with a colourful old core that makes a good base for journeys to nearby Shatrunjaya and Blackbuck National Park.

◉ Sights

Gandhi Smriti Museum   MUSEUM
(☉9am-1pm & 3-6pm Mon-Sat, closed 2nd & 4th Sat of the month) FREE Mahatma Gandhi attended university in Bhavnagar, and this dusty museum, by the clock tower, has a multitude of Gandhi photographs and documents. Unfortunately, explanatory placards aren't in English.

Barton Museum   MUSEUM
(Indian/foreigner ₹2/50; ☉9am-1pm & 3-6pm Mon-Sat, closed 2nd & 4th Sat of the month) Located beneath the Gandhi Smriti Museum, this dusty but interesting collection contains religious carvings, betel-nut cutters, and a skeleton in a cupboard.

Takhteshwar Temple   HINDU TEMPLE
Perched atop a small hillock, this temple is high enough to provide splendid views over the city and out onto the Gulf of Cambay.

Old City   AREA
North of Ganga Jalia Tank, Bhavnagar's old city is well worth a wander, especially in the early evening – it's busy with shops and cluttered with dilapidated elaborate wooden buildings leaning over the colourful crowded bazaars. Don't miss the vegetable market!

🛏 Sleeping

The budget hotels, mostly in the old city and near the train station, are fairly grim, but midrange hotels are reasonable.

Hotel Sun 'n' Shine   HOTEL $$
(☏2516131; www.hotelsunnshine.in; Panwadi Chowk, ST Rd; r incl breakfast from ₹2000, ste from ₹3800; ❋@◉) This well-run, three-star hotel is decent value. It has a Mediterranean vertigo-inducing atrium, a welcoming front desk, and the reliable RGB restaurant. The rooms are fresh and clean with comfortable beds and soft pillows: the more you pay, the more windows you get. Breakfast is substantial, and free airport transfers are offered.

Nilambag Palace Hotel   HERITAGE HOTEL $$$
(☏2424241; www.nilambagpalace.com; cottage s/d ₹2900/4100, palace r ₹5250-7000; ❋◉❂) In large gardens beside the Ahmedabad road, about 600m southwest of the bus station, this former maharaja's palace was built in 1859. The lobby looks like an understated regal living room, with a beautiful mosaic floor. The sizeable palace rooms retain a stately early 20th-century feel; the 'cottage' rooms are good-sized but rather ordinary.

Guests have use of a swimming pool (nonguests ₹100) in the Vijay Mahal, plus a gym and tennis facilities.

Bhavnagar

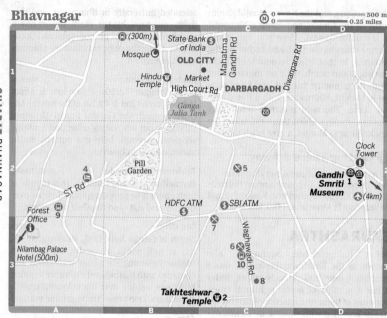

✗ Eating

Sankalp
SOUTH INDIAN **$**

(Waghawadi Rd; mains ₹80-160; ⊙11am-3pm & 6-11pm) First-class South Indian veg dishes served in clean, contemporary surroundings.

Tulsi Restaurant
INDIAN, CHINESE **$$**

(Kalanala Chowk; mains ₹120-170; ⊙noon-4pm & 7-11pm) Low-lit with plants and understat-ed decor, this cosy and clean place with well-prepared Punjabi and Chinese veg dishes is rightly popular. Service is friendly and efficient, and it's excellent value.

Rasoi
INDIAN, CHINESE **$$**

(thalis ₹190; ⊙11.30am-3pm & 7-10.45pm) This secluded bungalow and (in the evening) garden restaurant serves up great unlimited Gujarati thalis. It's behind the police post between two petrol stations just north of the Galaxy Cinema.

ⓘ Information

Forest Office (☎0278-2426425; Bahumali Bhavan, Annexe; ⊙10.30am-6.30pm Mon-Sat, closed 2nd & 4th Sat of the month) Book accommodation for Blackbuck National Park here. It's near the STC bus stand.

State Bank of India (Darbargadh; ⊙10.30am-4.30pm Mon-Fri) The State Bank of India changes cash and travellers cheques and has a 24-hour ATM and a lovely, ornately carved, old-city portico.

ⓘ Getting There & Around

AIR

Jet Airways (☎2433371; www.jetairways.com; Surat House, Waghawadi Rd) has daily flights to and from Mumbai. The airport is about 3.5km from town. A taxi to/from the airport costs around ₹150.

BUS

From the ST bus stand there are frequent services to Rajkot (₹130, four hours), Ahmedabad (₹120, five hours), Vadodara (₹200, four hours) and Palitana (₹37, two hours). There are eight daily buses to Diu (₹125, seven hours).

Private bus companies include **Tanna Travels** (☑ 2425218; Waghawadi Rd), with AC buses to Ahmedabad (₹240, four hours, 15 daily) and Mumbai (₹850, 14 hours, 4pm).

TRAIN

The 12972 Bhavnagar-Bandra Express departs at 8.30pm and arrives in Ahmedabad (sleeper/3AC/2AC ₹230/535/735) at 1.52am on its way to Mumbai.

Blackbuck National Park

★ **Blackbuck National Park**   NATURE RESERVE
(Velavadar NP; Indian/foreigner car ₹250/US$20, 4hr guide ₹100/US$10; ⊙ dawn-dusk 16 Oct-15 Jun) This beautiful, 34-sq-km park encompasses large areas of pale, custard-coloured grassland stretching between two seasonal rivers. Formerly called Velavadar National Park, it's famous for its blackbucks, beautiful, fast antelope that sport elegant spiralling horns – as long as 65cm in mature males. Some 1600 inhabit the park, which is also good for spotting birds such as wintering harriers from Siberia (about 2000 of them most years). If you're lucky, you may even spot wolves!

Pay your fees (convert the dollar rate into rupees) and pick up a mandatory guide (who is unlikely to speak English) at the reception centre about 65km from Bhavnagar, north of Valabhipur. The park has a good road network and is best explored by car. A taxi day trip from Bhavnagar costs about ₹2500.

🛏 Sleeping

Forest Department Guest House   HOTEL $$
(Indian/foreigner d ₹500/US$50, with AC ₹1500/US$75) Near the reception centre, book one of the four rooms here through the Forest Office (p706) in Bhavnagar.

Blackbuck Lodge   HOTEL $$$
(☑ 9978979728, 8154973478; www.theblackbucklodge.com; s/d incl breakfast ₹14,400/15,000 Oct-Mar, ₹9600/9000 Apr-Sep) These comfortable stone villas are just outside the park's western entrance. Packages with dinner included are also offered, as are safaris.

Palitana

☑ 02848 / POP 55,000

The hustling, dusty town of Palitana, 51km southwest of Bhavnagar, has grown rapidly to serve the pilgrim trade around Shatrunjaya. Your best bet for general information is the helpful manager at Hotel Shravak.

⊙ Sights & Activities

★ **Shatrunjaya**   SACRED SITE
(Place of Victory; ⊙ temples 6.30am-6pm) One of Jainism's holiest pilgrimage sites, Shatrunjaya is an incredible hilltop sea of temples, built over 900 years. It is said that Adinath (also known as Rishabha), the founder of Jainism, meditated and gave his first sermon beneath the rayan tree at the summit. The temples are grouped into *tunks* (enclosures), each with a central temple and many minor ones. The 500m climb up 3300 steps to the temples adds to the extraordinary experience.

The steps start on the southwest edge of Palitana about 3.5km from the bus stand (₹20 by autorickshaw). Most days, hundreds of pilgrims make the 1½-hour climb; crowds swell into the thousands around Kartik Purnima (p689), which marks the end of Chaturmas, a four-month period of spiritual retreat and material self-denial that coincides with the monsoon season.

As you near the top of the hill, the track forks. The main entrance, Ram Pole, is reached by bearing left, though the best views are to the right, where on a clear day you can see the Gulf of Cambay. Inside the Nav Tonk Gate, one path leads left to the Muslim shrine of Angar Pir – a Muslim saint who protected the temples from a Mughal attack; women who want children

---

ⓘ SHATRUNJAYA PRACTICALITIES

It's best to start the ascent around dawn, before it gets too hot. Dress respectfully (no shorts etc), leave behind leather items (including belts and bags), and don't eat or drink inside the temples. If you wish, you can be carried up and down the hill in a *dholi* (portable chair with two bearers), for about ₹1000 round trip. Photos may be taken on the trail and outside the temples, but not inside them.

come here and make offerings of miniature cradles. To the right, the second *tunk* you reach is the Chaumukhji Tunk, containing the **Chaumukh** (Four-Faced Shrine), built in 1618 by a wealthy Jain merchant. Images of Adinath, the first Jain *tirthankar* (great teacher; believed to have attained enlightenment here), face the four cardinal directions.

You can easily spend a couple of hours wandering among the hundreds of temples up here. The biggest and one of the most splendid and important, with a fantastic wealth of detailed carving, is the **Adinath Temple**, on the highest point on the far (south) side.

Shri Vishal Jain Museum   MUSEUM
(admission ₹10; ⊙8.30am-12.30pm & 3.30-8.30pm) This museum features some remarkable – if randomly displayed – exhibits of Jain artwork and artefacts up to 500 years old. In the basement is a surprising circular temple with mirror walls and centuries-old images of four *tirthankars*. It's 500m down the street from the foot of the Shatrunjaya steps.

🛏 Sleeping & Eating

Hotel Shravak   HOTEL $
(☑ 252428; s/d/tr ₹200/500/600, r with AC ₹900; ❋) The ultrabasic rooms at the friendly and helpful Shravak, opposite the bus stand, are the best bet in Palitana itself. They're shabby but clean, though bathrooms are hit or miss (mostly miss); doubles are much bigger than singles. Buckets of hot water are available from 5am to 10am.

★ **Vijay Vilas Palace**   HERITAGE HOTEL $$
(☑ 282371, 9427182809; vishwa_adpur@yahoo.co.in; Adpur village; r incl breakfast ₹3750; ❋) This small former palace built in 1906 sits surrounded by fields in the countryside beneath the western end of Shatrunjaya, 10km west of Palitana. There are six large, plain but nicely decorated rooms, with original furniture. Three have terraces/balconies looking towards Shatrunjaya – which can be climbed from here by a slightly shorter, steeper path than the one from Palitana.

Vijay Vilas is family-run, with delicious home-cooked food (a mix of Gujarati and Rajasthani, veg and nonveg). You can also just pop in for lunch (₹300) – call first.

Jagruti Restaurant   INDIAN $
(thalis ₹35-70; ⊙24hr) Across the laneway from Hotel Shravak, Jagruti is a busy thali house.

ℹ Getting There & Away

Plenty of ST buses run to/from Bhavnagar (₹37, 1½ hours, hourly) and Ahmedabad (₹150, five hours, hourly). For Diu, take a bus to Talaja (₹21, one hour, hourly), where you can change for Diu (₹90, 5½ hours, around six daily).

Four passenger trains run daily to/from Bhavnagar (2nd class ₹15, 1½ hours).

Diu

☑ 02875 / POP 52,056

Diu is different. This tiny island linked by a bridge to Gujarat's southern coast is infused with Portuguese history; its major architectural landmarks include three churches and a seafront fort; the streets of the main town are remarkably clean and quiet once you get off the tourist-packed waterfront strip; and alcohol is legal here. If you've been spending time immersed in the intensity of Gujarati cities, or just really need a beer, Diu offers a refreshing break.

Despite its draw as a seaside destination, Diu is not a great choice for a beach-centric vacation. Most of its sandy strips are littered with trash, and the throngs of families make them better for people-watching than sun-worshipping. Add in the random drunk-guy factor and any fantasies you have of a tropical paradise will surely be dashed. Diu, however, is one of the safest places in India to ride a scooter, with minimum traffic and excellent roads, and zipping along the coast with the wind in your hair is a joy.

Like Daman and Goa, Diu was a Portuguese colony until taken over by India in 1961. With Daman, it is still governed from Delhi as part of the Union Territory of Daman & Diu and is not part of Gujarat. It includes Diu Island, about 11km by 3km, separated from the mainland by a narrow channel, and two tiny mainland enclaves. One of these, housing the village of Ghoghla, is the entry point to Diu from Una.

Diu town sits at the east end of the island. The northern side of the island, facing Gujarat, is tidal marsh and salt pans, while the southern coast alternates between limestone cliffs, rocky coves and sandy beaches.

The island's main industries are fishing, tourism, alcohol and salt. Kalpana Distillery at Malala produces rum from sugar cane.

One custom of the Portuguese still very much respected by local businesses is that of the siesta, meaning you shouldn't count on much being open mid-afternoon.

Diu Town

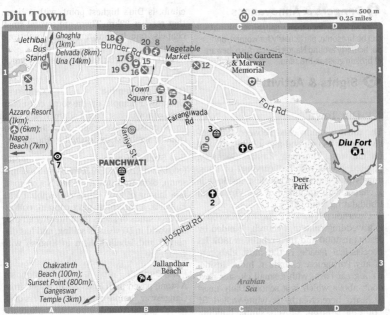

Diu Town

History

Diu was the first landing point for the Parsis when they fled from Persia in the 7th century AD, and it became a major port between the 14th and 16th centuries, when it was the trading post and naval base from which the Ottomans controlled the northern Arabian Sea shipping routes.

The Portuguese secured control of Diu in 1535 and kept it until India launched Operation Vijay in 1961. After the Indian Air Force unnecessarily bombed the airstrip and terminal near Nagoa Beach, it remained derelict until the late 1980s. Diu, Daman and Goa were administered as one union territory of India until 1987, when Goa became a state.

❶ Dangers & Annoyances

More an annoyance than a danger, drunk males can be tiresome, particularly for women, and particularly around Nagoa Beach. Also, beware of broken glass in the sand.

◉ Sights & Activities

◉ Diu Town

The town is sandwiched between the massive fort at its east end and a huge city wall on the west. The main Zampa Gateway, painted bright red, has carvings of lions, angels and a priest, while just inside it is a chapel with an image of the Virgin and Child dating from 1702.

Cavernous St Paul's Church (⊙8am-6pm) is a wedding cake of a church, founded by Jesuits in 1600 and then rebuilt in 1807. Its neoclassical facade is the most elaborate of any Portuguese church in India. Inside, it's a great barn, with a small cloister next door, above which is a school. Daily mass is heard here. Nearby is white-walled St Thomas' Church, a lovely, simple building that is now the Diu Museum (⊙9am-9pm) FREE, with a spooky, evocative collection of wooden Catholic saints going back to the 16th century. Once a year, on All Saints Day (1 November), this is used for a packed-out mass. The Portuguese-descended population mostly live in this area, still called Farangiwada (Foreigners' Quarter). The Church of St Francis of Assisi (Hospital), founded in 1593, has been converted into a hospital, but is also sometimes used for services.

Many other Diu buildings show a lingering Portuguese influence. The western part of town is a maze of narrow, winding streets and many houses are brightly painted, with the most impressive being in the Panchwati area, notably Nagar Sheth Haveli, an old merchant's house laden with stucco scrolls and fulsome fruit.

◉ Around the Island

★ Diu Fort   FORT
(⊙8am-6pm) Built in 1535, with additions made in 1541, this massive, well-preserved Portuguese fort with its double moat (one tidal) must once have been impregnable, but sea erosion and neglect are leading to a slow collapse. Cannonballs litter the place, and the ramparts have a superb array of cannons. The lighthouse, which you can climb, is Diu's highest point, with a beam that reaches 32km. There are several small chapels, one holding engraved tombstone fragments.

Part of the fort also serves as the island's jail.

Gangeswar Temple   HINDU TEMPLE
Gangeswar Temple, on the south coast 3km west of town, just past Fudam village, is a small coastal cave where five Shiva linga (phallic symbols) are washed by the waves.

Sea Shell Museum   MUSEUM
(adult/child ₹20/10; ⊙9.30am-5pm) This museum, 6km from town on the Nagoa road, is a labour of love. Captain Devjibhai Vira Fulbaria, a merchant navy captain, collected thousands of shells from literally all over the world in 50 years of sailing, and has displayed and labelled them in English with great care.

Parsi Bungali   HISTORIC SITE
A stone-paved path leads 200m inland from Gangeswar Temple to two Parsi 'towers of silence' – squat, round stone towers where the Parsis laid their dead out to be consumed by vultures. Climb the ramp slowly and make some noise, so as not to startle the groups of dogs that hang out inside!

★ Vanakbara   VILLAGE
At the extreme west of the island, Vanakbara is a fascinating little fishing village and the highlight of Diu It's great to wander around the port, packed with colourful fishing boats and bustling activity – best around 7am to 8am when the fishing fleet returns and sells off its catch.

Beaches
Nagoa Beach, on the south coast of the island 7km west of Diu town, is long, palm-fringed and safe for swimming – but trash-strewn and very busy, often with drunk men: foreign women receive a lot of unwanted attention. Two kilometres further west begins the sandy, 2.5km sweep of Gomptimata Beach. This is often empty, except on busy weekends, but it gets big waves – you need to be a strong swimmer here. Within walking distance of Diu town is the rocky Jallandhar Beach, on the town's southern shore; the longer, sandier Chakratirth Beach, west of Jallandhar; and pretty Sunset Point Beach, a small, gentle curve beyond Chakratirth that's popular for swimming and relatively hassle-free. Sunset Point itself

is a small headland at the south end of the beach, topped by the **INS Khukhri Memorial**, commemorating an Indian Navy frigate sunk off Diu during the 1971 India–Pakistan War. Unfortunately the region around Sunset Point is also a dumping ground, and any early-morning excursion will reveal that the tidal zone here is a popular toilet venue.

The best beach is **Ghoghla Beach**, north of Diu. A long stretch of sand, it's got less trash and fewer people than the others, along with gentle waves and some decent restaurants behind it.

☞ Tours

Boat Trips   BOATING

(per person ₹40, minimum ₹240; ⊙9.30am-1.pm & 3-6.30pm) You can take 20-minute boat trips around the harbour. Get tickets at the kiosk in front of the tourist office.

🛏 Sleeping

Rates at most hotels are extremely flexible, with discounts of up to 60% available at the more expensive places when things are quiet. Some only charge the full rates at peak holiday times such as Diwali and Christmas/New Year. We've quoted the highest prices here.

🛏 Diu Town

★Herança Goesa   GUESTHOUSE $

(📞253851; heranca_goesa@yahoo.com; Farangiwada; r ₹400-800) Behind the Diu Museum, this friendly home of a Portuguese-descended family has eight absolutely spotless rooms that represent incredible value. Take one of the upstairs rooms that captures the sea breeze and just relax. Good breakfasts are served and delicious fish/seafood dinners may be available if you ask in advance.

Hotel Super Silver   HOTEL $

(📞252020; Super Silver Complex; r ₹450, with AC ₹950; ❄) Super Silver has a nice central location and is good value, with simple, very clean rooms – though the bathrooms could use some help. The affable manager raises and lowers prices according to demand on any given day, but likes foreign tourists and is willing to give them a break.

Hotel Samrat   HOTEL $$

(📞252354; www.hotelsamratdiu.com; Old Collectorate Rd; r ₹1450, with AC from ₹2050; ❄⊠) Hotel Samrat is the best midrange choice downtown, with comfortable doubles, some

with street-facing balconies. Credit cards are accepted, and there's a swimming pool, and a decent Indian-Chinese restaurant with plenty of grog available.

★Azzaro Resort   HOTEL $$$

(📞255421; www.azzarodiu.com; Fudam Rd; d ₹4950-11,900; ❄@🛜⊠) A kilometre outside the city gate, this is hands down Diu's most luxurious hotel. It features tastefully luxurious rooms with high-tech lighting controls and stylish glass walls between the bedroom and bath. All look out onto the garden surrounding the sapphire-blue pool, many with balconies. There's a spa, a gym, two restaurants and a 24-hour coffee shop. In all, worth the money.

🛏 Nagoa Beach

Hoka Island Villa   HOTEL $$

(📞253036; www.resorthoka.com; r ₹2740-3170; ❄🛜⊠) Hoka is a great place to stay, with colourful, clean and cool rooms in a small, palm-shaded complex with a swimming pool. Some rooms have terraces over the palm trees. Management is helpful, you can hire mopeds, and the food is excellent. On the main road, pass the turn into Nagoa Beach, and it's on the left after 150m.

Radhika Beach Resort   HOTEL $$$

(📞252553; www.radhikaresort.com; d ₹5430-7580; ❄🛜⊠) An immaculate, smart, modern place and Diu's best-located upmarket option, with comfortable, condo-like villas in grassy grounds. Rooms are spacious and clean, and there's a very good multicuisine restaurant. The classic and VIP rooms are set around a large pool.

🍴 Eating

There's a daily **fish market** opposite Jethibai bus stand, and another one across the bridge in Ghoghla, which is active around 6.30pm. The fresh fish and seafood are delicious; most guesthouses and hotels will cook anything you buy.

Ram Vijay   ICE CREAM $

(scoops ₹25-30; ⊙8.30am-1.30pm & 3.30-9.30pm) For a rare treat head to this small, squeaky-clean, old-fashioned ice-cream parlour near the town square for delicious handmade ice cream and milkshakes. Going since 1933, this family enterprise started with soft drinks, and still makes its own brand (Dew) in Fudam village – try a ginger lemon soda and then all the ice creams!

O'Coqueiro MULTICUISINE $$
(Farangiwada Rd; breakfast ₹50-120, lunch & dinner ₹100-330; ⊙8am-9pm) Here, the dedicated Kailash Pandey has developed a soul-infused garden restaurant celebrating freshness and quality. The menu offers uncomplicated but very tasty pasta, chicken and seafood, plus a handful of Portuguese dishes learnt from a local Diu matriarch. There's also good coffee, cold beer, groovy music and friendly service.

Cat's Eye View MULTICUISINE $$
(Hoka Island Villa, Nagoa Beach; breakfast ₹50-150, lunch & dinner ₹90-290; ⊙8-10am, 12-2.30pm & 7-9.30pm; 🐾) The open-air restaurant at Hoka Island Villa has excellent food, with inviting breakfasts and delicious choices such as penne with tuna and tomato, fish and chips, and prawn coconut curry.

Sea View Restaurant SEAFOOD $$
(Ghoghla Beach; meals ₹100-240; ⊙8am-11pm) Just behind Ghoghla Beach, the open-air Sea View has a full menu of Indian and seafood, with the sand a stone's throw away. The prawn biryani (₹150) is big and spicy good.

Apana Foodland MULTICUISINE $$
(Apana Hotel, Fort Rd; mains ₹80-300; ⊙7am-10.30pm) This outdoor restaurant facing the town waterfront does everything: breakfasts, South Indian, Gujarati, Punjabi and Chinese, with plenty of chicken and mutton on the list. The fish dishes, including king-fish or prawns with rice, chips and salad, can be pre-ordered so you don't miss out. The Gujarati fruit salad is delicious.

🍷 Drinking & Nightlife

Apart from the restaurants (most of which serve beer), there are a number of bars around town, some on the seedy side. Drinks are blissfully cheap – around ₹50 for a Kingfisher or ₹150 for a bottle of port.

Casaluxo Bar BAR
(⊙9am-1pm & 4-9pm Tue-Sun) The almost pub-like Casaluxo Bar has a more salubrious air. It opened in 1963 and, except for some sexy swimsuit posters in the back room, might not have updated its decor since.

❶ Information

Many shops around town change money.

A to Z (Vaniya St, Panchwati; per hour ₹40; ⊙9am-9pm) The best internet cafe is near Panchwati Rd.

Post Office (⊙9am-5pm Mon-Sat) Upstairs, facing the town square.

State Bank of India (Main Bazaar; ⊙10am-4pm Mon-Fri) Changes cash and travellers cheques and has an ATM.

Tourist Office (☎252653; www.diutourism.co.in; Bunder Rd; ⊙9.30am-1.30pm & 2.30-6pm Mon-Sat) Has maps, bus schedules and hotel prices.

❶ Getting There & Away

AIR

Jet Airways (☎255030; www.jetairways.com) flies to/from Mumbai via Porbandar. There are several ticketing agents in town. The airport is 6km west of town, just before Nagoa Beach.

BUS & CAR

Visitors arriving in Diu by road may be charged a border tax of ₹50 per person, though the practice seems to be erratic.
From Jethibai bus stand there are buses to:

Ahmedabad ₹250, 12 hours, 7am
Bhavnagar ₹175, seven hours, nine daily
Junagadh ₹140, five hours, seven daily
Rajkot ₹175, six hours, six daily
Veraval ₹90, three hours, 12 daily

More frequent departures go from Una, 14km north of Diu. Buses run between Una bus stand and Diu (₹17, 40 minutes, half-hourly) between 6.30am to 8pm. Outside these hours, shared autorickshaws go to Ghoghla or Diu from Tower Chowk in Una (1km from the bus stand), for about the same fare. An autorickshaw costs ₹250. Una rickshaw-wallahs are unable to proceed further than the bus station in Diu, so cannot take you all the way to Nagoa Beach (an additional ₹100).

Ekta Travels (☎9898618424) runs private buses from the Diu bus stand to Mumbai at 11.30am (sleeper ₹1000, 22 hours) and to Ahmedabad at 7.30pm (seat/sleeper ₹400/500, 10 hours).

TRAIN

Delvada is the nearest railhead, 8km from Diu on the Una road. The 52951 MG Passenger at 2.25pm runs to Sasan Gir (2nd class ₹25, 3½ hours) and Junagadh (₹35, 6¼ hours), while the 52950 Passenger at 8.05am heads to Veraval (₹25, 3¼ hours). Half-hourly Diu–Una buses stop at Delvada (₹15, 20 minutes).

❶ Getting Around

Travelling by autorickshaw anywhere in Diu town should cost no more than ₹30. From the bus stand into town is ₹40. To Nagoa Beach and beyond pay ₹100 and to Sunset Point ₹50.

Scooters are a perfect option for exploring the island – the roads are deserted and in good condition. The going rate is ₹350 per day (not including fuel), and motorcycles can be had for ₹400. Most hotels can arrange rentals, although quality varies. You will normally have to show your driving licence and leave a deposit of ₹1500.

Local buses from Diu town to Nagoa and Vanakbara (both ₹10) leave Jethibai bus stand at 7am, 11am and 4pm. From Nagoa, they depart for Diu town from near the police post at 1pm, 5.30pm and 7pm.

Veraval

02876 / POP 153,696

Cluttered and chaotic, Veraval is one of India's major fishing ports; its busy harbour is full of bustle and boat building. It was also the major seaport for Mecca pilgrims before the rise of Surat. The main reason to come here now is to visit the Temple of Somnath, 6km southeast; while the town of Somnath is a nicer place to stay, Veraval is more convenient to public transport.

Sights

Bhalka Tirth HINDU TEMPLE

One kilometre from Veraval towards Somnath, Bhalka Tirth is where Krishna was mistaken for a deer (he was sleeping in a deerskin) and fatally wounded by an arrow. The temple here is an architecturally mundane affair, but it contains an image of Krishna reclining, a tulsi tree planted in his memory growing out through the roof, a relief of his footprint and two Shiva linga.

A sign outside tells us that this was where Krishna departed on his journey to Neejdham (final rest) at 2.27 and 30 seconds am on 18 February, 3102 BC.

Fishing Harbour AREA

About 2km from downtown Veraval towards Somnath, the harbour is a striking sight with hundreds of wooden dhows flying colourful flags.

Sleeping & Eating

Hotel Shyam HOTEL $

(7048221414, 221414; www.hotelshyamsomnath. com; Maa Complex; r ₹1000, with AC from ₹1400;) Virtually across the street from the bus stand, this brand-new hotel is Veraval's best. Rooms are modern, with sleek fixtures and colourfully patterned walls. Staff are ex-ceedingly friendly and discounts are usually available for the asking.

Hotel Kaveri HOTEL $

(220842; www.hotelkaveri.in; 2 Akar Complex, ST Rd; r ₹500, with AC from ₹850, ste from ₹1500;) Convenient to the bus stand, with a range of well-kept rooms.

Toran Tourist Bungalow HOTEL $

(246588; College Rd; s/d ₹400/500, with AC ₹700/900;) This state-government-run hotel, 1km west of the bus stand area, is not very conveniently situated. But it has size-able, quiet, clean rooms with white-tile walls and floors, and sea-view terraces.

Sagar INDIAN, CHINESE $$

(ST Rd; mains ₹100-135; 10am-3pm & 6.30-11pm) With air-con and fish tanks, this all-veg Punjabi-Chinese restaurant is a quiet oasis with reliable food and attentive service.

Information

There's an ATM just outside the bus stand, and others around town.

Cybertown (internet per hour ₹20; 8am-midnight) A hundred metres from the bus stand, opposite Hotel Kaveri.

JP Travels International (Satta Bazaar; 10am-8.30pm Mon-Sat) Changes travellers cheques and cash.

Getting There & Away

BUS

ST buses go to Ahmedabad (₹250, nine hours, 11 daily), including one AC Volvo service (₹733) at 9.15pm. Frequent buses go to Junagadh (₹83, 2½ hours), Rajkot (₹140, four hours) and Una (for Diu, ₹93, three hours), with buses direct to Diu (₹93, three hours) at 7.30am, 9.30am and 4.30pm. There's sporadic service throughout the day to Sasan Gir (₹35, 1½ hours, hourly). **Patel Tours & Travels** (222863), opposite the ST bus stand, offers a nightly non-AC jaunt to Ahmedabad (seat/sleeper ₹300/400) at 9.30pm.

TRAIN

The 11463 Jabalpur Express leaves at 9.50am for Junagadh (sleeper/3AC/2AC ₹140/485/690, 1¾ hours), Rajkot (₹140/485/690, four hours) and Ahmedabad (₹260/690/990, nine hours). Second-class-only trains with unreserved seating head to Sasan Gir (₹10) at 9.45am (two hours) and 1.55pm (1¼ hours). There's a **computerised reservation office** (8am-10pm Mon-Sat, to 2pm Sun) at the station.

ⓘ Getting Around

The best way to get to Somnath is by autorick-shaw, which costs ₹10/120 for shared/private.

Somnath
☑ 02876

Somnath's famous, phoenix-like temple stands in neat gardens above the beach, 6km southeast of Veraval. The sea below gives it a wistful charm. The small town of Somnath is an agglomeration of narrow, interesting market streets with no car traffic, so it's easy to walk around and enjoy. There's a State Bank ATM on your right as you approach the temple. Somnath celebrates Kartik Purnima (p689), marking Shiva's killing of the demon Tripurasura, with a large colourful fair.

⊙ Sights

Temple of Somnath   HINDU TEMPLE
(⊙6am-9pm) It's said that Somraj (the moon god) first built a temple here, made of gold; this was rebuilt by Ravana in silver, by Krishna in wood and by Bhimdev in stone. The current serene, symmetrical structure was built to traditional designs on the original coastal site: it's painted a creamy colour and boasts a little fine sculpture. The large, black Shiva lingam at its heart is one of the 12 most sacred Shiva shrines, known as *jyoti linga*.

A description of the temple by Al-Biruni, an Arab traveller, was so glowing that it prompted a visit in 1024 by a most unwelcome tourist – the legendary looter Mahmud of Ghazni from Afghanistan. At that time, the temple was so wealthy that it had 300 musicians, 500 dancing girls and even 300 barbers. Mahmud of Ghazni took the town and temple after a two-day battle in which it's said 70,000 Hindu defenders died. Having stripped the temple of its fabulous wealth, Mahmud destroyed it. So began a pattern of Muslim destruction and Hindu rebuilding that continued for centuries. The temple was again razed in 1297, 1394 and finally in 1706 by Aurangzeb, the notorious Mughal ruler. After that, the temple wasn't rebuilt until 1950.

Cameras, mobile phones and bags must be left at the cloakroom before entering. Colourful dioramas of the Shiva story line the north side of the temple garden, though it's hard to see them through the hazy glass. A

one-hour **sound-and-light show** highlights the temple nightly at 7.45pm.

Prabhas Patan Museum   MUSEUM
(Indian/foreigner ₹5/50; ⊙10.30am-5.30pm Thu-Tue, closed 2nd & 4th Sat of the month) This museum, 300m north of the Somnath temple, is laid out in courtyard-centred rooms and contains remains of the previous temples, some intricately carved, though many are very weathered.

🛏 Sleeping & Eating

Hotel Kailash   HOTEL $
(☑ 9228205381; r from ₹400, with AC from ₹800; ☀) This hotel just north of Somnath Temple is the best option close to the temple and the markets. Rooms are in good shape, have modern air-con units and flat-screen TVs.

New Bhabha Restaurant   INDIAN, CHINESE $
(mains ₹80-120) The pick of a poor bunch of eateries, vegetarian New Bhabha sits 50m north of the ST bus stand. You can eat in a small air-con room or outside open to the street.

ⓘ Getting There & Away

Somnath has fewer departures than Veraval, but buses run to Diu (₹65, three hours, daily at 10am and 5.15pm), and to Junagadh (₹90, two hours) throughout the day. There are eight regular daily buses to Ahmedabad (₹255, nine hours), plus one AC Volvo (₹800, 9pm). **Shyam Travels** (☑ 232670), just north of the ST bus stand, also runs several evening buses to Ahmedabad (seat/sleeper ₹350/450, nine hours), with one AC departure (₹500) at 9.45pm; it also serves other destinations including Bhuj and Dwarka.

Gir National Park & Wildlife Sanctuary
☑ 02877

The last refuge of the Asiatic lion (*Panthera leo persica*) is this forested, hilly, 1412-sq-km sanctuary about halfway between Veraval and Junagadh. It feels beguilingly uncommercial, and simply driving through the thick, undisturbed forests would be a joy even if there wasn't the excitement of lions and other wildlife to spot.

The sanctuary was set up in 1965, and a 259-sq-km core area was declared a national park in 1975. Since the late 1960s, lion numbers have increased from under 200 to over 400. The sanctuary's 37 other mammal species, most of which have also increased in numbers, include dainty chital (spotted deer), sambar (large deer), nilgais (large antelopes), chousinghas (four-horned antelopes), chinkaras (gazelles), crocodiles and rarely seen leopards. Sasan Gir is a great destination for birders too, with over 300 species, most of them resident.

While the wildlife has been lucky, more than half the sanctuary's human community of distinctively dressed *maldhari* (herders) have been resettled elsewhere, ostensibly because their cattle and buffalo were competing for food resources with the antelopes, deer and gazelles, while also being preyed upon by the lions and leopards. Around 1000 people still live in the park, however, and their livestock accounts for about a quarter of the lions' diet.

Gir is no longer big enough for the number of lions that currently live here; some may be moved to Madhya Pradesh to protect genetic diversity, but the Gujarat government opposes this plan, vying to remain the sole home of India's lions.

The sanctuary access point is Sasan Gir village, on a minor road and railway between Veraval and Junagadh (about 40km from each). The best time to visit is from December to April; the sanctuary is closed from 16 June to 15 October and possibly longer if there has been a heavy monsoon.

Safaris

Safaris (www.girlion.in; permit vehicle with up to 6 passengers Indian/foreigner ₹400/US$40 Mon-Fri, ₹500/US$50 Sat & Sun, guide 3hr ₹250, camera Indian/foreigner ₹100/600) into the sanctuary are made in 4WD jeeps – called Gypsy – and entry is strictly managed. Visiting hours are split into three, three-hour time slots – 6am to 9am, 9am to noon, and 3pm to 6pm – and

only 30 Gypsies are allowed in the park at any one time. Your best bet for seeing wildlife is early morning or a bit before sunset.

Most hotels and guesthouses in and around Sasan Gir have Gypsys and drivers or will arrange them for you, charging ₹1500 or more per vehicle for up to six passengers. Alternatively, you can hire an open 4WD and driver for around ₹1300 outside the sanctuary reception centre, in Sasan Gir village. Once you have a vehicle sorted, you must queue up at the reception centre to obtain a permit and a guide, and pay photography fees. Your driver will usually help with this.

Permit-issuing times are posted at the reception centre: at research time they were 5.30am, 8.30am and 2.30pm – but you'll want to be at the reception centre with your passport much earlier to ensure you get a permit. It's not unheard of for the early-morning queue to begin before midnight! If you can plan ahead, half of the permits issued each day can be booked online, from three months to 48 hours advance.

As a general rule, about one in every two safaris has a lion sighting. So if you're determined to see lions, allow for a couple of trips. You'll certainly see a variety of other wildlife, and the guides are adept spotters.

⊙ Sights & Activities

Gir Interpretation Zone   WILDLIFE WATCHING
(Indian/foreigner ₹75/1200 Mon-Fri, ₹95/1500 Sat & Sun; ⊙8-11am & 3-5pm) Twelve kilometres west of Sasan Gir village at Devalia, within the sanctuary precincts, is the Gir Interpretation Zone, better known as simply Devalia. The 4-sq-km fenced-off compound is home to a cross-section of Gir wildlife. Chances of seeing lions here are good but stage-managed, and you're only likely to

---

THE LAST WILD ASIATIC LIONS

The Asiatic lion *(Panthera leo persica)* once roared as far west as Syria and as far east as India's Bihar. Widespread hunting decimated the population, with the last sightings recorded near Delhi in 1834, in Bihar in 1840 and in Rajasthan in 1870. In Gujarat, too, they were almost hunted to extinction, with as few as 12 remaining in the 1870s. It was not until one of their erstwhile pursuers, the enlightened Nawab of Junagadh, decided to set up a protection zone at the beginning of the 20th century that the lions began slowly to recover. This zone now survives as the Sasan Gir Wildlife Sanctuary.

Separated from their African counterpart *(Panthera leo leo)* for centuries, Asiatic lions have developed unique characteristics. Their mane is less luxuriant and doesn't cover the top of the head or ears, while a prominent fold of skin runs the length of the abdomen. They are also purely predatory, unlike African lions which sometimes feed off carrion.

get 30 to 45 minutes looking for wildlife and only from a bus. An autorickshaw/taxi round trip to Devalia from Sasan Gir village costs around ₹120/200.

Gir Orientation Centre   EXHIBITION
(◷8am-6pm) FREE Next to the reception centre, this has an informative exhibition on the sanctuary and a small shop. It was being renovated at the time of research.

🛏 Sleeping & Eating

It's a good idea to make an advance booking. Sasan Gir has one main street and most accommodation is on it or nearby, with a few top-end options further away.

★Nitin Ratanghayara
Family Rooms   GUESTHOUSE $
(☑9979024670; ratanghayaranitin@yahoo.com; r ₹700, with AC ₹1200; ❄@🛜) At his family's courtyard-style home in Sasan, friendly, golden-toothed Nitin Ratanghayara has several very good rooms for travellers. They're well kept, and much better value than any of the budget joints on the main street. Plus, you get to eat his sister-in-law's home cooking, and can help her in the kitchen if you like. Look for his sign over his shop along Sasan's main drag.

Hotel Umang   HOTEL $
(☑285728; www.sasangirhotels.in; Rameshwar Society, SBS Rd; r ₹750, with AC ₹1250; ❄🛜) This is a quiet option with perfectly good rooms, helpful management and decent meals. Discounts are available when business is slow. It's 200m south off the main road near the town centre; follow the signs.

★Gateway Hotel   HOTEL $$$
(☑285551; www.thegatewayhotels.com; r incl breakfast from ₹8800, ste from ₹11,700; ❄@🛜➿) ⚓ The remodelling of an old government property by the Taj Group is easily the finest – and greenest – choice in town. The rooms and huge suites are lush with comforts – they even come with yoga mats! All overlook a river where buffaloes wade and lions have been spotted.

Booking online in advance gets serious discounts, and promotional packages that include all meals and safaris are offered.

Gir Birding Lodge   HOTEL $$$
(☑8882677766; www.girbirdinglodge.com; room or cottage incl meals s/d ₹5300/6300; ❄) This peaceful place is situated in a mango grove on the edge of the forest. The six cottages

are simple and sweet, with a few nice touches such as handmade wooden beds. The 16 hotel rooms are brand new and modern, if a bit plain. It's 2.5km from the village off the Junagadh road.

Bird and river walks are available; naturalist guides cost ₹2000 per day.

Amidhara Avezika Resort   HOTEL $$$
(☑285950; www.avezikahotels.com; r incl meals ₹5000-9000; ❄🛜➿) Two kilometres south of the village on the Veraval road, the regular hotel rooms here are surprisingly basic and the super deluxe rooms are alright but overpriced. Stay here for the cottages, which are modern, comfortable and great if you're travelling with kids. There's a pool, playground, gym and ping-pong tables.

Gir Rajwadi Hotel   INDIAN $
(mains ₹90-150; ◷11am-4pm & 7-11pm) This vegetarian joint is the best of several simple restaurants along the village's main street. Gujarati thali is ₹120.

❶ Getting There & Away

Buses run from Sasan Gir village to both Veraval (₹34, 1½ hours) and Junagadh (₹40, two hours) throughout the day.

Second-class unreserved-seating trains run to Junagadh (₹20, 5.58pm, 2¾ hours), Delvada (for Diu, ₹25, 9.58am, 3½ hours), and Veraval (₹10, 1½ hours, 11.58am and 4.27pm).

Junagadh
☑0285 / POP 320,250

Reached by few tourists, Junagadh is nestled against some of the most impressive topography in Gujarat. It's an ancient, fortified city (its name means 'old fort') with 2300 years of history, at the base of holy Girnar Hill. The Nawab of Junagadh opted to take his tiny state into Pakistan at the time of Partition – a wildly unpopular decision as the inhabitants were predominantly Hindu, so the nawab departed on his own. Junagadh makes a good jumping-off point for seeing the lions at Sasan Gir.

◉ Sights & Activities

While parts of the centre are as traffic-infested and hot as any other city, the area up towards Uparkot Fort and around Circle and Diwan Chowks is highly atmospheric, dotted with markets and half-abandoned palaces in

Euro-Mughal style with grass growing out of their upper storeys.

⭐**Girnar Hill** SACRED SITE
This sacred mountain, which rises dramatically from the plains, is covered with Jain and Hindu temples. Pilgrims from far and wide come to tackle the long climb up 10,000 stone steps to the summit, which is best begun at dawn. Be prepared to spend a full day if you want to reach the uppermost temples. Ascending in the early morning light is a magical experience, as pilgrims and porters begin to trudge up the well-maintained steps.

The Jain temples, a cluster of mosaic-decorated domes interspersed with elaborate stupas, are about two-thirds of the way up. The largest and oldest is the 12th-century **Temple of Neminath**, dedicated to the 22nd *tirthankar*: go through the first left-hand doorway after the first gate. Many temples are locked from around 11am to 3pm, but this one is open all day. The nearby triple **Temple of Mallinath**, dedicated to the ninth *tirthankar,* was erected in 1177 by two brothers. During festivals this temple is a sadhu magnet.

Further up are various Hindu temples. The first peak is topped by the **Temple of Amba Mata**, where newlyweds worship to ensure a happy marriage. Beyond here there is quite a lot of down as well as up to reach the other four peaks and further temples. The **Temple of Gorakhnath** is perched on Gujarat's highest peak at 1117m. The steep peak Dattatraya is topped by a shrine to a three-faced incarnation of Vishnu. Atop the final outcrop, Kalika, is a shrine to the goddess Kali.

The trail begins 4km east of the city at **Girnar Taleti**. A motorable road, which may or may not be open, leads to about the 3000th step, which leaves you only 7000 to go! Refreshment stalls on the ascent sell chalk, so you can graffiti your name on the rocks. If you can't face the walk, *dholis* carried by porters cost ₹3850 (round trip) if you weigh between 50kg and 70kg, and ₹4250 for heavier passengers. If your weight range isn't obvious, you suffer the indignity of being weighed on a huge beam scale before setting off. Note that while photography is permitted on the trail, it's not allowed inside the temples.

The Bhavnath Mela (p689), over five days in the month of Magha, brings folk music and dancing and throngs of *nagas* (naked sadhus or spiritual men) to Bhavnath Mahadev Temple at Girnar Taleti. It marks the time when Shiva is believed to have danced his cosmic dance of destruction.

An autorickshaw from town to Girnar Taleti costs about ₹70.

⭐**Uparkot Fort** FORT
(☉dawn-dusk) This ancient fort is believed to have been built in 319 BC by the Mauryan emperor Chandragupta, though it has been extended many times. In places the ramparts reach 20m high. It's been besieged 16 times, and legend has it that the fort once withstood a 12-year siege. The views over the city and east to Girnar Hill are superb, and there are a number of interesting sights within its walls.

The **Jumma Masjid**, the mosque inside the fort, was converted from a palace in the 15th century by Gujarat sultan Mahmud Begada and has a rare roofed courtyard with three octagonal openings which may once have been covered by domes.

Close to the mosque is a set of **Buddhist caves** (Indian/foreigner ₹5/100; ☉8am-6pm), not actually caves but monastic quarters carved out of the rock about 2000 years ago. The three-storey complex is quite eerie and the main hall contains pillars with weathered carvings.

The fort has two fine step-wells both cut from solid rock. **Adi Kadi Vav**, named after two slave girls who used to fetch water from it, is 41m deep and was cut in the 15th century. **Navghan Kuvo**, 52m deep and designed to help withstand sieges, is almost 1000 years old and its magnificent staircase spirals around the well shaft.

⭐**Mahabat Maqbara** MAUSOLEUM, MOSQUE
This stunning mausoleum of Nawab Mahabat Khan II of Junagadh (1851–82) seems to bubble up into the sky. One of Gujarat's most glorious examples of Euro-Indo-Islamic architecture, with French windows and Gothic columns, its lavish appeal is topped off by its silver inner doors.

Vazir's Mausoleum MAUSOLEUM
Boasting even more flourish than neighbouring Mahabat Maqbara, Vazir's Mausoleum sports four storybook minarets encircled by spiralling stairways.

Sakkarbaug Zoo ZOO, MUSEUM
(admission ₹20, camera/video ₹20/100; ☉9am-6pm Thu-Tue) If you don't make it to Sasan Gir Wildlife Sanctuary, Junagadh's zoo, 2km

Junagadh

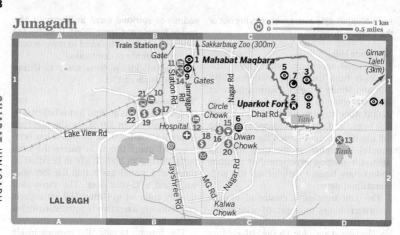

north of the centre, has Asiatic lions and a broad selection of other Indian wildlife.

Most of the animal pens are rather depressing; in the **'safari' park** (20min bus tour ₹25; ⊙bus tour 9am-1pm & 2.30-5.45pm) at the back, the big cats you view from a bus are in larger, more humane enclosures. Still, it's not a bad place to go, as it's shady and quiet, and the beauty of some of the animals is mesmerising despite the cages.

The zoo also houses the **Junagadh Museum**, with paintings, manuscripts, archaeological finds and more. An autorickshaw from the centre costs around ₹25.

Darbar Hall Museum   MUSEUM
(Diwan Chowk; Indian/foreigner ₹5/50; ⊙10am-1.15pm & 2.45-6pm Thu-Tue, closed 2nd & 4th Sat of the month) This museum displays weapons, armour, palanquins, chandeliers, and howdahs from the days of the nawabs, as well as a huge carpet woven in Junagadh's jail. There's a royal portrait gallery, including photos of the last nawab with his numerous beloved dogs. At the time of research, the museum was closed due to an internal dispute; no one could say when it will reopen.

Ashokan Edicts   HISTORIC SITE
(Indian/foreigner ₹5/100; ⊙dawn-dusk) Just outside town on the road to Girnar Hill, a white building on the right encloses a large boulder on which the Buddhist emperor Ashoka had 14 edicts inscribed in Brahmi script in the Pali language about 250 BC. The spidery lettering instructs people to be kind to women and animals and give to beggars, among other things, and is one of several inscriptions that Ashoka placed all around his

realm expounding his moral philosophy and achievements.

🛏 Sleeping

There are several cheap hotels around Kalwa Chowk which, because of the clientele they attract, are best avoided by females – even when travelling with a male companion.

Relief Hotel   HOTEL $
(☑ 2620280; www.reliefhotel.com; Chitta Khana Chowk; r ₹600-800, with AC ₹1200; ❈ @) Mr Sorathia (Junagadh's unofficial tourist officer) presides over the pick of the town's budget accommodation, which was undergoing a major renovation at the time of research. Most rooms, including all air-con rooms and the once-excellent restaurant, were being completely rebuilt and should be open by the time you read this. Note: this hotel closes during the month of Ramadan.

Hotel Vishala   HOTEL $
(☑ 2631599; www.hotelvishala.com; r from ₹940, with AC from ₹2080; ❈ 🤶) Almost opposite the bus station, Hotel Vishala has good-sized rooms that are comfortable and clean. Staff are friendly, and though there's some street noise during the day, it quietens down at night. There's room service and a rooftop veg restaurant.

Lotus Hotel   HOTEL $$
(☑ 2658500; www.thelotushotel.com; Station Rd; s/d from ₹1800/2280; ❈ 🤶) This luxurious and comfortable option occupies the totally renovated top floor of a former *dharamsala* (pilgrim's rest house). Pilgrims never had it so good, with split-system air-con and LCD TVs. Rooms are beautifully bright, spacious and pristine, the beds are great, and everything works – incredible value for such quality. There isn't a restaurant, but there is room service and Geeta Lodge is in the same building.

🍴 Eating & Drinking

Junagadh is famous for its fruit, especially for *kesar* (mangoes) and *chiku* (sapodilla), which are popular in milkshakes in November and December.

Garden Cafe   INDIAN $
(mains ₹90-140; ⊙ 6.30-10.30pm Thu-Tue) Something different: this restaurant has a lovely garden setting next to Jyoti Nursery on the eastern side of town, and serves reasonable Jain, Punjabi and South Indian food. It's

popular with families and young people, and worth the short rickshaw ride.

★ Geeta Lodge   GUJARATI $$
(Station Rd; thali ₹110; ⊙ 10am-3.30pm & 6.30-10pm) Geeta's army of waiters are constantly on the move serving up top-class, all-you-can-eat veg Gujarati thalis at a bargain price. Finish off with sweets, such as fruit salad or puréed mango, for ₹20.

Petals   MULTICUISINE $$
(Lotus Hotel, Station Rd; meals ₹140-290; ⊙ 7-10am, 11am-3pm & 7-11pm) The restaurant at the Lotus Hotel delivers a sleek first impression, with a modern, and very white, design. The menu ranges from Punjabi to sizzlers to pastas, and is very popular with middle-class families. If you're tired of thali, come on in!

Jay Ambe Juice Centre   JUICE BAR
(Diwan Chowk; snacks & drinks ₹20-50; ⊙ 10am-11.30pm) The perfect retreat for a fresh juice, milkshake or ice cream – try a custard-apple shake.

ⓘ Information

The very helpful management at Relief Hotel serves as an unofficial tourist information provider.

Bank of Baroda (cnr MG & Post Office Rds)
State Bank of India (Nagar Rd; ⊙ 11am-2pm Mon-Fri) Changes travellers cheques and cash and has an ATM.
X'S Internet Cafe (1st fl, Lake View Complex, Lake View Rd; per hour ₹20; ⊙ 9.30am-11pm)

ⓘ Getting There & Away

BUS

Buses leave the ST bus stand for the following destinations:
Ahmedabad ₹210, eight hours, half-hourly
Bhuj ₹170, seven hours, seven daily
Diu ₹140, five hours, 2pm and 5pm
Jamnagar ₹90, four hours, nine daily
Rajkot ₹93, two hours, hourly
Sasan Gir ₹55, two hours, hourly
Una (for Diu) ₹130, 4½ hours, eight daily
Veraval ₹100, 2½ hours, eight daily

Various private bus offices, including **Mahasagar Travels** (☑ 0285-2629199; Dhal Rd), are on Dhal Rd, near the railway tracks. Services go to:
Ahmedabad non-AC/AC/Volvo ₹350/400/420, eight hours
Jamnagar ₹100, four hours
Mumbai sleeper ₹1000, 19 hours

Rajkot non-AC/AC ₹100/120, two hours
Udaipur seat/sleeper ₹700/800, 14 hours

TRAIN

There's a **computerised reservation office** (⊙ 8am-10pm Mon-Sat, to 2pm Sun) at the station.

The Jabalpur Express (train 11463 or 11465) departs at 11.29am for Rajkot (sleeper/3AC/2AC ₹140/490/690, 2½ hours) and Ahmedabad (₹220/590/840, seven hours).

Second-class train 52952 heads to Sasan Gir (₹20, 2¾ hours) and Delvada (for Diu, ₹35, six hours) at 7.15am.

Gondal

📞 02825 / POP 112,064

Gondal is a small, leafy town, 38km south of Rajkot, that sports a string of palaces and a gentle river. It was once capital of a 1000-sq-km princely state ruled by Jadeja Rajputs who believe they are descendants of Krishna.

⊙ Sights & Activities

Naulakha Museum   MUSEUM

(Naulakha Palace; admission ₹20; ⊙ 9am-noon & 3-6pm) This eclectic museum in the old part of town is housed in a beautiful, 260-year-old riverside royal palace that was built in a mixture of styles, with striking gargoyles. It shows royal artefacts, including scales used to weigh Maharaja Bhagwat Sinhji in 1934 (his weight in silver was distributed to the poor), a nine-volume Gujarati dictionary compiled by the same revered maharaja, and Dinky Toy collections. Two stables full of mint-condition horse carriages can be seen for an extra ₹20.

Bhuvaneshwari Ayurvedic

Pharmacy   HISTORIC BUILDING

(www.bhuvaneshwaripith.com; Ghanshyam Bhuvan; ⊙ 9am-noon & 3-5pm Tue-Sat) Founded in 1910 by Gondal's royal physician, this pharmacy manufactures ayurvedic medicines and it's possible to see all the weird machinery involved, as well as buy medicines for treating hair loss, vertigo, insomnia etc. The founding physician, Brahmaleen Acharyashree, is said to have coined the title 'Mahatma' (Great Soul) for Gandhi. Also here is a temple to the goddess Bhuvaneshwari.

Udhyog Bharti Khadi

Gramodyog   HANDICRAFTS WORKSHOP

(Udhyog Bharti Chowk; ⊙ 9am-noon & 3-5pm Mon-Sat) A large *khadi* (homespun cloth) work-

shop where women work spinning cotton upstairs, while downstairs embroidered *salwar kameez* (traditional dresslike tunic and trouser combinations for women) and saris are on sale.

Vintage & Classic Car Collection   MUSEUM

(Orchard Palace Hotel, Palace Rd; Indian/foreigner ₹120/250; ⊙ 9am-noon & 3-6pm) This is the royal collection of cars – 32 impressive vehicles, from a 1907 car made by the New Engine Company Acton to racing cars raced by the present maharaja. All are still in working condition.

🛏 Sleeping & Eating

Orchard Palace   HERITAGE HOTEL $$$

(📞 220002; www.heritagepalacesgondal.com; Palace Rd; s/d ₹5200/6600; ❄) 🍴 This small palace, once the royal guesthouse, has seven well-kept, though hardly luxurious, high-ceilinged rooms of different sizes, filled with 1930s and '40s furniture. The parlours and patios, with more of the same, have an inviting, relaxed kind of charm. Guests get free admission to all of Gondal's attractions. The restaurant uses vegetables from the on-site organic garden. Reservations recommended.

Riverside Palace   HERITAGE HOTEL $$$

(📞 220002; www.heritagepalacesgondal.com; Ashapura Rd; s/d ₹5200/6600; ❄) This is the erstwhile ruling family's other palace-hotel, built in the 1880s and formerly the crown prince's abode. Adorned with hunting trophies and four-poster beds, it's kind of like a royal time machine you can sleep in, and has river views. There's a restaurant (₹400 to ₹700) here; nonguests should call in advance. Reservations recommended.

ℹ Getting There & Around

Buses run frequently to/from Rajkot (₹30, one hour) and Junagadh (₹65, two hours). Slow passenger trains between Rajkot (₹10, one hour) and Junagadh (₹15, 1½ hours) also stop at Gondal.

Hiring an autorickshaw to take you to all the sights and wait while you see them costs about ₹100 per hour.

Rajkot

📞 0281 / POP 1.28 MILLION

Rajkot is a large, hectic commercial and industrial city that isn't easy to love with its heavy traffic, lack of open spaces and scant worthwhile sights. But the old city, east of the newer centre, still has plenty of character, with narrow streets, markets, and farmers still selling ghee on street corners.

Rajkot was founded in 1612 by Jadeja Rajputs, and in colonial times it became the headquarters of the Western India States Agency, Britain's administrative centre for some 400 princely states in Saurashtra, Kachchh and northern Gujarat. After Independence Rajkot was capital of the short-lived state of Saurashtra.

◎ Sights

Watson Museum MUSEUM

(Jubilee Gardens; Indian/foreigner ₹5/50; ◎9am-12.45pm & 3-6pm Thu-Tue, closed 2nd & 4th Sat of the month) The Watson Museum is named after Colonel John Watson, a political agent (administrator) in the 1880s who gathered many historical artefacts and documents from around Saurashtra. It's a jumbled attic of a collection, featuring 3rd-century inscriptions, delicate ivory work, and taxidermy exhibits put together by someone with a bizarre sense of humour.

Kaba Gandhi No Delo HISTORIC BUILDING

(Ghee Kanta Rd; ◎9am-6pm) This is the house where Gandhi lived from the age of six (while his father was diwan of Rajkot), and it contains lots of interesting information on his life. The Mahatma's passion for the handloom is preserved in the form of a small weaving school.

Handicrafts Workshops

The Patola-weaving skill comes from Patan, and is a torturous process that involves dyeing each thread before it is woven. In Patan, both the warp and weft threads are dyed (double *ikat*), in Rajkot only the weft is dyed (single *ikat*), so the product is more affordable. You can visit workshops in people's houses in the Sarvoday Society area about 1km southwest of Shastri Maidan, including **Mayur Patola Art** (☑2464519; Sarvoday Society; ◎10am-6pm), behind Virani High School. Call for directions.

🛏 Sleeping

There are plenty of cheapies on Dhebar and Kanak Rds, either side of the ST bus stand, but many fill up early.

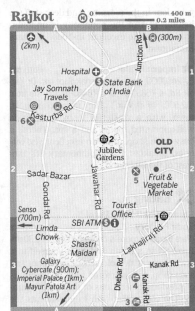

Hotel Bhakti HOTEL $

(☑2227744; Kanak Rd; s/d ₹700/950, s with AC ₹1000-1200, d with AC ₹1500-1800; ❄🛜) This reasonable semi-cheapie behind the bus station is a good deal for what you get, with rooms that are neat and in good shape. Discounts are usually available.

Hotel Kavery HOTEL $$

(☑2239331; www.hotelkavery.com; Kanak Rd; s ₹1350-1880, d ₹2000-2600, all incl breakfast; ❄🛜) The rooms fill up quickly at this popular midrange business hotel. Rooms are comfortable, a newspaper is delivered to your door in the morning, and desk staff are helpful. Part of the popularity is undoubtedly due to the excellent in-house Bukhara Restaurant.

★ **Imperial Palace** HOTEL $$$
(☑ 2480000; www.theimperialpalace.biz; Dr Yagnik Rd; s ₹5850-9100, d ₹6450-10,000, ste from ₹12,500; ✳@☎🖥) The numero uno in town, with a masterful lobby and lavish, well-appointed rooms and a spa. There's a busy wine shop, and two excellent veg eateries. Breakfast is complimentary. It's 1km west of the bus stand.

✕ Eating

Shree Shakti Vijay Patel
Soda Factory ICE CREAM $
(Para Bazaar; scoops & drinks ₹20-40; ☺8.30am-11pm) Sit in a booth and treat yourself to a few scoops at this old-school ice-cream and soda shop, with mirrored walls and pictures of previous generations of the owner's family. The cold coffee with ice cream hits the spot on a hot day!

Bukhara Restaurant MULTICUISINE $$
(Hotel Kavery, Kanak Rd; mains ₹115-200, thalis ₹120; ☺11.30am-3pm & 7-11pm) Bukhara is smart, cool and calm with good service and quality food, including a great Gujarati thali for lunch, and South Indian for dinner.

Senso MULTICUISINE $$
(Imperial Palace, Dr Yagnik Rd; mains ₹120-400; ☺24hr) The Imperial Palace's very good round-the-clock coffee shop does everything from Mediterranean and lasagne to sizzlers and South Indian – all without meat.

Temptations MULTICUISINE $$
(Kasturba Rd; mains ₹200-400; ☺noon-midnight) Hugely popular with families, Mexican, Italian, falafel, baked potatoes, *parathas* (thick flatbread with stuffings such as vegetables or paneer) and South Indian are served in a clean, bright air-conditioned cafe.

ℹ Information

There are ATMs all over town, including SBI on Jawahar Rd.

Buzz Cyber Café (Alaukik Bldg, Kasturba Rd; per hour ₹25; ☺8.30am-9pm) Tucked away opposite Temptations restaurant.

Galaxy Cybercafe (Dr Yagnik Rd; per hour ₹25; ☺8am-10pm) About 300m south of the Imperial Palace hotel.

State Bank of India (Kasturba Rd; ☺10am-4pm) Changes cash and travellers cheques and has an ATM.

Tourist Office (☑ 2234507; Bhavnagar House, Jawahar Rd; ☺10.30am-6pm Mon-Sat) Behind a State Bank of India building.

ℹ Getting There & Around

AIR

The airport is 2.5km northwest of the town centre. **Air India** (☑ 2234122; www.airindia.in) and **Jet Airways** (☑ 2450200; www.jetairways.com) have daily flights to Mumbai.

BUS

Services leaving from the ST bus stand connect Rajkot with Jamnagar (₹90, two hours, half-hourly), Junagadh (₹90, two hours, hourly) and Bhuj (₹250, seven hours, about hourly), among many other destinations. Ahmedabad is served by frequent ordinary buses (₹200, 4½ hours, half-hourly) as well as AC Volvos (₹390). Private buses operate to Ahmedabad, Bhavnagar, Una (for Diu), Mt Abu, Udaipur and Mumbai. Several offices are on Limda Chowk. Head to **Jay Somnath Travels** (☑ 6545979; Kasturba Rd) for buses to Bhuj (regular/AC/Volvo ₹250/300/350, seven hours).

TRAIN

The 19006 Saurashtra Mail leaves at 5.45pm and arrives in Ahmedabad (sleeper/3AC/2AC/1AC ₹180/485/690/1150) at 10.25pm and Mumbai (₹380/1030/1480/2505) at 7.10am. The 19005 departs at 10.30am and arrives at Jamnagar (₹140/485/690/1150) at 12.09pm. An autorickshaw to the station from the centre costs about ₹30.

Jamnagar

☑ 0288 / POP 529,308

Jamnagar is another little-touristed but interesting city, brimming with ornate, decaying buildings and colourful bazaars displaying the town's famous, brilliant-coloured *bandhani* (tie-dye) – produced through a laborious 500-year-old process involving thousands of tiny knots in a piece of folded fabric. Perhaps best of all, people here are exceedingly friendly.

Before Independence, Jamnagar was capital of the Nawanagar princely state. Today, Jamnagar is quite a boom town, with the world's biggest oil refinery, belonging to Reliance Petroleum, not far west of the city. The whole central area is one big commercial zone, with more brightly lit shops and stalls at night than you'll find in many a larger city.

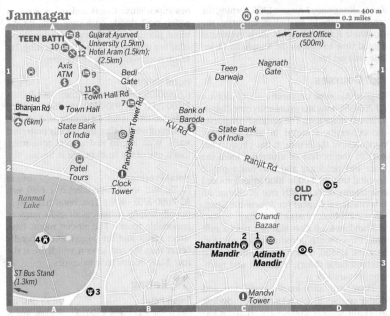

Jamnagar

◎ Sights

★ Old City
AREA

The heart of the old city is known as Chandi Bazaar (Silver Market; which it is, among other things) and it contains heaving markets and three beautiful Jain temples. The larger two, **Shantinath Mandir** and **Adinath Mandir**, dedicated to the 16th and first *tirthankars* (great Jain teachers), explode with fine murals, mirrored domes and elaborate chandeliers. The Shantinath Mandir is particularly beautiful, with coloured columns and a gilt-edged dome of concentric circles.

Around the temples spreads the old city with its lovely buildings of wood and stone, peeling, pastel-coloured shutters and crumbling wooden balconies. **Willingdon Crescent**, a European-style arcaded crescent, was built by Jam Ranjitsinhji to replace Jamnagar's worst slum. It now houses an assortment of shops, and is commonly known as Darbargadh, after the now-empty royal residence across the street. **Subhas market**, the vegetable market, has lots of local colour.

Ranmal Lake
LAKE

The promenades around Ranmal Lake make for a nice stroll when temperatures are moderate. Flamingos and other birds can some-

Jamnagar

◎ **Top Sights**
1 Adinath Mandir	C3
2 Shantinath Mandir	C3

◎ **Sights**
3 Bala Hanuman Temple	A3
4 Lakhota Palace	A3
5 Subhas Market	D2
6 Willingdon Crescent	D3

🛏 **Sleeping**
7 Hotel Ashiana	B1
8 Hotel Kalatit	A1
9 Hotel President	A1
10 Hotel Punit	A1

🍴 **Eating**
7 Seas Restaurant	(see 9)
11 Fresh Point	A1
12 Hotel Kalpana	A1

times be spotted on the water. The diminutive mid-19th-century **Lakhota Palace**, a fort on an island in the lake, houses a small museum that was closed indefinitely at research time.

Bala Hanuman Temple
HINDU TEMPLE

This temple on the southeastern side of Ranmal Lake has been the scene of continuous chanting of the prayer *Shri Ram, Jai Ram,*

Jai Jai Ram since 1 August 1964, earning the temple a place in an Indian favourite, the *Guinness Book of Records*. Early evening is a good time to visit as the temple and lakeside area get busy.

🎓 Courses

Gujarat Ayurved University   AYURVEDA
(☑ 2664866; www.ayurveduniversity.com; Chanakya Bhavan, Hospital Rd) The world's first ayurvedic university, founded in 1967, is 1.5km northwest of the centre. It has played a big part in the revival of ayurvedic medicine since Independence and also has a public hospital treating 800 to 1000 inpatients and outpatients daily, mostly free of charge. Its **International Center for Ayurvedic Studies** (☑ 2664866; icasjam@gmail.com; ⊙ office 10.30am-1pm & 3-6.30pm Mon-Sat) runs a full-time, three-month introductory course (registration US$20, tuition per month US$375) teaching basic theory, treatment and medicine preparation.

There are also longer certificate and degree courses in several subjects, including ayurvedic surgery. Courses are set up for foreign nationals with medical backgrounds; see the website for more information.

🛏 Sleeping

Hotel Punit   HOTEL $
(☑ 2670966; www.hotelpunit.com; Teen Batti; r ₹800-2000; ❋🛜) Currently the best budget spot in town; rooms are simple but in decent shape, with modern air-con units and LCD TVs. Just a quick walk from a number of restaurants and convenient to the old city.

Hotel Ashiana   HOTEL $
(☑ 2559110; www.ashianahotel.com; New Super Market; s ₹450-1300; d ₹500-1500; ❋🛜) Rambling, welcoming Ashiana has helpful management and a variety of rooms, from simple and run-down to large and comfortable. There's a roof terrace to enjoy in the evenings, and airport, train and bus station transfers. Enter by lift or stairs from inside the New Super Market shopping centre.

Hotel Aram   HERITAGE HOTEL $$
(☑ 2551701; www.hotelaram.com; Pandit Nehru Marg; r ₹2230-3960, ste ₹4320-7200; ❋@🛜) This former royal property has gotten an upgrade, creating an interesting mix of historic and contemporary. Rooms vary widely, from simple standards up to luxurious superdeluxe rooms and suites, some of which can't decide on a style. Still, it's the nicest place around. There's a good multicuisine veg restaurant with garden seating. It's 1.5km northwest of the city centre.

Hotel Kalatit   HOTEL $$
(☑ 2660105; www.hotelkalatit.com; Teen Batti; s ₹1600-2200, d ₹1950-2600, ste ₹5400; ❋🛜) This modern hotel feels new and stylish, with creative lighting and artfully patterned walls. With a gym and a good restaurant, this is one of the best options in town.

Hotel President   HOTEL $$
(☑ 2557491; www.hotelpresident.in; r ₹780, with AC ₹1790-2760; ❋🛜) This hotel has exceptionally helpful management and a range of reasonable rooms. The air-con rooms have street views and are bigger and generally better than the non air-con, which are at the rear. Many rooms have balconies.

🍴 Eating

Fresh Point   INDIAN, CHINESE $
(Town Hall Rd; mains ₹80-1100; ⊙ 10am-3pm & 6-11pm) A simple, friendly, bustling restaurant with generous serves of Punjabi, South Indian and Chinese in clean surroundings.

Hotel Kalpana   MULTICUISINE $$
(Teen Batti; mains ₹80-150; ⊙ 9am-11pm Tue-Sun) Clean and modern, with cushy booths, this place has a full list of Punjabi, Gujarati and Chinese food, along with pizza. If you want chicken or mutton, you'll get it here!

7 Seas Restaurant   MULTICUISINE $$
(Hotel President; mains ₹110-290; ⊙ 6-10am & 11am-11pm; 🛜) This cool, clean, efficient hotel restaurant has a nautical theme and a touch of class, offering a good range of veg and nonveg dishes, including seafood and tandoori options, and real breakfasts. The tandoori *bhindi* (okra) is a triumph.

ℹ Information

The city's website (www.jamnagar.org) is full of useful information for visitors.

The State Bank of India by the Town Hall roundabout, and Bank of Baroda and SBI on Ranjit Rd, change travellers cheques and cash between 10am and 4pm Monday to Friday. Hotel President will also change foreign currency.

Surf the internet at **IWorld** (Pancheshwar Tower Rd; 75min ₹30; ⊙ 7am-11pm).

Getting There & Away

AIR

Air India (✆ 1800-1801407; www.airindia.in) has daily flights to Mumbai.

BUS

ST buses run to Rajkot (₹54, two hours, half-hourly), Junagadh (₹108, four hours, about hourly) and Ahmedabad (₹140, seven hours, about hourly). There are also several morning and evening bus services to Bhuj (₹135, six hours)

There are numerous private companies, many based along Indira Gandhi Marg, including **Patel Tours** (✆ 2660243) which has 19 daily Volvo AC buses to Ahmedabad (₹550, seven hours) and four non-AC buses to Bhuj (seat/sleeper ₹300/400, six hours). Tickets can be booked at the convenient branch office, but buses leave from the main office on Indira Gandhi Marg.

TRAIN

One of the most useful train services is the 19006 Saurashtra Mail, which departs at 3.40pm for Rajkot (sleeper/3AC/2AC/1AC ₹140/485/690/1150, 1¾ hours), Ahmedabad (₹215/575/820/1375, seven hours) and Mumbai (₹410/1105/1595/2705, 16 hours).

Getting Around

An autorickshaw from the airport, 6km west, should be around ₹50, and a taxi ₹150. An autorickshaw from the ST bus stand to Bedi Gate costs ₹20.

Around Jamnagar

Khijadiya Bird Sanctuary

Khijadiya Bird Sanctuary WILDLIFE RESERVE
(vehicle with up to 6 people ₹900, camera ₹450; ☉ 7am-6pm) This small, 6-sq-km sanctuary, about 12km northeast of Jamnagar, encompasses both salt- and freshwater marshlands and hosts over 200 bird species, including rarities such as the Dalmatian pelican and painted stork. It's best visited between October and March and in the early morning or at sunset. The evening arrival of cranes for roosting can be spectacular.

Hiring a car to take you to/from Jamnagar and drive you around the sanctuary costs around ₹1400. Entry is only possible between 7am and noon and 3pm and 6pm. You'll have to show your passport and fill out some paperwork at the interpretation centre before going in.

Marine National Park

Marine National Park NATIONAL PARK
(up to 6 people ₹900, camera ₹450) This national park and the adjoining marine sanctuary encompass the intertidal zone and 42 small islands along some 120km of coast east and west of Jamnagar – an area rich in marine and bird life which faces growing challenges from industrialisation. Coral, octopus, anemones, puffer fish, sea horses, lobsters and crabs are among the marine life you may see in shallow water at low tide. The

GUJARAT AROUND JAMNAGAR

OFF THE BEATEN TRACK

WESTERN SAURASHTRA

Mahatma Gandhi was born in 1869 in the chaotic port town of Porbandar, 130km southwest of Jamnagar. You can visit **Gandhi's birthplace** (☉ 9am-noon & 3-6pm) – a 22-room, 220-year-old house – and a memorial next door, Kirti Mandir. **Dwarka**, 106km from Jamnagar at the western tip of the Kathiawar Peninsula, is one of the four holiest Hindu pilgrimage sites in India – Krishna is said to have set up his capital here after fleeing from Mathura. Its **Dwarkadhish Temple** is believed to have been founded over 2500 years ago, and has a fantastically carved, 78m-high spire. The town swells to breaking point for **Janmastami** (☉ Aug/Sep) in celebration of Krishna's birthday.

There are some good beaches on the ocean coast, including the beautiful, long, clean **Okhamadhi**, 22km south of Dwarka, where waves can be strong, and the calmer **Shivrajpur**, a long lagoon beach 12km north of Dwarka. En route to Porbandar, the **Barda Wildlife Sanctuary** is a hilly, forested area with stone-built villages, old temples and good hiking. A good contact for more information on visiting these and other off-the-beaten-track places in western Saurashtra is **Mustak Mepani** (✆ 9824227786) at Jamnagar's Hotel President..

best time to visit is December to March, when wintering birds are plentiful.

The park has two sections of the park: Narada and Poshitra. Narada is more interesting – from the entry gate, you park and hike 2.3km over rock and reef to the Gulf of Kachchh, where you can spot a variety of sea life. (You'll want to wear footwear with decent soles, as the terrain is sharp.) Narada is best reached from Jamnagar, which is 65km away; hiring a car to get you there and back costs about ₹1800. Poshitra's main draw is the coral; you won't see many animate creatures there. Hiring a vehicle from Jamnagar costs ₹4000 whether you go one-way or round-trip, it's closer to Dwarka, which is a reasonable base to visit from.

Narada and Poshitra are only open during low tide, so the entry schedule shifts daily. To figure out what time to go, phone the **Forest Office** (☑ 0288-2679357; Indira Gandhi Marg, Forest Colony; ☺ 10.30am-6pm Mon-Sat, closed 2nd & 4th Sat of the month) in Jamnagar, or call **Mustak Mepani** (☑ 9824227786) at Jamnagar's Hotel President (p724), a terrific resource who specialises in arranging tours and cars and drivers to both Marine National Park and Khijadiya Bird Sanctuary. Before you enter, you'll have to show your passport and fill out some paperwork.

KACHCHH (KUTCH)

Kachchh, India's wild west, is a geographic phenomenon. The flat, tortoise-shaped land (*kachbo* means tortoise in Gujarati), edged by the Gulf of Kachchh and Great and Little Ranns, is a seasonal island. During the dry season, the Ranns are vast expanses of hard, dried mud. Come the monsoon, they're flooded first by seawater, then by fresh river water. The salt in the soil makes the low-lying marsh area almost completely barren. Only on scattered 'islands' above the salt level is coarse grass which provides fodder for the region's wildlife.

The villages dotted across Kachchh's arid landscape are home to a jigsaw of tribal groups and sub-castes who produce some of India's finest handicrafts, above all their textiles which glitter with exquisite embroidery and mirrorwork.

A branch of the Indus River once entered the Great Rann until a massive earthquake in 1819 altered its course. Another mammoth earthquake in January 2001 again altered the landscape, killing nearly 30,000 people and completely destroying many villages. Although the effects of the tragedy will resonate for generations, the residents have determinedly rebuilt their lives and are welcoming to visitors. Tax breaks to encourage economic recovery have brought in new industrial plants, but by and large Kachchh still remains a refreshingly pristine, rural environment.

Bhuj

☑ 02832 / POP 147,123

The capital of Kachchh is an interesting city, mostly resurrected following the massive 2001 earthquake that destroyed much of the place. It sells amazing Kachchh handicrafts, and historic buildings such as the Aina Mahal and Prag Mahal possess an eerie beauty. Bhuj is an ideal springboard for visits to the surrounding villages, and textile tourism is attracting visitors from around the world.

The Jadeja Rajputs who took control of Kachchh in 1510 made Bhuj their capital 29 years later, and it has remained Kachchh's most important town ever since.

⊙ Sights

★ **Darbargadh** PALACES
This walled complex houses three palaces from which Kachchh was once ruled. The largest is the 19th-century **Prag Mahal** (New Palace; admission ₹20; ☺ 9.30am-noon & 3-6pm). It's in a sad state and most sections are closed, but it's worth visiting for its ghostly Durbar Hall, a wonderful piece of decayed magnificence with broken chandeliers, rotting hunting trophies covered in bird droppings, and gold-skirted classical statues that wouldn't look out of place decorating a nightclub.

The beautiful **Aina Mahal** (Old Palace; admission ₹10, camera ₹30; ☺ 9am-noon & 3-6pm Fri-Wed), built in the 1750s, was badly damaged in the 2001 earthquake, but the 1st and 2nd floors are open again and contain a fascinating museum with excellent explanatory information in English. The palace was built for Maharao Lakhpatji by Ramsingh Malam, a sailor from Dwarka who had learned European arts and crafts on his travels. The elaborately mirrored interior is a demonstration of the maharao's fascination with all things European – an inverted mirror of European Orientalism – with blue-and-white Delft-style tiling, a candelabra with Venetian-glass

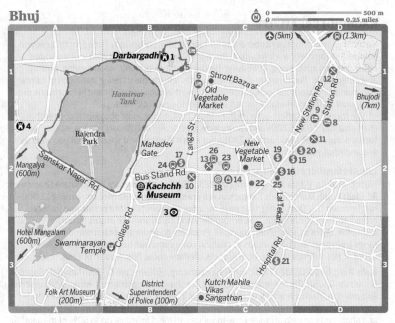

Bhuj

shades and the Hogarth lithograph series, *The Rake's Progress*. In the bedroom is a bed with solid gold legs (the king apparently auctioned his bed annually). In the Fuvara Mahal room, fountains played around the ruler while he sat watching dancers or composing poems.

The 17th-century **Rani Mahal**, the former main royal residence, is completely closed up, though you can still admire the latticed windows of its zenana (women's quarters).

KACHCHH CREATIVITY

Kachchh is one of India's richest areas for handicrafts, particularly famed for its beautiful, colourful embroidery work (of which there are at least 14 distinct styles), but it also has many artisans specialising in weaving, tie-dyeing, block printing, wood carving, pottery and other crafts. The diversity of Kachchh crafts reflects the differing traditions of its many communities. Numerous local cooperatives invest in social projects and help artisans produce work that is marketable yet still preserves their artistic heritage.

The tourist office offers autorickshaw tours that stop at most of the local cooperatives (half-/full day ₹600/1200) and can include visits to Ajir and Rabari villages; ask former–tourism director Pramod Jethi (p730) what's on the menu, and specify what you want to see and what you don't.

Local Handicrafts Cooperatives

Kutch Mahila Vikas Sangathan (☎02832-222124; www.kmvs.org.in; Gymkhana Ghanshyam Rd, Bhuj) Kutch Mahila Vikas Sangathan is a grass-roots organisation, comprising 12,000 rural women (1200 artisans), that pays members a dividend of the profits and invests money to meet social needs. The embroidery and patchwork are exquisite, employing the distinctive styles of several communities. Products go under the brand name Qasab and range from bags and bedspreads to cushion covers and wall hangings. Visit the Qasab outlet at Hotel Prince in Bhuj, or in Khavda, a village about 80km north of Bhuj.

Kala Raksha (☎02832-277237; www.kala-raksha.org; ☺10am-2pm & 3-6pm Mon-Sat) Based at Sumrasar Sheikh, 25km north of Bhuj, Kala Raksha is a nonprofit trust working to preserve and promote Kachchh arts. It works with about 1000 embroiderers and patchwork and appliqué artisans from six communities in some 25 villages. The trust has a small museum and shop, and can help arrange visits to villages to meet artisans. Up to 80% of the sale price goes to the artisans, who also help design and price the goods.

Vankar Vishram Valji (☎02832-240723; Bhujodi; ☺8am-8pm) Vankar Vishram Valji is a family operation and one of the leading weavers in Bhujodi; it sells beautiful blankets, shawls, stoles and rugs.

★**Kachchh Museum**   MUSEUM
(College Rd; Indian/foreigner ₹5/50; ☺10am-1pm & 2.30-5.30pm Thu-Tue, closed 2nd & 4th Sat of the month) Opposite Hamirsar Tank, Gujarat's oldest museum has eclectic displays spanning textiles, weapons, silverware, sculpture, wildlife, geography and dioramas of Kachchh tribal costumes and artefacts, with labelling in English and Gujarati.

Folk Art Museum   MUSEUM
(Bhartiya Sanskriti Darshan; near College Rd; admission ₹50, camera ₹200; ☺11am-1pm & 3-6pm Tue-Sun) This museum has excellent displays on traditional Kachchh culture, including reconstructed Rabari *bhungas* (mud-and-mirrorwork huts), musical instruments, many wood and stone carvings and much more. It's a further 700m south of the Kachchh Museum, off Mandvi Rd.

Sharad Baug Palace   PALACE
(admission ₹10, camera/video ₹20/100; ☺9am-noon & 3-6pm Sat-Thu) This graceful 1867 Italianate palace, set among shade trees full of

crows and bats, was the abode of the last Maharao of Kachchh, Madansingh, until his death in 1991. It lost most of its 3rd floor in the 2001 earthquake, and the remaining lower floors are closed. However, the adjacent former dining hall now houses the palace's eclectic museum collection. Standout exhibits are two huge stuffed tigers that the erstwhile maharao shot, and his coffin.

🛏 Sleeping

Hotel Gangaram   HOTEL **$**
(☎224231; off Shroff Bazaar; s/d ₹1000/1200, with AC ₹1200/1400; ❈ ☎) In the old city, near the Darbargadh, this is a great place run by a kindly manager and well away from the din of Bhuj's main thoroughfares. The rooms vary, so look at a few. Meals are delicious.

City Guest House   GUESTHOUSE **$**
(☎9913922669; abhasonara@yahoo.com; Langa St; d ₹500, s/d without bathroom from ₹300/400) Just off Shroff Bazaar, this is unusually bright and cheery for a budget guesthouse,

Shrujan (☑ 02832-240272; www.shrujan.org; Bhujodi; ☉ 10am-7.30pm) Shrujan, just past the Bhujodi turn-off, behind the GEB Substation, is a nonprofit trust working with over 3000 women embroiderers of nine communities in 114 villages. Its showroom sells top-class shawls, saris, cushion covers and more.

Dr Ismail Mohammad Khatri (☑ 02832-299786, 9427719313; dr.ismail2005@gmail.com; Ajrakhpur; ☉ 9am-5pm) Dr Ismail Mohammad Khatri in Ajrakhpur, 6km east of Bhujodi along the Bhachau road, heads a 10-generation-old block-printing business of real quality, using all-natural dyes in bold geometric designs. Go in the morning if you want to see a demonstration of the fascinating, highly skilled process. You can buy tablecloths, shawls, skirts, saris and other attractive products.

Parmarth (☑ 02832-273453; 106 Ramkrushn Nagar, New Dhaneti; ☉ 8.30am-9pm) Run by a delightful family whose work has won national awards, Parmarth specialises in Ahir embroidery. New Dhaneti is 17km east of Bhujodi, on the Bhachau road.

Khamir (☑ 02832-271272; www.khamir.org; Kukma Rd, Lakhond Crossroad, Kukma; ☉ 10am-5.30pm) Khamir is an umbrella organisation dedicated to preserving and encouraging Kachchh crafts in all their diversity. At the Kukma centre you can see demonstrations and buy some of the artisans' products. It's about 4km beyond Bhujodi, in the Anjar direction.

Textile Dealers

In Bhuj, textile dealers line Shroff Bazaar just east of the Darbargadh. However, plenty of so-called block-printed fabric is in fact screen-printed.

Mr AA Wazir (☑ 02832-224187; awazir1@rediffmail.com; Plot 107B, Lotus Colony, Bhuj) If you're interested in antique embroidery, contact Mr AA Wazir, opposite the General Hospital. He has a stunning collection of more than 3000 pieces, about half of which are for sale.

Bhoomi Handicrafts (☑ 02832-225808; Bus Stand Rd, Bhuj; ☉ 9am-9pm) Bhoomi Handicrafts, across from the bus stand, is popular with locals.

and has neat, basic rooms that are clean though have peeling paint. Try for one with a window. Bathrooms have either squat toilets or the hybrid variety. Breakfast is available, there are two airy rooftop terraces, and you can rent motorbikes for ₹500 per day.

Hotel Ilark　　　　　　　　HOTEL **$$**
(☑ 258999; www.hotelilark.com; Station Rd; s ₹2950-4880, d ₹3125-4800, ste from ₹5050; ❀ @ ☎) One of Bhuj's top hotels, with stylish wood-panelled, wood-furnished rooms that live up to the promise of the modern glass-and-red-paint exterior. Service is very professional. You can't go wrong here.

Hotel Mangalam　　　　　　HOTEL **$$**
(☑ 220303; www.mangalamhotels.com; Mangalam Cross Roads; s ₹1120, s with AC ₹1670-3420, d with AC ₹2820-3960; ❀ ☎) Towards the southern edge of town, the new Mangalam has big, bright rooms with comfy furnishings. Some have good views. Free airport transfers are offered, and there's an excellent restaurant on the ground floor.

Hotel Prince　　　　　　　HOTEL **$$$**
(☑ 220370; www.hotelprinceonline.com; Station Rd; r ₹4290-6690, ste ₹7890; ❀ ☎) Bhuj's most luxurious hotel is back after an extensive renovation that upgraded all but the cheapest class of rooms. New rooms are a modern melange of silver, cream and brass, with an abundance of faux-wood panelling. Two quality restaurants are on-site.

✖ Eating

★ **Shankar Vadapav**　　　STREET FOOD **$**
(Bus Stand Rd; snacks from ₹10) This food stall is a local legend. Try a *vadapav* (basically a spiced-fried-potato with chutney sandwich) or go big and get the *mirchvada* (fluffy fried dough covering a whole chilli pepper that's stuffed with a paste of spices and served on bread). The sign is in Gujarati; it's right next to the Gopi Gola Ghar ice-cream shop.

Hotel Nilam　　　　INDIAN, CHINESE **$$**
(Station Rd; mains ₹90-190; ☉ 8-10.30am & 11am-11pm) Good service by bow-tied, waistcoated

waiters complements tasty vegetarian North and South Indian and Chinese dishes at this long, white highly popular restaurant. There's Gujarati thali (₹160) at lunchtime and a limited menu between 4pm and 7pm.

Noorani Mahal   INDIAN $$
(Station Rd; mains ₹70-220; ⊙11am-3pm & 6-11pm) This popular nonveg place gets packed with families feasting on chicken, but there's also mutton and veg cooked in the tandoor and spicy North Indian curry.

★**Mangalya**   MUGHLAI $$
(Hotel Mangalam, Mangalam Cross Roads; mains around ₹150, buffet lunch ₹200) Creative twists on all-veg Mughlai cuisine are sure to please your palette. The tandoor options and paneer varieties are outstanding – try the delicious Mix Grill Platter if you can't decide. There are also dosas and other South Indian dishes. And if you feel like a taste of home, try the pizza!

Green Rock   MULTICUISINE $$
(Bus Stand Rd; mains ₹90-190, thalis ₹175-190; ⊙11am-3pm & 7-10.30pm) This 1st-floor, air-con place serves up tasty lunchtime thalis as well as an extensive all-veg menu.

ⓘ Information

Ashapura Money Changer (Station Rd; ⊙9.30am-7pm Mon-Sat) Changes currency and travellers cheques.

Om Cybercafe (Bus Stand Rd; per hour ₹30; ⊙9.15am-9pm Mon-Sat, 10am-4pm Sun) Across from the bus stand.

Pramod Jethi (☏9374235379; near Darbargadh; ⊙9am-noon & 3.30-6pm Mon-Sat) Pramod Jethi, the knowledgeable former curator of the Aina Mahal, knows all there is to know about Bhuj and surrounding villages. He's also

written a very useful guide to Kachchh (₹150), published in English. Feel free to phone him if his office is closed; he's available seven days a week. He offers tours but is happy to provide information for free.

State Bank of India (Hospital Rd; ⊙10am-4pm Mon-Fri, to 1pm Sat) Changes travellers cheques or currency. There's also an SBI ATM on Station Rd.

ⓘ Getting There & Away

AIR

Jet Airways (☏1800-225522; www.jetairways.com) has daily flights to Mumbai.

BUS

Numerous buses run from the ST bus stand to Ahmedabad (₹200, nine hours), Rajkot (₹153, seven hours), Jamnagar (₹173, seven hours) and Mandvi (₹40, two hours). Book private buses with **Hemal Travels** (Bus Stand Rd; ⊙9am-9pm), just outside the bus station, for Ahmedabad (without AC seat/sleeper ₹400/500, with AC seat/sleeper ₹500/600, nine hours, 9pm departures) and Jamnagar (seat/sleeper ₹300/400, six hours, 3pm and 9pm), or at **Jay Somnath Travels** (☏9979869670; Bus Stand Rd; ⊙8am-9pm) for Rajkot (without/with AC/Volvo ₹250/300/350, seven hours, six daily).

TRAIN

Bhuj station is 1.5km north of the centre and has a **reservations office** (⊙8am-8pm Mon-Sat, to 2pm Sun). The 14312 Ala Hazrat Express leaves at 12.25pm (Tuesday, Thursday, Sunday) and arrives at Ahmedabad (sleeper/3AC/2AC ₹225/600/855) at 7.40pm, continuing to Abu Road, Jaipur and Delhi. The 19116 Sayaji Express leaves at 10.15pm daily and hits Ahmedabad (sleeper/3AC/2AC/1AC ₹225/600/855/1430) at 5.05am and Mumbai/Bandra Station (₹415/1110/1605/2725) at 2.05pm.

EXPLORING KACHCHH

It is possible to get out to Kachchh's villages by public transport – for example, there are three buses a day to Khavda (₹50, two hours). You can also take autorickshaws to villages not too far from the city. But you'll have many more options and more flexibility if you hire a car and driver; most Bhuj hotels can organise this for you.

Thoughtfully themed and customised autorickshaw tours (half-/full day ₹600/1200) to villages outside Bhuj are organised by Pramod Jethi (☏9374235379; pramodjethi 2013@gmail.com; ⊙9am-noon & 3.30-6pm Mon-Sat), former curator of the Aina Mahal and expert on everything Kachchhi. Get specifics on your itinerary from Mr Jethi, so you can see what you want and skip what you don't. He can also arrange single and multiday tours around the region, and will accompany you as a personal guide for an extra ₹1500 per day – a bargain for such a friendly trove of knowledge! Find his small office 100m from the entry gate to the Darbargadh, or call, even on Sunday.

ⓘ Getting Around

The airport is 5km north of town – a taxi will cost around ₹200, an autorickshaw ₹100. Autorickshaws to the train station cost ₹30.

Around Bhuj

The local Jat, Ahir, Harijan, nomadic Rabari and other communities have distinct, colourful craft traditions that make their villages fascinating to visit.

Bhujodi, about 7km southeast of Bhuj, is a village of weavers, mostly using pit looms, operated by both feet and hands. You can look into many workshops, which produce attractive shawls, blankets and other products. The village is 1km off Hwy 42. You can take a bus towards Ahmedabad and ask the driver to drop you at the turn-off for Bhujodi (₹10). A return rickshaw from Bhuj is ₹300.

In the hills about 60km northwest of Bhuj is the eerie monastery at **Than**. The holy man Dhoramnath, as penance for a curse he had made, stood on his head on top of Dhinodhar hill for 12 years. The gods pleaded with him to stop, and he agreed, provided the first place he looked at became barren – hence the Great Rann. He then established the monastic order of Kanphata (Split Ears, because of large piercings through the ear's concha), whose monastery (dating back to at least the 12th century) stands at the foot of the hill. This is a laid-back place to explore the surrounding hills, and the architecture ranges from crumbling mud brick to Portuguese-style stucco, blue and whitewash bell towers, with a hint of basil and marigold in the air. There's one bus daily to Than from Bhuj (₹50, two hours) at 5pm, returning early next morning. The monastery and the temple atop Dhinodhar have very basic guest rooms with mattresses on the floor and simple food (pay by donation) but no drinking water.

You need a permit to visit the villages of Lakhpat, Dhorodo, Khavda, and Ludia, but these are easy to obtain. For Lakhpat, take a copy of your passport and visa (and the originals) to the office of the **District Superintendent of Police** (⊙10am-6pm Mon-Sat, closed 2nd & 4th Sat of the month), 800m south of Kachchh Museum in Bhuj, and you should get the permit (free of charge; maximum 10 days) straight away. Your driver will need a permit if you plan to stay overnight. For the other villages, get your permit at the police post on the way, in Bhirandiyara. It's free, unless you plan on going into the White Rann north of Dhorodo – for that, pay ₹100. Drivers also need permits for the White Rann.

Shaam-e-Sarhad Village Resort (☑02803-296222; www.hodka.in; s/d tent ₹2800/3200, bhunga ₹3800/4800, incl meals; ⊙Oct-Mar) ✐, just outside Hodka, in the beautiful Banni grasslands 70km north of Bhuj, is a fascinating and successful project in 'endogenous tourism'. Owned and operated by the Halepotra Maldharis, its accommodation consists of three *bhungas* (mud huts) with sloping roofs and groovy interiors, and six comfortable earth-floored tents, all with private bathroom and electricity. Local (non-English speaking) guides cost ₹300 per day for birdwatching or visits to villages in the area such as Hodka, Khavda (known for its pottery and textiles) or Ludia (known for its intricately decorated homes); to Kalo Dungar (Black Hill, Kachchh's highest point at 462m above sea level); or to the Great Rann itself, with its snow-glare of salt (you may need to provide your own transport). You can also stop by for a superb thali lunch (₹200) – call in advance.

Centre for Desert & Ocean (CEDO; ☑02835-221284, 9825248135; www.cedobirding.com) ✐, 53km northwest of Bhuj, is a wildlife conservation organisation run by passionate environmentalist Jugal Tiwari. It does birding and wildlife trips focusing on the wildlife-rich Banni grasslands (between Sumrasar Sheikh and Khavda). Accommodation is in plain but well-kept rooms with 24-hour solar-heated hot water; meals are Gujarati vegetarian. Staying costs ₹1750 to ₹2000 per person per day, including meals. Safaris cost ₹3600 per day for a car and driver; expert naturalist/birding guides cost an extra ₹1800 per day.

A long drive northeast from Bhuj is the fascinating and remote archaeological site of **Dholavira**, on a seasonal island in the Great Rann. Excavations have revealed a complex town of stone buildings 1 sq km in area, inhabited by the Harappan (Indus Valley) civilisation from around 2900 to 1500 BC. It's best to organise your own transport (₹4500 one-way or return): the only bus to Dholavira leaves Bhuj at 2pm (₹80, six hours) and starts back at 5am. The state-government-run **Toran Tourist Complex** (☑02837-277395; s/d ₹350/500, with AC ₹750/900; ❀) at Dholavira offers basic accommodation and meals.

Mandvi

☑ 02834 / POP 48,500

Mandvi is an hour down the road from Bhuj and is a busy little place with an amazing shipbuilding yard. Hundreds of men construct, by hand, these wooden beauties for faraway Arab merchants. The massive timbers apparently come from Malaysian rainforests. Mandvi suffered far less destruction than Bhuj in the 2001 earthquake, so the heart of town (around Mochi Bazaar) is lined with beautiful old buildings in faded pastel hues and temples with wildly sculpted, cartoonlike facades. There are also some sweeping beaches, including the glorious, long, clean private beach near Vijay Vilas Palace, and public Kashivishvanath Beach, with food stalls and camel rides, 2km from the centre just east of the Rukmavati River.

◉ Sights

Vijay Vilas Palace
PALACE

(admission Mon-Sat ₹25, Sun ₹35, vehicle ₹40, camera/video ₹50/200; ⊙7am-7pm) Vijay Vilas Palace is a 1920s palace reminiscent of a large English country house, 7km west of town amid extensive orchards, and set by a magnificent private beach. Originally a summer abode for the Kachchh rulers, its 1st floor (out of bounds to visitors) is now the erstwhile royal family's main residence. The view from the roof is worth the climb, and the gardens make a nice stroll.

Autorickshaws charge about ₹200/300 one-way/return from town. You can walk back to town along the beach if it's low tide.

Asher House
HISTORIC BUILDING

(☑ 9825311061; dilipchessasher@yahoo.com; Lakshmi Talkies; by donation) For a taste of Mandvi's past glory, call Dilip Asher, a chess instructor who is a loveable character and descendant of the town's once-richest merchant family. If he's around, he will give you an informal tour of his family's home, where he still lives with his sister who is blind. The house has definitely seen better days, but the Portuguese tiles, ceiling murals and other artworks – along with a dilapidated 1932 Chevrolet – still have a touch of magic.

Donations help with the much needed upkeep of the house.

🛏 Sleeping & Eating

Rukmavati Guest House
GUESTHOUSE $

(☑ 223558, 9429040484; www.rukmavatihotel.webs.com; Bridge Gate; s/d from ₹600/700, r with AC ₹1000; ❄🖵) The best Indian hospital to spend the night in, this former medical centre, near the bridge as you enter town, is light, bright, clean and welcoming to travellers. Some rooms have riverview balconies, and there's a nice shaded terrace. Owner Vinod is a gentleman, and the town's unofficial tourist officer. Guests can use the refrigerator and kitchen facilities.

Hotel Sea View
HOTEL $

(☑ 9825376063; www.hotelseaviewmandvi.com; cnr ST & Jain Dharamsala Rds; r ₹750, with AC ₹1200-2300; ❄) This small hotel facing the river has brightly decorated rooms with big windows that make the most of the views of the shipbuilding.

Beach at Mandvi Palace
HOTEL $$$

(☑ 9879013118, 277597; www.mandvibeach.com; s/d incl meals ₹7000/8500) A small tent resort in a peaceful location on a superb swathe of beach that stretches down from Vijay Vilas Palace. The luxurious air-cooled tents have big beds, white-tiled bathrooms and wooden furniture. Lunch (₹550, 10am to 3pm) and dinner (₹650, 7pm to 9pm) available and access to the private beach is included.

Vijay Vilas Heritage Resort
HERITAGE HOTEL $$$

(☑ 277700; www.vijayvilasheritageresort.com; Vijay Vilas Palace; r ₹9580, tent ₹8380) Part of the Vijay Vilas Palace property, this newly converted heritage hotel was once part of the residence of Kachchh's royal family. Rooms are spacious and maintain a period feeling, while being equipped with modern comforts. Luxury air-con tents surround the courtyard. From the hotel, walk 1.5km down a private road to the royal beach.

★ Osho Restaurant
GUJARATI $

(1st fl, Osho Hotel, Bhid Gate; thali ₹100; ⊙11.45am-3pm & 7-9pm) In the heart of the town, Osho is a massively popular place that dishes out one of the best thalis in all of Gujarat. All you can eat! Look for the big 'Osho Hotel' sign.

ℹ Getting There & Away

Regular buses to/from Bhuj (₹30) take 1½ to two hours. Or you can take faster shared 4WD taxis (₹35) which depart from the street south of Bhuj's main vegetable market. Several agencies near Hotel Sea View sell tickets for private buses to Ahmedabad, including Patel Tours & Travels (☑ 9925244272; non-AC seat/sleeper ₹370/470, 11 hours, 7.30pm) and Royal Express (☑ 232135; AC coach ₹650, 11 hours, 7.30pm).

Wild Ass Sanctuary

The barren, blindingly white land of the Little Rann is nature at its harshest and most compelling. It's best known as the home of the last remaining population of the chestnut-coloured Indian wild ass (also called khur), as well as bluebulls, blackbuck and chinkara. There's also a huge bird population from October to March (this is one of the few areas in India where flamingos breed in the wild).

The Little Rann is punctuated by desolate salt farms, where people eke out a living by pumping up groundwater and extracting the salt. Heat mirages disturb the vast horizon – bushes and trees seem to hover above the surface. Rain turns the desert into a sea of mud, and even during the dry season the solid-looking crust is often deceptive, so it's essential you take a local guide when exploring the area.

The 4953-sq-km **Wild Ass Sanctuary** (4WD safari with up to 6 passengers Indian/foreigner ₹350/1200 Mon-Fri, ₹435/1500 Sat-Sun, camera ₹100/600) covers a large part of the Little Rann. Easily accessible from Ahmedabad, it can be combined with trips to Nalsarovar Bird Sanctuary, Modhera and Patan. About 3000 khurs live in the sanctuary, surviving off the flat, grass-covered expanses or islands, known as *bets,* which rise up to around 3m. These remarkable, notoriously untamable creatures are capable of running at an average speed of 50km/h for long distances.

Desert Coursers (☑9426372113, 9427066070; www.desertcoursers.net), run by infectiously enthusiastic naturalist Dhanraj Malik, organises excellent Little Rann safaris and village tours from its **Camp Zainabad** (per person incl full board ₹1900-2800; ☉Oct-Mar; ❄), very close to the east edge of the Little Rann and just outside the small town of Zainabad, 105km northwest of Ahmedabad. The lodge has air-conditioned *koobas* (thatch-roofed huts) and excellent meals, in a peaceful, remote setting. The price includes a 4WD safari. Advance booking is advised.

To get to Zainabad from Ahmedabad, hiring a private car is easiest but you can also take a bus from Ahmedabad's ST bus stand to Dasada, 10km away (₹80, 2½ hours, about hourly), from where Desert Coursers does

free pick-ups. There are direct buses between Zainabad and Patan (₹75, 2½ hours, two daily) via Modhera. Desert Coursers can arrange taxis around the area if desired.

Rann Riders (☑9925236014; www.rannriders.com; s/d incl all meals & safari ₹6000/7200; ❄☎❄), near Dasada, is also family-run and offers luxurious cottage accommodation in pretty gardens, plus highly recommended 4WD and camel safaris and its own stable of indigenous horses for riding.

The simplest of the camps is the **Eco Tour Camp** (☑9825548090; www.littlerann.com; near Kidi Village; per person incl full board ₹1000-2000; ☉Oct-Apr), run by the personable Devjibhai Dhamecha, where you can stay in basic cement huts or round *koobas*. Situated right on the sanctuary's edge, you can walk right into it and see wild asses, bluebulls and a bevy of birds – no guide is needed. 4WD safaris (₹2000/3000 per vehicle) are offered by Devjibhai's son, Ajay, an enthusiastic guide who will take you through some of the less touristed parts of the sanctuary.

The camp is near Kidi village – Devjibhai arranges pickups (autorickshaw/taxi ₹600/1000) from the town of Dhrangadra, 45km away, on the main road and rail routes between Ahmedabhad (three hours) and Bhuj (5½ hours). The town of Halwad – also along the main highway – is much closer, but you have to arrange your own ride to the camp – a spot in the back of a *chakda* (half-motorcycle, half-pickup truck) should cost ₹20 from Halvad to Kidi. All buses between Ahmedabad and Bhuj stop at Dhrangadra; only some stop at the Halwad bus stand. The guides mentioned will arrange your permits for the reserve; the cost of these is normally additional to safari prices.

An hour south of Dhrangadhra on the Ahmedabad–Rajkot highway is **Sayla**, a peaceful, pastoral town that swells during the **Tarnetar Fair** (☉Aug/Sep). **Bell Guest House** (☑9724678145; www.bellguesthouse.com; s/d incl breakfast ₹3550/4700; ❄), presided over by the erstwhile ruling family of Sayla (and their yellow labs), is an ageing heritage hotel retreat down a lane off the Sayla roundabout on Hwy 8A. Rooms have modern ensuite bathrooms. You can look for bluebulls and peacocks in the surrounding countryside or take trips further afield to see wild asses, blackbuck, the birds of Nalsarovar or a variety of artisans in area villages.

Mumbai (Bombay)

022 / POP 21.1 MILLION

Best Places to Eat

➡ Peshawri (p763)

➡ Revival (p760)

➡ Dakshinayan (p762)

➡ Koh (p761)

➡ La Folie (p760)

Best Places to Stay

➡ Taj Mahal Palace, Mumbai (p756)

➡ Residency Hotel (p757)

➡ Abode Bombay (p756)

➡ Sea Shore Hotel (p755)

➡ Juhu Residency (p758)

Why Go?

Mumbai is big. It's full of dreamers and hard-labourers, starlets and gangsters, stray dogs and exotic birds, artists and servants, fisherfolk and *crorepatis* (millionaires) – and lots of people. It has India's most prolific film industry, some of Asia's biggest slums (as well as the world's most expensive home) and the largest tropical forest in an urban zone. Mumbai is India's financial powerhouse, fashion epicentre and a pulse point of religious tension. It's even evolved its own language, Bambaiyya Hindi, which is a mix of...everything.

If Mumbai is your introduction to India, prepare yourself. The city isn't a threatening place but its furious energy, limited public transport and punishing pollution makes it challenging for visitors. The heart of the city contains some of the grandest colonial-era architecture on the planet but explore a little more and you'll uncover unique bazaars, hidden temples, hipster enclaves and India's premier restaurants and nightlife.

When to Go
Mumbai (Bombay)

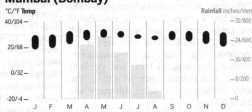

Dec & Jan The very best, least sticky weather.

Aug & Sep Mumbai goes crazy for Ganesh during its most exciting festival, Ganesh Chaturthi.

Oct–Apr There's very little rain, post-monsoon; the best time of year for festivals.

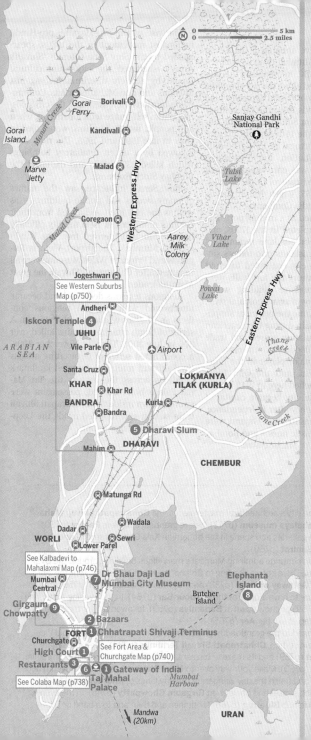

Mumbai Highlights

❶ Marvelling at the magnificence of Mumbai's colonial-era architecture: **Chhatrapati Shivaji Terminus** (p739), **High Court** (p743) and **Gateway of India** (p738)

❷ Investigating the labyrinthine lanes and stalls in Mumbai's ancient **bazaar district** (p769)

❸ Dining like a maharaja at one of India's best restaurants such as **Indigo** (p759)

❹ Feeling the love with the Krishna crowd at the unique **Iskcon Temple** (p749)

❺ Exploring the self-sufficient world of Asia's largest shantytown, **Dharavi Slum** (p755)

❻ Sleeping at the **Taj Mahal Palace, Mumbai** (p756), one of the world's iconic hotels, or having a drink at its bar, Mumbai's first

❼ Ogling the gorgeous Renaissance revival interiors of the **Dr Bhau Daji Lad Mumbai City Museum** (p745)

❽ Beholding the commanding triple-headed Shiva at **Elephanta Island** (p751)

❾ Catching the city's sea breeze among playing kids, big balloons and a hot-pink sunset at **Girgaum Chowpatty** (p745)

History

Koli fisherfolk have inhabited the seven islands that form Mumbai from as far back as the 2nd century BC. Remnants of this culture remain huddled along the city shoreline today. A succession of Hindu dynasties held sway over the islands from the 6th century AD until the Muslim Sultans of Gujarat annexed the area in the 14th century, eventually ceding it to Portugal in 1534. The only memorable contribution the Portuguese made to the area was christening it Bom Bahai. They handed control to the English government in 1665, which leased the islands to the East India Company.

Bombay flourished as a trading port. The city's fort was completed in the 1720s, and a century later ambitious land reclamation projects joined the islands into today's single landmass. The city continued to grow, and in the 19th century the fort walls were dismantled and massive building works transformed the city in grand colonial style. When Bombay became the principal supplier of cotton to Britain during the American Civil War, the population soared and trade boomed as money flooded into the city.

Bombay was a major player in the Independence movement, and the Quit India campaign was launched here in 1942 by Mahatma Gandhi. The city became capital of the Bombay presidency after Independence, but in 1960 Maharashtra and Gujarat were divided along linguistic lines – and Bombay became the capital of Maharashtra.

The rise of the pro-Marathi, pro-Hindu regionalist movement in the 1980s, spearheaded by the Shiv Sena (literally 'Shivaji's Army'), shattered the city's multicultural mould by actively discriminating against Muslims and non-Maharashtrians. Communalist tensions increased, and the city's cosmopolitan self-image took a battering when 900 people, mostly Muslims, were killed in riots in late 1992 and 1993. The riots were followed by a dozen retaliatory bombings which killed 257 people and damaged the Bombay Stock Exchange.

Shiv Sena's influence saw the names of many streets and public buildings – as well as the city itself – changed from their colonial monikers. In 1996 the city officially became Mumbai (derived from the Hindu goddess Mumba). The airport, Victoria Terminus and Prince of Wales Museum were all renamed after Chhatrapati Shivaji, the great Maratha leader.

Religious tensions deepened and became intertwined with national religious conflicts and India's relations with Pakistan. A series of bomb attacks on trains killed over 200 in July 2006. Then, in November 2008, a coordinated series of devastating attacks (by Pakistani militants) targeted landmark buildings across the city, as the Taj Mahal Palace hotel burned, passengers were gunned down inside the Chhatrapati Shivaji train station and 10 killed inside the Leopold Cafe backpacker haunt.

MUMBAI IN…

Two Days

Begin at one of the city's architectural masterpieces, the **Chhatrapati Shivaji Maharaj Vastu Sangrahalaya museum** (p742), before grabbing a drink in **Pantry** (p760) and exploring the galleries and scene in the bohemian Kala Ghoda district. Lunch Gujarati-style at **Samrat** (p760).

In the afternoon continue admiring Mumbai's marvellous buildings around the Oval Maiden and Marine Drive before heading to Colaba, the heart of the city. Tour the city's iconic sights, the **Gateway of India** (p738) and **Taj Mahal Palace hotel** (p756) around sunset, and be sure to have a drink at the **Harbour Bar** (p764). In the evening either fine dine at **Indigo** (p759) or chow down at **Bademiya** (p759), followed by (for those with the stamina) a nightcap at sky bar **Aer** (p765).

The next day, head to the granddaddy of Mumbai's colonial-era giants, the old Victoria Terminus train station, **Chhatrapati Shivaji Terminus** (p739). Then investigate **Crawford Market** (p769) and its maze of bazaars, hidden temples and unique street life. Lunch at **Revival** (p760). Make your way over to **Mani Bhavan** (p745), the museum dedicated to Gandhi, and finish the day wandering the tiny lanes of **Khotachiwadi** (p745) followed by a beach sunset and *bhelpuri* at **Girgaum Chowpatty** (p745). In the evening head to hip nightlife hub **Bluefrog** (p766) for dinner, and then bop to a band or DJ.

TOP FESTIVALS IN MUMBAI

Mumbai Sanskruti (⊙ Jan) This free, two-day celebration of Hindustani classical music is held on the steps of the gorgeous Asiatic Society Library in the Fort area.

Kala Ghoda Festival (www.kalaghodaassociation.com; ⊙ Feb) Getting bigger and more sophisticated each year, this two-week-long art fest held in Kala Ghoda and the Fort area sees tons of performances and exhibitions.

Elephanta Festival (www.maharashtratourism.gov.in; ⊙ Mar) This classical music and dance festival takes place on the waterfront Apollo Bunder at the Gateway of India.

Nariyal Poornima (⊙ Aug) This Koli celebration in Colaba marks the start of the fishing season and the retreat of monsoon winds.

Ganesh Chaturthi (⊙ Aug/Sep) Mumbai gets totally swept up by this 10- to 12-day celebration of the Hindu god Ganesh. On the festival's first, third, fifth, seventh and 11th days, families and communities take their Ganesh statues to the seashore at Chowpatty and Juhu beaches and auspiciously submerge them.

Mumbai Film Festival (MFF; www.mumbaifilmfest.org; ⊙ Oct) New films from the sub-continent and beyond are screened at the weeklong MFF at cinemas across Mumbai.

In late 2012, when the Sena's charismatic founder Bal Thackeray died (500,000 attended his funeral), the Shiv Sena mission begin to falter, and in the 2014 assembly elections, President Modi's BJP became the largest party in Mumbai.

Despite recent troubles Mumbaikars are a resilient bunch. Increased security is very much part of everyday life today and the city's status as the engine room of the Indian economy remains unchallenged. However, the Mumbai politicians certainly have their work cut out, with the megacity's feeble public transport, gridlocked streets, pollution and housing crisis all in desperate need of attention.

⊙ Sights

Mumbai is an island connected by bridges to the mainland. The city's commercial and cultural centre is at the southern, claw-shaped end of the island known as South Mumbai. The southernmost peninsula is Colaba, traditionally the travellers' nerve centre, with many of the major attractions.

Directly north of Colaba is the busy commercial area known as Fort, where the British fort once stood. This part of the city is bordered on the west by a series of interconnected grassy areas known as maidans (pronounced may-*dahns*).

Continuing north you enter 'the suburbs' which contain the airport and many of Mumbai's best restaurants, shopping and nightspots. The upmarket districts of Bandra, Juhu and Lower Parel are key areas.

⊙ Colaba

Along the city's southernmost peninsula, Colaba is a bustling district packed with elegant art deco and colonial-era mansions, budget-to-midrange lodgings, bars and restaurants, street stalls and a fisherman's quarter. Colaba Causeway (Shahid Bhagat Singh Marg) dissects the district.

If you're here in August, look out for the Koli festival Nariyal Poornima, which is big in Colaba.

★**Taj Mahal Palace, Mumbai** LANDMARK
(Map p738; Apollo Bunder) Mumbai's most famous landmark, this stunning hotel is a fairy-tale blend of Islamic and Renaissance styles, and India's second-most photographed monument. It was built in 1903 by the Parsi industrialist JN Tata, supposedly after he was refused entry to one of the European hotels on account of being 'a native'. Dozens were killed inside the hotel when it was targeted during the 2008 terrorist attacks, and images of its burning facade were beamed across the world. The fully restored hotel reopened on Independence Day 2010.

Much more than an iconic building, the Taj's history is intrinsically linked with the nation: it was the first hotel in India to employ women, the first to have electricity (and fans), and it also housed freedom-fighters (for no charge) during the struggle for independence.

Colaba

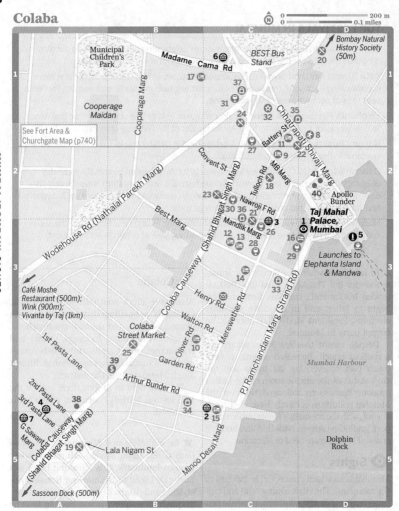

Today the Taj fronts the harbour and Gateway to India, but it was originally designed to face the city (the entrance has been changed).

Gateway of India   MONUMENT
(Map p738) This bold basalt arch of colonial-era triumph faces out to Mumbai Harbour from the tip of Apollo Bunder. Incorporating Islamic styles of 16th-century Gujarat, it was built to commemorate the 1911 royal visit of King George V, but wasn't completed until 1924. Ironically, the British builders of the gateway used it just 24 years later to parade the last British regiment as India marched towards independence. These days, the gateway is a favourite gathering spot for locals and a top place for people-watching. Giant-balloon sellers, photographers, vendors making *bhelpuri* (thin fried rounds of dough with rice, lentils, lemon juice, onion, herbs and chutney) and touts rub shoulders with locals and tourists, creating all the hubbub of a bazaar. In March, they are joined by classical dancers and musicians who perform during the Elephanta Festival (p737).

Boats depart from the gateway's wharfs for Elephanta Island.

Colaba

⊙ Top Sights
1 Taj Mahal Palace, Mumbai.................... D3

⊙ Sights
2 Chatterjee & Lal C4
3 Galerie Mirchandani +
   Steinruecke C3
4 Gallery Maskara A4
5 Gateway of India D3
6 National Gallery of Modern Art C1
7 Project 88 .... A5

⊙ Activities, Courses & Tours
8 Palm Spa.. D2

⊙ Sleeping
9 Abode Bombay C2
10 Bentley's Hotel...................................... B4
   Carlton Hotel .... (see 3)
11 Gordon House Hotel.............................. C2
12 Hotel Moti C3
   Hotel Suba Palace .... (see 11)
   India Guest House .... (see 15)
13 Regent Hotel.. C3
14 Salvation Army Red Shield
   Guest House C3
15 Sea Shore Hotel C4
16 Taj Mahal Palace, Mumbai.................... D3
17 YWCA B1

⊙ Eating
18 Bademiya.. C2
   Café Moshe....................................(see 22)
19 Colaba Market A5
20 Hotel OCH D1

21 Indigo C3
22 Indigo Delicatessen.................................C2
23 Olympia C2
24 Saharkari Bhandar Supermarket..........C2
25 Sufra...B4

⊙ Drinking & Nightlife
26 Busaba...C3
27 Cafe Mondegar C2
28 Colaba Social C3
29 Harbour Bar C3
30 Leopold Cafe...C2
31 Woodside Inn C1

⊙ Entertainment
32 Regal Cinema..C1

⊙ Shopping
33 Bombay Electric C3
34 Bungalow 8...B4
   Central Cottage Industries
   Emporium ....(see 2)
35 Central Cottage Industries
   Emporium...C1
36 Cottonworld Corp...................................C2
37 Phillips C1

⊙ Information
38 Akbar Travels..A4
39 Thomas Cook...B4

⊙ Transport
40 MTDC Booth D2
41 PNP Ticket Office D2

Sassoon Dock WATERFRONT
Sassoon Dock is a scene of intense and pungent activity at dawn (around 5am) when colourfully clad Koli fisher-folk sort the catch unloaded from fishing boats at the quay. The fish drying in the sun are *bombil*, used in the dish Bombay duck. Photography at the dock is prohibited.

⊙ Fort Area & Churchgate

Lined up in a row and vying for your attention with aristocratic pomp, many of Mumbai's majestic Victorian buildings pose on the edge of **Oval Maidan**. This land, and the **Cross** and **Azad Maidans** immediately to the north, was on the oceanfront in those days, and this series of grandiose structures faced west directly to the Arabian Sea.

Kala Ghoda, or 'Black Horse', is a hip, atmospheric subneighbourhood of Fort just north of Colaba. It contains many of Mumbai's museums and galleries alongside a wealth of colonial-era buildings and some of the city's best restaurants and cafes.

★**Chhatrapati Shivaji
Terminus** HISTORIC BUILDING
(Victoria Terminus; Map p740) Imposing, exuberant and overflowing with people, this monumental train station is the city's most extravagant Gothic building and an aphorism for colonial-ear India. It's a meringue of Victorian, Hindu and Islamic styles whipped into an imposing Daliesque structure of buttresses, domes, turrets, spires and stained-glass. As historian Christopher London put it, 'the Victoria Terminus is to the British Raj what the Taj Mahal is to the Mughal empire'.

Some of the architectural detail is incredible, with dog-faced gargoyles adorning the magnificent central tower and peacock-filled windows above the central courtyard. Designed by Frederick Stevens, it was completed in 1887, 34 years after the first train in India left this site.

Fort Area & Churchgate

MUMBAI (BOMBAY)

Enlargement

Mahatma Gandhi (MG) Rd

49

14

24

33

31

Master Rd

26

27

29

39

3

45

Dr VB Gandhi Marg

7

K Dubash Marg

46

15

Marine Dr

Girgaum Chowpatty (1.5km)

Metro Big (100m)

41

Bombay Hospital

New Marine Lines (Sir Vithaldas Thackersey Rd)

Maharshi Karve (MK) Rd

44

D Rd

38

C Rd

CHURCHGATE

B Rd

A Rd

28

Back Bay

Churchgate Train Station

Indiatourism

E Rd

13

Western Railways Reservation Office

Veer Nariman Rd

Brabourne Stadium

40

Dinsha Wachha Marg

35

J Tata Rd

Maharshi Karve Rd

37

Oval Maidan

56

Madame Cama Rd

Air India

8

19

Barrister Rajni Patel Marg

Jet Airways

See Colaba Map (p738)

Municipal Children's Park

NARIMAN POINT

42

55

36

43

J Bajaj Marg

59

57

Cooperage Maidan

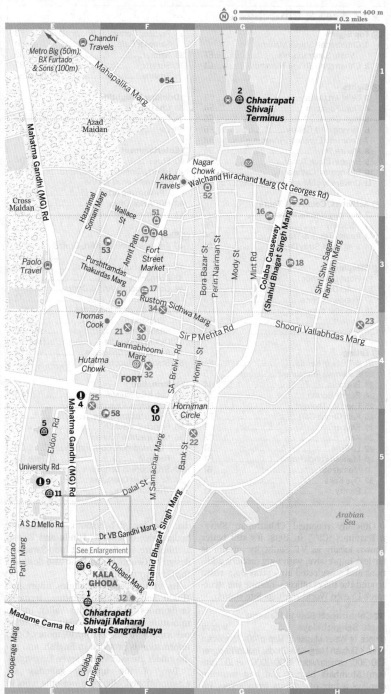

0   400 m
0   0.2 miles

Metro Big (50m);
BX Furtado
& Sons (100m)

Chandni
Travels

Mahapalika Marg

●54

2
Chhatrapati
Shivaji
Terminus

Azad
Maidan

Nagar
Chowk

Mahatma Gandhi (MG) Rd

Cross
Maidan

Akbar
Travels

Walchand Hirachand Marg (St Georges Rd)

52

20

Hazarimal
Somani Marg

Wallace
St

51

16

Colaba Causeway
(Shahid Bhagat Singh Marg)

47 48

Amrit Path

Paolo
Travel

53

Bora Bazar St

Perin Nariman St

Mody St

Mint Rd

18

Shri Shiv Sagar
Rangulam Marg

Purshttamdas
Thakurdas Marg

Fort
Street
Market

50

17

Rustom Sidhwa Marg

34

Thomas
Cook

21

30

Sir P Mehta Rd

Shoorji Vallabhdas Marg

23

Janmabhoomi
Marg

SA Brelvi Rd

Homji St

Hutatma
Chowk

@

32

FORT

4

25

58

10

Hornimans
Circle

5

Eldon Rd

University Rd

9

11

Mahatma Gandhi (MG) Rd

Dalal St

M Samachar Marg

Bank St

22

Arabian
Sea

A S D Mello Rd

Dr VB Gandhi Marg

Shahid Bhagat Singh Marg

See Enlargement

Bhaurao
Patil Marg

6

KALA
GHODA

K Dubash Marg

1

12

Madame Cama Rd

Chhatrapati
Shivaji Maharaj
Vastu Sangrahalaya

Cooperage Marg

Colaba
Causeway

Fort Area & Churchgate

Officially renamed Chhatrapati Shivaji Terminus (CST) in 1998, it's still better known locally as VT. Sadly, its interior is far less impressive, with ugly modern additions and a neglected air – stray dogs roam around the ticket offices – despite the structure's Unesco World Heritage Site status.

★**Chhatrapati Shivaji Maharaj Vastu Sangrahalaya** MUSEUM
(Prince of Wales Museum; Map p740; http://csmvs.in; K Dubash Marg, Kala Ghoda; Indian/foreigner ₹50/300, camera/video ₹200/1000; ⊙10.15am-6pm) Mumbai's biggest and best museum displays a mix of exhibits from across India. The domed behemoth, an intriguing hodgepodge of Islamic, Hindu and British architecture, is a flamboyant Indo-Saracenic design by George Wittet (who also designed the Gateway of India).

Its vast collection includes impressive Hindu and Buddhist sculpture, terracotta figurines from the Indus Valley, Indian miniature paintings, porcelain and some particularly vicious-looking weaponry. Good information is provided in English, and audio guides are available in seven languages.

Two of the upstairs galleries are air-conditioned, offering a welcome relief to

THE ART DISTRICT

India's contemporary art scene has exploded in recent years, and Mumbai, along with Delhi, is the centre of the action. A slew of galleries are showing incredible work in some gorgeous spaces across the city.

Kala Ghoda hosts a wonderful two-week festival (p737) each February, with some great exhibitions (as well as music, theatre, dance and literary events).

Year-round, the second Thursday of each month is 'Art Night Thursday', when galleries stay open late and the vibe is social. Gallery crawls are sometimes organised; check **Mumbai Boss** (www.mumbaiboss.com) for the latest or the free fold-up *Mumbai Art Map*, available at galleries and bookstores. To go more in depth, check out the magazine *Art India,* available at most English-language bookshops, which has news, background and criticism on work from across the country.

Or, just read nothing and go see pretty things on your own: many galleries are within walking distance of one another in Colaba and Fort. If street art is more your thing, don't miss the Great Wall of Mumbai (p749).

Chatterjee & Lal (Map p738; www.chatterjeeandlal.com; 1st fl, Kamal Mansion, Arthur Bunder Rd, Colaba; ⊙11am-7pm Tue-Sat) Work by emerging artists and historical material.

Galerie Mirchandani + Steinruecke (Map p738; www.galeriems.com; 1st fl, Sunny House, 16/18 Mereweather Rd, Colaba; ⊙11am-7pm Tue-Sat) Contemporary Indian art and sculpture; the gallery is just behind the Taj Mahal Palace hotel.

Gallery Maskara (Map p738; www.gallerymaskara.com; 6/7 3rd Pasta Lane, Colaba; ⊙11am-7pm Tue-Sat) This Colaba gallery showcases exciting contemporary art.

Jhaveri Contemporary (www.jhavericontemporary.com; Krishna Niwas, 58A Walkeshwar Rd, Walkeshwar, Malabar Hill; ⊙11am-6pm Tue-Sat) Cutting-edge photography and art from Indian and overseas artists.

Project 88 (Map p738; www.project88.in; BMP Building, NA Sawant Marg, Colaba; ⊙11am-7pm Tue-Sat) Well established gallery which features leading Indian artists.

the summer heat. There's a fine cafeteria at the entrance and the museum shop is also excellent.

Marine Drive   PROMENADE
(Map p740; Netaji Subhashchandra Bose Rd) Built on reclaimed land in 1920, Marine Dr arcs along the shore of the Arabian Sea from Nariman Point past Girgaum Chowpatty and continues to the foot of Malabar Hill. Lined with flaking art deco apartments, it's one of Mumbai's most popular promenades and sunset-watching spots. Its twinkling nighttime lights earned it the nickname 'the Queen's Necklace'.

Hundreds gather on the promenade around Nariman Point in the early evening to snack and chat, when it's a good place to meet Mumbaikars.

University of Mumbai   HISTORIC BUILDING
(Bombay University; Map p740; Bhaurao Patil Marg) Looking like a 15th-century French-Gothic mansion plopped incongruously among Mumbai's palm trees, this structure was designed by Gilbert Scott of London's St Pancras train station fame. There's an exquisite **University Library** and **Convocation Hall**, as well as the 80m-high **Rajabai Clock Tower** (Map p740), decorated with detailed carvings. Since the 2008 terror attacks, there's no public access to the grounds but it's still well worth admiring from the street.

High Court   HISTORIC BUILDING
(Map p740; Eldon Rd; ⊙10.45am-2pm & 2.45-5pm Mon-Fri) A hive of daily activity, packed with judges, barristers and other cogs in the Indian justice system, the High Court is an elegant 1848 neo-Gothic building. The design was inspired by a German castle and was obviously intended to dispel any doubts about the authority of the justice dispensed inside.

Visitors are permitted to explore the building and attend cases. Inside it's quite a spectacle, with court officials kitted out in starched white tunics offset with red cummerbunds and scarlet berets, while robed barristers strut about with their chests puffed out.

No photography is permitted; cameras have to be left with guards at the entrance.

Keneseth Eliyahoo Synagogue SYNAGOGUE
(Map p740; www.jacobsassoon.org; Dr VB Gandhi Marg, Kala Ghoda; camera/video ₹100/500; 11am-6pm Mon-Sat, 1-6pm Sun) Built in 1884, this unmistakable sky-blue synagogue still functions and is tenderly maintained by the city's dwindling Jewish community. It's protected by very heavy security, but the caretaker is welcoming (and will point out a photo of Madonna, who dropped by in 2008).

St Thomas' Cathedral CHURCH
(Map p740; Veer Nariman Rd; 7am-6pm) This charming cathedral, begun in 1672 and finished in 1718, is the oldest British-era building standing in Mumbai: it was once the eastern gateway of the East India Company's fort (the 'Churchgate'). The cathedral is a marriage of Byzantine and colonial-era architecture, and its airy interior is full of grandiose colonial-era memorials.

Jehangir Art Gallery ART GALLERY
(Map p740; www.jehangirartgallery.com; 161B MG Rd, Kala Ghoda; 11am-7pm) FREE Recently renovated, this excellent gallery hosts shows by local artists and the occasional big name; it's also home to Samovar Café (p761).

National Gallery of Modern Art MUSEUM
(NGMA; Map p738; www.ngmaindia.gov.in; MG Rd; Indian/foreigner ₹10/150; 11am-6pm Tue-Sun)

DHARAVI SLUM

Mumbaikars were ambivalent about the stereotypes in 2008's *Slumdog Millionaire*, but slums are very much a part of – some would say the foundation of – Mumbai city life. An astonishing 60% of Mumbai's population lives in slums, and one of the city's largest slums is Dharavi. Originally inhabited by fisher-folk when the area was still creeks, swamps and islands, it became attractive to migrant workers from South Mumbai and beyond when the swamp began to fill in due to natural and artificial causes. It now incorporates 2.2 sq km of land sandwiched between Mumbai's two major railway lines, and is home to perhaps as many as a million people.

While it may look a bit shambolic from the outside, the maze of dusty alleys and sewer-lined streets of this city-within-a-city are actually a collection of abutting settlements. Some parts of Dharavi have mixed populations, but in other parts inhabitants from different parts of India, and with different trades, have set up homes and tiny factories. Potters from Saurashtra (Gujarati) live in one area, Muslim tanners in another; embroidery workers from Uttar Pradesh work alongside metalsmiths; while other workers recycle plastics as women dry pappadams in the searing sun. Some of these thriving industries, as many as 20,000 in all, export their wares, and the annual turnover of business from Dharavi is thought to exceed US$700 million.

Up close, life in the slums is fascinating to witness. Residents pay rent, most houses have kitchens and electricity, and building materials range from flimsy corrugated-iron shacks to permanent multistorey concrete structures. Perhaps the biggest issue facing Dharavi residents is sanitation, as water supply is irregular – every household has a 200L drum for water storage. Very few dwellings have a private toilet or bathroom, so some neighbourhoods have constructed their own (to which every resident must contribute financially) while other residents are forced to use rundown public facilities.

Many families have been here for generations, and education achievements are higher than in many rural areas: around 15% of children complete a higher education and find white-collar jobs. Many choose to stay, though, in the neighbourhood they grew up in.

Slum tourism is a polarising subject, so you'll have to decide for yourself. If you opt to visit, Reality Tours & Travel (p755) does a illuminating tour, and puts a percentage of profits back into Dharavi. Some tourists opt to visit on their own, which is OK as well – just don't take photos. Take the train from Churchgate station to Mahim, exit on the west side and cross the bridge into Dharavi.

To learn more about Mumbai's slums, check out Katherine Boo's 2012 book *Behind the Beautiful Forevers*, about life in Annawadi, a slum near the airport, and *Rediscovering Dharavi*, Kalpana Sharma's sensitive and engrossing history of Dharavi's people, culture and industry.

KHOTACHIWADI

The storied *wadi* (hamlet) of **Khotachiwadi** (Map p746) is a bastion clinging onto Mumbai life as it was before high-rises. A Christian enclave of elegant two-storey wooden mansions, it's 500m northeast of Girgaum Chowpatty, lying amid Mumbai's predominantly Hindu and Muslim neighbourhoods. These winding lanes allow a wonderful glimpse into a quiet(ish) life free of rickshaws and taxis. It's not large, but you can spend a little while wandering the alleyways and admiring the old homes and, around Christmas, their decorations.

To find Khotachiwadi, aim for **St Teresa's Church** (Map p746), on the corner of Jagannath Shankarsheth Marg (JSS Marg) and Rajarammohan Roy Marg (RR Rd/Charni Rd), then head directly opposite the church on JSS Marg and duck down the second and third lanes on your left.

Well-curated shows of Indian and international artists in a bright and spacious exhibition space.

Delhi Art Gallery　　　ART GALLERY
(Map p740; www.delhiartgallery.com; 58 VB Gandhi Marg, Kala Ghoda; ⊙11am-7pm) FREE Spread over four floors of a beautifully restored cream colonial-era structure. Showcases important modern Indian art from its extensive collection and well-curated exhibitions.

◉ Kalbadevi to Mahalaxmi

★Dr Bhau Daji Lad Mumbai City Museum　　　MUSEUM
(Map p746; www.bdlmuseum.org; Dr Babasaheb Ambedkar Rd; Indian/foreigner ₹10/100; ⊙10am-6pm Thu-Tue) This gorgeous museum, built in Renaissance revival style in 1872 as the Victoria & Albert Museum, contains 3500-plus objects relating to Mumbai's history – photography and maps, textiles, books and manuscripts, *bidriware*, laquerware, weaponry and exquisite pottery.

The landmark building was renovated in 2008, with its Minton tile floors, gilded ceiling mouldings, ornate columns, chandeliers and staircases all restored to their former glory. Contemporary music, dance and drama feature in the new Plaza area, where there's a cafe and shop.

The museum is located in the lush gardens of Jijamata Udyan; skip the zoo.

Mani Bhavan　　　MUSEUM
(Map p746; ☎23805864; www.gandhi-manibhavan.org; 19 Laburnum Rd, Gamdevi; donation appreciated; ⊙9.30am-6pm) As poignant as it is tiny, this museum is in the building where Mahatma Gandhi stayed during visits to Bombay from 1917 to 1934. The leader for-

mulated his philosophy of satyagraha (nonviolent protest) and launched the 1932 Civil Disobedience campaign from here. Exhibitions include a photographic record of his life, along with dioramas and documents, such as letters he wrote to Adolf Hitler and Franklin D Roosevelt and tributes from Ho Chi Minh and Einstein.

Girgaum Chowpatty　　　BEACH
(Map p746) This city beach is a favourite evening spot for courting couples, families, political rallies and anyone out to enjoy what passes for fresh air. Evening *bhelpuri* at the throng of stalls at the beach's southern end is an essential part of the Mumbai experience. Forget about taking a dip: the water's toxic.

On the 10th day of the Ganesh Chaturthi festival (p737), in August or September, millions flock here to submerge huge Ganesh statues: it's joyful mayhem.

Mumba Devi Temple　　　HINDU TEMPLE
(Map p746; Bhuleshwar) Pay a visit to the city's patron goddess at this 18th-century temple, about 1km north of Chhatrapati Shivaji Terminus. Among the deities in residence is Bahuchar Maa, goddess of the transgender *hijras*, and *puja* (prayer) is held here several times a day.

Haji Ali Dargah　　　MOSQUE
(Map p746; www.hajialidargah.in; off V Desai Chowk) Floating like a sacred mirage off the coast, this Indo-Islamic shrine located on an offshore inlet is a striking sight. Built in the 19th century, it contains the tomb of the Muslim saint Pir Haji Ali Shah Bukhari. Legend has it that Haji Ali died while on a pilgrimage to Mecca and his casket miraculously floated back to this spot.

MUMBAI (BOMBAY)

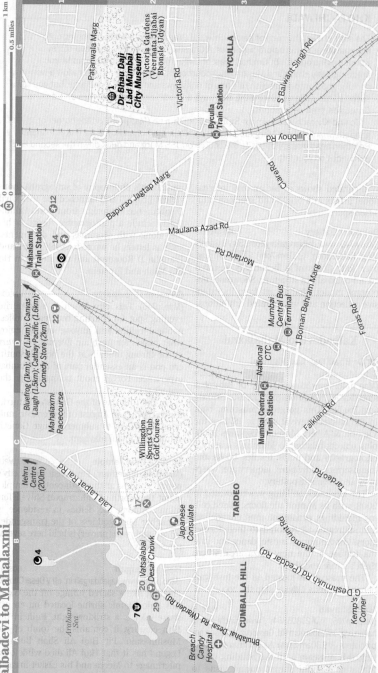

Kalbadevi to Mahalaxmi

1 km
0.5 miles

0
0

Arabian Sea

4

7
20 Vatsalabai
29 Desai Chowk

Bhulabhai Desai Rd (Warden Rd)

Nehru Centre (200m)

Lala Lajpat Rai Rd

21
17

Japanese Consulate

Breach Candy Hospital

Willingdon Sports Club Golf Course

Mahalaxmi Racecourse

Bluefrog (1km); Aer (1km); Canvas Laugh (1.5km); Cathay Pacific (1.6km); Comedy Store (2km)

22

6
14
Mahalaxmi Train Station

12

CUMBALLA HILL

G Deshmukh Rd (Peddar Rd)

Kemp's Corner

Altamount Rd

TARDEO

Tardeo Rd

Falkland Rd

Mumbai Central Train Station
National CTC

Mumbai Central Bus Terminal

J Bonan Behram Marg

Foras Rd

Maulana Azad Rd

Bapurao Jagtap Marg

Morland Rd

Clare Rd

J Jiljibhoy Rd

Byculla Train Station

BYCULLA

Victoria Rd

S Balwant Singh Rd

Patanwala Marg

1
Dr Bhau Daji Lad Mumbai City Museum

Victoria Gardens (Veermata Jijabai Bhonsle Udyan)

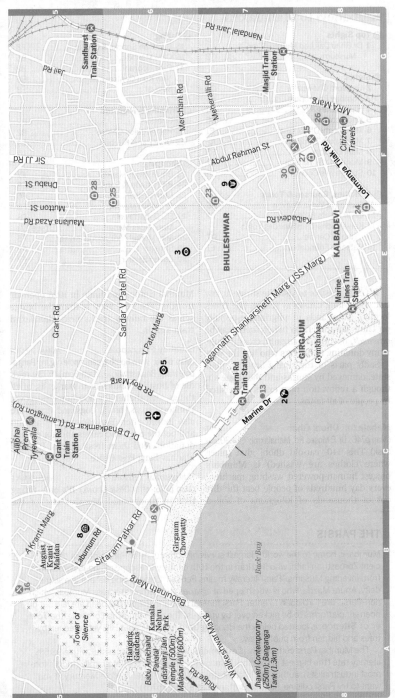

Kalbadevi to Mahalaxmi

⊙ Top Sights
1 Dr Bhau Daji Lad Mumbai City Museum G2

⊙ Sights
2 Girgaum Chowpatty D7
3 Bombay Panjrapole E6
4 Haji Ali Dargah B1
5 Khotachiwadi D6
6 Mahalaxmi Dhobi Ghat E1
7 Mahalaxmi Temple A2
8 Mani Bhavan B5
9 Mumba Devi Temple F7
10 St Teresa's Church C6

⊙ Activities, Courses & Tours
11 Bharatiya Vidya Bhavan B6
12 Child Rights & You E1
13 Kaivalyadhama Ishwardas Yogic Health Centre D7
14 Vatsalya Foundation E1

⊗ Eating
15 Badshah Snacks & Drinks F8
16 Café Moshe B5
17 Cafe Noorani B2
18 New Kulfi Centre B6
19 Revival F8

⊙ Drinking & Nightlife
20 Ghetto B2
21 Haji Ali Juice Centre B2
22 Olive Bar & Kitchen D1

⊙ Shopping
23 Bhuleshwar Market F7
24 BX Furtado & Sons E8
25 Chor Bazaar F6
26 Crawford Market F8
27 DD Dupattawala F8
    Mangaldas Market .... (see 27)
28 Mini Market/Bollywood Bazaar F5
29 Shrujan A2
30 Zaveri Bazaar F7

It's only possible to visit the shrine at low tide, via a long causeway (check tide times locally). Thousands of pilgrims, especially on Thursday and Friday (when there may be *qawwali,* devotional singing), cross it daily, many donating to beggars who line the way.

Sadly parts of the shrine are in a poor state, damaged by storms and the saline air, though a renovation plan exists. It's visited by people of all faiths.

Mahalaxmi Dhobi Ghat   GHAT
(Map p746; Dr E Moses Rd, Mahalaxmi; ⊙ 4.30am-dusk) This 140-year-old dhobi ghat (place where clothes are washed) is Mumbai's biggest human-powered washing machine: every day hundreds of people beat the dirt out of thousands of kilograms of soiled Mumbai clothes and linen in 1026 open-air troughs. The best view is from the bridge across the railway tracks near Mahalaxmi train station.

Bombay Panjrapole   ANIMAL SHELTER
(Map p746; www.bombaypanjrapole.org.in; Panjra-pole Marg, Bhuleshwar; ⊙ 11am-6pm) In the mid-dle of bustling Bhuleshwar market is, of all things, this shelter for 300 homeless cows. Donkeys, goats, birds, dogs and ducks are also looked after. You can wander around and pet the cows and calves and, for a small donation, feed them fresh greens. It's near Madhav Baug Post Office.

Mahalaxmi Temple   HINDU TEMPLE
(Map p746; off V Desai Chowk) It's only fitting that in money-mad Mumbai one of the

THE PARSIS

Mumbai is home to the world's largest surviving community of Parsis, people of the an-cient Zoroastrian faith, who fled Iran in the 10th century to escape religious persecution from invading Muslims. 'Parsi' literally means Perisan. Zoroastrians believe in a single deity, Ahura Mazda, who is worshipped at *agiaries* (fire temples) across Mumbai, which non-Parsis are forbidden to enter. Parsi funeral rites are unique: the dead are laid out on open-air platforms to be picked over by vultures. The most renowned of these, the **Tow-er of Silence**, is located below the Hanging Gardens in Malabar Hill, yet screened by trees and hidden from public view.

The Mumbai Parsi community is extremely influential and successful, with a 98.6% literacy rate (the highest in the city). Famous Parsis include the Tata family (India's fore-most industrialists), author Rohinton Mistry and Queen singer Freddie Mercury. If you want to try Parsi cuisine, head to Brittania restaurant (p761).

WORTH A TRIP

THE GREAT WALL OF MUMBAI

Starting as an initiative by artists to add colour to a suburban street in Bandra, the **Wall Project** (www.thewallproject.com) has introduced vibrant public art, murals and graffiti across the city. There's no official membership, and the art has been created by both amateurs and professionals.

The guidelines are that no advertising, political statements, religious content or obscene messaging should be used. Social messaging that's too preachy is not encouraged either.

Hundreds of individuals have joined the project, with most murals dealing with personal stories: their dreams, desire for change, criticisms and frustrations.

Perhaps the most spectacular stretch is a 2km canvas along **Senapati Bapat Marg** (Tulsi Pipe Rd), between the train stations of Mahim and Dadar on the Western Line, where the art parallels the tracks. It's a very thought-provoking and enriching experience to take in; allow an hour and a half to explore.

This particular wall had long been coveted by the Wall Project founders, but they expected firm opposition from the authorities. Instead they were actually approached by the city's Municipal Commissioner, who invited them to create something. Around 400 people contributed.

Many murals on Senapati Bapat Marg have a theme that's relevant to India and Mumbai such as the environment, pollution and pressures of metropolitan life. One mural of a Mumbai cityscape simply says 'Chaos is our Paradise'.

Bandra is another area rich in street art, where many walls and bridges have been customised: Chapel Lane is a good place to start investigating.

busiest and most colourful temples is dedicated to Mahalaxmi, the goddess of wealth. Perched on a headland, it is the focus for Mumbai's Navratri (Festival of Nine Nights) celebrations in September/October.

Babu Amichand Panalal
Adishwarji Jain Temple   JAIN TEMPLE
(Walkeshwar Marg, Malabar Hill; ⊗ 5am-9pm) This temple is renowned among Jains for its beauty – given how beautiful Jain temples are, that's saying a lot. Check out the paintings and especially the ecstatically colourful zodiac dome ceiling. It's a small, actively used temple; visitors should be sensitive and dress modestly.

Nehru Centre   CULTURAL COMPLEX
(☑ 24964676, 24964680; www.nehru-centre. org; Dr Annie Besant Rd, Worli; Discovery of India admission free, planetarium adult/child ₹50/25; ⊗ 10am-6pm Tue-Sun, Discovery of India 11am-5pm, planetarium English show 3pm) The Nehru Centre is a cultural complex that includes a planetarium, theatre, gallery and an interesting history exhibition, Discovery of India. The architecture is striking: the tower looks like a giant cylindrical pineapple, the planetarium like a UFO. High-quality dance, drama and live music events are held here.

The complex is just inland from Lala Lajpat Rai Rd.

Malabar Hill   AREA
(around BG Kher Marg) Mumbai's most exclusive neighbourhood, at the northern end of Back Bay, surprisingly contains one of Mumbai's most sacred oases. Concealed between apartment blocks is **Banganga Tank**, an enclave of serene temples, bathing pilgrims, meandering, traffic-free streets and picturesque old *dharamsalas* (pilgrims' rest houses). According to Hindu legend, Lord Ram created this tank by piercing the earth with his arrow. For some of the best views of Chowpatty, about 600m west, and the graceful arc of Marine Dr, visit **Kamala Nehru Park**.

⊙ Western Suburbs

★ **Iskcon Temple**   HINDU TEMPLE
(Map p750; www.iskconmumbai.com; Juhu Church Rd, Juhu; ⊗ 4.30am-1pm & 4-9pm) A focus for intense, celebratory worship in the sedate suburbs, this temple is a compelling place to visit. Iskcon Juhu has a key part in the Hare Krishna story, as founder AC Bhaktivedanta Swami Prabhupada spent extended periods here (you can visit his modest living

Western Suburbs

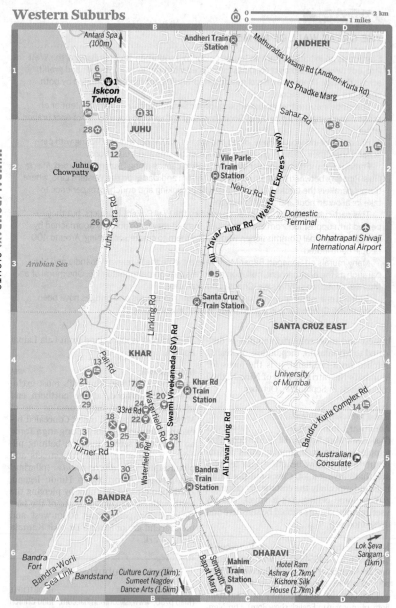

quarters in the adjacent building). The temple compound comes alive during prayer time as the faithful whip themselves into a devotional frenzy of joy, with *kirtan* dancing accompanied by crashing hand symbols and drumbeats.

Murals that are dotted around the compound detail the Hare Krishna narrative. The Iskcon (p758) hotel that is located here is also recommended, as is the canteen (meals ₹70).

Western Suburbs

◎ Top Sights
1 Iskcon Temple B1

◔ Activities, Courses & Tours
2 Humsafar Trust C3
3 Yoga Cara A5
4 Yoga House A5
5 Yoga Institute C3

◷ Sleeping
6 Anand Hotel A1
7 Hotel Neelkanth B4
8 Hotel Oriental Aster D2
9 Hotel Regal Enclave B4
10 Hotel Suba International D2
   Iskcon .... (see 1)
11 ITC Maratha D2
12 Juhu Residency B2
13 Le Sutra A4
14 Sofitel Mumbai BKC D4
15 Sun-n-Sand A1

◵ Eating
   Raaj Bhog .... (see 9)
   Dakshinayan .... (see 6)
16 Eat Around the Corner B5
   Peshawri .... (see 11)

Prithvi Cafe .... (see 28)
17 Salt Water Café B6
18 Soul Fry B5
19 Suzette B5
   Yoga House .... (see 4)

◔ Drinking & Nightlife
20 Hoppipola B4
21 Big Nasty A4
22 Bonobo B5
23 Daily B5
24 Elbo Room B5
   Olive Bar & Kitchen .... (see 13)
25 Toto's Garage B5
26 Trilogy A3

◷ Entertainment
27 Mehboob Studios A5
28 Prithvi Theatre A2

◶ Shopping
29 Indian Hippy A4
30 Play Clan B5
31 Shrujan B1

◉ Gorai Island

Global Pagoda BUDDHIST TEMPLE
(www.globalpagoda.org; Gorai; ◷ 9am-7pm, meditation classes 10am-6pm) Rising up like a mirage from polluted Gorai Creek is this breathtaking, golden 96m-high stupa modelled on Myanmar's Shwedagon Pagoda. Its dome, which houses relics of Buddha, was built entirely without supports using an ancient technique of interlocking stones, and the meditation hall beneath it seats 8000.

There's a museum dedicated to the life of the Buddha and his teaching, and 20-minute meditation classes are offered daily; an on-site meditation centre also offers 10-day courses.

To get here, take a train from Churchgate to Borivali (exit the station at the 'West' side), then take bus 294 (₹5) or an autorickshaw (₹40) to the ferry landing, where Esselworld ferries (return ₹50) depart every 30 minutes. The last ferry to the pagoda is at 5.30pm.

◉ Elephanta Island

★ **Elephanta Island** HINDU TEMPLE
(Gharapuri; Indian/foreigner ₹10/250; ◷ caves 9am-5pm Tue-Sun) Northeast of the Gateway of India in Mumbai Harbour, the rock-cut temples on Gharapuri, better known as Elephanta Island, are a Unesco World Heritage Site. Created between AD 450 and 750, the labyrinth of cave temples represent some of India's most impressive temple carving. The main Shiva-dedicated temple is an intriguing latticework of courtyards, halls, pillars and shrines; its magnum opus is a 6m-tall statue of Sadhashiva, depicting a three-faced Shiva as the destroyer, creator and preserver of the universe, his eyes closed in eternal contemplation.

It was the Portuguese who dubbed the island Elephanta because of a large stone elephant near the shore (this collapsed in 1814 and was moved by the British to Mumbai's Jijamata Udyan). There's a small museum on-site, with informative pictorial panels on the origin of the caves.

Pushy, expensive guides are available – but you don't really need one as Pramod Chandra's *A Guide to the Elephanta Caves,* widely held to be best, is more than sufficient.

Launches (Map p738) head to Gharapuri from the Gateway of India every half-hour from 9am to 3.30pm. Buy tickets (economy/deluxe ₹130/160) at the booths lining Apollo Bunder. The voyage takes about an hour.

The ferries dock at the end of a concrete pier, from where you can walk or take the miniature train (₹10) to the stairway (admission ₹10) leading up to the caves. It's lined with souvenir stalls and patrolled by pesky monkeys. Wear good shoes.

Activities

Mumbai has surprisingly good butterfly- and birdwatching opportunities. Sanjay Gandhi National Park is popular for woodland birds, while the mangroves of Godrej (13km east of Bandra) are rich in waders. The **Bombay Natural History Society** (BNHS; Map p740; 22821811; www.bnhs.org; Hornbill House, Shahid Bhagat Singh Marg; 9am-5.30pm Mon-Fri) runs excellent trips every weekend.

Outbound Adventure   OUTDOOR ADVENTURE
(26315019;   www.outboundadventure.com) This outfit runs one-day rafting trips on the Ulhas River from July to early September (₹2000 per person). After a good rain, rapids can get up to Grade III+, though usually the rafting is calmer. Also organises camping (from ₹1500 per person per day) and canoeing trips.

MUMBAI FOR CHILDREN

Kidzania (www.kidzania.in; 3rd flr, R City, LBS Marg, Ghatkopar West; child/adult Tue-Fri ₹950/500, Sat & Sun ₹950/700) is Mumbai's latest attraction, an educational activity centre where kids can learn all about piloting a plane, fighting fires, policing and get stuck into lots of art- and craft-making. It's on the outskirts on the city, 10km northeast of the Bandra Kurla Complex.

Little tykes with energy to burn will love the Gorai Island amusement parks, **Esselworld** (www.esselworld.in; adult/child ₹790/490; 11am-7pm, from 10am weekends) and **Water Kingdom** (www.waterkingdom.in; adult/child ₹690/490; 11am-7pm, from 10am weekends). Both have lots of rides, slides and shade. Combined tickets are ₹1190/990 (adult/child).

The free **Hanging Gardens**, in Malabar Hill, have animal topiaries, swings in the shade and coconut-wallahs. **Kamala Nehru Park**, across the street, has a two-storey 'boot house'. Bombay Natural History Society (p752) also conducts nature trips for kids.

Wild Escapes   TREKKING
(66635228; www.wild-escapes.com; treks from ₹780) Weekend trekking trips to forts, valleys and waterfalls around Maharashtra.

Yoga House   YOGA
(Map p750; 65545001; www.yogahouse.in; 53 Chimbai Rd, Bandra; class ₹700; 8am-10pm) A variety of yoga traditions are taught at this homey, Western-style yoga centre, housed in a Portuguese-style bungalow by the sea. There's also a charming cafe.

Yoga Cara   YOGA, MASSAGE
(Map p750; 022-26511464; www.yogacara. in; 1st fl, SBI Bldg, 18A New Kant Wadi Rd, Bandra; yoga per class/week ₹600/1500) Classic hatha and iyengar yoga institute. Massages (from ₹1850 per hour) and treatments are excellent here; the SoHum rejuvenating massage is recommended. Ayurvedic cooking classes are also offered.

Antara Spa   SPA
(022-66939999; www.theclubmumbai.com; 197 DN Nagar, Andheri West; 1hr massage from ₹2450; 10am-10pm) Luxury spa with skilled therapists offering a range of therapies and treatments, including Swedish, Thai and hot-stone massages.

Palm Spa   SPA
(Map p738; 022-66349898; www.thepalms spaindia.com; Chhatrapati Shivaji Marg, Colaba; 1hr massage from ₹3200; 9.30am-10.30pm) Indulge in a rub, scrub or tub at this renowned Colaba spa. The exfoliating lemongrass and green-tea scrub is ₹2500.

Child Rights & You   VOLUNTEERING
(CRY; Map p746; 23096845; www.cry.org; 89A Anand Estate, Sane Guruji Marg, Mahalaxmi) Raises funds for marginalised children. Volunteers can assist with campaigns (online and on the ground), research, surveys and media, as well as occasional fieldwork. A four-week commitment is required.

Lok Seva Sangam   VOLUNTEERING
(022-24070718; http://loksevasangam.word press.com; D/1, Everard Nagar Eastern Express Hwy, Sion) Works to improve lives in the city's slums. Medical staff who can speak Hindi/Marathi or those with fundraising skills are needed.

Vatsalya Foundation   VOLUNTEERING
(Map p746; 24962115; www.thevatsalyafoun dation.org; Anand Niketan, King George V Memorial, Dr E Moses Rd, Mahalaxmi) Works with

SANJAY GANDHI NATIONAL PARK

It's hard to believe that within 1½ hours of the teeming metropolis you can be surrounded by a 104-sq-km protected tropical forest. At **Sanjay Gandhi National Park** (☎28866449; Borivali; adult/child ₹30/15, vehicle ₹100, safari admission ₹50; ◷7.30am-6pm Tue-Sun, last entry 4pm) bright flora, birds, butterflies and elusive wild leopards replace pollution and concrete, all surrounded by forested hills on the city's northern edge. Urban development has muscled in on the fringes, but the heart of the park is still very peaceful.

A trekking ban is in force to protect wildlife, but you can still walk in the woods if you go with Bombay Natural History Society. On your own, you can cycle (hire bikes cost ₹20 per hour, ₹200 deposit) or take the shuttle to the Shilonda Waterfall, Vihar and Tulsi Lakes (where there's boating) and the most intriguing option, the **Kanheri Caves** (Indian/foreigner ₹5/100), a set of 109 dwellings and monastic structures for Buddhist monks 6km inside the park. The caves, not all of which are accessible, were developed over 1000 years, beginning in the 1st century BC, as part of a sprawling monastic university complex. Avoid the zoo-like lion and tiger 'safari' as the animals are in cages and enclosures.

Inside the park's main northern entrance is an information centre with a small exhibition on the park's wildlife. The best time to see birds is October to April and butterflies August to November.

The nearest station is Borivali, served by trains on the Western Railway line from Churchgate station (30 minutes, frequent).

MUMBAI (BOMBAY) COURSES

Mumbai's street children. There are long- and short-term opportunities in teaching English, computer skills and sports activities.

Welfare of Stray Dogs   VOLUNTEERING
(Map p740; ☎64222838; www.wsdindia.org; Yeshwant Chambers, B Bharucha Rd, Kala Ghoda) Operates sterilisation and antirabies programs. Volunteers can walk dogs, treat street dogs, manage stores, educate kids in school programs or fundraise.

≋ Courses

★ Yoga Institute   YOGA
(Map p750; ☎26122185; www.theyogainstitute. org; Shri Yogendra Marg, Prabhat Colony, Santa Cruz East; per 1st/2nd month ₹650/450) At its peaceful leafy campus near Santa Cruz, the respected Yoga Institute has daily classes as well as weekend and weeklong programs, and longer residential courses including teacher training (with the seven-day course a prerequisite).

**Kaivalyadhama Ishwardas
Yogic Health Centre**   YOGA
(Map p746; ☎22818417; www.kdhammumbai.org; 43 Marine Dr; ◷6am-7pm Mon-Sat) Several daily yoga classes as well as workshops; fees include a ₹800 monthly membership fee and a ₹600 admission fee.

★ Bharatiya Vidya
Bhavan   LANGUAGE COURSE, MUSIC
(Map p746; ☎23871860; www.bhavans.info; 2nd fl, cnr KM Munshi Marg & Ramabai Rd, Girgaum; per hour ₹500; ◷4-8pm) Excellent private Hindi, Marathi, Gujarati and Sanskrit language classes. Contact Professor Ghosh (a Grammy Award–winning composer and musician) for lessons in tabla, vocals, sitar or classical dance.

Sumeet Nagdev Dance Arts   DANCE
(SNDA; ☎24366777; www.sumeetnagdevdance arts.in; Silver Cascade Bldg, SB Marg, Dadar West; 1hr class ₹450) SNDA offers tons of dance classes, from samba and ballet to 'Indian Folk Bollywood'. Classes are also held at a **Chowpatty location** (Studio Balance, Krishna Kunj, 29/30 KM Munshi Marg).

☞ Tours

Fiona Fernandez' *Ten Heritage Walks of Mumbai* (₹395) has walking tours of the city, with fascinating historical background. The Government of India tourist office can provide a list of approved multilingual guides; most charge ₹750/1000 per half-/full day.

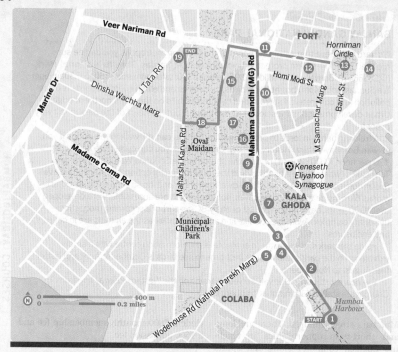

City Walk
Architectural Mumbai

START GATEWAY OF INDIA
END EROS CINEMA
LENGTH 2.5KM; 1½ HOURS

Mumbai's defining feature is its distinctive mix of colonial-era and art deco architecture. Starting from the ① **Gateway of India** (p738), walk up Chhatrapati Shivaji Marg past the art deco residential and-commercial complex ② **Dhunraj Mahal**, towards ③ **Regal Circle**. Walk the circle for views of the surrounding buildings – including the art deco ④ **Regal cinema** (p768) and the ⑤ **Majestic Hotel**, now the Sahakari Bhandar cooperative store. Continue up MG Rd, past the beautifully restored facade of the ⑥ **National Gallery of Modern Art** (p744). Opposite is the landmark ⑦ **Chhatrapati Shivaji Maharaj Vastu Sangrahalaya** (p742) built in glorious Indo-Saracenic style. Back across the road is the 'Romanesque Transitional' ⑧ **Elphinstone College** and the ⑨ **David Sassoon Library & Reading Room**, where members escape the afternoon heat

lazing on planters' chairs on the upper balcony. Continue north to admire the vertical art deco stylings of the ⑩ **New India Assurance Company Building**. On an island ahead lies ⑪ **Flora Fountain**, depicting the Roman goddess of flowers. Turn east down Veer Nariman Rd, walking towards ⑫ **St Thomas' Cathedral** (p744). Ahead lies the stately ⑬ **Horniman Circle**, an arcaded ring of buildings laid out in the 1860s around a beautifully kept botanical garden. It's overlooked from the east by the neoclassical ⑭ **Town Hall**, home to the Asiatic Society library. Backtrack to Flora Fountain, continuing west and turning south onto Bhaurao Patil Marg to see the august ⑮ **High Court** (p743) and the ornate ⑯ **University of Mumbai** (p743). The university's 80m-high ⑰ **Rajabai Clock Tower** (p743) is best observed from within the ⑱ **Oval Maidan**. Turn around to compare the colonial-era edifices with the row of art deco beauties lining Maharshi Karve (MK) Rd, culminating in the wedding-cake tower of the classic ⑲ **Eros Cinema** (p768).

A **cruise** on Mumbai Harbour is a good way to see the Gateway of India and Colaba harbourfont from the sea. Half-hour ferry rides (₹80) depart from the Gateway of India; tickets are sold on-site.

⭐ **Reality Tours & Travel**   SLUM TOUR
(Map p740; ☑9820822253; www.realitytour sandtravel.com; 1/26, Unique Business Service Centre, Akber House, Nowroji Fardonji Rd; most tours ₹750-1500) ✍ Compelling tours of the Dharavi slum, with 80% of post-tax profits going to the agency's own NGO, Reality Gives (www.realitygives.org). Street food, market, bicycle and Night Mumbai tours are also excellent.

Bombay Heritage Walks   WALKING TOUR
(☑23690992, 9821887321; www.bombayherit agewalks.com; per 2hr tour from ₹2500, for up to 5 people) Run by two enthusiastic architects, BHW has terrific tours of heritage neighbourhoods.

Mumbai Magic Tours   CITY TOUR
(☑9867707414; www.mumbaimagic.com; 2hr tour per person from ₹1750) Designed by the authors of the fabulous **Mumbai Magic blog** (www.mumbai-magic.blogspot.com), these city tours focus on food markets, traditional dance and music, and Jewish heritage, among others.

Nilambari Bus Tours   BUS TOUR
(MTDC; ☑020-22845678; www.maharashtratour ism.gov.in; 1hr tour lower/upper deck ₹60/180; ☉7pm & 8.15pm Sat & Sun) Maharashtra Tourism runs open-deck bus tours of illuminated heritage buildings on weekends. Buses depart from and can be booked at both the **MTDC booth** (Map p738) and the **MTDC office** (☑22841877; www.maharashtra tourism.gov.in; Madame Cama Rd, Nariman Point; ☉9.45am-5.30pm Mon-Sat).

🛏 Sleeping

Mumbai has the most expensive accommodation in India, and you'll never quite feel like you're getting your money's worth. Welcome to Mumbai real estate!

Colaba is compact, has the liveliest tourist scene and many budget and midrange options. The neighbouring Fort area is convenient for the main train stations (CST and Churchgate). Most of the top-end places are dotted along Marine Dr and out in the suburbs. Note that although there are very few hotels in the cosmopolitan areas of Juhu

SLEEPING PRICE RANGES

The following price ranges refer to a double room and are inclusive of tax:

$ less than ₹2500

$$ ₹2500 to ₹6000

$$$ more than ₹6000

and Bandra, many airport hotels are only a 15-minute taxi ride away.

No matter where you stay, always book ahead.

🛏 Colaba

⭐ **Sea Shore Hotel**   GUESTHOUSE **$**
(Map p738; ☑22874237; 4th fl, 1-49 Kamal Mansion, Arthur Bunder Rd; s/d without bathroom ₹700/1100; 🛜) This place is really making an effort, with small but immaculately clean and inviting rooms, all with flat-screen TVs, set off a railway-carriage-style corridor. Half the rooms even have harbour views (the others don't have a window). The modish communal bathrooms are well-scrubbed and have a little gleam and sparkle. Wi-fi in the reception area only.

Carlton Hotel   HOTEL **$**
(Map p738; ☑22020642; 1st fl, Florence House, Mereweather Rd; s/d/tr without bathroom from ₹1050/1550/2300, s/d with AC ₹2900/3200; ❄) Rooms here are a fair deal for the location, with original floor tiles, high ceilings, a contemporary touch or two, and some boasting balconies with colonial-era Colaba views; however, many lack private bathrooms. The building itself is rundown and staff could be more eager to please.

Bentley's Hotel   HOTEL **$**
(Map p738; ☑22841474; www.bentleyshotel.com; 17 Oliver Rd; r incl breakfast ₹1740-2490; ❄🛜) A welcoming Parsi-owned place in the heart of Colaba which travellers either love or hate, depending on which of the five apartment buildings they end up in. First choice are the spacious, colonial-style rooms in the main building; avoid Henry Rd and JA Allana Marg. Air-conditioning is ₹315 extra, wi-fi is reception-only.

India Guest House   GUESTHOUSE **$**
(Map p738; ☑22833769; 3rd fl, 1/49 Kamal Mansion, Arthur Bunder Rd; s/d without bath-

room from ₹400/500; ⊚) Run by the same people as the excellent Sea Shore Hotel, this overflow place is not as attractive but its boxrooms (some with partial sea views) are cheap as chapatis and enjoy a fine location. However, the design (partition walls, shared bathrooms at one end of the corridor) means that it feels more student house than hotel.

Salvation Army Red Shield
Guest House GUESTHOUSE $
(Map p738; ☑22841824; red_shield@vsnl.net; 30 Mereweather Rd; dm incl breakfast ₹350, d with fan/AC incl breakfast ₹1100/1500; ❈@) A Mumbai institution popular with rupee-pinching travellers. Accommodation is very spartan (and a little grubby) but doable for a night or so. Dorms cannot be reserved in advance: come just after the 9am kickout to ensure a spot. Curfew is midnight.

★YWCA GUESTHOUSE $$
(Map p738; ☑22025053; www.ywcaic.info; 18 Madame Cama Rd; s/d/tr with AC incl breakfast & dinner ₹2400/3640/5450; ❈@⊚) Efficiently managed, and within walking distance of all the sights in Colaba and Fort, the YMCA is a good deal and justifiably popular. The spacious, well-maintained rooms boast desks and wardrobes and multichanelled TVs (though wi-fi is restricted to the lobby). Tariffs include a buffet breakfast, dinner and a daily newspaper.

Hotel Suba Palace HOTEL $$
(Map p738; ☑22020636, 22020639; www.hotelsubapalace.com; Battery St; s/d with AC incl breakfast ₹5520/6340; ❈⊚) 'Palace' is pushing it a little but this modern, brilliantly located little place is certainly verging on boutique hotel territory with its contemporary decor: neutral tones are offset with zebra-print quilted headboards in the tasteful rooms. There's a good in-house restaurant and free wi-fi.

Regent Hotel HOTEL $$
(Map p738; ☑22021518; 8 Best Marg; s/d with AC incl breakfast ₹3920-4910; ❈@⊚) A dependable choice where staff go the extra mile to help out guests. Located just off Colaba's main drag and has well-furnished rooms with good-quality mattresses and modern marble-floored bathrooms.

Hotel Moti GUESTHOUSE $$
(Map p738; ☑22025714; hotelmotiinternational@yahoo.co.in; 10 Best Marg; d/tr with AC ₹3300/

4500; ❈@⊚) A gracefully crumbling, colonial-era building in prime Colaba, where owner Raj is generous with advice about the city. Rooms are simply furnished (many have some period charm, like ornate stucco ceilings), but all could be better maintained.

★Taj Mahal Palace,
Mumbai HERITAGE HOTEL $$$
(Map p738; ☑66653366; www.tajhotels.com; Apollo Bunder; s/d tower from ₹15,800/17,620, palace from ₹23,530, 25,990; ❈@⊚⊚) The grand dame of Mumbai is one of the world's most iconic hotels and has hosted a roster of presidents and royalty. Sweeping arches, staircases and domes and a glorious garden and pool ensure an unforgettable stay. Rooms in the adjacent tower lack the period details of the palace itself, but many have spectacular, full-frontal views of the Gateway to India.

With a myriad of excellent in-house eating and drinking options, plus spa and leisure facilities, it can be a wrench to leave the hotel premises. All guests are entitled to an exceptional guided tour, which provides illuminating context about the hotel's role in the city's history.

★Abode Bombay BOUTIQUE HOTEL $$$
(Map p738; ☑8080234066; www.abodeboutiquehotels.com; 1st fl, Lansdowne House, MB Marg; r with AC incl breakfast ₹5850-14,400; ❈⊚) Terrific new hip hotel, stylishly designed using colonial-era and art deco furniture, reclaimed teak flooring and original artwork; the luxury rooms have glorious free-standing bath tubs. Staff are very switched on to travellers' needs, and breakfast is excellent with fresh juice and delicious local and international choices. A little tricky to find, it's located behind the Regal Cinema.

Vivanta by Taj HOTEL $$$
(☑022-66650808; www.vivantabytaj.com; 90 Cuffe Pde; s/d from ₹8050/9230; ❈❈⊚) In a quiet, leafy neighbourhood 1.5km south of the Gateway, this towering hotel has relatively modest rates (for Mumbai!), considering its excellent facilities which include a large pool, excellent gym, lounge bar and lots of good dining choices.

Gordon House Hotel HOTEL $$$
(Map p738; ☑22894400; www.ghhotel.com; 5 Battery St; r incl breakfast ₹7700; ❈⊚) Light, airy, spacious and well-equipped rooms a stone's throw from the Gateway to India.

GROWING PAINS

Shoehorned into a narrow peninsula that juts into the Arabian Sea, Mumbai is one of the world's most congested and densely populated megacities. The numbers are startling: over 22 million live in the Mumbai conurbation and around 60% of these live in slums.

While the city is blessed with sea to the west and a large bay to the east, it's also cursed by the narrowness of the spit of land it calls home. Every day over six million commuters from the outer suburbs attempt to reach their workplaces in the south of the city via a network of antiquated suburban trains and buses. A desperately needed metro link to the heart of the city is planned (but not scheduled to be completed until at least 2020, if on time). For years the city planners invested in an ever-increasing number of flyovers, as car ownership has grown by 58% since 2000, while failing to build a single bus lane or cycle path. Gridlock is the norm and the pollution is punishing, with particulate and nitric oxide levels way above WHO danger levels.

The future of the city is in the balance. Mumbai is one of the least green cities on earth, with open spaces, parks and recreation grounds accounting for only 2.5% of its total area (Delhi has 20%, Chandigarh 35%). Yet on the eastern side of town, stretching north from the shoreline of Colaba, is a vast area of decaying docklands which has been long-slated for redevelopment. Will it be set aside for green space, parks and leisure facilities or luxury housing and concrete?

Design-wise each floor is themed: the decor ranges Mediterranean (think terracotta tiles, bold colours), Scandinavian (blond wood, clean lines) and Country (er...patchwork quilts?). There's a good Asian restaurant on the ground floor.

Fort Area & Churchgate

Traveller's Inn
HOTEL $

(Map p740; ☐22644685; 26 Adi Marzban Path; dm/d ₹630/1880, d with AC incl breakfast ₹2550; ❄@⑂) On a quiet, tree-lined street, this small hotel is a very sound choice with clean, if tiny, rooms with cable TV that represent good value. The three (fan-cooled) dorms can get Hades-hot in summer but are a steal for Mumbai – bring your own ice pack (and exorcist). The location's excellent, staff are helpful and there's free wi-fi in the lobby.

Hotel Lawrence
GUESTHOUSE $

(Map p740; ☐22843618; 3rd fl, ITTS House, 33 Sai Baba Marg, Kala Ghoda; s/d/tr without bathroom incl breakfast ₹850/950/1500) Run by kindly folk, this venerable place has been hosting shoestring travellers for years. Rooms are certainly basic but kept pretty tidy, as are the communal bathrooms. Boasts an excellent Kala Ghoda location, on a quiet little lane accessed by a ramshackle old lift.

Hotel Oasis
HOTEL $

(Map p740; ☐30227886, 30227889; www.hotel oasisindia.in; 276 Shahid Bhagat Singh Marg; r ₹1620-3050; ❄⑂) Hotel Oasis enjoys a convenient location near the CST and offers decent accommodation for the modest rates asked. Rooms are smallish, and some are low on natural light, but they have flat-screen TVs and in-room wi-fi.

★ Residency Hotel
HOTEL $$

(Map p740; ☐22625525; www.residencyhotel. com; 26 Rustom Sidhwa Marg, Fort; s/d with AC incl breakfast from ₹4430/4670; ❄@⑂) The best-run midranger in Mumbai, the Residency is the kind of dependable place where you can breathe a sigh of relief after a long journey and be certain you'll be looked after well. It's fine value too, with contemporary rooms that boast mood lighting, fridges, flat-screens and hip en suite bathrooms. Its Fort location is excellent and you'll find some fascinating books to browse over breakfast in the pleasant cafe. For the best rates, always book via the hotel's own website.

Welcome Hotel
HOTEL $$

(Map p740; ☐6631488; welcomehotel@gmail. com; 257 Shahid Bhagat Singh Marg; s/d incl breakfast from ₹3280/3890, without bathroom from ₹1810/2020; ❄⑂) Service is a little hit 'n' miss but rooms here are simple and comfortable, and shared bathrooms are well kept. Top-floor executive rooms are more boutique than midrange.

Trident
HOTEL $$$

(Oberoi Hotel; Map p740; ☑66324343; www.tridenthotels.com; Marine Dr; s/d from ₹15,300/17,000; ❋@🐾🏊) This Marine Dr landmark is part of the Oberoi Hotel complex, but offers better value and a pleasing contemporary look in its restaurants, bars and pool area. Upper-floor ocean-view rooms offer truly spectacular vistas of the Queen's Necklace. Wi-fi, surprisingly, costs extra.

🛏 Western & Northern Suburbs

★ Juhu Residency
BOUTIQUE HOTEL $$

(Map p750; ☑67834949; www.juhuresidency.com; 148B Juhu Tara Rd, Juhu; s/d with AC incl breakfast & wi-fi from ₹5850; ❋@🛰) Essential oil aromas greet you in the lobby at this excellent boutique hotel with an inviting, relaxing atmosphere (and a fine location, five minutes' walk from Juhu beach). The chocolate-and-coffee colour scheme in the modish rooms works well, each boasting marble floors, dark woods, artful bedspreads and flat-screen TVs. There are three restaurants – good ones – for just 18 rooms.

To top it all, free airport pick-ups are included.

Hotel Oriental Aster
HOTEL $$

(Map p750; ☑022-28232323; http://theorientalaster.com; 45 Tarun Bharat Society, Dr Karanjiya Road; r with AC & breakfast from ₹4700; ❋🛰) An efficiently run airport hotel with attractive modern rooms that have space and a splash of art on show; bathrooms are small but perfectly formed. There's 24-hour room service, and free wi-fi and airport transportation.

Anand Hotel
HOTEL $$

(Map p750; ☑26203372; anandhote@yahoo.co.in; Gandhigram Rd, Juhu; s/d with AC from ₹2580/4230; ❋🛰) Yes, the decor's in 50 shades of beige but the Anand's rooms are comfortable, spacious and represent decent value, considering the prime location on a quiet street next to Juhu beach. The excellent in-house Dakshinayan restaurant (p762) scores highly for authentic, inexpensive meals too. It's a particularly good deal for solo travellers.

Hotel Regal Enclave
HOTEL $$

(Map p750; ☑67261111; www.regalenclave.com; 4th Rd, Khar West; r with AC incl breakfast from ₹6000; ❋🛰) Enjoys a stellar location in an exceedingly leafy part of Khar, right near the station (some rooms have railway views)

and close to all of Bandra's best eating, drinking and shopping. Rooms are spacious and comfortable, with pleasant if unoriginal decor. Rates include airport pick-up.

Iskcon
GUESTHOUSE $$

(Map p750; ☑26206860; www.iskconmumbai.com/guest-house; Juhu Church Rd, Juhu; s/d ₹3100/3500, with AC ₹3400/4000; ❋@🛰) An intriguing place to stay inside Juhu's lively Iskcon complex. Though the hotel building is a slightly soulless concrete block, some rooms enjoy vistas over the Hare Krishna temple compound. Spartan decor is offset by the odd decorative flourish such as Gujarati *sankheda* (lacquered country wood) furniture, and staff are very welcoming.

Hotel Neelkanth
HOTEL $$

(Map p750; ☑26495566, 26495569; 354 Linking Rd, Khar West; s/d from ₹2460/3380; ❋🛰) Rooms at the friendly Neelkanth are inadvertently retro, with lots of marble and chrome-trimmed wooden furniture; check out the sublimely mod logo too. Yes, it's old-fashioned, but it's also decent value for this neighbourhood with great shopping nearby.

Hotel Suba International
BOUTIQUE HOTEL $$

(Map p750; ☑67076707; www.hotelsubainternational.com; Sahar Rd, Andheri East; r with AC incl breakfast from ₹6400; ❋🛰) A 'boutique business' hotel that's very close to the airport (free transfers are included) and boasts modish rooms with clean lines and stylish touches.

Le Sutra
BOUTIQUE HOTEL $$$

(Map p750; ☑022-66420025; www.lesutra.in; 14 Union Park, Khar West; s/d incl breakfast from ₹7900/10,450; ❋🛰) This hip hotel in the happening Khar area blends contemporary chic with traditional artefacts (textiles and hand-carved chairs) and some statement art in its lovely rooms. The in-house gallery, spa, cafe and restaurants (Out of the Blue and Olive) seal the deal. Check the website for special offers that include dinner or a spa treatment.

Sofitel Mumbai BKC
HOTEL $$$

(Map p750; ☑022-61175000; www.sofitel-mumbai-bkc.com; C-57, Bandra Kurla Complex Rd; s/d from ₹7720/8500; ❋🛰) Located in Mumbai's BKC business district, which is handy for the airport and close enough to Bandra, the Sofitel offers commodious comfort levels. Rooms have a mod-Indian design and facilities are excellent, with great restaurants and one of the best breakfast buffets in the city.

ITC Maratha
HOTEL $$$

(Map p750; ☑ 28303030; www.itchotels.in; Sahar Rd, Andheri East; s/d incl breakfast from ₹16,450/19,200; ✳@🅐🅢) The five-star hotel with the most luxurious Indian character, from the Rajasthani-style lattice windows around the atrium, to the rooms with their silk throw pillows and lush raspberry-and-grey colour schemes. Peshawri (p763), one of Mumbai's best restaurants, is located here.

Sun-n-Sand
HOTEL $$$

(Map p750; ☑ 66938888; www.sunnsandhotel.com; 39 Juhu Chowpatty; r with AC from ₹10,000; ✳@🅐🅢) A beachfront institution with well-maintained if slightly dated rooms that are big on browns and beiges. Rates (add ₹1000 or so for a sea view) are competitive given the location in exclusive Juhu and free airport transfers. Staff are eager to please.

✗ Eating

Flavours from all over India collide with international trends and taste buds in Mumbai. Colaba is home to most of the cheap tourist haunts, while Fort and Churchgate are more upscale, a trend that continues as you head north to Mahalaxmi and the western suburbs, where you'll find Mumbai's most international and expensive restaurants.

Sample Gujarati or Keralan thalis (all-you-can-eat meals), Mughlai kebabs, Goan vindaloo and Mangalorean seafood. And don't forget, if you see Bombay duck on a menu, it's actually *bombil* (fish dried in the sun and deep-fried).

✗ Colaba

Bademiya
MUGHLAI, FAST FOOD $

(Map p738; Tulloch Rd; light meals ₹60-150; ⊙8pm-1.30am) Formerly a tiny, outrageously popular late-night street stall, Bademiya now encompasses a (dingy) seating area too. Yes, prices have risen, but it remains a key Colaba hang-out for its trademark buzz and bustle, plus its delicious meat-heavy menu. Expect spicy, fresh-grilled kebabs, mutton and chicken curries, and tikka rolls.

Olympia
INDIAN $

(Map p738; Rahim Mansion, 1 Shahid Bhagat Singh Marg; meals ₹80-140; ⊙7am-midnight) While we didn't encounter any athletes at the Olympia, its *masala kheema* (spicy minced meat; ₹40) is certainly a breakfast of champions when munched with a couple of roti. A simple place renowned for its pocket-friendly meat dishes; the seekh kebab and chicken butter fry masala (₹80) are also great.

Hotel OCH
INDIAN $

(Map p738; Shahid Bhagat Singh Marg; mains ₹50-150; ⊙7am-10.30pm) A good Colaba cheapie, with decent lunch thalis and lots of Punjabi dishes in a large, cafeteria-like setting. Popular with families and cops working next door.

Sufra
MIDDLE EASTERN $$

(Map p738; 16A Cusrow Baug, Shahid Bhagat Singh Rd; meals ₹120-250; ⊙11am-11.45pm) Serves up excellent Arab dishes such as *kibbeh* (chicken, burgul and mint bites), falafel, shwarma, kebabs and fresh juices at very reasonable rates. It's a tiny place with just a few tables so best for a hit and run or takeaway.

★Indigo
FUSION, CONTINENTAL $$$

(Map p738; ☑ 66368980; www.foodindigo.com; 4 Mandlik Marg; mains ₹780-1250; ⊙noon-3pm & 6.30pm-midnight; 🕾) This incredibly classy

---

STREET FOOD

Mumbai's street cuisine is vaster than many Western culinary traditions. Stalls tend to get started in late afternoon, when chai complements much of the fried deliciousness; items are ₹10 to ₹25.

Most street food is vegetarian. Chowpatty Beach is a great place to try Mumbai's famous *bhelpuri*. Stalls offering samosas, *pav bhaji* (spiced vegetables and bread), *vada pav* (deep-fried spiced lentil-ball sandwich), *bhurji pav* (scrambled eggs and bread) and *dabeli* (a mixture of potatoes, spices, peanuts and pomegranate, also on bread) are spread through the city.

For a meaty meal, Mohammed Ali and Merchant Rds in Kalbadevi are famous for kebabs. In Colaba, Bademiya is a late-night Mumbai rite of passage, renowned for its chicken tikka rolls.

The office workers' district on the north side of Kala Ghoda is another good hunting ground for street snacks.

Colaba institution is a colonial-era property converted into a temple of fine dining. Serves inventive, expensive European and Asian cuisine and offers a long wine list, sleek ambience and a gorgeous rooftop deck. Favourites include the pulled duck tortellini, Kochi oysters, and pork belly with maple-glazed apple. Reserve ahead.

Indigo Delicatessen CAFE $$$
(Map p738; www.indigodeli.com; Pheroze Bldg, Chhatrapati Shivaji Marg; snacks/mains from ₹320/470; ⊙8.30am-midnight; 🛜) Bustling and fashionable cafe-restaurant with cool tunes and massive wooden tables. The menu includes all-day breakfasts (₹155 to ₹385) and international classics such as pork ribs, thincrust pizza and inventive sandwiches. It's busy so service can be stretched.

Self-Catering

Colaba Market MARKET
(Map p738; Lala Nigam St; ⊙7am-5pm) The Colaba market has fresh fruit and vegetables.

Saharkari Bhandar Supermarket SUPERMARKET
(Map p738; ☑22022248; cnr Colaba Causeway & Wodehouse Rd; ⊙10am-8.30pm) Well-stocked for self-caterers.

🍴 Fort Area & Churchgate

Pradeep Gomantak Bhojanalaya MAHARASHTRIAN $
(Map p740; Sheri House, Rustom Sidhwa Marg; mains ₹60-150; ⊙11am-4pm & 7.30-10pm) A simple but satisfying place that serves Malvani cuisine and gets very busy at lunchtime. Its *bombil* rice plate (₹70) and crab masala (₹65) are very flavoursome and prepared with real care and attention. Wash your meal down with *sol kadhi* (a soothing, spicy drink of coconut milk and kokum).

Badshah Snacks & Drinks INDIAN $
(Map p746; Lokmanya Tilak Rd; snacks & drinks ₹40-120; ⊙7am-12.30am) Opposite Crawford Market, Badshah's been serving snacks, fruit juices and its famous *falooda* (rose-flavoured drink made with milk, cream, nuts and vermicelli) to hungry bargain-hunters for more than 100 years.

★ La Folie CAFE $$
(Map p740; Ropewalk Lane, Kala Ghoda; croissants/cakes from ₹110/220; ⊙noon-11pm) Chocoholics and cake fetishistas look no further, this minuscule Kala Ghoda place will satisfy your cravings, and then some. Owner Sanjana Patel spent seven years in France studying the art (addiction?) of pastry- and chocolate-making, which was obviously time well spent. Try the delectable Madagascar cake (chocolate with raspberry mousse) with a latte (₹130) or the 70% cocoa Venezuelan-sourced chocolates.

Frankly, wherever you are dining in South Mumbai skip the dessert menu and head here instead.

★ Revival INDIAN $$
(Map p746; www.revivalindianthali.com; 361 Sheikh Memon St, Kalbadevi, opp Mangaldas market; mains ₹200-360, thali from ₹350; ⊙noon-4pm & 7.30-10.30pm, lunch only Sun; ❄🍽) Thali mecca near Crawford Market where waiters in silken dhoti come one after another to fill your plates with dozens of delectable (veg-only) curries, sides, chutneys, rotis and rice dishes in an all-you-can-eat gastro onslaught. The thali menu changes daily and the premises are air-conditioned.

Pantry CAFE $$
(Map p740; www.thepantry.in; B Bharucha Rd; snacks/meals from ₹200/270; ⊙8.30am-11pm; 🛜) Pantry is a bakery-cafe that offers a choice of fine pies and pastries, soups and sandwiches plus delicious mains (such as curry leaf chicken with burgal pilaf). Breakfasts are legendary: try the tomato scrambled eggs with parmesan and rosti, or some organic-flour waffles with fruit. The elegantly restored historic premises are also perfect for a coffee and slab of cake.

Samrat GUJARATI $$
(Map p740; ☑42135401; www.prashantcaterers.com; Prem Ct, J Tata Rd; thali ₹400, mains ₹160-290; ⊙noon-11pm; ❄) Samrat has an à la carte menu but most rightly opt for the famous Gujarati thali – a cavalcade of taste and texture, sweetness and spice that includes four curries, three chutneys, curd, rotis and other bits and pieces. Beer is available.

Oye Kake NORTH INDIAN $$
(Map p740; 13C Cawasji Patel St; mains ₹120-180; ⊙11am-4pm & 7-11pm) Intimate all-veg Punjabi place where the daily thali (₹170) is widly popular with local office workers and renowned for its authenticity. Signature dishes include the panner tikka masala, *sarson da saag* (mustard leaf curry) and the *parathas;* lassis are excellent too. Prepare to have to wait for a table.

DABBA-WALLAHS

A small miracle of logistics, Mumbai's 5000 *dabba-wallahs* (literally 'food container person'; also called tiffin-wallahs) work tirelessly to deliver hot lunches to office workers throughout the city.

Lunch boxes are picked up each day from restaurants and homes and carried on heads, bicycles and trains to a centralised sorting station. A sophisticated system of numbers and colours (many wallahs don't read) identifies the destination of each lunch. More than 200,000 meals are delivered – always on time, come (monsoon) rain or (searing) shine. This system has been used for over a century and there's only about one mistake per six million deliveries. (In a 2002 analysis, *Forbes Magazine* found that the *dabba-wallahs* had a six-sigma, or 99.99966%, reliability rating.)

Look for these master messengers midmorning at Churchgate and CST stations.

A Taste of Kerala   KERALAN $$
(Map p740; Prospect Chambers Annex, Pitha St, Fort; mains ₹70-170, thali from ₹110; ⊙6am-midnight) Inexpensive Keralan eatery with lots of coconut and southern goodness on the menu; try a thali (served on a banana leaf) or one of the seafood specials like the prawn pepper masala. It also serves Punjabi and meat dishes. Staff are very welcoming, and there's an air-conditioned dining room.

Café Moshe   CAFE $$
(Map p738; www.moshes.in; Chhatrapati Shivaji Marg; light meals ₹200-380; ⊙9am-midnight; 🛜) Moshe's menu has more than a nod to the Middle East, with excellent mezze, pita bread sandwiches and wraps, salads and outstanding hummus bowls (₹250 to ₹280) that have a choice of toppings. Desserts, juices and coffee also score highly.

Other outlets, all serving the same great food, include the flagship **restaurant** (7 Minoo Manor, Cuffe Pde; ⊙9am-midnight), in a heritage building, and the bookstore **cafe** (Map p746; Crossword, NS Patkar Marg) at Kemp's Corner.

Bademiya Restaurant   NORTH INDIAN $$
(Map p740; ☑22655657; Botawala Bldg, Horniman Circle; mains ₹110-220; ⊙11am-1am) The grown-up, sit-down version of Bademiya's legendary Colaba street-side stand (p759) has the classic rolls and rotis, plus biryanis, tikka masalas and dhals. Delivers.

Kala Ghoda Café   CAFE $$
(Map p740; www.kgcafe.in; 10 Ropewalk Lane, Kala Ghoda; light meal ₹100-280, dinner ₹380-530; ⊙8.30am-11.45pm; 🛜) 🍃 Tiny boho cafe with a handful of tables that's a favourite with creative types. There's usually interesting art or photography. Serves organic coffee and tea, sandwiches, salads and breakfasts.

Suzette   FRENCH $$
(Map p740; www.suzette.in; Atlanta Bldg, Vinayak K Shah Marg, Nariman Point; meals ₹300-450; ⊙9am-11pm Mon-Sat; 📞) This relaxed Parisian-style place with delectable crêpes, croques, salads, pasta and loungy music. On the crêpe front, sweet tooths should try the jaggery and butter; for a savoury flavour, order an *italie* (with pesto, mozzarella and mushrooms). The **Bandra branch** (Map p750; St John's St, Pali Naka; ⊙9am-11pm) has outdoor seating and is open daily.

Brittania   PARSI $$
(Map p740; Wakefield House, Ballard Estate; mains ₹150-550; ⊙noon-4pm Mon-Sat) This Parsi institution has been around since 1923 and retains a (faded) colonial-era feel. The signature dishes are the *dhansak* (meat with curried lentils and rice) and the berry *pulao* – spiced and boneless mutton or chicken, or veg or egg, buried in basmati rice and tart barberries that are imported from Iran. It's a little tricky to find. Cash only.

Samovar Café   CAFE $$
(Map p740; Jehangir Art Gallery, MG Rd, Kala Ghoda; snacks & meals ₹90-170; ⊙11am-7pm Mon-Sat) Inside the art gallery, this cafe is perfect for a snack (try the rolls; ₹100 to ₹120) or meal (the pepper mutton chops are great). It overlooks the gardens of the Chhatrapati Shivaji Maharaj Vastu Sangrahalaya museum. Cappuccinos and beers are also on offer.

★ Koh   THAI $$$
(Map p740; ☑39879999; InterContinental, Marine Dr; mains ₹850-1850; ⊙12.30-3pm & 7.30-midnight) Destination Thai restaurant with a

MUMBAI (BOMBAY) EATING

real wow factor, where celeb chef Ian Kitti-chai works his native cuisine into an international frenzy of flavour. The massamun curry (Thai Muslim-style spiced lamb shank with cucumber relish) is his signature (and most expensive) dish, but there are lots of sublime seafood and vegetarian choices too. Well worth a splurge.

★**Mamagoto**   ASIAN $$$
(Map p740; ☑ 022-67495660; www.mamagoto.in; 5 Surya Mahal, B Bharucha Marg; meals ₹350-550; ☺noon-11.30pm) Mamagoto means 'play with food' in Japanese and this zany little Kala Ghoda place is certainly fun, with a relaxed vibe, cool tunes and kooky decor (think pop and propaganda art). The menu really delivers, with punchy Pan-Asian flavours: combo meal deals (₹400 to ₹550) include a great juice, and the authentic Malay-style Penang curry is terrific.

There's also a branch in Bandra (☑ 022-26552600; www.mamagoto.in; 133 Gazebo House, Hill Rd, Bandra; ☺noon-11.30pm).

Burma Burma   ASIAN $$$
(Map p740; ☑ 022-40036600; www.burmaburma.in; Oak Lane, off MG Road; meals ₹330-500; ☺noon-3pm & 7-10.30pm) Sleek, stylish new restaurant that marries contemporary design with a few traditional artefacts (prayer wheels line one wall) and provides a beautiful setting for the cuisine of Myanmar. The menu is well priced, intricate and ambitious with inventive salads (try the tea leaf), curries and soups: *oh no khow suey* is a glorious coconut-enriched noodle broth. No alcohol is served.

Khyber   MUGHLAI, INDIAN $$$
(Map p740; ☑ 40396666; 145 MG Rd; mains ₹380-800; ☺12.30-4pm & 7.30-11.30pm) The much-acclaimed Khyber has a Northwest Frontier-themed design that incorporates murals featuring turbaned Mughal royalty, lots of exposed brickwork and oil lanterns – just the sort of place an Afghan warlord might feel at home. The meat-centric menu features gloriously tender kebabs, rich curries and lots of tandoori favourites roasted in Khyber's famous red masala sauce. Garlic or butter naan bread (₹95) is the perfect accompaniment.

Trishna   SEAFOOD $$$
(Map p740; ☑ 22703214; www.trishna.co.in; Ropewalk Lane, Kala Ghoda; mains ₹320-1110; ☺noon-3pm & 6.30pm-12.15am) Behind a modest entrance on a quiet Kala Ghoda lane is this often-lauded, intimate South Indian seafood restaurant. It's not a trendy place – the decor is old school, seating a little cramped and menu perhaps too long – but the cooking is superb, witness the Hyderabadi fish tikka, jumbo prawns with green pepper sauce, and outstanding crab dishes.

Mahesh Lunch Home   SEAFOOD $$$
(Map p740; ☑ 22023965; www.maheshlunchhome.com; Cowasji Patel St; mains ₹280-1300; ☺11.30am-4pm & 7pm-midnight) A great place to try Mangalorean or Chinese-style seafood in Mumbai. It's renowned for its ladyfish, pomfret, lobster, crab (try this with butter garlic pepper sauce) and salt-and-pepper squid (₹425). There's also a Juhu branch.

🍴 Kalbadevi to Mahalaxmi

New Kulfi Centre   ICE CREAM $
(Map p746; cnr Chowpatty Seaface & Sardar V Patel Rd; kulfi per 100gm ₹40-70; ☺10am-1am) Serves the best *kulfi* (Indian firm-textured ice cream) you'll have anywhere. Killer flavours include pistachio, *malai* (cream) and mango.

Cafe Noorani   NORTH INDIAN $$
(Map p746; Tardeo Rd, Haji Ali Circle; mains ₹80-300; ☺8am-11.30pm) Inexpensive, old-school eatery that's a requisite stop before or after visiting the Haji Ali mosque. Mughlai and Punjabi staples dominate, with kebabs chargrilled to perfection and great biriyanis; try the chicken kadai (₹200).

🍴 Western Suburbs

North Mumbai is home to the city's trendiest dining, centered on Bandra West and Juhu.

Hotel Ram Ashray   SOUTH INDIAN $
(Bhandarkar Rd, King's Circle, Matunga East; light meals ₹40-70; ☺5am-9.30pm) In the Tamil enclave of King's Circle, 80-year-old Ram Ashray is beloved by southern families for its spectacular dosas, *idli* (spongy, round, fermented rice cake) and *uttapa* (savoury rice pancake with toppings). Filter coffee is strong and flavoursome. The menu, written on a chalkboard, changes daily. It's just outside Matunga Rd train station's east exit.

★**Dakshinayan**   SOUTH INDIAN $$
(Map p750; Anand Hotel, Gandhigram Rd, Juhu; light meals ₹90-170; ☺11am-3pm & 6-11pm, from 8am Sun) With *rangoli* on the walls, serv-

ers in lungis and sari-clad women lunching (*chappals* off under the table), Dakshinayan channels Tamil Nadu. There are delicately textured dosas (₹110 to ₹165), *idli* and *uttapam*, village-fresh chutneys and perhaps the best *rasam* (tomato soup with spices and tamarind) in Mumbai. Finish off with a South Indian filter coffee – served in a stainless-steel set.

Chilli-heads should order *molagapudi idli* (₹110), a dozen *idli* coated in 'gunpowder' (potent spices).

★ Yoga House
CAFE $$
(Map p750; www.yogahouse.in; 53 Chimbai Rd, Bandra West; light meals ₹140-250; ⊙8am-10pm; 🛜) This haven of pastel shades, scatter cushions and greenery in Yoga House's seaside bungalow is the perfect retreat from Mumbai's mean streets. The menu is very creative and healthy – much of it raw vegan and all of it wholesome. Signature items include its famous salads (₹195 to ₹350), soups, 10-grain bread (₹130) and hash browns (with spinach, mozzarella and peppers).

Soul Fry
GOAN, SEAFOOD $$
(Map p750; ✆022-26046892; Silver Croft, Pali Mala Rd, Pali Hill; mains ₹140-390; ⊙noon-3pm & 7.30pm-midnight; ❄) Rightly famous for its terrific seafood, this lively, scruffy-yet-atmospheric Goan place by Pali market is just the place to escape Bandra's Bollywood set. Crab curry, tamarind prawns and Goan meat dishes such as chicken *xacuti* are authentic and loaded with coastal flavour. There's an air-conditioned interior and bench seating on the terrace. Be warned: Monday night is karaoke night.

Raaj Bhog
GUJARATI $$
(Map p750; 3rd Rd, Cosmos Commercial Center, Khar West; meals ₹180-300; ⊙11am-3.30pm & 7-11pm) Modestly priced restaurants are not easy to find in this part of town so this new Gujarati place by Khar station is a welcome addition. The (unlimited) deluxe thali (₹280) is filling and varied; it's served with basmati rice and rotis.

Prithvi Cafe
CAFE $$
(Map p750; Juhu Church Rd, Juhu; light meals ₹70-165; ⊙9am-11pm) A bohemian cafe on a large, shady terrace attached to the Prithvi Theatre that's something of a cultural hub of intellectuals, artists and theatre types. The snacky food – croissants, sandwiches, *chaat* (savoury snacks) and Punjabi standards – is OK, but it's the setting that's special.

★ Peshawri
NORTH INDIAN $$$
(Map p750; ✆28303030; ITC Maratha, Sahar Rd, Andheri East; meals ₹1100-2700; ⊙12.45-2.45pm & 7-11.45pm) Make this Northwest Frontier restaurant, outside the international airport, your first or last stop in Mumbai. The buttery *dhal bukhara* (a thick black dhal cooked for a day; ₹700) is perhaps the signature dish, but its kebabs are sublime: try the *peshawri* (chargrilled lamb marinated in yoghurt and spices).

Despite the five-star surrounds (and prices) you're encouraged to eat with your hands and the seating is low.

Culture Curry
SOUTH INDIAN, SEAFOOD $$$
(www.culturecurry.com; Kataria Rd, Matunga West; mains ₹260-500; ⊙noon-3.45pm & 7pm-12.30am) Exquisite dishes from all over the south, from Andhra and Coorg to Kerala, are the speciality here. Best for vegie and seafood dishes; the *prawn hirva rassa* (with green mango and coconut; ₹379) is a symphony of South Indian flavour. From Matunga Rd train station, it's about 750m west along Kataria Rd.

Salt Water Café
CAFE, FUSION $$$
(Map p750; www.saltwatercafe.in; 87 Chapel Rd, Bandra West; breakfasts ₹180-290, mains ₹410-650; ⊙12.30-3.30pm & 7.30-11.50pm; 🛜) A Bandra institution where filmi producers and expats socialise in the stylish air-conditioned dining room or buzzing terrace. Stick to the classic breakfasts, omelettes and sandwiches (₹350 to ₹410) as some of the zany fusion flavour combinations are perhaps too much of a culinary clash.

Eat Around the Corner
CAFE $$$
(Map p750; www.eataroundthecorner.in; cnr 24th & 30th Rds; light meals ₹250-400, mains ₹280-600; ⊙7am-1am; 🛜) Visually it's quite a concept, its minimalist interior replete with banquette and bench seating and a long, long display counter of tempting treats (falafel, soups, salads, cakes, pastries). Prices are high, not that the young, wealthy clientele seem bothered.

Drinking & Nightlife

Forget the capital, Mumbai is a city that really knows how to enjoy itself. Whatever your tipple and whatever your taste, you'll find it here – from dive bar to sky bar. Colaba is rich in unpretentious publike joints (but also has some very classy places), while

MUMBAI (BOMBAY) DRINKING & NIGHTLIFE

Bandra and Juhu are home turf for the filmi and model set. Some of the most intriguing new places are opening in midtown areas such as Lower Parel.

Wednesday and Thursday are big nights at some clubs, as well as the traditional Friday and Saturday; there's usually a cover charge. Dress codes apply, so don't rock up in shorts and sandals. The trend in Mumbai is towards resto-lounges as opposed to full-on nightclubs. You're also technically supposed to have a license to drink in Maharashtra; some bars require you to buy a temporary one, for a nominal fee.

🍷 Colaba

⭐ Harbour Bar
BAR

(Map p738; Taj Mahal Palace, Mumbai, Apollo Bunder; ⏰11am-11.45pm) With unmatched views of the Gateway of India and harbour, this timeless bar inside the Taj is an essential visit. Drinks aren't uber-expensive (₹395/800 for a beer/cocktail) given the surrounds and the fact they come with very generous portions of nibbles (including jumbo cashews).

⭐ Colaba Social
BAR

(Map p738; www.socialoffline.in; ground fl, Glen Rose Bldg, BK Boman Behram Marg, Apollo Bunder; ⏰9am-1.30am; 🛜) The Social opened with a

bang in late 2014, thanks to its stellar cocktail list (most are just ₹300 or so; try the Longest Island Ice Tea) and fab Colaba location. During the day it's a social-cum-workspace for laptop-toting, brunching creative types, but by 6pm the place is crammed with a raucous young crowd. Snacks (₹120 to ₹380) and espresso coffee are available.

Also hosts DJ and live-music events, art and photography exhibits and stand-up comedy acts.

Woodside Inn
PUB

(Map p738; Wodehouse Rd, Regal Circle; ⏰10am-1am) As close as you'll get to a London pub in Mumbai, this cosy place has a gregarious vibe and serves Gateway craft beers on draught (₹300); try the wheat beer. There's comfort food (mains ₹300 to ₹450) and a great daily happy hour (4pm to 8pm).

Cafe Mondegar
PUB

(Map p738; Metro House, 5A Shahid Bhagat Singh Rd; ⏰7.30pm-12.30am) Old-school bar that draws a mix of foreigners and locals who all cosy up together in the small space, bonding over the jukebox, which is cranked up to energise the crowd.

Busaba
LOUNGE

(Map p738; www.busaba.net; 4 Mandlik Marg; ⏰6.30pm-1am; 🛜) Sunken couches and contem-

---

QUEER MUMBAI

Mumbai's LGBTQ scene is still quite underground, especially for women, but it's gaining momentum. No dedicated LGBTQ bars/clubs have opened yet, but gay-friendly 'safe house' venues often host private gay parties (announced on Gay Bombay).

Humsafar Trust (Map p750; ☎022-26673800; www.humsafar.org; 3rd fl, Manthan Plaza Nehru Rd, Vakola, Santa Cruz East) Runs tons of programs and workshops; one of its support groups organises the monthly gathering 'Sunday High'. It's also closely connected to the erratically published but pioneering magazine **Bombay Dost** (www.bombaydost.co.in).

Galaxy (www.gaylaxymag.com) India's best gay e-zine; well worth consulting and has lots of Mumbai content.

Gay Bombay (www.gaybombay.org) A great place to start, with event listings including meet-ups in Bandra, GB-hosted bar and film nights, hiking trips and other info.

Kashish Mumbai International Queer Film Festival (www.mumbaiqueerfest.com) Excellent annual May event with a mix of Indian and foreign films; in 2014, 154 films from 31 countries were featured.

LABIA (Lesbian & Bisexuals in Action; labia_india@yahoo.com) Lesbian and bi support group based in Mumbai; provides a counselling service for women.

Queer Azaadi Mumbai (www.queerazaadi.wordpress.com) Organises Mumbai's Pride Parade, which is usually held in early February.

Queer Ink (www.queer-ink.com) Online publisher with excellent books, DVDs and merchandise. Also hosts a monthly arts event with speakers, workshops, poetry, comedy, music and a marketplace.

porary Buddha art give this restaurant-bar a loungey vibe. Cocktails are pricey (from ₹450) but potent and a DJ plays house on weekends. The upstairs **restaurant** (mains from ₹480) serves pan-Asian; its back room feels like a posh treehouse. Reserve ahead for dinner.

Leopold Cafe   BAR

(Map p738; www.leopoldcafe.com; cnr Colaba Causeway & Nawroji F Rd; ☉ 7.30am-12.30am) Love it or hate it, most tourists end up at this clichéd Mumbai travellers' institution at one time or another. Around since 1871, Leopold's has wobbly ceiling fans, crap service and a rambunctious atmosphere conducive to swapping tales with strangers. There's also food and a cheesy DJ upstairs on weekend nights.

Wink   NIGHTCLUB

(Vivanta by Taj, 90 Cuffe Pde; ☉ 6pm-1am) Saturday and Sunday are thumping here, but it's a classy place most nights with its sophisticated decor (low beige sofas, intricately carved screens), long whiskey list and famous Winktinis.

Fort Area & Churchgate

Dome   LOUNGE

(Map p740; Hotel InterContinental, 135 Marine Dr, Churchgate; ☉ 5.30pm-1.30am; 🕾) This white-on-white rooftop lounge has awesome views of Mumbai's crescent beach from its 8th-floor vantage. Cocktails (₹850 to ₹1200) beckon the hip young things of Mumbai each night. Indulge yourself with a Ki Garden (vodka, elderberry and cloudy apple juice) or nurse a Kingfisher (₹375).

Liv   NIGHTCLUB

(Map p740; 1st fl, 145 MG Rd, Kala Ghoda; cover per couple ₹3000; ☉ 10pm-1.30am Wed-Sat) Exclusive new Kala Ghoda club that draws an up-for-it crowd of SoBo (South Bombay) pretty young things with its out-there LED lighting and intimate feel. Musically, Wednesday is hip hop, on Friday it's Bollywood Boogie, while on Saturday EDM DJs let rip.

Kalbadevi to Mahalaxmi

Haji Ali Juice Centre   JUICE BAR

(Map p746; Lala Lajpatrai Rd, Haji Ali Circle; juices & snacks ₹30-180; ☉ 5am-1.30am) Serves fresh juices, milkshakes, mighty fine *falooda* and fruit salads. Strategically placed at the en-

trance to Haji Ali mosque, it's a great place to cool off after a visit.

Shiro   LOUNGE, NIGHTCLUB

(☑ 66511201; www.shiro.co.in; Bombay Dyeing Mills Compound, Worli; ☉ 7.30pm-1.30am) Visually this place is stunning, with water pouring from the hands of a towering Japanese goddess into lotus ponds, which reflect shimmering light on the walls. It's totally over the top, but the drinks (as well as the Asian-fusion dishes) are excellent. By 10.30pm or so it morphs into more of a club, with DJs spinning some mean salsa (Wednesday), disco (Friday) and house (Saturday). It's about 3km north of the Mahalaxmi Racecourse.

Ghetto   BAR

(Map p746; ☑ 23538418; 30 Bhulabhai Desai Marg, opp Tirupathi Apt; ☉ 7pm-1am) A grungy, graffiti-covered hang-out blaring classic and contemporary rock (Red Hot Chili Peppers, Rolling Stones) to a dedicated set of regulars. You can shoot pool here too.

Western Suburbs

★**Bonobo**   BAR

(Map p750; www.facebook.com/BonoboBandra; Kenilworth Mall, 33rd Rd, Bandra West, off Linking Rd; ☉ 6pm-1am; 🕾) The scenesters' first choice in Bandra, this bar champions underground and alternative music. DJs spin drum 'n' bass and electronica, big beats and funk tech-house, and musicians play folk and blues. There's a great rooftop terrace.

★**Aer**   LOUNGE

(Four Seasons Hotel, 34th fl, 114 Dr E Moses Rd, Worli; cover Fri & Sat after 8pm ₹2500; ☉ 5.30pm-midnight; 🕾) Boasting astounding sea, sunset and city views, Aer is Mumbai's premier sky bar. Drink prices are steep, but that's kind of the point: cocktails cost around ₹900, beers start at ₹350 and happy hour is 5.30pm to 8pm. A DJ spins house and lounge tunes nightly from 9pm.

Toto's Garage   BAR

(Map p750; ☑ 26005494; 30th Rd, Bandra West; ☉ 6pm-1am) Highly sociable, down-to-earth local dive done up in a car mechanic theme where you can go in your dirty clothes, drink draught beer (₹200 a glass) and listen to classic rock. Check out the upended VW Beetle above the bar. Always busy and has a good mix of guys and gals.

MUMBAI (BOMBAY) DRINKING & NIGHTLIFE

Daily BAR

(Map p750; SV Rd, Bandra; ⊘6pm-1.30am; 🛜) Hip and happening new Bandra bar that take its moniker from the good news stories the owners have collated (and suspended on pages from the ceiling). Attracts a lively crowd with decadent cocktails, sangria pitchers, snappy service and a cool indoor/outdoor design. Also hosts films and live music.

Trilogy NIGHTCLUB

(Map p750; www.trilogy.in; Hotel Sea Princess, Juhu Tara Rd, Juhu; cover per couple after 11pm ₹2000; ⊘10.30pm-3am Wed-Sat) This glam, glitzy Juhu club, like its clientele, is gorgeous, with two dance floors spectacularly illuminated by LED cube lights that are synced with the epic sound system. It's hip hop on Wednesday, house on Friday and EDM on Saturday.

Hoppipola BAR

(Map p750; 757 Ramee Guestline, MD Ali Quereshi Chowk, off SV Rd; ⊘noon-1am; 🛜) With its wacky design (including squadrons of toy planes suspended from the roof) and abundant board games, Hoppipola doesn't take itself too seriously, with decor that's more playschool than lounge bar. Get stuck into some test-tube shots or a tower of beer and it's perfect for a session of Jenga drinking games. Bar grub (from ₹200) is tasty too.

Olive Bar & Kitchen BAR

(Map p750; ☑26058228; www.olivebarandkitchen.com; 14 Union Park, Khar West; ⊘7.30pm-1am daily, plus noon-3.30pm Sat & Sun; 🛜) The watering hole of choice for Bandra's filmi elite and aspiring starlets, Olive is a Mediterranean-style bar-restaurant whose whitewashed walls, candle-lit terraces and rooms evoke Ibiza and Mykonos. It's the perfect setting for inspired Greek and Italian food (mains ₹600 to ₹1100) and vibing DJ sounds. Thursdays and weekends are packed. There's a second branch (Map p746; ☑40859595; Gate No 8, Mahalaxmi Racecourse; ⊘noon-3.30pm & 7.30pm-1.30am) in Mahalaxmi.

Big Nasty BAR

(Map p750; 1st fl, 12 Union Park, Khar West, above Shatranj Napoli; ⊘7pm-12.30am) The decor may be industrial, but the Nasty is fun and unpretentious. It's best known for its cheap(ish) drinks – beers from ₹220, wine from ₹350 and cocktails starting at ₹400.

Elbo Room PUB

(Map p750; St Theresa Rd, Khar West, off 33rd Rd; ⊘11am-1am) This publike place has a very so-cial vibe and an Italian-Indian menu that's best enjoyed on the plant-filled terrace.

⭐ Entertainment

Mumbai has an exciting live music scene, some terrific theatres, an emerging network of comedy clubs and, of course, cinemas and sporting action.

Consult **Mumbai Boss** (www.mumbaiboss.com), **Time Out Mumbai** (www.timeoutmumbai.net) and www.nh7.in for live-music listings. Unfortunately, Hindi films aren't shown with English subtitles. The cinemas we've listed all show English-language movies, along with some Bollywood numbers.

Mumbai has some great arts festivals, the major ones include the excellent Mumbai Film Festival (p737) in October, May's **Kashish-Mumbai International Queer Film Festival** (www.mumbaiqueerfest.com), Prithvi Theatre's November festival for excellent drama and music, and Mumbai Sanskruti (p737), which sees two days of Hindustani classical music. The National Centre for the Performing Arts hosts numerous cultural festivals throughout the year.

⭐ **Bluefrog** LIVE MUSIC

(☑61586158; www.bluefrog.co.in; D/2 Mathuradas Mills Compound, Senapati Bapat Marg, Lower Parel; admission ₹300-1200; ⊘6.30pm-1.30am Tue-Sat, from 11.30am Sun) Mumbai cultural mecca, a world-class venue for concerts (everything from indie to Mexican), stand-up comedy and lots of DJ-driven clubby nights (hip hop, house and techno). There's also a restaurant with space-age pod seating (book ahead for dinner) in the intimate main room. Happy hour is 6.30pm to 9pm.

National Centre for the Performing Arts THEATRE, LIVE MUSIC

(NCPA; Map p740; ☑66223737, box office 22824567; www.ncpamumbai.com; Marine Dr & Sri V Saha Rd, Nariman Point; tickets ₹200-800; ⊘box office 9am-7pm) This vast cultural centre is the hub of Mumbai's high-brow music, theatre and dance scene. In any given week, it might host experimental plays, poetry readings, photography exhibitions, a jazz band from Chicago or Indian classical music. Many performances are free. The box office (Map p740) is at the end of NCPA Marg.

Prithvi Theatre THEATRE

(Map p750; ☑26149546; www.prithvitheatre.org; Juhu Church Rd, Juhu; tickets ₹80-300) A Juhu institution that's a great place to see both

BOLLYWOOD DREAMS

Mumbai is the glittering epicentre of India's gargantuan Hindi-language film industry. From silent beginnings, with a cast of all-male actors (some in drag) in the 1913 epic *Raja Harishchandra,* and the first talkie, *Lama Ara* (1931), it now churns out more than 1000 films a year – more than Hollywood. Not surprising considering it has a captive audience of one-sixth of the world's population.

Every part of India has its regional film industry, but Bollywood continues to entrance the nation with its escapist formula in which all-singing, all-dancing lovers fight and conquer the forces keeping them apart. These days, Hollywood-inspired thrillers and action extravaganzas vie for moviegoers' attention alongside the more family-oriented saccharine formulas.

Bollywood stars can attain near godlike status in India and star-spotting is a favourite pastime in Mumbai's posher establishments. You can also see the stars' homes as well as a film/TV studio with **Bollywood Tours** (www.bollywoodtours.in; 8hr tour per person ₹6000), but you're not guaranteed to see a dance number and you may spend much of it in traffic.

Extra, Extra!

Studios sometimes want Westerners as extras to add a whiff of international flair (or provocative dress, which locals often won't wear) to a film.

If you're game, just hang around Colaba (especially the Salvation Army hostel) where studio scouts, recruiting for the following day's shooting, will find you. A day's work, which can be up to 16 hours, pays ₹500. You'll get lunch, snacks and (usually) transport. The day can be long and hot with loads of standing around the set; not everyone has a positive experience. Complaints range from lack of food and water to dangerous situations and intimidation when extras don't comply with the director's orders. Others describe the behind-the-scenes peek as a fascinating experience. Before agreeing to anything, always ask for the scout's identification and go with your gut.

MUMBAI (BOMBAY) ENTERTAINMENT

Hindi- and English-language theatre or an arthouse film, and there's a cafe (p763) for drinks. Its excellent international theatre festival in November showcases contemporary Indian theatre and includes international productions.

Canvas Laugh
COMEDY

(☑022-43485000; www.canvaslaughclub.com; 3rd fl, Palladium Mall, Phoenix Mills, Lower Parel; tickets ₹200-750) Popular comedy club that hosts around 50 shows per month, with twice-nightly programs on weekends. All comedians use English. It's 1km north of Mahalaxmi train station.

Comedy Store
COMEDY

(☑022-39895050; www.thecomedystore.in; D2 Mathuradas Mills Compound, Senapati Bapat Marg, Lower Parel; tickets from ₹400; ⊙8pm-midnight Tue & Sun) Stand-up comedy (in English) featuring established and upcoming Indian comedians that's always a good night out. It's based at the Bluefrog, but the Comedy Store also pops up at other venues across town; check the website for details.

Liberty Cinema
CINEMA, LIVE MUSIC

(Map p740; ☑9820027841; www.thelibertycinema.com; 41/42 New Marine Lines, near Bombay Hospital) Stunning art deco Liberty was once the queen of Hindi film – think red-carpet openings with Dev Anand. It fell on hard times in recent years, but is rebounding.

Mehboob Studios
LIVE MUSIC, GALLERY

(Map p750; ☑022-26421628; 100 Hill Rd, Bandra West) As well as live music, these famous film studios also host the annual Times Litfest (in December), art exhibitions and film screenings.

Wankhede Stadium
SPORTS

(Mumbai Cricket Association; Map p740; ☑22795500; www.mumbaicricket.com; D Rd, Churchgate; ⊙ticket office 11.30am-7pm Mon-Sat) Test matches and one-day internationals are played a few times a year in season (October to April). Contact the Cricket Association for ticket information; for a test match you'll probably have to pay for the full five days.

D Y Patil Stadium
SPORTS

(☑022-27731545; Yashwantrao Chavan Marg, Nerul, Navi Mumbai) A 55,000-capacity stadium that hosts the ISL's Mumbai City FC football team, plus occasional IPL cricket matches. It's 21km east of central Mumbai. Tickets are available at the gate.

Regal Cinema
CINEMA

(Map p738; ☑ 22021017; Shahid Bhagat Singh Rd, Regal Circle, Colaba; tickets ₹130-180) A faded art deco masterpiece that's good for both Hollywood and Bollywood blockbusters.

Eros
CINEMA

(Map p740; ☑ 22822335; www.eroscinema.co.in; Maharshi Karve Rd, Churchgate; tickets ₹100-170) To experience Bollywood blockbusters in situ, the Eros is the place.

Metro Big
CINEMA

(☑ 39894040; www.bigcinemas.com; MG Rd, New Marine Lines, Fort; tickets ₹130-600) This grand dame of Bombay talkies was just renovated into a multiplex.

🛍 Shopping

Mumbai is India's great marketplace, with some of the best shopping in the country.

Be sure to spend a day at the markets north of CST for the classic Mumbai shopping experience. In Fort, booksellers, with surprisingly good wares (not all pirated), set up shop daily on the sidewalks around Flora Fountain. Snap up a bargain backpacking wardrobe at Fashion Street (MG Rd), the strip of stalls lining MG Rd between Cross and Azad Maidans. Hone your bargaining skills. Kemp's Corner has many good shops for designer threads.

🛍 Colaba

Bungalow 8
CLOTHING, ACCESSORIES

(Map p738; www.bungaloweight.com; 1st, 2nd & 3rd fls, Grants Bldg, Arthur Bunder Rd; ☺10.30am-7.30pm) Original, high-end, artisanal clothing, jewellery, home decor and other objects of beauty, spread across three loftlike floors.

Phillips
ANTIQUES

(Map p738; www.phillipsantiques.com; Wodehouse Rd, Colaba; ☺10am-7pm Mon-Sat) Art deco and colonial-era furniture, wooden ceremonial masks, silver, Victorian glass and also high-quality reproductions of old photos, maps and paintings.

Cottonworld Corp
CLOTHING

(Map p738; ☑ 22850060; www.cottonworld.net; Mandlik Marg; ☺10.30am-8pm Mon-Sat, noon-8pm Sun) Stylish Indian-Western-hybrid

goods made from cotton, linen and natural materials (including er...paper made from rhino and elephant dung). Yes, you read that right. Only in India.

Bombay Electric
CLOTHING

(Map p738; www.bombayelectric.in; 1 Reay House, Best Marg; ☺11am-9pm) High fashion is the calling at this trendy, slightly overhyped unisex boutique, which it sells at top rupee alongside arty accessories and a handful of fashionable antiques.

Central Cottage
Industries Emporium
HANDICRAFTS, SOUVENIRS

(Map p738; ☑ 22027537; www.cottageemporium.in; Chhatrapati Shivaji Marg; ☺10am-6pm) Fair-trade souvenirs including pashminas. Second branch in Colaba (Map p738; Kamal Mansion, Arthur Bunder Rd; ☺11am-7pm Mon-Sat).

🛍 Fort Area & Churchgate

★Kitab Khana
BOOKS

(Map p740; www.kitabkhana.in; Somaiya Bhavan, 45/47 MG Rd, Fort; ☺10.30am-7.30pm) This bookstore has a brilliantly curated selection of books, all of which are 20% off all the time. There's a great little cafe (Map p740; www.cafefoodforthought.com; light meals ₹120-180) at the back.

★Contemporary Arts & Crafts
HOMEWARES

(Map p740; www.cac.co.in; 210 Dr Dadabhai Naoroji Rd, Fort; ☺10.30am-7.30pm) Modish, high-quality takes on traditional crafts: these are not your usual handmade souvenirs.

Artisans' Centre for
Art, Craft & Design
CLOTHING, ACCESSORIES

(Map p740; ☑ 22673040; 1st fl, 52-56 Dr VB Gandhi Marg, Kala Ghoda; ☺11am-7pm) Exhibits high-end handmade goods – from couture and jewellery to handicrafts and luxury *khadi* (homespun cloth).

Khadi & Village
Industries Emporium
CLOTHING

(Khadi Bhavan; Map p740; 286 Dr Dadabhai Naoroji Rd, Fort; ☺10.30am-6.30pm Mon-Sat) A dusty, 1940s time warp full of traditional Indian clothing, silk and *khadi,* and shoes.

Chimanlals
HANDICRAFTS

(Map p740; www.chimanlals.com; Wallace St, Fort; ☺9.30am-6pm Mon-Fri, to 5pm Sat) The beautiful traditional printed papers here will make you start writing letters.

BAZAAR DISTRICT

Mumbai's main market district is one of Asia's most fascinating, an incredibly dense combination of humanity and commerce that's a total assault on the senses. If you've just got off a plane from the West, or a taxi from Bandra – hold on tight. This working-class district stretches north of Crawford Market up as far as Chor Bazaar, a 2.5km walk away. Such are the crowds (and narrowness of the lanes), allow yourself two to three hours to explore it thoroughly.

You can buy just about anything here, but as the stores and stalls are very much geared to local tastes, most of the fun is simply taking in the street life and investigating the souklike lanes rather than buying souvenirs. The markets merge into each other in an amoeba-like mass, but there are some key landmarks so you can orientate yourself.

Crawford Market (Mahatma Phule Market; Map p746; cnr DN & Lokmanya Tilak Rds) Crawford Market is the largest in Mumbai, and contains the last whiff of British Bombay before the tumult of the central bazaars begins. Bas-reliefs by Rudyard Kipling's father, Lockwood Kipling, adorn the Norman Gothic exterior. Fruit and vegetables, meat and fish are mainly traded, but it's also an excellent place to stock up on spices. If you're lucky to be here during alphonso mango season (May to June) be sure to indulge.

Mangaldas Market (Map p746) Mangaldas Market, traditionally home to traders from Gujarat, is a minitown, complete with lanes of fabrics. Even if you're not the type to have your clothes tailored, drop by DD Dupattawala (Map p746; Shop No 217, 4th Lane, Mangaldas Market; ⊙9.30am-6.30pm) for pretty scarves and dupattas at fixed prices. Zaveri Bazaar (Map p746) for jewellery and Bhuleshwar Market (Map p746; cnr Sheikh Menon St & M Devi Marg) for fruit and veg are just north of here. Just a few metres further along Sheikh Menon Rd from Bhuleshwar is a Jain pigeon-feeding station, flower market and a religious market.

Chor Bazaar (Map p746) Chor Bazaar is known for its antiques, though nowadays much of it is reproductions; the main area of activity is Mutton St, where shops specialise in 'antiques' and miscellaneous junk. Dhabu St, to the east, is lined with fine leather goods.

Royal Music Collection   MUSIC STORE
(Map p740; 192 Kitab Mahal, Dr Dadabhai Naoroji Rd, Fort; ⊙11am-9pm Mon-Sat) Brilliant street stall selling vintage vinyl (from ₹250).

Fabindia   CLOTHING, HOMEWARES
(Map p740; www.fabindia.com; Jeroo Bldg, 137 MG Rd, Kala Ghoda; ⊙10am-8pm) Ethically sourced cotton and silk fashions and homewares in a modern-meets-traditional Indian shop.

Chetana Book Centre   BOOKS
(Map p740; www.chetana.com; K Dubash Marg, Kala Ghoda; ⊙10.30am-7.30pm Mon-Sat) This great spirituality bookstore has lots of books on Hinduism and a whole section on 'Afterlife/Death/Psychic'.

Standard Supply Co   PHOTOGRAPHY
(Map p740; ☏22612468; Walchand Hirachand Marg, Fort; ⊙10am-7pm Mon-Sat) Everything for digital and film photography.

Oxford Bookstore   BOOKS
(Map p740; www.oxfordbookstore.com; Apeejay House, 3 Dinsha Wachha Marg, Churchgate;

⊙8am-10pm) Spacious store with a good selection of travel books and a tea bar (teas ₹35-80; ⊙10am-10pm).

Kalbadevi to Mahalaxmi

Shrujan   HANDICRAFTS
(Map p746; www.shrujan.org; Sagar Villa, Bhulabhai Desai Marg, Breach Candy, opp Navroze Apts; ⊙10am-7.30pm Mon-Sat) Nonprofit that sells the intricately-embroidered clothing, bags, cushions covers and shawls of 3500 women in 114 villages in Kutch, Gujarat. There's also a (hard-to-find) Juhu branch (Map p750; Hatkesh Society, 6th North South Rd, JVPD Scheme; ⊙10am-7.30pm Mon-Sat).

Mini Market/Bollywood Bazaar   ANTIQUES, SOUVENIRS
(Map p746; ☏23472427; 33/31 Mutton St; ⊙11am-8pm Sat-Thu) Sells vintage Bollywood posters and other movie ephemera.

BX Furtado & Sons   MUSIC STORE
(Map p746; www.furtadosonline.com; Jer Mahal, Dhobi Talao; ⊙10.30am-7.30pm Mon-Sat) *The*

place in town for musical instruments: sitars, tablas, accordions and local and imported guitars.

Western Suburbs

Indian Hippy ART
(Map p750; ☑8080822022; www.hippy.in; 17/C Sherly Rajan Rd, Bandra West, off Carter Rd; portraits from ₹10,000; ⊙by appointment) Because you need to have your portrait hand-painted in the style of a vintage Bollywood poster. Bring (or email) a photo. Also sells LP clocks, vintage film posters and all manner of (frankly bizarre) Bollywood-themed products.

Play Clan SOUVENIRS, CLOTHING
(Map p750; www.theplayclan.com; Libra Towers, Hill Rd, Bandra West; ⊙11am-8.30pm) Kitschy, design-y goods that are pricey but the best in town. Check out the eye masks and cartoon Hanuman cushion covers.

Kishore Silk House CLOTHING, HANDICRAFTS
(Bhandarkar Rd, Matunga East; ⊙10am-8.30pm Tue-Sun) Handwoven saris and dhotis from Tamil Nadu and Kerala.

❶ Information

EMERGENCY
Call the **police** (☑100) for emergencies.

INTERNET ACCESS
Anita CyberCafé (Map p740; Cowasji Patel Rd, Fort; per hour ₹30; ⊙9am-10pm Mon-Sat, 2-10pm Sun) Opposite one of Mumbai's best chai stalls (open evenings).

Portasia (Map p740; Kitab Mahal, Dr Dadabhai Naoroji Rd, Fort; per hour ₹30; ⊙9am-9pm Mon-Sat) Its entrance is down a little alley.

MEDIA
To find out what's going on in Mumbai, check out the highly informative **Mumbai Boss** (www.mumbaiboss.com). The *Hindustan Times* is the best paper; its *Café* insert has a good what's-on guide. **Time Out Mumbai** (www.timeoutmum bai.net) no longer publishes a Mumbai magazine but its website is worth consulting.

MEDICAL SERVICES
Bombay Hospital (Map p740; ☑22067676, ambulance 22067309; www.bombayhospital. com; 12 New Marine Lines) A private hospital with the latest medical technology and equipment.

Breach Candy Hospital (Map p746; ☑23672888, emergency 23667809; www. breachcandyhospital.org; 60 Bhulabhai Desai Marg, Breach Candy) The best in Mumbai, if not India. It's 2km northwest of Chowpatty Beach.

MONEY
ATMs are everywhere, and foreign-exchange offices changing cash are also plentiful.

Thomas Cook (Map p738; ☑66092608; Colaba Causeway; ⊙9.30am-6pm) Has a branch in the Fort area also.

POST
Main post office (Map p740; Walchand Hirachand Marg; ⊙10am-7pm Mon-Sat, to 4pm Sun) The main post office is an imposing building beside CST. Poste restante (⊙10am-3pm Mon-Sat) is at the 'Delivery Department'. Letters should be addressed c/o Poste Restante, Mumbai GPO, Mumbai 400 001. Bring your passport to collect mail. Opposite the post office are parcel-wallahs who will stitch up your parcel for ₹40.

TELEPHONE
Call ☑197 for directory assistance.

TOURIST INFORMATION
Indiatourism (Government of India Tourist Office; Map p740; ☑22074333; www.incred ibleindia.com; Western Railways Reservation Complex, 123 Maharshi Karve Rd; ⊙8.30am-6pm Mon-Fri, to 2pm Sat) Provides information for the entire country, as well as contacts for Mumbai guides and homestays.

Maharashtra Tourism Development Corporation Booth (MTDC; ☑22841877; Apollo Bunder; ⊙8.30am-4pm Tue-Fri, to 9pm Sat & Sun) For city bus tours.

Maharashtra Tourism Development Corporation (MTDC; Map p740; ☑22044040; www. maharashtratourism.gov.in; Madame Cama Rd, Nariman Point; ⊙10am-5pm Mon-Sat, closed 2nd & 4th Sat) The MTDC's head office has helpful staff and lots of pamphlets to give away.

TRAVEL AGENCIES
Akbar Travels (www.akbartravelsonline.com; ⊙10am-7pm Mon-Fri, to 6pm Sat); Colaba (Map p738; ☑22823434; 30 Alipur Trust Bldg, Shahid Bhagat Singh Marg); Fort (Map p740; ☑22633434; 167/169 Dr Dadabhai Naoroji Rd) Extremely helpful and can book car/drivers and buses. Also has good exchange rates.

Thomas Cook (Map p740; ☑61603333; www. thomascook.in; 324 Dr Dadabhai Naoroji Rd, Fort; ⊙9.30am-6pm Mon-Sat) Flight and hotel bookings, plus foreign exchange.

VISAS
Foreigners' Regional Registration Office (FRRO; Map p740; ☑22620446; www.immigra

tionindia.nic.in; Annexe Bldg No 2, CID, Badaruddin Tyabji Marg, near Special Branch; ⏱9.30am-1pm Mon-Fri) Tourist and transit visas can no longer be extended except in emergency situations; check the latest online.

Getting There & Away

AIR

Mumbai's **Chhatrapati Shivaji International Airport** (BOM; Map p750; ☎66851010; www.csia.in), about 30km from the city centre, was nearing the end of a $2 billion modernisation program at the time of research. The impressive international terminal is complete, while its new domestic terminal should be fully operational some time in 2015, creating a fully integrated airport.

At the time of writing, the airport still comprised of one international terminal and a separate domestic terminal (also known locally as Santa Cruz airport) 5km away. A free shuttle bus runs between the two terminals every half-hour (journey time 15 minutes) for ticket-holders. Both terminals have ATMs, foreign-exchange counters and tourist-information booths.

Travel agencies and airlines' websites are usually best for booking flights. The following airlines have offices in town and/or at the airport:

Air India (Map p740; ☎27580777, airport 28318666; www.airindia.com; Air India Bldg, cnr Marine Dr & Madame Cama Rd, Nariman Point; ⏱9.30am-6.30pm Mon-Fri, to 5.15pm Sat & Sun) International and domestic routes.

Jet Airways (Map p740; ☎022-39893333; www.jetairways.com; B1, Amarchand Mansion, Madam Cama Rd, Colaba; ⏱9am-6pm Mon-Sat) India's second-largest domestic carrier.

Major nonstop domestic flights from Mumbai include the following:

DESTINATION	FARE (₹)	DURATION (HR)
Bengaluru	3700	1½
Chennai	5800	2
Delhi	5900	2
Goa	3300	1
Hyderabad	4200	1½
Jaipur	4300	1¾
Kochi	5700	2
Kolkata	6100	2¾
Nagpur	4200	1½

BUS

Numerous private operators and state governments run long-distance buses to and from Mumbai.

Long-distance government-run buses depart from the **Mumbai Central bus terminal** (Map

AIRPORT ARRIVAL

Many international flights arrive after midnight. Beat the daytime traffic by heading straight to your hotel, and carry detailed landmark directions: many airport taxi drivers don't speak English and may not use official street names.

p746; ☎enquiry 23024075; Jehangir Boman Behram Rd) right by Mumbai Central train station. They're cheaper and more frequent than private services, but standards are usually lower. The **MSRTC** (Maharashtra State Road Transport Corporation; ☎1800221250; www.msrtc.gov.in) website theoretically has schedules and is supposed to permit online booking, though in practice it's next to useless.

Private buses are usually more comfortable and simpler to book (if a bit more costly). Most depart from Dr Anadrao Nair Rd near Mumbai Central train station, but many buses to southern destinations depart from Paltan Rd, near Crawford Market. Check departure times and prices with **Citizen Travels** (Map p746; ☎23459695; www.citizenbus.com; D Block, Sitaram Bldg, Paltan Rd) or **National CTC** (Map p746; ☎23015652; Dr Anadrao Nair Rd). Fares to popular destinations (such as Goa) are up to 75% higher during holiday periods.

Private buses to Goa vary in price from ₹350 (bad choice) to ₹2600. Many leave from way out in the suburbs but **Chandni Travels** (Map p740; ☎22713901, 22676840) has six daily from in front of Azad Maidan and **Paolo Travel** (Map p740; ☎0832-6637777; www.paulotravels.com), with an 8pm daily departure from Fashion St, are convenient to the centre.

TRAIN

Three train systems operate out of Mumbai, but the most important services for travellers are Central Railways and Western Railways. Tickets for either system can be bought from any station that has computerised ticketing.

Central Railways (☎139), handling services to the east, south, plus a few trains to the north, operates from CST (also known as 'VT'). Foreign-tourist–quota tickets and Indrail passes can be bought at Counter 52.

Some Central Railways trains depart from Dadar (D), a few stations north of CST, or Lokmanya Tilak (LTT), 16km north of CST.

Western Railways (☎139) has services to the north from Mumbai Central train station, usually called Bombay Central (BCT). The **reservation centre** (Map p740; ⏱8am-8pm Mon-Sat, to 2pm Sun), opposite Churchgate station, has foreign-tourist–quota tickets.

ⓘ Getting Around

TO/FROM THE AIRPORTS

International

Prepaid Taxi Taxis with set fares cost ₹700/800 (non-AC/AC) to Colaba and Fort and ₹450/550 to Bandra. The journey to Colaba takes about an hour at night (via the Sealink) and 1½ to two hours during the day.

Autorickshaws Available but they only go as far south as Bandra (daytime/night around ₹180/240).

Train If you arrive during the day (but not during 'rush hour' – 6am to 11am) and are not weighed down with luggage, consider the train: take an autorickshaw (around ₹60) to Andheri train station and then the Churchgate or CST train (₹9, 45 minutes).

Taxi From South Mumbai to the international airport should be around ₹500. Allow two hours for the trip if you travel between 4pm and 8pm.

Domestic

There's a prepaid taxi counter in the arrivals hall. A non-AC/AC taxi costs ₹600/700 to Colaba or Fort and ₹370/480 to Bandra.

Alternatively, if it's not rush hour, catch an autorickshaw (around ₹45) to Vile Parle station, where you can get a train to Churchgate (₹8, 45 minutes).

BOAT

PNP (☑ 22885220) and **Maldar Catamarans** (☑ 22829695) run regular ferries to Mandwa (one way ₹125 to ₹155), useful for access to Murud-Janjira and other parts of the Konkan Coast, avoiding the long bus trip out of Mumbai. Buy **tickets** (Map p738) near the Gateway of India.

BUS

Few travellers bother with city buses but **BEST** (www.bestundertaking.com) has a useful search facility for hardcore shoestringers and masochists – you'll also need to read the buses'

Devanagiri numerals and beware of pickpockets. Fares start at ₹5.

CAR

Cars with driver can be hired for moderate rates. Air-conditioned cars start at ₹1550/1800 for half/full-day rental of around 80km.
Clear Car Rental (☑ 0888-8855220; www.clearcarrental.com)

Metro

The first section of Line 1, Mumbai's new **metro** (www.mumbaimetroone.com) opened in 2014. Initially it only connected seven stations in the far northern suburbs, well away from anywhere of interest to visitors. However Line 1 is scheduled to be extended south as far as Jacob Circle (5km north of Chhatrapati Shivaji Terminus) sometime in 2015, bringing it past Lower Parel.

Single fares cost between ₹10 and ₹20, with monthly Trip Passes (from ₹600) also available. Access to stations is by escalator, carriages are air-conditioned, and there are seats reserved for women and the disabled. Line 3 (a 33km underground line connecting Cuffe Pde south of Colaba, all the main railway terminals, Bandra and the airport) will be the next line to be constructed. It's been approved but won't open for many years.

MOTORCYCLE

Allibhai Premji Tyrewalla (Map p746; ☑ 23099313, 23099417; www.premjis.com; 205 Dr D Bhadkamkar (Lamington) Rd; ☺ 10am-7pm Mon-Sat) Sells new and used motorcycles with a guaranteed buy-back option. Long-term rental schemes (two months or more) start at around ₹25,000, with a buy-back price of around 60% after three months.

TAXI & AUTORICKSHAW

Mumbai's black-and-yellow taxis are inexpensive and the most convenient way to get around southern Mumbai; drivers *almost* always use the meter without prompting. The minimum fare is ₹21 (for up to 1.6km), a 5km trip costs about ₹50.

MAJOR LONG-DISTANCE BUS ROUTES

DESTINATION	PRIVATE NON-AC/AC SLEEPER (₹)	GOVERNMENT NON-AC (₹)	DURATION (HR)
Ahmedabad	400-650/500-2300	N/A	7-12
Aurangabad	400/550-900	472 (five daily)	9-11
Hyderabad	800-2500 (all AC)	N/A	16
Mahabaleshwar	400-2100 (all AC)	335 (three daily)	7-8
Panaji (Panjim)	600-750/700-2700	2400	14-16
Pune	250-735 (all AC)	224 (half-hourly)	3-5
Udaipur	800-1200/1500-2050	N/A	13-16

Consult www.makemytrip.com for latest schedules and prices

MAJOR TRAINS FROM MUMBAI

DESTINATION	TRAIN NO & NAME	SAMPLE FARE (₹)	DURATION (HR)	DEPARTURE
Agra	12137 Punjab Mail	580/1515/2195/3760 (A)	22	7.40pm CST
Ahmedabad	12901 Gujarat Mail	315/805/1135/1915 (A)	9	10pm BCT
	12009 Shatabdi Exp	960/1870 (C)	7	6.25am BCT
Aurangabad	11401 Nandigram Exp	235/620/885 (B)	7	4.35pm CST
	17617 Tapovan Exp	140/500 (C)	7	6.15am CST
Bengaluru	16529 Udyan Exp	505/1355/1975/3375 (A)	25	8.05am CST
Chennai	12163 Chennai Exp	570/1485/2145/3670 (A)	23½	8.30am CST
Delhi	12951 Rajdhani Exp	2030/2810/4680 (D)	16	4.35pm BCT
Hyderabad	12701 Hussain-sagar Exp	425/1115/1590/2695 (A)	14½	9.50pm CST
Indore	12961 Avantika Exp	440/1150/1640/2780 (A)	14	7.05pm BCT
Jaipur	12955 Jaipur Exp	535/1405/2025/3455 (A)	18	6.50pm BCT
Kochi	16345 Netravati Exp	615/1635/2400 (B)	25½	11.40am LTT
Madgaon (Goa)	10103 Mandovi Exp	390/1055/1520/2575 (A)	12	7.10am CST
	12133 Mangalore Exp	420/1100/1570 (B)	9	10pm CST
Pune	11301 Udyan Exp	485/690/1150 (D)	3½	8.05am CST

Station abbreviations: CST (Chhatrapati Shivaji Terminus); BCT (Mumbai Central); LTT (Lokmanya Tilak); D (Dadar). Fares: (A) sleeper/3AC/2AC/1AC, (B) sleeper/3AC/2AC, (C) sleeper/CC, (D) 3AC/2AC/1AC.

Autorickshaws are the name of the game north of Bandra. The minimum fare is ₹17, up to 1.6km, a 3km trip is about ₹30.

Both taxis and autorickshaws tack 25% onto the fare between midnight and 5am.

Tip: Mumbaikars tend to navigate by landmarks, not street names (especially new names), so have some details before heading out.

TRAIN

Mumbai's suburban train network is one of the world's busiest; forget travelling during rush hours. Trains run from 4am to 1am and there are three main lines:

Western Line The most useful; operates out of Churchgate north to Charni Rd (for Girgaum Chowpatty), Mumbai Central, Mahalaxmi (for the Dhobi Ghat), Bandra, Vile Parle (for the domestic airport), Andheri (for the international airport) and Borivali (for Sanjay Gandhi National Park), among others.

Central Line Runs from CST to Byculla (for Veermata Jijabai Bhonsle Udyan, formerly Victoria Gardens), Dadar and as far as Neral (for Matheran).

From Churchgate, 2nd-/1st-class fares are ₹5/48 to Mumbai Central, ₹8/85 to Vile Parle, and ₹9/116 to Borivali.

To avoid the queues, buy a **coupon book** (₹50), good for use on either train line, then 'validate' the coupons at the machines before boarding.

'Tourist tickets' permit unlimited travel in 2nd/1st class for one (₹75/225), three (₹115/415) or five (₹135/485) days.

Watch your valuables, and gals, stick to the ladies-only carriages except late at night, when it's more important to avoid empty cars.

Maharashtra

Best Places to Eat

➜ Malaka Spice (p805)
➜ Chaitanya (p797)
➜ Dario's (p805)
➜ Bhoj (p783)
➜ Little Italy (p809)

Best Places to Stay

➜ Hotel Sunderban (p804)
➜ Verandah in the Forest (p799)
➜ Beyond (p777)
➜ Hotel Panchavati (p781)
➜ Hotel Plaza (p791)

Why Go?

India's third-largest state, Maharashtra showcases many of India's iconic attractions. There are lazy, palm-fringed beaches, lofty, cool-green mountains, World Heritage Sites and bustling cosmopolitan cities. In the far east of the state are some of the nation's most impressive national parks, including the Tadoba-Andhari Tiger Reserve.

Inland lie the extraordinary cave temples of Ellora and Ajanta, undoubtedly Maharashtra's greatest monuments, hewn by hand from solid rock. Matheran, a colonial-era hill station served by a toy train, has a certain allure. Pilgrims and inquisitive souls are drawn to cosmopolitan Pune, a city famous for its 'sex guru' and alternative spiritualism. And westwards, the romantic Konkan Coast fringing the Arabian Sea is lined with spectacular, crumbling forts and sandy beaches, some of the best around the pretty resort of Malvan, which is fast becoming one of India's premier diving centres.

When to Go
Nasik

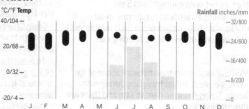

Jan It's party time at Nasik's wineries, marked by grape harvesting and crushing galas.

Sep The frenzied, energetic Ganesh Chaturthi celebrations reach fever pitch.

Dec Clear skies, mild temperatures; the secluded beaches of Murud, Ganpatipule and Tarkali are lovely.

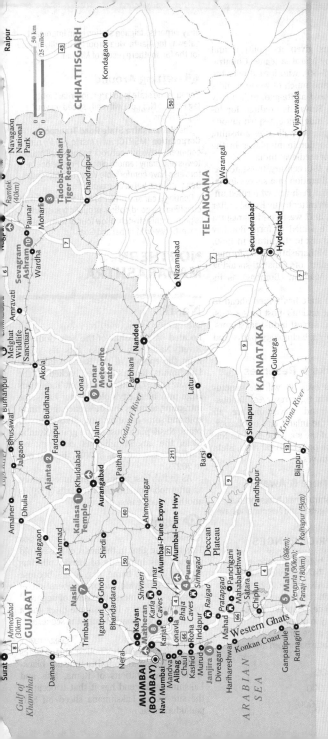

Maharashtra Highlights

1 Being amazed by the intricate beauty of the **Kailasa Temple** (p786) at Ellora

2 Wandering through ancient cave galleries at **Ajanta** (p788)

3 Searching for big cats inside **Tadoba-Andhari Tiger Reserve** (p793)

4 Delving into new-age spiritualism and modern Indian cuisine in diverse, progressive **Pune** (p801)

5 Diving or snorkelling in the big blue off **Malvan** (p797)

6 Wondering at the might of a lost civilisation at the colossal fort of **Janjira** (p794)

7 Sipping in the wine country around **Nasik** (p779)

8 Exploring the spectacular viewpoints at the hill station of **Matheran** (p798)

9 Contemplating the power of nature at the primordial **Lonar Meteorite Crater** (p793)

10 Learning about the Gandhian way of life at the **Sevagram Ashram** (p792)

History

Maharashtra was given its political and ethnic identity by Maratha leader Chhatrapati Shivaji (1627–80), who lorded over the Deccan plateau and much of western India from his stronghold at Raigad. Still highly respected today, Shivaji is credited for instilling a strong, independent spirit among the region's people, as well as establishing Maharashtra as a dominant player in the power relations of medieval India.

From the early 18th century, the state was under the administration of a succession of ministers called the Peshwas, who ruled until 1819, ceding thereafter to the British. After Independence in 1947, western Maharashtra and Gujarat were joined to form Bombay state. But it was back to the future in 1960, when modern Maharashtra was formed with the exclusion of Gujarati-speaking areas and with Mumbai (Bombay) as its capital.

Since then the state has forged ahead to become one of the nation's most prosperous, with one of India's largest industrial sectors, partly thanks to its technology parks and software exports.

National Parks & Reserves

Maharashtra has over 30 wildlife sanctuaries, including six tiger reserves: Tadoba-Andhari, Pench and Navagaon are all grouped around the inland city of Nagpur. In the far south of the state the Malvan National Marine Park protects coral reefs, islets and coastal mangroves.

ⓘ Getting There & Away

Mumbai is Maharashtra's main transport hub, though Pune, Aurangabad and Nagpur also have busy airports. Jalgaon station is an important gateway for Ajanta. Goa airport is handily placed for the far southern resort of Malvan.

ⓘ Getting Around

Because the state is so large, internal flights (eg Pune to Nagpur) will really speed up your explorations.

The **Maharashtra State Road Transport Corporation** (MSRTC; www.msrtc.gov.in) runs a comprehensive bus network spanning all major towns and many remote places. Private operators also have comfortable Volvo and Mercedes Benz services between major cities.

Renting a car and driver to explore the Konkan coastline is a good option as public transport is poor on this stretch: allow four or five days to travel between Mumbai and Goa.

NORTHERN MAHARASHTRA

Nasik

📞 0253 / POP 1.57 MILLION / ELEV 565M

Located on the banks of the holy Godavari River, Nasik (or Nashik) gets its name from the episode in the Ramayana where Lakshmana, Rama's brother, hacked off the *nasika* (nose) of Ravana's sister. Today this large provincial city's old quarter has some intriguing temples that reference the Hindu epic and some huge bathing ghats. Every 12 years, Nasik plays host to the grand Kumbh Mela, the largest religious gathering on Earth (the last one was in 2015, the next one in 2027).

As India's best wines are produced locally, an afternoon touring the vineyards (p779) is another good reason to drop by.

⊙ Sights

Ramkund   GHAT

This bathing ghat in the heart of Nasik's old quarter sees hundreds of Hindu pilgrims arriving daily to bathe, pray and – because the waters provide *moksha* (liberation of the soul) – to immerse the ashes of departed friends and family. It's a shame litter and a scruffy adjacent market taint the scene.

Kala Rama Temple   HINDU TEMPLE

(⊙ 6am-10pm) The city's holiest shrine dates back to 1794 and contains unusual black-stone representations of Rama, Sita and Lakshmana. Legend has it that it occupies the site where Lakshmana sliced off Surpanakha's nose.

Gumpha Panchavati   HINDU TEMPLE
(⊙6am-9.30pm) Sita is said to have hid in this cavelike temple while being assailed by the evil Ravana. You'll have to stoop and shuffle into the cave as the entrance is very narrow.

🛌 Sleeping

Hotel Samrat   HOTEL $
(☑2577211; www.hotelsamratnasik.com; Old Agra Rd; s/d from ₹950/1330, with AC ₹1580/1820; ✳🛜) Offering good value, with comfortable rooms that have large windows and pine furniture; the budget options have garish colour schemes, the upmarket rooms are more restrained. Located right next to the bus stand, its spick-and-span vegetarian restaurant is open 24 hours, making it popular as a refuelling stop.

Hotel Abhishek   HOTEL $
(☑2514201; www.hotelabhishek.com; Panchavati Karanja; s/d from ₹370/490, with AC ₹770/830; ✳🛜) Found just off the Panchavati Karanja roundabout, this decent budget place offers clean if ageing rooms, hot showers (mornings only) and appetising vegetarian food. Service varies a bit according to who is on reception duty.

Hotel Panchavati   HOTEL $
(☑2575771; www.panchavatihotels.com; 430 Chandak Wadi, Vakil Wadi Rd; s/d incl breakfast ₹1300/1500, with AC from ₹1500/1900; ✳🛜) This hotel in a sprawling complex contains a multitude of different room categories, two good restaurants and a bar. Rooms are perhaps a little dated (expect uniquely Indian mismatched decor) but spacious, kept clean and pretty well maintained. Wi-fi access is only in the lobby.

Ibis   HOTEL $$
(☑0253-6635555; www.ibis.com; Trimback Rd; s/d ₹2580/2760; ✳🛜) Sleek, modern, well-equipped, smallish rooms that boast fine-quality beds and linen; wi-fi is fast and reliable. With a good restaurant, gym and 24-hour room service, it all adds up to a great package. Located 4km west of the centre.

Ginger   HOTEL $$
(☑0253-6616333; www.gingerhotels.com; Plot P20, Satpur MIDC, Trimbak Rd; s/d ₹3060/3670; ✳🛜) Primarily a business hotel, it features DIY service, but there are luxe features and conveniences aplenty, and rooms have blonde wood, high cleanliness standards and swish ensuites, and are fresh and in-

TOP STATE FESTIVALS

Naag Panchami (⊙Jul/Aug) A traditional snake-worshipping festival, held in Pune and Kolhapur.

Ganesh Chaturthi (⊙Aug/Sep) Celebrated with fervour all across Maharashtra; Pune goes particularly hysteric in honour of the elephant-headed deity.

Dussehra (⊙Sep & Oct) A Hindu festival, but it also marks the Buddhist celebration of the anniversary of the famous humanist and Dalit leader BR Ambedkar's conversion to Buddhism.

Ellora Ajanta Aurangabad Festival (⊙Nov) Aurangabad's cultural festival brings together the best classical and folk performers from across the region, while promoting a number of artistic traditions and handicrafts on the side.

Kalidas Festival (⊙Nov) Commemorates the literary genius of legendary poet Kalidas through spirited music, dance and theatre in Nagpur.

Sawai Gandharva Sangeet Mahotsav (⊙Dec) An extravaganza of unforgettable performances by some of the heftiest names in Indian classical music in Pune.

viting. It's around 4km west of the central district.

★Beyond   RESORT $$$
(☑09970090010; www.sulawines.com; Gangapur-Savargaon Rd; d/ste incl breakfast from ₹7750; ✳✳) Sula Vineyards' luxury resort is set by a lake and bordered by rolling hills, where you can roam the landscape on bicycles, go kayaking on the still waters or laze the hours away at the spa or games room. Its 32 beautifully designed, contemporary rooms are pricey but very tasteful and the in-house dining options are great.

🍴 Eating

Shilpa's Food Lounge   INDIAN, MULTICUISINE $
(Vakil Wadi Rd; meals ₹60-150; ⊙8.30am-11pm; 🛜) A clean, modern and welcoming new place in the heart of town with good selection of Indian, continental and Chinese food, plus air-con. The *misal pav* (₹45), an unusual Maharashtrian breakfast prepared

Nasik

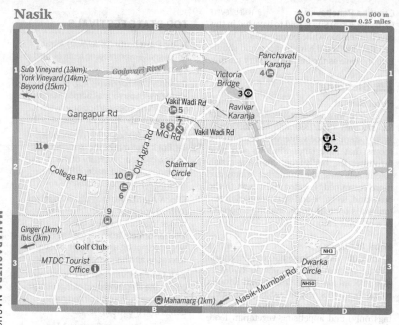

with bean sprouts and served with bread, is the best in town.

Khyber MUGHLAI, MULTICUISINE **$$**
(Hotel Panchavati, 430 Chandak Wadi, Vakil Wadi Rd; mains ₹180-300; ⊙11.30am-11.30pm) At the Hotel Panchavati, this restaurant is known for its delectable Afghani-style dishes, including *murgh shaan-e-khyber* (chicken marinated with herbs and cooked in a creamy gravy).

Soleil by La Plage FRENCH, INDIAN **$$$**
(⊡7722020927; Sula Vineyards, Gangapur-Savargaon Rd; meals ₹600-1100; ⊙12.30-3.30pm & 7.30-10.30pm) Spectacular new restaurant on the Sula estate, created by the French owners of a famous Goan establishment. The design is urban and bohemian, with hip seating and lots of space for a serious gastronomic feast. Stick to Gallic classics like the *coq au vin*, though Indian and international dishes are also available (as are Sula wines, of course).

ℹ Information

Cyber Café (Vakil Wadi Rd; per hour ₹20; ⊙10am-10pm) Staff are friendly and helpful.
MTDC Tourist Office (⊡2570059; www.maharashtratourism.gov.in; T/I, Golf Club, Old Agra Rd; ⊙10.30am-5.30pm Mon-Sat) About 1km south of the Old Central bus stand; helpful staff.

ℹ Getting There & Around

BUS

The **New Central bus stand** has services to Aurangabad (semideluxe ₹292, 4½ hours) and Pune (semideluxe/deluxe ₹308/570, 4½ hours). Nasik's **Old Central bus stand** (CBS; ⊡0253-

2309310) has buses to Trimbak (₹35, 45 minutes). South of town, the **Mahamarg bus stand** has services to Mumbai Central (semi deluxe ₹278, four hours) and Shirdi (₹114, 2½ hours). Private bus agents based near the CBS run buses to Pune, Mumbai, Aurangabad and Ahmedabad. Most buses depart from Old Agra Rd, and most Mumbai-bound buses terminate at Dadar in Mumbai.

TRAIN

The Nasik Rd train station is 8km southeast of the town centre, but a useful **railway reservation office** (1st fl, Commissioner's Office, Canada Corner; ⊙8am-8pm Mon-Sat) is 500m west of the Old Central bus stand. There are around 15 daily trains to Mumbai so you won't have to wait long; these include the daily Pushpak Express (1st/2nd/3rd class ₹1230/735/535, 4½ hours, 3.15pm). There are four daily departures to Aurangabad; try the Tapovan Express (2nd class/chair ₹85/320, 3½ hours, 9.50am). An autorickshaw to the station costs about ₹125.

Around Nasik

Bhandardara

The picturesque village of Bhandardara is nestled deep in the folds of the Sahyadris, about 70km from Nasik. A little-visited place surrounded by craggy mountains, it is one of Maharashtra's best escapes from the bustle of urban India.

Most of Bhandardara's habitation is thrown around **Arthur Lake**, a horseshoe-shaped reservoir fed by the waters of the Pravara River. The lake is barraged on one side by the imposing **Wilson Dam**, a colonial-era structure dating back to 1910. If you like walking, consider a hike to the summit of **Mt Kalsubai**, which at 1646m was once used as an observation point by the Marathas. Alternatively, you could hike to the ruins of the **Ratangad Fort**, another of Shivaji's erstwhile strongholds, which has wonderful views of the surrounding ranges.

The charming **Anandvan Resort** (☑9920311221; www.anandvanresorts.com; d from ₹7350; ❊), a hilltop hotel with a choice of comfy cottages and villas overlooking Arthur Lake, allows you to sleep in style, while the **MTDC Holiday Resort** (☑0242-4257032; budget/deluxe r from ₹1100/4000; ❊), further down the hill, has both renovated comfortable rooms and reasonable budget options.

Bhandardara can be accessed by taking a local bus from Nasik's Mahamarg bus stand

GRAPES OF NASIK

From wimpy raisins to full-bodied wines, the grapes of Nasik have come a long way. The surrounding region had been producing table grapes since ancient times. However, it was only in the early 1990s that a couple of entrepreneurs realised that Nasik, with its fertile soils and temperate climate, boasted good conditions for wine cultivation. In 1997 industry pioneer Sula Vineyards fearlessly invested in a crop of sauvignon blanc and chenin blanc, and the first batch of domestic wines hit the shelves in 2000. Nasik hasn't looked back.

These days, the wine list in most of Nasik's wineries has stretched to include shiraz, merlot, cabernet, semillon and zinfandel as well as a few sparkling wines, and most of these drops can be sampled first-hand by visiting one of the estates.

During harvest season (January to March), some wineries also organise grape-crushing festivals, marked by unbridled revelry. Events are usually advertised on the wineries' websites.

Sula Vineyards (☑09970090010; www.sulawines.com; Gangapur-Savargaon Rd, Govardhan; ⊙11am-10pm) Sula Vineyards, 15km west of Nasik, offers a slick, professional tour (around 45 minutes) of its impressive estate and high-tech facilities. This is rounded off with a wine-tasting session (four/six wines ₹150/250) that features its best drops and offers excellent tasting tips. The cafe here has commanding views of the countryside (though only snacks are sold and it does get very busy); for meals the neighbouring French restaurant Soleil by La Plage is recommended.

York Winery (☑0253-2230700; www.yorkwinery.com; Gangapur-Savargaon Rd, Gangavarhe; ⊙noon-10pm, tours 12.30-6pm) A further kilometre from Sula Vineyards, York Winery offers tours and wine-tasting sessions (₹100) in a top-floor room that has scenic views of the lake and surrounding hills. Five reds, a rosé and chenin blanc are produced. There's a large garden where continental snacks (olives, cheeses) are offered.

to Ghoti (₹38, one hour), from where an auto-rickshaw ride costs ₹90. A taxi from Nasik can also drop you at your resort for about ₹1500.

Igatpuri

Heard of *vipassana*, haven't you? Well head to Igatpuri to see where (and how) it all happens. Located about 44km south of Nasik, this village is home to the headquarters of the world's largest *vipassana* meditation institution, the **Vipassana International Academy** (☎02553-244076; www.dhamma.org; donations accepted), which institutionalises this strict form of meditation first taught by Gautama Buddha in the 6th century BC and reintroduced to India by teacher SN Goenka in the 1960s. Ten-day residential courses (advance bookings compulsory) are held throughout the year, though teachers warn that it requires rigorous discipline. Basic accommodation, food and meditation instruction are provided free of charge, but donations upon completion are accepted. Consult the academy website for detailed transport information; options from Nasik include share taxi and state bus links (both leave from the New Central bus stand).

Trimbak

Trimbakeshwar Temple HINDU TEMPLE
(entrance ₹200 to avoid queue; ⊙5.30am-9pm) The moody Trimbakeshwar Temple stands in the centre of Trimbak, 33km west of Nasik. It's one of India's most sacred temples, containing a *jyoti linga*, one of the

TOP YOGA & MEDITATION CENTRES

The Vipassana International Academy in Igatpuri has long been a destination for those wishing to put mind over matter through an austere form of Buddhist meditation. The boundaries of yoga, on the other hand, are constantly pushed at the Ramamani Iyengar Memorial Yoga Institute (p804) in Pune and the Kaivalyadhama Yoga Hospital (p799) in Lonavla. For a more lavish and indulgent form of spiritual engagement, there's the superluxurious Osho International Meditation Resort (p803) in Pune, where one can meditate in style, while flexing a few muscles in the unique game of zennis (Zen tennis).

12 most important shrines to Shiva. Only Hindus are allowed in, but non-Hindus can peek into the courtyard. Nearby, the waters of the Godavari River flow into the **Gangadwar bathing tank**, where all are welcome to wash away their sins. Regular buses run from the Old Central bus stand in Nasik to Trimbak (₹30, 45 minutes).

Aurangabad

☑0240 / POP 1.28 MILLION / ELEV 515M

Aurangabad lay low through most of the tumultuous history of medieval India and only hit the spotlight when the last Mughal emperor, Aurangzeb, made the city his capital from 1653 to 1707. With the emperor's death came the city's rapid decline, but the brief period of glory saw the building of some fascinating monuments, including a Taj Mahal replica (Bibi-qa-Maqbara), and these continue to draw a steady trickle of visitors. Alongside other historic relics, such as a group of ancient Buddhist caves, these Mughal relics make Aurangabad a good choice for a weekend excursion from Mumbai. But the real reason for traipsing here is because the town is an excellent base for exploring the World Heritage Sites of Ellora and Ajanta.

Silk fabrics were once Aurangabad's chief revenue generator, and the town is still known across the world for its hand-woven Himroo and Paithani saris.

The train station, cheap hotels and restaurants are clumped together in the south of the town along Station Rd East and Station Rd West. The MSRTC bus stand is 1.5km to the north of the train station. Northeast of the bus stand is the buzzing old town, with its narrow streets and Muslim quarter.

◉ Sights

★**Bibi-qa-Maqbara** MONUMENT
(Indian/foreigner ₹5/100; ⊙dawn-10pm) Built by Aurangzeb's son Azam Khan in 1679 as a mausoleum for his mother Rabia-ud-Daurani, Bibi-qa-Maqbara is widely known as the poor man's Taj. With its four minarets flanking a central onion-domed mausoleum, the white structure certainly does bear a striking resemblance to Agra's Taj Mahal. It is much less grand, however, and apart from having a few marble adornments, namely the plinth and dome, much of the structure is finished in lime mortar.

Apparently the prince conceived the entire mausoleum in white marble, but was thwarted by his frugal father who opposed his extravagant idea of draining state coffers for the purpose. However, despite the use of cheaper material and the obvious weathering, it's a sight far more impressive than the average gravestone.

The Bibi's formal gardens are a delight to explore, with the Deccan hills providing a scenic backdrop.

Aurangabad Caves CAVES
(Indian/foreigner ₹5/100; ⊙ dawn-dusk) Architecturally speaking, the Aurangabad Caves aren't a patch on Ellora or Ajanta, but they do throw some light on early Buddhist architecture and, above all, make for a quiet and peaceful outing. Carved out of the hillside in the 6th or 7th century AD, the 10 caves, comprising two groups 1km apart (retain your ticket for entry into both sets), are all Buddhist. Cave 7, with its sculptures of scantily clad lovers in suggestive positions, is a perennial favourite.

The caves are about 2km north of Bibi-qa-Maqbara. A return autorickshaw from the mausoleum shouldn't cost more than ₹180 including waiting time.

Panchakki GARDENS
(Indian/foreigner ₹5/20; ⊙ 6.15am-9.15pm) The garden complex of Panchakki, literally meaning 'water wheel', takes its name from the ancient hydromill which, in its day, was considered a marvel of engineering. It's still in working condition but is today really only of minor interest (unless you're a hydro-engineer perhaps).

Baba Shah Muzaffar, a Sufi saint and spiritual guide to Aurangzeb, is buried here. His memorial garden, flanked by a series of fish-filled tanks, is at the rear of the complex.

Shivaji Museum MUSEUM
(Dr Ambedkar Rd; admission ₹5; ⊙ 10.30am-6pm Fri-Wed) This simple museum is dedicated to the life of the Maratha hero Shivaji. Its collection includes a 500-year-old chain-mail suit and a copy of the Quran, handwritten by Aurangzeb.

☞ Tours

Classic Tours (☑ 2337788; www.classictours. info; MTDC Holiday Resort, Station Rd East) and the **Indian Tourism Development Corporation** (ITDC; ☑ 2331143; MTDC Holiday Resort, Station Rd East) both run daily bus tours to the Ajanta and Ellora Caves. Be aware that these are mass-market tours popular with domes-

tic tourists and designed to cover as much ground as possible in a short period of time. The trip to Ajanta Caves costs ₹450 and the tour to Ellora Caves, ₹325; prices include a guide but don't cover admission fees. The Ellora tour also includes all the other major Aurangabad sites along with Daulatabad Fort and Aurangzeb's tomb in Khuldabad, which is a lot to swallow in a day. All tours start and end at the MTDC Holiday Resort.

Ashoka Tours & Travels TOURS
(☑ 2359102, 9890340816; www.touristaurangabad. com; Hotel Panchavati, Station Rd West; ⊙ 8am-8pm) The stand-out Aurangabad agency, with excellent city and regional tours and decent car hire at fair rates. Prices for an aircon car and up to four people are ₹2400 for Ellora and ₹1400 for Ajanta. Run by Ashok T Kadam, a knowledgeable former autorickshaw driver.

🛏 Sleeping

★ Hotel Panchavati HOTEL $
(☑ 2328755; www.hotelpanchavati.com; Station Rd West; s/d ₹1000/1130, with AC ₹1150/1250; ✳@☎) The best budget hotel in town, the Panchavati is run by ever-helpful, switched-on managers who understand travellers' needs. Rooms are compact but thoughtfully appointed, with comfortable beds that have paisley-style bedspreads and 24-hour hot water (and room service). There are two restaurants and a bar, and it's a great place to hook up with other traveller.

Also home to the ever-reliable Ashoka Tours & Travels, which offers trips to Ellora and Ajanta.

Hotel Oberoi HOTEL $
(☑ 2323841; www.hoteloberoi.in; Osmanpura Circle, Station Rd East; s/d ₹900/1000, with AC ₹1260/1380; ✳☎) Cheekily named, and nothing to do with the five-star chain, this renovated hotel is owned by the same people behind Hotel Panchavati so there's good service and helpful staff. The spacious rooms are modern with flat-screen TVs and comfy beds, and the attractive bathrooms are in good shape. Call for a free pick-up from the train or bus stations.

Hotel Regal Plaza HOTEL $
(☑ 0240-2329322; www.hotelregalplaza.com; Station Rd West; s/d ₹870/990, with AC ₹1110/1200; ✳☎) Its mirror facade is a bit bling but staff here take care of guests and the light, airy rooms are in good shape and all have

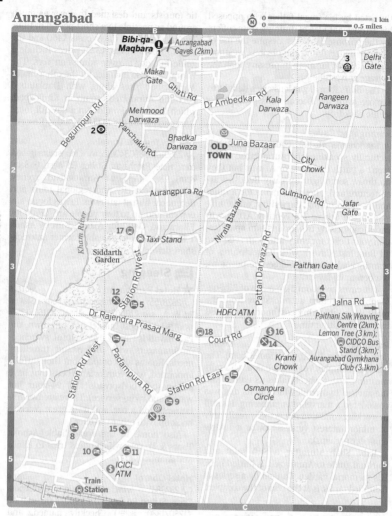

Bibi-qa-Maqbara
Aurangabad Caves (2km)
Makai Gate
Ghati Rd
Dr Ambedkar Rd
Kala Darwaza
Delhi Gate
Rangeen Darwaza
Begumpura Rd
Mehmood Darwaza
Panchakki Rd
Bhadkal Darwaza
Juna Bazaar
OLD TOWN
City Chowk
Aurangpura Rd
Gulmandi Rd
Jafar Gate
Kham River
Nirala Bazaar
Taxi Stand
Siddarth Garden
Station Rd West
Pattan Darwaza Rd
Paithan Gate
Dr Rajendra Prasad Marg
HDFC ATM
Paithani Silk Weaving Centre (2km);
Lemon Tree (3 km);
CIDCO Bus Stand (3km);
Aurangabad Gymkhana Club (3.1km)
Jalna Rd
Court Rd
Kranti Chowk
Station Rd West
Padampura Rd
Station Rd East
Osmanpura Circle
ICICI ATM
Train Station

cable TV. Pick-ups and drop-offs from bus and train stations are complimentary and value-for-money tours are offered. There's a dining room for Indian and Chinese meals.

MTDC Holiday Resort
HOTEL $

(☎ 2331513; Station Rd East; d from ₹1420, with AC from ₹1980; ✳) Very close to the train station, this curiously disorganised state-owned hotel has rooms that vary quite a bit: all are spacious but maintenance is an issue so take a look at a few. There's a well-stocked bar, a restaurant and a couple of travel agencies (for Ellora and Ajanta tours) on-site.

Keys Hotel
HOTEL $$

(☎ 0240-6654000; www.keyshotels.com; Padampura Circle; r/ste from ₹3160/4560; ✳✺) A modern, inviting hotel a kilometre from the train station where the rooms have a contemporary look, featuring laminate flooring, attractive wooden desks and wardrobes, and good beds with luxury linen. There's a gym (with free weights) and the in-house restaurant is a good bet for a bite.

Aurangabad Gymkhana Club
HOTEL $$

(☎ 0240-2476501; Mukunwadi Circle, Airport Rd; s/d from ₹2560/2860; ✳✺✺) Near the airport, this large hotel is perfect for exercise

Aurangabad

junkies with a 40m pool and one of the best gyms in the city. Its design is a little odd, with rooms around a covered courtyard but all are very spacious (the renovated ones are modern and worth the extra rupees). In-house dining is very tasty and good value. Service is a little chaotic but well-meaning.

Hotel Green Olive   HOTEL $$
(☑0240-2329490; www.dasilvascoffee.com; 13/3 Bhagya Nagar, off Station Rd West; r from ₹3700; ❋⊚) Impressive newcomer with a boutique-ish feel thanks to its stylish, well-equipped and well-maintained rooms. The staff here look after guests well and can organise transport and tours.

Hotel Amarpreet   HOTEL $$
(☑6621133; www.amarpreethotel.com; Jalna Rd; s/d from ₹3880/5170; ❋⊚◈⊠) Dated though spacious rooms, but the all-smiles management makes up for it with polite service, excellent housekeeping and a great selection

of food and booze. Located on a busy road, so ask for a room away from the traffic.

VITS   HOTEL $$
(☑2350701; www.vitshotelaurangabad.com; Station Rd East; r/ste incl breakfast ₹4680/8190; ❋⊚◈⊠) Handy to the train station, this city-centre landmark is now looking dated but its location is still a winner. Rooms are well-equipped and decent value, but the dining situation and complimentary breakfast is poor (a renovation of the cafe is planned, management says). There's a small gym.

⭐**Lemon Tree**   HOTEL $$$
(☑6603030; www.lemontreehotels.com; R7/2 Chikalthana, Airport Rd; r incl breakfast from ₹5590; ❋⊚◈⊠) The Lemon Tree offers elegance and class, looking more like a billionaire's luxury whitewashed Mediterranean villa than an Indian hotel. It's well designed too: all rooms face inwards, overlooking perhaps the best pool on the Deccan plateau, all 50m of it. The standard rooms, though not large, are brightened by vivid tropical tones offset against snow-white walls. Located near the airport, 6km from the centre.

✖ Eating

Swad Veg Restaurant   INDIAN $
(Kanchan Chamber, Station Rd East; mains ₹70-130) Swad offers a great range of Indian snacks and staples, such as dosas, plus a few pizzas, ice creams and shakes. Try the Gujarati thali (₹170), an endless train of dishes that diners gobble up under the benevolent gaze of patron saint swami Yogiraj Hanstirth.

Kailash   INDIAN $
(Station Rd East; mains ₹85-120; ⊙8am-11pm) This busy pure-veg restaurant looks and feels vaguely like an Indian take on an American diner, with big portions in familial surrounds. There's lots of Punjabi and South Indian food, as well as rice and noodle dishes, and an air-conditioned section.

⭐**Bhoj**   INDIAN $$
(Station Rd West; thalis ₹180; ⊙11am-3pm & 7-11pm) Rightly famous for its delicious unlimited Rajasthani and Gujarati thalis, Bhoj is a wonderful place to refuel and relax after a hard day on the road (or rail). It's on the 1st floor of a somewhat scruffy little shopping arcade, but the decor, ambience, service and presentation are all first rate.

MAHARASHTRA AURANGABAD

Hotel Panchavati
MULTICUISINE **$$**

(Station Rd West; mains ₹60-280; ⊙7am-10pm; 🖼) This budget hotel's restaurant has Chinese and Korean food in addition to an extensive Indian menu and cold beer. Ambience isn't a selling point here, but it's air-conditioned and staff are friendly.

Tandoor
NORTH INDIAN **$$**

(Shyam Chambers, Station Rd East; mains ₹160-290) Offers fine tandoori dishes and flavoursome North Indian veg and nonveg options in a weirdly Pharaonic atmosphere. Try the wonderful sizzler kebabs. A few Chinese dishes are also on offer, but patrons clearly prefer the dishes coming out of the tandoor.

🔒 Shopping

Himroo material is a traditional Aurangabad speciality made from cotton, silk and silver threads. Most of today's Himroo shawls and saris are produced using power looms, but some showrooms still stock handloomed cloth.

Himroo saris start at around ₹1200, for a cotton and silk blend. Paithani saris, which are of a superior quality, range from ₹5000 to ₹300,000 – but some of them take more than a year to make. Make sure you get authentic Himroo, not 'Aurangabad silk'.

Paithani Silk Weaving Centre
TEXTILES

(www.paithanisilk.com; 54, P-1, Town Center, Lokmat Nagar; ⊙11.30am-8pm) One of the best places to come and watch weavers at work is the Paithani Silk Weaving Centre where you'll find good-quality items for sale. It's about 6km east of Kranti Chowk (behind the Air India office), so take a taxi.

ℹ️ Information

MTDC Office (✉2331513; MTDC Holiday Resort, Station Rd East; ⊙10am-5.30pm Mon-Sat) Quite helpful and has a stock of brochures.
Post Office (Juna Bazaar; ⊙10am-6pm Mon-Sat)
Sai Internet Café (Station Rd East; per hour ₹15; ⊙8am-10pm) Has reliable connections; one of several on this block.
State Bank of India (Kranti Chowk; ⊙11am-5pm Mon-Fri, to 1pm Sat) Handles foreign exchange.

ℹ️ Getting There & Away

AIR

The airport is 10km east of town. Daily direct flights go to Delhi (around ₹8500) and Mumbai (around ₹4500) with both Air India and Jet Airways.

BUS

Buses leave about every half-hour from the **MSRTC bus stand** (Station Rd West) to Pune (semideluxe/deluxe ₹330/620, five hours) and roughly hourly to Nasik (semideluxe ₹290, 4½ hours) between 8am and 10pm. Private bus agents are clustered on Dr Rajendra Prasad Marg and Court Rd; a few sit closer to the bus stand. Deluxe overnight bus destinations include Mumbai (with/without AC from ₹550/350, sleeper ₹900 to ₹1500, 7½ to 9½ hours), Ahmedabad (seat ₹400, sleeper ₹800 to ₹1050, 13 to 15 hours) and Nagpur (sleeper with AC ₹600, without AC ₹700 to ₹1050, 8½ to 10 hours).

Ordinary buses head to Ellora from the MSRTC bus stand every half-hour (₹30, one hour) and hourly to Jalgaon (₹155, four hours) via Fardapur (₹95, 2½ hours), which is the drop-off point for Ajanta.

From the **CIDCO bus stand** (Airport Rd), by the Lemon Tree hotel junction, ordinary buses leave for the Lonar meteorite crater (every two hours, 4½ hours, ₹172).

TRAIN

Aurangabad's **train station** (Station Rd East) is not on a main line, but it has four daily direct trains to/from Mumbai. The Tapovan Express (2nd class/chair ₹140/500, 7½ hours) departs Aurangabad at 2.35pm; the Janshatabdi Express (2nd class/chair ₹172/575, 6½ hours) departs Aurangabad at 6am. For Hyderabad, trains include the Ajanta express (sleeper/2nd class/1st class ₹805/1150/1925, 10 hours, 10.45pm). To reach northern or eastern India, take a bus to Jalgaon and board a train there.

ℹ️ Getting Around

Autorickshaws are common here. The taxi stand is next to the MSRTC bus stand; shared 4WDs also depart from here for Ellora and Daulatabad but are usually very packed. Renting a car and driver is a much better option.

Ashoka Tours & Travels (p781) rates for return trip with a car/driver to Ellora are ₹1250/1400 in a car/AC car; to Ajanta it's ₹2080/2400.

Around Aurangabad

Daulatabad

This one's straight out of a Tolkien fantasy. A most beguiling structure, the 12th-century hilltop fortress of Daulatabad is located about 15km north of Aurangabad, en route to Ellora. Now in ruins, the citadel was originally conceived as an impregnable fort by the Yadava kings. Its most infamous high point came in 1328, when it was named

Daulatabad (City of Fortune) by eccentric Delhi sultan Mohammed Tughlaq and made the capital – he even marched the entire population of Delhi 1100km south to populate it. Ironically, Daulatabad – despite being better positioned strategically than Delhi – soon proved untenable as a capital due to an acute water crisis, and Tughlaq forced the weary inhabitants all the way back to Delhi, which had by then been reduced to a ghost town.

Daulatabad's central bastion sits atop a 200m-high craggy outcrop known as Devagiri (Hill of the Gods), surrounded by a 5km **fort** (Indian/foreigner ₹10/100; ⊙6am-6pm). The climb to the summit takes about an hour, and leads past an ingenious series of defences, including multiple doorways designed with odd angles and spike-studded doors to prevent elephant charges. A tower of victory, known as the Chand Minar (Tower of the Moon), built in 1435, soars 60m above the ground to the right; it's closed to visitors. Higher up, you can walk into the Chini Mahal, where Abul Hasan Tana Shah, king of Golconda, was held captive for 12 years before his death in 1699. Nearby, there's a 6m cannon, cast from five different metals and engraved with Aurangzeb's name.

Part of the ascent goes through a pitch-black, bat-infested, water-seeping, spiralling tunnel. Guides (₹500) are available near the ticket counter to show you around, and their torch-bearing assistants will lead you through the dark passageway for a small tip. On the way down you'll be left to your own devices, so carry a torch.

As the fort is in ruins (with crumbling staircases and sheer drops) and involves a steep ascent, the elderly, children and those suffering from vertigo or claustrophobia will find it a tough challenge. Allow 2½ hours to explore the structure, and bring water.

Khuldabad

Time permitting, take a pit stop in the scruffy-walled settlement of Khuldabad (Heavenly Abode), a quaint little Muslim pilgrimage village just 3km from Ellora. Buried deep in the pages of history, Khuldabad is where a number of historic figures lie interred, including emperor Aurangzeb, the last of the Mughal greats. Despite matching the legendary King Solomon in terms of state riches, Aurangzeb was an ascetic in his personal life, and insisted that

he be buried in a simple tomb, which you'll find in the courtyard of the **Alamgir Dargah** (⊙7am-8pm).

Generally a calm place, Khuldabad is swamped with pilgrims every April when a robe said to have been worn by the Prophet Mohammed, and kept within the dargah (shrine), is shown to the public. Across the road from the Alamgir Dargah, another shrine is said to contain strands of the Prophet's beard.

Ellora
📄 02437

Give a man a hammer and chisel, and he'll create art for posterity. Come to the World Heritage **Ellora cave temples** (Indian/ foreigner ₹10/250; ⊙dawn-dusk Wed-Mon), 30km northwest of Aurangabad, and you'll know exactly what we mean. The epitome of ancient Indian rock-cut architecture, these caves were chipped out laboriously over five centuries by generations of Buddhist, Hindu and Jain monks. Monasteries, chapels, temples – the caves served every purpose, and they were stylishly embellished with a profusion of remarkably detailed sculptures. Unlike the caves at Ajanta, which are carved into a sheer rock face, the Ellora caves line a 2km-long escarpment, the gentle slope of which allowed architects to build elaborate courtyards in front of the shrines, and render them with sculptures of a surreal quality.

Ellora has 34 caves in all: 12 Buddhist (AD 600–800), 17 Hindu (AD 600–900) and five Jain (AD 800–1000) – though the exact timescales of these caves' construction is the subject of academic debate. Undoubtedly the grandest is the awesome Kailasa Temple (Cave 16), the world's largest monolithic sculpture, hewn top to bottom against a rocky slope by 7000 labourers over a period of 150 years. Dedicated to Lord Shiva, it is clearly among the best that ancient Indian architecture has to offer.

The established academic theory is that the site represents the renaissance of Hinduism under the Chalukya and Rashtrakuta dynasties, the subsequent decline of Indian Buddhism and a brief resurgence of Jainism under official patronage. However, due to the absence of inscriptional evidence, it's been impossible to accurately date most of Ellora's monuments. Some scholars argue that some Hindu temples predate those in

MAHARASHTRA ELLORA

Ellora Caves

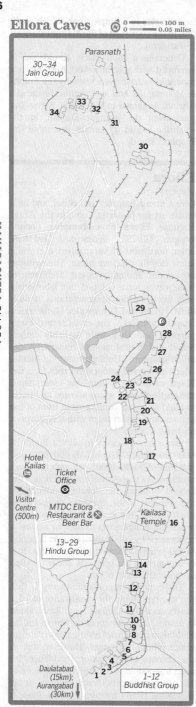

the Buddhist group. What is certain is that their coexistence at one site indicates a lengthy period of religious tolerance.

Official guides can be hired at the ticket office in front of the Kailasa Temple for ₹1070 (up to five people). Guides have an extensive knowledge of cave architecture so are worth the investment. If your tight itinerary forces you to choose between Ellora or Ajanta, Ellora wins hands down in terms of architecture (though Ajanta's setting is more beautiful and more of a pleasure to explore).

Ellora is very popular with domestic tourists; if you can visit on a weekday, it's far less crowded. The whole complex is in desperate need of reorganising: currently the car park is far too close to the temples so expect plenty of background honking and beeping as you tour the caves.

◉ Sights

★ Kailasa Temple   HINDU TEMPLE
One of Incredible India's greatest monuments, this astonishing temple, carved from solid rock, was built by King Krishna I in AD 760 to represent Mt Kailasa (Kailash), Shiva's Himalayan abode. To say that the assignment was daring would be an understatement. Three huge trenches were bored into the sheer cliff face, a process that entailed removing 200,000 tonnes of rock by hammer and chisel, before the temple could begin to take shape, and its remarkable sculptural decoration added.

Covering twice the area of the Parthenon in Athens and being half as high again, Kailasa is an engineering marvel that was executed straight from the head with zero margin for error. Modern draughtsmen might have a lesson or two to learn here.

The temple houses several intricately carved panels, depicting scenes from the Ramayana, the Mahabharata and the adventures of Krishna. Also worth admiring are the immense monolithic pillars that stand in the courtyard, flanking the entrance on both sides, and the southeastern gallery that has 10 giant and fabulous panels depicting the different avatars of Lord Vishnu.

After you're done with the main enclosure, bypass the hordes of snack-munching day trippers to explore the temple's many dank, bat-urine-soaked corners with their numerous forgotten carvings. Afterwards, hike up a foot trail to the south of the complex that takes you to the top perimeter of the 'cave', from where you can get a bird's-eye view of the entire temple complex.

Buddhist Caves

Calm and contemplation infuse the 12 Buddhist caves, which stretch to the south of Kailasa. All are Buddhist *viharas* (monasteries) used for study and worship, but the multi-storeyed structures also included cooking, living and sleeping areas.

The one exception is Cave 10, which is a *chaitya* (assembly hall). While the earliest caves are simple, Caves 11 and 12 are more ambitious; both have three stories and are on par with the more impressive Hindu temples.

Cave 1, the simplest *vihara*, may have been a granary. **Cave 2** is notable for its ornate pillars and the imposing seated Buddha, which faces the setting sun. **Cave 3** and **Cave 4** are unfinished and not well preserved.

Cave 5 is the largest *vihara* in this group, at 18m wide and 36m long; the rows of stone benches hint that it may once have been an assembly hall.

Cave 6 is an ornate *vihara* with wonderful images of Tara, consort of the Bodhisattva Avalokiteshvara, and of the Buddhist goddess of learning, Mahamayuri, looking remarkably similar to Saraswati, her Hindu equivalent. **Cave 7** is an unadorned hall, but from here you can pass through a doorway to **Cave 8**, the first cave in which the sanctum is detached from the rear wall. **Cave 9** is notable for its wonderfully carved fascia.

Cave 10 is the only *chaitya* in the Buddhist group and one of the finest in India. Its ceiling features ribs carved into the stonework; the grooves were once fitted with wooden panels. The balcony and upper gallery offer a closer view of the ceiling and a frieze depicting amorous couples. A decorative window gently illuminates an enormous figure of the teaching Buddha.

Cave 11, the Do Thal (Two Storey) Cave, is entered through its third basement level, not discovered until 1876. Like Cave 12, it possibly owes its size to competition with Hindu caves of the same period.

Cave 12, the huge Tin Thal (Three Storey) Cave, is entered through a courtyard. The locked shrine on the top floor contains a large Buddha figure flanked by his seven previous incarnations. The walls are carved with relief pictures.

Hindu Caves

Drama and excitement characterise the Hindu group (Caves 13 to 29). In terms of scale, creative vision and skill of execution, these caves are in a league of their own.

All these temples were cut from the top down, so it was never necessary to use scaffolding – the builders began with the roof and moved down to the floor. Highlights include caves 14, 15, 16, 21 and 29.

Cave 13 is a simple cave, most likely a granary. **Cave 14**, the Ravana-ki-Khai, is a Buddhist *vihara* converted to a temple dedicated to Shiva sometime in the 7th century.

Cave 15, the Das Avatara (Ten Incarnations of Vishnu) Cave, is one of the finest at Ellora. The two-storey temple contains a mesmerising Shiva Nataraja, and Shiva emerging from a lingam (phallic image) while Vishnu and Brahma pay homage.

Caves 17 to 20 and **caves 22 to 28** are simple monasteries.

Cave 21, known as the Rameshvara Cave, features interesting interpretations of familiar Shaivite scenes depicted in the earlier temples. The figure of the goddess Ganga, standing on her Makara (mythical sea creature), is particularly notable.

The large **Cave 29**, the Dumar Lena, is thought to be a transitional model between the simpler hollowed-out caves and the fully developed temples exemplified by the Kailasa. It has views over a nearby waterfall.

Jain Caves

The five Jain caves, the last created at Ellora, may lack the ambitious size of the best Hindu temples, but they are exceptionally detailed, with some remarkable paintings and carvings.

The caves are 1km north of the last Hindu temple (Cave 29) at the end of the bitumen road; autorickshaws run here from the main car park.

Cave 30, the Chhota Kailasa (Little Kailasa), is a poor imitation of the great Kailasa Temple and stands by itself some distance from the other Jain temples.

In contrast, **Cave 32**, the Indra Sabha (Assembly Hall of Indra), is the finest of the Jain temples. Its ground-floor plan is similar to that of the Kailasa, but the upstairs area is as ornate and richly decorated as the downstairs is plain. There are images of the Jain *tirthankars* (great teachers) Parasnath and Gomateshvara, the latter surrounded by wildlife. Inside the shrine is a seated figure of Mahavira, the last *tirthankar* and founder of the Jain religion.

Cave 31 is really an extension of Cave 32. **Cave 33**, the Jagannath Sabha, is similar in plan to 32 and has some well-preserved sculptures. The final temple, the small **Cave 34**, also has interesting sculptures. On the hilltop over the Jain temples, a 5m-high image of Parasnath looks down on Ellora.

🛏 Sleeping & Eating

Hotel Kailas   HOTEL $$
(🖉244446; www.hotelkailas.com; r ₹2110, with AC from ₹3510; ❀) The sole decent hotel near the site, with attractive cottages set in leafy grounds. The restaurant (mains ₹110 to ₹250) is excellent, with a menu chalked up on a blackboard that includes sandwiches, breakfasts, curries and tandoori favourites.

MTDC Ellora Restaurant
& Beer Bar   INDIAN $
(mains/thalis from ₹90/110; ⊗8am-5pm) Located within the temple complex, this is a good place for lunch.

ℹ Information

Ellora Visitor Centre (⊗9am-5.30pm Wed-Mon) Ellora's impressive new visitor centre, 750m west of the site, is worth dropping by to put the caves in historical context. It features modern displays and information panels, a 15-minute video presentation, and two galleries: one on the Kailasa Temple (with a diorama of the temple) and other dedicated to the site itself. A cafe, craft centre and restaurant are planned.

ℹ Getting There & Away

Note that the temples are closed on Tuesday. Buses regularly ply the road between Aurangabad and Ellora (₹30, one hour); the last bus departs from Ellora at 8pm. Share 4WDs are also an option, but get packed; they leave when full and stop outside the bus stand in Aurangabad (₹70). A full-day tour to Ellora, with stops en route, costs ₹1400 in an AC car; try Ashoka Tours & Travels (p781). Autorickshaws ask for ₹700.

Ajanta
🖉02438

Superbly set in a remote river valley 105km northeast of Aurangabad, the remarkable cave temples of Ajanta are this region's second World Heritage Site. Much older than Ellora, these secluded caves date from around the 2nd century BC to the 6th century AD and were among the earliest monastic institutions to be constructed in the country. Ironically, it was Ellora's rise that brought about Ajanta's downfall, and historians believe the site was abandoned once the focus had shifted to Ellora.

Ajanta was deserted for about a millenium, as the Deccan forest claimed and shielded the caves, with roots and shoots choking the sculptures, until 1819, when a British hunting party led by officer John Smith stumbled upon them purely by chance.

One of the primary reasons to visit Ajanta is to admire its renowned 'frescoes', actually temperas, which adorn many of the caves' interiors. With few other examples from ancient times matching their artistic excellence and fine execution, these paintings are of unfathomable heritage value. It's believed that the natural pigments for these paintings were mixed with animal glue and vegetable gum, to bind them to the dry surface. Many caves have small, craterlike holes in their floors, which acted as palettes during paint jobs. Despite their age, the paintings in most caves remain finely preserved today, and many attribute it to their relative isolation from humanity for centuries. However, it would be a tad optimistic to say that decay hasn't set in.

◎ Sights

★ Ajanta Caves   CAVE
(Indian/foreigner ₹10/250, video ₹25, authorised guide ₹750; ⊗9am-5.30pm Tue-Sun) Ajanta's caves line a steep face of a horseshoe-shaped gorge bordering the Waghore River. Five of the caves are *chaityas* (prayer halls) while others are *viharas* (monasteries). Caves 8, 9, 10, 12, 13 and part of 15 are early Buddhist caves, while the others date from around the 5th century AD (Mahayana period). In the austere early Buddhist school, the Buddha was never represented directly but always alluded to by a symbol such as the footprint or wheel of law.

During busy periods, viewers are allotted 15 minutes within the caves, many of which have to be entered barefoot (socks or shoe covers allowed). Caves 3, 5, 8, 22, 28, 29 and 30 remain either closed or inaccessible.

Cave 1   CAVE
Cave 1, a Mahayana *vihara,* was one of the last to be excavated and is the most beautifully decorated. This is where you'll find a rendition of the Bodhisattva Padmapani, the most famous and iconic of the Ajanta artworks. A verandah in front leads to a large congregation hall, housing sculptures and narrative murals known for their splendid perspective and elaborate detailing of dress,

Ajanta Caves

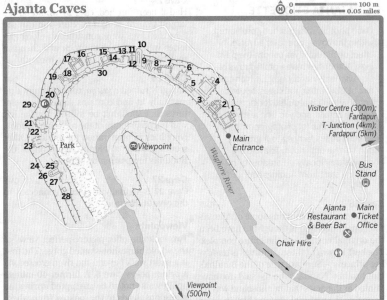

daily life and facial expressions. The colours in the paintings were created from local minerals, with the exception of the vibrant blue made from Central Asian lapis lazuli. Look up to the ceiling to see the carving of four deer sharing a common head.

Cave 2   CAVE
Cave 2 is a late Mahayana *vihara* with deliriously ornamented columns and capitals, and some fine paintings. The ceiling is decorated with geometric and floral patterns. The murals depict scenes from the Jataka tales, including Buddha's mother's dream of a six-tusked elephant, which heralded his conception.

Cave 4   CAVE
Cave 4 is the largest *vihara* at Ajanta and is supported by 28 pillars. Although never completed, the cave has some impressive sculptures: four statues surround a huge central Buddha, and there are scenes of people fleeing from the 'eight great dangers' to the protection of Avalokitesvara.

Cave 6   CAVE
Cave 6 is the only two-storey *vihara* at Ajanta, but parts of the lower storey have collapsed. Inside is a seated Buddha figure and an intricately carved door to the shrine.

Upstairs the hall is surrounded by cells with fine paintings on the doorways.

Cave 7   CAVE
Cave 7 has an atypical design, with porches before the verandah leading directly to the four cells and the elaborately sculptured shrine.

Cave 9   CAVE
Cave 9 is one of the earliest *chaityas* at Ajanta. Although it dates from the early Buddhist period, the two figures flanking the entrance door were probably later Mahayana additions. Columns run down both sides of the cave and around the 3m-high dagoba at the far end.

Cave 10   CAVE
Cave 10 is thought to be the oldest cave (200 BC) and was the first one to be spotted by the British hunting party. Similar in design to cave 9, it is the largest *chaitya*. The facade has collapsed and the paintings inside have been damaged, in some cases by graffiti dating from soon after their rediscovery. One of the pillars to the right bears the engraved name of Smith, who left his mark here for posterity.

ⓘ AJANTA ETIQUETTE

Flash photography is strictly prohibited within the caves, due to its adverse effect on natural dyes used in the paintings. Authorities have installed rows of tiny pigment-friendly lights, which cast a faint glow within the caves, but additional lighting is required for glimpsing minute details, and you'll have to rely on long exposures for photographs.

Most buses ferrying tour groups don't arrive until noon. To avoid the crowds stay locally in Fardapur or make an early start from Aurangabad.

Cave 16   CAVE
Cave 16, a *vihara,* contains some of Ajanta's finest paintings and is thought to have been the original entrance to the entire complex. The best known of these paintings is the 'dying princess' – Sundari, wife of the Buddha's half-brother Nanda, who is said to have fainted at the news that her husband was renouncing the material life (and her) in order to become a monk. Carved figures appear to support the ceiling, and there's a statue of the Buddha seated on a lion throne teaching the Noble Eightfold Path.

Cave 17   CAVE
With carved dwarfs supporting the pillars, cave 17 has Ajanta's best-preserved and most varied paintings. Famous images include a princess applying make-up, a seductive prince using the old trick of plying his lover with wine, and the Buddha returning home from his enlightenment to beg from his wife and astonished son. A detailed panel tells of Prince Simhala's expedition to Sri Lanka: with 500 companions he is shipwrecked on an island where ogresses appear as enchanting women, only to seize and devour their victims. Simhala escapes on a flying horse and returns to conquer the island.

Cave 19   CAVE
Cave 19, a magnificent *chaitya,* has a remarkably detailed facade; its dominant feature is an impressive horseshoe-shaped window. Two fine, standing Buddha figures flank the entrance. Inside is a three-tiered dagoba with a figure of the Buddha on the front. Outside the cave, to the west, sits a striking image of the Naga king with seven cobra hoods around his head. His wife, hooded by a single cobra, sits by his side.

Cave 24   CAVE
Had it been finished, cave 24 would be the largest *vihara* at Ajanta. Here you can see how the caves were constructed – long galleries were cut into the rock and then the rock between them was broken through.

Cave 26   CAVE
A largely ruined *chaitya,* cave 26 is now dramatically lit and contains some fine sculptures that shouldn't be missed. On the left wall is a huge figure of the reclining Buddha, lying back in preparation for nirvana. Other scenes include a lengthy depiction of the Buddha's temptation by Maya.

Cave 27   CAVE
Cave 27 is virtually a *vihara* connected to the cave 26 *chaitya.*

Viewpoints
Two lookouts offer picture-perfect views of the whole horseshoe-shaped gorge. The first is a short walk beyond the river, crossed via a bridge below cave 8. A further 40-minute uphill walk (not to be attempted during the monsoons) leads to the lookout from where the British party first spotted the caves.

🛏 Sleeping & Eating

Accommodation options close to the caves are quite limited. Aurangabad (or even Jalgaon) has far more choice, while Fardapur is the closest option and most convenient for arriving at the caves early morning.

MTDC Holiday Resort Fardapur   HOTEL **$$**
(✆ 244230; Aurangabad-Jalgaon Rd, Fardapur; d ₹1480, with AC ₹1860; ❄) Recently renovated, this government hotel is now a good option set amid lawns in a peaceful location off the main road in Fardapur, 5km from the caves. Rooms are in good shape and well-equipped; there's a bar garden and restaurant (order ahead for your meal).

MTDC Ajanta Tourist Complex   HOTEL **$$**
(✆ 09422204325; Fardapur T-junction; cottage ₹2320; ❄) Located just behind the shopping 'plaza' and the bus stand, these five cottages nestled amid grassy lawns have some charm, though maintenance could be better. There's no restaurant here.

Ajanta Restaurant & Beer Bar   FAST FOOD **$**
(mains ₹90-150, thalis from ₹130; ⏰ 9am-5.30pm Tue-Sun) This cafe-restaurant right by the main ticket office at the caves serves a decent vegetarian thali and cold drinks, including beer.

ℹ Information

A cloakroom is available at the Fardapur T-junction (but not at the caves), where you can leave gear (₹10 per item for four hours).

Ajanta Visitor Centre (⊘ 9am-5.30pm Tue-Sun) This state-of-the-art new facility is one of India's very best, with highly impressive replicas of four caves (1, 2, 16 and 17) in real scale, audio guides available in many languages, excellent painting and sculpture galleries, story of Buddhism in India, an audio-visual arena and large cafe.

ℹ Getting There & Away

Note that the caves are closed on Monday. Buses from Aurangabad or Jalgaon will drop you at the Fardapur T-junction (where the highway meets the road to the caves), 4km from the site. From here, after paying an 'amenities' fee (₹10), walk to the departure point for the buses (with/without AC ₹20/15), which zoom up to the caves. Buses return half-hourly to the T-junction; the last bus is at 5pm.

All MSRTC buses passing through Fardapur stop at the T-junction. After the caves close you can board buses to either Aurangabad or Jalgaon outside the MTDC Holiday Resort in Fardapur, 1km down the main road towards Jalgaon. Taxis are available in Fardapur; ₹1300/1600 should get you to Jalgaon/Aurangabad.

Jalgaon

📞 0257 / POP 468,300 / ELEV 208M

Apart from being a handy base for exploring Ajanta 60km away, the industrial city of Jalgaon is really nothing more than a convenient transit town. It has rail connections to all major cities across India.

🛏 Sleeping & Eating

★ **Hotel Plaza**   HOTEL $
(📞 9370027354, 2227354; hotelplaza_jal@yahoo. com; Station Rd; dm ₹250, s/d from ₹550/750, r with AC from ₹1300; 🏢@🛜) Offering brilliant value, this extremely well-managed and presented hotel is only a short hop from the station. Rooms vary in size and layout, but with whitewashed walls, a minimalist feel and almost Swiss-clean bathrooms, they're a steal at this price. The effusive owner is a mine of useful information and can assist with train reservations, car hire and recommendations.

Hotel Royal Palace   HOTEL $$
(📞 2233555; www.hotelroyalpalace.in; Mahabal Rd, Jai Nagar; s/d incl breakfast from ₹2520/2680; 🏢🛜) Rooms here don't quite reach the heights promised by the chintzy lobby

but they're decent value and comfortable enough, particularly if you like beige-on-beige colour schemes. The in-house restaurant is a pure-veg affair with North Indian, coastal, Chinese and Continental food. Free pick-ups are offered from the train station.

Hotel Arya   INDIAN $
(Navi Peth; mains ₹50-100; ⊘ 8.30am-10.50pm) Delicious vegetarian food, particularly Punjabi cuisine, though a few Chinese and South Indian dishes are also offered. It's a short walk south along Station Rd, left at MG Rd, and left at the clock tower. You may have to queue for a table at lunchtime.

ℹ Information

Banks, ATMs and internet cafes are on Nehru Rd, which runs along the top of Station Rd.

ℹ Getting There & Around

Several express trains connecting Mumbai (sleeper/2AC ₹280/1000, eight hours), Delhi (sleeper/2AC ₹530/1970, 18 hours), Ahmedabad (sleeper/2AC ₹345/1322, 14 hours) and Varanasi (sleeper/2AC ₹515/1950, 20 hours) stop at Jalgaon train station. Eight daily trains head for Nagpur (sleeper/2AC ₹290/1090, seven to nine hours).

Buses to Fardapur (₹60, 1½ hours) depart half-hourly from the bus stand starting at 6am, continuing to Aurangabad (₹155, four hours).

Jalgaon's train station and bus stand are about 2km apart (₹25 by autorickshaw). Private bus companies on Station Rd offer services to Aurangabad (₹170 to ₹200, 3½ hours) and Mumbai (₹450 to ₹650, 9½ hours).

Nagpur

📞 0712 / POP 2.43 MILLION / ELEV 305M

Way off the main tourist routes, the isolated city of Nagpur lacks must-see sites but is an important gateway to several reserves and parks including Tadoba-Andhari Tiger Reserve and Pench National Park. It's also close to the temples of Ramtek and the ashrams of Sevagram. Summer is the best time to taste the city's famous oranges.

🛏 Sleeping & Eating

Nagpur's hotels are not great value and cater primarily to business travellers. Central Ave is noisy but close to the train station.

Hotel Blue Moon   HOTEL $
(📞 0712 2726061; Central Ave; s/d from ₹650/850, with AC ₹1100/1350; 🏢) Large, plain rooms that don't win any awards for imagination

but are one of the better budget options in this pricey city. It's one of the closest hotels to the train station. Staff are helpful.

Legend Inn   HOTEL **$$**
(📞 6658666; www.thelegendinn.com; 15 Modern Society, Wardha Rd; s/d from ₹3300/3700; ❄️ 📶) On the main highway for the Tadoba-Andhari Tiger Reserve, this is an efficiently run hotel with well-appointed and -presented rooms, a good restaurant and smiley staff. Free pick-ups are included from the airport, 1km away. The 'gym' is two running machines in the basement. Rates drop by 10% in summer.

Peanut Hotel   HOTEL **$$**
(📞 0712-3250320; www.peanuthotels.com; Bharti House, 43 Kachipura Garden, New Ramdaspeth; s/d from ₹2790/2960, with AC from ₹3090/3260; ❄️ 📶) Located on a leafy residential street, this new hotel's modern, whitewashed rooms have a contemporary look and are kept spick and span; all are no smoking. It's 2km southeast of the train station.

Krishnum   SOUTH INDIAN **$**
(Central Ave; mains ₹50-80; ⏱ 11.30am-10pm) This popular place dishes out South Indian snacks and generous thalis, as well as freshly squeezed fruit juices. There are branches in other parts of town.

Picadilly Checkers   FAST FOOD **$**
(VCA Complex, Civil Lines; mains ₹60-80; ⏱ 11am-10pm) A favourite eating joint for Nagpur's college brigade, with a good range of vegetarian quick bites on offer.

ℹ️ Information

Numerous ATMs line Central Ave.
Computrek (18 Central Ave; per hour ₹20; ⏱ 10am-10pm) Internet access on the main drag.
MTDC (📞 2533325; near MLA Hostel, Civil Lines; ⏱ 10am-5.45pm Mon-Sat) Staff here can help with getting to national parks near Nagpur.

ℹ️ Getting There & Around

AIR

The airport is 7km southwest of the centre. Domestic airlines, including Air India, Indigo and Jet Airways, fly daily to Delhi (from ₹5500, 1½ hours), Mumbai (from ₹4400, 1½ hours) and Kolkata (from ₹7500, 1½ hours), as well as Ahmedabad, Bengaluru, Chennai, Jaipur and Pune. Taxis/autorickshaws from the airport to the city centre cost ₹380/200.

BUS

The main MSRTC bus stand is 2km south of the train station. Ordinary buses head for Wardha (₹88, three hours) and Ramtek (₹45, 1½ hours). There are two buses to Jalgaon (₹650, 10 hours) and four daily to Pune (₹1070, 16 hours).

TRAIN

From Mumbai's CST, the Duronto Express runs daily to Nagpur (sleeper/2AC ₹470/1830, 10 hours, 9.15pm). From Nagpur, it departs at 8.50pm and arrives at 7.50am the following morning. Heading north to Kolkata is the Gitanjali Express (sleeper/2AC ₹480/1920, 17½ hours, 7.05pm). Several expresses bound for Delhi and Mumbai stop at Jalgaon (sleeper/2AC ₹280/1020, eight hours), for Ajanta caves.

Around Nagpur

Ramtek

About 40km northeast of Nagpur, Ramtek is believed to be the place where Lord Rama, of the epic Ramayana, spent some time during his exile with his wife Sita and brother Lakshmana. The place is marked by a cluster of **temples** (⏱ 6am-9pm) about 600 years old, which sit atop the Hill of Rama and have their own population of resident monkeys. Autorickshaws will cart you the 5km from the bus stand to the temple complex for ₹80. You can return to town via the 700 steps at the back of the complex. On the road to the temples you'll pass the delightful **Ambala Tank**, lined with small shrines. Boat rides around the lake are available.

Buses run half-hourly between Ramtek and the MSRTC bus stand in Nagpur (₹52, 1½ hours). The last bus to Nagpur is at 7pm.

Sevagram
📞 07152
About 85km from Nagpur, Sevagram (Village of Service) was chosen by Mahatma Gandhi as his base during the Indian Independence Movement. Throughout the freedom struggle, the village played host to several nationalist leaders, who would regularly come to visit the Mahatma at his **Sevagram Ashram** (📞 07152-284753; www.gandhiashramsevagram.org; ⏱ 9am-noon & 2-6pm). The overseers of this peaceful ashram, built on 40 hectares of farmland, have carefully restored the original huts where Gandhi lived and worked, and which now house some of his personal effects.

LONAR METEORITE CRATER

If you like off-beat adventures, travel to Lonar to explore a prehistoric natural wonder. About 50,000 years ago, a meteorite slammed into the earth here, leaving behind a massive crater, 2km across and 170m deep. In scientific jargon, it's the only hypervelocity natural-impact crater in basaltic rock in the world. In lay terms, it's as tranquil and relaxing a spot as you could hope to find, with a shallow green lake at its base and wilderness all around. The lake water is supposedly alkaline and excellent for the skin. Scientists think that the meteorite is still embedded about 600m below the southeastern rim of the crater.

crater's edge is home to several Hindu temples as well as wildlife, including langurs, peacocks, deer and numerous birds.

The **MTDC Tourist Complex** (☑ 07260221602; d ₹1300, with AC ₹2590; ﹡) has a prime location just across the road from the crater, and offers newly renovated deluxe rooms that are in excellent shape, with stylish ensuite bathrooms. There are regular buses between Lonar and the CIDCO bus stand in Aurangabad (p784).

Very basic lodging is available in the **Yatri Nivas** (☑ 284753; d ₹100), across the road from the entry gate; advance booking is recommended. Simple vegetarian meals can be served in the ashram's dining hall with prior notice.

Just 3km from Sevagram, Paunar village is home to the **Brahmavidya Mandir Ashram** (☑ 07152-288388; ⊙ 6am-noon & 2-8pm). Founded by Vinoba Bhave, a nationalist and disciple of Gandhi, the ashram is run almost entirely by women. Modelled on *swaraj* (self-sufficiency), it's operated on a social system of consensus, with no central management.

Sevagram can be reached by taking a Wardha-bound bus from Nagpur (₹85, three hours).

Tadoba-Andhari Tiger Reserve

One of the best places to see tigers in India, the seldom-visited **Tadoba-Andhari Tiger Reserve** (⊙ dawn-dusk Wed-Mon), 150km south of Nagpur, is now much more accessible thanks to the upgrading of state highways. Seeing fewer visitors than most other forest reserves in India, this is a place where you can get up close with wildlife without having to jostle past truckloads of shutter-happy tourists. Mammals in the reserve include gaurs, chitals, nilgais, sloth bears and leopards as well as very healthy tiger numbers (estimated at around 120, with 24 cubs born in 2014). Of the 280 bird species logged in the park, there's a raptor population that includes crested serpent eagles, oriental honey buzzards and rare species of

owls. The park also remains open throughout the year, unlike many in India.

Walking safaris (₹850) in the buffer zone allow you to look for tracks, observe birds and insects at close quarters, and catch the scents and sounds of wild India. Guides from the Gond tribe accompany you through the forest.

Guided canoe trips (₹1200 per person) on the Irai and Tadoba lakes allow you the chance explore inlets, islands and bays, with a chance of seeing crocodiles and magnificent birdlife, including the grey-headed fish eagle, ospreys and storks. Electric pontoon boats (₹800 per person) also operate.

Four state buses ply the road between Nagpur and Chandrapur (₹138, 3½ hours).

The nearest train station of Wardha (connected by trains from Hyderabad and Nagpur) is 40km from the reserve.

🛏 Sleeping & Eating

Tiger Trails Jungle Lodge　　　LODGE **$$$**
(☑ 0712-6541327; www.tigertrails.in; Khutwanda Gate; s/d incl all meals ₹9500/15,000; ﹡ ﹡ ☕) The Tiger Trails Jungle Lodge is owned by passionate enthusiasts who have spent decades studying tigers inside the national park. A special lodge, it's located in the wildlife-rich buffer zone. Accommodation is spacious and divided between rooms in an older block (with big roof terrace) and more modern, better-appointed options. Camera traps around the property regularly 'catch' tigers. All safari tours (from ₹4500) are with expert guides, accommodation is spacious and comfortable, and meals generous and tasty.

THE LEGEND OF BABA AMTE

The legend of Murlidhar Devidas 'Baba' Amte (1914–2008) is oft-repeated in humanitarian circles around the world. Hailing from an upper-class Brahmin family in Wardha, Amte was snugly ensconced in material riches and on his way to becoming a successful lawyer when he witnessed a leper die unattended in the streets one night. It was an incident that changed him forever.

Soon after, Amte renounced worldly comforts, embracing an austere life through which he actively worked for the benefit of leprosy patients and those belonging to marginalised communities. In the primitive forested backyards of eastern Maharashtra, he set up his ashram called **Anandwan** (Forest of Joy; ☑ 07176-282034; www.anandwan. in). A true Gandhian, Amte believed in self-sufficiency, and his lifelong efforts saw several awards being conferred upon him, including the Ramon Magsaysay Award in 1985.

Amte's work has been continued by his sons Vikas and Prakash and their wives – the latter couple also won the Magsaysay Award in 2008. The family now runs many ashrams in these remote parts to care for the needy, both humans and animals. Over 2500 people are currently cared for, including 1500 leprosy patients. Animals in the 'orphanage' include otters, eagles, crocodiles, monkeys, wild boars, deer, hyenas, snakes, leopards and lions. There's also a school for tribal people.

Volunteering opportunities are available and donations welcome (via website).

Svasara
LODGE $$$
(☑ 9370 008008; www.svasararesorts.com; Kolara Gate; d incl all meals ₹14,000; ☒) Svasara is a beautifully designed new luxury lodge where the gorgeous suites and facilities really take the jungle out of the location. The food is great and safaris are well organised and lead by enthusiastic staff.

MTDC Resort
HOTEL $
(☑ 02168-260318; Bombay Point Rd; d from ₹1645) The MTDC Resort has recently been renovated and now has comfortable, well-furnished rooms and cottages, some overlooking the Irai lake, and good dining facilities. Staff are helpful and arrange good jungle safaris in 4WDs (₹2700 per vehicle, plus ₹300 for a mandatory guide). Bookings and packages can be made at the MTDC's Nagpur office.

SOUTHERN MAHARASHTRA

Konkan Coast

A little-developed shoreline running south from Mumbai all the way to Goa, this picturesque strip of coast is peppered with postcard beaches, fishing villages and magnificent ruined forts. Travelling through this tropical backwater can be sheer bliss. However, remember that accommodation is scant and transport limited and a little unreliable. The best option, if you've got the funds, is to rent a car in Mumbai and drift slowly down the coast to Goa. What you'll get in return is an experience that money can't buy.

Murud
☑ 02144 / POP 13,100

The sleepy fishing hamlet of Murud – 165km from Mumbai – should be on any itinerary of the Konkan Coast. The relaxed pace of life, fresh seafood, stupendous offshore Janjira fort (and the chance to feel the warm surf rush past your feet) makes the trip here well worthwhile.

Murud's beach is fun for a run or game of cricket with locals. Peer through the gates of the off-limits Ahmedganj Palace, estate of the Siddi Nawab of Murud, or scramble around the decaying mosque and tombs on the south side of town.

◎ Sights

★ Janjira
FORT
(⊙ 7am-dusk) The commanding, brooding fortress of Janjira, built on an island 500m offshore, is the most magnificent of the string of forts which line the Konkan coastline. This citadel was completed in 1571 by the Siddis, descendants of slaves from the Horn of Africa, and was the capital of a princely state.

Over the centuries Siddi alignment with Mughals provoked conflict with local kings, including Shivaji and his son Sambhaji, who attempted to tunnel to it. However, no outsider (including British, French and Portuguese colonists) ever made it past the fort's 12m-high granite walls which, when seen during high tide, seem to rise straight from the sea. Unconquered through history, the fort is finally falling to forces of nature as its mighty walls slowly crumble and wilderness reclaims its innards.

Still, there's a lot to see today, including the remarkable close-fitting stonework that's protected the citadel against centuries of attack by storms, colonists and gunpowder. You approach the fort via a brooding grey-stone gateway, and then can explore its ramparts (complete with giant cannons) and 19 bastions, large parts of which are intact. Its inner keep, palaces and mosque are in ruins, though the fort's huge twin reservoirs remain. As many of the surviving walls and structures are in poor shape, tread carefully as you explore the site, which is unfortunately littered with trash.

The only way to reach Janjira is by boat (₹20 return, 20 minutes) from Rajpuri port. Boats depart from 7am to 4.45pm daily and allow you 45 minutes to explore the fort. To get to Rajpuri from Murud, take an autorickshaw (₹75) or hire a bicycle.

🛏 Sleeping & Eating

Devakinandan Lodge GUESTHOUSE $
(☑ 9273524061; r ₹1000-1200) This simple little guesthouse has clean, basic rooms with TV and attached bathrooms with hot water. You'll find a few hammocks scattered in its beach-facing garden. The family owners are friendly but speak very little English.

Sea Shell Resort HOTEL $$
(☑ 274306; www.seashellmurud.com; Darbar Rd; r with/without AC from ₹2500/2000; ❇ ❇) Set back from the beachside road, this cheery place has neat, spacious breezy sea-facing rooms with hot-water bathrooms and a multi-cuisine restaurant. Staff can be a bit vacant on reception but dolphin safaris can be arranged. The pool is tiny.

Golden Swan Beach Resort HOTEL $$
(☑ 274078; www.goldenswan.com; Darbar Rd; s/d incl breakfast from ₹3800; ❇ 🖤) Rates are a little steep (particularly the cheaper options), but these seafront cottages and rooms occupy a fine spot on a great stretch of beach, with distant views of Ahmedganj Palace and Kasa Fort. There are also rooms in a charming old bungalow a short walk away. The in-house restaurant is superb, try the Szechwan chicken. Rates increase on weekends.

New Sea Rock Restaurant INDIAN $
(Rajpuri; mains ₹50-180; ⊙7am-8pm) Perched on a cliff overlooking the beach at Rajpuri, this joint has an awesome view of Janjira. A perfect place to steal a million-dollar sunset for the price of a chai (₹10), though you will probably be tempted to try the Indian or Chinese mains.

Hotel Vinayak INDIAN $
(Darbar Rd; mains ₹70-150; ⊙8am-10pm) Its sea-facing terrace is the perfect place to tuck into a delicious and fiery Malvani thali (₹80 to ₹180), served with pink kokam syrup to smother the spices. Fresh fish (₹100 to ₹250), prawn dishes and good breakfasts are also available.

ℹ Getting There & Around

Ferries and catamarans (₹95 to ₹160, one hour) from the Gateway of India in Mumbai cruise to Mandva pier between 6am and 7pm. The ticket includes a free shuttle bus to Alibag (30 minutes). Rickety local buses from Alibag head down the coast to Murud (₹52, two hours). Alternatively, hourly buses from Mumbai Central bus stand take almost six hours to Murud (ordinary/ semideluxe ₹158/212).

The nearest railhead is at Roha, two hours away and poorly connected.

Bicycles (₹75 per hour) and cars (from ₹1500 per day) can be hired at the Golden Swan Beach Resort.

Around Murud

RAIGAD FORT

Alone on a high and remote hilltop, 24km off Hwy 66, the enthralling **Raigad Fort** (Indian/foreigner ₹5/100; ⊙8am-5.30pm) served as Shivaji's capital from 1648 until his death in 1680. The fort was later sacked by the British, and some colonial structures added, but monuments such as the royal court, plinths of royal chambers, the main marketplace and Shivaji's tomb still remain, and it's worth an excursion.

You can hike a crazy 1475 steps to the top. But for a more 'levitating' experience, take the vertigo-inducing **ropeway** (www.raigadropeway.com; return ₹200; ⊙8.30am-5.30pm) – actually a cable car – which climbs up the cliff and offers a bird's-eye view of the deep gorges below. Be warned this is a very popular attraction with domestic tourists and you may have to wait up to an hour for a ride during holiday times. Guides (₹200) are available within the fort complex. **Sarja Restaurant** (snacks ₹30-100), adjoining the

OFF THE BEATEN TRACK

THE ROAD TO RUINS

A scenic coastal road parallels the shoreline north of Murud, skirting headlands, beaches and rocky shores. Just a couple of kilometres from town, the clifftop **Nawab's Palace** is an extraordinary Victorian Gothic-Mughal structure that's been abandoned for years but would make a perfect heritage hotel. You can peek through its gates (complete with coat of arms) from the roadside for a glimpse of the palace.

Sixteen kilometres north of Murud, **Kashid Beach** is a beautiful sandy cove where you can take a dip and sip on tender coconuts. It's a peaceful spot, though expect a smattering of camel-ride-wallahs and banana boats on weekends. The road continues north, gripping the contours of the exposed shoreline, affording superb oceanic views until you reach the tiny traditional fishing village of **Korlai**, 31km from Murud. Perched on the rocky headland above the village are the ruined remains of **Korlai Fort**, which once guarded the giant Kundaliker river estuary and still affords panoramic vistas.

Share autorickshaws (₹100) run as far as Kashid Beach. Cars and bicycles can be hired at the Golden Swan Beach Resort in Murud.

ropeway's base terminal, is a good place for lunch or snacks.

Autorickshaws (₹180, 45 minutes) shuttle up to Raigad from the town of Mahad on Hwy 66 (look out for the 'Raigad Ropeway' sign). Mahad is located 158km south of Mumbai and 88km from Murud. The Mahad–Raigad road is paved and in good condition. Taxis charge ₹2000 for a day trip here from Murud.

Ganpatipule
☑ 02357

The tiny beach resort of Ganpatipule has been luring a steady stream of sea-lovers over the years with its warm waters and wonderful stretches of sand. Located about 375km from Mumbai, it's a village that snoozes through much of the year, except during holidays such as Diwali or Ganesh Chaturthi. These are times when hordes of boisterous tourists turn up to visit the seaside **Ganesha Temple** (⊙ 6am-9pm) housing a monolithic orange Ganesh.

Activities on and off the beach at Ganpatipule include camel and boat rides (dolphins are sometimes encountered in the morning). Away from a small crowded section near the temple, you'll find the beach is perfect for a long walk along the sand.

🛏 Sleeping & Eating

There are plenty of guesthouses in Ganpatipule but at the time of research we couldn't find one that would rent out rooms to foreigners. We were told this is because Mumbai bomb plotter David Healey spent time in the town.

MTDC Resort HOTEL **$$**
(☑ 235248; d from ₹2250, with AC ₹2550; ❄ 🛜) Spread over prime beachfront, this huge operation is something of a holiday camp for Mumbaiker families. Its concrete rooms and cottages would benefit from a little updating, but all boast magnificent full-frontal ocean views. It also packs in a decent restaurant that serves cold beer.

Bhau Joshi Bhojnalay INDIAN **$**
(mains ₹50-80; ⊙ 11am-10.30pm) A clean, orderly restaurant inland from the beach that offers delicious Maharashtrian food including *baingan masala* (eggplant curry; ₹80) and okra and tomato dishes.

ℹ Information

There are several ATMs in Ganpatipule including one about 400m inland from the MTDC Resort.

ℹ Getting There & Around

Ganpatipule has limited transport links. Ratnagiri, 40km to the south, is the nearest major town. Hourly buses (₹50, 1½ hours) connect the two places; autorickshaws/taxis cost ₹400/750.

Several buses leave Ganpatipule for Mumbai (₹400 to ₹650, 10 hours) between 6.30pm and 10pm; there are also three daily buses to both Pune (₹350) and Kolhapur (₹145).

Ratnagiri train station is on the Konkan Railway line. From Ratnagiri, the Mandovi Express goes daily to Mumbai (2nd class/1st class ₹160/1670, 7½ hours, 2.10pm). The return train heading for Goa (2nd class/1st class ₹120/1400, 5½ hours) is at 1.10pm. From Ratnagiri's old bus stand, buses leave for Goa (semideluxe ₹270, six hours) and Kolhapur (₹160, four hours).

Malvan

☑ 02365

A government tourism promo parades the emerging Malvan region as comparable to Tahiti, which is a tad ambitious, but it does boast near-white sands, sparkling seas and jungle-fringed backwaters. Offshore there are coral reefs, sea caves and vibrant marine life – diving is becoming a huge draw with the opening of a new world-class diving school.

Malvan town is one of the prettiest on the Konkan Coast. It's a mellow place with a good stock of old wooden buildings and a busy little harbour and bazaar. Stretching directly south of the centre is lovely Tarkali beach, home to many hotels and guesthouses.

◎ Sights & Activities

There are several dodgy dive shops operating in Malvan, which allow unqualified diving; if you want to dive, stick with a registered operator.

The southern end of Tarkali beach is bordered by the broad, beautiful Karli river. Several boat operators (you'll find them moored on the northern bank) offer multi-stop boat trips along this backwater, to Seagull Island, Golden Rock, Dolphin Point and cove beaches. A three-hour trip with a maximum of six people costs ₹1800 per boat.

Sindhudurg Fort   FORT

Built by Shivaji and dating from 1664, this monstrous fort lies on an offshore island and can be reached by frequent ferries (9am to 5.30pm, ₹50) from Malvan's harbour. It's not as impressive as Janjira up the coast, and today lies mostly in ruins, but it remains a powerful presence. You can explore its ramparts and the coastal views are impressive. Boatmen allow you one hour on the island.

Tarkali Beach   BEACH

A golden arc south of Marvan, this crescent-shaped sandy beach is a vision of tropical India, fringed by coconut palms and casuarina trees, plus the odd cow. At dusk (between October and February) fishermen work together to haul in huge, kilometre-long nets that are packed with sardines.

★ IISDA   DIVING

(Indian Institute of Scuba Diving & Aquasports; ☑ 02365-248790; www.iisda.gov.in; Tarkali Beach; per dive ₹3000, PADI Open Water ₹22,000) This state-of-the-art new PADI diving cen-

tre is India's finest, run by marine biologist and all-round diving pro Dr Sarang Kulkarni. It offers professional instruction, a 20m-long and 8m-deep pool for training, air-conditioned classrooms and comfortable sleeping quarters for students. IISDA is also a marine conservation centre and there's even a restaurant, bar and tennis court. Located 7km south of Malvan.

🛏 Sleeping & Eating

MTDC Holiday Resort   BUNGALOW $$

(☑ 252390; Tarkali Beach; bungalow/boathouse from ₹3110/5400; ❊🐾) The MTDC Holiday Resort enjoys a wonderful location on a lovely stretch of clean sand 5km south of Malvan town. Its concrete bungalows and boathouses (actually boat-shaped wooden cabins with huge front decks) are a little tired, but spacious. There's a restaurant for seafood, local and Chinese grub. No beer, and wi-fi limited to the reception area only.

★ Chaitanya   MALVANI, INDIAN $$

(☑ 02365-252172; 502 Dr Vallabh Marg; mains ₹70-250; ☉ 11am-11pm) On Malvan's main drag, this great, family-run place specialises in Konkan cuisine including *bangda tikhale* (fish in thick coconut sauce), prawns malvani and very flavoursome crab masala; staff will keep topping up the *sol kadhi* (coconut and fruit digestive) bowl as you eat. Its vegetarian dishes are excellent. It's always packed with locals and has an air-con section.

Athithi Bamboo   INDIAN $$

(Church St; mains ₹60-240; ☉ noon-3.30pm & 8-10.30pm) On the north side of the harbour, this large casual place offers excellent thalis (from ₹60) and lots of fresh fish. There's no

---

KONKAN SPECIALITIES

Often called Malvani cuisine, this coastal region has many special dishes and snacks you should try.

dhondas – cucumber cakes made from cucumber and palm sugar

kaju chi aamti – spicy cashew-nut curry

kombdi vade – spicy chicken prepared with lime and coconut

mori masala – shark curry

sol kadhi – pink-coloured, slightly sour digestive made from coconut milk and kokum fruit; accompanies many meals

MALVAN NATIONAL MARINE PARK

The shoreline around Malvan is incredibly diverse, with rich wetlands, sandy and rocky beaches, mangroves and river estuaries. But underwater it's arguably even more compelling, with coral and caves that shelter abundant marine life and extensive forests of *sargassum* seaweed which acts as a nursery for juvenile fish. Rocky offshore islands attract schools of snapper and large grouper, butterfly fish, yellow-striped fusiliers and lobster. Pods of dolphins are regularly seen between November and February. And the world's largest fish, the whale shark, even puts in an appearance every now and then.

Presently only a small section is protected as the **Malvan National Marine Park**, which encompasses the Sindhudurg Fort, yet such is its rich diversity that marine biologists, including IISDA's director Dr Sarang Kulkarni, feel it's essential that the boundaries are extended. The reef extends for 16km offshore and has been described as India's Great Barrier Reef. A submerged plateau, the **Angria Bank** is 40km long and 20km wide, with healthy coral and an abundance of sealife: nurse sharks are seen on almost every dive. IISDA has plans to operate day trips and liveaboard excursions to Angria; consult its website for information.

sign in English and you sit under a tin roof (so it gets very hot during the day), but the seafood is surf-fresh and cooking is Konkan-authentic.

ℹ Information

There are numerous ATMs in Malvan.
Bank of India ATM (Dr Vallabh Marg)
Scorpion Cyber (Dr Vallabh Marg; ⊙10am-10pm) Several terminals for internet access.

ℹ Getting There & Away

The closest train station is Kudal, 38km away. Frequent buses (₹30, one hour) cover the route from Malvan bus stand, or an autorickshaw is about ₹500. Malvan has ordinary buses to:
Kolhapur ₹170, five hours, seven daily
Mumbai ₹500, 12 hours, one daily
Panaji ₹110, 3½ hours, four daily
Ratnagiri ₹165, five hours, three daily

Malvan is only 80km from northern Goa; taxis charge ₹1200 for the two-hour trip.

Matheran

☏ 02148 / POP 5750 / ELEV 803M
Matheran, literally 'Jungle Above', is a tiny patch of peace and quiet capping a craggy Sahyadri summit within spitting distance of Mumbai's heat and grime. Endowed with shady forests criss-crossed with foot trails and breathtaking lookouts, it still retains an elegance and colonial-era ambience, though creeping commercialism and illegal construction are marring its appeal.

Getting to Matheran is really half the fun. While speedier options are available by

road, nothing beats arriving in town on the narrow-gauge toy train that chugs up to the heart of the settlement. Motor vehicles are banned within Matheran, making it an ideal place to give your ears and lungs a rest and your feet some exercise.

◉ Sights & Activities

You can walk along shady forest paths to most of Matheran's viewpoints in a matter of hours; it's a place well suited to stress-free ambling. To catch the sunrise, head to **Panorama Point**, while **Porcupine Point** (also known as Sunset Point) is the most popular (read: packed) as the sun drops. **Louisa Point** and **Little Chowk Point** also have stunning views of the Sahyadris.

If you're here on a weekend or public holiday you might want to avoid the most crowded section around **Echo Point**, **Charlotte Lake** and **Honeymoon Point**, which get rammed with day trippers.

You can reach the valley below One Tree Hill down the path known as **Shivaji's Ladder**, supposedly trod upon by the Maratha leader himself. Horse-wallahs will hustle you constantly for rides (about ₹300 per hour).

🛏 Sleeping & Eating

Hotels in Matheran are generally overpriced and many places have a minimum two-night stay. Checkout times vary wildly (as early as 7am), as do high- and low-season rates. Matheran shuts shop during the monsoons.

Hope Hall Hotel HOTEL $
(☏ 230253; www.hopehallmatheran.com; MG Rd; d Mon-Fri ₹1370, Sat & Sun ₹1710) Run by a

very hospitable family, this long-running place has been hosting happy travellers for years; the house dates back to 1875. Spacious rooms with high ceilings and arty touches are in two blocks at the rear of the leafy garden. Good breakfasts and drinks are available. Ask Maria to show you her amazing mineral and crystal collection. Rates double during peak holiday periods.

MTDC Resort LODGE $$
(☑ 02148-230277; d ₹1580, with AC ₹5050; ✸) This government-run place offers functional, economy rooms, disappointing family rooms, and modern, very attractive air-conditioned rooms in the Shruti villa. The downside is it's located next to the Dasturi car park, so you're away from the midtown action. There's a good restaurant.

★ **Verandah in the Forest** HERITAGE HOTEL $$$
(☑ 230296; www.neemranahotels.com; Barr House; d incl breakfast from ₹5880) This deliciously preserved 19th-century bungalow thrives on undiluted nostalgia, with quaintly luxurious rooms. Find yourself reminiscing about bygone times in the company of ornate candelabras, oriental rugs, antique teak furniture, Victorian canvases and grandfather clocks. The verandah has a lovely aspect over Matheran's wooded hillsides, and the in-house restaurant offers fine Indian food and a terrific four-course c ontinental dinner (₹600).

Hotel Woodlands HOTEL $$$
(☑ 230271; www.woodlandsmatheran.com; Chinoy Rd; r from ₹5540) A venerable old homestead with historic charm and enough modern comforts thrown in to keep the most fussy guest satisfied. The forested setting is very relaxing and the playground should keep the kids occupied. But it's the verandah that steals the show; a great place to kick back.

Shabbir Bhai INDIAN $
(Merry Rd; mains ₹70-120; ⊙ 10am-10pm) Known locally as the 'Byrianiwala', this funky joint has a full North Indian menu, but it's all about the spicy biryanis: chicken, mutton and veg. To find it, take the footpath uphill beside the Jama Masjid on MG Rd.

ℹ Information

Entry to Matheran costs ₹40 (₹20 for children), which you pay on arrival at the train station or the Dasturi car park.
Union Bank of India (MG Rd; ⊙ 10am-2pm Mon-Fri, to noon Sat) Has an ATM.

ℹ Getting There & Away

TAXI
Buses (₹25) and shared taxis (₹75) run from Neral to Matheran's Dasturi car park (30 minutes). Horses (₹300) and hand-pulled rickshaws (₹400) wait here to whisk you (relatively speaking) to Matheran's main bazaar. You can also walk this stretch in a little under an hour (around 3.5km uphill) and your luggage can be hauled for around ₹220.

TRAIN
The toy train (2nd class/1st class ₹35/225) chugs between Matheran and Neral Junction five times daily. The service is suspended during monsoons.

From Mumbai's CST station there are two daily express trains to Neral Junction at 7am and 8.40am (2nd class/1st class ₹45/205, 1½ hours). Other expresses from Mumbai stop at Karjat, down the line from Neral, from where you can backtrack on a local train or catch a bus to Matheran (₹30). From Pune, there are at least 13 daily departures to Karjat. Note: trains from Pune don't stop at Neral Junction.

ℹ Getting Around

Apart from hand-pulled rickshaws and horses, walking is the only other transport option in Matheran.

Lonavla

☑ 02114 / POP 57,400 / ELEV 625M
Lonavla is an overdeveloped (and overpriced) resort town about 106km southeast of Mumbai. It's far from attractive, with its main drag consisting almost exclusively of garishly lit shops flogging *chikki*, the rockhard, brittle sweet made in the area.

The main reason to come here is to visit the nearby Karla and Bhaja caves which, after those at Ellora and Ajanta, are the best in Maharashtra.

Hotels, restaurants and the main road to the caves lie north of the train station. Most of the Lonavla township and its markets are located south of the station.

🏃 Activities

Kaivalyadhama Yoga Hospital YOGA
(☑ 273039; www.kdham.com; 2-week course incl full board US$800) This progressive yoga centre is located in neatly kept grounds about 2km from Lonavla, en route to the Karla and Bhaja Caves. Founded in 1924 by Swami Kuvalayanandji, it combines yoga courses with

naturopathic therapies. Courses cover full board, yoga classes, programs and lectures.

Nirvana Adventures PARAGLIDING
(☎ 022-26053724; www.flynirvana.com) Mumbai-based Nirvana Adventures offers paragliding courses (two-day learner course ₹8500 per person including full board) and short tandem flights (from ₹2500) in a charming rural setting near the town of Kamshet, 25km from Lonavla.

🛌 Sleeping & Eating

Lonavla's hotels tend to have inflated prices, low standards and early checkouts.

★ Ferreira Resort HOTEL $
(☎ 272689; www.ferreiraresortlonavala.blogspot. co.uk; DT Shahani Rd; s/d Sun-Thu ₹1350/1500, Fri & Sat ₹1600/1800 ; ❀ 🖤) It's certainly not a resort, but it is something of a rarity in Lonavla: a family-run, well-priced place in a quiet residential location that's close to the train station. All the 16 clean, well presented air-con rooms have a balcony and there's a little lawned garden and small restaurant. The owners are helpful and informative about the region.

Citrus HOTEL $$$
(☎ 398100; www.citrushotels.com; DT Shahani Rd; r from ₹6380; ❀ 🖤 🖤) The design and decor of the rooms here don't quite reach the hip hotel target market, but are spacious and well presented and have a modish feel. The garden area has a generously sized pool and loungers. It's a little overpriced, but that's Lonavla.

Biso ITALIAN $$
(Citrus Hotel, DT Shahani Rd; mains ₹230-340; ❀ noon-3.30pm & 7-10.30pm; 🖤) This could be a delightfully redeeming feature of your Lonavla trip. A top-class alfresco restaurant with an excellent selection of pastas, wood-fired pizzas and desserts.

ℹ Information

There are numerous ATMs in town.
Balaji Cyber Café (1st fl, Khandelwal Bldg, New Bazaar; per hour ₹15; ❀ 12.30-10.30pm) Has internet access. Located immediately south of the train station.

ℹ Getting There & Away

Lonavla is serviced by MSRTC buses departing from the bus stand to Dadar in Mumbai (ordinary/semideluxe ₹76/118, two hours) and Pune (ordinary/semideluxe ₹66/105, two hours). Luxury AC buses (₹200 to ₹330) also travel to both cities.

All express trains from Mumbai's CST to Pune stop at Lonavla (2nd class ₹75 to ₹90, chair ₹255 to ₹305, 2½ to three hours).

Karla & Bhaja Caves

While they pale in comparison to Ajanta or Ellora, the Karla and Bhaja rock-cut caves, which date from around the 2nd century BC, are among the better examples of Buddhist cave architecture in India. They are also low on commercial tourism, making them ideal places for a quiet excursion. Karla has the most impressive single cave, but Bhaja is a quieter site to explore.

◉ Sights

Karla Cave CAVE
(Indian/foreigner ₹5/100; ❀ 9am-5pm) Karla Cave, the largest early *chaitya* (Buddhist temple) in India, is reached by a 20-minute climb from a mini-bazaar at the base of a hill. Completed in 80 BC, the *chaitya* is around 40m long and 15m high, and sports a vaulted interior and intricately executed sculptures of Buddha, human and animal figures. Excluding Ellora's Kailasa Temple, this is probably the most impressive cave temple in the state.

A semicircular 'sun window' filters light in towards a dagoba or stupa (the cave's representation of the Buddha), protected by a carved wooden umbrella, the only remaining example of its kind. The cave's roof also retains ancient teak buttresses. The 37 pillars forming the aisles are topped by kneeling elephants. The carved elephant heads on the sides of the vestibule once had ivory tusks. There's a **Hindu temple** in front of the cave, thronged by pilgrims whose presence adds colour to the scene.

Bhaja Caves CAVE
(Indian/foreigner ₹5/100; ❀ 9am-6pm) It's a 3km jaunt from the main road, on the other side of the expressway, to the Bhaja Caves, where the setting is lusher, greener and quieter than at Karla Cave. Thought to date from around 200 BC, 10 of the 18 caves here are *viharas* (Buddhist monasteries), while Cave 12 is an open *chaitya* (Buddhist temple), earlier than that at Karla, containing a simple dagoba. Beyond this is a strange huddle of 14 stupas, five inside and nine outside a smaller cave.

🛏 Sleeping & Eating

MTDC Karla Resort   HOTEL $$
(☑02114-282230; d ₹1740, with AC from ₹2090; ❄) Set off the highway, close to the Karla–Bhaja access point, this large resort in a rural location attracts weekending Mumbai families thanks to its water park (closed in winter) and play facilities. It's much more peaceful during the week. There's a wide choice of rooms and cottages, from economy to smart, and a restaurant.

❶ Getting There & Around

Karla is 11km east of Lonavla, and Bhaja 9km. Both can be visited on a local bus (₹16, 30 minutes) to the access point, from where it's about a 6km return walk on each side to the two sites. But that would be exhausting and hot. Autorickshaws charge around ₹500 from Lonavla for the tour, including waiting time.

Pune

☑020 / POP 5.14 MILLION / ELEV 535M

A thriving, vibrant metropolis, Pune is a centre of academia and business that epitomises 'New India' with its baffling mix of capitalism, spiritualism, ancient and modern. It's also globally famous, or notorious, for an ashram, the Osho International Meditation Resort, founded by the late guru Bhagwan Shree Rajneesh.

Pune was initially given pride of place by Shivaji and the ruling Peshwas, who made it their capital. The British took the city in 1817 and, thanks to its cool and dry climate, soon made it the Bombay Presidency's monsoon capital. Globalisation knocked on Pune's doors in the 1990s, following which it went in for an image overhaul. However, some colonial-era charm was retained in a few old buildings and residential areas, bringing about a pleasant coexistence of the old and new, which (despite the pollution and traffic) makes Pune a worthwhile place to explore.

In August/September Ganesh Chaturthi (p777) brings on a tide of festivities across the city, and provides a fantastic window for exploring the city's cultural side. On a more sombre note, the fatal 2010 terrorist attack on the German Bakery, a once favourite haunt for travellers and ashramites, remains a painful memory in this peace-loving city.

The city sits at the confluence of the Mutha and Mula rivers. Mahatma Gandhi (MG) Rd, about 1km south of Pune train station, is the main commercial street. The leafy upmarket suburb of Koregaon Park, northeast of the train station, is home to numerous hotels, restaurants, coffee shops and, of course, the Osho ashram.

◉ Sights & Activities

Aga Khan Palace   PALACE
(Ahmednagar Rd; Indian/foreigner ₹5/100; ⊙9am-5.30pm) The grand Aga Khan Palace is set in a peaceful wooded 6.5-hectare plot northeast of the centre. Built in 1892 by Sultan Aga Khan III, this graceful building was where Mahatma Gandhi and other prominent nationalist leaders were interned by the British following Gandhi's Quit India campaign in 1942. The main palace now houses the **Gandhi National Memorial** where you can peek into the room where the Mahatma used to stay. Photos and paintings exhibit moments in his extraordinary life.

Both Kasturba Gandhi, the Mahatma's wife, and Mahadeobhai Desai, his secretary for 35 years, died here in confinement. You'll find their shrines (containing their ashes) in a quiet garden to the rear.

Raja Dinkar Kelkar Museum   MUSEUM
(www.rajakelkarmuseum.com; Bajirao Rd, 1377-1378 Natu Baug; Indian/foreigner ₹50/200; ⊙10am-5.30pm) An oddball of a museum that's one of Pune's true delights, housing only a fraction of the 20,000-odd objects of Indian daily life painstakingly collected by Dinkar Kelkar (who died in 1990). The quirky pan-Indian collection includes hundreds of hookah pipes, writing instruments, lamps, textiles, toys, entire doors and windows, kitchen utensils, furniture, puppets, jewellery, betel-nut cutters and an amazing gallery of musical instruments.

Tribal Cultural Museum   MUSEUM
(28 Queen's Garden; Indian/foreigner ₹10/200; ⊙10.30am-5.30pm Mon-Sat) This small museum showcases artefacts (jewellery, utensils, musical instruments, even black-magic accessories) from remote tribal belts. Highlights include some demonic-looking papier-mâché festival masks and superb monochrome Warli paintings.

Shaniwar Wada   FORT
(Shivaji Rd; Indian/foreigner ₹5/100; ⊙8am-6pm) The remains of this fortressed palace of the Peshwa rulers are located in the old part of the city. Built in 1732, Shaniwar Wada was destroyed in a fire in 1828, but the massive walls and ramparts remain, as does a mighty fortified gateway. In the evenings, there's a

Pune

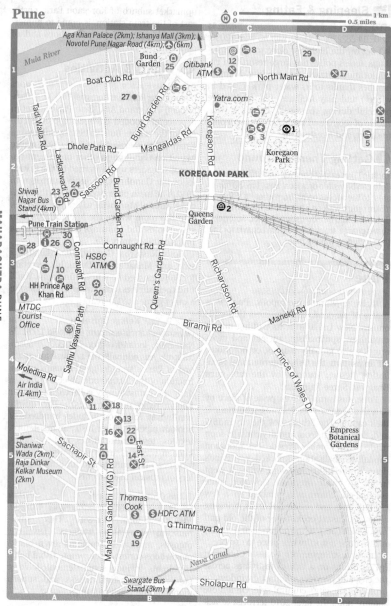

45-minute sound-and-light show (in English at 8.30pm; ₹25) though a minimum of 10 people is needed for the show to commence.

Pateleshvara Cave Temple   HINDU TEMPLE
(Jangali Maharaj Rd; ☺6am-9.30pm) Set across the river is the curious rock-cut Pateleshvara Cave Temple, a small and unfinished (though actively used) 8th-century temple, similar in style to the grander caves at Elephanta Island. Adjacent is the **Jangali Maharaj Temple** (☺6am-9.30pm), dedicated to a Hindu ascetic who died here in 1818.

Pune

MAHARASHTRA PUNE

Osho Teerth Gardens   GARDENS

(⊘ 6-9am & 3-6pm) The 5-hectare Osho Teerth gardens are a verdant escape from urban living with giant bamboo, jogging trails, a gurgling brook and smooching couples. You don't have to be an Osho member as they're accessible to all.

Osho International
Meditation Resort   MEDITATION

(☑ 66019999; www.osho.com; 17 Koregaon Park) Indelibly linked with Pune's identity, this iconic ashram-resort, located in a leafy, up-scale northern suburb, has been drawing thousands of *sanyasins* (seekers) since the death of Osho in 1990. With its swimming pool, sauna and spa, 'zennis' and boutique guesthouse, it is, to some, the ultimate place to indulge in some luxe meditation. Alternately, detractors point fingers at the blatant commercialisation and high cost and accuse it of marketing a warped version of the mystic East to rich, gullible Westerners.

To make up your own mind you'll have to cough up the (steep) registration and daily meditation fees. Tours of the facilities are no longer permitted – the only way to access Osho is to pay an initial ₹1400, which covers registration (passport required) and a mandatory on-the-spot HIV test (sterile needles used). You'll also need two robes (one ma-

roon and one white, ₹500 to ₹700 per robe) and attend a welcome session (daily at 9am). Note that the rules and regulations are very strict, even pedantic: swimmers are only allowed to wear, and have to pay for, Osho maroon swimwear and there are mandatory (Osho maroon) clothes for the gym. Indian nationals are also lectured about behaviour (eg not hassling foreign women) in special etiquette classes.

Once you've got all this out the way, you can then pay for a meditation pass (₹760/1560 per day Indian/foreigner, with discounts for longer stays). Oh, that's apart from the fee to enter the Basho Spa (where the pool, Jacuzzi, gym, saunas and tennis courts are all located), which will be a further ₹280.

The main centre for meditation and the nightly white-robed spiritual dance in the Osho Auditorium (no coughing or sneezing, please). The Osho Samadhi, where the guru's ashes are kept, is also open for meditation. The commune's 'Multiversity' runs a plethora of courses in meditation and other esoteric techniques. In the evenings, as well as meditation sessions, there's a 'nightlife' program, with parties, cinema and theatre and 'creativity nights'. Photography is not permitted anywhere in the ashram.

Ramamani Iyengar Memorial Yoga Institute
YOGA

(☑ 25656134; www.bksiyengar.com; 1107 B/1 Hare Krishna Mandir Rd, Model Colony) To attend classes at this famous institute, 7km northwest of the train station, you need to have been practising yoga for at least eight years.

🛏 Sleeping

Pune's main accommodation hubs are around the train station, where budget places proliferate, and leafy Koregaon Park, where you'll find good midrange options. Many upmarket places are on the road to the airport, 6km or so from the centre.

Hotel Homeland
HOTEL $

(☑ 26123203; www.hotelhomeland.net; 18 Wilson Garden; s/d ₹1040/1250, with AC from ₹1410/1620; ❄) A landmark art deco building that's very convenient to the train station, yet tucked away from the associated din. Rooms are in good shape with freshly painted walls, and there's a coffee shop and restaurant. Be sure to book ahead.

Hotel Surya Villa
HOTEL $

(☑ 26124501; www.hotelsuryavilla.com; 294/2 Koregaon Park; s/d from ₹1340/1670, with AC ₹1670/2350; ❄🛜) The Surya's functional, tiled rooms are well kept and generously proportioned, and though a little Spartan, they do have bathrooms with hot water, wi-fi and cable TV. It enjoys a good location on a quiet street in Koregaon Park, close to popular cafes.

★ Hotel Sunderban
HOTEL $$

(☑ 26124949; www.tghotels.com; 19 Koregaon Park; s/d incl breakfast from ₹3300/3850; ❄🛜) Set around a manicured lawn right next to the Osho Resort, this renovated art deco bungalow effortlessly combines colonial-era class with boutique appeal. Deluxe rooms in the main building sport antique furniture, while even the cheapest options are beautifully presented (though lack a private bathroom). The priciest rooms are across the lawns, in a sleek, glass-fronted building.

An additional draw is the in-house fine-dining restaurant, Dario's.

Novotel Pune Nagar Road
HOTEL $$

(☑ 67056000; www.novotel.com; Weikfield IT City Infopark, Pune-Nagar Rd; s/d from ₹4330/4650; ❄🛜🏊) Around 5km northeast of the centre, handily placed for the airport and tech parks, this contemporary-chic hotel gets everything right, with an excellent restaurant-cafe, a rooftop pool big enough for laps, good gym, superb service and commodious rooms. It's fine value.

— proper:

Hotel Lotus
HOTEL $$

(26139701; www.hotelsuryavilla.com; Lane 5, Koregaon Park; s/d ₹1640/2230, with AC ₹2230/2820; ❄🛜) Hotel Lotus is good value for the quiet, Koregaon Park location, and though the rooms are not that spacious, they are light and airy, most with balconies. There's no restaurant, though they offer room service and there are plenty of good eating options close by.

Samrat Hotel
HOTEL $$

(26137964; thesamrathotel@vsnl.net; 17 Wilson Garden; s/d from ₹2110/2530, with AC from ₹2930/3390; ❄🛜) It's not quite as grand as its fancy lobby would indicate, but with a central location just a few steps from the train station and spacious, well-maintained rooms, the Samrat represents decent value. Complimentary airport pick-up.

Hotel Srimaan
HOTEL $$

(26136565; srimaan@vsnl.com; 361/5 Bund Garden Rd; s/d ₹3120/3600; ❄@🛜) With a good location opposite the Pune Central shopping mall, free wi-fi and a well-regarded Italian restaurant, this business hotel is a solid choice. Rooms are compact but quite luxurious for the price.

Osho Meditation Resort Guesthouse
GUESTHOUSE $$$

(66019900; www.osho.com; Koregaon Park; s/d ₹6930/7510; ❄🛜) This uberchic place will only allow you in if you come to meditate at the Osho International Meditation Resort. The rooms and common spaces are an exercise in modern minimalist aesthetics with several ultra-luxe features – including purified fresh air supplied in all rooms!

🍴 Eating

Kayani Bakery
BAKERY $

(6 East St; cakes & biscuits per kg from ₹200; 7.30am-1pm & 3.30-8pm) A Raj-era institution that seems to be stuck in a time warp, where those in the know queue (in the loose sense of the word) for Shrewsbury biscuits (₹320 per kilogram), bread, Madeira (₹100) and sponge cakes (₹40).

Juice World
CAFE $

(2436/B East St; snacks ₹60-80; 11am-11.30pm) This casual cafe with outdoor seating serves wholesome snacks such as *pav bhaji* (spiced vegetables and bread) and delicious fresh fruit juices and shakes. On a hot day it's impossible to walk past its fruit displays and not drop in for a drink.

Coffee House
CAFE $

(2A Moledina Rd; mains ₹60-140; 8am-11.30pm) A calm and clean, coffee-coloured, almost art deco retreat with a huge menu and satisfying filter coffee. Dishes include dosas and other excellent South Indian menu items, plus North Indian curries and Chinese.

German Bakery
BAKERY $$

(North Main Rd; cakes ₹40-170, mains ₹160-190; 6.30am-11.30pm; 🛜) A Pune institution famous for its traveller-geared grub, including omelettes, breakfasts, Greek salad, cappuccinos and lots of sweet treats (try the mango cheesecake). Located on a very busy traffic-plagued corner, it's running again after the fatal terrorist attack here in 2010.

Prem's
MULTICUISINE $$

(North Main Rd, Koregaon Park; mains ₹140-340; 8am-11.30pm; 🛜) In a quiet, tree-canopied courtyard, Prem's is perfect for a lazy, beery daytime drinking session, with lots of imported beers to try, perhaps with one of its famous sizzlers. The morning after? Well, Prem's is the logical choice again, with the city's best breakfast selection: eggs Benedict with smoked salmon (₹160), cereals, pancakes and detox shots.

Mayur
INDIAN $$

(www.mayurthali.com; 2434 East St; dishes/thalis from ₹60/300; 8am-11pm) Famous throughout Pune for its sweet, spicy and unlimited Gujarati-style thalis, which are lovingly prepared, as well as good lassis and juices!

⭐ Malaka Spice
ASIAN FUSION $$$

(www.malakaspice.com; Lane 5, Koregaon Park, North Main Rd; mains ₹280-730; 11.30am-11.30pm; 🛜) Mouth-watering Southeast Asian fare that's been given a creative tweak or two by star chefs. Choose from the classic or street menu, both strong on seafood, vegetarian, chicken, duck and mutton offerings. Eat alfresco or in the air-con room (which doubles as an art gallery).

⭐ Dario's
ITALIAN $$$

(www.darios.in; Hotel Sunderban, 19 Koregaon Park; mains ₹310-380; 11.30am-3pm & 7-11pm; 🛜) At the rear of Hotel Sunderban, this Italian place is perhaps the most elegant dining experience in Pune, with fine art in the stunning air-con dining room and a gorgeous courtyard for alfresco meals. Expensive but worth a splurge with homemade pasta, milanesas, fish and fine salads: try a Bosco (₹450) with milanesas and mushrooms.

The Place: Touche the Sizzler
MULTICUISINE $$$

(7 Moledina Rd; mains ₹330-480; 11.30am-3.30pm & 7-10.45pm) The perfect old-school eating option where the menu evokes the days of the Raj, Queen Victoria and all that old chap: shrimp cocktails, Russian salads, steak cordon bleu and a few options from the tandoor. The smoking sizzlers (veg, seafood, beef, chicken) can't be beat.

🍷 Drinking & Entertainment

1000 Oaks
NIGHTCLUB

(2417 East St; 7pm-late) An old favourite with a cosy pub-style bar, a compact dance floor and a charming terrace for those who prefer it quieter. Pitchers (₹700 to ₹750) of Long Island iced tea and sangria are very popular. There's live music on Sunday.

Hoppipola – All Day Bar & Bonhomie
BAR

(ITI Park, Aundh; noon-11pm Tue-Sun, 5-11pm Mon;) Hip new bar in the university zone that attracts a young arty, studenty crowd with its zany decor, chillout garden, wine and cocktail selection and good bar food: try the rasta chicken. There's a relaxed vibe during the week, but it gets rammed on weekends. It's around 6km west of the centre.

⭐ Bluefrog
NIGHTCLUB, LIVE MUSIC

(020-40054001; www.bluefrog.co.in; Ishanya Mall, off Airport Rd, Yerwada; 6pm-12.30am Tue-Fri, 1pm Sat & Sun) This new Pune branch of Mumbai's famous Bluefrog has really shaken up the city's nightlife, with exciting electronic DJs, live music from all over the world, theatre and stand-up comedy, depending on the night. The seriously stylish venue has hip semicircular seating pods, a sweeping bar, full range of cocktails (₹450) and good grub (₹300 to ₹700)

Inox
CINEMA

(www.inoxmovies.com; Bund Garden Rd) A multiplex where you can take in the latest blockbuster from Hollywood or Mumbai.

🔒 Shopping

Bombay Store
SOUVENIRS

(www.thebombaystore.com; 322 MG Rd; 10.30am-8.30pm Mon-Sat) Stocks quality handicrafts, souvenirs, quirky bags, hip accessories and contemporary furnishings.

Ishanya Mall
MALL

(www.ishanya.com; off Airport Rd, Yerwada; 11am-10pm) Huge new mall that's richly endowed with interior design and fashion stores. Shop till you drop then head to the food court (or Bluefrog, which is also located here).

Fabindia
CLOTHING

(www.fabindia.com; Sakar 10, Sassoon Rd; 10am-8pm) For Indian saris, silks and cottons, as well as linen shirts for men and diverse accessories including bags and jewellery.

Crossword
BOOKS

(www.crossword.in; 1st fl, Sohrab Hall, Ladkatwadi Rd; 10.30am-9pm) An excellent collection of fiction, nonfiction and magazines. There's a smaller branch on East St.

Pune Central
MALL

(Bund Garden Rd, Koregaon Park; 10am-10pm) This centrally located mall is full of global labels and premium Indian tags.

ℹ️ Information

You'll find several internet cafes along Pune's main thoroughfares and there are dozens of ATMs spread through the city and at the train station.

Main Post Office (Sadhu Vaswani Path; 10am-6pm Mon-Sat)

MTDC Tourist Office (26126867; I Block, Central Bldg, Dr Annie Besant Rd; 10am-

MAHABALESHWAR

Once a summer capital under the British, today the hill station of Mahabaleshwar (1327m) is an over-developed mess, tainted by an ugly building boom and traffic chaos as tourists attempt a mad dash to tick off its viewpoints. There's no massive reason to visit, though the town can be used as a base to visit the impressive Pratapgad fort (p808) an hour or so away. Don't even consider dropping by during the monsoon when the whole town virtually shuts down (and a staggering 6m of rain falls).

From Mahabaleshwar bus stand, state buses leave roughly hourly for Pune (semideluxe ₹240, 3½ hours). Luxury buses can be booked via agents in the bazaar for Goa (₹1300 to ₹1780, 12 hours, some with a changeover in Surur); Mumbai (₹525 to ₹800, 7½ hours) and Pune (₹630 to ₹790, 3½ hours).

For the Pratapgad fort, a state bus (₹130 return, one hour, 9.15am) does a daily round-trip, with a waiting time of around one hour; taxi drivers charge a fixed ₹1000 return.

MAJOR TRAINS FROM PUNE

DESTINATION	TRAIN NO & NAME	FARE (₹)	DURATION (HR)	DEPARTURE
Bengaluru	16529 Udyan Express	455/1765	21	11.45am
Chennai	12163 Chennai Express	515/1950	19½	12.10am
Delhi	11077 Jhelum Express	615/2400	27½	5.20pm
Hyderabad	17031 Hyderabad Express	330/1280	13½	4.35pm
Mumbai CST	12124 Deccan Queen	105/370	3½	7.15am

Express fares are sleeper/2AC; Deccan Queen fares are 2nd class/chair

5.30pm Mon-Sat, closed 2nd & 4th Sat) Buried in a government complex south of the train station. There's also an MTDC desk (☺10am-5.30pm Mon-Sat) at the train station.

Shivam Computers (Koregaon Park; per hour ₹20; ☺10am-10pm) Quick connections and helpful staff.

Thomas Cook (☑66007903; 2418 G Thimmaya Rd; ☺9.30am-6pm Mon-Sat) Cashes travellers cheques and exchanges foreign currency.

Yatra.com (☑020-65006748; www.yatra.com; Koregaon Park Rd; ☺10am-8pm Mon-Sat) The city office of the internet ticketing company.

ⓘ Getting There & Away

AIR

Airlines listed below fly daily from Pune to Mumbai (from ₹5400, 45 minutes), Delhi (from ₹5800, two hours), Jaipur (from ₹3800, 1½ hours), Bengaluru (from ₹2100, 1½ hours), Nagpur (from ₹2400, 1½ hours), Goa (from ₹2500, one hour) and Chennai (from ₹3700, 1½ hours).

Air India (☑26052147; www.airindia.in; 39 Dr B Ambedkar Rd)

GoAir (☑9223222111; www.goair.in)

IndiGo (☑9910383838; www.goindigo.in)

Jet Airways (☑022-39893333; www.jetairways.com; 243 Century Arcade, Narangi Baug Rd)

BUS

Buses leave the **Pune train station stand** (☑020-26126218) for Mumbai, Goa, Belgaum, Kolhapur (₹350, five hours, hourly), Mahabaleshwar and Lonavla (₹170, 2½ hours, hourly). Deluxe buses shuttle from here to Dadar (Mumbai; ₹330, 3½ hours) every hour. From the **Shivaji Nagar bus stand** (☑020-25536970) buses go to Aurangabad (from ₹270, five to six hours, every 45 minutes), Ahmedabad and Nasik, while buses for Sinhagad, Bengaluru and Mangalore leave from the **Swargate bus stand** (☑020-24441591).

Private buses head to Panaji in Goa (ordinary from ₹300, AC sleeper ₹700 to ₹1200, 11 hours), Nasik (semideluxe/deluxe ₹270/550, 5½

hours) and Aurangabad (₹250/550, 5½ hours). Pune has three bus stands.

TAXI

Shared taxis (up to four passengers) link Pune with Mumbai airport around the clock. They leave from the **taxi stand** (☑02026121090) in front of Pune train station (₹475 per seat, 2½ hours). To rent a car and driver try **Simran Travels** (☑26153222; North Main Rd , Koregaon Park).

TRAIN

Pune train station (sometimes called Pune Junction) is in the heart of the city, on HH Prince Aga Khan Rd. There are very regular, roughly hourly, services to Mumbai, and good links to cities including Delhi, Chennai and Hyderabad.

ⓘ Getting Around

The modern airport is 8km northeast of the city. From the centre of town, an autorickshaw costs about ₹120 and a taxi ₹280.

Autorickshaws can be found everywhere; a trip from the train station to Koregaon Park costs about ₹40 (more at night).

Around Pune

Sinhagad

The ruined **Sinhagad** (Lion Fort; ☺dawn-dusk) **FREE**, situated about 24km southwest of Pune, was wrested by Maratha leader Shivaji from the Bijapur kings in 1670. In the epic battle (where he lost his son Sambhaji), Shivaji is said to have used monitor lizards yoked with ropes to scale the fort's craggy walls. Today, it's in a poor state, but worth visiting for the sweeping views and opportunity to hike in the hills. From Sinhagad village, shared 4WDs (₹50) can cart you 10km to the base of the summit. Bus 50 runs frequently to Sinhagad village from Swargate (₹27, 45 minutes).

WORTH A TRIP

PRATAPGAD FORT

The spectacular **Pratapgad Fort** (Indian/foreigner ₹10/100; ☉9am-dusk), built by Shivaji in 1656 (and still owned by his descendents), straddles a high mountain ridge 24km northwest of the town of Mahabaleshwar. In 1659, Shivaji agreed to meet Bijapuri general Afzal Khan here, in an attempt to end a stalemate. Despite a no-arms agreement, Shivaji, upon greeting Khan, disembowelled his enemy with a set of iron *baghnakh* (tiger's claws). Khan's tomb marks the site of this painful encounter at the base of the fort. Pratapgad is reached by a 500-step climb that affords brilliant views. For ₹200 a guide will take you to 20 points of interest, taking nearly two hours.

From the bus stand in Mahabaleshwar, 120km south of Pune, a state bus (₹130 return, one hour, 9.15am) does a daily shuttle to the fort, with a waiting time of around one hour. Taxi drivers in Mahabaleshwar charge a fixed ₹1000 return.

Shivneri

Situated 90km northwest of Pune, above the village of Junnar, **Shivneri Fort** (☉dawn-dusk) **FREE** holds the distinction of being the birthplace of Shivaji. Within the ramparts of this ruined fort are the old royal stables, a mosque dating back to the Mughal era and several rock-cut reservoirs. The most important structure is Shivkunj, the pavilion in which Shivaji was born.

About 4km from Shivneri, on the other side of Junnar, is an interesting group of Hinayana Buddhist caves called **Lenyadri** (Indian/foreigner ₹5/100; ☉dawn-dusk). Of the 30-odd caves, cave 7 is the most impressive, and interestingly houses an image of the Hindu god Ganesh.

Hourly buses (₹85, two hours) connect Pune's Shivaji Nagar terminus with Junnar. A cab from Pune is about ₹2600.

Kolhapur

☏0231 / POP 561,300 / ELEV 550M

A little-visited city, Kolhapur is the perfect place to get intimate with the flamboyant side of India. Only a few hours from Goa, this historic settlement boasts an intensely fascinating temple complex. In August, Kolhapur is at its vibrant best, when **Naag Panchami** (☉Jul/Aug), a snake-worshipping festival, is held in tandem with one at Pune. Gastronomes take note: the town is also the birthplace of the famed, spicy Kolhapuri cuisine, especially chicken and mutton dishes.

The old town around the Mahalaxmi Temple is 3km southwest of the bus and train stations, while the 'new' palace is a similar distance to the north. Rankala Lake, a popular spot for evening strolls, is 5km southwest of the stations.

◉ Sights

The atmospheric old town quarter around the Mahalaxmi Temple and Old Palace has a huge (traffic-free) plaza and is accessed by a monumental gateway.

★**Mahalaxmi Temple**　HINDU TEMPLE
(☉5am-10.30pm) One of Maharashtra's most important and vibrant places of worship, the Mahalaxmi Temple is dedicated to Amba Bai (Mother Goddess). The temple's origins date back to AD 10, but much of the present structure is from the 18th century. It draws an unceasing tide of humanity, as pilgrims press to enter the holy inner sanctuary and bands of musicians and worshippers chant devotions. Non-Hindus are welcome and it's a fantastic place for people-watching.

★**Shree Chhatrapati Shahu Museum**　MUSEUM
(Indian/foreigner incl coffee ₹20/75; ☉9.30am-5.30pm) 'Bizarre' takes on a whole new meaning at this 'new' palace, an Indo-Saracenic behemoth designed by British architect 'Mad' Charles Mant for the Kolhapur kings in 1884. The madcap museum features countless trophies from the kings' trigger-happy jungle safaris, including walking sticks made from leopard vertebrae and ashtrays fashioned out of tiger skulls and rhino feet. The armoury houses enough weapons to stage a mini-coup. The horror-house effect is brought full circle by the taxidermy section. Don't miss the highly ornate Durbar Hall, where the rulers held court sessions, and dotted around the palace you'll find dozens of portraits of the portly maharajas to admire. Photography is prohibited inside. There's a little cafe by the entrance for snacks (and where foreigners may claim their com-

plimentary coffee). A rickshaw from the train station will cost ₹35.

Old Palace
HISTORIC BUILDING

In the heart of the old town this palace was once the ruling Chatrapati's main residence, and is still occupied by some in the family. You can enter the building's front courtyard but there's little to see today except a temple dedicated to the deity Bhavani Mata.

Motibag Thalim
COURTYARD

Kolhapur is famed for the calibre of its Kushti wrestlers, and at the Motibag Thalim, young athletes train in an earthen pit. The *akhara* (training ground) is reached through a low doorway and passage beside the entrance to Bhavani Mandap (ask for directions). You are free to walk in and watch, as long as you don't mind the sight of sweaty, semi-naked men and the stench of urine emanating from the loos.

Kasbagh Maidan
SPORTS ARENA

Professional wrestling bouts are held between June and December in this red-earth arena a short walk south of Motibag Thalim.

🛏 Sleeping & Eating

Hotel Pavillion
HOTEL $

(📞2652751; www.hotelpavillion.co.in; 392 Assembly Rd; s/d incl breakfast ₹1460/1730, with AC from ₹1920/2240; ❄@) Located at the far end of a leafy park-cum-office-area, this hotel guarantees a peaceful stay. Its large, well-equipped rooms are perhaps a little dated but many have windows that open out to delightful views of seasonal blossoms.

Hotel Panchshil
HOTEL $$

(📞2537517; www.hotelpanchshilkolhapur.com; 517 A2 Shivaji Park; s/d ₹3400/3740; ❄🛜) The ageing lobby and location on a busy road are a little off-putting but the rooms have been given the full makeover treatment and are very inviting, comfortable and stylish. The Little Italy restaurant downstairs is another excellent reason to check in.

Hotel K Tree
HOTEL $$

(📞0231-2526990; www.hotelktree.com; 65 E, Shivaji Park; s/d incl breakfast from ₹3230/3880; ❄🛜) With high service standards and very inviting modish rooms, this new hotel is fine value. It's located on a quiet side street, so there's little traffic noise and the multicusine restaurant has an extensive menu.

Surabhi
INDIAN $

(Hotel Sahyadri Bldg; mains ₹70-100; ⏱10am-10pm) A great place to savour Kolhapur's legendary snacks such as spicy *misal* (puffed rice tossed with fried rounds of dough, lentils, onions, herbs and chutneys), thalis and lassi. It's close to the bustling bus stand.

★ Little Italy
ITALIAN $$

(📞0231-2537133; www.littleitaly.in; 517 A2 Shivaji Park; mains ₹250-450) If you've been clocking up some hard yards on India's roads, this authentic, professionally run restaurant is just the place to head to sustain you for the next trip. All the flavours are to savour, with a delicious, veg-only menu of antipasta, thin-crust pizzas (from a wood-fired oven), *al dente* pasta and a great wine list (by the glass available).

ℹ Information

Axis Bank ATM Near the Mahalaxmi Temple.
Internet Zone (Kedar Complex, Station Rd; per hour ₹20; ⏱8am-11pm)
MTDC Tourist Office (📞2652935; Assembly Rd; ⏱10am-5.30pm Mon-Sat) Located opposite the Collector's Office.
State Bank of India (Udyamnagar; ⏱10am-2pm Mon-Sat) A short autorickshaw ride southwest of the train station near Hutatma Park. Handles foreign exchange and has an ATM.

ℹ Getting There & Around

From the bus stand, services head regularly to Pune (semideluxe/deluxe ₹280/500, five hours), Ratnagiri (ordinary/semideluxe ₹120/154, four hours) and ordinary-only buses to Malvan (₹170, five hours). Most private bus agents are on the western side of the square at Mahalaxmi Chambers, across from the bus stand. There are over a dozen daily dozen services to Panaji (semideluxe ₹400, AC sleeper ₹800 to ₹1050, 5½ hours). Overnight AC services head to Mumbai (seat ₹450, sleeper ₹600 to ₹1250, nine hours).

The train station, known as Chattrapati Shahu Maharaj Terminus, is 10 minutes' walk west of the bus stand. Three daily expresses, including the 10.50pm Sahyadri Express, go to Mumbai (sleeper/2AC ₹305/1165, 13 hours) via Pune (₹210/805, eight hours). The Rani Chennama Express makes the long voyage to Bengaluru (sleeper/2AC ₹4000/1555, 17½ hours, 2.20pm). There are no direct trains to Goa.

Autorickshaws are abundant in Kolhapur and many drivers carry conversion charts to calculate fares from the outdated meters.

Kolhapur airport was not operational at the time of research.

Goa

♪ 0832 / POP 1.46 MILLION

Best Places to Eat

➡ Ruta's World Cafe (p843)

➡ Go With the Flow (p830)

➡ Black Sheep Bistro (p818)

➡ Bomra's (p826)

➡ Ourem 88 (p853)

Best Beaches

➡ Palolem (p849)

➡ Mandrem (p839)

➡ Cola & Khancola (p848)

➡ Anjuna (p831)

➡ Arambol (p840)

Why Go?

Goa is like no other state in India. It could be the Portuguese colonial influence, the endless beaches, the glorious whitewashed churches or the relaxed culture of *susegad* – a uniquely Goan term that translates as 'laid-backness' and is evident in all aspects of daily life and in the Goan people themselves.

But Goa is far more than its old-school reputation as a hippie haven or its contemporary status as a beach getaway. Goa is as naturally and culturally rich as it is compact; you can go birdwatching in a butterfly-filled forest, marvel at centuries-old cathedrals, trek out to milky waterfalls and aromatic spice farms or meander the capital's charming alleyways. Add a dash of Portuguese-influenced food and architecture, infuse with a colourful blend of religious traditions, pepper with parties and beach shacks, and you've got a recipe that makes Goa easy to enjoy and extremely hard to leave.

When to Go
Goa (Panaji)

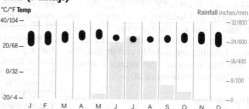

Sep–Nov	Dec–Feb Festivals,	Mar–Apr
Post-monsoon, some shacks are up but crowds are still down	Christmas and great weather; peak prices and crowds from mid-Dec to early Jan.	Carnival and Easter celebrations as the season winds down.

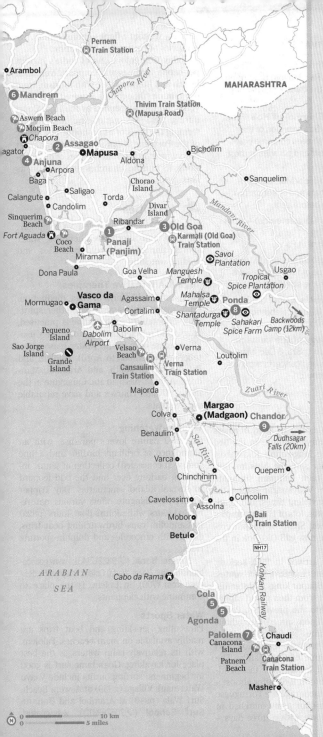

1 Wander the Portuguese-era quarters of **Panaji** (p814), cruise the Mandovi and linger over lunch at one of its traditional Goan restaurants

2 Open up your chakras and join one of the **yoga** (p835) retreats around Assagao and Anjuna

3 Bask in the glory of the grand Se Cathedral and Basilica of Bom Jesus at historic **Old Goa** (p821)

4 Bargain hard at **Anjuna's flea market** (p834) then watch the sunset at a beachside bar

5 Indulge in barefoot luxury on the white-sand beach at **Agonda** (p848) or hidden **Cola Beach** (p848), in the state's sleepy south

6 Worship the sun and sleep in style at smooth and soulful **Mandrem Beach** (p839)

7 Kayak out to see playful dolphins at sunset from **Palolem Beach** (p849)

8 Spend a day learning about the spices that first made Goa famous at a **spice plantation** (p823) near Ponda

9 Dream of times gone by in the mansions of **Chandor** (p845)

STATE FESTIVALS

Feast of the Three Kings (p845; 6 Jan, Chandor & Reis Magos) Boys re-enact the story of the three kings bearing gifts for Christ.

Shigmotsav (Shigmo) of Holi (Feb/Mar; statewide) Goa's version of the Hindu festival Holi sees coloured powders thrown about and parades in most towns.

Sabado Gordo (Feb/Mar; Panaji) A procession of floats and street parties on the Saturday before Lent.

Carnival (p815; Mar; statewide) A four-day festival kicking off Lent; the party's particularly jubilant in Panaji.

Fama de Menino Jesus (2nd Mon in Oct; Colva) Statue of the baby Jesus is paraded through the streets of Colva.

Feast of St Francis Xavier (p821; 3 Dec; Old Goa) A 10-day celebration of Goa's patron saint

Feast of Our Lady of the Immaculate Conception (p815; 8 Dec; Margao, Panaji) Fairs and concerts around Panaji's famous church.

History

Goa went through a dizzying array of rulers from Ashoka's Mauryan empire in the 3rd century BC to the long-ruling Kadambas. Subsequent conflict saw the Muslim Delhi sultanate and then Bahmani sultanate fighting the Hindu Vijayanagar empire for control; these were violent times, and in addition to many deaths, lots of Hindu temples were razed. The Adil Shahs of Bijapur created the capital we now call Old Goa in the 15th century.

The Portuguese arrived in 1510, seeking control of the region's lucrative spice routes. They defeated the Bijapur kings and steadily pushed their power from their grand capital at Old Goa out into the provinces. Portuguese rule and religion spread throughout the state – sometimes by force – and the Goan Inquisition brought repression and brutality in the name of Christianity. The Portuguese resisted India's 1947 Independence from Britain but in 1961, after almost a decade in talks to encourage the Portuguese to withdraw, the Indian Army marched in and took Goa by force within three days – virtually without a fight – ending almost five centuries of Portuguese occupation.

Today Goa enjoys one of India's highest per-capita incomes and comparatively high health and literacy rates, with tourism, iron-ore mining (though this is mired in controversy and was suspended by the High Court during 2013–14), agriculture and fishing forming the basis of its economy. The legacy of the Portuguese can still be found almost everywhere, in the state's scores of old mansions, its cuisine, churches and even in its language.

🏃 Activities

In season Goa has a whole host of options for yoga and alternative therapies, water sports, paragliding, cooking classes and wildlife-watching.

Yoga & Alternative Therapies

Every imaginable form of yoga, meditation, reiki, ayurvedic massage and other spiritually orientated health regime is practised, taught and relished in Goa, though they usually operate only in the winter season (October or November to April). Palolem and Patnem, in the south, and Arambol, Mandrem, Anjuna, Assagao and Calangute in the north, all offer courses and have reputable yoga retreats.

Wildlife-Watching

Goa is a nature lover's paradise, with an abundance of brilliant birdlife and a fine (but well concealed) collection of fauna, including barking deer and the odd leopard in several inland sanctuaries. Day Tripper (p827) in Calangute offers various nature-related tours, while John's Boat Tours (p825) in Candolim runs birdwatching boat trips, along with crocodile- and dolphin-spotting rides.

Jungle Book (☑9822121431; www.goaecotourism.com; Bazar Wada, Colem; elephant rides/wash from ₹700), in Colem, is the place to commune with elephants.

Water Sports

Parasailing, jet-skiing and boat trips are readily available on main beaches. Palolem, with its relatively calm waters, is the best place for kayaking. Goa's tame surf is good for beginners: surfing outfits include Vaayu Waterman's Village (p839) at Aswem Beach, Surf Wala (p840) at Arambol and Banana Surf School (☑7057998120; www.goasurf.

com; Utorda Beach; lessons €45-250; ⊙7.30am-12.30pm Oct-Mar) at Utorda.

Goa has four scuba diving outfits where you can gain PADI certification and go on dive trips to Grande Island and further afield. Goa Aquatics (p827), Barracuda Diving (p827) and **Goa Diving** (☑9049442647; www.goadiving.com; courses from ₹11,000, one-/two-tank dive ₹3000/5000) are recommended.

ⓘ Information

The Goa Tourism Development Corporation (p820) provides maps and information, operates hotels throughout the state and runs a host of one-day and multiday tours.

ⓘ Getting There & Away

AIR

Goa's only airport, Dabolim, is served directly by domestic flights, a handful of international flights from the Middle East; and seasonal package-holiday charters, mostly from Russia, Europe and Britain.

Unless you're on a charter you'll generally have to fly in to a major Indian city and change to a domestic flight with Jet Airways, Air India, SpiceJet or IndiGo.

BUS

Plenty of long-distance interstate buses – both state-run and private – operate to and from Panaji, Margao, Mapusa and Chaudi, near Palolem. Fares for private operators are only slightly higher than for Kadamba government buses, and they fluctuate throughout the year. Long-distance buses may be standard, air-conditioned (AC), Volvo (the most comfortable seater buses) and sleeper. For fares, timetables and online booking see www.goakadamba.com.

TRAIN

The **Konkan Railway**, the main train line running through Goa, connects Mumbai and Mangalore, though the rail line continues all the way south to Trivandrum. The biggest station in Goa is Margao's Madgaon station. See the Margao section (p844) for useful trains. Other smaller stations on the line include Pernem for Arambol, Thivim for Mapusa and the northern beaches, Karmali (Old Goa) for Panaji, and Canacona for Palolem.

ⓘ Getting Around

TO/FROM THE AIRPORT

Dabolim's prepaid taxi counter in the arrivals hall makes arriving easy; buy your ticket here and you'll be ushered to a cab. Real budgeteers without much luggage can try walking out to the main road and waving down one of the frequent buses heading east from Vasco da Gama to Margao and catch onward transport from there.

BUS

Goa's extensive network of local buses run frequently and fares range from ₹5 to ₹40. Travelling between north, central and south Goa you'll need to change buses at either Panaji or Margao.

CAR & MOTORCYCLE

It's easy in Goa to organise a private car with a driver for long-distance day trips. Expect to pay from ₹2000 for a full day out on the road (usually defined as eight hours and 80km). It's also possible, if you have the nerves and the need to feel independent, to procure a self-drive car. A

SLEEPING PRICES IN GOA

Accommodation prices in Goa vary considerably depending on the season and demand. High-season prices run from November to late February, but prices climb higher to a peak rate during the crowded Christmas and New Year period (around 22 December to 3 January). Mid-season is October and March to April, and low season is the monsoon (May to September). These seasonal dates can vary a little depending on the monsoon and the granting of shack licences, which are renewed every couple of years. As well as hotels, seasonal beach huts and guesthouses, throughout Goa's coastal belt are private rooms and whole houses to let, generally for stays of a week or more.

All accommodation rates listed are for the high season – but not the peak Christmas period, when you'll almost certainly have to book ahead anyway. Always call ahead for rates and ask about discounts. Most accommodation places have an 11am or noon checkout. To compare or book beach huts in South Goa, check out www.beachhutbooking.com.

Accommodation price ranges used in this chapter are as follows:

$ below ₹1200

$$ ₹1200 to ₹5000

$$$ above ₹5000

GOA PANAJI (PANJIM)

small Maruti will cost from ₹900 to ₹1200 per day and a large jeep around ₹2000, excluding petrol and usually with a kilometre limit. Your best bet for rental is online at sites such as www.goa2u.com and www.mygoatour.com.

You'll rarely go far on a Goan road without seeing a tourist whizzing by on a scooter or motorbike, and renting one is a breeze. You'll likely pay from ₹200 to ₹300 per day for a scooter, ₹400 for a smaller Yamaha motorbike, and ₹500 for a Royal Enfield Bullet. These prices can drop considerably if you're renting for more than a few days or if it's an off-peak period – it's all supply and demand, so bargain if there are lots of machines around.

Bear in mind that Goan roads – while better than many Indian roads – can be tricky, filled with human, bovine, canine, feline, mechanical and avian obstacles, as well as potholes, speed-breakers and hairpin bends. Take it slowly, avoid riding at night (when black cows and drunk tourists can prove dangerous), don't attempt a north–south day trip on a 50cc scooter, and ask for a helmet – in theory, compulsory, though the law is still routinely ignored by Goans and tourists alike.

TAXI & AUTORICKSHAW

Taxis are widely available for town-hopping, but the local union cartel means prices are high, especially at night. A new initiative by Goa Tourism is the **Women Taxi Service** (☎0832-2437437), with female drivers, phone-only bookings and only females, couples or families accepted as passengers. The vehicles are fitted with GPS monitoring, martial-arts trained drivers and accurate meters. Fares can even by paid with a credit card.

Unlike elsewhere in India, autorickshaws are not much cheaper than taxis and are not as common, but they're still good for short trips if you can find one. Motorcycle taxis, known as 'pilots', are also a licensed form of taxi in Goa, identified by a yellow front mudguard. They're only really common around major taxi stands and beach resorts and cost half the price of a taxi.

DRUGS

Acid, ecstasy, cocaine, charas (hashish), marijuana and most other forms of drugs are illegal in India (though still available in Goa), and purchasing or carrying drugs is fraught with danger. Goa's Fort Aguada jail is filled with prisoners, including some foreigners, serving lengthy sentences for drug offences. Being caught in possession of even a small quantity of illegal substances can mean a 10-year stretch.

CENTRAL GOA

Panaji (Panjim)
POP 115,000

One of India's most relaxed state capitals, Panaji (Panjim) overlooks the mouth of the broad Mandovi River, where party boats and floating casinos cast neon reflections in the night. A glorious whitewashed church lords over the city centre, a broad tree-lined boulevard skirts the river and grand colonial-era buildings rub shoulders with arty boutiques, old-school bookshops and backstreet bars.

But it's the tangle of narrow streets in the old quarter of Fontainhas that really steal the show. Nowhere is the Portuguese influence felt more strongly than here, where the late afternoon sun lights up yellow houses with purple doors, and around each corner you'll find crumbling ochre-coloured mansions with wrought-iron balconies, terracotta-tiled roofs and oyster-shell windows. Panjim is a place for walking, enjoying the peace of the afternoon siesta, eating well and meeting real Goans. A day or two in the capital really is an essential part of your Goan experience.

⊙ Sights & Activities

One of the great pleasures of Panaji is long, leisurely strolls through the sleepy Portuguese-era districts of Sao Tomé, Fontainhas and Altinho. Riverside Campal Gardens, west of the centre, and Miramar Beach, 2km further on, are also popular spots.

★ **Church of Our Lady of the Immaculate Conception** CHURCH
(cnr Emilio Gracia & Jose Falcao Rds; ⊙10am-12.30pm & 3-5.30pm Mon-Sat, 11am-12.30pm & 3.30-5pm Sun, English Mass 8am) Panaji's spiritual, as well as geographical, centre is this elevated, pearly white church, built in 1619 over an older, smaller 1540 chapel and stacked like a fancy white wedding cake. When Panaji was little more than a sleepy fishing village, this church was the first port of call for sailors from Lisbon, who would give thanks for a safe crossing, before continuing to Ela (Old Goa) further east up the river. The church is beautifully illuminated at night.

Goa State Museum MUSEUM
(☎0832-2438006; www.goamusem.gov.in; EDC Complex, Patto; ⊙9.30am-5.30pm Mon-Sat)

FREE This spacious museum east of town houses an eclectic, if not extensive, collection of items tracing aspects of Goan history. As well as some beautiful Hindu and Jain sculptures and bronzes, there are nice examples of Portuguese-era furniture, coins, an intricately carved chariot and a pair of quirky antique rotary lottery machines.

Goa State Central Library　　　　LIBRARY
(Sanskruti Bhavan, Patto; ⊙9am-7.30pm Mon-Fri, 9.30am-5.45pm Sat & Sun) FREE Panaji's ultra-modern new state library, near the state museum, has six floors of reading material, a bookshop and gallery. The 2nd floor features a children's book section and internet browsing (free, but technically only for academic research). The 4th floor has Goan history books and the 6th a large collection of Portuguese books.

Houses of Goa Museum　　　　MUSEUM
(☑0832-2410711; www.archgoa.org; near Nisha's Play School, Torda; adult/child ₹100/25; ⊙10am-7.30pm Tue-Sun) This multilevel museum was created by a well-known local architect, Gerard da Cunha, to illuminate the history of Goan architecture. Interesting displays on building practices and European and local design will change the way you see those old Goan homes. The triangular building is an architectural oddity in itself, and the museum traces Goan architectural traditions, building materials and styles in an indepth but accessible style. From Panaji, a taxi or rickshaw will cost you about ₹400 one-way.

☞ Tours

Goa Tourism and several private companies offer cruises on the Mandovi River from Santa Monica Jetty. With bars and DJs playing loud music, these can get rowdy on weekends but are an entertaining perspective on the capital.

Heritage walking tours (☑9823025748; per person ₹500, per person for five or more ₹250), covering the old Portuguese quarter, are conducted by experienced local guides on demand.

Mandovi River Cruises　　　　CRUISE
(sunset cruise ₹200, dinner cruise ₹650, backwater cruise ₹900; ⊙sunset cruise 6pm, sundown cruise 7.15pm, dinner cruise 8.45pm Wed & Sat, backwater cruise 9.30am-4pm Tue & Fri) Goa Tourism operates a range of entertaining hour-long cruises along the Mandovi River aboard the *Santa Monica* or *Shantadurga*. All include

ⓘ **EMERGENCIES**

Dialling ☑108 will connect you to the police, fire brigade or medical services.

a live band and usually performances of Goan folk songs and dances. There are also twice-weekly, two-hour dinner cruises and a twice-weekly, all-day backwater cruise, which takes you down the Mandovi to Old Goa, stopping for lunch at a spice plantation and then heading back past Divar and Chorao Islands. All cruises depart from the Santa Monica Jetty next to the Mandovi Bridge, where you can purchase tickets.

☆☆ Festivals & Events

International Film Festival of India　　　　FILM FESTIVAL
(www.iffi.nic.in; Panaji; ⊙Nov) Film screenings and Bollywood glitterati everywhere.

Feast of Our Lady of the Immaculate Conception　　　　RELIGIOUS
(Margao, Panaji; ⊙8 Dec) Fairs and concerts are held, as is a beautiful church service at Panaji's Church of Our Lady of the Immaculate Conception.

Carnival　　　　RELIGIOUS
(statewide; ⊙Mar) A four-day festival kicking off Lent; the party's particularly jubilant in Panaji.

🛏 Sleeping

As in the rest of Goa, prices vary in Panaji depending on supply and demand.

★**Old Quarter Hostel**　　　　HOSTEL $
(☑0832-6517606; www.thehostelcrowd.com; 31st Jan Rd, Fontainhas; dm ₹450, d with AC from ₹2000; ❄@) Backpackers rejoice! This cool new hostel in an old Portuguese-style house in historic Fontainhas offers slick four-bed dorms with lockers and two comfortable doubles upstairs, along with a cafe, arty murals, good wi-fi and bikes. Noon checkout.

Pousada Guest House　　　　GUESTHOUSE $
(☑9850998213, 0832-2422618; sabrinateles@yahoo.com; Luis de Menezes Rd; s/d from ₹800/1050, d with AC ₹1575; ❄@) The five rooms in this bright-yellow place are simple but clean and come with comfy spring-mattress beds and TV. Owner Sabrina is friendly and no-nonsense, and it's one of Panaji's better budget guesthouses.

GOA PANAJI (PANJIM)

Panaji (Panjim)

GOA PANAJI (PANJIM)

N

0   0.2 miles
0   400 m

Mandovi Bridge

Belim (2km);
Houses of Goa Museum (4km);
Torda (4km);
Mapusa (13km)

Private Bus Stand (80m);
Old Goa (9km);
Kamali (12km);
Ponda

PATTO

Santa Monica Jetty

New Patto Bridge

Old Patto Bridge

Ourem Creek

Mandovi River

Dabolim (29km);
Vasco da Gama (32km);
Margao (34km)

Goa Tourism Development Corporation

Dr Alvaro Costa Rd

ATMs

MG Rd

Footbridge

Ourem Rd

31st January Rd

Emilio Gracia Rd

GP Rd

CA Rd

St Sebastian Rd

Rua de Natal

SAO TOMÉ

Statue of Abbé Faria

Steps

Avenida Dom Joao Castro

Jose Falcao Rd

Church of Our Lady of the Immaculate Conception

FONTAINHAS

31st January Rd

Fountain

Baba's Wood Cafe (400m)

Dabolim (29km);
Margao (34km)

Panaji Jetty

Ferry to Betim

Dayanand Bandodkar Marg

DR RS Rd

MG Rd

Ormuz Rd

Municipal Gardens (Church Square)

Cunha-Rivara Rd

Jama Masjid

Avenida Pe Agnelo

Mahalaxmi Temple

ALTINHO

Cafe Bodega (100m)

Azad Maidan

Malaca Rd

Menezes Braganza Rd

Dr Pisurlekar Rd

Dr P Shirgaonkar Rd

Forest Department

Swami Vivekanand Rd

Dr Dada Vaidya Rd

Dr Atmaram Borkar Rd

Campal Gardens (400m); Kala Academy (800m); Goa Marriott Resort (1.8km)

Heliodoro Salgado Rd

Municipal Market

General Bernado Guedes Rd

18th June Rd

Gen Costa Alvares Rd

Caculo Mall (1km);
Vintage Hospitals (1.5km)

Panaji (Panjim)

⊙ Top Sights
1 Church of Our Lady of the
  Immaculate Conception D2

⊙ Sights
2 Goa State Central Library F4
3 Goa State Museum F4

⊙ Activities, Courses & Tours
4 Mandovi River Cruises G2

🛏 Sleeping
5 Afonso Guesthouse E3
6 Casa Nova E2
7 Casa Paradiso D2
8 Mayfair Hotel B3
9 Old Quarter Hostel E4
10 Panjim Inn E4
11 Panjim Pousada E4
12 Pousada Guest House E2

⊗ Eating
13 Anandashram E2
14 Black Sheep Bistro B3
15 Hotel Venite E2
16 Hotel Vihar E2
17 Upper House C2
  Verandah .... (see 10)
18 Viva Panjim E3

⊙ Drinking & Nightlife
19 Cafe Mojo B2
20 Riverfront & Down the Road F2

⊙ Entertainment
21 Casino Pride C1
22 Deltin Royale E1
23 INOX Cinema A2

⊚ Shopping
24 Khadi Gramodyog Bhavan C2
  Marcou Artifacts .... (see 18)
25 Municipal Market A2
26 Singbal's Book House D2

ⓘ Information
Government of India
  Tourist Office .... (see 26)

ⓘ Transport
27 Kadamba Bus Stand G3
  Konkan Railway
  Reservation Office .... (see 27)
28 Paulo Travels G3
29 Private Bus Agents G3

★ **Panjim Inn** — HERITAGE HOTEL **$$**
(☏ 0832-2226523, 9823025748; www.panjiminn.
com; 31st Jan Rd; s ₹3400-6000, d ₹3900-6500,
ste ₹5950; ❋ 🛜) One of the original herit-
age hotels in Fontainhas, the Panjim Inn
has been a long-standing favourite for its
character and charm, friendly owners and
helpful staff. This beautiful 19th-century
mansion has 12 charismatic rooms in
the original house, along with 12 newer
rooms with modern touches, but all have
four-poster beds, colonial-era furniture and
artworks. Buffet breakfast is included, and
the restaurant serves excellent Goan food.

Panjim Pousada — GUESTHOUSE **$$**
(☏ 0832-2226523; www.panjiminn.com; 31st Jan
Rd; s ₹3400-4400, d ₹3900-4900; ❋ 🛜) In an
old Hindu mansion, the nine divine rooms
at Panjim Pousada are set off by a stunning
central courtyard, with antique furnishings
and lovely art on the walls. Various doorways and staircases lead to the rooms; those
on the upper level are the best.

Afonso Guesthouse — GUESTHOUSE **$$**
(☏ 9764300165, 0832-2222359; www.afonsoguest-
house.com; St Sebastian Rd; d ₹1800-3000; ❋ 🛜)

Run by the friendly Jeanette, this pretty
Portuguese-style townhouse offers spacious,
well-kept rooms with timber ceilings. The
rooftop terrace makes for sunny breakfast-
ing (extra) with Fontainhas views. Add ₹200
for air-con. It's a simple, serene stay in the
heart of the most atmospheric part of town.
Checkout is 9am and bookings are accepted
online but not by phone.

Casa Paradiso — HOTEL **$$**
(☏ 0832-3290180; www.casaparadisogoa.com;
Jose Falcao Rd; d/tr with AC ₹1911/2200; ❋) A
neat and welcoming little stay in the heart
of the city. Up a small flight of stairs, the
simple but clean rooms come with TV, hot
water and noon checkout.

Mayfair Hotel — HOTEL **$$**
(☏ 0832-2223317; manishafernz@yahoo.com; Dr
Dada Vaidya Rd; s/d from ₹1105/1330, d with AC
₹1690; ❋ 🛜) The oyster-shell windows and
mosaic tiling in the lobby of this popular
corner hotel are promising but the rooms
are not quite as bright. Ask to see a few as
there are new and old wings with rooms
of varying quality, some overlooking a po-
tentially nice back garden. Friendly family

owners have been sheltering travellers for many years. Noon checkout.

Casa Nova
GUESTHOUSE $$

(📞 9423889181; www.goaholidayaccommodation.com; Gomes Pereira Rd; ste ₹4300; ❄️🛜) In a gorgeous Portuguese-style house (c 1831) in Fontainhas, Casa Nova comprises just one stylish, exceptionally comfy apartment, accessed via a little alley and complete with arched windows, wood-beam ceilings, and mod-cons such as a kitchenette and wi-fi.

Goa Marriott Resort
INTERNATIONAL $$$

(📞 0832-2463333; www.marriott.com; Miramar Beach; d ₹7000-15,000; ❄️🛜🏊) Miramar's plush Goa Marriot Resort is the best in the Panaji area. Fve-star treatment begins in the lobby and extends to the rooms-with-a-view. The 24-hour Waterfront Terrace & Bar is a great place for a sundowner overlooking the pool, while its Simply Grills restaurant is a favourite with well-heeled Panjimites.

Eating

You'll never go hungry in Panaji, where food is enjoyed fully and frequently. A stroll down 18th June or 31st January Rds will turn up a number of cheap canteen-style options, as will a circuit of the Municipal Gardens.

★ Viva Panjim
GOAN $

(📞 0832-2422405; 31st Jan Rd; mains ₹100-170; ⏱️11.30am-3.30pm & 7-11pm Mon-Sat, 7-11pm Sun) Well known to tourists, this little side-street eatery, in an old Portuguese-style house

---

GOAN CUISINE

Goan cuisine is a tantalising fusion of Portuguese and South Indian flavours. Goans tend to be hearty meat and fish eaters, and fresh seafood is a staple: the quintessential Goan lunch of 'fish-curry-rice' is fried mackerel steeped in coconut, tamarind and chilli sauce. Traditional dishes include vindaloo (a fiery dish in a marinade of vinegar and garlic), *xacuti* (a spicy chicken or meat dish cooked in red coconut sauce) and *cafreal* (dry-fried chicken marinated in a green masala paste and sprinkled with toddy vinegar). For dessert try the layered coconut cake, bebinca.

The traditional Goan alcoholic drink is feni, a double-distilled fiery liquour made from the cashew fruit or palm toddy.

---

and with a few tables out on the laneway, still delivers tasty Goan classics at reasonable prices. There's a whole page devoted to pork dishes, along with tasty *xacuti* and *cafrial*-style dishes, seafood such as kingfish vindaloo and crab *xec xec,* and desserts such as *bebinca* (richly layered Goan dessert made from egg yolk and coconut).

Hotel Vihar
VEGAN $

(MG Rd; mains ₹40-100; ⏱️7.30am-10pm) A vast menu of 'pure veg' food, great big thalis and a plethora of fresh juices make this clean, simple canteen a popular place for locals and visitors alike.

Anandashram
INDIAN, GOAN $

(31st Jan Rd; thalis ₹80-130, seafood ₹200-350; ⏱️noon-3.30pm & 7.30-10.30pm Mon-Sat) This little place is renowned locally for seafood, serving up simple but tasty fish curries, as well as veg and nonveg thalis for lunch and dinner.

Hotel Venite
GOAN $$

(31st Jan Rd; mains ₹210-260; ⏱️9am-10.30pm) With its cute rickety balconies overhanging the cobbled street, Venite has long been among the most atmospheric of Panaji's old-school Goan restaurants. The menu is traditional, with spicy sausages, fish curry rice, pepper steak and *bebinca* featuring, but Venite is popular with tourists and prices are consequently rather inflated. It's not to be missed though.

★ Cafe Bodega
CAFE $$

(📞 0832-2421315; Altinho; mains ₹120-320; ⏱️10am-7pm Mon-Sat, to 4pm Sun; 🛜) It's well worth a trip up to Altinho Hill for this serene cafe-gallery in a lavender-and-white Portuguese-style mansion in the grounds of Sunaparanta Centre for the Arts. Enjoy good coffee, juices and fresh-baked cakes around the inner courtyard or lunch on super pizzas and sandwiches.

Verandah
GOAN $$

(📞 0832-2226523; 31st Jan Rd; mains ₹180-360; ⏱️11am-11pm) The breezy 1st-floor restaurant at Panjim Inn is indeed on the balcony, with just a handful of finely carved tables and fine Fontainhas street views. Goan cuisine is the speciality, but there's also a range of Indian and continental dishes and local wines.

★ Black Sheep Bistro
EUROPEAN, TAPAS $$$

(📞 0832-2222901; www.blacksheepbistro.in; Swami Vivekanand Rd; tapas ₹180-225, mains

₹320-450) One of the new breed of Panaji boutique restaurants, Black Sheep's impressive pale-yellow facade gives way to a sexy dark-wood bar and loungy dining room. The tapas dishes are light, fresh and expertly prepared in keeping with their farm-to-table philosophy. Salads, pasta, local seafood and dishes like lamb osso bucco also grace the menu, while an internationally trained sommelier matches food to wine.

Baba's Wood Cafe   ITALIAN $$$
(0832-3256213; 49 Mala, Fontainhas; pizza & pasta ₹300-500; ⊙noon-3pm & 7-11.30pm) Sharing an interesting premises with a wood-craft gallery, this upmarket Italian restaurant in a quiet street near the Maruti Temple has a lovely little alfresco dining area and a menu featuring more than 20 different pasta dishes from ravioli to carbonara. Pizzas are wood-fired and the pasta is homemade, while desserts include tiramisu and chocolate fondue. Good for a splurge.

Upper House   GOAN $$$
(☑0832-2426475; www.theupperhousegoa.com; Cunha-Rivara Rd; mains ₹220-440; ⊙11am-10pm) Climbing the stairs to the Upper House is like stepping into a cool European restaurant, with a modern but elegant dining space overlooking the Municipal Gardens, a chic neon-lit cocktail bar and a more formal restaurant at the back. The food is very much Goan though, with regional specialities such as crab *xec xec*, fish curry rice and pork vindaloo prepared to a high standard at relatively high prices.

Drinking & Nightlife

Panaji's simple little bars with a few plastic tables and chairs are a great way to get chatting with locals over a glass of feni.

Cafe Mojo   BAR
(www.cafemojo.in; Menezes Braganza Rd; ⊙10am-4am Mon-Thu, to 6am Fri-Sun) The decor is cosy English pub, the clientele young and up for a party, and the hook is the e-beer system. Each table has it's own beer tap and LCD screen: you buy a card (₹1000), swipe it at your table and start pouring – it automatically deducts what you drink (you can also use the card for spirits, cocktails or food). Wednesday night is ladies night, Thursday karaoke and the weekends go till late.

Riverfront & Down the Road   BAR
(cnr MG & Ourem Rds; ⊙11am-1am) This restaurant's balcony overlooking the creek and Old Patto Bridge makes for a cosy beer or cocktail spot with carved barrels for furniture. The ground-floor bar (from 6pm) is the only real nightspot on the Old Quarter side of town, with occasional live music.

☆ Entertainment

Several casino boats sit moored on the Mandovi, offering a surprisingly entertaining night out.

Kala Academy   CULTURAL CENTRE
(☑0832-2420452; http://kalaacademygoa.org; Dayanand Bandodkar Marg) On the west side of the city, in Campal, is Goa's premier cultural centre, which features a program of dance, theatre, music and art exhibitions throughout the year. Many shows are in Konkani, but there are occasional English-language productions. The website has an up-to-date calendar of events.

INOX Cinema   CINEMA
(☑0832-2420900; www.inoxmovies.com; Old GMC Heritage Precinct; tickets ₹180-200) This comfortable, plush multiplex cinema shows Hollywood and Bollywood blockbusters. Book online to choose your seats in advance.

Deltin Royale   CASINO
(☑8698599999; www.deltingroup.com/deltin-royale; Noah's Ark, RND Jetty, Dayanand Bandodkar Marg; weekday/weekend ₹2500/3000, premium weekend ₹4000-4500; ⊙24hr, entertainment 9pm-1am) Goa's biggest luxury floating casino, Deltin Royal has 123 tables, the Vegas Restaurant, a Whisky Bar and a creche. Entry includes gaming chips worth ₹1500/2000 weekday/weekend and to the full value of your ticket with the premium package. Unlimited food and drinks included.

Casino Pride   CASINO
(☑0832-6516666; www.bestgoacasino.com; Dayanand Bandodkar Marg; weekday/weekend ₹1500/2000; ⊙24hr, entertainment 9-11pm) These two casino boats are loosely modelled on Mississippi-style paddle boats. *Pride I* has 40 gaming tables, kids' play room and an outdoor party deck. Admission includes ₹1000 coupon for gaming. Unlimited dinner buffet is included, as well as free drinks if you're playing a table. *Pride II* is the same deal but smaller.

🔒 Shopping

Panaji's covered **municipal market** (Heljogordo Salgado Rd; ⊙from 7.30am) is a great place for people-watching and buying necessities.

Caculo Mall MALL

(📞0832-2222068; 16 Shanta, St Inez; ⊙8am-11pm) Goa's biggest mall is four levels of air-conditioned family shopping heaven with brand-name stores, food court, kids' toys, Time Zone arcade games and a movie theatre.

Singbal's Book House BOOKS

(Church Sq; ⊙9.30am-1pm & 3.30-7.30pm Mon-Sat) On the corner opposite Panaji's main church, Singbal's has an excellent selection of international magazines and newspapers, and lots of books on Goa and travel.

Marcou Artifacts CRAFTS

(📞0832-2220204; www.marcouartifacts.com; 31st Jan Rd; ⊙9am-8pm) This small shop showcases one-off painted tiles, fish figurines and hand-crafted Portuguese and Goan ceramics at reasonable prices. Also showrooms at the Hotel Delmon and Margao's market.

Khadi Gramodyog Bhavan HANDICRAFTS

(Dr Atmaram Borkar Rd; ⊙9am-noon & 3-7pm Mon-Sat) 🖉 Goa's only outpost of the government's Khadi & Village Industries Commission has an excellent range of hand-woven cottons, oils, soaps, spices and other handmade products that come straight from (and directly benefit) regional villages.

ℹ Information

Goa Tourism Development Corporation

(Goa Tourism, GTDC; 📞0832-2437132; www.goa-tourism.com; Paryatan Bhavan, Dr Alvaro Costa Rd; ⊙9.30am-5.45pm Mon-Sat) Better known as Goa Tourism, the GTDC office is in the slick new Paryatan Bhavan building across the Ourem Creek and near the bus stand. However, it's more corporate office than tourist office and is of little use to casual visitors, unless you want to book one of GTDC's host of tours.

Government of India Tourist Office (📞0832-2223412; www.incredibleindia.com; Communidade Bldg, Church Sq; ⊙9.30am-1.30pm & 2.30-6pm Mon-Fri, 10am-1pm Sat) The staff at this central tourist office can be helpful, especially for information outside Goa. This office is expected to move to the same building as Goa Tourism by the time you read this.

Main Post Office (MG Rd; ⊙9.30am-5.30pm Mon-Sat) Offers swift parcel services and Western Union money transfers.

Vintage Hospitals (📞0832-6644401, ambulance 9764442220; www.vintagehospitals.com; Caculo Enclave, St Inez; ⊙24hr) Central Panaji's best hospital in an emergency; it's just west of the centre near Caculo Mall.

ℹ Getting There & Away

A taxi from Panaji to Dabolim Airport takes about an hour, and costs ₹670 (₹770 for AC).

BUS

All government buses depart from the huge and busy **Kadamba bus stand** (📞interstate enquiries 0832-2438035, local enquiries 0832-2438034; www.goakadamba.com; ⊙reservations 8am-8pm), with local services heading out every few minutes. To get to south Goan beaches, take an express bus to Margao and change there; for far northern beaches, change at Mapusa. Kadamba station has an ATM, internet cafe, food outlets and even a Ganesh temple. Destinations include:

Calangute (₹20, 45 minutes)

Candolim (₹15, 35 minutes)

Mapusa (₹15, 30 minutes)

Margao (express shuttle; ₹30, 35 minutes)

Old Goa (₹10, 15 minutes)

Private operators have booths outside Kadamba, but the buses depart from the private interstate bus stand next to New Patto Bridge. One reliable company is **Paulo Travels** (📞0832-2438531; www.phmgoa.com; G1, Kardozo Bldg). Some high-season government and private long-distance fares include the following:

Bengaluru (₹600 to ₹1200, 14 to 15 hours, around 30 daily)

Hampi (private sleeper; ₹900 to ₹1100, 10 to 11 hours, 2-3 daily)

Mumbai (₹350 to ₹1100, 12 to 14 hours, frequent)

Pune (₹325 to ₹1000, 11 hours, frequent)

TRAIN

Panaji's closest train station is Karmali (Old Goa), 12km to the east, where many long-distance services stop (check timetables). A taxi there costs ₹350. Panaji's **Konkan Railway reservation office** (📞0832-2712940; www.konkanrailway.com; ⊙8am-8pm Mon-Sat) is on the 1st floor of the Kadamba bus stand. See the Margao section (p844) for major trains.

ℹ Getting Around

Panaji is generally a pleasure to explore on foot. Frequent buses run between Kadamba and the municipal market and on to Miramar and Dona Paula.

To Old Goa, an autorickshaw/taxi should cost around ₹300/350.

Scooters and motorbikes can easily be hired from around the post office from around ₹200/300 per day.

A useful shortcut across the river to the northern beaches is the free vehicle **ferry** (⊙every 20 min 6am-10pm) to Betim.

Old Goa

From the 16th to the 18th centuries, when Old Goa's population exceeded that of Lisbon or London, Goa's former capital was considered the 'Rome of the East'. You can still sense that grandeur as you wander what's left of the city, with its towering churches and cathedrals and majestic convents. Its rise under the Portuguese, from 1510, was meteoric, but cholera and malaria outbreaks forced the abandonment of the city in the 1600s. In 1843 the capital was officially shifted to Panaji.

Some of the most imposing churches and cathedrals are still in use and are remarkably well preserved, while other historical buildings have become museums or ruined sites. It's a fascinating day trip, but it can get crowded: consider visiting on a weekday morning, when you can take in Mass at Sé Cathedral or the Basilica of Bom Jesus (remember to cover shoulders and legs in the churches; no beachwear).

The major event of the year is the 10 day Novena leading up to the **Feast of St Francis Xavier** on 3 December. Once every decade on this date, the Exposition sees the casket containing St Francis' body carried through Old Goa's streets; the next one is 2024.

◉ Sights

★ Basilica of Bom Jesus
CHURCH
(⊙ 7.30am-6.30pm) Famous throughout the Roman Catholic world, the imposing Basilica of Bom Jesus contains the tomb and mortal remains of St Francis Xavier, the so-called Apostle of the Indies. St Francis Xavier's missionary voyages throughout the East became legendary. His 'incorrupt' body is in the mausoleum to the right, in a glass-sided coffin amid a shower of gilt stars.

Construction on the basilica began in 1594 and was completed in 1605, to create an elaborate late-Renaissance structure, fronted by a facade combining elements of Doric, Ionic and Corinthian design.

★ Sé Cathedral
CATHEDRAL
(⊙ 9am-6pm; Mass 7am & 6pm Mon-Sat, 7.15am, 10am & 4pm Sun) At over 76m long and

GOA OLD GOA

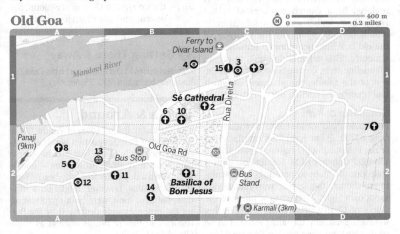

Old Goa

0 ——— 400 m
0 ——— 0.2 miles

Ferry to Divar Island

Mandovi River

Sé Cathedral

Rua Direita

Panaji (9km)

Old Goa Rd

Bus Stop

Basilica of Bom Jesus

Bus Stand

↓ Karmali (3km)

Old Goa

55m wide, the cavenerous Sé Cathedral is the largest church in Asia. Building work commenced in 1562, on the orders of King Dom Sebastiao of Portugal, and the finishing touches where finally made some 90 years later. The exterior of the cathedral is notable for its plain style, in the Tuscan tradition. Also of note is its rather lopsided look resulting from the loss of one of its bell towers, which collapsed in 1776 after being struck by lightning. The remaining tower houses the famous **Sino de Ouro** (Golden Bell), the largest in Asia and renowned for its rich tone, which once tolled to accompany the Inquisition's notoriously cruel *autos-da-fé* (trials of faith), held out the front of the cathedral on what was then the market square.

Church of St Francis of Assisi   CHURCH

West of the Sé Cathedral, the Church of St Francis of Assisi is no longer in use for worship, and consequently exudes a more mournful air than its neighbours.

The church started life as a small chapel, built on this site by eight Franciscan friars on their arrival in 1517. In 1521 it was replaced by a church consecrated to the Holy Ghost, which was then subsequently rebuilt in 1661, with only the doorway of the old building incorporated into the new structure. This original doorway, in ornate Manueline style, contrasts strongly with the rest of the facade, the plainness of which had become the fashion by the 17th century.

Museum of Christian Art   MUSEUM

(www.museumofchristianart.com; admission ₹50, camera ₹100; ⊙9am-6pm) This excellent museum, in a stunningly restored space within the 1627 Convent of St Monica, contains a collection of statues, paintings and sculptures, though the setting warrants a visit in its own right. Interestingly, many of the works of Goan Christian art made during the Portuguese era, including some of those on display here, were produced by local Hindu artists.

Church of St Cajetan   CHURCH

(⊙9am-5.30pm) Modelled on the original design of St Peter's in Rome, the Church of St Cajetan was built by Italian friars of the Order of Theatines, who were sent by Pope Urban III to preach Christianity in the kingdom of Golconda (near Hyderabad). The friars were not permitted to work in Golconda, so settled at Old Goa in 1640. The construction of the church began in 1655.

Church of Our Lady of the Mount   CHURCH

This church is often overlooked due to its location on a wooded hilltop, some 2km east of the central area. A sealed road leads to an overgrown flight of steps (don't walk it solo) and the hill on which the church stands commands an excellent view of Old Goa, with the church spires seemingly rising out a sea of palms.

Monastery of St Augustine   HISTORIC SITE

The melancholy, evocative ruins of this once vast and impressive Augustinian monastery are all that remain of a huge structure founded in 1572 and abandoned in 1835. The building's facade came tumbling down in 1942; all that remains, amid piles of rubble, is the towering skeletal belfry, though the bell itself was rescued and now hangs in Panaji's Church of Our Lady of the Immaculate Conception.

Other Sights

There are plenty of other monuments in Old Goa to explore, including the Viceroy's Arch, Adil Shah Palace Gateway, Chapel of St Anthony, Chapel of St Catherine, Albuquerque's Steps, the Convent & Church of St John, Sisters' Convent and the Church of Our Lady of the Rosary.

ⓘ Getting There & Away

Frequent buses to Old Goa depart from Panaji's Kadamba bus stand (₹10, 25 minutes).

Ponda & Around

The workaday inland town of Ponda, 29km southeast of Panaji, has two big drawcards in the vicinity – Goa's best Hindu temple complexes and spice plantations – and is well worth a day away from the beach. Temple aficionados, however, might be a little disappointed; most were built or rebuilt after the originals were destroyed by the Portuguese, so they're not as ancient as those elsewhere in India.

The 18th-century hilltop **Mangueshi Temple** at Priol, 5km northwest of Ponda, is dedicated to Manguesh, a god known only in Goa, while 1km away at Mardol is the **Mahalsa Temple**, also dedicated to a specifically Goan deity. The 1738 **Shantadurga Temple**, meanwhile, just west of Ponda, is dedicated to Shantadurga, the goddess of peace, and is one of the most famous shrines in Goa.

There are regular buses to Ponda from Panaji (₹20, 1½ hours) and Margao (₹18, one

SPICE UP YOUR LIFE

The Ponda region is the centre of commercial spice farms, producing vanilla, pepper, cardamom, nutmeg, chilli and tumeric, along with crops such as cashew, betel nut, coconut, pineapple and papaya. Farms offer a guided tour of the plantation, buffet thali-style lunch, and in some cases elephant rides and cultural shows.

Savoi Plantation (☑0832-2340272, 9822133309; adult/child ₹600/300; ⊗9am-4.30pm) This 200-year-old plantation is the least touristy farm, where you'll find a warm welcome from knowledgeable guides keen to walk you through the 40-hectare plantation at your own pace.

Sahakari Spice Farm (☑0832-2312394; www.sahakarifarms.com; admission incl lunch ₹400; ⊗8am-4.30pm) Well-touristed farm 2km from Ponda; good place for elephant rides and bathing (₹700 each) in the small river.

Pascoal Organic Spice Village (☑0832-2344268; www.pascoalfarm.com; farm tour & lunch adult/child ₹400/200; ⊗9am-4pm) About 7km from Ponda, Pascoal offers bamboo river-rafting, elephant rides and cultural shows, along with farm tours and lunch.

Tropical Spice Plantation (☑0832-2340329; www.tropicalspiceplantation.com; Keri; admission incl lunch ₹400; ⊗9am-4pm) One of the busiest farms frequented by tour groups, 5km north of Ponda. Feed the elephants and enjoy a banana-leaf buffet lunch.

Butterfly Conservatory of Goa (☑0832-2985174; www.bcogoa.org; Priol; admission ₹100; ⊗9am-4.30pm) Near the spice farms, this small butterfly sanctuary, 5km north of Ponda, houses more than 100 species of free-flying butterflies.

hour), after which you'll need to arrange a taxi to visit the temples or spice farms. Taxis from Panaji charge ₹1500 for a day trip to the area (up to eight hours and 80km).

NORTH GOA

Mapusa

POP 40,100

The pleasantly bustling market town of Mapusa (pronounced 'Mapsa') is the largest in northern Goa and a transport hub for local and interstate buses. The main reason for travellers to visit is for the busy **Mapusa Market** (⊗8am-6.30pm Mon-Sat), which attracts scores of buyers and sellers from neighbouring towns and villages. It's a good place to pick up the usual embroidered bedsheets and the like at prices lower than in the beach resorts. The market operates daily, but Friday is the biggest day.

Mapusa is also home to the rewarding little **Other India Bookstore** (☑0832-2263306; www.otherindiabookstore.com; Mapusa Clinic Rd; ⊗9am-5pm Mon-Fri, to 1pm Sat), specialising in 'dissenting wisdom' and alternative press – a small but spectacular selection of books on nature, environment, politics, education and natural health.

Volunteering

If you're interested in volunteering while in Goa, there are a couple of well-established charity organisations around Mapusa.

El Shaddai　　　VOLUNTEERING
(☑0832-2461068, 0832-6513286; www.childrescue.net; El Shaddai House, Socol Vaddo, Assagao) El Shaddai is a British-founded charity that aids impoverished and homeless children throughout Goa. Volunteers able to commit to more than four weeks' work with El Shaddai can apply through the website. There's a rigorous vetting process, so start well in advance. Volunteers are also welcome to visit one of the Assagao schools between 4.30pm and 6.30pm (call ahead). For more information, there's a stall at the Anjuna flea market.

Mango Tree Goa　　　VOLUNTEERING
(☑9881261886; www.mangotreegoa.org; 'The Mango House', near Vrundavan Hospital, Karaswada, Mapusa) Offers placements for volunteers providing support for disadvantaged children around Mapusa.

Sleeping & Eating

There's little reason to stay the night in Mapusa when the beaches of the north coast are so close and most long-distance transport departs in the evening.

Hotel Vilena
HOTEL $

(☑ 0832-2263115; Feira Baixa Rd; d with/without bathroom ₹840/630, with AC ₹1575; ❀) Mapusa's best budget choice, with 14 plain double rooms, is not much to look at, but staff are welcoming.

Hotel Vrundavan
INDIAN $

(thalis from ₹75; ☺ 7am-10pm Wed-Mon) This all-veg place bordering the Municipal Gardens is a great place for a hot chai, *pau bhaji* (bread with spicy veg) or a quick breakfast.

Ruta's World Cafe
INTERNATIONAL $$

(☑ 0832-2250757; www.caferuta.com; St Xavier's College Rd, opp Ashirwad Bldg; mains ₹110-270; ☺ 10am-8pm Mon-Sat) The second branch of Ruta's excellent brand of fresh and tasty American-inspired cuisine has given travellers a good culinary reason to visit Mapusa. Sandwiches, salads and comfort foods such as jambalaya. It's north of the centre, in the same Portuguese-style house as Fabindia.

Pub
PUB

(near the market; mains from ₹100; ☺ 10am-4pm & 7-11pm Mon-Sat) Don't be put off by the dingy entrance or stairwell: once you're upstairs, this breezy place opposite the market is great for watching the milling crowds over a cold beer or feni. Eclectic daily specials make it a good spot for lunch.

ⓘ Getting There & Away

If you're coming to Goa by bus from Mumbai, Mapusa's **Kadamba bus stand** (☑ 0832-2232161) is the jumping-off point for the northern beaches. Local services run every few minutes; for buses to the southern beaches, take a bus to Panaji, then Margao, and change there.

Local services include the following:

Anjuna (₹15, 20 minutes)
Arambol (₹27, 1½ hours)
Calangute/Candolim (₹10/12, 20/35 minutes)
Panjim (₹15, 20 minutes)
Thivim (₹15, 20 minutes)

Interstate services run out of the same lot, but private operators have their offices next to the bus stand. There's generally little difference in price between private services and the Kadamba buses, but shop around as there are various standards of bus. Long-distance services include the following:

Bengaluru (private; AC or sleeper ₹1400, 13-14hr)
Mumbai (private; non-AC ₹700, AC ₹1200, 12-15hr)
Pune (private; non-AC from ₹650, AC ₹1200, sleeper ₹1000, 11-13hr)

There's a prepaid taxi stand outside the bus terminal where you can catch taxis to Anjuna

---

GREEN GOA

Goa's environment has suffered from an onslaught of tourism over the last 40 years, but also from the effects of logging, mining and local customs (rare turtle eggs have traditionally been considered a delicacy). Construction proceeds regardless of what the local infrastructure or ecosystem can sustain, while plastic bottles pile up in vast mountains. There are, however, a few easy ways to minimise your impact on Goa's environment:

➡ Take a bag when shopping and refill water bottles with filtered water where possible.

➡ Rent a bicycle instead of a scooter, for short trips at least; bicycle rentals are declining as a result of our scooter infatuation and the bikes are poor quality, but they'll bounce back if the demand is there.

➡ Goa Tourism now employs cleaners to comb the beaches each morning picking up litter but do your part by disposing of cigarette butts, litter and plastic bottles.

Turtles are protected by the **Forest Department** (www.forest.goa.gov.in), which operates information huts on beaches such as Agonda, Galgibag and Morjim, where turtles arrive to lay eggs. Also doing good work over many years is the **Goa Foundation** (☑ 0832-2256479; www.goafoundation.org; St Britto's Apts, G-8 Feira Alta, Mapusa), the state's main environmental pressure group based in Mapusa. It has spearheaded a number of conservation projects since its inauguration in 1986, including pressure to stop illegal mining, and its website is a great place to learn more about Goan environmental issues. The group's excellent *Fish Curry & Rice* (₹600), a sourcebook on Goa's environment and lifestyle, is sold at Mapusa's Other India Bookstore. The Foundation occasionally runs volunteer projects.

(₹300), Calangute (₹300), Arambol (₹500) and Panaji (₹500); autorickshaws typically charge ₹50 less than taxis.

Thivim, about 12km northeast of town, is the nearest train station on the Konkan Railway. Local buses meet trains; an autorickshaw into Mapusa from Thivim costs around ₹200.

Candolim, Sinquerim & Fort Aguada

POP 8600

Candolim's long and languid beach, which curves round as far as smaller Sinquerim beach in the south, is largely the preserve of mature, slow-roasting tourists from the UK, Russia and Scandinavia (and elsewhere in India), and is fringed with seasonal beach shacks, all offering sun beds and shade in exchange for your custom.

Back from the beach, busy Fort Aguada Rd is among one of the best resort strips in Goa for shops and services, and is home to dozens of restaurants, bars and hotels, but it lacks the personality of many other beach towns and independent travellers might find it a bit soulless.

⊙ Sights & Activities

Fort Aguada FORT

(⊙8.30am-5.30pm) FREE Standing on the headland overlooking the mouth of the Mandovi River, Fort Aguada occupies a magnificent and successful position, confirmed by the fact it was never taken by force. A highly popular spot to watch the sunset, with uninterrupted views both north and south, the fort was built in 1612, following the increasing threat to Goa's Portuguese overlords by the Dutch, among others.

John's Boat Tours TOUR

(☑0832-6520190, 9822182814; www.johnboattours.com; Fort Aguada Rd, Candolim; ⊙9am-9pm) A respected and well-organised Candolim-based operator offering a wide variety of boat and jeep excursions, as well as overnight houseboat cruises (₹5500 per person including meals). Choose from dolphin-watching cruises (₹1000), a return boat trip to the Wednesday Anjuna flea market (₹800), or the renowned 'Crocodile Dundee' river trip, to catch a glimpse of the Mandovi's mugger crocodile.

Sinquerim Dolphin Trips BOAT TOUR

(per person ₹300; ⊙8.30am-5pm) The boatmen on the Nerul River below Fort Agua-

da have banded together, so trips are now fixed price. A one-hour dolphin-spotting and sightseeing trip costs ₹300 per person with a minimum of 10 passengers. Trips pass Nerul (Coco) Beach, Fort Aguada Jail, the fort, and 'Jimmy Millionaire's House.'

🛏 Sleeping

Candolim has a good range of accommodation; the southern end is dominated by the five-star Taj hotels, while the best budget and midrange choices are in the lush laneways back from the northern beach.

Dona Florina HOTEL $

(☑9923049076, 0832-2489051; www.donaflorina.co.in; Monteiro's Rd, Escrivao Vaddo; r ₹1000-2000; ❄🖤) Friendly Dona Florina is a good value, spotless guesthouse in a pleasant tangle of laneways and family-run hotels just back from the beach. Front-facing upper-floor rooms have sea views, there's daily yoga on the roof terrace, and the lack of vehicle access ensures a peaceful experience.

Zostel HOSTEL $

(☑917726864942; www.zostel.com; Candolim; dm ₹450-550, d ₹1800; ❄🖤) The first Goan addition to this funky Indian hostel chain has popped up on the Candolim–Calangute border, bringing budget dorm beds to package-tour central. There are six- and eight-bed dorms with aircon, a 10-bed dorm and a female-only dorm, all in a whitewashed two-storey house set back from Fort Aguada Rd. Facilities include a kitchen, free wi-fi, common room and lockers. There's just one double room.

★Bougainvillea Guest House GUESTHOUSE $$

(☑0832-2479842, 9822151969; www.bougainvilleagoa.com; Sinquerim; r ₹2500, penthouse ₹6000; ❄🖤) A lush, plant-filled garden leads the way to this gorgeous family-run guesthouse, located off Fort Aguada Rd. The eight light-filled suite rooms are spacious and spotless, with fridge, flat-screen TV and either balcony or private sit-out; the top-floor penthouse has its own rooftop terrace. This is the kind of place guests come back to year after year. Book ahead.

D'Mello's Sea View Home HOTEL $$

(☑0832-2489650; www.dmellos.com; Monteiro's Rd, Escrivao Vaddo; d ₹1200-1700; ❄@🖤) D'Mello's has grown up from small beginnings but is still family-run and occupies four buildings around a lovely garden. The front building has the sea view rooms so check out a few, but all are clean and well-maintained. Add ₹500 if you want air-con. Wi-fi is available in the central area.

★ **Marbella Guest House** BOUTIQUE HOTEL $$$
(☑ 0832-2479551, 9822100811; www.marbella-goa.com; Sinquerim; r ₹3400-4200, ste ₹4900-6400; ✷ ☎) This stunning Portuguese-era villa, filled with antiques and enveloped in a peaceful courtyard garden, is a romantic and sophisticated old-world remnant. Rooms are individually themed, including Moghul, Rajasthani and Bouganvillea. The penthouse suite is a dream of polished tiles, four-poster bed with separate living room, dining room and terrace. Its kitchen serves up some imaginative dishes. Located off Fort Aguada Rd. No kids under 12.

✗ Eating & Drinking

Candolim's plentiful beach shacks are always popular places to eat or relax with a beer, and there are some excellent restaurants along Fort Aguada Rd.

Viva Goa! GOAN, SEAFOOD $
(Fort Aguada Rd; mains ₹90-180; ☺ 11am-midnight) This inexpensive, locals-oriented little place, also popular with in-the-know tourists, serves fresh fish and Goan seafood specialities such as a spicy mussel fry. Check market price of seafood before ordering.

Zappa's CAFE $
(☑ 9767019410; Candolim; mains ₹40-120; ☺ 8am-2pm) A tiny cafe sandwiched between the beach and busy Fort Aguada Rd, Zappa's serves up tasty breakfast and brunch dishes and some of the freshest pasta dishes in town. The owner has spent many years living and cooking in Europe. Zappa's beach shack is directly west.

★ **Café Chocolatti** CAFE, BAKERY $$
(409A Fort Aguada Rd; sweets ₹50-200, mains ₹270-420; ☺ 9am-5.30pm) The lovely garden tearoom at Café Chocolatti may be on the main Fort Aguada Rd but it's a divine and peaceful retreat where chocolate brownies, waffles and banoffee pie with a strong cup of coffee or organic green tea seem like heaven. Also a great range of salads, paninis, crepes and quiches for lunch. Take away a bag of chocolate truffles, homemade by the in-house chocolatier.

Stone House STEAKHOUSE, SEAFOOD $$
(Fort Aguada Rd; mains ₹150-500; ☺ 11am-3pm & 7pm-midnight) Surf 'n' turf's the thing at this venerable old Candolim venue, inhabiting a stone house and its leafy front courtyard, with the improbable-sounding 'Swedish Lobster' topping the list. It's also a popular blues bar with live music most nights of the week in season.

★ **Bomra's** BURMESE $$$
(☑ 9767591056; www.bomras.com; 247 Fort Aguada Rd; mains from ₹300; ☺ noon-2pm & 7-11pm) Wonderfully unusual food is on offer at this sleek little place serving interesting modern Burmese cuisine with a fusion twist. Aromatic curries include straw mushroom, lychee, water-chestnut, spinach, and coconut curry and duck curry with sweet tamarind and groundnut shoot. Decor is palm-thatch style huts in a lovely courtyard garden.

Tuscany Gardens ITALIAN $$$
(☑ 0832-6454026; www.tuscanygardens.in; Fort Aguada Rd; mains ₹240-410; ☺ 1-11pm) You can easily be transported to Tuscany at Candolim's cosy, romantic Italian restaurant, where perfect antipasti, pasta, pizza and risotto are the order of the day. Try the chicken breast stuffed with gorgonzola and ham, the seafood pizza or buffalo mozzarella salad.

Bob's Inn BAR
(Fort Aguada Rd, Candolim; ☺ noon-4pm & 7pm-midnight) The African wall hangings, palm-thatch, communal tables and terracotta sculptures are a nice backdrop to the *rava* (semolina) fried mussels or the prawns 'chilly fry' with potatoes, but this Candolim institution is really just a great place to drop in for a drink.

LPK Waterfront CLUB
(www.lpkwaterfront.com; couples ₹1500; ☺ 9.30pm-4am) The initials stand for Love, Peace and Karma: welcome to North Goa's biggest new club, the whimsical, sculpted waterfront LPK. It's actually across the Nerul River from Candolim (so technically in Nerul) but its club nights attract party-goers from all over with huge indoor and outdoor dance areas.

🛍 Shopping

Newton's SUPERMARKET
(Fort Aguada Rd; ☺ 9am-midnight) If you're desperately missing Edam cheese or Pot Noodles, or just want to do some self-catering, Newton's is Goa's biggest supermarket. There's a good line in toiletries,

wines, children's toys and luxury food items. The downside is that it's usually packed and security guards won't allow bags inside.

❶ Getting There & Away

Buses run frequently to Panaji (₹15, 35 minutes) and Mapusa (₹12, 35 minutes) and stop at the turn-off near John's Boat Tours. Calangute buses (₹5, 15 minutes) start at the Fort Aguada bus stop and can be flagged down on Fort Aguada Rd.

Calangute & Baga

POP 15,800

Love it or loathe it, Calangute and Baga are Goa's most popular beaches – at least with the cashed-up domestic tour crowd and European package tourists. Once a refuge of wealthy Goans, and later a 1960s hot spot for naked, revelling hippies, Calangute has adapted its scant charms to extended Indian families, groups of Indian bachelors and partying foreigners. This is Goa's most crowded beach stretch – from the traffic-clogged streets to the Arabian Sea, which fills up with people, boats and jet skis – though the southern beach is more relaxed. Baga, to the north, is notorious for drinking and dancing, while Northern Baga, across the Baga River, is surprisingly tranquil, with a few budget guesthouses and some top-notch restaurants.

🏃 Activities

Water Sports

You'll find numerous jet-ski and parasailing operators on Calangute and Baga beaches. Parasailing costs around ₹800 per ride, jet-skiing costs ₹1500 per 15 minutes.

Two local scuba diving operators are recommended: **Goa Aquatics** (Map p828; ☑ 9822685025; www.goaaquatics.com; 136/1 Gaura Vaddo; dive trip from ₹5000, dive course ₹14,000-25,000) in Calangute and **Barracuda Diving** (Map p828; ☑ 9822182402, 0832-2279409; www.barracudadiving.com; Sun Village Resort; dive trip/course from ₹4500/6000) in Baga.

👉 Tours

Day Tripper TOUR
(Map p828; ☑ 0832-2276726; www.daytrippergoa.com; Gaura Vaddo, Calangute; ⊙ 9am-5.30pm Mon-Sat Nov-Apr) Calangute-based Day Tripper is one of Goa's biggest and most reliable tour agencies. It runs a wide variety of minibus and boat trips around Goa, in-cluding two-hour dolphin trips (₹500 per person), trips to Dudhsagar Falls (₹1530), a houseboat stay (₹5300 per person) and also interstate tours to Hampi and the Kali River (for rafting and birdwatching trips) in Karnataka.

GTDC Tours TOUR
(Goa Tourism Development Corporation; Map p828; ☑ 0832-2276024; ⊙ www.goa-tourism.com) Goa Tourism's tours can be booked online or at the refurbished GTDC Calangute Residency hotel beside the beach. The full-day North Goa tour (₹225, 9.30am to 6pm daily) departs from Calangute or Mapusa and takes in the Mandovi estuary, Candolim, Calangute, Anjuna and inland to Mayem Lake.

🛏 Sleeping

Calangute and Baga's sleeping options are plentiful, lining the main roads and laneways down to the beach for several kilometres. Generally, the quietest hotels are in south Calangute, and across the bridge north of Baga.

🛏 Calangute

★ **Ospy's Shelter** GUESTHOUSE $
(Map p828; ☑ 7798100981, 0832-2279505; ospeys.shelter@gmail.com; d ₹800-900) Tucked away between the beach and St Anthony's Chapel, in a quiet, lush little area full of palms and sandy paths, Ospey's is a traveller favourite

---

BACKWOODS CAMP

In a forest near Bhagwan Mahaveer Sanctuary, full of butterflies and birds, **Backwoods Camp** (☑ 9822139859; www.backwoodsgoa.com; Matkan, Tambdi Surla; 1-/2-/3-day ₹4500/7500/11,000) is a magical, serene spot. The resort is about 1km from Tambdi Surla temple in the state's far east, and for birdwatching enthusiasts it offers one of Goa's richest sources birding, with everything from Ceylon frogmouths and Asian fairy bluebirds to puff-throated babblers and Indian pittas putting in a regular appearance. Accommodation is in comfortable tents on raised platforms, bungalows and farmhouse rooms. Rates include three guided birdwatching walks daily.

GOA CALANGUTE & BAGA

Calangute & Baga

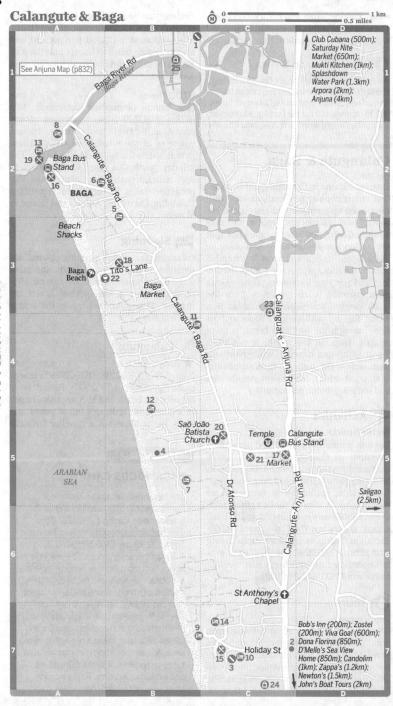

See Anjuna Map (p832)

Baga River Rd
Baga River

Calangute - Baga Rd

BAGA

Baga Bus Stand

Beach Shacks

Baga Beach

Tito's Lane

Baga Market

Calangute - Baga Rd

Calangute - Anjuna Rd

ARABIAN SEA

São João Batista Church

Temple

Calangute Bus Stand

Market

Dr Afonso Rd

Calangute - Anjuna Rd

Saligao (2.5km)

St Anthony's Chapel

Holiday St

0   1 km
0   0.5 miles

Club Cubana (500m);
Saturday Nite
Market (650m);
Mukti Kitchen (1km);
Splashdown
Water Park (1.3km);
Arpora (2km);
Anjuna (4km)

Bob's Inn (200m); Zostel
(200m); Viva Goa! (600m);
Dona Florina (850m);
D'Mello's Sea View
Home (850m); Candolim
(1km); Zappa's (1.2km);
Newton's (1.5km);
John's Boat Tours (2km)

Calangute & Baga

and only a two-minute walk from the beach. Spotless upstairs rooms have fridges and balconies and the whole place has a cosy family feel. Take the road directly west of the chapel – but it's tough to find, so call ahead.

Johnny's Hotel
HOTEL **$**

(Map p828; ☑ 0832-2277458; www.johnnyshotel. com; s ₹400-600, d ₹700-900, with AC ₹1000-1200; ❄☎) The 15 simple rooms at this backpacker-popular place make for a sociable stay, with a downstairs restaurant-bar and regular yoga and reiki classes. A range of apartments and houses are available for longer stays. It's down a lane lined with unremarkable midrange hotels and is just a short walk to the beach.

Coco Banana
GUESTHOUSE **$**

(Map p828; ☑ 0832-2279068; www.cocobananagoa. com; d ₹950, with AC ₹1500; ❄☎) Among the palms south of the main entrance to Calangute Beach, colourful Coco Banana has been

providing a soothing retreat for travellers for many years. Run by the friendly Walter, rooms are spacious and spotless and the vibe mellow. For families or groups, ask about the self-contained apartments at nearby Casa Leyla.

Hotel Golden Eye
HOTEL **$$**

(Map p828; ☑ 9822132850, 0832-2277308; www. hotelgoldeneye.com; Holiday St; d ₹2000, with AC ₹2500, sea-facing rooms from ₹4500, apt ₹5000-8000; ❄☎) This popular beachfront hotel at the end of 'Holiday St' has a fine range of rooms and apartments, from tidy ones at the back to the boutique sea-facing rooms with modern decor, air-con and cable TV. Unlike some midrangers it's welcoming to independent walk-in travellers, though you'll need to book ahead in season. The Flying Dolphin beach shack is out front.

Hotel Seagull
HOTEL **$$**

(Map p828; ☑ 0832-2179969; Holiday St; d with AC ₹2500; ❄☎☒) Bright, friendly and welcoming, the Seagull's rooms, set in a cheerful blue-and-white house in south Calangute, are light and airy with air-con and a small pool out back. Downstairs is the fine Blue Mariposa bar-restaurant, serving Goan, Indian and continental dishes.

Baga

★ Indian Kitchen
GUESTHOUSE **$**

(Map p828; ☑ 9822149615, 0832-2277555; www.indiankitchen-goa.com; s/d/chalet ₹770/990/1500; ❄@☎☒) If a colourful budget stay is what you're after, look no further than this family-run guesthouse, which offers a range of rooms from basic to more spacious, comfy apartments, but all with lots of effort at individual charm. There's a neat central courtyard and, surprisingly for a budget place, a sparklingly clean pool out the back. Each room has its own terrace or sit-out.

Melissa Guest House
GUESTHOUSE **$**

(Map p828; ☑ 9822180095, 0832-2279583; Baga River Rd; d ₹800) Across the Baga River, Melissa Guest House has just four neat little rooms, all with attached bathrooms and hot-water showers, in a tatty garden. Good value for the location.

Divine Guest House
GUESTHOUSE **$$**

(Map p828; ☑ 0832-2279546, 9370273464; www. indivinehome.com; Baga River Rd; s ₹600, d ₹1200-1300, with AC ₹1650-3000; ❄@☎) Not the bargain it once was, Divine still sits pretty on the relatively quiet headland north of the Baga River. The 'Praise the Lord' gatepost offers a little gentle proselytising from the friendly family, while the rooms are homey and bright with the odd individual touches. Wi-fi is prepaid.

Alidia Beach Cottages
GUESTHOUSE $$

(Map p828; ☑ 0832-2279014; Calungute-Baga Rd, Saunta Waddo; d ₹2000, with AC from ₹3300; ❉ 🛜 🏊) Set back behind a whitewashed church off busy Baga Rd, this convivial but quiet place has well kept Mediterranean-style rooms orbiting a gorgeous pool. The cheaper, non-air-con rooms at the back are not as good, but all are in reasonably good condition, staff are eager to please, and there's a path leading directly to Baga Beach.

Cavala Seaside Resort
HOTEL $$

(Map p828; ☑ 0832-2276090; www.cavala. com; Calungute-Baga Rd; s/d incl breakfast from ₹1500/3000, d & ste with AC ₹3500-5500; ❉ 🛜 🏊) Idiosyncratic, ivy-clad Cavala has been harbouring Baga-bound travellers for over 25 years and is often full. Perhaps as a result service is indifferent, but there's a big range of rooms, pool and a bar-restaurant with frequent live music.

🍴 Eating

Calangute and Baga boast probably the greatest concentration of dining options anywhere in Goa, with everything from the simplest street food to the finest filet steak. The beach shacks are an obvious go-to, but there are some interesting gems along the 'Strip' and some excellent upmarket offerings on the north side of the Baga River.

🍴 Calangute

Plantain Leaf
INDIAN $

(Map p828; ☑ 0832-2279860; veg thali ₹100, mains ₹90-270; ⊙ 8am-11pm) In the heart of Calangute's busy market area, 1st-floor Plantain Leaf has consistently been the area's best veg restaurant for many years. It's gone through a change though, dumping the classic South Indian banana leaf thalis, adding nonveg (meat) to the menu and expanding its repertoire to more North Indian flavours. It's still a good place for a thali, along with seafood (fish thali ₹150), kebabs and biriyani, and just sneaks in to the budget category.

Cafe Sussegado Souza
GOAN $$

(Map p828; ☑ 8652839651; Calangute-Anjuna Rd; mains ₹160-280; ⊙ noon-midnight) In a little yellow Portuguese-style house just south of the Calangute market area, Cafe Sussegado is the place to come for Goan food such as fish curry rice, chicken *xacuti* and pork *sorpotel* (a vinegary stew made from liver, heart and kidneys), with a shot of feni to be going on with. Authentic, busy and good atmosphere.

Infantaria
BAKERY, ITALIAN $$

(Map p828; Calangute-Baga Rd; pastries ₹50-200, mains ₹160-440; ⊙ 7.30am-midnight) Infanteria began life as Calangute's best bakery but has developed into an extremely popular Italian-cum-Indian restaurant. The bakery roots are still there, though, with homemade cakes, croissants, little flaky pastries and real coffee. Get in early for breakfast before the good stuff runs out. For lunch and dinner it's Goan and Italian specialities and a full bar. Regular live music in season.

A Reverie
INTERNATIONAL $$$

(Map p828; ☑ 9823505550; www.areverie.com; Holiday St; mains ₹475-700; ⊙ 7pm-late) A gorgeous award-winning lounge bar, all armchairs, cool jazz and whimsical outdoor space, this is the place to spoil yourself, with the likes of Serrano ham, grilled asparagus, French wines and Italian cheeses. Although fine dining, A Reverie likes to style itself as 'fun dining' and doesn't take itself too seriously. On the snack list, check out the Indian taco truck (₹275), wasabi prawns or barbecue pulled-pork rolls.

🍴 Baga

Britto's
MULTICUISINE, BAR $$

(Map p828; ☑ 0832-2277331; Baga Beach; mains ₹180-460; ⊙ 8.30am-midnight) Long-running Britto's is an arena-sized Baga institution at the north end of the beachfront, with a sandy floor if you've forgotten you're on the beach. It's a good spot for breakfast and gets busy for lunch and dinner. The drinks list is longer than the food menu and young Indian tourists are fond of ordering the iced Kingfisher mini-kegs. All good fun and live music most nights in season.

⭐ Go With the Flow
INTERNATIONAL, BRAZILIAN $$$

(Map p828; ☑ 7507771556; www.gowiththeflow goa.com; Baga River Rd; mains ₹200-650; ⊙ from 6pm Mon-Sat) Stepping into the fantasy neon-lit garden of illuminated white-wicker furniture is wow factor enough, but the food is equally out of this world. With a global menu leaning towards European and South American flavours, Brazilian chef Guto brings a wealth of experience and culinary imagination to the table. Try some of the small bites (ask about a tasting plate) or go straight for the pork belly or duck ravioli.

★ **Fiesta**   CONTINENTAL $$$
(Map p828; ☑ 0832-2279894; www.fiestagoa.in; Tito's Lane; mains ₹250-600; ⊘ 7pm-late) Follow the lamplights off happening Tito's Lane: there's something magical about stepping into Fiesta's candlelit split-level tropical garden. Soft music and exotic furnishings add to an upmarket Mediterranean-style dining experience that starts with homemade pizza and pasta and extends to French-influenced seafood dishes and some of the finest desserts around. Worth a splurge.

🍷 Drinking & Nightlife

Baga's boisterous club scene – centred on Tito's Lane – has long been well known among the tourist crowd looking for a late night out. Some find the scene a little sleazy here and the bar staff indifferent. Solo women are welcomed into clubs (usually free) but should exercise care and take taxis to and from venues.

Club Cubana   CLUB
(☑ 9823539000; www.clubcubanagoa.com; Arpora; ⊘ 9.30pm-4am) Billing itself as the 'nightclub in the sky,' this hilltop place in Arpora (a few kilometres north of Baga) has been providing a late-night pool party scene for more than a decade. As with most clubs it's couples or ladies only (though solo males can usually pay a premium to get in) and, depending on the night, it's open bar with a cover charge of ₹1000 to ₹2000. Wednesday is ladies night.

Café Mambo   CLUB
(Map p828; ☑ 7507333003; www.cafemambogoa. com; Tito's Lane, Baga; cover charge couples ₹500; ⊘ 10.30pm-3am) Part of the Tito's empire, Mambo is one of Baga's most happening clubs with an indoor/outdoor beachfront location and nightly DJs pumping out house, hip-hop and Latino tunes. Couples or females only.

Shopping

Both **Mackie's Saturday Nite Bazaar** (Map p828; www.mackiesnitebazaar.com; ⊘ from 6pm Sat Nov-Apr), in Baga, and the larger **Saturday Nite Market** (www.snmgoa.com; Arpora; ⊘ from 6pm Sat Nov-Mar), in Arpora, about 2km northeast of Baga, set up in season and are fun alternatives to Anjuna's Wednesday market, with food stalls, entertainment and the usual souvenir stalls. They have been cancelled from time to time in recent years for reasons unclear. Ask around to see when they're on.

Karma Collection   SOUVENIRS
(Map p828; www.karmacollectiongoa.com; Calangute-Arpora Rd; ⊘ 9.30am-10.30pm) Beautiful home furnishings, textiles, ornaments, bags and other enticing stuff – some of it antique – has been sourced from across India, Pakistan and Afghanistan and gathered at Karma Collection, which makes for a mouth-watering browse. Fixed prices, though it's not cheap.

Literati Bookshop & Cafe   BOOKS
(Map p828; ☑ 0832-2277740; www.literati-goa. com; Calangute; ⊘ 10am-6.30pm Mon-Sat) A refreshingly different bookstore, in the owners' South Calangute home, and a very pleasant Italian-style garden cafe. Come for a fine espresso and browse the range of books by Goan and Indian authors as well as antiquarium literature. Check the website for readings and other events.

ℹ️ Information

Currency exchange offices, ATMs, pharmacies and internet cafes cluster around Calangute's main market and bus stand area, and along the Baga and Candolim roads.

ℹ️ Getting There & Around

Frequent buses to Panaji (₹20, 45 minutes) and Mapusa (₹10) depart from the Baga and Calangute bus stands, and a local bus (₹5) runs between the Baga and Calangute stands every few minutes; catch it anywhere along the way. Taxis charge an extortionate ₹100 between Calangute and Baga. A prepaid taxi from Dabolim Airport to Calangute costs ₹750.

Anjuna

Good old Anjuna. The stalwart of India's hippy scene still drags out the sarongs and sandalwood each Wednesday for its famous, and once infamous, flea market. With its

GOA ANJUNA

raggedy beach, rice paddies and cheap guesthouses huddled in relatively peaceful pockets, it continues to pull in backpackers and long-term hippies, while midrange tourists are also increasingly making their way here. The village itself might be a bit frayed around the edges – if your only introduction is the tatty cliff-tops around the bus stand you may be unimpressed. But look further and you may come to appreciate Anjuna's haphazard charm, and see why it remains a favourite of both long-stayers and first-timers.

◉ Sights & Activities

Anjuna's charismatic little **beach** runs for almost 2km from the northern village area to the flea market. The northern end is mostly cliffs lined with cheap cafes and basic guesthouses, but the beach proper is a nice stretch of sand (when the tide is out) with a bunch of multistorey beach bars at the southern end.

There's lots of yoga, reiki and ayurvedic massage offered around Anjuna and nearby Assagao; look for notices at Artjuna Cafe and the German Bakery. Drop-in classes are organised by **Brahmani Yoga** (☑ 9545620578; www.brahmaniyoga.com; Tito's White House, Aguada-Siolim Rd; classes ₹600, 10-class pass ₹4500), at Tito's White House.

Splashdown Water Park   SWIMMING
(☑ 0832-2273008;   www.splashdowngoa.com; Anjuna-Baga Rd, Arpora; weekdays/weekends ₹380/420, spectators ₹260/300; ⊙ 10.30am-6pm) This fabulous collection of pools, fountains and waterslides will keep kids (and adults) happy all day long. A nice cafe and bar overlook over the action. It's in Arpora, roughly halfway between Anjuna and Baga.

Mukti Kitchen   COOKING
(☑ 08007359170; www.muktikitchen.com; Anjuna-Baga Rd, Arpora; veg/nonveg ₹1500/1800; ⊙ 11am-2pm & 5-8pm) Mukti shares her cooking skills twice daily at these recommended classes on

Anjuna

Vagator Beach (3.5km)

Hotel Bougainvillea (250m); Brahmani Yoga (650m); Assagao (5km); Mapusa (7km)

Bus Stand

HDFC ATM

Clifftop Bars & Restaurants

St Anthony's Chapel

Anjuna Beach

ARABIAN SEA

Anjuna–Mapusa Rd (Anjuna Beach Rd)

Bank of Baroda

MAZAL WADDO

Baga River

Market Rd

Market Rd

See Calangute & Baga Map (p828)

Baga River Rd

the Anjuna Rd in Arpora. Courses include five dishes which can be tailored – veg or nonveg, Goan, Indian or ayurvedic. Minimum four people, maximum six; book one day ahead.

🛏 Sleeping

Most accommodation and other useful services are sprinkled along the beach cliffs, on the Anjuna-Mapusa Rd leading to the bus stand or down shady inland lanes.

Prison Hostel
HOSTEL $

(☏0832-2273745; www.thehostelcrowd.com; 940 Market Rd; dm ₹350-400, with AC ₹450, d ₹1400; ❉🛜) Cell-like rooms are not uncommon in India but this quirky new backpacker hostel on Anjuna's Market Rd goes a step further and is themed like a jail. Apart from the bars on the windows and B&W decor, there's no sense of incarceration here, however. Clean four- to 10-bed dorms have individual lockers and bed-lights, there's a good kitchen, and breakfast and wi-fi are included. Expect loud music and partying guests.

Red Door Hostel
HOSTEL $

(☏0832-2274423; reddoorhostels@gmail.com; dm without/with AC ₹500/600, d without/with AC ₹1600/2000; ❉🛜) A recent addition to North Goa's hostel scene, Red Door is a welcoming place close to Anjuna's central crossroads. Clean four- and six-bed dorms plus a few private rooms. Facilities include lockers, free wi-fi, garden and good communal areas, including a well-equipped kitchen. Laidback vibe and resident pet dogs.

Vilanova
GUESTHOUSE $

(☏0832-6450389, 9225904244; mendonca90@rediffmail.com; Anjuna Beach Rd; d ₹600-700, with AC ₹1200; ❉) Big, clean rooms have a fridge, TV, 24-hour hot water and window screens and are set in three Portuguese-style bungalows in a cute little compound. Good vibes and a comfortable family atmosphere, with friendly staff and a good restaurant.

Florinda's
GUESTHOUSE $

(☏9890216520; s/d ₹500/700, with AC ₹1500; ❉🛜) One of the better budget places near the beach, Florinda's has clean rooms, with 24-hour hot water, window screens and mosquito nets, set around a pretty garden. The few air-con rooms fill up fast.

Paradise
GUESTHOUSE $

(☏9922541714; janet_965@hotmail.com; Anjuna-Mapusa Rd; d ₹800-1000, with AC ₹2000; ❉@🛜) This friendly place is fronted by an old Portuguese home and offers neat, clean rooms with well-decorated options in the newer annexe. The better rooms have TV, fridge and hammocks on the balcony. Friendly owner Janet and family also run the pharmacy, general store, restaurant, internet cafe, Connexions travel agency and money exchange!

Peace Land
GUESTHOUSE $

(San Miguel's; ☏9822685255, 0832-2273700; s/d from ₹600/800, with AC ₹1200-1500; ❉🛜) A good budget deal with small but tidy rooms arranged around a tranquil courtyard garden back from the main Anjuna road. It's run by a friendly family and there's a pool table, chillout area, hammocks and a decent restaurant.

Sea Horse
HUT $$

(☏9764465078; www.vistapraiaanjuna.com; ☺hut without/with AC ₹1500/1800; ❉🛜) A line-up of timber cabins behind the beach restaurant of the same name, Sea Horse is decent value for the location. The huts are small and have modern bathrooms but get a little hot – go for the air-con rooms if it's humid. Staff are friendly and accommodating. The same owners have a pricier beachfront set-up called Praia Anjuna.

Banyan Soul
BOUTIQUE HOTEL $$

(☑9820707283; www.thebanyansoul.com; d ₹2200; ※ 🛜) A slinky 12-room option, tucked down the lane off Market Rd, and lovingly conceived and run by Sumit, a young Mumbai escapee. Rooms are chic and well equipped with air-con and TV, and there's a lovely library and shady seating area beneath a banyan tree.

Palacete Rodrigues
HERITAGE HOTEL $$

(☑0832-2273358; www.palacetegoa.com; Mazal Vaddo; d & ste ₹3000-6000; ※ 🛜 ※) This lovely family-run mansion, filled with antiques and ornate furniture, is as quirky as you'll find in Anjuna – perhaps too over-the-top for some. Some of the 14 rooms and suites are themed and decorated along ethnic cultural lines: French, Chinese, Japanese and Goan.

Casa Anjuna
HERITAGE HOTEL $$$

(☑0832-2274123-5; www.casaboutiquehotels. com; D'Mello Vaddo 66; r from ₹7700; ※ 🛜 ※) This heritage hotel is enclosed in lovely plant-filled gardens around an inviting pool, managing to shield itself from the hype of central Anjuna. All rooms have antique furnishings and period touches; like many upmarket places it's better value out of season when rates halve.

✖ Eating & Drinking

The southern end of Anjuna beach boasts a string of super-sized semipermanent beach shacks serving all day food and drinks and partying late into the night – good ones include Cafe Lilliput, Curlies, Shiva Garden and Janet & John's. Oxford Arcade (Anjuna-Vagator Rd; ⊙8.30am-9pm) is an excellent, modern supermarket where you can stock up on imported goods and cheap booze.

★ Artjuna Cafe
CAFE $

(☑0832-2274794; www.artjuna.com; Market Rd; mains ₹80-290; ⊙8am-10.30pm) Artjuna is right up there with our favourite cafes in Anjuna. Along with all-day breakfast, outstanding espresso coffee, salads, sandwiches and Middle Eastern surprises such as baba ganoush, tahini and felafel, this sweet garden cafe has an excellent craft and lifestyle shop, yoga classes and one of Anjuna's best noticeboards. Great meeting place.

Burger Factory
BURGERS $$

(Anjuna-Mapusa Rd; burgers ₹250-450; ⊙noon-11pm) There's no mistaking what's on offer at this little alfresco diner/kitchen. The straightforward menu is chalked up on a blackboard at the side, and though the burgers aren't cheap, they are interesting and expertly crafted. Choose between beef or chicken burgers and toppings such as cheddar, wasabi and mayo or beetroot and aioli.

Om Made Cafe
MEDITERRANEAN $$

(D'Mello Vaddo; dishes ₹120-250; ⊙9am-sunset) A highlight on Anjuna's same-same clifftop strip, this cheery little place offers striped deckchairs from which to enjoy the views and the super breakfasts, sandwiches and salads. The food is fresh and organic.

Dhum Biryani & Kebabs
INDIAN $$

(Anjuna-Mapusa Rd; mains ₹180-350; ⊙9am-1am) Loved by visitors and locals alike, Dhum Biryani serves up consistently good kebabs as well as biryani and other usual suspects.

Martha's Breakfast Home
CAFE $$

(meals ₹60-300; ⊙7.30am-1.30pm) As the name suggests, welcoming Martha's speciality is breakfast, served up in a quiet garden on the way down to the flea-market site. Omelettes, fresh juice and cereal are *de rigueur*, but the stars of the show are the waffles with maple syrup and strawberries (in season). There are some nice rooms (₹700) here and a two-bedroom house to rent (₹10,000 per week). Located off Market Rd.

ANJUNA'S FLEA MARKET EXPERIENCE

Anjuna's Wednesday **flea market** (⊙8am-late Wed Nov-late Mar) is as much part of the Goan experience as a day on the beach. More than three decades ago it was the sole preserve of hippies smoking jumbo joints and convening to compare experiences on the heady Indian circuit. Nowadays, things are far more mainstream with stalls carrying crafts from Kashmir and Karnataka, mirrored textiles from Rajasthan, spices from Kerala and Tibetan trinkets. There are a couple of bars with live music and cold beer.

The market is still good fun and shows no sign of waning in popularity, so dive in and enjoy the ride. The best time to visit is early (from 8am) or late afternoon (around 4pm till close just after sunset).

YOGA RETREATS

The Anjuna/Vagator/Assagao area has a number of yoga retreats where you can immerse yourself in courses, classes and a zen vibe during the October–March season.

Purple Valley Yoga Retreat (☑0832-2268363; www.yogagoa.com; 142 Bairo Alto, Assagao; dm/s one week from £600/750, two weeks £980/1200; ☎) Popular yoga resort in Assagao offering one- and two-week residential and nonresidential Ashtanga courses.

Swan Yoga Retreat (☑0832-2268024, 8007360677; www.swan-yoga-goa.com; Assagao; per person one week from ₹17,500) In a peaceful jungle corner of Assagao, Swan Retreat is a very zen yoga experience. Minimum week-long yoga retreats start every Saturday and include eco-accommodation, ayurvedic veg meals, meditation, daily classes and an optional afternoon 'masterclass'.

Yoga Magic (☑0832-6523796; www.yogamagic.net; Anjuna; s/d lodge ₹6750/9000, ste ₹9000/12,000; ☎) ✦ Solar lighting, vegetable farming and compost toilets are just some of the worthy initiatives practised in this luxurious yoga resort. The lodge features dramatic Rajasthani tents under a thatched shelter.

German Bakery MULTICUISINE $$
(www.german-bakery.in; bread & pastries ₹50-90, mains ₹100-450; ⊙8.30am-11pm; ☎) Leafy and filled with prayer flags, occasional live music and garden lights, German Bakery is a long-standing favourite for hearty and healthy breakfast, fresh-baked bread and organic food, but these days the menu runs to pasta, burgers and pricey seafood. Prices are up and service is down though. Healthy juices (think wheatgrass) and espresso coffee.

Heidi's Beer Garden GERMAN $$
(☑9886376922; Market Rd; mains ₹100-400; ⊙11am-11pm) It may well be Goa's first German-style beer garden and restaurant, which is reason enough to call into Heidi's. Another is the range of some 40 international beers from Germany, Belgium, Mexico, Japan, Portugal and more. The imported beers are relatively expensive, but you can still order local beers, including a Goan draught. The food is mostly German and European, including bratwurst sausages and the acclaimed German thali (₹400).

Curlies BAR
(www.curliesgoa.com; ⊙9am-3am) At the southern end of Anjuna Beach, Curlies mixes laid-back beach-bar vibe with sophisticated night spot – the party nights here are notorious. There's a parachute silk-covered rooftop lounge bar and an enclosed late-night dance club. on Thursday and Saturday.

❶ Information

Anjuna has three ATMs, clustered together on the main road to the beach, and another down near the bus stand. Free wi-fi is common in guesthouses and cafes.

❶ Getting There & Away

Buses to Mapusa (₹15) depart every half-hour or so from the main **bus stand** near the beach; some from Mapusa continue on to Vagator and Chapora. Two daily buses to Calangute depart from the main crossroads. Taxis and autos gather at both stops, and you can hire scooters and motorcycles easily from the crossroads.

Vagator & Chapora

Vagator's twin beaches are small by Goan standards but the dramatic red-stone cliffs, rolling green hills, patches of forest and a crumbling 17th-century Portuguese fort provide Vagator and its diminutive neighbour Chapora with one of the prettiest settings on the north Goan coast. Once known for wild trance parties and heady, hippy lifestyle, Vagator has slowed down, but it's still the place of choice for many backpackers and partygoers, and tiny Chapora – reminiscent of *Star Wars'* Mos Eisley Cantina – remains a fave for longstayers and charas smokers.

🛏 Sleeping

🛏 Vagator

You'll see lots of signs for 'Rooms to Let' in private homes and guesthouses.

★ **Jungle Hostel** HOSTEL $
(☑0832-2273006; www.thehostelcrowd.com; Vagator Beach Rd; dm ₹450, with AC ₹500, s/d

Vagator & Chapora

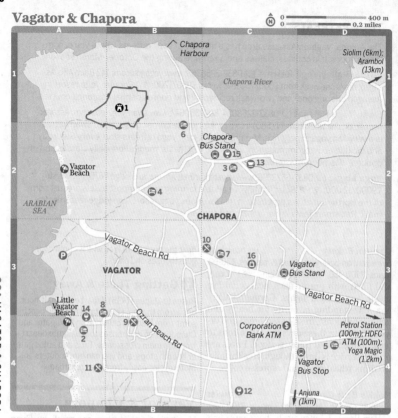

Vagator & Chapora

₹900/1400; ✳ @ 🕿) True backpacker hostels are on the rise in Goa, but this was one of the originals, bringing the dorm experience and an international vibe to Vagator. The six-bed dorms are clean and bright and things like lockers, wi-fi, breakfast, communal kitchen and travel advice are free.

Bean Me Up   GUESTHOUSE **$**
(Enterprise Guest House; ☎ 7769095356; www. beanmeup.in; 1639/2 Deulvaddo; d ₹1200, without

bathroom ₹900; 🕾) Set around a leafy, parachute-silky courtyard that's home to Vagator's best vegan restaurant (p837), rooms at the Enterprise Guest House look simple but are themed with individual exotic decor, earthy shades, mosquito nets and shared verandahs. The mellow yoga-friendly vibe matches the clientele.

Shalom GUESTHOUSE $
(📲919881578459, 0832-2273166; www.shalom guesthousegoa.com; d ₹800-1400, with AC ₹1800; ❈🕾) Arranged around a placid garden not far from the path down to Little Vagator Beach, this established place run by a friendly family (whose home is onsite) offers a variety of extremely well-kept rooms and a two-bedroom apartment for long-stayers.

Alcove Resort HOTEL $$
(📲0832-2274491; www.alcovegoa.com; Little Vagator Beach; d ₹3300, with AC ₹3850, cottage ₹4400/4950; ❈@🕾🏊) The location overlooking Little Vagator Beach is hard to beat at this price. Attractively furnished rooms, slightly larger cottages and four suites surrounding a decent central pool, restaurant and bar, make this a good place for those who want a touch of affordable luxury.

🛏 Chapora

Head down the road to the harbour and you'll find lots of rooms – and whole homes – for rent.

Casa de Olga GUESTHOUSE $
(📲0832-2274355, 9822157145; eadsouza@yahoo. co.in; r ₹600-1200, without bathroom from ₹300) This welcoming family-run homestay, set around a nice garden on the way to Chapora harbour, offers spotless rooms of varying sizes in a three-storey building. The best are the brand-new top-floor rooms with swanky bathrooms, TV and balcony. Budget travellers will be happy with the compact ground-floor rooms with shared bathroom.

Baba GUESTHOUSE $
(📲0832-2273339; babavilla11@yahoo.in; d ₹500, without bathroom ₹250) At this price, and with its laid-back Chapora location, Baba is often full with long-stayers but you might be lucky as a walk-in. The 14 rooms are clean and simple but serviceable. Located behind the Baba Restaurant on the main street.

Baba Place GUESTHOUSE $
(📲9822156511; babaplace11@yahoo.com; Chapora Fort Rd; d without/with AC ₹800/1200; ❈🕾) Brand new at the time of research, Baba Place features a rooftop terrace with views of Chapora Fort, immaculate, decent-sized rooms with verandah, and a nice, quiet Chapora location.

🍴 Eating

🍴 Vagator

⭐ Bean Me Up Soya Station VEGAN $$
(www.beanmeup.in; 1639/2 Deulvaddo; mains ₹180-350; ⊗8am-11pm; 🕾) Bean Me Up has gone all vegan, but even nonveg travellers will be blown away by the taste, variety and filling plates on offer in this relaxed garden restaurant. The extensive menu includes vegan pizzas, ice creams and innovative salads. Ingredients are as diverse as coconut, cashew milk and cashew cheese, quinoa, tofu and lentil dhal.

Bluebird GOAN $$
(www.bluebirdgoa.com; Ozran Beach Rd; mains ₹250-370; ⊗8.30am-11pm) Bluebird specialises in Goan cuisine, with genuine vindaloos, chicken *cafrial*, fish curry rice and Goan sausages among the temptations, as well as some delicately spiced seafood dishes. Dine in the lovely open garden cafe. The attached guesthouse has some nice rooms.

Mango Tree Bar & Cafe MULTICUISINE $$
(Vagator Beach Rd; mains ₹120-550; ⊗24hr) With loud reggae, crappy service, dark-wood furniture, a sometimes rambunctious bar scene, ancient expats leaning over the bar, draught beer and an overall great vibe, the Mango Tree is a classic Vagator meeting place. It's open late (24 hours if it's busy enough), the food is pretty good – from Goan to European, pizza, Thai and Mexican – and films or sports are sometimes shown on the big screen.

⭐ Thalassa GREEK $$$
(📲9850033537; www.thalassagoa.com; mains ₹300-750; ⊗4pm-midnight) Authentic and ridiculously good Greek food is served alfresco on a breezy terrace to the sound of the sea just below. Kebabs, souvlaki and thoughtful seafood dishes are the speciality, but vegie dishes are also excellent; the *spanakorizo*

WHERE'S THE PARTY?

Goa was long legendary among Western visitors for its all-night, open-air trance parties, until a central government 'noise pollution' ban on loud music in open spaces between 10pm and 6am largely curbed its often notorious, drug-laden party scene (late nights are still allowed in sound-proof interior spaces). If you're looking for the remainder of the real party scene, though, you'll need to keep your ear close to the ground, and wait out for word in Vagator or Anjuna. Authorities tend to turn a blind eye to parties during the peak Christmas–New Year period.

(spinach and rice cooked with Greek olive oil and herbs and topped with feta) is outstanding. Wash it all down with a jug of sangria. It's very popular around sunset – book ahead for a beachside table.

✗ Chapora

Tiny Chapora's eating scene is not as evolved as Vagator's. **Scarlet Cold Drinks** (juices & snacks ₹30-80; ⊙8.30am-midnight) and **Jai Ganesh Fruit Juice Centre** (Chapora; juices ₹40-80; ⊙8.30am-midnight) are both popular meeting places side by side in close proximity to the thickest gusts of charas (hasish) smoke. Scarlet has an exceptionally good noticeboard, while Jai Ganesh has cold coffee and avocado lassis.

🍷 Drinking & Entertainment

Vagator's party scene is hanging on, especially over the peak Christmas/New Year period. The Russians, having taken the party crown away from the Israelis, seem to create nightlife in various spots around town.

Paulo's Antique Bar BAR
(Chapora; ⊙11.30am-11pm) In season this hole-in-the-wall bar on Chapora's main street overflows with good music and cold beer at night. Even during the afternoon the few tables on the verandah are a good spot to watch the world go by.

Nine Bar BAR
(⊙6pm-4am) Once the hallowed epicentre of Goa's trance scene, the open-air Nine Bar, on the clifftop overlooking Little Vagator Beach, has now moved into an indoor space so the parties can still go all night. Look out for flyers and local advice to see when the big party nights are on.

Hilltop CLUB
(☑0832-2273665; ⊙sunset-late) Hilltop is a long-serving Vagator trance and party ven-

ue that's deserted by day but comes alive from sunset. Its edge-of-town neon-lit coconut grove location allows it, on occasion, to bypass the 10pm noise regulations to host concerts, parties and the occasional international DJ. Sunday sessions (5pm to 10pm) are legendary here, and in season there's usually an evening market and techno party on Friday night.

🛍 Shopping

Rainbow Bookshop BOOKS
(Vagator Beach Rd; ⊙10am-2pm & 3-7pm) Long-running shop stocking a good range of secondhand and new books.

ℹ Information

Vagator's closest ATM is the HDFC at the petrol station on the back road to Anjuna and Mapusa. Plenty of internet places are scattered around town and lots of accommodation places offer wi-fi.

ℹ Getting There & Away

Frequent buses run from Chapora, through Vagator, to Mapusa (₹10) throughout the day, many via Anjuna. The buses start in Chapora village, but there are a couple of other stops in Chapora and Vagator. Scooters/motorbikes can easily be hired for around ₹200/300 per day in high season.

Morjim & Aswem

Morjim and Aswem, a peaceful strip of uncrowded sand stretching north from the Chapora river mouth, are two North Goan beaches where sunbathing doesn't attract hordes of hawkers, dogs and onlookers. The water, though, does suffer from a bit of river run-off pollution and the sand is more black than golden. Rare olive ridley turtles nest at Morjim's southern end from November to February, so this is a protected area, but it's developing rapidly due mainly to a heavy influx of Russian visitors.

🏃 Activities

Vaayu Waterman's Village SURFING
(📞 9850050403; www.vaayuvision.org; Aswem; surfboard hire per hr ₹500, lessons ₹2700) Goa's only surf shop is also an activity and art centre where you can arrange lessons and hire equipment for surfing, kiteboarding, stand up paddleboarding, kayaking and wakeboarding. Enthusiastic young owners also run an art gallery, cafe and funky accommodation across the road from Aswem beach.

🛌 Sleeping & Eating

★ Wanderers Hostel HOSTEL $
(📞 9619235302; www.wanderershostel.com; Morjim; dm incl breakfast ₹500, luxury tent d ₹2000; ❄ 🎇 🛜) This relatively new hostel about five minutes' walk back from Morjim Beach is a real find. The main building, decorated with original travellers murals, has 40 beds in spotless air-con dorms with lockers, bed lights and free wi-fi, full kitchen, clean bathrooms, cosy communal areas and a pool table. In the garden next door is a tent village with swimming pool and yoga retreat centre (classes free to guests).

Goan Café & Resort RESORT $$
(📞 0832-2244394; www.goancafe.com; apt & cottage from ₹1800, with AC ₹2200, treehouse without/with bathroom from ₹1200/1700; ❄ 🎇) Fronting Morijm Beach, this excellent family-run resort has a fine array of beachfront stilted 'treehouse' huts and more solid rooms (some with AC) at the back. The **Friends Corner** restaurant is good; it's not licensed but you're welcome to BYO.

Meems' Beach Resort RESORT $$
(📞 0832-2247015; www.meemsbeachresort.com; r ₹2000, with AC ₹2500, f ₹4000; ❄ 🎇) A solid guesthouse with 11 very clean rooms, Meems' is just across the road from the beach. A feature here is the atmospheric garden restaurant with low tables and floor cushions, specialising in Kashmiri cuisine and Vietnamese barbecue.

Yab Yum HUTS $$$
(📞 0832-6510392; www.yabyumresorts.com; hut from ₹5800; 🎇) 🏄 This top-notch choice has unusual, stylish, dome-shaped huts – some look like giant hairy coconuts – made of a combination of all-natural local materials, including mud, stone and mango wood. A whole host of yoga and massage options are available, and it's all set in one of the most secluded beachfront jungle gardens you'll find in Goa.

La Plage MEDITERRANEAN $$
(mains ₹210-400; ⏱ 9am-10pm Nov-Mar) Rnowned in these parts, La Plage takes beach shack to the next level with its inspired gourmet French-Mediterranean food. Along with excellent salads, seafood and fabulous desserts (try the chocolate thali), La Plage stocks great wines. It's usually open from late November to April.

ℹ Getting There & Around

Although local buses run between Siolim and Morjim, unless you have your own transport it's easiest to take a taxi from Arambol, Mapusa or Anjuna.

Mandrem

Mellow Mandrem has developed in recent years from an in-the-know piece of beach heaven for those seeking a change from the traveller scenes of Arambol and Anjuna to a fairly mainstream but still incredibly lovely hangout. An unusual feature of Mandrem is the narrow river inlet separating the white-sand beach from most of the accommodation strip and road – rickety bamboo bridges connect you to the beach, where seasonal shack restaurants set up. Development here is still low-key compared to most resorts in Goa and the beaches are largely free of hawkers and tourist crowds. There's plenty of yoga, meditation and ayurveda on offer, good dining and space to lay down with a good book. Many travellers believe there's no better place in North Goa.

🏃 Activities

Himalaya Yoga Valley YOGA
(📞 9960657852; www.yogagoaindia.com; Mandrem Beach) The winter home of a popular Dharamsala outfit, HYV specialises in hatha and ashtanga residential teacher-training courses, but also has daily drop-in classes (₹400; 1½ hours; 8am, 10am and 3pm daily) and 10-day yoga refresher courses.

Oceanic Yoga YOGA
(📞 9049247422; www.oceanicyoga.com; Junas Waddo, Mandrem; drop-in class ₹300-400) Oceanic officers drop-in classes, seven-day yoga

and meditation retreats, reiki and yoga teacher-training courses.

🛏 Sleeping & Eating

★ **Dunes Holiday Village**   BEACH HUT $
(☑ 0832-2247219; www.dunesgoa.com; r & hut ₹900-1100; @ 🛜) The pretty huts here are peppered around a palm-filled lane leading to the beach; at night, globe lamps light up the place like a palm-tree dreamland. Huts range from basic to more sturdy 'treehouses' (huts on stilts). It's a friendly, good-value place with a decent beach restaurant, massage, yoga classes and a marked absence of trance.

★ **Mandala**   RESORT $$
(☑ 9158266093; www.themandalagoa.com; r & hut ₹1600-5500; ✳ 🛜) Mandala is a very shanti and beautifully designed eco-village with a range of huts and a couple of quirky air-con rooms in the 'Art House.' Pride of place goes to the barn-sized two-storey villas inspired by the design of a Keralan houseboat. There are no beach views or even direct beach access but the location, overlooking the tidal lagoon, is serene with a large garden, daily yoga sessions and an organic restaurant.

Beach Street   RESORT $$
(Lazy Dog; ☑ 0832-3223911; Mandrem Beach; r & hut ₹3300-4400; 🛜 ✳) This large and relatively new beachfront villa has neat and tidy rooms, while the seasonal beachfront huts are spacious and well designed. The pool is a nice touch but it's only a short walk over the bamboo bridge to the beach.

❶ Getting There & Around

It's a nightmare trying to get anywhere in a hurry on public transport. Most travellers taxi to their chosen accommodation, then either hire a scooter/motorbike or use taxis from there.

Arambol (Harmal)

With its craggy cliffs, sweeping beach and remote northerly location, Arambol first emerged in the 1960s as a mellow paradise for long-haired long-stayers, and ever since travellers have been drifting up to this blissed-out corner of Goa. As a result, in high season the beach and the road leading down to it (known as Glastonbury St) can get pretty crowded – with huts, people and nonstop stalls selling the usual tourist stuff.

Further north around the headland is the near-deserted Querim (Keri) beach where the Terekhol River meets the coast.

🏃 Activities

Follow the cliff path north of Arambol Beach to pretty Kalacha Beach, which meets the small 'sweetwater' lake, a great spot for swimming.

Arambol Paragliding   PARAGLIDING
(10min flight ₹1500; ☺ noon-6pm) The headland above Kalacha Beach (Sweetwater Lake) is an ideal launching point for paragliding. There are a number of independent operators: ask around at the shack restaurants on the beach, arrange a pilot, then make the short hike to the top of the headland. Most flights are around 10 minutes, but if conditions are right you can stay up much longer.

Himalayan Iyengar Yoga Centre   YOGA
(www.hiyogacentre.com; Madhlo Vaddo; 5-day yoga course ₹4000; ☺ 9am-6pm Tue-Sun Nov-Mar) Arambol's reputable Himalayan Iyengar Yoga Centre, which runs five-day courses in hatha yoga from mid-November to mid-March, is the winter centre of the iyengar yoga school in Dharamkot, near Dharamsala in north India. First-time students must take the introductory five-day course, then can continue with more advanced five-day courses at a reduced rate.

Surf Wala   SURFING
(www.surfwala.com; Surf Club; 1½hr lesson from ₹2000, 3-/5-day course ₹5000/8000) If you're a beginner looking to get up on a board, join the international team of surfers based at Arambol's Surf Club. Prices include board hire, wax and rashie. Check the website for instructor contact details – between them they speak English, Russian, Hindi, Konkani and Japanese! Board-only rental is ₹500.

🛏 Sleeping

Arambol is known for its sea-facing, cliff-hugging budget huts – trawl the cliffside to the north of Arambol's main beach for the best hut options. It's almost impossible to book in advance: simply turn up early in the day to check who's checking out. The beach stretch is also lined with shack restaurants with hut accommodation at the back, much like Palolem.

Chilli's   HOTEL $
(☑ 9921882424; d ₹600, apt with AC ₹1000; ☺ year-round; ✳) Near the beach entrance

on Glastonbury St, this clean and friendly canary-yellow place is one of Arambol's better non-beachfront bargains. Chilli's offers 10 decent, no-frills rooms, all with attached bathroom, fan and a hot-water shower. The top-floor apartment with AC and TV is great value. Owner Derek hires out motorbikes and scooters and free advice.

Shree Sai Cottages   HUT $
(☑ 0832-3262823, 9420767358; shreesai_cottages @yahoo.com; hut without bathroom ₹400-600) A good example of what's on offer along the cliffs, Shree Sai has simple, cute, sea-facing huts on the cliffs overlooking Kalacha Beach.

Om Ganesh   BEACH HUT $
(☑ 9404436447; r & hut ₹400-800) Popular seasonal huts along the cliff path and a good restaurant, Om Ganesh has been around for a while and also has solid rooms in a building on the hillside.

Arambol Plaza Beach Resort   HOTEL $$
(☑ 9545550731, 0832-2242052; Arambol Beach Rd; r & cottage ₹1800-2500; ❋ ☎ ☲) On the road between the upper village and the beach, Arambol Plaza is a reasonable mid-range choice with cute timber cottages around a decent pool. All rooms are air-con but avoid the poorly maintained rooms in the building at the side.

Surf Club   GUESTHOUSE $$
(www.surfclubgoa.com; d ₹1200-1600; ☎) In its own space at the end of a lane, on the very southern end of Arambol Beach, the Surf Club is one of those cool little hang-outs that offer a bit of everything: simple but clean rooms, a funky bar with live music, surf lessons and a seasonal kindergarten.

✕ Eating & Drinking

Beach shacks with chairs and tables on the sand and parachute-silk canopies line the beach at Arambol. There are more restaurants and cafes lining the main road from the village to the beach. For simpler fare, head up to Arambol village, by the bus stop, where small local joints will whip you up a thali and a chai for less than ₹50.

Shimon   MIDDLE EASTERN $
(meals ₹100-160; ☺ 9am-11pm) Just back from the beach, and understandably popular with Israeli backpackers, Shimon is the place to fill up on exceptional falafel. For something more unusual go for *sabich,* crisp slices of eggplant stuffed into pita bread along with

boiled egg, boiled potato and salad. The East-meets-Middle-East thali (₹360) comprises a little bit of almost everything on the menu.

Dylan's Toasted & Roasted   CAFE $
(☑ 9604780316; www.dylanscoffee.com; coffee & desserts from ₹60; ☺ 9am-11pm late Nov-Apr) The Goa (winter) incarnation of a Manali institution, Dylan's is a fine place for an espresso, chocolate chip cookies and old-school dessert. A nice hang-out just back from the southern beach entrance.

Fellini   ITALIAN $$
(mains ₹180-350; ☺ from 6.30pm) On the left-hand side just before the beach, this unsignposted but long-standing Italian joint is perfect if you're craving a carbonara or calzone. More than 20 wood-fired, thin-crust pizza varieties are on the menu, but save space for a very decent rendition of tiramisu.

Double Dutch   MULTICUISINE $$
(mains ₹110-390, steaks ₹420-470; ☺ 7am-10pm) In a peaceful garden set back from the main road to the Glastonbury St beach entrance, Double Dutch has long been popular for its steaks, salads, Thai and Indonesian dishes, and famous apple pies. It's a very relaxed meeting place with secondhand books, newspapers and a useful noticeboard for current Arambolic affairs.

ⓘ Information

The nearest ATM is in Arambol village near the bus stop.

ⓘ Getting There & Around

Buses to Mapusa (₹30, one hour) depart from Arambol village every half-hour. A taxi to Mapusa or Anjuna should cost around ₹600. If you're heading north to Mumbai, travel agents can book bus tickets and you can board at a stop on the highway in the main village.

Lots of places in Arambol rent scooters and motorbikes, for ₹250 and ₹350, respectively, per day.

SOUTH GOA

Margao (Madgaon)

POP 94,400

Margao (also called Madgaon) is the capital of south Goa and for travellers is chiefly a transport hub, with the state's major train

Margao (Madgaon)

Panaji (33km)

Market

Kadamba
Bus Stand

Chandor
(15km);
Ponda
(17km)

Colva
(6km)

Fatorda Stadium
(200m)

Church of
the Holy
Spirit

**LARGO
DE IGREJA**

**MONTE
HILL**

Damodar
Temple

7
Paulo Travels
3

Padre Miranda Rd

Abade Faria Rd

Bank

9

5
2

Valaulikar Rd

Municipal
Gardens

Bank

Miguel LF Rd

Central
Bus Stand

Isidoro Baptista Rd

8

6
1

Luis Miranda Rd

Erasmo Carvalho Rd

4

Rue F de Loiola

10
Station Rd

(2km);
Palolem (37km)

0 ____ 200 m
0 ____ 0.1 miles

Margao (Madgaon)

and bus stations. Although lacking much of Panaji's charm, it's a bustling market town of a manageable size for getting things done, or for simply enjoying the busy energy of urban India without big-city hassles.

◎ Sights

It's worth a walk around the **Largo de Igreja** district, home to lots of atmospherically crumbling and restored old Portuguese-era homes, and the richly decorated 17th-century **Church of the Holy Spirit**, particularly impressive when a Sunday morning service is taking place.

The city's business district orbits the rectangular **Municipal Gardens**, a mini-oasis of lawns, flowers and paths. At the southern end the Municipal Building is home to the **Municipal Library** (Abade Faria Rd; ⊙8am-8pm Mon-Fri, 9am-noon & 4-7pm Sat & Sun), which has some great books on Goa and a retro reading room where locals gather to read the daily paper.

🛏 Sleeping

Hotel Tanish   HOTEL $
(☑0832-2735858; www.hoteltanishgoa.com; Reliance Trade Centre, Valaulikar Rd; s/d ₹900/1200, s/d/ste with AC ₹1100/1500/2000; ❉) Oddly situated inside a modern mall, this top-floor hotel offers good views of the surrounding countryside, with stylish, well-equipped rooms. Suites come with a bathtub, a big TV and a view all the way to Colva; just make sure you get an outside-facing room, as some overlook the mall interior.

Om Shiv Hotel   HOTEL $$
(☑0832-2710294; www.omshivhotel.com; Cine Lata Rd; d ₹2750-3850, ste ₹5000; ❉@🛜) In a bright-yellow building tucked away behind the Bank of India, Om Shiv does a decent line in fading 'executive' rooms, all of which have air-con and balcony. The suites have good views, there's a gym and the 7th-floor **Rockon Pub**.

Nanutel Margao   HOTEL $$
(☑0832-6722222; Padre Miranda Rd; s/d incl breakfast ₹3780/4100, ste ₹4750-5300; ❉🛜❉) Margao's best business class hotel by some margin, Nanutel is modern and slick with a lovely pool, good restaurant, bar and coffee shop, and clean air-con rooms. The location, between the Municipal Gardens and Largo de Igreja district, is convenient for everything.

🍴 Eating

Swad   INDIAN $
(New Market; ₹50-10; ⊙7.30am-8pm) Some of Margao's best veg food is dished up at the family-friendly, lunch-break favourite Swad, across from Lotus Inn. The thalis, South Indian tiffins and other mains are all reliably tasty.

Café Tato   INDIAN $
(Valaulikar Rd; thalis ₹90; ⊙7am-10pm Mon-Sat) A favourite local lunch spot: tasty vegetarian fare in a bustling backstreet canteen, and delicious all-you-can-eat thalis.

★Ruta's World Cafè   AMERICAN, INTERNATIONAL $$
(☑0832-2710757; www.caferuta.com; Fr Miranda Rd; mains ₹150-350; ⊙10am-7pm Mon-Sat) Ruta's is a quality addition to Margao's otherwise average dining scene and an excellent reason to get off the beach. After years working as an award-winning cook, teacher and recipe book author on the San Francisco scene, chef Ruta Kahate has brought some of her culinary magic to Goa (there's another restaurant in Mapusa; p824).

★Longhuino's   GOAN, MULTICUISINE $$
(Luis Miranda Rd; mains ₹95-205; ⊙8.30am-10pm) A local institution since 1950, quaint old Longhuino's has been serving up tasty Indian, Goan and Chinese dishes, popular with locals and tourists alike. Go for a Goan dish such as *ambot tik,* and leave room for the retro desserts like rum balls and tiramasu. Service is as languid as the slowly

whirring ceiling fans but it's a great place to watch the world go by over a coffee or beer.

 Shopping

MMC New Market   MARKET
(⊙ 8.30am-9pm Mon-Sat) Margao's crowded, covered canopy of colourful stalls is a fun place to wander around, sniffing spices, sampling soaps and browsing the household merchandise.

Golden Heart Emporium   BOOKS
(Confidant House, Abade Faria Rd; ⊙ 10am-1.30pm & 4-7pm Mon-Sat) One of Goa's best bookshops, Golden Heart is crammed from floor to ceiling with fiction, nonfiction, children's books, and illustrated volumes on the state's food, architecture and history. It also stocks otherwise hard-to-get titles by local Goan authors. It's situated down a little lane off Abade Faria Rd, on the right-hand side as you're heading north.

ℹ **Information**

Banks offering currency exchange and 24-hour ATMs are all around town, especially near the municipal gardens and along Luis Miranda Rd. There's a handy HDFC ATM and an internet cafe in the Caro Centre near Longuinhos.

ℹ **Getting There & Around**

BUS

Long-distance buses depart from Kadamba bus stand and a private stand, both about 2km north of the Municipal Gardens. Shuttle buses (₹30, 35 minutes) run to Panaji every few minutes. For North Goa destinations head to Panaji and change there. Local buses to Benaulim (₹10, 20 minutes), Colva (₹10, 20 minutes) and Palolem (₹40, one

MAJOR TRAINS FROM MARGAO (MADGAON)

DESTINATION	TRAIN	FARE (₹)	DURATION (HR)	DEPARTURES
Bangalore	02779 Vasco da Gama-SBC Link (D)	360/970	15	3.50pm
Chennai (Madras; via Yesvantpur)	17312 Vasco-da-Gama-Chennai Express (C)	475/1275/1850	21	3.20pm Thu
Delhi	12431 Rajdhani Express (A)	2110/3050	27	10.10am Wed, Fri, Sat
Ernakulum	12618 Lakshadweep Express (C)	445/1165/1665	14½	7.20pm
	16345 Netravati Express (C)	415/1120/1620	15	11.10pm
Hubli	02779 Vasco-da-Gama-SBC Link (D)	160/485	6½	3.50pm
Mangalore	12133 Mangalore Express (C)	290/735/1035	5½	7.10am
Mumbai (Bombay)	10112 Konkan Kanya Express (C)	390/1055/1250	12	6pm
	10104 Mandovi Express (C)	390/1055/1520	12	9.15am
Pune	12779 Goa Express (C)	335/930/1315	12	3.50pm
Thiruvananthapuram	12432 Rajdhani Express (A)	1775/2420	19	12.45pm Mon, Wed, Thu
	16345 Netravati Express (C)	480/1290/1875	19½	11.10pm

Fares: (A) 3AC/2AC, (B) 2S/CC, (C) sleeper/3AC/2AC, (D) sleeper/3AC

hour) stop at the bus stop on the east side of the Municipal Gardens every 15 minutes or so.

Private buses ply interstate routes several times daily, most departing between 5.30pm and 7.30pm, and can be booked at offices around town; try **Paulo Travel.** (☑ 0832-2702405; ww.phmgoa.com; Hotel Nanutel, Padre Miranda Rd)

TAXI

Taxis go to Palolem (₹900), Panaji (₹800), Dabolim airport (₹600), Calangute (₹1000) and Anjuna (₹1200). Except for the train station, where there's a prepaid booth, you'll have to negotiate the fare with the driver.

TRAIN

Margao's well-organised train station, about 2km south of town, serves the Konkan Railway and other routes. Its **reservation hall** (☑ PNR enquiry 0832-2700730, information 0832-2712790; ☺8am-2pm & 2.15-8pm Mon-Sat, 8am-2pm Sun) is on the 1st floor. A taxi or autorickshaw to or from the town centre should cost around ₹100.

Chandor

The lush village of Chandor, 15km east of Margao, makes a perfect day away from the beaches, and it's here more than anywhere else in the state that the once opulent lifestyles of Goa's former landowners, who found favour with the Portuguese aristocracy, are still visible in its quietly decaying colonial-era mansions. Chandor hosts the colourful **Feast of the Three Kings** on the 6 January, during which local boys re-enact the arrival of the three kings from the Christmas story.

Braganza House, built in the 17th century, is possibly the best example of what Goa's scores of once grand and glorious mansions have today become. Built on land granted by the King of Portugal, the house was divided from the outset into two wings, to house two sides of the same family. The **West Wing** (☑ 0832-2784201; donation ₹150; ☺9am-5pm) belongs to one set of the family's descendants, the Menezes-Bragança, and is filled with gorgeous chandeliers, Italian marble floors, rosewood furniture, and antique treasures from Macau, Portugal, China and Europe. Despite the passing of the elderly Mrs Aida Menezes-Bragança in 2012, the grand old home, which requires considerable upkeep, remains open to the public. Next door, the **East Wing** (☑ 0832-2784227;

WORTH A TRIP

HAMPI

The surreal ruins of the Vijayanagar empire at Hampi (p896), in Karanakata, are a popular detour or overnight trip from Goa. Hampi can be reached by train from Margao to Hospet on the VSG Howrah Express which departs at 7.10am Tuesday, Thursday, Friday and Saturday (sleeper/3AC/2AC ₹235/620/885, eight hours). More convenient are the overnight sleeper buses direct to Hampi from Margao and Panaji operated by Paulo Travel (₹900 to ₹1100, 10 to 11 hours, 2-3 daily).

donation ₹100; ☺10am-6pm) is owned by the Braganza-Pereiras, descendants of the other half of the family. It's nowhere near as grand, but it's beautiful in its own lived-in way, and has a small but striking family chapel that contains a carefully hidden fingernail of St Francis Xavier – a relic that's understandably a source of great pride. Both homes are open daily, and there's almost always someone around to let you in. Donations are requested and expected.

About 1km east of Chandor's church, the original building of the **Fernandes House** (☑0832-2784245; donation ₹200; ☺9am-6pm), also known as Casa Grande, dates back more than 500 years, while the Portuguese section was tacked on by the Fernandes family in 1821. The secret basement hideaway, full of gun holes and with an escape tunnel to the river, was used by the family to flee attackers.

Colva & Benaulim

POP 12,000

Colva and Benaulim boast broad, open beaches, but are no longer the first place backpackers head in south Goa – most tourists here are of the domestic or ageing European varieties. There's no party scene as in north Goa and they lack the beauty and traveller vibe of Palolem. Still, these are the closest beaches to the major transport hubs of Margao and Dabolim airport. Benaulim has the greater charm, with only a small strip of shops and a village vibe, though out of high season it sometimes has the melancholy feel of a deserted seaside town.

GOA CHANDOR

◉ Sights & Activities

The beach entrance at Colva, and to a lesser extent Benaulim, throng with operators keen to sell you **parasailing** (per ride ₹800), **jet-skiing** (per 15 minutes s/d ₹300/500), and one-hour **dolphin-watching trips** (per person from ₹300).

★ Goa Chitra   MUSEUM
(☑0832-6570877; www.goachitra.com; St John the Baptist Rd, Mondo Vaddo, Benaulim; admission ₹200; ⏱9am-6pm Tue-Sun) Artist and restorer Victor Hugo Gomes first noticed the slow extinction of traditional objects – from farming tools to kitchen utensils to altarpieces – as a child in Benaulim. He created this ethnographic museum from the more than 4000 cast-off objects that he collected from across the state over 20 years (he often had to find elderly people to explain their uses). Admission to this fascinating museum is via a one-hour guided tour, held on the hour. Goa Chitra is 3km east of Maria Hall – ask locally for directions.

🛏 Sleeping

🛏 Colva

Colva still has a few basic budget guesthouses among the palm groves back from the beach; ask around locally.

Sam's Guesthouse   HOTEL $
(☑0832-2788753; r ₹650; 🖥) Away from the fray, north of Colva's main drag on the road running parallel to the beach, Sam's is a big, cheerful place with friendly owners and spacious rooms that are a steal at this price. Rooms are around a pleasant garden courtyard and there's a good restaurant and a whacky bar.

Colmar Beach Resort   RESORT $
(☑022-67354666 in Mumbai; www.colmarbeachresort.net; d ₹700, with AC from ₹1100, poolside cottage ₹1500; ❄🖥🏊) Colmar Beach Resort is the closest budget place to Colva's beach and, provided you're not expecting too much, it can make a reasonable stay. The cottages around the small pool are the pick, while the ageing rooms at the back are cheaper and a bit grimy. The beach is right in front and the restaurant-bar is quite good.

La Ben   HOTEL $
(☑0832-2788040; www.laben.net; Colva Beach Rd; r ₹1100, with AC ₹1400; ❄🖥) Neat, clean and not entirely devoid of atmosphere. If you're not desperately seeking anything with character, La Ben has decent, good-value rooms and has been around for ages. A great addition is the Garden Restaurant.

Skylark Resort   HOTEL $$
(☑0832-2788052; www.skylarkresortgoa.com; d ₹2885-3639, f ₹4270; ❄🖥🏊) A serious step up from the budget places, Skylark's clean, fresh rooms are graced with bits and pieces of locally made teak furniture and block-print bedspreads, while the lovely pool makes a pleasant place to lounge. The best (and more expensive) rooms are those facing the pool.

🛏 Benaulim

There are lots of homes around town advertising simple rooms to let. This, combined with a couple of decent budget options, make Benaulim a better (and quieter) bet for backpackers than Colva.

Rosario's Inn   GUESTHOUSE $
(☑0832-2770636; r ₹450, with AC ₹450 800; ❄) Across a football field flitting with young players and dragonflies, family-run Rosario's

---

PUPPY LOVE

International Animal Rescue (Animal Tracks; ☑0832-2268272; www.internationalanimalrescuegoa.org.in; Madungo Vaddo, Assagao; ⏱9am-4pm) runs the Animal Tracks rescue facility in Assagao, North Goa. At Colva's **Goa Animal Welfare Trust Shop** (☑0832-2653677; www.gawt.org; ⏱9.30am-1pm & 4-7pm Mon-Sat), next to Skylark Resort, you can pick up some gifts, donate clothes and other stuff you don't want, and borrow books from the lending library. You can also learn more about the work of **GAWT** (☑0832-2653677; www.gawt.org; Old Police Station, Curchorem; ⏱9am-5.30pm Mon-Sat, 10am-1pm Sun), which operates a shelter in Curchorem (near Margao). At Chapolim, a few kilometres northeast of Palolem, the **Animal Rescue Centre** (☑0832-2644171; Chapolim; ⏱10am-1pm & 2.30-5pm Mon-Sat) also takes in sick, injured or stray animals. Volunteers are welcome at the shelters, even for a few hours, to walk or play with the dogs.

is a large establishment with very clean, simple rooms and a restaurant. Excellent value.

D'Souza Guest House
GUESTHOUSE $

(☑0832-277 0583; d ₹600) With just three rooms, this blue-painted house in the back lanes is run by a local Goan family and comes with bundles of homey atmosphere and a lovely garden. It's often full so book ahead.

Palm Grove Cottages
HOTEL $$

(☑0832-2770059; www.palmgrovegoa.com; Vaswado; d incl breakfast ₹2020-3700; ❋🕾) Old-fashioned, secluded charm and Benaulim's leafiest garden wecomes you at Palm Grove Cottages, a great midrange choice. The quiet AC rooms, some with a balcony, all have a nice feel but the best are the spacious deluxe rooms in a separate Portuguese-style building. The Palm Garden Restaurant here is exceptionally good.

Anthy's Guesthouse
GUESTHOUSE $$

(☑0832-2771680; anthysguesthouse@rediffmail. com; Sernabatim Beach; d ₹1300, with AC ₹1700; ❋) One of a handful of places lining Sernabatim Beach itself, Anthy's is a firm favourite with travellers for its good restaurant, book exchange, and its well-kept chalet-style rooms, which stretch back from the beach surrounded by a garden.

Blue Corner
BEACH HUTS $$

(☑9850455770; www.bluecornergoa.com; huts ₹1600) Behind the beach shack restaurant a short walk north of the main beach entrance is this group of sturdy cocohuts – not so common around here – with fan and verandah. The restaurant gets good reviews.

🍴 Eating & Drinking

🍴 Colva

Colva's beach has a string of shacks offering the standard fare and fresh seafood.

Sagar Kinara
INDIAN $

(Colva Beach Rd; mains ₹60-180; ☺7am-10.30pm) A pure-veg restaurant upstairs (nonveg is separate, downstairs) with tastes to please even committed carnivores, this place is clean, efficient and offers cheap and delicious North and South Indian cuisine all day.

Leda Lounge & Restaurant
BAR

(☺7.30am-midnight) Part sports bar, part music venue, part cocktail bar, Leda is Colva's best nightspot by a long shot. There's live music from Thursday to Sunday, fancy

DUDHSAGAR FALLS

On the eastern border with Karnataka, Dudhsagar Falls (603m) are Goa's most impressive waterfalls, and the second highest in India, best seen as soon as possible after the rains. The main access is the village of Colem, from where jeeps (₹400 per person for six passengers) make the bumpy but scenic 40-minute drive to the car park from where it's a short scramble to the falls

A nice way to get here is the 8.15am train to Kulem (Colem) from Margao (check return times), then pick up a jeep. An easier option (especially if coming from your beach resort rather than Margao) is to take a taxi, book with a travel agent, or take a full-day GTDC tour from Panaji, Mapusa or Calangute (₹1200, Wed & Sun).

drinks (Mojitos, Long Island iced teas) and good food (mains ₹270 to ₹600).

🍴 Benaulim

Pedro's Bar & Restaurant
GOAN, MULTICUISINE $$

(Vasvaddo Beach Rd; mains ₹110-350; ☺7am-midnight) Set amid a large, shady garden on the beachfront and popular with local and international travellers, Pedro's offers standard Indian, Chinese and Italian dishes, as well as Goan choices and 'sizzlers.'

Johncy Restaurant
GOAN, MULTICUISINE $$

(Vasvaddo Beach Rd; mains ₹110-350; ☺7am-midnight) Unlike most beach shacks, Johncy has been around forever, dispensing standard Goan, Indian and Western favourites from its location just back from the sand.

Club Zoya
CLUB

(☑9822661388; www.clubzoya.com; ☺from 8pm) The party scene has hit sleepy little Benaulim in the form of barn-sized Club Zoya, with international DJs, big light shows and a cocktail bar featuring speciality flavoured and infused vodka drinks. Something's on most nights here in season but check the website for upcoming events and DJs.

ℹ Information

Colva has several ATMs strung along the east–west Colva Beach Rd. Benaulim has a HDFC ATM on the back road to Colva.

ℹ Getting There & Around

Scooters can be rented at Colva and Benaulim for around ₹250.

COLVA

Buses run from Colva to Margao every few minutes (₹10, 20 minutes) until around 7pm. An autorickshaw/taxi to Margao costs ₹200/250.

BENAULIM

Buses from Benaulim to Margao are also frequent (₹10, 20 minutes); they stop at the Maria Hall crossroads, 1.2km east of the beach. Some from Margao continue south to Varca and Cavelossim.

Benaulim to Agonda

Immediately south of Benaulim are the beach resorts of **Varca** and **Cavelossim**, with wide, pristine sands and a line of flashy five-star hotels set amid landscaped private grounds fronting the beach. About 3km south of Cavelossim, at the end of the peninsula, **Mobor** and its beach is one of the prettiest spots along this stretch of coast, with simple beach shacks serving good food. The pick here is **Blue Whale** (mains ₹100-350).

Cross the Sal River from Cavelossim to Assolna on the huge new bridge and continue south to the rustic but charming fishing village of **Betul**.

From Betul the road winds over gorgeous, undulating hills thick with palm groves. It's worth detouring to the bleak old Portuguese fort of **Cabo da Rama**, which has a small church within the fort walls, stupendous views and several old buildings rapidly becoming one with the trees.

Back on the main road to Agonda, look out for the turn-off to the right (west) to **Cola Beach**, one of south Goa's most gorgeous hidden beach gems complete with emerald-green lagoon. It's reached via a rough 2km dirt road from the highway, but it's not totally deserted – a couple of busy hut villages and a tent resort set up in season. About 500m north of the Cola turn-off is another jungle-strewn path to **Khancola** (or Kakolem) beach, with steep steps leading to a secluded beach and just a handful of huts.

Agonda is another 2.5km south of the Cola Beach turnoff.

Agonda

Agonda Beach is a fine 2km stretch of white sand framed between two forested headlands. Travellers have been drifting here for years and seasonal hut villages – some very luxurious – now occupy almost all available beachfront space, but it's still much more low-key than Palolem and a good choice if you're after some relaxation. Rare Olive Ridley turtles nest at the northern end, which is protected by the Forest Department.

There's lots of yoga and ayurveda in Agonda and a community feel among the shops and cafes in the street running parallel to the beach. There's a HDFC ATM near the church crossroads.

🛏 Sleeping & Eating

Some of Goa's most sophisticated and luxurious beach huts, along with beachfront restaurants and bars, set up along the foreshore from November to May, and there are a few more permanent places on the sideroad running parallel to the beach.

Fatima Guesthouse　　　GUESTHOUSE $
(☑0832-2647477; d ₹600-700, with AC ₹800; ❄🖵) An ever-popular two-storey guesthouse with clean rooms, a good restaurant and highly obliging staff, on the southern stretch of Agonda's beach road. The rooftop yoga classes and extended courses (and the budget price) mean it's often full.

Abba's Gloryland　　　GUESTHOUSE $
(☑9404312232, 0832-2647822; www.abbasgloryland.com; hut/r ₹1000/1200; 🖵) Set back from the road at the northern end of the beach, this friendly, family-run place offers cool, tiled rooms in a pink building, and neat bamboo huts with slate floors. A good budget option with no sea views but only a short walk from the beach.

Agonda White Sand　　　BEACH HUTS $$
(☑9823548277; www.agondawhitesand.com; Agonda Beach; hut from ₹3800; 🖵) Beautifully designed and constructed cottages with open-air bathrooms and spring mattresses surround a central bar and restaurant at this stylish beachfront place. Less than 100m away the same owners have a pair of amazing five-star sea-facing villas (₹7000 to ₹9000) with enormous beds and cavernous bathrooms large enough to contain a garden and fish pond!

★**H2O Agonda**　　　BEACH HUTS $$$
(☑9423836994; www.h2oagonda.com; d incl breakfast ₹4500-6500; ❄🖵) With its purple and mauve muslin curtains and Arabian nights ambience, H2O is among the most

impressive of Agonda's luxury cottage set-ups. From the hotel-style reception, walk through a leafy garden to the spacious cottages with air-con, TV and enormous open-air bathrooms. The more expensive sea-facing cottages, with zebra print spreads on king-size beds, are worth paying extra for.

Fatima Thali Shop SOUTH INDIAN $
(veg/fish thali ₹80/100) Beloved by locals and visitors, tiny Fatima, with just four tables, is an Agonda institution, with filling South Indian thalis whipped up inside its improbably small kitchen. It's also a cosy spot for breakfast, salads and chai.

Palolem & Around

Palolem is undoubtedly one of Goa's most postcard-perfect beaches: a gentle curve of palm-fringed sand facing a calm bay. But in season it's bursting at the seams.

If you want to see what Palolem looked like 10 or 15 years ago, turn up in September or early October, before the beach huts start to go up. Once the hammering and sawing starts, the beachfront is transformed into a toy-town of colourful and increasingly sophisticated timber and bamboo huts fronted by palm-thatch restaurants. It's still a great place to be and is popular with backpackers, long-stayers and families. Aside from being one of the safest swimming and kayaking beaches in Goa, Palolem is a great place to learn to cook, drop in to yoga classes or hire a motorbike and cruise to surrounding beaches, waterfalls and wildlife parks. At night you can listen to live rock or reggae as the sun sets or dance in silence at a headphone party.

Further south is the small rocky cove of **Colomb Bay**, with several basic places to stay, and then peaceful and pretty **Patnem Beach**, a more relaxed version of Palolem with just a dozen or so beach hut villages and shack restaurants.

🏃 Activities

Yoga
There are courses and classes on offer at numerous places in Palolem and Patnem. Bhakti Kutir (p851) and Space Goa (p852) offer daily drop-in yoga classes, while Butterfly Book Shop (p853) arranges daily yoga (₹300) and cooking classes (₹1200).

In Patnem, **Bamboo Yoga Retreat** (☑9765379887; www.bamboo-yoga-retreat.com; Patnam Beach; s/d from ₹5300/7400; 🕾) is recommended but exclusive to guests. About 4km further south Shamana Retreat is a new outfit with an attractively remote jungle location.

Beach Activities
Kayaks are available for rent on Palolem beaches (₹150 per hour), as well as a few stand-up paddleboards (₹500). Fishermen and other boat operators hanging around the beach offer dolphin-spotting trips or rides to tiny **Butterfly Beach**, north of Palolem, for around ₹1200 for two people.

Trekking
Cotigao Wildlife Sanctuary NATURE RESERVE
(☑0832-2965601; adult/child ₹20/10, camera/video ₹30/150; ☉7am-5.30pm) About 9km

---

WORTH A TRIP

DAYTRIPPING DOWN SOUTH

Goa's far south is tailor-made for daytripping. Hire a motorbike or charter a taxi and try these road trips from Palolem, Patnem or Agonda.

➡ **Tanshikar Spice Farm** (☑0832-2608358, 9421184114; www.tanshikarspicefarm.com; Netravali; spice tour incl lunch ₹450; ecohuts inc meals ₹1500 per person; ☉10am-4pm) About 35km inland from Palolem via forest and farms is this excellent spice plantation, along with jungle treks to waterfalls and the enigmatic 'bubble lake'.

➡ **Talpona & Galgibag** These two near-deserted beach gems are scenically framed (naturally) by the Talpona and Galgibag rivers. Olive Ridley turtles nest on Galgibag and there are a couple of excellent shack restaurants and huts. The winding country drive here is half the fun.

➡ **Polem Beach** Goa's most southerly beach, 25km south of Palolem, has just one set of beach huts and a real castaway feel. A trip here should be combined with the detour to Talpona and Galgibag.

Palolem

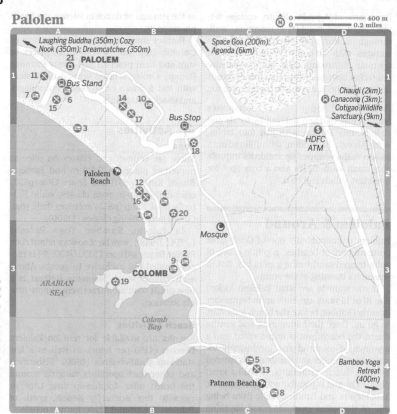

ARABIAN
SEA

COLOMB

Colomb
Bay

Laughing Buddha (350m); Cozy
Nook (350m); Dreamcatcher (350m)

Space Goa (200m);
Agonda (6km)

Chaudi (2km);
Canacona (3km);
Cotigao Wildlife
Sanctuary (9km)

HDFC
ATM

Palolem
Beach

Mosque

Bamboo Yoga
Retreat
(400m)

Patnem Beach

southeast of Palolem, and a good day trip, is the beautiful, remote-feeling Cotigao Wildlife Sanctuary, Goa's second-largest sanctuary and easily its most accessible, if you have your own transport. Don't expect to bump into its more exotic residents (including gaurs, sambars, leopards and spotted deer), but frogs, snakes, monkeys, insects and blazingly plumed birds are in no short supply.

Goa Jungle Adventure OUTDOORS
(☏ 9850485641; www.goajungle.com; trekking & canyoning trips ₹1890-3590) This adventure company, run by an experienced French guide, will take you out for thrilling trekking and canyoning trips in the Netravali area at the base of the Western Ghats, where you climb, jump and abseil into remote waterfilled plunges. Trips run from a half-day to several days, and extended rafting trips into Karnataka are also sometimes offered.

🛏 Sleeping

🛏 Palolem

Most of Palolem's accommodation is of the seasonal beach-hut variety, though there are plenty of old-fashioned guesthouses or family homes to be found back from the beach with decent rooms from ₹600. It's still possible to find a basic palm-thatch hut without bathroom somewhere near the beach for ₹700, but most of the huts these days are made of plywood or timber and come with attached bathrooms and multiple levels. The very best seafacing rooms feature aircon, flat-screen TVs and balconies and command more than ₹5000! Since the huts are dismantled and rebuilt each year, standards and ownership can vary – the places listed here are either permanent guesthouses or well-established hut operations.

Palolem

🛏 Sleeping

✖ Eating

🎭 Entertainment

🛍 Shopping

My Soulmate   GUESTHOUSE $

(📞9823785250; mysolmte@gmail.com; d ₹1000, with AC ₹1500; ❄) This friendly and spotless two-storey guesthouse in a good location just off the main Palolem Beach road is a good nonbeach bet. Neat rooms come with TV and hot water and the newer ones have sexy circular beds. Good cafe, nice staff.

Sevas   HUT $

(📞9422065437; www.sevaspalolemgoa.com; s/d hut ₹600/800, family cottage ₹1600; @🛜) Hidden in the jungle on the Colomb Bay side of Palolem, Sevas has a range of simple palm-thatch huts with open-air bathrooms, larger family huts and rooms set in a lovely shaded garden area. Wi-fi is ₹100 per day.

★ Ciaran's   HUT $$

(📞0832-2643477; www.ciarans.com; hut incl breakfast ₹3000-4000, r with AC ₹4500; ❄🛜) Ciaran's has some of the most impressive huts on the beachfront. Affable owner John has worked hard over the years to maintain a high standard and his beautifully designed cottages around a plant-filled garden and

pond are top-notch. The sea-view cottages are the more expensive and there are some air-con rooms – including a Jacuzzi room. There's a popular multicuisine restaurant, tapas restaurant and quality spa centre.

Art Resort   HUT $$

(📞9665982344; www.art-resort-goa.com; Ourem Rd; hut ₹1500-2500; 🛜) The nicely designed cottages behind an excellent beachfront restaurant have a Bedouin camp feel with screened sit-outs and modern art works sprinkled around. The resort hosts art exhibitions and has regular live music.

Cozy Nook   HUT $$

(📞0832-2643550, 9822584760; www.cozynook goa.com; hut ₹2500-3500) This long-running operation at the northern end of the beach has well-designed cottages, including some treehouses, and a funky bar.

Dreamcatcher   HUT $$

(📞0832-2644873; www.dreamcatcher.in; hut ₹1750-2500) Probably the largest resort in Palolem, Dreamcatcher's 60 sturdy huts are nevertheless secluded, set in a coconut grove just back from the far northern end of the beach. One of the highlights here is the riverside restaurant and cocktail bar, and the wide range of holistic treatments, massage and yoga on offer, with daily drop-in yoga and reiki courses available. Access it from the back road running parallel to the beach.

Kate's Cottages   GUESTHOUSE $$

(📞9822165261; www.katescottagesgoa.com; Ourem Rd; d ₹3000-5000; ❄🛜) The two stunning rooms above Fern's restaurant are beautifully designed with heavy timber finishes, huge four-poster beds, TV, modern bathrooms and views to the ocean from the balcony. There are also a couple of cheaper ground-floor cottages.

Village Guesthouse   GUESTHOUSE $$

(📞9960487627, 0832-2645767; www.village guesthousegoa.com; d incl breakfast ₹3400-4300; ❄🛜) The Village is a lovely expat-run boutique hotel with eight spotless and spacious air-con rooms that are a cut above most Palolem hotels. Nicely furnished with sparkling bathrooms, four-poster beds, TV and homely touches, it makes a good base if you value peace more than being on the beach. Breakfast is served in the rear garden.

Bhakti Kutir   COTTAGE $$

(📞0832-2643469, 9823627258; www.bhakti kutir.com; Colomb Bay; cottage ₹2200-3300; @)

Ensconced in a thick wooded grove in the Colomb Bay area south of Palolem, Bhakti's well-equipped rustic cottages are a little worn and you might find yourself sharing with local wildlife but this is still a popular eco and spiritual retreat with an ayurvedic massage centre and daily drop-in yoga classes.

Palolem Beach Resort RESORT $$
(☑0832-2645775, 9764442778; www.cubagoa.com/palolem; r ₹3000, with AC ₹4000, cottages ₹3000; ▣ 🛜) You can't beat the location, on the beachfront at the main road entrance to the beach, but Palolem Beach Resort has lifted its prices in keeping with most places in Palolem. It's good value in the fringe seasons when it's one of the only beachfront places open. There are average permanent rooms (air-con ones are better), seasonal huts at the front and a friendly beachfront restaurant.

🛏 Patnem

Long-stayers will love Patnem's choice of village homes and apartments available for rent. A very basic house can cost ₹10,000 per month, while a fully equipped apartment can run up to ₹40,000.

Mickys HUT $
(☑9850484884; www.mickyhuts.com; Patnem Beach; r & hut ₹800-1500, without bathroom hut ₹400; 🛜) If you don't mind huts so basic they don't even have electricity, you can sleep cheap here. Fear not: there are also better huts with power and attached bath; rooms are available most of the year (closed only August and September). It's run by a friendly family at the northern end of the beach.

Mickys Naughty Corner is a cruisy beachfront cafe in front of the accommodation.

Papaya's HUT $$
(☑9923079447; www.papayasgoa.com; hut ₹3000, with AC ₹4000; ▣🛜) Solid huts constructed with natural materials head back into the palm grove from Papaya's popular restaurant, which does great versions of all the beachfront classics. Each hut is lovingly built, with lots of wood, four-poster beds and floating muslin.

🍴 Eating

With limited beach space, restaurant shacks are banned from the sand at Palolem and Patnem, but there are plenty of beach-facing restaurants on the periphery, all offering all-day dining and fresh seafood. Palolem also has some interesting dining choices back along the main road to the beach.

Little World Cafe CAFE $
(chai ₹10, snacks ₹70-120; ⏱8am-6pm) This shanti little cafe serves up Palolem's best masala chai, along with healthy juices.

Shiv Sai INDIAN $
(thalis ₹70-90, mains ₹60-150; ⏱9am-11pm) A thoroughly local lunch joint on the parallel beach road, Shiv Sai serves tasty thalis of the vegie, fish and Gujarati kinds.

★ Space Goa CAFE $$
(☑80063283333; www.thespacegoa.com; mains ₹90-250; ⏱8.30am-5pm) On the Agonda road, Space Goa combines an excellent organic whole-food cafe with a gourmet deli, craft shop and a wellness centre offering reiki and reflexology. The food is fresh and delicious,

---

SILENT PARTIES

Considerately sidestepping the statewide ban on loud music after 10pm, Palolem is the home of popular silent rave parties where guests don a pair of headphones and dance the night away in inward bliss but outward quiet. You get the choice of two or three channels featuring inhouse Goan and international DJs playing hip hop, house, electro and funk. The concept came from British expats (now operating at Alpha Bar) but others jumped on the bandwagon and at last count there were four events, all operating on different nights.

Silent Noise @ Alpha Bar (www.silentnoise.in; cover charge ₹500; ⏱9pm-4am Thu Nov-Apr) The original headphone party organisers.

Deafbeat (Cleopatra's, Palolem Beach Rd; ₹500, before 11pm free; ⏱from 9pm Wed)

Laughing Buddha (cover charge ₹400; ⏱from 10pm Tue)

Neptune Point (www.neptunepoint.com; Neptune's Point, Colomb Bay; cover charge ₹600; ⏱9am-4am Sat Nov-Apr) South of Palolem at Colomb Bay

with fabulous salads, paninis and meze, and the desserts – such as chocolate beetroot cake – are divine. Drop-in morning yoga classes are ₹500.

★**Café Inn** CAFE **$$**
(Palolem Beach Rd; meals ₹150-550; ⊙10am-11pm; 🖘) If you're craving a cappuccino, semi-open-air Café Inn, which grinds its own blend of beans to perfection, is one of Palolem's favourite hang-outs – and it's not even on the beach. Its breakfasts are immense, and comfort-food burgers and panini sandwiches hit the spot. From 6pm there's an excellent barbecue. Free wi-fi.

German Bakery BAKERY, MULTICUISINE **$$**
(Ourem Rd; pastries ₹25-80, mains ₹80-210; ⊙7am-10pm) Tasty baked treats are the stars at the Nepali-run German Bakery, but there is also an excellent range of set breakfasts and croissants with yak cheese. It's set in a peaceful garden festooned with flags.

Fern's By Kate's GOAN **$$**
(☑9822165261; mains ₹200-450; ⊙8.30am-10.30pm; 🖘) Back from the beach, this solid timber place with a vague nautical feel serves up excellent authentic Goan food such as local sausages, fish curry rice and shark *amok tik*.

★**Home** CONTINENTAL **$$**
(☑0832-2643916; www.homeispatnem.com; Patnem Beach; mains ₹180-290; ⊙8.30am-9.30pm; 🖘) Standing out from the beach shacks like a beacon, this bright white, relaxed vegetarian restaurant is run by a British couple and serves up Patnem's best breakfasts, pastas, risotto and salads, continental-style. A highlight here is the dessert menu – awesome chocolate brownies, apple tart and cheesecake. Home also rents out eight nicely decorated, light rooms (from ₹1500).

Magic Italy ITALIAN **$$**
(☑88057 67705; Palolem Beach Rd; mains ₹180-460; ⊙5pm-midnight) On the main beach road, Magic Italy has been around for a while and the quality of its pizza and pasta remains high, with imported Italian ingredients like ham, salami, cheese and olive oil, imaginative wood-fired pizzas and home-made pasta. Sit at tables, or Arabian-style on floor cushions. Busy but chilled.

★**Ourem 88** FUSION **$$$**
(☑8698827679; mains ₹440-650; ⊙6-10pm Tue-Sat) Big things come in small packages at British-run Ourem 88, a gastro sensation with just a handful of tables and a small but masterful menu. Try tender calamari stuffed with Goan sausage, slow-roasted pork belly, fluffy souffle or fillet steak with Béarnaise sauce. Worth a splurge.

🍸 Drinking & Nightlife

Leopard Valley CLUB
(www.leopardvalley.com; Palolem-Agonda Rd; admission from ₹600; ⊙9pm-4.30am Fri) South Goa's biggest new outdoor dance club is a sight (and sound) to behold, with 3D laser light shows, pyrotechnics and state-of-the-art sound systems blasting local and international DJs. It's in an isolated but easily reached location between Palolem and Agonda, but given noise restrictions we don't know if it will endure. Friday night at time of research but possibly Sunday too.

🛍 Shopping

Butterfly Book Shop BOOKS
(☑9341738801; ⊙9am-10.30pm) The best of several good bookshops in town, this cute and cosy place stocks best sellers, classics, and a good range of books on yoga, meditation and spirituality. This is also the base for yoga classes and cooking courses.

ℹ Information

Palolem's main road is lined with travel agencies, internet places and money changers. The nearest ATM is about 1.5km away, where the main highway meets Palolem Beach Rd, or head to nearby Chaudi.

ℹ Getting There & Around

Frequent buses run to nearby Chaudi (₹7) from the bus stop on the corner of the road down to the beach. There are hourly buses to Margao (₹40, one hour) from the same place. From Chaudi you can also pick up regular buses to Margao, from where you can change for Panaji, or south to Polem Beach and Karwar (Karnataka). Local buses run regularly to Agonda (₹10).

The closest train station is Canacona, 2km from Palolem's beach entrance, which is useful for trains south to Gokarna and Mangalore.

An autorickshaw from Palolem to Patnem should cost ₹80, to Chaudi ₹120 and to Agonda ₹250. A taxi to Dabolim Airport is around ₹1200.

Scooters and motorbikes can easily be hired along the main road leading to the beach from ₹200. Mountain bikes (₹100 per day) can be hired from Seema Bike Hire on Ourem Rd.

GOA PALOLEM & AROUND

Karnataka & Bengaluru

Best Places to Eat

➜ Karavalli (p864)

➜ Koshy's Bar &
Restaurant (p864)

➜ Sapphire (p878)

➜ Lalith Bar &
Restaurant (p890)

Best Places to Stay

➜ Casa Piccola Cottage
(p862)

➜ Green Hotel (p876)

➜ Golden Mist (p885)

➜ Dhole's Den (p882)

➜ Waterwoods Lodge (p883)

Why Go?

Blessed with a a diverse makeup conforming to all the romance of quintessential India, Karnataka delivers with its winning blend of palaces, tiger reserves, megacities, ancient ruins, beaches and legendary hang-outs.

At its nerve centre is the silicon-capital Bengaluru (Bangalore), overfed with the good life. Scattered around the epicurean city are rolling hills dotted with spice and coffee plantations, the regal splendour of Mysuru (Mysore), and jungles teeming with monkeys, tigers and Asia's biggest population of elephants.

If that all sounds too mainstream, head to the countercultural enclave of tranquil Hampi with hammocks, psychedelic sunsets and boulder-strewn ruins. Or the blissful beaches of Gokarna, a beach haven minus the doof doof. Otherwise leave the tourist trail behind entirely, and take a journey to the stunning Islamic ruins of northern Karnataka.

When to Go
Bengaluru

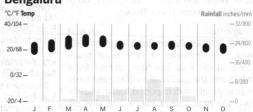

Mar–May The best season to watch tigers and elephants in Karnataka's pristine national parks.

Oct Mysuru's Dussehra (Dasara) carnival brings night-long celebrations and a jumbo parade.

Dec & Jan The coolest time to explore the northern districts' forts, palaces, caves and temples.

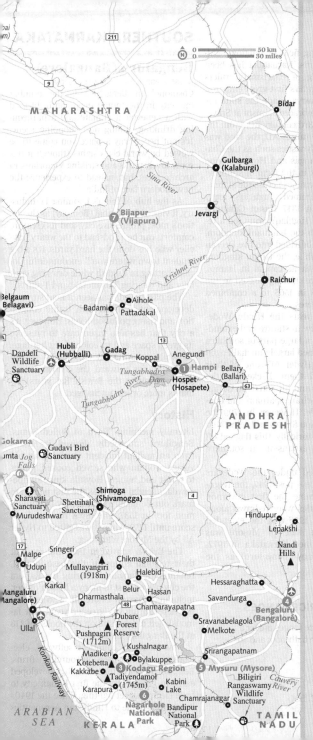

Karnataka & Bengaluru Highlights

1 Marvelling at the gravity-defying boulders, and wandering among the melancholic ruins of **Hampi** (p896)

2 Hitting **Gokarna** (p893) for its beautiful beaches and legendary chilled-out atmosphere minus the resorts

3 Savouring aromatic coffee while recharging your soul in the cool highlands of the **Kodagu Region** (p883)

4 Drinking yourself under the table, or tucking into top-notch global cuisine in **Bengaluru** (p863)

5 Being bowled over by the grandiose **royal palace** (p871) in Mysuru

6 Spying on lazy tuskers in the forests bordering serene Kabini Lake at **Nagarhole National Park** (p883)

7 Strolling in the peaceful manicured grounds of exquisite 16th-century Islamic monuments in **Bijapur** (p906)

History

A rambling playing field of religions, cultures and kingdoms, Karnataka has been ruled by a string of charismatic rulers through history. India's first great emperor, Chandragupta Maurya, made the state his retreat when he embraced Jainism at Sravanabelagola in the 3rd century BC. From the 6th to the 14th centuries AD, the land was under a series of dynasties such as the Chalukyas, Cholas, Gangas and Hoysalas, who left a lasting mark in the form of stunning cave shrines and temples across the state.

In 1327 Mohammed Tughlaq's army sacked Halebid. In 1347 Hasan Gangu, a Persian general in Tughlaq's army, led a rebellion to establish the Bahmani kingdom, which was later subdivided into five Deccan sultanates. Meanwhile, the Hindu kingdom of Vijayanagar, with its capital in Hampi, rose to prominence. Having peaked in the early 1550s, it fell in 1565 to a combined effort of the sultanates.

In subsequent years the Hindu Wodeyars of Mysore grew in stature and extended their rule over a large part of southern India. They remained largely unchallenged until 1761, when Hyder Ali (one of their generals) deposed them. Backed by the French, Hyder Ali and his son Tipu Sultan set up capital in Srirangapatnam and consolidated their rule. However, in 1799 the British defeated Tipu Sultan and reinstated the Wodeyars. Historically, this flagged off British territorial expansion in southern India.

Mysore remained under the Wodeyars until Independence – post-1947, the reigning maharaja became the first governor. The state boundaries were redrawn along linguistic lines in 1956 and the extended Kannada-speaking state of Mysore was born. It was renamed Karnataka in 1972, with Bangalore (now Bengaluru) as the capital.

SOUTHERN KARNATAKA

Bengaluru (Bangalore)

✑ 080 / POP 10.2 MILLION / ELEV 920M

Cosmopolitan Bengaluru is the number one city in the Indian deep south, blessed with a benevolent climate and a burgeoning drinking, dining and shopping scene. It's not necessarily a place you come to be wowed by world-class sights (though it has some lovely parks and striking Victorian-era architecture), but instead to experience the new modern face of India.

As the hub of India's booming IT industry, it vies with Mumbai (Bombay) as the nation's most progressive city, and its creature comforts can be a godsend to the weary traveller who has done the hard yards. It's a big student town where you'll encounter hip locals chatting in English while drinking craft beer and wearing '80s metal band T-shirts.

The past decade has seen a mad surge of development, coupled with traffic congestion and rising pollution levels. However, it's a city that has also taken care to preserve its green space and its colonial-era heritage. So while urbanisation continually pushes its boundaries outward, the central district (dating back to the British Raj years) remains more or less unchanged.

History

Literally meaning 'Town of Boiled Beans', Bengaluru supposedly derived its name from an ancient incident involving an old village woman who served cooked pulses to a lost and hungry Hoysala king. Kempegowda, a feudal lord, was the first person to mark out Bengaluru's extents by building a mud fort in 1537. The town remained obscure until 1759, when it was gifted to Hyder Ali by the Mysore maharaja.

The British arrived in 1809 and made it their regional administrative base in 1831, renaming it Bangalore. During the Raj era the city played host to many a British officer, including Winston Churchill, who enjoyed life here during his greener years and famously left a debt (still on the books) of ₹13 at the Bangalore Club.

Now home to countless software, electronics and business-outsourcing firms, Bengaluru's knack for technology developed early. In 1905 it was the first Indian city to have electric street lighting. Since the 1940s it has been home to Hindustan Aeronautics

Ltd (HAL), India's largest aerospace company. And if you can't do without email, you owe it all to a Bangalorean – Sabeer Bhatia, the inventor of Hotmail, grew up here.

The city's name was changed back to Bengaluru in November 2006, though few care to use it in practice.

ℹ Orientation

Finding your way around Bengaluru can be difficult at times. In certain areas, roads are named after their widths (eg 80ft Rd). The city also follows a system of mains and crosses: 3rd Cross, 5th Main, Residency Rd, for example, refers to the third lane on the fifth street branching off Residency Rd. New affluent pockets are springing up across the city, including the ritzy suburbs of Indirangar, JP Nagar, Koramangala and Whitefield – all with Western-style malls, nightlife and restaurants.

◉ Sights

★ National Gallery of Modern Art
ART GALLERY

(NGMA; ☎080-22342338; www.ngmaindia.gov.in/ngma_bangaluru.asp; 49 Palace Rd; Indian/foreigner ₹10/150; ⏱10am-5pm Tue-Sun) Housed in a century-year-old mansion – the former vacation home of the Raja of Mysore – this world-class art museum showcases an impressive permanent collection as well as changing exhibitions. The Old Wing exhibits works from pre-Independence, including paintings by Raja Ravi Varma and Abanindranath Tagore (nephew of Rabindranath Tagore, and founder of the avant-garde Bengal School art movement). Interconnected by a walk bridge, the sleek New Wing focuses on contemporary post-Independence works.

Lalbagh Botanical Gardens
GARDENS

(☎9888947670; www.horticulture.kar.nic.in/lalbagh.htm; Lalbagh Rd; admission ₹10; ⏱6am-7pm) Spread over 97 hectares of landscaped terrain, the expansive Lalbagh Botanical Gardens were laid out in 1760 by the famous Mysore ruler Hyder Ali. As well as amazing centuries-old trees it claims to have the world's most diverse species of plants. Bangalore Walks (p861) has guided tours.

Cubbon Park
GARDENS

(www.horticulture.kar.nic.in/cubbon.htm; Kasturba Rd) In the heart of Bengaluru's business district is Cubbon Park, a sprawling 120-hectare garden where Bengaluru's residents converge to steal a moment from the rat race that rages outside.

It's surrounded by wonderful colonial-era architecture, including the red-painted Gothic-style State Central Library (Cubbon Park); the colossal neo-Dravidian-style Vidhana Soudha (Dr Ambedkar Rd), built in 1954 and which serves as the legislative chambers of the state government; and neoclassical Attara Kacheri (High Court; Cubbon Park) built in 1864 and housing the High Court. The latter two are closed to the public.

Karnataka Chitrakala Parishath
ART GALLERY

(www.karnatakachitrakalaparishath.com; Kumarakrupa Rd; admission ₹50; ⏱10am-5.30pm Mon-Sat) A superb gallery with a wide range of Indian and international contemporary art on show, as well as permanent displays of Mysore-style paintings and folk and tribal art from across Asia. A section is devoted to Russian master Nicholas Roerich, known for his vivid paintings of the Himalaya.

Government Museum
MUSEUM

(Kasturba Rd; admission ₹4; ⏱10am-5pm Tue-Sun, closed every 2nd Sat) In a beautiful red colonial-era building dating from 1877, you'll find a dusty collection of 12th-century stone carvings and artefacts excavated from Halebid, Hampi and Attriampakham. Your ticket also gets you into the Venkatappa Art Gallery (Kasturba Rd; ⏱10am-5pm Tue-Sun) FREE next door, where you can see works and personal memorabilia of K Venkatappa (1887–1962), court painter to the Wodeyars.

Bangalore Palace
PALACE

(Palace Rd; Indian/foreigner ₹225/450, camera/video ₹675/1405; ⏱10am-5.30pm) The private residence of the Wodeyars, erstwhile maharajas of the state, Bangalore Palace preserves a slice of bygone royal splendour. Still the residence of the current maharaja, an audio guide provides a detailed explanation of the building, vaguely designed to resemble Windsor Castle, and you can marvel at the lavish interiors and galleries featuring grisly hunting memorabilia, family photos and a collection of nude portraits.

Visvesvaraya Industrial & Technical Museum
MUSEUM

(www.vismuseum.gov.in; Kasturba Rd; adult/child ₹40/free; ⏱10.30am-5pm) One mainly for kids, this hands-on science museum makes you feel a bit like you're on a school excursion, but there are some cool electrical and engineering displays, plus kitschy fun-house

Bengaluru (Bangalore)

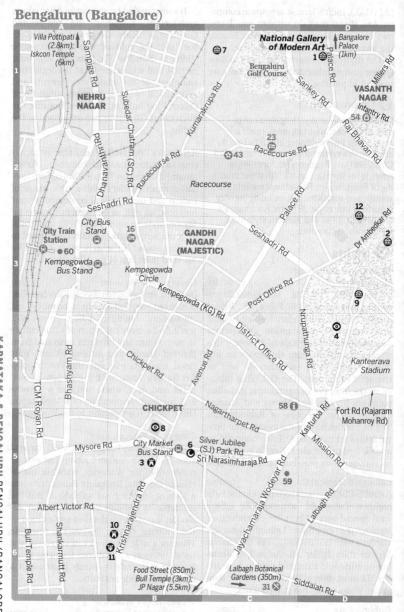

Villa Pottipati (2.8km); Iskcon Temple (6km)

National Gallery of Modern Art

Bangalore Palace (1km)

Bengaluru Golf Course

NEHRU NAGAR

VASANTH NAGAR

Infantry Rd

Racecourse Rd

Racecourse

Seshadri Rd

City Train Station

City Bus Stand

Kempegowda Bus Stand

Kempegowda Circle

GANDHI NAGAR (MAJESTIC)

Kempegowda (KG) Rd

Post Office Rd

District Office Rd

Chickpet Rd

Avenue Rd

Kanteerava Stadium

Fort Rd (Rajaram Mohanroy Rd)

CHICKPET

Nagartharpet Rd

Mysore Rd

City Market Bus Stand

Silver Jubilee (SJ) Park Rd

Sri Narasimharaja Rd

Albert Victor Rd

Food Street (850m); Bull Temple (3km); JP Nagar (5.5km)

Lalbagh Botanical Gardens (350m)

Siddaiah Rd

KARNATAKA & BENGALURU BENGALURU (BANGALORE)

mirrors and a walk-on piano. There's also a replica of the Wright brothers' 1903 flyer.

Tipu Sultan's Palace PALACE
(Albert Victor Rd; Indian/foreigner ₹5/100, video ₹25; ⊙8.30am-5.30pm) Situated close to the vibrant Krishnarajendra Market is the elegant palace of Tipu Sultan, which is notable for its teak pillars and ornamental frescoes. Though it is not as beautiful (or as well maintained) as Tipu's summer palace in Srirangapatnam, near to Mysuru, it's an in-

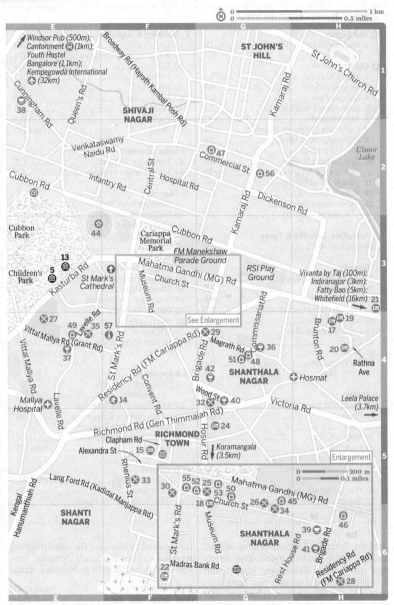

teresting monument, and worth an outing when combined with other nearby sights such as the ornate 17th-century **Venkataraman Temple** (Krishnarajendra Rd; ⏰ 8.30am-6pm) that is located next door, and the

massive **Jamia Masjid** (SJ Park Rd), as well as the fort and market.

Krishnarajendra Market MARKET
(City Market; Silver Jubilee Park Rd; ⏰ 6am-10pm)
For a taste of traditional urban India, dive

Bengaluru (Bangalore)

into the bustling Krishnarajendra Market and the dense grid of commercial streets that surround it. Weave your way around this lively colourful market past fresh produce, piles of vibrant dyes, spices and copperware. The colourful **flower market** in the centre is the highlight.

Bangalore Fort FORT
(KR Rd) The remnants of this 1761 fort is a peaceful escape from the chaotic city surrounds, with its manicured lawn and stone pink walls. The fort remained in use until the destruction by the British in 1791, and today

the gate and bastions are the only structures remaining. There's a small dungeon here, and Ganesh temple with its Mooshak statue.

Bull Temple HINDU TEMPLE
(Bull Temple Rd, Basavangudi; ⊙7am-8.30pm) Built by Kempegowda in the 16th-century Dravidian style, the Bull Temple contains a huge granite monolith of Nandi (Shiva's bull) and is one of Bengaluru's most atmospheric. Nearby is the **Swee Dodda Ganapathi Temple** (Bull Temple Rd; ⊙7am-8.30pm), with an equally enormous Ganesh idol. The temples are 1km south of Tipu Sultan's Palace.

Iskcon Temple · HINDU TEMPLE

(www.iskconbangalore.org; Chord Rd, Hare Krishna Hill; ⊙ 7.30am-1pm & 4.15-8.30pm Mon-Fri, to 1pm Sat, to 2pm Sun) Built by the International Society of Krishna Consciousness (Iskcon), also referred to as the Hare Krishnas, this shiny temple, inaugurated in 1997, is lavishly decorated in a mix of ultracontemporary and traditional styles. There are many food stalls here so bring an appetite. It's around 10km northwest from the centre of town.

🏃 Activities

Ayurvedagram · AYURVEDA, YOGA

(📞 080-65651090; www.ayurvedagram.com; Hemmandanhalli, Whitefield; 1-day package from ₹4000) Set over three hectares of tranquil gardens with heritage homes transplanted from Kerala, this centre specialises in specifically tailored ayurvedic treatments, yoga and rejuvenation programs. It's in the outer suburb of Whitefield, around 25km from central Bengaluru.

Soukya · YOGA

(📞 080-28017000; www.soukya.com; Soukya Rd, Samethanahalli, Whitefield; 7-day package per day incl treatments, meals & accommodation from ₹8800; ⊙ 6am-8.30pm) Internationally renowned retreat on a picture-perfect 12-hectare organic farm running long-term programs in ayurvedic therapy and yoga, as well as medical and therapeutic skin treatments (₹3300 per hour).

Equilibrium · ROCK CLIMBING

(www.facebook.com/EquilibriumClimbingStation; 6th fl, Devatha Plaza, 606 Residency Rd; from ₹150; ⊙ 6am-11pm) India's first indoor climbing centre is more indoor bouldering, which will suit those en route to Hampi, a world-renowned climbing destination. It also arranges weekend climbing excursions.

👉 Tours

In a city lacking in blockbuster sights, there are a couple of companies offering fantastic grassroots tours to get under Bengaluru's skin.

★ Bangalore Walks · WALKING TOUR

(📞 9845523660; www.bangalorewalks.com; adult/child ₹500/300; ⊙ 7-10am Sat & Sun) Highly recommended tours with the choice of a walk through Lalbagh Gardens, a medieval Old City history walk or 19th-century Victorian walk. There's a delicious breakfast en route. Book in advance.

Bus Tours · SIGHTSEEING

(www.karnatakaholidays.net; half-day non AC/AC ₹230/255, full day non AC/AC ₹385/485) The government tourism department runs city bus tours, all of which begin at Badami House. The basic half-day city tour runs twice daily

---

TOP STATE FESTIVALS

Udupi Paryaya (⊙ Jan/Feb) Held even-numbered years, with a procession and ritual marking the handover of swamis at Udupi's Krishna Temple in January.

Classical Dance Festival (⊙ Jan/Feb) Some of India's best classical dance performances take place in Pattadakal.

Vijaya Utsav (p899) A three-day extravaganza of culture, heritage and the arts in Hampi.

Tibetan New Year (⊙ Jan/Feb) Lamas in Tibetan refugee settlements in Bylakuppe take shifts leading nonstop prayers that span the weeklong celebrations.

Vairamudi Festival (⊙ Mar/Apr) Lord Vishnu is adorned with jewels at Cheluvanarayana Temple in Melkote, including a diamond-studded crown belonging to Mysuru's former maharajas, attracting 400,000 pilgrims.

Ganesh Chaturthi (p892) Families march their Ganesh idols to the sea in Gokarna at sunset in September.

Dussehra (p878) Mysore Palace is lit up in the evenings and a vibrant procession hits town to the delight of thousands.

Lakshadeepotsava (p891) Thousands and thousands of lamps light up the Jain pilgrimage town of Dharmasthala in November, offering spectacular photo ops.

Huthri (Madikeri; Nov/Dec) The Kodava community in Madikeri celebrates the start of the harvesting season with ceremony, music, traditional dances and feasting for a week.

KARNATAKA & BENGALURU BENGALURU (BANGALORE)

at 7.30am and 2pm, while the full-day tour departs at 7.15am Wednesday to Sunday.

The day trips around Bengaluru are worth considering, particularly the daily departure to the hard-to-get-to Belur, Halebid and Sravanabelagola (non AC/AC ₹800/850) departing 6.30am and returning 10pm.

🛏 Sleeping

Decent budget rooms are in short supply but a stack of dive lodges line Subedar Chatram (SC) Rd, east of the bus stands and around the train station.

🛏 MG Road Area

Hotel Ajantha   HOTEL $$
(☑ 080-25584321; www.hotelajantha.in; 22A MG Rd; s/d incl breakfast with fan ₹1450/1990, with AC ₹2200/2630; ❄️🛜) An old budget favourite Ajantha is no longer the steal it once was, but it's still affordable for the MG Rd area with a range of par-for-the-course rooms in a compound.

St Mark's Inn   HOTEL $$
(☑ 080-41122783; www.stmarkshotels.com; St Marks Rd; s/d incl breakfast ₹2500/2800; ❄️🛜) A top-value designer hotel with immaculate rooms decked out with modern decor, big comfy beds, in-room safe and sparkling stainless-steel bathroom fittings, plus free wi-fi and buffet breakfast.

Hotel Empire International   HOTEL $$
(☑ 080-42678888; www.hotelempire.in; 36 Church St; s/d incl breakfast from ₹1780/2140; ❄️) The slightly shabby Hotel Empire remains excellent value for its handy central location in happening Church St. Rooms vary in size and decency so ask to check out a few before committing, but they are generally spacious

with speedy wi-fi. Its hotel in up-and-coming Kormangala (☑ 080-40222777; www.hotelempire.in; 103 Industrial Area; s/d ₹2135/2570) is another good choice.

Tom's Hotel   HOTEL $$
(☑ 080-25575875; www.hoteltoms.com; 1/5 Hosur Rd; s/d incl breakfast with fan ₹1900/2080, with AC ₹2310/2560; ❄️@🛜) Long favoured for its low tariffs, bright and cheerful Tom's allows you to stay in a central location in spacious clean rooms with friendly staff.

⭐ Casa Piccola Cottage   HERITAGE HOTEL $$$
(☑ 080-22990337; www.casacottage.com; 2 Clapham Rd; r incl breakfast from ₹4300; ❄️🛜) Within a beautifully renovated heritage building, Casa Piccola's atmospheric rooms offer a tranquil sanctuary from the city madness. Its personalised brand of hospitality has garnered it a solid reputation and rooms come with tiled floors, spotless bathrooms and traditional bedspreads, and garden surrounds of papaya and avocado trees. Also offers furnished apartments.

Oberoi   HOTEL $$$
(☑ 080-41358222; www.oberoihotels.com; 39 MG Rd; s/d from ₹12,000/13,000; ❄️@🛜) Staking its claim as one of Bengaluru's most luxurious hotels, the colossal Oberoi is set over more than a hectare of lush gardens around an enchanting 120-year-old tree. It mixes colonial-era ambience with modern touches, from tablet-controlled devices to TVs in bathrooms.

Laika Boutique Stay   B&B $$$
(☑ 9482806630; www.laikabangalore.in; Rathna Rd; r incl breakfast ₹4780; ❄️🛜) Hidden down a leafy side street, this homely guesthouse is a wonderful choice for those seeking a more local experience combined with style and comfort.

TOURING KARNATAKA

There are some unique ways of getting around Karnataka.

Golden Chariot (☑ 11-42866600; www.thegoldenchariot.co.in; s/d 7 nights incl full board & activities US$5278/7630; 🛜) Beginning in Bengaluru, this luxurious train journey takes you through the romance of Karnataka, visiting palaces, temples, ancient ruins and wildlife. Its AC cabins are equipped with mod cons, plus several bars and restaurants.

goMowgli (☑ 9008730975; www.gomowgli.in; per day from ₹1700) Set up by a bunch of local travellers, this hop-on-hop-off bus journeys across Karnataka aiming to provide more enriching cultural experiences.

Art of Bicycle (☑ 8129945707; www.artofbicycletrips.com; per person from ₹2250) Cycling tours in the countryside around Bengaluru and beyond, including to Nandi Hills or 10-day journeys to Gokarna.

Vivanta by Taj
HOTEL $$$

(☑080-66604444; www.vivantabytaj.com; 41/3, MG Rd; s/d from ₹10,000/12,000; ❄@🔊🏊) Mixing boutique chic with five-star standards, Vivanta has an appealing casualness without skimping on professionalism. The pick of the rooms have rooftop views and a grassy lawn area. Its luxurious pool is perfect for those wanting to lounge around.

Jüsta MG Rd
BOUTIQUE HOTEL $$$

(☑080-41135555; www.justahotels.com/mg-road-bangalore; 21/14 Craig Park Layout, MG Rd; s/d incl breakfast ₹3980/4670; ❄🔊) A wonderful alternative to Bengaluru's plethora of generic business hotels, this intimate art hotel has slick and spacious rooms with Japanese-inspired motifs throughout.

🛏 Other Areas

Hotel Adora
HOTEL $

(☑080-22200024; 47 SC Rd; s/d ₹600/832, with AC ₹990/1560; ❄) A largish budget option with unfussy rooms near the train and Kempegowda bus stations. Downstairs is a good veg restaurant.

Youth Hostel Bangalore
HOSTEL $

(☑080-25924040; www.youthhostelbangalore.com; 65/2 Millers Rd; dm/d ₹150/650, d with AC ₹850; ❄🔊) Strictly for those on a tight budget, this *very* basic hostel is popular with Indian students, and allows you to opt for extras such as bucket hot water (₹15), wi-fi (per hour ₹20) and downstairs security lockers (per day ₹20). Discounts for YHA members. It's close to Cantonment train station, north of the city.

Mass Residency
GUESTHOUSE $$

(☑9945091735; massresidency@yahoo.com; 18, 2nd Main Rd, 11th Cross, JP Nagar; r incl breakfast with fan/AC ₹1600/2000; ❄🔊) In a laid-back neighbourhood away from the city centre, this welcoming guesthouse is run by two brothers who are world travellers themselves. It has comfortable enough rooms, but wins rave reviews for its warm hospitality and free neighbourhood walking tours.

★ Villa Pottipati
HERITAGE GUESTHOUSE $$$

(☑080-41144725; www.villa-pottipati.neemrana-hotels.com; 142 8th Cross, 4th Main, Malleswaram; s/d incl breakfast from ₹3300/4400; ❄@🔊🏊) On the city's outskirts, this heritage building was once the garden home of the wealthy expat Andhra family. Needless to say, it's flooded with memories and quaintness such as antique furniture, knick-knacks and arched doorways. Its garden is full of ancient trees and a dunk-sized pool.

★ Leela Palace
HOTEL $$$

(☑080-25211234; www.theleela.com; 23 HAL Airport Rd; s/d from ₹19,000/20,500) Modelled on Mysore Palace, the astonishing Leela isn't actually a palace (it was built in 2003), but it certainly feels fit for royalty. Gleaming marble, thick luxuriant carpets, regal balconies and period features are done superbly, as are its stately grounds with beautiful gardens, waterfalls, classy restaurants, bars and boutique galleries. It's within the Leela Galleria complex, 5km east of MG Rd.

Taj West End
HERITAGE HOTEL $$$

(☑080-66605660; www.tajhotels.com; Racecourse Rd; s/d incl breakfast from ₹24,000/25,500; ❄🔊🏊) The West End saga flashbacks to 1887, when it was incepted by a British family as a 10-room hostel for passing army officers. Since then, nostalgia has been a permanent resident at this lovely property which – spread over eight hectares of tropical gardens – has evolved as a definitive icon of Indian luxury hospitality.

🍴 Eating

Bengaluru's adventurous dining scene keeps pace with the whims and rising standards of its hungry, moneyed locals and IT expats. You'll find high-end dining, gastropubs and cheap local favourites.

🍴 MG Road Area

Khan Saheb
INDIAN $

(www.khansaheb.co; 9A Block, Brigade Rd; rolls from ₹60; ⊘noon-11.30pm) A tasty cheap eat famous for its rolls filled with anything from charcoal-grilled meats and tandoori prawns to paneer and mushroom tikka.

★ Koshy's Bar & Restaurant
INDIAN $$

(39 St Mark's Rd; mains ₹160-350; ⊘9am-11pm) They say half of Bengaluru's court cases are argued around Koshy's tables, and many hard-hitting newspaper articles written over its steaming coffees. Serving the city's intelligentsia for decades, this buzzy and joyful resto-pub is where you can put away tasty North Indian dishes in between fervent discussions and mugs of beer.

Queen's Restaurant
INDIAN $$

(7 Church St; mains ₹140-240; ◷12.30-3.30pm & 7-10.30pm Tue-Sun) Intimate and atmospheric, reputed Queen's interior is rustic village-style, with painted motifs adorning earthy walls. It serves quick and tasty Indian dishes such as a range of vegetable and dhal preparations, to go with fluffy, hot chapati.

Church St Social
GASTROPUB $$

(46/1 Church St; mains ₹150-350; ◷9am-11pm Mon-Thu, to 1am Fri & Sat) Bringing hipsterism to Bengaluru, this industrial warehouse-style space serves cocktails in beakers to go with a menu of all-day breakfasts, jalapeño mac 'n' cheese, southern fried chicken burgers and inventive Indian classics.

★ Karavalli
SEAFOOD $$$

(☑080-66604545; Gateway Hotel, 66 Residency Rd; mains ₹500-1500; ◷12.30-3pm & 6.30-11pm) The Arabian Sea may be 400km away, but you'll have to come only as far as this classy spot to savour South India's finest coastal cuisines. The decor is a stylish mash of traditional thatched roof, vintage woodwork and beaten brassware. In the garden seating enjoy superb fiery Mangalorean fish dishes or its signature lobster *balchao* (₹1495).

Sunny's
ITALIAN $$$

(☑080-41329366; www.sunnysbangalore.in; 50 Lavelle Rd; mains ₹380-730; ◷12.30-3pm & 7-11pm; ☎) A well-established fixture on Bengaluru's restaurant scene, classy Sunny's is all about authentic charcoal thin-crust pizzas, homemade pastas, imported cheese and some of the best desserts in the city.

DON'T MISS

FOOD STREET

For a local eating experience, head to VV Puram, aka **Food Street** (Sajjan Rao Circle, VW Puram; ◷from 5pm), with its strip of hole-in-the-wall eateries cooking up classic street-food dishes. Things kick off in the early evening when the stalls fire up and people stand around watching rotis being handmade and spun in the air or *bhaji* (vegetable fritters) dunked into hot oil before being dished up on paper plates, where you can eat standing in the street.

It's all-vegetarian with a range of dosas (lentil-flour pancake), curries, roti and deep-fried goodies.

Ebony
MULTICUISINE $$$

(☑41783333; www.ebonywithaview.com; 13th fl, Barton Centre, 84 MG Rd; mains ₹300-500; ◷12.30-3pm & 7-11pm) While there's a delectable menu of Indian, Thai and European dishes, here it's all about the romantic views from its luxurious rooftop, making it a good spot to treat yourself for a night out.

Fava
MEDITERRANEAN $$$

(www.fava.in; UB City, 24 Vittal Mallya Rd; mains ₹350-850; ◷11am-11pm) Dine alfresco on Fava's canopy-covered decking, feasting on large plates of mezze, fish kebabs, zatar sausages or something from the organic menu.

★ Olive Beach
MEDITERRANEAN $$$

(☑080-41128400; www.olivebarandkitchen.com; 16 Wood St, Ashoknagar; mains ₹530-800; ◷noon-11.30pm) A white-washed villa straight from the coast of Santorini, Olive Beach does a menu that evokes wistful memories of sunny Mediterranean getaways. Things change seasonally, but expect Moroccan lamb tagines, caramelised pork belly and savoury tarts, as well as fantastic cocktails.

✗ Other Areas

★ Mavalli Tiffin Rooms
SOUTH INDIAN $

(MTR; www.mavallitiffinrooms.com; Lalbagh Rd; dosa from ₹50, meals from ₹130; ◷6.30-11am, 12.30-2.45pm, 3.30-7.30pm & 8-9.30pm) A legendary name in South Indian comfort food, this super-popular eatery has had Bengaluru eating out of its hands since 1924. Head to the dining room upstairs, queue for a table, and then admire the dated images of southern beauties etched on smoky glass as waiters bring you savoury local fare, capped by frothing filter coffee served in silverware. It's a definitive Bengaluru experience.

Gramin
INDIAN $

(☑080-41104104; 20, 7th Block Raheja Arcade, Koramangala; mains ₹90-180; ◷12.30-3.30pm & 7-11pm) Translating to 'from the village', Gramin offers a wide choice of flavourful rural North Indian fare at this cosy, eclectic all-veg place popular with locals. Try the excellent range of lentils and curries best had with oven-fresh rotis, accompanied by sweet rose-flavoured lassi served in a copper vessel.

Windsor Pub
INDIAN $$

(7 Kodava Samaja Bldg, 1st Main Vasanthnagar; mains ₹250-350; ◷11.30am-3pm & 6-11pm) Its dark pub interior may not inspire, but it has a fantastic menu of regional favourites

such as flavoursome Mangalorean fish, or the tangy *pandhi* (pork) masala from Kodagu's hills. It also does draught beer and a soundtrack of blues, jazz and '70s rock. It's near Bangalore Palace.

★**Fatty Bao** ASIAN $$$
(www.facebook.com/thefattybao; 610 12th Main Rd, Indiranagar; mains ₹380-650; ⊙11am-3.30pm & 7-11pm) This hip rooftop restaurant serves up Asian hawker food to a crowd of fashionable, young Bangalorean foodies in a vibrant setting with colourful chairs and wooden bench tables. There's ramen, Thai curries and Malaysian street food, as well as Asian-inspired cocktails such as lemongrass mojitos. There's a branch of Monkey Bar is downstairs..

 Drinking & Nightlife

Bars & Lounges
Bengaluru's rock-steady reputation and wide choice of chic watering holes makes it the place to indulge in a spirited session of pub-hopping in what's the original beer town of India. Many microbreweries have sprung up in the past few years, producing quality locally made ales. All serve food too.

The trendiest nightclubs will typically charge a cover of around ₹1000 per couple, but it's often redeemable against drinks or food.

Monkey Bar PUB
(www.monkeybarindia.com; 14/1 Wood St, Ashoknagar; ⊙noon-11pm) From the owners of Olive Beach comes this vintage gastropub that draws a mixed, jovial crowd to knock back drinks around the bar or at wooden booth seating. Otherwise head down to the basement to join the 'party' crew shooting pool, playing foosball and rocking out to bangin' tunes. There's also a branch in **Indiranagar** (925 12th Main Rd, Indiranagar).

Plan B PUB
(20 Castle St, Ashoknagar; ⊙11am-11.30pm Sun-Thu, to 1am Fri & Sat) It may not have fancy craft beer on tap, but this popular student hang-out instead has 3.5L beer towers and 15 different burgers. It also runs the industrial chic **Plan B Loaded** (13 Rhenius St, Richmond Town) gastropub.

Pecos BAR
(Rest House Rd; ⊙10.30am-11pm) Hendrix, The Grateful Dead and Frank Zappa posters adorn the walls of this divey, narrow tri-level

bar. It's a throwback to simpler times where cassettes line the shelves behind the bar, sport is on the TV and the only thing to quench your thirst is one choice of cheap beer on tap. No wonder it's an all-time favourite with students. There are now several branches in the immediate area.

Shiro BAR
(www.shiro.co.in; UB City, 24 Vittal Mallya Rd; ⊙12.30-11.30pm Sun-Thu, to 1am Fri & Sat) A sophisticated lounge for getting sloshed in style, Shiro has elegant interiors complemented by the monumental Buddha busts and Apsara figurines or outdoor seating.

13th Floor BAR
(13th fl, Barton Centre, 84 MG Rd; ⊙5-11pm Sun-Thu, to 1am Fri & Sat) Forget your superstitions and head up to 13th Floor's terrace, with all of Bengaluru glittering at your feet. Happy hour is 5pm to 7pm.

Microbreweries
Biere Club MICROBREWERY
(www.thebiereclub.com; 20/2 Vittal Mallya Rd; ⊙11am-11.30pm Sun-Thu, to 1am Fri & Sat) Beer lovers rejoice as South India's first microbrewery serves up handcrafted beers on tap, six of which are brewed on-site. Large copper boilers sit behind the bar.

Arbor Brewing Company MICROBREWERY
(www.arborbrewing.com; 8 Magrath; noon-11.30pm Sun-Thu, to 1am Fri & Sat) This classic brewpub

with roots in Michigan, USA, was one of the first microbreweries to get the ball rolling in Bengaluru with its eight beers brewed on-site including IPA, pilsner and Belgian beers.

Toit Brewpub
MICROBREWERY
(www.toit.in; 298 100ft Rd, Indiranagar; ☉noon-11.30pm Sun-Thu, to 1am Fri & Sat) A brick-walled gastropub split over three levels where lively punters sample its quality beers brewed on-site, including two seasonals and an Irish red ale on tap.

Brewski
MICROBREWERY
(www.brewsky.in; 4th & 5th Fl Goenka Chambers, 19th Main Rd, JP Nagar; ☉noon-11.30pm Mon-Thu, to 1am Fri & Sat) This rooftop brewery is a cool new spot with city views and a funky restaurant with vintage decor. It brews six beers including a golden ale, wheat beer and stout.

Barleyz
MICROBREWERY
(www.barleyz.com; 100ft Rd, Koramangala; ☉11am-11.30pm Sun-Thu, to 1am Fri & Sat) A suave rooftop beer garden with potted plants, Astroturf and tables with built-in BBQ grills. Offers free tastings of its six beers, and does growlers for takeaway. There's also excellent wood-fired pizza.

Big Pitcher
MICROBREWERY, CLUB
(www.bigpitcher.in; 4121 HAL Airport Rd; ☉noon-11.30pm Sun-Thu, to 1am Fri & Sat) More nightclub than pub, with six floors, but its Brazilian brewer does six beers. Head up to its glamorous rooftop for wonderful views.

Vapour
MICROBREWERY, BAR
(www.vapour.in; 773 100ft Rd, Indiranagar) Multilevel complex divided into several bars and restaurants, though its highlight is the rooftop with big screen to enjoy its six microbrews, including a rice beer and guest ale.

Cafes

Dyu Art Cafe
CAFE
(www.dyuartcafe.yolasite.com; 23 MIG, KHB Colony, Koramangala; ☉10am-10.30pm; 🐾) An atmospheric cafe-gallery in a leafy neighbourhood with a peaceful courtyard reminiscent of a Zen temple. It has coffee beans from Kerala and does good filtered, espresso and iced coffee, to go with homemade cakes.

Matteo
CAFE
(www.matteocoffea.com; Church St; ☉9am-11pm; 🐾) The coolest rendezvous in the city centre where arty locals lounge on retro couches sipping first-rate brews while chatting,

plugged into free wi-fi, or browsing a great selection of newspapers and mags.

Infinitea
CAFE
(www.infinitea.in; 2 Shah Sultan Complex, Cunningham Rd; pot of tea from ₹100; ☉11am-11pm; 🐾) This smart yet homely cafe has an impressive menu of steaming cuppas, including orthodox teas from the best estates, and a few selections such as blooming flowers. Order your pot and team it with a delectable sweet or light lunch. Sells loose tea by the gram.

☆ Entertainment

Live Music

Humming Tree
LIVE MUSIC
(www.facebook.com/thehummingtree; 12th Main Rd, Indiranagar; ☉11am-11.30pm Sun-Thu, to 1am Fri & Sat) One of Bengaluru's premier live-music venues, this warehouse-style venue has bands (starting around 9pm), DJs and a rooftop bar. Cover charge is anything from free to ₹300.

B Flat
LIVE MUSIC
(☎8041739250; www.facebook.com/thebflat bar; 776 100ft Rd, Indiranagar; cover charge ₹300; ☉6.30-11.30pm Sun-Thu, to 1am Fri & Sat) A pub and live-music venue that features some of India's best blues and jazz bands.

Sport

M Chinnaswamy Stadium
SPORTS
(www.ksca.co.in; MG Rd) For a taste of India's sporting passion, attend one of the regular cricket matches at M Chinnaswamy Stadium. Check online for the upcoming schedule of Tests, one-dayers and Twenty20s.

Bangalore Turf Club
HORSE RACING
(www.bangaloreraces.com; Racecourse Rd) Horse racing is big in Bengaluru and can make for a fun day out. Races are generally held on Friday and Saturday afternoons.

Theatre

Ranga Shankara
THEATRE
(☎26592777; www.rangashankara.org; 36/2 8th Cross, JP Nagar) Interesting theatre (in a variety of languages and genres) and dance are held at this cultural centre.

Shopping

Bengaluru's shopping options are abundant, ranging from teeming bazaars to glitzy malls. Some good shopping areas include Commercial St, Vittal Mallya Rd and the MG Rd area.

Mysore Saree Udyog CLOTHING
(www.mysoresareeudyog.com; 1st fl, 316 Kamaraj Rd; ⊕10.30am-11pm) A great choice for top-quality silk saris and men's shirts, this busy store has been in business for over 70 years and has something to suit all budgets. Most garments are made with Mysore silk; also stocks 100% *pashmina* (wool shawls).

Cauvery Arts & Crafts Emporium SOUVENIRS
(49 MG Rd; ⊕10am-9pm) Large government-run emporium famous for it expansive collection of quality sandalwood and rosewood products as well as textiles.

Kynkyny Art Gallery ART
(www.kynkyny.com; Embassy Sq, 148 Infantry Rd; ⊕10am-7pm Mon-Sat) This sophisticated commercial gallery inside a stunning colonial-era building sells works by contemporary Indian artists, priced suitably for all budgets. Also sells designer furniture.

Forest Essentials COSMETICS
(www.forestessentialsindia.com; 4/1 Lavelle Junction Bldg, Vittal Mallya Rd; ⊕10am-9pm) Smell the lemongrass as you browse the shelves at this tranquil store selling all-organic ayurvedic essential oils and beauty products.

Fabindia CLOTHING, HOMEWARES
(www.fabindia.com; 54 17th Main, Koramangala; ⊕10am-8pm) Commercial St (152 Commercial St; ⊕10am-8.30pm); Garuda Mall (Garuda Mall, McGrath Rd; ⊕10am-8pm); MG Rd (1 MG Rd; ⊕10am-8pm) Hugely successful chain with a range of traditional clothing, homewares and accessories in traditional cotton prints and silks. Quality skincare products too.

UB City MALL
(www.ubcitybangalore.in; 24 Vittal Mallya Rd; ⊕11am-9pm) Global haute couture (Louis Vuitton, Jimmy Choo, Burberry) and Indian high fashion come to roost at this towering mall in the central district.

Garuda Mall MALL
(McGrath Rd) A modern mall with all the usual food and clothing chains.

Forum MALL
(www.theforumexperience.com/forumbangalore. htm; Hosur Rd, Koramangala; ⊕10am-11pm) Shiny mall complex in Koramangala.

Leela Galleria MALL
(23 Airport Rd, Kodihalli) A glamorous mall with high end shops. It's nearby to the ritzy suburb of Indiranagar.

Indiana Crockery HOMEWARES
(97/1 MG Rd; ⊕10.30am-9pm) Good spot to buy thali trays, brass utensils and chai cups for that dinner party back home.

Goobe's Book Republic BOOKS
(www.goobes.wordpress.com; 11 Church St; ⊕10.30am-9pm Mon-Sat, noon-9pm Sun) Great little bookstore selling new and secondhand, cult and mainstream books and comics.

Gangarams Book Bureau BOOKS
(2nd fl, 48 Church St; ⊕10am-8pm Mon-Sat) Excellent selection of Indian titles, guidebooks and Penguin classics.

Bookworm BOOKS
(Shrungar Shopping Complex, MG Rd; ⊕10am-9pm) Great secondhand bookstore filled with contemporary and classic literature as well as travel guidebooks.

Blossom Book House BOOKS
(www.blossombookhouse.com; 84/6 Church St; ⊕10.30am-9.30pm) Great deals on new and secondhand books.

Magazines BOOKS
(41/1 Rayan Tower, Church St; ⊕10am-10pm) Huge collection of international magazines.

ⓘ Information

INTERNET ACCESS
Being an IT city, internet cafes are plentiful in Bengaluru, as is wi-fi access in hotels.

LEFT LUGGAGE
The City train station and Kempegowda bus stand have 24-hour cloakrooms (per day ₹10).

MAPS
The tourist offices give out decent city maps and you can find maps at most major bookstores.

MEDIA
Time Out Bengaluru (www.timeout.com/bangalore), *What's Up Bangalore* (www.whatsupguides.com) and *Explocity* (www.bangalore.explocity.com) cover all the latest events, nightlife, dining and shopping in the city; magazines are available in major bookshops.

MEDICAL SERVICES
Hosmat (☑25593796; www.hosmatnet.com) For critical injuries and general illnesses.
Mallya Hospital (☑22277979; www.mallyahospital.net; 2 Vittal Mallya Rd) Emergency services and 24-hour pharmacy.

MONEY
ATMs are everywhere, as are moneychangers around MG Rd.

POST

Main post office (Cubbon Rd; ⊙10am-7pm Mon-Sat, to 1pm Sun)

TOURIST INFORMATION

Government of India tourist office (GITO; ☑25585417; 2nd level, 48 Church St; ⊙9.30am-6pm Mon-Fri, 9am-1pm Sat) Very helpful for Bengaluru and beyond.

Karnataka State Tourism Development Corporation (KSTDC) Badami House (☑080-43344334; www.karnatakaholidays.net; Kasturba Rd; ⊙10am-7pm Mon-Sat); Karnataka Tourism House (☑41329211; 8 Papanna Lane, St Mark's Rd; ⊙10am-7pm Mon-Sat) Mainly for booking tours and government-run accommodation around Karnataka, but also has a useful website.

TRAVEL AGENCIES

Skyway (☑22111401; www.skywaytour.com; 8 Papanna Lane, St Mark's Rd; ⊙9am-6pm Mon-Sat) Thoroughly professional and reliable outfit for booking long-distance taxis and air tickets.

⊙ Getting There & Away

AIR

International flights arrive at Bengaluru's **Kempegowda International Airport** (www.bengaluruairport.com). Domestic flights also leave here with daily flights to major cities across India, including Chennai (₹2600, two hours), Mumbai (₹4000, two hours), Hyderabad (₹3000, one hour), Delhi (₹6100, 2½ hours) and Goa (₹2500, one hour).

AirAsia (☑1860-5008000; www.airasia.com)
Air India (☑22978427; www.airindia.com; Unity Bldg, JC Rd)
GoAir (☑47406091; www.goair.in)
IndiGo (☑9910383838; www.goindigo.in)
Jet Airways (☑39893333; www.jetairways.com; Unity Bldg, JC Rd)
SpiceJet (☑18001803333; www.spicejet.com)

BUS

Bengaluru's huge, well-organised **Kempegowda bus stand** (Gubbi Thotadappa Rd), also commonly known as either the Central or Majestic, is directly in front of the City train station.

Karnataka State Road Transport Corporation (KSRTC; ☑44554422; www.ksrtc.in) buses run from here throughout Karnataka.

The KSRTC website lists current schedules and fares. At the time of research booking online wasn't possible using an international credit card, but check if things have changed. Otherwise KSRTC has convenient booking counters

around town, or computerised advance booking at the station. It's wise to book long-distance journeys in advance.

Private bus operators line the street facing Kempegowda bus stand, or you can book through a travel agency.

Interstate bus operators also run from Kempegowda bus stand.

TRAIN

Bengaluru's **City train station** (www.bangalorecityrailwaystation.in; Gubbi Thotadappa Rd) is the main train hub. There's also **Cantonment train station** (Station Rd), a sensible spot to disembark if you're arriving and headed for the MG Rd area, while **Yeshvantpur train station** (Rahman Khan Rd), 8km northwest of downtown, is the starting point for trains to Goa.

If you have a local phone number, tickets can be booked online at www.irctc.co.in. If a train is booked out, foreign travellers can use the foreign-tourist quota. The computerised **reservation office** (☑139; ⊙8am-8pm Mon-Sat, to 2pm Sun), on the left facing the station, has separate counters for credit-card purchase, women and foreigners. Luggage can be left at the 24-hour cloakroom on Platform 1 at the City train station.

⊙ Getting Around

TO/FROM THE AIRPORT

The swish Kempegowda International Airport is in Hebbal, about 40km north from the MG Rd area. Metered AC taxis from the airport to the city centre cost between ₹750 and ₹1000.

Flybus KSRTC runs the Flybus to Mysuru (₹750, four hours) departing the airport at 10.30am and 9pm.

Vayu Vajra (☑18004251663; www.mybmtc.com) Vayu Vajra's airport shuttle service has an AC bus to Kempegowda (Central Majestic) bus stand or MG Rd (₹210), departing hourly from 6.10am to 10.25pm.

AUTORICKSHAW

The city's autorickshaw drivers are legally required to use their meters; few comply. After 10pm, 50% is added to the metered rate. Flag fall is ₹25 for the first 2km and then ₹13 for each extra kilometre.

BUS

Bengaluru has a thorough local bus network, operated by the **Bangalore Metropolitan Transport Corporation** (BMTC; www.mybmtc.com), with a useful website for timetable and fares. Red AC Vajra buses criss-cross the city, while green Big10 deluxe buses connect the suburbs.

Ordinary buses run from the City bus stand, next to Kempegowda (Central Majestic) bus stand; a few operate from the City Market bus stand.

To get from the City train station to the MG Rd area, catch any bus from Platform 17 or 18 at the City bus stand. For the City Market bus stand, take bus 31, 31E, 35 or 49 from Platform 8.

TAXI
Standard rates for a long-haul Tata Indica cab are ₹8.5 per kilometre for a minimum of 250km, plus a daily allowance of ₹200 for the driver. An eight-hour day rental is around ₹2000.

Olacabs (☏ 33553355; www.olacabs.com) Professional, efficient company with modern air-con cars. Online and phone bookings.
Meru Cabs (☏ 44224422; www.merucabs.com)

METRO
Bengaluru's shiny new AC metro service, known as Namma Metro, is still very much a work in progress, but it does have a few lines up and running. The most relevant to tourists is Line 1 from MG Rd to Indiranagar (₹13), running every 15 minutes, 6am to 10pm. For the latest updates on the service, log on to www.bmrc.co.in.

TRANSPORT FROM BENGALURU

Major Bus Services from Bengaluru

DESTINATION	FARE (₹)	DURATION (HR)	FREQUENCY
Chennai	390 (R)/690 (V)/757 (S)	7-8	hourly, 5.35am-11.45pm
Ernakulam	587 (R)/1012 (V)/1062 (S)	10-12	7 daily, 4-9.45pm
Hampi	546 (R)	8½	1 daily, 11pm
Hospet	326 (R)/566 (V)/695 (S)	8	14 buses, 4.30-11pm, hourly
Hyderabad	672 (R)/812 (V)/1012 (S)	9½-11	23 daily, 7.30am-10.30pm
Mumbai	1690 (V)	17½-19	4 daily, 3-9pm
Mysuru	190 (R)/270 (V)	3	Every 10min, 24hr
Ooty	256 (R)/490 (V)	8	9 daily, 6.15am-11.15pm
Panaji	1190 (V)	13	4 daily, 6.20-8pm
Gorkana	562 (R)	12	2 daily, from 9pm

Fares: (R) Rajahamsa Semideluxe, (V) Airavath AC Volvo, (S) AC Sleeper

Major Trains from Bengaluru

DESTINATION	TRAIN NO & NAME	FARE (₹)	DURATION (HR)	DEPARTURES
Chennai	12658 Chennai Mail	260/920	6½	10.40pm
	12028 Shatabdi	785/1510	5	6am & 4.25pm Wed-Mon
Delhi	12627 Karnataka Exp	815/3110	39	7.20pm
	12649 Sampark Kranti Exp	795/3030	35	10.10pm Mon, Wed, Fri, Sat & Sun
Hospet	16592 Hampi Exp	255/970	9½	10pm
Hubli	16589 Rani Chennamma Exp	270/1040	8½	9.15pm
Kolkata	12864 YPR Howrah Exp	740/2820	34½	7.35pm
Mumbai	11302 Udyan Exp	505/1975	23½	8.30pm
Mysuru	12007 Shatabdi	435/825	2	11am Thu-Tue
	12614 Tippu Exp	90/305	2½	3pm
Trivandrum	16526 Kanyakumari Exp	420/1630	16½	8pm

Fares: Shatabdi fares are AC chair/AC executive; Express (Exp/Mail) fares are 2nd-class/AC chair for day trains and sleeper/2AC for night trains.

Around Bengaluru

If Bengaluru's mayhem and traffic jams are doing your head in, then head to the hills for some fresh air, rural culture and lovely scenery.

Nandi Hills

Rising to 1455m, **Nandi Hills** (admission ₹10, car ₹150; ⊙6am-6pm), 60km north of Bengaluru, were once the summer retreat of Tipu Sultan (his palace is still here). Today it's the Bengaluru techie's favourite weekend getaway, and is predictably congested on Saturday and Sunday; aim to visit midweek. Nonetheless, it's a good place for a leisurely hike, panoramic views of sweeping plains and two notable **Chola temples**. It's a 2km hike to the top from the entrance gate for those without a vehicle. Macaques run amok, so avoid carrying food.

At the top of Nandi Hills, **Hotel Mayura Pine Top** (☑8970650019; mains ₹80-160; ⊙10.30am-8pm) does good Indian dishes which can be enjoyed with excellent views from it's glassed-in restaurant. Its **rooms** (fan/AC ₹1500/3000) also feature stellar views.

Around Nandi Hills is one of India's premier wine-growing regions.

Buses head to Nandi Hills (₹65, two hours) from Bengaluru's Kempegowda (Central Majestic) bus stand.

KARNATAKA CITY NAME CHANGES

From 1 November 2014 the Karnataka government officially announced the name changes of 12 cities across the state, returning to their precolonial titles. The following are most relevant to tourists:

➡ Bangalore to Bengaluru
➡ Mysore to Mysuru
➡ Mangalore to Mangaluru
➡ Hospet to Hosapete
➡ Hubli to Hubballi
➡ Bijapur to Vijapura
➡ Gulbarga to Kalaburgi
➡ Shimoga to Shivamogga

Hessaraghatta

Located 30km northwest of Bengaluru, Hessaraghatta is home to **Nrityagram** (☑080-28466313; www.nrityagram.org; self-guided tour ₹50; ⊙10am-2pm Tue-Sun), a leading dance academy established in 1990 to revive and popularise Indian classical dance. The brainchild and living legacy of celebrated dancer Protima Gauri Bedi (1948–98), the complex was designed like a village by Goa-based architect Gerard da Cunha. You can take a self-guided tour, or book a tour, lecture and demonstration and vegetarian meal (₹1500 to ₹2000, minimum 10 people). Note the early 2pm closure.

From Bengaluru's City Market, buses 266, 253, 253D and 253E run to Hessaraghatta (₹25, one hour), with bus 266 continuing on to Nrityagram. From Hessaraghatta an autorickshaw will cost ₹70.

🛏 Sleeping

Taj Kuteeram HOTEL $$$
(☑080-28466326; www.tajhotels.com; d from ₹4800; ❄@🛜) Opposite Nrityagram dance village, Kuteeram isn't as luxurious as other Taj Group hotel offerings, but it's still very nice with a balance of comfort and rustic charm, and designs by renowned architect Gerard da Cunha. It also offers ayurveda and yoga sessions.

Janapada Loka Folk Arts Museum

Janapada Loka Folk Arts Museum MUSEUM (Bangaluru-Mysuru Rd; Indian/foreigner ₹20/100; ⊙9am-5.30pm) A worthwhile stopover between Bengaluru and Mysuru, this museum is dedicated to the preservation of rural local culture. It has a wonderful collection of folkart objects, including 500-year-old shadow puppets, festival costumes, musical instruments and a superb temple chariot and a replica of a traditional village. It's situated 53km south of Bengaluru, 3km from Ramnagar; any Mysuru–Bengaluru bus can drop you here.

Mysuru (Mysore)

☑0821 / POP 895,000 / ELEV 707M
One of South India's most famous tourist destinations, Mysuru (which recently changed its name from Mysore) is known for its glittering royal heritage and magnif-

WHISKEY & WINE

In a country not known for being a big exponent of fine wines and liquors (anyone who has stepped foot into one of India's ubiquitous 'wine shops' can attest to this), Bengaluru (Bangalore) is very much an exception to the rule. It's a city that's not only gained a thirst for craft beer (p865), but has on its doorstep one of India's premier wine-growing regions in Nandi Hills. While an emerging industry, it's fast gaining a reputation internationally with some 18 wineries in the area. Also a few clicks out of town is India's first single-malt whiskey distillery, where you're also able to sample the goods.

Grover Wineries (☑9379627188; www.groverzampa.in; 1½hr tour Mon-Fri ₹850, Sat & Sun ₹1000) Highly recommended tours of Grover Wineries where you'll learn about India's wine industry that produces quality white and red varietals. Prices include tastings of five wines in the cellar rooms accompanied by cheese and crackers, followed by lunch. From February to May you'll also see grape crushing and visit its vineyards. It's located on the approach to Nandi Hills, around 40km north of Bengaluru; you'll need to hire a car to get here.

Amrut (☑080-23100402; www.amrutdistilleries.com; Mysuru Rd; tour free) Established in 1948, India's first producer of single malt whiskey, Amrut offers free distillery tours run by knowledgeable guides. You get taken through the entire process before tasting its world-class single malts and blends. It's 20km outside Bangaluru on the road to Mysuru; pre-bookings essential.

icent monuments and buildings. Its World Heritage–listed palace may be what brings most travellers here, but it's also a thriving centre for the production of premium silk, sandalwood and incense. These days ashtanga yoga is another drawcard, attracting visitors worldwide with its reputation as one of India's best places to practise yoga.

History

Mysuru owes its name to the mythical Mahisuru, a place where the demon Mahisasura was slain by the goddess Chamundi. Its regal history began in 1399, when the Wodeyar dynasty of Mysuru was founded, though they remained in service of the Vijayanagar empire until the mid-16th century. With the fall of Vijayanagar in 1565, the Wodeyars declared their sovereignty, which – save a brief period of Hyder Ali and Tipu Sultan's supremacy in the late 18th century – remained unscathed until Independence in 1947.

◉ Sights

Mysuru isn't known as the City of Palaces for nothing, being home to a total of seven and an abundance of majestic heritage architecture dating from the Wodeyars dynasty and British rule. The majority of grand buildings are owned by the state, and used as anything from hospitals, colleges and government buildings to heritage hotels. Visit www.karnatakatourism.org/Mysore/en for list of notable buildings.

★ **Mysore Palace** PALACE
(Maharaja's Palace; www.mysorepalace.gov.in; Indian/foreigner incl audio guide ₹40/200, child under 10yr free; ⊘10am-5.30pm) Among the grandest of India's royal buildings, this fantastic palace was the former seat of the Wodeyar maharajas. The old palace was gutted by fire in 1897; the one you see now was completed in 1912 by English architect Henry Irwin at a cost of ₹4.5 million. The interior of this Indo-Saracenic marvel – a kaleidoscope of stained glass, mirrors and gaudy colours – is lavish and undoubtedly over the top. The decor is further embellished by carved wooden doors, mosaic floors and a series of paintings depicting life in Mysore during the Edwardian Raj era.

The way into the palace takes you past a fine collection of sculptures and artefacts. Don't forget to check out the armoury, with an intriguing collection of 700-plus weapons.

Every Sunday and national holiday, from 7pm to 7.45pm, the palace is illuminated by nearly 100,000 light bulbs that accent its majestic profile against the night.

Entrance to the palace grounds is at the South Gate on Purandara Dasa Rd. While you are allowed to snap the palace's exterior, photography within is strictly prohibited.

Mysuru (Mysore)

Cameras must be deposited in lockers at the palace entrance. See illustrated highlight (p874) for more detail.

Devaraja Market
MARKET

(Sayyaji Rao Rd; ⏰6am-8.30pm) Dating from Tipu Sultan's reign, this lively bazaar has local traders selling traditional items such as flower garlands, spices and conical piles of *kumkum* (coloured powder used for bindi dots), all of which makes for some great photo ops. Refresh your bargaining skills before shopping.

Chamundi Hill
VIEWPOINT

At a height of 1062m, on the summit of Chamundi Hill, stands the **Sri Chamundeswari Temple** (⏰7am-2pm, 3.30-6pm & 7.30-9pm), dominated by a towering 40m-high *gopuram* (gateway tower). It's a fine half-day excursion, offering spectacular views of the city below. Queues are long at weekends, so visit during the week. From Central bus

stand take bus 100 (₹17, 25 minutes) or 201 (₹28, AC) that rumbles up the narrow road to the summit. A return autorickshaw trip will cost about ₹400.

Alternatively, you can take the foot trail comprising 1000-plus steps that Hindu pilgrims use to visit the temple. One-third of the way down is a 5m-high statue of **Nandi** (Shiva's bull) that was carved out of solid rock in 1659.

Jaganmohan Palace
PALACE

(Jaganmohan Palace Rd; adult/child ₹120/60; ⏰8.30am-5pm) Built in 1861 as the royal auditorium, this stunning palace just west of the Mysore Palace, houses the **Jayachamarajendra Art Gallery**. Set over three floors it has a huge collection of Indian paintings, including works by noted artist Raja Ravi Varma and traditional Japanese art. There's also regal memorabilia from the Mysore royal family, weapons and rare musical instruments.

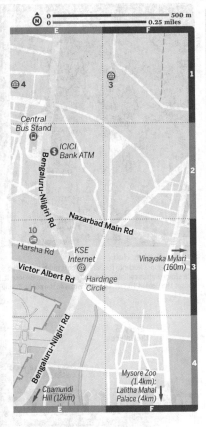

Indira Gandhi Rashtriya Manav Sangrahalaya   MUSEUM
(National Museum of Mankind; ☎ 2526531; www.igrms.com; Wellington Lodge, Irwin Rd; ⊙10am-5.30pm Tue-Sun) FREE Lovely arts and cultural centre that presents rotating exhibitions showcasing arts from rural India.

Government House   HISTORIC BUILDING
(Irwin Rd) Dating from 1805, Government House, formerly the British Residency, is a Tuscan Doric building set in 20 hectares of gardens.

Jayalakshmi Vilas Mansion Museum Complex   MUSEUM
(Mysore University Campus; ⊙10.15am-5pm Mon-Sat) FREE Housed in a grand mansion, on the university campus west of town, this museum specialises in folklore, with artefacts, stone tablets and sculptures, including rural costumes and a wooden puppet of the 10-headed demon king Ravana.

St Philomena's Cathedral   CHURCH
(St Philomena St; ⊙8am-5pm) The beauty of towering St Philomena's Cathedral, built between 1933 and 1941 in neo-Gothic style, is emphasised by lovely stained-glass windows. It's on the northern outskirts of town.

Rail Museum   MUSEUM
(KRS Rd; adult/child ₹15/10, camera/video ₹20/30; ⊙9.30am-6.30pm Tue-Sun) Behind the train station, this open-air museum's main exhibit is the Mysore maharani's saloon, a wood-panelled beauty dating from 1899 that provides an insight into the way in which the royals once rode the railways. A toy train (₹10) rides the track around the museum.

Mysore Zoo   ZOO
(Indiranagar; adult/child ₹50/20, camera ₹20; ⊙8.30am-5.30pm Wed-Mon) Unlike many other pitiful zoos in India, Mysore Zoo conforms to much higher standards, set in pretty gardens that date from 1892. Highlights include white tigers, lowland gorillas and rhinos. It's situated around 2km southeast of Mysore Palace.

(Continued on p876)

Mysore Palace

The interior of Mysore Palace houses opulent halls, royal paintings, intricate decorative details, as well as sculptures and ceremonial objects. There is a lot of hidden detail and much to take in, so be sure to allow yourself at least a few hours for the experience. A guide can also be invaluable.

After entering the palace the first exhibit is the **Doll's Pavilion** ❶, which showcases the maharaja's fine collection of traditional dolls and sculptures acquired from around the world. Opposite the **Elephant Gate** ❷ you'll see the seven cannons that were used for special occasions, such as the birthdays of the maharajas. Today the cannons are still fired as part of Dasara festivities.

At the end of the Doll's Pavilion you'll find the **Golden Howdah** ❸. Note the fly whisks on either side; the bristles are made from fine ivory.

Make sure you check out the paintings depicting the Dasara procession in the halls on your way to the **Marriage Pavilion** ❹ and look into the courtyard to see what was once the wrestling arena. It's now used during Dasara only. In the Marriage Pavilion, take a few minutes to scan the entire space. You can see the influence of three religions in the design of the hall: the glass ceiling represents Christianity, stone carvings along the hallway ceilings are Hindu design and the top-floor balcony roof (the traditional ladies' gallery) has Islamic-style arches.

When you move through to the **Private Durbar Hall** ❺, take note of the intricate ivory motifs depicting Krishna in the rosewood doors. The **Public Durbar Hall** ❻ is usually the last stop where you can admire the panoramic views of the gardens through the Islamic arches.

Private Durbar Hall

Rosewood doors lead into this hall, which is richly decorated with stained-glass ceilings, steel grill work and chandeliers. It houses the Golden Throne, only on display to the public during Dasara.

Entry to the Palace

Doll's Pavilion

The first exhibit, the Doll's Pavilion, displays the gift collection of 19th- and early-20th-century dolls, statues and Hindu idols that were given to the maharaja by dignitaries from around the world.

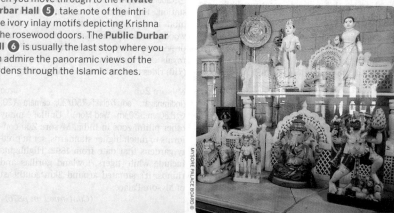

Public Durbar Hall
The open-air hall contains a priceless collection of paintings by Raja Ravi Varma and opens into an expansive balcony supported by massive pillars with an ornate painted ceiling of 10 incarnations of Vishnu.

Marriage Pavilion
This lavish hall used for royal weddings features themes of Christianity, Hindu and Islam in its design. The highlight is the octagonal painted glass ceiling featuring peacock motifs, the bronze chandelier and the colonnaded turquoise pillars.

Elephant Gate
Next to the Doll's Pavilion, this brass gate has four bronze elephants inlaid at the bottom, an intricate double-headed eagle up the top and a hybrid lion-elephant creature (the state emblem of Karnataka) in the centre.

Golden Howdah
At the far end of the Doll's Pavilion, a wooden elephant howdah decorated with 80kg of gold was used to carry the maharaja in the Dasara festival. It now carries the idol of goddess Chamundeswari.

(Continued from p873)

Karanji Lake Nature Park
PARK,

(Indiranagar; admission ₹25, camera ₹20; ☻8.30am-5.30pm) Next to the zoo, this nature park is the place to spy on various bird species, including herons, rose-ringed parakeets, painted storks and butterflies.

🏃 Activities

Emerge Spa
AYURVEDA

(📞2522500; www.thewindflower.com; Windflower Spa & Resort, Maharanapratap Rd, Nazarbad; Abhayanga massage ₹2150; ☻7am-9pm) Slick, out-of-town resort offering pampering ayurvedic sessions. Try the one-hour Abhayanga massage, which involves two therapists. It's located 3km southeast of Mysore Palace; rates include pick-up and drop-off.

Indus Valley Ayurvedic Centre
AYURVEDA

(📞2473263; www.ayurindus.com; Lalithadripura) Set on 10 hectares of gardens, 16km east of town, this classy centre derives its therapies from ancient scriptures and prescriptions. The overnight package (single/double including full board US$180/320) includes one session each of ayurveda, yoga and beauty therapy.

Swaasthya Ayurveda Centre
AYURVEDA

(📞9845913471, 6557557; www.swaasthya.com; 726/B, 6th Cross, opp Yoganarsimhaswamy Temple; treatments from ₹250) Situated around 15km north of Mysuru, Swaasthya Ayurveda Centre has professional ayurveda therapists providing traditional treatments and all-inclusive packages that include accommodation and food. Also a retreat in (Kodagu) Coorg.

🐚 Courses

Shruthi Musical Works
MUSIC

(📞9845249518; 1189 3rd Cross, Irwin Rd; per hour ₹400; ☻10.30am-9pm Mon-Sat, to 2pm Sun) Music teacher Jayashankar gets good reviews for his tabla instruction.

👉 Tours

KSTDC Transport Office
BUS TOUR

(city tour ₹210) KSTDC runs a daily Mysuru city tour, taking in city sights (excluding the palace), Chamundi Hill, Srirangapatnam and Brindavan Gardens. It starts daily at 8.30am, ends at 8.30pm and is likely to leave you breathless! Other tours go to Belur, Halebid and Sravanabelagola (₹550) on Tuesday and Thursday from 7.30am to 9pm.

All tours leave from the KSTDC transport office (p879) next to Hotel Mayura Hoysala,

from where bookings are made, or at travel agencies around town.

Royal Mysore Walks
WALKING

(📞9632044188; www.royalmysorewalks.com; 2hr walk ₹600-1500) An excellent way to familiarise yourself with Mysuru's epic history and heritage, these weekend walks offer a range of themes from royal history to food walks.

🛏 Sleeping

Mysuru attracts tourists t hroughout the year and can fill up very quickly during Dussehra (p878). Booking early is recommended.

Hotel Maurya
HOTEL $

(📞2426677; 9/5 Hanumantha Rao St; s/d from ₹180/330; ✺🛜) Maurya is your classic cheap Indian hotel with large, unremarkable rooms but it's still a good budget choice. It offers TV and AC too.

Mysore Youth Hostel
HOSTEL $

(📞2544704; www.yhmysore.com; Gangothri Layout; dm ₹130) On a patch of green lawn 3km west of town, this hostel has clean, well-maintained male and female dorms. OK, there's a 10.30pm curfew, no alcohol allowed, bucket hot water and no towels, but you can't go past these prices. Discounts are available for students. Take a city bus to Maruthi Temple, from where it's a short walk; an autorickshaw costs ₹60.

★Parklane Hotel
HOTEL $$

(📞4003500; www.parklanemysore.com; 2720 Harsha Rd; r from ₹2000; ✺@🛜) Travellers' central on Mysuru's tourist circuit, the Parklane is over-the-top kitsch but it's hard to dislike with its massive and immaculate rooms, ultracomfortable and thoughtfully outfitted with mobile-chargers and considerate toiletry kits. Its lively open-air restaurant is always buzzing, and it has a small rooftop pool too.

Hotel Mayura Hoysala
HOTEL $$

(📞2426160; www.karnatakaholidays.net; 2 Jhansi Lakshmi Bai Rd; s/d incl breakfast from ₹1350/1500, with AC ₹2480/2750; ✺) The potential of this beautiful historic building remains unrealised as this government-owned hotel continues to offer its blend of moth-balled heritage. It's still worthy of consideration, especially at these rates. The bar here is popular with Mysuru's tipplers.

★Green Hotel
HERITAGE GUESTHOUSE $$$

(📞4255000; www.greenhotelindia.com; 2270 Vinoba Rd, Jayalakshmipuram; s/d incl breakfast from ₹3880/4480; 🖭) 🖉 The character-filled Green Hotel has unndergone several fascinating reincarnations over the years. It was originally built as the Chittaranjan Palace in the 1920s by the marajah for his three daughters, before becoming a major film studio from the 1950s to 1987. Today its 31-rooms, set among charming gardens, are all run on solar power and those in the Palace building include themes such as a Writers room or kitschy Bollywood decor.

Dinner in the evenings is also wonderfully atmospheric with candle-lit tables set up on the lawn. Best of all, the profits are

MYSURU (MYSORE) ASHTANGA YOGA

What Rishikesh is to North India, Mysuru is to the South. This world-famous centre for yoga attracts thousands of international students each year to learn, practise or become certified in teaching ashtanga.

For the most part students are required to be austerely committed to the art, and will need at least a month. While in more recent times there's a growing trend for drop-in classes or week-long courses, for long-term students you'll need to register far in advance, as courses are often booked out.

Yoga Centres

Ashtanga Yoga Research Institute (AYRI; 📞 9880185500; www.kpjayi.org; 235 8th Cross, 3rd Stage, Gokulam; 1st/2nd month ₹33,700/22,500) Founded by the renowned ashtanga teacher K Pattabhi Jois, who taught Madonna her yoga moves. He has since passed away and the reigns have been handed over to his son, who is proving very popular. You need to register two months in advance.

IndeaYoga (Ānanda Yoga India; 📞 2416779; www.indeayoga.com; 144E 7th Main, Gokulam; 4/8 weeks US$1200/1600) Very popular school offering hatha and ashtanga yoga with a young guru, Bharath Shetty, who practised under the late BKS Iyengar from Pune. Also does drop-in classes.

Mystic School (📞 4288490; www.mysoreyoga.in; 100 3rd A Main Rd, Gokulam) Gets good feedback for its diverse program covering hatha and asthanga, meditation and lectures. Suitable for short- and long-term students at all levels. Offers accommodation too.

Atma Vikasa Centre (📞 2341978; www.atmavikasayoga.com; 18, 80ft Rd, Ramakrishnanagar) Backbending expert Yogacharya Venkatesh offers courses in yoga, Sanskrit and meditation. It's located in a peaceful suburb 5km southwest of the palace.

Sleeping & Eating

Most foreign yoga students congregate in the upmarket residential suburb of Gokulam. Few yoga centres offer accommodation, so you'll need to make your own arrangements; check out Facebook groups, **Ashtanga Community in Mysore** and **Mysore Yoga Community Group** for accommodation rentals. Expect to pay ₹12,000 to ₹15,000 per month for a private apartment.

Mystic School & Om Cafe (📞 4288490; www.mysoreyoga.in; 100 3rd Main Rd, Gokulam; r with/without kitchen per month ₹25,000/18,000; 🖭🖩🖩) This is the most stylish accommodation in Gokulam offering squeaky-clean studios with kitchenettes, as well as an atmospheric rooftop cafe (8am to 8.30pm), Finnish sauna and plunge pool.

Urban Oasis (📞 2410713; www.urbanoasis.co.in; 7 Contour Rd, 3rd Stage, Gokulam; r from ₹1800, monthly from ₹30,000; 🖭🖩) More of a business hotel, but popular with students for its clean, modern rooms.

Anokhi Garden Guest House (📞 9620793762; www.anokhigarden.com; 408 Contour Rd, 3rd Stage, Gokulam; s/d from ₹2000/3000; ⏰cafe 8am-12.30pm Thu-Sun; 🖩) French-run boutique guesthouse in a leafy property, with a lovely cafe that does vegetarian and vegan meals.

Anu's Bamboo Hut (📞 9900909428; anugan@gmail.com; 365, 2nd Main, 3rd Stage, Gokulam; lunch buffet ₹250; ⏰1-3pm & 5-7pm Fri-Wed) Rooftop shack cafe catering to yoga students with healthy vegetarian lunch buffets and evening smoothies. A great source of info; also offers cooking classes (₹450).

distributed to charity and environmental projects across India. It's 3km west of town.

★ **Lalitha Mahal Palace** HERITAGE HOTEL **$$$**
(☎2526100; www.lalithamahalpalace.in; r incl breakfast ₹4830-12,080; ❄@⊛) A former maharaja's guesthouse built in 1921, this majestic heritage building has been operating as a hotel since 1974. Old-world charm comes in bucket loads from the 1920s birdcage elevator to mosaic tiled floors. The heritage classic rooms are where you'll feel the history. Spacious four-poster beds sit next to antique furniture, claw-foot baths sit on marble bathroom floors, and shuttered windows look out to stately landscaped gardens. It's around 5km from the centre of town.

Royal Orchid Metropole HERITAGE HOTEL **$$$**
(☎4255566; www.royalorchidhotels.com; 5 Jhansi Lakshmi Bai Rd; s/d incl breakfast from ₹7170/8540; ❄⊛⊛) Originally built by the Wodeyars to serve as the residence of the maharaja's British guests, this is undoubtedly one of Mysuru's leading heritage hotels. The charming colonial-era structure has 30 rooms oozing historical character, and there are magic shows and snake-charming performances when tour groups pass through.

✖ Eating & Drinking

Malgudi Café CAFE **$**
(Green Hotel; 2270 Vinoba Rd, Jayalakshmipuram; cakes from ₹40, sandwiches ₹60; ⊙10am-7pm; ⊛) Set around an inner courtyard within the Green Hotel, this ambient cafe brews excellent coffees and Himalayan teas to be enjoyed with tasty cakes and sandwiches. Staff come from underprivileged backgrounds and are mostly women, and profits assist with disadvantaged communities, so you can do your bit by ordering a second cuppa.

Hotel RRR SOUTH INDIAN **$**
(Gandhi Sq; mains ₹90-130; ⊙11.30am-4.30pm & 7-11pm) Classic Andhra-style food is ladled out at this ever-busy eatery, and you may have to queue for a table during lunch. One item to try is the piping-hot veg thali (₹90) served on banana leaves.

Vinayaka Mylari SOUTH INDIAN **$**
(769 Nazarbad Main Rd; mains ₹30-50; ⊙6.30am-1.30pm & 4-8pm) Local foodies say this is one of the best eateries in town to try South Indian classics of *masala dosa* (curried vegetables in a crisp pancake) and *idlis* (South Indian spongy, round, fermented rice cakes). There's a similar branch up the road, Hotel Mylari, run by the owner's brother, and both are as good as each other.

Cafe Aramane SOUTH INDIAN **$**
(Sayyaji Rao Rd; mains ₹90-110; ⊙7am-10.30pm) ✐ In a character-filled heritage building, this typically busy South Indian eatery rolls out steaming breakfast platters for Mysuru's office-goers, and welcomes them back in the evenings with aromatic filter coffee and a convoy of delicious snacks, including speciality *dosas* each day of the week.

★ **Sapphire** INDIAN **$$**
(Lalitha Mahal Palace; mains ₹250-1000; ⊙12.30-7.45pm & 8-11pm) Dine in absolute royal Indian-style in the grand ballroom of the Lalitha Mahal Palace hotel. And grand it is, with high stained-glass ceilings, lace tablecloths and polished teak floors. Order the royal Mysore silver thali (₹485) which gets you an assortment of vegetables, breads and

---

DUSSEHRA JAMBOREE

Mysuru is at its carnivalesque best during the 10-day **Dussehra** (Dasara ; ⊙Sep/Oct) festival held September or October. During this time the Mysore Palace is dramatically lit up every evening, while the town is transformed into a gigantic fairground, with concerts, dance performances, sporting demonstrations and cultural events.

On the last day the celebrations are capped off in grand style. A dazzling procession of richly costumed elephants, garlanded idols, liveried retainers and cavalry, marches through the streets to the rhythms of clanging brass bands.

Mysuru is choc-a-bloc with tourists during the festival, especially on the final day. To bypass suffocating crowds, consider buying a **Dasara VIP Gold Card** (₹7500 for two adults). Though expensive, it assures you good seats at the final day gala and helps you beat the entry queues at other events and performances, while providing discounts on accommodation, dining and shopping. It's also possible to buy tickets (₹250 to ₹1000) just for entering the palace and Bannimantap for the final day's parades. Contact the the **Dasara Information Centre** (☎0821-2423800; www.mysoredasara.gov.in) for more details.

sweets served on lavish brassware. Week-ends are buffet menu only. The nonguest ₹1000 entrance fee is refundable if you're here to eat.

Parklane Hotel MULTICUISINE $$
(2720 Harsha Rd, Parklane Hotel; mains ₹100-140) Mysuru's most social restaurant with outdoor tables, lit up moodily by countless lanterns. The menu does delicious regional dishes from across India accompanied by live traditional music.

Tiger Trail INDIAN $$$
(Royal Orchid Metropole, 5 Jhansi Lakshmi Bai Rd; mains ₹250-750; ⊙7.30am-11.30pm) This so-phisticated restaurant works up delectable Indian dishes in a courtyard that twinkles with torches and fairy lights at night and a menu comprising jungle recipes collected from different tiger reserves across India. Also has a lunch buffet from ₹450.

Pelican Pub PUB
(Hunsur Rd; mains ₹100-190; ⊙11am-11pm) A popular watering hole located on the fringes of upmarket Gokulam, this laid-back joint serves beer for ₹65 a mug in the indoor clas-sic pub or alfresco-style garden setting out back. There's live music Wednesday.

🛍 Shopping

Mysuru is a great place to shop for its famed sandalwood products, silk saris and wooden toys. It is also one of India's major incense-manufacturing centres.

Look for the butterfly-esque 'Silk Mark'; it's an endorsement for quality silk.

Government Silk Weaving Factory CLOTHING
(☑8025586550; www.ksicsilk.com; Mananthody Rd, Ashokapuram; ⊙8.30am-4pm Mon-Sat, out-let 10.30am-7pm daily) Given that Mysuru's prized silk is made under its very sheds, this government-run outlet is the best and cheapest place to shop for the exclusive tex-tile. Behind the showroom is the factory, where you can drop by to see how the fabric is made. It's around 2km south of town.

Sandalwood Oil Factory SOUVENIRS
(Mananthody Rd, Ashokapuram; ⊙outlet 9.30am-6.30pm, factory closed Sun) A quality-assured place for sandalwood products including incense, soap, cosmetics and the prohibi-tively expensive pure sandalwood oil (if in

stock). Guided tours are available to show you around the factory.

Cauvery Arts & Crafts Emporium CRAFTS, SOUVENIRS
(Sayyaji Rao Rd; ⊙10.30am-8pm) Not the cheapest place, but the selection at this gov-ernment emporium is extensive and there's no pressure to buy.

Sumangali Silks CLOTHING
(off Gandhi Sq; ⊙10.30am-8.30pm) Excep-tionally popular with Indian ladies, this multi-level store stocks silk saris, with quality of varying degrees depending on how much you want to spend.

Sri Sharada Grand Musical Works MUSIC STORE
(2006 Seebaiah Rd) Sells a variety of tradition-al musical instruments including tabla sets and assorted percussion instruments.

ℹ Information

Most hotels have wi-fi access, otherwise internet cafes charge around ₹50 per hour.

The City bus stand's left-luggage cloakroom is open from 6am to 11pm and costs ₹10 per bag for 12 hours.

Government Hospital (☑4269806; Dhanvan-thri Rd) Has a 24-hour pharmacy.

Karnataka Tourism (☑2422096; www.karna takatourism.org; 1st fl, Hotel Mayura Hoysala, 2 Jhansi Lakshmi Bai Rd; ⊙10am-5.30pm Mon-Sat) Extremely helpful and has plenty of brochures.

KSTDC Transport Office (☑2423652; www.karnatakaholidays.net; Yatri Navas Bldg, 2 Jhansi Lakshmi Bai Rd; ⊙8.30am-8.30pm) Offers general tourist information and provides a useful map. Has counters at the train station and Central bus stand, as well as this main office.

Main Post Office (cnr Irwin & Ashoka Rds; ⊙10am-6pm Mon-Sat)

Thomas Cook (☑2420090; Silver Tower, 9/2 Ashoka Rd; ⊙9.30am-6pm Mon-Sat) Foreign currency.

ℹ Getting There & Away

BUS

The **Central bus stand** (Bengaluru-Nilgiri Rd) handles all KSRTC long-distance buses. The **City bus stand** (Sayyaji Rao Rd) is for city, Sriran-gapatnam and Chamundi Hill buses.

TRAIN

Train tickets can be bought from Mysuru's **railway reservation office** (☑131; ⊙8am-8pm Mon-Sat, to 2pm Sun).

ⓘ Getting Around

Agencies at hotels and around town rent cabs from ₹8 per kilometre, with a minimum of 250km per day, plus a daily allowance of ₹200 for the driver.

Count on around ₹800 for a day's sightseeing in an autorickshaw.

Around Mysuru (Mysore)

Consider one of KSTDC's tours (p876) for visiting sights around Mysuru.

Srirangapatnam

🎵 08236

Steeped in bloody history, the fort town of Srirangapatnam, 16km from Mysuru, is built on an island straddling the Cauvery River. The seat of Hyder Ali and Tipu Sultan's power, this town was the de facto capital of much of southern India during the 18th century. Srirangapatnam's glory days ended when the British waged an epic war against Tipu Sultan in 1799, when he was defeated and killed. His sword and the ring he wore in battle are now displayed in the British Museum in London. The ramparts, battlements and some of the gates of the fort still stand, as do a clutch of monuments. The island is now linked to the mainland by bridge.

⊙ Sights

Daria Daulat Bagh   PALACE
(Summer Palace; Indian/foreigner ₹20/100; ⊙9am-5pm) Set within lovely manicured grounds, Srirangapatnam's star attraction is Tipu's summer palace, 1km east of the fort. Built largely out of teak, the palace may not look like much from the outside, but the lavish decoration that covers every inch of its interiors is impressive. The ceilings are embellished with floral designs, while the walls bear murals depicting courtly life and Tipu's campaigns against the British. There's a small museum within displaying artefacts and interesting paintings.

Gumbaz   MAUSOLEUM
(⊙8am-6.30pm) FREE Located within a serene garden, the historically significant Gumbaz is the resting place of the legendary Tipu Sultan, his equally famed father, Hyder Ali, and his wife. The interior of the onion-dome mausoleum is painted in tiger-like motif as a tribute to the sultan. Across from the tomb is the Masjid-E-Aska tomb.

Sri Ranganathaswamy Temple   HINDU TEMPLE
(⊙7.30am-1pm & 4-8pm) Constructed in 894 AD, this attractive Vaishnavite temple has a mix of Hoysala and Vijayanagar design. Within are cavernous walkways, pillars and the centerpiece 4.5m-long reclining statue of Ranganatha, a manifestation of Vishnu.

Jamia Masjid   MOSQUE
This cream-coloured mosque with two minarets was built by the sultan in 1787 and features an interesting blend of Islamic and Hindu architecture. Climb the stairs at the back for panoramic views of the site.

Colonel Bailey's Dungeon   HISTORIC SITE
FREE North of the island, on the banks of the Cauvery, is this well-preserved 18th-century

KSRTC BUSES FROM MYSURU (MYSORE)

DESTINATION	FARE (₹)	DURATION (HR)	FREQUENCY
Bandipur	78 (O)/200 (V)	2	via Ooty every 30min 6.30am-3.30pm
Bengaluru	133 (O)/190 (R)/270 (V)	3	every 20min
Channarayapatna	84 (O)	2	hourly
Chennai	586 (R)/916 (R)	10-12	5 daily from 5pm
Ernakulam	620-820 (V)	9-11	4 daily from 5pm
Gokarna	481 (O)	12	1 daily
Hassan	114 (O)	3	hourly
Hospet	386 (O)/551 (R)	10-12	6 daily
Mangaluru	249 (O)/391 (R)/502 (V)	6	hourly
Ooty	131 (O)/193 (R)/351 (V)	4-5	12 daily

Fares: (O) Ordinary, (R) Rajahamsa Semideluxe, (V) Airavath AC Volvo

MAJOR TRAINS FROM MYSURU (MYSORE)

DESTINATION	TRAIN NO & NAME	FARE (₹)	DURATION (HR)	DEPARTURE TIME
Bengaluru	16215 Chamundi Express	2nd class/AC 75/255	2½	6.45am
Bengaluru	12613 Tippu Express	2nd class/AC chair 90/305	2½	11.15am
Bengaluru	12008 Shatabdi Express	AC chair/AC executive chair 370/765	2	2.15pm daily Thu-Tue
Chennai	12008 Shatabdi Express	AC chair/AC executive chair 935/1830	7	2.15pm daily Thu-Tue
Hosapete (for Hampi)	16592 Hampi Express	3AC/2AC sleeper 1000/1440	11½	6.40pm
Hubli	17301 Mysore Dharwad Express	sleeper/2AC 275/1055	9½	10.30pm

white-walled dungeon used to hold British prisoners of war, including Colonel Bailey who died here in 1780. Jutting out from the walls are stone fixtures used to chain prisoners. East along the river from here is **Thomas Inman's Dungeon**, hidden away beneath undulating terrain, with a more undiscovered feel that's fun to explore.

🛏 Sleeping & Eating

Mayura River View   HOTEL $$
(📞0823-6252114; d with fan/AC from ₹2000/2500; ❄) There's not much atmosphere here, but these government bungalows have a nice location on a quiet patch of riverbank. Day-trippers can pop in for lunch (mains ₹150 to ₹120) to gaze at the river while guzzling beer.

ℹ Getting There & Away

Take buses 313 or 313A (₹25 to ₹30, 45 minutes) that depart every hour from Mysuru's City bus stand. Passenger trains travelling from Mysuru to Bengaluru (₹2, 20 minutes) also stop here. Bus 307 (₹18, 30 minutes) heading to Brindavan Gardens is just across from Srirangapatnam's main bus stand. A return autorickshaw will cost from Mysuru ₹700, and a taxi around ₹1000.

ℹ Getting Around

The sights are spread out, so hiring an autorickshaw (₹300 for three hours) is the best option for getting around.

Melkote

Life in the devout Hindu town of Melkote (also called Melukote), about 50km north of Mysuru, revolves around the atmospheric 12th-century **Cheluvanarayana Temple** (Raja St; ☺8am-1pm & 5-8pm), with its rose-coloured *gopuram* (gateway tower) and ornately carved pillars. Get a workout on the hike up to the hilltop **Yoganarasimha Temple**, which offers fine views of the surrounding hills.

Three KSRTC buses shuttle daily between Mysuru and Melkote (₹100, 1½ hours).

Somnathpur

The astonishingly beautiful **Keshava Temple** (Indian/foreigner ₹5/100; ☺8.30am-5.30pm) is one of the finest examples of Hoysala architecture, on par with the masterpieces of Belur and Halebid. Built in AD 1268, this star-shaped temple, 33km from Mysuru, is adorned with superb stone sculptures depicting various scenes from the Ramayana, Mahabharata and Bhagavad Gita, and the life and times of the Hoysala kings.

Somnathpur is 12km south of Bannur and 10km north of Tirumakudal Narsipur. Take one of the half-hourly buses from Mysuru to either village (₹40, 30 minutes) and change there.

Bandipur National Park

📞 08229

Part of the Nilgiri Biosphere Reserve, **Bandipur National Park** (Indian/foreigner ₹75/1000, video ₹1000; ☺6am-9.30am & 4-6pm) is one of South India's most famous wilderness areas. Covering 880 sq km, it was once the Mysore maharajas' private wildlife reserve, and is now a protected zone for over 100 species of mammals, including tigers, elephants, leopards, gaur (Indian bison), chital (spotted deer), sambars, sloth bears, dhole (wild dogs), mongoose and langurs. It's also home to an impressive 350 species of birds.

Only 80km south of Mysuru on the Ooty road, it's easily accessible from Bengaluru and Mysuru.

🏃 Activities

Only government vehicles are permitted to run safaris within the park.

Bandipur Safari Lodge   JEEP SAFARI
(☑ 08229-236043; 2hr safari per person ₹2500; ◷ 6.30am & 4.30pm) Easily the best option is with Bandipur Safari Lodge who have open-air 4WDs and minibuses, accompanied by knowledgeable guides.

Forest Department Safari   JEEP SAFARI
(☑ 08229-236051; 1hr safari per person incl permit ₹1100; ◷ hourly departures 6am-9.30am & 3.30-6.30pm) The forest department has rushed, impersonal bus drives arranged at the park headquarters. Avoid crowded weekends.

🛏 Sleeping & Eating

Forest Department
Bungalows   GUESTHOUSE $$
(☑ 08229-236051; www.bandipurtigerreserve.in; 9-/20-bed dm ₹680/1000, bungalow foreigner from ₹3000; 🛜) Basic lodging at the park HQ is convenient for location and atmosphere, but the downside is foreigners have to pay an additional ₹1000 per night for park entry fees. Dorms are rented out in the entirety, so you won't need to share with strangers. You can book online.

Tiger Ranch   LODGE $$
(☑ 8095408505; www.tigerranch.net; Mangala Village; cottage incl full board ₹1510) The only place in Bandipur offering a genuine wilderness experience, Tiger Ranch has a reputation as somewhere you either love or hate (many find it a bit too rustic). Either way you're guaranteed a memorable stay in basic but attractive cottages that blend wonderfully into nature. It has an atmospheric thatched-roof dining hall, and evenings can be enjoyed around the bonfire. Animals visit occasionally, so you should be vigilant at night, and be warned monkeys and rodents can be serious a nuisance, so do not leave food (or any of your valuables!) lying around your room. There's no alcohol here, so bring your own. It's located 10km from the park; call ahead to arrange a pickup (₹300).

MC Resort   HOTEL $$
(☑ 9019954162; www.mcresort.in; Bangaluru-Ooty Rd, Melukamanahally; r incl full board ₹2500; 🛜🍽) Slightly tacky but low-key resort with reasonable rooms, swimming pool, wi-fi and convenient location near the park. Rates are inclusive of meals making it a good deal.

Hotel Bandipur Plaza   HOTEL $$
(☑ 08229-233200; Ooty-Mysuru Hwy; r ₹1500) Its highway location may not be what you hope for when visiting a national park, but its rooms are functional and more affordable in an otherwise pricey destination. It's nearby Bandipur Safari Lodge, so convenient for safaris into the park.

★ Dhole's Den   LODGE $$$
(☑ 08229-236062; www.dholesden.com; Kaniyanapura Village; camping/s/d incl full board from ₹3000/9000/10,000; 🛜) 🌿 With a boutique design that's lifted straight from the pages of an architectural magazine, Dhole's effectively mixes comfort with lovely pastoral surrounds. Stylish rooms are decked out with art and colourful fabrics, plus couches and deck chairs. The bungalows are worth the upgrade for extra space and privacy. It's environmentally conscious with solar power, tank water and organic vegies. Camping is available for those on a budget. It's a 20-minute drive from the park headquarters.

Serai   RESORT, LODGE $$$
(☑ 08229-236075; www.theserai.in; Kaniyanapura Village; r incl full board from ₹20,000; ❄🛜🍽) Backing on to the park, this luxurious resort has Mediterrean-inspired villas spread over 15 hectares of landscaped property that's in harmony with the natural surrounds. Thatched-roof rooms feature elegant touches such as stone-wall showers and wildlife photography on the walls. Its glassed-in restaurant and infinity pool both maximise outlooks to Nilgiri Hills.

Bandipur Safari Lodge   COTTAGES $$$
(☑ 08229-233001; www.junglelodges.com; Mysuru-Ooty Rd; r incl full board & safari Indian/foreigner ₹6420/8700; ❄) This sprawling government-owned camp has well-maintained, comfortable cottages, but it lacks character and 'safari' atmosphere.

ℹ Getting There & Away

Buses between Mysore and Ooty can drop you at Bandipur (₹78, 2½ hours), an 88km journey. Skyway (p868) can arrange an taxi from Mysuru for about ₹2000.

Nagarhole National Park & Around

Blessed with rich wildlife, attractive jungle and a scenic lake, **Nagarhole National Park** (Rajiv Gandhi National Park; Indian/foreigner ₹200/1000, video ₹1000; ⊙6am-6pm), pronounced 'nag-ar-hole-eh', is one of Karnataka's best wildlife getaways. Adjoining **Kabini Lake**, it forms an important animal corridor that runs through neighbouring Bandipur National Park – making up a part of the Nilgiri Bioshpere Reserve. Despite sharing the same wildlife, it sees much fewer visitors than Bandipur, making it all the more appealing. Set over 643 sq km, Nagarhole features a good blend of dense jungle and open sightlines along the river bank, which makes for fantastic wildlife-watching. Its lush forests are home to tigers, leopards, elephants, gaur, barking deer, dhole, bonnet macaques and common langurs, plus 270 species of birds. The park can remain closed for long stretches between July and October, when rains transform the forests into a slush-pit.

The traditional inhabitants of the land, the hunter-gatherer Jenu Kuruba people, still live in the park, despite government efforts to relocate them.

The best time to view wildlife is during summer (April to May), though winter (November to February) is more comfortable.

Government-run **4WD safaris** (Kabini River Lodge; 2½hr 4WD safari ₹2000) and **boat trips** (Kabini River Lodge; per person ₹2000) are conducted from Kabini River Lodge between 6.30am and 9.30am and 3.15pm and 6.15pm, which are good ways to see animals.

⊨ Sleeping & Eating

Many places screen wildlife docos in the evening.

Karapur Hotel   GUESTHOUSE **$$**
(☑9945904840; Karapura roundabout; r ₹1000) The only cheapish option close to Kabini is this simple lodge with a few rooms above a shop in Karapura, 3km from the park.

★**Waterwoods Lodge**   GUESTHOUSE **$$$**
(☑082-28264421; www.waterwoods.in; s/d incl full board ₹6500/8500; ❋᠆᠎) Situated on a grassy embankment overlooking scenic Kabini Lake, Waterwoods has undergone extensive renovations to evolve from intimate guesthouse to stunning boutique lodge. Most rooms have balconies with views, swing chairs, hardwood floors and designer flair. It's kid-friendly with trampoline, infinity pool, free canoe hire and wood-fired pizzas.

Bison Resort   LODGE **$$$**
(☑080-41278708; www.thebisonresort.com; Gundathur Village; s/d incl full board from US$315/350, camping per person from ₹2500; ❋) Inspired by the luxury safari lodges in Africa, Bison succeeds in replicating the classic wilderness experience with a stunning waterfront location and choice between canvas-walled cottages, stilted bungalows or bush camping. Adding to the experience is the wooden-decked swimming pool sundowners, nightly bonfires, bush dinners and expert naturalists.

KAAV Safari Lodge   LODGE **$$$**
(☑08228-264492; www.kaav.com; Mallali Cross, Kabini; s/d incl full board ₹13,000/16,000; ❋᠎᠆) A swish designer hotel, KAAV has open-plan rooms with polished concrete floors, modern bathrooms, king-sized beds and spacious balconies that open directly to the national park. Otherwise head up to the viewing tower to lounge on plush day beds, or take a dip in its infinity pool.

Kabini River Lodge   LODGE **$$$**
(☑08228-264405; www.junglelodges.co; per person India/foreigner incl full board & activities from ₹6280/11,420; ❋) Located in the serene, tree-lined grounds of the former Mysore maharaja's hunting lodge, these now government-run bungalows have a prime location beside the lake with a choice between large tented cottages and bungalows. It has an atmospheric colonial-style bar.

ℹ Getting There & Away

The park's main entrance is 93km southwest of Mysuru. A few buses depart daily from Mysore to Karapuram (₹65, 2½ hours), around 3km from Kabini Lake.

Kodagu (Coorg) Region

Nestled amid ageless hills that line the southernmost edge of Karnataka is the luscious Kodagu (Coorg) region, gifted with emerald landscapes and acres of plantations. A major centre for coffee and spice production, this rural expanse is also home to the unique Kodava race, believed to have descended from migrating Persians and Kurds, or perhaps even

Greeks left behind from Alexander the Great's armies. The uneven terrain and cool climate make it a fantastic area for trekking, birdwatching or lazily ambling down little-trodden paths winding around carpeted hills. All in all, Kodagu is rejuvenation guaranteed.

Kodagu was a state in its own right until 1956, when it merged with Karnataka. The region's chief town and transport hub is Madikeri, but for an authentic Kodagu experience, you have to venture into the plantations. Avoid weekends, when places can quickly get filled up.

Activities

Exploring the region by foot is a highlight for many visitors. Treks are part cultural experience, part nature encounter, involving hill climbs, plantation visits, forest walks and homestays.

The best season for trekking is October to March; there are no treks during monsoon. The most popular peaks are the seven-day trek to Tadiyendamol (1745m), and to Pushpagiri (1712m) and Kotebetta (1620m). As well as good walking shoes you'll need insect repellant. A trekking guide is essential for navigating the labyrinth of forest tracks.

V-Track   TREKKING
(☑ 08272-229102, 08272-229974; v_track@rediffmail.com; College Rd, Madekeri, opp Corporation Bank; ☺ 10am-2pm & 4.30-8pm Mon-Sat) Veteran guides Raja Shekhar and Ganesh can arrange one- to weeklong treks, which include guide, accommodation and food. Rates are ₹950 to ₹1150 per person per day, depending upon group size.

Coorg Trails   TREKKING
(☑ 08272-220491, 9886665459; www.coorgtrails.com; Main Rd; ☺ 9am-8.30pm) Another recommended outfit, Coorg Trails can arrange day treks around Madikeri for ₹450 per person, and a 16km trek to Kotebetta, including an overnight stay in a village (from ₹850).

Madikeri (Mercara)

☑ 08272 / POP 32,500 / ELEV 1525M

Also known as Mercara, this congested market town is spread out along a series of ridges. The only reason for coming here is to organise treks or sort out the practicalities of travel.

◉ Sights & Activities

Madikeri Fort   HISTORIC SITE
Originally Tipu Sultan's fort in the 16th century, before Raja Lingarajendra II took over in 1812, today it's the less glamorous site of the municipal headquarters. Within the fort's walls are the hexagonal palace (now the dusty district commissioner's office) and colonial-era church, which houses a quirky museum (☺ 10am-5.30pm Sun-Fri) FREE displaying eclectic exhibits.

Raja's Seat   VIEWPOINT
(MG Rd; entry ₹5; ☺ 5.30am-7.30pm) The place to come to watch the sunset, as the raja himself did, with fantastic outlooks to rolling hills and endless valleys.

Raja's Tombs   HISTORIC BUILDING
(Gaddige) FREE The quietly beautiful Raja's Tombs are built in Indo-Sarcenic style with domed tombs that serve as the resting place for Kodava royalty and dignitaries. Located 7km from town, an autorickshaw costs ₹200 return.

Abbi Falls   WATERFALL
A spectacular sight after the rainy season, these 21.3m-high falls can pack a punch. It's ₹250 for a return autorickshaw, including stop off at Raja's Tombs.

Coorg Sky Adventures   SCENIC FLIGHT
(☑ 9448954384; www.coorgskyadventures.com; 10-/30min ₹2500/4850) Head up into the skies via a microlight flight for tremendous views of Coorg's lush scenery.

Ayurjeevan   AYURVEDA
(☑ 944974779; www.ayurjeevancoorg.com; Kohinoor Rd, Madikeri; 1hr from ₹1200; ☺ 7am-7pm) An ayurvedic 'hospital' that offers a range of intriguing and rejuvenating techniques. It's a short walk from the State Bank India.

🛏 Sleeping & Eating

With fantastic guesthouses in the surrounding plantations, there's no reason to stay in Madikeri, though you may have to spend a night if you arrive late.

Hotel Chitra   HOTEL $
(☑ 08272-225372; www.hotelchitra.co.in; School Rd; dm ₹250, d from ₹750, with AC ₹1620; ❄) A short walk off Madikeri's main traffic intersection is this austere hotel, providing low-cost, no-frills rooms. Friendly service

coupled with spacious rooms and dorms make it a good budget option.

Hotel Mayura Valley View HOTEL $$
(✏228387; d incl breakfast from ₹2400; ✻) On the hilltop past Raja's Seat, this government hotel is one of Madikeri's best, with large bright rooms and fantastic valley views. Its restaurant-bar with terrace overlooking the valley is a great spot for a beer.

★**Coorg Cuisine** INDIAN $$
(Main Rd; mains ₹100-120; ☺noon-4pm & 7-10pm) Finally a place that makes an effort to serve regional dishes, cooking up unique Kodava specialities such as *pandhi barthadh* (pork dry fry) and *kadambuttu* (rice dumplings), and some tasty veg options too. It's above a shop on the 1st floor on the main road.

ℹ Information

State Bank of India (✏229959; College Rd) and **HDFC Bank** (Racecourse Rd) have ATMs.
Cyber Inn (Kohinoor Rd; per hour ₹20; ☺9am-9pm)
Travel Coorg (✏08272-321009; www.travelcoorg.in; ☺24hr) Provides a good overview of things to do, as well as arranging homestays, trekking guides and other activities. It's outside the KSRTC bus stand.

ℹ Getting There & Away

Regular buses depart from the KSRTC bus stand for Bengaluru (fan/AC ₹400/485, six hours), stopping in Mysuru (₹200/250, 3½ hours) en route. Deluxe buses go to Mangaluru (₹200/280, four hours, three daily), while frequent ordinary buses head to Hassan (₹120, four hours).

Around Madikeri

Spread around Madikeri are Kodagu's enchanting and leafy spice and coffee plantations. Numerous estates here offer 'homestays', which are actually more like B&Bs (and normally closed during monsoon). Some seriously luxurious high-end resorts have opened up too.

✖ Activities

★**Jiva Spa** AYURVEDA
(✏0827-2665800; www.tajhotels.com/jivaspas/index.html; Vivanta, Galibeedu) Surrounded by rainforest, Jiva Spa at the stunning Vivanta hotel (p886) is *the* place to treat yourself with a range of rejuvenating treatments

amid lavish atmosphere. Appointments essential.

Swaasthya Ayurveda Retreat Village AYURVEDA
(www.swaasthya.com; Bekkesodlur Village; s/d incl full board & yoga class ₹2500/4000; ☎) For an exceptionally peaceful and refreshing ayurvedic vacation, head to south Coorg to soothe your soul among the lush greenery on 1.6 hectares of coffee and spice plantations.

🛏 Sleeping

★**Golden Mist** HOMESTAY $$
(✏9448903670, 08272-265629; www.golden-mist.net; Galibeedu; s/d incl full board ₹2500/4000; @☎) One of Coorg's finest plantation stays, the friendly Indian-German-managed Golden Mist has character-filled loft-style cottages on its lovely property of rice paddies and tea-, coffee- and spice-plantations. Meals are tasty rustic dishes made from the farm's organic produce, including homemade cheese and bread. Rates include highly recommended walks and plantation tours. A rickshaw costs ₹170 from Madikeri.

Rainforest Retreat GUESTHOUSE $$
(✏08272-265638, 08272-265639; www.rainforestours.com; Galibeedu; dm incl breakfast ₹1000, s/d tent ₹1500/2000, cottage from ₹2500/4000) ✐ A nature-soaked refuge immersed within forest and plantations, Rainforest Retreat is supported by an NGO that devotes

ℹ SPICE OF LIFE

If you have space in your bag, pick up some local spices and natural produce from Madikeri's main market. Here you'll find coffee beans, vanilla, nutmeg, lemongrass, pepper and cardamom, which all come in from the plantations. Sickly sweet 'wines' are also widely available.

Several chocolatiers also try their hand at handmade truffles using spices such as cardamom, pepper and coffee. Don't expect Belgian quality, but there are some interesting varieites such as betel-nut chocolate from **Choci Coorg** (www.chocicoorg.com; opp bus stand, Madikeri; ☺9am-9.30pm) or fiery birdseye chilli chocolate from **Chocotila** (Green Acres; ✏08272-238525; Yavakopadi Village, Kabbinakad).

itself to exploring organic and ecofriendly ways of life. Accommodation is lazy camping (pre-pitched tents with beds), cottages with solar power or private dorms. Rates include plantation tours, birdwatching and treks. Check the website for volunteering opportunities. An autorickshaw from Madikeri is ₹200.

★ **Vivanta** HOTEL $$$
(☑ 08272-665800; www.vivantabytaj.com; Galibeedu; r from ₹13,000; @ 🛜 ☀) Another stunner by the Taj Group, built across 73 hectares of misty rainforest. Its stylish design incorporates principles of space and minimalism, and effectively blends itself into its environment. Old cattle tracks lead to rooms, with pricier ones featuring private indoor pools, fireplaces and butlers. Meanwhile the 9000 sq ft presidential suite, costing a cool lakh (₹100,000), is the size of a small village.

Other highlights are its stunning views from the lobby and infinity pool, the outdoor ampitheatre surrounded by water, ayurvedic spa and game console room.

Kakkabe

☑ 08272
About 40km from Madikeri, the village of Kakkabe is an ideal base to plan an assault on Kodagu's highest peak, Tadiyendamol.

At the bottom of the summit, 3km from Kakkabe, is the picturesque **Nalakunad Palace** (🕘 9am-5pm) **FREE**, the restored hunting lodge of a Kodagu king dating from 1794. The caretaker will happily show you around.

Regular buses run to Kabbinakad from Madikeri (₹50, 1½ hours) or it's around ₹500 for an autorickshaw.

🛏 Sleeping & Eating

Honey Valley Estate GUESTHOUSE $
(☑ 08272-238339; www.honeyvalleyindia.in; r with/without bathroom from ₹800/550) Located 3km from Kakkabe this wonderful trekking guesthouse sits at 1250m above sea level, transporting you into a lovely cool, fresh climate with plenty of birdlife. The owners' friendliness, ecomindedness and local knowledge of 18 trekking routes is a plus. It's accessible by jeep (inclusive of rates) or by a one-hour uphill walk.

DON'T MISS

BYLAKUPPE

Tiny Bylakuppe was among the first refugee camps set up in South India to house thousands of Tibetans who fled following the 1959 Chinese invasion. Over 10,000 Tibetans live here (including some 3300 monks), making it South India's largest Tibetan settlement.

The area's highlight is the atmospheric **Namdroling Monastery** (www.palyul.org), home to the spectacular **Golden Temple** (Padmasambhava Buddhist Vihara; 🕘 7am-8pm), presided over by three 18m-high gold-plated Buddha statues. The temple is at its dramatic best when prayers are in session and it rings out with gongs, drums and the drone of hundreds of young monks chanting. You're welcome to sit and meditate; look for the small blue guest cushions lying around. The **Zangdogpalri Temple** (🕘 7am-8pm), a similarly ornate affair, is next door.

Foreigners are not allowed to stay overnight in Bylakuppe without a Protected Area Permit (PAP) from the Ministry of Home Affairs in Delhi, which can take up to five months to process. Contact the **Tibet Bureau Office** (☑ 11-26479737; www.tibetbureau.in; New Delhi) for details. Day-trippers are welcome to visit, however.

If you have a permit, the simple **Paljor Dhargey Ling Guest House** (☑ 8223-258686; pdguesthouse@yahoo.com; d ₹500) is opposite the Golden Temple. For delicious momos (Tibetan dumplings) or thukpa (noodle soup), pop into the Tibetan-run **Malaya Restaurant** (opp Golden Temple; momos ₹60-90; 🕘 7am-9pm). Otherwise there are many hotels in nearby Kushnalagar, including **Ice Berg** (☑ 9880260544; Main Rd; s/d from ₹600/800), with clean functional rooms.

Autorickshaws (shared/solo ₹15/40) run to Bylakuppe from Kushalnagar, 6km away. Buses frequently run 34km to Kushalnagar from Madikeri (₹40, 45 minutes) and Hassan (₹78, 2½ hours). Most buses on the Mysuru–Madikeri route stop at Kushalnagar (₹85 to ₹180, two hours).

Chingaara GUESTHOUSE $$
(☑08272-204488; www.chingaara.com; Kabbini-akad; r incl half board ₹1800-2900) Run by the same family as Honey Valley Estate (from which it's just up the hill), this delightful farmhouse has roaming donkeys and is surrounded by verdant coffee plantations. Attractive rooms are spacious, and most have good views – room 9 especially. It's 2.5km up a steep hill; call ahead to get Chingaara's jeep to pick you up from Kabbinakad junction.

⭐**Tamara Resort** RESORT $$$
(☑0827-2238000; www.thetamara.com; Yavaka-padi Village; r incl meals & activities from ₹21,500; ❈🛜) Immersed within 70 hectares of coffee plantations, this romantic nature resort has stilted cottages that soar above the lush green surrounds. Luxurious rooms all have teak floorboards, balconies, king-sized beds, chessboard coffee tables and French-press plungers with Coorg coffee. Its memorable restaurant is raised above the plantations with a glass-bottom floor to look down upon.

Additional highlights are its spa, yoga classes and coffee cupping sessions. It's popular with honeymooners.

Belur & Halebid

☑ 08177 / ELEV 968M

The Hoysala temples at Halebid (also known as Halebeedu) and Belur (also called Beluru) are the apex of one of the most artistically exuberant periods of ancient Hindu cultural development. Architecturally, they are South India's answer to Khajuraho in Madhya Pradesh and Konark near Puri in Odisha.

Only 16km lie between Belur and Halebid; they are connected by frequent buses from 6.30am to 7pm (₹25, 40 minutes).

To get here you'll need to pass through the busy transport hub of Hassan – easily accessible from Mysuru and Bengaluru, with buses departing regularly to Mysore (₹115, three hours), Bengaluru (semideluxe/deluxe ₹195/392, 3½ hours) and Mangaluru (₹166/380, 3½ hours). From Hassan's well-organised train station, several passenger trains head to Mysuru daily (2nd class ₹140, 2½hours). For Bengaluru, there's the red-eye 2.50am 16518 Bangalore Express (sleeper ₹180, 5½ hours). It's also possible to visit on day trip from Bengaluru or Mysuru with a KSTDC tour (p861).

Belur

The **Channakeshava Temple** (Temple Rd; ⏱7.30am-7.30pm) was commissioned in AD 1116 to commemorate the Hoysalas' victory over the neighbouring Cholas. It took more than a century to build, and is currently the only one among the three major Hoysala sites still in daily use – try to be there for the ritual *puja* (prayer) ceremonies at around 8.45am and 6.45pm. Some parts of the temple, such as the exterior lower friezes, were not sculpted to completion and are thus less elaborate than those of the other Hoysala temples. However, the work higher up is unsurpassed in detail and artistry, and is a glowing tribute to human skill. Particularly intriguing are the angled bracket figures depicting women in ritual dancing poses. While the front of the temple is reserved for images depicting erotic sections from the Kamasutra, the back is strictly for gods. The roof of the inner sanctum is held up by rows of exquisitely sculpted pillars, no two of which are identical in design.

Scattered around the temple complex are other smaller temples, a marriage hall which is still used, and the seven-storey *gopuram*, which has sensual sculptures explicitly portraying the activities of dancing girls. Guides can be hired for ₹250.

Hotel Mayura Velapuri (☑0817-7222209; Kempegowda Rd; d with fan/AC from ₹1000/1350; ❈), a state-run hotel gleaming with post-renovation glory, is located on the way to the temple. Its restaurant-bar serves a variety of Indian dishes (from ₹80) to go with beer. The cheaper **Sumukha Residency** (☑08177-222181; Temple Rd; s/d ₹350/730) is another option.

There's an Axis ATM on the road leading to the temple.

There are frequent buses to/from Hassan (₹40 to ₹90, 45 minutes), 38km away.

Halebid

Construction of the stunning **Hoysaleswara Temple** (⏱dawn-dusk), Halebid's claim to fame, began around AD 1121 and went on for more than 190 years. It was never completed, but nonetheless stands today as a masterpiece of Hoysala architecture. The interior of its inner sanctum, chiselled out of black stone, is marvellous. On the outside, the temple's richly sculpted walls are covered with a flurry of Hindu deities, sages, stylised animals and friezes depicting the life of the Hoysala rulers. Two statues of

Nandi (Shiva's bull) sit to the left of the main temple, facing the inner sanctum. Guides are available for ₹250.

The temple is in large gardens, adjacent to which is a small museum (admission ₹5; ⊙9am-5pm Sat-Thu) with a collection of beautiful sculptures from around Halebid.

Take some time out to visit the nearby, smaller Kedareswara Temple, or a little-visited enclosure containing three Jain temples about 500m away.

Hotel Mayura Shanthala (☑0817-7273224; d incl breakfast with AC from ₹1500; ❀🛜), set in a leafy garden opposite the temple complex, is the best sleeping option.

Regular buses depart for Hassan (₹35, one hour), 33km away, while buses to Belur are ₹25 for the 15km journey.

Sravanabelagola
☑ 08176

Atop the bald rock of Vindhyagiri Hill, the 17.5m-high statue of the Jain deity Gomateshvara (Bahubali) is visible long before you reach the pilgrimage town of Sravanabelagola. Viewing the statue close up is the main reason for heading to this sedate town, whose name means 'Monk of the White Pond'.

◉ Sights

Gomateshvara Statue   JAIN MONUMENT
(Bahubali; ⊙6.30am-6.30pm) A steep climb up 614 steps takes you to the top of Vindhyagiri Hill, the summit of which is lorded over by the towering naked statue of the Jain deity Gomateshvara (Bahubali). Commissioned by a military commander in the service of the Ganga king Rachamalla and carved out of a single piece of granite by the sculptor Aristenemi in AD 98, it is said to be the world's tallest monolithic statue. Leave your shoes at the foot of the hill.

Bahubali was the son of emperor Vrishabhadeva, who later became the first Jain *tirthankar* (revered teacher) Adinath. Embroiled in fierce competition with his brother Bharatha to succeed his father, Bahubali realised the futility of material gains and renounced his kingdom. As a recluse, he meditated in complete stillness in the forest until he attained enlightenment. His lengthy meditative spell is denoted by vines curling around his legs and an ant hill at his feet.

Every 12 years, millions flock here to attend the Mastakabhisheka (⊙Feb; 2018) ceremo-

ny, when the statue is dowsed in holy waters, pastes, powders, precious metals and stones.

Jain Temples
Apart from the Bahubali statue, there are several interesting Jain temples in town. The Chandragupta Basti (Chandragupta Community; ⊙6am-6pm), on Chandragiri Hill opposite Vindhyagiri, is believed to have been built by Emperor Ashoka. The Bhandari Basti (Bhandari Community; ⊙6am-6pm), in the southeast corner of town, is Sravanabelagola's largest temple. Nearby, Chandranatha Basti (Chandranatha Community; ⊙6am-6pm) has well-preserved paintings depicting Jain tales.

🛏 Sleeping & Eating

The local Jain organisation SDJMI (☑08176-257258) handles bookings for its 15 guesthouses (double/triple ₹250/310). The office is behind the Vidyananda Nilaya Dharamsala, past the post office.

Hotel Raghu   HOTEL $
(☑08176-257238; s/d from ₹400/500, d with AC ₹900; ❀) Basic but clean rooms with a popular vegetarian restaurant downstairs, which works up an awesome veg thali (₹80).

ℹ Getting There & Away

There are no direct buses from Sravanabelagola to Hassan or Belur – you must go to Channarayapatna (₹43, 20 minutes) and catch an onward connection there. Three daily buses run direct to Bengaluru (₹156, 3½ hours) and Mysuru (₹85, 2½ hours).

KARNATAKA COAST

Mangaluru (Mangalore)
☑ 0824 / POP 484,785

Alternating from relaxed coastal town to hectic nightmare, Mangaluru (more commonly known as Mangalore) has a Jekyll and Hyde thing going, but it's a pleasant enough place to break up your trip. While there's not a lot to do here, it has an appealing off-the-beaten-path feel, and the spicy seafood dishes are sensational.

It sits at the estuaries of the picturesque Netravathi and Gurupur Rivers on the Arabian Sea coast and has been a major pit stop on international trade routes since the 6th century AD. It was ruled by the Portuguese during the 16th and 17th centuries, before the British took over a century later.

Mangaluru (Mangalore)

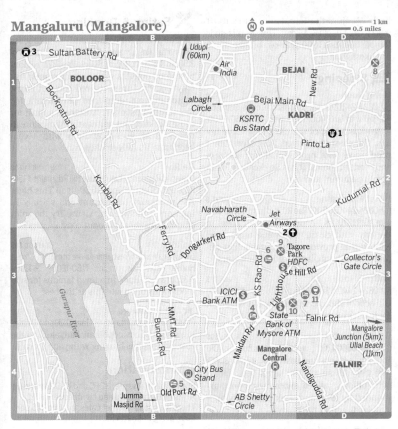

Sights

Ullal Beach
BEACH

While it's no Om Beach, this stretch of golden sand is a good place to escape the city heat. It's about an hour's drive south of town. An autorickshaw is ₹200 one way, or catch the frequent bus 44A or 44C (₹10) from the City bus stand.

St Aloysius College Chapel
CHURCH

(Lighthouse Hill; ⊙9am-6pm) Catholicism's roots in Mangaluru date back to the arrival of the Portuguese in the early 1500s, and one of the most impressive legacies is the 1880 Sistine Chapel–like St Aloysius chapel, with its walls and ceilings painted with brilliant frescoes.

Sultan's Battery
FORT

(Sultan Battery Rd; ⊙6am-6pm) The only remnant of Tipu Sultan's fort is this small lookout with views over scenic backwaters. It's

Mangaluru (Mangalore)

⊙ Sights
1 Kadri Manjunatha Temple	D2
2 St Aloysius College Chapel	C3
3 Sultan's Battery	A1

⊖ Sleeping
4 Adarsh Hotel	C3
5 Gateway Hotel	B4
6 Hotel Manorama	C3
7 Hotel Roopa	D3

⊗ Eating
8 Gajalee	D1
9 Kadal	C3
10 Lalith Bar & Restaurant	C3

⊖ Drinking & Nightlife
11 Liquid Lounge	D3

4km from the city centre on the headland of the old port; bus 16 will get you there.

Kadri Manjunatha Temple HINDU TEMPLE
(Kadri; ⊙ 6am-1pm & 4-8pm) This Kerala-style temple houses a 1000-year-old bronze statue of Lokeshwara.

🛏 Sleeping

Hotel Roopa HOTEL $
(☑ 0824-2421272; www.roopahotel.com; Balmatta Rd; s/d with fan ₹400/1000, with AC ₹1250/1500; ❄🛜) Easily one of the city's best value hotels, the centrally located Roopa combines good prices with professional management and modern rooms. It has an excellent basement restaurant and bar.

Hotel Manorama HOTEL $
(☑ 0824-2440306; KS Rao Rd; s/d from ₹600/630, with AC ₹1070; ❄) A decent budget hotel in the city with clean, good-value rooms and a lobby that provides a memorable first impression with its display of Hindu statues.

Adarsh Hotel HOTEL $
(☑ 0824-2440878; Market Rd; s/d ₹310/460) Old-school cheapie with divey but well-kept rooms. It's often booked out.

Gateway Hotel HOTEL $$$
(☑ 0824-6660420; www.tajhotels.com; Old Port Rd; s/d incl breakfast from ₹7170/8060; ❄@🛜☲) Plasma TVs, large beds laden with pillows, and a swimming pool surrounded by lawn and deck chairs, it's high standards across the board.

Summer Sands Beach Resort HOTEL $$$
(☑ 8861373737; www.summersands.in; Ullal Beach; d incl half board ₹6780; ❄@☲) Set amid palm groves on a remote patch along Ullal Beach, Summer Sands offers kitschy bungalows in a tropical-resort-style set-up. Its restaurant has a great seafood selection.

🍴 Eating & Drinking

★**Lalith Bar & Restaurant** SEAFOOD $$
(Balmatta Rd; mains ₹150-400; ⊙ 11.30am-3.30pm & 6.30-11.30pm) Specialising in regional seafood delights such as spicy masala fish fry smothered in saucy red coconut curry, or scrumptious deep-fried prawn rava fry, this scruffy upstairs restaurant is a must for those seeking out authentic Mangalorean dishes. It all goes beautifully with a cold beer, from its fully stocked bar.

Kadal SOUTH INDIAN $$
(Nalapad Residency, Lighthouse Hill Rd; mains ₹150-220; ⊙ 11.30am-3.30pm & 6.30-11pm) This high-rise restaurant has elegant and warmly lit interiors with sweeping views. Try the spicy chicken *uruval* (a coconut coastal curry).

Gajalee SEAFOOD $$$
(www.gajalee.com/rest_mangalore.html; Circuit House, Kadri Hills; mains ₹150-1200; ⊙ 11am-3.30pm & 6.30-11pm) In a town famous for seafood, locals often cite this as the best.

★**Liquid Lounge** PUB
(☑ 4255175; Balmatta Rd; ⊙ 11am-11.30pm) Bringing a slice of cosmopolitan Bangalore to the coast, this pub is buzzing with young locals.

ℹ️ Information

State Bank of Mysore, HDFC and ICICI Bank have ATMs on Balmatta Rd and Lighthouse Hill Rd. There are cheap internet cafes, costing ₹15 per hour, along Balmatta Rd.

ℹ️ Getting There & Away

AIR
The **airport** (☑ 0824-2254252; www.mangaloreairport.com) is precariously perched atop a plateau in Bajpe, about 20km northeast of town.

MAJOR TRAINS FROM MANGALORE CENTRAL

DESTINATION	TRAIN NO & NAME	FARE (₹)	DURATION (HR)	DEPARTURE TIME
Bengaluru	16524 Bangalore Express	sleeper/2AC 300/1150	11½	8.55pm
Chennai	12686 Chennai Express	sleeper/2AC 460/1715	15½	4.20pm
Gokarna	16523 Karwar Express	sleeper/2AC 205/770	4½	8.20am
Gokarna	56640 Madgaon Passenger	2nd-class 75	4	5.50am
Thiruvananthapuram	16630 Malabar Express	sleeper/2AC 345/1335	15	6.20pm

There are daily flights to Mumbai, Bengaluru, Hyderabad and Chennai.

Air India (☎ 2451046; Hathill Rd)
Jet Airways (☎ 2441181; Ram Bhavan Complex, KS Rao Rd)
SpiceJet (☎ 1800-1803333)

BUS

The **KSRTC bus stand** (☎ 0824-2211243; Bejai Main Rd) is 3km from the city centre. Deluxe buses depart half-hourly to Bengaluru (₹370 to ₹720, eight to nine hours), via Madikeri (₹140 to ₹300, five hours) and Mysuru (₹260 to ₹500, seven hours).

Dharmasthala ₹72, 2½ hours, 2.20pm daily
Ernakulam ₹793, nine hours, night bus
Gokarna ₹234, 5½ hours, 12.45pm daily
Hassan ₹65 to ₹356, five hours, 10 daily
Panaji ₹352 to ₹580, 8½ hours, twice daily

For Udupi (₹55, 1½ hours) head to the **City bus stand** (State Bank stand).

TRAIN

The main train station Mangalore Central is south of the city centre.

Mangalore Junction (aka Kankanadi), 5km east of Mangaluru, has the 1.55pm 12134 Mumbai Express, stopping at Margao in Goa (sleeper/2AC ₹290/1035, five hours), continuing to Mumbai (sleeper/2AC ₹540/2045, 14½ hours).

ⓘ Getting Around

To get to the airport, take buses 47B or 47C from the City bus stand, or catch a taxi (₹500).

An autorickshaw to Mangalore Junction (Kankanadi) train station costs around ₹80, or take bus 9 or 11B.

Dharmasthala

Inland from Mangaluru are a string of Jain temple towns, such as Venur, Mudabidri and Karkal. The most interesting among them is Dharmasthala, 75km east of Mangaluru by the Netravathi River. Some 10,000 pilgrims pass through this town every day. During holidays and major festivals such as the five-day pilgrim festival of **Lakshadeepotsava** (☉ Nov), the footfall can go up tenfold.

The **Manjunatha Temple** (☉ 6.30am-2pm & 5-9pm) is Dharmasthala's main shrine, devoted to Shiva. Men have to enter bare-chested with legs covered. Simple free meals are available in the temple's **kitchen** (☉ 11.30am-2.15pm & 7.30-10pm), attached to a hall that can seat up to 3000.

Associated sights in town include the 12m-high **statue of Bahubali** at Ratnagiri

Hill, and the **Manjusha Museum** (admission ₹5; ☉ 9am-1pm & 4.30-9pm), which houses an eclectic collection of everything from artefacts to quirky collections of vintage cameras, telephones and typewriters. Don't forget to visit the fantastic **Car Museum** (admission ₹3; ☉ 8.30am-1pm & 2-7pm), home to 48 vintage autos, including a 1903 Renault and 1920s Studebaker President used by Mahatma Gandhi.

Should you wish to stay, contact the helpful **temple office** (☎ 0825-6277121; www.shridharmasthala.org) for accommodation in pilgrim lodges (per person ₹50).

There are frequent buses to Dharmasthala from Mangaluru (₹72, 2½ hours).

Udupi (Udipi)

☎ 0820

Udupi is a buzzing yet relaxed pilgrim town that's home to the atmospheric 13th-century **Krishna Temple** (Car St; ☉ 3.30am-10pm), which draws thousands of Hindu pilgrims throughout the year. Surrounded by eight maths (monasteries), it's a hive of ritual activity, with temple musicians playing at the entrance, elephants on hand for *puja*, and pilgrims constantly passing through. Non-Hindus are welcome inside the temple; men must enter bare-chested. Come late afternoon for the best atmosphere.

Udupi is famed for its vegetarian food, and recognised across India for its sumptuous thali and as the birthplace of the humble dosa.

ICICI (Car St) has an ATM near the temple.

🛏 Sleeping & Eating

Shri Vidyasamuda Choultry HOTEL $
(☎ 2520820; Car St; r ₹150-300) There are several pilgrim hotels near the temple, but this simple offering is the best with views looking over the ghat.

Hotel Sriram Residency HOTEL $$
(☎ 2530761; www.hotelsriramresidency.com; r with fan/AC from ₹940/1680; ❄) Udupi's most modern hotel is set over numerous floors, along with multiple restaurants and bars. It's a short walk from the temple complex.

Woodlands INDIAN $
(Dr UR Rao Complex; dosas from ₹60, thalis from ₹90; ☉ 8am-3.15pm & 5.30-10.30pm) In the town that's famous for its vegetarian fare, Woodlands is regarded as one of the best places to sample the goods. It's a short walk south of Krishna Temple.

❶ Getting There & Away

Udupi is 58km north of Mangaluru along the coast; regular buses ply the route (₹56, 1½ hours). Buses also head to Gokarna (₹180, six hours) and Bengaluru (₹410 to ₹870, 10 hours). Regular buses head to Malpe (₹8, 30 minutes).

Malpe

📵 0820

A fishing harbour on the west coast 4km from Udupi, Malpe has nice beaches ideal for flopping about in the surf. The **Paradise Isle Beach Resort** (📵 0820-2538777; www.theparadiseisle.com; r with fan/AC from ₹2000/4750; ✱@🌐✱) has decent rooms; ask for one with a sea view. It can also organise **houseboat cruises** (per couple ₹4000; ☺Oct-Mar) on backwaters that are similarly scenic to Kerala's, yet all a bit undeveloped.

From Malpe pier you can take a government ferry (₹100 return, 45 minutes, departing when full from 9am to 5.30pm) or charter a private ferry from Malpe Beach to tiny **St Mary's Island**. It's known for where Portuguese explorer Vasco da Gama supposedly landed in 1498, and for curious hexagonal basalt formations No boats run from June to mid-October. Buses to Udupi are ₹8, and an autorickshaw ₹80.

Jog Falls

📵 08186

Nominally the highest waterfalls in India, Jog Falls only come to life during the monsoon. The tallest of the four falls is the Raja, which drops 293m. For a good view of the falls, bypass the area close to the bus stand and hike to the foot of the falls down a 1200-plus-step path. Watch out for leeches during the wet season.

Hotel Mayura Gerusoppa (📵 08186-244732; d with fan/AC from ₹1800/2200; ✱), near the car park, has a few enormous, musty double rooms. Stalls near the bus stand serve thalis and noodle dishes.

Jog Falls isn't the easiest place to reach without a car, so most people hire a taxi; a return trip from Gokarna costs around ₹2000. Otherwise you can get a string of buses which head via Kumta and turn off at Honavar (₹66); or Shimoga (Shivamogga) if coming via Bengaluru (₹468, nine hours).

Gokarna

📵 08386

A regular nominee among travellers' favourite beaches in India, Gokarna is a more laid-back and less-commercialised version of Goa. It attracts a crowd for a low-key, chilled-out beach holiday and not for full-scale parties. Most accommodation is in thatched bamboo huts along its several stretches of blissful coast.

There are two Gokarnas; adjacent to the beaches is the sacred Hindu pilgrim town of Gokarna, full of ancient temples that come to life during festivals such as **Shivaratri** (☺Feb/Mar) and **Ganesh Chaturthi** (☺Sep). While its lively bazaar is an interesting place to visit, most foreign tourists don't hang

---

RANI ABBAKKA THE WARRIOR QUEEN

The legendary exploits of Rani Abbakka, one of India's first freedom fighters – who happened to be a female – is one that gets surprisingly little attention outside the Mangaluru region. An Indian Joan of Arc, her inspiring story is just waiting to be picked up by a Bollywood/Hollywood screenwriter.

As the Portuguese consolidated power along India's western coastline in the 16th century, seizing towns across Goa and down to Mangalore, their attempts to take Ullal proved more of a challenge. This was thanks to its 'fearless queen' who proved to be a major thorn in their grand plans to control the lucrative spice trade. Her efforts to continually repel their advances is the stuff of local legend.

Well trained in the art of war, both in strategy and combat, she knew how to brandish a sword. And while she was eventually defeated, it was a result of her treacherous ex-husband, who conspired against her in leaking intelligence to the enemy.

Her efforts to rally her people to defeat the powerful Portuguese is not forgotten by locals: she's immortalised in a bronze statue on horseback at the roundabout on the road to Ullal beach, and has an annual festival dedicated to her.

The shore temple that looks over the beautiful Someshwara beach a few kilometres south from Ullal was the former site of her fort, but only sections of its wall remains intact.

SURFING SWAMIS

While there has always been a spiritual bond between surfer and Mother ocean, the- **Surfing Ashram** (Mantra Surf Club; ☑ 9880659130; www.surfingindia.net; 6-64 Kolachikambla, Mulki; s/d incl full board from ₹3000/4500; 🖥) at Mulki, 30km north of Mangaluru, takes things to a whole new plane. At this Hare Krishna ashram, which was established by its American guru who's been surfing since 1963 (and living in India for four decades), devotees follow a daily ritual of *puja* (prayers), chanting, mediation and vegetarian diet in between catching barrels.

There's surf year-round, but the best waves are May to June and September to October. The swamis can also assist with information on surfing across India. Board hire is ₹700 per day (also bodyboards and stand-up paddleboards) and lessons are ₹2500 per day.

Accommodation is pricey, but it has a homely beach-house feel, and rates include meals.

All are welcome to visit, but it's important to be aware that it's strictly a place of worship and there are guidelines to abide by, including abstinence from meat, alcohol, tobacco and sex during your stay. See the website for more details.

around overnight, instead making a bee-line straight to the adjoining beaches.

Note that bag searches and passport checks by the police are common upon arrival.

◉ Sights & Activities

Temples

Foreigners and non-Hindus are not allowed inside Gokarna's temples. However, there are plenty of colourful rituals to be witnessed around town. At the western end of Car St is the **Mahabaleshwara Temple**, home to a revered lingam. Nearby is the **Ganapati Temple**, while at the other end of the street is the **Venkataraman Temple**. About 100m further south is **Koorti Teertha**, the large temple tank where locals, pilgrims and immaculately dressed Brahmins perform their ablutions.

Beaches & Surfing

The best beaches are due south of Gokarna town, with Om Beach and Kudle Beach being the most popular. Don't walk around the paths after dark, and not alone at any time – it's easy to slip or get lost, and muggings have occurred.

Om Beach   BEACH
Gokarna's most famous beach twists and turns over several kilometres in a way that's said to resemble the outline of an Om symbol. It's a great mix of lovely long beach and smaller shady patches of sand, perfect for sunbathing and swimming. It's a 20-minute walk to Kudle Beach; an autorickhaw to Gokarna town is about ₹150.

Kudle Beach   BEACH
Lined with rows of restaurants and guesthouses, Kudle Beach has emerged as a popular alternative to Om Beach. It's one of Gokarna's longest beaches, with plenty of room to stretch out on its attractive sands.

It's a 20-minute hike from both Gokarna town or Om Beach along a path that heads atop along the barren headland with expansive sea views. Otherwise it's a ₹60 autorickshaw ride to town.

Gokarna Beach   BEACH
While Gokarna's main town beach isn't meant for casual bathing, and is more popular with domestic tourists, walk up a bit and you'll find a long stretch of pristine sand that seems to go forever – perfect for those seeking isolation.

Cocopelli Surf School   SURFING
(☑ 8105764969; www.cocopelli.org; Gokarna Beach; lesson per person ₹2000, board rental per 2hr ₹750; ◷ Oct-May) Offers lessons by internationally certified instructors and rents boards. Has accommodation along here too.

Half Moon & Paradise Beach   BEACH
Well hidden away south of Om Beach lie the small sandy coves of Half Moon Beach and Paradise Beach. **Half Moon** is the more attractive, with a lovely sweep of powdery sand and basic hut accommodation. **Paradise Beach** is a mix of sand and rocks, and a haven with the long-term 'turn-on-tune-in-drop-out' crowd; unfortunately the government routinely destroys all the huts out this

way, leaving it in a ramshackle state – hence it's BYO everything here.

From Om Beach, these beaches are a 30-minute and one-hour walk, respectively. Watch out for snakes and don't walk it after dark. A fishing boat from Om Beach will cost around ₹700, which can fit 10 people. For Paradise Beach you can also grab a bus to Velikom from Gokarna (₹12, 20 minutes), from where it's a 15-minute walk.

🛏 Sleeping & Eating

With a few exceptions, the choice here is basic, but perfectly comfortable, beach shacks. Most close from May to August.

🛏 Om Beach

Om Shree Ganesh   BUNGALOW $
(☑ 8386-257310; www.omshreeganesh.com; hut ₹500, without bathroom ₹300) A winning combination of cheap bungalows, friendly management and beachside location makes this place justifiably popular. Its atmospheric double-storey restaurant rocks at night and does tasty dishes such as tandoori prawns, mushroom tikka and *momos*.

Sangham   BUNGALOW $
(☑ 9448101099; r with/without bathroom ₹500/300) A blissful spot overlooking the water with a sandy path leading to the bungalows out back among banana trees; life's definitely a beach at Sangham.

Moksha Cafe   BUNGALOW $
(☑ 9741358997; Om Beach; r with/without bathroom ₹600/300) In the middle of Om Beach, these graffiti-splashed bungalows are as good as any with private porches, hammocks and sandy garden full of coconut palms.

Dolphin Bay Cafe   BUNGALOW $
(☑ 9742440708; r from ₹200; ⊗ 8am-10pm) Literally plonked on the beach, Dolphin Bay is your classic chilled-out shack **restaurant** (mains ₹80-180) that makes Gokarna so great. It has a choice of sandy-floor huts or sturdier concrete rooms.

Dolphin Shanti   GUESTHOUSE $
(☑ 9740930133; r from ₹200) Occupying the last plot of land on Om Beach (heading towards Half Moon beach), this mellow guesthouse sits perched upon the rocks with fantastic ocean views, and lives up to its name with dolphins often spotted. Rooms are ultra basic yet appealing.

Nirvana Café   GUESTHOUSE $
(☑ 329851; d ₹250, cottage ₹400-600; @) Towards the southern end of Om, Nirvana has popular el cheapo huts and spacious cottages set among a shady landscaped garden. Internet costs ₹60 per hour and hammocks are for sale if you need one.

Namaste Café   GUESTHOUSE $
(☑ 08386-257141; www.namastegokarna.com; Om Beach; r with fan/AC from ₹800/1500; ❄ ⑳) At the beginning of Om, this long-standing guesthouse has a very different vibe to the others, with a proper resort feel. It's an excellent choice, especially if you're after the comforts of AC, wi-fi, hot water, cold beer and romantic open-air restaurant with dreamy sea views. These days it's more popular with domestic travellers.

SwaSwara   HOTEL $$$
(☑ 08386-257132; www.swaswara.com; Om Beach; s/d 5 nights €1730/2300; ❄ @ ⑳ ✈) One of South India's finest retreats, this health resort offers a holiday based around yoga and ayurveda. No short stays are possible, but once you've set eyes upon its elegant private villas – some with forest views, others with

FORMULA BUFFALO

Call it an indigenous take on the Grand Prix, Kambla, or traditional buffalo racing, is a hugely popular pastime among villagers along the southern Karnataka coast. Popularised in the early 20th century and born out of local farmers habitually racing their buffaloes home after a day in the fields, the races have now hit the big time. Thousands of spectators attend each edition, and racing buffaloes are pampered and prepared like thoroughbreds.

Kambla events are held between November and March, usually on weekends. Parallel tracks are laid out in a paddy field, along which buffaloes hurtle towards the finish line. In most cases the man rides on a board fixed to a ploughshare, literally surfing his way down the track behind the beasts. The faster creatures can cover the 120m-odd distance through water and mud in around 14 seconds!

river – you'll be happy to stay put. All have small garden courtyards full of basil and lemongrass, open-air showers and sitting areas.

Kudle Beach

Sea Rock Cafe   GUESTHOUSE $
(☑ 7829486382; Kudle Beach; r from ₹300) Yet more chilled-out bungalows, with an option of more-comfortable rooms and a beachside restaurant where the good times roll.

Ganga View   GUESTHOUSE $
(☑ 9591978042; Kudle Beach; r from ₹250; 🛜) At the end of Kudle, relaxed Ganga is a perennial favourite. Also has rooms up the hill with soaring views. Wi-fi costs ₹50 per hour.

Goutami Prasad   GUESTHOUSE $
(☑ 9972382302; Kudle Beach; hut from ₹200, r from ₹500) Relaxed, family-run guesthouse with a prime spot in the centre of Kudle Beach. Choose between basic huts with sandy floors or more comfortable, spotless rooms.

Uma Garden   GUESTHOUSE $
(☑ 9916720728; Kudle Beach; r without bathroom ₹250) Tucked around the corner at the beginning of Kudle, this bucolic guesthouse has a laid-back owner and sea-facing vegetarian restaurant.

Strawberry Farmhouse   GUESTHOUSE $$
(☑ 7829367584; Kudle Beach; r from ₹700; ❄) A kitschy guesthouse at the northern section of Kudle with over-the-top bright cottages (some with AC) and prime position looking out to the water.

Half Moon Beach

Half Moon Garden Cafe   BUNGALOW $
(☑ 9743615820; Half Moon Beach; hut ₹200) A throwback to the hippie days, this hideaway has a blissful beach and bare-bones huts without electricity.

Gokarna Beach

This seemingly endless stretch of beach is the place for a more isolated relaxed beachside hang-out.

Hema Shree Garden   BUNGALOW $
(☑ 9845983223; Gokarna Beach; r from ₹250) A superchilled beach guesthouse that's a 20-minute walk along Gokarna Beach with a variety of rooms around its tropical garden, plus some bungalows looking directly to the ocean.

MURUDESHWAR

A worthwhile stopover for those taking the coastal route from Gokarna to Mangaluru, is Murudeshwar, a beachside pilgrimage town. It's most notable for its colossal seashore statue of **Lord Shiva** (Murudeshwar), which sits directly on the shore overlooking the Arabian Sea, making for spectacular photo-ops. For the best views, take the lift 20 stories to the top of the skyscraper-like **Shri Murudeshwar Temple** (lift ₹10; ⊙ lift 7.45am-12.30pm & 3.15-6.45pm).

It's 3km off the main highway, accessed by train or bus passing up and down the coast. If you want to stay the night, **Hotel Kawari's Palm Grove** (☑ 08385-260178; r with fan/AC from ₹500/1000; ❄) has decent enough rooms 500m from the action.

Namaste Garden   BUNGALOW $
(☑ 9448906436; Gokarna Beach; r ₹500) Delightfully simple huts with hammocks, beachside tables and umbrellas. It's in the middle of Gokarna Beach, 10 minutes from town.

Gokarna Town

Shree Shakti Hotel   HOTEL $
(☑ 9036043088; Gokarna Beach Rd; s/d ₹300/600) On Gokarna's main strip, this friendly hotel is excellent value with immaculate lime-green rooms above a restaurant which does excellent food, including homemade ice cream.

Greenland Guesthouse   GUESTHOUSE $
(☑ 9019651420; www.gokarnagreenland.in; Gokarna Town; r from ₹200) Hidden down a jungle path outside town, this mellow family-run guesthouse has clean rooms in vibrant colours. Will suit those not wanting a beach shack, but somewhere with character.

Hotel Gokarna International   HOTEL $
(☑ 9739629390; Main Rd; r with fan/AC from ₹450/1000; @) This typical institutional Indian hotel is worth a look if you want large AC rooms with TV and balcony.

🛍 Shopping

Shree Radhakrishna Bookstore   BOOKS
(Car St, Gokarna Town; ⊙ 10am-6pm) Secondhand novels, postcards and maps.

ℹ️ Information

Axis Bank (Main St, Gokarna Town)

SBI (Main St, Gokarna Town)

Shama Internet Centre (Car St, Gokarna Town; per hour ₹40; ⊙10am-11pm)

Sub post office (1st fl, cnr Car & Main Sts, Gokarna Town; ⊙10am-4pm Mon-Sat)

ℹ️ Getting There & Away

BUS

A mix of local and private buses depart daily to Bengaluru (₹509, 12 hours) and Mysuru (from ₹550, 12 hours), as well as Mangaluru (₹240, 6½ hours) and Hubli (₹190, four hours), mostly transferring at Kumta (₹34, one hour), or Honnavar (₹55, two hours) for Jog Falls.

For Hampi, **Paolo Travels** (📞 0832-6637777; www.phmgoa.com) is a popular choice which heads via Hospet (fan/AC ₹1100/1600, seven hours). Note if you're coming from Hampi, you'll be dropped at Ankola from where there's a free transfer for the 26km journey to Gokarna.

There are also regular buses to Panaji (₹116, four hours) and Mumbai (₹900, 12 hours).

TRAIN

Many express trains stop at Gokarna Road station, 9km from town; however, double check your ticket as some stop at Ankola, 26km away. Many of the hotels and small travel agencies in Gokarna can book tickets.

The 3am 12619 Matsyagandha Express goes to Mangaluru (sleeper ₹235, 4½ hours); the return train leaves Kumta around 6.30pm for Margao (Madgaon; sleeper ₹170, 2½ hours) and Mumbai (sleeper/2AC, ₹465/1735, 12 hours).

Autorickshaws charge ₹200 to go to Gokarna Road station (or ₹500 to Ankola); a bus from Gokarna charges ₹40, every 30 minutes.

CENTRAL KARNATAKA

Hampi

📞 08394

Unreal and bewitching, the forlorn ruins of Hampi dot an unearthly landscape that will leave you spellbound the moment you cast your eyes on it. Heaps of giant boulders perch precariously over miles of undulating terrain, their rusty hues offset by jade-green palm groves, banana plantations and paddy fields. While it's possible to see the ancient ruins and temples of this World Heritage Site in a day or two, this goes against Hampi's relaxed grain. Plan on lingering for a while.

The main travellers' ghetto has traditionally been Hampi Bazaar, a village crammed with budget lodges, shops and restaurants, and towered over by the majestic Virupaksha Temple. However, recent demolitions have seen tranquil Virupapur Gaddi across the river become the new hang-out. Both offer different experiences, and it's recommended to spend a few nights at each.

Hampi is generally a safe, peaceful place, but don't wander around the ruins after dark or alone, as it can be dangerous terrain to get lost in, especially at night.

History

Hampi and its neighbouring areas find mention in the Hindu epic Ramayana as Kishkinda, the realm of the monkey gods. In 1336 Telugu prince Harihararaya chose Hampi as the site for his new capital Vijayanagar, which – over the next couple of centuries – grew into one of the largest Hindu empires in Indian history. By the 16th century it was a thriving metropolis of about 500,000 people, its busy bazaars dabbling in international commerce, brimming with precious stones and merchants from faraway lands. All this, however, ended in a stroke in 1565, when a confederacy of Deccan sultanates razed Vijayanagar to the ground, striking it a death blow from which it never recovered.

◉ Sights

Set over 36 sq km, there are some 3700 monuments to explore in Hampi, and it would take months if you were to do it justice. The ruins are divided into two main areas: the **Sacred Centre**, around Hampi Bazaar with its temples, and the **Royal Centre**, towards Kamalapuram, where the Vijayanagara royalty lived and governed.

Sacred Centre

⭐ **Virupaksha Temple**   HINDU TEMPLE
(Map p901; admission ₹2, camera ₹50; ⊙dawn-dusk)
The focal point of Hampi Bazaar is the Virupaksha Temple, one of the city's oldest structures, and Hampi's only remaining working temple. The main *gopuram* (gateway tower), almost 50m high, was built in 1442, with a smaller one added in 1510. The main shrine is dedicated to Virupaksha, an incarnation of Shiva.

If Lakshmi, the **temple elephant**, and her attendant are around, she'll smooch (bless) you for a coin; she gets her morning bath at 8am down by the river ghats.

To the south, overlooking Virupaksha Temple, **Hemakuta Hill** has a few early ruins, including monolithic sculptures of

Narasimha (Vishnu in his man-lion incarnation) and Ganesha. At the east end of the recently abandonded Hampi Bazaar is a monolithic **Nandi statue**, around which stand colonnaded blocks of the ancient marketplace. Overlooking the site is Matanga Hill, whose summit affords dramatic views of the terrain at sunrise.

Within the now-derelict bazaar is the **Hampi Heritage Gallery** (Map p901; ⊘ 10am-1pm & 3-6pm Tue-Sun) **FREE**, exhibiting interesting historical photos of the ruins.

★ **Vittala Temple**   HINDU TEMPLE
(Map p898; Indian/foreigner ₹10/250, child under 15 free; ⊘ 8.30am-5.30pm) The undisputed highlight of the Hampi ruins, the 16th-century Vittala Temple stands amid the boulders 2km from Hampi Bazaar. Work possibly started on the temple during the reign of Krishnadevaraya (r 1509-29). It was never finished or consecrated, yet the temple's incredible sculptural work remains the pinnacle of Vijayanagar art.

The ornate **stone chariot** that stands in the courtyard is the temple's showpiece and represents Vishnu's vehicle with an image of Garuda within. Its wheels were once capable of turning. The outer 'musical' pillars reverberate when tapped. They were supposedly designed to replicate 81 different Indian instruments, but authorities have placed them out of tourists' bounds for fear of further damage, so no more do-re-mi.

As well as the main temple, whose sanctum was illuminated using a design of reflective waters, you'll find the marriage hall and prayer hall, the structures to the left and right upon entry, respectively.

Lakshimi Narasmiha   HINDU TEMPLE
(Map p898) An interesting stop off along the road to the Virupaksha Temple is the 6.7m monolithic statue of the bulging-eyed Lakshimi Narasmiha in a cross-legged lotus position and topped by a hood of seven snakes.

Krishna Temple   HINDU TEMPLE
(Map p898) Built in 1513, the Krisha Temple is fronted by a D-cupped *apsara* and 10 incarnations of Vishnu. It's on the road to the Virupaksha Temple.

Sule Bazaar   HISTORIC SITE
(Map p898) Halfway along the path from Hampi Bazaar to Vittala Temple, a track to the right leads over the rocks to deserted Sule Bazaar, one of ancient Hampi's principle centres of commerce and reputedly its red-light district. At the southern end of this area is the beautiful 16th-century **Achyutaraya Temple** (Map p898).

Royal Centre & Around

While it can be accessed by a 2km foot trail from the Achyutaraya Temple, the **Royal Centre** is best reached via the Hampi–Kamalapuram road. A number of Hampi's major sites stand here.

Mahanavami-diiba   RUIN
(Map p898) The Mahanavami-diiba is a 12m-high three-tired platform with intricate carvings and panoramic vistas of the walled complex of ruined temples, stepped tanks and the King's audience hall. The platform was used as a Royal viewing area for the Dasara festivities, religious ceremonies and processions.

Hazarama Temple   HINDU TEMPLE
(Map p898) Hazarama Temple features exquisite carvings that depict scenes from the Ramayana, and polished black granite pillars.

Zenana Enclosure   RUIN
(Map p898; Indian/foreigner ₹10/250; ⊘ 8.30am-5.30pm) Northeast of the Royal Centre within the walled ladies' quarters is the Zenana Enclosure. Its peaceful grounds and manicured lawns feel like an oasis amid the arid surrounds. Here is the **Lotus Mahal** (Map p898), a delicately designed pavilion which was supposedly the queen's recreational mansion. It overlooks the 11 grand **Elephant Stables** (Map p898; ⊘ 8.30am-5.30pm) with arched entrances and domed chambers. There's also a small museum and army barracks within the high-walled enclosure.

Queen's Bath   RUIN
(Map p898; ⊘ 8.30am-5.30pm) South of the Royal Centre you'll find various temples and elaborate waterworks, including the Queen's Bath, deceptively plain on the outside but amazing within, with its Indo-Islamic architecture.

Archaeological Museum   MUSEUM
(Map p898; Kamalapuram; ⊘ 10am-5pm Sat-Thu) Worth popping in for its quality collection of sculptures from local ruins, plus neolithic tools, fascinating coins, 16th-century weaponry and a large floor model of the Vijayanagar ruins.

KARNATAKA & BENGALURU HAMPI

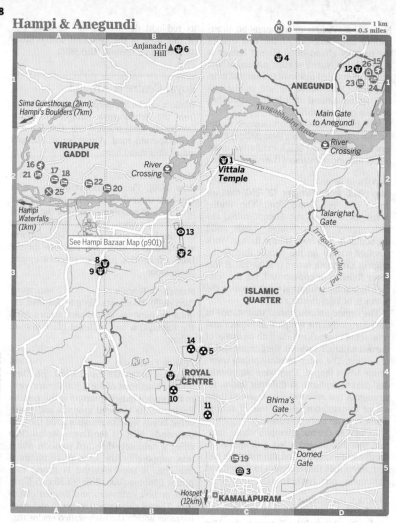

See Hampi Bazaar Map (p901)

Activities

Hampi Waterfalls
WATERFALL

About a 2km walk west of Hampi Bazaar, past banana plantations, you can scramble over boulders to reach the attractive Hampi 'waterfalls,' a series of small whirlpools among the rocks amid superb scenery.

Bouldering & Rock Climbing

Hampi is the undisputed bouldering capital of India. The entire landscape is a climber's adventure playground made of granite crags and boulders, some bearing the marks of ancient stonemasons. *Golden Boulders* (2013) by Gerald Krug and Christiane Hupe has information about bouldering in Hampi.

Tom & Jerry
BOULDERING

(☎ 8277792588, 9482746697; luckykoushik1@gmail.com; Virupapur Gaddi; 2½hr class ₹500) Two local lads who are doing great work in catering to climbers' needs, providing quality mats, shoes and local knowledge. They also organise climbing trips upcountry to Badami.

Thimmaclimb
BOULDERING

(Map p898; ☎ 8762776498; www.thimmaclimb.wix.com/hampi-bouldering; Shiva Guesthouse, Virupap-

Hampi & Anegundi

◉ Top Sights
1 Vittala Temple C2

◎ Sights
2 Achyutaraya Temple B3
3 Archaeological Museum C5
4 Durga Temple C1
5 Elephant Stables C4
6 Hanuman Temple B1
7 Hazarama Temple B4
8 Krishna Temple A3
9 Lakshimi Narasmiha A3
    Lotus Mahal .... (see 14)
10 Mahanavami-diiba B4
11 Queen's Bath C4
12 Ranganatha Temple D1
13 Sule Bazaar B3
14 Zenana Enclosure B4

◉ Activities, Courses & Tours
15 Kishkinda Trust D1
16 Thimmaclimb A2

🛌 Sleeping
17 Gopi Guesthouse A2
18 Hema Guest House A2
19 Hotel Mayura
    Bhuvaneshwari C5
20 Manju's Place B2
    Peshagar Guest
    House .... (see 26)
21 Shanthi A2
22 Sunny Guesthouse A2
23 Uramma Cottage D1
24 Uramma House D1

✕ Eating
    Hoova Craft Shop &
    Café .... (see 26)
25 Laughing Buddha A2

🛍 Shopping
26 Banana Fibre Craft
    Workshop D1

ur Gaddi; class from ₹350-500) A small operation run by local pro Thimma, who guides, runs lessons and stocks professional equipment for hire and sale.

Birdwatching
Get in touch with **Kishkinda Trust** (TKT; ☑08533-267777; www.thekishkindatrust.org) in Anegundi for info on birdwatching in the area, which has over 230 species, including the greater flamingo. *The Birds of Hampi* (2014) by Samad Kottur is the definitive guide.

🎎 Festivals & Events

Vijaya Utsav   RELIGIOUS
(Hampi Festival; ☉Jan) Hampi's three-day extravaganza of culture, heritage and the arts in January.

Virupaksha Car Festival   RELIGIOUS FESTIVAL
(☉Mar/Apr) The Virupaksha Car Festival in March/April is a big event, with a colourful procession characterised by a giant wooden chariot (the temple car from Virupaksha Temple) being pulled along the main strip of Hampi bazaar.

🛌 Sleeping

Most guesthouses are cosy family-run digs, perfect for the budget traveller. A handful of places also have larger, more-comfortable rooms with air-con and TV.

🛌 Hampi Bazaar

⭐ **Padma Guest House**   GUESTHOUSE $
(Map p901; ☑08394-241331; padmaguest house@gmail.com; d from ₹800; ❈ 🛜) In a quiet corner of Hampi Bazaar, this amiable guesthouse feels more like a homestay, with basic, squeaky-clean rooms, many of which have views of Virupaksha Temple.

Archana Guest House   GUESTHOUSE $
(Map p901; ☑08394-241547; addihampi@yahoo. com; d from ₹600; 🛜) On the riverfront, quiet and cheerful Archana is one of the few places in the bazaar with a view. It's set over two houses opposite each other, with rooms painted in vivid purple and green, and has an open-air restaurant overlooking the river.

Pushpa Guest House   GUESTHOUSE $
(Map p901; ☑9448795120; pushpaguest house99@yahoo.in; d from ₹850, with AC from ₹1200; ❈🛜) The highly recommendable Pushpa is a top all-rounder that gets you a comfortable, attractive and spotless room.

ⓘ HAMPI RUINS TICKET

The ₹250 ticket for Vittala Temple entitles you to same-day admission into most of the paid sites across the ruins (including around the Royal Centre and the Archaeological Museum), so don't lose your ticket.

KARNATAKA & BENGALURU HAMPI

It has a lovely sit-out on the 1st floor, and reliable travel agency.

Vicky's
GUESTHOUSE $

(Map p901; ☑ 9480561010; vikkyhampi@yahoo. co.in; r ₹600; 🗺) An old faithful done up in pop purple and green, with decent rooms and friendly owner.

Netra Guesthouse
GUESTHOUSE $

(Map p901; ☑ 9480569326; r with/without bathroom from ₹400/250) Basic but relaxed rooms for shoestringers, with ambient restaurant.

Ganesh Guesthouse
GUESTHOUSE $

(Map p901; vishnuhampi@gmail.com; r ₹400-800, with AC ₹1200-2000; ❄️🗺) The small family-run Ganesh has been around for 20 years, yet only has downstairs rooms, giving it an appealing intimacy. Also has a nice rooftop restaurant.

Kiran Guest House
GUESTHOUSE $

(Map p901; ☑ 9448143906; kiranhampi2012@ gmail.com; r ₹400-600; 🗺) Chilled-out guesthouse on the riverfront and banana groves.

Ranjana Guest House
GUESTHOUSE $$

(Map p901; ☑ 08394-241696; ranjanaguesthouse@gmail.com; r from ₹1000; ❄️) Run by a tight-knit family, Ranjana prides itself on well-appointed rooms and killer temple views from its sunny rooftop terrace.

Gopi Guest House
GUESTHOUSE $$

(Map p901; ☑ 08394-241695; www.gopiguesthouse.com; r with AC ₹1200; ❄️@🗺) Split over two properties on the same street, long-standing Gopi offers quality rooms that are almost upscale for Hampi's standards. Its rooftop cafe is a nice place to hang out.

🏠 Virupapur Gaddi

Many travellers prefer the tranquility of Virupapur Gaddi, across the river from Hampi Bazaar.

Hema Guest House
GUESTHOUSE $

(Map p898; ☑ 8762395470; rockyhampi@gmail. com; Virupapur Gaddi; d ₹350; 🗺) Rows of cute and comfy colourful cottages situated in a shady grove, all with hammocks, and perpetually full restaurant.

Sunny Guesthouse
GUESTHOUSE $

(Map p898; ☑ 9448566368; www.sunnyguesthouse.com; r ₹200-750; @🗺) Sunny both in name and disposition, this popular guesthouse is a hit among backpackers for its cheap rooms, tropical garden, hammocks and chilled-out restaurant.

Gopi Guesthouse
GUESTHOUSE $

(Map p898; ☑ 9481871816; www.hampiisland. com; Virupapura Gaddi; r ₹300-1200; 🗺) A classic Hampi set-up with basic huts and hammocks in its garden as well as a chilled-out restaurant. Also has plush rooms with tiled floors and hot water.

Shanthi
GUESTHOUSE $

(Map p898; ☑ 9449260162; shanthi.hampi@gmail. com; cottage ₹800-1500; @) A more upmarket choice, Shanthi's earth-themed, thatched cottages have rice-field, river and sunset views, with couch swings dangling in their front porches.

Manju's Place
GUESTHOUSE $

(Map p898; ☑ 9449247712; r ₹300, without bathroom from ₹100) The place for those who like

---

DEMOLISHMENT OF HAMPI BAZAAR

While in 1865 it was the Deccan sultanates who levelled Vijayanagar, today a different battle rages in Hampi, between conservationists bent on protecting Hampi's architectural heritage and the locals who have settled there.

In mid-2012 the government's master plan that had been in the works since the mid-2000s, and which aims to classify all of Hampi's ruins as protected monuments, was dramatically and forcefully put into action. Overnight shops, hotels and homes in Hampi Bazaar were bulldozed, reducing the atmospheric main strip to rubble overnight, as villagers who'd made the site a living monument were evicted.

While villagers were compensated with a small plot of land in Kaddirampur, 4km from the bazaar (where there is talk of new guesthouses eventually opening up), many locals remain displaced years later as they await their pay out.

While at the time of research, rubble from the demolished buildings remained, iconic hang-outs had been destroyed (including riverside restaurants such as the Mango Tree) and the main temple road resembled a bombed-out town; guesthouses and restaurants on the fringes of the bazaar remain intact.

Hampi Bazaar

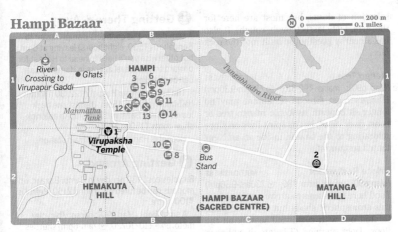

Hampi Bazaar

things quiet, with attractive mud-brick huts in a bucolic setting among rice fields.

Sima Guesthouse　　　　　GUESTHOUSE $
(☑ 9481664504; r with shared bathroom ₹200-300) A quirky guesthouse that is situated away from the crowds, low-key Sima has *very* basic but memorable rooms incorporated into boulder faces. Unexpectedly has a tiny skate ramp, along with a couple of boards.

Hampi's Boulders　　　　　LODGE $$$
(☑ 9448034202; www.hampisboulders.com; Narayanpet; r incl full board from ₹7000; ❄ 🛜 🏊) The only luxury option in these parts, this 'eco-wilderness' resort sits amid leafy gardens 7km west of Virupapur Gaddi. There's a choice of themed rooms, but by far the best are the chic cottages with elegant furnishing, river views and outdoor showers. Rates include guided walks and transfer from Hampi.

🛏 Kamalapuram

Hotel Mayura Bhuvaneshwari　HOTEL $$
(Map p898; ☑ 08394-241574, 8970650025; s/d from ₹1620/1800; ❄ 🛜) This tidy government operation, which is located about 3km south of the Royal Centre, has well-appointed but dated rooms, a lovely big garden, much-appreciated bar, and good multicuisine restaurant.

❌ Eating

Due to Hampi's religious significance, meat is strictly off the menu in all restaurants, and alcohol is banned (though some restaurants can order it for you).

Ravi's Rose　　　　　MULTICUISINE $
(Map p901; mains from ₹100; ⊙ 8am-10pm) This slightly sketchy rooftop-restaurant is the bazaar's most social hang-out, with a good

selection of dosas, but most are here for the, erm, tasty lassis (cough, cough). It also has a nearby guesthouse built into the rock face.

Mango Tree   MULTICUISINE **$$**
(Map p901; mains ₹90-310; ⊘7.30am-9.30pm) Hampi's most famous restaurant may no longer sit beneath its iconic mango tree or boast river views, but its spirit lives on since relocating to the bazaar, inside an ambient tented restaurant.

Prince Restaurant   MULTICUISINE **$$**
(Map p901; mains from ₹80; ⊘7.30am-9.30pm) Food here takes ages to arrive, so thankfully this atmospheric shady hut is a good place to chill out with cushioned seating on the floor. Does *momos* (Tibetan dumplings), pizzas etc.

★**Laughing Buddha**   MULTICUISINE **$**
(Map p898; mains from ₹80; ⊘8am-10pm; 🖥) Now that Hampi's famous riverside restaurants have closed on the other side, Laughing Buddha has taken over as the most atmospheric place to eat, with serene river views that span beyond to the temples and ruins. Its menu is curries, burgers, pizzas, you know the drill...

🛍 Shopping

Akash Art Gallery & Bookstore   BOOKS
(Map p901; Hampi Bazaar) ⊘6am-9pm) This gallery and bookstore has an excellent selection of books on Hampi and India, plus secondhand fiction. Pick up the free map it offers.

ℹ Information

There's no ATM in Hampi; the closest is 3km away in Kamalapuram – an autorickshaw costs ₹100 for a return trip.

Internet (per hour ₹40) is ubiquitous in Hampi Bazaar, though most guesthouses have free wi-fi these days. A good tourist resource for Hampi is www.hampi.in.

Tourist office (Map p901; 📞241339; ⊘10am-5.30pm Sat-Thu) This dingy office inside Virupaksha Temple has brochures but is more useful for arranging cycling tours (per person ₹400 including bike and guide), walking guides (half-/full day ₹600/1000) and bus tours (₹350, seven hours), all of which head to the ruins.

ℹ Getting There & Away

A semideluxe bus connects Hampi Bazaar to Bengaluru (₹550, eight hours) leaving at 8pm, but otherwise you'll have to head to Hospet for onward travel. Travel agents in Hampi Bazaar can book tickets.

The first bus from Hospet (₹22, 30 minutes, half-hourly) is at 5.45am; the last one back leaves Hampi Bazaar at 7.30pm. An autorickshaw costs ₹150 to ₹200.

Hospet is Hampi's nearest train station.

ℹ Getting Around

Bicycles cost ₹30 per day in Hampi Bazaar, while mopeds can be hired for around ₹150. Petrol is ₹100 a litre.

A small **boat** (Map p901; person/bicycle/motorbike ₹10/10/20; ⊘7am-6pm) shuttles frequently across the river to Virupapur Gaddi. A large backpack will cost ₹10 extra, while a special trip after 6pm is ₹50 to ₹100 per person depending on how late you cross.

Walking the ruins is possible, but expect to cover at least 7km just to see the major sites. Autorickshaws and taxis are available for sightseeing. Hiring an autorickshaw for the day costs ₹750.

Around Hampi

Anegundi

Across the Tungabhadra River, about 5km northeast of Hampi Bazaar, sits Anegundi, an ancient fortified village that's part of the Hampi World Heritage Site but predates Hampi by way of human habitation. Gifted with a landscape similar to Hampi, Anegundi has been spared the blight of commercialisation, and thus continues to preserve the local atmosphere minus the touristy vibe.

👁 Sights & Activities

Mythically referred to as Kishkinda, the kingdom of the monkey gods, Anegundi retains many of its historic monuments, such as sections of its defensive wall and gates, and the Ranganatha Temple (Map p898; ⊘dawn-dusk) devoted to Rama. Also worth visiting is the Durga Temple (Map p898; ⊘dawn-dusk), an ancient shrine closer to the village.

Hanuman Temple   HINDU TEMPLE
(Map p898; ⊘dawn-dusk) The whitewashed Hanuman Temple, accessible by a 570-step

climb up the Anjanadri Hill, has fine views of the rugged terrain around. Many believe this is the birthplace of Hanuman, the Hindu monkey god who was Rama's devotee and helped him in his mission against Ravana. The hike up is pleasant, though you'll be courted by impish monkeys, and within the temple you'll find a large group of chillum-puffing sadhus.

Kishkinda Trust CULTURAL PROGRAMS, OUTDOOR ADVENTURE

(TKT; Map p898; ☑ 08533-267777; www.tktkishkinda.org; Main Rd, Anegundi) For cultural events, activities and volunteering opportunities, get in touch with Kishkinda Trust, an NGO based in Anegundi that works with local people.

Sleeping & Eating

A great place to escape the hippies in Hampi, Anegundi has fantastic homestays in restored heritage buildings. Most guesthouses in Anegundi are managed by **Uramma Heritage Homes** (☑ 9449972230; www.urammaheritagehomes.com; Anegundi).

Peshagar Guest House GUESTHOUSE $

(Map p898; ☑ 09449972230; www.urammaheritagehomes.com; s/d ₹450/850) Six simple rooms done up in rural motifs open around a pleasant common area in this heritage house with courtyard garden and basic rooftop.

★ **Uramma Cottage** COTTAGE $$

(Map p898; ☑ 08533-267792; www.urammaheritagehomes.com; s/d from ₹2000/2500; ❄🏠) Delightful thatched-roof cottages with rustic farmhouse charm that are both comfortable and attractive and set in a relaxed landscaped garden setting.

Uramma House GUESTHOUSE $$

(Map p898; ☑ 09449972230; www.urammaheritagehomes.com; s/d ₹2000/3500, house for 4 people ₹7000; 🏠) This 4th-century heritage house is a gem, with traditional-style rooms featuring boutique touches.

Hoova Craft Shop & Café CAFE $

(Map p898; mains ₹60-100; ☺ 8.30am-9.30pm) A lovely place for an unhurried local meal.

Shopping

Banana Fibre Craft Workshop HANDICRAFTS

(Map p898; ☺ 10am-1pm & 2-5pm Mon-Sat) Watch on at this small workshop as workers ply their trade making a range of handicrafts and accessories using the bark of a banana tree, and recycled materials. Of course they sell it all too.

ⓘ Getting There & Away

Anegundi is 7km from Hampi, and reached by crossing the river on a coracle (₹10) from the pier east of the Vittala Temple. By far the most convenient way is to hire a moped or bicycle (if you're feeling energetic) from Virupapur Gaddi. An autorickshaw costs ₹200.

Hospet (Hosapete)

☑ 08394 / POP 164,200

A hectic, dusty regional centre, Hospet (renamed as Hosapete in 2014) is certainly nothing to write home about, and notable only as a transport hub for Hampi.

Sleeping & Eating

Hotel Malligi HOTEL $$

(☑ 08394-228101; www.malligihotels.com; Jabunatha Rd; r ₹990-5000; ❄@🛜🏊) Hotel Malligi has built a reputation around clean and well-serviced rooms, aquamarine swimming pool and a good multicuisine restaurant.

Udupi Sri Krishna Bhavan SOUTH INDIAN $

(Bus Stand; thali ₹45, mains ₹50-70; ☺ 6.30am-10.30pm) Opposite the bus stand, this clean spot dishes out Indian vegie fare, including thalis.

DAROJI SLOTH BEAR SANCTUARY

About 30km south of Hampi, amid a scrubby undulated terrain, lies the **Daroji Sloth Bear Sanctuary** (₹25; ☺ 9.30am-6pm), which nurses a population of around 150 free-ranging sloth bears in an area of 83 sq km. You have a very good chance of spotting them, as honey is slathered on the rocks to coincide with the arrival of visitors. However, you can only see them from afar at the viewing platform. Bring binoculars, or there's no point turning up. Generally 4pm to 6pm is the best time to visit.

The sanctuary is also home to leopards, wild boars, hyenas, jackals and others animals, but you're unlikely to see anything other than peacocks. You'll need to arrange transport to get here, which should cost around ₹600 for an autorickshaw and ₹1000 for a car.

ℹ️ Information

You'll find ATMs along the main drag and Shanbagh Circle. Internet joints (₹40 per hour) are common.

ℹ️ Getting There & Away

BUS

Hospet's bus stand has services to Hampi from Bay 10 every half-hour (₹22, 30 minutes). Overnight private sleeper buses ply to/from Goa (10 hours) and Gokarna (eight hours) for ₹850 to ₹1150, and to Bengaluru (₹340 to ₹700, 6½ hours) and Mysuru (₹380 to ₹605, 8½ hours).

TRAIN

Hospet's train station is a ₹20 autorickshaw ride from town. The 18047 Amaravathi Express and KCG YPR Express head to Margao (Magdaon), Goa (sleeper/2AC ₹225/855, 7½ hours) at 6.30am on Monday, Wednesday, Thursday and Saturday. The 16591 Hampi Express departs nightly at 9pm for Bengaluru (3AC/2AC/1AC ₹680/970/1635, nine hours) and Mysore (₹860/1240/2075, 12½ hours).

Hubli (Hubballi)

📞 0836 / POP 943,857

Prosperous Hubli (recently renamed as Hubballi) is a hub for rail routes for Mumbai, Bengaluru, Goa and northern Karnataka. The train station is a 15-minute walk from the old bus stand. Most hotels sit along this stretch.

🛏️ Sleeping & Eating

Hotel Ajanta   HOTEL $

(📞 0836-2362216; Jayachamaraj Nagar; s/d from ₹390/510) This well-run place near the train station has basic, functional rooms. Its popular ground-floor restaurant serves delicious regional-style thalis for ₹55.

Ananth Residency   HOTEL $$

(📞 0836-2262251; ananthresidencyhubli@yahoo. co.uk; Jayachamaraj Nagar; d from ₹1600; ❄️) A comfortable option that sports a sleek business-hotel look, and cheerful restaurant with chilled beer.

ℹ️ Information

There's an ATM opposite the bus stand. On the same stretch are several internet cafes, charging ₹30 per hour.

ℹ️ Getting There & Away

AIR

The airport is around 5km from the centre of town. SpiceJet has daily flights to Bengaluru.

BUS

There are frequent morning semideluxe servies to Bengaluru (semideluxe/AC Volvo/sleeper ₹434/650/690, 8½ hours) until around 9.30am, Bijapur (₹165 to ₹250, seven hours) and Hospet (₹144 to ₹237, four hours). There's an 8am bus to Gokarna (₹161, four hours) and regular connections to Mangaluru (₹356 to ₹600, 9½ hours), Mumbai (semideluxe/sleeper ₹700/1100, 11 hours), Mysuru (₹450, 10 hours) and Panaji (₹171 to ₹304, seven hours).

TRAIN

From the train station, plenty of expresses head to Hospet (sleeper/2AC class ₹140/690, 2½ hours, six daily), Bengaluru (sleeper/2AC ₹300/1085, eight hours, four daily) and Mumbai (sleeper/2AC ₹380/1480, 15½ hours). The 11pm 06948 Hubli-Vasco Link Express goes to Goa (sleeper/3AC ₹160/485, 6½ hours).

NORTHERN KARNATAKA

Badami

📞 08357 / POP 26,000

Once the capital of the mighty Chalukya empire, today Badami is famous for its magnificent rock-cut cave temples, and red sandstone cliffs that resemble the Wild West. While the dusty main road is an eyesore that will have you wanting to get the hell out of there, its backstreets are a lovely area to explore with old houses, carved wooden doorways and the occasional Chalukyan ruin.

History

From about AD 540 to 757, Badami was the capital of an enormous kingdom stretching from Kanchipuram in Tamil Nadu to the Narmada River in Gujarat. It eventually fell to the Rashtrakutas, and changed hands several times thereafter, with each dynasty sculpturally embellishing Badami in their own way.

The sculptural legacy left by the Chalukyan artisans in Badami includes some of the earliest and finest examples of Dravidian temples and rock-cut caves.

⊙ Sights & Activities

The bluffs and horseshoe-shaped red sandstone cliff of Badami offer some great low-altitude climbing. For more information, visit www.indiaclimb.com.

Badami's caves overlook the 5th-century Agastyatirtha Tank and the waterside Bhutanatha temples. On the other side of the tank is an archaeological museum (admission ₹5; ⊙9am-5pm Sat-Thu), which houses superb examples of local sculpture, including a remarkably explicit Lajja-Gauri image of a fertility cult that once flourished in the area. The stairway behind the museum climbs through a sandstone chasm and fortified gateways to reach the ruins of the North Fort.

Cave Temples   CAVE

(Indian/foreigner ₹5/100, video camera ₹25, tour guide ₹300; ⊙6am-6pm) Badami's highlights are its beautiful cave temples. Cave One, just above the entrance to the complex, is dedicated to Shiva. It's the oldest of the four caves, probably carved in the latter half of the 6th century. On the wall to the right of the porch is a captivating image of Nataraja striking 81 dance moves in the one pose. On the right of the porch area is a huge figure of Ardhanarishvara. On the opposite wall is a large image of Harihara, half Shiva and half Vishnu.

Dedicated to Vishnu, Cave Two is simpler in design. As with caves one and three, the front edge of the platform is decorated with images of pot-bellied dwarfs in various poses. Four pillars support the verandah, their tops carved with a bracket in the shape of a yali (mythical lion creature). On the left wall of the porch is the bull-headed figure of Varaha, the emblem of the Chalukya empire. To his left is Naga, a snake with a human face. On the right wall is a large sculpture of Trivikrama, another incarnation of Vishnu.

Between the second and third caves are two sets of steps to the right. The first leads to a natural cave with a small image of Padmapani (an incarnation of the Buddha). The second set of steps – sadly, barred by a gate – leads to the hilltop South Fort.

Cave Three, carved in AD 578, is the largest and most impressive. On the left wall is a carving of Vishnu, to whom the cave is dedicated, sitting on a snake. Nearby is an image of Varaha with four hands. The pillars have carved brackets in the shape of yalis.

The ceiling panels contain images, including Indra riding an elephant, Shiva on a bull and Brahma on a swan. Keep an eye out for the image of drunken revellers, in particular one lady being propped up by her husband. There's also original colour on the ceiling; the divots on the floor at the cave's entrance were used as paint palettes.

Dedicated to Jainism, Cave Four is the smallest of the set and dates between the 7th and 8th centuries. The right wall has an image of Suparshvanatha (the seventh Jain *tirthankar*) surrounded by 24 Jain *tirthankars*. The inner sanctum contains an image of Adinath, the first Jain *tirthankar*.

🛏 Sleeping & Eating

Mookambika Deluxe   HOTEL $

(☑08357-220067; hotelmookambika@yahoo.com; Station Rd; d with fan/AC from ₹850/1750; ❉) A friendly hotel with comfy rooms done up in matt orange and green. Staff are a good source of travel info.

Hotel Mayura Chalukya   HOTEL $$

(☑08357-220046; Ramdurg Rd; d with fan/AC from ₹1000/1500; ❉) Away from the bustle, this stock-standard government hotel has large, clean rooms with an OK restaurant serving Indian staples.

Krishna Heritage   HOTEL $$$

(☑08357-221300; www.krishnaheritagebadami. com; Ramdurg Rd; r incl breakfast from ₹3500) An upmarket resort 2km from town set on sprawling grounds with a distinct African feel; including a roaming flock of guinea fowl. Rooms are massive with open-air showers and balconies.

Golden Caves Cuisine   MULTICUISINE $

(Station Rd; mains ₹60-120; ⊙8.30am-11.30pm) Produces good North and South Indian fare, with a pleasant outdoor area that's perfect for beers on a balmy evening.

ⓘ Information

There are ATMs on the main road.

Hotel Rajsangam (Station Rd; per hour ₹20) Internet is available at Hotel Rajsangam in the town centre.

KSTDC tourist office (☑220414; Ramdurg Rd; ⊙10am-5.30pm Mon-Sat) The KSTDC tourist office, adjoining Hotel Mayura Chalukya, has brochures on Badami, but otherwise isn't useful.

KARNATAKA & BENGALURU BADAMI

ℹ️ Getting There & Away

Buses regularly shuffle off from Badami's bus stand on Station Rd to Kerur (₹25, 45 minutes), which has connections to Bijapur and Hubli. Buses to Hospet (₹180, six hours) also leave from here.

Several trains run to Bijapur including the 11424 Solapur Express (₹70, 3½ hours, 5.30pm), while the Hubli Express goes to Hubli (2nd class ₹75, 3½ hours, 11am). For Bengaluru, take the 16536 Gol Gumbaz Express (2nd class ₹330, 13 hours, 7.15pm).

ℹ️ Getting Around

Theoretically you can visit Aihole and Pattadakal in a day from Badami if you get moving early. It's much easier and less stressful to arrange an autorickshaw or taxi for the day; it costs around ₹900/1500 for a day trip to Pattadakal, Aihole and nearby Mahakuta.

Start with Aihole (₹40, one hour), then move to Pattadakal (₹23, 30 minutes), and finally return to Badami (₹23, one hour). The last bus from Pattadakal to Badami is at 4pm.

Around Badami

There's no accommodation or restaurants at either Pattadakal or Aihole.

Pattadakal

A secondary capital of the Badami Chalukyas, Pattadakal is known for its temples, which are collectively a World Heritage Site.

Pattadakal is 20km from Badami, with buses (₹23) departing every 30 minutes until about 5pm. There's a morning and afternoon bus to Aiole (₹20), 13km away.

Barring a few that date back to the 3rd century AD, most of Pattadakal's **temples** (Indian/foreigner ₹10/250, video camera ₹25; ⊙6am-6pm) were built during the 7th and 8th centuries AD. Historians believe Pattadakal served as an important trial ground for the development of South Indian temple architecture. A guide here costs about ₹250.

The main **Virupaksha Temple** is a massive structure, its columns covered with intricate carvings depicting episodes from the Ramayana and Mahabharata. A giant stone sculpture of **Nandi** (Shiva's bull) sits to the temple's east. The **Mallikarjuna Temple**, next to the Virupaksha Temple, is almost identical in design. About 500m south of the main enclosure is the Jain **Papanatha Temple**, its entrance flanked by elephant sculptures.

Aihole

Some 100 temples, built between the 4th and 6th centuries AD, speck the ancient Chalukyan regional capital of Aihole (*ay*-ho-leh). Most, however, are either in ruins or engulfed by the modern village. Aihole documents the embryonic stage of South Indian Hindu architecture, from the earliest simple shrines, such as the most ancient Ladkhan Temple, to the later and more complex buildings, such as the Meguti Temple.

Aihole is about 40km from Badami and 13km from Pattadakal.

The most impressive of all the temples in Aihole is the 7th-century **Durga Temple** (Indian/foreigner ₹5/100, camera ₹25; ⊙8am-6pm), notable for its semicircular apse (inspired by Buddhist architecture) and the remains of the curvilinear *sikhara* (temple spire). The interiors house intricate stone carvings. The small **museum** (admission ₹5; ⊙9am-5pm Sat-Thu) behind the temple contains further examples of Chalukyan sculpture.

To the south of the Durga Temple are several other temple clusters, including early examples. About 600m to the southeast, on a low hillock, is the Jain **Meguti Temple**. Watch out for snakes if you're venturing up.

Bijapur (Vijapura)

📞 08352 / POP 326,360 / ELEV 593M

A fascinating open-air museum dating back to the Deccan's Islamic era, dusty Bijapur (renamed Vijapura in 2014) tells a glorious tale dating back some 600 years. Blessed with a heap of mosques, mausoleums, palaces and fortifications, it was the capital of the Adil Shahi kings from 1489 to 1686, and one of the five splinter states formed after the Islamic Bahmani kingdom broke up in 1482. Despite its strong Islamic character, Bijapur is also a centre for the Lingayat brand of Shaivism, which emphasises a single personalised god. The **Lingayat Siddeshwara Festival** runs for eight days in January/February.

⊙ Sights

⭐ **Golgumbaz**   MONUMENT

(Indian/foreigner ₹5/100, camera ₹25; ⊙6am-6pm) Set in tranquil gardens, the magnificent Golgumbaz mausoleum houses the tombs of emperor Mohammed Adil Shah (r 1627–56), his two wives, his mistress (Rambha), one of his daughters and a grandson.

Bijapur (Vijapura)

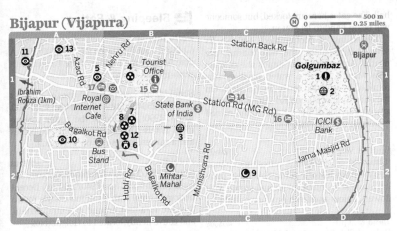

Bijapur (Vijapura)

Octagonal seven-storey towers stand at each corner of the monument, which is capped by an enormous dome. An astounding 38m in diameter, it's said to be the largest dome in the world after St Peter's Basilica in Rome.

Climb the steep, narrow stairs up one of the towers to reach the 'whispering gallery' within the dome. An engineering marvel, its acoustics are such that if you whisper into the wall, a person on the opposite side of the gallery can hear you clearly. Unfortunately people like to test this out by hollering (its unnerving acoustics have the nightmarish effect of a bad acid trip).

The **archaeological museum** (admission ₹5; ⊙10am-5pm Sat-Thu) has an excellent collection of Persian carpets, weapons and scrolls dating back to Bijapur's heyday.

★ Ibrahim Rouza   MONUMENT
(Indian/foreigner ₹5/100, video ₹25; ⊙6am-6pm) The beautiful Ibrahim Rouza is among the most elegant and finely proportioned Islamic monuments in India. Its 24m-high minarets are said to have inspired those of the Taj Mahal, and its tale is similarly poignant: built by emperor Ibrahim Adil Shah II (r 1580–1627) as a future mausoleum for his queen, Taj Sultana. Ironically, he died before her, and was thus the first person to be rested there. Also interred here with Ibrahim Adil Shah are his queen, children and mother.

For a tip (₹150 is fine), caretakers can show you around the monument, including the dark labyrinth around the catacomb where the actual graves are located.

Citadel   FORT
Surrounded by fortified walls and a wide moat, the citadel once contained the palaces, pleasure gardens and durbar (royal court) of the Adil Shahi kings. Now mainly in ruins, the most impressive of the remaining fragments is the colossal archway of **Gagan Mahal**, built by Ali Adil Shah I around 1561 as a dual-purpose royal residency and durbar

hall. The gates here are locked, but someone will be on hand to let you in.

The ruins of Mohammed Adil Shah's seven-storey palace, the Sat Manzil, are nearby. Across the road stands the delicate Jala Manzil, once a water pavilion surrounded by secluded courts and gardens. On the other side of Station Rd (MG Rd) are the graceful arches of Bara Kaman, the ruined mausoleum of Ali Roza.

Central Market
MARKET

(Station Rd; ⊙9am-9pm) A refreshing change in pace from historic ruins, this lively market is an explosion of colour and scents with flowers, spices and fresh produce on sale.

Jama Masjid
MOSQUE

(Jama Masjid Rd; ⊙9am-5.30pm) Constructed by Ali Adil Shah I (r 1557–80), the finely proportioned Jama Masjid has graceful arches, a fine dome and a vast inner courtyard with room for more than 2200 worshippers. Women should cover their heads and not wear revealing clothing.

Asar Mahal
HISTORIC BUILDING

FREE Built by Mohammed Adil Shah in about 1646 to serve as a Hall of Justice, the Asar Mahal once housed two hairs from Prophet Mohammed's beard. The rooms on the upper storey are decorated with frescoes and a square tank graces the front. It's out of bounds for women.

Upli Buruj
HISTORIC SITE

Upli Buruj is a 16th-century, 24m-high watchtower near the western walls of the city. An external flight of stairs leads to the top, where you'll find two hefty cannons and good views of other monuments.

Malik-e-Maidan
HISTORIC SITE

(Monarch of the Plains) Perched upon a platform is this beast of a cannon – over 4m long, almost 1.5m in diameter and estimated to weigh 55 tonnes. Cast in 1549, it was supposedly brought to Bijapur as a war trophy thanks to the efforts of 10 elephants, 400 oxen and hundreds of men!

Jod Gumbad
HISTORIC SITE

In the southwest of the city, off Bagalkot Rd, stand the twin Jod Gumbad tombs with handsome bulbous domes. An Adil Shahi general and his spiritual adviser, Abdul Razzaq Qadiri, are buried here.

🛏 Sleeping & Eating

Hotel Tourist
HOTEL $

(☑08352-250655; Station Rd; s/d ₹180/350) A dive bang in the middle of the bazaar, with scrawny (but clean) rooms.

Hotel Mayura Adil Shahi Annexe
HOTEL $

(☑08352-250401; Station Rd; s/d from ₹540/600, with AC ₹990; ⊛) One of the better government hotels with massive rooms, balconies and a garden. Prices rise on weekends.

Hotel Pearl
HOTEL $$

(☑08352-256002; www.hotelpearlbijapur.com; Station Rd; d with fan/AC from ₹940/1300; ⊛) Decent midrange hotel with clean motel-style rooms that are arranged around a central atrium, and conveniently located to Golgumbaz.

Hotel Madhuvan International
HOTEL $$

(☑08352-255571; Station Rd; d with fan/AC ₹1000/1400; ⊛🕾) Hidden down a lane off Station Rd, this pleasant hotel boasts lime-green walls, tinted windows and a lovely garden restaurant (mains ₹60-80; ⊙9am-11am, noon-4pm & 7-11pm).

ℹ Information

You'll find ATMs about town, including State Bank of India (Station Rd) and ICICI Bank (Station Rd).

Royal Internet Cafe (Station Rd, below Hotel Pearl; per hour ₹30; ⊙9.30am-9.30pm)

Tourist office (☑08352-250359; Hotel Mayura Adil Shahi Annexe, Station Rd; ⊙10am-5.30pm Mon-Sat) Has a good brochure on Bijapur with useful map.

ℹ Getting There & Away

BUS

The following services leave from the bus stand (☑08352-251344):

Bengaluru Ordinary/sleeper ₹577/692, 12 hours

Bidar ₹270, seven hours, three evening buses

Gubarga (Kalaburgi) ₹155 to ₹240, four hours

Hospet ₹240 to ₹340, five hours

Hubli ₹163, six hours

Hyderabad ₹367 to ₹604, eight to 10 hours, four daily

Mumbai ₹610, 12 hours, five daily, via Pune (₹380 to ₹430, 10 hours)

TRAIN

Trains from Bijapur station:

Badami 17320 Hubli-Secunderabad Express, sleeper/2AC ₹140/690, 3½ hours, several daily night trains

KARNATAKA & BENGALURU BIJAPUR (VIJAPURA)

Bengaluru 16536 Golgumbaz Express, sleeper/2AC ₹375/1455, 15½ hours, 5pm

Hyderabad 17319 Secunderabad Express, sleeper/2AC ₹250/955, 9½ hours, 2am

Mumbai 51030 BJP BB Fast Passenger, sleeper ₹215, 13 hours, four weekly

ℹ Getting Around

Given the amount to see and the distance to cover, ₹500 is a fair price to hire an autorickshaw for a day of sightseeing. Expect to pay ₹40 to get from the train station to the town centre, and ₹50 between Golgumbaz and Ibrahim Rouza.

Bidar

📞 08482 / POP 211,944 / ELEV 664M

Despite being home to amazing ruins and monuments, Bidar, hidden away in Karnataka's far northeastern corner, gets very little tourist traffic – which of course makes it all the more appealing. It's a city drenched in history, with the old-walled town being the first capital of Bahmani kingdom (1428–87) and later the capital of the Barid Shahi dynasty.

◉ Sights

Bidar Fort   FORT
(⊙9am-5pm) Keep aside a few hours for peacefully wandering around the remnants of this magnificent 15th-century fort, the largest in South India – and once the administrative capital of much of the region. Surrounded by a triple moat hewn out of solid red rock and 5.5km of defensive walls (the second longest in India), the fort has a fairytale entrance that twists in an elaborate chicane through three gateways.

Guides from the archaeological office have the keys to unlock the most interesting ruins within the fort. These include the **Rangin Mahal** (Painted Palace), with elaborate tilework, teak pillars and panels with mother-of-pearl inlay, **Solah Khamba Mosque** (Sixteen-Pillared Mosque), and **Tarkash Mahal** with exquisitive Islamic inscriptions and wonderful rooftop views. There's a small **museum** in the former royal bath with local artefacts.

Bahmani Tombs   HISTORIC SITE
(⊙dawn-dusk) FREE The huge domed tombs of the Bahmani kings in Ashtur, 3km east of Bidar, were built to house the remains of the sultans, of which the painted interior of Ahmad Shah Bahman's tomb is the most impressive.

Choukhandi   HISTORIC BUILDING
(⊙dawn-dusk) FREE Located 500m from the Badami Tombs is the serene mausoleum of Sufi saint Syed Kirmani Baba, who travelled here from Persia during the golden age of the Bahmani empire. An uncanny air of calm hangs within the monument, and its polygonal courtyard houses rows of medieval graves.

Khwaja Mahmud Gawan Madrasa   RUIN, HISTORIC SITE
(⊙dawn-dusk) FREE Dominating the heart of the old town are the ruins of Khwaja Mahmud Gawan Madrasa, a college for advanced learning built in 1472. To get an idea of its former grandeur, check out the remnants of coloured tiles on the front gate and one of the minarets which still stands intact.

🛏 Sleeping & Eating

Hotel Mayura   HOTEL $
(📞08482-228142; Udgir Rd; d with fan/AC from ₹900/2000; ※) Smart and friendly, with cheerful and well-appointed rooms, bar and restaurant, this is the best hotel to camp at in Bidar. It's bang opposite the central bus stand. Look out for its NBC-peacock symbol.

Hotel Mayura Barid Shahi   HOTEL $
(📞08482-221740; Udgir Rd; s/d ₹500/600, r with AC ₹1000; ※) Otherwise featureless with simple, institutional rooms, this place scores due to its central location and garden bar-restaurant.

★ **Jyothi Fort**   INDIAN $
(Bidar Fort; mains ₹70-110; ⊙9am-5pm) A peaceful setting at the fort's entry with tables set up on the grass under sprawling tamarind trees. It has delicious vegetarian meals.

ℹ Information

You can find **ATMs** (Udgir Rd) and **internet** (per hour ₹ 20; ⊙9am-9pm) on the main road and opposite Hotel Mayura Barid Shahi.

ℹ Getting There & Away

From the bus stand, frequent buses run to Gulbarga (₹115, three hours) and two evening buses to Bijapur (₹280, seven hours). There are also buses to Hyderabad (₹143, four hours, 6.30pm) and Bengaluru (semideluxe/AC ₹700/900, 12 hours, six daily).

Trains head to Hyderabad (sleeper ₹120, five hours, three daily) and Bengaluru (sleeper ₹722 to ₹1012, 13 to 17 hours, twice daily).

ℹ Getting Around

You can arrange a day tour in an autorickshaw for around ₹400.

Telangana & Andhra Pradesh

Why Go?

Hyderabad, the fascinating capital of Telangana, is reason enough on its own to visit this region. Its old quarter of colourful markets, teahouses, biryani restaurants and narrow lanes is studded with the monuments and palaces of bygone dynasties. On the city's fringes rise the fabled Golconda fort and magnificent tombs of departed royalty. Meanwhile Hyderabad's newer districts are lit up by the classy restaurants, hotels, boutiques and bars of IT-fuelled economic advance.

The other attractions of these two states (which were one state until they split in 2014) are less brazen, but dig around and you will unearth gems – like the wonderful medieval temple sculptures of Palampet, the beauty of ancient Buddhist sites such as Sankaram and Guntupalli hidden in deep countryside, the cheery coastal holiday vibe of Visakhapatnam, and the positive vibrations emanating from the vast pilgrim crowds at Tirumala Temple.

Best Places to Eat

→ Southern Spice (p922)

→ Hotel Shadab (p922)

→ SO (p922)

→ Shah Ghouse Cafe (p922)

→ Sea Inn (p933)

Best Off the Beaten Track

→ Guntupalli (p933)

→ Sankaram (p935)

→ Moula Ali Dargah (p917)

→ Bhongir Fort (p928)

When to Go
Hyderabad

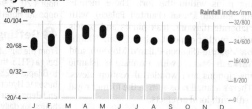

May–Jun Join locals digging into *haleem*, a Ramadan (Ramzan) favourite.

Nov–Feb Explore Hyderabad's sights in perfect 20-25°C weather.

Dec–Apr Best time to enjoy Vizag's coastal attractions – little rain, not *too* hot.

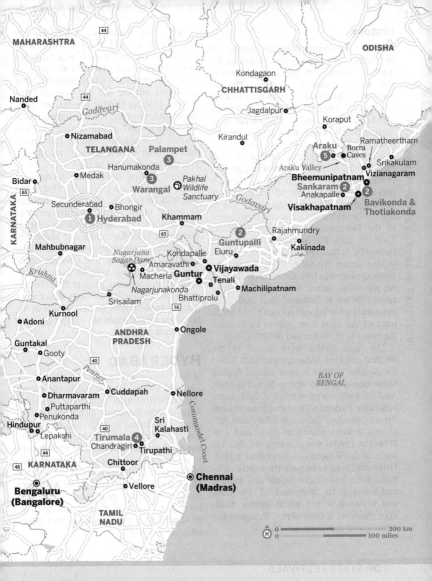

Telangana & Andhra Pradesh Highlights

1 Exploring the markets, feasting on the food and gazing on the architectural marvels of historical and contemporary **Hyderabad** (p912)

2 Absorbing the meditative vibrations of monks past at beautiful **Sankaram** (p935), **Bavikonda** (p935),

Thotlakonda (p935), and **Guntupalli** (p933), destinations on a 2300-year-old monastic trail

3 Enjoying the genius of Kakatiya sculptors at **Palampet** (p929) and **Warangal** (p928)

4 Finding devotion you didn't know you had alongside thousands of Hindu pilgrims at **Tirumala** (p936)

5 Enjoying the lush green forests and wide green valleys as your train chugs through the spectacular Eastern Ghats up to **Araku** (p935)

History

From the 3rd century BC to 3rd century AD the Satavahana empire, also known as the Andhras, ruled over much of the Deccan plateau from a base in this region. The Satavahanas helped Buddhism to flourish after it arrived with emperor Ashoka's missionary monks, and today Andhra Pradesh has more ancient Buddhist sites than almost any other Indian state.

The Hindu Kakatiyas, based at Warangal, ruled most of Telangana and Andhra Pradesh from the 12th to 14th centuries, a period that saw the rise of Telugu culture and language. Warangal eventually fell to the Muslim Delhi Sultanate and then passed to the Deccan-based Bahmani Sultanate. Then, in 1518, the Bahmanis' governor at Golconda, Sultan Quli Qutb Shah, claimed independence. His Qutb Shahi dynasty developed Golconda into the massive fortress we see today. But a water shortage there caused Sultan Mohammed Quli Qutb Shah to relocate a few kilometres east to the south bank of the Musi River, where he founded the new city of Hyderabad in 1591.

The Qutb Shahis were ousted by the Mughal emperor Aurangzeb in 1687. When the Mughal empire in turn started fraying at the edges, its local viceroy Nizam ul-Mulk Asaf Jah took control of much of the Deccan, launching Hyderabad's second great Muslim dynasty, the Asaf Jahis – the famously fabulously wealthy nizams of Hyderabad – in 1724. His capital was Aurangabad, but his son Asaf Jah II moved to Hyderabad in 1763. Hyderabad rose to become the centre of Islamic India and a focus for the arts, culture and learning. Its abundance of rare gems and minerals – the world-famous Kohinoor diamond is from here – furnished the nizams with enormous wealth.

The whole region was effectively under British control from around 1800, but while Andhra Pradesh was governed from Madras (now Chennai), the princely state of Hyderabad – which included large territories outside the city populated by Telugu-speaking Hindus – remained nominally independent. Come Indian Independence in 1947, nizam Osman Ali Khan wanted to retain sovereignty, but Indian military intervention saw Hyderabad state join the Indian union in 1948.

When Indian states were reorganised along linguistic lines in 1956, Hyderabad was split three ways. What's now Telangana joined other Telugu-speaking areas to form Andhra Pradesh state; other districts became parts of Karnataka and Maharashtra. Telangana was never completely happy with this arrangement, and after prolonged campaigning, it was split off from Andhra Pradesh as a separate state in 2014. Hyderabad remains capital of both states until Andhra Pradesh gets its new capital at Vijayawada up and running, with a time limit of 10 years.

HYDERABAD

📞 040 / POP 6.81 MILLION

The Old City of Hyderabad is everything you might dream an Indian old city to be – narrow lanes thronged with markets, chai shops, wandering animals, autorickshaws, a whirl of noise, colour, languages and religions dotted with stately old architecture in varying states of repair. Two unbelievably wealthy Muslim royal houses, the Qutb Shahs and the Asaf Jahs, came and went from this city of pearls and diamonds, leaving a legacy of magnificent palaces, mosques and tombs and a majority population in poverty.

TOP STATE FESTIVALS

Sankranti (p919; ⊙ Jan) This important Telugu festival marks the end of harvest season. Kite-flying abounds, doorsteps are decorated with colourful *kolams* (rice-flour designs) and men adorn cattle with bells and fresh horn paint.

Brahmotsavam (Venkateshwara Temple, Tirumala; ⊙ Sep/Oct) This nine-day festival sees the Venkateshwara temple at Tirumala (p936) awash in vast crowds of worshippers. Special *pujas* and chariot processions are held, and it's an auspicious time for *darshan* (deity-viewing).

Muharram (Hyderabad; ⊙ Sep/Oct) Commemorates the martyrdom of Mohammed's grandson Hussain. A huge procession throngs the Old City in Hyderabad (p919).

Hyderabad's other pole is far younger – its Hi-Tech City, or 'Cyberabad', out west, which since the 1990s has propelled the city into the modern world with its accoutrements of glittery malls, multiplexes, clubs, pubs and sleek restaurants to sit alongside the traditional biryani joints and teahouses.

Between the old and the new lie, in both material and geographical terms, dense inner city areas like Abids, north of the Old City, and leafy middle-class areas like Banjara Hills and Jubilee Hills. In the northeast, site of one of Hyderabad's three main train stations, is Secunderabad, the former British military cantonment still referred to as Hyderabad's 'twin city', though they are effectively one now.

One thing you have to accept wherever you are in Hyderabad: the traffic is appalling. Happily a new Metro Rail rapid transit system, coming on stream as we speak, should ease things.

Hyderabad's Muslim population (Urdu-speaking) is concentrated mostly in the Old City and nearby areas north of the Musi River. The majority of the population are Telugu-speaking Hindus and there's also a growing number of migrants from other parts of India attracted by the IT boom.

◎ Sights

◉ Old City

★ Charminar
MONUMENT

(Map p920; Indian/foreigner ₹5/100; ⊘9am-5.30pm) Hyderabad's principal landmark and city symbol was built by Mohammed Quli Qutb Shah in 1591 to commemorate the founding of Hyderabad and the end of epidemics caused by Golconda's water shortage. The beautiful four-column, 56m-high structure has four arches facing the cardinal points, with minarets atop each column (hence the name Charminar, 'four minarets'). It stands at the heart of Hyderabad's most atmospheric area (also known as Charminar), a labyrinth of lanes crowded with shops, stalls, markets and shoppers.

The Charminar's second floor, home to Hyderabad's oldest mosque, and the upper columns, are not open to the public. The structure is illuminated from 7pm to 9pm.

★ Chowmahalla Palace
PALACE

(Map p920; www.chowmahalla.com; Indian/foreigner ₹40/150, camera ₹50; ⊘10am-5pm Sat-Thu)

This opulent 18th- and 19th-century palace, the main residence of several nizams, comprises four garden courtyards in a line from north to south. Most dazzling is the Khilwat Mubarak at the end of the first courtyard, a magnificent durbar hall where nizams held ceremonies under 19 enormous chandeliers of Belgian crystal. Its side rooms today house photos and historical exhibits extolling the nizams' virtues. Its balcony once served as seating for the royal women, who attended durbars in purdah.

Several other halls contain interesting exhibits of nizams' personal possessions, arts, crafts and costumes, and in the southernmost courtyard you'll find a 1911 yellow Rolls-Royce which was preserved for very special occasions and has travelled only 356 miles in more than a century.

Salar Jung Museum
MUSEUM

(Map p920; www.salarjungmuseum.in; Salar Jung Rd; Indian/foreigner ₹10/150, camera ₹50; ⊘10am-5pm Sat-Thu) This vast and varied collection was put together by Mir Yousuf Ali Khan (Salar Jung III), who was briefly grand vizier to the seventh nizam, Osman Ali Khan (r 1911–48), before devoting his large fortune to amassing Asian and European art and craftworks. The 40-plus galleries include early South Indian bronzes and wood and stone sculptures, Indian miniature paintings, European fine art, historic manuscripts, a room of jade and another room of very fancy walking sticks.

A special highlight is the remarkable *Veiled Rebecca* by 19th-century Italian sculptor Benzoni. The museum is very popular, and can be bedlam on Sundays.

HEH The Nizam's Museum
MUSEUM

(Purani Haveli; Map p920; off Dur-e-Sharwah Hospital Rd; adult/child ₹80/15, camera ₹150; ⊘10am-5pm Sat-Thu) The Purani Haveli was a home of the sixth nizam, Mahbub Ali Khan (r 1869–1911). He was rumoured to have never worn the same thing twice: hence the 54m-long, two-storey Burmese teak

Hyderabad

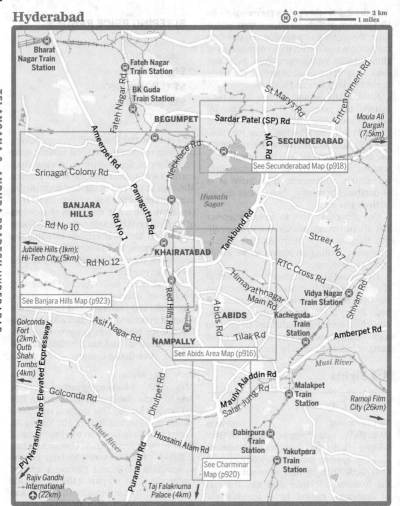

wardrobe. Much of the museum, occupying just one wing of the long palace compound, is devoted to personal effects of the seventh nizam, Osman Ali Khan, including his silver cradle, gold-burnished throne and lavish Silver Jubilee gifts.

Mecca Masjid
MOSQUE

(Map p920; Shah Ali Banda Rd, Charminar; ⏰4.30am-9pm) This mosque is one of the world's largest, with 10,000 men praying here at major Muslim festivals, and also one of Hyderabad's oldest buildings, begun in 1617 by the city's founder Mohammed Quli Qutb Shah. Women are not allowed inside the main prayer hall, and male tourists are unlikely to be let in either (they can look through the railings). Female tourists, even with headscarves, may not even be allowed into the vast courtyard if their clothing is judged too skimpy or tight.

Several bricks embedded above the prayer hall's central arch are made with soil from Mecca, hence the mosque's name. An enclosure alongside the courtyard contains the tombs of several Hyderabad nizams.

Badshahi Ashurkhana   MUSLIM SACRED SITE
(Map p920; High Court Rd) The 1594 Badshahi Ashurkhana (literally 'royal house of mourning') was one of the first structures built by the Qutb Shahs in their new city of Hyderabad. In a courtyard set back from the road, its walls are practically glowing with intricate, brightly coloured tile mosaics. The Ashurkhana is packed during Muharram, as well as on Thursdays, when local Shiites gather to commemorate the martyrdom of Hussain Ibn Ali. Visitors should remove shoes and dress modestly (including a headscarf for women).

⊙ Abids Area

State Museum   MUSEUM
(Map p916; Public Gardens Rd, Nampally; admission ₹10, camera/video ₹100/500; ⊙10.30am-4.30pm Sat-Thu, closed 2nd Sat of month) This sprawling museum, in a fanciful 1920 building constructed by the seventh nizam as a playhouse for one of his daughters, hosts a collection of important archaeological finds as well as an exhibit on the region's Buddhist history, with relics of the Buddha himself. There's also an interesting decorative-arts gallery, where you can learn about Bidriware inlaid metalwork and *kalamkari* textile painting, plus a bronze sculpture gallery and a 4500-year-old Egyptian mummy

British Residency   HISTORIC BUILDING
(Koti Women's College; Koti) This palatial Palladian residence, built in 1803-06 by James Achilles Kirkpatrick, the British Resident (official East India Company representative) in Hyderabad, features in William Dalrymple's brilliant historical love story *White Mughals*. It's sadly dilapidated today, though long-mooted restoration plans may at last be coming to fruition. If you enter the grounds a caretaker will probably offer to open up the grand original building (tip ₹50 to ₹100 when you've finished).

Kirkpatrick became enchanted by Hyderabad courtly culture, converted to Islam and married Khair-un-Nissa, a teenage relative of the Hyderabad prime minister. The Residency and its extensive gardens became the Osmania University College for Women, known as Koti Women's College, in 1949. Inside the grand classical portico, you can admire the Durbar Hall, with Islamic geometric designs on its high ceiling above the

chandeliers and classical columns, and the elaborate curving staircase behind. In the overgrown gardens to the southwest you'll find a British cemetery and, if you're lucky, the surviving entrance to the Residency's zenana (women's quarters) and a model of the Residency building made by Kirkpatrick for Khair-un-Nissa – though our guide refused to venture beyond the cemetery for fear of snakes! Detours (p918) does fascinating White Mughals tours which include the Residency.

Birla Mandir   HINDU TEMPLE
(Map p916; ⊙7am-noon & 2-9pm) The ethereal Birla Mandir, constructed of white Rajasthani marble in 1976, graces Kalabahad (Black Mountain), one of two rocky hills overlooking Hussain Sagar. Dedicated to Venkateshwara, it's a popular Hindu worship centre, with a relaxed atmosphere and affords magnificent views over the city, especially at sunset.

Birla Modern Art Gallery   MUSEUM
(Map p916; www.birlasciencecentre.org; Naubat Pahad Lane, Adarsh Nagar; admission ₹50; ⊙10.30am-6pm) This skilfully curated collection of modern and contemporary art is the best of its kind in South India. Look for paintings by superstars Jogen Chowdhury, Tyeb Mehta and Arpita Singh. Also here is the fun **Birla Science Centre** (Map p916; museum/planetarium ₹50/50; ⊙10.30am-8pm, planetarium shows 11.30am, 4pm & 6pm), comprising a museum of science, dolls and archaeology, and a planetarium.

⊙ Other Areas

★**Golconda Fort**   FORT
(Indian/foreigner ₹5/100, sound-and-light show adult ₹70-130; ⊙9am-5pm, English-language sound-and-light show 6.30pm Nov-Feb, 7pm Mar-Oct) It was the Qutb Shahs in the 16th century who made Golconda into the massive fortress whose substantial ruins we see today. The mighty citadel is built on a 120m-high granite hill, surrounded by crenellated ramparts of large masonry blocks, with another ring of crenellated ramparts, 11km in perimeter, outside it. Morning visits are best for relative peace and quiet.

By the time of the Qutb Shahs, Golconda fort had already existed for at least three centuries under the Kakatiyas and Bahmani sultanate, and was already famed for its diamonds, which were mostly mined in

Abids Area

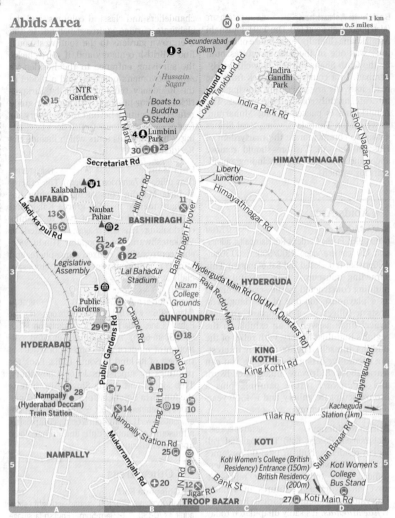

the Krishna River valley, but cut and traded here. The Qutb Shahs moved to their new city of Hyderabad in 1591, but maintained Golconda as a citadel until the Mughal emperor Aurangzeb took it in 1687 after a year-long siege, ending Qutb Shahi rule.

Golconda's massive gates were studded with iron spikes to obstruct war elephants. Within the fort, a series of concealed glazed earthenware pipes ensured a reliable water supply, while the ingenious acoustics guaranteed that even the smallest sound from the entrance would echo across the fort complex.

Guides charge at least ₹600 per 90-minute tour. Small ₹20 guide booklets are also available. Inside the citadel gate, an anticlockwise circuit leads through gardens and up past mostly minor buildings to the top of the hill, where you'll find the functioning Hindu Jagadamba Mahakali Temple and the three-storey durbar hall, with fine panoramas. You then descend to the old palace buildings in the southeastern part of the fort and return to the entrance passing the elegant three-arched Taramati Mosque.

Golconda is about 10km west from Abids or the Charminar: autorickshaws charge

Abids Area

⊚ Sights
1	Birla Mandir	A2
	Birla Modern Art Gallery	(see 2)
2	Birla Science Centre	B3
3	Buddha Statue & Hussain Sagar	B1
4	Lumbini Park	B2
5	State Museum	B3

⊜ Sleeping
6	Hotel Harsha	B4
7	Hotel Rajmata	B4
8	Hotel Suhail	B5
9	Royalton Hotel	B4
10	Taj Mahal Hotel	B4

⊗ Eating
	Dakshina Mandapa	(see 10)
11	Gufaa	B2
12	Kamat Andhra Meals	B5
13	Kamat Hotel	A2
14	Kamat Hotel	B4
	Kamat Jowar Bhakri	(see 12)
	Kamat Restaurant	(see 12)
15	Paradise	A1

⊕ Entertainment
16	Ravindra Bharathi Theatre	A3

⊜ Shopping
17	Fabindia	B3
18	Lepakshi	B4

⊙ Information
19	Aloe Vera Home	B4
20	Care Hospital	B5
21	State Bank of India	A3
22	Telangana Tourism	B3
23	Telangana Tourism	B2

⊙ Transport
24	Air India	B3
25	GPO Abids Bus Stop	B5
26	Jet Airways	B3
27	Koti Bus Stand	D5
28	Nampally Reservation Complex	A4
29	Public Gardens Bus Stop	B4
30	Secretariat Bus Stop (Pushpak)	B2

TELANGANA & ANDHRA PRADESH HYDERABAD

around ₹400 return, including waiting. Buses 65G and 66G run from Charminar bus stop to Golconda via GPO Abids hourly; the journey takes about an hour. Bus 142K goes from Koti bus stop via GPO Abids about every 90 minutes.

★ **Qutb Shahi Tombs**   HISTORIC SITE
(Tolichowki;   adult/child   ₹10/5,   camera/video ₹20/100;   ⊙9.30am-5.30pm Sat-Thu) These 21 magnificent domed granite tombs, with almost as many mosques, sit serenely in landscaped gardens about 2km northwest of Golconda Fort, where many of their occupants spent large parts of their lives. Seven of the eight Qutb Shahi rulers were buried here, as well as family members and a few physicians, courtesans and other favourites. An exhibition near the entrance provides helpful explanatory information.

The tombs' great domes are mounted on cubical bases, many of which have beautiful colonnades and delicate lime stucco ornamentation. You could easily spend half a day taking photos and wandering in and out of the mausoleums. Among the finest is that of Mohammed Quli, the founder of Hyderabad, standing 42m tall on a platform near the edge of the complex, with views back towards Golconda.

The tombs are an easy walk from Golconda, or about ₹30 by autorickshaw. Infrequent buses 80S and 142K also link the two places.

Paigah Tombs   HISTORIC SITE
(Santoshnagar;   ⊙9.30am-5pm)   FREE   The aristocratic Paigah family, purportedly descendents of the second Caliph of Islam, were fierce loyalists of the nizams, serving as statespeople, philanthropists and generals under and alongside them. The Paigahs' necropolis, in a quiet neighbourhood 4km southeast of Charminar, is a small compound of exquisite mausoleums made of marble and lime stucco. It's signposted down a small lane opposite Owaisi Hospital on the Inner Ring Rd.

The complex contains 27 carved-marble tombs in enclosures with delicately carved walls and pillars, stunning geometrically patterned filigree screens and, overhead, tall, graceful turrets. At the western end a handsome mosque is reflected in its large ablutions pool.

Moula Ali Dargah   MUSLIM SACRED SITE
Out on the city's northeastern fringes, the dramatic rock mound of Moula Ali hill is a wonderful change of pace, with distant views, cool breezes and at the top, up 500 steps, a dargah (shrine to a Sufi saint) containing what's believed to be a handprint of Ali, the son-in-law of the Prophet Mohammed. The dargah's reputed healing properties make it a pilgrimage site for the sick.

Secunderabad

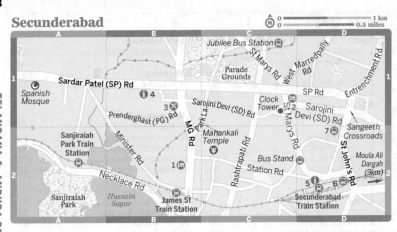

Secunderabad

🛏 Sleeping

🍴 Eating

ℹ Information

ℹ Transport

Visitors are normally allowed inside the dargah, which is covered in thousands of tiny mirrors, only during the three-day Moula Ali *urs* festival during Muharram, but you can admire them it outside at other times.

Moula Ali hill is 9km northeast of Secunderabad – around ₹110 one-way by autorickshaw, or take bus 16A or 16C from Rathifile bus stand to ECIL bus stand, and an autorickshaw 2km from there.

Buddha Statue & Hussain Sagar MONUMENT
(Map p916; boats adult/child ₹55/35) Set picturesquely on a plinth in the Hussain Sagar, a lake created by the Qutb Shahs, is one of the world's largest free-standing stone Buddha statues (18m tall). It's an especially magnificent sight when illuminated at night.

Frequent boats make the 30-minute return trip to the statue from both **Eat Street** (Map p923; ⊙launches 3-8pm) and popular **Lumbini Park** (Map p916; admission ₹10; ⊙9am-9pm). The Tankbund Rd promenade, on the eastern shore of Hussain Sagar, has great views of the statue.

🎫 Tours

★Detours CULTURE, FOOD
(☑9000850505; www.detoursindia.com; per person 3hr walk ₹2500, half-/full day tour incl transport & admissions from ₹3500/5500) Fascinating and entertaining individual and small-group tours led by the enthusiastic, knowledgeable Jonty Rajagopalan and her small team. Options cover off-the-beaten-track corners of Hyderabad and original angles on the classic sights, plus markets, food (with cooking lessons and eating included), wedding culture, religion and crafts.

Telangana Tourism SIGHTSEEING
(☑1800-42546464; www.telanganatourism.gov. in) On weekends Telangana Tourism does an afternoon-and-evening tour to Chowmahalla Palace, Falaknuma Palace and the Golconda sound-and-light show for ₹3100/2000 with/without high tea at Falaknuma. It also offers daily bus tours of city sights (from ₹350 plus admission tickets) and Ramoji Film City (₹1250/1100 AC/non-AC), evening Golconda sound-and-light trips, and out-of-town trips. Book at any Telangana Tourism office (p925).

Heritage Walks WALKING TOUR
(Map p920; ☑9849728841; www.aptdc.in/heritage_walks; per person ₹50; ⊙7.30-9am Sun) These Sunday-morning walks from the Charminar were designed and are sometimes led by architect Madhu Vottery, whose *Guide to Heritage of Hyderabad* is part of a movement to foster Hyderabad's rich architectural heritage.

★ Festivals & Events

Sankranti HINDU
(regionwide; ⊙Jan) Hyderabad's skies fill with kites during this important Telugu harvest festival.

Muharram MUSLIM
(⊙Sep/Oct) Muharram is the first month of the Islamic year and commemorates the martyrdom of Mohammed's grandson Hussain with mass mourning and all-night sermons. Black-clad Shiite throngs gather at Badshahi Ashurkhana, and a massive Old City procession on the 10th day draws crowds from around the region.

🛏 Sleeping

The inner-city Abids area is convenient for Nampally station and the Old City. For more space and greenery head to middle-class Banjara Hills, about 4km northwest of Abids. At top-end hotels good discounts are often available from the rack rates quoted here.

Golden Glory Guesthouse GUESTHOUSE $
(Map p923; ☑040-23554765; www.goldengloryguesthouse.com; off Rd No 3, Banjara Hills; s/d incl breakfast ₹900/1240, with AC ₹1240/1690; ❋🛜) This well-run place has a nice location on a leafy residential street in Banjara Hills. The 22 rooms are modest, but clean and homey, and some have balconies. There's free wi-fi

throughout, and several moderately priced eateries are nearby.

Hotel Rajmata HOTEL $
(Map p916; ☑040-66665555; royalrajmata@gmail.com; Public Gardens Rd; s/d ₹900/1020, AC ₹2030/2250; ❋🛜) The Rajmata, popular with families, is only 250m from Nampally station, but set back from the busy main road, which keeps things quiet. Standard quarters are aged but roomy; air-con rooms are overpriced but fresh.

Hotel Suhail HOTEL $
(Map p916; ☑040-24610299; www.hotelsuhail.in; Troop Bazar; s/d/tr from ₹600/800/1100, air-con ₹1100/1365/1600; ❋@🛜) Better than most comparable places in Abids, the Suhail has friendly staff and large, quiet rooms with balconies and hot water. It's tucked away on a lane off Bank St.

YMCA International Guest House HOSTEL $
(Map p918; ☑040-27801190; secunderabadymca@yahoo.co.in; St Mary's Rd, Secunderabad; dm ₹125, s/d ₹500/600, without bathroom ₹350/450, r with AC ₹950; ❋) This friendly hostel in a quiet spot in Secunderabad has basic rooms, some with balconies. The sheets are cleaner than the walls, and the shared bathrooms are fine.

Taj Mahal Hotel HOTEL $$
(Map p916; ☑040-24758250; www.hoteltajmahalindia.com; Abids Rd; incl breakfast s ₹1690-3150, d ₹2420-3150; ❋🛜) The original 1924 building houses the reception and a few bedrooms ('heritage' rooms have some character, others are plain); the majority of rooms are in a modern block at the side and reasonably attractive in simple contemporary greys and reds. It adds up to good value, with helpful reception, free wi-fi and air-con in all rooms.

KITSCHABAD

Along with Hyderabad's world-class sights are some attractions that err on the quirky side.

Ramoji Film City (www.ramojifilmcity.com; adult/child from ₹800/700; ⊙8.30am-10pm) The Telangana/Andhra Pradesh film industry, 'Tollywood', is massive, and so is the 6.7-sq-km Film City, where films and TV shows in Telugu, Tamil and Hindi, among others, are made. The day-visit ticket includes a bus tour, funfair rides and shows. Take bus 206 or 209 from Koti Women's College (1½ hours, 30km) or a Telangana Tourism (p918) tour.

Sudha Cars Museum (www.sudhacars.com; Bahadurpura; Indian/foreigner ₹50/200, camera ₹50; ⊙9.30am-6.30pm) The eccentric creations of auto-enthusiast K Sudhakar include cars in the shape of a cricket bat, hamburger and snooker table, among other wacky designs. And they all work. The museum is 3km west of Charminar.

Charminar 🅝 ⓝ
0 ──────── 0.5 km
0 ──────── 0.25 miles

painstakingly mending such nizam-esque indulgences as embossed-leather wallpaper and 24-carat-gold ceiling trim. The rooms are stunning, and it's astoundingly opulent.

Non-guests can come for lunch/dinner (from ₹2420/3025) or 'high tea' (₹2240), served from 3.30pm to 5pm on the Jade Room terrace. Guests (including those just there to eat) get a free palace tour at 5pm. Book meals two days ahead, or you won't get past the outer gate of the 1.2km driveway.

The Taj group also runs three of Hyderabad's other best hotels, in Banjara Hills: the opulent **Taj Krishna** (Map p923; ☑040-66662323; www.tajhotels.com; Rd No 1; s/d from ₹44,970; ✳ @ 🛜 ☲), stylish **Taj Deccan** (Map p923; ☑040-66669999; www.tajhotels.com; Rd No 1; s/d from ₹12,930/14,060; ✳ @ 🛜 ☲) and lakeside **Taj Banjara** (Map p923; ☑040-66669999; www.tajhotels.com; Rd No 1; s/d from ₹9560/10,680; ✳ @ 🛜 ☲).

Hotel Harsha   HOTEL $$
(Map p916; ☑040-23201188; www.hotelharsha.net; Public Gardens Rd; s/d incl breakfast from ₹2020/2240; ✳ 🛜) Rooms don't have tons of character and can be noisy but they're big, clean, comfy and in good shape. Nampally station is close, check-out is 24 hours and staff are all smiles. One of the city's best deals. Wi-fi is ₹110 per hour.

Raj Classic Inn   HOTEL $$
(Map p918; ☑040-27815291; rajclassicinn@gmail.com; 50 MG Rd, Secunderabad; s/d incl breakfast from ₹1580/1920; ✳ 🛜) Clean, spacious rooms a short ride from Secunderabad.

★ Taj Falaknuma Palace HERITAGE HOTEL $$$
(☑040-66298585; www.tajhotels.com; Engine Bowli, Falaknuma; s/d from ₹41,600/43,290; ✳ @ 🛜) The Taj group took more than a decade to restore the former residence of the sixth nizam, an 1884 neoclassical palace on a panoramic hilltop south of the city,

Fortune Park Vallabha   HOTEL $$$
(Map p923; ☑040-39884444; www.fortunehotels.in; Rd No 12, Banjara Hills; s/d incl breakfast from ₹5060/6190; ✳ @ 🛜) Fortune Park provides

large, comfy, contemporary rooms with stained-glass panels, tea/coffee makers and a good array of toiletries, plus a terrific breakfast buffet and free morning yoga sessions. It's a pleasure to stay in, except for the hard-to-fathom wi-fi charging system!

Royalton Hotel   HOTEL **$$$**
(Map p916; ☑040-67122000; www.royaltonhotel.in; Fateh Sultan Lane, Abids; s/d incl breakfast from ₹5060/5650; ❋ ❀) In a relatively quiet part of Abids, Royalton's gargantuan black lobby chandelier and mirrored lifts give off a slight Manhattan vibe. Rooms have tasteful textiles, glass showers and tea/coffee makers. The hotel is vegetarian, and alcohol-free.

Marigold   HOTEL **$$$**
(Map p923; ☑040-67363636; www.marigoldhotels.com; Ameerpet Rd, Greenlands; s/d incl breakfast from ₹6750/7870; ❋@❀❀) The Marigold is as practical as it is stylish. Rooms are smart but not try-hard, with golds, neutrals and fresh flowers, while the lobby has vanishing-edge fountains and artful chandeliers. The rooftop pool is a great feature.

The **GreenPark** (Map p923; ☑040-66515151; www.hotelgreenpark.com; Ameerpet Rd, Greenlands; s/d incl breakfast from ₹5630/6750; ❋@❀), under the same ownership next door, is a notch lower in style and comfort but still a worthy alternative.

✖ Eating

In the early evenings, look out for *mirchi bhajji* (chilli fritters), served at street stalls with tea. The Hyderabadi style is famous: chillis are stripped of their seeds, stuffed with tamarind, sesame and spices, dipped in chickpea batter and fried.

Per local usage, we use the term 'meal' instead of 'thali'.

✖ Old City & Abids Area

Govind Dosa   STREET FOOD **$**
(Map p920; Charkaman; snacks ₹30-60; ⊙6am-noon) Probably the city's most famous breakfast cook, cheery Govind's street-corner stand is permanently surrounded by happy Hyderabadis savouring his delicious dosas and *idlis* (spongy fermented rice cakes), including unusual dosas with *upma* (a seasoned semolina porridge) and *tawa idlis* topped with chilli powder and spices.

Kamat Andhra Meals   ANDHRA **$**
(Map p916; Troop Bazar; meals ₹90; ⊙11am-4pm & 7-11pm) This small, simple restaurant does authentic and delicious veg Andhra meals on banana leaves, topped up till your tongue falls off from the heat. In the same compound, the Maharashtrian **Kamat Jowar Bhakri** (Map p916; meals ₹130-180; ⊙noon-4pm & 7-11pm) and the South and North Indian **Kamat Restaurant** (Map p916; meals & mains ₹75-180; ⊙7am-10.30pm) are also good. No relation to Kamat Hotel.

Nimrah   CAFE **$**
(Map p920; Charminar; baked goods ₹2-10; ⊙5.30am-11pm) Irani cafes – old-fashioned teahouses founded by 19th-century Persian immigrants and serving super-thick, super-sweet Irani chai – are an endangered breed in India these days, but Hyderabad still has a goodly number. Nimrah, almost underneath the Charminar's arches, has a particularly tasty range of Irani baked goods to accompany your chai pick-me-up.

The classic dunk is Osmania biscuits (melt-in-the-mouth shortbreads). Nimrah also offers *dil khush* ('happy heart') and *dil pasand,* types of pie/pastry with sweet coconut-y fillings, and more.

TELANGANA & ANDHRA PRADESH HYDERABAD

HYDERABAD CUISINE

Hyderabad has a food culture all its own and Hyderabadis take great pride and pleasure in it. It was the Mughals who brought the tasty biryanis, skewer kebabs and *haleem* (a thick Ramadan soup of pounded, spiced wheat with goat, chicken or beef, and lentils). Mutton (goat or lamb) is the classic biryani base, though chicken, egg and vegetable biryanis are plentiful too. Biryanis come in vast quantity and one serve may satisfy two people.

If you're in Hyderabad during Ramadan (known locally as Ramzan), look out for the clay ovens called *bhattis.* You'll probably hear them before you see them. Men gather around, taking turns to vigorously pound *haleem* inside purpose-built structures. Come nightfall, the serious business of eating begins. The taste is worth the wait.

Andhra cuisine, found in Telangana as well as Andhra Pradesh, is more curry- and pilau-based, often with coconut and/or cashew flavours, and famous across India for its delicious spicy hotness. Vegetarians are well catered for, but you'll find plenty of fish, seafood and meat dishes too.

★**Hotel Shadab**　　HYDERABADI $$
(Map p920; High Court Rd, Charminar; mains ₹140-300; ⏲noon-11.30pm) This hopping restaurant, packed with Old City families and good vibes, is the capital of biryani, kebabs and mutton and, during Ramadan, *haleem* (thick soup of spiced wheat with goat, chicken or beef). Head upstairs to the air-con room.

★**Shah Ghouse Cafe**　　HYDERABADI $$
(Shah Ali Banda Rd; mains ₹100-190; ⏲noon-2am) During Ramadan, Hyderabadis line up for Shah Ghouse's famous *haleem,* and at any time of year the biryani is near-perfect. Don't expect ambience: just good, hard-working, traditional food, in a no-frills upstairs dining hall.

Dakshina Mandapa　　SOUTH INDIAN $$
(Map p916; Taj Mahal Hotel, Abids Rd; mains & meals ₹160-195; ⏲7am-10.30pm) A beloved spot for South Indian vegetarian meals. You may have to wait for a lunch table, but order the South Indian thali and you'll be brought heap after heap of rice and refills of exquisite, burn-your-tongue-off veg dishes. The air-con room upstairs does a very good ₹300 lunch buffet (noon to 3pm).

Kamat Hotel　　SOUTH INDIAN $$
(Map p916; Secretariat Rd, Saifabad; meals ₹95-170, mains ₹150-200; ⏲8am-10pm) Each Kamat is slightly different, but they're all good for South Indian fare. There's another **branch** (Map p916; Nampally Station Rd; meals & mains ₹70-165; ⏲7am-10pm) near Nampally station.

Gufaa　　NORTH INDIAN $$$
(Map p916; Ohri's Cuisine Court, Bashirbagh Rd; mains ₹250-600; ⏲11am-3.30pm & 7-11.30pm) Gufaa ('Cave') has faux-rock walls, zebra-striped furniture and a Bollywood oldies soundtrack. And it serves Peshawari food (good veg and nonveg kebabs and curries). Somehow it all works, and even the dhal here is special. A good drinks menu too.

🍴 **Banjara Hills & Jubilee Hills**

★**Southern Spice**　　SOUTH INDIAN $$
(Map p923; Rd No 3; mains ₹170-500, thalis ₹210-320; ⏲noon-3.30pm & 7-10.30pm) Southern Spice does a fine Andhra meal as well as specialities from all over the south, in several cosy, warm-toned rooms. It's a good place to

sample typical Andhra dishes such as *natu kodi iguru* ('country chicken') or *chapa pulusu,* a tasty, spicy fish dish.

Chutneys　　SOUTH INDIAN $$
(Map p923; Shilpa Arcade, Rd No 3; mains & meals ₹240-300; ⏲7am-11pm) Chutneys is famous for its South Indian meals and all-day dosas, *idlis* and *uttapams.* Its dishes are low on chilli, so you can get the full 'Andhra meals' experience without the pain. It's a bustling place with teams of purple-shirted waiters.

★**SO**　　ASIAN, MEDITERRANEAN $$$
(☎040-23558004; www.notjustso.com; Aryan's, Rd No 92, near Apollo Hospital, Jubilee Hills; mains ₹375-625; ⏲noon-11pm; 🛜) On a quiet Jubilee Hills rooftop, with candles, loungy playlists and sugarcane and banana plants, SO is one of the most atmospheric eating spots in town. And the pan-Asian and Mediterranean dishes are exquisite. Downstairs are the highly popular **Little Italy** (☑23558001; www.littleitaly.in; mains ₹350-600; ⏲noon-3pm & 7-11pm) and MOB (p924). It's on a side-road off the south side of KBR National Park, 4km west of Banjara Hills' Rd No 1.

Fusion 9　　CONTINENTAL $$$
(Map p923; ☑040-65577722; www.fusion9.in; Rd No 1; mains ₹550-975; ⏲12.30-3.30pm & 7-11.30pm) Soft lighting and cosy decor set off oven-roasted seabass or Moroccan veg tagine with lemon couscous. One of the best international menus in town. Downstairs, **Deli 9** (Map p923; snacks ₹40-230; ⏲9.30am-10.30pm; 🛜) has quiches, cakes, crepes and free wi-fi.

Firdaus　　INDIAN $$$
(Map p923; ☑040-66662323; Taj Krishna, Rd No 1; mains ₹500-1100; ⏲12.30-3pm & 7.30-11.45pm) For a refined evening of top-class Hyderabadi and other dishes to the strains of live *ghazals* (classical Urdu love songs, accompanied by harmonium and tabla), book a table at elegant Firdaus. It even serves *haleem* outside Ramadan.

Barbeque Nation　　INDIAN $$$
(Map p923; ☑040-64566692; www.barbeque-nation.com; ANR Centre, Rd No 1; veg/nonveg lunch ₹620/745, dinner ₹940/1060; ⏲noon-3.30pm & 6.30-10.30pm) All-you-can-eat kebabs, curries, salads and desserts in unpretentious surrounds, with many veg and nonveg options. A great-value place to come when you're hungry! Prices go up ₹150 for Sunday lunch, and down ₹240 for Monday and Tuesday dinner and before 7pm any night.

Banjara Hills

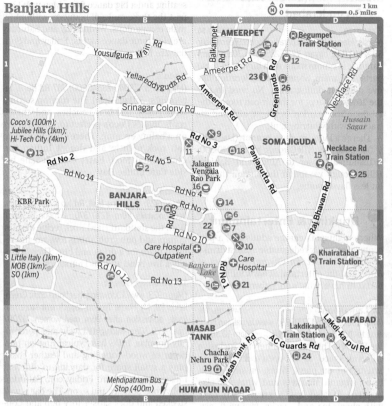

Banjara Hills

🛏 Sleeping
1	Fortune Park Vallabha	B3
2	Golden Glory Guesthouse	B2
3	GreenPark	C1
4	Marigold	C1
5	Taj Banjara	C3
6	Taj Deccan	C3
7	Taj Krishna	C3

🍴 Eating
8	Barbeque Nation	C3
9	Chutneys	C2
10	Deli 9	C3
	Firdaus	(see 7)
	Fusion 9	(see 10)
11	Southern Spice	B2

🍸 Drinking & Nightlife
12	10 Downing Street	C1
13	Coco's	A2
14	Hard Rock Cafe	C2
15	Kismet	D2
16	Lamakaan	C2

🛍 Shopping
17	Fabindia	B2
18	Himalaya Book World	C2
19	Malkha	C4
20	Suvasa	B3

ℹ Information
	Citibank ATM	(see 14)
21	Citibank ATM	C3
22	Citibank ATM	C3
	Indiatourism	(see 23)
23	Telangana Tourism	C1

ℹ Transport
24	AC Guards Bus Stop (Pushpak)	D4
25	Eat Street Boating	D2
26	Paryatak Bhavan Bus Stop (Pushpak)	C1

TELANGANA & ANDHRA PRADESH HYDERABAD

🍴 Secunderabad

Paradise
HYDERABADI $$

(Persis; Map p918; www.paradisefoodcourt.com; cnr SD & MG Rds; biryani ₹220-285; ⏱11.30am-11pm) Paradise is synonymous with biryani in these parts. The main, Secunderabad location has five different dining areas. No need to pay the 20% surcharge for the air-con rooms: the 1st-floor 'roof garden' is bright, airy and attractive, with whirring fans.

There's a large, modern **branch** (Map p916; ☎040-66661188; NTR Gardens; mains ₹240-500; ⏱11am-11pm) closer to Abids and Banjara Hills, though we found the biryani there a bit less flavoursome.

🍷 Drinking & Entertainment

Where nightspots charge admission, a percentage is usually redeemable against drinks or food. The *Deccan Chronicle, Times of India* and the entertaining www.fullhyderabad.com have 'what's on' information.

★ Lamakaan
CAFE, THEATRE

(Map p923; ☎9642731329; www.lamakaan.com; next to JVR Park, Banjara Hills; ⏱10am-10.30pm Tue-Sun; 📶) This non-commercial 'inclusive cultural space' is an open centre where artists put on plays, films, music, exhibitions, organic markets and whatever else inspires. It also has a great Irani cafe, with cheap tea and snacks, free wi-fi, artsy types collaborating on the leafy patio and a bulletin board of Hyderabad's most interesting possibilities.

★ MOB
BAR

(www.facebook.com/itismob; Aryan's, Rd No 92, near Apollo Hospital, Jubilee Hills; ⏱noon-11.30pm; 📶) A refreshingly mixed-gender, mixed-age crowd flocks to this pub-like space for the simple pleasures of conversation, terrific Belgian beer (tap or bottled) and tasty finger food. You can dine at SO (p922) or Little Italy (p922) in the same building. Packed on Friday and Saturday evenings. It's on a side-road off the south side of KBR National Park, 4km west of Banjara Hills' Rd No 1.

Kismet
CLUB

(Map p923; ☎040-23456789; www.theparkhotels.com/hyderabad; The Park, Somajiguda; admission per couple ₹500-2000; ⏱9pm-midnight or later Wed-Sun) *The* happening nightclub, glamorous Kismet is all curves, with loungey booth seating and a big dance floor. Men won't get past the three ranks of bouncers without female companions. Wednesday and Saturday are electronic dance nights; Friday and Sunday are Bollywood.

Coco's
BAR

(Map p923; ☎040-23540600; 217 Rd No 2, Jubilee Hills; ⏱11am-11pm) The rooftop setting, with rustic bamboo couches and thatch roofs, makes Coco's perfect for a cold drink on a balmy evening. There's live blues and soft rock nightly, and decent Indian and Continental food. Enter down a lane beside Café Coffee Day.

Hard Rock Cafe
BAR

(Map p923; GVK One Mall, Rd No 1, Banjara Hills; beer/cocktails from ₹210/370; ⏱noon-11.30pm) With the standard Hard Rock recipe of stars' guitars and pub grub, this is a warm and relaxed place for a drink and bite. There's usually a live band at 9pm Thursdays.

10 Downing Street
BAR

(Map p923; www.10downingstreetindia.com; Greenlands Rd, My Home Tycoon department store rear yard; admission after 9pm men/women ₹1200/free; ⏱11.30am-midnight) Lively and perennially popular, 10DS has 'typical English pub' decor of wood panelling and leather sofas, plus a small space for dancing to different music nightly – retro Friday, club Saturday, Bollywood Sunday, and so on. The bar is well stocked and does satisfactory pub and Continental food.

Ravindra Bharathi Theatre
THEATRE

(Map p916; ☎040-23233672; www.ravindrabharathi.org; Ladki-ka-pul Rd, Saifabad) Regular music, dance and drama performances.

🛍 Shopping

Charminar (p925) is the most exciting place to shop: you'll find exquisite pearls, slippers, gold and fabrics alongside billions of bangles.

Malkha
CLOTHING

(Map p923; www.malkha.in; Khadi Bhavan, Masab Tank Rd, opposite NMDC bus stop, Humayun Nagar; ⏱10am-7pm Mon-Sat) Unlike industrial cotton, Malkha cloth is made near the cotton fields, by hand and with natural dyes, reducing strain to the cotton and the environment and putting primary producers in control. The result is gorgeous; pick up shawls or fabric at reasonable prices.

Himalaya Book World   BOOKS
(Map p923; Panjagutta Circle, Banjara Hills; ⊙10.30am-10pm) A fine selection of English-language fiction and nonfiction by Indian and international authors.

Fabindia   CLOTHING
(Map p923; www.fabindia.com; Rd No 9, Banjara Hills; ⊙11am-8.30pm Tue-Sun) 🌿 Lovely women's and some men's clothes in artisanal fabrics with contemporary prints and colours, at fair prices. Has a branch (Map p916; Fateh Maidan; ⊙10.30am-8.30pm) in Bashirbagh.

Lepakshi   HANDICRAFTS
(Map p916; www.lepakshihandicrafts.gov.in; Abids Rd, Gunfoundry; ⊙10am-8pm Mon-Sat) Big selection of Telangana, Andhra and other crafts.

Suvasa   CLOTHING
(Map p923; www.suvasa.in; Rd No 12, Banjara Hills; ⊙11am-7.30pm) Suvasa's block-printed kurtas (long shirts with a short or no collar), baggy *salwar* pants and dupattas (scarves) are a step up in cut and prints from most mainstream boutiques. A Suvasa kurta plus some *churidhars* (leggings) equals your new favourite travel outfit.

Hyderabad Perfumers   PERFUME
(Map p920; Patthargatti; ⊙10am-8.30pm Mon-Sat) This fourth-generation family business can whip something up for you on the spot.

ℹ️ Information

INTERNET ACCESS
Aloe Vera Home (Map p916; Chirag Ali Lane; per hour ₹20; ⊙6am-10pm) Small room in a side lane.

MEDICAL SERVICES
Care Hospital (📞emergency 105711; www.care-hospitals.com) A reputable private hospital with several branches, including 24-hour pharmacies, in Banjara Hills (Map p923; 📞30418888; Rd No 1); Banjara Hills Outpatient (Map p923; 📞39310444; 4th Lane, Rd No 10); Nampally (Map p916; 📞30417777; Mukarramjahi Rd).

MONEY
Citibank ATM (Map p923; Prashanthi Mansion, Rd No 1, Banjara Hills) Citibank ATMs allow withdrawals up to ₹40,000, saving on bank charges. Also at City Center Mall (Map p923; Rd No 1, Banjara Hills) and GVK One Mall (Map p923; Rd No 1, Banjara Hills).
State Bank of India (Map p916; HACA Bhavan, Saifabad; ⊙10.30am-4pm Mon-Fri) Currency exchange.

POST
General Post Office (Map p916; Abids Circle; ⊙8am-7.30pm Mon-Sat, 10am-1pm Sun)

TOURIST INFORMATION
Indiatourism (Map p923; 📞040-23409199; www.incredibleindia.org; Tourism Plaza, Greenlands Rd; ⊙9.30am-6pm Mon-Fri, 9.30am-1pm Sat) Very helpful, with information on Hyderabad, Telangana and beyond.
Telangana Tourism (📞1800 42546464; www.telanganatourism.gov.in) Tourist information and bookings for state-government-run tours and hotels in Telangana. Branches at Bashirbagh (Map p916; 📞66745986; Shakar Bhavan; ⊙6.30am-8.30pm), Tankbund Rd (Map p916; 📞65581555; ⊙6.30am-8.30pm), Greenlands Rd (Map p923; 📞040-23414334; Tourism Plaza; ⊙7am-8pm), Hyderabad airport (📞040-24253215), Secunderabad (Map p918;

CHARMINAR MARKETS

Hyderabadis and visitors of every stripe flock to the Charminar area's labyrinthine lanes to browse, buy and wander. Patthargatti, the broad avenue leading in from the Musi River, is lined with shops selling clothes (especially wedding outfits), perfumes and Hyderabad's famous pearls. Laad Bazar (Map p920), running west from the Charminar, is famed for its sparkling bangle shops: lac bangles, made from a resinous insect secretion and encrusted with colourful beads or stones, are a Hyderabad speciality. In Laad Bazar you'll also find perfumers, wedding goods and fabrics.

Laad Bazar opens into Mehboob Chowk (Map p920), a square with a 19th-century clock tower and mosque, shops selling antiquarian books and antiques, a livestock market on its south side, and a market in exotic birds, Chiddi Bazar (Map p920), just southwest.

A short distance north, the Patel Market (Map p920), selling cloth fabrics, cranks into action from around 11am in the back lanes between Patthargatti and Rikab Gunj. Further north again and on the other side of Patthargatti, the wholesale vegetable market Mir Alam Mandi (Map p920) trades in all kinds of fresh stuff from 6.30am to 6.30pm daily.

040-27893100; Yatri Nivas Hotel, SP Rd; ⊙6.30am-8.30pm) and Secunderabad station (Map p918; ☑27801614; ⊙10am-8pm). The Andhra Pradesh Tourism Development Corporation (APTDC; ☑1800 42545454; www.aptdc. gov.in), with the same functions for Andhra Pradesh state, shares the same offices, for the moment at least.

❶ Getting There & Away

AIR

Hyderabad's massive, modern, efficient **Rajiv Gandhi International Airport** (☑040-66546370; www.hyderabad.aero; Shamshabad) is 25km southwest of the city centre. It has direct daily flights to 19 Indian cities (on Air Costa, Air India, IndiGo, Jet Airways or Spice-Jet), Chicago, London and several Southeast Asian and Gulf destinations. Only two domestic airlines have city airline offices:

Air India (Map p916; ☑040-23389711; HACA Bhavan, Saifabad; ⊙9.45am-1.15pm & 2-5pm Mon-Sat)

Jet Airways (Map p916; ☑040-39893333; Summit Apts, Hill Fort Rd)

BUS

The main terminal is the 74-platform **Mahatma Gandhi bus station** (MGBS, Imlibun Bus Station; Map p920; ☑040-24614406; ⊙advance booking offices 8am-10.30pm) near Abids. Air-con services by the TSRTC (www.tsrtcbus. in) are quite good; for Karnataka, go with KSRTC near platform 30. Many long-distance services depart in the evening. When booking ahead, women should request seats up front as these are reserved for women.

Secunderabad's **Jubilee bus station** (Map p918; ☑040-27802203) is smaller; frequent city buses run here from St Mary's Rd near Secunderabad station. Useful routes from here include:

Bengaluru (ordinary/Volvo AC/sleeper ₹610/1000/1600, 10 to 12 hours, seven daily)
Vijayawada (non-AC/AC ₹310/450, five to seven hours, 11 daily)
Mumbai ('express' ₹600, 14 hours, 2pm)

TRAIN

Secunderabad, **Nampally** (officially called Hyderabad Deccan), and **Kacheguda** are Hyderabad's three major train stations. Most through trains stop at Kacheguda.

The reservation complexes at **Nampally** (Map p916; ☑040-27829999; ⊙8am-8pm Mon-Sat, 8am-2pm Sun) and **Secunderabad** (Rathifile; Map p918; St John's Rd; ⊙8am-8pm Mon-Sat, 8am-2pm Sun), both in separate buildings away from the stations, have foreign-tourist-quota counters (bring passport and visa photocopies, along with originals). For inquiries and PNR status, phone ☑139.

There are around 20 trains a day each to Warangal (sleeper/3AC/2AC ₹170/535/735, 2½ hours) and Vijayawada (₹190/495/720, six hours), mostly from Secunderabad.

❶ Getting Around

TO/FROM THE AIRPORT

Bus

The TSRTC's Pushpak air-conditioned bus service runs between about 4am and 11pm to and from various stops in the city, including **AC Guards** (Map p923; ₹200, two or three buses hourly) and **Secretariat** (Map p916; ₹200, about hourly), both about 1.5km from Abids, **Paryatak Bhavan** (Map p923) on Greenlands Rd (₹250, about hourly), and **Secunderabad** (Map p918; ₹250, twice hourly). The trip takes about one hour. Contact **TSRTC** (Telangana State Road

BUSES FROM MAHATMA GANDHI BUS STATION

DESTINATION	FARE (₹)	DURATION (HR)	FREQUENCY
Bengaluru	720-1010	9-11	21 buses 5-10.30pm
Bidar	150	4½	hourly 5am-10pm
Chennai	700-1200	12-14	4 buses 6.30-9pm
Hospet	355-850	8-11	9 daily
Mumbai	1100 (AC)	14	6.30pm Thu & Sun
Mysore	1130-1210	12-14	4 buses 5-7.45pm
Tirupati	700-1000	12	half-hourly 1.30-10pm
Vijayawada	350-480	6	half-hourly
Visakhapatnam	730-1100	13	hourly 2-10pm
Warangal	155-195	4	half-hourly

MAJOR TRAINS FROM HYDERABAD & SECUNDERABAD

DESTINATION	TRAIN NO & NAME	FARE (₹)	DURATION (HR)	DEPARTURE TIME & STATION
Bengaluru	22692 or 22694 Rajdhani	1815/1330 (B)	12	6.50pm Secunderabad
	12785 Bangalore Exp	370/970/1370 (A)	11½	7.05pm Kacheguda
Chennai	12604 Hyderabad–Chennai Exp	405/1055/1500 (A)	13	5.20pm Nampally
	12760 Charminar Exp	425/1115/1590 (A)	14	6.30pm Nampally
Delhi	12723 AP Exp	670/1745/2545 (A)	27	6.25am Nampally
	22691 or 22693 Rajdhani	2360/3245 (B)	22	7.50am Secunderabad
Kolkata	12704 Falaknuma Exp	630/1650/2395 (A)	26	4pm Secunderabad
Mumbai	12702 Hussainsagar Exp	425/1115/1590 (A)	14½	2.45pm Nampally
	17032 Mumbai Exp	395/1070/1545 (A)	16½	8.40pm Nampally
Tirupati	12734 Narayanadri Exp	385/1005/1430 (A)	12	6.05pm Secunderabad
	12797 Venkatadri Exp	375/980/1385 (A)	11½	8.05pm Kacheguda
Visakhapatnam	12728 Godavari Exp	405/1055/1500 (A)	12½	5.15pm Nampally

Fares: (A) sleeper/3AC/2AC, (B) 3AC/2AC

Transport Corporation; ☑ 1800 2004599; http://tsrtcbus.in) or check http://hyderabad.aero for timings.

Taxi

The prepaid taxi booth is on the lowest level of the terminal; ignore touts on the way down. Fares to Abids or Banjara Hills are ₹600 to ₹700. **Meru Cabs** (☑ 040-44224422) and **Sky Cabs** (☑ 040-49494949) 'radio taxis', with counters in the arrivals area, charge ₹21 per kilometre (₹26 at night), which works out much the same. Meru and Sky also provide reliable service for trips within the city.

AUTORICKSHAW

Official fares are ₹20 for the first 1.6km, then ₹11 for each additional kilometre, with a 50% surcharge between 11pm and 5am. But most drivers won't use their meters so you must negotiate and will probably end up paying ₹20 to ₹25 per kilometre (more after dark).

BUS

City buses (₹6 to ₹12 for most rides) run everywhere but you'll usually need local help in finding the right stop and right bus; www.hyderabadbusroutes.com gives routes with some stops mapped, but can be inaccurate.

CAR

Arrange car hire through your hotel. The going rate for a small AC car such as an Indica, with a driver, is ₹1000 to ₹1200 per day for city sightseeing (eight hours/80km maximum), and ₹2800 to ₹3200 per day for out-of-town trips (up to 300km).

METRO RAIL

Hyderabad Metro Rail (www.hmr.gov.in), a 72km rapid transit network being phased into operation between 2015 and 2017, will make getting around the city a whole lot easier! Trains will run on elevated tracks above Hyderabad's streets, with 66 stations on three lines.

SELECTED HYDERABAD CITY BUS ROUTES

65G, 66G	Charminar–Golconda Fort, via Afzalgunj, GPO Abids; both about hourly
49M	Secunderabad Junction–Mehdipatnam via Rd No 1 (Banjara Hills); frequent
8A	Charminar–Secunderabad Junction via Afzalgunj, GPO Abids; frequent
40, 86	Secunderabad Junction–Koti Bus Stop; both frequent
127K	Koti Bus Stop–Jubilee Hills via GPO Abids, Public Gardens, Rd Nos 1 & 12 (Banjara Hills); frequent

TRAIN

MMTS suburban trains (www.mmtstraintimings.in; fares ₹5-11) are convenient for the three main stations, but infrequent (every 30 to 45 minutes). There are two routes: Hyderabad (Nampally) to Lingampalli (northwest of Banjara Hills) stops at Necklace Rd, Begumpet and Hi-Tech City; Falaknuma (south of Old City) to Lingampalli stops at Kacheguda and Secunderabad stations and joins the Hyderabad–Lingampalli line at Begumpet.

TELANGANA

The most interesting spots to visit in the newly created state of Telangana, outside its capital Hyderabad, lie in and around the state's second city, Warangal.

Bhongir

Most Hyderabad–Warangal buses and trains stop at Bhongir, 60km from Hyderabad. It's worth stopping to climb the fantastical-looking 12th-century Chalukyan **hill fort** (admission ₹3, camera ₹10; ⊙10am-5pm), sitting on what resembles a gargantuan stone egg right above the bus station. You can leave backpacks at the ticket office.

Warangal

☎0870 / POP 620,000

Warangal was the capital of the Kakatiya kingdom, which ruled most of present-day Telangana and Andhra Pradesh from the 12th to early 14th centuries. **Telangana Tourism** (☎0870-2571339; opposite Indian Oil, Nakkalgutta, Hanumakonda; ⊙10.30am-5pm Mon-Sat) is helpful.

◉ Sights

Fort
FORT

Warangal's fort, on the southern edge of town, was a massive construction with three circles of walls (the outermost 7km around). Most of it is now either fields or buildings, but at the centre is a huge, reassembled Shaivite **Svayambhu Temple** (Indian/foreigner ₹5/100; ⊙9am-6pm), with handsome, large *torana* gateways at its cardinal points. An autorickshaw from Warangal station costs around ₹300 return.

The ticket also covers the Kush Mahal (Shitab Khan Mahal), a 16th-century royal hall 400m west. Almost opposite the Svayambhu entrance is a **park** (admission ₹10; ⊙7am-7pm) containing the high rock Ekashila Gutta, topped by another Kakatiya temple overlooking a small lake.

1000-Pillared Temple
HINDU TEMPLE

(⊙6am-6pm) Six kilometres northwest of Warangal station in the adjoining town of Hanumakonda (Hanamkonda), the 1000-Pillared Temple, constructed in 1163, is a fine example of Kakatiya architecture and sculpture, in a leafy setting. Unusually, the cross-shaped building has shrines to the sun god Surya (to the right as you enter), Vishnu (centre) and Shiva (left). Despite the name, it certainly does not have 1000 pillars. Behind rises Hanumakonda Hill, site of the original Kakatiya capital.

Other ancient temples in Hanumakonda include the lakeside Bhadrakali Temple, 2km southeast of the 1000-Pillared Temple, whose idol of the mother goddess Kali sits with a weapon in each of her eight hands, and the small Siddeshwara Temple on the south side of Hanumakonda Hill.

⌂ Sleeping & Eating

Vijaya Lodge
HOTEL $

(☎0870-2501222; Station Rd; s ₹260, d ₹450-700) About 350m from Warangal's train and bus stations, the Vijaya is well organised, with helpful staff. Rooms are borderline dreary, with showers by bucket, but workable. The upper floors are better.

Hotel Ashoka
HOTEL $$

(☎0870-2578491; hotelashoka_wgl@yahoo.co.in; Main Rd, Hanumakonda; r ₹1580-2250; ❀@) Straightforward, well-kept, air-con rooms at a busy, well-run hotel near the Hanumakonda bus stand and 1000-Pillared Temple. Also here are the good veg restaurant **Kanishka** (meals ₹110; ⊙ 6.30am-10.30pm) plus a nonveg restaurant, a pub and a bar-restaurant.

Hotel Landmark HOTEL $$
(☎ 0870-2546333; Nakkalagutta; r ₹1800; ❄ 🛜)
A decent alternative, 2km out of town along the Hyderabad road.

Sri Geetha Bhavan ANDHRA $
(Market Rd, Hanumakonda; mains ₹80-95; ⊙ 6am-11pm) Really good South Indian meals (₹80) in pleasant air-con surroundings.

ⓘ Getting There & Around

Buses to Hyderabad (₹130 to ₹195, four hours) leave about three times hourly from **Hanumakonda bus stand** (☎ 9959226056; New Bus Stand Rd) and hourly from **Warangal bus stand** (☎ 2565595; Station Rd), opposite the train station.

From Warangal several trains daily run to the Hyderabad (sleeper/3AC/2AC ₹170/535/735, three hours), Vijayawada (₹190/535/735, three hours) and Chennai (₹375/980/1385, 11½ hours).

Shared autorickshaws (₹15) ply fixed routes around Warangal and Hanumakonda.

Palampet

In lovely green countryside 65km northeast of Warangal, the stunning Ramappa Temple (camera ₹25; ⊙ 6am-6pm) FREE, built in 1213, is the outstanding gem of Kakatiya architecture, covered in wonderfully detailed carvings of animals, lovers, wrestlers, musicians, dancers, deities and Hindu legends. Brackets on its external pillars support superb black-basalt carvings of mythical creatures and sinuous women twined with snakes. The large temple tank, Ramappa Cheruvu, 1km south, is popular with migrating birds.

The easiest way to get here is by taxi (around ₹1800 return from Warangal), but buses also run half-hourly from Hanumakonda to Mulugu (₹50, one hour), then a further 13km to Palampet (₹20).

ANDHRA PRADESH

The recently reduced state of Andhra Pradesh stretches 850km along the Bay of Bengal between Tamil Nadu and Odisha, and inland up into the picturesque Eastern Ghats. It's the proud standard-bearer of a long tradition of Telugu language and culture, and is one of India's wealthiest states.

Explorers will discover one of India's most visited temples (at Tirumala), some fascinating and remote ancient sites from the earliest days of South Indian Buddhism, and one of the nicest stretches of India's east coast, north of Visakhapatnam – and you'll be able to enjoy the spicily delicious Andhra cuisine everywhere. Andhra's tourism websites are www.aptourism.gov.in and www.aptdc.gov.in.

Vijayawada
☎ 0866 / POP 1.05 MILLION

Centrally located in the new Andhra Pradesh, the commercial and industrial city of Vijayawada, on the north bank of the Krishna River, is to be Andhra's new capital. The state government has ambitious plans to construct a showpiece capital complex encompassing 17 existing villages on the south side of the river, at a cost of over 1 trillion rupees (US$16 billion).

Vijayawada is a good base for visiting some fascinating old Buddhist sites in the lush and green surrounding area. The city is considered by many to be the heart of Andhra culture and language, and its 12th-century Kanaka Durga Temple (Durga Temple Ghat Rd, Indrakeeladri Hill) draws many pilgrims. The 1.3km-long Prakasam Barrage across the Krishna here feeds three irrigation canals which run through the city.

⊙ Sights

★ Undavalli Cave Temples HINDU TEMPLE
(Indian/foreigner ₹5/100; ⊙ 9am-5pm) Just 6km southwest of downtown Vijayawada, on the south side of the Krishna River, this stunning four-storey cave temple was probably originally carved out of the hillside for Buddhist monks in the 2nd century AD, then converted to Hindu use in the 7th century. The shrines are now empty except those on the third level, one of which houses a huge reclining Vishnu. Three gnome-like stone Vasihnavite gurus or preachers gaze out over the rice paddies from the terrace. Bus 301 (₹20, 20 minutes) runs here every 20 minutes from Vijayawada bus station; autorickshaws ask ₹250 return.

🛏 Sleeping & Eating

Hotel Sripada HOTEL $
(☎ 0866-6644222; hotelsripada@rediffmail.com; Gandhi Nagar; s ₹900-1460, d ₹1010-1690; ❄) One of the few cheaper hotels in Vijayawada

authorised to accept foreign guests, the Sripada has small but bright rooms in reasonable condition, a decent restaurant and helpful staff. Near the train station.

Hotel Southern Grand   HOTEL $$

(☎0866-6677777; www.hotelsoutherngrand.com; Papaiah St, Gandhi Nagar; incl breakfast s ₹1910-2360, d ₹2250-2700; ❋ ⊛) Rates here are very reasonable for such neat, spotless and contemporary rooms. Just 600m from the train station, the hotel also has an excellent veg restaurant, Arya Bhavan (Hotel Southern Grand, Papaiah St, Gandhi Nagar; mains ₹120-165, thalis ₹105-160; ⊙7am-11pm), a useful travel desk, Southern Travels (☎0870-6677777; Hotel Southern Grand, Papaiah St, Gandhi Nagar), and offers free airport and station transfers.

Gateway Hotel   HOTEL $$$

(☎0866-6644444; www.thegatewayhotels.com; MG Rd; s/d from ₹5060/5900; ❋ ⊛ ⊛) This classy Taj group hotel has six floors of well-equipped, contemporary rooms around its high atrium lobby, plus two stylish restaurants, a bar and Vijayawada's only hotel pool. Check the website for discounts. It's 3km southeast of the train station.

★ Minerva Coffee Shop   INDIAN $$

(Museum Rd; mains ₹180-220, meals ₹140-220; ⊙7am-11pm) Round the corner from the large Big Bazaar shop, this outpost of the excellent Minerva chain does great North and South Indian veg cuisine in bright, spotless surroundings, with good, friendly service. Meals (thalis) are only available from 11.30am to 3.30pm but top-notch dosas, *idlis* and *uttapams* (₹35 to ₹70) are served all day. There's another branch (MG Rd; meals ₹185-220; ⊙7am-11pm) with similarly excellent food in airy surrounds on MG Rd.

ⓘ Information

Department of Tourism (☎0866-2578880; train station; ⊙10am-5pm)

ⓘ Getting There & Around

The train and bus stations have prepaid autorickshaw stands.

BUS

Services from the large **Pandit Nehru Bus Station** (Arjuna St) include:
Chennai (non-AC/AC ₹450/750, eight to 10 hours, seven daily)

STATE OF GOOD KARMA

Lying at a nexus of major Indian land routes and sea routes across the Bay of Bengal, Andhra Pradesh played an important role in the early history of Buddhism. Andhra and Telangana have about 150 known Buddhist stupas, monasteries, caves and other sites. They speak of a time when Andhra Pradesh, or 'Andhradesa', was a hotbed of Buddhist activity, when Indian monks set off for Sri Lanka and Southeast Asia to spread the Buddha's teachings, and monks came from far and wide to learn from renowned Buddhist teachers.

Andhradesa's Buddhist culture lasted around 1500 years from the Buddha's own lifetime in the 6th century BC. The dharma really took off in the 3rd century BC under the Mauryan emperor Ashoka, who dispatched monks across his empire to teach and construct stupas enshrining relics of the Buddha. (Being near these was thought to help progress on the path to enlightenment.)

After Ashoka's death in 232 BC, succeeding rulers of central Andhra Pradesh, the Satavahanas and then the Ikshvakus, continued to support Buddhism. At their capital Amaravathi, the Satavahanas adorned Ashoka's stupa with elegant decoration. They built monasteries across the Krishna Valley and exported the dharma through their sophisticated maritime network. It was under Satavahana rule that Nagarjuna, considered the progenitor of Mahayana Buddhism, is believed to have lived, in the 2nd or 3rd centuries AD. The monk, equal parts logician, philosopher and meditator, wrote several ground-breaking works that shaped Buddhist thought.

Today, even in ruins, you can get a sense of how large some of the stupas were, how expansive the monastic complexes, and of how the monks lived, sleeping in caves and fetching rainwater from stone-cut cisterns. Many of the sites have stunning views across seascapes or countryside. The complexes at Nagarjunakonda (p931) and Amaravathi (p931) have good infrastructure and helpful museums on-site. For a bit more adventure, head out from Vijayawada to Guntupalli (p933) or Bhattiprolu, or from Visakhapatnam to Thotlakonda (p935), Bavikonda (p935) and Sankaram (p935).

Eluru (₹45, 1½ hours, half-hourly)

Hyderabad (non-AC/AC ₹310/450, five to seven hours, half-hourly)

Tirupati (non-AC/AC ₹420/570, nine hours, half-hourly)

Visakhapatnam (non-AC/AC ₹415/550, eight hours, half-hourly)

TRAIN

Vijayawada Junction station is on the main Chennai–Kolkata and Chennai–Delhi railway lines. The 12841/12842 Coromandel Express between Chennai and Kolkata is quick for journeys up and down the coast. Typical journey times and sleeper/3AC/2AC fares:

Chennai (₹290/735/1035, seven hours, 13 daily)

Hyderabad (₹190/495/720, 6½ hours, 20 daily)

Tirupati (₹235/635/905, seven hours, 12 daily)

Warangal (₹190/535/735, three hours, 24 daily)

Around Vijayawada

Amaravathi

Amaravathi, 43km west of Vijayawada, was the earliest centre of Buddhism in the southern half of India. India's biggest **stupa** (Indian/foreigner ₹5/100; ◷7am-7pm), 27m high and 49m across, was constructed here in the 3rd century BC. Amaravathi flourished as a capital of the Satavahana kingdom which ruled from Andhra across the Deccan for four or five centuries, becoming the fountainhead of Buddhist art in South India. All that remains of the stupa now are its circular base and a few parts of the surrounding stone railing. The great hemispherical dome is gone – but the next-door **museum** (admission ₹5; ◷9am-5pm Sat-Thu) has a model of the stupa and some of the intricate marble carvings depicting the Buddha's life with which the Satavahanas covered and surrounded it. A section of reconstructed stone railing gives you an idea of the stupa's massive scale.

About 1km away, on the edge of town, is the 20m-high **Dhyana Buddha** statue, erected on the site where the Dalai Lama spoke in 2006.

Bus 301 from Vijayawada bus station runs to Amaravathi (₹60, two hours) every 20 minutes, via Unduvalli, through some lovely countryside.

Eluru

The city of Eluru, 60km east of Vijayawada on the road and railway to Visakhapatnam, is the jumping-off point for the remote old Buddhist site of Guntupalli (p933) and the Dhamma Vijaya meditation centre at Vijayarai. Buses depart Eluru for Vijayarai (₹15, 20 minutes) half-hourly.

Dhamma Vijaya   MEDITATION
(☑9441449044; www.dhamma.org; Eluru-Chinta lapudi Rd, Vijayarai) Monthly intensive 10-day *vipassana* silent meditation courses are offered in lush palm- and cocoa-forested grounds; apply in advance. Payment is by donation.

Nagarjunakonda

A road trip of about 180km west from Vijayawada or 170km southeast from Hyderabad, followed by a 45-minute boat trip over Nagarjuna Sagar reservoir, brings you to the unique island of Nagarjunakonda, peppered with ancient Buddhist structures. Until 1960, when the big Nagarjunasagar Dam was built on the Krishna River, the island was the top of a hill in the Krishna valley. The Ikshvaku Dynasty had its capital here in the 3rd and 4th centuries AD, when the area was probably the most important Buddhist centre in South India, with some 30 monasteries nearby. Excavations in the 1950s, in anticipation of the dam, unearthed stupas, *viharas* (monasteries), *chaitya-grihas* (prayer halls with stupas), *mandapas* (pillared pavilions) and many outstanding white-marble sculptures. The finds were reassembled on Nagarjunakonda.

◉ Sights & Activities

Nagarjunakonda Museum   MUSEUM
(incl monuments Indian/foreigner ₹10/105; ◷9am-4pm Sat-Thu) The thoughtfully laid-out Nagarjunakonda Museum has Buddha statues and some superbly detailed carvings depicting the Buddha's lives and local contemporary life. The reassembled remains of several buildings, including stupa bases, walls of monastery complexes and pits for horse sacrifice, are arranged along a 1km path running along the island. The largest stupa, in the Chamtasri Chaitya Griha group, contained a bone fragment thought to be from the Buddha himself.

Sri Parvata Arama   MUSEUM
(Buddhavanam) 8km north of the dam is this Buddhism theme park, featuring a re-creation of the huge Amaravathi stupa. It has been under construction by the state tourism authorities for several years and was scheduled to open in late 2015. Coming by bus from Hyderabad, alight at Buddha Park.

Dhamma Nagajjuna   MEDITATION
(✆ 9440139329, 9348456780; www.nagajjuna. dhamma.org; Hill Colony) Keeping the Buddha's teachings alive in the region, Dhamma Na-gajjuna, 8km north of the dam, offers 10-day *vipassana* silent meditation courses in charming flower-filled grounds overlooking Nagarjuna Sagar. Apply in advance; pay-ment is by donation. Coming by bus from Hyderabad, alight at Buddha Park.

🛌 Sleeping & Eating

Nagarjuna Resort   HOTEL $
(✆ 08642-242471; Vijayapuri South; r ₹800 with AC ₹1500; ☀) The most convenient place to stay, across the road from the boat launch, has spacious, slightly shabby rooms with geysers and balconies with good views.

Haritha Vijaya Vihar   HOTEL $$
(✆ 08680-277362/3; r with AC incl breakfast Mon-Thu ₹1350-1690, Fri-Sun ₹2480-2810; ☀☁) Six kilometres north of the dam is Telangana Tourism's Haritha Vijaya Vihar, with decent rooms, nice gardens and lovely lake views.

Hotel Siddhartha   INDIAN $$
(Buddhavanam, Hill Colony; mains ₹110-210; ☺6am-11pm) The best food in the Nagarjuna area is at Hotel Siddhartha, where curries, biryanis, fish dishes and lots of snacks are served in an airy pavilion.

❶ Getting There & Away

The easiest way to visit Nagarjunakonda, other than with a private vehicle, is a bus tour from Hy-derabad with Telangana Tourism (p918) (₹550), running on weekends only.

Public buses from Hyderabad's Mahatma Gandhi Bus Station run hourly to Hill Colony/Na-garjuna Sagar (₹200, four hours): alight at Pylon and catch an autorickshaw (₹15/100 shared/private) 8km to Vijayapuri South.

Boats (₹100 return) depart for the island from Vijayapuri South, 7km south of the dam, theoret-ically at 9.30am, 11.30am and 1.30pm, and stay for one or two hours. The first two boats may not go if not enough people turn up, but the 1.30pm boat goes every day and starts back from the island at 4.30pm.

Visakhapatnam

☎ 0891 / POP 1.73 MILLION

Visit Visakhapatnam – also called Vizag (*vie-zag*) – during the December-to-February holiday season and you'll see domestic tourism in rare form: balloons, fairy floss (cotton candy) and, of course, weddings! This is where Andhra Pradesh comes to have fun by the sea, and the crowds only enhance the area's kitschy atmosphere. The pedestrian promenade along Ramakrishna Beach has appeal, nearby Rushikonda beach is Andhra's best, and the surrounding area contains one of Andhra's most important Hindu temples, several ancient Buddhist sites, and the rural Araku Valley.

The beach-resort vibe exists despite the fact that Vizag is Andhra Pradesh's largest city, famous for steel and its big port.

If you visit in mid-January you may coin-cide with **Visakha Utsav**, an annual festival with food stalls on Ramakrishna Beach, ex-hibitions and cultural events.

◉ Sights & Activities

Ramakrishna Beach   BEACH
Ramakrishna (RK) Beach stretches 4km up the coast from the large port area in the south of town, overlooking the Bay of Bengal with its mammoth ships and brightly painted fish-ing boats.

Submarine Museum   MUSEUM
(Beach Rd; adult/child ₹40/20, camera ₹50; ☺2-8.30pm Tue-Sat, 10am-12.30pm & 2-8.30pm Sun) Towards the north end of the RK Beach promenade you'll find the 91m-long, Soviet-built, Indian navy submarine *Kur-sura,* now a facinating museum.

Kailasagiri Hill   PARK
(admission ₹5, cable car round-trip adult/child ₹75/40; ☺11am-8pm) Kailasagiri Hill, rising above Beach Rd in the north of town, has a cable car with panoramic views, attractive gardens, a sculpture park, playgrounds, a toy train, a marble Shiva and Parvati and several cafes. Bus 10K runs there from the RTC Complex and Ramakrishna Beach.

Rushikonda   BEACH
Rushikonda, 10km north of town, is one of the nicest stretches of India's east coast, and the best beach for swimming. To avoid unwanted attention, women should go for modest swimming attire (T-shirts

GUNTUPALLI

Getting here is a very scenic adventure. The former Buddhist **monastic compound** (Indian/foreigner ₹5/100; ⊙10am-5pm), high on a hilltop overlooking a vast expanse of forest and paddy fields, is specially noteworthy for its circular rock-cut *chaitya-griha* shrine. The cave's domed ceiling is carved with 'wooden beams' designed to look like those in a hut. The *chaitya-griha* has a well-preserved stupa and, like the monks' dwellings lining the same cliff, a gorgeous arched facade also designed to look like wood. Check out the stone 'beds' in the monks' cells, and the compound's 60-plus votive stupas. The monastery was active from the 2nd century BC to 3rd century AD.

From Eluru, on the Vijayawada–Visakhapatnam road and railway, take a bus 35km north to Kamavarapukota (₹35, one hour, half-hourly), then a local bus or autorickshaw 10km west to Guntupalli. A taxi from Eluru costs around ₹1500 return.

and shorts). Weekends are busy and festive. Surfers and kayakers can rent decent boards and kayaks from local surf pioneer **Melville Smythe** (☑9848561052; per hr surfboard ₹400-600, 2-person kayak ₹300, surf tuition ₹200), by the jet-ski hut.

You can reach Rushikonda by bus 900K from the train station or RTC Complex, or a shared autorickshaw up Beach Rd.

Simhachalam Temple   HINDU TEMPLE
(⊙7-11.30am,   12.30-2.30pm,   3.30-7pm) Andhra's second most visited temple (after Tirumala) is a 16km drive northwest of town. Large but tranquil and orderly, it's dedicated to Varahalakshmi Narasimha, a combination of Vishnu's boar and lion-man avatars. A ₹100 ticket will get you to the deity (and a sip of holy water) much quicker than a ₹20 one. Buses 6A and 28 go here from the RTC Complex and train station.

The temple's architecture bears much Odishan influence, including the 13th-century main shrine with its carved stone panels (the lion-man can be seen disembowelling a demon on the rear wall).

🛏 Sleeping

Beach Rd is the place to stay, but it's low on inexpensive hotels.

SKML Beach Guest House   GUESTHOUSE $
(☑9848355131; ramkisg.1074@gmail.com; Beach Rd, Varun Beach; r ₹1000-1200, with AC ₹1600-2000) SKML is towards the less select southern end of Ramakrishna Beach but its 12 rooms are clean and decent. Best are the two top-floor 'suites' with sea views, a terrace and a bit of art.

Hotel Morya   HOTEL $
(☑0891-2731112; www.hotelmorya.com; Bowdara Rd; s/d from ₹480/620, r with AC ₹1570; ﹡) A reasonable cheapie 600m south of the train station. Standard rooms are small and lack ventilation, but the others are good-sized, and check-out is 24 hours. You can't miss its bright neon sign at night.

Haritha Beach Resort   HOTEL $$
(☑0891-2788826; www.aptdc.gov.in; Rushikonda; r with AC incl breakfast ₹1920-2810; ﹡) Rooms at this state-run hotel are bare if clean, but the executive and luxury categories are large, with balconies overlooking its prime asset – the hillside location facing Rushikonda Beach. Just below, and with beach access, **Vihar** (Rushikonda; mains ₹100-240; ⊙11am-10.30pm) is great for a beer or meal.

★ Park   HOTEL $$$
(☑0891-3045678;   www.theparkhotels.com; Beach Rd; s/d incl breakfast from ₹8150/10,480; ﹡@🛜🏊) Vizag's best hotel is elegant and tasteful, but also warm and inviting. The large and lovely beachfront gardens contain a fine pool and three of the hotel's four restaurants. Rooms are cosy and sophisticated.

Ambica Sea Green   HOTEL $$$
(☑0891-2821818;   www.ambicaseagreen.com; Beach Rd; r incl breakfast from ₹5060; ﹡🛜) The very comfy, well-equipped rooms here all have sea views and are much less pricey than other top-end Beach Rd hotels. There's reliable free wi-fi and breakfast is a big buffet.

🍴 Eating

★ Sea Inn   ANDHRA $$
(Beach Rd, Rushikonda; mains ₹90-180; ⊙noon-4pm) The chef here cooks Andhra-style curries the way her mum did, with fish, seafood,

chicken or veg, and serves them up in a simple, semi-open-air dining room with bench seating, about 300m north of the Haritha Resort turn-off.

Dharani INDIAN $$

(Daspalla Hotel, Suryabagh; thalis & mains ₹170-220; ⊙ noon-3.30pm & 7-10.30pm) Words don't do justice to the super-deliciousness of the meals at this family veg restaurant. Be sure to try the Daspalla special filter coffee: you'll die. The fabulous Daspalla Hotel has several other restaurants too, including Andhra nonveg and North Indian veg options.

Little Italy ITALIAN $$

(1st fl, South Wing, ATR Towers, Vutagedda Rd, Paandurangapuram; mains ₹230-400; ⊙ noon-3pm & 7-11pm) This all-veg spot 500m back from Ramakrishna Beach does fine thin-crust pizza and reasonable salads in a neat, tranquil ambience. No alcohol, but good mocktails.

Vista MULTICUISINE $$$

(The Park, Beach Rd; mains ₹350-900; ⊙ dinner 7.30-11pm) Of the Park's four restaurants, the indoor Vista is our overall pick for its long, truly global menu and excellent all-you-can-eat dinner buffet (₹900). If you prefer alfresco dining, **Bamboo Bay** (The Park, Beach Rd; mains ₹450-970; ⊙ 7.30-11pm) does good Andhra, Chettinad and Mughlai food.

❶ Information

The RTC Complex has several internet cafes (per hour ₹20).

APTDC (☑ 0891-2788820; www.aptdc.gov. in; RTC Complex; ⊙ 6.30am-9.30pm) Tours, hotel bookings, tourist information. Has a train station office (p934) too.

❶ Getting There & Away

AIR

Direct flights by **Air India** (☑ 0891-2746501; www.airindia.com; LIC Building Complex, Jeevan Prakash Marg), **Air Costa** (www.aircosta.in), **Indigo** (www.goindigo.in) or **SpiceJet** (www.spicejet.com) go daily to Bengaluru, Bhubaneswar, Chennai, Delhi, Hyderabad, Kolkata and Mumbai.

BOAT

Boats depart roughly twice-monthly for Port Blair (p1088) in the Andaman Islands. See www. and.nic.in for expected schedules. Tickets for the 56-hour journey (₹2268 to ₹8841) go on sale two or three days before departure at **AV Bhanojirow, Garuda Pattabhiramayya & Co**

(☑ 0891-2565597; ops@avbgpr.com; Harbour Approach Rd, Next to NMDC, Port Area; ⊙ 9am-5pm). Bring your passport, two photocopies, and two photos.

BUS

Services from Vizag's well-organised **RTC Complex** (☑ 2746400) include the following:

Vijayawada (general/superluxury'/AC ₹356/425/610, eight hours, hourly 5am to midnight)

Hyderabad (non-AC/AC ₹727/1120, 13 hours, about hourly 2.30pm to 9pm)

Jagdalpur (₹227, eight hours, two daily)

CAR

Genial, English-speaking **Srinivasa 'Srinu' Rao** (☑ 7382468137) is a good driver for out-of-town trips. He charges around ₹3000 for an Araku Valley day trip and ₹1400 to Sankaram and back.

Reliable **Guide Tours & Travels** (☑ 9848265559, 0891-2754477; Shop 15, Sudarshan Plaza; ⊙ 7am-10pm), opposite the RTC Complex, charges around ₹3200 plus tolls for a day trip up to 300km.

TRAIN

Visakhapatnam station, on the western edge of town, is on the main Kolkata–Chennai line. The 12841/12842 Coromandel Express is fastest in both directions – 12½ hours to Chennai (sleeper/3AC/2AC ₹425/1115/1590) and 14 hours to Kolkata (₹460/1200/1715). Over 20 daily trains run to Vijayawada (₹255/645/900, seven hours) and about 10 to Bhubaneswar (₹290/750/1050, seven hours). The daily 58538 Visakhapatnam-Koraput Passenger and the 18512 Visakhapatnam–Koraput Intercity Express (Monday and Friday only) head near Chatikona, Onkadelli and Chandoori Sai in Odisha. The **reservation centre** (⊙ 8am-10pm Mon-Sat, to 2pm Sun) is 300m south of the main building.

❶ Getting Around

To Visakahapatnam airport, 12km west of downtown, take an autorickshaw (₹250), taxi (₹400), or bus 38 from the RTC Complex (₹15, 30 minutes). The arrivals hall has a prepaid taxi booth.

The train station has a prepaid autorickshaw booth but otherwise you have to negotiate fares. Rides to Ramakrishna Beach should cost ₹60 from the train station and ₹50 from the RTC Complex. Shared autorickshaws run right along Beach Rd from the port at the south end of town to Rushikonda, 10km north of Vizag, and Bheemunipatnam, 25km north, charging between ₹5 (for a 1km hop) and ₹40 (Vizag to Bheemunipatnam): flag down any autorickshaw.

Around Visakhapatnam

Sankaram

Forty kilometres southwest of Vizag, this stunning Buddhist complex (⊙8am-5pm) FREE, also known by the names of its two parts, Bojjannakonda and Lingalakonda, occupies a rocky outcrop about 300m long. Used by monks from the 2nd to 9th centuries AD, the outcrop is covered with rock-cut caves, stupas, ruins of monastery structures and reliefs of the Buddha. Bojjannakonda, the eastern part, has a pair of rock-cut shrines with several gorgeous carvings of the Buddha inside and outside. Above sit the ruins of a huge stupa and a monastery. Lingalakonda, at the western end, is piled with tiers of rock-cut stupas, some of them enormous. Both parts afford fabulous views over the surrounding rice paddies.

A car from Vizag costs ₹1400. Or take a bus (₹42, 1½ hours, every half-hour from the RTC Complex) or train (₹35, one hour) to Anakapalle, 3km away, and then an autorickshaw (₹120 return including waiting).

Bavikonda & Thotlakonda

Bavikonda (⊙9am-5pm) FREE and Thotlakonda (pedestrian/car ₹5/30; ⊙8am-5.30pm) were Buddhist monasteries on scenic hilltop sites north of Vizag that each hosted up to 150 monks, with the help of massive rainwater tanks. The site was excavated in the 1980s and 90s.

The monasteries flourished from around the 3rd century BC to the 3rd century AD, and had votive stupas, congregation halls, *chaitya-grihas, viharas* and refectories. Thotlakonda has sea views, and Bavikonda has special importance because a relic vessel found in its Mahachaitya stupa contained a piece of bone believed to be from the Buddha himself.

Bavikonda and Thotlakonda are reached from turnoffs 14km and 15km, respectively, from Vizag on Bheemunipatnam road: Bavikonda is 3km off the main road and Thotlakonda 1.25km. Vizag autorickshaw drivers charge around ₹600 return to see both: you can also reach the turnoffs by shared autorickshaw or bus 900K. An autorickshaw from the main road to Bavikonda and back costs ₹100 to ₹150.

Bheemunipatnam

This former Dutch settlement, 25km north of Vizag, is the oldest municipality in mainland India, with bizarre sculptures on the beach, an 1861 lighthouse, an interesting Dutch cemetery, and Bheemli Beach, where local grommets surf not-very-clean waters on crude homemade boards. From Vizag, catch bus 900K or a shared autorickshaw.

Araku Valley

☑ 08936 / ELEV 975M

Andhra's best train ride is through the beautiful, lushly forested Eastern Ghats to the Araku Valley, centred on Araku town, 115km north of Vizag. The area is home to isolated tribal communities and known for its tasty organic coffee and lovely green countryside. The 58501 Visakhapatnam Kirandul Passenger train (₹30, four hours) leaves Vizag at 6.50am; train 58502 returns from Araku at 2.50pm. Hourly buses from Vizag (₹70 to ₹105) take 4½ hours, and a taxi day trip costs between ₹3000 to ₹4000. The APTDC runs a variety of tours that all include a tribal dance performance and a visit to the million-year-old limestone Borra Caves (adult/child ₹60/45, camera ₹100; ⊙10am-1pm & 2-5pm), 38km before Araku.

At Araku town, the Museum of Habitat (admission ₹10; ⊙8am-1.30pm & 2.30-8pm), next to the bus station and 2km east of the train station, has extensive exhibits on eastern Andhra Pradesh's tribal peoples, including mock-ups of hunting, ceremonial and other scenes. Next door, you can sample and buy local coffee and chocolate-covered coffee beans at Araku Valley Coffee House (coffee ₹25-95; ⊙8.30am-9pm), and browse tribal crafts at Araku Aadiwasi Arts & Crafts (⊙8am-8pm). On Fridays villagers crowd into Araku for the weekly market.

The oddly unfriendly Hotel Rajadhani (☑08936-249580; www.hotelrajadhani.com; r ₹800, with AC ₹1200; ❄), halfway between the train and bus stations, has clean, reasonably-sized rooms and the Vasundhara Restaurant (⊙6am-11pm), serving good Indian meals. The APTDC has two decent hotels: Hill Resort Mayuri (Mayuri; ☑08936-249204; incl breakfast cottage ₹893, r ₹1349-2361; ❄) just behind the museum, and Valley Resort (☑08936-249202; r incl breakfast ₹1130-2030, with AC ₹2250; ❄), 1km east, which is favoured by Tollywood film crews.

Tirumala & Tirupati

POP 287,000 (TIRUPATI), 7700 (TIRUMALA)

The holy hill of Tirumala is, on any given day, thronged with tens of thousands of blissed-out devotees, many of whom have made long journeys to see the powerful Lord Venkateshwara here, at his home. Around 60,000 pilgrims come each day, and *darshan* runs 24/7. The efficient **Tirumala Tirupati Devasthanams** (TTD; ☑ 0877-2277777, 0877-2233333; www.tirumala.org) (TTD) brilliantly administers the multitudes, employing 20,000 people to do so. Despite the crowds, a sense of order, serenity and ease mostly prevails, and a trip to the Holy Hill can be fulfilling, even if you're not a pilgrim.

'It is believed that Lord Sri Venkateshwara enjoys festivals', according to the TTD. And so do his devotees: *darshan* queues during the annual nine-day **Brahmotsavam festival** (☉ late Sep/early Oct) can run up to several kilometres.

Tirupati, the town at the bottom of the hill, has many hotels and restaurants and is the main transport nexus for Tirumala. You'll find most of your worldly needs around the Tirupati bus station (TP Area) and, 700m west, the train station.

◉ Sights

Venkateshwara Temple   HINDU TEMPLE
Devotees flock to Tirumala to see Venkateshwara, an avatar of Vishnu. 'Ordinary *darshan*' requires a wait of anywhere from two to eight hours in claustrophobic metal cages ringing the temple. Special-entry *darshan* tickets (₹300) will get you through the queue faster, though you'll still have to brave the cages, which is part of the fun, kind of... Head to the Seeghra Darshan counters at Vaikuntam Queue Complex 1 for these.

There are different hours for special-entry *darshan* each day: check the website. Upon entry, you'll have to sign a form declaring your faith in Lord Venkateshwara.

Among the many powers attributed to Venkateshwara is the granting of any wish made before the idol at Tirumala. Legends about the hill itself and the surrounding area appear in the *Puranas*, and the temple's history may date back 2000 years. The main temple is an atmospheric place, though you'll be pressed between hundreds of devotees when you see it. Venkateshwara inspires bliss and love among his visitors from the back of the dark and magical inner sanctum; it smells of incense, resonates with chanting and may make you religious. You'll have a moment to say a prayer and then you'll be shoved out again. Don't forget to collect your delicious *ladoo* from the counter: Tirumala *ladoos* (sweet balls made with chickpea flour, cardamom and dried fruits) are famous across India.

Many pilgrims donate their hair to the deity – in gratitude for a wish fulfilled, or to renounce ego – so hundreds of barbers attend to devotees. Tirumala and Tirupati are filled with tonsured men, women and children.

🛏 Sleeping & Eating

The TTD runs vast **dormitories** (beds free) and **guesthouses** (r ₹50-3000) near the temple in Tirumala, intended for pilgrims. To stay, check in at the Central Reception Office. Huge **dining halls** (meals free) on the hill feed thousands of pilgrims daily; veg restaurants also serve meals for ₹25.

Hotel Annapurna   HOTEL $
(☑ 0877-2250666; 349 G Car St, Tirupati; r ₹1240 with AC ₹1920; ❄) Rooms at the Annapurna are clean, simple and pink. Since it's on a corner across from the train station, the front rooms can be noisy. Its veg **restaurant** (mains ₹110-210; ☉ 5.30am-11pm) has fresh juices and excellent food.

Hotel Mamata Residency   HOTEL $
(☑ 0877-2225873; 1st fl, 170 TP Area, Tirupati; s/d/tr/q ₹400/600/800/1000, AC ₹750/999/1249/1499; ❄) A spick-and-span cheapie between the train and bus stations, but you may find all the AC rooms are full.

Hotel Regalia   HOTEL $$
(☑ 0877-2238699; Ramanuja Circle, Tirupati; r incl breakfast ₹2360; ❄ 🛜) On the east side of town, 1.5km from the train station (₹30 by autorickshaw), the Regalia provides attractive, spotless, contemporary rooms, and the included breakfast is a big buffet.

★ **Minerva Grand**   HOTEL $$
(☑ 0877-6688888; http://minervahotels.in; Renigunta Rd, Tirupati; s/d with AC from ₹3150/3830; ☉ restaurants 7am-11.30pm; ❄ 🛜) The Minerva has the best rooms in town – comfy business-style abodes with desks, plump pillows and good mattresses. Its two restaurants, both with icy AC, are tops too: the veg-only **Minerva Coffee Shop** (Minerva Grand, Renigunta Rd; thalis ₹185-220; ☉ 7am-11.30pm) does superb thalis and dynamite

filter coffee, while the Blue Fox (Minerva Grand, Renigunta Rd; mains ₹205-370; ☺7am-11.30pm) does veg and nonveg dishes and serves alcohol.

Maya INDIAN $$
(☎0877-2225521; bhimasdeluxe@rediffmail.com; Bhimas Deluxe Hotel, 34-38 G Car St, Tirupati; meals & mains ₹130-190; ☺6am-10pm) Great veg meals in the basement of the Bhimas Deluxe, near the train station.

ℹ Getting There & Away

It's possible to visit Tirumala on a (very) long day trip from Chennai. The APSRTC runs 51 daily buses direct to Tirumala (₹165 to ₹219, five hours) from Chennai's CMBT bus station.

AIR

Tirupati Airport (www.tirupatiairport.com) is at Renigunta, 14km east of town. **Air India** (☎0877-2283981, airport 0877-2283992; www.airindia.in; Srinivasam Pilgrim Amenities Complex, Tirumala By-Pass Road,Tirumala Bypass Rd; ☺9.30am-5.30pm), **SpiceJet** (☎9871803333; www.spicejet.com) and **Air Costa** (☎9949852229; www.aircosta.in) all fly to Hyderabad daily.

BUS

Tirupati's **bus station** (☎0877-2289900) is a wonder of logistics. Useful services, all once or twice hourly, include the following:
Bengaluru (express/Volvo/night Volvo ₹230/400/450, four to six hours)
Chennai (express/Volvo ₹121/222, four hours)
Hyderabad (superluxury/Volvo ₹610/950, 10 to 12 hours)
Vijayawada (express/superluxury ₹350/460, nine hours)

TRAIN

There are numerous daily departures to main destinations; the **reservation office** (☺8am-8pm Mon-Sat, 8am-2pm Sun) is opposite the station's east end. Typical journey times and fares for sleeper/3AC/2AC:
Bengaluru (₹250/635/885, seven hours)
Chennai (₹140/485/690, three to four hours)
Hyderabad (₹380/1030/1480, 13 hours)
Vijayawada (₹235/635/905, seven hours)

ℹ Getting Around

There's a prepaid taxi booth outside the east end of the train station.

BUS

There's a stand for buses to Tirumala opposite the train station, with departures every few minutes. The scenic one-hour trip costs ₹45/82 one-way/return.

WALKING

The TTD has constructed probably the best footpath in India for pilgrims to walk up to Tirumala. It's about 12km from the start of the path at Alipiri on the north side of Tirupati (₹50 by autorickshaw), and takes three to six hours. You can leave your luggage at Alipiri and it will be transported free to the reception centre. There are rest points along the way, and a few canteens.

Around Tirumala & Tirupati

Chandragiri Fort

This fort 15km west of Tirupati dates back 1000 years, but its heyday came in the late 16th century when the rulers of the declining Vijayanagar Empire, having fled from Hampi, made it their capital. At the heart of a 1.5km-long stout-walled enclosure beneath a rocky hill, the palace area (Indian/foreigner ₹10/100; ☺9am-5pm Sat-Thu) contains nice gardens and the Raja Mahal, a heavily restored Vijayanagar palace reminiscent of Hampi buildings, with an interesting museum of bronze and stone sculptures. The upper fort on the hillside is frustratingly out of bounds. Buses for Chandragiri (₹10) leave Tirupati hourly. Prepaid taxis are ₹500 return.

Sri Kalahasti

Sri Kalahasti, 37km east of Tirupati, is known for its important Sri Kalahasteeswara Temple and for being, along with Machilipatnam near Vijayawada, a centre for the ancient textile-painting art of *kalamkari*. Cotton cloth is primed with *myrabalam* (resin) and cow's milk; figures are drawn with a pointed bamboo stick dipped in fermented jaggery and water; and the dyes are made from cow dung, ground seeds, plants and flowers. You can see artists at work, and buy some of their products, in the Agraharam neighbourhood, 2.5km from the bus stand. Sri Vijayalakshmi Fine Kalamkari Arts (☎9441138380; Door No 15-890; ☺daily) is a 40-year-old family business employing over 60 artists. *Dupatta* scarves start around ₹1500.

Buses leave Tirupati for Sri Kalahasti every 10 minutes (₹35, one hour); a prepaid taxi is ₹900 return.

Kerala

Best Wildlife-Watching

➡ Wayanad Wildlife
Sanctuary (p993)

➡ Periyar Wildlife
Sanctuary (p966)

➡ Thattekkad Bird
Sanctuary (p973)

➡ Parambikulam Wildlife
Sanctuary (p974)

Best Homestays

➡ Green Woods
Bethlehem (p979)

➡ Varnam Homestay (p994)

➡ Tranquil (p995)

➡ Graceful Homestay (p943)

➡ Reds Residency (p979)

Why Go?

A sliver of a coastal state in India's deep south, Kerala is shaped by its layered landscape: almost 600km of glorious Arabian Sea coast and beaches; a languid network of glistening backwaters; and the spice- and tea-covered hills of the Western Ghats. Just setting foot on this swathe of soul-quenching, palm-shaded green will slow your subcontinental stride to a blissed-out amble. Kerala is a world away from the frenzy of elsewhere, as if India had passed through the Looking Glass and become an altogether more laid-back place.

Besides its famous backwaters, elegant houseboats, ayurvedic treatments and delicately spiced, tastebud-tingling cuisine, Kerala is home to wild elephants, exotic birds and the odd tiger, while vibrant traditions such as Kathakali plays, temple festivals and snake-boat races frequently bring even the smallest villages to life. It's hard to deny Kerala's liberal use of the slogan 'God's Own Country'.

When to Go
Thiruvananthapuram

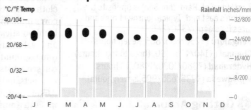

Dec–Feb Perfect beach and backwater weather. Ernakulathappan Utsavam festival in Kochi.

Apr Kathakali at Kottayam and Kollam festivals, and the elephant procession in Thrissur.

Aug–Oct End of the monsoon period: Onam festival, snake-boat races.

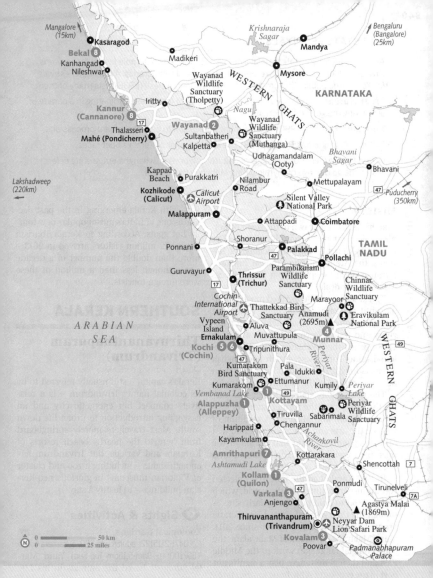

Kerala Highlights

1 Cruising in a houseboat or punted canoe through slippery **backwaters** (p964) from Alappuzha, Kollam or Kottayam

2 Spotting wild elephants at **Wayanad** (p993) amid mountain scenery and epic forest treks

3 Watching days slip away at the clifftop beach resort

of **Varkala** (p950) or having some laid-back beach fun in **Kovalam** (p946)

4 Bedding down in a remote resort and trekking through emerald tea plantations around **Munnar** (p970)

5 Feeling the history and relaxing in a homestay in calm **Fort Cochin** (p974)

6 Experience a performance of **Kathakali** (p985) or the martial arts **kalarippayat** (p985) in Kochi

7 Calling in for a cuddle at the **ashram** (p957) of 'The Hugging Mother' in Amrithapuri

8 Exploring unspoilt beaches and *theyyam* rituals at **Kannur** (p996) and **Bekal** (p998)

History

Traders have been drawn to the scent of Kerala's spices for more than 3000 years. The coast was known to the Phoenicians, the Romans, the Arabs and the Chinese, and was a transit point for spices from the Moluccas (eastern Indonesia).

The kingdom of Cheras ruled much of Kerala until the early Middle Ages, competing with kingdoms and small fiefdoms for territory and trade. Vasco da Gama's arrival in 1498 opened the floodgates to European colonialism as Portuguese, Dutch and English interests fought Arab traders, and then each other, for control of the lucrative spice trade.

The present-day state of Kerala was created in 1956 from the former states of Travancore, Kochi and Malabar. A tradition of valuing the arts and education resulted in a post-Independence state that is one of the most progressive in India, with the nation's highest literacy rate.

In 1957 Kerala had the first freely elected communist government in the world, which has gone on to hold power regularly since – though the Congress-led United Democratic Front (UDF) has been in power since 2011. Many Malayalis (speakers of Malayalam, the state's official language) work in the Middle East and their remittances play a significant part in the economy. A big hope for the state's future is the relatively recent boom in tourism, with Kerala emerging in the past decade as one of India's most popular new tourist hot spots. According to Kerala Tourism almost 12 million visitors arrived in 2013 – more than double the number of a decade ago – though less than a million of these were foreign tourists.

SOUTHERN KERALA

Thiruvananthapuram (Trivandrum)

☑ 0471 / POP 958,000

Kerala's capital – still usually referred to by its colonial name, Trivandrum – is a relatively compact but energetic city and an easy-going introduction to urban life down south. Most travellers merely springboard from here to the nearby beach resorts of Kovalam and Varkala, but Trivandrum has enough sights – including a zoo and cluster of Victorian museums in glorious neo-Keralan buildings – to justify a stay.

◉ Sights & Activities

Zoological Gardens   ZOO
(☑ 0471-2115122; adult/child ₹20/5, camera/video ₹50/100; ⊘ 9am-5.15pm Tue-Sun) Yann Martel famously based the animals in his *Life of Pi* on those he observed in Trivandrum's zoological gardens. Shaded paths meander through woodland, lakes and native forest, where tigers, macaques and hippos gather in reasonably large open enclosures.

★ Napier Museum   MUSEUM
(adult/child ₹10/5; ⊘ 10am-5pm Tue & Thu-Sun, 1-5pm Wed) Housed in an 1880 wooden building designed by Robert Chisholm, a British architect whose Fair Isle–style version of the Keralan vernacular shows his enthusiasm

for local craft, this museum has an eclectic display of bronzes, Buddhist sculptures, temple carts and ivory carvings. The carnivalesque interior is stunning and worth a look in its own right.

Natural History Museum   MUSEUM
(adult/child ₹20/5; ⊙10am-4.45pm Tue & Thu-Sun, 1-4.45pm Wed) In the zoological park complex, the Natural History Museum has hundreds of stuffed animals and birds, and a fine skeleton collection.

Shri Chitra Art Gallery   ART GALLERY
(adult/child ₹20/5; ⊙10am-4.45pm Tue-Sun) Inside the grounds of the zoo itself, this gallery has paintings by the Rajput, Mughal and Tanjore schools, and portraits by renowned artist Ravi Varma (1848–1906).

★**Museum of History & Heritage**   MUSEUM
(☑9567019037; www.museumkeralam.org; Park View; adult/child Indian ₹20/10, foreigner ₹200/50, camera ₹25; ⊙10am-5.30pm Tue-Sun) In a lovely heritage building within the Kerala Tourism complex, this beautifully presented museum traces Keralan history and culture through superb static displays and interactive audiovisual presentations. Exhibits range from Iron Age implements to bronze and terracotta sculptures, murals, *dhulichitra* (floor paintings) to recreations of traditional Keralan homes.

Shri Padmanabhaswamy Temple   HINDU TEMPLE
(⊙inner sanctum 3.30am-7.30pm; Hindus only) Trivandrum's spiritual heart is this 260-year-old temple in the Fort area. The main entrance is the 30m-tall, seven-tier eastern *gopuram* (gateway tower). In the inner sanctum (Hindus only), the deity Padmanabha reclines on the sacred serpent and is made from over 10,000 *salagramam* (sacred stones) that were purportedly transported from Nepal by elephant.

The path around to the right of the gate offers good views of the *gopuram*.

Puthe Maliga Palace Museum   MUSEUM
(Fort; Indian/foreigner ₹15/50, camera/video ₹30/250; ⊙9.30am-12.45pm & 3-4.45pm Tue-Sun) The 200-year-old palace of the Travancore maharajas has carved wooden ceilings, marble sculptures and imported Belgian glass. Inside you'll find Kathakali images, an armoury, portraits of maharajas, ornate thrones and other artefacts. Admission includes an informative one-hour guided tour,

though you can just visit the outside of the palace grounds (free), where you'll also find the Chitrali Museum (admission ₹50) containing loads of historical memorabilia, photographs and portraits from the Travancore dynasty.

📖 **Courses**

Ayushmanbhava Ayurvedic Centre   AYURVEDA, YOGA
(☑0471-2556060; www.ayushmanbhava.com; Pothujanam; massage from ₹800; ⊙yoga classes 6.30am) This centre, 5km west of MG Rd, offers massage, daily therapeutic-yoga classes, as well as longer ayurvedic treatments. Also accommodation and a herbal garden.

Margi Kathakali School   CULTURAL PROGRAM
(☑0471-2478806; www.margitheatre.org; Fort) Conducts courses in Kathakali and Kootiattam (traditional Sanskrit drama) for beginner and advanced students. Fees average ₹300 per two-hour class. Visitors can peek at uncostumed practice sessions held from 10am to noon Monday to Friday. It's in an unmarked building behind the Fort School, 200m west of the fort.

CVN Kalari Sangham   MARTIAL ARTS
(☑0471-2474182; www.cvnkalari.in; South Rd; 15-day/1-month course ₹1000/2000) Long-term courses in *kalarippayat* for serious students (aged under 30) with some experience in martial arts. Training sessions are held Monday to Saturday from 7am to 8.30am.

THE INDIAN COFFEE HOUSE STORY

The Indian Coffee House is a place stuck in time. Its India-wide branches feature old-India prices and waiters dressed in starched white with peacock-style headdresses. It was started by the Coffee Board in the early 1940s, during British rule. In the 1950s the Board began to close down cafes across India, making employees redundant. At this point, the Keralan-born communist leader Ayillyath Kuttiari Gopalan Nambiar began to support the workers and founded with them the India Coffee Board Worker's Co-operative Society. The Coffee House has remained ever since, always atmospheric, and always offering bargain snacks and drinks such as Indian filter coffee, rose milk and *idlis*. It's still run by its employees, all of whom share ownership.

Thiruvananthapuram (Trivandrum)

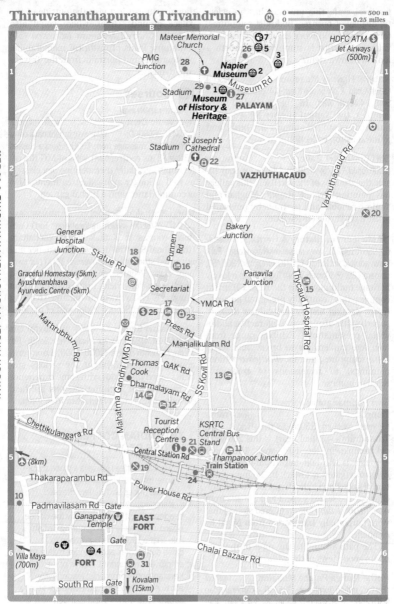

Tours

KTDC Tours

BUS TOUR

(☎ 0471-2330031; www.ktdc.com) The KTDC runs several tours, all leaving from the Tourist Reception Centre at the Hotel Chaithram on Central Station Rd. The City Tour (₹300) includes the zoo, museums and other local sights; the Kanyakumari Day Tour (₹700) visits Padmanabhapuram Palace, Kanyakumari in Tamil Nadu and the nearby Suchindram Temple. Other trips include Neyyar Dam (₹400) and Kovalam (₹200).

Thiruvananthapuram (Trivandrum)

🛏 Sleeping

There are several decent budget and mid-range hotels along Manjalikulam Rd, north of Central Station Rd.

Princess Inn
HOTEL $

(☏0471-2339150; princess_inn@yahoo.com; Manjalikulam Rd; s/d from ₹450/550, with AC from ₹950/1130; ❋🖥) In a glass-fronted building, the Princess Inn promises a relatively quiet sleep in a central side-street location. It's comfortable, with satellite TV and immaculate bathrooms; it's worth paying a little more for the spacious 'deluxe' rooms.

YMCA International Guesthouse
HOTEL $

(☏0471-2330059; www.ymcatvm.org; YMCA Rd; s/d ₹790/1130, with AC ₹1270/1690; ❋) Centrally located, this is a good budget deal, although prices have crept up and it's often full with groups. Rooms are spacious and clean with tiled bathrooms and TV. Both men and women accepted.

Hotel Regency
HOTEL $

(☏0471-2330377; www.hotelregency.com; Manjalikulam Cross Rd; s/d ₹620/1000, with AC ₹1180/1500; ❋🖥) This tidy, welcoming place offers small but spotless rooms with satellite TVs; the deluxe rooms are larger and there's wi-fi available in the lobby.

Greenland Lodge
HOTEL $

(☏0471-2328114; Thampanoor Junction; s/d ₹430/680, with AC ₹900/1130; ❋) Close to the muted mayhem of the train station and bus stand, pastel-coloured Greenland is an acceptable budget option for the location. Rooms are cleanish but variable so ask to see a few. Officious staff demand a hefty two-night advance deposit.

★ Graceful Homestay
HOMESTAY $$

(☏9847249556, 0417-2444358; www.graceful-homestay.com; Pothujanam Rd, Philip's Hill; incl breakfast downstairs s/d ₹1450/1650, upstairs & ste s/d ₹2200/2750; @🖥) In Trivandrum's leafy western suburbs, this lovely, serene house set in a couple of hectares of garden is owned by Sylvia and run by her brother Giles. The four rooms are all neatly furnished with individual character and access to kitchen, living areas and balconies. The pick of the rooms has an amazing covered terrace with views overlooking a sea of palms. It's around 6km from the train station and 5km from the airport; call ahead for directions.

★ Varikatt Heritage
HOMESTAY $$

(☏9895239055, 0417-2336057; www.varikat theritage.com; Punnen Rd; r/ste incl breakfast ₹4000/5000; 🖥) Trivandrum's most charismatic place to stay is the 250-year-old home of Colonel Roy Kuncheria. It's a wonderful Indo-Saracenic bungalow with four rooms flanked by verandahs facing a pretty garden. Every antique – and the home itself – has a family story attached. Lunch and dinner available (₹500).

Vivanta by Taj HOTEL $$$

(☎0417-6612345; www.vivantabytaj.com; Thycaud Hospital Rd; s/d incl breakfast from ₹9000/11,800; ✳@🖥🏊) The lobby here is bigger than most hotels in town, so the Taj doesn't disappoint with the wow factor. Rooms are sufficiently plush, the lawn and pool area is well-maintained, and there's a spa, 24-hour gym and several good restaurants, including Smoke on the Water poolside grill.

Hyacinth by Sparsa HOTEL $$$

(☎0471-2552999; Manorama Rd; d incl breakfast ₹4800-7200, ste ₹10,800; ✳🖥) A white, modern luxury hotel close to the city centre, Hyacinth is more boutique chic than five-star flash. It features functional, well-appointed rooms, a rooftop pool, a fitness centre and several good restaurants.

🍴 Eating

★ Indian Coffee House INDIAN $

(Maveli Cafe; Central Station Rd; snacks ₹10-60; ⏲7am-10.30pm) This branch of Indian Coffee House serves its strong coffee and snacks in a crazy red-brick tower that looks like a cross between a lighthouse and a pigeon coop, and has a spiralling interior lined with concrete benches and tables. You have to admire the hard-working waiters.

Ariya Nivaas INDIAN $

(Manorama Rd; mains ₹30-140, thalis ₹100; ⏲6.45am-10pm, lunch 11.30am-3pm) Trivandrum's best all-you-can-eat South Indian veg thalis

mean Ariya Nivaas is always busy at lunchtime, but service is snappy and the food fresh.

Ananda Bhavan SOUTH INDIAN $

(☎0417-2477646; MG Rd; dishes ₹12-40; ⏲lunch & dinner) Classic cheap veg place specialising in tiffin snacks and dosas.

Azad Restaurant INDIAN $

(MG Rd; dishes ₹50-200; ⏲11am-11.30pm) Busy family favourite serving up authentic Keralan fish dishes, like fish *molee,* and excellent biryanis and tandoori. There's another branch in Press Rd.

Cherries & Berries CAFE $$

(☎0471-2735433; www.cherriesandberries.in; Carmel Towers, Cotton Hill; dishes ₹100-200; ⏲10am-10pm; 🖥) For serious comfort food, icy air-con and free wi-fi that really works, take a trip east of the centre to Cherries & Berries. The menu includes waffles, mini-pizzas, hot dogs, toasties, good coffee and indulgent chocolate-bar milkshakes – try the Kit Kat shake (₹150).

★ Villa Maya KERALAN $$$

(☎0471-2578901; www.villamaya.in; 120 Airport Rd, Injakkal; starters ₹350-600, mains ₹450-1050; ⏲11am-11pm) Villa Maya is more an experience than a restaurant. Dining is either in the magnificent 18th-century Dutch mansion or in private curtained niches in the tranquil courtyard garden, where you'll be lulled by lily ponds and trickling fountains. The Keralan cuisine itself is expertly crafted, delicately spiced and beautifully presented. Seafood is a speciality, with dishes like stuffed crab with lobster butter, but there

BUSES FROM TRIVANDRUM (KSRTC BUS STAND)

DESTINATION	FARE (₹)	DURATION (HR)	FREQUENCY
Alleppey	120, AC 211	3½	every 15min
Chennai	595	17	10 daily
Ernakulam (Kochi)	167, AC 281	5½	every 20min
Kanyakumari	67-81	2	6 daily
Kollam	60	1½	every 15min
Kumily (for Periyar)	231	8	2 daily
Munnar	235	8	3 daily
Neyyar Dam	34	1½	every 40min
Thrissur	225	7½	every 30min
Udhagamandalam (Ooty)	510	14	1 daily
Varkala	60	1¼	hourly

MAJOR TRAINS FROM TRIVANDRUM

DESTINATION	TRAIN NO & NAME	FARE (₹)	DURATION (HR)	DEPARTURE
Bengaluru	16525 Bangalore Express	420/1120/1630	18	12.45pm
Chennai	12696 Chennai Express	470/1230/1760	16½	5.20pm
Coimbatore	17229 Sabari Express	255/680/970	9¼	7.15am
Mumbai	16346 Netravathi Express	670/1785/2625	31	9.50am
Mangalore	16604 Maveli Express	340/910/1310	12½	7.30pm

Fares: sleeper/3AC/2AC

are some tantalising veg dishes too. Between lunch and dinner (3pm to 7pm) you can order snacks like sandwiches, pizzas and calzones. Ask the friendly staff for a free tour of the historic manor.

🛍 Shopping

Connemara Market   MARKET
(MG Rd; ⊙from 7am) Vendors sell vegetables, fish, live goats, fabric, clothes, spices and more at this busy market.

SMSM Institute   HANDICRAFTS
(www.keralahandicrafts.in; YMCA Rd; ⊙9am-8pm Mon-Sat) Kerala Government–run handicraft emporium with an Aladdin's cave of fix-priced goodies.

ℹ Information

ABC Internet (MG Rd, Capital Centre; per 30min ₹20; ⊙9am-9pm) One of several good internet places in this small mall.

KIMS (Kerala Institute of Medical Sciences; ☑0471-3041000, emergency 0471-3041144; www.kimskerala.com; Kumarapuram; ⊙24hr) Best choice for medical problems; about 7km northwest of Trivandrum railway station.

Main Post Office (☑0471-2473071; MG Rd) Trivandrum's central post office.

Tourist Facilitation Centre (☑0471-2321132; Museum Rd; ⊙24hr) Near the zoo; supplies maps and brochures.

Tourist Reception Centre (KTDC Hotel Chaithram; ☑0471-2330031; Central Station Rd; ⊙7am-9pm) Arranges KTDC-run tours.

ℹ Getting There & Away

AIR

Trivandrum's airport serves international destinations with direct flights to/from Colombo in

Sri Lanka, Male in the Maldives and major Gulf regions such as Dubai, Sharjah, Muscat, Bahrain and Kuwait.

Within India, **Air India** (☑2317341; Mascot Sq), **Jet Airways** (☑2728864; Sasthamangalam Junction), **IndiGo** (www.goindigo.in) and **SpiceJet** (☑09871803333; www.spicejet.com; Trivandrum airport) fly between Trivandrum and Mumbai (Bombay), Kochi, Bengaluru (Bangalore), Chennai (Madras) and Delhi.

All airline bookings can be made at the efficient **Airtravel Enterprises** (☑3011300; www.ate.travel; MG Rd, New Corporation Bldg).

BUS

State-run and private buses use Trivandrum's giant new concave **KSRTC Central Bus Stand** (☑0471-2462290; www.keralatc.com; Central Station Rd, Thampanoor), opposite the train station.

Buses leave for Kovalam beach (₹15, 30 minutes, every 20 minutes) between 6am and 9pm from the southern end of the East Fort bus stand on MG Rd.

TRAIN

Trains are often heavily booked, so it's worth visiting the **reservation office** (☑139; ⊙8am-8pm Mon-Sat, to 2pm Sun) at the main train station or booking online. While most major trains arrive at **Trivandrum Central Station** close to the city centre, some express services terminate at **Vikram Sarabhai Station** (Kochuveli), about 7km north of the city – check in advance.

Within Kerala there are frequent express trains to Varkala (2nd/sleeper/3AC ₹45/140/485, one hour), Kollam (₹55/170/535, 1¼ hour) and Ernakulam (₹95/195/535, 4½ hours), with trains passing through either Alleppey (₹80/170/535, three hours) or Kottayam (₹80/140/485, 3½ hours). There are also numerous daily services to Kanyakumari (2nd/sleeper/3AC ₹80/140/485, three hours).

❶ Getting Around

The **airport** (📞 2501424) is 10km from the city and 15km from Kovalam; take local bus 14 from the East Fort and City Bus stand (₹9). Prepaid taxi vouchers from the airport cost ₹350 to the city and ₹500 to Kovalam.

Autorickshaws are the easiest way to get around, with short hops costing ₹30 to ₹50.

Around Trivandrum

Neyyar Wildlife Sanctuary

Surrounding an idyllic lake created by the 1964 Neyyar Dam 35km north of Trivandrum, the main attraction at this sanctuary is the **Lion Safari Park** (📞0471-2272182, 9744347582; Indian/foreigner ₹200/300; ⊗9am-4pm Tue-Sun). Admission includes a boat ride across the lake, a lion safari and a visit to a **deer park** and **Crocodile Production Centre** (named for Australian legend Steve Irwin). The fertile forest lining the shore is home to gaurs, sambar deer, sloth, elephants, lion-tailed macaques and the odd tiger.

Get here from Trivandrum's KSRTC bus stand by frequent bus (₹34, 1½ hours). A taxi is about ₹1000 return (with two hours' waiting time) from Trivandrum, or ₹1400 from Kovalam. The KTDC office in Trivandrum also runs tours to Neyyar Dam (₹400).

Sivananda Yoga Vedanta Dhanwantari Ashram

Just before Neyyar Dam, the superbly located **Sivananda Yoga Vedanta Dhanwantari Ashram** (📞0471-2273093; www.sivananda.org.in/neyyardam; dm & tent ₹750, tw ₹950-1200, with AC ₹1700), established in 1978, is renowned for its hatha yoga courses. Courses start on the 1st and 16th of each month, run for a minimum of two weeks and include various levels of accommodation and vegetarian meals. Low season (May to September) rates are ₹100 less. There's an exacting schedule (5.30am to 10pm) of yoga practice, meditation and chanting. Bookings essential. Month-long yoga-teacher training and ayurvedic massage courses are also available.

Kovalam

📞 0471

Once a calm fishing village clustered around its crescent beaches, Kovalam today is Kerala's most developed resort. The main stretch, **Lighthouse Beach**, is touristy with hotels and restaurants built up along the shore, while **Hawah Beach** to the north is usually crowded with day trippers heading straight from the taxi stand to the sand. Neither beach is particularly clean, but at less than 15km from the capital it's a convenient place to have some fun by the sea, there's some promising surf, and it makes a good base for ayurvedic treatments and yoga courses.

About 2km further north, **Samudra Beach** has several upmarket resorts, restaurants and a peaceful but steep beach.

❶ Dangers & Annoyances

There are strong rips at both ends of Lighthouse Beach that carry away several swimmers every year. Swim only between the flags in the area patrolled by lifeguards and avoid swimming during the monsoon.

◉ Sights & Activities

Vizhinjam Lighthouse   LIGHTHOUSE
(Indian/foreigner ₹10/25, camera/video ₹20/25; ⊗10am-5pm) Kovalam's most distinguishing feature is the working candy-striped lighthouse at the southern end of the beach. Climb the spiral staircase for vertigo-inducing views up and down the coast.

Kovalam Surf Club   SURFING
(📞9847347367; www.kovalamsurfclub.com; Lighthouse Beach; 1½ hr lessons ₹1000, board rental half-/full day ₹500/1000) This surf shop and club on Lighthouse Beach offers lessons (from introductory to performance), board rental and a community focus.

Santhigiri   AYURVEDA
(📞0471-2482800;   www.santhigiriashram.org; Lighthouse Beach Rd; from ₹1100; ⊗9am-8pm) Recommended massages and ayurvedic treatments.

🛏 Sleeping

Kovalam is packed with hotels and guesthouses, though true budget places are becoming a dying breed in high season. Beachfront properties are the most expensive and sought-after, but look out for smaller places tucked away in the labyrinth of sandy paths behind the beach among the palm groves and rice paddies; they're usually much better value. All places offer big discounts outside the December–January high season; book ahead in peak times.

Kovalam

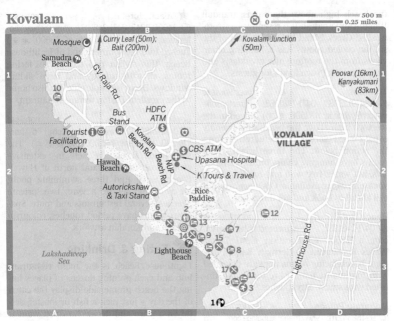

Kovalam

◉ Sights
1	Vizhinjam Lighthouse	C3

◉ Activities, Courses & Tours
2	Kovalam Surf Club	B2
3	Santhigiri	C3

◉ Sleeping
4	Beach Hotel	C3
5	Beach Hotel II	C3
6	Dwaraka Lodge	B2
7	Green Valley Cottages	C3
8	Hotel Greenland	C3
9	Jeevan Ayurvedic Beach Resort	C3
10	Leela	A1
11	Maharaju Palace	C3
12	Paradesh Inn	C2
	Sea Flower	(see 5)
	Treetops	(see 12)
13	Wilson Ayurvedic Resort	B3

◉ Eating
	Fusion	(see 5)
14	Malabar Cafe	B3
15	Suprabhatham	C3
16	Swiss Cafe	B3
17	Varsha Restaurant	C3
	Waves Restaurant & German Bakery	(see 4)

Green Valley Cottages GUESTHOUSE $
(☎0471-2480636; indira_ravi@hotmail.com; r ₹700-1000) Back amongst the palm trees and overlooking a lily pond, this serene complex feels a little faded but it's quiet and good value. The 22 rooms are simple, but the upper rooms have good views from the front terraces.

Hotel Greenland GUESTHOUSE $
(☎0471-2486442; hotelgreenlandin@yahoo.com; r ₹500-1400) This friendly family-run place has refurbished rooms in a multilevel complex just back from the beach. It's not flash but rooms have lots of natural light and the larger upstairs rooms have balconies.

Dwaraka Lodge GUESTHOUSE $
(☎0471-2480411; d ₹500) With regular licks of paint helping to cover up the war wounds of this tired old-timer attached to Rock Cafe, friendly Dwaraka is the cheapest oceanside property.

Paradesh Inn GUESTHOUSE $$
(☎9995362952; inn.paradesh@yahoo.com; Avaduthura; d incl breakfast from ₹1800; @) Back from

KERALA KOVALAM

the beach high above the palms, tranquil Italian-run Paradesh Inn resembles a white-washed Greek island hideaway. Each of the six fan-cooled rooms has a hanging chair, views from the rooftop, nice breakfasts and *satya* cooking ('yoga food') for guests.

Treetops   GUESTHOUSE $$
(☑ 9847912398, 0471-2481363; treetopsofkovalam@yahoo.in; d ₹1500; @ 🛜) Indeed in the treetops high above the beach, this friendly expat-owned place is a peaceful retreat from the action below. The three bright, clean rooms have hanging chairs on the terraces, TVs, hot water, free wi-fi and rooftop views; yoga classes are available. Open year-round; call ahead to book and get directions.

Beach Hotel   GUESTHOUSE $$
(☑ 0471-2481937; www.thebeachhotel-kovalam.com; d ₹2850; 🛜) Location alert! Below Waves Restaurant & German Bakery, the eight beach-facing rooms here are designed with minimalist flair, ochre tones and finished with smart, arty touches.

Maharaju Palace   GUESTHOUSE $$
(☑ 9946854270; www.maharajupalace.com; s/d incl breakfast ₹2600/3300, cottage ₹4200/5300; ❄ 🛜) More of a peaceful retreat than a palace, this quirky Dutch-owned place in a lane just back from the beach has more character than most, with timber furnishings, including the odd four-poster bed, and a separate cottage in the garden. The lovely breakfast terrace is hung with chintzy chandeliers.

Jeevan Ayurvedic Beach Resort   RESORT $$
(☑ 9846898498, 0471-2480662; www.jeevanresort.net; d ₹1800-4200, with AC ₹2400-12,000; ❄ 🏊) Beachfront Jeevan is an inviting sort of place with one of the only seafront pools on this strip. Expect decent-sized rooms with bathtubs. All but the cheapest ground-floor rooms have sea views and balconies.

Wilson Ayurvedic Resort   HOTEL $$
(☑ 0471-2480051; Lighthouse Beach; d ₹750-1250, with AC ₹2000-3500; ❄ 🛜 🏊) Wilson has clean and reasonably well-maintained rooms orbiting a pool just back from Lighthouse Beach. It has a leafy holiday-resort vibe and offers ayurvedic treatments.

Sea Flower   HOTEL $$
(☑ 0471-2480554; www.seaflowerkovalam.com; d ₹2300; 🛜) At the southern end of Lighthouse Beach, this friendly little place is handy for Lighthouse Rd and is reasonably priced for the beachfront location. Rooms are simple but fresh, with balconies and sea views.

★ Beach Hotel II   HOTEL $$$
(☑ 9400031243, 0471-2481937; www.thebeachhotel-kovalam.com; d ₹4500, with AC ₹5600; ❄ 🛜) Tucked into the southern end of Lighthouse Beach, this stylish pad has 10 sea-facing rooms, all with balcony and large sliding windows. Decor is simple chic. It's also home to the excellent Fusion terrace restaurant.

Leela   HOTEL $$$
(☑ 0471-2480101; www.theleela.com; d from ₹16,200, ste from ₹40,000; ❄ @ 🛜 🏊) The sumptuous Leela is set in extensive grounds on the headland north of Hawah Beach. You'll find three swimming pools, an ayurvedic centre, a gym, two 'private beaches', several restaurants and more. Spacious rooms have period touches, colourful textiles and Keralan artwork.

✕ Eating & Drinking

Lighthouse Beach is the main restaurant hub and each evening dozens of places lining the beach promenade display the catch of the day – just pick a fish or lobster, settle on a price and decide how you want it prepared. Market price varies enormously depending on the day's catch, but at the time of research it was around ₹350 per fish fillet, ₹900 per half kilo of tiger prawns, and ₹3500 per kilo of lobster. Unlicensed places might serve alcohol in mugs, or with the bottles hidden discreetly out of sight (or not, depending on current government rules).

Samudra Beach, to the north, is quieter but also has some restaurants worth seeking out. For a romantic dining splurge, the restaurants at Leela and Vivanta by Taj are pricey but top class.

Suprabhatham   KERALAN $
(meals ₹80-230; ⊙ 7am-10pm) This little veg place hidden back from the beach doesn't look like much, but it dishes up excellent, inexpensive Keralan cooking, vegetarian thalis and fresh fruit juices in a rustic setting.

Varsha Restaurant   SOUTH INDIAN $
(mains ₹100-175; ⊙ 8am-10pm) This little restaurant just back from Lighthouse Beach serves some of Kovalam's best vegetarian food at budget prices. Dishes are fresh and carefully prepared. A great spot for breakfast and lunch in particular.

Waves Restaurant &
German Bakery   MULTICUISINE $$
(Beach Hotel; breakfast ₹80-450, mains ₹250-450; ⊙ 7.30am-11pm; 🛜) With its broad, burnt-

KERALA GOING DRY?

In an effort to curb high per capita alcohol consumption and perceived associated social problems (including India's highest suicide rate), the Keralan government is going dry. In 2014, the government announced a 10-year plan to move towards full prohibition by gradually closing down bars (except those in five-star hotels) and state-run liquor outlets. At the time of writing, almost 700 bars had been closed, mostly in three- and four-star hotels, though many government-run liquour outlets were still dispensing bottles of IMFL rum and brandy to long queues. The plan is to close 10% of these outlets each year over 10 years.

It remains to be seen how this ban might affect the tourism industry or how far the government will take it. The general consensus is that while hard liquour bars will remain closed, 'beer parlours' would open in their place and that a Kingfisher will still be available at tourist places. It's also likely that the black market will boom.

orange balcony, ambient soundtrack and wide-roaming menu, Waves is usually busy with foreigners. It morphs into the German Bakery, a great spot for breakfast with fresh bread, croissants, pastries and decent coffee, while dinner turns up Thai curries, German sausages, pizza and seafood. There's a small bookshop attached. Wi-fi is ₹40.

Swiss Cafe   CAFE $$
(mains ₹110-490; ⊘ 7.15am-10pm) Swiss Cafe stands out for tasty Euro dishes like rosti, schnitzel, pasta and pizza, unusual dishes like roast lamb in whisky sauce as well as the usual fresh seafood and Indian staples. The balcony, with its wicker chairs, is a good place to take in the action.

Malabar Cafe   INDIAN $$
(mains ₹110-450; ⊘ 8am-11pm) The busy tables tell a story: with candlelight at night and views through pot plants to the crashing waves, Malabar offers tasty food and good service.

Fusion   MULTICUISINE $$
(mains ₹150-450; ⊘ 7.30am-10.30pm; 🐦) The terrace restaurant at Beach Hotel II is one of the best dining experiences on Lighthouse Beach with an inventive East-meets-West menu – a range of Continental dishes, Asian fusion, and interesting seafood numbers like lobster steamed in vodka. Also serves French press coffee and herbal teas.

Curry Leaf   MULTICUISINE $$
(Samudra Beach; mains ₹100-350; ⊘ 8am-8.30pm) On a small hilltop overlooking Samudra Beach, this new two-storey restaurant boasts enviable ocean and sunset views, eager staff and good food ranging from fresh seafood and tandoori to continental dishes. It requires a bit of a walk along paths or up-

hill from the beach, but the uncrowded location is part of the charm.

Bait   SEAFOOD $$$
(Vivanta by Taj; mains ₹300-750; ⊘ 12.30-3pm & 6-10.30pm) The seafood restaurant at the Taj off Samudra Beach is designed as an upmarket alfresco beach shack. Watch the chefs at work in the open kitchen; the seafood and spicy preparations are top-notch.

ℹ Information

About 500m uphill from Lighthouse Beach are HDFC and Axis ATMs, and there are Federal Bank and ICICI ATMs at Kovalam Junction. There are several small internet cafes charging around ₹30 per hour.

Global Internet (Leo Restaurant; internet/wi-fi per hour ₹40/30; ⊘ 9am-9pm; 🐦) Check your email on the terminals or hook up to the wi-fi in the restaurant.

Post Office (Kovalam Beach Rd; ⊘ 9am-1pm Mon-Sat) Near Leela Hotel.

Tourist Facilitation Centre (☎ 0471-2480085; Kovalam Beach Rd; ⊘ 9.30am-5pm) Helpful; in the entrance to Government Guesthouse near the bus stand.

Upasana Hospital (☎ 0471-2480632) Has English-speaking doctors who can take care of minor injuries.

ℹ Getting There & Around

BUS

Buses start and finish at an unofficial stand on the main road outside the entrance to Leela resort and all buses pass through Kovalam Junction, about 1.5km north of Lighthouse Beach. Buses connect Kovalam and Trivandrum every 20 minutes between 5.30am and 10pm (₹15, 30 minutes). For northbound onward travel it's easiest to take any bus to Trivandrum and change there, but there are two buses daily to Ernakulam (₹210, 5½ hours), stopping at Kallambalam (for Varkala, ₹750, 1½ hours), Kollam (₹85, 2½ hours) and Alleppey (₹125, four hours). There are also a couple of buses for Kanyakumari (₹80, two hours).

TAXI

A taxi between Trivandrum and Kovalam beach is around ₹400; an autorickshaw should cost ₹300. From the bus stand to the north end of Lighthouse Beach costs around ₹50.

MOTORCYCLE

K Tours & Travel (🖋 8089493376, 0471-2127003; scooters/Enfields per day from ₹400/600) next door to Devi Garden Restaurant just above Hawa Beach, rents out scooters and Enfields.

Around Kovalam

Poovar

About 16km southeast of Kovalam, almost at the Tamil Nadu border, Poovar is the gateway to a region of beaches, estuaries, villages and upmarket resorts that comprise the 'mini backwaters' of Kerala's far south.

Boat operators along the Neyyar River will take you on 1½- to two-hour cruises through the waterways visiting the beach, bird-filled mangrove swamps and forested Poovar Island for around ₹2500 for two people. Travel agents in Kovalam can also arrange these trips.

Poovar Island Resort   RESORT $$$
(🖋 0471-2212068, 9895799044; www.poovarislandresorts.com; s/d cottage from ₹9600/10,800, floating cottage from ₹15,000/16,200; ❄🖥🏊) Accessible only by boat, this resort is popular for its romantic 'floating' cottages moored on the water's edge – though most of the rooms are on land and designed in Keralan architectural style. It's a soothing, peaceful and very well-appointed place to retreat from the mainland or beach resorts.

Varkala

🖋 0470 / POP 42,270

Perched almost perilously along the edge of 15m-high red laterite cliffs, the resort of Varkala has a naturally beautiful setting and the cliff-top stretch has steadily grown into

---

AYURVEDIC RESORTS

Between Kovalam and Poovar, amid seemingly endless swaying palms, laid-back village life and some empty golden-sand beaches, are a string of upmarket ayurvedic resorts that are worth a look if you're serious about immersing yourself in ayurvedic treatments. They're all between 6km and 10km southeast of Kovalam.

Dr Franklin's Panchakarma Institute (🖋 0471-2480870; www.dr-franklin.com; Chowara; s/d hut €23/30, r from €28/37, with AC €41/60; @🖥🏊) For those serious about ayurvedic treatment, this is a reputable and less expensive alternative to the flashier resorts. Daily treatment with full meal plan costs €70. Accommodation is comfortable but not resort style.

Niraamaya Surya Samudra (🖋 0471-2480413; www.niraamaya.in; Pulinkudi; r incl breakfast ₹18,000-32,000; ❄🖥🏊) The latest incarnation of Surya Samudra offers A-list-style seclusion. The 22 transplanted traditional Keralan homes come with four-poster beds and open-air bathrooms, set in a palm grove above sparkling seas. There's an infinity pool carved out of a single block of granite, renowned Niraamaya Spa, ayurvedic treatments, gym and spectacular outdoor yoga platforms.

Bethsaida Hermitage (🖋 0471-2267554; www.bethsaidahermitage.com; Pulinkudi; s €90-150, d €150-165; ❄🖥🏊) This charitable organisation helps support two nearby orphanages and several other worthy causes. As a bonus, it's also a luxurious and remote beachside escape, with sculpted gardens, seductively slung hammocks, putting-green-perfect lawns, palms galore and professional ayurvedic treatments and yoga classes.

Thapovan Heritage Home (🖋 0471-2480453; www.thapovan.com; s/d hillside from ₹3200/4000, cottages ₹5300/6700, beachfront s/d cottage ₹5600/7000; ❄🖥) Two properties only 100m apart – one consists of beachfront cottages in Keralan style, and the other is the gorgeous hilltop location where Keralan teak cottages are filled with hand-crafted furniture and set among perfectly manicured grounds with wonderful views to the ocean and swaying palm groves. Ayurvedic treatments range from one-hour massages to 28-day treatment marathons, as well as yoga and meditation sessions.

Kerala's most popular backpacker hang-out. A small strand of beach nuzzles Varkala's cliff edge, where restaurants play innocuous trance music and stalls sell T-shirts, baggy trousers and silver jewellery. It's touristy and the sales pitch can be tiring, but Varkala is still a great place to watch the days slowly turn into weeks, and it's not hard to escape the crowds further north or south where the beaches are cleaner and quieter.

Despite its backpacker vibe, Varkala is essentially a temple town, and the main Papanasham beach is a holy place where Hindus come to make offerings for passed loved ones, assisted by priests who set up shop beneath the Hindustan Hotel.

ⓘ Dangers & Annoyances

The beaches at Varkala have strong currents; even experienced swimmers have been swept away. During the monsoon the beach all but disappears and the cliffs themselves are slowly being eroded. Take care walking on the cliff path, especially at night – much of it is unfenced and it can be slippery in parts.

If women wear bikinis or even swimsuits on the beach at Varkala, they are likely to feel uncomfortably exposed to stares. Wearing a sarong when out of the water will help avoid offending local sensibilities. Dress conservatively if going into Varkala town.

◎ Sights

Janardhana Temple　　　　HINDU TEMPLE
Varkala is a temple town and Janardhana Temple is the main event – its technicolour Hindu spectacle sits hovering above Beach Rd. It's closed to non-Hindus, but you may be invited into the temple grounds where there is a huge banyan tree and shrines to Ayyappan, Hanuman and other deities.

Sivagiri Mutt　　　　ASHRAM
(☑ 0470-2602807; www.sivagirimutt.org) Sivagiri Mutt is the headquarters of the Shri Narayana Dharma Sanghom Trust, the ashram devoted to Shri Narayana Guru (1855–1928), Kerala's most prominent guru. This is a popular pilgrimage site and the resident swami is happy to talk to visitors.

Ponnumthuruthu Island　　　　ISLAND
(boat ride ₹250 per person) About 10km south of Varkala, this island in the middle of a backwater lake is home to the Shiva-Parvati Hindu Temple, also known as the Golden Temple. The main reason to venture down here is the scenic punt-powered boat ride to and around the island.

Kappil Beach　　　　BEACH
About 9km north of Varkala by road, Kappil Beach is a prettty and, as yet, undeveloped stretch of sand. It's also the start of a mini network of backwaters. The Kappil Lake Boat Club, near the bridge, hires out boats for short trips on the lake.

🏃 Activities

The gently undulating path from the northern clifftop continues for a photogenic 7km to Kappil Beach, passing a subtley changing beach landscape, including Odayam Beach and the fishing village of Edava. The walk is best done early in the morning.

Yoga (per session ₹300 to ₹400) is offered at several guesthouses, and boogie boards (₹100) can be hired from places along the beach; be wary of strong currents. Many of the resorts and hotels along the north cliff offer ayurvedic treatments and massage.

Laksmi's　　　　BEAUTY & MASSAGE
(☑ 9895948080; Clafouti Beach Resort; manicure/pedicure ₹600-1000, henna ₹500, massage ₹1200; ⊙ 9am-7pm) This tiny place offers quality ladies-only treatments such as threading and waxing, manicures and massage.

Haridas Yoga　　　　YOGA
(www.pranayogavidya.com; Hotel Green Palace; classes ₹300; ⊙ 8am & 4.30pm Aug-May) Recommended drop-in 1½-hour hatha yoga classes with experienced teachers.

Eden Garden　　　　MASSAGE
(☑ 0470-2603910; www.edengarden.in; massages from ₹1000) Offers a more upmarket ayurvedic experience, including single treatments and packages.

Soul & Surf　　　　SURFING, YOGA
(☑ 9895580106; www.soulandsurf.com; South Cliff; surf lessons ₹2300, surf guides ₹1150; ⊙ Oct-May) This UK outfit organises surfing trips and yoga retreats in season, with accommodation at their South Cliff pad. They also run the Papanasam Surf School for beginners, with 1½-hour lessons. If you already surf and there's space, join one of the regular surf tours (₹1150). Board rental is ₹850/1600 for a half/full day.

🛌 Sleeping

Most places to stay are crammed in along the north cliff where backpackers tend to congregate, but there are some nice

Varkala

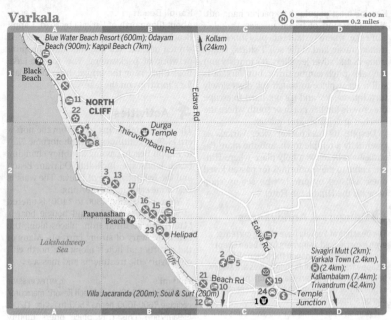

Varkala

places down by the southern cliffs. Less-developed Odayam Beach, about 1km further north of Varkala's Black Beach, is a tranquil alternative.

Practically all accommodation places can be reached by taxi or autorickshaw via the network of lanes leading to the cliffs, but the commission racket is alive and well – make sure your driver takes you to the place you've asked for.

★ **Jicky's** GUESTHOUSE **$**
(📞 9846179325, 0470-2606994; www.jickys.com; s ₹500, d ₹800-1200, AC cottage ₹3000; ❄ 🛜)
In the palm groves just back from the cliffs and taxi stand, family-run Jicky's remains as friendly as they come and has blossomed into several buildings offering plenty of choice for travellers. The rooms in the main whitewashed building are fresh, and nearby are two charming octagonal double cottages,

and some larger air-con rooms. Offers good off-season discounts.

★ **Kaiya House** GUESTHOUSE **$$**
(☑ 9746126909, 9995187913; www.kaiyahouse.com; d incl breakfast ₹2750, d with AC ₹3300; ✳🛜) What Kaiya House lacks in sea views it makes up for with charm, welcoming owners and sheer relaxation. Each of the five rooms is thoughtfully furnished and themed (African, Indian, Chinese, Japanese and English) with four-poster beds and artworks on the walls. There's a lovely rooftop terrace and rear courtyard with calming vibe. Expat owner Debra will welcome you with tea, advice and free walking tours. The clifftop is a 10-minute walk away.

Eden Garden RESORT **$$**
(☑ 0470-2603910; www.edengarden.in; cottages ₹1500-2000, deluxe ₹4500; 🛜) Stylish rooms come with high wooden ceilings and attractive furniture, set around a lush lily pond. There are also bamboo cottages and deluxe organically-shaped cottages like white space-mushrooms with intricate paintwork, round beds, and mosaic circular baths. Ayurvedic packages from three to 30 days.

Kerala Bamboo House RESORT **$$**
(☑ 9895270993; www.keralabamboohouse.com; huts d ₹2500-3500, r with AC ₹5000; ✳🛜) For that simple bamboo-hut experience, this popular place squishes together dozens of pretty Balinese-style huts and a neatly maintained garden about half-way along the North Cliff walk. Ayurvedic treatments, yoga and cooking classes (₹600 per person, minimum two people) are on offer.

Puthooram RESORT **$$**
(☑ 9895675805, 0470-3202007; www.puthooram.com; r ₹400-1350, with AC ₹1650-3300; ✳@) Puthooram's wood-lined bungalows are set around a charming little garden of pot plants. Room prices and standards vary so check out a few; rooms with sea view are pricier.

Omsam Guesthouse GUESTHOUSE **$$**
(☑ 0470-2604455; www.omsamguesthome.com; South Cliff; d ₹2500-3500, d with AC ₹4500; ✳🛜) The seven rooms in this beautful Keralan-style guesthouse are a delight, with heavy timber stylings and furniture. Good location south of the main beach.

Sea Pearl Chalets RESORT **$$**
(☑ 0470-2660105; www.seapearlchalets.com; d ₹2030) Perched on Varkala's quieter southern cliff, these basic, pod-like huts have un-

beatable views and are surrounded by prim lawns. Worth checking out before they tumble into the ocean.

Krishnatheeram RESORT **$$$**
(Ayur Holy Beach Resort; ☑ 0470-2601305; www.krishnatheeram.com; r ₹5000, with AC ₹6000; ✳🛜🏊) Overlooking Black Beach and one of the few northern beachfront resorts with a pool, this neat ayurvedic resort specialises in yoga therapy, with daily classes and professional ayurvedic treatments.

Villa Jacaranda GUESTHOUSE **$$$**
(☑ 0470-2610296; www.villa-jacaranda.biz; d incl breakfast ₹5200-7000; 🛜) The ultimate in understated luxury, this romantic retreat back from the southern beach has just four spacious, bright rooms in a large two-storey house, each with a balcony and decorated with a chic blend of minimalist modern and period touches. The top-floor room has its own rooftop garden with sea views.

Blue Water Beach Resort COTTAGES **$$$**
(☑ 0470-2664422, 9446848534; www.bluewaterstay.com; Odayam Beach; cottages ₹5000, with AC ₹7500; ✳🛜) At quiet Odayam Beach, north of Varkala, Blue Water has sturdy individual timber cottages with tiled roofs arranged in a pleasant lawn area sloping to the beach.

Gateway Hotel Janardhanapuram HOTEL **$$$**
(☑ 0470-6673300; www.thegatewayhotels.com; d incl breakfast from ₹9000, ste ₹12,500; ✳@🛜🏊) Varkala's flashiest hotel, the rebadged Gateway, is looking hot with gleaming linen and mocha cushions in rooms overlooking the garden, while the more expensive rooms have sea views and balconies. There's a fantastic pool with bar (nonguests ₹500), tennis court and the well-regarded GAD restaurant.

✖ Eating & Drinking

Most restaurants in Varkala offer the same traveller menu of Indian, Asian and continental fare to a soundtrack of easy-listening trance and Bob Marley, but the quality of the cliffside 'shacks' has improved one of sight over the years and most offer free wi-fi. Join in the nightly Varkala saunter till you find a place that suits.

Sreepadman SOUTH INDIAN **$**
(thalis ₹75; ⏰ 5am-10pm) For cheap and authentic Keralan fare – think dosas and thalis – where you can rub shoulders with rickshaw drivers and pilgrims rather than

tourists, pull up a seat at hole-in-the-wall Sreepadman, opposite the Janardhana Temple and overlooking the large bathing tank.

Oottupura Vegetarian Restaurant INDIAN $
(mains ₹45-100) Near the taxi stand, this budget eatery has a respectable range of cheap veg dishes, including breakfast *puttu* (flour with milk, bananas and honey).

Coffee Temple CAFE $
(coffee ₹70-100, mains ₹80-250; ⊙6am-7pm; ☎) For your early-morning coffee fix it's hard to beat this English-run place, where the beans are freshly ground, there's fresh bread and a daily paper. The menu has also expanded into crêpes and Mexican burritos, fajitas and tacos – and it's no worse for that.

Juice Shack CAFE $
(juices from ₹70, snacks ₹80-250; ⊙6am-8.30pm; ☎) It certainly looks a bit 'shack-like' next to the fancy neighbours, but this funky little health-juice bar still turns out great juices, smoothies and snacks such as Mexican wraps.

Cafe Italiano ITALIAN $$
(mains ₹200-400; ⊙7am-11pm; ☎) As well as good pizza, pasta and crêpes, two-storey Italiano is worth a visit for its library and book exchange and for the tree growing through the upper deck.

Café del Mar MULTICUISINE $$
(dishes ₹120-450; ⊙9am-10pm; ☎) It doesn't have the big balcony of some of its neighbours, but Café del Mar is usually busy thanks to efficient service, good coffee and consistently good food.

God's Own Country Kitchen MULTICUISINE $$
(North Cliff; mains ₹80-400; ⊙8.30am-10pm; ☎) This fun place doesn't really need to play on Kerala Tourism's tagline – the food is good, there's a great little upper-floor deck and there's live music some nights in season.

Trattorias MULTICUISINE $$
(meals ₹100-400; ⊙8.30am-11pm) Trattorias aims to specialise in Italian with a decent range of pasta and pizza but also offers Japanese – including sushi – and Thai dishes. This was one of the original places with an Italian coffee machine, and the wicker chairs and sea-facing terrace are cosy.

Wait n Watch INDIAN $$
(Hindustan Beach Retreat; mains ₹120-280; ⊙11am-10pm; ☎) The top-floor restaurant and cocktail bar at this ugly beachfront hotel block offers tasty-enough Indian fare and seafood, but the main reason to take the elevator is for the view from the balcony (with just a couple of tables) over the action of the beach. There's another alfresco restaurant by the pool.

AYURVEDA

With its roots in Sanskrit, the word ayurveda comes from *ayu* (life) and *veda* (knowledge); the knowledge or science of life. Principles of ayurvedic medicine were first documented in the Vedas some 2000 years ago, but may have been practised centuries earlier.

Ayurveda sees the world as having an intrinsic order and balance. It argues that we possess three *doshas* (humours): *vata* (wind or air); *pitta* (fire); and *kapha* (water/earth), known together as the *tridoshas*. Deficiency or excess in any of them can result in disease: an excess of *vata* may result in dizziness and debility; an increase in *pitta* may lead to fever, inflammation and infection. *Kapha* is essential for hydration.

Ayurvedic treatment aims to restore the balance, and hence good health, principally through two methods: panchakarma (internal purification), and herbal massage. Panchakarma is used to treat serious ailments, and is an intense detox regime, a combination of five types of therapies to rid the body of built-up endotoxins. These include: *vaman* (therapeutic vomiting); *virechan* (purgation); *vasti* (enemas); *nasya* (elimination of toxins through the nose); and *raktamoksha* (detoxification of the blood). Before panchakarma begins, the body is first prepared over several days with a special diet, oil massages (*snehana*) and herbal steam baths (*swedana*). Although it may sound pretty grim, panchakarma purification might only use a few of these treatments at a time, with therapies like bloodletting and leeches only used in rare cases. Still, this is no spa holiday. The herbs used in ayurveda grow in abundance in Kerala's humid climate – the monsoon is thought to be the best time of year for treatment, when there is less dust in the air, the pores are open and the body is most receptive to treatment – and every village has its own ayurvedic pharmacy.

☆ Entertainment

Kathakali performances are organised during high season – look out for notices locally.

Rock n Roll Cafe — LIVE MUSIC

(☑8136858684; ⏱24hr) Music is the thing at this otherwise unremarkable restaurant-bar. There's live music, DJs or movies on most nights in season, as well as tabla lessons. There's also cold beer, a good cocktail list and food is available from 6pm.

❶ Information

A 24-hour ATM at Temple Junction takes Visa cards, and there are several more ATMs in Varkala town. Many of the travel agents lining the cliff do cash advances on credit cards and change travellers cheques. Most restaurants and cafes offer free wi-fi.

❶ Getting There & Away

There are frequent local and express trains to Trivandrum (2nd/sleeper/3AC ₹45/140/485, one hour) and Kollam (2nd/sleeper/3AC ₹45/140/485, 40 minutes), as well as seven daily services to Alleppey (2nd/sleeper/3AC ₹95/140/485, two hours). From Temple Junction, three daily buses pass by on their way to Trivandrum (₹60, 1½ to two hours), with one heading to Kollam (₹40, one hour).

❶ Getting Around

It's about 2.5km from the train station to Varkala Beach, with autorickshaws going to Temple Junction for ₹80 and North Cliff for ₹100. Local buses also travel regularly between the train station and Temple Junction (₹5).

A few places along the cliff hire out scooters/motorbikes for ₹350/450 per day.

Kollam (Quilon)

☑0474 / POP 349,000

Kollam (Quilon) is the southern approach to Kerala's backwaters and one end of the popular backwater ferry trip to Alleppey. One of the oldest ports in the Arabian Sea, it was once a major commercial hub that saw Roman, Arab, Chinese and later Portuguese, Dutch and British traders jostle into port – eager to get their hands on spices and the region's cashew crops. The centre of town is reasonably hectic, but surrounding it are the calm waterways of Ashtamudi Lake, fringed with coconut palms, cashew plantations and traditional villages – a great place to get a feel for the backwaters without the crowds.

◉ Sights & Activities

The best thing to do from Kollam is explore the backwaters around **Munroe Island** by canoe, via a network of canals off Ashtamudi Lake about 15km north of Kollam.

There's a rowdy **fishing harbour** at Kollam Beach where customers and fisherfolk alike pontificate on the value of the day's catch; there's also an evening fish market from 5pm to 9pm. There's an average **beach** 2km south of town, marked at the northern end by the **Thangassery Lighthouse**.

★**Canal Cruise** — BOATING

(www.dtpckollam.com; tours per person ₹500; ⏱9am-1.30pm & 2-6.30pm) Excellent tours through the canals of Munroe Island are organised by the DTPC and a few private operators. After a 25km drive to the starting point, you take a three-hour trip via punted canoe to observe daily village life, see *kettuvallam* (rice barge) construction, toddy (palm beer) tapping, coir-making (coconut fibre), prawn and fish farming, and do some birdwatching on spice-garden visits.

Houseboat Cruises — BOATING

(www.dtpckollam.com; overnight cruise ₹5000-9200, Kollam to Alappuzha cruise ₹14,000) Kollam has far fewer houseboats than Alleppey, which can mean a less touristy experience. The DTPC organises houseboat cruise packages, both locally and to Alleppey and Kochi.

Santhigiri Ayurveda Centre — AYURVEDA

(☑9287242407, 0474-2763014; www.santhigiriashram.com; Asramam Rd, Kadappakada; massage from ₹1200) An ayurvedic centre with more of an institutional than a spa vibe, popular for its seven- to 21-day treatment packages.

✦ Festivals & Events

The Kollam region hosts many festivals and boat regattas – in November and December there are temple festivals somewhere in the region virtually every day.

Kollam Pooram — RELIGIOUS

(Apr) Colourful annual temple festival featuring elephants and mock sword fights.

President's Trophy Boat Race — BOAT RACE

(⏱1 Nov) On Ashtamudi Lake, this is the most prestigious regatta in Kollam region.

Kottamkulangara Chamaya Vilakku — RELIGIOUS

(⏱Mar/Apr) Local men dress as women and carry lamps to the temple at Chavara, 15km north of Kollam.

KERALA KOLLAM (QUILON)

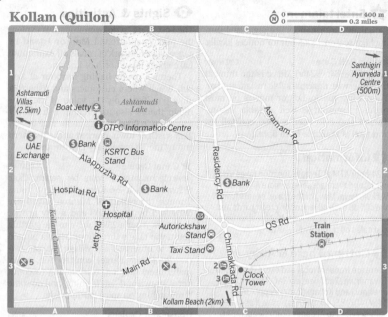

Kollam (Quilon)

Kollam (Quilon)

🛏 Sleeping

The DTPC office keeps a list of homestays in and around Kollam.

Munroe Island Backwaters Homestay
HOMESTAY $

(☏ 9048176186; Munroe Island; cottage ₹1200) The three colourful cottages built in Keralan style and hidden away in the backwaters of Munroe Island about 25km north (by road) of Kollam allow travellers to delve into the village experience. The friendly family can arrange canoe tours and meals..

Karuna Residency
GUESTHOUSE $

(☏ 0474-2760066; Main Rd; dm ₹150, s/d ₹400/600) This little budgeteer is starting to show its age and is very basic, but it's still in reasonable condition and the owner is accustomed to travellers.

⭐ Ashtamudi Villas
GUESTHOUSE $$

(☏ 9847132449, 0474-2706090; www.ashtamudivillas.com; near Kadavoor Church, Mathilil; d ₹1500-2000; 🛜) These charming brick cottages on the water's edge are easily the best choice for a relaxing, affordable stay in Kollam. Ebullient host Prabhath Joseph offers a warm welcome and pulls out all the stops with thoughtful architectural design, colourful decor, gleaming bathrooms, hammocks swinging between palm trees by the lake and a library of books on Kerala. Access is by road or boat – call ahead for directions.

Nani Hotel
HOTEL $$

(☏ 0474-2751141; www.hotelnani.com; Chinnakada Rd; d incl breakfast ₹1460, with AC ₹2250-3650; ❄@🛜) This boutique business hotel is a surprise in Kollam's busy centre, and very good value. Built by a cashew magnate, its beautifully designed architecture mixes traditional Keralan elements and modern lines for a sleek look. Even the cheaper rooms have flat-screen TVs, feathery pillows and sumptuous bathrooms.

Eating

Hotel Guru Prasad
INDIAN $

(Main Rd; meals ₹10-45; ☺11am-3pm) In a neat colonial building, this busy lunch place draws (mostly male) punters with cheap thalis.

Wok & Grill
MULTICUISINE $$

(☎0474-2753400; mains ₹120-290; ☺11am-3pm & 6-10pm) The combination of Thai, Chinese, Arabic and North Indian cuisines offers some tasty, meaty dishes at this modern, clean restaurant. Choose from Kung Pao chicken, green curry, ginger garlic prawns and shwarma rolls.

Prasadam
MULTICUISINE $$

(☎0474-2751141; Nani Hotel, Chinnakada Rd; mains ₹160-250, lunch thalis ₹125; ☺8am-10pm) The restaurant at the Nani Hotel has a slightly formal feel with high-backed chairs amid intricate copper-relief artwork depicting Kollam history. Meals, including Keralan dishes such as Travancore egg masala, as well as tandoori and Chinese, are beautifully prepared, and the tasty thalis are excellent value at lunchtime.

ℹ Information

DTPC Information Centre (☎0474-2745625; www.dtpckollam.com; ☺8am-7pm) Helpful and can organise backwater trips; near the KSRTC bus stand and boat jetty.

ℹ Getting There & Away

BOAT

Many travellers take the canal boat to or from Alleppey (₹400; eight hours; 10.30am) as part of the classic backwaters tour (p964). From the main boat jetty there are frequent public ferry services across Ashtamudi Lake to Guhanandapuram (one hour). Fares are around ₹10 return, or ₹3 for a short hop.

BUS

Kollam is on the Trivandrum–Kollam–Alleppey–Ernakulam bus route, with buses departing every 10 or 20 minutes to Trivandrum (₹70, two hours), Alleppey (₹80, 2½ hours), Kumily (₹125, five hours, 7.50am) and Ernakulam (Kochi, ₹150, 3½ hours). Buses depart from the **KSRTC bus stand** (☎0474-2752008), conveniently near the boat jetty.

TRAIN

There are frequent trains to Ernakulam (sleeper/3AC ₹140/485, 3½ hours, six daily), Trivandrum (₹140/485, one hour) via Varkala (₹36/165, 30 minutes), and Alappuzha (Alleppey; ₹170/535, 1½ hours).

Around Kollam

Krishnapuram Palace Museum
MUSEUM

(☎0479-2441133; admission ₹10, camera/video ₹25/250; ☺9.30am-4.30pm Tue-Sun) Two kilometres south of Kayamkulam (between

---

MATHA AMRITHANANDAMAYI MISSION

The incongruously pink **Matha Amrithanandamayi Mission** (☎04762897578; www.amritapuri.org; Amrithapuri) is the famous ashram of one of India's few female gurus, Amrithanandamayi, also known as Amma (Mother) or 'The Hugging Mother' because of the *darshan* (audience) she offers, often hugging thousands of people in marathon all-night sessions.

The ashram runs official tours at 4pm and 5pm daily. It's a huge complex, with about 3000 people living there permanently – monks, nuns, students and families, both Indian and foreign. It offers food, ayurvedic treatments, yoga and meditation. Amma travels around for much of the year, so you might be out of luck if in need of a cuddle. A busy time of year at the ashram is around Amma's birthday on 27 September.

Visitors should dress conservatively and there is a strict code of behaviour. With prior arrangement – register online – you can stay at the ashram in a triple room for ₹250 per person, or ₹500 for a single (including simple vegetarian meals).

Since the ashram is on the main canal between Kollam and Alleppey, many travellers break the ferry ride by getting off here, staying a day or two, then picking up another cruise. Alternatively, cross to the other side of the canal and grab a rickshaw 10km south to Karunagappally or 12km north to Kayankulam (around ₹200), from where you can catch onward buses or trains.

If you're not taking the cruise, catch a train to either Karunagappally or Kayankulam and take an autorickshaw (around ₹200) to Vallickavu and cross the pedestrian bridge from there. If you intend to stay a while, you can book online for an ashram taxi – they pick up from as far away as Kochi or Trivandrum.

Kollam and Alleppey), this restored palace is a fine example of grand Keralan architecture. Inside are paintings, antique furniture, sculptures and a renowned 3m-high mural depicting the Gajendra Moksha (liberation of Gajendra, chief of the elephants) as told in the Mahabharata.

Buses (₹26, one hour) leave Kollam every few minutes for Kayamkulam. Get off at the bus stand near the temple gate, 2km before the palace.

Alappuzha (Alleppey)

☑ 0477 / POP 74,200

Alappuzha – still better known as Alleppey – is the hub of Kerala's backwaters, home to a vast network of waterways and more than a thousand houseboats. Wandering around the small but chaotic city centre, with its modest grid of canals, you'd be hard-pressed to agree with the 'Venice of the East' tag. But step out of this mini-mayhem – west to the beach or in practically any other direction towards the backwaters – and Alleppey is graceful and greenery-fringed, disappearing into a watery world of villages, punted canoes, toddy shops and, of course, houseboats. Float along and gaze over paddy fields of succulent green, curvaceous rice barges and village life along the banks. This is one of Kerala's most mesmerisingly beautiful and relaxing experiences.

◉ Sights & Activities

Alleppey Beach   BEACH

Alleppey's main beach is about 2km west of the city centre; there's no shelter at the beach itself and swimming is fraught due to strong currents, but the sunsets are good and there are a few places to stop for a drink or snack, including a good coffee shop. The beach stretches up and down the coast.

RKK Memorial Museum   MUSEUM

(☑ 0477-2242923; www.rkkmuseum.com; NH47, near Powerhouse Bridge; Indian/foreigner ₹150/350; ⊗9am-5pm Tue-Sun) The Revi Karuna Karan (RKK) Memorial Museum, in a grand building fronted by Greco-Roman columns, contains a lavish collection of crystal, porcelain, ivory, Keralan antiques, furniture and artworks from the personal collection of wealthy businessman Revi Karuna Karan. The museum was created as a memorial after he passed away in 2003.

Kerala Kayaking   KAYAKING

(☑ 0477-2245001, 9846585674; www.keralakayaking.com; 4/7/10hr per person ₹1500/3000/4500) The original kayaking outfit in Alleppey. The young crew here offer excellent guided kayaking trips through narrow backwater canals. Paddles in single or double kayaks include a support boat and motorboat transport to your starting point. There are four-hour morning and afternoon trips, seven- or 10-hour day trips, and multiday village tours can also be arranged.

Shree Krishna Ayurveda Panchkarma Centre   AYURVEDA

(☑ 09847119060; www.krishnayurveda.com; 3/5/7-day treatments from €275/420/590) For ayurvedic treatments; one-hour rejuvenation massages are ₹1000, but it specialises in three-, five- and seven-night packages with accommodation and yoga classes. Rates are cheaper with two people sharing accommodation. It's near the Nehru race finishing point.

Elephant Camp   ELEPHANTS

(☑ 9249905525; 30/60min program ₹400/1000; ⊗8am-5.30pm) This small elephant camp near the north end of Punnamada Lake offers elephant experiences from 30 minutes to two hours. Longer sessions include feeding, bathing and a trunk shower.

☞ Tours

Any guesthouse, hotel, travel agent or the DTPC can arrange canoe or houseboat tours of the backwaters (see p964).

Kashmiri-style *shikaras* (covered boats) gather along the North Canal on the road to the houseboat dock. They charge ₹300 to ₹400 per hour for motorised canal and backwater trips. Punt-powered dugout canoes are slower but more ecofriendly. They charge from ₹250 per hour and most tours require four to five hours with village visits, walks and a visit to a toddy bar.

✸ Festivals & Events

Nehru Trophy Boat Race   BOAT RACE

(www.nehrutrophy.nic.in; tickets ₹50-2000; ⊗2nd Sat in Aug) This is the most popular and fiercely contested of Kerala's boat race regattas. Thousands of people, many aboard houseboats, gather around the starting and finishing points on Alleppey's Punnamada Lake to watch snakeboats with up to 100 rowers battle it out.

🛏 Sleeping

Even if you're not planning on boarding a houseboat, Alleppey has some of the most charming and best-value accommodation in Kerala, from heritage homes and resorts to family-run homestays with backwater views.

The rickshaw-commission racketeers are at work here, particularly at the train and bus stations; ask to be dropped off at a landmark close to your destination, or if you're booked in, call ahead to say you're on the way.

Matthews Residency   GUESTHOUSE $
(☑ 9447667888, 0477-2235938; www.palmyres-idency.com; off Finishing Point Rd; r ₹450-750; @ 🛜) One of the better budget deals, this place has six spotless rooms with Italian marble floors, three with garden-facing verandahs. It's north of the canal five minutes' walk from the bus stand but set well back from the road amid lush greenery.

★ Mandala Beach House   GUESTHOUSE $
(☑ 8589868589; www.mandalabeachhouse.com; Alleppey Beach; d ₹600-900, cottages ₹750, ste ₹2000; 🛜) Beachfront accommodation on a budget doesn't get much better than this in Alleppey. Super laid-back Mandala sits on the edge of the sand and has a range of simple rooms – the best being the glass-fronted 'penthouse' with unbeatable sunset views. Impromptu parties are known to crank up here in season, and there's a quieter nearby annexe.

Johnson's   GUESTHOUSE $
(☑ 9846466399, 0477-2245825; www.johnsons-kerala.com; d ₹500-850; @ 🛜) This backpacker favourite in a tumbledown mansion is as quirky as its owner, the gregarious Johnson Gilbert. It's a rambling residence with themed rooms filled with funky furniture, loads of plants outside and a canoe-shaped fish tank for a table. Johnson also hires out his eco-houseboat (www.ecohouseboat.com; ₹7000-13,000) and has a secluded riverside guesthouse in the backwaters.

Nanni Beach Residence   GUESTHOUSE $
(☑ 9895039767; www.nannitours.com; Cullan Rd; d ₹250-600) A very good deal, this easy-going guesthouse is a short walk from the beach and 1.5km north of the train station. Rooms are simple and the upstairs ones are spacious. Young owner Shibu is a good source of local information and works hard making the place homely.

Palmy Lake Resort   HOMESTAY $
(☑ 9447667888, 0477-2235938; www.palmyre-sorts.com; Punnamada Rd East; cottages d ₹1000) With six individual cottages, there's some lakeside charm, swinging hammocks and a sense of calm at this welcoming family homestay with homecooked meals.

Paradise Inn   GUESTHOUSE $
(dm ₹250, d from ₹600, with AC ₹1250; ❄ 🛜) This double-storey guesthouse north of the main canal offers daily yoga classes (₹300) in its rooftop shala, budget dorms and a restaurant. Owner Antony organises tours.

Vedanta Wake Up!   HOSTEL $
(☑ 0477-2231133; www.vedantawakeup.com; Punnamuda Rd; dm ₹700, d with AC ₹2000; ❄ 🛜) In a good location just north of the houseboat dock, this new hostel has neat and clean air-con dorms, cosy common areas, a cafe and the usual extras like lockers and wi-fi. It's a good place to meet other travellers, especially if you're looking to get a houseboat group together.

Cherukara Nest   HOMESTAY $$
(☑ 9947059628, 0477-2251509; www.cheru-karanest.com; d/tr incl breakfast ₹900/1100, with AC ₹1500, AC cottages ₹1500; ❄ @ 🛜) Set in well-tended gardens, with a pigeon coop at the back, this lovely heritage home has the sort of welcoming family atmosphere that makes you want to stay. In the main house there are four large characterful rooms, with high ceilings, lots of polished wood touches and antediluvian doors with ornate locks – check out the spacious split-level air-con room. Owner Tony also has a good-value houseboat (2/4-people ₹6000/8000) – one of the few that still uses punting power.

Gowri Residence   GUESTHOUSE $$
(☑ 9847055371, 0477-2236371; www.gowriresi-dence.com; Mullackal Rd; d ₹600-1200, AC cottages ₹1500-2000; ❄ 🛜) This rambling complex about 800m north of North Canal has an array of rooms and cottages in a large garden: traditional wood-panelled rooms in the main house, and several types of bungalows made from either stone, wood, bamboo or thatch – the best have cathedral ceilings, air-con and flat-screen TVs. Overall the place is looking a little faded.

Tharavad   HOMESTAY $$
(☑ 0477-242044; www.tharavadheritageresort.com; d ₹2500-3500; ❄) In a quiet canalside location between the town centre and beach, this

Alappuzha (Alleppey)

500 m
0.25 miles

Punnamada Lake

Houseboat Dock

Punnamada Rd

Bank

KSRTC Bus Stand

DTPC Tourist Reception Centre

Vedanta Wake Up! (700m); Palmy Lake Resort (450m); Malayalam (1.3km); Palmgrove Lake Resort (1.8km)

Sona Heritage Home (280m);

Boat Jetty

Bank

South Canal

Mullackal Rd.

UAE Exchange

Bank

Mermaid Statue

Gowri Residence (550m)

@Mailbox

Bank

CCSB Rd

North Canal

Vazhicherry Bridge

Cullan Rd

CCNB Rd

YMCA Rd

AC Rd

Palace Rd

VCSB (Boat Jetty) Rd

VP Rd

Zachariya Bazar

CCNB Rd

Train Station

Alappuzha (Alleppey)

charming ancestral home has lots of glossy teak and antiques, shuttered windows, five characterful rooms and well-maintained gardens.

Sona Heritage Home   GUESTHOUSE **$$**
(☑0477-2235211; www.sonahome.com; Lakeside, Finishing Point; r ₹800-900, with AC ₹1400-1500; ❄🛜) Run by the affable Joseph, this beautiful old heritage home has high-ceilinged rooms with faded flowered curtains, Christian motifs and four-poster beds overlooking a well-kept garden.

Malayalam   RESORT **$$**
(☑9496829424, 0477-2234591; malayalamresorts @yahoo.com; Punnamada; r ₹1600-2500; 🛜) This little family-run pad has four cute bamboo cottages and a pair of spacious two-storey four-room houses facing the lake near the Nehru Trophy starting point. Views from the upstairs rooms with balcony are sweet. Walk past the Keraleeyam resort reception and along the canal bank.

Palmgrove Lake Resort   RESORT **$$**
(☑0477-2235004; www.palmgrovelakeresort.com; Punnamada; cottages d ₹2800-3300, ste ₹4000; ❄🛜) Close to the starting point of the Neh-

ru Trophy Snake Boat Race on Punnamada Lake, the stylish but ageing individual double cottages here are set in a palm-filled garden with lake views. They're all air-con and the owners are planning on building some new ones.

Punnamada Homestay   HOMESTAY **$$**
(☑9847044688, 0484-2371761; d incl meals ₹3000; 🛜) This attractive heritage-style family home is about 8km north of Alleppey in a peaceful location close to Punnamada Lake. The two rooms are neat, well-furnished and have private balconies, while the home-cooking is first-rate.

★**Raheem Residency**   HOTEL **$$$**
(☑0477-2239767; www.raheemresidency.com; Beach Rd; d €120-150; ❄🛜🏊) This thoughtfully renovated 1860s heritage home is a joy to visit, let alone stay in. The 10 rooms have been restored to their former glory and have bathtubs, antique furniture and period fixtures. The common areas are airy and comfortable, and there are pretty indoor courtyards, a well-stocked library, a great little pool and an excellent restaurant. Creative types should enquire about Raheem's writers' retreats.

🍴 Eating & Drinking

★**Mushroom**   ARABIAN, INDIAN **$**
(mains ₹70-140; ☺noon-midnight) Breezy open-air restaurant with wrought-iron chairs specialising in cheap, tasty and spicy halal meals like chicken kali mirch, fish tandoori and chilli mushrooms. Lots of locals and travellers give it a good vibe. It's near the South Police Station.

Kream Korner Art Cafe   MULTICUISINE **$**
(☑0477-2252781; www.kreamkornerartcafe.com; Mullackal Rd; dishes ₹40-250; ☺9am-10pm) The most colourful dining space in town, this food-meets-art restaurant greets you with brightly painted tables and contemporary local art on the walls. It's a relaxed, airy place popular with Indian and foreign families for its inexpensive and tasty menu of Indian and Chinese dishes.

Thaff   INDIAN **$**
(YMCA Rd; meals ₹45-120; ☺9am-9pm Sun-Thu, 9am-10pm Sat & Sun) This popular restaurant serves tasty South Indian bites, with some North Indian and Chinese flavours mixed in. It does succulent spit-roasted-chicken, biryanis and brain-freezing ice-cream shakes.

KERALA ALAPPUZHA (ALLEPPEY)

There's another busy hole-in-wall location on Punnamada Rd.

Le Coffee Time
CAFE

(Alleppey Beach; coffee & snacks ₹70-150; ⊙ 8.30am-5pm; ☎) Friendly beachfront place with a genuine Italian espresso machine, some shady tables and free wi-fi.

Dreamers
MULTICUISINE $$

(☎ 8086752586; www.dreamersrestaurant. com; Alleppey Beach; mains ₹130-450; ⊙ 11am-10.30pm) Designed to vaguely resemble a *kettuvallam* (rice barge), Dreamers, across from Alleppey Beach, is a rustic but cool little restaurant with an upper deck, serving a wide variety of dishes from Tibetan momos and Thai curries to seafood and pizzas.

Harbour Restaurant
MULTICUISINE $$

(☎ 0484-2230767; Beach Rd; meals ₹120-300; ⊙ 10am-10pm) This enjoyable beachside place is run by the nearby Raheem Residency. It's more casual and budget-conscious than the hotel's restaurant, but promises a range of well-prepared Indian, Chinese and continental dishes, and some of the coldest beer in town.

Royale Park Hotel
INDIAN $$

(YMCA Rd; meals ₹120-250; ⊙ 7am-10.30pm, bar from 10.30am; ☎) There's an extensive menu at this air-con hotel restaurant, and the food, including veg and fish thalis, is consistently good. You can order from the same menu in the surprisingly nice upstairs bar and wash down your meal with a cold Kingfisher.

Chakara Restaurant
MULTICUISINE $$$

(☎ 0477-2230767; Beach Rd; mini Kerala meal ₹500, mains from ₹450; ⊙ 12.30-3pm & 7-10pm) The restaurant at Raheem Residency is Alleppey's finest, with seating on a bijou open rooftop, reached via a spiral staircase, with views over to the beach. The menu creatively combines traditional Keralan and European cuisine, specialising in locally caught fish.

ⓘ Information

DTPC Tourist Reception Centre (☎ 0477-2253308; www.dtpcalappuzha.com; Boat Jetty Rd; ⊙ 9am-5pm) Close to the bus stand and boat jetty. Staff are helpful and can advise on homestays and houseboats.

Tourist Police (☎ 0477-2251161; ⊙ 24hr) Next door to the DTPC.

UAE Exchange (cnr Cullan & Mullackal Rds; ⊙ 9.30am-6pm Mon-Fri, to 4pm Sat, to 1pm Sun) Changes cash and travellers cheques.

ⓘ Getting There & Away

BOAT
Ferries run to Kottayam (₹10) from the boat jetty on VCSB (Boat Jetty) Rd.

BUS
From the KSRTC bus stand, frequent buses head to Trivandrum (₹122, 3½ hours, every 20 minutes), Kollam (₹70, 2½ hours) and Ernakulam (Kochi, ₹52, 1½ hours). Buses to Kottayam (₹43, 1¼ hours, every 30 minutes) are much faster than the ferry. One bus daily leaves for Kumily at 6.40am (₹120, 5½ hours). The Varkala bus (₹89, 3½ hours) leaves at 9am and 10.40am daily.

TRAIN
There are numerous daily trains to Ernakulam (2nd-class/sleeper/3AC ₹50/170/535, 1½ hours) and Trivandrum (₹80/140/485, three hours) via Kollam (₹66/140/485, 1½ hours). Six trains a day stop at Varkala (2nd-class/AC chair ₹65/255, two hours). The train station is 4km west of town.

ⓘ Getting Around

An autorickshaw from the train station to the boat jetty and KSRTC bus stand is around ₹60. Several guesthouses around town hire out scooters for ₹300 per day.

Around Alleppey

Kattoor & Marari Beaches

The beaches at Kattoor and Marari, 10km and 14km north of Alleppey respectively, are a popular beachside alternative to the backwaters. Marari is the flashier of the two, with some exclusive five-star beachfront accommodation, while Kattoor, sometimes known as 'Secret Beach', is more of a fishing village, where development is at a minimum and sandy back lanes lead down to near-deserted sands.

🛏 Sleeping

★ **Secret Beach Inn**
HOMESTAY $

(☎ 9447786931; www.secretbeach.in; Kattoor Beach; r ₹350-1000; ☎) It almost seems a shame to mention this special little homestay, but with just two rooms it will never feel crowded. The location is sublime, with a small lagoon separating the property from a near-deserted piece of Kattoor Beach; get there by floating mat or walk through the village. Home-cooked meals are available and the talented and welcoming

WORTH A TRIP

GREEN PALM HOMES

Green Palm Homes (☎9495557675, 0477-2724497; www.greenpalmhomes.com; Chennamkary; r without bathroom incl full board ₹2250, with bathroom ₹3250-4000; ❄) Just 12km from Alleppey on a backwater island, Green Palm Homes is a series of homestays that seem a universe away, set in a picturesque village, where you sleep in simple rooms in villagers' homes among rice paddies (though 'premium' rooms with attached bathroom and air-con are available). It's splendidly quiet, there are no roads in sight and you can take a guided walk, hire bicycles (₹50 per hour) and canoes (₹100 per hour), or take cooking classes with your hosts (₹150).

To get here, call ahead and catch one of the hourly ferries from Alleppey to Chennamkary (₹10, 1¼ hours).

young owner Vimal is an accredited yoga and kalarippayat instructor.

A Beach Symphony BOUTIQUE COTTAGES $$$
(☎9744297123; www.abeachsymphony.com; cottages ₹13,000-16,500; ❄📶🏊) With just four individually designed cottages, this is one of Marari's most exclusive beachfront resorts. The Keralan-style cottages are plush and private – Violin Cottage even has its own plunge pool in a private garden.

Kottayam

☎0481 / POP 335,000

Conveniently placed between the Western Ghats and the backwaters, Kottayam is renowned for being the centre of Kerala's spice and rubber trade, rather than for its aesthetic appeal. For most travellers it's a hub town, well connected to both the mountains and the backwaters, with many travellers taking the public c anal cruise to or from Alleppey before heading east to Kumily or north to Kochi. The city itself has a crazy, traffic-clogged centre, but you don't have to go far to be in the villages and waterways.

The **Thirunakkara Utsavam festival** is held in March at the Thirunakkara Shiva Temple.

Sleeping

There's enough accommodation in Kottayam to justify a stay if you're coming off the Alleppey ferry but there are better lakeside stays (at a price) at Kumarakom.

Homestead Hotel HOTEL $
(☎0481-2560467; KK Rd; s/d from ₹500/860, d with AC ₹1690; ❄) In a little compound back from busy KK Rd, Homestead has reasonably well-maintained budget rooms – though some are a little musty and come with eye-watering green decor.

Ambassador Hotel HOTEL $
(☎0481-2563293; ambassadorhotelktm@yahoo.in; KK Rd; s/d from ₹400/560, with AC from ₹950; ❄) This old-school place is one of the better budget hotels in the town centre. Rooms with TV are spartan but fairly clean, spacious and quiet for this price. It has a bar, an adequate restaurant, a pastry counter and a boat-shaped fish tank in the lobby.

Windsor Castle & Lake Village Resort HOTEL $$$
(☎0481-2363637; www.thewindsorcastle.net; MC Rd; s/d from ₹3600/5200, Lake Village cottages ₹7200; ❄📶🏊) This grandiose white box has some of Kottayam's best hotel rooms, but the more interesting accommodation is in the Lake Village behind the hotel. Deluxe cottages, strewn around the private backwaters and manicured gardens, are top-notch. There's a pleasant restaurant overlooking landscaped waterways.

Eating

Thali SOUTH INDIAN $
(1st fl, KK Rd; meals ₹40-140; ⏲8am-8pm) A lovely, spotlessly kept 1st-floor dining room with slatted blinds, Thali is a swankier version of the typical Keralan set-meal place. The food here is great, including Malabar fish curry and thalis.

Meenachil MULTICUISINE $
(2nd fl, KK Rd; dishes ₹60-170; ⏲noon-3pm & 6-9.30pm) A favourite place in Kottayam to fill up on Indian and Chinese fare. The family atmosphere is friendly, the dining room modern and tidy, and the menu expansive.

★**Nalekattu** SOUTH INDIAN $$$
(Windsor Castle Hotel; MC Rd, dishes ₹190-500; ⏲noon-3pm & 7-10pm) The traditional Keralan restaurant at the Windsor Castle overlooks

KERALA'S BACKWATERS

The undisputed highlight of a trip to Kerala is travelling through the 900km network of water-ways that fringe the coast and trickle inland. Long before the advent of roads, these waters were the slippery highways of Kerala, and many villagers still use paddle-power as their main form of transport. Trips through the backwaters traverse palm-fringed lakes studded with cantilevered Chinese fishing nets, and wind their way along narrow, shady canals where coir (coconut fibre), copra (dried coconut kernels) and cashews are loaded onto boats. Along the way are isolated villages where farming life continues as it has for eons.

Tourist Cruises

The popular tourist cruise between Kollam and Alleppey (₹400) departs from either end at 10.30am, arriving at 6.30pm, daily from July to March and every second day at other times. Generally, there's a 1pm lunch stop and a brief afternoon chai stop. Bring drinks, snacks, sun-screen and a hat. It's a scenic and leisurely way – the journey takes eight hours – to get between the two towns, but the boat travels along only the major canals – you won't have many close-up views of the village life that makes the backwaters so magical. Another option is to take the trip halfway (₹200) and get off at the Matha Amrithanandamayi Mission (p957).

Houseboats

If the stars align, renting a houseboat designed like a *kettuvallam* (rice barge) could well be one of the highlights of your trip to India. It can be an expensive experience (depending on your budget) but for a couple on a romantic overnight jaunt or split between a group of travellers, it's usually worth every rupee. Drifting through quiet canals lined with coconut palms, eating delicious Keralan food, meeting local villagers and sleeping on the water – it's a world away from the usual clamour of India.

Houseboats cater for couples (one or two double bedrooms) and groups (up to seven bedrooms!). Food (and an onboard chef to cook it) is generally included in the quoted cost, as is a driver/captain. Houseboats can be chartered through a multitude of private opera-tors in Alleppey, Kollam and Kottayam. This is the biggest business in Kerala and the quality of boats varies widely, from rust buckets to floating palaces of varying cleanliness – try to inspect the boat before agreeing on a price. Travel-agency reps will be pushing you to book a boat as soon as you set foot in Kerala, but it's better to wait till you reach a backwater hub: choice is greater in Alleppey (an extraordinary 1000-plus boats), and you're much more likely to be able to bargain down a price if you turn up and see what's on offer. Most guesthouses and homestays can also book you on a houseboat.

some picturesque backwaters and serves tasty Keralan specialities like *chemeen* (prawn curry).

ⓘ Information

DTPC Office (☏ 0481-2560479; www.dtpckot-tayam.com; ◷10am-5pm Mon-Sat) At the boat jetty. Offers daily backwater trips to Allepey and Kumarakom for ₹350. Private operators nearby offer similar trips.

ⓘ Getting There & Away

BOAT

Daily ferries run to Alleppey from the jetty (₹10).

BUS

The **KSRTC bus stand** has buses to Trivandrum (₹120, four hours, every 20 minutes), Alleppey (₹43, 1¼ hours, hourly) and Ernakulam (Kochi, ₹56, two hours, every 20 minutes). There are

also frequent buses to nearby Kumarakom (₹15, 30 minutes, every 15 minutes), to Thrissur (₹105, four hours, hourly), Calicut (₹190, seven hours, 13 daily), Kumily for Periyar Wildlife Sanctuary (₹93, four hours, every 30 minutes) and Munnar (₹119, five hours, five daily). There are also buses to Kollam (₹75, three hours, four daily), where you can change for Varkala.

TRAIN

Kottayam is well served by frequent trains run-ning between Trivandrum (2nd-class/sleeper/3AC ₹80/140/485, 3½ hours) and Ernakulam (₹55/140/485, 1½ hours).

ⓘ Getting Around

The KSRTC bus stand is 1km south of the centre; the boat jetty is a further 2km (at Kodimatha). An autorickshaw from the jetty to the KSRTC bus stand is around ₹50, and from the bus stand to the train station about ₹40.

In the busy high season, when prices peak, you're likely to get caught in backwater-gridlock – some travellers are disappointed by the number of boats on the water. It's possible to travel by houseboat between Alleppey and Kollam and part way to Kochi – though these trips spend more time on open lakes and large canals than true backwaters and take longer than most travellers expect. Expect a boat for two people for 24 hours to cost about ₹6000 to ₹8000 at the budget level; for four people, ₹10,000 to ₹12,000; for larger boats or for air-conditioning expect to pay from ₹15,000 to ₹30,000. Shop around to negotiate a bargain – though this will be harder in the peak season. Prices triple from around 20 December to 5 January.

Village Tours & Canoe Boats

More and more travellers are opting for village tours or canal-boat trips. Village tours usually involve small groups of five to six people, a knowledgeable guide and an open canoe or covered *kettuvallam*. The tours (from Kochi, Kollam or Alleppey) last from 2½ to six hours and cost from around ₹400 to ₹800 per person. They include visits to villages to watch coir-making, boat building, toddy (palm beer) tapping and fish farming. The Munroe Island trip from Kollam (p"oCanal CruiseBoating" on page 955) is an excellent tour of this type; the Tourist Desk in Ernakulam also organises recommended tours.

Public Ferries

If you want the local backwater transport experience for just a few rupees, there are State Water Transport (www.swtd.gov.in) boats between Alleppey and Kottayam (₹19, 2½ hours) five times daily starting from Alleppey at 7.30am. The trip crosses Vembanad Lake and has a more varied landscape than the Kollam–Alleppey cruise.

Environmental Issues

Pollution from houseboat motors is becoming a major problem as boat numbers increase. The Keralan authorities have introduced an ecofriendly accreditation system for houseboat operators. Among the criteria an operator must meet before being issued with the 'Green Palm Certificate' are the installation of solar panels and sanitary tanks for the disposal of waste – ask operators whether they have the requisite certification. Consider choosing one of the few remaining punting, rather than motorised, boats if possible, though these can only operate in shallow water.

Around Kottayam

Kumarakom

📞 0481

Kumarakom, 16km west of Kottayam and on the shore of vast Vembanad Lake – Kerala's largest lake – is an unhurried backwater village with a smattering of dazzling top-end sleeping options and a renowned bird sanctuary. You can arrange houseboats on Kumarakom's less-crowded canals, but expect to pay considerably more than in Alleppey.

◉ Sights

Kumarakom Bird Sanctuary   NATURE RESERVE
(Indian/foreigner ₹50/150; ☺6am-5pm) This reserve on the 5-hectare site of a former rubber plantation is the haunt of a variety of domestic and migratory birds. October to February is the time for travelling birds like the garganey teal, osprey, marsh harrier and steppey eagle; May to July is the breeding season for local species such as the Indian shag, pond herons, egrets and darters. Early morning is the best viewing time. A guide costs ₹300 for a two-hour tour (₹400 from 6am to 8am).

🛏 Sleeping

Cruise 'N Lake   RESORT $$
(📞9846036375, 0481-2525804; www.kumarakom.com/cruisenlake; Puthenpura Tourist Enclave, Cheepunkal; d ₹1500, with AC ₹2000; ❄) Location, location. Surrounded by backwaters on one side and a lawn of rice paddies on the other, this is the ideal affordable Kumarakom getaway. The rooms in two separate buildings are plain but all have verandahs facing the water. Go a couple of kilometres

past the sanctuary to Cheepunkal and take a left; it's then 2km down a rugged dirt road. Management can arrange pick-ups from Kottayam, and houseboats and all meals are available from here.

Tharavadu Heritage Home GUESTHOUSE $$
(☑ 0481-2525230; www.tharavaduheritage.com; d from ₹1150, bamboo cottage ₹1680, d with AC ₹2650-3000; ❉ @) Rooms are either in the superbly restored 1870s teak family mansion or in equally comfortable individual creek-side bamboo cottages. All are excellently crafted and come with arty touches. It's 4km before the bird sanctuary.

Sree Vallabha Temple

Devotees make offerings at this temple, 2km from Tiruvilla, in the form of traditional, regular all-night **Kathakali** performances that are open to all. Around 10km east of here, the **Aranmula Boat Race**, one of Kerala's biggest snake-boat races, is held during Onam in August/September.

THE WESTERN GHATS

Periyar Wildlife Sanctuary
☑ 04869

South India's most popular wildlife sanctuary, **Periyar** (☑ 04869-224571; www.periyar tigerreserve.org; Indian/foreigner ₹25/450; ☺ 6am-6pm; last entry 5pm) encompasses 777 sq km and a 26-sq-km artificial lake created by the British in 1895. The vast region is home to bison, sambar, wild boar, langur, 900 to 1000 elephants and 35 to 40 hard-to-spot tigers. Firmly established on both the Indian and foreigner tourist trails, the place can sometimes feel a bit like Disneyland-in-the-Ghats, but its mountain scenery and jungle walks make for an enjoyable visit.

Kumily is the closest town and home to a growing strip of hotels, homestays, spice shops, chocolate shops and Kashmiri emporiums. Thekkady, 4km from Kumily, is the sanctuary centre with the KTDC hotels and boat jetty. Confusingly, when people refer to the sanctuary they tend to use Thekkady, Kumily and Periyar interchangeably.

◉ Sights & Activities

Various tours and trips access Periyar Wildlife Sanctuary, all arranged through the Ec-

otourism Centre. Most hotels and agencies around town can arrange all-day jeep **jungle safaris** (per person ₹1600-2000; ☺ 5am-6.30pm) which cover over 40km of trails in jungle bordering the park, though many travellers complain that at least 30km of the trip is on sealed roads.

Cooking classes (₹300-450) are offered by local homestays. There are recommended four-hour classes at **Bar-B-Que** (☑ 04869-320705; KK Rd; ₹500), about 1km from the bazaar on the road to Kottayam.

Several spice plantations are open to visitors and most hotels can arrange tours (₹450/750 by autorickshaw/taxi).

Periyar Lake Cruise BOATING
(adult/child ₹150/50; ☺ departures 7.30am, 9.30am, 11.15am, 1.45pm & 3.30pm) These 1½-hour boat trips around the lake are the main way to tour the sanctuary without taking a guided walk. You might see deer, boar and birdlife but it's generally more of a cruise – often a rowdy one – than a wildlife-spotting experience. Boats are operated by the forest department and the KTDC – the ticket counters are together in the main building above the boat jetty, and you must buy a ticket before boarding the boat. In high season get to the ticket office 1½ hours before each trip to buy tickets. The first and last departures offer the best prospects for wildlife spotting, and October to March are generally the best time to see animals.

Ecotourism Centre OUTDOOR ADVENTURE
(☑ 8547603066, 04869-224571; www.periyartiger reserve.org; Thekkady Rd; ☺ 9am-1pm & 2-5pm) The main operator of explorations into the park is the Ecotourism Centre, run by the Forest Department. These include border hikes (₹1500), 2½-hour nature walks (₹300), half-/full day bamboo rafting (₹1500/200) and 'jungle patrols' (₹1000), which cover 4km to 5km and are the best way to experience the park close up, accompanied by a trained tribal guide. Rates are per person and trips usually require a minimum of four. There are also overnight 'tiger trail' treks (₹5000 per person) run by former poachers retrained as guides, covering 20km to 30km.

Gavi Ecotourism OUTDOOR ADVENTURE
(☑ 04869-223270, 994792399; www.kfdcecotourism.com; treks per person from ₹1000; ☺ 9am-8pm) This Forest Department venture offers jeep safaris, treks and boating to Gavi, a cardamom plantation and jungle area bordering the sanctuary about 45km from Kumily. Hotels can help organise similar jeep trips.

Connemara Tea Factory TEA FACTORY
(Vandiperiyar; tours ₹100; ⊙tours hourly 9am-4pm) About 13km from Kumily, this 75-year-old working tea factory and plantation offers interesting guided tours of the tea-making process and tea garden and ends with some tea-tastings. Regular buses from Kumily pass by the entrance.

Abraham's Spice Garden SPICE GARDEN
(☑04869-222919; www.abrahamspice.com; Spring Valley; tours ₹100; ⊙7am-6.30pm) Abraham's Spice Garden is a family-run farm operating for more than 50 years. It's 3km from Kumily on the Kottayam Rd.

Highrange Spices SPICE GARDEN
(☑04869-222117; tours ₹100; ⊙7am-6pm) Highrange Spices, 3km from Kumily, has 4 hectares of spice garden where you can see ayurvedic herbs and vegetables growing.

Spice Walk SPICE PLANTATION
(☑04869-222449; www.spicewalk.com; Churakulam Coffee Estate; tours ₹150; ⊙8.45am-5.30pm) Part of Churakulam Coffee Estate, Spice Walk is a 44-hectare plantation surrounding a small lake. Informative walks take around one hour and include explanations of coffee and cardamom processing, but there's also fishing and boating and a small cafe at the front. It's only 2km from Kumily.

Elephant Junction ELEPHANT RIDES
(₹400-5000; ⊙8.30am-6pm) In a lovely 16-hectare patch of forest about 2km from Kumily, you can wash, feed and ride elephants. Programs start from a half-hour ride (₹400) up to full day that includes elephant bathing, plantation tours, breakfast and lunch. This is a better option for interacting with elephants than the touristy operation in Kumily village.

Santhigiri Ayurveda AYURVEDA
(☑8113018007, 04869-223979; www.santhigiri-ashram.org; Munnar Rd, Vandanmedu Junction; ⊙8am-8pm) An authentic place for the ayurvedic experience, offering top-notch massage (₹900 to ₹1800) and long-term treatments lasting seven to 14 days.

Kumily & Periyar Wildlife Sanctuary

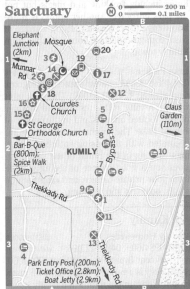

Kumily & Periyar Wildlife Sanctuary

🛏 Sleeping

🛏 Inside the Sanctuary

The KTDC runs three steeply priced hotels in the park, including Periyar House, Aranya Nivas and the grand Lake Palace. Note that there's effectively a curfew at these places – guests are not permitted to roam the sanctuary after 6pm.

The Ecotourism Centre can arrange tented accommodation inside the park at the **Jungle Camp** (per person incl meals ₹2000). Rates include trekking and meals but not the park entry fee. Another option is **Bamboo Grove** (d incl breakfast ₹1500), a group of basic cottages and tree houses not far from Kumily town.

Lake Palace
HOTEL $$$

(✆04869-223887; www.lakepalacethekkady.com; r incl all meals ₹24,000-30,000) There's a faint whiff of royalty at this restored old summer palace, located on an island in the middle of Periyar Lake. The six charismatic rooms are decorated with flair using antique furnishings. Staying in the midst of the sanctuary gives you a good chance of seeing wildlife from your private terrace, and rates include meals, boat trip and trekking.

🛏 Kumily

Mickey Homestay
GUESTHOUSE $

(✆9447284160, 04869-223196; www.mickey-homestay.com; Bypass Rd; r & cottages ₹700-1000; ☎) Mickey is a genuine homestay with just a handful of intimate rooms in a family house and a rear cottage, all with homely touches that make them some of the cosiest in town. Balconies have rattan furniture and hanging bamboo seats, and the whole place is surrounded by greenery.

★ Green View Homestay
HOMESTAY $$

(✆9447432008, 04869-224617; www.suresh-greenview.com; Bypass Rd; r incl breakfast ₹500-1750; ☎) It has grown from its humble homestay origins but Green View is a lovely place that manages to retain its personal and friendly family welcome from owners Suresh and Sulekha. The two buildings house several classes of well-maintained rooms with private balconies – the best are the upper-floor rooms overlooking a lovely rear spice garden. Excellent vegetarian meals and cooking lessons (veg/nonveg ₹350/450) are available.

El-Paradiso
HOMESTAY $$

(✆9447431950, 04869-222350; www.goelparadiso.com; Bypass Rd; d ₹950-1850, q ₹2500; @☎) This immaculate family homestay has fresh rooms with balconies and hanging chairs, or opening onto a terrace overlooking greenery at the back. Cooking classes (₹400) are a speciality here.

Tranquilou
HOMESTAY $$

(✆04869-223269; www.tranquilouhomestay.com; off Bypass Rd; r incl breakfast ₹1200-2800; @☎) Another of Kumily's friendly family homestays in a peaceful location. Neatly furnished rooms surround a pleasant garden; the two doubles that adjoin a shared sitting room are a good family option.

Claus Garden
HOMESTAY $$

(✆9567862421, 04869-222320; www.homestay.in; Thekkumkadu; d/tr/f ₹1600/1800/2000; ☎) Set well away from the hustle and bustle and up a steep hill with good views, this German-run place has gently curving balconies, spotless rooms and a rooftop overlooking a lush green garden. The family option is two rooms sharing a bathroom. Organic breakfast with fresh-baked bread is available for ₹250.

Chrissie's Hotel
GUESTHOUSE $$

(✆9447601304, 04869-224155; www.chrissies.in; Bypass Rd; r ₹1920-2400, f ₹3840; ☎) This four-storey building behind the popular expat-run restaurant of the same name somehow manages to blend in with the forest-green surrounds. The chic rooms are spacious and bright, with cheery furnishings, lamps and colourful pillows. Yoga, shiatsu and reiki classes can be arranged. Wi-fi in lobby only.

Spice Village
HOTEL $$$

(✆0484-3011711; www.cghearth.com; Thekkady Rd; villas ₹18,700-24,000; ☎☎☀) 𝄢 This CGH Earth place takes its green credentials very seriously and has captivating, spacious cottages that are smart yet cosily rustic, in pristinely kept grounds. Its restaurant does lavish lunch and dinner buffets (₹1400 to ₹1800), there's a colonial-style bar and you can find the **Wildlife Interpretation Centre** (✆04869-222028; ◷6am-6pm) here, which has a resident naturalist showing slides and answering questions about the park. Good value out of high season when rates halve.

✗ Eating

There are a few good cheap veg restaurants in Kumily's busy bazaar area, and some decent traveller-oriented restaurants on the road to the wildlife sanctuary. Most homestays will offer home-cooked meals on request.

Shri Krishna INDIAN $
(KK Rd; meals ₹70-130; ⊙lunch & dinner) A local favourite in the bazaar, serving up spicy pure veg meals including several takes on the lunchtime thali.

Chrissie's Cafe MULTICUISINE $$
(www.chrissies.in; Bypass Rd; meals ₹150-350; ⊙8am-10pm) A perennially popular traveller haunt, this clean, airy 1st-floor and rooftop cafe satisfies with cakes and snacks, excellent coffee, well-prepared Western faves like pizza and pasta, and even a Middle Eastern platter (₹275).

Ebony's Cafe MULTICUISINE $$
(Bypass Rd; meals ₹90-200; ⊙8.30am-9.30pm) This fading rooftop joint with lots of pot plants, check tablecloths and traveller-friendly tunes serves up a simple assortment of Indian and continental food from mashed potato to basic pasta.

French Restaurant & Bakery CAFE, BAKERY $$
(meals ₹90-200; ⊙8am-9.30pm) This family-run shack set back from the main road is a good spot for breakfast or lunch, mainly for the fluffy tuna or cheese baguettes baked on site, but also pasta and noodle dishes.

Ambadi Restaurant INDIAN $$
(dishes ₹100-250; ⊙7.30am-9.30pm) At the English manor-style hotel of the same name, Ambadi has a more formal feel than most with an almost church-like decor, but the broad menu of North and South Indian dishes is very reasonably priced and the food is good.

☆ Entertainment

Mudra Cultural Centre CULTURAL SHOWS
(☏9446072901; www.mudraculturalcentre.com; Lake Rd; admission ₹200, video ₹200; ⊙Kathakali 5pm & 7pm; kalari 6pm & 7.15pm) Kathakali shows at this cultural centre are highly entertaining. Make-up and costume starts 30 minutes before each show; use of still cameras is free and welcome. Arrive early for a good seat. There also two *kalarippayat* (martial arts) performances nightly.

Kadathanadan Kalari Centre CULTURAL PROGRAM
(www.kalaripayattu.co.in; Thekkady Rd; tickets ₹200; ⊙shows 6-7pm) Hour-long demonstrations of the exciting Keralan martial art of *kalarippayat* are staged here every evening. Tickets are available from the box office throughout the day.

❶ Information

There's a Federal Bank ATM accepting international cards at the junction with the road to Kottayam, and several internet cafes in the bazaar area.

DTPC Office (☏04869-222620; ⊙10am-5pm Mon-Sat) Uphill behind the bus stand; you can pick up a map but that's about it.

Ecotourism Centre (☏8547603066, 04869-224571; www.periyartigerreserve.org; ⊙9am-1pm & 2-5pm) For park tours, information and guided walks.

Mt Sinai Cyber Cafe (☏04869-222170; Thekkady Junction; per hour ₹20; ⊙9am-10pm) Reliable internet cafe upstairs in Kumily's main bazaar.

❶ Getting There & Away

Kumily's KSRTC bus stand is at the eastern edge of town.

Eleven buses daily operate between Ernakulam (Kochi) and Kumily (₹145, five hours). Buses leave every 30 minutes for Kottayam (₹84, four hours), with two direct buses to Trivandrum at 8.45am and 11am (₹210, eight hours) and one daily bus to Alleppey at 1.10pm (₹120, 5½ hours). Private buses to Munnar (₹80, four to five hours) also leave from the bus stand at 6am, 9.45am and noon.

SABARIMALA

Deep in the Western Ghats, about 20km west of Gavi and some 50km from the town of Erumeli, is a place called Sabarimala, home to the Ayyappan temple. It's said to be one of the world's most visited pilgrimage centres, with anywhere between 40 and 60 million Hindu devotees trekking here each year. Followers believe the god Ayyappan meditated at this spot. Non-Hindus can join the pilgrimage but strict rules apply, and women aged 12 to 50 are only allowed as far as the Pampa checkpoint. For information see www.sabarimala.kerala. gov.in or www.sabarimala.org.

Tamil Nadu buses leave every 30 minutes to Madurai (₹90, four hours) from the Tamil Nadu bus stand just over the border.

ⓘ Getting Around

It's only about 1.5km from Kumily bus stand to the main park entrance, but it's another 3km from there to Periyar Lake; you might catch a bus (almost as rare as the tigers), but will more likely take an autorickshaw from the entry post (₹70) or set off on foot – but bear in mind there's no walking path so you'll have to dodge traffic on the road. Autorickshaws will take you on short hops around town for ₹30.

Kumily town is small enough to explore on foot but some guesthouses hire bicycles (₹200) and most can arrange scooter hire (₹500) if you want to explore further afield.

Munnar

☑ 04865 / POP 68,200 / ELEV 1524M

The rolling hills around Munnar, South India's largest tea-growing region, are carpeted in emerald-green tea plantations, contoured, clipped and sculpted like ornamental hedges. The low mountain scenery is magnificent – you're often up above the clouds watching veils of mist clinging to the mountaintops. Munnar town itself is a scruffy administration centre, not unlike a North Indian hill station, but wander just a few kilometres out of town and you'll be engulfed in a sea of a thousand shades of green.

Once known as the High Range of Travancore, today Munnar is the commercial centre of some of the world's highest tea-growing estates. The majority of the plantations are operated by corporate giant Tata, with some in the hands of local co-operative Kannan Devan Hills Plantation Company (KDHP).

◉ Sights & Activities

The main reason to visit Munnar is to explore the lush, tea-filled hillocks that surround it. Hotels, homestays, travel agencies, autorickshaw drivers and practically every passerby will want to organise a day of sightseeing for you: shop around, though rates are fairly standard. The best way to experience the hills is on a guided trek, which can range from a half-day 'soft trekking' around tea plantations (from ₹600 per person) to more arduous full-day mountain treks (from ₹800), which open up some stupendous views. Trekking guides can easily be organised through hotels and guesthouses or the DTPC.

Bear in mind that the tea plantations are private property and trekking around without a licensed guide is trespassing.

Tea Museum   MUSEUM
(☑ 04865-230561; adult/child ₹80/35, camera ₹20; ◉ 9am-4pm Tue-Sun) About 1.5km northwest of town, this museum is as close as you'll get to a working tea factory around Munnar. It's a demo model of the real thing, but it still shows the basic process. A collection of old bits and pieces from the colonial era, including photographs and a 1905 tea-roller, are also kept here. A 30-minute video explaining the history of Munnar, its tea estates and the programs put in place for its workers screens hourly. The walk to or from town follows the busy road with views of tea plantations; an autorickshaw charges ₹25 from the bazaar.

Nimi's Lip Smacking Classes   COOKING
(☑ 9745513373, 9447330773; www.nimisrecipes. com; classes ₹1500; ◉ 5pm Mon-Fri, 2pm Sat & Sun) Nimi Sunilkumar has earned a solid reputation for Keralan cooking, publishing her own cookbook, website and blog, and now offers daily cooking classes in Munnar. You'll learn traditional Keralan recipes and the cost includes a copy of her book *Lip Smacking Dishes of Kerala*. She's based in an unassuming building next to the DTPC.

☞ Tours

The DTPC (p973) runs three fairly rushed but inexpensive full-day tours to points around Munnar. The Sandal Valley Tour (per person ₹400; ◉ tour 9am-6pm) visits Chinnar Wildlife Sanctuary, several viewpoints, waterfalls, plantations, a sandalwood forest and villages. The Tea Valley tour (per person ₹400; ◉ tour 10am-6pm) visits Echo Point, Top Station and Rajamalai (for Eravikulam National Park), among other places. The Village Sightseeing Tour (per person ₹400; ◉ 9.30am-6pm) covers Devikulam, Anayirankal Dam, Ponmudy and a farm tour among others. You can hire a taxi to visit the main local sights for around ₹1300.

🛏 Sleeping

Munnar has plenty of accommodation but it seems a shame to stay in Munnar town when the views and peace are out in the hills and valleys. There are some good budget options just south of the town centre; if you really want to feel the serenity and are willing to pay a bit more, head for the hills.

📖 Around Town

⭐ JJ Cottage
HOMESTAY $

(📞 9447228599, 04865-230104; jjcottagemunnar@gmail.com; d ₹350-800; @ 🛜) The sweet family at this little purple place 2km south of town (but easy walking distance from the main bus stand) will go out of its way to make sure your stay is comfortable. The varied and uncomplicated rooms are ruthlessly clean, bright and good value, and have TV and hot water. The one deluxe room on the top floor has a separate sitting room and sweeping views.

Green View
GUESTHOUSE $

(📞 9447825447, 04865-230940; www.greenviewmunnar.com; d ₹500-800; @ 🛜) This tidy guesthouse has 10 fresh budget rooms, a friendly welcome and reliable tours and treks. The best rooms are on the upper floor and there's a super rooftop garden where you can sample 15 kinds of tea. The young owner organises trekking trips (www.munnartrekking.com) and also runs **Green Woods Anachal** (📞 04865-230189; Anachal; d incl breakfast ₹750), a four-room budget house out in the spice plantations, 10km outside of Munnar.

Zina Cottages
GUESTHOUSE $

(📞 04865-230349; r ₹700-1000) On the outskirts of town but immersed in lush tea plantations and with some fine views, this fading 50-year-old house offers an interesting location with good walks from your doorstep but slightly run-down rooms. They offer pickup from town.

Kaippallil Inn
GUESTHOUSE $

(📞 9495029259; kaippallilinn@gmail.com; r ₹350-800) A stiff walk uphill from the bazaar, Kaippallil is a reasonable budget bet in the town centre, thanks mainly to the serene Benoy, who offers free yoga, reiki and meditation sessions and plenty of tea. It looks a little tatty from the outside but the rooms are clean enough and the top ones have little corner balconies with city views.

Royal Retreat
HOTEL $$

(📞 8281611100, 04865-230240; www.royalretreat.co.in; d ₹3000-3600, ste ₹4400; @ 🛜) Away from the bustle just south of the main bus stand, Royal Retreat is an average but reliable midranger with neat ground-level rooms facing a pretty garden and others with tea plantation views.

Munnar

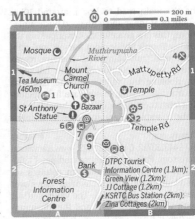

Munnar

📖 Munnar Hills

⭐ Green Valley Vista
GUESTHOUSE $$

(📞 9447432008, 04865-263261; www.greenvalleyvista.com; Chithirapuram; d incl breakfast ₹1500-2000; 🛜) The valley views are superb, facilities top-notch and the welcome warm at this new guesthouse. There are three levels but all rooms face the valley and have private balconies with dreamy greenery views, as well as flat-screen TVs and modern bathrooms with hot water. Staff can organise trekking, jeep safaris and village tours. It's about 11km south of Munnar.

⭐ Rose Gardens
HOMESTAY $$

(📞 9447378524, 04864-278243; www.munnarhomestays.com; NH49 Rd, Karadipara; r incl breakfast ₹4500; @ 🛜) Despite its handy location on the main road to Kochi, around 10km south of Munnar and with good bus connections, this is a peaceful spot overlooking the owner Tomy's idyllic plant nursery and mini spice and fruit plantation. The five rooms are large and comfortable with balconies overlooking the valley, and the family is charming. Cooking lessons are free, including fresh coconut pancakes for breakfast and delicately spiced Keralan dishes for dinner.

Aranyaka   RESORT $$
(☏9443133722, 04865-230023; www.aranyakaresorts.com; Pallivasal Tea Estate; cottages ₹4800-6000; ☞) These neat modern cottages set in a landscaped garden have fine views over the Pallivasal Tea Estate. The valley setting, with views of waterfalls and the Muthirappuzhayar River, feels remote but is only 8km from Munnar town.

Dew Drops   GUESTHOUSE $$
(☏04842-216455; wilsonhomes2003@yahoo.co.in; Kallar; r incl breakfast ₹2800-3150) Set in thick forest around 20km south of Munnar, this remote-feeling place lies on 97 hectares of spice plantation and farmland (not tea plantations). There are eight bright, simple rooms each with a verandah. The peace here is zen but some find it a little isolated

Bracknell Forest   GUESTHOUSE $$$
(☏9446951963; www.bracknellforestmunnar.com; Bison Valley Rd, Ottamaram; r incl breakfast ₹5000-6000; @☞) A remote-feeling 9.5km southeast of Munnar, this place houses 11 neat rooms with balconies and views of a lush valley and cardamom plantation. It's surrounded by deep forest on all sides. The small restaurant has wraparound views. A transfer from Munnar costs around ₹400 but call ahead for directions.

Windermere Estate   RESORT $$$
(☏0484-2425237; www.windermeremunnar.com; Pothamedu; s/d incl breakfast from ₹8300/9600, villa ₹18,300/21,600; ✳@☞) Windermere is a charming boutique-meets-country-retreat 4km southeast of Munnar. There are supremely spacious garden and valley view rooms, but the best are the suite-like 'Plantation Villas' with spectacular views, surrounded by 26 hectares of cardamom and coffee plantations. There's a cosy library above the country-style restaurant.

✖ Eating

Early-morning food stalls in the bazaar serve breakfast snacks and cheap meals, but some of the best food is served up at the homestays and resorts.

Rapsy Restaurant   INDIAN $
(Bazaar; dishes ₹50-140; ☺8am-9pm) This spotless glass-fronted sanctuary from the bazaar is packed at lunchtime, with locals lining up for Rapsy's famous *paratha* (flaky fried bread) or biryani. It also makes a decent stab at fancy international dishes like Spanish omelette, Israeli *shakshuka* (eggs with tomatoes and spices) and Mexican salsa.

SN Restaurant   INDIAN $
(AM Rd; meals ₹50-110; ☺7.30am-10pm) Just south of the DTPC office, SN is a cheery place with a warm orange interior; it appears to be perpetually packed with people digging into thalis, *masala dosas* (thin pancake stuffed with curried vegetables) and other Indian veg and nonveg dishes.

Sree Mahaveer Bhojanalaya   NORTH INDIAN $$
(Mattupetty Rd; meals ₹100-250; ☺8.30am-10.30pm) This pure veg restaurant attached to SN Annex Hotel has a nice deep-orange look with slatted blinds at the windows. It's madly popular with families for its great range of thalis: take your pick from Rajasthani, Gujarati, Punjabi and more, plus a dazzling array of veg dishes.

Eastend   INDIAN $$
(Temple Rd; dishes ₹110-250; ☺7.30am-10.30am, noon-3.30pm & 6.30-10.30pm) In the slightly fancy hotel of the same name, this brightly lit, smartish place serves Chinese, North and South Indian and Kerala specialities, including occasional lunch and dinner buffets.

☆ Entertainment

Punarjani Traditional Village   CULTURAL SHOWS
(☏04865-216161; www.punarjanimunnar.org; 2nd Mile, Pallivasal; tickets ₹200-300; ☺shows 5pm & 6pm) Touristy but entertaining daily performances of Kathakali (5pm) and kalari (6pm). Arrive at 4pm if you want to see the ritual Kathakali make-up session. Tickets are available on the day but for the best seats consider booking a day in advance. It's about 8km south of Munnar town.

Thirumeny Cultural Centre   CULTURAL PROGRAM
(☏9447827696; Temple Rd; shows ₹200; ☺Kathakali shows 5-6pm & 7-8pm; kalari 6-7pm & 8-9pm) On the road behind the East End Hotel, this small theatre stages one-hour Kathakali shows and *kalari* (martial arts) demonstrations twice nightly.

ℹ️ Information

There are ATMs near the bridge, south of the bazaar.

DTPC Tourist Information Office (☎04865-231516; keralatourismmunnardtpc@gmail.com; Alway-Munnar Rd; �
8.30am-6.30pm) Marginally helpful; operates a number of tours and can arrange trekking guides.

Forest Information Centre (☎04865-231587; enpmunnar@gmail.com; �
10am-5pm) Wildlife Warden's Office, for accommodation bookings in Chinnar Wildlife Sanctuary.

Olivia Communications (per hour ₹35; �
9am-9pm) Cramped but surprisingly fast internet cafe in the bazaar.

ℹ️ Getting There & Away

Roads around Munnar are in poor condition and can be affected by monsoon rains. The main **KSRTC bus station** (AM Rd) is south of town, but it's best to catch buses from stands in Munnar town (where more frequent private buses also depart). The main stand is in the bazaar.

There are around 13 daily buses to Ernakulam (Kochi, ₹114, 5½ hours), two direct buses to Alleppey (₹158, five hours) at 6.20am and 1.10pm, and four to Trivandrum (₹231, nine hours). Private buses go to Kumily (₹80, four hours) at 11.25am, 12.20pm and 2.25pm.

A taxi to Ernakulam costs around ₹3000, and to Kumily ₹2500.

ℹ️ Getting Around

Gokulam Bike Hire (☎9447237165; per day ₹300-350; �
7.30am-7.30pm), in the former bus stand south of town, has motorbikes and scooters for hire. Call ahead.

Autorickshaws ply the hills around Munnar with bone-shuddering efficiency; they charge up to ₹800 for a day's sightseeing.

Around Munnar

Top Station

High above Kerala's border with Tamil Nadu, Top Station is popular for its spectacular views over the Western Ghats. From Munnar, four daily buses (₹40, from 7.30am, 1½ hours) make the steep 32km climb in around an hour, or book a return taxi (₹1000).

Eravikulam National Park

Eravikulam National Park　　NATIONAL PARK
(☎04865-231587; www.eravikulam.org; Indian/foreigner ₹75/250, camera/video ₹25/2000; �
8am-5pm Mar-Dec) Eravikulam National Park, 16km from Munnar, is home to the endangered, but almost tame, Nilgiri tahr (a type of mountain goat). From Munnar, an autorickshaw/taxi costs around ₹300/400 return; a government bus takes you the final 4km from the checkpoint (₹40).

Chinnar Wildlife Sanctuary

Chinnar Wildlife Sanctuary　　NATURE RESERVE
(www.chinnar.org; Indian/foreigner ₹100/150, camera/video ₹25/150; ☉7am-6pm) About 60km northeast of Munnar, this wildlife sanctuary hosts deer, leopards, elephants and the endangered grizzled giant squirrel. Trekking and tree house or hut accommodation within the sanctuary are available, as well as ecotour programs like river-trekking, cultural visits (two tribal groups inhabit the sanctuary) and waterfall treks (around ₹600 per person). For details contact the Forest Information Centre in Munnar. Buses from Munnar can drop you off at Chinnar (₹40, 1½ hours), or taxi hire for the day will cost around ₹1500.

Thattekkad Bird Sanctuary

Thattekkad Bird Sanctuary　　NATURE RESERVE
(☎04852588302; Indian/foreigner ₹25/165, camera/video ₹25/150; ☉6.30am-6pm) , cut through by two rivers and two streams, Thattekkad Bird Sanctuary is home to over 320 fluttering species – unusual in that they are mostly forest, rather than water birds – including Malabar grey hornbills, Ripley owls, jungle nightjars, grey drongos, darters and rarer species like the Sri Lankan frogmouth. There are kingfishers, flycatchers, warblers, sunbirds and flower peckers.

Thattekkad is on the Ernakulam–Munnar road. Take a direct bus from either Ernakulam (₹35, two hours) or Munnar (₹60, three hours) to Kothamangalam, from where a Thattekkad bus travels the final 12km (₹8, 25 minutes), or catch an autorickshaw for around ₹250.

🛏️ Sleeping

Jungle Bird Homestay　　HOMESTAY $$
(☎0485-2588143, 9947506188; www.junglebird-homestay.blogspot.com.au; per person incl meals ₹1300) A good budget option is this homestay inside the park, run by the enthusiastic Ms Sudah and son Gireesh, who

KERALA AROUND MUNNAR

OFF THE BEATEN TRACK

PARAMBIKULAM WILDLIFE SANCTUARY

Parambikulam Wildlife Sanctuary (☑ 04253-245025, 9442201690; www.parambikulam. org; Indian/foreigner ₹10/150, camera/video ₹25/150; ⊙ 7am-6pm; last entry 4pm) Possibly the most protected environment in South India – nestled behind three dams in a valley surrounded by Keralan and Tamil Nadu sanctuaries – Parambikulam Wildlife Sanctuary constitutes 285 sq km of Kipling-storybook scenery and wildlife-spotting goodness. Far less touristed than Periyar, it's home to elephants, bison, gaur, sloths, sambar, crocodiles, tigers, panthers and some of the largest teak trees in Asia. The sanctuary is best avoided during monsoon (June to August) and it sometimes closes in March and April.

Contact the Information Centre in Anappady to arrange tours of the park, hikes (one-/two-day trek from ₹3000/6000, shorter treks from ₹600) and accommodation in tree-top huts (₹3000 to ₹5000) or niche tents (₹6000).

You have to enter the park from Pollachi (40km from Coimbatore and 49km from Palakkad) in Tamil Nadu. There are two buses in either direction between Pollachi and Parambikulam via Annamalai daily (₹19, 1½ hours).

will meet guests at the gate. They also offer expert guided birdwatching trips (₹750 for three hours).

Soma Birds Lagoon RESORT $$$
(☑ 0471-2268101; www.somabirdslagoon.com; Palamatton, Thattekkad; s/d incl breakfast €75/85, with AC from €97/113; ❄ ⚞) For accommodation with a little more style, the lovely Soma Birds Lagoon, set deep in the villages near Thattekkad, is a low-key resort on a seasonal lake among spacious and manicured grounds. The basic rooms and cottages here are roomy, with lots of wood trim and lamp lighting. Popular with visiting ornithologists, it's 16km from Kothamangalam.

Hornbill Camp TENTED CAMP $$$
(☑ 0484-2092280; www.thehornbillcamp.com; d full board US$100) About 8km by road from Thattekkad Bird Sanctuary, the tented Hornbill Camp has accommodation in large permanent tents, in a sublimely peaceful location facing the Periyar River. Kayaking, cycling and a spice-garden tour, as well as all meals, are included in the price. Birdwatching guides cost ₹1500.

CENTRAL KERALA

Kochi (Cochin)

☑ 0484 / POP 601,600

Serene Kochi has been drawing traders and explorers to its shores for over 600 years. Nowhere else in India could you find such an intriguing mix: giant fishing nets from China, a 400-year-old synagogue, ancient mosques, Portuguese houses and the crumbling remains of the British Raj. The result is an unlikely blend of medieval Portugal, Holland and an English village grafted onto the tropical Malabar Coast. It's a delightful place to spend some time and nap in some of India's finest homestays and heritage accommodation. Kochi is also a centre for Keralan arts and one of the best places to see Kathakali and *kalarippayat* (p985).

Mainland Ernakulam is the hectic transport and cosmopolitan hub of Kochi, while the historical towns of Fort Cochin and Mattancherry, though well-touristed, remain wonderfully atmospheric – thick with the smell of the past. Other islands, including Willingdon and Vypeen, are linked by a network of ferries and bridges.

◉ Sights

◉ Fort Cochin

Fort Cochin has a couple of small, sandy beaches which are only really good for people-watching in the evening and gazing out at the incoming tankers. A popular promenade winds around from Mahatma Gandhi Beach to the Chinese fishing nets and fish market. This part of Fort Cochin's foreshore is rubbish-strewn and grubby but locals are working towards cleaning it up.

Look out along the shore for the scant remains of Fort Immanuel, the 16th-century Portuguese fort from which the area takes its name.

Kochi (Cochin)

Chinese Fishing Nets
LANDMARK

(Map p976) The unofficial emblems of Kerala's backwaters, and perhaps the most photographed, are the half-dozen or so giant cantilevered Chinese fishing nets on Fort Cochin's northeastern shore. A legacy of traders from the AD 1400 court of Kublai Khan, these enormous, spiderlike contraptions require at least four people to operate their counterweights at high tide. Modern fishing techniques are making these labour-intensive methods less and less profitable, but they still supply the fresh seafood you'll see for sale. Smaller fishing nets are dotted around the shores of Vembanad Lake.

Indo-Portuguese Museum
MUSEUM

(Map p976; ☎0484-2215400; Indian/foreigner ₹10/25; ☺9am-1pm & 2-6pm Tue-Sun) This museum in the garden of the Bishop's House preserves the heritage of one of India's earliest Catholic communities, including vestments, silver processional crosses and altarpieces from the Cochin diocese. The basement contains remnants of the Portuguese Fort Immanuel.

Maritime Museum
MUSEUM

(Beach Rd; adult/child ₹40/20, camera/video ₹100/150; ☺9.30am-12.30pm & 2.30-5.30pm Tue-Sun) In a pair of former bomb shelters, this museum traces the history of the Indi-

an navy, as well as maritime trade dating back to the Portuguese and Dutch, through a series of rather dry relief murals and information panels. There's plenty of naval memorabilia, including a couple of model battleships outside in the garden.

St Francis Church
CHURCH

(Map p976; Church Rd; ☺8.30am-5pm) Constructed in 1503 by Portuguese Franciscan friars, this is believed to be India's oldest European-built church. The edifice that stands here today was built in the mid-16th century to replace the original wooden structure. Explorer Vasco da Gama, who died in Cochin in 1524, was buried in this spot for 14 years before his remains were taken to Lisbon – you can still visit his tombstone in the church.

Santa Cruz Basilica
CHURCH

(Map p976; cnr Bastion St & KB Jacob Rd; ☺7am-8.30pm) The imposing Catholic basilica was originally built on this site in 1506, though the current building dates to 1902. Inside are artefacts from the different eras in Kochi and a striking pastel-coloured interior.

Dutch Cemetery
HISTORIC SITE

(Map p976; Beach Rd) Consecrated in 1724, this cemetery near Kochi beach contains

KERALA KOCHI (COCHIN)

Fort Cochin

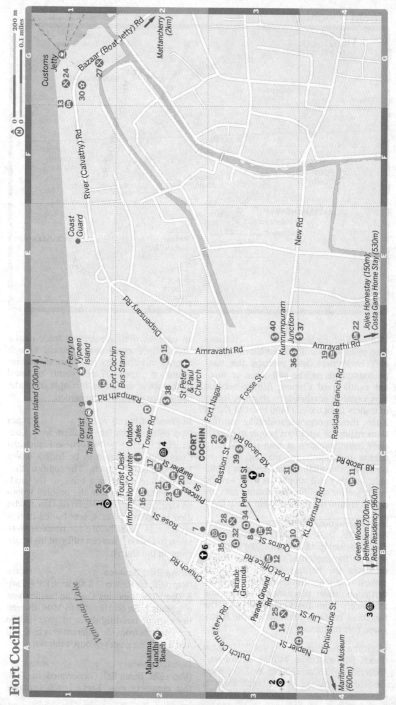

Vembanad Lake

Customs Jetty

Bazaar (Boat Jetty) Rd

Mattancherry (2km)

River (Calvathy) Rd

Coast Guard

Ferry to Vypeen Island

Vypeen Island (300m)

Dispensary Rd

Fort Cochin Bus Stand

Rampath Rd

Amravathi Rd

Tourist Taxi Stand

Tourist Desk Information Counter

Outdoor Cafes

Tower Rd

St Peter & Paul Church

Kuruntumpuram Junction

Amravathi Rd

Jojies Homestay (150m);
Costa Gama Home Stay (530m)

New Rd

Fort Nagar

Bastion St

Burgher St

Princess St

Rose St

FORT COCHIN

Peter Celli St

KB Jacob Rd

Fosse St

Residale Branch Rd

KB Jacob Rd

KL Bernard Rd

Quiros St

Post Office Rd

Church Rd

Parade Grounds

Parade Ground Rd

Dutch Cemetery Rd

Mahatma Gandhi Beach

Napier St

Lily St

Elphinstone St

Green Woods Bethlehem (700m);
Reds Residency (960m)

Maritime Museum (600m)

Dutch Cemetery Rd

200 m
0.1 miles

Fort Cochin

⊙ Sights
1 Chinese Fishing Nets	B1
2 Dutch Cemetery	A3
3 Indo-Portuguese Museum	A4
4 Kashi Art Gallery	C2
5 Santa Cruz Basilica	C3
6 St Francis Church	B2

⊙ Activities, Courses & Tours
7 Art of Bicycle Trips	B2
8 Cook & Eat	B3
9 KTDC	C1
10 SVM Ayurveda Centre	B3

⊜ Sleeping
11 Daffodil	C4
12 Delight Home Stay	B3
13 Fort House Hotel	G1
14 Malabar House	A3
15 Noah's Ark	D2
16 Old Harbour Hotel	C2
17 Princess Inn	C2
18 Raintree Lodge	B3
19 Saj Homestay	D4
20 Sonnetta Residency	C2
21 Spice Fort	C2
22 Tea Bungalow	D4
23 Walton's Homestay	C2

⊗ Eating
24 Arca Nova	G1
25 Dal Roti	A3
26 Fishmongers	C1
Kashi Art Cafe	(see 4)
Malabar Junction	(see 14)
Oy's Restaurant	(see 17)
27 Solar Cafe	G1
28 Teapot	B3
29 Upstairs Italian	C3

⊛ Entertainment
30 Greenix Village	G1
31 Kerala Kathakali Centre	C3

⊜ Shopping
32 Cinnamon	B3
33 Fabindia	A4
Idiom Bookshop	(see 7)
34 Niraamaya	B3
35 Tribes India	B3

⊕ Information
36 Federal Bank ATM	D3
37 ICICI ATM	D4
38 SBI ATM	D2
39 South India Bank ATM	C3
40 UAE Exchange	D3

KERALA KOCHI (COCHIN)

the worn and dilapidated graves of Dutch traders and soldiers. Its gates are normally locked but a caretaker might let you in, or ask at St Francis Church.

Kashi Art Gallery ART GALLERY
(Map p976; ☑ 0484-2215769; www.kashiartgallery.com; Burgher St; ⊙ 8.30am-7.30pm) The pioneer of Fort Cochin's art revival, Kashi displays changing exhibitions of local artists; most travellers come for the good cafe.

⊙ Mattancherry & Jew Town

About 3km southeast of Fort Cochin, Mattancherry is the old bazaar district and centre of the spice trade. These days it's packed with spice shops and pricey Kashmiri-run emporiums that autorickshaw drivers will fall over backwards to take you to for a healthy commission – any offer of a cheap tour of the district will inevitably lead to a few shops. In the midst of this, Jew Town is a bustling port area with a fine synagogue. Scores of small firms huddle together in dilapidated old buildings and the air is filled with the biting aromas of ginger, cardamom, cumin, turmeric and cloves, though the lanes around the Dutch Palace and synagogue are

packed with antique and tourist-curio shops rather than spices.

★ Mattancherry Palace MUSEUM
(Dutch Palace; Map p978; ☑ 0484-2226085; Palace Rd; adult/child ₹5/free; ⊙ 9am-5pm Sat-Thu) Mattancherry Palace was a generous gift presented to the Raja of Kochi, Veera Kerala Varma (1537–61), as a gesture of goodwill by the Portuguese in 1555. The Dutch renovated the palace in 1663, hence its alternative name, the Dutch Palace. The star attractions here are the astonishingly preserved Hindu murals, depicting scenes from the Ramayana, Mahabharata and Puranic legends in intricate detail.

★ Pardesi Synagogue SYNAGOGUE
(Map p978; admission ₹5; ⊙ 10am-1pm & 3-5pm Sun-Thu, closed Jewish holidays) Originally built in 1568, this synagogue was partially destroyed by the Portuguese in 1662, and rebuilt two years later when the Dutch took Kochi. It features an ornate gold pulpit and elaborate hand-painted, willow-pattern floor tiles from Canton, China, which were added in 1762. It's magnificently illuminated by Belgian chandeliers and coloured-glass lamps. The graceful clock tower was built in 1760.

Mattancherry

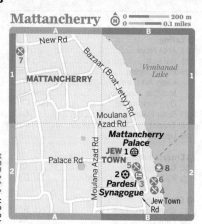

```
0 ——————— 200 m
0 ——————— 0.1 miles
```

There is an upstairs balcony for women, who worshipped separately according to Orthodox rites. Note that shorts, sleeveless tops, bags and cameras are not allowed inside.

◉ Ernakulam

Kerala Folklore Museum — MUSEUM
(☎0484-2665452; www.keralafolkloremuseum. org; Folklore Junction, Thevara; Indian/foreigner ₹100/200, camera ₹100; ◷9.30am-6pm) Created in Keralan style from ancient temples and beautiful old houses collected by its owner, an antique dealer, the museum includes over 4000 artefacts and covers three architectural styles: Malabar on the ground-floor, Kochi on the 1st, Travancore on the 2nd. Upstairs is a beautiful wood-lined theatre with a 17th-century wooden ceiling. It's about 6km south of Ernakulam Junction

train station. A rickshaw from Ernakulam should cost ₹90, or you can take any bus to Thivara from where it's a ₹25 rickshaw ride. An autorickshaw from Fort Cochin should cost ₹200.

🏃 Activities

Ayur Dara — AYURVEDA
(☎0484-2502362, 9447721041; www.ayurdara. com; Murikkumpadam, Vypeen Island; ◷9am-5.30pm) Run by third-generation ayurvedic practitioner Dr Subhash, this delightful waterside treatment centre specialises in treatments of one to three weeks (₹1500 per day). By appointment only. It's 3km from the Vypeen Island ferry.

SVM Ayurveda Centre — AYURVEDA
(Kerala Ayurveda Pharmacy Ltd; Map p976; ☎9847371667; www.svmayurveda.com; Quieros St; massage from ₹900, rejuvenation from ₹1200; ◷9.30am-7pm) A small Fort Cochin centre, offering relaxing massages and Hatha yoga daily. Longer rejuvenation packages are also available.

🎓 Courses

The Kerala Kathakali Centre (p984) has lessons in classical Kathakali dance, music and make-up (short and long-term courses from ₹350 per hour).

For a crash course in the martial art of *kalarippayat*, Ens Kalari (p984) is a famed training centre which offers short intensive courses from one week to one month.

Cook & Eat — COOKING
(Map p976; ☎0484-2215377; www.leelahomestay. com; Quiros St; classes ₹700; ◷11am & 6pm) Mrs Leelu Roy runs popular two-hour cooking classes in her big family kitchen at Leelu Homestay, teaching five dishes and her homemade garam masala to classes of five to 10 people.

👉 Tours

Tourist Desk Information Counter — TOURS
(Map p980; ☎9847044688, 0484-2371761; www. touristdesk.in; Ernakulam Boat Jetty & Tower Rd, Fort Cochin) This excellent private tour agency runs the popular full-day **Water Valley Tour** (₹850, departs 8am) by houseboat through local backwater canals and lagoons. A canoe trip through smaller canals and villages is included, as is lunch and hotel pick-ups. It also offers a **sunset dinner cruise** (₹750) by canoe from Narakkal Village on Vypeen Island, with the option of an overnight stay

at a beach bungalow, and an overnight **Munnar Hill Station Tour** (₹3000) with transport, accommodation and meals. Staff here are a good source of information on local temple festivals.

KTDC BOAT TOUR
(Map p976; ☑ 0484-2353234; Marine Dr, Kochi; ☺ 10am-5pm Mon-Sat) The KTDC has half-day **backwater tours** (₹600) at 8.30am and 2pm, and full-day **houseboat backwater trips** (₹700) visiting local weaving factories, spice gardens and toddy tappers.

Elephant Training Camp ELEPHANT RIDE
(Kodanuda; ☺ 7am-6pm) Most hotels and tourist offices can arrange the day trip out to the elephant training camp at Kodanadu, 50km from Kochi. Here you can go for a ride (₹200), or help out with washing the gentle beasts if you arrive by 8am. Entry is free, though the elephant trainers will expect a small tip. A return trip out here in a taxi should cost around ₹1200.

Art of Bicycle Trips BICYCLE TOUR
(Map p976; ☑ 9656703909; www.artofbicycletrips. com; Bastion St; tours ₹1450-4200; ☺ 9am-6pm) Guided bicycle tours on quality mountain bikes include a morning tour of the historic Fort area (₹1450), a half-day ride towards the backwaters (₹2450) and a full-day trip south towards Alleppey with backwater canoeing (₹4200). A great way to see the area at a slow place.

Kerala Bike Tours BICYCLE TOUR
(☑ 04842356652, 9388476817; www.keralabike-tours.com; Kirushupaly Rd, Ravipuram) Organises motorcycle tours around Kerala and the Western Ghats and hires out touring-quality Enfield Bullets (from US$155 per week) with unlimited mileage, full insurance and free recovery/maintenance options.

🎉 Festivals & Events

Ernakulathappan Utsavam FESTIVAL
(Shiva Temple, Ernakulam, Kochi; ☺ Jan/Feb) Eight days of festivities culminating in a parade of 15 splendidly decorated elephants, plus music and fireworks.

Cochin Carnival FESTIVAL
(www.cochincarnival.org; ☺ 21 Dec) The Cochin Carnival is Fort Cochin's biggest bash, a 10-day festival culminating on New Year's Eve. Street parades, colourful costumes, embellished elephants, music, folk dancing and lots of fun.

🛏 Sleeping

Fort Cochin can feel a bit touristy and crowded in season but, with some of Kerala's finest accommodation, it's a great place to escape the noise and chaos of the mainland. This is India's homestay capital, with dozens of family houses offering clean budget rooms, home-cooked meals and a hearty welcome.

Ernakulam is cheaper and more convenient for onward travel, but the ambience and accommodation choices are less inspiring. Regardless of where you stay, book ahead during December and January. At other times you may be able to bargain for a discount. Go on line at www.fortcochin homestays.com to check out a few places.

🛏 Fort Cochin

★ **Green Woods Bethlehem** HOMESTAY $
(☑ 9846014924, 0484-3247791; greenwoodsbethlehem1@vsnl.net; d incl breakfast ₹1000-1200, with AC ₹1500; ❄ ☎) With a smile that brightens weary travellers, welcoming owner Sheeba looks ready to sign your adoption papers the minute you walk through her front door. Down a quiet laneway and with a walled garden thick with plants and palms, this is one of Kochi's most serene homestays. The rooms are humble but cosy; breakfast is served in the fantastic, leafy rooftop cafe, where cooking classes and demonstrations are often held.

Princess Inn GUESTHOUSE $
(Map p976; ☑ 0484-2217073; princessinnfortkochi@gmail.com; Princess St; s/d/tr ₹400/600/1000) Sticking to its budget guns, the friendly Princess Inn spruces up its otherwise dull, tiny rooms with cheery bright colours. The communal spaces are welcoming, and the three large, front-facing rooms are good value for this location.

Costa Gama Home Stay HOMESTAY $
(☑ 0484-2216122; www.stayincochin.com; Thamaraparambu Rd; r ₹800, with AC ₹1200; ❄ ☎) With just three rooms, this cosy little place gets good reviews. Across the road are another three rooms in a heritage-style building with a nice terrace.

★ **Reds Residency** HOMESTAY $$
(☑ 9388643747, 0484-3204060; www.redsresidency.in; 11/372 A, KJ Herschel Rd; d incl breakfast ₹900-1200, with AC from ₹1200, AC rooftop cottage ₹1500; ❄ @ ☎) Reds is a lovely homestay with hotel-quality rooms but a true family

Ernakulam

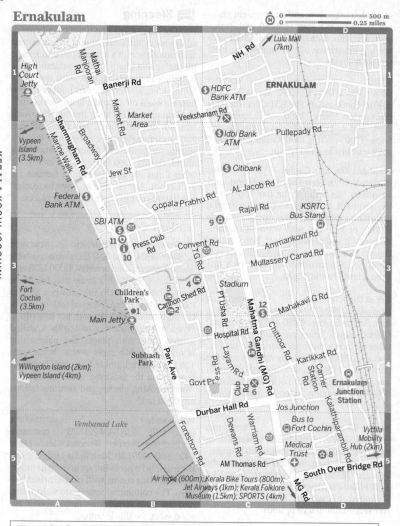

KERALA KOCHI (COCHIN)

Ernakulam

Activities, Courses & Tours
1 Tourist Desk Information
  Counter B3

Sleeping
2 Boat Jetty Bungalow B3
3 Grand Hotel C4
4 John's Residency B3
5 Saas Tower B3

Eating
6 Chillies C4
7 Frys Village Restaurant C1
  Grand Pavilion ....(see 3)

Entertainment
8 See India Foundation D5

Shopping
9 Centre Square Mall C3

Information
10 KTDC Tourist Reception Centre B3
  Tourist Desk Information
  Counter ....(see 1)
11 Tourist Police (Ernakulam).................B3
12 UAE Exchange C3

welcome from knowledgeable hosts Philip and Maryann. The seven rooms – including a triple and four-bed family room – are modern and immaculate, and there's a brilliant self-contained 'penthouse' cottage with kitchen on the rooftop. It's in a peaceful location south of the centre.

Walton's Homestay   GUESTHOUSE $$
(Map p976; ☑9249721935, 0484-2215309; www.waltonshomestay.com; Princess St; r incl breakfast ₹1600-3000; ❀⊜) The fastidious Mr Walton offers big wood-furnished rooms in his lovely old house that's painted a nautical white with blue trim and buried behind a bookstore. Downstairs rooms open onto a lush garden while upstairs rooms have balcony, and there's a communal breakfast room.

Jojies Homestay   HOMESTAY $$
(☑9567045544; 1/1276 Chirattapallam, off KB Jacob Road; d ₹1500-2500; ⊜) Clean, friendly and welcoming homestay popular with travellers thanks to helpful owners and big breakfasts.

Raintree Lodge   GUESTHOUSE $$
(Map p976; ☑9847029000, 0484-3251489; www.fortcochin.com; Peter Celli St; r ₹2800; ❀⊜) The intimate and elegant rooms at this historic place flirt with boutique-hotel status. Each of the five rooms has a great blend of contemporary style and heritage carved-wood furniture and the front upstairs rooms have gorgeous vine-covered Romeo-and-Juliet balconies. Good value.

Delight Home Stay   GUESTHOUSE $$
(Map p976; ☑98461121421, 0484-2217658; www.delightfulhomestay.com; Post Office Rd; r incl breakfast ₹1600-1800, with AC ₹2500; ❀⊜) And delightful it is. This grand house's exterior is adorned with frilly white woodwork, and the six rooms are spacious and polished. There's a charming little garden, elegant breakfast room and an imposing sitting room covered in wall-to-wall teak. Good food is served and cooking classes are offered in the open kitchen.

Daffodil   GUESTHOUSE $$
(Map p976; ☑9895262296, 0484-2218686; www.daffodilhomestay.com; Njaliparambu Junction; d incl breakfast ₹1600, with AC ₹2500; ❀@⊜) Run by a welcoming local couple, Daffodil has eight big and brightly painted modern rooms with a sense of privacy, but the best feature is the carved-wood Keralan balcony upstairs.

Saj Homestay   HOMESTAY $$
(Map p976; ☑9847002182; www.sajhome.com; Amravathi Rd, near Kunnumpuram Junction; d incl breakfast from ₹900, with AC ₹2200; ❀⊜) There are six upstairs rooms at this welcoming homestay run by helpful Saj. It can be a bit street-noisy at the front but the rooms are clean and travellers rave about the breakfast.

Noah's Ark   HOMESTAY $$
(Map p976; ☑9745365260, 0484-2215481; www.noahsarkcochin.com; 1/508 Fort Cochin Hospital Rd; r ₹2800-3500; ❀@⊜) This large modern family home, with a sweeping spiral staircase from the reception room and four immaculate, upmarket rooms – two with a balcony – comes with a friendly welcome but plenty of privacy.

Sonnetta Residency   GUESTHOUSE $$
(Map p976; ☑9895543555, 0484-2215744; www.sonnettaresidency.com; 1/387 Princess St; d/f ₹1575/2250, with AC ₹2250/2800; ❀⊜) Right in the thick of the Fort Cochin action, the six rooms at this friendly Portuguese-era place are immaculately kept and well-presented, with nice, chintzy touches like curtains, colourful bedspreads and indoor plants. Every room has air-con but you can choose not to use it at the cheaper rate.

★Malabar House   HOTEL $$$
(Map p976; ☑0484-2216666; www.malabarhouse.com; Parade Ground Rd; r €240, ste incl breakfast €330-380; ❀@⊠) What may just be one of the fanciest boutique hotels in Kerala, Malabar flaunts its uber-hip blend of modern colours and period fittings like it's not even trying. While the suites are huge and lavishly appointed, the standard rooms are more snug. The award-winning restaurant and wine bar are top-notch.

★Brunton Boatyard   HOTEL $$$
(☑0484-2215461; bruntonboatyard@cghearth.com; River Rd; r/ste ₹26,000/34,000; ❀@⊜⊠) This imposing hotel faithfully reproduces 16th- and 17th-century Dutch and Portuguese architecture in its grand complex. All of the rooms look out over the harbour, and have bathtubs and balconies with a refreshing sea breeze that beats air-con any day. The hotel is also home to the excellent History Restaurant and Armoury Bar, along with a couple of open-air cafes.

Spice Fort   BOUTIQUE HOTEL $$$
(Map p976; ☑9364455440; www.duneecogroup.com; Princess St; r ₹8500-11,000; ❀⊜⊠) The

chic red-and-white spice-themed rooms here have TVs built into the bed heads, cool tones and immaculate bathrooms. They all orbit an inviting pool in a heritage courtyard shielded from busy Princess St. Great location, excellent restaurant, friendly staff.

Tea Bungalow HOTEL $$$
(Map p976; ☎0484-3019200; www.teabungalow.in; 1/1901 Kunumpuram; r ₹15,000-18,000; ❄@🛜☳) This mustard-coloured colonial building was built in 1912 as headquarters of a UK spice trading company before being taken over by Brooke Bond tea. The 10 graceful boutique rooms – all named after sea ports – are decorated with flashes of strong colour and carved colonial-era wooden furniture, and have Bassetta-tiled bathrooms. Off-season rates drop by 60%.

Old Harbour Hotel HOTEL $$$
(Map p976; ☎0484-2218006; www.oldharbourhotel.com; 1/328 Tower Rd; r/ste ₹10,200/17,600; ❄@☳) Set around an idyllic garden with lily ponds and a small pool, the dignified Old Harbour is housed in a 300-year-old Dutch/Portuguese-era heritage building. The elegant mix of period and modern styles lend it a more intimate feel than some of the more grandiose competition. There are 13 rooms and suites, some facing directly onto the garden, and some with open-air bathrooms.

Fort House Hotel HOTEL $$$
(Map p976; ☎0484-2217103; www.hotelforthouse.com; 2/6A Calvathy Rd; r incl breakfast ₹5500; ❄@) Close to the ferry point, this is one of the few truly waterfront hotels, though the 16 smart air-con rooms are set back in a lush garden, with the restaurant taking prime waterside position.

🛏 Mattancherry & Jew Town

Caza Maria HOMESTAY $$
(Map p978; ☎9846050901; cazamaria@rediffmail.com; Jew Town Rd; r incl breakfast ₹4500; ❄) Right in the heart of Jew Town, this unique place has just two large heritage rooms overlooking the bazaar. Fit for a maharaja, the rooms feature an idiosyncratic style, with each high-ceilinged room painted in bright colours, filled to the brim with antiques.

🛏 Ernakulam

John's Residency HOTEL $
(Map p980; ☎0484-2355395; TD Rd; s/d from ₹550/650, with AC ₹1600; ❄) John's is a genuine backpacker place with helpful staff, local

information and a quiet location that's still a short walk from the boat jetty. Rooms are small (deluxe rooms are bigger) but decorated with flashes of colour that give them a welcoming funky feel in this price bracket.

Boat Jetty Bungalow HOTEL $
(Map p980; ☎0484-2373211; www.boatjettybungalow.com; Cannon Shed Rd; s/d ₹430/735, with AC ₹960/1465; ❄) This 140-year-old former jettty manager's house has been refurbished and opened in 2014 as a very good value hotel with 22 compact and clean rooms with TV. It's a short walk to the boat jetty to Fort Cochin.

Saas Tower HOTEL $$
(Map p980; ☎0484-2365319; www.saastower.com; Cannon Shed Rd; s/d ₹1200/1800, with AC from ₹2100/2400, ste from ₹3600; ❄@) The flashy lobby is more promising than the rooms in this midrange business hotel but if you're after a step up from the budget hotels near the jetty, it isn't a bad option. Clean rooms filled with wooden furniture, a restaurant, business centre and a day spa with ayurvedic treatments.

Grand Hotel HOTEL $$
(Map p980; ☎9895721014, 0484-2382061; www.grandhotelkerala.com; MG Rd; s/d incl breakfast from ₹3250/4000, ste ₹6000; ❄@🛜) This 1960s hotel, with its polished original art deco fittings, exudes the sort of retro cool that modern hotels would love to recreate. The spacious rooms have gleaming parquet floors and large modern bathrooms, and there's a good restaurant and Ernakulam's most sophisticated bar.

🛏 Around Kochi

Kallancherry Retreat HOMESTAY $
(☎0484-2240564, 9847446683; www.kallancherryretreat.com; Kumbalanghi Village; r without/with AC ₹800/1000, cottage without/with AC ₹1000/1500; ❄🛜) Escape the Kochi tourist crowds to this serene budget waterfront homestay and expansive garden in the village of Kumbalanghi, about 15km south of Fort Cochin. Rooms are either in the family home or in a sublime lakefront cottage. Offers Chinese fishing nets on your doorstep, boat trips, village tours and home-cooked meals.

★Olavipe HOMESTAY $$$
(☎0478-2522255; www.olavipe.com; Olavipe; s/d incl meals ₹5100/8500) This gorgeous 1890s traditional Syrian-Christian home is on a

16-hectare farm surrounded by backwaters, 28km south of Kochi. A restored mansion of rosewood and glistening teak, it has several large and breezy rooms beautifully decorated in original period decor.

✗ Eating & Drinking

Some of Fort Cochin's best dining can be found in the homestays, but there are lots of good restaurants and cafes.

✗ Fort Cochin

Behind the Chinese fishing nets are **fishmongers** (Map p976; seafood per kilo ₹200-1000) from whom you can buy the day's catch – fresh fish, prawns, crab and lobster – then take your selection to one of the row of simple but popular restaurants on nearby Tower Rd where they will cook it and serve it to you for an additional charge. Market price varies but you'll easily get a feel for prices if you wander along and bargain.

Teapot   CAFE $
(Map p976; Peter Celli St; mains ₹70-140; ⊘8.30am-8.30pm) This atmospheric cafe is the perfect venue for 'high tea', with 16 types of tea, sandwiches, cakes and a few meals served in chic, airy rooms. Witty tea-themed accents include loads of antique teapots, tea chests for tables and a tea-tree-based table.

Solar Cafe   CAFE $
(Map p976; Bazaar Rd; meals ₹80-130; ⊘8am-8pm) This arty upstairs cafe serves organic breakfasts and lunches, cinnamon coffee and fresh juice, in a lime-bright, book-lined setting opposite the Customs Jetty.

Oy's Restaurant   MULTICUISINE $
(Map p976; www.oys.co.in; Burgher St; mains ₹50-200; ⊘8.30am-10pm; 🛜) Oy's has made a name for itself among travellers with loungy decor, chill-out soundtrack, cafe comfort food and Asian–focused dishes.

★ Dal Roti   INDIAN $$
(Map p976; ☑9746459244; 1/293 Lily St; meals ₹100-230; ⊘noon-3.30pm & 6.30-10.30pm Wed-Mon) There's a lot to like about busy Dal Roti. Friendly and knowledgeable owner Ramesh will hold your hand through his expansive North Indian menu, which even sports its own glossary, and help you dive into his delicious range of vegetarian, eggetarian and nonvegetarian options. From *kati* rolls (flatbrad rolled with stuffing) to seven types of thali, you won't go hungry. No alcohol.

Kashi Art Cafe   CAFE $$
(Map p976; Burgher St; breakfast & snacks ₹90-250; ⊘8.30am-10pm) An institution in Fort Cochin, this natural-light-filled place has a zen-but-casual vibe and solid wood tables that spread out into a semi-courtyard space. The coffee is as strong as it should be and the daily continental breakfast and lunch specials are excellent. A small gallery shows off local artists.

Arca Nova   SEAFOOD $$
(Map p976; 2/6A Calvathy Rd; mains ₹190-650; ⊘7.30am-10.30pm) The waterside restaurant at the Fort House Hotel is a prime choice for a leisurely lunch. It specialises in fish dishes and you can sit out at tables overlooking the water or in the serenely spacious covered garden area.

Upstairs Italian   ITALIAN $$$
(Map p976; ☑9745682608; Bastion St; mains ₹250-600; ⊘10am-11pm) For authentic Italian fare – Gorgonzola, prosciutto, olive oil, Parmesan cheese – head upstairs to this cosy little place serving Kochi's best pizza, pasta and antipasto. Pricey but worth a splurge.

★ Malabar Junction   INTERNATIONAL $$$
(Map p976; ☑0484-2216666; Parade Ground Rd; mains ₹360-680, 5-course degustation ₹2000; ⊘lunch & dinner) Set in an open-sided pavilion, the restaurant at Malabar House is movie-star cool, with white-tableclothed tables in a courtyard close to the small pool. There's a seafood-based, European-style menu – the signature dish is the impressive seafood platter with grilled vegetables. Upstairs, the wine bar serves upmarket tapas-style snacks and fine wine by the glass.

✗ Mattancherry & Jew Town

Ramathula Hotel   INDIAN $
(Kayikka's; Map p978; Kayees Junction, Mattancherry; biryani ₹40-60; ⊘lunch & dinner) This place is legendary for its chicken and mutton biryanis – get here early or miss out. It's better known by the chef's name, Kayikka's.

Caza Maria   MULTICUISINE $$
(Map p978; Bazaar Rd; mains ₹210-700; ⊘9am-8pm) This enchanting 1st-floor place is a bright-blue, antique-filled heritage space with soft music and a changing daily menu of North Indian, South Indian and French dishes.

Café Jew Town

CAFE $$

(Map p978; Bazaar Rd; snacks ₹120-200; ⊙9am-6pm) Walk through chic antique shops and galleries to reach this sweet Swiss-owned cafe; the few tables proffer good cakes, snacks and Italian coffee.

Cafe Crafters

CAFE $$

(Map p978; Jew Town Rd; mains ₹100-280; ⊙9.30am-6.30pm) In the heart of Mattancherry's Jewish Quarter, this charming little 1st-floor restaurant cooks up Keralan seafood and continental efforts like sandwiches and burgers. Prime position is the small balcony overlooking the street.

★ Ginger House

INDIAN $$$

(Map p978; Bazaar Rd; mains ₹190-700; ⊙8.30am-6pm) Hidden behind a massive antique-filled godown (warehouse) is this fantastic waterfront restaurant, where you can feast on Indian dishes and snacks – ginger prawns, ginger ice cream, ginger lassi ... you get the picture. To get to the restaurant, walk through the astonishing Heritage Arts showroom with amazing sculptures and antiques – check out the giant snake-boat canoe. If you ask, the owner might show you the rest of the collection upstairs.

✗ Ernakulam

Ernakulam's mega shopping malls provide food-court dining. Another interesting development is the leafy Panampilly Ave, in a residential area south of the main train station, which is lined with modern fine-dining and fast-food restaurants.

Frys Village Restaurant

KERALAN $

(Map p980; Chittoor Rd; mains ₹80-150; ⊙noon-3.30pm & 7-10.30pm) This brightly decorated and breezy place with an arched ceiling is a great family restaurant with authentic Keralan food, especially seafood like *pollichathu* or crab roast. Fish and veg thalis are available for lunch.

Chillies

INDIAN $$

(Map p980; Layam Rd; meals ₹130-280; thali ₹140; ⊙11.30am-3.30pm & 7.30-11pm) A dark, buzzing 1st-floor place, serving Kochi's best spicy Andhra cuisine on banana leaves. Try a thali, for all-you-can-eat joy.

Grand Pavilion

INDIAN $$$

(Map p980; MG Rd; meals ₹250-370) The restaurant at the Grand Hotel is as elegant and retro-stylish as the hotel itself, with cream-coloured furniture and stiff tablecloths. It serves a tome of a menu that covers dishes from most of the Asian continent.

☆ Entertainment

There are several places in Kochi where you can view Kathakali. The performances are designed for tourists, but they're a good introduction to this intriguing art form. The standard program starts with the intricate make-up application and costume-fitting, followed by a demonstration and commentary on the dance and then the performance – usually two hours in all. The fast-paced traditional martial art of *kalarippayat* can also be easily seen, often at the same theatres.

☆ Fort Cochin

Kerala Kathakali Centre

CULTURAL PROGRAM

(Map p976; ☎0484-2217552; www.kathakalicentre.com; KB Jacob Rd; shows ₹250-300; ⊙make-up from 5pm, show 6-7.30pm) In an intimate, wood-lined theatre, this recommended place provides a useful introduction to Kathakali, complete with handy translations of the night's story. The centre also hosts performances of *kalarippayat* at 4pm to 5pm daily, traditional music at 8pm to 9pm Sunday to Friday and classical dance at 8pm to 9pm Saturday.

Greenix Village

CULTURAL PROGRAM

(Map p976; ☎9349372050, 0484-2217000; www.greenix.in; Kalvathy Rd; shows ₹300-500; ⊙10am-6pm, shows from 5pm) This touristy 'cultural village' seeks to put the full gamut of Keralan music and arts under one roof with a small cultural museum, yoga classes (₹450), performances of Kathakali and *kalarippayat* (₹300) and other cultural shows in an impressive complex.

☆ Ernakulam

See India Foundation

CULTURAL PROGRAM

(Map p980; ☎0484-2376471; devankathakali@yahoo.com; Kalathiparambil Lane; admission ₹300; ⊙make-up 6pm, show 7-8pm) One of the oldest Kathakali theatres in Kerala, it has small-scale shows with an emphasis on the religious and philosophical roots of Kathakali.

Ens Kalari

CULTURAL PROGRAM

(☎0484-2700810; www.enskalari.org.in; Nettoor; admission by donation; ⊙demonstrations 7.15-8.15pm) If you want to see real professionals have a go at *kalarippayat,* it's best to travel out to this renowned *kalarippayat* learning centre, 8km southeast of Ernakulam. There are one-hour demonstrations daily (one day's notice required).

Shopping

Broadway in Ernakulam is good for local shopping, spice shops and clothing. On Jew Town Rd in Mattancherry you'll find a plethora of Gujarati-run shops selling genuine antiques mingled with knock-offs and copies. Most of the shops in Fort Cochin are identikit Kashmiri-run shops selling a mixed bag of North Indian crafts. Many shops around Fort Cochin and Mattancherry operate lucrative commission rackets, with autorickshaw drivers getting huge kickbacks for dropping tourists at their door.

Lulu Mall　　　　　　　　　　　　MALL
(☑0484-2727777; www.lulu.in; NH47, Edapally; ◷9am-11pm; ☏) India's largest shopping mall, Lulu is an attraction in its own right with people coming from all over to shop here, hang out in the food courts or cinema, and go ice-skating or ten-pin bowling. Sprawling over seven hectares, the state-of-the-art aircon mall has more than 215 brand outlets from Calvin Klein to KFC. It's in Edapally, about 9km from the boat jetty.

Niraamaya　　　　　　　　　　CLOTHING
(Map p976; Quiros St, Fort Cochin; ◷10am-5.30pm Mon-Sat) Popular throughout Kerala, Niraamaya sells 'ayurvedic' clothing and fabrics – all made of organic cotton, coloured with natural herb dyes or infused with ayurvedic oils. There's another branch in Mattancherry.

Centre Square Mall　　　　　　MALL
(Map p980; ☑0484-4041888; MG Rd, Ernakulam; ◷10am-11pm) In central Ernakulam, this flashy new mall is smaller than Lulu but still has five floors of shopping, including a top-floor food court and bowling alley, as well as a cinema.

Idiom Bookshop　　　　　　　BOOKS
(Map p976; Bastion St; ◷10.30am-9pm Mon-Sat) Huge range of quality new and used books in Fort Cochin.

TRADITIONAL KERALAN ARTS

Kathakali

The art form of Kathakali crystallised at around the same time as Shakespeare was scribbling his plays. The Kathakali performance is the dramatised presentation of a play, usually based on the Hindu epics the Ramayana, the Mahabharata and the Puranas. All the great themes are covered – righteousness and evil, frailty and courage, poverty and prosperity, war and peace.

Drummers and singers accompany the actors, who tell the story through their precise movements, particularly *mudras* (hand gestures) and facial expressions.

Preparation for the performance is lengthy and disciplined. Paint, fantastic costumes, ornamental headpieces and meditation transform the actors both physically and mentally into the gods, heroes and demons they are about to play. Dancers even stain their eyes red with seeds from the *chundanga* plant to maximise the drama.

Traditional performances can last for many hours, but you can see cut-down performances in tourist hot spots all over the state, and there are Kathakali schools in Trivandrum (p941) and near Thrissur that encourage visitors.

Kalarippayat

Kalarippayat (or *kalari*) is an ancient tradition of martial arts training and discipline, still taught throughout Kerala. Some believe it is the forerunner of all martial arts, with roots tracing back to the 12th-century skirmishes among Kerala's feudal principalities.

Masters of *kalarippayat,* called Gurukkal, teach their craft inside a special arena called a *kalari.* You can see often *kalarippayat* performances at the same venues as Kathakali.

The three main schools of *kalarippayat* can be divided into northern and central, both practised in northern Kerala and Malabar region, and southern *kalarippayat.* As well as open hand combat and grappling, demonstrations of the martial art are often associated with the use of weapons, including sword and shield (*valum parichayum*), short stick (*kurunthadi*) and long stick (*neduvadi*)..

Fabindia   CLOTHING, HOMEWARES
(Map p976; ☑ 0484-2217077; www.fabindia.com;
Napier St, Fort Cochin; ☺ 10.30am-8.30pm) Fine
Indian textiles, fabrics, clothes and house-
hold linen from this renowned brand.

Cinnamon   CLOTHING
(Map p976; Post Office Rd, Fort Cochin; ☺ 10am-
7pm Mon-Sat) Cinnamon sells gorgeous
Indian-designed clothing, jewellery and
homewares in an ultrachic white retail
space.

Tribes India   HANDICRAFTS
(Map p976; ☑ 0484-2215077; Post Office Rd, Head
Post Office, Fort Cochin; ☺ 10am-6.30pm Mon-Sat)
Tucked behind the post office, this TRIFED
(Ministry of Tribal Affairs) enterprise sells
tribal artefacts, paintings, shawls, figurines
etc, at reasonable fixed prices and the profits
go towards supporting the artisans.

❶ Information

INTERNET ACCESS
There are several internet cafes around Princess
St in Fort Cochin charging ₹40 per hour; many
homestays and hotels offer free wi-fi.

MEDICAL SERVICES
Lakeshore Hospital (☑ 0484-2701032; www.
lakeshorehospital.com; NH Bypass, Marudu)
Modern hospital 8km southeast of Ernakulam.

Medical Trust (Map p980; ☑ 0484-2358001;
www.medicaltrusthospital.com; MG Rd) Central
hospital.

MONEY
UAE Exchange (☺ 9.30am-6pm Mon-Fri, to
2pm Sat) Ernakulam (Map p980; ☑ 2383317;
MG Rd, Perumpillil Bldg); Ernakulam
(☑ 3067008; Chettupuzha Towers, PT Usha Rd
Junction); Fort Cochin (Map p976; ☑ 2216231;
Amravathi Rd) Foreign exchange and travellers
cheques.

POST
College Post Office (Map p980; ☑ 0484-
2369302; Convent Rd, Ernakulam; ☺ 9am-5pm
Mon-Sat)

Ernakulam Post Office (Map p980; ☑ 0484-
2355467; Hospital Rd; ☺ 9am-8pm Mon-Sat,
10am-5pm Sun) Also branches on MG Rd and
Broadway.

Main Post Office (Map p976; Post Office Rd,
Fort Cochin; ☺ 9am-5pm Mon-Fri, to 3pm Sat).

TOURIST INFORMATION
There's a tourist information counter at the
airport. Many places distribute a free brochure
that includes a map and walking tour entitled
Historical Places in Fort Cochin.

KTDC Tourist Reception Centre (Map p980;
☑ 0484-2353234; Shanmugham Rd, Ernakulam; ☺ 8am-7pm) Also organises tours. There's
another office at the jetty at Fort Cochin.

Tourist Desk Information Counter (www.
touristdesk.in) Ernakulam (Map p980;
☑ 9847044688, 0484-2371761; Boat Jetty;

MAJOR BUSES FROM ERNAKULAM

The following bus services operate from the KSRTC bus stand and Vyttila Mobility Hub.

DESTINATION	FARE (₹)	DURATION (HR)	FREQUENCY
Alleppey	52	1½	every 10min
Bengaluru	4600-1100	14	4 daily
Calicut	170	5	hourly
Chennai	590	16	1 daily, 2pm
Coimbatore	150	4½	hourly
Kannur	220-250	8	5 daily
Kanyakumari	230	8	2 daily
Kollam	114	3½	every 30min
Kothamangalam	40	2	every 10min
Kottayam	57	2	every 30min
Kumily (for Periyar)	130	5	8 daily
Mangalore	335	12	6.30pm & 9.30pm
Munnar	100	4½	every 30min
Thrissur	55	2	every 10min
Trivandrum	170	5	every 30min

MAJOR TRAINS FROM ERNAKULAM

DESTINATION	TRAIN NO & NAME	FARE (₹)	DURATION (HR)	DEPARTURE
Bengaluru	16525 Bangalore Express (A)	345/930/1335	13	5.35pm
Chennai	12624 Chennai Mail (A)	395/1035/1470	12	7.30pm
Delhi	12625 Kerala Express (B)	885/2275/3375	46	3.45pm
Goa (Madgaon)	16346 Netravathi Express (B)	415/1120/1620	15	2.10pm
Mumbai	16346 Netravathi Express (B)	615/1635/2400	27	2.10pm

Fares: sleeper/3AC/2AC; (A) departs from Ernakulam Town (B) departs Ernakulam Junction

⊘ 8am-6pm); Fort Cochin (Map p976; ☑ 0484-2216129; Tower Rd, Fort Cochin; ⊘ 8am-7pm) At this private tour agency, with offices at Ernakalum's ferry terminal and in Fort Cochin, the staff are extremely knowledgeable and helpful about Kochi and beyond. They run several popular and recommended tours, including a festival tour, and publish information on festivals and cultural events.

Tourist Police Ernakulam (Map p980; ☑ 0484-2353234; Shanmugham Rd; ⊘ 8am-6pm); Fort Cochin (Map p976; ☑ 0484-2215055; ⊘ 24hr)

❶ Getting There & Away

AIR

Kochi International Airport is a popular hub, with international flights to/from the Gulf States, Sri Lanka, the Maldives, Malaysia and Singapore.

On domestic routes, Jet Airways, Air India, Indigo and Spicejet fly direct daily to Chennai, Mumbai, Bengalaru, Hyderabad, Delhi and Trivandrum (but not Goa). Air India flies to Delhi daily and to Agatti in the Lakshadweep islands six times a week.

BUS

All long-distance services operate from Ernakulam. The **KSRTC bus stand** (Map p980; ☑ 2372033; ⊘ reservations 6am-10pm) still has a few services but most state-run and private buses pull into the massive new **Vyttila Mobility Hub** (☑ 2306611; www.vyttilamobilityhub.com; ⊘ 24hr), a state-of-the-art transport terminal about 2km east of Ernakulam Junction train station. Numerous private bus companies have super-deluxe, air-con, video and Volvo buses to long-distance destinations such as Bengaluru, Chennai, Mangalore, Trivandrum and Coimbatore; prices vary depending on the standard but the best buses are about 50% higher than government buses. Agents in Ernakulam and

Fort Cochin sell tickets. Private buses also use the Kaloor bus stand, 1km north of the city.

A prepaid autorickshaw from Vyttila costs ₹73 to the boat jetty, ₹190 to Fort Cochin and ₹370 to the airport.

TRAIN

Ernakulam has two train stations, Ernakulam Town and Ernakulam Junction. Reservations for both are made at the Ernakulam Junction **reservations office** (☑ 132; ⊘ 8am-8pm Mon-Sat, 8am-2pm Sun).

There are local and express trains to Trivandrum (2nd-class/sleeper/3AC ₹95/195/535, 4½ hours), via either Alleppey (₹50/170/535, 1½ hours) or Kottayam (₹55/140/485, 1½ hours). Trains also run to Thrissur (2nd/AC chair ₹60/255, 1½ hours), Calicut (sleeper/3AC/2AC ₹140/485/690, 4½ hours) and Kannur (₹220/535/735, 6½ hours).

❶ Getting Around

An above-ground **metro** (www.kochmetro.org) is under construction in Ernakalum, which will connect the airport with the city when completed. The first phase is due in 2016.

TO/FROM THE AIRPORT

Kochi International Airport (☑ 2610125; www.cochinairport.com) is at Nedumbassery, 30km northeast of Ernakulam. Air-con buses run between the airport and Fort Cochin (₹80, one hour, eight daily), some going via Ernakulam. Taxis to/from Ernakulam cost around ₹850, and to/from Fort Cochin around ₹1200, depending on the time of night.

BOAT

Ferries are the fastest and most enjoyable form of transport between Fort Cochin and the mainland. The jetty on the eastern side of Willingdon Island is called Embarkation; the west one, opposite Mattancherry, is Terminus; and the main stop at Fort Cochin is Customs, with another stop at the Mattancherry Jetty near the synagogue. One-way fares are ₹4 (₹6 between Ernakulam and Mattancherry).

Ernakulam

There are services to both Fort Cochin jetties (Customs and Mattancherry) every 25 to 50 minutes from Ernakulam's main jetty between 4.40am and 9.10pm.

Ferries also run every 20 minutes or so to Willingdon and Vypeen Islands.

Fort Cochin

Ferries run from Customs Jetty to Ernakulam regularly between 5am and 9.50pm. Ferries also hop between Customs Jetty and Willingdon Island 18 times a day.

Car and passenger ferries cross to Vypeen Island from Fort Cochin virtually nonstop.

LOCAL TRANSPORT

There are no regular bus services between Fort Cochin and Mattancherry Palace, but it's an enjoyable 30-minute walk through the busy warehouse area along Bazaar Rd. Autorickshaws should cost around ₹70, much less if you promise to look in a shop. Most short autorickshaw trips around Ernakulam shouldn't cost more than ₹50.

To get to Fort Cochin after ferries (and buses) stop running you'll need to catch a taxi or auto-rickshaw – Ernakulam Town train station to Fort Cochin should cost around ₹400; prepaid auto-rickshaws during the day cost ₹250.

Scooters (₹300 per day) and Enfields (₹400 to ₹600) can be hired from agents in Fort Cochin.

Around Kochi

Cherai Beach

On Vypeen Island and 25km from Fort Cochin, Cherai Beach makes a nice day trip or getaway from Kochi, especially if you hire a scooter or motorbike in Fort Cochin. The main beach entrance can get busy at times but with miles of lazy backwaters just a few hundred metres from the seafront, it's a pleasant place to explore.

To get here from Fort Cochin, catch the vehicle-ferry to Vypeen Island (₹3) and either hire an autorickshaw from the jetty (around ₹400) or catch one of the frequent buses (₹15, one hour) and get off at Cherai village, 1km from the beach. Buses also go here direct from Ernakulam via the Vallar-padam bridge.

🛏 Sleeping & Eating

Brighton Beach House   GUESTHOUSE $$
(☑ 9946565555; www.brightonbeachhouse.org; d ₹2000-2500) Brighton Beach House has five basic rooms in a small building right near the shore. The beach is rocky here, but the place is filled with hammocks to loll in, and has a neat, elevated stilt-restaurant that serves perfect sunset views with dinner.

Cherai Beach Resort   RESORT $$
(☑ 0484-2416949; www.cheraibeachresorts.com; villas from ₹3500, with AC from ₹4500; ❄@) This collection of distinctive cottages scattered around a meandering lagoon has the beach on one side and backwaters on the other. Bungalows are individually designed using natural materials, with either curving walls or split-levels or lookouts onto the backwaters. There's even a tree growing inside one room.

Les 3 Elephants   RESORT $$$
(☑ 0484-2480005, 9349174341; www.3elephants.in; Convent St; cottages ₹5000-10,000; ❄🛜) Hidden back from the beach but with the backwaters on your doorstep, Les 3 Elephants is a superb French-run ecoresort. The 11 beautifully designed boutique cottages are all different but have private sitouts, thoughtful personal touches and lovely backwater views out to Chinese fishing nets. The restaurant serves home-cooked French-Indian fare. Worth the trip.

Chilliout Cafe   CAFE $$
(mains ₹160-320; ⊙ 9am-late Oct-May) For continental-style comfort food by the beach (think burgers, pizzas and barbecue) Chilliout Cafe is a cool hang-out with sea breezes and a relaxed vibe.

Tripunithura

At Tripunithura, 16km southeast of Ernakulam, **Hill Palace Museum** (☑ 0484-2781113; admission ₹20; ⊙ 9am-12.30pm & 2-4.30pm Tue-Sun) was formerly the residence of the Kochi royal family and is an impressive 49-building palace complex. It now houses the collections of the royal families, as well as 19th-century oil paintings, old coins, sculptures and paintings, and temple models. From Ernakulam catch the bus to Tripunithura from MG Rd or Shanmugham Rd, behind the Tourist Reception Centre (₹5 to ₹10, 45 minutes); an autorickshaw should cost around ₹300 return with one-hour waiting time.

Parur & Chennamangalam

Nowhere is the tightly woven religious cloth that is India more apparent than in Parur, 35km north of Kochi. Here, one of the oldest synagogues (admission ₹5; ⊙9am-5pm Tue-Sun) in Kerala, at Chennamangalam, 8km from Parur, has been fastidiously renovated. Inside you can see door and ceiling wood reliefs in dazzling colours, while just outside lies one of the oldest tombstones in India, inscribed with the Hebrew date corresponding to 1269. The Jesuits first arrived in Chennamangalam in 1577 and there's a Jesuit church and the ruins of a Jesuit college nearby. Aloso here is a Hindu temple on a hill overlooking the Periyar River, a 16th-century mosque, and Muslim and Jewish burial grounds.

In Parur town, you'll find the agraharam (place of Brahmins) – a small street of closely packed and brightly coloured houses originally settled by Tamil Brahmins.

Parur is compact, but Chennamangalam is best visited with a guide. Travel agencies in Fort Cochin can organise tours.

Thrissur (Trichur)

☏0487 / POP 315,600

While the rest of Kerala has its fair share of celebrations, untouristy, slightly chaotic Thrissur is the cultural cherry on the festival cake. With a list of energetic festivals as long as a temple elephant's trunk, the region supports several institutions that nurse the dying classical Keralan performing arts back to health. Centred on a large park (known as the 'Round') and temple complex, Thrissur is home to a Nestorian Christian community whose denomination dates to the 3rd century AD.

◉ Sights & Activities

Thrissur is renowned for its central temple, as well as for its numerous impressive churches, including the massive Our Lady of Lourdes Cathedral, towering, whitewashed Puttanpalli (New) Church and the Chaldian (Nestorian) Church.

Vadakkunathan Kshetram Temple
HINDU TEMPLE

Finished in classic Keralan architecture and one of the oldest Hindu temples in the

Thrissur (Trichur)

Thrissur (Trichur)

◉ Sights
1 Archaeology Museum	B1
2 Vadakkunathan Kshetram Temple	B2

◉ Sleeping
3 Hotel Luciya Palace	A3
4 Pathans Hotel	A3
5 YMCA International Guesthouse	B2

◉ Eating
6 India Gate	B1
7 Navaratna Restaurant	A2
Pathans Restaurant	(see 4)

ⓘ Transport
8 KSRTC Bus Stand	A4
9 Priyadarshini (North) Bus Stand	B1
10 Sakthan Thampuran Bus Stand	B4

state, Vadakkunathan Kshetram Temple crowns the hill at the epicentre of Thrissur.

Only Hindus are allowed inside, though the mound surrounding the temple has sweeping views and the surroudning park is a popular spot to linger.

Archaeology Museum MUSEUM
(adult/child ₹20/5, camera/video ₹50/250; ⊘9.30am-1pm & 2-4.30pm Tue-Sun) The refurbished Archaeology Museum is housed in the wonderful 200-year-old Sakthan Thampuran Palace. Its mix of artefacts include 12th-century Keralan bronze sculptures, giant earthenware pots, weaponry, coins and a lovely carved chessboard. To the side is a shady heritage garden.

✦✦ Festivals & Events

In a state where festivals are a way of life, Thrissur stands out for temple revelry.

Thypooya Maholsavam FESTIVAL
(⊘Jan/Feb) The festival stars a *kavadiyattam* (a form of ritualistic dance) procession in which dancers carry tall, ornate structures called *kavadis*.

Uthralikavu Pooram FESTIVAL
(⊘Mar/Apr) The climactic day of this event sees 20 elephants circling the shrine.

Thrissur Pooram FESTIVAL
(⊘Apr/May) At Vadakkumnathan Kshetram Temple, this is the largest and most colourful and biggest of Kerala's temple festivals with wonderful processions of caparisoned elephants.

🛏 Sleeping

Pathans Hotel HOTEL $
(⊘0487-2425620; www.pathansresidentialhotel. in; Round South; ⊘s/d from ₹587/784, with AC ₹1045/1450; ✸) No-frills rooms at no-frills prices and the location is unbeatable across from the central park. The basic, cleanish and secure rooms are on the 5th and 6th floors (served by a painfully slow lift) and have TVs and occasional hot water.

YMCA International Guesthouse GUESTHOUSE $
(⊘0487-2331190; www.ymcathrissur.org; Palace Rd; d ₹700, with AC ₹1050) Clean, comfortable and secure. A good budget choice when it's not full with school groups.

Hotel Luciya Palace HOTEL $$
(⊘0487-2424731; www.hotelluciyapalace.com; Marar Rd; s/d with AC ₹2250/3100, ste ₹5625; ✸) In a cream, colonial-themed building, this is

one of the few places in town that has some character and the spacious, modern air-con rooms are good value. It's in a quiet cul-de-sac but close to the temple and town centre action, and has a neat lawn garden, a decent restaurant and a busy bar.

🍴 Eating & Drinking

India Gate INDIAN $
(Palace Rd; dishes ₹80-130; ⊘8am-10pm) In the Kalliyath Royal Square building, this bright, pure-veg place has a vintage feel and an extraordinary range of dosas, including jam, cheese and cashew versions. In the same complex is a Chinese restaurant (China Gate) and a fast-food joint (Celebrations).

Pathans Restaurant INDIAN $
(1st fl, Round South; dishes ₹30-80; ⊘6.30am-9.30pm) On the 1st floor of the Pathans Hotel building, this easy-going place opens early for a cheap breakfast and is popular with families for lunch (thalis ₹50).

Navaratna Restaurant MULTICUISINE $$
(Round West; dishes ₹100-180; ⊘noon-9.30pm) Cool, dark and intimate, this is one of the classiest dining experiences in town, with seating on raised platforms. Downstairs is veg and upstairs is nonveg, with lots of North Indian specialities, Chinese and a few Keralan dishes.

ℹ Information

There are several ATMs and internet cafes around town.
DTPC Office (⊘0487-2320800; Palace Rd; ⊘10am-5pm Mon-Sat) You might be able to pick up some local brochures from this tourist office.

ℹ Getting There & Away

BUS

State buses leave around every 30 minutes from the KSRTC bus stand bound for Trivandrum (₹214, 7½ hours), Ernakulam (Kochi, ₹65, two hours), Calicut (₹102, 3½ hours), Palakkad (₹57, 1½ hours) and Kottayam (₹105, four hours). Hourly buses go to Coimbatore (₹94, three hours).

Regular services also chug along to Guruvayur (₹26, one hour), Irinjalakuda (₹25, one hour) and Cheruthuruthy (₹28, 1½ hours). Two private bus stands (Sakthan Thampuran and Priyadarshini) have more frequent buses to these destinations, though the chaos involved in navigating each station hardly makes using them worthwhile.

TRAIN

Services run regularly to Ernakulam (2nd-class/ AC chair ₹60/255, 1½ hours), Calicut (₹70/255, three hours) and Coimbatore (₹90/305, three hours).

Around Thrissur

Kerala Kalamandalam CULTURAL PROGRAM
(📞04884262418; www.kalamandalam.org; courses per month ₹2500; ⊙ Jun-Mar) Using an ancient Gurukula system of learning, students undergo intensive study in Kathakali, *mohiniyattam* (dance of the enchantress), Kootiattam, percussion, voice and violin. A Day with the Masters (₹1000, including lunch) is a morning program allowing visitors to tour the theatre and classes and see various art and cultural presentations. Email to book in advance. It's 26km north of Thrissur.

Natana Kairali Research & Performing Centre for Traditional Arts CULTURAL PROGRAM
(📞0480-2825559; www.natanakairali.org) This school, 20km south of Thrissur near Irinjalakuda, offers training in traditional arts, including rare forms of puppetry and dance..

🛏 Sleeping

River Retreat GUESTHOUSE $$
(📞0488-4262244; www.riverretreat.in; Palace Rd, Cheruthuruthy; d from ₹3480-6540, ste ₹7800, cottage ₹8580; ❄ 🛜 🛋) River Retreat is an excellent hotel and ayurvedic resort in the former summer palace of the Maharajas of Cochin. Along with ayurvedic treatments, facilities include a pool, gym and business centre. It's about 30km north of Thrissur.

NORTHERN KERALA

Kozhikode (Calicut)

📞 0495 / POP 432,100

Northern Kerala's largest city, Calicut was always a prosperous trading town and was once the capital of the formidable Zamorin dynasty. Vasco da Gama first landed near here in 1498, on his way to snatch a share of the subcontinent for king and country (Portugal that is). These days, trade depends mostly on exporting Indian labour to the Middle East, while agriculture and the timber industry are economic mainstays. For travellers it's mainly a jumping-off

point for Wayanad or for the long trip over the ghats to Mysuru (Mysore) or Bengaluru (Bangalore.)

👁 Sights

Mananchira Square, a large central park, was the former courtyard of the Zamorins and preserves the original spring-fed tank. South of the centre, the 650-year-old **Kuttichira Mosque** is in an attractive wooden four-storey building that is supported by impressive wooden pillars and painted brilliant aquamarine, blue and white. The central **Church of South India** was established by Swiss missionaries in 1842 and has unique Euro-Keralan architecture.

About 1km west of Mananchira Square is Kozhikode Beach – not much for swimming but good enough for a sunset promenade.

🛏 Sleeping

Alakapuri HOTEL $
(📞0495-2723451; MM Ali Rd; s/d from ₹700/1300, with AC from ₹1600; ❄) Built motel-style around a green lawn (complete with fountain!) this place is set back from a busy market area. Various rooms are a little scuffed and dingy, but reasonable value.

Beach Hotel HOTEL $$
(📞9745062055, 0495-2762055; www.beachheritage.com; Beach Rd; r with seaview or AC inc breakfast ₹3500; ❄ 📶) Built in 1890 to house the Malabar British Club, this is a slightly worn but charming 10-room hotel. Some have bathtubs and secluded sea-facing verandahs; others have original polished wooden floors and private balconies. All are tastefully furnished and drip with character.

Hyson Heritage HOTEL $$
(📞0495-4081000; www.hysonheritage.com; Bank Rd; s/d inc breakfast from ₹2700/3600; ❄ 🛜) You get a bit of swank for your rupee at this central business hotel. Rooms are spick and span and shielded from the main road. There's a good restaurant and a gym.

⭐ **Harivihar** BOUTIQUE HOMESTAY $$$
(📞9388676054, 0495-2765865; www.harivihar.com; Bilathikulam; s/d incl meals €110/140; 🛜) In northern Calicut, the ancestral home of the Kadathanadu royal family is as serene as it gets, a traditional Keralan family compound with pristine lawns. The seven rooms are large and beautifully furnished with dark-wood antiques. There's an ayurvedic

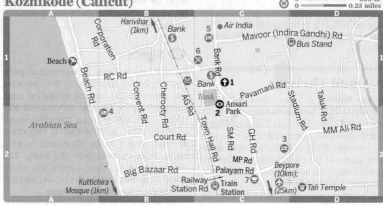

Kozhikode (Calicut)

and yoga centre, with packages available. The pure veg food is delicious and cooking classes are available. It's hard to find (taxi drivers are largely baffled), so call ahead.

🍴 Eating & Drinking

Paragon Restaurant　　　　　INDIAN $$
(Kannur Rd; dishes ₹125-340; ⊙8am-midnight, lunch from noon) You might struggle to find a seat at this always-packed restaurant, founded in 1939. The overwhelming menu is famous for fish dishes such as fish in tamarind sauce, and its legendary chicken biryani.

Salkaram & Hut　　　　　INDIAN $$
(Beach Rd; mains ₹110-290; ⊙7am-10.30pm) At the back of the Beach Hotel are two restaurants with the same menu: the air-con Salkaram, and the cool open-sided bamboo 'hut' restaurant-bar serving a big range of fish and chicken dishes and Malabari cuisine. It's a breezy place for a cold beer..

Indian Coffee House　　　　　CAFE
(GH Rd; ₹10-60; ⊙8am-9pm) For tasty snacks and good coffee.

ⓘ Information

There are HDFC and State Bank of India ATMs in town, and several internet cafes.

ⓘ Getting There & Away

AIR

Calicut airport is about 25km south of the city in Karipur. It serves major domestic routes as well as international flights to the Gulf.

Spicejet has the best domestic connections with direct flights to Mumbai, Bangalore and Chennai. **Air India** (📞2771974; 5/2521 Bank Rd, Eroth Centre) flies to Kochi and Coimbatore. **Jet Airways** (📞271 2375; Calicut Airport) has one daily flight to Mumbai. Flights to Goa go via Bangalore or Mumbai.

BUS

The new KSRTC **bus stand** (Mavoor Rd) has government buses to Bengaluru (Bangalore, via Mysore, ₹335-500, eight hours, 10 daily), Mangalore (₹300, seven hours, three daily) and to Ooty (₹130, 5½ hours, 5am & 6.45am). There are frequent buses to Thrissur (₹100, 3½ hours) and Kochi (₹180, four hours, eight daily). For Wayanad district, buses leave every 15 minutes heading to Sultanbatheri (₹75, three hours) via Kalpetta (₹60, two hours). Private buses for various long-distance locations also use this stand.

TRAIN

The train station is 1km south of Mananchira Sq. There are frequent trains to Kannur (2nd-class/

sleeper/3AC ₹60/140/485, two hours), Mangalore (sleeper/3AC/2AC ₹195/535/735, five hours), Ernakulam (₹165/485/690, 4½ hours) via Thrissur (₹200/535/735, three hours), and all the way to Trivandrum (₹275/705/985, 11 hours).

Heading southeast, trains go to Coimbatore (sleeper/3AC/2AC ₹170/535/735, 4½ hours), via Palakkad (₹140/485/690, 3½ hours).

❶ Getting Around

Calicut has a glut of autorickshaws and most are happy to use the meter. It costs about ₹40 from the station to the KSRTC bus stand or most hotels. An autorickshaw/taxi to the airport costs around ₹400/600.

Wayanad Wildlife Sanctuary

☑ 04936 / POP 816,500

Many Keralans rate the Wayanad region as the most beautiful part of their state. Encompassing part of a remote forest reserve that spills into Tamil Nadu and Karnataka, Wayanad's landscape combines epic mountain scenery, rice paddies of ludicrous green, skinny betel nut trees, bamboo, red earth, spiky ginger fields, and rubber, cardamom and coffee plantations. Foreign travellers are making it here in increasing numbers, partly because it provides easy access between Mysuru (Mysore) or Bengaluru (Bangalore) and Kerala, but it's still fantastically unspoilt and satisfyingly remote. It's also an excellent place to spot wild elephants.

The 345-sq-km sanctuary has two separate pockets – Muthanga in the east bordering Tamil Nadu, and Tholpetty in the north bordering Karnataka. Three main towns in Wayanad district make good bases and transport hubs for exploring the sanctuary – Kalpetta in the south, Sultanbatheri (Sultan Battery) in the east and Mananthavadi in the northwest – though the best of the accommodation is scattered throughout the region. Most hotels and homestays can arrange guided jeep tours to various parts of Wayanad.

◉ Sights & Activities

★ Wayanad Wildlife Sanctuary
NATURE RESERVE

(www.wayanadsanctuary.org; admission to each part Indian/foreigner ₹115/300, camera/video ₹40/225; ☺ 7-10am & 3-5pm) Entry to both parts of the sanctuary is only permitted as part of a jeep safari, which can be arranged at the sanctuary entrances. At the time of research there was no trekking in the park for safety reasons. Both Tholpetty and Muthanga close during the June to August monsoon period.

At Tholpetty (☑ 04935-250853; jeep tours ₹500; ☺ 7-10am & 3-5pm), the two-hour jeep tours can be rough going but are a great way to spot wildlife. Similar tours are available at Muthanga (☑ 0493-6271010; jeep tours ₹500). At both locations arrive at least an hour before the morning or afternoon openings to register and secure a vehicle, as there are a limited number of guides and jeeps permitted in the park at one time.

Thirunelly Temple
HINDU TEMPLE

(☺ dawn-dusk) Thought to be one of the oldest on the subcontinent, Thirunelly Temple is 10km from Tholpetty. Non-Hindus cannot enter, but it's worth visiting for the otherworldly cocktail of ancient and intricate pillars. Follow the path behind the temple to the stream known as Papanasini, where Hindus believe you can wash away all your sins.

Edakal Caves
CAVES

(adult/child ₹20/10, camera ₹30; ☺ 9am-4pm Tue-Sun) The highlight of these remote hilltop 'caves' – more accurately a small series of caverns – is the ancient collection of petroglyphs in the top cave, thought to date back over 3000 years. From the car park near Ambalavayal it's a steep 20-minute walk up a winding road to the ticket window, then another steep climb up to the light-filled top chamber. On a clear day there are exceptional views out over the Wayanad district. The caves get crowded on weekends and are closed Monday.

Wayanad Heritage Museum
MUSEUM

(Ambalavayal; admission ₹20; ☺ 9am-5pm) In the small village of Ambalavayal, about 5km from Edva Caves, this museum exhibits headgear, weapons, pottery, carved stone and other artefacts dating back to the 15th century that shed light on Wayanad's significant Adivasi population.

Uravu
HANDICRAFTS CENTRE

(☑ 0493-6231400; www.uravu.net; Thrikkaippetta; ☺ 8.30am-5pm Mon-Sat) ✎ Around 6km southeast of Kalpetta a collective of workers create all sorts of artefacts from bamboo. You can visit the artists' workshops, where they work on looms, paintings and carvings, and support their work by buying vases, lampshades, bangles and baskets.

Kannur Ayurvedic Centre   AYURVEDA
(☑0436203001; www.ayurvedawayanad.com; Kalpetta; massage from ₹1200, yoga & meditation ₹1200; ☺yoga classes 6-7am) For rejuvenation and curative ayurvedic treatments, visit this small, government-certified and family-run clinic, in the backstreets of Kalpetta. Accommodation and yoga classes available.

Trekking
There are some top opportunities for independent trekking around the district (though not in the wildlife sanctuary itself). Top treks include **Chembra Peak** (2100m), the area's tallest summit; **Vellarimala**, with great views and lots of wildlife-spotting opportunities; and **Pakshipathalam**, a seven-hour return mountain trek in the northern Brahmagiri Hills that takes you to a formation of large boulders high in the forest. Permits and guides are mandatory and can be arranged at forest offices in South or North Wayanad or through your accommodation. The standard cost for permit and guide is ₹2500 for up to five people – try to arrange a group in advance. The **DTPC office** in Kalpetta also organises trekking guides and transport.

🛏 Sleeping & Eating
There's plenty of accommodation in Wayanad's towns, but the isolated homestays or resort accommodation scattered throughout the region are better choices.

🛏 Kalpetta
PPS Residency   HOTEL $
(☑04936-203431; www.ppstouristhome.com; Kalpetta; s/d ₹400/500, d with AC ₹1500; ❄) This friendly budget place in the middle of Kalpetta has a variety of reasonably clean rooms in a motel-like compound as well as a multicuisine restaurant. Helpful management can arrange trips around Wayanad.

Haritagiri   HOTEL $$
(☑04936-203145; www.hotelharitagiri.com; Kalpetta; s/d incl breakfast from ₹1450/1850, with AC from ₹1850/2500; ❄🛜🏊) Set back from Kalpetta's busy main streets, this is a comfortable midrange option, and some of the rooms have balconies. There are two restaurants, a gym and an ayurvedic 'village' on-site.

🛏 Sultanbatheri
Mint Flower Residency   HOTEL $$
(☑04936-222206, 9745222206; www.mintflower residency.com; Sultan Batheri; s/d ₹830/1375, with AC ₹1075/1670) The new budget annexe of Mint Flower Hotel is in great condition. It's no-frills but rooms are spotless and come with hot water and TV.

Issac's Hotel Regency   HOTEL $$
(☑04936-220512; www.issacsregency.com; Sultanbatheri; s/d/tr from ₹1150/1600/1800, with AC from ₹1550/2000/2250; ❄@🏊) This quiet and no-nonsense place near the local bus stand has routine, large and relatively tidy rooms in a U-shaped building.

🛏 Around Wayanad
★**Varnam Homestay**   HOMESTAY $$
(☑9745745860, 04935-215666; www.varnam homestay.com; Kadungamalayil House, Payyampally; s/d incl meals ₹1500/2400, villa ₹1800/3000; ❄🛜) This oasis of peace and calm is a lovely place to stay only a few kilometres from Karikulum in northern Wayanad. Varghese and Beena will look after you with Wayanad stories, local information and delicious home-cooking with organic farm-fresh ingredients. Rooms are in a traditional family home or a newer elevated 'tree house' villa, and the property is surrounded by jungle and spice plantations. Forest drives and trekking to tribal villages can be arranged.

Greenex Farms   RESORT $$
(☑9645091512; www.greenexfarms.com; Chundale Estate Rd, Moovatty; r ₹2250-4500) Greenex Farms is a wonderfully remote-feeling place surrounded by spice and tea plantations about 8km southwest of Kalpetta. Each of the private cottages is individually designed with separate lounge, bathroom, balconies and superb views.

Pachyderm Palace   GUESTHOUSE $$
(☑9847044688, reservations 0484-2371761; www. touristdesk.in/pachydermpalace.htm; Tholpetty; s/d incl meals ₹2000/4000, tree house ₹4000) This fine old Keralan house lies just outside the gate of Tholpetty Wildlife Sanctuary – handy for early-morning treks, tours and wildlife viewing. The varied rooms include two secluded stilt-bungalow 'tree houses' surrounded by forest and another private cottage. Venu is a stupendous cook, and his son Dilip is a great guide who can organise village and mountain treks.

Wayanad District

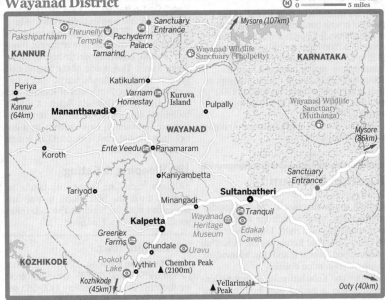

Ente Veedu   HOMESTAY $$

(☎ 9446834834, 0493-5220008; www.enteveedu. co.in; Panamaram; r incl breakfast ₹2500-3500, with AC ₹3500-4000; @ 🖥) Isolated and set in a lovely location overlooking sprawling banana plantations and rice paddies, this homestay halfway between Kalpetta and Mananthavady is definitely worth seeking out. There are several large rooms, two bamboo-lined rooms with private balconies, hammocks and wicker lounges to enjoy the sensational views. Lunch and dinner are available for ₹250/350 veg/nonveg.

★**Tranquil**   HOMESTAY $$$

(☎ 04936220244; www.tranquilresort.com; Kuppamudi Estate, Kolagapara; full board s/d from ₹14,400/13,750, tree house ₹17,750/24,600, tree villa ₹18,300/26,400; 🖥 🏊) This wonderfully serene and exclusive homestay is in the middle of an incredibly lush 160 hectares of pepper, coffee, vanilla and cardamom plantations. The elegant house has sweeping verandahs filled with plants and handsome furniture, and there are two tree houses that may be the finest in the state. A network of marked walking trails meander around the plantation.

ℹ Information

The **DTPC office** (☎ 04936202134; www.dtpc-wayanad.com; Kalpetta; ⊙ 10am-5pm Mon-Sat) at Kalpetta can help organise tours, permits and trekking. There are UAE Exchange offices in Kalpetta and Sultanbatheri, and ATMs can be found in each of the three main towns.

ℹ Getting There & Away

Although remote, Wayanad is easily accessible by bus from Calicut and Kannur in Kerala, and from Mysore (Karnataka) and Ooty (Tamil Nadu). Buses brave the winding roads – including nine spectacular hairpin bends – between Calicut and Kalpetta (₹60 to ₹76, two hours) every 15 minutes, with some continuing on to Sultanbatheri (₹80, three hours) and others to Mananthavadi (₹87, three hours). Hourly buses run between Kannur and Mananthavadi (₹70, 2½ hours).

From Sultanbatheri, an 8am bus heads out for Ooty (₹100, four hours), with a second one passing through town at around 12.45pm. Buses run from Kalpetta to Mysore (₹130 to ₹160, four hours, hourly), via Sultanbatheri, but note that the border gate is closed between 7pm and 6am. There are four daily buses to Mysore (₹144, three hours) on the northern route from Mananthavadi, where the border is open 24 hours.

ℹ️ Getting Around

The Wayanad district is quite spread out but plenty of private buses connect the main towns of Mananthavadi, Kalpetta and Sultanbatheri every 10 to 20 minutes during daylight hours (₹15 to ₹25, 45 minutes to one hour). From Mananthavadi, regular buses also head to Tholpetty (₹15, one hour). You can hire jeeps or taxis to get between towns for ₹600 to ₹800 each way, or hire a vehicle to tour the region for around ₹2000 per day.

There are plenty of autorickshaws and taxis for short hops within the towns.

Kannur & Around

📞 0497 / POP 1.2 MILLION

Kerala's northern coast is far less tourist-ed than the south, which for many is an attraction in its own right. The main draw in this part of coastal Kerala are the beautiful, undeveloped beaches and the enthralling *theyyam* possession rituals.

Under the Kolathiri rajas, Kannur (Cannanore) was a major port bristling with international trade – explorer Marco Polo christened it a 'great emporium of spice trade'. Since then, the usual colonial suspects, including the Portuguese, Dutch and British, have had a go at exerting their influence on the region. Today it is an unexciting, though agreeable, town known mostly for its weaving industry and cashew trade.

This is a predominantly Muslim area, so local sensibilities should be kept in mind: wear a sarong over your bikini on the beach.

👁️ Sights & Activities

Kannur's main town beach is the 4km-long **Payyambalam Beach** (beach park ₹5, camera ₹25), which starts about 1.5km east of the train station, just past the military cantonment. The beach park gets busy in the evening when families and couples come down to watch the sunset and picnic.

Loknath Weavers'
Co-operative   HANDICRAFTS WORKSHOP
(📞0497-2726330; ⏰8.30am-5.30pm Mon-Sat) FREE Established in 1955, this is one of the oldest cooperatives in Kannur and occupies a large building busily clicking with the sound of looms. You can stop by for a quick (free) tour; the shop here displays the fruits of the workers' labours (with the obligatory sales pitch). It's 4km south of Kannur town.

Kerala Dinesh
Beedi Co-Operative   HANDICRAFTS WORKSHOP
(📞0497-2835280; www.keraladinesh.com; ⏰8am-6pm Tue-Sat) FREE The Kannur region is known for the manufacture of *beedis,* those tiny Indian cigarettes deftly rolled inside green leaves. This is one of the largest and purportedly best manufacturers, with a factory at Thottada, 7km south of Kannur and about 4km from Thottada Beach. A skilled individual can roll up to 1000 a day! Visitors are welcome to look around; an autorickshaw should cost around ₹120 return from Kannur town.

🛏️ Sleeping & Eating

Although there are plenty of hotels in Kannur town, the best places to stay are homestays near the beach at Thottada (8km south) and towards Thalassery.

🛏️ Kannur Town

Hotel Meridian Palace   HOTEL $
(📞9995999547, 0497-2701676; www.hotelmeridianpalace.com; Bellard Rd; s/d from ₹400/550, deluxe ₹850/1000, with AC ₹1400-1700; ❄️) In the market area opposite the main train station, this is hardly palatial but it's friendly enough and offers a cornucopia of clean budget rooms and a Punjabi restaurant.

Mascot Beach Resort   HOTEL $$
(📞0497-2708445;   www.mascotresort.com;   d ₹2400, with AC from ₹3600, ste ₹7200; ❄️@🛜🏊) All rooms are sea-facing at this compact, slightly faded midrange hotel looking over the small, rocky Baby Beach. Facilities are good, including a pool with a view and the seaside Mermaid restaurant.

Hotel Odhen's   MALABAR $
(Onden Rd; meals ₹30-60; ⏰8.30am-5pm) This popular local restaurant in Kannur's market area is usually packed at lunchtime. The speciality is Malabar cuisine, including tasty seafood curries and banana-leaf thalis.

🛏️ Thottada Beach & Around

⭐**Blue Mermaid Homestay**   HOMESTAY $$
(📞9497300234; www.bluemermaid.in; Thottada Beach; s/d inc breakfast & dinner ₹2000/3000, d with AC ₹3600; ❄️🛜) With a prime location among the palms facing Thottada Beach, Blue Mermaid is a charming and immaculate guesthouse with rooms in a traditional home, bright air-con rooms in a newer building and a whimsical stilted 'honeymoon cottage'. Friendly young owners cook

up fine Keralan meals, with breakfast and dinner included.

Waves Beach Resort
HOMESTAY $$

(☎9495050850; www.wavesbeachresort.co.in; Adikadalayai, Thottada Beach; s/d incl meals ₹2000/3000; 🖢) Crashing waves will lull you to sleep at this very cute pair of hexagonal laterite brick huts overlooking a semi-private little crescent beach. There are four rooms here (two up, two down). The welcoming owners, Seema and Arun, also have rooms in two other nearby properties, including cheaper rooms in an old Keralan house.

Costa Malabari
GUESTHOUSE $$

(☎09447775691, reservations 0484-2371761; www.touristdesk.in/costamalabari; Thottada Beach; s/d incl meals ₹3000-3500; 🗙🖢) Surrounded by lush greenery on a hill back from the beach, Costa Malabari pioneered tourism in this area. There are spacious rooms in an old hand-loom factory, and extra rooms are offered in two other nearby bungalows. The home-cooked Keralan food is plentiful. Manager Kurien is an expert on the *theyyam* ritual and can help arrange a visit.

Kannur Beach House
HOMESTAY $$

(☎0497-2708360, 9847184535; www.kannurbeachhouse.com; Thottada Beach; s/d ₹2400/3400) The original beachfront homestay is a traditional Keralan building with handsome wooden shutters, but the rooms are looking a little worn. Still, you can enjoy sensational ocean sunset views from your porch or balcony. A small lagoon separates the house from the beach. Breakfast and dinner included.

Ezhara Beach House
HOMESTAY $$

(☎0497-2835022; www.ezharabeachhouse.com; 7/347 Ezhara Kadappuram; s/d incl meals ₹1250/2500; 🖢) Fronting the unspoilt Kizhunna Ezhara beach, midway between Kannur and Thalassery railway stations (11km from each) the blue Ezhara Beach House is run by no-nonsense Hyacinth. The five rooms are simple but the house has character.

ℹ Getting There & Away

BUS

Kannur has several bus stands: the enormous central bus stand – is the place to catch private and some government buses, but most long-distance buses still use the KSRTC bus stand near the Caltex junction, 1km northeast of the train station.

There are daily buses to Mysore (₹200, eight hours, six daily), Madikeri (₹80, 2½ hours, 11am) and Ooty (via Wayanad, ₹225, nine hours, 7.30am & 10pm). For the Wayanad region, buses leave every hour from the central bus stand to Mananthavadi (₹80, 2½ hours).

For Thottada Beach, take bus No 29 (₹8) from Plaza Junction opposite the train station and get off at Adikatalayi village.

THEYYAM

Kerala's most popular ritualistic art form, *theyyam* is believed to pre-date Hinduism, originating from folk dances performed during harvest celebrations. An intensely local ritual, it's often performed in *kavus* (sacred groves) throughout northern Kerala.

Theyyam refers both to the shape of the deity/hero portrayed, and to the actual ritual. There are around 450 different *theyyams,* each with a distinct costume, made up of face paint, bracelets, breastplates, skirts, garlands and exuberant, intricately crafted headdresses that can be up to 6m or 7m tall. During performances, each protagonist loses his physical identity and speaks, moves and blesses the devotees as if he were that deity. Frenzied dancing and wild drumming create an atmosphere in which a deity indeed might, if it so desired, manifest itself in human form.

During October to May there are annual rituals at each of the hundreds of *kavus*. *Theyyams* are often held to bring good fortune to important events such as marriages and housewarmings. The best place for visitors to see *theyyam* is in village temples in the Kannur region of northern Kerala (most frequently between late November and mid-April). In peak times (December to February) there should be a *theyyam* ritual happening somewhere almost every night.

Although tourists are welcome to attend, this is not a dance performance but a religious ritual, and the usual rules of temple behaviour apply: dress appropriately, avoid disturbing participants and villagers; refrain from displays of public affection. Photography is permitted, but avoid using a flash. For details on where and when, ask at your guesthouse or contact Kurien at Costa Malabari in Thottada Beach..

TRAIN

There are frequent daily trains to Calicut (2nd-class/AC chair ₹60/255, 1½ hours), Ernakulam (sleeper/3AC/2AC ₹₹220/535/735, 6½ hours) and Alleppey (₹245/625/870). Heading north there are express trains to Mangalore (sleeper/3AC/2AC ₹140/485/690, three hours) and up to Goa (sleeper/3AC/2AC ₹350/910/1285, eight hours).

Bekal & Around

♪ 0467

Bekal and nearby Palakunnu and Udma, in Kerala's far north, have some long white-sand beaches begging for DIY exploration. The area is gradually being colonised by glitzy five-star resorts catering to fresh-from-the-Gulf millionaires, but it's still worth the trip for off-the-beaten-track adventurers.

The laterite-brick Bekal Fort (Indian/foreigner ₹5/100; ⊘8am-5pm), built between 1645 and 1660, sits on Bekal's rocky headland and houses a small Hindu temple and plenty of goats. Next door, Bekal Beach (admission ₹5) encompasses a grassy park and a long, beautiful stretch of sand that turns into a circus on weekends and holidays when local families descend here for rambunctious leisure time. Isolated Kappil Beach, 6km north of Bekal, is a beautiful, lonely stretch of fine sand and calm water, but beware of shifting sandbars.

Apart from the five-star Vivanta by Taj and Lalit hotels in Bekal, there are lots of cheap, poor-quality hotels scattered between Kanhangad (12km south) and Kasaragod (10km north), with a few notable exceptions.

Nirvana@Bekal   COTTAGES $$

(✆9446463088, 0467-2272900; www.nirvana-bekal.com; Bekal Fort Rd; d incl breakfast ₹1800-4700; ✴) Right below the walls of Bekal Fort, these laterite brick cottages in a beachfront palm-filled garden are the best value in town. There's a restaurant, ayurvedic treatments and even a cricket bowling machine!

★ Neeleshwar Hermitage   RESORT $$$

(✆0467-2287510; www.neeleshwarhermitage.com; Ozhinhavalappu, Neeleshwar; s/d cottages from ₹13,300/15,800, seaview ₹21,000/22,800; ✴✺🌐) This spectacular beachfront ecoresort consists of 16 beautifully designed thatch-roof cottages modelled on Keralan fisherman's huts but with modern comforts like iPod docks and a five-star price tag. Built according to the principles of Kerala Vastu, the resort has an infinity pool, nearly 5 hectares of lush gardens fragrant with frangipani, superb organic food and yoga programs.

ⓘ Getting There & Around

A couple of local trains stop at Fort Bekal station, right on Bekal Beach. Kanhangad, 12km south, and Kasaragod, 10km to the north, are major train stops. Frequent buses run from Bekal to both Kanhangad and Kasaragod (around ₹12, 20 minutes), from where you can pick up major trains to Mangalore, Goa or south to Kochi. An autorickshaw from Bekal Junction to Kappil Beach is around ₹60.

OFF THE BEATEN TRACK

VALIYAPARAMBA BACKWATERS

Kerala's 'northern backwaters' offer an intriguing alternative to better-known waterways down south. This large body of water is fed by five rivers and fringed by ludicrously green groves of nodding palms. One of the nearest towns is Payyanur, 50km north of Kannur. It's possible to catch the ferry from Kotti, from where KSWTD operates local ferries to the surrounding islands. The 2½-hour trip (₹10) from Kotti takes you to the Ayitti Jetty, 8km from Payyanur, from where you can also catch the return ferry.

You can stay at the peaceful Valiyaparamba Retreat (✆0484-2371761; www.touristdesk.in/valiyaparambaretreat.htm; d incl meals ₹3000), a secluded place 15km north of Payyanur and 3km from Ayitti Jetty. It has two simple rooms and two stilted bungalows, fronted by an empty golden-sand beach. Kochi's Tourist Desk (p986) also runs day trips on a traditional houseboat around the Valiyaparamba Backwaters.

Around 22km south of Bekal, Bekal Boat Stay (✆0467-2282633, 9447469747; www.bekalboatstay.com; Kottappuram, Nileshwar) offers overnight houseboat trips (₹6000 to ₹8000) around the Valiyaparamba backwaters. Day cruises (₹4000 for up to six people) are also available. It's about 2km from Nileshwar – get off any bus between Kannur and Bekal and take an autorickshaw from there (₹30).

LAKSHADWEEP

POP 64,500

Comprising a string of 36 palm-covered, white-sand-skirted coral islands 300km off the coast of Kerala, Lakshadweep is as stunning as it is isolated. Only 10 of these islands are inhabited, mostly by Sunni Muslim fishermen, and foreigners are only allowed to stay on a few of these. With fishing and coir production the main sources of income, local life on the islands remains highly traditional, and a caste system divides the islanders between Koya (land owners), Malmi (sailors) and Melachery (farmers).

The real attraction of the islands lies under the water: the 4200 sq km of pristine archipelago lagoons, unspoiled coral reefs and warm tropical waters.

Lakshadweep can only be visited on a prearranged package trip. At the time of research, resorts on Kadmat, Minicoy, Kavaratti, Agatti and Bangaram islands were open to tourists – though most visits to the islands are boat-based packages which include a cruise from Kochi, island visits, watersports, and nights spent on board. Packages include permits and meals, and can be arranged though SPORTS.

🛏 Sleeping

Kadmat Beach Resort   RESORT $$$

(☎0484-4011134; www.kadmat.com; 3/4 night d from €605/693; 🌣) Kadmat Beach Resort has 28 modern air-con cottages facing the beach. The island can be reached by overnight boat from Kochi, or by boat transfer from Agatti airport on Tuesday and Saturday.

Minicoy Island Resort   RESORT $$$

(☎0484-2668387; www.lakshadweeptourism.com; s/d with AC from ₹5000/6000; 🌣) The remote island of Minicoy, the second-largest island in Lakshadweep and the closest geographically to the Maldives, offers acommodation in modern cottages or a 20-room guesthouse. Booking is via SPORTS – check out the Swaying Palms and Coral Reef packages.

ⓘ Information

SPORTS (Society for the Promotion of Recreational Tourism & Sports; ☎9495984001,

DIVING

Lakshadweep is a scuba diver's dream, with excellent visibility and amazing marine life living on undisturbed coral reefs. The best time to dive is between November and mid-May when seas are calm and visibility is 20m to 40m. There are dive centres on Kadmat, Kavaratti, Minicoy and Agatti islands, and SPORTS can organise dive packages or courses.

Based on Agatti Island, **Dive Lakshadweep** (☎9446055972; www.divelakshadweep.com; Agatti Island; s dive ₹3000, PADI open water course ₹24,000) offers a variety of PADI courses and dive packages, including Discover Scuba (₹1700) dives for beginners.

0484-2668387; www.lakshadweeptourism. com; IG Rd, Willingdon Island; ⏱10am-5pm Mon-Sat) SPORTS is the main organisation for tourist information and booking package tours.

PERMITS

At the time of writing, foreigners were allowed to stay at the government resorts on Kadmat and Minicoy islands, Agatti (which has a private resort and the only airport), Kavaratti and Bangaram (tent resort); enquire at SPORTS. Visits require a special permit (one month's notice) which can be organised by tour operators or SPORTS in Kochi.

ⓘ Getting There & Away

Air India flies between Kochi and Agatti Island (from ₹7000 return) daily except Sunday. Boat transport between Agatti and Kadmat or Kavaratti is included in the package tours available.

Six passenger ships – MV *Kavaratti*, MV *Arabian Sea*, MV *Lakshadweep Sea*, MV *Bharat Seema*, MV *Amindivi* and MV *Minicoy* operate between Kochi and Lakshadweep, taking 14 to 20 hours.

Cruise packages start from a weekend package (adult/child ₹6185/7216) to a five-day three-island cruise from ₹17,000/24,000.

See the package section of www.lakshadweep tourism.com for more details.

Tamil Nadu & Chennai

Best Temples

➡ Meenakshi Amman Temple (p1057)

➡ Brihadishwara Temple (p1047)

➡ Arunachaleshwar Temple (p1032)

➡ Sri Ranganathaswamy Temple (p1051)

➡ Nataraja Temple (p1043)

Best Places to Stay

➡ Visalam (p1056)

➡ Les Hibiscus (p1038)

➡ Bungalow on the Beach (p1043)

➡ Sinna Dorai's Bungalow (p1074)

➡ 180° McIver (p1074)

Why Go?

Tamil Nadu is the homeland of one of humanity's living classical civilisations, stretching back uninterrupted for two millennia and very much alive today in the Tamils' language, dance, poetry and Hindu religion.

But this state, with its age-old trading vocation, is as dynamic as it is immersed in tradition. Fire-worshipping devotees who smear tikka on their brows in the famously spectacular Tamil temples might rush off to IT offices to develop new software applications – and then unwind at a swanky night-time haunt in rapidly modernising Chennai (Madras). When the heat and noise of Tamil Nadu's temple towns overwhelm, escape to the very end of India where three seas mingle, or up to the cool, forest-clad, wild-life-prowled Western Ghats. It's all packed into a state that remains proudly distinct from the rest of India, while at the same time being among the most welcoming.

When to Go

Chennai

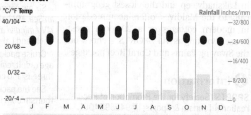

Jan Pongal (harvest) celebrations spill into the streets and while the weather is at its (relative) coolest.

Jul–Sep Hit the hill stations after the crowded 'season' but while the weather is still good.

Nov–Dec The full-moon festival of lights.

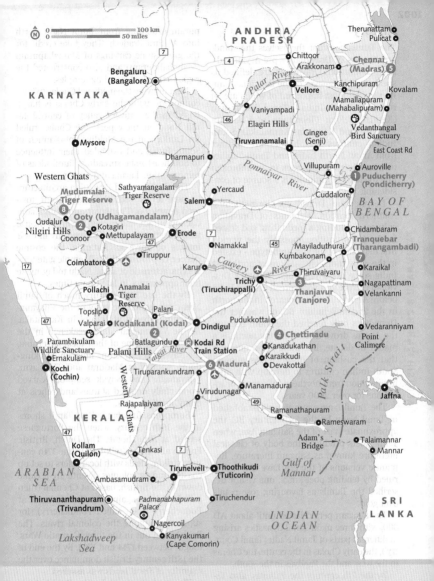

Tamil Nadu Highlights

1 Soaking up the unique Franco-Indian flair and yoga scene of **Puducherry** (Pondicherry; p1034)

2 Climbing into the cool, misty forests of the Western Ghats at **Kodaikanal** (p1066) or **Ooty** (p1076)

3 Admiring the magnificence of Chola architecture at Thanjavur's **Brihadishwara Temple** (p1047)

4 Spending the night in an opulent mansion in **Chettinadu** (p1054)

5 Exploring the countless faces of the traditional but cosmopolitan capital **Chennai** (Madras; p1003)

6 Getting lost in the colour of Madurai's **Meenakshi Amman Temple** (p1057)

7 Relaxing at tranquil **Tranquebar** (p1043), a quirky old Danish colony

8 Tracking down rare, exotic wildlife at **Mudumalai Tiger Reserve** (p1082)

History

The Tamils consider themselves the standard bearers of Dravidian – pre-Aryan Indian – civilisation. Dravidians are defined as speakers of languages of the Dravidian family, the four most important of which are all rooted in South India – Tamil, Malayalam (Kerala), Telugu (Telangana and Andhra Pradesh) and Kannada (Karnataka). South Indian cultures and history are distinct from Aryan North India, and Tamils' ability to trace their identity back in an unbroken line to classical antiquity is a source of considerable pride.

Despite the Dravidians' long-standing southern location, elements of Dravidian culture – including a meditating god seated in the lotus position, possibly the world's first depiction of the yogi archetype – existed in the early Indus civilisations of northwest India some 4000 years ago. Whether Dravidian culture was widespread around India before Aryan cultures appeared in the north in the 2nd millennium BC, or whether the Dravidians only reached the south because the Aryans drove them from the north, is a matter of debate. But there is no question that the cushion of distance has allowed South Indian cultures to develop with little interruption from northern influences or invasions for over 2000 years.

The Tamil language was well established in Tamil Nadu by the 3rd century BC, the approximate start of the Sangam Age, when Tamil poets produced the body of classical literature known as Sangam literature. Romantic versions of the era have the region ruled by feuding poet-kings; one visitor described the Tamils as favouring rose petals over gold.

The Sangam period lasted until about AD 300, with three main Tamil dynasties arising in different parts of Tamil Nadu (Tamil Country'): the early Cholas in the centre, the Cheras in the west and the Pandyas in the south.

By the 7th century the Pallavas, also Tamil, established an empire based at Kanchipuram extending from Tamil Nadu north into Andhra Pradesh. They take credit for the great stone carvings of Mamallapuram (Mahabalipuram) and also constructed the region's first free-standing temples.

Next up were the medieval Cholas (whose connection with the early Cholas is hazy). Based in the Cauvery valley of central Tamil Nadu, at their peak the Cholas ruled Sri Lanka and the Maldives plus much of South India, and extended their influence to Southeast Asia, spreading Tamil ideas of reincarnation, karma and yogic practice.

The Cholas raised Dravidian architecture to new levels with the magnificent towered temples of Thanjavur and Gangaikondacholapuram, and carried the art of bronze image casting to its peak, especially in their images of Shiva as Nataraja, the cosmic dancer. *Gopurams,* the tall temple gate towers characteristic of Tamil Nadu today, make their appearance in late Chola times.

By the late 14th century much of Tamil Nadu was under the sway of the Vijayanagar empire based at Hampi in Karnataka. As the Vijayanagar state weakened in the 16th century, some of their local governors, the Nayaks, set up strong independent kingdoms, notably at Madurai and Thanjavur. Vijayanagar and Nayak sculptors carved wonderfully detailed statues and reliefs at many Tamil temples.

Europeans first landed on Tamil shores in the 16th century, when the Portuguese settled at San Thome. The Dutch, British, French and Danes followed in the 17th century, striking deals with local rulers to set up coastal trading colonies. Eventually it came down to the British, based at Chennai (then called Madras), against the French, based at Puducherry (then called Pondicherry), for supremacy among the colonial rivals. The British won out in the three Carnatic Wars, fought between 1744 and 1763. By the end of the 18th century British dominance over the majority of Tamil lands was assured.

The area governed by the British from Madras, the Madras Presidency, included parts of Andhra Pradesh, Kerala and Karnataka, an arrangement that continued after Indian ndependence in 1947, until Kerala, Karnataka, Andhra Pradesh and present-day Tamil Nadu (130,058 sq km) were created on linguistic lines in the 1950s. It wasn't until 1968 that the current state (population 72.1 million) was officially named Tamil Nadu.

SLEEPING PRICES

Accommodation price ranges for this chapter are as follows:

$ below ₹1100

$$ ₹1100 to ₹5000

$$$ above ₹5000

TOP STATE FESTIVALS

Pongal (statewide; ☻ mid-Jan) marks the end of the harvest season and is one of Tamil Nadu's most important festivals, named after a rice-and-lentil dish cooked at this time in new clay pots. Animals, especially cows, are honoured for their contributions.

Other important festivals include:

International Yoga Festival (p1038; ☻ 4–7 Jan) Shows, workshops and competitions in Puducherry.

Thyagaraja Aradhana (p1049; ☻ Jan) Carnatic music in Thiruvaiyaru.

Teppam (Float) Festival (p1058; ☻ Jan/Feb) Meenakshi temple deities are paraded around Madurai.

Natyanjali Dance Festival (p1044; ☻ Feb/Mar) Five days of professional classical dance in Chidambaram.

Chithirai Festival (p1059; ☻ Apr/May) Two-week event in Madurai celebrating the marriage of Meenakshi to Sundareswarar (Shiva).

Karthikai Deepam Festival (p1033; statewide; ☻ Nov/Dec) Festival of lights.

Chennai Festival of Music & Dance (p1009; ☻ mid-Dec–mid-Jan) A huge celebration of South Indian music and dance in the state capital.

Mamallapuram Dance Festival (p1025; ☻ Dec–Jan) Four weekends of classical and folk dance from across India on open-air stages in Mamallapuram.

CHENNAI (MADRAS)

☑ 044 / POP 8.7 MILLION

With its withering southern heat, roaring traffic and scarcity of outstanding sights, the 'capital of the south' has always been the rather dowdy sibling among India's four biggest cities. But if you have time to explore Chennai's diverse neighbourhoods and role as keeper of South Indian artistic and religious traditions, the odds are this 400-sq-km conglomerate of urban villages will sneak its way into your heart.

Among Chennai's greatest assets are its people, who are infectiously enthusiastic about their hometown; they won't hit you with a lot of hustle and hassle. Recent years have added a new layer of cosmopolitan glamour, in the shape of luxury hotels, sparkling boutiques, classy contemporary restaurants and a sprinkling of swanky bars and clubs open well into the night.

Even if you're just caught here between connections, it's well worth poking around the museums, exploring the temples or taking a sunset saunter along Marina Beach.

The old British Fort St George and the jumble of narrow streets and bazaars that is George Town constitute the historic hub of the city. The two main train stations, Egmore and Central, sit inland from the fort. Much of the best eating, drinking, shopping and accommodation lies in the leafier southern and southwestern suburbs such as Nungambakkam, T Nagar (Thyagaraya Nagar), Alwarpet and, increasingly, Velachery and Guindy. The major thoroughfare linking northern with southern Chennai is Anna Salai (Mount Rd).

History

The southern neighbourhood of Mylapore existed long before the rest of Chennai and there is evidence that it traded with Roman and even Chinese and Greek merchants. The Portuguese established their San Thome settlement on the coast nearby in 1523. Another century passed before Francis Day and the British East India Company rocked up in 1639, searching for a good southeast Indian trading base, and struck a deal with the local Vijayanagar ruler to build a fort-cum-trading-post at Madraspatnam fishing village. This was Fort St George, erected between 1640 and 1653.

The three Carnatic Wars between 1744 and 1763 saw Britain and its colonialist rival France allying with competing South Indian princes in their efforts to get the upper hand over the locals – and each other. The French occupied Fort St George from 1746 to 1749 but the British eventually won out, and the French withdrew to Pondicherry.

As capital of the Madras Presidency, one of the four major divisions of British India,

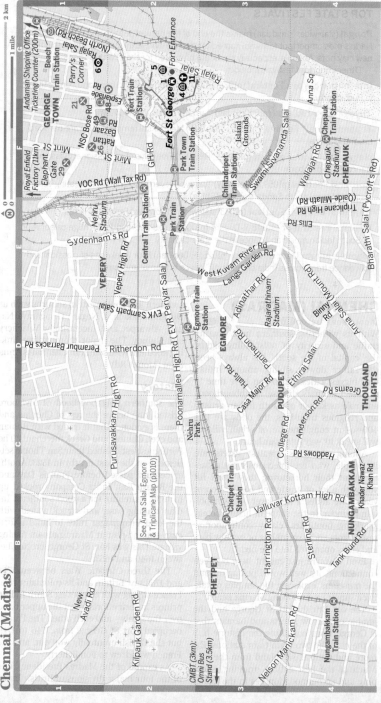

Chennai (Madras)

TAMIL NADU & CHENNAI

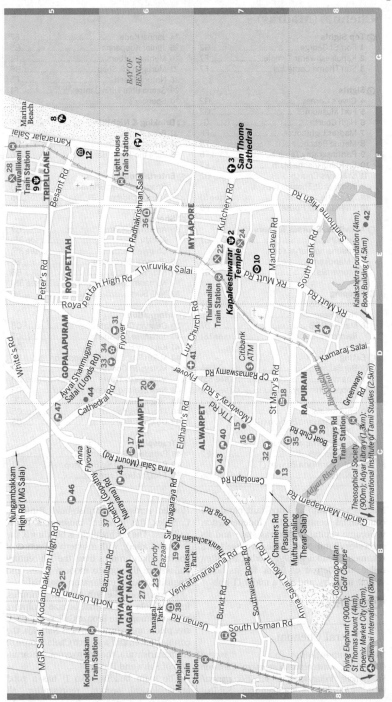

TAMIL NADU & CHENNAI

Madras grew into an important naval and commercial centre. After Independence, it became capital of Madras state and its successor Tamil Nadu. The city itself was renamed Chennai in 1996. Today, it's often called 'the Detroit of India' for its boom vehicle industry, and it is a major IT hub.

◉ Sights

◉ Central Chennai

★ Government Museum   MUSEUM
(Map p1010; www.chennaimuseum.org; Pantheon Rd, Egmore; Indian/foreigner ₹15/250, camera/video ₹200/500; ⊙9.30am-5pm Sat-Thu)

Housed across the British-built Pantheon Complex, this excellent museum is Chennai's best. The big highlight is building 3, the **Bronze Gallery**, with a superb collection of South Indian bronzes from the 7th-century Pallava era through to modern times, and English-language explanatory material.

It was from the 9th to 11th centuries, in the Chola period, that bronze sculpture peaked. Among the Bronze Gallery's impressive pieces are many of Shiva as Nataraja, the cosmic dancer, and a superb Chola bronze of Ardhanarishvara, the androgynous incarnation of Shiva and Parvati.

The main building (No 1) has a good archaeological section representing all the major South Indian periods from 2nd-century-BC Buddhist sculptures to 16th-century- Vijayanagar work, with special rooms devoted to Hindu, Buddhist and Jain sculpture. Building 2, the **Anthropology Galleries**, traces South Indian human history back to prehistoric times, displaying tribal artefacts from across the region.

The museum also includes the **National Art Gallery**, **Contemporary Art Gallery** and **Children's Museum**, on the same ticket. You may find some sections temporarily closed for renovation.

High Court   NOTABLE BUILDING
(Map p1004; Parry's Corner) Completed in 1892, this imposing red Indo-Saracenic structure is said to be the largest judicial building in the world after the Courts of London. Depending on current regulations, you may or may not be allowed to wander the grounds on Sundays until 1pm. If you fancy trying, take your passport.

★**Fort St George**   FORT
(Map p1004; Rajaji Salai; ⊗9am-5pm) Finished in 1653 by the British East India Company, the fort has undergone many facelifts over the years. Inside the vast perimeter walls is now a precinct housing Tamil Nadu's Legislative Assembly & Secretariat, and a smattering of older buildings. One of these, the **Fort Museum** (Map p1004; Indian/foreigner ₹5/100; ⊗9am-5pm Sat-Thu), has displays on Chennai's origins and the fort itself, and interesting military memorabilia and artwork from colonial times. The 1st-floor portrait gallery of colonial-era VIPs includes a very assured-looking Robert Clive (Clive of India).

Also within the fort is **St Mary's Church** (Map p1004; ⊗10am-5pm Mon-Sat), completed in 1680, and India's oldest surviving British church. To its right is the former Admiralty House (Clive's House). **Clive's Corner** (Map p1004; ⊗9am-6pm) `FREE`, at the end of the building, houses a quirky memorial museum to Robert Clive.

Marina Beach   BEACH
(Map p1004) Take an early-morning or evening stroll (you really don't want to roast here at any other time) along the 3km-long main stretch of Marina Beach and you'll pass cricket matches, flying kites, fortune-tellers, fish markets, corn-roasters and families enjoying the sea breeze. Don't swim: strong rips make it dangerous. At its southern end, the newly reopened, ridiculously popular **Madras Lighthouse** (Map p1004; Marina Beach; Indian/foreigner ₹20/50, camera ₹25; ⊗10am-1pm & 3-5pm Tue-Sun) is India's only lighthouse with a lift; the panoramic city and beach views are fabulous.

Parthasarathy Temple   HINDU TEMPLE
(Map p1004; Singarachari St, Triplicane; ⊗6am-noon & 4-9pm) Built under the 8th-century Pallavas and unusually dedicated to Krishna (a form of Vishnu) as the charioteer Parthasarathy, this is one of Chennai's oldest temples. Most of its elaborate carvings, however, date from its 16th-century Vijayanagar expansion, including the fine colonnade fronting the main entrance. It's special for its shrines dedicated to five of the incarnations of Vishnu.

Vivekananda House   MUSEUM
(Vivekanandar Illam, Ice House; Map p1004; www.vivekanandahouse.org; Kamarajar Salai; adult/child ₹10/5; ⊗10am-12.15pm & 3-7.15pm Thu-Tue) The marshmallow-pink Vivekananda House is

TAMIL NADU & CHENNAI CHENNAI (MADRAS)

DRAVIDIAN PRIDE

Since before Indian Independence in 1947, Tamil politicians have railed against caste (which they see as favouring light-skinned Brahmins) and the Hindi language (seen as North Indian cultural imperialism). The pre-Independence 'Self Respect' movement and Justice Party, influenced by Marxism, mixed South Indian communal values with class-war rhetoric, and spawned Tamil political parties that remain the major powers in Tamil Nadu today. In the early post-Independence decades there was even a movement for an independent Dravida Nadu nation comprising the four main South Indian peoples, but there was little solidarity between different groups. Today Dravidian politics is largely restricted to Tamil Nadu, where parties are often led by former film stars.

During the conflict in nearby Sri Lanka, many Indian Tamil politicians loudly defended the Tamil Tigers, the organisation that assassinated Rajiv Gandhi in a village near Chennai (Madras) in 1991. There is still considerable prejudice among the generally tolerant Tamils towards anything Sinhalese. The most obvious sign of Tamil pride that you'll see today is the white shirt and white *mundu* (sarong), worn by any Tamil public figure worth their salt.

interesting not only for its displays on the famous 'wandering monk', Swami Vivekananda, but also for its semicircular form, built in 1842 to store ice imported from the USA. Vivekananda stayed here briefly in 1897 and preached his ascetic Hindu philosophy to adoring crowds. The displays include a photo exhibition on the swami's life and the room where Vivekananda stayed, now used for meditation. Free weekly one-hour meditation classes may be available.

⊙ Southern Chennai

★**Kapaleeshwarar Temple**   HINDU TEMPLE
(Map p1004; Ponnambala Vathiar St, Mylapore; ⊙5.30am-12.15pm & 4-9.30pm) The Mylapore neighbourhood is one of Chennai's most characterful and traditional; it predated colonial Madras by several centuries. The Kapaleeshwarar Temple is Chennai's most active and impressive temple, believed to have been built after the Portuguese destroyed the seaside original in 1566. It displays the main architectural elements of many a Tamil Nadu temple – a rainbow-coloured *gopuram* (gateway tower), pillared *mandapas* (pillared pavilions), and a huge tank – and is dedicated to the state's most popular deity, Shiva.

Legend tells that in an angry fit Shiva turned his consort Parvati into a peacock, and commanded her to worship him here to regain her normal form. Parvati supposedly did so at a spot just outside the northeast corner of the temple's central block, where a shrine commemorates the event. Hence the name Mylapore, or 'town of peacocks'.

The temple's colourful Brahmotsavam festival (in March/April) sees the deities paraded around Mylapore's streets.

★**San Thome Cathedral**   CHURCH
(Map p1004; www.santhomechurch.com; Santhome High Rd; ⊙6am-7.30pm) This soaring Roman Catholic cathedral, a stone's throw from the beach, was founded by the Portuguese in the 16th century, then rebuilt in neo-Gothic style in 1896, and is said to mark the final resting place of St Thomas the Apostle. It's believed 'Doubting Thomas' brought Christianity to the subcontinent in AD 52 and was killed at St Thomas Mount, Chennai, in AD 72. Behind the cathedral is the entrance to the **tomb of St Thomas** (Map p1004; admission free; ⊙6am-8pm).

Although most of St Thomas' mortal remains are apparently now in Italy, a small cross on the tomb wall contains a tiny bone fragment marked 'Relic of St Thomas'. The museum above displays Thomas-related artefacts including the lancehead believed to have killed him.

St Thomas' Pole, at the beach end of the street on the cathedral's south side, is said to have miraculously saved the cathedral from the 2004 tsunami.

Sri Ramakrishna Math   RELIGIOUS COMPLEX
(Map p1004; www.chennaimath.org; 31 RK Mutt Rd; ⊙Universal Temple 4.30-11.45am & 3-9pm, evening prayers 6.30-7.30pm) The tranquil, flowery grounds of the Ramakrishna Math are a world away from the chaos outside. Orange-robed monks glide around and there's a reverential feel. The Math is a monastic order following the teachings of the 19th-century sage Sri Ramakrishna, who preached the essential unity of all religions. The Universal Temple here is a handsome modern building incorporating architectural elements from several different religions. It's open to all, to worship, pray or meditate.

Theosophical Society   GARDEN
(www.ts-adyar.org; south end of Thiru Vi Ka Bridge, Adyar; ⊙grounds 8.30-10am & 2-4pm Mon-Sat) FREE Between the Adyar River and the coast, the 100-hectare grounds of the Theosophical Society provide a peaceful, green, vehicle-free retreat from the city. A lovely spot just to wander, they contain a church, mosque, Buddhist shrine, Zoroastrian temple and Hindu temple as well as a huge variety of native and introduced flora, including the offshoots of a 400-year-old banyan tree torn down by a storm in the 1980s.

The **Adyar Library** (1yr reader's card ₹50, deposit ₹250; ⊙9am-5pm Tue-Sun) here has a huge collection of religion and philosophy books (some on display), from 1000-year-old Buddhist scrolls to handmade 19th-century Bibles.

Kalakshetra Foundation   ARTS SCHOOL
(☑044-24521169; www.kalakshetra.in; Muthulakshmi St, Thiruvanmiyur; Indian/foreigner incl craft centre ₹100/500; ⊙campus 9-11.30am Mon-Fri Jul-Feb, craft centre 9am-1pm & 2-5pm Mon-Sat, all closed 2nd & 4th Sat of month) Founded in 1936, Kalakshetra is a leading serious school of Tamil classical dance and music (sponsoring many students from disadvantaged backgrounds), set in beautiful, shady grounds in far south Chennai. During morning class times visitors can (quietly) wander the grounds, and visit the **Rukmini**

Devi Museum. Across the road is the **Kalakshetra Craft Centre** where you can see Kanchipuram-style hand-loom weaving, textile block-printing and the fascinating, rare art of *kalamkari* (hand-painting on textiles with vegetable dyes).

The Thiruvanmiyur bus stand, terminus of many city bus routes, is 500m west of the Kalakshetra entrance.

While here it's also worth visiting the **Book Building** (☑ 044-24426696; www.tarabooks.com; Plot 9, CGE Colony, Kuppam Beach Rd, Thiruvanmiyur; ⊘ 10am-7.30pm Mon-Sat), 700m south of Kalakshetra, where Tara Books stages free exhibitions, talks and workshops, as well as displaying its own highly original handmade books. With prior notice, you can visit the book-making workshop (10 minutes' drive away).

St Thomas Mount   SACRED SITE
(Parangi Malai; off Lawrence Rd; camera ₹10; ⊘ 6am-8pm) The reputed site of St Thomas' martyrdom in AD 72 rises in the southwest of the city, 2.5km north of St Thomas Mount train station. The Church of Our Lady of Expectation, built atop the 'mount' by the Portuguese in 1523, contains what are supposedly a fragment of Thomas' finger bone and a cross he carved; the city views are wonderful.

🏃 Activities

Krishnamacharya Yoga Mandiram   YOGA, MEDITATION
(Map p1004; ☑ 044-24952900; www.kym.org; 31 4th Cross St, RK Nagar; class US$30; ⊘ 8am-7pm) Highly regarded, serious two-week and month-long yoga and yoga therapy courses, and teacher training.

📖 Courses

International Institute of Tamil Studies   LANGUAGE
(☑ 044-22542781; www.ulakaththamizh.org; CIT Campus, 2nd Main Rd, Tharamani) Runs intensive three-month and six-month courses in Tamil.

Kalakshetra Foundation   TEXTILE PAINTING
(☑ 044-24521169; www.kalakshetra.in; Muthulakshmi St, Thiruvanmiyur; per week ₹2500) Kalakshetra's crafts centre offers one-week to one-month courses in the fascinating old art of *kalamkari* – hand-painting of textiles using vegetable inks – which survives in only a handful of places. Courses run from 10am to 1pm Monday to Friday.

🧭 Tours

The Tamil Nadu Tourism Development Corporation (p1018) conducts half-day city tours (non-AC/AC ₹300/370) and day trips to Mamallapuram (₹450/550). Book ahead for weekends and holidays; be ready for cancellations on quiet weekdays. Every full moon there's an overnight pilgrimage trip to Tiruvannamalai (₹600/780).

⭐ Detours   WALKING TOURS
(Map p1004; ☑ 9000850505, 9840060393; www.detoursindia.com; RM Towers, 108 Chamiers Rd, Alwarpet) A fantastic way to explore Chennai is with Detours' off-beat, in-depth history, faith, and food tours, run by local experts. Four-hour early-morning food walks cost ₹5000 to ₹6000 per person.

Storytrails   WALKING TOURS
(Map p1004; ☑ 9962201244, 044-45010202; www.storytrails.in; 21/2 1st Cross St, TTK Rd, Alwarpet; 3hr tour for up to 4 people ₹3500) Entertaining neighbourhood walking tours on themes such as dance, temples, jewellery and bazaars.

Royal Enfield Factory   FACTORY TOUR
(☑ 044-42230400; www.royalenfield.com; Tiruvottiyur High Rd, Tiruvottiyur; per person ₹600) The classic Enfield Bullet motorcycle has been manufactured since 1955 in far northern Chennai. Two-hour tours run on the second and fourth Saturdays of each month at 10.30am. Bookings essential.

🎊 Festivals & Events

Chennai Festival of Music & Dance   MUSIC, DANCE
(Madras Music & Dance Season; ⊘ mid-Dec–mid-Jan) One of the largest of its type in the

---

TRADITIONAL TRADERS

Even as Chennai expands relentlessly to the south, west and north, George Town, the local settlement that grew up near the British Fort St George, remains the city's wholesale centre. Many of its narrow streets are entirely devoted to selling one particular product, as they have for hundreds of years – flowers in Badrian St, paper goods in Anderson St, jewellery on NSC Bose Rd. Even if you aren't buying, wander the mazelike streets to see Indian life flowing seamlessly from the past into the present.

Anna Salai, Egmore & Triplicane

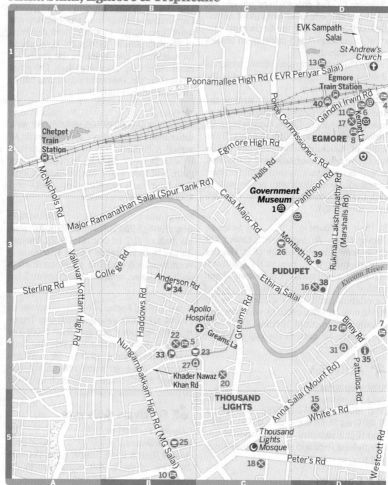

world, this festival celebrates South Indian music and dance.

🛏 Sleeping

Hotels in Chennai are pricier than in the rest of Tamil Nadu and don't, as a rule, offer much bang for your buck. The Triplicane High Rd area is best for budget accommodation. There are some cheapies in Egmore, along with a few good midrange options. The number of top-end hotels has risen dramatically over the past couple of years, mostly in the more middle-class southern areas.

Many hotels in Chennai fill up by noon, so call ahead. The most expensive hotels have good discounts online.

🛏 Egmore & Around

New Lakshmi Lodge   HOTEL **$**
(Map p1010; ☎044-42148725, 044-28194576; www.nll.co.in; 16 Kennet Lane; s/d ₹500/880, r with AC ₹1400-1500; ✱) With small and bare but spotless, pastel-walled rooms spread over four floors around a central parking courtyard, this huge block is not a bad budget

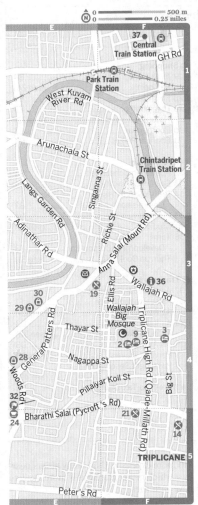

✳ 🛜) Spread across two residential buildings engulfed by greenery in upmarket Wallace Garden, Hanu Reddy is exactly the kind of peaceful homey hideaway that central Chennai needs. The eight cosy, unpretentious rooms come with air-con, free wi-fi, tea/coffee sets, and splashes of colourful artwork; the teensy terraces have bamboo lounging chairs. Service hits the perfect personal-yet-professional balance.

YWCA International Guest House
GUESTHOUSE **$$**

(Map p1010; 📞044-25324234; igh@ywcamadras.org; 1086 Poonamallee High Rd; incl breakfast s ₹1500-1980, d ₹1800-2400, s/d without AC ₹900/1350; ✳@🛜) The YWCA guesthouse, set in shady grounds, offers very good value along with a calm atmosphere. Efficiently run by helpful staff, it has good-sized, brilliantly clean rooms, spacious common areas and solid-value meals (₹175/275 for veg/nonveg lunch or dinner). Wi-fi (in the lobby) costs ₹100 per day. Renovations were underway at the time of research.

Hotel Chandra Park
HOTEL **$$**

(Map p1010; 📞044-40506060; www.hotelchandrapark.com; 9 Gandhi Irwin Rd; incl breakfast s ₹1320-2280, d ₹1500-2580; ✳🛜) Chandra Park's prices remain mysteriously lower than most similar establishments. Standard rooms are small but have air-con, clean towels and tight, white sheets. Throw in a decent (if male-dominated) bar, a hearty buffet breakfast, and free wi-fi, and this is excellent value by Chennai standards.

Fortel
HOTEL **$$$**

(Map p1010; 📞044-30242424; www.fortelhotels.com; 3 Gandhi Irwin Rd; incl breakfast s ₹4200-6600, d ₹4800-7200; ✳🛜) Conveniently close to Egmore train station, the Fortel is cool and stylish in a wood, mirrors and white walls way, with cushion-laden beds, free wi-fi and a good restaurant, Madras Masala. Most station-facing rooms have views of St Andrew's Church rising through trees. It's worth asking about discounts.

🛏 Triplicane & Around

Paradise Guest House
HOTEL **$**

(Map p1010; 📞044-28594252; paradisegh@hotmail.com; 17 Vallabha Agraharam St; r ₹500, with AC ₹800-1000; ✳🛜) Paradise offers some of Triplicane's best-value digs – simple rooms with clean tiles, a breezy rooftop, friendly staff and hot water by the steaming bucket. Wi-fi costs ₹50 per hour.

choice. Book ahead, as it's often full. Go for the upper floors for more privacy.

Raj Residency
HOTEL **$**

(Map p1010; 📞044-28192219; www.rajresidencyhotel.com; 2/22 Kennet Lane; s ₹840-1020, d ₹1020-1180, with AC s ₹1180-1310, d ₹1310-1550; ✳🛜) The non-AC rooms here are reasonable value, a bit dingy and worn but clean enough, in shades of brown.

★ Hanu Reddy Residences
B&B **$$**

(Map p1010; 📞044-45038413; www.hanureddyresidences.com; 6A/24 3rd St, Wallace Garden, Nungambakkam; r incl breakfast ₹3600-4200;

Anna Salai, Egmore & Triplicane

◉ Top Sights
1 Government Museum	C3

🛏 Sleeping
2 Broad Lands Lodge	F4
3 Cristal Guest House	F4
4 Fortel	D1
5 Hanu Reddy Residences	B4
6 Hotel Chandra Park	D2
7 La Woods	D4
8 New Lakshmi Lodge	D2
9 Paradise Guest House	F4
10 Park Hotel	B5
11 Raj Residency	D2
12 Vivanta by Taj – Connemara	D4
13 YWCA International Guest House	D1

🍽 Eating
14 A2B	F5
15 Amethyst	D5
16 Annalakshmi	D3
17 Hotel Saravana Bhavan	D2
18 Hotel Saravana Bhavan (Thousand Lights)	C5
19 Hotel Saravana Bhavan (Triplicane)	E3
Madras Masala	(see 4)
20 Nilgiri's	C4
Raintree	(see 12)
21 Ratna Café	F5
22 Tuscana Pizzeria	B4

🍷 Drinking & Nightlife
23 Café Coffee Day	B4
24 Café Coffee Day	E5
25 Café Coffee Day	B5
26 Café Coffee Day (Egmore)	C3

Leather Bar	(see 10)
Pasha	(see 10)

🛍 Shopping
27 Evoluzione	B4
Fabindia	(see 24)
28 Fabindia	E4
29 Higginbothams	E3
Naturally Auroville	(see 23)
30 Poompuhar	E3
31 Spencer Plaza	D4

ℹ Information
32 Australian Consulate	E4
33 Belgian Consulate	B4
34 British Deputy High Commission	B3
35 Indiatourism	D4
Studio	(see 21)
36 Tamil Nadu Tourism Development Corporation	F3
Thomas Cook	(see 31)

ℹ Transport
37 Advanced Computerised Reservation Office	F1
Air Asia	(see 25)
38 Air India	D3
Air India Express	(see 38)
39 Jet Airways	D3
Parveen Travels	(see 11)
Passenger Reservation Office	(see 40)
40 Pre-Paid Taxi Stand	D1

TAMIL NADU & CHENNAI CHENNAI (MADRAS)

Broad Lands Lodge GUESTHOUSE $
(Map p1010; ☑ 044-28545573; broadlandshotel@
yahoo.com; 18 Vallabha Agraharam St; s ₹400-450,
d ₹500-1000; ❋ 🗟) In business since 1951,
Broad Lands was a hippie-era stalwart and
probably hasn't had a fresh coat of pale-blue
paint since. But this laid-back colonial-era
mansion, with leafy courtyards and rooms
up rambling staircases, still has its devotees, who don't seem to mind the bare-
bone, idiosyncratic rooms, dank bathrooms,
or high-volume muezzins of Wallajah Big
Mosque. Reception-only wi-fi (a 21st-century
concession) is free.

Cristal Guest House HOTEL $
(Map p1010; ☑ 044-28513011; 34 CNK Rd; r ₹400,
with AC ₹750; ❋) The clean, pink abodes in
this modern building aren't quite the cheapest rooms in Chennai, but they're only about

₹10 more expensive than many others nearby – which means the hotel is more likely to
have vacancies.

La Woods HOTEL $$
(Map p1010; ☑ 044-28608040; www.lawoodsho
tel.com; 1 Woods Rd; r incl breakfast ₹3500; ❋ 🗟)
Wonderfully erratic colour schemes throw
fresh whites against lime-greens and tur-
quoises at this friendly modern hotel, new
in 2013. The shiny, well-kept, contemporary
rooms are perfectly comfy, with free wi-fi
and mountains of pillows, as well as kettles,
hairdryers, and 'global' plug sockets.

**Vivanta by Taj –
Connemara** HERITAGE HOTEL $$$
(Map p1010; ☑ 044-66000000; www.vivantabytaj.
com; Binny Rd; r incl breakfast ₹11,990-14,390;
❋ @ 🗟 ⏅) The top-end Taj Group has four

hotels in and around Chennai, but this is the only one with historical ambience, built in the 1850s as the British governor's residence. There's a beautiful pool in tropical gardens, and even the smallest, cream-coloured rooms are very comfy and airy, with all mod cons. Chettinadu Raintree restaurant is one of Chennai's best.

🛏 Southern Chennai

★ Footprint B&B
B&B $$
(Map p1004; ☑9840037483; www.chennaibedandbreakfast.com; Gayatri Apts, 16 South St, Alwarpet (behind Sheraton Park Hotel); r incl breakfast ₹4500; ❋@🛜) This is a beautifully comfortable, relaxed base for your Chennai explorations, spread over four apartments on a quiet street in a leafy neighbourhood. Bowls of wild roses and old-Madras photos set the scene for 12 cosy, spotless rooms, with king-size or wide twin beds. Breakfasts (Western or Indian) are generous, wi-fi is free and the welcoming owners are full of Tamil Nadu tips. Book ahead.

Madras B&B
B&B $$
(Map p1004; ☑9677135753; madrasbnb@gmail.com; Flat 1/3, Nandini Apts, 72/45 1st Main Rd, RA Puram; r incl breakfast ₹3000; ❋🛜) Like a cosy self-service lodge, this friendly little place has just three (soon to be seven) good-sized, straightforward but comfy and stylish rooms in a peaceful, private apartment, which makes it popular with yoga students. Help yourself to the fully equipped kitchen, free wi-fi, library, and relaxed communal lounge with flower bowls. Bookings recommended.

★ Park Hotel
BOUTIQUE HOTEL $$$
(Map p1010; ☑044-42676000; www.thepark hotels.com; 601 Anna Salai; s ₹12,590-14,990, d ₹13,790-16,190, ste from ₹19,190; ❋@🛜🏊) We love this superchic boutique hotel, which flaunts design everywhere you look, from the towering lobby's bamboo, steel and gold cushions to the posters from classic South Indian movies shot in Gemini Studios, the site's previous incarnation. Rooms have lovely lush bedding and stylish touches such as feathered lamps and glass-walled bathrooms. There are three restaurants, a rooftop pool, a luxury spa, and three packed-out nightspots too!

Hyatt Regency
HOTEL $$$
(Map p1004; ☑044-61001234; www.chennai.regency.hyatt.com; 365 Anna Salai; incl breakfast s ₹10,190-11,990, d ₹11,390-13,190; ❋@🛜🏊)

Smart, swish, and bang up to date, this towering, triangular beauty of a hotel is the most central of Chennai's top-end newbies. Contemporary art surrounds the sun-flooded atrium, local chefs head up three good restaurants and a popular bar, and glossy all-modern rooms have walk-through bathrooms and fabulous sea/city panoramas through massive picture windows. The pool is fringed by flowery gardens.

Raintree
HOTEL $$$
(Map p1004; ☑044-42252525; www.raintree hotels.com; 120 St Mary's Rd, Alwarpet; s/d ₹9590/10,790; ❋@🛜🏊) 🍃 At this 'ecosensitive' hotel, floors are bamboo or rubber, water and electricity conservation hold pride of place, and the AC-generated heat warms the bathroom water. The sleek, minimalist rooms are comfy and stylish, with free wi-fi; freshly revamped rooms should be ready for 2015. The rooftop supports a sea-view infinity pool (doubling as insulation) along with a restaurant.

🍴 Eating

Chennai is packed with inexpensive 'meals' joints ('messes'), serving thalis for lunch and dinner, and tiffin (snacks) such as *idlis* (spongy, round fermented rice cakes), *vadas* (deep-fried lentil-flour doughnuts) and dosas. It's perfectly possible to eat every meal at Chennai's 24 Saravana Bhavan restaurants, where you can count on quality vegetarian food. In the Muslim area around

---

TYPICALLY TAMIL FOOD

Tamil Nadu's favourite foods are overwhelmingly vegetarian, full of coconut and chilli. You'll find dosas, *idlis* (spongy, round fermented rice cakes) and *vadas* (deep-fried lentil-flour doughnuts), all served with coconut chutney and *sambar* (lentil broth). Almost as ubiquitous is the *uttapam*, a thick, savoury rice pancake with finely chopped onions, green chillies and coriander. South Indian 'meals' – thalis based around rice, lentil dishes, *rasam* (hot and sour tamarind soup) and chutneys, often served on banana leaves – are also good. The main local exception to the all-veg diet is Chettinad food, from the Chettinad region south of Trichy. For a tea-growing state, Tamil Nadu adores its filter coffee, with milk, sugar, and a dash of chicory.

Triplicane High Rd you'll find great biryani stops every few steps.

Classier Indian restaurants are on the rise, and international cuisines have really taken off in Chennai, so there's plenty of up-market dining, especially at top-end hotels.

Useful, well-stocked supermarkets include Spencer's (Map p1004; 15 EVK Sampath Salai, Vepery; ⊘ 7.30am-9.30pm), not too far from Egmore and Central stations; Big Bazaar at T Nagar (Map p1004; 34 Sir Thyagaraya Rd; ⊘ 10.30am-9.30pm) and Express Avenue Mall (Express Avenue, White's Rd; ⊘ 10am-9pm); and Nilgiri's (Map p1010; 25 Shafee Mohammed Rd, Thousand Lights West; ⊘ 8.30am-9.30pm) off Nungambakkam's Khader Nawaz Khan Rd.

✗ Egmore

★ **Hotel Saravana Bhavan**   INDIAN $
(Map p1010; www.saravanabhavan.com; 21 Kennet Lane; mains ₹75-140; ⊘ 6am-10pm) Dependably delish, South Indian thali 'meals' at this famous Chennai vegetarian chain run around ₹80 to ₹100. It's also excellent for South Indian breakfasts (*idlis* and *vadas* from ₹33), filter coffee and other Indian vegetarian fare. Branches include George Town (Map p1004; 209 NSC Bose Rd; ⊘ 6am-10pm), Triplicane (Map p1010; Shanthi Theatre Complex, 44 Anna Salai; ⊘ 7am-11pm), Thousand Lights (Map p1010; 293 Peter's Rd; mains ₹115-175; ⊘ 7.30am-11pm), Mylapore (Map p1004; 70 North Mada St; ⊘ 6am-10pm) and T Nagar (Map p1004; 102 Sir Thyagaraya Rd; ⊘ 7am-10.30pm), along with London, Paris, and New York!

The Thousand Lights branch, more upscale, does a ₹300 lunch and dinner buffet.

Annalakshmi   INDIAN $$
(Map p1010; ☑ 044-28525109; www.annalakshmichennai.co.in; 1st fl, Sigapi Achi Bldg, 18/3 Rukmani Lakshmipathy Rd; mains ₹180-280, set/buffet lunch ₹750/400; ⊘ noon-2.30pm & 7-9pm Tue-Sun) Very fine South and North Indian vegetarian fare in a beautiful dining room decorated with carvings and paintings, inside a high-rise behind the Air India building. The buffet lunch is served in another part of the same block. Annalakshmi is run and staffed by devotees of Swami Shanthanand Saraswathi, and proceeds support medical programs for the poor.

Madras Masala   MULTICUISINE $$
(Map p1010; Fortel, 3 Gandhi Irwin Rd; mains ₹188-375; ⊘ 7am-11pm) Reincarnated from its former Continental-focused life, this restaurant

at the Fortel hotel has an impressive range of Indian veg and nonveg dishes, including great biryanis. It's tranquil, tasteful and friendly, with red crushed-velvet booths and local-life paintings.

✗ Triplicane & Around

Ratna Café   SOUTH INDIAN $
(Map p1010; 255 Triplicane High Rd; dishes ₹50-110; ⊘ 6am-10.45pm) Though often crowded and cramped, Ratna is famous for its scrumptious *idlis* and the hearty doses of its signature *sambar* (lentil broth) that go with them – people have been sitting down to this ₹30 dish at all hours since 1948. There's a new AC room out the back.

A2B   SOUTH INDIAN $
(Map p1010; 47/23 Bharathi Salai; mains ₹90-130; ⊘ 7am-11pm) Tuck into South Indian classics or veg biryani in the clean AC hall upstairs, or go for the sweets downstairs. Nearby Natural Fresh (Map p1004; 35 Bharathi Salai; scoop ₹53; ⊘ 11am-11pm) does excellent ice cream.

★ **Amethyst**   MULTICUISINE, CAFE $$$
(Map p1010; ☑ 044-45991633; www.amethystchennai.com; White's Rd, Royapettah; mains ₹240-450; ⊘ 10am-11pm; ☎) Set in an exquisitely converted warehouse with a wraparound verandah from which tables spill out into lush gardens, Amethyst is a nostalgically posh haven that's outrageously popular with expats and well-off Chennaiites. Top-notch, European-flavoured treats range over quiches, pasta, crepes, creative salads (watermelon and feta), and even afternoon tea. Fight for your table, then check out the stunning Indian couture boutique.

✗ Nungambakkam & Around

Tuscana Pizzeria   ITALIAN $$$
(Map p1010; ☑ 044-45038008; www.tuscanakryptos.in; 19, 3rd St, Wallace Garden; pizzas & pasta ₹480-780; ⊘ noon-11pm) This, my pizza-loving friends, is the real deal, and Chennai has well and truly embraced it. Tuscana turns out authentic thin-crust pizzas with toppings such as prosciutto and mozzarella, as well as creative takes such as spiced paneer masala pizza, and tasty pastas. It even has whole-wheat and gluten-free options. Best to book ahead.

Raintree   CHETTINADU $$$
(Map p1010; www.vivantabytaj.com; Vivanta by Taj – Connemara, Binny Rd; mains ₹500-1000; ⊘ 12.30-

CHENNAI STREET FOOD

Chennai may not have the same killer street food reputation as Delhi or Mumbai (Bombay), but there are some sensational streetside delicacies around, especially in Mylapore, George Town, Egmore and T Nagar (Thyagaraya Nagar).

Jannal Kadai (Map p1004; Ponnambala Vathiar St, Mylapore; bajjis ₹20; ⊙ 7.30-10am & 5.30-8.45pm Mon-Sat, 7.30-10am Sun) You take what you're given from the chap in the 'window shop', a fast and furious hole-in-the-wall famous for its hot crispy *bajjis* (vegetable fritters), *bondas* (mashed potato patty) and *vadas* (deep-fried lentil-flour doughnuts). Look for the navy-blue windows opposite Pixel Service.

Seena Bhai Tiffin Centre (Map p1004; 11/1 NSC Bose Rd; idlis & uttapams ₹40; ⊙6pm-midnight) Nothing but deliciously griddled, ghee-coated *idlis* and *uttapams* (thick, savoury rice pancakes with onions, chillies and coriander) at this 35-year-old eatery in the thick of George Town.

Mehta Brothers (Map p1004; 310 Mint St; dishes ₹15-25; ⊙4-9pm Mon-Sat) This tiny spot pulls in the crowds with the deep-fried delights of its signature Maharashtrian *vada pavs*, spiced potato fritters in buns, doused in garlicky chutney.

2.45pm & 7.30-11.45pm) This 25-year-old wood-ceilinged restaurant is probably the best place in Chennai to savour the delicious flavours of Tamil Nadu's Chettinadu region. Chettinad cuisine is famously meat-heavy and superbly spicy without being chilli-laden, but veg dishes are good too. When the weather behaves, you can dine outside in the leafy garden with water lilies.

✕ Southern Chennai

Murugan Idli Shop   SOUTH INDIAN **$**
(Map p1004; 77 GN Chetty Rd, T Nagar; dishes ₹50-85; ⊙ 7am-11.30pm) Those in the know generally agree this particular branch of the small Madurai-born chain serves some of the best *idlis* and South Indian meals in town. We heartily agree.

Chamiers   MULTICUISINE, CAFE **$$**
(Map p1004; 106 Chamiers Rd, RA Puram; mains ₹295-380, breakfasts ₹195-335; ⊙8am-11.30pm; 🛜) This 1st-floor cafe feels a continent away from Chennai, except that Chennaiites love it too. Flowery wallpaper, leaves through the windows, wicker chairs, wi-fi (per hour ₹100), wonderful carrot cake and cappuccino, English breakfasts, American pancakes, pasta, quiches, quesadillas, salads...

Junior Kuppanna   SOUTH INDIAN **$$**
(Map p1004; 4 Kannaiya St, North Usman Rd, T Nagar; mains ₹130-190, thalis veg/nonveg ₹160/190; ⊙noon-4pm & 7-11pm) From an impeccably clean kitchen (which you can tour if you like), come limitless, flavour-packed lunchtime thalis, dished up traditional-style on banana leaves. This typical, frenzied Chennai 'mess' also has a full menu, and carnivores tiring of the pure-veg lifestyle can seek solace in specialities like mutton brains and pan-fried seer fish. Arrive early: it's popular.

Enté Keralam   KERALAN **$$**
(Map p1004; ☎044-32216591; http://entekeralam.in; 1 Kasturi Estate 1st St, Poes Garden; mains ₹215-450; ⊙noon-3pm & 7-11pm) A calm ambience seeps through the four orange-toned rooms of this Keralan restaurant, holding just three or four tables each. Try the lightly spiced *pachakkari* vegetable stew with light, fluffy *appam* (rice pancake) or *kozhi porichatu* (deep-fried marinated chicken) and wind up with tender coconut ice cream or *paal ada payasam*, a kind of sweet rice pudding.

★**Dakshin**   SOUTH INDIAN **$$$**
(Map p1004; ☎044-24994101; Sheraton Park Hotel, 132 TTK Rd, Alwarpet; mains ₹690-1670; ⊙12.30-2.45pm & 7-11.15pm) Widely considered Chennai's finest South Indian restaurant, Dakshin specialises in the cuisines of Kerala, Tamil Nadu, Andhra Pradesh and Karnataka. Traditional sculptures and mirrored pillars set the temple-inspired scene, and flute and tabla musicians play nightly except Monday. Food suggestion: the Andhra Pradesh fish curry – and perhaps a little something from the impressive whiskey and wine list.

★**Copper Chimney**   NORTH INDIAN **$$$**
(Map p1004; ☎044-28115770; 74 Cathedral Rd, Gopalapuram; mains ₹290-700; ⊙noon-3pm & 7-11pm) Meat-eaters will drool over the yummy North Indian tandoori dishes served

here in stylishly minimalist surroundings, but the veg food is fantastic too (even some Jain specialities). The *machchi* tikka – skewers of tandoori-baked fish – is superb, as is the spiced paneer kebab.

Drinking & Nightlife

Chennai nightlife is on the up, but you'll need a full wallet for a night out here. Chennai has possibly the most liberal licensing laws in India – for five-star hotels. Bars and clubs in these hotels serve alcohol 24 hours a day, seven days a week, so that's where most of the after-dark fun happens. Solo guys ('stags') can be turned away. Dress codes are strict: no shorts and sandals.

Other hotel bars, mostly male-dominated, generally close at midnight. If you're buying your own alcohol, look for 'premium' TASMAC government liquor stores inside malls. For listings see www.timescity.com/chennai.

Zara the Tapas Bar BAR
(Map p1004; ☑ 044-28111462; zaratapasbar.in; 71 Cathedral Rd; cocktails ₹430-550, tapas ₹230-380; ⊗12.30pm-midnight) Where else in the world can you find DJs playing club music beneath bullfighting posters next to TVs showing cricket? Zara is packed with a young, fashionable crowd most nights, and it's a good idea to book a table. And the tapas? The *jamón serrano* is sacrilegiously minced into a paste, but the *tortilla española* is authentically good. Live bands on Tuesdays.

Pasha NIGHTCLUB
(Map p1010; Park Hotel, 601 Anna Salai; per couple ₹2000 incl ₹1500 drink voucher, women free; ⊗8.30pm-2.30am) A stylish, early-20s bunch packs into this glitzy, two-level, Persian-themed club, where popular Bollywood night takes over on Wednesdays and Saturdays. See big-name international DJs take to the decks. Dress code: smart casual.

Flying Elephant BAR, RESTAURANT
(☑044-71771234; Park Hyatt, 39 Velachery Rd, Guindy; per couple ₹3000 incl ₹2000 drink voucher, women free; ⊗11pm-3am Sat, restaurant 7-11pm

daily) Slickly contemporary and favoured by the elite, the Park Hyatt's high-energy, restaurant morphs into Chennai's hottest new party pad from 11pm on Saturday. Drinks are pricey (by any standards) but it's all very glam, with a sunken bar. The world fusion food (mains ₹650 to ₹1670), whipped up in five live kitchens, is good too. Head to the Guindy area, towards the airport.

Brew Room CAFE
(Map p1004; Savera Hotel, Dr Radhakrishnan Salai; coffees ₹100-175, dishes ₹250-350; ⊗8am-10pm; ⊛) The trendy home-brew cafe has hit Chennai, and Chennai loves it. Decked out in neorustic style, Brew Room does coffee like you've never had here, from double espresso and Italian cappuccino to French press and Americano. The contemporary Continental menu includes great vegetarian and vegan choices – even tofu!

Leather Bar BAR
(Map p1010; Park Hotel, 601 Anna Salai; ⊗24hr) 'Leather' refers to furniture, floor and wall coverings rather than anything kinky. This tiny, chic pad has mixologists dishing up fancy drinks and DJs spinning dance tunes from around 9pm.

Dublin PUB, NIGHTCLUB
(Map p1004; Sheraton Park Hotel, 132 TTK Rd, Alwarpet; per couple ₹2000 incl ₹1000 drink voucher; ⊗from 8pm Wed-Sat) Belting out beats from hip-hop to Bollywood, this long-running, three-floor party place is an Irish pub until 10pm, then it becomes a packed-out club that goes to 3am on Friday and Saturday. No unaccompanied men (stags).

Café Coffee Day CAFE
(Map p1010; www.cafecoffeeday.com; Ispahani Centre, 123 Nungambakkam High Rd; ⊗10am-10.30pm; ⊛) Reliably good hot and cold coffees and teas for ₹60 to ₹120. Also at **Egmore** (Map p1010; Alsa Mall, Montieth Rd; ⊗11am-9pm), **Nungambakkam** (Map p1010; Khader Nawaz Khan Rd, Nungambakkam; ⊗9am-11pm) and **Express Avenue Mall** (Map p1010; 3rd fl, Express Avenue Mall, White's Rd; ⊗9.30am-10pm).

☆ Entertainment

There's *bharatanatyam* (Tamil classical dance) and/or a Carnatic music concert going on somewhere in Chennai almost every evening. Check listings in the *Hindu* or *Times of India,* or on www.timescity.com/chennai. The **Music Academy** (Map p1004;

ℹ ATMS

Citibank ATMs are best for withdrawing large amounts of cash with foreign cards in Tamil Nadu. Axis Bank, Canara Bank, HDFC Bank, ICICI Bank and State Bank of India ATMs are other options.

044-28112231; www.musicacademymadras.in; 168 (old 306) TTK Rd, Royapettah) is the most popular venue; the Kalakshetra Foundation (p1008) and **Bharatiya Vidya Bhavan** (Map p1004; 044-24643420; www.bhavanchennai.org; East Mada St, Mylapore) also stage many events.

Shopping

T Nagar has great shopping, especially at Pondy Bazaar and in the Panagal Park area. Many of the finest Kanchipuram silks turn up in Chennai, and the streets around Panagal Park are filled with silk shops; if you're lucky enough to be attending an Indian wedding, this is where you buy your sari.

Nungambakkam's Khader Nawaz Khan Rd is a lovely lane of increasingly upmarket designer boutiques, cafes and galleries.

Chennai's shopping malls are full of major international and Indian apparel chains. The best include **Express Avenue** (White's Rd, Royapettah; ⊙10am-9pm), **Chennai Citi Centre** (Map p1004; 10 Dr Radhakrishnan Salai, Mylapore; ⊙10am-11.30pm), **Spencer Plaza** (Map p1010; Anna Salai; ⊙10.30am-9pm), and the new **Phoenix Market City** (142 Velachery Main Rd, Velachery; ⊙11am-10pm). Spencer Plaza is a bit downmarket from the others, with smaller craft and souvenir shops.

Central Chennai

★**Higginbothams**   BOOKS
(Map p1010; higginbothams@vsnl.com; 116 Anna Salai; ⊙9am-8pm) Open since 1844, this grand white building is reckoned to be India's oldest bookshop. It has a brilliant English-language selection, including Lonely Planet books, and a good range of maps.

Naturally Auroville   HANDICRAFTS
(Map p1010; 8 Khader Nawaz Khan Rd, Nungambakkam; ⊙10.30am-9pm) Colourful handicrafts and home-decor trinkets, including bedspreads, incense, scented candles, and handmade-paper notebooks, all from Auroville, near Puducherry.

Starmark   BOOKS
(www.starmark.in; 2nd fl, Express Avenue, White's Rd; ⊙10.30am-9.30pm) Smart new bookshop with an excellent collection of English, Indian and Tamil fiction and nonfiction, India travel books and Lonely Planet guides.

Evoluzione   CLOTHING
(Map p1010; www.evoluzionestyle.com; 3 Khader Nawaz Khan Rd, Nungambakkam; ⊙10.30-7.30pm

ⓘ **HOLIDAY TRANSPORT**

All kinds of transport in, to and from Tamil Nadu get booked up weeks in advance for periods around major celebrations, including Pongal, Karthikai Deepam, Gandhi Jayanti and Diwali. Plan ahead.

Mon-Sat, noon-6pm Sun) This high-end boutique showcases neotraditional creations by cutting-edge Indian designers. Great for browsing, even if your budget won't allow the fabulously glittery wedding gowns!

Poompuhar   HANDICRAFTS
(Map p1010; 108 Anna Salai; ⊙10am-8pm Mon-Sat, 11am-7pm Sun) This large branch of the fixed-price state-government handicrafts chain is good for everything from cheap technicolour plaster deities to a ₹200,000, metre-high bronze Nataraja.

Southern Chennai

★**Nalli Silks**   TEXTILES
(Map p1004; www.nallisilks.com; 9 Nageswaran Rd, T Nagar; ⊙9am-9pm) Set up in 1928, the huge supercolourful granddaddy of Chennai silk shops sparkles with wedding saris and all kinds of Kanchipuram silks, as well as silk dhotis (long loincloths) for the boys. There's a jewellery branch next door.

Fabindia   CLOTHING, HANDICRAFTS
(www.fabindia.com; 35 TTK Rd, Mylapore; ⊙10.30am-8.30pm) This fair-trade, nationwide chain sells stylishly contemporary village-made clothes and crafts. Perfect for picking up a kurta (long shirt with short/no collar) to throw over leggings. This branch also has incense, ceramics, table and bed linen, and natural beauty products. Also at **Woods Rd** (Map p1010; 3 Woods Rd; ⊙10.30am-8.30pm), **Express Avenue** (Map p1010; 1st fl, Express Avenue Mall, White's Rd; ⊙11am-9pm) and **T Nagar** (Map p1004; 44 GN Chetty Rd, T Nagar; ⊙10.30am-8.30pm).

Chamiers   CLOTHING, HANDICRAFTS
(Map p1004; 106 Chamiers Rd, RA Puram; ⊙10am-8pm) On the ground floor of this popular cafe-cum-boutique-complex, **Anokhi** has wonderful, East-meets-West block-printed clothes, bedding and accesories in light fabrics, at decent prices. Elegant **Amethyst Room** next door takes things upmarket with beautiful Indian-design couture.

NONSTOP DOMESTIC FLIGHTS FROM CHENNAI

DESTINATION	AIRLINES	FARE FROM (₹, ONE WAY)	DURATION (HR)	FREQUENCY (DAILY)
Bengaluru	AI, I8, SG, S2, 6E, 9W	990	1	17
Delhi	AI, SG, 6E, 9W	3776	2¾	24
Goa	AI, SG, 6E	1577	1¼-2	3-4
Hyderabad	AI, SG, 6E, 9W	1576	1-1½	13
Kochi	AI, SG, 6E, 9W	1576	1-1½	7
Kolkata	AI, SG, 6E	2777	2-2¾	9
Mumbai	AI, G8, SG, 6E, 9W	2775	2	22
Port Blair	AI, G8, SG, 9W	6684	2-2¼	4
Trivandrum	AI, SG, 6E	2172	1½	4

Airline codes: AI – Air India, G8 – Go Air, I8 – AirAsia India, SG – SpiceJet, 6E – IndiGo, 9W – Jet Airways

Kumaran Silks   TEXTILES
(Map p1004; www.kumaransilksonline.com; 12 Nageswaran Rd, T Nagar; ⏲9am-9pm) Saris, saris (including 'budget saris') and plenty of Kanchipuram silk.

ℹ Information

INTERNET ACCESS
'Browsing centres' are dotted all over town. Plenty of cafes have wi-fi.

Internet (Map p1010; 6 Gandhi Irwin Rd, Egmore; per hour ₹30; ⏲8am-10pm) In the Hotel Imperial yard.

Studio (Map p1010; Theetharappan St, Triplicane; per hour ₹15; ⏲9.30am-10.30pm) You'll need your passport.

LEFT LUGGAGE
Egmore and Central train stations have left-luggage offices (signed 'Cloakroom') for people with journey tickets. The airport also has left-luggage facilities.

MEDICAL SERVICES
Apollo Hospital (Map p1010; ☎044-28296569, emergency 044-28293333; www.apollohospitals.com; 21 Greams Lane) State-of-the-art, expensive hospital, popular with 'medical tourists'.

Kauvery Hospital (Map p1004; ☎044-40006000; www.kauveryhospital.com; 199 Luz Church Rd, Mylapore) Good, private, general hospital.

MONEY
ATMs are everywhere, including at Central train station, the airport and the main bus station.

Thomas Cook (Map p1010; Phase I, Spencer Plaza, Anna Salai; ⏲9.30am-6.30pm) Changes foreign cash and American Express travellers cheques.

POST
DHL (Map p1010; ☎044-42148886; www.dhl.co.in; 85 VVV Sq, Pantheon Rd, Egmore; ⏲9am-10pm Mon-Sat) Secure international parcel delivery; several branches around town.

Main post office (Map p1004; Rajaji Salai, George Town; ⏲8am-8.30pm Mon-Sat, 10am-6pm Sun)

TOURIST INFORMATION
Indiatourism (Map p1010; ☎044-28460285; www.incredibleindia.org; 154 Anna Salai; ⏲9am-6pm Mon-Fri) Helpful on all of India, as well as Chennai.

Tamil Nadu Tourism Development Corporation (TTDC; Map p1010; ☎044-25383333; www.tamilnadutourism.org; Tamil Nadu Tourism Complex, 2 Wallajah Rd, Triplicane; ⏲10am-6pm) The state tourism body's main office takes bookings for its own bus tours, answers questions and hands out leaflets. In the same building are state tourist offices from all over India, mostly open 10am to 6pm. The TTDC has counters at Central and Egmore stations.

TRAVEL AGENCIES
Milesworth Travel (Map p1004; ☎044-24320522; http://milesworth.com; RM Towers, 108 Chamiers Rd, Alwarpet; ⏲9.30am-6pm Mon-Sat) A very professional, welcoming agency that will help with all your travel needs.

ℹ Getting There & Away

AIR
Chennai International Airport is situated at Tirusulam in the far southwest of the city. The international terminal is about 500m west of the domestic terminal; the two are linked by a raised walkway.

There are direct flights to cities all over India, including Trichy (Tiruchirappalli), Madurai, Coimbatore and Thoothikudi (Tuticorin) within Tamil Nadu. Internationally, Chennai has plenty of direct flights to/from Colombo, Singapore, Kuala Lumpur and the Gulf states. The best fares from Europe are often on Jet Airways (via Mumbai or Delhi), Qatar Airways (via Doha) or Emirates (via Dubai). Cathay Pacific flies to Hong Kong, and Maldivian to Male.

Airline Offices

Air Asia (Map p1010; ☑ 044-33008000; www.airasia.com; Ispahani Centre, 123 Nungambak-kam High Rd; ☺ 9.30am-6pm Mon-Sat)

Air India (Map p1010; ☑ 044-23453375; www.airindia.com; 19 Rukmani Lakshmipathy Rd, Egmore; ☺ 9.45am-1pm & 1.45-5.15pm Mon-Sat)

Air India Express (Map p1010; ☑ 044-23453375; www.airindiaexpress.in; 19 Rukmani Lakshmipathy Rd, Egmore; ☺ 9.45am-1pm & 1.45-5.15pm Mon-Sat)

Jet Airways (Map p1010; ☑ 044-39893333; www.jetairways.com; 43/44 Montieth Rd, Egmore; ☺10am-6pm Mon-Fri)

BOAT

Passenger ships sail from George Town harbour direct to Port Blair in the Andaman Islands (p1084) once weekly. The **Andaman Shipping Office Ticketing Counter** (☑ 044-25226873; www.and.nic.in; 2nd fl, Shipping Corporation of India, Jawahar Bldg, 17 Rajaji Salai, George Town; ☺10am-1pm & 2-4pm Mon-Fri, 10am-12.30pm Sat) sells tickets (₹2270 to ₹8850) for the 60-hour trip. Book several days ahead,

and take three copies each of your passport data page and Indian visa along with the original. It can be a long process.

BUS

Most government buses operate from the large but surprisingly orderly **CMBT** (Chennai Mofussil Bus Terminus; Jawaharlal Nehru Rd, Koyambedu), 6km west of the centre. The most comfortable and expensive are the AC buses (and best of these are the Volvo AC services), followed by the UD (Ultra Deluxe), and these can generally be reserved in advance. There's a computerised reservation centre at the left end of the main hall, where you can book up to 60 days ahead.

The **T Nagar Bus Terminus** (Map p1004; South Usman Rd) is handy for bus 599 to Mamallapuram (₹27, 1½ hours, every 30 minutes).

Private buses generally offer greater comfort than non-AC government buses to many destinations, at up to double the price. Service information is available at www.redbus.in, and tickets can be booked through many travel agencies. Their main terminal is the **Omni bus stand** (off Kaliamman Koil St, Koyambedu), 500m west of the CMBT, but some companies also pick up and drop off elsewhere in the city. Parveen Travels, for example, runs services to Bengaluru, Ernakulam (Kochi), Kodaikanal, Madurai, Ooty, Puducherry, Trichy and Thiruvananthapuram (Trivandrum) departing from its **Egmore office** (Map p1010; ☑ 044-28192577; www.parveentravels.com; 11/5 Kennet Lane, Egmore).

GOVERNMENT BUSES FROM CMBT

DESTINATION	FARE (₹)	DURATION (HR)	FREQUENCY
Bengaluru	360-700	8	60 daily
Coimbatore	405	11	16 daily
Ernakulam (Kochi)	590	16	3pm
Hyderabad	730-1200	12	5 daily 6.30pm
Kodaikanal	390	13	5pm
Kumbakonom	190-275	7	every 30min 4am-midnight
Madurai	355-430	10	every 15min 4am-midnight
Mamallapuram	80	2	every 30min 4am-midnight
Mysuru	630-1050	10	6 daily
Ooty	415	13	4.30pm, 5.45pm, 7.15pm
Puducherry	95-200	4	every 30min 4am-midnight
Rameswaram	420-445	13	5pm, 5.30pm, 5.45pm
Thanjavur	220-325	8½	every 30min 5am-11pm
Tirupathi	162-232	4	21 daily
Trichy	190-285	7	every 15min 2am-midnight
Trivandrum	565	15	12 daily

CAR

Renting a car with a driver is the easiest way of getting anywhere and is easily arranged through most travel agents, midrange or top-end hotels, or the airport's prepaid taxi desks. Sample rates for non-AC cars are ₹700/800 for up to five hours and 50km, and ₹1400/1600 for up to 10 hours and 100km.

TRAIN

Interstate trains and those heading west generally depart from Central station, while trains heading south mostly leave from Egmore. The **advance reservations office** (Map p1010; 1st fl, Chennai Central local station; ◷ 8am-8pm Mon-Sat, 8am-2pm Sun), with its incredibly helpful Foreign Tourist Cell, is on the 1st floor in a separate 11-storey building just west of the main Central station building. Egmore station has its own **Passenger Reservation Office** (Map p1010; Chennai Egmore station; ◷ 8am-8pm Mon-Sat, 8am-2pm Sun).

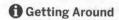

Getting Around

TO/FROM THE AIRPORT

The Chennai Metro Rail system, expected to open in late 2015, will provide a cheap, easy link between the airport and city. Meanwhile, the cheapest option is a suburban train to/from Tirusulam station opposite the parking areas of the domestic terminal, accessed by a pedestrian subway under the highway. Trains run every 10 to 20 minutes from 4am to midnight to/from Chennai Beach station (₹5, 42 minutes) with stops including Kodambakkam, Egmore, Chennai Park and Chennai Fort.

Prepaid taxi kiosks outside the airport's international terminal charge ₹480/580 for a non-AC/AC cab to Egmore, and ₹400/500 to T Nagar. Rates are slightly lower at prepaid taxi kiosks outside the domestic terminal.

From the CMBT, city buses 70 and 170 to Tambaram stop on the highway across from the airport.

MAJOR TRAINS FROM CHENNAI

DESTINATION	TRAIN NO & NAME	FARE (₹)	DURATION (HR)	DEPARTURE
Bengaluru	12007 Shatabdi Express*	529/1155 (A)	5	6am CC
	12609 Chennai-Bangalore Express	110/535 (B)	6½	1.35pm CC
Coimbatore	12675 Kovai Express	180/655 (B)	7½	6.15am CC
	12671 Nilgiri Express	315/805/1135 (C)	7¾	9.15pm CC
Delhi	12621 Tamil Nadu Express	780/2020/2970 (C)	33	10pm CC
Goa	17311 Vasco Express (Friday only)	475/1275/1850 (C)	22	1.50pm CC
Hyderabad	12759 Charminar Express	425/1115/1590 (C)	13½	6.10pm CC
Kochi	16041 Alleppey Express	395/1035/1470 (C)	11½	8.45pm CC
Kolkata	12842 Coromandel Express	665/1730/2520 (C)	27	8.45am CC
Madurai	12635 Vaigai Express	180/655 (B)	8	1.20pm CE
	12637 Pandyan Express	315/805/1135 (C)	9	9.20pm CE
Mumbai	11042 Mumbai Express	540/1440/2100 (C)	26	11.55am CC
Mysore	12007 Shatabdi Express*	915/1805 (A)	7	6am CC
	16021 Kaveri Express	285/755/1085 (C)	10	9pm CC
Tirupathi	16053 Tirupathi Express	80/285 (B)	3½	2.10pm CC
Trichy	12635 Vaigai Express	145/510 (B)	5	1.20pm CE
Trivandrum	12695 Trivandrum Mail	470/1230/1760 (C)	16	3.25pm CC

Departure Codes: CC – Chennai Central, CE – Chennai Egmore

*Daily except Wednesday

Fares: (A) chair/executive; (B) 2nd/chair; (C) sleeper/3AC/2AC

CHENNAI BUS ROUTES

BUS NO	ROUTE
A1	Central–Anna Salai–RK Mutt Rd (Mylapore)–Theosophical Society–Thiruvanmiyur
1B	Parry's–Central–Anna Salai–Airport
10A	Parry's–Central–Egmore (S)–Pantheon Rd–T Nagar
11	Rattan–Central–Anna Salai–T Nagar
12	T Nagar–Pondy Bazaar–Eldham's Rd–Dr Radhakrishnan Salai–Vivekananda House
15B & 15F	Broadway–Central–CMBT
21H	Broadway–Fort St George–Kamarajar Salai–San Thome Cathedral–Theosophical Society
M27	CMBT–T Nagar
27B	CMBT–Egmore (S)–Bharathi Salai (Triplicane)
27D	Egmore (S)–Anna Salai–Cathedral Rd–Dr Radhakrishnan Salai–San Thome Cathedral
32 & 32A	Central–Vivekananda House

Routes operate in both directions.

Broadway – Broadway Bus Terminus, George Town

Central – Central Station

Egmore (S) – Egmore station (south side)

Parry's – Parry's Corner

AUTORICKSHAW
Fixed autorickshaw fares are ₹25 for the first 1.8km (minimum charge), then ₹12 per kilometre. Some drivers still refuse to use their meters and quote astronomical fares, while others take unnecessarily long routes or ask for 'meter plus extra', but most will go by the meter if you insist. Avoid paying upfront, and always establish the meter is on before getting into a rickshaw. Rates rise by up to 50% from 11pm to 5am.

There are prepaid autorickshaw booths outside the CMBT (₹125 to Egmore) and Central station, and 24-hour prepaid stands with fare charts outside the north and south exits of Egmore station.

Tempting offers of ₹50 'city tours' by autorickshaw drivers sound too good to be true. They are. You'll spend the day being dragged from one shop or emporium to another.

BUS
Chennai's city bus system is worth getting to know, although buses get packed to overflowing at busy times. Fares are between ₹3 and ₹14 (up to double for express and deluxe services, and multiplied by five for Volvo AC services). Route information is online at http://busroutes.in/chennai.

METRO RAIL
Chennai Metro Rail, a new, part-underground rapid transit system, is expected to open in late 2015 and should make moving around the city much easier. Line 1 goes from the airport to Teynampet, Thousand Lights, Central train station, the High Court and Washermanpet in northern Chennai, running beneath Anna Salai for several kilometres. Line 2 goes from Central train station west to Egmore and the CMBT then south to St Thomas Mount.

TAXI
Both airport terminals have prepaid taxi kiosks. There's a **prepaid taxi stand** (Map p1010; Egmore Station; ⊙4am-1pm) outside the south side of Egmore station; a ride of 7km, such as to Alwarpet, costs about ₹240.

Relatively reliable **Fast Track** (☑6000 6000) taxis charge ₹100 for up to 4km, then ₹18 per kilometre (with a 25% hike in rates between 11pm and 5am); bookings are taken by phone.

TRAIN
Efficient, cheap suburban trains run from Beach station to Fort, Park (near Central station), Egmore, Chetpet, Nungambakkam, Kodambakkam, Mambalam, Saidapet, Guindy, St Thomas Mount, Tirusulam (for the airport), and on down to Tambaram. At Egmore station, the suburban platforms (10 and 11) and ticket office are on the north side of the station. A second line branches south after Fort to Park Town, Chepauk, Tiruvallikeni (for Marina Beach), Light House and Thirumailai (near Kapaleeshwarar Temple). Trains run from 4am to midnight, several times hourly; rides cost ₹5 to ₹10.

NORTHERN TAMIL NADU

Chennai to Mamallapuram

Chennai's sprawl peters out after an hour or so heading south on the East Coast Road (ECR), at which point Tamil Nadu becomes red dirt, blue skies, palm trees, and green fields, sprinkled with towns and villages (or, if you take the 'IT Expressway' inland, huge new buildings).

Swimming along the coast is dangerous due to strong currents.

👁 Sights & Activities

**Cholamandal
Artists' Village**　　ARTIST COLONY, MUSEUM
(☑044-24490092; www.cholamandalartistsvillage.in; Injambakkam; museum ₹20; ☺museum 9.30am-6.30pm) There's a tropical bohemian groove floating around Injambakkam village, site of the Cholamandal Artists' Village, 10km south of the Adyar River. This 3-hectare artists' cooperative – founded in 1966 by artists of the Madras Movement, pioneers of modern art in South India – is a serene muse away from the world, and the art in its museum is very much worth lingering over. Look especially for work by KCS Paniker, SG Vasudev, M Senathipathi and S Nandagopal.

**DakshinaChitra
Museum**　　ARTS & CRAFTS CENTRE
(☑044-27472603; www.dakshinachitra.net; East Coast Rd, Muttukadu; Indian adult/student ₹100/50, foreign ₹250/70; ☺10am-6pm Wed-Mon) DakshinaChitra, 22km south of the Adyar River, offers a fantastic insight into South India's traditional arts and crafts. Like a treasure chest of local art and architecture, this jumble of open-air museum, preserved village, artisan workshops (pottery, silk weaving, basket making), and a new tribal art gallery is set among an exquisite collection of traditional South Indian homes.

Covelong Point　　SURFING
(☑9840975916; www.covelongpoint.com) The fishing village of Kovalam, 20km north of Mamallapuram, has recently sprung into the spotlight for having probably the best surfing waves on the Tamil Nadu coast. For classes or surf companionship, head to 'social surfing school' Covelong Point, run by Kovalam's original local surf pioneer Murthy. Kovalam also hosts the hugely popular **Covelong Point Surf & Music Festival** (www.covelongpoint.com; ☺Sep), now into its second year.

Madras Crocodile Bank　　ZOO
(☑044-27472447; www.madrascrocodilebank.org; Vadanemmeli; adult/child ₹35/10, camera/video ₹20/100; ☺8.30am-5.30pm Tue-Sun) ✪ Madras Crocodile Bank, 6km south down the ECR from Kovalam, is a fascinating peek into the reptile world, and an incredible conservation and research trust. Founded by croc/snake-man Romulus Whitaker, the Bank has thousands of reptiles, including 18 of the world's 23 species of crocodilian (crocodiles and similar creatures), and does crucial work in maintaining genetic reserves of these animals, several of which are endangered.

Tiger Cave　　SACRED HINDU SITE
(Saluvankuppam; admission free; ☺6am-6pm) Just 5km north of Mamallapuram, the Tiger Cave is an unfinished but impressive rock-cut shrine, probably dating from the 7th century and dedicated to Durga (a form of Devi, Shiva's wife). What's special is the 'necklace' of 11 monstrous tigerlike heads framing its central shrine-cavity. At the north end of the parklike complex is a rock-cut Shiva shrine from the same era. Beyond the fence lies the more recently excavated **Subrahmanya Temple**, comprising an 8th-century granite shrine built over a Sangam-era brick temple dedicated to Murugan, which is one of the oldest known temples in Tamil Nadu.

ℹ Getting There & Away

To reach these places, take any bus heading south from Chennai to Mamallapuram and ask to be let off at the appropriate point(s). The TTDC's Chennai–Mamallapuram round-trip bus tour (₹450 to ₹550, 10 hours) visits several of the sites and Mamallapuram itself. A full-day taxi tour from Chennai costs around ₹3000.

Mamallapuram (Mahabalipuram)

☑044 / POP 15,172

Mamallapuram was the major seaport of the ancient Pallava kingdom based at Kanchipuram, and a wander round the town's magnificent, World Heritage–listed temples and carvings inflames the imagination, especially at sunset.

And then, in addition to ancient archaeological wonders and coastal beauty, there's the traveller ghetto of Othavadai and Othavadai Cross Sts. Restaurants serve pasta, pizza and pancakes, shops sell hand sanitiser and things from Tibet, and you know you have landed, once again, in the great Kingdom of Backpackistan.

'Mahabs', as most call it, is under two hours by bus from Chennai, and many travellers make a beeline straight here. The town is small and laid-back, and its sights can be explored on foot or by bicycle.

◉ Sights

You can easily spend a full day exploring Mamallapuram's marvellous temples and rock carvings. Most of them were carved from the rock during the 7th-century reign of Pallava king Narasimhavarman I, whose nickname Mamalla (Great Wrestler) gave the town its name. Apart from the Shore Temple and the Five Rathas, admission is free. Official Archaeological Survey of India guides can be hired at sites for around ₹100.

★Shore Temple   HINDU TEMPLE
(combined 1-day ticket with Five Rathas Indian/foreigner ₹10/250, video ₹25; ⊙6am-6pm) Standing like a magnificent fist of rock-cut elegance overlooking the sea, the two-towered Shore Temple symbolises the heights of Pallava architecture and the maritime ambitions of the Pallava kings. Its small size belies its excellent proportion and the supreme quality of the carvings, many of which have been eroded into vaguely Impressionist embellishments. Built under Narasimhavarman II in the 8th century, it's the earliest significant free-standing stone temple in Tamil Nadu.

The two towers rise above shrines to Shiva and their original linga (phallic symbols of Shiva) captured the sunrise and sunset. Between the Shiva shrines is one to Vishnu, shown sleeping. Rows of Nandi (Shiva's vehicle) statues frame the temple courtyard.

★Five Rathas   HINDU TEMPLE
(Pancha Ratha; Five Rathas Rd; combined 1-day ticket with Shore Temple Indian/foreigner ₹10/250, video ₹25; ⊙6am-6pm) Huddled together at the southern end of Mamallapuram, the Five Rathas look like buildings, but they were, astonishingly, all carved from single large rocks. Each of these 7th-century temples was dedicated to a Hindu god and is now named after one or more of the Pandavas, the five hero-brothers of the epic Mahabharata, or their common wife, Draupadi. The *rathas* were hidden in the sand until excavated by the British 200 years ago.

Ratha is Sanskrit for chariot, and may refer to the temples' form or to their function as vehicles for the gods. It's thought they didn't originally serve as places of worship, but were created as architectural models.

The first *ratha* on the left after you enter the gate is the **Draupadi Ratha**, in the form of a stylised South Indian hut. It's dedicated to the demon-fighting goddess Durga, who looks out from inside, standing on a lotus. A huge sculpted lion, Durga's mount, stands guard outside.

Next, on the same plinth, is the 'chariot' of the most important Pandava, the **Arjuna Ratha**, dedicated to Shiva. Its pilasters, miniature roof shrines, and small octagonal dome make it a precursor of many later temples in South India. A huge Nandi, Shiva's vehicle, stands behind. Shiva and other gods are depicted on the temple's outer walls.

The barrel-roofed **Bhima Ratha** was never completed, as is evidenced by the missing colonnade on its north side. Inside is a shrine to Vishnu. The **Dharmaraja Ratha**, tallest of the temples, is similar in form to the Arjuna Ratha but one storey higher. The carvings on its outer walls mostly represent gods, including the androgynous Ardhanarishvara (half Shiva, half Parvati) on the east side. King Narasimhavarman I appears at the west end of the south side.

The **Nakula-Sahadeva Ratha** (named after two twin Pandavas) stands aside from the other four and is dedicated to Indra. The life-size stone elephant beside it is one of the most perfectly sculpted elephants in India. Approaching from the gate to the north you see its back end first, hence its nickname Gajaprishthakara (elephant's backside).

★Arjuna's Penance   HINDU, MONUMENT
(West Raja St) The crowning masterpiece of Mamallapuram's stonework, this giant relief carving is one of India's greatest ancient art works. Inscribed on two huge, adjacent boulders, the Penance bursts with scenes of Hindu myth and everyday vignettes of South Indian life. In the centre *nagas* (snake-beings), descend a once water-filled cleft, representing the Ganges. To the left Arjuna (hero of the Mahabharata) performs self-mortification (fasting on one leg), so that the four-armed Shiva will grant him his most powerful weapon, the god-slaying Pasupata.

Mamallapuram (Mahabalipuram)

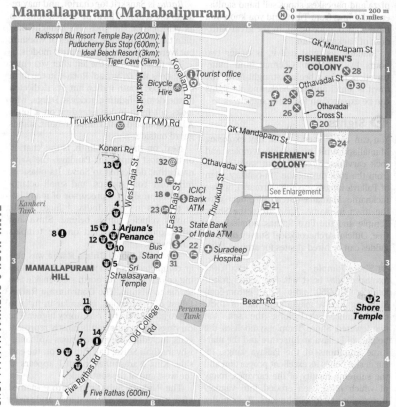

Some scholars believe the carving shows not Arjuna but the sage Bagiratha, who did severe penance to obtain Shiva's help in bringing the Ganges to earth. Shiva is attended by dwarves, and celestial beings fly across the upper parts of the carving. Below Arjuna/Bagiratha is a temple to Vishnu, mythical ancestor of the Pallava kings. The many wonderfully carved animals include a herd of elephants and – humour amid the holy – a cat mimicking Arjuna's penance to a crowd of mice.

South along the road from Arjuna's Penance are the unfinished **Panch Pandava Mandapa** (☉6.30am-6pm) cave temple; the **Krishna Mandapa** (☉6.30am-6pm), which famously depicts Krishna lifting Govardhana Hill to protect cows and villagers from a storm sent by Indra; an **unfinished relief carving** of similar size to Arjuna's Penance; and the **Dharmaraja Cave Temple** (☉6.30am-6pm).

🏃 Activities

Beaches

The beach fronting the village isn't exactly pristine, but south of the Shore Temple it clears into finer sand. You'll also be further away from the leers of men who spend their days gawking at tourists. Like most of Tamil Nadu's coast, these beaches aren't great for swimming, due to dangerous rips.

Surfing

Mumu Surf School SURFING
(☎9789844191; http://mumusurfer.wix.com; 42 Fishermen's Colony; 90min group/private class ₹750/1000; ☉7.30am-6pm) Popular, well-organised school for all levels and board rental (per hour ₹150 to ₹300).

Therapies

Numerous places in town offer massage, reiki, yoga and ayurveda, at similar rates. Ask fellow travellers, question the therapist care-

Mamallapuram (Mahabalipuram)

fully and if you have any misgivings, don't proceed.

Sri Durga — AYURVEDA, YOGA
(☑9840288280; www.sridurgaayurveda.com; 35 Othavadai St; 45min massage ₹750, 1hr yoga ₹200) Recommended massages and ayurvedic treatments (male therapists for men, female for women), and yoga at 7am and 6pm.

☞ Tours

Travel XS — CYCLING, BIRDWATCHING
(☑044-27443360; www.travel-xs.com; 123 East Raja St; bicycle tours ₹450-500; ☺9.30am-6pm Mon-Fri, 9.30am-2pm Sat) Runs half-day bicycle tours to nearby villages, visiting local potters and observing activities such as *kolam* drawing (the 'welcome' patterns outside doorways, also called *rangoli*), and organises day trips to places including Kanchipuram and Vedanthangal Bird Sanctuary.

✦✧ Festivals & Events

Mamallapuram Dance Festival — DANCE
(☺late Dec-late Jan) A four-week, weekend-only dance festival showcasing classical and folk dances from all over India, with many performances on an open-air stage against the imposing backdrop of Arjuna's Penance.

Dances include *bharatanatyam* (from Tamil Nadu), Kuchipudi (Andhra Pradesh) tribal dance, and Kathakali (Kerala).

🛏 Sleeping

Hotel Daphne — HOTEL $
(☑9894282876; www.moonrakersrestaurants. com; 24 Othavadai Cross St; r ₹500-1500; ❖☀) Most rooms here are perfectly acceptable if nothing fancy, but the top-floor AC rooms 13 and 14 are great value, with four-poster beds, balconies and cane swing chairs. The courtyard and free wi-fi are other drawcards.

**Tina Blue View Lodge &
Restaurant** — GUESTHOUSE $
(☑9840727270, 044-27442319; 48 Othavadai St; s/d/tr ₹500/600/900) Frayed and faded Tina is one of Mamallapuram's originals and kind of looks it, but remains deservedly popular for its whitewashed walls, blue flourishes and tropical garden, as well as tireless original owner Xavier.

Sri Harul Guest House — GUESTHOUSE $
(Sea View Guest House; ☑9384620173; sriharul@ gmail.com; 181 Bajanai Koil St, Fishermen's Colony; r ₹800-900) Surf crashes onto the rocks right below your balcony if you land one of the half-dozen sea-view rooms at Sri Harul, one

of the better seafront budget deals. Rooms are basic, medium-sized and quite clean, and you can hang out at the rooftop cafe.

Greenwoods Beach Resort GUESTHOUSE $
(☎044-27442212; greenwoods_resort@yahoo.com; 7 Othavadai Cross St; r ₹500-800, with AC ₹1200; ❋☎) Perhaps the most characterful of the Othavadai Cross St cheapies and definitely not on the beach, Greenwoods is run by an enthusiastic family who put up backpackers in plain, clean-ish rooms up staircases around a pretty leafy courtyard.

Butterball Bed 'n Breakfast B&B $$
(☎9094792525; 9/26 East Raja St; s/d incl breakfast ₹1700/2000; ❋☎) There's a great view of the eponymous giant rock from the roof terrace, and a lovely lawn. The smallish but clean, pleasant rooms have old English prints, writing desks and blue-tiled bathrooms, and breakfast is served in its **Burger Shack** (9/26 East Raja St; mains ₹120-300; ⊙10am-10pm) restaurant out the front.

Hotel Mahabs HOTEL $$
(☎044-27442645; www.hotelmahabs.com; 68 East Raja St; r ₹2140-2930; ❋@☎☒) Friendly Mahabs is centred on a pretty mural-lined pool

(₹300 for nonguests) surrounded by tropical greenery. Boring brown is the room theme, but they're very clean and comfy. There's a decent in-house restaurant.

Hotel Mamalla Heritage HOTEL $$
(☎044-27442060; www.hotelmamallaheritage.com; 104 East Raja St; incl breakfast s ₹2400-2640, d ₹2640-2880; ❋☎☒) King of tour group packages, the Mamalla has big, comfortable, forgettable rooms rising around a nice pool, and a quality rooftop veg restaurant.

★**Radisson Blu Resort Temple Bay** RESORT $$$
(☎044-27443636; www.radissonblu.com/hotel-mamallapuram; 57 Kovalam Rd; r incl breakfast from ₹9880; ❋@☎☒) The Radisson's 144 luxurious chalets, villas and bungalows are strewn across manicured gardens stretching 500m to the beach. Somewhere in the midst is India's longest swimming pool, all 220m of it. Rooms range from large to enormous; the most expensive have private pools. The Radisson also offers Mamallapuram's finest (and priciest) dining and a top-notch ayurvedic spa. Best rates online.

MAMALLAPURAM HILL

Many interesting monuments are scattered across the rock-strewn hill on the west side of town. It takes about an hour to walk round the main ones. The hill area is open from 6am to 6pm and has two entrances: a northern one on West Raja St, and a southern one just off Five Rathas Rd.

Straight ahead inside the northern entrance you can't miss the huge boulder with the inspired name of **Krishna's Butterball**, immovable but apparently balancing precariously. Pass between the rocks north of here to the **Trimurti Cave Temple**, honouring the Hindu 'trinity': Brahma (left), Shiva (centre) and Vishnu (right). On the back of the same rock is a beautiful group of carved elephants.

Back south of Krishna's Butterball you reach the **Ganesh Ratha**, carved from a single rock with lion-shaped pillar bases. Once a Shiva temple, it became a shrine to Ganesh (Shiva's elephant-headed son) after the original lingam was removed. Southwest of here, the **Varaha Mandapa** houses some of Mamallapuram's finest carvings. The left panel shows Vishnu's boar avatar, Varaha, lifting the earth out of the oceans. The outward-facing panels show Vishnu's consort Lakshmi (washed by elephants) and Durga, while the right-hand panel has Vishnu in his eight-armed giant form, Trivikrama, overcoming the demon king Bali.

A little further south, then up to the left, is the 16th-century **Raya Gopura** (Olakkanatha Temple), probably an unfinished *gopuram* (gateway tower). West just up the hill is the finely carved **Lion Throne**. The main path continues south to the **Ramanuja Mandapa** and up to Mamallapuram's **lighthouse** (Indian/foreigner ₹10/25, camera ₹20; ⊙10am-1pm & 2-5.30pm). Just southwest of the lighthouse is the **Mahishamardini Mandapa**, carved from the rock with excellent scenes from the Puranas (Sanskrit stories from the 5th century AD). The left-side panel shows Vishnu sleeping on the coils of a snake; on the right, Durga bestrides her lion vehicle while killing the demon-buffalo Mahisha. Inside the central shrine, Murugan is depicted sitting between his parents Shiva and Parvati.

Ideal Beach Resort
RESORT $$$

(☎044-27442240; www.idealresort.com; East Coast Rd; s/d from ₹6000/6600; ❂@❂❂) With a landscaped garden setting and its own stretch of (pretty nice) beach, this laid-back resort, 3km north of town, is popular with weekending families and couples. It's quiet and secluded, there's a lovely pool-side restaurant, and some rooms come with open-air showers. Nonguests can get pool/beach day passes for ₹400.

✖ Eating

Eateries on Othavadai and Othavadai Cross Sts provide semi-open-air settings, decent Western mains and bland Indian curries. Most will serve you a beer. For Indian food, there are cheap veg places near the bus stand.

Le Yogi
MULTICUISINE $$

(19 Othavadai St; mains ₹100-200; ☺7.30am-11pm) This is some of the best Western food in town; the pasta, pizza, sizzlers and crepes are genuine and tasty (if small), service is good, and the chilled-out setting, with bamboo posts and pretty lamps dangling from a thatched roof, has a touch of the romantic.

Gecko Restaurant
MULTICUISINE $$

(www.gecko-web.com; 37 Othavadai St; mains ₹150-270; ☺9am-10pm; ☎) Two friendly brothers run this cute blue-and-yellow-walled spot sprinkled with colourful artwork and wood carvings. The offerings and prices aren't that different from other tourist-oriented spots, but there's more love put into the cooking here and it's tastier.

Freshly 'n Hot
CAFE $$

(Othavadai Cross St; mains ₹70-200; ☺7am-9pm) Yes, the name makes no sense, but this tiny place is relaxed, fresh and friendly. A comparatively small menu of perfectly OK pizza, pasta, sandwiches and crepes accompanies a long list of coffees. The iced coffees are great.

Moonrakers
MULTICUISINE $$

(34 Othavadai St; mains ₹100-180; ☺10am-10pm; ☎) You'll probably end up here at some point; it's the kind of place that's dominated the backpacker-ghetto streetscape forever. The food won't win any prizes but it's fine, and the three floors of tables keep busy (probably partly thanks to the free wi-fi).

Water's Edge Cafe
MULTICUISINE $$$

(Radisson Blu Resort Temple Bay, 57 Kovalam Rd; mains ₹480-900; ☺24hr) The Radisson's poolside 'cafe' offers everything from American pancakes to grilled tofu, Indian veg dishes, and a fantastic breakfast buffet (₹970). Also here is **The Wharf** (mains ₹550-1600; ☺noon-3pm & 7-11pm), which looks like a beach shack but is actually a gourmet seaside restaurant.

🛍 Shopping

The roar of electric stone-grinders has just about replaced the tink-tink of chisels in Mamallapuram's stone-carving workshops, enabling them to turn out ever more granite sculptures of varying quality, from ₹100 pendants to a ₹400,000 Ganesh that needs to be lifted with a crane. There are also some decent art galleries, tailors and antique shops.

Southern Arts & Crafts
ANTIQUES, HANDICRAFTS

(☎044-27443675; www.southernarts.in; 72 East Raja St; ☺9am-7.30pm) Expensive but beautiful curios acquired from local homes, along with quality new sculptures.

Apollo Books
BOOKS

(150 Fishermen's Colony; ☺9am-9.30pm) Good collection of books in several languages, to sell and swap.

ⓘ Information

Head to East Raja St for ATMs.

AM Communications (East Raja St; per hour ₹30; ☺11am-9pm)

Ruby Forex (East Raja St; ☺9.30am-7pm Mon-Sat) Currency exchange.

Suradeep Hospital (☎044-27442448; 15 Thirukula St; ☺24hr) Recommended by travellers.

Tourist office (☎044-27442232; Kovalam Rd; ☺10am-5.45pm Mon-Fri)

ⓘ Getting There & Away

From the **bus stand** (East Raja St), bus 599 heads to Chennai's T Nagar Bus Terminus (₹27, 1½ hours) every 30 minutes from 7am to 8.30pm, and AC bus 588C (588C on weekends) runs to Chennai's CMBT (₹85, two hours) every two hours, 6am to 8pm. For Chennai airport take bus 515 to Tambaram (₹40, 1½ hours, every 30 minutes), then a taxi, autorickshaw or suburban train. There are also nine daily buses to Kanchipuram (₹40, two hours). Buses to Puducherry (₹60, two hours) stop about every 30 minutes at the junction of Kovalam Rd and the Mamallapuram bypass, 1km north of the town centre.

Taxis are available from the bus stand, travel agents and hotels. It's about ₹1500 to Chennai or the airport, or ₹2000 to Puducherry.

You can make train reservations at the **Southern Railway Reservation Centre** (1st fl, 32 East Raja St; ☺10am-1pm & 2.30-5pm Mon-Sat, 8am-1pm Sun).

ⓘ Getting Around

The easiest way to get around is by walking, though on a hot day it's a hike to see all the monuments. You can hire bicycles at some guesthouses and rental stalls for about ₹80 per day.

Kanchipuram

☑ 044 / POP 164,384

Kanchipuram, 80km southwest of Chennai, was capital of the Pallava dynasty during the 6th to 8th centuries, when the Pallavas created the great stone monuments of Mamallapuram. Today a typically hectic modern Indian town, it's famed for its numerous important and vibrant temples, some dating from Pallava, Chola or Vijayanagar times, and also for its high-quality silk saris, woven on hand looms by thousands of families in the city and nearby villages. Silk and sari shops are strung along Gandhi Rd, southeast of the centre, though their wares are generally no cheaper than at Chennai silk shops. Kanchi is easily visited in a day trip from Mamallapuram or Chennai.

◎ Sights

All temples have free admission, though you may have to pay small amounts for shoe-keeping and/or cameras. Ignore claims that there's an entrance fee for non-Hindus.

Kailasanatha Temple   HINDU TEMPLE
(⊙6am-noon & 4-8pm) Kanchi's oldest temple is its most impressive, not for its size but for its weight of historical presence and the intricacy of its stonework. As much monument as living temple, Kailasanatha is quieter than other temples in town, and has seen a lot of restoration. Dedicated to Shiva, it was built in the 8th century by the Pallava king Narasimhavarman II, who also gave us Mamallapuram's Shore Temple.

The low-slung sandstone compound has fascinating carvings, including many of the half-animal deities in vogue in early Dravidian architecture. Note the rearing lions on the outer walls. The inner sanctum is centred on a large 16-sided lingam, which non-Hindus can view from about 8m away. The tower rising above it is a precursor of the great *vimanas* of later Chola temples. An autorickshaw from the centre costs ₹40, but walking is nice.

Ekambareshwara Temple   HINDU TEMPLE
(Ekambaranathar Temple; phone-camera/camera/video ₹10/20/100; ⊙6am-12.30pm & 4-8.30pm)
Of the five South Indian Shiva temples associated with the five elements, this 12-hectare precinct is the shrine of earth. You enter beneath the 59m-high, unpainted south *gopuram,* whose lively carvings were chiselled in 1509 under Vijayanagar rule. Inside, a columned hall leads left into the central compound, which Nandi faces from the right. The inner sanctum (Hindus only) contains a lingam made of earth and a mirror chamber whose central Shiva image is reflected in endless repetition.

According to legend, the goddess Kamakshi (She Whose Eyes Awaken Desire; a form of Parvati, Shiva's consort) worshipped

---

WORTH A TRIP

VEDANTHANGAL BIRD SANCTUARY

Vedanthangal Bird Sanctuary (admission ₹10, camera/video ₹100/250; ⊙6am-6pm), 55km southwest of Mamallapuram, is a spectacular 30-hectare breeding ground for many kinds of water birds, which migrate here from November to February. Some years as many as 100,000 birds mass at Vedanthangal Lake and its marshy surrounds. The top viewing times are dawn and late afternoon.

The lushly shaded, 4.5-hectare lodge of **Karadi Malai Camp** (☑8012033087; www.draco-india.com; Pambukudivanam, Chengalpattu; r incl breakfast ₹5000; ✆) borders the Vallam Reserve Forest, 30km northeast of Vedanthangal on the Chengalpattu–Tirupporur road, and makes the perfect Vedanthangal base. Owned by snake-man Rom Whitaker and writer Janaki Lenin, it's packed with wildlife (you can help track the local leopard), and has three simple, comfy bamboo huts on stilts.

Some visitors make a taxi day trip to Vedanthangal from Mamallapuram, for around ₹2200. On public transport, first go to Chengalpattu, an hour's bus ride from Mamallapuram en route to Kanchipuram, then take a bus to Vedanthangal via Padalam (possibly changing buses again). Most Vedanthangal buses go to the sanctuary entrance, but some stop at the village bus station, 1km away.

Shiva under a mango tree here. In a court-yard behind the inner sanctum you can see a mango tree said to be 2500 years old, with four branches representing the four Vedas (sacred Hindu texts).

Tamil Nadu is home to three more of South India's five elemental Shiva temples: Arunachaleshwar Temple in Tiruvan-namalai (fire), Nataraja Temple in Chid-ambaram (space) and Sri Jambukeshwara Temple in Trichy (water). The fifth is Sri Kalahasteeswara Temple (air), in Andhra Pradesh.

Kamakshi Amman Temple   HINDU TEMPLE
(⊙ 5.30am-noon & 4-8pm) This imposing tem-ple, dedicated to Kamakshi/Parvati, is one of India's most important places of *shakti* (female energy/deities) worship, said to mark the spot where Parvati's midriff fell to earth. It's thought to have been founded by the Pallavas. The entire main building inside is off-limits to non-Hindus, but the small, square marriage hall, to the right inside the temple's southeast entrance, has wonderful-ly ornate pillars. You might catch the temple elephant giving blessings just inside this entrance.

Each February/March carriages bear-ing the temple deities are hauled around Kanchipuram.

Varadaraja Perumal Temple   HINDU TEMPLE
(Devarajaswami Temple; 100-pillared hall ₹1, camera/video ₹5/100; ⊙ 7.30am-noon & 3.30-8pm) The enormous 11th-century Chola-built Varadaraja Perumal Temple in southeast Kanchi is dedicated to Vishnu. Non-Hindus cannot enter the central compound, but the artistic highlight is the 16th-century '100-pillared' marriage hall, just inside the western entrance. Its pillars (actually 96) are superbly carved with animals and monsters; at its corners hang four stone chains, each carved from a single ro ck.

Every 40 years the waters of the temple tank are drained, revealing a huge wooden statue of Vishnu that is worshipped for 48 days. Next viewing: 2019.

Volunteering

RIDE   VOLUNTEERING
(Rural Institute for Development Education; ☑ 044-27268223; www.rideindia.org; 48 Periyar Nagar, Little Kanchipuram) Kanchipuram's famous silk-weaving industry has tradi-tionally depended heavily on child labour. The NGO RIDE has been a leader in re-

Kanchipuram

⊙ Sights
1 Ekambareshwara Temple A1
2 Kamakshi Amman Temple A1

⊖ Sleeping
3 GRT Regency B3
4 Sree Sakthi Residency B2

⊗ Eating
Dakshin .... (see 3)
Sangeetha Restaurant .... (see 4)
5 Saravana Bhavan A2

ⓘ Information
6 Axis Bank ATM B3
7 State Bank of India ATM B2

ducing the industry's child labour num-bers from over 40,000 in 1997 to less than 1000 by 2010 (by its own estimates), and empowering the rural poor. It welcomes volunteers (one week minimum); pay be-tween ₹3500 and ₹7000 per week for food and accommodation.

☞ Tours

RIDE offers fascinating, original **tours** (per person incl lunch half/full day ₹600/900) cover-ing diverse themes from silk weaving and temples to Indian cookery classes with market visits.

🛏 Sleeping & Eating

RIDE   GUESTHOUSE **$**
(Rural Institute for Development Education; 📞 044-27268223; www.rideindia.org; 48 Periyar Nagar, Little Kanchipuram; per person ₹750; ❄) This NGO has simple, clean rooms for travellers at its base in a residential area 5km southeast of Kanchipuram (signposted from the main road 1km past Varadaraja Perumal Temple). If it's quiet, the friendly owners put you up in their own colourful home next door. Home-cooked lunch and dinner are available (₹250). Book a day ahead.

GRT Regency   HOTEL **$$**
(📞 044-27225250; www.grthotels.com; 487 Gandhi Rd; s/d incl breakfast ₹3420/4200; ❄ 🛜) The GRT has the cleanest and comfiest rooms you'll find in Kanchi, boasting marble floors and tea/coffee makers. The hotel's **Dakshin** (mains ₹190-400; ⏱7am-11pm) restaurant is a tad overpriced but offers a big multicuisine menu including breakfast omelettes, good seafood and tasty tandoori.

Sree Sakthi Residency   HOTEL **$$**
(📞 044-27233799; www.sreesakthiresidency.com; 71 Nellukara St; s ₹1560-1800, d ₹1920-2160; ❄ 🛜) Simple blonde-wood furniture and coloured walls make the clean rooms fairly modern; the 'premiums' were new in 2014. The ground-floor **Sangeetha Restaurant** (71 Nellukara St; mains ₹85-135; ⏱6am-10.30pm) does good vegetarian food.

Saravana Bhavan   SOUTH INDIAN **$$**
(66 Nellukara St; mains ₹80-200, meals ₹80-110; ⏱6am-10.30pm) A reliable veg restaurant with a welcome AC hall, and thalis on the 1st floor.

ℹ Information

Web Space (Ulagalandhar Mada Veedhi; per hour ₹30; ⏱10am-10pm)

ℹ Getting There & Away

Suburban trains to Kanchipuram (₹25, 2½ hours) leave Chennai's Egmore station (platform 10) six to eight times daily. A full-day taxi from Mamallapuram costs around ₹1800.

The busy bus stand is in the centre of town. Departures include:

Chennai (₹47, two hours, every five minutes 4am to 10pm)

Mamallapuram (₹41, two hours, eight daily)

Puducherry (₹75, three hours, 15 daily)

Tiruvannamalai (₹65, three hours, hourly 5am to 8.30pm)

Vellore (₹41, two hours, every five minutes 4am to 10.30pm)

ℹ Getting Around

Bicycle hire (per hour ₹5) is available at stalls around the bus stand. An autorickshaw for a half-day tour of the five main temples (₹400 to ₹500) will inevitably involve stopping at a silk shop.

Vellore

📞 0416 / POP 185,803

For a dusty bazaar town, Vellore feels a bit cosmopolitan, thanks to a couple of tertiary institutions and the American-founded Christian Medical College (CMC), one of India's finest hospitals, attracting both medical students and patients from across the country. On the main Chennai–Bengaluru road, Vellore is worth a stop mainly for its massive Vijayanagar fort. Many Indians come to visit the golden Sripuram Temple 10km south of town.

Central Vellore is bounded on the north by Ida Scudder Rd (Arcot Rd), home to the hospital and cheap hotels and eateries; and on the west by Officer's Line (Anna Salai), with Vellore Fort on its west side.

◉ Sights

Vellore Fort   FORT
A circuit of the moat-surrounded ramparts (nearly 2km) of Vellore's splendid fort is the most peaceful experience in town. The fort was built in the 16th century and passed through Maratha and Mughal hands before the British occupied it in 1760. These days it houses, among other things, the magnificent Vijayanagar-era Jalakantesvara Temple, two museums, two parade grounds, a church, government offices, and a police recruiting school.

Inside, the **Jalakantesvara Temple** (⏱6.30am-1pm & 3-8.30pm), a gem of late Vijayanagar architecture, dates from around 1566, and was once occupied as a garrison. Check out the small, detailed sculptures – especially the *yali* (mythical lion creatures) – on the walls and columns of the marriage hall in the southwest corner. The dusty exhibits in the **Government Museum** (Indian/foreigner ₹5/100; ⏱9.30am-5pm Sat-Thu) have seen better days, but the **Archaeological Survey Museum** (⏱9am-5pm Sat-Thu) FREE has a good collection of Pallava, Chola and Nayak stone sculptures, plus displays on the 1806 Vellore Mutiny, the earliest anti-British uprising by Indian troops. Next door, pretty **St John's Church** (1846) opens only for Sunday services.

🛏 Sleeping & Eating

Vellore's cheap hotels are concentrated along Ida Scudder Rd and in the busy, narrow streets just south. The cheapest are pretty grim; the better ones fill up fast.

Hotel Solai   HOTEL $
(☑0416-2222996; hotelsolai@gmail.com; 26 Babu Rao St; s/d ₹380/660, with AC ₹715/1056; ❄) If you can get a room, this newish hotel near the hospital is probably the best value, with

clean rooms, reasonably airy walkways, enthusiastic staff, and a back-up generator.

GRT Regency Sameera   HOTEL $$
(☑0416-2206466; www.grthotels.com; 145 Green Circle, New Bypass Rd; incl breakfast s ₹3600-5700, d ₹4440-5700; ❄☎) Mirrored cupboards, in-room tea/coffee sets, and splashes of colour make the GRT's smart modern rooms pretty characterful, for Vellore. The free wi-fi, two restaurants, and 24-hour cafe are extra bonuses. It's 1.5km north of central Vellore, near the Chennai–Bengaluru road (surprisingly not too noisy).

Darling Residency   HOTEL $$
(☑0416-2213001;   www.darlingresidency.com; 11/8 Officer's Line; incl breakfast s ₹2400-2640, d ₹2760-3000; ❄@☎) It's not five-star, but

TAMIL NADU & CHENNAI VELLORE

TAMIL NADU TEMPLES

Tamil Nadu is a gold mine for anyone wanting to explore Indian temple culture. Not only does it have some of the country's most spectacular temple architecture and sculpture, but few parts of India are as fervent in their worship of the Hindu gods as Tamil Nadu. Its 5000-odd temples are constantly abuzz with worshippers flocking in for *puja* (offering or prayer), and colourful temple festivals abound. Among the plethora of Hindu deities, Shiva probably has most Tamil temples dedicated to him, in a multitude of forms including Nataraja, the cosmic dancer, who dances in a ring of fire with two of his four hands holding the flame of destruction and the drum of creation, while the third makes the *abhaya mudra* (fear not) gesture and the fourth points to the dwarf of ignorance being trampled beneath Shiva's foot. Tamils also have a soft spot for Shiva's peacock-riding son Murugan (also Kartikeya or Skanda), who is intricately associated with their cultural identity.

The special significance of many Tamil temples makes them goals of countless Hindu pilgrims from all over India. The Pancha Sabhai Sthalangal are the five temples where Shiva is believed to have performed his cosmic dance (chief among them Chidambaram). Then there's the Pancha Bootha Sthalangal, the five temples where Shiva is worshipped as one of the five elements – land, water, sky/space, fire and air (this last in Andhra Pradesh). Each of the nine Navagraha temples in the Kumbakonam area is the abode of one of the nine celestial bodies of Hindu astronomy – key sites given the importance of astrology in Hindu faith.

Typical Tamil temple design features tall layered entrance towers called *gopurams*, encrusted with often colourfully painted sculptures of gods and demons; halls of richly carved columns called *mandapas;* a sacred water tank; and a series of compounds (*prakarams),* one within the next, with the innermost containing the central sanctum where the temple's main deity resides. The earliest Tamil temples were small rock-cut shrines; the first free-standing temples were built in the 8th century AD; *gopurams* first appeared around the 12th century.

Admission to most temples is free, but non-Hindus are often not allowed inside inner sanctums, which can be disappointing for travellers. At other temples priests may invite you in and in no time you are doing *puja,* having an auspicious *tilak* mark daubed on your forehead and being asked for a donation.

Temple touts can be a nuisance, but there are also many excellent guides who deserve both your time and rupees; use your judgement, talk to other travellers and be on the lookout for badge-wearing official guides.

A South Indian Journey by Michael Wood is a great read if you're interested in Tamil culture. **TempleNet** (www.templenet.com) is one of the best online resources.

rooms are clean and comfortable if forgettable (those at the back are quieter), reception is friendly and the hotel's four restaurants include the cool, breezy Aaranya Roof Garden Restaurant (mains ₹150-250; ⊙11.30am-11pm). It's 1.5km south of Vellore Fort entrance.

Hotel Arthy   INDIAN $
(Ida Scudder Rd; dishes ₹50-70, meals ₹70-85; ⊙6am-10.30pm) Cheap veg restaurants line Ida Scudder Rd, but this is one of the cleanest and most popular, with tasty North and South Indian favourites including good thalis, cheap, yummy biryani, and enough dosas to last you a lifetime.

ℹ Information

Canara Bank ATM (Officer's Line) Opposite Vellore Fort entrance.
Sri Apollo (Ida Scudder Rd; internet per hour ₹30; ⊙8.30am-9pm)
State Bank of India ATM (Officer's Line) About 700m south of Vellore Fort entrance.

ℹ Getting There & Away

BUS

Buses use the New bus stand, 1.5km north of central Vellore. Departures include:
Bengaluru (₹138, five hours, every 30 minutes)
Chennai (AC Volvo buses ₹160, 2½ hours, hourly; other buses ₹81, three hours, every 10 minutes)
Kanchipuram (₹47, two hours, every 10 minutes)
Tiruvannamalai (₹50, two hours, every 10 minutes)

TRAIN

Vellore's main station is 5km north at Katpadi. There are at least 20 daily superfast or express trains to/from Chennai Central (2nd class/AC chair ₹90/305, 1½ to 2¼ hours) and 10 to/from Bengaluru's Bangalore City station (₹115/415, three to five hours). Buses 1 and 2 shuttle between the station and town.

Tiruvannamalai

☑ 04175 / POP 145,278

There are temple towns, there are mountain towns, and then there are temple-mountain towns where God appears as a phallus of fire. Welcome to Tiruvannamalai, one of Tamil Nadu's holiest destinations. Set below boulder-strewn Mt Arunachala, this is one of South India's five 'elemental' cities of Shiva; here the god is worshipped in his fire

incarnation as Arunachaleshwar. At every full moon 'Tiru' swells with thousands of pilgrims who come to circumnavigate the base of Arunachala in a purifying ritual known as Girivalam, but at any time you'll see Shaivite priests, sadhus (spiritual men) and devotees gathered around the Arunachaleshwar Temple. Tiru's reputation for strong spiritual energies has produced numerous ashrams, and it now attracts ever-growing numbers of spiritual-minded travellers. Around the main cluster of ashrams, on and near Chengam Rd about 2km southwest of the centre, you'll find a few chilled-out cafes and the better sleeping options.

⊙ Sights & Activities

★ **Arunachaleshwar Temple**   HINDU TEMPLE
(Annamalaiyar Temple; www.arunachaleswarar.com; ⊙5.30am-12.30pm & 4-9pm) This 10-hectare temple is one of the largest in India. Its oldest parts date back to the 9th century and the site was a place of worship long before that. Four huge, unpainted white *gopurams* mark the entrances, with the main, eastern one rising 13 storeys and an astonishing 66m. During festivals the Arunachaleshwar is awash in golden flames and the roasting scent of burning ghee, as befits the fire incarnation of the Destroyer of the Universe.

Inside the complex are five more *gopurams*, a 1000-pillared hall with impressive carvings, two tanks and a profusion of sub-temples and shrines. There's a helpful temple model inside the second *gopuram* from the east, where the temple elephant gives blessings. To reach the innermost sanctum, with its huge lingam, worshippers must pass through five surrounding *prakarams* (compounds).

Mt Arunachala   MOUNTAIN
This 800m-high extinct volcano dominates Tiruvannamalai and local conceptions of the element of fire, which supposedly finds its sacred abode in Arunachala's heart. Devout barefoot pilgrims, especially on full-moon and festival days, make the 14km circumambulation of the mountain, stopping at eight famous linga along the route. The inner path was closed at research time, but it's still possible to circle around on the main road, or climb the hill past two caves where Sri Ramana Maharshi lived and meditated from 1899 to 1922.

The hot ascent to the top opens up superb views of Tiruvannamalai, and takes five or six hours round-trip: start early and take water. An unsigned path across the road from the northwest corner of Arunachaleshwar Temple leads the way up past homes and the two caves, **Virupaksha** (about 20 minutes up) and **Skandasramam** (30 minutes). Women are advised not to do the hike alone.

If you aren't that devoted, buy a Giripradakshina map (₹15) from the bookshop at Sri Ramana Ashram (p1033), hire a bicycle on the roadside nearby (per day ₹40), and ride your way around. Or make an autorickshaw circuit for about ₹250 (up to double at busy times).

Sri Ramana Ashram   ASHRAM
(Sri Ramanasramam; ☑9244937292; www.sriramanamaharshi.org; Chengam Rd; ☺office 7.30am-12.30pm & 2-6.30pm) This tranquil ashram, 2km southwest of the centre in green grounds filled with peacocks, draws devotees of Sri Ramana Maharshi, one of the first Hindu gurus to gain an international following, who died here in 1950 after half a century in contemplation. Visitors can meditate or attend daily *pujas* (prayers) and chantings, mostly in the samadhi hall where the guru's body is enshrined.

A limited amount of free accommodation (donations accepted; three to four weeks) is available *for devotees only:* write or email a month ahead.

Sri Seshadri Swamigal Ashram   ASHRAM
(☑04175-236999; www.tiruvarunaimahan.org; Chengam Rd; ☺office 9am-1pm & 4-8.30pm) Dedicated to a contemporary and helper of Sri Ramana, with meditation platforms and some accommodation. It's in the southwest of town next to Sri Ramana Ashram.

Sri Anantha Niketan   ASHRAM
(☑09003480013; www.sriananthaniketan.com; Periya Paliyapattu Village; admission by donation) A place for organised retreats rather than a permanent community, Sri Anantha Ni-

ketan has tree-shaded grounds, wonderful Arunachala views, homey rooms and weekend chanting in an attractive meditation hall. It's just off the Krishnagiri road, 7km west of town. Book well ahead for November to February.

🛏 Sleeping & Eating

Most visitors stay in the less hectic Chengam Rd area, but there are also typical temple-town options near the Arunachaleshwar Temple. During Karthikai Deepam (November/December) prices can multiply several times. Hotels get heavily booked at full moon.

Hill View Residency   HOTEL **$**
(☑9442712441; hillviewresidency@gmail.com; 120 Seshatri Mada St; r from ₹400, with AC from ₹800) Extremely good value, Hill View has large, clean, cool, marble-floored rooms around two small garden patios, up a lane off Chengam Rd, but limited English is spoken (so booking ahead is tricky). Upstairs under a big palm roof, **Tasty Café** (dishes ₹70-170; ☺8am-10pm) does well-prepared Indian and Continental food.

Arunachala Ramana Home   HOTEL **$**
(☑9486722892; www.arunachalaramanahome.co.in; 70 Ramana Nagar; s/d ₹500/600, with AC d ₹1200; ❋) Basic, clean and friendly, this popular place is down a lane off Chengam Rd.

Sunshine Guest House   GUESTHOUSE **$$**
(☑04175-235335; http://sunshineguesthouseindia.com; 5 Annamalai Nagar, Perumbakkam Rd; s/d ₹500/700, with AC ₹1400/1970; ❋🛜) In a blissfully quiet spot 1km southwest of the main ashram area, this colourful new-build fronted by pretty gardens offers excellent value. Simple but tasteful, spotless rooms, each done up after a different Hindu god, feel like walking into an Indian trinkets shop: print-design sheets, sequined fabrics,

TAMIL NADU & CHENNAI TIRUVANNAMALAI

THE LINGAM OF FIRE

Legend has it Shiva appeared as the original lingam of fire on Mt Arunachala to restore light to the world after his consort Parvati playfully plunged everything into darkness by closing his eyes. The **Karthikai Deepam Festival** (statewide; ☺Nov/Dec) celebrates this legend throughout India but becomes particularly significant at Tiruvannamalai. The lighting of a huge fire atop Mt Arunachala on the full moon night, from a 30m wick immersed in 3 tonnes of ghee, culminates a 10-day festival for which hundreds of thousands of people converge on Tiruvannamalai. Huge crowds scale the mountain or circumnavigate its base, chanting Shiva's name. The sun is relentless, the rocks are jagged and the journey is barefoot – none of which deters the thousands of pilgrims who joyfully make their way to the top and the abode of their deity.

dangling cane chairs, and in-room water filters. Fresh breakfasts cost ₹150.

Hotel Arunachala   HOTEL $$
(Arunachala Inn; ☑04175-228300; www.hotelarunachala.in; 5 Vada Sannathi St; s/d ₹500/990, with AC ₹1125/1690, deluxe d ₹2250; ❋) This place right next to the Arunachaleshwar Temple's east entrance is clean and fine with pretentions to luxury in the marblesque floors, ugly furniture, and keen management. Best are the recently revamped 'deluxe' rooms. Pure-veg **Hotel Sri Arul Jothi** (dishes ₹40-80; ⊙5.30am-10.30pm) downstairs has good South Indian dishes, including thalis (₹80 to ₹100).

★ **Dreaming Tree**   CAFE, ORGANIC $$
(☑8870057753; www.dreamingtree.in; Ramana Nagar; mains ₹150-250; ⊙9am-4.30pm Mon-Sat) 🌿 Superchilled Dreaming Tree dishes out huge portions of exquisite, health-focused veg fare, prepped with mostly organic ingredients, on a breezy hut-like rooftop with hammocks. Fabulous 'hippie salads' and grilled paneer-veg baguettes, good breakfasts, and all kinds of cakes, juices, lassis and organic coffees. Signs lead the way (about 500m) across the road from Sri Ramana Ashram.

Shanti Café   CAFE $$
(www.shanticafe.com; 115A Chengam Rd; dishes ₹60-200, drinks ₹30-70; ⊙8.30am-8.30pm) This popular and relaxed cafe with floor-cushion seating, up a lane off Chengam Rd, serves wonderful croissants, cakes, baguettes, pancakes, juices, coffees and breakfasts. There's an **internet cafe** (per hour ₹25; ⊙8.30am-1.30pm & 3-7pm Mon-Sat) downstairs.

🛍 Shopping

**Shantimalai Handicrafts
Development Society**   HANDICRAFTS
(www.smhds.org; 83/1 Chengam Rd; ⊙9am-7pm Mon-Sat) Beautiful bedspreads, incense, oils, bangles, scarves and cards, all made by local village women.

ℹ Getting There & Around

A taxi to Puducherry with a two- to three-hour stop at Gingee costs around ₹2800.

The bus stand is 800m north of the Arunachaleshwar Temple, and a ₹50 to ₹60 autorickshaw ride from the main ashram area.

Chennai (₹110, four hours, every 15 minutes)
Puducherry (₹63, three hours, about hourly)
Trichy (₹125, six hours, about hourly)
Vellore (₹50, two hours, every 15 minutes)

Gingee (Senji)

With three separate hilltop citadels and a 6km perimeter of cliffs and thick walls, the ruins of enormous **Gingee Fort** (☑04145-222072; Indian/foreigner ₹5/100; ⊙8am-5pm) rise out of the Tamil plain, 37km east of Tiruvannamalai, like something misplaced from *The Lord of the Rings*. The fort was constructed mainly in the 16th century by the Vijayanagars and later occupied by the Marathas, Mughals, French and the British before being abandoned in the 19th century.

Today, few foreigners make it here, but Gingee is popular with domestic tourists for its starring role in various films. The main road from Tiruvannamalai towards Puducherry slices through the fort, just before Gingee town. The easiest citadel to reach, **Krishnagiri**, lies north of the road. To the south are the highest of the three, **Rajagiri**, and the most distant and least interesting, **Chakklidurg**. Ticket offices are at the foot of Krishnagiri and Rajagiri.

Remains of numerous buildings stand in the site's lower parts, especially at the bottom of Rajagiri, where the main landmark of the old palace area is the white, restored, seven-storey **Kalyana Mahal** (Marriage Hall). Just east of the palace area is an 18th-century **mosque**; southeast of that is the abandoned 16th-century **Venkataramana Temple**.

It's a good hike to the top of Krishnagiri and even more so to the top of more popular Rajagiri (over 150m above the plain), and you need at least half a day to cover both hills. Start early and bring water; hill-climbing entry ends at 2.30pm.

Gingee is on the Tiruvannamalai–Puducherry bus route, with buses from Tiruvannamalai (₹23, one hour) about every 15 minutes. Get off at the fort to save a trip back out from Gingee town.

Puducherry (Pondicherry)

☑0413 / POP 244,377

Puducherry (formerly called Pondicherry and generally referred to as 'Pondy') was under French rule until 1954 and some people here still speak French (and English with French accents). Hotels, restaurants and 'lifestyle' shops sell a seductive vision of the French-subcontinental aesthetic, enhanced by Gallic creative types whose presence has in turn attracted Indian artists and designers. Thus Pondy's vibe: less faded colonial-era *ville,* more a bohemian-chic, New Age–cum–Old World hang-out on the international travel trail.

If you've come from Chennai or some of Tamil Nadu's inland cities, Pondy may well seem a sea of tranquility. The older part of this former French colony (where you'll probably spend most of your time) is full of quiet, clean, shady cobbled streets, lined with bougainvillea-draped colonial-era townhouses numbered in an almost logical manner. The newer side of town is typically, hectically South Indian.

Part of the vibe stems from the presence of the internationally famous Sri Aurobindo Ashram and its offshoot just out of town, Auroville, which draw large numbers of spiritually minded visitors.

Enjoy the shopping, the French food (hello steak!), the beer (*au revoir* Tamil Nadu alcohol taxes – Pondy is a Union Territory), the sea air and plenty of yoga and meditation.

Puducherry is split from north to south by a partially covered canal. The 'French' part of town is on the east side (towards the sea). Nehru (JN) St and Lal Bahadur Shastri St (Rue Bussy) are the main east–west streets; Mahatma Gandhi (MG) Rd and Mission St (Cathedral St) are the chief north–south thoroughfares. Many streets change names as they go along and often have English, French and Tamil names simultaneously.

◎ Sights

★ French Quarter   NEIGHBOURHOOD
Pocketed away just behind the seafront is a series of cobbled streets, white-and-mustard buildings in various states of romantic dishevelment, and a slight sense of Gallic glory gone by, otherwise known as the French Quarter. A do-it-yourself heritage walk could start at the **French Consulate** (☑ 0413-2231000; 2 Marine St) near the north end of seafront Goubert Ave, then gradually head south.

Turn inland south of the French Consulate to shady **Bharathi Park**, with the neoclassical governor's residence, **Raj Nivas**, facing its north side. Return to the seafront at the **Gandhi Memorial**, pass the **Hôtel de Ville** (City Hall) and then potter south through the 'white town' – Dumas, Romain Rolland, Suffren and Labourdonnais Sts. Towards the southern end of Dumas St, wander into the beautiful **École Française D'Extrême-Orient**. A lot of restoration has been going on in this area: if you're interested in Pondy's architectural heritage check out **Intach Pondicherry** (www.intachpondicherry.org).

Seafront   PROMENADE
(Goubert Ave) Pondy is a seaside town, but that doesn't make it a beach destination; the city's sand is a thin strip of dirty brown that slurps into a seawall of jagged rocks. But Goubert Ave (Beach Rd) is a killer stroll, especially at dawn and dusk when half the town takes a romantic wander there. In a stroke of genius the city council has banned traffic here from 6pm to 7.30am.

There are a few sandy beaches north and south of town, but they aren't good for sunbathing due to crowds of men, and possible undertow or rip tides make swimming risky.

Sri Aurobindo Ashram   ASHRAM
(www.sriaurobindoashram.org; Marine St; ⊘general visits 8am-noon & 2-6pm) Founded in 1926 by Sri Aurobindo and a French-born woman known as 'the Mother', this spiritual community now has about 1200 members working in its many departments. Aurobindo's teachings focus on an 'integral yoga' as the path towards a 'supramental consciousness which will divinise human nature'; devotees work in the world, rather than retreating from it. General visits to the main ashram building are cursory – you just see the flower-festooned samadhi of Aurobindo and the Mother, then the bookshop, then you leave.

Ashram accommodation guests can access other areas and activities. Evening meditation around the samadhi is open to people with passes – which you can only get if you're staying at an ashram guesthouse or from the ashram's **Bureau Central** (☑ 0413-2233604; bureaucentral@sriaurobindoashram.org; Ambour Salai; ⊘ 6-7.30am, 9am-noon & 3-7pm), where there are also interesting exhibitions on Sri Aurobindo and the Mother.

Sri Manakula Vinayagar Temple   HINDU TEMPLE
(Manakula Vinayagar Koil St; ⊘ 5.45am-12.30pm & 4-9pm) Pondy may have more churches than most towns, but this is still India, and the Hindu faith reigns supreme. Don't miss the chance to watch tourists, pilgrims and the curious get a head pat from the temple elephant at this temple dedicated to Ganesh, which also contains over 40 painted friezes.

Puducherry Museum   MUSEUM
(St Louis St; Indian/foreigner ₹10/50; ⊘10am-1pm & 2-5pm Tue-Sun) God knows how this cute

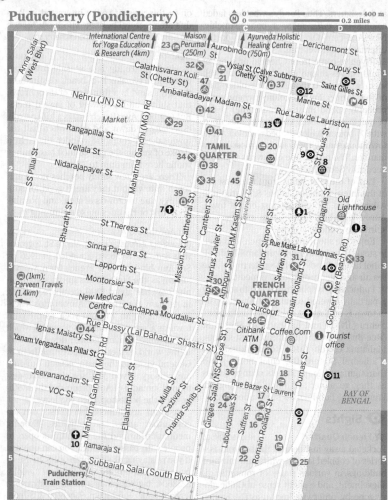

little museum keeps its artefacts from disintegrating, considering there's a whole floor of French-era furniture sitting in the South Indian humidity. On the ground floor look especially for the Chola, Vijayanagar and Nayak bronzes, and the pieces of ancient Greek and Spanish pottery and amphorae (storage vessels) excavated from Arikamedu, a once-major trading port just south of Puducherry. Upstairs is Governor Dupleix' bed.

Institut Français de Pondichéry LIBRARY
(☎0413-2231609; www.ifpindia.org; 11 St Louis St; ◷9am-1pm & 2-5.30pm Mon-Fri) This grand neoclassical colonial-era building is also a flourishing research institution devoted to Indian culture, history and ecology. Visitors can browse books in the beach-facing library.

Activities

Sita ARTS, COOKING
(☎0413-4200718; www.pondicherry-arts.com; 22 Candappa Moudaliar St; classes ₹300-1000) This energetic Franco-Indian cultural centre runs a host of activities, which visitors can join (even for just a single session): Indian or

Puducherry (Pondicherry)

French cooking, *bharatanatyam* or Bollywood dance, Tamil language, *kolam* making, *mehndi* (henna 'tattoos'), yoga, pilates, ayurveda and more.

Kallialay Surf School   SURFING
(☎9442992874; www.surfschoolindia.com; Serenity Beach, Tandriankuppam; 1hr private class ₹1400, board rental per 90min ₹400-600) Surfing is soaring in popularity along Tamil Nadu's coast, and this long-standing, well-equipped, Spanish-run school, 5km north of Puducherry, offers everything from beginner sessions to intensive 'surf camps'.

Yoga & Ayurveda
You can practise (and study) yoga at Sri Aurobindo Ashram (p1035) and Auroville. Sita offers yoga, ayurvedic massages, and courses in practising ayurveda.

International Centre for Yoga Education & Research   YOGA
(Ananda Ashram; ☎0413-2241561; www.icyer.com; 16A Mettu St, Chinnamudaliarchavady, Kottuppam) Annual six-month yoga-teacher-training and 10-lesson, one-to-one introductory courses (₹8000).

⌲ Tours
A wonderful way to see Pondy is with Sita's popular early-morning guided **bicycle tours** (per person from ₹1200), which include breakfast.

Shanti Travel (p1041) offers recommended two-hour **walking tours** (per person ₹500) of Puducherry that are available with either English- or French-speaking guides.

PUDUCHERRY'S CATHEDRALS

Pondy has one of the best collections of over-the-top cathedrals in India. *Merci*, French missionaries. **Our Lady of Immaculate Conception Cathedral** (Mission St; ⊙ 7-11am & 4-8.30pm), completed in 1791, is a robin's-egg-blue-and-cloud-white typically Jesuit edifice in a Goa-like Portuguese style, while the brown-and-white grandiosity of the **Sacred Heart Basilica** (Subbayah Salai; ⊙ 7-11am & 4-8.30pm) is set off by stained glass and a Gothic sense of proportion. The twin towers and dome of the mellow-pink-and-cream **Notre Dame des Anges** (Dumas St; ⊙ 6-10am & 4-7pm), built in the 1850s, look sublime in the late-afternoon light. The smooth limestone interior was made using eggshell plaster.

✸ Festivals & Events

International Yoga Festival   YOGA
(⊙ 4-7 Jan) Puducherry's ashrams and yoga culture are put on show with workshops, demonstrations and competitions, attracting experts from all over India and beyond.

Bastille Day   PARADE
(⊙ 14 Jul) Street parades and a bit of French pomp and ceremony are part of the fun at this celebration.

🛏 Sleeping

If you've been saving for a splurge, this is the place for it: Puducherry's lodgings are as good as South India gets. Local heritage houses combine colonial-era romanticism with comfort and, dare we say, French playfulness. Most of these rooms would cost five times as much back in Europe. Book ahead for weekends.

Sri Aurobindo Ashram (p1035) runs several simple but clean guesthouses. They're primarily intended for ashram guests, but many accept other travellers willing to follow their rules: 10.30pm curfew and no smoking, alcohol or drugs. The ashram's Bureau Central (p1035) has a list.

Kailash Guest House   GUESTHOUSE $
(☑ 0413-2224485; http://kailashguesthouse.in; 43 Vysial St; s/d ₹800/1000, with AC d ₹1250; ❄) The best value for money in this price range, Kailash has simple, superclean rooms with well mosquito-proofed windows, friendly management, and superb city views from the top floors. It's geared to traveller needs, with loungey communal areas, clothes-drying facilities, and a bar on the way.

Park Guest House   ASHRAM GUESTHOUSE $
(☑ 0413-2233644; parkgh@sriaurobindoashram.org; 1 Goubert Ave; r ₹800, with AC ₹900; ❄) The most sought-after ashram guesthouse in town thanks to its wonderful seafront position. All front rooms face the sea and have a porch or balcony, and there's a garden for yoga or meditation. The best-value AC rooms around, but no advance bookings.

International Guest House   ASHRAM GUESTHOUSE $
(☑ 0413-2336699; ingh@aurosociety.org; 47 NSC Bose St; s/d ₹500/650, with AC ₹700/1050; ❄) The sparse, clean rooms here, adorned with a single photo of the Mother, make for good-value ashram lodgings. Predictably it's very popular: book three weeks ahead.

★ Les Hibiscus   GUESTHOUSE $$
(☑ 9442066763, 0413-2227480; www.leshibiscus.in; 49 Suffren St; s/d incl breakfast ₹2400/2700; ❄ @ 🖤) A strong contender for our favourite Tamil Nadu hotel, Hibiscus has just four pristine, high-ceilinged rooms with gorgeous antique beds, coffee-makers and a mix of quaint Indian art and old-Pondy photos, at incredibly reasonable prices. The whole place is immaculately tasteful, breakfast is fabulous, internet is free and management is genuinely friendly and helpful. Make sure you book ahead.

Gratitude   GUESTHOUSE $$
(☑ 0413-2225029; www.gratitudeheritage.in; 52 Romain Rolland St; s ₹3375-5510, d ₹4240-6470, all incl breakfast; ❄ 🖤) A wonderfully tranquil 19th-century house (no TVs, no children) with welcoming staff, sun-yellow Gratitude has been painstakingly restored to a state probably even more charming than the original. The nine spotless, individually styled rooms are spread over two floors around a tropically shaded courtyard. There's a lovely roof terrace for yoga and massages.

Maison Tamoule   HERITAGE HOTEL $$
(☑ 0413-2223738; www.neemranahotels.com; 44 Vysial St; r incl breakfast ₹3220-5370; ❄ 🖤) The old Tamil Quarter has almost as many mansions as the French Quarter but is off most tourists' radars. Reincarnated under efficient new management, this excellent

heritage choice, on a quiet, tree-shaded street, mixes a soaring sense of space with a sunken teak-columned atrium, gorgeous Chettinad-tiled floors, and 10 elegantly styled rooms featuring big bath tubs (though single beds are a tad small).

Hotel de Pondichéry   HERITAGE HOTEL $$

(☑ 0413-2227409; www.hoteldepondicherry.com; 38 Dumas St; incl breakfast s ₹2000, d ₹3000-5000; ❈ 🕤) A colourful heritage spot with 14 comfy, quiet, high-ceilinged, colonial-style rooms and a dash of original modern art. Their excellent restaurant, Le Club, takes up the pretty front courtyard. Staff are lovely and there's free wi-fi in the lobby.

Coloniale Heritage Guest House   GUESTHOUSE $$

(☑ 0413-2224720; www.colonialeheritage.com; 54 Romain Rolland St; r incl breakfast ₹2000-3300; ❈ 🕤) This colonial-era home with six comfy rooms (some up steep stairs) is chock-full of character thanks to the owner's amazing collection of gem-studded Tanjore paintings, Ravi Varma lithographs and other 19th- and 20th-century South Indian art. One room even has a swing. Breakfast is served in a sunken patio beside the leafy garden.

Nilla Guesthouse   GUESTHOUSE $$

(☑ 9994653006; www.nillaguesthouse.com; 18 Labourdonnais St; r ₹1500-2100; ❈ 🕤) A simple but brilliantly characterful and well-kept home run by a welcoming host, with just five fresh, colourful, heritage-style rooms, handy communal kitchens, and free wi-fi in the loungey terrace area.

★ Villa Shanti   HERITAGE HOTEL $$$

(☑ 0413-4200028; www.lavillashanti.com; 14 Suffren St; r incl breakfast ₹7870-10,117; ❈ 🕤) Set in a 100-year-old building revamped by two French architects, Villa Shanti puts an exquisitely contemporary twist on the traditional Pondy heritage hotel. Beautiful fresh rooms combine super-chic design with typically Tamil materials and colonial-style elegance: four-poster beds, Chettinadu tiles, Tamil murals. The courtyard houses a popular restaurant and cocktail bar, so book upper-floor beds for early snoozing.

Maison Perumal   HERITAGE HOTEL $$$

(☑ 0413-2227519; www.cghearth.com; 44 Perumal Koil St; r incl breakfast ₹8360-10,450; ❈ 🕤) Cool peaceful rooms with colourful flourishes sit above two pillared patios in this renovated 130-year-old building lined with photos of old Chettiar families and pocketed away in Pondy's less touristic Tamil Quarter. The excellent Tamil/French **restaurant** (dinner ₹990, lunch mains ₹275-400; ⊙12.30-2pm & 7.30-10.30pm) cooks everything from market-fresh ingredients, and staff are delightful. From March to October rates dip by 30%.

Hotel De L'Orient   HERITAGE HOTEL $$$

(☑ 0413-2343067; www.neemranahotels.com; 17 Romain Rolland St; r incl breakfast ₹3760-8060; ❈ 🕤) This grand restored 18th-century mansion has breezy verandahs, keen staff, and charming rooms in all shapes and sizes, kitted out with antique furniture; some are cosy attics, others palatial. A place to get that old Pondy feel while enjoying polished service and French, Italian or creole (French-Indian) food in the courtyard **Carte Blanche Restaurant** (mains ₹300-580; ⊙7.30-10.30am, noon-3pm & 7-9.30pm).

✖ Eating

Puducherry is a culinary highlight of Tamil Nadu; you get great South Indian cooking plus well-prepped French and Italian cuisine. If you've been missing cheese or have a craving for pâté, you're in luck, and *everyone* in the French Quarter does good brewed coffee and crepes.

Baker Street   CAFE $

(123 Rue Bussy; items ₹40-130; ⊙7am-9pm; 🕤) A popular upmarket, French-style bakery with delectable cakes, croissants and biscuits. Baguettes, brownies and quiches aren't bad either. Eat in or take away.

Indian Coffee House   SOUTH INDIAN $

(125 Nehru St; dishes ₹30-60; ⊙6.30am-10pm) Snack to your heart's content on cheap, South Indian favourites – dosas, *vadas, uttapams* and ₹15 filter coffee – at this Pondy institution. It's also, incidentally, where Yann Martel's novel *Life of Pi* begins.

Surguru   SOUTH INDIAN $

(235 (old 99) Mission St; mains ₹70-120; ⊙7am-10.30pm) Simple South Indian in a relatively posh setting. Surguru is the fix for thali (lunchtime only) and dosa addicts who like their veg with good strong AC.

★ La Pasta   ITALIAN $$

(☑ 9994670282; http://lapastapondy.blogspot.com; 55 Vysial St; mains ₹230-350; ⊙noon-2pm & 5-9pm Tue-Sat) Pasta lovers should make a pilgrimage to this little spot with just four check-cloth tables, where an Italian whips up her own authentically yummy sauces and concocts her own perfect pasta in an open-plan kitchen as big as the dining area. No alcohol: it's all about the food.

Café des Arts
CAFE $$

(10 Suffren St; dishes ₹130-230; ⊙8.30am-7pm Wed-Mon; 🛜) This bohemian, vintage-style cafe would look perfectly at home in Europe, but this is Pondy, so there's a cycle-rickshaw in the garden. Refreshingly light dishes range from crisp salads, baguettes and toasties to crepes, and the coffees and fresh juices are great. The old-townhouse setting is lovely, with low tables and lounge chairs spilling out in front of a quirky boutique.

Kasha Ki Aasha
CAFE $$

(23 Rue Surcouf; mains ₹150-250; ⊙10am-8pm Mon-Sat) You'll get a great pancake breakfast, good lunches and delicious cakes on the low-key rooftop of this colonial-era-house-cum-craft-shop-cum-cafe run by an all-female team. Fusion food includes chips with chutney, 'European-style thali' and 'Indian enchilada', and the pretty fabrics and leather sandals downstairs come direct from their makers.

Le Café
CAFE $$

(Goubert Ave; dishes ₹50-225; ⊙24hr) This seafront spot is good for baguettes, croissants, salads, cakes and organic South Indian coffee (hot or iced), plus welcome fresh breezes from the Bay of Bengal. It's popular, so you often have to wait for, or share, a table. But hey, it's all about the location.

Le Club
CONTINENTAL, INDIAN $$$

(📞0413-2339745; 38 Dumas St; mains ₹300-500; ⊙noon-3.30pm & 7-11pm Tue-Sun) The steaks (with sauces like blue cheese or Béarnaise), pizzas and crepes are all top-class at this popular romantically lit garden restaurant. Tempting local options include creole prawn curry, veg-paneer kebabs, and Malabar-style fish, and there are plenty of wines, mojitos and margaritas to wash it all down.

Villa Shanti
CONTINENTAL, INDIAN $$$

(📞0413-4200028; 14 Suffren St; mains ₹225-495; ⊙12.30-2.30pm & 7-10.30pm) Smart candle-lit tables in a palm-dotted pillared courtyard attached to a colourful bar create a casually fancy vibe at this stylish, packed-out hotel restaurant. The building's contemporary Franco-Indian flair runs right through the North Indian/European menu and, while portions are small, flavours are superb and there are some deliciously creative veg dishes. Good cocktails too. Reserve for weekends.

Self-Catering

Nilgiri's
SUPERMARKET

(23 Rangapillai St; ⊙9.30am-9pm) Well-stocked AC shop for groceries and toiletries.

🍷 Drinking & Nightlife

Although Pondy is one of the better places in Tamil Nadu to knock back a beer, closing time is a strictly enforced 11pm. Despite low taxes on alcohol, you'll really only find cheap beer in 'liquor shops' and their attached darkened bars. Hotel restaurants and bars make good drinking spots.

L'e-Space
BAR, CAFE

(2 Labourdonnais St; cocktails ₹200; ⊙5-11pm) A quirky little semi-open-air upstairs bar-cafe-lounge that's friendly and sociable, and does good cocktails (assuming that the barman hasn't disappeared).

🔒 Shopping

With all the yoga yuppies congregating here, Pondy specialises in the boutique-chic-meets-Indian-bazaar school of fashion and souvenirs, and there's some beautiful and original stuff, a lot of it produced by Sri Aurobindo Ashram or Auroville. Nehru St and MG Rd are the shopping hotspots.

★Kalki
CLOTHING, ACCESSORIES

(134 Mission St; ⊙9.30am-8.30pm) Gorgeous, jewel-coloured silk and cotton fashions, as well as accessories, incense, essential oils, handmade-paper trinkets and more, mostly made at Auroville, where there's another branch (Visitors Centre; ⊙9.30am-6pm).

Fabindia
CLOTHING, TEXTILES

(www.fabindia.com; 223 Mission St; ⊙10.30am-8.30pm) Going strong since 1960, the Fabindia chain stocks stunning handmade products predominantly made by villagers using traditional craft techniques, and promotes rural employment. This branch has a wonderful collection of cotton and silk garments in contemporary Indian style, along with quality fabrics, tablecloths, oils, beauty products, and even furniture.

La Maison Rose
CLOTHING, HOMEWARES

(www.lamaisonrosepondicherry.com; 8 Romain Rolland St; ⊙10am-7.30pm) This restored baby-pink mansion houses three luxurious boutiques packed with exquisite East-meets-West fashion, fabrics, jewellery, homewares and furniture. Flop over fresh juices and French-inspired dishes under the mango tree in the fairy-light-flooded courtyard cafe-restaurant (8 Romain Rolland St; mains ₹300-470; ☺noon-3pm, 7-10pm).

Auroshikha
INCENSE
(www.auroshikha.com; 28 Marine St; ☺9am-1pm & 3-7pm Tue-Sun) An endless array of incense, perfumed candles and essential oils, made by Sri Aurobindo Ashram.

La Boutique d'Auroville
HANDICRAFTS
(38 Nehru St; ☺9.30am-8pm) It's fun browsing through the crafts here, including jewellery, clothes, shawls, handmade cards and pretty wooden trays.

Hidesign
LEATHER GOODS
(www.hidesign.com; 69 Nehru St; ☺9am-10pm) Established in Pondy in the 1970s, Hidesign sells beautifully made designer leather bags, briefcases, purses and belts in all kinds of colours, at very reasonable prices, and now has outlets across the world. The top-floor cafe, Le Hidesign (69 Nehru St; mains ₹120-180; ☺9am-9.30pm; ☎), serves delicious tapas and excellent coffee.

Geethanjali
ANTIQUES
(www.geethanjaliartifacts.com; 20 Rue Bussy; ☺10.30am-8.30pm) The kind of place where Indiana Jones gets the sweats, this antique and curio shop sells sculptures, carved doors, wooden chests, paintings and furniture culled from Puducherry's colonial and even precolonial history. It ships to Europe for ₹20,000 per cubic metre – make sure to check that your purchases aren't subject to export restrictions.

Focus
BOOKS
(204 Mission St; ☺9.30am-1.30pm & 3.30-9pm Mon-Sat) A great collection of India-related and other English-language books (including Lonely Planet guides).

Librairie Kailash
BOOKS
(169 Rue Bussy; ☺9am-1pm & 3-7.30pm Mon-Sat) Good selection of India and Asia titles in French.

ℹ Information

ATMs are everywhere and there are numerous currency-exchange offices on Mission St near the corner of Nehru St.

Rue Bussy between Bharathi St and MG Rd is packed with clinics and pharmacies.

Coffee.Com (11A Romain Rolland St; per hour ₹80; ☺10.30am-10pm) A genuine internet cafe, with good coffee and light food (₹60 to ₹300).

New Medical Centre (☎0413-2225287; www.nmcpondy.com; 470 MG Rd; ☺24hr) Recommended private clinic and hospital.

Shanti Travel (☎0413-4210401; www.shantitravel.com; 13 Romain Rolland St; ☺10am-1.30pm & 2.30-7pm) Professional agency offering transport tickets, walking tours, day trips and Chennai airport pick-ups.

Tourist office (☎0413-2339497; http://tourism.puducherry.gov.in; 40 Goubert Ave; ☺9am-1pm & 2-7pm)

ℹ Getting There & Away

BUS
The bus stand (Maraimalai Adigal Salai) is in the west of town, 2km from the French Quarter. For Kumbakonam, change at Chidambaram. Further services run from Villupuram (₹18, one hour, every 10 minutes), 38km west of Puducherry. Private bus companies, operating mostly overnight to various destinations, have offices along Maraimalai Adigal Salai west of the bus stand. **Parveen Travels** (☎0413-2201919; www.parveentravels.com; 288 Maraimalai Adigal Salai) runs an 11pm semisleeper service to Kodaikanal (₹610, eight hours).

BUSES FROM PUDUCHERRY (PONDICHERRY) BUS STAND

DESTINATION	FARE (₹)	DURATION (HR)	FREQUENCY (DAILY)
Bengaluru	310	7	8pm & 10pm
Chennai	97 (Volvo AC 190)	4	every 30min (6 Volvo AC 6.30am-6pm)
Chidambaram	60	2	48
Mamallapuram	80	2	36
Tiruvannamalai	47-62	3	11
Trichy	112	5	4.40am, 10am, 8pm, 10pm

TAMIL NADU & CHENNAI PUDUCHERRY (PONDICHERRY)

TRAIN

Puducherry station has just a few services. Two daily trains go to Chennai Egmore, with unreserved seating only (₹45 to ₹75, four to five hours). You can connect at Villupuram for many more services north and south. The station has a computerised booking office for trains throughout India.

❶ Getting Around

Pondy's flat streets are great for getting around on foot. Autorickshaws are plentiful. Official metered fares are ₹40 for up to 2km and then ₹15 per kilometre, but most drivers refuse to use their meters. A trip from the bus stand to the French Quarter costs around ₹60.

A good way to explore Pondy and around is by rented bicycle or motorbike from various outlets (per day bicyle/scooter/motorbike ₹50/200/250) on northern Mission St, between Nehru and Chetty Sts.

Auroville

🕿 0413 / POP 2345

Auroville, 'the City of Dawn', is one of those ideas that anyone with idealistic leanings will love: an international community dedicated to peace, harmony, sustainable living, and 'divine consciousness', where people from across the globe, ignoring creed, colour and nationality, work together to build a universal, cash-free, nonreligious township and realise good old human unity.

Outside opinions of Auroville's inhabitants range from admiration to accusations of self-indulgent escapism. Imagine over 100 small settlements scattered across the Tamil countryside, with 2300-odd residents of 43 nationalities. Nearly 60% of Aurovillians are foreign, and most new members require more funds than most Indians are ever likely to have. But the vibe you'll receive on a visit will probably be positive, and the energy driving the place is palpable.

Some 12km northwest of Puducherry, Auroville was founded in 1968 on the inspiration of 'the Mother', co-founder of Puducherry's Sri Aurobindo Ashram, and her philosophy still guides it. Aurovillians run a huge variety of projects ranging from schools and IT to organic farming, renewable energy and handicrafts production, employing 4000 to 5000 people from nearby villages.

The Auroville website (www.auroville.org) is an encyclopedic resource.

◉ Sights & Activities

Auroville isn't really geared for tourism – most inhabitants are just busy getting on with their lives – but it does have a good visitors centre (🕿 0413-2622239; ◷ 9am-1pm & 1.30-5pm) with information services, exhibitions and Auroville products. You can buy a handbook and map (₹20), and watch a 10-minute video. Free passes for external viewing of the Matrimandir (◷ passes issued 9.30am-4.45pm Mon-Sat, 9.30am-12.45pm Sun), Auroville's 'soul', a 1km walk away through the woodlands, are also handed out here.

The large, golden, almost spherical Matrimandir is often said to resemble a golf ball, on a bed of lotus petals. You might equally feel that its grand simplicity, surrounded by pristine green parkland, does indeed evoke the divine consciousness it's supposed to represent. The orb's main inner chamber, lined with white marble, houses a large glass crystal that suffuses a beam of sunlight around the chamber. It's a place for individual silent concentration and if, after viewing the Matrimandir from the gardens, you want to meditate inside, you must book in person at least one day ahead at the Matrimandir access office (🕿 0413-2622204; Visitors Centre; ◷ 10-11am & 2-3pm Wed-Mon).

Visitors are perfectly free to wander round Auroville's 10-sq-km network of roads and tracks. With two million trees planted since Auroville's foundation, it's a lovely shaded area.

If you're interested in getting to know Auroville, residents recommend you stay at least 10 days and join one of their introduction and orientation programs. To get seriously involved, you normally need to come as a volunteer for two to 12 months. Contact the Auroville Guest Service (🕿 0413-2622675; www.aurovilleguestservice.org; Solar Kitchen Bldg, 2km east of Visitors Centre; ◷ 9.30am-1pm Mon-Sat) for advice on active participation.

🛏 Sleeping & Eating

Auroville has over 50 guesthouses (per person ₹250-4500) of hugely varied comfort levels, offering from two to 50 beds. The Guest Accommodation Service (🕿 0413-2622704; www.aurovilleguesthouses.org; Visitors Centre; ◷ 9.30am-12.30pm & 2-5pm) can advise you, but bookings are done directly with individual guesthouses. For the peak seasons, December to March and August and September, reservations three or four months ahead are recommended.

The **Right Path Cafe** (Visitors Centre; mains ₹175-295; ⊙8am-8.30pm Tue-Sun, 8am-4.45pm Mon), open to all, serves decent Indian and Continental food.

ⓘ Getting There & Away

The main turning to Auroville from the East Coast Rd is at Periyar Mudaliarchavadi village, 6km north of Puducherry. From there it's about 6km west to the visitors centre. An autorickshaw one way from Puducherry is about ₹250, or you can take a Kottukuppam bus northbound on Ambour Salai to the Auroville turnoff (₹6 to ₹20, every 10 minutes), then an autorickshaw for ₹150. Otherwise, rent a bicycle or motorcycle from outlets on northern Mission St in Puducherry.

CENTRAL TAMIL NADU

Chidambaram

☎04144 / POP 62,153

There's basically one reason to visit Chidambaram: the great temple complex of Nataraja, Shiva as the Dancer of the Universe. One of the holiest of all Shiva sites, this also happens to be a Dravidian architectural highlight.

Most accommodation is close to the temple or the bus stand (500m southeast of the temple). The train station is about 1km further southeast.

⊙ Sights

★**Nataraja Temple**   HINDU TEMPLE
(⊙inner compound 6am-noon & 4.30-10pm) According to legend, Shiva and Kali got into a dance-off judged by Vishnu. Shiva dropped

TAMIL NADU & CHENNAI CHIDAMBARAM

OFF THE BEATEN TRACK

TRANQUIL TRANQUEBAR (THARANGAMBADI)

South of Chidambaram the many-armed delta of the Cauvery River stretches 180km along the coast and deep into the hinterland. The Cauvery is the beating heart of Tamil agriculture and its valley was the heartland of the Chola empire. Today the delta is one of the prettiest, poorest and most traditional parts of Tamil Nadu.

The tiny coastal town of Tharangambadi, still mostly known by its old name Tranquebar, is easily the most appealing base. A great place to recharge from the hot, crowded towns inland, this former Danish colony is quiet, neat, and set right on a long sandy beach with a few fishing boats and delicious sea breezes. It's said the air here is especially ozone-rich. The old part of town inside the 1791 Landporten gate makes a brilliantly peaceful stroll, and has been significantly restored since the 2004 tsunami, which killed about 800 people here. Intach Pondicherry (www.intachpondicherry.org) has a good downloadable map. The old Danish fort, **Dansborg** (Indian/foreigner ₹5/50, camera/video ₹30/100; ⊙10am-1pm & 2-5.30pm Sat-Thu), dates from 1624 and contains an interesting little museum. Other notable buildings include **New Jerusalem Church** (Tamil Evangelical Lutheran Church; King's St), an intriguing mix of Indian and European styles built in 1718, and the 14th-century seafront **Masilamani Nathar Temple**, now in kaleidoscopic colours.

All accommodation is run by the **Bungalow on the Beach** (☎04364-288065; www.neemranahotels.com; 24 King's St; r incl breakfast ₹5400-8990, budget r ₹990; ❄🖤❄), in the former residence of the British administrator (Denmark sold Tranquebar to the British East India Company in 1845). There are 17 beautiful old-world rooms spread across the main building and two other heritage locations in town, plus five simple, clean budget rooms in the Hotel Tamil Nadu, opposite the main building; you get wonderful temple views from budget room 5, and all rooms are AC. The main building has a fantastic swimming pool and a good multicuisine **restaurant** (mains ₹150-300; ⊙7.30-9.30am, 12.30-2.30pm & 7-9.30pm). Booking ahead is strongly recommended.

Buses in this region get incredibly crowded, but Tranquebar has regular connections with Chidambaram (₹30, two hours, hourly) and Karaikal (₹11, 30 minutes, half-hourly). From Karaikal buses go to Kumbakonam (₹36, 2¼ hours, half-hourly 4.15am to 10.15pm), Thanjavur (₹64, 3½ hours, hourly 4.15am to 10.15pm) and Puducherry (₹85, four hours, half-hourly 4.15am to midnight).

an earring and picked it up with his foot, a move that Kali could not duplicate, so Shiva won the title Nataraja (Lord of the Dance). It is in this form that he is worshipped at this great temple, which draws an endless stream of worshippers. It was built during Chola times (Chidambaram was a Chola capital), but the main shrines date back to at least the 6th century.

The high-walled 22-hectare complex has four towering *gopurams* decked out in Dravidian stone and stucco work. The main entrance is through the east (oldest) *gopuram*, off East Car St. The 108 sacred positions of classical Tamil dance are carved in its passageway. To your right through the *gopuram* are the 1000-pillared Raja Sabha (King's Hall; ⊙festival days), and the large Sivaganga tank.

You enter the central compound (no cameras) from the east. In its southern part (left from the entrance) is the 13th-century Nritta Sabha (Dance Hall), shaped like a chariot with 56 finely carved pillars. Some say this is the very spot where Shiva outdanced Kali.

North of the Nritta Sabha, through a door, you enter the inner courtyard. Right in front is the Kanaka Sabha pavilion, where many temple rituals are performed. At *puja* times devotees crowd into and around the pavilion to witness the rites performed by the temple's hereditary Brahmin priests, the Dikshithars, who shave off some of their hair but grow the rest of it long (thus representing both Shiva and Parvati) and tie it into topknots.

Behind (north of) the Kanaka Sabha is the innermost sanctum, the golden-roofed Chit Sabha (Wisdom Hall), which holds the temple's central bronze image of Nataraja – Shiva the cosmic dancer, ending one cycle of creation, beginning another and uniting all opposites.

Priests may offer to guide you around the temple complex. Since they work as a kind of cooperative to fund the temple, you may wish to support this magnificent building by hiring one (for anything between ₹30 and ₹300, depending on language skills and knowledge). Unusually for Tamil Nadu, the temple is privately funded and managed.

★ Festivals & Events

Of the town's many festivals, the two largest are the 10-day chariot festivals (⊙ Jun-Jul & Dec-Jan).

Natyanjali Dance Festival   DANCE
(⊙ Feb-Mar) Chidambaram's five-day dance festival attracts 300 to 400 classical dancers from all over India to the Nataraja Temple.

🛏 Sleeping & Eating

Many cheap pilgrims' lodges are clustered around the temple, but some are pretty grim. If there's anywhere really nice to stay in Chidambaram, we haven't found it yet. There are plenty of cheap veg eats surrounding the temple, but the best places for meals are hotels.

Hotel Saradharam   HOTEL $$
(☏ 04144-221336;   www.hotelsaradharam.co.in;
19 VGP St; r incl breakfast ₹1100, with AC ₹2160;
❋ @ 🛜) The busy, friendly Saradharam is as good as it gets, and is conveniently located opposite the bus stand. It's a bit worn but comfortable enough, and a welcome respite from the town-centre frenzy. There's free wi-fi in the lobby, and the hotel has three restaurants – two vegetarian, plus the good multicuisine, AC Anupallavi (mains ₹130-250; ⊙ 7-10am, noon-3pm & 6-10.45pm).

ℹ Information

ICICI Bank ATM (Hotel Saradharam, VGP St)

ℹ Getting There & Away

Three or more daily trains head to Trichy (2nd-class/3AC/2AC ₹80/485/690, 3½ hours) via Kumbakonam and Thanjavur, and six to Chennai (₹105/485/690, 5½ hours). Universal Travels (⊙ 10am-midnight), opposite the bus stand, has three daily Volvo AC buses to Chennai (₹500, five hours).

Government buses from the bus stand include:
Chennai (₹180, six hours, every 30 minutes)
Kumbakonam (₹40, three hours, every 30 minutes)
Puducherry (₹40 to ₹50, two hours, every 30 minutes)
Thanjavur (₹60, four hours, every 30 minutes)
Tranquebar (Tharangambadi; ₹30, two hours, every 30 minutes)

Kumbakonam

☏ 0435 / POP 140,156
At first glance Kumbakonam is just another Indian junction town, but then you notice the dozens of colourful *gopurams* pointing skyward from its 18 temples, a reminder that this was once a seat of medieval South Indian power. And with another two magnif-

Kumbakonam

icent World Heritage–listed Chola temples (p1046) nearby, it's worth staying the night.

⊙ Sights

Most of the temples are dedicated to Shiva or Vishnu.

Nageshwara Temple   HINDU TEMPLE
(⊙6.30am-noon & 4.30-8.30pm) Founded by the Cholas in 886, this is Kumbakonam's oldest temple, and is dedicated to Shiva in the guise of Nagaraja, the serpent king. On three days of the year (in April or May) the sun's rays fall on the lingam. The Nataraja shrine just to the right in front of the inner sanctum is fashioned like a horse-drawn chariot.

Sarangapani Temple   HINDU TEMPLE
(⊙6.30am-noon & 4.30-8.30pm) Sarangapani is the largest Vishnu temple, with a 45m-high eastern *gopuram* as its main entrance (photography is not permitted inside). Past the temple cowshed (Krishna the cowherd is one of Vishnu's forms), another *gopuram* and a pillared hall, you reach the inner sanctuary, a 12th-century Chola creation styled like a chariot with big carved elephants, horses and wheels.

Kumbeshwara Temple   HINDU TEMPLE
(⊙6.30am-noon & 4.30-8.30pm) Kumbeshwara Temple, entered via a nine-storey *gopuram* and with a long porticoed *mandapa*, is Kumbakonam's biggest Shiva temple. It dates from the 17th and 18th centuries and contains a lingam said to have been made by Shiva himself when he mixed the nectar of immortality with sand.

Mahamaham Tank   WATER TANK
(⊙6.30am-noon & 4.30-8.30pm) Surrounded by 17 pavilions, the huge Mahamaham Tank is one of Kumbakonam's most sacred sites. It's believed that every 12 years the waters of India's holiest rivers, including the Ganges, flow into it, and at this time a festival is held; the next is due in 2016.

⌐ Sleeping & Eating

Pandian Hotel   HOTEL **$**
(☑ 0435-2430397; 52 Sarangapani Koil Sannadhi St; s/d ₹350/660, d with AC ₹990; ☒) It's slightly institutional, but you're generally getting fair value at this clean-enough budget standby.

DON'T MISS

CHOLA TEMPLES NEAR KUMBAKONAM

Two of the three great monuments of Chola civilisation stand in villages near Kumbakonam: the Airavatesvara Temple in Darasuram and the Gangaikondacholapuram temple. Unlike the also World Heritage–listed Brihadishwara Temple at Thanjavur, today these temples receive relatively few worshippers (and visitors). They are wonderful both for their overall form (with pyramidal towers rising at the heart of rectangular walled compounds) and for the exquisite detail of their carved stone.

From Kumbakonam, frequent buses heading to nearby villages will drop you at Darasuram; buses to Gangaikondacholapuram (₹21, 1½ hours) run every half-hour. A return autorickshaw to Darasuram costs about ₹150. A half-day car trip to both temples, with Hotel Raya's is ₹1100 (₹1250 with AC).

Airavatesvara Temple (⊙6am-8pm) Only 3km west of Kumbakonam in Darasuram, this temple dedicated to Shiva was constructed by Rajaraja II (1146–63). The steps of the Rajagambhira Hall are carved with vivid elephants and horses pulling chariots. This pavilion's 108 all-different pillars have detailed carvings including dancers, acrobats and the five-in-one beast Yali (elephant's head, lion's body, goat's horns, pig's ears and a cow's backside). Inside the main shrine (⊙6am-noon & 4-8pm), you can honour the central lingam and get a *tilak* (forehead) mark for ₹10.

On the outside of the shrine are several fine carved images of Shiva. Four *mandapas* frame the corners of the courtyard complex.

Gangaikondacholapuram Temple (⊙6am-noon & 4-8pm) The temple at Gangaikondacholapuram ('City of the Chola who Conquered the Ganges'), 35km north of Kumbakonam, is dedicated to Shiva. It was built by Rajendra I in the 11th century when he moved the Chola capital here from Thanjavur, and has many similarities to the earlier Brihadishwara at Thanjavur. Its beautiful 49m-tall tower, however, has a slightly concave curve, making it the 'feminine' counterpart to the mildly convex Thanjavur one. The complex's artistic highlights are the wonderfully graceful sculptures around the tower's exterior.

A massive Nandi (Shiva's vehicle) faces the temple from the surrounding gardens. The main shrine, beneath the tower, contains a huge lingam and is approached through a long, gloomy 17th-century hall. The fine carvings on the tower's exterior include Shiva as the beggar Bhikshatana, immediately left of the southern steps; Ardhanarishvara (Shiva as half-man, half-woman) and Shiva as Nataraja, on the south side; and Shiva with Ganga, Shiva emerging from the lingam, and Vishnu with Lakshmi and Bhudevi (the first three images on the west side). Most famous of all is the striking panel of Shiva garlanding the head of his follower, Chandesvara, beside the northern steps.

Hotel Raya's   HOTEL **$$**
(☑ 0435-2423170; www.hotelrayas.com; 18 Head Post Office Rd; r ₹1200, with AC ₹1440-1560; ❋) Friendly service and reliably spacious, spotless rooms make Raya's your top lodging option in town, but the new annexe (r ₹1800; ❋) has the best, brightest rooms. It runs a convenient car service for out-of-town trips, and **Sathars Restaurant** (mains ₹110-195; ⊙11.30am-11.30pm) here does good veg and nonveg fare in clean surroundings.

Mantra Veppathur   RESORT **$$$**
(☑ 0435-2462261; www.mantraveppathur.com; 536/537A, 1 Bagavathapuram Main Rd Extension, Srisailapathipuram Village; r incl breakfast ₹8400-10,790; ❋ ⊛ ❋) 🖉 Lost in the riverside jungle, 10km northeast of Kumbakonam, this is a welcome retreat from temple-town chaos. Comfy rustic-style rooms fronted by porches with rocking chairs have open-air showers; yoga, meditation, and ayurveda are offered; and the organic farm fuels the Indian-focused restaurant, where you can eat out on a turquoise-tiled verandah.

Hotel Sri Venkkatramana   INDIAN **$**
(TSR Big St; thalis ₹60-100; ⊙5.30am-10.30pm Mon-Sat) Serves good fresh veg food; very popular with locals.

Taj Samudra   INDIAN **$$**
(80 Nageswaran South St; mains ₹115-185; ⊙noon-3pm & 7-11pm) Here you can get tasty veg and

nonveg dishes from all over India, brought by friendly waiters, against an almost stylish backdrop.

ℹ Information

Speed Systems (Sarangapani Koil Sannadhi St; internet per hour ₹20; ⊙ 9.30am-9.30pm) Take your passport.

ℹ Getting There & Away

Thirteen daily trains head to Thanjavur (2nd-class/3AC/2AC ₹45/485/690, 30 minutes to one hour) and eight to Trichy (₹60/485/690, two to 2½ hours). Five daily trains to/from Chennai Egmore include the overnight Mannai Express (sleeper/3AC/2AC/1AC ₹210/555/790/1315, 6½ hours) and the daytime Chennai Express/Trichy Express (₹210/555/790/1315, six to seven hours).

Government buses from the bus stand include:

Chennai (₹185 to ₹230, 6½ to eight hours, every 15 minutes)

Chidambaram (₹44, 2½ to three hours, every 20 minutes)

Karaikal (₹34, 2¼ hours, every 30 minutes)

Thanjavur (₹30, 1½ hours, every 10 minutes)

Thanjavur (Tanjore)

♪ 04362 / POP 222,943

Here are the ochre foundation blocks of perhaps the most remarkable civilisation of Dravidian history, one of the few kingdoms to expand Hinduism beyond India, a bedrock for aesthetic styles that spread from Madurai to the Mekong. A dizzying historical legacy was forged from Thanjavur, capital of the great Chola empire during its heyday. Today, this is a crowded, hectic, modern Indian town but the past is still very much present. Every day thousands of people worship at the Cholas' grand Brihadishwara Temple, and Thanjavur's labyrinthine royal palace preserves memories of other powerful dynasties from later centuries.

◉ Sights

⭐ **Brihadishwara Temple**   HINDU TEMPLE

(⊙6am-8.30pm) Come here twice: in the morning, when the tawny granite begins to assert its dominance over the white dawn sunshine, and in the evening, when the rocks capture a hot palette of reds, oranges, yellows and pinks on the crowning glory of Chola temple architecture. The World Heritage–listed Brihadishwara Temple was built between 1003 and 1010 by Rajaraja I (king of kings). The outer fortifications were put up by Thanjavur's later Nayak and British regimes.

You enter through a Nayak gate, followed by two original *gopurams* with elaborate stucco sculptures. You might find the temple elephant under one of the *gopurams,* dispensing good luck with a dab of his trunk to anyone who puts a rupee in it. Several shrines are dotted around the extensive grassy areas of the walled temple compound, including one of India's largest statues of Nandi (Shiva's sacred bull) facing the main temple building. Cut from a single rock, this 16th-century Nayak creation is 6m long.

A long, columned assembly hall leads to the **central shrine** (⊙8.30am-12.30pm & 4-8.30pm) with its 4m-high Shiva lingam, beneath the superb 61m-high *vimana* (tower). The assembly hall's southern steps are flanked by two huge *dvarapalas* (temple guardians). Many lovely, graceful deity images stand in niches around the *vimana's* lower levels, including Shiva emerging from the lingam (beside the southern steps); Shiva as the beggar Bhikshatana (first image, south side); Harihara (half Shiva, half Vishnu) on the west wall; and Ardhanarishvara (Shiva as half-man, half-woman), leaning on Nandi, on the north side. Between the deity images are panels showing classical dance poses.

The compound also contains a helpful interpretation centre along the south wall and, in the colonnade along the west and north walls, hundreds more linga. Both west and north walls are lined with exquisite lime-plaster Chola frescoes, for years buried under later Nayak-era murals. North of the temple compound, but still within the outer fortifications, are a **park** (admission ₹5) containing the **Sivaganga tank**, and 18th-century **Schwartz's Church**.

⭐ **Royal Palace**   PALACE

(Indian/foreigner   ₹30/150, camera ₹50/100; ⊙9am-6pm) Thanjavur's royal palace is a mixed bag of ruin and renovation, superb art and random royal paraphernalia. The mazelike complex was constructed partly by the Nayaks who took over Thanjavur in 1535, and partly by a local Maratha dynasty that ruled from 1676 to 1855. The two don't-miss sections are the Saraswati Mahal Library Museum and the Art Gallery.

Seven different sections of the palace can be visited – and you'll need three

TAMIL NADU & CHENNAI THANJAVUR (TANJORE)

Thanjavur (Tanjore)

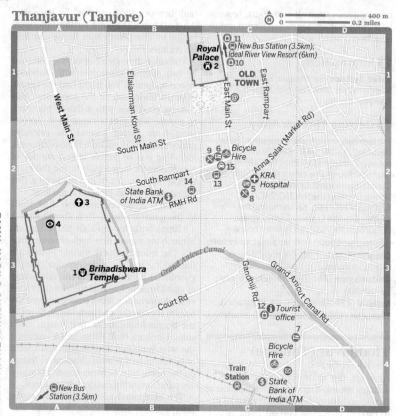

different tickets to see them all! The Art Gallery and Saraswati Mahal Library Museum are included in the 'full' ticket, along with the Mahratta Dharbar Hall, the bell tower, and the Saarjah Madi. The main entrance is from the north, via a lane off East Main St. On the way in you'll come to the main ticket office, followed by the Maratha Palace complex.

Past the ticket office, a passage to the left leads to, first, the Royal Palace Museum, a small miscellany of sculptures, weaponry, elephant bells and rajas' headgears; second, the Maharaja Serfoji Memorial Hall, commemorating the enlightened Maratha scholar-king Serfoji II (1798–1832), with a better collection overlooking a once-splendid, now crumbling courtyard; and third, the Mahratta Dharbar Hall, where Maratha rulers gave audience in a grand but faded pavilion adorned with colourful murals, including their own portraits behind the dais.

As you exit the passage, the fabulous little Sarawasti Mahal Library Museum is on your left. Perhaps Serfoji II's greatest contribution to posterity, this is testimony both to the 19th-century obsession with knowledge accumulation and to an eclectic mind that collected prints of Chinese torture methods, Audubon-style paintings of Indian flora and fauna, world atlases and rare medieval books. Serfoji amassed more than 65,000 books and 50,000 palm-leaf paper manuscripts in Indian and European languages, though most aren't displayed.

Leaving the library, turn left for the Art Gallery, set around the Nayak Palace courtyard. This contains a collection of superb, mainly Chola, bronzes and stone carvings, and one of its rooms, the 1600 Nayak Durbar Hall, has a statue of Serfoji II. From the courtyard, steps lead part of the way up a large *gopuram*-like tower to a whale skeleton said to have been washed up in Tranquebar. The renovated **Saarjah Madi** is best admired from East Main St for its ornate balconies.

★ Festivals & Events

Thyagaraja Aradhana — MUSIC
(◉Jan) At Thiruvaiyaru, 13km north of Thanjavur, this important five-day Carnatic music festival honours the saint and composer Thyagaraja.

🛏 Sleeping

Hotel Ramnath — HOTEL $
(☎04362-272567; hotel_ramnath@yahoo.com; 1335 South Rampart; r ₹1000, with AC ₹1300; ❄🤶) The best of a bunch of cheapies facing the local bus stand downtown (not quite as noisy as you'd think), the Ramnath is a decent 'upmarket budget' option with clean, smallish, pine-furnished rooms.

Hotel Valli — HOTEL $
(☎04362-231584; www.hotelvalli.com; 2948 MKM Rd; s/d ₹605/825, r with AC ₹1460; ❄) Near the train station, green-painted Valli offers good-value, spick-and-span rooms, friendly staff, and a basic restaurant. It's in a reasonably peaceful leafy spot beyond a bunch of greasy backstreet workshops.

Hotel Gnanam — HOTEL $$
(☎04362-278501; www.hotelgnanam.com; Anna Salai; s/d incl breakfast ₹2640/3000; ❄🤶) Easily the best value in town, the Gnanam has stylish, comfy rooms (some with balconies or lovely clean bath-tubs) and ultraefficient receptionists, and is perfect for anyone needing good food, free wi-fi and other modern amenities in Thanjavur's geographic centre.

Ideal River View Resort — RESORT $$$
(☎04362-250533; www.idealresort.com; Vennar Bank, Palliagraharam; s/d ₹6000/6600; ◉7-10am, 12.30-3pm & 7.30-10pm; ❄🤶🏊) Brightly furnished cottages with roomy balconies sprawling across tropical gardens on the banks of the Vennar River, 7km northwest of central Thanjavur, make this tranquil resort by far the most atmospheric sleeping spot around. You can hire bikes, do yoga, or just enjoy the pool. The semi-open-air Indian/Sri Lankan/Continental **restaurant** (mains ₹175-450) overlooks the river.

✕ Eating

Sri Venkata Lodge — SOUTH INDIAN $
(Gandhiji Rd; thalis ₹50; ◉5.15am-10.15pm) A friendly, popular, veg-only place near the centre of everything, that does a nice thali.

Vasanta Bhavan — INDIAN $
(1338 South Rampart; mains ₹65-85; ◉6am-11pm) The most popular of several veg places facing the local bus stand downtown, Vasanta Bhavan doles out biryani and North Indian curries as well as your usual southern favourites, in AC comfort.

Sahana — INDIAN $$
(Hotel Gnanam; Anna Salai; mains ₹95-160; ◉7am-10.30pm) This classy hotel restaurant does a very nice line in fresh, tasty, mainly Indian veg dishes, along with a decent multicuisine breakfast buffet.

Diana — MULTICUISINE $$
(Hotel Gnanam; Anna Salai; mains ₹160-400; ◉11am-3pm & 6.30-10.30pm) The Hotel Gnanam's smart-ish nonveg restaurant is very good, with a wide range of northern dishes and local Chettinadu fare – and even beer.

🛍 Shopping

Thanjavur is good for handicrafts shopping, especially near the palace, where outlets such as **Kandiya Heritage** (634 East Main St; ◉7am-7pm Mon-Sat) and **Chola Art Galerie**

(78/799 East Main St; ⊙9am-7pm) sell antiques, reproduction bronzes, brightly painted wooden horses, old European pottery, jewellery and more. For fixed prices, try state-run **Poompuhar** (Gandhiji Rd; ⊙10am-8pm Mon-Sat).

ⓘ Information

Sify iWay (927 East Main St; internet per hour ₹25; ⊙10am-9pm)

Tourist office (☑ 04362-230984; Gandhiji Rd; ⊙10am-5.45pm Mon-Fri) One of Tamil Nadu's more helpful offices.

ⓘ Getting There & Away

BUS

The downtown **SETC bus stand** (⊙reservation office 7.30am-8.30pm) has express buses to Chennai (₹260, eight hours) hourly from 5.30am to 12.30pm, and five times between 8pm and 10.45pm. Buses for other cities leave from the New Bus Station, 5km southwest of the centre. Many arriving buses will drop you off in the city centre on the way out there. Services from the New Bus Station include:

Chidambaram (₹90, four hours, every 30 minutes)

Kumbakonam (₹22 to ₹29, 1½ hours, every five minutes)

Madurai (₹90, four hours, every 20 minutes)

Trichy (₹24 to ₹31, 1½ hours, every 10 minutes)

TRAIN

The station is central enough, at the end of Gandhiji Rd. Five daily trains head to Chennai Egmore (seven to eight hours) including the 10.45pm Mannai Express (sleeper/3AC/2AC/1AC ₹225/600/855/1430). Seventeen trains go to Trichy (2nd-class/3AC/2AC ₹45/485/690, 1½ hours) and 12 to Kumbakonam (₹45/485/690, 30 minutes to 1¼ hours).

ⓘ Getting Around

You can hire bikes (per hour ₹6) from stalls opposite the local bus stand and train station. Bus 74 (₹6) shuttles between the New Bus Station and the local bus stand; autorickshaws cost ₹100.

Trichy (Tiruchirappalli)

☑ 0431 / POP 847,387

Welcome to (more or less) the geographic centre of Tamil Nadu. Tiruchirappalli, universally known as Trichy or Tiruchi, isn't just a travel junction; it also mixes up a heaving bazaar with some major must-see temples.

It's a huge, crowded, busy city, and the fact that most hotels are clumped together around the big bus station isn't exactly a plus point. But Trichy has a strong character and long history, and a sneaky way of overturning first impressions.

Trichy may have been a capital of the early Cholas in the 3rd century BC. It passed through the hands of the Pallavas, medieval Cholas, Pandyas, Delhi Sultanate and Vijayanagars before the Madurai Nayaks brought it to prominence, making it a capital in the 17th century and building its famous Rock Fort Temple.

Trichy stretches a long way from north to south, and most of what's interesting to travellers is split into three distinct areas. The Trichy Junction, or Cantonment, area in the south has most of the hotels and restaurants and the main bus and train stations. The Rock Fort Temple and main bazaar are 4km north of here; the other important temples are in Srirangam, a further 4km north, across the Cauvery River. Luckily, the whole lot is connected by a good bus service.

◉ Sights

★ **Rock Fort Temple**   HINDU TEMPLE
(Map p1051; admission ₹3, camera/video ₹20/100; ⊙6am-8pm) The Rock Fort Temple, perched 83m high on a massive outcrop, lords over Trichy with stony arrogance. The ancient rock was first hewn by the Pallavas and Pandyas, who cut small cave temples on its south side, but it was the war-savvy Nayaks who later made strategic use of the naturally fortified position. There are over 400 stone-cut steps to climb to the top.

From NSB Rd on the south side, you pass between small shops and cross a street before entering the temple precinct itself. Then it's 180 steps up to the Thayumanaswamy Temple, the rock's biggest temple, on the left (closed to non-Hindus). A gold-topped tower rises over its sanctum, which houses a 2m-high Shiva lingam. Further up, you pass the 6th-century Pallava cave temple on the left – it's usually railed off but if you get inside, note the famous Gangadhara panel on the left, showing Shiva restraining the waters of the Ganges with a single strand of his hair. From here it's just another 183 steps to the small Uchipillaiyar Temple at the summit, dedicated to Ganesh. The view is wonderful, with eagles wheeling beneath and Trichy sprawling all around. Back at the bottom, check out the lower rock-cut

Trichy (Tiruchirappalli)

self-enclosed city. It has 49 separate shrines, all dedicated to Vishnu, and reaching the inner sanctum from the south, as most worshippers do, requires passing through seven *gopurams*. The first, the **Rajagopuram** (Map p1051), was added in 1987, and is one of Asia's tallest temple towers at 73m high.

You pass through streets with shops, restaurants, motorbikes and cars until you reach the temple proper at the fourth *gopuram*. Inside is the ticket desk for the nearby **roof viewpoint** (ticket ₹10; ⊙6am-5pm), which gives semipanoramic views of the complex. Take no notice of would-be guides who spin all kinds of stories to get you to hire them. Non-Hindus cannot pass the sixth *gopuram* so won't see the innermost sanctum whose image shows Vishnu as Lord Ranganatha, reclining on a five-headed snake.

Turn right just before the fifth *gopuram* to the small but intriguing **Art Museum** (admission ₹5; ⊙9am-1pm & 2-6pm), with good bronzes, tusks of bygone temple elephants, and a collection of superb 17th-century Nayak ivory figurines depicting gods, demons, and kings and queens (some erotically engaged). Continue round to the left past the museum to the **Sesha Mandapa**, a 16th-century pillared hall with magnificently detailed Vijayanagar carvings of rearing horses in battle. Inside the fifth *gopuram* is the **Garuda Mandapa**, with a shrine to Vishnu's man-eagle vehicle.

cave temple, with particularly fine pillars (right past five or six houses as you exit the temple precinct, then right again down a small lane).

The stone steps get scorchingly hot in the midday sun and it's a barefoot climb, so time your visit carefully.

★ **Sri Ranganathaswamy Temple**   HINDU TEMPLE
(Map p1051; camera/video ₹50/100; ⊙6am-9pm) All right temple-philes, here's the one you've been waiting for: quite possibly the biggest temple in India – so large, it feels like a

TAMIL NADU & CHENNAI TRICHY (TIRUCHIRAPPALLI)

The temple's most important festival is the 21-day Vaikunta Ekadasi (Paradise Festival) in December/January, when the celebrated Vaishnavaite text, Tiruvaimozhi, is recited before an image of Vishnu.

Bus 1 from the Central Bus Station or the Rock Fort stops south of the Rajagopuram.

Sri Jambukeshwara Temple   HINDU TEMPLE

(Tiruvanakoil; camera/video ₹30/200; ⊙5am-9pm) If you're visiting Tamil Nadu's five elemental temples of Shiva, you need to see Sri Jambukeshwara, dedicated to Shiva, Parvati and the medium of water. The liquid element is realised in the central shrine (closed to non-Hindus), whose Shiva lingam reputedly issues a nonstop trickle of water. If you're taking bus 1, ask for 'Tiruvanakoil'; the temple is 350m east of the main road.

Lourdes Church   CHURCH

(Map p1051; College Rd; ⊙8am-8.30pm) The hush of this 19th-century neo-Gothic church makes an interesting contrast to the frenetic activity of Trichy's Hindu temples. In the cool, green campus of Jesuit St Joseph's College next door, the dusty St Joseph's College Museum (Map p1051; ⊙9am-noon & 2-4pm Mon-Sat) FREE contains the creepy natural history collections of the Jesuit priests' Western Ghats excursions in the 1870s. Ask at reception as you approach the museum and someone will probably let you in.

🛏 Sleeping & Eating

Most hotels are near the Central Bus Station, a short walk north from Trichy Junction train station.

The top eateries are usually in the better hotels, but there are some decent cheaper places too.

Hotel Abbirami   HOTEL $

(Map p1053; ☎0431-2415001; 10 McDonald's Rd; r ₹770-990, with AC ₹1439-1919; ☀) Most appealing are the 1st- and 4th-floor renovated rooms, with light wood and colourful glass panels. Older rooms have darker wood and are a bit worn, but still well-kept. It's a busy place with friendly staff.

Hotel Mathura   HOTEL $

(Map p1053; ☎0431-2414737; www.hotelmathura.com; 1 Rockins Rd; r ₹700, with AC ₹1100; ☀) Rooms are very basic but tolerably clean. Many of the non-ACs are in better shape than those with AC. The 2nd floor, at least, has had a decent coat of paint.

Hotel Ramyas   HOTEL $$

(Map p1053; ☎0431-2414646; www.ramyas.com; 13-D/2 Williams Rd; s/d ₹990/1680, with AC s ₹2100-2700, d ₹2400-3300, all incl breakfast; ☀@⊛) Excellent rooms, service and facilities make this business-oriented hotel great value. 'Business' singles are small but it's only another ₹200-odd for a good 'executive'. Turquoise-clad Meridian (Map p1053; mains ₹100-215; ⊙11.30am-3pm & 6.30-11pm) does tasty multicuisine fare, breakfast is a nice buffet, and the Chola Bar (Map p1053; ⊙11am-3.30pm & 6.30-11pm) is less dingy than most hotel bars (though still male-dominated). Best is the lovely Thendral (Map p1053; mains ₹100-230; ⊙7-9.30am & 6.30-11pm) roof-garden restaurant.

Grand Gardenia   HOTEL $$

(☎0431-4045000; www.grandgardenia.com; 22-25 Mannarpuram Junction; s ₹3000, d ₹3600-4800, all incl breakfast; ☀⊛) Elegant modern rooms come with free wi-fi, comfy beds, and glassed-in showers at this sparkly corporate-style hotel, currently your smartest option in Trichy. Kannappa (mains ₹95-180; ⊙11.30am-11.30pm) serves up excellent Chettinadu food and the rooftop terrace hosts a good multicuisine restaurant (mains ₹115-220; ⊙7.30-10am, noon-3pm & 7-10.45pm) and a gym. Comfort and amenities outweigh the uninspiring location, near the highway 1km south of Trichy Junction station.

Femina Hotel   HOTEL $$

(Map p1053; ☎0431-2414501; www.feminahotel.net; 109 Williams Rd; s ₹1600-3600, d ₹2040-4200, all incl breakfast; ☀@⊛) It's hard to tell where the enormous Femina begins and ends. From outside it looks 1950s, but renovations have turned the interior quite contemporary. Facilities are good and staff helpful. Renovated deluxe rooms are cosy and modern, while standard rooms are a tad worn but very spacious. There's a nice outdoor pool and eateries include the Round the Clock (Map p1053; mains ₹80-120; ⊙24hr) coffee-shop-cum-veg-restaurant.

Breeze Residency   HOTEL $$

(Map p1053; ☎0431-2414414; www.breeze residency.com; 3/14 McDonald's Rd; s/d ₹3000/3480, ste ₹4200-6000, all incl breakfast; ☀@⊛) The Breeze is huge, semiluxurious and in a quiet leafy location. The best rooms are on the top floors but all are well appointed. Facilities include a gym, the Madras Restaurant (Map p1053; lunch/

dinner buffet ₹400/450; ☺noon-3.30pm & 7-11pm), a 24-hour coffee shop, and a bizarre Wild West theme bar.

Hotel Royal Sathyam `HOTEL $$`
(Map p1051; ☎0431-4011414; http://sathyamgrouphotels.in; 42A Singarathope; s ₹1440-1920, d ₹1680-3000, all incl breakfast; 🅰🖥) The classiest option if you want to be close to the temple and market action. Rooms are small but smart, with extra-comfy mattresses and a fresh wood-and-whitewash theme, and it's a friendly place.

Vasanta Bhavan `INDIAN $`
(Map p1051; 3 NSB Rd; mains ₹60-85, thalis ₹60-120; ☺7am-10.30pm) A great spot for a meal with a view and, if you're lucky, a breeze near the Rock Fort. Tables on the outer gallery overlook the Teppakulam Tank. It's good for North Indian veg food – of the paneer and naan genre – as well as South Indian. People crowd in for the lunchtime thalis. There's another branch (Map p1053; Rockins Rd; mains ₹40-85, thalis ₹80; ☺6am-11pm) in the Cantonment.

DiMora `MULTICUISINE $$`
(Map p1051; ☎0431-2762656; 4th fl, Ambigai City Center, Shastri Rd; mains ₹150-440; ☺noon-4pm & 7-11.30pm) Waiters in all-black take your order on mobile phones to a soundtrack of trancey lounge music that makes this smart, popular top-floor restaurant feel more Chennai than Trichy. The menu roams all over the world, but it's great for pastas, wood-fired pizzas and fresh juices, as well tandoori and other Indian dishes.

🛍 Shopping

The main bazaar, immediately south of the Rock Fort, is as chaotic and crowded as you could want.

Saratha's `CLOTHING`
(Map p1051; 45 NSB Rd; ☺9am-9.30pm) Bursting with clothing of every conceivable kind and colour, Saratha's claims to be (and might well be) the 'largest textile showroom in India'.

ℹ Information

Indian Panorama (☎0431-4226122; www.indianpanorama.in; 5 Annai Ave, Srirangam) Trichy-based and covering all of India, this professional, reliable travel agency/tour operator is run by an Indian–New Zealander couple.

KMC Speciality Hospital (Kauvery Hospital; Map p1053; ☎0431-4077777; www.kmcspecialityhospital.in; 6 Royal Rd) Large, well-equipped, private hospital.

Tourist office (Map p1053; ☎0431-2460136; McDonald's Rd; ☺10am-5.45pm Mon-Fri)

Trichy Junction Area

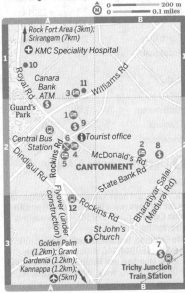

Trichy Junction Area

😴 Sleeping
1	Hotel Ramyas	A2
2	Breeze Residency	B2
3	Femina Hotel	A1
4	Hotel Abbirami	A2
5	Hotel Mathura	A2

🍴 Eating
	Meridian	(see 1)
	Madras Restaurant	(see 2)
	Round the Clock	(see 3)
	Thendral	(see 1)
6	Vasanta Bhavan	A2

🍷 Drinking & Nightlife
	Chola Bar	(see 1)

ℹ Information
7	State Bank of India ATM	B3
8	State Bank of India ATM	B2
9	State Bank of India ATM	A2

🚍 Transport
10	Air Asia	A1
	Femina Travels	(see 3)
11	Mihin Lanka	A1
12	Parveen Travels	A3
	SriLankan Airlines	(see 3)

GOVERNMENT BUSES FROM TRICHY (TIRUCHIRAPPALLI)

DESTINATION	FARE (₹)	DURATION (HR)	FREQUENCY
Bengaluru	350 Ultra Deluxe (UD)	9	6 UD daily
Chennai	211 regular, 260 UD, 325 AC	6-7	15 UD, 4 AC daily
Coimbatore	116 regular, 126 Deluxe (D)	5-6	every 10min, 3 D daily
Kodaikanal	126	5	6.40am, 8.40am, 11am, 11.40am, 12.40pm
Madurai	80	2½	every 15min
Ooty	260 UD	8	10.15pm UD
Rameswaram	170	6½	hourly
Thanjavur	31	1½	every 10min
Trivandrum	365	9	4 daily

ⓘ Getting There & Away

AIR

Trichy's airport has four daily flights to Chennai on **Jet Airways** (www.jetairways.com) and **Air India Express** (☎ 0431-2341744; www.airindi aexpress.in).

To Colombo, **SriLankan Airlines** (Map p1053; ☎ 0431-2460844; 14C Williams Rd; ◷ 9am-5.30pm Mon-Sat) and **Mihin Lanka** (Map p1053; ☎ 0431-4200070; www.mihinlanka.com; 14C Williams Rd; ◷ 9am-5.30 Mon-Fri) each fly twice daily.

Air Asia (Map p1053; ☎ 0431-4540394; www.airasia.com; 18/3-5 Ivory Plaza, Royal Rd; ◷ 9.30am-5pm Mon-Fri, 9.30am-1pm Sat) flies to Kuala Lumpur three times daily, **Tiger Air** (www.tigerair.com) to Singapore daily, and Air India Express daily to Singapore and Dubai.

BUS

Government buses use the busy but orderly **Central Bus Station** (Map p1053; Rockins Rd). The best services for longer trips are the UD (Ultra Deluxe), with the softest seats. There's a booking office for these in the southwest corner of the station. For Kodaikanal, a good option is to take one of the frequent buses to Dindigul (₹48, two hours) and change there.

Private bus companies have offices near the Central Bus Station, including **Parveen Travels** (Map p1053; ☎ 0431-2419811; www.parveen travels.com; 12 Ashby Complex; ◷ 24hr) which offers AC services to Chennai (₹560 to ₹680, six hours, seven daily) and Trivandrum (Thiru-vananthapuram; ₹1100 to ₹1200, seven hours, 12.30am and 1am), plus non-AC semisleeper services to Puducherry (₹500, four hours, midnight) and Kodaikanal (₹500, 4½ hours, 2.30am).

TAXI

Travel agencies and hotels provide cars with drivers. Efficient, reasonably priced **Femina Travels** (Map p1053; ☎ 0431-2418532; 109 Williams Rd; ◷ 6am-10pm) charges ₹1900 for up to 10 hours and 100km (AC).

TRAIN

Trichy Junction station is on the main Chennai–Madurai line. Of 16 daily express services to Chennai, the best daytime option is the Vaigai Express (2nd/chair class ₹145/510, 5¾ hours) departing at 9am. The overnight Pandyan Express (sleeper/3AC/2AC/1AC ₹245/625/870/1450, 6½ hours) leaves at 11.10pm. Thirteen daily trains to Madurai include the 7.15am Tirunelveli Express (2nd/chair class ₹95/340, 2¼ hours) and the 1.15pm Guruvaya Express (2nd-class/sleeper/3AC/2AC ₹80/140/485/690, three hours). Eighteen trains head to Thanjavur (2nd-class/sleeper/3AC ₹45/140/485, 40 minutes to 1½ hours).

ⓘ Getting Around

The 5km ride between the airport and Central Bus Station area costs about ₹300 by taxi and ₹150 by autorickshaw; there's a prepaid taxi stand at the airport. Or take bus K1.

Bus 1 from Rockins Rd outside the Central Bus Station goes every few minutes to Sri Ranganathaswamy Temple (₹6) and back, stopping near the Rock Fort Temple and Sri Jambukeshwara Temple en route.

SOUTHERN TAMIL NADU

Chettinadu

The Chettiars, a community of traders based in and around Karaikkudi, 95km south of Trichy, hit the big time back in the 19th century as financiers and entrepreneurs in colonial-era Sri Lanka and Southeast Asia.

They lavished their fortunes on building at least 10,000, maybe even 30,000 opulent mansions in the 75 towns and villages of their arid rural homeland, Chettinadu. No expense was spared on finding the finest materials for these palatial homes – Burmese teak, Italian marble, Indian rosewood, English steel, and art and sculpture from everywhere. In the aftermath of WWII, the Chettiars' business networks came crashing down and many families left Chettinadu. Disused mansions fell into decay and were demolished or sold off piecemeal. Awareness of their value started to revive around the turn of the 21st century, with Chettinadu making it onto Unesco's tentative World Heritage list in 2014. Several mansions have now been turned into gorgeous heritage hotels where you can enjoy authentic Chettinad cuisine, known throughout India for its brilliant use of spices.

⊙ Sights & Activities

Hotels give cooking demos or classes, and provide bicycles or bullock carts for rural rambles. They can also arrange visits to sari-weavers, temples, private mansions, the Athangudi tileworkers (producing the colourful handmade tiles in most Chettiar mansions), and shrines of the popular pre-Hindu deity Ayyanar (identifiable by their large terracotta horses, Ayyanar's vehicle). The antique shops in Karaikkudi's Muneeswaran Koil St give you an idea of how much of the Chettiar heritage is still being flogged.

The nondescript town of Pudukkottai, 51km south of Trichy and 44km north of Karaikkudi, has historical significance in inverse proportion to its current obscurity: it was the capital of the only princely state in Tamil Nadu to remain officially independent throughout British rule.

Vijayalaya Cholisvaram   HINDU TEMPLE
(Narthamalai) This small but stunning 8th-century temple stands on a dramatically deserted rock slope 1km southwest of Narthamalai village, about 16km north of Pudukkottai. Reminiscent of the Shore Temple at Mamallapuram, without the crowds, it was probably built in late Pallava times. The caretaker, if present, will open two rock-cut Shiva shrines in the rock face behind, one with 12 impressively large reliefs of Vishnu.

The Narthamalai turn-off is 7km south of Keeranur on the Trichy–Pudukkottai road; it's 2km west to the village.

Pudukkottai Museum   MUSEUM
(Thirukokarnam, Pudukkottai; Indian/foreigner ₹5/100, camera/video ₹20/100; ☺9.30am-5pm Sat-Thu) The relics of bygone days are on display in this wonderful museum, 4km north of Pudukkottai train station. Its eclectic collection includes musical instruments, megalithic burial artefacts, and some remarkable paintings, sculptures and miniatures.

Thirumayam Fort   FORT
(Thirumayam; Indian/foreigner ₹5/100; ☺10am-5.30pm) Simple and imposing, the renovated Thirumayam Fort, about 20km south of Pudukkottai, is worth a climb for the 360-degree views from the battlements over the surrounding countryside. There's a rock-cut Shiva shrine up some metal steps on the west side of the small hill.

Mansions
Lakshmi House   HISTORIC BUILDING
(Athangudi Periya Veedu; Athangudi Rd, Athangudi; admission ₹100; ☺9am-5pm) With perhaps the most exquisitely painted wood-carved ceilings in Chettinadu, Lakshmi House is a popular film set. Take in the especially fine materials (Belgian marble, English iron), Chettiar history panels, and curious statues of British rulers and Hindu gods above the front entrance. Athangudi is 15km northwest of Karaikkudi.

CVCT House   HISTORIC BUILDING
(CVCT St, Kanadukathan; admission ₹100, camera ₹50; ☺9am-5pm) Backed by the typical succession of pillar-lined courtyards, the impressive reception hall of this 'twin house' is shared by two branches of the same family. Don't miss the fabulous views over neighbouring mansions from the rooftop terrace. On the same street, **VVRM House** (CVCT St, Kanadukathan) is one of Chettinadu's oldest mansions, built in 1870 with distinctive egg-plaster walls, teak columns and intricate wood carvings; a ₹100 group 'donation' is expected. Kanadukathan is 9km south of Thirumayam.

PKACT House   HISTORIC BUILDING
(Trichy Main Rd, Kottaiyur, opp. ICICI Bank ATM; admission ₹50; ☺10am-5pm) Run by the Chennai-based **M.Rm.Rm. Cultural Foundation** (Map p1004; mrmrmculturalfoundation.moonfruit.com), this particularly well-preserved early-1900s mansion mixes modern and traditional architecture. Unusually, you can tour the whole house; upstairs,

there's a superb collection of Ravi Varma prints. Kottaiyur is 6km north of Karaikkudi.

Sleeping & Eating

To get a feel for the palatial life, book into one of Chettinadu's top-end hotels; they're pricey but the experience is fantastic.

★ **Visalam**　　　HERITAGE HOTEL $$$
(☎04565-273301; www.cghearth.com; Local Fund Rd, Kanadukathan; r incl breakfast ₹6500-13,000; ❋@☎❄) Stunningly restored and professionally run by a Malayali hotel chain, Visalam is a relatively young Chettiar mansion, done in the fashionable art-deco style of the 1930s. It's still decorated with the original owners' photos, furniture and paintings. The garden is lovely, the rooms large and full of character, and the pool setting is magical, overflowing with bougainvillea and with a low-key cafe alongside it. Kanadukathan is 9km south of Thirumayam.

★ **Saratha Vilas**　　BOUTIQUE HOTEL $$$
(☎9884203175, 9884936158; www.sarathavilas.com; 832 Main Rd, Kothamangalam; r incl breakfast ₹8000-11,000; ❋@☎) A different type of Chettiar charm inhabits this stylishly renovated, French-run mansion from 1910, 6km east of Kanadukathan. Rooms combine traditional and contemporary with distinct French panache, and the food is an exquisite mix of Chettinad and French. Most of the furnishings were personally designed by the knowledgeable architect owners, who are very active players in the preservation and promotion of Chettinadu heritage.

They're also the founders of local conservation NGO ArcHeS.

Bangala　　　BOUTIQUE HOTEL $$$
(☎04565-220221; www.thebangala.com; Devakottai Rd, Karaikkudi; r ₹6500-7000; ❋☎❄) This lovingly restored whitewashed 'bungalow' isn't a typical mansion but has all the requisite charm, with colourful rooms, quirky decorations, antique furniture, old family photos, and a beautiful pool. It's famous for its food: the ₹1000 set meals are actually Chettiar wedding feasts worth every paisa (available to nonguests from 12.30pm to 2.30pm and 8pm to 10pm; call two hours ahead).

Chettinadu Mansion　　HERITAGE HOTEL $$$
(☎04565-273080; www.chettinadmansion.com; 11 AR St, SARM House, Kanadukathan; s/d incl breakfast ₹5000/6400, half-board ₹5700/7800; ❋☎❄) Slightly shabbier than other Chettiar joints, but friendly and well managed,

this colourful century-old house is still owned (and lived in) by the original family. Of its 126 rooms, just 12 are open to guests – all sizeable with free wi-fi, wacky colour schemes and private balconies looking over other mansions.

The owners also run **Chettinadu Court** (☎9443495598; www.deshadan.com; Raja's St, Kanadukathan; s/d incl breakfast ₹3400/4500; ❋☎❄) a few blocks away, which has eight pleasant rooms sporting a few heritage touches. The two share an off-site pool.

❶ Getting There & Away

Car is by far the best way to get to and around Chettinadu. Renting one with a driver from Trichy, Thanjavur or Madurai for two days costs around ₹5000. Otherwise there are buses about every five minutes from Trichy to Pudukkottai (₹25, 1½ hours) and Karaikkudi (₹85, 2½ hours); you can hop off and on along the way. From Madurai, buses run to Karaikkudi (₹37, two hours) and Pudukkottai (₹57, 2½ hours) every 10 minutes. There are also buses from Thanjavur and Rameswaram.

Madurai

☎0452 / POP 1.02 MILLION

Chennai may be the capital of Tamil Nadu, but Madurai claims its soul. Madurai is Tamil-born and Tamil-rooted, one of the oldest cities in India, a metropolis that traded with ancient Rome and was a great capital long before Chennai was even dreamt of.

Tourists, Indian and foreign, usually come here to see the Meenakshi Amman Temple, a labyrinthine structure ranking among the greatest temples of India. Otherwise, Madurai, perhaps appropriately given her age, captures many of India's glaring dichotomies, with a centre dominated by a medieval temple and an economy increasingly driven by IT, all overlaid with the energy and excitement of a big Indian city and slotted into a much more manageable package than Chennai's sprawl.

History

Legend has it that Shiva showered drops of nectar (*madhuram*) from his locks onto the city, giving rise to the name Madurai – 'the City of Nectar'.

Ancient documents record the existence of Madurai from the 3rd century BC. It was a trading town, especially in spices, and according to legend was the home of the third *sangam* (gathering of Tamil scholars and poets). Over the centuries Madurai came under the sway of the Cholas, Pandyas, local Muslim sultans, Hindu Vijayanagar kings, and the Nayaks, who ruled until 1736 and set out the old city in a lotus shape. Under Tirumalai Nayak (1623–59) the bulk of the Meenakshi Amman Temple was built, and Madurai became the hub of Tamil culture, playing an important role in the development of the Tamil language.

In 1840 the British East India Company razed Madurai's fort and filled in its moat. The four broad Veli streets were constructed on top and to this day define the old city's limits.

◉ Sights

★ **Meenakshi Amman Temple**   HINDU TEMPLE
(Indian/foreigner ₹5/50, phone camera ₹50; ⊙4am-12.30pm & 4-9.30pm) The abode of the triple-breasted warrior goddess Meenakshi ('fish-eyed' – an epithet for perfect eyes in classical Tamil poetry) is considered by many to be the height of South Indian temple architecture, as vital to the aesthetic heritage of this region as the Taj Mahal is to North India. It's not so much a 17th-century temple as a 6-hectare complex with 12 tall *gopurams,* encrusted with a staggering array of gods, goddesses, demons and heroes (1511 of them on the south *gopuram* alone).

According to legend, the beautiful Meenakshi (a version of Parvati) was born with three breasts and this prophecy: her superfluous breast would melt away when she met her husband. The event came to pass when she met Shiva and took her place as his consort. The existing temple was built during the 17th-century reign of Tirumalai Nayak, but its origins go back 2000 years to when Madurai was a Pandyan capital.

The four streets surrounding the temple are pedestrian-only. Dress codes and security are strict for the temple itself: no women's shoulders, or legs of either gender, may be exposed, and no cameras are allowed inside (but you *can* use phone cameras). Despite this the temple has a happier, more joyful atmosphere than some of Tamil Nadu's more solemn shrines, and is adorned with especially colourful ceiling and wall paintings. Every evening at 9pm, a frenetic, incense-clouded procession carries an icon of Sundareswarar (Shiva) to Meenakshi's shrine to spend the night; visitors are welcome to follow along.

Before entering the temple, have a look around the Pudhu Mandapa. The main temple entrance is through the eastern (oldest) gopuram. First, on the right, you'll come to the Thousand Pillared Hall, now housing an Art Museum. Moving on into the temple, you'll reach a Nandi shrine surrounded by more beautifully carved columns. Ahead is the main Shiva shrine, flanked on each side by massive *dvarapalas,* and further ahead to the left in a separate enclosure is the main Meenakshi shrine, both open only to Hindus. However , anyone wander round the Golden Lotus Tank, then leave the temple via a Hall of flower sellers and the arch-ceilinged Ashta Shakti Mandapa – this is actually used as the temple entrance by most worshippers and is lined with relief carvings of the goddess's eight attributes, with perhaps the loveliest of all the temple's vibrantly painted ceilings.

➡ **Pudhu Mandapa**
(East Chitrai St) This 16th-century pillared hall stands outside the temple, opposite the eastern *gopuram.* It's filled with colourful textile and crafts stalls and tailors at sewing machines, partly hiding some of the lovely pillar sculptures, but it's easy to find the triple-breasted Meenakshi near the southeast corner, facing Sundareswarar (opposite), and their marriage, accompanied by Vishnu, just inside the western entrance. A particularly handsome light-blue Nandi (Shiva's vehicle) sits outside the *mandapa*'s eastern entrance.

➡ **Art Museum**
(Indian/foreigner ₹5/50, phone camera ₹50; ⊙6.30am-1pm & 4-9pm) Inside the temple's eastern *gopuram,* is the Nayak-period Thousand Pillar Hall (with 985 columns) on the right. This is now the Art Museum, where you can admire at your leisure a Shiva shrine with a large bronze Nataraja at the end of a corridor of superbly carved pillars, plus many other fine bronzes and colourfully painted panels. Some of the best carvings, including Krishna with his flute and Ganesh dancing with a woman on his knee, are immediately inside the museum entrance.

Gandhi Memorial Museum   MUSEUM
(Gandhi Museum Rd; camera ₹50; ⊙10am-1pm & 2-5.45pm Sat-Thu) FREE Housed in a 17th-century Nayak queen's palace, this excellent museum contains an impressively moving and comprehensive account of India's struggle for independence from 1757 to

Madurai

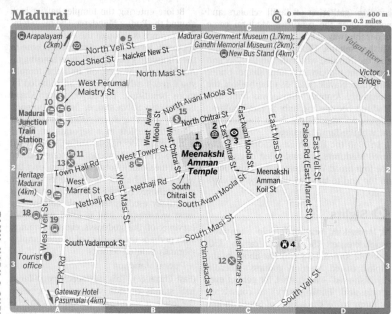

1947, and the English-language text spares no detail about British rule. Included in the exhibition is the blood-stained dhoti that Gandhi was wearing when he was assassinated in Delhi in 1948; it was here in Madurai, in 1921, that he first took up wearing the dhoti as a sign of native pride.

The small **Madurai Government Museum** (Indian/foreigner ₹5/100, camera ₹20; ⏱9.30am-5pm Sat-Thu) is next door, and the **Gandhian Literary Society Bookshop** (⏱10am-1pm & 2.30-6.30pm Mon-Sat) behind. **Yoga** (one-month unlimited membership ₹100; ⏱6am, 10.30am & 5pm Mon-Fri) takes place within the museum's grounds; no bookings needed.

Bus 75 from **Periyar Bus Stand** (West Veli St) goes to the Tamukkam bus stop on Alagarkoil Rd, 600m from the museum.

Tirumalai Nayak Palace PALACE
(Palace Rd; Indian/foreigner ₹10/50, camera/video ₹30/100; ⏱9am-1.30pm & 2-5pm) What the Meenakshi Amman Temple is to Nayak religious architecture, Tirumalai Nayak's crumbling palace is to the secular. Although it's said to be only a quarter of its original size, its massive scale and hybrid Dravidian-Islamic style still testify to the lofty aspirations of its creator. You enter from the east – a large courtyard surround-

ed by tall columns topped with fancy stucco work leads through to the grand throne chamber with its 25m-high dome; two stone-carved horses frame the steps up.

👉 Tours

Foodies Day Out FOOD TOUR
(☑9840992340; www.foodiesdayout.com; 2nd fl, 393 Anna Nagar Main Rd; per person ₹2000) For a fantastic evening exploring Madurai's culinary specialities with a local food enthusiast, contact Foodies Day Out. Minimum two people; vegetarian tours available.

Storytrails WALKING TOUR
(☑7373675756; www.storytrails.in; 35 Krishnarayar Tank Rd; 2hr tour for up to 4 people ₹2500) This Chennai-based organisation runs highly rated story-based neighbourhood walking tours.

🎎 Festivals & Events

Teppam (Float) Festival RELIGIOUS
(⏱Jan/Feb) A popular event held on the full moon of the Tamil month of Thai, when Meenakshi temple deities are paraded around town in elaborate procession and floated in a brightly lit 'mini-temple' on the huge Mariamman Teppakkulam tank, 3km east of the old city.

TAMIL NADU & CHENNAI MADURAI

Madurai

The evening culminates in Shiva's seduction of his wife, whereupon the icons are brought back to the temple to make love and, in so doing, regenerate the universe. Meenakshi's diamond nose stud is removed so it doesn't irritate her lover. Due to low rainfall, the 2013 and 2014 celebrations were 'dry' floats.

Chithirai Festival RELIGIOUS
(☉Apr/May) The highlight of Madurai's busy festival calendar is this two-week event celebrating the marriage of Meenakshi to Sundareswarar (Shiva). The deities are wheeled around the Meenakshi Amman Temple in massive chariots forming part of long, colourful processions.

🛏 Sleeping

Budget hotels in central Madurai are mostly dreary and unloved, but there is a big choice of perfectly fine, near-identical midrange places along West Perumal Maistry St, near the train station. Most have rooftop restaurants with temple and sunset views.

Hotel West Tower HOTEL $
(☑0452-2349600; 42/60 West Tower St; s/d ₹500/800, with AC ₹1200/1800; ⊛) The West Tower's best asset is that it's very near the temple, but it's also acceptably clean and friendly.

TM Lodge HOTEL $
(☑0452-2341651; www.tmlodge.in; 50 West Perumal Maistry St; s/d ₹440/660, r with AC ₹1300; ⊛) The walls are a bit grubby, but the sheets are clean. TM is efficiently run, even with a lift operator!

Madurai Residency HOTEL $$
(☑0452-4380000; www.madurairesidency.com; 15 West Marret St; s ₹2380-2860, d ₹2760-3220, all incl breakfast; ⊛🛜) The service is stellar and the rooms are comfy and fresh at this winner, which has one of the the highest rooftop restaurants in town. It's very popular, so book at least a day ahead.

Royal Court HOTEL $$
(☑0452-4356666; www.royalcourtindia.com; 4 West Veli St; s ₹3960-4910, d ₹4800-5640, all incl breakfast; ⊛@🛜) The Royal Court blends a bit of white-sheeted, hardwood-floored colonial elegance with comfort, good eating options, free wi-fi and friendy yet professional service. Rooms come with tea/coffee sets. It's an excellent, central choice for someone in need of a treat.

Hotel Park Plaza HOTEL $$
(☑0452-3011111; www.hotelparkplaza.net; 114 West Perumal Maistry St; s/d incl half-board ₹2880/3480; ⊛🛜) The Plaza's rooms are comfortable and simply but smartly done up, with free wi-fi. Four have temple views. It also boasts a good multicuisine rooftop **Temple View** (☉5pm-midnight) restaurant and the (inappropriately named) **Sky High Bar** – on the 1st floor.

Hotel Supreme HOTEL $$
(☑0452-2343151; www.hotelsupreme.in; 110 West Perumal Maistry St; s ₹2390-3270, d ₹2710-3470, all incl breakfast; ⊛🛜) The Supreme is a well-presented, slightly faded hotel with friendly service, that's very popular with domestic tourists. There's good food at the rooftop Surya restaurant and free in-room wi-fi, and the spaceship-themed basement bar will make you wonder if someone laced your lassi last night.

TAMIL NADU & CHENNAI MADURAI

Gateway Hotel Pasumalai   HOTEL $$$

(☎0452-6633000; www.thegatewayhotels.com; 40 TPK Rd, Pasumalai; s ₹6000-8390, d ₹7200-9600; @🛜🏊) A stunning escape from the city scramble, the Gateway sprawls across hilltop gardens 5km southwest of the centre. The views, outdoor pool and 45 resident peacocks are wonderful, and rooms are luxuriously comfy and equipped with glassed-in showers and do-it-yourself yoga kits. The Garden All Day restaurant is excellent.

Heritage Madurai   HERITAGE HOTEL $$$

(☎0452-3244187; www.heritagemadurai.com; 11 Melakkal Main Rd, Kochadai; s ₹5880-8820, d ₹6470-9410; ❄🛜🏊) This leafy haven, 4km west of central Madurai, originally housed the old Madurai Club. It's been impeccably tarted up, with intricate woodwork, a lovely sunken pool and airy, terracotta-floored 'deluxe' rooms. Best are the comfy 'villas' featuring private mini-swimming-pools. There's a good Chettinad restaurant, along with a spa, bar and 24-hour cafe.

✖ Eating

The hotel-rooftop restaurants along West Perumal Maistry St offer breezy night-time dining and temple views (don't forget the mosquito repellent); most of the hotels also have AC restaurants open for breakfast and lunch. Look out for Madurai's famous summer drink *jigarthanda* (boiled milk, almond essence, rose syrup and vanilla ice cream).

Murugan Idli Shop   SOUTH INDIAN $

(196 West Masi St; dishes ₹11-40; ⏰7am-midnight) Though it now has Chennai branches, Murugan is Madurai born and bred. Here you can put the fluffy signature *idlis* to the test, and feast on South Indian favourites such as dosas and *uttapams*.

Sri Sabareesh   INDIAN $

(49A West Perumal Maistry St; mains ₹57-85; ⏰6.30am-11.30pm) Decked with old-Madurai photos, Sri Sabareesh is a popular pure-veg spot that does decent South Indian thalis for ₹80. It's quite characterful and contemporary for a cheapie on this street.

Surya   MULTICUISINE $$

(110 West Perumal Maistry St; mains ₹80-190; ⏰4-11.30pm) The Hotel Supreme's rooftop restaurant offers excellent service, good pure-veg food and superb city and temple views, but the winner here has got to be the iced coffee, which might have been brewed by a god when you sip it on a hot, dusty day.

Garden All Day   MULTICUISINE $$$

(Gateway Hotel, 40 TPK Rd, Pasumalai; mains ₹300-525; ⏰7am-10.30pm) If you fancy splashing out, the panoramic all-day restaurant at the Gateway Hotel (5km southwest of central Madurai) does a fantastic multicuisine dinner buffet (₹800 to ₹1000). Outside in the gardens or inside in AC comfort.

GOVERNMENT BUSES FROM MADURAI

DESTINATION	FARE (₹)	DURATION (HR)	FREQUENCY
Bengaluru	440-750	9	9pm, 9.15pm, 9.30pm, 9.45pm
Chennai	325	9-10	every 30min 4am-11.30pm
Coimbatore	125	6	every 15min
Ernakulam (Kochi)	325	9	9am & 9pm
Kanyakumari	180	6	every 2hrs 6am-10pm, hourly 10pm-6am
Kodaikanal	62	4	14 buses 1.30am-2.50pm & 5.50pm
Mysuru	300-440	10	4 buses 4.30-9pm
Ooty	180	9	7.30am & 9pm
Puducherry	250	8	9pm
Rameswaram	85-110	5	every 30min 6am-midnight
Trichy	75-90	3	every 15min

Shopping

Madurai teems with cloth stalls and tailors' shops, as you might notice upon being approached by tailor touts. A great place for getting clothes made up is the Pudhu Mandapa. Here you'll find rows of tailors busily treadling away and capable of whipping up a good replica of whatever you're wearing in an hour or two. A cotton top or shirt can cost ₹350. Drivers, guides and touts will also be keen to lead you to the Kashmiri craft shops in North Chitrai St, offering to show you the temple view from the rooftop – the views are good, and so is the inevitable sales pitch.

❶ Information

State Bank of India (West Veli St) Foreign-exchange desks and ATM.

Supreme Web (110 West Perumal Maistry St; per hour ₹30; ☺7.30am-9.30pm) Take your passport.

Tourist office (☑0452-2334757; 1 West Veli St; ☺10am-5.45pm Mon-Fri)

❶ Getting There & Away

AIR

SpiceJet (www.spicejet.com) flies at least once daily to Bengaluru, Chennai, Colombo, Delhi, Dubai, Hyderabad and Mumbai (Bombay). Further Chennai flights are operated by **Jet Airways** (www.jetairways.com) three or four times daily, and **Air India** (☑0452-2690333; www.airindia.com) once daily.

BUS

Most government buses arrive and depart from the **New bus stand** (Melur Rd), 4km northeast of the old city. Services to Coimbatore, Kodaikanal and Ooty go from the **Arapalayam bus stand** (Puttuthoppu Main Rd), 2km northwest of the old city. Tickets for more expensive (and more comfortable) private buses are sold by agencies on the south side of the **Shopping Complex bus stand** (btwn West Veli St & TPK Rd). Most travel overnight.

TRAIN

From Madurai Junction station, 13 daily trains head north to Trichy and 10 to Chennai, the fastest being the 7am Vaigai Express (Trichy 2nd/chair class ₹93/340, two hours; Chennai ₹180/655, 7¾ hours). A good overnight train for Chennai is the 8.35pm Pandyan Express (sleeper/3AC/2AC/1AC ₹315/805/1135/1915, nine hours). To Kanyakumari the only daily train departs at 1.55am (sleeper/3AC/2AC/1AC ₹210/535/735/1230, five hours), though there's a later train some days (at varying times). Trivandrum (Thiruvananthapuram; three trains

daily), Coimbatore (three daily), Bengaluru (two daily) and Mumbai (Bombay; one daily) are other destinations.

❶ Getting Around

The airport is 12km south of town; taxis cost ₹300 to the centre. Alternatively, bus 10A runs to/from the Shopping Complex bus stand. From the New Bus Stand, bus 75 (₹11) shuttles into the city; an autorickshaw is ₹100.

Fixed-rate railway permit taxis congregate out the front of the train station. There's also a Fast Track taxi **booking counter** (☑0452-2888999; Madurai Junction; ☺24hr) here; fares start at ₹75 for the first 3km, then ₹15 per kilometre.

Rameswaram

☑04573 / POP 44,856

Rameswaram was once the southernmost point of sacred India; to leave its boundaries was to abandon caste and fall below the status of the lowliest skinner of sacred cows. Then Rama, incarnation of Vishnu and hero of the Ramayana, led an army of monkeys and bears across a monkey-built bridge to the island of (Sri) Lanka, where he defeated the demon Ravana and rescued his wife, Sita. Afterwards, prince and princess came to this spot to offer thanks to Shiva.

If all this seems like so much folklore, it's absolute truth for millions of Hindus, who flock to the Ramanathaswamy Temple to worship where a god worshipped a god.

Apart from these pilgrims, Rameswaram is a small fishing town on a conch-shaped island, Pamban, connected to the mainland by 2km-long road and rail bridges. The town smells of drying fish and, if you aren't a pilgrim, the temple alone barely merits the journey here. But the eastern point of the island, Dhanushkodi, only 30km from Sri Lanka, has a natural magic and beauty that add considerably to Rameswaram's appeal.

Most hotels and eateries are clustered around the Ramanathaswamy Temple, which is surrounded by North, East, South and West Car Sts. Middle St heads west towards the bus stand (around 2km). The train station is 1.5km southwest of the temple.

◉ Sights

Ramanathaswamy Temple   HINDU TEMPLE
(☺5am-1pm & 3-8pm) Housing the world's most sacred sand mound (a lingam said to have been created by Rama's wife Sita, so that he could worship Shiva), this temple is

one of India's holiest shrines. Dating mainly from the 16th to 18th centuries, it's notable for its long, exquisite 1000-pillar halls and 22 *theerthams* (temple tanks), in which pilgrims bathe before visiting the deity. Attendants tip pails of water over the (often fully dressed) faithful, who then rush on to the next *theertham*.

The legend goes that, when Rama decided to worship Shiva, he figured he'd need a lingam to do the thing properly. Being a god, he sent Hanuman to find the biggest lingam around – a Himalayan mountain. But the monkey took too long, so Sita made the simple lingam of sand now enshrined in the temple's inner sanctum.

Cameras and phones are forbidden inside the temple. Only Hindus may enter the inner shrine.

🛏 Sleeping & Eating

Most hotels are geared towards pilgrims, and some cheapies (which are mostly pretty grim) refuse to take single travellers, but there's a string of reasonable midrange hotels. Book ahead before festivals. Budget travellers can try the **rooms booking office** (East Car St; ⏰24hr), opposite the main, eastern temple entrance, which often scores doubles for as low as ₹300 a night.

Inexpensive vegetarian restaurants such as **Vasantha Bhavan** (East Car St; dishes ₹30-50; ⏰7am-10pm) and **Ananda Bhavan** (West Car St; ⏰6.30am-10.30pm) serve thali lunches for ₹50 to ₹70, and evening dosas and *uttapams* for about ₹40. You might find fish in some restaurants, but no real meats.

Hotel Venkatesh
HOTEL $
(☎04573-221296; SV Koil St; r ₹495-660, with AC ₹880; ❄) Open to single travellers, the lemon-walled rooms here are tolerably clean and not bad value. It's on the westward continuation of South Car St.

Daiwik Hotels
HOTEL $$
(☎04573-223222; www.daiwikhotels.com; Madurai-Rameswaram Hwy; r ₹4330-5570; ❄ @ 🛜) Fresh, comfy and gleaming, 'India's first four-star pilgrim hotel', 200m west of the bus station, is your swankiest choice in Rameswaram. Bright, airy rooms come smartly decked out with huge mirrors and local-life photos, and the vegetarian **Ahaan** (mains ₹140-270; ⏰7am-10pm) restaurant is very good.

Hotel Sri Saravana
HOTEL $$
(☎04573-223367; www.srisaravanahotel.com; 1/9A South Car St; r ₹1400-2810; ❄) The best of the town-centre hotels, Sri Saravana is friendly and clean with decent service and spacious, colourful rooms. Those towards the top have sea views (and higher rates).

ℹ Information

Micro Net Browsing (West Car St; per hour ₹30; ⏰8.30am-8pm)
State Bank of India ATM (South Car St)

ℹ Getting There & Around

Buses run to Madurai (₹110, four hours) every 10 minutes, and to Trichy (₹180, 6½ hours) hourly. 'Ultra Deluxe' (UD) services are scheduled three times daily to Chennai (₹450, 13 hours) and once daily to Kanyakumari (₹250, eight hours), but don't always run.

WORTH A TRIP

DHANUSHKODI

The promontory stretches 22km southeast from Rameswaram, narrowing to a thin strip of sand dunes about halfway along. Near the end stands the ghost town of Dhanushkodi. Once a thriving port, Dhanushkodi was washed away by the tidal waves of a monster cyclone in 1964. The shells of its train station, church, post office and other ruins still stand among a scattering of fishers' shacks, and Adam's Bridge (or Rama's Bridge), the chain of reefs, sandbanks and islets that almost connects India with Sri Lanka, stretches away to the east. For many, this is the final stop of a long prilgrimage. Go for sunrise, when the atmosphere is at its most magical, with pilgrims performing *pujas* (prayers).

Autorickshaws charge about ₹400 round trip (including waiting time) to Moonram Chattram, a collection of fishers' huts about 14km from town. From there to Dhanushkodi it's a hot 4km beach walk, or a ₹100 two-hour round trip in a truck or minibus which goes when it fills up with 12 to 20 customers (6am to 6pm). Many hotels organise private jeeps to whizz you along to Danushkodi (around ₹1500 return). It's tempting to swim, but beware of strong rips.

The three daily trains to/from Madurai (₹35, four hours) have unreserved seating only. The Rameswaram–Chennai Express departs daily at 8pm (sleeper/3AC/2AC ₹330/890/1280, 12½ hours) via Trichy. The Rameswaram–Kanyakumari Express leaves at 8.45pm Monday, Thursday and Saturday, reaching Kanyakumari (sleeper/3AC ₹275/705) at 4.05am.

Bus 1 (₹4) shuttles between the bus stand and East Car St. Autorickshaws to the centre from the bus stand or train station cost ₹40.

Kanyakumari (Cape Comorin)

📞 04652 / POP 22,453

This is it, the end of India. There's a sense of accomplishment on making it to the tip of the subcontinent's 'V', past the final dramatic flourish of the Western Ghats and the green fields, glinting rice paddies and slow-looping wind turbines of India's deep south. Like all edges, there's a sense of the surreal here. At certain times of year you can see the sun set and the moon rise over three seas simultaneously. The Temple of the Virgin Sea Goddess, Swami Vivekananda's legacy and the 'Land's End' symbolism draw crowds of pilgrims and tourists to Kanyakumari, but it remains a small-scale, refreshing respite from the hectic Indian road.

◎ Sights & Activities

Kumari Amman Temple   HINDU TEMPLE
(⊙ 4.30am-12.15pm & 4-8.15pm) The legends say the *kanya* (virgin) goddess Kumari, a manifestation of the Great Goddess Devi, single-handedly conquered demons and secured freedom for the world. At this temple at the tip of the subcontinent, pilgrims give her thanks in an intimately spaced, beautifully decorated temple, where the crash of waves from three seas can be heard behind the twilight glow of oil fires clutched in vulva-shaped votive candles (referencing the sacred femininity of the goddess).

It's believed that the sea-facing door of the temple stays locked to prevent the shimmer of the goddess's diamond nose-stud leading ships astray. You'll probably be asked for an ₹10 donation to enter the inner precinct, where men must remove their shirts, and cameras are forbidden.

The shoreline around the temple has a couple of tiny beaches, and bathing ghats where some worshippers immerse themselves before visiting the temple. The *mandapa* south of the temple is popular for sunset-watching and daytime shade. A small souvenir-shop bazaar leads back from here to the main road.

Vivekananda Memorial   MONUMENT
(admission ₹10; ⊙ 8am-4pm) Four hundred metres offshore is the rock where the famous Hindu apostle Swami Vivekananda meditated from 25 to 27 December 1892, and decided to take his moral message beyond India's shores. A two-*mandapa* memorial to Vivekananda, built in 1970, reflects temple architectural styles from across India. With all the tourist crowds this brings, Vivekananda would no doubt choose somewhere else to meditate today. Ferries shuttle out to the Vivekananda island (₹34 return) between 7.45am and 4pm.

Thiruvalluvar Statue   MONUMENT
(⊙ 7.45am-4pm) FREE Looking like an Indian Colossus of Rhodes, the towering statue on the smaller island next to the Vivekananda Memorial is of the ancient Tamil poet Thiruvalluvar. The work of more than 5000 sculptors, it was erected in 2000 and honours the poet's 133-chapter work Thirukural – hence its height of exactly 133ft (40.5m). Vivekananda rock ferries (₹34 return) usually continue to Thiruvalluvar between 2pm and 4pm.

Swami Vivekananda Wandering Monk Exhibition   MUSEUM
(Main Rd; admission ₹10; ⊙ 9am-12.30pm & 4-8.30pm) This excellent exhibition details Swami Vivekananda's wisdom, sayings and encounters with the mighty and the lowly during his five years as a wandering monk around India from 1888 to 1893.

Your ticket also covers the 'Awake! Awake!' Vivekananda-inspired exhibition (Vivekanandapuram; ⊙ 9am-1pm & 4-8pm Wed-Mon, 9am-1pm Tue) in Vivekanandapuram, a peaceful ashram 1km north of town, with various yoga retreats. The spiritual organisation Vivekananda Kendra (www.vivekanandakendra.org), devoted to carrying out Vivekananda's teachings, has its headquarters here.

Gandhi Memorial   MONUMENT
(⊙ 7am-7pm) FREE Appropriately placed at the end of the nation that Gandhi fathered, this cream-and-blue memorial is designed in the form of an Odishan temple embellished by Hindu, Christian and Muslim architects. The central plinth was used to store some of the Mahatma's ashes before they were

immersed in the sea, and each year, on Gandhi's birthday (2 October), the sun's rays fall on the stone. Exhibits are limited to a few photos; the tower is a popular sunset-gazing spot.

Kamaraj Memorial MONUMENT
(⊙7am-6.45pm) FREE This memorial near the shoreline commemorates K Kamaraj, known as the 'Gandhi of the South'. One of the most powerful and respected politicians of post-Independence India, Kamaraj held the chief ministership of both Madras state and its successor, Tamil Nadu. The dusty photos inside have captions.

🛏 Sleeping

As befits a holiday destination, many Kanyakumari hoteliers have gone for bright, playful decor; after the bland statewide sameness of midrange hotels, it's exciting to find a huge neon-coloured tiger painted on your bedhead.

Hotel Narmadha HOTEL $
(☑04652-246365; Kovalam Rd; r ₹400-600) This long, colourful concrete block conceals friendly staff, a back-up generator and a range of cheap rooms, some of which are cleaner and have less grim bathrooms than

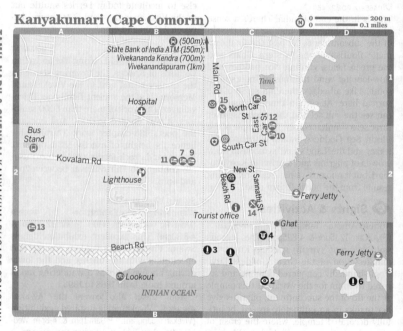

Kanyakumari (Cape Comorin)

Kanyakumari (Cape Comorin)

⊙ Sights
1	Gandhi Memorial	C3
2	Ghat	C3
3	Kamaraj Memorial	C3
4	Kumari Amman Temple	C3
5	Swami Vivekananda Wandering Monk Exhibition	C2
6	Thiruvalluvar Statue	D3

🛏 Sleeping
7	Hotel Narmadha	B2
8	Hotel Sivamurugan	C1
9	Hotel Tri Sea	B2
10	Lakshmi Tourist Home	C2
11	Santhi Residency	B2
12	Seashore Hotel	C2
13	Sparsa Resort	A3

⊗ Eating
	Auroma	(see 13)
14	Hotel Saravana	C2
15	Sangam Restaurant	C1
	Seashore Hotel	(see 12)

others; the ₹600 sea-view doubles with spearmint-stripe sheets are good value.

Lakshmi Tourist Home   HOTEL **$**
(✆04652-246333; East Car St; r ₹750-1000, with AC ₹1350) Basic but well-kept, this relatively helpful family hotel is a decent town-centre deal. The better (and pricier) rooms come with sea views and hot water, but most are neat and clean.

Hotel Tri Sea   HOTEL **$$**
(✆04652-246586; www.hoteltrisea.in; Kovalam Rd; d ₹1180-2590; ❄🌐❄) You can't miss the high-rise Tri Sea, whose sea-view rooms are huge, spotless and airy, with particularly hectic colour schemes. The top-floor triples are even grander. Reception is super-efficient and the rooftop pool, sunrise and sunset viewing platforms and free in-room wifi are welcome bonuses, though the restaurant is a sad afterthought.

Hotel Sivamurugan   HOTEL **$$**
(✆04652-246862; www.hotelsivamurugan.com; 2/93 North Car St; r ₹1375, with AC ₹2250-2700; ❄🌐) A welcoming, well-appointed hotel, with spacious, spotless, marble-floored rooms and free wi-fi (lobby only). The 'super-deluxes' have sea glimpses past a couple of buildings. Rates stay fixed year-round (a novelty for Kanyakumari) and there's 24-hour hot water, which not all competitors can claim.

Santhi Residency   HOTEL **$$**
(Kovalam Rd; r ₹1000, with AC ₹1500; ❄) A smaller, older restored house with leafy courtyards, Santhi has an unusually restrained style for Kanyakumari (the only decoration in each room is a picture of Jesus). It's quiet and clean with tight-fit rooms and bathrooms.

Sparsa Resort   HOTEL **$$$**
(✆04652-247041; www.sparsaresorts.com; 6/112B Beach Rd; r incl breakfast ₹5400-7200; ❄🌐❄) Located away from the temple frenzy, elegant Sparsa is a good few notches above your average Kanyakumari hotel. Fresh, orange-walled rooms with low, dark-wood beds, lounge chairs and mood-lighting make for a contemporary oriental vibe and there's a lovely pool that is surrounded by palms, as well as good Indian cooking at Auroma (mains ₹150-380; ◷7-10am, noon-3pm, 7-10.30pm).

Seashore Hotel   HOTEL **$$$**
(✆04652-246704; http://theseashorehotel.com; East Car St; r ₹4140-7800; ❄🌐) The fanciest hotel in town centre has shiny, spacious rooms with gold curtains and cushions, glassed-in showers, free wi-fi and useful equipment including kettles and hair-dryers. It's lost some of its original sparkle, but all rooms except the cheapest have panoramic sea views, and the 7th-floor restaurant is one of Kanyakumari's best.

🍴 Eating

Hotel Saravana   INDIAN **$**
(Sannathi St; mains ₹89-120; ◷6.30am-10pm) A clean, popular spot with plenty of North and South Indian vegetarian dishes, lunchtime thalis and crispy dosas.

Seashore Hotel   MULTICUISINE **$$**
(East Car St; mains ₹190-380; ◷7am-10.30pm) Amazingly, the classy 7th-floor restaurant at the Seashore Hotel is the only one in Kanyakumari with a proper sea view. There's grilled fish and plenty of pan-Indian veg and nonveg choices, plus the odd Continental creation; try the veg or seafood sizzlers. Service is spot-on and it's great for brekkie (buffet or à la carte).

Sangam Restaurant   INDIAN **$$**
(Main Rd; mains ₹90-280; ◷7am-11pm) It's as if the Sangam started in Kashmir, trekked the length of India, and stopped off here to offer top veg and nonveg picks from every province along the way. The food is good, the seats are soft and the joint is bustling.

ⓘ Information

Tourist office (✆04652-246276; Beach Rd; ◷10am-5.45pm Mon-Fri)
Xerox, Internet, Fax (Main Rd; internet per hour ₹30; ◷9.30am-10pm Mon-Sat) Staffed by women.

ⓘ Getting There & Away

BUS

The sedate **bus stand** (Kovalam Rd) is a 10-minute walk west of the centre. Ordinary buses run 11 times daily to Madurai (₹165, six hours) and at least seven times daily to Trivandrum (₹71, 2½ hours). Two daily buses, 6am and 2pm, go to Kovalam (₹80, three hours). The most comfortable buses are the 'Ultra Deluxe' (UD), which include the following:

Chennai (₹540, 12 to 14 hours, eight daily)
Kodaikanal (₹310, 10 hours, 8.15pm)
Madurai (₹220, four hours, eight daily)

TAMIL NADU & CHENNAI KANYAKUMARI (CAPE COMORIN)

OFF THE BEATEN TRACK

PADMANABHAPURAM PALACE

With a forest's worth of intricately carved rosewood ceilings and polished-teak beams, the **Padmanabhapuram Palace** (☎ 04651-250255; Padmanabhapuram; Indian/foreigner ₹35/300, camera/video ₹50/2000; ⏱ 9am-1pm & 2-4.30pm Tue-Sun), 35km northwest of Kanyakumari near the Kerala border, is considered the finest example of traditional Keralan architecture today. Asia's largest wooden palace complex, it was once the capital of Travancore, an unstable princely state taking in parts of both Tamil Nadu and Kerala. As the egos of successive rulers left their mark, it expanded into the magnificent conglomeration of 14 palaces it is today; the oldest sections date back to 1550.

Direct buses leave from Kanyakumari bus stand at 7.15am, 11am, 1pm, 1.30pm and 4.45pm (₹21, two hours); buses also run every 10 minutes between 4.30am and 10pm to Thuckalay, from where it's a short autorickshaw ride or 15-minute walk. Taxis between Kanyakumari and Kovalam (Kerala), stopping at Padmanabhapuram, cost ₹3000.

From Trivandrum (Thiruvananthapuram) take any bus towards Kanyakumari and get off at Thuckalay (₹50, 1½ hours, eight daily). The Kerala Tourist Development Corporation (KTDC; p942) runs full-day Kanyakumari tours from Trivandrum (₹700) covering Padmanabhapuram.

TAXI

Drivers ask ₹2000 to Kovalam.

TRAIN

The train station is a walkable distance north of the centre. The one daily northbound train, the Kanyakumari Express, departs at 5.20pm for Chennai (sleeper/3AC/2AC/1AC ₹415/1085/1545/2610, 13½ hours) via Madurai (₹210/535/735/1230, 4½ hours) and Trichy (₹275/705/985/1655, 7¼ hours). Two daily express trains depart at 6.50am and 10.30am for Trivandrum (Thiruvananthapuram; 2nd-class/sleeper/3AC/2AC ₹60/140/485/690, 2¼ hours), both continuing to Kollam (Quilon) and Ernakulam (Kochi). More trains go from Nagercoil Junction, 15km northwest of Kanyakumari.

For real train buffs, the Vivek Express runs all the way to Dibrugarh in Assam, 4236km and 80 hours – the longest single train ride in India. It departs from Kanyakumari at 11pm Thursday (sleeper/3AC/2AC ₹1085/2810/4235).

THE WESTERN GHATS

Welcome to the lush Western Ghats, some of the most welcome heat relief in India. Rising like an impassable bulwark of evergreen and deciduous tangle from north of Mumbai to the tip of Tamil Nadu, the World Heritage-listed Ghats (with an average elevation of 915m) contain 27% of India's flowering plants and an incredible array of endemic wildlife. In Tamil Nadu they rise to 2000m and more in the Palani Hills around Kodaikanal and the Nilgiris around Ooty. British influence lingers a little stronger up in these hills, where the colonists built their 'hill stations' to escape the sweltering plains and covered slopes in neatly trimmed tea bushes. It's not just the air and (relative) lack of pollution that's refreshing – there's a certain acceptance of quirkiness and eccentricity here that is rarer in the lowlands. Think organic farms, handlebar-moustached trekking guides and leopard-print earmuffs.

Kodaikanal (Kodai)

☎ 04542 / POP 36,500 / ELEV 2100M

There are few more refreshing Tamil Nadu moments than boarding a bus in the heat-soaked plains and disembarking in the sharp pinch of a Kodaikanal night or morning. This misty hill station, 120km northwest of Madurai in the Palani Hills, is more relaxed and intimate than its big sister Ooty (Kodai is the 'Princess of Hill Stations', while Ooty is the 'Queen'). It's not all cold either; during the day the weather can be more like deep spring than early winter. The renowned Kodaikanal International School provides a bit of cosmopolitan flair, with students from around the globe.

Centred on a beautiful lake, Kodai rambles up and down hillsides with patches of *shola* (virgin) forest, unique to the Western Ghats in South India, and evergreen broadleaf trees such as magnolia, mahogany, myrtle and rhododendron. Another of its plant specialities is the *kurinji* shrub, whose lilac-blue blossoms appear only every 12 years: next due 2018.

Kodai is popular with honeymooners and groups, who flock to the spectacular viewpoints and waterfalls in and around town.

Sights & Activities

Sacred Heart Natural Science Museum   MUSEUM

(Sacred Heart College, Law's Ghat Rd; adult/child ₹15/10, camera ₹20; ☺9am-6pm) In the grounds of a former Jesuit seminary 4km downhill east of town, this museum has a ghoulishly intriguing miscellany of flora and fauna put together over more than 100 years by priests and trainees. Displays range over bottled snakes, human embryos (!), giant moths and stuffed animal carcasses. You can also see pressed *kurinji* flowers (*Strobilanthes kunthiana)* in case you aren't around for their flowering.

Parks & Waterfalls

Bryant Park (adult/child ₹30/15, camera/video ₹50/100; ☺9am-6pm), landscaped and stocked by the British officer after whom it's named, is pretty, and usually busy with both tourists and canoodling couples.

Several natural beauty spots around Kodai (crowded with souvenir and snack stalls) are very popular with Indian tourists. They're best visited by taxi unless you like strolling along busy roads. Taxi drivers offer three-hour 12-stop tours for around ₹1200. On clear days, Green Valley View (6km from the centre), Pillar Rocks (7km) and less visited Moir's Point (13km), all along the same road west of town, have spectacular views to the plains far below.

To go beyond Moir's Point to forest-fringed Berijam Lake (☺closed Tues) requires a ₹150 Forest Department permit. Taxi drivers can organise this, often the same day, and do four-hour 'forest tours' to Berijam for ₹1800.

The river that empties Kodaikanal Lake tumbles dramatically down Silver Cascade, on the Madurai road 7km from town. Compact Bear Shola Falls are in a pocket of forest on the northwest edge of town.

Walking

Assuming it's not cloaked in opaque mist, the views from paved Coaker's Walk (admission ₹10; ☺7.30am-7pm) are beautiful, all the way down to the plains 2000m below. The stroll takes five minutes.

The 5km Kodaikanal Lake circuit is lovely in the early morning before the crowds roll in. A walk along Lower Shola Rd takes you through the Bombay Shola, the nearest surviving patch of *shola* to central Kodai.

Most serious trekking routes around Kodai require Forest Department permits which can only be obtained with time, patience and luck. Contact Kodai's District Forest Office (☎04542-240287; Muthaliarpuram; ☺8am-5.45pm Mon-Fri, permits issued 8-10am Mon, Wed, Thu & Fri). The tourist office and guesthouses like Greenlands Youth Hostel will put you in touch with local guides, including the very experienced Vijay Kumar (☎9965524279; thenaturetrails@gmail.com), who can help with permits and offer interesting off-road routes (₹500 to ₹800 per half-day).

A good trek, if you can organise it, is the two-day Kodai–Munnar route into Kerala via Bodi and Top Station (though it involves some bus/rickshaw transport). Guides charge ₹4000 to ₹5000 per person.

Boating, Cycling & Horse Riding

If you're sappy in love like a bad Bollywood song, the thing to do in Kodai is rent a pedal boat (₹60 per half-hour for two people), rowboat (₹90 including boatman) or Kashmiri *shikara* ('honeymoon boat'; ₹350 including boatman) from the Kodaikanal Boat & Rowing Club (☺9am-5.30pm) or Tamil Nadu Tourist Development Corporation (☺9am-5.30pm).

Bicycle-rental (per hour/day ₹20/300) and horse-riding (per 500m/2 hours ₹50/1000) stands are dotted around the lake.

Sleeping

Some hotels hike prices by up to 100% during the 'season' (April to June). There are some lovely heritage places, and good-value midrange options if you can live without colonial-era ambience. Most hotels have a 9am or 10am checkout from April to June.

Sri Vignesh Guest House   GUESTHOUSE $

(☎9094972524; umaarkrishnan@gmail.com; Lake Rd; r ₹700-800) Up a steep driveway and surrounded by colourful, neat gardens, this simple but characterful Raj-era home is run by a friendly local couple, who welcome 'peaceful' guests (no packs of boys!). Rooms are clean and very basic, and there's hot water until noon.

TAMIL NADU & CHENNAI KODAIKANAL (KODAI)

Kodaikanal (Kodai)

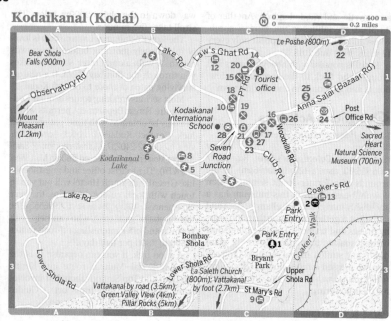

Snooze Inn
HOTEL $

(☏04542-240837; www.jayarajgroup.com; Anna Salai; r ₹770-970; ☏) Rooms don't have quite as much character as the outside suggests, but this is a decent-value budget choice with clean bathrooms, free wi-fi and plenty of blankets.

Greenlands Youth Hostel
HOSTEL $

(☏04542-240899; www.greenlandskodaikanal. com; St Mary's Rd; dm ₹300, d ₹600-2025; ☏) This long-running and sociable budget favourite has a pretty garden and wonderful views, but the accommodation is very bare and basic, hot water only runs from 8am to 10am, and washing in the dorms (minimum 10 people for a booking) is by buckets.

Villa Retreat
HOTEL $$

(☏04542-240940; www.villaretreat.com; Club Rd; r incl breakfast ₹3480-5280; ☏) You can take in the fantastic Coaker's Walk views from your garden breakfast table at this lovely old stone-built family hotel, right next to the walk's northern end. It's a friendly place with comfy, good-sized rooms and free wi-fi in the dining room, where there's often a roaring fire on cold nights. Prices feel a tad steep, but service is incredibly attentive.

Hilltop Towers
HOTEL $$

(☏04542-240413; www.hilltopgroup.in; Club Rd; r incl breakfast ₹2220-2760; ☏) Although it's bland on the outside, rustic flourishes like polished teak floors, plus keen staff, in-room tea/coffee sets and free wi-fi make the Hilltop a good midrange choice.

Mount Pleasant
BOUTIQUE HOTEL $$

(☏04542-242023, 9655126023; www.kodaikanal-heritage.com; 19/12-20 Observatory Rd; r incl breakfast ₹1900-3100; ☏) Despite being out on the fringe of Kodai's spaghetti-like street map, 2km west of the centre, Mount Pleasant is worth finding for its quiet setting, tasty buffet dinners, homey rooms and the welcoming Keralan owner's quirky taste – colourful wall weavings, coconut-wood beds, coir matting. Book ahead.

★ Carlton Hotel
HOTEL $$$

(☏04542-240056; www.krahejahospitality.com; Lake Rd; s/d/cottage incl half-board ₹9560/ 10,570/16,290; ☏) The cream of Kodai's hotels is a magnificent five-star colonial-era mansion overlooking the lake. Rooms are spacious with extra comfy beds and, for some, huge private balconies. The grounds and common areas get the old hill-station ambience spot on: open stone walls, billiards, evening bingo by the fireplace, and a bar that

Kodaikanal (Kodai)

makes you want to demand a Scotch now, dammit, from the eager staff.

Le Poshe HOTEL **$$$**
(www.leposhehotel.com; 25 Sivanadi Rd; s ₹5040-7440, d ₹5400-7790, all incl breakfast; 🛜) This stylish new addition to Kodai's hotel scene feels like you've stumbled into a flashy furniture showroom. Warm woods and whites give a fresh alpine-chalet-chic theme to the cosy, minimalist rooms sporting glassed-in

showers and tea/coffee makers. Staff are charming, views are lovely, and perks include a good restaurant, a spa and a gym. It's 2km north of town.

Vattakanal

Little Vattakanal village ('Vatta'), about 4.5km southwest of Kodai centre, is a great rural retreat for budget travellers. It's very popular, particularly with groups of Israeli travellers, and there's a laid-back party vibe when things gets busy. Altaf's Cafe has a few sizeable three-bed rooms for six people (sometimes more!) with private bathroom for ₹1200.

Kodai Heaven GUESTHOUSE **$**
(☑ 9865207207; www.kodaiheaven.com; Dolphin's Nose Rd, Vattakanal; r ₹1000-2500) Simple, hillside sharing rooms for two to six people.

Eating & Drinking

PT Rd is the best place for cheap restaurants and it's here that most travellers and students from the international school hang out.

Tava INDIAN **$**
(PT Rd; mains ₹75-110; ⊙11am-8.45pm Thu-Tue) Clean, fast and cheap, pure-veg Tava has a wide menu; try the spicy, cauliflower-stuffed *gobi paratha* or *sev puri* (crisp, puffy fried bread with potato and chutney).

Altaf's Cafe MULTICUISINE **$$**
(☑ 9487120846; Vattakanal; dishes ₹60-220; ⊙8.30am-9.30pm) This semi-open-air cafe whips up Italian, Indian and Middle Eastern dishes including breakfasts and *sabich* (Israeli aubergine-and-egg pita sandwiches), for the hungry travellers at Vattakanal.

Pot Luck CAFE **$**
(PT Rd; snacks & light meals ₹50-160; ⊙11am-7.30pm Wed-Mon) Pancakes, toasties, coffee, omelettes and quesadillas served up on a tiny, pretty terrace attached to a pottery shop.

Hotel Astoria INDIAN **$$**
(Anna Salai; mains ₹100-130; ⊙7am-10pm) This veg restaurant is always packed with locals and tourists, especially at lunchtime when it serves excellent all-you-can-eat thalis.

★ Carlton Hotel MULTICUISINE **$$$**
(Lake Rd; buffet lunch/dinner ₹750/850; ⊙7-10am, 1-3pm & 7.30-11pm) Definitely the place to come for a splash-out buffet fill-up: a

TAMIL NADU & CHENNAI KODAIKANAL (KODAI)

WORTH A TRIP

VATTAKANAL WALK

This is a lovely walk of about 4.5km (each way) from central Kodai, on which you might spot gaur (bison) or giant squirrels in the forested bits. From the south end of Coaker's Walk, follow St Mary's Rd west then southwest, passing La Saleth Church after 1.2km. At a fork 400m after the church, go left downhill on what quickly becomes an unpaved track passing through the Pambar Shola forest. After 450m you emerge on a bridge above some falls. Across the bridge you'll find snack stalls selling fruit, tea, coffee, bread omelettes and roasted corn with lime and masala. Follow the road 1km downhill, with panoramas opening up as you go, to Vattakanal village. Take the steep path down past Altaf's Cafe and in about 15 minutes you'll reach the Dolphin's Nose, a narrow rock lookout overhanging a precipitous drop, and a couple more snack stalls.

huge variety of excellent Indian and Continental dishes in limitless quantity.

Cloud Street MULTICUISINE $$$
(PT Rd; mains ₹250-500; ☻9am-9pm) Why yes, that is a real Italian-style wood-fire pizza oven. And yes, that's hummus and falafel on the menu, along with oven-baked pasta and nachos. It's all great food in a simple, relaxed setting, but it's a bit pricier than you'd expect.

Cafe Cariappa CAFE
(PT Rd; coffees ₹70-110; ☻6am-11pm Mon-Sat) A caffeine addict's dream, this cute, wood-panelled cafe does fantastic cappuccino, espresso, mocha, and macchiato, all infused with locally grown organic Palani Hills coffee.

Self-Catering

Pastry Corner BAKERY $
(Anna Salai; ☻10am-2pm & 3-6pm) Pick up yummy muffins, croissants and sandwiches at this hugely popular bakery, or squeeze onto the benches with a cuppa.

Eco Nut ORGANIC $
(PT Rd; ☻10.30am-6pm Mon-Sat) This tiny shop sells local organic food – wholewheat bread, muffins, muesli, spices – as well as oils, herbs and herbal remedies.

🛍 Shopping

Shops and stalls all over town sell homemade chocolate, spices, natural oils and handicrafts. Some also reflect a low-key but long-term commitment to social justice.

Re Shop HANDICRAFTS
(www.bluemangoindia.com; Seven Rd Junction; ☻10am-7pm Mon-Sat) Stylish jewellery, fabrics, cards and more, at reasonable prices,

made by and benefiting marginalised village women around Tamil Nadu.

Cottage Craft Shop HANDICRAFTS
(PT Rd; ☻10am-7pm Mon-Sat, 1.30-7pm Sun) Sells incense, embroidery, hats, bags and other goods crafted by disadvantaged groups across India, with about 80% of the purchase price returned to the makers.

ℹ Information

Hi-Tech Internet (Seven Rd Junction; per hour ₹60; ☻9am-8pm Mon-Sat)
Tourist office (☎04542-241675; PT Rd; ☻10am-5.45pm Mon-Sat) Doesn't look too promising but they're helpful enough.

ℹ Getting There & Away

The nearest train station is Kodai Road, down in the plains about 80km east of Kodaikanal. There are eight daily trains to/from Chennai Egmore including the overnight Pandyan Express (sleeper/3AC/2AC/1AC ₹295/760/1065/1800, eight hours), departing Chennai at 9.20pm and departing Kodai Road northbound at 9.10pm. For most closer destinations, it's quicker and easier to get a bus. Taxis to/from the station cost ₹1200. Direct buses from Kodaikanal to Kodai Road leave daily at 3pm and 4pm (₹55, three hours); there are also plenty of buses between the station and Batlagundu, on the Kodai–Madurai bus route. Kodai's post office has a **train booking desk** (Head Post Office, Post Office Rd; ☻9am-2pm & 3-4pm Mon-Sat).

Government buses from Kodai's **bus stand** (Anna Salai) include:
Bengaluru (₹600 to ₹750, 12 hours, 5.30pm and 6pm)
Chennai (₹480, 12 hours, 6.30pm)
Coimbatore (₹120, six hours, 8.30am and 4.30pm)
Madurai (₹62, four hours, 15 daily)
Trichy (₹111, six hours, four daily)

Raja's Tours & Travels (📞 04542-242422; Anna Salai) runs 20-seat minibuses with push-back seats to Ooty (₹400, eight hours, 7pm) and Kochi (Cochin; ₹800, 11 hours, 6pm), along with overnight AC sleeper buses to Chennai (₹1100, 12 hours) and Bengaluru (₹950, 12 hours) at 6pm.

❶ Getting Around

Central Kodaikanal is compact and easy to get around on foot. There are no autorickshaws (believe it or not), but plenty of taxis. Trips within town generally cost ₹150.

Around Kodaikanal

There are some fabulous country escapes in the Palani Hills below Kodaikanal.

Elephant Valley   FARMSTAY **$$**
(📞 9244103418; www.duneecogroup.com; Ganesh Puram; r incl breakfast ₹3300-7200; 📶) 🐾 Deep in the valley 22km from Kodaikanal, off the Kodai–Palani road, this ecofriendly French-run retreat sprawls across 49 hectares of mountain jungle and organic farm. Elephants, peacocks and bison wander through regularly, and comfy local-material cottages, including a treehouse, sit either side of a river. The French-Indian restaurant does wonderful meals packed with garden-fresh veg, and home-grown coffee. Wildlife spotting peaks April to July.

Coimbatore

📞 0422 / POP 1.05 MILLION

This big business and junction city – Tamil Nadu's second largest, often known as the Manchester of India for its textile industry – is friendly enough and increasingly cosmopolitan, but the lack of interesting sights means that for most travellers it's just a stepping stone towards Ooty or Kerala. It has plenty of accommodation and eating options if you're spending the night.

🛏 Sleeping

Sree Subbu   HOTEL **$**
(📞 0422-2300006; Geetha Hall Rd; s ₹370-480, d ₹660) If you don't need AC and price is the priority, Sree Subbu does a decent budget job.

Legend's Inn   HOTEL **$$**
(📞 0422-4350000; www.legendsinn.com; Geetha Hall Rd; r ₹1440, s/d with AC ₹1800/2040; 📶) One of a good 10 places on this lane opposite the train station, this is a great-value midrange choice, with spacious, clean, comfortable rooms and 24-hour checkout. It gets busy, so book ahead.

Hotel ESS Grande   HOTEL **$$**
(📞 0422-2230271; www.hotelessgrande.co.in; 358-360 Nehru St; s ₹2160-2520, d ₹2520-2880, all incl breakfast; 📶 @) Handy for a few of the bus stands, the friendly ESS has small but very clean, fresh rooms, all with cable internet. There are several other midrange and budget hotels on this street.

CAG Pride   HOTEL **$$**
(📞 0422-4317777; www.cagpride.com; 312 Bharathiyar Rd; s ₹4080-4560, d ₹4800-5280, all incl breakfast & dinner; 📶📶) Touches of modern art add colour to the glossy, cosy rooms here, the best of which have freshly revamped bathrooms (renovations were still underway at research time). It's smart, helpful and near the central bus stations.

Residency   HOTEL **$$$**
(📞 0422-2241414; www.theresidency.com; 1076 Avinashi Rd; s/d incl breakfast from ₹6600/7080; 📶 @📶📶) Opening through a soaring lobby, the Residency is top choice for its friendly staff, elegant and well-equipped rooms, swimming pool, free wi-fi and excellent eating and drinking options, including good-value buffet meals at the **Pavilion** (buffet breakfast/lunch/dinner ₹470/950/950; ⏱7-10am, 12.30-3pm & 7pm-midnight) restaurant. Check online for discounts.

🍴 Eating

Junior Kuppanna   SOUTH INDIAN **$$**
(177 Sarojini Rd; dishes ₹120-180) Your favourite South Indian thalis come piled onto banana leaves with traditional flourish, and starving carnivores will love the long menu of mostly nonveg southern specialities, all from a perfectly spotless kitchen.

Hot Chocolate   CONTINENTAL **$$**
(734 Avinashi Rd; mains ₹120-330; ⏱10.30am-10.30pm) Not bad at all if you're craving pasta, wraps, sandwiches or cakes.

That's Y On The Go   MULTICUISINE **$$**
(167 Racecourse Rd; mains ₹220-480; ⏱12.30-3pm & 7-10.30pm) Colourful, contemporary, and filled with cartoons and turquoise sofas, this is a great place for tasty global fare from Italian and Middle Eastern to Southeast Asian and North Indian.

Coibatore

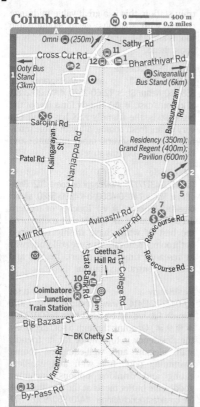

Coimbatore

ℹ Information

State Bank of India ATM (Coimbatore Junction) One of several ATMs outside the train station.

Travel Gate (Geetha Hall Rd; per hour ₹30; ⏰ 8.30am-9.30pm) Cramped internet cafe.

ℹ Getting There & Away

AIR

The airport is 10km east of town, with daily direct flights to domestic destinations including Bengaluru, Chennai, Delhi, Hyderabad and Mumbai on **Air India** (☎ 0422-2303933; www.airindia.com), **IndiGo** (www.goindigo.in), **Jet Airways** (www.jetairways.com) or **SpiceJet** (www.spicejet.com).

SilkAir (☎ 0422-4370271; www.silkair.com) flies four times weekly to/from Singapore.

BUS

From the **SETC bus stand** (Thiruvalluvar Bus Stand; Bharathiyar Rd), express or superfast government buses head to Bengaluru (₹375 to ₹750, nine hours, seven daily), Chennai (₹400, 11 hours, 10 buses 5.30pm to 10pm), Ernakulam (Kochi; ₹152 to ₹174, 5½ hours, six daily), Mysore (₹160 to ₹381, six hours, 21 daily) and Trivandrum (₹312 to ₹344, 10½ hours, six daily).

The **Ooty bus stand** (New bus stand; Mettupalayam (MTP) Rd), northwest of the centre, has services to Ooty (₹53, four hours) via Mettupalayam (₹17, one hour) and Coonoor (₹40, three hours) every 20 minutes, plus hourly buses to Kotagiri (₹32, three hours, 5.20am to 7.20pm), 16 buses daily to Mysuru (₹160 to ₹381, six hours) and six to Bengaluru (₹375 to ₹750, nine hours).

From the **Singanallur bus stand** (Kamaraj Rd), 6km east of the centre, buses go to Trichy (₹130, six hours) and Madurai (₹130, six hours) every 10 minutes. City bus 140 (₹11) shuttles between here and the **Town bus stand** (cnr Dr Nanjappa & Bharathiyar Rds).

Ukkadam bus station (NH Rd), southwest of the centre, has buses to southern destinations including Pollachi (₹23, 1¼ hours, every 5 minutes), Kodaikanal (₹120, six hours, 10am) and Munnar (₹140, 6½ hours, 8.15am), plus some services to Madurai.

Private buses to Bengaluru, Chennai, Ernakulam, Puducherry, Trichy and Trivandrum start from the **Omni bus stand** (Sathy Rd), 500m north of the Town bus stand. Agencies on Sathy Rd sell tickets.

TAXI

A taxi up the hill to Ooty (three hours) costs about ₹2100; Ooty buses often get so crowded that it's worth considering.

TRAIN

Coimbatore Junction is on the main line between Chennai and Ernakulam (Kochi, Kerala), with at least 13 daily trains in each direction. The 5.15am Nilgiri Express to Mettupalayam connects with the miniature railway departure from Mettupalayam to Ooty at 7.10am. The whole trip to Ooty takes about seven hours.

❶ Getting Around

For the airport take bus 20 (₹11) from the Town bus stand. Many buses run between the train station and the Town bus stand. Autorickshaws charge ₹60 from the train station to the Ukkadam bus station, ₹80 to the SETC or Town Bus Stands, and ₹150 out to the Ooty bus stand.

Around Coimbatore

The **Isha Yoga Center** (☏0422-2515345; www.ishafoundation.org), an ashram in **Poondi**, 30km west of Coimbatore, is also a yoga and rejuvenation retreat and place of pilgrimage. The centrepiece is a multireligious temple housing the Dhyanalinga, believed to be unique in embodying all seven chakras of spiritual energy. Visitors are welcome to meditate or for yoga courses, which you should book in advance.

The commercial town of **Mettupalayam**, 40km north of Coimbatore, is the starting point for the miniature train to Ooty. If you need to stay the night before catching the 7.10am train, there's plenty of accommodation. **Hotel EMS Mayura** (☏04254-227936; hotelemsmayura@gmail.com; 212 Coimbatore Rd; r ₹1200, with AC ₹1800; ❄), a fine, bland midrange hotel with a decent restaurant, is just 300m from the bus station and 1km from the train station.

Coonoor

☏0423 / POP 45,494 / ELEV 1720M

Coonoor is one of the three Nilgiri hill stations – Ooty, Kotagiri and Coonoor – that are situated high above the southern plains. Smaller and quieter than Ooty, it has some fantastic heritage hotels and guesthouses, from which you can do exactly the same kind of things as you would do from bigger, busier Ooty. From upper Coonoor, 1km to 2km above the town centre, you can look down over the sea of red-tile rooftops to the slopes beyond and soak up the peace, cool climate and beautiful scenery. But you get none of the above in central Coonoor, which is a bustling, honking mess.

❂ Sights & Activities

Sim's Park   PARK
(adult/child ₹30/15, camera/video ₹50/100; ⊙8am-6.30pm) Upper Coonoor's 12-hectare Sim's Park, established in 1874, is a peaceful oasis of sloping manicured lawns with more than 1000 plant species from several continents, including magnolias, tree ferns, roses and camellias. Kotagiri-bound buses will drop you here.

Highfield Tea Estate   TEA ESTATE
(Walker's Hill Rd; ⊙8am-9pm) **FREE** This 50-year-old estate (2km northeast of upper Coonoor) is one of few Nilgiri working tea factories open to visitors. Self-appointed guides jump in quickly, but you're perfectly welcome to watch the full tea-making process independently.

MAJOR TRAINS FROM COIMBATORE

DESTINATION	TRAIN NO & NAME	FARE (₹)	DURATION (HR)	DEPARTURE
Bengaluru	16525 Bangalore Express	260/690/990 (B)	8½	10.55pm
Chennai Central	12676 Kovai Express	180/655 (A)	7½	2.55pm
	22640 Chennai Express	315/805/1135 (B)	7½	10.15pm
Ernakulam (Kochi)	12677 Ernakulam Express	105/385 (A)	3¾	1.10pm
Madurai	16610 Nagercoil Express	205/540 (C)	5½	8.30pm

Fares: (A) 2nd-class/AC chair; (B) sleeper/3AC/2AC; (C) sleeper/3AC

ANAMALAI TIGER RESERVE

A pristine 850-sq-km reserve of tropical jungle, *shola* forest and grassland rising to 2400m and spilling over into Kerala in the Western Ghats between Kodaikanal and Coimbatore, **Anamalai Tiger Reserve** (Indira Gandhi Wildlife Sanctuary & National Park; admission ₹20, camera/video ₹50/200; ⊙ Jun-Feb) is well off most tourists' radar. Declared a tiger reserve in 2007, it's home to all kinds of exotic endemic wildlife, much of it rare and endangered – including leopards and a few elusive tigers, though you'll probably mostly spot lion-tailed macaques, peacocks, langurs, spotted deer, elephants – or crocodiles at Amaravathi Crocodile Farm.

The reserve's **Reception and Interpretation Centre** (☑ 04253-245002; Topslip; ⊙ 6.30am-3.30pm) is at Topslip, 35km southwest of Pollachi. From here you can head off on **elephant rides** (per hour ₹800-1500), official one-hour **minibus jungle 'safaris'** (per person from ₹120) or **guided treks** (per 2 h ₹2000). Most people visit on day trips, but for those staying the night Topslip has **Forest Department accommodation** (r ₹500-2500) of varying comfort levels. Book several days ahead through the **District Forest Office** (☑ 04259-225356, 04259-238360; 365/1 Meenkarai Rd, Pollachi; ⊙ 10am-5.45pm Mon-Fri) in Pollachi; phone reservations are accepted.

The tiny tea-plantation town of **Valparai**, on the fringes of the reserve 65km south from Pollachi and reached via a spectacular 40-hairpin-bend road, makes a beautifully peaceful Anamalai base where you're just as likely to see wildlife. Our pick of the accommodation is **Sinna Dorai's Bungalow** (☑ 9443077516; www.sinnadorai.com; Valparai; r incl full-board ₹7500; ☎). Exquisitely located on a rambling tea estate, Sinna Dorai has just six huge rooms bursting with local early-20th-century history. A cosy library, wonderful homemade meals, and charming service make you feel right at home. After-dark wildlife-spotting drives, on which you may well find elephants, bison, lion-tailed macaques, and leopards, run regularly, and experienced trekkers will lead you along local paths. It's well signposted from central Valparai.

Several daily buses connect Pollachi with Topslip (₹40, 1½ hours) and Valparai (₹42, three hours). Buses to Pollachi run from Coimbatore's Ukkadam bus station (p1072), which also has four daily services to Valparai (₹65, four hours). From Kodaikanal, buses head to Pollachi (₹100, six hours) at 8.30am and 4.30pm.

Dolphin's Nose — VIEWPOINT

About 10km from town, this viewpoint exposes a vast panorama encompassing Catherine Falls across the valley. On the same road, **Lamb's Rock**, a favourite picnic spot in a pretty patch of forest, has amazing views past tea and coffee plantations to the hazy plains. The easiest way to see these sights is a rickshaw tour for around ₹600, or walk the 6km or so back into town from Lamb's Rock (mostly downhill).

🛌 Sleeping & Eating

You'll need a rickshaw, car or great legs to reach these places.

YWCA Wyoming Guesthouse — HOSTEL $

(☑ 0423-2234426; www.ywcaagooty.com; Bedford; dm/s/d ₹165/414/972) A ramshackle, 150-year-old gem, the Wyoming is draughty and creaky but oozes colonial-era character with wooden terraces and serene town views through trees. The rooms are good and clean, with geysers, and you get a friendly welcome. Meals available at two hours' notice.

★ 180° McIver — BOUTIQUE HOTEL $$

(☑ 0423-2233323; www.serendipityo.com; Orange Grove Rd; r incl breakfast ₹4200-6540; ☎) A classic 1890s British bungalow at the top of town has been turned into something special with a soupçon of French taste. The six lovely, airy rooms sport antique furniture, working fireplaces and big fresh bathrooms. On-site restaurant **La Belle Vie** (mains ₹200-450; ⊙ 12.30-3.30pm & 7.30-10.30pm) attracts diners for its European-Indian food and 'tea boutique'. The panoramas from the wraparound lawn are fabulous.

Acres Wild — FARMSTAY $$

(☑ 9443232621; www.acres-wild.com; Upper Meanjee Estate, Kanni Mariamman Kovil St; r incl breakfast ₹3600-5400; ☎) 🐾 This beautifully positioned farm on the southeast edge of town is run on sustainable lines with solar heating, rainwater harvesting and cheese like you've never tasted in India from the milk of its own cows. Guests can take cheese-making courses. The five rooms, in three cottages, are large and stylish, with kitchens and fireplaces.

Your friendly Mumbaikar hosts are full of ideas for things to do away from tourist crowds. Book ahead.

Gateway Hotel   HERITAGE HOTEL **$$$**
(☑0423-2225400;   www.thegatewayhotels.com; Church Rd, Upper Coonoor; s ₹5710-9910, d ₹6310-10,520, all incl breakfast; 🖝) A colonial-era priory turned gorgeous heritage hotel, the Taj-Group Gateway has homey cream-coloured rooms immersed in greenery. You get wonderful mountain views from those at the back while the good multicuisine **restaurant** (mains ₹400-600; ⊙7.30-10.30am, 12.30-3pm & 7.30-10.30pm) overlooks the gardens. Evening bonfires are lit on the lawn and there's free daily yoga along with an ayurvedic spa.

Self-Catering

Tulsi Mall   SUPERMARKET
(31 Mount Pleasant Rd; ⊙10am-8.30pm Wed-Mon) Well-stocked supermarket with a good range of Western products.

🛍 Shopping

Green Shop   HANDICRAFTS, FOOD
(www.lastforest.in;   Jograj Bldg, Bedford Circle; ⊙9.30am-7pm Mon-Sat) 🌿 Beautiful fairtrade local tribal crafts, clothes and fabrics, plus organic treats such as wild honey, nuts, chocolates and tea.

ⓘ Getting There & Away

Coonoor is on the miniature train line between Mettupalayam (27km) and Ooty (19km), with three daily trains just to/from Ooty as well as the daily Mettupalayam–Ooty–Mettupalayam service. Buses to and from Ooty (₹10, one hour) run every 10 minutes; buses to Kotagiri (₹11, one hour) and Coimbatore (₹45, 2½ hours) go every 20 minutes.

Kotagiri

☑ 04266 / POP 28,200 / ELEV 1800M
The oldest and smallest of the three Nilgiri hill stations, Kotagiri is a quiet, unassuming place with a forgettable town centre – its appeal is the escape to red dirt tracks in the pines, blue skies and the high green walls of the Nilgiris.

◉ Sights & Activities

You can visit **Catherine Falls**, 8km south, off the Mettupalayam road (the last 3km is on foot; the falls only flow after rain), **Elk Falls** (6km) and **Kodanad Viewpoint** (19km north), where there's a view over both the Coimbatore Plains and the Mysore Plateau. A half-day taxi tour to all three costs around ₹1000.

Sullivan Memorial   MUSEUM
(☑9488771571; www.sullivanmemorial.org; Kannerimukku; adult/child ₹20/10; ⊙10am-5pm) If you're interested in the history of the Nilgiris, check out this wonderful little museum, 2km north of Kotagiri centre. The house built in 1819 by John Sullivan, founder of Ooty, has been refurbished and filled with fascinating photos, newspaper cuttings and artefacts about local tribal groups, European settlement and icons like the toy train. It also contains the **Nilgiri Documentation Centre** (www.nilgiridocumentation.org), dedicated to preserving the region's heritage.

Keystone Foundation   VOLUNTEERING
(☑04266-272277; www.keystone-foundation.org; Groves Hill Rd) 🌿 This Kotagiri-based NGO works to improve environmental conditions in the Nilgiris while involving, and improving living standards for, indigenous communities.

🛏 Sleeping & Eating

The Kotagiri-based Keystone Foundation's **Green Shop** (Johnstone Sq; ⊙9.30am-7pm Mon-Sat) has picnic goodies (organic chocolates, wild honey).

La Maison   HERITAGE GUESTHOUSE **$$$**
(☑9585857732;   www.lamaison.in;   Hadatharai; s/d ₹7760/8890; 🖝) Flower-draped, French-owned La Maison is a beautifully renovated 1890s Scottish bungalow superbly located on a hilltop surrounded by tea plantations, 5km southwest of Kotagiri. The design is quirky French-chic all the way: antique furniture, tribal handicrafts, old-Ooty paintings. Hike to waterfalls, visit tribal villages, tuck into excellent homecooked meals (₹750), or laze in the valley-facing jacuzzi.

ⓘ Getting There & Away

Buses run half-hourly to/from Ooty (₹15, 1½ hours), crossing one of Tamil Nadu's highest passes, and to Mettupalayam (₹16 to ₹22, 1½ hours). Buses to Coimbatore (₹30, 2½ hours) leave hourly.

Ooty (Udhagamandalam)

📱 0423 / POP 88,430 / ELEV 2240M

Ooty may be a bit hectic for some tastes, and the town centre is an ugly mess, but it doesn't take long to get up into the quieter, greener areas where tall pines rise above what could almost be English country lanes. Ooty, 'the Queen of Hill Stations', mixes up Indian bustle and Hindu temples with lovely parks and gardens and charming Raj-era bungalows, the latter providing its most atmospheric (and most expensive) places to stay.

The town was established by the British in the early 19th century as the summer headquarters of the Madras government, and memorably nicknamed 'Snooty Ooty'. Development ploughed through a few decades ago, but somehow old Ooty survives. You just have to walk a bit further out to find it.

The journey up here on the celebrated miniature train is romantic and the scenery stunning. Even the road up from the plains is impressive. From April to June (the *very* busy 'season') Ooty is a welcome relief from the hot plains, and in the colder months (October to March) you'll need warm clothing, which you can buy cheap here, as overnight temperatures occasionally drop to 0°C.

The train and bus stations are at the west end of Ooty's racecourse, in almost the lowest part of town. To their west is the lake, while the streets of the town snake upwards all around. From the bus station it's a 20-minute walk to Ooty's commercial centre, Charing Cross. Like Kodaikanal, Ooty has an international school whose students can be seen around town.

🔘 Sights

Botanical Gardens GARDEN
(adult/child ₹30/15, camera/video ₹50/100; ⊙7am-6.30pm) Established in 1848, these pretty gardens are a living gallery of the natural flora of the Nilgiris. Look out for a fossilised tree trunk believed to be 20 million years old, and on busy days, around 20 million Indian tourists.

St Stephen's Church CHURCH
(⊙10.30am-5pm, services 8am & 11am Sun) Perched above the town centre, the immaculate St Stephen's, built in 1829, is the oldest church in the Nilgiris. It has lovely stained glass, huge wooden beams hauled by elephant from the palace of Tipu Sultan 120km away, and the sometimes kitschy, sometimes touching slabs and plaques donated by colonial-era churchgoers. In the quiet, overgrown cemetery you'll find headstones commemorating many an Ooty Brit.

Nilgiri Library LIBRARY
(📱0423-2441699; Hospital Rd; ⊙10am-1pm & 2.30-6pm) This quaint little haven in a crumbling 1867 building has more than 30,000 books, including rare titles on the Nilgiris and hill tribes and 19th-century British journals. Visitors can consult books in the reading room with a temporary one-month membership (₹500). Upstairs is a portrait of Queen Victoria presented to Ooty on her 1887 Golden Jubilee.

Rose Garden GARDEN
(Selbourne Rd; adult/child ₹30/15, camera/video ₹50/100; ⊙7.30am-6.30pm) With terraced lawns and over 20,000 rose bushes of more than 2000 varieties – best between May and July – the Rose Garden is a lovely place for a stroll, and has good Ooty views from its hillside location.

Doddabetta Lookout VIEWPOINT
(admission ₹5, camera/video ₹10/50; ⊙8am-5.30pm) This is it: the highest point (2633m) of the Nilgiris and one of the best viewpoints around, assuming it's a clear day (go early for better chances of mist-free views). It's about 7km from the town centre. Kotagiri buses will drop you at the Doddabetta junction, then you have a steep-ish 3km walk or a quick jeep ride. Taxis do the round trip from Charing Cross for ₹500.

🏃 Activities

Hiking & Trekking

The best of Ooty is out in the beautiful Nilgiris. Ooty's tourist office and many accommodation places can put you in touch with local guides who do day hikes for ₹400 to ₹600 per person. You'll normally drive out of town and walk around hills, tribal villages and tea plantations.

More serious trekking in the best forest areas with plenty of wildlife – such as beyond Avalanche to the south or Parsons Valley to the west, in Mukurthi National Park, or down to Walakkad and Sairandhri in Kerala's Silent Valley National Park – requires Tamil Nadu Forest Department permits. At the time of research, the **Office of the Field Director** (📱0423-2444098, Mudumalai accom-

Nilgiri Hills

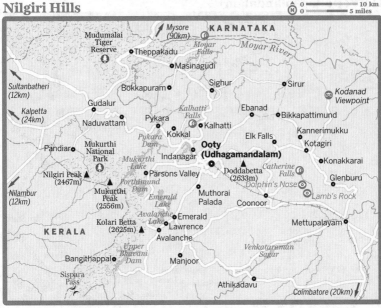

modation bookings 0423-2445971; fdmtr@tn.nic.in; Mount Stuart Hill; ⊙10am-5.45pm Mon-Fri) was not issuing permits due to rising concerns about man–animal conflict in the region; in January 2014, a tiger killed three people in the Doddabetta area, and there have been several elephant-related foreigner fatalities in recent years.

The **Nilgiri Wildlife & Environment Association** (📞 0423-2447167; www.nwea.in; Mount Stuart Hill; ⊙10am-1pm & 2-5pm Mon-Fri, 10am-1pm Sat), the **District Forest Office Nilgiris South Division** (📞 0423-2444083; dfosouth@sancharnet.in; Mount Stuart Hill; ⊙10am-5.45pm Mon-Fri), and the **District Forest Office Nilgiris North Division** (📞 0423-2443968; dfonorth_ooty@yahoo.co.in; Mount Stuart Hill; ⊙10am-5.45pm Mon-Fri) can help with trekking updates and advice.

Boating

Rowboats can be rented from the **Boathouse** (admission ₹10, camera/video ₹20/125; ⊙9am-6pm) by Ooty's lake. Prices start from ₹120 (plus a ₹120 deposit) for a two-seater pedal boat (30 minutes).

Horse Racing

Ooty's racecourse dominates the valley between Charing Cross and the lake. Racing season runs from mid-April to mid-June, and on the two or three race days (₹10 per person) each week the town is a hive of activity. Racing happens between about 10.30am and 2.30pm.

👉 Tours

Fixed taxi tour rates are ₹800 for four hours tootling around Ooty, ₹1200 to Coonoor (four hours), or ₹1800 to Mudumalai Tiger Reserve (full-day).

🛏 Sleeping

Ooty has some gorgeous colonial-era homes at the high end and some decent backpacker crashpads, but there isn't much in the lower midrange. Be warned: it's a sellers' market during the 'season' (1 April to 15 June), when hotels hike rates and checkout time is often 9am. Book well ahead for public holidays.

YWCA Anandagiri   HOSTEL $
(📞 0423-2444262; www.ywcaagooty.com; Ettines Rd; dm ₹200, s ₹400-1300, d ₹800-1400) This former brewery and sprawling complex of cottages is dotted with flower gardens. A fresh coat of paint and some smartening up has increased rates, but with clean, characterful rooms and spacious common areas including a restaurant (book ahead

Ooty (Udhagamandalam)

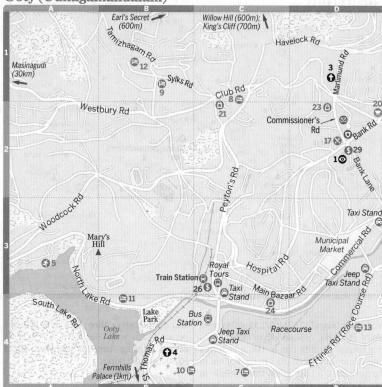

for good-value meals), you've still got some excellent budget accommodation going on. High ceilings can mean cold nights, so do ask for extra blankets.

Hotel Sweekar HOTEL $
(☑ 0423-2442348; hotelsweekar@gmail.com; 236 Race View Rd; r ₹500-600) The Sweekar hosts guests in small, basic but clean rooms in a traditional Ooty cottage at the end of a flower-lined path. Hot water only runs until noon (at best), but the Sweekar is good value for its price, and incredibly popular. It's run by a very helpful and efficient Bahai manager.

Reflections Guest House GUESTHOUSE $
(☑ 0423-2443834; www.reflectionsguesthouse ooty.com; 1B North Lake Rd; r ₹770-990; ☎) A long-standing budget haunt, Reflections sits across the road from Ooty's lake, and most of its 12 clean, decent rooms have lake views. It also serves Indian and Continental food at

fair prices (₹60 to ₹180), and can organise guided day treks. Hot showers are available for two hours daily; towels on request.

★**Lymond House** HERITAGE HOTEL $$
(☑ 0423-2223377; http://serendipityo.com; 77 Sylks Rd; r incl breakfast ₹4800-5400; ☎) What is it about this 1850s British bungalow that gives it the edge over its peers? The cosy cottage set-up with fresh flowers, four-poster beds, fireplaces and comfy lounges? The contemporary fittings thrown in with rich old-world style in the big rooms and bathrooms? The good food and pretty gardens? All of it, no doubt – plus an informal but wonderfully efficient management style.

Hotel Welbeck Residency HOTEL $$
(☑ 0423-2223300; www.welbeck.in; Welbeck Circle, Club Rd; r ₹3240-4620; @☎) An attractive older building that's been thoroughly spruced up with comfortable rooms, a touch of colonial-era class (a 1920 Austin saloon

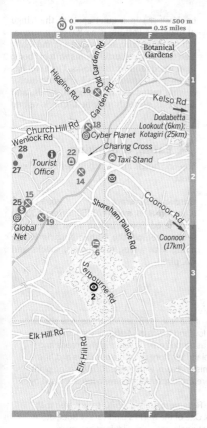

TAMIL NADU & CHENNAI OOTY (UDHAGAMANDALAM)

at the front door!), a decent restaurant and very keen staff.

Mount View Hotel HOTEL $$
(☎0423-2443307; www.hotelmountviewooty.com; Ettines Rd; r ₹1970-3940; 🛜) Perched on a quiet (bumpy) driveway handy for the bus and train stations, the nine enormous, high-ceilinged, wood-lined rooms in this elegant old bungalow have been done up comfortably enough. It's just a shame they still won't use the fireplaces.

★ Savoy Hotel HERITAGE HOTEL $$$
(☎0423-2225500; www.tajhotels.com; 77 Sylks Rd; s ₹5950-11,900, d ₹6550-12,500, all incl breakfast; @🛜) The Savoy is one of Ooty's oldest hotels, with parts dating back to 1829. Big cottages are set around a beautiful lawned garden; the pretty rooms have spacious bathrooms, log fires and bay windows. Staff are efficient and modern facilities include a bar (even cocktails), an ayurveda centre,

wi-fi, and an excellent multicuisine dining room (p1081). Half-board arrangements are compulsory from April to June.

Fernhills Palace HERITAGE HOTEL $$$
(☎0423-2443911; www.fernhillspalace.co.in; Fern Hill; r incl breakfast ₹13,190-32,380; @🛜) The Maharaja of Mysore's exquisite Anglo-Indian summer palace has been lovingly restored in gorgeous, completely over-the-top princely

colonial style. If you can afford it, it's worth the splurge. All 19 rooms are big suites, with antique furnishings, teak flourishes, fireplaces and jacuzzis. Play billiards, walk in the huge, forest-fringed grounds and dine on regal fare beneath Raj-inspired murals.

King's Cliff HERITAGE HOTEL **$$$**
(☑ 0423-2452888; www.littlearth.in; Havelock Rd; r incl breakfast ₹2600-6930; ☎) High above Ooty on Strawberry Hill is this classic colonial-era house with wood panelling, antique furnishings, a snug lounge, and good Indian/ Continental cooking at the **Earl's Secret** (mains ₹340-600; ☺ 8-10am, noon-3pm & 7-10pm) restaurant. The cheaper rooms don't have quite the same old-world charm as the most expensive ones.

Fortune Sullivan Court HOTEL **$$$**
(☑ 0423-2441415; www.fortunehotels.in; 123 Selbourne Rd; s ₹6000-7200, d ₹6600-7800, all incl breakfast; ☎) In a quiet spot on the fringe of town, the Fortune is no Raj-era mansion, but twirling staircases around a grand lobby lead to comfy, colourful rooms with big beds, light woods and writing desks. The hotel has its own bar, spa and small gym, the multicuisine restaurant does decent meals, and service is perfectly polished. Check online for discounts.

🍴 Eating & Drinking

Top-end hotels are your best bet for a classy meal.

Garden Restaurant SOUTH INDIAN **$**
(Commercial Rd; mains ₹70-150; ☺ 7am-9.30pm) Very good South Indian food in a clean setting behind the Nahar Nilgiris Hotel, along with juices, milkshakes, snacks and OK pizza.

THE NILGIRIS & THEIR TRIBES

The forest-clothed, waterfall-threaded walls of the Nilgiris (Blue Mountains) rise abruptly from the surrounding plains between the lowland towns of Mettupalayam (to the southeast) and Gudalur (to the northwest), ascended only by winding ghat roads and the famous Nilgiri Mountain Railway. The upland territory, a jumble of valleys and hills with over 20 peaks above 2000m, is a botanist's dream, with over 2300 flowering plant species, although a lot of the native *shola* forest and grasslands have been displaced by tea, eucalyptus and cattle.

The Unesco-designated Nilgiri Biosphere Reserve is a larger, 5520-sq-km area that also includes parts of Kerala and Karnataka. One of the world's biodiversity hotspots, it contains several important tiger reserves, national parks and wildlife sanctuaries.

The Nilgiris' tribal inhabitants were left pretty much to themselves in their isolated homeland until the British arrived two centuries ago. Today, the effects of colonialism and migration have reduced many tribal cultures to the point of collapse, and some have assimilated to the point of invisibility. Others, however, continue at least a semi-traditional lifestyle. Organisations such as the Keystone Foundation (p1075) work to promote traditional crafts and activities.

Best known of the tribes, thanks to anthropologists' interest and their proximity to Ooty, are the Toda, who number just over 1000. Some still inhabit tiny villages (*munds*) of their traditional barrel-shaped huts made of bamboo, cane and grass. Toda women style their hair in long, shoulder-length ringlets, and are skilled embroiderers; both sexes wear distinctive black-and-red-embroidered shawls. Central to Toda life is the water buffalo, which provides milk and ghee for consumption and bartering. Traditionally, it is only at funerals that the strictly vegetarian Toda kill a buffalo, to accompany the deceased.

The 350,000-strong Badaga are thought to have migrated into the Nilgiris from Karnataka around AD 1600, and are thus not usually considered truly indigenous. Their traditional dress is of white cloth with a border of narrow coloured stripes. They worship the mother goddess Hetti Amman, to whom their December/January Hettai Habba festival is dedicated.

The Kota, traditionally cultivators, live in seven settlements in the Kotagiri area. They have adapted relatively well to modernity, with a significant number holding government jobs.

The Kurumba inhabit the thick forests of the south and are gatherers of forest products such as bamboo and wild honey, though many of them now work in agriculture.

Kabab Corner   NORTH INDIAN $$

(Commercial Rd; mains ₹140-360; ⊙1-10pm) This is the place for meat-eaters who are tiring of South Indian pure-veg food. It doesn't look much from outside, but here you can tear apart perfectly grilled and spiced chunks of lamb, chicken and, if you like, paneer, sopping up the juices with pillowy triangles of naan. Also on **Club Rd** (Club Rd; mains ₹140-360; ⊙12.30-10pm).

Shinkow's Chinese Restaurant   CHINESE $$

(38/83 Commissioner's Rd; mains ₹120-250; ⊙noon-3.45pm & 6.30-9.45pm) Shinkow's is an Ooty institution and the simple menu of chicken, pork, beef, fish, noodles and rice dishes is reliably good and quick to arrive at your check-print table.

Savoy   MULTICUISINE $$$

(☑0423-2225500; 77 Sylks Rd; mains ₹325-675; ⊙12.30-3pm & 7.30-10pm) All wood walls, intimate lighting and smart red velvets, the Savoy's dining room dishes up excellent contemporary Continental, Indian and pan-Asian cuisine – including all-day breakfasts, yummy salads, pastas and kebabs, and wonderfully chocolatey desserts.

Willy's Coffee Pub   CAFE

(KCR Arcade, Walsham Rd; dishes ₹40-90; ⊙10am-9.30pm; 🛜) Climb the stairs and join the international students for board games, wi-fi, a lending library and reasonably priced pizzas, chips, toasties, cakes and cookies.

Café Coffee Day   CAFE

(Church Hill Rd; coffee ₹60-110; ⊙9am-11pm) Dependably good coffee, tea and cakes. There's another **branch** (Garden Rd; ⊙9am-10.45pm) on Garden Rd.

Self-Catering

Modern Stores   SUPERMARKET

(144 Garden Rd; ⊙9.30am-8.30pm) This mini-supermarket stocks all kinds of Western foods from muesli to marmalade, as well as Nilgiri-produced bread and cheese.

Virtue Bakes   BAKERY

(Garden Rd; ⊙10.30am-8.30pm) Great cakes, pastries, croissants and bread to go.

🛍 Shopping

The main shopping street is Commercial Rd, where you'll find Kashmiri shops as well as outlets for Keralan crafts and *khadi* (hand-spun cloth). Near the botanical gardens entrance, Tibetan refugees sell jumpers and shawls, which you'll appreciate on a chilly Ooty evening.

K Mahaveer Chand   JEWELLERY

(291 Main Bazaar Rd; ⊙10am-8pm) K Mahaveer Chand has been selling particularly beautiful Toda tribal and silver jewellery for around 40 years.

Green Shop   HANDICRAFTS, FOOD

(www.lastforest.in; Sargan Villa, off Club Rd; ⊙10am-7pm Mon-Sat) 🌿 Run by Kotagiri's Keystone Foundation (p1075), this fair-trade and organic-oriented shop sells gorgeous tribal crafts and clothes, and wild honey and other produce harvested by local indigenous farmers.

Higginbothams   BOOKS

(☑0423-2443736; Commercial Rd; ⊙9am-1pm & 3.30-7.30pm) A good English-language book selection (including Lonely Planet guides), with another **branch** (☑0423-2442546; Commissioner's Rd; ⊙9.30am-1pm & 2-6pm Mon-Sat) up the hill.

ℹ Information

Cyber Planet (Garden Rd; per hour ₹30; ⊙10am-6pm)

Global Net (Commercial Rd; per hour ₹30; ⊙10am-10pm)

Tourist office (☑0423-2443977; Wenlock Rd; ⊙10am-5.45pm Mon-Fri)

ℹ Getting There & Away

The fun way to arrive in Ooty is on the miniature train from Mettupalayam. Buses also run regularly up and down the mountain from other parts of Tamil Nadu, from Kerala and from Mysuru and Bengaluru in Karnataka. Taxis cluster at several stands around town and there are fixed one-way fares to many destinations, including Coonoor (₹750), Kotagiri (₹850), Coimbatore (₹1700) and Mudumalai Tiger Reserve (₹1250).

BUS

For Kochi (Cochin, Kerala) take the 7am or 8am bus to Palakkad (₹95, six hours) and change there. **Royal Tours** (☑0423-2446150), opposite the train station, runs a 9am minibus to Kodaikanal (₹600, eight hours).

The Tamil Nadu and Karnataka state bus companies have reservation offices at the busy bus station. Departures include:

Bengaluru (₹391 to ₹650, eight hours, nine daily)

Chennai (₹462, 14 hours, 4.30pm & 5.45pm)

Coimbatore (₹56, four hours, every 30 minutes, 5.30am to 8.40pm)

Mysuru (₹136, five hours, about every 45 minutes, 6.30am to 5.45pm)

TRAIN

The miniature (or 'toy') train from Mettupalayam to Ooty – one of the Mountain Railways of India given World Heritage status by Unesco – is the best way to get here. Called the Nilgiri Mountain Railway, it requires special cog wheels on the locomotive, meshing with a third, 'toothed' rail on the ground, to manage the exceptionally steep gradients. There are wonderful forest, waterfall, mountainside and tea plantation views along the way. The section between Mettupalayam and Coonoor uses steam engines, which push, rather than pull, the train up the hill.

For the high season (April to June), book the train several weeks ahead; at other times a few days ahead is advisable (though not always essential). The train departs Mettupalayam for Ooty at 7.10am daily (1st/2nd class ₹205/30, five hours). From Ooty to Mettupalayam the train leaves at 2pm and takes 3½ hours. Departures and arrivals at Mettupalayam connect with the Nilgiri Express to/from Chennai Central. There are also three daily passenger trains each way just between Ooty and Coonoor (₹25, 1¼ hours).

Ooty is usually listed as Udhagamandalam in train timetables.

ⓘ Getting Around

There are autorickshaws and taxis everywhere. Autorickshaw fare charts are posted outside the bus station and botanical gardens and elsewhere. An autorickshaw from the train or bus station to Charing Cross costs about ₹60.

There are jeep taxi stands near the bus station and municipal market: expect to pay about 1.5 times local taxi fares.

Mudumalai Tiger Reserve

📋 0423

In the foothills of the Nilgiris, this 321-sq-km reserve is like a classical Indian landscape painting given life: thin, spindly trees and light-slotted leaves concealing spotted chital deer and grunting wild boar. Also here are around 50 tigers, giving Mudumalai the highest tiger population density in India – though you'll be very lucky to see one. Overall the reserve is Tamil Nadu's best wildlife-spotting place. The creatures you're most likely to see include deer, peacocks, wild boar, langurs and Malabar giant squirrels. There's also a good chance of sighting wild elephants (the park has several hundred) and gaur (Indian bison).

Along with Karnataka's Bandipur and Nagarhole, Kerala's Wayanad and Tamil Nadu's newly created Sathyamangalam Tiger Reserve, Mudumalai forms part of an unbroken chain of protected areas comprising an important wildlife refuge.

Mudumalai sometimes closes for fire risk in April, May or June. Rainy July and August are the least favourable months for visiting.

The reserve's **reception centre** (📞0423-2526235; ⏱6-10am & 2-5.30pm), and some reserve-run accommodation, is at Theppakadu, on the main road between Ooty and Mysuru. The closest village to Theppakadu is Masinagudi, 7km east.

◉ Sights & Activities

Hiking in the reserve is not allowed and private vehicles are only permitted on the main Ooty–Gudalur–Theppakadu–Mysuru-road and the Theppakadu–Masinagudi and Masinagudi–Moyar River roads. Some wildlife can be spotted from these roads, but the best way to see the reserve is on the official 45-minute **minibus tours** (per person ₹135; ⏱hourly 7-10am & 2-6pm), which make a 15km loop in camouflage-striped 15- or 26-seat buses. Book at the reception centre a couple of hours ahead.

Half-hour **elephant rides** (up to four people ₹860; ⏱7-8am & 4-5pm Sep-Jun) are also available from the reception centre; reserve 30 minutes ahead. From 8.30am to 9am and 5.30pm to 6pm you can watch the reserve's working elephants being fed at the nearby **elephant camp** (minibus-tour customers free, others ₹15).

Some operators may offer treks in the buffer zone around the reserve, but these are potentially dangerous and the reserve authorities advise very strongly against them; tourists have died from getting too close to wild elephants on illegal treks. Jeep safaris organised through the better resorts, with expert guides, are a safer option.

🛏 Sleeping & Eating

The reserve runs simple lodgings along a track just above the Moyar River at Theppakadu. Better accommodation is provided by numerous lodges and forest resorts outside the park's fringes, many of them welcoming family-run businesses offering high standards and breathtaking views. Most of the best cluster in Bokkapuram village, 5km from Masinagudi at the foot of the mountains.

📖 Theppakadu

For this reserve-run accommodation you should book in advance (by phone or in person) with the Office of the Field Director (p1076) in Ooty, though the reception centre accepts walk-ins if there are vacancies.

Sylvan Lodge   LODGE $
(d ₹780) Plain, well-scrubbed rooms, and ₹70 meals.

Theppakadu Log House   LODGE $$
(r ₹1360-2200) The best of the reserve-owned accommodation, with comfortable well-maintained rooms that have private bathrooms. Meals cost around ₹70.

📖 Bokkapuram & Around

Don't wander outside your resort at night – leopards, among other wild animals, are around.

Wilds at Northernhay   LODGE $$
(☎9843149490; www.serendipityo.com; Singara; r incl breakfast ₹4800-5400) A wonderful lodge 8km southwest of Masinagudi, in a converted coffee warehouse on a coffee plantation filled with tall trees that give it a deep-in-the-forest feel. Cosy rooms (some up in the trees) and excellent meals complement the morning and evening jeep safaris (per hour ₹3000), on which you should see a good variety of wildlife.

Jungle Retreat   RESORT $$
(☎0423-2526469; www.jungleretreat.com; Bokkapuram; dm ₹1000, r ₹4000-5400; 🛜🏊) One of the most stylish resorts around, with accommodation in lovingly built stone cottages or a high treehouse, all spread out for maximum seclusion. The bar, restaurant and common area is great for meeting travellers, and staff are knowledgeable and friendly. The pool has a stunning setting – leopards and elephants often drop by for a drink. Three daily meals cost ₹1700.

Bamboo Banks Farm   LODGE $$
(☎0423-2526211; www.bamboobanks.com; Masinagudi; full-board d ₹6140; 🛜🏊) This friendly family-owned operation has seven simple, comfy cottages tucked into its own patch of unkempt jungle, 2km south of Masinagudi. Geese waddle around, there's a peaceful grassy pool area with hammocks, meals are good South Indian buffets, and the efficient owners can organise horse riding and private safaris.

Jungle Hut   RESORT $$$
(☎0423-2526463; www.junglehut.in; Bokkapuram; full-board s ₹4400-6900, d ₹6600-9000; ❄🛜🏊) Along with ecofriendly touches and a sociable lounge, this welcoming 28-year-old resort has probably the best food in Bokkapuram (if you're visiting from another resort after dark, don't walk home alone!). Spacious rooms in cottages are scattered around large grounds, where a herd of 200-odd chital deer grazes morning and evening. Jeep safaris, treks and birdwatching can be organised.

❶ Getting There & Around

A taxi day trip to Mudumalai from Ooty costs around ₹1800. Do go at least one way by the alternative Sighur Ghat road with its spectacular 36-hairpin-bend hill. A one-way taxi from Ooty to Theppakadu should be ₹1250.

Buses between Ooty and Mysuru go via Gudalur and stop at Theppakadu (₹37, three hours from Ooty). Smaller buses that can handle the Sighur Ghat road run from Ooty to Masinagudi (₹17, 1½ hours, 10 daily). Local buses run several times daily between Masinagudi and Theppakadu (₹5); shared jeeps also ply this route for ₹10 per person if there are enough passengers, or you can have one to yourself for about ₹120. Costs are similar for jeeps between Masinagudi and Bokkapuram.

TAMIL NADU & CHENNAI MUDUMALAI TIGER RESERVE

Andaman Islands

Best Beaches

- ➡ Radhanagar (p1093)
- ➡ Merk Bay (p1099)
- ➡ Ross & Smith Islands (p1101)
- ➡ Butler Bay (p1102)
- ➡ Lalaji Bay (p1099)

Best Places to Stay

- ➡ Emerald Gecko (p1095)
- ➡ Aashiaanaa Rest Home (p1090)
- ➡ Pristine Beach Resort (p1101)
- ➡ Blue View (p1102)
- ➡ Blue Planet (p1100)

Why Go?

Long fabled among travellers for its legendary beaches, world-class diving and far-flung location in the middle of nowhere, the Andaman Islands are still the ideal place to get away from it all.

Lovely opaque emerald waters are surrounded by primeval jungle and mangrove forest, and snow-white beaches that melt under flame-and-purple sunsets. The population is a friendly masala of South and Southeast Asian settlers, as well as Negrito ethnic groups whose arrival here still has anthropologists baffled. Adding to the intrigue is its remote location, some 1370km from the mainland, meaning the islands are geographically more Southeast Asia – 150km from Indonesia and 190km from Myanmar.

While the archipelago comprises some 300 islands, only a dozen or so are open to tourists, Havelock by far being the most popular for its beaches and diving. The Nicobars are strictly off limits to tourists, as are the tribal areas.

When to Go
Port Blair

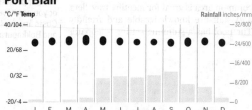

Dec–Mar Perfect sunny days, optimal diving conditions and turtle nesting.

Oct–Dec & Mar–mid-May Weather is a mixed bag, but fewer tourists and lower costs.

Feb–Aug Pumping waves on Little Andaman for experienced surfers.

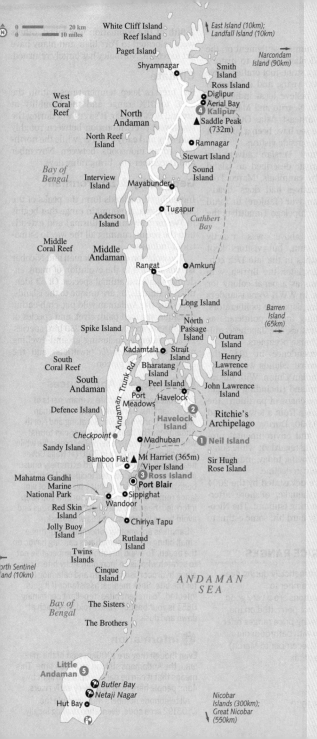

Andaman Islands Highlights

1 Disconnecting from the mainland and easing into the blissfully mellow pace of life on **Neil Island** (p1096)

2 Diving, snorkelling and socialising on **Havelock Island** (p1093)

3 Glimpsing Port Blair's colonial history at **Ross Island** (p1090)

4 Experiencing the true wilds of Northern Andaman in **Kalipur** (p1100), while island-hopping to pristine beaches and coral reefs

5 Finding Butler Bay and paradise on **Little Andaman** (p1101)

History

The date of initial human settlement on the Andamans and Nicobars is lost to history. Anthropologists say stone-tool crafters have lived here for 2000 years, and scholars of human migration believe local indigenous tribes have roots in Negrito and Malay ethnic groups in Southeast Asia. Otherwise, these specks in the sea have been a constant source of legend to outside visitors.

The 10th-century Persian adventurer Buzurg Ibn Shahriyar described an island chain inhabited by cannibals, Marco Polo added that the natives had dogs' heads, and tablets in Thanjavur (Tanjore) in Tamil Nadu named the archipelago Timaittivu: the Impure Islands.

None of the above was exactly tourism-brochure stuff, but visitors kept coming: the Marathas in the late 17th century and, 200 years later, the British, who used the Andamans as a penal colony for political dissidents. In WWII some islanders greeted the invading Japanese as liberators, but despite installing Indian politicians as (puppet) administrators, the Japanese military proved to be harsh occupiers.

Following Independence in 1947, the Andaman and Nicobar Islands were incorporated into the Indian Union. With migration from the mainland (including Bengali refugees fleeing the chaos of partition), the population has grown from a few thousand to more than 350,000. During this influx, tribal land rights and environmental protection were often disregarded; while some conditions are improving today, indigenous tribes remain largely in decline.

The islands were devastated by the 2004 Indian Ocean earthquake, offshore aftershocks and the resulting tsunami. The Nicobars were especially hard hit; some estimate a fifth of the population was killed, others were relocated to Port Blair and many have yet to return. Normalcy has largely returned.

Climate

Sea breezes keep temperatures within the 23°C to 31°C range and the humidity at around 80% all year. It's very wet during the southwest (wet) monsoon between roughly mid-May and early October, while the northeast (dry) monsoons between November and December also bring rainy days.

Geography & Environment

Incredibly the islands form the peaks of the Arakan Yoma, a mountain range that begins in Western Myanmar (Burma) and extends into the ocean, running all the way to Sumatra in Indonesia.

The isolation of the Andaman and Nicobar Islands has led to the evolution of many endemic plant and animal species. Of 62 identified mammals, 32 are unique to the islands, including the Andaman wild pig, crab-eating macaque, masked palm civet, and species of tree shrews and bats. Of the 250 bird species, 18 are endemic, including ground-dwelling megapodes, *hawabills* (swiftlets) and the emerald Nicobar pigeon.

❶ Dangers & Annoyances

Crocodiles are a way of life in many parts of the Andamans, particularly Little Andaman, Wandoor, Corbyn's Cove, Baratang and North Andamans. The death of an American tourist who was attacked by a saltwater crocodile while snorkelling in Havelock in 2010 (at Neils Cove near Beach 7) was considered extremely unusual, and remains an isolated incident. There have been no sightings since, but a high level of vigilance remains in place. It's important you keep informed, heed any warnings by authorities and avoid being in the water at dawn or dusk.

Sandflies are another hindrance, with these small biting insects sometimes causing havoc on the beach. To avoid infection, it's imperative not to scratch what is an incredibly itchy bite. Bring along hydrocortisone cream and calamine lotion for the bite. Seek medical assistance if it gets infected. To prevent bites, repellant containing DEET is your best bet, and avoid the beach at dawn and dusk.

❶ Information

Even though they are 1000km east of the mainland, the Andamans still run on Indian time. This means that it can be dark by 5pm and light by 4am; people here tend to be very early risers.

All telephone numbers must include the ☎ 03192 area code, even when dialling locally.

SLEEPING PRICE RANGES

Tariffs can rise dramatically during peak season of mid-December to January – reservations are a very good idea. Camping is not permitted on the islands. The following price ranges refer to a double room with bathroom during the high season (December to March) and are inclusive of tax:

$ less than ₹800

$$ ₹800 to ₹2500

$$$ more than ₹2500

PERMITS

All foreigners need a permit to visit the Andaman Islands; it's issued free on arrival from Port Blair's airport or Haddo Jetty. The 30-day permit allows foreigners to stay in Port Blair, South and Middle Andaman (excluding tribal areas), North Andaman (Diglipur), Long Island, North Passage, Little Andaman (excluding tribal areas), and Havelock and Neil Islands. It's possible to get a 15-day extension from the **Immigration Office** (☑ 03192-237793; ☺ 8.30am-1pm & 2-5pm Mon-Fri, to 1pm Sat) in Port Blair, or at police stations elsewhere.

Keep your permit on you at all times – you won't be able to travel without it. Police frequently ask to see it, especially when you're disembarking on other islands, and hotels will need permit details. You'll also need it to pass immigration when departing the Andamans.

The permit also allows day trips to Jolly Buoy, South Cinque, Red Skin, Ross, Narcondam, Interview and Rutland Islands, as well as the Brothers and the Sisters. For most day permits it's not the hassle but the cost. For areas such as Mahatma Gandhi Marine National Park, and Ross and Smith Islands near Diglipur, the permits cost ₹50/500 for Indians/foreigners. Students with valid ID pay minimal entry fees, so don't forget to bring your card.

The Nicobar Islands are off-limits to all except Indian nationals engaged in research, government business or trade.

❶ Getting There & Away

AIR

There are daily flights to Port Blair from Delhi, Kolkata and Chennai, though flights from Delhi and Kolkata are often routed through Chennai. Round-trip fares are between US$250 and US$600, depending on how early you book; some airlines offer one-way flights for as low as US$80, but these need to be booked months in advance.

Air India (☑ 03192-233108; www.airindia.com)

GoAir (☑ 03192-231540, reservations 092-23222111; www.goair.in)

Jet Airways (☑ 1800-225522, 03192-230545; www.jetairways.com)

SpiceJet (☑ 0987-1803333; www.spicejet.com)

BOAT

Depending on who you ask, the infamous boat to Port Blair is either the only *real* way to get to the Andamans or a hassle and a half. The truth lies somewhere in between. There are usually three to four sailings a month between Port Blair and Chennai (three days) and Kolkata (four to five days), plus a monthly ferry to Visakhapatnam (four days). All ferries arrive at Haddo Jetty.

Take sailing times with a large grain of salt – travellers have reported sitting on the boat at Kolkata harbour for up to 12 hours, or waiting to

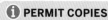

❶ PERMIT COPIES

At the time of research it was a requirement to produce a photocopy of your permit when booking ferry tickets. While you're not always asked to provide it, it's worth taking five or so copies before arriving at Port Blair's ferry office: you'll likely need them later in your trip.

dock near Port Blair for several hours. With holdups and variable weather and sea conditions, the trip can take a day or two extra.

Assistant Director of Shipping Services (☑ 044-25226873; 17 Rajaji Salai, Jawahar Bldg, Chennai Port; ☺ 10am-1pm & 2-4pm Mon-Fri, to 12.30pm Sat) has boats from Chennai, **Shipping Corporation of India** (☑ 033-22543505/7, in Kolkata 033-22543400; www.shipindia.com; 13 Strand Rd, Kolkata; ☺ 9am-1pm & 2-5pm Mon-Fri, to noon Sat) departs from Kolkata, and **Pattabhiramayya & Co** (☑ 0891-2565597; ops@avbgpr.com; Harbour Approach Rd, next to NMDC, Port Area; ☺ 9am-5pm) from Visakhapatnam.

You can organise your return ticket at the ferry booking office (p1091) at Phoenix Bay. Bring two passport photos and a photocopy of your permit. Schedules and fares can be found at www.andamans.gov.in or www.shipindia.com. Otherwise enquire at Phoenix Bay's info office.

Classes vary slightly between boats, but the cheapest are bunk (₹2270), followed by 2nd-class (six beds, ₹5817), 1st class (four beds, ₹7319) and deluxe cabins (two beds, ₹8841). Higher-end tickets cost as much as, if not more than, a plane ticket. If you go bunk, prepare for waking up to a chorus of men 'hwwaaaaching' and spitting, little privacy and toilets that tend to get...unpleasant after three days at sea. That said, it's a good way to meet locals, and one for proponents of slow, adventure travel.

Food (tiffin for breakfast, thalis for lunch and dinner) costs around ₹150/200 per day for bunk/cabin class, though bring something (fruit in particular) to supplement your diet. Some bedding is supplied, but if you're travelling bunk class bring a sleeping sheet. Many travellers take a hammock to string up on deck.

There is no ferry between Port Blair and Thailand, but private yachts can get clearance. You can't legally get from the Andamans to Myanmar by sea. Be aware you risk imprisonment or worse from the Indian and Burmese navies if you try it.

❶ Getting Around

AIR

Two modes of air transport link Port Blair with the other islands. If your budget allows it, it's worth it for the views.

> **ℹ FERRY CANCELLATIONS**
>
> Bad weather can play havoc with your itinerary, with ferry services often cancelled if the sea is rough. Build in a few days' buffer to avoid being marooned..

Interisland Helicopter While the interisland helicopter service isn't for tourists, you can chance your luck by applying one day before at the Directorate of Civil Aviation office (☑ 03192-233601; VIP Rd Port Blair Helipad) at the helipad near the airport. It runs to/from Port Blair to Little Andaman (₹2625, 35 minutes), Havelock (₹1500, 20 minutes), Diglipur (₹4125, one hour) and Mayabunder (₹3375, 45 minutes). The 5kg baggage limit precludes most tourists from using this service.

Sea Plane (☑ 09531828222; andamanseaplane@gmail.com; ⊙ Mon-Sat) The amphibious Sea Plane links Port Blair with Havelock (₹4100), Little Andaman (₹7170) and Diglipur (₹10,500), landing and taking off on the water, and the runway in Port Blair. It operates January to April. Note the 5kg baggage limit.

BOAT

Most islands can only be reached by water. While this sounds romantic, ferry ticket offices can be hell: expect hot waits, slow service, queue-jumping and a rugby scrum to the ticket window. To hold your spot and advance in line, you need to be a little aggressive (but not a jerk) or be a woman; ladies' queues are a godsend for women travellers, but they really only apply in Port Blair. You can buy tickets the day you travel by arriving at the appropriate jetty an hour beforehand, but this is risky, and normally one or two days in advance is recommended. You can't pre-book ferry tickets until you've been issued your island permit (p1087) upon arrival in the Andamans.

There are regular boat services to Havelock and Neil Islands (three to four per day), as well as Rangat, Mayabunder, Diglipur and Little Andaman. A schedule of interisland sailing times can be found at www.andamans.gov.in.

Two private ferry companies also run to Havelock and Neil Islands from Port Blair.

Makruzz Ferry (☑ 03192-212355; www.makruzz.com)

Coastal Cruise (☑ 03192-241333; www.coastalcruise.in; 13 RP Rd, Aberdeen Bazaar)

CAR & MOTORCYCLE

A car with driver costs ₹550 per 35km, or around ₹10,000 for a return trip to Diglipur from Port Blair (including stopovers along the way). Motorbikes and scooters are available for hire from Port Blair and all the islands from around ₹300 to ₹400 per day. Due to restrictions in travel within tribal areas, it's not permitted for foreigners to drive their own vehicles to North and Middle Andaman.

BUS

All roads – and ferries – lead to Port Blair, and you'll inevitably spend a night or two here booking onward travel. The main island group – South, Middle and North Andaman – is connected by road, with ferry crossings and bridges. Buses run south from Port Blair to Wandoor, and north to Baratang, Rangat, Mayabunder and Diglipur, 325km north of the capital.

Port Blair

POP 100,600

Though surrounded by attractive lush forest and rugged coastline, Port Blair is more or less your typical Indian town that serves as the provincial capital of the Andamans. It's a vibrant mix of Indian Ocean inhabitants – Bengalis, Tamils, Telugus, Nicobarese and Burmese. Most travellers don't hang around any longer than necessary (usually one or two days while waiting to book onward travel in the islands, or returning for departure), but PB's fascinating history makes for some worthwhile sightseeing.

◉ Sights

★ Cellular Jail National Memorial   HISTORIC BUILDING

(GB Pant Rd; admission ₹10, camera/video ₹25/100, sound-and-light show adult/child ₹50/25; ⊙ 8.45am-12.30pm & 1.30-5pm) A former British prison, the evocative Cellular Jail National Memorial now serves as a shrine to the political dissidents it once jailed. Construction of the jail began in 1896 and it was completed in 1906 – the original seven wings (several of which were destroyed by the Japanese during WWII) contained 698 cells radiating from a central tower. Like many political prisons, Cellular Jail became something of a university for freedom fighters, who exchanged books, ideas and debates despite walls and wardens. Guides (₹200) are available to show you around.

There's a fairly cheesy **sound-and-light show** detailing the jail's history in English at 7.15pm on Monday, Wednesday and Friday.

Anthropological Museum   MUSEUM

(MG Rd; admission ₹10, camera ₹20; ⊙ 9am-1pm & 1.30-4.30pm Tue-Sun) This museum provides a thorough and sympathetic portrait of the islands' indigenous tribal communities. The glass display cases may be old school, but they don't feel anywhere near as ancient as the simple geometric patterns etched into a

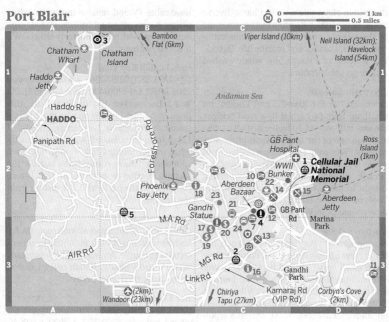

Port Blair

Port Blair

◎ Top Sights
1 Cellular Jail National Memorial D2

◎ Sights
2 Anthropological Museum C3
3 Chatham Saw Mill A1
4 Clock Tower C2
5 Samudrika Marine Museum B2

🛏 Sleeping
6 Aashiaanaa Rest Home C2
  Amina Lodge .... (see 7)
7 Azad Lodge C2
8 Da Bay Inn B1
9 Fortune Resort – Bay Island C2
10 Hotel Lalaji Bay View C2
11 Hotel Sinclairs Bayview D3
12 J Hotel C2

🍽 Eating
13 Annapurna C3
  Bayview .... (see 11)
  Excel Restaurant .... (see 10)
  Gagan Restaurant .... (see 4)
14 Lighthouse Residency C2
15 New Lighthouse Restaurant D2

🍷 Drinking & Nightlife
  Nico Bar .... (see 9)

ℹ Information
16 Andaman & Nicobar Tourism C3
17 Axis Bank ATM C3
  Axis Bank ATM .... (see 12)
18 Directorate of Shipping
    Information Office C2
  E-Cafe .... (see 4)
19 ICICI ATM C3
  Immigration Office .... (see 16)
  Island Travels .... (see 14)
20 State Bank of India C3

ℹ Transport
21 Bus Stand C2
22 Coastal Cruise C2
  Ferry Booking Office .... (see 18)
23 Saro Tours C2
24 Taxi & Autorickshaw Stand C3

Jarawa chest guard, a skull left in a Sentinelese lean-to, or the totemic spirits represented by Nicobarese shamanic sculptures.

Samudrika Marine Museum   MUSEUM
(Haddo Rd; adult/child ₹20/10, camera/video ₹20/50; ⊙9am-1pm & 2-5pm Tue-Sun) Run by

the Indian Navy, this museum has a diverse range of exhibits with informative coverage of the islands' ecosystem, tribal communities, plants, animals and marine life. Outside is a skeleton of a young blue whale washed ashore on the Nicobars.

Chatham Saw Mill
HISTORIC SITE

(admission ₹10; ⊙ 8.30am-2.30pm) Located on Chatham Island (reached by a road bridge), the saw mill was set up by the British in 1883 and was one of the largest wood processors in Asia. The mill is still operational, and while it may not be to everyone's taste, especially conservationists, it's an interesting insight to the island's history and economy. Look out for the bomb crater, left by Japanese ordnance in WWII.

Corbyn's Cove
BEACH

No one comes to Port Blair for the beach, but if you need a break from town, Corbyn's Cove has a small curve of sand backed by palms. The coastal road here is a scenic journey, and passes several Japanese WWII bunkers along the way. Located 7km south of town, an autorickshaw costs ₹200, or rent a scooter. Crocodiles are occasionally spotted.

🛏 Sleeping

Get in touch with the tourist office (p1091) for a list of homestay options in Port Blair.

★ Aashiaanaa Rest Home
GUESTHOUSE $

(☑ 09474217008; shads_maria@hotmail.com; Marine Hill; r without bathroom ₹300, with AC from ₹900; ❄ 🖥 🛜) Port Blair's most comfortable budget choice has homely rooms decked out in aquamarine and mauve, and a convenient location uphill from Phoenix Bay jetty. Most

have cable TV and reliable hot water, while pricier rooms get you a balcony and air-con. Staff can help with booking ferry tickets. Wi-fi is ₹60 per hour.

Hotel Lalaji Bay View
GUESTHOUSE $

(☑ 9476005820, 03192-236333; www.lalajibay-view.com; RP Rd; s/d ₹300/400, r with AC from ₹1200; ❄ 🖥 🛜) Backpacker HQ in Port Blair, this popular budget hotel is run by the friendly young entrepreneur Nirman (grandson of Lalaji from Long Island) who knows exactly what makes tourists tick. Rooms are cosy, spotless and have comfy beds, but it's the sociable rooftop restaurant-bar that brings people in, with (paid) wi-fi. It's just up from the mosque.

Amina Lodge
GUESTHOUSE $

(☑ 9933258703; aminalodge@ymail.com; MA Rd, Aberdeen Bazaar; s/d ₹450/600) Run by an entertaining couple, Amina has spotless rooms with TV and a handy, though noisy, location in the bazaar. Prices are fixed.

Azad Lodge
GUESTHOUSE $

(☑ 03192-242646; MA Rd, Aberdeen Bazaar; s/d without bathroom ₹200/300, d ₹500, r with AC ₹850) An old budget favourite with basic and clean rooms.

Da Bay Inn
HOTEL $$

(☑ 9647200473; Foreshore Rd; sea-facing r incl breakfast ₹3000) Overlooking the bay, this hotel is only recommended if you get one of the sea-facing rooms. Decor is garish, but otherwise a comfortable choice.

★ Hotel Sinclairs Bayview
HOTEL $$$

(☑ 03192-227824; www.sinclairshotels.com/portblair; South Point; s/d incl breakfast from

---

DON'T MISS

ROSS ISLAND
....

Just a 20-minute boat ride from Port Blair, visiting Ross Island (not to be confused with its namesake island in North Andaman) feels like discovering a jungle-clad Lost City, à la Angkor Wat, except here the ruins are Victorian English rather than ancient Khmer. The former administrative headquarters for the British in the Andamans, Ross Island in its day was fondly called the 'Paris of the East' (along with Pondicherry, Saigon etc etc...), but the cute title, vibrant social scene and tropical gardens were all wiped out by the double whammy of a 1941 earthquake and invasion by the Japanese.

Today the old English architecture is still standing, despite an invading wave of fast-growing jungle vegetation. Landscaped paths cross the island and most of the buildings are labelled. There's a small **museum** with historical displays and resident spotted deer. A sound-and-light show was also on the cards at the time of research.

Ferries to Ross Island (₹100, 20 minutes) depart hourly from Aberdeen Jetty behind the aquarium in Port Blair, between 8.30am and 2pm every day except Wednesday.

₹8100/8600; ❄ 🛜 ❄) Located on the road to Corbyn's Cove, 2km outside town, Sinclairs' large modern rooms open right out to the water. It has a nice seaside garden with hammocks to lounge in, and a Japanese WWII bunker onsite. Free airport transfer.

Fortune Resort – Bay Island   HOTEL $$$
(☑ 03192-234101; www.fortunehotels.in; Marine Hill; s/d incl breakfast from ₹7090/7630; ❄ 🛜 ❄) One of PB's finest, with lovely bay views, tropical garden, and modern rooms with polished floors; ask for one that's sea-facing.

J Hotel   HOTEL $$$
(☑ 03192-246000; www.jhotel.in; Aberdeen Bazaar; r incl breakfast from ₹4300; ❄ 🛜) A slick designer hotel in the heart of the bazaar, with modern rooms and chic rooftop restaurant. Lack of natural light is a downside until you remember the 5am sunrise!

✕ Eating & Drinking

⭐ Excel Restaurant   INTERNATIONAL, INDIAN $
(Hotel Lalaji Bay View, RP Rd; mains from ₹100; ☺ 7am-11pm; 🛜) This alluring bamboo rooftop restaurant above Hotel Lalaji Bay View (not to be confused with the seedy downstairs bar), brings a 'Havelock' menu to the city, with grilled fish, burgers, Israeli dishes etc. Wi-fi access (₹60 per hour) and a fully stocked bar makes it *the* place to hang out.

Gagan Restaurant   INDIAN $
(Clock Tower, Aberdeen Bazaar; mains from ₹90-200; ☺ 7am-10pm) Popular with locals, this hole-in-the-wall Bengali restaurant serves up great food at good prices, including Nicobari fish, crab curries, coconut chicken, and dosas for breakfast.

Annapurna   INDIAN $
(MG Rd; mains ₹100-150; ☺ 6.30am-10.30pm) An excellent veg option that looks like a high-school cafeteria and serves delicious dosas and rich North Indian–style curries.

Lighthouse Residency   SEAFOOD $$
(MA Rd; mains ₹80-800; ☺ 11am-11pm) Select your meal from the display of red snapper, crab or tiger prawns to barbecue (served with rice and chips), and head to its rooftop for a cold Kingfisher beer. There's a cheaper **second branch** (Marina Park; mains ₹80-400) in an outdoor shack near the water.

Bayview   MULTICUISINE $$$
(Hotel Sinclairs Bayview; mains ₹110-500; ☺ 11am-11pm) Right on the water with a lovely cool sea breeze, the Bayview is a top spot to grab lunch out of town.

Nico Bar   BAR
(Marine Hill; ☺ 11am-11pm) The closest you'll get to the Nicobars, Fortune Bay Hotel's bar is the spot for sea breezes and scenic views (the picture on the ₹20 note is based on this spot). A great place to while away an afternoon or balmy evening with a drink.

ℹ Information

There are several ATMs around town. You can find internet cafes, with wi-fi and computer terminals (₹40 per hour), in Aberdeen Bazaar near the clock tower.

Aberdeen Police Station (☑ 03192-232400; MG Rd)

Andaman & Nicobar Tourism (☑ 03192-232694; www.andamans.gov.in; Kamaraj Rd; ☺ 8.30am-1pm & 2-5pm) The main island tourist office has brochures and is the place to book permits for areas around Port Blair. Its website has useful info such as ferry schedules.

GB Pant Hospital (☑ emergency 03192-232102, 03192-233473; GB Pant Rd)

Island Travels (☑ 03192-233358; islandtravels@yahoo.com; Aberdeen Bazaar; ☺ 9am-1pm & 2-6pm Mon-Sat) Reliable travel agency for booking flights. Also has foreign-exchange facilities.

Main Post Office (MG Rd; ☺ 9am-7pm Mon-Sat)

State Bank of India (MA Rd; ☺ 9am-noon & 1-3pm Mon-Fri, 10am-noon Sat) Foreign currency can be changed here.

ℹ Getting There & Away

BOAT
Most interisland ferries depart from **Phoenix Bay Jetty**. Tickets can be purchased from its **ferry booking office** (☺ 9am-1pm & 2-4pm Mon-Fri, to noon Sat). Ferries can be pre-booked one to three days in advance; if they are sold out you can chance your luck with a same-day ticket issued an hour before departure from outside the ticket office at the end door. There's a **ferry information office** (☑ 03192-245555; Phoenix Bay Jetty; ☺ 5.30am-6.30pm) outside the ticket office for enquiries.

Ferries to Havelock (₹195, 2½ hours) depart daily at 6.20am, 11am, 1pm and 2pm; with several heading via Neil Island; all book out fast.

Otherwise there are private, pricier ferries. Makruzz (p1088) has daily departures to Havelock (₹975 to ₹1700, 1½ hours) at 8.15am and 2pm, which continue to Neil Island (₹1315 to ₹2224, 2½ hours). Tickets are available for the airport or travel agents in town. Coastal Cruise (p1088) heads to Neil Island (₹875 to ₹1200) via Havelock (₹875 to ₹1200) at 7.30am.

There are also daily boats to Little Andaman, which also regularly sell out, and several boats a week to Diglipur and Long Island.

New arrivals should make the jetty their first port of call to book tickets.

BUS

Government buses run all day from the **bus stand** at Aberdeen Bazaar to Wandoor (₹20, one hour) and Chiriya Tapu (₹20, one hour). Buses to Diglipur run at 4am (to Aerial Bay) and 7am (₹265, 12 hours), and 9.45am for Mayabunder (₹200, 10 hours) all via Rangat (₹160, six hours) and Baratang (₹190, three hours). More comfortable, but pricier, private buses have 'offices' (a guy with a ticket book) across from the main bus stand.

ⓘ Getting Around

TO & FROM THE AIRPORT

A taxi or autorickshaw from the airport to Aberdeen Bazaar costs around ₹100 for the 4km trip. There are also hourly buses (₹10) between the airport and main bus stand.

AUTORICKSHAW

Aberdeen Bazaar to Phoenix Bay Jetty is about ₹30, and to Haddo Jetty it's around ₹50.

MOTORBIKE

You can hire a scooter from various spots in Port Blair for around ₹400 per day. Try **Saro Tours** (☑ 9933291466; www.rentabikeandaman.com; Marine Rd).

Around Port Blair

There are eco-related volunteering opportunities around Port Blair. See the Volunteering chapter (p46).

Wandoor

Wandoor, a tiny speck of a village 29km southwest of Port Blair, is a good spot to see the interior of the island. It's best known as a jumping-off point for snorkelling at Mahatma Gandhi Marine National Park. Buses run from Port Blair to Wandoor (₹20, one hour).

🏃 Activities

Wandoor has a nice beach, though at the time of research, swimming was prohibited due to crocodiles.

Mahatma Gandhi Marine National Park SNORKELLING
(permit Indian/foreigner ₹50/500; ⊘ Tue-Sun) Popular with Indian tourists, the half-day snorkelling trips to Mahatma Gandhi Marine National Park are a good option for those wanting to get underwater while in Port Blair. The park comprises 15 islands of mangrove creeks, tropical rainforest and reefs supporting 50 types of coral and plenty of colourful fish. Boats depart 9am from Wandoor Jetty, costing ₹750 in addition to the ₹500 permit which you need to arrange at the tourist office (p1091) in Port Blair.

Depending upon the time of year, the marine park's snorkelling sites alternate between Jolly Buoy and Red Skin, allowing the other to regenerate.

🛏 Sleeping

Anugama Resort RESORT $$$
(☑ 03192-280068; www.anugamaresort.com; Wandoor; r with fan/AC incl breakfast ₹3000/3500; ❄🐾) Run by an enthusiastic Singaporean diver, Anugama has basic but comfortable cottages in a bucolic setting among forest and mud flats. It's a good spot for outdoor lovers with activities such as snorkelling, bike hire and nature walks exploring mangrove and intertidal zones.

Chiriya Tapu

Chiriya Tapu, 30km south of Port Blair, is a tiny village fringed by beaches and mangroves, and famous for celestial sunsets. It also has Munda Pahar Beach, popular with Indian day-trippers. Hourly buses head from Port Blair (₹20, one hour); the last bus back is at 6pm.

⊙ Sights & Activities

Chiriya Tapu Biological Park ZOO
(Indian/foreigner ₹20/50; ⊘9am-4pm Tue-Sun) A pleasant place to stroll in a forested setting with natural enclosures for indigenous species such as crab-eating macaques, Andaman wild pigs and salt-water crocs.

Diving

Dive companies based in Chiriya Tapu can arrange trips to Cinque and Rutland Islands, both known for their abundance of fish, colourful soft corals and excellent visibility. Cinque also has a blinding white sandbar beach. There's a WWII British minesweeper wreck dive too.

Lacadives DIVING
(☑ 03192-281013; www.lacadives.com; per dive Rutland Island ₹2000, Cinque Island ₹8000; ⊘Oct-May) Long-established Indian dive company, which can arrange budget diver accommodation. Boats carry up to 10 people.

Infinity Scuba DIVING
(✆ 03192-281183; www.infinityscubandamans.com; 2 dives incl lunch Rutland Island ₹3500, Cinque Island ₹4000) Set up by Baath, an ex-Navy commando, Infinity also arranges popular fishing and live-aboard trips.

🛏 Sleeping & Eating

⭐ **Wildgrass Resort** RESORT $$$
(✆ 9474204508; www.wildgrassresorts.com; r incl breakfast ₹4000; ❄) Run by the Infinity Scuba team, Wildgrass offers romantic cottages with an island ambience and lush jungle backdrop. It also has an atmospheric bamboo restaurant that's good for day-trippers.

Havelock Island

POP 5500

With snow-white beaches, teal shallows, a coast crammed with beach huts and some of the best diving in South Asia, Havelock has a well-deserved reputation as a backpacker paradise. For many, Havelock *is* the Andamans, and it's what lures most tourists across the Bay of Bengal, many of whom are content to stay here for the whole trip.

◉ Sights & Activities

Beaches

Radhanagar BEACH
(Beach 7) One of India's prettiest and most famous stretches of sand is the critically acclaimed Radhanagar. It's a beautiful curve of sugar fronted by perfectly spiraled waves, all backed by native forest. It's on the northwestern side of the island, about 12km from the jetty. Late afternoon is the best time to visit to avoid the heat and crowds, as well as for its sunset.

Neils Cove BEACH
Northwest of Radhanagar is the gorgeous 'lagoon' at Neils Cove, another gem of sheltered sand and crystalline water. Swimming is prohibited at dusk and dawn; take heed of any warnings regarding crocodiles.

Beach 5 BEACH
On the north-eastern coast of the island, the palm-ringed Beach 5 has your more classic tropical vibe, with the bonus of shady patches and fewer sandflies. Swimming is difficult at low tide when the water becomes shallow. Most accommodation is out this way.

Kalapathar BEACH
Hidden away 5km south of Beach 5, you'll find the low-key Kalapathar, a pristine beach. You'll have to walk a bit to get away from package tourists.

Diving & Snorkelling

Havelock is the premier spot for diving in the Andamans. It's world renowned for its crystal-clear waters, corals, schools of fish, turtles and kaleidoscope of colourful marine life. Diving here is suitable for all levels.

The main dive season is roughly November to April, but trips run year-round.

All companies offer fully equipped boat dives, and prices vary depending on the location, number of participants and duration of the course. Diving starts from around ₹5000 for a two-tank dive, with options of Discover Scuba (one hour ₹4500), PADI open-water (four dives ₹21,700) and advanced (three dives ₹13,500) courses.

While coral bleaching has been a major issue since 2010 (mainly due to El Niño weather patterns), diving remains world-class. The shallows may not have bright corals, but all the colourful fish are still here, and for depths beyond 16m, corals remain as vivid as ever. The Andamans recovered from a similar bleaching in 1998, and today things are likewise slowly repairing themselves.

Popular sites are **Dixon's Pinnacle** and **Pilot Reef** with colourful soft coral, **South Button** for macro dives (to see small critters) and rock formations, **Jackson Bar** or **Johhny's Gorge** for deeper dives with schools of snapper, sharks, rays and turtles, and **Minerva's Delight** for a bit of everything. There's also a **wreck dive** to SS *Inchcket*, a 1950s cargo carrier. Keep an eye out for trips further afield such as **Barren Island**, home to India's only active volcano, whose ash produces an eerie underwater spectacle for divers.

Dive companies can arrange **snorkelling** trips, but it's cheaper to organise a boat through your guesthouse. Snorkelling gear is widely available on Havelock but is generally low quality.

Most boats head to **Elephant Beach** for snorkelling, which can also be reached by a 40-minute walk through a muddy elephant logging trail; it's well marked (off the cross-island road), but turns to bog if it's been raining. At high tide it's also impossible to reach – ask locally for more info. Lots of snorkelling charters, and even jet skis, come out this way, so be prepared as it can be a bit of a circus. If you head here around 6am, you'll have the place to yourself.

Prices are standardised, so find a dive operator you feel comfortable with.

Havelock Island

Andaman Bubbles DIVING
(☎03192-282140; www.andamanbubbles.com; No 5 Village) Quality outfit with professional staff.

Barefoot Scuba DIVING
(☎9566088560; www.diveandamans.com; No 3 Village) Popular, long-established company with budget dive-accommodation packages.

Dive India DIVING
(☎9932082205; www.diveindia.com; btwn No 3 & 5 Village) The original PADI company in Havelock, and still one of the best.

Ocean Tribe DIVING
(☎03192-210004; www.ocean-tribe.com; No 3 Village) Run by legendary local Karen divers, including Dixon, Johnny and Jackson, all who have had dive sites named after them.

Other Activities
Most come to Havelock for lazing on the beach, diving or snorkelling.

Some resorts can organise guided **jungle treks** for keen walkers or birdwatchers, but be warned the forest floor turns to glug after rain. The inside rainforest is a spectacular, emerald-coloured hinterland cavern, and the **birdwatching** – especially on the forest fringes – is rewarding; look out for the blue-black racket-tailed drongo or golden oriole.

Yoga (per 1½ hours, ₹500) is available during season at Flying Elephant (p1095).

Captain Hook's FISHING
(☎9434280543; www.andamansportsfishing.com; Beach 3; half-/full day for 2 people incl lunch from ₹6000/20,000) Sport fishing is growing in popularity, with Captain Hook's running catch-and-release fishing trips where you can reel in giant trevally, and kayaking trips.

Andaman Kayak Tours KAYAKING
(☎9933269653; www.andamankayaktours.com; 2½hr cruise ₹2500) Tours explore Havelock's mangroves by sea kayak, and runs memorable

Havelock Island

night trips gliding among bio-luminescence. Minimum two people.

⊨ Sleeping

Orient Legend Resort GUESTHOUSE $
(☑03192-282389; Beach 5; hut without bathroom ₹300-500, r with bathroom ₹800-2000, with AC ₹3000) This popular place on Beach 5 covers most budgets, from doghouse A-frame huts and concrete rooms to double-storey cottages.

Coconut Grove GUESTHOUSE $
(☑9474269977; hut ₹400, without bathroom ₹300; ✱) Popular with Israeli travellers, Coconut Grove has an appealing communal vibe with psychedelic-painted huts arranged in a circular outlay.

Sea View Beach Resort BUNGALOW $
(☑943429877; Beach 2; r ₹600-1000) Chilled out beach bungalows, backing on to the Ocean Tribe dive shop, offer the quintessential Havelock experience away from the crowds.

Dreamland Resort GUESTHOUSE $
(☑9474224164; Beach 7; hut without bathroom ₹400) In a prime location, only 50m from Beach 7, Dreamland is an old backpacker favourite now popular with Indian families.

Pellicon Beach Resort BUNGALOW $
(☑9932081673; www.pelliconbeachresort.com; Beach 5; hut from ₹500) Attractive beachside bungalows as well as Nicobari huts with private porches on a peaceful plot of land close to the beach.

Sunrise Beach Resort BUNGALOW $
(☑9474206183; Beach 6; r ₹600-1000, with AC ₹4000) Offers the same thatched goodness as every other resort on Havelock – what sets it apart is its budget A-frame huts with water views. Has a bar too.

★ **Emerald Gecko** BUNGALOW $$
(☑9474250821; www.emerald-gecko.com; Beach 5; hut ₹1600-3200) On an island where very little thought goes into design, Emerald Gecko stands miles ahead. Double-storey bungalows look to the water, while pricier rooms have ambient lighting and outdoor bathrooms all lovingly constructed from bamboo rafts drifted ashore from Myanmar. It has one of Havelock's best restaurants (BYO alcohol), friendly staff and free filtered water.

Wild Orchid RESORT $$$
(☑03192-282472; www.wildorchidandaman. com; Beach 5; r incl breakfast from ₹5600; ✱@🕏) One of the Andamans' premier resorts, with modern and thoughtfully furnished Andamanese-style cottages, all set around a fabulous tropical garden.

Barefoot at Havelock RESORT $$$
(☑044-24341001; www.barefootindia.com; Beach 7; tented cottage incl breakfast ₹5050, Nicobari cottage ₹8920, with AC ₹11,820; ✱) Luxurious resort boasting beautifully designed timber and bamboo-thatched cottages just back from the famed Radhanagar Beach.

Flying Elephant BUNGALOW, RETREAT $$$
(☑9474250821; www.flying-elephant.in; Kalapathar; r ₹4000) Hidden away on Kalapathar beach, in a pastoral setting among rice paddies and betel palms, this yoga and meditation retreat has elegant bamboo duplexes with outdoor stone-garden bathrooms.

ANDAMAN ISLANDS HAVELOCK ISLAND

Symphony Palms Beach Resort RESORT $$$
(📞 03192-214315; www.symphonypalmshavelock.
com; Beach 5; r incl breakfast from ₹10,000; ❄)
Only recommended for its seaside luxury
rooms (not the resort across the road), Sym-
phony Palms is like an upmarket version of
Havelock's bungalow resorts. It has a private
beach with sun lounges.

✖ Eating & Drinking

There are *dhabas* (snack bars) near the
jetty or head to the main bazaar (No 3
Village) for local meals. Alcohol is available
from a **store** (Beach 3; ⊙8am-noon & 3-8pm)
next to the ATM at No 3 Village.

Welcome Restaurant INDIAN, SEAFOOD $
(No 3 Village; mains from ₹150; ⊙7.30am-9pm) In
the market, this eatery does delicious sea-
food curries and prawn rolls with *parathas*.

Rony's INDIAN $
(Beach 5; mains ₹110-250; ⊙7am-11pm) Popular
family-run place serving up seafood curries,
pizzas and other backpacker favs.

Fat Martin's SOUTH INDIAN $
(Beach 5; mains ₹60-120; ⊙7.30am-10pm)
Squeaky-clean open-air cafe with a good se-
lection of chapati rolls and dosas, including
paneer tikka and nutella dosas.

★ Red Snapper SEAFOOD, MULTICUISINE $$
(Wild Orchid; mains ₹250-900; ⊙7.30-10am, noon-
2.30pm & 6-9.30pm) Easily Havelock's best
restaurant and bar, with its atmospheric
polished-bamboo decor and thatched-roof
exuding a romantic island ambience. Pick
from lavish seafood platters, BBQ fish and
handmade pastas, accompanied by delicious
cheese-and-olive naan. The breezy outdoor
deck seating is a good spot for a beer.

Anju-coco Resto INDIAN, CONTINENTAL $$
(Beach 5; mains ₹200-900; ⊙8am-10.30pm) One
of Havelock's best, Anju-coco offers a varied
menu, with standouts being its big break-
fasts and BBQ fish.

Full Moon Cafe MULTICUISINE $$
(Dive India, Beach 5; mains ₹200-450; 🍃) Run by
an Irish-Indian couple, this busy thatched-
roof restaurant shares a site with Dive India on Beach 5. It does excellent seafood,
healthy salads and refreshing cardamom
lime fizzes. Free water refills.

B3 – Barefoot Bar & Restaurant PIZZERIA $$
(Village No 1; mains ₹200-900; ⊙11am-3.30pm &
6-9pm) Modern decor with cult movie post-
ers on the walls, B3 has a Western-heavy
menu, with the best pizzas in Havelock.
Its outside decking makes it a good place
to wait for your ferry. There's no alcohol.
Downstairs has the sophisticated **Dakshin**
(Village No 1; mains ₹80-150; ⊙6-10am & 11.30-
3pm), specialising in South Indian cuisine.

Cicada LIVE MUSIC
(Beach 5) Run by the team from Emerald
Gecko, this live music venue has an appeal-
ing jungle location accessed down a path off
the main road across from Beach 5.

ℹ Information

There are two ATMs side by side in No 3 Village.
Satellite internet is insanely slow and pricey at
around ₹300 per hour.

Havelock Tourist Service (Beach 3;
⊙9.30am-8pm) A private operator which can
arrange air tickets, info for government and
private ferries, and sundries for tourists.

ℹ Getting There & Away

Government ferries run from Havelock to Port
Blair three times a day (₹378, 2½ hours) at
9am, 2pm and 4pm. You're best to book tickets
from the **jetty** (⊙9.15am-noon & 2-4pm Mon-
Fri, to noon Sat) at least two days in advance
(most hotels can arrange this for a fee). One to
two ferries a day link Havelock with Neil Island
(₹378, one hour 10 minutes), while four boats a
week head to Long Island (₹378, two hours) en
route to Rangat.

Makruzz (p1088) and Coastal Cruise (p1088)
have daily services to Port Blair via Neil Island.

ℹ Getting Around

A local bus (₹10, 40 minutes) connects the jetty,
villages and Radhanagar on a roughly hourly
circuit until 6pm. You can rent a scooter (per 24
hours from ₹250) or bicycle (per day ₹60).

An autorickshaw from the jetty to No 3 Village
is ₹50, to No 5 ₹80 and to No 7 ₹500.

Neil Island

Happy to laze in the shadows of its more fa-
mous island neighbour, tranquil Neil is still
the place for that added bit of relaxation. Its
beaches may not be as luxurious as Have-
lock's, but they have ample character and
are a perfect distance apart to explore by
bicycle; cycling through picturesque villag-
es you'll get many friendly hellos. The main
bazaar has a mellow vibe and is a popular
gathering spot in the early evening. In Neil
Island you're about 40km from Port Blair, a
short ferry ride from Havelock, and several
universes away from life at home.

◉ Sights & Activitieses

Neil Island's five beaches (numbered one to five) all have their unique charms, though they aren't necessarily great for swimming.

Beach 1   BEACH
(Laxmanpur) Beach 1 is a long sweep of sandy beach and mangrove, a 40-minute walk west of the jetty and village. There's a good sunset viewpoint out this way accessed via Pearl Park Beach Resort (p1097). Dugongs are sometime spotted here.

Beach 2   BEACH
On the north side of the island, Beach 2 has the Natural Bridge rock formation, accessible only at low tide by walking around the rocky cove. To get here by bicycle, take the side road that runs through the bazaar, then take a left where the road forks.

Beach 3   BEACH
(RamNagar) Beach 3 is a secluded powdery sand and rocky cove, which is best accessed via Blue Sea restaurant (p1098). There's also good snorkelling here.

Beach 4   BEACH
(Bharatpur) The best swimming beach, though its proximity to the jetty is a turn-off, as are rowdy day-trippers who descend upon the beach in motorised boats.

Beach 5   BEACH
(Sitapur) The more rugged Beach 5, 5km from the village on the eastern side of Neil, is a nice place to walk along the sand, with small limestone caves accessible at low tide.

Diving & Snorkelling

Neil Island offers some excellent dive sites, with colourful fish, large schools of Jack, turtles, sharks, rays, and soft and hard corals.

The island's best snorkelling is around the coral reef at the far (western) end of Beach 1 at high tide; if you're extremely lucky you may spot a dugong feeding in the shallows at high tide. Beach 3 also has good snorkelling. Gear costs around ₹150 to hire and available from many guesthouses.

There are two dive operators on Neil Island. Those interested in free diving can contact Sanjay at Gayan Garden (p1097).

India Scuba Explorers   DIVING
(☑ 9474238646; www.indiascubaexplorers.com; Beach 1; per 1/2 dives ₹3000/5000) Neil's first dive shop set up by a young husband-wife team is popular for its personalised service.

Dive India   DIVING
(☑ 8001222206; www.diveindia.com/neil.html; per 1/2 dives ₹3000/5000) Established in Havelock, this professional company has recently opened here.

🛏 Sleeping

These days Beach 3 and 5 are the most popular with backpackers. Beach 1 attracts package tourists, but still has excellent choices.

🛏 Beach 1

Sunset Garden Guesthouse   BUNGALOW $
(☑ 9933294573; Beach 1; hut ₹250-400) Ideal for those wanting to get away from it all, these bamboo huts are in a secluded spot accessed via a 15-minute walk through rice fields.

Gayan Garden   BUNGALOW $
(Beach 1; r ₹300) Bamboo cottages halfway between the bazaar and Beach 1 with a relaxed garden, seafood restaurant and filtered coffee. Offers cooking classes too.

Tango Beach Resort   HOTEL $
(☑ 9474212842; www.tangobeachandaman. com; Beach 1; hut ₹500, cottage with fan/AC from ₹1200/4000; ❄) Famous for its sea breeze, this Beach 1 classic is pricier than most, but its sea-facing rooms are still a fine choice.

Pearl Park Beach Resort   BUNGALOW $$
(☑ 9434260132; www.andamanpearlpark.com; Beach 1; s/d incl breakfast with fan from ₹1500/1800, with AC from ₹2500/3200; ❄🐾) Neil's original bamboo-bungalow 'resort' now caters more for domestic tourists and is grossly overpriced, but it still has pleasant huts arranged around a flower-filled garden.

Seashell   RESORT $$$
(☑ 9933239625; www.seashellneil.com; Beach 1; cottage incl breakfast ₹8590) Upmarket tented cottages leading down to the beach.

🛏 Beach 3

★ Kalapani   BUNGALOW $
(☑ 9474274991; Beach 3; hut ₹400, without bathroom ₹200) Run by the delightful Prakash and Bina, laid-back Kalapani has blissfully simple and clean bungalows with quality mattresses. Motorbikes, bicycles and snorkelling gear are available for hire.

Breakwater Beach Resort   BUNGALOW $
(☑ 9933292654; www.neilislandaccommodation. in; Beach 3; hut ₹500-1000, without bathroom ₹300) Wins rave reviews for its chilled-out ambience and delicious food.

📖 Beach 5

Sunrise Beach Resort BUNGALOW $
(📞 9933266900; Beach 5; r without bathroom ₹200-400) Thatched and concrete bungalows a one-minute walk from the beach.

Emerald Gecko BUNGALOW $$
(Beach 5; r ₹1000-3000) Still under construction when we visited, but if it's anything close to its sister guesthouse in Havelock (p1095), it'll be a wonderful addition to Neil.

✕ Eating

Moonshine INTERNATIONAL, INDIAN $
(Beach 1; mains ₹90-250) On the road to Beach 1, this backpacker favourite has excellent homemade pastas, fish thalis and cold beer.

Blue Sea SEAFOOD, INDIAN $
(Beach 3; mains from ₹100; ⊙ 6am-11pm) Old-school beach shack with sandy floor, dangling beach curios and a blue whale skull centrepiece, serving all the usual dishes. The path here leads to arguably Neil's best beach.

Chand Restaurant INDIAN, CONTINENTAL $
(Bazaar; mains ₹70-200; ⊙ 6am-10.30pm) The best place in the market with a good mix of international and Indian dishes, strong filtered coffee and delicious seafood.

ℹ Information

There's no ATM or moneychanging facilities on Neil, so bring plenty of cash. There's wi-fi access at Pearl Park Beach Resort (p1097) on Beach 1 for ₹200 per 24 hours.

ℹ Getting There & Around

A ferry heads to Port Blair two or three times a day (₹378, two hours). There are also one or two daily ferries to Havelock (₹378, one hour), and three ferries a week to Long Island (₹378, five hours). Makruzz (p1088) and Coastal Cruise (p1088) also have ferries to/from Port Blair (from ₹875, one hour) and Havelock (from ₹710).

Hiring a bicycle (per day from ₹80) is the best way to get about; roads are flat and distances short. You'll be able to find one in the bazaar or at a guesthouse. An autorickshaw will take you from the jetty to Beach 1 or 3 for ₹70 to ₹100.

Middle & North Andaman

The Andamans aren't just sun and sand. They are also jungle that feels as primeval as the Jurassic, a green tangle of ancient forest that could have been birthed in Mother Nature's subconscious. This wild, antediluvian side of the islands can be seen on a long bus ride up the Andaman Trunk Rd (ATR), crossing tannin-red rivers prowled by saltwater crocodiles on roll-on, roll-off ferries.

But there's a negative side to riding the ATR: the road cuts through the homeland of the Jarawa (p1099) and has brought the tribe into incessant contact with the outside world. Modern India and tribal life do not seem able to coexist – every time Jarawa and settlers interact, misunderstandings have led to friction, confusion and, at worst, violent attacks and death. Indian anthropologists and indigenous rights groups such as Survival International have called for the ATR to be closed; its status continues to be under review. At present, vehicles are permitted to travel only in convoys at set times from 6am to 3pm. Photography is strictly prohibited, as is stopping or any other interaction with the Jarawa people who are becoming increasingly reliant on handouts from passing traffic.

The first place of interest north of Port Blair are the **limestone caves** (⊙ Tue-Sun) at Baratang. It's a 45-minute boat trip (₹450) from the jetty, a scenic trip through mangrove forest. A permit is required, organised at the jetty.

Rangat & Around

Rangat is the next main town, a transport hub with not much else going for it. If you do get stuck here, UK Nest has clean budget rooms, while Priya International is a more upmarket choice with handy tourist information on things to do in the area. There's an ATM nearby. The turtle breeding grounds at **Dhaninallah Mangrove** is the most popular sight, viewed early evening (mid-December to April) from the 1km-long boardwalk, a 45-minute drive from Rangat.

Ferries depart Long Island (₹11) from Yeratta Jetty, 8km from Rangat, at 9am and 3.30pm. Rangat Bay, 5km outside town, has ferries to/from Port Blair (₹378, six hours) and Havelock (₹378, two hours). A daily bus goes to Port Blair (₹145, seven hours) and Diglipur (₹65, four hours).

Long Island

With its friendly island community and lovely slow pace of life, Long Island is perfect for those wanting to take the pace down a few more notches. Other than the odd

ISLAND INDIGENES

The Andaman and Nicobar Islands' indigenous peoples constitute 12% of the population and, in most cases, their numbers are decreasing. The Onge, Sentinelese, Andamanese and Jarawa are all of Negrito ethnicity, and share a strong resemblance to people from Africa. Tragically, numerous groups have become extinct over the past century. In February 2010 the last speaker of the Bo language passed away, bringing an end to a culture and language that originated 65,000 years ago.

The *Land of the Naked People* (2003) by Madhusree Mukerjee provides an interesting anthropological account. It's important to note that these ethnic groups live in areas strictly off limits to foreigners, and people have been arrested for trying to visit these areas.

Jarawa

The 250 remaining Jarawa occupy the 639-sq-km reserve on South and Middle Andaman Islands (p1098). In 1953 the chief commissioner requested that an armed sea plane bomb Jarawa settlements, and their territory has been consistently disrupted by the Andaman Trunk Rd, forest clearance and settler and tourist encroachment. In 2012, a video went viral showing an exchange between Jarawa and tourists, whereby a policeman orders them to dance in exchange for food. This resulted in a government inquest that saw to the end of the so-called 'human safari' tours.

Nicobarese

The 30,000 Nicobarese are the only indigenous people whose numbers are not decreasing. The majority have converted to Christianity and been partly assimilated into contemporary Indian society. Living in village units led by a head man, they farm pigs and cultivate coconuts, yams and bananas. The Nicobarese, who probably descended from people of Malaysia and Myanmar, inhabit a number of islands in the Nicobar group, centred on Car Nicobar, the region worst affected by the 2004 tsunami.

Onge

Two-thirds of Little Andaman's Onge Island was taken over by the Forest Department and 'settled' in 1977. The 100 or so remaining members of the Onge tribe live in a 25-sq-km reserve covering Dugong Creek and South Bay. Anthropologists say the Onge population has declined due to demoralisation through loss of territory.

Sentinelese

The Sentinelese, unlike the other tribes on these islands, have consistently repelled outside contact. For years, contact parties arrived on the beaches of North Sentinel Island with gifts of coconuts, bananas, pigs and red plastic buckets, only to be showered with arrows, though some encounters have been a little less hostile. About 150 Sentinelese remain.

Andamanese

As they now number only about 50, it seems impossible the Andamanese can escape extinction. There were around 7000 Andamanese in the mid-19th century, but friendliness to colonisers was their undoing, and by 1971 all but 19 of the population had been swept away by measles, syphilis and influenza epidemics. They have been resettled on Strait Island.

Shompen

Only about 250 Shompen remain in the forests on Great Nicobar. Seminomadic hunter-gatherers who live along the riverbanks, they have resisted integration.

ANDAMAN ISLANDS MIDDLE & NORTH ANDAMAN

motorcycle, there's no motorised vehicles on the island, and at certain times you may be the only tourist here.

◎ Sights & Activities

Beaches

There's a nice beach close to Blue Planet (p1100), reached via the yellow arrows.

Lalaji Bay   BEACH

A 1½-hour trek in the jungle will lead you to the secluded Lalaji Bay, a beautiful white-sand beach with good swimming and snorkelling; follow the red arrows to get here. Hiring a *dunghi* (motorised boat; ₹2500 return for two persons) is also an option. Inconveniently, you need a permit (free) from the Forest Office near the jetty to visit.

Diving & Snorkelling

Blue Planet (p1100) has a dive shop (December to March), charging ₹4000 for two dives, and visits Campbell Shoal for its schools of trevally and barracuda.

You can also get a *dunghi* to North Passage Island for snorkelling at the stunning **Merk Bay** (₹3500 for two people) with blinding white sand and translucent waters.

There's excellent offshore **snorkelling** at Lalaji Bay with colourful corals out front from the rest huts. There's also good snorkelling at the 'Blue Planet' beach, directly out from the blue Hindu temple; swim beyond the sea grass to get to the coral. Blue Planet hires snorkelling gear for ₹100.

🛏 Sleeping

⭐ **Blue Planet** GUESTHOUSE $
(☎ 9474212180; www.blueplanetandamans.com; r from ₹1500, without bathroom ₹500; @) The only place to stay on the island, so fortunately it's a gem, with thatched-bamboo rooms and hammocks set around a lovely Padauk tree. Food is delicious and there's free filtered water. It's a 15-minute walk from the jetty; follow the blue arrow markers. It also has wonderful double-storey bamboo cottages (from ₹3000) at a nearby location.

ℹ Getting There & Away

There are four ferries a week to Havelock, Neil and Port Blair (₹195). From Yeratta, there are two daily boats to Long Island (₹11, one hour) at 9am and 3.30pm, returning at 7am and 2pm. A bus meets ferries at Yeratta. If you can't get a ferry here from Port Blair, jump on a bus to Rangat to get the ferry from Yeratta.

Diglipur & Around

Those who make it this far north are rewarded with some impressive attractions in the area. It's a giant outdoor adventure playground designed for nature lovers: home to a world-famous turtle nesting site, Andaman's highest peak and a network of caves to go with white-sand beaches and some of the best snorkelling in the Andamans.

However, don't expect much of Diglipur (population 70,000), the second largest town in the Andamans, a sprawling, gritty bazaar town with an ATM and internet access (per hour ₹40). Instead head straight for the tranquil coastal village of **Kalipur**.

Ferries and some buses arrive at **Aerial Bay**, from where it's 11km to Diglipur, and 8km to Kalipur in the other direction.

🏃 Activities

Diglipur has huge tourist potential, and those who hang around will have plenty to discover. In season most come to see the turtles (p1101). Get in touch with Pristine Beach Resort (p1101), who are involved with the DARTED grassroots tourist initiative to promote Alfred Caves, mud volcanoes and crocodile habitats.

MAYABUNDER & AROUND

In 'upper' Middle Andaman, Mayabunder is most famous for its villages inhabited by Karen, members of a Burmese hill tribe who were relocated here during the British colonial period. It's a low-key destination for travellers looking for an experience away from the crowds.

You can go on a range of day tours, with the highlight being jungle trekking at creepy **Interview Island** (boat hire ₹3000, up to six people), inhabited by a population of 36 wild elephants, descendants of working elephants released after a logging company closed in the 1950s. You'll feel very isolated here. Armed guards accompany you in case of elephant encounters. A permit (₹500) is required, which is best organised by emailing a copy of your arrival permit to Sea'n'Sand guesthouse. Other trips include **turtle nesting** at Dhaninallah Mangrove; **Forty One Caves**, where *hawabills* (swiftlets) make their highly prized edible nests; and snorkelling off **Avis Island** (boat hire ₹1500).

Sea'n'Sand (☎ 03192-273454; titusinseansand@yahoo.com; r from ₹750; ❀) is easily the best place to stay with comfortable rooms. Hosts Titus and Elizabeth (and their extended Karen family) are an excellent source for everything Mayabunder. Go the top level for water views. The food here is sensational.

Mayabunder, 71km north of Rangat (₹70, two hours), is linked by daily buses from Port Blair (₹200, 10 hours) and Diglipur (₹55, two hours) and by thrice-weekly ferries. There's an ATM here.

Ross & Smith Islands   BEACH, SNORKELLING
(⊘ closed Tue) Like lovely tropical counter-weights, the twin islands of Smith and Ross are connected by a narrow sandbar of dazzling white sand, and are up there with the best in the Andamans for both swimming and snorkelling. No permits are required for Smith Island, which is accessed by boat (₹2500, fits five people) from Aerial Bay. While theoretically you need a permit for Ross Island (₹500), as it's walkable from Smith permits generally aren't checked. Enquire with Pristine Resort for more info.

Ross and Smith are closed Tuesday for beach cleaning; volunteers are welcome (₹250, covering permit, transport and food).

Saddle Peak   TREKKING
(Indian/foreigner ₹25/250) At 732m Saddle Peak is the highest point in the Andamans. You can trek through subtropical forest to the top and back from Kalipur in about six to seven hours; the views from the peaks onto the archipelago are incredible. It's a demanding trek, so bring plenty of water (around 4L). A permit (₹250) is required from the Forest Office at the trailhead, open 6am to 2pm. A local guide (300₹) will make sure you don't get lost, but otherwise follow the red arrows marked on the trees.

Craggy Island   SNORKELLING
A small island off Kalipur, Craggy is a good spot for snorkelling. Strong swimmers can make it across (flippers recommended), otherwise a *dunghi* is available (₹2500 return).

Excelsior Island   SNORKELLING
Recently opened for tourism, Excelsior has beautiful beaches, snorkelling plus resident spotted deer. Permits are required (₹500); boats cost ₹4500 and fit seven people.

🛏 Sleeping & Eating

⭐ **Pristine Beach Resort**   GUESTHOUSE $
(📱9474286787;   www.andamanpristineresorts.com; hut ₹600-1000, r ₹3000-4500; ✴@) Huddled among the palms between paddy fields and the beach, this relaxing resort has simple bamboo huts, more romantic bamboo 'tree houses' and upmarket rooms. Its attractive restaurant-bar serves up delicious fish Nicobari and cold beer. Alex, the superfriendly owner, is a top source of information. It also rents bicycles/motorcycles (per day ₹100/250) and snorkelling gear (₹100).

TURTLE NESTING IN KALIPUR
∙∙∙∙∙∙∙∙∙∙∙∙∙∙∙∙∙∙∙∙∙∙∙∙∙∙∙∙∙∙∙∙∙∙∙∙∙∙
Reputedly the only beach in the world where leatherback, hawksbill, olive ridley marine and green turtles all nest along the same coastline, Kalipur is a fantastic place to observe this evening show from mid-December and April. Turtles can be witnessed most nights, and you can assist with collecting eggs, or with the release of hatchlings. Contact Pristine Beach Resort (p1101).

The Dhaninallah Mangrove boardwalk north of Rangat is another good spot to see turtles.

Sion   INDIAN $
(Diglipur; mains ₹60-150; ⊘10am-10pm) If you have time to kill in Diglipur, this rooftop restaurant serving excellent seafood dishes is the place to head.

ℹ Getting There & Around

Diglipur, located about 80km north of Mayabunder, is served by daily buses to Port Blair (₹255, 12 hours) at 5am, 7am and a 10.40pm night bus. There are also buses to Mayabunder (₹55, 2½ hours) and Rangat (₹100, 4½ hours).

Ferries to Port Blair (seat/bunk ₹110/350, nine hours) depart three times a week.

Buses run the 18km journey from Diglipur to Kalipur (₹15, 30 mintues) every 45 minutes; an autorickshaw costs ₹200.

Little Andaman

As far south as you can go in the islands, Little Andaman has an appealing end-of-the-world feel. It's a gorgeous fist of mangroves, jungle and teal, ringed by beaches as fresh as bread out of the oven. It rates as many traveller's favourite spot in the Andamans.

Badly hit by the 2004 tsunami, Little Andaman has slowly rebuilt itself. Located about 120km south of Port Blair, the main settlement here is **Hut Bay**, a pleasant small town with smiling Bengalis and Tamils.

👁 Sights & Activities

Little Andaman Lighthouse   LIGHTHOUSE
Located 14km east of Hut Bay, Little Andaman lighthouse makes for a worthwhile excursion. Exactly 200 steps spiral

up to magnificent views over the coastline and forest. The easiest way to get here is by motorcycle. Otherwise take a sweaty bicycle journey or autorickshaw until the road becomes unpassable; from there, walk for an hour along the blissful stretch of deserted beach.

Beaches

Come prepared for sandflies (p1086); crocodiles are also about.

Butler Bay   BEACH

(entry ₹20) Little Andaman's best beach is Butler Bay, a spectacular curve with lifeguards and good surf at the 14km mark.

Netaji Nagar   BEACH

The sprawling and rugged Netaji Nagar, stretching 8km to 12km north of Hut Bay, is where most accommodation is located. The downside is the occasional rubbish that washes ashore from Thailand and Myanmar.

Kalapathar   BEACH

Located before Butler Bay is Kalapathar lagoon, a popular enclosed swimming area with shady patches of sand. Look for the cave in the cliff face that you can scramble through for stunning ocean views. It's accessed via a side road that runs past modern housing constructed after the 2004 tsunami.

Surfing

Intrepid surfing travellers have been whispering about Little Andaman since it first opened to foreigners several years ago. The reef breaks are legendary, but best suited for more experienced surfers. The most accessible is Jarawa Point, a left reef break on Butler Bay. Beginners should stick to beach breaks along Km8 to Km11. February to April brings the best waves.

Surfing Little Andaman   SURFING

(☑ 9933269762; www.surfinglittleandaman.com; Hut Bay; board rental half-/full day ₹500/900, 2hr lesson ₹1000) Run by Basque surfer Varuna, here you can hire boards, arrange lessons and get the lowdown on everything about surfing in Little Andaman.

Waterfalls

Inland, the White Surf and Whisper Wave waterfalls offer a jungle experience for when you're done lazing on the beach. The latter involves a 4km forest trek and a guide is highly recommended. They are pleasant falls and you may be tempted to swim in the rock pools, but beware of crocodiles.

🛏 Sleeping & Eating

There are cheap thali places in town. No guesthouses serve alcohol, but you can stock up from a 'wine shop' in Hut Bay. Accommodation options are across from the beach.

⭐ Blue View   BUNGALOW $

(☑ 9734480840; www.blueviewresort.net; Km11.5, Netaji Nagar; r without bathroom ₹200-500; ☺ Oct-May) Blue View's simple thatched bungalows are still the pick, mainly for the legendary hospitality of Azad and his lovely wife Papia. Food here is amazing, and surfboards and bicycles/motorbikes (per day ₹50/300) are available for hire.

Aastha Eco Resort   BUNGALOW $

(Km10, Netaji Nagar; r ₹200-400) Set among betel and coconut palms, Aastha has the best rooms on the island with its atmospheric Nicobari huts and comfortable thatched cottages, all with clean bathrooms.

Hawwa Beach Resort   BUNGALOW $

(☑ 9775181290; Km8, Netaji Nagar; s/d ₹300/400) This laid-back, family-run resort has five pink cottages with quality mattresses and spotless attached bathrooms.

Hotel Sea Land   HOTEL $

(☑ 9679534673; Hut Bay; s/d ₹300/500, with AC ₹800) Sea Land offers comfortable, air-con concrete rooms, but lacks atmosphere.

Palm Groove   INDIAN $

(Hut Bay; mains ₹60-135; ☺ 7am-9pm) Attractive heritage-style bungalow where a good selection of biriyanis and thalis can be had in the outdoor garden gazebo.

ℹ Information

There's an ATM in Hut Bay and village at 16Km, but no internet.

ℹ Getting There & Around

Ferries land at Hut Bay Jetty. Buses (₹10, depart hourly) to Netaji Nagar usually coincide with ferry arrivals, but often leaves before you clear immigration, leaving pricey jeeps (per person ₹100) as the other option. An autorickshaw from the jetty to Netaji Nagar is ₹250, or ₹70 to town. Motorbikes and bicycles are popular for getting around, and are available from most lodges; otherwise, shared jeeps (₹20) and buses are handy.

Boats sail to Port Blair daily, alternating between afternoon and evening departures on vessels ranging from big ferries with four-/two-bed rooms (₹230/320, six to 8½ hours) to faster 5½-hour government boats (₹35); all have air-con. The ferry office is closed Sunday. You can get here by helicopter and seaplane (p1087).

Understand India

India Today

With so many states, languages, religions, traditions, opinions and people – so many people! – India always has lots going on. The political, economic and social systems of the world's largest democracy are complex and, while mostly functional, there are hitches. Ongoing conflicts with neighbouring Pakistan have been constant challenges, as have bouts of unrest on the domestic front, from communal discord to violence against women. But Indians are eager for change – and travelling ever closer towards it.

Best in Film

Fire (1996), **Earth** (1998) and **Water** (2005) Trilogy directed by Deepa Mehta.

Pather Panchali (1955) Haunting masterpiece from Satyajit Ray.

Pyaasa (Thirst; 1957) and **Kaagaz Ke Phool** (Paper Flowers; 1959) For a taste of nostalgia.

Gandhi (1982) The classic.

Lagaan (2001) Written and directed by Ashutosh Gowariker.

Best in Print

Midnight's Children Salman Rushdie's allegory about Independence and Partition.

A Fine Balance Rohinton Mistry's beautifully written, tragic tale set in Mumbai.

White Tiger Aravind Adiga's Booker-winning novel about class struggle in globalised India.

Behind the Beautiful Forevers Katherine Boo's mind-stirring account of life in one of Mumbai's slums.

Shantaram Gregory David Roberts' vivid experiences of his life in India. A traveller favourite!

The Political Landscape

When the Congress Party regained power in 2004, it was under the leadership of Sonia Gandhi – the Italian-born wife of the late Rajiv Gandhi, who served as prime minister from 1984 to 1989. A planned national agitation campaign against Sonia Gandhi's foreign origins by the opposition Bharatiya Janata Party (BJP) was subverted when she stepped aside to allow Manmohan Singh to be sworn in as prime minister. However, despite Singh's formidable fiscal reputation (in 1991, Singh, then finance minister, floated the rupee against a basket of 'hard' currencies; state subsidies were phased out and the economy was opened up to foreign investment) many deemed his decision-making power, as prime minister, to be stymied under Sonia Gandhi.

In January 2013, Rahul Gandhi, Sonia's son, assumed the post of vice president of the Congress Party. The move didn't surprise anyone: the Nehru-Gandhi name has become synonymous with the party. But he wasn't widely seen as a strong or strategic figure, and in 2014 the Congress-led United Progressive Alliance (UPA) suffered a huge defeat with the BJP-led National Democratic Alliance (NDA) winning by a landslide under the charismatic leadership of its prime ministerial candidate, Narendra Modi. The election went down in history as the world's biggest, with approximately 814.5 million people eligible to vote (a rise of around 100 million voters since the 2009 election), according to the Election Commission of India.

With the BJP securing 282 seats (in the 543-seat Parliament) on its very own, this was the first time since the 1984 election that a party held enough seats to govern outright. Reasons for Modi's success at the federal elections include his former economic reputation as chief minister of the state of Gujarat, his appeal to 'ordinary' Indians due to his working class origins, and his masterful political campaigning which involved savvy use of digital technology, including social media.

Since coming to power, Modi has set about to not only resurrect India's ailing economy but to also address social issues such as sanitation, gender equality, poverty and health. Apart from vowing to build millions of toilets, largely in rural areas, he launched the Swachh Bharat Abhiyan (Clean India Mission) in 2014, a national cleanliness awareness drive that has seen politicians (including the PM himself) along with revered celebrities – from Bollywood stars to cricket icons – publicly sweeping streets and clearing rubbish in a bid to encourage all citizens to do so.

On the fiscal front, both the World Bank and International Monetary Fund forecast that India's economy was on track to become the world's fastest-growing (expected to overtake China in 2016/17) citing renewed investment confidence – under the business-friendly BJP government – as being one of the reasons. Another economic achievement under the new government has been India breaking a Guinness World Record for the most bank accounts opened in one week – 18,096,130 – a scheme (known as the Pradhan Mantri Jan-Dhan Yojana) aimed to proffer socio-economic opportunities for the poor, who were often denied banking access in the past.

To read more about Indian politics see the History chapter.

The Kashmir Impasse

Decades of border skirmishes between India and Pakistan, over the disputed territory of Kashmir, have resulted in many casualties and diplomatic stalemates. The impasse over Kashmir has plagued bilateral relations between the two South Asian neighbours ever since Partition in 1947. The predominantly Muslim Kashmir Valley is claimed by both countries (as well as a section of less powerful Kashmiris themselves).

Three India–Pakistan wars – in 1947, 1965 and 1971 – resolved little, and by 1989 Kashmir had its own Pakistan-backed armed insurgency. Tens of thousands were killed in the conflicts, and India has maintained hundreds of thousands of troops in Indian-administered Kashmir ever since. India–Pakistan relations sunk even lower in 1998 when both governments tested nuclear devices in a muscle-flexing show: nukes were now in the picture.

Talks that might have created an autonomous region were derailed in 2008, when terrorists killed at least 163 people at 10 sites around Mumbai (Bombay) during three days of coordinated bombings and shootings. The one sniper caught alive, a Pakistani, had ties to Lashkar-e-Taiba, a militant group that formed to assist the Pakistani army in Kashmir in the 1990s. Pakistan denied involvement. In late 2012, India executed the Pakistani sniper, and in early 2013, a Kashmiri man convicted for involvement in a 2001 terrorist attack on India's Parliament was also hanged.

POPULATION: **1.2 BILLION**

GDP: **US$2.05 TRILLION (2014)**

UNEMPLOYMENT RATE: **8.8% (2013)**

LITERACY RATE: **65/82% (FEMALE/MALE)**

GENDER RATIO: **940/1000 (FEMALE/MALE)**

if India were 100 people

55 would speak one of 21 other official languages
41 would speak Hindi
4 would speak one of 400 other official languages

belief systems
(% of population)

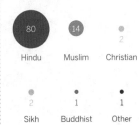

80 Hindu

14 Muslim

2 Christian

2 Sikh

1 Buddhist

1 Other

population per sq km

INDIA   CHINA   USA

👤 ≈ 30 people

Dos & Don'ts

Dress modestly Avoid stares by avoiding tight, sheer and skimpy clothes.

Shoes It's polite to remove shoes before entering homes and places of worship.

Photos Best to ask before photographing people, ceremonies or sacred sites.

Bad vibes Avoid pointing soles of feet towards people or deities, or touching anyone with your feet.

Niceties

Namaste Saying *namaste* with hands together in a prayer gesture is a respectful Hindu greeting.

Shake don't hug Shaking hands is fine but hugs between strangers is not the norm.

Head wobble It can mean 'yes', 'maybe' or a polite way of saying 'I have no idea'.

Pure touch The right hand is for eating and shaking hands; the left hand is the 'toilet' hand.

When India's BJP won the federal elections, in 2014, Pakistan's Prime Minister, Nawaz Sharif, was invited to attend Narendra Modi's Prime Ministerial oath-taking ceremony. But it wasn't long before relations between the two nations soured, after Islamabad faltered on certain diplomatic matters and violated cross-border ceasefires. At the time of writing, there had been no formal resumption of dialogue.

Violence Against Women

In December 2012, a 23-year-old paramedic and her male friend boarded a bus on their way home from the movies in Delhi only to find that it was a fake city bus, with blackened windows, where six men awaited them. The men beat the two friends, and raped the woman so brutally that she died 12 days later. The woman became known in India as Nirbhaya, or 'fearless one', and the event set off massive protests and soul-searching nationwide. Within weeks, India passed a package of new but controversial laws to deter violence against women: rape now carries a seven-year minimum sentence, with the death penalty in cases where the victim dies.

But in the months following the murder, more crimes took place, including violent rapes of girls as young as three. And while some Indian politicians condemned the rapists, others made comments that downplayed rape or blamed the victim. Many in India are also now reflecting on other abuses of women (tens of thousands die over dowry disputes alone each year), widespread police and justice-system mishandling of cases, and the greater issue of gender inequality. Although the violence situation has a long way to go, many are hopeful that change will follow now that the issues are out in the open.

Since becoming prime minister, Narendra Modi has been actively trying to change the national psyche regarding gender equality. On his first Indepedence Day address to the nation, in 2014, Modi spoke out about rape. In this speech he said: "I want to ask parents when your daughter turns 10 or 12 years old, you ask, 'Where are you going? When will you return?' Do the parents dare to ask their sons, 'Where are you going? Why are you going? Who are your friends?' After all, the rapist is also someone's son." Then, in 2015, Modi launched the Beti Bachao Beti Padhao (Save the Daughter, Teach the Daughter) campaign which aims to work towards gender equality by discouraging female infanticide and encouraging education, among other things. With programs, such as this one, it's hoped the way in which society views gender issues will improve. Time, as ever, shall tell.

See also the Women in India section (p1126) in The Way of Life chapter.

History

Throughout thousands of years of great civilisations, invasions, the birth of religions and countless cataclysms, India has proved itself to be, in the words of its first prime minister, Jawaharlal Nehru, 'a bundle of contradictions held together by strong but invisible threads'. Indian history has always been a work-in-progress, an evolution that can prove elusive for those seeking to grasp its essence. India's history is also not solely that of a nation, but of a collection of many different countries contained within the subcontinent, seldom dominated by a single power. And yet, a vibrant, diverse country has emerged out of this many-faceted past, as enduring and grounded as it is dynamic.

Indus Valley Civilisation

The Indus Valley, straddling the modern India–Pakistan border, is the cradle of civilisation on the Indian subcontinent. The first inhabitants of this region were nomadic tribes who cultivated land and kept domestic animals. Over thousands of years, an urban culture began to emerge from these tribes, particularly from 3500 BC. By 2500 BC large cities were well established, the focal points of what became known as the Harappan culture, which would flourish for more than 1000 years.

The great cities of the Mature Harappan period were Moenjodaro and Harappa in present-day Pakistan, and Lothal near Ahmedabad. Lothal can be visited (p700), and from the precise, carefully laid-out street plan, some sense of this sophisticated 4500-year-old civilisation is still evident. Harappan cities were astoundingly uniform, despite being spread across an enormous area. Even their brickwork and streets had a standard size. They often had a separate acropolis, suggesting a religious function, and the great tank at Moenjodaro may have been used for ritual bathing purposes. The major Harappan cities were also notable for their size – estimates put the population of Moenjodaro at as high as 50,000.

By the middle of the 3rd millennium BC, the Indus Valley culture was arguably the equal of other great civilisations emerging at the time. The Harappans traded with Mesopotamia, and developed a system of weights and measures, along with highly developed art in the form of terracotta and bronze figurines. Recovered relics, including models of bullock carts

To learn more about the ancient Indus Valley civilisations, ramble around Harappa (www.harappa.com), which presents an accessible yet scholarly multimedia overview.

TIMELINE	10,000 BC	2600–1700 BC	1500 BC
	Stone Age paintings first made in the Bhimbetka rock shelters, in what is now Madhya Pradesh; the art continues here for many centuries. Settlements thought to exist across subcontinent.	The Indus Valley civilisation's heyday. Spanning parts of Rajasthan, Gujarat and Sindh province in present-day Pakistan, it takes shape around metropolises such as Harappa and Moenjodaro.	The Indo-Aryan civilisation takes root in the fertile plains of the Indo-Gangetic basin. Settlers speak an early form of Sanskrit, from which several Indian vernaculars, including Hindi, later evolve.

and jewellery, offer the earliest evidence of a distinctive Indian culture. Indeed, many elements of Harappan culture would later become assimilated into Hinduism: clay figurines found at these sites suggest worship of a Mother goddess (later personified as Kali) and a male three-faced god sitting in the pose of a yogi (believed to be the historic Shiva) attended by four animals. Black stone pillars (associated with phallic worship of Shiva) and animal figures (the most prominent being the humped bull; later Shiva's mount, Nandi) have also been discovered. The 'dancing girl', a small bronze statuette of a young girl, whose insouciant gaze has endured over 4500 years, may be seen in the National Museum (p71) in Delhi, and is the most famous Harappan work of art to have been discovered. It indicates a well-developed society, both in its skillful sculpture and the indication of the opportunity for leisure pursuits.

Early Invasions & the Rise of Religions

The Harappan civilisation fell into decline from the beginning of the 2nd millennium BC. Some historians attribute the end of the empire to floods or decreased rainfall, which threatened the Harappans' agricultural base. Despite a lack of archaeological proof or written reports in the ancient Indian texts, an enduring, if contentious, theory is that an Aryan invasion put paid to the Harappans. A rival theory claims that it was the Aryans (from a Sanskrit word for 'noble') who were the original inhabitants of India. There's no clear evidence that the Aryans came from elsewhere, and it's even questionable whether the Aryans were a distinct race, so the 'invasion' could simply have been an invasion of new ideas from neighbouring cultures.

Those who defend the traditional invasion theory believe that from around 1500 BC Aryan tribes from Afghanistan and Central Asia began to filter into northwest India. Despite their military superiority, their progress was gradual, with successive tribes fighting over territory and new arrivals pushing further east into the Ganges plain. Eventually these tribes controlled northern India as far as the Vindhya Hills. Many of the original inhabitants of northern India, the Dravidians, the theory goes, were pushed south.

What is certain is that the Aryans were responsible for the great Sanskrit literary tradition. The Hindu sacred scriptures, the Vedas, were written during this period of transition (1500–1200 BC), and the caste system became formalised. These compositions are of seminal importance in terms of India's spirituality and history.

As Aryan culture spread across the Ganges plain in the late 7th century BC, its followers were absorbed into 16 major kingdoms, which were, in turn, amalgamated into four large states. Out of these states arose the Nanda dynasty, which came to power in 364 BC, ruling over huge swathes of North India.

During this period, the Indian heartland narrowly avoided two invasions from the west which, if successful, could have significantly altered

---

RK Narayan's 1973 *Ramayana* is a condensed and novelistic retelling of the 3rd century BC classic. The renowned novelist took on the *Mahabharata* in 1978.

History Good Reads

A Traveller's History of India, SinhaRaja Tammita-Delgoda

Empires of the Indus, Alice Albinia

India: a History, John Keay

1500–1200 BC	599–528 BC	563–483 BC	400–321 BC
The Rig-Veda, the first and longest of Hinduism's canonical texts, the Vedas, is written; three more books follow. Earliest forms of priestly Brahmanical Hinduism emerge.	The life of Mahavir, the 24th and last *tirthankar* (enlightened teacher) who established Jainism. Like the Buddha, he preaches compassion and a path to enlightenment for all castes.	The life of Siddhartha Gautama. The prince is born in modern-day Nepal and attains enlightenment beneath the Bodhi Tree in Bodhgaya (Bihar), thereby transforming into the Buddha (Awakened One).	Nanda dynasty evolves from the wealthy region of Magadha (roughly, today's Bihar) and grows to encompass a huge area, from Bengal to Punjab. It falls to Maurya in 321 BC.

the path of Indian history. The first was by the Persian king Darius (521–486 BC), who annexed Punjab and Sindh (on either side of the modern India–Pakistan border). Alexander the Great advanced to India from Greece in 326 BC, an achievement in itself, but he turned back in the Punjab, without ever extending his power deeper into India.

The period is also distinguished by the rise of two of India's most significant religions, Buddhism and Jainism, which arose around 500 BC in the northern plains. Both the Buddha and Jainism's Mahavir questioned the Vedas and were critical of the caste system, attracting followers from the lower castes.

The Mauryan Empire & its Aftermath

If the Harappan culture was the cradle of Indian civilisation, Chandragupta Maurya was the founder of the first great Indian empire, probably the most extensive ever forged, stretching from Bengal to Afghanistan and Gujarat. He came to power in 321 BC, having seized the throne from the Nandas, and he soon expanded the empire to include the Indus Valley previously conquered by Alexander the Great.

From its capital at Pataliputra (modern-day Patna), with its many-pillared palace, the Mauryan empire encompassed much of North India and reached as far south as modern-day Karnataka. There is much documentation of this period in contemporary Jain and Buddhist texts, plus the intensely detailed depiction of Indian statecraft in the ancient text known as the *Arthasastra*. The empire reached its peak under emperor Ashoka (p1110). Such was Ashoka's power to lead and unite that after his death in 232 BC, no one could be found to hold the disparate elements of the Mauryan empire together. The empire rapidly disintegrated, collapsing altogether in 184 BC.

None of the empires that immediately followed could match the stability or enduring historical legacy of the Mauryans, although the post-Ashokan era did produce at least one line of royalty whose patronage of the arts and ability to maintain a relatively high degree of social cohesion were substantial. The Satavahanas eventually controlled all of Maharashtra, Madhya Pradesh, Chhattisgarh, Karnataka and Andhra Pradesh. Under their rule, between 230 BC and AD 200, the arts, especially literature and philosophy, blossomed; the Buddha's teaching thrived; and the subcontinent enjoyed a period of considerable prosperity. South India may have lacked vast and fertile agricultural plains on the scale of North India, but it compensated by building strategic trade links via the Indian Ocean. Trade across the subcontinent grew during this time – with the Roman Empire (overland, and by sea through the southern ports) and with China (overland).

The Golden Age of the Guptas

The empires that followed the Mauryans may have claimed large areas of Indian territory as their own, but many secured only nominal power over

Mauryan Remains

Junagadh (Gujarat)

Allahabad Fort (Uttar Pradesh)

Sarnath (Uttar Pradesh)

Sanchi (Madhya Pradesh)

Bodhgaya (Bihar)

Vaishali (Bihar)

Amaravathi (Andhra Pradesh)

HISTORY THE MAURYAN EMPIRE & ITS AFTERMATH

Emperor Ashoka's ability to rule was assisted by a standing army consisting of roughly 9000 elephants, 30,000 cavalry and 600,000 infantry.

326 BC	321–185 BC	c 300 BC	c 300 BC
Alexander the Great invades India. He defeats King Porus in Punjab to enter the subcontinent, but a rebellion within his army keeps him from advancing beyond the Punjab.	Rule of the Maurya kings. Founded by Chandragupta Maurya, this pan-Indian empire is ruled from Pataliputra (present-day Patna) and briefly adopts Buddhism during the reign of Emperor Ashoka.	Buddhism spreads across subcontinent and beyond via Ashoka's monastic ambassadors: monks travel to Sri Lanka and Southeast Asia. Amaravathi, Sanchi and other stupas are erected.	Bhakti movement emerges in Hinduism, following first mention in the 5th-century-BC Bhagavad Gita. It emphasises individual devotion and union with the Divine, challenging traditional hierarchy of Brahmanism.

AN ENLIGHTENED EMPEROR

Apart from the Mughals and then the British many centuries later, no other power controlled more Indian territory than the Mauryan empire. It's therefore fitting that it provided India with one of its most important historical figures.

Emperor Ashoka's rule was characterised by flourishing art and sculpture, while his reputation as a philosopher-king was enhanced by the notably expressive rock-hewn edicts he used to both instruct his people, express remorse at the human suffering resulting from his battles, and delineate the enormous span of his territory. Some of these moral teachings can still be seen, particularly the Ashokan Edicts (p718) at Junagadh in Gujarat. Most of them mention and define the concept of *dhamma*, variously as good behaviour, obedience, generosity and goodness.

Ashoka's reign also represented an undoubted historical high point for Buddhism: he embraced the Buddha's teaching in 262 BC, declaring it the state religion and cutting a radical swathe through the spiritual and social body of Hinduism. The emperor also built thousands of stupas and monasteries across the region, the extant highlights of which are visible at Sarnath (p403) in Uttar Pradesh – on the spot where Buddha delivered his first sermon expounding the Noble Eightfold Path, or Middle Way to Enlightenment – and Sanchi (p652) in Madhya Pradesh. Ashoka also sent missions abroad, and he is revered in Sri Lanka because he sent his son and daughter to carry the Buddha's teaching to the island.

After his death and the empire's disintegration, his vision endured as an aspiration, if not a reality. One of this emperor's many legacies is the Indian national flag: its central design is the Ashoka Chakra, a wheel with 24 spokes.

their realms. Throughout the subcontinent, small tribes and kingdoms effectively controlled territory and dominated local affairs.

In AD 319, Chandragupta I, the third king of one of these tribes, the little-known Guptas, came to prominence by a fortuitous marriage to the daughter of one of the most powerful tribes in the north, the Liccavis. The Gupta empire grew rapidly and under Chandragupta II (r 375–413) achieved its greatest extent. The Chinese pilgrim Fa-hsien, visiting India at the time, described a people 'rich and contented', ruled over by enlightened and just kings.

The concepts of zero and infinity are widely believed to have been devised by eminent Indian mathematicians during the reign of the Guptas.

Poetry, literature, astronomy, medicine and the arts flourished, with some of the finest work done at Ajanta, Ellora, Sanchi and Sarnath. The Guptas were tolerant of, and even supported, Buddhist practice and art. Towards the end of the Gupta period, Hinduism became the dominant religious force, however, and its revival eclipsed Jainism and Buddhism; the latter in particular went into decline in India with the Hun invasion and would never again be India's dominant tradition.

The invasions of the Huns at the beginning of the 6th century signalled the end of this era, and in 510 the Gupta army was defeated by the

c 235 BC	230 BC–AD 220	AD 52	1st Century
Start of Early Chola reign in the south; it's unknown if they were related to the later Chola dynasty.	The Satavahana empire, of Andhra origin, rules over a huge central Indian area. Their interest in art and maritime trade influences artistic development regionally and in Southeast Asia.	Possible arrival of St Thomas the Apostle on the coast of Kerala. Christianity thought to have been introduced to India with his preaching in Kerala and Tamil Nadu.	International trade booms: the region's elaborate overland trade networks connect with ports linked to maritime routes. Trade to Africa, the Gulf, Socotra, Southeast Asia, China and even Rome thrives.

Hun leader Toramana. Power in North India again devolved to a number of separate Hindu kingdoms.

The Hindu South

Southern India has always laid claim to its own unique history. Insulated by distance from the political developments in the north, a separate set of powerful kingdoms emerged, among them the Satavahanas – who, though predominantly Hindu, probably practiced Buddhist meditation and patronised Buddhist art at Amaravathi and Sanchi – as well as the Kalingas and Vakatakas. But it was from the tribal territories on the fertile coastal plains that the greatest southern empires – the Cholas, Pandyas, Chalukyas, Cheras and Pallavas – came into their own.

The Chalukyas ruled mainly over the Deccan region of south-central India, although their power occasionally extended further north. In the far south, the Pallavas ruled from the 4th to 9th centuries and pioneered Dravidian architecture, with its exuberant, almost baroque, style. The surviving architectural high points of Pallava rule can be found across Tamil Nadu, including in the erstwhile Pallava capital at Kanchipuram (p1028).

The south's prosperity was based on long-established trading links with other civilisations, among them the Egyptians and Romans. In return for spices, pearls, ivory and silk, the Indians received Roman gold. Indian merchants also extended their influence to Southeast Asia. In 850, the Cholas rose to power and superseded the Pallavas. They soon set about turning the south's far-reaching trade influence into territorial conquest. Under the reign of Rajaraja Chola I (985–1014) they controlled almost the whole of South India, the Deccan plateau, Sri Lanka, parts of the Malay peninsula and the Sumatran-based Srivijaya kingdom.

Not all of their attention was focused overseas, however, and the Cholas left behind some of the finest examples of Dravidian architecture, most notably the sublime Brihadishwara Temple (p1047) in Thanjavur and Chidambaram's stunning Nataraja Temple (p1043).

Throughout, Hinduism remained the bedrock of South Indian culture.

The Muslim North

The first Muslims to reach India were some newly converted merchants crossing the Arabian sea in the early 7th century who established communities in some southern ports, and some small, pioneering Arabian forces in 663 from the north. Sporadic skirmishes took place over the ensuing centuries, but no major confrontations took place until the late 10th century. But at this point wave after wave of land assaults had begun convulsing the north.

At the vanguard of Islamic expansion was Mahmud of Ghazni. In the early 11th century, Mahmud turned Ghazni (in today's Afghanistan) into one of the world's most glorious capital cities, which he largely funded by

HISTORY THE HINDU SOUTH

Mahvir and the Buddha were contemporaries, and their teachings overlapped. The Buddha lays out the discrepancies (and his critiques) in the *Sankha Sutta* and *Devadaha Sutta*, referring to Mahvir as Nigantha ('free from bonds') Nataputta. Read them at the Theravada resource, www. accesstoinsight. com.

A History of South India from Prehistoric Times to the Fall of Vijayanagar by KA Nilakanta Sastri is arguably the most comprehensive (if heavy-going) history of this region.

319–510	4th–9th Centuries	500–600	610
The golden era of the Gupta dynasty, the second of India's great empires after the Mauryas. The period is marked by a creative surge in literature and the arts.	The Pallavas enter the shifting landscape of southern power centres, establishing dominance in Andhra Pradesh and northern Tamil Nadu from their base in Kanchipuram.	The emergence of the Rajputs in Rajasthan. Hailing from three principal races supposedly of celestial origin, they form 36 clans which spread across the region to secure their own kingdoms.	Prophet Mohammed establishes Islam. He soon invites the people of Mecca to adopt the new religion under the command of God, and his call is met with eager response.

Pallava Architecture in Tamil Nadu

Shore Temple, Mamallapuram

Five Rathas, Mamallapuram

Temples, Kanchipuram

Rock Fort Temple, Trichy (Tiruchirappalli)

plundering his neighbours' territories. From 1001 to 1025, Mahmud conducted 17 raids into India, most infamously on the famous Shiva Temple of Somnath (p714) in Gujarat. The Hindu force of 70,000 died trying to defend the temple, which eventually fell in early 1026. In the aftermath of his victory, Mahmud transported a massive haul of gold and other booty back to his capital. These raids effectively shattered the balance of power in North India, allowing subsequent invaders to claim the territory for themselves.

Following Mahmud's death in 1033, Ghazni was seized by the Seljuqs and then fell to the Ghurs of western Afghanistan, who similarly had their eyes on the great Indian prize. The Ghur style of warfare was brutal.

In 1191 Mohammed of Ghur advanced into India. Although defeated in a major battle against a confederacy of Hindu rulers, he returned the following year and routed his enemies. One of his generals, Qutb ud-din Aibak, captured Delhi and was appointed governor; it was during his reign that the great Delhi landmark, the Qutb Minar Complex (p102), containing India's first mosque, was built. A separate Islamic empire was established in Bengal, and within a short time almost the whole of North India was under Muslim control.

Following Mohammed's death in 1206, Qutb ud-din Aibak became the first sultan of Delhi. His successor, Iltutmish, brought Bengal back under central control and defended the empire from an attempted Mongol invasion. Ala-ud-din Khilji came to power in 1296 and pushed the borders of the empire inexorably south, while simultaneously fending off further attacks by the Mongols.

North Meets South

Ala-ud-din died in 1320, and Mohammed Tughlaq ascended the throne in 1324. In 1328, Tughlaq took the southern strongholds of the Hoysala empire, which had centres at Belur, Halebid and Somnathpur. However, while the empire of the pre-Mughal Muslims would achieve its greatest extent under Tughlaq's rule, his overreaching ambition also sowed the seeds of its disintegration. Unlike his forebears, Tughlaq dreamed not only of extending his indirect influence over South India, but of controlling it directly as part of his empire.

After a series of successful campaigns Tughlaq decided to move the capital from Delhi to a more central location. The new capital was called Daulatabad and was near Aurangabad in Maharashtra. Tughlaq sought to populate the new capital by forcefully marching the entire population of Delhi 1100km south, resulting in great loss of life. However, he soon realised that this left the north undefended, and so the entire capital was moved north again. The superb hilltop fortress of Daulatabad (p784) stands as the last surviving monument to his megalomanic vision.

The days of the Ghur empire were numbered. The last of the great sultans of Delhi, Firoz Shah, died in 1388, and the fate of the sultanate was

In its 800-year history, the Qutb Minar has been damaged by two lightning strikes and one earthquake, and has been repaired or built up by four sultans, one British major and one governor general.

850	12th–19th Centuries	1192	1206
The Medieval Cholas, a Tamil dynasty, accreted power across South India, Sri Lanka and the Maldives in the 9th to 13th centuries.	Africans are brought to the Konkan Coast as part of trade with the Gulf; the slaves become servants, dock workers and soldiers and are known as Siddis or Habshis.	Prithviraj Chauhan loses Delhi to Mohammed of Ghori. The defeat effectively ends Hindu supremacy in the region, exposing the subcontinent to subsequent Muslim rulers marching in from the northwest.	Ghori is murdered during prayer while returning to Ghazni from Lahore. In the absence of an heir, his kingdom is usurped by his generals. The Delhi Sultanate is born.

sealed when Timur (Tamerlane) made a devastating raid from Samarkand (in Central Asia) into India in 1398. Timur's sacking of Delhi was truly merciless; some accounts say his soldiers slaughtered every Hindu inhabitant.

After Tughlaq's withdrawal from the south, several splinter kingdoms arose. The two most significant were the Islamic Bahmani sultanate, which emerged in 1345 with its capital at Gulbarga, and later Bidar, and the Hindu Vijayanagar empire, founded in 1336 with its capital at Hampi. The battles between the two were among the bloodiest communal violence in Indian history and ultimately resolved nothing in the two centuries before the Mughals ushered in a more enlightened age.

The Mughals

Even as Vijayanagar was experiencing its last days, the next great Indian empire was being founded. The Mughal empire was massive, at its height covering almost the entire subcontinent. Its significance, however, lay not only in its size. Mughal emperors presided over a golden age of arts and literature and had a passion for building that resulted in some of the finest architecture in India, including Shah Jahan's sublime Taj Mahal (p352).

The founder of the Mughal line, Babur (r 1526–30), was a descendant of both Genghis Khan and Timur (Tamerlane). In 1525, he marched into Punjab from his capital at Kabul. With technological superiority brought by firearms, and consummate skill in simultaneously employing artillery and cavalry, Babur defeated the larger armies of the sultan of Delhi at the Battle of Panipat in 1526.

Despite this initial success, Babur's son, Humayun (r 1530–56) was defeated by a powerful ruler of eastern India, Sher Shah, in 1539 and forced to withdraw to Iran. Humayun spent much time outside India, a fact reflected in the design of his tomb in Delhi, which was designed by Persian architects and influenced by Iranian style. Following Sher Shah's death in 1545, Humayun returned to claim his kingdom, eventually conquering Delhi in 1555. He died the following year and was succeeded by his young son Akbar (r 1556–1605) who, during his 49-year reign, managed to extend and consolidate the empire until he ruled over a mammoth area.

True to his name, Akbar (which means 'great' in Arabic) was probably the greatest of the Mughals: he not only had the military ability required of a ruler at that time, but was also a wise leader and a man of culture. He saw, as previous Muslim rulers had not, that the number of Hindus in India was too great to subjugate. Although Akbar's tolerance of other cultures was relative – vast massacres of Hindus at Panipat and Chitrod tarnish his legacy – he remains known for integrating Hindus into his empire and skilfully using them as advisers, generals and administrators. Akbar also had a deep interest in religious matters, and spent many hours in discussion with religious experts of all persuasions, including Christians and Parsis.

Architecture of the Deccan Sultanate

Citadel, Golgumbaz, Ibrahim Rouza, Jama Masjid (Bijapur)

Fort, Bahmani Tombs (Bidar)

Golconda Fort, Qutb Shahi Tombs, Charminar (Hyderabad)

Persian was the official language of several empires, from Mahmud of Ghazni to the Delhi Sultanate to the Mughals. Urdu, which combines Persian, Arabic and indigenous languages, evolved over hundreds of years and came into its own during Mughal reign.

13th Century	1321	1336	1345
The Pandyas, a Tamil dynasty dating to the 6th century BC, assumes control of Chola territory, expanding into Andhra Pradesh, Kalinga (Odisha [Orissa]) and Sri Lanka from their Madurai capital.	The Tughlaqs come to power in Delhi. Mohammed bin Tughlaq expands his empire but becomes known for inelegant schemes: moving the capital to Daulatabad and creating forgery-prone currency.	Foundation of the mighty Vijayanagar empire, named after its capital city, the ruins of which can be seen today in the vicinity of Hampi (in Karnataka).	Bahmani Sultanate is established in the Deccan following a revolt against the Tughlaqs of Delhi. The capital is set up at Gulbarga, in today's northern Karnataka, later shifting to Bidar.

THE STRUGGLE FOR THE SOUL OF INDIA

Founded as an alliance of Hindu kingdoms banding together to counter the threat from the Muslims, the Vijayanagar empire rapidly grew into one of India's wealthiest and greatest Hindu empires. Under the rule of Bukka I (c 1343–79), the majority of South India was brought under its control.

The Vijayanagars and the Bahmani sultanate, which was also based in South India, were evenly matched. The Vijayanagar armies occasionally got the upper hand, but generally the Bahmanis inflicted the worst defeats. The atrocities committed by both sides almost defy belief. In 1366, Bukka I responded to a perceived slight by capturing the Muslim stronghold of Mudkal and slaughtering every inhabitant bar one, who managed to escape and carry news of the attack to Mohammad Shah, the sultan. Mohammad swore that he would not rest until he had killed 100,000 Hindus. Instead, according to the Muslim historian Firishtah, 500,000 'infidels' were killed in the ensuing campaign.

Somehow, Vijayanagar survived. In 1484, the Bahmani sultanate began to disintegrate, and five separate kingdoms, based on the major cities – Berar, Ahmadnagar, Bidar, Bijapur and Golconda – were formed. Bijapur and Bidar still bear exceptional traces of this period of Islamic rule. With little opposition from the north, the Hindu empire enjoyed a golden age of almost supreme power in the south. In 1520, the Vijayanagar king Krishnadevaraya even took Bijapur.

Like Bahmani, however, Vijayanagar's fault lines were soon laid bare. A series of uprisings divided the kingdom fatally, just at a time when the Muslim sultanates were beginning to form a new alliance. In 1565, Hampi was destroyed at the Battle of Talikota. Although the last of the Vijayanagar line escaped and the dynasty limped on for several years, real power passed to local Muslim rulers or Hindu chiefs once loyal to the Vijayanagar kings. One of India's grisliest periods came to an end when the Bahmani kingdoms fell to the Mughals.

Jehangir (r 1605–27) ascended to the throne following Akbar's death. Despite several challenges to Jehangir's authority, the empire remained more or less intact. In periods of stability Jehangir spent time in his beloved Kashmir, eventually dying en route there in 1627. He was succeeded by his son, Shah Jahan (r 1627–58), who secured his position by executing all male relatives who stood in his way. During his reign, some of the most vivid and permanent reminders of the Mughals' glory were constructed; in addition to the Taj Mahal, he oversaw the construction of the mighty Red Fort (p60) (Lal Qila) in Delhi and converted the Agra Fort (p353) into a palace that would later become his prison.

The last of the great Mughals, Aurangzeb (r 1658–1707), imprisoned his father (Shah Jahan) and succeeded to the throne after a two-year struggle against his brothers. Aurangzeb devoted his resources to extend-

1398	1469	1484	1498
Timur (Tamerlane) invades Delhi, on the pretext that the Delhi Sultans are too tolerant with their Hindu subjects. He executes tens of thousands of Hindus before the battle for Delhi.	Guru Nanak, founder of the Sikh faith, which has millions of followers within and beyond India to the present day, is born in a village near Lahore (in modern-day Pakistan).	Bahmani Sultanate begins to break up following independence movements; Berar is the first to revolt. By 1518 there are five Deccan sultanates: Berar, Ahmadnagar, Bidar, Bijapur and Golconda.	Vasco da Gama discovers the sea route from Europe to India. The first European to reach India by sea, he engages in trade with the local nobility of Kerala.

ing the empire's boundaries, and thus fell into much the same trap as that of Mohammed Tughlaq some 300 years earlier. A combination of decaying court life and dissatisfaction among the Hindu population at inflated taxes and religious intolerance weakened the Mughal grip.

The empire was also facing serious challenges from the Marathas in central India and, more significantly, the British in Bengal. With Aurangzeb's death in 1707, the empire's fortunes rapidly declined, and Delhi was sacked by Persia's Nadir Shah in 1739. Mughal 'emperors' continued to rule right up until the First War of Independence (Indian Uprising) in 1857, but they were emperors without an empire.

The Rajputs & the Marathas

Throughout the Mughal period, there remained strong Hindu powers, most notably the Rajputs. Centred in Rajasthan, the Rajputs were a proud warrior caste with a passionate belief in the dictates of chivalry, both in battle and state affairs. The Rajputs opposed every foreign incursion into their territory, but they were never united. When they weren't battling foreign oppression, they squandered their energies fighting one another. This eventually led to their territories becoming vassal states of the Mughal empire. Their prowess in battle, however, was acknowledged, and some of the best military men in the Mughal armies were Rajputs.

The Marathas were less picaresque but ultimately more effective. They first rose to prominence under their great leader Shivaji, also known as Chhatrapati Shivaji Maharaj, who gathered popular support by championing the Hindu cause against the Muslim rulers. Between 1646 and 1680 Shivaji performed heroic acts in confronting the Mughals across most of central India. Shivaji was captured by the Mughals and taken to Agra, but, naturally, he managed to escape and continue his adventures. Tales of his larger-than-life exploits are still popular with wandering storytellers. He is a particular hero in Maharashtra, where many of his wildest adventures took place. (Today, you'll see Shivaji's name all over Mumbai.) He's also revered for the fact that, as a lower-caste Shudra, he showed that great leaders don't have to be of the Kshatriya (soldier) caste.

Shivaji's son was captured, blinded and executed by Aurangzeb, and his grandson wasn't made of the same sturdy stuff, so the Maratha empire continued under the Peshwas, hereditary government ministers who became the real rulers. They gradually took over more of the weakening Mughal empire's powers.

The expansion of Maratha power came to an abrupt halt in 1761 at Panipat. In the town where Babur had won the battle that established the Mughal empire more than 200 years earlier, the Marathas were defeated by Ahmad Shah Durrani from Afghanistan. Maratha expansion to the

White Mughals by William Dalrymple tells the true story of an East India Company soldier who married an Indian Muslim princess, a tragic love story interwoven with harem politics, intrigue and espionage.

Amar Chitra Katha, a hugely popular publisher of comic books about Indian folklore, mythology and history, has several books about Shivaji, including *Shivaji – The Great Maratha, Tales of Shivaji* and *Tanaji, the Maratha Lion,* about Shivaji's close friend and fellow warrior.

1510	**1526**	**1542–45**	**1556**
Portuguese forces capture Goa under the command of Alfonso de Albuquerque, whose initial attempt was thwarted by then-ruler, Sultan Adil Shah of Bijapur. He succeeds following Shah's death.	Babur becomes the first Mughal emperor after conquering Delhi. He stuns Rajasthan by routing its confederate force, gaining an edge with the introduction of matchlock muskets in his army.	St Francis Xavier's first mission to India. He preaches Catholicism in Goa, Tamil Nadu and Sri Lanka, returning in 1548–49 and 1552 in between travels in the Far East.	Hemu, a Hindu general in Adil Shah Suri's army, seizes Delhi after Humayun's death. He rules for barely a month before losing to Akbar in the Second Battle of Panipat.

west was halted, and although they consolidated their control over central India, they were to fall to India's final imperial power – the British.

The Rise of European Power

The Portuguese sought a sea route to the East so they could trade directly in spices. They also hoped to find the kingdom of legendary Christian ruler Prester John, thought to contain the fountain of youth. In India they found spices and the Syrian Orthodox community, but not Prester John.

In 1498, Vasco da Gama arrived on the coast of modern-day Kerala, having sailed around the Cape of Good Hope. Pioneering this route gave the Portuguese a century-long monopoly over Indian and far-Eastern trade with Europe. In 1510, they captured Goa, followed by Diu in 1531; Goa was last colony in India to be returned to the Indian people, following an Indian Army invasion in 1961. In its heyday, the trade flowing through 'Golden Goa' was said to rival that passing through Lisbon. However, the Portuguese didn't have the resources to maintain a worldwide empire and they were quickly eclipsed and isolated after the arrival of the British and French.

In 1600, Queen Elizabeth I granted a charter to a London trading company that gave it a monopoly on British trade with India. In 1613, representatives of the East India Company established their first trading post at Surat in Gujarat. Further British trading posts, administered and governed by representatives of the company, were established at Madras (Chennai) in 1639, Bombay (Mumbai) in 1661 and Calcutta (Kolkata) in 1690. For nearly 250 years a commercial trading company and not the British government 'ruled' over British India.

By 1672, the French had established themselves at Pondicherry (Puducherry), an enclave they held even after the British departed and where architectural traces of the French era remain. The stage was set for more than a century of rivalry between the British and French for control of Indian trade. At one stage, the French appeared to hold the upper hand, even taking Madras in 1746. But they were outmaneuvered by the British, and by the 1750s were no longer a serious influence on the subcontinent. Serious French aspirations effectively ended in 1750 when the directors of the French East India Company decided that their representatives were playing too much politics and doing too little trading. Key representatives were sacked, and a settlement designed to end all ongoing political disputes was made with the British. The decision effectively removed France as a serious influence on the subcontinent.

Britain's Surge to Power

The transformation of the British from traders to governors began almost by accident. Having been granted a licence to trade in Bengal by the Mughals, and following the establishment of a new trading post at Calcutta (Kolkata)

The word Pakistan was originally an acronym thought of by a group of Cambridge Muslims to define a homeland consisting of P(unjab), A(fghania), K(ashmir), I(ran), S(ind), T(urkharistan), A(fghanistan) and (Baluchia)N. It also conflates the terms *pak*, a Persian word meaning 'pure/clean', and *sthāna*, an Indo-Aryan term meaning 'place'.

1560–1812	1600	1631	1672
Portuguese Inquisition in Goa. Trials focus on converted Hindus and Muslims thought to have 'relapsed'. Thousands were tried and several dozen were likely executed before it was abolished in 1812.	Britain's Queen Elizabeth I grants the first trading charter to the East India Company, with the maiden voyage taking place in 1601 under the command of Sir James Lancaster.	Construction of the Taj Mahal begins after Shah Jahan, overcome with grief following the death of his wife Mumtaz Mahal, vows to build the most beautiful mausoleum in the world.	The French East India Company establishes an outpost at Pondicherry (Puducherry), which the French, Dutch and British fight over repeatedly in the coming century.

in 1690, business began to expand rapidly. Under the apprehensive gaze of the nawab (local ruler), British trading activities became extensive and the 'factories' took on an increasingly permanent (and fortified) appearance.

Eventually the nawab decided that British power had grown large enough. In June 1756, he attacked Calcutta and, having taken the city, locked his British prisoners in a tiny cell. The space was so cramped and airless that many were dead by the following morning.

Six months later, Robert Clive, an employee in the military service of the East India Company, led an expedition to retake Calcutta and entered into an agreement with one of the nawab's generals to overthrow the nawab himself. He did this in June 1757, at the Battle of Plassey (now called Palashi), and the general who had assisted him was placed on the throne. With the British effectively in control of Bengal, the company's agents engaged in a period of unbridled profiteering. When a subsequent nawab finally took up arms to protect his own interests, he was defeated at the Battle of Baksar in 1764, a victory that confirmed the British as the paramount power in east India.

In 1771, Warren Hastings was made governor in Bengal. During his tenure, the company greatly expanded its control. He was aided by the fact that India was experiencing a power vacuum created by the disintegration of the Mughal empire. The Marathas, the only real Indian power to step into this gap, were divided among themselves. Hastings concluded a series of treaties with local rulers, including one with the main Maratha leader. From 1784 onwards, the British government in London began to take a more direct role in supervising affairs in India, although the territory was still notionally administered by the East India Company until 1858.

In the south, the picture was confused by the strong British–French rivalry, and one ruler was played off against another. This was never clearer than in the series of Mysore wars in which Hyder Ali and his son, Tipu Sultan, waged a brave and determined campaign against the British. In the Fourth Mysore War (1789–99), Tipu Sultan was killed at Srirangapatnam, and British power took another step forward. The long-running struggle with the Marathas was concluded a few years later, leaving only Punjab (held by the Sikhs) outside British control. Punjab finally fell in 1849 after the two Sikh Wars.

By the early 19th century, India was effectively under British control, although there remained a patchwork of states, many nominally independent and governed by their own rulers, the maharajas (or similarly titled princes) and nawabs. While these 'princely states' administered their own territories, a system of central government was developed. British bureaucratic models were replicated in the Indian government and civil service – a legacy that still exists today. Trade and profit continued to be the main focus of British rule in India, with far-reaching effects. Iron and coal mining were developed, and tea, coffee and cotton became key crops. A start was made on the vast rail network that's still in use today,

Makers of Modern India, edited by Ramachandra Guha, is a fascinating collection of speeches and writings by 19 of modern India's most influential activists and thinkers.

Plain Tales from the Raj by Charles Allen (ed) is a fascinating series of interviews with people who played a role in British India on both sides of the table.

1674	1707	1757	1801
Shivaji establishes the Maratha kingdom, spanning western India and parts of the Deccan and North India. He assumes the imperial title of Chhatrapati, which means 'Great Protector'.	Death of Aurangzeb, the last of the Mughal greats. His demise triggers the gradual collapse of the Mughal empire, as anarchy and rebellion erupt across the country.	The East India Company registers its first military victory on Indian soil. Siraj-ud-Daulah, nawab of Bengal, is defeated by Robert Clive in the Battle of Plassey.	Ranjit Singh becomes maharaja (Great King) of the newly united Sikhs and forges a powerful new kingdom from his capital in Lahore (in present-day Pakistan).

irrigation projects were undertaken, and the Mughal-era zamindar (landowner) system was encouraged, further contributing to the development of an impoverished and landless peasantry.

The British also imposed English as the language of administration. For them, this was critical in a country with so many different languages, but it also kept the new rulers at arm's length from the Indian populace.

The Road to Independence

Opposition to the British increased at the turn of the 20th century, spearheaded by the Indian National Congress, the country's oldest political party, also known as the Congress Party and Congress.

It met for the first time in 1885 and soon began to push for participation in the government of India. A highly unpopular attempt by the British to partition Bengal in 1905 resulted in mass demonstrations and brought to light Hindu opposition to the division; the Muslim community formed its own league and campaigned for protected rights in any future political settlement. As pressure rose, a split emerged in Hindu circles between moderates and radicals, the latter resorting to violence to publicise their aims.

With the outbreak of WWI, the political situation eased. India contributed hugely to the war: more than one million Indian volunteers were enlisted and sent overseas, suffering more than 100,000 casualties. The contribution was sanctioned by Congress leaders, largely with the expectation that it would be rewarded after the war. No such rewards transpired and disillusion followed. Disturbances were particularly persistent in Punjab, and in April 1919, following riots in Amritsar, a British army contingent was sent to quell the unrest. Under direct orders of the officer in charge, they ruthlessly fired into a crowd of unarmed protesters at Jallianwala Bagh (p214). News of the massacre spread rapidly throughout India, turning huge numbers of otherwise apolitical Indians into Congress supporters.

At this time, the Congress movement found a new leader in Mohandas Gandhi. Not everyone involved in the struggle agreed with or followed Gandhi's policy of nonviolence, yet the Congress Party and Gandhi remained at the forefront of the push for independence.

As political power-sharing began to look more likely, and the mass movement led by Gandhi gained momentum, the Muslim reaction was to consider its own immediate future. The large Muslim minority realised that an independent India would be dominated by Hindus and that, while Gandhi's approach was fair-minded, others in the Congress Party might not be so willing to share power. By the 1930s Muslims were raising the possibility of a separate Islamic state.

Political events were partially disrupted by WWII, when large numbers of Congress supporters were jailed to prevent disruption to the war effort.

Colonial-era Architecture

Colaba and Kala Ghoda, Mumbai (British)

BBD Bagh and environs, Kolkata (British)

Old Goa and Panjim, Goa (Portuguese)

Puducherry, Tamil Nadu (French)

1835–1858	1857	1858	1869
Life of Lakshmi Bai, Rani of Jhansi. The queen of the Maratha state led her army against the British, who seized Jhansi after her husband's death. She died in battle.	The First War of Independence (Indian Uprising) against the British. With no national leader, freedom fighters coerce the Mughal king, Bahadur Shah Zafar, to proclaim himself emperor of India.	British government assumes control over India – with power officially transferred from the East India Company to the Crown – beginning the period known as the British Raj.	Opening of Suez Canal accelerates trade from Europe and makes Bombay (Mumbai) India's first port of call; trip from England goes from three months to three weeks.

THE FIRST WAR OF INDEPENDENCE: THE INDIAN UPRISING

In 1857, half a century after having established firm control of India, the British suffered a setback. To this day, the causes of the Indian Uprising are the subject of debate. The key factors included the influx of cheap goods, such as textiles, from Britain that destroyed many livelihoods; the dispossession of territories from many rulers; and taxes imposed on landowners.

The incident that's popularly held to have sparked the Indian Uprising, however, took place at an army barracks in Meerut in Uttar Pradesh on 10 May 1857. A rumour leaked out that a new type of bullet was greased with what Hindus claimed was cow fat, while Muslims maintained that it came from pigs; pigs are considered unclean to Muslims, and cows are sacred to Hindus. Since loading a rifle involved biting off the end of the waxed cartridge, these rumours provoked considerable unrest.

In Meerut, the situation was handled with a singular lack of judgment. The commanding officer lined up his soldiers and ordered them to bite off the ends of their issued bullets. Those who refused were immediately marched off to prison. The following morning, the soldiers of the garrison rebelled, shot their officers and marched to Delhi. Of the 74 Indian battalions of the Bengal army, seven (one of them Gurkhas) remained loyal, 20 were disarmed and the other 47 mutinied. The soldiers and peasants rallied around the ageing Mughal emperor in Delhi. They held Delhi for some months and besieged the British residency in Lucknow for five months before they were finally suppressed.

Almost immediately the East India Company was wound up and direct control of the country was assumed by the British government, which announced its support for the existing rulers of the princely states, claiming they would not interfere in local matters as long as the states remained loyal to the British.

Mahatma Gandhi

One of the great figures of the 20th century, Mohandas Karamchand Gandhi was born on 2 October 1869 in Porbandar, Gujarat. After studying in London (1888–91), he worked as a barrister in South Africa. Here, the young Gandhi became politicised, railing against the discrimination he encountered. He soon became the spokesperson for the Indian community and championed equality for all.

Gandhi returned to India in 1915 with the doctrine of *ahimsa* (non-violence) central to his political plans, and committed to a simple and disciplined lifestyle. He set up the Sabarmati Ashram in Ahmedabad, which was innovative for its admission of Untouchables.

Within a year, Gandhi had won his first victory, defending farmers in Bihar from exploitation. This was when it's said he first received the title 'Mahatma' (Great Soul) from an admirer (often said to be Bengali poet Rabindranath Tagore). The passage of the discriminatory Rowlatt Acts, which allowed certain political cases to be tried without juries, in 1919 spurred him to

1885	1919	1930	1940
The Indian National Congress, India's first home-grown political organisation, is set up. It brings educated Indians together and plays a key role in India's enduring freedom struggle.	The massacre, on 13 April, of unarmed Indian protesters at Jallianwala Bagh in Amritsar (Punjab). Gandhi responds with his program of civil (nonviolent) disobedience against the British government.	Salt Satyagraha begins on 12 March. Gandhi embarks on a 24-day walk from his Sabarmati Ashram near Ahmedabad to the coastal village of Dandi to protest the British salt tax.	The Muslim League adopts its Lahore Resolution, which champions greater Muslim autonomy in India. Campaigns for the creation of a separate Islamic nation are spearheaded by Mohammed Ali Jinnah.

The Proudest Day – India's Long Road to Independence by Anthony Read and David Fisher is an engaging account of India's pre-Independence period.

further action, and he organised a national protest. In the days that followed this *hartal* (strike), feelings ran high throughout the country. After the massacre of unarmed protesters in Amritsar, Gandhi, deeply shocked, began to organise his program of civil (nonviolent) disobedience against the British.

By 1920 Gandhi was a key figure in the Indian National Congress, and he coordinated a national campaign of noncooperation or *satyagraha* (nonviolent protest) to British rule, with the effect of raising nationalist feeling while earning the lasting enmity of the British. In early 1930, Gandhi captured the imagination of the country, and the world, when he led a march of several thousand followers from Ahmedabad to Dandi on the coast of Gujarat. On arrival, Gandhi ceremoniously made salt by evaporating sea water, thus publicly defying the much-hated salt tax; not for the first time, he was imprisoned. Released in 1931 to represent the Indian National Congress at the second Round Table Conference in London, he won the hearts of many British people but failed to gain any real concessions from the government.

Disillusioned with politics, he resigned his parliamentary seat in 1934. He returned spectacularly to the fray in 1942 with the Quit India campaign, in which he urged the British to leave India immediately. His actions were deemed subversive, and he and most of the Congress leadership were imprisoned.

In the frantic independence bargaining that followed the end of WWII, Gandhi was largely excluded and watched helplessly as plans were made to partition the country – a dire tragedy in his eyes. Gandhi stood almost alone in urging tolerance and the preservation of a single India, and his work on behalf of members of all communities drew resentment from some Hindu hardliners. On his way to a prayer meeting in Delhi on 30 January 1948, he was assassinated by a Hindu zealot, Nathuram Godse.

Gandhian Sites

Raj Ghat, Delhi

Gandhi Smriti, Delhi

Anand Bhavan, Allahabad

Sabarmati Ashram, Ahmedabad

Kaba Gandhi No Delo, Rajkot

Mani Bhavan, Mumbai

Gandhi National Memorial, Pune

Independence & the Partition of India

The Labour Party victory in the British elections in July 1945 dramatically altered the political landscape. For the first time, Indian independence was accepted as a legitimate goal. This new goodwill did not, however, translate into any new wisdom as to how to reconcile the divergent wishes of the two major Indian parties. Mohammed Ali Jinnah, the leader of the Muslim League, championed a separate Islamic state, while the Congress Party, led by Jawaharlal Nehru, campaigned for an independent greater India.

In early 1946, a British mission failed to bring the two sides together – indeed, there was evidence that the British deliberately fostered resentment on both sides to discourage a unified resistence – and the country slid closer towards civil war. A 'Direct Action Day', called by the Muslim League in August 1946, led to the slaughter of Hindus in Calcutta, which prompted reprisals against Muslims. In February 1947, the nervous British government made the momentous decision that Independence

1942	1947	1947–48	1948
Mahatma Gandhi launches the Quit India campaign, demanding that the British leave India without delay and allow the country to get on with the business of self-governance.	India gains independence on 15 August. Pakistan is formed a day earlier. Partition is followed by mass cross-border exodus, as Hindus and Muslims migrate to their respective nations.	First war between India and Pakistan takes place after the (procrastinating) maharaja of Kashmir signs the Instrument of Accession that cedes his state to India. Pakistan challenges the document's legality.	Mahatma Gandhi is assassinated in New Delhi by Nathuram Godse on 30 January. Godse and his co-conspirator, Narayan Apte, are later tried, convicted and executed (by hanging).

would come by June 1948. In the meantime, the viceroy, Lord Archibald Wavell, was replaced by Lord Louis Mountbatten.

The new viceroy encouraged the rival factions to agree upon a united India, but to no avail. A decision was made to divide the country, with Gandhi the only staunch opponent. Faced with increasing civil violence, Mountbatten made the precipitous decision to bring forward Independence to 15 August 1947.

Dividing the country into separate Hindu and Muslim territories was immensely tricky; the dividing line proved almost impossible to draw. Some areas were clearly Hindu or Muslim, but others had evenly mixed populations, and there were 'islands' of communities in areas predominantly settled by other religions. Moreover, the two overwhelmingly Muslim regions were on opposite sides of the country and, therefore, Pakistan would inevitably have an eastern and western half divided by a hostile India. The instability of this arrangement was self-evident, but it was 25 years before the split finally came and East Pakistan became Bangladesh.

An independent British referee was given the odious task of drawing the borders, well aware that the effects would be catastrophic for countless people. The decisions were fraught with impossible dilemmas. Calcutta, with its Hindu majority, port facilities and jute mills, was divided from East Bengal, which had a Muslim majority, large-scale jute production, no mills and no port facilities. One million Bengalis became refugees in the mass movement across the new border.

The problem was worse in Punjab, where intercommunity antagonisms were already running at fever pitch. Punjab, one of the most fertile and affluent regions of the country, had large Muslim, Hindu and Sikh communities. The Sikhs had already campaigned unsuccessfully for their own state and now saw their homeland divided down the middle. The new border ran straight between Punjab's two major cities, Lahore and Amritsar. Prior to Independence, Lahore's population of 1.2 million included approximately 500,000 Hindus and 100,000 Sikhs. When the dust had finally settled, roughly 1000 Hindus and Sikhs remained.

Punjab contained all the ingredients for an epic disaster, but the resulting bloodshed was far worse than anticipated. Huge population exchanges took place. Trains full of Muslims, fleeing westward, were held up and slaughtered by Hindu and Sikh mobs. Hindus and Sikhs fleeing to the east suffered the same fate at Muslim hands. The army that was sent to maintain order proved totally inadequate and, at times, all too ready to join the sectarian carnage. By the time the Punjab chaos had run its course, more than 10 million people had changed sides and at least 500,000 had been killed.

India and Pakistan became sovereign nations under the British Commonwealth in August 1947, but the violence, migrations and the integration of a few states, especially Kashmir, continued. The Constitution of India was at

A golden oldie, *Gandhi*, directed by Richard Attenborough, is one of the few movies that adeptly captures the grand canvas that is India whilst tracing the country's rocky road to Independence.

A Princess Remembers by Gayatri Devi and Santha Rama Rau is the captivating memoir of the former maharani of Jaipur, the glamorous Gayatri Devi (1919–2009).

HISTORY INDEPENDENCE & THE PARTITION OF INDIA

1948	1948–56	1949	1950
Asaf Jah VII, Hyderabad's last nizam, surrenders to the Indian government on 17 September. The Muslim dynasty was receiving support from Pakistan but had refused to join either new nation.	Rajasthan takes shape, as the princely states form a beeline to sign the Instrument of Accession, giving up their territories which are incorporated into the newly formed Republic of India.	The Constitution of India, drafted over two years by a 308-member Constituent Assembly, is adopted. The Assembly is chaired by BR Ambedkar and includes members from scheduled castes.	Constitution goes into effect on 26 January, and India becomes a republic. The date commemorates the Declaration of Independence, put forth by the Indian National Congress in 1930.

THE KASHMIR CONFLICT

Kashmir is the most enduring symbol of the turbulent partition of India. In the lead up to Independence, the delicate task of drawing the India–Pakistan border was complicated by the fact that India's 'princely states' were nominally independent. As part of the settlement process, local rulers were asked which country they wished to belong to. Kashmir was a predominantly Muslim state with a Hindu maharaja, Hari Singh, who tried to delay his decision. A ragtag Pashtun (Pakistani) army crossed the border, intent on racing to Srinagar and annexing Kashmir for Pakistan. In the face of this advance, the maharaja panicked and requested armed assistance from India. The Indian army arrived only just in time to prevent the fall of Srinagar, and the maharaja signed the Instrument of Accession, tying Kashmir to India, in October 1947. The legality of the document was immediately disputed by Pakistan, and the two nations went to war, just two months after Independence.

In 1948, the fledgling UN Security Council called for a referendum (which remains a central plank of Pakistani policy) to decide the status of Kashmir. A UN-brokered ceasefire in 1949 kept the countries on either side of a demarcation line, called the Cease-Fire Line (later to become the Line of Control, or LOC), with little else resolved. Two-thirds of Kashmir fell on the Indian side of the LOC, which remains the frontier, but neither side accepts this as the official border. The Indian state of Jammu and Kashmir, as it has stood since that time, incorporates Ladakh (divided between Muslims and Buddhists), Jammu (with a Hindu majority) and the 130km-long, 55km-wide Kashmir Valley (with a Muslim majority and most of the state's inhabitants). On the Pakistani side, over three million Kashmiris live in Azad (Free) Kashmir, known to Indians as Pakistan Occupied Kashmir (POK). Since the frontier was drawn, incursions across the LOC have occurred with dangerous regularity.

In 1989-90, the majority of Kashmiri Pandits (*pandit* means scholar, usually referring to a particular Hindu community of Brahmins), fled their homes following persecution and murder by extremists among the Muslim majority. Up to 170,000 left, many settling in refugee camps around Jammu. In 2014, President Mukherjee, when outlining the Modi government's five-year programme, pledged the Pandits would be helped to return ' to the land of their ancestors with full dignity, security and assured livelihood'.

last adopted in November 1949 and went into effect on 26 January, 1950, and, after untold struggles, independent India officially became a Republic.

After Independence

Jawaharlal Nehru tried to steer India towards a policy of nonalignment, balancing cordial relations with Britain and Commonwealth membership with moves towards the former USSR. The latter was due partly to conflicts with China, and US support for its arch-enemy Pakistan.

The 1960s and 1970s were tumultuous times for India. A border war with China in what was then known as the North-East Frontier Area (NEFA; now the Northeast States) and Ladakh, resulted in the loss of

1961	1962	1965	1966
Indian troops annexe Goa in a campaign lasting just 48 hours. The era of European colonialism in India is over.	Border war (known as the Sino-Indian War) with China over the North-East Frontier Area and Ladakh. China successfully captures the disputed territory and ends the war with a unilateral ceasefire.	Skirmishes in Kashmir and Gujarat's disputed Rann of Kutch flare into the Second India-Pakistan War, which involved the biggest tank battles since WWII. The war ends with a UN-mandated ceasefire.	Indira Gandhi, daughter of Jawaharlal Nehru, becomes prime minister of India, remembered today for her heavy-handed rule. She has been India's only female prime minister.

Aksai Chin (Ladakh) and smaller NEFA areas. Wars with Pakistan in 1965 (over Kashmir) and 1971 (over Bangladesh) also contributed to a sense among many Indians of having enemies on all sides.

In the midst of it all, the hugely popular Nehru died in 1964 and his daughter Indira Gandhi (no relation to Mahatma Gandhi) was elected as prime minister in 1966. Indira Gandhi, like Nehru before her, loomed large over the country she governed. Unlike Nehru, however, she was always a profoundly controversial figure whose historical legacy remains hotly disputed.

In 1975, facing serious opposition and unrest, she declared a state of emergency (which later became known as the Emergency). Freed of parliamentary constraints, Gandhi was able to boost the economy, control inflation remarkably well and decisively increase efficiency. On the negative side, political opponents often found themselves in prison, India's judicial system was turned into a puppet theatre and the press was fettered.

Gandhi's government was bundled out of office in the 1977 elections, but the 1980 election brought Indira Gandhi back to power with a larger majority than ever before, firmly laying the foundation for the Nehru-Gandhi family dynasty that would continue to dominate Indian politics for decades. Indira Gandhi was assassinated in 1984 by one of her Sikh bodyguards after her decision to attack the Golden Temple which was being occupied by fundamentalist Sikh preacher, Sant Jarnail Singh Bhindranwale. Her son Rajiv took over and was subsequently killed in a suicide bomb attack in 1991. His widow, Sonia, later became president, with Manmohan Singh as Prime Minister. However, the Congress party lost popularity as the economy slowed, and have been accused of cronyism and corruption.

The 2014 Federal elections saw the unpopular Congress party suffer a humiliating defeat under the shaky leadership of Rahul Gandhi, Indira's grandson. The BJP, headed by Narendra Modi, swept to power in a landslide victory (for more on this see India Today, p1104). Modi, former chief minister of Gujarat, who oversaw the state's transformation into an economic powerhouse, is a forceful, charismatic premier, hugely popular with business leaders and the BJP's Hindu-nationalist traditionalists, as well as with the ordinary man on the street.

However, some continue to ask questions about Modi's role in the deadly riots in Gujarat in 2002, which killed nearly 1000 people, most of them Muslims. Despite an official inquiry in 2014 which cleared the prime minister of any wrong-doing, allegations still circulate that the Gujarat government was complicit in the violence, which was triggered by a deadly arson attack on a train carrying Hindu pilgrims from Ayodhya. Nevertheless, as prime minister, Modi has thus far offered vision and hope, and a secular approach, which has inspired the country and provided new impetus both at home and abroad.

Deepa Mehta's 1998 film *Earth* is a dramatic retelling of the violence of Partition through the eyes of a young girl in Lahore.

The results of the 2011 census found India's population had increased by 181 million over 10 years.

1971	1972	1975	2014
East Pakistan champions independence from West Pakistan. India gets involved, sparking the Third India-Pakistan War. West Pakistan surrenders, losing sovereignty of East Pakistan, which becomes Bangladesh.	The Simla Agreement between India and Pakistan attempts to normalise relations. The Kashmiri ceasefire line is formalised: the 'Line of Control' remains the de-facto border between the two countries.	In a questionable move, Prime Minister Indira Gandhi declares a state of emergency under Article 352 of the Indian Constitution, in response to growing civil unrest and political opposition.	Narendra Modi, born into a Gujarati grocery family, achieves a historic landslide victory for the BJP, routing the Congress Party.

The Way of Life

Spirituality is the common thread in the richly diverse tapestry that is India. It, along with family, lies at the heart of society, and these two tenets intertwine in ceremonies to celebrate life's milestones. Despite the rising number of nuclear families – primarily in the more cosmopolitan cities such as Mumbai, Bengaluru and Delhi – the extended family remains a cornerstone in both urban and rural India, with males – usually the breadwinners – considered the head of the household.

Marriage, Birth & Death

Different religions practice different traditions, but for all communities, marriage, birth and death are important and marked with traditional ceremonies according to the faith. Hindus are in the majority in India. Barely 15% of the population are Muslim (though, at 180 million, Indian Muslims roughly equal the population of Pakistan).

Marriage is an exceptionally auspicious event for Indians – for most Indians, the idea of being unmarried by their mid-30s is unpalatable. Although 'love marriages' have spiralled upwards in recent times (mainly in urban hubs), most Indian marriages are still arranged, be the family Hindu, Muslim, Sikh or Buddhist. Discreet enquiries are made within the community. If a suitable match is not found, the help of professional matchmakers may be sought, or advertisements may be placed in newspapers and/or on the internet. In Hindu families, the horoscopes of both potential partners are checked and, if propitious, there's a meeting between the two families.

Dowry, although illegal, is still a key issue in more than a few arranged marriages (mostly in conservative communities), with some families plunging into debt to raise the required cash and merchandise (from cars and computers to refrigerators and televisions). Health workers claim that India's high rate of abortion of female foetuses (sex identification medical tests are banned in India, but they still clandestinely occur in some clinics) is predominantly due to the financial burden of providing a daughter's dowry. Muslim grooms have to pay what is called a *mehr* to the bride.

The Hindu wedding ceremony is officiated over by a priest and the marriage is formalised when the couple walk around a sacred fire seven times. Muslim ceremonies involve the reading of the Qu'ran, and traditionally the husband and wife view each other via mirrors. Despite the existence of nuclear families, it's still the norm for a wife to live with her husband's family once married and assume the household duties outlined by her mother-in-law. Not surprisingly, the mother–daughter-in-law relationship can be a tricky one, as portrayed in various Indian TV soap operas.

Divorce and remarriage is becoming more common (primarily in bigger cities), but divorce is still not granted by courts as a matter of routine and is not looked upon very favourably by society. Among the higher castes, in more traditional areas, widows are traditionally expected not to remarry and are expected to wear white and live pious, celibate lives. It is still legal for Muslim males in India to obtain oral divorce according to sharia law (by uttering the word *talaq* meaning 'divorce' three times).

The Wonder That Was India by AL Basham gives descriptions of Indian civilisations, major religions and social customs – a good thematic approach to weave the disparate strands together.

The birth of a child is another momentous occasion, with its own set of special ceremonies which take place at various auspicious times during the early years of childhood. For Hindus these include the casting of the child's first horoscope, name-giving, feeding the first solid food, and the first hair cutting.

Hindus cremate their dead, and funeral ceremonies are designed to purify and console both the living and the deceased. An important aspect of the proceedings is the *sharadda,* paying respect to one's ancestors by offering water and rice cakes. It's an observance that's repeated at each anniversary of the death. After the cremation, the ashes are collected and, 13 days after the death (when blood relatives are deemed ritually pure), a member of the family usually scatters them in a holy river such as the Ganges or in the ocean. Sikhs similarly wash then cremate their dead. Muslims also prepare their dead carefully, but bury them, while the minority Zoroastrian Parsi community place their dead in 'Towers of Silence' (stone towers) to be devoured by birds.

Matchmaking has, inevitably, gone online, with popular sites including www.shaadi.com, www.bharatmatrimony.com and, in a sign of the times, www.second-shaadi.com – for those seeking a partner again.

The Caste System

Although the Indian constitution does not recognise the caste system, caste still wields powerful influence, especially in rural India, where the caste you are born into largely determines your social standing in the community. It can also influence your vocational and marriage prospects. Castes are further divided into thousands of *jati,* groups of 'families' or social communities, which are sometimes but not always linked to occupation. Conservative Hindus will only marry someone of the same *jati,* and you'll often see caste as a criteria in matrimonial adverts, 'Mahar seeks Mahar', etc. In some traditional areas, young men and women who fall in love outside their caste have been murdered.

According to tradition, caste is the basic social structure of Hindu society. Living a righteous life and fulfilling your dharma (moral duty) raises your chances of being reborn into a higher caste and thus into better circumstances. Hindus are born into one of four varnas (castes): Brahmin (priests and scholars), Kshatriya (soldiers and administrators), Vaishya (merchants) and Shudra (labourers). The Brahmins were said to have emerged from the mouth of Lord Brahma at the moment of creation, Kshatriyas were said to have come from his arms, Vaishyas from his thighs and Shudras from his feet. Beneath the four main castes are the

---

INDIAN ATTIRE

Widely worn by Indian women, the elegant sari comes in a single piece (between 5m and 9m long and 1m wide) and is ingeniously tucked and pleated into place without the need for pins or buttons. Worn with the sari is the choli (tight-fitting blouse) and a drawstring petticoat. The *palloo* is the part of the sari draped over the shoulder. Also commonly worn is the *salwar kameez,* a traditional dresslike tunic and trouser combination accompanied by a dupatta (long scarf). Saris and *salwar kameez* come in a fantastic range of fabrics, colours and designs.

Traditional attire for men includes the dhoti, and in the south, the *lungi* and the *mundu.* The dhoti is a loose, long loincloth pulled up between the legs. The *lungi* is more like a sarong, with its end usually sewn up like a tube. The *mundu* is like a lungi but is always white. A kurta (shirt) is a long tunic or shirt worn mainly by men, usually with no collar. Kurta pyjama are a cotton shirt and trousers set worn for relaxing or sleeping. *Churidar* are close-fitting trousers often worn under a kurta. A *sherwani* is a long coat-like men's garment, which originated as a fusion of the *salwar kameez* with the British frock coat.

There are regional and religious variations in costume – for example, you may see Muslim women wearing the all-enveloping burka.

RANGOLIS

Rangolis, the striking and breathtakingly intricate chalk, rice-paste or coloured powder designs (also called *kolams*) that adorn thresholds, especially in South India, are both auspicious and symbolic. *Rangolis* are traditionally drawn at sunrise and are sometimes made of rice-flour paste, which may be eaten by little creatures – symbolising a reverence for even the smallest living things. Deities are deemed to be attracted to a beautiful *rangoli,* which may also signal to sadhus (ascetics) that they will be offered food at a particular house. Some people believe that *rangolis* protect against the evil eye.

Dalits (formerly known as Untouchables), who hold menial jobs such as sweepers and latrine cleaners. Many of India's complex codes of ritual purity were devised to prevent physical contact between people of higher castes and Dalits. A less rigid system exists in Islamic communities in India, with society divided into *ashraf* (high born), *ajlaf* (low born) and *arzal* (equivalent to the Dalits).

The word 'pariah' is derived from the name of a Tamil Dalit group, the Paraiyars. Some Dalit leaders, such as the renowned Dr BR Ambedkar (1891–1956), sought to change their status by adopting another faith; in his case it was Buddhism. At the bottom of the social heap are the Denotified Tribes. They were known as the Criminal Tribes until 1952, when a reforming law officially recognised 198 tribes and castes. Many are nomadic or seminomadic tribes, forced by the wider community to eke out a living on society's fringes.

Based on Rabindranath Tagore's novel, *Chokher Bali* (directed by Rituparno Ghosh) is a poignant film about a young widow living in early-20th-century Bengal who challenges the 'rules of widowhood' – something unthinkable in that era.

To improve the Dalits' position, the government reserves considerable numbers of public-sector jobs, parliamentary seats and university places for them. Today these quotas account for almost 25% of government jobs and university (student) positions. The situation varies regionally, as different political leaders chase caste vote-banks by promising to include them in reservations. The reservation system, while generally regarded in a favourable light, has also been criticised for unfairly blocking tertiary and employment opportunities for those who would have otherwise got positions on merit. On the other hand, there are still regular examples of discrimination against Dalits in daily life, for example, higher castes denying them entry into certain temples.

Pilgrimage

Devout Hindus are expected to go on a *yatra* (pilgrimage) at least once a year. Pilgrimages are undertaken to implore the gods or goddesses to grant a wish, to take the ashes of a cremated relative to a holy river, or to gain spiritual merit. India has thousands of holy sites to which pilgrims travel; the elderly often make Varanasi their final one, as it's believed that dying in this sacred city releases a person from the cycle of rebirth. Sufi shrines in India attract thousands of Muslims to commemorate holy days, such as the birthday of a sufi saint, and many Muslims also make the hajj to Mecca in Saudi Arabia.

Sati: A Study of Widow Burning in India by Sakuntala Narasimhan explores the history of *sati* (a widow's suicide on her husband's funeral pyre; now banned) on the subcontinent.

Most festivals in India have religious roots and are thus a magnet for throngs of pilgrims. Remember that most festivals are spiritual occasions, even those that have a carnivalesque sheen. Also be aware that there are deaths at festivals every year because of stampedes, so be cautious in crowds.

Women in India

According to the most recent census, in 2011, India's population is comprised of 586 million women, with an estimated 68% of those working (mostly as labourers) in the agricultural sector.

Women in India are entitled to vote and own property. While the percentage of women in politics has risen over the past decade, they're still notably underrepresented in the national parliament, accounting for 11% of parliamentary members.

Although the professions are male dominated, women are steadily making inroads, especially in urban centres. Kerala was India's first state to break societal norms by recruiting female police officers in 1938. It was also the first state to establish an all-female police station (1973). For village women it's much more difficult to get ahead, but groups such as the Self-Employed Women's Association (SEWA) in Gujarat have shown what's possible, organising socially disadvantaged women into unions and offering microfinance loans.

In low-income families, especially, girls can be regarded as a serious financial liability because at marriage a dowry must often be supplied.

For the urban middle-class woman, life is much more comfortable, but pressures still exist. Broadly speaking, she is far more likely to receive a tertiary education, but once married is still usually expected to 'fit in' with her in-laws and be a homemaker above all else. Like her village counterpart, if she fails to live up to expectations – even if it's just not being able to produce a grandson – the consequences can sometimes be dire, as demonstrated by the extreme practice of 'bride burning', wherein a wife is doused with flammable liquid and set alight. In 2013, the National Crime Records Bureau (NCRB) figures reported 8083 incidences, almost one every hour.

Although the constitution allows for divorcees (and widows) to remarry, relatively few reportedly do so, simply because divorcees are traditionally considered outcasts from society, most evidently so beyond big cities. Divorce rates in India are among the world's lowest, though they are steadily rising. Most divorces take place in urban centres and are deemed less socially unacceptable among those occupying the upper echelons of society.

In October 2006, following women's civil rights campaigns, the Indian parliament passed a landmark bill (on top of existing legislation) which gives women who are suffering domestic violence increased protection and rights. Prior to this legislation, although women could lodge police complaints against abusive spouses, they weren't automatically entitled to a share of the marital property or to ongoing financial support. Critics

If you want to learn more about India's caste system, these two books are a good start: *Interrogating Caste* by Dipankar Gupta and *Translating Caste* edited by Tapan Basu.

Read more about India's tribal communities at www.tribal.nic.in, a site maintained by the Indian government's Ministry of Tribal Affairs.

THE WAY OF LIFE WOMEN IN INDIA

ADIVASIS

India's Adivasis (tribal communities; Adivasi translates to 'original inhabitant' in Sanskrit) have origins that precede the Vedic Aryans and the Dravidians of the south. These groups range from the Gondi of the central plains to the animist tribes of the Northeast States. Today, they constitute less than 10% of the population and are comprised of more than 400 different tribal groups. The literacy rate for Adivasis is significantly below the national average.

Historically, contact between Adivasis and Hindu villagers on the plains rarely led to friction as there was little or no competition for resources and land. However, in recent decades an increasing number of Adivasis have been dispossessed of their ancestral land and turned into impoverished labourers. Although they still have political representation thanks to a parliamentary quota system, the dispossession and exploitation of Adivasis have reportedly sometimes been with the connivance of officialdom – an accusation the government denies. Whatever the arguments, unless more is done, the Adivasis' future is an uncertain one.

Read more about Adivasis in *Archaeology and History: Early Settlements in the Andaman Islands* by Zarine Cooper, *The Tribals of India* by Sunil Janah and *Tribes of India: The Struggle for Survival* by Christoph von Fürer-Haimendorf.

claim that many women, especially those outside India's larger cities, are still reluctant to seek legal protection because of the social stigma involved. And despite legal reforms, conviction rates remain low enough for perpetrators to feel a sense of impunity.

India remains an extremely prudish and conservative society, and despite the highly sexualised images of women churned out in Bollywood movies (although kissing is still rarely seen on screen), it's considered by many traditionally minded people that a woman is somehow wanton if she so much as goes out after dark.

According to India's National Crime Records Bureau (NCRB), reported incidences of rape have gone up over 50% in the last 10 years, but it's believed that only a small percentage of sexual assaults are reported, largely due to family pressure and/or shame, especially if the perpetrator is known to the family (which is true in many cases).

Following the highly publicised gang-rape and murder of a 23-year-old Indian physiotherapy student in Delhi in December 2012, tens of thousands of people protested in the capital, and beyond, demanding swift government action to address the country's escalating gender-based violence. It took a further year before legal amendments were made to existing laws to address the problem of sexual violence, including stiffer punishments such as life imprisonment and the death penalty (but there is still limited recognition of marital rape, and government permission is necessary before security forces can be prosecuted for criminal offences). Despite the action taken, more shocking cases are horrifyingly regular occurrences. The NCRB reported that in 2013, 309,546 crimes were against women. Of these, 33,707 were rape and 70,739 were molestation. The conviction rate for rape was 27.1% in 2013. It's doubtless that sexual violence is a pervasive social problem in India. For information on safety for female visitors, see Women & Solo Travellers, p1176.

India has the world's second largest diaspora – over 25 million people – with Indian banks holding upwards of US$70 billion in Non-Resident Indian (NRI) accounts.

Sport

Cricket has long been engraved on the nation's heart, with the first recorded match in 1721, and India's first test match victory in 1952 in Chennai against England. It's not only a national sporting obsession, but a matter of enormous patriotism, especially evident whenever India plays against Pakistan. Matches between these South Asian neighbours – which have had rocky relations since Independence – attract especially passionate support, and the players of both sides are under immense pressure to do their respective countries proud. The most celebrated Indian cricketer of recent years is Sachin Tendulkar – fondly dubbed the 'Little Master' – who, in 2012, became the world's only player to score 100 international centuries, retiring on a high the following year. Cricket – especially the

HIJRAS

India's most visible nonheterosexual group is the *hijras*, a caste of transvestites and eunuchs who dress in women's clothing. Some are gay, some are hermaphrodites and some were unfortunate enough to be kidnapped and castrated. *Hijras* have long had a place in Indian culture, and in 2014 the Indian Supreme Court recognised *hijras* as a third gender and as a class entitled to reservation in education and jobs. Conversely, in 2013, homosexuality was ruled to be unlawful (having been legal since 2009).

Hijras work mainly as uninvited entertainers at weddings and celebrations of the birth of male children, and possibly as prostitutes. In 2014, Padmini Prakash became India's first transgender daily television news show anchor, indicating a new level of acceptance.

Read more about *hijras* in *The Invisibles* by Zia Jaffrey and *Ardhanarishvara the Androgyne* by Dr Alka Pande.

Twenty20 format (www.cricket20.com) – is big business in India, attracting lucrative sponsorship deals and celebrity status for its players. The sport has not been without its murky side though, with Indian cricketers among those embroiled in match-fixing scandals over past years. International games are played at various centres – see Indian newspapers or check online for details about matches that coincide with your visit. Keep your finger on the cricketing pulse at www.espncricinfo.com (rated most highly by many cricket aficionados) and www.cricbuzz.com.

The launch of the Indian Super League (ISL; www.indiansuperleague.com) in 2013 has achieved its aim of promoting football as a big-time, big-money sport. With games attracting huge crowds and international players, such as the legendary Juventus footballer Alessandro del Piero (who was signed for the Delhi Dynamos in 2014) or Marco Materazzi (of World Cup headbutt fame) as trainer of Chennai, the ISL has become an international talking point. The first week of the ISL in 2014 had 170.6m viewers in the first week – the figures for the first phase of the Indian Premier League cricket was 184m, which gives a sense of football's growth in popularity. The I-League is the longer-running domestic league, but it has never attracted such media attention or funding.

The country is also known for its historical links to horse polo, which intermittently thrived on the subcontinent (especially among nobility) until Independence, after which patronage steeply declined due to dwindling funds. Today there's a renewed interest in polo thanks to beefed-up sponsorship and, although it still remains an elite sport, it's attracting more attention from the country's burgeoning upper middle class. The origins of polo are not completely clear. Believed to have its roots in Persia and China around 2000 years ago, on the subcontinent it's thought to have first been played in Baltistan (in present-day Pakistan). Some say that Emperor Akbar (who reigned in India from 1556 to 1605) first introduced rules to the game, but that polo, as it's played today, was largely influenced by a British cavalry regiment stationed in India during the 1870s. A set of international rules was implemented after WWI. The world's oldest surviving polo club, established in 1862, is in Kolkata (Calcutta Polo Club; www.calcuttapolo.com). Polo takes place during the cooler winter months in major cities, including Delhi, Jaipur, Mumbai and Kolkata. It is also occasionally played in Ladakh and Manipur.

Although officially the national sport, field hockey no longer enjoys the same fervent following it once did, though currently India's national men's/women's hockey world rankings are 9/13 respectively. During its golden era, between 1928 and 1956, India won six consecutive Olympic gold medals in hockey; it later bagged two further Olympic gold medals, one in 1964 and the other in 1980. Recent initiatives to ignite renewed interest in the game have had mixed results. Tap into India's hockey scene at Indian Hockey (www.indianhockey.com) and Indian Field Hockey (www.bharatiyahockey.org).

Kabaddi is another popular competitive sport in the region. Two teams occupy two sides of a court. A raider runs into the opposing side, taking a breath and try to tag one or more members of the opposite team. The raider chants 'kabaddi' repeatedly to show that they have not taken a breath, returning to the home half before exhaling.

Other sports gaining ground in India include tennis (the country's star performers are Sania Mirza, Leander Paes and Mahesh Bhupathi – to delve deeper, click www.aitatennis.com) and horse racing, which is reasonably popular in the larger cities such as Mumbai, Delhi, Kolkata and Bengaluru.

If you're interested in catching a sports match during your time in India, consult local newspapers (or ask at a tourist office) for current details about dates and venues.

Cricket lovers are likely to be bowled over by *The Illustrated History of Indian Cricket* by Boria Majumdar and *The States of Indian Cricket* by Ramachandra Guha.

Several of the Indian Super League teams are co-owned by Bollywood superstars, for example, Pune by Hrithik Roshan, and Chennai by Abhishek Bachchan.

Spiritual India

From elaborate city shrines to simple village temples, spirituality suffuses almost every facet of life in India. The nation's major faith, Hinduism, is practised by around 80% of the population and it is one of the world's oldest extant religions, with roots extending beyond 1000 BC. Buddhism, Jainism and Zoroastrianism have a similarly historic pedigree in India. The mind-stirring sight of sacred architecture, and the soul-warming sound of bhajans (devotional songs) and qawwali (Islamic devotional singing) are bound to burn bright in your memory long after you've left India.

Hinduism

Hinduism has no founder or central authority and it isn't a proselytising religion. Essentially, Hindus believe in Brahman, who is eternal, uncreated and infinite. Everything that exists emanates from Brahman and will ultimately return to it. The multitude of gods and goddesses are merely manifestations – knowable aspects of this formless phenomenon.

Hindus believe that earthly life is cyclical: you are born again and again (a process known as samsara), the quality of these rebirths being dependent upon your karma (conduct or action) in previous lives. Living a righteous life and fulfilling your dharma (moral code of behaviour; social duty) will enhance your chances of being born into a higher caste and better circumstances. Alternatively, if enough bad karma has accumulated, rebirth may take animal form. But it's only as a human that you can gain sufficient self-knowledge to escape the cycle of reincarnation and achieve moksha (liberation).

Gods & Goddesses

All Hindu deities are regarded as a manifestation of Brahman, who is often described as having three main representations, the Trimurti: Brahma, Vishnu and Shiva.

The Hindu pantheon is said to have a staggering 330 million deities; those worshipped are a matter of personal choice or tradition.

Brahman

The One; the ultimate reality. Brahman is formless, eternal and the source of all existence. Brahman is *nirguna* (without attributes), as opposed to all the other gods and goddesses, which are manifestations of Brahman and therefore *saguna* (with attributes).

Brahma

Only during the creation of the universe does Brahma play an active role. At other times he is in meditation. His consort is Saraswati, the goddess of learning, and his vehicle is a swan. He is sometimes shown sitting on a lotus that rises from Vishnu's navel, symbolising the interdependence of the gods. Brahma is generally depicted with four (crowned and bearded) heads, each turned towards a point of the compass. Worship of Brahma was eclipsed by the rise of cults devoted to Shiva and Vishnu. Today, India has few Brahma temples.

Vishnu

The preserver or sustainer, Vishnu is associated with 'right action'. He protects and sustains all that is good in the world. He is usually depicted with four arms, holding a lotus, a conch shell (it can be blown like a trumpet so symbolises the cosmic vibration from which existence emanates), a discus and a mace. His consort is Lakshmi, the goddess of wealth, and his vehicle is Garuda, the man-bird creature. The Ganges is said to flow from his feet.

Shiva is sometimes characterised as the lord of yoga, a Himalaya-dwelling ascetic with matted hair, an ash-smeared body, a penchant for chillum (hash pipe) smoking, and a third eye symbolising wisdom.

Shiva

Shiva is the destroyer – to deliver salvation – without whom creation couldn't occur. Shiva's creative role is phallically symbolised by his representation as the frequently worshipped lingam. With 1008 names, Shiva takes many forms, including Nataraja, lord of the *tandava* (cosmic victory dance), who paces out the creation and destruction of the cosmos.

Sometimes Shiva has snakes draped around his neck and is shown holding a trident (representative of the Trimurti) as a weapon while riding Nandi, his bull. Nandi symbolises power and potency, justice and moral order. Shiva's consort, Parvati, is capable of taking many forms, including blood-thirsty Durga and Kali.

Other Prominent Deities

Elephant-headed Ganesh is the god of good fortune, remover of obstacles, and patron of scribes (the broken tusk he holds was used to write sections of the Mahabharata). His animal vehicle is Mooshak (a ratlike creature). How Ganesh came to have an elephant's head is a story with several variations. One legend says that Ganesh was born to Parvati in the absence of his father Shiva, and so grew up not knowing him. One day, as Ganesh stood guard while his mother bathed, Shiva returned and asked to be let into Parvati's presence. Ganesh, who didn't recognise Shiva, refused. Enraged, Shiva lopped off Ganesh's head, only to later discover, much to his horror, that he had slaughtered his own son. He vowed to replace Ganesh's head with that of the first creature he came across, which happened to be an elephant.

Another prominent deity, Krishna is an incarnation of Vishnu sent to earth to fight for good and combat evil. His dalliances with the *gopis* (milkmaids) and his love for Radha have inspired countless paintings and songs. Depicted with blue-hued skin, Krishna is often seen playing the flute.

Hanuman is the hero of the Ramayana and loyal ally of Rama. He embodies the concept of *bhakti* (devotion). He's the king of the monkeys, but is capable of taking on other forms.

Among Shaivites (followers of the Shiva movement), *shakti*, the divine creative power of women, is worshipped as a force in its own right. The concept of *shakti* is embodied in the ancient goddess Devi (divine

THE SACRED SEVEN

The number seven has special significance in Hinduism. There are seven sacred Indian cities, which are all major pilgrimage centres: Varanasi, associated with Shiva; Haridwar, where the Ganges enters the plains from the Himalaya; Ayodhya, birthplace of Rama; Dwarka, with the legendary capital of Krishna thought to be off the Gujarat coast; Mathura, birthplace of Krishna; Kanchipuram, site of the historic Shiva temples; and Ujjain, venue of the Kumbh Mela every 12 years.

There are also seven sacred rivers: the Ganges (Ganga), Saraswati (thought to be underground), Yamuna, Indus, Narmada, Godavari and Cauvery.

> ## OM
> ....
> The word 'Om' has significance for several religions, and is one of Hinduism's most vener-
> ated symbols. Pronounced 'aum', it's a highly propitious mantra (sacred word or syllable).
> The 'three' shape symbolises the creation, maintenance and destruction of the universe
> (and thus the holy Trimurti). The inverted *chandra* (crescent or half moon) represents the
> discursive mind and the *bindu* (dot) within it, Brahman.
>
> Buddhists believe that, if intoned often enough with complete concentration, it will
> lead to a state of blissful emptiness.

mother), who is also manifested as Durga and, in a fiercer evil-destroying
incarnation, Kali. Other widely worshipped goddesses include Lakshmi,
the goddess of wealth, and Saraswati, the goddess of learning.

Sacred Texts

Hindu sacred texts fall into two categories: those believed to be the word
of god (*shruti*, meaning 'heard') and those produced by people (*smriti*,
meaning 'remembered'). The Vedas are regarded as *shruti* knowledge
and are considered the authoritative basis for Hinduism. The oldest of
the Vedic texts, the Rig-Veda, was compiled over 3000 years ago. Within
its 1028 verses are prayers for prosperity and longevity, as well as an
explanation of the universe's origins. The Upanishads, the last parts of
the Vedas, reflect on the mystery of death and emphasise the oneness of
the universe. The oldest of the Vedic texts were written in Vedic Sanskrit
(related to Old Persian). Later texts were composed in classical Sanskrit,
but many have been translated into the vernacular.

Two recom-
mended publica-
tions containing
English trans-
lations of holy
Hindu texts
are *The Bhaga-
vad Gita* by S
Radhakrishnan
and *The Valmiki
Ramayana* by
Romesh Dutt.

The *smriti* texts comprise a collection of literature spanning centuries and include expositions on the proper performance of domestic ceremonies as well as the proper pursuit of government, economics and
religious law. Among its well-known works are the Ramayana and Mahabharata, as well as the Puranas, which expand on the epics and promote the notion of the Trimurti. Unlike the Vedas, reading the Puranas is
not restricted to initiated higher-caste males.

The Mahabharata

Thought to have been composed around 1000 BC, the Mahabharata
focuses on the exploits of Krishna. By about 500 BC, the Mahabharata
had evolved into a far more complex creation with substantial additions,
including the Bhagavad Gita (where Krishna proffers advice to Arjuna
before a battle).

The story centres on conflict between the heroic gods (Pandavas) and
the demons (Kauravas). Overseeing events is Krishna, who has taken on
human form. Krishna acts as charioteer for the Pandava hero Arjuna,
who eventually triumphs in a great battle against the Kauravas.

The Ramayana

Composed around the 3rd or 2nd century BC, the Ramayana is believed
to be largely the work of one person, the poet Valmiki. Like the Mahabharata, it centres on conflict between the gods and the demons.

The story goes that Dasharatha, the childless king of Ayodhya, called
upon the gods to provide him with a son. His wife duly gave birth to a
boy. But this child, named Rama, was in fact an incarnation of Vishnu,
who had assumed human form to overthrow the demon king of Lanka
(now Sri Lanka), Ravana.

As an adult, Rama, who won the hand of the princess Sita in a competition, was chosen by his father to inherit his kingdom. At the last minute

Rama's stepmother intervened and demanded her son, Barathan, take Rama's place. Rama, Sita and Rama's brother, Lakshmana, were exiled and went off to the forests, where Rama and Lakshmana battled demons and dark forces. Ravana's sister attempted to seduce Rama but she was rejected and, in revenge, Ravana captured Sita and spirited her away to his palace in Lanka.

Rama, assisted by an army of monkeys led by the loyal monkey god Hanuman, eventually found the palace, killed Ravana and rescued Sita. All returned victorious to Ayodhya, where Rama was welcomed by Barathan and crowned king.

Did you know that blood-drinking Kali is another form of milk-giving Gauri? *Myth = Mithya: A Handbook of Hindu Mythology* by Devdutt Pattanaik sheds light on this and other fascinating Hindu folklore.

Naturally Sacred

Animals, particularly snakes and cows, have long been worshipped on the subcontinent. For Hindus, the cow represents fertility and nurturing, while snakes (especially cobras) are associated with fertility and welfare. Naga stones (snake stones) serve the dual purpose of protecting humans from snakes and appeasing snake gods.

Plants can also have sacred associations, such as the banyan tree, which symbolises the Trimurti, while mango trees are symbolic of love – Shiva is believed to have married Parvati under one. Meanwhile, the lotus flower is said to have emerged from the primeval waters and is connected to the mythical centre of the earth through its stem. Often found in the most polluted of waters, the lotus has the remarkable ability to blossom above murky depths. The centre of the lotus corresponds to the centre of the universe, the navel of the earth: all is held together by the stem and the eternal waters. The fragile yet resolute lotus is an embodiment of beauty and strength and a reminder to Hindus of how their own lives should be. So revered has the lotus become that today it's India's national flower. The Rudraksha (meaning 'Shiva's eye') tree is said to have sprung from Shiva's tears, and its seeds are used as prayer beads.

Worship

Worship and ritual play a paramount role in Hinduism. In Hindu homes you'll often find a dedicated worship area, where members of the family

ANATOMY OF A GOMPA

Parts of India, such as Sikkim and Ladakh, are known for their ornate, colourful gompas (Tibetan-style Buddhist monasteries). The focal point of a gompa is the *dukhang* (prayer hall), where monks assemble to chant passages from the sacred scriptures (morning prayers are a particularly atmospheric time to visit gompas). The walls may be covered in vivid murals or *thangkas* (cloth paintings) of bodhisattvas (enlightened beings) and *dharmapalas* (protector deities). By the entrance to the *dukhang*, you'll usually find a mural depicting the Wheel of Life, a graphical representation of the core elements of Buddhist philosophy (see www.buddhanet.net/wheel1.htm for an interactive description of the Wheel of Life).

Most gompas hold *chaam* dances (ritual masked dances to celebrate the victory of good over evil) during major festivals. Dances to ward off evil feature masks of Mahakala, the Great Protector, usually dramatically adorned with a headdress of human skulls. The Durdag dance features skull masks depicting the Lords of the Cremation Grounds, while Shawa dancers wear masks of wild-eyed stags. These characters are often depicted with a third eye in the centre of their foreheads, signifying the need for inner reflection.

Another interesting activity at Buddhist monasteries is the production of butter sculptures, elaborate models made from coloured butter and dough. The sculptures are deliberately designed to decay, symbolising the impermanence of human existence. Many gompas also produce exquisite sand mandalas – geometric patterns made from sprinkled coloured sand, then destroyed to symbolise the futility of the physical plane.

pray to the deities of their choice. Beyond the home, Hindus worship at temples. *Puja* is a focal point of worship and ranges from silent prayer to elaborate ceremonies. Devotees leave the temple with a handful of *prasad* (temple-blessed food used in religious ceremonies) which is shared among others. Other forms of worship include *aarti* (the auspicious lighting of lamps or candles) and the playing of bhajans (devotional songs).

Islam

Islam is India's largest minority religion, followed by approximately 13.4% of the population. It's believed that Islam was introduced to northern India by Muslim conquerors (in the 16th and 17th centuries the Mughal empire controlled much of North India) and to the south by Arab traders.

Islam was founded in Arabia by the Prophet Mohammed in the 7th century AD. The Arabic term *islam* means to surrender, and believers (Muslims) undertake to surrender to the will of Allah (God), which is revealed in the scriptures, the Quran. In this monotheistic religion, God's word is conveyed through prophets (messengers), of whom Mohammed was the most recent.

Following Mohammed's death, a succession dispute split the movement, and the legacy today is the Sunnis and the Shiites. Most Muslims in India are Sunnis. The Sunnis emphasise the 'well-trodden' path or the orthodox way. Shiites believe that only imams (exemplary leaders) can reveal the true meaning of the Quran. India also has a long tradition of Sufism, a mystical interpretation of Islam that dates back to the earliest days of the religion.

All Muslims, however, share a belief in the Five Pillars of Islam: the shahada (declaration of faith: 'There is no God but Allah; Mohammed is his prophet'); prayer (ideally five times a day); the zakat (tax), in the form of a charitable donation; fasting (during Ramadan) for all except the sick, young children, pregnant women, the elderly and those undertaking arduous journeys; and the hajj (pilgrimage) to Mecca, which every Muslim aspires to do at least once.

Sikhism

Sikhism, founded in Punjab by Guru Nanak in the 15th century, began as a reaction against the caste system and Brahmin domination of ritual, but evolved into a militarised religion resisting the Islamic domination of the Punjab. Sikhs believe in one god and although they reject the worship of idols, some keep pictures of the 10 gurus as a point of focus. The Sikhs' holy book, the Guru Granth Sahib, contains the teachings of the 10 Sikh gurus, several of whom were executed by the Mughals. Like Hindus and Buddhists, Sikhs believe in rebirth and karma. In Sikhism, there's no ascetic or monastic tradition ending the cycles of rebirth. Almost 2% of India's citizens are Sikhs, with most living in Punjab.

Born in present-day Pakistan, Guru Nanak (1469–1539) was largely dissatisfied with both Muslim and Hindu religious practices. He believed in family life and the value of hard work – he married, had two sons and worked as a farmer when not travelling around, preaching and singing self-composed *kirtan* (Sikh devotional songs) with his Muslim musician, Mardana. He is said to have performed miracles and he encouraged meditation on God's name as a prime path to enlightenment.

Nanak believed in equality centuries before it became socially fashionable and campaigned against the caste system. He was a practical guru – 'a person who makes an honest living and shares earnings with others recognises the way to God'. He appointed his most talented disciple to be his successor, not one of his sons. His *kirtan* are still sung in gurdwaras (Sikh temples) today, and his picture is kept in millions of homes on and beyond the subcontinent.

Unravelling the basic tenets of Hinduism are two books, both called *Hinduism: An Introduction* – one is by Shakunthala Jagannathan, the other by Dharam Vir Singh.

To grasp the intricacies of Sikhism, read Volume One (1469–1839) or Volume Two (1839–2004) of *A History of the Sikhs* by Khushwant Singh.

Sikhs strive to follow the spiritual lead of the Khalsa, the five Sikh warriors anointed by Guru Gobind Singh as perfectly embodying the principles of the Sikh faith. Wearing a *dastar*, or turban, is mandatory for baptised Sikh men, and devout Sikhs uphold the 'Five Ks' - *kesh* (leaving hair uncut), *kanga* (carrying a wooden comb), *kara* (wearing an iron bracelet), *kacchera* (wearing cotton shorts) and *kirpan* (carrying a dagger or sword).

Buddhism

Less than 1% of the country's population is Buddhist. Bodhgaya, in the state of Bihar, where the Buddha achieved enlightenment, is one of Buddhism's most sacred sites, drawing pilgrims from across the world.

Buddhism arose in the 6th century BC as a reaction against the strictures of Brahminical Hinduism. Buddha (Awakened One) is believed to have lived from about 563 to 483 BC. Formerly a prince (Siddhartha Gautama) from the Nepali plains, the Buddha, at the age of 29, embarked on a quest for emancipation from the world of suffering. He achieved nirvana (the state of full awareness) at Bodhgaya (Bihar), aged 35. Critical of the caste system and the unthinking worship of gods, the Buddha urged his disciples to seek truth within their own experiences.

The Buddha taught that existence is based on Four Noble Truths: that life is rooted in suffering, that suffering is caused by craving, that one can find release from suffering by eliminating craving, and that the way to eliminate craving is by following the Noble Eightfold Path. This path consists of right understanding, right intention, right speech, right action, right livelihood, right effort, right awareness and right concentration. By successfully complying with these one can attain nirvana.

Buddhism had somewhat waned in parts of India by the turn of the 20th century. However, it saw a revival in the 1950s among intellectuals and Dalits who were disillusioned with the caste system. The number of

Tribal religions have so merged with Hinduism and other mainstream religions that very few are now clearly identifiable, though animist traditions persist in the Northeast. Some basic tenets of Hinduism are believed to have originated in tribal culture.

RELIGIOUS ETIQUETTE

Whenever visiting a sacred site, dress and behave respectfully – don't wear shorts or sleeveless tops (this applies to men and women) – and refrain from smoking. Loud and intrusive behaviour isn't appreciated, and neither are public displays of affection or kidding around.

Before entering a holy place, remove your shoes (tip the shoe-minder a few rupees when retrieving them) and check if photography is allowed. You're permitted to wear socks in most places of worship – often necessary during warmer months, when floors can be uncomfortably hot.

Religious etiquette advises against touching locals on the head, or directing the soles of your feet at a person, religious shrine or image of a deity. Protocol also advises against touching someone with your feet or touching a carving of a deity.

Head cover (for women and sometimes men) is required at some places of worship – especially gurdwaras (Sikh temples) and mosques – so carry a scarf just to be on the safe side. There are some sites that don't admit women and some that deny entry to non-adherents of their faith – enquire in advance. Women may be required to sit apart from men. Jain temples request the removal of leather items you may be wearing or carrying and may also request that menstruating women not enter. When walking around any Buddhist sacred site (chortens, stupas, temples, gompas) go clockwise. Don't touch them with your left hand. Turn prayer wheels clockwise, with your right hand.

Taking photos inside a shrine, at a funeral, at a religious ceremony or of people taking a holy dip can be offensive – ask first. Flash photography may be prohibited in certain areas of a shrine, or may not be permitted at all.

followers has been further increased with the influx of Tibetan refugees. Both the current Dalai Lama and the 17th Karmapa reside in India.

Jainism

Jainism arose in the 6th century BC as a reaction against the caste restraints and rituals of Hinduism. It was founded by Mahavira, a contemporary of the Buddha.

Jains believe that liberation can be attained by achieving complete purity of the soul. Purity means shedding all *karman*, matter generated by one's actions that binds itself to the soul. By following various austerities (eg fasting and meditation), one can shed *karman* and purify the soul. Right conduct is essential, and fundamental to this is *ahimsa* (nonviolence) in thought and deed towards any living thing.

> A sadhu is someone who has surrendered all material possessions in pursuit of spirituality through meditation, the study of sacred texts, self-mortification and pilgrimage. Explore further in *Sadhus: India's Mystic Holy Men* by Dolf Hartsuiker.

The religious disciplines of followers are less severe than for monks (some Jain monks go naked). The slightly less ascetic maintain a bare minimum of possessions which include a broom to sweep the path before them to avoid stepping on any living creature, and a piece of cloth tied over their mouth to prevent the accidental inhalation of insects.

Today, around 0.4% of India's population is Jain, with the majority living in Gujarat and Mumbai. Some notable Jain holy sites include Sravanabelagola, Palitana, Ranakpur and the temples of Mt Abu.

Christianity

There are various theories circulating about Christ's link to the Indian subcontinent. Some, for instance, believe that Jesus spent his 'lost years' in India, while others say that Christianity came to South India with St Thomas the Apostle, who allegedly died in Chennai in the first century AD. However, many scholars attest it's more likely Christianity is traced to around the 4th century with a Syrian merchant, Thomas Cana, who set out for Kerala with around 400 families. India's Christian community today stands at about 2.3% of the population, with the bulk residing in South India.

Catholicism established a strong presence in South India in the wake of Vasco da Gama's visit in 1498, and orders that have been active – not always welcomed – in the region include the Dominicans, Franciscans and Jesuits. Protestant missionaries are believed to have begun arriving – with a conversion agenda – from around the 18th century, particularly in India's tribal regions.

Zoroastrianism

> The Zoroastrian funerary ritual involves the 'Towers of Silence' where the corpse is laid out and exposed to vultures that pick the bones clean.

Zoroastrianism, founded by Zoroaster (Zarathustra), had its inception in Persia in the 6th century BC and is based on the concept of dualism, whereby good and evil are locked in a continuous battle. Zoroastrianism isn't quite monotheistic: good and evil entities coexist, although believers are urged to honour only the good. Both body and soul are united in this struggle of good versus evil. Although humanity is mortal, it has components that are timeless, such as the soul. On the day of judgement the errant soul is not called to account for every misdemeanour – but a pleasant afterlife does depend on one's deeds, words and thoughts during earthly existence.

Zoroastrianism was eclipsed in Persia by the rise of Islam in the 7th century and its followers, many of whom openly resisted this, suffered persecution. Over the following centuries some immigrated to India, where they became known as Parsis. Historically, Parsis settled in Gujarat and became farmers; however, during British rule they moved into commerce, forming a prosperous community in Mumbai.

In recent decades the Parsi population has been spiralling downward; there are now believed to be only between 40,000 and 45,000 Parsis left in India, with most residing in Mumbai.

Delicious India

India's culinary terrain – with its especially impressive vegetarian cuisine – is a feast for all the senses, not just the sense of taste. Local cooks make full use of the fresh local ingredients available, be they fragrant spices or desert vegetables, and you can delight in everything from sensational street food to work-of-art thalis, from creative contemporary masterpieces to family-run stalls that have served up one specialty for over 50 years. Indeed, it's the sheer diversity of what's on offer that makes eating your way through India so deliciously rewarding.

A Culinary Carnival

India's culinary story is an ancient one, and the food you'll find here today reflects millennia of regional and global influences.

Land of Spices

Christopher Columbus was actually searching for the black pepper of Kerala's Malabar Coast when he stumbled upon America. The region still grows the finest quality of the world's favourite spice, and it's integral to most savoury Indian dishes.

Turmeric is the essence of the majority of Indian curries, but coriander seeds are the most widely used spice and lend flavour and body to just about every dish. Indian 'wet' dishes – commonly known as curries in the West – usually begin with the crackle of cumin seeds in hot oil. Tamarind is sometimes known as the 'Indian date' and is a popular souring agent in the south. The green cardamom of Kerala's Western Ghats is regarded as the world's best, and you'll find it in curries, desserts and warming chai (tea). Saffron, the dried stigmas of crocus flowers grown in Kashmir, is so light it takes more than 1500 hand-plucked flowers to yield just one gram.

Spotlighting rice, *Finest Rice Recipes* by Sabina Sehgal Saikia shows just how versatile this humble grain is, with classy creations such as rice-crusted crab cakes.

Rice Paradise

Rice is a staple, especially in South India. Long-grain white rice varieties are the most popular, served hot with just about any 'wet' cooked dish. From Assam's sticky rice in the far northeast to Kerala's red grains in the extreme south, you'll find countless regional varieties that locals will claim to be the best in India, though this honour is usually conceded to basmati, a fragrant long-grain variety which is widely exported around the world. Rice is usually served after you have finished with the rotis (breads), usually accompanied by curd to enrich the mix.

Ghee is the Hindi word for 'fat'. It's made by melting butter and removing the water and milk solids – ghee is the clear butter fat that remains. It's better for high-heat cooking than butter and keeps for longer.

Flippin' Fantastic Bread

While rice is paramount in the south, wheat is the mainstay in the north. Roti, the generic term for Indian-style bread, is a name used interchangeably with chapati to describe the most common variety, an irresistible unleavened round bread made with whole-wheat flour and cooked on a *tawa* (hotplate). It may be smothered with ghee (clarified butter) or oil. In some places, rotis are bigger and thicker than chapatis and sometimes cooked in a tandoor. *Paratha* is a layered pan-fried flat bread, that may also be stuffed, and makes for a hearty and popular breakfast. *Puri* – puffy fried bread pillows – are another popular sauce soaker-upper. Naan is a larger, thicker bread, baked in a tandoor and usually eaten with meaty sauces or kebabs. In Punjab, look out for naan-like *kulcha*, flavoured with herbs and spices.

> Thali means 'plate' in Hindi, and is the name of a complete meal, a selection of dishes in small metal bowls served on a larger metal dish, plus bread, rice, chutneys and dessert. Unlimited thali means you get refills.

Dhal-icious!

The whole of India is united in its love for dhal (curried lentils or pulses). You may encounter up to 60 different pulses: the most common are *channa* (chickpeas); tiny yellow or green ovals called *moong* (mung beans); salmon-coloured *masoor* (red lentils); the ochre-coloured southern favourite, *tuvar* (yellow lentils; also known as *arhar*); *rajma* (kidney beans); *urad* (black gram or lentils); and *lobhia* (black-eyed peas).

Meaty Matters

Although India probably has more vegetarians than the rest of the world combined, it still has an extensive repertoire of carnivorous fare. Chicken, lamb and mutton (sometimes actually goat) are the mainstays; religious taboos make beef forbidden to devout Hindus and pork to Muslims.

In northern India, you'll come across meat-dominated Mughlai cuisine, which includes rich curries, kebabs, koftas (meatballs) and biryanis. This spicy cuisine traces its history back to the (Islamic) Mughal empire that once reigned supreme. In the south, you'll find the meaty Chettinadu cuisine of Tamil Nadu, which is beautifully spiced without being too fiery.

Tandoori meat dishes are another North Indian favourite. The name is derived from the clay oven, or tandoor, in which the marinated meat is cooked.

Deep-Sea Delights

> The *Penguin Food Guide to India* by Charmaine O'Brien is an engrossing and evocative read.

India has around 7500km of coastline, so it's no surprise that seafood is an important ingredient, especially on the west coast, from Mumbai down to Kerala. Kerala is the biggest fishing state, while Goa boasts particularly succulent prawns and fiery fish curries, and the fishing communities of the Konkan Coast – sandwiched between Goa and Mumbai – are renowned for their seafood recipes. Few main meals in Odisha (Orissa) exclude fish, and in West Bengal, puddled with ponds and lakes, fish is king. The far-flung Andaman Islands also won't disappoint seafood lovers with the day's catch featuring on most menus.

The Fruits (& Vegetables) of Mother Nature

Vegetables are usually served at each main meal across India, and *sabzi* (vegetables) is a word recognised in every Indian vernacular.

PAAN

Meals are often rounded off with *paan*, a fragrant mixture of betel nut (also called areca nut), lime paste, spices and condiments wrapped in an edible, silky *paan* leaf. Peddled by *paan*-wallahs, who are usually strategically positioned outside busy restaurants, *paan* is eaten as a digestive and mouth-freshener. The betel nut is mildly narcotic and some aficionados eat *paan* the same way heavy smokers consume cigarettes – over the years these people's teeth can become rotted red and black. Usually the gloopy red juice is spat out, which is not always particularly sightly.

There are two basic types of *paan*: *mitha* (sweet) and *saadha* (with tobacco, which has similar health risks to other forms of tobacco use). A parcel of *mitha paan* is a splendid way to finish a meal. Pop the whole parcel in your mouth and chew slowly, allowing the juices to oooooooze.

Thali, Mumbai

They're generally cooked *sukhi* (dry) or *tari* (in a sauce), and within these two categories they can be fried, roasted, curried, stuffed, baked, mashed and combined (made into koftas) or dipped in chickpea-flour batter to make a deep-fried *pakora* (fritter).

Potatoes are ubiquitous and popularly cooked with various masalas (spice mixes), with other vegetables, or mashed and fried for the street snack *aloo tikki* (mashed-potato patties). Onions are fried with other vegetables, ground into a paste for cooking with meats, and served raw as relishes, but are avoided by Jains. Heads of cauliflower are usually cooked dry on their own, with potatoes to make *aloo gobi* (potato-and-cauliflower curry), or with other vegetables such as carrots and beans. Fresh green peas turn up stir-fried with other vegetables in pilaus and biryanis and in one of North India's signature dishes, the magnificent *mattar paneer* (unfermented cheese and pea curry). *Baigan* (eggplant/aubergine) can be curried or sliced and deep-fried. Also popular is *saag* (a generic term for leafy greens), which can include mustard, spinach and fenugreek. Something a little more unusual is the bumpy-skinned *karela* (bitter gourd) which, like the delectable *bhindi* (okra), is commonly prepared dry with spices.

India's fruit basket is also bountiful. Along the southern coast are super-luscious tropical fruits such as pineapples and papayas. Mangoes abound during summer (especially April and May), with India offering more than 500 varieties – the pick of the juicy bunch is the sweet Alphonso. Citrus fruit, such as oranges (often yellow-green in India), tangerines, pink and white grapefruits, kumquats and sweet limes are widely grown. Himachal Pradesh produces crisp apples in autumn, while plump strawberries are especially good in Kashmir during summer. You'll find

The Anger of Aubergines: Stories of Women and Food by Bulbul Sharma is an amusing culinary analysis of social relationships interspersed with enticing recipes.

DOSA

Savoury dosas (also spelt dosai), a family of large, crispy, papery rice-flour crêpes, usually served with a bowl of hot *sambar* (soupy lentil dish) and another bowl of cooling coconut *chatni* (chutney), are a South Indian breakfast speciality that can be eaten at any time of day. The most popular is the *masala dosa* (stuffed with spiced potatoes), but there are also other fantastic dosa varieties – the *rava* dosa (batter made with semolina), the Mysore dosa (like *masala dosa* but with more vegetables and chilli in the filling), and the *pessarettu* dosa (batter made with mung-bean dhal) from Andhra Pradesh. Nowadays, dosas are readily found in almost every corner of South India, from Tamil Nadu to the Himalaya.

fruit inventively fashioned into a *chatni* (chutney) or pickle, and also flavouring lassi, *kulfi* and other sweet treats.

Vegetarians & Vegans

India is king when it comes to vegetarian fare. There's little understanding of veganism (the term 'pure vegetarian' means without eggs), and animal products such as milk, butter, ghee and curd are included in most Indian dishes. If you are vegan, your first problem is likely to be getting the cook to understand your requirements, though big hotels and larger cities are getting better at catering to vegans.

For further information, surf the web – try Indian Vegan (www.indian-vegan.com) and Vegan World Network (www.vegansworldnetwork.org).

Pickles, Chutneys & Relishes

Pickles, chutneys and relishes are accompaniments that add zing to meals. A relish can be anything from a tiny pickled onion to a delicately crafted fusion of fruit, nuts and spices. One of the most popular side dishes is yoghurt-based raita, which makes a tongue-cooling counter to spicy food. *Chatnis* can come in any number of varieties (sweet or savoury) and can be made from many different vegetables, fruits, herbs and spices.

Sweet at Heart

India has a colourful kaleidoscope of, often sticky and squishy, *mithai* (Indian sweets), most of them sinfully sugary. The main categories are *barfi* (a fudgelike milk-based sweet), soft *halwa* (sweet made with vegetables, cereals, lentils, nuts or fruit), *ladoos* (sweet balls made with gram flour and semolina), and those made from *chhana* (unpressed paneer), such as *rasgullas*. There are also simpler – but equally scrumptious – offerings such as crunchy *jalebis* (coils of deep-fried batter dunked in sugar syrup; served hot) that you'll see all over the country.

Kheer (called *payasam* in the south) is one of the most popular after-meal desserts. It's a creamy rice pudding with a light, delicate flavour, enhanced with cardamom, saffron, pistachios, flaked almonds, chopped cashews or slivered dried fruit. Other favourites include hot *gulab jamuns* and refreshing *kulfi*.

Each year, an estimated 14 tonnes of pure silver is converted into the edible foil that decorates many Indian sweets, especially during the Diwali festival.

Technically speaking, there's no such thing as an Indian 'curry' – the word, an anglicised derivative of the Tamil word *kari* (sauce), was used by the British as a term for any spiced dish.

Where to Fill Up?

You can eat well in India everywhere from ramshackle street *dhabas* (snack bars) to otherworldly five-star hotels. Most midrange restaurants serve a few basic genres: South Indian (which usually means the vegetarian food of Tamil Nadu and Karnataka) and North Indian (which largely comprises Punjabi/Mughlai fare), and often Indian interpretations of Chinese dishes. You'll also find the cuisines of neighbouring regions and states. Indians frequently migrate in search of work and these restaurants cater to the large communities seeking the familiar tastes of home.

Not to be confused with burger joints and pizzerias, restaurants in the south advertising 'fast food' are some of India's best. They serve the whole gamut of tiffin (snack) items and often have separate sweet counters. Many upmarket hotels have outstanding restaurants, usually with pan-Indian menus so you can explore various regional cuisines. Meanwhile, the independent restaurant dining scene keeps mushrooming in India's larger cities, with every kind of cuisine available, from Mexican and Mediterranean to Japanese and Italian.

Dhabas are oases to millions of truck drivers, bus passengers and sundry travellers going anywhere by road. The original *dhabas* dot the North Indian landscape, but you'll find versions of them throughout the country. The rough-and-ready but satisfying food served in these happy-go-lucky shacks has become a genre of its own, known as '*dhaba* food'.

Got the munchies? Grab *Street Foods of India* by Vimla and Deb Kumar Mukerji, which has recipes of much-loved Indian snacks, from samosas and *bhelpuri* to *jalebis* and *kulfi*.

DELICIOUS INDIA WHERE TO FILL UP?

Street Food

Whatever the time of day, street food vendors are frying, boiling, roasting, peeling, simmering, mixing, juicing or baking different types of food and drink to lure peckish passers-by. Small operations usually have one special that they serve all day, while other vendors have different dishes for breakfast, lunch and dinner. The fare varies as you venture between neighbourhoods, towns and regions; it can be as simple as puffed rice or peanuts roasted in hot sand, or as complex as the riot of different flavours known as *chaat* (savoury snack). Fabulous calvalcades of taste include *chole bhature* (puffed bread served with spicy chickpeas and dipped in fragrant sauce) in north India, *aloo tikki*, which are renowned in Lucknow, *gol gappa/Panipuri/gup chup* (puffed spheres of bread with a spicy filling), all over India, and *idli sambar* (rice patties served with delectable sauce and chutney) in Chennai and the south.

Check out Pamela Timms' Eatanddust.com for an outsider's take on Indian street food, plus her book *Korma, Kheer & Kismet.*

STREET FOOD: TIPS

Tucking into street eats is a highlight of travelling in India, but to avoid tummy troubles:

➡ Give yourself a few days to adjust to the local cuisine, especially if you're unaccustomed to spicy food.

➡ If locals are avoiding a particular vendor, you should too. Also note the profile of the customers – any place popular with families will probably be your safest bet.

➡ Check how and where the vendor is cleaning the utensils, and how and where the food is covered. If the vendor is cooking in oil, have a peek to check it's clean. If the pots or surfaces are dirty, there are food scraps about or too many buzzing flies, don't be shy to make a hasty retreat.

➡ Don't be put off when you order some deep-fried snack and the cook throws it back into the wok. It's common practice to partly cook the snacks first and then finish them off once they've been ordered. Frying them hot again kills germs.

➡ Unless a place is reputable (and busy), it's best to avoid eating meat from the street.

➡ The hygiene standard at juice stalls varies, so exercise caution. Have the vendor press the juice in front of you and steer clear of anything stored in a jug or served in a glass (unless you're confident with the washing standards).

➡ Don't be tempted by glistening pre-sliced melon and other fruit, which keeps its luscious veneer with regular dousing of (often dubious) water.

Street food, Jaipur

Railway Snack Attack

One of the thrills of travelling by rail in India is the culinary circus that greets you at almost every station. Roving vendors accost arriving trains, yelling and scampering up and down the carriages; fruit, *namkin* (savoury nibbles), omelettes, nuts and sweets are offered through the grills on the windows; and platform cooks try to lure you from the train with the sizzle of spicy goodies such as samosas. Frequent rail travellers know which station is famous for which food item: Lonavla station in Maharashtra is known for *chikki* (rock-hard toffee-like confectionery), Agra for *peitha* (square sweet made from pumpkin and glucose, usually flavoured with rose water, coconut or saffron) and Dhaund near Delhi for biryani.

Daily Dining Habits

Containing handy tips, including how to best store spices, Monisha Bharadwaj's *The Indian Spice Kitchen* is a slick cookbook with more than 200 traditional recipes.

Three main meals a day is the norm in India. Breakfast is usually fairly light, maybe *idlis* (South Indian spongy fermented rice cake) and *sambar* in the south, and *parathas* in the north. Lunch can be substantial (perhaps a thali) or light, especially for time-strapped office workers. Dinner is usually the main meal of the day. It's generally comprised of a few different preparations – several curried vegetables (maybe also meat) dishes and dhal, accompanied by rice and/or chapatis. Dishes are served all at once rather than as courses. Desserts are optional and most prevalent during festivals or other special occasions. Fruit may wrap up a meal. In many Indian homes dinner can be a rather late affair (post-9pm) depending on personal preference and the season (eg late dinners during the warmer months). Restaurants usually spring to life after 9pm in the cities, but in smaller towns they're busy earlier.

Spiritual Sustenance

For many in India, food is considered just as critical for fine-tuning the spirit as it is for sustaining the body. Broadly speaking, Hindus traditionally avoid foods that are thought to inhibit physical and spiritual development, although there are few hard-and-fast rules. The taboo on eating beef (the cow is holy to Hindus) is the most rigid restriction. Jains avoid foods such as garlic and onions, which, apart from harming insects in their extraction from the ground, are thought to heat the blood and arouse sexual desire. You may come across vegetarian restaurants that make it a point to advertise the absence of onion and garlic in their dishes for this reason. Devout Hindus may also avoid garlic and onions. These items are also banned from many ashrams.

Some foods, such as dairy products, are considered innately pure and are eaten to cleanse the body, mind and spirit. Ayurveda, the ancient science of life, health and longevity, also influences food customs.

Pork is taboo for Muslims and stimulants such as alcohol are avoided by the most devout. Halal is the term for all permitted foods, and *haram* for those prohibited. Fasting is considered an opportunity to earn the approval of Allah, to wipe the sin-slate clean and to understand the suffering of the poor.

Buddhists subscribe to the philosophy of ahimsa (nonviolence) and are mostly vegetarian. Jainism's central tenet is strict vegetarianism, and rigid restrictions are in place to avoid injury to any living creature – Jains abstain from eating vegetables that grow underground because of the potential to harm insects during cultivation and harvesting.

India's Sikh, Christian and Parsi communities have few restrictions on what they can eat.

Food which is first offered to the gods at temples then shared among devotees is known as *prasad*.

For India-wide restaurant reviews and recommendations, check out the excellent Zomato (zomato.com).

Cooking Courses

You might find yourself so inspired by Indian food that you want to take home a little Indian kitchen know-how, via a cooking course, such as those offered in Delhi, Udaipur, and McLeod Ganj. Courses are popular in Goa and Kerala, with the best in Palolem, Anjuna and Siolim in Goa, and at homestays in Kumily (Periyar) and Kochi in Kerala. Some courses are professionally run, others are informal. Most require at least a few days' advance notice.

Drinks, Anyone?

Gujarat, Nagaland and Mizoram are India's only dry states but there are drinking laws in place all over the country, and each state may have regular dry days when the sale of alcohol from liquor shops is banned. Kerala, where alcohol consumption was twice the national average, is moving towards complete prohibition by 2024, with hundreds of bars being

FEASTING INDIAN-STYLE

Most people in India eat with their right hand. In the south, they use as much of the hand as is necessary, while elsewhere they use the tips of the fingers. The left hand is reserved for unsanitary actions such as removing shoes. You can use your left hand for holding drinks and serving yourself from a communal bowl, but it shouldn't be used for bringing food to your mouth. Before and after a meal, it's good manners to wash your hands.

Once your meal is served, mix the food with your fingers. If you are having dhal and *sabzi* (vegetables), only mix the dhal into your rice and have the *sabzi* in small scoops with each mouthful. If you are having fish or meat curry, mix the gravy into your rice. Scoop up lumps of the mix and, with your knuckles facing the dish, use your thumb to shovel the food into your mouth.

Chai (tea) being made by a street vendor

closed down. In Goa, because of the Portuguese influence, alcohol taxes are lower and the drinking culture less restricted. On Gandhi's birthday (2 October), you'll find it hard to get an alcoholic drink anywhere.

You'll find excellent watering holes in most big cities, especially Mumbai, Bengaluru (the craft beer capital of India), Kolkata and Delhi, which are usually at their liveliest on weekends. The more upmarket bars serve an impressive selection of domestic and imported drinks as well as draught beer. Many bars turn into music-thumping nightclubs anytime after 8pm, although there are quiet lounge-bars to be found in most large cities. In smaller towns, the bar scene can be a seedy, male-dominated affair – not the kind of place thirsty female travellers should venture into alone.

Wine-drinking is steadily on the rise, despite the domestic wine-producing industry still being relatively new. The favourable climate and soil conditions in certain areas – such as parts of Maharashtra and Karnataka – have spawned some commendable Indian wineries, such as those of the Grover and Sula Vineyards.

Stringent licensing laws and religious restrictions mean some restaurants won't serve alcohol, but places that depend on the tourist rupee may covertly serve you beer in teapots and disguised glasses – however, don't assume anything, at the risk of causing offence.

Very few vegetarian restaurants serve alcohol.

The subcontinent's wine industry is an ever evolving one – take a cyber-sip of Indian wine at www.indianwine.com.

Nonalcoholic Beverages

Chai (tea), the much-loved drink of the masses, is made with copious amounts of milk and sugar. A glass of steaming, frothy chai is the perfect antidote to the vicissitudes of life on the Indian road; the disembodied voice droning 'garam chai, garam chai' (hot tea, hot tea) is likely to become one of the most familiar and welcome sounds of your trip. Masala chai adds cardamom, ginger and other spices.

While chai is the traditional choice of most of the nation, South Indians have long shared their loyalty with coffee. In recent years, though, the number of coffee-drinking North Indians has skyrocketed, with ever-multiplying branches of slick coffee chains, such as Barista and Café Coffee Day.

Masala soda is the quintessentially Indian soft drink. It's a freshly opened bottle of fizzy soda, pepped up with lime, spices, salt and sugar. You can also plump for a plainer lime soda, which is soda with fresh lime, served sweet (with sugar) or salted as you prefer. Also refreshing is *jal jeera,* made of lime juice, cumin, mint and rock salt. Sweet and savoury lassi, a yoghurt-based drink, is especially popular nationwide and is another wonderfully cooling beverage.

Falooda is a rose-flavoured drink made with milk, cream, nuts and strands of vermicelli, while *badam* milk (served hot or cold) is flavoured with almonds and saffron.

Homegrown Brews

An estimated three-quarters of India's drinking population quaffs 'country liquor', such as the notorious arak (liquor distilled from coconut-palm sap, potatoes or rice) of the south. This is widely known as the poor-man's drink and millions are addicted to the stuff. Each year, many people are blinded or even killed by the methyl alcohol in illegal arak.

An interesting local drink is a clear spirit with a heady pungent flavour called *mahua,* distilled from the flower of the *mahua* tree. It's brewed in makeshift village stalls all over central India during March and April, when the trees bloom. *Mahua* is safe to drink as long as it comes from a trustworthy source. There have been cases of people being blinded after drinking *mahua* adulterated with methyl alcohol.

Rice beer is brewed all over east and northeast India, while in the Himalayas you'll find a grain alcohol called *raksi,* which is strong, has a mild charcoal flavour and tastes vaguely like Scotch whisky.

Toddy, the sap from the palm tree, is drunk in coastal areas, especially Kerala, while feni is the primo Indian spirit, and the preserve of laid-back Goa. Coconut feni is light and rather unexceptional but the more popular cashew feni – made from the fruit of the cashew tree – is worth a try.

If you fancy sipping booze of the blue-blood ilk, traditional royal liqueurs of Rajasthan (once reserved for private consumption among nobility) are sold at some liquor shops, especially in Delhi and Jaipur. Ingredients range from aniseed, cardamom and saffron to rose, dates and mint.

Menu Decoder

achar	pickle
aloo	potato; also *alu*
aloo tikki	mashed-potato patty
appam	South Indian rice pancake
arak	liquor distilled from coconut milk, potatoes or rice
baigan	eggplant/aubergine; also known as *brinjal*
barfi	fudgelike sweet made from milk
bebinca	Goan 16-layer cake
besan	chickpea flour
betel	nut of the betel tree; also called areca nut
bhajia	vegetable fritters
bhang lassi	blend of lassi and bhang (a derivative of marijuana)

bhelpuri	thin fried rounds of dough with puffed rice, lentils, lemon juice, onion, herbs and chutney
bhindi	okra
biryani	fragrant spiced steamed rice with meat or vegetables
bonda	mashed-potato patty
chaat	savoury snack, may be seasoned with *chaat* masala
chach	buttermilk beverage
chai	tea
channa	spiced chickpeas
chapati	round unleavened Indian-style bread; also known as roti
chawal	rice
cheiku	small, sweet brown fruit
dahi	curd/yoghurt
dhal	spiced lentil dish
dhal makhani	black lentils and red kidney beans with cream and butter
dhansak	Parsi dish; meat, usually chicken or lamb, with curried lentils, pumpkin or gourd and rice
dosa	large South Indian savoury crepe
falooda	rose-flavoured drink made with milk, cream, nuts and vermicelli
faluda	long chickpea-flour noodles
feni	Goan liquor distilled from cashew fruit or coconut palm toddy
ghee	clarified butter
gobi	cauliflower
gulab jamun	deep-fried balls of dough soaked in rose-flavoured syrup
halwa	soft sweet made with vegetables, lentils, nuts or fruit
idli	South Indian spongy, round fermented rice cake
imli	tamarind
jaggery	hard brown, sugarlikesweetener made from palm sap
jalebi	orange-coloured coils of deep-fried batter dunked in sugar syrup; served hot
karela	bitter gourd
keema	spiced minced meat
kheer	creamy rice pudding
khichdi	blend of lightly spiced rice and lentils; also *khichri*
kofta	minced vegetables or meat; often ball-shaped
korma	currylike braised dish
kulcha	soft leavened Indian-style bread
kulfi	flavoured (often with pistachio) firm-textured ice cream
ladoo	sweet ball made with gram flour and semolina; also *ladu*
lassi	yoghurt-and-iced-water drink
malai kofta	paneer cooked in a creamy sauce of cashews and tomato
masala dosa	large South Indian savoury crepe (dosa) stuffed with spiced potatoes
mattar paneer	unfermented cheese and pea curry
methi	fenugreek
mishti doi	Bengali sweet; curd sweetened with jaggery

mithai	Indian sweets
momo	savoury Tibetan dumpling
naan	tandoor-cooked flat bread
namak	salt
namkin	savoury nibbles
noon chai	salt tea (Kashmir)
pakora	bite-sized vegetable pieces in batter
palak paneer	unfermented cheese chunks in a puréed spinach gravy
paneer	soft, unfermented cheese made from milk curd
pani	water
pappadam	thin, crispy lentil or chickpea-flour circle-shaped wafer; also pappad
paratha/ parantha	flaky flatbread (thicker than chapati); often stuffed
phulka	a chapati that puffs up on an open flame
pilau	rice cooked in spiced stock; also *pulau*, *pilao* or *pilaf*
pudina	mint
puri	flat savoury dough that puffs up when deep-fried; also *poori*
raita	mildly spiced yoghurt, often containing shredded cucumber or diced pineapple
rasam	dhal-based broth flavoured with tamarind
rasgulla	cream-cheese balls flavoured with rose-water
rogan josh	rich, spicy lamb curry
saag	leafy greens
sabzi	vegetables
sambar	South Indian soupy lentil dish with cubed vegetables
samosa	deep-fried pastry triangles filled with spiced vegetables
sonf	aniseed; used as a digestive and mouth-freshener; also *saunf*
tandoor	clay oven
tawa	flat hotplate/iron griddle
thali	all-you-can-eat meal; stainless steel (sometimes silver) compartmentalised plate
thukpa	Tibetan noodle soup
tiffin	snack; also refers to meal container often made of stainless steel
tikka	spiced, often marinated, chunks of chicken, paneer etc
toddy	alcoholic drink, tapped from palm trees
tsampa	Tibetan staple of roast-barley flour
upma	*rava* (semolina) cooked with onions, spices, chili peppers and coconut
uttapam	thick savoury South Indian rice pancake with finely chopped onions, green chillies, coriander and coconut
vada	South Indian doughnut-shaped deep-fried lentil savoury
vindaloo	Goan dish; fiery curry in a marinade of vinegar and garlic
wazwan	traditional Kashmiri banquet

The Great Indian Bazaar

India's bazaars and shops sell a staggering range of goodies: from woodwork to silks, chunky tribal jewellery to finely embroidered shawls, sparkling gemstones to rustic village handicrafts. The array of arts and handicrafts is vast, with every region – sometimes every village – having its own traditions, some of them ancient. Be prepared to encounter – and bring home – some spectacular items. India's shopping opportunities are as inspiring and multifarious as the country itself.

Bronze Figures, Pottery, Stone Carving & Terracotta

In southern India and parts of the Himalaya, small images of deities are created by the age-old lost-wax process. A wax figure is made, a mould is formed around it, and the wax is melted, poured out and replaced with molten metal; the mould is then broken open to reveal the figure inside. Figures of Shiva as dancing Nataraja are the most popular, but you can also find images of Buddha and numerous deities from the Hindu pantheon.

The West Bengalese also employ the lost-wax process to make Dokra tribal bell sculptures, while in Chhattisgarh's Bastar region, the Ghadwa Tribe has an interesting twist on the lost-wax process: a fine wax thread covers the metal mould, leaving a lattice-like design on the final product.

In Buddhist areas, you'll find striking bronze statues of Buddha and the Tantric deities, finished off with finely polished and painted faces.

Rajasthan is a treasure trove of handicrafts. Its capital, Jaipur, is known for its blockprinting and its blue-glazed pottery with pretty floral and geometric motifs.

In Mamallapuram in Tamil Nadu, craftsmen using local granite and soapstone have revived the ancient artistry of the Pallava sculptors; souvenirs range from tiny stone elephants to enormous deity statues weighing half a tonne. Tamil Nadu is also known for bronzeware from Thanjavur and Trichy (Tiruchirappalli).

A number of places produce attractive terracotta items, ranging from vases and decorative flowerpots to images of deities, and children's toys.

Outside temples you can buy small clay effigies of Hindu deities.

Carpets, Carpets, Carpets!

Carpet-making is a living craft in India, with workshops throughout producing fine wool and silkwork. The finest carpets are produced in Kashmir, Ladakh, Himachal Pradesh, Sikkim and West Bengal. Carpet-making is also a major revenue earner for Tibetan refugees; most refugee settlements have cooperative carpet workshops. You can also find reproductions of tribal Turkmen and Afghan designs in states such as Uttar Pradesh. Antique carpets usually aren't antique – unless you buy from an internationally reputable dealer; stick to 'new' carpets.

In both Kashmir and Rajasthan, you'll find coarsely woven woollen *numdas* (or *namdas*), which are cheaper than knotted carpets. Various regions manufacture flat-weave *dhurries* (kilim-like cotton rugs), including Kashmir, Himachal Pradesh, Rajasthan and Uttar Pradesh. Kashmiris also produce *gabbas* (rugs with appliqué), made from chain-stitched wool or silk.

Children have been employed as carpet weavers in the subcontinent for centuries. Child labour maintains a cycle of poverty, by driving down adult wages, reducing adult work opportunities, and depriving children of their education. The carpets produced by Tibetan refugee cooperatives are almost always made by adults; government emporiums and charitable cooperatives are usually the best places to buy.

Costs & Postage

The price of a carpet is determined by the number and the size of the hand-tied knots, the range of dyes and colours, the intricacy of the design and the material. Silk carpets cost more and look more luxurious, but wool carpets usually last longer. Expect to pay upwards of US$250 for a good quality 90cm by 1.5m (or 90cm by 1.8m, depending on the region) wool carpet, and around US$2000 for a similar-sized carpet in silk. Tibetan carpets are cheaper, reflecting the relative simplicity of the designs; many refugee cooperatives sell the same size for around US$100.

Some people buy carpets thinking that they can be sold for a profit back home, but unless you really know your carpets, you're better off just buying a carpet because you love it. Many places can ship carpets home for a fee – although it may be safest to send things independently to avoid scams – or you can carry them in the plane's hold (allow 5kg to 10kg of your baggage allowance for a 90cm by 1.5m carpet, and check that your airline allows outsized baggage). Shipping to Europe for a carpet of this size would cost around ₹4000).

Be cautious when buying items that include international delivery, and avoid being led to shops by smooth-talking touts, but don't worry about too much else – except your luggage space!

Jewellery

Virtually every town in India has at least one bangle shop selling an extraordinary variety, ranging from colourful plastic and glass to brass and silver.

Heavy folk-art silver jewellery can be bought in various parts of the country, particularly in Rajasthan; Jaipur, Udaipur and Pushkar are good places to find silver jewellery pitched at foreign tastes. Jaipur is also renowned for its precious and semiprecious gems (and its gem scams). Chunky Tibetan jewellery made from silver (or white metal) and semiprecious stones is sold all over India. Many pieces feature Buddhist motifs and text in Tibetan script, including the famous mantra *Om Mani Padme Hum* (Hail to the Jewel in the Lotus). Some of the pieces sold in Tibetan centres, such as McLeod Ganj and Leh, are genuine antiques, but there's a huge industry in India, Nepal and China making artificially aged souvenirs. For creative types, loose beads of agate, turquoise, carnelian and silver are widely available. Buddhist meditation beaded strings made of gems or wood also make good souvenirs.

Pearls are produced by most Indian seaside states, but they're a particular speciality of Hyderabad. You'll find them at most state emporiums across the country. Prices vary depending on the colour and shape: you pay more for pure white pearls or rare colours such as black, and perfectly round pearls are generally more expensive than misshapen or elongated pearls. A single strand of seeded pearls can cost as little as ₹500, but better-quality pearls start at around ₹1000.

Throughout India you can find finely crafted gold and silver rings, anklets, earrings, toe rings, necklaces and bangles, and pieces can often be made to order.

Leatherwork

As cows are sacred in India, leatherwork is made from buffalos, camels, goats or some other animal skin. Kanpur in Uttar Pradesh is the country's major leatherwork centre.

Most large cities offer a smart range of modern leather footwear at very reasonable prices, some stitched with zillions of sparkly sequins – marvellous partywear!

The states of Punjab and Rajasthan (especially Jaipur) are famed for jootis (traditional, often pointy-toed slip-on shoes).

Chappals, those wonderful (often curly-toed) leather sandals, are sold throughout India but are particularly good in the Maharashtrian cities of Kolhapur, Pune and Matheran.

In Bikaner in Rajasthan, artisans decorate camel hide with gold to produce beautiful mirror frames, boxes and bottles, while in Indore in Madhya Pradesh, craftspeople stretch leather over wire-and-cloth frameworks to make cute toy animals.

Cuttack in Odisha (Orissa) is famed for its lacelike silver-filigree ornaments known as *tarakasi*. A silver framework is made and then filled in with delicate curls and ribbons of silver.

Metal & Marble

You'll find copper and brassware throughout India. Candleholders, trays, bowls, tankards and ashtrays are particularly popular buys. In Rajasthan and Uttar Pradesh, the brass is inlaid with exquisite designs in red, green and blue enamel.

Many Tibetan religious objects are created by inlaying silver in copper; prayer wheels, ceremonial horns and traditional document cases are all inexpensive buys. Resist the urge to buy *kangling* (Tibetan horns) and *kapala* (ceremonial bowls) made from inlaid human leg bones and skulls – they are illegal!

In all Indian towns you can find *kadhai* (Indian woks, also known as *balti*) and other cookware for incredibly low prices. Beaten-brass pots are particularly attractive, while steel storage vessels, copper-bottomed cooking pans and steel thali trays are also popular souvenirs. Be sure to have your name engraved on them (free of charge).

The people of Bastar in Chhattisgarh use an iron-smelting technique similar to the one discovered 35,000 years ago to create abstract sculptures of spindly animal and human figures. These are often also made into functional items such as lamp stands and coat racks.

A sizeable cottage industry has sprung up in Agra reproducing the ancient Mughal art form of pietra dura (inlaying marble with semiprecious stones).

THE ART OF HAGGLING

Government emporiums, fair-trade cooperatives, department stores and modern shopping centres almost always charge fixed prices. Anywhere else you need to bargain. Shopkeepers in tourist hubs are accustomed to travellers who have lots of money and little time to spend it, so you can often expect to be charged double or triple the going rate. Souvenir shops are generally the most notorious.

The first 'rule' to haggling is to never show too much interest in the item you've got your heart set upon. Second, resist purchasing the first thing that takes your fancy. Wander around several shops and price items, but don't make it too obvious: if you return to the first shop, the vendor will know it's because they are the cheapest (resulting in less haggling leeway).

Decide how much you would be happy paying, and then express a casual interest in buying. If you have absolutely no idea of the going rate, a common approach is to start by slashing the price by half. The vendor will, most likely, look aghast, but you can now work up and down respectively in small increments until you reach a mutually agreeable price. You'll find that many shopkeepers lower their so-called 'final price' if you head out of the store saying you'll 'think about it'.

Haggling is a way of life in India and is usually taken in good spirit. It should never turn ugly. Always keep in mind how much a rupee is worth in your home currency, and how much you'd pay for the item back home, to put things in perspective. If you're not sure of the 'right' price for an item, think about how much it is worth to you. If a vendor seems to be charging an unreasonably high price, look elsewhere.

Musical Instruments

Quality Indian musical instruments are mostly available in the larger cities, especially Kolkata (Calcutta), Varanasi and Delhi. Prices vary according to the quality and sound of the instrument.

Decent tabla sets (pair of drums) with a wooden tabla (tuned treble drum) and metal *dugi* or *bayan* (bass tone drums) cost upwards of ₹5000. Cheaper sets are generally heavier and often sound inferior.

Sitars range anywhere from ₹5000 to ₹20,000 (sometimes even more). The sound of each sitar will vary with the wood used and the shape of the gourd, so try a few. Note that some cheaper sitars can warp in colder or hotter climates. On any sitar, make sure the strings ring clearly and check the gourd carefully for damage. Spare string sets, sitar plectrums and a screw-in 'amplifier' gourd are sensible additions.

Other popular instruments include the *shehnai* (Indian flute), the *sarod* (like an Indian lute), the harmonium and the *esraj* (similar to an upright violin). Conventional violins are great value – prices start at ₹3500, while Kolkata is known for its quality acoustic guitars (from ₹2500).

> *Bidri*, a method of damascening where silver wire is inlaid in gunmetal (a zinc alloy) and rubbed with soil from Bidar, Karnataka, is used to make jewellery, boxes and ornaments.

THE GREAT INDIAN BAZAAR MUSICAL INSTRUMENTS

Paintings

Miniatures

Reproductions of Indian miniature paintings are widely available, but the quality varies: the cheaper ones have less detail and are made with inferior materials. Udaipur and Bikaner in Rajasthan have a particularly good range of shops specialising in modern reproductions on paper and silk, or you can browse Delhi's numerous state emporiums.

In regions such as Kerala and Tamil Nadu, you'll find miniature paintings on leaf skeletons that portray domestic life, rural scenes and deities.

Folk Art

In Andhra Pradesh, *cheriyal* paintings, in bright, primary colours, were originally made as scrolls for travelling storytellers.

The artists' community of Raghurajpur near Puri (Odisha) preserves the age-old art of *patachitra* (cloth) painting. Cotton or tassar (silk cloth) is covered with a mixture of gum and chalk; it's then polished, and images of deities and scenes from Hindu legends are painted on with exceedingly fine brushes. Odisha also produces *chitra pothi*, where images are etched onto dried palm-leaf sections with a fine stylus.

Bihar's unique folk art is Mithila (or Madhubani) painting, an ancient art form preserved by the women of Madhubani. These captivating paintings are most easily found in Patna, but are also sold in big city emporiums.

Thangkas

Exquisite *thangkas* (rectangular Tibetan paintings on cloth) of Tantric Buddhist deities and ceremonial mandalas are sold in Tibetan Buddhist areas, including Sikkim, parts of Himachal Pradesh and Ladakh. Some perfectly reproduce the glory of the murals in India's medieval gompas (Tibetan Buddhist monasteries); others are simpler. Prices vary, but bank on at least ₹4000 for a decent-quality *thangka* of A3 size, and a lot more (up to around ₹30,000) for large intricate *thangkas*. The selling of antique *thangkas* is illegal, and you would be unlikely to find the real thing anyway.

> In towns with Buddhist communities, such as McLeod Ganj, Leh, Manali, Gangtok, Kalimpong, Darjeeling, and Delhi, keep an eye out for 'Buddha shops' selling prayer flags, singing bowls and prayer wheels.

Contemporary Art

India is a major centre of contemporary art, and its larger cities are well stocked with independent galleries. Delhi, Mumbai and Kolkata are the best places to look for shops and galleries selling contemporary paintings by local artists.

Textiles

Shawls

Indian shawls are famously warm and lightweight – they're often better than the best down jackets. It's worth buying one to use as a blanket on cold night journeys. Shawls are made from all sorts of wool, and many are embroidered with intricate designs.

The undisputed capital of the Indian shawl is the Kullu Valley in Himachal Pradesh, with dozens of women's cooperatives producing fine woollen pieces. These may be made from wool (from ₹700), angora (mohair) or *pashmina* (the downy hair of the pashmina goat).

Ladakh and Kashmir are major centres for *pashmina* production – you'll pay at least ₹6000 for the authentic article. Be aware that many so-called *pashminas* are actually made from a mixture of wool and silk, however, these 'fake' pashminas are often very beautiful even so, and a lot less expensive, costing around ₹1200. Shawls from the Northeast States are famously warm, with bold geometric designs. In Sikkim and West Bengal, you may also find embroidered Bhutanese shawls. Gujarat's Kutch region produces some particularly distinctive woollen shawls, patterned with subtle embroidery and mirrorwork. Handmade shawls and tweeds can also be found in Ranikhet and Almora in Uttarakhand.

In Andhra Pradesh, intricately drawn, graphic cloth paintings called *kalamkari* depict deities and historic events.

Saris

Saris are a very popular souvenir, especially given that they can be easily adapted to other purposes (from cushion covers to skirts). Real silk saris are the most expensive, and the silk usually needs to be washed before it becomes soft. The 'silk capital' of India is Kanchipuram in Tamil Nadu (Kanchipuram silk is also widely available in Chennai), but you can also find fine silk saris (and cheaper scarves) in centres including Varanasi, Mysore and Kolkata. Assam is renowned for its muga, endi and pat silks (produced by different species of silkworms), which are widely available in Guwahati. You'll pay upwards of ₹3000 for a quality embroidered silk sari.

Patan in Gujarat is the centre for the ancient and laborious craft of *patola*-making. Every thread in these fine silk saris is individually hand-dyed before weaving, and patterned borders are woven with real gold. Slightly less involved versions are produced in Rajkot. Gold thread is also used in the famous *kota doria* saris of Kota in Rajasthan.

Aurangabad, in Maharashtra, is the traditional centre for the production of *himroo* shawls, sheets and saris, made from a blend of cotton, silk and silver thread. Silk and gold-thread saris produced at Paithan (near Aurangabad) are some of India's finest – prices range from around ₹7000 to a mind-blowing ₹300,000. Other regions famous for sari production include Madhya Pradesh for its cotton Maheshwari saris (from Maheshwar) and silk Chanderi saris (from Chanderi), and West Bengal, for its *baluchari* saris from Bishnupur, which employ a traditional form of weaving with untwisted silk thread.

Be aware that it's illegal to buy *shahtoosh* shawls, as rare Tibetan antelopes are slaughtered to provide the wool. If you come across anyone selling these shawls, inform local authorities.

Khadi & Embroidery

Textile production is India's major industry and around 40% takes place at the village level, where it's known as *khadi* (homespun cloth) – hence the government-backed *khadi* emporiums around the country. These superstores sell all sorts of items made from *khadi*, including the popular Nehru jackets and kurta pyjamas (long shirt and loose-fitting trousers), with sales benefiting rural communities. *Khadi* has recently become increasingly chic, with India's designers referencing the fabrics in their collections.

You'll find a truly amazing variety of weaving and embroidery techniques around India. In tourist centres such as Goa, Rajasthan and Himachal Pradesh, textiles are stitched into popular items such as shoulder

PUTTING YOUR MONEY WHERE IT COUNTS

Overall, a small proportion of the money brought to India by tourism reaches people in rural areas. Travellers can make a greater contribution by shopping at community cooperatives set up to protect and promote traditional cottage industries and provide education, training and a sustainable livelihood at the grassroots level. Many of these projects focus on refugees, low-caste women, tribal people and others living on society's fringes.

The quality of products sold at cooperatives is high and the prices are usually fixed, which means you won't have to haggle. A share of the sales money is channelled directly into social projects such as schools, healthcare, training and other advocacy programs for socially disadvantaged groups. Shopping at the national network of Khadi and Village Industries Commission emporiums will also contribute to rural communities.

Wherever you travel, keep your eyes peeled for fair-trade cooperatives.

bags, cushion covers, clothes and much more. In Adivasi (tribal) areas of Gujarat and Rajasthan, small pieces of mirrored glass are embroidered onto fabric, creating eye-catching bags, cushion covers and wall hangings. The region of Kutch is particularly renowned for its embroidery.

Appliqué, Tie-dye & Blockprint

Appliqué is an ancient art in India, with most states producing their own version, often featuring abstract or anthropomorphic patterns. The traditional lampshades and pandals (tents) used in weddings and festivals are usually produced using the same technique.

Gujarat has a diversity of textile traditions: Jamnagar is famous for its vibrant *bandhani* (tie-dye work) used for saris and scarves, among other things, and Vadodara is renowned for block-printed fabrics, used for bedspreads and clothing. Ahmedabad is a good place to buy Gujarati textiles.

Block-printed and woven textiles are sold by fabric shops all over India: each region has its own speciality. The India-wide retail chain-stores Fabindia (www.fabindia.com) and Anokhi (www.anokhi.com) strive to preserve traditional patterns and fabrics, transforming them into home-decor items and Indian- and Western-style fashions. The latter has the Anokhi Museum of Hand Printing (p125), which demostrates the crafts.

Odisha has a reputation for bright appliqué and *ikat* (a Southeast Asian technique where thread is tie-dyed before weaving). The town of Pipli, between Bhubaneswar and Puri, produces striking appliqué work. The techniques used to create *kalamkari* cloth paintings in Andhra Pradesh (a centre for this ancient art is Sri Kalahasti) and Gujarat are also used to make lovely wall hangings and lampshades.

Indian Textiles, by John Gillow and Nicholas Barnard, explores India's beautiful regional textiles and includes sections on tie-dye, weaving, beadwork, brocades and even camel girths.

Woodcarving

Woodcarving is an ancient art form throughout India. In Kashmir, walnut wood is used to make finely carved wooden screens, tables, jewellery boxes and trays, inspired by the decorative trim of houseboats. Willow cricket bats are another Kashmiri speciality.

Wood inlay is one of Bihar's oldest crafts – you'll find lovely wooden wall hangings, tabletops, trays and boxes inlaid with metals and bone.

Sandalwood carvings of Hindu deities are one of Karnataka's specialities, but you'll pay a king's ransom for the real thing – a 10cm-high Ganesh costs around ₹3000 in sandalwood, compared to roughly ₹300 in kadamb wood. However, the sandalwood will release fragrance for years.

In Udaipur in Rajasthan, you can buy brightly painted figures of Hindu deities carved from mango wood. In many parts of Rajasthan you can also find fabric printing blocks carved from teak wood.

Buddhist woodcarvings are a speciality of Sikkim, Ladakh, Arunachal Pradesh and all Tibetan refugee areas. You'll find wall plaques of the eight lucky signs, dragons and *chaam* masks, used for ritual dances. Most of the masks are cheap reproductions, but you can sometimes find genuine *chaam* masks made from lightweight whitewood or papier mâché from ₹3000 upwards.

Other Great Finds

It's little surprise that Indian spices are snapped up by tourists. Virtually all towns have shops and bazaars selling locally made spices at great prices. Karnataka, Kerala, Uttar Pradesh, Rajasthan and Tamil Nadu produce most of the spices that go into garam masala (the 'hot mix' used to flavour Indian dishes), while the Northeast States and Sikkim are known for black cardamom and cinnamon bark. Note that some countries, such as Australia, have stringent rules regarding the import of animal and plant products. Check with your country's embassy for details.

Attar (essential oil, mostly made from flowers) shops can be found around the country. Mysore in Karnataka is famous for its sandalwood oil, while Mumbai is a major centre for the trade of traditional fragrances, including valuable *oud,* made from a rare mould that grows on the bark of the agarwood tree. In Tamil Nadu, Ooty and Kodaikanal produce aromatic and medicinal oils from herbs, flowers and eucalyptus.

Indian incense is exported worldwide, with Bengaluru and Mysore, both in Karnataka, being major producers. Incense from Auroville in Tamil Nadu is also well regarded.

A speciality of Goa is feni (liquor distilled from coconut milk or cashews): a head-spinning spirit that often comes in decorative bottles.

Quality Indian tea is sold in Darjeeling and Kalimpong (both in West Bengal), Assam and Sikkim, as well as parts of South India, such as Munnar in Kerala and the Ooty area in Tamil Nadu's Western Ghats. There are also top tea retailers in Delhi and other urban hubs.

In Bhopal in Madhya Pradesh, colourful *jari* shoulder bags, embroidered with beads, are a speciality. Also on the portables front, the Northeast States are noted for their beautiful hand-woven baskets and wickerwork – each tribe has its own unique basket shape.

Jodhpur in Rajasthan, among other places, is famed for its antiques (though be aware that exporting antiques is prohibited).

Artisans in Jammu and Kashmir have been producing lacquered papier mâché for centuries, and papier-mâché bowls, boxes, letter holders, coasters, trays and Christmas decorations are now sold across India, and make extremely inexpensive yet beautiful gifts (those with more intricate work command higher prices). In Rajasthan, look for colourful papier-mâché puppets, typically sold as a pair and often depicting a husband and wife, as well as beautiful little temples carved from mango wood, brightly painted with religious stories.

Fine-quality handmade paper – often fashioned into cards, boxes and notebooks – is worth seeking out. Puducherry in Tamil Nadu, Delhi, Jaipur and Mumbai are good places to start.

Hats are also popular: the Assamese make decorated reed-pith sun hats, and Tibetan refugees produce woollen hats, gloves and scarves, sold nationwide. Traditional caps worn by men and women of Himalayan tribes are available in many Himachal Pradesh towns.

India has a phenomenal range of books at very competitive prices, including leather-bound titles. Asian Educational Services publishes old (from the 17th century) and out-of-stock titles, in original typeface. Delhi's Sunday Book Market is a particularly good place to discover unexpected treasures.

Crafts aren't necessarily confined to their region of origin; artists migrate and are sometimes influenced by regional aesthetics, resulting in some interesting stylistic combinations. For example, you can visit a community of Rajasthani potters on the outskirts of Delhi.

The Arts

Over the millennia India's many ethnic groups have spawned a rich artistic heritage, and today, you'll experience art, both lofty and humble, around every corner: from intricately painted trucks on dusty roads to harmonic chanting from an ancient temple to wedding-season hands adorned with *mehndi* (henna). The wealth of creative expression is a highlight of travelling here, and today's artists fuse ancient and modern influences to create art, dance, literature and music that are as evocative as they are beautiful.

Dance

The ancient Indian art of dance is traditionally linked to mythology and classical literature. Dance can be divided into two main forms: classical and folk. Classical dance is essentially based on well-defined traditional disciplines. Some classical dance styles:

➡ **Bharatanatyam** (also spelt Bharata Natyam) Originated in Tamil Nadu, and has been embraced throughout India.

➡ **Kathak** Has Hindu and Islamic influences and was particularly popular with the Mughals. Kathak suffered a period of notoriety when it moved from the courts into houses where *nautch* (dancing) girls tantalised audiences with renditions of the Krishna-and-Radha love story. It was restored as a serious art form in the early 20th century.

➡ **Kathakali** Has its roots in Kerala; sometimes referred to as 'dance' but essentially is a kind of drama based on mythological subjects.

➡ **Kuchipudi** A 17th-century dance-drama that originated in the Andhra Pradesh village from which it takes its name. The story centres on the envious wife of Krishna.

➡ **Odissi** From Odisha (Orissa); thought to be India's oldest classical dance form. It was originally a temple art, and was later also performed at royal courts.

➡ **Manipuri** Has a delicate, lyrical flavour; hails from Manipur. It attracted a wider audience in the 1920s when acclaimed Bengali writer Rabindranath Tagore invited one of its most revered exponents to teach at Shantiniketan (West Bengal).

India's second major dance form, folk, is widespread and varied. It ranges from the high-spirited bhangra dance of Punjab to the theatrical dummy-horse dances of Karnataka and Tamil Nadu, and the graceful fishers' dance of Odisha. In Gujarat, the colourful group dance known as *garba* is performed during Navratri (Hindu festival held in September or October).

Pioneers of modern dance forms in India include Uday Shankar (older brother of the late sitar master Ravi), who once partnered with Russian ballerina Anna Pavlova. Rabindranath Tagore was another innovator; in 1901 he set up a school at Shantiniketan in West Bengal that promoted the arts, including dance.

The dance you'll most commonly see, though, is in films. Dance has featured in Indian movies since the dawn of 'talkies' and often combines traditional, folk, modern and contemporary choreography.

Indian Classical Dance by Leela Venkataraman and Avinash Pasricha is a lavishly illustrated book covering various Indian dance forms, including Bharata Natyam, Odissi, Kuchipudi and Kathakali.

Music

Indian classical music traces its roots back to Vedic times, when religious poems chanted by priests were first collated in an anthology called the Rig-Veda. Over the millennia classical music has been shaped by many influences, and the legacy today is Carnatic (characteristic of South India) and Hindustani (the classical style of North India) music. With common origins, they share a number of features. Both use the raga (the melodic shape of the music) and *tala* (the rhythmic meter characterised by the number of beats); *tintal,* for example, has a *tala* of 16 beats. The audience follows the *tala* by clapping at the appropriate beat, which in *tintal* is at beats one, five and 13. There's no clap at the beat of nine; that's the *khali* (empty section), which is indicated by a wave of the hand. Both the raga and the *tala* are used as a basis for composition and improvisation.

Both Carnatic and Hindustani music are performed by small ensembles, generally comprising three to six musicians, and both have many instruments in common. There's no fixed pitch, but there are differences between the two styles. Hindustani has been more heavily influenced by Persian musical conventions (a result of Mughal rule); Carnatic music, as it developed in South India, cleaves more closely to theory. The most striking difference, at least for those unfamiliar with India's classical forms, is Carnatic's greater use of voice.

One of the best-known Indian instruments is the sitar (large stringed instrument), with which the soloist plays the raga. Other stringed instruments include the sarod (which is plucked) and the *sarangi* (which is played with a bow). Also popular is the tabla (twin drums), which provides the *tala*. The drone, which runs on two basic notes, is provided by the oboe-like *shehnai* or the stringed *tampura* (also spelt tamboura). The hand-pumped keyboard harmonium is used as a secondary melody instrument for vocal music.

Indian regional folk music is widespread and varied. Wandering musicians, magicians, snake charmers and storytellers often use song to entertain their audiences; the storyteller usually sings the tales from the great epics.

In North India you may come across *qawwali* (Sufi devotional singing), performed in mosques or at musical concerts. *Qawwali* concerts usually take the form of a *mehfil* (gathering) with a lead singer, a second singer, harmonium and tabla players, and a thunderous chorus of junior singers and clappers, all sitting cross-legged on the floor. The singers whip up the audience with lines of poetry, dramatic hand gestures and religious phrases as the two voices weave in and out, bouncing off each other to create an improvised, surging sound. On command the chorus dives in with a hypnotic and rhythmic refrain. Members of the audience often sway and shout out in ecstatic appreciation.

A completely different genre altogether, filmi (music from films) includes modern, slower-paced love serenades, along with hyperactive dance songs. To ascertain the latest filmi favourites, as well as in-vogue Indian pop singers, enquire at music stores, or invest in a portable radio.

To tune into the melodious world of Hindustani classical music, including a glossary of musical terms, get a copy of *Nād: Understanding Raga Music* by Sandeep Bagchee.

Painting

Around 1500 years ago artists covered the walls and ceilings of the Ajanta caves in Maharashtra, western India, with scenes from the Buddha's past lives. The figures are endowed with an unusual freedom and grace, and contrast with the next major style that emerged from this part of India in the 11th century.

India's Jain community created some particularly lavish temple art. However, after the conquest of Gujarat by the Delhi Sultanate in 1299, the Jains turned their attention to illustrated manuscripts, which could

Get arty with *Indian Art* by Roy C Craven, *Contemporary Indian Art: Other Realities* edited by Yashodhara Dalmia, and *Indian Miniature Painting* by Dr Daljeet and Professor PC Jain.

MAGICAL MEHNDI

Mehndi is the traditional art of painting a woman's hands (and sometimes feet) with intricate henna designs for auspicious ceremonies, such as marriage. If quality henna is used, the design, which is orange-brown, can last up to one month.

In touristy areas, *mehndi*-wallahs are adept at applying henna tattoo 'bands' on the arms, legs and lower back. If you get *mehndi* applied, allow at least a few hours for the design process and required drying time (during drying you can't use your hennaed hands).

It's always wise to request the artist to do a 'test' spot on your arm before proceeding: nowadays some dyes contain chemicals that can cause allergies. (Avoid 'black henna', which is mixed with some chemicals that may be harmful.) If good-quality henna is used, you should not feel any pain during or after the application.

be hidden away. These manuscripts are the only known form of Indian painting that survived the Islamic conquest of North India.

The Indo-Persian style – characterised by geometric design coupled with flowing form – developed from Islamic royal courts, although the depiction of the elongated eye is one convention that seems to have been retained from indigenous sources. The Persian influence blossomed when artisans fled to India following the 1507 Uzbek attack on Herat (in present-day Afghanistan), and with trade and gift-swapping between the Persian city of Shiraz, an established centre for miniature production, and Indian provincial sultans.

The 1526 victory by Babur at the Battle of Panipat ushered in the era of the Mughals in India. Although Babur and his son Humayun were both patrons of the arts, it's Humayun's son Akbar who is generally credited with developing the characteristic Mughal style. This painting style, often in colourful miniature form, largely depicts court life, architecture, battle and hunting scenes, as well as detailed portraits. Akbar recruited artists from far and wide, and artistic endeavour first centred on the production of illustrated manuscripts (topics varied from history to mythology), but later broadened into portraiture and the glorification of everyday events. European painting styles influenced some artists, and this influence occasionally reveals itself in experiments with motifs and perspective.

Akbar's son Jehangir also patronised painting, but he preferred portraiture, and his fascination with natural science resulted in a vibrant legacy of paintings of flowers and animals. Under Jehangir's son Shah Jahan, the Mughal style became less fluid and, although the bright colouring was eye-catching, the paintings lacked the vigour of before.

Miniature painting flowered first at the Mughal court in the 16th century, as well as the Deccan sultanates (Golconda, Bijapur, Bidar etc). As Mughal power and wealth declined, many artists moved to Rajasthan where the Rajasthani school developed from the late 17th century. Later, artists from Rajasthan moved into the Himalayan foothills of Punjab, Himachal Pradesh and Uttarakhand, where the Pahari (Hill Country) school flourished in the 18th and early 19th centuries. The subject matter ranged from royal processions to shikhar (hunting expeditions), with many artists influenced by Mughal styles. The intense colours, still evident today in miniatures and frescoes in some Indian palaces, were often derived from crushed semiprecious stones, while the gold and silver colouring is finely pounded pure gold and silver leaf.

By the 19th century, painting in North India was notably influenced by Western styles (especially English watercolours), giving rise to what has been dubbed the Company School, which had its centre in Delhi. Meanwhile, in the south, painter Ravi Varma painted schmaltzy mythological

Encyclopedia of Indian Cinema by Ashish Rajadhyaksha and Paul Willemen chronicles India's dynamic cinematic history, spanning from 1897 to the 21st century.

scenes and portraits of women, which were hugely popular and gave Indian subjects a very Western treatment. Look out for the distinctive stylised works of Jamini Roy, depicting village life and culture.

The Madras Movement pioneered modern art in South India in the 1960s, and in 21st-century India, paintings by modern and contemporary Indian artists have been selling at record numbers (and prices) around the world. One very successful online art auction house is the Mumbai-based Saffronart (www.saffronart.com), or you can see and buy art at the Delhi Art Gallery (p745). Delhi and Mumbai are currently India's contemporary-art centres.

Cinema

India's film industry was born in the late 19th century – the first major Indian-made motion picture, *Panorama of Calcutta,* was screened in 1899. India's first real feature film, *Raja Harishchandra,* was made during the silent era in 1913 and it's ultimately from this film that Indian cinema traces its vibrant lineage.

Today, India's film industry is the biggest in the world – twice as big as Hollywood. Mumbai (Bombay), the Hindi-language film capital, aka 'Bollywood', is the biggest producer (p767), but India's other major film-producing cities – Chennai (Kollywood), Hyderabad (Tollywood) and Bengaluru (Sandalwood) – also have a huge output. A number of other centres produce films in their own regional vernaculars too. Big-budget films are often partly or entirely shot abroad, with some countries vigorously wooing Indian production companies because of the potential spin-off tourism revenue these films generate.

An average of 2000 feature films are produced annually in India. Apart from hundreds of millions of local Bolly-, Tolly- and Kollywood buffs, there are also millions of Non-Resident Indian (NRI) fans, who have played a significant role in catapulting Indian cinema onto the international stage.

Broadly speaking, there are two categories of Indian films. Most prominent is the mainstream 'masala' movie – named for its 'spice mix' of elements. Designed to have something for every member of the family, the films tend to have a mix of romance, action, slapstick humour and moral themes. Three hours and still running, these blockbusters are often tear-jerkers and are packed with dramatic twists interspersed with numerous song-and-dance performances. There is no explicit sex, and not even much kissing (although smooching is creeping into some Bollywood movies) in Indian films made for the local market; however, lack of nudity is often compensated for by heroines dressed in skimpy or body-hugging attire, and the lack of overt eroticism is more than made up for with heaps of intense flirting and loaded innuendos.

The second Indian film genre is art house, which adopts Indian 'reality' as its base. Generally speaking they are, or at least are supposed to be, socially and politically relevant. Usually made on infinitely smaller budgets than their commercial cousins, these films are the ones that win kudos at global film festivals and award ceremonies, such as the Lunchbox (Critics' Week Viewers Choice Award, Cannes 2013). The late Bengali director Satyajit Ray, most famous for his 1950s work, is the father of Indian art films, winning many awards for movies such as Pather Panchali, which portrays the poverty of a Bengal family.

Literature

India has a long tradition of Sanskrit literature, although works in the vernacular have contributed to a particularly rich legacy. In fact, it's claimed there are as many literary traditions as there are written languages.

Haider, an updated film version of Hamlet set in Kashmir (with songs), made waves in 2014, irking both hardline Hindus and Muslims, with some calling for it to be banned.

In 2013, *Dabba* (Lunchbox), a non-Bollywood romantic comedy directed and written by Ritesh Batra, won the Grand Rail d'Or at Cannes International Critics' Week.

Hobnob with acclaimed local and international writers at Asia's biggest literary event, the Jaipur Literature Festival (www.jaipurliteraturefestival.org), held in late January in Jaipur (Rajasthan).

Bengalis are traditionally credited with producing some of India's most celebrated literature, a movement often referred to as the Indian or Bengal Renaissance, which flourished from the 19th century with works by Bankim Chandra Chatterjee. But the man who to this day is mostly credited with first propelling India's cultural richness onto the world stage is the Bengali Rabindranath Tagore, with works such as *Gitanjali* (Song Offerings), *Gora* (Fair-Faced) and *Ghare-Baire* (The Home and the World).

One of the earliest Indian authors writing in English to receive an international audience, in the 1930s, is RK Narayan, whose deceptively simple writing about small-town life is subtly hilarious. Keralan Kamala Das (aka Kamala Suraiyya) wrote poetry, such as Summer in Calcutta, in English, and her memoir, My Story, in Malayalam, which she later translated to English; her frank approach to love and sexuality, especially in the 1960s and '70s, broke ground for women writers.

India has an ever-growing list of internationally acclaimed contemporary authors. Particularly prominent writers include Vikram Seth, best known for his epic novel *A Suitable Boy,* and Amitav Ghosh, who has won a number of accolades; his *Sea of Poppies* was shortlisted for the 2008 Man Booker Prize. Indeed, recent years have seen a number of Indian-born authors win the prestigious Man Booker Prize, the most recent being Aravind Adiga, who won in 2008 for his debut novel, *The White Tiger*. The prize went to Kiran Desai in 2006 for *The Inheritance of Loss;* Kiran Desai is the daughter of the award-winning Indian novelist Anita Desai, who has thrice been a Booker Prize nominee. In 1997 Arundhati Roy won the Booker Prize for her novel *The God of Small Things,* while Mumbai-born Salman Rushdie took this coveted award in 1981 for *Midnight's Children*.

The brilliant and prolific writer and artist Rabindranath Tagore won the Nobel Prize in Literature in 1913 for *Gitanjali*. For a taste of Tagore's work, read *Selected Short Stories*.

THE ARTS LITERATURE

Sacred Architecture

India has a remarkable assortment of historic and contemporary sacred architecture that draws inspiration from a variety of religious denominations. Although few of the wooden and occasionally brick temples built in early times have weathered the vagaries of nature, by the advent of the Guptas (4th to 6th centuries AD) of North India, sacred structures of a new type – better engineered to withstand the elements – were being constructed, and these largely set the standard for temples for several hundred years.

For Hindus, the square is a perfect shape, and complex rules govern the location, design and building of each temple, based on numerology, astrology, astronomy and religious principles. Essentially, a temple represents a map of the universe. At the centre is an unadorned space, the *garbhagriha* (inner sanctum), which is symbolic

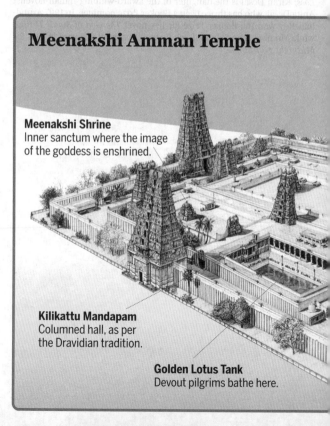

Meenakshi Amman Temple

Meenakshi Shrine
Inner sanctum where the image of the goddess is enshrined.

Kilikattu Mandapam
Columned hall, as per the Dravidian tradition.

Golden Lotus Tank
Devout pilgrims bathe here.

of the 'womb-cave' from which the universe is believed to have emerged. This provides a residence for the deity to which the temple is dedicated.

Above a Hindu temple's shrine rises a tower superstructure known as a *vimana* in South India, and a *sikhara* in North India. The *sikhara* is curvilinear and topped with a grooved disk, on which sits a pot-shaped finial, while the *vimana* is stepped, with the grooved disk being replaced by a solid dome. Some temples have a *mandapa* (forechamber) connected to the sanctum by vestibules. The *mandapa* may also contain *vimanas* or *sikharas*.

A *gopuram* is a soaring pyramidal gateway tower of a Dravidian temple. The towering *gopurams* of various South Indian temple complexes, such as the nine-storey *gopurams* of Madurai's Sri Meenakshi Temple, took ornamentation and monumentalism to new levels.

Commonly used for ritual bathing and religious ceremonies, as well as adding aesthetic appeal, temple tanks have long been a focal point of temple activity. These often-vast, angular, engineered reservoirs of water, sometimes fed by rain, sometimes fed – via a complicated drainage system – by rivers, serve both sacred and secular purposes. The waters of some temple tanks are believed to have healing properties, while others are said to have the power to wash away sins. Devotees (as well as travellers) may be required to wash their feet in a temple tank before entering a place of worship.

Masterpieces of Traditional Indian Architecture by Satish Grover and *The History of Architecture in India* by Christopher Tadgell proffer interesting insights into temple architecture.

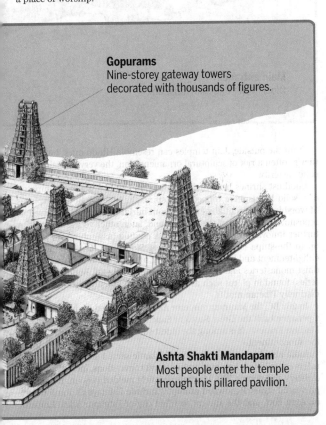

Gopurams
Nine-storey gateway towers decorated with thousands of figures.

Ashta Shakti Mandapam
Most people enter the temple through this pillared pavilion.

Golden Temple

Pilgrim accommodation

Main entrance
Clock tower and Sikh museum.

From the outside, Jain temples can resemble Hindu ones, but inside they're often a riot of sculptural ornamentation, the very opposite of ascetic austerity.

Buddhist shrines have their own unique features. Stupas, composed of a solid hemisphere topped by a spire, characterise Buddhist places of worship and essentially evolved from burial mounds. They served as repositories for relics of the Buddha and, later, other venerated souls. A further innovation is the addition of a *chaitya* (assembly hall) leading up to the stupa itself. Bodhgaya, where Siddhartha Gautama attained enlightenment and became the Buddha, has a collection of notable Buddhist monasteries and temples. The gompas (Tibetan Buddhist monasteries) found in places such as Ladakh and Sikkim are characterised by distinctly Tibetan motifs.

The focal point of a gompa is the *dukhang* (prayer hall), where monks assemble to chant passages from sacred scriptures.

In 262 BC, the Mauryan emperor Ashoka embraced Buddhism, and as a penance built the Great Stupa at Sanchi, in the central Indian state of Madhya Pradesh. It is among the oldest surviving Buddhist structures in the subcontinent.

India also has a rich collection of Islamic sacred sites, as its Muslim rulers contributed their own architectural conventions, including arched cloisters and domes. The Mughals uniquely melded Persian, Indian and provincial styles. Renowned examples include Humayun's Tomb in Delhi, Agra Fort, and the ancient fortified city of Fatehpur Sikri. Emperor

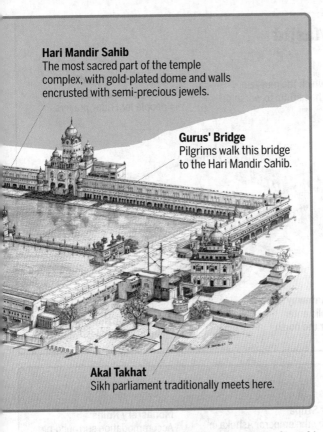

Hari Mandir Sahib
The most sacred part of the temple complex, with gold-plated dome and walls encrusted with semi-precious jewels.

Gurus' Bridge
Pilgrims walk this bridge to the Hari Mandir Sahib.

Akal Takhat
Sikh parliament traditionally meets here.

Shah Jahan was responsible for some of India's most spectacular architectural creations, most notably the milky white Taj Mahal.

Islamic art eschews any hint of idolatry or portrayal of God, and it has evolved a vibrant heritage of calligraphic and decorative designs. In terms of mosque architecture, the basic design elements are similar worldwide. A large hall is dedicated to communal prayer and within the hall is a mihrab (niche) indicating the direction of Mecca. The faithful are called to prayer from minarets, placed at cardinal points. Delhi's formidable 17th-century Jama Masjid is India's biggest mosque, its courtyard able to hold 25,000 people.

The Sikh faith was founded by Guru Nanak, the first of 10 gurus, in the 15th century. Sikh temples, called gurdwaras, can usually be identified by their bud-like *gumbads* (domes) and *nishan sahib* (a flagpole flying a triangular flag with the Sikh insignia). Amritsar's stunning Golden Temple is Sikhism's holiest shrine.

Discover more about India's diverse temple architecture (in addition to other temple-related information) at Temple Net (www.templenet.com).

Jama Masjid

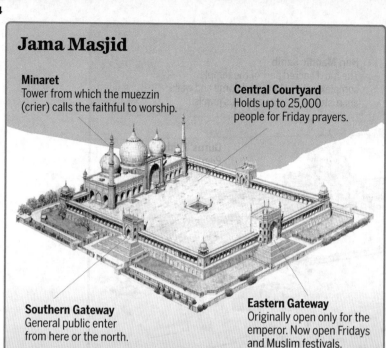

Minaret
Tower from which the muezzin (crier) calls the faithful to worship.

Central Courtyard
Holds up to 25,000 people for Friday prayers.

Southern Gateway
General public enter from here or the north.

Eastern Gateway
Originally open only for the emperor. Now open Fridays and Muslim festivals.

Sanchi

Great Stupa
Built by the emperor Ashoka in the 2nd century BC to enshrine relics of the Buddha.

Monastery Ruins
Accommodation surrounding a central courtyard.

Stupa Three
Contained the relics of two important disciples of the Buddha.

Processional path
Pilgrims circumambulated the stupa along this path.

India's Wildlife & Parks

The wildlife of India comprises a fascinating melting pot of animals from Europe, Asia and ancient Gondwanaland, all swirled together in a bewildering mix of habitats ranging from steamy mangrove forests and jungles to sandy deserts and icy alpine mountains.

India is celebrated for its big, bold, exalted species – tigers, elephants, rhinos, leopards, bears and monkeys. But there is much much more, including a mesmerising collection of colourful birds and some of the world's most endangered and intriguing wildlife, such as the Ganges river dolphin and the Asiatic lion.

India's Iconic Species

If you had to pick India's most charismatic species, the list would inevitably include tigers, elephants and rhinos, all of which are scarce and in need of stringent protection.

Asian elephants – a thoroughly different species to the larger African elephant – are revered in Hindu custom and were able to be domesticated and put to work in India, and many still survive in the wild. Because they migrate long distances in search of food, these 3000kg animals require huge parks; inter-species conflicts often erupt when herds of elephants attempt to follow ancestral paths that are now occupied by villages and farms. Some of the best parks for elephant viewing are Corbett Tiger Reserve (p441) in Uttarakhand and Nagarhole National Park (p883) in Karnataka.

There are far fewer one-horned rhinos left and two-thirds (just shy of 2000) of the world's total population can be found in Kaziranga National Park (p572), where they serenely wander lush alluvial grasslands at the base of the Himalaya. They may look sedate but rhinos are unpredictably dangerous, built like battering rams, covered in plates of armour-like skin and use their sharp teeth to tear off chunks of flesh when they attack – so let's just say that it's safest to watch them from the back of an elephant.

And the tiger – fixed in the subcontinent's subconscious as the mythological mount of Durga, the powerful, demon-slaying goddess, while prowling the west's image of India as Mowgli's jungle nemesis. This awesome, iconic animal is critically endangered but can be seen, if you're lucky, at tiger reserves around the country. Your best chance of spotting one is in Madhya Pradesh.

Tourism & Conservation

Wildlife-watching has become one of the country's prime tourist activities, and there are hundreds of national parks and wildlife sanctuaries offering opportunities to spot rare and unusual creatures. Your visit helps notify the government and local people that protecting endangered species and fragile ecosystems is important, and of economic value. So take some time to track down a rhino or spot a tiger on safari.

Resources

Wildlife, conservation and environment awareness-raising at www.sanctuaryasia.com

The Wildlife Trust of India news at www.wti.org.in

Top birdwatching information and photo galleries at www.birding.in

Books

Mammals of India by Vivek Menon

A Guide to the Birds of India and Pocket Guide to Birds of the Indian Subcontinent by Richard Grimmett, Carol Inskipp and Tim Inskipp

Treasures of Indian Wildlife by AS Kothari and BF Chappgar

The Maneaters of Kumaon and The Man-eating Leopard of Rudraprayag by Jim Corbett

PROJECT TIGER

When naturalist Jim Corbett first raised the alarm in the 1930s, no one believed that tigers would ever be threatened. At the time, it was believed there were 40,000 tigers in India, although no one had ever conducted a census. Then came Independence, which put guns into the hands of villagers who pushed into formerly off-limits hunting reserves seeking highly profitable tiger skins. By the time an official count was made in 1972, there were only 1800 tigers left, and the international outcry prompted Indira Gandhi to make the tiger the national symbol of India and set up **Project Tiger** (http://projecttiger.nic.in). It has since established 47 tiger reserves totaling over 68,676 sq km that protect not only this top predator but all animals that share its habitat. After an initial round of successes, relentless poaching over the past decade has caused tiger numbers to plummet, from 3600 in 2002 to around 1700 in 2011. Despite countless rupees and high-tech equipment devoted to saving this majestic animal, out of 63 wild tiger deaths in 2013, only one was from old age, while 48 were from poaching. Fortunately, the most recent tiger census results, from January 2015, show an encouraging rise in India's tiger population, to at least 2220 – a gain of over 500 in just four years.

Cats & Dogs

India is justifiably famous for its tigers, but is also home to 14 other species of cats, so don't miss any opportunities to see one of the other gorgeous felines.

Protection efforts have been successfully made on behalf of the Asiatic lion, a close relative of the more familiar African lion. A hundred years ago there were only 20 of these lions left in the world, but their population of 400-plus now seems to be doing fairly well in Gujarat's Sasan Gir National Park. Some 300 of India's 1150 leopards also roam in Gir.

An estimated 400 to 700 snow leopards survive in the alpine altitudes of Ladakh, Sikkim, Uttarakhand, Arunachal Pradesh, and Himachal Pradesh – where it is the official state animal. This much-celebrated big cat is so elusive that many locals claim it can appear and disappear at will. Your chances of seeing one are small, but if you want to seek this ghost-like feline, try the Spiti region for starters.

Other wild cats include the clouded leopard and its smaller cousin, the marbled cat, both of which lurk in the jungles of northeast India. They are strikingly marked with rosettes and rings for camouflage in the dappled light of their forest homes.

India is also home to about 1000 Indian wolves, which can best be seen in Gujarat's Blackbuck National Park. Jackals, foxes, and dholes (wild dogs) can be spotted in enclaves around the country. The rare, and most ancient, breed of wolf – the Spitian – howls over Spiti Valley.

India's national animal is the tiger, its national bird is the peacock and its national flower is the lotus. The national emblem of India is a column topped by three Asiatic lions.

Adaptation the Key to Success

By far the most abundant forms of wildlife you'll see in India are deer (nine species), antelope (six species), goats and sheep (10 species), and primates (15 species). In the open grasslands of many parks look for the stocky nilgai, India's largest antelope, or elegantly horned blackbucks. If you're heading for the mountains, keep your eyes open in the Himalaya for blue sheep – with partially curled horns – or the rare argali, with fully curled horns, found in Ladakh. The deserts of Rajasthan and Gujarat are home to arid land species such as chinkaras (Indian gazelles); while the mangrove swamps of the Sundarban Delta have chitals (spotted deer), who cope with their brackish environment by excreting salt from their nasal glands. Chitals are also the most abundant deer in central India's high-profile tiger reserves.

For memorable wildlife shots, a camera with a long lens – at least 300mm – is essential.

India's primates range from the extremely rare hoolock gibbon and golden langur of the northeast to species that are so common as to be pests – most notably the stocky and aggressive rhesus macaque and the elegant grey (Hanuman) langur. In the south, the pesky monkeys that loiter around temples and tourist sites are bonnet macaques.

Endangered Species

Despite having amazing biodiversity, India faces a growing challenge from its exploding human population. Wildlife is severely threatened by poaching and habitat loss. A recent count suggested India had over 500 threatened species, including 247 species of plants, 53 species of mammals, 78 species of birds, 22 species of reptiles, 68 species of amphibians, 35 species of fish and 22 species of invertebrates. In 2012, the International Union for Conservation of Nature released a list of the 100 most threatened species in the world. It included four Indian species; a spider, a turtle and two birds – the great Indian bustard and white-bellied heron.

Although much touted as a success, even the well-resourced Project Tiger faces an uphill battle every day. Every good news story seems to be followed by yet another story of poaching gangs or tiger or leopard attacks on villagers. All of India's wild cats, from leopards to snow leopards, panthers and jungle cats are facing extinction from habitat loss and poaching for the lucrative trade in skins and body parts for Chinese medicine (a whole tiger carcass can fetch upwards of UK£32,000). Government estimates suggest that India is losing 1% of its tigers every year to poachers. Still, conservation efforts are seeing some notable successes, with a nearly 30% increase in the country's tiger population over the past four years alone.

Even highly protected rhinos are poached for the illegal medicine trade – rhino horn is highly valued as an aphrodisiac in China and as a material for making handles for daggers in the Gulf. Elephants are regularly poached for ivory. From 2000 to 2008, some 320 elephants were poached; do not support this illegal trade by buying ivory souvenirs. Various species of deer are threatened by hunting for food and trophies, and the chiru, or Tibetan antelope, is nearly extinct because its hair is woven into wool for expensive shahtoosh shawls.

India's bear species remain under threat, although sloth bears are experiencing a reprieve with the recent demise of the dancing bear industry. In the rivers, India's famous freshwater dolphins are in dire straits from pollution, habitat alteration and direct human competition. The sea-turtle populations that nest on the Orissa coast also face environmental challenges.

Threatened primate species clinging on in rainforests in the south include lion-tailed macaques, glossy black Nilgiri langurs and the slender loris, an adept insect-catcher with huge eyes for nocturnal hunting.

Birds

With well over 1000 species of birds, India is a birdwatcher's dream. Many birds are thinly spread over this vast country, but wherever critical habitat has been preserved in the midst of dense human activity, you might see phenomenal numbers of birds in one location. Winter can be

India has some of the richest biodiversity in the world. There are 397 species of mammals, 1250 bird species, 460 types of reptiles, 240 amphibian species and 2546 fish species – among the highest species count for any country.

India has 238 species of snake, of which about 50 are poisonous. Of the various species of cobra, the king cobra is the world's largest venomous snake, attaining a length of 5m.

INDIA'S WILDLIFE & PARKS ENDANGERED SPECIES

ANIMAL ATTACKS

Human/animal conflict is on the rise in India, as wildlife habitat shrinks and human settlement expands. In recent years, about 80 people are killed or injured annually by tigers, and its not unusual to hear of leopard attacks in villages and cities across northern India – even in Mumbai! While such attacks get lots of press coverage and cause great panic, around 46,000 Indians die each year from snakebite, and 20,000 die from rabid dog bites. It's rare for tigers to turn into true maneaters; those that do are generally old, injured, or both.

a particularly good time, as wetlands throughout the country host northern migrants arriving to kick back in the lush subtropical warmth of the Indian peninsula. Throughout the year, wherever you may be travelling, look for colourful kingfishers, barbets, sunbirds, parakeets and magpies, or the blue flash of an Indian roller. Keen types will take a special trip into the Himalaya in search of one of India's (and the world's) mostly highly sought-after birds, the enigmatic ibisbill.

Once considered the premier duck-hunting destination in the British Empire when royal hunting parties would shoot 4000 ducks in a single day, the seasonal wetlands of Rajasthan's Keoladeo Ghana were elevated to national park status in 1982, and the park is rightly famous for its migratory avian visitors. Now whittled down to a relatively small pocket of habitat amid a sea of villages and agricultural fields, this is still one of the finest birdwatching destinations in the world. Even better, Keoladeo Ghana and its abundant birdlife are ridiculously easy to explore: just hop on a bike at the gate and tootle around the flat tracks that weave among the park's clearly defined ponds and marshes. In the winter there are so many ducks, herons, storks, cranes, egrets and raptors packing themselves into the park that your foremost problem will be trying to identify individual animals amid the chaos.

Plants

Once upon a time India was almost entirely covered in forest; now its total forest cover is estimated to be around 20%. Despite widespread clearing of native habitats, the country still boasts 49,219 plant species, of which some 5200 are endemic. Species on the southern peninsula show Malaysian ancestry, while desert plants in Rajasthan are more clearly allied with the Middle East, and the conifer forests of the Himalaya derive from European and Siberian origins. The Forest Survey of India has set an optimistic target of returning to 33% cover.

Outside of the mountain forests found in the Himalaya, nearly all the lowland forests of India are subtypes of tropical forest, with native sal forests forming the mainstay of the timber industry. Some of these tropical forests are true rainforest, staying green year-round – such as in the Western Ghats and in the northeast states – but most forests are deciduous; during the hot, dry months of April and May, many forests lose their canopies, as leaves wither and fall from the trees. This is often the best time to view wildlife, as the cover is thinner, and animals seek out scarce waterholes.

High-value trees such as Indian rosewood, Malabar kino and teak have been virtually cleared from the Western Ghats, and sandalwood is endangered across India due to illegal logging for the incense and wood-carving industries. A bigger threat to forested lands is firewood harvesting, often carried out by landless peasants who squat on gazetted government land.

Several trees have significant religious value in India, including the silk-cotton tree, a huge tree with spiny bark and large red flowers under which Pitamaha (Brahma), the god of creation, sat after his labours. Two well-known figs, the banyan and peepal, grow to immense size by dangling roots from their branches and fusing into massive multi-trunked jungles of trunks and stems – one giant is nearly 200m across. It is said

Top Parks North

Corbett Tiger Reserve

Kaziranga National Park

Keoladeo Ghana National Park

Ranthambhore National Park

Top Parks Central

Bandhavgarh National Park

Kanha National Park

Panna National Park

Sunderbans Tiger Reserve

Top Parks South

Mahatma Gandhi Marine National Park

Nagarhole National Park

Periyar Wildlife Sanctuary

BIG & SMALL

India's largest contiguous protected area is the Nanda Devi Biosphere Reserve, in Uttarakhand; covering 2237 sq.km. It includes India's second-highest peak (Nanda Devi – 7817m) and the famous Valley of Flowers. India's smallest national park is South Button Island, in the Andamans, at less than 5 sq.km.

PARKS & PEOPLE

While national parks and wildlife sanctuaries have been crucial to protecting the habitats of India's endangered species, their creation has had some tragic consequences. As a result of the Wildlife Protection Act of 1972, which banned people from living in parks, about 1.6 million Adivasis and other forest-dwellers have been evicted from their traditional lands. Many were resettled into villages and forced to abandon their age-old ways of life, resulting in profound personal suffering and irreplaceable cultural losses. Today, the Forest Rights Act of 2006 forbids the displacement of forest-dwellers from national parks (except in so-called "critical wildlife habitat"), and should protect the four-million-or-so people who still live in them. It's still too early to tell how successful the law will be at helping tribes remain in parks – and how their continued presence will impact fragile wildlife habitat.

For more on the Forest Rights Act and issues surrounding 'people in parks', visit www.forestrightsact.com; also see the Van Gujjar Project at www.traditionalculturesproject.org.

that Buddha achieved enlightenment while sitting under a peepal (also known as the Bodhi tree).

The foothills and slopes of the Himalaya preserve classic montane species, including blue pine and deodar (Himalayan cedar), and deciduous forests of apple, chestnut, birch, plum and cinnamon. Above the snowline, hardy plants such as anemones, edelweiss and gentians can be prolific, and one fabulous place to see such flowers is at the Valley of Flowers National Park.

India's hot deserts have their own unique species – the khejri tree and various strains of scrub acacia. The hardy sea-buckthorn bush is the main fruiting shrub in the high-altitude deserts of the Himalaya.

> Around 2000 plant species are described in Ayurveda (traditional Indian herbal medicine) texts.

National Parks & Wildlife Sanctuaries

Prior to 1972 India only had five national parks. The Wildlife Protection Act was introduced that year to set aside land for parks and stem the abuse of wildlife. The act was followed by a string of similar pieces of legislation with bold ambitions but few teeth with which to enforce them.

India now has about 100 national parks and 500 wildlife sanctuaries, which constitute around 5% of India's territory. An additional 70 parks have been authorised on paper but not yet implemented on the ground or only implemented to varying degrees. There are also 14 biosphere reserves, overlapping many of the national parks and sanctuaries, providing safe migration channels for wildlife and allowing scientists to monitor biodiversity.

We strongly recommend visiting at least one national park or sanctuary on your travels – the experience of coming face-to-face with a wild elephant, rhino or tiger will stay with you for a lifetime, while your visit adds momentum to efforts to protect India's natural resources. Wildlife reserves tend to be off the beaten track and infrastructure can be limited – book transport and accommodation in advance, and check opening times, permit requirements and entry fees before you visit. Many parks close to conduct a census of wildlife in the low season, and monsoon rains can make wildlife-viewing tracks inaccessible.

Almost all parks offer jeep/van tours, but you can also search for wildlife on guided treks, boat trips and elephant safaris. New rules introduced in 2012 put an end to 'tiger shows', whereby resting tigers became sitting ducks for tourists that were radioed in, taken off their jeep and put on elephants to get close to the, presumably peeved, resting tiger. Also, in many reserves, safari vehicle visits have been reduced and some tiger sanctuaries may be closed to safaris one day a week. These new rules still are in flux, so do find out the latest situation before booking your safari.

> Located almost perfectly in the centre of the country, Bandhavgarh National Park is one dynamic example of what the original Indian landscape might have been like. Here you can explore meadows, forests and rocky ridges in a thrilling search for tigers, leopards and other big fauna.

The Landscape

India is an incredibly diverse country with everything from steamy jungles and tropical beaches to arid deserts and the soaring icy peaks of the Himalaya. At 3,287,263 sq km, it is the second-largest Asian country after China, and forms the vast bulk of the South Asian subcontinent – an ancient block of earth crust that carried a wealth of unique plants and animals like a lifeboat across a prehistoric ocean before slamming into Asia about 40 million years ago.

The Lie of The Land

Look for the three major geographic features that define modern-day India: Himalayan peaks and hills along the northern borders, the floodplains of the Indus and Ganges Rivers in the north, and the elevated Deccan Plateau that forms the core of India's triangular southern peninsula.

India is home to 18% of the world's population crowded together on 2.5% of the world's landmass – making it the second-most densely populated among the 10 most populous countries on earth (after Bangladesh).

The Himalaya

As the world's highest mountains – with the highest peak in India (Khangchendzonga) reaching 8598m – the Himalaya create an almost impregnable boundary separating India from its neighbours to the north. These mountains formed when the Indian subcontinent broke away from Gondwanaland, a supercontinent in the Southern Hemisphere that included Africa, Antarctica, Australia and South America. All by itself, India drifted north and finally slammed slowly, but with immense force, into the Eurasian continent about 40 million years ago, buckling the ancient seafloor upward to form the Himalaya and many lesser ranges that stretch 2500km from Afghanistan to Myanmar (Burma).

When the Himalaya reached its great heights during the Pleistocene (less than 150,000 years ago), it blocked and altered weather systems, creating the monsoon climate that dominates India today, as well as forming a dry rainshadow to the north.

Although it looks like a continuous range on a map, the Himalaya is actually a series of interlocking ridges, separated by countless valleys. Until technology enabled roadbuilding into the Himalaya, many of these valleys were virtually isolated, creating a diverse array of mountain cultures.

The Indo-Gangetic Plains

Covering most of northern India, the vast alluvial plains of the sacred Ganges River are so flat that they drop a mere 200m between Delhi and the waterlogged wetlands of West Bengal, where the river joins forces with the Brahmaputra River from India's northeast, before dumping into the sea in Bangladesh. Vast quantities of eroded sediments from the neighbouring highlands accumulate on the plains to a depth of nearly 2km, creating fertile, well-watered agricultural land. This densely populated region was once extensively forested and rich in wildlife.

Gujarat in the far west of India is separated from Sindh (Pakistan) by the Rann of Kutch, a brackish marshland that becomes a huge inland sea during the wet season; the waters recede in the dry season, leaving isolated islands perched on an expansive plain.

It is estimated that India's population will reach 1.3 billion people by 2016.

The Deccan Plateau

South of the Indo-Gangetic (northern) plain, the land rises to the Deccan Plateau, marking the divide between the Mughal heartlands of North India and the Dravidian civilisations of the south. The Deccan is bound on either side by the Western and Eastern Ghats, which come together in their southern reaches to form the Nilgiri Hills in Tamil Nadu.

On the Deccan's western border, the Western Ghats drop sharply down to a narrow coastal lowland, forming a luxuriant slope of rainforest.

The Islands

Offshore from India are a series of island groups, politically part of India but geographically linked to the landmasses of Southeast Asia and islands of the Indian Ocean. The Andaman and Nicobar Islands sit far out in the Bay of Bengal, while the coral atolls of Lakshadweep (300km west of Kerala) are a northerly extension of the Maldives islands, with a land area of just 32 sq km.

Environmental Issues

With well over a billion people, ever-expanding industrial and urban centres, and growth in chemical-intensive farming, India's environment is under tremendous pressure. An estimated 65% of the land is degraded in some way, most of it seriously, and the government has been consistently falling short of the majority of its environmental protection goals. Many current problems are a direct result of the Green Revolution of the 1960s, when chemical fertilisers and pesticides enabled huge growth in agricultural output but at enormous cost to the environment.

Despite numerous environmental laws, corruption continues to exacerbate environmental degradation – exemplified by the flagrant flouting of laws by companies involved in hydroelectricity and mining. Usually, the people most affected are low-caste rural farmers and Adivasis (tribal people) who have limited political representation and few resources to fight big businesses.

Agricultural production has been reduced by soil degradation from over-farming, rising soil salinity, loss of tree cover and poor irrigation. The human cost is heart-rending, and lurking behind all these problems is a basic Malthusian truth: there are far too many people for India to support.

As anywhere, tourists tread a fine line between providing an incentive for change and making the problem worse. For example, many of the environmental problems in Goa are a direct result of irresponsible

> Get the inside track on Indian environmental issues at Down to Earth (www.downtoearth.org.in), an online magazine that delves into stories overlooked by mainstream media.

STRADDLING THE FUTURE

India is grappling with a major dilemma: how to develop, modernise and grow economically, without destroying what's left of its environment, or adding to the global climate problem. The current government, led by Narendra Modi, offers mixed signals as to its priorities. On one hand, Modi has made it his personal mission to clean the Ganges River by 2019, has launched the much-publicised Swachh Bharat campaign to reduce trash pollution nationwide, and supports large-scale solar power generation. But his government has also pledged to increase domestic coal mining and double its use, adding significantly to India's greenhouse gas emissions. Meanwhile, the committee that's rewriting India's environmental regulations has proposed abandoning environmental inspections, saying, according to the New York Times, that "India should rely on business owners to voluntarily disclose the pollution that their projects will generate and then monitor their own compliance". Also according to the New York Times, Modi's environment minister defended decisions to cut regulations, saying that the government was "not phasing out important environmental protections, just 'those which, in the name of caring for nature, were stopping progress'".

development for tourism. Always consider your environmental impact while travelling in India.

Climate Change

The Andaman and Nicobar Islands comprise 572 islands and are the peaks of a vast submerged mountain range extending almost 1000km between Myanmar (Burma) and Sumatra.

Changing climate patterns – linked to global carbon emissions – have been creating dangerous extremes of weather in India. While India's per capita carbon emissions still rank far behind that of the USA, Australia and Europe, the sheer size of its population makes it a major polluter.

It has been estimated that by 2030, India will see a 30% increase in the severity of its floods and droughts. In the mountain deserts of Ladakh, increased rainfall is changing time-honoured farming patterns, while glaciers on nearby peaks are melting at alarming rates. In 2013, devastating flooding hit Uttarakhand – with unconfirmed estimates of between 6000 and 50,000 people killed over the course of a couple of days. In 2014, massive floods struck the Kashmir Valley, inundating Srinagar, wreaking widespread damage and loss of life. Conversely, other areas are experiencing reduced rainfall, causing drought and riots over access to water. Islands in the Lakshadweep group as well as the low-lying plains of the Ganges delta are being inundated by rising sea levels.

Deforestation

Noise pollution in major cities has been measured at over 90 decibels – more than one and a half times the recognised 'safe' limit. Bring earplugs!

Since Independence, over 50,000 sq km of India's forests have been cleared for logging and farming, or destroyed by urban expansion, mining, industrialisation and river dams. Even in the well-funded, highly protected Project Tiger parks, the amount of forest cover classified as 'degraded' has tripled due to illegal logging. The number of mangrove forests has halved since the early 1990s, reducing the nursery grounds for the fish that stock the Indian Ocean and Bay of Bengal.

India's first Five Year Plan in 1951 recognised the importance of forests for soil conservation, and various policies have been introduced to increase forest cover. Almost all have been flouted by officials or criminals and by ordinary people clearing forests for firewood and grazing in forest areas. What can you do? Try to minimise the use of wood-burning stoves while you travel. Further, you could support the numerous charities working with rural communities to encourage tree planting.

Water Resources

Arguably the biggest threat to public health in India is inadequate access to clean drinking water and proper sanitation. With the population set to double by 2050, agricultural, industrial and domestic water usage are all expected to spiral, despite government policies designed to control water use. The World Health Organisation estimates that, out of more than 3000 cities and towns in India, only eight have adequate waste-water treatment facilities. Many cities dump untreated sewage and partially cremated bodies directly into rivers, while open defecation is a simple fact of life in most rural (and many urban) areas.

Downstream of Varanasi, the Ganges River is a black, septic mess with 3000 times the acceptable limit of faecal coliform bacteria.

Rivers are also affected by run-off, industrial pollution and sewage contamination – the Sabarmati, Yamuna and Ganges are among the most polluted rivers on earth. At least 70% of the freshwater sources in India are now polluted in some way. In recent years, drought has devastated parts of the subcontinent (particularly Rajasthan and Gujarat) and has been a driving force for rural-to-urban migration.

Water distribution is another volatile issue. Since 1947 an estimated 35 million people in India have been displaced by major dams, mostly built to provide hydroelectricity for this increasingly power-hungry nation. While hydroelectricity is one of the greener power sources, valleys across India are being sacrificed to create new power plants, and displaced people rarely receive adequate compensation.

Survival
Guide

Scams

India has a deserved reputation for scams. Of course, most can be easily avoided with a little common sense and an appropriate amount of caution. Scams tend to be more of a problem in the big cities of arrival (such as Delhi or Mumbai), or very touristy spots (such as Rajasthan), though in Goa and Kerala they are rare. Chat with fellow travellers to keep abreast of the latest cons. Look at the India branch of Lonely Planet's Thorn Tree Travel Forum (www.lonelyplanet.com/thorntree), where travellers post warnings about problems they have encountered on the road.

Contaminated Food & Drink

➡ The late 1990s saw a scam in North India where travellers died after consuming food laced with dangerous bacteria from restaurants linked to dodgy medical clinics; we've heard no recent reports but the scam could resurface. In unrelated incidents, some clinics have also given more treatment than necessary to procure larger payments.

➡ Most bottled water is legit, but ensure the seal is intact and the bottom of the bottle hasn't been tampered with. While in transit, try to carry packed food. If you eat at bus or train stations, buy cooked food only from fast-moving places.

Credit-Card Con

Be careful when paying for souvenirs with a credit card. While government shops are usually legitimate, private souvenir shops have been known to run off extra copies of the credit-card imprint slip and use them for phoney transactions later. Ask the trader to process the transaction in front of you. Memorising the CVV/CVC2 number and scratching it off the card is also a good idea, to avoid misuse. In some restaurants, waiters will ask you for your PIN with the intention of taking your credit card to the machine – never give your PIN to anyone, and ask to use the machine in person.

Druggings

Occasionally, tourists (especially solo travellers) are drugged and robbed during train or bus journeys. A spiked drink is the most commonly used method for sending them off to sleep – chocolates, chai from a co-conspiring vendor and 'homemade' Indian food are also known to be used. Use your instincts, and if you're unsure, politely decline drinks or food offered by strangers.

Gem Scams

This classic scam involves charming con artists who promise foolproof 'get rich quick' schemes. Travellers are asked to carry or mail gems home and then sell them to the trader's (nonexistent) overseas representatives at a profit. Without exception, the goods – if they arrive at all – are worth a fraction of what you paid, and the 'representatives' never materialise.

KEEPING SAFE

➡ A good travel-insurance policy is essential.

➡ Email copies of your passport identity page, visa and airline tickets to yourself, and keep copies on you.

➡ Keep your money and passport in a concealed money belt or a secure place under your shirt.

➡ Store at least US$100 separately from your main stash.

➡ Don't publicly display large wads of cash when paying for services or checking into hotels.

➡ If you can't lock your hotel room securely from the inside, stay somewhere else.

Don't believe hard-luck stories about an inability to obtain an export licence, or the testimonials they show you from other travellers – they are fake. Travellers have reported this con happening in Agra, Delhi, and Jaisalmer among other places, but it's particularly prevalent in Jaipur. Carpets, curios and *pashminas* are other favourites for this con.

Overpricing

Always agree on prices beforehand while availing services that don't have regulated tariffs. This particularly applies to friendly neighbourhood guides, snack bars at places of touristy interest, and autorickshaws and taxis without meters.

Photography

Use your instincts (better still, ask for permission) while photographing people. The common argument – sometimes voiced after you've snapped your photos – is you're going to sell them to glossy international magazines, so it's only fair that you pay a fee.

Theft

Theft is a risk in India, as anywhere else. Keep luggage locked and chained on buses and trains. Remember that snatchings often occur when a train is pulling out of the station, as it's too late for you to give chase.

Touts & Commission Agents

➡ Touts come in many avatars and operate in mysterious ways. Cabbies and autorickshaw drivers will often try to coerce you to stay at a budget hotel of their choice, only to collect a commission (included within your room tariff) from the receptionists afterward.

➡ Wherever possible, arrange hotel bookings (if only for

OTHER TOP SCAMS

➡ Gunk (dirt, paint, poo) suddenly appears on your shoes, only for a shoe cleaner to magically appear and offer to clean it off – for a price.

➡ Some shops are selling overpriced SIM cards and not activating them; it's best to buy your SIM from an official shop (Airtel, Vodafone etc) and check it works before leaving the area (activation can take 24 hours).

➡ Shops and restaurants 'borrow' the name of their more successful and popular competitor.

➡ Touts claim to be 'government-approved' guides or agents, and sting you for large sums of cash. Enquire at the local tourist office about licensed guides and ask to see identification from guides themselves.

➡ Artificial 'tourist offices' that are actually dodgy travel agencies whose aim is to sell you overpriced tours, tickets and tourist services.

the first night), and request a hotel pick-up. You'll often hear stories about hotels of your choice being 'full' or 'closed' – check things out yourself. Reconfirm and double-check your booking the day before you arrive.

➡ Be very sceptical of phrases like 'my brother's shop' and 'special deal at my friend's place'. Many fraudsters operate in collusion with souvenir stalls, so be careful while making expensive purchases in private stores.

➡ Avoid friendly people and 'officials' in train and bus stations who offer unsolicited help, then guide you to a commission-paying travel agent. Look confident, and if anyone asks if this is your first trip to India, say you've been here several times, even if you haven't. Telling touts that you have already prepaid your transfer/tour/onward journey may help dissuade them.

Transport Scams

➡ Upon arriving at train stations and airports, if you haven't prearranged pick-up, book transport from government-approved booths. All major airports now have radio cab, prepaid taxi and

airport shuttle bus counters in the arrival lounge. Never go with a loitering cabbie who offers you a cheap ride into town, especially at night.

➡ While booking multiday sightseeing tours, stick to itineraries offered by tourism departments, or those that come recommended either in this guidebook or by friends who've personally used them. Be extremely wary of anyone in Delhi offering houseboat tours to Kashmir – we've received many complaints over the years about dodgy deals.

➡ When buying a bus, train or plane ticket anywhere other than the registered office of the transport company, make sure you're getting the ticket class you paid for. Use official online booking facilities where possible.

➡ Some tricksters pose as Indian Railways officials and insist you pay to have your e-ticket validated on the platform; ignore them.

➡ Train station touts (even in uniform or with 'official' badges) may tell you that your intended train is cancelled/flooded/broken down or that your ticket is invalid. Do not respond to any 'official' approaches at train stations.

Women & Solo Travellers

There are extra considerations for women and solo travellers when visiting India – from cost to safety. As with anywhere else in the world, it pays to be prepared.

Women Travellers

Although Bollywood might suggest otherwise, India remains a conservative society. Female travellers should be aware that their behaviour and attire choice are likely to be under constant scrutiny.

Unwanted Attention

Unwanted attention from men is a common problem.

➡ Be prepared to be stared at; it's something you'll simply have to live with, so don't allow it to get the better of you.

➡ Refrain from returning male stares; this can be considered encouragement.

➡ Dark glasses, phones, books or electronic tablets are useful props for averting unwanted conversations.

Clothing

Avoiding culturally inappropriate clothing will help avert undesirable attention.

➡ Steer clear of sleeveless tops, shorts, short skirts (ankle-length skirts are recommended) and anything else that's skimpy, see-through or tight-fitting.

➡ Wearing Indian-style clothes is viewed favourably.

➡ Draping a dupatta (long scarf) over T-shirts is another good way to avoid stares – it's shorthand for modesty, and also handy if you visit a shrine that requires your head to be covered.

➡ Wearing a salwar kameez (traditional dresslike tunic and trousers) will help you blend in; a smart alternative is a kurta (long shirt) worn over jeans or trousers.

➡ Avoid going out in public wearing a choli (sari blouse) or a sari petticoat (which some foreign women mistake for a skirt); it's like strutting around half-dressed.

➡ Aside from at pools, many Indian women wear long shorts and a T-shirt when swimming in public view; it's wise to wear a sarong from the beach to your hotel.

Health & Hygiene

➡ Sanitary pads are widely available but tampons are usually restricted to pharmacies in big cities and tourist towns (even then, the choice may be limited). Carry additional stocks for travel off the beaten track.

Sexual Harassment

Many female travellers have reported some form of sexual harassment while in India, such as lewd comments, invasion of privacy and even groping. Serious sexual assaults do happen but are rare; follow similar safety precautions as you would at home.

➡ Women travellers have experienced provocative gestures, jeering, getting 'accidentally' bumped into on the street and being followed.

➡ Incidents are common at exuberant (and crowded) public events such as the Holi festival. If a crowd is gathering, make yourself scarce or find a safer place overlooking the event so that you're away from wandering hands.

➡ Women travelling with a male partner will receive far less hassle.

Staying Safe

The following tips will help you avoid uncomfortable or dangerous situations during your journey:

➡ Always be aware of your surroundings. If it feels wrong, trust your instincts. Tread with care. Don't be scared, but don't be reckless either.

➡ If travelling after 9pm, use a recommended, registered taxi service.

➡ Don't organise your travel in such a way that means you're hanging out at bus/train stations or arriving late at night. Arrive in towns before dark.

➡ Keep conversations with unknown men short – getting involved in an inane conversation with someone you barely know can be misinterpreted as a sign of sexual interest.

- Some women wear a pseudo wedding ring, or announce early on in the conversation that they're married or engaged (regardless of the reality).

- If you feel that a guy is encroaching on your space, he probably is. A firm request to keep away usually does the trick, especially if your tone is loud and curt enough to draw the attention of passers-by.

- The silent treatment can also be very effective.

- Follow local women's cues and instead of shaking hands say *namaste* – the traditional, respectful Hindu greeting.

- Avoid wearing expensive-looking jewellery and carrying flashy accessories.

- Check the reputation of any teacher or therapist before going to a solo session (get recommendations from travellers). Some women have reported being molested by masseurs and other therapists. If you feel uneasy at any time, leave.

- Female filmgoers may attract less attention and lessen the chances of harassment by going to the cinema with a companion.

- Lone women may want to invest in a good-quality hotel in a better neighbourhood.

- At hotels keep your door locked, as staff (particularly at budget and midrange places) can knock and walk in without waiting for your permission.

- Avoid wandering alone in isolated areas even during daylight. Steer clear of gallis (narrow lanes) and deserted roads.

- When on rickshaws alone, call/text someone, or pretend to, to indicate someone knows where you are.

- Act confidently in public; to avoid looking lost (and thus more vulnerable) consult maps at your hotel (or at a restaurant) rather than on the street.

Taxis & Public Transport

Being female has some advantages; women can usually queue-jump for buses and trains without consequence and on trains there are special ladies-only carriages. There are also women-only waiting rooms at some stations.

- Solo women should prearrange an airport pick-up from their hotel, especially if their flight is scheduled to arrive after dark.

- Delhi and some other cities have licensed prepaid radio cab services such as Easycabs – they're more expensive than the regular prepaid taxis, but promote themselves as being safe, with drivers who have been vetted as part of their recruitment.

- If you do catch a regular prepaid taxi, make a point of writing down the registration and driver's name – in front of the driver – and giving it to one of the airport police.

- Avoid taking taxis alone late at night and never agree to have more than one man (the driver) in the car – ignore claims that this is 'just my brother' etc.

- Solo women have reported less hassle by choosing more expensive classes on trains.

- If you're travelling overnight in a three-tier carriage, try to book the uppermost berth, which will give you more privacy (and distance from potential gropers).

- On public transport, don't hesitate to return any errant limbs, put an item of luggage between you and others, be vocal (attracting public attention, thus shaming the pest), or simply find a new spot.

Solo Travellers

One of the joys of travelling solo in India is that you're more likely to be 'adopted' by families, especially if you're commuting together on a long rail journey. It's a great opportunity to make friends and get a deeper understanding of local culture. If you're keen to hook up with fellow travellers, tourist hubs such as Goa, Rajasthan, Kerala, Manali, McLeod Ganj, Leh, Agra and Varanasi are some popular places to do so. You may also be able to find travel companions on Lonely Planet's **Thorn Tree Travel Forum** (www.lonelyplanet.com/thorntree).

Cost

The most significant issue facing solo travellers is cost.

- Single-room accommodation rates are sometimes not much lower than double rates.

- Some midrange and top-end places don't even offer a single tariff.

- It's always worth trying to negotiate a lower rate for single occupancy.

Safety

Most solo travellers experience no major problems in India but, like anywhere else, it's wise to stay on your toes in unfamiliar surroundings.

- Some less honourable souls (locals and travellers alike) view lone tourists as an easy target for theft and sexual assault.

- Single men wandering around isolated areas have been mugged, even during the day.

Transport

- You'll save money if you find others to share taxis and autorickshaws, as well as when hiring a car for longer trips.

- Solo bus travellers may be able to get the 'co-pilot' (near the driver) seat on buses, which not only has a good view out front, but is also handy if you've got a big bag.

Directory A–Z

Accommodation

Accommodation in India ranges from backpacker dives with bucket showers to opulent palaces with plunge pools. We've listed reviews first by price range and then by author preference.

Categories

Budget (₹) covers everything from hostels, hotels and guesthouses in urban areas to traditional homestays in villages. Midrange hotels (₹₹) tend to offer extras such as cable/satellite TV and air-conditioning. Top-end places (₹₹₹) stretch from luxury five-star chains to gorgeous heritage palaces.

Costs

Given that the cost of budget, midrange and top-end hotels varies so much across India, it would be misleading for us to provide a 'national' price strategy. Most establishments raise tariffs annually, so prices may have risen by the time you read this. Prices are highest in large cities (eg Delhi, Mumbai) and lowest in rural areas (eg Bihar, Andhra Pradesh). Costs are also seasonal – hotel prices can drop by 20% to 50% outside of peak season.

Price Icons

Lonely Planet price indicators refer to the cost of a double room, including private bathroom, unless otherwise noted.

Reservations

➡ It's a good idea to book ahead, online or by phone, especially when travelling to more popular destinations. Some hotels require a credit-card deposit at the time of booking.

➡ Some budget options won't take reservations as they don't know when people are going to check-out; call ahead or just turn up around check-out time.

➡ Other places may want a deposit at check-in – ask for a receipt and be wary of any request to sign a blank impression of your credit card. If the hotel insists, pay cash.

➡ Verify the check-out time when you check-in – some hotels have a fixed check-out time (usually 10am or noon), while others offer 24-hour check-out. In some places, check-out can be as early as 9am. Sometimes you can request to check in early and the hotel will oblige if the room is empty.

Seasons

➡ Rates given are full price in high season. High season usually coincides with the best weather for the area's sights and activities – normally spring and autumn in the mountains (March to May and September to November), and the cooler months in the plains (around November to mid-February).

➡ In areas popular with foreign tourists, there's an additional peak period over Christmas and New Year; make reservations well in advance.

➡ At other times you may find significant discounts; if the hotel seems quiet, ask for one.

➡ Some hotels in places such as Goa close during the monsoon period, or in hill stations such as Manali during winter.

➡ Many temple towns have additional peak seasons around major festivals and pilgrimages.

Taxes & Service Charges

➡ State governments slap a variety of taxes on hotel

BOOK YOUR STAY ONLINE

For more accommodation reviews by Lonely Planet authors, check out http://lonelyplanet.com/hotels/. You'll find independent reviews, as well as recommendations on the best places to stay. Best of all, you can book online.

accommodation (except at the cheaper hotels), and these are added to the cost of your room.

➜ Taxes vary from state to state. Even within a state prices can vary, with more expensive hotels levying higher taxes.

➜ Many upmarket hotels also add an additional 'service charge' (usually around 10%).

➜ Rates quoted in this book include taxes.

➜ Some upscale restaurants may add a service charge (between 10% and 13%) on meals.

Budget & Midrange Hotels

➜ Sometimes you'll luck out and find these in atmospheric old houses or heritage buildings, but the majority of budget and midrange hotels are modern-style concrete blocks with varying degrees of comfort. Some are charming, clean and good value; others less so. Room quality can vary considerably within a hotel so try to inspect a few rooms first.

➜ Shared bathrooms (often with squat toilets) are usually only found in the cheapest lodgings. Most rooms have ceiling fans and better rooms have electric mosquito killers and/or window nets, though cheaper rooms may lack windows altogether.

➜ If you're mostly staying in budget places, bring your own sheet or sleeping-bag liner, towel and soap. Sheets and bedclothes at cheap hotels can be stained, worn and in need of a wash, and towels and toiletries are often not supplied.

➜ An insect repellent and a torch (flashlight) are essential accessories in many budget hotels. Sound pollution can be irksome (especially in urban hubs);

SAMPLE ACCOMMODATION COSTS

CATEGORY	MUMBAI	RAJASTHAN	SIKKIM
₹ budget	<₹2500	<₹1000	<₹1500
₹₹ midrange	₹2500-6000	₹1000-5000	₹1500-4000
₹₹₹ top end	<₹6000	<₹5000	<₹4000

pack earplugs and request a room that doesn't face a busy road.

➜ It's wise to keep your door locked at all times, as some staff (particularly in budget hotels) may knock and walk in without awaiting your permission. Blackouts are common (especially during summer and the monsoon) so double-check that the hotel has a back-up generator if you're paying for electric 'extras' such as air-conditioners, TVs and wi-fi.

➜ A room with a TV generally guarantees a working power socket for charging your phone, ipad etc.

➜ Note that some hotels lock their doors at night. Members of staff might sleep in the lobby but waking them up can be a challenge. Let the hotel know in advance if you'll be arriving late at night or leaving early in the morning.

➜ Away from tourist areas, cheaper hotels may not take foreigners because they don't have the necessary foreigner-registration forms.

Camping

There are few official camping sites in India. On the other hand, wild camping is often the only accommodation option on trekking routes.

In some mountain or desert areas you'll also find summer-only tented camps, with accommodation in semipermanent 'Swiss tents' with attached bathrooms.

Dormitory Accommodation

There's a burgeoning number of great backpacker hostels across India, notably in Delhi, Varanasi and Goa.

A number of hotels have cheap dormitories, though these may be mixed gender and, in less touristy places, full of drunken males – not ideal conditions for women. The handful of hostels run by the YMCA, YWCA and Salvation Army or associated with HI or YHAI (Youth Hostels Association of India) are more traveller-friendly.

Government Accommodation & Tourist Bungalows

The Indian government maintains a network of guesthouses for travelling officials and public workers, known variously as rest houses, dak bungalows, circuit houses, PWD (Public Works Department) bungalows and forest rest houses. These places may accept travellers if no government employees need the rooms, but permission is sometimes required from local officials.

'Tourist bungalows' are run by state governments – rooms are usually mid-priced (some with cheap dorms) and have varying standards of cleanliness and service.

Some state governments also run chains of more expensive hotels, including some lovely heritage properties. Check with the local state tourism office.

Homestays & B&Bs

These family-run guest-houses will appeal to those seeking a small-scale, more homey setting with home-cooked meals.

Standards range from mud-and-stone village huts with hole-in-the-floor toilets to comfortable middle-class homes in cities.

In places like Ladakh, homestays are increasingly the way to go but standards are fairly simple.

Be aware that some hotels market themselves as 'homestays' but are run like hotels with little (or no) interaction with the family.

Contact the local tourist office for a full list of participating families.

Railway Retiring Rooms

Most large train stations have basic rooms for travellers holding an ongoing train ticket or Indrail Pass. Some are grim, others are surprisingly pleasant but suffer from the noise of passengers and trains.

They're useful for early-morning train departures and there's usually a choice of dormitories or private rooms (24-hour check-out) depending on the class you're travelling in.

Some smaller stations may have only waiting rooms (again divided by class).

Temples & Pilgrims' Rest Houses

Accommodation is available at some ashrams (spiritual retreats), gurdwaras (Sikh temples) and *dharamsalas* (pilgrims' guesthouses) for a donation or a nominal fee. Vegetarian meals are usually available at the refectories.

These places have been established for genuine pilgrims so please exercise judgement about the appropriateness of staying.

Always abide by any protocols. Smoking and drinking within the premises are a complete no-no.

Top-End & Heritage Hotels

India has plenty of top-end properties, from modern five-star chain hotels to glorious palaces, and luxury eco- and forest resorts.

You can browse members of the Indian Heritage Hotels Association on the tourist board website **Incredible India** (www.incredibleindia.org).

Customs Regulations

Technically you're supposed to declare any amount of cash over US$5000, or total amount of currency over US$10,000 on arrival.

Indian rupees shouldn't be taken out of India; however, this is rarely policed.

Officials very occasionally ask tourists to enter expensive items such as video cameras and laptop computers on a 'Tourist Baggage Re-export' form to ensure they're taken out of India at the time of departure.

Electricity

230V/50Hz. Plugs have two round pins or, less commonly, three pins.

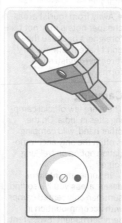

230V/50Hz

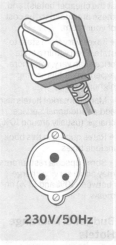

230V/50Hz

Embassies & Consulates

Most foreign diplomatic missions are based in Delhi, but there are various consulates in other Indian cities.

➡ **Australian**: Delhi (Map p72; ☎011-41399900, 011-41399900; www.india.highcommission.gov.au; 1/50G Shantipath, Chanakyapuri), Mumbai (Map p750; 10th fl, A Wing, Crescenzo Bldg, G Block, Plot C 38-39, Bandra Kurla Complex, Mumbai), Chennai (Map p1010; ☎044-45921300; 9th fl, Express Chambers, Express Avenue Estate, White's Rd, Royapettah)

➡ **Bangladeshi**: Delhi (Map p72; ☎011-24121394; www.bdhcdelhi.org; EP39 Dr Radakrishnan Marg, Chanakyapuri), Kolkata (☎033-40127500; 9 Circus Ave)

➡ **Bhutanese**: Delhi (Map p72; ☎011-26889230; www.bhutan.gov.bt; Chandragupta Marg, Chanakyapuri), Kolkata (Map p456; Tivoli Court, Ballygunge Circular Rd)

➡ **Canadian**: Delhi (Map p72; ☎011-41782000; www.canadainternational.gc.ca/india-inde; 7/8 Shantipath, Chanakyapuri), Mumbai (www.canadainternational.gc.ca; 21st fl, Tower 2, Indiabulls Finance Centre, Senapati Bapat Marg, Elphinstone Rd West)

➔ **Chinese**: Delhi (Map p72; ☑26112345; www.in.chinaembassy.org; 50-D Shantipath, Chanakyapuri)

➔ **French**: Delhi (Map p72; ☑011-24196100; http://ambafrance-in.org; 2/50E Shantipath, Chanakyapuri), Mumbai (Map p740; ☑022-66694000; 7th fl, Hoechst House, Nariman Point, Mumbai),

➔ **German**: Delhi (Map p72; ☑011-44199199; www.new-delhi.diplo.de; 6/50G Shantipath, Chanakyapuri), Kolkata (Map p468; ☑24791141; 1 Hastings Park Rd, Alipore)

➔ **Israeli**: Delhi (Map p72; ☑011-30414500, 011-30414500; http://delhi.mfa.gov.il; 3 Aurangzeb Rd), Mumbai (☑022-61600500; Marathon Futurex, 1301, A Wing, N M Joshi Marg, Lower Parel, Mumbai)

➔ **Japanese**: Delhi (Map p72; ☑011-26876581; www.in.embjapan.go.jp; 50G Shantipath, Chanakyapuri), Mumbai (Map p746; ☑022-23517101; 1 ML Dahanukar Marg, Cumballa Hill), Chennai (Map p1004; ☑044-24323860; 12/1 1st St, Cenotaph Rd, Teynampet)

➔ **Malaysian**: Delhi (Map p72; ☑011-26111291/97; www.kln.gov.my/web/ind_new-delhi/home; 50M Satya Marg, Chanakyapuri)

➔ **Myanmar**: Delhi (Map p72; ☑011-24678822; http://myanmedelhi.com; 3/50F Nyaya Marg), Kolkata (Map p468; ☑033-24851658; mcgkolcg@gmail.com; 57K Ballygunge Circular Rd)

➔ **Nepali**: Delhi (Map p72; ☑011-23476200; www.nepalembassy.in; Mandi House, Barakhamba Rd), Kolkata (☑033-24561224; 1 National Library Ave, Alipore)

➔ **Netherlands**: Delhi (Map p72; ☑011-24197600; http://india.nlembassy.org; 6/50F Shantipath, Chanakyapuri), Mumbai (Map p740; ☑022-

PRACTICALITIES

Newspapers & Magazines

English-language dailies include the *Hindustan Times*, *Times of India*, *Indian Express*, *Hindu*, *Statesman*, *Telegraph*, *Daily News & Analysis* (DNA) and *Economic Times*. Regional English-language and local-vernacular publications are found nationwide. Incisive current-affairs magazines include *Frontline*, *India Today*, *Week*, *Open*, *Tehelka*, *Outlook* and *Motherland*.

Radio

Government-controlled All India Radio (AIR), India's national broadcaster, has over 220 stations broadcasting local and international news. Private FM channels broadcast music, current affairs, talkback and more.

TV & Video

The national (government) TV broadcaster is Doordarshan. More people watch satellite and cable TV; English-language channels include BBC, CNN, Star World, HBO, National Geographic and Discovery.

Weights & Measures

Officially India is metric. Terms you're likely to hear are lakhs (one lakh = 100,000) and crores (one crore = 10 million).

22194200; Forbes Bldg, Chaaranjit Rai Marg, Fort)

➔ **New Zealand**: Delhi (Map p72; ☑011-46883170, 011-46883170; www.nzembassy.com/india; Sir Edmund Hillary Marg, Chanakyapuri), Mumbai (☑022-61316666; Level 2, Maker Maxity, 3 North Ave, Bandra Kurla Complex, Mumbai), Chennai (Map p1004; ☑044-28112472; Rane Holdings Ltd, Maithri, 132 Cathedral Rd, Gopalapuram)

➔ **Pakistani**: Delhi (Map p72; ☑011-24676004; www.mofa.gov.pk/india; 2/50G Shantipath, Chanakyapuri)

➔ **Singaporean**: Delhi (Map p72; ☑011-46000915, 011-46000915; www.mfa.gov.sg/newdelhi; E6 Chandragupta Marg, Chanakyapuri), Mumbai (Map p740; ☑022-22043205,; 152 Makers Chambers IV, 14th fl, 222 Jamnalal Bajaj Rd, Nariman Point), Chennai (Map p1004; ☑044-28158207; 17A North Boag Rd, T Nagar)

➔ **Sri Lankan**: Delhi (Map p72; ☑011-23010202; www.slhcindia.org; 27 Kautilya Marg, Chanakyapuri), Mumbai (Map p740; ☑022-22045861; Mulla House, 34 Homi Modi St, Fort), Chennai (☑044-28241896; www.sldhcchennai.org; 56 Sterling Rd, Nungambakkam)

➔ **Thai**: Delhi (Map p76; ☑011-4977 4100; www.thaiemb.org.in; 56N Nyaya Marg, Chanakyapuri), Kolkata (☑033-24407836; 18B Mandeville Gardens, Ballygunge), Mumbai (Map p740; ☑022-22823535; Dalamal House, 1st fl, Jamnalal Bajaj Marg, Nariman Point), Chennai (Map p1004; ☑044-42300760; 3 1st Main Rd, Vidyodaya Colony, T Nagar)

➔ **UK**: Delhi (Map p72; ☑011-24192100; Shantipath), Kolkata (Map p456; ☑033-22885172; www.gov.uk/government/world/organisations/british-deputy-high-commission-kolkata; 1A Ho Chi Minh Sarani),

EATING PRICE RANGES

Prices in this book reflect the cost of a standard main meal (unless otherwise indicated). Reviews are listed by author preference within the following price categories.

₹ **budget** less than ₹100

₹₹ **midrange** ₹100-300

₹₹₹ **top end** more than ₹300

Mumbai (☎022-66502222; Naman Chambers, C/32 G Block Bandra Kurla Complex, Bandra East), Chennai (Map p1010; ☎044-42192151; 20 Anderson Rd)

➡ **US**: Delhi (Map p72; ☎011-24198000; http://newdelhi. usembassy.gov/; Shantipath), Kolkata (Map p456; ☎033-39842400; http://kolkata. usconsulate.gov/; 5/1 Ho Chi Minh Sarani), Mumbai, (☎022-26724000; C49, G Block, Bandra Kurla Complex, Mumbai) Chennai (Map p1004; ☎044-28574000; 220 Anna Salai, Gemini Circle)

Gay & Lesbian Travellers

Homosexuality was made illegal in India in 2013, after having only been decriminalised since 2009. Gay and lesbian visitors should be discreet in this conservative country. Public displays of affection are frowned upon for both homosexual and and heterosexual couples.

Despite the ban, there are gay scenes (and Gay Pride marches) in a number of cities including Mumbai, Delhi, Kolkata, Chennai and Bengaluru (Bangalore), as well as a holiday gay scene in Goa.

Websites & Publications

Gay Bombay (www.gaybombay.org) Lists gay events as well as offering support and advice.

Gay Delhi (www.gaydelhi.org) LGBT support group, also organises social events in Delhi.

Gaysi Zine (http://gaysifamily. com/) This is a thoughtful monthly magazine and website featuring gay writing and issues.

Indian Dost (www.indian-dost.com/gay.php) News and information including contact groups in India.

Indja Pink (www.indjapink. co.in) India's first 'gay travel boutique' founded by a well-known Indian fashion designer.

Queer Azaadi Mumbai (http://queerazaadi.wordpress. com) Mumbai's queer pride blog, with news.

Queer Ink (www.queer-ink. com) Online bookstore specialising in gay- and lesbian-interest books from the subcontinent.

Support Groups

Chennai Dost (www. chennai-dost.blogspot.com) Community space for stories and information; organises events, including parties, exhibitions, campaigns, film festivals and Chennai Rainbow Pride (June).

Humsafar Trust (☎022-26673800; www.humsafar.org; Old BMC Bldg, 1st fl, Nehru Rd, Vakola, Santa Cruz East) Gay and transgender support groups and advocacy. The drop-in centre hosts workshops and has a library – pick up a copy of LGBT magazine Bombay Dost.

Queer Campus Hyderabad (www.facebook. com/qcampushyd) Student-focused group holds weekly meetings and monthly events including carnival days and film festivals.

Wajood Society (www. wajoodsociety.com) Hyderabad queer-support group, involved in organising events such as Queer Pride (February).

Insurance

➡ Comprehensive travel insurance to cover theft, loss and medical problems (as well as air evacuation) is strongly recommended.

➡ Some policies exclude potentially dangerous activities such as scuba diving, skiing, motorcycling, paragliding and even trekking: read the fine print.

➡ Some trekking agents may only accept customers who have cover for emergency helicopter evacuation.

➡ If you plan to hire a motorcycle in India, make sure the rental policy includes at least third-party insurance.

➡ Check in advance whether your insurance policy will pay doctors and hospitals directly or reimburse you later (keep all documentation for your claim).

➡ It's crucial to get a police report in India if you've had anything stolen; insurance companies may refuse to reimburse you without one.

➡ Worldwide travel insurance is available at www. lonelyplanet.com/bookings. You can buy, extend and claim online anytime – even if you're already on the road.

Internet Access

Internet cafes are widespread and connections are usually reasonably fast, except in more remote areas. Wi-fi access is widely available; it's usually free but some places charge.

Practicalities

➡ Internet charges vary regionally; charges range from ₹15 to ₹100 per hour;

often with a 15- to 30-minute minimum.

➡ Bandwidth load tends to be lowest in the early morning and early afternoon.

➡ Some internet cafes may ask to see your passport.

Security

Using online banking on any nonsecure system is unwise. If you have no choice but to do this, it's wise to change all passwords (email, netbanking, credit card 3-D Secure code etc) when you get back home.

Laptops

The simplest way to connect to the internet, when away from a wi-fi connection, is to use your smartphone as a personal wi-fi hotspot (use a local SIM to avoid roaming charges). However, if this isn't an option, companies that offer prepaid wireless 2G/3G modem sticks (called dongles) include Reliance, Airtel, Tata Docomo and Vodafone. To organise a connection you have to submit your identity proof and address in India, and activation can take up to 24 hours. A nonrefundable activation fee (around ₹2000) has to be paid, which includes the price of the dongle and around 10GB of data. A 20GB recharge costs around ₹1000.

➡ Make sure the areas you will be travelling to are covered by your service provider.

➡ Consider purchasing a fuse-protected universal AC adaptor to protect your circuit board from power surges.

➡ Plug adaptors are widely available throughout India, but bring spare plug fuses from home.

Language Courses

The following places offer language courses, some requiring a minimum time commitment.

➡ **Delhi** Hindi classes at Delhi's **Central Hindi Directorate** (Map p76; ☑26178454; www.hindinideshalaya.nic.in; West Block VII, RK Puram, Vivekanand Marg; 60hr basic course ₹6000). Hindi, Urdu and Sanskrit classes at **Zabaan** (http://zabaan.com).

➡ **Himachal Pradesh** Three-month courses in Tibetan at the **Library of Tibetan Works & Archives** (Map p319; ☑9218422467; www.ltwa.net; Gangchen Kyishong; ⊘9am-1pm & 2-5pm Mon-Sat, closed 2nd & 4th Sat of month), in McLeod Ganj. Several other places in McLeod Ganj offer courses in Tibetan and Hindi.

➡ **Mumbai (Bombay)** Beginners' courses in Hindi, Marathi and Sanskrit at **Bharatiya Vidya Bhavan** (Map p746; ☑23871860; www.bhavans.info; 2nd fl, cnr KM Munshi Marg & Ramabai Rd, Girgaum; per hour ₹500; ⊘4-8pm).

➡ **Tamil Nadu** Tamil courses at **International Institute of Tamil Studies** (☑044-22542781; www.ulakaththamizh.org; CIT Campus, 2nd Main Rd, Tharamani), in Chennai.

➡ **Uttar Pradesh** Hindi courses at **Pragati Hindi** (Map p394; ☑9335376488; www.pragatihindi.com; B-7/176 Harar Bagh), in Varanasi.

➡ **Uttarakhand** Hindi courses at the **Landour Language School** (☑0135-2631487; www.landourlanguageschool.com; Landour; group per hour ₹285, private per hour ₹460; ⊘Feb-Dec), in Mussoorie.

➡ **West Bengal** Tibetan courses at the **Manjushree Centre of Tibetan Culture** (Map p502; ☑0354-2252977; www.manjushree-culture.org; 12 Gandhi Rd; 3-/6-/9-month courses US$230/340/450, plus registration US$30; ⊘mid-Mar–mid-Dec), in Darjeeling.

Legal Matters

If you're in a sticky legal situation, contact your embassy immediately. However, be aware that all your embassy may be able to do is monitor your treatment in custody and arrange a lawyer. In the Indian justice system, the burden of proof can often be on the accused and stints in prison before trial are not unheard of.

Antisocial Behaviour

➡ Smoking in public places is illegal but this is rarely enforced; if caught you'll be fined ₹200, which could rise to ₹20,000 if proposed changes go ahead.

➡ People can smoke inside their homes and in most open spaces such as streets (heed any signs stating otherwise).

➡ Some Indian cities have banned spitting and littering, but this is also enforced irregularly.

WARNING: BHANG LASSI

Although it's rarely printed in menus, some restaurants in popular tourist centres will clandestinely whip up bhang lassi, a yoghurt and iced-water beverage laced with cannabis (and occasionally other narcotics). Commonly dubbed 'special lassi', this often potent concoction can cause varying degrees of ecstasy, drawn-out delirium, hallucination, nausea and paranoia. Some travellers have been ill for several days, robbed or hurt in accidents after drinking this fickle brew. A few towns have legal (controlled) bhang outlets such as the Bhang Shop in Jaisalmer.

Drugs

➡ Indian law does not distinguish between 'hard' and 'soft' drugs; possession of any illegal drug is regarded as a criminal offence, which will result in a custodial sentence. This may be up to a year for possession of a small amount for personal use, to a minimum of 10 years if it's deemed the purpose was for sale or distribution. There's also usually a hefty fine on top of any sentence.

➡ Cases can take months, even years, to appear before a court while the accused may have to wait in prison.

➡ Be aware that travellers have been targeted in sting operations in Manali, Goa and other backpacker enclaves.

➡ Marijuana grows wild in various parts of India, but consuming it is still an offence, except in towns where bhang is legally sold for religious rituals.

➡ Police are getting particularly tough on foreigners who use drugs, so you should take this risk very seriously.

➡ Pharmacutical drugs that are restricted in other countries may be available over the counter or via prescription. Be aware that to take these without professional guidance can be dangerous.

Police

You should always carry your passport; police are entitled to ask you for identification at any time.

If you're arrested for an alleged offence and asked for a bribe, be aware that it is illegal to pay a bribe in India. Many people deal with an on-the-spot fine by just paying it to avoid trumped up charges. Corruption is rife so the less you have to do with local police the better; try to avoid all potentially risky situations.

Maps

Maps available inside India are of variable quality. Throughout India, most state-government tourist offices stock basic local maps. These are some of the better map series, which should be available at good bookshops:

Eicher (http://maps.eicher-world.com/)

Leomann Maps Useful trekking maps for Jammu & Kashmir, Himachal Pradesh and Uttarakhand.

Nelles (www.nelles-verlag.de)

Nest & Wings (www.nest-wings.in)

Survey of India (www.surveyofindia.gov.in)

TTK (www.ttkmaps.com)

Money

The Indian rupee (₹) is divided into 100 paise, but only 50 paise coins are legal tender and these are rarely seen. Coins come in denominations of ₹1, ₹2, ₹5 and ₹10 (the 1s and 2s look almost identical); notes come in ₹5, ₹10, ₹20, ₹50, ₹100, ₹500 and ₹1000 (this last is handy for paying large bills but can pose problems when getting change for small services). The Indian rupee is linked to a basket of currencies and has been subject to fluctuations in recent years.

ATMs

➡ ATMs are found in most urban centres.

➡ Visa, MasterCard, Cirrus, Maestro and Plus are the most commonly accepted cards.

➡ ATMs at Axis Bank, Citibank, HDFC, HSBC, ICICI and State Bank of India recognise foreign cards. Other banks may accept major cards (Visa, Mastercard etc).

➡ Citibank ATMs generally allow you to withdraw up to ₹40,000 in one transaction (most others have a limit of ₹10,000 to ₹15,000), which reduces transaction charges.

➡ Before your trip, check whether your card can access banking networks in India and ask for details of charges.

PROHIBITED EXPORTS

To protect India's cultural heritage, the export of certain antiques is prohibited, especially those which are verifiably more than 100 years old. Reputable antique dealers know the laws and can make arrangements for an export-clearance certificate for old items that are OK to export. Detailed information on prohibited items can be found on the government webpage www.asi.nic.in/pdf_data/8.pdf. The rules may seem stringent but the loss of ancient artworks in places such as Ladakh, Himachal Pradesh, Gujarat and Rajasthan, due to the international trade in antiques, has been alarming. Look for quality reproductions instead.

The Indian Wildlife Protection Act bans any form of wildlife trade. Don't buy any product that endangers threatened species and habitats – doing so can result in heavy fines and even imprisonment. This includes ivory, shahtoosh shawls (made from the down of chirus or rare Tibetan antelopes) and anything made from the fur, skin, horns or shell of any endangered species. Products made from certain rare plants are also banned.

➼ Notify your bank that you'll be using your card in India to avoid having it blocked; take along your bank's phone number in case.

➼ Always keep the emergency lost-and-stolen numbers for your credit cards in a safe place, separate from your cards, and report any loss or theft immediately.

➼ Away from major towns, always carry cash (including a stock of rupees).

Black Market

Black-market moneychangers exist but legal moneychangers are so common that there's no reason to use illegal services, except perhaps to change small amounts of cash at land border crossings. If someone approaches you on the street and offers to change money, you're probably being set up for a scam.

Cash

➼ Major currencies such as US dollars, pounds sterling and euros are easy to change throughout India, although some bank branches insist on travellers cheques only.

➼ Some banks also accept other currencies such as Australian and Canadian dollars, and Swiss francs.

➼ Private moneychangers deal with a wider range of currencies, but Pakistani, Nepali and Bangladeshi currency can be harder to change away from the border.

➼ When travelling off the beaten track, always carry an adequate stock of rupees.

➼ Whenever changing money, check every note. Don't accept any filthy, ripped or disintegrating notes, as these may be difficult to use.

➼ It can be tough getting change in India so keep a stock of smaller currency; ₹10, ₹20 and ₹50 notes are helpful.

➼ Officially you cannot take rupees out of India, but this is laxly enforced. You can change any leftover rupees back into foreign currency most easily at the airport (some banks have a ₹1000 minimum). You may have to present encashment certificates or credit-card/ATM receipts, and show your passport and airline ticket.

Credit Cards

➼ Credit cards are accepted at a growing number of shops, upmarket restaurants, and midrange and top-end hotels, and they can usually be used to pay for flights and train tickets.

➼ Cash advances on major credit cards are also possible at some banks.

➼ MasterCard and Visa are the most widely accepted cards.

Encashment Certificates

➼ Indian law states that all foreign currency must be changed at official moneychangers or banks.

➼ For every (official) foreign-exchange transaction, you'll receive an encashment certificate (receipt), which will allow you to change rupees back into foreign currency when departing India.

➼ Encashment certificates should cover the amount of rupees you intend to change back to foreign currency.

➼ Printed receipts from ATMs are also accepted as evidence of an international transaction at most banks.

International Transfers

If you run out of money, someone back home can wire you cash via moneychangers affiliated with **Moneygram** (www.moneygram.com) or **Western Union** (www.westernunion.com). A fee is added to the transaction.

To collect the cash, bring your passport and the name and reference number of the person who sent the funds.

Moneychangers

Private moneychangers are usually open for longer hours than banks and are found almost everywhere (many also double as internet cafes and travel agents).

Upmarket hotels may also change money, but their rates are usually not as competitive.

Tipping, Baksheesh & Bargaining

➼ In tourist restaurants or hotels, a service fee is usually added to your bill and tipping is optional. Elsewhere, a tip is appreciated.

➼ Hotel bellboys and train/airport porters appreciate anything around ₹50; hotel staff should be given similar gratuities for services above and beyond the call of duty.

➼ It's not mandatory to tip taxi or rickshaw drivers, but it's good to tip drivers who are honest about the fare.

➼ If you hire a car with driver for more than a couple of days, a tip is recommended for good service.

➼ Baksheesh can loosely be defined as a 'tip'; it covers everything from alms for beggars to bribes.

➼ Many Indians implore tourists not to hand out sweets, pens or money to children, as it encourages them to beg. To make a lasting difference, consider donating to a reputable school or charitable organisation.

➼ Except in fixed-price shops (such as government emporia and fair-trade cooperatives), bargaining is the norm.

Travellers Cheques

➼ Travellers cheques are becoming harder and harder to change, as credit cards become more widely accepted. They are often more hassle than they are worth.

➜ All major brands are accepted, but some banks may only accept cheques from American Express (Amex) and Thomas Cook.

➜ Euros, pounds sterling and US dollars are the safest currencies, especially in smaller towns.

➜ Keep a record of the cheques' serial numbers separate from your cheques, along with the proof-of-purchase slips, encashment certificates and photocopied passport details. If you lose your cheques, contact the Amex or Thomas Cook office in Delhi.

➜ To replace lost travellers cheques, you need the proof-of-purchase slip and the numbers of the missing cheques (some places require a photocopy of the police report and a passport photo). If you don't have the numbers of your missing cheques, the issuing company (eg Amex) will contact the place where you bought them.

Opening Hours

➜ Official business hours are from 10am to 5pm Monday to Friday but many offices open later and close earlier.

➜ Most offices have an official lunch hour from around 1pm.

➜ Bank opening hours vary from town to town, so check locally; foreign-exchange offices may open longer and operate daily.

➜ Some larger post offices are open a full day on Saturday and a half-day on Sunday.

➜ In some places with six-day weeks, establishments may be closed on the second and fourth Saturdays of the month.

➜ Due to sporadic bouts of volatility, curfews can sometimes apply in certain areas, notably parts of Kashmir and the Northeast Region.

➜ Business hours vary wildly from state to state. Also, in remote areas such as the Northeast Region, shops may open and close depending on the weather, local political situation or the proprietor's mood.

Permits

Access to certain parts of India – particularly disputed border areas – is controlled by an often-complicated permit system.

A permit known as an Inner-Line Permit (ILP) or a Restricted Area Permit (RAP) is required to visit Arunachal Pradesh, Sikkim and certain parts of Himachal Pradesh, Ladakh and Uttarakhand that lie close to the disputed border with China/Tibet. Nagaland and Mizoram have reintroduced Restricted Area Permits (RAP) for foreign travellers (and Meghalaya and Manipur are considering doing so). Permits are also necessary for travel to the Andaman and Lakshadweep Islands, and some parts of Kutch in Gujarat.

Obtaining the ILP/RAP is usually a formality, but travel agents must apply on your behalf for certain areas, including many trekking routes passing close to the border.

Permits are issued by regional magistrates and district commissioners, either directly to travellers (for free) or through travel agents (for a fee). You also need to pay an Environmental Tax of ₹300; ensure you keep the receipt.

In Odisha (Orissa), foreign tourists require permission to visit some tribal regions. You can obtain this from the district collector, which may take a couple of days. Government-approved tourist agencies can speed up the process but you'll be tied to them throughout your visit.

Double-check with tourism officials to see if permit requirements have undergone any changes before you head out to these areas.

STANDARD HOURS

We've only listed business hours where they differ from the following standards. Minor post offices tend to open shorter hours than major ones Monday to Saturday, and not at all on Sunday.

BUSINESS	OPENING HOURS
Airline offices	9.30am-5.30pm Mon-Sat
Nationalised banks	10am-2pm or 4pm Mon-Fri, to noon or 1pm Sat
Government offices	9.30am-1pm & 2-5.30pm Mon-Fri
Post offices	9am-8pm Mon-Sat, 10am-4pm Sun
Museums	10am-5pm Tue-Sun
Restaurants	lunch noon-3pm, dinner 7-10pm or 11pm
Sights	10am-5pm or dawn-dusk
Shops	10am-7pm or 8pm, some closed Sun

Photography

For useful tips and techniques on travel photography, check out Lonely Planet's guide to *Travel Photography*.

Digital

Memory cards for digital cameras are available from photographic shops in most large cities and towns. However, the quality of memory cards is variable – some don't carry the advertised amount of data. Expect to pay upwards of ₹200 for a 4GB card.

To be safe, regularly back up your memory card. If your camera isn't wi-fi-enabled, take a memory card reader with you. Alternatively some internet cafes will write your pictures to CD. Some photographic shops make prints from digital photographs for roughly the standard print-and-processing charge.

Restrictions

➡ India is touchy about anyone taking photographs of military installations – this can include train stations, bridges, airports, military sites and sensitive border regions.

➡ Photography from the air is mostly OK, unless you're taking off from (or landing in) airports actively shared by defence forces.

➡ Many places of worship – such as monasteries, temples and mosques – also prohibit photography. Taking photos inside a shrine, at a funeral, at a religious ceremony or of people publicly bathing (including rivers) can also be offensive – ask first.

➡ Flash photography may be prohibited in certain areas of a shrine or historical monument, or may not be permitted at all.

➡ Exercise sensitivity when taking photos of people, especially women, who may find it offensive – obtain permission in advance.

➡ It is not uncommon these days for people in touristy areas to demand a posing fee in return for being photographed. Exercise your discretion in these situations. In any case, ask first to avoid misunderstandings later.

Post

India has the biggest postal network on earth, with over 155,015 post offices. Mail and poste-restante services are generally good, although the speed of delivery will depend on the efficiency of any given office. Airmail is faster and more reliable than sea mail, although it's best to use courier services (such as DHL and TNT) to send and receive items of value – expect to pay around ₹3000 per kilogram to Europe, Australia or the USA. Smaller private couriers are often cheaper, but goods may be repacked into large packages to cut costs and things sometimes go missing.

Receiving Mail

➡ To claim mail you'll need to show your passport.

➡ Ask senders to address letters to you with your surname in capital letters and underlined, followed by poste restante, GPO (main post office), and the city or town in question.

➡ Many 'lost' letters are simply misfiled under given/first names, so check under both your names and ask senders to provide a return address.

➡ Letters sent via poste restante are generally held for one to two months before being returned.

➡ It's best to have any parcels sent to you by registered post.

Sending Mail
LETTERS

➡ Posting airmail letters/aerogrammes to anywhere overseas costs ₹25/15.

➡ International airmail postcards cost around ₹12.

➡ For postcards, stick on the stamps *before* writing on them, as post offices can give you as many as four stamps per card.

➡ Sending a letter overseas by registered post costs an extra ₹50.

PARCELS

➡ Posting parcels can either be relatively straightforward or involve multiple counters and lots of queuing; get to the post office in the morning.

➡ Prices depend on weight (including packing material). Packing the article safely is your responsibility, but you can usually find someone near the post office providing this service.

➡ An airmail package (unregistered) costs around ₹400 TO ₹850 (up to 250g) to any country and ₹50 to ₹150 per additional 250g (up to a maximum of 2kg; different charges apply for higher weights).

➡ Parcel post has a maximum of 20kg to 30kg depending on the destination.

➡ Airmail takes one to three weeks, sea mail two to four months and Surface Air-Lifted (SAL) – a curious hybrid where parcels travel by both air and sea – around one month.

➡ Express mail service (EMS; delivery within three days) costs around 30% more than the normal airmail price.

➡ All parcels sent through the government postal service must be packed up in white linen and the seams sealed with wax – agents outside the post office usually offer this service for a small fee.

➡ Customs declaration forms, available from the post office, must be stitched or pasted to the parcel. No duty is payable by the recipient for gifts under the value of ₹1000.

➡ Carry a permanent marker to write on the parcel any information requested by the desk.

➡ You can send printed matter via surface mail 'Bulk Bag' for ₹350 (maximum 5kg, plus ₹100 for each additional kilo). The parcel has to be packed with an opening so it may be checked by the customs.

➡ **India Post** (www.indiapost. gov.in) has an online calculator for domestic and international postal tariffs.

Public Holidays

There are three official national public holidays – Republic and Independence Days and Gandhi's birthday (Gandhi Jayanti) – plus a lot of other holidays celebrated nationally or locally, many of them marking important days in various religions and falling on variable dates. The most important are the 18 'gazetted holidays' (listed) which are observed by central-government offices throughout India. On these days most businesses (offices, shops etc), banks and tourist sites close, but transport is usually unaffected. It's wise to make transport and hotel reservations well in advance if you intend visiting during major festivals.

Republic Day 26 January

Holi March

Ram Navami March/April

Mahavir Jayanti March/April

Good Friday March/April

Dr BL Ambedkar's Birthday 14 April

Buddha Jayanti May

Eid al-Fitr June/July

Independence Day 15 August

Janmastami Aug/Sep

Eid al-Adha September

Dussehra September/October

Gandhi Jayanti 2 October

Muharram October

Diwali October/November

Guru Nanak Jayanti November

Eid-Milad-un-Nabi December

Christmas Day 25 December

Safe Travel

Travellers to India's major cities may fall prey to petty and opportunistic crime, but most problems can be avoided with a bit of common sense and an appropriate amount of caution. Also have a look at the India branch of Lonely Planet's **Thorn Tree forum** (www.lonely-planet.com/thorntree), where travellers often post timely warnings about problems they've encountered on the road. Always check your government's travel advisory warnings.

Rebel Violence

India has a number of (sometimes armed) dissident groups championing various causes, who have employed the same tried and tested techniques of rebel groups everywhere: assassinations and bomb attacks on government infrastructure, public transport, religious centres, tourist sites and markets.

Certain areas are prone to insurgent violence – specifically Kashmir, states in the Northeast Region such as Assam, Manipur and Nagaland, remote tribal regions in Bihar, Jharkhand, Chhattisgarh and, less frequently, parts of West Bengal. However, while troubles in Kashmir may prove little more than an inconvenience to travellers, travelling in rural Bihar might put you at risk. Read the latest government travel advisory for up-to-the-minute reports on where is considered unsafe.

Curfews and strikes can close the roads (as well as banks, shops etc) for days on end in sensitive regions like Kashmir or Assam.

International terrorism is as much of a risk in Europe or the US, so this is no reason not to go to India, but it makes sense to check the local security situation carefully before travelling (especially in high-risk areas).

Telephone

➡ There are few payphones in India (apart from in airports), but private STD/ISD/PCO call booths do the same job, offering inexpensive local, interstate and international calls at lower prices than calls made from hotel rooms.

➡ These booths are found around the country. A digital meter displays how much the call is costing and usually

---

USEFUL GOVERNMENT RESOURCES

The following government websites offer travel advice and information on current hotspots.

Australian Department of Foreign Affairs (www.smarttraveller.gov.au)

British Foreign Office (www.gov.uk/fco)

Canadian Department of Foreign Affairs (www.voyage.gc.ca)

German Foreign Office (www.auswaertiges-amt.de)

Japan Ministry of Foreign Affairs (www.mofa.go.jp)

Netherlands Ministry of Foreign Affairs (www.government.nl)

Swiss Department of Foreign Affairs (www.eda.admin.ch)

US State Department (http://travel.state.gov)

provides a printed receipt when the call is finished.

→ Costs vary depending on the operator and destination but can be from ₹1 per minute for local calls and between ₹5 and ₹10 for international calls.

→ Some booths also offer a 'call-back' service – you ring home, provide the phone number of the booth and wait for people at home to call you back, for a fee of around ₹20 on top of the cost of the preliminary call.

→ Getting a line can be difficult in remote country and mountain areas – an engaged signal may just mean that the exchange is overloaded or broken, so keep trying.

→ Useful online resources include the **Yellow Pages** (www.yellowpages.co.in) and **Justdial** (www.justdial.com).

Mobile Phones

→ Indian mobile phone numbers usually have 10 digits, mostly beginning with 9 (but sometimes also with 7 or 8).

→ There's roaming coverage for international GSM phones in most cities and large towns.

→ To avoid expensive roaming costs (often highest for incoming calls), get hooked up to the local mobile-phone network by applying for a local prepaid SIM card.

→ Mobiles bought in some countries may be locked to a particular network; you'll have to get the phone unlocked or buy a local phone (available from ₹2000) to use an Indian SIM card.

GETTING CONNECTED

→ Getting connected is inexpensive and fairly straightforward in many areas. It's easiest to obtain a local SIM card when you arrive if you're flying into a large city.

→ Foreigners must supply between one and five passport photos, and photocopies of their passport identity and visa pages. Often mobile shops can arrange all this for you, or you can ask your hotel to help you. It's best to try to do this in tourist centres and cities, as in many regions – for example, Tamil Nadu, Andhra Pradesh, Telangana and most of Himachal Pradesh – it's a great deal more difficult.

→ You must also supply a residential address, which can be the address of your hotel. Usually the phone company will call your hotel (warn the hotel a call will come through) any time up to 24 hours after your application to verify that you are staying there. It's a good idea to obtain the SIM card somewhere where you're staying for a day or two so that you can return to the vendor if there's any problem. Obtain your SIM card from a reputable branded phone store to avoid scams.

→ Another option is to get a friendly local to obtain a connection in their name.

→ Prepaid mobile phone kits (SIM card and phone number, plus an allocation of calls) are available in most towns for about ₹200 from a phone shop, local STD/ISD/PCO booth or grocery store.

→ SIMs are sold as regular size, but most places have machines to cut them down to the required size if necessary.

→ You must then purchase more credit, sold as direct credit. You pay the vendor and the credit is deposited straight into your account, minus some taxes and a service charge.

CHARGES

→ Calls made within the state or city where you bought the SIM card are less than ₹1 a minute. You can call internationally for less than ₹10 a minute.

→ SMS messaging is even cheaper. International outgoing messages cost ₹5. Incoming calls and messages are free.

→ Unreliable signals and problems with international texting (messages or replies not coming through or being delayed) are not uncommon.

→ The leading service providers are Airtel, Vodafone, Reliance, Idea and BSNL. Coverage varies from region to region – Airtel has wide coverage, for example, but BSNL is the only network that works in remote Himachal areas.

JAMMU & KASHMIR AND ASSAM

→ Due to ongoing terrorist threats, mobile phone use in Jammu & Kashmir, as well as Assam, is more strictly controlled.

→ Roaming on foreign mobiles won't work in Jammu & Kashmir, nor will pay-as-you-go SIM cards purchased elsewhere in India.

→ Airtel and AirCell both offer prepaid SIM cards; you'll need four or five photos, your passport, address (your hotel) and to wait at least 48 hours.

→ You may be able to tip a local to apply for a SIM in their name and sell it on to you.

→ Foreign mobile roaming won't work and domestic SIM cards are difficult to procure in Assam (except in Guwahati), but you can use a SIM card purchased elsewhere. Airtel and BSNL work best here, Vodafone is not recommended.

Phone Codes

→ Calling India from abroad: dial your country's international access code, then ☎91 (India's country code), then the area code (without the initial zero), then the local number. For mobile phones, the area code and initial zero are not required.

➜ Calling internationally from India: dial ⌨00 (the international access code), then the country code of the country you're calling, then the area code (without the initial zero) and the local number.

➜ Land-phone numbers have an area code followed by up to eight digits.

➜ Toll-free numbers begin with ⌨1800.

➜ To make interstate calls to a mobile phone, add 0 before the 10-digit number.

➜ To call a land phone from a mobile phone, you always have to add the area code (with the initial zero).

➜ Some call-centre numbers might require the initial zero (eg calling an airline ticketing service based in Delhi from Karnataka).

➜ A Home Country Direct service, which gives you access to the international operator in your home country, exists for the US (⌨000 117) and the UK (⌨000 4417).

➜ To access an international operator elsewhere, dial ⌨000 127. The operator can place an international call and allow you to make collect calls.

Time

India uses the 12-hour clock and the local standard time, known as Indian Standard Time (IST), is 5½ hours ahead of GMT/UTC. The half-hour was added to maximise daylight hours over such a vast country.

Toilets

Public toilets are most easily found in major cities and tourist sites; the cleanest (usually with sit-down and squat choices) are often at modern restaurants, shopping complexes and cinemas.

Beyond urban centres, toilets are of the squat variety and locals may use the 'hand-and-water' technique, which involves carrying out ablutions with a small jug of water and the left hand. It's always a good idea to carry your own toilet paper and hand sanitiser, just in case.

Tourist Information

In addition to Government of India tourist offices (also known as 'India Tourism'), each state maintains its own network of tourist offices. These vary in their efficiency and usefulness – some are run by enthusiastic souls who go out of their way to help, others are little more than a means of drumming up business for State Tourism Development Corporation tours.

The first stop for information should be the tourism website of the Government of India, **Incredible India** (www.incredibleindia.org); for details of its regional offices around India, click on the 'Help Desk' tab at the top of the homepage.

Travellers with Disabilities

India's crowded public transport, crush of humanity and variable infrastructure can test even the hardiest able-bodied traveller. If you have a physical disability or are vision impaired, these can pose even more of a challenge. If your mobility is considerably restricted, you may like to ease the stress by travelling with an able-bodied companion.

Accessibility Some restaurants and offices have ramps but most tend to have at least one step. Staircases are often steep; lifts frequently stop at mezzanines between floors.

Accommodation Wheelchair-friendly hotels are almost exclusively top-end. Make enquiries before travelling and book ground-floor rooms at hotels that lack adequate facilities.

Footpaths Where pavements exist, they can be riddled with holes, littered with debris and packed with pedestrians. If using crutches, bring along spare rubber caps.

Transport Hiring a car with driver will make moving around a lot easier; if you use a wheelchair, make sure the car-hire company can provide an appropriate vehicle.

For further advice pertaining to your specific requirements, consult your doctor before heading to India.

The following organisations may proffer further information:

Accessible Journeys (www.disabilitytravel.com)

Access-Able Travel Source (www.access-able.com)

Global Access News (www.globalaccessnews.com)

Mobility International USA (www.miusa.org)

Visas

Visa on Arrival

Citizens of Australia, Brazil, Cambodia, Cook Islands, Djibouti, Fiji, Finland, Germany, Guyana, Indonesia, Israel, Japan, Jordan, Kenya, Kiribati, Laos, Luxembourg, Marshall Islands, Mauritius, Mexico, Micronesia, Myanmar, Nauru, New Zealand, Niue Island, Norway, Oman, Palau, Palestine, Papua New Guinea, Philippines, Republic of Korea, Russia, Samoa, Singapore, Solomon Islands,Thailand, Tonga, Tuvalu, UAE, Ukraine, USA, Vanuatu, and Vietnam are currently granted a 30-day single-entry visa on arrival (VOA) at Bengaluru, Chennai, Kochi (Cochin), Delhi, Goa, Hyderabad, Kolkata, Mumbai and Trivandrum airports.

However, to participate in the scheme, you need to apply online at https://indianvisaonline.gov.in for an Electronic Travel Authority (ETA), a minimum of four and a maximum of 30 days before you are due to travel. The fee is US$60, and you have to upload a photograph as well as a copy of your passport. Travellers have reported being asked for documentation showing their hotel confirmation at the airport, though this is not specified on the VOA website. The VOA is valid from the date of arrival.

It's intended that the scheme will be rolled out to 180 nations, including the UK and China, so check online for any updates.

Other Visas

If you want to stay longer than 30 days, or are not covered by the VOA scheme, you must get a visa before arriving in India (apart from Nepali or Bhutanese citizens). Visas are available at Indian missions worldwide, though in many countries, applications are processed by a separate private company. In some countries, including the UK, you must apply in person at the designated office as well as filing an application online.

Note that your passport needs to be valid for at least six months beyond your intended stay in India, with at least two blank pages. Most people are issued with a standard six-month tourist visa, which for most nationalities permits multiple entry.

➟ Student and business visas have strict conditions (consult the Indian embassy for details).

➟ Tourist visas are valid from the date of issue, not the date you arrive in India.

➟ Five- and 10-year tourist visas are available to US citizens *only* under a bilateral arrangement; however, you can still only stay in the country for up to 180 days continuously.

➟ Currently you are required to submit two passport photographs with your visa application; these must be in colour and must be 5.08cm by 5.08 cm (2in by 2in; larger than regular passport photos).

➟ An onward travel ticket is a requirement for some visas, but this isn't always enforced (check in advance).

➟ Additional restrictions apply to travellers from Bangladesh and Pakistan, as well as certain Eastern European, African and central Asian countries. Check any special conditions for your nationality with the Indian embassy in your country.

➟ Visas are priced in the local currency and may have an added service fee.

➟ Extended visas are possible for people of Indian origin (excluding those in Pakistan and Bangladesh) who hold a non-Indian passport and live abroad.

➟ For visas lasting more than six months, you're supposed to register at the **Foreigners' Regional Registration Office** (FRRO; Map p76; ☎011-26711443; frrodil@nic.in; Level 2, East Block 8, Sector 1, Rama Krishna (RK) Puram, Delhi; ◷9.30am-3pm Mon-Fri) in Delhi within 14 days of arriving in India; enquire about these special conditions when you apply for your visa.

Re-Entry Requirements

Most tourists are permitted to transit freely between India and its neighbouring countries. However, citizens of China, Pakistan, Iraq, Iran, Afghanistan, Bangladesh and Sudan are barred from re-entering India within two months of the date of their previous exit.

Visa Extensions

India has traditionally been stringent with visa extensions. At the time of writing, the government was granting extensions only in circumstances such as medical emergencies or theft of passport just before the applicant planned to leave the country (at the end of their visa).

If you do need to extend your visa due to any such exigency, you should contact the Foreigners' Regional Registration Office in Delhi. This is also the place to come for a replacement visa, and if you need your lost/stolen passport replaced (required before you can leave the country). Regional FRROs are even less likely to grant an extension.

Assuming you meet the stringent criteria, the FRRO is permitted to issue an extension of 14 days (free for nationals of most countries; enquire on application). You must bring your confirmed air ticket, one passport photo (take two, just in case) and a photocopy of your passport identity and visa pages. Note that this system is designed to get you out of the country promptly with the correct official stamps, not to give you two extra weeks of travel and leisure.

Transport

GETTING THERE & AWAY

Plenty of international airlines service India, and overland routes to and from Nepal, Bangladesh, Bhutan and Pakistan are all currently open. Flights, tours and other tickets can be booked online at www.lonelyplanet.com/bookings.

Entering India

Entering India by air or land is relatively straightforward, with standard immigration and customs procedures. A frustrating law barring re-entry into India within two months of the previous date of departure has now been done away with (except for citizens of some Asian countries), thus allowing most travellers to combine their India tour with side trips to neighbouring countries.

Passport

To enter India you need a valid passport and an onward/return ticket. You'll also need a visa, which some nationalities can now obtain on arrival. Other nationalities or those wishing to stay more than 30 days need to get their visa beforehand. See the Visa section (p1190) for details. Your passport should be valid for at least six months beyond your intended stay in India. If your passport is lost or stolen, immediately contact your country's representative. Keep photocopies of your airline ticket and the identity and visa pages of your passport in case of emergency. Better yet, scan and email copies to yourself. Check with the Indian embassy in your home country for any special conditions that may exist for your nationality.

Air

Airports & Airlines

India has six main gateways for international flights; however, a number of other cities such as Goa, Kochi (Cochin), Lucknow and Trivandrum also service international carriers. For detailed information, see www.aai.aero.

India's national carrier is **Air India** (☑1800-1801407; www.airindia.com), which operates international and domestic flights. Air travel in India has had a relatively decent safety record in recent years.

International airports include the following:

Bengaluru (Bangalore; BLR; ☑1800 4254425; www.bengaluruairport.com; Kempegowda International Airport)

Chennai (Madras; MAA; ☑044-22560551; www.aai.aero/chennai; Chennai International Airport)

CLIMATE CHANGE & TRAVEL

Every form of transport that relies on carbon-based fuel generates CO_2, the main cause of human-induced climate change. Modern travel is dependent on aeroplanes, which might use less fuel per kilometre per person than most cars but travel much greater distances. The altitude at which aircraft emit gases (including CO_2) and particles also contributes to their climate change impact. Many websites offer 'carbon calculators' that allow people to estimate the carbon emissions generated by their journey and, for those who wish to do so, to offset the impact of the greenhouse gases emitted with contributions to portfolios of climate-friendly initiatives throughout the world. Lonely Planet offsets the carbon footprint of all staff and author travel.

Delhi (New Delhi; DEL; ☎0124-3376000; www.newdelhiairport.in; Indira Gandhi International Airport)

Hyderabad (HYD; ☎040-66546370; http://hyderabad.aero; Rajiv Gandhi International Airport)

Kolkata (Calcutta; CCU; ☎033-25118036; www.aai.aero/kolkata; Kolkata, Netaji Subhash Chandra Bose International Airport)

Mumbai (Bombay; BOM; ☎022-66851010; www.csia.in; Chhatrapati Shivaji International Airport)

Tickets

Departure tax and other charges are included in airline tickets. You are required to show a copy of your ticket and your passport in order to enter the airport, whether flying internationally or within India.

Land

Border Crossings

Although most visitors fly into India, it is possible to travel overland between India and Bangladesh, Bhutan, Nepal, Pakistan and Myanmar (though the border is only open occasionally and this route is not recommended). The overland route from Nepal is the most popular. For more on these routes, check for up-to-date information on Lonely Planet's **Thorntree forum** (www.lonelyplanet.com/thorntree) or see the 'Europe to India overland' section on www.seat61.com/India.htm.

If you enter India by bus or train, you'll be required to disembark at the border for standard immigration and customs checks.

You *must* have a valid Indian visa in advance, as no visas are available at the border crossings.

Drivers of cars and motorbikes will need the vehicle's registration papers, liability insurance and an international drivers' permit in addition to their domestic licence. You'll also need a *Carnet de Passage en Douane*, which acts as a temporary waiver of import duty on the vehicle.

For travellers wishing to visit Tibet from India, the only way to do so is to exit to Nepal and then enter Tibet through the border crossing at Kodari as part of an organised tour. Alternately, you could fly to Lhasa from Kathmandu.

To find out the latest requirements for the paperwork and other important driving information, contact your local automobile association.

BANGLADESH

Foreigners can use four land crossings between Bangladesh and India, all in West Bengal or the Northeast States.

Heading from Bangladesh to India, you have to prepay the exit tax, which can be done at a Sonali Bank branch (either in Dhaka, another big city or at the closest branch to the border).

Exiting Bangladesh overland is complicated by red tape – if you enter the country by air, you require a road permit (or 'change of route' permit) to leave by land.

OVERLAND TO/FROM BANGLADESH

ROUTE/BORDER TOWNS	TRANSPORT	VISAS	MORE INFORMATION
Kolkata–Dhaka/Petrapole (India) & Benapole (Bangladesh)	Regular daily Kolkata–Dhaka buses; twice-weekly train via Darsana border post.	Obtain in advance. To buy a train ticket, Darsana must be marked on your Bangladesh visa.	p1180
Siliguri–Chengrabandha/Chengrabandha (India) & Burimari (Bangladesh)	Regular direct Siliguri–Chengrabandha buses; then bus to Rangpur, Bogra & Dhaka.	Obtain in advance.	p499
Shillong–Sylhet/Dawki (India) & Tamabil (Bangladesh)	Jeeps run from Shillong to Dawki. From Dawki walk (1.5km) or take a taxi to Tamabil bus station for regular buses to Sylhet.	Obtain in advance.	p593
Agartala–Dhaka/Agartala, 3km from border along Akhaura Rd (India) & Akhaura, 5km from border (Bangladesh)	Akhaura is on Dhaka–Comilla train line. Dhaka–Sylhet trains run from Ajampur train station, 3km further north.	Obtain in advance.	p593

OVERLAND TO/FROM NEPAL

ROUTE/BORDER TOWNS	TRANSPORT	VISAS	MORE INFORMATION
Delhi, Varanasi–Kathmandu/Sunauli (India) & Bhairawa (Nepal)	Trains from Delhi to Gorakhpur, half-hourly buses to border. Buses from Varanasi to Sunauli leave early morning & evening (uncomfortable ride). Buses & jeeps from Bhairawa to Kathmandu.	Nepali available at border. Indian must be acquired in advance.	p405
Kolkata (Patna & the eastern plains)–Kathmandu, Pokhara/Raxaul (India) & Birganj (Nepal)	Daily buses from Patna & Kolkata to Raxaul. Mithila Express train daily from Kolkata. Regular day/night buses from Birganj to Kathmandu & Pokhara.	As above. (6am-6pm)	p527
West Bengal–Eastern Nepal/Panitanki (India) & Kakarbhitta (Nepal)	Regular buses from Kakarbhitta to Kathmandu (17hr) & other destinations. Bhadrapur airport (23km away) flights to Kathmandu.	As above. (7am-7pm)	p499
Jamunaha, Uttar Pradesh–Nepalganj, Western Nepal/Rupaidiha (India) & Nepalganj (Nepal)	Good gateway for Nepal's Royal Bardia National Park. Flights to Kathmandu.	As above.	
Uttarakhand–Western Nepal/Banbassa (India) & Mahendranagar (Nepal)	Border is 5km from Banbassa, then an autorickshaw to Mahendranagar. From there, buses to Kathmadu & Pokhara (1 daily).	As above. (6am-6pm)	p452

To apply for visa extensions and change of route permits you will need to visit the **Immigration and Passport Office** (☎00-88-2-8159525; www.dip.gov.bd; Agargaon Rd; ⊗Sat-Thu) in Dhaka.

Note that some travellers have reported problems exiting Bangladesh overland with the visa issued on arrival at Dhaka airport.

BHUTAN

Phuentsholing is the main entry and exit point between India and Bhutan, although the eastern checkpost at Samdrup Jongkhar is also used.

As entry requirements need advance planning and are subject to change, we recommend you consult a travel agent or Bhutanese embassy for up-to-the-minute details. Also see www.tourism.gov.bt and Lonely Planet's *Bhutan*.

NEPAL

Political and weather conditions permitting, there are five land border crossings between India and Nepal. Check the current security status before crossing into Nepal; local newspapers and websites are good sources of information.

Multiple-entry visas (15-/30-/90-days US$25/40/100 – US dollars cash, not rupees) are available at the Nepal immigration post (you need two passport photos). You can now save time by applying online at http://online.nepalimmigration.gov.np/tourist-visa. Your receipt, which you must produce at the border within 15 days of your application, outlines the border procedures.

Travellers have reported being harassed crossing into India at the Sunauli border and having to pay inflated prices for bus and train tickets. Consider taking a taxi to Gorakpur and getting a train or bus from there.

OVERLAND TO/FROM BHUTAN

ROUTE/BORDER TOWNS	TRANSPORT	VISAS	MORE INFORMATION
Siliguri–Kolkata–Phuentsholing/Jaigon (India) & Phuentsholing (Bhutan)	From Kolkata, direct bus at 7pm thrice weekly. From Siliguri daily buses and possibly shared jeeps to Jaigon/Phuentsholing.	Non-Indian nationals need visa & tour booking with registered operator.	p499, p1180

PAKISTAN

Given the rocky relationship between India and Pakistan, crossing by land depends on the current state of relations between the two countries – check locally.

If the crossings are open, you can reach Pakistan from Delhi, Amritsar (Punjab) and Rajasthan by bus or train. The bus route from Srinagar to Pakistan-administered Kashmir is currently only open to Indian citizens.

You must have a visa in order to enter Pakistan. It is easiest to obtain this before you travel from the Pakistan mission that is located in your home country. At the time of writing, the **Pakistan Embassy** (☏011-26110601; www.mofa.gov.pk; 2/50G Shantipath, Chanakyapuri) in Delhi was not issuing tourist visas for most nationalities, but this could change.

Sea

There are several sea routes between India and surrounding islands but none leave Indian sovereign territory. After a 28-year hiatus, a ferry service between southern India and Sri Lanka restarted in 2011, linking Thoothikudi (Tuticorin) in Tamil Nadu with Colombo, but was suspended after five months. A new service between the same ports, or on the old route between Rameswaram and Talaimannar, may start; check for updates before you leave.

GETTING AROUND

Air

Airlines in India

Transporting vast numbers of passengers annually, India has a very competitive domestic airline industry. In a crowded marketplace, many players have suffered huge financial losses and run into trouble. Major carriers are Air India, IndiGo, Spice Jet and Jet Airways.

Airline seats can be booked cheaply over the internet or through travel agencies. Apart from airline sites, bookings can be made through reliable ticketing portals such as **Cleartrip** (www.cleartrip.com), **Make My Trip** (www.makemytrip.com) and **Yatra** (www.yatra.com). Domestic airlines set rupee fares for Indian citizens, while foreigners may be charged US dollar fares (usually payable in rupees).

Security norms require you to produce your ticket and your passport at the time of entering an airport.

Keep in mind, however, that fares fluctuate dramatically, affected by holidays, festivals and seasons.

OVERLAND TO/FROM PAKISTAN

There is usually a direct bus or train from Delhi to Lahore, but at the time of writing, the Lahore Bus Service, which departs from Delhi (6am daily), terminates at Wagah due to security concerns. When it goes on to Lahore, the entire journey takes 12 hours. Advance bookings are essential. There are twice weekly trains between Lahore and Attari (on the Indian side of the border), where there is a customs and immigration stop. There are buses from Amritsar to Attari. Check the border is open before you leave; usual hours are 10am to 3.30pm daily, but arrive at least an hour before closure. From Wagah there are buses and taxis on to Lahore. Security on this route has been tightened but it is still a concern.

A Jodhpur–Karachi train leaves every Saturday (Friday in the opposite direction). Advance booking only. Customs/immigration is at Munabao (Indian border), where you physically change trains. Expect extremely tight security.

Security at airports is stringent. In smaller airports, all hold baggage must be X-rayed prior to check-in (major airports now have in-line baggage screening facilities). Every item of cabin baggage needs a label, which must be stamped as part of the security check (don't forget to collect tags at the check-in counter). Flights to sensitive destinations, such as Srinagar and Ladakh, have extra security restrictions. You may also have to allow for a spot-check of your cabin baggage on the tarmac before you board.

Keeping peak-hour congestion in mind, the recommended check-in time for domestic flights is two hours before departure – the deadline is 45 minutes. The usual baggage allowance is 20kg (10kg for smaller aircraft) in economy class.

At the time of writing, the following airlines were operating across various destinations in India:

Air India (☎1800-1801407; www.airindia.com) India's national carrier operates many domestic and international flights.

GoAir (☎020-2566-2111; www.goair.in) Reliable low-cost carrier servicing Goa, Kochi (Cochin), Jaipur, Delhi and Bagdogra, among other destinations.

IndiGo (☎099-10383838; www.goindigo.in) Reliable and popular, with myriad flights across India and to select overseas destinations.

Jet Airways (☎1800-225522; www.jetairways.com) Operates flights across India and to select overseas destinations.

Spice Jet (☎098-71803333; www.spicejet.com) Domestic and some regional flights.

Bicycle

There are no restrictions on bringing a bicycle into the country. However, bicycles sent by sea can take a few weeks to clear customs in India, so it's better to fly them in. It may be cheaper – and less hassle – to hire or buy a bicycle locally. Read up on bicycle touring before you travel: Rob Van Der Plas' *Bicycle Touring Manual*, Stephen Lord's *Adventure Cycle-Touring Handbook* and Laura Stone's *Himalaya by Bike* are good places to start. The **Cycling Federation of India** (☎011-23753528; www.cyclingfederationofindia.org) can provide local information.

Hire

➡ Tourist centres and traveller hang-outs are the easiest spots to find bicycles for hire – enquire locally.

➡ Prices vary: between ₹40 and ₹100 per day for a roadworthy, Indian-made bicycle; mountain bikes, where available, are usually upwards of ₹400 per day.

➡ Hire places may require a cash security deposit (avoid leaving your airline ticket or passport).

Practicalities

➡ Mountain bikes with off-road tyres give the best protection against India's puncture-inducing roads.

➡ Roadside cycle mechanics abound but you should still bring spare tyres, brake cables, lubricating oil, chain repair kit and plenty of puncture-repair patches.

➡ Bikes can often be carried for free, or for a small luggage fee, on the roof of public buses – handy for uphill stretches.

➡ Contact your airline for information about transporting your bike and customs formalities in your home country.

Purchase

➡ Delhi's **Jhandewalan Cycle Market** (Map p64) has imported and domestic, new and second-hand bikes, and spare parts.

➡ Mountain bikes with reputable brands that include Hero and Atlas generally start at around ₹7000.

➡ Reselling is usually fairly easy – ask at local cycle shops or put up an advert on travel noticeboards. If you purchased a new bike and it's still in reasonable condition, you should be able to recoup around 50% of what you originally paid.

Road Rules

➡ Vehicles drive on the left in India but otherwise road rules are virtually nonexistent.

➡ Cities and national highways can be hazardous

RIDING THE RAILS WITH YOUR WHEELS

For long hauls, transporting your bike or motorbike by train can be a convenient option. Buy a standard train ticket for the journey, then take your bike to the station parcel office with your passport, registration papers, driver's licence and insurance documents. Packing-wallahs will wrap your bike in protective sacking for around ₹200 to ₹500 and you must fill out various forms and pay the shipping fee, which varies according to the route and train type – plus an insurance fee of 1% of the declared value of the bike. Bring the same paperwork to collect your bike from the goods office at the other end. If the bike is left waiting at the destination for more than 24 hours, you'll pay a storage fee of around ₹100 per day.

places to cycle so, where possible, stick to back roads.

⇒ Be conservative about the distance you expect to cover – an experienced cyclist can manage around 60km to 100km a day on the plains, 40km to 60km on all-weather mountain roads and 40km or less on dirt roads.

Boat

Scheduled ferries connect mainland India to the Andaman Islands, with departures to Port Blair from Chennai, Kolkata and Visakhapatnam; see www.andamans.gov.in.

Between October and May, there are cruise packages from Kochi (Kerala) to the Lakshadweep islands; see the Kerala chapter (p999) for details. There's also a popular day-long canal ferry between Kollam and Alleppey.

There are also numerous shorter ferry services across rivers, from chain pontoons to coracles and various boat cruises.

Bus

Buses go almost everywhere in India and are the only way to get around many mountainous areas. They tend to be the cheapest way to travel. Services are fast and frequent.

Roads in mountainous or curvy terrain can be perilous; buses are often driven with wilful abandon, and accidents are always a risk.

Avoid night buses unless there's no alternative: driving conditions are more hazardous and drivers may be inebriated or overtired.

All buses make snack and toilet stops (some more frequently than others), providing a break but possibly adding hours to journey times.

Shared jeeps complement the bus service in many mountain areas.

Classes

State-owned and private bus companies both offer several types of buses, graded loosely as 'ordinary', 'semideluxe', 'deluxe' or 'superdeluxe'. These are usually open to interpretation, and the exact grade of luxury offered in a particular class varies.

In general, ordinary buses tend to be ageing rattletraps while the deluxe grades range from less decrepit versions of ordinary buses to flashy Volvo buses with air-con and reclining (locally called 'push-back') two-by-two seating.

Buses run by the state government are usually more reliable (if there's a breakdown, another bus will be sent to pick up passengers), and seats can usually be booked up to a month in advance. Many state governments now operate superdeluxe buses.

Private buses are either more expensive (but more comfortable), or cheaper but with kamikaze drivers and intense overcrowding.

Travel agencies in many tourist towns offer relatively expensive private two-by-two buses, which tend to leave and terminate at conveniently central stops.

Take earplugs on long-distance buses, to muffle the often deafening music or movies played in some buses.

On any bus, try to sit up-front to minimise the bumpy effect of potholes. Never sit directly above the wheels.

Costs

The cheapest buses are 'ordinary' government buses, but prices vary from state to state.

Add around 50% to the ordinary fare for deluxe services, double the fare for air-conditioning, and triple or quadruple the fare for a two-by-two superdeluxe service.

Rajasthan Roadways offer discounts for female travellers.

Luggage

Luggage is stored in compartments underneath the bus (sometimes for a small fee) or carried on the roof.

Arrive at least an hour before departure time – some buses cover roof-stored bags with a canvas sheet, making last-minute additions inconvenient/impossible.

If your bags go on the roof, make sure they're securely locked, and tied to the metal baggage rack – unsecured bags can fall off on rough roads.

Theft is a (minor) risk: watch your bags at snack and toilet stops. Never leave day-packs or valuables unattended inside the bus.

Reservations

Most deluxe buses can be booked in advance – government buses up to a month ahead – at the bus station or local travel agencies.

Online bookings are now possible in many states including the Punjab, Karnataka and Rajasthan, or at the excellent portals **Cleartrip** (www.cleartrip.com), **Makemytrip** (www.makemytrip.com), and **Redbus** (www.redbus.in).

Reservations are rarely possible on 'ordinary' buses; travellers can be left behind in the mad rush for a seat.

To secure a seat, send a travelling companion ahead to claim some space, or pass a book or article of clothing through an open window and place it on an empty seat. This 'reservation' method rarely fails.

If you board a bus midway through its journey, you may have to stand until a seat becomes free.

Many buses only depart when full – passengers might suddenly leave yours to join one that looks nearer to departing.

Many bus stations have a separate women's queue (not always obvious when signs are in Hindi and men join the melee).

Women have an unspoken right to elbow their way to the front of any bus queue in India, so don't be shy, ladies!

Car

Few people bother with self-drive car hire – not only because of the hair-raising driving conditions, but also because hiring a car with driver is potentially affordable in India, particularly if several people share the cost. **Hertz** (www.hertz.com) is one of the few international companies with representatives in India.

Hiring a Car & Driver

Most towns have taxi stands or car-hire companies where you can arrange short or long tours.

Not all hire cars are licensed to travel beyond their home state. Those that are will pay extra state taxes, which are added to the hire charge.

Ask for a driver who speaks some English and knows the region you intend visiting. Try to see the car and meet the driver before paying anything.

A wide range of cars now ply as taxis. From a proletarian Tata Indica hatchback to a comfy Toyota Innova SUV, there's a model to suit every pocket.

Hire charges for multiday trips cover the driver's meals and accommodation, and

drivers should make their own sleeping and eating arrangements.

It's essential to set the ground rules from day one; politely but firmly let the driver know that you're boss to avoid difficulties later.

Costs

Car hire costs depend on the distance and the terrain (driving on mountain roads uses more petrol, hence the higher cost).

One-way trips usually cost the same as return ones (to cover the petrol and driver charges for getting back).

Hire charges vary from state to state. Some taxi unions set a maximum time limit or a maximum kilometre distance for day trips – if you go over, you'll have to pay extra. Prices also vary according to the make and model of the taxi.

To avoid misunderstandings, get *in writing* what you've been promised (quotes should include petrol, sightseeing stops, all your chosen destinations, and meals and accommodation for the driver). If a driver asks you for money for petrol en route because he is short of cash, get receipts for reimbursement later. If you're travelling by the kilometre, check the odometer reading before you set out so as to avoid confusions later.

For sightseeing day trips around a single city, expect to pay upwards of

₹1000/1200 for a non-aircon/air-con car with an eight-hour, 80km limit per day (extra charges apply for longer trips). For multiday trips, operators usually peg a 250km minimum running distance per day and charge around ₹8/10 per km for a non-air-con/air-con car, for anything over this.

A tip is customary at the end of your journey; at least ₹150-200 per day is fair.

Hitching

Hitching is never entirely safe, and we don't recommend it. Travellers who hitch should understand that they are taking a small but potentially serious risk. However, for a negotiable fee, truck drivers supplement the bus service in some remote areas. As drivers rarely speak English, you may have difficulty explaining where you wish to go, and working out a fair price to pay. Be aware that truck drivers have a reputation for driving under the influence of alcohol. Women are strongly advised against hitching. Always use your instincts.

Local Transport

Buses, cycle-rickshaws, autorickshaws, taxis, boats and urban trains provide transport around India's cities.

Costs for public transport vary from town to town.

For any transport without a fixed fare, agree on the price *before* you start your journey and make sure that it covers your luggage and every passenger.

Even where meters exist, drivers may refuse to use them, demanding an elevated 'fixed' fare. Insist on the meter; if that fails, find another vehicle. Or just bargain hard.

Fares usually increase at night (by up to 100%) and some drivers charge a few rupees extra for luggage.

Carry plenty of small bills for taxi and rickshaw fares as drivers rarely have change.

In some places, taxi/ autorickshaw drivers are involved in the commission racket.

Autorickshaw, Tempo & Vikram

Similar to the *tuk-tuks* of Southeast Asia, the Indian autorickshaw is a three-wheeled motorised contraption with a tin or canvas roof and sides, with room for two passengers (although you'll often see many more squeezed in) and limited luggage.

They are also referred to as autos, scooters and riks.

Autorickshaws are mostly cheaper than taxis and usually have a meter, although getting it turned on can be a challenge.

Travelling by auto is great fun but, thanks to the open windows, can be noisy and hot (or severely cold!).

Tempos and *vikrams* (large tempos) are outsized autorickshaws with room for more passengers, shuttling on fixed routes for a fixed fare.

In country areas, you may also see the fearsome-looking 'three-wheeler' – a crude tractor-like tempo with a front wheel on an articulated arm – or the Magic, a cute minivan that can take in up to a dozen passengers.

Boat

Various kinds of local boats offer transport across and down rivers in India, from big car ferries to wooden canoes and wicker coracles. Most of the larger boats carry bicycles and motorcycles for a fee.

Bus

Urban buses range from fume-belching, human-stuffed mechanical monsters that travel at breakneck speed to sanitised air-conditioned vehicles with comfortable seating and

---

MANNING THE METER

Getting a metered ride is only half the battle. Meters are almost always outdated, so fares are calculated using a combination of the meter reading and a complicated 'fare adjustment card'. Predictably, this system is open to abuse. To get a rough estimate of fares in advance, try the portal www.taxiautofare.com.

---

smoother ride quality. In any case, it's usually far more convenient to opt for an autorickshaw or taxi, as they are quicker and more frequent.

Cycle-Rickshaw

A cycle-rickshaw is a pedal cycle with two rear wheels, supporting a bench seat for passengers. Most have a canopy that can be raised in wet weather or lowered to provide extra space for luggage.

Fares must be agreed upon in advance – speak to locals to get an idea of what is a fair price for the distance you intend to travel.

Kolkata is the last bastion of the hand-pulled rickshaw, known as the *tana* rickshaw. This is a hand-cart on two wheels pulled directly by the rickshaw-wallah.

Metro

New metro systems are starting to transform urban transport in the biggest cities. Kolkata was the first, opening in 1984. Delhi's metro opened in 2002, and increases its reach year on year. Bengaluru's metro opened in 2011, Mumbai's in 2014, and the Chennai and Hyderabad metros were expected to start operating in 2015. They will become increasingly useful to visitors as their networks expand over the coming years. Mumbai, Hyderabad and Chennai, among other cities, also have useful suburban trains leaving from ordinary train stations.

Taxi

Most towns have taxis, and these are usually metered, however, getting drivers to use the meter can be a hassle. To avoid fare-setting shenanigans, use prepaid taxis where possible. Radio cars are the most efficient option in larger cities.

Prepaid Taxis & Radio Cabs

Most major Indian airports and train stations now incorporate prepaid-taxi and radio-cab booths. Here, you can book a taxi for a fixed price (which will include baggage) and thus avoid commission scams. Hold onto your receipt until you reach your destination, as proof of payment.

Radio cabs cost marginally more than prepaid taxis, but are air-conditioned and manned by the company's chauffeurs. Cabs have electronic, receipt-generating fare meters and are fitted with GPS units, so the company can monitor the vehicle's movement around town. These minimise chances of errant driving or unreasonable demands for extra cash by the driver afterward.

Smaller airports and stations may have prepaid autorickshaw booths instead.

Other Local Transport

In some towns, *tongas* (horse-drawn two-wheelers) and *victorias* (horse-drawn carriages) still operate. Kolkata has a tram network, and Mumbai, Delhi, Kolkata and Chennai, among other centres, have suburban trains that leave from ordinary train stations.

Motorcycle

Despite traffic challenges, India is an amazing country for long-distance motorcycle touring. However, it can be quite an undertaking; there are some popular motorcycle tours for those who don't want the rigmarole of going it alone.

The most preferred starting point for motorcycle tours is Delhi, as well as Manali, and popular destinations include Rajasthan, South India and Ladakh. Weather is an important factor and you should check for the best times to visit different areas. To cross from neighbouring countries, check the latest regulations and paperwork requirements from the relevant diplomatic mission.

Driving Licence

To hire a motorcycle in India, technically you're required to have a valid international drivers' permit in addition to your domestic licence. In tourist areas, some places may rent out a motorcycle without asking for a driving permit/licence, but you won't be covered by insurance in the event of an accident, and may also face a fine.

Hire

The classic way to motorcycle around India is on a Royal Enfield, built to both vintage and modern specs. As well as making a satisfying chugging sound, these bikes are fully manual, making them easy to repair (parts can be found almost everywhere in India). On the other hand, Enfields are often less reliable than many of the newer, Japanese-designed bikes.

Plenty of places rent out motorcycles for local trips and longer tours. Japanese- and Indian-made bikes in the 100cc to 150cc range are

cheaper than the big 350cc to 500cc Enfields.

As security, you'll need to leave a large cash deposit (ensure you get a receipt that stipulates the refundable amount) or your passport/air ticket. We strongly advise not leaving these documents, in particular your passport, which you need for hotel check-ins and if stopped by the police.

For three weeks' hire, a 500cc Enfield costs from ₹22,000; a 350cc costs ₹15,000. The price includes excellent advice and an invaluable crash course in Enfield mechanics and repairs.

As for accessories, helmets are available for ₹500 to ₹2000; extras (panniers, luggage racks, protection bars, rear-view mirrors, lockable fuel caps, petrol filters, extra tools) are also easy to come by.

A useful website for Enfield models is www.royalenfield.com.

The following dealers come recommended:

Lalli Motorbike Exports (Map p64; ☑28750869; www.lallisingh.com; 1740-A/55 Hari Singh Nalwa St, Abdul Aziz Rd; Delhi; ⓜKarol Bagh) Run by the knowledgeable Lalli Singh, this outfit sells and rents out Enfields and parts, and buyers get a crash course in running and maintaining these lovable but temperamental machines. He can also recommend other reputable dealers in the area.

Anu Auto Works (Royal Moto Touring; Map p310; ☑9816163378; www.royal-mototouring.com; Vashisht Rd; Manali) Rents Enfields and takes tours over high Himalayan passes to Ladakh and Spiti from mid-May to mid-September. Typical Enfield rental rates are ₹1500 per day for a 500cc, ₹1200 to ₹1300 per day for 350cc. Discounts usually available for rentals of about 18 days or more.

Allibhai Premji Tyrewalla (☑022-23099313; www.premjis.com; 205 Dr D Bhadkamkar (Lamington) Rd, Mumbai) Sells

new and second-hand motorcycles with a buy-back option.

Rajasthan Auto Centre (☑9829188064; Sanjay Bazaar, Sanganeri Gate, Jaipur) Comes recommended as a place for hiring, fixing or purchasing a motorcycle. To hire a 350cc Bullet costs ₹500 to ₹600 per day (including helmet).

Purchase

For longer tours, purchasing a new motorcycle may sound like a great idea. However, selling motor vehicles to foreigners comes with reams of complicated paperwork, and in many situations, procuring a motorcycle might not be possible or feasible at all.

Second-hand bikes are widely available, though, and paperwork is simpler than for a new machine. The Delhi government is in the process of creating a new rule to ban all 15-year-old privately owned vehicles from the Delhi roads. There are strong objections to this from the public, so it's debatable whether the rule will be passed.

To find a second-hand motorcycle, check travellers' noticeboards and ask motorcycle mechanics and other bikers. A well looked-after second-hand 350cc Enfield costs ₹50,000-105,000. The 500cc model ranges between ₹85,000-135,000. You will also have to pay for insurance.

OWNERSHIP PAPERS

There's plenty of paperwork associated with owning a motorcycle. The process is complicated and time-consuming, so it's wise to seek advice from the agent selling the bike.

Registration papers are signed by the local registration authority when the bike is first sold; you need these when you buy a second-hand bike.

Foreign nationals cannot change the name on the registration but you must fill out forms for change of ownership and transfer of insurance.

Registration must be renewed every 15 years (for around ₹5000); make absolutely sure that it states the 'road-worthiness' of the vehicle, and that there are no outstanding debts or criminal proceedings associated with the bike.

Insurance

Only hire a bike that has third-party insurance – if you hit someone without insurance the consequences can be very costly. Reputable companies will include third-party cover in their policies; those that don't probably aren't trustworthy.

You must also arrange insurance if you buy a motorcycle (usually you can organise this through the person selling the bike).

The minimum level of cover is third-party insurance – available for around ₹800 to ₹1500 per year. This will cover repair and medical costs for any other vehicles, people or property you might hit, but no cover for your own machine. Comprehensive insurance (recommended) costs ₹1200 to ₹3500 per year.

Fuel, Spare Parts & Extras

Petrol and engine oil are widely available in the plains, but petrol stations are rarer in the mountains. If travelling to remote regions, carry enough extra fuel (seek local advice about fuel availability before setting off). At the time of writing, petrol cost around ₹55 per litre in different states.

If you're going to remote regions it's also important to carry basic spares (valves, fuel lines, piston rings etc). Parts for Indian and Japanese machines are widely available in cities and larger towns; Delhi's Karol Bagh is a good place to find parts for all Indian and imported bikes.

Get your machine serviced regularly (particularly older ones). Indian roads and engine vibration work things loose quite quickly.

Check the engine and gearbox oil level regularly (at least every 500km) and clean the oil filter every few thousand kilometres.

Given the road conditions, the chances are you'll make at least a couple of visits to a puncture-wallah – start your trip with new tyres and carry spanners to remove your own wheels.

It's a good idea to bring your own protective equipment (jackets, gloves etc).

Road Conditions

Given the varied road conditions, India can be challenging for novice riders. Hazards range from cows and chickens crossing the carriageway to broken-down trucks, unruly traffic, pedestrians on the road, and ubiquitous potholes and unmarked speed humps. Rural roads sometimes have grain crops strewn across them to be threshed by passing vehicles – a serious sliding hazard for bikers.

Try not to cover too much territory in one day and never ride in the dark – many vehicles drive without lights, and dynamo-powered motorcycle headlamps are useless at low revs while negotiating around potholes.

On busy national highways, expect to average 40km/h to 50km/h without stops; on winding back roads and dirt tracks this can drop to 10km/h.

Organised Motorcycle Tours

Dozens of companies offer organised motorcycle tours around India with a support vehicle, mechanic and guide. Below are some reputable outfits (see websites for contact details, itineraries and prices):

Blazing Trails (www.blazing trailstours.com)

Classic Bike Adventure (www.classic-bike-india.com; Assagao) This well-established Goan company organises motorbike tours on Enfields through the Himalaya, Nepal, South India and Goa.

Ferris Wheels (www.ferris-wheels.com.au)

H-C Travel (www.hctravel.com)

Himalayan Roadrunners (www.ridehigh.com)

Kerala Bike Tours (📞04842356652, 9388476817; www.keralabiketours.com; Kirushupaly Rd, Ravipuram) Organises motorcycle tours around Kerala and the Western Ghats and hires out touring-quality Enfield Bullets (from US$155 per week) with unlimited mileage, full insurance and free recovery/maintenance options.

Lalli Singh Tours (www.lallisingh.com)

Moto Discovery (www.motodiscovery.com)

Royal Expeditions (www.royalexpeditions.com)

Saffron Road Motorcycle Tours (www.saffronroad.com)

Wheel of India (www.wheelofindia.com)

Shared Jeeps

In mountain areas shared jeeps supplement the bus services, charging similar fixed fares.

Although nominally designed for five to six passengers, most shared jeeps squeeze in more. The seats beside and immediately behind the driver are more expensive than the cramped bench seats at the rear.

Jeeps only leave when full; people often bail out of a half-full jeep and pile into one with more passengers that's ready to depart. Drivers will leave immediately if you pay for all the empty seats and 'reserve' a vehicle for yourself.

Jeeps run from jeep stands and 'passenger stations' at the junctions of major roads; ask locals to point you in the right direction.

In some states, jeeps are known as 'sumos' after the Tata Sumo, a popular vehicle.

Travel sickness, particularly on winding mountain roads, may mean you are asked to give up your window seat to queasy fellow passengers.

Tours

Tours are available all over India, run by tourist offices, local transport companies and travel agencies. Organised tours can be an inexpensive way to see several places on one trip, although you rarely get much time at each place. If you arrange a tailor-made tour, you'll have more freedom about where you go and how long you stay.

Drivers may double as guides, or you can hire a qualified local guide for a fee. In tourist towns, be wary of touts claiming to be professional guides.

International Tour Agencies

Many international companies offer tours to India, from straightforward sightseeing trips to adventure tours and activity-based holidays. To find current tours that match your interests, quiz travel agents and surf the web. Some good places to start your tour hunt:

Dragoman (www.dragoman. com) One of several reputable overland tour companies offering trips on customised vehicles.

Exodus (www.exodus.co.uk) A wide array of specialist trips, including tours with a holistic, wildlife and adventure focus.

India Wildlife Tours (www. india-wildlife-tours.com) All sorts of wildlife tours, plus jeep/horse/camel safaris and birdwatching.

Indian Encounter (www. indianencounters.com) Special-interest tours that include wildlife spotting, river-rafting and ayurvedic treatments.

Intrepid Travel (www. intrepidtravel.com) Endless possibilities from wildlife tours to sacred rambles.

Peregrine Adventures (www.peregrineadventures. com) Popular cultural and trekking tours.

Sacred India Tours (www. sacredindiatours.com) Includes tours with a holistic focus such as yoga and ayurveda, as well as architectural and cultural tours.

Shanti Travel (www.shanti travel.com/en) A range of tours including family and adventure tours, run by a Franco-Indian team.

World Expeditions (www. worldexpeditions.com) An array of options that includes trekking and cycling tours.

Train

Travelling by train is a quintessential Indian experience. Trains offer a smoother ride than buses and are especially recommended for long journeys that include overnight travel. India's rail network is one of the largest and busiest in the world and Indian Railways is the largest utility employer on earth, with roughly 1.5 million workers. There are around 6900 train stations scattered across the country.

We've listed useful trains but there are hundreds more. The best way of sourcing updated railway information is to use relevant internet sites such as **Indian Railways** (www.indianrail.gov. in) and the excellent **India Rail Info** (http://indiarailinfo. com), with added offline browsing support, as well as the user-friendly **Erail** (www. erail.in). There's also *Trains at a Glance* (₹45), available at many train station bookstands and better bookshops/newsstands, however it's published annually so it's not as up to date as websites. Nevertheless, it offers comprehensive timetables covering all the main lines. For more information see p34.

Booking Tickets in India

You can either book tickets through a travel agency or hotel (for a commission), or in person at the train station. You can also book online through **IRCTC** (www. irctc.co.in), the e-ticketing division of Indian Railways, or portals such as **Cleartrip** (www.cleartrip.com), **Make My Trip** (www.makemytrip. com) and **Yatra** (www.yatra. com). Remember, however, that online booking of train tickets has its share of glitches: travellers have reported problems with registering themselves on some portals and using certain overseas credit cards. Big stations often have English-speaking staff who can help with reser-

EXPRESS TRAIN FARES IN RUPEES

DISTANCE (KM)	1AC	2AC	3AC	FIRST CLASS	CHAIR CAR (CC)	SECOND (II)
100	1047	613	428	262	205	48
200	1047	613	428	412	282	73
300	1047	613	561	558	378	103
400	1460	843	591	690	467	128
500	1794	1058	733	843	577	151
1000	2940	1708	1352	1371	931	258
1500	3787	2188	1487	1753	1189	334
2000	4620	2659	1797	2127	1443	412

vations. At smaller stations, the stationmaster and his deputy usually speak English. It's also worth approaching tourist-office staff if you need advice.

AT THE STATION

Get a reservation slip from the information window, fill in the name of the departure station, destination station, the class you want to travel and the name and number of the train. Join the long queue for the ticket window where your ticket will be printed. Women should take advantage of the separate women's queue – if there isn't one, go to the front of the regular queue.

TOURIST RESERVATION BUREAU

Larger cities and major tourist centres have an International Tourist Bureau, which allows you to book tickets in relative peace – check www.indianrail.gov.in for a list of these stations.

Reservations

Bookings open up to 60 days before departure and you must make a reservation for chair-car, sleeper, 1AC, 2AC and 3AC carriages. No reservations are required for general (2nd class) compartments; you have to grab seats here the moment the train pulls in.

Trains are always busy so it's wise to book as far in advance as possible, especially for overnight journeys. There may be additional services to certain destinations during major festivals but it's still worth booking well in advance.

Reserved tickets show your seat/berth and carriage number. Carriage numbers are written on the side of the train (station staff and porters can point you in the right direction). A list of names and berths is posted on the side of each reserved carriage.

FARE FINDER

Go to www.indiarailinfo.com or erail.in and type in the name of the two destinations. You'll promptly get a list of every train (with the name, number, arrival/departure times and journey details) plying the route, as well as fares for each available class.

Refunds are available on any ticket, even after departure, with a penalty – rules are complicated, check when you book.

Trains can be delayed at any stage of the journey; to avoid stress, factor some leeway into your plans.

Be mindful of potential drugging and theft; a padlock and chain are useful for securing your baggage to luggage racks for longer journeys.

If the train you want to travel on is sold out, enquire about other options.

TOURIST QUOTA

A special (albeit small) tourist quota is set aside for foreign tourists travelling between popular stations. These seats can only be booked at dedicated reservation offices in major cities, and you need to show your passport and visa as ID. Tickets can be paid for in rupees (some offices may ask to see foreign exchange certificates – ATM receipts will suffice).

TATKAL TICKETS

Indian Railways holds back a small number of tickets on key trains and releases them at 10am one day before the train is due to depart. A charge of ₹10 to ₹400 is added to each ticket price. First AC tickets are excluded from the scheme.

RESERVATION AGAINST CANCELLATION (RAC)

Even when a train is fully booked, Indian Railways sells a handful of seats in each class as 'Reservation Against Cancellation' (RAC).

This means that if you have an RAC ticket and someone cancels before the departure date, you will get his or her seat (or berth). You'll have to check the reservation list at the station on the day of travel to see if you've been allocated a confirmed seat/berth. Even if no one cancels, you can still board the train as an RAC ticket holder and travel without a seat.

WAITLIST (WL)

If the RAC quota is maxed out as well, you will be handed a waitlisted ticket (marked WL). This means that if there are enough cancellations, you may eventually move up the order to land a confirmed berth, or at least an RAC seat. Check your booking status at www.indianrail.gov.in/pnr_Enq.html by entering your ticket's PNR number. You can't board the train on a waitlisted ticket, but a refund is available – ask the ticket office about your chances.

Costs

Fares are calculated by distance and class of travel; Rajdhani and Shatabdi trains are slightly more expensive, but the price includes meals. Most air-conditioned carriages have a catering service (meals are brought to your seat). In unreserved classes it's a good idea to carry portable snacks. Male/female seniors (those over 60/58) get 40/50% off all fares in all classes on all types of train. Children below the age of six travel free, those aged between six and 12 are charged half price, up to 300km.

Health

Hygiene is generally poor in most regions so food and water-borne illnesses are fairly common. A number of insect-borne diseases are present, particularly in tropical areas. Medical care is basic in various areas (especially beyond the larger cities) so it's essential to be well prepared.

Pre-existing medical conditions and accidental injury (especially traffic accidents) account for most that are life-threatening. Becoming ill in some way, however, is common. Fortunately, most travellers' illnesses can be prevented with some common-sense behaviour or treated with a well-stocked travellers' medical kit – however, never hesitate to consult a doctor while on the road, as self-diagnosis can be hazardous.

The following information is a general guide only and certainly does not replace the advice of a doctor trained in travel medicine.

BEFORE YOU GO

You can buy many medications over the counter in India without a doctor's prescription, but it can be difficult to find some of the newer drugs, particularly the latest antidepressant drugs, blood-pressure medications and contraceptive pills. Bring the following:

➡ medications in their original, labelled containers

➡ a signed, dated letter from your doctor describing your medical conditions and medications, including generic names

➡ a doctor's letter documenting the necessity of any syringes you bring

➡ if you have a heart condition, a copy of your ECG taken just prior to travelling

➡ any regular medication (double your ordinary needs)

Insurance

Don't travel without health insurance. Emergency evacuation is expensive. Consider the following when buying insurance:

➡ You may require extra cover for adventure activities such as rock climbing.

➡ In India, doctors usually require immediate payment in cash. Your insurance plan may make payments directly to providers or it will reimburse you later for overseas health expenditures. If you do have to claim later, make sure you keep all relevant documentation.

➡ Some policies ask that you telephone back (reverse charges) to a centre in your home country where an immediate assessment of your problem will be made.

Vaccinations

Specialised travel-medicine clinics are your best source of up-to-date information; they stock all available vaccines and can give specific recommendations for your trip. Most vaccines don't give immunity until at least two weeks after they're given, so visit a doctor well before departure. Ask your doctor for an International Certificate of Vaccination (sometimes known as the 'yellow booklet'), which will list all the vaccinations you've received.

Medical checklist

Recommended items for a personal medical kit:

➡ Antifungal cream, eg clotrimazole

➡ Antibacterial cream, eg mupirocin

➡ Antibiotic for skin infections, eg amoxicillin/clavulanate or cephalexin

➡ Antihistamine – there are many options, eg cetirizine for daytime and promethazine for night

➡ Antiseptic, eg Betadine

➡ Antispasmodic for stomach cramps, eg Buscopam

➡ Contraceptive

➡ Decongestant, eg pseudoephedrine

➡ DEET-based insect repellent

➡ Diarrhoea medication – consider an oral rehydration solution (eg Gastrolyte), diarrhoea 'stopper' (eg loperamide) and antinausea medication (eg prochlorperazine). Antibiotics for diarrhoea include ciprofloxacin; for bacterial diarrhoea azithromycin; for giardia or amoebic dysentery tinidazole

➡ First-aid items such as elastoplasts, bandages, gauze, thermometer (but not mercury), sterile needles and syringes, and tweezers

⇒ Ibuprofen or another anti-inflammatory

⇒ Iodine tablets (unless you're pregnant or have a thyroid problem) to purify water

⇒ Migraine medication if you suffer from migraines

⇒ Paracetamol

⇒ Pyrethrin to impregnate clothing and mosquito nets

⇒ Steroid cream for allergic or itchy rashes, eg 1% to 2% hydrocortisone

⇒ High-factor sunscreen

⇒ Throat lozenges

⇒ Thrush (vaginal yeast infection) treatment, eg clotrimazole pessaries or Diflucan tablet

⇒ Ural or equivalent if prone to urine infections

Websites

There is lots of travel-health advice on the internet; www.lonelyplanet.com is a good place to start. Other options:

Centers for Disease Control and Prevention (CDC; www.cdc.gov) Travel health advice.

MD Travel Health (www.mdtravelhealth.com) Travel-health recommendations for every country, updated daily.

World Health Organization (WHO; www.who.int/ith) Its helpful book *International Travel & Health* is revised annually and is available online.

Further Reading

Lonely Planet's *Healthy Travel – Asia & India* is pocket sized with useful information, including pre-trip planning, first aid, immunisation

REQUIRED & RECOMMENDED VACCINATIONS

The only vaccine required by international regulations is **yellow fever**. Proof of vaccination will only be required if you have visited a country in the yellow-fever zone within the six days prior to entering India. If you are travelling to India from Africa or South America, you should check to see if you require proof of vaccination.

The World Health Organization (WHO) recommends the following vaccinations for travellers to India (as well as being up to date with measles, mumps and rubella vaccinations):

Adult diphtheria & tetanus Single booster recommended if none in the previous 10 years. Side effects include sore arm and fever.

Hepatitis A Provides almost 100% protection for up to a year; a booster after 12 months provides at least another 20 years' protection. Mild side effects such as headache and sore arm occur in 5% to 10% of people.

Hepatitis B Now considered routine for most travellers. Given as three shots over six months. A rapid schedule is also available, as is a combined vaccination with Hepatitis A. Side effects are mild and uncommon, usually headache and sore arm. In 95% of people lifetime protection results.

Polio Only one booster is required as an adult for lifetime protection. Inactivated polio vaccine is safe during pregnancy.

Typhoid Recommended for all travellers to India, even those only visiting urban areas. The vaccine offers around 70% protection, lasts for two to three years and comes as a single shot. Tablets are also available, but the injection is usually recommended as it has fewer side effects. Sore arm and fever may occur.

Varicella If you haven't had chickenpox, discuss this vaccination with your doctor.

These immunisations are recommended for long-term travellers (more than one month) or those at special risk (seek further advice from your doctor):

Japanese B Encephalitis Three injections in all. Booster recommended after two years. Sore arm and headache are the most common side effects. In rare cases, an allergic reaction comprising hives and swelling can occur up to 10 days after any of the three doses.

Meningitis Single injection. There are two types of vaccination: the quadravalent vaccine gives two to three years' protection; meningitis group C vaccine gives around 10 years' protection. Recommended for long-term backpackers aged under 25.

Rabies Three injections in all. A booster after one year will then provide 10 years' protection. Side effects are rare – occasionally headache and sore arm.

Tuberculosis (TB) Adult long-term travellers are usually recommended to have a TB skin test before and after travel, rather than vaccination. Only one vaccine given in a lifetime.

information, and what to do if you get sick on the road. Other good references include *Travellers' Health* by Dr Richard Dawood and *Travelling Well* by Dr Deborah Mills – check out the website (www.travellingwell.com.au) too.

IN INDIA

Availability of Health Care

Medical care is hugely variable in India. Some cities now have clinics catering specifically to travellers and expatriates; these clinics are usually more expensive than local medical facilities, and offer a higher standard of care. Additionally, they know the local system, including reputable local hospitals and specialists. They may also liaise with insurance companies should you require evacuation. It is usually difficult to find reliable medical care in rural areas.

Self-treatment may be appropriate if your problem is minor (eg traveller's diarrhoea), you are carrying the relevant medication, and you cannot attend a recommended clinic. If you suspect a serious disease, especially malaria, travel to the nearest quality facility.

Before buying medication over the counter, check the use-by date, and ensure the packet is sealed and properly stored (eg not exposed to the sunshine).

Infectious Diseases

Malaria

This is a potentially deadly disease. Before you travel, seek expert advice according to your itinerary (rural areas are especially risky) and on medication and side effects.

Malaria is caused by a parasite transmitted by the bite of an infected mosquito. The most important symptom of malaria is fever, but general symptoms, such as headache, diarrhoea, cough or chills, may also occur. Diagnosis can only be properly made by taking a blood sample.

Two strategies should be combined to prevent malaria: mosquito avoidance and antimalarial medications. Most people who catch malaria are taking inadequate or no antimalarial medication.

Travellers are advised to prevent mosquito bites by taking these steps:

➡ Use a DEET-based insect repellent on exposed skin. Wash this off at night – as long as you are sleeping under a mosquito net. Natural repellents such as citronella can be effective, but must be applied more frequently than products containing DEET.

➡ Sleep under a mosquito net impregnated with pyrethrin.

➡ Choose accommodation with proper screens and fans (if not air-conditioned).

➡ Impregnate clothing with pyrethrin in high-risk areas.

➡ Wear long sleeves and trousers in light colours.

➡ Use mosquito coils.

➡ Spray your room with insect repellent before going out for your evening meal.

There are a variety of medications available:

Chloroquine & Paludrine combination Limited effectiveness in many parts of South Asia. Common side effects include nausea (40% of people) and mouth ulcers.

Doxycycline (daily tablet) A broad-spectrum antibiotic that helps prevent a variety of tropical diseases, including leptospirosis, tick-borne disease and typhus. Potential side effects include photosensitivity (a tendency to sunburn), thrush (in women), indigestion, heartburn, nausea and interference with the contraceptive pill. More serious side effects include ulceration of the oesophagus – take your tablet with a meal and a large glass of water, and never lie down within half an hour of taking it. It must be taken for four weeks after leaving the risk area.

Lariam (mefloquine) This weekly tablet suits many people. Serious side effects are rare but include depression, anxiety, psychosis and seizures. Anyone with a history of depression, anxiety, other psychological disorders or epilepsy should not take Lariam. It is considered safe in the second and third trimesters of pregnancy. Tablets must be taken for four weeks after leaving the risk area.

Malarone A combination of atovaquone and proguanil. Side effects are uncommon and mild, most commonly nausea and headache. It is the best tablet for scuba divers and for those on short trips to high-risk areas. It must be taken for one week after leaving the risk area.

Other diseases

Avian Flu 'Bird flu' or Influenza A (H5N1) is a subtype of the type A influenza virus. Contact with dead or sick birds is the principal source of infection and bird-to-human transmission does not

---

HEALTH ADVISORIES

It's a good idea to consult your government's travel-health website before departure, if one is available:

➡ **Australia** (www.smartraveller.gov.au)

➡ **Canada** (www.travelhealth.gc.ca)

➡ **New Zealand** (www.mfat.govt.nz/travel)

➡ **UK** (www.fco.gov.uk/en/travelling-and-living-overseas)

➡ **US** (www.cdc.gov/travel)

easily occur. Symptoms include high fever and flu-like symptoms with rapid deterioration, leading to respiratory failure and death in many cases. Immediate medical care should be sought if bird flu is suspected. Check www.who.int/en/or www.avianinfluenza.com.au.

Dengue Fever This mosquito-borne disease is becomingly increasingly problematic, especially in the cities. As there is no vaccine available it can only be prevented by avoiding mosquito bites at all times. Symptoms include high fever, severe headache and body ache and sometimes a rash and diarrhoea. Treatment is rest and paracetamol – do not take aspirin or ibuprofen as it increases the likelihood of haemorrhaging. Make sure you see a doctor to be diagnosed and monitored.

Hepatitis A This food- and water-borne virus infects the liver, causing jaundice (yellow skin and eyes), nausea and lethargy. There is no specific treatment for hepatitis A; just allow time for the liver to heal. All travellers to India should be vaccinated against hepatitis A.

Hepatitis B This sexually transmitted disease is spread by body fluids and can be prevented by vaccination. The long-term consequences can include liver cancer and cirrhosis.

Hepatitis E Transmitted through contaminated food and water, hepatitis E has similar symptoms to hepatitis A, but is far less common. It is a severe problem in pregnant women and can result in the death of both mother and baby. There is no commercially available vaccine, and prevention is by following safe eating and drinking guidelines.

HIV Spread via contaminated body fluids. Avoid unsafe sex, unsterile needles (including in medical facilities) and procedures such as tattoos. The growth rate of HIV in India is one of the highest in the world.

Influenza Present year-round in the tropics, influenza (flu) symptoms include fever, muscle aches, a runny nose, cough and sore throat. It can be severe in people over the age of 65 or in those with medical conditions such as heart disease or diabetes – vaccination is recommended for these individuals. There is no specific treatment, just rest and paracetamol.

Japanese B Encephalitis This viral disease is transmitted by mosquitoes and is rare in travellers. Most cases occur in rural areas and vaccination is recommended for travellers spending more than one month outside of cities. There is no treatment, and it may result in permanent brain damage or death. Ask your doctor for further details.

Rabies This fatal disease is spread by the bite or possibly even the lick of an infected animal – most commonly a dog or monkey. You should seek medical advice immediately after any animal bite and commence postexposure treatment. Having pretravel vaccination means the postbite treatment is greatly simplified. If an animal bites you, gently wash the wound with soap and water, and apply iodine-based antiseptic. If you are not prevaccinated you will need to receive rabies immunoglobulin as soon as possible, and this is very difficult to obtain in much of India.

Tuberculosis While TB is rare in travellers, those who have significant contact with the local population (such as medical and aid workers and long-term travellers) should take precautions. Vaccination is usually only given to children under the age of five, but adults at risk are recommended to have pre- and post-travel TB testing. The main symptoms are fever, cough, weight loss, night sweats and fatigue.

Typhoid This bacterial infection is also spread via food and water. It gives a high and progressive fever and headache, and may be accompanied by a dry cough and stomach pain. It is diagnosed by blood tests and treated with antibiotics. Vaccination is recommended for all travellers who are spending more than a week in India. Be aware that vaccination is not 100% effective, so you must still be careful with what you eat and drink.

Travellers' Diarrhoea

This is by far the most common problem affecting travellers in India – between 30% and 70% of people will suffer from it within two weeks of starting their trip. It's usually caused by a bacteria, and thus responds promptly to treatment with antibiotics.

Travellers' diarrhoea is defined as the passage of more than three watery bowel actions within 24 hours, plus at least one other symptom, such as fever, cramps, nausea, vomiting or feeling generally unwell.

Treatment consists of staying well hydrated; rehydration solutions like Gastrolyte are the best for this. Antibiotics such as ciprofloxacin or azithromycin should kill the bacteria quickly. Seek medical attention quickly if you do not respond to an appropriate antibiotic.

Loperamide is just a 'stopper' and doesn't get to the cause of the problem. It can be helpful, though (eg if you have to go on a long bus ride). Don't take loperamide if you have a fever or blood in your stools.

Amoebic Dysentery Amoebic dysentery is very rare in travellers but is quite often misdiagnosed by poor-quality labs. Symptoms are similar to bacterial diarrhoea: fever, bloody diarrhoea and generally feeling unwell. You should always seek reliable medical care if you have blood in your diarrhoea. Treatment involves two drugs: tinidazole or metronidazole to kill the parasite in your gut and then a second drug to kill the cysts. If left untreated complications such as liver or gut abscesses can occur.

Giardiasis Giardia is a parasite that is relatively common in travellers. Symptoms include nausea, bloating, excess gas, fatigue and intermittent diarrhoea. The parasite will eventually go away if left untreated but this can take months; the best advice is to seek medical treatment. The treatment of choice is tinidazole, with metronidazole being a second-line option.

Environmental Hazards

Air Pollution

Air pollution, particularly vehicle pollution, is an increasing problem in most of India's urban hubs. If you have severe respiratory problems, speak with your doctor before travelling to India.

Diving & Surfing

Divers and surfers should seek specialised advice before they travel to ensure their medical kit contains treatment for coral cuts and tropical ear infections. Divers should ensure their insurance covers them for decompression illness – get specialised dive insurance through an organisation such as Divers Alert Network (www.danasiapacific.org). Certain medical conditions are incompatible with diving; check with your doctor.

Food

Dining out brings with it the possibility of contracting diarrhoea. Ways to help avoid food-related illness:

➡ eat only freshly cooked food

➡ avoid shellfish and buffets

➡ peel fruit

➡ cook vegetables

➡ soak salads in iodine water for at least 20 minutes

➡ eat in busy restaurants with a high turnover of customers

Heat

Many parts of India, especially down south, are hot and humid throughout the year. For most visitors it takes around two weeks to comfortably adapt to the hot climate. Swelling of the feet and ankles is common, as are muscle cramps caused by excessive sweating. Prevent these by avoiding dehydration and excessive activity in the heat. Don't eat salt tablets (they aggravate the gut); drinking rehydration solution or eating salty food helps. Treat cramps by resting, rehydrating with double-strength rehydration solution and gently stretching.

Dehydration is the main contributor to heat exhaustion. Recovery is usually rapid and it is common to feel weak for some days afterwards. Symptoms include:

➡ feeling weak

➡ headache

➡ irritability

➡ nausea or vomiting

➡ sweaty skin

➡ a fast, weak pulse

➡ normal or slightly elevated body temperature.

Treatment:

➡ get out of the heat

➡ fan the sufferer

➡ apply cool, wet cloths to the skin

➡ lay the sufferer flat with their legs raised

➡ rehydrate with water containing one-quarter teaspoon of salt per litre.

Heat stroke is a serious medical emergency. Symptoms include:

➡ weakness

➡ nausea

➡ a hot dry body

➡ temperature of over 41°C

➡ dizziness

➡ confusion

➡ loss of coordination

➡ seizures

➡ eventual collapse.

Treatment:

➡ get out of the heat

➡ fan the sufferer

➡ apply wet cloths to the skin or ice to the body, especially to the groin and armpits.

Prickly heat is a common skin rash in the tropics, caused by sweat trapped under the skin. Treat it by moving out of the heat for a few hours and by having cool showers. Creams and ointments clog the skin so they should be avoided. Locally bought prickly-heat powder can be helpful.

Altitude Sickness

If you are going to altitudes above 3000m, Acute Mountain Sickness (AMS) is an issue. The biggest risk factor is going too high too quickly – follow a conservative acclimatisation schedule found in good trekking guides, and *never* go to a higher altitude when you have any symptoms that could be altitude related. There is no way to

DRINKING WATER

➡ Never drink tap water.

➡ Bottled water is generally safe – check the seal is intact at purchase.

➡ Avoid ice unless you know it has been made hygienically.

➡ Be careful of fresh juices served at street stalls in particular – they may have been watered down or may be served in unhygienic jugs/glasses.

➡ Boiling water is the most efficient method of purifying it.

➡ The best chemical purifier is iodine. It should not be used by pregnant women or those with thyroid problems.

➡ Water filters should also filter out most viruses. Ensure your filter has a chemical barrier such as iodine and a small pore size (less than four microns).

predict who will get altitude sickness and it is quite often the younger, fitter members of a group who succumb.

Symptoms usually develop during the first 24 hours at altitude but may be delayed up to three weeks. Mild symptoms include:

➡ headache
➡ lethargy
➡ dizziness
➡ difficulty sleeping
➡ loss of appetite.

AMS may become more severe without warning and can be fatal. Severe symptoms include:

➡ breathlessness
➡ a dry, irritative cough (which may progress to the production of pink, frothy sputum)
➡ severe headache
➡ lack of coordination and balance
➡ confusion
➡ irrational behaviour
➡ vomiting
➡ drowsiness
➡ unconsciousness.

Treat mild symptoms by resting at the same altitude until recovery, which usually takes a day or two. Paracetamol or aspirin can be taken for headaches. If symptoms persist or become worse, immediate descent is necessary; even 500m can help. Drug treatments should never be used to avoid descent or to enable further ascent.

The drugs acetazolamide and dexamethasone are recommended by some doctors for the prevention of AMS; however, their use is controversial. They can reduce the symptoms, but they may also mask warning signs; severe and fatal AMS has occurred in people taking these drugs.

To prevent acute mountain sickness:

➡ ascend slowly – have frequent rest days, spending

CARBON-MONOXIDE POISONING

Some mountain areas rely on charcoal burners for warmth, but these should be avoided due to the risk of fatal carbon-monoxide poisoning. The thick, mattress-like blankets used in many mountain areas are amazingly warm once you get beneath the covers. If you're still cold, improvise a hot-water bottle by filling your drinking-water bottle with boiled water and covering it with a sock.

two to three nights at each rise of 1000m

➡ sleep at a lower altitude than the greatest height reached during the day, if possible. Above 3000m, don't increase sleeping altitude by more than 300m daily

➡ drink extra fluids

➡ eat light, high-carbohydrate meals

➡ avoid alcohol and sedatives

Insect Bites & Stings

Bedbugs Don't carry disease but their bites can be very itchy. They usually live in furniture and walls and then migrate to the bed at night. You can treat the itch with an antihistamine.

Lice Most commonly appear on the head and pubic areas. You may need numerous applications of an antilice shampoo such as pyrethrin. Pubic lice are usually contracted from sexual contact.

Ticks Contracted walking in rural areas. Ticks are commonly found behind the ears, on the belly and in armpits. If you have had a tick bite and have a rash at the site of the bite or elsewhere, fever or muscle aches, you should see a doctor. Doxycycline prevents tick-borne diseases.

Leeches Found in humid rainforest areas. They do not transmit any disease but their bites are often intensely itchy for weeks and can easily become infected. Apply an iodine-based antiseptic to any leech bite to help prevent infection.

Bee and wasp stings Anyone with a serious bee or wasp allergy should carry an injection of adrenalin (eg an Epipen). For others pain is the main problem –

apply ice to the sting and take painkillers.

Skin Problems

Fungal rashes There are two common fungal rashes that affect travellers. The first occurs in moist areas, such as the groin, armpits and between the toes. It starts as a red patch that slowly spreads and is usually itchy. Treatment involves keeping the skin dry, avoiding chafing and using an antifungal cream such as clotrimazole or Lamisil. The second, *Tinea versicolor*, causes light-coloured patches, most commonly on the back, chest and shoulders. Consult a doctor.

Cuts and scratches These become easily infected in humid climates. Immediately wash all wounds in clean water and apply antiseptic. If you develop signs of infection (increasing pain and redness), see a doctor.

Women's Health

For gynaecological health issues, seek out a female doctor.

Birth control Bring adequate supplies of your own form of contraception.

Sanitary products Pads, rarely tampons, are readily available.

Thrush Heat, humidity and antibiotics can all contribute to thrush. Treatment is with antifungal creams and pessaries such as clotrimazole. A practical alternative is a single tablet of fluconazole (Diflucan).

Urinary-tract infections These can be precipitated by dehydration or long bus journeys without toilet stops; bring suitable antibiotics.

Language

The number of languages spoken in India helps explain why English is still widely spoken here, and why it's still in official use. Another 22 languages are recognised in the constitution, and more than 1600 minor languages are spoken throughout the country.

Major efforts have been made to promote Hindi as the national language of India and to gradually phase out English. However, English remains popular, and while Hindi is the predominant language in the north, it bears little relation to the Dravidian languages of the south such as Tamil. Consequently, very few people in the south speak Hindi.

Many educated Indians speak English as virtually their first language and for a large number of Indians it's their second tongue. Although you'll find it easy to get around India with English, it's always good to know a little of the local language.

HINDI

Hindi has about 600 million speakers worldwide, of which 180 million are in India. It developed from Classical Sanskrit, and is written in the Devanagari script. In 1947 it was granted official status along with English.

Most Hindi sounds are similar to their English counterparts. The main difference is that Hindi has both 'aspirated' consonants (pronounced with a puff of air, like saying 'h' after the sound) and unaspirated ones, as well as 'retroflex' (pronounced with the tongue bent backwards) and nonretroflex consonants. Our simplified pronunciation guides don't include these distinctions – read them as if they were English and you'll be understood.

Pronouncing the vowels correctly is important, especially their length (eg a and aa). The consonant combination ng after a vowel indicates nasalisation (ie the vowel is pronounced 'through the nose'). Note also that au is pronounced as the 'ow' in 'how'. Word stress is very light – we've indicated the stressed syllables with italics.

Basics

Hindi verbs change form depending on the gender of the speaker (or the subject of the sentence in general), so it's the verbs, not the pronouns 'he' or 'she' (as is the case in English) which show whether the subject of the sentence is masculine or feminine. In these phrases we include the options for male and female speakers, marked 'm' and 'f' respectively.

Hello./Goodbye.	नमस्ते ।	na·ma·ste
Yes.	जी हाँ ।	jee haang
No.	जी नहीं ।	jee na·heeng
Excuse me.	सुनिये ।	su·ni·ye
Sorry.	माफ़ कीजिये ।	maaf kee·ji·ye
Please ...	कृपया ...	kri·pa·yaa ...
Thank you.	थैंक्यू ।	thayn·kyoo
You're welcome.	कोई बात नहीं ।	ko·ee baat na·heeng

How are you?	आप कैसे/कैसी हैं?	aap kay·se/kay·see hayng (m/f)
Fine. And you?	मैं ठीक हूँ । आप सुनाइये ।	mayng teek hoong aap su·naa·i·ye

WANT MORE?

For in-depth language information and handy phrases, check out Lonely Planet's *Hindi, Urdu & Bengali Phrasebook* and *India Phrasebook*. You'll find them at **shop.lonelyplanet.com**, or you can buy Lonely Planet's iPhone phrasebooks at the Apple App Store.

What's your name?
आप का नाम क्या है?   aap kaa naam kyaa hay

My name is ...
मेरा नाम ... है।   me·raa naam ... hay

Do you speak English?
क्या आपको अंग्रेज़ी   kyaa aap ko an·gre·zee
आती है?   aa·tee hay

I don't understand.
मैं नहीं समझा/   mayng na·heeng sam·jaa/
समझी।   sam·jee (m/f)

Accommodation

Where's a ...?	... कहाँ है?	... ka·haang hay
guesthouse	गेस्ट हाउस	gest haa·us
hotel	होटल	ho·tal
youth hostel	यूथ हास्टल	yoot haas·tal
Do you have a ... room?	क्या ... कमरा है?	kyaa ... kam·raa hay
single	सिंगल	sin·gal
double	डबल	da·bal
How much is it per ...?	... के लिये कितने पैसे लगते हैं?	... ke li·ye kit·ne pay·se lag·te hayng
night	एक रात	ek raat
person	हर व्यक्ति	har vyak·ti
air-con	ए० सी०	e see
bathroom	बाथरूम	baat·room
hot water	गर्म पानी	garm paa·nee
mosquito net	मसहरी	mas·ha·ree
washerman	धोबी	do·bee
window	खिड़की	kir·kee

Directions

Where's ...?
... कहाँ है?   ... ka·haang hay

How far is it?
वह कितनी दूर है?   voh kit·nee door hay

What's the address?
पता क्या है?   pa·taa kyaa hay

Can you show me (on the map)?
(नक्शे में) दिखा   (nak·she meng) di·kaa
सकते है?   sak·te hayng

Turn left/right.
लेफ्ट/राइट मुड़िये।   left/raa·it mu·ri·ye

NUMBERS – HINDI

1	१	एक	ek
2	२	दो	do
3	३	तीन	teen
4	४	चार	chaar
5	५	पाँच	paanch
6	६	छह	chay
7	७	सात	saat
8	८	आठ	aat
9	९	नौ	nau
10	१०	दस	das
20	२०	बीस	bees
30	३०	तीस	tees
40	४०	चालीस	chaa·lees
50	५०	पचास	pa·chaas
60	६०	साठ	saat
70	७०	सत्तर	sat·tar
80	८०	अस्सी	as·see
90	९०	नब्बे	nab·be
100	१००	सौ	sau
1000	१०००	एक हज़ार	ek ha·zaar

at the corner	कोने पर	ko·ne par
at the traffic lights	सिगनल पर	sig·nal par
behind ...	... के पीछे	... ke pee·che
in front of ...	... के सामन	... ke saam·ne
near ...	... के पास	... ke paas
opposite ...	... के सामने	... ke saam·ne
straight ahead	सीधे	see·de

Eating & Drinking

What would you recommend?
आपके ख्याल में   aap ke kyaal meng
क्या अच्छा होगा?   kyaa ach·chaa ho·gaa

Do you have vegetarian food?
क्या आप का खाना   kyaa aap kaa kaa·naa
शाकाहारी है?   shaa·kaa·haa·ree hay

I don't eat (meat).
मैं (गोश्त) नहीं   mayng (gosht) na·heeng
खाता/खाती।   kaa·taa/kaa·tee (m/f)

I'll have ...
मुझे ... दीजिये।   mu·je ... dee·ji·ye

That was delicious.
बहुत मज़ेदार हुआ।   ba·hut ma·ze·daar hu·aa

Please bring the menu/bill.
मेन्यू/बिल लाइये।   men·yoo/bil laa·i·ye

Key Words

bottle	बोतल	*bo·tal*
bowl	कटोरी	*ka·to·ree*
breakfast	नाश्ता	*naash·taa*
dessert	मीठा	*mee·taa*
dinner	रात का खाना	*raat kaa kaa·naa*
drinks	पीने की चीज़ें	*pee·ne kee chee·zeng*
food	खाना	*kaa·naa*
fork	काँटा	*kaan·taa*
glass	गिलास	*glaas*
knife	चाकू	*chaa·koo*
local eatery	ढाबा	*daa·baa*
lunch	दिन का खाना	*din kaa kaa·naa*
market	बाज़ार	*baa·zaar*
plate	प्लेट	*plet*
restaurant	रेस्टोरेंट	*res·to·rent*
set meal	थाली	*taa·lee*
snack	नाश्ता	*naash·taa*
spoon	चम्मच	*cham·mach*

Meat & Fish

beef	गाय का गोश्त	*gaai kaa gosht*
chicken	मुर्गी	*mur·gee*
duck	बतख़	*ba·tak*
fish	मछली	*mach·lee*
goat	बकरा	*bak·raa*
lobster	बड़ी झींगा	*ba·ree jeeng·gaa*
meat	गोश्त	*gosht*
meatballs	कोफ़्ता	*kof·taa*
pork	सुअर का गोश्त	*su·ar kaa gosht*
prawn	झींगी मछली	*jeeng·gee mach·lee*
seafood	मछली	*mach·lee*

Fruit & Vegetables

apple	सेब	*seb*
apricot	खुबानी	*ku·baa·nee*
banana	केला	*ke·laa*
capsicum	मिर्च	*mirch*
carrot	गाजर	*gaa·jar*
cauliflower	फूल गोभी	*pool go·bee*
corn	मक्का	*mak·kaa*
cucumber	ककड़ी	*kak·ree*
date	खजूर	*ka·joor*
eggplant	बैंगन	*bayng·gan*
fruit	फल	*pal*
garlic	लहसुन	*leh·sun*
grape	अंगूर	*an·goor*
grapefruit	चकोतरा	*cha·kot·raa*

lemon	निम्बू	*nim·boo*
lentils	दाल	daal
mandarin	संतरा	*san·ta·raa*
mango	आम	aam
mushroom	खुम्भी	*kum·bee*
nuts	मेवे	*me·ve*
orange	नारंगी	*naa·ran·gee*
papaya	पपीता	*pa·pee·taa*
peach	आड़ू	*aa·roo*
peas	मटर	*ma·tar*
pineapple	अनन्नास	*a·nan·naas*
potato	आलू	*aa·loo*
pumpkin	कद्दू	*kad·doo*
spinach	पालक	*paa·lak*
vegetables	सब्ज़ी	*sab·zee*
watermelon	तरबूज़	*tar·booz*

Other

bread	चपाती/नान/रोटी	*cha·paa·tee/naan/ro·tee*
butter	मक्खन	*mak·kan*
chilli	मिर्च	mirch
chutney	चटनी	*chat·nee*
egg	अंडे	*an·de*
honey	मधु	*ma·dhu*
ice	बर्फ़	barf
ice cream	कुल्फ़ी	*kul·fee*
pappadams	पपड़	*pa·par*
pepper	काली मिर्च	*kaa·lee mirch*
relish	अचार	*a·chaar*
rice	चावल	*chaa·val*
salt	नमक	*na·mak*
spices	मिर्च मसाला	*mirch ma·saa·laa*
sugar	चीनी	*chee·nee*
tofu	टोफू	*to·foo*

Drinks

beer	बियर	*bi·yar*
coffee	कॉफ़ी	*kaa·fee*
(sugarcane) juice	(गन्ने का) रस	*(gan·ne kaa) ras*
milk	दूध	dood
red wine	लाल शराब	*laal sha·raab*
sweet fruit drink	शरबत	*shar·bat*
tea	चाय	chaai
water	पानी	*paa·nee*
white wine	सफ़ेद शराब	*sa·fed sha·raab*
yoghurt	लस्सी	*las·see*

Emergencies

Help!
मदद कीजिये!   *ma·dad kee·ji·ye*

Go away!
जाओ!   *jaa·o*

I'm lost.
मैं रास्ता भूल   mayng *raas·*taa bool
गया/गयी हूँ ।   ga·*yaa*/ga·*yee* hoong (m/f)

Call a doctor!
डॉक्टर को बुलाओ!   *daak·*tar ko bu·*laa·*o

Call the police!
पुलिस को बुलाओ!   pu·*lis* ko bu·*laa·*o

I'm ill.
मैं बीमार हूँ ।   mayng *bee·*maar hoong

Where is the toilet?
टॉइलेट कहाँ है?   *taa·*i·let ka·*haang* hay

Shopping & Services

I'd like to buy ...
मुझे ... चाहिये ।   mu·*je* ... *chaa·*hi·ye

I'm just looking.
सिर्फ़ देखने आया/   sirf *dek·*ne aa·*yaa/*
आयी हूँ ।   aa·*yee* hoong (m/f)

Can I look at it?
दिखाइये ।   di·*kaa·*i·ye

How much is it?
कितने का है?   *kit·*ne kaa hay

It's too expensive.
यह बहुत महँगा/   yeh ba·*hut* ma·*han·*gaa/
महँगी है (m/f)   ma·*han·*gee hay (m/f)

There's a mistake in the bill.
बिल में गलती है ।   bil meng *gal·*tee hay

bank	बैंक	baynk
post office	डाक ख़ाना	daak *kaa·*naa
public phone	सार्वजनिक फ़ोन	*saar·*va·ja·nik fon
tourist office	पर्यटन ऑफ़िस	*par·*ya·tan *aa·*fis

Time & Dates

What time is it?
टाइम क्या है?   *taa·*im kyaa hay

It's (10) o'clock.
(दस) बजे हैं ।   (das) ba·*je* hayng

Half past (10).
साढ़े (दस) ।   *saa·*re (das)

morning	सुबह	su·*bah*
afternoon	दोपहर	*do·*pa·har
evening	शाम	shaam
Monday	सोमवार	*som·*vaar
Tuesday	मंगलवार	man·*gal·*vaar
Wednesday	बुधवार	*bud·*vaar
Thursday	गुरुवार	gu·ru·*vaar*
Friday	शुक्रवार	*shuk·*ra·vaar
Saturday	शनिवार	sha·ni·*vaar*
Sunday	रविवार	ra·vi·*vaar*

Transport

When's the ... (bus)?
... (बस) कब जाती है?   ... (bas) kab *jaa·*tee hay

first	पहली	*peh·*lee
last	आख़िरी	*aa·*ki·ree
bicycle	साइकिल	*saa·*i·kil
rickshaw	रिक्शा	*rik·*shaa
boat	जहाज़	ja·*haaz*
bus	बस	bas
plane	हवाई जहाज़	ha·*vaa·*ee ja·*haaz*
train	ट्रेन	tren

a ... ticket
... के लिये टिकट दीजिये ।   ... ke li·*ye* ... ti·*kat* dee·ji·ye

one-way	एक तरफ़ा	ek ta·ra·*faa*
return	आने जाने का	*aa·*ne *jaa·*ne kaa
bus stop	बस स्टॉप	bas *is·*taap
ticket office	टिकटघर	ti·*kat·*gar
timetable	समय सारणी	sa·*mai saa·*ra·nee
train station	स्टेशन	*ste·*shan

Does it stop at ...?
क्या ... में रुकती है?   kyaa ... meng *ruk·*tee hay

Please tell me when we get to ...
जब ... आता है,   jab ... *aa·*taa hay,
मुझे बताइये ।   mu·*je* ba·*taa·*i·ye

Please go straight to this address.
इसी जगह को   *is·*ee ja·*gah* ko
फ़ौरन जाइए ।   *fau·*ran *jaa·*i·ye

Please stop here.
यहाँ रुकिये ।   ya·*haang* ru·ki·ye

TAMIL

Tamil is the official language in the South Indian state of Tamil Nadu. It's one of the major Dravidian languages of South India, with records of its existence going back more than 2000 years. Tamil has about 62 million speakers in India.

Like Hindi, the Tamil sound system includes a number of 'retroflex' consonants (pronounced with the tongue bent backwards). Unlike Hindi, however, Tamil has no 'aspirated' sounds (pronounced with a puff of air). Our simplified pronunciation guides don't distinguish the retroflex consonants from their nonretroflex counterparts – just read the guides as if they were English and you'll be understood. Note that aw is pronounced as in 'law' and ow as in 'how'. The stressed syllables are indicated with italics.

Basics

Hello.	வணக்கம்.	va·*nak*·kam
Goodbye.	போய் வருகிறேன்.	po·i va·*ru*·ki·reyn
Yes./No.	ஆமாம்./இல்லை.	aa·maam/*il*·lai
Excuse me.	தயவு செய்து.	ta·ya·vu sei·*du*
Sorry.	மன்னிக்கவும்.	man·*nik*·ka·vum
Please.	தயவு செய்து.	ta·ya·vu chey·*tu*
Thank you.	நன்றி.	nan·*dri*

Do you speak English?

நீங்கள் ஆங்கிலம் பேசுவீர்களா? — neeng·kal aang·ki·lam pey·chu·*veer*·ka·la

I don't understand.

எனக்கு விளங்கவில்லை. — e·*nak*·ku vi·*lang*·ka·vil·*lai*

Accommodation

Where's a ... nearby?	அருகே ஒரு ... எங்கே உள்ளது?	a·ru·*ke* o·*ru* ... eng·ke *ul*·la·tu
guesthouse	விருந்தினர் இல்லம	vi·*run*·ti·nar *il*·lam
hotel	ஹோட்டல	*hot*·tal

Do you have a ... room?	உங்களிடம் ஓர் ... அறை உள்ளதா?	ung·ka·li·tam awr ... a·*rai* *ul*·la·taa
single	தன	ta·*ni*
double	இரட்டை	i·rat·*tai*

How much is it per ...?	ஓர் ... என்னவிலை?	awr ... en·na·vi·lai
night	இரவுக்கு	i·ra·*vuk*·ku
person	ஒருவருக்கு	o·ru·va·*ruk*·ku

NUMBERS – TAMIL

1	ஒன்று	on·*dru*
2	இரண்டு	i·*ran*·tu
3	மூன்று	moon·dru
4	நான்கு	naan·*ku*
5	ஐந்து	ain·*tu*
6	ஆறு	aa·ru
7	ஏழு	ey·zu
8	எட்டு	et·*tu*
9	ஒன்பது	on·pa·*tu*
10	பத்து	pat·*tu*
20	இருபது	i·ru·pa·*tu*
30	முப்பது	mup·pa·*tu*
40	நாற்பது	naar·pa·*tu*
50	ஐம்பது	aim·pa·*tu*
60	அறுபது	a·ru·pa·*tu*
70	எழுபது	e·zu·pa·*tu*
80	எண்பது	en·pa·*tu*
90	தொன்னூறு	ton·noo·*ru*
100	நூறு	noo·*ru*
1000	ஓராயிரம்	aw·raa·yi·ram

air-conditioned	குளிர்சாதன வசதியுடையது	ku·*lir*·chaa·ta·na va·*cha*·ti·yu·*tai*·ya·tu
bathroom	குளியலறை	ku·*li*·ya·la·rai
bed	படுக்கை	pa·*tuk*·kai
window	சன்னல	*chan*·nal

Eating & Drinking

Can you recommend a ...?	நீங்கள் ஒரு ... பரிந்துரைக்க முடியுமா?	neeng·kal o·ru ... pa·rin·tu·*raik*·ka mu·ti·*yu*·maa
bar	பார்	paar
dish	உணவு வகை	u·na·vu va·*kai*
place to eat	உணவகம்	u·na·va·*ham*

I'd like (a/the) ..., please.	எனக்கு தயவு செய்து ... கொடுங்கள்.	e·*nak*·ku ta·ya·vu chey·*tu* ... ko·*tung*·kal
bill	வீலைச்சீட்டு	vi·*laich*·cheet·tu
menu	உணவுப்– பட்டியல்	u·na·*vup*– pat·ti·yal
that dish	அந்த உணவு வகை	an·ta u·na·vu va·*hai*

Do you have vegetarian food?

உங்களிடம சைவ உணவு உள்ளதா? — ung·ka·li·tam chai·va u·na·vu *ul*·la·taa

Emergencies

Help!
உதவ! u·ta·vi

Go away!
போய் வீடு! pow·i vi·tu

Call a doctor!
ஐ அழைக்கவும் i a·zai·ka·vum
ஒரு மருத்துவர்! o·ru ma·rut·tu·var

Call the police!
ஐ அழைக்கவும் i a·zai·ka·vum
போலீஸ்! pow·lees

I'm lost.
நான் வழி தவறி naan va·zi ta·va·ri
போய்விட்டேன். pow·i·vit·teyn

Where are the toilets?
கழிவறைகள் எங்கே? ka·zi·va·rai·kal eng·key

Shopping & Services

Where's the market?
எங்கே சந்தை eng·key chan·tai
இருக்கிறது? i·ruk·ki·ra·tu

Can I look at it?
நான் இதைப் naan i·taip
பார்க்கலாமா? paark·ka·laa·maa

How much is it?
இது என்ன விலை? i·tu en·na vi·lai

That's too expensive.
அது அதிக விலையாக a·tu a·ti·ka vi·lai·yaa·ka
இருக்கிறது. i·ruk·ki·ra·tu

bank	வங்கி	vang·ki
internet	இணையம்	i·nai·yam
post office	தபால்	ta·paal
	நிலையம்	ni·lai·yam
tourist office	சுற்றுப்பயண	chut·rup·pa·ya·na
	அலுவலகம்	a·lu·va·la·kam

Time & Dates

What time is it?
மணி என்ன? ma·ni en·na

It's (two) o'clock.
மணீ (இரண்டு). ma·ni (i·ran·tu)

Half past (two).
(இரண்டு) முப்பது. (i·ran·tu) mup·pa·tu

yesterday	நேற்று	neyt·tru
today	இன்று	in·dru
tomorrow	நாளை	naa·lai
morning	காலை	kaa·lai
evening	மாலை	maa·lai
night	இரவு	i·ra·vu

Monday	திங்கள்	ting·kal
Tuesday	செவ்வாய்	chev·vai
Wednesday	புதன்	pu·tan
Thursday	வீயாழன்	vi·yaa·zan
Friday	வெள்ளி	vel·li
Saturday	சனி	cha·ni
Sunday	ஞாயிறு	nyaa·yi·ru

Transport & Directions

Where's the ...?
... எங்கே இருக்கிறது? ... eng·key i·ruk·ki·ra·tu

What's the address?
விலாசம் என்ன? vi·laa·cham en·na

Can you show me (on the map)?
எனக்கு (வரைபடத்தில்) e·nak·ku (va·rai·pa·tat·til)
காட்ட முடியுமா? kaat·ta mu·ti·yu·maa

Is this the ... to (New Delhi)?	இது தானா (புது– டில்லிக்குப்) புறப்படும் ...?	i·tu taa·naa (pu·tu til·lik·kup) pu·rap·pa·tum ...
bus	பஸ்	pas
plane	வீமானம்	vi·maa·nam
train	இரயில்	i·ra·yil
One ... ticket (to Madurai), please.	(மதுரைக்கு) தயவு செய்து ... டிக்கட் கொடுங்கள்.	(ma·tu·raik·ku) ta·ya·vu chey·tu ... tik·kat ko·tung·kal
one-way	ஒரு வழிப்பயண	o·ru va·zip·pa·ya·na
return	இரு வழிப்பயண	i·ru va·zip·pa·ya·na
bicycle	சைக்கிள்	chaik·kil
boat	படகு	pa·ta·ku
bus stop	பஸ் நிறுத்தும்	pas ni·rut·tum
economy class	சீக்கன வகுப்பு	chik·ka·na va·kup·pu
first class	முதல் வகுப்பு	mu·tal va·kup·pu
motorcycle	மோட்டார் சைக்கிள்	mowt·taar chaik·kil
train station	நிலையம்	ni·lai·yam

What time's the first/last bus?
எத்தனை மணிக்கு et·ta·nai ma·nik·ku
முதல்/இறுதி mu·tal/i·ru·ti
பஸ் வரும்? pas va·rum

How long does the trip take?
பயணம் எவ்வளவு pa·ya·nam ev·va·la·vu
நேரம் எடுக்கும்? ney·ram e·tuk·kum

GLOSSARY

Adivasis – tribal people

Ardhanarishvara – *Shiva*'s half-male, half-female form

Arjuna – Mahabharata hero and military commander; he had the *Bhagavad Gita* related to him by *Krishna*.

Aryan – Sanskrit for 'noble'; those who migrated from Persia and settled in northern India

ashram – spiritual community or retreat

ASI – Archaeological Survey of India; an organisation involved in monument preservation

autorickshaw – noisy, three-wheeled, motorised contraption for transporting passengers, livestock etc for short distances; found throughout the country, they are cheaper than taxis

Avalokitesvara – in Mahayana Buddhism, the *bodhisattva* of compassion

avatar – incarnation, usually of a deity

ayurveda – ancient and complex science of Indian herbal medicine and holistic healing

azad – Urdu for 'free', as in Azad Jammu and Kashmir

Baba – religious master or father; term of respect

bagh – garden

bahadur – brave or chivalrous; an honorific title

baksheesh – tip, donation (alms) or bribe

banyan – Indian fig tree; spiritual to many Indians

baoli – see *baori*

baori – well, particularly a step-well with landings and galleries; in Gujarat it is more commonly referred to as a *baoli*

barasingha – deer

basti – slum

bearer – like a butler

Bhagavad Gita – Hindu Song of the Divine One; Krishna's lessons to *Arjuna*, the main thrust of which was to emphasise the philosophy of *bhakti*; it is part of the Mahabharata

bhajan – devotional song

bhakti – surrendering to the gods; faith, devotion

bhang – dried leaves and flowering shoots of the marijuana plant

bhangra – rhythmic Punjabi music/dance

Bharat – Hindi for India

bhavan – house, building; also spelt bhawan

Bhima – Mahabharata hero; the brother of Hanuman, husband of Hadimba, father of Ghatotkach, and renowned for his great strength

bindi – forehead mark (often dot-shaped) made from *kumkum*, worn by women

BJP – Bharatiya Janata Party

Bodhi Tree – tree under which *Buddha* sat when he attained enlightenment

bodhisattva – enlightened beings

Bollywood – India's answer to Hollywood; the film industry of Mumbai (Bombay)

Brahma – Hindu god; worshipped as the creator in the Trimurti

Brahmanism – early form of Hinduism that evolved from Vedism (see *Vedas*); named after *Brahmin* priests and *Brahma*

Brahmin – member of the priest/scholar caste, the highest Hindu caste

Buddha – Awakened One; the originator of *Buddhism*; also regarded by Hindus as the ninth incarnation of *Vishnu*

Buddhism – see *Early Buddhism*

cantonment – administrative and military area of a Raj-era town

Carnatic music – classical music of South India

caste – a Hindu's hereditary station (social standing) in life; there are four main castes: Brahmin, Kshatriya, Vaishya and Shudra

chaam – ritual masked dance performed by some Buddhist monks in gompas to celebrate the victory of good over evil and of Buddhism over preexisting religions

chaitya – prayer room; assembly hall

chakra – focus of one's spiritual power; disc-like weapon of *Vishnu*

Chamunda – form of Durga; armed with a scimitar, noose and mace, and clothed in elephant hide, her mission was to kill the demons Chanda and Munda

chandra – moon, or the moon as a god

Chandragupta – Indian ruler in the 3rd century BC

chappals – sandals or leather thonglike footwear; flip-flops

char dham – four pilgrimage destinations of Badrinath, Kedarnath, Yamunotri and Gangotri

charas – resin of the marijuana plant; also referred to as hashish

charbagh – formal Persian garden, divided into quarters (literally 'four gardens')

chedi – see *chaitya*

chhatri – cenotaph (literally 'umbrella'),or pavilion

chikan – embroidered cloth (speciality of Lucknow)

chillum – pipe of a hookah; commonly used to describe the pipes used for smoking ganja (marijuana)

chinkara – gazelle

chital – spotted deer

chogyal – king

choli – sari blouse

chorten – Tibetan for stupa

choultry – pilgrim's rest house; also called dharamsala

chowk – town square, intersection or marketplace

Cong (I) – Congress Party of India; also known as Congress (I)

coracle – a small, traditional keel-less boat, often round or oval in shape, comprising a wickerwork or lath frame over which greased cloth or hide is stretched

dagoba – see *stupa*

Dalit – preferred term for India's Untouchable caste; see also *Harijan*

dargah – shrine or place of burial of a Muslim saint

darshan – offering or audience with a deity

deul – temple sanctuary

Devi – *Shiva*'s wife; goddess

dhaba – basic restaurant or snack bar

dham – holiest pilgrimage places of India

dharamsala – pilgrim's rest house

dharma – for Hindus, the moral code of behaviour or social duty; for Buddhists, following the law of nature, or path, as taught by Buddha

dhobi – person who washes clothes; commonly referred to as dhobi-wallah

dhobi ghat – place where clothes are washed

dhoti – long loincloth worn by men; like a lungi, but the ankle-length cloth is then pulled up between the legs

Digambara – 'Sky-Clad'; Jain group that demonstrates disdain for worldly goods by going naked

diwan – principal officer in a princely state; royal court or council

Diwan-i-Am – hall of public audience

Diwan-i-Khas – hall of private audience

dowry – money and/or goods given by a bride's parents to their son-in-law's family; it's illegal but still widely exists in many arranged marriages

Draupadi – wife of the five Pandava princes in the Mahabharata

Dravidian – general term for the cultures and languages of the deep south of India, including Tamil, Malayalam, Telugu and Kannada

dukhang – Tibetan prayer hall

dun – valley

dupatta – long scarf for women often worn with the *salwar kameez*

durbar – royal court; also a government

Durga – the Inaccessible; a form of *Shiva*'s wife, Devi, a beautiful, fierce woman riding a tiger/lion; a major goddess of the *Shakti* order

Early Buddhism – any of the schools of Buddhism established directly after Buddha's death and before the advent of Mahayana; a modern form is the Theravada (Teaching of the Elders) practised in Sri Lanka and Southeast Asia; Early Buddhism differed from the Mahayana in that it did not teach the *bodhisattva* ideal

gabba – appliquéd Kashmiri rug

gali – lane or alleyway

Ganesh – Hindu god of good fortune; elephant-headed son of *Shiva* and Parvati, he is also known as Ganpati and his vehicle is Mooshak (a ratlike creature)

Ganga – Hindu goddess representing the sacred Ganges River; said to flow from *Vishnu*'s toe

ganj – market

gaon – village

garh – fort

Garuda – man-bird vehicle of *Vishnu*

gaur – Indian bison

Gayatri – sacred verse of Rig-Veda repeated mentally by Brahmins twice a day

geyser – hot-water unit found in many bathrooms

ghat – steps or landing on a river; a range of hills or a road up hills

giri – hill

gompa – Tibetan Buddhist monastery

Gopala – see *Govinda*

gopi – milkmaid; Krishna was fond of gopis

gopuram – soaring pyramidal gateway tower of Dravidian temples

Govinda – Krishna as a cowherd; also just cowherd

gumbad – dome on an Islamic tomb or mosque

gurdwara – Sikh temple

guru – holy teacher; in Sanskrit literally 'goe' (darkness) and 'roe' (to dispel)

Guru Granth Sahib – Sikh holy book

haat – village market

haj – Muslim pilgrimage to Mecca

haji – Muslim who has made the haj

hammam – Turkish bath; public bathhouse

Hanuman – Hindu monkey god, prominent in the Ramayana, and a follower of Rama

Hari – another name for *Vishnu*

Harijan – name (no longer considered acceptable) given by Mahatma Gandhi to India's Untouchable caste, meaning 'children of god'

hashish – see *charas*

hathi – elephant

haveli – traditional, often ornately decorated, residences, particularly those found in Rajasthan and Gujarat

hijab – headscarf used by Muslim women

hijra – eunuch, transvestite

hookah – water pipe used for smoking marijuana or strong tobacco

howdah – seat for carrying people on an elephant's back

ikat – fabric made with thread which is tie-dyed before weaving

imam – Muslim religious leader

imambara – tomb dedicated to a Shiite Muslim holy man

Indo-Saracenic – style of colonial architecture that integrated Western designs with Islamic, Hindu and Jain influences

Indra – significant and prestigious Vedic god; god of rain, thunder, lightning and war

jagamohan – assembly hall

Jagannath – Lord of the Universe; a form of Krishna

jali – carved lattice (often marble) screen; also refers to the holes or spaces produced through carving timber or stone

Jataka – tale from Buddha's various lives

jauhar – ritual mass suicide by immolation, traditionally performed by Rajput women at times of military defeat to avoid being dishonoured by their captors

jhula – bridge

ji – honorific that can be added to the end of almost anything as a form of respect; thus 'Babaji', 'Gandhiji'

jooti – traditional, often pointy-toed, slip-in shoes; commonly found in North India

juggernaut – huge, extravagantly decorated temple 'car' dragged through the streets during certain Hindu festivals

jyoti linga – naturally occurring lingam believed to derive currents of *Shakti*

kabaddi – traditional game (similar to tag)

Kailasa – sacred Himalayan mountain; home of *Shiva*

Kali – ominous-looking evil-destroying form of Devi; commonly depicted with dark skin, dripping with blood, and wearing a necklace of skulls

Kama – Hindu god of love

Kama Sutra – ancient Sanskrit text largely covering the subjects of love and sexuality

kameez – woman's shirtlike tunic; see also *salwar kameez*

karma – Hindu, Buddhist and Sikh principle of retributive justice for past deeds

khadi – homespun cloth; Mahatma Gandhi encouraged people to spin this rather than buy English cloth

Khalsa – Sikh brotherhood

Khan – Muslim honorific title

khur – Asiatic wild ass

kirtan – Sikh devotional singing

koil – Hindu temple

kolam – see *rangoli*

kot – fort

kothi – residence or mansion

kotwali – police station

Krishna – *Vishnu's* eighth incarnation, often coloured blue; he revealed the *Bhagavad Gita* to *Arjuna*

kumkum – coloured powder used for *bindi* dots

kund – lake or tank; Toda village

kurta – long shirt with either short collar or no collar

Lakshmana – half-brother and aide of Rama in the Ramayana

Lakshmi – *Vishnu's* consort, Hindu goddess of wealth; she sprang forth from the ocean holding a lotus

lama – Tibetan Buddhist priest or monk

Laxmi – see *Lakshmi*

lingam – phallic symbol; auspicious symbol of *Shiva*; plural 'linga'

lok – people

Lok Sabha – lower house in the Indian parliament (House of the People)

Losar – Tibetan New Year

lungi – worn by men, this loose, coloured garment (similar to a sarong) is pleated by the wearer at the waist to fit

madrasa – Islamic seminary

maha – prefix meaning 'great'

Mahabharata – Great Hindu Vedic epic poem of the Bharata dynasty; containing approximately 10,000 verses describing the battle between the Pandavas and the Kauravas

Mahakala – Great Time; *Shiva* and one of 12 jyoti linga (sacred shrines)

mahal – house or palace

maharaja – literally 'great king'; princely ruler

maharana – see *maharaja*

maharani – wife of a princely ruler or a ruler in her own right

maharao – see *maharaja*

maharawal – see *maharaja*

mahatma – literally 'great soul'

Mahavir – last tirthankar

Mahayana – the 'greater-vehicle' of Buddhism; a later adaptation of the teaching that lays emphasis on the *bodhisattva* ideal, teaching the renunciation of nirvana in order to help other beings along the way to enlightenment

maidan – open (often grassed) area; parade ground

Maitreya – future Buddha

mandal – shrine

mandala – circle; symbol used in Hindu and Buddhist art to symbolise the universe

mandapa – pillared pavilion, temple forechamber

mandi – market

mandir – temple

mani stone – stone carved with the Tibetan-Buddhist mantra 'Om mani padme hum' ('Hail the jewel in the lotus')

mani walls – Tibetan stone walls with sacred inscriptions

mantra – sacred word or syllable used by Buddhists and Hindus to aid concentration; metrical psalms of praise found in the *Vedas*

Maratha – central Indian people who controlled much of India at various times and fought the Mughals and Rajputs

marg – road

masjid – mosque

mata – mother

math – monastery

maya – illusion

mehndi – henna; ornate henna designs on women's hands (and often feet), traditionally for certain festivals or ceremonies (eg marriage)

mela – fair or festival

mithuna – pairs of men and women; often seen in temple sculpture

Moghul – see *Mughal*

monsoon – rainy season

muezzin – one who calls Muslims to prayer, traditionally from the minaret of a mosque

Mughal – Muslim dynasty of subcontinental emperors from Babur to Aurangzeb

Mumbaikar – resident of Mumbai (Bombay)

namaste – traditional Hindu greeting (hello or goodbye), often accompanied by a respectful small bow with the hands together at the chest or head level

Nanda – cowherd who raised Krishna

Nandi – bull, vehicle of *Shiva*

Narayan – incarnation of *Vishnu* the creator

Nataraja – *Shiva* as the cosmic dancer

nawab – Muslim ruling prince or powerful landowner

Naxalites – ultra-leftist political movement begun in West Bengal as a peasant rebellion; characterised by violence

nilgai – antelope

nirvana – ultimate aim of Buddhists and the final release from the cycle of existence

niwas – house, building

nizam – hereditary title of the rulers of Hyderabad

nullah – ditch or small stream

Om – sacred invocation representing the essence of the divine principle; for Buddhists, if repeated often enough with complete concentration, it leads to a state of emptiness

Osho – the late Bhagwan Shree Rajneesh, a popular, controversial guru

paan – mixture of betel nut and leaves for chewing

padma – lotus; another name for the Hindu goddess Lakshmi

pagoda – see *stupa*

paise – the Indian rupee is divided into 100 paise

palanquin – boxlike enclosure carried on poles on four bearer's shoulders; the occupant sits inside on a seat

Pali – the language, related to Sanskrit, in which the Buddhist scriptures were recorded; scholars still refer to the original Pali texts

pandal – marquee; temple shrine

Parsi – adherent of the Zoroastrian faith

Partition – formal division of British India in 1947 into two separate countries, India and Pakistan

Parvati – another form of Devi

pashmina – fine woollen shawl

PCO – Public Call Office, from where you can make local, interstate and international phone calls

peepul – fig tree, especially a bo tree

peon – lowest-grade clerical worker

pietra dura – marble inlay work characteristic of the Taj Mahal

pradesh – state

pranayama – study of breath control; meditative practice

prasad – temple-blessed food offering

puja – literally 'respect'; offering or prayers

pukka – proper; a Raj-era term

punka – cloth fan, swung by pulling a cord

Puranas – set of 18 encyclopaedic Sanskrit stories, written in verse, relating to the three gods, dating from the 5th century AD

purdah – custom among some conservative Muslims (also adopted by some Hindus, especially the Rajputs) of keeping women in seclusion; veiled

Purnima – full moon; considered to be an auspicious time

qawwali – Islamic devotional singing

qila – fort

Quran – the holy book of Islam, also spelt Koran

Radha – Krishna's consort and the most revered of the gopis

raga – any of several conventional patterns of melody and rhythm that form the basis for freely interpreted compositions

railhead – station or town at the end of a railway line; termination point

raj – rule or sovereignty; British Raj (sometimes just Raj) refers to British rule

raja – king; sometimes rana

rajkumar – prince

Rajput – Hindu warrior caste, former rulers of northwestern India

Rama – seventh incarnation of *Vishnu*

Ramadan – Islamic holy month of sunrise-to-sunset fasting (no eating, drinking or smoking); also referred to as Ramazan

Ramayana – story of Rama and Sita and their conflict with Ravana; one of India's best-known epics

rana – king; sometimes raja

rangoli – elaborate chalk, rice-paste or coloured powder design; also known as kolam

rani – female ruler or wife of a king

ranns – deserts

rath – temple chariot or car used in religious festivals

rathas – rock-cut Dravidian temples

Ravana – demon king of Lanka who abducted Sita; the titanic battle between him and Rama is told in the Ramayana

rickshaw – small, two- or three-wheeled passenger vehicle

Rig-Veda – original and longest of the four main *Vedas*

rishi – any poet, philosopher, saint or sage; originally a sage to whom the hymns of the *Vedas* were revealed

Road – railway town that serves as a communication point to a larger town off the line, eg Mt Abu and Abu Road

Rukmani – wife of Krishna; died on his funeral pyre

sadar – main

sadhu – ascetic, holy person, one who is trying to achieve enlightenment; often addressed as 'swamiji' or 'babaji'

sagar – lake, reservoir

sahib – respectful title applied to a gentleman

salai – road

salwar – trousers usually worn with a kameez

salwar kameez – traditional dresslike tunic and trouser combination for women

samadhi – in Hinduism, ecstatic state, sometimes defined as 'ecstasy, trance, communion with God'; in Buddhism, concentration; also a place where a holy man has been cremated/buried, usually venerated as a shrine

sambar – deer

samsara – Buddhists, Hindus and Sikhs believe earthly life is cyclical; you are born again and again, the quality of these rebirths being dependent upon your karma in previous lives

sangha – community of Buddhist monks and nuns

Saraswati – wife of Brahma, goddess of learning; sits on a white swan, holding a veena (a type of string instrument)

Sat Sri Akal – Sikh greeting

Sati – wife of *Shiva*; became a sati ('honourable woman') by immolating herself; although banned more than a century ago, the act of sati is still (very) occasionally performed

satra – Hindu Vaishnavaite monastery and centre for art

satyagraha – nonviolent protest involving a hunger strike, popularised by Mahatma Gandhi; from Sanskrit, literally meaning 'insistence on truth'

Scheduled Castes – official term used for the Untouchable or Dalit caste

Shaivism – worship of *Shiva*

Shaivite – follower of *Shiva*

shakti – creative energies perceived as female deities; devotees follow Shaktism order

sheesha – see *hookah*

shikara – gondola-like boat used on lakes in Srinagar (Kashmir)

shikhar – hunting expedition

Shiva – Destroyer; also the Creator, in which form he is worshipped as a lingam

shola – virgin forest

shree – see *shri*

shri – honorific male prefix; Indian equivalent of 'Respected Sir'

Shudra – caste of labourers

sikhara – Hindu temple-spire or temple

Singh – literally 'lion'; a surname adopted by Sikhs

Sita – Hindu goddess of agriculture; more commonly associated with the Ramayana

sitar – Indian stringed instrument

Siva – see *Shiva*

sree – see *shri*

sri – see *shri*

stupa – Buddhist religious monument composed of a solid hemisphere topped by a spire, containing relics of Buddha; also known as a *dagoba* or *pagoda*

Subhadra – Krishna's incestuous sister

Sufi – Muslim mystic

Sufism – Islamic mysticism

Surya – the sun; a major deity in the *Vedas*

sutra – string; list of rules expressed in verse

swami – title of respect meaning 'lord of the self'; given to initiated Hindu monks

tabla – twin drums

tal – lake

tank – reservoir; pool or large receptacle of holy water found at some temples

tantric Buddhism – Tibetan Buddhism with strong sexual and occult overtones

tempo – noisy three-wheeler public transport vehicle, bigger than an *autorickshaw*; see *Vikram*

thakur – nobleman

thangka – Tibetan cloth painting

theertham – temple tank

Theravada – orthodox form of Buddhism practised in Sri Lanka and Southeast Asia that is characterised by its adherence to the Pali canon; literally 'dwelling'

tikka – mark Hindus put on their foreheads

tirthankars – the 24 great Jain teachers

tonga – two-wheeled horse or pony carriage

torana – architrave over a temple entrance

trekkers – jeeps; hikers

Trimurti – triple form or three-faced; the Hindu triad of *Brahma*, *Shiva* and *Vishnu*

Untouchable – lowest caste or 'casteless', for whom the most menial tasks are reserved; the name derives from the belief that higher castes risk defilement if they touch one; formerly known as *Harijan*, now *Dalit*

Upanishads – esoteric doctrine; ancient texts forming part of the *Vedas*; delving into weighty matters such as the nature of the universe and soul

urs – death anniversary of a revered Muslim; festival in memory of a Muslim saint

Valmiki – author of the Ramayana

Vedas – Hindu sacred books; collection of hymns composed in preclassical Sanskrit during the second millennium BC and divided into four books: Rig-Veda, Yajur-Veda, Sama-Veda and Atharva-Veda

vihara – Buddhist monastery, generally with central court or hall off which open residential cells, usually with a Buddha shrine at one end; resting place

vikram – tempo or a larger version of the standard tempo

vimana – principal part of Hindu temple; a tower over the sanctum

vipassana – insight meditation technique of Theravada Buddhism in which mind and body are closely examined as changing phenomena

Vishnu – part of the Trimurti; Vishnu is the Preserver and Restorer who so far has nine *avatars*: the fish Matsya; the tortoise Kurma; the wild boar Naraha; Narasimha; Vamana; Parasurama; Rama; Krishna; and Buddha

wallah – man; added onto almost anything, eg dhobi-wallah, chai-wallah, taxi-wallah

yakshi – maiden

yali – mythical lion creature

yatra – pilgrimage

yatri – pilgrim

yogini – female goddess attendants

yoni – female fertility symbol; female genitalia

zenana – area of an upperclass home where women are secluded; women's quarters

Behind the Scenes

SEND US YOUR FEEDBACK

We love to hear from travellers – your comments keep us on our toes and help make our books better. Our well-travelled team reads every word on what you loved or loathed about this book. Although we cannot reply individually to your submissions, we always guarantee that your feedback goes straight to the appropriate authors, in time for the next edition. Each person who sends us information is thanked in the next edition – the most useful submissions are rewarded with a selection of digital PDF chapters.

Visit **lonelyplanet.com/contact** to submit your updates and suggestions or to ask for help. Our award-winning website also features inspirational travel stories, news and discussions.

Note: We may edit, reproduce and incorporate your comments in Lonely Planet products such as guidebooks, websites and digital products, so let us know if you don't want your comments reproduced or your name acknowledged. For a copy of our privacy policy visit lonelyplanet.com/privacy.

OUR READERS

Many thanks to the travellers who used the last edition and wrote to us with helpful hints, useful advice and interesting anecdotes:

A Aar Nuss, Adi Bloom, Alerta Suvion, Alex Jones, Alexa Owen, Alice Bell, Alwin Siegersma, Amy Benson, Andrea Andersen, Andrew Johnson, Andy Brown, Anne D'heygers, Anne & Michel Ropion, Avril Ingram **B** Bar Sayada, Behemoth Lopez, Benoit Valdelievre, Bernhard Bouzek, Bronte Rhodes **C** Carrie Campbell, Catherine Heintz, Cerafin Lampion, Charlotte Bibby, Charlotte De Val, Chris Beales, Cindy Bendat, Cord Rehren, Craig Wilson, Cyriac Schmit **D** Daniel Brewer, David Hanslian **E** Emily Crawford, Estela Roman **F** Faezah Sani, François Béga, Francois-Alexandre Tremblay, Frank Damato **G** Gayle Wells, Geoff Spencer, Gerard Hengeveld, Ginevra Massari, Graeme Spedding, Guenter Gloeckle, Guy Kohn, Guy Saunders **H** Hanna Tadesse, Hans Heckel, Hidde Jansen, Hironobu Ichikawa, Hoel Achermann, Holly Pearson **I** Ian Curwen, Indara Rodriguez, Indrani Ganguly, Itamar Weissbein **J** Jadwiga Rudy, James Clark, James Nolan, James Wales, Jay Prasuna, Jeffrey Gold, Jessica Smith, Jessica Tracey, Jo Kirkpatrick, Joanna Schmidt, John Fuhrman, Jon Dean, Jon Vegard, Jordan Thomas, Jozef Avgoustakis, Julian Vadas, Jyoti Careswell **K** Kacie Youso, Kamal Paliwal, Kate Vallance, Ken Badenoch, Ken Lau, Kevin Parsons, Kevin Yuih, Koisty Jones **L** Laska Pare, Laura Monfort, Laurent Guillet, Lenita Canon, Lily Martens, Linda Johansson, Linda Vega & Rowan Fraser, Lisa Chung, Lodewijk Portielje **M** Maarten Dallinga, Marcel Ottiger, Marcel Phaf, Maria Morera, Mark Anderson, Mark Bell, Markus Kremmler, Marta Rasi, Martin Salamanca, Mary Fairfield, Matan Gilat, Michael Snaith, Michal Sasson, Mick Radford, Milena Schulz, Molshree Aggarwal **N** Nadav Atik, Niccki Brooks, Nicholas Tippins, Nikesh Jethva, Noele Phillips, Ntsiki Anderson **O** Oliver Heard, Olwen Herbison, Orian Shalev **P** Patrick Berg, Pernilla Becker, Peter Walker, Petra O'Neill, Philippa Watts **R** Rachel Hirschi, Rachel Savin, Rafael Higuerars, Reinout Hekel, Renata Grabowska, Richard Gordon, Richard Jenkins, Rishabh Jain, Robin Hedges, Robyn Williams, Rod Little, Roya Rouzbehani, Rupert Hart, Ryrie Bridges **S** Sajid Chougle, Sam Burns, Sanne van Heuveln, Shah Singh, Shelby Sangster, Sion Massip, Sue Sullman, Suzanne Jacob & David Lloyd **T** Tania Sadler, Tanneke Huttner, Terry Rugg, Tom Salman, Tom Stuart, Tony Walmsley **U** Uwe Müller **V** Veronika Stalz, Viacheslav Shuper, Vishvas Vasuki **W** William Cousins **X** Xaver Reinhardt & Jaqueline Mayer **Y** Yulia Yulish, Yuma Nakamura

AUTHOR THANKS

Sarina Singh

Coordinating a book of this scale was a delight thanks to a dedicated team of accomplished writers and editorial staff – massive thanks to you all. Gratitude, also, to our many readers who took the time to send in their feedback and share travel experiences. Finally, warm thanks to my parents for being so incredibly awesome.

Michael Benanav

Huge thanks to Lalji, Neeta, Sonal, Ashwin and their families, for their hospitality and ever-deeper insights into all things Gujarati. In Uttarakhand, thanks go to Manto and Debopam for help getting beneath the surface of the state. A special thanks to Adina, for running down a few details for me, for picking up that book about Rajula Malushahi, and for entertaining musings on the terrace in Kasar Devi. And thanks to Kelly and Luke, for keeping everything cool back home.

Abigail Blasi

Thank you Joe Bindloss and Sarina Singh, CE and CA supreme, and to my wonderful co-authors. Thanks in Delhi to Sarah Fotheringham, to Nicolas Thompson and Danish Abbas, to Dilliwala Mayank Austen Soofi, to Rajinder and Surinder Budhraja, to Niranjan and Jyoti Desai, my Delhi family, and to Luca for holding the fort.

Paul Clammer

Thanks – and apologies – to everyone I met on the road who helped with research, without realising that Rajasthan is a place best covered anonymously for Lonely Planet. I wish I could have told you what I was doing! It would have been immeasurably harder however if I hadn't had a confidante along the way, so my biggest thanks and love go to Robyn – sidekick and constant companion, in India as she is everywhere else I go. In Fatehpur and Bikaner, thank you Jean for the limericks and the gin, and in Pushkar, Anna Voss for the fairy lights and being a lovely neighbour. Thank you also to fellow authors Sarina Singh, and Daniel McCrohan for the kebabs, Karim's and Kingfishers in Delhi.

Mark Elliott

Many thanks to Rouf and family in Srinagar, Najum, Hamza and Muzamil in Kargil, Rajesh, Mowgli, Jai and Bunny in Kolkata, high-flying Simone, Aadil in Anantnag, Selim and Chamba in Leh, Stenzin Motup, Jaweed Ahmad, Zalina and Nabila, Lal Kumar, Sumit, Tony and Inge, Sophie, Tim and the crazy Nimaling yoga gang. Bless you Kate for joining the Himalayan adventures and making the treks so much more memorable. Eternal thanks as ever to my beloved parents.

Paul Harding

Thanks to Hannah and Layla for accompanying me to Goa and putting up with my absence while in Kerala. Cheers to Joe for entrusting me with such a great part of India. In India, thanks to all who offered advice and company but especially to all the friends in Goa and Kerala that I met up with again – you all know who you are!

Trent Holden

Thanks first up to Joe Bindloss for giving me the opportunity again to work again on India – a seriously dream gig. As well as to my co-authors, especially Sarina for all the help and tips along the way. A shout out to all the good folk I met along the road and shared a beer with. But as always my biggest thanks goes to my beautiful girlfriend Kate, and my family and friends who I all miss back home in Melbourne.

Anirban Mahapatra

My thanks, as always, to the entire editorial and production team at Lonely Planet, and to my awesome fellow authors for making this colossal project a reality. On the ground (in no particular order), my sincerest thanks to Sangey, Oken, Aaron, Audrey, Babul, Monjit,

THIS BOOK

This 16th edition of Lonely Planet's *India* guidebook was researched and written by Sarina Singh, Abigail Blasi, Michael Benanav, Paul Clammer, Mark Elliott, Paul Harding, Trent Holden, Anirban Mahapatra, Daniel McCrohan, Isabella Noble, John Noble, Kevin Raub and Iain Stewart.

This guidebook was produced by the following:

Destination Editor
Joe Bindloss

Product Editors Kate Mathews, Alison Ridgway

Book Designer
Katherine Marsh

Assisting Book Designer
Clara Monitto

Assisting Editors Kate Chapman, Nigel Chin, Melanie Dankell, Kate Evans, Carly Hall, Gabbi Innes, Kellie Langdon, Rosie Nicholson, Samantha Forge, Paul Harding, Victoria Harrison, Kate Kiely, Lauren O'Connell, Kathryn Rowan, Gabrielle Stefanos, Ross Taylor, Jeanette Wall

Cover Researcher
Naomi Parker

Thanks to Lonely Planet Cartography, Wayne Murphy, Ellie Simpson

Jyoti, Anit, Nino, Kanno, Bambang, Hoihnu, Yishey, Hemanta, Rahul, Norden, Hemlata, Rintu, Binod, Ajay and Boomoni for all their help in fields as diverse as spirited long-distance driving, logistical troubleshooting, local knowledge, culinary prowess and, above all, for being great hosts, co-travellers and friends in general. Finally, hats off to Castleton Tea Estate, for their awesome teas that kept me awake through the wee writing hours.

Daniel McCrohan

My biggest thanks goes to my uncle, David Campos, who had to put up with me dragging him round half of India, just so that I could have some company on my trip! All my love, too, to the rest of my family back home, especially my darling wife and our two amazing children. In Punjab, thank you to Bimla Lyall MBE for a fascinating introduction to Sikhism (and for being the first person I've met who's got an MBE!). In Odisha, thanks to John Duncan and the rest of the Southampton University research team. And many thanks to my colleagues Kevin Raub, Mark Elliott and Trent Holden for tips and advice.

Isabella Noble

Cheers to everyone who helped out in Tamil Nadu, Ashish and Rucha Gupta for endless hospitality, Bernard Dragon and Rom Whitaker, and Junaid Sait for saving the day when I forgot to book Ooty accommodation. Special thanks to fellow authors Abi and Sarina for girl support, and to Andrew for Pondy fun and keeping me sane in Trichy. At home, huge thanks to Jacky and Paps for the laughs and advice. Mostly, to Susan Forsyth, for being there always.

John Noble

Thanks to everybody in India who answered my questions, pointed me in the right direction and helped with the logistics of a fabulous trip, especially Sumit Raj Vashisht, Jakamur Chauhan, Jonty Rajagopalan, Ashish and Rucha Gupta, Praveen Sood, the Dhami family of Chamba, Karanbir Singh Bedi, Ankit Sood and Vaneet Rana. Thanks also to Alice McGuigan and Sarina Singh and the fantastic author team, especially Isabella Noble with whom it was wonderful to share so much of this project!

Kevin Raub

Thanks to my wife, Adriana Schmidt Raub, who gladly ships me off to India without her! Joe Bindloss; at LP On the road, Anil Whadwa, Mini-Google, Shiron Haider, Shibab Haider, Naghma Haider, Aisha Khan, Mukal Kumar, Guatam Singh, Megha Singh, Naheed Varma, Harish Rijhwani, Malika Rijhwani, Rochikant Mishra, Nicole Seregni, Fernanda Polacow, Marta Delellis, Rashi Rajoria, R.K. Rai, Saptarishi Saigal, Awesh Ali, Eli Rasaero and Ivan and Pixie Lamech.

Iain Stewart

It was great to hang with Laksh in Bandra and have a virtual beer with Paul Harding by the sea. Thanks to the good folk at the MTDC all over the state, particularly Mr Shaker and Mrs Singh in Mumbai. I'm also very grateful to Aditya in Nagpur and Tadoba, Maria in Matheran and the merry musicians of Kolhapur.

ACKNOWLEDGMENTS

Climate map data adapted from Peel MC, Finlayson BL & McMahon TA (2007) 'Updated World Map of the Köppen-Geiger Climate Classification', Hydrology and Earth System Sciences, 11, 163344.

Illustrations pp1160-1, pp1162-3, p1164 by Kelli Hamblet; pp370-1, pp874-5 by Michael Weldon; pp623, pp356-7, pp640-1 by Javier Zarracina.

Cover photograph: Taj Mahal, Agra/Peter Adams/AWL.

Index

INDEX H

Map Legend

Sights

- Beach
- Bird Sanctuary
- Buddhist
- Castle/Palace
- Christian
- Confucian
- Hindu
- Islamic
- Jain
- Jewish
- Monument
- Museum/Gallery/Historic Building
- Ruin
- Shinto
- Sikh
- Taoist
- Winery/Vineyard
- Zoo/Wildlife Sanctuary
- Other Sight

Activities, Courses & Tours

- Bodysurfing
- Diving
- Canoeing/Kayaking
- Course/Tour
- Sento Hot Baths/Onsen
- Skiing
- Snorkelling
- Surfing
- Swimming/Pool
- Walking
- Windsurfing
- Other Activity

Sleeping

- Sleeping
- Camping

Eating

- Eating

Drinking & Nightlife

- Drinking & Nightlife
- Cafe

Entertainment

- Entertainment

Shopping

- Shopping

Information

- Bank
- Embassy/Consulate
- Hospital/Medical
- @ Internet
- Police
- Post Office
- Telephone
- Toilet
- Tourist Information
- Other Information

Geographic

- Beach
- Hut/Shelter
- Lighthouse
- Lookout
- ▲ Mountain/Volcano
- Oasis
- Park
-)(Pass
- Picnic Area
- Waterfall

Population

- Capital (National)
- Capital (State/Province)
- City/Large Town
- Town/Village

Transport

- Airport
- Border crossing
- Bus
- Cable car/Funicular
- Cycling
- Ferry
- Metro station
- Monorail
- Parking
- Petrol station
- Subway station
- Taxi
- Train station/Railway
- Tram
- Underground station
- Other Transport

Routes

- Tollway
- Freeway
- Primary
- Secondary
- Tertiary
- Lane
- Unsealed road
- Road under construction
- Plaza/Mall
- Steps
-)- - Tunnel
- Pedestrian overpass
- Walking Tour
- Walking Tour detour
- Path/Walking Trail

Boundaries

- International
- State/Province
- Disputed
- Regional/Suburb
- Marine Park
- Cliff
- Wall

Hydrography

- River, Creek
- Intermittent River
- Canal
- Water
- Dry/Salt/Intermittent Lake
- Reef

Areas

- Airport/Runway
- Beach/Desert
- + + Cemetery (Christian)
- × × Cemetery (Other)
- Glacier
- Mudflat
- Park/Forest
- Sight (Building)
- Sportsground
- Swamp/Mangrove

Note: Not all symbols displayed above appear on the maps in this book

Isabella Noble

Tamil Nadu & Chennai Isabella's first experience of South India was a masala dosa at Shimla's Indian Coffee House. She has been travelling to India for over five years, but loves the ever-so-slightly more laid-back pace of the friendly South. This time she got lost in Valparai's tea plantations, checked out Chennai's countless bars, then got stuck in the Nilgiris thanks to landslide. Between trips, Isabella lives in London with a wardrobe of Indian shawls. She tweets @isabellamnoble.

Read more about Isabella at:
http://auth.lonelyplanet.com/profiles/isabellanoble

John Noble

Himachal Pradesh, Telangana & Andhra Pradesh John, from England, has written about 20-odd countries for Lonely Planet, including covering six very different Indian states for editions of this book. He loves returning to the subcontinent because, in a nutshell, there's never a dull moment there! Biggest thrills of this trip: getting back into the Himalaya (the world's most wonderful landscapes) and travelling the unbelievable Kinnaur-Spiti loop, and, as a long-time fan of William Dalrymple's *White Mughals*, exploring fascinating Hyderabad. He tweets @john_a_noble and Instagrams as johnnoble11.

Read more about John at:
http://auth.lonelyplanet.com/profiles/ewoodrover

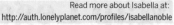

Kevin Raub

Agra & the Taj Mahal, Uttar Pradesh, Madhya Pradesh & Chhattisgarh Kevin Raub grew up in Atlanta and started his career as a music journalist in New York, working for *Men's Journal* and *Rolling Stone* magazines. He ditched the rock 'n' roll lifestyle for travel writing and moved to Brazil. On his 8th epic Indian journey, Kevin was only out-spiced by an Indian chef once and never outsmarted by a rickshaw driver. This is Kevin's 30th Lonely Planet guide. Follow him on Twitter (@RaubOnTheRoad).

Read more about Kevin at:
http://auth.lonelyplanet.com/profiles/kraub

Iain Stewart

Mumbai (Bombay), Maharashtra Iain grew up in Leicester, a very Indian town transplanted to the Midlands, UK (complete with its own curry mile). He first visited India in 1991 and explored the sights at totally the wrong time of year with temperatures approaching 50°C in parts. For this trip he wised up and travelled post-monsoon: bar-hopping in Mumbai, meandering down the Konkan coast and having several near-misses with tigers in Tadoba.

Paul Clammer

Rajasthan Paul Clammer has contributed to over 25 Lonely Planet guidebooks, and worked as a tour guide in countries from Turkey to Morocco. In a previous life he may even have been a molecular biologist. He first covered India for LP back in 2004, up in the Himalayas, so jumped at the chance to explore Rajasthan in more depth this time around, staying on to write the chapter in a converted temple in Pushkar, where it was necessary to lock the doors to stop monkeys stealing his notes. Follow @paulclammer on Twitter.

Mark Elliott

Jammu & Kashmir, Kolkata (Calcutta) Mark has been making forays to the subcontinent since a 1984 ultra-budget adventure that lined his stomach for all eventualities. In various trips to J&K he has been stuck in two Kashmiri curfews, luckily sidestepped the 2010 Leh flash-floods and narrowly dodged the Srinagar deluge of 2014. He remains passionately enamoured of the region's people and landscapes while considering Kolkata India's most inspiring mega-city.

Paul Harding

Goa, Kerala Paul first landed in India in the mid-90s and has returned regularly over the years, usually writing about it. He still has a soft spot for the south, where the pace of life is slower, the food tastier and the beer (usually) colder. For this edition he was fortunate enough to return to Goa and Kerala where he researched beaches and backwaters, homestays and bamboo huts, seafood curries and chicken xacutis. This was Paul's 9th assignment on India and the second with his intrepid young daughter.

Trent Holden

Karnataka & Bengaluru, Andaman Islands On his third time co-authoring the India book, Trent was assigned with the not-so-shabby task of testing out Bengaluru's microbreweries, searching for tigers in Bandipur NP and checking out Hampi's ruins before hitting the beaches in Gokarna. He then returned to the Andaman Islands for more sun, surf and sand. A freelance travel writer based in London, Trent also covers destinations such as Nepal, Zimbabwe and Japan. In between travels he writes about food and music. You can catch him on Twitter @hombreholden.

Anirban Mahapatra

West Bengal & Darjeeling, Sikkim, Northeast States Anirban started his career as a newspaper reporter in 2004, but transitioned into travel journalism some years later after realising that all the good things in life awaited him on the open road. A Lonely Planet author since 2007, he specialises on India and the Subcontinent, and loves to trundle routinely through the hinterlands of East and Northeast India, sampling the awesome culture and cuisine of the region. A closet Buddhist (and probably a reborn lama), he takes special interest in Himalayan traditions. Apart from writing, Anirban currently also works on photographic and video projects. He lives in Kolkata.

Daniel McCrohan

Haryana & Punjab, Bihar & Jharkhand, Odisha Daniel has been writing for Lonely Planet about India and China for almost a decade now. Originally from the UK, he's based in Beijing these days, but has been travelling to India, on and off, since the early 1990s. This is his 23rd Lonely Planet book, and his fourth successive stint on India. Daniel is also the creator of the smartphone app Beijing on a Budget, a host on the travel show Best in China and a 'travel ninja' for planmy. travel. You can contact him through his website, danielmccrohan.com.

Read more about Daniel at:
http://auth.lonelyplanet.com/profiles/danielmccrohan

OUR STORY

A beat-up old car, a few dollars in the pocket and a sense of adventure. In 1972 that's all Tony and Maureen Wheeler needed for the trip of a lifetime – across Europe and Asia overland to Australia. It took several months, and at the end – broke but inspired – they sat at their kitchen table writing and stapling together their first travel guide, *Across Asia on the Cheap*. Within a week they'd sold 1500 copies. Lonely Planet was born.

Today, Lonely Planet has offices in Franklin, London, Melbourne, Oakland, Beijing and Delhi, with more than 600 staff and writers. We share Tony's belief that 'a great guidebook should do three things: inform, educate and amuse'.

OUR WRITERS

Sarina Singh

Coordinating Author After finishing a business degree in Melbourne, Sarina travelled to India where she pursued a hotel corporate traineeship before becoming a journalist. After five years she returned to Australia and completed postgraduate journalism qualifications before authoring Lonely Planet's first edition of *Rajasthan*. Apart from numerous Lonely Planet books she has written for a raft of newspapers and magazines, and has been a scriptwriter and travel columnist. Sarina is also the author of two prestigious publications – *Polo in India* and *India: Essential Encounters*. Her award-nominated documentary film premiered at the Melbourne International Film Festival before being screened internationally. Sarina wrote the Welcome to India, India's Top 17 and the India Today chapters.

Michael Benanav

Uttarakhand, Gujarat As a writer and photojournalist who covers issues affecting traditional cultures, Michael knew he hit the motherlode when he first visited Gujarat, criss-crossing the state on his way to remote tribal villages. In Uttarakhand, he's migrated with nomadic water buffalo herders in the Himalaya and joined religious worshippers on mountainous pilgrimage trails. The abundance of fascinating stories in these states – and the friendships he's formed in them - keep drawing him back. You can see his work at www.michaelbenanav.com. Michael also wrote the Trekking, India's Wildlife & Parks and The Landscape chapters.

Abigail Blasi

Delhi This is Abigail's sixth India title for Lonely Planet, and she was delighted to return to explore Delhi again, learning to love Paharganj, exploring the city's enclaves, and cycling through the mayhem of Old Delhi. She fell in love with the country on her first visit in 1994, and since then she's explored and written on India from north to south and back again. She's covered plenty of other places for Lonely Planet too, from Mauritania and Mali to Rome and Lisbon. Abigail also wrote the Need to Know, If You Like, Month by Month, Itineraries, Booking Trains, Yoga, Spas & Spiritual Pursuits, Volunteering, Travel with Children, Regions at a Glance, History, The Way of Life, Spiritual India, Delicious India, The Great Indian Bazaar, The Arts, Sacred Architecture, Scams, Women & Solo Travellers, Directory, Transport and Health chapters.

OVER PAGE MORE WRITERS

Published by Lonely Planet Publications Pty Ltd
ABN 36 005 607 983
16th edition – October 2015
ISBN 978 1 74321 676 7
© Lonely Planet 2015 Photographs © as indicated 2015
10 9 8 7 6 5 4 3 2 1
Printed in Singapore